D0771370

NEW WEBSTER'S DICTIONARY

AND

ROGET'S THESAURUS

NEW WEBSTER'S DICTIONARY

AND

ROGET'S THESAURUS

Book Essentials, Inc.
New York, New York, 10016

This book is not published by the original publishers
of WEBSTER'S DICTIONARY, or by their successors.

Created and manufactured for Book Essentials, Inc. by Ottenheimer
Publishers, Inc.
Copyright © 1991, 1992 Ottenheimer Publishers, Inc.
All Rights Reserved
Printed in the United States of America

Map pages copyright © Bartholomew, a division of
HarperCollins Publishers, 1992. All rights reserved.

CONTENTS

DICTIONARY

KEY TO THIS DICTIONARY

The entries in this Dictionary are arranged in groups, derived and related words being placed under the main entry.

A. Each main entry, in bold-face type, is syllabified, with the phonetic spelling and accented syllable shown in parentheses. The part of speech, in italics, follows; then the definition.
   Ex.: **cross** (kraws) *a.* intersecting; interchanged...

B. Subentries are shown in bold-face type following the definition of the main entry.

   1. If a hyphen precedes the subentry, the ending (or the word) is added to the main entry.
      Ex.: **-ing** (read **crossing**)
   2. If a dash precedes the subentry, a hyphenated word is indicated.
      Ex.: **—examination** (read **cross-examination**)
   3. If a dash and a space precede the subentry, the words form a spaced compound expression.
      Ex.: **— reference** (read **cross reference**)

C. The etymology of the main entry is found in brackets following the entry paragraph.

Note: Irregularities of verb forms, plurals and comparisons are included as sub-entries to facilitate word usage.

PRONUNCIATION GUIDE

These pronunciation symbols are used for the sounds indicated by the bold face letter or letters in the key words.

Vowels and diphthongs:

- a—b**a**t
- ȧ—b**o**tany
- ạ—**a**bout, sod**a** (unstressed)
- ā—b**ai**t
- aw—b**ou**ght
- e—b**e**t
- ē—b**ee**t
- i—b**i**t
- i·—cit**y** (final syllable)
- ī—b**i**te
- ō—b**oa**t
- oo—b**oo**k
- ȯȯ—b**oo**t
- oi—b**oi**l
- ou—b**ou**t
- u—b**u**t
- ū—b**u**tte
- ur—B**er**t (stressed)
- er—blubb**er** (unstressed)

Consonants:

- b—**b**ill
- ch—**ch**ur**ch**
- d—**d**ill
- f—**f**ill
- g—**g**et
- h—**h**ill
- hw—**wh**eel
- j—**j**u**dg**e
- k—**k**ill
- l—**l**ily
- m—**m**ill
- n—**n**il
- ng—si**ng**
- ngg—fi**ng**er
- p—**p**ill
- r—**r**ill
- s—**s**ill
- sh—**sh**all, **s**ure
- t—**t**ill
- th—**th**in
- TH—**th**en
- v—**v**illa
- w—**w**ill
- y—**y**et
- z—**z**illion
- zh—plea**s**ure

ABBREVIATIONS USED IN THIS DICTIONARY

a. adjective
abbrev. abbreviation
ablat. ablative; ablatival
Aborig. Aboriginal
acc. accusative
A.D. Anno Domini (in the year of Our Lord)
adv. adverb
Aero. Aeronautics
Afr. Africa; African
Agric. Agriculture
Alg. Algebra
alt. alternative
Amer. America; American
Anat. Anatomy
Anglo-Ind. Anglo-Indian
Anthropol. Anthropology
Ar. Arabic
Arch. Archaic
Archaeol. Archaeology
Archit. Architecture
Arith. Arithmetic
Astrol. Astrology
Astron. Astronomy
aux. auxiliary
Aviat. Aviation

Bacter. Bacteriology
B.C. before Christ
Bib. Biblical
Biol. Biology
Bot. Botany
Br., Brit. British
Braz. Brazilian
Bret. Breton
Build. Building

c. about (L. = *Circa)*
C. Centigrade; Central
Can. Canada; Canadian
Cap. capital letter
Carib. Caribbean
Carp. Carpentry
Celt. Celtic
cent. century
Cent. Central
cf. compare (L. = *confer*)
ch. Chapter
Chem. Chemistry
Chin. Chinese
Class. Myth. Classical Mythology
Colloq. Colloquial; Colloquialism
Comm. Commerce; Commercial
comp. comparative
conj. conjunction
conn. connected
contr. contraction
corrupt. corruption

Dan. Danish
dat. dative
def. art. definite article
demons. demonstrative
der. derivation; derived
Dial. Dialect; Dialectal
Dict. Dictionary
dim. diminutive
Dut. Dutch
Dyn. Dynamics

E. East; English
Eccl. Ecclesiastical
e.g. for example (L. = *exemplia gratia)*
E.Ind. East Indian
Elect. Electricity
Embryol. Embryology
Engin. Engineering
Entom. Entomology
esp. especially
Ethnol. Ethnology
etym. etymology

F, Fahr. Fahrenheit
fem. feminine
fig. figuratively
Finn. Finnish
Flem. Flemish
Fort. Fortification
fr. from
Fr. French
freq. frequentative

Gael. Gaelic
gen. genitive
Geog. Geography
Geol. Geology
Geom. Geometry
Ger. German
Gk. Greek
Gk. Myth. Greek Mythology
Gram. Grammar

Heb. Hebrew
Her. Heraldry
Hind. Hindustani
Hist. History
Hort. Horticulture
Hung. Hungarian

i. intransitive
Ice. Icelandic
i.e. that is (L. = *id est)*
imit. imitation; imitative
imper. imperative
impers. impersonal
Ind. Indian
indef. art. indefinite article
indic. indicative
infin. infinitive
interj. interjection
interrog. interrogative
Ir. Irish
It. Italian

Jap. Japanese

L. Latin
l.c. lower case letter
L.Ger. Low German
lit. literally
Lit. Literature
L.L. Low (Late) Latin

masc. masculine
Math. Mathematics
M.E. Middle English
Mech. Mechanics
Med. Medicine
Metal. Metallurgy
Meteor. Meteorology
Mex. Mexican

M.H.Ger. Middle High German
Mil. Military
Min. Mineralogy
Mod. Modern
Mus. Music
Myth. Mythology

n. noun
N. North; Norse
Nat.Hist. Natural History
Naut. Nautical
neg. negative
neut. neuter
nom. nominative
Norw. Norwegian
n.pl. noun plural
n.sing. noun singular
N.T. New Testament

obj. object; objective
obs. obsolete
O.E. Old English
O.Fr. Old French
O.H.Ger. Old High German
O.L.Ger. Old Low German
O.N. Old Norse
Onomat. Onomatopoeic
opp. opposite; opposed
Opt. Optics
orig. originally
Ornith. Ornithology
O.T. Old Testament

Paint. Painting
pa.p. past participle
pass. passive
pa.t. past tense
Path. Pathology
perh. perhaps
pers. person
Pers. Persian
pert. pertaining
Peruv. Peruvian
Pharm. Pharmacy
Philol. Philology
Philos. Philosophy
Phon. Phonetics
Photog. Photography
Phys. Physics
Physiol. Physiology
pl. plural
Poet. Poetry; poetical
Pol. Polish
Port. Portuguese
poss. possessive
pref. prefix
prep. preposition
pres. present
Print. Printing
prob. probably
pron. pronoun
Pros. Prosody
Prov. Provincial
pr.p. present participle
Psych. psychology

q.v. which see (L. = *quod vide)*

R. River
R.C. Roman Catholic

recip. reciprocal
redup. reduplication
ref. reference; referring
refl. reflexive
rel. related; relative
Rhet. Rhetoric
Rom. Roman
Rom.Myth. Roman Mythology
Russ. Russian

S. South
S.Afr. South African
S.Amer. South American
Sans. Sanskrit
Scand. Scandinavian
Scot. Scots; Scottish
Sculp. Sculpture
sing. singular
Singh. Singhalese
Slav. Slavonic
Sp. Spanish
St. Saint
superl. superlative
Surg. Surgery
Sw. Swedish
Syn. Synonym

t. transitive
Teleg. Telegraphy
Teut. Teutonic
Theat. Theatre
Theol. Theology
Trig. Trigonometry
Turk. Turkish

U.S.(A.) United States (of America)
usu. usually

v. verb
var. variant; variation
v.i. verb intransitive
v.t. verb transitive
vulg. vulgar

W. Welsh; West

Yid. Yiddish

Zool. Zoology

A

A (ā, ạ) *indef. art.*, meaning *one* (See *an*) [contr. of O.E. *ān*, one].
A-1 (ā·wun′) first-rate; excellent; physically fit.
aard·vark (ȧrd′·vark) *n.* animal resembling the ant-eater, found in parts of Africa [Dut. *aarde*, earth; *vark*, a pig].
A.B. (ā·bē′) Bachelor of Arts [L. *Artium Baccalaureus*].
ab- (ab) *prefix* meaning *from, away, off* [L.].
a·ba·cá (ȧb′·ạ·kȧ) *n.* Manila hemp, or the plant producing it [Malay].
a·back (ạ·bak′) *adv.* backwards; on the back; (*Naut.*) against the masts, of sails pressed back by the wind. **taken —,** taken by surprise; disconcerted [O.E. *on bacc*].
a·ba·cus (ȧb′·ạ·kạs) *n.* an instrument with parallel wires on which arithmetical calculations are made with sliding balls or beads; a counting-frame; (*Archit.*) a tablet crowning a column and its capital [L., fr. Gk. *abax*, a reckoning-board].
a·baft (ạ·baft′) *adv., prep.* (*Naut.*) at or towards the stern; behind [O.E. *aeftan*, behind].
ab·a·lo·ne (ab·ạ·lō′·nē) *n.* the name of several species of limpet-like molluscs or "earshells," yielding mother-of-pearl [Sp.].
a·ban·don (ạ·ban′·dạn) *v.t.* to give up wholly and finally; to relinquish; to surrender; *n.* careless freedom; a yielding to unrestrained impulse; dash. **-ed** *a.* deserted; forsaken; unrestrained; given up entirely to, esp. wickedness. **-edly** *adv.* **-ment** *n.* the act of abandoning, or state of being abandoned; (*Law*) the relinquishing of an interest or claim [O.Fr. *abandoner*].
a·base (ạ·bās′) *v.t.* to bring low; to cast down; to humble. **-ment** *n.* humiliation [L. *ad*, to; L.L. *bassare*, to lower].
a·bash (ạ·bash′) *v.t.* to strike with shame or fear; to excite a consciousness of guilt, inferiority, etc. **-ment** *n.* confusion from shame, etc. [O.Fr. *esbahir*, to astound].
a·bate (ạ·bāt′) *v.t.* to beat down, lessen; (*Law*) to put an end to, as a nuisance; to annul, as a writ; *v.i.* to decrease, subside, decline. **-able** *a.* **-ment** *n.* **-r** *n.* [*L. ad, batere*, for *batuere*, to strike].
a·bat·toir (a·bạ·twȧr′) *n.* a slaughter-house [Fr. *abattre*, to fell].
ab·ba·cy (ab′·ạ·si·) *n.* the office or dignity of an abbot; the building under the control of an abbot; an abbey. **abbatial** (ạ·bā′·shal) *a.* pert. to an abbot, or an abbey. **abbé** (ab′·i.) *n.* designation of and mode of address for an R.C. priest in France; an abbot. **abbey** *n.* a church establishment forming the dwelling-place of a community of monks or nuns. **abbot** *n.* (*fem.* **abbess**) the head of an abbey or monastery. **abbotship** *n.* [Syriac *abba*, father; Heb. *ab*, father].
ab·bre·vi·ate (ạ·brē′·vi·āt) *v.t.* to shorten, reduce by contraction or omission. **abbreviation** *n.* the act of abbreviating; a shortened form. **abbreviator** *n.* **abbreviatory** *a.* [L. *abbreviare*, fr. *brevis*, short].
A·b·c (ā·bē·sē′) *n.* the first three letters of the alphabet; the alphabet; the rudiments of any subject; a primer.
ab·di·cate (ab′·di·kāt) *v.t., v.i.* formally to give up power or office. **abdication** *n.* [L. *ab*, from; *dicare*, to proclaim].
ab·do·men (ab·dō′·mạn, ab′·dạ·mạn) *n.* the lower part of the trunk of the body; the belly. **abdominal** *a.* **abdominous** *a.* having a big belly; paunchy [L.].
ab·duct (ab·dukt′) *v.t.* to take away by fraud or force; to kidnap; (*Anat.*) to draw, e.g. a limb away from its natural position. **abducent** (ab·dū′·sent) *a.* (*Anat.*) abducting. **-tion** *n.* [L. *ab*, from; *ducere, ductum*, to lead].
a·beam (ạ·bēm′) *adv.* (*Naut.*) at right angles to a ship's length; hence, straight across a ship; abreast [fr. *beam*].
a·bed (ạ·bed′) *adv.* in bed (fr. *on bed*].
a·bele (ạ·bēl′) *n.* the white poplar-tree [L. *albus*, white].
ab·er·rate (ab′·ẹr·āt) *v.i.* to deviate from the right path or normal course. **aberrant** (ab·-e′·rạnt) *a.* deviating from the normal. **aberration** (ab·ạ·rā′·shun) *n.* a wandering, esp. mental disorder, forgetfulness; mental instability or peculiarity; moral lapse [L. *ab*, from; *errare*, to wander].
a·bet (ạ·bet′) *v.t.* to encourage or aid, esp. in doing wrong. *pr.p.* **-ting.** *pa.p., pa.t.* **-ted. -ment** *n.* **-ter, -tor** *n.* [O.Fr. *abeter*, to incite].
a·bey·ance (ạ·bā′·ạns) *n.* a state of suspension or temporary inactivity; the condition of not being in use or action. Also **abeyancy** [O.Fr. *abeance*, expectation].
ab·hor (ab·hawr′) *v.t.* to hate extremely. *pr.p.* **-ring.** *pa.p., pa.t.* **-red. -rence** *n.* detestation; loathing. **-rent** *a.* detestable; abominable; repugnant. **-rer** *n.* [L. *ab*, from; *horrere*, to shiver].
a·bide [ạ·bīd′) *v.i.* to stay; reside; continue firm or stable; *v.t.* to tolerate; bear; wait for. *pa.p., pa.t.* **-d, abode. abidance** *n.* **abiding** *a.* lasting; enduring [O.E. *abidan*].
a·bil·i·ty (ạ·bil′·i·ti·) *n.* quality, state, or condition of being able; power to act; skill; capacity; competence [L. *habilitas*, cleverness].
ab·i·o·gen·e·sis (ab·i·ō·jen′·ạ·sis) *n.* (*Biol.*) the theory of spontaneous generation from non-living matter [Gk. *a-*; neg.; *bios*, life; *genesis*, birth].
ab·ject (ab′·jekt, ab·jekt′) *a.* base; mean and worthless; contemptible; miserable. **-ly** *adv.* **-tion, -ness** *n.* degradation; abasement; servility [L. *ab*, away; *jacere, jactum*, to throw].
ab·jure (ab·joor′) *v.t.* to renounce upon oath; to abandon allegiance to a cause, doctrine, or principle; repudiate; forswear. **abjuration** *n.* [L. *abjurare*, to deny on oath].
ab·la·tive (ab′·lạ·tiv) *n.* the sixth case of Latin nouns and pronouns expressing *time when;* originally implied *separation from; a.* **ablatival** *a.* [L. *ab*, from; *ferre, latum*, to carry].
ab·laut (ab′·lout) *n.* (*Philol.*) variation of root vowel in certain related words, as *sink, sank, sunk* [Ger. = derived sound].
a·blaze (ạ·blāz′) *a.* on fire; aglow; gleaming.
a·ble (ā′·bl) *a.* having skill, strength to perform a task; competent; talented; vigorous. **—bodied** *a.* of sound body; robust; (of a seaman) having all-round knowledge of seamanship (*abbrev.* **A.B.**). **ability** *n.* the state of being able. **-ness** *n.* **ably** *adv.* competently [L. *habilis*, manageable].
a·bloom (ạ·blo͝om′) *adv., a.* in bloom.
ab·lu·tion (ab·lo͞o′·shạn) *n.* cleansing or washing; (usu. *pl.*) the purification of the body or of sacred vessels before certain religious ceremonies, e.g., Eucharist; the wine and water used. **-ary** *a.* pert. to cleansing [L. *ab*, from; *luere, lutum*, to wash].

ab·ne·gate (ab′·ne·gāt) *v.t.* to deny; surrender; relinquish. **abnegation** *n.* denying; renunciation [L. *ab*, away; *negare*, to deny].

ab·nor·mal (ab·nawr′·mạl) *a.* contrary to rule, or system; deviating from a recognized standard; exceptional; psychologically maladjusted. Also **-ity, -ism** *n.* the state of being abnormal; deformity; idiosyncrasy. **-ly** *adv.* **abnormity** *n.* abnormality; monstrosity [L. *ab*, from; *norma*, rule].

a·board (ạ·bōrd′) *adv.* and *prep.* (*Naut.*) on board; within a vessel; on a train.

a·bode (ạ·bōd′) *n.* residence, permanent or temporary; a dwelling place [from *abide*].

a·bol·ish (ạ·bål′·ish) *v.t.* to do away with; to repeal; to obliterate. **-ment** *n.* [L. *abolescere*, to destroy].

ab·o·li·tion (ab·ạ·lish′·an) *n.* the act of abolishing, as of laws, taxes, etc. **-al** *a.* **-ist** *n.* **-ism** *n.* the policy of an abolitionist [L. *abolescere*, to destroy].

A-bomb (ā′·bȧm) *n.* atomic bomb.

a·bom·i·nate (a·bȧm′·i·nāt) *v.t.* to loathe; detest extremely; abhor. **abominable** *a.* loathsome; morally detestable; odious. **abominableness** *n.* **abominably** *adv.* **abomination** *n.* the act or object of loathing; a despicable practice [L. *abominari*, to detest].

ab·o·rig·i·nes (ab·ạ·rij′·i·nēz) *n.pl.* the original inhabitants of a country. **aboriginal** *a.* [L. *ab origine*, from the beginning].

a·bort (ạb·awrt′) *v.i.* to miscarry in giving birth; (*Fig.*) to fail to come to fruition. **abortifacient** (ȧ·bawr′·ti·fā·shạnt) *n.* a drug causing abortion; *a.* capable of producing abortion. **-ion** *n.* miscarriage; one born permaturely. **-ionist** *n.* **-ive** *a.* prematurely produced; undeveloped; imperfect; rudimentary. **-ively** *adv.* [L. *aboriri, abortus*, to miscarry].

a·bound (ạ·bound′) *v.i.* to be in great plenty (used with preps. *with* and *in*). **-ing** *a.* plentiful [L. *abundare*, to overflow].

a·bout (ạ·bout′) *adv.* and *prep.* on every side; concerning; approximately; (before an infin.) on the point of. **to bring about,** to effect. **about face,** *n.* and *v.* turn in opposite direction [O.E. *būtan*, outside].

a·bove (ạ·buv′) *adv.* and *prep.* and *a.* higher than; more in number, quantity or degree. **above board,** open or openly; honorably. [O.E. *abufan*, upwards].

ab·ra·ca·dab·ra (ab′·rạ·kạ·dab′·rạ) *n.* corruption of sacred Gnostic term, derived from ancient Egyptian magical formula; a catchword; gibberish.

a·brade (ạ·brād′) *v.t.* to rub or wear off; to scrape or grate off; to graze (of skin). **abradant** *n.* a substance, e.g. emery powder, for polishing. **abrading** *n.* soil-erosion. **abrasion** n. a rubbing or scraping off; a grazing of the skin. **abrasive** *a.* tending to abrade; scouring; *n.* something used for scouring. [L. *ab*, from; *radere, rasum*, to scrape].

ab·re·ac·tion (ab·rē·ak′·shạn) *n.* in psychoanalysis, elimination of a morbid complex by expression through conscious association with the original cause. **abreact** *v.t.* [L. *ab*, from; and *reaction*].

a·breast (ạ·brest′) *adv.* side by side; on a line with [E.].

a·bridge (ạ·brij′) *v.t.* to shorten; curtail; reduce; diminish; epitomize. **-ment** *n.* a cutting-off; a summary; a précis; an abstract of evidence. **-r** *n.* [Fr. *abréger;* L. *abbreviare*, to shorten].

a·broad (ạ·brawd′) *adv.* and *a.* at large, over a wide space; beyond or out of a house, camp, or other enclosure; in foreign countries; overseas [E.].

ab·ro·gate (ab′·rạ·gāt) *v.t.* to annul; repeal (a law); do away with; put an end to; cancel. **abrogation** *n.* [L. *ab*, away; *rogare*, to ask].

ab·rupt (ạ·brupt′) *a.* broken off; steep; precipitous; describing a sudden change of subject, etc. in speech or writing; curt; unceremonious; brusque; (*Bot.*) without a terminal leaf. **-ly** *adv.* **-ness** *n.* [L. *ab*, away; *rumpere, ruptum*, to break].

ab·scess (ab′·ses) *n.* gathering of pus in any infected organ or tissue of the body [L. *abscessus*, a going away].

ab·scind (ab·sind′) *v.t.* to cut off; pare away; separate; rend apart. **absciss, abscissa** *n.* (*Geom.*) the distance of a point from a fixed line measured horizontally; one of the elements of reference by which a point, as of a curve, is referred to a system of fixed rectilineal coordinate axes; *pl.* **abscissas, abscissae. abscission** *n.* act or process of cutting off [L. *ab*, away; *scindere, scissum*, to cut].

ab·scond (ab·skȧnd′) *v.i.* to take oneself off; to flee from justice. **-ence** *n.* **-er** *n.* [L. *abs*, away; *condere*, to hide].

ab·sence (ab′·sạns) *n.* being absent; failure to appear when cited to a court of law; inattention to prevailing conditions. **absent** *a.* not present; inattentive. **absent** (ab·sent′) *v.t.* to withdraw (oneself); deliberately to fail to appear. **absentee** *n.* one who is not present. **absently** *adv.* casually; forgetfully. **absent-minded** *a.* abstracted; absorbed; pre-occupied [L. *ab*, away; *esse*, to be].

ab·sinthe, ab·sinth (ab′·sinth) *n.* a green-colored liqueur flavored with wormwood and other aromatics [L. *absinthium*, wormwood].

ab·so·lute (ab′·sạ·lòòt) *a.* unconditional; without restraint; (*Gram.*) not dependent; pure. **-ly** *adv.* positively; very; entirely. **-ness** *n.* **absolution** *n.* a remission of sin after confession, pronounced by the R. C. Church; formal acquittal by a judge. **absolutism** *n.* unrestricted and unlimited rule; arbitrary government. **absolutist** *n.* **absolutory, absolvatory** *a.* **absolute alcohol,** alcohol free from water. **absolute pressure** (*Phys.*) pressure of gas, steam, or liquid measured as excess over zero pressure, i.e. over atmospheric pressure. **absolute zero** (*Phys.*) the lowest possible temperature —273.1° C. **nominative (ablative) absolute,** a grammatical construction consisting of a substantive and a participle independent of the main sentence [L. *absolutus*, freed].

ab·solve (ab·sȧlv′) *v.t.* to set free from an obligation, guilt, debt, penalty; to pardon; acquit. **-r** *n.* [L. *ab*, away; *solvere*, to loosen].

ab·sorb (ab·sawrb′) *v.t.* to swallow up; drink in; soak up; to engage one's whole attention. **-ability** *n.* **-able** *a.* **-ing** *a.* **-ent** *a.* absorbing; *n.* anything which absorbs. **-ency** *n.* [L. *ab*, away; *sorbere, sorptum*, to suck].

ab·sorp·tion (ab·sawrp′·shạn) *n.* the act of absorbing. **absorptive** *a.* able to absorb [fr. *absorb*].

ab·stain (ab·stān′) *v.i.* to forbear; to refrain. **-er** *n.* one who abstains, esp. from alcohol [L. *abs*, from; *tenere*, to hold].

ab·ste·mi·ous (ab·stē′·mi·ạs) *a.* showing moderation in the use of food and drink. **-ly** *adv.* **-ness** *n.* [L. *abs*, from; *temetum*, strong drink].

ab·sten·tion (ab·sten′·shạn) *n.* the act of abstaining or refraining from. **-ist** *n.* [L. *abs*, from; *tenere*, to hold].

ab·sti·nence (ab′·sti·nạns) *n.* voluntary forbearance from using or doing something. Also **abstinency. abstinent** *a.* temperate; refraining from. **abstinently** *adv.* [L. *abs*, from; *tenere*, to hold].

ab·stract (ab·strakt′) *v.t.* to separate from; remove, summarize; reduce. **-ed** *a.* **-edly** *adv.* *a.* not concrete, theoretical. (ab′·strakt) *n.* that which comprises in itself the essential qualities of a larger thing, or of several things; a summary. **-ion** *n.* abstracting or separating; a theoretical idea. **in the abstract,** without reference to particular cases [L. *abs*, from; *trahere, tractum*, to draw].

ab·struse (ab·stro͝os′) *a.* hidden; difficult or hard to be understood. **-ly** *adv.* **-ness** *n.* [L. *abs,* from; *trudere, trusum,* to thrust].
ab·surd (ab·surd′) *a.* contrary to reason; ridiculous; silly. **-ly** *adv.* **-ity** *n.* that which is absurd. Also **-ness** [L. *absurdus,* out of tune].
a·bun·dance (a·bun′·dạns) *n.* ample sufficiency; great plenty. **abundant** *a.* fully sufficient; plentiful. **abundantly** *adv.* [L. *abundare,* to overflow].
a·buse (ạ·būz′) *v.t.* to make a wrong use of; to ill-treat; to violate; revile; malign. **abuse** (ạ·būs′) *n.* ill-usage; improper treatment; a corrupt practice; rude language. **abusive** *a.* practicing abuse; rude; insulting. **abusiveness** *n.* [Fr. *abuser*].
a·but (ạ·but′) *v.i.* to end; to touch with one end; to border on; to adjoin. *pr.p.* **-ting.** *pa.p.* **-ted.** **-ment** *n.* (*Archit.*) the support at end of an arch or bridge [O.Fr. *abouter,* to join at the end].
a·byss (ạ·bis′) *n.* any deep chasm; a gulf. formerly, **abysm** (ạ·bizm′) *n.* **abysmal** *a.* bottomless; vast; profound. **abysmally** *adv.* **abyssal** *a.* inhabiting, or characteristic of, the depths of the ocean; abysmal [Gk. *abussos,* bottomless].
a·ca·cia (ạ·kā′·shạ) *n.* thorny, leguminous tree or shrub, yielding gum arabic [Gk. *akakia,* from *akē,* a sharp point].
a·cad·e·my (ạ·kad′·ạ·mi·) *n.* a place of education or specialized training; popularly a school; a society of men united for the promotion of the arts and sciences. **academic, academical** *a.* belonging to an academy or other institution of learning. **academician** (ạ·kad·-ạ·mish′·ạn) *n.* a member of an academy or society for promoting the arts and sciences [Gk. *akademeia*].
a·can·thus (ạ·kan′·thạs) *n.* a prickly plant, also called 'bear's breech' or 'brank-ursine'; (*Archit.*) an ornament like this leaf, esp. on the capitals of Corinthian pillars [Gk. *ake,* a point; *anthos,* a flower].
a cap·pel·la (á kạ·pel′·ạ) *mus.* singing without instrumental accompaniment [It.].
a·cat·a·lec·tic (ạ·kat·ạ·lek′·tik) *a.* not stopping short; complete in syllables; *n.* a verse that has the complete number of syllables.
a·cat·a·lep·sy (ạ·kat·ạ·lep′·si·) *n.* incomprehensibility; **acatalepsia** *n.* (*Med.*) uncertainty in the diagnosis of a disease. **acataleptic** *a.* [Gk. *a-,* neg.; *kata,* down; *lepsis,* a seizing].
a·cat·a·pha·si·a (ạ·kat·ạ·fā′·zi·ạ) *n.* difficulty or inability in expressing ideas logically.
ac·cede (ak·sēd′) *v.i.* to agree; assent; consent; to arrive at a certain state or condition; to succeed as heir. **-r** *n.* [L. *ad,* to; *cedere,* to go].
ac·cel·er·an·do (ak·sel·ạ·ran′·dō) *a.* and *n.* (*Mus.*) a direction to quicken the time [It. fr. L. *celer,* swift].
ac·cel·er·ate (ak·sel′·ạ·rāt) *v.t.* and *i.* to cause to move faster; to become swifter. **acceleration** *n.* an increase in speed, action, etc.; the rate of increase in the velocity of a moving body. **accelerative** *a.* quickening. **accelerator** *n.* a mechanism for increasing speed. **acceleratory** *a.* [L. *celer,* swift].
ac·cent (ak′·sent) *n.* stress on a syllable or syllables of a word; a mark to show this; inflection of the voice; manner of speech; pronunciation and inflection of the voice peculiar to a country, town, or individual. **accent** (ak·sent′) *v.t.* to utter, pronounce, or mark with accent; to emphasize; to stress. **-ual** *a.* **-uate** *v.t.* to accent; to stress; to make more prominent. **-uation** *n.* [Fr. fr. L. *accentus,* a tone].
ac·cept (ak·sept′) *v.t.* to take; receive; admit; believe; to agree to; (*Comm.*) to agree to pay a bill. **-able** *a.* welcome; pleasing; agreeable. **-ably** *adv.* **-ability** *n.* **-ance** *n.* the act of accepting. **-ation** *n.* the usual meaning of a word, statement, etc. **-ed** *a.* **-er, -or** *n.* [L. *acceptare*].
ac·cess (ak′·ses) *n.* a coming to the means or way of approach; admission; entrance; attack; fit. **-ary** *a.* (*Law.* See accessory). **-ible** *a.* easy of access or approach; approachable. **-ibility** *n.* **-ion** *n.* increase; a coming to, esp. to a throne, office, or dignity. **-ory** (ak·ses′·ạ·ri·), **-ary** *a.* aiding; contributing; additional; *n.* an additional, secondary piece of equipment; an accompaniment; (*Law*) one implicated in a felony (though not as a principal); a confederate [L. *accedere, accessum,* to go to].
ac·ci·dence (ak′·si·dans) *n.* the part of grammar dealing with changes in the form of words, e.g. plurals, etc. [fr. *accidents*].
ac·ci·dent (ak′·si·dent) *n.* chance; a mishap; a casualty; contingency; a quality not essential. **-al** *a.* **-ally** *adv.* [L. *ad,* to; *cadere,* to fall].
ac·claim (a·klām′) *v.t.* and *i.* to receive with applause, etc.; cheer; to hail as; **acclamation** (ak·lạ·mā′·shạn) *n.* general applause. **acclamatory** (ạ·klam′·ạ·tōr·i·) *a.* [L. *acclamare,* to shout to].
ac·cli·ma·tize (ạ·klī′·mạ·tīz) *v.t.* to accustom to a new climate. Also **acclimate** (ạ·klī′·mit). **acclimatization** *n.* Also **acclimatation, acclimation** (ak·li·mā′·shun) *n.* [fr. *climate*].
ac·cliv·i·ty (ạ·kliv′·i·ti·) *n.* an upward slope [L. *ad,* to; *clivus,* a slope].
ac·co·lade (ak′·ạ·lād) *n.* a ceremony used in conferring knighthood, consisting now of a tap given on the shoulder; award, praise [L. *ad,* to; *collum,* the neck].
ac·com·mo·date (ạ·kȧm·ạ·dāt) *v.t.* to render fit or suitable; adapt; adjust; reconcile; provide room for. **accommodating** *a.* obliging. **accommodation** *n.* (usually pl.) a loan of money; convenience; room or space for; lodgings. **accommodative** *a.* obliging; supplying accommodation; adaptive [L. *accommodare,* to fit].
ac·com·pa·ny (ạ·kum′·pạ·ni·) *v.t.* to go with; (*Mus.*) to play the accompaniment. **accompaniment** *n.* that which goes with; (*Mus.*) the instrumental parts played with a vocal or other instrumental part. **accompanist** *n.* [Fr. *accompagner*].
ac·com·plice (ạ·kȧm′·plis) *n.* a companion in evil deeds; an associate in crime [Earlier *complice,* fr. L. *complex,* woven together].
ac·com·plish (ạ·kȧm′·plish) *v.t.* to carry out; to finish; to complete; to perform. **-ed** *a.* complete; perfect; having accomplishments; hence, talented. **-ment** *n.* completion; finish; that which makes for culture, elegant manners, etc. [L. *ad,* to; *complere,* to complete].
ac·cord (a·kawrd′) *n.* agreement; harmony; *v.t.* to grant; settle; compose; *v.i.* to agree; to agree in pitch and tone. **-ance** *n.* **-ant** *a.* corresponding. **-ing** *a.* in accordance; agreeing; suitable. **-ingly** *adv.* **of one's own accord,** of one's own free will; voluntarily [L. *ad,* to; *cor, cordis,* the heart].
ac·cor·di·on (a·kawr′·di·ạn) *n.* wind instrument fitted with bellows and button keyboards; in the **piano-accordion** the right hand keyboard is like that of a piano. **accordion-pleated** *a.* having narrow folds like those of the bellows of an accordion.
ac·cost (ạ·kawst′) *v.t.* to speak first to; to address; to approach [L. *ad,* to; *costa,* a rib].
ac·count (ạ·kount′) *n.* a reckoning; a record; a report; a description; a statement of debts and credits in money transactions; value; advantage; profit; *v.t.* to reckon, judge; *v.i.* to give a reason; to give a financial reckoning. **-able** *a.* liable to be held responsible; able to be explained. **-ably** *adv.* **-ability** *n.* **-ancy** *n.* the profession of an accountant. **-ant** *n.* one skilled in recording financial transactions, esp. as a profession. **-ing** *n.* or *a.* [O.Fr. *aconter,* to reckon].
ac·cou·ter (ạ·ko͞o′·tẹr) *v.t.* to furnish with dress or equipment, esp. military; to equip.

-ments *n.pl.* dress; military dress and equipment [Fr. *accoutrer,* to dress].

ac·cred·it (ạ·kred′·it) *v.t.* to give trust or confidence to; to vouch for; to recommend; to furnish with credentials, as an envoy or ambassador. **-ed** *a.* **-ation** *n.* [Fr. *accréditer*].

ac·crete (ạ·krēt′) *v.i.* to grow together; *v.t.* to add by growth. **accretion** *n.* an increase in growth, esp. by an addition of parts externally. **accretive** *a.* [L. *ad,* to; *crescere,* to grow].

ac·crue (ạ·kròò′) to increase; to result naturally; to come as an addition, e.g. interest, profit, etc. **accrual** *n.* [Fr. *accrue,* an extension, from L. *ad,* to; *crescere,* to grow].

ac·cu·mu·late (ạ·kū′·mū·lāt) *v.t.* to heap up; to collect; *v.i.* to grow into a mass; to increase. **accumulation** *n.* a collection; a mass; a pile. **accumulative** *a.* **accumulatively** *adv.* **accumulator** *n.* one who, or that which, collects; an apparatus for the storage of electricity [L. *ad,* to; *cumulus,* a heap].

ac·cu·rate (ak′·ū·rit) *a.* correct. **-ly** *adv.* **-ness** *n.* **accuracy** *n.* correctness; exactness; precision [L. *ad,* to; *cura,* care].

ac·curse (ạ·kurs′) *v.t.* to doom to destruction; to curse. **-ed** *a.* under a curse. **-dness** *n.*

ac·cuse (ạ·kūz′) *v.t.* to charge with a crime or fault; to blame. **-d** *a.* charged with a crime; *n.* one so charged. **-r** *n.* **accusation** (ak·ū·zā′·shun) *n.* a charge. **accusative** *a.* producing or containing accusations; (*Gram.*) of the case which forms the direct object of a transitive verb (the objective case); *n.* the accusative case. **accusatory** *a.* [L. *accusare*].

ac·cus·tom (ạ·kus′·tạm) *v.t.* to make familiar by use; to familiarize; to habituate. **-ed** *a.* often practiced; usual; ordinary [O.Fr. *acostumer*].

ace (ās) *n.* a card with only one spot; a single point; the best, highest; an outstanding fighter pilot; an expert player; an unreturnable service in tennis [L. *as,* a unit].

ac·er·bate (as′·ẹr·bāt) *v.t.* to make bitter; to exasperate; *a.* embittered; severe; exasperated. **acerbity** *n.* sourness of taste, with bitterness and astringency; hence bitterness, or severity in persons [L. *acerbus,* bitter].

a·ce·tic (ạ·set′·ik, ạ·sē′·tik) *a.* pert. to acetic acid, the acid in vinegar. **acetate** *n.* (*Chem.*) a salt formed by acetic acid; also a rayon material made from the acetic ester of cellulose. **acetify** *v.t.* and *v.i.* to turn into vinegar. **acetification** *n.* **acetous** (ạ·sē′·tạs) *a.* sour. [L. *acetum,* vinegar].

a·cet·y·lene (a·set′·i·lēn) *n.* a highly inflammable gas used as an illuminant [L. *acetum,* vinegar].

ache (āk) *n.* a continuous dull, heavy pain; often found compounded in such words as *earache, headache; v.i.* to be in pain. **aching** *a.* and *n.* [O.E. *acan*].

a·chieve (ạ·chēv′) *v.t.* to bring to a successful end; to accomplish. **achievable** *a.* **-ment** *n.* performing; a performance; an exploit; a feat. **-r,** *n.* [O.Fr. *à chef,* to a head].

ach·ro·ma·si·a (ak·rō·mā′·zi·ạ) *n.* (*Med.*) absence of color. **achromate** *a.* without color; showing color-blindness [Gk. *a-,* neg.; *chroma,* color].

ach·ro·ma·tic (ak·rạ·mat′·ik) *a.* (*Opt.*) free from color; transmitting light without decomposing it; of a lens, giving an image free from color around the edges. **-ity** (ak·rō·mạ·ti′·si·ti·) **achromatism** (ạ·krō′·mạ·tizm) *n.* **achromatize** *v.t.* to deprive of color. **achromatous** *a.* [Gr. *a-,* neg.; *chroma,* color].

ac·id (as′·id) *a.* sour; sharp to the taste; having the taste of vinegar; *n.* a sour substance; (*Chem.*) a substance which contains hydrogen replaceable by a metal, is generally sour and reacts with a base to form salt and water. **-ify** *v.t.* and *i.* to make or become sour; to turn into an acid. **-ity** *n.* the state or quality of being acid; sourness; sharpness. **-osis** (as·i·dō′·sis) *n.* (*Med.*) fatty-acid poisoning in the blood, due to over-production of acids in it. **-ulate** *v.t.* to make slightly acid or sour; (*Fig.*) to embitter. **-ulated, -ulous** *a.* slightly sour; sourish; severe. **acid test** (*Fig.*) a conclusive proof of genuineness (referring to the test of gold by acid) [L. *acidus,* sour].

ack-ack (ak′·ak) *a.* (*Mil. slang*) anti-aircraft; *n.* anti-aircraft fire.

ac·know·ledge (ak·nȧl′·ij) *v.t.* to admit as true; to give a receipt for; to give thanks for; to reward. **-ment** *n.* [M.E. *knowlechen,* to perceive].

ac·me (ak′·mē) *n.* the highest point, the top; perfection [Gk. *akmē,* the top].

ac·ne (ak′·nē) *n.* a skin disease characterized by hard, reddish pimples often appearing as blackheads [fr. Gk. *akmē,* a point].

ac·o·lyte (ak′·ạ·līt) *n.* a candidate for priesthood in the R. C. Church; a lesser church officer; an assistant; a novice [Gk. *akolouthos,* a follower].

ac·o·nite (ak′·ạ·nīt) *n.* (*Bot.*) wolf's-bane or monk's-hood; a poisonous drug extracted from it [Gk. *akoniton*].

a·corn (ā′·kawrn) *n.* the seed or fruit of the oak. [O.E. *aecern,* fruit of the open country].

a·cous·tic (ạ·kòò′·stik, ạ·kou′·stik) *a.* pert. to the sense of hearing. **acoustics** *n.pl.* the science of sounds; the estimation of audibility in a theater, etc. [Gk. *akouein,* to hear].

ac·quaint (ạ·kwānt′) *v.t.* to make fully known or familiar; to inform. **-ance** *n.* familiar knowledge; a person known slightly. **-anceship** *n.* **-ed** *a.* [O.Fr. *acointier;* L. *cognoscere, cognitum,* to know].

ac·qui·esce (ak·wi·es′) *v.i.* to agree in silence; to assent without objection. **-nce** *n.* **-ent** *a.* submissive; consenting [L. *ad,* to; *quiescere,* to keep quiet].

ac·quire (ạ·kwīr′) *v.t.* to gain; to obtain; to get. **acquirable** *a.* **-ment** *n.* **acquisition** (ak·wi·zi′·shạn) *n.* the act of acquiring; the thing acquired. **acquisitive** *a.* grasping; greedy for gain. **acquisitiveness** *n.* [L. *ad,* to; *quaerere,* to seek].

ac·quit (ạ·kwit′) *v.t.* to set free; release; declare innocent; to conduct oneself; to discharge a debt. *pr.p.* **-ting.** *pa.p.* and *pa.t.* **-ted. -tal.** *n.* judicial release; declaration of 'not guilty.' **-tance** *n.* [Fr. *aquitter,* fr. L. *quies,* rest].

a·cre (ā′·kẹr) *n.* a measure of land containing 4840 square yards. **-age** (ā′·crē·ij) *n.* extent of a piece of land in acres [O.E. *aecer,* a field].

ac·rid (ak′·rid) *a.* bitter; sharp; pungent; harsh; ill-tempered. **-ly** *adv.* **-ness, -ity** *n.* [L. *acer,* sharp].

ac·ri·mo·ny (ak′·ri·mōn·i·) *n.* bitterness of temper or of language. **acrimonious** (ak·ri·mō′·ni·us) *a.* sharp; bitter; stinging; sarcastic. **acrimoniously** *adv.* [L. *acer,* sharp].

ac·ro·bat (ak′·rạ·bat) *n.* one skilled in gymnastic feats; a rope-dancer; a tumbler. **-ic** *a.* **-ics** *n.pl.* skill of an acrobat. [Gk. *akrobatein,* to walk on tiptoe].

ac·ro·nym (ak′·rạ·nim) *n.* a word formed from initials, e.g., *radar.*

ac·ro·pho·bi·a (ak·rạ·fō′·bi·ạ) *n.* a morbid fear of heights. [Gk. *akros,* extreme; *phobia,* fear].

a·crop·o·lis (ạ·krȧp′·ạ·lis) *n.* the fortified summit of a Greek city; a citadel, esp. the citadel of Athens, on which stands the Parthenon [Gk. *akros,* topmost; *polis,* city].

a·cross (ạ·kraws′) *adv.* and *prep.* from side to side; transversely; athwart; at an angle with [*a,* and *cross*].

a·cros·tic (ạ·kraws′·tik) *n.* a composition in verse, in which the first, and sometimes last, letters of the lines read in order form a name, a sentence, or title [Gk. *akros,* extreme; *stichos,* a line].

act (akt) *v.t.* to perform, esp. upon stage; to behave as; *v.i.* to exert energy; to fulfil a function; to operate. *n.* deed; performance; actuality; action; a decree, law, edict, or judgment; principal division of a play. **-ing** *a.* performing a duty; performing on the stage; serving for, as *Acting Captain.* **-or** *n.* one who performs. **-ress** *n.* a female actor [L. *agere, actum,* to do].

ACTH Adreno-corticotropic-hormone used in the treatment of rheumatic diseases.

ac·tin·i·a (ak·tin′·i·ạ) *n.* the sea anemone. *pl.* **actiniae** [Gk. *aktis,* a ray].

ac·tin·ism (ak′·ti·nizm) *n.* the radiation of light or heat; the property possessed by the sun's ray, of producing chemical changes, as in photography. **actinic** *a.* pert. to actinism. **actiniform** *a.* having a ray-like structure [Gk. *aktis,* a ray].

ac·tin·i·um (ak·tin′·i·um) *n.* a radio-active element; symbol **Ac** [Gk. *aktis,* a ray].

ac·ti·nol·o·gy (ak·ti·nál′·ạ·ji·) *n.* that branch of science concerned with chemical action of light [Gk. *aktis,* a ray; *logos,* word].

ac·ti·no·ther·a·py (ak·tin·ạ·ther′·ạ·pi·) *n.* the treatment of disease by natural or artificial light rays; often known as 'sunlight treatment' [Gk. *aktis,* a ray; *therapeia,* service].

ac·tion (ak′·shạn) *n.* a thing done; behavior; physical movement; function; a battle; the development of events in a play, etc.; legal proceedings; (*Chem.*) effect. **-able** *a.* affording grounds for legal proceedings. **-ably** *adv.* **reflex action,** an involuntary motor reaction to a sensory impulse [L. *agere, actum,* to do].

ac·ti·vate (ak′·ti·vāt) *v.t.* to make active. **activation** *n.*

ac·tive (ak′·tiv) *a.* having the power to act; agile; busy; alert; (*Gram.*) implying action by the subject. **-ly** *adv.* vigorously. **activism** *n.* policy of those who, by energetic action, seek to fulfil the promises of a political program. **activist** *n.* one who advocates or practices activism. **activity, -ness** *n.* [L. *agere, actum,* to do].

ac·tu·al (ak′·choo·ạl) *a.* existing now or as a fact; real; effectual. **-ize** *v.t.* to make real in fact or by vivid description. **-ist** *n.* a realist. **-ity** (ak·choo·al′·ạ·ti·) *n.* reality, existence. **-ly** *adv.* [L. *actualis,* active].

ac·tu·a·ry (ak′·choo·ar·i·) *n.* registrar or clerk; an official who calculates for insurance companies. **actuarial** *a.* **actuarially** *adv.* [L. *actuarius,* a clerk].

ac·tu·ate (ak′·choo·āt) *v.t.* to put into action; incite; motivate; influence. **actuation** *n.* **actuator** *n.* [L. *actus,* action].

a·cu·men (ạ·kū′·mạn) *n.* quickness of perception or discernment; sharpness; penetration. **acuminous** *a.* [L. *acumen,* a point].

a·cute (ạ·kūt′) *a.* sharp; pointed; sagacious; subtle; penetrating; (*Med.*) of disease with severe symptoms and sharp crisis; (*Geom.*) less than a right angle. **-ly** *adv.* **-ness** *n.* **acute accent,** a mark (′) over a letter, as in French, to indicate pronunciation [L. *acutus,* sharp].

ad (ad) *n.* (*Colloq.*) advertisement.

A.D. (ā dē) in the year of our Lord [L. *anno Domini*].

ad·age (ad′·ij) *n.* saying or maxim that has obtained credit by long use; a proverb; a byword. **adagial** *a.* [L. *adagium,* proverb].

a·da·gio (ạ·dá′·jō) *adv.* (*Mus.*) slowly and expressively; *n.* a slow movement, in a symphony or sonata. **adagio cantabile,** slowly and in a singing manner [It.].

ad·a·mant (ad′·ạ·mạnt) *n.* a stone of impenetrable hardness; the diamond; *a.* very hard; unyielding. **adamantine** (a·dạ·man′·tin) *a.* [Gk. *a-,* neg.; *damaein,* subdue].

Ad·am's ap·ple (ad′·ạmz a′·pl) *m.* projection of cartilege at the front of one's throat.

a·dapt (ạ·dapt′) *v.t.* to make fit or suitable; to make to correspond. **-ability, -ableness** *n.* the quality of being adaptable. **-able** *a.* may be adapted; versatile; **-ation** (a·dap·tā′·shạn) *n.* the gradual process of adjustment to new physical conditions exhibited by living organisms. **-er** *n.* any appliance which makes possible a union of two different parts of an apparatus. **-ive** *a.* **-ively** *adv.* **-iveness** *n.* **-or** *n.* a device to make possible the use of a machine, tool, etc. with modification [L. *ad,* to; *aptare,* to fit].

add (ad) *v.t.* to join, unite to form one sum or whole; to annex; to increase; to say further. **-able, -ible** *a.* **-er** *n.* a machine which adds; a comptometer. **-ibility** *n.* **-ition** *n.* the act of adding; anything added; the branch of arithmetic which deals with adding. **-itional** *a.* supplementary; extra. **-itionally** *adv.* **-itive** *a.* to be added; of the nature of an addition [L. *ad,* to; *dare,* to give].

ad·dend (ad′·end) *n.* number to be added.

ad·den·dum (ạ·den′·dạm) *n.* a thing to be added; an appendix; *pl.* **addenda** [L.].

ad·der (ad′·ẹr) *n.* a venomous serpent [M.E. *an addere* for *a naddere,* fr. O.E. *naeddre,* snake].

ad·dict (ạ·dikt′) *v.t.* to apply habitually; habituate. **addict** (ad′·ikt) *n.* one addicted to evil habit, e.g. drug-taking. **-ed** *a.* devoted, wholly given over to. **-ion, -ness,** *n.* [L. *addicere,* to assign].

ad·dle (ad′·l) *v.t.* to corrupt; putrify; confuse; to make addled. **addle, addled,** *a.* diseased, e.g. an egg; putrid; unfruitful. **-brained, -headed, -pated** *a.* confused [O.E. *adela,* filth].

ad·dress (ạ·dres′) *v.t.* to direct in writing, as a letter; to apply (oneself); to make a speech; to present a congratulatory message or petition; accost; *n.* a formal speech; manner of speaking; direction of a letter; skill. **-es** *n.pl.* attentions in courtship. **-ee** *n.* person to whom a communication is sent. **-er** *n.* **-ograph** *n.* a machine for addressing envelopes, etc. [Fr. *adresser*].

ad·duce (ạ·dūs′) *v.t.* to bring forward as proof; to cite; to quote. **-nt** *a.* **-r** *n.* **adducible** *a.* **adduction** (a·duk′·shạn) *n.* drawing together or bringing forward. **adductive** *a.* tending to bring together. **adductor** *n.* adducent muscle [L. *ad,* to; *ducere,* to lead].

ad·en (o) - (ȧd′·n-(o)) a combining form. **-itis** *n.* inflammation of the lymphatic glands. **-oid, -oidal** *a.* glandular; gland-shaped. **-oids** *n.pl.* a swelling of tissue between nose and throat [fr. Gk. *aden,* a gland].

a·dept (ạ·dept′) *n.* one skilled in any art; an expert; *a.* well skilled; expert [L. *adeptus,* having attained].

ad·e·quate (ad′·ạ·kwit) *a.* equal to; sufficient. **adequacy. -ness** *n.* **-ly** *adv.* [L. *adaequatus,* made equal to].

ad·here (ạd·hēr′) *v.i.* to stick fast; to be devoted to; to hold to (an opinion). **-nce** *n.* state of adhering; steady attachment. **-nt** *a.* united with or to; *n.* supporter of person or cause. **adhesion** *n.* act of adhering. **adhesive** *a.* sticky; tenacious; *n.* an agent which sticks things together. **adhesively** *adv.* **adhesiveness** *n.* [L. *ad,* to; *haerere,* to stick].

ad·hib·it (ạd·hib′·it) *v.t.* to use or apply; to attach [L. *adhibitus,* added to].

a·dieu (ạ·dū′) *interj.* good-bye; farewell; *n.* a farewell; a leave-taking. *pl.* **adieus, adieux** (ạ·dūz′) [Fr. meaning, *"to God"*].

ad in·fi·ni·tum (ad in·fạ·nī′·tạm) to infinity, without limit [L.].

ad in·ter·im (ad in′·tẹr·im) in the meantime [L].

a·di·os (ȧ·dōs′) good-bye [Sp.].

ad·i·pose (ad′·i·pōs) *a.* pert. to animal fat; fatty. **adiposity** (ad·i·pás′·i·ti·) *n.* fatness. **adipic** *a.* pert. to, or derived from, fatty substances [L. *adeps,* soft fat].

ad·it (ad′·it) *n.* horizontal or inclined entrance into a mine [L. *aditus,* an entrance].

ad·ja·cent (ạ·jā′·sạnt) *a.* lying close to; adjoining, bordering on. **-ly** *adv.* **adjacency** *n.* [L. *ad,* to; *jacere,* to lie].

ad·jec·tive (ad′·jik·tiv) *n.* a word used with a noun to qualify, limit, or define it; *a.* pert. to an adjective. **adjectival** (ad·jik·tī′·v'l) *a.* **adjectivally** *adv.* [L. *adjicere,* to add].

ad·join (ạ·join′) *v.t.* to join or unite to; to be next or contiguous to; *v.i.* to be next to. **-ing** *a.* [L. *adjungere,* to join to].

ad·journ (ạ·jurn′) *v.t.* to put off to another day; to postpone. **-ment** *n.* [L. *diurnus,* daily].

ad·judge (ạ·juj′) *v.t.* to settle judicially; to pronounce judgment; to award; to regard or deem. **adjudgment** *n.* **adjudicate** (ạ·jòò′·di·kāt) *v.t.* to settle judicially; *v.i.* to pronounce judgment. **adjudication** *n.* **adjudicator** *n.* a judge [L. *adjudicare,* to award as a judge].

ad·junct (ad′·jungkt) *n.* something joined to another thing, but not essential to it; (*Gram.*) a word or phrase added to modify meaning; *a.* added to; united with. **-ive, -ively** *adv.* [L. *adjunctus,* united to].

ad·jure (ạd·jòor′) *v.t.* to charge or bind, under oath; to entreat earnestly. **adjuration** *n.* a solemn command on oath; an earnest appeal. **adjuratory** *a.* [L. *adjurare,* to confirm by oath].

ad·just (ạ·just′) *v.t.* to adapt; to put in working order; to accommodate. **-able** *a.* **-ment** *n.* **-er, -or** *n.* arrangement; settlement; adaptation [L. *ad,* to; *justus,* just].

ad·ju·tant (aj′·ạ·tạnt) *n.* an assistant; staff officer who helps the commanding officer issue orders. **adjutancy** *n.* the office of an adjutant. **adjutant bird** a species of Indian stork [L. *ad,* to; *juvare,* to help].

ad lib (ad lib′) *v.i.* and *v.t.* (*Colloq.*) to improvise something not in the script [L. *abbrev.* for *ad libitum,* at pleasure].

ad·min·is·ter (ạd·min′·is·tẹr) *v.t.* to manage public affairs or an estate; to dispense, as justice or relief; to give, as medicine; to apply, as punishment or reproof; (*Law*) to settle the estate of one who has died intestate; *v.i.* to give aid (to). **administrable** *a.* **administrant** *a.* executive; *n.* one who administers. **administration** *n.* the executive part of a government; dispensation; direction. **administrative** *a.* **administrator** *n.* (*fem.* **administratrix**) one who directs; executes affairs of any kind [L. *ad,* to; *ministrare,* to give service].

ad·mi·ral (ad′·mi·rạl) *n.* a naval officer of the highest rank (graded as—admiral, vice-admiral, or rear-admiral). **-ty** *n.* rank or authority of an admiral; maritime law [Fr. *amiral,* fr. Ar. *amir-al-bahr,* prince of the sea].

ad·mi·ral (ad′·mi·rạl) *n.* a species of butterfly, esp. the red admiral.

ad·mire (ạd·mīr′) *v.t.* to regard with wonder and approval, esteem, or affection; to prize highly; *v.i.* to wonder; to marvel. **-r** *n.* **admiring** *a.* **admiringly** *adv.* **admirable** (ad′·mi·rạ·bl) *a.* excellent; praiseworthy. **admirably** *adv.* **admiration** *n.* wonder mingled with esteem, love, or veneration [L. *ad,* to; *mirari,* to wonder].

ad·mis·si·ble (ạd·mis′·i·bl) *a.* allowable. **admissibly** *adv.* **admissibility** *n.* **admission** *n.* permission to enter; the price paid for this [L. (part.) *admissus,* allowed to go].

ad·mit (ạd·mit′) *v.t.* to grant entrance; to concede as true; to acknowledge. *pr.p.* **-ting.** *pa.p.* and *pa.t.* **-ted.** **-tance** *n.* permission to enter [L. *ad,* to; *mittere,* to send].

ad·mix (ạd·miks′) *v.t.* to mingle with something else **-ture** *n.* [L. *admiscere,* to mix].

ad·mon·ish (ạd·mȧn′·ish) *v.t.* to reprove gently; to instruct or direct. **-er** *n.* **admonition** (ad·mạ·ni′·shan) *n.* rebuke. **admonitory** *a.* [L. *ad,* to; *monere, monitum,* to warn].

ad nau·se·am (ad naw′·shi·ạm, also ·nawz·) to a sickening degree [L.].

a·do (ạ·dòò′) *n.* fuss; bustle; trouble.

a·do·be (ạ·dō′·bi·) *n.* sun-dried brick [Sp.].

ad·o·les·cence (ạd·ạ·les′·ens) *n.* stage between childhood and manhood; youth. **adolescent** *a.* growing up; *n.* a young man or woman [L. *adolescere,* to grow up].

a·dopt (ạ·dȧpt′) *v.t.* to receive the child of another and treat it as one's own; to select and accept as one's own, e.g. a view. **-er** *n.* **-able** *a.* **-ion** *n.* **-ive** *a.* that adopts or is adopted [L. *ad,* to; *optare,* to choose].

a·dore (ạ·dōr′) *v.t.* to worship; to love deeply; **-r** *n.* a lover. **adorable** *a.* **adorably** *adv.* **adorableness** *n.* **adoration** (ad·ạ·rā′·shạn) *n.* profound veneration; ardent devotion [L. *ad,* to; *orare,* to pray].

a·dorn (ạ·dawrn′) *v.t.* to decorate; to deck or ornament; to set off to advantage. **-ing** *a.* beautifying; ornamental. **-ment** *n.* ornament; embellishment [L. *ad,* to; *ornare,* to deck].

ad·re·nal (ad·rē′·nạl) *n.* a small, ductless gland situated close to upper end of each kidney (same as *supra-renal*). **adrenalin** (ad·ren′·ạl·in) *n.* the hormone of the adrenal glands; the most effective hemostatic agent known [L. *ad,* to; *renes,* kidneys].

a·drift (ạ·drift′) *adv.* and *a.* floating at random; at mercy of the wind and tide; (*Fig.*) at a loss.

a·droit (ạ·droit′) *a.* dexterous; skillful; ingenious; adept. **-ly** *adv.* **-ness** *n.* [Fr.].

ad·sorb (ad·sawrb′) *v.t.* said of solids, to condense and hold a gas on the surface. **adsorption** *n.* [L. *ad,* to; *sorbere,* to drink in].

ad·u·late (aj′·ū·lāt) *v.t.* to praise or flatter in a servile manner; to fawn; to cringe. **adulation** *n.* **adulator** *n.* **adulatory** (aj·ạ·lạ·tawr′·i·) *a.* excessively [L. *adulari,* to flatter].

a·dult (ạ·dult′, ad′·ult) *a.* grown to maturity, or to full size and strength; appropriate for a grown-up; *n.* a grown-up person. **-ness** *n.* **-hood** *n.* [L. *adultus,* grown up].

a·dul·ter·ate (ạ·dul′·tạ·rāt) *v.t.* to debase by addition of inferior materials; to vitiate; to corrupt. *a.* debased; guilty of adultery. **adulteration** *n.* the act of debasing a substance [L. *adulterare,* to defile].

a·dul·ter·y (ạ·dul′·tẹr·i·) *n.* violation of the marriage vows. **adulterer** *n.* (*fem.* **adulteress**). **adulterous** *a.* pert. to or guilty of adultery. **adulterously** *adv.* [L. *adulterare,* to defile].

ad·um·brate (ạd·um′·brāt) *v.t.* to shadow forth; to give faint outline of; to forecast; to typify. **adumbral** *a.* shady. **adumbrant** *a.* showing a slight resemblance. **adumbrative** *a.* **adumbration** *n.* [L. *ad,* to; *umbra,* a shade].

ad·vance (ạd·vans′) *v.t.* to bring or push forward; to raise in status, price, or value; to propose as a claim; to supply beforehand, esp. money; *v.i.* to go forward; to improve; to rise in rank, etc. *a.* before the time, as in *advance-booking* *n.* a forward movement; gradual approach; a paying out of money before due; an increase in price; expansion of knowledge. **-d** *a.* in the front rank; progressive; well on in years; beyond the elementary stage (in education). **-ment** *n.* promotion; improvement; success; the state of being progressive in opinion; a loan of money. **-r** *n.* a promoter [Fr. *avancer,* to go forward].

ad·van·tage (ạd·van′·tij) *n.* any state or means favorable to some desired end; upper-hand; profit; in tennis, a point gained after deuce; *v.t.* to benefit, to promote the interests of; to profit. **-able** *a.* able to be turned to advantage. **-ous** (ạd·van·tā′·jus) *a.* beneficial; opportune; convenient. **-ously** (ạd·van·tā′·jus·li·) *adv.* [Fr. *avantage*].

ad·vent (ad′·vent) *n.* arrival; approach; the anticipated coming of Christ; the four weeks from the Sunday nearest to St. Andrew's Day (30th Nov.) to Christmas. **-ual** *adv.* pertaining to the season of Advent [L. *ad,* to; *venire,* to come].

ad·ven·ti·tious (ad·ven·tish′·ạs) *a.* accidental; out of the proper place; extraneous. **-ly** *adv.* [L. *ad,* to; *venire,* to come].
ad·ven·ture (ạd·ven′·chẹr) *n.* risk; bold undertaking; chance; trading enterprise of a speculative nature; *v.t.* to risk. *v.i.* to venture; to dare. **-r** *n.* (*fem.* **adventuress**). **-some** *a.* bold; daring; enterprising; facing risk. **-someness** *n.* **adventurous** *a.* inclined to take risks; perilous; hazardous. **adventurously** *adv.* [L. *adventurus,* about to arrive].
ad·verb (ad′·vurb) *n.* a word used to modify a verb, adjective, or other adverb. **-ial** *a.* **-ially** *adv.* [L. *ad,* to; *verbum,* a word].
ad·ver·sa·ry (ad′·vẹr·ser·i·) *n.* an opponent; one who strives against us; an enemy [L. *adversus,* opposite to].
ad·ver·sa·tive (ạd·vẹrs′·ạ·tiv) *a.* expressing opposition; not favorable [L. *adversus*].
ad·verse (ad·vurs′) *a.* contrary; opposite in position; unfortunate; opposed. **-ly** *adv.* **-ness** *n.* **adversity** *n.* adverse circumstances; misfortune [L. *adversus,* opposite to].
ad·vert (ạd·vurt′) *v.i.* to turn the mind or attention to; to remark upon; allude; refer. **-ence, -ency** *n.* [L. *ad,* to; *vertere,* to turn].
ad·vẹr·tise (ad′·vẹr·tīz) *v.t.* and *v.i.* to give public notice of; to inform; to make known through agency of the press. **-ment** *n.* a public intimation in the press; legal notification. **-r** *n.* one who advertises; **advertising** *n.* and *a.* [Fr. *avertir,* from L. *ad,* to; *vertere,* to turn].
ad·vice (ạd·vīs′) *n.* opinion offered as to what one should do; counsel; information [Fr. *avis*].
ad·vise (ạd·vīz′) *v.t.* to give advice to; to counsel; to give information to; to consult (with). *v.i.* to deliberate. **advisability, advisableness** *n.* expediency. **advisable** *a.* prudent; expedient. **advisably** *adv.* **advised** *a.* acting with due deliberation; cautious; prudent; judicious. **advisedly** *adv.* purposely. **advisedness, -ment** *n.* deliberate consideration. **-r** or **advisor** *n.* **advisory** *a.* having power to advise; containing advice [Fr. *avis*].
ad·vo·cate (ad′·vạ·kit) *n.* a vocal supporter of any cause; one who pleads or speaks for another. (ad′·vạ·kāt) *v.t.* to recommend; to maintain by argument. **advocacy** *n.* a pleading for; judicial pleading. **advocator** *n.* an intercessor; a pleader [L. *ad,* to; *vocare,* to call].
adz, adze (adz) *n.* a carpenter's tool for chipping, having a thin arching blade set at right angles to the handle [O.E. *adesa*].
ae·gis (ē′·jis) *n.* originally the shield of Jupiter; (*Fig.*) protection [Gk. *aigis*].
ae·on, eon (ē′·ȧn) *n.* an infinitely long period of time; an age [Gk. *aion,* an age].
aer·ate (ā′·ẹr·āt) *v.t.* to charge with carbon dioxide or other gas; to supply with air. **aeration** *n.* the act of exposing to the action of the air; saturation with a gas. **aerator** *n.* **aerated waters,** beverages charged with carbon dioxide [Gk. *aer,* air].
aer·i·al (ār′·i·ạl) *a.* pert. to, consisting of, air; *n.* and *a.* (*Radio and Television*) an insulated wire or wires, generally elevated above the ground and connected to a transmitting or receiving set. **-ly** *adv.* [Gk. *aēr,* air].
aer·i·al·ist (ār′·i·ạl·ist) *n.* high wire acrobat.
a·er·ie, a·er·y (ā′·ri·, e′·ri·) *n.* the nest of a bird of prey, esp. of the eagle [O.Fr. *aire*].
a·er·o (ā′·er·ō) a combining form from Gk. *aēr,* air, used in many derivatives.
a·er·o·dy·nam·ics (er·ạ·dī·nam′·iks) *n.pl.* the science that treats of gases in motion [Gk. *aēr,* air; *dunamis,* power].
aer·o·lite (er′·ạ·lit) *n.* a meteorite; a meteoric stone. Also **aerolith, aerolithic** *a.* **aerology** *n.* the science which treats of the air and its phenomena [Gk. *aēr,* air; *lithos,* stone; *logos,* discourse].
a·er·o·meter (er·ȧm′·ạ·tẹr) *n.* an instrument for measuring the weight or density of air and other gases. **aerometry** *n.* this science [Gk. *aēr,* air; *metron,* a measure].
aer·o·naut (ār′·ạ·nawt) *n.* a balloonist. **-ic** *a.* pert. to aeronautics. **-ics** *n.* the science of flight. [Gk. *aēr,* air; *nautes,* a sailor].
aer·o·sol (ār′·ạ·sȧl) *n.* a smoke, suspension of insoluble particles in a gas.
aer·o·stat (ār′·ạ·stat) *n.* a generic term for all lighter than air flying machines. **-ics** *n.* the science that treats of the equilibrium of gases, or of the buoyancy of bodies sustained in them; the science of air-navigation [Gk. *aēr,* air; *statos,* standing].
aes·thet·ics (es·thet′·iks) *n.* the laws and principles determining the beautiful in nature, art, taste, etc. **aesthetic, aesthetical** *a.* **aesthetically** *adv.* **aesthete** (es′·thēt) *n.* a disciple of aestheticism; a lover of the beautiful. **aestheticism** *n.* [Gk. *aisthanesthai,* to perceive].
a·far (ạ·fȧr′) *adv.* from, at, or to a distance; far away [E. *far*].
af·fa·ble (af′·ạ·bl) *a.* ready to converse; easy to speak to; courteous; friendly. **affably** *adv.* **affability** *n.* [L. *ad,* to; *fari,* to speak].
af·fair (ạ·fār′) *n.* what is to be done; a business or matter; a concern; a thing; (*Mil.*) a minor engagement. **affairs** *n.pl.* public or private business; finances. **affair of honor,** a duel [L. *ad,* to; *facere,* to do].
af·fect (ạ·fekt′) *v.t.* to act upon; to produce a change in; to put on a pretense of; to influence. **-ed** *a.* inclined or disposed; not natural. **-edly** *adv.* **-edness** *n.* **-ing** *a.* moving; pathetic. **-ingly** *adv.* **-ation** *n.* a striving after artificial appearance or manners. **affective** *a.* **affectively** *adv.* [L. *affectare,* to apply onself to].
af·fec·tion (ạ·fek′·shạn) *n.* disposition of mind; good-will; tender attachment; disease. **-ate** *a.* loving. **-ately** *adv.* [L. *affectare,* to apply oneself to].
af·fer·ent (af′·ẹr·ạnt) *a.* conveying to, esp. of nerves carrying sensations to the centers [L. *ad,* to; *ferre,* to carry].
af·fi·ance (ạ·fī′·ạns) *n.* plighted faith; betrothal; the marriage contract; reliance; confidence; *v.t.* to betroth [O.Fr. *afiance,* trust].
af·fi·da·vit (af·i·dā′·vit) *n.* (*Law*) a written statement of evidence on oath [L.L. = he pledged his faith, from L. *ad,* to; *fides,* faith].
af·fil·i·ate (ạ·fil′·i·āt) *v.t.* to adopt as a son; to receive into fellowship; to unite a society, firm, or political party with another, but without loss of identity. **affiliation** *n.* act of being affiliated; relationship. (ạ·fil′·i·ạt) *n.* one who affiliates [L. *ad,* to; *filius,* a son].
af·fin·i·ty (ạ·fin′·i·ti·) *n.* relationship by marriage; close agreement; resemblance; attraction; similarity. **affined** (ạ·fīnd′) *a.* **affinitive** *a.* closely related [L. *affinis,* related].
af·firm (ạ·furm′) *v.t.* to assert positively; to confirm; to aver; to strengthen; to ratify a judgment; *v.i.* (*Law*) to make a solemn promise to tell the truth without oath; to ratify a law. **-able** *a.* **-ably** *adv.* **-ance** *n.* **-ant, -er** *n.* **-ative** *a.* ratifying; *n.* positive; speaking in favor of a motion or subject of debate. **in the affirmative,** yes. **-atively** *adv.* [L. *affirmare,* to assert].
af·fix (ạ·fiks′) *v.t.* to fasten to; to attach; to append to. **affix** (a′·fiks) *n.* addition to either end of word to modify meaning or use (includes *prefix* and *suffix*) [L. *affigere*].
af·la·tus (ạ·flā′·tạs) *n.* inspiration; impelling inner force [L. a blast].
af·flict (a·flikt′) *v.t.* to give continued pain to; to cause distress or grief to. **-ed** *a.* distressed in mind; diseased. **-ing** *a.* distressing. **-ingly** *adv.* **-ion** *n.* a cause of continued pain of body or mind. **-ive** *a.* causing distress. **-ively** *adv.* [L. *affligere*].
af·flu·ence (af′·lòò·ạns) *n.* abundance, esp. riches. **affluent** *a.* wealthy; flowing to; *n.*

tributary of river. **affluently** *adv.* **afflux, affluxion** *n.* flowing to; that which flows to [L. *ad,* towards; *fluere,* to flow].

af·ford (ą·fōrd′) *v.t.* to yield, supply, or produce; to be able to bear expense [O.E. *geforthian,* to further].

af·for·est (ą·får′·est) *v.t.* to plant trees on a big scale. **-ation** *n.* [fr. *forest*].

af·fran·chise (ą·fran′·chīz) *v.t.* to enfranchise; to free from slavery; to liberate. **-ment** *n.* [Fr. *affranchir,* to make free].

af·fray (ą·frā′) *n.* a noisy quarrel or fight in public; *v.t.* to frighten; to startle [Fr. *effrayer,* to frighten].

af·fright, af·fright·en (ą·frīt′, -ąn) *v.t.* to impress with sudden and lively fear [O.E. *afyrhtan,* to terrify].

af·front (ą·frunt′) *v.t.* to confront; to meet face to face; to insult one to the face; to abash. **-ed** *a.* [L. *ad,* to; *frons, frontis,* forehead].

a·field (ą·fēld′) *adv.* to or in the field; abroad; off the beaten track; astray [E.].

a·fire (a·fīr′) *adv., a.* on fire.

a·flame (ą·flām′) *adv., a.* flaming; on fire; glowing; ablaze [E.].

a·float (ą·flōt′) *adv., a.* borne on the water; not aground or anchored.

a·flut·ter (ą·flut′·ęr) *a.* fluttering

a·foot (ą·foot′) *adv.* on foot; astir [E.].

a·fore (ą·fōr′) *adv., prep.* before. **-hand** *adv.* beforehand; before; *a.* provided; prepared. **-mentioned** *a.* spoken of, or named before. **-said** *a.* said or mentioned before. **-thought** *a.* thought of beforehand; premeditated. **-time** *adv.* in times past; at a former time; previously [O.E. *on foran,* in front].

a·foul (ą·foul′) *adv.* in collision, in a tangle.

a·fraid (ą·frād′) *a.* filled with fear; frightened [orig. *affrayed*].

a·fresh (ą·fresh′) *adv.* anew; over again.

aft (aft) *adv., a.* (*Naut.*) toward, or at, the stern. **fore and aft,** lengthwise [O.E. *afta,* behind].

af·ter (af′·tąr) *prep.* behind; later; in pursuit of; in imitation of; according to; *adv.* behind; *a.* in the rear; succeeding. **-birth** *n.* (*Med.*) the placenta, etc. expelled from uterus after childbirth. **-crop** *n.* a later crop in same year from same soil. **-damp** *n.* a gas formed in a mine after an explosion of fire-damp; choke-damp. **-deck** *n.* weather deck aft of midship house. **-effect** *n.* a secondary result, an effect coming after. **-glow** *n.* a glow in the sky after sunset. **-math** *n.* result; consequence. **-most** *a.* hindmost; nearest to stern. **-noon** *n.* time from noon to evening. **-pains** *n.pl.* pains succeeding childbirth. **-thought** *n.* reflection after an act; an idea occurring later. **-ward(s)** *adv.* later; subsequently [O.E. *aefter,* farther away].

a·gain (ą·gen′) *adv.* another time; once more; in return; moreover [O.E. *ongean*].

a·gainst (ą·genst′) *prep.* in contact with; opposite to; in opposition to; in preparation for; in exchange for [fr. *again*].

a·gape (ą·gāp′) *a., adv.* open-mouthed, as in wonder, expectation, etc.; gaping.

ag·ate (ag′·it) *n.* a precious stone, composed of layers of quartz of different colors [Gk. *Achatēs*].

age (āj) *n.* the length of time a person or thing has existed; a period of time; periods of history; maturity; (*Colloq.*) a long time; *v.t.* to cause to grow old; *v.i.* to grow old. *pr.p.* **aging. -d** *a.* of the age of. **aged** (āj′·ed) *a.* **-less** *a.* **-long** *a.* **to come of —,** to attain one's 21st birthday [Fr. *âge,* fr. L. *aetas,* age].

age·ism (āj′·izm) *n.* the discrimination on the basis of (old) age. **ageist** *a., n.*

a·gen·cy (ā′·jen·si·) *n.* instrumentality; a mode of exerting power; office or duties of an agent [L. *agere,* to do].

a·gen·da (ą·jen′dą) *n.* literally, things to be done; the items of business to be discussed at a meeting [L. *pl.* of *agendum*].

a·gent (ā′·jent) *n.* a person or thing that exerts power or has the power to act; one entrusted with the business of another; a deputy or substitute [L. *agere,* to do].

ag·glom·er·ate (ą·glåm′·ą·rāt) *v.t., v.i.* to collect into a mass; *a.* heaped up; *n.* (*Geol.*) a mass of compacted volcanic debris. **agglomeration** *n.* **agglomerative** *a.* [L. *ad,* to; *glomus,* mass or ball].

ag·glu·ti·nate (ą·glòò′·ti·nāt) *v.t.* to unite with glue; *a.* united, as with glue. **agglutination** *n.* **agglutinative** *a.* having a tendency to cause adhesion; (*Philol.*) applied to languages which are non-inflectional [L. *ad,* to; *gluten,* glue].

ag·gran·dize (ą·gran′·dīz) *v.t.* to make greater in size, power, rank, wealth, etc.; to promote; to increase; to exalt. **aggrandizement** *n.* [L. *ad,* to; *grandis,* great].

ag·gra·vate (ag′·rą·vāt) *v.t.* to make more grave, worse; (*Colloq.*) to irritate. **aggravating** *a.* making worse; provoking. **aggravatingly** *adv.* **aggravation** *n.* [L. *aggravare,* to make heavier].

ag·gre·gate (ag′·rą·gāt) *v.t.* to collect into a total; to accumulate into a heap; (ag′·rą·git) *n.* a sum or assemblage of particulars; the sum total; *a.* collected together. **aggregation** *n.* the act of aggregating; a combined whole. **aggregative** *a.* collective; accumulative [L. *aggregare,* to form into a flock, fr. *grex, gregis,* a flock].

ag·gress (ą·gres′) *v.i.* to attack; to start a quarrel. **-ion** *n.* a first act of hostility; an unprovoked attack. **-ive** *a.* **-ively** *adv.* **-iveness** *n.* **-or** *n.* the one who first attacks [L. *aggredi,* to attack].

ag·grieve (ą·grēv′) *v.t.* to give pain or sorrow to; to bear heavily upon; to vex; to afflict. **-d** *a.* [L. *aggravare,* to make heavier].

a·ghast (ą·gast′) *a.* struck with amazement, horror, terror; transfixed with fright [earlier *agast,* fr. O.E. *gaestan,* to terrify].

ag·ile (aj′·il) *a.* having the power of quick motion; nimble. **-ly** *adv.* **-ness, agility** *n.* [L. *agilis,* fr. *agere,* to do].

ag·i·tate (aj′·i·tāt) *v.t.* to throw into violent motion; to stir up; to disturb, excite, upset; to debate earnestly; *v.i.* to cause a disturbance. **agitatedly** *adv.* **agitation** *n.* violent and irregular motion; perturbation; inciting to public disturbance. **agitator** *n.* [L. *agitare,* to keep in motion].

a·gleam (ą·glēm′) *adv., a.* gleaming.

a·glow (ą·glō′) *adv., a.* glowing.

AGM (ā·jē·em′) *n.* air-to-ground missile.

ag·nate (ag′·nāt) *n.* any male relation on the father's side. *a.* related on the father's side; akin; allied. **agnatic** *a.* **agnation** *n.* [L. *ad,* to; *natus,* born].

ag·no·men (ag·nō′·mąn) *n.* an additional name given by the Romans, generally because of some famous exploit, as Alexander the Great [L. *ad,* to; *nomen,* name].

ag·nos·tic (ąg·nås′tik) *n.* one who believes that God, life hereafter, etc., can neither be proved nor disproved; *a.* pert. to agnosticism. **-ism** *n.* [Gk. *a-,* neg.; *gnostikos,* knowing].

ago (ą·gō′), **a·gone** (ą·gawn′) *adv., a.* past; gone; in time past [O.E. *agan,* to pass away].

a·gog (ą·gåg′) *a., adv.* eagerly excited; expectantly [Fr. *en gogues,* in a merry mood].

a·gon·ic (ą·gån′·ik) *a.* not forming an angle [Gk. *a-,* neg.; *gonia,* an angle].

ag·o·ny (ag′·ą·ni·) *n.* extreme physical or mental pain; the death struggle; throes; pang. **agonize** *v.t.* to distress with great pain; to torture. *v.i.* to writhe in torment. **agonizing** *a.* **agonizingly** *adv.* **— column,** section of newspaper containing advertisements for lost relatives, personal messages, etc. [Gk. *agon,* a contest].

ag·o·ra (ag′·ą·rą) *n.* forum, public square, or market of ancient Greek towns. **-phobia** *n.*

fear of open spaces [Gk. *agora*, a market place; *phobia*, fear].

a·gou·ti (ạ·go͝o'·ti·) *n.* a genus of rodents or gnawing animals, natives of S. America, allied to the guinea-pig [Native].

a·grar·i·an (ạ·grar'·i·ạn) *a.* relating to lands, their management and distribution; (*Bot.*) growing in a field. *n.* one who favors an equal division of property. **-ize** *v.t.* **-ism** *n.* an equal division of land or property [L. *ager*, a field].

a·gree (ạ·grē') *v.i.* to be of one mind; to acquiesce; to resemble; (*Gram.*) to correspond in gender, case, or number. *pr.p.* **-ing.** *pa.p.* **-d. -able** *a.* consenting; favorable; suitable; pleasant; congenial. **-ably** *adv.* **-ableness** *n.* **-ment** *n.* agreeing; bargain; a written statement accepting certain conditions [L. *ad*, to; *gratus*, pleasing].

ag·ri·cul·ture (ag'·ri·kul·chẹr) *n.* the science and practice of the cultivation of the soil. **agricultural** *a.* **agriculturist** or **agriculturalist** *n.* one skilled in agriculture; a farmer [L. *ager*, a field; *colere, cultum*, to till].

a·gron·o·my (a·grȧn'·ạ·mi·) *n.* rural economy; husbandry. **agronomial, agronomic, agronomical** *a.* **agronomics** *n.pl.* the science of management of farms. **agronomist** *n.* [Gk. *agros*, field; *nemein*, to deal out].

a·ground (ạ·ground') *adv.* and *a.* on the ground; stranded; run ashore; beached.

a·gue (ā'·gū) *n.* (*Med.*) intermittent malarial fever, marked by fits of shivering, burning, sweating. **agued, aguish** *a.* [L. *acuta febris*, acute fever].

a·head (ạ·hed') *adv.* farther forward; in advance; in front; head foremost [E.].

a·hoy (ạ·hoi') *interj.* used in hailing, as in *ship ahoy* [form of *interj. hoy*].

aid (ād) *v.t.* and *v.i.* to help; to relieve. *n.* help; assistance; the person or thing which aids; auxiliary; assistant. **aide** *n.* [Fr. *aider*].

aide-de-camp (ād·de·kamp') *n.* an officer attached to the personal staff of a general to assist him in his military routine. *pl.* **aides-de-camp** [Fr.].

AIDS (ādz') *n.* acquired immune deficiency syndrome.

ai·grette (ā'·gret) *n.* a tuft or spray, as of feathers, diamonds, etc.; the small white heron; an egret [Fr.].

ai·guille (ā·gwēl') *n.* (*Geol.*) a sharp, slender rock; a drill for boring rock. **aiguillette, aiguillet** (ā·gwē·let') *n.* the tag of a shoe-lace; *pl.* ornamental spangles of a dancer's dress [Fr. = a needle].

ail (āl) *v.t.* to trouble; disturb; to pain; afflict. *v.i.* to feel pain; to be ill. **-ing** *a.* **-ment** *n.* illness. [O.E. *eglan*, to pain].

ai·le·ron (ā'·lạ·rȧn) *n.* adjustable flaps near the tips of the wings of an airplane for balance and lateral control [Fr.].

aim (ām) *v.t.* to point at; to direct; to endeavor after; to intend; *n.* direction; end; purpose; intention. **-less** *a.* without aim or purpose. **-lessly** *adv.* **-lessness** *n.* [O.Fr. *esmer*, esteem].

ain't (ānt) (*Colloq.*) contracted form of *am not*, extended to *is not*, or *are not*.

air (ār) *n.* the atmosphere; a gas; a light breeze; a tune; manner, bearing of a person; carriage; appearance; mien. *v.t.* to expose to air or heat, for drying or warming; to parade before the public. **airs** *n.pl.* an affected manner. **-ing** *n.* a ride or walk in the open air. **-y** *a.* of air; exposed to the air; light-hearted. **-ily** *adv.* gaily; merrily; lightly. **-iness** *n.* openness to the air; gaiety. **air base** *n.* a place for housing, or directing operations of, aircraft. **airborne** *a.* carried by aircraft; supported by the air (of aircraft). **air brake** *n.* brake worked by compressed air. **air condenser** *n.* an electrical condenser insulated between the plates by air. **air-condition** *v.t.* to provide a building, etc. with air through a filtering apparatus. **air conditioning** *n.* **air cool** *v.t.* to cool by air, to air condition. **aircraft** *n.* all kinds of machines for flying. **aircraft carrier,** an armed vessel built to carry aircraft. **airdrome** *n.* an airport. **airfield** *n.* tract of land, used for accommodation and maintenance of aircraft. **airfoil** *n.* any surface wing, etc. to help in lifting or controlling an aircraft. **air force,** the whole of a nation's aircraft. **air gun** *n.* a gun discharged by elastic force of air. **air lift** *n.* large-scale transport operation by aircraft. **air line** *n.* a service of aircraft plying regularly; a telephone line above ground level. **air liner** *n.* a large passenger airplane flying on a definite route. **air load** *n.* cargo carried by aircraft. **air lock** *n.* the stoppage of the flow of liquid in a pipe caused by the presence of air; a small chamber to allow the passage of men or materials at the top of a caisson. **air mail** *n.* the transport of letters, parcels, etc., by airplane. **airman** *n.* an aviator. **air-minded** *adj.* interested in aviation; **airplane** *n.* a heavier than air aircraft. **airport** *n.* a terminal station for passenger airplanes. **air pressure** *n.* pressure of atmosphere. **air pump** *n.* a machine for exhausting the air from a closed vessel. **air raid** *n.* an attack by hostile aircraft. **air rifle** *n.* a rifled air gun. **air sacs** *n. pl.* air-cells in the bodies of birds. **air ship** *n.* lighter-than-air machine, developed from balloon. **airsick** *adj.* ill from air travel. **airstrip** *n.* concrete runway on an airfield. **airtight** *a.* admitting no air. **airway** *n.* a prepared route for travel by airplane; a ventilating passage [Gk. *aēr*, air].

aire·dale (ār'·dāl) *n.* a kind of large terrier, with a close, wiry coat of tan and black [originally fr. *Airedale*, Yorkshire].

aisle (īl) *n.* the wing of a building; any lateral division of a church; the passage-ways between rows [L. *ala*, a wing].

aitch·bone (āch'·bōn) *n.* the rump bone of an ox; the cut of beef surrounding it [L. *natis*, the rump; *E.* bone].

a·jar (ạ·jȧr') *adv.* partly open, as a door [M.E. *on char*, on the turn].

a·kim·bo (ạ·kim'·bō) *adv.* with a crook; bent. **with arms akimbo,** with hands on hips and elbows turned outward [M.E. *in kenebow*, into a crooked bend].

a·kin (ạ·kin') *a.* related by blood; allied by nature; having the same properties.

-al (ạl) a *suffix* to *n.* to form *a.*; or to form *n.* from *v.*

à la (ȧ·lȧ), according to [Fr.].

al·a·bas·ter (al'·ạ·bas·tẹr) *n.* gypsum; a semi-transparent kind of soft marble-like mineral; *a.* made of, or white as, alabaster. **alabastrian, alabastrine** *a.* [Gk. *alabastros*].

a·lack (ạ·lak') *interj.* (*Arch.*) an exclamation expressive of sorrow. **alack-a-day** (ạ·lak'·-ạ·dā) *interj.* an exclamation of regret [E.].

a·lac·ri·ty (ạ·lak'·ri·ti·) *n.* cheerful readiness; eagerness; briskness [L. *alacer*, brisk].

a·lar (ā'·lẹr) *a.* wing-like; pert. to wings; having wings [L. *ala*, a wing].

a·larm (ạ·lȧrm') *n.* sound giving notice of danger; a mechanical contrivance to rouse from sleep; a summons to arms; sudden fear or apprehension; dismay; trepidation. *v.t.* to fill with apprehension; to call to arms. **-ingly** *adv.* **-ist** *n.* one given to exciting alarm, esp. needlessly. **alarum** *n.* an old spelling of 'alarm' [O.Fr. *a l'arme*, to arms].

a·las (ạ·las') *interj.* an exclamation of sorrow, pity, etc. [O.Fr. *a las*, ah weary].

a·late (āl'·āt) *a.* having wings; winged. Also **-d** *a.* [L. *ala*, a wing].

alb (alb) *n.* a vestment of white linen, reaching to the feet, worn by R.C. clergy officiating at the Eucharist [L. *albus*, white].

al·ba·core (al'·bạ·kōr) *n.* tunny fish [Ar. *al*, the; *bukr*, a young camel].

al·ba·tross (al'·bạ·traws) *n.* a large web-footed sea-bird commonest in the South Seas [fr. obsolete *alcatras*, a frigate-bird].

al·be·it (awl·bē′·it) *conj.* although; even though; notwithstanding that [E. *al* = although, *be*, and *it*].

al·bi·no (al·bī′·nō) *n.* a person, or animal, with an abnormal whiteness of the skin and hair, and a pink color in the eyes. **albinism** *n.* [L. *albus*, white].

al·bum (al′·bạm) *n.* a book for autographs, photographs, stamps, etc.; a book of selections [L. *album*, a white tablet].

al·bu·men (al·bū′·mạn) *n.* white of egg; a similar substance found in the tissues of animals and plants. **albumin** *n.* any of a class of proteins, necessary for growth in the body. **albuminoid** *n.* a substance resembling albumen. **albuminous** *a.* [L. *albumen*, white of egg].

al·bur·num (al·bur′·nạm) *n.* sapwood, part of tree under bark and outside heart up which sap rises [L. *albus*, white].

al·che·my (al′·kạ·mi·) *n.* the forerunner of modern chemistry. Its chief aims were (*a*) transmuting the baser metals into gold, and (*b*) discovery of an elixir of life. **alchemic** *a.* **alchemist** *n.* [Ar. *al*, the; *kimia* fr. Gk. *chumeia*, alloying of metals].

al·co·hol (al′·kạ·hȧl) *n.* pure spirit; a liquid of strong pungent taste, the intoxicating element in fermented or distilled liquor. **-ism** *n.* a morbid condition caused by over-indulgence in alcoholic liquor. **-ic** *a.* pert. to alcohol; *n.* one addicted to the immoderate use of alcohol; a habitual drunkard. **absolute alcohol,** alcohol entirely free from water [Ar. *al-koh'l*, powder of antimony to stain the eyelids].

al·cove (al′·kōv) *n.* a recess in a room; a covered seat in a garden [Sp. *alcoba*].

al·de·hyde (al′·dạ·hīd) *n.* a liquid produced by the oxidation of alcohol [fr. letters of *al*cohol *dehyd*rogenatum, i.e. alcohol without hydrogen].

al·der (awl′·dẹr) *n.* a tree of birch family, growing in marshy soil [O.F. *alor*].

al·der·man (awl′·dẹr·mạn) *n.* a civic dignitary. *pl.* **aldermen** [O.E. *ealdorman*].

ale (āl) *n.* liquor made from malt by fermentation; a festivity (from the amount of ale drunk at it. **alehouse** *n.* a place where ale is sold [O.E. *ealu*].

a·lem·bic (ạ·lem′·bik) *n.* a vessel of glass or metal formerly used in distillation; (*Fig.*) a refining medium, as in the *alembic of the mind* [Ar. *al-ambig*, a cup].

a·lert (ạ·lurt′) *a.* watchful; vigilant; brisk; nimble; active; *n.* a signal by sirens of air attack; period of air-raid. **-ly** *adv.* **-ness** *n.* [It. *all' erta*, on the look-out].

al·ex·an·drine (al·eg·zan′·drin) *n.* a verse of six iambic feet, probably from O.Fr. poems dealing with Alexander the Great; found as ninth line of Spenserian Stanza.

a·lex·i·a (ạ·lek′·si·ạ) *n.* inability to understand written language.

al·fal·fa (al·fal′·fạ) *n.* plant of the pea family, valued as fodder [Sp. *alfalfa*, three-leaved grass].

al·fres·co (al·fres′·kō) *a.* and *adv.* in the fresh air, as an *alfresco meal* [It.].

al·ga (al·gạ) *n.* (Bot.) one of the **algae** (al′·jē) *pl.* plants found in sea-water, and in slow-moving fresh or stagnant water. **algal, algoid, algous** *a.* **algology** *n.* scientific study of marine plants [L. *alga*, seaweed].

al·ge·bra (al′·je·brạ) *n.* a branch of mathematics in which calculations are made by using letters to represent numbers or quantities and symbols to denote arithmetical operations of these numbers; a kind of abstract arithmetic used in almost all branches of science. **-ic(al)** (al·je·brā′·ik(ạl)) *a.* **-ically** *adv.* **-ist** *n.* [Ar. *al'jebr*, joining together of fragment].

al·gid (al′·jid) *a.* cold. **algid cholera** Asiatic cholera. **-ity, -ness** *n.* coldness. **algific** *a.* causing cold [L. *algere*, to be cold].

a·li·as (ā′·li·ạs) *adv.* otherwise; *n.* an assumed name [L. *alias*, at another time].

al·i·bi (al′·i·bī) *n.* (*Law*) a plea that the prisoner was elsewhere when the crime was committed; excuse [L. *alibi*, elsewhere].

al·ien (āl′·yạn) *a.* of another country; foreign; different in nature; estranged; *n.* a non-naturalized foreigner. **-able** *a.* (of property) capable of being sold or handed over. **-ability** *n.* **-ate** *v.t.* to transfer to another; estrange; **-ation** *n.* (*Med.*) insanity. **-ator** *n.* **-ism** *n.* study of mental diseases. **-ist** *n.* specialist in treatment of mental diseases; a psychiatrist [L. *alienus*, belonging to another].

a·lif·er·ous (al·if′·ẹr·ạs) *a.* having wings.

a·light (ạ·līt′) *adv.* or *a.* on fire; illuminated; kindled [O.E. *on; lēoht*, light].

a·light (ạ·līt′) *v.i.* to dismount; to finish one's journey; to fall; to descend. **-ing** *n.* [O.E. *alihtan*, to descend].

a·lign (ạ·līn′) *v.t.* to adjust by a line; to line up; to range; *v.i.* to form in a line; to fall in, as troops. Also **aline, -ment** *n.* [Fr. *aligner*, to put in line].

a·like (ạ·līk′) *a.* having likeness; similar; *adv.* similarly; equally [O.E. *gelic*, like].

al·i·ment (al′·i·mạnt) *n.* nourishment; nutriment; (*Law*) provision for maintenance. *v.t.* to maintain. **-al** *a.* **-ally** *adv.* **-ary** *a.* pert. to food; nutritive. **-ation** *n.* the process of introducing nutriment into the body. **-ary canal,** the large intestine [L. *alimentum*, nourishment].

al·i·mo·ny (al′·i·mō·ni·) *n.* means of living, esp. an allowance made to a wife out of her husband's income, after legal separation [L. *alimonia*, sustenance].

al·i·quant (a′·li·kwạnt) *a.* (of a number) not dividing without remainder [L. *aliquantus*, considerable].

al·i·quot (al′·i·kwạt) *a.* dividing exactly, or without remainder [L. *aliquot*, some].

a·live (ạ·līv′) *a.* having life; existent; active; alert; thronged with [O.E. *on life*, living].

al·ka·li (al′·kạ·lī) *n.* one of a class of chemical compounds which combine with acids to form salts—used with fats to form soap. **alkalify** (al′·kạ·li·fī), **alkalize** *v.t.* to render alkaline; *v.i.* to become alkaline; *pa.p.* **-fied. -fiable** *a.* capable of being converted into an alkali. **-metry** (al·kạ·lim′·ạ·tri·) *n.* the quantitative estimation of the strength of alkalis. **-ne** *a.* pert. to alkali; with qualities of alkali. **-nity** (al·kạ·lin′·i·ti·) *n.* **alkaloid** *n.* nitrogenous organic compound which acts chemically like an alkali; *a.* resembling an alkali in properties [Ar. *al*, the; *qaliy*, calcined ashes].

all (awl) *a.* the whole of; every one of; *n.* whole amount; whole duration of; *adv.* wholly; entirely. **all-American** *adj.* chosen best in U.S.; *n.* player so chosen. **all-around** *adj.* versatile, having many abilities. **all-fours** *n.* hands and feet. **all-hail!** *interj.* welcome! good health! **all-in** *a.* exhausted. **all out** *adj.* total. **all-powerful** *a.* omnipotent. **all but,** nearly; almost. **all in all,** in all respects [O.E. *all. eall*].

al·lay (ạ·lā′) *v.t.* to lighten; to make quiet; to lessen grief or pain. **-er** *n.* **-ment** *n.* [O.E. *alecgan*, to put down].

al·le·ga·tion (al·ạ·gā′·shạn) *n.* affirmation; that which is positively asserted; the act of alleging [L. *allegare*, to allege]. **allege** (ạ·lej′) *v.t.* to bring forward with positiveness; to plea, or excuse; to declare; affirm; cite. **allegeable** *a.* **allegedly** *adv.* [L. *allegare*, to allege].

al·le·giance (a·lē′·jạns) *n.* the duty of a subject to his government or superior; loyalty; an oath of homage. **allegiant** *a.* loyal; *n.* one who owes allegiance [fr. O.Fr. *ligeance*].

al·le·go·ry (al′·ạ·gō·ri·) *n.* a narrative in which abstract ideas are personified; a description to convey a different meaning from that which is expressed; a continued metaphor. **allegoric, (-al)** *a.* **allegorically** *adv.* **allegorize** *v.t.* to write in allegorical form; *v.i.* to use figurative language. **allegorist** *n.* [Gk. *allos*, other; *agoreuein*, to speak].

al·le·gret·to (al·ļa·gret′·tō) *a.* (*Mus.*) livelier than *andante* but not so quick as *allegro* [It. dim. of *allegro*, gay].

al·le·gro (ą·lā′·grō) *a.* (*Mus.*) brisk, gay, sprightly (movement). **allegro vivace** (vē-·vȧtch′·e), allegro in an even more spirited manner [It. *allegro*, gay].

al·le·lu·iah (al·ą·lòò′·yą) *interj.* hallelujah; *n.* song of praise to the Almighty [Heb.].

al·ler·gy (al′·ẹr·ji·) *n.* hyper-sensitivity to particular substances; susceptibility to ill-effects from eating some foods. **allergen** *n.* a substance which induces allergy. **allergic** *a.* [Gk. *allos*, other; *ergon*, work].

al·le·vi·ate (ą·lē′·vi·āt) *v.t.* to make light; to lighten; to ease; to afford relief; to mitigate. **alleviation** *n.* **alleviative** *a.* **alleviator** *n.* [L. *alleviare* fr. *levis*, light].

al·ley (al′·i·) *n.* a narrow passage between buildings; a garden path; a long, narrow passage for bowling. **alley-way** *n.* an alley [Fr. *aller*, to go].

al·li·ance (ą·lī′·ąns) *n.* persons, parties, or states allied together for a common purpose; union by marriage [Fr. *allier*].

al·li·ga·tor (al′·i·gā·tẹr) *n.* a reptile distinguished from crocodile by a broad flat head, depressed muzzle and unequal teeth [Sp. *el lagarto*, the lizard].

al·lit·er·ate (ą·lit′·ẹr·āt) *v.i.* to begin each word with the same letter or sound. **alliteration** *n.* recurrence of a letter or letters at the beginning of words in close succession; head rhyme. **alliterative** *adj.* [L. *ad*, to; *littera*, letter].

al·lo·cate (al′·ō·kāt) *v.t.* to distribute; to assign to each his share; to place. **allocation** *n.* **allocatur** *n.* (*Law*) a certificate that costs have been allowed [L. *ad*, to; *locus*, a place].

al·lo·cu·tion (al·ō·kū′·shąn) *n.* a formal address, esp. of the Pope to his clergy [L. *ad*, to; *locutio*, a speech].

al·lot (ą·lȧt′) *v.t.* to divide by lot; to distribute as shares. *pr.p* **-ting.** *pa.p.* and *pa.t.* **-ted. -ment** *n.* what is alloted; distribution; a share; a portion [L. *ad, to;* O.E. *hlot*, a share].

al·lot·ro·py (ą·lȧt′·rą·pi·) *n.* property of some chemical substances of being found in two or more different forms, e.g. coal, graphite, and diamond are all carbon. **allotropic** *a.* **allotropism** *n.* [Gk. *allos*, other; *tropos*, manner].

al·low (ą·lou′) *v.t.* to acknowledge; to permit; to give; to set apart; *v.i.* to provide. **-able** *a.* permissible; lawful; acceptable. **-ance** *n.* what is allowed; permission; a stated quantity to be added or deducted; a rebate; a grant. **-edly** *adv.* **to make allowance for,** to take into consideration [O.Fr. *allouer*].

al·loy (ą·loi′) *v.t.* to melt together two or more metals; to reduce the purity of a metal by mixing with a less valuable one; to debase. **alloy** (al′·oi, ą·loi′) *n.* any mixture of metals e.g. copper and zinc to form brass; a combination; an amalgam; (*Fig.*) evil mixed with good [L. *ad*, to; *ligare*, to join].

all right (awl rīt) satisfactory, yes, certainly.

all·spice (awl′·spīs) *n.* a spice [E. *all*, and *spice*].

al·lude (ą·lòòd′) *v.i.* to refer indirectly to; to hint at; to suggest; to mention lightly [L. *ad*, at; *ludere*, to play].

al·lure (ą·loor′) *v.t.* to tempt by a lure, offer, or promise. **-ment** *n.* that which allures. **alluring** *a.* enticing; attractive; fascinating. **alluringly** *adv.* [L. *ad*, to; Fr. *leurre*, bait].

al·lu·sion (ą·lòò′·zhun) *n.* a passing or indirect reference; a hint; a suggestion. **allusive** *a.* referring to indirectly; marked by allusions; symbolical. **allusively** *adv.* [fr. *allude*].

al·lu·vi·on (ą·lòò′·vi·ąn) *n.* land formed by washed-up earth and sand. **alluvium** *n.* water-borne matter deposited on low-lying lands. [L. *alluvio*, an overflowing].

al·ly (a·lī′) *v.t.* to join by treaty, marriage, or friendship; *pr.p.* **-ing;** *pa.p.* and *pa.t.* **allied. ally** (ą·lī′, or a′·lī) *n.* a person, family, country, etc., bound to another, esp. of nations in war-time; a partner. *pl.* **allies** (ą·līz′, or a′·līz) [L. *ad*, to; *ligare*, to bind].

al·ma ma·ter (al′·mą mȧ′·tẹr) *n.* college or school one attended [L. fostering mother].

al·ma·nac (awl′·mą·nak) *n.* a calendar of days, weeks and months, to which astronomical and other information is added [etym. uncertain].

al·might·y (awl·mīt′·i·) *a.* all-powerful; omnipotent. **The Almighty,** the Supreme Being; God; **almightiness** *n.* [O.E. *ealmihtig*].

al·mond (ȧ′·mąnd) *n.* the kernel of the nut of the almond-tree [Gk. *amugdalē*, an almond].

al·mon·er (ȧ′·, ȧl′·mąn·ẹr) *n.* one who distributes alms or bounty. **almonry** *n.* a place for distributing alms [O.Fr. *almosnier*].

al·most (awl′·mōst) *adv.* very nearly; all but [O.E. *eallmoest*].

alms (ȧmz) *n.* gift offered to relieve the poor; a charitable donation. **alms-house** *n.* a building, usually erected and endowed by private charity, for housing the aged poor [Gk. *eleēmosunē*, pity].

al·oe (al′·ō) *n.* a bitter plant used in medicine; a purgative drug, made from the juice of several species of aloe. **— wood** [Gk. *aloe*, a bitter herb].

a·loft (ą·lawft′) *adv.* on high; (*Naut.*) on the yards or rigging [O.N. *a lopt*, in the air].

a·lo·ha (ą·lō′·ą, ȧ·lō′·hȧ) *n.*, *interj.* greetings, farewell [Hawaiian].

a·lone (ą·lōn′) *a.* solitary; single; *adv.* by oneself; singly [E. *all* and *one*].

a·long (ą·lawng′) *adv.* in a line with; through out the length of; lengthwise; onward; in the company of (followed by *with*); *prep.* by the side of. **-side** *adv.* by the side of, esp. of a ship [O.E. *andlang*].

a·loof (ą·lòòf′) *a.* reserved in manner, almost unsociable; *adv.* at a distance; apart. **-ness** *n* [fr. Dut. *to loef*, to windward].

al·o·pe·ci·a (al·ą·pē′·shi·ą) *n.* disease causing loss of hair [Gk. *alopekia*, fox-mange].

a·loud (ą·loud′) *adv.* with a loud voice or noise; loudly; audibly [fr. E. *loud*].

alp (alp) *n.* a high mountain; mountain pasture-land. **Alps** *n.pl.* the mountains of Switzerland. **alpine** *a.* pert. to the Alps; *n.* a plant that grows on high ground. **alpinist** (al′·pin·ist) *n.* [L. *Alpes*].

al·pac·a (al·pak′·ą) *n.* a sheeplike animal of Peru; a species of llama; a thin kind of cloth made of the wool of the alpaca [Sp.].

al·pen·horn, alp·horn (al′·pen·hawrn, alp′·hawrn) *n.* a long wooden horn curving towards a wide mouth-piece, used by Swiss herds. **alpenstock** *n.* a long, stout staff, shod with iron, used by mountaineers [Ger.=horn (stick) of the Alps].

al·pha (al′·fą) *n.* the first letter of Greek alphabet. **alpha and omega,** the first and the last. **alpha particle,** a helium nucleus travelling at high speed, given out when atoms of Uranium, Radium, etc., undergo radioactive breakdown. **alpha rays,** streams of alpha particles [Gk.].

al·pha·bet (al′·fą·bet) *n.* letters of a language arranged in order; first principles. **-ic, -al** *a.* **-ically** *adv.* **-ize** *v.* [Gk. *alpha*, *beta*, the first two Greek letters].

al·read·y (awl·red′·i·) *adv.* before this; even now; even then; previously to the time specified [E. *all ready*, prepared].

al·so (awl′·sō) *adv.* and *conj.* in like manner; likewise; further.

al·tar (awl′·tẹr) *n.* a table or raised structure in a place of worship, on which gifts and sacrifices are offered to a deity; the communion table [L. *altare*].

al·ter (awl′·tẹr) *v.t.* to change; *v.i.* to become different. **-ably** *adv.* **-ability** *n.* **-ation** *n.* the act of altering; change; modification [L. *alter,* other].

al·ter·cate (awl′·tẹr·kāt) *v.i.* to contend in words; to wrangle. **altercation** *n.* a dispute; a controversy [L. *altercari,* to wrangle].

al·ter·nate (awl·tẹr′·nit) *a.* occuring by turns; one following the other in succession. **-ly** *adv.* by turns. **alternate** (awl′·tẹr·nāt) *v.t.* to cause to follow by turns; *v.i.* to happen by turns. **alternation** *n.* **alternative** *a.* offering a choice of two things; *n.* a choice of two things. **alternatively** *adv.* **alternator** *n.* (*Elect.*) a dynamo for producing alternating current. **alternating current** (*Elect.*) a current which reverses its direction of flow at fixed periods. *Abbrev.* **A.C.** [L. *alternare,* fr. *alter,* other].

al·though (awl·THō′) *conj.* admitting that; notwithstanding that [E. *all* and *though*].

al·tim·e·ter (al·tim′·ạ·tẹr) *n.* an instrument for taking altitudes; in aviation, barometer to show height [L. *altus,* high; Gk. *metron,* a measure].

al·ti·tude (al′·ti·tūd) *n.* height; perpendicular elevation above a given level [L. *altitudo*].

al·to (al′·tō) *n.* (*Mus.*) part once sung by highest male voice or counter-tenor, now sung by lowest female voice; singer with voice higher than tenor, lower than soprano; contralto [L. *altus,* high].

al·to·geth·er (awl·tạ·geTH′·ẹr) *adv.* wholly, entirely, quite; on the whole [E.].

al·tru·ism (al′·trŏŏ·izm) *n.* the principle of living for the good of others (opp. to *egoism*). **altruist** *n.* **altruistic** *a.* unselfish. **altruistically** *adv.* [L. *alter,* another].

al·um (al′·ạm) *n.* a double sulphate of alumina and potash; a mineral salt used as a styptic, astringent, etc., as a mordant in dyeing, and in tanning [L. *alumen*].

a·lu·mi·num (ạ·lòò′·mi·nạm) *n.* a whitish metal produced largely from bauxite; it is strong, light, malleable. **alumina, alumine** *n.* an oxide of aluminum; the clay, loam, etc., from which alum is obtained. **aluminate** *v.t.* to impregnate with alum. **aluminic** *a.* **aluminiferous** *a.* containing alum or alumina. **aluminite** *n.* a sulphate of alumina [L. *alumen,* alum].

a·lum·nus (ạ·lum′·nus) *n.* (*fem.* **alumna,** *pl.* **alumnae**) a graduate or former student of a school, college, or university. *pl.* **alumni** [L. *alumnus,* foster-child].

al·ve·o·lar (al·vē′·ō·lẹr) *a.* pert. to or resembling the sockets of the teeth. **alveolate** *a.* pitted; honeycombed. **alveolus** *n.* (*pl.* **alveoli**) a tooth socket; a cell in a honeycomb [L. *alveolus,* a small cavity].

al·ways (awl′·wāz) *adv.* at all times; perpetually; invariably; regularly [O.E. *ealne weg,* the whole way].

a·lys·sum (a′·li·sạm) *n.* a species of rock plant with white or yellow flowers; madwort [Gk. *alussos,* curing madness].

am (am) the *first person sing. pres. indic.* of the verb **to be.**

a. m. (ā em) before noon [L. *ante meridiem*].

a·mah (à′·mạ) *n.* a nurse, in the Orient [Port. *ama*].

a·main (ạ·mān′) *adv.* (*Arch.*) with all strength or force [E. *on; main,* strength].

a·mal·gam (ạ·mal′·gạm) *n.* a compound of mercury with another metal; a mixture of different substances. **-ate** *v.t.* to mix a metal with quicksilver; to compound; to consolidate; to combine (esp. of business firms); *v.i.* to coalesce; to blend; to fuse. **-ation** *n.* the act or results of amalgamating. **-ative** *a.* **-ator** *n.* [Gk. *malagma,* an emollient].

a·man·u·en·sis (ạ·man·ū·en′·sis) *n.* one who writes what another dictates, or copies what another has written; a secretary. *pl.* **amanuenses** [L. *ab,* from; *manus,* hand].

am·a·ranth (am′·ạ·ranth) *n.* an imaginary purple flower which never fades; 'love-lies-bleeding'; a purplish color; also a real flower. **amaranthine** *a.* never-fading; purplish [Gk. *amaranthos,* never-fading].

am·a·ryl·lis (a′·mạ·ril·ạs) *n.* a plant, the belladonna lily [Gk.].

a·mass (ạ·mas′) *v.t.* to heap up; to collect; accumulate [L. *ad,* to; *massa,* a lump].

am·a·teur (am′·ạ·tẹr) *n.* one who cultivates any study, art, or sport for the love of it, and not for money; *a.* like an amateur. **amateurish** *a.* unskilled; clumsy. **amateurism, amateurishness** *n.* [L. *amare,* to love].

am·a·tive (am′·ạ·tiv) *a.* pert. to love; amorous [L. *amare,* to love].

am·a·tol (am′·ạ·tȧl) *n.* explosive of ammonium nitrate of trinitrotoluene (**T.N.T.**) [name from parts of names of ingredients].

am·a·to·ry (am′·ạ·tōr·i·) *a.* pert. to or causing love. **amatorial** *a.* amorous; affectionate. **amatorially** *adv.* [L. *amare,* to love].

a·maze (ạ·māz′) *v.t.* to fill with astonishment or wonder; to confound; to perplex. **-dly** (ạ·māz·ạd·li′) *adv.* **-ment** *n.* astonishment, surprise. **amazing** *a.* causing amazement, wonder, or surprise. **amazingly** *adv.* [O.E. *amasian,* to confound].

Am·a·zon (am′·ạz·ȧn) *n.* one of a mythical race of female warriors of Scythia; a masculine woman. **Amazonian** *a* [Gk. *a-,* neg. and *mazos,* breast].

am·bages (am′·bājz) *n.pl.* circumlocution; subterfuge; evasion; used in *pl.* [L. *ambages,* a winding].

am·bas·sa·dor (am·bas′·ạ·dẹr) *n.* an envoy of highest rank sent to a foreign country; (*Fig.*) an intermediary; a messenger. **ambassadress** *n. fem.* **ambassadorial** *a.* **-ship** *n.* [L. *ambactus,* vassal].

am·ber (am′·bẹr) *n.* a yellowish, brittle fossil resin of vegetable origin, used in making jewelry, etc.; *a.* of or like, amber [Ar. *anbar,* ambergris].

am·ber·gris (am′·bẹr·grēs) *n.* a fragrant, ash-colored. waxy substance, derived from a biliary secretion of the spermaceti whale [Fr. *ambre gris,* grey amber].

am·bi·dex·ter (am·bi·leks′·tẹr) *n.* one able to use either hand with equal dexterity; a double-dealer. **ambidexterity** *n.* **ambidextrous** *a.* able to use either hand equally skilfully. **ambidextrously** *adv.* [L. *ambo,* both; *dexter,* right hand].

am·bi·ent (am′·bi·ạnt) *a.* encompassing on all sides [L. *ambire,* to go round].

am·bi·gu·i·ty (am·bi·gū′·i·ti·) *n.* any statement that may be interpreted in more than one way. **ambiguous** *a.* doubtful or uncertain; equivocal; susceptible of two or more meanings. **ambiguously** *adv.* **ambiguousness** *n.* [L. *ambigere,* to waver].

am·bit (am′·bit) *n.* circuit or compass; sphere of action; scope [L. *ambire,* to go round].

am·bi·tion (am·bish′·ạn) *n.* an eager desire for the attainment of honor, fame, or power; aim; aspiration. **ambitious** *a.* ardently desirous of acquiring power, rank, office, etc. **ambitiously** *adv.* [L. *ambitio,* going about for votes].

am·biv·a·lence, am·biv·a·len·cy (am·biv′·ạ·lạns, -i·) *n.* in psychoanalysis, the simultaneous operation in the mind of two conflicting wishes. **ambivalent** *a.* [L. *ambo,* both; *valere,* to be strong].

am·ble (am′·bl) *v.i.* to move along easily and gently; *n.* a peculiar gait of a horse; a stroll. **ambler** *n.* **ambling** *a.* **amblingly** *adv.* [L. *ambulare,* to walk].

am·bro·sia (am·brō′·si·ạ) *n.* (*Myth.*) the food of the Ancient Greek gods which conferred immortality; an exquisite dish. **ambrosial** *a.* [Gk. *a-*, neg.; *brotos*, mortal].

am·bu·lance (am′·bū·lạns) *n.* a covered vehicle for the transport of the injured or sick; a hospital unit in the field [Fr. *ambulance*].

am·bu·lant (am′·bū·lạnt) *a.* walking. **ambulate** *v.i.* to walk backwards and forwards. **ambulation** *n.* walking. **ambulatory** *a.* having power of walking; used for walking; moving from place to place; *n.* a cloister for walking exercise [L. *ambulare*, to walk].

am·bush (am′·boosh) same as **ambuscade** (am·bạs·kād′) *n.* a surprise attack; the place of ambush; the force concealed; *v.i.* to lie in wait; *v.t.* to attack from a concealed position [L. *in*; Late L. *boscus*, a wood].

a·me·ba. See **amoeba.**

a·mel·io·rate (ạ·mēl′·yẹr·āt) *v.t., v.t.* to make better; to improve. **amelioration** *n.* **ameliorative** *a.* [L. *ad*, to; *melior*, better].

A·men (ā·men′, ȧ′·men) *adv., interj.* so be it; truly; verily (uttered at the end of a prayer) [Heb. = certainly].

a·me·na·ble (ạ·mē′·nạ·bl, ạ·men′·ạ·bl) *a.* liable to be brought to account; easily led; willing to yield or obey. **amenability, -ness** *n.* the state of being amenable. **amenably** *adv.* [Fr. *amener*, to lead near].

a·mend (ạ·mend′) *v.t.* to change for the better; to improve; to alter in detail as a law, etc.; *v.i.* to grow better. **-able** *a.* **-atory** *a.* **-ment** *n.* the act of amending; a change for the better. **amends** *n.pl.* reparation for loss or injury; compensation [L. *emendare*, to remove a fault].

a·men·i·ty (ạ·men′·i·ti·) *n.* pleasantness, as in climate, manners, or disposition. **amenities** *n.pl.* pleasant ways or manners; agreeable surroundings [L. *amoenus*, agreeable].

A·mer·i·can (a·mer′·i·kạn) *n.* in, of, or characteristic of the United States or America. *n.* a native, citizen, or resident of America or the United States. **-a** *n.pl.* collection of facts, books, data pert. to America. **-ism** *n.* **-ize** *v.t., v.i.* **-ization** *n.* [fr. *Amerigo* Vespucci, Italian navigator].

am·er·i·ci·um (am.ẹr.ish′.i.ạm) *n.* a radioactive metallic element (*abbrev.* **Am**) [fr. *America*].

Am·er·ind (am′·ẹr·ind) *n., a.* American Indian or Eskimo. **-ian** *a., n.* **-ic** *a.* [fr. *American Indian*].

am·e·thyst (am′·ạ·thist) *n.* a kind of quartz; violet, purple, or blue color [Gk. *a-*, neg.; *methein*, to be drunken].

a·mi·a·ble (ā′·mi·ạ·bl) *a.* worthy of love or affection; sweet-tempered. **amiably** *adv.* **amiability, -ness** *n.* [L. *amicabilis*, friendly].

am·i·ca·ble (am′·i·kạ·bl) *a.* friendly; peaceable. **amicably** *adv.* **amicability, -ness** *n.* [L. *amicabilis*, friendly].

a·mid (ạ·mid′), **a·midst** (ạ·midst′) *prep.* in the middle of; among [O.E. *on middan*].

am·i·no ac·ids (ạ·mē′·nō as′·idz) *n.pl.* a group of nitrogenous organic compounds, basic constituents of proteins.

a·miss (ạ·mis′) *a.* wrong; faulty; improper; *adv.* in a faulty manner [fr. *miss*, a failure].

am·i·ty (am′·i·ti·) *n.* friendship [Fr. *ami*, a friend, fr. L. *amicus*].

am·me·ter (am′·mē·tẹr) *n.* an instrument used to measure the strength of an electric current in amperes [fr. *ampere;* Gk. *metron*, a measure].

am·mo (am′·ō) *n.* (*Army Slang*) ammunition.

am·mo·ni·a (a·mō·ni·a) *n.* a pungent, alkaline gas, very soluble in water; a solution of this gas in water, for household use. **ammoniac(al)** *a.* **ammoniated** *a.* combined with, containing, ammonia. **ammonium** *n.* hypothetical base of ammonia [Fr. *sal ammoniac*].

am·mu·ni·tion (am.ū.nish′.ạn) *n.* military projectiles and missiles of all kinds; originally, military stores; *a.* [O.Fr. *l'amunition*, for *la munition*].

am·ne·sia (am·nē′·zhi·ạ) *n.* memory loss [Gk.]

am·nes·ty (am′·nes·ti·) *n.* an act of oblivion; a general pardon of political offenders [Gk. *amnesia*, a forgetting].

am·ni·o·cen·te·sis (am·ni·ō·sen·tē′·sis) *n.* the extraction of a sample of fluid from the uterus to diagnose genetic defects, diseases, and the sex of the fetus [N.L., fr. *amnion*, a membrane; Gk. *kentein*, to puncture].

a·moe·ba (ạ·mē′·bạ) *n.* a minute animalcule of the simplest structure constantly changing in shape. *pl.* **-e, -s** [Gk. *amoibē*, change].

a·mok (ạ·mȧk′). See **amuck.**

a·mong (ạ·mung′), **a·mongst** (ạ·mungst′) *prep.* mixed with; making part of; amidst [M.E. *amonge*].

a·mor·al (ā·mȧr′ạl) *a.* non-moral; heedless of morals [Gk. *a-*, neg.; and E. *moral*].

am·o·rous (am′·ẹr·ạs) *a.* having a propensity for love and sexual enjoyment; in love; pert. to love. **-ly** *adv.* **-ness** *n.* [L. *amor*, love].

a·mor·phous (ạ·mawr′·fạs) *a.* without regular shape; shapeless; irregular; uncrystallized [Gk. *a-*, neg.; *morphe*, form].

a·mor·tize (am′·ẹr·tīz) *v.t.* to pay off a debt usually by periodic payments. **amortization** *n.*

a·mount (ạ·mount′) *v.i.* to rise to; to result in; to come to (in value or meaning); to be equal to; *n.* the sum total; the whole, or aggregate [O.Fr. *amonter*, to mount up].

am·pere (am′·pir) *n.* the unit of electric current (*abbrev.* **amp.**). **amperage** *n.* strength of electric current in amperes [named after André *Ampère*, a French physicist, 1775-1836].

am·per·sand (am′·per·sand) *n.* the name given to the sign & [fr. *and per se and*, i.e. 'and' by itself = 'and.'].

am·phet·a·mine (am·fet′·ạ·mēn) *n.* a drug used to relieve hay fever and head colds and to control weight gain and depression [I.S.V., *a*lpha; *m*ethyl; *ph*enyl; *et*hyl; *amine*].

Am·phib·i·a (am·fib′·i·ạ) *n.pl.* animals that can live either on land or in water, as frogs, toads, newts, etc. **amphibian** *n.* an animal of the class Amphibia; *a.* **amphibious** *a.* [Gk. *amphi*, on both sides; *bios*, life].

am·phi·the·a·ter (am′·fi·thē·ạ·tẹr) *n.* an edifice, having tiers of seats, encircling an arena, used for sports or spectacles; a rising gallery in a theater, concert-hall, etc. [Gk. *amphi*, on both sides; *theatron*, a theater].

am·pho·ra (am′·fạ·rạ) *n.* a two-handled earthenware vessel or jar, used by the ancient Greeks and Romans; 6 gallons [Gk. *amphi*, on both sides; *pherein*, to bear].

am·ple (am′·pl) *a.* of full dimensions; of adequate size; of sufficient quantity; abundant; copious. **amply** *adv.* **-ness** *n.* [L. *amplus*].

am·pli·fy (am′·pli·fī) *v.t.* to make larger; to extend; to enlarge; *v.i.* to dilate; to expatiate upon. **amplification** *n.* **amplifier** *n.* an apparatus which increases the volume of sound [L. *amplus*, large; *facere*, to make].

am·pli·tude (am′·pli·tūd) *n.* largeness; extent; abundance; (*Radio*) (of a wave) vertical distance between its highest and lowest levels; **— modulation (AM)** radio transmission by changing the amplitude of waves; (*Elect.*) maximum value of an alternating current [L. *amplus*, large].

am·poule (am′·pȯȯl) also **ampule** (am′·pūl) *n.* a small sealed glass container holding hypodermic dose [Fr.].

am·pul·la (am·pūl′·ạ) *n.* a sacred vessel for holding oil; cruet holding wine and water for Mass. *pl.* **-e** [L. *ampulla*].

am·pu·tate (am′·pū·tāt) *v.t.* to cut off, as a limb of the body, or a bough of a tree. **amputation** *n.* **amputee** *n.* one who has lost a limb through amputation [L. *amputare*, to cut off].

a·muck, a·mok (ạ·muk′, ạ·mȧk′) *adv.* to rush about frantically or murderously [Malay *amuq*, rushing in frenzy].

am·u·let (am′·yą·lit) *n.* a talisman; a charm; *a.* [Fr. *amulette,* fr. L. *amuletum*].

a·muse (ą·mūz′) *v.t.* to entertain agreeably; to occupy pleasantly; to divert. **-ment** *n.* anything which entertains or pleases; a pastime. **amusing** *a.* [Fr. *amuser,* to entertain].

an (an) *a.* the form of the indefinite article used before a vowel sound. See **a.** Also *Arch. conj.* if = a form of *and* [O.E. *an,* one].

an·a·bap·tist (an·ą·bap′·tist) *n.* one who denies the validity of infant baptism and advocates re-baptism of adults (by immersion) [Gk. *ana,* again; *baptizein,* to dip].

a·nab·a·sis (ą·nab′·ą·sis) *n.* a military expedition. *pl.* **anabases** [Gk.].

a·nab·o·lism (ąn·ab′·ąl·izm) *n.* (*Physiol.*) the constructive form of metabolism; the building-up of tissues by plant or animal which process alternates with the breaking down (katabolism) in the chemical routine [Gk. *ana,* up; *bole,* a throwing].

a·nach·ro·nism (ąn·ak′·rąn·izm) *n.* a chronological error; post- or ante-dating of an event or thing. **anachronistic** *a.* **anachronous** *a.* [Gk. *ana,* back; *chronos,* time].

an·a·con·da (an·ą·kȧn′·dą) *n.* a gigantic, non-venomous snake of tropical S. America.

a·nae·mia See **anemia.**

an·aes·the·sia, anesthesia See **anesthesia.**

an·a·glyph (an′·ą·glif) *n.* a figure or ornament cut in low relief; a cameo. **anaglyphic** *a.* [Gk. *ana,* up; *gluphein,* to engrave].

an·a·gram (an′·ą·gram) *n.* a transposition of the letters of a word or phrase to form a new word or phrase. **anagrammatic, -al** *a.* **anagrammatically** *adv.* **anagrammatize** *v.t.* to form anagrams. **anagrammatism** *n.* [Gk. *ana-,* again; *gramma,* letter].

a·nal (ā′·nąl) *a.* pert. to or near the anus.

an·a·lects, an·a·lec·ta (an′·ą·lekts, an·ą·lek′·tą) *n.pl.* an anthology of short literary fragments. **analectic** *a.* [Gk. *analektos,* choice].

an·a·lep·sis (an·ą·lep′·sis) *n.* (*Med.*) restoration of strength after disease. Also **analepsy. analeptic** *a.* [Gk. *ana,* up; *lēpsis,* a taking].

an·al·ge·sia (an·ąl·jē′·zi·ą) *n.* (*Med.*) absence of pain while retaining tactile sense; painlessness. **analgesic** *a.* insensible to or alleviating pain; *n.* a drug which relieves pain [Gk. *an-,* neg.; *algēsis,* pain].

a·nal·o·gy (ą·nal′·ą·ji·) *n.* resemblance in essentials between things or statements otherwise different; relationship; likeness; parallelism; correspondence. **analogic, -al** *a.* **analogically** *adv.* **analogize** *v.t.* to explain by analogy. **analogism** *n.* an argument proceeding from cause to effect; investigation by, or reasoning from, analogy. **analogist** *n.* **analogous** (ą·nal′·ą·gus) *a.* having analogy. **analogously** *adv.* **analogue** *n.* a word or thing resembling another [Gk. *analogia,* proportion].

a·nal·y·sis (ą·nal′·i·sis) *n.* the resolution, separating, or breaking up of anything into its constituent elements; a synopsis; (*Chem.*) determination of elements comprising a compound or mixture; (*Gram.*) logical arrangement of a sentence into its component parts; (*Math.*) theory of real and complex numbers. *pl.* **analyses. analyzable** *a.* **analyzation** *n.* **analyze** *v.t.* to take to pieces; to examine critically part by part. **analyst** *n.* one skilled in analysis; an analytical chemist. **analytic, -al** *a.* **analytically** *adv.* **analytics** *n.pl.* the technique of logical analysis [Gk. *ana,* up; *lusis,* a loosening].

an·a·pest, an·a·paest (an′·ą·pest) *n.* in prosody, a foot of three syllables, two short or unaccented followed by one long or accented syllable (⏑⏑—). **anapestic** *a.* [Gk. *anapaistos* reversed].

an·ar·chy (an′·ęr·ki·) *n.* want of government in society; lawless disorder in a country; a political theory, which would dispense with all laws, founding authority on the individual conscience. **anarchic, anarchically** *adv.* **anarchize** *v.t.* **anarchism** *n.* confusion, chaos. **anarchist** *n.* [Gk. *an-,* neg.; *archein,* to rule].

a·nath·e·ma (ą·nath′·ą·mą) *n.* the word used in the R.C. church as part of the formula in excommunication; something highly distasteful to one; accursed thing. **-tic** *a.* **-tization** *n.* **-ize** *v.t.* to pronounce a curse against; to excommunicate [Gk.].

a·nat·o·my (ą·nat′·ą·mi·) *n., pl.* **-mies,** art of dissecting an animal or a plant; study of form or structure of an animal; the body; a skeleton. **anatomic, -al** *a.* **anatomically** *adv.* **anatomize** *v.t.* to dissect; to lay open the interior structure for examining each part. **anatomist** *n.* [Gk. *ana,* up; *tome,* cutting].

an·ces·tor (an′·ses·tęr) *n.* (*fem.***ancestress**) forefather; progenitor; forebear. **ancestral** *a.* **ancestry** *n.* lineage [L. *ante,* before; *cedere, cessum,* to go].

an·chor (ang′·kęr) *n.* a heavy iron instrument by which a ship is held fast to the sea-bottom; a molder's chaplet; *v.t.* to place at anchor; to weight down; *v.i.* to cast anchor; to stop; **anchorage** *n.* a sheltered place where a ship may anchor; dues chargeable on ships which wish to anchor in harbor. **anchored** *a.* at anchor; firmly fixed. **to cast anchor,** to let down anchor. **to weigh anchor,** to raise anchor preparatory to sailing [L. *ancora*].

an·chor·ite, an·chor·et (ang′·kę·rīt, -ret) *n.* one who lives apart, renouncing the world for religious reasons; a hermit. **anchoress, anchoritess** *n.* a female hermit. **anchorage** *n.* home of anchorite [Gk. *anachorētēs,* one who retires].

an·cho·vy (an′·chō·vi·; an·chō′·vi·) *n.* small fish of the herring family [Sp. *anchova*].

an·cient (ān′·shąnt) *a.* very old; antique; venerable; former; *n.* an aged or venerable person; one who lived in olden times. **-ly** *adv.* **-ness** *n.* **-ry** *n.* ancestry; seniority [L. *ante,* before].

an·cil·lar·y (an′·sąl·er·i·) *a.* giving help to; attending upon; auxiliary; subordinate [L. *ancilla,* a maid-servant].

and (and) *conj.* added to; together with; a word that joins words, clauses, or sentences [O.E.].

an·dan·te (an·dan′·ti·, ȧn·dȧn′·ti·) *a.* or *adv.* (*Mus.*) moving rather slowly, but in a steady, flowing manner, faster than *larghetto,* but slower than *allegretto; n.* a moderately slow, flowing movement [It. *andare,* to go].

and·i·ron (and′·ī·ęrn) *n.* a utensil for supporting logs in a fireplace; a firedoy [O.Fr. *andier*].

an·dro·gen (an′·drą·jąn) *n.* male sex hormone [Gk. *andros* man, and *gen*].

an·drog·y·nous (an·drȧj′·i·nus) *a.* having the characteristics of both sexes; hermaphrodite. Also **androgynal. androgyny** *n.* [Gk. *aner, andros,* a man; *kephale,* the head; *gune,* a woman].

an·ec·dote (an′·ik·dōt) *n.* a biographical incident; a brief account of any fact or happening (often amusing); **anecdotage** *n.* anecdotes collectively. **anecdotal** *a.* **anecdotist** *n.* a writer or teller of anecdotes [Gk. *anekdotos,* not published].

an·e·lec·tric (an·i·lek′·trik) *a.* non-electric; *n.* a body that does not become electric; a conductor of electricity [Gk. *an-,* neg., and *electric*].

a·ne·mi·a (a·nē′·mi·ą) *n.* Also **anaemia** (a·nē′·mi·a) *n.* disease characterized by a deficiency of blood or of hemoglobin. **anemic** *a.* [Gk. *an-,* neg.; *haima,* blood].

a·nem·o·ne (ą·nem′·ą·nē) *n.* plant of crow-foot family; wind-flower. **sea-anemone** *n.* name given to certain plant-like marine animals [Gk. *anemos,* wind].

a·nent (ą·nent′) *prep.* concerning; about; in respect of; as to [O.E. *on; efen,* even].

an·e·roid (an′·e·roid) *a.* denoting a barometer

depending for its action on the pressure of the atmosphere on a metallic box almost exhausted of air, without the use of mercury or other fluid [Gk. *a-*, neg.; *neres*, wet; *eidos*, form].

an·es·the·sia, an·aes·the·sia (an·ạs·thē′·zh·ạ) *n.* absence of sensibility to external impressions, particularly touch. Also **anesthesis. anesthetic** *n.* a drug which induces insensibility to pain; *a.* producing loss of feeling and sensation. **anesthetically** *adv.* **anesthetize** *v.t.* **anesthetist** *n.* [Gk. *an-*, not; *aisthesis*, feeling].

an·eu·rism (an′·yạ·rizm) *n.* (*Med.*) a local widening or dilatation in the course of an artery [Gk. *ana*, up; *eurus*, wide].

a·new (ạ·nū′) *adv.* in a new form or manner; newly; over again; afresh [M.E. *of newe*].

an·gel (ān′·jel) *n.* a heavenly messenger; a spirit who conveys God's will to man; a guardian spirit; (*Colloq.*) a lovable person; a dear. **angel fish** *n.* a bright-colored tropical fish. **angel food cake** *n.* a spongy, light, white cake. **angelic(al)** (an·jel′·ic) *a.* like an angel. **angelically** *adv.* [Gk. *angelos*, a messenger].

an·ge·lus (an′·jạ·lạs) *n.* a short devotional service in the R.C. Church held morning, noon, and sunset; the bell rung to remind the faithful to recite the prayer [L.].

an·ger (ang′·gẹr) *n.* a strong passion or emotion excited by injury; rage; *v.t.* to excite to wrath; to enrage. **angry** (ang′·gri·) *a.* roused to anger; displeased; enraged; inflamed. **angrily** *adv.* **angriness** *n.* [O.N. *angr*, trouble].

an·gi·na (an·jī′·nạ, an′·ji·nạ) *n.* (*Med.*) inflammation of the throat, e.g., quinsy. **angina pectoris,** a heart disease characterized by attacks of agonizing pain [L.].

an·gi·o·sperm (an′·ji·ō·spurm) *n.* (*Bot.*) a plant whose seeds are enclosed in a seed-vessel [Gk. *nageion*, a vessel; *sperma*, a seed].

an·gle (ang′·gl) *n.* a fish-hook; a rod and line for fishing; *v.i.* to fish with rod, line, and hook; (*Fig.*) to use artifice. **angler** *n.* one who angles. **angling** *n.* [O.E. *angul*].

an·gle (ang′·gl) *n.* a corner; the point at which two lines meet; (*Geom.*) the amount of turning made by revolving a straight line in a plane, round a point in itself, from one direction to another. **acute angle,** one less than 90°. **obtuse angle,** greater than 90° but less than 180°. **right angle,** a quarter of a complete revolution, i.e. 90°. (*Fig.*) a point of view. [L. *angulus*, a corner].

An·gli·can (ang′·gli·cạn) *a.* English; of, or belonging to, Church of England; *n.* a member of Church of England. **Anglicanism** *n.* [L. *Angli*, the Angles].

an·gli·cize (ang′·glạ·sīz) *v.t.* to make or express in English idiom. **anglicism** *n.* an English idiom; an English custom or characteristic. **anglify** *v.t.* to make English [L. *Angli*, the Angles].

An·glo- (ang′·glō) *prefix* fr. L. *Anglus*, an Angle, combining to form many compound words. **Anglo-American** *a.* involving English and Americans. **Anglo-Saxon** *a.* pert. to Anglo-Saxons or their language; *n.* one of the nations formed by the union of the Angles, Saxons. **Anglophile** (ang′·glō·fīl) *a.* favoring anything English; *n.* a supporter of English customs, manners, or policy.

An·go·ra (ang·gō′·rạ) *n.* a Turkish province in Asia minor, famous for a breed of goats; cloth made from hair of these goats.

an·guish (ang′·gwish) *n.* acute pain of body or of mind; grief; anxiety; moral torment. **-ment** *n.* [L. *angustia*, straitness].

an·gu·lar (ang′·gū·lạr) *a.* having angles; sharp-cornered; (of people) not plump; gawky; irascible. **angularity** *n.* **-ly** *adv.* **angulate** *a.* having angles [L. *angulus*, a corner].

an·hy·dride (an·hī′·drīd) *n.* (*Chem.*) a compound formed from an acid by evaporation of water. **anhydrous** *a.* entirely without water [Gk. *an-*, neg.; *hudor*, water].

an·il (an′·il) *n.* a West Indian shrub from the leaves and stalks of which indigo is made. **aniline** (an′·il·īn, or -in) *n.* a product orig. obtained from indigo, now mainly from coal-tar, and used in the manufacture of brilliant dyes, colored inks, soaps, explosives, etc.; *a.* pert. to anil or aniline [Fr. fr. Sans. *nila*, dark blue].

an·ile (an′·īl) *a.* like an old woman; imbecile. **anility** *n.* senility [L. *anus*, an old woman].

an·i·mad·vert (an·i·mad·vurt′) *v.t.* to turn the mind to; to consider disparagingly; to comment on censoriously; to reprove. **animadversion** *n.* [L. *animus*, the mind; *vertere*, to turn].

an·i·mal (an′·i·mạl) *n.* a living creature having sensation and power of voluntary motion; a living organism, distinct from plants; *a.* pert. to or got from animals. **-cule** *n.* a very minute animal (*pl.* **-cules** or **-cula**). **-culine** *a.* pert. to animalcula. **-ism** *n.* sensuality. **— magnetism,** mesmerism, hypnotism. **— spirits,** natural buoyance [L. *anima*, breath].

an·i·mate (an′·i·māt) *v.t.* to give natural life to; to endow with spirit or vigor; to energize; to inspire; to make alive; *a.* living or organic. **-d** *a.* **-dly** *adv.* **animating** *a.* inspiring. **animation** *n.* the state of possessing life or spirit; vivacity. **animator** *n.* one who or that which animates; a movie cartoonist [L. *animatus*, filled with life].

an·i·mism (an′·i·mizm) *n.* the belief that all forms of organic life have their origin in the soul; that all natural objects have a soul. **animist** *n.* **animistic** *a.* [L. *anima*, life or soul].

an·i·mos·i·ty (an·i·mȧs′·i·ti·) *n.* violent hatred; active enmity; acrimony; orig. meant *courage* [L. *animosus*, full of spirit].

an·i·mus (an′·i·mạs) *n.* animosity; temper; grudge; (*Law*) intention, purpose [L. *animus*, spirit, temper].

an·ise (an′·is) *n.* an herb with pungent smell and bearing aromatic seeds. **aniseed** *n.* seed of anise used for flavoring and in manufacture of liqueurs [Gk. *anis*].

an·kle (ang′·kl) *n.* the joint connecting the foot with the leg. **anklet** *n.* a sock which reaches just above the ankle; an ornament for the ankle [M.E. *ancle*].

an·nals (an′·ạlz) *n.pl.* history of events recorded each year; a yearly chronicle. **annalize** *v.t.* to write annals; to record chronologically. **annalist** n. [L. *annus*, a year].

an·neal (ạ·nēl′) *v.t.* to heat, and then cool slowly, for the purpose of rendering less brittle; to heat in order to fix colors. **-ing** *n.* [O.E. *an; aclan*, to kindle].

an·nex (an′·eks) *v.t.* to unite at the end; to subjoin; to bind to; to take additional territory under control; *n.* something joined on; building attached to, or sufficiently near, main building to be considered part of it. **annexation** *n.* the act of annexing; what is annexed. **annexion, annexment** *n.* [L. *ad*, to; *nectere*, to bind].

an·ni·hi·late (ạ·nī′·hil·āt) *v.t.* to reduce to nothing; to destroy; to make null and void. **annihilable** *a.* **annihilation** *n.* **annihilator** *n.* [L. *ad*, to; *nihil*, nothing].

an·ni·ver·sa·ry (an·i·vur′·sạ·ri·) *a.* yearly; annual; *n.* day on which event is yearly celebrated [L. *annus*, year; *vertere*, to turn].

an·no·tate (an′·ō·tāt) *v.t.* to mark in writing; to write explanatory notes, esp. upon literary text. **annotation** *n.* a written commentary. **annotator** *n.* **annotatory** *a.* [L. *annatotus*, marked with notes].

an·nounce (ạ·nouns′) *v.t.* to give first public notice of; to proclaim; to promulgate; to publish. **-ment** *n.* giving public notice; proclamation; declaration. **-r** *n.* a broadcasting official who gives the news, etc. [L. *ad*, to; *nuntiare*, to announce].

an·noy (ạ·noi′) *v.t.* to injure, disturb continually; to torment; tease; vex; pester; molest; trouble. **-ance** *n.* [fr. L. *in odio,* in hatred].

an·nu·al (an′·ū·ạl) *a.* yearly; performed in the course of a year; *n.* a periodical published once a year; a plant which completes its life-cycle within a year. **-ly** *adv.* [L. *annus,* a year].

an·nu·i·ty (ạ·nū′·i·ti·) *n.* a fixed sum of money payable each year for a number of years, or for life. **annuitant** *n.* one in receipt of an annuity [L. *annus,* a year].

an·nul (ạ·nul′) *v.t.* to make void; to nullify; repeal; cancel; *pr.p.* **-ling;** *pa.t.* and *pa.p.* **-led. -ment** *n.* [L. *ad,* to; *nullus,* none].

an·nu·lar (an′·ū·lạr) *a.* ring-shaped; like a ring. **annulated** *a.* having rings or belts. **annulet** *n.* a little ring. **annularly** *adv.* **annulose** *a.* ringed. **annulation** *n.* ring-like formation [L. *annulus,* a ring].

an·num (a′·nạm) *n.* year [L.].

an·nun·ci·ate (ạ·nun′·sī·āt) *v.t.* to announce; to make known; to proclaim. **annunciation** *n.* an announcing; (*cap.*) a holy day (March 25) in R.C. Church. **annunciator** *n.* **annunciatory** *a.* [L. *ad,* to; *nuntiare,* to announce].

an·ode (an′·ōd) *n.* positive electrode of a voltaic current; (*Radio*) plate of an electron tube [Gk. *anodos,* way up].

an·o·dyne (an′·ō·dīn) *n.* a drug or measures which relieve pain [Gk. *an-,* neg.; *odunē,* pain].

a·noint (ạ·noint′) *v.t.* to pour oil upon; to rub over with an ointment or oil; to consecrate by unction. **-ed** *a.* consecrated; *n.* a consecrated person. **-ment** *n.* consecration; a salve. **the Lord's anointed,** Christ [L. *in,* on; *ungere,* to anoint].

a·nom·a·ly (ạ·nȧm′·ạ·li·) *n.* deviation from the common rule or type; irregularity. **anomalism** *n.* **anomalistic** *a.* **anomalous** *a.* irregular; incongruous [Gk. *anomalos,* not even].

a·non (ạ·nȧn′) *adv.* quickly; at once; forthwith; soon. **ever and anon,** every now and then [O.E. *on,* in; *an,* one].

a·non·y·mous (ạ·nȧn′·i·mạs) *a.* applied to a writing or work of which the author is not named. **anonym** *n.* one who remains anonymous. **-ly** *adv.* **anonymity** *n.* [Gk. *an-,* neg.; *onoma,* name].

an·o·rex·ia (an·ạ·rek′·sē·a) *n.* prolonged loss of appetite; **anorectic** *a.* [N.L. fr. Gk. *a-* + *orexis,* appetite, fr. *oregein*].

an·oth·er (ạ·nuTH′·ẹr) *a.* not the same; different; one more; *pron.* any one else [E.].

an·swer (an′·sẹr) *v.t.* to speak or write in return; to vindicate; to witness for; *v.i.* to reply; to suit; to suffer the consequence of; *n.* something said or written in return to a question, etc.; the solution of a problem; response. **-able** *a.* capable of being answered; responsible. **-er** *n.* **to answer for,** to be responsible for [O.E. *andswarian,* to swear back].

ant (ant) *n.* a small mebranous-winged insect living in colonies in wood or the ground; an emmet. **ant-bear** *n.* the great ant-eater of South America. **ant-eater** *n.* one of several quadrupeds, e.g. ant-bear, aardvark, that feed chiefly on ants. **ant-hill** *n.* a mound raised by a colony of ants or termites [O.E. *aemette*].

ant- (ant) a combining form fr. Gk. *anti,* against, used to form compounds. **-acid** (ant·-as′·id) *a.* counteracting acidity; *n.* a remedy for acidity of the stomach.

an·tag·o·nize (an·tag′·ạ·nīz) *v.t.* to contend violently against; to act in opposition; to oppose; to make hostile. **antagonism** *n.* opposition; hostility; hatred; dislike. **antagonist** *n.* **antagonistic** *a.* **antagonistically** *adv.* [Gk. *anti,* against; *agon,* a contest].

ant·arc·tic (ant·ȧrk′·tik) *a.* opposite to arctic pole; relating to southern pole or region near it [Gk. *anti,* against; E. *arctic*].

an·te (an′·te) *n.* in poker, a player's stake [L. *ante,* before].

an·te- (an′·te) *prefix* fr. L. *ante,* meaning *before* (place, time, or order), combining to form derivatives. **antebellum** *a.* [L.] before the war (esp. U.S. Civil War). **antecedent** (an·tạ·sēd′·ạnt) *a.* going before in time, place, rank, etc.; preceding; prior; *n.* that which goes before; (*Gram.*) the noun or pronoun to which a relative refers. **antichamber** *n.* a chamber leading to the chief apartment. **antecursor** *n.* a forerunner [L. *cedere,* to go; *camera,* a room; *currere,* to run].

an·te·date (an′·tạ·dāt) *v.t.* to date before the true time; to precede in time [L. *ante,* before, E. *date*].

an·te·di·lu·vi·an. (an·tȧ·di·lȯȯ′·vi·ạn) *a.* pert. to before the Flood; ancient; antiquated [L. *ante,* before; *diluvium,* a flood].

an·te·lope (an′·tạ·lōp) *n.* (*pl.* **-lope, lopes**) a hoofed ruminant, notable for its graceful and agile movement [Gk. *antholops*].

an·te·me·rid·i·an (an·te·mẹ·rid′·i·ạn) *a.* before noon (abbrev. **a.m.**) [L. *ante meridiem* = before midday, the period of time between midnight and noon].

an·ten·na (an·ten′·ạ) *n.* feeler of an insect, crustacean, etc. *pl.* **antennae** (an·ten′·ē). **antenna** *n.* (*Radio*) a wire for sending or receiving electric waves; an aerial. *pl.* **antennas. -ry** *a.* [L. *antenna,* a sailyard].

an·te·pe·nult (an·te·pē′·nạlt) *n.* last syllable but two of word. **antepenultimate** *a.* [L. *ante,* before; *paene,* almost; *ultimus,* last].

an·te·ri·or (an·tē′·ri·ẹr) *a.* before; occurring earlier. **anteriority** *n.* [L. *ante,* before].

an·te·room (an′·te·rȯȯm) *n.* a room giving entry to another [L. *ante,* before; E. *room*].

an·them (an′·thạm) *n.* a hymn sung in alternate part; Church music adapted to passages from the Scriptures; song of praise [Gk. *antiphonon,* a response sung].

an·ther (an′·thẹr) *n.* the little sac in a flower, containing the pollen or fertilizing dust. **-al** *a.* [Gk. *anthēros,* flowery].

an·thol·o·gy (an·thȧl′·ạ·ji·) *n.* orig. a collection of flowers; a collection of literary passages or poetry. **anthologist** *n.* [Gk. *anthos,* a flower; *legein,* to gather].

an·thra·cene (an′·thrạ·sēn) *n.* product from distillation of coal-tar, used in manufacture of dyes. **anthracite** *n.* coal, nearly pure carbon, burning without smoke or flame [Gk. *anthrax,* coal].

an·thrax (an′·thrax) *n.* a carbuncle; a malignant disease in cattle and sheep; a malignant pustule [Gk. *anthrax,* coal].

an·thro·po- (an′·thrạ·pō) *prefix* fr. Gr. *anthropos,* meaning man, combining to form derivatives. **anthropogency** (·poj′·en·i·) *n.* science of development of man. **anthropoid** *a.* man-like [Gk. *genesthai,* to be born; *graphein,* to write; *eidos,* form; *lithos,* a stone].

an·thro·pol·o·gy (an·thrạ·pȧl′·ạ·ji·) *n.* study of man, including all aspects of his evolution, physical and social. **anthropological** *a.* **anthropologically** *adv.* **anthropologist** *n.* [Gk. *anthropos,* man; *logos,* discourse].

an·thro·pom·e·try (an·thrạ·pȧm′·e·tri·) *n.* the scientific measurement of the human body [Gk. *anthropos,* man; *metron,* a measure].

an·thro·po·mor·phism (an·thrạ·pạ·mawr′·-fizm) *n.* the conception of God as a human being with human attributes. **anthropomorphist** *n.* **anthropomorphize** *v.t.* to invest with human qualities. **anthropomorphic** *a.* [Gk. *anthropos,* man; *morphe,* form].

an·thro·po·mor·pho·sis (an·thrạ·pạ·mawr′·-fō·sis) *n.* transformation into human shape [Gk. *anthropos,* man; *morphe,* form].

an·ti- (an′·ti) *prefix* fr. Gk. *anti,* meaning *against, opposite, instead of,* combining to form derivations; contracted to **ant-** before a vowel. **anti-aircraft** *a.* used against aircraft.

an·ti·bi·ot·ic (an·ti·bī·ȧt′·ik) *n.* substance which acts as an antibacterial agent [Gk. *anti,* against; *bios*, life].

an·ti·bod·y (an′·ti·bȧd·i·) *n.* a substance in blood which counteracts growth and harmful action of bacteria; anti-toxin.

an·tic (an′·tik) *a.* odd; grotesque; *n.* a buffoon; a comical action [L. *antiquus*, old].

An·ti·christ (an′·ti·krīst) *n.* a name given in the New Testament to various incarnations of opposition to Christ.

an·tic·i·pate (an·tis′·ạ·pāt) *v.t.* to be before another; to be beforehand in thought or action; to enjoy prematurely; to forestall. **anticipant** *a.* anticipating; (*Med.*) occurring before the regular time. **anticipation** *n.* the act of anticipating. **anticipative** *a.* full of expectation. **anticipatively, anticipatorily** *adv.* **anticipatory** *a.* happening in advance [L. *ante*, before; *capere*, to take].

an·ti·cli·max (an·ti·klī′·maks) *n.* a sentence or figure of speech in which ideas are arranged in descending order of importance (opp. of *climax*); a sudden drop from the dignified to the trivial.

an·ti·cy·clone (an′·ti·sī′·klōn) *n.* a spiral flow of air (clockwise in N. Hemisphere, anti-clockwise in S. Hemisphere) around a high-pressure region.

an·ti·dote (an′·ti·dōt) *n.* a remedy counteracting a poison or an evil. **antidotal** *a.* [Gk. *anti*, against; *doton*, given].

an·ti·freeze (an′·ti·frēz) *n.* a substance added to water in automobile radiators to prevent freezing in very cold weather.

an·ti·gen (an′·ti·jạn) *n.* a substance producing antibodies in the blood-stream [Gk. *anti*, against; *genesthai*, to be born].

an·ti·his·ta·mine (an·ti·his′·tạ·mēn) *n.* any of several drugs used to treat allergies.

an·ti·knock (an·ti·nȧk′) *n.* a substance added to fuel to eliminate or decrease the knocking noise in an internal-combustion engine.

an·ti·log·a·rithm (an·ti·lȧg′·ạ·rithm) *n.* the complement of a logarithm or of a sine, tangent, or secant; the number corresponding to a logarithm (*abbrev.* **antilog**).

an·til·o·gy (an·til′·ạ·ji·) *n.* a contradiction in terms, or in two separate passages of a book. **antilogous** *a.* [Gk. *logos*, a discourse].

an·ti·ma·cas·sar (an·ti·ma·kas′·ẹr) *n.* an ornamental covering for chair backs, etc. [Gk. *Macassar oil* from Celebes].

an·ti·mat·ter (an′·tī·mat·ẹr, an·ti-) *n.* matter consisting of the counterparts of ordinary matter, but with reversed electrical charges, e.g. positrons instead of electrons.

an·ti·mis·sile (an′·tī·mis·l, an′·ti-) *a.* (missile) designed to intercept hostile guided missiles.

an·ti·mo·ny (an′·ti·mōn·i·) *n.* a whitish, brittle chemical element. **antimonial** *a.* **antimoniate** *n.* a salt of antimonic acid. **antimonic, antimonious** *a.* of or containing antimony. **antimonite** *n.* stibnite [L. *antimonium*].

an·ti·pas·to (ȧn·ti·pȧs′tō) *n.* an appetizer course; hors d'oeuvres [It.]

an·tip·a·thy (an·tip′·ạ·thi·) *n.* opposition; aversion; dislike; enmity; hatred. **antipathetic(al)** *a.* **antipathic** *a.* hostile to; having an opposite nature. **antipathist** *n.* [Gk. *anti*, against; *pathos*, feeling].

an·ti·phon (an′·ti·fȧn) *n.* the chant, or alternate singing, in choirs; an anthem; a response. Also **antiphony. -al** *n.* a book of antiphons; *a.* **-ally** *adv.* **-ic(al)** *a.* [doublet of *anthem*].

an·ti·phra·sis (an·tif′·rạ·sis) *n.* (*Rhet.*) use of words in a sense opposite to their proper meaning. **antiphrastic(al)** *a.* pert. to antiphrasis. **antiphrastically** *adv.* [Gk. *anti*, against; *phrazein*, speak].

an·tip·o·des (an·tip′·ạ·dēz) *n.pl.* those living on opposite side of globe; regions directly opposite any given point on globe; (*Fig.*) anything diametrically opposed to anything else [Gk. *anti*, against; *pous*, a foot].

an·ti·pope (an′·ti·pōp) *n.* one who usurps the papal office; rival to Pope properly elected by Cardinals. **antipapal** *a.*

an·ti·pro·ton (an·ti·prō′·tȧn) *n.* the anti-particle of the proton, with negative charge.

an·ti·py·ret·ic (an·ti·pī·ret′·ik) *n.* any agent which lowers temperature in fevers; *a.* counteracting fever [Gk. *anti*, against; *puretos*, fever].

an·tique (an·tēk′) *a.* ancient; old-fashioned; obsolete; aged; *n.* relic of bygone times; ancient work of art; the style of ancient art. **antiquarian** *n.* student of antiquity or antiquities; a collector of relics of former times; *a.* pert. to old times or objects; out-of-date; obsolete. **antiquarianism** *n.* study of antiquities. **antiquary** *n.* an antiquarian. **antiquate** *v.t.* to render obsolete. **antiquated** *a.* very old; out of date. **antiquity** *n.* ancient times; former ages; great age; the people of ancient times. **antiquities** *n.pl.* the remains and relics of ancient times; manners and customs of ancient times [Fr., fr. L. *antiquus*, ancient].

an·ti-Sem·ite (an·ti·sem′īt, an·tī-) *n.* a person who hates, or is prejudiced against, Jews. **anti-Semitic** *a.* **anti-Semitism** *n.*

an·ti·sep·sis (an·ti·sep′sis) *n.* prevention of sepsis; destruction or arresting of growth of living micro-organisms which cause putrefaction. **antiseptic** *n.* a disinfectant; a substance which destroys bacteria; *a.* [Gk. *anti*, against; *sepsis*, putrefaction].

an·ti·so·cial (an·ti·sō′·shạl) *a.* averse to social intercourse; opposed to social order.

an·ti·the·ism (an·ti·thē′·izm) *n.* opposition to the belief in the existence of God. **antitheist** *n.* **antitheistic** *a.*

an·tith·e·sis (an·tith′·ạ·sis) *n.* a direct opposition of words or ideas; (*Rhet.*) a figure in which words or thoughts are set in contrast. *pl.* **antitheses. antithetic(al)** *a.* [Gk. *anti*, opposite; *thesis*, placing].

an·ti·tox·in (an·ti·tȧk′·sin) *n.* a toxin which neutralizes another toxin in the blood serum. **antitoxic** *a.* [Gk. *anti*, against; *toxikon*, arrow-poison].

an·ti·trust (an·ti·trust′) *a.* opposed to trusts or monopolies.

ant·ler (ant′·lẹr) *n* .a horn of an animal of the deer family. **-ed** *a.* [L. *ante*, before; *oculus*, the eye].

an·to·nym (an′·tạ·nim) *n.* a word of contrary meaning (opp. of *synonym*) [Gk. *anti*, against; *onoma*, a name].

an·trum (an′·trum) *n.* a cavity, esp. sinus of the upper jaw. *pl.* **antra** [Gk. *ántron*].

a·nus (ā′·nạs) *n.* the lower orifice of the alimentary canal [L.]

an·vil (an′·vil) *n.* an iron block, usually steel-faced, upon which blacksmith's forgings are hammered and shaped. **-led** *a.* [O.E. *anfilte*].

anx·i·e·ty (ang·zī′·e·ti·) *n.* distress of mind; disquietude; uneasiness; eagerness (to serve, etc.). **anxious** (angk′·shạs) *a.* uneasy; eager. **anxiously** *adv.* [L. *anxius*, anxious].

an·y (en′·i·) *a.* one out of many; some; *adv.* to any extent; at all. **-body** *n.* any person; an ordinary person. **-how** *adv.* at any rate; in a careless manner; in any case. **-one** pron. any person. **-thing** *n.* any one thing, no matter what. **-way** *adv.* in any way or manner; anyhow; carelessly. **-where** *adv.* in any place. **-wise** *adv.* in any way [O.E. *an*, one].

A-one (ā·wun′) *a.* (*Colloq.*) first class, excellent.

a·or·ta (ā·awr′·tạ) *n.* the great artery leading from the left ventricle of the heart. **aortal, aortic** *a.* [Gk. *aorte*].

a·pace (ạ·pās′) *adv.* at a quick pace; hastily; swiftly; fast [Middle Fr. *a pas*, at pace].

A·pach·e (ạ·pa′·chi·) *n.* one of a tribe of American Indians. **apache** (ạ·pȧsh′) *n.* a bandit of the Paris underworld, a street hooligan [Amer. Ind. *e patch*, an enemy].

ap·a·nage See **appanage.**
a·part (ạ·pårt′) *adv.* separately; aside, asunder; at a distance [Fr. *à part,* aside].
a·part·heid (ạ·pårt′·hād) *n.* racial segregation [S. Afr.].
a·part·ment (ạ·part′·ment) *n.* a room in a house; a suite of rooms; lodgings [Fr. *appartement,* a suite of rooms].
ap·a·thy (ap′·ạth·i·) *n.* want of feeling; indifference. **apathetic** *a.* void of feeling; indifferent; insensible [Gr. *c*-, neg.; *pathos,* feeling].
ape (āp) *n.* a monkey, esp. one without a tail; one of the larger species, e.g. chimpanzee, gorilla, etc.; a mimic; *v.t.* to imitate; to mimic. **-r** *n.* one who apes; a servile imitator. **apery** *n.* mimicry. **apish** *a.* ape-like; inclined to imitate in a foolish manner [O.E. *apa*].
a·pe·ri·tif (a·pā′·rē·tif) *n.* alcoholic drink taken before meals [L. *aperire,* to open].
ap·er·ture (a′·pẹr·chẹr) *n.* an opening; a hole [L. *aperire,* to open].
a·pex (ā′·peks) *n.* the top, peak, or summit of anything. *pl.* **apexes** or **apices.**
a·pha·sia (ạ·fā′·zi·ạ) *n.* loss of power of expressing ideas in words, often due to brain disease; loss of power of remembering words. **aphasic** *a.* [Gk. *a*-, neg.; *phasis,* speech].
ap·er·ture (a′·pẹr·chẹr) *n.* an opening; a hole
a·phe·li·on (ạ·fē′·li·ạn) *n.* point of planet's orbit most distant from sun [Gk. *apo,* away; *helios,* the sun].
aph·o·rism (af′·ẹr·izm) *n.* a pithy saying; a maxim. **aphoristic** *a.* **aphoristically** *adv.* **aphorize** *v.t.* and *i.* to make or use aphorisms. **aphorist** *n.* [Gk. *aphorismos,* a definition].
a·phra·sia (ạ·frā′·zi·ạ) *n.* inability to use connected language; speechlessness [Gk. *a*-, neg.; *phrasis,* speech].
Aph·ro·di·te (af·rạ·di′·tē) *n.* (*Myth.*) the Greek goddess of love and beauty. **aphrodisiac** (af·rō·diz′·i·ak) *a.* exciting sexual desire; *n* anything which so excites.
a·pi·ar·y (ā′·pi·er·i·) *n.* place where bees are kept. **apiarian** (ā·pi·e′·ri·ạn) *a.* pert. to bees or to bee-keeping. **apiarist** *n.* one who keeps or studies bees. **apiculture** *n.* [L. *apis,* a bee].
a·piece (ạ·pēs′) *adv.* for each one; to each one [orig. two words].
a·plomb (ạ·plåm′) *n.* perpendicularity; uprightness; (*Fig.*) self-assurance; coolness [L. *ad,* to; *plumbum,* lead].
a·poc·a·lypse (ạ·påk′·ạ·lips) *n.* an unveiling of hidden things; revelation; disclosure **Apocalypse** *n.* (*Bib.*) the last book of the New Testament, called the Revelation of St. John. **apocalyptic, -al** pert. to revelation; of style, allegorical; obscure. **apocalyptically** *adv.* [Gk. *apokalupsis,* unveiling].
a·poc·ry·pha (ạ·påk′·ri·fạ) *n.pl.* originally hidden or secret things not suitable to be seen by the uninitiated. **Apocrypha** *n.pl.* (*Bib.*) the collective name for the fourteen books not included in the Old Testament, but incorporated in the Vulgate of the R.C. Church. **apocryphal** *a.* spurious; unauthentic; pert. to the Apocrypha [Gk. *apo,* away; *kruptein,* to hide].
a·pod·o·sis (ạ·påd′·ạ·sis) *n.* (*Gram.*) the clause, in a conditional sentence, which expresses result as distinct from the *protasis. pl.* **apodoses** [Gk. *apo,* back; *didonai,* to give].
ap·o·gee (ap′·ạ·jē) *n.* that point in the orbit of a heavenly body at the greatest distance from the earth (opposed to *perigee*); the culmination; climax; highest point; zenith. **apogeal** (ap·ạ·jē′·ạl), **apogean** *a.* [Gk. *apo,* from; *ge,* the earth].
ap·o·logue (ap′·ạ·lawg) *n.* a parable; a fable [Gk. *apo,* from; *logos,* speech].
a·pol·o·gy (ạ·pål′·ạ·ji·) *n.* something spoken in defense; expression of regret at offense; an excuse; a poor substitute (with for). **apologize** *v.i.* to make an apology, or excuse; to express regret. **apologist** *n.* one who makes an apology; a defender of a cause. **apologetic** (ạ·pål·ạ·jet′·ik), **apologetical** *a.* **apologetically** *adv.* **apologetics** *n.* the branch of theology charged with the defense of Christianity. **apologia** (ap·ạ·lō·ji·ạ) *n.* a defense in writing of the author's principles, etc. [Gk. *apologia,* a speaking away].
ap·o·thegm (a′·pạ·thėm) *n.* a short, pithy saying, a maxim; a proverb. **apothegmatic** (a·pạ·theg·mat′·ik), **apothegmatical** *a.* [Gk. *apo,* from; *phthengesthai,* to utter].
ap·o·plex·y (ap′·ạ·plek·si·) *n.* a sudden loss of consciousness, sensation, and voluntary motion, due generally to rupture of a blood-vessel in the brain. **apoplectic** *a.* [Gk. *apoplexia*].
a·pos·ta·sy, a·pos·ta·cy (ạ·pås′·tạ·si·) *n.* the act of renouncing one's faith, principles, or party; desertion of a cause. **apostate** *n.* renegade; traitor; deserter; *a.* false; traitorous. **apostatic, -al** *a.* **apostatize** *v.i.* to abandon one's faith [Gk. *apo,* apart; *stasis,* a standing].
a pos·te·ri·o·ri (á·pås·tir′·i·ōr·i) from effect to cause [L. from the subsequent].
a·pos·tle (a·pås′·l) *n.* one sent out to preach or advocate a cause; one of the twelve disciples of Christ sent to preach the Gospel. **apostolate** (ạ·pås′·tạ·lạt) *n.* the office or dignity or mission of an apostle. **apostolic, apostolical** *a.* **apostolically** *adv.* **apostolicism** *n.* **Apostles' Creed,** creed supposedly used by apostles, summarizing Christian faith. **Apostolic Church,** church derived from, and incorporating the spirit of, the apostles. **Apostolic see,** the jurisdiction of the Pope. **Apostolic succession,** the derivation of spiritual authority in an unbroken line from the Apostles, through bishops [Gk. *apo,* away; *stellein,* to send].
a·pos·tro·phe (ạ·pạs′·trạ·fi) *n.* an address delivered to the absent or the dead, or to an inanimate thing, as if present; a mark (') indicating possessive case, or omission of one or more letters of a word. **apostrophic** *a.* **apostrophize** *v.t.* and *i.* to address by, or to use, apostrophe [Gk. *apostrophē,* a turning away].
a·poth·e·car·y (a·påth′·ạ·ker·i·) *n.* one who prepares or sells drugs for medicines [Gk. *apothēkē,* a store house].
a·poth·e·o·sis (a·på·thi·ō′·sis or a·på·thē′·ạ·sis) *n.* the act of raising a mortal to the rank of the gods; deification. **apotheosize** *v.t.* to exalt to the dignity of a god [Gk. *apo,* apart; *theos,* a god].
ap·pall (a·pawl′) *v.t.* to overwhelm with sudden fear; to confound; to scare; to terrify; **-ing** *a.* shocking. [O.Fr. *apalir,* to make pale].
ap·pa·ra·tus (ap·ạ·rā′·tạs or ·rat′·ạs) *n.* things provided as a means to an end; collection of implements or utensils for effecting an experiment, or given work. *s.* and *pl.* [L. *ad,* to; *parare,* to prepare].
ap·par·el (ạ·par′·el) *n.* clothing; dress; garments; (*Naut.*) rigging, etc.; *v.t.* to dress; *pr.p.* [O.Fr. *apareiller,* to dress].
ap·par·ent (ạ·par′·ạnt) *a.* visible; evident; obvious. **-ly** *adv.* [L. *apparere,* to appear].
ap·pa·ri·tion (ap·ạ·rish′·ạn) *n.* appearance (esp. inexplicable); ghost. **-al** *a.* [Fr. fr. L. *apparitio,* appearance].
ap·peal (ạ·pēl′) *v.i.* to invoke; to call to witness; to solicit aid; (*Law*) to reopen a case before a higher court; to be pleasing to mind or senses. *n.* an urgent call for sympathy or aid; personal attraction. **-able, -ing** *a.* **-ingly** *adv.* **-ingness** *n.* [O.Fr. *apeler,* to call].
ap·pear (ạ·pēr′) *v.i.* to come in sight; to become visible; to seem; to be obvious or manifest. **-ance** *n.* a coming in sight; semblance; outward look or show; likeness; personal presence. **-er** *n.* [L. *apparere,* to appear].
ap·pease (ạ·pēz′) *v.t.* to quiet; to calm; to pacify; to satisfy (hunger, etc.); to dispel anger or hatred. **appeasable** *a.* **-ment** *n.* pacifying; policy of making substantial concessions in order to preserve peace. **-r** *n.* [Fr. *apaiser;* O.Fr. *a pais,* at peace].

ap·pel·lant (ą·pel′·ąnt) *n.* (*Law*) one who appeals to a higher court against the verdict of a lower tribunal; one who makes any appeal. **appellancy** *n.* an appeal. **appellate** *a.* (*Law*) pert. to appeals; having power to hear and give decision on appeals. **appellation** *n.* name; title; designation. **appellational** *a.* **appellative** *a.* naming; common to many; pert. to the common noun; *n. common* noun as distinct from *proper* noun. **appellatively** *adv.* **appellee** *n.* (*Law*) the defendant in an appeal [L. *appellare,* to call].

ap·pend (ą·pend′) *v.t.* to hang or attach to; to add. **-age** *n.* something added. **-ant** *n.* an adjunct or unessential thing; *a.* hanging to; annexed [L. *appendere,* to hang on].

ap·pen·di·ci·tis (ą·pen·di·sī′·tis) *n.* (*Path.*) inflammation of the appendix vermiformis. **appendectomy** (a·pen·dek′·tą·mi·) *n.* surgical removal of appendix [fr. *appendix*].

ap·pen·di·cle (ą·pen′·di·kl) n. a small appendage. **appendicular** *a.* [L. *appendicula*].

ap·pen·dix (ą·pen′·diks) *n.* thing added; an adjunct; supplement at end of book; (*Med.*) the blind tube extending from caecum into pelvis. *pl.* **-es, appendices** [L. *ad,* to; *pendere,* to hang].

ap·per·cep·tion (ap·ęr·sep′·shąn) *n.* (*Philos.*) an act of voluntary consciousness; a mental perception of self as a conscious agent; spontaneous thought [L. *ad,* to; *percipere, perceptum,* to perceive].

ap·per·tain (ap·ęr·tān′) *v.i.* to belong by nature; to relate. **-ing** *a.* **-ment** *n.* **appertinent** (ą·pur′·tą·nąnt) *a.* belonging to [L. *ad,* to; *pertinere,* to belong].

ap·pe·tite (ap′·ą·tīt) *n.* desire as for food, drink, rest, etc. **appetitive** *a.* **appetize** *v.t.* to create an appetite. **appetizer** *n.* something taken before a meal to create appetite. **appetizing** *a.* [L. *ad,* to; *petere,* to seek].

ap·plaud (ą·plawd′) *v.t.* and *v. i.* to praise by clapping; to acclaim; commend; extol. **-er** *n.* **applause** *n.* approval publicly expressed [L. *ad,* to; *plaudere,* to clap].

ap·ple (ap′·l) *n.* fruit of the apple-tree; the apple-tree. **—faced, —cheeked** *a.* of rosy hue. chubby. **— jack** *n.* brandy distilled from hard cider. **—pie order,** perfect order. **— polisher** *n.* (*slang*) flatterer, one who seeks favors by gifts, etc. [O.E. *aeppel*].

ap·pli·ance See under **apply.**

ap·pli·cant (ap′·li·kąnt) *n.* one who applies; a candidate; a petitioner. **applicability** *n.* the quality of being suitable. **applicable** *a.* suitable; adapted. **applicableness** *n.* **applicably** *adv.* **applicate** *a.* applied or put to some use. **application** *n.* the act of applying; the thing applied; close attention. **applicatory** *a.* [L. *applicare,* to attach to].

ap·plied (a·plīd′) *pa.p.* and *pa.t.* of **apply.**

ap·pli·qué (ap·li·kā′) *n.* any ornamentation, sewn or fixed on a material or metal [Fr.].

ap·ply (ą·plī′) *v.t.* to place one thing upon another; to employ for a particular purpose; to fix the attention upon; to administer a remedy; *v.i.* to agree with; to be relevant; to have recourse to; to become a candidate. **appliance** *n.* act of applying; thing applied; an instrument or tool [L. *ad,* to; *plicare,* to fold].

ap·point (ą·point′) *v.t.* to set apart; to assign; to ordain; to decree; to designate for an office; to fix (a date); to equip. **-ed** *a.* established, furnished. **-ee** *n.* the person appointed. **-ment** *n.* the act of appointing; a new situation; date. **-ments** *n.pl.* equipment; furnishings; fittings [Fr. *à point,* fitly].

ap·por·tion (ą·pōr′·shąn) *v.t.* to divide and share in just proportion. **-ment** *n.* [L. *ad,* to; *portio,* a share].

ap·po·site (ap′·ą·zit) *a.* appropriate; well adapted. **-ly** *adv.* **-ness** *n.* **apposition** (ap·ą·zish′·ąn) *n.* the act of placing beside; (*Gram.*) the relation to a noun (or pronoun) of a noun, adjective, or clause, added by way of explanation. **appositional** *a.* [L. *appositus,* put near].

ap·praise (ą·prāz′) *v.t.* to put a price upon; to fix the value of. **appraisal** *n.* the act of appraising; a valuation. **-ment** *n.* **-r** *n.* **appraising** *a.* [L. *ad,* to; *pretium,* price].

ap·pre·ci·ate (ą·prē′·shi·āt) *v.t.* to value justly; *v.i.* to rise in value. **appreciation** (ą·prē·shi·ā′·shąn) *n.* the setting of a value on; a just estimate; rise in value. **appreciative, appreciatory** *a.* **appreciatively** *adv.* **appreciable** *a.* that may be estimated. **appreciably** *adv.* [L. *ad,* to; *pretium,* price].

ap·pre·hend (ap·ri·hend′) *v.t.* to seize; to arrest; to understand; to fear. **apprehensible** *a.* **apprehension** *n.* **apprehensive** *a.* filled with dread; suspicious. **apprehensively** *adv.* [L. *ad,* to; *prehendere,* to grasp].

ap·pren·tice (ą·pren′·tis) *n.* one bound to another to learn a trade or art; beginner; *v.t.* to bind as apprentice. **-ship** *n.* [L. *ad,* to; *prehendere,* to grasp].

ap·prise (ą·prīz′) *v.t.* to inform; to tell; to give notice [Fr. *apprendre,* to inform].

ap·proach (ą·prōch′) *v.i.* to come near; *v.t.* to come near to; to enter into negotiations with; to resemble; (*Golf*) to play a shot intended to reach the green; *n.* the act of drawing near; access; a road; approximation; negotiation. **-es** *n.pl.* the works thrown up by besiegers in their advances towards a fortress. **-able** *a.* accessible. **-ability** *n.* [L. *ad,* to; *prope,* near].

ap·pro·ba·tion (ap·rą·bā′·shąn) *n.* approval; sanction. **approbate** *v.t.* to approve of. **approbative, approbatory** *a.* approving [L. *ad,* to; *probare,* to test].

ap·pro·pri·ate (ą·prō′·pri·āt) *v.t.* to take as one's own; to set apart for a particular purpose; to claim; *a.* suitable; fitting. **-ly** *adv.* **-ness** *n.* **appropriation** *n.* the act of setting apart. **appropriative** *a.* **appropriator** *n.* [L. *ad,* to; *proprius,* one's own].

ap·prove (ą·prōōv′) *v.t.* to be pleased with; to commend; to accept; to sanction officially. **approval** *n.* **approving** *a.* [L. *ad,* to; *probare,* to test].

ap·prox·i·mate (ą·pråk′·si′·māt) *v.t.* to come near to; to bring near; *a.* near to; nearly correct; not quite exact. **-ly** *adv.* **approximation** *n.* a coming near; a close estimate [L. *ad,* to; *proximus,* near].

ap·pur·te·nance (ą·pur′·tą·nąns) *n.* that which appertains or is annexed to another thing; adjunct; accessory. **appurtenant** *a.* [O.Fr. *apartenance,* a belonging].

a·pri·cot (ā′·pri·kåt) *n.* an oval, orange-yellow fruit [L. *praecox,* early ripe].

A·pril (ā′·pril) *n.* the fourth month of the year [L. *Aprilis,* fr. *aperire,* to open].

a pri·o·ri (ā·pri·ō′·ri·) from cause to effect [L. from something prior].

a·pron (ā′·prąn) *n.* a covering or protection worn in front to protect the clothes; concrete-surfaced area in front of aircraft hangar [O.Fr. *naperon,* a cloth].

a·pro·pos (a·prą·pō′) *adv.* at the right time; *adj.* apt, relevant [Fr.].

apse (aps) *n.* semi-circular recess at east end of church. **apsidal** *a.* [Gk. *hapsis,* loop].

ap·sis (ap′·sis) *n.* the point at which a planet is nearest to, or farthest from, the sun; *pl.* **apsides** (ap′·si·dēz). **apsidal** *a.* [Gk. *hapsis,* a loop, a vault].

apt (apt) *a.* fit; suitable; prompt; quick-witted. **-ly** *adv.* **aptitude** *n.* natural capacity for; suitableness; faculty for learning; talent. **-ness** *n.* fitness; appropriateness [L. *aptus,* fit].

aq·ua (ak′·wą, ā′·kwa) *n.* L. = water. **aqua fortis** *n.* nitric acid. **aqua pura,** pure water. **aqua vitae,** any distilled alcoholic liquor.

aq·ua·ma·rine (ak·wa·ma·rēn) *n.* a semi-precious stone; *a.* of a sea-green color [L. *aqua,* water; *mare,* the sea].

aq·ua·plane (ak′·wạ·plān) *n.* a plank or boat towed by a fast motor-boat [L. *aqua*, water; *planus*, flat].

a·quar·i·um (ạ·kwā′·ri·ạm) *n.* a glass tank in which is kept living specimens of water animals and plants; *pl.* **-s**, or **aquaria** [L. *aqua*, water].

A·quar·i·us (ạ·kwā′·ri·us) *n.* (*Astron.*) the Waterbearer, the 11th sign of the Zodiac.

a·quat·ic (ạ·kwat′·ik) *a.* growing or living in water; practiced on, or in, water [L. *aqua*, water].

aq·ua·tint (ak′·wạ·tint) *n.* an etching process; *v.i.* [L. *aqua*, water, and *tint*].

aq·ue·duct (ak′·we·dukt) *n.* a course, channel, or bridge for conveying water either under or above ground [L. *aqua*, water; *ducere*, to lead].

a·que·ous (ā′·kwi·ạs) *a.* watery; made of, or from, water. **-ly** *adv.* [L. *aqua*, water; *ferre*, to bear].

aq·ui·line (ak′·wi·līn, ·lin) *a.* belonging to the eagle; curving; hooked like the beak of an eagle [L. *aquila*, an eagle].

Ar·ab (ar′·ạb) *n.* native of Arabia; an Arab horse. **street arab,** a homeless urchin of the streets. **Arabian** (ạ·rā′·bi·ạn) *n.* the native of Arabia; *a.* relating to Arabia. **Arabic** (ar′·a·-bik) *n.* the language of the Arabians.

ar·a·besque (ar·ạ·besk′) *n.* an ornament after the Arabian manner, with intricate interlacing of foliage, fruits, etc. **arabesqued** *a.* [It. *Arabesco*, Arabian-like]. [L. *arare*, to plough].

ar·a·ble (ar′·ạ·bl) *a.* fit for ploughing or tillage

a·rach·nid (a·rak′·nid) *n.* one of the *Arachnida*, the spiders, scorpions, mites, etc. **arachnoid** *a.* resembling *Arachnida;* cobweb-like. **arachnoidal** *a.* [Gk. *arachne*, a spider].

ar·bi·ter (ȧr′·bi·tẹr) *n.* (*fem.* **arbitress**) an umpire; a judge in a dispute; one who has supreme control. **arbitrable** *a.* capable of settlement by discussion. **arbitrage** *n.* **arbitral** *a.* pertaining to an arbiter or arbitration. **arbitrament** *n.* decision; authoritative judgment; award of arbitration. **arbitrary** *a.* guided by will only; high-handed; despotic; absolute. **arbitrarily** *adv.* **arbitrariness** *n.* **arbitrate** *v.t.* and *v.i.* to hear and give an authoritative decision in a dispute. **arbitration** *n.* a method of settling disputes between persons, parties and nations by an agreement on both sides to accept the findings of a third party. **arbitrator** *n.* (*fem.* **arbitratrix**) a referee; an umpire [L. *arbiter*, a judge].

ar·bor (ȧr′·bẹr) *n.* the Latin word for a *tree.* **arboraceous** *a.* tree-like; wooded; **arboreal** *a.* living in trees. **arboreous** *a.* wooded. **arborescent** *a.* growing like a tree. **arboretum** *n.* botanical garden for special planting and growing of trees; (*pl.* **arboreta**). **arborous** *a.* formed by trees [L. *arbor*, a tree].

ar·bor (ȧr′·bẹr) *n.* a garden seat sheltered or enclosed by trees; a bower; a shady retreat. [L. *arbor*, a tree].

ar·bu·tus (ȧr·bū′·tạs) *n.* evergreen shrub with scarlet berries. [L. *arbutus*, the wild strawberry tree].

arc (ȧrk) *n.* a curved line or any part of a curve forming segment of a circle; the arc-shaped band of light formed by passage of an electric current between two carbon points. **— lamp,** *n.* an electric lamp making use of electric arc, used in spotlights, searchlights, etc. **— welding,** *n.* a method of joining metals by use of electric arc [L. *arcus*, bow].

ar·cade (ȧr·kād′) *n.* a series of arches, generally supported by pillars; a walk, arched above; a covered street, usually with shops on both sides [L. *arcus*, bow].

Ar·ca·di·a (ȧr·kā′·di·ạ) *n.* region in the Peloponnesus conceived by poets to be a land of shepherds and shepherdesses. **Arcadian** *a.* **Arcady** *n.* an ideal rustic place.

ar·ca·num (ȧr·kā′·num) *n.* a secret; mystery. *pl.* **arcana** [L. *arcanum*, secret].

arch (ȧrch) *a.* cunning; sly; mischievous; roguish. **-ness** *n.* [Gk. *archein*, to rule].

arch (ȧrch) *prefix* used as *a.* chief; first of a class, as in *arch-bishop*, etc. **-angel** *n.* an angel of supreme order. **-deacon** *n.* a Church dignitary next below bishop. **-duke** *n.* a grand duke. **-duchess** *n.* **-duchy** *n.* the territory of an archduke. **-ducal** *a.* **-enemy** *n.* chief enemy [Gk. *archein*, to rule].

arch (ȧrch) *n.* an arc of a circle; a structure for support; *v.t.* or *v.i.* to form an arch; to bend into an arch. **-ed** *a.* **-way** *n.* arched passage or entrance [L. *arca*, a chest, and *arcus*, a bow].

ar·chae·ol·o·gy, archeology (ȧr·kē·ȧl′·ạ·-ji·) *n.* the study of human antiquities. **archaeologist** *n.* **archaeological** *a.* [Gk. *archaios*, ancient; *logos*, a discourse].

ar·cha·ic (ȧr·kā′·ik) *a.* antiquated; ancient; antique; obsolete; primitive. **archaically** *adv.* **archaism** *n.* a word, expression or idiom out of date. **archaist** *n.* an antiquary; one who revives the use of archaisms in his writings. **archaistic** *a.* [Gk. *archaios*, ancient].

ar·che·an (ȧr·kē′·an) *a.* pert. to the oldest period of geological time [Gk. *archaios*, ancient].

arch·er (ȧrch′·ẹr) *n.* one who shoots with a bow; a bowman. **-y** *n.* art and practice of shooting with bow and arrow [L. *arcus*, a bow].

ar·che·type (ȧr′·kẹ·tīp) *n.* the original pattern or model from which a thing is made or copied; prototype. **archetypal** *a.* [Gk. *archi-*, chief; *tupos*, a model].

ar·chi·pel·a·go (ȧr·ki·pel′·ạ·gō) *n.* name originally of Aegean Sea; a group of islands; a stretch of water scattered with isles; *pl.* **archipelagoes. archipelagic** (·aj′·ik) *a.* [Gk. *archi-*, chief; *pelagos*, the sea].

ar·chi·tect (ȧr′·ka·tekt) *n.* one skilled in the art of building; designer or contriver. **architectonics** *n.pl.* the science or art of architecture. **architectural** *a.* **architecturally** *adv.* **architecture** *n.* the art of building; a distinct style of designing buildings [Gk. *archi-*, chief; *tekton*, worker].

ar·chives (ȧr′·kīvz) *n.pl.* place in which public or historical records, charters and documents are stored and preserved; public records. **archival** *a.* **archivist** *n.* a keeper of archives [Gk. *archeion*, a town-hall].

arc·tic (ȧrk′·tik) *a.* pert. to the regions near the N. Pole; northern; extremely cold; frigid [Gk. *arktos*, a bear].

ar·dent (ȧr′·dạnt) *a.* burning; passionate; eager. **-ly** *adv.* **ardency** *n.* warmth of passion; zeal. **ardor** (ȧr′·dẹr) *n.* heat; warmth of affection; eagerness; zeal [L. *ardere*, to burn].

ar·du·ous (ȧr′·dū·ạs) *a.* high and lofty; steep; difficult to overcome; laborious; strenuous. **-ly** *adv.* [L. *arduus*, steep].

are (ȧr) present indicative plural of the verb **to be** [O.E. *aron*].

are (ār) *n.* metric unit of land measure containing 100 square meters, about 119.6 square yards [Fr. fr. L. *area*].

a·re·a (ā′·ri·ạ) *n.* an open space; a tract of land; a region; scope; total outside surface of a thing; superficial extent [L. *area*, open space].

a·re·na (ạ·rē′·nạ) *n.* oval space of a Roman amphitheater, any place of public contest; a battlefield. **arenaceous** (ar·ạ·nā′·shạs), *a.* like sand; sandy [L. *arena*, sand].

ar·e·om·e·ter (a·rc·ȧm′·e·tẹr) *n.* an instrument for measuring the specific gravity of fluids [Gk. *araios*, rare; *metron*, a measure].

a·rete (ạ·rāt′) *n.* a sharp mountain ridge; a rocky spur [Fr. = a fish-bone].

ar·gent (ȧr′·jent) *a.* made of, or like, silver; silvery; *n.* white or silver color in heraldry. **-iferous** *a.* bearing silver. **-ine** *a.* pert. to, or like, silver; sounding like silver; *n.* a variety of carbonate of lime [L. *argentum*, silver].

ar·gil (ȧr′·jil) *n.* pure clay; potter's earth. [L. *argilla*, white clay].

ar·gon (ȧr′·gȧn) *n.* an inert gas used for filling electric light bulbs [Gk. *argos*, inactive].

ar·go·sy (ȧr′·gạ·si·) *n.* a large, richly-laden merchant ship [earlier *ragusye*, a ship of *Ragusa*, a Dalmatian port].

ar·got (ȧr′·gō, ȧr′·gạt) *n.* slang; cant [Fr.]. tious. [L. *arguere*, to chide].

ar·gue (ȧr′·gū) *v.t.* to prove by reasoning; to discuss; to persuade by debate; *v.i.* to prove; to offer reasons; to dispute. **arguable** *a.* capable of being argued. **-r** *n.* one who argues. **argument** *n.* a reason offered in proof for or against a thing; the subject of a speech, etc. **argumentation** *n.* arguing, reasoning. **argumentative** *a.* given to arguing; contentious. **argumentatively** *adv.* **argumentativeness** *n.* [L. *arguere*, to chide].

a·ri·a (ȧ′·ri·ạ, a′·ri·ạ) *n.* (*Mus.*) a melody as distinct from harmony; a solo part in a cantata, opera, oratorio, etc., with musical accompaniment [It. *aria*, an air].

ar·id (ar′·id) *a.* dry; parched; barren; (*Fig.*) uninteresting. **aridity** *n.* absence of moisture; dryness; barrenness [L. *aridus*].

a·right (ạ·rīt′) *adv.* rightly [E. *on right*].

a·rise (ạ·rīz′) *v.t.* to come up; to stand up; to get up; to come into view; to spring up; to occur; *pr.p.* **arising.** *pa.p.* **arisen** (ạ·rizn′). *pa.t.* **arose** [O.E. *arisan*].

ar·is·toc·ra·cy (ar·is·tȧk′·rạ·si·) *n.* originally the rule of the best; later, the rule of an hereditary upper class; privileged class in a state; the nobility; upper classes. **aristocrat** (a·ris′·tạ·krat) *n.* a member of the aristocracy. **aristocratic** *a.* **aristocratically** *adv.* [Gk. *aristos*, best; *kratos*, power].

Ar·is·tot·le (ar·is·tȧt′·l) *n.* (384-322 B.C.), a great Greek philosopher, pupil and disciple of Plato. **Aristotelian** (ar·is·tạ·tē′·li·ạn) *n.* a follower of Aristotle.

a·rith·me·tic (ạ·rith′·mạ·tik) *n.* the science of numbers; the art of reckoning by figures; a work on this subject. **arithmetical** *a.* **arithmetically** *adv.* **arithmetician** (ạ·rith·mạ·tish′·ạn) *n.* one skilled in arithmetic. **arithmetical progression,** a series of numbers which increase or decrease by a common difference, e.g. 2, 4, 6, 8, or 21, 18, 15, 12 [Gk. *arithmos*, number].

ark (ȧrk) *n.* the large floating vessel in which Noah lived during the Flood (Genesis 6-8); vessel of bulrushes in which the infant Moses was placed (Exodus 2). **ark of the Covenant,** the chest containing the two Tables of the Law, a pot of manna, and Aaron's rod (Exodus 25); a chest; a coffer [O.E. *arc*, a box].

arm (ȧrm) *n.* the limb extending from shoulders to hand; anything projecting from main body, as a branch; *v.t.* to give an arm to for support. **-less** *a.* without arms. **-ful** *n.* as much as the arms can hold. **—chair** *n.* a chair with arms. **—pit** *n.* the cavity under the shoulder. **at arm's length,** at a safe distance. **with open arms,** cordially [O.E. *earm*].

arm (ȧrm) *n.* a weapon; a branch of the army, e.g. infantry, artillery, etc.; *pl.* all weapons; exploits; military profession; armor; heraldic bearings; *v.t.* to equip with weapons; *v.i.* to take up arms. **-ed** (ȧrmd, or ȧrm′·ed) *a.* equipped with, or supported by, arms; fortified; strengthened. **armed neutrality,** the condition of holding aloof from a contest, while ready to repel attack. **small arms,** weapons that can be carried by hand, e.g. pistols, revolvers, shotguns, rifles, etc. **under arms,** enlisted for military service; fully equipped for battle. **up in arms,** eager to give battle; roused to anger. **to lay down arms,** to surrender [L. *arma*, weapons].

ar·ma·da (ȧr·mȧ′·dạ, ȧr·mā′·dạ) *n.* a fleet of armed ships [Sp. *armar*, to arm].

ar·ma·dil·lo (ȧr·mạ·dil′·ō) *n.* an animal, having the body encased in armor-like covering of small, bony shell plates [Sp. dimin. of *armado*, a man-in-armor].

Ar·ma·ged·don (ȧr·mạ·ged′·ạn) *n.* the scene of the last battle between the powers of good and evil, before Day of Judgment; final decisive battle between great nations. [Or. *Megiddo*, in Palestine].

ar·ma·ment (ȧr′·mạ·mạnt) *n.* land, naval, or air forces equipped for war; munitions; the process of equipping forces in time of war [L. pl. *armamenta*, equipment].

ar·ma·ture (ȧr′·mạ·chẹr) *n.* armor; protective covering (of plants); part of magnet or dynamo which rotates in electrical generator; coil of wire in electric motor which breaks magnetic field [L. *armare*, to arm].

ar·mi·stice (ȧr′·mis·tis) *n.* a temporary or lasting cessation of hostilities; a truce [L. *arma*, weapons; *sistere*, to cause to stop].

arm·let (ȧrm′·lit) *n.* a small arm, as of sea; band worn round arm. [O.E. *earm*].

ar·mor (ȧr′·mẹr) *n.* defensive covering for the body in battle; orig. chain-mail, etc.; steel plates used to protect ships of war, tanks, cars, etc. **-bearer** *n.* one who carried arms of a superior. **—clad** *a.* **-ed car,** a metal-plated car with machine-gun in revolving turret. **-ed division,** a mobile unit with tanks, armored cars, etc. [L. *armare*, to arm].

ar·mor·y (ar′·mẹr·i·) *n.* place where arms are stored; building for headquarters and drill area of National Guard unit; arsenal; (*Arch.*) science of heraldry. [L. *arma*, weapons or arms].

ar·my (ȧr′·mi·) *n.* a body of men trained and equipped for war; a military force commanded by a general; an organized body for some special purpose, e.g. *Salvation Army;* large number of people. **army corps,** a large unit comprising various branches of the service. **standing army,** the regular army in peacetime [L. *arma*, weapons].

a·ro·ma (ạ·rō′·mạ) *n.* fragrance in plants; perfume or flavor; charm; atmosphere. **aromatic** *a.* fragrant; spicy; *n.* a plant, drug with fragrant smell [Gk. *aroma*, spice].

a·round (ạ·round′) *adv.* in a circle; near; *prep.* on all sides of; about [E. *a*, on; *round*].

a·rouse (ạ·rouz′) *v.t.* to excite to action; to awaken; *v.i.* to wake; to become active. **arousal** *n.* [E. *a*, on, and *rouse*].

ar·peg·gi·o (ȧr·pe′·ji·ō) *n.* (*Mus.*) the sounding of notes of a chord in quick succession [It. *arpeggiare*, to play the harp].

ar·que·bus (ȧr′·kwi·bạs) *n.* an ancient form of handgun. Also **harqueous. arquebusier** *n.* [O.H.Ger. *Haken*, hook; *Büchse*, a gun].

ar·raign (a·rān′) *v.t.* to call or set a prisoner at the bar; to call to account; to accuse publicly. **-ment** *n.* [L. *ad*, to; *ratio*, account].

ar·range (ạ·rānj′) *v.t.* to put into order; to settle terms; to prepare; to adapt; to adjust; *v.i.* to make agreement; to take steps. **-ment** *n.* act of arranging; the way or manner in which things are placed; needful preparation; (*Mus.*) transcription or adaptation of a piece of music to an instrument other than that for which it was originally composed. **-r** *n.* [Fr. *rang*, rank]. [utter. **-ly** *adv.* (doublet of errant).

ar·rant (ar′·ạnt) *a.* notorious; unmitigated;

ar·ras (ar′·ạs) *n.* tapestry; large tapestries, used as wall hangings [fr. the city of *Arras*, France, where first woven].

ar·ray (ạr·rā′) *v.t.* to set in order; to draw up, as troops for battle; to dress; to equip; *n.* order; equipment; fine apparel [O.Fr. *aréer*].

ar·rear (ạ·rēr′) *n.* the state of being behind. **-s** *n.pl.* moneys still owing; work still to be overtaken. **-age** *n.* [Fr. *arrière*, behind].

ar·rest (ạ·rest′) *v.t.* to stop; to check; to hinder; to seize by authority of law; to engage the attention; *n.* the apprehending of a person by the authority of law; any seizure, physical or moral; stoppage. **arrestation** *n.* act of arresting. **-er, -or** *n.* one who, or that which, arrests. **-ing.** *a.* impressive; striking. **-ive** *a.* calculated to draw attention. **-ment** *n.* an arrest of a criminal; the seizure of a person's wages, etc. in debt claims [O.Fr. *arester*].

ar·rive (ạ·rīv′) *v.i.* to reach a point; to come to; to attain to any aim or object. **arrival** *n.* act of arriving [Fr. *arriver*, to arrive].

ar·ro·gance (ar′·ạ·gạns) *n.* insolent pride; intolerable presumption; overbearing manner. **arrogant** *a.* presuming on one's rank or power; haughty; proud. **arrogantly** *adv.* **arrogate** *v.t.* to claim unduly; to take upon one's self without authority; to demand overbearingly; to presume [L. *ad*, for; *rogare*, to ask].

ar·row (ar′·ō) *n.* a barbed missile shot from a bow; a sign ➳ to show direction. **-y** *a.* of, like an arrow. **—grass** *n.* small, erect, grass-like plants [O. E. *arwe*].

ar·row·root (ar′·ō·ròòt) *n.* a nutritious starch used in puddings, cookies, etc. [So-called because used to counteract the poison of arrows].

ar·roy·o (ạ·roi′·ō) *n.* gulch, small watercourse having steep sides and usually dry [Sp.].

ar·se·nal (àr′·sạn·ạl) *n.* factory for military and naval arms and stores; an armory [It. *arsenale*, fr. Ar. *al-sina'ah*, workshop].

ar·se·nic (àr′·sạ·nik) *n.* a semi-metallic element; the poisonous, whitish, or steel-grey powder of white oxide of arsenic. **arsenic, arsenical** *a.* pert. to arsenic. [Gk. *arsēn*, male. The alchemists classed metals as male and female].

arsenous *a.* [Gk. *arsēn*, male. The alchemists classed metals as male and female].

ar·son (àr′·sạn) *n.* the crime of intentionally setting on fire houses, buildings, ships, or other property [L. *ardere*, *arsum*, to burn].

art (àrt) *n.* skill; human skill as opposed to nature; skill applied to music, painting, poetry, etc.; any of the subjects of this skill; a system of rules; a profession or craft; cunning; trick. **arts** *n.pl.* certain branches of learning, languages, history, etc. as distinct from natural science. **-ful** *a.* exhibiting art or skill; crafty; cunning. **-fully** *adv.* **-fulness** *n.* **-less** *a.* free from art; guileless. **-lessly** *adv.* **-lessness** *n.* **-y** *a.* (*Colloq.*) affectedly artistic. **black art,** magic. **fine arts,** painting, sculpture, architecture, music. **useful arts,** those in which the hands, rather than the mind, are used [L. *ars*, *artis*].

ar·ter·y (àr′·te·ri·) *n.* a vessel carrying blood from the heart; (*Fig.*) any essential channel of communication. **arterial** (àr·tē′·ri·ạl) *a.* pert. to an artery; pert. to a first-class road. **arterialize** *v.t.* to change venous blood into arterial blood by oxygenization. **arterialization** *n.* **arteriole** *n.* a small artery. **arteriosclerosis** *n.* (*Med.*) a hardening of the arteries [Gk. *arteria*, the windpipe, an artery; *logos*, discourse; *skleros*, hard].

ar·te·sian well (àr·tē′·zhạn wel) *n.* a well bored deep enough so that water rises to the surface of the ground by internal pressure (the first such well was sunk at *Artois* in the 12th cent.) [Fr. *Artésien*].

ar·thri·tis (àr·thrī′·tis) *n.* inflammation of a joint; gout. **arthritic(al)** (àr·thrit′·ik) *a.*

ar·thro·pod (àr′·thrạ·pàd) *n.* an animal with segmented body and jointed limbs, e.g. a spider, crustacean, etc. **arthropodal** *a.* [Gk. *arthron*, a joint; *pous*, *podos*, a foot].

ar·ti·choke (àr′·ti·chōk) *n.* a plant with thistlelike head, which can be cooked and the fleshy base eaten. **Jerusalem artichoke** *n.* an entirely different plant, bearing edible tubers which resemble the potato in appearance [It. *articiocco*, fr. Ar., Jerusalem is corrupt. of It. *girasole*, sun-flower].

ar·ti·cle (àr′·ti·kl) *n.* a clause or term in a contract, treaty, etc.; a literary composition in a journal, etc.; a paragraph or section; a point of faith; a rule or condition; an item; a commodity or object; (*Gram.*) one of the words *a*, *an* (the indefinite article) and *the* (the definite article); *v.t.* to apprentice; to accuse specifically [L. *articulus*, a little joint].

ar·tic·u·lar (àr·tik′·yoo·lạr) *a.* pert. to the joints [L. *articulus*, a little joint].

ar·tic·u·late (àr·tik′·yoo·lāt) *v.t.* to connect by a joint; to utter clearly-defined sounds; *v.i.* to be connected by joints; to speak in distinct syllables or words; *a.* jointed; of speech, clear, distinct. **-ly** *adv.* **-ness** *n.* **articulation** *n.* the act of articulating; a consonant; a joint between two or more bones [L. *articulus*, a little joint, fr. *artus*, a limb].

ar·ti·fact (àr′·ti·fakt) *n.* object made by man [L. *ars*, *artis*, art; *facere*, to make].

ar·ti·fice (àr′·ti·fis) *n.* an artful or skilful contrivance; a ruse; a trick; cunning. **artificer** *n.* a skilled workman; an inventor. **artificial** (àr·ti·fish′·ạl) *a.* made by art; manufactured; affected in manners. **artificially** *adv.* **artificiality** *n.* [L. *artificium*, a trade, fr. *ars*, art; *facere*, to make].

ar·til·lery (àr·til′·ạ·ri·) *n.* cannon; troops trained in the use of guns; a branch of the armed forces. **artilleryman** *n.* a soldier serving in the artillery [Fr. *artillerie*, fr. O.Fr. *artillier*, to equip].

ar·ti·san (àr′·ti·zạn) *n.* a craftsman; a mechanic [Fr. fr. L. *ars*, *artis*, art].

art·ist (àr′·tist) *n.* one who practices one of the fine arts, e.g. painting, sculpture, etc.; applicable to any craftsman whose work is of high standard. **-ic(al),** *a.* **-ically** *adv.* **artistry** (ar′·tis·tri·) *n.* artistic ability or effect; beauty of work [L. *ars*, *artis*, art].

ar·tiste (àr·tēst′) *n.* an expert in some art, not one of the fine arts; often applied to a member of the theatrical profession [L. *ars*, *artis*, art].

Ar·y·an (ā′·ri·ạn) *n.* the progenitors of the Indo-European group, i.e. Celtic, Teutonic, etc. [Sans. *Arya*, noble].

as (az) *adv.* like; in like manner; similar to; for example; *conj.* since; because; when; while; *pron.* that [form of *also*].

as·bes·tos (as·bes′·tạs) *n.* a fibrous non-inflammable mineral, used in manufacture of fire-proof materials [Gk. *a-*, neg.; *sbestos*, to be quenched].

as·cend (ạ·send′) *v.t.* to climb, to mount; to walk up; *v.i.* to rise; to arise; to soar; to climb; to mount; to go back in time. **-able, -ible** *a.* **-ancy, -ency** *n.* superior or controlling influence; authority; domination [L. *ad*, to; *scendere*, to climb].

as·cent (a·sent′) *n.* the act of rising; the way by which one rises; a slope; a way up [L. *ad*, to; *scandere*, to climb].

as·cer·tain (as·ẹr·tān′) *v.t.* to get to know; to find out for a certainty. **-able** *a.* **-ment** *n.* [L. *ad*, to; *certus*, sure].

as·cet·ic (ạ·set′·ik) *a.* sternly self-denying; austere; strict; *n.* one who practices rigorous self-denial; a hermit; an anchorite. **asceticism** *n.* **-ally** *adv.* [Gk. *askein*, to exercise].

as·cot (as′·kạt) *n.* a kind of scarf or broad tie.

as·cribe (as·krīb′) *v.t.* to attribute; to impute; to assign. **ascribable** *a.* **ascription** *n.* [L. *ascribere*, to add in writing].

a·sep·sis (ạ·sep′·sis) *n.* freedom from putrefaction; freeing from bacteria by use of antiseptics. **aseptic** *a.* not liable to putrefaction; sterilized [Gk. *a-*, neg.; *sepsis*, decay].

a·sex·u·al (ā·sek′·shoo·ạl) *a.* without sex; lacking sexual instinct or reproductive organs. **asexuality** *n.* [L. *a*, away; *sexus*, sex].

ash (ash) *n.* a genus of trees of the olive family having a tough, hard, elastic wood. **-en** *a.* [O.E. *aesce*, the ash-tree].

ash (ash) *n.* the dry white or greyish dust left after a substance has been burned. **-es** *n.pl.* the remains of a human body after cremation;

(*Fig.*) a dead body; (*Chem.*) potash. (*Naval Slang*) a depth-charge; a multiple arc lamp used in theaters. **-en** *a.* of the color of ashes; pale. — **tray** *n.* receptacle for cigarette ash. **-y** *a.* **Ash Wednesday,** the first day of Lent [M.E. *asche*, ash].

a·shamed (ạ·shāmd′) *a.* affected by shame; covered with confusion, caused by awareness of guilt [O.E. *ascamian*, to be ashamed].

a·shore (ạ·shōr′) *adv.* on or to shore; on land, opp. to *aboard* [E. *a*, on; M. E. *shore* fr. O.E. *sciran*, to cut].

A·sian, A·si·at·ic (ā′·zhạn, ā·zhi·at′·ik) *a.* pert. to Asia or to the people of Asia [Gk. *Asia*, a part of Lydia].

a·side (ạ·sīd′) *n.* something said in an undertone, esp. on stage by an actor and supposed not to be heard by the other actors; *adv.* on or to one side; apart; dismissed from use [O.E. *a*, on; *sid*, broad].

as·i·nine (as′·in·īn) *a.* pert. to an ass; stupid. **asininity** *n.* [L. *asinus*, an ass].

ask (ask) *v.t.* to seek information; to interrogate; *v.i.* (*for, about*) to request; to inquire. **-er** *n.* [O.E. *ascian*, to seek].

a·skance, a·skant (ạ·skans′, ạ·skant′) *adv.* towards one corner of the eye; awry; with disdain or suspicioun; not straightforward.

a·skew (ạ·skū′) *adv.* askant; aside; awry; obliquely; off the straight [See **skew**].

a·slant (ạ·slant′) *adv.* in a slanting direction.

a·sleep (ạ·slēp′) *adv.* and *a.* in a state of sleep; at rest; benumbed; dormant; dead.

a·slope (ạ·slōp′) *a.* sloping; tilted; oblique. *adv.* with a slope [O.E. *slūpan*, to slip].

a·so·cial (ā·sō′·shạl) *a.* not social, selfish [Gk. *a-*, neg.; social].

asp, as·pic (asp, asp′·ik) *n.* a small, hooded, poisonous serpent [Gk. *aspis*].

as·par·a·gus (ạs·par′·ạ·gạs) *n.* a succulent vegetable with tender shoots [Gk.].

as·par·tame (as·par′·tām) *n.* a low-calorie, non-carbohydrate sweetener.

as·pect (as′·pekt) *n.* look; appearance; position or situation; view [L. *aspicere*, look at].

as·pen (as′·pin) *n.* a tree known also as the trembling poplar; *a.* trembling [O.E. *aespe*].

as·per·ate (as·per′·āt) *v.t.* to make harsh or uneven; to roughen [L.].

as·per·i·ty (as·per′·i·ti·) *n.* roughness of surface, manner, or speech; harshness; crabbedness; sharpness; acrimony [L. *asper*, rough].

as·perse (ạs·purs′) *v.t.* to slander; to defame; to vilify; to calumniate; to bespatter (with). **-er** *n.* **aspersion** *n.* slander. **aspersive, aspersory** *a.* [L. *ad*, to; *spargere*, to sprinkle].

as·phalt (as′·fawlt), *n.* a black, hard, tar-like substance, used for paving, roofing, etc. **asphalt** *v.t.* to cover with asphalt. **asphaltic** *a.* bituminous [Gk. *asphaltos*].

as·phyx·i·a, as·phyx·y (ạs·fik′·si·ạ, -si·) *n.* suspended animation due to lack of oxygen in the blood; it is caused by obstructed breathing, as in drowning, inhalation of gases, etc. **-te** *v.t.* to suffocate. **-tion** *n.* [Gk. *asphuxia*, pulse stoppage].

as·pic (as′·pik) *n.* savory jelly containing pieces of fish, fowl, egg, etc. [Fr.].

as·pi·rate (as′·pi·rāt) *v.t.* to pronounce with a full breathing sound; to prefix the sound *h* to a word or letter; *n.* a letter marked with a note of breathing; a breathed sound; *a.* pronounced with a rough breathing. **aspiration** *n.* act of breathing; (*Med.*) the removal of fluids from a cavity in the body by suction [L. *aspiratus*, breathed upon].

as·pire (ạs·pīr′) *v.i.* to desire with eagerness; to strive towards something higher (usually followed by *to* or *after*). **aspirant** *a.* ambitious; *n.* one who aspires; a candidate. **aspiration** *n.* **-r** *n.* [L. *ad*, to; *spirare*, breathe].

as·pi·rin (as′·pi·rin) *n.* a drug used for relief of headache, fever, etc.

ass (as) *n.* a quadruped of the horse family; a donkey; (*Fig.*) a stupid person [L. *asinus*].

as·sail (ạ·sāl′) *v.t.* to leap or fall on; to attack; to assault; to ply with arguments, reproaches, etc. **-able** *a.* **-ant** *a.* and *n.* [L. *ad*, to; *salire*, to leap].

as·sas·sin (ạ·sas′·in) *n.* one who murders by secret or treacherous assault, esp. a hired murdered. **-ate** *v.t.* to murder by guile or by sudden violence. **-ation** *n.* **-ator** *n.* [Moslem ***hashish***, an intoxicating drug].

as·sault (ạ·sawlt′) *n.* a violent onset or attack; *v.t.* to attack violently, both physically and with words or arguments; to storm. **-able** *a.* **-er** *n.* **assault and battery** (*Law*) violent attacking and beating a person [L. *ad*, to; *salire*, to leap].

as·say (ạ·sā′) *n.* trial; test; examination; analysis of the amount of metal in ores or coins, or of ingredients in drugs; *v.t.* to test. **-er** *n.* [Fr. *essayer*, to try].

as·sem·ble (ạ·sem′·bl) *v.t.* to bring or call together; to collect; to fit together the parts, e.g. of a machine; *v.i.* to meet together. **assemblage** *n.* a group, gathering. **assembly** *n.* a meeting; a company gathered; the putting together of all the different parts to make a complete machine [L. *ad*, to; *simul*, together].

as·sent (ạ·sent′) *v.i.* to agree; to admit; to concur; *n.* acquiescence; approval. **assentation** *n.* servile assent; obsequiousness. **-er, -or** *n.* one who assents. **assentient** (ạ·sen′·shạnt) *a.* giving assent; *n.* one who assents [L. *ad*, to; *sentire*, to think].

as·sert (ạ·surt′) *v.t.* to declare strongly; to maintain or defend by argument. **-er, -or** *n.* **assertion** *n.* the act of asserting; affirmation; declaration. **-ive** *a.* positive; self-confident. **-ively** *adv.* **-iveness** *n.* **-ory** *a.* affirmative [L. *asserere*, to claim].

as·sess (ạ·ses′) *v.t.* to fix the amount of a tax or fine; to tax or fine; to estimate for damage, taxation, etc.; to rate; to appraise. **-able** *a.* **-ment** *n.* assessing; valuation for taxation; a tax; evaluation of merits. **-or** *n.* [L. *assidere*, assessum, to sit by a judge].

as·sets (as′·ets) *n.pl.* funds or property available for payment of debts, etc.; the estate of an insolvent or deceased person; the entire property of a business company, association, society, etc.; *n.sing.* an item of such property; a thing of value [Fr. *assez*, enough].

as·sev·er·ate (ạ·sev′·ẹr·āt) *v.t.* and *i.* to assert positively or solemnly; to aver. **asseveration** *n.* [L. *asseverare*, fr. *severus*, serious].

as·sid·u·ous (ạ·sid′·joo·us) *a.* constant in application or attention; diligent; hard-working. **-ly** *adv.* **-ness, assiduity** (as·i·dū′·i·ti·) *n.* close application; unremitting attention: devotion [L. *assiduus*, constantly near].

as·sign (ạ·sīn′) *v.t.* to allot; to apportion; to give out; to fix; to transfer; to ascribe. **-able** *a.* **assignation** (a·sig·nā′·shạn) *n.* the act of assigning; an appointment, esp. if made by lovers; a tryst; (*Law*) an assignment, or the deed by which it is made. **assignee** (a·sī·nē′) *n.* one to whom something is assigned; a person appointed to act for another. **-ment** *n.* an allotting to a particular person or use; a transfer of legal title or interest; a task assigned. [L. *assignare*, to allot by sign (*signuum*)].

as·sim·i·late (ạ·sim′·i·lāt) *v.t.* to make similar; to change into a like substance; to absorb into the system; to digest; *v.i.* to become similar; to be absorbed. **assimilation** *n.* the act of assimilating; (*Fig.*) full comprehension of anything. **assimilative** *a.* capable of assimilating [L. *assimilare*, to make like].

as·sist (ạ·sist′) *v.t.* to help; to aid; to give support to; *v.i.* to lend aid; to be present. **-ance** *n.* help; aid. **-ant** *a.* helping; acting under the direction of a superior; *n.* one who assists; a helper [L. *assistere*, to stand by].

as·size (ạ·sīz′) *v.t.* to fix the rate of; to assess; *n.* orig. the regulation of a court fixing selling price of bread, ale, etc.; edict; a sitting of a court of justice. **-ment** *n.* inspection of weights and measures. **-r** *n.* [O.Fr. *assise,* an assembly of judges].

as·so·ci·ate (ạ·sō′·shi·āt) *v.t.* to join with as a friend, colleague, confederate or partner; to class together; (*reflex.*) to express agreement with; *v.i.* (foll. by *with*) to keep company; to combine; *n.* (ạ·sō′·shi·it) a companion; a coadjutor; a member of a group; a junior member; *a.* affiliated. **associable** *a.* companionable. **associableness, associability,** *n.* friendly, companionable quality; sympathy; **-ship** *n.* **associative** *a.* [L. *associare,* fr. *socius,* an ally].

as·so·nance (as′·ạ·nạns) *n.* a resemblance of sounds; imperfect rhyme in which vowel sounds are same, but consonants following are different, e.g *blunder, slumber.* **assonant(al)** *a.* **assonate** *v.t.* to correspond in sound [L. *ad,* to; *sonare,* to sound].

as·sort (a·sawrt′) *v.t.* to classify; to arrange; *v.i.* to suit or agree or match (foll. by *with*). **-ed** *a.* classified; varied. **-edness, -ment** *n.* act of arranging in groups; a miscellaneous collection [Fr. *assortir,* to match].

as·suage (ạ·swāj′) *v.t.* to soften; to allay; to mitigate. **-ment** *n.* **-r** *n.* **assuasive** *a.* [L. *ad,* to; *suavis,* sweet].

as·sume (a·sȯȯm′) *v.t.* to take upon oneself; to take for granted; to appropriate; to usurp; *v.i.* to claim unduly; to be pretentious or arrogant. **assumable** *a.* **assumed** *a.* supposed; feigned; hypothetical. **assumedly** *adv.* **assuming** *a.* arrogant. **assumingly** *adv.* **assumption** *n.* the act of taking to or upon oneself by force or right; the act of taking for granted; the thing supposed to be true, or to have happened. **assumptive** *a.* [L. *ad,* to; *sumere,* to take].

as·sure (a·shoor′) *v.t.* to make sure or certain; to affirm; to ensure; to convince. **assurable** *a.* **assurance** *n.* the act of assuring; promise; self-confidence; presumption; *Br.* insurance. **-d** *a.* certain, safe; confident. **assuredly** *adv.* **assuredness** *n.* certainty. **-r** *n.* **assuringly** *adv.* confidently [L. *ad,* to; *securus,* safe].

as·ter (as′·tẹr) *n.* a genus of plants so called because the expanded flowers of various hues are like stars [Gk. *aster,* star].

as·ter·isk (as′·tạ·risk) *n.* the mark (*) used in printing to indicate words for reference or words omitted. **asterism** *n.* small cluster of stars; three asterisks (***), indicating point or passage of special interest [Gk. *asterikos,* a little star]. [hinder part of ship; behind.

a·stern (ạ·sturn′) *adv.* in, at, or toward the

as·ter·oid (as′·tẹr·oid) *a.* star-shaped; *n.* one of the smaller planets; (*Zool.*) star-fish. **asteroidal** *a.* [Gk. *aster,* a star; *eidos,* a form].

asth·ma (az′·mạ, as′·mạ) *n.* a chronic disorder of the respiratory organs, marked by cough, labored breathing and feeling of suffocation. **asthmatic(al)** *a.* **asthmatically** *adv.* [Gk. *asthma,* panting].

a·stig·ma·tism (ạ·stig′·mạ·tizm) *n.* a defect of eye, attended with dimness of vision, due to malformation of lens of eye. **astigmatic** *a.* [Gk. *a-,* neg.; *stigma,* point]. [in motion [E.].

a·stir (ạ·stur′) *adv.* or *a.* on the move; alert;

as·ton·ish (ạ·stȧn′·ish) *v.t.* to impress with sudden surprise, wonder or admiration; to strike with sudden terror; to amaze; to astound. **-ed** *a.* **-ing** *a.* **-ingly** *adv.* **-ment** *n.* [Formerly, also *astony,* fr. O.Fr. *astroner*].

as·tound (ạ·stound′) *v.t.* to strike dumb with terror or amazement; to astonish greatly; to stun. **-ing** *a.* [By-form of *astony, astonish*].

as·tra·khan (as′·trạ·kan) *n.* the skin of the young Persian lamb with soft, curling ringlets of wool; a cheap fabric, made in imitation [*Astrakhan,* city on the Caspian Sea].

as·tral (as′·tral) *a.* pert. to the stars; star-shaped [Gk. *astron,* star].

a·stray (ạ·strā′) *adv.* out of the right way; in the wrong direction.

a·strict (ạ·strikt′) *v.t.* to bind fast; to confine; to restrict; to contract. **-ion** *n.* restriction; (*Med.*) constipation. **-ive** *a.* astringent [L. *astrictus,* drawn close].

a·stride (ạ·strīd′) *adv.* straddling; with the legs apart; *prep.* with one foot on each side of an object.

as·tringe (ạ·strinj′) *v.t.* to bind together; to draw together; to astrict; to constipate. **-ncy** *n.* the condition of being astringent. **-nt** *a.* binding; strengthening; constricting; contracting; *n.* a drug which causes contraction of the muscular fiber-tissues. **-ntly** *adv.* [L. *ad,* to; *stringere,* to bind].

as·tro- (as′·trō) *prefix* used in the construction of compound words having some reference to stars [Gk. *astron,* star].

as·tro·labe (as′·trạ·lāb) *n.* instrument for finding altitude of stars, etc. [Gk. *astron,* star; *lambanein,* to take].

as·trol·o·gy (ạ·strȧl′·ạ·ji·) *n.* science which professes to interpret the influence of heavenly bodies on human affairs. **astrologer** *n.* **astrologic(al)** *a.* [Gk. *astron,* a star; *logos,* a discourse].

as·trom·e·try (ạ·strȧm′·ạ·tri·) *n.* the determination of the magnitudes of the fixed stars [Gk. *astron,* a star; *metron,* measure].

as·tro·naut (as′·trạ·nawt) *n.* a space traveler; **-ical** *a.* **-ics** *n.* science of traveling outside the earth's atmosphere [Gk. *astron,* a star; *nautilos,* a sailor].

as·tron·o·my (ạ·strȧn′·ạ·mi·) *n.* the science which studies the heavenly bodies. **astronomer** *n.* one versed in astronomy. **astronomic(al)** *a.* pert. to astronomy; boundless, countless, prodigious. [Gk. *astron,* a star; *nomos,* law].

as·tro·phys·ics (ạs·trō·fiz′·iks) *n.* (*Astron.*) the study of the physical components of the stars by means of the spectroscope and other instruments [Gk. *astron,* a star; *phusis,* nature].

as·tute (ạ·stȯȯt′) *a.* cunning; shrewd; sagacious; crafty; wily; sly; subtle; keen. **-ly** *adv.* **-ness** *n.* [L. *astutus*].

a·sun·der (ạ·sun′·dẹr) *adv.* apart; into different pieces; in a divided state.

a·sy·lum (ạ·sī′·lạm) *n.* a sanctuary; refuge for criminals, debtors, and others liable to be pursued; any place of refuge; an institution for the deaf and dumb, the blind, or the insane; the protection afforded by such places [Gk. *asulon,* inviolate].

a·sym·me·try (ā·sim′·ạ·tri·) *n.* want of symmetry. **asymmetric(al)** *a.*

as·ymp·tote (as′·im·tōt) *n.* (*Math.*) a straight line that continually approaches a curve but never meets it within a finite distance [Gk. *a-,* neg.; *sun,* with; *ptosis,* a falling].

a·syn·chro·nism (ā·sin′·krạ·nizm) *n.* lack of synchronim; want of correspondence in time. **asynchronous** *a.* not simultaneous.

a·syn·de·ton (ạ·sin′·dạ·tạn) *n.* (*Rhet.*) the omission of conjunctions. **asyndetic** *a.* [Gk. *asyndetos,* unjoined].

at (at) *prep.* denoting rest in a place, presence, or nearness; near to, by, in; engaged on; in the direction of [O.E. *aet*].

At·a·brine (at′·ạ·brin) *n.* an anti-malarial drug [Trademark].

at·a·vism (at′·ạ·vizm) *n.* the recurrence in living organisms of hereditary characteristics, diseases, etc. which have skipped one or more generations; reversion to type. **atavistic** [L. *atavus,* a great-grandfather's grandfather].

a·tax·i·a (ạ·tak′·si·ạ) *n.* (*Med.*) irregularity of bodily functions; irregularity of movement, due to defective muscular control. **ataxic** *a.* [Gk. *a-,* neg.; *taxis,* order].

ate (āt) *pa.t.* of **eat.**

at·el·ier (at·ạl·yā′) *n.* a workshop, esp. of an artist; hence, a studio [Fr. = a workshop].

a·the·ism (ā′·thē·izm) *n.* disbelief in the existence of God. **atheist** *n.* one who denies the existence of God. **atheistic, -al** *a.* **athiestically** *adv.* [Gk. *a-*, neg.; *theos*, a god] .

A·the·na, A·the·ne (a·thē′·na, -nē) *n.* (*Myth.*) Greek goddess of wisdom, art, industries, and prudent warfare. **Athenian** *a.* pert. to Athens. *n.* native of Athens.

a·thirst (ạ·thurst′) *a.* thirsty; eager [fr. *thirst*].

ath·lete (ath′·lēt) *n.* one trained to physical exercises, feats or contests of strength, etc.; a man strong and active by training. **athletic** (ath·let′·ik) *a.* pert. to physical exercises, contests, etc.; strong; vigorous; muscular. **athletics** *n.pl.* athletic sports [Gk. *athlētēs*, a contestant for a prize].

a·thwart (ạ·thwawrt′) *prep.* across; from side to side; *adv.* crosswise in opposition [O.N. *a* and *thvert*, across].

a·tilt (ạ·tilt′) *a., adv.* tilted.

a·tin·gle (ạ·ting′·gạl) *a.* tingling.

At·lan·tic (at·lan′·tik) *a.* pert. to the ocean (named after Mt. *Atlas*) separating Europe and Africa from America; *n.* the ocean itself.

At·las (at′·lạs) *n.* (*Myth.*) a Titan, condemned by Zeus to carry the world on his shoulders. **atlas** *n.* a book of maps.

at·mos·phere (at′·mạs·fēr) *n.* the mass of air, clouds, gases, and vapor, surrounding the earth or other heavenly body; any similar mass; atmospheric pressure; the air in any place, esp. if enclosed, e.g. in a theater; (*Fig.*) any surrounding influence. **atmospheric, atmospherical** *a.* pert. to, or depending on, the atmosphere. **atmospherically** *adv.* [Gk. *atmos*, vapor; *sphaira*, a ball].

at·oll (at′·ȧl, ạ·tȧl′) *n.* a ring-shaped coral reef surrounding a lagoon [Native].

at·om (at′·ạm) *n.* the smallest unit. **-ary** constituent of a chemical element; (*Fig.*) anything very small; a tiny bit. **atomic, atomical** *a.* pert to the atom. **atomicity** *n.* the number of atoms in the molecule of any element; **atomization** *n.* the changing of any liquid into the form of fine spray. **atomize** *v.t.* to reduce to atoms. **atomizer** *n.* an instrument for reducing a liquid to the form of spray. **atomy** *n.* an atom; a tiny being; (*Anat.*) a skeleton. **atom (atomic) bomb,** a bomb of unimaginable destructive power, whose energy is derived from the nuclear disintegration of atoms of elements of high atomic mass, e.g. uranium 235. **atomic energy,** energy derived from the disintegration of the nucleus of an atom. **atomic fission,** the action of disintegrating; the disintegration of the atom. **atomic pile,** apparatus for producing energy by the disintegration of atoms. **atomic weight,** the weight of an atom of an element, [Gk. *a-*, neg.; *tome*, a cuttnig].

a·tonal (ā·tōn′·ạl) *a.* (*Mus.*) without tone; unreferred to any scale or tonic. **atonality** *n.* **atonic** (ā·tȧn′·ik) *a.* without tone; unaccented; (*Med.*) lacking tone or energy. **atony** (at′·ạ·ni·) *n.* lack of tone or accent [Gk. *a-*, neg; *tonos*, tone].

a·tone (ạ·tōn′) *v.t.* to appease; to expiate (*rare*); *v.i.* to make amends or reparation for an offense; to satisfy by giving an equivalent (with *for*). **-ment** *n.* amends; reconciliation, esp. the reconciliation of God and man [E. (to set) *at one*].

a·top (ạ·tȧp′) *a., adv.* on or at the top; *prep.* [on top of.

a·tri·um (ā′·tri·um) *n.* the principal room of an ancient Roman house; (*Anat.*) an auricle of the heart [L. = a hall].

a·tro·cious (ạ·trō′·shạs) *a.* savagely brutal; extremely cruel; very wicked; grievous; (*Colloq.*) of work, etc., of very poor quality. **-ly** *adv.* **-ness** *n.* **atrocity** (ạ·trȧs′i·ti·) *n.* extreme wickedness; a brutal act [L. *atrox*, fierce].

a·tro·phy (at′·rạ·fi·) *n.* a wasting away through lack of nutrition or use; emaciation. Also *v.t.* and *i.* to waste away; to cause to waste away. **atrophic, atrophied** *a.* [Gk. *a-*, neg.; *trophē*, nourishment].

at·ro·pin, at·ro·pine (at′·rạ·pēn, ·pin) *n.* a poisonous alkaloid obtained from the deadly nightshade, used as a drug to dilate the pupil of the eye [Gk. *Atropos*, one of the *Fates*].

at·tach (ạ·tach′) *v.t.* to bind, fasten, or tie; to take by legal authority; to bind by affection; to assign, e.g. an officer to a regiment; *v.i.* to adhere; to be ascribed to. **-able** *a.* **-ed** *a.* fixed; fond of. **-ment** *n.* [Fr. *attacher*].

at·ta·ché (at·ạ·shā′) *n.* one attached to the staff of an ambassador. **— case,** *n.* small hand-case [Fr. *attacher*].

at·tack (ạ·tak′) *v.t.* to fall on with force; to assail with hostile criticism in words or writing; to set to work on; to begin to affect (of illness); *n.* a violent onset or assault [Fr. *attaquer*].

at·tain (ạ·tān′) *v.t.* to reach by exertion; to obtain by effort; to accomplish; to achieve; *v.i.* to arrive at (generally foll. by *to*). **-able** *a.* **-ability, -ableness** *n.* **-ment** *n.* [L. *attingere*, to reach].

at·taint (ạ·tānt′) *v.t.* to stain or disgrace; to accuse of; to find guilty; to deprive of civil rights for treason; *n.* a taint or disgrace. **attainder** *n.* loss of civil rights after sentence of death or outlawry for treason or felony. **-ment** *n.* [O.Fr. *ataint*, convicted].

at·tar (at′·ẹr) *n.* a fragrant oil obtained from flower-petals [Pers. *atar*, fragrance].

at·tempt (ạ·tempt′) *v.t.* to try; to endeavor to do; to attack; *n.* trial; an effort, esp. unsuccessful; an assault. *a.* [L. *ad*, to; *temptare*, to try].

at·tend (ạ·tend′) *v.t.* to accompany; to be present with or at; to give medical care to; *v.i.* to be present; to pay attention; to take care of; to wait on. **-ance** *n.* the act of attending; persons present. **-ant** *a.* being present; consequent; *n.* one who accompanies as friend or servant; a caretaker. **attention** *n.* careful observation; watching; act of civility; command issued, as in a military sense, to ensure readiness to act. **attentions** *n.pl.* courtship. **attentive** *a.* full of attention. **attentively** *adv.* [L. *ad*, to; *tendere*, to stretch].

at·ten·u·ate (ạ·ten′·ū·āt) *v.t.* to make thin or fine, to make slender; to weaken the potency of; *a.* slender; thin; (*Bot.*) tapering. **attenuant** *a.* tending to make thin, esp. of liquids; diluting. **-d** *a.* **attenuation** *n.* **attenuator** *n.* [L. *ad*, to; *tenuis*, thin].

at·test (ạ·test′) *v.t.* and *v.i.* to bear witness to; to vouch for; to certify; (*Law*) to witness officially (a signature). **-able, -ative** *a.* **-ation** *n.* [L. *attestari*, to bear witness].

At·tic (a′·tik) *a.* pert. to *Attica* or Athens; resembling the refined and elegant style of the Athenian writers. **attic** *n.* a room under the roof of a house where ceiling follows line of the roof (common in Greek archit.); a garret [Gk. *Attikos*, pert. to Attica].

at·tire (ạ·tīr′) *v.i.* to dress; to array in splendid garments; *n.* apparel; dress. **-ment, attiring** *n.* [O.Fr. *atirier*, to put in order].

at·ti·tude (at′·ạ·tôōd) *n.* posture of a person; pose (in portrait); (*Fig.*) mental or moral disposition [L. *aptus*, fit].

at·tor·ney (ạ·tur′·ni·) *n.* one put in the *turn* or place of another; one legally authorized by another to transact business; lawyer; solicitor. **attorn** *v.t.* to transfer; *v.i.* to transfer homage; to acknowledge a new landlord. **-ship** *n.* **-dom** *n.* **— general** *n.* chief law officer of a state or nation. **power, letter** or **warrant of attorney,** a legal authorization by which one person may act for another [O.Fr. *atorner*, to direct].

at·tract (ạ·trakt′) *v.t.* and *v.i.* to draw toward; to cause to approach; (*Fig.*) to allure; to provoke notice. **-able** *a.* **-ile** *a.* attractive. **attraction** *n.* the act of drawing to; the force which draws together bodies or particles; the affinity existing between one chemical body and another; (*Fig.*) that which allures, or fascinates. **-ive** *a.* **-ively** *adv.* **-iveness** *n.* [L. *ad*, to;

trahere, tractum, to draw].

at·tri·bute (ạ·trib′·yoot) *v.t.* to consider as belonging to; to ascribe to. **attribute** (at′·rạ·būt) *n.* something inherent in a person or thing; an inseparable property; (*Gram.*) a qualifying word used, not as part of predicate, but adjectivally, as in *red* hair. **attributable** *a.* that may be ascribed to. **attribution** *n.* the act of ascribing to; the quality attributed. **attributive** *a.* [L. *ad,* to; *tribuere,* to bestow].

at·tri·tion (ạ·trish′·ạn) *n.* the act of wearing away by friction; state of being worn; (*Mil.*) deliberate exhaustion of enemy's men and resources before making an attack. **attrite** *a.* worn away by rubbing or friction; (*Theol.*) penitent through fear [L. *attritus,* rubbed away].

at·tune (ạ·tōōn′) *v.t.* to put in tune; to make musical; to make one instrument accord with another; (*Fig.*) to bring into spiritual harmony; to fit for a purpose. *a.* in harmony. **-ment** *n.* [L. *ad,* to; *tune*].

a·typ·i·cal (ā·tip′·ạ·kạl) *a.* not typical; abnormal. **-ly** *adv.* [Gk. *a-,* neg.; typical].

au·burn (aw′·burn) *a.* reddish brown; *n.* rich chestnut color [L.L. *alburnus,* blond].

auc·tion (awk′·shạn) *n.* a method of public sale whereby the object for sale is secured by highest bidder; *v.t.* to sell by auction. **-eer** *n.* one licensed to sell by auction; *v.i.* to sell by auction [L. *augere, auctum,* to increase].

auc·tion bridge (awk′·shạn brij′) *n.* a card game in which the players bid.

au·da·cious (aw·dā′·shạs) *a.* bold, fearless; impudent; insolent. **-ly** *adv.* **-ness** *n.* **audacity** (aw·da′·si·ti·) *n.* boldness, effrontery, impudence. [L. *audix,* bold].

au·di·ble (aw′·dạ·bl) *a.* capable of being heard. **audibly** *adv.* **audibility** *n.* [L. *audire,* to hear].

au·di·ence (aw′·di·ạns) *n.* the act of hearing; an assembly of hearers or spectators; a ceremonial reception or interview; a judicial hearing. **audient** *a.* listening [L. *audire,* to hear].

au·di·o (aw′·di·ō) *a.* electronic apparatus using audible frequencies (between 15-20,000 cycles) [L. *audire,* hear].

au·dit (aw′·dit) *n.* an examination, by qualified persons, of accounts of a business, public office, or undertaking; *v.t.* to test and vouch for the accuracy of accounts; listen. **audition** *n.* the act, or sense, of hearing; hearing given to a performer as test. **-or** *n.* a hearer; one authorized to investigate the financial condition of a company or society. **auditorium** *n.* the body of a concert hall or theater where the audience are seated; the nave of a church. **-ory** *a.* pert. to the sense of hearing; *n.* a lecture room; an audience [L. *audire,* to hear].

au·ger (aw′·gẹr) *n.* a boring tool for woodwork, like a large gimlet. [*An auger* for *a nauger,* fr. O.E. *nafu,* nave; *gār,* dart].

aught (awt) *n.* anything; any part; zero; *adv.* to any extent [O.E. *awiht,* fr. *a,* ever, and *wiht,* thing].

aug·ment (awg·ment′) *v.t.* to increase; to add to; to make larger; to enlarge; *v.i.* to grow larger. **augment** *n.* an increase; a prefix added to the past tense of verbs to distinguish them from other tenses. **-able** *a.* **-ation** *n.* act of enlarging; an increase. **-ative** *a.* increasing; *n.* a word which expresses with increased force the idea conveyed by the simpler word. **-er** *n.* [L. *augumentum,* an increase].

au·gur (aw′·gẹr) *n.* a soothsayer; a diviner; a member of a college of priests in Rome who claimed to be able to foretell events by observing the flight or other actions of birds; *v.t.* to foretell; to presage; to prognosticate. **-al** *a.* **-ship** *n.* **-y** *n.* divination; omen [L.].

au·gust (aw·gust′) *a.* majestic; imposing; sublime; grand; magnificent; sacred. **-ly** *adv.* **-ness** *n.* [a title first bestowed on the Emperor Octavianus by the Roman Senate, fr. L. *augere,* to increase].

Au·gust (aw′·gạst) *n.* the eighth month of the year [in honor of the Emperor *Augustus*].

Au·gus·tan (aw·gus′·tạn) *a.* classic; refined; pertaining to the Emperor *Augustus,* 31 B.C.-A.D. 14; *n.* a writer of the Augustan age.

Au·gus·tine (aw·gạs·tēn′) *n.* a member of a monastic order which follows rules framed by St. Augustine (354-430) or deduced from his writings; a Black Friar.

auk (awk) *n.* a marine bird, of the Arctic regions [Ice. *alka*].

aunt (ant, ȧnt) *n.* a father's or a mother's sister; also applied to an uncle's wife [L. *amita,* a father's sister].

au·ra (aw′·rạ) *n.* a subtle invisible essence or fluid said to emanate from human and animal bodies, and even from things; the atmosphere surrounding a person; character; personality; (*Path.*) a premonitory symptom of epilepsy and hysteria, as of cold air rising to the head. **-l** *a.* pert. to the air, or to an aura [L. *aura,* a breeze].

au·ral (aw′·rạl) *a.* pert. to the ear, or sense of hearing. **-ly** *adv.* [L. *auris,* the ear].

au·re·ole (aw′·ri·ōl), **au·re·ola** (aw·rē′·ạ·lạ) *n.* a radiance around a sacred figure, in art; a halo; a nimbus [L. *aureus,* golden].

Au·re·o·my·cin (aw′·ri·ō·mī′·sin) *n.* an antibiotic [Trademark].

au·ric (aw′·rik) *a.* pert. to gold; (*Chem.*) applied to compounds in which gold is trivalent. **aureate** *a.* golden [L. *aurum,* gold].

au·ri·cle (aw′·ri·kl) *n.* the external ear; each of the two upper cavities of the heart. **auricula** (aw·rik′·yoo·lạ) *n.* a part like an ear. **auricular** *a.* pert. to ear, or to hearing; (confession) told in the ear. **auriculate, auriform** *a.* ear-shaped [L. *auris,* the ear].

au·rif·er·ous (aw·rif′·ạ·rạs) *a.* yielding gold [L. *aurum,* gold; *ferre,* to bear].

Au·ro·ra (aw·raw′·rạ) *n.* (*Myth.*) the Roman goddess of the dawn. **aurora** *n.* the dawn; the rosy tint in the sky before the sun rises; an orange-red color. **aurora borealis** (bō·ri·a′·lis) *n.* a luminous phenomenon, supposed to be of electrical origin, seen at night in the northern sky. Also called 'northern lights.'

aus·cul·ta·tion (aws·kul·tā′·shạn) *n.* (*Med.*) listening to the movement of heart and lungs either directly with the ear, or with a stethoscope. **auscultate** *v.t., v.i.* to examine thus [L. *auscultare,* to listen to].

aus·pice (aw′·spis) *n.* favoring influence; an omen based on observing birds; augury; divination. **-s** *n.pl.* protection; patronage esp. **under the -s of. auspicate** *v.t.* to predict; to inaugurate in favorable conditions. **auspicious** (aw·spi′·shạs) *a.* giving promise of success; favorable; propitious. **auspiciously** *adv.* **auspiciousness** *n.* [L. *auspicium,* fr. *avis,* a bird; *specere,* to behold].

aus·tere (aw·stēr′) *a.* harsh; severe; strict; simple and without luxury. **-ly** *adv.* **-ness, austerity** *n.* severity; extreme simplicity; asceticism [Gk. *austeros,* harsh].

aus·tral (aws′·trạl) *a.* southern [L. *auster,* the south wind].

au·tar·chy (aw′·tȧr·ki·) *n.* absolute power; despotism; dictatorship. **autarchic** *a.* [Gk. *autos,* self; *archein,* to rule].

au·then·tic (aw·then′·tik) *a.* genuine; real; not of doubtful origin; trustworthy; of attested authority. Also **-al. -ally** *adv.* **-ate** *vt.* to prove to be genuine; to confirm. **-ation** *n.* **-ity** *n.* (aw·then·tis′·ạ·ti·) the quality of genuineness [Gk. *authentikos,* warranted, fr. *authentein,* to have full power].

au·thor (aw′·thẹr) *n.* (*fem.* **-ess**) the beginner or originator of anything; the writer of a book, article, etc. **-ial** *a.* pert. to an author. **-ship** *n.* the quality or function of being an author; source; origin [L. *auctor*].

au·thor·i·ty (aw·thár′·i·ti·) *n.* legal power or right; accepted source of information; a writing by an expert on a particular subject; the writer himself; justification; influence; permission; a body or group of persons in control (often *pl.*). **authoritarian** *a.* advocating obedience to authority as opposed to individual liberty; *n.* an advocate of authority. **authoritative** *a.* having the weight of authority; justified. **authoritatively** *adv.* [L. *auctoritas*].

au·thor·ize (aw′·tha·rīz) *v.t.* to clothe with authority; to empower; to sanction; to make legal; to justify. **authorization** *n.* [L. *auctorari*].

au·to- (aw′·tō) a combining form fr. Gk. *autos*, self, used in many derivatives and meaning *self, oneself, by oneself*, etc.

au·to (aw′·tō) *n.* (*Colloq.*) abbrev. for automobile. **-ist** *n.* a motorist. **-mobile** (aw·tȧ·-mȧ′·bēl) *n.* a road vehicle driven by mechanical power. **-motive** *a.* pertaining to automobiles; self-propelling [Gk. *autos*, self; L. *mobilis*, mobile].

au·to·bahn (aw′·tạ·bȧn) in Germany, a highway specially constructed for motor traffic [Ger. *Bahn*, a road].

au·to·bi·og·raphy (aw·tạ·bī·ȧg′·rạ·fi·) *n.* the story of a person's life, written by himself. **autobiographer** *n.* **autobiographic** *a.* [Gk. *autos*, self; *bios*, life; *graphein*, to write].

au·to·crat (aw′·tạ·krat) *n.* monarch who rules by his own absolute right; despot. **-ic** *a.* **-ically** *adv.* **autocracy** (aw·tok′·rạ·si·) *n.* uncontrolled power; a state ruled thusly [Gk. *autos*, self; *kratein*, to rule].

au·to·gi·ro (aw·tạ·ji··rō) *n.* airplane using horizontal revolving wings for vertical ascent and descent [Gk. *autos*, self; *guros*, a ring].

au·to·graph (aw′·tạ·graf) *n.* a person's own handwriting or signature; an original manuscript; *a.* written in one's own handwriting; *v.t.* to write with one's own hand; to write one's signature [Gk. *autos*, self; *graphein*, to write].

au·to·mat·ic (aw·tạ·mat′·ik) *a.* self-acting; mechanical; not voluntary; done unconsciously; *n.* an automatic pistol. **automat** *n.* a restaurant which serves food using automatic devices. **-ally** *adv.* mechanically. **automate** *v.t.* **automation** (aw·tạ·mā′·shạn) *n.* the automatic control of production processes by electronic apparatus. **automatism** *n.* involuntary action; power of self-movement without external stimulus. **automaton** (aw·tám′·ạ·tan) *n.* [Gk. *automatso*, self-acting].

au·to·mo·bile. See **auto.**

au·ton·o·my (aw·tán′·ạ·mi·) *n.* the right of self-government; independence; **autonomous, autonomic** *a.* [Gk. *autos*, self; *nomos*, a law].

au·top·sy (aw′·tȧp·si·) *n.* the dissection and examination of a dead body; a post-mortem examination; personal observation. **autoptic, (al)** *a.* self-observed. **autoptically** *adv.* [Gk. *autos*, self; *opsis*, sight].

au·to·sug·ges·tion (aw·tō·sạg·jes′·chạn) *n.* a mental process similar to hypnotism but applied by the subject to himself.

au·tumn (aw′·tạm) *n.* the third season of the year, generally applied to September, October, and November; fall; the season of decay; the time of declining powers. **-al** *a.* [L. *autumnus*].

aux·il·ia·ry (awg·zil′·yạ·ri·) *a.* helping; assisting; subsidiary; *n.* a helper; (*Gram.*) a verb which helps to form moods, tenses, or voice of another verb, e.g. *be, have, shall, will, may* [L. *auxilium*, help].

a·vail (ạ·vāl′) *v.i.* to profit by; to take advantage of; *v.t.* to benefit; to profit; *n.* advantage; profit; benefit; utility. **-able** *a.* capable of being used to advantage; procurable. **-ability -ability** *n.* [L. *ad*, to; *valere*, to be strong].

av·a·lanche (av′·ạ·lansh) *n.* mass of snow and ice moving down from a height and gathering momentum in its descent; (*Fig.*) tremendous downpour [O.Fr. *a val*, into the valley].

av·a·rice (av′·ạ·ris) *n.* excessive love of money; greed; miserliness; cupidity. **avaricious** *a.* covetous; grasping. **avariciously** *adv.* **avariciousness** *n.* [L. *avarus*, greedy].

a·vast (a·vast′) *interj.* cease! hold! stop! enough! [Dut. *houd vast*, hold fast].

a·ve (ȧ′ vi, ȧ′·vā) *interj.* hail! farewell; *n.* an Ave Maria or Hail Mary; angel Gabriel's salutation (Luke 1) [L.].

a·venge (ạ·venj′) *v.t.* and *v.i.* to take satisfaction for an injury to; to punish a wrong-doer; to seek retribution. **-ful** *a.* desiring retribution. **-ment** *n.* **-r.** *n.* (*fem.* **-ress**) one who avenges [O.Fr. *avengier*, to seek retribution].

av·e·nue (av′·e·nòò) *n.* a wide street with houses and row of trees down each side; (*Fig.*) a means towards, as in *avenue to fame* [L. *ad*, to; *venire*, to come].

a·ver (ạ·vur′) *v.t.* to declare positively; to avouch; to assert; to allege. *pr.p.* **-ring**; *pa.p.* **-red.** **-ment** *n.* the act of averring; a positive assertion; (*Law*) proof of a plea [L. *ad*, to; *verus*, true].

av·er·age (av′·ạ·rij) *a.* containing a mean proportion; ordinary; normal; *n.* a medial estimate obtained by dividing the sum of a number of quantities by the number of quantities; *v.t.* to reduce to a mean [O.Fr. *average*, cattle or possessions; fr. L. *habere*, to have].

a·verse (ạ·vurs′) *a.* reluctant (to do) or disinclined for; unwilling; set against (foll. by *to*). **-ly** *adv.* with repugnance. **-ness** *n.* **aversion** *n.* a strong dislike; instinctive antipathy; object of dislike [L. *aversus*, turned away].

a·vert (ạ·vurt′) *v.t.* to turn away from or aside; to ward off. **-ed** *a.* **-edly** *adv.* **-ible** *a.* capable of being avoided [L. *a*, from; *vertere*, to turn].

a·vi·an (ā′·vi·ạn) *a.* pert. to birds. **aviary** *n.* an enclosed space for breeding, rearing and keeping of birds [L. *avis*, a bird].

a·vi·a·tion (ā·vi·ā′·shạn) *n.* the art of flying aircraft. **aviate** *v.i.* to fly. **aviator** *n.* (*fem.* **aviatress, axiatrix**) [L. *avis*, a bird].

av·id (av′·id) *a.* eager; greedy; desirous (foll. by *of* or *for*). **avidity** *n.* greediness; eagerness; hunger; (*Fig.*) zest [L. *avidus*, greedy].

a·vo·ca·do (av·ạ·kȧ′·dō) *n.* the alligator pear; juicy eible fruit [Mex.].

av·o·ca·tion (av·ạ·kȧ′·shạn) *n.* a distraction; a minor plausable occupation; a hobby; a side interest; **avocative** *a.* calling off; *n.* a dissuasion [L. *a*, away; *vocare*, to call].

a·void (ạ·void′) *v.t.* to shun; to elude; to keep clear of; to eschew; to abstain from; to escape; (*Law*) to invalidate; to annul. **-able** *a.* **-ance** *n.* the act of shunning [L. *ex*, out; and *void*].

av·oir·du·pois (av·ẹr·dạ·poiz′) *n.* a common system of weights; (*Colloq.*) heaviness [corrupt. of O.Fr. *avoir de pois*, goods by weight i.e. not by numbers].

a·vouch (ạ·vouch′) *v.t.* to declare positively; to guarantee [L. *ad*, to; *vocare*, to call].

a·vow (ạ·vou′) *v.t.* to declare openly; to own; to confess freely; to acknowledge. **-able** *a.* **-al** *n.* an open declaration or admission. **-ance,** evidence; testimony. **-edly** *adv.* [Fr. *avouer*].

aw (aw) *interj.* sound of protest; dislike.

a·wait (ạ·wāt′) *v.t.* to wait for; be in store for; attend; be ready for.

a·wake (ạ·wāk′) *v.t.* to rouse from sleep; to stir up; *v.i.* to cease from sleep; to bestir oneself; *pa.t.* **awoke;** *pa.p.* **awoke, awaked;** *a.* not asleep; alert; vigilant; alive. **awaken** *v.t.* and *v.i.* to rouse from sleep; to awake; to excite. **awak(en)ing** *n.* a revival of interest or conscience [O.E. *awacian*].

a·ward (ạ·wawrd′) *v.t.* to adjudge; to determine (a point submitted); to decide authoritatively; to assign judicially; *n.* judgment; the recorded decision of an arbitrator in a court of law; thing awarded; prize [fr. O. Fr. *eswarder*].

a·ware (ạ·wār′) *a.* watchful; mindful; conscious of; possessing knowledge of; sensible. **-ness** *n.*

[O.E. *gewaer*, conscious].

a·wash (ą·wȧsh′) *adv* (*Naut.*) level with the surface of the water; washed by the waves.

a·way (ą·wā′) *adv.* absent; at a distance; on the way; apart; be gone! [O.E. *onweg*, on the way].

awe (aw) *n.* wonder mingled with veneration and dread; *v.t.* to inspire with awe. **-some** *a.* **-struck, -stricken** *a.* **awful** *a.* full of awe; filling with fear and admiration; impressive; venerable; majestic, dreadful; terrible; horrible; ugly; unsightly. **awfulness** *n.* **awfully** *adv.* (*Colloq.*) very, extremely [O.E. *ege*, awe].

a·weigh (ą·wā′) *adj* (anchor) clearing the bottom; atrip.

aw·ful. See **awe.**

a·while (ą·wh.l′) *adv.* for a while.

awk·ward (awk′·węrd) *a.* unskilful; ungainly; clumsy; difficult to manage; inconvenient; embarrassing. **-ly** *adv.* **-ness** *n.* **— age** *n.* adolescence [M.E. *awk*, wrong; and *ward*].

awl (awl) *n.* a small pointed instrument for boring holes in leather [O.E. *awel*].

awn·ing (aw′·ning) *n.* a covering of canvas, etc. to shelter from the sun's rays.

a·woke. See **awake.**

a·wry (ą·ri′) *adv., a.* twisted to one side; crooked (See *wry*) [earlier, *on wry*].

ax, axe (aks) *n.* tool for cutting, chopping, or hewing. **an — to grind,** a private end or purpose to serve [O.E. *aex*].

ax·es (ak′·ses) *pl.* of **axe** and **axis.**

ax·i·om (ak′·si·ąm) *n.* a necessary and self-evident proposition, requiring no proof. **-atic(al)** *a.* self-evident. **-atically** *adv.* [Gk. *axioma*, fr. *axioein*, to require].

ax·is (ak′·sis) *n.* the imaginary line round which a solid body rotates or a geometrical figure is symmetrically disposed. *pl.* **axes** (ak′·sēs). **axial** *a.* forming the axis. **axially** *adv.* [L. *axis*, an axle].

ax·le, ax·le-tree (ak′·sl·trē) *n.* a bar of wood or iron rod on which a wheel, or a system of wheels, turns [O.N. *oxul-tre*].

ay, aye (ī) *adv.* yes; yea. **ayes** (īz) *n.pl.* affirmative votes or voters [*yea*].

ay·at·ol·lah (ȧ·yȧ·tȧl′·ą) *n.* a high-ranking imam in the Shiite branch of Islam.

aye, ay (ā) *adv.* always; ever [O.N. *ei*].

a·za·le·a (ą·zā′·li·ą) *n.* a genus of plants allied to the rhododendron [Gk. *azaleos*, dry].

a·zo·ic (ą·zō′·ik] *a.* pert. to that part of geologic time before animal life existed [Gk. *a-*, neg.; *zoe*, life].

Az·tec (az′·tek) *n.* a member of a people dominant in Mexican empire at the time of the Sp. conquest; their language; *a.* pert to the race or its language.

az·ure (azh′·ęr) *n.* sky blue; the sky; *a.* sky-blue [Fr. *azur*, from Ar.].

B

Ba·al (bā′·ąl) *n.* a false deity. *pl.* **Baalim. -ist** *n.* a worshipper of Baal [Heb.].

babble (ba′·bl) *v.t., v.i.* to chatter senselessly; to prate; to reveal secrets; *n.* prattling; idle talk; murmuring of running water. **-r** *n.* **babbling** *n.* [imit. origin].

babe (bāb) *n.* an infant; a young child [earlier *baban*, imit. of baby speech].

ba·bel (bā′·bąl) *n.* a confusion of unintelligible sounds; noisy babble of many people talking at the same time; uproar, at a public meeting. **-dom** *n.* uproar [Heb. = confusion].

ba·boon (ba·bôôn′) *n.* a species of monkey with large body, big canine teeth, and capacious cheek-pouches [Fr. *babouin*].

ba·by (bā′·bi·) *n.* an infant; a young child; *a.* pert. to a baby; small, as in *baby grand* (piano). **-hood** *n.* the period of infancy. **-ish** *a.* infantile; behaving like a young child. [earlier *baban*, imit of baby speech].

bac·ca·lau·re·ate (bak·ą·law′·ri·ąt) *n.* the university degree of bachelor; an address to a graduating class [fr. L. *baccalarius*].

Bac·chus (bak·′ąs) *n.* (*Myth.*) the god of wine. **bacchanal** *n.* a worshipper of Bacchus; a drunken reveller; an orgy in honor of Bacchus; *a.* pert. to Bacchus; riotous; drunken. **bacchanalia** *n.pl.* feasts in honor of Bacchus; drunken revels. **bacchanalian** *n.* and *a.* **bacchic** *a.* relating to Bacchus; jovial due to intoxication [L.].

bach·e·lor (bach′·ą·lęr) *n.* an unmarried man; a celibate; one who has taken the first degree at a university; a monk who performed menial duties. **-hood, -ism, -ship** *n.* [M.L. *baccalarius*, a small farmer].

ba·cil·lus (bą·sil′·ąs) *n.* microscopic, rod-like organisms capable of causing certain diseases. *pl.* **bacilli, bacillar, bacillary** *a.* **bacilliform** *a.* of a rod-like shape [L. *baculus*, a rod].

back (bak) *n.* the upper or hinder part of the trunk of an animal; the hinder part of an object; a football player whose position is behind the line of scrimmage; *a.* of the back; at the rear of; not current (as a magazine); reversed; remote; *adv.* to or toward a former place, state, condition, or time; away from the front; in return; *v.t.* to get, or ride, upon the back of; to provide with a back; to force backward; to place a bet on; to support; to endorse (a check, etc.); *v.i.* to move or go back; of the wind, to change direction counter-clockwise. **-bite** *v.t.* to speak evil of someone in his absence. **backbiter** *n.* **-bone** *n.* the spine or vertebral column; firmness; courage. **backboned** *a.* **-er** *n.* supporter; **-field** *n.* the backs as in football who play behind the line. **-fire** *n.* in internal combustion engines, premature ignition of fuel; *v.i.* to do this; to go awry; **-ground** *n.* part behind foreground of a picture or stage setting; knowledge gained by experience. **—hand** *n.* writing sloped from left to right; a stroke in tennis with the hand turned backwards. **-handed** *a.* with the back of the hand; deceitful; indirect; sarcastic; doubtful. **-ing** *n.* support; sympathy; providing anything with a support; **-lash** *n.* the jarring reaction of a machine due to the degree of play; **-log** *n.* an accumulation, a reserve amount. **— number** *n.* a copy of an out-of-date publication; one behind the times or unprogressive. **-side** *n.* back or hinder part; the rear side; the buttocks; the rump. **-sight** *n.* the rear sight of a rifle. **-slide** *v.i.* to slide backwards; to lapse from a high moral standard. **-stage** *adv.* behind the stage, in the wings, etc. **-stays** *n.pl.* ropes supporting the upper mast. **— talk** *n.* insolent reply; impertinence. **-track** *v.i.* to retreat; to return over the same route. **-ward** *adv.* with the back in advance; towards, or on, the back; to a worse state; in a reverse direction; *a.* directed to the back or rear; dull; behind in one's education; shy; unwilling; late. **-wash** *n.* backward current; (*Slang*) the dire consequences. **-water** *n.* water held back by a dam; water thrown back by a paddle-wheel; a by-way in a river or creek. **-woods** *n.pl.* outlying forest districts or remote undeveloped country. **-woodsman** *n.* [O.E. *bacc*].

back·gam·mon (bak·gam′·ąn) *n.* a game played by two with 15 pieces each on a special board [E. fr. *back* and M.E. *gamen*, play].

ba·con (bā′·kn) *n.* back and sides of hogs after being salted and smoked [O.Fr.].

bac·te·ri·um (bak·ti′·ri·ąm) *n.* group of non-spore forming bacteria. *pl.* **bacteria. bacterial** *a.* **bactericide** *n.* any agent capable of destroying bacteria. **bactericidal** *a.* **bacteriology** *n.* the study of bacteria [Gk. *bakterion*, a little stick].

bad (bad) *a.* ill or evil; wicked. **-dish** *a.* rather bad. **-ly** *adv.* **-ness** *n.* **bad blood,** ill feeling. **bad lands** *n.pl.*, badly eroded, barren land esp. in the Dakotas. **to go bad,** to rot or decay [M.E. *badde*].

bade (bad) past tense of the verb **bid.**

badge (baj) *n.* an emblem, usually symbolic, worn to distinguish members of societies, regiments, etc.; token; mark; symbol [M.E. *bage*].

badg·er (baj'·ẹr) *n.* a greyish-brown hibernating animal; *v.t.* to follow hotly as dogs do the badger; to tease, by persistent questioning; to pester or annoy [from the white stripe or *badge* on the animal's forehead].

bad·i·nage (bad·ạ·nij') *n.* playful or sportive talk; banter [Fr. *badin,* frivolous].

bad·min·ton (bad'·min·tạn) *n.* a game similar to tennis with the substitution of shuttlecocks for tennis balls [fr. *Badminton* House in Gloucestershire where the game was invented].

baf·fle (baf'·l) *v.t.* to frustrate; to confuse; to check or turn, as wind baffles a ship. **-r** *n.* **baffling** *a.* disconcerting; confusing.

baf·fle (baf'·l) *n.* a plate for regulating the flow of a liquid or gas; a metal plate used between the cylinders of an air-cooled motor engine to break up a stream of heated gases; a baffle-plate; a rigid mounting usually of wood, holding the reproducing diaphragm of a radio receiver.

bag (bag) *n.* a sack or pouch; content of a sack; results of one's fishing or hunting; an udder; *v.t.* to put into a bag; to seize; *v.i.* to hang loosely; to bulge or swell out. *pr.p.* **-ging.** *pa.p.* **-ged. -gage,** *n.* tents and stores of an army; luggage; a dissolute woman. **bag and baggage,** with all one's belongings. **-ging** *n.* cloth or material for bags. **-giness** *n.* the state of being baggy (as trousers). **-gy** *a.* hanging loosely; puffy. **in the bag,** certain, assured. **to let the cat out of the bag,** to reveal a secret unwittingly [O.N. *baggi*].

bag·a·telle (bag·ạ·tel') *n.* a trifle; a thing of little worth or importance; a game played with balls and a cue on a board; a short piece of music in light style [Fr.].

ba·gel (bā·'gl) *n.* a doughnut-shaped roll.

bag·pipe (bag'·pīp) *n.* musical reed instrument, common to Scotland. **-r** *n.* [M.E. *baggepipe*].

bail (bāl) *n.* (*Law*) security taken by the court that a person charged will attend at a future date to answer to the charge; one who furnishes this security; *v.t.* to obtain the release of a person from prison by giving security against his reappearance. **-able** *a.* **— bond** *n.* a bond given by a person who is being bailed and his surety. **-ee** *n.* the holder of goods in trust who must obey the direction with which the delivery to him is made. **bail out** *v.i.* to jump from an aircraft and descend by parachute [O.Fr. *bailler*].

bail (bāl) *n.* a scoop; a shallow vessel for clearing water out of a boat; *v.t.* to empty of water with some kind of water scoop. **-er** *n.* [F. *baille,* bucket].

bail·iff (bā'·lif) *n.* an under-officer of a sheriff; a minor officer of a court; (*Br.*) land-owner's agent [O.Fr. *baillir*].

bail·i·wick (bāl'·a·wik) *n.* bailiff's jurisdiction; (*Fig.*) one's special domain, or area of skill, work, etc. [O.Fr., *baillif,* a justice; O.E. *wice,* office].

bairn (bern) *n.* (*Scot.*) a child (O.E. *bearn*].

bait (bāt) *n.* food set to entice fish or an animal; a lure; snare; *v.t.* to put food on a hook or in a trap as a lure; to set dogs on an animal; to harass; to tease. **-er** *n.* **-ing** *a.* and *n.* [Icel. *beita,* to cause to bite].

baize (bāz) *n.* a woolen or cotton cloth with long nap [O.Fr.].

bake (bāk) *v.t.* to harden by heat; to cook in an oven or over a fire; *v.i.* to work at baking; to be baked. **-house** *n.* **bakery** *n.* a bakehouse.**baking** *n.* a batch of bread, etc. **a baker's dozen,** thirteen [O.E. *basan*].

Ba·ke·lite (bāk'·ạ·līt) *n.* a hard, strong synthetic resin used as a substitute for wood, bone, celluloid, etc. [L. H. *Baekeland,* the inventor; Trademark].

bal·a·lai·ka (bal·a·lī'·kạ) *n.* an old Slavic stringed instrument [Russ.].

bal·ance (bal'·ạns) *n.* an apparatus for determining the weight, or comparing the masses, of bodies; a poised beam with two opposite scales; any condition of equilibrium; part of a watch or clock which regulates the beats; a sense of proportion and discretion; poise; payment still due, or cash in hand; *v.t.* to weigh, as in a balance; to render equal in proportion, etc.; to adjust, as an account; *v.i.* to be of the same weight; to be in equipoise. **— sheet** *a.* statement of the assets and liabilities of a company [L. *bis,* twice; *lanx,* a plate].

bal·co·ny (bal'·kạ·ni·) *n.* a platform or gallery projecting from a building; a gallery in a theater or concert hall [It. *balcone*].

bald (bawld) *a.* destitute of hair or feathers on the crown of the head; bare; unadorned; undisguised; without literary style; monotonous. **-head, -pate** *n.* one destitute of hair. **-ly** *adv.* **-ness** *n.* [M.E. *balled*].

bal·der·dash (bawl'·dẹr·dash) *n.* a jargon of meaningless words jumbled together; nonsense.

bale (bāl) *n.* that which causes sorrow or ruin; evil; misery; mischief; injury; woe. **-ful** *a.* **-fully** *adv.* [O.E. *bealu,* evil].

bale (bāl) *n.* a package, compactly compressed, in a protecting cover; *v.t.* to pack in bales. **-r** *n.* one employed in baling goods [O.Fr. *balle*].

ba·leen (bạ·lēn') *n.* whalebone [L. *balaena,* a whale].

balk (bawk) *n.* a crossbeam or rafter, of squared timber, stretching from wall to wall; an unploughed ridge of land; a barrier or check; a disappointment; a part of a billiard table; (*Baseball*) an uncompleted pitch, entitling base runners to advance one base; *v.t.* to frustrate; to bar the way; *v.i.* to stop abruptly; refuse to move. **-y** *a.* [O.E. *balca,* a ridge].

ball (bawl) *n.* any round body; a sphere; a globe; the earth; bullet or shot; a delivery outside the strike zone by a pitcher; the heavy piece of a pendulum; *v.t., v.i.* to form into a ball. **— bearings** *n.* hardened steel balls interposed in channels or 'races' between the rotating and stationary surfaces of a bearing to lessen friction. **—point pen** *n.* fountain pen with a tiny ball point leaving a fine trace of ink on the paper. **—race** *n.* the grooves in which the balls of a ball-bearing run. **— and socket** *n.* a joint formed by a ball partly enclosed in a cup and so adjusted that it can move freely in all directions [Scand. origin].

ball (bawl) *n.* a social gathering for the purpose of dancing; an assembly. **-room** *n.* [L.L. *ballare,* to dance].

bal·lad (bal'·ạd) *n.* a story in verse, of popular origin, generally patriotic and sung orig. to the harp; a concert-room melody, usually sentimental. **-ist** *n.* a composer or singer of ballads. **-ry** *n.* collected ballads; folk songs. **-eer** *n.* [L.L. *ballare,* to dance].

bal·lade (bạ·lȧd') *n.* a short poem of one to three triplet stanzas of eight lines, each with the same rhymes and refrain, and an envoy of four or five lines [Fr.].

bal·last (bal'·ạst) *n.* heavy material taken on board ship to increase the vessel's draft and steadiness; sandy material dredged from river beds used for concrete; that which renders anything steady; *v.t.* to load with ballast; to steady [obs. *last,* burden].

bal·le·ri·na (bal·ạ·rē'·nạ) *n.* a female ballet dancer [It.].

bal·let (bal'·ā) *n.* a representation, consisting of dancing and miming, aiming to express an idea or tell a story, to the accompaniment of music. **-omane** (bal·ạt·ạ·mān') *n.* an enthusiast for ballet [Fr.].

bal·lis·ta, balista (bạ·lis′·tạ) *n.* an ancient military contrivance for hurling huge stones. **ballistic** *a.* pert. to a projectile and its flight. **ballistics** *n.pl.* scientific study of motion of projectiles [Gk. *ballein,* to throw].

bal·loon (bạ·lòòn′) *n.* bag designed to float in the air and unequipped for mechanical propulsion; anything inflated. **-ing** *n.* **ist** *n.* [Fr. *ballon*].

bal·lot (bal′·ạt) *n.* secret voting; slip of paper used in secret voting; *v.t.* to vote on by ballot; to draw lots [Fr. *ballotte,* little ball].

bal·ly·hoo (bal′·i·hòò)*n.* (*Slang*) advertising; bombast.

balm (bȧm) a fragrant plant; any fragrant or healing ointment; anything which soothes pain. **-iness** *n.* **-y** *a.* fragrant; bearing balm [Fr. *balsamum*].

ba·lo·ney, boloney (bạl·ō′·ni·) *n.* (*Slang*) misleading talk; nonsense; (*Colloq.*) bologna sausage [etym. unknown].

bal·sa, (bawl′·sạ) *n.* the extremely light wood of a W. Indian tree [Sp.].

bal·sam (bawl′·sạm) *n.* a name applied to many aromatic resins and oils with stimulant and tonic properties; a soothing ointment; a healing agent. **-ic** *n.* soothing, oily. **-ous** *a.* soothing. **-y** *a.* [Gk. *balsamon*].

bal·us·ter (bal′·ạs·tẹr) *n.* a stone or wooden shaft turned and molded, used to support a handrail. **-ed** *a.* provided with balusters. **balustrade** *n.* a row of balusters supporting a railing [Gk. *balaustion,* the pomegranate, whose flowers it resembles].

bam·bi·no (bam·bē′·nō) *n.* a child or baby [It.].

bam·boo (bam·bòò′) *n.* a genus of immense grasses in the tropics [Malay].

bam·boo·zle (bam·bòò′·zl) *v.t.* (*Slang*) to mystify; to trick; hoax; cheat; swindle. **-r** *n.*

ban (ban) *n.* proclamation; a sentence of outlawry; excommunication; a curse; a prohibition; *v.t.* to prohibit; to curse; *pr.p.* **-ning.** *pa.t.* and *pa.p.* **-ned** [O.E. *bannan,* to summon, curse].

ba·nal (bān′·ạl, bạn·ȧl′, ban′·ạl) *a.* trite, trivial, petty, vulgar, commonplace. **-ity** *n.*

ba·nan·a (bạ·na′·nạ) *n.* the edible fruit of a tropical plant [Sp.].

band (band) *n.* a cord, tie, or fillet; part of a clerical, legal, or university vestment consisting of two pieces of cambric or linen joined together and worn under the chin; an ornamental strip separating moldings on a building or dividing a wall space; an endless belt used for driving wheels or rollers. **-box** *n.* a light cardboard box for millinery. [O.E. *bindan,* to bind].

band (band) *n.* players of musical instruments in combined performance; a company united for common purpose; a number of armed men; *v.t.* to bind together; *v.i.* to associate, join together. **-master** *n.* director of a military or brass band. **bandsman** *n.* a member of a brass band. **-stand** *n.* an open-air structure suitable for musical performances. **to climb aboard the band wagon,** to participate in a movement when its success is assured. [Fr.].

band·age (band′·ij) *n.* a strip of cloth, used for binding up wounds, etc. *v.t.* to bind with a bandage [Fr. *bande*].

ban·dan·na, ban·dan·a (ban·dan′·ạ)*n.* a large patterned silk or cotton handkerchief [Hind.].

ban·deau (ban′·dō) *n.* a narrow band worn by women to bind the hair; narrow brassiere; *pl.* **bandeaux** [Fr.].

ban·dit (ban′·dit) *n.* robber; brigand; outlaw; highwayman; *pl.* **-s, -ti. -ry** *n.* [It. *bandito,* fr. *bandire,* to outlaw].

ban·do·leer, ban·do·lier (ban·dạ·lēr′) *n.* a broad belt worn over the shoulder and fitted with pockets to hold cartridges [It. *bandoliera*].

ban·dy (ban′·di·) *a.* crooked; bent; bandied; bandy-legged; *v.t.* to beat to and fro; to toss from one to another, as 'to bandy words.' **bandied** *a.* **—legged** *a.* having crooked legs, bending outwards [Fr. *bander,* to bend].

bane (bān) *n.* any cause of ruin; destruction; mischief; noxious substance; poison. **-ful** *a.* **-fulness** *n.* [O.E. *bana,* a murdered].

bang (bang) *v.t.* to beat, as with a club; to handle roughly; to make a loud noise; *n.* a blow with a club or a fist; a loud noise; an explosion. **-ing** *n.* [Scand. *banga,* to hammer].

bang (bang) *v.t.* to cut the front hair square across; *n.* a straight fringe over the forehead or at the end of a horse's tail [nasal variant of *bag*-(cut)].

ban·gle (bang′·gl) *n.* an ornamental ring worn round arm or ankle; bracelet [Urdu, *bangri,* a bracelet].

ban·ish (ban′·ish) *v.t.* to condemn to exile; to drive away; to expel; to cast from the mind. **-ment** *n.* exile [fr. *ban*].

ban·is·ter (ban′·is·tẹr) *n.* Same as **baluster.**

ban·jo (ban′·jō) *n.* a stringed musical instrument [Gk. *pandoura,* a musical instrument].

bank (bangk) *n.* a ridge of earth; a shoal; a sandbank; the edge of a stream or lake; the raised edge of a road, etc.; a mass of heavy clouds or fog; *v.t.* to raise a mound; to dike; to cover a fire with small coal to procure slow combustion; to tilt about the longitudinal axis when turning. **to bank on** *v.t.* to depend on [O.E. *banc,* a bench].

bank (bangk) *n.* a bench on which rowers sit; a tier of oars; a row of objects [Fr. *banc*].

bank (bangk) *n.* an establishment where money is received for custody and repaid on demand; money-box; the money at stake in games of chance; a pool; *v.t.* to deposit money in a bank. **-book** *n.* a pass-book in which a customer's dealings with a bank are recorded. **-er** *n.* one employed in banking; in games of chance the proprietor against whom the other players stake. **— note** *n.* a promissory note on bank of issue promising to pay its face value to bearer on demand. **— rate** *n.* the rate of discount, fixed by a bank or banks [Fr. *banque*].

bank·rupt (bangk′·rupt) *n.* insolvent person compelled to place his affairs in the hands of creditors; *v.t.* to cause to go bankrupt; *a.* insolvent, unable to pay debts; lacking in (ideas, etc.). **-cy** *n.* [E. *bank; ruptus,* broken].

ban·ner (ban′·ẹr) *n.* a flag or ensign. **-ed** *a.* [Fr. *bannière*].

ban·nock (bạn′·ạk) *n.* (*Scot.*) a flat, thick, cake of oatmeal or barley [Gael. *bonnach*].

banns (banz) *n.pl.* proclamation of intended marriage [fr. *ban*].

ban·quet (bang′·kwet) *n.* a feast; a rich repast; something specially delicious; *v.t.* to entertain at a banquet. **-ing** *n.* [Fr. dim. of *banc,* bench].

ban·shee (ban′·shē) *n.* in Ireland and W. Highlands of Scotland, a fairy-elf who, by shrieks and wailing, foretells the approaching death of a member of a family [Ir. *bean sidhe,* woman of the fairies].

ban·tam (ban′·tạm) *n.* a variety of the small common domestic fowl; *a.* of very light weight; plucky. **-weight,** a boxer weighing less than 118 lbs. [fr. *Bantam,* a village in Java].

ban·ter (ban′·tẹr) *v.i.* to make good-natured fun of someone; to joke, jest; to rally; *n.* wit at expense of another; chaff; pleasantry. **-er** *n.*

Ban·tu (ban′·tòò) *n.* an African language.

ban·yan (ban′·yạn) *n.* the Indian fig; a tree whose branches, bending to the ground, take root and form new stocks, till they become a forest. Hence—**to flourish like the banyan-tree** [Port.].

bap·tize (bap′·tīz) *v.t.* to administer the sacrament of baptism to; to christen; give a name to. **baptism** *n.* sacrament by which a person is initiated into the membership of the Christian Church. **baptismal** *a.* **Baptist** *n.* one who baptizes; one who insists that the rite of initiation is duly administered only by immersion upon personal profession of faith. **bap-**

tistery, baptistry *n.* an ancient circular building in which baptisms took place [Gk. *baptizein*, to immerse].

bar (bȧr) *n.* a long piece of any solid material, used as barrier; the bolt of a door; a sand-bank; part of a tavern with a counter for the sale of liquor; a public-house; the rail before the judge's seat where prisoners appear; members of the legal profession allowed to plead in court; (*Her.*) a band crossing the shield; (*Mus.*) a perpendicular line drawn across the stave immediately before the primary accent; *v.t.* to fasten or mark with a bar; to obstruct; to prevent; to exclude; *prep.* except. **-maid, -man, -tender** *n.* a bar attendant. **-ring** *prep.* excepting; *n.* exclusion of any kind. *pr.p.* **-ring.** *pa.p.* **-red.** [Fr. *barre*].

barb (bȧrb) *n.* a hooked hair; the spike of an arrow, fish-hook, etc.; a horse of great speed and endurance, originally from Barbary; *v.t.* to furnish with barbs or prongs, as an arrow; to trim the beard. **-ed** *a.* bearded; furnished with a barb or barbs. **-ed wire** *n.* a wire armed with sharp points used for defensive purposes [L. *barba*, beard].

bar·bar·i·an (bȧr·be′·ri·ạn) *n.* orig. one who could not speak Greek, now an uncivilized being without culture; a cruel, brutal man; *a.* savage; rude. **barbaric** *a.* uncivilized; rude; nobly savage. **barbarize** *v.t.* to render barbarous. **barbarism** *n.* incorrect use of idiom or word; want of civilization. **barbarity** *n.* cruelty; savagery. **barbarous** *a.* uncivilized or savage [Gk. *barbaros*, foreign].

bar·be·cue (bȧr′·bi-kū) *n.* a grid-iron on which meat is roasted over an open fire; an animal so roasted; a lavish open-air feast [Haitian].

bar·ber (bȧr′·bẹr) *n.* one who shaves or trims and dresses the hair; a hair-dresser [L. *barba*, beard].

bar·ber·ry (bȧr′·bẹr·i·) *n.* (*Bot.*) a shrub with clusters of red berries [M.L. *berberis*].

bar·bi·tu·rates (bār-bit′·ū·rātz) *n.* (*Med.*) derivatives of barbituric acid, non-habit forming, hypnotic and sedative drugs.

bar·ca·role, bar·ca·rolle, (bȧr′·kạ·rōl) *n.* a musical composition written in imitation of the gondoliers' songs of Venice. [It. *barca*, a boat].

bard (bȧrd) *n.* a Celtic minstrel who celebrated in song the great deeds of heroes; a poet. **-ic** *a.* pert. to bards or their poetry [Celt.].

bare (bār) *a.* without covering; naked; empty; open to view; paltry; *v.t.* to strip off or uncover. **-ly** *adv.* openly; poorly; scarcely. **-ness** *n.* **-facedness** *n.* sheer impudence. [O.E. *baer*].

bar·gain (bȧr′·gin] *n.* an agreement between parties in buying and selling; a profitable transaction; something purchased cheaply. *v.i.* to make a contract; to chaffer. **-er** *n.* one who haggles over the price. **into the bargain,** over and above what is agreed upon [O.Fr. *bargaigner*].

barge (bȧrj) *n.* flat-bottomed boat; a ship's boat; *v.i.* to push forward roughly. **-man** *n.* [L. *barca*, a boat].

bar·i·tone (bar′·ạ-tōn) *n.* the male human voice between tenor and bass [Gk. *barys*, heavy; *tonos*, tone].

bar·i·um (bār′·i·ạm) *n.* metallic element (symbol *Ba*). **baric** *a.* [fr. Gk. *barys*, heavy].

bark (bȧrk) *n.* the outer covering of a tree; rind; waste tan used in manufacturing white-lead; *v.t.* to strip off bark; to graze the skin. [Scand.].

bark (bȧrk) *v.t.* to utter a cry like a dog; to yelp; (*Slang*) to advertise by shouting; to speak sharply; **-er,** *n.* **to bark up the wrong tree,** to be on the wrong trail [O.E. *beorcan*].

bark, barque (bȧrk) *n.* a three masted vessel; a small sailing-ship; (*Poet.*) a ship [Fr. *barque*].

bar·ley (bȧr′·li·) *n.* a cereal, the grain being used for malt-making, bread, and food for cattle. **-corn** *n.* a grain of barley; the third part of an inch. **John Barleycorn** (*Fig.*) whisky. **— flour** *n.* flour made by grinding barley. **— sugar** *n.* a confection made from sugar boiled till brittle in barley water. [O.E. *bere*, barley].

barm (bȧrm) *n.* the froth on fermenting malt liquors, used in making bread; yeast. **-y** *a.* pert. to barm; light-headed, flighty, or giddy [O.E. *beorma*, yeast].

barn (bȧrn) *n.* a covered farm-building for storing grain, hay, etc. and for stabling live stock; *v.t.* to store in a barn. **— dance** *n.* a lively dance in 4-4 time, resembling the schottische. **-yard** *a.* pert. to domestic fowls. *n.* open enclosure attached to barn. **-stormer** *n.* an itinerant actor [O.E. *bere*, barley; *ern*, a place].

bar·na·cle (bȧr′·nạ·kl) *n.* a shell-fish which attaches itself to the bottoms of ships and to rocks. **-d** *a.* [O.Fr. *bernac*].

ba·rom·e·ter (bạ·rȧm′·ạ·tẹr) *n.* an instrument for recording the weight or pressure of the atmosphere which indicates impending weather changes. **barometric, barometrical** *a.* [Gk. *baros*, weight; *metron*, measure].

bar·on (bar′·ạn) *n.* a title of nobility, the lowest of the British peerage to sit in the House of Lords; a commercial magnate. (*fem.* **baroness)** [L.L. *baro*, a man].

bar·o·net (bar′·ạ·net) *n.* hereditary title ranking below a baron and above a knight but without privilege of peerage. **baronetcy** *n.* the rank of a baronet [dim. of *baron*].

ba·roque (bạ-rōk′) *n.* orig. a jeweller's trade term for ill-shaped pearls; (*Art.*) a florid style of the late Renaissance; *a.* over-lavish; extravagantly ornamented [Port. *barrocco*].

bar·o·scope (bar′·ạ·skōp) *n.* an instrument giving rough indications of variations in the atmospheric pressure [Gk. *baros*, weight; *skopein*, to see].

bar·rack (bar′·ạk) *n.* a building for the accommodation of soldiers (generally used in the plural) [Sp. *barraca*, a tent].

bar·ra·cuda (bar·ạ·ko͝o′·dạ) *n.* a large edible pike-like fish, found in the Atlantic [Sp.].

bar·rage (bạ-razh′) *n.* an artificial bar erected across a stream to regulate its flow; a screen of continuous military fire produced to protect the advance of troops or to stop hostile attacks; heavy prolonged attack.

bar·ra·try (bar′·ạ·tri·) *n.* fraudulent breach of duty by the master of a ship entailing loss by the owners or insurers of ship or cargo; habitually inciting riot or stirring up suits and quarrels [O.Fr. *barat*, fraud].

bar·rel (bar′·ạl) *n.* a cylindrical wooden container consisting of staves bound by hoops; a measure of capacity; anything cylindrical, as a gun-barrel; *v.t.* to stow in barrels. **— organ** *n.* street-organ played by rotating a wooden barrel [Fr. *baril*].

bar·ren (bar′·ạn) *a.* incapable of producing off-spring or fruit; empty, lacking. **-ly** *adv.* **-ness** *n.* sterility [O.Fr.].

bar·rette (bạ·ret′) *n.* small bar or clasp worn to hold hair in place [Fr. *barre*].

bar·ri·cade (bar′·i·kād) *n.* a make-shift fortification, built as an obstruction; an obstruction which hinders free passage; *v.t.* to build this; formerly **barricado** [Fr. *barrica*, a cask].

bar·ri·er (bar′·i·ẹr) *n.* a chain of military posts to protect frontiers; a railing, fence, or wall; any obstruction; a line of separation [O.Fr. *barrière*].

bar·ris·ter (bar′·is·tẹr) *n.* (*Br.*) a member of the highest branch of the legal profession, with exclusive right of practicing in the superior courts of England [fr. *bar*].

bar·row (bar′·ō) *n.* a small kind of light frame provided with two shafts, for carrying loads [O.E. *beran*, to hear].

bar·row (bar′·ō) *n.* an artificial mound of stone, wood, or earth, piled up over the remains of the dead; a hillock [O.E. *beorg,* a mound].

bar·ter (bȧr′·tẹr) *v.t.* to exchange or give in exchange; *v.i.* to traffic by exchange of one kind of goods for another; *n.* direct exchange of commodities [O.Fr. *barater,* to haggle].

bas·al. See **base.**

bas·al me·tab·o·lism (bās′·l mạ·tab′·ạl·izm) *n.* the energy used by a body in a state of total rest [Gk. *basis,* base; *metabolē,* change].

ba·salt (bạ·sawlt′) *n.* an igneous rock of a greenish-black color. **-ic** *a.* [L. *basaltes,* black basalt].

bas·cule (bas′·kūl) *n.* a balancing lever. **—bridge** *n.* a counterpoise bridge [Fr. *bas,* down; *cul,* the posterior].

base (bās) *a.* of humble birth or of low degree; morally low. **-ly** *adv.* **-born** *a.* illegitimate [Fr. *bas,* low].

base (bās) *n.* bottom; support; starting-place; fixed point; supply point of an army; station at baseball; main ingredient; (*Chem*) a substance capable of combining with an acid to form a salt; *v.t.* to put on a base; to found. **basal** *a.* situated at the base. **-less** *a.* having no foundation. **-lessness** *n.* **-ly** *adv.* **-ment** *n.* the lowest story of a building. **basic** *a.* **-board** *n.* a skirting board covering the lower part of a wall [Gk. *basis*].

base (*Mus.*). See **bass.**

base·ball (bās′·bawl) *n.* ball game, played by two teams of nine players in which a player after batting must make the complete circuit of four bases to score a run; the ball used.

bash (bash) *v.t.* (*Colloq.*) to smash in; to beat in; to knock out of shape; to beat; *n.* a severe blow; a dent. **-ing** *n.* a thrashing [orig. uncertain].

bash·ful (bash′·ful) *a.* shy; not desiring to attract notice. **-ly** *adv.* **-ness** *n.* [fr. *abashfull*].

ba·sic (bā′·sik) *a.* relating to a base; primary; containing a small amount of silica. **— slag** *n.* a by-product in the manufacture of steel, used as a manure [Gk. *basis,* a base].

bas·il (baz′·il) *n.* aromatic culinary plant; sweet basil [Gk. *basilikos,* royal].

ba·sil·i·ca (bạ·sil′·i·kạ) *n.* a public building or hall of the Romans, later often converted into a church by early Christians; a spacious church built on the model of the original basilicas. **-n** *a.* [Gk. *basilikos,* royal].

bas·i·lisk (bas′·ạ·lisk) *n.* a fabulous creature; a cockatrice; (*Zool.*) a harmless tree-dwelling American lizard [Gk. *basilikos,* royal].

ba·sin (bā′·sn) *n.* a wide, hollow, bowl-shaped container; a sink; a land-locked bay with a good anchorage; the whole tract of country drained by a river [Fr. *bassin*].

ba·sis (bā′·sis) *n.* that on which a thing rests; foundation. *pl.* **bases** [Gk.].

bask (bask) *v.i.* to sun onesefl; to lie in warmth or sunshine (Scand.].

bas·ket (bas′·kit) *n.* a container made of willow, cane, rushes, or other flexible materials, interwoven. **-bal** *n.* a game where a ball has to be thrown through a basket. **-ful** *n.* **-ry,** **-work** *n.* wickerwork [M.E.].

Basque (bask) *n.* a native or the language of the Basque country (Western Pyrenees); part of a lady's dress, resembling a jacket with a short skirt; *a.* relating to the Basques [Fr.].

bas-re·lief, bass-re·lief (bȧ-, bȧs·rạ·lēf′) *n., a.* low relief, sculpture in which figures or objects are raised slightly upon a flat surface, like embossed work [Fr.].

bass (bas) *n.* name applied to any perch-like fish [M.E. *barse, bace*].

bass (bas) *n.* the basswood or linden tree or its inner barks; fiber; matting [O.E. *baest*].

bass, base (bās) *n.* (*Mus.*) the lowest part of harmony, whether vocal or instrumental; the deepest quality of the human voice or a stringed instrument; *a.* low. **— clef** *n.* the sign on the fourth line of the bass stave. **double-bass** *n.* the largest of the stringed instruments [It. *basso,* low].

bas·set (bas′·it) *n.* a hound formerly used in badger hunting; (*Geol.*) emergence of strata at the surface; out-crop. **— horn** *n.* a rich-toned wind instrument [Fr. *bas,* low].

bas·si·net, bas·si·nette (bas·ạ·net′) *n.* a baby's basket with a hood [Fr. dim. of *bassin*].

bas·so (bas′·ō) *n.* a bass singer; the bass part of a harmony [It. = low].

bas·soon (bạ·sóòn′) *n.* a wood-wind musical instrument with a double reed mouthpiece; organ reed stop of that name. **double —** *n.* one which sounds an octave lower. **-ist** *n.* [It. *basso,* low].

bast (bast) *n.* inner bark of a tree, used for binding purposes; raffia, matting, cordage, etc., made of the bark [O.E. *baest*].

bas·tard (bas′·tẹrd) *n.* a child born out of wedlock; an ımpure, coarse brown refuse product of sugar-refining, used to color beer; *a.* illegitimate; false; counterfeit; **-y** *n.* act of begetting a bastard; being a bastard. **-ize** *v.t.* to render illegitimate [O.Fr. *bastard,* from *fils de bast,* son of a pack-saddle].

baste (bāst) *v.t.* to sew loosely with long stitches; to moisten (meat) with butter, drippings, etc. while cooking [O.Fr. *bastir,* to stitch loosely].

bas·tille (bas·tēl′) *n.* originally a tower or bastion; a state prison. **Bastille** *n.* the famous state prison of Paris [Fr. *bastille,* a building].

bas·ti·na·do (bas·ti·nā′·do) *n.* an oriental form of punishment by heating the soles of the feet [Sp. *bastón,* a stick].

bas·tion (bas′·chạn) *n.* a stronghold of defense [Fr.].

bat (bat) *n.* a club or stick; a shaped club used in cricket or baseball; a piece of a brick; wad of clay; *v.i.* to strike or hit with a bat. *pr.p.* **-ting.** *pa.p.* **-ted. -ter, -man** *n* [O.E. *batt,* club].

bat (bat) *n.* nocturnal, flying mammal. **-ty** *a.* (*Slang*) crazy. **bats, to have bats in the belfry,** to be crazy or eccentric [Scand. *bakke*].

bat (bat) *v.t.* (*Colloq.*) to wink. **never -ted an eyelid,** showed no emotion whatever; never slept. [var. of *bate,* flutter].

batch (bach) *n.* the quantity of bread baked at one time; a number of articles received or disjatched at one time; a set of similar articles [M.E. *batche,* fr. bake].

bate (bāt) *v.t.* to lessen; to abate [form of [*abate*].

bath (bath) *n.* a vessel or place to bathe in; the water in which to bathe; *v.t.* to wash oneself. **-s** *n.pl.* hot or mineral springs resorted to by invalids. **-house** *n.* **-room** *n.* **blood—***n.* a massacre [O.E. *baeth*].

bathe (bāTH) *v.t.* to wash by immersion; *v.i.* to be immersed; to swim. *pr.p.* **bathing. -r** *n.* **bathing** *n.* **bathing-pool** *n.* [O.E. *bathian*].

ba·thet·ic. See **bathos.**

bath·i·nette (bath′·i·net) *n.* portable folding bathtub for babies.

ba·thom·e·ter (bạ·thȧm′·ạ·tẹr) *n.* a spring balance for determining the depth of water [Gk. *bathos,* depth; *metron,* measure].

ba·thos (bā′·thȧs) *n.* a term for ludicrous descent from the sublime to the ridiculous; anticlimax. **bathetic** *a.* [Gk. *bathos,* depth].

bath·y- (bath′·i·) *prefix* from Gk. *bathus,* deep, used in the construction of compound terms relating to sea-depths. **-sphere** *n.* a form of deep-sea diving-bell [Gk. *bathos,* deep; *metron,* measure; *sphaira,* a ball].

ba·tik (bạ·tēk′, bat′·ik) *n.* a technique for dyeing fabrics by applying wax to the parts that are not to be dyed; cloth dyed in this way [Javenese = painted].

ba·tiste (ba·tēst′) *n.* a fine kind of linen cloth from Flanders; a variety of cambric [Fr.].

ba·ton (bạ·tȧn′) *n.* a short staff or club; a truncheon, symbolic of authority or used as an offensive weapon; in music, wand used by conductor in beating time; a marshal's staff. *v.t.* to strike with a baton [Fr. *baton*].

batt, batt·ing (bat, bat′·ing) *n.* fiber wadded into sheets [O.E. *batt*].

bat·tal·ion (bạ-tal′·yạn) *n.* a military tactical and administrative unit of command consisting of three or more companies or similar units. **-s** *n.pl.* great numbers, swarms [Fr. *bataillon,* cf. **battle**].

bat·ten (bat′·n) *v.t.* to fatten; *v.i.* to grow fat in luxury [Icel. *batna,* to grow better].

bat·ten (bat′·n) *n.* a piece of wood nailed on a surface to give it strength; board used on ships to fasten down the hatch-covers in stormy weather; *v.t.* to fasten or form with battens [a form of *bâton*].

bat·ter (bat′·ẹr) *v.t.* to strike or beat continuously; to assault; to wear by hard use; *n.* a mixture moistened to a paste and briskly beaten up. **-ing ram** *n.* a suspended beam used to breach walls [Fr. *battre,* to beat].

bat·ter·y (bat′·ẹr·i·) *n.* act of battering; a place where cannon are mounted; a division of artillery; electric cells which store electric current; the pitcher and catcher in baseball [Fr. *battre,* to beat].

bat·tle (bat′·l) *n.* an encounter between enemies; struggle of any kind; *v.i.* to fight on a large scale. **—axe** *n.* primitive weapon; (*Slang*) cantankerous woman. **— cry** *n.* a war-shout; a slogan. **-field, -ground** *n.* scene of battle. **-r** *n.* one who take part in a battle. **— royal** *n.* a regular melée where firsts are freely used. **-ship** *n.* the largest and most heavily armed of fast warships [Fr. *bataille*].

bat·tle·ment (bat′·l·mạnt) *n.* a protective parapet on a wall [M.E. *batilment*].

bau·ble (baw′·bl) *n.* a trifling piece of finery; a gew-gaw; a stick with a fool's head on the end, carried by jesters of former times; *a.* trifling [O.Fr. *baubel,* a toy].

baulk (bawk) See **balk.**

baux·ite (bȧk′·sīt, bō′·zīt) *n.* a hydrated oxide of aluminum and ferric oxide; the principal source of aluminum [fr. *Baux,* near Arles, S. France].

bawd (bawd) *n.* a procurer or procuress of women for immoral purposes. **-ily** *adv.* **-iness** *n.* **-ry** *n.* **-y** *a.* obscene; filthy; unchaste. **—house,** *n.* a brothel (O.Fr. *baud,* gay].

bawl (bawl) *v.t.* to shout, to proclaim; *v.i.* to shout out with a loud voice; *n.* a loud, prolonged cry. **bawl out** (*Colloq.*) reprimand [M.L. *laulare,* to bark].

bay (bā) *a.* reddish-brown; *n.* a chestnut horse. **-ard** *n.* a bay horse; a spirited horse; one foolishly self-confident; a knight of good fame [L. *badius,* chestnut-colored].

bay (bā) *n.* an inlet of the sea [Fr. *baie*].

bay (bā) *n.* the subdivision longitudinally of a building by piers, arches, girders, etc. **— window** *n.* a window projecting beyond the wall. **sick —,** ship's hospital [Fr. *baie*].

bay (bā) *n.* the laurel tree. **-s** *n.pl.* the victor's garland or crown. **— rum** *n.* an aromatic liquid used as a perfume and cosmetic for the hair [Fr. *baie,* berry].

bay (bā) *n.* barking, esp. of hounds in pursuit of prey; *v.t.* to bark at. **at bay,** said of a hunted animal, when all escape is cut off [O.Fr. *baier,* to bark].

bay·ber·ry (bā′·ber·i·) *n.* evergreen shrub, used for making bay rum; one variety used in candle making [*bay* and *berry*].

bay·o·net (bā′·ạ·net) *n.* a short spear-like weapon attached to the muzzle of a rifle; *v.t.* to stab with a bayonet, [fr. *Bayonne,* the town where first made].

ba·zaar, bazar (bạ·zȧr′) *n.* an Oriental market-place; a sale where articles are sold for charity; shop selling miscellaneous goods [Pers.].

ba·zoo·ka (bạ·zòò′·kạ) *n.* a portable light rocket-gun.

B.C. before Christ.

be (bē) *v.i.* and *aux.* (*pres. indic.* **am;** *past indic.* **was;** *past part.* **been**), to exist; to live; to have a state, existence, or quality; to remain; to happen; to belong [O.E. *beon*].

be- *prefix* used in the construction of compound words, as *becalm,* etc.

beach (bēch) *n.* the shore of the sea or of a lake, esp. where sandy or pebbly; the shore; *v.t.* to run or haul a boat up on to a beach. **-comber** *n.* a long, rolling wave; a lounger who frequents beaches or seaports; scrounger. **-head** *n.* a footing gained on hostile shores by an army.

bea·con (bē′·kn) *n.* a fire lit on a high eminence, usually as a warning; a warning light; a floating buoy; traffic sign indicating a pedestrian crossing; *v.t.* to mark a channel by beacons [O.E. *beacn*].

bead (bēd) *n.* a little ball pierced for stringing; any small spherical object such as a front sight on a gun; *v.t.* to furnish with beads; *v.i.* to string beads. **-s** *n.pl.* a rosary, a necklace; flange of a tire; **-ed** *a.* in bead form. **-ing** *n.* a small rounded molding imitating beads. **-y** *a.* bead-like. **to draw a bead on,** to aim a gun at. [O.E. *gebed,* a prayer].

bea·gle (bē′·gl) *n.* the smallest hound used in hunting; (*Fig.*) a spy or informer.

beak (bēk) *n.* the horny bill of a bird, turtle, etc.; anything shaped like a beak (*Slang*) a beak-shaped nose [Fr. *bec.*].

beak·er (bē′·kẹr) *n.* a large drinking-cup or vessel; a tumbler-shaped vessel of thin glass used by chemists [Scand. *bikarr*].

beam (bēm) *n.* a strong, horizontal piece of timber or reinforced concrete for spanning and supporting weights; the part of a balance from which the scales hang; the cross-timber of a ship; the extreme width, measured athwartships, of a ship; wooden cylinder on which the warp is wound in a loom; the pole of a carriage; the shaft of an anchor; a sharply defined ray of light; the sparkle in a person's eyes manifesting extreme pleasure or interest; *v.t.* to emit beams of light; *v.i.* to send forth rays of light; to shine; to smile benignly. **-ing** *a.* radiantly happy; shining; *n.* rays of light; manifestation of pleasure by smiling. **-less** *a.* [O.E. *beam,* a tree].

bean (bēn) *n.* the flat, kidney-shaped seed of various plants, chiefly of the genus *Phaseolus;* (*Slang*) head. **-bag** *n.* a toy, a small cloth bag partly filled with beans. **full of beans,** in good fettle; energetic. [O.E. *bean*].

bear (bār) *v.t.* to support or to carry; to endure; to suffer; to behave; to give birth to; *v.i.* to produce (as fruit); to endure; to press; *pa.t.* **bore;** *pa.p.* **borne** or **born. -able** *a.* able to be borne; tolerable. **-ably** *adv.* **-er** *n.* carrier or messenger; a person who helps to carry a coffin; a presenter of a check. **-ing** *n.* the manner in which a person acts or behaves; the direction in which one thing lies from another; relation to or connection with; **-ings** *n.pl.* machine surfaces carrying a moving part and bearing friction. **to bear out,** to corroborate. **to bear with,** to endure patiently. **to bring to bear,** to apply pressure. **to lose one's bearings,** to lose all sense of direction [O.E. *beran*].

bear (bār) *n.* a carnivorous mammal of the Ursidae order; a rough, boorish person; one who sells stocks before he has bought them, in the hope of a fall in price before settlement; (*Astron.*) one of two constellations in the northern hemisphere, called respectively the **Great Bear** and the **Lesser Bear. — baiting** *n.* a form of sport where dogs were employed to worry the animal. **-like** *a.* **skin** *n.* [O.E. *bera*].

beard (bērd) *n.* the hair that grows on the chin and cheeks; the awns or prickles of an ear of corn; the gills of oysters; the barb of an arrow; *v.t.* to pluck the beard of; to confront or defy someone. **-ed** *a.* **-less** *a.* [O.E.].

beast (bēst) *n.* any inferior animal as opposed

to man; a four-footed animal especially if wild; cattle; person of brutal nature or of dirty habits. **-ly** *a.* like a beast in form or nature; filthy; displeasing. **-liness** *n.* [L. *bestia*].

beat (bēt) *v.t.* to strike or hit repeatedly; to pommel; to crush;to defeat; to be too difficult for; to spread flat and thin with a tool, as gold leaf; to drive game out of cover; to mark time in music; *v.i.* to throb; to dash against as waves, wind, etc. *pa.t.* **beat;** *pa.p.* **-en;** *n.* a recurrent stroke; a pulse throb; (*Mus.*) the divisions in a bar, the movement of a conductor's baton; zig-zag sailing of a ship working up against the wind; the round or course followed repeatedly by someone, e.g. a policeman, a postman; *a.* (*Colloq.*) exhausted. **-en** *a.* hammered into shape by a tool; worn by continual use. **-er** *n.* **-ing** *n.* act of giving blows; a thrashing; throbbing; driving out game. **-nik** *n.* (*Colloq.*) one who rebels against the conventions of society. **to beat about the bush,** to approach a subject in a round about way. **to beat a tatoo,** to sound the drums at roll-call. **dead beat** *n.* (*Colloq.*) one with a reputation for not paying his bills; (*Slang*) a loafer; sponger [O.E. *beatan*].

be·at·i·fy (bē·at′·ạ·fī) *v.t.* to render supremely blessed or happy; to bless with celestial enjoyment (preliminary to canonization in R.C. Church). **beatific(al)** *a.* having power of making happy or blessed. **beatifically** *adv.* **beatification** *n.* [L. *betaus*, happy].

be·at·i·tude (bē·at′·ạ·tūd) *n.* highest form of heavenly happiness; supreme blessedness. **the beatitudes** (*Bib.*) blessings spoken in regard to particular virtues (Matt. 5) [L. *beatus*, happy].

beau (bō) *n.* a fop; dandy; sweetheart; suitor. *pl.* **beaux** (bōz). **— monde** *n.* the fashionable world and its people [Fr.].

beau·ty (bū′·ti·) *n.* the inherent quality in an object of pleasing the eye, ear, or mind; a particular grace or excellence; a beautiful woman; a fine specimen. **beauteous** *a.* full of beauty; very handsome. **beauteously** *adv.* **beauteousness** *n.* **beautician** *n.* expert in use of cosmetics. **beautifier** *n.* a cosmetic; a decorator. **beautiful** *a.* highly pleasing to eye, ear, or mind; handsone; lovely; fine; excellent. **beautifully** *adv.* **beautifulness** *n.* **beautify** *v.t.* to make beautiful. **beautiless** *a.* lacking beauty. **— spot** *n.* a place noted for its attractive surroundings; a patch placed on the face to heighten beauty [Fr. *beauté*].

bea·ver (bē′·vẹr) *n.* an amphibious, four-footed rodent valued for its fur and for castoreum, an extract from its glands used in medicine; the fur of the beaver; a beaver hat; *a.* made of beaver fur [O.E. *beofor*].

be·bop (bē′·bȧp) *n.* (*Slang*) jazz music characterized by improvization. [**-ed** *a.*

be·calm (bē·kȧm′) *v.t.* to make calm or quiet.

be·came (bi·kām′) past tense of **become.**

be·cause (bi·kawz′) *adv.* and *conj.* for the reason that; since [E. *by*, and *cause*].

beck (bek) *n.* sign or gesture of the head or hand; a nod; *v.i.* to make such a gesture; *v.t.* to call by a nod or a sign; to beckon. **at one's beck and call,** entirely at someone's disposal [fr. *beckon*].

beck·on (bek′·n) *v.t.* and *v.i.* to make a sign with the hand or head; to summon with hand or finger [O.E. *becnan*].

be·come (bi·kum′) *v.t.* to pass from one state to another; to suit or be suitable to; *pa.t.* **became;** *pa.p.* **become. becoming** *a.* appropriate or fit [O.E. *becuman*].

bed (bed) *n.* a couch on which to sleep or take rest; a plot of ground in which plants are cultivated; channel of a stream; the bearing surface of anything; a thin layer of mortar between two surfaces; a layer of rock; stratum; *v.t.* to place in bed; to plant out; to arrange in layers; *pr.p.* **-ding;** *pa.p.* **-ded. -bug** *n.* bloodsucking insect. **-clothes** *n.pl.* bed coverings, clothes worn to bed. **-ding** *n.* materials of a bed. **-fast** *a.* confined to bed; bed-ridden. **-fellow** *n.* one who sleeps in the same bed with another. **-pan** *n.* a pan for warming a bed; pan used as toilet. **-plate** *n.* the foundation plate of an engine lathe, etc. **-post** *n.* one of the upright supports of a bed. **-rid, -ridden** *a.* permanently confined to bed by age or infirmity. **-rock** *n.* the solid rock beneath loose material as sand, etc.; fundamentals. **-room** *n.* a room for sleeping. **-sore** *n.* ulcer caused by constant pressure on a part of the body of a bed-ridden patient. **-spread** *n.* a covering of fine material for a bed. **-stead** *n.* the framework, of iron or wood, of a bed. **-ticking** *n.* the cloth case for holding the feathers, hair, etc. of a mattress. **bed and board,** food and lodging [O.E. *bedd*].

be·daub (bi·dawb′) *v.t.* to smear.

be·daz·zle (bi·daz′·l) *v.t.* to overpower by employing too strong a light or by a magnificent show.

be·deck (bē·dek′) *v.t.* to deck, adorn, ornament.

be·dev·il (bi·dev′·l) *v.t.* to beat with devilish malignity; to torment; to throw into confusion, to confound; to bewitch.

be·dew (bi·dū′) *v.t.* to moisten with dew.

be·dight (bi·dīt′) *a.* decked out with ornaments; adorned; arrayed (*Poet.*).

be·dim (bi·dim′) *v.t.* to make dim; to darken. *pr.p.* **-ming;** *pa.t.* **-med. bedimmed** *a.*

be·diz·en (bi·diz′·n, bi·dī′·zn) *v.t.* to dress gaudily or with false taste. **-ed** *a.*

bed·lam (bed′lạm) *n.* a mad-house; a lunatic asylum; a mental institution; a scene of uproar; pandemonium. **-ite** *n.* a lunatic [corrupt. of *Bethlehem*, an asylum].

Bed·ou·in (bed′·oo·in) *n.* Arab; nomad [Ar. *bādāwin*, dwellers in the desert].

be·drag·gle (bi·drag′·l) *v.t.* to soil by trailing in the wet or mud. **-d** *a.*

bee (bē) *n.* highest form of insect belonging to the order Hymenoptera; the honey-bee; a social gathering for amusement or mutual help, e.g. a spelling-bee; a busy person. **-culture** *n.* the rearing of bees, apiculture. **-hive** *n.* a case or box where the bees are housed; *a.* shaped like a bee-hive. **-keeper** *n.* **-line** *n.* the shortest route from one place to another. **-swax** *n.* the wax secreted by bees; a floor-polish; *v.t.* to polish with beeswax [O.E. *bēo*].

beech (bēch) *n.* a tree of the temperate and sub-frigid zones, greatly valued for its wood. **-coal** *n.* charcoal made from beechwood. **-en** *a.* made of beech. **beechnut** *n.* the triangular, edible nut of the beech [O.E. *béce*].

beef (bēf) *n.* the flesh of an ox, bull, or cow; flesh and muscle; muscular strength; vigor; *a.* consisting of beef; *v.i.* (*Slang*) to make complaints. **beeves** (bēvz) *n.pl.* oxen. **-eater** *n.* one of the Yeomen of the Guard; a Warder of the Tower of London. **-iness** *n.* tendency to put on flesh. **-steak** *n.* a thick slice of beef. **-y** *a.* stolid; fat; stout [Fr. *boeuf*, ox].

been (bin) *pa.p.* of the verb **be.**

beer (bēr) *n.* an alcoholic beverage made by brewing and fermentation of cereals. **-y** *a.* pert. to the taste or smell of beer; discolored with beer slops [O.E. *beor*].

beest·ings, biest·ings (bēs′·tingz) *n.* the first milk taken from a cow after calving, thicker than ordinary milk [O.E. *bysting*].

beet (bēt) *n.* a garden or field plant having a succulent tap root, the red variety being used as a vegetable, the white yielding sugar. **— sugar** *n.* crystallized sugar extracted from beetroot [O.E. *bēte*, fr. L. *bēta*].

bee·tle (bē′·tl) *n.* heavy wooden mallet for beating down paving-stones or driving in piles; wooden utensil for beating linen, mashing potatoes or stirring porridge, etc. [O.E. *betel*, a mallet].

bee·tle (bē′·tl) *n.* name of a large order of insects, Coleoptera [O.E. *bitula*, a biter].

bee·tle (bē′·tl) *v.i.* to be prominent; to jut out; to overhang. **beetling** *a.* overhanging. **—browed** *a.* with overhanging brows; scowling. **-head** *n.* a dull, stupid person [O.E. *bitel*].

beeves (bēvz) *n.pl.* cattle, oxen [See **beef**].

be·fall (bi·fawl′) *v.t.* to happen to; *v.i.* to come to pass; to happen; *pr.p.* **-ing;** *pa.t.* **befell;** *pa.p.* **-en** [O.E. *befeallan*].

be·fit (bi·fit′) *v.t.* to fit or be suitable to; to become; be right for; *pr.p.* **-ting;** *pa.t., pa.p.* **-ted. -ting** *a.* **-tingly** *adv.*

be·fog (bi·fawg′) *v.t.* to envelop in a fog; perplex. *pr.p.* **-ging.** *pa.t.* **-ged.**

be·fore (bi·fōr′) *prep.* in front of; preceding; in the presence of; prior to; previous to; superior to; *adv.* in front of; in advance; a short time ago; already. *conj.* sooner than; rather than. **-hand** *adv.* previously. **-time** *adv.* of old; formerly [O.E. *beforan*].

be·foul (bi·foul′) *v.t.* to foul, soil, dirty.

be·friend (bi·frend′) *v.t.* to act as a friend to; to favor; to help a stranger.

be·fud·dle (bi·fu′·dl) *v.t.* to confuse.

beg (beg) *v.t.* to ask earnestly and humbly; to ask for alms; to practice begging; to beseech; *pr.p.* **-ging;** *pa.t.* and *pa.p.* **-ged. -gar** *n.* one who solicits alms; a mendicant; *v.t.* to reduce to beggary; to ruin financially. **-garliness** *n.* **-garly** *a.* like a beggar; poor; mean; squalid; worthless; meagre; trifling; *adv.* meanly. **-gary** *n.* extreme poverty. **-ging** *n.* soliciting alms; *a.* pert. to begging; imploring; soliciting. **to beg the question,** to assume truth of thing to be proved [M.E. *beggen*].

be·gan (bi·gan′) *pa.t.* of **begin.**

be·get (bi·get′) *v.t.* to generate; to procreate; to produce or to cause; to get; give rise to. *pr.p.* **-ting;** *pa.t.* **begot, begat;** *pa.p.* **begot, begotten** [O.E. *begitan*, fr. *get*].

be·gin (bi·gin′) *v.t.* to enter on; to start, to commence; *v.i.* to take the first step; to set about. *pr.p.* **-ning;** *pa.t.* **began;** *pa.p.* **begun. -ner** *n.* one who begins; novice. **-ning** *n.* source; first part [O.E. *beginnan*].

be·gird (bi·gurd′) *v.t.* to gird or bind with a girdle or band; *pa.t.* **begirt** or **-ed.**

be·gone (bi·gawn′) *interj.* go away! depart! **woebegone** *a.* gloomy and miserable.

be·go·ni·a (bi·gōn′·yạ) *n.* a genus of tropical plants [Michel *Bégon*, Fr. botanist].

be·got (bi·gȧt′) **begotten** *pa.p.* of **beget.**

be·grime (bi·grīm′) *v.t.* to soil with grime.

be·grudge (bi·gruj′) *v.t.* to grudge; to allow reluctantly. **begrudgingly** *adv.*

be·guile (bi·gīl′) *v.t.* to cheat or deceive by trickery; to ensnare; to delude; to while away (time); to amuse or divert. **-ment** *n.* **-r** *n.* **beguilingly** *adv.*

be·gum (bē′·gạm) *n.* the Hindustani name given to a Moslem princess.

be·gun (bi·gun′) *pa.p.* of **begin.**

be·half (bi·haf′) *n.* favor; advantage; benefit; support; vindication; defense [O.E. *be healfe*, by the side].

be·have (bi·hāv′) *v.t.* and *v.i.* to conduct oneself; to act. **behavior** *n.* bearing or conduct; deportment. **behaviorism** *n.* theory that man's actions are automatic responses to stimuli and not dictated by consciousness.

be·head (bi·hed′) *v.t.* to sever the head from the body. **-al, -ing** *n.*

be·held (bi·held′) *pa.p.* of **behold.**

be·hest (bi·hest′) *n.* that which is willed or ordered [O.E. *behaes*].

be·hind (bi·hīnd′) *prep.* at the back of; in the rear (of); after; late; farther back than; in an inferior position; *n.* rump; buttocks; posterior. **-hand** *adv.* and *a.* late; backward; in arrears [O.E. *behindan*].

be·hold (bi·hōld′) *v.t.* to look at; to fix the eyes upon; to observe carefully; *v.i.* to look; fix the attention. *pa.t.* and *pa.p.* **beheld. -en** *a.* obliged (to); owing a debt of gratitude (to). **-er** *n.* an on-looker; spectator [O.E. *behealdan*].

be·hoof (bi·hȯȯf′) *n.* advantage; benefit; profit; use. **behoove, behove** *v.t.* to be necessary, convenient for; to befit [O.E. *behōf*].

beige (bāzh) *n.* very light brown color of unbleached wool [Fr.].

be·ing (bē′·ing) *n.* existence; that which exists; [an animal [fr. *to be*].

be·la·bor (bi·lā′·bẹr) *v.t.* to beat soundly; to cudgel; to exert much labor upon; to assail verbally.

be·late (bi·lāt′) *v.t.* to cause to be late; to retard. **-d** *a.* **-dness** *n.*]

be·lay (bi·lā′) *v.t.* to make fast a rope, by winding it round a fixed pin or cleat; *n.* in mountaineering, a rock to which a climber anchors himself by a rope. **-ing-pin** *n.* a pin or cleat, to which running rigging may be belayed [Dut. *beleggen*].

belch (belch) *v.t.* to emit wind from the stomach by way of the mouth; to cast forth; *n.* eructation [O.E. *bealcam*].

bel·dam (bel′·dạm) *n.* a grandmother; an ugly, old wọman; a hag; an irate woman. Also **beldame** [orig. *grandmother*, Fr. *belle dame*].

be·lea·guer (bi·lē′·gẹr) *v.t.* to surround with an army so as to preclude escape. **-ment** *n.* [Dut. *belegeren*, to besiege].

bel·fry (bel′·fri·) *n.* a bell-tower, or a part of a steeple, where bells are hung. Orig. a watch-tower, a bell being the signal [Fr. *beffroi*].

Ba·li·al (bēl′·yạl) *n.* Satan; the devil [Heb. = that which is without profit or worth].

be·lie (bi·lī′) *v.t.* to give the lie to; to falsify; to speak falsely of; to misrepresent; *pr.p.* **belying** [O.E. *beleogan*, to deceive].

be·lieve (bi·lēv′) *v.t.* to regard as true; to trust; *v.i.* to have faith (in); to think; to suppose. **belief** *n.* that which is believed; full acceptance of a thing as true; faith; a firm persuasion of the truth of a body of religious tenets. **believable** *a.* credible. **-r** *n.* **to make believe,** to pretend; to fancy [M.E. *beleven*].

be·lit·tle (bi·lit′·l) *v.t.* to make small; to think lightly of; to disparage. **-ment** *n.*

bell (bel) *n.* a hollow, cup-shaped metal vessel which gives forth a clear, musical note when struck; anything shaped like a bell; *v.t.* to provide with a bell. **bells** *n.pl.* (*Naut.*) half hours of a watch at sea, struck on a ship's bell. **-boy** *n.* page-boy in hotel. **-buoy** *n.* a buoy which by its swaying rings a bell attached.

bell (bel) *n.* the cry of an animal; the bellow of the stag in rutting time. Also **-ing;** *v.i.* to bellow; to roar [O.E. *bellan*, to roar].

bel·la·don·na (bel·ạ·dȧn′·ạ) *n.* deadly nightshade from which drugs, hyoscine and atropine, are obtained [It. = fair lady].

belle (bel) *n.* a particularly beautiful woman [Fr. *belle*, fair].

belles-let·tres (bel·let′·r) *n.pl.* polite literature, i.e. literature which includes poetry, the drama, criticism, aesthetics, etc. [Fr.].

bel·li·cose (bel′·ạ·kōs) *a.* pugnacious; contentious; war-like; quarrelsome. **-ly** *adv.* **bellicosity** *n.* [L. *bellum*, war].

bel·lig·er·ence (be·lij′·ẹr·ạns) *n.* the state of being at war; warlike attitude. **belligerency** *n.* a state of war. **belligerent** *n.* a nation, party, or person taking part in war; a contending party; *a.* waging war; pugnacious; bellicose [L. *bellum*, war; *gerere*, to carry on].

bel·low (bel′·ō) *v.i.* to roar like a bull; to shout loudly; to make an outcry; to roar, as of cannon; *n.* a loud hollow roar, as of a bull, cannon, etc.; any deep cry [O.E. *bellan*, to bellow].

bel·lows (bel′·ōz, bel′·ạz) *n.pl.* an instrument for producing a strong blast of air (to stimulate a fire, to work an organ, etc.) [fr. O.E. *bielg*, belly; the full O.E. name was *blaestbelg*, blast-bag].

bel·ly (bel′·i·) *n.* part of the body which contains bowels; abdomen; stomach; part of anything bulging like a paunch; *a.* ventral; abdominal; *v.i.* to swell out; to bulge. **-ache** *n.* abdominal pains. **-band** *n.* a band under the belly of a horse to secure saddle. **-ful** *n.* sufficiency of food, etc. [O.E. *belg*].

be·long (bi·lawng′) *v.i.* to pertain to; be connected with; to be property or attribute of; to be resident or native of. **-ings** *n.pl.* what belongs to one; possessions [M.E. *belongen*].

be·loved (bi·luv′·ad, bi·luvd′) *a.* greatly loved; *n.* one very dear to others.

be·low (bi·lō′) *prep.* under; beneath; of inferior rank or status; on a lower level than; unworthy of; *adv.* in a lower place; beneath; on earth or hell, as opposed to heaven [*by*, and *low*].

belt (belt) *n.* a band, girdle, or zone, used for encircling; a zone given over to the raising of one plant, e.g. wheat—*v.t.* to encircle, as with a belt; to thrash with a belt. **-ed** *a.* wearing a belt, esp. as a mark of honor, as in 'a belted knight'; thrashed with a belt. **conveyor —** *n.* an endless belt used for conveying material from one place to another. **-ing** *n.* material for skirt or bodice bands; a thrashing [E.].

be·moan (bi·mōn′) *v.t.* to express deep grief for, by moaning; to lament; to mourn for.

be·muse (bi·mūz′) *v.t.* to put into a state of confusion; to stupefy; to daze. **-d** *a.*

ben (ben) *n.* a geographical term, a mountain peak, as Ben Lomond [Gael]; son of [Heb.].

bench (bensh) *n.* a long seat; a table on which woodwork is done; the seat in court of a judge or magistrate; collective name for the body of judges sitting in judgment; *v.t.* to furnish with benches; to place, for exhibit, on a bench [M.E. *benche* fr. O.E. *benç*].

bend (bend) *v.t.* to curve; to arch; to turn out of direct course; to incline; to sway; to subdue or make submissive; to tie, make fast—of ropes and sails; *v.i.* to be moved out of a straight line; to stoop; to lean, to incline; to bow; to yield; *pa.t.* **bent,** *pa.p.* **bent** or **-ed;** *n.* a curve; crook; curvature; turn. **-er** *n.* an instrument for bending; a hard drinker; a drinking spree. **the bends,** aenoembolism. **to be bent upon,** to be determined upon [O.E. *bendan*].

be·neath (bi·nēth′) *prep.* under; below; lower than; unworthy of; below the level of; *adv.* below [O.E. *beneothan*].

ben·e·dict (ben′·a·dikt) *n.* a man newly married, esp. if considered a confirmed bachelor.

Ben·e·dict (ben′·a·dikt) *n.* the founder of Western monasticism. **Benedictine** *a.* pert. to St. Benedict or his monastic order; *n.* a Black Friar; a cordial or liqueur originally distilled by the Benedictine monks.

ben·e·dic·tion (ben·a·dik′·shan) *n.* a blessing of a formal character; the blessing at the end of a religious service. **benedictory** *a.* imparting a blessing [L. *bene*, well; *dicere*, to speak].

ben·e·fac·tion (ben·a·fak′·shan) *n.* act of doing good; a benefit conferred; donation. **benefactor** *n.* (*fem.* **benefactress**) one who helps others; a donor; a patron. **benefactory** *a* [L. *bene*, well; *facere, factum*, to do].

ben·e·fice (ben′·a·fis) *n.* an ecclesiastical living. **-d** *a.* in enjoyment of a benefice [L. *beneficium*].

be·nef·i·cence (ba·nef′·i·sens) *n.* habitual practice of doing good; charity. **beneficent** *a.* kindly disposed; generous; doing good. **beneficently** *adv.* [L. *beneficium*].

ben·e·fi·cial (ben·a·fish′·al) *a.* conferring benefits; advantageous; helpful. **-ly** *adv.* **-ness** *n.* **beneficiary** *n.* one who benefits from the act of another; a holder of an ecclesiastical benefice [L.L. *beneficialis*].

ben·e·fit (ben′·a·fit) *n.* an act of kindness; a favor conferred; an advantage; profit; interest; a theatrical or other exhibition, the proceeds of which go to charity or an individual; a payment or allowance such as given by an insurance company or public agency; *v.t.* to do good to; to be useful to; to profit; *v.i.* to gain advantage (from). **fringe benefits,** such things as health insurance paid in addition to regular salary [L. *bene*, well; *facere*, to do].

Ben·e·lux (ben′·a·luks) *n.* the economic bloc of the three countries *Be*lgium, the *Ne*therlands, and *Lux*emburg.

be·nev·o·lence (ba·nev′·a·lans) *n.* disposition to do good; love of mankind; an act of kindness; generosity. **benevolent** *a.* of a kindly nature [L. *bene*, well; *velle*, to wish].

be·night·ed (bi·nīt′·ad) *a.* overtaken by night; enveloped in moral or mental darkness; ignorant; unenlightened; lost.

be·nign (bi·nīn′) *a.* of a kindly disposition; mild, not malignant (of disease); propitious (of climate). **-ancy** (bi·nig′·nan·si·) *n.* benignant quality. **-ant** *a.* kind; gracious; favorable; beneficial. **-antly** *adv.* **-ity** *n.* **-ly** *adv.* in benign fashion [L. *benignus*, kind].

ben·i·son (ben′·i·zn) *n.* benediction; blessing [L. *benedictio*. Doublet of *benediction*].

Ben·ja·min (ben′·ja·min) *n.* (*Bib.*) a youngest son; a favorite child [Heb. = son of the right hand].

ben·ja·min (ben′·ja·min) *n.* benzoin, a kind or resin or gum used as a medicine [corrupt. of *benzoin*].

bent (bent) *pa.t.* and *pa.p.* of **bend.**

bent (bent) *n.* (of mind), leaning, bias, or inclination for; a tendency [fr. *bend*].

bent (bent) *n.* bent grass; any stiff, wiry, coarse grass. **-y** *a.* overrun with bent [O.E. *beonet*].

be·numb (bi·num′) *v.t.* to make numb, through cold or fear; to deprive of all sensation; to deaden. **-ed** *a.* [O.E. *beniman*, to deprive].

Ben·ze·drine (ben′·za·drēn) *n.* amphetamine, a synthetic drug [Trademark].

be·queath (bi·kwēTH′) *v.t.* to leave by will, said of personal property; to leave to those who follow on, as a problem, trouble, etc. **bequest** *n.* that which is left by will; legacy [O.E. *becwethan*].

be·rate (bi·rāt′) *v.t.* to scold vigorously.

be·reave (bi·rēv′) *v.t.* to make destitute; to deprive of; *pa.p.* **-d** or **bereft. -d** *a.* robbed by death, esp. of a relative. **-ment** *n.* loss, esp. by death [E. pref. *be*; O.E. *rēafian*, to spoil].

be·ret (ber′·ā, ber′·it) *n.* a soft, round tight-fitting cap without any peak [Fr. fr. L.L. *birretum*, a cap].

berg (burg) *n.* a large mass or mountain of ice; an iceberg [Ger. = a mountain].

ber·i·ber·i (ber′·i·ber′·i·) *n.* a nervous disease due to deficiency of vitamin B [Singh.].

ber·lin (bur′·lin) *n.* a four-wheeled closed carriage with two seats [Fr. *Berlin*, Germany].

ber·ry (ber′·i·) *n.* a small, pulpy, juicy fruit; strictly a simple fruit with succulent pericarp. **-ing** *n.* **berried** *a.* [O.E. *berie*].

ber·serk, ber·serk·er (ber′·surk, ·ker) *n.* a battle-frenzied Norse warrior; *a.* frenzied. **to go berserk,** to go mad with fury [Scand. = poss. bare of sark or shirt of mail].

berth (burth) *n.* the place where a ship is anchored or moored; a sleeping-place on a ship, etc.; a situation or job. *v.t.* to bring to anchorage. **-age** *n.* dock or harbor dues. **to give a wide berth to,** to steer clear of; to shun; to avoid [Doublet of *birth*].

ber'yl (ber′·il) *n.* a group of green or bluish-green precious stones of exceptional hardness. **-lium** *n.* a rare metal of the magnesium group [Gk. *bērullos*].

be·seech (bi·sēch′) *v.t.* to ask or entreat earnestly; to solicit; beg; implore; *pa.t.* and *pa.p.* **besought. -er** *n.* **-ing** *a.* [M.E. *sechen*, to seek]

be·seem (bi·sēm′) *v.t.* to be fit for; to befit; to suit, to become. **beseeming** *a.*

be·set (bi·set′) *v.t.* to place on, in, or around; to hem in on all sides; to surround; to enclose; to assail; *pr.p.* **-ting.** *pa.t.* and *pa.p.* **beset, -ment** *n.* **-ter** *n.* **-ting** *a.* customary; habitual, as in 'besetting sin' [O.E. *besettan*].

be·shrew (bi′·shrōō′) *v.t.* (*Arch.*) to wish some slight evil to befall one; to curse; to rate.

be·side (bi·sīd′) *prep.* and *adv.* at the side of;

over and above; in addition to; apart from; distinct from. **-s** *adv.* moreover; *prep.* over and above. **— oneself,** out of one's wits [O.E. *bi sidan*].

be·siege (bi·sēj′) *v.t.* to lay siege to; to surround with armed forces; to pay court to; to beleaguer. **-ment** *n.* **-r** *n.* **besieging** *a.* **besiegingly** *adv.* [M. E. *asege*, fr. Fr. *assiéger*].

be·smear (bi·smir′) *v.t.* to smear over; to soil; to bedaub [O.E. *besmerian*].

be·smirch (bi·smurch′) *v.t.* to soil; to sully; to tarnish one's reputation, etc.

be·sot (bi·sạt′) *v.t.* to make sottish by drink; to make stupid. **-ted** *a.* [O.E.].

be·sought (bi·sawt′) *pa.t.* and *pa.p.* of **beseech.**

be·spat·ter (bi·spat′·ẹr) *v.t.* to sprinkle or splash with mud, ink, etc.; to defame.

be·speak (bi·spēk′) *v.t.* to order, speak for, or engage beforehand; to foretell; to indicate; *pa.t.* **bespoke.** *pa.p.* **bespoke** and **bespoken. bespoke, bespoken** *a.* ordered beforehand; of goods [O.E. *besprecan*].

be·speck·le (bi·spek′·l) *v.t.* to mark with speckles or spots; to variegate. **-d** *a.*

Bes·se·mer (bes′·ạm·ẹr) *a.* applied to steel prepared by the Bessemer process of forcing atmospheric air into molten cast iron [Sir H. *Bessemer*, (1813-98), the inventor].

best (best) *a. superl.* good in the highest degree; excellent beyond all others; most suitable, advantageous, advisable, or appropriate; *adv.* in the most excellent manner; *n.* utmost; highest endeavor; perfection. **— man,** chief attendant to the groom at a wedding. **— seller,** a current popular book with an enormous sale. **to make the best of,** to resign oneself to conditions, etc. [O.E. *bet(e)st*].

bes·tial (bēs′·tyạl) *a.* pert. to a beast; having the instincts of a beast; like a repulsive beast. **-ity** *n.* beastly depravity [Fr. fr. L. *bestialis*].

be·stir (bi·stur′) *v.t.* to rouse into vigorous action; to exert (oneself); to stimulate. *pr.p.* **-ring.** *pa.t.* **-red** [O.E. *bestyrian*].

be·stow (bi′·stō′) *v.t.* to lay up in store; to expend, as energy; to give ceremoniously; to confer; to award; grant; present; impart. **-al** *n.* **-er** *n.* **-ment** *n.* bestowing; what is bestowed [M.E. *bestowen*, to place].

be·strew (bi·strŏŏ′) *v.t.* to scatter over; to besprinkle. *pa.p.* **-ed, -n.**

be·stride (bi′·strīd′) *v.t.* to stride over; to stand or sit with the legs extended across. *pr.p.* **bestriding;** *pa.t.* **bestrode, bestrid;** *pa.p.* **bestrid, bestridden.** [O.E. *bestridan*].

bet (bet) *n.* a stake or wager on some problematical event; *v.t.* to stake money upon some contingency; *pr.p.* **-ting;** *pa.t.* and *pa.p.* **bet** or **-ted. -ter, -tor** *n.* [fr. *abet*].

be·ta (bā′·tạ, bē′·tạ) *n.* the second letter of the Greek alphabet, printed thus, β. **— particles,** fast electrons emitted when certain atoms undergo radioactive breakdown. **— rays,** streams of beta particles emanated by radioactive substances.

be·take (bi·tāk′) *v.t.* to have recourse to; (with reflexive) to go, to repair to; to make one's way; *pr.p.* **betaking;** *pa.t.* **betook;** *pa.p.* **-en** [M.E. *betaken*].

be·tel (bē′·tl) *n.* a species of pepper. **— nut** *n.* the nut of the areca palm [Port. *betle*].

be·think (bi·thingk′) *v.t.*) to call to mind; to remind oneself; to cogitate. *pa.t.* **bethought.**

be·tide (bi·tīd′) *v.t.* to happen to; *v.i.* to occur; happen [M.E. *betiden*, to happen].

be·times (bi·tīmz′) *adv.* in good time; seasonably; soon; early; forward [M.E.].

be·token (bi·tō′·kn) *v.t.* to show by some visible sign; to foreshow [M.E. *betacnien*].

be·took (bi·to͝ok′) *pa.t.* of **betake.**

be·tray (bi·trā′) *v.t.* to give up treacherously; to be disloyal to; to disclose (a secret); to seduce; to show signs of; deceive. **-al** *n.* **-er** *n.* a traitor; a seducer [L. *tradere*, to give up].

be·troth (bi·trōTH′, ·trawTH′) *v.t.* to promise to give or take in marriage; to affiance. **-al** *n.* an agreement with a view to marriage. **-ed** *n.* a person engaged to be married; fiancé, (*fem.*) fiancée. **-ment** *n.* the state of being betrothed [M.E. *bitreuthien*].

bet·ter (bet′·ẹr) *a.* (compar. of *good*), showing a greater degree of excellence; improved in health; *adv.* (compar. of *well*), in a more excellent or superior manner; more fully; *v.t.* and *i.* to make better; to amend; to raise one's worldly position. **-ment** *n.* improvement; enhanced value of property due to local improvements. **-s** *n.pl.* one's superiors in rank or wealth. **— half,** a jocular term for spouse. **— off,** in more prosperous circumstances. **to get the better of,** to gain an advnatage over. **to think better of,** to reconsider [O.E. *betera*].

be·tween (bi·twēn′) *prep.* in the middle of two (of space, time, etc.); in the middle or intermediate space; shared by two; *adv.* midway. **go-between** *n.* an intermediary [O.E. *betweonum*, by twain].

be·twixt (bi·twikst′) *prep.* between; midway.

bev·el (bev′·l) *n.* an angle, not being a right angle, formed by two surfaces; an adjustable instrument used in building, etc. for testing angles; *a.* having the form of a bevel; slanting; *v.t.* to cut to a bevel angle. **-led** *a.* **-ing, -ment** *n.* [Fr. *biveau*, carpenter's rule].

bev·er·age (bev′·a·rij) *n.* a refreshing liquid suitable for drinking [O.Fr. *bevrage*].

bev·y (bev′·i·) *n.* a flock of birds; an assembly; a collection or group.

be·wail (bi·wāl′) *v.t.* to express grief for; to lament; deplore; mourn over.

be·ware (bi·wār′) *v.i.* to be wary of; to be on one's guard; to be alive to impending danger; to take care (lest).

be·wil·der (bi·wil′·dẹr) *v.t.* to lead astray or into confusion; to confound; perplex; puzzle. **-ed** *a.* **-ing** *a.* confusing. **-ment** *n.* [fr. obs. *wildern*, wilderness].

be·witch (bi·wich′) *v.t.* to gain power over, by sorcery; to charm; captivate; entrance. **-er** *n.* **-ery, -ment** *n.* power to bewitch; enchantment. **-ing** *a.* [M.E. *bewicchen*].

be·wray (bi·rā′) *v.t.* to divulge; to disclose; to reveal without intent [O.E. *wregan*, to accuse].

be·yond (bi·yạnd′) *prep.* on the farther side of; out of reach of; above; past in time; later than; superior to; *adv.* farther off; at a distance; *n.* the future life [O.E. *geond*, across].

bez·el (bez′·ạl) *n.* the piece of metal under the setting holding the jewel of a ring; the groove in which the glass of a watch is set; the sloped cutting edge of a tool; the sloping facets of a cut gem. Also **basil** or **bezil** [O.Fr. bisel].

bi-, (bī) *prefix* used in the construction of compound nouns, indicating two, twice, or double [L. *bis*, twice].

bi·an·nu·al (bī·an′·yoo·ạl) *a.* happening twice a year. **-ly** *adv.*

bi·as (bī′·ạs) *n.* prejudice; prepossession that sways the mind; a diagonal line of direction; *v.t.* to influence; to prejudice; to prepossess (often unduly; *pa.t.* and *pa.p.* **-sed** or **-ed** [Fr. *biais*, oblique].

bib (bib) *n.* piece of cloth worn mainly by children over the breast when eating; part of a workman's overalls to protect chest; *v.t.* and *v.i.* to sip; tipple; drink frequently. *pr.p.* **-bing;** *pa.t.* and *pa.p.* **-bed. -acious** *a.* addicted to tippling. **-ber** *n.* a person given to frequent and excessive imbibing of liquor or wines; a tippler [L. *bibere*, to drink].

Bi·ble (bī′·bl) *n.* the volume which contains the Scriptures of the Old and/or New Testament; an authoritative book on a specific subject. **biblical** *a.* scriptural [Gk. *biblia*, books].

bib·li·o- (bib′·li·ō) *prefix* from Gk. *biblion*, a book, used in the formation of compound words referring to books. **-graphy** *n.* expert knowledge of history of books; a list of books on a specific subject. **-grapher** *n.* one who compiles lists of books for further study of a subject; one interested in various editions of certain books. **-graphic(al)** *a.* **-logy** *n.* knowledge of the production and distribution of books. **-mania** *n.* a mania for possessing rare books. **-maniac** *n.* **-phile** *n.* a lover of books. **-pole, -polist** *n.* a dealer in books, esp. rare books. **-poly** *n.* **-theca** *n.* a library. **-thecary** *n.* a librarian [Gk. *biblion*, a book].

bib·u·lous (bib′·ū·lạs) *a.* given to excessive or frequent drinking; absorbent; spongy. **-ly** *adv.* [L. *bibere*, to drink].

bi·cam·er·al (bī·kam′·ạ·rạl) *a.* pert. to or containing two legislative or other chambers [L. *bis*, twice; *camera*, chamber].

bi·car·bon·ate (bī·kȧr′·bạ·nāt) *n.* a salt or compound containing two equivalents of carbonic acid to one of a base—usually applied loosely for 'bicarbonate of soda.'

bice (bīs) *n.* a blue or green pigment [Fr. *bis*].

bi·ceps (bī′·seps) *n.* two-headed muscle of arm or leg; a flexor muscle. **biciptial** *a.* [L. *bis*, twice; *caput*, head].

bick·er (bik′·ẹr) *v.i.* to bandy words; to wrangle; to move quickly and lightly. **-ing** *n.* **-ment** *n.* [M.E. *biker(en)*].

bi·cus·pid (bī·kus′·pid) *n.* a tooth with two fangs; *a.* having two cusps or fangs. Also **-ate** [L. *bis*, twice; *cuspis*, a point].

bi·cy·cle (bī′·sī·kl) *n.* a vehicle with two wheels, one in front of the other, propelled by pedals; *v.i.* to cycle. **bicyclist** *n.* one who rides a bicycle. **bike** *n.* (*Colloq.*) [L. *bis*, twice; Gk. *kuklos*, a wheel].

bid (bid) *v.t.* to ask; to invite; to order or direct; to offer a price; to give, as good-bye; *pr.p.* **bidding**; *pa.t.* **bid** or **bade**; *pa.p.* **bid, -den**; *n.* an offer of a price, esp. at auctions; an attempt. **-dable** *a.* compliant; docile; obedient; submissive; willing; (*Cards*) that may be bid without undue risk. **-der** *n.* **-ding** *n.* invitation; command; offer at an auction; series of bids at cards [confusion of O.E. *beodam*, offer, and *biddan*, request].

bid·dy (bid′·i·) *n.* chicken; hen [orig. uncert.].

bide (bīd) *v.i.* to dwell permanently; abide; remain; continue; tarry; sojourn; reside. *v.t.* to endure; put up with; suffer; tolerate; bear [O.E. *bidan*, to remain].

bi·en·ni·al (bī·en′·i·ạl) *a.* happening once in two years; lasting for only two years; *n.* a plant which requires two seasons to bloom. **-ly** *adv.* [L. *bis*, twice; *annus*, a year].

bier (bēr) *n.* a frame or carriage for conveying the dead to the grave; a coffin; grave; tomb [O.E. *baer*].

bi·fa·cial (bī·fā′·shạl) *a.* having two like [faces or opposite surfaces.

bi·fo·cal (bī·fō′·kạl) *a.* having two foci; *n.pl.* spectacles with a small lens for reading, set into a larger lens for distant vision [L. *bis*, twice; E. *focal*].

bi·fo·li·ate (bī·fō′·li·āt) *a.* (*Bot.*) having two leaflets springing from the same point L. *bis*, twice; *folium*, leaf].

bi·fur·cate (bī′·fur·kāt) *v.t.* to divide into two; *v.i.* to fork. **bifurcate, -d** *a.* **bifurcation** *n.* **bifurcous** *a.* [L. *bis*, twice; *furca*, a fork].

big (big) *a.* bulky; massive; huge; great; pregnant; generous; magnamimous; important. **—hearted** *a.* **-ness** *n.* size; bulk; largeness; importance. **— shot** *n.* (*Colloq.*) **-wig** *n.* (*Colloq.*) a person of great importance or influence.

big·a·my (big′·ạ·mi·) *n.* the crime of having two wives or husbands at one time. **bigamist** *n.* **bigamous** *a.* **bigamously** *adv.* [L. *bis*, twice; Gk. *gamos*, marriage].

big·horn (big′·hawrn) *n.* a Rocky Mountain wild sheep.

bight (bīt) *n.* a curve; a loop of a rope when folded; a bend in the sea-coast; an open bay [O.E. *byht*].

big·ot (big′·ạt) *n.* one obstinately and unreasably wedded to a particular belief or creed; dogmatist. **-ed** *a.* **-ry** *n.* the blind zeal of a bigot [Fr. of unknown origin].

bike (bīk) *n.* (*Colloq.*) a bicycle.

bi·ki·ni (bi·kē′·ni·) *n.* a scanty two-piece bathing suit [*Bikini*, Pacific island].

bi·lat·er·al (bī·lat′·ạ·rạl) *a.* having two sides; affecting two parties. **-ly** *adv.* [L. *bis*, twice; *latus, lateris*, side].

bil·bo (bil′·bō) *n.* formerly a rapier or sword. **bilboes** *n.pl.* shackles for the feet, formerly used for prisoners on ships [fr. *Bilbao*, Spain].

bile (bīl) *n.* a greenish, viscous, bitter fluid secreted by the liver; gall; general disorder of health due to faulty secretion of bile; bad temper. **biliary** (bil′·yẹr·i·) *a.* pert. to the bile. **bilious** *a.* pert. to the bile; affected by bile; choleric; peevish; crabbed; ill-humored. **biliousness** *n.* a disturbance of the digestive system associated with an excess of bile [L. *bilis*].

bilge (bilj) *n.* the swelling part of a cask; the broadest part of a ship's bottom nearest the keel, acting as a sump; (*Colloq.*) nonsense; *v.i.* to spring a leak. **— water** *n.* evil-smelling water which gathers in a ship's botton.

bi·lin·gual (bī·ling′·gwạl) *a.* speaking, or written in, two languages. Also **bilinguar. bilinguist** *n.* a person who can speak fluently in two languages [L. *bis*, twice; *lingua*, tongue].

bilk (bilk) *v.t.* to defraud, to swindle. **-er** *n.*

bill (bil) *n.* a kind of axle with two sharp pointed spikes mounted on a long staff; a hook-shaped pruning instrument. **-hook** *n.* a small bill with a hooked end for lopping branches [O.E. *bil*].

bill (bil) *n.* printed notice for public display; an account of money owed; a written engagement to pay money under the hand of the granter; a declaration of certain facts in legal proceedings; the draft of a proposed law; *v.t.* to announce by posters; to cover with posters; to placard; to send a statement of money owed. **-board** *n.* a signboard for advertising. **-fold** *n.* a wallet. **-ing** *n.* advertising; invoicing [L.L. *billa* = *bulla*, a seal].

bil·let (bil′·it) *n.* a short note; an order requisitioning accommodation for soldiers; the quarters occupied by soldiers in private houses, etc.; *v.t.* to quarter or lodge troops. **billet-doux** (bil·i·dòò′) *n.* a love letter; *pl.* **billets-doux** [Fr. = a note] .

bil·liard (bil′·yẹrd) *a.* pert. to billiards. **billiards,** *n.* a table game played with three balls which are hit by a cue [Fr. *bille*, log].

bil·lion (bil′·yan) *n.* a thousand millions (10^9). **-aire** *n.* a fabulously wealthy person. **-th** *a.* [L. *bis*, twice; *million*].

bil·low (bil′·ō) *n.* a great, swelling wave of the sea; a surge of flame, smoke, cloud, etc.; a breaker; *v.i.* to swell or roll, as waves. **-ed, -y** *a.* [O.N. *bylgja*].

bil·ly (bil′·i·) *n.* (*Colloq.*) a policeman's stick.

bil·ly·goat (bil′·i·gōt) *n.* a he-goat; a tufted beard [*billy* = *Willie*].

bi·met·al·lism (bī·met′·ạl·izm) *n.* in currency, the use of both gold and silver coins at a fixed relative value.

bi·month·ly (bī·munth′·li·) *a.* once in two months or twice in a month; *n.* a periodical which appears once in two months or twice a month.

bin (bin) *n.* a box or enclosed place with a lid, for corn, bread, etc.; a receptacle for bottles of wine; *v.t.* to store in a bin. *pr.p.* **-ning.** *pa.t.* **-ned.** [O.E. *binn*, crib].

bi·na·ry (bī′·nạ·ri·) *a.* composed of two; two-fold; double; dual; *n.* a double star. **binate** *a.* growing in pairs [L. *bini*, two by two].

bind (bīnd) *v.t.* to tie together as with a band, cord, etc.; to constrain by moral influence; to secure together and enclose in a cover; to place under legal obligation; to be obligatory; to apprentice; to constipate; *pa.t.* and *pa.p.* **bound. -er** *n.* a person who binds; a machine for binding, as sheaves, books, etc.; cover in filing and loose-leaf systems. **-ery** *n.* a bookbinding establishment. **-ing** *a.* obligatory; constipating; *n.* act of fastening; anything which binds [O.E. *bindan*].

binge (binj) *n.* (*Slang*) a spree

bin·na·cle (bin′·ą·kl) *n.* the box containing the compass of a ship [earlier *bittacle*, fr. L. *habitaculum*, little dwelling].

bin·o·cle (bin′·ą·kl) *n.* a telescope fitted with two tubes. **binoculars** *n.pl.* field-glasses [L. *bini*, two by two; *oculus*, eye].

bi·no·mi·al (bī·nō′·mi·ąl) *n.* an algebraic expression involving two terms connected by the sign plus (+) or minus (—), e.g. a + b, or c — d; *a.* [L. *bis*, twice; *nomen*, name].

bi·nom·i·nal (bī·nȧm′·i·nal) *a.* (*Bot.*) having two names, the first indicating the genus, the second indicating the species.

bi·o- (bī′·ō) *prefix* used in the construction of compound terms, to express having organic life [Gk. *bios*, life].

bi·o·chem·is·try (bī·ō·kem′·is·tri·) *n.* physiology considered from the chemical point of view; the chemistry of living things.

bi·o·de·grad·a·ble (bī·ō·di·grād′·ą·bl) *a.* (detergent, container, etc.) capable of being absorbed by the organic environment when thrown out or disposed of [Gk. *bios*, life; L. *de*, down; *gradus*, a step].

bi·o·dy·nam·ics (bī·ō·dī·nam′·iks) *n.* the science which investigates the vital forces; the energy of living functions.

bi·o·feed·back (bī·ō·fēd′·bak) *n.* a method of controlling one's involuntary nervous-system functions, such as the heartbeat, through an electronic monitoring device [Gk. *bios*, life].

bi·o·gen (bī′·ą·jen] *n.* a hypothetical protein molecule assumed to be the primary source of all living matter. **-esis** *n.* the theory that life develops only from living organisms [Gk. *bios*, life; *genesis*, beginning].

bi·og·ra·phy (bī·ȧg′·rą·fi·) *n.* the detailed story of a person's life; the section of literature devoted to the writing of such stories. **biographic(al)** *a.* [Gk. *bios*, life; *graphein*, to write].

bi·ol·o·gy (bī·ȧl′·ą·ji·) *n.* the science of life, whether animal or vegetable. **biologic(al)** *a.* **biologically** *adv.* **biologist** *n.* **biological warfare** *n.* a method of fighting in which disease bacteria would be used [Gk. *bios*, life; *logos*, a discourse].

bi·o·me·chan·ics (bī·ō·mą·kan′·iks) *n.* a branch of science, combining biology and mechanical engineering, that studies parts of living organisms as mechanical devices, e.g., the eye or the leg. **biomechanical** *a.* **biomechanician** *n.* [Gk. *bios*, life; and *mechanics*].

bi·o·nom·ics (bī·ą·nȧm′iks) *n.* study of influence of environment on organisms; ecology [Gk. *bios*, life; *nomos*, law].

bi·o·phys·ics (bī·ō·fiz′iks) *n.* physics of living organisms. [of living tissue for diagnosis.

bi·op·sy (bī′·ȧp·si·) *n.* the excision of a piece

bi·ot·ic (bī·ȧt′·ik) *a.* (*Biol.*) relating to life; vital. **-s** *n.* the functions, properties, and activities of living things [Gk. *bios*, life].

bi·o·tin (bī′·ą·tin) *n.* a constituent of the vitamin B_2 complex essential to many forms of life [Gk. *bios*, life].

bi·par·ti·san (bī·pȧr′·ti·ząn) *a.* pert. to, representing, or composed of, members of two parties [L. *bis*, twice; *partire*, to divide].

bi·par·tite (bī·pȧr′·tit) *a.* consisting of two corresponding parts; shared by the two parties concerned [L. *bis*, twice; *partire*, to divide].

bi·ped (bī′·ped) *n.* a two-footed animal; *a.* **-al** *a.* [L. *bis*, twice; *pse*, a foot].

bi·plane (bī′·plān) *n.* an airplane or glider having two main wings.

bi·po·lar (bī·pōl′·ęr) *a.* having two poles [L.].

bi·quad·rate (bī·kwȧd′·rāt, -rit) *n.* (*Math.*) the value of the fourth power of a number. **biquadratic** *n.* the fourth power; *a.* [L. *bis*, twice; *quadratus*, squared].

birch (burch) *n.* a tree with slim branches and silvery bark-scales; the hard, close-grained wood of the birch; *v.t.* flog with a birch-rod. **-en** *a.* **-rod** *n.* a rod of birch twigs for inflicting punishment [O.E. *birce*].

bird (burd) *n.* a feathered animal with wings. **— cage** *n.* a cage made of wire and wood for keeping birds. **-call** *n.* the sounds made by a bird; instrument used to allure birds by imitating their notes [O.E. *brid*, a bird].

bird·ie (burd′·i·) *n.* (*Golf*) holing a ball in one stroke under par.

bi·ret·ta (bi·ret′·ą) *n.* a flat, square, stiff cap worn by Catholic clergy [It. *berretta*].

birr (bur) *n.* a whirring noise like that of a revolving wheel; an energetic push; a pronounced accent; strongly trilling the consonant *r*. Also **burr** [Scand. *burr*].

birth (burth) *n.* act of coming into life or of being born; the delivery of a newly born child alive; descent; origin. **— control** *n* restriction of conception. **-day** *n.* the day on which one is born; the anniversary of that day. **-mark** *n.* peculiar mark on the body at birth. **-place** *n.* the place where a person is born. **— rate** *n.* the ration of births to the total population. **-right** *n.* anything to which one is entitled by birth [M.E. *birthe*, perh. fr. Scand.].

bis (bis) *adv.* twice; *interj.* (*Mus*) perform the bar or passage twice.

bis·cuit (bis′·kit) *n.* a quick bread in small soft cakes; stoneware, earthenware, porcelain, etc. after firing but before being glazed [L. *bis*, twice; *coctus*, cooked].

bi·sect (bī·sekt′) *v.t.* to divide into two equal parts. **-ion** *n.* one of two equal parts. **-or** *n.* a bisecting line. **bisegment** *n.* one of two segments of a bisected line [L. *bis*, twice; *secare*, to cut].

bi·sex·u·al (bī sek′·shoo·ąl) *a.* responding sexually to both sexes; having the organs of both sexes; *n.* [L. *bis*, twice].

bish·op (bish′·ąp) *n.* a clergyman of high rank; chessman moving diagonally. **-ric** *n.* diocese, jurisdiction, or office of a bishop. **-'s lawn** *n.* a fine kind of linen [Gr. *episkopos*, overseer].

bis·muth (biz′·mąth) *n.* a reddish-white metal the salts of which are used in medicine.

bi·son (bī′·sąn) *n.* the large buffalo of Western N. Am. [L.].

bisque (bisk) *n.* one of various kinds of soup; unglazed porcelain [Fr.].

bis·tro (bis′·trō) *n.* a small tavern or café [Fr.]

bi·sul·phate (bī·sul′·fāt) *n.* a salt of sulphuric acid in which one-half of the hydrogen in the acid is replaced by a metal.

bit (bit) *pa.t.* of **bite.**

bit (bit) *n.* a mouthful; a morsel; small piece of anything; a fragment; a boring tool generally for use in brace; part of bridle which is placed in a horse's mouth; *v.t.* to put the bit in the mouth of a horse [O.E. *bita*].

bitch (bich) *n.* the female of the dog, wolf, or fox; (*Colloq.*) an opprobrious term for a woman; *v.i.* (*Slang*) to complain [O.E. *bicce*].

bite (bit) *v.t.* to cut, crush, seize, or wound with the teeth; to pinch with cold; to eat into, as acid; to corrode, to gnaw; to champ; to nip; to defraud; to cheat; *v.i.* to be given to biting; to be pungent; *pr.p.* **biting;** *pa.t.* **bid;** *pa.p.* **bit, bitten;** *n.* act of biting; a portion bitten off; food; morsel; sharp, pungent taste; the nibble of a fish at a hook; the grip of an edged tool on metal. **-r** *n.* **biting** *a.* sharp; severe; sarcastic; caustic; pungent; chilling [O.E. *bitan*].

bitt (bit) *n.* a post for securing cables, etc. usually *pl.; v.t.* to put around a bitt [Scand.].

bit·ter (bit′·ęr) *a.* biting or acrid to the taste; causing pain or smart to the feelings; *n.* bitter beer. **-ly** *adv.* **-ness** *n.* the quality of being bitter to the taste; animosity. **-s** *n.* alcoholic liquor containing bitter flavorings. **-sweet** *n.* the woody nightshade whose root, when chewed, tastes first bitter then sweet [O.E. *biter*].

bit·tern (bit′·ẹrn) *n.* a wading marsh-bird of the heron family [O.Fr. *butor*].

bi·tu·men (bi·tū′·men) *n.* an inflammable, mineral pitch, as asphalt, petroleum, etc. **bituminize** *v.t.* to prepare or treat with bitumen. **bituminous** *a.* [L.].

bi·valve (bī′·valv) *a.* having two valves; *n.* animal with a shell of two parts. **bivalvous** *a.*

biv·ou·ac (biv′·o̤o̤·ak) *n.* encampment in the open air, without cover; *v.i.* to encamp without covering. *pr.p.* **-king.** *pa.t., pa.p.* **-ked** [Fr.].

bi-week·ly (bī·wēk′·li·) *a.* occurring once in every two weeks; occurring twice in each week; *n.* a periodical issued twice a week or once in two weeks [L. *bis,* twice].

bi·zarre (bi·zår′) *a.* odd; eccentric; strange [Fr.].

blab (blab) *v.t.* to reveal imprudently secrets entrusted to one; *v.i.* to tell tales; *pr.p.* **-bing;** *pa.t., pa.p.* **-bed;** *n.* a chatterer; a gossip; a tell-tale. Also **-ber** [Scand. *blabbre,* to babble].

black (blak) *a.* of the darkest color; dark; nightlike; destitute of light; funereal; ominous; *n.* the darkest color; a person of African descent; mourning; *v.t.* to make black. **-en** *v.t.* to make black; to polish with blacking; to defame; *v.i.* to grow or turn black. **-ly** *adv.* **-ness** *n.* **— art** *n.* magic; necromancy. **-ball** *v.t.* to reject a candidate for admission to a club by putting a black ball in the ballot box. **-berry** *n.* a fruit-bearing shrub, the bramble. **-bird** *n.* any of a number of birds which have predominantly black plumage. **-board** *n.* a board painted black, a slate, or any dark surface to write on with chalk. **-bread** *n.* rye bread. **— diamonds** (*Colloq.*) coal. **— eye** *n.* discoloration due to a blow. **-face** *a.* (*Theat.*) having a blackened face, as in a ministrel show; *n.* (*Print.*) boldface. **-flag** *n.* flag associated with pirates. **— friar** *n.* a Dominican friar, from his black mantle. **— frost** *n.* severe frost. **-guard** (blag′·ẹrd) *n.* orig. a menial of the scullery; a low scoundrel; *a.* low; vile; *v.t.* to treat as a blackguard; to revile; *v.i.* to act in a vile manner. **-guardism** *n.* **-guardly** *a.* **-head** *n.* a small black-topped mass which plugs the mouths of the follicles of the skin. **— hole** *n.* a hypothetical collapsed star that is invisible because its density is so great that even light cannot escape its gravitational pull. **-ing** *n.* an old form of boot polish. **-jack** *n.* a short, leather-covered club with a heavy head on an elastic shaft; the flag of a pirate; a miner's name for zincblende. **— lead** *n.* graphite, as used in pencils, etc. **—list** *n.* any list of undesirable persons; *v.t.* to place on such a list. **-mail** *n.* extortion of money by threats of exposure or denunciation; hush-money; orig. moneys paid over to robbers to obviate constant pillaging. **— mark** *n.* a mark of censure or failure. **— market** *n.* a clandestine market for the sale of goods whose distribution is regulated, and which are not on free sale. **-out** *n.* temporary loss of vision or memory; a total cutting off of all lights. **— sheep** *n.* a loose, dissolute member of a respectable family [O.E. *blaec*].

blad·der (blad′·ẹr) *n.* a thin musculo-membranous bag, in the pelvis, serving as a reservoir for urine; the windbag of a bagpipe; any membranous sac. **-ed** *a.* swollen like a bladder. **-wort** *n.* water-plant with floating leaves. **-y** *a.* thin and inflated; blistered [O.E. *blaedre,* a blister].

blade (blād) *n.* the leaf, or flat part of the leaf, of a plant; the cutting part of a knife, or tool; the broad part of an oar; a sword; (*Colloq.*) a dashing fellow. **-bone** *n.* the upper bone in shoulder, scapula. **-d** *a.* [O.E. *blaed*].

blame (blām) *v.t.* to express disapprobation of; to censure; *n.* fault. **-less** *a.* **-lessness** *n.* [O.Fr. *blasmer,* to speak evil of].

blanch (blanch) *v.t.* to whiten; to bleach; to strip (the husk); *v.i.* to become white; to turn pale; to gloss over. **-ing** *n.* [Fr. *blanc,* white].

blanc-mange (blą·mánzh′) *n.* a pudding [Fr. *blanc,* white; *manger,* to eat].

bland (bland) *a.* mild; gentle; affable. **-ly** *adv.* **-ness** *n.* [L. *blandus,* flattering].

blan·dish (blan′·dish) *v.t.* to flatter and coax; to wheedle. **-ment** *n.* [L. *blandus*].

blank (blangk) *a.* without writing or any marks; empty; confused; *n.* an empty space; a lottery ticket not drawing a prize; the white disc of a target. **-ly** *adv.* **— verse,** unrhymed heroic [Fr. *blanc,* white].

blan·ket (blang′·kit) *n.* a loosely woven woollen bedcover; a covering; a thick canopy of cloud; *v.t.* to cover with a blanket; to toss in a blanket. **-ing** *n.* thick material for blankets; tossing in a blanket. **a wet blanket,** one who depresses others; kill-joy [Fr. *blanc,* white].

blare (blār) *v.t.* and *v.i.* to sound loudly; to trumpet; *n.* a long, prolonged noise [O.E. *blaesan,* to blow].

blar·ney (blår′·ni·) *n.* coaxing, cajoling talk; outrageous flattery; blandishing [fr. *Blarney-stone,* near Cork, Ireland].

bla·sé (blá′·sā) *a.* surfeited with everything; absolutely bored; sophisticated [Fr.].

blas·pheme (blas·fēm′) *v.t.* to speak irreverently of God; to desecrate by impious talk; *v.i.* to take God's name in vain; to curse and swear. **-r** *n.* **blaspheming** *n.* impious talk. **blasphemous** *a.* **blasphemously** *adv.* **blasphemy** *n.* irreverence in speaking of sacred matters; profane talk [Gk. *blasphēmein*].

blast (blast) *n.* a gust or puff of air; a forced stream of air; the blowing of a wind instrument; an explosion of gunpowder in rending rocks; a blight affecting plants or cattle. *v.t.* to injure, as by a noxious wind; to blight; to split, as by gunpowder; to abuse vehemently. **-ed** *a.* blighted; accursed; (*Colloq.*) confounded; infernal. **-er** *n.* **— furnace** *n.* a smelting-furnace in which hot air is furnished by bellows or other apparatus. **-ing** *n.* a blast; explosion [O.E. *blaest*].

bla·tant (blā′·tąnt) *a.* offensively noisy; loud-(voiced); brawling; obtrusive. **blatancy** *n.* **-ly** *adv.* [coined by Spenser].

blath·er, blether (bla′·THẹr) *n.* one who talks nonsense; *v.i.* to talk nonsense. **-s** nonsensical, foolish talk. **-ing** *n.* **-skite** *n.* one who talks sheer nonsense [Scand. *blathra,* to talk nonsense].

blaze (blāz) *n.* bright flame; a big conflagration; outburst of activity or zeal; display; *v.i.* to burn brightly; to glow with anger. **-r** *n.* sports jacket of bright color. **-s** *pl.* hell, as in **'Go to blazes'** [O.E. *blaese,* a flame].

blaze (blāz) *n.* white mark upon a horse's forehead; a mark on a tree made by pathfinders; *v.t.* to mark a trail [L.G. *blāse,* white mark on head of horse].

blaze (blāz) *v.t.* to proclaim; spread abroad [O.E. *blaesan,* to blow].

bla·zon (blā′zn) *v.t.* to make known to everybody; to display armorial bearings in their proper colors; to embellish; *n.* art of drawing or explaining coats of arms. **-er** *n.* **-ment** *n.* **-ry** *n.* art of describing or explaining coats of arms in heraldic terms [Fr. *blason,* shield].

bleach (blēch) *v.t.* to whiten by exposure to sunlight and air, or by chemical action; *v.i.* to become whiter or paler; *n.* a decolorizing, chemical agent. **-er** *n.* one who, or that which, bleaches. **bleachers** *n.pl.* outdoor, uncovered seat for a spectator in a stadium [O.E. *blaecan,* fr. *blaec,* pale].

bleak (blēk) *a.* without color; pale; desolate and exposed. **-ly** *adv.* **-ness** *n.* [O.E. *blaec,* pale].

blear (blēr) *a.* dim or watery, due to inflammation of the eye or tears; *v.i.* to dim or blur. **-y** *a.* dim [M.E. *bleren,* to have sore eyes].

bleat (blēt) *v.i.* to cry as a sheep; to talk in a complaining, whining fashion; *n.* the sound made by a sheep [O.E. *blaetan*].

bleed (blēd) *v.t.* to draw blood surgically; to extort money from someone; *v.i.* to lose blood; to die in battle; *pa.t.* and *pa.p.* **bled. -er** *n.* a person who is afflicted by haemophilia, excessive bleeding. **-ing** *n.* [O.E. *bledan*].

blem·ish (blem′·ish) *n.* any deformity, physical or moral; flaw; disfigurement; *v.i.* to mark with a flaw; to mar or disfigure [Fr. *blémir*].

blench (blensh) *v.i.* to start back from lack of courage; to flinch [O.E. *blencan*, to deceive].

blend (blend) *v.t.* to mix allied articles together smoothly and inseparably; *v.i.* to intermix; to mingle well; *pa.p.* **-ed** or **blent;** *n.* a mixture. **-er** *n.* **-ing** *n.* [Scand. *blanda*, to mix].

blende (blend) *n.* an ore of zinc, consisting of zinc and sulphur; name given to certain lustrous minerals [Ger. *blenden*].

bless (bles) *v.t.* to consecrate; glorify; sanctify; praise; to give thanks to; invoke happiness on; magnify *pa.p.* **-ed** or **blest. blessed** (bles′·id), **blest** *a.* happy; favored with blessings; hallowed. **-edness** *n.* happiness; heavenly joy; felicity. **-ing** *n.* a source of happiness or gratitude; benefaction; boon; benediction; prayer [O.E. *bletsian*, to consecrate (with blood)].

blew (blòò) *pa.t.* of **blow.**

blight (blīt) *n.* disease of plants caused by certain fungi or parasitic bacteria; anything which has an adverse effect, injures, or destroys; *v.t.* to affect with blight.

blimp (blimp) *n.* a small non-rigid airship.

blind (blīnd) *a.* destitute of sight; ignorant; undiscerning; reckless; unaware of; heedless; at random; invisible; concealed; closed at one end; (*Slang*) drunk; *v.t.* to deprive of sight; to dazzle; to darken or obscure; to hide; to deceive; *n.* a window-covering or screen; something intended to mislead. **— date** *n.* a date arranged with someone not previously known; the person involved. **-ed** *a.* rendered sightless; dazzled; oblivious to all other factors. **-ers** *n.pl.* a horse's blinkers. **-fold** *a.; v.t.* to cover the eyes with something; to mislead. **-ing** *a.* **— landing** *n.* grounding an aircraft by depending on radio signals. **-ly** *adv.* **-ness** *n.* lacking power of sight; ignorance; obstinacy [O.E. *blind*].

blink (blingk) *v.i.* to wink; to look with the eyes half-shut; to glimmer, as a candle; *v.t.* to shut out of sight, as a fact or question; to ignore; *n.* a glimpse; a glance. **-ard** *n.* one who blinks; a stupid person. **-ers** *n.pl.* pieces of leather preventing a horse from seeing to either side [M.E. *blenken*].

bliss (blis) *n.* the acme of happiness; perfect felicity; heavenly rapture. **-ful** *a.* supremely happy; enjoyable. **-fully** *adv.* **-fulness** *n.* **-less** *a.* [O.E. *bliths*, fr. *blithe*].

blis·ter (blis′·tẹr) *n.* a vesicle of the skin filled with a clear or blood-stained serum; a pustule; any like swelling as on plants, paint or steel; a plaster applied to skin to raise a blister; *v.t.* to raise blisters upon; to wither up with scorn and sarcasm; *v.i.* to rise in blisters. **-y** *a.* [O.Fr. *blestre*].

blithe (blīTH) *a.* gay; happy; gladsome; jolly; merry; sprightly. **-ly** *adv.* **-ness** *n.* **-some** *a.* merry; cheerful [O.E. *blithe*, joyous].

blitz (blits) *n.* a heavy, sudden attack by enemy bombers; *v.t.* to bomb from the air. **-ed** *a.* also **blitz-krieg** [Ger. *Blitz*, lightning; *krieg*, war]. [Ger. *bletz*, lightening].

bliz·zard (bliz′·ẹrd) *n.* a blinding snowstorm

bloat (blōt) *v.t.* to cause to have an unhealthy swollen appearance; to swell or puff out; to cure fish by salting and smoking. **-ed** *a.* swollen. **-edness** *n.* **bloater** *n.* a herring—salted, smoked, and dried [fr. Scand. *blautr*, soft].

blob (blȧb) *n.* anything small and globular; small, round mass [var. of *bleb*, blister (?)].

bloc (blȧk) *n.* a combination of two or more countries or political parties [Fr.].

block (blȧk) *n.* a solid mass of matter; a roughly squared piece of wood, stone, etc.; the large piece of wood on which persons were beheaded; the wheel of a pulley with its case of wood; a number of buildings forming one compact mass; an obstruction, esp. on roads; mounted plate for printing; *v.t.* to shut in, to enclose; to obstruct; to shape (a hat); to sketch out roughly. **-buster** *n.* a heavy explosive bomb. **-ing** *n.* the process of stamping bookcovers with a decorative pattern. **-head** *n.* a dullard. **-house** *n.* an improvised fort made of logs; a fortified place. **— letters** *n.* a form of script where the letters are printed instead of in the usual cursive style. **block and tackle,** a pulley enclosed in a block used for lifting weights [Fr. *bloc*].

block·ade (blȧ·kād′) *n.* prevention of imports into countries usually during a war; *v.t.* to shut up hostile troops in a town by surrounding it; to prevent trade with a hostile country. **— runner** *n.* a vessel employed to slip through to a blockaded country [fr. *block*].

blond (blȧnd) *n.* (*fem.* **blonde**) a person of fair complexion and generally, light blue eyes; *a.* fair; light golden-brown [Fr.].

blood (blud) *n.* the red, viscid fluid which circulates in the body of men and animals; relationship, consanguinity, kindred; honorable birth; descent; a rake, man about town; *v.t.* (*Med.*) to let blood, to bleed. **— bank** *n.* a store of blood for use in a transfusion. **— count** *n.* the number of red and white cells in a specific quantity of blood. **-curdling** *a.* terrifying. **-hound** *n.* a hound, with keen sense and perseverance. **-ily** *adv.* **-less** *a.* without blood; anemic; spiritless. **-lessness** *n.* **-letting** *n.* the withdrawal of blood to allay fever; phlebotomy. **-mobile** *n.* a mobile unit for collecting blood for blood banks. **-money** *n.* money paid for betraying another; wages earned at a sweated rate of labor. **— plasma,** the fluid part of blood. **— poisoning** *n.* a condition due to circulation of bacteria in blood stream. **—pressure** *n.* the pressure exerted by the blood on the walls of the arteries. **—red** *a.* crimson. **— serum** *n.* the fluid part of the blood after the fibrin and the corpuscles have been eliminated. **-shed** *n.* the shedding of blood; slaughter. **-shot** *a.* of the eyes, red or congested with blood. **-stain** *n.* the dried and darkened stain left on clothing, floors, etc. after contact with blood. **-stone** *n.* a semi-precious stone, a variety of crystalline silica, dark green in color with red spots. Also called heliotrope. **-sucker** *n.* an animal which sucks blood, esp. the leech; an extortioner. **— test** *n.* an examination of the blood often to determine to which of the four groups it belongs. **-thirsty** *a.* eager to shed blood. **—transfusion** *n.* the transference of blood from one person to another. **— vessel** *n.* an artery or vein through which blood flows. **-y** *a.* pert. to blood; stained with or containing blood; ruthless in shedding blood; (*Br.*) used vulgarly as an expletive to add an intensive force; *v.t.* to make bloody [O.E. *blod*].

bloom (blòòm) *n.* a flower; a blossom; state of freshness and vigor; flush of youth; powdery coating on freshly picked fruit;*v.i.* to blossom; to glow with youthful vigor; to flourish; *v.t.* to cause to blossom or flourish.

bloom·ers (blòò′·mẹrz) *n.pl.* women's loose trousers gathered at the knee, worn for sports; an undergarment of the same design [Mrs. *Bloomer*, of New York, 1849].

blos·som (blȧs′·ạm) *n.* the flower of a plant, esp. a tree; *v.i.* to put forth blossoms; to flourish. **-ed** *a.* **-y** *a.* rich in blossoms [O.E. *blostm*].

blot (blȧt) *v.t.* to spot or bespatter esp. with ink; to stain with infamy; to obliterate; to dry with blotting-paper; *pr.p.* **-ting;** *pa.p.* **-ted;** *n.* a spot or stain, as of ink; blemish; disgrace. **-ter** *n.* a blotting-pad. **-ting-paper** *n.* a kind of unsized paper for drying ink [Scand.].

blotch (blȧch) *n.* an irregular, colored spot; an eruption upon the skin; pimple; *v.t.* to mark with blotches; to make spotted. **-y** *a.* [O.Fr. *bloche*].

blot·to (blȧt′·ō) *a.* (*Slang*) very drunk.

blouse (blous, blouz) *n.* a light, loose upper garment; *v.i.* and *v.t.* to drape loosely [Fr.].

blow (blō) *n.* a mass or bed of flowers; *v.i.* to blossom [O.*E.* *blowan,* to blossom].

blow (blō) *n.* a stroke; a knock; a thump; a smack; a rap; sudden calamity.

blow (blō) *v.i.* to produce a current of air; to move, as air; to breathe hard or quickly; to puff; to pant; (*Slang*) to brag; (*Slang*) to squander; to spout (of whales); *v.t.* to direct a current of air on; to sound a wind instrument; to put out of breath; *pa.t.* **blew;** *pa.p.* **-n;** *n.* a high wind. **-fly** *n.* insect, e.g., blue-bottle which blows eggs in meat. **-lamp** *n.* a portable lamp for applying intense local heat. **-n** *a.* swelled ;tired; out of breath; tainted. **-out** *n.* (*Slang*) a feast or big meal; a burst tire. **—pipe** *n.* an instrument for concentrating the heat of a flame on some point, by blowing; a blowgun. **-y** *a.* windy [O.E. *blawan*].

blub·ber (blub′·ẹr) *n.* the fat of whales and other marine animals; *v.i.* to weep unrestrainedly. **-ed** *a.* swollen by weeping. **-ing** *n.* [imit. formation, with first meaning of *bubble*].

bludg·eon (bluj′·ạn) *n.* a short cudgel with one end loaded; *v.t.* to knock out with a club [probably Celt., fr. *plug*].

blue (blòò) *n.* the color of the clear sky; one of the seven primary colors; a dye or pigment; indigo powder used in laundering; the sea; *n.pl.* (*Slang*) a fit of depression; a very slow jazz dance of Negro origin. **blue** *a.* of the color blue; azure; livid; melancholy; glum; *v.t.* to make or dye blue. **bluish** *a.* slightly blue. **-bell** *n.* the wild hyacinth. **-berry** *n.* a shrub with edible small berries. **-bird** *n.* a migratory bird of N. Am. belonging to the thrush family. **— blood** *n.* an aristocrat. **-bonnet** *n.* Scottish trooper, from the blue woolen cap at one time in general use. **— book** *n.* a directory of socially prominent people; a college examination book. **-bottle** *n.* the cornflower; a large fly whose larvae are often parasites of domestic animals. **Blue Cross,** a system of nonprofit health insurance. **-grass** *n.* meadow grass of Kentucky which forms thick turf. **-heat,** about 550° F. **-jacket** *n.* a sailor. **-jay** *n.* a crested bird of the eastern U.S. and Canada. **— laws** *n.* laws restricting activities on Sunday. **— pencil** *v.t.* to edit, to alter. **-print** *n.* a simple photographic reproduction of technical drawings leaving white lines of plan on a blue background; (*Fig.*) any projected plan with its details. **— ribbon,** first prize; an emblem of temperance [Fr. *bleu*].

bluff (bluf) *a.* steep and broad; rough and ready; frank and hearty in manner; *n.* a high bank or cliff presenting a steep front; a headland; a cluster of trees on the prairie. **-ness** *n.* steepness; a frank, blunt manner of speech.

bluff (bluf) *n.* an attempt to mislead in regard to one's real purpose; *v.t.* to mislead one by giving a wrong impression. **-er** *n.* **-ing** *n., a.*

blun·der (blun′·dẹr) *v.i.* to make a gross mistake; to err through thoughtlessness; to flounder about; *n.* a gross mistake. **-er** *n.* **-head** *n.* one continually blundering. **-ing** *n.* and *a.* continually making mistakes; bungling; clumsy; fumbling. **-ingly** *adv.* [M.E. *blondren,* to confuse].

blun·der·buss (blun′·dẹr·bus) *n.* an obsolete short gun with a bell-shaped muzzle and a wide bore [Dut. *donderbus,* thunder-box].

blunt (blunt) *a.* having a dull edge or point; dull; brusque in speech; *v.t.* to render less sharp; to weaken appetite or desire. **-ly** *adv.* **-ness** [origin unknown].

blur (blur) *n.* a spot; stain; smudge; whatever dims without effacing; *v.t.* to smear; to make indistinct. *pr.p.* **-ring;** *pa.t.* and *pa.p.* **-red.**

blurb (blurb) *n.* an advertisement, esp. extravagant in praise [word invented by Gelett Burgess].

blurt (blurt) *n.* a sudden outburst. **to blurt out** *v.t.* to give information suddenly, indiscreetly, or tactlessly [imit.].

blush (blush) *v.i.* to redden in the face, from shame, modesty, or confusion; *n.* a rosy tint; a red color suffusing the face; first glance or view. **-ing** *n.* a rosy glow on the face; *a.* modest; coy; bashful. **-ingly** *adv.* [O.E. *blyscan,* to shine].

blus·ter (blus′·tẹr) *v.i.* to blow in boisterous gusts, of wind; to talk with violence and noise; to bully or swagger; *n.* fitful noise and violence. **-er** *n.* **-ous** *a.* **-y** *a.* stormy.

bo·a (bo′·ạ) *n.* a genus of constricting, nonvenomous serpents; a long round coil of fur or feathers for the neck. **—constrictor** *n.* a serpent which crushes its victims [L.].

boar (bōr) *n.* the male of the swine. **—hound** *n.* a large dog used in hunting boars [O.E. *bar*].

board (bōrd) *n.* a long, narrow strip of timber; a table, hence food or diet; council-table; council itself; a thick paper made by pasting together several layers (card-board, paste-board, etc.); *v.t.* to cover with boards; to supply with meals and lodging for payment; to embark on a ship, airplane, etc.; *v.i.* to be a lodger. **-s** *n.pl.* the stage in a theater; the covers of a book. **-er** *n.* one who boards a vehicle; one rereiving food and lodging. **-ing** *n.* a wooden fence, floor, etc.; entering a vehicle; obtaining food and lodging. **-ing-house** *n.* a house in which boarders are accommodated. **-ing-school** *n.* a school in which the students are in residence [O.E. *bord*].

boast (bōst) *v.t.* to speak with vanity of; to be unduly proud of; *v.i.* to brag; to vaunt; to praise oneself extravagantly; *n.* a statement, expressive of pride or vain glory; that which is boasted of. **-er** *n.* **-ful** *a.* **-fully** *adv.* **-fulness, -ing** *n.* indulging in boasting. **-ingly** *adv.* [M.E. *bost*].

boat (bōt) *n.* a small vessel, generally undecked, moved by oars or sails or small motor; a ship; anything resembling a boat, e.g. a sauce-boat; *v.t.* to carry in a boat; *v.i.* to row or sail about in a boat. **boatswain** (bō′·sun) *n.* a ship's officer [O.E. *bat*].

bob (bȧb) *n.* a short, jerking motion; anything which swings when suspended; a jerk; a pendant; the weight of a pendulum; hair cut short and square across; a docked tail; *v.t.* to move with a jerk; to cut hair semi-short; *v.i.* to dangle; to move up and down or in and out; *pr.p.* **-bing;** *pa.p.* **-bed.**

bob·bin (bȧb′·in) *n.* a cylinder or spool on which thread is wound [Fr. *bobine*].

bob-o-link (bȧb′·a·lingk) *n.* a common North American songbird.

bob·by-sox (bȧb′·i·sȧks) *n.* (*Colloq.*) ankle socks, usually worn by girls in their teens. **-er** *n.* a girl in her teens.

bob·sled, bob·sleigh (bȧb′·sled, ·slā) *n.* two small sleds coupled together; a long toboggan; *v.i.* to use a bobsled.

bock (bȧk) *n.* dark beer [Ger. fr. *Eimbeck* where first brewed].

bode (bōd) *v.t.* and *v.i.* to portend; to presage; to foretell; to foreshadow; to be an omen of. **-ful** *a.* **-ment** *n.* an omen; portent; presentiment. **boding** *a.* ominous; *n.* an omen; a presentiment [O.E. *bodian,* to announce].

bod·ice (bȧd′·is) *n.* that part of a woman's dress above the waist, with or without sleeves, and close-fitting [orig. *pl. bodies*].

bod·kin (bȧd′·kin) *n.* (*Obs.*) a short, sharp dagger or stiletto; an instrument for piercing holes in material; a large blunt needle; a pin for dressing hair [M.E. *boidekin*].

bod·y (bȧd′·i·) *n.* the frame of a human being or of an animal; the main part of anything; coachwork, seating and upholstery of a car; an assemblage of things or persons; a solid substance; strength or consistency of a liquid; *v.t.* to produce in definite shape; *pa.t.* and *pa.p.* **bodied. bodied** *a.* used in compounds, e.g. able-bodied. **bodiless** *a.* possessing no body. **bodily** *a.* pert. to the body; *adv.* physically, in the body, in the flesh; altogether; completely; in the mass. **-guard** *n.* life-guard of an important individual; an escort [O.E. *bodig*].

Boe·o·tian (bē·ō′·shạn) *a.* pert. to *Boeotia* in ancient Greece; boorish, dull, stupid, as the inhabitants were so considered.

Boer (bōr) *n.* a S. African of Dutch descent [Dut. cf. *boor*].

bo·gey (bō′·gi·) *n.* (*Golf*) one over par for hole. See *bogle* [fr. imaginary partner, Colonel *Bogey*].

bog·gle (bȧg′·l) *v.i.* to stop or shrink back through fear; to hesitate; to equivocate; to bungle.

bo·gle (bō′·gl′) *n.* a ghost or demon; a fearsome apparition, imp, or hobgoblin associated with the nursery. **bogey, bogy** *n.* the devil; a bugbear; a goblin. **bogeyman, boggard** *n.* [fr. *bug*].

bo·gus (bō′·gus) *a.* sham; counterfeit; spurious; false [etym. unknown].

Bo·he·mi·an (bō·hē′·mi·ạn) *a.* pert. to Bohemia or its inhabitants; pert. to the gypsies; unconventional; *n.* a native of Bohemia; a gypsy; one who leads a loose and unsettled life [Fr. *bohémien*, gypsy].

boil (boil) *v.t.* to bring to a seething condition, by heating; to cook, by boiling; *v.i.* to be agitated by the action of heat; to seethe; to reach boiling-point. **-er** *n.* one who boils; a vessel for boiling. **-ing point,** the temperature at which a liquid boils; of water 212° Fahr. [Fr. *bouillir*, to boil].

boil (boil) *n.* local inflammation of the skin round a hair follicle [O.E. *bule*, sore].

bois·ter·ous (bois′·tẹr·ạs) *a.* wild; noisy; hearty; turbulent; stormy; windy. **-ly** *adv.* **-ness** *n.* [M.E. *boistous*].

bo·la, bo·las (bol′·ạ) *n.* a missile used by S. American cowboys, consisting of two or three stone balls attached to the ends of a rope, to entangle the feet of cattle [Sp.].

bold (bōld) *a.* daring; ready to meet danger; courageous; brave; intrepid; valorous; fearless; cheeky. **—faced** *a.* impudent; forward; brazen; of letters, printed with heavy thick strokes. **-ly** *adv.* **-ness** *n.* [O.E. *bald*].

bole (bōl) *n.* the trunk of a tree. **bolling** *n.* a tree with the top and branches cut off; a pollard [Scand. *bolr*].

bo·le·ro (bō·le′·rō) *n.* a national Spanish dance, in triple time; the music for this dance; a short jacket, usually without sleeves, worn over a blouse [Sp.].

boll (bōl) *n.* a seed capsule of cotton, flax, etc. **-weevil, -worm,** larvae of various moths destructive of cotton crops [O.E. *bolla*].

bol·lard (bȧl′·ẹrd) *n.* a strong post on a wharf, etc., for making fast hawsers [fr. *bole*].

bo·lo·gna (bạ·lō′·ni, ·nạ) *n.* a large smoked, seasoned type of sausage.

bo·lo·ney See **baloney.**

Bol·she·vik (bȧl′·shạ·vik, also bōl·) *n.* a member of the Communist Party; a violent revolutionary. **bolshevism** *n.* theory and practice of Russian or other communism. **bolshevist** *n.* and *a.* **bolshevistic** *a.* **bolshevize** *v.t.* [Russ. *bolshe*, comp. of *veliki*, great].

bol·ster (bōl′·stẹr) *n.* a long round bed-pillow; anything designated as a support; *v.t.* to sustain; to support; to prop. **-er** *n.* **to bolster up,** to support a weak case or person [O.E.].

bolt (bōlt) *n.* a bar for fastening a door, window, etc.; part of a lock which engages with the keeper; a metal pin with a head at one end and screw threads at the other to receive a nut; a roll of cloth; a thunderbolt; an arrow; a sudden rush; *v.t.* to fasten with a bolt; to swallow food hurriedly; to expel suddenly; *v.i.* to rush away; to start suddenly forward [E.].

bomb (bȧm) *n.* a cast-iron container filled with high explosives, gas, incendiary contents, or smoke-producing substances exploding by percussion or by a timing mechanism. **-er** *n.* an airplane for bombs. **-proof** *a.* secure against small bomb splinters. **-shell** *n.* a bomb; something devastating and quite unexpected. **atom(ic) bomb,** a bomb depending on the release of atomic energy. **bomb sight,** instrument for aiming bombs [Gk. *bombos*, a booming sound].

bom·bard (bȧm′·bȧrd) *n.* an early mortar with a wide bore, using stone-shot. **bombard** (bạm.-bard′) *v.t.* to batter with heavy artillery fire; to ply with many questions. **-ier** *n.* a gunner in the artillery. **-ment** *n.* a sustained attack with guns, bombs, etc. [O.Fr. *bombarde*].

bom·bast (bȧm′·bast) *n.* inflated, high-sounding language. **-ic** *a.* **-ically** *adv.* [O.Fr. *bombace*, cotton-wool].

bom·ba·zine, bom·ba·sine (bȧm·bạ.zēn′) *n.* a twilled fabric of silk and worsted or cotton [Fr. *bombasin*].

bombe (bōmb) *n.* a melon-shaped or round mold of ice cream [Fr.].

bo·nan·za (bō′·nan′·zạ) *n.* an exceptionally rich and persistent vein of ore; a profitable enterprise [Sp.].

bon bon (bȧn′·bȧn) *n.* a fondant candy. **-nere** (nyār) *n.* candy dish [Fr. *bon*, good].

bond (bȧnd) *n.* that which binds, a band, a link, a tie; an oath or promise; obligation; duty; the arrangement of bricks or stones in a wall so that successive courses interlock and give stability. **-s** *n.pl.* fetters; chains; captivity. **-age** *n.* a state of being bound; slavery; political subjection [O.E. *bindan*, to bind].

bond (bȧnd) *n.* a legal engagement in writing to fulfill certain conditions; a certificate of ownership of capital lent to a government, municipality, etc.; a mortgage on a house, etc.; *v.t.* to put dutiable articles on or under bond. **-ed** *a.* placed in bond; mortgaged. **-ed warehouse,** a warehouse for holding goods in bond [O.E. *bindan*, to bind].

bone (bōn) *n.* the hard tissue which forms the skeleton of mammals, birds, reptiles and fishes. **-r** *n.* (*Slang*) a mistake. *v.t.* to remove the bones; to filet (fish); to stiffen corsets with whale-bone, etc. **-s** *n.pl.* human remains; corpse; dice; castanets. **— ash** *n.* calcined bones. **-black** *n*: finely ground animal charcoal. **— china** *n.* china in which bone ash is used. **-dry** *a.* absolutely dry. **—head** *n.* (*Slang*) a stupid person. **— meal** *n.* a fertilizer for dry soils, made from ground bones. **boniness** *n.* **bony** *a.* full of bones [O.E. *ban*].

bon·fire (bȧn′·fīr) *n.* orig. a fire for burning bones; a large fire specially built and lit to express public joy [fr. *bone* and *fire*].

bon·ho·mie (bon′·ạ·mē) *n.* frank and simple good nature; geniality [Fr.].

bo·ni·to (bạ·nē′·tō) *n.* a fish of the striped tunny kind [Sp.].

bon·net (bȧn′·et) *n.* a woman's head-gear, often tied under the chin. **-ed** *a.*

bon·ny (bȧn′·i·) *a.* pretty [Fr. *bon, bonne*].

bo·nus (bō′·nạs) *n.* something over and above that which is due [L. *bonus*, good].

boo (bȯȯ) *interj.* an exclamation of disapproval or contempt, often used to startle. **-es** *n.pl.* *v.t.* and *v.i.* to hoot; to show disapproval; *pr.t.* (he) **booes;** *pa.t.* **-ed** [imit.].

book (book) *n.* a number of sheets of paper, etc. bound together; a literary composition or treatise, written or printed; a record of betting transactions; the words of a play, the libretto; *v.t.* to put into a book; to obtain, or give, a business order, ticket (theater, etc.). **-s** *n.pl.* record of business transactions, especially financial; ledgers. **-binder** *n.* one who binds books. **-binding** *n.* **-case** *n.* a case with shelving for books. **— club** *n.* a club to distribute specially chosen books to subscribers. **— ends** *n. pl.* weighted props to keep books upright on a shelf. **-ie** *n.* (*Slang*) a bet taker. **-ing** *n.* entering in a book a business transaction; recording field observations in surveying; an engagement to perform. **-ing-clerk** *n.* a clerk who issues railway, etc., tickets or registers orders. **-ish** *a.* fond of books and study. **-ishness** *n.* **— jacket** *n.* an attractively printed outer paper wrapper of a book. **-keeper** *n.* **-keeping** *n.* the art of keeping a systematic account of financial transactions. **— learning, -lore** *n.* knowledge acquired by extensive reading. **-let** *n.* a small book; a pamphlet. **-maker** *n.* one who compiles a book from various sources; a professional betting-man who accepts bets. **-mark** *n.* something placed in a book to mark a particular page. **the Book of Books,** the Holy Bible. **-plate** *n.* a label, often illustrated, pasted on the front end-papers of a book to denote ownership. **-seller** *n.* one who sells books. **-selling** *n.* **-shelf** *n.* a shelf for displaying books. **-shop, -stall, -stand** *n.* a place for exhibiting books and periodicals for sale. **-worm** *n.* one who reads intensively; larvae of insects which bore holes through the pages and bindings [O.E. *boc*, a book, the beech].

boom (bȯȯm) *n.* light spar for stretching bottom of a sail [*Dut.*].

boom (bȯȯm) *v.i.* to make a deep hollow sound; to be extremely popular and successful; to flourish; *n.* a hollow roar; the cry of the bittern; a sudden advance in popular favor; a sudden demand for an article; economic prosperity. **-er** *n.* **-ing.** *a.* [M.E. *bommen*].

boom·er·ang (bȯȯ′·mạ·rang) *n.* a curved wooden missile used by the natives of Australia

boon (bȯȯn) *n.* some good thing given or asked for; a benefit [Fr. *bon*, good].

boon (bȯȯn) *a.* gay; merry; jolly [Fr. *bon*].

boor (boor) *n.* a peasant; a rustic; a churl; lout; clown, bumpkin. **-ish** *a.* **-ishly** *adv.* **-ishness** *n.* [Dut. *boer*, peasant].

boost (bȯȯst) *v.t.* to raise by pushing from beneath; to give a lift to; to help forward; to advertise on a big scale; to increase the output or power of a machine; *n.* a push up. **-er** *n.*

boot (bȯȯt) *n.* a covering for the foot and leg; a kick; an instrument of judicial torture in which the leg was crushed; *v.t.* to put on boots; to kick. **-black** *n.* one who polishes the shoes of passers-by. **-ee** *n.* a knitted boot. **-leg** *v.t.* to sell illicitly alcoholic liquor; to smuggle. **-legger** *n.* **-legging** *n.* **-licker** *n.* (*Colloq.*) a hanger-on; a flatterer; a sycophant. **-licking** *n.* [Fr. *botte*].

booth (bȯȯth) *n.* a temporary structure of boards or other materials; a covered stall at a market or fair; a small restaurant compartment [O.N. *buth*, a dwelling].

boo·ty (bȯȯ′·ti·) *n.* spoils of war [Fr. *butin*].

booze (bȯȯz) *n.* (*Colloq.*) alcoholic liquor; *v.i.* to drink excessively. **-r.** *n.* one who drinks to excess. **-y** *a.* a little intoxicated [Dut.].

bo·rax (bō·raks) *n.* hydrated sodium borate, used in the manufacture of enamels and glazes, as a softener for hard water, an antiseptic, a soldering flx, etc. **boracic** *a.* **boracic acid,** white powder used as an antiseptic or for checking excessive perspiration. **borate** *n.* a salt of boracic acid [Ar. *būraq.*]

bor·deaux (bawr·dō′) *n.* red or white wines of *Bordeaux*, France [Fr.].

bor·der (bawrd′·er) *n.* the outer part or edge of anything; the exterior limit of a place; a frontier; an ornamental design around the outside edge of anything; a flower-bed; *v.t.* to adorn with a border; to adjoin; *v.i.* to touch at the edge; to come near. **-ing** *n.* material for a border. **-land** *n.* land continguous to a frontier; an indeterminate state or condition. **-line** *a.* on the verge of [Fr. *bordure*].

bore (bōr) *v.t.* to make a hole in; to pierce; to drill; to weary by uninteresting talk; to fatigue; n. the hole made by boring; the inside diameter measurement of a cylinder; the hollow interior part of a gun barrel; a thing or person that wearies one. **-dom** *n.* the state of being bored; ennui. **-r** *n.* tool for drilling; insect [O.E. *borian*, to pierce].

bore (bōr) *pa.t.* of **bear.**

Bo·re·as (bō′·ri·ạs) *n.* (*Myth.*) the god of the North wind. **boreal** *a.* northern [Gk.].

bo·ric (bōr′·ik) *a.* pert. to boron [shortened form of *boracic*].

born (bawrn) *pa.p.* of **bear,** to bring forth; *a.* natural; innate; perfect.

borne (bōrn) *pa.p.* of **bear,** to carry.

bo·ron (bō′·rȧn) *n.* a non-metallic element whose compounds are useful in the arts and medicine [fr. *borax*].

bor·ough (bur′·ō) *n.* an incorporated town [O.E. *burg, burh*, a fort, a manor-house].

bor·row (bȧr′·ō) *v.t.* to obtain on loan or trust; to adopt from abroad. **-ed** *a.* **-er** *n.* **-ing** *n.* [O.E. *borgian*, fr. *borg*, a pledge].

bor·zoi (bawr′·zoi) *n.* the Russian wolf-hound, remarkable for grace and swiftness [Russ].

bosh (bȧsh) *n.* empty talk; nonsense [Turk.].

bosk (bosk) n. (*Arch.*) a thicket or small wood. **-y** *a.* bushy; covered with underbrush. **-iness** *n.*

bos·om (boo′·zum) *n.* the breast of a human being; part of the dress over the breast; the heart; embrace; enclosure; a shirtfront; *v.t.* to press to the bosom; *a.* intimate; cherished [O.E. *bosm*].

boss (baws) *n.* a prominent circular projection on any article; a knob; a round, slightly raised ornament; *v.t.* to emboss; to provide with bosses. **-ed** *a.* embossed. **-y** *a.* containing, or ornamented with, bosses [Fr. *bosse*, a hump].

boss (baws) *n.* master; employer; one in charge; *v.t.* to manage; to supervise; (*Colloq.*) to browbeat. **-iness** *n.* **-y** *a.* fussy and masterful. **-ism** *n.* [Dut. *baas*, master].

bo·s'un See **boatswain** (under **boat**).

bot, bott (bȧt) *n.* usually *pl.* **bots, botts,** larvae of species of gad-fly found in intestines of horses, etc., causing tumor-like swellings [Gael. *botus*, belly-worm].

bot·a·ny (bȧt′·ạ·ni·) *n.* that branch of biology which is concerned with the structure and growth of plants. **botanic, botanical** *a.* pert. to botany. **botanically** *adv.* **botanic garden,** a garden where plants are scientifically studied. **botanist** *n.*; **botanize** *v.i.* to study plants; to search for and collect plants for further study [Gk. *botanē*, herb].

botch (bȧch) *n.* a clumsy patch of a garment; bungled work; *v.t.* to bungle; to patch clumsily; to blunder; spoil. **-er** *n.* a bungler. **-ery, -work** *n.* **-ily** *adv.* **-y** *a.* [M.E. *bocchen*, to patch].

both (bōth) *a.* and *pron.* the one and the other; *conj.* (foll. by *and*) as well [O.E. *bā*].

both·er (bȧTH′·ẹr) *v.t.* to annoy; worry; trouble; vex; perplex; flurry; tease; plague; *v.i.* to fuss; to be troublesome; *n.* trouble; annoyance; fuss; worry; *interj.* an excalmation of annoyance. **-ation** *n.* trouble and worry; a mild imprecation. **-some** *a.* troublesome.

bot·tle (bȧt′·l) *n.* a vessel with a narrow neck for holding liquids; its contents; hard drinking; a thermionic valve; *v.t.* to put into bottles; to restrain; to curb. **-d** *a.* enclosed in bottles; of a bottle shape. **-d-up** *a.* confined; not allowed to speak. **— green** *a.* of a dark-green color. **bottling** *n.* and *a.* **-neck** *n.* a narrow outlet which impedes the smooth flow of traffic or production of goods. **-nose** *n.* a whale with a beaked snout. **— party** *n.* one where the guests provide the liquid refreshments. **-r** *n.* [O.Fr. *botel*, fr. *botte*, a truss].

bot·tom (bȧt′·ạm) *n.* the lowest part of anything; the posterior of human body; the base; bed or channel of a river or lake; foundation or groundwork; origin; *v.t.* to put a bottom on an article; to lay a foundation for a road, etc.

-less *a.* **-less pit,** hell [O.E. *botm*].
bot·u·lism (bàch′·ạ·lizm) *n.* a rare and dangerous form of food poisoning caused by spoiled foods [L. *botulus*, a sausage].
bou·cle (bòò′·klā′) *n.* a woven material with raised pile; *a.* pert. to such material [Fr.].
bou·doir (bòò′·dwàr) *n.* a lady's private room.
bouf·fant (bòò·fànt′) *a.* puffed out, full, as in draperies, skirts, hair [Fr.].
bou·gain·vil·le·a (bòò′·gạn·vil′·i·ạ) *n.* a S. American plant with great masses of red or lilac bracts [Louis *Bougainville* (1729-1814)].
bough (bou) *n.* an arm or large branch of a tree [O.E. *bog, boh*].
bought (bawt) *pa.t.* and *pa.p.* of **buy.**
bouil·lon (bòòl′·yàn) *n.* broth; stock. **bouillabaisse** (bòò·ya·bes′) *n.* a Provençal fish soup or stew [Fr. *bouillir*, to boil].
boul·der (bōl′·dẹr) *n.* a rock torn from its bed, and rounded by water. **—clay** *n.* a stiff clay of the glacial or ice-drift age [M.E. *bulderston*].
boul·e·vard (bòòl′·ạ·vàrd) *n.* a street or promenade planted with trees. **-ier** *n.* one who haunts the boulevards; a man-about-town [Fr. fr. Ger. *Bollwerk*].
bounce (bouns) *v.i.* to move with a bound and rebound; to leap or spring suddenly; *v.t.* to cause to rebound, as a ball; to eject; *n.* a sudden spring or leap; rebound; **-r** *n.* (*Slang*) one who expels disorderly persons. **bouncing** *a.* vigorous; big [Dut. *bonzen*, to strike].
bound (bound) *pa.t.* and *pa.p.* of **bind.**
bound (bound) *v.i.* to leap; jump; spring; skip; frisk; *n.* a leap; jump [Fr. *bondir*, to leap].
bound (bound) *a.* tending to go or on the way, as in *homeward bound* [Scand.].
bound (bound) *n.* usually in *pl.* limit or boundary; confines; precincts; *v.t.* to restrain; to form the boundary of; to set bounds to. **-ed** *a.* restricted; bordered; cramped. **-less** *a.* without limits; wide and spacious; vast; infinite. **-lessness** *n.* [O.E. *bindan*, to bind].
bound·a·ry (bound′·ạr·i·) *n.* a border or limit; a dividing line; barrier.
boun·ty (boun′·ti·) *n.* liberality; generosity; munificence; a payment formerly made to men enlisting voluntarily in the army or navy; a premium offered by a government. **bounteous, bountiful** *a.* generous; liberal; ample; plentiful. **bounteously, bountifully** *adv.;* **bounteousness, bountifulness** *n.* [Fr. *bonté*, goodness].
bou·quet (bō′·kā, bòò′·kā) *n.* a nosegay; a bunch of flowers; a perfume; the aromatic flavor and aroma of wine; (*fig.*) a compliment [Fr.].
bour·bon (bur′·bạn) *n.* a whisky distilled from corn and rye [*Bourbon*, Kentucky].
bour·geois (boor·zhwà) *n.* a member of middle-class society; *a.* of commercial or non-manual classes; middle-class; conventional; humdrum; stodgy. **bourgeoisie** (boor′·zhwà·zē) *n.* [Fr.].
bourgeon See **burgeon.**
bourn (bōrn) *n.* a stream; a burn [O.E. *burna*].
bourn, bourne (bōrn, boorn) *n.* a boundary; a limit; a realm; a domain; goal. **last bourne,** the grave [Fr. *borne*, limit].
bourse (boors) *n.* the stock exchange, esp. in Paris [Fr.]. [See **purse**].
bout (bout) *n.* a turn; a conflict; contest; continuous drinking [Doublet of *bight*].
bou·ton·nier (bòò′·tạn·yēr) *n.* a flower or flowers worn in a buttonhole or on a lapel [Fr.]
bo·vine (bō′·vīn) *a.* pert. to cattle; ox-like; dull; stupid; stolid; obtuse [L. *bovinus*].
bow (bou) *v.i.* to bend body in respect, assent, etc.; to submit; *v.t.* to bend downwards; to cause to stoop; to crush; to subdue; *n.* an inclination of head or body; the rounded forward part of a ship; the stem or prow. **-line** (bō′·lin) *n.* a rope used to keep the weather edge of the sail tight forward; knot used for tying a rope to a post. **-man** *n.* the one who rows the foremost oar in a boat. **-sprit** (bō′·sprit) *n.* a large spar projecting over the stem of a vessel [O.E. *bugan*, to bend].
bow (bō) *n.* anything bent or curved; weapon from which an arrow is discharged; any curved instrument, as a fiddle-stick; a lace or ribbon tied in a slip-knot; a rainbow; *v.t.* to manipulate ithe bow of a violin, etc. **-ed** *a.* bent like a bow; crooked. **-er** *n.* **-legged** *a.* having crooked legs. **-man** *n.* an archer. **— tie** *n.* a small bow-shaped tie [O.E. *boga*].
bowd·ler·ize (boud′·lẹr·īz) *v.t.* to leave out indelicate words or passages in a book in the alleged interest of moral purity. **bowdlerism** *n.* [fr. T. *Bowdler's* expurgated edition of Shakespeare, 1818].
bow·el (bou′·ạl) *n.* an entrail; the entrails; the inside of everything; (*Fig.*) the seat of pity, tenderness, etc. **-s** *n.pl.* the intestines [O.Fr. *boel*].
bow·er (bou′·ẹr) *n.* a shady recess; an arbor; (*Poetic*) a small country dwelling; a boudoir. **-y** a. shady [O.E. *bur*, dwelling].
bow·ie-knife (bō′·i·nīf) *n.* a long hunting-knife, the point double-edged, the blade straight and single-edged at the hilt [invented by Col. James *Bowie*].
bowl (bōl) *n.* a round vessel; a deep basin; a drinking-cup; the hollow part of anything, as a pipe for smoking; a stadium [O.E. *bolle*].
bowl (bōl) *n.* anything rounded by art; a ball rolled in certain games; a ball with bias; *pl.* a game played on a bowling-green with bowls; *v.t.* to roll, as a bowl; *v.i.* to play with bowls; to move rapidly and smoothly; to deliver a ball. **-er** *n.* one who bowls. **-ing** *n.* [O.Fr. *boule*].
bow·ler (bōl′·ẹr) *n.* (*Br.*) a derby [fr. name of original maker].
bow·sprit (bō′·sprit) *n.* See **bow.**
box (bàks) *n.* a small case or chest, generally with a lid; its contents; a compartment. **— kite** *n.* a kite consisting of a square frame strength. **— office** *n.* ticket office at a theater. **— pleat** *n.* a double fold with material turned under on both sides with knife edges [O.E.].
box (bàks) *n.* a small evergreen shrub. **—berry** *n.* the wintergreen. **-en** *a.* made of or like boxwood. **-wood** *n.* a tree [L. *buxus*].
box (bàks) *n.* a blow on the head or the ears; *v.t.* to buffet; *v.i.* to fight with the fists. **-er** *n.* a pugilist. **-ing** *n.* the sport of fighting with fists.
boy (boi) *n.* a male child; a lad. **-hood** *n.* **-ish** *a.* boy-like; puerile. **-ishly** *adv.* **-ishness** *n.* the natural actions of a boy [M.E. *boi, boy*].
boy·cott (boi′·kàt) *n.* a method of coercion by refusing to deal with; *v.t.* to act as above; to ostracize. **-er** *n.* **-ing** *n.* [fr. Capt. *Boycott*].
bra (brà) See **brassiere.**
brace (brās) *n.* a rod or bar crossing a space diagonally to connect two structural parts; a pair; a support; a fastener; a carpenter's tool for boring; a printer's mark ({) used in bracketing words; *v.t.* to furnish with braces; to support; to tighten; to nerve or strengthen. **-s** *n.pl.* suspenders; an arm guard; wires for straightening teeth. **and bit,** small interchangeable boring tool fitted into the socket of a brace. **-r** *n.* a wrist-guard of leather or metal, used esp. by archers; (*Colloq.*) stimulating drink. **bracing** *a.* strengthening; invigorating; refreshing [Fr. *bras*, arm].
brace·let (brās′·let) *n.* an encircling ornament for the wrist. **-s** *n. pl.* (*Colloq.*) handcuffs.
bra·chi·al (brā′·ki·ạl, brak′·i·ạl) *a.* belonging to the arm; of the nature of an arm; resembling an arm [L. *brachium*, arm].
brack·en (brak′·ạn) *n.* a large coarse species of fern [M.E. *braken*].
brack·et (brak′·it) *n.* a projecting support fastened to a wall; one of two hooks, [ ], { }, or ( ), used to enclose explanatory words; *v.t.* to place within brackets; to couple names together as of equal merit, etc. [Fr. *braguette*, fr. L. *bracae*, breeches].

brack·ish (brak′·ish) *a.* somewhat salty; distasteful. **-ness** *n.* [Dut. *brak,* briny].

bract (brakt) *n.* a leaf in the axil of which a flower or inflorescence arises. **-eal** *a.* of the nature of a bract. **-eate** *a.* having bracts; bracteal [L. *bractea,* a thin plate].

brad (brad) *n.* a cut nail tapering in width with a small head projecting at one end. **-awl** *n.* a small hand-boring tool [Scand.].

brag (brag) *v.i.* to boast; to praise oneself or one's belongings; *pr.p.* **-ging;** *pa.t., pa.p.* **-ged;** *n.* boasting; bragging. **-gadocio** (brag·ą·dō′·shi·ō) *n.* a boasting fellow. **-gart** *a.* boastful; *n.* a boaster. **-ging** *a., n.* **-gingly** *adv.*

Brah·ma (brȧ′·mą) *n.* the 1st aspect of the Trimurti, or Hindu Trinity, the Creator. **brahman** *n.* a person of the highest or priestly caste among the Hindus; also **brahmin.**

braid (brād) *v.t.* to plait, entwine, or interweave; to bind with braid; *n.* a narrow ribbon or tape used as a dress-trimming or in upholstery; a tress of hair. **-ed** *a.* **-ing** *n.* [O.E. *bregdan*].

braille (brāl) *n.* a system of printing books in relief to be read by the blind; also the letters used, consisting of raised dots in combination [Louis *Braille,* inventor].

brain (brān) *n.* the whitish, soft mass in the skull in which are the nerve centers; intellect; mental capacity; understanding; intelligence; *v.t.* to dash out the brains of. **— drain** *n.* (*Slang*) the migration of highly professional personnel to another country because of better opportunities. **-ed** *a.* having the brains beaten out; used in compound terms, as *feather-brained.* **-less** *a.* witless; stupid. **—storm** *n.* (*Colloq.*) a sudden idea, inspiration. **— trust** *n.* body of experts engaged in research or planning. **-wash** *v.t.* (*Colloq.*) to effect a radical change in beliefs by intensive indoctrination. **— wave** *n.* (*Colloq.*) a spontaneous bright idea. **-y** *a.* highly intellectual; clever [O.E. *braegen*].

braise (brāz) *v.t.* to cook meat by browning in fat and simmering in a covered dish with a small amount of liquid [Fr.].

brake (brāk) *n.* instrument for breaking flax or hemp; a harrow; any device for checking speed; any restraining influence or curb; *v.t.* to pound or crush flax, hemp, etc., by beating; to check by applying a brake. **braking** *n.* **— shoe** *n.* the surface ofa block brake.

bram·ble (bram′·bl) *n.* a prickly hedge-plant; the wild blackberry [O.E. *brembel*].

bran (bran) *n.* the ground husk of wheat and other grain, separated from the flour [O. Fr.].

branch (branch) *n.* a limb of a tree or shrub; a bough; a department of a business, etc.; a line of family descent; an off-shoot; ramification; section; part; sub-division; *a.* pert. to a subsidiary section of any business; *v.t.* to divide, as into branches; *v.i.* to spread, in branches; to diverge. **-ed** *a.* **-ing** *a.* shooting out; starting from. **-y** *a.* [Fr. *branche*].

bran·chi·ae (brang′·ki·ē) *n.pl.* the breathing organs of fishes, the gills. **branchial** *a.* pert. to gills. **branchiate** *a.* furnished with gills [Gk. *branchia,* gills].

brand (brand) *n.* a burning, or partly burnt, piece of wood; an iron used for burning marks on; a mark made by a hot iron; a trademark; a grade; a sword; a mark of infamy; stigma; *v.t.* to burn a mark on; to fix a stamp on; to designate a commodity by a special name or trademark; to stigmatize; to reproach. **-ed** *a.* **-er** *n.* **-ing-iron** *n.* [O.E.].

bran·dish (bran′·dish) *v.t.* to flourish or wave, as a weapon [Fr. *brand,* sword].

bran.dy (bran′·di·) *n.* a spirit distilled from wine [Dut. *brandewijn,* burnt wine].

brant (brant) *n.* small dark wild goose.

brash (brash) *a.* hasty; insolent; **-ness** *n.*

brass (bras) *n.* a yellow alloy of two parts of copper to one of zinc; (*Colloq.*) money; effrontery; impudence; obstinacy; *a.* brazen; made of brass. **-es** *n.pl.* the brass instruments of an orchestra. **— band** *n.* musicians who perform on brass instruments; (*Colloq.*) a military band. **— hat** *n.* (*Colloq.*) staff-officer (from gold braid on hat). **-iness** *n.* bold; impudent. **-y** *a.* pert. sole. **— knuckles** *n.pl.* metal pieces fitted across the knuckles, used in fighting. **to get down to brass tacks** (*Colloq.*) to return to essentials, fundamentals [O.E. *braes*].

bras·sard (bras′·ȧrd) *n.* a band worn around arm to signify special duty; armor for upper arm [Fr. *bras,* arm].

bras·si·ere (brą·zēr′) *n.* a woman's undergarment supporting the breasts; short form **bra** [Fr.]. [offspring [O.E. *bratt,* a pinafore].

brat (brat) *n.* a child (used contemptuously);

bra·va·do (bra·vȧ′·dō) *n.* showy bravery [Sp.].

brave (brāv) *a.* courageous; noble; fearless; *n.* an Indian warrior; *v.t.* to encounter with courage. **-ly** *adv.* **-ry** *n.* courage; heroism [Fr.].

bra·vo (brȧ′·vō) *interj.* an expression of applause, well done!; *pl.* **-es** [It.].

brawl (brawl) *v.i.* to flow noisily, as water; to squabble noisily; *n.* a noisy quarrel. **-er** *n.* [Fr. fr. Scand.].

brawn (brawn) *n.* muscular strength. esp. of the arms and legs; muscles; the flesh of a boar; a preparation of meat made from pigs' head. **-er** *n.* a boar fattened for the table. **-iness** *n.* **-y** *a.* muscular; sinewy; athletic; robust; stout [O.Fr. *braon,* fleshy part].

bray (brā) *n.* the harsh noise of a donkey; any harsh, strident noise; continual complaining; *v.i.* to utter a harsh noise, like a donkey [Fr. *braire*].

bray (brā) *v.t.* to pound; to powder; to pulverize; to grind small [O.Fr. *breier*].

braze (brāz) *v.t.* to solder metals with a hard alloy; to make or ornament with brass.**brazing** *n.* [Fr. *braser,* to solder].

bra·zen (brā′·zn) *a.* pert. to, or made of, brass; impudent; shameless; sounding like a brass instrument; *v.t.* to face a situation in a bold, impudent manner. **-ly** *adv.* [M.E. *brasen*].

bra·zier (brāzh′·yęr) *n.* a portable iron container to hold burning coals; a worker in brass [Fr. *brasier*].

Bra·zil·i·an (brą·zil′·yąn) *n.* a native of Brazil, in S. America; *a.* pert. to Brazil.

breach (brēch) *n.* a break or opening, esp. in a wall; a hole or gap; non-fulfillment of a contract, promise, etc.; an infringement of a rule, duty, etc.; a quarrel; *v.t.* to make a breach or gap in something. **— of promise,** the non-fulfillment of a promise, esp. of marriage [Fr. *brèche*].

bread (bred) *n.* form of food prepared by baking dough made from a cereal; food in general. **— winner** *n.* one who earns a living for his dependents [O.E.].

breadth (bredth) *n.* distance from side to side; width; freedom from narrowness of mind [O.E. *braedu*].

break (brāk) *v.t.* to shatter by force; to mitigate (a blow, a fall); to tame (a horse, etc.); to wean from (a habit); to bankrupt; to weaken or impair (health); to subdue (a person's temper); to violate (promises, etc.); to interrupt (friendship, silence, monotony, etc.); *v.i.* to divide into several parts; to open (as an abscess); curl over (as waves); to burst forth (as a storm); to dawn (as an idea, day, etc.); to crack or falter (as the voice); to make the first stroke at billiards; to change (as a horse); *pa.t.* **broke;** *pa.p.* **broken** [O.E. *brecan*].

break (brāk) *n.* the act or state of being broken; a fracture; a gap; an opening; dawn; separation; interruption; a breathing space; (*Slang*) a chance, good luck; a sudden fall in price; a scoring sequence at billiards. **-able** *a.* fragile. **-age** *n.* act of breaking; an allowance for articles broken. **-down** *n.* loss of health; an accident to machinery; suspension of negotiations; *v.t.* to divide into small categories. **-er** *n.* one who breaks; a long wave or crest as it breaks into foam. **-fast** (brek·fast) *n.* the first meal of the day. **-neck** *a.* dangerous to life and limb. **-up** *n.* disintegration; collapse; separation. **-water** *n.* a strong structure to break the force of the waves [O.E. *brecan*, to break].

breast (brest) *n.* the external part of the thorax or chest between neck and abdomen; bosom; seat of the affections and passions; *v.t.* to bear the breast against; to oppose, face, or meet boldly (a wave); to mount (a hill, etc.). **-s** *n.pl.* the milk or mammary glands of women and female animals. **-bone** *n.* the sternum, the flat narrow bone to which the first seven ribs are attached. **-plate** *n.* a metal plate or piece of armor for protecting the chest. **— stroke** *n.* a long-distance stroke in swimming [O.E. *breost*].

breath (breth) *n.* air respired by the lungs; the act of breathing freely; life; respite; a single respiration, or the time of making it; a very slight breeze; whisper; fragrance. **-less** *a.* out of breath; panting; dead; eager and excited; expectant. **-lessness** *n.* **under one's breath,** in a low voice or whisper. **with bated breath,** breath held from fear or excitement [O.E. *braeth*, exhalation].

breathe (brēTH) *v.t.* to draw in and give out air from the lungs; to infuse or inspire, as life, courage, etc.; *v.i.* to inhale and emit air—hence to live; to take breath. **breathable** *a.* **-d** (brēTHd) *a.* (*Phon.*) uttered with breath only. **-r** *n.* a short spell of rest. **breathing** *n.* respiration; a mark (') placed over a vowel in Greek grammar giving it the sound of *h.* **breathing-space, breathing-time,** *n.* a pause; relaxation; a short respirte [fr. *breath*].

bred *pa.t.* and *pa.p.* of **breed.**

breech (brēch) *n.* the buttocks; the hinder part, esp. of a gun-barrel; *v.t.* to put (a young child for the first time) into breeches; to whip; to flog. **-es** *n.pl.* trousers, esp. those which fit tightly around knees. **-es-buoy** *n.* an apparatus consisting of a canvas bag slung along a rope, used for saving persons from a wreck. **-ing** *n.* that part of the harness which passes round a horse's haunches [O.E. *brec*].

breed (brēd) *v.t.* to beget; to engender; to generate; to propagate; to hatch; to train or bring up; *v.i.* to be produced; to be with young; to increase in number; *pa.t.* and *pa.p.* **bred;** *n.* a race of animals from the same stock; kind; sort. **-er** *n.* one who breeds cattle or other live stock. **-ing** *n.* producing; the rearing of live stock; manners; deportment; courtesy [O.E. *bredan*, to nourish].

breeze (brēz) *n.* a wind of moderate strength. **breezy** *a.* windy; gusty; of a person, animated and brisk [Fr. *brise*].

br'er (brur, brer) *n.* brother; used in the animal stories of Uncle Remus [S. Dial.].

breth·ren (breTH'·rin) *n.pl.* members of the same society or profession [See **brother**].

Bre·ton (bret'·an) *n.* pert. to Brittany; *a.* one of the Celtic dialects, spoken in Brittany; a native of Brittany; a hat with turned-up brim [O.Fr.].

breve (brēv) *n.* the longest note now used in music; a mark distinguishing short vowels; a writ issued by a court [It. fr. L. *brevis*, short].

bre·vet (brev'·et) *a.* a commission, which entitles an officer to an honorary rank in the army above his actual rank. **-cy** *n.* brevet rank [Fr. fr. L. *brevis*, short].

bre·vi·ar·y (brēv'·i·e·ri·) *n.* a book containing the daily service of the R.C. Church [L. *brevis*, short].

brev·i·ty (brev'·a̤·ti·) *n.* shortness; conciseness; briefness; terseness [L. *brevis*, short].

brew (bro̤o) *v.t.* to prepare a fermented liquor, from malt, hops, etc.; to infuse (tea); to plot; concoct; mix; *v.i.* to perform the operations of brewing; to be impending; *n.* something brewed; a particular brand or quality of beer. **-er** *n.* **-ery** *n.* a place where brewing is carried on [O.E. *breowan*].

bri·ar See **brier.**

bribe (brīb) *n.* anything bestowed, with a view to influence judgment and conduct; *v.t.* to influence by gifts; *v.i.* to practice bribery. **bribable** *a.* **bribery** *n.* [Fr. *bribe*, fragment].

bric-à-brac (brik'·a̤·brak) *n.* curios; ornamental articles; knickknacks [Fr.].

brick (brik) *n.* a building material made from a special clay molded into a rectangular block and hardened by drying in the sun or firing in a kiln; (*Colloq.*) a sterling friend; *v.t.* to lay, or pave, with bricks. **-bat** *n.* a fragment of a brick. **-bats** *n.pl.* uncomplimentary comments. **-kiln** *n.* a kiln in which bricks are baked or burnt. **-layer** *n.* one who is skilled in building with bricks. **-laying** *n.* **— red** *a.* of a dull scarlet color like brick [Fr. *brique*].

bride (brīd) *n.*a woman about to be, or just, married. **bridal** *n.* wedding; *a.* pert. to a bride or a wedding; nuptial; connubial; conjugal. **bridal-suite** *n.* apartments set aside for a honeymoon couple. **-groom** *n.* a man newly-married, or about to be married. **-s maid** *n.* an unmarried woman who acts as attendant on a bride [O.E. *bryd*].

bridge (brij) *n.* a structure spanning a river or a valley, etc., in order to afford passage; a support for the strings of a violin; the hurricane deck or bridge deck of a vessel; the bone of the nose, etc.; mounting for false teeth; (*Mus.*) connecting passage; *v.t.* to build a bridge or bridges over. **-head** *n.* a work protecting the end of a bridge nearest the enemy; a footing gained by an attacking force on the far bank of a river. [O.E. *brycg*].

bridge (brij) *n.* a card game for four players.

bri·dle (brī'·dl) *n.* the headgear of a beast of burden, of a horse; a curb; constraint; *v.t.* to put a bridle upon; to check; subdue; curb; control. **— path** *n.* a narrow track used by riders on horseback [O.E. *bridel*].

brief (brēf) *a.* short in duration; using few words; *n.* an abridged statement of a case; an outline of an argument; a writ, summoning one to answer in an action; *v.t.* to instruct or retain counsel by giving him a brief; to inform personnel of the details of an impending action. **— case** *n.* a small flat case for carrying papers, cash, etc. **-ly** *adv.* **-ness** *n.* **-s** *n.pl.* undershorts [Fr. *bref*, fr. L. *brevis*, short].

bri·er, bri·ar (brī'·e̤r) *n.* the heath of S. France; a pipe made from the root of this brier [Fr. *bruyère*, heather].

bri·er (brī'·e̤r) *n.* any prickly bush; a tangled mass of them; a smoking pipe [O.E.].

brig (brig) *n.* a sailing-ship with two masts, both square-rigged; (*Slang*) guardhouse [shortened *brigatine*, q.v. but not to be confused with it].

bri·gade (bri·gād)') *n.* a sub-division of an army under the command of a general officer; a group of people organized for a specific purpose, such as a *fire brigade*. **brigadier-general** *n.* [It. *brigata*, a troop].

brig·and (brig'·a̤nd) *n.* a lawless fellow who lives by plunder; bandit; highwayman. **-age** *n.* [O.Fr. *brigand*, a foot-soldier].

bright (brīt) *a.* shining; full of light or splendor; cheerful; vivacious; sparkling; luminous; radiant; clear; clever; intelligent. **-en** *v.t.* to make bright; *v.i.* to grow bright. **-ly** *adv.* **-ness** *n.* [O.E. *beorht*].

bril·liant (bril'·ya̤nt) *a.* glittering; sparkling; radiant; shining; illustrious; distinguished; splendid; very clever; *n.* a polished diamond cut to a definite pattern. **-ly** *adv.* **-ness** *n.* **brilliance** *n.* **brilliancy** *a.* [Fr. *brillant*].

brim (brim) *n.* rim or border; the rim of a hat; *v.i.* to be full to the brim. **-ful** *a.* **-med** *a.* **-ming** *a.* [M.E. *brimme*].

brim·stone (brim'·stōn) *n.* sulphur; hellfire; *a.*

lemon-colored [M.E. *brenston* = burning-stone].
brin·dle, brindled (brin′·dl, ·dld) *a.* streaked with dark stripes, or spots, on a gray or tan ground [Scand.].
brine (brīn) *n.* water containing an admixture of salt; sea-water; the sea. **brinish** *a.* salty, like brine. **briny** *a.* [O.E. *bryne*].
bring (bring) *v.t.* to carry; to fetch, to convey from one person or place to another; to transfer; to transport; to draw; to lead; to prevail on; *pa.t.* and *pa.p.* **brought** (brawt) [O.E. *bringan*].
brink (bringk) *n.* edge, margin of a steep slope; verge [M.E. *brenk*].
bri·o (brē′·ō) *n.* (*Mus.*) liveliness; vivacity [It.].
bri·quette (bri·ket′) *n.* a brick of compressed coal dust. Also **briquet** [Fr.].
brisk (brisk) *a.* full of activity; *v.t.* and *i.* to enliven; to cheer up. **-ly** *adv.* **-ness** *n.* [Celt.].
bris·ket (bris′·kit) *a.* part of animal's breast which lies next to ribs [O.Fr.].
bris·tle (bris′·l) *n.* a very stiff, erect, coarse hair, as of swine; a quill; *v.t.* to erect the bristles of; *v.i.* to stand up erect, like bristles; to show anger; to be surrounded with. **-d** (bris′·ld) *a.* provided with bristles [O.E. *bryst*].
Bri·tan·ni·a (bri·tan′·yạ) *n.* Great Britain personified; a female figure forming an emblem of Great Britain. **Britannic** *a.* pert. to Great Britain [L.].
Brit·ish (brit′·ish) *a.* of or pertaining to Britain; *n.* the inhabitants of Britain. **-er** *n.* a British subject [fr. *Briton*].
Brit·on (brit′·ạn) *n.* a native of Britain [L. *Brito*].
brit·tle (brit′·l) *a.* easily broken; apt to break; frail; fragile [fr. O.E. *breotan*, to break].
broach (brōch) *n.* a roasting-spit; a tapered, hardened-steel bit for enlarging holes in metal; *v.t.* to pierce; to tap, as a cask; to open; to approach a subject [Fr. *broche*, a roasting-spit].
broad (brawd) *a.* wide, ample, open; outspoken, unrestrained; coarse, indelicate, gross; tolerant, literal-minded; with a marked local dialect; plain, unmistakable (hint); full (daylight); *n.* (*Slang*) coarse for a woman. **broad, -ly** *adv.* **-brim** *n.* a wide-brimmed hat, much affected by Quakers, and so a Quaker. **-cast** *v.t.* to scatter seed; *n.* a casting of seed from the hand in sowing [See **broadcast**]. **-cloth** *n.* a finely woven woollen, cotton, or rayon cloth for clothing. **-en** *vt.* and *v.i.* to make or grow broad. **— jump** *n.* (*Sports*) a horizontal jump from rest or from a run. **-loom** *n.* woven on a wide loom, of carpets and rugs. **—minded** *a.* tolerant. **-ness** *n.* **-side** *n.* a sheet of paper printed on one side of the paper only; the whole side of a ship above water-line; a volley from the gun on one side of a naval craft; violent abuse [O.E. *brad*].
broad·cast (brawd′·kast) *n.* a transmission by radio of lectures, music, etc.; a program; *a.*; *v.t.* to disseminate by radio-telephone transmitter, news, plays, music, etc., for reception by receiving apparatus. **-er** *n.* a person or organization broadcasting [O.E. *brad*, and Dan. *kaste*].
bro·cade (brō·kād′) *n.* a fabric woven with elaborate design; *v.t.* to make brocade; to ornament a fabric with raised designs. **-d** *a.* [Sp. *brocado*].
broc·co·li (bråk′·ạ·li·) *n.* a variety of the cauliflower [It. pl. dim. fr. *brocco*, a shoot].
bro·chette (brō·shet′) *n.* skewer.
bro·chure (brō·shoor′) *n.* a printed work of a few sheets of paper; a booklet; a pamphlet [Fr. *brocher*, to stitch].
brogue (brōg) *n.* a stout, comfortable, ordinary shoe. Also **brogan** [Ir. *brog*].
brogue (brōg) *n.* a mode of pronunciation peculiar to Irish speakers [Ir. *brog*, shoe].
broi·der (broi′·dẹr) *v.t.* to adorn with figured needlework; to embroider [Fr. *broder*].
broil (broil) *n.* a noisy quarrel; contention; altercation [Fr. *brouiller*, to trouble].
broil (broil) *v.t.* to cook on a gridiron over coals, or directly under gas or electric heat in a stove; to grill, *v.i.* to suffer discomfort through heat; to be overheated [Fr. *brûler*, to burn].
broke (brōk) *pa.t.* and old *pa.p.* of **break;** *a.* (*Colloq.*) penniless; ruined; degraded. **-n** *pa.p.* of **break;** *a.* shattered; fractured; severed; separated; parted; abrupt; rough; impaired; exhausted; spent. **-n English,** imperfect English, as spoken by a non-native. **-n hearted** *a.* crushed with grief; inconsolable. **-nly** *adv.* intermittently. **-nness** *n.* [*break*].
brok·er (brōk′·ẹr) *n.* a person employed in the negotiation of commercial transactions between other parties in the interests of one of the principals; a pawn-broker; a dealer in second-hand goods; an agent. **-age, brokage,** *n.* the business of a broker; the commission charged by a broker [M.E. *brocour*].
bro·mide (brō′·mīd) *n.* a compound of bromine with some other element; a sedative drug, employed to induce sleep [See **bromine**].
bro·mine (brō′·mēn, -min) *n.* one of the elements, related to chlorine, iodine, and fluorine. **bromic** *a.* [Gk. fr. *bromos*, stench].
bron·chi, bron·chi·a (brång′·kī, ·ki·ạ) *n.pl.* the two tubes forming the lower end of the trachea. **-al** *a.* pert. to the bronchi. **bronchitis,** *n.* inflammation of the bronchial tubes. [Gr. *bronchia*].
bron·chus (brång′·kus) *n.* one of the bifurcations of the windpipe; *pl.* see **bronchi** [Gk. *bronchos*, windpipe].
bron·co (brång′·kō) *n.* an unbroken, or partly broken horse. **— buster** *n.* [Sp. rough].
bronze (brånz) *n.* an alloy of copper, tin, and zinc; a work of art cast in bronze; the color of bronze; *a.* made of or colored like bronze; *v.t.* to give the appearance of bronze to; to sunburn; to harden. **Bronze Age,** pre-historic period between the Stone and Iron Ages. **bronzy** *a.* [It. *bronzo*].
brooch (brōch, brŏŏch) *n.* an ornamental clasp with a pin for attaching it to a garment [Fr. *broche*, a spike, a brooch].
brood (brŏŏd) *v.t.* to sit upon, as a hen on eggs; to ponder; *v.i.* to sit upon to hatch; to meditate moodily; *n.* off-spring; a family of young, esp. of birds; a tribe; a race. **-er** *n.* an appliance for rearing incubator-hatched chickens by artificial heat. **— mare** *n.* a mare kept for breeding. **-y** *a.* wishing to sit, as a hen; moody; sullen [O.E. *brod*].
brook (brook) *n.* a small stream. **-let** *n.* a [streamlet [O.E. *broc*].
brook (brook) *v.t.* to bear; to endure; to support [O.E. *brucan*, use, enjoy].
broom (brŏŏm, broom) *n.* a wild evergreen shrub producing yellow flowers and pods; an implement for sweeping [O.E. *brom*].
broth (brawth) *n.* water in which meat has been boiled with vegetables [O.E. *brodh*].
broth·el (bråth′·ạl) *n.* house of prostitution [O.E. *brothen*, degenerate].
broth·er (bruTH′·ẹr) *n.* a male born of the same parents; one closely resembling another in manner or character; an associate or fellow-member of a corporate body; *pl.* **-s, brethren. -hood** *n.* the state of being a brother; an association of men of the same religious order, profession, or society; the mutual regard resulting from this association. **—in-law** *n.* the brother of one's husband or wife; a sister's husband. **—like, -ly** *a.* like a brother, affectionate. **-liness** *n.* [O.E. *brothor*].
brough·am (brŏŏm, brō′·ạm) *n.* a closed horse-carriage with two or four wheels, with an elevated seat for the driver [fr. Lord *Brougham*].
brought (brawt) *pa.t.* and *pa.p.* of **bring.**
brow (brou) *n.* the ridge over the eyes; the eyebrow; the forehead; the rounded top of a hill. **-beat** *v.t.* to bully or over-rule a person by over-bearing speech. **-beater** *n.* [O.E. *bru*].

brown (broun) *n.* a dark color inclining to red or yellow; a mixture of black, red, and yellow; *a.* of a brown color; swarthy; sunburnt; *v.t.* to give a brown color to; to sunbathe; to grill or roast brown. **— betty** *n.* a spiced, bread and apple pudding. **-out** *n.* a reduction of electric power as a conservation measure or because of plant failure. **— shirt** *n.* a member of the German Nazi party. **-stone** *n.* a reddish-brown sandstone used in building. **— sugar** *n.* unrefined or partly refined sugar [O.E. *brun*].

brown·ie (broun′·i·) *n.* a member of the junior section of the Girl scouts; a chocolate cookie.

browse (brouz) *v.t., v.i.* to nibble; to glance through a book shop, etc. [O.Fr. *broust*, a shoot].

bruise (bro͝oz) *v.t.* to injure by striking or crushing; to contuse; to pound or pulverize; *n.* a contusion. **-r** *n.* a prize-fighter; (*Colloq.*) a tough bully [O.E. *brysan*, to break].

bruit (bro͝ot) *v.t.* to report; to rumor [Fr.].

bru·mal (bro͝o′·mạl) *a* relating to winter [L. *bruma*, winter].

brume (bro͝om) *n.* mist, fog, vapor. **brumous** [*a.* foggy [Fr. *brume*, fog].

brunch (brunch) *n.* (*Colloq.*) *br*eakfast and *lunch* combined [Portmanteau word].

bru·nette (bro͝o·net′) *n.* a woman with dark brown hair or brown complexion; *a.* [Fr.].

brunt (brunt) *n.* the main shock of onset; the force of a blow [E., conn. with *burn*].

brush (brush) *n.* an implement made of bristles, twigs, feathers, etc.; the smaller trees of a forest, brushwood; a sharp skirmish; the bushy tail of a fox or squirrel; (*Elect.*) the stationary contact pieces which collect current from the commutator of a dynamo; *v.t.* to remove dust, etc., with a brush; to touch lightly in passing; *v.i.* to touch with light contact. **-off** *n.* (*Slang*) an abrupt refusal. **-wood** *n.* small branches broken or cut from trees; thicket of small trees and shrubs. **-y** *a.* rough, shaggy [O.Fr. *brosse*, brushwood].

brusque (brusk), *a.* blunt; abrupt in speech. **-ness** *n.* [Fr.].

brute (bro͝ot) *a.* irrational; ferocious; brutal; *n.* a beast; one of lower animals; a low-bred, unfeeling person. **brutal** *a.* savage; inhuman. **brutalism, brutality** *n.* inhumanity; savagery; **brutalize** *v.t.* to make brutal, cruel, or coarse; to treat with brutality; *v.i.* to become brutal. **brutally** *adv.* **brutish** *a.* [L. *brutus*, dull; stupid].

bry·ol·o·gy (brī·ȧl′·ạ·ji·) *n.* the science of mosses [Gk. *bruon*, moss; *logos*, discourse].

Bry·thon·ic (brith·ȧn′·ik) *a.* term embracing the Welsh, Cornish, and Breton group of Celtic languages [W. *Brython*, a Briton].

B.S. (bē·es′) *n.* Bachelor of Science [L. *Baccalaureus Scientiae*].

B.T.U. (bē·tē·ū′) *n.* British thermal unit, the amount of heat needed to raise one pound of water one degree Fahrenheit.

bub·ble (bub′·l) *n.* a hollow globe of water or other liquid blown out with air or gas; a globule of air or gas in liquid or solid substances; a small bladder-like excrescence on surface of paint, metals, etc.; *v.i.* to rise in bubbles; to effervesce; to make a noise like bubbles; to gurgle; *v.t.* to cause to bubble. **bubbly** *a.* [earlier *burble*, of imit. origin].

bu·bo (bū′·bō) *n.* lymphatic swelling of the glands in the groin or armpit. **-nic** *a. pl.* **-es. -nic plague** *n.* the Black Death of the 14th cent. [Gk. *boubon*, the groin].

buc·ca·neer (buk·ạ·nir′) *n.* a pirate; *v.i.* to play the buccaneer [Fr. *boucanier*, a grill].

buck (buk) *n.* the male of the rabbit, hare, sheep, goat, and deer; a spirited young dandy; *v.i.* to try to unseat a rider by jumping vertically with arched back and head down; to foil all attempts at improvement. **-shot** *n.* large leaden shot for big game. **-skin** *n.* a soft leather made of deerskin or sheepskin. **-tooth** *n.* a tooth which protrudes. **— up!** (*Colloq.*) hurry up! cheer up! [M.E. *bukke*, a he-goat].

buck·board (buk·bōrd) *n.* a four-wheeled vehicle in which a long elastic board takes the place of steel springs.

buck·et (buk′·it) *n.* a vessel for carrying water; *v.t.* to handle anything in a bucket. **-ful** *n.* the quantity held by a bucket. **— seat** *n.* a small round-backed seat for one [O.E. *buc*, pitcher].

buck·le (buk′·l) *n.* a metal clasp with a rim and tongue, for fastening straps, bands, etc.; a bend, bulge, or kink; *v.t.* and *v.i.* to fasten or clasp with a buckle; to twist out of shape; to bend; to gird with a shield and sword [M.E. *bokel*].

buck·ram (buk′·rạm) *n.* a coarse linen or cotton cloth stiffened with glue and sizing; *a.* made of buckram [O.Fr. *boucaran*, goat's skin].

buck·wheat (buk′·hwēt) *n.* an herb, the seeds of which are ground into flour or fed to animals [O.E. *boc*, beech tree].

bu·co·lic (bū·kȧl′·ik) *a.* rustic; countrified; *n.* a pastoral poem [Gk. *boukolos*, cowherd].

bud (bud) *n.* the shoot or sprout on a plant containing an unexpanded leaf, branch, or flower; *v.i.* to put forth buds; to begin to grow; *v.t.* to graft by budding. **-ding** *n.* the act of inserting the bud of one tree under the bark of another, for propagation. **-let** *n.* a little bud. **to nip in the bud,** to destroy at the beginning. *pr.p.* **-ding.** *pa.t.* **-ded** [M.E. *budde*].

Bud·dhism (boo′·dizm) *n.* the chief religion of E. Asia. **Buddhist** *n.* a worshipper of Buddha [Sans. *buddha*, wise].

bud·dy (bud′·i·) *n.* a person; a bosom friend; a comrade [fr. *body*].

budge (buj) *v.t.* and *i.* to move; to stir [Fr. *bouger*, to move].

budg·et (buj′·it) *n.* a plan for systematic spending; *v.t.* to plan one's expenditures of money, time, etc. **-ary** *a.* [Fr. *bougette*].

buff (buf) *n.* a soft, yellow leather prepared from the skin of the buffalo, elk, and other animals; a revolving wooden disc covered with layers of leather or cloth used with an abrasive for polishing; a buff-wheel; a polishing pad or stick; a light yellow-tan color; (*Colloq.*) a fan or devotee; *a.* made of, or colored like, buff leather; *v.t.* to polish with a buff. **-y** *a.* of a buff color [Fr. *buffle*, buffalo].

buf·fa·lo (buf′·ạ·lō) *n.* a ruminating horned animal, resembling an ox, but larger and more powerful [Port. *bufalo*].

buf·fer (buf′·ẹr) *n.* a resilient cushion or apparatus to deaden the concussion between a moving body and one on which it strikes; a polisher. **— state,** a country lying between two powerful and rival nations [O.Fr. *bouffe*, a slap].

buf·fet (buf′·ā) *n.* a cupboard for displaying fine china, plate, etc.; a freshment bar; *a.* (a meal) spread on tables or a counter from which guests serve themselves [Fr.].

buf·fet (buf′·it) *n.* a blow with the fist; a slap; a cuff on the ears; *v.t.* to strike with the fist; to contend against. **-s** *n.pl.* hardships [O.Fr. *buffet*, a slap].

buf·foon (bu·fo͝on′) *n.* a person who acts the clown by his clumsy attempts at humor; a fool. **-ery** *n.* the silly, vulgar antics or practical jokes of a buffoon. **-ish** *a.* [Fr. *bouffon*].

bug (bug) *n.* name applied to various insects; a difficulty or a defect in a mechanism; a concealed microphone; (*Slang*) an enthusiast. **-aboo** *n.* a terrifying object; an imaginary fear. **-bear** *n.* anything that frightens or annoys. **-gy** *a.* crazy; swarming with bugs [corrupt. of O.E. *budda*, bettle].

bug·gy (bug′·i·) *n.* a word applied to various [types of carriages.

bu·gle (bū′·gl) *n.* a wind instrument used because of its penetrating note for conveying orders by certain calls; long glass bead; *v.i.* to sound a call. **-r** *n.* [for *bugle-horn* fr. L. *buculus*, dim. of *box*, ox].

build (bild) *v.t.* to erect a structure; to construct a public work, as a railway, etc.; to fabricate; to establish (a reputation, etc.); to raise (hopes); *v.i.* to exercise the art or work of building; to depend with *on, upon; pa.t.* and *pa.p.* **built;** *n.* form; construction; physique; style of construction. **-er** *n.* **-ing** *n.* [O.E. *byldan*].

bulb (bulb) *n.* a modified leaf-bud emitting roots from its base and formed of fleshy leaf scales containing a reserve supply of food; any globular form, shaped like a bulb; a dilated glass tube containing filament for electric lighting; *v.i.* to form bulbs; to bulge. **-aceous, -ar, -ed, -ose, -y** *a.* pert. to bulbs. **-iform** *a.* shaped like a bulb. **-osity** *n.* the state of being bulbous. **-ous** *a.* having the appearance of a bulb; growing from bulbs [L. *bulbus*].

bulge (bulj) *n.* anything rounded which juts out; the part of a cask which swells out; an outer protective hull, below the water-line; *v.i.* to swell out. **bulgy** *a.* [O.Fr. *boulge*].

bu·lim·ia (bū·lim′·ē·à) *n.* an abnormal craving for food; **bulimic** *a.* [N.L. fr. Gk. *boulimia* great hunger].

bulk (bulk) *n.* size; the main body; the majority; the largest portion; unpackaged goods; *v.i.* to pile up; *v.i.* to be of some importance; to swell. **-age** *n.* roughage. **-iness** *n.* **-y** *a.* voluminous and clumsy in shape, so difficult to handle. **in bulk,** unpackaged, in large quantity [O.N. *bulki,* heap, cargo].

bulk·head (bulk′·hed) *n.* a partition in a ship made with boards, etc., to form separate compartments; a horizontal or sloping cover to outside step leading to the cellar of a building.

bull (bool) *n.* the male of any bovine; the male of numerous animals as elephant, whale, seal, moose, elk, deer; a sign of the zodiac, the constellation Taurus; a speculator who buys stocks or shares to make a profit by selling at a higher rate before time of settlement arrives; *v.t.* to attempt to bring about a rise in the price of stocks and shares; *a.* to denote a male animal. **-baiting** *n.* an ancient sport of setting ferocious dogs on a bull tied to a stake. **-dog** *n.* a breed of dog formerly used for bull-baiting; a person who displays obstinate courage; **-dozer** *n.* a tractor with an attached horizontal blade in front. **-fight** *n.* the national sport of certain Latin races, esp. in Spain and consisting of a combat between men and specially bred bulls. **-finch** *n.* a bird of the thrush family with a thicker head and neck. **-frog** *n.* a large, dusky-brown frog. **-headed** *n.* obstinate, headstrong. **— pen,** fenced enclosure; (*Sports*) where baseball pitchers practice. **— ring** *n.* the arena in which a bull-fight is held. **bull's-eye** *n.* the central spot of a target; a shot that hits the center of the target; a small circular window. **— session** (*Colloq.*) informal discussion. **— terrier** *n.* a cross between bulldog and terrier. **to take the bull by the horns,** to face a difficulty resolutely [M.E. *bole*].

bull (bool) *n.* the seal appended to the edicts of the pope; papal edict. **-ary** *n.* a collection of papal bulls [L. *bulla,* a bubble, a seal].

bul·let (bool′·it) *n.* a small projectile to be discharged from a gun. **—headed** *a.* round-headed; stubborn [L. *bulla,* a bubble, a knob].

bul·le·tin (bool′·ạ·tin) *n.* a periodical report or publication; a brief statement of facts issued by authority. **-board** *n.* [Fr.].

bul·lion (bool′·yạn) *n.* uncoined, refined gold or silver, generally in ingots; the precious metals, including coined metal, when exported or imported [etym. uncertain].

bul·ly (bool′·i·) *n.* noisy, over-bearing person who tyrannizes the weak; *v.t.* to domineer; intimidate; ill-treat; *v.i.* to bluster.

bul·rush (bool′·rush) *n.* name applied to several species of marsh plants [O.E. *bulrysche*].

bul·wark (bool′·wẹrk) *n.* an outwork for defense; sea defense wall; *pl.* a railing round the deck of a ship; any defense of a ship; *v.t.* to fortify with a rampart [Ger. *Bollwerk*].

bum (bum) *n.* an idle, dissolute person; *a.* worthless, bad; *v.i.* to loaf; to sponge on others; cadge [Ger. *bummeln,* to loaf].

bum·ble-bee (bum′·bạl·bē) *n.* a large, hairy, social bee [E. *bumble* = keep bumming].

bum·bling (bum′·bling) *a.* noisy and blundering [See **bumble-bee**].

bump (bump) *n.* a dull, heavy blow; a thump; a swelling resulting from a bump or blow; one of the protuberances on the skull, said by phrenologists to give an indication of mental qualities, character, etc.; *v.t.* to strike against; *v.i.* to collide. **-y** *a.* covered with bumps [imit.].

bump·er (bum′·pẹr) *n.* a cup or glass filled to the brim, esp. when toasting a guest; (*Auto.*) a horizontal bar in front and rear of car; a buffer; *a.* very large; excellent [fr. *bump*].

bump·kin (bump′·kin) *n.* an awkward, stupid person; a country lout; yokel [E. = *bumkin,* a thick log, fr. Dut.].

bump·tious (bump′·shạs) *a.* rudely self-assertive; self-important. **-ness** *n.* [fr. *bump*].

bun (bun) *n.* a kind of bread roll, light in texture and slightly sweetened; hair twisted into a knot at the back of a woman's head [O.Fr. *bugne*].

bunch (bunch) *n.* a cluster of similar things, tied or growing together; a tuft or knot; a bouquet of flowers; a lump or protruberance; (*Slang*) a group, gang, or party; *v.t.* to tie up or gather together; to crowd; *v.i.* to swell out like a bunch. **bunched** *a.* crowded together. **-y** *a.* growing in bunches [Dan. *bunke,* a heap].

bun·dle (bun′·dl) *n.* a number of things bound together; a package; a definite number of things; *v.t.* to make up into a bundle or roll; *v.i.* to dress warmly [O.E. *byndel*].

bung (bung) *n.* the stopper for an opening in a cask; a large cork; *v.t.* to close or stop up; (*Slang*) to bruise.

bun·ga·low (bung′·gạ·lō) *n.* a house in India of a single floor; small detached one-storied house [Hind. *bangla,* fr. *Banga,* Bengalese].

bun·gle (bung′·gl) *v.t.* to make or mend clumsily; to manage clumsily; to botch; *v.i.* to act awkwardly; *n.* a blundering performance. **-r** *n.* **bungling** *a.* [etym. uncertain].

bun·ion (bun′·yạn) *n.* an inflamed swelling occurring on the foot.

bunk (bungk) *n.* a box-like structure used as a seat by day and a bed at night; a sleeping-berth on board ship; in a camp, etc.; *v.i.* to sleep in a bunk [Scand.].

bunk (bungk) *n.* (*Colloq.*) humbug; nonsense; [fr. *bunkum*].

bunk·er (bung′·kẹr) *n.* a large hopper or bin for holding coal, etc.; storage room on board ship for coal or oil fuel; an underground fortification; a sand-pit placed as an obstacle on a golf course [Scand.].

bun·ny (bun′·i·) *n.* a pet name for a rabbit. **-hug** *n.* a kind of jazz dance [etym. unknown].

Bun·sen burn·er (bun′·sạn bur′·nẹr) *n.* a gas burner in which a strong current of air produces a weakly luminous, but very hot, flame [fr. the inventor, Prof. *Bunsen*].

bunt (bunt) *n.* the middle or furled part of a sail. **-line** *n.* a rope fastened to the bottom of a sail used to haul it up [Scand.].

bunt (bunt) *v.t.* to butt with horns or head; (baseball) to bounce ball a short distance off the bat.

bun·ting (bun′·ting) *n.* a group of birds of the finch family, including the indigo-, reed-, and snow-buntings; coarse woolen fabric of which flags are made; flags in general.

buoy (boi) *n.* any floating body of wood or iron employed to point out the particular situation of a ship's anchor, a shoal, a navigable channel, etc.; a life-buoy; *v.t.* to fix buoys. **to buoy up,** to keep afloat; to sustain (hopes, etc.). **-age** *n.* a series of buoys in position; the providing of buoys. **-ancy** *n.* capacity for floating in water or air; cheerfulness. **-ant** *a.* floating lightly; lighthearted; hopeful; of stocks and shares, tending to increase in price [Dut. *boci*].

bur (bur) *n.* the rough, sticky seed-case of certain plants with hooked spines to help in its distribution; a burr. See **burr.**

bur·ble (bur′·bl) *v.i.* to bubble up; to gurgle, as of running water; (*Colloq.*) to talk idly.

bur·den (bur′·dn) *n.* that which is borne or carried; anything difficult to bear, as care, sorrow, etc.; *v.t.* to load; to oppress; to encumber. Also (*Arch.*) **burthen. -ous, -some** *a.* heavy, onerous; felt as a burden [O.E. *burthen*].

bur·den (bur′·dn) *n.* the refrain of a song; a chorus [Fr. *bourdon*, deep murmur].

bur·dock (bur′·dȧk) *n.* a coarse reed with wide leaves and prickly burs [Dan. *borre*, a bur].

bu·reau (bū′·rō) *n.* a small chest of drawers; an office, esp. for public business; a government department [Fr.].

bu·reau·c·ra·cy (bū·rȧ′·krạ·si·) *n.* administration by bureaus, often excessively numerous and powerful; the officials engaged in such an administration; identified with officialdom and 'red tape.' **bureaucrat** *n.* one who advocates or takes part in such a system of government. **bureaucratic** *a.* [Fr. *bureau;* Gk. *kratein*, to govern].

bu·rette (bū·ret′) *n.* a graduated glass tube provided with a stop-cock at the lower end, used for delivering accurately measured quantities of liquid [Fr.].

burg (burg) *n.* (*Colloq.*) a town or village; a common ending of the names of cities in Holland or Germany [O.E. *burh*].

bur·geon (bur′·jạn) *v.i.* to sprout; to bud; to put forth branches [Fr.].

bur·glar (burg′·lẹr) *n.* one who is guilty of house-breaking. **-y** *n.* breaking and entering into a dwelling-house originally between 9 p.m. and 6 a.m. with intent to commit a felony but extended by statute to include daytime.

Bur·gun·dy (bur′·gạn·di·) *n.* name given to various wines, red or white [*Burgundy*, Fr.].

bur·i·al (ber′·i·ạl) *n.* the act of burying; interment; entombment. **— ground,** a cemetery [O.E. *byrgels*, tomb]. [See **bury**].

burke (burk) *v.t.* to murder, esp. by smothering; to put an end to quietly [fr. *Burke*].

burl (burl) *n.* a knot in wood, thread or yarn. **-ed** *a.* [L. *burra*, coarse].

bur·lap (bur′·lap) *n.* gunny sacking; a coarsely woven canvas of flax, hemp, or jute, used for packing and as a wall covering, etc.

bur·lesque (bur·lesk′) *n.* distorting, exaggerating, and ridiculing a work of art; travesty; parody; theatrical performance featuring vulgar comedy and dancing; *a.* comical; ludicrous; risqué; *v.t.* to turn into burlesque [It. *burlesco*].

bur·ly (bur′·li·) *a.* of stout build; big and sturdy. **burliness** *n.* [M.E. *borlich*, massive].

burn (burn) *v.t.* to consume with fire; to subject to the action of fire; to char; to scorch; *v.i.* to be on fire; to flame; flare; blaze; glow; be excited or inflamed with passion; *pa.t.* and *pa.p.* **-ed** or **-t;** *n.* injury or damage caused by burning. **-er** *n.* part of a lamp or gas jet from which the flame issues. **-ing** *n.* act of consuming by fire; inflammation; *a.* flaming; scorching; parching, ardent; excessive. **-ing-glass** *n.* a convex lens which causes intense heat by bending the rays of the sun and concentrating them upon a single point. **burning question,** a topic of universal discussion. **burnt-offering** *n.* a sacrifice of a living person or animal by burning. **burnt sienna,** a fine, reddish-brown pigment from calcined Sienna earth. **burnt umber,** a brown pigment obtained from calcined umber [O.E. *baernan*].

bur·nish (bur′·nish) *v.t.* to polish by continual rubbing; *n.* polish; gloss; luster [O.Fr. *burnisant*, polishing].

burnoose (bur·nôôs′) *n.* a hooded cloak worn by Arabs. Also **burnous** [Ar.].

burnt *pa.t.* and *pa.p.* of **burn.**

burr (bur) *n.* a tool for cutting or drilling; a rough edge left on metal by a cutting tool. Also **bur** [Dan. *borre*].

burr (bur) *n.* the trilled guttural sound of *r*, as heard in Northumberland and Scotland; *v.t.*, *v.i.* to roll the 'r' sound [imit.].

bur·ro (bur′·ō) *n.* a donkey [Sp.].

bur·row (bur′·ō) *n.* a hole dug in the ground by certain small animals to serve as an abode or for concealment; *v.i.* to tunnel through earth; to search assiduously; to live in a burrow [var. of *borough*].

bur·sar (bur′·sẹr) *n.* a treasurer of a college. **-y** *n.* (in Scotland) a scholarship [L.L. *bursa*, Fr. *bourse*, a purse].

bur·sa (bur′·sạ) *n.* a sac or cavity, especially between joints; **-l** *a.;* **bursitis** *n.* [LL. = *a purse, bag*].

burst (burst) *v.t.* to fly asunder; to break into pieces; to break open violently; to break suddenly into some expression of feeling; to split; *v.i.* to shatter; to break violently; *pa.t., pa.p.* **burst;** *n.* a bursting; an explosion; an outbreak; spurt [O.E. *berstan*].

bur·y (ber′·i·) *v.t.* to inter in a grave; to put underground; to hide or conceal by covering; *pa.p.* **buried. -ing** *n.* burial; interment. **to — the hatchet,** to cease from strife; to restore friendly relations [O.E. *byrigan*].

bus (bus) *n.* a vehicle for public conveyance; *v.t. pl.* **-es** [L. *omnibus*, for all and sundry].

bush (boosh) *n.* a shrub; a low woody plant with numerous branches near ground-level; a thicket of small trees and shrubs; the interior of a country; the backwoods; *v.i.* to grow thick or bushy; *v.t.* to plant bushes about. **—fighting** *n.* guerilla warfare where advantage is taken of trees and bushes. **-iness** *n.* the quality of being bushy. **-man** *n.* bush dweller. **Bushman** *n.* member of a nomadic people of southern Africa. **-master** *n.* a large venomous snake. **-whacker** *n.* one skilled in travelling through brush or woods; a guerilla. **-y** *a.* full of bushes; thick and spreading [M.E. *busch*].

bush (boosh) *n.* the internal lining of a bearing, to form a plain bearing surface for a pin or shaft. **-ing** *n.* a removable lining to reduce friction [Dut. *bus*, a box].

bush·el (boosh′·ạl) *n.* a dry measure of 4 pecks, for corn, fruit, etc. [O.Fr. *boissel*, a little box].

busi·ness (biz′·nis) *n.* employment; profession; vocation; any occupation for a livelihood; trade; firm; concern; action on the stage, apart from dialogue. **-like** *a.* practical; systematic; methodical. **-man** *n.* [fr. *busy*].

bus·kin (busk′·in) *n.* a kind of half-boot worn by ancient Greeks and Roman tragic actors.

buss (bus) *n.* a hearty kiss; *v.t.* to kiss, esp. boisterously [Fr. *baiser*, to kiss].

bust (bust) *n.* sculptured representation of a person from the waist upwards; the upper part of the human body; a woman's bosom. **-ed** *a.* breasted [Fr. *buste*].

bust (bust) *v.i., v.t.* (*Slang*) to burst; to break; to arrest; *n.* (*Slang*) a failure; a spree or binge; an arrest [fr. *burst*].

bus·tle (bus′·l) *v.i.* to busy oneself with much stir and movement; *n.* great stir. **-r** *n.* [O.E. *bysig*, busy].

bus·tle (bus′·l) *n.* a stuffed pad worn by ladies to support and elevate the back of the skirt just below the waist [Fr. *buste*].

bus·y (biz′·i·) *a.* having plenty to do; active and earnest in work; diligent; industrious; officious; meddling; *v.t.* to make or keep busy; to occupy (oneself). **busily** *adv.* **-body** *n.* a person who meddles in other people's business. **-ness** *n.* state of being busy [O.E. *bysig*].

but (but) *conj.* yet; unless; that not; nevertheless; notwithstanding; *prep.* except; without; *adv.* only. **all —,** nearly [O.E. *butan*, outside].

bu·tane (bū′·tān) *n.* a natural gas used in refrigeration and as a fuel [L. *butyrum*, butter].

butch·er (booch′·ẹr) *n.* one who slaughters animals for food or retails the meat; one who recklessly destroys human life; *v.t.* to slaughter animals for food; to murder in cold blood; to spoil work. **-ing,** *n.* killing for food or lust of blood. **-y** *n.* wanton slaughter [O.Fr. *bochier,* one who kills goats].

but·ler (but′·lẹr) *n.* a male servant who has charge of the liquors, plate, etc. **-y** *n.* a butler's pantry [O.Fr. *bouteillier,* a bottler].

butt (but) *n.* the lower end of a tree-trunk providing the strongest timber; the end of anything; one continually subject to ridicule; (*Slang*) a cigarette; *v.t.* to strike by thrusting the head downwards; to abut on; to protrude. **-s** *n.pl.* a mound with targets where shooting is practiced. **-er** *n.* an animal, e.g. the goat, which butts. **to butt in** (*Colloq.*) to intervene without permission [Fr. *but,* end].

butt (but) *n.* a large cake. **-ery** *n.* [Fr. *bote*].

butte (būt) *n.* a steep hill standing alone [Fr.].

but·ter (but′·ẹr) *n.* the fatty ingredients of milk, emulsified by churning; gross flattery; *v.t.* to spread with butter; to flatter. **-cup** *n.* plant with cup-shaped, glossy, yellow flowers. **-fingers** *n.* (*Colloq.*) one who has failed to hold a catch or who drops things easily. **-milk** *n.* the fluid residue after butter has been churned from cream. **-scotch** *n.* a kind of taffy with butter as an ingredient. **-y** *a.* [O.E. *butere*].

but·ter·fly (but′·ẹr·flī) *n.* the common name of all diurnal, lepidopterous insects; a gay, flighty woman [O.E. *buter-flege*].

but·tock (but′·ạk) *n.* the rump; rounded lower posterior part of the body; hip; haunch (usually in *pl.*) [prob. dim. of *butt,* thick end].

but·ton (but′·n) *n.* a knob or stud for fastening clothing; a bud; the safety knob at the end of a fencing foil; a small round protuberance, e.g. that of an electric bell; an emblem of membership; *v.t.* to fasten with buttons; *v.i.* to be fastened by a button. **-hole** *n.* the hole or loop in which a button is fastened; *v.t.* to detain a person in talk again his will. **-hook** *n.* a hook for pulling a button through a buttonhole [Fr. *bouton,* bud].

but·tress (but′·ris) *n.* a projecting support to a wall; any prop or support; *v.t.* to support [O.Fr. *bouter,* to thrust].

bu·tyl (bū′·til) *n.* an alcohol radical; a highly elastic synthetic rubber, made from butane, a natural gas [L. *butyrum,* butter].

buy (bī) *v.t.* to obtain by payment; to purchase; to pay a price for; to bribe; *pa.t.* and *pa.p.* **bought.** **-er** *n.* a purchaser [O.E. *bycgan*].

buzz (buz) *v.i.* to make a humming or hissing sound; *v.t.* to spread news abroad secretly; to tap out signals by means of a buzzer. **-er** *n.* one who buzzes; an apparatus used for telephonic signaling. **-ingly** *adv.* [imit. word].

buz·zard (bus′·ẹrd) *n.* a genus of birds of the hawk family (O.Fr. *busard*].

by (bī) *prep.* near; beside; in the neighborhood of; past; through the agency of; according to; *adv.* near; in the neighborhood; close; out of the way; beyond. **by and by,** soon; in the near future. **-name** *n.* a nick-name. **—pass** *n.* a road for the diversion of traffic from crowded centers; *v.t.* to avoid a place by going round it. **—path** *n.* a side path. **-play** *n.* action carried on apart from the main part of a play; diversion. **—product** *n.* secondary product obtained during manufacture of principal commodity. **-road** *n.* a less frequented side road. **-stander** *n.* an onlooker. **-way** *n.* a secluded path or road. **-word** *n.* a common saying; a proverb [O.E. *bi*].

bye (bī) *n.* anything subordinate; having no opponent in a round of competition. **-bye** (*Colloq.*) good-bye [var. of *by*].

by·law, bye-law (bī′·law) *n.* a local law made by an association [M.E. *bilaw,* fr. *bi,* a borough]

byte (bīt) *n.* a short group of adjacent binary digits processed by a computer as a unit.

Byz·an·tine (biz·an′·tin, biz′·ạn·tīn, -tin) relating to *Byzantium,* the original name for Constantinople; pert. to Asiatic architecture with Grecian characteristics.

C

cab (kab) *n.* a taxicab; the covered part of a locomotive; driver's accomodation on a truck. **-by** *n.* a taxi driver [short for Fr. *cabriolet,* a light carriage].

ca·bal (ka·bal′) *n.* a secret scheming faction in a state. **-istic** *a.* [Heb. *gabbalah*].

cab·a·la, cabbala (kab′·ạ·la) *n.* occultism. **cabalism** *n.* **cabalist, cabalistic(al)** *a.* mysterious; occult [Heb. *gabbalah,* mystical interpretation].

cab·a·ret (ka′·ba·rā, -ret) *n.* restaurant providing entertainment and space for dancing [Fr. *cabaret,* a tavern].

cab·bage (kab′·ij) *n.* a garden vegetable of Brassica family [L. *caput,* the head].

cab·in (kab′·in) *n.* a small house; a hut; an apartment in a ship; the space in an airplane for the pilot and passengers; *v.t.* to confine in a cabin; *v.i.* to live in a cabin; to lodge. **boy,** a boy who waits on the officers of a ship [Fr. *cabine,* a cabin; *cabane,* a hut].

cab·i·net (kab′·ạ·net) *n.* a private room; a council of ministers who advise the chief executive; a chest or case for holding or displaying objects; **—maker** *n.* a maker of cabinets and other furniture [Fr. *cabinet,* fr. *cabine*].

ca·ble (kā′·bl) *n.* a large, strong rope or chain; a stranded insulated conductor of electricity; a submarine telegraph line; a message sent by such line; *v.t.* to fasten with a cable; to send a message by cable. **car** *n.* a car pulled by a moving cable. **—gram** *n.* a telegram sent by cable; a cable [fr. L.L. *capulum,* a halter].

ca·boo·dle (ka·bòò′·dl) *n.* (*Slang*) collection.

ca-boose (kạ·bòòs′) *n.* a car attached to a freight train for the crew [Dut. *kombuis*].

cab·ri·o·let (kab·ri·ạ·lā′) *n.* a light one-horse carriage with a hood [Fr. fr. L. *caper,* a goat].

ca·ca·o (kạ·kā′·ō, kạ·ká′·ō) *n.* a tropical tree from the seeds of which cocoa and chocolate are prepared [Mex.].

cache (kash) *n.* orig. a hole in the ground for storing or hiding provisions, etc.; any hiding-place; articles so hidden; *v.t.* to put in a cache; to conceal [Fr. *cacher,* to hide].

ca·chet (ka′·shā) *n.* a seal, as on a lette; distinctive mark [Fr. *cacher,* to hide].

cach·in·na·tion (kak·i·nā′·shạn) *n.* loud, immoderate, or hysterical laughter. **cachinnate** *v.i.* [L. *cachinnare,* to laugh loudly].

ca·chou (kạ·shòò′) *n.* a tablet or pellet, used to perfume the breath [Fr.].

cack·le (kak′·l) *v.i.* to make a noise like a hen or goose; to gossip noisily; *n.* [imit.].

cac·o- (kak′·ạ) a combining form fr. Gk. *kakos,* bad, used in derivatives.

ca·cog·raphy (kạ·kág′·rạ·fi·) *n.* bad writing or spelling [Gk. *kakos,* bad; *graphia,* writing].

ca·coph·o·ny (kạ·káf′·ạ·ni·) *n.* a harsh or disagreeable sound; a discord; a use of ill-sounding words. **cacophonous** *a.* [Gk. *kakos,* bad; *phōnē,* sound].

cac·tus (kak′·tạs) *n.* an American desert plant with thick, fleshy, prickly stems, generally no leaves but frequently producing showy flowers. *pl.* **-es,** or **cacti.** [Gk. *kaktos,* a cardoon].

cad (kad) *n.* a low, mean, vulgar fellow. **-dish** *a.* ill-bred, mean [short for Fr. *cadet,* junior].

ca·dav·er (kạ·da′·vẹr) *n.* (*Med.*) a corpse. **-ous** *a.* corpse-like; gaunt; sickly-looking [L.].

cad·die, cad·dy (kad′·i·) *n.* an attendant who carries a golfer's clubs; *v.i.* [fr. Fr. *cadet*].

cad·dis, cad·dice (kad′·is) *n.* worm-like aquatic larva of caddis-fly [etym. unknown].

cad·dy (kad′·ɪ·) *n.* a small box for holding tea [Malay *kati,* a weight, 1⅓ lbs. (for tea)].
ca·dence (kā′·dens) *n.* a fall of the voice in reading or speaking; a modulation; the beat of any rhythmical action; (*Mus.*) the subsiding of a melody towards a close. **-d** *a.* rhythmical. **cadency** *n.* [L. *cadere,* to fall].
ca·den·za (ką·den′·zą) *n.* (*Mus.*) an ornamental passage for a voice or solo instrument in an aria or concerto [It.].
ca·det (ką·det′) *n.* a youth in training for commissioned ranks in the armed forces. **-ship** *n.* [Fr. *cadet,* younger].
cadge (kaj) *v.t., v.i.* to peddle goods; to beg. **-r** *n.* a peddlar; a beggar; a sponger.
cad·mi·um (kad′·mi·ąm) *n.* (*Chem.*) a soft, bluish-white metal of zinc group. **cadmia** *n.* an oxide of zinc [Gk. *kadmeia*].
ca·dre (kȧ′·dri·) *n.* the framework of a military unit [Fr. = a frame].
ca·du·ce·us (ką·dū′·si·ąs) *n.* the staff carried by Mercury, messenger of the gods; the emblem of the medical profession.
cae·cum (sē′·kąm) *n.* (*Med.*) the first part of the large intestine, opening into the colon. *pl.* **caeca. caecal** *a.* [L. *caecus,* blind].
Cae·sar (sē′·zęr) *n.* one who acts like Julius Caesar (100-44 B.C.), Roman emperor and dictator; hence, autocrat; dictator. **-ean, -ian** *a.* pert. to Julius Caesar. **-ian section** (*Med.*) delivery of child through an opening cut in abdominal wall [Julius Caesar is said to have been born thus].
cae·si·um. See cesium.
cae·su·ra, cesura (sē·zū′·rą) *n.* a break or division in a line of poetry; in English prosody, the natural pause of the voice. **-l** *a.* [L. *caedere, caesum,* to cut].
ca·fé (ką·fā′) *n.* a coffee-house; a restaurant, usually licensed for the sale of light refreshments only. **— so·ci·e·ty** *n.* fashionable people frequenting fashionable night clubs [Fr. *café,* coffee].
caf·e·te·ri·a (kaf·i·tir′·i·ą) *n.* a restaurant where the customers help themselves [Amer.-Sp. = a coffee-shop].
caf·feine (kaf·ēn′) *n.* the stimulating alkaloid in coffee and tea [Fr. *café,* coffee].
cage (kāj) *n.* a place of confinement; a box-like enclosure, with bars of iron or wire; *v.t.* to confine in a cage; to imprison. **-ling** *n.* a bird kept in a cage. **-work** *n.* open frame-work. **-y** *a.* cautious, wary [L. *cavea,* hollow].
ca·hoot (ka·ho͝ot′) *n.* (*Slang*) league or partnership (*usu. pl., in cahoots*).
cai·man. See **cayman.**
cairn (kern) *n.* a rounded or conical pile of stones [Gael. *carn,* a heap].
cais·son (kā′·sȧn) *n.* an ammunition chest or wagon; (*Engin.*) a water-tight chamber of sheet-iron or wood, used for workmen in laying the foundations of piers or bridges, quay-walls, etc.; an apparatus for raising sunken vessels [Fr. *caisse,* a case].
ca·jole (ką·jōl′) *v.t.* to persuade by flattery; to wheedle. **-r** *n.* **-ry** *n.* cajoling [Fr. *cajoler*].
cake (kāk) *n.* a piece of dough baked; fancy bread; a flattish mass of matter, esp. soap, tobacco, etc.; *v.t.* to make into a cake; *v.i.* to become a flat, doughy mass. **caky** *a.* **-walk** *n.* a black American dance [O.N. *kaka*].
cal·a·bash (kal′·ą·bash) *n.* the bottle-gourd tree; the fruit of this tree; a vessel made from the gourd, or the gourd itself; a species of pear [Ar.].
cal·a·boose (kal′·ą·bo͞os) *n.* (*Slang*) a prison; a jail [Sp.].
cal·a·mine (kal′·ą·mīn) *n.* a silicate of zinc, used as a pigment in painting pottery and in skin ointments [Gk. *kadmeia*].
ca·lam·i·ty (ką·lam′·ą·ti·) *n.* any great misfortune; disaster; affliction; mischance. **calamitous** *a.* producing distress and misery. **calamitously** *adv.* [Fr. *calamité*].
cal·a·mus (kal′·ą·mąs) *n.* a reed used in ancient times as a pen, or made into a musical instrument [L. fr. Gk.].
ca·lash (ka·lash′) *n.* a light carriage with low wheels, and a top or hood that can be raised or lowered; a silk hood [Fr. *calèche*].
cal·car·e·ous (kal·ke′·ri·ąs) *a.* chalky [L. *calx, calcis,* lime].
cal·cif·er·ol (kal·sif′·ą·ràl) *n.* crystalline vitamine D. used in fortifying margarine. **calciferous** *a.* containing carbonate of lime [L. *calx, calcis,* lime; *ferre,* to bear].
cal·ci·fy (kal′·si·fī) *v.t.* and *i.* to turn into lime; to harden or petrify, by a deposit of lime. **calcification** *n.* [L. *calx,* lime; *facere,* to make].
cal·ci·mine (kal′·si·mīn) *n.* a white or tinted wash for ceiling and walls.
cal·cine (kal′·sīn, -sin) *v.t.* to reduce to powder by heat; to expel water and other volatile substances by heat; *v.i.* to be turned into powder. **calcinable** *a.* **calcination** *n.* **calcinatory** *n.* a vessel used in calcination [Fr. *calciner*].
cal·ci·um (kal·si·ąm) *n.* the metallic base of lime. **calcic** *a.* containing calcium. **calcite** *n.* native carbonate of lime [L. *calx, calcis,* lime].
cal·cu·late (kal′·kyą·lāt) *v.t.* to count; to estimate; to compute; to plan; to expect; *v.i.* to make a calculation. **calculable** *a.* **-d** *a.* adapted to a purpose; intended to produce a certain effect. **calculating** *a.* capable of performing calculations; shrewd in matters of self-interest; scheming. **calculation** *n.* **calculative** *a.* tending to calculate. **calculator** *n.* one who computes; a machine which does automatic computations [L. *calculare,* to count].
cal·cu·lus (kal′·kyą·ląs) *n.* a branch of higher mathematics concerned with the properties of continuously varying quantities; *n.* a hard concretion which forms, esp. in kidney, bladder, etc. usually called stone or gravel; *pl.* **calculi. calculose, calculous** *a.* hard, like stone; gritty [L. *calculus,* a pebble].
cal·dron, cauldron (kawl′·drąn) *n.* a large metal kettle or boiler [L. *caldera,* warm pot].
cal·a·fac·tion (kal·ą·fak′·shąn) *n.* the act of heating, the state of being heated. **calefacient** (kal·ą·fā′·shi·ąnt) *a.* making warm; *n.* a heat-giving remedy. **calefactor** *n.* that which gives heat. **calefactory** *a.* [L. *calere,* to be warm; *facere,* to make].
cal·en·dar (kal′·ąn·dęr) *n.* a table of days, months or seasons; an almanac; a list of criminal cases; a list of saints; *v.t.* to enter in a list [L. *Calendae,* the calends].
cal·en·der (kal′·ąn·dęr) *n.* a hot press with rollers, used to make cloth, etc. smooth and glossy [Fr. *calandre,* a cylinder].
cal·ends (kal′·endz) *n.pl.* the first day of each month, among the Romans. **at the Greek calends,** never (because the Greeks had no calends). Also **kalends** [L. *Calendae*].
calf (kaf) *n.* the young of the cow, and of some other mammals, such as elephant, whale, etc.; a mass of ice detached from a glacier, iceberg, or floe; *pl.* **calves** (kavz). **—love, a** youthful, transitory attachment to one of the opposite sex. **—skin** *n.* a fine, light-colored leather made from the skin of a calf. **calve** (kav) *v.i.* to bring forth a calf [O.E. *cealf*].
calf (kaf) *n.* the thick, fleshy part of the leg below the knee; *pl.* **calves** [O.N. *kalfi*].
cal·i·ber (kal′·ą·bęr) *n.* the diameter of the bore of a cannon, gun, etc.; the internal diameter of a tube or cylinder; (*Fig.*) capacity; quality of mind; character. **calibrate** *v.t.* to determine the caliber of a firearm tube or other cylindrical object. **calibration** *n.* [Fr. *calibre*].
cal·i·co (kal′·ą·kō) *n.* white cotton cloth, first made in *Calicut* in India; printed cotton cloth; *a.* made of calico.
cal·i·pers, callipers (kal′·i·pęrz) *n.* a two-legged instrument for measuring diameters [Fr. *calibre*].

ca·liph, ca·lif (kal′·if, kā′·lif) *n.* a title given to the successors of Mohammed [Ar. *khalifah,* a successor].
ca·lix See **calyx.**
calk, caulk (kawk) *v. t.* to press tarred oakum into the seams between the planks of a boat to prevent leaks; to fill or close joints or crevices to make air- or water-tight. **-er** *n.* **-ing** *n.* [L.L. *calicare,* to stop up with lime, *calx*].
calk (kawk) *n.* a pointed stud on a horse-shoe to prevent slipping; *v.t.* [L. *calcar,* a spur].
call (kawl) *v.t.* to announce; to name; to summon; to name, as for office; to utter in a loud voice; *v.i.* to speak in a loud voice; to cry out; to make a brief visit; *n.* a shout; a summons or invitation; a short visit; a public claim; a requisition; authorized command; an invitation, as to be minister of a church; a note blown on a horn, bugle, etc.; the characteristic cry of a bird or animal. **-er** *n.* one who calls. **-ing** *n.* a person's usual occupation. **at call,** on demand. **on call,** of a person, ready if summoned. **-boy** *n.* a boy who calls actors to go on the stage; a bellboy. **to call down,** to rebuke. **to call up** (*Mil.*) to summon to military service; to telephone [O.E. *ceallian*].
cal·ligra·phy (ką·lig′·rą·fi·) *n.* the art of beautiful writing; penmanship. **calligrapher, calligraphist** *n.* **calligraphic** *a.* [Gk. *kallos,* beauty; *graphein,* to write].
cal·li·o·pe (ką·lī′·ą·pē) *n.* musical instrument with steam whistles, played like an organ.
cal'lis·then·ics (kal·is·then′·iks) *n.pl.* light gymnastic exercises to promote beauty and grace of movement. **callisthenic** *a.* [Gk. *kallos,* beauty; *sthenos,* strength].
cal·lous (kal′·us) *a.* hardened; hardened in mind; unfeeling; having a callus; **-ly** *adv.* **-ness** *n.* **callosity** *n.* a horny hardness of the skin [L. *callus,* hard skin].
cal·low (kal′·ō) *a.* pert. to the condition of a young bird; unfledged; (*Fig.*) inexperienced; raw. **-ness** *n.* [L. *calvus,* bald].
cal·lus (kal′·ąs) *n.* a hardened or thickened part of the skin [L. = hard skin].
calm (kȧm) *a.* still; quiet; at rest; *n.* the state of being calm; *v.t. to make calm.* **-ly** *adv.* **-ness** *n.* [Fr. *calme*].
cal·o·mel (kal′·ą·mel) *n.* (*Med.*) sub-chloride of mercury, used as a purgative [Gk. *kalos,* fair; *melas,* black].
ca·lor·ic (ką·lawr′·ik) *n.* heat; *a.* pert. to heat; heat-producing. **caloricity** *n.* the power of animals to develop heat. **calorifacient** *a.* heat-producing. **calorific** *a.* pert. to heat; heat-producing. **calorification** *n.* the production of heat [L. *calor,* heat].
cal·o·rie, calory (kal′·ęr·i·) *n.* (*Phys.*) the unit of heat; the unit of heat or energy produced by any food substance. **calorimeter** *n.* a scientific instrument for determining the amount of heat produced by any substance [L. *calor,* heat].
cal·u·met (kal′·yoo·met) *n.* the 'pipe of peace' of the N. Amer. Indians [L. *calamus,* a reed].
ca·lum·ni·ate (ką·lum′·ni·āt) *v.t.* to accuse falsely; to slander; *v.i.* to utter slanders. **calumniation** *n.* false and slanderous representations. **calumniator** *n.* **calumniatory, calumnious** *a.* slanderous. **calumniously** *adv.* **calumny** *n.* a false accusation; malicious slander; libel [L. *calumnia*].
Cal·va·ry (kal′·vą·ri·) *n.* the place of Christ's crucifixion [L. *calvaria,* a skull].
calve (kav) See **calf.**
Cal·vin·ism (kal′·vin·izm) *n.* the doctrines of John *Calvin,* which lay special stress on the sovereignty of God in the conferring of grace. **Calvinist** *n.* **Calvinistic** *a.*
calx (kalks) *n.* the crumbly substance that remains after the calcination of a metal or mineral; *pl.* **calxes, calces** (kalk′·siz, kal′·sēz) [L. = lime].
ca·lyp·so (ką·lip′·sō) *n.* an improvised song in native rhythm from the West Indies.
ca·lyx, ca·lix (kā′·liks) *n.* a cup-shaped cavity; the outer covering or leaf-like envelope of a flower [Gk. *kalux,* a husk, a cup].
cam (kam) *n.* a projecting part of a wheel used to give an alternating or variable motion to another wheel or piece. **-shaft** *n.* the shaft on which cams are formed for opening the valves [Dut. *kam,* a comb].
ca·ma·ra·de·rie (kȧm·ą·rȧd′·ą·rē) *n.* good-fellowship [Fr. *comarade,* a companion].
cam·ber (kam′·bęr) *n.* a slight convexity of an upper surface, as of a ship's deck, a bridge, a road surface [Fr. *cambrer,* to arch].
Cam·bri·an (kam′·bri·ąn) *a.* Welsh; pert. to Cambria or Wales; *n.* a Welshman. [L. fr. *Cymru,* Wales].
cam·bric (kām′·brik) *n.* a fine white linen fabric first made at *Cambrai,* in N. France.
came (kām) *pa.t. of the verb* **come.**
cam·el (kam′·ąl) *n.* a large ruminant animal of Asia and Africa, with one or two humps, used as a beast of burden. **-eer** *n.* a camel driver [Gk. *kamēlos*].
ca·mel·lia (ką·mēl′·yą) *a.* a species of Asiatic shrub with showy flowers and elegant dark-green, laurel-like leaves [fr. *Kamel,* botanist].
Cam·em·bert (ka′·mąm·ber) *n.* a small, soft, rich cheese [fr. a village in Normandy].
cam·e·o (kam′·i·ō) *n.* a gem stone of two layers cut in ornamental relief [etym. unknown].
cam·e·ra (kam′·ą·rą) *n.* device for taking photographs. **-man** *n.* a professional motion picture or press photographer [L. *camera,* a vault]
cam·e·ra (kam′·ą·rą) *n.* a judge's private room; hence (*Law*) 'to hear a case' **in camera** [L. *camera,* a room].
cam·i·sole (kam′·ą·sōl) *n.* a lady's under-bodice; light dressing-jacket [Fr.].
cam·o·mile, chamomile (kam′·ą·mīl) *n.* an aromatic creeping plant whose flowers are used medicinally [Gk. *chamaimēlon,* the earth-apple].
cam·ou·flage (kam′·ą·flazh) *n.* (*Mil.*) a method of visual deception of the enemy by disguising; any form of disguise; *v.t.* to cover with camouflage material; to disguise [Fr.].
camp (kamp) *n.* the area of ground where soldiers or other groups of people are lodged in huts or tents; permanent barracks near a suitable exercise ground; group in agreement; *v.t.* and *i.* to pitch tents. **-er** *n.* one who lives in a camp in open country, esp. living in a tent. **-ing** *n.* the act of living in camp. **— chair** *n.* a light, portable chair with folding legs. **— follower** *n.* a non-combatant who follows the troops, *i.e.,* a prostitute, washer woman, etc. **— meeting** *n.* a religious meeting in the open air. **— out** *v.* to live without conveniences [L. *campus,* a field].
cam·paign (kam·pān′) *n.* a series of operations in a particular theater of war; hence, in politics, business, etc. an organized series of operations (meetings, canvassing, etc.); *v.i.* to serve in a war; to conduct, or assist in political, etc. operations. **-er** *n.* [L. *campus,* a plain].
cam·pa·ni·le (kam·pą·nē·li·, kam′·pą·nīl) *n.* a bell-tower constructed beside a church, but not necessarily attached to it. **campanology** *n.* the art of bell-ringing, or of bell-founding; bell-lore. [It. *campana,* a bell].
cam·phor (kam′·fęr) *n.* a whitish substance with an aromatic taste and smell, obtained from the camphor laurel-tree. **-aceous** (kam.-fęr·ā′·shąs) *a.* resembling camphor. **-ate** *v.t.* to impregnate with camphor. **-ate, -ic** *a.* pert. to camphor [Malay, *kapur,* chalk].
cam·pus (kam′·pąs) *n.* the grounds of a college or school [L. *campus,* a plain].
can (kan) *pres. indic.* of a defective, intransitive verb meaning, to be able, to have the power, to be allowed. *pa.p., pa.t.* **could** (kood) [O.E. *cunnan,* to know].
can (kan) *n.* a metal vessel or container for holding liquids, etc.; *v.t.* to put into a can for

the purpose of preserving; *pr.p.* **-ning.** *pa.p.* and *pa.t.* **-ned. -nery** *n.* a factory where foods are preserved by canning [O.E. *canne*].

Ca·na·di·an (kạ·nā′·di·ạn) *n.* an inhabitant of Canada; *a.* pert. to Canada.

ca·naille (kạ·nāl′) *n.* the dregs of society; the mob; rabble [Fr. fr. I. *canis*, a dog].

ca·nal (kạ·nal′) *n.* an artificial watercourse for transport, drainage or irrigation purposes; a duct in the body; a groove. **canalize** *v.t.* to make a canal through; to convert into a canal [L. *canalis*].

can·a·pé (ka′·nạ·pi·) *n.* a small piece of toast or bread, with anchovies, etc. on it served as an appetizer [Fr. *canapé*, a sofa].

ca·nard (ka·nȧrd′) *n.* a false rumor; an absurd or extravagant piece of news [Fr.].

ca·nar·y (kạ·nā′·ri·) *n.* a yellow singing bird, a species of finch; a pale-yellow color; a light wine made in the Canary Islands [Fr. *canari*].

ca·nas·ta (kạ·nas′·tạ) *n.* a card game played with two packs.

can-can (kan′·kan) *n.* a kind of dance, once popular in music-halls in France [Fr.].

can·cel (kan′·sạl) *v.t.* to cross out; to blot out; to annul; to suppress; (*Math.*) to strike out common factors; to balance; to offset. **-lation** *n.* the act of canceling [L. *cancellatus*, latticed].

can·cer (kan′·sẹr) *n.* (*Med.*) a malignant growth or tumor. **-ate** *v.i.* to grow into a cancer.**-ation** *n.* **-ous** *a.* pert. to or resembling cancer [L. *cancer*, a crab].

can·de·la·brum (kan·dạ·lȧ′·brạm) *n.* a branched and highly ornamented candle-stick; a chandelier. **candelabra** *n.sing.* and *pl.* [L. fr. *candela*, a candle].

can·did (kan′·did) *a.* fair; open; frank. **-ly** *adv.* **-ness** *n.* frankness; ingenuousness [L. *candidus*, white].

can·di·date (kan′·dạ·dāt) *n.* one who seeks an appointment, office, honor, etc. **candidature, candidacy** *n.* the position of being a candidate [L. *candidus*, white (one wearing a white toga)].

can·dle (kan′·dl) *n.* a stick of tallow, wax, etc. with a wick inside, used for light. **power,** the unit of luminosity. **-stick** *n.* an instrument for holding a candle [L. *candela*].

Can·dle·mas (kan′·dl·mạs) *n.* a religious festival to commemorate the Purification of the Virgin and the presentation of Jesus in the temple [*candle* and *mass*].

can·dor (kan′·dẹr) *n.* candidness; sincerity; frankness [L. *candor*, whiteness].

can·dy (kan′·di·) *n.* a kind of sweetmeat made of sugar; *v.t.* to preserve in sugar; to form into crystals, as sugar; *v.i.* to become candied. **candied** (kan′·did) *a.* [Ar. *qand*, sugar].

can·dy·tuft (kan′·di·tuft) *n.* a large genus of herbs or shrubs [fr. *Candia*].

cane (kān) *n.* the stem of a small palm or long, strong reed; the bamboo, etc.; the sugar-cane; a walking-stick; *v.t.* to beat with a cane; to fix a cane bottom to, e.g. a chair. **-brake** *n.* a dense growth of canes. **— sugar** *n.* sugar from the sugar-cane [Gk. *kanna*, a reed].

ca·nine (kā′·nīn) *a.* of, or pert. to a dog. **teeth,** the two pointed teeth in each jaw, one on each side, between the incisors and the molars [L. *canis*, a dog].

can·is·ter (kan′·is·tẹr) *n.* a small case or box for holding tea, coffee, etc. **— shot** *n.* a number of small iron balls enclosed in a case of a size to fit the gun-barrel (an early form of shrapnel) [L. *canistrum*, a wicker basket].

can·ker (kang′·kẹr) *n.* ulceration of the mouth; a disease of trees; a disease affecting horses' feet; (*Fig.*) anything that eats away, corrupts, etc.; *v.t.* to consume; to gnaw at; to corrupt; *v.i.* to decay, to become cankered. **-ed** *a.* corrupted; malignant. **-ous** *a.* corrupting like a canker. **-y** *a.* cankered. **-worm** *n.* a destructive caterpillar [L. *cancer*, a crab].

can·nel-coal (kan′·el-kōl) *n.* a kind of coal, burning with a clear, smokeless flame, used in the manufacture of gas. Also **candle-coal.**

can·ni·bal (kan′·ạ·bạl) *n.* one who eats human flesh; *a.* relating to this practice. **-ism** *n.* the practice of eating human flesh. **-istic** *a.* **cannibalize** *v.t.* to dismantle in the hope of getting spare parts to be used for re-conditioning. [Sp. *canibal* = *Caribal*, a Carib].

can·non (kan′·ạn) *n.* a large gun; *v.i.* to cannonade. **-ade** *n.* an attack with cannon; the firing of cannon; *v.t.* to bombard. **-eer, -ier** (kan·ạn·ir′) *n.* one who loads or fires cannon; an artilleryman. **— ball** *n.* an iron ball to be discharged by cannon. **— shot** *n.* a cannonball; the range of a cannon [L. *canna*, a tube].

can·not (kan′·ȧt) combination of *can* and *not*, therefore, = not to be able.

can·ny (kan′·i·) *a.* (*Scot.*) cautious; thrifty.

ca·noe (ka·nòò′) *n.* a light, narrow boat propelled by a hand paddle.**-ist** *n.* [Haiti, *canoa*].

can·on (kan′·ạn) *n.* a law or rule, esp. of the church; the books of the Scriptures accepted by the Church as of divine authority; rules of faith; a standard; the list of saints; a church dignitary, esp. one connected with a cathedral; (*Mus.*) a form of composition in which the melody is repeated at set intervals by the other parts. **-ess** *n.* a member of a religious association of women. **canonic, canonical** *a.* **canonicals** *n.pl.* official dress worn by a clergyman. **canonically** *adv.* **-ization** *n.* **-ize** *v.t.* to place in the list of saints. **-ist** *n.* one skilled in canon law. **-ry** *n.* the office of canon. [Gk. *kanōn*, a rule].

can·o·py (kan′·ạ·pi·) *n.* a covering fixed above a bed, or a dais, or carried on poles above the head; any overhanging shelter [Gk. *kōnōpion*, a couch with mosquito curtains].

cant (kant) *n.* an inclination from the level; a tilted position; *v.t.* to tilt; to jerk; to toss; *v.i.* to have, or take a leaning position [O.Fr.].

cant (kant) *n.* an insincere or conventional mode of speaking; an expression peculiar to a group [L. *cantare*, to sing].

can't (kant) *v.* contr. of **cannot.**

can·ta·bi·le (kȧn·tȧ′·bi·lā) *adv.* (*Mus.*) in a flowing, graceful, style, like singing [It.].

can·ta·loupe, can·ta·loup (kan′·tạ·lōp) *n.* a variety of muskmelon, having a furrowed rind [*Cantalupo*, a town in Italy].

can·tan·ker·ous (kan·tang′·kẹr·ạs) *a.* perverse; ill-natured; quarrelsome. **-ly** *adv.*

can·ta·ta (kan·tȧ′·tạ) *n.* a short musical composition in oratorio or lyric drama form. **cantatrice, cantatrici** (kan′·tạ·trēs, kan-tā·-trē′·chā) a professional female singer [It.].

can·teen (kan·tēn′) *n.* a small container for carrying water; a store and refreshment-room in camps and barracks for soldiers, sailors, etc.; a similar place in a social or institutional club [It. *cantina*, a cellar].

can·ter (kan′·tẹr) *v.i.* to move at an easy gallop; *n.* an easy gallop or gait [fr. *Canterbury gallop*, easy pace of the pilgrims].

can·ti·cle (kan′·ti·kl) *n.* a little song; a nonmetrical hymn. **Canticles** (*Bib.*) the Song of Songs [L. *canticulum*, a little song].

can·ti·lev·er (kan′·ti·lēv·ẹr) *n.* a bracket for supporting a cornice or balcony. **cantilever bridge,** a bridge built on the same principle [fr. *cant*, an angle; Fr. *lever*, to raise].

can·to (kan′·tō) *n.* a division or part of a poem. **-r** *n.* a precentor; the leader of the singing, esp. in a synagogue [It. fr. L. *canere*, to sing].

can·ton (kan′·tȧn) *n.* a small district (in Switzerland, administered by a separate government); a section of something; *v.t.* to divide into districts, as territory. **-al** *a.* **-ment** *n.* quarters for troops [Fr.].

can·vas (kan′·vạs) *n.* a coarse cloth made of hemp, for sails, tents, etc.; the sails of a vessel; a special prepared material for painting on; painting [O.Fr. *canevas;* L. *cannabis*, hemp].

can·vass (kan′·vạs) *v.t.* to sift; to examine

thoroughly; to solicit support, or votes, or contributions; *v.i.* to solicit votes; *n.* a close examination (by discussion); a scrutiny; solicitation; a seeking to obtain votes. **-er** *n.* [fr. *canvas* = to sift, as through canvas].

can·yon (kan′·yạn) *n.* a ravine; a deep gorge. Also **cañon** [Sp.].

cap (kap) *n.* a brimless covering, for the head; the top or highest point; a small lid used as a cover; *v.t.* to cover the top or end of; to surpass; (*University, etc.*) to confer a degree on; *pr.p.* **-ping.** *pa.p.* and *pa.t.* **-ped** [O.E. *cappe*, a hood].

ca·pa·ble (kā′·pạ·bl) *a.* competent; gifted; skillful. **capably** *adv.* **-ness** *n.* **capability** *n.* power [L. *capere*, to hold].

ca·pa·cious (kạ·pā′·shạs) *a.* roomy; spacious; **-ly** *adv.* **-ness** *n.* [L. *capere*, to hold].

ca·pac·i·ty (kạ·pas′·i·ti·) *n.* power of holding or grasping; room; volume; power of mind; character; ability; cubic content. **capacitate** *v.t.* to render capable [L. *capacitas*].

cap·à·pie (kap·ạ·pē′) *adv.* from head to foot [O.Fr. fr. L. *caput*, the head; *pes*, the foot].

ca·par·i·son (kạ·par′·ạ·sạn) *n.* a covering laid over a horse; trappings; harness; *v.t.* to cover with a decorated cloth; to adorn with rich dress [O.Fr. *caparasson*, preparation].

cape (kāp) *n.* a covering for the shoulders [L.L. *cappa*].

cape (kāp) *n.* a point of land running out into the sea; a headland [L. *caput*, the head].

ca·per (kā′·pẹr) *v.i.* to leap about like a goat, in a sprightly manner; to skip; to dance; to frolic; *n.* a frolicsome skip [L. *caper*, a goat].

ca·per (kā′·pẹr) *n.* a herb or shrub whose flower-buds when pickled in vinegar are used in sauces [Gk. *kapparis*].

cap·il·lar·y (kap′·ạ·ler·i·) *a.* resembling a hair; as fine as a hair; descriptive of the very fine bore of a tube or similar passage; *n.* one of the microscopic blood-vessels connecting the arteries and veins. **capillarity** *n.* **capilliform** *a.* hair-shaped [L. *capillus*, hair].

cap·i·tal (kap′·ạ·tạl) *a.* pert. to the head; involving the forfeiture of life; first in importance; chief; principal; excellent; *n.* (*Archit.*) the head of a column, pillaster, etc.; the city or town which is the seat of government in a state or nation; the estimated total value of a business, property, stock, etc.; ready money; **— punishment** *n.* the death penalty; **-ize** *n.* to take advantage of. **-ization** *n.* to provide with capital letters; to supply with capital [L. *caput*, the head].

cap·i·tal·ism (kap′·ạ·tạl·izm) *n.* form of economic, industrial, and social organization of society involving ownership, control, and direction of production by privately owned business organizations. **capitalist** *n.*

cap·i·ta·tion (kap·ạ·ta′·shạn) *n.* a census; a tax or grant per head [L. *capitatio*, a poll-tax].

Cap·i·tol (kap′·ạ·tạl) *n.* the temple of Jupiter in Rome; the building used by the U.S. Congress in Washington for its sessions; a state legislature building [L. *Capitolium*].

ca·pit·u·late (kạ·pit′·ū·lāt) *v.i.* to surrender; to draw up terms of an agreement. **capitulation** *n.* **capitulator** *n.* [L.L. *capitulare*, to draw up a treaty].

ca·pon (kā′·pȧn) *n.* a young castrated cock fed for the table. **caponize** *v.t.* [O.E. *capun*].

ca·price (kạ·prēs′) *n.* illogical change of feeling or opinion; a whim; a fancy. **capricious** (kạ·pri′·shạs) *a.* [L. *caper*, a goat].

cap·si·cum (kap′·sạ·kạm) *n.* a genus of tropical plants, whose fruits when dried and ground give Cayenne pepper [L. *capsa*, a box].

cap·size (kap·sīz′) *v.t.* and *i.* to overturn.

cap·stan (kap′·stạn) *n.* a heavy cable-holder revolving on an upright spindle [L. *capistrum*, a halter].

cap·stone (kap′·stōn) *n.* a finishing stone.

cap·sule (kap′·sạl) *n.* the seed-vessel of a plant; a small gelatinous case containing medicine; a metal cap placed over the mouth of a corked bottle; *a.* condensed [L. *capsa*, a box].

cap·tain (kap′·tin) *n.* in the army, an officer commanding a company of infantry; in the navy, an officer in command of a man-of-war; the master of a merchant ship or other vessel; in sport, the leader of a team; *v.t.* to command; to lead. **-cy** *n.* the rank or commission of a captain [L. *caput*, the head].

cap·tion (kap′·shạn) *n.* the heading of a newspaper, chapter, page, etc.; the title of an illustration [fr. L. *capere*, to take].

cap·tious (kap′·shạs) *a.* apt to find fault; difficult to please. **-ly** *adv.* **-ness** *n.* fault-finding [L. *captiosus*, deceiving].

cap·ti·vate (kap′·tạ·vāt) *v.t.* to capture the fancy of. **captivating** *a.* winning, charming. **captivation** *n.* [L. *captivus*, captive].

cap·tive (kap′·tiv) *n.* a prisoner; one held in captivity; *a.* made prisoner. **captivity** *n.* imprisonment; bondage; servitude. **captor** *n.* one who takes a prisoner or a prize. **capture** *n.* the act of seizing by force or stratagem; arrest; the thing seized; the prize; *v.t.* to take captive; to take possession of [L. *capere*, to take].

Cap·u·chin (kap′·yoo·chin) *n.* a Franciscan monk (from the hood he wears); a hooded cloak for women; a hooded pigeon; a long-tailed S. American monkey. **capuche** (kạ-pȯȯsh′) *n.* a hood; a cowl [It. *cappucino*, a cow].

car (kȧr) *n.* any kind of vehicle on wheels; abbrev. for motor-car; automobile; the part of a balloon in which the aeronauts sit [L. *carrus*].

car·a·cole (kar′·ạ·kōl) *v.i.* to wheel [Sp.].

ca·rafe (kạ·rȧf′) *n.* a glass water-bottle or decanter [Fr.].

car·a·mel (kar′·ạ·mel) *n.* burnt sugar, used for coloring and in cooking; a kind of candy [Sp. *caramelo*].

car·at (kar′·ạt) *n.* a measure of weight for gold and precious stones, the standard carat being 3.16 grains troy [Gk. *keration*, a carob-tree seed].

car·a·van (kar′·ạ·van, kar·ạ·van′) *n.* parties of merchants , pilgrims, or others traveling together for greater security, esp. across deserts. **-eer** *n.* the leader of a caravan. **-sary, -serai** *n.* a large Eastern inn, with a court in the middle; a large inn [Pers. *karwan*].

car·a·vel (kar′·ạ·vel) *n.* a light sailing-ship. Also **carvel** [L. *carabus*, a wicker boat].

car·a·way (kar′·ạ·wā) *n.* a biennial aromatic plant; its seed, used as a flavoring for bread, cakes, etc. [Gk. *karon*].

car·bide (kȧr′·bīd) *n.* a compound of carbon with certain elements, including calcium, manganese, iron, etc. [L. *carbo*, coal].

car·bine, carabine (kȧr′·(a)·bīn) *n.* a short rifle. **carbineer, carabineer** *n.* a soldier armed with a carbine [etym. uncertain].

car·bo·hy·drate (kȧr·bō·hī′·drāt) *n.* a substance, such as sugar, starch, cellulose, etc. composed of carbon, hydrogen, and oxygen [L. *carbo*, coal; Gk. *hudō*, water].

car·bol·ic (kȧr·bȧl′·ik) *a.* derived from carbon; *n.* carbolic acid. **carbolated** *a.* treated with or containing, carbolic acid. **carbolic acid,** a poisonous acid distilled from coal tar [L. *carbo*, coal].

car·bon (kȧr′·bạn) *n.* a non-metallic element existing pure in nature as diamond, graphite, charcoal, etc. and as a compound of animal and vegetable substances; a thin rod of hard carbon used in an electric arc-lamp; a copy made by using carbon paper. **-aceous** (kȧr.bạn·ā′·-shus) *a.* pert. to, or composed of, coal. **-ize** *v.t.* to make into carbon; to coat with carbon. **-ization** *n.* **— paper,** type of paper used for duplicating written work [L. *carbo*, coal]. carbon dioxide. **-d** *a.* **carbonation** *n.*

car·bo·run·dum (cȧr·bạ·run′·dạm) *n.* silicon

carbide, a black, crystalline substance, of exceptional hardness.

car·boy (kår′·boi) *n.* a large, globular glass bottle, encased in basket-work [Pers. *garabah*].

car·bun·cle (kår′·bung·kl) *n.* a variety of garnet; an inflamed bunion or boil. **carbuncular** *a.* [L. *carbunculus*, a small coal].

car·bu·ret·or (kår′·bạ·rā·tẹr) *n.* an apparatus in an internal-combustion engine to convert liquid gasoline into vaporized form. **carburation** *n.* **carburize** *v.t.*, cause to unite with carbon [L. *carbo*, coal].

car·cass, carcase (kår′·kạs) *n.* the dead body of man or animal, esp. of the latter; the framework or shell of anything [It. *carcassa*, the framework of a ship, etc.].

car·ci·no·ma (kår·si·nō′·mạ) *n.* a cancer.

card (kård) *n.* pastebord; a small piece of pasteboard often with figures, pictures, etc. on it for playing games; a piece of pasteboard having on it a person's name and address; an ornamented piece of paper or cardboard with a greeting, such as a birthday card; (*Slang*) a humorous fellow. **-board** *n.* finely finished pasteboard. **-sharp** *n.* one who cheats at cards [L. *charta*, paper].

card (kård) *n.* a toothed instrument for combing wool, flax, etc.; *v.t.* to comb, as wool, flax, etc. **-er** *n.* one who cards [L. *carduus*, a thistle].

car·di·ac See **cardio-**

car·di·gan (kår′·di·gạn) *n.* a knitted jacket or jacketlike sweater [fr. an Earl of *Cardigan*].

car·di·nal (kår′·di·nạl) *a.* chief; main; of great importance; fundamental; (*Color*) deep scarlet. **-ly** *adv.* **— numbers,** 1, 2, 3, 4, 5, etc. [L. *cardo*, a hinge].

car·di·nal (kår′·di·nạl) *n.* the highest rank next to the Pope, in the Catholic Church. **-ate, -ship** *n.* the office of a cardinal [L. *cardo*, a hinge].

car·di·o- (kår′·di·ạ) *prefix* from Gk. *kardia*, the heart, combining to form derivatives. **cardiac** *a.* pert. to the heart; *n.* a heart stimulant. **-gram** *n.* the graphic tracing of the movements of the heart as recorded by an instrument called the **cardiograph. cardiology** *n.* (*Med.*) the branch of medicine which deals with the functions and diseases of the heart.

care (ker, kār) *n.* concern or anxiety; an object of anxiety; pains or heed; caution; charge or oversight; trouble; grief (formerly); *v.i.* to be anxious, concerned; to be affected with solicitude; to have a fondness (with *for*). **-ful** *a.* full of care or solicitude; cautious or watchful; painstaking. **-fully** *adv.* **-fulness** *n.* **-less** *a.* heedless; thoughtless; regardless. **-lessly** *adv.* **-lessness** *n.* **-worn** *a.* showing the wearing effects of care. **-taker** *n.* one who takes over the care of anything or anyone [O.E. *caru*].

ca·reen (kạ·rēn′) *v.t.* to turn a ship over on one side; *v.i.* to lean over [L. *caring*, a keel].

ca·reer (kạ·rēr′) *n.* rapid motion; a course of action; profession; conduct in life, or progress through life; *v.i.* to speed along; to rush wildly. **-ist** *n.* one who makes his personal advancement his one aim in life [Fr. *carrière*, orig. a chariot course].

ca·ress (kạ·res′) *v.t.* to treat with affection; to fondle; to kiss; *n.* a loving touch; an embrace. **-ing** *a.* [L. *carus*, dear].

car·et (kar′·ạt, kā′·rạt) *n.* a mark (‸) which shows where something should be inserted [L. *caret*, is wanting].

car·go (kår′·gō) *n.* the freight of a ship; the goods or merchandise carried [Sp. fr. *cargar*, to load].

car·i·bou (kar′·i·bòò) *n.* the N. American reindeer [Canadian Fr.].

car·i·ca·ture (kar′·i·kạ·cher) *n.* a ludicrous exaggeration (usually in picture form) of peculiar personal characteristics; *v.t.* to exaggerate or distort, in words or in pictorial form. **caricaturist** *n.* [It. *caricare*, to load].

car·ies (kār′·ēz) *n.* decay of bone, teeth, etc. **carious** *a.* [L.].

car·il·lon (kar′·i·lån, kạ·ril′·yạn) *n.* a set or peal of bells of different tones; a melody played on such bells [Fr.].

car·i·ole (kar′·i·ōl) *n.* a small, open, two-wheeled carriage or light cart. Also **carriole** [L. *carrus*].

Car·mel·ite (kår′·mel·īt) *n.* a begging friar of the order of Our Lady of Mount Carmel, established in the 12th cent. [fr. Mount *Carmel*].

car·mine (kår′·min, mīn) *n.* a brilliant crimson, prepared from cochineal. Also *a.* [Fr. or Sp. *carmin*].

car·nage (kår′·nij) *n.* slaughter; massacre; bloodshed [L. *caro, carnis*, flesh].

car·nal (kår′·nạl) *a.* pert. to the flesh; sensual; animal; worldly; material, as opposed to spiritual. **-ize** *v.t.* to make carnal. **carnality** *n.* fleshly lust. **-ly** *adv.* **— knowledge,** sexual intercouse [L. *caro, carnis*, flesh].

car·na·tion (kår·nā′·shạn) *n.* a flesh-color; a variety of the clove-pink, noted for its beauty and sweet scent [L. *carnatio*, fleshiness].

car·nel·ian (kår·nēl′·yạn) *n.* a variety of light-red chalcedony, used for jewelry. Also **cornelian** [L. *cornu*, horn].

car·ni·val (kår′·nạ·vạl) *n.* a traveling show with amusements such as merry-go-rounds, etc. [L. *carnem levare*, to take away flesh].

car·niv·o·ra (kår·niv′·ạ·rạ) *n.pl.* animals that feed on flesh. **carnivore** (kar′·ni·vōr) *n.* a flesh-eating animal. **carnivorous** *a.* **carnivorously** *adv.* **carnivorousness** *n.* [L. *caro, carnis*, flesh; *vorare*, to devour].

car·ol (kar′·al) *n.* a song of joy, esp. a Christmas hymn; *v.i.* to sing a carol [O.Fr. *carole*].

ca·rot·id (kạ·råt′·id) *n.* each of the two main arteries in the neck conveying blood to the head; *a.* pert. to these [Gk. *karōtides*].

ca·rouse (kạ·rouz′) *v.i.* to revel; to drink deeply; to hold a drinking-party. **carousal** *n.* a noisy drinking-party. **-r** *n.* [O.Fr. *carous*, fr. Ger. *gar aus* (drink) right to the bottom (of the glass)].

car·ou·sel See **carrousel.**

carp (kårp) *v.i.* to catch at small faults or errors; to find fault petulantly and without reason [O.N. *karpa*, to chatter].

carp (kårp) *n.* a fresh-water fish [Fr. *carpe*].

car·pel (kår′·pạl) *n.* (*Bot.*) the seed-bearing part of a plant; part of a compound ovary. **-lary** *a.* [Gk. *karpos*, fruit].

car·pen·ter (kår′·pạn·tẹr) *n.* a worker in lumber as used in building of houses, ships, etc. **carpentry** *n.* [L.L. *carpentarius*, a cartwright]

car·pet (kår′·pit) *n.* a woven or felted covering for floors; **-ing** *n.* a covering similar to a carpet. **-bag** *n.* a 19th cent. traveling bag made of carpet. **-bagger** *n.* a political adventurer. [L.L. *carpita*, patchwork].

car·ra·way See **caraway.**

car·riage (kar′·ij) *n.* the act of carrying passengers or goods; the cost of carrying; a vehicle for passengers; a wheeled or moving support or conveyor; one's posture or bearing; conduct. **-able** (kar′·ij·ạ·bl) *a.* carriable; passable for carriages [O.Fr. *cariage*, luggage].

car·ri·er (kar′·i·ẹr) *n.* one who carries; one who carries goods for hire, often called a 'common carrier'; a receptacle for carrying objects; a pigeon used for carrying messages; (*Med.*) one who, without showing symptoms of disease, can convey infection to others [O.Fr. *carier*, to loa].

car·ri·ole See **cariole.**

car·ri·on (kar′·i·ạn) *n.* dead, rotting flesh; anything putrid [L. *caro*, flesh].

car·rot (kar′·ạt) *n.* a plant cultivated for its edible root. **-y** *a.* reddish-yellow; red-haired [L. *carota*].

car·rou·sel, car·ou·sel (kar·ạ·sel′) *n.* a merry-go-round; military ornament [Fr.].

car·ry (kar′·i·) *v.t.* to convey; to transport; to

impel; to transfer; to obtain possession of by force; to behave; *v.i.* to reach, of a projectile; *n.* range. [O.Fr. *carier* fr. *car,* a vehicle].

cart (kårt) *n.* a two-wheeled vehicle used for the transport of heavy goods; a small four-wheeled vehicle pulled by hand; *v.t.* to convey in a cart. **-age** *n.* carting; the price paid for carting. **-er** *n.* **-wright** *n.* builder or maker of carts [O.N. *kartr,* a cart].

carte blanche (kårt.blånsh) *n.* full authority.

car·tel (kår′.tel) *n.* an international industrial combination for regulating volume and price of output; a trust; an agreement between states at war for exchange of prisoners; a challenge [Fr. fr. L. *cartello*].

car·ti·lage (kår′.ti.lij) *n.* (Anat.) gristle; a strong, transparent tissue in the body, very elastic and softer than bone. **cartilaginous** (kår.ti.la′.ji.nạs) *a.* [L. *cartilago,* gristle].

car·tog·ra·phy (kår.tåg′.rạ.fi.) *n.* the art of making charts or maps. **cartographer** *n.* [L. *charta,* chart; Gr. *graphein,* to draw].

car·ton (kår′.tạn) *n.* a pasteboard box [Fr. *carton,* pasteboard].

car·toon (kår.tòòn′) *n.* a design drawn on strong paper for transference to mosaics, tapestries, frescoes, etc.; an illustration treating current affairs in an amusing fashion; a pictorial caricature; a comic strip; movie comics. **-ist** *n.* [Fr. *carton,* pasteboard].

car·tridge (kår′.trij) *n.* a case made of metal, cardboard, etc. to contain the charge for a gun. [Fr. *cartouche,* fr. L. *charta,* paper].

carve (kårv) *v.t.* and *i.* to fashion artistically by cutting; to hew out, as a path, a career, etc.; to cut in pieces or slices, as meat, etc.; to divide. **-r** *n.* one who carves; a large knife for carving. **carving** *n.* [O.E. *ceorfan*].

car·y·at·id (kar.i.at′.id) *n.* (*Archit.*) a draped, female figure used in place of a column. **caryatides** (kar.i.at′.i.dēz) [Gk. *Karuatis,* a woman of *Caryae* in Laconia].

cas·cade (kas.kåd′) *n.* a waterfall; anything resembling this; a wavy fall of lace; *v.i.* to fall in cascades [L. *cadere,* to fall].

cas·car·a (kas-ke′.rạ) *n.* **cascara sagrada,** a fluid extracted from dried California buckthorn bark and used as a laxative [Sp. *cascara,* bark; *sagrada,* sacred].

case (kās) *n.* a receptacle; a covering; a sheath; anything which encloses or contains; a box and its contents; a set; (*Print.*) a frame for holding type; *v.t.* to put in a case. **casing** *n.* a case or covering. **-room** *n.* (*Print.*) the room in which type is set. **— shot** *n.* canister shot; small projectiles put in cases or canisters, to be shot from cannon. **-harden** *v.t.* to heat soft steel in contact with carbonaceous material, so that carbon is absorbed, and a surface of harder steel produced. **lower case** (*Print.*) denoting small letters. **upper case** (*Print.*) denoting capital letters [O.Fr. *casse*].

case (kās) *n.* an event, occurrence, or circumstance; a state or condition of things or persons; a question of facts or principles requiring investigation or solution; (*Med.*) a patient under treatment; (*Gram.*) an inflection or terminal change in nouns, pronouns, etc. **casal** *a.* (*Gram.*) pert. to case [L. *cadere,* to fall].

ca·se·in (kā′.si.in) *n.* the curd or cheesy part of milk, a protein [L. *caseus,* cheese].

case·ment (kās′.ment) *n.* a window-frame; a window, or part of a window, opening on hinges [fr. *encase*].

cash (kash) *n.* money, esp. ready money; coin; also, paper-money, bank-note, etc.; *v.t.* to turn into, or exchange for, money. **—register** *n.* an automatic money-till which registers and indicates the amount paid for goods sold [O.Fr. *casse,* a box].

cash·ew (ka′.shòò) *n.* a tropical American tree whose fruit, the cashew-nut, is eaten raw or roasted [Fr. *acajou*].

cash·ier (kash.ir′) *n.* one who has charge of the cash [O.Fr. *casse,* a box].

cash·ier (kash.ir′) *v.t.* to dismiss from office in disgrace; to discard [Fr. *casser,* to annul, to dismiss].

cash·mere (kash′.mir) *n.* a shawl made from the hair of the Kashmir (Cashmere) goat; the material; *a.* [fr. *Cashmere,* in India].

ca·si·no (kạ.sē′.nō) *n.* a public assembly-room or building for dancing, gambling, etc. [It. *casino,* a little house].

cask (kask) *n.* a large wooden vessel for holding liquor; a barrel; *v.t.* to put in a cask [Sp. *casco,* a potsherd, a cask].

cas·ket (kas′.kit) *n.* a coffin; a small cask or case; a small box.. [*casco,* a helmet].

casque (kask) *n.* a sort of military helmet [Sp.

cas·se·role (kas′.ạ.rōl) *n.* a covered baking dish in which food is both cooked and served; a food mixture cooked in such a dish [Fr.].

cas·sia (kash′.ạ) *n.* a genus of plants, including senna, whose pods are used medicinally as a laxative; a cheap kind of cinnamon [L. *casia*].

cas·si·mere (kas′.ạ.mir) *n.* a thin twilled, wollen cloth [form of *cashmere*].

cas·sock (kas′.ạk) *n.* a long, close-fitting black gown worn by clergymen [Fr. *casaque*].

cast (kast) *v.t.* to fling; to hurl; to direct or bestow, as a glance; to project, as a shadow; to shed, as a skin; to reckon or compute (with *up*); to shape in a mold (as metal); to distribute the parts of a play among the actors; to throw a line in angling; to forecast (to cast a horoscope); to let down (an anchor); to give (a vote); to give birth prematurely; *n.* the act of casting; a throw; the distance a thing is thrown; a mold or form; a change of direction; that which is shed or ejected; a reckoning; a forecast; the actors appearing in a play; expression (of the face); squint (of the eye). **—down** *a.* depressed. **-ing** *n.* an article cast in a mold; the act of foundling and molding. **-ing-vote** *n.* the vote of a chairman, which decides a question when votes are equally divided. **—iron** *a.* made of cast iron; rigid; indefatigable; unshakable; (*Slang*) irrefutable [O.N. *kasta*].

cas·ta·nets (kas′.tạ.nets) *n.pl.* two small concave shells of ivory or hard wood, fastened to the thumb and clicked in time to dances and music of a Spanish type [L. *castanea,* a chestnut-tree].

cast·a·way (kast′.ạ.wā) *n.* a shipwrecked person; an outcast [fr. to *cast away*].

caste (kast) *n.* an exclusive social order [L. *castus,* pure].

cas·tel·lat·ed (kas′.tạ.lā.tạd) *a.* adorned with turrets and battlements like a castle [L. *castellatus*].

cast·er, castor (kas′.tẹr) *n.* a small bottle with perforated top for sugar, pepper, etc.; a stand for a set of such bottles; a small swivelled wheel on the foot of a chair-leg, etc. [fr. *cast*].

cas·ti·gate (kas′.tạ.gāt) *v.t.* to correct; to rebuke severely; to chastise; to punish. **castigation** *n.* severe chastisement; discipline. **castigator** *n.* [L. *castigare,* to punish].

castle (kas′.l) *n.* a fortified residence; a stronghold, esp. of nobleman; any imposing mansion; a piece (also called rook) in chess. **-d** *a.* having a castle; built like a castle [L. *castellum*].

cas·tor (kas′.tẹr) *n.* the beaver; a hat made of beaver fur. See **caster** [Gk. *kastor*].

cas·tor·oil (kas′.tẹr.oil) *n.* an oil used as a cathartic.

cas·trate (kas′.trāt) *v.t.* to deprive of the testicles; to emasculate; to render incapable of generation; to render imperfect. **castration** *n.* [L. *castrare*].

cas·u·al (kazh′.òò.ạl) *a.* accidental; incidental; occasional; offhand or careless; *n.* a casual or occasional worker, etc. **-ly** *adv.* **-ness** *n.* **-ty** *n.* an accident, mishap. **-ties** *n.pl.* (*Mil.*) losses caused by death, wounds, capture, etc. [L. *casuc*, accident, chance].

cas·u·ist (kazh′·òò·ist) *n.* one versed in casuistry. **-ry** *n.* the science of dealing with problems of right or wrong conduct by applying principles drawn from the Scriptures, etc.; the use of specious reasoning and fallacious argument, esp. on matters of morals. **casuistic, casuistical** *a.* **casuistically** *adv.* [Fr. *casuiste*].

cat (kat) *n.* a small domestic quadruped, of the family of felines; the undomesticated cat, usually called wild-cat; related carnivores such as the lion, tiger, leopard, lynx, etc.; a spiteful woman; strong tackle used to hoist an achor; *v.t.* and *i.* to hoist an anchor. **-ty, -tish** *a.* spiteful. **-bird** *n.* a gray N. Am. songbird having a cry similar to a cat's mew. **— burglary,** a burglar who makes his entry by climbing to windows, roofs, etc. **-call** *n.* a cat-like cry, used by audiences to express disapproval. **—eyed** *a.* able to see in the dark. **— nap** *n.* a very short, light sleep. **-'s-eye** *n.* a gem with reflections like those from a cat's eye. **cat's-paw** *n.* a dupe of another; (*Naut.*) a light breeze. **cat-o-nine-tails** *n.* a whip with nine thongs or lashes. **tabby cat,** a female cat; a striped cat. **tom cat,** a male cat [O.E. *catt*].

cat·a- (kat′·ạ) a combining form fr. Gk. *kata*, meaning down, away, against, fully, used to form derivatives.

cat·a·chre·sis (kat·ạ·krē′·sis) (*Rhet.*) a figure by which one word is wrongly used for another [Gk. *katachresis*, misuse].

cat·a·clysm (kat′·ạ·klizm) *n.* a social or political upheaval; a catastrophe; a sudden and violent alteration in earth's surface. **-al** *a.* **-ic** *a.* [Gk. *kata*, down; *kluzein*, to wash over].

cat·a·combs (kat′·ạ·kōmz) *n.pl.* underground passageways with niches for tombs [Gr. *kata*, down; *kumbē*, a cavity].

cat·a·falque (kat′·ạ·falk) *n.* a structure on which a coffin is placed for a lying-in-state [It.]

cat·a·lec·tic (kat·ạ·lek′·tik) *a.* lacking a syllable at the end of a verse; applied to an incomplete foot in prosody [Gk. *kata*, down; *legein*, to stop].

cat·a·lep·sy (kat′·ạ·lep·si·) *n.* (*Med.*) suspension of senses and bodily powers, with muscular rigidity; a trance. **cataleptic** *a.* [Gk. *kata*, down; *lēpsis*, a seizure].

cat·a·logue (kat′·ạ·lawg) *n.* a list, usually alphabetical, of names, books, goods, etc.; a descriptive price-list; also **catalog.** *v.t.* to make such a list. **-r** *n.* [Gk. *kata*, throughout; *legein*, to choose].

ca·tal·y·sis (kạ·tal′·ạ·sis) *n.* (*Chem.*) the chemical change effected in one substance by the aid of another which itself undergoes no change. **catalyst** *n.* a substance producing such a change. **catalytic** *a.* [Gk. *kata*, down; *lusis*, a loosening].

cat·a·ma·ran (kat·ạ·mạ·ran′) *n.* a raft consisting of pieces of wood lashed together; a craft with twin parallel hulls; (*Colloq.*) a quarrelsome person [Tamil = a tied tree].

cat·a·pult (kat′·ạ·pult) *n.* a siege engine for hurling stones, arrows, etc.; a device for launching airplanes from the deck of a ship; *v.t.* [Gk. *kata*, against; *pallein*, to hurl].

cat·a·ract (kat′·ạ·rakt) *n.* a waterfall; the flow of a large body of water over a precipice; a torrent; (*Med.*) a disease of the eye, characterized by an opaque condition in the lens [Gk. *katarrhaktēs*].

ca·tarrh (kạ·tȧr′) *n.* (*Med.*) inflammation of the mucous membranes of the body. **-al** *a.* [Gk. *katarrhein*, to flow down].

ca·tas·ta·sis (kạ·tas′·tạ·sis) *n.* part of drama where action has reached its height [Gk.].

ca·tas·tro·phe (kạ·tas′·trạ·fe) *n.* a disaster; a calamity; a decisive event in drama; the denouement; the culmination. **catastrophic** *a.* *katastrophē*, an overturning].

catch (kach) *v.t.* to take hold of; to seize; to grasp; to arrest; to trap; to get a disease by infection or contagion; to detect; to understand; to come upon unexpectedly; *v.i.* to seize, and keep hold; to grasp at; *pa.t.* and *pa.p.* **caught** (kawt) *n.* a seizure; anything that holds, stops, etc.; that which is caught; a sudden advantage; gain; the total amount of fish taken by a fisherman; a form of musical composition (a round). **-able** *a.* able to be caught. **-er** *n.* **-ing** *a.* **-y** *a.* containing a hidden difficulty; (*Mus.*) (usually of light music) captivating; attractive. **-all** *n.* a receptacle for miscellaneous objects [L. *capere*, to take].

catch·fly (kach′·flī) *n.* the name of certain plants to whose stems insects adhere.

catch·ment (kach′·ment) *n.* drainage area [fr. *catch*].

catch·pen·ny (kach′·pen·i·) *n.* something of little value and usually showy, made to sell quickly; *a.* cheap and showy.

catch·up, catsup, ketchup (kach′ạp, kat′·sạp, kech′·ạp) *n.* a bottled sauce made from tomatoes, vinegar, sugar and spices [E. Ind.].

catch·word (kach′·wurd) *n.* a word or short phrase that takes the popular fancy; a slogan; (*Theat.*) an actor's cue; the first word in the column of a dictionary, etc., repeated above the column as a reference.

cat·e·chize (kat′·e·kīz) *v.t.* to instruct by question and answer, esp. in Christian doctrine; to question; to examine orally. **catechism** (kat′·e·kizm) *n.* a set form of question and answer to teach the tenets of religion; a book containing this system. **catechist** *n.* one who catechizes. **catechetical** *a.* consisting of question and answer. **catechetically** *adv.* **catechesis** (kat′ạ·kē′·sis) *n.* oral instruction as given to catechumens [Gk. *katēchizein*, to teach by word of mouth].

cat·e·chu·men (kat·ạ·kū′·mạn) *n.* one being instructed in the fundamentals of a subject, esp. religion [See **catechize**].

cat·e·go·ry (kat′·ạ·gōr·i·) *n.* a class, group, or division; in logic, any fundamental conception. **categorical** *a.* pert. to a category; admitting no conditions; absolute; precise. **categorically** *adv.* **categorize** *v.t.* to place in a category [Gk. *katēgoria*, an assertion].

ca·te·na (kạ·tē′·nạ) *n.* a chain; a series of connected things. **catenate** *v.t.* to connect in a series of links. **catenary** (ka′·tạ·ne·ri·) *n.* the curve of a chain, wire, etc., hanging freely between two supports. **catenation** *n.* [L. = a chain].

ca·ter (kā′·tẹr) *v.i.* to buy or procure food; to provide food, entertainment, etc. **-er** *n.* [O.Fr. *acat*, a purchase].

cat·er-cor·nered (kat′·ạ·kȧwrn′·ẹrd) *a.* diagonal [F. *quatre*, four, cornered].

cat·er·pil·lar (kat′·ẹr·pil·ẹr) *n.* the grub or larva of butterflies and moths [O.Fr. *chatepelose*, lit. a hairy cat].

cat·er·waul (kat′·ẹr·wawl) *v.i.* to cry like cats in heat [E. *cat*, and imit. sound].

ca·thar·tic (kạ·thȧr′·tik) *a.* (*Med.*) purgative; cleansing the bowels; *n.* a purging medicine. **catharize** *v.t.* to cleanse; to purify. **catharsis** *n.* purgation, also of the emotions, through art [Gk. *katharos*, pure].

Ca·thay (ka·thā′) *n.* an old name for China or Chinese Tartary.

ca·the·dral (kạ·thē′·drạl) *n.* the principal church in a diocese, which contains the bishop's throne; *a.* pert. to a cathedral [Gk. *kata*, down; *hedra*, a seat].

cath·ode (kath′·ōd) *n.* the negative pole of an electric cell; the conductor by which an electric current leaves an electrolyte, and passes over to the negative pole; opp. of *anode*. **— rays,** negative ions or electrons [Gk. *kathodos*, descent].

cath·o·lic (kath′·ạ·lik) *a.* universal; embracing

all Christians; pert. to Roman Catholics; liberal or comprehensive in understanding and sympathies; *n.* a member of the Church Universal, or of the R.C. Church. **-ism** (kạ.thȧl′.ạ.sizm) *n.* the faith and practice of Catholic Church, or of R.C. Church; breadth of view; catholicity. **-ity** (.lis′.ạ.ti.) *n.* [Gk. *katholikos*, general].
cat·nip (kat′.nip) *n.* an aromatic plant with blue flowers, attractive to cats [*cat* and *mint*].
CAT scan·ner (kat′.skan′.ẹr) *n.* a diagnostic device that combines a computer with an X-ray tube that rotates around the patient, giving a detailed cross-sectional view of any part of the body. **CAT scan** *v.t., v.i.* [fr. computed axial tomography].
cat·sup. See **catchup.**
cat·tle (kat′.l) *n.pl.* domestic livestock, esp. cows and bulls [L.L. *capitale*, stock.]
Cau·ca·sian (kaw.kā′.zhạn) *a.* belonging to *Caucasia;* Indo-European, i.e. pert. to the white race. *n.* [fr. the *Caucasus*, mountains near the Black Sea.]
cau·cus (kaw′.kạs) *n.* a meeting of leaders of a political party to decide policies, etc.
cau·dal (kaw′.dạl) *a.* pert. to a tail [L. *cauda*].
caught (kawt) *pa.p., pa.t.* of **catch.**
caul (kawl) *n.* a net, etc. worn on the head; the membrane covering the head of some babies at birth [etym. unknown].
caul·dron. See **caldron.**
cau·li·flow·er (kaw′.lạ.flou.ẹr) *n.* a variety of cabbage [L. *caulis*, a stalk; and *flower*].
caulk. See **calk.**
cau·sal (kaw′zạl) *a.* relating to a cause or causes. **-ity** *n.* the manner in which a cause works; the relation of cause and effect. **causation** *n.* agency by which an effect is produced. **causative** *a.* [L. *causa*, cause].
cause (kawz) *n.* that which produces a result or effect; the origin or motive of an action; an action or lawsuit in court; principle supported by a person or party; *v.t.* to produce; to be the occasion of; to induce. **-r** *n.* **-less** *a.* without reason or motive [L. *causa*].
cau·se·rie (kō′.zạ.rē) *n.* a chat; an informal article or essay [Fr. = a talk].
cause·way (kawz′.wā) *n.* a raised paved road [L.L. *calciata*, trodden, fr. *calx*, a heel].
caus·tic (kaws′.tik) *a.* burning; (*Fig.*) biting, bitter, satirical; *n.* a substance that corrodes and destroys animal tissue. **-ally** *adv.* **-ity** *n.* [Gr. *kaustos*, burned].
cau·ter (kaw′.tẹr) *n.* a hot, searing iron. **-ize** *v.t.* to sear animal tissue in order to destroy diseased tissue, or promote healing. **-ization** *n.* **-y** *n.* the act of cauterizing; a hot iron for searing [Gk. *kautērion*, a branding-iron].
cau·tion (kaw′.shạn) *n.* carefulness; prudence; wariness; a warning; (*Colloq.*) an odd or droll person; *v.t.* to advise to take care; to warn or admonish. **cautious** *a.* wary; prudent; discreet. **cautiously** *adv.* **-ary** *a.* containing a warning. **-er** *n.* [L. *cavere, cautum*, to beware].
cav·al·cade (kav′.ạl.kād′) *n.* procession on horseback [L.L. *caballus*, a horse].
cav·a·lier (kav.ạ.lir′) *n.* a horseman; a knight; a gallant; an attendant escort to a lady; *a.* gay and offhand; supercilious; haughty and discourteous. **-ly** *adv.* [L.L. *caballus*, a horse].
cav·al·ry (kav′.ạl.ri.) *n.* horse-soldiery [L.L. *caballus*, a horse].
cave (kāv) *n.* a small chamber hollowed out of the earth horizontally, either by nature or by man; a den. **— man** *n.* a very masculine male of primitive ways. **to — in** (of ground) to fall in, to subside; (*Fig.*) to yield; to admit defeat [L. *cavus*, hollow].
ca·ve·at (kā′.vi.at) *n.* a warning; a legal notice to stop proceedings [L. = let him beware, fr. *cavere*, to beware].
cav·en·dish (kav′.ạn.dish) *n.* tobacco pressed into plugs [fr. *Cavendish*, the first maker].
cav·ern (kav′.ẹrn) *n.* a deep, hollow place under the earth; a large dark cave. **-ed** *a.* full of caverns. **-ous** *a.* hollow; deep-set [L. *caverna*].
cav·i·ar, caviare (kav′.i.ȧr) *n.* a delicacy made from the roes of the sturgeon [Turk.].
cav·il (kav′.il) *v.i.* (with 'at') to raise frivolous objections; to find fault unreasonably. *n.* a frivolous objection. **-er** *n.* [L. *cavilla*, raillery].
cav·i·ty (kav′.i.ti.) *n.* a hole; a hollow place of any size [L. *cavus*, hollow].
ca·vort (kạ.vawrt′) *v.i.* (*Colloq.*) to prance; to frisk about [etym. uncertain].
caw (kaw) *v.i.* to cry like a crow or raven; *n.* the sound made by the crow, rook, or raven.
cay·enne (kā.yen′) *n.* a pungent red pepper [fr. *Cayenne*, in S. America].
CB (sē.bē′) *n.* abbrev. of citizens' *b*and, short-wave frequencies for private two-way radio communication.
cease (sēs) *v.t.* to put a stop to; *v.i.* to stop; to discontinue. **-less** *a.* without stopping. **-lessly** *adv.* [L. *cessare*, to cease].
ce·dar (sē′.dẹr) *n.* species of coniferous, evergreen trees yielding durable, fragrant wood. **-n, cedrine** *a.* [Gk. *kedros*].
cede (sēd) *v.t.* to yield; to surrender; to give up, esp. territory [L. *cedere*].
ce·dil·la (sạ.dil′.ạ) *n.* a small sign used, principally in French, as a pronunciation mark. It is placed under 'ç', when followed by a, o, or u, to indicate that the 's' sound is to be used [Gk. *zēta*, z].
ceil·ing (sē′.ling) *n.* the interior part of the roof of a room; (*Fig.*) the upper limit of production, wages, prices, etc. [Fr. *ciel*, the sky].
cel·e·brate (sel′.ạ.brāt) *v.t.* to make famous; to mark by ceremony, as an event or festival; to observe with solemn rites. **-d** *a.* renowned; famous. **celebration** *n.* the act of celebrating. **celebrant** *n.* one who celebrates. **celebrity** (sẹ.leb′.rạ.ti.) *n.* renown; fame; a person of distinction [L. *celebrare*].
ce·ler·i·ty (sạ.ler′.ạ.ti.) *n.* rapidity of motion; speed; swiftness [L. *celer*, swift].
cel·er·y (sel′.ẹr.i.) *n.* an edible plant cultivated for eating with salads or as a cooked vegetable [Fr. *céléri*, fr. Gk. *selinon*, parsley].
ce·les·ta (sạ.les′tạ) *n.* (*Mus.*) a small piano-like instrument [Fr.].
ce·les·tial (sạ.les′.chạl) *a.* heavenly; divine; blessed; *n.* an inhabitant of heaven. **-ly** *adv.* [L. *caelum*, heaven].
cel·i·ba·cy (sel′.ạ.ba.si.) *n.* single life; the unmarried state. **celibate** *n.* one unmarried; *a.* [L. *caelebs*, unmarried].
cell (sel) *n.* a small room, as in a prison or monastery; a small cavity; the basic unit in the structure of living matter; a small group of members of a political party; a division of a voltaic or galvanic battery. **-ed** (seld) *a.* furnished with, or containing, cells; contained in cells. **-ular** *a.* consisting of, or containing, cells, as *cellular tissue*. **-ulated** *a.* having a cellular structure [L. *cella*, a small room].
cel·lar (sel′.ẹr) *n.* an underground room, the lowest story under a building; a storeroom, esp. for wines, liquors. [L. *cellarium*, a pantry].
cel·lo, 'cel·lo (chel′.ō) *n.* (*Mus.*) a contraction for violoncello, a stringed musical instrument. **cellist, 'cellist** *n.* a player on the violoncello.
cel·lo·phane (sel′.ạ.fān) *n.* a tough, transparent, waterproof material used as wrapping tissue, etc. [fr. *cellulose* and Gk. *phainein*, to show].
Cel·lu·loid (sel′.yạ.loid) *n.* a hard compound used in the manufacture of imitation ivory, coral, amber, etc. [L. *cellula*, a little cell; Trademark].
cel·lu·lose (sel′.yạ.lōs) *n.* a chemical substance, one of the carbohydrates, forming the chief constituent of the walls of plant cells; an essential part of wood, paper, linen, cotton, etc. [L. *cellula*, a little cell].
Celt, Kelt (selt, kelt) *n.* one of a race, including the Highlanders of Scotland, the Irish, Welsh, Bretons, Manx, and Cornish. **Celtic, Keltic** *n.* the language spoken by the Celts. *a.* pert. to the Celts [L. *Celticus*].

ce·ment (sạ·ment′) *n.* a plastic mixture that can unite two bodies; mortar; a material used in making concrete for building or paving; a bond or union; *v.t.* to unite by using cement; to join closely. **-ation** *n.* the act of cementing; the conversion of iron into steel [L. *caementum,* stone for building].

cem·e·ter·y (sem′·ạ·ter·i·) *n.* a graveyard; a burying ground [Gk. *koimētērion,* a sleeping-room].

ce·no·bite, coenobite (sē′·nạ·bīt) *n.* member of a religious order, dwelling in community [Gk. *koinos,* common; *bios,* life].

cen·o·taph (sen′·ạ·taf) *n.* a monument erected to one buried elsewhere; an empty sepulcher [Gk. *kenos,* empty, *taphos,* a tomb].

Cen·o·zo·ic (sēn·ạ·zō′·ik) *a.* (*Geol.*) belonging to the third or Tertiary period; the present period of geologic time. Also **Cainozoic** [Gk. *kainos,* recent; *zōē,* life].

cen·ser (sen′·sẹr) *n.* a metal vessel in which incense is burned. **cense** *v.t.* to perfume with incense [L. *incendere,* to burn].

cen·sor (sen′·sẹr) *n.* a Roman official who looked after property, taxes, and the people's morals; one appointed to examine books, plays, newspaper articles, etc. before publication, and ban them if containing anything objectionable; also, in time of war or crisis, to examine letters, etc., and erase anything calculated to convey information to the enemy; one who blames or finds fault; *v.t.* to blame or reprove; to subject to examination by the censor. **-ial** *a.* pert. to correction of morals; pert. to a censor. **-ious** *a.* apt to find fault. **-iously** *adv.* **-iousness** *n.* **-ship** *n.* the office of a censor; the act of censoring [L. *censere,* to estimate].

cen·sure (sen′·shẹr) *n.* the act of finding fault; disapproval; *v.t.* to reprove; to express disapproval of; to criticize adversely. **censurable** *a.* [L. *censura,* opinion].

cen·sus (sen′·sạs) *n.* an official numbering of the inhabitants of a country. **censual** *a.* [L. *census,* register].

cent (sent) *n.* a hundredth, as 10 per *cent;* a U.S. coin worth the hundredth part of a dollar [L. *centum*].

cen·taur (sen′·tawr) *n.* (*fem.* **centauress**) (*Myth.*) a fabulous being, half man and half horse [Gk. *kentaurion*].

cen·te·nar·y (sen′·te·ner·i·, sen·ten·ạr·i·) *n.* a period of a hundred years; a century; the commemoration of a hundredth anniversary; a centennial. **centenarian** (sen·tạ·ne′·ri·ạn) *n.* a person a hundred years old [L. *centum,* a hundred].

cen·ten·ni·al (sen·ten′·i·ạl) *a.* pert. to a period of 100 years; happening once in a hundred years; *n.* a hundredth anniversary [L. *centum; annus,* a year].

cen·ter (sen′·tẹr) *n.* the mid-point of anything; pivot; axis; a point to which things move or are drawn; a point of concentration; *v.t.* and *i.* to place in the center; to be fixed. **-piece** *n.* an ornament or cloth covering for the center of a table. **centric(al)** *a.* placed in center or middle. **centrically** *adv.* **centricity** (sen·tris′·i·ti·) *n.* the state of being centric. **center of gravity,** the point in a body about which it will balance [L. *centrum*].

cen·ti- (sen′·ti) *prefix* fr. L. *centum,* a hundred, combining to form derivatives. **-grade** *a.* divided into 100 degrees, as the centigrade thermometer on which freezing-point is marked 0°, and boiling-point 100°. **-meter** (sen′·ti·mē·tẹr) *n.* 100th part of a meter = .394 inch.

cen·ti·pede (sen′·ti·pēd) *n.* an insect, of flat and elongated shape, with a segmented body [L. *centum,* a hundred; *pes, pedis,* a foot].

cen·tral (sen′·trạl) *a.* relating to, or placed in, the center; chief; important. **-ly** *adv.* **-ize** *v.t.* to draw to a central point; to concentrate; to put under one control. **-ization** *n.* **-ism** *n.* centralization, esp. of government. **centrality** *n.* the state of being central. **— heating,** heating of a building or group of buildings from one central furnace [L. *centralis,* fr. L. *centrum*].

cen·tri·fu·gal (sen·trif′·yoo·gạl) *a.* tending to move away from the center of a revolving body [L. *centrum,* the center; *fugere,* to flee].

cen·trip·e·tal (sen·trip′·ạ·tạl) *a.* tending to move towards the center [L. *centrum,* the center; *petere,* to seek].

cen·tu·ple (sen′·too·pl) *a.* hundredfold. [L. *centum,* a hundred; *plicare,* to fold].

cen·tu·ry (sen′·chạ·ri·) *n.* a period of a hundred years; a set of a hundred; a company of a Roman legion numbering a hundred soldiers under the command of a **centurion** [L. *centuria*].

ce·ram·ic (sạr·am′·ik) *a.* pert. to pottery. **ceramics** *n.pl.* the art of molding, modelling, and baking clay; the study of pottery as an art [Gk. *keramos,* pottery].

cere (sir) *v.t.* (*Obs.*) to cover with wax; *n.* the wax-like membrane at base of bill in some birds. **ceraceous** (si·rā′·shạs) *a.* waxy. **cerate** *n.* an ointment of wax, oil, etc. **-cloth** *n.* a cloth smeared with melted wax in which dead bodies used to be wrapped. **-ment** *n.* (usually *pl.*) graveclothes [L. *cera,* wax].

ce·re·al (si′·ri·ạl) *a.* pert. to edible grain; *n.* any edible grain (wheat, barley, oats, etc.); a breakfast food made of such grains. [L. *Ceres,* Roman goddess of corn].

ce·re·brum (ser′·ạ·brạm) *n.* the upper and larger division of the brain. **cerebellum** *n.* the part of the brain behind and below the cerebrum. **cerebral** *a.* pert. to the brain. **cerebral hemorrhage,** rupture of an artery of the brain with a consequent escape of blood. **cerebral palsy** *n.* paralysis from cerebral lesion, chiefly characterized by spasms. **cerebrate** *v.i.* to have the brain in action. **cerebration** *n.* **cerebrospinal** *a.* pert. to both brain and spinal cord [L. *cerebrum,* the brain].

ce·re·mo·ny (ser′·ạ·mō·ni·) *n.* a sacred rite; formal observance; formality; usage of courtesy; prescribed rule; a public or private function. **ceremonial** *a.* pert. to ceremony; formal; *n.* an outward observance; usage followed in performing rites. **ceremonially** *adv.* **ceremonious** *a.* full of ceremony; particular in observing forms. **ceremoniously** *adv.* **ceremoniousness** *n.* **master of ceremonies** *n.* at public functions, etc. one whose business it is to see that all forms, rules, and courtesies are observed [L. *caerimonia,* a rite].

ce·rise (sạr·ēs′) *n.* and *a.* light clear red; cherry-colored [Fr. = cherry].

ce·ri·um (sir′·ē·am) *n.* a metallic element, malleable and ductile, one of the rare-earth group [N.L. fr. *Ceres*].

cer·tain (sur′·tin) *a.* sure; settled; undoubted; inevitable; one; constant; of moderate quantity, degree, etc. **-ly** *adv.* **-ty** *n.* the quality of being certain. **certitude** *n.* freedom from doubt; certainty. **certes** (sur′·tēz) *adv.* (*Arch.*) certainly; in truth [L. *certus*].

cer·ti·fi·cate (sẹr·tif′·ạ·kạt) *n.* a written testimony to the truth of a fact; a testimonial or written statement of qualifications or of accomplishment; *v.i.* (sẹr·ti·fạ·kāt) to attest by a certificate; to furnish with a certificate. **certify** (sur′·ti·fī) *v.t.* to testify to in writing; to vouch for the truth of. **certifiable** *a.* able to be vouched for. **certification** *n.* the act of certifying. **certified** *a.* [L. *certus,* certain; *facere,* to make].

ce·ru·le·an (sạ·ròò′·li·ạn) *a.* sky-blue; deep blue. **ceruleous** *a.* sky-blue [L. *caeruleus*].

ce·ruse (si′·ròòs) *n.* white lead. **cerussite** *n.* a carbonate of lead [L. *cerussa,* white lead].

cer·vi·cal (sẹr′·vi·kạl) *a.* pert. to the neck or neck of the uterus [L. *cervix,* the neck].

ce·si·um, caesium (sē′·zi·ạm) *n.* a silver-white alkaline metal belonging to the sodium and potassium family [L. *caesius,* bluish-gray].

ces·sa·tion (se·sā′·shạn) *n.* stoppage; discontinuance [L. *cessare,* to cease].
ces·sion (se′·shạn) *n.* act of surrendering, as by treated; something yielded, ceded [L. *cessio*].
cess·pool (ses′·pòol) *n.* a pit or hollow for collection of drainage water or sewage.
chafe (chāf) *v.t.* to warm by rubbing; to wear away by rubbing; to irritate; to vex; *v.i.* to be worn by rubbing or friction; to rage or fret; *n.* friction; injury caused by rubbing. **-r** *n.* one who chafes. **chafing dish** *n.* a dish and heating apparatus for cooking or keeping food warm on the table [Fr. *chauffer,* to warm].
chaff (chaf) *n.* the husk of grains; straw cut small for cattle-feeding; worthless matter; refuse. **-y** *a.* [O.E. *ceaf*].
chaff (chaf) *n.* banter; jesting talk; *v.t.* to tease; to make fun of (without spite) [form of *chafe,* to irritate].
cha·grin (shạ·grin′) *n.* ill-humor; vexation; mortification; *v.t.* to vex deeply [Fr.].
chain (chān) *n.* a series of metal rings or links connected and forming a flexible cable; a fetter; a succession of things or events; a mountain range; a measure such as used by engineers or surveyors; *v.t.* to fasten or connect with a chain; to fetter; to restrain. **— bridge** *n.* a suspension bridge. **-drive** *n.* the transmitting of driving-power by means of chain-gear. **— gang** *n.* a number of convicts chained together. **— reaction** *n.* in nuclear physics, a self-sustaining process in which some neutrons from one splitting atom are able to split more atoms, setting free still more neutrons which carry on the reaction indefinitely [L. *catena,* a chain.
chair (chār) *n.* a seat with a back, legs, and sometimes arms, usually for one person; a portable covered vehicle for carrying one person, e.g. a sedan; an official seat occupied by the president of a meeting, a university professor, a bishop, etc.; *v.t.* to install in a chair or office; to provide with chairs. **to take the chair,** to act as chairman of a meeting; to preside. **-man** *n.* the presiding officer of a meeting, board, committee, etc. **-manship** *n.* **-woman** *n.* [Fr. *chaire,* a pulpit, fr. Gk. *kathedra*].
chaise (shāz) *n.* a light, one-horse carriage; a posting-carriage. **— longue** (lawng) *n.* an elongated seat with backrest at one end and support for legs [Fr. *chaise,* a chair, a seat].
chal·ced·o·ny (kal′·se·dō·ni·) *n.* a whitish or bluish-white variety of quartz. **chalcedonic** *a.* [fr. *Chalcedon,* a town in Asia Minor].
cha·let (shạ·lā′) *n.* a timber-built house in the Alps; a country residence like a Swiss mountain cottage [Fr.].
chal·ice (chal′·is) *n.* a wine-cup; a goblet; a [communion-cup L. *calix*].
chalk (chawk) *n.* a soft, white, carbonate of lime; a chalk-like material used for marking; *v.t.* to rub or mark with chalk. **-y** *a.* containing or like chalk. **-iness** *n.* **— up** *v.t.* to score; to earn. **French chalk,** tailor's chalk [L. *calx,* limestone].
chal·lenge (chal′·inj) *n.* an invitation to a contest, esp. to a duel; defiance; the warning call of a sentry; exception taken to a juror; *v.t.* to call upon a person to settle a dispute by fighting; to defy; to summon to answer; to call in question. **-able** *a.* **-r** *n.* [L. *calumnia.* Doublet of E. *calumny*].
chal·lis, challie (sha′·li·) *n.* a lightweight [fabric.
cham·ber (chām′·bẹr) *n.* a room, esp. one used for lodging, privacy, or study; a place where an assembly, such as a legislature meets, and the assembly itself; a cavity; the cavity at the rear end of the bore of a gun; a vessel for urine; *v.t.* to shut up or confine, as in a chamber; *v.i.* to occupy as a chamber. **-ed** *a.* **-s** *n.pl.* a room or rooms where a judge hears cases not requiring action in court. **-maid** *n.* a woman servant who has the care of bedrooms, esp. in hotels, etc. **— music** *n.* music suitable for performance in a house or small hall [L. *camera,* a room].
cham·ber·lain (chām′·bẹr·lin) *n.* court official. **-ship** *n.* [fr. *chamber*].
cham·bray (sham′·brā) *n.* a fine cotton material, a variety of gingham [fr. *Cambrai,* Fr.].
cha·me·le·on (kạ·mēl′·yạn) *n.* a small lizard, which changes color with its surroundings; (*Fig.*) an inconstant person [Gk. *chamai,* on the ground; *leōn,* a lion].
cham·fer (cham′·fẹr) *v.t.* to cut a groove in; to bevel; *n.* a groove; a bevel. **-ed** *a.* [O.Fr. *chanfraindre,* edge and fragile].
cham·ois (sham′·i·) *n.* a goat-like species of antelope; a kind of soft leather [L.L. *camox*].
champ (champ) *v.t.* and *i.* to bite, chew, or munch noisily. **to champ at the bit** (*Fig.*) to be impatient; *n.* (*Slang*) champion.
cham·pagne (sham·pān′) *n.* a light effervescent, white wine, made in the province of *Champagne* in N.E. France, or elsewhere.
cham·pi·on (cham′·pi·ạn) *n.* one who fought in single combat to defend the honor of another; a defender of any cause; one capable of defeating his competitors in any form of sport; *a.* first-class; *v.t.* to defend; to maintain or support. **-ship** *n.* the position of a champion; defense; advocacy [L.L. *campio,* a fighter in the arena].
chance (chans) *n.* an unforeseen occurrence; risk; likelihood; opportunity; possibility; *a.* accidental; *v.t.* to risk; *v.i.* to happen. **by —,** accidentally [O.Fr. *cheance,* fall of dice].
chan·cel (chan′·sạl) *n.* the east part of a church, where the altar is placed, orig. shut off from the nave [L. *cancelli,* lattice-work].
chan·cel·lor (chan′·sạ·ler) *n.* the title of various high officials in the state, and in the law; the head of a university; the chief secretary of an embassy. **-ship** *n.* the office of chancellor. **chancellery** *n.* the premises of a chancellor. [Fr. *chancelier,* orig. keeper of a barrier].
chan·cer·y (chan′·sẹr·i·) *n.* the office of a chancellor; a chancellery; a court of equity [orig. *chancellory*].
chan·de·lier (chan·dạ·lir′) *n.* a branched framework for holding lights, esp. one hanging from the ceiling; orig. for holding candles [L. *candela,* a candle].
chand·ler (chand′·lẹr) *n.* orig. a candle-maker; now a grocer or dealer in small wares [L. *candela,* a candle].
change (chānj) *v.t.* to alter or make different; to put one thing for another; to shift; to quit one state for another; to exchange, as money; to convert; *v.i.* to become different; to change one's clothes; *n.* the act of changing; alteration; that which makes for variety; money of small denomination given in exchange for money of larger; balance of money returned after payment; fresh clothing; an exchange. **-able** *a.* variable; fickle; unsteady. **-ful** *a.* **-fully** *adv.* **-fulness** *n.* **-less** *a.* unchanging; constant. **-ling** *n.* a child left in place of another taken by the fairies [L. *cambire,* to barter].
chan·nel (chan′·ạl) *n.* a waterway; the deeper part of a river, harbor, etc.; a strait; a groove or furrow; means of access; *a.* frequency band for transmission of radio, television, etc.; *v.t.* to form a channel; to groove or furrow; to direct in a particular course [L. *canalis*].
chant (chant) *v.t.* and *i.* to sing; to celebrate in song; to intone; *n.* a song; melody; sacred words recited in a singing manner. **-er** *n.* (*fem.* **-euse** or **-ress**). **-y** (shan′·ti·) *n.* a sailor's song [L. *cantare,* to sing].
chant·i·cleer (chant′·i·klir) *n.* a cock, rooster [O.Fr. *chanté-cler,* sing-clear].
cha·os (kā′·ås) *n.* complete confusion; state of the universe before creation. **chaotic** *a.* [Gk.].
chap (chap) *v.t.* to cleave; to split; to crack; *v.i.* to become cracked, red, and rough (as the skin in cold weather); *pr.t.* **-ping.** *pa.t.* **-ped.**

n. a chink; a crack in the skin [related to *chip, chop*].

chap (chap) *n.* (*Colloq.*) a fellow; (*Br.*) a peddler O.E. *caep*, a bargain].

chap·el (chap′·ạl) *n.* a private church; a subordinate place of worship; a division of a church with its own altar [L.L. *cappella*, a sanctuary for relics].

chap·e·ron (shap′·ạ·rōn) *n.* a kind of hood; a mature person who escorts an unmarried lady in public or is in attendance at social gatherings of young people; *v.t.* to escort, accompany. **-age** *n.* [Fr. = a hood].

chap·lain (chap′·lin) *n.* a clergyman. **-cy** *n.* [Fr. *chapelain*].

chap·let (chap′·lit) *n.* a garland or wreath for the head; a string of beads; a division of the rosary [O.Fr. *chapelet*].

chaps (shaps) *n.pl.* leather over-trousers worn by a cowboy [fr. Sp. *chaparejos*].

chap·ter (chap′·tẹr) *n.* a divison of a book or treatise; a bishop's council in a diocese; an organized branch of a society, fraternity, or military order; *v.t.* to divide into chapters [L. *caput*, the head].

char (chȧr) *n.* a species of trout [Celt.].

char (chȧr) *v.t.* to reduce to charcoal; to burn to a black cinder; *pr.p.* **-ring.** *pa.p.* and *pa.t.* **-red.** **-coal** *n.* the residue of partially burnt animal or vegetable matter, esp. wood.

char, chare (chȧr) *n.* a job; work done by the day; *v.i.* to work by the day; to do small jobs. **-woman** *n.* [O.E. *cerr.*]

char·ac·ter (kar′·ik·tẹr) *n.* a mark, letter, figure, sign, stamp; any distinctive mark; an essential feature; nature; the total of qualities making up an individuality; moral excellence; (*Colloq.*) a person noted for eccentricity; a personage in a play or novel; *v.t.* to characterize; to portray; to represent. **-ize** *v.t.* to depict the peculiar qualities of; to distinguish; to give character to. **-istic** *a.* serving to mark the character of; peculiar; distinctive; *n.* that which distinguishes a person or thing from another; **-istically** *adv.* **-ization** *n.* the act or characterizing literary or dramatic portrayal of character [Gk. *charactēr*, an engraved mark].

cha·rade (shạ·rād′) *n.* a game, consisting of the interpretation (usually dramatic) of a word for others to guess [Fr.].

chard (chȧrd) *n.* leafy vegetable.

charge (chȧrj) *n.* a load or burden; price or cost; care or trust; an earnest exhortation, as of a judge or bishop; accusation or allegation; a clergyman's parish or the people of that parish; the amount of powder, etc., that a gun is fitted to hold; an impetuous onset or attack, or the signal for it; custody; electrical contents of accumulator or battery; *v.t.* to lay a task, command, trust upon; to ask as payment; to accuse; to load, as a gun; *v.i.* to make an onset. **-able** *a.* **-r** *n.* a large, flat dish; a warhorse [L.L. *carricare*, to load a cart].

char·gé d'af·fairs (shȧr·zhā′·da·fer′) *n.* a minor diplomatic emissary; a deputy ambassador [Fr. = charged with business].

char·i·ot (char′·i·ạt) *n.* in ancient times, a two-wheeled cart used in warfare; a four-wheeled state carriage. **-eer** *n.* [Fr. dim. of *char*, a car, cart].

char·i·ty (char′·i·ti·) *n.* (*Bib.*) love and goodwill to men; liberality to the poor; leniency in judging others, any act of kindness; alms; a charitable cause or institution. **charitable** *a.* pert. to charity; liberal to the poor; generous. **charitably** *adv.* [L. *caritas*, affection].

cha·riv·a·ri (shȧ·ri·vȧ′·ri·) *n.* a mock serenade. Also **shivaree** (shi′·vạ·ri·) [Fr.].

char·la·tan (shȧr′·lạ·tạn) *n.* a quack or imposter [It. *ciarlare*, to prate, chatter].

char·lotte (shȧr′·lạt) *n.* (*Cookery*) a kind of pudding made by lining a mold with bread or cake and filling it [Fr.].

charm (chȧrm) *n.* a magic spell; anything supposed to possess magic power; a talisman; a trinket worn on a bracelet; attractiveness; *v.t.* to subjugate by magic; to attract irresistibly; *v.i.* to please greatly; to be fascinating. **-er** *n.* **-ing** *a.* attractive; alluring; delightful [Fr. *charme*, fr. L. *carmen*, a song].

char·nel (chȧr′·nel) *a.* containing dead bodies. **— house** *n.* a place where the bodies or bones of the dead are deposited; a sepulcher [L. *caro, carnis*, flesh].

chart (chȧrt) *n.* a map of part of the sea, showing currents, depths, islands, coasts, etc.; a diagram giving information in tabular form; a graph; *v.t.* to represent on a chart; to map; to delineate. **-er** *n.* [L. *charta*, a paper].

char·ter (chȧr′·ter) *n.* a formal document confirming privileges, titles, or rights; an act of incorporation; the hiring of a vessel; *v.t.* to establish by charter; to hire, as a ship. **-ed** *a.* **— member** *n.* one of the original members [L. *charta*, a paper].

char·treuse (shȧr·trẹz′) *n.* a liqueur; a light yellowish-green color [Fr.].

char·y (chȧr′·i·) *a.* careful; sparing. **charily** *adv.* [O.E. *cearig*, full of care].

chase (chās) *v.t.* to pursue; to run after; to hunt; to drive away; *v.i.* to hasten; to hurry; *n.* pursuit; hunting of enemy, game, etc.; what is pursued or hunted. **-r** *n.* one who chases; a mild beverage taken after liquor [L. *captare*, to seize].

chase (chās) *v.t.* to enchase; to engrave metal. **-r** *n.* [abbrev. of *enchase*].

chase (chās) *n.* (*Print.*) an iron frame to hold type when set up; a wide groove [L. *capsa*, a box. Doublet of *case*].

chasm (kazm) *n.* a deep opening in the earth; a cleft [Gk. *chasma*].

chassé (sha·sā′) *n.* in dancing, a rapid gliding step to the right or left [Fr.].

chas·sis (sha′·si·) *n.* the framework and undercarriage of an automobile, including the engine; the framework on which a gun is moved; landing gear of an airplane [Fr. *chassis*, a frame].

chaste (chāst) *a.* pure; virtuous; undefiled; pure and simple in taste and style. **-ly** *adv.* **-ness** *n.* **chastity** *n.* purity; virginity [L. *castus*, pure].

chas·ten (chā′·sn) *v.t.* to correct by punishment; to subdue [L. *castigare*, to punish].

chas·tise (chas′·tīz) *v.t.* to inflict pain in order to reform; to punish. **-ment** *n.* [L. *castigare*, to punish].

chas·u·ble (chaz′·yoo·bl) *n.* a sleeveless vestment worn over the alb by the priest during Mass [L.L. *casula*, a mantle].

chat (chat) *v.i.* to talk idly or familiarly; *n.* light, informal talk; *pr.p.* **-ting;** *pa.p.* and *pa.t.* **-ted.** **-ter** *v.i.* to talk idly or rapidly; to rattle together, of the teeth. **-terbox** *n.* one who chatters excessively. **-terer** *n.* one who chatters. **-tiness** *n.* **-ty** *a.* talkative; gossipy.

cha·teau (sha·tō′) *n.* a castle; a country-seat, esp. in France; a mansion; *pl.* **chateaux** (sha·-tōz′). **chatelain** (sha′·tạ·len) *n.* the mistress of a castle or other fashionable household; a chain fastened around a lady's waist, with keys, seals, etc. attached [O.Fr. *chastel*. Doublet of *castle*].

chat·tel (chat′·l) *n.*, usually in *pl.* **chattels,** any kind of property, except land and buildings. **— mortgage** *n.* a mortgage on personal property [O.Fr. *chatel*, a castle].

chat·ter See **chat.**

chauf·feur (shō·fur′·, shō′·fẹr) *n.* the paid driver of private automobile; *v.t.* to drive [Fr. = a stoker].

chau·vin·ism (shō′·vin·izm) *n.* absurdly exaggerated patriotism; blind enthusiasm for a cause. **chauvinist** *n.* **chauvinistic** *a.* [fr. Nicolas *Chauvin*].

chaw (chaw) *n.* (*Dial.*) See **chew.**

cheap (chēp) *a.* low in price; of low cost, as

compared with the value, or the usual cost; contemptible, inferior, vulgar. **-ly** *adv.* **-ness** *n.* **-en** *v.t.* to bring down the price; to lessen the value; to belittle [O.E. *ceap*, a bargain].

cheat (chēt) *v.t.* to deceive; to defraud; to trick; *v.i.* to practice trickery; *n.* a fraud; one who cheats; an impostor. **-er** *n.* [short for *escheat*].

check (chek) *n.* a stop; a restraint; an interruption in progress; an obstacle, obstruction; control or supervision, or one employed to carry out such; a mark placed against items in a list; an order to a bank to pay money; a term in chess to indicate that opponent's king must be moved or guarded; a pattern of squares in cloth, etc.; *v.t.* to restrain; to hinder; to chide or reprove; to verify; to put a mark against, in a list; to leave articles in the custody of another; in chess, to put in check; *v.i.* to come to a sudden stop; to pause. **-ers** *n.pl.* a board game for 2. **-book** *n.* book of blank checks or orders on a bank. **-mate** *n.* the final movement in chess, when the king can be neither moved or protected; complete defeat. **-room** *n.* a place where articles may be left under the temporary protection of others. **-up** *n.* a medical examination [fr. Pers. *shah*, king].

check·er (chek′·ẹr) *v.t.* to variegate with cross lines; to diversify; *v.i.* to produce a checkered effect, esp. of alternate light and shade; *n.* a square; a pattern like a chess-board; a piece in the game of checkers. **-ed** *a.* [Fr. *échiquier*].

Ched·dar (ched′·ạr) *n.* a kind of hard, smooth cheese [fr. *Cheddar*, in Somerset].

cheek (chēk) *n.* the fleshy wall or side of the mouth; each side of the face below the eyes; (*Colloq.*) insolence or impudence. **-bone** *n.* the bone below the outer corner of the eye. **-y** *a.* [O.E. *ceace*, the cheek, jaw].

cheep (chēp) *v.i.* to chirp, as a small bird; *n.* a small shrill sound [imit. origin].

cheer (chēr) *n.* good spirits; disposition; state of mind; gaiety; expression of approval, or encouragement, by shouting; rich food; *v.t.* to render cheerful; to comfort; to hearten or encourage; to salute with cheers; *v.i.* to shout hurrah. **-er** *n.* **-ful** *a.* having good spirits. **-fully** *adv.* **-fulness** *n.* **-ily** *adv.* with cheerfulness. **-iness** *n.* **-io!** *interj.* an informal salutation at parting. **-less** *a.* gloomy; comfortless. **-lessness** *n.* **-y** *a.* in good spirits; promoting cheerfulness [O.Fr. *chiere*, countenance; L.L. *cara*, the face].

cheese (chēz) *n.* a curd of milk, separated from the whey, and prepared in several ways as food; a solid mass or cake of this food. **-cloth** *n.* a thin loosely woven cotton cloth, orig. used for wrapping cheese. **cheese it** (*Slang*) Look out! Run! [O.E. *cese*, *cyse*, curdled milk].

chee·tah (chē′·tạ) *n.* the hunting leopard of India and Africa [Hind.].

chef (shef) *n.* a head cook. **chef-d'oeuvre** (shā·devr′) *n.* a masterpiece, esp. in art or literature [Fr.].

chei·ro- See **chiro-**.

chem·i·cal (kem′·i·kạl) *a.* pert. to, or made by, chemistry; *n.* a substance used in chemistry, or produced by chemical processes. **-ly** *adv.* according to chemical principles [fr. *Alchemy*].

che·mise (shạm·ēz′) *n.* a woman's undershirt [Fr. *chemise*, a shirt].

chem·ist (kem′·ist) *n.* a person versed in chemistry or professionally engaged in it. **-ry** *n.* the study of the various substances which compose the universe, their combinations, and the processes by which they act one upon another [shortened form of *alchemist*].

chem·o·ther·a·peu·tics (kem′·ō·ther·a·pū′·tiks) *n.* (*Med.*) the use of chemical compounds in the treatment of disease. **chemotherapy** *n.* [E. *chemical;* Gk. *therapeuein*, to heal].

chem·ur·gy (kem′·ẹr·ji·) *n.* applied chemistry directed to developing industrial uses for agricultural produce.

che·nille (shạ·nēl′) *n.* a soft plush-like cord of silk, wool, worsted, etc. used for ornamental trimmings, fringes, etc.; a soft, velvety fabric [Fr. = a caterpillar].

cher·ish (cher′·ish) *v.t.* to hold dear; to treat tenderly; to foster [L. *carus*, dear].

che·root (shạ·ròòt′) *n.* a kind of cigar, open at both ends [Hind.].

cher·ry (cher′·i·) *n.* the bright red fruit of a tree akin to the plum; a cherry tree; *a.* pert. to a cherry; red [Gk. *kerasos*].

cher·ub (cher′·ạb) *n.* a winged creature with a human face; an angel; a celestial spirit; a beautiful child. *pl.* **-im** (cher′·ạ·bim) or **-s. -ic** (chạ·ròò′·bik) *a.* [Heb. *kerub*].

chess (ches) *n.* a game played by two persons on a board of 64 squares, with 32 pieces or 'men.' **-man** *n.* a piece used in the game [Pers. *shah*, a king].

chest (chest) *n.* a large box; a coffer; a trunk; part of the body enclosed by ribs and breastbone; *v.t.* to place in a chest. **— of drawers** *n.* a piece of furniture fitted with drawers. **-y** *a.* having a large chest; conceited [O.E.].

ches·ter·field (ches′·tẹr·fēld) *n.* a long overcoat; a heavily padded sofa [after Earl of *Chesterfield*].

chest·nut (ches′·nut) *n.* the nut of a forest tree; the tree itself, or its timber; a reddish-brown color; (*Colloq.*) a stale joke or story; *a.* reddish-brown [L. *castanea*].

che·val (shạ·val′) *n.* a support or frame. **— glass** *n.* a large mirror within a supporting frame. **-ier** (shev·ạ·lir′) *n.* orig. a horseman; a cavalier [Fr. *cheval*, a horse].

Chev·i·ot (chev′·i·ạt) *n.* famous breed of sheep; its wool [fr. *Cheviot* Hills, Eng. & Scot.].

chev·ron (shev′·rạn) *n.* a V-shaped bar worn on the sleeve to designate rank [Fr. *chevron*, a rafter].

chew (chòò) *v.t.* to bite and crush with the teeth; to masticate; to ruminate; to champ; *n.* action of chewing; a quid of tobacco. **-ing gum** *n.* a sweet and flavored substance for chewing prepared from chicle, the gum of a Mexican rubber-tree [O.E. *ceowan*].

Chi·an·ti (kē·an′·ti·) *n.* an Italian red or white wine [fr. *Chianti* hills in Italy].

chi·a·ro·scu·ro (ki·ạr·ạ·skyoo′·rō) *n.* the reproduction in art of the effects of light and shade in nature [It. = bright, dark].

chic (shēk) *n.* style and elegance; effectiveness; *a.* stylish; modish [Fr.].

chi·cane (shi·kān′) *n.* trick or artifice; sharp practice, esp. in legal proceedings; (*Cards*) a bridge hand with no trumps in it; *v.i.* to use trickery. **-ry** *n.* trickery. **-r** *n.* [Fr.].

Chi·ca·no (chi·kán′·ō) *n.* an American of Mexican descent; *a.* [Sp. *Mejicano*, a Mexican].

chick·en (chik′·ạn) *n.* a common domestic fowl. **chick** *n.* a young chicken. **-en-hearted** *a.* cowardly; timid. **-en-pox** *n.* a mild, contagious, eruptive disease. **-weed** *n.* weed with small white blossoms [O.E. *cicen*].

chic·le (chik′·l) *n.* a gum-like, milky juice obtained from several Central American trees [Sp. Amer.].

chic·o·ry (chik′·ạ·ri·) *n.* a plant whose taproot when roasted and ground is used to mix with coffee and whose greens are used for salad [Fr. *chicorée*].

chide (chīd) *v.t.* to scold; to rebuke; *v.i.* to find fault. *pr.p.* **chiding.** *pa.p.* **-d, chid.** *pa.t.* **chid** [O.E. *cidạn*].

chief (chēf) *a.* foremost in importance; principal; main; at the head; most influential; *n.* a head or leader; a principal person or thing. **-ly** *adv.* principally; for the most part. **-tain** *n.* the head of a clan or tribe; a commander [Fr. *chef.*, fr. L. *caput*, the head].

chif·fon (shi·fán′) *n.* a thin, soft, gauzy material. **-ier** (shif·ạn·ēr′) *n.* a high narrow chest of drawers [Fr. *chiffon*, a rag].

chig·ger (chig′·ẹr) *n.* a parasitic mite larva.

chi·gnon (shēn′·yáng) *n.* a rolled-up pad or

bun of hair at the back of a woman's head or on the nape of the neck [Fr.].

chil·blain (chil′.blān) *n.* an inflammatory swelling caused by cold and bad circulation [fr. *chill* and *blain*].

child (chīld) *n.* a very young person of either sex; offspring; descendant. **-ren** (chil′.drin) *n.pl.* offspring, descendants. **-birth** *n.* the act of bearing a child. **-bearing** *n.* producing children. **-bed** *n.* childbirth. **-hood** *n.* the state of being a child; the time during which one is a child. **-ish** *a.* pert. to a child; silly; trifling. **-ishly** *adv.* **-ishness** *n.* **-less** *a.* **-lessness** *n.* **-like** *a.* like a child; innocent; trustful. **with child,** pregnant [O.E. *cild*].

chil·i (chil′.i.) *n.* the red pepper, or fruit of the capsicum, called Cayenne pepper when dried and ground [Mex.].

chill (chil) *a.* cold; tending to cause shivering; cool in manner or feeling; discouraging; *n.* a feeling of coldness, attended with shivering; illness caused by cold; discouragement; *v.t.* to cool; to cause to shiver; to benumb; to dispirit; to keep cold; *v.i.* to grow cold. **-y** *a.* cold; creating cold; depressing; ungenial. **-iness** *n.* [O.E. *cele, ciele,* coldness].

chime (chīm) *n.* the musical sound of bells; a set of bells tuned to the musical scale (usu. *pl.*); *v.t., v.i.* to sound harmoniously; to be in harmony; to agree with [M.E. *chimbe,* orig. *cymbal*].

chi·me·ra, chi·mae·ra (ki.mi′.rạ) *n.* a fabulous, fire-breathing monster; a creature of the imagination. **chimeric(al)** *a.* [Gk. *chimaira*].

chim·ney (chim′.ni.) *n.* the passage through which the smoke of a fireplace, etc., is carried off; a glass tube around the flame of a lamp. **— sweep** *n.* one who removes the soot from chimneys [Gk. *kaminos,* a furnace].

chim·pan·zee (chim.pan′.zē) *n.* a large African anthropoid ape [W. Africa].

chin (chin) *n.* the part of the face below the mouth; *v.t.* (*Colloq.*) to chat; to raise oneself on a horizontal bar so that the chin is level with the bar. *pr.t.* **-ning.** *pa.t.* **-ned** [O.E. *cin*].

Chi·na (chī′.nạ) *n.* a vast country in E. Asia. **china, chinaware** *n.* a translucent, vitreous ceramic ware; porcelain. **Chinese** (chī.nēz′) *n.* a native, the natives, or the language of China; *a.*

chin·chil·la (chin.chil′.ạ) *n.* a small animal, with very fine, soft fur; the fur itself; a heavy woolen material used esp. for coats [Sp.].

chine (chīn) *n.* the backbone or spine of an animal; a piece of the backbone, with the flesh, cut for cooking [Fr. *échine,* the spine].

chink (chingk) *n.* a small cleft, rent, or fissure; a gap or crack; *v.t.* to open; *v.i.* to crack [O.E. *cinu,* a fissure].

chink (chingk) *n.* the sound of a piece of metal when struck; the ring of coin; *v.i.* to ring.

Chi·nook (chi.nook′) *n.* a tribe of N.W. American Indians. **chinook** *n.* a wind.

chintz (chints) *n.* a printed cotton cloth, glazed or unglazed [Hind. *chint*].

chip (chip) *v.t.* to chop off into small pieces; to break little pieces from; to shape by cutting off pieces, *v.i.* to break or fly off in small pieces; *pr.p.* **-ping;** *pa.p., pa.t.* **-ped;** *n.* a piece of wood, etc. separated from a larger body by an axe, etc.; a fragment; a counter, instead of money, used in gambling. **-s** *n.pl.* fried slices of potato. **-per** *a.* (*Colloq.*) cheerful; lively. **— shot** *n.* (*Golf*) a short, lofted shot onto the green. **— in** *v.t.* to contribute [cf. *chop*].

chip·munk (chip′.mungk) *n.* a burrowing ground-squirrel [Algoukian].

chip·pen·dale (chip′.pạn.dāl) *n.* a style of furniture [fr. cabinet-maker *Chippendale*].

chi·ro- (kī′.rō) *prefix* fr. Gk. *cheir,* the handy.

chi·ro·man·cy (kī′.rō.man.si.) *n.* divination by inspection of the hand; palmistry [Gk. *cheir,* the hand; *manteia,* divination].

chi·rop·o·dist (ki.ráp′.ạ.dist) *n.* one skilled in the treatment of diseases of the feet. **chiropody** *n.* [Gk. *cheir,* hand; *podos,* foot].

chi·ro·prac·tic (ki.rạ.prak′.tik) *n.* a method of healing which relies upon the removal of nerve interference by manual adjustment of the spine. **chiropractor** *n.* [Gk. *cheir,* the hand; *prassein,* to do].

chirp, chir·rup (churp, chir′.ạp) *n.* a short, sharp note, as of a bird or cricket; *v.i.* to make such a sound; to twitter; to talk gaily.

chis·el (chiz′.al) *n.* a tool sharpened to a cutting edge at the end, used in carpentry, sculpture, etc.; *v.i.* to cut or carve with this tool; (*Slang*) to cheat [O.Fr. *cisel*].

chit (chit) *n.* an informal note; a voucher; a permit or pass [Hind. *chitthi*].

chit-chat (chit′.chat) *n.* prattle; trivial talk.

chit·ter·lings (chit′.ẹr.lingz) *n.pl.* the smaller intestines of swine, etc., used as food.

chiv·al·ry (shiv′.ạl.ri.) *n.* the system of knighthood in medieval times; the qualities of a knight, viz. dignity, courtesy, bravery, generosity, gallantry. **chivalric, chivalrous** *a.* pert. to chivalry. **chivalrously** *adv.* [Fr. *chevalerie,* fr. *cheval,* a horse].

chive (chīv) *n.* a small herb of the onion kind [L. *cepa,* an onion].

chla·myd·ia (klȧ·mid′·ē·ȧ) *n.* a contagious venereal disease; **chlamydial** *adj.* [N.L. fr. Gk. *chlamyd-, chlamys*].

chlor-, chlo·ro- (klōr) combining forms fr. Gk. *chloros,* green; also denoting chlorine.

chlo·rine (klō′.rēn) *n.* a heavy gas of yellowish-green color used in disinfecting, bleaching, and poison-gas warfare. **chloral** *n.* a sleep-producing drug. **chlorate** *n.* a salt of chloric acid. **chloric** *a.* pert. to chlorine. **chloride** *n.* a compound of chlorine with another element. **chlorinate** *v.t.* disinfect, bleach, or combine with chlorine. **chlorination** *n.* **chlorite** *n.* a mineral of a green color, soft and friable. **chloroform** *n.* a colorless, volatile liquid used as an anesthetic; *v.t.* to make insensible by using chloroform [Gk. *chloros,* pale-green].

chlo·ro·phyll (klō′.ra.fil) *n.* (*Bot.*) the green coloring matter of plants [Gk. *chloros,* pale-green; *phullon,* a leaf].

chock (chák) *n.* a wedge to steady a wheel or a cask lying on its side; *v.t.* to make fast, with a block or wedge. **-ful** *a.* packed [fr. *choke*].

choc·o·late (chák′.ạ.lit) *a.* a paste or hard cake made from the powdered seeds of the cacao plant, mixed with sugar, etc.; a beverage made by pouring boiling water or milk over this; candy; *a.* dark brown [Mex. Sp.].

choice (chois) *n.* the act of choosing; the power or opportunity of choosing; selection; the thing chosen; alternative; *a.* worthy of being chosen; rare; superior [Fr. *choisir,* to choose].

choir (kwīr) *n.* a company of singers, esp. belonging to a church; that part of the church set apart for them [L. *chorus*].

choke (chōk) *v.t.* to stop the breath as by compression of the windpipe; to stifle or smother; *v.i.* to have the wind-pipe stopped; to be suffocated; *n.* the act of choking; an obstructing piece in mechanism; a valve regulating the proportion of gas to air in a motor. **-r.** *n.* one who chokes; something worn closely about the neck, as beads, etc. [M.E. *choken*].

chol·er (kál′.ẹr) *n.* bile; anger; wrath. **choleric** *a.* passionate; easily angered. **cholera** *n.* deadly, epidemic, bilious disease, marked by purgings, vomiting and gripping pains. [Fr. *colère,* anger, fr. Gk. *cholē,* bile].

cho·les·ter·ol (kạ.les′.tạ.rōl) *n.* a fatlike substance found in bile, gallstones, blood, and the brain, also in egg yolks, etc. [Gk. *cholē,* bile; *stereos,* solid].

cho·lic (kol′.ik) *a.* pert. to, or obtained from, bile [Gk. *cholē,* bile].

choose (chòòz) *v.t.* to pick out; to select; to take one thing in preference to another; *v.i.* to decide; to think fit. *pa.p.* **chosen;** *pa.t.* **chose. choosey** *a.* (*Slang*) fastidious, difficult to please [O.E. *ceosan*].

chop (cháp) *n.* (usually *pl.*) the jaw of an animal; the jaw of a vice [etym. uncertain].

chop (cháp) *v.t.* to cut into pieces; to mince, by striking repeatedly with a sharp instrument; to sever by blows; *v.i.* to make a quick stroke or repeated strokes with a sharp instrument, as an axe; *n.* the act of chopping; a piece chopped off; a thick slice of meat attached to a rib or other bone; a cutlet. *pr.p.* **-ping.** *pa.p.* and *pa.t.* **-ped. -per** *n.* one who chops; a large heavy knife; cleaver. **-py** *a.* full of fissures; of the sea, having short, broken waves.

chop sticks (cháp stiks) *n.* one of two small sticks of wood, ivory, etc. used by the Chinese in taking food.

chop su·ey (cháp sòò′·i·) also **chop sooey.** A Chinese-American dish of meat, bean sprouts, etc. [fr. Chin.].

cho·ral (kō′·ral) *a.* pert. or belonging to a choir or chorus. **-ly** *adv.* **choric** *a.* pert. to a chorus, esp. Greek dramatic chorus. [Gk. *choros*, a band of dancers and singers].

cho·rale (kō·rál′) *n.* a simple, dignified melody sung to religious words [Gk. *choros*].

chord (kawrd) *n.* the string of a musical instument; (*Mus.*) a series of tones having a harmonic relation to each other, and sounded simultaneously; (*Geom.*) a straight line between two points in the circumference of a circle [Gk. *chordē*, a string].

chore (chōr) *n.* any odd job, or occasional piece of housework; (*pl.*) routine work [O.E. *cerr*, work].

cho·re·a (kō·rē′·a) *n.* (*Med.*) uncontrollable spasms of limbs, body and facial muscles; St. Vitus's dance [Gk. *choreia*, a dancing].

cho·re·og·ra·phy (kō·ri·á′·gra·fi·) *n.* ballet dancing; the art of creating dance compositions for ballet. **choreographer** *n.* **choreographic** *a.* [Gk. *choros*, dance; *graphein*, to write].

chor·is·ter (kawr′·is·tər) *n.* a choir member.

cho·rog·ra·phy (kō·rág′·ra·fi·) *n.* the art of making a map, or writing a description, of a region or country. **chorology** *n.* the study of the geographical distribution of plants and animals [Gk. *chora*, land; *graphein*, to write].

chor·tle (chawr′·tl) *v.i.* to chuckle gleefully. **chortling** *n.* [invented by Lewis Carroll from *ch*uckle and sn*ort*].

cho·rus (kō′·ras) *n.* orig. a band of singers and dancers; a combination of voices singing together; what is sung or spoken by the chorus; in a Greek play, certain performers who witness the action, and at intervals express their feelings regarding it; the refrain; *v.t.* to join in the refrain; to call out or sing together. **choric** *a.* pert. to a chorus [Gk. *choros*, a band of dancers and singers].

chose (chōz) *pa.t.* of **choose.**

chosen (chō′·zn)*pa.p.* of **choose.**

chow·der (chou′·dər) *n.* a stew made of fish, pork, onions, etc. [Fr. *chaudièr*, a pot].

Christ (krīst) *n.* The Anointed—a name given to Jesus of Nazareth. **-like, -ly** *a.* resembling Christ [Gk. = anointed].

chris·ten (kris′·n) *v.t.* to baptize in the name of Christ; to give a name to. **Christendon** *n.* all Christian countries; the whole body of Christians. **-ing** *n.* baptism [Gk.].

Chris·tian (kris′·chan) *n.* a follower or disciple of Christ; a professed adherent of the Church of Christ; *a.* pert. to Christ or his religion. **-ize** *v.t.* to make Christian; to convert to Christianity. **Christianity** *n.* the religion of the followers of Christ. **— era,** the era counting from the birth of Christ. **— name,** the name given at baptism; individual name, as opposed to surname or family name. **— Science,** a religious doctrine of faith-healing founded in America by Mrs. Mary Eddy [Gk. *Christos*, anointed].

Christ·mas (kris′·mas) the annual celebration of the birth of Christ, observed on Dec. 25 [E. *Christ* and *Mass*].

chrom- (krōm) combing form fr. Gk. *chroma*, color; word element referring to chromium.

chro·mat·ic (krō·mat′·ik) *a.* pert. to color; (*Mus.*) proceeding by semitones. **-s** *n.* the science of colors; (*Mus.*) chromatic notes. **-ally** *adv.* [Gk. *chroma*, color].

chrome, chro·mi·um (krōm, krō′·mi·um) *n.* a metal, very resistant to corrosion, used generally for plating other metals. **chromic** *a.* pert. to, or obtained from, chrome or chromium. **chromate** *n.* a salt of chromic acid. **chromite** *n.* a mineral, the chief source of chromium [Gk. *chroma*, color].

chro·mo·some (krō′·ma·sōm) *n.* (*Biol.*) one of the gene-carrying bodies in the tissue of a cell, regarded as the transmitter of hereditary factors from parent to child [Gk. *chroma*, color; *soma*, a body].

chron·ic (krán′·ik) *a.* continuing for a long time; of disease, deep-seated and lasting; confirmed; inveterate. **-ally** [Gk. *chronos*, time].

chron·i·cle (kran′·i·kl) *n.* a register of events in order of time; a history or account; *v.t.* to record in order of time. **-r** *n.* [Gk. *chronika*, annals, fr. *chronos*, time].

chro·no- (krán′·a) a combining form fr. Gk. *chronos*, time. **-graph** *n.* an instrument for measuring and recording time very exactly. **chronology** (kra·ná′·la·ji·) *n.* the science that treats of historical dates and arranges them in order; a table of events and dates. **chronologer, chronologist** *n.* one who records historical events, etc. **chronological** *a.* arranged in order of time. **chronologically** *alv.* **chronometer** *n.* a very accurate watch or time-keeper. **-metric, -metrical** *a.* **chronometry** *n.* the process of measuring time by instruments.

chrys·a·lis (kris′·a·lis) *n.* the case in which a caterpillar encloses itself before it becomes a butterfly or moth; *pl.***chrysalides** (kris·al′·i·-dēz) **chrysalid** *a.* [Gk. *chrusos*, gold].

chrys·an·the·mum (kris·an′·tha·mam) *n.* a mop-headed garden flower [Gk. *chrusos*, gold; *anthemon*, a flower].

chry·so- (kris′·a) a combining form fr. Gk. *chrusos*, gold. **chrysocracy** (kris·ák′·ra·si·) *n.* the rule of wealth. **chrysolite** *n.* a yellowish-green precious stone. **chrysoprase** (kris′·a·prāz) used as a gem.

chub (chub) *n.* a fish of the carp family, small and fat. **-by** *a.* round and plump. **-biness** *n.* [M.E. *chubbe*].

chuck (chuk) *v.t.* (*Colloq.*) to throw; to toss; to tap under the chin; *n.* a toss; a pat under the chin.

chuck (chuk) *n.* in machinery, part of a lathe for holding an object while it is being operated on; a cut of beef from the neck to the shoulder blade [etym. uncertain].

chuck·le (chuk′·l) *v.i.* to laugh in a suppressed manner; *n.* a short, quiet laugh [imit. origin].

chuck·le·head (chuk′·l·hed) *n.* a dolt, a lout [E. *chock*, a block].

chug (chug) *n.* an explosive sound made by an engine exhaust; *v.i.* to make an explosive sound. *pa.p., pa.t.* **-ged.** *pr.p.* **-ging.**

chum (chum) *n.* an intimate friend; a pal; a roommate; *v.i.* to be friendly (with); to share a room with. *pr.p.* **-ming.** *pa.p.* and *pa.t.* **med. -my** *a.* friendly; sociable.

chump (chump) *n.* a lump of wood; the thick end of anything; (*Slang*) a blockhead.

chunk (chungk) *n.* a short, thick piece of wood, etc. **-y** *a.* [etym. uncertain].

church (church) *n.* building for Christian worship; collective body of Christians; a denomination or sect of the Christian religion; the clergy; the church service; *v.t.* to bring to church. **-goer** *n.* one who attends church regularly. **-ly** *a.* **-man** *n.* an ecclesiastic; a member of a church. **-warden** *n.* an officer entrusted with the interests of the church or parish. **-yard** *n.* the ground adjoining a church [O.E. *circe*, belonging to the Lord].

churl (churl) *n.* a countryman. **-ish** *a.* **-ishly** *adv.* **-ishness** *n.* [O.E. *ceorl*, a man].

churn (churn) *n.* a vessel in which cream is violently stirred to produce butter; *v.t.* to agitate cream so as to produce butter; to stir up violently; *v.i.* to produce butter [O.E. *cyrin*].

chute (shòòt) *n.* a rapid descent in a river; a rapid; a sloping contrivance for transferring coal, rubbish, etc. to a lower level [Fr. *chute*, a fall].

chut·ney, chutnee (chut′·ni·) *n.* an E. Indian condiment, generally made with mangoes, peppers and spices [Hind. *chatni*].

ci·ca·da, cicala (si·kȧ′·dạ, si·kȧ′·lạ) *n.* an insect, the male of which emits a shrill, chirping sound [L. *cicada*, a cricket].

cic·a·trix, cicatrice (sik′·ạ·triks) *n.* a scar left after a healed wound; *pl.* **cicatrices** (sik·-ạ·trī′·sēz). **cicatrize** (sik′·ạ·trīz) *v.t.* to heal and induce the formation of new tissue [L.].

cic·e·ro·ne (sis·ạ·rō′·ni·; It. chē·chā·rō′·nā) *n.* one who shows strangers over a place, as a cathedral, etc.; a guide [It. fr. L. *Cicero*].

ci·der (sī′·dẹr) *n.* a drink made from the juice of apples [Heb. *shakȧr*, to be intoxicated].

ci·gar (si·gȧr′) *n.* tobacco leaf made up in a roll for smoking. **-ette** *n.* finely cut tobacco rolled in thin paper [Sp. *cigarillo*].

cil·i·a (sil′·i·ạ) *n.pl.* the eyelashes; (*Anat.*) hair-like, vibratile processes. **ciliary, ciliate, ciliated, ciliferous, ciliform** *a.* [L.].

cinch (sinch) *n.* a saddle-girth; (*Slang*) a certainty; *v.t.* to fasten a cinch around; to tighten (girth) [L. *cingula*, a girth].

cin·cho·na (sin·kō′·nạ) *n.* a genus of trees from which quinine is extracted; the bark. **-ceous** (sin·kạ·nā′·shạs) *a.* [Sp. fr. Countess of *Chinchon*, who was cured by it in 1638].

cinc·ture (singk′·chẹr) *n.* a belt; a girdle; a zone; *v.t.* to encircle. **-d** *a.* [L. *cinctura*, a girdle]

cin·der (sin′·dẹr) *n.* the remains of burned coal; any partially burned combustible substance [O.E. *sinder*].

cin·e·ma (sin′·ạ·mạ) *n.* a hall or theater where moving pictures are shown; a motion picture; **-scope** *n.* a wide, panoramic motion picture screen. **-tography** *n.* **-tographer** *n.* [Gk. *kinema*, movement].

cin·er·ar·y (sin′·ạ·re·ri·) *a.* pert. to ashes; made to hold ashes. **cinerarium** *n.* (*pl.* **-raria**) *n.* a place for ashes after cremation. **cineration** *n.* a reducing to ashes; incineration [L. *cinerarius*, ashy].

cin·na·bar (sin′·ạ·bȧr) *n.* red sulphide of mercury used as a pigment; vermilion; *a.* vermilion colored [Gk. *kinnabari*, vermilion].

cin·na·mon (sin′·ạ·mạn) *n.* the inner bark of a laurel tree of Ceylon; an aromatic substance obtained from the bark, used as a spice; *n.* and *a.* a light-brown color [Heb. *qinnamon*].

ci·pher, cy·pher (sī′·fẹr) *n.* the arithmetical symbol 0; any figure; a person of no account; a secret writing; a code; the key to a code; *v.i.* to write in cipher; to work at arithmetic [Fr. *chiffre*, a figure].

cir·ca (sur′·kạ) *prep.* about; around; approximately; (*abbrev.*) **ca.** or **c.** [L. *circa, circiter*].

cir·cle (sur′·kl) *n.* a plane figure bounded by a singel curved line called its circumference, every point of which is equally distant from a point within called the center; the curved line that bounds such a figure, a circumference; a round body; a sphere; an orb; a ring; the company associated with a person; a society group; club or group, esp. literary; a never-ending series; *v.t.* to move or revolve round; to encompass, as by a circle; to surround; *v.i.* to move in a circle [L. *circulus*].

cir·cuit (sur′·kit) *n.* the act of moving round; the space enclosed within a fixed limit; area; (*Law*) the round made by judges holding court; the district thus visited; the path of an electric current. **-eer** (sur·ki·tir′) one who moves in a circuit. **circuitous** (sur·kū′·i·tạs) *a.* indirect [L. *circuitus*, a going round].

cir·cu·lar (sur′·kyạ·lạr) *a.* in the form of a circle; round; moving in a circle; roundabout; addressed to a circle of people; *n.* a notice sent out in quantities. **-ly** *adv.* **circularity** *n.* **-ize** *v.t.* to send circulars to [L. *circularis*].

cir·cu·late (sur′·kyạ·lāt) *v.t.* to cause to pass round as in a circle; to spread abroad; *v.i.* to move around and return to the same point; to be spread abroad. **circulation** *n.* the act of moving around; the flow of blood from, and back to, the heart; the extent of sale of a newspaper, etc.; the money circulating in a country; currency. **circulative, circulatory** *a.* circulating. **circulator** *n.* [L. *circulare*].

cir·cum- (sur·kạm) *prefix* fr. Latin meaning *round, about*, combining to form many derivatives as in **-ambient** *a.* surrounding; enclosing. **-ambiency** *n.* environment. **-ambulate** *v.t.* and *i.* to walk around or about [L. *ambire*, to go round; *ambulare*, to walk].

cir·cum·cise (sur′·kạm·sīz) *v.t.* to cut off the foreskin. **circumcision** *n.* [L. *circum; caedere*, to cut].

cir·cum·fer·ence (sẹr·kum′·fẹr·ạns) *n.* the line that bounds a circle; the distance around; area. **circumferential** *a.* [L. *circum; ferre*, to carry].

cir·cum·flex (sur′·kạm·fleks) *n.* an accent mark placed over a vowel to denote length, contraction, etc. [L. *circum; flectere*, to bend].

cir·cum·flu·ent (sur·kạm′·flòò·ạnt) *a.* flowing round. **circumfluence** *n.* [L. *circum; fluere*, to flow].

cir·cum·ja·cent (sur·kạm·jā′·sạnt) *a.* bordering on every side [L. *circum*; *facere*, to lie].

cir·cum·lo·cu·tion (sur·kạm·lō·kū′·shạn) *n.* a roundabout manner of speaking. **circumlocutory** *a.* [L. *circum*; *locutos*, to speak].

cir·cum·nav·i·gate (sur·kạm·nav′·i·gāt) *v.t.* to sail around. **circumnavigable** *a.* capable of being sailed round. **circumnavigation** *n.* **circumnavigator** *n.* one who sails around, esp. the world [L. *circum; navigare*, to sail].

cir·cum·scribe (sur′·kạm·skrīb) *v.t.* to draw a circle around; to enclose within limits; to confine; to define. **circumscription** *n.* limitation. **circumscriptive** *a.* confined or limited in space [L. *circum; scribere*, to write].

cir·cum·spect (sur′·kạm·spekt) *a.* watchful on all sides; prudent; discreet. **-ly** *adv.* **circumspection** *n.* caution; prudence; discretion; tact. **-ive** *a.* [L. *circum*; *spicere*, to look].

cir·cum·stance (sur′·kạm·stans) *n.* a particular fact, event, or case; anything attending on, relative to, or affecting, a fact or event; accident; incident; particular; *v.t.* to place in a particular situation. **-s** *n.pl.* worldly estate; condition as to pecuniary resources; situation; position; details. **circumstantial** *a.* accidental; not essential; full of details; minute. **circumstantially** *adv.* **circumstantiality** *n.* minuteness of detail. **circumstantiate** *v.t.* to detail exactly [L. *circum*; *stare*, to stand].

cir·cum·vent (sur·kạm·vent′) *v.t.* to get around by stratagem; to outwit; to go around. **-ion** *n.* **-ive** *a.* [L. *circum*; *venire*, to come].

cir·cus (sur′·kạs) *n.* a travelling company of performers, animals, etc.; a circular enclosure for performances; the performance itself [L.].

cir·rho·sis (si·rō′·sis) *n.* (*Med.*) hardening and enlargement of the liver. **cirrhotic** *a.* [Gk. *kirrhos*, tawny].

cir·rus (sir′·ạs) *n.* a tendril; a curled filament; a lofty, fleecy cloud; *pl.* **cirri** (sir′·ī) (L. *cirrus*, a curl of hair].

cis·tern (sis′·tęrn) *n.* a large tank for holding water; a reservoir [L. *cisterna*].

cit·a·del (sit′·ą·del) *n.* a fortress or castle in or near a city [It. *cittadella*].

cite (sīt) *v.t.* to summon; to quote; to name; to bring forward as proof. **citation** *n.* an official notice to appear; the act of quoting; the passage or words quoted; the mention of gallantry in military orders. **citator** *n.* **citatory** *a.* [L. *citare*].

cith·a·ra (sith′·ą·rą) *n.* the ancient Greek lyre. **cithern, cittern** *n.* a kind of flat-backed guitar [Gk. *kithara*].

cit·i·zen (sit′·i·zn) *n.* an inhabitant of a city; a member of a state; *a.* having the character of a citizen. **-ry** *n.* citizens collectively. **-ship** *n.* the state of being a citizen; the rights and duties of a citizen [O.Fr. *citeain*].

cit·ron (sit′·rąn) *n.* the fruit of the citron tree, resembling a lemon; the tree itself; the preserved rind of the fruit; a yellow color. **citrate** *n.* a salt of citric acid. **citric** *a.* extracted from the citron lemon, etc. **citrus fruits,** citrons, lemons, oranges, etc. [L. *citrus*, a citron-tree].

cit·ron·el·la (sit·rą·nel′·ą) *n.* a sharp smelling oil to keep insects away [See **citron**].

cit·tern, cithern *See* **cithara.**

cit·y (sit′·i·) *n.* a large town; a corporate town; the business or shopping center of a town; *a.* pert. to a city [L. *civitas*, a city].

civ·et (siv′·it) *n.* a perfume, with a strong musk-like smell; the animal from which this perfume is obtained. Also, **— cat.** [Ar. *zabad*].

civ·ic (siv′·ik) *a.* pert. to a city or a citizen. **-s** *n.pl.* the study of civic affairs, municipal or national [L. *civis*, a citizen].

civ·il (siv′·il) *a.* pert. to city, state, or citizen; lay, as opposed to military, etc.; polite. **-ly** *adv.* **civilian** (są·vil′·yąn) *n.* one whose employment is non-military; *a.* pert. to civilian life (e.g. civilian dress). **civility** *n.* courtesy; politeness; *pl.* acts of politeness. **civil defense,** an organization to deal with civilians during air raids, etc. **civil engineer,** one who plans bridges, roads, dams, canals, etc. **civil service,** the government positions obtained by examination. **civil war,** war between citizens of the same country [L. *civis*, a citizen].

civ·i·lize (siv′·il·īz) *v.t.* to reclaim from a savage state; to refine; to enlighten. **-d** *a.* **civilization** *n.* the act of civilizing, or state of being civilized [L. *civilis*].

clack (klak) *v.i.* to make a sudden, sharp noise, as by striking; to talk rapidly and continually; to chatter; *n.* a sharp, repeated, rattling sound; continual talk [imit. origin].

clad (klad) *pa.p.* and *pa.t.* of **clothe;** a. clothed.

claim (klām) *v.t.* to demand as a right, or as due; to call for; to assert as true; *n.* the demand of a right or supposed right; a title; the thing claimed. **-ant** *n.* one who claims. **—jumper** *n.* one who seizes a piece of land marked out by a settler or miner [L. *clamare*, to shout].

clair·voy·ance (kler·voi′·ąns) *n.* the power of seeing things not normally perceptible to the senses; second sight. **clairvoyant** *n.* one who claims the power of clairvoyance. Also *a.* [Fr.].

clam (klam) *n.* an edible bivalve shell-fish; (*Colloq.*) a reticent person [O.E. *clam*, a bond].

cla·mant (klā′·mąnt) *a.* crying out; clamorous. **clamancy** *n.* [L. *clamare*, to cry out].

clam·ber (klam′·bęr) *v.i.* to climb with difficulty, holding on with the hands [cf. Ger. *klammern*, to cling to].

clam·my (kla′·mi·) *a.* sticky and moist; cold and damp. **clamminess** *n.* [O.E. *claeman*, to anoint].

clam·or (klam′·ęr) *n.* loud shouting; tumult; outcry; uproar; *v.i.* to shout loudly; to utter loud complaints or demands. **-ous** *a.* [L. *clamare*, to cry out].

clamp (klamp) *n.* any appliance with parts brought together by a screw for holding anything; a brace; *v.t.* to make firm [Dut. *klamp*].

clan (klan) *n.* a tribe bearing the same surname, united under a chieftain; a set or clique of persons having a common interest. **-nish** *a.* disposed to associate only with members of the same sect or clique. **-nishly** *adv.* **-nishness** *n.* [Gael. *clann*, children].

clan·des·tine (klan·des′·tin) *a.* secret, and contrary to law, morals, etc. **-ly** *adv.* **-ness** *n.* [L. *clandestinus*, fr. *clam*, secretly].

clang (klang) *v.t.* to strike with a ringing, metallic sound; *v.i.* to give forth a ringing, metallic sound; *n.* a sharp, ringing sound. **-ing** *n.* a clang [L. *clangere*].

clan·gor (klang′·ęr) *n.* a loud harsh, ringing sound. **-ous** *a.* **-ously** *adv.* [L. *clangere*].

clank (klangk) *n.* a brief, hard, metallic sound; *v.t.* and *i.* to produce such a sound [imit.].

clap (klap) *v.t.* to bring together with a sharp sound; to strike the hands together in approval; to slap; *v.i.* to strike the hands together in applause; *n.* a sudden, sharp noise caused by impact; applause; a slap or pat; *pr.p.* **-ping.** *pa.p.* and *pa.t.* **-ped. -per** *n.* one who claps; the tongue of a bell. **-board** *n.* thin board used to cover wooden houses. **-trap** *n.* in speech-making, tricks to win applause; *a.* cheap and showy [M.E. *clap*].

clar·et (klar′·it) *n.* any red Bordeaux wine; *a.* a purplish-red. [Fr. *clairet*, fr. *clair*, clear].

clar·i·fy (klar ·i·fī) *v.t.* to make clear or pure; to explain or clear up; to remove possibility of error; *v.i.* to become clear. **clarification** *n.* **clarity** *n.* clearness; lucidity of mind [L. *clarus*, clear; *facere*, to make].

clar·i·on (klar′·i·ąn) *n.* trumpet with shrill piercing note; its sound. **clarinet, clarionet** *n.* a wood wind instrument. **clarinettist** *n.* [Fr. *clairon*].

clash (klash) *v.t.* to strike noisily together; *v.i.* to dash noisily together; to collide; to conflict; to disagree; *n.* a loud noise; a conflict [imit.].

clasp (klasp) *v.t.* to shut or fasten together with a catch or hook; to embrace; to grasp; to surround and cling to; *n.* a catch or hook for fastening; a close embrace; a grasping of the hands [M.E. *clapse*, fr. *clyppan*, to embrace].

class (klas) *n.* an order or division or grouping of persons or things possessing the same characteristics or status; a group of pupils or students taught together; a grouping of plants or animals; rank or standing in society. *v.t.* to arrange in classes; to rank together; *v.i.* to rank. **-able, -ible** *a.* **-y** *a.* (*Colloq.*) high-class [L. *classis*].

clas·sic (klas′·ik) *n.* a work, writer of recognized worth; an ancient Latin or Greek writer or book; *a.* of model excellence in literature or art; conforming to standards of Greek and Roman art. **-s** *n.pl.* ancient Latin or Greek literature. **-al** *a.* **-ally** *adv.* **ality, -alness** *n.* the quality of being classical. **classicism** (klas′·i·sizm) *n.* classic principles in art and literature; classic style; a classical idiom. **classicist** *n.* [L. *classicus*, of the first rank].

clas·si·fy (klas′·i·fī) *v.t.* to arrange in classes; to put into a class. **classifiable** *a.* **classification** *n.* the act of classifying [L. *classis*, a class; *facere*, to make].

clat·ter (klat′·ęr) *v.t.* to strike and so make a rattling noise; *v.i.* to make rattling sounds; to prattle; to talk rapidly and idly; *n.* a repeated rattling noise; noisy and idle talk [fr. *clack*].

clause (klawz) *n.* (*Gram.*) a subordinate part of a sentence; (*Law*) an article or distinct portion of a document, contract, etc.; a paragraph; a subdivision [L. *claudere*, to shut].

claus·tral (klaws′·trąl) *a.* pert. to a cloister; cloister-like; secluded. **claustration** *n.* the state of being confined in a cloister [L. *claustrum*, a bar or bolt].

claus·tro·pho·bi·a (klaws·trą·fō′·bi·ą) *n.* (*Med.*) a morbid dread of confined spaces [L. *claustrum*, bolt, Gk. *phobia*, fear].

clav·i·chord (kla′·vi·kawrd) *n.* a medieval musical instrument like a spinet [L. *clavis*, a key; *chorda*, a string].
clav·i·cle (klav′·i·kl) *n.* the collarbone. **clavicular** *a.* [L. *clavicula*, dim. fr. *clavis*, a key].
cla·vi·er (kla′·vyẹr) *n.* (*Mus.*) a stringed musical instrument with a keyboard [L. *clavis*, a key].
claw (klaw) *n.* a sharp, hooked nail, as of a beast or bird; anything like this; *v.t.* to pull, tear, or scratch with claws or nails; to grasp [O.E. *clawu*].
clay (klā) *n.* soft earth, consisting of alumina and silica, with water used in making pottery, bricks, etc.; earth in general; the human body. **-ey** *a.* consisting of clay; like clay [O.E. *claeg*].
clean (klēn) *a.* free from dirt, stain, or any defilement; pure; guiltless; *v.t.* to free from dirt; to purify; *adv.* so as to leave no dirt; quite; entirely. **-er** *n.* one who, or that which, cleans. **-liness** (klen′·li·nes) *n.* freedom from dirt; purity. **-ly** (klen′·li) *a.* habitually clean in persons and habits; pure. **-ly** (klēn′·li·) *adv.* in a clean manner; neatly. **-ness** (klēn′·nes) *n.* **—cut** *a.* well-shaped; definite. [O.E. *claene*].
clear (klēr) *a.* bright; free from cloud; undimmed; pure; free from obstruction; plain; distinct; manifest; without defect or drawback; transparent; *adv.* clearly; wholly; *v.t.* to make bright or clear; to make evident; to free from accusation; to acquit; to pass over or through; to cleanse; to empty; to make as profit; to free by payment of dues; to settle a debt; to free from difficulty, obstruction, suspicion, etc.; *v.i.* to become clear, bright, transparent, free; (*Naut.*) to leave a port. **-age** *n.* clearance. **-ance** *n.* the act of clearing; a certificate that a ship has been cleared at the custom house; in machinery, distance by which one part is clear of another. **-ing** *n.* a tract of land cleared of wood. **-ing-house** *n.* an office maintained by several banks for balancing accounts, exchanging checks, etc. **-ly** *adv.* **-ness** *n.* **—cut** *a.* sharply defined. **—eyed, —seeing, —sighted** *a.* having acuteness of sight or intellect [L. *clarus*, clear].
clear·sto·ry See **clerestory.**
cleat (klēt) *n.* a wedge; (*Naut.*) a piece of wood or iron with two projecting ends, round which ropes are fastened; a piece of metal fastened to a shoe [O.E. *cleat*].
cleave (klēv) *v.t.* to split asunder; to cut in two; *v.i.* to fall apart; to split; to open; to crack asunder; *pa.p.* **cloven** or **cleft.** *pa.t.* **clove** or **cleft. cleavage** *n.* of rocks, the quality of splitting naturally; (*Fig.*) separation due to a difference of opinions, etc.; a rupture .**-r** *n.* one who, or that which, cleaves; a butcher's chopper [O.E. *cleofan*].
cleave (klēv) *v.i.* to adhere closely; to stick; to agree; to be faithful to [O.E. *clifian*].
clef (klef) *n.* (*Mus.*) a sign used to indicate the pitch [Fr., fr. L. *clavis*, a key].
cleft (kleft) *pa.p.* and *pa.t.* of the verb **cleave;** *n.* a fissure or split; a chasm; a chink [O. E. *cleofan*].
clem·a·tis (klem′·ạ·tis) *n.* a woody vine [Gk. *klēmatis*, fr. *klēima*, a twig].
clem·en·cy (klem′·en·si·) *n.* leniency; mildness; gentleness; mercy. **clement** *a.* mild; compassionate [L. *clemens*].
clench, clinch (klensh, klinsh) *v.t.* to grasp firmly; to close together tightly (the hands, the teeth); to confirm (a bargain); *n.* a firm closing; decisive proof; a firm grip. **-er** *n.* an unanswerable argument [O.E. *clencean*].
clere·sto·ry (klēr′·stō·ri·) *n.* the upper part of the central nave of churches, which rises clear of the other buildings and has its own row of windows [fr. *clear* and *story*].
cler·gy (klur′·ji·) *n.* the body of men ordained for religious service. **-man** *n.* a minister [Fr. *clergé* fr. L. *clericus*].
cler·ic (kler′·ik) *n.* a clerk or clergyman; *a.* clerical. **clerical** *a.* belonging to the clergy; pert. to a clerk or copyist [L. *clericus*].
clerk (klurk) *n.* one who is employed to do correspondence, keep accounts, etc. in an office; salesman or saleswoman; *v.i.* to act as a clerk or secretary. **-ship** *n.* [O.E. *clerc*, a priest].
clev·er (klev′·ẹr) *a.* able; skillful; ingenious; intelligent. **-ly** *adv.* **-ness** *n.*
clew, clue (klòò) *n.* a ball of thread or cord; (*Myth.*) a ball of thread used as a guide through a maze; hence, anything that serves to guide one in an involved affair or helps to solve a mystery; (*Naut.*) the lower corner of a sail [O.E. *cliven*].
cli·ché (klē·shā′) *n.* (*Print.*) an electrotype or stereotype plate; a stereotyped or hackneyed phrase [Fr.].
click (klik) *n.* a slight, short sound, as of a latch in a door; *v.i.* to make such a sound; (*Slang*) to be successful [imit. origin].
cli·ent (klī′·ạnt) *n.* one who employs another (esp. a lawyer) professionally as his agent; a customer. **clientele** (klī′·en·tel) *n.* clients or customers collectively [L. *cliens*, a follower].
cliff (klif) *n.* a high rock-face; the sheer side of a mountain [O.E. *clif*].
cli·mac·ter·ic (klī·mak′·tạ·rik) *n.* a period in human life in which a change takes place in the constitution; the menopause; any critical period; *a.* pert. to a climacteric; critical. **-al** *a.* [Gk. *klimakiēr*, rung of a ladder].
cli·mate (klī′·mit) *n.* the general atmospherical conditions (temperature, moisture, etc.) of a country or region. **climatic** *a.* **climatical** *a.* [Gk. *klima, klimatos*, slope].
cli·max (klī′·maks) *n.* an arrangement of words, phrases, etc. such that they rise in rhetorical force and impressiveness; acme; the point of greatest excitement or tension in a play, story, etc. **climactic** *a.* [Gk. = a ladder].
climb (klīm) *v.t.* and *i.* to go up, ascend (as a hill, tree, etc.); to grow upward as a plant by tendrils; to rise in the social scale; to slope upward; *n.* an ascent. **-er** *n.* [O.E. *climban*].
clime (klīm) *n.* a region or country; (*Poet.*) climate [Gk. *klima*, fr. *klinein*, to slope]
clinch (klinsh) *v.t.* and *i.* to grapple or struggle at close quarters in wrestling or boxing; to fasten with a rivet; (*Fig.*) to settle or conclude, as an agreement; *n.* a close holding in wrestling or boxing; a rivet. **-er** *n.* [fr. *clench*].
cling (kling) *v.i.* to adhere or stick close to; to be attached firmly to; *pa.p.* and *pa.t.* **clung** [O.E. *clingan*].
clin·ic (klin′·ik) *n.* the teaching of medical subjects at the bedside; an institution where non-resident patients attend for treatment. **-al** *a.* [Gk. *klinē*, a bed].
clink (klingk) *n.* a slight, sharp, tinkling sound; (*Slang*) prison [imit. origin].
clink·er (kling′·kẹr) *n.* a mass of slag or cinders from furnaces; a kind of brick [Dut.].
clink·er·built (kling′·kẹr·bilt) *a.* (*Naut.*) built with overlapping boards or plates (opp. of *carvel-built*) [fr. *clench*].
clip (klip) *v.t.* to grip tightly. *pr.p.* **-ping.** *pa.t.*, *pa.p.* **-ped.** *n.* any device for grasping or holding a thing firmly [O.E. *clyppan*, to embrace].
clip (klip) *v.t.* to cut with scissors or shears; to prune or cut short; to shear sheep; to pare the edge of a coin; to shorten or slur words; *v.i.* to move quickly; *n.* act of clipping; a season's shearing of wool; a rapid pace; (*Colloq.*) a sharp blow. *pr.p.* **-ping.** *pa.p.* and *pa.t.* **-ped. -per** *n.* one who clips; a fast sailing-vessel, with a long sharp bow; fast, long distance airliner. **-pers** *n.* a two-bladed instrument for cutting hair, shearing sheep, etc. **-ping** *n.* an item cut from a newspaper, etc. [Scand.].
clique (klik) *n.* a narrow circle of persons with common interests; a coterie. **cliquish** *a.* **cliquishness** *n.* [Fr.].
cloak (klōk) *n.* a long, loose, outer garment;

something that conceals; a pretext; *v.t.* to cover with a cloak; to hide; to mask or dissemble. **-room** *n.* a room where coats, hats, etc. may be temporarily left [O.Fr. *cloque*].

clob·ber (klȧb′·ęr) *v.t.* (*Slang*) to beat decisively.

cloche (klōsh) *n.* glass covering used for intensive cultivation of vegetables, etc.; a close-fitting bell-shaped hat [Fr. = a bell].

clock (klȧk) *n.* a device which measures time. **-wise** *adv.* in the direction of the hands of a clock. **counterclockwise** *adv.* circling in the opposite direction. **-work** *n.* the movements or machinery of a clock; regular movement as of clock; *a.* mechanically regular. **o'clock,** by the clock [Fr. *cloche,* a bell].

clock (klȧk) *n.* an ornament worked on a stocking on each side of the ankle.

clod (klȧd) *n.* a lump of earth clay, or turf; the earth; a dull, stupid fellow. **-hopper** *n.* a rustic; a boor; a clumsy, heavy shoe [O.E. fr. *clot*].

clog (klȧg) *n.* a strong, clumsy shoe with a thick wooden sole; an impediment; an obstruction; *v.t.* to hinder; to encumber; to choke up; *v.i.* to become choked, encumbered. *pr.p.* **-ging.** *pa.p. pa.t.* **-ged** [M.E. *clogge,* a block of wood].

clois·ter (klois′·tęr) *n.* covered arcade running along one or more walls of the inner court of a monastery or college; a monastery or nunnery; a secluded spot; *v.t.* to confine. **-al, cloistral** *a.* **-ed** *a.* [L. *claustrum,* enclosed place].

close (klōz) *v.t.* to shut; to stop up; to finish; to conclude; to complete (a wireless circuit); *v.i.* to come together; to unite; to end. **closing** *a.* ending; *n.* the act of shutting; the end; the conclusion. **closure** (klō′·zhęr) *n.* the act of shutting; a closing; the close of a debate. [L. *claudere,* to shut].

close (klōs) *a.* shut up; confined; tight; stifling; near at hand; secret; niggardly; familiar; intimate; compact; crowded; searching; *adv.* in a close manner or state; nearly; tightly; *n.* an enclosed place; the precinct of a cathedral; (*Mus.*) a cadence. **-ly** *adv.* **-ness** *n.* **— by,** near. **— call,** a very narrow escape. **—fisted** or **—handed** *a.* miserly, penurious. **—mouthed** *a.* uncommunicative. **— quarters** *n.pl.* a crowded space. **a close shave,** a very narrow escape. **—up** *n.* a close view of anything [L. *claudere,* to shut].

clos·et (klȧz′·it) *n.* a small room or recess for storing things; a small private room; a lavatory; a water closet; *v.t.* to take into a private room for consultation [L. *claudere,* to shut].

clot (klȧt) *n.* a mass or lump, esp. of a soft, slimy character; (*Med.*) a coagulated mass of blood; *v.t.* to form into clots; *v.i.* to coagulate. *pr. p.* **-ting.** *pa.p.* and *pa.t.* **-ted** [O.E. *clod*].

cloth (klawth) *n.* any woven fabric of wool, hair, silk, cotton, flax, or oher fibers; a cover for a table. *pl.* **cloths** (klawTHz). **the Cloth** (*Fig.*) clergymen [O.E. *clath*].

clothe (klōTH) *v.t.* to put garments on; to cover as with a garment; to furnish raiment; (*Fig.*) to surround with; to wrap up in. *pr.p.* **clothing.** *pa.p.* and *pa.t.* **-d** or **clad. -s** *n. pl.* garments; wearing apparel; short for bedclothes, i.e. sheets, blankets, etc. **clothier** (klōTH′·yęr) *n.* one who makes, or sells, clothes; a tailor; an outfitter. **clothing** *n.* garments in general; dress; wearing-apparel; raiment. **clotheshorse** *n.* a frame for hanging clothes; one who like clothes [O.E. *clath*].

clo·ture (klō′·chęr) *n.* closure, applied to parliamentary debate [L. *clasura,* closure].

cloud (kloud) *n.* a body of visible vapor floating in the atmosphere; a mass of smoke, flying dust, etc.; that which has a dark, threatening aspect; a state of obscurity or impending trouble; a great multitude; *v.t.* to overspread with clouds; to darken; to sadden; to defame; v.i. to grow cloudy; to be blurred. **-y** *a.* darkened with clouds; overcast; hazy; dim; blurred; indistinct; gloomy. **-ily** *adv.* **-iness** *n.* **-burst** *n.* a violent downpour of rain; a deluge [O.E. *clud*].

clout (klout) *n.* the center of the target at which archers shoot; (*Colloq.*) a slap or blow; a piece of old cloth used for cleaning, scouring, etc.; *v.t.* (*Colloq.*) to strike with the open hand [O.E. *clut*].

clove (klōv) *n.* the flower-bud of the clove-tree, used as a spice; also yields oil [Fr. *clou,* a nail, fr. L. *clavus*].

clove (klōv) *pa.t.* of **cleave.**

clove hitch (klōv′·hich) *n.* (*Naut.*) a hitch used to secure a rope around a spar.

clo·ven (klōv′·n) *pa.p.* of **cleave.** Also *a.* split; divided into two parts [fr. *cleave*].

clo·ver (klō·vęr) *n.* a common field plant of the trefoil family, used for fodder. **-leaf** *n.* a highway intersection in the shape of a four-leaf clover [O.E. *clafre*].

clown (kloun) *n.* the fool or buffoon in a play or circus; a peasant or rustic; an ill-bred man; a boor; *v.i.* to play the fool; to behave like a fool. **-ishly** *adv.* **-ishness** *n.*

cloy (kloi) *v.t.* to induce a sensation of loathing by overmuch of anything, esp. of sweetness, sentimentality, or flattery; to satiate. **-ing** *a.* satiating; disgusting [Fr. *clouer,* to nail].

club (klub) *n.* a heavy stick, thickening towards one end, used as a weapon; a cudgel; a stick used in the game of golf; an association of people united in pursuance of a common interest; the premises in which such an association meets; *v.t.* to beat with a club; to gather into a club; *v.i.* to form a club; to unite for a common end; to pay shares in a common expense. *pr.p.* **-bing.** *pa.p.* and *pa.t.* **-bed. -foot** *n.* a congenitally deformed or crooked foot; talipes [O.N. *klubba*].

clump (klump) *n.* a shapeless mass of any substance; a cluster of trees or shrubs; a heavy extra sole on a shoe; a tramping sound; *v.t.* to put in a clump or group; *v.i.* to tramp heavily [Dut. *klomp*].

clum·sy (klum′·zi·) *a.* ill-made; awkward; ungainly. **clumsily** *adv.* **clumsiness** *n.* [M.E. *clumsen,* to benumb].

clung (klung) *pa.p.* and *pa.t.* of **cling.**

clus·ter (klus′·tęr) *n.* a bunch; a number of things growing together, as grapes; a collection; *v.t.* to collect into a bunch; *v.i.* to grow, or be, in clusters [O.E. *clyster*].

clutch (kluch) *v.t.* and *i.* to seize or grip with the hand; to grasp; *n.* a grasp; a tight grip; a set of eggs hatched at one time; a brood of chicks; the coupling of two working parts, used in motor vehicles to connect or disconnect engine and transmission gear. **-es** *n.pl.* the claws; the hands; power [O.E. *clyccan*].

clut·ter (klut′·ęr) *n.* crowded confusion; disorder; noise; *v.t.* to crowd together in disorder; to make untidy [origin uncertain].

co- (kō) *prefix* meaning together, joint, etc. [fr. L. *cum,* with].

coach (kōch) *n.* a railroad passenger car; a tutor who prepares students for examination; a trainer in athletics; *v.i.* to travel in a coach; *v.t.* to tutor or train [Fr. *coche,* a coach].

co·ac·tion (kō·ak′·shąn) *n.* compulsion [L. *cogere, coactum,* to compel].

co·ad·ju·tant (kō·aj′·oo·tąnt) *a.* assisting; *n.* an assistant. **coadjutor** (·tąr) *n.* an assistant; an associate and destined successor [L. *co-,* together; *adjuvare,* to help].

co·ag·u·late (kō·ag′·yą·lāt) *v.t.* to cause to curdle or congeal; to solidify; *v.i.* to curdle; to clot. **coagulant** *n.* a substance that causes coagulation. **coagulation** *n.* **coagulative** *a.* [L. *co-,* together; *agere,* to drive].

coal (kōl) *n.* a black substance used for fuel, composed of mineralized vegetable matter; a piece of this substance; *v.t.* to supply with coal; *v.i.* to take in coal. **-s** *n.pl.* glowing embers. **— bin** *n.* a recess for storing coal. **— field** *n.* a district where coal abounds. **— gas** *n.* gases produced from the distillation of coal or from burning coal. — **mine,** — **pit** *n.* the excavation from which coal is dug. — **oil** *n.* kerosene. — **tar** *n.* a thick, sticky substance, produced during the distilling of coal [O.E. *col*].

co·a·lesce (kō·ạ·les′) *v.t.* to grow together; to unite into one body or mass; to fuse. **coalescent** *a.* coalescing. **coalescence** *n.* [L. *co-*, together; *alescere*, to grow up].

co·a·li·tion (kō·ạ·lish′·ạn) *n.* a union or combination of persons, parties, or states into one body; a league. **-ist** *n.* [L. *co-*, together; *alescere*, to grow up].

coarse (kōrs) *a.* rough, rude; not refined; without grace or elegance; ill-mannered; vulgar; inferior. **-ly** *adv.* **-n** *v.t.* and *i.* to make or become coarse. **-ness** *n.* [M.E. *cors; Fr. gros*].

coast (kōst) *n.* land bordering the sea; the seashore; the country near the shore; *v.t.* and *i.* to sail near or along the coast; to run shut off, or on a bicycle without pedaling; to toboggan. **-al** *a.* pert. to the coast. **-er** *n.* a vessel trading between towns along the coast; a small tray placed under glasses to protect a table. **-guard** *n.* a service organized orig. to prevent smuggling; since 1925, largely a life-saving service; a member of this service. **-line** *n.* the outline of a coast. **-wards** *adv.* toward the coast. **-wise** *adv.* along the coast [L. *costa*, a rib].

coat (kōt) *n.* an outer garment; a jacket; an overcoat; the fur or skin of an animal; a covering; a layer spread over another, as paint; *v.t.* to cover with a coat; to clothe. **-ed** *a.* **-ing** *n.* any covering; a layer; cloth for making coats [Fr. *cotte*, an overall].

coax (kōks) *v.t.* to win over by fond pleading or flattery. **-ingly** *adv.* [etym. uncertain].

co-ax·i·al (kō·ak′·si·ạl) *a.* having a common axis [fr. *axis*].

cob (kob) *n.* a corn-cob; a male swan.

co·balt (kō′·bawlt) *n.* a metallic element classified with iron and nickel, and used as an ingredient of many alloys. — **blue** *n.* a pigment containing an oxide of cobalt; *a.* a dark-blue color. **-ic** *a.* [Ger. *Kobalt*].

co·balt bomb *n.* a type of atomic bomb equal in power to the hydrogen bomb and with more lethal and lasting effects.

cob·ble (kȧb′·l) *v.t.* to mend or patch coarsely; to mend boots or shoes. **-r** *n.* a mender of shoes; a deep-dish fruit pie with a biscuit crust.

cob·ble (kȧb′·l) *n.* a stone rounded by the action of water; *v.t.* to pave with cobbles. **-stone** *n.* a rounded stone used in paving.

co·bra (kō′·brạ) *n.* the venomous 'hooded' snake of Africa and India. **cobric** *a.* [L. *colubra*, a snake].

cob·web (kȧb′·web) *n.* a spider's web; anything flimsy, transparent, and fragile; a trap or entanglement [O.E. *coppe*, a spider].

co·ca (kō′·kạ) *n.* a Peruvian plant or its dried leaf, which is a nerve stimulant. **cocaine** (kō·kān′) *n.* a drug made from coca leaves, used as a local anesthetic [Native].

coc·cyx (kȧk′·siks) *n.* the triangular bone ending spinal column. *pl.* **coccyges** (kȧk′·si·jēz). **coccygeal** *a.* [Gk. *kokkux*, cuckoo].

coch·i·neal (kȧk′·i·nēl) *n.* a scarlet dye-stuff, made from the dried bodies of insects [L. *coccineus*, scarlet].

coch·le·a (kȧk′·li·a) *n.* a spiral passage of the inner ear [Gk. *kochlias*, a snail from the shape of its shell].

cock (kȧk) *n.* the male of birds, esp. of the domestic fowl; a weather-cock; a tap to regulate the flow of fluids; the hammer of a firearm; the cocked position of a hammer (of a firearm); a chief or leader; *v.t.* to draw back the hammer of a gun; to set up, set erect, set at an angle, as a hat; *v.i.* (*Dial.*) to swagger. **-crow** *n.* early morning. **-erel** *n.* a young cock; a swaggering youth. **-eyed** *a.* squinting; (*Slang*) on a slant; foolish. **-scomb** *n.* the comb of a cock; a flowering plant. **-sure** *a.* quite sure. **-tail** *n.* a horse not of pure breed; a drink concocted of liquor, bitters, sugar, etc; a mixture of fruit, or of seafood, served as an appetizer. **-y** *a.* vain and confident; full of self-assurance. **-ily** *adv.* **-iness** *n.* [O.E. *coc*].

cock (kȧk) *n.* a pile of hay [O.E. *coc*].

cock·ade (kȧ·kād′) *n.* a knot of ribbons, a rosette or badge, often worn on the hat [Fr. *cocarde*, fr. *coq*, a cock].

cock·a·too (kȧk·ạ·to̍o̍′) *n.* a kind of parrot with a crested head [Malay].

cock·a·trice (kȧk′·ạ·tris) *n.* a fabulous animal represented as a cock with a dragon's tail; a fabulous serpent imagined to possess the powers of the basilisk, whose glance deals death [O.Fr. *cocatrice*].

cock·er (kȧk′·ẹr) *n.* a cocker spaniel, a small variety of spaniel, used for retrieving game.

cock·le (kȧk′·l) *n.* a weed that grows among corn; the corn rose [O.E. *coccel*].

cock·le (kȧk′·l) *n.* a bivalve shell-fish, with a thick ribbed shell; *v.t.* to cause to pucker; to wrinkle. **-shell** *n.* the shell of a cockle; a shallow boat [Fr. *coquille*].

Cock·ney (kȧk′·ni·) *n.* a native of London. **-dom** *n.* the home of cockneys. **-fied** *a.* like a cockney.

cock·pit (kȧk′·pit) *n.* in aircraft, a compartment in the fuselage for the pilot and controls; the pit or ring in which game cocks fought, hence any arena of frequent strife.

cock·roach (kȧk′·rōch) *n.* a black or brown beetle infesting houses [Sp. *cucaracha*].

cock·swain See **coxswain.**

co·co, co·coa (kō′·kō) *n.* a palm tree producing the coconut. **-nut,** the fruit of the coco palm [Sp. and Pot. *coco*, a bugbear].

co·coa (kō′·kō) *n.* a powder made from the kernels of the cacao or chocolate plant; a beverage from this [corrupt. fr. *cacao*].

co·coon (kạ·ko̍o̍n′) *n.* the silky envelope which the silkworm and other larvae spin for themselves before passing into the pupa stage [O.Fr. *coque*, a shell].

cod, cod·fish (kȧd, kȧd′·fish) *n.* a large fish from northern seas, much used as food.

co·da (kō′·dạ) *n.* (*Mus.*) a short passage added at the end of a composition to round it off [It. fr. L. *cauda*, a tail].

cod·dle (kȧd′·l) *v.t.* to boil gently; to pamper or spoil [etym. uncertain].

code (kōd) *n.* an orderly collection of laws; a system of words, symbols, or numbers adopted for secrecy or economy; a cipher; *v.t.* to put into the form of a code. **codify** (kȧ′·di·fī) *v.t.* to collect laws, etc. into a digest. **codification** *n.* act of collecting laws. [L. *codex*, a book].

co·dex (kō′·deks) *n.* an ancient manuscript of a book, esp. of the Bible; a collection of manuscripts; *pl.* **codices** [L. *codex*, a book].

codg·er (kȧj′·ẹr) *n.* (*Colloq.*) an eccentric.

cod·i·cil (kȧd′·ạ·sil) *n.* a supplement or appendix to a will [L. *codicillus*, dim. of *codex*, a book].

co·ed·u·ca·tion (kō·ed·ū·kā′·shạn) *n.* the education of boys and girls together in mixed classes. **-al** *a.* **co-ed** *n.* (*Colloq.*) a female student at a coeducational college or university.

co·ef·fi·cient (kō·ạ·fish′·ạnt) *a.* cooperating; combining; *n.* that which unites with something else to produce a result; (*Math.*) a number or other factor placed before another as a multiplier; (*Phys.*) a constant number or factor measuring some specified property of a substance. **coefficiency** *n.*

co·e·qual (kō·ē′·kwal) *a.* equal; of the same rank or power as another; *n.* a person having equality with another.

co·erce (kō·urs′) *v.t.* to compel by force; to constrain; to restrain. **coercible** *a.* **coercive** *a.* having power to compel. **coercively** *adv.* **coercion** (kō·ur′·shạn) *n.* coercing; state of being coerced; compulsory force; restraint [L. *coercere*].

co·e·val (kō·ē′·val) *a.* of same age; *n.* contemporary [L *co-*, together; *aevum*, age].
co·ex·ist (kō·ig·zist′) *v.i.* to exist at the same time or together. **-ence** *n.* **-ent** *a.*
cof·fee (kawf′·i·) *n.* an evergreen shrub, valuable for its berries; the seeds of the berries, esp. when ground and roasted; a drink from this. **-bean** *n.* the seed of the berry. **-house** *n.* a restaurant where coffee and other refreshments are supplied [Ar. *qahwah*].
cof·fer (kawf′·ęr, kȧf′·ęr) *n.* a chest for valuables; a large money-box; an ornamental panel in a ceiling or archway; *v.t.* to put in a coffer; to hoard (money, etc.). **-dam** *n.* in engineering, a watertight, box-like, iron structure, used in the construction of the underwater foundations of bridges, etc. [Fr. *coffre*, a box].
cof·fin (kawf′·in) *n.* a box or casket in which the dead are enclosed before burial; *v.t.* to place in a coffin [Gk. *kophinos*, a basket].
cog (kȧg) *n.* one of a series of teeth on a wheel; *v.t.* to fit a wheel with cogs. *pr.p.* **-ging.** *pa.p.* and *pa.t.* **-ged** [M.E. *cogge*].
co·gent (kō′·jant) *a.* having great force; powerful; convincing. **-ly** *adv.* **cogence, cogency** *n.* force; convincing power [L. *cogere*, to force].
cog·i·tate (kȧj′·i·tāt) *v.i.* to reflect deeply; to meditate. **cogitable** *a.* **cogitation** *n.* contemplation. **cogitative** *a.* [L. *cogitare*].
co·gnac (kōn′·yak) *n.* a French brandy, so called from the town of *Cognac* in S.W. France; brandy in general.
cog·nate (kȧg′·nāt) *a.* allied by blood or birth; of the same stock; from the same origin, formation, etc.; *n.* a relative by birth; anything of the same origin, kind, nature, or effect [L. *cognatus*, born together].
cog·ni·zance (kȧg·na·zans) *n.* knowledge; perception. **cognizable** *a.* capable of being perceived or known. **cognizably** *adv.* **cognizant** *a.* having cognizance or knowledge of; competent to take judicial notice [L. *cognoscere*, to know].
cog·ni·tion (kȧg·ni·shan) *n.* awareness; state of being able to perceive objects or to remember ideas. **cognitive** *a.* [L. *cogniscere*, to know].
cog·no·men (kȧg·nō′·men) *n.* a surname; a nickname [L. *nomen*, a name].
co·ha·bit (kō·hab′·it) *v.i.* to live together as husband and wife (usually of unmarried persons). **-ation, -ant** *n.*
co·here (kō·hir′) *v.i.* to stick together; to be connected; to follow regularly in natural order; to be consistent; to coalesce; to adhere. **-nce, -ncy** *n.* **-nt** *a.* sticking together; connected; consistent. **-ntly** *adv.* **cohesible** *a.* capable of cohesion. **cohesion** *n.* the act of sticking together. **cohesive** *a.* having the power of cohering. **cohesiveness, cohesibility** *n.* [L. *cohaerere*, to stick together].
co·hort (kō′·hawrt) *n.* a division of a Roman legion, from 300 to 600 soldiers; a company of persons; an associate [L. *cohors*].
coif (koif) *n.* a headdress in the form of a close-fitting cap, worn by nuns. **-feur** (kwȧ·-fur′) (*fem.* **coiffeuse**) *n.* a hairdresser. **coiffure** (kwȧ·fyoor′) *n.* a headdress; a style of dressing the hair [Fr. *coiffe*].
coign (koin) *n.* a corner; a corner-stone; a wedge [same as *coin*, fr. L. *cuneus*, a wedge].
coil (koil) *v.t.* to wind in rings, as a rope; to twist into a spiral shape; *v.i.* to take on a spiral shape; *n.* the spiral of rings into which anything is wound; one of the rings of the spiral [L. *colligere*, to gather].
coil (koil) *n.* turmoil; tumult; fuss.
coin (koin) *n.* a piece of stamped metal issued by government authority to be used as money; money; a wedge or cornerstone; *v.t.* to make into money; to mint; or invent or fabricate, as a word or phrase. **-age** *n.* the act of coining; money coined; currency. **-er** *n.* one who makes coins; an inventor [L. *cuneus*, a wedge].
co·in·cide (kō-in-sīd′) *v.i.* to correspond in detail; to happen at the same time; to agree (in opinion). **coincidence** (kō·in′·si·dęns) *n.* correspondence in nature, circumstances, etc. **coincident, coincidental** *a.* occupying the same space; agreeing; simultaneous. **coincidently** *adv.* [L. *co-*, together; *incidere*, to happen].
coir (koir) *n.* the fiber from the husk of the coconut, used for cordage, matting, etc. [Malay, *kayar*, cord].
co·i·tion (kō′·i·shan) *n.* sexual intercourse; copulation. Also **coitus** (kō·i·tas) [L. *co-*, together; *ire, itum*, to go].
coke (kōk) *n.* coal half burnt, and used as fuel; *v.t.* to turn into coke [origin uncertain].
col·an·der (kȧl′·an·dęr) *n.* a vessel with a perforated bottom, used for draining off liquids in cookery; a sieve. Also **cullender** [L. *colare*, to strain].
cold (kōld) *a.* wanting in heat; chill; deficient in the emotions; spiritless; *n.* absence of warmth; chilliness; cold weather; a disorder of the nose, throat and chest, often caused by cold, and characterized by running at the nose, hoarseness and coughing; catarrh. **-ly** *adv.* **-ish** *a.* somewhat cold. **-ness** *n.* **—blooded** *a.* having cold blood, like fish; susceptible to cold; callous or heartless. Also **—hearted** (hårt′·ad). **— war,** campaign carried on by means of economic pressure, press, radio, etc. [O.E. *ceald*].
cole (kōl) *n.* a name for plants of the cabbage family. **—slaw** *n.* a salad of finely sliced or chopped cabbage. **-wort** *n.* any kind of cabbage whose leaves do not form a compact head [L. *caulis*, a stalk, esp. a cabbage stalk].
Co·le·op·ter·a (kōl·i·ȧp′·tęr·a) *n.pl.* the order of insects, such as beetles, whose outer wings form a horny sheath or covering for the true wings [Gk. *koleos*, a sheath; *pteron*, a wing].
col·ic (kȧl′·ik) *n.* severe paroxysmal pain in the abdomen [Gk. *kolon*, the lower intestine].
co·li·se·um (kȧ·la·sē′·am) *n.* a stadium, amphitheater, or large auditorium [M.L. *colosseum*].
col·lab·o·rate (ka·lab′·a·rāt) *v.i.* to work or labor together; to act jointly, esp. in works of literature, art, science. **collaboration** *n.* joint labor; (*World War* 2) willing cooperation with the enemy given by an inhabitant of an occupied country. **collaborator** *n.* [L. *co-*, *laborare*, to work].
col·lapse (ka·laps′) *v.i.* to fall in; to break down; to fail suddenly; to lose strength; to give way under physical or mental strain; *v.t.* to cause to collapse (as of a lung); *n.* a falling in or down; a sudden and complete failure; a breakdown. **collapsable, collapsible** *a.* [L. *collabi, collapsus*, to fall to pieces].
col·lar (kȧl′·ęr) *n.* something worn around the neck; the part of a garment that fits around the neck; *v.t.* to seize by the collar; to arrest; to capture; to grab; to put a collar on. **-bone** *n.* the bone from the shoulders to the breast-bone; the clavicle [L. *collum*, the neck].
col·late (kȧ·lāt′) *v.t.* to compare critically; to arrange in order, as the sheets of a book for binding; to appoint to a benefice. **collation** *n.* the act of collating; a lunch or repast. **collative** *a.* **collator** *n.* [L. *conferre, collatum*, to bring together].
col·lat·e·ral (kal·at′·a·ral) *a.* side by side; running parallel; subordinately connected; descended from the same ancestor but through a different line; additional (of a security); *n.* a collateral relative; a kinsman; additional security. **-ly** *adv.* **-ness** [L. *con; latus*, the side].
col·league (kȧl′·ēg) *n.* as associate or companion [L. *collega*, an associate].
col·lect (ka·lekt′) *v.t.* to bring together; to gather; to assemble; to receive payment of; *v.i.* to be assembled; to come together. **collect**

(kål′.ekt) *n.* a very short prayer. **-able, -ible** *a.* **-ed** *a.* not disconcerted; cool; self-possessed. **-edly** *adv.* **-edness** *n.* **collection** *n.* the act of collecting; a contribution or sum of money gather at a meeting for a religious, charitable, etc. object; assemblage. **-ive** *a.* formed by gathering; gathered into a mass, sum, or body; expressing a collection or aggregate. **-ively** *adv.* **-ivism** *n.* a term embracing all systems on the Socialistic doctrine of the state, municipal, cooperative, etc. control of the economic life of the country. **-ivist** *n.* **-or** *n.* one who collects; an officer appointed to receive taxes, customs, duties, tolls, etc. [L. *colligere, collectum,* to gather together].

col·leen (kål′.ēn) *n.* a girl [Ir. *cailin*].

col·lege (kål′.ij) *n.* an institution for higher education; the buildings, etc. of such an institution; an association of professional men, e.g. of physicians; an assembly, as of electors or cardinals. **collegial** *a.* pert. to a college. **collegian** (kạ.lē′.ji.ạn) *n.* a member of a college; a student. **collegiate** *a.* pert. to, or instituted like, a college; corporate [L. *collegium,* a society].

col·let (kål′.it) *n.* a collar; a neckband; the rim in which the stone of a ring is set [Fr. fr. L. *collum,* the neck].

col·lide (kạ.līd′) *v.i.* to strike or dash together; to clash; to come into conflict. **collision** *n.* (kạ.lizh′.ạn) *n.* the act of striking together; a violent impact; a clash; conflict [L. *collidere,* to dash together].

col·lie (kål′.i.) *n.* a breed of sheep dog.

col·lier·y (kål′.yạ.ri.) *n.* a coal mine [fr. coal]

col·lin·e·ar (kạ.lin′.i.ẹr) *a.* in the same straight line; aligned [L. *collineare*].

col·lo·cate (kål′.ō.kāt) *v.t.* to set or place together; to arrange. **collocation** *n.* [L. *collocare,* to place together].

col·lo·di·on (kạ.lō′.di.ạn) *n.* a solution of guncotton in ether, used in preparing photographic plates and in surgery [Gk. *kollla,* glue; *eidos,* form].

col·loid (kål′.oid) *a.* like glue; gelatinous; *n.* a glue-like, non-crystalline substance unable to pass through animal membranes. **-al** *a.* like a colloid [Gk. *kolla,* glue; *eidos,* form].

col·lo·quy (kål′.ạ.kwi.) *n.* conversation; dialogue; discussion; a conference, esp. political; a debate. **colloquial** (kạ.lō′.kwi.ạl) *a.* pert. to, or used in, ordinary conversation. **colloquially** *adv.* **colloquialism** *n.* an expression used in cordinary conversation, but not regarded as slang [L. *colloqui,* to speak together].

col·lu·sion (kạ.lòò′.zhạn) *n.* a secret agreement between two or more persons for a fraudulent purpose, usually in connection with legal proceedings. **collusive** *a.* [L. *colludere, collusum,* to play together].

co·logne (kạ.lōn′) *n.* a perfumed toilet water.

co·lon (kō′.lạn) *n.* a punctuation mark (:), separating parts of a sentence that are almost independent and complete in themselves; (*Anat.*) that part of the large intestine extending from the caecum to the rectum. **colonic** *a.* [Gk. *kolon,* a limb or member].

colo·nel (kur′.nạl) *n.* the officer ranking between lieutenant colonel and a brigadier general, usually commanding a regiment. **-cy, -ship** *n.* the rank or quality of colonel [L. *columna,* a column. The pronunciation is due to a Sp. form *coronel,* one also used].

col·on·nade (kål.ạ.nād′) *n.* a series of colums arranged symmetrically [L. *columna,* a column].

col·o·ny (kål′.ạn.i.) *n.* a body of people who settle in a new country but remain subject to the parent state; the country thus occupied; a group of people living in a community for a common purpose; a group of animals or plants living and growing together. **colonial** *a.* pert. to a colony; *n.* a colonist. **colonize** *v.t.* to plant or establish a colony; *v.i.* to settle. **colonist** *n.* **colonization** *n.* [L. *colonia*].

col·o·phon (kål′.ạ.fån) *n.* individual device or inscription used by publishers and printers on the title pages of books, etc. [Gk. *colophon,* the finish].

col·or (kul′.ẹr) *n.* any hue or tint as distinguished from white; paint; complexion; a flush; outward appearance; kind or general character; vividness in writing; (*Mus.*) variety of timbre; *v.t.* to paint or tinge with color; *v.i.* to blush. **-s** *n.pl.* a flag or standard; a colored badge, device, rosette, etc. used as a distinguishing mark. **-able** *a.* capable of being colored; specious; plausible. **-ably** *adv.* **-ed** *a.* having color; biased; (*usu. offensive*) of non-white origin. **-ful** *a.* having plenty of color. **—blind** *a.* unable to distinguish colors. **— line** *n.* discrimination in social, political, and economic status based on skin pigmentation [L. *color,* color].

col·or·a·tion (kul.ạ.rā′.shạn) *n.* coloring; arrangement or disposition of colors in art [L. *color,* color].

col·or·a·tu·ra [kål.ạr.ạ.tū′.rạ) *n.* (*Mus.*) ornamental runs and trills in vocal music [It.].

co·los·sus (kạ.lås′.us) *n.* a gigantic statue, esp. that of Apollo at Rhodes; hence any person of great stature or enormous strength. **colossal** *a.* of enormous size [Gk. *kolossos*].

colt (kōlt) *n.* young horse, esp. a male [O.E.].

Colt (kōlt) *n.* a repeating rifle; also a revolver [invented by Samuel *Colt*].

col·ter (kōl′.tẹr) *n.* the sharp blade of iron placed at the front end of a plow to act as a cutter. Also **coulter** [O.E. *culter*].

col·um·bine (kål′.ạm.bīn) *a.* of, or like, a dove; dove-colored; *n.* a small bell-shaped flower, with five spurred petals [L. *columba,* a dove].

col·umn (kål′.ạm) *n.* a round pillar; a support; a body of troops drawn up in deep files; a division of a page; a perpendicular line of figures. **-ar** (kạ.lum′.nẹr) *a.* formed in columns; having the form of columns. **-ated, -ed** *a.* furnished with, or supported on, columns. **-ist** *n.* a writer who contributes articles to a newspaper. **fifth —** *n.* group of people residing in a country who are in sympathy with and assist its enemies [L. *columna*].

co·ma (kō′.mạ) *n.* (*Med.*) a deep sleep or stupor generally resulting from injury to the brain or alcoholic or narcotic poisoning; (*Fig.*) lethargy; drowsiness. **-tose** *a.* lethargic; drowsy [Gk. *koma*].

comb (kōm) *n.* a toothed instrument for separating, cleansing, adjusting, or fastening hair, dressing wool, etc.; a decoration for a lady's hair; a cock's crest; the crest of a wave; the cell structure in which bees store their honey; *v.t.* to separate, cleanse, dress, etc. with a comb; *v.i.* to roll over or break with a white foam (said of waves). **-er** *n.* one who, or that which, combs; a long, curling wave. **-ing** *n.* **-ings** *n.pl.* hair, wool, etc. removed by combing [O.E. *camb*].

com·bat (kạm.bat′) *v.t.* to fight against; to oppose by force; to contend with; *v.i.* to struggle; to contend; (kåm′.bat) *n.* a fight; a struggle; a contest. **-ant** *a.* contending; disposed to contend; *n.* one engaged in a fight. **-ive** *a.* disposed to combat; quarrelsome [Fr. *combattre,* to fight].

com·bine (kạm.bīn′) *v.t.* to join together; to unite; to connect; *v.i.* to form a union; to cooperate; (*Chem.*) to unite and form a new compound; (kåm′.bīn) *n.* an association formed to further political or commercial interests; a trust; a syndicate; a harvester; an agricultural machine that reaps, threshes, and bags the grain in one operation. **combinable** *a.* capable of combining. **combinative, combinatory** *a.* tending to combine. **combination** (kåm.bạ.nā′.shạn) *n.* union or connection; association of persons; alliance; chemical union; series of letters or numbers for operating a lock; an undergarment combining vest and pants. [L.L. *combinare*].

com·bus·tion (kąm·bus′·chąn) *n.* the act of fire on inflammable substances; the act of burning; chemical action accompanied by heat and light. **combustible** *a.* liable to take fire; inflammable; *n.* a substance that burns readily [L. *comburere,* to burn up].

come (kum) *v.i.* to approach; to arrive; to arrive at some state or condition; to move towards; to reach; to happen (to); to originate (from); to occur; to turn out to be; to appear. *pr.p.* **coming.** *pa.p.* **come.** *pa.t.* **came.** **-back** *n.* a return to a former activity; (*Slang*) a retort [O.E. *cuman*].

com·e·dy (kȧm′·ą·di·) *n.* a play dealing with the lighter side of life; the humorous element in literature, life, or an incident.

co·me·di·an (ką·mē′·di·ąn) *n.* an actor in comedy; an entertainer whose songs or stories are light and humorous; (*Colloq.*) a funny person; a comic. **comedienne** (kąm·ē·di·en′) *n. fem.* [Gk. *komoidia,* fr. *komos,* revel; *odē,* song].

come·ly (kum′·li·) *a.* good-looking; graceful. **comeliness** *n.* [O.E. *cyme,* fair].

co·mes·ti·ble (ką·mes′·ti·bl) *a.* fit for eating. [L. *comedere,* to eat up].

com·et (kȧm′·it) *n.* a heavenly body consisting of a diffuse, nebulous head, a nucleus, and a tail [Gk. *komētēs,* long-haired].

come·up·pance (kum·up′·ąns) *n.* (*Slang*) deserved punishment.

com·fort (kum′·fęrt) *v.t.* to allay grief or trouble; to console, cheer, gladden; *n.* solace or consolation; ease of body or mind, or whatever causes it. **-s** *n.pl.* appurtenances or circumstances which give greater ease to life. **-able** *a.* promoting or enjoying comfort. **-ably** *adv.* **-er** *n.* one who comforts; a quilted bedcover. **-less** *a.* **Job's comforter,** one who, in seeking to comfort, achieves the opposite [L. *confortare,* to strengthen].

com·ic (kȧm′·ik) *a.* pert. to comedy; mirth-provoking; funny; *n.* that which induces amusement or laughter; (*Colloq.*) a comedian; (*Colloq.*) (*pl.*) a comic magazine or newspaper strip. **-al** *a.* droll; ludicrous. **-ally** *adv.* **-ality** *n.* [Gk. *komos,* revel].

com·in·form (kȧm′·in·fawrm) *n.* *Com*munist *Inform*ation Bureau.

Com·in·tern (kȧm′·in·turn) *n.* *Com*munist *Intern*ational, the international association of Communist parties.

com·i·ty (kȧm′·ą·ti·) *n.* courtesy; civility; suavity of manners [L. *comitas*].

com·ma (kȧm′·ą) *n.* a punctuation mark (,), used to mark the shortest pauses in the division of a sentence [Gk. fr. *komma,* short clause].

com·mand (ką·mand′) *v.t.* to order or demand with authority; to govern or control; to have at one's disposal; to overlook or have a view over; *v i.* to be at the head; *n.* an order; the body of troops under an officer; a district or region under a commander; a word of command; mastery or facility. **-ing** *a.* fitted to control; impressive or imperious. **-ant** *n.* officer in charge of a military station or a body of troops. **-eer** (ką·mąn·dēr′) *v.t.* to seize for military purposes; to take forcible possession of. **-er** (ka·man′·dęr) *n.* a leader; a commanding officer; in the navy, an officer ranking between a lieutenant commander and a captain. **-ment** *n.* a command; precept. **-er-in-chief,** the officer in supreme command of the forces of a state [L. *commendare,* to entrust].

com·man·do (ką·man′·dō) *n.* (*Mil.*) a selected body of men, who undergo special training for particularly dangerous enterprises against the enemy; a member of this body [Sp.].

com·mem·o·rate (ką·mem′·ą·rāt) *v.t.* to call to remembrance; to celebrate the memory of someone or something by a solemn act of devotion. **commemoration** *n.* **commemorative, commemoratory** *a.* [L. *commemorare*].

com·mence (ką·mens′) *v.t.* to begin, to start, to originate; *v.i.* to originate; to take rise; to begin. **-ment** *n.* beginning; the ceremony of conferring degrees in colleges and universities [Fr. *commencer*].

com·mend (ką·mend′) *v.t.* to praise; to speak favorably of; to present as worthy; to entrust to. **-able** *a.* **-ably** *adv.* **-ableness** *n.* **-ation** *n.* the act of commending; praise; approval. **-atory** *a.* [L. *commendare,* to entrust].

com·men·su·rate (ką·men′·shą·rit) *a.* equal in extent; proportionate; adequate. **-ly** *adv.* **-ness** *n.* **commensuration** *n.* **commensurable** *a.* having a common measure; suitably proportioned. **commensurably** *adv.* **commensurability** *n.* [L. *con-; mensura,* a measure].

com·ment (kȧ′·ment) *v.t.* and *i.* to make remarks, notes, criticisms; *n.* a note; a collection of notes; an explanation; a critical remark; an observation. **-ary** (kȧ·mąn·te′·ri) *n.* a series of notes; an exposition of a book; an historical narrative. **running commentary,** the description of an event while in actual progress, broadcast by an eye-witness. **-ate** *v.t.* to annotate; to interpret the meaning of. **-ator** *n.* an annotator; an expositor; one who speaks a commentary, either on events for broadcasting, or with a film [L. *comminisci, commentus,* to contrive].

com·merce (kȧm′·urs) *n.* buying and selling; trade; social or personal intercourse. **commercial** (ką·mur′·shąl) *a.* pert. to commerce; (*Radio*) broadcast program paid for by an advertiser. **commercialism** *n.* business principles, methods, or viewpoint. **commercialize** *v.t.* **commercially** *adv.* [L. *con-; merx,* merchandise].

com·min·gle (ką·ming′·gl) *v.t.* and *i.* to mingle together.

com·mis·er·ate (ką·miz′·ą·rāt) *v.t.* and *i.* to have compassion for; to condole with; to pity; to sympathize. **commiseration** *n.* [L. *commiserari,* to bewail with].

com·mis·sar (kȧm′·i·sȧr) *n.* one of the heads of a Soviet government department or commissariat [L. *committere,* to entrust].

com·mis·sar·i·at (kȧm·i·sa′·ri·ąt) *n.* the army department which supplies food, stores, equipment, transport; any of the governmental divisions of the U.S.S.R. [L. *committere,* to entrust]

com·mis·sa·ry (kȧm′·i·ser·i·) *n.* one to whom duty is assigned; a deputy; a commissioner; (*Mil.*) a store which supplies food and equipment. **commissarial** *a.* [L. *committere,* to entrust].

com·mis·sion (ką·mish′·ąn) *n.* the act of committing; something entrusted to be done; payment by a percentage for doing something; a group of people authorized to deal with specified matters; a legal warrant to execute some office, trust, or duty; the power under such warrant; the document that contains it; the thing to be done as agent for another; (*Mil., Naval, etc.*) a warrant of appointment, by the head of a state, to the rank of officer in the army, navy, etc.; *v.t.* to give power to; to authorize; to give an order for; to appoint to the rank of officer. **-ed** *a.* **-er** *n.* one holding a commission to act; the head of a governmental department [L. *committere,* to entrust].

com·mit (ką·mit′) *v.t.* to entrust; to give in charge; to perform; to be guilty of; to pledge or bind; to send for trial or confinement; *pr.p.* **-ting,** *pa.p.* and *pa.t.* **-ted.** **-tal** *a.* **-ment** *n.* [L. *committere*].

com·mit·tee (ką·mit′·i·) *n.* a number of persons appointed to attend any particular business by a legislative body, court, society, etc. [L. *committere,* to entrust].

com·mode (ką·mōd′) *n.* a chest of drawers; a small piece of furniture containing a chamber pot [L. *commodus*, suitable].

com·mo·di·ous (ka̩·mō′·di·a̩s) *a.* convenient; roomy; spacious. **-ly** *adv.* **-ness** *n.* **commodity** *n.* any useful thing; an article of trade. **commodities** *n.pl.* goods [L. *commodus*, suitable].

com·mo·dore (kȧm′·a̩·dōr) *n.* (*Naval*) the rank just below rear admiral; captain of a convoy of ships [etym. uncertain].

com·mon (kȧm′·a̩n) *a.* shared by or belonging to all, or to several; public; general; ordinary; usual; frequent; vulgar; inferior; of little value; of low social status; *n.* a tract of land belonging to a community for public use. **commons** *n.pl.* the lower House of Parliament, called the **House of Commons;** (*l.c.*) a dining room at a university. **-alty** *n.* the general body of the people with reference to rank, position, etc. **-er** *n.* one of the common people, i.e. not a member of the nobility. **-ly** *adv.* in a common manner; usually; jointly; meanly. **-ness** *n.* **-place** *a.* ordinary; trite; hackneyed; *n.* a common topic; a trite remark. **— sense** *n.* sound and practical understanding; well-balanced judgment. **— law,** (*Eng.*) law based on usage and custom, and confirmed by judicial decision; the unwritten law as distinguished from statute law. **the common good,** the welfare of the community as a whole [L. *communis*].

com·mon·weal (kȧm′·a̩n·wēl) *n.* the public welfare; the common good. **commonwealth** (welth) *n.* the whole body of people; a republican or democratic state. **Commonwealth** *n.* since 1947 the comprehensive term for all territories within the British Empire, including the Dominions [*common* and *weal*].

com·mo·tion (ka̩·mō′·sha̩n) *n.* violent motion; agitation; tumult; public disorder [L. *commorere, motum*, to move].

com·mune (ka̩·mūn′) *v.i.* to converse together intimately; to have spiritual intercourse (*with*); (*Eccl.*) to receive the communion. **communion** (ka̩m·ūn′·ya̩n) *n.* the act of communing; (*Christianity*) the celebration of the Lord's Supper [L. *communish*, common].

com·mune (kȧm′·ūn) *n.* a small administrative district (esp. in France) governed by a mayor. **communal** *a.* pert. to a commune or community; for common use. **communalize** *v.t.* to make over for common use. **communalism** *n.* a system by which small local governments have large powers. **communism** *n.* the theory of a social system in which everything is held in common, private property being abolished. **communist** *n.* **communistic** *a.* [L. *communis*, common].

com·mu·ni·cate (ka̩·mū′·na̩·kāt) *v.t.* to impart information; to reveal; to convey; *v.i.* to have connection with; to have dealings, correspondence, with. **communicable** *a.* **communicably** *adv.* **communication** *n.* the act of making known; intercourse by speech, correspondence, messages, etc.; information; means of passing from one place to another; a connecting passage. **communicant** *n.* one who imparts information; one who receives communion. **communicative** *a.* ready to converse or to impart information; talkative. [L. *communicare*]. [announcement [Fr.].

com·mu·ni·qué (ka̩·mū′·ni·kā) *n.* an official

com·mu·ni·ty (ka̩·mū′·na̩·ti·) *n.* a locality where people reside; people having common interests; the public, or people in general; common possession or enjoyment [L. *communis*].

com·mute (ka̩·mūt′) *v.t.* to exchange; to substitute; to mitigate a sentence; travel regularly between home and work. **commutable** *a.* exchangeable. **commutability** *n.* **commutation** *n.* **commutator** *n.* (*Elect.*) a device for reversing the direction of an electric current. **-r** *n.* [L. *con.; mutare*, to change].

com·pact (ka̩m·pakt′) *a.* firm; solid; closely packed; condensed; terse; *v.t.* to press closely together; to make firm. **compact** (kȧm′·pakt) *n.* a pocket vanity-case. **-ly** *adv.* **-ness** *n.* **-ed** *a.* firmly united [L. *con-; pangere, pactum*, to fix].

com·pact (ka̩m′·pakt) *n.* an agreement or contract; a mutual bargain; a league or covenant [L. *con-; pactus*, to make an agreement].

com·pan·ion (ka̩m·pan′·ya̩n) *n.* one who is in another's company, habitually or for the moment; comrade; an associate or partner; a match or mate. **-able** *a.* fitted to be a companion; sociable. **-ably** *adv.* **-ability, -ableness** *n.* **-ship** *n.* [L. *companium*, fellowship, fr. *con-, panis*, bread].

com·pan·ion (ka̩m·pan′·ya̩n) *n.* (*Naut.*) a skylight on upper deck, to let light into cabin below. **-way,** cabin staircase [O.Fr. *compagne*].

com·pa·ny (kum′·pa·ni·) *n.* a gathering of persons; an assembly; a group; an association of persons in business, etc.; visitors; a division of a regiment; a ship's crew [L. *con-; panis*, bread]

com·pare (ka̩m·pār′) *v.t.* to notice or point out the likeness and differences of two or more things; to liken or contrast; (*Gram.*) to state the comparative and superlative of an adjective or adverb; *v.i.* to be like; to compete with. **comparable** (kȧm′·pa̩r·a̩·bl) *a.* capable of being compared; of equal regard or value. **comparably** *adv.* **comparative** (ka̩m·par′·a̩·tiv) *a.* estimated by comparison; not absolute; relative; partial; (*Gram.*) expressing 'more'. **comparatively** *adv.* **comparison** *n.* the act of comparing [L. *comparare*, to match].

com·part·ment (ka̩m·pȧrt′·ma̩nt) *n.* a part divided off; a section; a division of a railway car [L. *compartiri*, to divide].

com·pass (kum′·pa̩s) *n.* an instrument for showing directions (north, east, etc.); (*Mus.*) the range of a voice in the musical scale; circuit; a circumference; measurement around; space; area; scope; reach; *v.t.* to go round; to surround; to contrive; to attain; to accomplish. **-es** *n.pl.* a mathematical instrument for drawing circles, measuring, etc. [L. *con-; passus*, a step].

com·pas·sion (ka̩m·pash′·a̩n) *n.* sympathy with the distress or suffering of another; pity. **-ate** *a.* full of sympathy; showing pity; merciful; *v.t.* to pity. **-ately** *adv.* **-ateness** *n.* [L. *con-; pati, passus*, to suffer].

com·pat·i·ble (ka̩m·pat′·a̩·bl) *a.* consistent; agreeing with; capable of harmonious union. **compatibly** *adv.* **compatibility** *n.* [L. *con-; pati*, to suffer].

com·pa·tri·ot (ka̩m·pā′·tri·a̩t) *n.* one of the same country; a fellow countryman [L. *con-;* and *patriot*].

com·peer (ka̩m·pir′) *n.* an equal; a companion; an associate [L. *con-; par*, equal].

com·pel (ka̩m·pel′) *v.t.* to force; to overpower; to bring about by force; *pr.p.* **-ling.** *pa.p.* and *pa.t.* **-led. -lable** *a.* [L. *compellere*, to drive together].

com·pen·di·um (ka̩m·pen′·di·a̩m) *n.* an abridgement or summary; an abstract. Also **compend.** *pl.* **-s,** or **compendia. compendious** *a.* abridged. **compendiously** *adv.* [L.].

com·pen·sate (kȧm′·pa̩n·sāt) *v.t.* to recompense suitably; to reward; to pay; *v.i.* to make amends; to make up for. **compensation** *n.* recompense; payment for some loss, injury, etc. **compensative, compensatory** *a.* [L. *compensare*, to weigh together].

com·pete (ka̩m·pēt′) *v.i.* to strive against others to win something; to vie with. **competition** (kȧm·pa̩·tish′·a̩n) *n.* the act of competing; a contest. **competitive** *a.* **competitively** *adv.* **competitor** *n.* one who competes. **competitory** *a.* [L. *competere*, to seek with].

com·pe·tent (kȧm′·pa̩·tant) *a.* able; properly qualified; proper; suitable; skillful. **-ly** *adv.* **competence, competency** *n.* the state of being fit or capable; sufficiency, esp. of means of subsistence [L. *competere*, to seek together].

com·pile (ka̩m·pīl′) *v.t.* to put together literary

materials into one book or works; to collect or amass. **-r** *n.* **compilation** *n.* [L. *compilare,* to plunder].

com·pla·cent (kạm·plā′·sạnt) *a.* self-satisfied; pleased or gratified. **-ly** *adv.* **complacence, complacency** *n.* self-satisfaction [L. *complacere,* to please greatly].

com·plain (kạm·plān′) *v.i.* to express distress, grief, dissatisfaction; to lament; to grumble; to be ailing. **-ant** *n.* a complainer; (*Law*) a plaintiff; one who brings an action against another. **complaint** *n.* the expression of distress, dissatisfaction, etc.; a malady or ailment [L. *con-; plangere,* to bewail].

com·plai·sant (kạm·plā′·zạnt) *a.* desirous to please; affable; obliging; gracious. **-ly** *adv.* **complaisance** *n.* [L. *complacere,* to please greatly].

com·ple·ment (kȧm′·plạ·mạnt) *n.* that which supplies a deficiency; something completing a whole; the full quantity or number; *v.t.* to complete; to supply a deficiency. **-al, -ary** *a.* completing [L. *complere,* to fill up].

com·plete (kạm·plēt′) *a.* entire; finished; perfect, with no part lacking; *v.t.* to bring to a state of entirety; to make perfect; to fulfill; to accomplish. **-ly** *adv.* **-ness** *n.* **completion** (kạm·plē′·shạn) *n.* the act of completing; fulfilment; conclusion [L. *complere,* to fill up].

com·plex (kȧm′·pleks) *a.* consisting of two or more parts; not simple; involved or intricate; *n.* a complicated whole; (*Psych.*) a group of repressed emotional ideas responsible for abnormal mental condition; (*Colloq.*) an obsession. **-ly** *adv.* **-ness, -ity** *n.* [L. *complectere,* to interweave].

com·plex·ion (kạm·plek′·shạn) *n.* color of the skin, esp. of the face; aspect or appearance; quality or texture; character [L. *complexio*].

com·pli·ance (kạm·plī′·ạns) *n.* submission; a yielding; acquiescence. **compliant** *a.* yielding; obedient; civil. **compliantly** *adv.* **compliable** *a.* inclined to comply [fr. *comply*].

com·pli·cate (kȧm′·plạ·kāt) *v.t.* to fold or twist together; to entangle; to make intricate. **-d** *a.* tangled; involved. **complication** *n.* [L. *con-; plicare,* to fold].

com·plic·i·ty (kạm·plis′·ạ·ti·) *n.* the state of being an accomplice, of having a share in the guilt [Fr. *complice,* an accomplice].

com·pli·ment (kȧm′·plạ·mạnt) *n.* an expression of regard or admiration; flattering speech; a formal greeting (usually *pl.*); *v.t.* to express approbation; to congratulate; to express respect for. **-ary** *a.* expressing praise, admiration; free, a *complimentary* ticket [L. *complete,* to fill up].

com·ply (kạm·plī′·) *v.i.* to yield to; to agree; to consent; to conform; to adapt oneself to. **complier** *n.* [L. *complere,* to fill up].

com·po·nent (kạm·pō′·nạnt) *a.* constituting; composing; making up; helping to form a compound; *n.* a part helping to make a whole [L. *componere,* to put together].

com·port (kạm·pōrt′) *v.t.* to behave; to conduct oneself; *v.i.* to agree; to accord; to suit [L. *comportare,* to carry together].

com·pose (kạm·pōz′) *v.t.* to form by uniting parts; to arrange; to put in order; to write; to invent; to adjust; to calm; to soothe; to set up the types in proper order for printing; *v.i.* to practice composition. **-d** *a.* sedate; quiet; calm. **-dly** *adv.* **-dness** *n.* **-r** *n.* one who composes; an author. **composite** (kạm·pȧz′·it) *a.* made up of distinct parts or elements. **composition** (kȧm·pạ·zish′·ạn) *n.* the act of composing; the thing formed by composing; a pupil's essay; a literary, musical, artistic, etc. work; the organization of the parts of a work of art. **compositor** (kạm·pȧz′·ạ·tẹr) *n.* a typesetter. **composure** (kạm·pō′·zhẹr) *n.* calmness [Fr. *composer*].

com·post (kȧm′·pōst) *n.* a fertilizing mixture; a composition for plaster work, etc. [L. *componere.* to put together].

com·pote (kȧm′·pōt) *n.* fruit stewed or preserved in syrup; a stemmed candy dish [Fr.].

com·pound (kȧm·pound′) *v.t.* to put together, as elements or parts, to form a whole; to combine; to compromise; to make a settlement of debt by partial payment. **to compound a felony** (*Law*) to refrain, for some consideration, from prosecuting [L. *componere,* to put together].

com·pound (kȧm′·pound) *a.* composed of elements, ingredients, or parts; not simple; composite; *n.* a mixture; a joining; a substance to which something has been added; a word, etc. made up of parts; (*Chem.*) a substance composed of two or more elements, which are always present in the same fixed proportions. **— fracture,** a fracture of a bone where a portion pierces the skin, making a surface wound. **— interest,** interest paid on capital plus accumulated interest [L. *componere,* to put together].

com·pound (kȧm′·pound) *n.* in the Orient, an enclosure about a house; in S. Africa, an enclosed area in which native laborers reside [Malay, *kampong,* an enclosure].

com·pre·hend (kȧm·pri·hend′) *v.t.* to understand; to grasp with the mind; to take in; to include; to comprise. **comprehensible** (kȧm·-pri·hen′·sạ·bl) *a.* understandable; conceivable. **comprehensibly** *adv.* **comprehensibility, comprehensibleness** *n.* **comprehension** *n.* the act of comprehending; the capacity of the mind to perceive and understand. **comprehensive** *a.* including much within narrow limits; extensive; large; capacious; inclusive [L. *comprehendere,* to grasp].

com·press (kạm·pres′) *v.t.* to press together; to reduce the volume by pressure; to condense. **-ed** *a.* **-ible** *a.* **-ibility** *n.* **-ion** (kạm·presh′·-ạn) *n.* the act or effect of compressing. **-ive** *a.* tending to compress. **-or** *n.* [L. *compressus,* pressed together].

com·press (kȧm′·pres) *n.* (*Med.*) a pad to make pressure on a wound; a wet pad to reduce inflammation.

com·prise (kạm·prīz′) *v.t.* to include; to be composed of; to consist of [Fr. *comprendre,* to include] .

com·pro·mise (kȧm′·prạ·mīz) *n.* a settling of matters by mutual adjustment, each side making some concessions; a middle course; *v.t.* and *i.* to settle by making mutual concessions; to commit oneself; to expose to the risk of scandal or disgrace [L. *con-; promittere,* to promise].

comp·tom·e·ter (kȧm(p)·tȧm′·ạ·tẹr) *n.* a calculating machine [Trade Name].

comp·trol·ler (kạn·trōl′·ẹr) *n.* a form of controller [L.].

com·pul·sion (kạm·pul′·shạn) *n.* the act or effect of compelling; force; constraint; violence; (*Psych.*) an irresistible impulse. **compulsive** *a.* exercising compulsion. **compulsory** *a.* compelling; constraining; obligatory; enforced [L. *compulsus,* driven together].

com·punc·tion (kạm·pungk′·shạn) *n.* remorse of conscience; scruple. **compuctious** *a.* conscience-stricken; regretful; remorseful [L. *con-; pungere,* to prick].

com·pute (kạm·pūt′) *v.t.* to count; to calculate; to estimate. **computable** *a.* **computation** *n.* calculation; reckoning [L. *con-; putare,* to reckon].

com·put·er (kạm·pūt′·er) *n.* an electronic device which retrieves, stores, and processes data.

com·rade (kȧm′·rad) *n.* a close friend or companion; a mate; an associate. **-ship** *n.* close friendship; fellowship; affectionate association [Sp. *camarada,* a room-mate].

con (kȧn) (*Naut.*) *v.t.* and *i.* to superintend the steering of a vessel [L. *conducere,* to guide].

con (kȧn) *adv.* (*abbrev.* of **contra**), against, e.g. in the phrase **pro and con,** for and against. **the pro and con** *n.* Also *pl.* **the pros and cons,** the advantages and disadvantages [L.].

con (kȧn) *a.* (*Slang*) confidence; *v.t.* to swindle. *pr.p.* **-ning.** *pa.t.* **-ned.**
con- prefix fr. L. *cum*, with, together.
con·cat·e·nate (kạn·kat′·ạ·nāt) *v.i.* to link together; to unite in a series. **concatenation** *n.* a series of things depending on each other; a connected chain, as of circumstances [L. *con-*; *catena*, a chain].
con·cave (kȧn′·kāv) *a.* hollow and curved inwards, as the inner surface of a vault. **concavity** (kȧn·kav′·i·ti·) *n.* hollowness [L. *con-*; *cavus*, hollow].
con·ceal (kạn·sēl′) *v.t.* to hide or secrete; to mask or disguise; to withhold from knowledge. **-ment** *n.* [L. *con-*; *celare*, to hide].
con·cede (kạn·sēd′) *v.t.* to yield; to admit to be true; to grant; to surrender; *v.i.* to admit [L. *concedere*, to yield].
con·ceit (kạn·sēt′) *n.* over-estimation of self-vanity; opinion; fanciful thought. **-ed** *a.* vain. **-edly** *adv.* [fr. *conceive*].
con·ceive (kạn·sēv′) *v.t.* to form an idea in the mind; to think; to imagine; to understand; *v.i.* to become pregnant; to have a notion. **conceivable** *a.* that may be believed, imagined, or understood. **conceivably** *adv.* [L. *con-*; *capere*, to take, seize].
con·cen·trate (kȧn′·sen·trāt) *v.i.* to bring to a common center; to reduce to small space; to increase in strength; to condense; *v.i.* to come together; to devote all attention. **concentration** *n.* the act of concentrating; increased strength; the fixation of the mind on something. **concentration camp,** a place of detention. [L. *con-*; *centrum*, the center].
con·cen·tric (kạn·sen′·trik) *a.* having the center. **-al** *a.* **-ally** *adv.* **concentricity** (kȧn·-sạn·tris′·ạ·ti·) *n.*
con·cept (kȧn′·sept) *n.* an abstract notion; a mental impression of an object. **conception** (kạn·sep′·shạn) *n.* the act of conceiving; the thing conceived; a mental picture; an idea; a notion; (*Med.*) the beginning of pregnancy. **conceptive** *a.* pert. to conception; capable of conceiving. **conceptual** *a.* pert. to conception or to a concept [L. *concipere*, to conceive].
con·cern (kạn·surn′) *v.t.* to relate or belong to; to be of importance to; to be the business of; to make uneasy; *n.* that which relates or belongs to one; interest in, or care for, any person or thing; worry; a business establishment. **-ed** *a.* interested; worried; anxious; troubled; involved. **-ing** *prep.* regarding; with respect to. **-ment** *n.* [L. *con-; cernere*, to distinguish].
con·cert (kạn·surt′) *v.t.* to plan together; to arrange; to design. **-ed** *a.* mutually planned; (*Mus.*) arranged in parts. **concert** (kȧn′·sẹrt) *n.* agreement in a plan; harmony; a musical entertainment. **concertina** (·tē′·nạ) *n.* a small hexagonal accordion. **concerto** (kạn·-cher′·tō) *n.* a musical composition arranged for a solo instrument with orchestral accompaniment [Fr. *concerter*].
con·ces·sion (kạn·sesh′·ạn) *n.* the act of conceding; a special privilege; a grant; an admission. **-aire** *n.* one who holds a concession. **-ary** *a.* [L. *con-*; *cedere*, to yield].
conch (kȧnk, kȧnch) *n.* a seashell; the spiral shell used as a trumpet by the Tritons [L. *concha*, a shell].
con·chol·o·gy (kȧng·kȧl′·ạ·ji·) *n.* the scientific study of shells and shellfish. **conchologist** *n.* [Gk. *konchē*, a shell; *logos*, discourse].
con·cil·i·ate (kạn·sil′·i·āt) *v.t.* to win over to goodwill; to appease; to make peace; to pacify. **conciliation** *n.* **conciliative** *a.* conciliatory. **conciliatory** *a.* tending to pacify [L. *conciliare*, to bring together].
con·cise (kạn·sīs′) *a.* brief; condensed; comprehensive. **-ly** *adv.* in few words; tersely. **-ness** *n.* [L. *concisus*, fr. *caedere*, to cut].
con·clave (kȧn′·klāv) *n.* a private meeting of cardinals for the election of a pope; where they meet; any secret meeting [L. *conclave*, a room; fr. *clavis*, a key].
con·clude (kạn·klòòd′) *v.t.* to bring to an end; to close; to finish; to complete; to make a final judgment of; to infer; *v.i.* to come to an end [L. *concludere*].
con·clu·sion (kạn·klòò′·zhạn) *n.* the end; the last part of anything; the final judgment; inference; result from experiment. **conclusive** *a.* final; convincing [L. *concludere*, to end].
con·coct (kạn·kȧkt′) *v.t.* to make a mixture; to make up, esp. a story. **concoction** *n.* [L. *concoctus*, cooked].
con·com·i·tant (kạn·kȧm′·ạ·tant) *a.* accompanying; attending; going along with; *n.* an accompanying circumstance. **concomitance, concomitancy** *n.* the state of being concomitant; coexistence [L. *concomitari*, to go with as companion].
con·cord (kȧn′·kawrd) *n.* agreement; union between persons, as in opinions, etc.; harmony; unison; consonance; *v.i.* to agree. **concordance** *n.* agreement; an index to the words of a book (esp. of the Bible) with references to the places of their occurrence. **concordant** *a.* harmonious [L. *con-*; *cor*, *cordis*, the heart].
con·cor·dat (kȧn-kawr′·dat) *n.* an agreement between the Pope and a sovereign or government on religious questions; a pact; a treaty [L. *con-*; *cor*, *cordis*, the heart].
con·course (kȧn′·kōrs) *n.* a gathering together; an assembly; a crowd; a promenade or roadway in a park; a large space in a railroad station [L. *concursus*, running together].
con·cres·cence (kȧn·kres′·ạns) *n.* a growing together [L. *con-*; *crescere*, to grow].
con·crete (kȧn′·krēt) *a.* made of concrete; consisting of matter, facts, etc.; solid; not abstract; specific; *n.* a mixture of sand, cement, etc., used in building; anything real or specific; *v.t.* to form into a solid mass; *v.i.* to unite into a mass; to harden. **-ly** *adv.* **-ness** *n.* **concretion** *n.* the state of being concrete; a mass formed of parts pressed together [L. *concrescere*, to grow together].
con·cu·bine (kȧng′·kū·bīn) *n.* a woman who lives with a man without being his lawful wife. **concubinage** (kȧn·kū′·bạ·nij) *n.* the living together of a man and a woman not legally married [L. *con-*; *cubare*, to lie].
con·cu·pis·cence (kȧn·kū′·pạs·ạns) *n.* violent sexual desire; lust. **concupiscent, concupiscible** *a.* lustful [L. *con-*; *cupere*, to desire].
con·cur (kạn·kur′) *v.i.* to agree; to express agreement; to meet in the same point; to coincide. *pr.p.* **-ring** *pa.p.* and *pa.t.* **-red. -rence** *n.* **-rent** *a.* acting in conjunction; agreeing; taking place at the same time; accompanying; *n.* a joint or contributory cause. **-rently** *adv.* [L. *concurrere*, to run together].
con·cus·sion (kạn·kush′·ạn) *n.* act of shaking by sudden striking; shock; (*Med.*) a violent disturbance of the brain caused by a blow or fall [L. *concussio*, a shaking together].
con·demn (kạn·dem′) *v.t.* to blame; to censure; to pronounce guilty; to sentence; to reprove; to declare unfit for use. **-ation** *n.* **-atory** *a.* [L. *condemnare*].
con·dense (kạn·dens′) *v.t.* to make more dense, close, or compact; to make more solid; to concentrate; to change a vapor or gas into liquid or solid; to pack into few words; *v.i.* to become more dense or compact; to pass from vapor to liquid or solid. **condensation** *n.* the act of condensing; the state of being condensed; conciseness; in psycho-analysis, the symbolization of two or more ideas by one symbol. **-d** *a.* compressed; concise; (of milk) evaporated and preserved in cans.**-r** *n.* one who, or that which, condenses; an apparatus for changing vapor or gas into liquid or solid; (*Elect.*) a device for accumulating and holding an electric charge [L. *condensare*, fr. *densus*, *dense*].
con·de·scend (kȧn·dạ·send′) *v.i.* to come down from one's position, rank, or dignity; to stoop;

to deign; to be gracious or affable to inferiors; to patronize. **-ing** *a.* **condescension** *n.* [L. *condescendere,* to come down].

con·dign (kạn·dīn′) *a.* deserved; adequate. **-ly** *adv.* [L. *dignus,* worthy].

con·di·ment (kȧn′·dạ·mạnt) *n.* a relish; seasoning for food [L. *condire,* to pickle].

con·di·tion (kạn·dish′·ạn) *n.* a thing on which a statement, happening, or existing depends; state or circumstances of anything; position as to worldly circumstances; rank; disposition; a prerequisite; a stipulation; *v.t.* to stipulate; to impose conditions on; to render fit and in good health; *v.i.* to make terms. **-al** *a.* depending on conditions; not absolute. **-ally** *adv.* **-ed** *a.* **-ed reflex** *n.* (*Psych.*) an automatic response [L.].

con·dole (kạn·dōl′) *v.i.* to grieve with; to offer sympathy. **-nce, -ment** *n.* an expression of sympathy [L. *condolere,* to suffer with].

con·dom (kȧn′·dum) *n.* a sheath worn over the penis to prevent conception or infection during coitus.

con·do·min·i·um (kȧn·dạ·min′·i·ạm) *n.* joint rule of a country by two or more countries; an apartment house of individually owned apartments; an apartment in such a house; a multi-house complex of individually owned houses; a house in such a complex [L. *con-;* and *dominium,* dominion].

con·duce (kạn·dūs′) *v.i.* to lead to some end or result; to help; to promote. **conducive** *a.* having a tendency to promote, help, or forward. **conduciveness** *n.* [L. *conducere,* to bring together, to lead].

con·duct (kȧn′·dukt) *n.* the act of guiding; guidance; management; behavior; (kạn·dukt′) *v.t.* to guide; to lead; to direct; to manage; to behave. **-ance** *n.* (*Elect.*) the property of a body for conducting electricity. **-ible** *a.* **-tion** *n.* the act of conducting; the transmission or flow of heat from one body to another. **-tive** *a.* able to transmit heat, electricity, etc. **-ivity** *n.* the quality of being conductive. **-or** *n.* a guide; the leader of a choir or orchestra; one in charge of a bus, train, etc. who collects fares; a substance capable of transmitting heat, electricity, etc. [L. *conducere,* to lead].

con·duit (kȧn′·dit, -doo·it) *n.* a pipe or channel for conveying fluids [Fr. fr. *conduire,* to lead].

cone (kōn) *n.* a solid body tapering to a point from a circular base; anything of this shape; the fruit of the fir, etc. **conic(al)** (kȧn′·ik, -i·kal) *a.* having the form of, or pert. to, a cone. **conically** *adv.* **conics** *n.* (*Geom.*) the branch dealing with conic sections [Gk. *kōnos*].

confab (kạn′·fab) *n.* (*Colloq.*) a chat.

con·fab·u·late (kạn·fab′·yạ·lāt) *v.i.* to chat. **confabulation** *n.* [L. *confabulari*].

con·fec·tion (kạn·fek′·shạn) *n.* the act of compounding different substances into one compound; candy, ice cream, etc. **-ary** *a.* **-er** *n.* one who makes or sells confections. **-er's sugar** *n.* finely powdered sugar. **-ery** *n.* candies, etc.; a shop where these are sold [L. *conficere,* to make up].

con·fed·er·ate (kạn·fed′·ẹr·it) *a.* united in a league; bound by treaty; allied; *n.* an ally; an accomplice; (kạn·fed′·ẹr·āt) *v.t., v.i.* to unite in a league. **confederacy** *n.* a union; an alliance. **confederation** *n.* the act of forming a confederacy; an alliance [L. *con-; foedus,* a league].

con·fer (kạn·fur′) *v.t.* to bestow upon; to grant; to award; *v.i.* to consult together; to take advice; to discuss. *pr.p.* **-ring.** *pa.p., pa.t.* **-red.** **-ee** *n.* one who takes part in a conference; a recipient of an award. **-ence** *n.* a meeting; a consultation [L. *conferre,* to bring together].

con·fess (kạn·fes′) *v.t.* to admit; to own; to acknowledge; to grant; to declare one's sins orally to a priest; (of a priest) to hear the sins of; to make confession; plead guilty. **-edly** *adv.* admittedly. **confession** (kạn·fesh′·ạn) *n.* admission; avowal of sins; declaring one's sins to priest. **confessional** *n.* the stall where a priest sits to hear confessions; *a.* pert. to confession. **-or** *n.* a priest who hears confessions. **confession of faith,** a statement of religious beliefs [L. *confiteri, confessus,* to acknowledge].

con·fet·ti (kạn·fet′·i·) *n.pl.* small bits of colored paper, for throwing at weddings, carnivals, etc. [It.].

con·fide (kạn·fīd′) *v.t.* to hand over to the charge of; to entrust to; to tell a secret to; *v.i.* to put faith in; to rely on. **confidant** *n.* (*fem.* **confidante**) a person in whom one can confide [L. *con-; fidere,* to trust].

con·fi·dence (kȧn′·fạ·dạns) *n.* that in which faith is put; belief; trust; feeling of security; self-reliance; presumption; intimacy; a secret. **confident** *a.* having assurance; bold. **confidently** *adv.* **confidential** (kạn·fȧ·den′·shạl) *a.* treated with confidence; private; secret. **confidentially** *adv.* [L. *con-; fidere,* to trust].

con·fig·u·ra·tion (kạn·fig·yạ·rā′·shạn) *n.* outward shape, form, or figure; grouping; outline; aspect [L. *con-; figurare,* to fashion].

con·fine (kạn·fīn′) *v.t.* to keep within bounds; to limit; to enclose; to imprison; *v.i.* to have a common boundary; **confine** (kȧn′·fīn) *n.* usually in *pl.* **confines,** boundary; limit. **-ment** *n.* imprisonment; restraint; detention; childbirth [L. *confinis,* having a common frontier].

con·firm (kạn·furm′) *v.t.* to make strong; to settle; to make valid by formal assent; to ratify; to make certain; to verify. **confirmation** *n.* the act of making strong, valid, certain, etc.; proof; a religious rite. **-ative** *a.* **-atory** *a.* **-ed** *a.* [L. *confirmare*].

con·fis·cate (kȧn′·fis·kāt) *v.t.* to seize by authority; to take possession of without compensation; *a.* forfeited. **confiscation** *n.* **confiscator** *n.* **confiscatory** *a.* [L. *confiscare*].

con·fla·gra·tion (kȧn·flạ·grā′·shạn) *n.* a destructive fire [L. *con-; flagrare,* to blaze].

con·flict (kạn·flikt′) *v.i.* to dash together; to clash; to be at odds with; to be inconsistent with; to differ. **conflict** (kȧn′·flikt) *n.* a prolonged struggle; a trial of strength; strong disagreement. **-ing** *a.* differing; contradictory [L. *confligere, conflictum,* to strike against].

con·flu·ence (kȧn′·flòò·ans) *n.* a flowing together; the meeting of two or more rivers, streams, etc.; a large assemblage; a crowd. **confluent** *a.* Also **conflux** [L. *confluere,* to flow together].

con·form (kạn·fawrm′) *v.t.* to make like; to bring into agreement; *v.i.* to comply; to agree; *a.* in accord. **-able** *a.* corresponding in form; similar; submissive. **-ably** *adv.* **-ation** *n.* the manner in which a body is formed or shaped; structure. **-ist** *n.* one who complies with usage or custom. **-ity** *n.* [L. *conformare,* to give the same shape].

con·found (kạn·found′) *v.t.* to mix up; to bring to confusion; to bewilder. **-ed** *a.* confused; baffled; perplexed; (*Colloq.*) odious [L. *confundere,* to pour together].

con·front (kạn·frunt′) *v.t.* to face boldly; to oppose; to bring face to face; to compare. **confrontation** *n.* [Fr. *confronter,* fr. *front,* the brow].

Con·fu·cius (kạn·fū′·shạs) *n.* Chinese philosopher.

con·fuse (kạn·fūz′) *v.t.* to mix up; to jumble together; to muddle; to perplex; hence, to mistake one thing for another. **-d** *a.* mixed up; perplexed. **confusedly** *adv.* **confusion** *n.* the state of being confused; disorder; bewilderment [L. *confundere,* to pour together].

con·fute (kạn·fūt′) *v.t.* to prove to be wrong; to disprove. **confutable** *a.* **confutation** *n.* [L. *confutare*].

con·geal (kạn·jēl′) *v.t.* and *i.* to freeze, as a fluid; to stiffen; to solidify; to curdle; to coagulate; *v.i.* to become stiff or solidified, from cold.

-**able** *a.* -**ment** *n.* a thing congealed; a clot. **congelation** *n.* [L. *con-; gelare,* to freeze].
con·gen·ial (kạn·jēn'·yạl) *a.* allied in disposition and tastes; kindred; agreeable. **-ly** *adv.* **congeniality** *n.* [L. *con-; genius,* spirit].
con·gen·i·tal (kạn·jen'·ạ·tạl) *a.* existing at the time of birth [L. *con-; genitus,* born].
con·gest (kạn·jest') *v.t.* to collect into a mass; to produce a hampering accumulation; to overcrowd. **-ed** *a.* overcrowded. **congestion** *n.* [L. *con-; gerere, gestum,* to bring, to carry].
con·glom·er·ate (kạn·glȧm'·ẹr·it) *a.* gathered into a mass; clustered; *v.t.* (·rāt') to bring together into a united mass; *n.* (*Geol.*) rock composed of fragments of rock cemented together. **conglomeration** *n.* a mixed collection; a cluster [L. *con-; glomus,* a mass].
con·grat·u·late (kạn·gra'·chạ·lāt) *v.t.* to wish joy to; to compliment; to felicitate. **congratulation** *n.* an expression of pleasure at the good fortune of someone; felicitation. **congratulatory** *a.* [L. *congratulari*].
con·gre·gate (kȧng'·grạ·gāt) *v.t.* to gather into a crowd or assembly; *v.i.* to meet together, in a body; (·git) *a.* assembled; collective. **congregation** *n.* the act of assembling; an assemblage; a gathering of persons for worship; a religious body. **congregational** *a.* **Congregationalism** *n.* a system of church government that gives independence to each local church [L. *con-; grex,* a flock].
con·gress (kȧng'·grạs) *n.* a meeting together of persons; a formal assembly, e.g. of envoys or representatives of governments. **Congress** *n.* the legislative body of the United States. **-man** *n.* a member of the U.S. House of Representatives. **-woman** *n.* **congressional** *a.* [L. *congredi, congressus,* to meet].
con·gru·ent (kȧng'·groo·ạnt) *a.* agreeing together; corresponding. **congruence, congruency** *n.* suitableness. **congruity** *n.* **congruous** *a.* accordant; suitable [L. *congruere,* to run together].
con·ic See **cone.**
co·nif·e·rae (kō·nif'·ạ·rē) *n.pl.* an order of trees bearing a cone-shaped fruit. **coniferous** *a.* [L. *conus,* a cone; *ferre,* to bear].
con·jec·ture (kạn·jek'·chẹr) *n.* a guess; an opinion founded on insufficient proof; surmise; inference; *v.t.* to guess; to surmise; to infer on insufficient grounds. **conjecturable** *a.* **conjectural** *a.* [L. *con-; jacere,* to throw].
con·join (kạn·join') *v.t.* to join together; *a.* united; concerted; associated [L. *conjungere,* join together].
con·ju·gal (kȧn'·joo·gạl) *a.* pert. to marriage; connubial; matrimonial. **-ly** *adv.* **conjugality** (kȧn'·jạ·gal'·i·ti·) *n.* the married state [L. *conjux, conjugis,* a spouse].
con·ju·gate (kȧn'·joog·āt) *v.t.* (*Gram.*) to recite or write all the different parts of a verb. **conjugation** *n.* the act of uniting; (*Gram.*) a class of verbs inflected in the same manner; (*Biol.*) the fusion of cells or individuals for reproduction [L. *con-; jugum,* a yoke].
con·junct (kạn·jungkt') *a.* joined together; united; associated. **-ly** *adv.* **conjunction** *n.* union; concurrence of events; (*Gram.*) a word used to join clauses, etc. **conjunctive** *a.* closely connected; serving to connect [L. *con-; jungere,* to join].
con·junc·ti·vi·tis (kạn·jungk·tạ·vī'·tạs) *n.* inflammation of the mucous membrane lining the eyelid [L. *con-; jungere,* to join].
con·jure (kạn·joor') *v.t.* to call on by a sacred name; solemnly to implore. **conjure** (kun'·jẹr) *v.i.* to practice magic; to practice the arts of a conjurer; (*Fig.*) to imagine. **conjuration** *n.* the act of calling upon or summoning by a sacred name. **conjurer, conjuror** *n.* a magician; a juggler [L. *con-; jurare,* to swear].
conk (kȧnk) (*Slang*) a blow; **— out,** fail suddenly.
con·nect (kạ·nekt') *v.t.* to fasten together; to associate; to relate; to attach; to join; *v.i.* to unite; to have a close relation. **-ed** *a.* joined; coherent. **-edly** *adv.* **connection** *n.* a link; the act of uniting, or state of being united; that which connects; a kinsman. **-ive** *a.* binding; *n.* a connecting word. **-or** *n.* **well connected,** of good family [L. *con-; nectere,* to bind].
con·nive (kạ·nīv') *v.i.* to wink at; to pretend not to see; to co-operate secretly (with 'at'). **connivance** *n.* consent in wrong-doing. **-r** *n.* [L. *connivere,* to shut the eyes].
con·nois·seur (kȧn·ạ·sur') *n.* an expert, esp. in fine arts [Fr. *connaître,* to know].
con·note (kạ·nōt') *v.t.* to mean; to imply; to signify; to have a meaning in addition to the primary meaning. **connotate** *v.t.* to connote. **connotation** *n.* a secondary implied meaning. **connotative** *a.* [L. *con-; notare,* to mark].
con·nu·bi·al (kạ·nū'·bi·ạl) *a.* pert. to marriage. **connubiality** *n.* [L. *con-; nubere,* to marry].
co·noid (kō'·noid) *n.* any object shaped like a cone [Gk. *konos,* a cọne; *eidos,* form].
con·quer (kȧng'·kẹr) *v.t.* to reduce by force, as of arms; to overcome; to subjugate or subdue; to vanquish; to surmount; *v.i.* to be victorious; to prevail. **-able** *a.* **-or** *n.* **conquest** (kȧng'·kwest) *n.* the act of conquering; that which is conquered [L. *con-; quaerere,* to seek].
con·quis·ta·dor (kȧn·kwis'·tạ·dawr) *n.* a conqueror, applied to the Spanish conquerors of Mexico and Peru in the 16th cent. [Sp.].
con·san·guin·e·ous (kȧn·sang·gwin'·i·ạs) *a.* of the same blood; related by birth. **consanguinity** *n.* [L. *con-; sanguis,* blood].
con·science (kȧn'·shạns) *n.* the faculty by which we know right from wrong. **conscientious** (kȧn·shi·en'·shạs) *a.* governed by dictates of conscience. **conscientiously** *adv.* **conscientiousness** *n.* **conscionable** (kȧn'·shạn·a·bl) *a.* governed by conscience. **—stricken** *a.* seized with scruples. **conscientious objector,** a man who refuses to serve in the armed forces, on moral or religious grounds [L. *conscire,* to be well aware].
con·scious (kȧn'·shạs) *a.* having inward knowledge (of); aware (of); having the use of one's faculties. **-ly** *adv.* **-ness** *n.* the state of being mentally awake to one's surroundings [L. *conscire,* to be aware].
con·script (kạn·skript') *v.t.* to enroll compulsorily for service in the armed forces. **conscript** (kan'·skript) *n.* one compelled to serve as a soldier, sailor, or airman, etc. **conscription** *n.* [L. *con-; scribere,* to write].
con·se·crate (kȧn'·sạ·krāt) *v.t.* to set apart for sacred uses; to dedicate. **consecration** *n.* [L. *con-; sacrare,* to hallow].
con·sec·u·tive (kạn·sek'·yạ·tiv) *a.* following one another in unbroken order; successive; resulting; (*Gram.*) expressing consequence. **-ly** *adv.* **-ness** *n.* [L. *con-; sequi,* to follow].
con·sen·sus (kạn·sen'·sạs) *n.* a general agreement; unanimity [L.].
con·sent (kạn·sent') *n.* agreement; assent; permission; *v.i.* to agree. **consentient** (kạn·sen'·shant) *a.* united in opinion. **consentience** *n.* [L. *con-; sentire,* to feel].
con·se·quent (kȧn'·sạ·kwent) *a.* following as a result; *n.* effect. **-ly** *adv.* therefore; as a result; by logical sequence. **consequence** *n.* that which naturally follows; result; importance; value. **consequential** (kȧn·sạ·kwen'·shal) *a.* [L. *con-; sequi,* to follow].
con·serve (kạn·surv') *v.t.* to keep safe; to preserve, to maintain; *n.* anything conserved; fruit, etc. prepared with sugar. **conservation** *n.* preservation; safe-guarding; protection; the official safe-guarding of forests, rivers, ports, etc.; the area so protected. **conservative** *a.* tending to conserve; disposed to maintain existing institutions; hostile to change; *n.* one opposed to hasty changes or innovations.

n. a greenhouse for plants; a school of music. **conservatory** [L. *con-; servare,* to keep].

con·sid·er (kạn·sid′·ẹr) *v.t.* to reflect upon carefully; to examine carefully; to be of opinion; to regard as; *v.i.* to deliberate seriously. **-able** *a.* worthy of attention; moderately large. **-ably** *adv.* **-ate** *a.* thoughful for others; circumspect. **-ately** *adv.* **-ateness** *n.* **-ation** *n.* the act of considering; deliberation; fee or recompense; thoughtful regard for others. **-ed** *a.* carefully thought out. **-ing** *prep.* in view of; taking into account [L. *considerare,* observe].

con·sign (kạn·sīn′) *v.t.* to give, transfer, or deliver in a formal manner; to entrust (goods) to a carrier for transport by rail, ship, etc.; *v.i.* to agree. **consignee** (càn·sī·nē′) *n.* the person to whom goods are consigned. **-er, -or** *n.* the person who consigns goods. **-ment** *n.* [L. *consignare,* to seal].

con·sist (kan·sist′) *v.i.* to be composed of; to be in a fixed or permanent state; to be compatible with. **-ence, -ency** *n.* a condition of being fixed; a degree of firmness or density; agreement or harmony. **consistent** *a.* compatible; constant in adhering to principles, etc. [L. *con-; sistere,* to stand].

con·sis·to·ry (kạn·sis′·tạr·i·) *a.* pert. to an ecclesiastical court; *n.* any solemn assembly or council [L. *consistorium,* a council].

con·sole (kạn·sōl′) *v.t.* to comfort in distress; to solace; to encourage. **consolable** *a.* able to be consoled. **consolation** *n.* the act of comforting; that which comforts; solace; encouragement. **consolatory** *a.* [L. *consolari*].

con·sol·i·date (kạn·sàl′·ạ·dāt) *v.t.* and *i.* to make solid; to make firm; to combine into a connected whole; to strengthen. **consolidation** *n.* the act of making or becoming compact and firm [L. *con-; solidus,* solid].

con·som·mé (kàn·sạ·mā′) *n.* a clear meat soup [Fr.].

con·so·nant (kàn′·sạ·nạnt) *a.* agreeing with; in accord; *n.* a sound (or letter) making a syllable only with a vowel; a non-vowel. **-ly** *adv.* **consonance, consonancy** *n.* agreement; harmony [L. *consonare,* to sound with].

con·sort (kàn′·sawrt) *n.* a companion or partner; a wife or husband. **consort** (kạn·sawrt′) *v.t.* to join; *v.i.* to keep company; to associate; to agree [L. *consors,* fr. *sors,* fate].

con·sor·ti·um (kạn·sawr′·shi·ạm) *n.* an association for a common end; an agreement between countries for mutual assistance and joint action [L.].

con·spec·tus (kạn·spek′·tạs) *n.* a general sketch or outline of a subject; a synopsis [L. fr. *conspicere,* to look at].

con·spic·u·ous (kạn·spik′·yoo·ạs) *a.* easy to be seen; very noticeable. **-ly** *adv.* **-ness, conspicuity** *n.* [L. *conspicere,* to catch sight of].

con·spire (kạn·spīr′) *v.i..* to unite for an evil purpose; to plot together. **conspiracy** (kạn·-spir′·ạ·si·) *n.* a combination of persons for an evil purpose; a plot. **conspirator** *n.* (*fem.* **conspiratress**). **conspiratorial** *a.* [L. *conspirare,* lit. to breathe together].

con·sta·ble (kàn′·stạ·bl, kun·stạ′·bl) *n.* a peace officer; a high officer in the Middle Ages. **constabulary** (kạn·stab′·yạ·ler·i·) *a.* pert. to constables; *n.* [L.L. *comes stabuli,* count of the stable, marshal].

con·stant (kàn′·stạnt) *a.* fixed; steadfast; invariable, permanent; *n.* that which is not subject to change. **-ly** *adv.* **constancy** *n.* steadfastness; resolution; fidelity [L. *constare,* to stand firm].

con·stel·la·tion (kàn·stạ·lā′·shạn) *n.* a group of fixed stars; an assemblage of notable persons or things [L. *con-; stella,* a star].

con·ster·na·tion (kạn·stẹr′·nā′·shạn) *n.* amazement or terror that throws the mind into confusion. **consternate** *v.t.* to fill with alarm or dismay [L. *con-; sternere,* to strew].

con·sti·pate (kàn′·stạ·pāt) *v.t.* to clog or make sluggish. **constipation** *n.* insufficient; irregular evacuation of the bowels [L. *con-; stipare,* to pack].

con·sti·tute (kàn′sti·tòòt) *v.t.* to appoint to an office or function; to establish; to set up; to form; to compose. **constitution** *n.* the act of constituting; the natural state of body or mind; composition; the system or body of laws under which a state exists. **constitutional** *a* pert. to the constitution; due to a person's physical or mental composition; *n.* a walk for the benefit of health. **constitutionally** *adv.* **constitutionalist** *n.* one who upholds constitutional government. **constitutionality** *n.* **constitutive** (kàn′·sti·tū·tiv) *a.* having powers to enact or establish. **constituent** (kạn·-stich′·òò·ạnt) *a.* serving to compose or make up; an element; *n.* a voter [L. *constituere,* to place together].

con·strain (kạn·strān′) *v.t.* to force or compel; to confine; to restrain; to limit. **-t** *n.* compelling force; restraining force; unnaturalness or embarrassment of manner [L. *con-; stingere,* to press].

con·strict (kạn·strikt′) *v.t.* to draw together; to cramp; to cause to shrink or contract; to squeeze. **-ion** *n.* **-ive** *a.* [L. *con-; stringere,* to bind].

con·struct (kạn·strukt′) *v.t.* to build; to fabricate; to devise or invent; to compile. **-ion** *n.* the act of building; erection; structure; interpretation or meaning. **-ive** *a.* **-iveness** *n.* **-or** *n.* [L. *construere,* to build].

con·strue (kạn·stròò′) *v.t.* to interpret; to put a construction upon; to deduce; to explain the structure of a sentence and the connection of the words in it; to translate. **construable** *a.* **-r** *n.* [L. *construere,* to build].

con·sub·stan·ti·ate (kàn-sạb·stan′·shi·āt) *v.t., v.i.* to unite in one substance or nature. **consubstantial** *a.* **consubstantiation** *n.* (*Theol.*) the doctrine of the substantial union of Christ's body and blood with the elements of the sacrament [L. *consubstantialis,* of like nature].

con·sul (kàn′·sạl) *n.* an officer appointed by a government to represent it in a foreign country. **-ar** *a.* **-ate** *n.* the offices of a consul. **-ship** *n.* [L.].

con·sult (kan·sult′) *v.t.* to ask advice of; to seek the opinion of; to look for information; to refer to; *v.i.* to confer. **-ant** *n.* one who consults; one who gives expert advice. **-ing** *a.* **-ation** *n.* the act of consulting; a council or conference. **-ative** *a.* advisory [L. *consulere*].

con·sume (kạn·sòòm′) *v.t.* to waste; to destroy; to use up; to eat or drink up; *v.i.* to waste away. **consumable** *a.* **-r** *n.* **-rism** *n.* a movement of consumers demanding fairness in products, packaging, and advertising [L. *consumere,* to use up].

con·sum·mate (kàn′·sạm·āt) *v.t.* to complete; to finish; to perfect; (*Law*) to complete marriage by sexual intercourse; (kạn·sum′·it) *a.* complete; perfect. **-ly** *adv.* **consummation** *n.* [L. *consummare*].

con·sump·tion (kạn·sump′·shạn) *n.* the act of consuming: the amount consumed; (*Med.*) pulmonary tuberculosis. **consumptive** *a.* destructive; wasteful; wasting; affected with, or inclined to, pulmonary tuberculosis; *n.* (*Med.*) a person suffering from consumption [L. *consumere, consumptum,* to use up].

con·tact (kàn′·takt) *n.* a touching; (*Colloq.*) a meeting; *v.t.* to get in touch with a person. **-ual** (kạn·tak′·choo·al) *a.* implying contact. **— lens** *n.* an invisible eye-glass fitting over the eyeball [L. *tangere, tactum,* to touch].

con·ta·gion (kạn·tā′·jạn) *n.* the transmission of a disease from one person to another; physical or moral pestilence. **contagious** *a.* communicable [L. *contagio,* fr. *tangere,* to touch].

con·tain (kạn·tān′) *v.t.* to hold; to have room for; to comprise; to include; to restrain. **-able**

a. **-er** *n.* [L. *con-; tenere,* to hold].

con·tam·i·nate (kạn·tam′·ạ·nāt) *v.t.* to soil; to taint; to corrupt; to infect. **contaminable** *a.* **contamination** *n.* pollution; taint; (*War*) the result of coming into contact with liquid gases or radioactive particles [L. *contamen,* contagion].

con·temn (kạn·tem′) *v.t.* to despise; to scorn. **-er** *n.* [L. *contemnere*].

con·tem·plate (kȧn′·tem·plāt) *v.t.* to look at with attention; to meditate on; to have in view; to intend; *v.i.* to think studiously; to reflect. **contemplation** *n.* **contemplative** *a.* **contemplatively** *adv.* [L. *contemplari,* to observe].

con·tem·po·ra·ne·ous (kạn·tem·pạ·rā′·ni·-ạs) *a.* having or happening at the same time. **-ly** *adv.* **-ness** *n.* **contemporary** *a.* living or happening at the same time; contemporaneous; present-day; *n.* one who lives at the same time as another; a person approximately of one's own age [L. *con-; tempus, temporis,* time].

con·tempt (kạn·temt′) *n.* scorn; disgrace; disregard; open disrespect to court orders or rule. **-ible** *a.* worthy of contempt; despicable. **-ibleness** *n.* **-ibly** *adv.* **-uous** *a.* expressing contempt or disdain; scornful. **-uously** *adv.* **-uousness** *n.* [L. *contemnere, contemptum,* to despise].

con·tend (kạn·tend′) *v.i.* to fight or struggle with; to strive for; to dispute; to assert strongly; **-er** *n.* [L. *con-; tendere,* to stretch].

con·tent (kạn·tent′) *a.* satisfied; pleased; willing; *v.t.* to satisfy the mind of; to please; to appease; *n.* satisfaction; freedom from anxiety. **-edly** *adv.* **-edness** *n.* **-ment** *n.* satisfaction; pleasure; ease of mind [L. *contentus*].

con·tent (kȧn′·tent) *n.* that which is contained; extent or area; volume. **-s** *n.pl.* an index of the topics treated in a book [L. *continere, contentum,* to contain].

con·ten·tion (kạn·ten′·shạn) *n.* strife; debate; subject matter of argument or discussion. **contentious** *a.* quarrelsome [L. *con-; tendere, tentum,* to stretch].

con·ter·mi·nous (kạn·tur′·mạn·ạs) *a.* having the same boundary; bordering; touching. Also **conterminable, conterminal.**

con·test (kạn·test′) *v.t.* to strive for; to question or resist, as a claim; to dispute; to oppose; *v.i.* to contend or vie (with). **contest** (kȧn′·-test) *n.* struggle; conflict; competition; dispute; strike. **-able** *a.* **-ant** *n.* a disputant; a competitor [L. *contestari,* to call to witness].

con·text (kȧn′·tekst) *n.* that which comes immediately before or after a passage or word quoted, and therefore helps to explain it; the setting of a text. **-ual** *a.* pert. to the context. **contexture** *n.* the weaving of parts into one body; structure; style of composition in writing [L. *con-; texere,* to weave].

con·ti·gu·i·ty (kạn·ti·gū′·ạ·ti·) *n.* the state of being contiguous. **contiguous** *a.* touching; near; adjacent [L. *contiguous,* touching].

con·ti·nent (kạn′·tin·ȧnt) *n.* one of the large divisions of unbroken land. **-al** *a.* pert. to a continent [L. *con-; tenere,* to hold].

con·ti·nent (kȧn′·tin·ạnt) *a.* chaste; temperate; moderate. **continence, continency** *n.* [L. *con-; tenere,* hold].

con·tin·gent (kạn·tin′·jạnt) *a.* liable to happen, but not sure to do so; possible; dependent; *n.* contingency; a quota, esp. of troops. **-ly** *adv.* **contingence, contingency** *n.* [L. *contingere,* to happen].

con·tin·ue (kạn·tin′·ū) *v.t.* to prolong or extend in duration; to go on with; to persist in; to resume; *v.i.* to remain in a state or place; to persevere; to last. **continual** *a.* lasting; without interruption; often repeated; unceasing. **continually** *adv.* **continuance** *n.* a remaining in existence; duration; uninterrupted succession. **continuant** *a.* **continuate** *a.* uninterrupted. **continuation** *n.* the act of continuing. **continuity** (kȧn·ti·nȯȯ′·i·ti·) *n.* the state of being continuous; uninterrupted succession; close union. **continuous** *a.* united without break; uninterrupted; constant. **continuously** *adv.* [L. *continuare*].

con·tort (kạn·tawrt′) *v.t.* to twist violently; to writhe; to bend out of shape. **contortion** *n.* a twisting; writhing. **contortionist** *n.* one who practices contortion. **contortive** *a.* [L. *con-; torquere, tortum,* to twist].

con·tour (kȧn′·toor) *n.* a bounding line; outline; *v.t.* to draw the contour of [L. *con-; tornare,* to round off].

con·tra- Latin *prefix* meaning against, contrary, in opposition to, used to form many compounds.

con·tra·band (kȧn′·trạ·band) *a.* prohibited by law or treaty; *n.* goods, the exportation or importation of which is forbidden; smuggled goods. **contraband of war,** goods not to be supplied by a neutral to a belligerent [L. *contra;* L.L. *bandum,* a ban].

con·tra·bass (kȧn′·tra·bās) *n.* (*Mus.*) the double-bass. Also **contrabasso.**

con·tra·cep·tion (kȧn·trạ·sep′·shạn) *n.* the prevention of conception; by artificial means; birth control. **contraceptive** *a.* and *n.* a drug or appliance for preventing conception [L. *contra;* and *conception*].

con·tract (kạn·trakt′) *v.t.* to draw together; to shorten; to reduce to a less volume; to incur or bring on; *v.i.* to become smaller; to become shorter; to agree upon; to become involved in. **contract** (kȧn′·trakt) *n.* a bargain; an agreement. **-ed** *a.* drawn together; narrow; mean. **-ible** *a.* **-ile** *a.* tending to contract; producing contraction. **-ility** *n.* **-ion** *n.* the act of contracting; the shortening of a word by the omission of a letter or syllable. **-or** *n.* one who undertakes to execute work for a fixed sum. **-ual** *a.* implying, or connected with, a contract [L. *contractus,* drawn together].

con·tra·dict (kȧn·trạ·dikt′) *v.t.* to assert the contrary of; to deny. **contradiction** *n.* denial; direct opposition; discrepancy of statements. **contradictious** *a.* inclined to contradict. **-ive** *a.* containing contradiction. **-ory** *a.* implying a denial; diametrically opposed; inconsistent [L. *contradicere,* to speak against].

con·tra·dis·tinc·tion (kȧn·trạ·dis·tingk′·-shạn) *n.* direct contrast. **contradistinctive** *a.* **contradistinguish** *v.t.* to note the difference between two things by contrasting their different qualities.

con·tral·to (kạn·tral′·tō) *n.* the lowest of the three female voices; a singer of that voice [It. *contra; alto*].

con·trap·tion (kạn·trap′·shạn) *n.* (*Colloq.*) a device; a gadget [perh. fr. *contrivance*].

con·tra·pun·tal (kȧn·trạ·pun′·tạl) *a.* pert. to counterpoint [See **counterpoint**].

con·tra·ry (kȧn′·tre·ri·) *a.* opposed; opposing; different; adverse; self-willed; *n.* something the exact opposite of. **contrariety** (kȧn·tra·-rī′·ạ·ti·) *n.* something contrary. **contrarily** *adv.* **contrariness** *n.* **contrariwise** *adv.* on the contrary [L. *contrarius,* fr. *contra,* against].

con·trast (kạn·trast′) *v.t.* to bring out differences; to set in opposition for the purpose of comparing; *v.i.* to be or stand in opposition. **contrast** (kȧn′·trast) *n.* a striking difference; a comparison to show their relative excellence [L. *contra; stare,* to stand].

con·tra·vene (kȧn·trạ·vēn′) *v.t.* to oppose; to break or infringe, as a law. **contravention** *n.* [L. *contravenire,* to come against].

con·tri·bute (kạn·trib′·yoot) *v.t.* to give or pay to a common fund; to help to a common result; to write for a newspaper, magazine, etc.; *v.i.* to lend assistance. **contributable** *a.*

contribution (kȧn·tri·bū′·shạn) *n.* that which is contributed. **contributive** *a.* **contributory** *a.* [L. *contribuere*].

con·trite (kȧn′·trīt) *a.* penitent; remorseful. **-ly** *adv.* **-ness** *n.* **contrition** (kạn·trish′·ạn) *n.* remorse [L. *con-*; *terere*, to grind].

con·trive (kạn·trīv′) *v.t.* and *i.* to plan; to effect or bring about; to invent. **contrivance** *n.* the act of planning; the thing contrived; artifice or device; mechanical invention. **-r** *n.* [L. *con-*; O.Fr. *trover*, to find].

con·trol (kạn·trōl) *v.t.* to have under command; to regulate; to check; to restrain; to direct; *n.* authority or power; government; restraint; in spiritualism, the spirit supposed to control the medium; the control system of levers, switches, etc. in aircraft, motor vehicles, etc. *pr.p* **-ling.** *pa.p.* and *pa.t.* **-led.** **-lable** *a.* **-ler** *n.* one who controls. **-lership** *n.* **-ment** *n.* [L. *contra*, against; *rotulus*, a roll].

con·tro·vert (kȧn′·trạ·vurt) *v.t.* to oppose or dispute by argument; to deny or refute. **-ible** *adv.* **controversy** *n.* disputation; argument, esp. by published writings; debate. **controversial** *a.* consisting of controversy; leading to controversy; likely to provoke argument. **controversially** *adv.* **controversialist** *n.* [L. *contra; vertere*, to turn].

con·tu·ma·cy (kȧn′·tyoo·mạ·si·) *n.* contempt of orders or authority; stubborn disobedience. **contumacious** *a.* rebellious. **-ly** *adv.* **-ness** *n.* [L. *contumacia*].

con·tu·me·ly (kȧn′·tyoo·mạ·li·) *n.* insult; affront; indignity; disdainful insolence. **contumelious** (kȧn·tū·mē′·li·us) *a.* insolent; haughtily disdainful [L. *contumelia*].

con·tuse (kạn·tūz′) *v.t.* to bruise or injure without breaking the skin. **contusion** *n.* a bruise [L. *con-; tundere, tusum*, to beat].

co·nun·drum (kạ·nun′·drạm) *n.* a riddle; anything that puzzles [etym. unknown].

con·va·lesce (kȧn·vạ·les′) *v.i.* to recover from illness. **convalescent** *a.* **convalescence** *n.* [L. *convalescere*].

con·vec·tion (kạn·vek′·shạn) *n.* the act or process of transmission, esp. of heat by means of currents in liquids or gases [L. *con-; vehere, vectum*, to carry].

con·vene (kạn·vēn′) *v.t.* to call together; *v.i.* to come together or assemble. **-r** *n.* **convenable** *a.* [L. *con-; venire*, to come].

con·ven·ient (kạn·vēn′·yạnt) *a.* fit; suitable; affording saving of trouble; handy or easy of access. **-ly** *adv.* **convenience** *n.* that which is convenient; any appliance which makes for comfort [L. *con-*; *venire*, to come].

con·vent (kȧn′·vent) *n.* a community, esp. of nuns, devoted to a religious life; a nunnery. **conventual** *a.* [L. *con-; venire*, to come].

con·ven·ti·cle (kạn·ven′·tạ·kl) *n.* secret gathering, esp. for worship [L. *con-*; *venire*, to come].

con·ven·tion (kạn·ven′·shạn) *n.* the act of coming together; a formal assembly of representatives; a provisional treaty; accepted usage, custom, or rule. **-al** *a.* formed by agreement or compact; sanctioned by usage; customary. **-ally** *adv.* **-alism** *n.* that which is established by usage. **-ality** *n.* [L. *con-; venire*, to come].

con·verge (kạn·vurj′) *v.i.* to tend to one point; to tend to meet; to approach. **convergent** *a.* **convergence, convergency** *n.* coming together [L. *con-; vergere*, to incline].

con·verse (kạn·vurs′) *v.i.* to talk with. **conversable** *a.* disposed to talk; affable. **conversably** *adv.* **conversance, conversancy** *n.* the state of being acquainted with. **conversant** *a.* familiar or acquainted with by use or study. **conversation** *n.* talk. **conversational** *a.* **conversation(al)ist** *n.* one who excels in conversation [L. *conversari*, to dwell with].

con·verse (kạn·vurs′) *a.* opposite; turned around; reversed in order or relation; *n.* (kȧn′·vurs) the opposite; the contrary **-ly** *adv.* [L. *conversus*, turned about].

con·vert (kạn·vurt′) *v.t.* to apply to another purpose; to change; to cause to adopt a religion, an opinion, etc.; *v.i.* to be turned or changed. **convert** (kȧn′·vurt) *n.* a converted person; one who has turned from sin to holiness. **conversion** *n.* a change from one state to another. **-er** *n.* one who, or that which, converts; (*Elect.*) a machine for changing alternating current into direct current, or altering the pressure of direct current; an iron retort. **-ible** *a.* capable of change; transformable; transmutable; *n.* (*Colloq.*) an automobile with a folding top [L. *convertere*, to turn about].

con·vex (kȧn·veks′) *a.* curving outwards; the opposite of *concave*; bulging. **-ity, -ness** *n.* [L. *convexus*, arched].

con·vey (kạn·vā′) *v.t.* to carry; to transport; to transfer; to make over by deed; to impart; to communicate. **-able** *a.* **-ance** *n.* the act of conveying; a means of transit; a vehicle; the transference of property; the legal document by which property, titles, etc., are transferred. **-ancing** *n.* **-er, -or** *n.* [L. *con-; via*, a way].

con·vict (kạn·vikt′) *v.t.* to prove guilty; to pronounce guilty. **convict** (kȧn′·vict) *n.* a person serving a sentence. **-ion** *n.* the act of convicting; a verdict of guilty; the state of being convinced; a firm belief [L. *convincere, convictum*, to prove guilty].

con·vince (kạn·vins′) *v.t.* to bring to a belief; to persuade by argument; to satisfy by proof. **convincible** *a.* **convincing** *a.* **convincingly** *adv.* [L. *convincere*, to prove].

con·viv·i·al (kạn·viv′·i·ạl) *a.* festive; jovial; social; merry. **-ly** *adv.* **conviviality** *n.* [L. *convivium*, a feast].

con·voke (kạn·vōk′) *v.t.* to call together; to convene; to assemble. **convocation** *n.* the act of calling together; an assembly [L. *convocare*, to call together].

con·volve (kạn·vȧlv′) *v.t.* and *i.* to roll or wind together; to twist; to coil. **convolute** (kȧn′·vạ·lȯȯt), **convoluted** *a.* rolled together; involved; spiral. **convolution** *n.* the act of rolling together; the state of being coiled; a turn of a coil; a fold of the brain [L. *convolvere*, to roll together].

con·voy (kạn·voi′) *v.t.* to accompany or escort for protection, by land, sea, or air. **convoy** (kȧn′·voi) *n.* the act of convoying; escort; escorting protection [L. *con-; via*, a way].

con·vulse (kạn·vuls′) *v.t.* to shake violently; to affect with violent and irregular spasms; to cause violent disturbance. **convulsion** *n.* any violent agitation; *pl.* (*Med.*) violent and involuntary contractions of the muscles; spasms; fits of laughter. **convulsive** *a.* characterized by convulsion; spasmodic; jerky [L. *con-; vellere, velsum*, to pluck].

coo (kòò) *v.i.* to make a low, melodius sound like the note of a dove; to act in a loving manner [imit.].

cook (kook) *v.t.* to prepare food by boiling, roasting, baking, etc.; (*Colloq.*) to concoct; to falsify; *v.i.* to prepare food by the action of heat; to undergo cooking; *n.* one whose occupation is to cook food. **-ery** *n.* the art or process of cooking. **-er** *n.* **-out** *n.* meal cooked and eaten outdoors [O.E. *coc*].

cook·y, cook·ie (kook′·i·) *n.* a small sweet cake made of stiff dough which is rolled, dropped, or sliced, and baked [Dut. *koek*, cake].

cool (kòòl) *a.* slightly cold; self-possessed; dispassionate; chilly or frigid in manner; impudent; *n.* a moderate state of cold; *v.t.* to cause to cool; to moderate or calm; *v.i.* to become cool; to lose one's ardor or affection. **-er** *n.* a container for cooling; (*Slang*) jail. **-ish** *a.*

fairly cool. **-ly** *adv.* **-ness** *n.* **—headed** *a.* calm; self-possessed. **— one's heels,** to wait a long time [O.E. *col*].

coo·lie (kòò′·li·) *n.* an Asiatic laborer. Also **cooly** [prob. *Kuli,* name of tribe].

coon (kòòn) *n.* a raccoon [abbrev. of *raccoon*].

coop (kòòp) *n.* pen for poultry; (*Slang*) jail; *v.t.* to put up in a coop; confine [M.E. *cupe,* a basket].

coop·er (kòòp′·ęr) *n.* a maker of casks or barrels [L. *cupa,* a cask]. shop [L. *cupa,* a cask].

co·op·er·ate (kō·àp′·ą·rāt) *v.i.* to act jointly with other; to unite for a common effort. **co-operation** *n.* **co-operative** *a.* **co-operator** *n.* **co-operative store,** the shop of a co-operative society, where members make their purchases and share the profits. Also **co-op** *n.* short form [L. *co-*; *operari,* to work].

co·opt (kō·àpt′) *v.t.* to choose or elect into a body or committee by the votes of its own members. **-ion, -ation** *n.* [L. *co-; optare,* to choose].

co·or·di·nate (kō·awr′·di·nāt) *a.* equal in degree, rank, importance, etc.; *v.t.* to make equal in degree, etc.; to bring into order as parts of a whole; to adjust; *n.* a person or thing of the same rank, importance, etc. as another. **-ly** *adv.* in the same order. **-ness** *n.* **coordination** *n.* **coordinative** *a.* [L. *co-*; *ordo,* rank, order].

coot (kòòt) *n.* a small water-fowl of the rail family [M.E. *cote*].

cop (kàp) *v.t.* (*Slang*) to catch or arrest. *pr.p.* **-ping.** *pa.t.* **-ped.** *n.* (*Slang*) a policeman..

co·part·ner (kō·pàrt′·nęr) *n.* a partner; an associate. **-ship** *n.*

cope (kōp) *n.* cloak or mantle; a long, sleeveless vestment worn by ecclesiastics during divine service; *v.t.* to dress with a cope. **coping** *n.* the highest course of masonry in a wall [form of *cape*].

cope (kōp) *v.i.* to contend, esp. on equal terms or with success; to deal successfully (with) [L. *colaphus,* a blow with the fist].

Co·per·ni·can (kō·pur′·ni·kąn) *a.* pert. to *Copernicus* the founder of modern astronomy.

cop·i·er (kàp′·i·ęr) *n.* See **copy.**

co·pi·ous (kō′·pi·ąs) *a.* abundant; plentiful; of style, not concise. **-ly** *adv.* **-ness** *n.* [L. *copia,* plenty].

cop·per (kàp′·ęr) *n.* a red-colored metal; a copper coin; *a.* copper-colored; made of copper; *v.t.* to cover with copper. **-y** *a.* made of copper; like copper. **-head** *n.* a poisonous N. American snake [L. *Cyprium aes,* bronze from the island of Cyprus].

cop·pice, copse (kàp′·is) *n.* a wood of small trees. Also **copsewood** *n.* [O.Fr. *coper,* to cut].

cop·ra (kàp′·rą) *n.* the dried kernel of the coconut palm [Malay.].

cop·u·la (kàp′·yą·lą) *n.* a connecting link; a bond; (*Gram.*) the word uniting the subject and predicate. **copulate** *v.i.* to unite sexually. **copulation** *n.* **-tive** *a.* pert. to copulation; serving to unite [L. = a bond].

cop·y (kàp′·i·) *n.* an imitation of an original; a writing like another writing; an exact reproduction; a transcript; a single specimen; anything to be imitated; the manuscript, etc. placed in the compositor's hands; the basic matter for a journalistic article; *v.t.* to write, print, etc. in imitation of an original; to imitate. **-ist** *n.* **copier** *n.* one who copies; an imitator. **-book** *n.* a book in which copies are written for learners to imitate. **-writer** *n.* a writer of advertisements. **-right** *n.* the legal exclusive right which an author, musician, or artist has to print, publish, and sell his own works, during a certain period of time; *a.* protected by the law of copyright [L. *copia,* abundance].

co·quet (kō·ket′) *v.i.* to attempt to attract the notice, admiration, or love of; to flirt with. *pr.p.* **-ting.** *pa.p.* and *pa.t.* **-ted. coquetry** (kō′·ket·ri·) *n.* affectation of amorous advances; trifling in love; airy graces to attract admirers. **coquette** *n.* a flirt. **-tish** *a.* [Fr. *coquet,* dim. of *coq,* a cock].

cor·al (kàr′·, kawr′·ąl) *n.* a hard reddish yellow, white, etc. substance growing on the bottom of tropical seas, and composed of the skeletons of zoophytes; *a.* coral-colored; made of coral [Gk. *korallion*].

cord (kawrd) *n.* a thick string or a thin rope of several strands; anything like a cord (e.g. spinal cord, vocal cord); a cubic measure esp. for fuel wood; *v.t.* to bind with a cord or rope. **-age** *n.* an assemblage of ropes and cords, esp. the rigging of a ship. **-ed** *a.* **-ing** *n.* ribbed surface [Gk. *chordē*].

cor·dial (kawr′·jal) *a.* expressing warmth of heart; sincere; stimulating; *n.* anything that invigorates or strengthens; a refreshing drink or medicine. **-ly** *adv.* **-ity** *n.* [L. *cor, cordis,* the heart].

cord·ite (kawrd′·īt) *n.* a smokeless explosive [fr. *cord*].

cor·don (kawr′·dąn) *n.* a line of military posts enclosing an area to prevent passage; hence, a circle of persons round any place or thing to prevent access; a tasseled cord or ribbon worn as a badge of honor. **— bleu,** a person of great distinction in his field [Fr.].

cor·do·van (kawr′·dą·vąn) *n.* Spanish leather; goatskin tanned and dressed [fr. *Cordoba,* in Spain].

cor·du·roy (kawr′·dą·roi·) *n.* a thick cotton fabric, corded or ribbed on the surface. *n.pl.* trousers made of this fabric [Fr. *corde du roi,* king's cord].

core (kōr) *n.* the heart or inner part, esp. of fruit; *v.t.* to take out the core [L. *cor,* the heart].

co·res·pon·dent (kō·ri·spàn′·dąnt) *n.* in a divorce suit the man or woman charged along with the respondent as guilty of adultery.

cork (kawrk) *n.* the outer bark of the cork-tree; a stopper for a bottle, cask, etc.; *a.* made of cork; *v.t.* to stop up with a cork; to stop up generally; to give wine, beer, etc. a corky taste. **-er** *n.* (*Slang*) anything first-class. **-ing** *a.* (*Slang*) excellent. **-screw** *n.* a tool for drawing corks from bottles; *a.* shaped like a corkscrew; with a spiral twist. [L. *cortex,* bark].

cor·mo·rant (kawr′·mą·rąnt) *n.* a voracious seabird; gluttonous person [Fr. *cormoran*].

corn (kawrn) *n.* a single seed of oats, wheat, rye, barley, maize, etc.; an inclusive term for grain of all kinds; *v.t.* to preserve meat by salting. **-cob** *n.* the head or seed-pod in which are encased the grains of the maize plant; a tobacco pipe with the bowl made from a corncob.**-flour** *n.* a foodstuff consisting of the finely ground starch granules of Indian corn (maize). **-flower** *n.* an annual weed growing in cornfields and bearing blue flowers. **-husk** *n.* the outer leaves enclosing an ear of corn. **-starch** *n.* a starch used for thickening puddings, sauces, etc. **-y** *a.* (*Slang*) trite, old-fashioned, unsophisticated [O.E. *corn*].

corn (kawrn) *n.* a horny growth of the skin, usually on toes and feet. **-y** *a.* pert. to a corn [L. *cornu,* a horn].

cor·ne·a (kawr′·ni·ą)*n.* the transparent membrane which forms part of the outer coat of the eyeball [L. *corneus,* horny].

cor·ner (kawr′·nęr) *n.* the point where two lines meet; the part of a room where two sides meet; an angle; a nook; an embarrassing position; *v t.* to drive into a corner; to put into a position of difficulty, leaving no escape; to establish a monopoly. **-stone** *n.* the stone which lies at the corner of two walls, and unites them; in an important edifice a corner foundation stone laid with ceremony; something of funda-

mental importance; **-wise** *adv.* diagonally; with the corner in front. **to corner the market,** to obtain a monopoly [L. *cornu,* a horn].
cor·net (kawr·net′) *n.* a kind of trumpet with valves; a cone of paper [L. *cornu,* a horn].
cor·nice (kawr′·nis) *n.* an ornamental molding around the top of the walls of a room [Fr. *corniche,* a ledge].
cor·nu·co·pi·a (kawr·nạ·kō′·pi·ạ) *n.* the horn of plenty, an emblem of abundance [L. *cornu,* a horn; *copia,* plenty].
cor·ol·lar·y (kȧr′·, kawr′·ạ·ler·i·) *n.* an inference from a preceding statement; a deduction; a consequence [L. *corolla,* a garland].
co·ro·na (kạ·rō′·nạ) *n.* the flat projecting part of a cornice; a top or crown; a halo around a heavenly body; a make of cigar (Trade Name). **-l** (kawr′·ạ·nạl) *a.* pert. to a corona; *n.* a crown; a wreath. **coronary** *a.* resembling a crown or circlet; (*Anat.*) encircling, as of a vessel or nerve; pertaining to the arteries which supply the heart tissues. **coronary thrombosis** (*Med.*) a heart condition caused by a blood clot in a coronary artery. **coronate** *v.t.* to crown. **coronation** *n.* the crowning of a sovereign. **coronet** *n.* a small crown worn by the nobility [L. *corona,* a crown].
cor·o·ner (kȧr′·, kawr′·ạ·nẹr) *n.* a legal officer appointed to hold an inquest in cases of death [L. *corona,* a crown].
cor·po·ral (kawr′·pạ·rạl) *n.* non-commissioned officer of a company or troop, next below a sergeant [L. *caput,* the head].
cor·po·ral (kawr′·pạ·ral) *a.* belonging or relating to the body; bodily; *n.* a communion ti·) *n.* the state of having a body; bodily subcloth. **-ly** *adv.* **corporality** (kawr·pạ·ral′·ạ·-stance. **corporate** (kawr′·pạ·rit) *a.* united legally in a body; pertaining to a corporation. **corporately** *adv.* **corporateness** *n.* **corporation** (kawr·pạ·rā′·shạn) *n.* united body; a legal, municipal, mercantile, or professional association. **corporative** *a.* **corporeal** (kawr·paw′·ri·ạl) *a.* pert. to the body; having a body; bodily; physical. **corporeally** *adv.* **corporal punishment,** punishment inflicted on the body [L. *corpus,* body].
corps (kawr) *n.* a division of an army forming a unit; any organized body of persons. *pl.* **corps** (kawrz) [Fr. fr. L. *corpus,* a body].
corpse (kawrps) *n.* a dead body, esp. of a human being [L. *corpus,* the body].
cor·pu·lence (kawr′·pyạ·lạns) *n.* excessive fatness; fleshiness; stoutness. Also **corpulency** *n.* **corpulent** *a.* [L. *corpus,* the body].
cor·pus (kawr′·pạs) *n.* a body; the main substance of anything. *pl.* **corpora** [L. = a body].
cor·pus·cle (kawr′·pus·l) *n.* a little body; a minute particle; (*Anat.*) an organic cell, either moving freely, as in the blood, or intimately connected with others, as bone-corpuscles [L. *corpusculum,* dim. of *corpus,* a body].
cor·ral (kạ·ral′) *n.* an enclosure for cattle, or for defense; *v.t.* to drive into a corral [Sp. fr. *corro,* a circle].
cor·rect (ka·rekt′) *a.* right; free from faults; accurate; *v.t.* to make right; to indicate the errors in; to bring to the standard of truth; to punish; to counteract. **-ly** *adv.* **-tion** *n.* amendment; a change to remedy a fault; punishment. **itude** *n.* **-ional** *a.* **-ive** *a.* having power to correct; *n.* that which corrects or counteracts. **-ness** *n.* **-or** *n.* [L. *corrigere,* to make right].
cor·re·late (kȧr′·, kawr′·ạ·lat) *v.i.* to be mutually related, as father and son; *v.t.* to place in reciprocal relations; *n.* a correlative; either of two things or words necessarily implying the other. **correlation** *n.* reciprocal relation. **correlative** *a.* reciprocally related; *n.* one who, or that which, is correspondingly related to another person of thing. **correlativity** *n.*
cor·re·spond (kȧr′·, kawr·ạ·spȧnd′) *v.i.* to exchange letters; to answer or agree with in some respect; to be congruous. **-ence** *n.* exchange of letters; the letters themselves; mutual adaptation of one thing to another; suitability. **-ent** *a.* suitable; conformable; congruous; *n.* one with whom intercouse is maintained by exchange of letters. **-ing** *a.* **-ingly** *adv.* [L. *correspondere,* answer with].
cor·ri·dor (kȧr′·, kawr′·ạ·dẹr) *n.* a gallery or passage in a building [L. *currere,* to run].
cor·ri·gen·dum (kawr·ạ·jen′·dạm) *n.* something to be corrected, esp. a misprint in a book; *pl.* **corrigenda** [L. = to be corrected].
cor·ri·gi·ble (kȧr′·, kawr·′ạ·jạbl) *a.* capable of being corrected [L. *corrigere,* to correct].
cor·rob·o·rate (kạ·rȧb′·ạ·rāt) *v.t.* to add strength to; to confirm; to support a statement, etc. **corroborant** *a.* giving strength. **corroboration** *n.* **corroborative** *a.* confirming; strengthening [L. *con-*; *robur, roboris,* strength]
cor·rode (kạ·rōd′) *v.t.* to eat away by degrees (by chemical action, disease, etc.); to rust. **corrodent** *a.* corrosive; *n.* a substance which eats away. **corrodible, corrosible** *a.* capable of being corroded. **corrosion** *n.* **corrosive** *a.* having the power of corroding; fretting or vexing; *n.* any corrosive substance [L. *con-*; *rodere,* to gnaw].
cor·ru·gate (kȧr′·, kawr′·ạ·gāt) *v.t.* to form into folds or alternate furrows and ridges. **corrugation** *n.* **— iron,** sheet-iron, corrugated to increase its rigidity [L. *con-*; *ruga,* a wrinkle].
cor·rupt (kạ·rupt′) *v.t.* and *i.* to make rotten; to rot; to defile; to contaminate; to make evil; to bribe; *a.* putrid; depraved; tainted with vice or sin; influenced by bribery; spoiled, by mistakes, or altered for the worse (of words, literary passages, etc.). **-er** *n.* **-ible** *a.* capable of being corrupted **.corruption** *n.* **-ive** *a.* **-ly** *adv.* **-ness** *n.* [L. *corrumpere, corruptum*].
cor·sage (kawr′·sȧj) *n.* a small bouquet worn by a lady; the bodice of a lady's dress [L. *corpus,* the body].
cor·sair (kawr′·sār) *n.* a pirate; a pirate's vessel [Fr. *corraire*].
cor·set (kawr′·sit) *n.* undergarment; girdle. **corselet** (kawr′·sạ·let), **corselette** (kawrs′·-lit) *n.* a corset. **corslet, corselet** *n.* a piece of armor to cover the trunk of the body [Fr. *corselet,* double dim. of O.Fr. *cors,* the body, fr. L. *corpus,* the body] .
cor·tège (kawr·tezh′) *n.* a train of attendants or procession; a funeral procession [Fr.].
cor·tex (kawr′·teks) *n.* bark; sheath or skin of a plant. (*Anat.*) the outer covering of an organ, esp. the outer layer of gray matter of the brain; *pl.* **cortices** (kawr′·ti·sēz). **cortical** *a.* **corticate, corticated** *a.* [L. = the bark of tree].
cor·ti·sone (kawr′·ti·zōn) *n.* a substance produced in the adrenal glands [fr. *cortex*].
co·run·dum (kạ·run′·dạm) *n.* common mineral noted for hardness [Hind. *kurand*].
cor·us·cate (kȧr′· kawr′·ạs·kāt) *v.i.* to flash; to sparkle, to glitter; to gleam. **coruscation** *n.* [L. *coruscare,* to glitter, vibrate].
cor·y·bant·ic (kawr′·ạ·bant·ik) *a.* rural estate; *a.* frenzied and delirious [*Myth.* goddess Cybele].
co·se·cant (kō·sē′·kạnt) *n.* (*Trig.*) the secant of the complement of an angle. (*Abbrev.*) **cosec** [L. *co-*; *secare,* to cut].
co·sig·na·to·ry (kō·sig′·nạ·tōr·i·) *a.* signing jointly; *n.* a joint signer of a document.
co·sine (kō′·sin) *n.* (*Trig.*) the sine of the complement of an angle. (*Abbrev.*) **cos.**
cos·met·ic (kȧz·met′·ik) *a.* making for beauty, esp. of the skin; *n.* any substance helping to improve or enhance the appearance [Gk. *kosmein,* to arrange, adorn].
cos·mic (kȧz′·mik) *a.* See **cosmos.**
cos·mo- (koz′·mō) a combining form from Gk. *kosmos,* the universe.

cos·mog·o·ny (kȧs·mȧg′·ą·ni·) *n.* a theory of the creation of the universe and its inhabitants. [Gk. *kosmos,* the universe; *gignesthai,* to be born].

cos·mol·o·gy (kȧs·mȧl′·ą·ji·) *n.* the science of the laws which control the universe. **cosmological** *a.* **cosmologist** *n.* [Gk. *kosmos,* the universe; *logos,* discourse].

cos·mo·naut (kȧz′·mą·nȧt) *n.* a space traveler.

cos·mo·pol·i·tan (kȧs·mą·pȧl′·i·tąn) *a.* relating to all parts of the world; free from national prejudice; *n.* a cosmopolitan person; a citizen of the world. Also **cosmopolite** *n.* [Gk. *kosmos,* the universe; *politēs,* a citizen].

cos·mos (kȧz′·mąs) *n.* the ordered universe; order (as opposed to 'chaos'); a genus of flowering plant. **cosmic, cosmical** *a.* pert. to the universe, or to the earth as a part of the universe; orderly. **cosmically** *adv.* **cosmic rays,** radiations of great penetrating power, coming to the earth from outer space [Gk. *kosmos,* order].

Cos·sack (kȧs′·k) *n.* member of S. Russ. tribe [Turk. *quazzaq,* an adventurer].

cost (kawst) *v.i.* to entail the payment, loss, or sacrifice of; to cause to bear or suffer; *n.* price; the amount paid, or to be paid, for anything; expenditure of time, labor, etc.; suffering undergone for any end. **-liness** *n.* great cost or expense; expensiveness. **-ly** *a.* very expensive. **— price,** the wholesale, as opposed to the retail, price [L. *constare,* fr. *stare,* to stand].

cos·tal (kȧs′·tąl) *a.* pert. to the ribs or to the side of the body [L. *costa,* a rib].

cos·tive (kȧs′·tiv) *a.* having sluggish motion; constipated. **-ness** *n.* [L. *con-; stipare,* to press together].

cos·tume (kȧs′·tūm) *n.* dress peculiar or appropriate, as to country, period, office, or character; a person's dress or attire. **-r** *n.* one who makes or deals in costumes. Also **costumier** (kȧs·tūm′·i·ęr) *n.* [It. *costume,* custom, fashion].

co·sy See **cozy.**

cot (kȧt) *n.* a cottage [O.E. *cot*].

cot (kȧt) *n.* a light, portable bed; (*Naut.*) a swinging bed on board ship [Hind. *khat*].

co·tan·gent (kō·tan′·jąnt) *n.* (*Trig.*) the tangent of the complement of an angle; (*Abbrev.*) **cot.**

cote (kōt) *n.* a shelter or enclosure for animals or birds; a sheep-fold [O.E. *cote*].

co·te·rie (kō′·ti·ri·) *n.* a set or circle of persons usually with common interests [Fr.].

co·til·lion, cotillon (kō·til′·yąn) *n.* a lively dance, of French origin; a complex dance of elaborate figures; music for the dance [Fr. *cotillon,* a petticoat].

cot·tage (kȧt′·ij) *n.* a small dwelling house, esp. in the country or at a resort. **-r** *n.* one who inhabits a cottage. **— cheese** *n.* a soft, white cheese [O.E. *cot*].

cot·ter (kȧt′·ęr) *n.* a pin or wedge used for tightening or fastening; a split pin.

cot·ton (kȧt′·n) *n.* a soft, downy, substance, resembling wool; cloth or thread made of cotton; *a.* made of cotton; *v.i.* (*Colloq.*) to become friendly; to take to. **— gin** *n.* a machine for separating the seeds from cotton. **-mouth** *n.* the water moccasin. **-tail** *n.* American rabbit. **-wood** *n.* a type of American poplar tree. **-y** *a.* [Ar. *qutum*].

cot·y·le·don (kȧt·ą·lē′·dąn) *n.* (*Bot.*) seed-lobe or primary leaf of the embryo plant [Gk. *kotulēdōn,* a cup-shaped cavity].

couch (kouch) *v.t.* to cause to lie down, esp. on a bed; to phrase; to express; to lower a lance, spear, etc. for action; *v.i.* to lie down; to crouch; *n.* a sofa; davenport. **couchant** (kouch′·ąnt) *a.* lying down [Fr. *coucher,* fr. L. *collocare,* to place together].

cou·gar (kòò′·gęr) *n.* the puma or American panther [Native S. Amer.)].

cough (kawf) *n.* noisy, violent, explosive effort to expel irritating matter from the lungs; *v.i.* to make such an effort; *v.t.* to expel from the lungs by a cough. **— up** (*Slang*) hand over [M.E. *coughen*].

could (kood) *p.at.* of the verb **can.**

cou·lomb (kòò·lȧm′) *n.* the quantity transferred by a current of one ampere in one second [Charles de *Coulomb,* a French physicist].

coul·ter See **colter.**

coun·cil (koun′·sal) *n.* an assembly summoned for consultation or advice; a municipal body; the deliberation carried on in such an assembly. **-man** *n.* **-lor** *n.* [L. *concilium*].

coun·sel (koun′·sąl) *n.* advice; opinion; deliberation together; one who gives advice, esp. legal; a lawyer; an advocate; *v.t.* to advise; admonish; recommend. **-or** *n.* an adviser; a trial lawyer. **-orship** *n.* [L. *consulere,* to consult].

count (kount) *n.* (*fem.* **countess**) a title of nobility [L. *comes, comitis,* companion].

count (kount) *v.t.* to number; to reckon; to sum up; to consider or esteem; to include; to recite the numerals in regular succession; *v.i.* to depend or rely (with 'on'); *n.* the act of reckoning; the number ascertained by counting; (*Law*) a charge in an indictment. **-able** *a.* **— down** *n.* the last check before a missile is launched. **-less** *a.* not capable of being counted; innumerable. **-er** *n.* one who counts; a token or disc of metal, wood, etc. is used in reckoning; a table on which money is counted, goods displayed, or business transacted [L. *computare*].

coun·te·nance (koun′·tą·nąns) *n.* the face; the features; aspect; look; appearance; encouragement; support; *v.i.* to favor; to support; to encourage; to approve. **to keep one's countenance,** to preserve one's composure [L. *continentia,* manner of holding oneself].

count·er (koun′·tęr) *a.* contrary; opposite; opposed; adverse; reciprocal; *adv.* in opposition; the opposite way; *n.* that which is opposite; a return blow or parry; *v.t.* and *i.* to parry; to oppose; to hinder; to do any act which opposes another; to make a counter-move. **-attack** *n.* an attack launched to recapture a position or to stop and drive back an enemy attack. **-attraction** *n.* rival attraction. **-claim** *n.* (*Law*) a claim set up by the defendant in a suit to counter that of the plaintiff. **-clockwise** *adv.* revolving in a direction opposite to the movement of the hands of a clock. **-espionage** *n.* spying directed against the enemy's system of espionage. **-irritant** *n.* a substance, the application of which, by inducing superficial irritation, relieves a more deep-seated irritation. **-tenor** *n.* a high tenor; a man's voice singing alto [L. *contra,* against].

coun·ter·act (koun·tęr·akt′) *v.t.* to act in opposition to; to hinder; to defeat.

coun·ter·bal·ance (koun′·tęr·bal·ąns) *v.t.* to act against with equal power or effect; to neutralize; *n.* equal opposing weight, power, or agency; a weight balancing another.

coun·ter·charge (koun′·tęr·chȧrj) *n.* a charge brought in opposition to another.

coun·ter·check (koun·tęr·chek′) *v.t.* to check by an opposing check; to reprimand.

coun·ter·feit (koun′·tęr·fit) *v.t.* to copy without authority; to imitate with intent to deceive; to forge; to feign; *a.* sham; forged; false; *n.* an imitation; a forgery; an impostor.**-er** *n.*

coun·ter·mand (koun·tęr·mand′) *v.t.* to cancel an order; *n.* a contrary order [L. *contra; mandare,* to command].

coun·ter·march (koun′·tęr·mārch) *v.i.* to march back; *n.* a marching back.

coun·ter·mine (koun′·tęr·mīn) *n.* (*Mil.*) to destroy enemy mines; any scheme to frustrate the designs of an opponent.

coun·ter·pane (koun′·tęr·pān) *n.* a coverlet; a quilt [L. *culcita puncta,* a stitched quilt].

coun·ter·part (koun′·tẹr·pȧrt) *n.* a duplicate; something complementary or correlative.

coun·ter·point (koun′·tẹr·point) *n.* (*Mus.*) the art of combining melodies; the addition of a subsidiary melody to another so as to form a perfect melody.

coun·ter·poise (koun′·tẹr·poiz) *v.t.* to act against with equal weight or power; *n.* a weight sufficient to balance another.

coun·ter·sign (koun′·tẹr·sīn) *v.t.* to sign a document already signed by another; to ratify; to attest authenticity; *n.* a password.

coun·try (kun′·tri·) *n.* a region; a district; a tract of land; the territory of a nation; the nation itself; land of birth, residence, etc.; rural districts as opposed to town; *a.* rural; rustic; pert. to territory distant from a city. **countrified** *a.* **countrify** *v.t.* to make rural. **— club** *n.* a club with grounds, a house, and facilities for outdoor sports. **-man** *n.* one who lives in the country; a rustic; one born in the same country; a compatriot. **-side** *n.* any rural district [L.L. *contrata*].

coun·ty (koun′·ti·) *n.* a division of a country or state for administrative purposes; the inhabitants of a county. **— seat,** the chief town or capital of a county [Fr. *comté,* fr. *comte,* a count].

coup (kòò) *n.* lit. a stroke or blow; then, a successful stroke or move *pl.* (kòòz) [Fr.].

coup de grâce (kòò·dạ·grȧs) *n.* blow, shot, etc. that brings death to a sufferer [Fr.].

coup d'é·tat (kòò·dā·tȧ′) *n.* lit. a stroke of state; a sudden and revolutionary change of government achieved by force [Fr.].

coupe (kòòp) *n.* a two-seat automobile with enclosed body [Fr. *couper,* to cut].

cou·ple (kup′·l) *n.* two things of the same kind taken together; two; a pair; a brace; husband and wife; a leash for two hounds; that which joins two things together; *v.t.* to join together; (*Colloq.*) to marry; *v.i.* to connect. **couplet** *n.* a pair of lines of verse. **coupling** *n.* a connection; that which couples, esp. the device joining railroad cars [L. *copula,* a bond].

cou·pon (kòò′·pȧn) *n.* an interest certificate attached to a bond; a dividend warrant; a negotiable ticket or voucher; a pass [Fr. *couper,* to cut off].

cour·age (kur′·ȧj) *n.* bravery; fearlessness; daring. **courageous** (kạ·rā′·jạs) *a.* full of courage. **courageously** *adv.* **courageousness** *n.* [O.Fr. *corage,* fr. L. *cor,* the heart].

cour·i·er (koo′·ri·ẹr) *n.* a runner or messenger; a state messenger; a tourist guide who accompanies travelers [L. *currere,* to run].

course (kōrs) *n.* the act of passing from one point to another; progress or movement, both in space and in time; the ground traversed; way or direction; line of conduct; the track or ground on which a race is run; career; a series (of lessons, lectures, etc.); each of the successive divisions of a meal; a continuous line of masonry at one level in a building; *v.t.* to hunt; to pursue; to chase; *v.i.* to run swiftly; to gallop. **-r** *n.* one who courses or hunts; a swift horse [L. *cursus,* running].

court (kōrt) *n.* an uncovered area enclosed by buildings, or by buildings and railings; a yard; the residence of a sovereign; the retinue of a sovereign; the homage or attention paid to a sovereign; a legal tribunal; the judge or judges, as distinguished from the counsel; the hall where justice is administered; (*Sport*) a space, usually rectangular, laid out for certain sports, as tennis, etc. **courteous** (kurt′·i·ạs) *a.* polite; well-bred; of courtlike manners. **courteously** *adv.* **courteousness** *n.* **courtier** (kōrt′·yẹr) one who frequents the courts of princes; one with the manners of a frequenter of courts. **-ly** *a.* elegant; flattering; with the manners of a courtier. **-liness** *n.* **—martial** *n.* a court of military or naval officers for the trial of persons in the army or navy; *pl.* **-s-martial.** [L. *cohors,* an enclosure].

court (kōrt) *v.t.* to seek the favor of; to try to gain the affections of; to seek in marriage; *v.i.* to woo; to play the lover. **-ship** *n.* [L. *cohors,* an enclosure].

cour·te·san (kōr′·tạ·zạn) *n.* a prostitute [It. *cortigiana*].

cour·te·sy (kur′·tạ·si·) *n.* politeness of manners; urbanity [O.Fr. *cortoisie*].

cou·sin (kuz′·n) *n.* formerly any kinsman; now, the son or daughter of an uncle or aunt [Fr. fr. L. *consobrinus*].

cou·tu·rier (koo·tu·rya') *n.* a man dressmaker. **-rieré** (·ryār′) *n. fem.*

cove (kōv) *n.* a small bay [O.E. *cofa,* a chamber].

cov·e·nant (kuv′·ạ·nạnt) *n.* a mutual and solemn agreement; a contract; a compact; a written agreement; *v.t.* to agree to by covenant; *v.i.* to enter into an agreement. **-er** *n.* one who makes a covenant or agreement. **Covenanters** later [L. *cno-*; *venire,* to come].

cov·er (kuv′·ẹr) *v.t.* to be over the whole top of; to overspread; to enclose; to include; to protect; to put hat on; to point a revolver, gun, etc. at; to wager an equal sum of money; *n.* anything that covers; a lid; a wrapper; an envelope; a binding; a cloak; disguise; concealment; shelter; defense. **-ing** *n.* **-let** *n.* a bedcover. **covert** *a.* covered over; concealed; sheltered; secret; veiled; *n.* a thicket; a place sheltering game. **covertly** *adv.* secretly; in private. **coverture** (kuv′·ẹr·chẹr) *n.* covering; shelter; defense. [Fr. *couvrir,* to cover].

cov·et (kuv′·it) *v.t.* to long to possess, esp. what belongs to another; to desire unreasonably or unlawfully; *v.i.* to have strong desire. **-able** *a.* that may be coveted. **-ous** *a.* very desirous; excessively eager; avaricious for gain. **-ously** *adv.* **-ousness** *n.* [L. *cupiditas,* desire].

cov·ey (kuv′·i·) *n.* a brood of partridges or quail; (*Fig.*) a company; a set [Fr. *couveé,* fr. *couver,* to brood].

cow (kou) *n.* the female of a bovine animal; the female elephant, whale, etc. **-ish** *a.* **-boy** *n.* a boy who herds cows; on the western plains, a herdsman employed on a ranch to look after cattle. **-catcher** *n.* a frame in front of a locomotive to remove obstructions. **-herd** *n.* one who herds cows. **-hide** *n.* the hide of a cow; leather made from the hide of a cow. **-lick** *n.* a tuft of hair not easily flattened [O.E. *cu*].

cow (kou) *v.t.* to frighten into submission; to overawe [O.N. *kuga,* to oppress].

cow·ard (kou′·ẹrd) *n.* one given to fear; one who lacks courage. **-ly** *a.* lacking in courage; afraid. **-ice** (·dis) *n.* want of courage; fear. [Fr. *couard,* fr. L. *cauda,* a tail].

cow·er (kou′·ẹr) *v.i.* to crouch down through fear, shame, cold [etym. uncertain].

cowl (koul) *n.* a monk's hooded cloak; the hood itself; a hooded top for a chimney. **-ed** *a.* [L. *cucullus,* the hood of a cloak].

cow·slip (kou′·slip) *n.* the marsh marigold [OE. *cu-slyppe,* cow dung].

cox·comb (kȧks′·kōm) *n.* one given to showing off; a fool; a fop. **-ry** *n.*

cox·swain (kȧk′·sn), **cox** (kȧks) *n.* the steersman of a boat. **to cox** *vt.* and *i.* to act as coxswain [fr. *cock*-boat and *swain*].

coy (koi) *a.* shy; modest; pretending to be shy. **-ly** *adv.* **-ness** *n.* [Fr. *coi,* fr. L. *quietus*].

coy·o·te (kī′·ōt) *n.* the Amer. prairie wolf [Mex.]

coz·en (kuz′·n) *v.t.* to flatter in order to cheat; to defraud [Fr. *cousiner,* to play the part of *cousin,* in order to sponge on people].

co·zy (kō′·zi·) *a.* snug; comfortable; *n.* a covering to keep a teapot hot (*tea cozy*). Also **cosy. cozily** *adv.* **coziness** *n.*

crab (krab) *n.* an edible crustacean; a disagreeable person; *v.t.* to fish for crabs; (*Slang*) to complain. *pr.p.* **-bing.** *pa.t.* **-bed.** **-biness** *n.* **-by** *a.* **— grass** *n.* rapid growing coarse grass

[O.E. *crabbd*, snatcher].
crab·bed (krab′·ạd) *a.* harsh; austere; fault-finding; perverse; bad-tempered; of writing, hard to read. **-ly** *adv.* **-ness** *n.*
crack (krak) *v.t.* to break with a sharp noise, either wholly or partially; to split or break; to produce a sudden sharp sound; to snap; *v.i.* to break partially; to burst open in chinks; to give forth a sudden, sharp sound; *n.* a partial break; fissure; a sharp noise; a flaw; a break in the voice; a mental flaw; (*Colloq.*) *a.* superior; special; expert. **-ed** *a.* **-er** *n.* one who cracks, that which cracks; a fire-cracker; a thin crisp biscuit.**-er-jack** (*Slang*) *n.* a person or thing of exceptional quality. **— up** *n.* a collision; a defeat; a breakdown [O.E. *cracian*].
crack (krak) *n.* small chips of highly purified cocaine used for smoking.
crack·le (krak′·l) *v.i.* to produce slight but repeated cracking sounds; *n.* a noise composed of frequent, slight cracking sounds; over-all fine cracks in porcelain glaze. **crackling** *n.* a succession of small sharp reports; rind of roasted pork [O.E. *cracian*, to crack].
cra·dle (krā′·dl) *n.* a bed for infants that can be rocked; infancy; the place of origin of anyone or anything; a framework used as a support; *v.t.* to place or rock in a cradle; to tend or train in infancy; to support on a cradle (as a vessel) [O.E. *cradol*].
craft (kraft) *n.* skill or dexterity; a skilled trade; cunning, artifice, or guile; a vessel; vessels collectively. **-y** *a.* cunning; artful. **-ily** *adv.* **-iness** *n.* **-sman** *n.* one engaged in a craft or trade. **-smanship** *n.* [O.E. *craeft*].
crag (krag) *n.* a steep, rugged rock or peak. **-ged** (krag′·ạd) *a.* **-gy** *a.* full of crags; rough; rugged. **-giness** *n.* [W. *craig*, a rock].
cram (kram) *v.t.* and *i.* to stuff; to pack tightly; (*Colloq.*) to prepare hastily for an examination. *pr.p.* **-ming.** *pa.t.* **-med.** *n.* (*Colloq.*) a crush or crowd of people [O.E. *crammian*].
cramp (kramp) *n.* a painful contraction of muscles of the body; that which restrains; a clamp for holding masonry, timbers, etc. together; *v.t.* to affect with cramp; to restrict or hamper; to hold with a cramp; *a.* narrow; cramped; restricted [O.Fr. *crampe*].
cran·ber·ry (kran′·ber·i·) *n.* a red, sour, berry [prob. orig. *crane-berry*].
crane (krān) *n.* a tall wading-bird with long legs, neck, and bill; a machine for lifting and lowering heavy weights; *v.t.* to stretch out the neck to look at something [O.E. *cran*].
cra·ni·um (krā′·ni·ạm) *n.* the skull. *pl.* **crania. cranial** *a.* pert. to the skull. **craniology** *n.* the study of skulls. **craniological** *a.* [Gk. *kranion*, the skull].
crank (krangk) *n.* a handle attached to a shaft for turning it; the bent portion of an axis, used to change horizontal or vertical into rotatory motion, etc.; a fanciful twist or whimsy in speech; (*Colloq.*) a faddist; an eccentric or crotchety person; *v.t.* to provide with a crank; to shape like a crank; to operate by a crank; *v.i.* to turn the crank as in starting an automobile engine (usually with 'up'). **-case** *n.* the housing for a crankshaft. **-shaft** *n.* (*Mach.*) a shaft driven by or driving a crank. **-y** *a.* shaky or in bad condition, of machinery; (*Fig.*) irritable or crotchety; bad-tempered. **-iness** *n.* [O.E. *cranc.*]
cran·ny (kran′·i·) *n.* an open crack; a small opening; a crevice; a chink [Fr. *cran*, a notch].
crash (krash) *n.* a violent fall or impact accompanied by loud noise; a burst of mixed, loud sound, e.g. of thunder, breaking crockery, etc.; bankruptcy; a sudden collapse or downfall; *v.i.* to make a crash; to fall, come with, strike with, a crash; to collapse; *v.t.* to break into pieces. **—helmet** *n.* a padded helmet worn by aviators and racing motorists [imit. of the sound].
crash (krash) *n.* a coarse linen cloth.
cra·sis (krā′·sis) *n.* (*Gram.*) union of two vowels into one long vowel or diphthong [Gk.].
crass (kras) *a.* thick; gross; dense; stupid. **-ly** *adv.* **-ness** *n.* [L. *crassus*, coarse].
crate (krāt) *n.* a wicker hamper, or open-work packing-case [L. *cratis*, a hurdle].
cra·ter (krā′·tẹr) *n.* the cup-shaped mouth of a volcano; the cavity resulting from the explosion of a large shell, bomb, mine, etc. [Gk. *kratēr*, a mixing-bowl].
cra·vat (krạ·vat′) *n.* a man's necktie or scarf [Fr. *cravate*, Croation (scarf)].
crave (krāv) *v.t.* and *i.* to have a very strong desire for; to long for; to ask with earnestness, submission, or humility; to beg. **-r.** *n.* **craving** *n.* an inordinate desire [O.E. *crafian*, to crave].
cra·ven (krāv′·n) *a.* cowardly; spiritless; chicken-hearted; *n.* a spiritless fellow; a coward [O.Fr. *cravanter*, to overthrow].
craw (kraw) *n.* crop or first stomach of fowls; stomach of any animal [M.E. *crawe*].
craw·fish, crayfish (kraw′·, krā′·fish) *n.* a fresh-water crustacean, resembling the lobster but smaller [Fr. *écrevisse*].
crawl (krawl) *v.i.* to move along the ground on the belly or on the hands and knees; to move very slowly; to move abjectly; to swim with an overarm stroke; *n.* a crawling motion; swimming stroke [O.N. *krafla*, to claw].
cray·on (krā′·ạn) *n.* a coloring pencil; a drawing made with crayons; *v.t.* to draw with crayons [Fr. *crayon*, a pencil; *craie*, chalk].
craze (krāz) *n.* a strong, habitual desire or passion; a general or individual mania; a very common fashion; *v.t.* to make crazy; (*Pottery*) to crackle. **-d** *a.* weak in mind. **craziness** *n.* **crazy** *a.* insane; extremely foolish; madly eager (for); falling to pieces. **crazily** *adv.* [Fr. *écraser*, to break].
creak (krēk) *n.* a harsh, grating sound; *v.i.* to make a sharp, harsh, grating sound. **-y** *a.* [imit. sound].
cream (krēm) *n.* the fatty substance that rises to the surface of milk; the best part of anything; anything resembling cream; *v.t.* to take off the cream; to add cream to; *v.i.* to become covered with cream; to froth. **-y** *a.* full of cream; resembling cream. **-ery** *n.* a butter and cheese factory; a center to which milk is sent for distribution. **-iness** *n.* **— cheese** *n.* a soft, smooth, white cheese. **— of tartar,** acid potassium tartrate, a component of baking powder [Gk. *chrisma*, unguent].
crease (krēs) *n.* a line or mark made by folding anything; *v.t.* to make a crease or mark on; *v.i.* to become creased [etym. uncertain].
cre·ate (krē·āt′) *v.t.* to bring into existence out of nothing; to originate; to make. **creation** (krē·ā′·shạn) *n.* the act of creating, esp. of bringing the world into being; the world; anything created; any original production of the human mind. **creative** *a.* capable of creation; original. **creator** *n.* one who creates; a maker. **Creator** *n.* God. **creature** (krē′·chẹr) *n.* anything created; any living being [L. *craere*].
cre·dence (krē′·dạns) *n.* trust; belief; (*Eccles.*) a small altar table. **credentials** (kri·den′·shạlz) *n.pl.* testimonials showing that a person is entitled to belief or credit. **credible** (kred′·ạ·bl) *a.* worthy of belief. **credibility** *n.* [L. *credere*, to believe].
cre·den·za (krạ·den′·zạ) *n.* a sideboard [fr. *credence*].
cred·it (kred′·it) *n.* belief; trust; trustworthiness; honor or reputation; anything that procures esteem or honor; the amount at a person's disposal in a bank; in commerce, the general system of buying, borrowing and lending based on good faith and confidence; *v.t.* to believe; to put trust in. **-able** *a.* reliable; meriting credit. **-ably** *adv.* **-ableness** *n.* **-or** *n.* one to whom money is due [L. *credere*, to believe].
cred·u·lous (kre′·jạ·lạs) *a.* too prone to believe. **-ly** *adv.* **-ness** *n.* **credulity** (krạ·dū′·-

lą·ti·) *n.* gullibility [L. *credulus,* believing].
creed (krēd) *n.* a statement of religious belief; any statement of principles. **credo** (krē′·dō) *n.* a creed [L. *credere,* to believe].
creek (krēk) *n.* a small inlet; a branch or small tributary of a river [O.N. *kriki*].
creel (krēl) *n.* an angler's basket [Celt.].
creep (krēp) *v.i.* to move along with the body close to the ground, like a worm or reptile; to spread, like certain plants, by clinging. *pa.t., pa.p.* **crept. -er** *n.* esp. a creeping plant; a genus of small birds. **-y** *a.* causing a creeping sensation on the skin [O.E. *creopan*].
cre·mate (krē′·māt) *v.t.* to consume by burning, esp. the dead; to reduce to ashes. **cremation** (krē·mā′·shąn) *n.* the act of cremating the dead. **cremator** *n.* **crematorium** *n.* an establishment for the cremation of bodies. **crematory** *a.* or *n.* [L. *cremare,* to burn].
cre·nate (krē′·nāt) *a.* with the edge notched. **-d** *a.* [L. *crena,* a notch].
Cre·ole (krē′·ōl) *n.* a native of Spanish America or the W. Indies, of European parentage; a white person descended from the French or Spanish settlers of Louisiana; a native of mixed parentage [Fr. fr. Sp. *criollo*].
cre·o·sote (krē′·ą·sōt) *n.* an oily liquid obtained from the distillation of coal tar, extensively used to preserve wood from decay [Gk. *sōtēr,* preserver].
crepe (krāp) *n.* a thin crinkled fabric or paper; mourning cloth; a kind of rough-surfaced rubber used for the soles of shoes, etc. [Fr.].
crept (krept) *pa.p.* and *pa.t.* of **creep.**
cre·pus·cu·lar (kri·pus′·kyą·lęr) *a.* pert. to twilight; dim. [L. *crepusculum,* twilight].
cre·scen·do (krą·shen′·dō) *n.* (*Mus.*) a gradual increase in loudness; *adv.* with increase in loudness. (*Abbrev.*) **cresc.** [It.].
cres·cent (kres′·ąnt) *a.* like the young moon in shape; increasing; *n.* the moon in first quarter; a crescent-shaped object [L. *crescere,* to grow].
cress (kres) *n.* various salad greens[O.E. *cerse, cresse,* creeper].
cres·set (kres′·it) *n.* an iron basket or cage-like container, filled with inflammable material used as a torch [O.Fr. *craisse,* grease].
crest (krest) *n.* the comb or tuft on a bird's head; the plume or top of a helmet; the top of a mountain, ridge, etc.; the highest part of a wave; a badge above the shield of a coat of arms; *v.t.* to reach the top of. **-fallen** *a.* dispirited; dejected [L. *crista*].
cre·tin·ism (krēt′·in·izm) *n.* condition caused by thyroid deficiency; a form of idiocy. **cretin** *n.* one suffering from cretinism. **cretinous** *a.* [Swiss *crestin,* a Christian].
cre·tonne (kri·tȧn) *n.* a strong, unglazed printed cotton cloth [*Creton,* in France].
cre·vasse (krą·vas′) *n.* a deep open chasm in a glacier; a fissure; a cleft [Fr.].
crev·ice (krev′·is) *n.* a cleft; a narrow fissure; a crack [Fr. *crever,* to burst].
crew (kròo) *n.* a group of workmen; a ship's or boat's company [earlier *crue, accrue,* a reinforcement].
crew·el (kròò′·ąl) *n.* embroidery yarn. **-work** *n.*
crib (krib) *n.* a manger; a stall for cattle; a child's bed with barred sides; a hut or small dwelling; a key or translation (used by students); an enclosure for storing grain [O.E. *cribb,* an oxstall].
crib·bage (krib′·ij) *n.* (*Cards*) a game played by two or four players.
crick (krik) *n.* neck or back spasm or cramp.
crick·et (krik′·it) *n.* a small, brown, chirping insect [Fr. *criquer,* to creak].
crick·et (krik′·it) *n.* a game played with bats, ball, and wickets; (*Colloq.*) fair play.
cri·er (krī′·ęr) *n.* See **cry.**
crime (krīm) *n.* a violation of the law (usually of a serious nature); an offense. **criminal** (krim′·ą·nąl) *a.* guilty of, or pert. to, crime; wicked; *n.* one guilty of a crime. **criminality** *n.* guiltiness. **criminally** *adv.* **criminate** *v.t.* to charge with a crime. **crimination** *n.* **criminative, criminatory** *a.* accusing. **criminologist** *n.* **criminology** *n.* science dealing with the cause and treatment of crime and criminals [L. *crimen,* a charge].
crimp (krimp) *v.t.* to form into curls or pleats; to wrinkle; to decoy or press into military or naval service; *n.* an agent who procures men for service as soldiers or sailors; a small waves, as in hair [O.E. *crimpan,* to curl].
crim·son (krim′·zn) *a.* of a rich deep red color; *n.* the color itself [O.Sp. *cremesin,* fr. Arab. *qirmiz,* the cochineal insect].
cringe (krinj) *v.t.* to shrink; to cower; to behave obsequiously [M.E. *crengen*].
crin·kle (kring′·kl) *v.t.* to wrinkle; to make a series of bends or twists in a line or surface; to rustle **crinkly** *adv.* [O.E. *crincan*].
crin·o·line (krin′·ą·lin) *n.* a hoop skirt; a stiff, coarse fabric petticoat [L. *crinis,* hair; *linum,* flax].
crip·ple (krip′·l) *n.* a person without the use of a limb or limbs; a lame person; *a.* lame; *v.t.* to lame [O.E. *crypel*].
cri·sis (krī′·sis) *n.* the decisive moment; the turning point, esp. in an illness; emergency; a time of difficulty or danger; *pl.* **crises** (krī′·sēz) [Gk. *krisis,* decision].
crisp (krisp) *a.* brittle; breaking with a short snap; of hair, curly; sharp; *v.t.* to make crisp; **-ly** *adv.* **-ness** *n.* [L. *crispus,* curled].
criss·cross (kris′·kraws) *a.* crossing; arranged in crossing lines; *adv.* crossing one another in different directions; *v.t.* and *i.* to mark or be marked with cross lines [corrupt. of *Christ's-cross*].
cri·te·ri·on (krī·tir′·i·ąn) *n.* a standard of judging; a rule or test by which opinions may be judged. *pl.* **criteria** [Gk.].
crit·ic (krit′·ik) *n.* one who expressed a reasoned judgment on any matter, esp. on art or literature; one whose profession it is to write reviews; one given to expressing adverse judgment or finding fault. **-al** *a.* pert. to criticism or critics; captious or fault-finding; pert. to a crisis; crucial; decisive. **-ally** *adv.* **criticism** *n.* the art of making a reasoned judgment, a critical appreciation. **criticize** *v.t.* and *i.* to pass judgment; to censure. **critique** (kri·tēk′) *n.* criticism; review [Gk. *krinein,* to judge].
croak (krōk) *v.t.* and *i.* to make a low, hoarse noise in the throat; (*Slang*) to die; *n.* the hoarse, harsh sound made by a frog or a crow. **-y** *a.* [imit].
cro·chet (krō·shā′) *n.* a kind of needlework consisting of loops; *v.t.* and *i.* to work in crochet [Fr. *crochet,* a small hook].
crock (krȧk) *n.* an earthenware pot or pitcher; a piece of broken earthenware. **-ery** *n.* vessels and dishes of all kinds, generally made of earthenware [Gael. *crog,* a pitcher].
croc·o·dile (krȧk′·ą·dīl) *n.* a large, amphibious reptile of the lizard kind. **— tears,** hypocritical tears; sham grief [Gk. *krokodilos,* a lizard].
cro·cus (krō′·kąs) *n.* a bulbous plant; saffron [Gk. *krokos,* crocus, saffron].
crone (krōn) *n.* a wizened old woman.
cro·ny (krō′·ni·) *n.* an intimate friend; a chum [earlier *chrony,* a contemporary, fr. Gk.].
crook (krook) *n.* any hook, bend, or sharp turn; a shepherd's or a bishop's staff; a thief; a swindler; *v.t.* to bend into a crook; to curve; to pervert; *v.i.* to be bent or curved. **-ed** *a.* bent; twisted; (*Fig.*) not straightforward. **-edly** *adv.* **-edness** *n.* **by hook or by crook,** by some means or other; by fair or foul [O.N. *krokr*].
croon (kròòn) *v.t.* and *i.* to sing or hum softly; to sing in a sentimental manner. **-er** *n.* **-ing** *n.* [imit.].
crop (krȧp) *n.* the cultivated produce of any plant or plants, in a farm, field, country, etc.; a harvest; the best ore; a pouch in a bird's gul-

let: the craw; a hunting-whip; a closely-cut head of hair; *v.t.* to reap the produce of a field. *pr.p.* **-ping.** *pa.p.* and *pa.t.* **-ped.** **—eared** *a.* with clipped ears; with hair cut close to head. **-per** *n.* one who, or that which, crops; (*Colloq.*) a heavy fall. **to crop up,** to appear unexpectedly [O.E. *cropp*, the head of a plant, ear of corn, etc.].

cro·quet (krō′·kā) *n.* an outdoor game played with balls, mallets and hoops.

cro·quette (krō·ket′) *n.* (*Cookery*) a ball of finely minced meat, fish, etc. seasoned and fried [Fr. *croquer*, to mince].

cro·sier, cro·zier (krō′·zhẹr) *n.* the pastoral staff of a bishop [O.Fr. *crosse*, a crook].

cross (kraws) *n.* a stake used for crucifixion, consisting of two pieces of timber placed upon one another in the shape † or ×; in particular, **the Cross,** the one on which Christ was crucified; a model or picture of this; anything in the shape of a cross; (*Fig.*) (the Cross being the symbol of suffering) affliction; tribulation; a misfortune; *v.t.* to mark with a cross; to make the sign of the cross. **-let** *n.* a small cross. **-wise** *adv.* in the form of a cross [L. *crux*, a cross].

cross (kraws) *a.* transverse; intersecting; interchanged; contrary, adverse; out of temper; dishonest; *n.* an intermixture of breeds or stocks, esp. in cattle-breeding; *v.t.* to place so as to intersect; to pass from one side to the other of; to pass over; to thwart; to oppose; to clash; to modify the breed of animals, plants, etc. by intermixture; *v.i.* to intersect; to move or pass from one side to the other; *adv.* across. **-ing** *n.* the act of passing across; an intersection; a place of crossing; the intermixture of breeds. **-ly** *adv.* **—action** *n.* (*Law*) an action brought by a defendant against a plaintiff on points pert. to the same case. **-bones** *n. pl.* two thigh bones crossed and surmounted by a skull, used as symbol of death, a sign of deadly danger, or the flag of a pirate ship. **-breed** *n.* parents of different breeds; a hybrid. **—examination** *n.* the examination of a witness by counsel on the other side. **—eyed** *a.* with eyes turned in toward the nose. **—grained** *a.* of wood, having the grain running across, or irregularly; of a person, ill-natured. **-hatching** *n.* in drawing, etching, etc. the art of shading by parallel intersecting lines. **— reference** *n.* in a book, e.g. a dictonary, the directing of the reader to another part for related information [L. *crux*, a cross].

cross·bill (kraws′·bil) *n.* a bird of the Finch family, whose mandibles cross.

cross·bow (kraws′·bō) *n.* a medieval weapon. **-man** *n.*

crotch (kråch) *n.* a fork or bifurcation; the angle where the legs branch off from the human body. **-ed** *a.* [etym. uncertain].

crotch·et (kråch′·at) *n.* a small hook. **-y** *a.* full of whims, or fads [Fr. *crochet*, dim. of *croc*. a hook].

crouch (krouch) *v.i.* to huddle down close to the ground; to stoop low; to cringe or fawn servilely [prob. Fr. *croc*, a hook, crook].

croup (kroop) *n.* the rump or hindquarters of a horse [Fr. *croupe*].

croup (kròòp) *n.* (*Med.*) acute inflammation of the windpipe, accompanied by a hoarse cough. **-y** *a.* [O.E. *kropan*, to cry].

crou·pi·er (kròò′·pi·ẹr) *n.* one who assists the chairman at a public banquet; an official in charge of a gaming table [Fr.].

crou·ton (kròò′·tån) *n.* a small cube of toasted bread used in soups, etc. [Fr. *croûte*].

crow (krō) *n.* a large bird, usually wholly black, of the genus Corvus; the cry of the cock; the name of a tribe of American Indians; a crowbar; *v.i.* to give the shrill cry of the cock; to utter a sound of pleasure. **crow's-foot** *n.* a wrinkle about the outer corners of the eyes in adults. **crow's-nest** *n.* a box or perch for the lookout man near the top of the mast [O.E. *crawan*].

crowd (kroud) *v.t.* to press or drive together; to fill or occupy by crushing together; *v.i.* to be numerous; to gather in numbers; *n.* a number of things or persons collected into a close body; a dense multitude or throng; (*Colloq.*) a set or clique [O.E. *crudan*].

crown (kroun) *n.* the diadem or state headdress worn by a sovereign; the sovereign; royalty; anything resembling a crown; something achieved or consummated; the topmost part of the head; the upper part of a hat; the summit; (*Br.*) a five-shilling piece (stamped with a crown); *v.t.* to invest with a crown or with royal dignity; to bestow upon as a mark of honor; to top or surmount; to complete. **— prince** *n.* the heir apparent to the throne. **— wheel** *n.* a wheel with cogs at right angles to its plane [L. *corona*, a crown].

cro·zier. See **crosier.**

cru·cial (kròò′·shạl) *a.* decisive; critical; cross-shaped [L. *crux*, a cross].

cru·ci·ble (kròò′·si·bl) *n.* vessel capable of withstanding great heat, used for melting metals, etc.; (*Fig.*) a severe test [L.L. *crucibulum*].

cru·ci·fy (kròò′·sạ·fī) *v.t.* to put to death by nailing to a cross; to torture; to mortify. **crucifier** *n.* **crucifix** *n.* a cross; an image of Christ on the Cross. **crucifixion** (kròò′·sạ·-fik′·shạn) *n.* **cruciform** *a.* cross-shaped [L. *crux*, a cross; *figere*, to fix].

crude (kròòd) *a.* in the natural or raw state; unripe; rough; unfinished. **-ly** *adv.* **-ness** *n.* **crudity** *n.* [L. *crudis*, raw].

cru·el (kròò′·el) *a.* hard-hearted. **-ly** *adv.* **-ty** *n.* the quality of being cruel (See *crude*).

cru·et (kròò′·it) *n.* a small stoppered bottle for holding vinegar, oil, etc. [O.Fr. *cruie*, a pot].

cruise (kròòz) *v.i.* to move about without precise destination; in motoring and aviation, to go at a normal operating speed; *n.* an organized pleasure-sail. **-r** *n.* **— missile** *n.* a jet-powered, long-range, remote-controlled missile that can be launched from an airplane, a submarine, etc. [L. *crux*, a cross].

crumb (krum) *n.* a small particle; a bit, esp. of bread; *v.t.* to reduce to crumbs; to cover with crumbs. **-y** *a.* **crummy** *a.* (*Slang*) inferior [O.E. *cruma*].

crum·ble (krum′·bl) *v.t.* to break into crumbs or fragments; *v.i.* to fall into crumbs. **crumbly** *a.* [O.E. *cruma*].

crum·ple (krum′·pl) *v.t.* to wrinkle; to crease; to rumple; *v.i.* to become wrinkled or creased; to shrink irregularly; to collapse.

crunch (krunch) *n.* the sound made by chewing crisp food, treading on gravel, hard snow, etc.; (*Colloq.*) a financial strain or cutback or a stress of any kind; *v.t.*, *v.i.* to chew, tread, etc. with a crunchy sound. **-y** *a.* [imit. origin].

cru·sade (kròò·sād′) *n.* a medieval Christian war to recover the Holy Land from the Saracens; a campaign against any evil or vice; *v.i.* to join in a crusade. **-r** *n.* [Fr. *croisade*, fr. L. *crux*, a cross].

crush (krush) *v.t.* to press between two hard bodies so as to break, bruise, or crumple; to break into fragments; to squeeze out by pressure; to defeat utterly; *v.i.* to be broken or compressed by weight or force; *n.* violent pressure; a closely packed crowd of people [O.Fr. *cruissir*].

crust (krust) *n.* the hard outer coat or covering of anything; the outer part of baked bread; pastry, etc. forming the covering of a pie; a deposit from wine collected on the interior of bottles; *v.t.* to cover with a crust; *v.i.* to gather into a crust; to form a crust. **-ated** *a.* covered with a crust; incrusted. **-ation** *n.* **-ily** *adv.* in a crusty manner; peevishly; morosely. **-iness** *n.* **-y** *a.* having a crust; like a crust; hard; peevish; surly [L. *crusta*].

Crus·ta·ce·a (krus·tā′·shi·ạ) *n.pl.* (*Zool.*) a

class of mainly aquatic animals including lobsters, crabs, shrimps, prawns, etc. **-n** *a.* pert. to the crustacea. **crustaceous** *a.* having a hard shell [L. *crusta,* a rind].

crutch (kruch) *n.* a staff with a cross-piece to go under the armpit for the use of cripples; a support; *v.t.* to support; to aid [O.E. *cryce*].

crux (kruks) *n.* a perplexing problem; a knotty point; the real issue [L. *crux,* a cross].

cry (krī) *v.t.* to call out; to proclaim; *v.i.* to call loudly; to exclaim vehemently; to weep; *n.* a loud utterance; the shedding of tears. **crier** *n.* one who cries; a public announcer. **-ing** *a.* **a far —,** a great distance. **to — wolf,** to give a false alarm [L. *quiritare,* to wail].

cry·o·lite (krī′·ạ·līt) *n.* a mineral used in making aluminum [Gr. *kruos,* frost; *lithos,* stone].

cry·on·ics (krī·ȧn′·iks) *n.* the practice of freezing dead humans with the intention of reviving them when technology has greatly advanced. **cryonic** *a.* [Gk. *kruos,* frost].

crypt (kript) *n.* a cell or chapel under a church, or underground, used for burial. **-ic(al)** *a.* hidden; secret; mysterious. **-ically** *adv.* [Gk. *kruptein,* to conceal].

cryp·to- *prefix* fr. Gk. *kruptos,* hidden, secret.

cryp·to·gram (krip′·tạ·gram) *n.* a writing in secret characters. Also **cryptograph. cryptology** *n.* a secret language. **cryptonym** (krip′·tạ·nim) *n.* a secret name [Gk. *kruptos,* hidden; *graphein,* to write].

crys·tal (kris′·tạl) *n.* a transparent, colorless quartz; an ornament made from it; a ball cut from it for crystal gazing; a superior sort of glass; a table article made from such glass with ornamental cutting; (*Chem.*) a mineral body which has assumed a regular geometrical form; *a.* consisting of, or like, crystal; clear; transparent. **-line** *a.* **-lize** *v.t.* to cause to form crystals; (*Fig.*) to cause to assume a definite shape; *v.i.* to be formed into crystals; (*Fig.*) to become definite in shape. **-lizable** *a.* **-lization** *n.* [Gk. *krustallos,* fr. *kruos,* frost].

cub (kub) *n.* the young of the bear, fox, wolf, etc.; a junior Boy Scout; *v.i.* to bring forth young (of animals) [etym. unknown].

cub·by hole (kub′·i·hōl) *n.* a small place for storage or hiding [dial. E. *cub,* a pen or shed].

cube (kūb) *n.* (*Geom.*) a solid body with six equal square sides; (*Math.*) the product of a number multiplied twice by itself, as $4 \times 4 \times 4 = 64$, 'the cube of 4,' or '4, to the third power'; *v.t.* to raise to the third power. **cubic(al)** *a.* having the form of a cube; of three dimensions, e.g., *cubic foot.* **cuboid** *a.* resembling a cube in shape. **— root** *n.* the number which gives the stated number if raised to the third power, or cubed, e.g. 4 is the cube root of 64 [Gk. *kubos*].

cu·bi·cle (kū·bi·kl) *n.* a small partitioned compartment [L. *cubiculum,* a bedroom].

cub·ism (kū′·bizm) *n.* (*Art*) a phase of modern art based on geometrical forms. **cubist** *n.*

cu·bit (kū′·bit) *n.* a measure of length, about 18 inches. **-al** *a.* [L. *cubitum,* the elbow].

cuck·old (kuk′·ạld) *n.* a man whose wife is unfaithful to him; *v.t.* to be unfaithful (to one's husband) [O.Fr. *cucu,* a cuckoo].

cuck·oo (koo′·ko̤o̤) *n.* a migratory bird named from its call; the call of the bird; a fool; *a.* (*Slang*) crazy; foolish [imit. origin].

cu·cum·ber (kū′·kum·bẹr) *n.* plant of the gourd family and its fruit [L. *cucumis*].

cud (kud) *n.* food brought up by ruminating animals, from their first stomach, and chewed a second time. **to chew the —** (*Fig.*), to meditate [O.E. *cudu*].

cud·dle (kud′·l) *v.t.* to caress; to hug; to fondle; *v.i.* to lie close or snug; to nestle; *n.* a close embrace. **-some** *a.* [etym. uncertain].

cudg·el (kuj·ạl) *n.* a short thick stick; *v.t.* to beat with a cudgel [O.E. *cycgel,* club].

cue (kū) *n.* the last words of an actor's speech as a signal to the next actor to speak; a hint [earlier 'q,' standing for L. *quando,* when (i.e. to come on)].

cue (kū) *n.* a long tapering rod used in pool, billiards, etc. [Fr. *queue,* pigtail].

cuff (kuf) *n.* a blow with the open hand; *v.t.* to strike with the open hand [etym. uncertain].

cuff (kuf) *n.* the ending of a sleeve; the turned-up end of a trouser leg; the wrist-band of a sleeve [M.E. *cuffe*].

cui·rass (kwi·ras′) *n.* metal or leather armor, consisting of a breastplate and backplate [Fr. *cuir,* leather].

cui·sine (kwi·zēn′) *n.* literally a kitchen; style of cooking [Fr. fr. *cuire,* to cook].

cul-de-sac (kool′·dạ·sak′) *n.* a blind alley [Fr. *cul,* bottom; *sac,* a bag].

cu·li·nar·y (kū′·li·ner·i·) *a.* pert. to the kitchen or cookery [L. *culina,* a kitchen].

cull (kul) *v.t.* to select, or pick out; to gather [Fr. *cueillir,* to gather].

cul·mi·nate (kul′·mạ·nāt) *v.i.* to reach the highest point (with 'in'); to reach a climax. **culmination** *n.* the attainment of the highest point; climax [L. *culmen,* summit].

cu·lottes (koo·lots′) *n.pl.* knee length trousers resembling a skirt [Fr.].

cul·pa·ble (kul′·pạ·bl) *a.* deserving blame or censure. **culpably** *adv.* **culpability, -ness** *n.* [L. *culpa,* fault].

cul·prit (kul′·prit) *n.* one accused of a crime; a criminal; an offender [L. *culpa,* a fault].

cult (kult) *n.* a system of religious worship, or rites and ceremonies [L. *cultus,* worship].

cul·ti·vate (kul′·tạ·vāt) *v.t.* to prepare for the raising of crops; to till; to produce by tillage, labor, or care; to train; to foster. **-d** *a.* [L. *colere, cultum,* to till].

cul·ture (kul′·chẹr) *n.* tillage or cultivation; mental training and development; refinement; civilization; the propagation of bacteria and other micro-organisms in artificial media; *v.t.* to cultivate. **cultural** *a.* pert. to culture. **-d** *a.* educated and refined [L. *colere,* to cultivate].

cul·vert (kul′·vẹrt) *n.* an arched drain or conduit for the passage of water under a road, railway, or canal [Fr. *couler,* to flow].

cum·ber (kum′·bẹr) *v.t.* to burden or hinder with a useless load. **-some** *a.* burdensome; clumsy and unmanageable. **cumbrous** *a.* [O.Fr. *combrer,* to hinder].

cum·mer·bund (kum′·ẹr·bund) *n.* a broad sash worn as a belt [Pers. *kamarband,* a loin band].

cu·mu·late (kū′·myạ·lāt) *v.t.* to heap together; *a.* heaped up. **cumulation** *n.* **cumulative** *a.* becoming greater by successive additions; gaining force or effect by additions. **cumulatively** *adv.* [L. *cumulus,* a heap].

cu·mu·lus (kū′·myạ·lạs) *n.* a heap; a piled-up cloud mass with rounded outlines. *pl.* **cumuli** [L. *cumulus,* a heap].

cu·ne·i·form, cuniform (kū′·ni·ạ·fawrm) *a.* wedge-shaped [L. *cuneus,* a wedge].

cun·ning (kun′·ing) *a.* wily; sly; artful; *n.* craft or skill; guile; deceit. **-ly** *adv.* [O.E. *cunnan,*to know].

cup (kup) *n.* a drinking vessel; the contents of a cup; anything resembling a teacup in shape; an ornamental vessel given as a prize for sport, etc.; *v.t.* to let blood; to hold, as in a cup; to form into a cup shape. *pr.p.* **-ping.** *pa.t.* **-ped. -ful** *n.* the quantity that a cup holds, 8 fluid oz. **cupboard** (kub′·ẹrd) *n.* a small closet with shelves for cups, plates, etc. **loving cup** *n.* a large cup; trophy, given as a prize [L. *cupa,* a tub].

cu·pid·i·ty (kū·pid′·ạ·ti·) *n.* an eager desire for possession; greed [L. *cupidus,* desirous].

cu·po·la (kū′·pạ·lạ) *n.* a spherical vault or small domed tower on the top of a building [It. *cupola,* fr. L. *cupa,* a tub].

cu·pre·ous (kū′·pri·ạs) *a.* of, pert. to, or containing copper [L. *cuprum,* copper].

cur (kur) *n.* a dog of mixed breed; a mongrel;

[O.N. *kurra*, to grumble].
cu·rate (kjoo'·rit) *n.* (*chiefly Br.*) an assistant to a vicar or rector. **curacy** *n.* [L. *cura*, care].
cu·ra·tor (kyoo·rā'·tẹr) *n.* a superintendent, as of a museum, library, etc.; a guardian. **-ship** *n.* [L. fr. *curare*, to care].
curb (kurb) *n.* a chain or strap attached to the bit of a bridle to give control with the reins; any check or means of restraint; an edging to a pavement or sidewalk; *v.t.* to apply a curb to (a horse); to restrain; to confine. **-ing** *n.* [Fr. *courber*, fr. L. *curvare*, to bend].
curd (kurd) *n.* the cheesy part of milk; coagulated milk; the coagulated part of any liquid. **-le** *v.t.* and *i.* to turn into curd; to coagulate [O.E. *crudan*, to press].
cure (kūr) *v.t.* to heal; to restore to health; to remedy; to preserve fish, skins, etc. by salting, drying, etc.; *n.* the act of healing; that which heals; a remedy. **curable** *a.* **curative** *a.* **cure-all** *n.* a remedy for all ills; a panacea [L. *cura*, care].
cu·rette (kū·ret') *n.* instrument for scraping body tissue. **-ment** *n.* [Fr. *curer*, to cleanse].
cur·few (kur'·fū) *n.* the time after which persons may not be out of doors [Fr. *couvre-feu* = cover fire].
cur·ie (kyoo'·ri) *n.* (*Chem.*) the standard unit of emanation from one gram of radium. **curium** (kyoo'·ri·ạm) *n.* a radioactive, inert, gaseous element [fr. M. and Mme. *Curie*, discoverers of radium].
cu·ri·o (kyoo'·ri·ō) *n.* a rare or curious object; a curiosity [abbrev. of *curiosity*].
cu·ri·ous (kyoo'·ri·ạs) *a.* eager to know; inquisitive; (*Colloq.*) puzzling; strange. **-ly** *adv.* **curiosity** *n.* eagerness to know; inquisitiveness; a strange or rare object; a novelty [L. *curiosus*, inquisitive].
curl (kurl) *v.t.* to twist into ringlets; to coil; to bend into spiral or curved shape; *v.i.* to take a spiral or curved shape or path; to turn into ringlets; to ripple; to play at the game of curling; *n.* a ringlet of hair; anything of a similar shape. **-y** *a.* having curls; tending to curl; full of ripples. **-icue** *n.* a lock of hair; a fancy curve in writing. **-iness** *n.* **-ing** *n.* a game like bowls played on ice with large, rounded stones. **-er** *n.* a pin used as a fastener to retain a curl or wave in position [M.E. *crul*, curly].
cur·lew (kur'·lòò) *n.* a long-billed wading bird [Fr. *courlieu*, imit. of its cry].
cur·mudg·eon (kẹr·muj'·ạn) *n.* a grasping ill-natured fellow; a churl [origin unknown].
cur·rant (kur'·ạnt) *n.* the fruit of various plants allied to the gooseberry.
cur·rent (kur'·ạnt) *a.* belonging to the present time; in circulation or general use; *n.* a flowing body of water or air in motion; the flow of a river, etc.; tendency; drift; transmission of electricity through a conductor. **-ly** *adv.* in a current manner; commonly. **currency** *n.* money in use or circulation [L. *currere*, to run].
cur·ric·u·lum (ku·rik'·yạ·lạm) *n.* a specified course of study at a school, college, university, etc.; *pl.* **curricula** [L. *curriculum*, a running, a race-course].
cur·ry (kur'·i·) *n.* (*Cookery*) a highly-flavored and pungent condiment much used in the East. **— powder** *n.* [Tamil].
cur·ry (kur'·i·) *v.t.* to dress leather; to comb, rub down, and clean a horse; to beat or thrash. **currier** *n.* one who dresses tanned leather. **to curry favor,** to try to win favor by flattery. [O.Fr. *correer*, to prepare].
curse (kurs) *v.t.* to utter a wish of evil against; to invoke evil upon; to swear at; to torment; *v.i.* to utter blasphemous words; to swear; *n.* the invocation of evil or injury upon a person; profane words or oaths. **cursed** (kurs'·ạd, kurst) *a.* hateful. **cursedly** *adv.* [O.E. *cursian*].
cur·sive (kur'·siv) *a.* written with a running hand, i.e. with all the letters joined; flowing. **-ly** *adv.* **cursory** *a.* characterized by haste; careless; superficial [L. *currere*, to run].
cur·sor (kur'·sẹr) *n.* a bright figure on a computer display indicating the present position.
curt (kurt) *a.* short; concise to the point of rudeness; abrupt; terse. *n.* [L. *curtus*, shortened].
cur·tail (kur·tāl') *v.t.* to cut short; to abridge; to diminish. **-ment** *n.* [L. *curtus*, shortened].
cur·tain (kur'·tin) *n.* a drapery; a screen in front of stage of a theater; anything that shuts off or conceals; *v.t.* to enclose or furnish with curtains. **— raiser** *n.* a short play preceding the main piece in a theater. **iron curtain** (*Fig.*) any hindrance to obtaining information about conditions in a country [L.L. *cortina*].
curt·sy, curtsey (kurt'·si·) *n.* a gesture of civility or respect made by women or girls; *v.i.* to make a curtsy [form of *courtesy*].
curve (kurv) *n.* a bending without angles; that which is bent; an arch; *a.* bent; *v.t.* and *i.* to bend. **curvate** *a.* curved. **curvature** *n.* [L. *curvus*, crooked].
cush·ion (koosh'·ạn) *n.* any stuffed or padded surface used as a rest or protector; *v.t.* to seat on a cushion; to provide or protect with a cushion [Fr. *coussin*, a cushion, fr. L. *coxa*, the hip].
cusp (kusp) *n.* a point or horn of a crescent, as of the moon; a prominence on a molar tooth; the point at which the two branches of a curve have a common tangent. **-id** *n.* a canine tooth. **-idal** *n.* ending in a point [L. *cuspis*, a point].
cus·pi·dor (kus'·pạ·dawr) *n.* a spittoon [Port.].
cus·tard (kus'·tẹrd) *n.* a sweet dish made with milk and eggs [M.E. *crystade*, a pie with a crust].
cus·to·dy (kus'·tạ·di·) *n.* a keeping or guarding; care; guardianship; imprisonment. **custodial** (kus·tō'·di·ạl) *a.* **custodian, custodier** *n.* a keeper; a caretaker [L. *custodia*, fr. *custos*, a keeper].
cus·tom (kus'·tạm) *n.* fashion; usage; habit; business patronage; toll, tax, or tribute; **-s** *n.pl.* duties levied on imports. **-able** *a.* liable to duty. **-ary** *a.* according to custom; established by common usage; usual; habitual. **-arily** *adv.* **-er** *n.* one who enters a shop to buy. **-house** *n.* office where customs are paid. [O.Fr. *coustume* fr. L. *consuetudo*].
cut (kut) *v.t.* to severe, penetrate, or wound with an edged instrument; to divide; to separate; to intersect; to cross; to mow; to hew; to carve; to trim; to shape; to reduce; to abridge; intentionally to ignore a person; (*Sports*) to hit the ball obliquely in order to impart spin to it. *pr.p.* **-ting.** *pa.p.* and *pa.t.* **cut** *n.* an act of cutting; opening made with an edged instrument; a gash; a wound; a piece cut off, as e.g. a joint of meat; a notch; a reduction, esp. in salary or wages. **-ter** *n.* he who, or that which, cuts; a warship's rowing and sailing boat. **-ting** *n.* an incision; a small branch, slip, etc. cut from a plant, bush, etc. *a.* sarcastic. **— glass** *n.* glass ornamented with cut designs. **-off** *n.* a road that is a short cut; a device to shut off. **—rate** *a.* below usual price. **-throat** *n.* a murderer; *a.* merciless. **to cut a caper,** to frisk about; to gambol.
cu·ta·ne·ous (kū·tā'·ni·ạs) *a.* belonging to, or affecting, the skin [L. *cutis*, the skin].
cute (kūt) *a.* (*Colloq.*) attractive [short for *acute*].
cu·ti·cle (kū'·ti·kl) *n.* the epidermis, esp. around the fingernails and toenails [L. *cutis*, skin].
cut·las (kut'·lạs) *n.* a short, broad-bladed, curving sword [O.Fr. *coutel*, a knife fr. L. *culter*, a ploughshare].
cut·ler (kut'·lẹr) *n.* one who makes, repairs, or deals in knives and cutting implements. **-y** *n.* business of a cutler; cutting instruments, esp. tableware [Fr. *coutelier*; *couteau*, a knife].
cut·let (kut'·lit) *n.* a piece of meat or chop from the rib bones [Fr. *cotelette*, fr. *côte*, a rib].
cy·a·nide (sī'·ạ·nīd) *n.* a poisonous compound.
cy·an·o·gen (sī·an'·ạ·jen) *n.* (*Chem.*) a color-

less, poisonous gas. **cyanic** *a.* blue [Gk. *kuanos*, blue, and root *gen*].

cy·ber·net·ics (sī·bẹr·net′·iks) *n.* the study of the self-organizing machine or mechanical brain [Gk. *kubornasis*, a pilot].

cyc·la·men (sik′·lạ·mạn) *n.* a tuberous plant of the Primrose family [Gk. *kuklaminos*].

cy·cle (sī′·kl) *n.* a regularly recurring succession of events or phenomena, or the period of time occupied by such a succession; a body of myths or legends, relating to some period, person, or event; a series of songs dealing with various phases of the same subject, and meant to be sung one after the other; a bicycle or tricycle; *v.i.* to pass through a cycle of changes; to ride a bicycle or tricycle. **cyclist** *n.* one who rides a bicycle or tricycle. **cycloid** *n.* (*Geom.*) a curve traced by a point in a circle when the circle revolves along a straight line [Gk. *kuklos*, a circle].

cy·clone (sī′·klōn) *n.* a violent storm characterized by strong winds. **cyclonic** [Gk. *kuklos*, a circle].

cy·clo·pe·di·a See **encyclopedia.**

cy·clo·ram·a (sī·klạ·rȧ′·mạ) *n.* circular panorama [Gk. *kuklos*, a circle; *orama*, a view].

cy·clo·tron (sī′·klạ·trȧn) *n.* a radio oscillator developed to disintegrate atoms, in order to study their internal structure [Gk. *kuklos*, a circle].

cyg·net (sig′·nit) *n.* a young swan [Fr. *cygne*, a swan].

cyl·in·der (sil′·in·dẹr) *n.* a roller-like body with straight sides, the ends being equal, parallel circles; any object of similar shape. **cylindric, cylindrical** *a.* **cylindriform** *a.* [Gk. *kulindros*, a roller].

cym·bal (sim′·bạl) *n.* musical percussion instrument [Gk. *kumbalon*].

cyn·ic (sin′·ik) *n.* one of a set of Greek philosophers who regarded virtue as the supreme good and despised all comfort or refinement; one who believes man's conduct is based on self-interest. **cynic(al)** *a.* sneering; distrustful of people's motives. **cynically** *adv.* **cynicalness** *n.* **cynicism** (sin′·i·sizm) *n.* principles of a cynic; disbelief in goodness; misanthropy [Gk. *kunikos*, doglike, fr. *kuon*, a dog].

cy·no·sure (sī′·nō·, sin′·ō·shoor) *n.* (*Astron.*) the constellation of the Lesser Bear, containing the Pole-star; hence, something to which all eyes are turned; a guiding star [Gk. *kuon*, a dog; *oura*, a tail].

cy·press (sī′·prạs) *n.* a slender coniferous tree with evergreen foliage [L. *cypressus*].

cyst (sist) *n.* (*Med.*) a bladder or membranous sac containing liquid secretion or morbid matter; **-ic** *a.* pert. to cysts [Gk. *kustis*, a bladder].

Czar (zȧr) *n.* a title used by various Slavonic rulers, esp. by the Emperors of Russia. **Czarina** (zȧ·rē′·nạ) *n.* the wife of a Czar. (Other forms are **Tsar, Tzar, Tsarina, Tzarina,** etc.) [fr. L. *Caesar*].

Czech (chek) *n.* a member of the Slavonic race of people inhabiting the western region of Czechoslovakia; the language spoken by them; *a.* pert. to the people or their language. **Czechoslovak** (chek·ạ·slō′·vak, chek·ạ·slō·vak′), **Czechoslovakian** *a.* pert. to the country, the people, or the language of Czechoslovakia; *n.* a native of the country; the language.

D

dab (dab) *n.* Eur. flatfish.

dab (dab) *v.t.* to pat gently and intermittently, **-bing.** *pa.p.* and *pa.t.* **-bed.** *n.* a gentle blow with a soft substance; a small lump of anything soft, as butter [M.E. *dabban*, to strike].

dab·ble (dab′·l) *v.t.* to wet by little dips; to moisten; *v.i.* to play in water; to pursue a subject superficially [M.E. *dabban*, to strike].

dace (dās) *n.* a small fresh-water river fish. Also **dart, dare** [O.Fr. *dars*, dart].

dach·shund (daks′·hoont) *n.* dog with long body, short legs, and drooping ears [Ger. *Dachs*, a badger; *Hund*, a dog].

dac·tyl (dak′·til) *n.* a metrical foot in poetry, consisting of one accented syllable followed by two unaccented syllables (— u u). **-ic** *a.* pert. to or consisting of a dactyl. **-iography** *n.* the history of gem engraving. **-ogram** *n.* a finger print. **-ography** *n.* the science of finger prints. **-ology** *n.* the finger language of the deaf and dumb [Gk. *daktulos*, a finger].

dad, dada, daddy (dad, dȧ′·da, dad′·i·) *n.* father, a word used by little children [W. *tad*, a father].

da·da·ism (dȧ′·dạ·izm) *n.* a school of art and literature which aims at suppressing all relation between thought and expression.

dad·dy-long-legs (dad′·i·lawng′·legz) *n.* a flying insect; a harvestman [fr. *dad*].

da·do (dā′·dō) *n.* (*Archit.*) the part of a pedestal between the base and cornice; the lower part or wide skirting of the walls of a room [It. *dado*, a pedestal].

dae·mon (dē′·mạn) *n.* an inspiring influence; a divinity; genius. **-ic** *a.* more than human; supernatural [Gk. *daimon*, spirit].

daf·fo·dil (daf′·ạ·dil) *n.* a spring plant of the genus Narcissus; the yellow color of the daffodil [Gk. *asphodelos*, a lily flower].

daft (daft) *a.* insane; foolish. **-ness** *n.* [M.E. *daft*, mild].

dag·ger (dag′·ẹr) *n.* a short, two-edged sword used in close combat; a mark of reference in typography (†) or (‡) [M.F. *daggen*, to slit].

dag·gle (dag′·l) *v.t.* to trail through mud; to bedraggle [Scand. *dagg*, dew].

da·guerre·o·type (dạ·ger′·ạ·tīp) *n.* in photography, an early method of taking pictures on plates of silver or silvered copper [fr. Louis *Daguerre* of Paris, the 19th cent. inventor].

dahl·ia (dal′·yạ) *n.* a genus of plants with large, brightly colored flowers [fr. *Dahl*, a Swedish botanist].

dai·ly (dā′·li·) *a.* or *adv.* happening each day; *n.* a newspaper published each day or each weekday [O.E. *daeg*, day].

dain·ty (dān′·ti·) *a.* pleasing to the taste; refined; pretty and delicate; scrupulous; *n.* a delicacy. **daintily** *adv.* [L. *dignus*, worthy].

dair·y (dā′·ri·) *n.* the place where milk and cream are kept cool, butter is churned, and cheese is made; the shop where milk and its products are sold; a dairy farm. **-ing** *n.* the business of conducting a dairy. **-maid, -man** *n.* [Icel. *deigja*, a dairymaid].

da·is (dā′·is) *n.* the raised platform at the end of a room, esp. of dining hall [O.Fr. *deis*, fr. L.L. *discus*, a table].

dai·sy (dā′·zi·) *n.* a common wild flower; (*Slang*) a person or thing unusually pleasing. **daisied** *a.* [O.E. *daeg*, a day; *eage*, an eye].

dale (dāl) *n.* a low place between hills; a valley or vale; a glen [O.E. *dael*, a valley].

dal·ly (dal′·i·) *v.i.* to waste time; to trifle; to fondle or interchange caresses. **dalliance** *n.* the act of trifling and wasting time; flirtation [M.E. *dalien*, to play].

Dal·ma·tian (dal·mā′·shạn) *n.* a breed of large white dogs with black or liver-colored spots [fr. *Dalmatia*].

dam (dam) *n.* a female parent—used of animals [form of *dame*].

dam (dam) *n.* a barrier of earth, stones, etc. to obstruct the flow of water; the water confined by a dam; *v.t.* to confine water by a dam; to block up [M.E. *dam*, an obstruction].

dam·age (dam′·ij) *n.* any injury or harm to person, property, or reputation; *v.t.* to harm;

to hurt. **-s** *n.pl.* legal compensation paid to injured party. **-able** *a.* [L. *damnum,* loss].

dam·ask (dam′·ạsk) *n.* a figured silk or linen fabric, orig. made at Damascus; steel ornamented with wavy pattern; a rose-pink color, like that of damask rose; *a.* woven with figured pattern like damask [fr. *Damascus,* in Syria].

dame (dām) *n.* (*Arch.*) a noble lady; (*Slang*) a woman. **Dame** *n.* (*Br.*) title of the wife of a knight or baronet [Fr. *dame,* a lady].

damn (dam) *v.t.* to consign to everlasting punishment; (*Colloq.*) to condemn irritably (used as interjection); to destroy the reputation of; *n.* an oath; a curse; (*Colloq.*) a trifle. **-able** *a.* **-ably** *adv.* **-ation** *n.* **-ed** *a.* odious [L. *damnare,* to condemn].

dam·o·sel, damozel (dam′·ō·zel) *n.* archaic and poetic var. of *damsel* [O.Fr. *damoisele,* a maiden].

damp (damp) *n.* moist air; humidity; fog; vapor; noxious gases in coal mines, wells, etc. (as fire-damp, choke-damp); *a.* slightly moist; *v.t.* to moisten slightly; to retard combustion (to *damp* down a fire). **-en** *v.t.* to moisten; (*Fig.*) to depress. **-er** *n.* one who or that which damps; a contrivance in a flue to regulate the draft; a device to minimize vibration. **-ish** *a.* [Ger. *Dampf,* steam].

dam·sel (dam′·sạl) *n.* a young unmarried woman [M.E. *damizel,* Fr. *demoiselle,* a maiden].

dam·son (dam′·zạn) *n.* a small dark plum [O.Fr. *damascene,* of Damascus].

dance (dans) *v.t.* and *v.i.* to move with measured steps; to move rhythmically; to caper; *n.* a lively and rhythmical movement with certain steps and gestures; a social gathering for the purpose of dancing. **-r** *n.* one who dances. **danseuse** *n.* a female dancer, esp. in ballet. **to lead someone a dance,** to lead someone in vain pursuit. **St. Vitus's dance** (*Med.*) nervous disorder accompanied by twitching of muscles [Fr. *danser,* to dance].

dan·de·li·on (dan·dạ·lī′·ạn) *n.* a plant with large yellow flowers, and tooth-edged leaves [Fr. *dent de lion,* lion-toothed].

dan·der (dan′·dẹr) *n.* (*Colloq.*) anger; passion; temper [fr. *dandriff*].

dan·dle (dan′·dl) *v.t.* to move up and down in affectionate play, as an infant; to pet; to caress [It. *dondolare,* to swing].

dan·druff, dandriff (dan′·drạf, ·drif) *n.* a disease affecting the scalp and producing scurf or small scales of skin under the hair.

dan·dy (dan′·di·) *n.* one who affects special finery in dress; a fop; *a.* (*Colloq.*) fine; first-rate. **dandify** *v.t.* to make like a dandy. **dandified** *a.* foppish [etym. poss. Scots corrupt. of St. Andrew].

Dane (dān) *n.* a native of Denmark; a breed of dog, large and smooth coated, usually *great Dane.* **Danish** *a.* pert. to Denmark or the Danes; *n.* the language of the Danes [O.E. *Dene,* a Dane].

dan·ger (dān′·jẹr) *n.* exposure to injury or evil; peril; hazard; jeopardy. **-ous** *a.* **-ously** *adv.* **dangerousness** *n.* [M.E. *danger,* power].

dan·gle (dang′·l) *v.t.* to swing loosely or carelessly; (*Fig.*) to use as a bait; *v.i.* to hang loosely [Scand. *dangle,* to swing].

dank (dangk) *a.* unpleasantly damp or moist. **-ness** *n.* [Scand. *danka,* moist].

dap·per (dap′·ẹr) *a.* neat; trim; smart; little and active [Dut. *dapper,* brave].

dap·ple (dap′·l) *n.* a spot; *a.* spotted, applied to horses and deer. **-d** *a.* spotted, esp. of pattern made by sunlight through trees.

dare (dār) *v.i.* to have courage for; to venture (to); to be audacious enough; *v.i.* to defy; to challenge. **daring** *n.* audacity; a bold action; *a.* bold; courageous; audacious. **daringly** *adv.* **—devil** *n.* a foolhardy, reckless fellow. **I dare say,** I presume [M.E. *durran,* to dare].

dark (dȧrk) *a.* lacking light; black; somber; evil; unenlightened; *n.* absence of light; gloom; obscurity; evil. **-en** *v.t.* to obstruct light; to render dim; to cloud; (*Fig.*) to sully; *v.i.* to grow dark. **-ish** *a.* rather dark. **-le** *v.i.* to grow dark; to lie hid. **-ling** *adv.* in the dark. **-ly** *adv.* **-ness** *n.* **— horse** *n.* (*Fig.*) one unexpectedly nominated for an office. **to -en a door,** to enter a door [O.E. *deorc,* dark].

dar·ling (dȧr′·ling) *n.* a beloved or lovable one; *a.* cherished [dim. of O.E. *deore,* dear].

darn (dȧrn) *v.t.* to mend; to repair a hole by weaving threads at right angles to one another; *n.* the place darned. **-ing-needle** *n.* [prob. O.E. *dernan,* to hide].

dart (dȧrt) *n.* a pointed arrow-like weapon; anything similar which pierces or wounds; a small seam or intake in garment to make it fit more closely; a sharp, forward movement; *v.t.* to send forward quickly; to throw suddenly; *v.i.* to run forward swiftly; to move like a dart. **-s** *n. pl.* a popular game using darts and dartboard [M.E. *dart,* a javelin].

Dar·win·i·an (dȧr·win′·i·ạn) *a.* pert. to *Darwin* or to his Theory of Evolution; *n.*

dash (dash) *v.t.* to throw violently; to cast down; to shatter; *v.i.* to rush forward or move violently; to strike violently against; *n.* a violent clashing of two bodies; a rapid movement; a mark of punctuation (—) to denote parenthesis; a small amount, as a *dash of soda.* **-ing** *a.* daring; spirited; showy. **-y** *a.* showy [M.E. *daschen,* to strike down].

das·tard (das′·tẹrd) *n.* mean or cowardly fellow; *a.* cowardly. **-ly** *a.* **-liness** *n.* [M.E. *dastard,* a stupid or mean person].

da·ta (dā′·tạ) *n.pl.* things known and from which inferences may be deduced. *sing.* **datum.** **— bank** *n.* a collection of information stored in a computer system, for instant retrieval or rearrangement. **— processing** *n.* the computer analysis and storing of information [L. *data,* things given].

date (dāt) *n.* period of time of an event; epoch; duration; (*Colloq.*) appointment; *v.t.* to note or fix the time of; to refer to as a starting point; *v.i.* to reckon back to a given time (foll. by *from* or *back to*). **—line** *n.* approximately the 180° parallel of longitude on each side of which the date of the day differs [L. *datum,* a thing given].

date (dāt) *n.* the stone fruit of the Eastern date palm. **— palm** *n.* tree bearing date fruit [Gk. *daktulos*].

da·tive (dā′·tiv) *n.* the case of a noun which is the indirect object of a verb, or which is preceded by certain prepositions [L. *dare,* to give].

da·tum (dā′·tum) *n.* a fact given. *pl.* **data** [L. *dare,* to give].

daub (dawb) *v.t.* to smear with mud or plaster; to soil; to paint crudely; *n.* a crude painting; a smudge. **-er** *n.* one who daubs; *n.* a daub; rough cast for exterior of houses [O.Fr. *dauber,* to plaster].

daugh·ter (daw′·tẹr) *n.* a female child; *a.* like a daughter. **—in-law** *n.* the wife of one's son [O.E. *dohtor*].

daunt (dawnt, dȧnt) *v.t.* to subdue the courage of; to dismay; to dishearten; to disconcert. **-less** *a.* fearless; intrepid [O.Fr., fr. L. *domare,* to tame].

dau·phin (daw′·fin) *n.* (*fem.* **dauphiness**) the French Crown prince [O.Fr. *daulphin*].

da·ven·port (dav′·ạn·pōrt) *n.* a sofa [fr. the name of the maker].

dav·it (da′·vit) *n.* any cranelike device for lowering life-boats over side of ship [orig. unknown].

daw (daw) *n.* a bird of the crow family; a jackdaw [imit.].

daw·dle (daw′·dl) *v.i.* to loiter; to move very slowly [prob. conn. with *dandle*].

dawn (dawn) *v.i.* to grow towards daylight; to begin to be visible; (*Fig.*) to come to the mind; *n.* daybreak; morning half-light; beginning [O.E. *daeg,* a day].

day (dā) *n.* the period from sunrise to sunset; the period of the sun's revolution on its axis; 24 hrs.; time of life; epoch. **— bed** *n.* a divan. **-book** *n.* a book kept to record daily transactions. **-break** *n.* dawn. **-dream** *n.* a reverie; *v.i.* to indulge in reveries [O.E. *daeg*, a day].
daze (dāz) *v.t.* to confuse; to stupefy; to bewilder; to stun; *n.* the state of being bewildered; stupefaction. **dazzle** *v.t.* to daze with sudden light; to make temporarily blind; to confuse mentally; *n.* brilliancy. **dazzling** *a.* [M.E. *dasen*, to stupefy].
dea·con (dē′·kạn) *n.* an assistant to a priest or minister; a layman elected to certain duties in the church. **-ess** *n.* **-hood** *n.* the office of deacon. **-ry** *n.* the body of deacons. **-ship** *n.* office of deacon [Gk. *diakonos*, a servant].
dead (ded) *a.* without life; *adv.* wholly; *n.* the most death-like time. **-en** *v.t.* to benumb. **-ness** *n.* **—beat** *a.* without oscillation, applied to measuring instruments in which the pointer comes to rest. **—end** *n.* a street with only one entrance. **-fall** *n.* a trap, esp. for large animals. **— heat** *n.* a race where two or more competitors reach the winning post at exactly the same time. **— language,** a language no longer spoken.**—letter** *n.* an undelivered or unclaimed letter.**—line** *n.* a time limit, as for a payment or news story. **-liness** *n.* **-lock** *n.* a state of affairs which renders further progress impossible; an impasse. **-ly** *a.* causing death; virulent; lethal; *adv.* completely.**—pan** (*Slang*) *n.* an immobile face.**—reckoning** *n.* (*Naut.*) the steering of a vessel by compass and not by the stars.**—weight** *n.* the unrelieved weight of inert objects [O.E. *dead*, dead].

deaf (def) *a.* lacking partially or wholly the sense of hearing; heedless; unwilling to listen. **-en** *v.t.* to make deaf; to stun with sound. **-ening** *a.* very loud; thunderous, as applause. **-ly** *adv.* **—mute** *n.* one who is deaf and dumb. **—mutism** *n.* **-ness** *n.* [O.E. *deaf*, deaf].
deal (dēl) *v.t.* to divide; to dole out; to distribute, as in card games; *v.i.* to traffic; to act; to give one's business to; to behave towards; *n.* a part or portion; distribution of playing cards; a business transaction; a bargain. *pa.p.* **dealt** (delt). **-er** *n.* **-ing** *n.* buying and selling; traffic; treatment; *pl.* intercourse or relations with others. **a raw deal,** iniquitously unfair treatment. **a square deal,** fair treatment [O.E. *daelen*, to divide].
dean (dēn) *n.* a dignitary in cathedral or collegiate churches; (in universities) the head of a faculty; an official of a college with disciplinary authority [O.Fr. *deien*, fr. L. *decanus*, an official].
dear (dēr) *a.* precious; much loved; highly esteemed or valued; costly; expensive; scarce; *interj.* expressing sorrow, pity or wonder, as in *'Oh, dear!'* **-ly** *adv.* [O.E. *deore*, precious].
dearth (durth) *n.* scarcity; lack [M.E. *derthe*].
death (deth) *n.* extinction of life; manner of dying; state of being dead; decease; dissolution; (*Fig.*) termination. **— blow** *n.* a fatal stroke. **-less** *a.* immortal. **-lessness** *n.* **-like** *a.* **-ly** *adv.; a.* like death. **— mask** *n.* a plaster cast of a person's face taken immediately after death. **— rate** *n.* the mortality rate per thousand of the population at a given time. **—throes** *n.pl.* last struggle before death. **— warrant** *n.* an official document authorizing execution of a criminal. **-watch** *n.* a vigil [O.E. *death*, death].
de·ba·cle (dā·bȧk′·ạl) *n.* a sudden collapse; a rout; the breaking up of ice in a river [Fr.].
de·bar (di·bȧr)′ *v.t.* to cut off from entrance; to hinder; to prohibit; to exclude; *pr.p.* **-ring.** *pa.t., pa.p.* **-red. -ment** *n.* [L. *de*; and *bar*].
de·bark (di·bȧrk′) *v.t.* and *v.i.* to disembark, oppos. of *embark*. **-ation, -ment** *n.* [Fr. *débarquer*, to disembark].
de·base (di·bās′) *v.t.* to reduce to a lower state; to disagree; to degrade; to adulterate. **-ment** *n.* **debasing** *a.* corrupting, esp. in moral sense.
de·bate (di·bāt′) *n.* controversy; wrangle; argument; dispute; *v.t.* to discuss; to dispute; to contend; to argue in detail; *v.i.* to take part in a discussion; to reflect. **debatable** *a.* **-r** *n.* [L. *de*, from; *batuere*, to strike or beat].
de·bauch (di·bawch′) *v.t.* to corrupt; to make depraved; to seduce; to pervert; *n.* excess in eating and drinking. **-ed** *a.* **-ee** *n.* a dissipated person. **-ery** *n.* moral corruption. **-ment** *n.* [O.Fr. *debaucher*, to corrupt].
de·ben·ture (di·ben′·chạr) *n.* a certificate acknowledging a debt and guaranteeing repayment of loan with interest [L. *debentur mihi*, first words of certificate meaning 'these sums are owing to me.'].
de·bil·i·tate (di·bil′·ạ·tāt) *v.t.* to weaken; to make infirm; to enervate. **debilitation, debility** *n.* [L. *debilitare*, to weaken].
deb·it (deb′·it) *n.* an item entered on debtor side of an account (oppos. of *credit*); *v.t.* to charge with debt [L. *debere*, *debitum*, to owe].
deb·o·nair (deb′·ạ·nār) *a.* bearing oneself cheerfully and well; sprightly; spruce [Fr. *de bon air*, of amiable disposition].
de·bris, dé·bris (dạ·brē′, dā′·brē) *n.* fragments (taken collectively); rubble; ruins [Fr. *briser*, to break].
debt (det) *n.* something owed to another; a liability; an obligation. **-or** *n.* one who owes a debt [L. *debere*, *debitum*, to owe].
de·bunk (dạ·bungk′) *v.t.* (*Slang*) to remove false sentiment from.
de·but, dé·but (di·bū′, dā·bū′) *n.* a first appearance in public, socially or as an artist. **debutante** *n.* one, esp. a girl, making her first appearance in society; abbrev. **deb.** [Fr. *début*, a first stroke, aim, or goal].
dec·a- *prefix* fr. Gk. *deka*, ten.
dec·ade (dek′·ād) *n.* a group of ten things; a period of ten years [Gk. *deka*, ten].
de·ca·dence (dek′·ạ·dạns, di·kā′·dạns) **decadency** *n.* deterioration; degeneration; decay; a falling off in moral or aesthetic standards.
dec·a·dent (dek′·ạ·dạnt) *a.* deteriorating [L. *decadentia*, a falling away].
de·caf·fein·at·ed (dē·kaf′·i·nāt·ed) adj. without caffeine.
dec·a·gram(me) (dek′·ạ·gram) *n.* in the metric system, a weight of 10 grams, i.e. 0.353 oz. [Gk. *deka*, ten; *gramma*, a weight].
dec·a·he·dron (dek·ạ·hē′·drạn) *n.* a solid figure of a body having ten sides. **decahedral** *a.* [Gk. *deka*, ten; *hedra*, face of a solid].
de·cal·ci·fy (dē·cal′·si·fī) *v.t.* to deprive bones (esp. teeth) of lime.
de·cal·i·ter (dek′·ạ·lē·tẹr) *n.* a measure of capacity equal to 10 liters—about 2.64 imperial gallons [Gk. *dega*, ten; Fr. *litre*].
Dec·a·logue (dek′·ạ·lawg) *n.* the Ten Commandments [Gk. *deka*, ten; *logos*, a word of discourse].
dec·a·me·ter (dek′·ạ·mē·tẹr) *n.* in the metric system a measure of ten meters, or 32.8 ft. [Gk. *deka*, ten; *metron*, measure].
de·camp (dē·kamp′) *v.i.* to move away from a camping ground; to move off suddenly or secretly [Fr. *décamper*, to break camp].
de·cant (di·kant′) *v.t.* to pour off liquid without disturbing sediment, esp. used of wines. **-er** *n.* a slender necked glass bottle into which wine is decanted [L. *de*, from; *canthus*, rim of a cup].
de·cap·i·tate (di·kap′·i·tāt) *v.t.* to cut off the head; to behead. **decapitation** *n.* [L. *de*, from; *caput*, head].
dec·a·pod (dek′·ạ·pȧd) *n.* a shellfish of the crab family having five pairs of legs; a ten-footed crustacean; *a.* having ten legs. **-al, -ous** *a.* [Gk. *deka*, ten; *pous*, a foot].
de·car·bon·ize (dē·kȧr′·bạ·nīz) *v.t.* to deprive of carbon; to remove a deposit of carbon, as from a motor cylinder. Also **decarbonate, decarburize. decarbonization, decarburi-**

zation *n.*

dec·a·syl·lab·ic (dek·ạ·si·lab′·ik) *a.* having ten syllables. **decasyllable** *n.* [Gk. *deka,* ten; syllable].

de·cath·lon (di·kath′·lȧn) *n.* a group of ten different contests at Olympic games [Gk. *deka,* ten; *athlon,* a contest].

de·cay (di·kā′) *v.i.* to rot away; to become decomposed; to waste away; to deteriorate; *v.t.* to impair; *n.* gradual decline or corruption; deterioration. **-ed** *a.* rotting. [L. *de,* down; *cadere,* to fall].

de·cease (di·sēs′) *n.* death; *v.i.* to die. **-d** *a.* dead; *n.* a dead person [L. *decessus,* a departure].

de·ceit (di·sēt′) *n.* fraud; duplicity; wile. **-ful** *a.* crafty; fraudulent. **-fulness** *n.* **deceive** *v.t.* to delude; to cheat. **deceivable** *a.* **deceivably** *adv.* **deceiver** *n.* [L. *decipere, deceptum,* to beguile].

de·cel·er·ate (dē·sel′·ẹr·āt) *v.t.* and *v.i.* to reduce speed [L. *de,* from; *celer,* swift].

De·cem·ber (di·sem′·bēr) *n.* orig. the tenth month of the Roman calendar; the twelfth month of the year [L. *decem,* ten].

de·cen·nial (di·sen′·i·ạl) *a.* lasting for ten years or happening every ten years. **decennary** *n.* [L. *decem,* ten; *annus,* a year].

de·cent (dē′·sent) *a.* fitting or becoming; modest; suitable; comely; sufficient. **decency** *n.* the state or quality of being decent. **-ly** *adv.* [L. *decere,* to be fitting].

de·cen·tral·ize (dē·sen′·trạl·īz) *v.t.* to remove from the center or point of concentration and distribute among small areas; esp. to enlarge powers of local government at expense of central authority. **decentralization** *n.*

de·cep·tion (di·sep′·shạn) *n.* the act of deceiving; fraud; illusion. **deceptible** *a.* **deceptibility** *n.* **deceptive** *a.* causing a false impression. **deceptively** *adv.* [L. *deceptus,* deceived].

dec·i·bel (des′·ạ·bel) *n.* one transmission unit; one tenth of a bel; the smallest variation in sound that the human ear can detect [L. *decem,* ten; *bel,* a coined word].

de·cide (di·sīd′) *v.t.* to determine the result of; to make up one's mind about; to settle an issue; *v.t.* to give a decision; to come to a conclusion. **-d** *a.* clear; not ambiguous; determined. **decidedly** *adv.* **decision** (di·sizh′·ạn) *n.* the act of settling; determination; settlement; judgment. **decisive** *a.* conclusive; resolute. **decisively** *adv.* **decisiveness** *n.* [L. *decidere,* to cut off].

de·cid·u·ous (di·sid′·yoo·ạs) *a.* (of trees) shedding leaves in autumn, oppos. of coniferous or evergreen; not lasting; liable to fall; (used also of a deer's horns) [L. *decidere,* to fall down].

dec·i·mal (des′·ạ·mạl) *a.* pert. to tens; numbered or proceeding by tens; *n.* some power of 10. **-ization** *n.* **-ize** *v.t.* to reduce to the decimal system. **— fraction,** a fraction the (unexpressed) denominator of which is 10 or a power of 10 [L. *decimus,* tenth].

dec·i·mate (des′·ạ·māt) *v.t.* to kill (as in Ancient Rome) every tenth man, chosen by lot, as punishment; to reduce the numbers of, very considerably. **decimation** *n.* [L. *decimus,* tenth].

de·ci·pher (di·sī′·fẹr) *v.t.* to read a cipher; to make out what is illegible, unintelligible or written in strange symbols.

de·ci·sion See **decide.**

deck (dek) *v.t.* to adorn; to cover; to dress up; to cover with a deck (of a ship); *n.* a covering; the horizontal platform extending from one side of ship to the other; a pack of cards, or part of pack remaining after dealing. **—chair** *n.* a light-weight, collapsible chair, made partly of canvas. **— hand** *n.* a person employed on deck of ship. **-ing** *n.* adornment. **hurricane-deck** *n.* a half-deck. **main-deck** *n.* deck below the upper deck. **quarter-deck** *n.* part of the deck abaft the main mast. **double-decker** *n.* a vehicle, as bus, or ferry, with upper and lower passenger-decks [Dut. *dekkan,* to cover].

deck·le (dek′·l) *n.* the gauge on a paper-making machine. **—edge** *n.* untrimmed edge of paper. **—edged** *a.* [Ger. *deckel,* cover].

de·claim (di·klām′) *v.t.* to recite in a rhetorical manner; *v.i.* to make a formal speech. **declamation** *n.* a set speech; a rhetorical and dramatic address. **declamatory** (di·klam′·ạ·tōr·i·) *a.* pert. to a declamation; ostentatiously rhetorical [L. *declamare,* to shout out].

de·clare (di·kler′) *v.t.* to proclaim; to make clear; to state publicly; to state in the presence of a witness; *v.i.* to make a declaration; (at Customs) to admit possession of dutiable goods. **declarable** *a.* **declaration** *n.* the act of declaring; a solemn statement. **declaratory** *a.* making clear or manifest; explanatory [L. *declarare,* to make clear].

de·clen·sion (di·klen′·shạn) *n.* the act of falling away; (*Fig.*) deterioration; (*Gram.*) the inflection of nouns, pronouns, adjectives; a class of nouns, etc. so inflected. **-al** *a.* [L. *declinare,* to fall away].

de·cline (di·klīn′) *v.t.* to bend downward; to refuse; to avoid; (*Gram.*) to give inflections of a word in oblique cases; *v.i.* to slope; to hang down; to fall in value or quantity; to pine away; to languish; *n.* a downward slope; a falling off. **declinable** *a.* able to be inflected. **declination** (de·kli·nā′·shạn) *n.* a sloping away [L. *declinare,* to fall away].

de·cliv·i·ty (di·kliv′·ạ·ti·) *n.* a downward slope; a gradual descent. **declivitous, declivous** *a.* [L. *declivis,* sloping down].

de·code (dē·kōd′) *v.t.* to translate a message in code into ordinary language.

de·col·le·tage (dā·kạl·tazh′) *n.* the line of a woman's low cut evening dress; the neck and shoulders of a person wearing such a dress. **décolleté** *a.* low-necked [Fr.].

de·com·pose (dē·kạm·pōz′) *v.t.* to break up into elements; to separate the constituent parts of; *v.i.* to decay; to rot. **decomposition** *n.* act of decomposing; decay; putrefaction.

de·con·tam·i·nate (dē·kạn·tam′·ạ·nāt) *v.t.* to cleanse from effects of poison gas, etc. **decontamination** *n.*

de·con·trol (dē·kạn·trōl′) *v.t.* to release from government or state control.

de·cor (dā·kawr′) *n.* the decoration, or setting of a theater, stage, or room [Fr.].

dec·o·rate (dek′·ạ·rāt) *v.t.* to beautify; to embellish; to honor a person by giving a medal or badge of honor. **-d** *a.* **decoration** *n.* an ornament; a badge of honor; insignia. **decorative** *a.* **decorativeness** *n.* **decorator** *n.* [L. *decus,* an ornament].

dec·o·rous (dek′·ạ·rạs) *a.* seemly; decent; staid. **-ly** *adv.* **-ness** *n.* **decorum** (di·kōr′·ạm) *n.* behavior, etc. in keeping with social conventions [L. *decus,* an ornament].

de·coy (di·koi′) *v.t.* to lead into a snare; (*Fig.*) to allure; to entice by specially tempting means; (dē′·koi) *n.* a device for leading wild birds into a snare; an enticement [Dut. *kooi,* a cage].

de·crease (di·krēs′) *v.t.* to lessen; to make smaller; to reduce gradually; *v.i.* to become less; to wane; to abate; (dē·crēs′) *n.* gradual diminution; a lessening [L. *de,* from; *crescere,* to grow].

de·cree (di·krē′) *n.* an order made by a competent authority; an edict; decision in a law court; an established law; (*Theol.*) divine purpose; *v.t.* to determine judicially; to order; *v.i.* to decide authoritatively. **decretal** *a.* pert. to a decree; *n.* an order given by a high authority, esp. the Pope. **decretive** *a.* [L. *decretum,* decreed].

de·cre·ment (dek′·rạ·mạnt) *n.* the act or state of decreasing; the quantity lost by decrease [L. *decrementum,* a decrease].

de·crep·it (di·krep′·it) *a.* worn out or enfeebled by old age; infirm; broken down; (of things) ramshackle. **-ude, -ness** *n.* [L. *decrepitus*, very old].

de·cres·cent (di·kres′·ạnt) *a.* becoming gradually less; waning.

de·cre·tal See **decree.**

de·cry (di·krī′) *v.t.* to bring into disrepute; to abuse. **decrial** *n.* act of decrying [L. *de*, from; Fr. *crier*, to cry].

ded·i·cate (ded′·i·kāt) *v.t.* to set apart and consecrate to a holy purpose; to give oneself wholly to a worthy purpose; to inscribe a book or other object to someone as mark of appreciation or admiration. **-d** *a.* devoted. **dedication** *n.* **dedicatory** *a.* containing a dedication; complimentary [L. *dedicare*, to announce].

de·duce (di·dūs′) *v.t.* to draw from; to reach a conclusion by deductive reasoning; to infer; to trace down. **deducible** *a.* inferred. **deduct** *v.t.* to remove; to subtract. **deductible** *a.* **deduction** *n.* the act or process of deducting; the amount subtracted; the inference or conclusion arrived at. **deductive** *a.* capable of being deduced. **deductively** *adv.* [L. *deducere*, to lead down].

deed (dēd) *n.* that which is done; an act; exploit; achievement; a legal document or contract; *v.t.* to convey by deed [O.E. *daed; don*, to do].

deem (dēm) *v.t.* to believe on consideration; to judge [O.E. *dēman*, to judge].

deep (dēp) *a.* extending far below the surface; low in situation; dark; intense; abstruse; low in pitch; sagacious; *adv.* to a great depth; *n.* that which is deep; the sea. **-en** *v.t.* to make deep; *v.i.* to become deeper. **-most** *a.* deepest. **-ness** *n.* depth. **—rooted** *a.* firmly established. **—seated** *a.* not superficial. **depth** *n.* the quality of being deep [O.E. *deop*, deep].

deer (dir) *n.* any of the ruminant quadrupeds, such as stag, roebuck, fallow deer, etc. [O.E. *dēor*, an animal].

de·face (di·fās′) *v.t.* to destroy or mar the external appearance of; to disfigure. **-able** *a.* **-ment** *n.* [Fr. *défacer*, to mar].

de·fal·cate (di·fal′·kāt) *v.t.* to misappropriate money; to embezzle. **defalcation** *n.* **defalcator** *n.* [L. *de*, from; *falx*, a sickle].

de·fame (di·fȧm′) *v.t.* to harm or destroy the good name or reputation of; to slander. **defamation** *n.* **defamatory** *a.* [L. *diffamare*, to spread an evil report].

de·fault (di·fawlt′) *n.* fault; neglect; defect; failure to appear in a law court when summoned; failure to account for money held in trust; *v.i.* to fail to meet an obligation. **-er** *n.* [O.Fr. *defaillir*, to fail].

de·fea·sance (di·fē′·zạns) *n.* defeat; a rendering null and void. **defeasible** *a.* capable of being annulled [O.Fr. *desfaire*, to undo].

de·feat (di·fēt′) *v.t.* to overcome; to subdue; to conquer; *n.* act of defeating; overthrow; conquest. **-ism** *n.* the attitude of mind of those who accept defeat as inevitable. **-ist** *n.; a.* pert. to defeatism [O.Fr. *desfait*, undone].

def·e·cate (def′·ạ·kāt) *v.t.* to clear or strain impurities from, as lees, dregs, etc.; *v.i.* to void excrement from the bowels. **defecation** *n.* [L. *de*, from; *faex*, dregs].

de·fect (dē·fekt′ di·fekt′) *n.* a want; an imperfection; absence of something necessary for completeness. **defection** *n.* a failure in duty; the act of abandoning allegiance to a cause. **-ive** *a.* incomplete; imperfect; faulty; (*Gram.*) not having all the parts to make the complete conjugation of a verb. **-ively** *adv.* **-iveness** *n.*

de·fend (dē·fend′) *v.t.* to protect; to ward off attack; to maintain; to justify; to vindicate; (*Law*) to state the case of an accused person (by counsel). **-able** *a.* **-ant** *n.* one who defends; the accused in a criminal case; the one prosecuted in a civil case. **-er** *n.* [L. *defendere*, to protect].

de·fense (di·fens′) *n.* the act of defending; that which shields or protects; vindication; justification; (*Law*) a plea or reply to a charge. **-less** *a.* open to attack. **-lessly** *adv.* **-lessness** *n.* **Civil Defense,** an organization in World War 2 and since, for protection of civilians. **defensible** *a.* **defensibility** *n.* **defensive** *a.* serving to defend; resisting attack; *n.* the position of defending against attack. **defensively** *adv.* [L. *defendere*, to protect].

de·fer (di·fur′) *v.i.* to submit; to yield or bow to the opinion of another. **deference** (def′·ẹr·ans) *n.* the act of deferring. **deferential** *a.* showing deference [L. *deferre*, to bring before].

de·fer (di·fur′) *v.t.* to put off; to postpone; *v.i.* to delay. *pr.p.* **-ring**; *pa.p.* **-red. -able, -rable** *a.* **-ment** *n.* delay; postponement [L. *deferre*, to postpone].

de·fi·ance (di·fī′·ạns) *n.* the act of defying; a challenge to combat; contempt; opposition. **defiant** *a.* aggressively hostile; insolent. **defiantly** *adv.* [Fr. *défier*, to challenge].

de·fi·cient (di·fish′·ạnt) *a.* wanting; failing; lacking a full supply; incomplete. **deficiency, deficience** *n.* shortcoming, shortage; defect. **-ly** *adv.* **deficit** (def′·ạ·sit) *n.* shortage or deficiency of revenue; excess of expenditure over income [L. *deficere*, to be wanting].

de·file (di·fīl′) *n.* a narrow pass; *v.i.* to march by files [Fr. *défiler*, to thread].

de·file (di·fīl′) *v.t.* to make unclean; soil; to dirty; to desecrate. **-ment** *n.* the act of defiling [L. *de.*; O.E. *fylan*, to pollute].

de·fine (di·fīn′) *v.t.* to determine the boundaries of; to state the exact meaning of; to circumscribe; to designate; to specify. **definable** *a.* **definite** (def′·ạ·nit) *a.* fixed or defined; exact; precise; specific; restricted. **definitely** *adv.* **definiteness** *n.* **definition** *n.* description of a thing by its properties; explanation of the exact meaning of a word or term; distinctness. **definitive** *a.* limiting; determining; final; positive [L. *de*, down; *finis*, end].

de·flate (di·flāt′) *v.t.* to empty of air or gas; to reduce inflated currency. **deflation** *n.* [L. *de*, down, *flare*, to blow].

de·flect (di·flekt′) *v.t.* to turn aside; to divert from the right direction; *v.i.* to swerve; to deviate. **-ed** *a.* **deflection** *n.* **-or** *n.* [L. *de*, from; *flectere*, to bend].

de·flow·er (di·flour′) *v.t.* to deprive of flowers; to ravish. [O.Fr. *defleurer*, to strip of flowers].

de·fo·li·a·tion (di·fō·li·ā′·shạn) *n.* the shedding of leaves. **defoliate** *v.t.* to deprive of leaves. **defoliate, defoliated** *a.* [L. *de*, *folium*, leaf].

de·for·est (dē·fawr′·ạst) *v.t.* to deprive of forests. **-ation** *n.*

de·form (di·fawrm′) *v.t.* to mar or alter the form of; to make misshapen; to disfigure. **-ed** *a.* **-ation** *n.* **-ity** *n.* the state of being disfigured; a malformation [L. *deformare*, disfigure].

de·fraud (di·frawd′) *v.t.* to deprive of, by fraud; cheat [L. *defraudare*].

de·fray (di·frā′) *v.t.* to bear the cost of; to provide the money for, as in to *defray the expenses*. **-al** *n.* [O.Fr. *desfrayer*, to pay the cost].

de·frock (dē·frok′) *v.t.* to unfrock, as of a priest deprived of ecclesiastical status.

deft (deft) *a.* dexterous; adroit; handy. **-ly** *adv.* **-ness** *n.* [O.E. *gedaeftan*, to make smooth].

de·funct (di·fungkt′) *a.* dead; deceased; (of things) obsolete; *n.* a dead person [L. *defunctus*, finished].

de·fy (di·fī′) *v.t.* to challenge; to dare; to resist authority [L. *dis*, away; *fidere*, to trust].

de·gen·er·ate (di·jen′·ẹr·āt) *v.i.* to decline from a noble to a lower state of development to become worse physically and morally; *n.* a person of low moral standards; *a.* having become less than one's kind. **degeneracy** *n.* **-ly** *adv.* **-ness** *n.* **degeneration** *n.* **degenerative** *a.* [L. *degenere*, unlike one's race].

de·grade (di·grād′) *v.t.* to reduce in status; to

lower the moral reputation of; to disgrace. **degradation** (deg·rạ·dā′·shạn) *n.* the act of degrading; the state or process of being degraded; abasement [L. *de,* down; *gradus,* a step].

de·gree (di·grē′) *n.* a step upward or downward; station or status; extent, as in *degree of proficiency;* rank to which one is admitted by a university; the 360th part of a revolution; a measured space on a thermometer, protractor, etc. (*Gram.*) modification of adjectives and adverbs by adding of suffix —*er* (comparative), and —*est* (superlative) to indicate intensifying of meaning. **third degree** (*U.S.*) a long, searching cross-examination by police of a suspect [L. *de,* down; *gradus,* a step].

de·gres·sion (di·gresh′·ạn) *n.* a going down; a lowering of rate of taxation on certain wage levels [L. *degredi,* to go down].

de·hy·drate (dē·hī′·drāt) *v.t.* to remove water from; *v.i.* to lose water; **dehydration** *n.* the process of reducing bulk and weight of food by removing water from products (e.g. dried eggs, milk, potatoes, etc.) [L. *de,* from; Gk. *hydor,* water].

de·i·cide (dē′·ạ·sīd) *n.* the killing of a god [L. *deus,* god; *caedere,* to kill].

de·i·fy (dē′·ạ·fī) *v.t.* to make a god of; to exalt to the rank of divinity; to worship. **deific, -al** *a.* making godlike. **deification** *n.* **deiform** *a.* of godlike form [L. *deus,* a god; *facere,* to make].

deign (dān) *v.i.* to condescend; to stoop; *v.t.* to condescend to do; to grant [L. *dignari,* to deem worthy].

de·ism (dē′·izm) *n.* belief, on purely rational grounds, in the existence of God without accepting the revelation implied in religious dogma. **deist** *n.* **deistic, -al** *a.* **deity** *n.* God, the Supreme Being; a pagan god or goddess [L. *deus,* god].

de·ject (di·jekt′) *v.t.* to cast down; to dishearten; to depress; to dispirit. **-ed** *a.* downcast; moody; in low spirits. **-edly** *adv.* **-edness** *n.* **-ion** *n.* lowness of spirits; (*Med.*) evacuation of the bowels [L. *de,* down; *jacere,* to throw].

de·lay (di·lā′) *v.t.* to put off; to postpone; to stop temporarily; *v.i.* to linger; to dawdle; to procrastinate; *n.* a stoppage; tardiness. **-er** *n.* [O.Fr. *delaier,* to prolong].

de·lec·ta·ble (di·lek′·tạ·bl) *a.* highly pleasing; delightful; enjoyable. **-ness** *n.* **delectably** *adv.* **delectation** *n.* pleasure; delight [L. *delectare,* to delight].

del·e·gate (del′·ạ·gāt) *v.t.* to entrust authority to a deputy. *n.* also (del′·ạ·git) a deputy; a representative. **delegation** *n.* act of delegating; body of delegates. **delegacy** *n.* [L. *de,* from; *legare,* to send].

de·lete (di·lēt′) *v.t.* to erase; to strike out (word or passage). **delenda** *n.pl.* things to be blotted out. **deletion** *n.* [L. *delere,* to blot out].

del·e·te·ri·ous (del·ạ·tē′·ri·ạs) *a.* capable of harming or destroying health; pernicious. **-ly** *adv.* **-ness** *n.* [Gk. *dēleisthai,* to harm].

delft (delft) *n.* glazed earthenware, orig. made at *Delft* in Holland. Also **delf, delft-ware.**

de·lib·er·ate (di·lib′·ạ·rāt) *v.t.* to weigh in the mind; to discuss; *v.i.* to consider carefully; to take counsel; to hesitate; *a.* (di·lib′·ạ·rit) carefully considered; slow. **-ly** *adv.* **-ness** *n.* **deliberation** *n.* the act of carefully considering; slowness of action or speech. **deliberative** *a.* [L. *deliberare,* to ponder].

del·i·cate (del′·ạ·kạt) *a.* dainty; frail; exquisitely wrought; nicely adjusted; highly sensitive or perceptive. **delicacy** *n.* fineness of shape, color, texture, or feeling; something which pleases the palate; a dainty; tact. **-ly** *adv.* **-ness** *n.* [L. *delicatus,* delightful].

del·i·ca·tes·sen (del·ạ·kạ·tes′·ạn) *n.pl.* a shop selling cold cooked meats and other foods requiring little or no preparation [Ger.].

de·li·cious (di·lish′·ạs) *a.* extremely pleasing to the taste or sense of smell; delightful. **-ly** *adv.* [L. *deliciae,* delight].

de·light (di·līt′) *v.t.* to give great pleasure to; to charm; *v.i.* to take delight; *n.* the source of pleasure; great satisfaction; joy. **-ed** *a.* **-edly** *adv.* **-ful** *a.* [L. *delectare,* to delight].

de·lim·it (di·lim′·it) *v.t.* to fix the limit or boundaries of. **-ation** *n.*

de·lin·e·ate (di·lin′·i·āt) *v.t.* to draw an outline; to sketch; to portray; (*Fig.*) to describe clearly in words. **delineation** *n.* the act of delineating; a portrayal in line or words; a sketch. **delineator** *n.* [L. *de,* from; *linea,* a line].

de·lin·quent (di·ling′·kwạnt) *n.* one who fails in duty; an offender or criminal, esp. of a young person; *a.* failing in duty. **delinquency** *n.* [L. *de,* from; *linquere,* to leave].

del·i·quesce (del·ạ·kwes′) *v.i.* to liquefy by absorbing moisture from the air. **deliquescence** *n.* **deliquescent** *a.* [L. *deliquescere,* to melt away].

de·lir·i·ous (di·lir′·i·ạs) *a.* wandering in the mind; light-headed; raving; incoherent. **deliration** *n.* madness. **-ly** *adv.* **-ness** *n.* **delirium** *n.* mental disturbance caused by grave physical illness or nervous shock; strong excitement. **delirium tremens** (*abbrev.* D.T.) violent delirium resulting from excessive alcoholism [L. *delirus,* crazy].

de·liv·er (di·liv′·ẹr) *v.t.* to liberate from danger, captivity, restraint; to save; to distribute or hand over; to pronounce (as a speech); to execute (as an attack); to give birth to a child (used passively). **-able** *a.* **-ance** *n.* liberation; state of being delivered; the formal statement of an opinion. **-er** *n.* **-y** *n.* the act of delivering; the style of utterance of a public speech or sermon; (*Med.*) the act of giving birth [L. *de,* from; *liberare,* to set free].

dell (del) *n.* a small, deep valley; a hollow [M.E. *delle,* a dell].

Del·phic, Del·phian (del′·fik, del′·fi·ạn) *a.* pert. to the town of *Delphia* in Ancient Greece, to the oracle of Apollo in that town; oracular.

del·phin·i·um (del·fin′·i·ạm) *n.* a genus of flowering plants [Gk. *delphinion,* larkspur].

del·ta (del′·tạ) *n.* the fourth letter of the Greek alphabet, Δ (small letter $= \delta$); (*Geog.*) a triangular tract of alluvium at the mouth of a large river. **delta rays,** rays from radioactive metals much less powerful and penetrating than the *alpha* rays [Gk.].

de·lude (di·lòòd′) *v.t.* to lead into error; to mislead; to deceive. **deludable** *a.* **-r** *n.* **delusion** *n.* the act of deluding; that which deludes; a mistaken belief. **delusive** *a.* **delusory** *a.* [L. *de; ludere,* to play].

de·luge (del′·ūj) *n.* a great flow of water; torrential rain; a flood; *v.t.* to flood; to inundate [L. *diluvium,* a washing away].

de luxe (di looks′) *a.* sumptuous; of superlative quality [Fr.].

delve (delv) *v.t.* and *v.i.* to carry on intensive research [O.E. *delfan,* to dig].

dem·a·gogue (dem′·ạ·gȧg) *n.* an unprincipled agitator. **demagogic, -al** (dem·a·gȧj′(g)·ik·ạl) *n.* **demagogy** (dem′·a·gȧj(g)·i·) *n.* the beliefs and actions of a demogague. Also **demagoguery** [Gk. *dēmos,* the people; *agein,* to lead].

de·mand (di·mand′) *v.t.* to ask authoritatively or peremptorily; to question; to require; *n.* the act of demanding; urgent claim; earnest inquiry; (*Econ.*) the requirement of purchaser or consumer, oppos. of *supply.* **-ant** *n.* a plaintiff [L. *demandare,* to entrust].

de·mar·ca·tion, demarkation (dē·mȧr·kā′·shun) *n.* the act of marking a line or boundary; a boundary. **demarcate** *v.t.* [Fr.].

de·mean (di·mēn′) *v.t.* to conduct or comport oneself. **demeanor** *n.* behavior; conduct [O.Fr. *demener,* to conduct].

de·mean (di·mēn′) *v.t.* to make mean; to debase; to degrade (used reflexively).

de·ment·ed (di·men′·tạd) *a.* insane; crazy;

suffering from dementia. **dement** *v.t.* to drive mad. **dementia** (di·men′·shi·ạ) *n.* incipient loss of reason; insanity marked by complete mental deterioration. **dementia praecox,** insanity in adolescence [L. *de,* from; *mens,* the mind].

de·mer·it (dē·mer′·it) *n.* a fault; a mark against one's record [L. *de,* from; *merere,* to deserve].

de·mesne (di·mān′, di·mēn′) *n.* a manor house and the estate adjacent to it; private ownership of land. Also **domain** [Fr.].

dem·i- *prefix* signifying *half* [L. *dimidium,* half; Fr. *demi*].

demi·i·god (dem′·i·gạd) *n.* a classical hero half human, half divine.

dem·i·john (dem′·ạ·jȧn) *n.* a glass bottle with large body, slender neck, and enclosed in wicker work [prob. fr. Fr. *dame-Jeanne*].

dem·i·monde (dem′·i·mạnd) *n.* a class of women of doubtful reputation; prostitutes. [Fr. *demi,* half; *monde,* world].

de·mise (di·mīz′) *n.* death; transmission by will to a successor; the conveyance of property; *v.t.* to bequeath; to transmit to a successor [L. *demittere,* to send down].

dem·i·tasse (de·mạ·tȧs′) *n.* a small-sized cup, esp. for after-dinner coffee [Fr.].

de·mo·bi·lize (dē·mō′·bạ·līz) *v.t.* to dismiss (troops); to disband. **demobilization** *n.*

de·moc·ra·cy (dạ·mȧk′·rạ·si·) *n.* a form of government for the people by the will of the majority of the people (based on conception of the equality of man); a state having this form of government. **democrat** (dem′·ạ·krat) *n.* one who adheres to democracy; member of Democratic party (opp. of Republican party). **democratic, democratical** *a.* [Gk. *dēmos,* the people; *kratein,* to rule].

de·mog·ra·phy (di·mȧg′·rạ·fi·) *n.* science of vital and social statistics [Gk. *dēmos,* people; *graphein,* to write].

de·mol·ish (di·mȧl′·ish) *v.t.* to destroy; to pull down (of a building); to ruin. **-er** *n.* **demolition** (dem·ạ·li′·shạn) *n.* the act or process of pulling down; destruction [L. *de,* down; *moles,* a heap].

de·mon (dē′·mạn) *n.* a spirit (esp. evil); a devil; sometimes like *daemon,* a friendly spirit. **demoniac** *a.* pert. to a demon; possessed of an evil spirit; devilish—also **demoniacal;** *n.* a human being possessed of an evil spirit. **-olatry, -ism** *n.* the worship of evil spirits. **-olater** *n.* [Gk. *daimon,* a spirit].

de·mon·e·ti·za·tion (dē·mȧn·ạ·tī·zā′·shạn) *n.* the act of demonetizing. **demonetize** *v.t.* to diminish or deprive of monetary value [L. *de,* down; *moneta,* money].

dem·on·strate (dem′·ạn·strāt) *v.t.* to prove by pointing out; to exhibit; to explain by specimens or experiment. **demonstrable** *a.* capable of being demonstrated. **demonstrably** *adv.* **demonstration** *n.* the act of making clear, esp. by practical exposition; proof beyond doubt; a display of emotion. **demonstrative** *a.* proving by evidence; exhibiting with clearness; inclined to show one's feelings openly;; (*Gram.*) of an adjective or pronoun which points out, as *this* or *that.* **demonstrator** *n.* [L. *demonstrare,* to show].

de·mor·al·ize (di·mawr′·ạl·īz) *v.t.* to injure the morale of; to corrupt; to throw into confusion.

de·mos (dē′·mạs) *n.* the people [Gk.].

de·mur (di·mur′) *v.i.* to object. *pr.p.* **-ring;** *pa.p.* **-red;** *n.* statement of objections. **-rable** *a.* **-rage** *n.* undue detention of a ship, railroad car, etc.; compensation paid for such detention. **-rer** *n.* one who demurs; (*Law*) a plea that a case has insufficient evidence to justify its being pursued further [L. *de; morari,* to delay].

de·mure (di·mūr′) *a.* grave; staid; shy; seemingly modest. **-ly** *adv.* **-ness** *n.* [O.Fr. *de murs,* of good manners].

den (den) *n.* a cave or hollow place; lair or cage of a wild beast; disreputable haunt; a private sanctum, study or workshop [O.E. *denn,* a cave].

de·nar·i·us (di·nạr′·i·ạs) *n.* a Roman silver coin; the 'penny' of the N.T. *pl.* **denarii. denary** *a.* containing ten [L.].

de·na·ture (dē·nā′·chẹr) *v.t.* to make unfit for eating or drinking by adulteration. **denaturant** *n.* that which changes the nature of a thing. **denaturation** *n.*

den·dri-, dendro- *prefix* from Gk. *dendron,* a tree, as in **-form** (den′·dri·fawrm) *a.* having the shape or appearance of a tree. **-tic, -tical** *a.* tree-like; arborescent. **dendroid, dendroidal** *a.* having the shape of a tree.

de·ni·al (di·nī′·ạl) *n.* the act of denying; a flat contradiction; a refusal [L. *de; negare,* to deny].

den·i·gra·tion (den·ạ·grā′·shạn) *n.* a blackening of; defamation of a person's character. **denigrate** *v.t.* [L. *de; nigrare,* to blacken].

den·im (den′·im) *n.* a stout cotton twill cloth [Fr. serge *de Nimes*].

den·i·zen (den′·ạ·zn) *n.* a dweller (human or animal); anything successfully naturalized; *v.t.* to make a denizen of [L. *de intus,* from within].

de·nom·i·nate (di·nȧm′·ạ·nāt) *v.t.* to give a name to; to designate; to style. **denominable** *a.* **denomination** *n.* the act of naming; a title; a class; a religious sect; (*Arith.*) unit of measure (money, length, etc.). **denominational** *a.* **denominative** *a.* conferring or having a distinctive name; (*Gram.*) a verb made from a noun or adjective. **denominatively** *adv.* **denominator** *n.* the one who, or that which, designates a class; the divisor; the number below the line in a fraction [L. *de; nominare,* to name].

de·note (di·nōt′) *v.t.* to signify or imply; to express by a sign; to mean; to be the symbol of; (*Logic*) to indicate the objects to which a term refers. **denotable** *a.* **denotation** *n.* [L. *denotare,* to mark].

dé·noue·ment (dā·nȯȯ′·mạng) *n.* the unraveling of the complication of a dramatic plot; the issue or outcome of a situation [Fr. fr. L. *de,* from; *nodare,* to tie with knots].

de·nounce (di·nouns′) *v.t.* to inform against; to accuse in public; to repudiate, as a treaty. **-ment** *n.* **-er** *n.* [L. *de; nuntiare,* to announce].

dense (dens) *a.* compact; thick, crowded; (of vegetation) impenetrable, luxuriant; (*Fig.*) stupid. **-ly** *adv.* **-ness** *n.* **density** *n.* the quality of being dense; (*Chem.*) the mass per unit volume of a substance [L. *densus,* thick].

dent (dent) *n.* a small depression made (by a blow) in a surface; *v.t.* to mark by a blow or pressure [O.E. *dynt,* a stroke].

den·tal (den′·tạl) *a.* pert. to the teeth or to dentistry; *n.* and *a.* a consonant sound (e.g. *d* or *t*) made by tip of tongue behind the upper front teeth. **dentate** *a.* toothed; sharply notched (e.g. leaf]. **dentiform** *a.* having the shape of a tooth. **dentifrice** *n.* powder, paste, or liquid used to clean and whiten teeth. **dentist** *n.* a medically trained specialist in the care of the teeth (also *dental surgeon*). **dentistry** *n.* **dentition** *n.* arrangement of teeth. **dentoid** *a.* tooth-like. **denture** *n.* set or part set of teeth, esp. artificial teeth [L. *dens,* a tooth].

den·ti·cle (den′·tạ·kl) *n.* a small tooth or projection. **denticular, denticulate, denticulated** *a.* having notches or sharp prejections [L. *dens,* tooth].

de·nude (di·nūd′) *v.t.* to lay bare; to strip. **denudation** *n.* [L. *denudare,* to make bare].

de·nun·ci·ate (di·nun′·si·āt) *v.t.* Same as **denounce. denunciation** *n.* **denunciator** *n.* [L. *de; nuntiare,* to announce].

de·ny (di·nī′) *v.t.* to declare to be untrue; to gainsay; to refuse a request; to disavow; to disown; to withhold; (*reflex.*) to abstain from [L. *de; negare,* to deny].

de·o·dor·ize (dē·ō′·dạ·rīz) *v.t.* to deprive of

odor. **deodorant, deodorizer** *n.* something which destroys an odor [L. *de,* from; *odor,* smell].

de•ox•i•dize (dē•āks′•ą•dīz) *v.t.* to remove oxygen from; to reduce from the state of an oxide.

de•part (di•pårt′) *v.i.* to go away; to leave; to die; to deviate (as from a policy); *v.t.* to leave (e.g. *to depart this life*). **-ed** *n.* (*sing.* and *pl.*) the dead. **-ment** *n.* a section of a business or administration; a special branch of the arts or science; an administrative district of a country, as in France. **-mental** *a.* pert. to a department.; affecting only a section of a business, etc. **-ure** *n.* the act of going away; divergence from rule [L. *de,* from; *partiri,* to part].

de•pend (di•pend′) *v.i.* to rely on; to be sustained by; to be contingent on; to hang; (*Law*) to be awaiting final judgment. **-able** *a.* trustworthy. **-ably** *adv.* **-ant, -ent** *n.* one who is supported, esp. financially by another; a retainer; a subordinate; *a.* hanging down; relying on for support or favor; varying according to; (spellings -ant, -ent are interchangeable in noun and adjective, but *-ant* is more common in noun, and *-ent* in adjective). **-ence** *n.* **-ency** *n.* **-ently, -antly** *adv.* [L. *dependere,* to hang down].

de•pict (di•pikt′) *v.t.* to portray; to present a visual image of; to describe in words. **-tion** *n.* **-ive** *a.* [L. *de; pingere, pictum,* to paint].

dep•i•late (dep′•ą•lāt) *v.t.* to remove hair from. **depilation** *n.* **depilatory** *n.* agent for removing superfluous hair from body; *a.* able to remove hair [L. *de,* from; *pilus,* a hair].

de•plete (di•plēt′) *v.t.* to empty; to diminish; to reduce. **depletion** *n.* **depletive, depletory** *a.* [L. *de,* from; *plere,* to fill].

de•plore (di•plōr′) *v.t.* to suffer remorse for; to regret; to express disapproval of. **deplorable** *a.* **deplorably** *adv.* [L. *de; plorare,* to weep].

de•ploy (di•ploi′) *v.t.* to spread out; to extend troops in line; *v.i.* to extend from column into line. **-ment** *n.* [Fr. *déployer,* to spread out].

de•po•lar•ize (dē•pō′•lą•rīz) *v.t.* to deprive of polarity [Gk. *poloz,* pivot].

de•pone (di•pōn′) *v.t.* to give evidence under oath, in a law court. **deponent** *n.* [L. *de,* down; *ponere,* to lay].

de•port (di•pōrt′) *v.t.* to carry away; to expel; to banish into exile (of undesirable aliens); (reflex.) to behave; to bear oneself. **-ation** *n.* the compulsory removal of people from one country to another. **-ment** *n.* conduct of a person [L. *de,* from; *portare,* to carry].

de•pose (di•pōz′) *v.t.* to remove from a throne; to oust from a high position; to degrade; (*Law*) to state upon oath. **deposable** *a.* **deposal** *n.* **deposition** (de•pą•zi′•shąn) *n.* removal of someone from a high position; (*Law*) act of deponing; a written declaration by a witness [L. *de,* down; *ponere,* to place].

de•po•sit (di•påz′•it) *v.t.* to lay down; to entrust; to let fall (as a sediment); to lodge (in a bank); to store; *n.* that which is deposted or laid down; sediment falling to the bottom of a fluid; money placed in safe-keeping of a bank (usually with interest); a security; partial payment. **-ary** *n.* one with whom anything is left in trust. **-or** *n.* **-ory** *n.* [L. *de,* down; *ponere,* to place].

de•pot (dē′•pō) *n.* a railway station; (*Mil.*) (de′•pō) a storage center for supplies and materials; (formerly) training center for recruits [Fr. *dépôt*].

de•prave (di•prāv′) *v.t.* to make bad or worse; to corrupt; to pervert. **depravation** *n.* **-d** *a.* immoral; vicious. **depravity** *n.* [L. *de; pravus,* vicious].

dep•re•cate (dep′•rą•kāt) *v.t.* to express disapproval of. **deprecatingly** *adv.* **deprecation** *n.* **deprecative, deprecatory** *a.* **deprecator** *n.* [L. *de,* from; *precari,* to pray].

de•pre•ci•ate (di•prē′•shi•āt) *v.t.* to lower in value; (*Fig.*) to disparage; to underrate; *v.i.* to lose quality; to diminish in market value. **depreciation** *n.* decline in value. **depreciative, depreciatory** *a.* **depreciator** *n.* [L. *de,* down; *pretium,* price].

dep•re•date (dep′•ri•dāt) *v.t.* to plunder; to lay waste. **depredation** *n.* the act of laying waste; pillaging [L. *de,* from; *praeda,* plunder].

de•press (di•pres′) *v.t.* to deject or cast a gloom over; to press down; to lower; to diminish the vigor of. **-ed** *a.* dejected; pressed down. **-ible** *a.* **depression** *n.* a hollow; a dip; a sinking; dejection; despondency; a slump (in trade); in meteorology, an area of low barometric pressure. **-or** *n.* [L. *depressus,* pressed down].

de•prive (di•prīv′) *v.t.* to take away; to dispossess; to debar a person from **deprivation** *n.* the act of depriving; the state of being deprived or dispossessed. **deprivable** *a.* **depriver** *n.* [L. *de,* from; *privare,* to deprive].

depth (depth) *n.* deepness; distance measured downwards from surface; distance from front to back, as of a shelf, etc.; profundity or penetration, as of mind [O.E. *deop,* deep].

de•pute (di•pūt′) *v.t.* to send with commission to act for another; to delegate duties to another. **deputation** *n.* the act of deputing; persons authorized to transact business for others; **deputize** *v.i.* to appoint as deputy. **deputy** *n.* (dep′•yoo•ti•) one who is appointed to act for another [L. *deputare,* to esteem, to allot].

de•range (di•rānj′) *v.t.* to put out of order or place; to upset; to make insane. **-d** *a.* mentally unstable; insane. **-ment** *n.* [Fr. *déranger,* to disturb].

der•by (dur′•bi•) *n.* a man's felt hat, with stiff rounded crown and narrow brim.

der•e•lict (der′•ą•likt) *a.* forsaken; abandoned and disclaimed by owner, esp. used of ships; *n.* a ship abandoned by captain and crew; a person abandoned by society. **dereliction** *n.* [L. *de,* from; *relinquere,* to leave].

de•ride (di•rīd′) *v.t.* to ridicule; to mock; to laugh at with scorn.**-r** *n.* **deridingly** *adv.* **derision** (di•rizh′•ąn) *n.* mockery; ridicule. **derisive** *a.* **derisively** *adv.* **derisiveness** *n.* **derisory** *a.* [L. *de,* down; *ridere,* to laugh].

de•rive (dą•rīv′) *v.t.* to obtain or draw from a source; to trace the etymology (of a word); to trace the descent or origin(of a person); *v.i.* to have as an origin; to proceed (foll. by *from*). **derivable** *a.* **derivation** (der•ą•vā′•shąn) *n.* act of deriving or process of being derived; tracing of a word back to its roots; etymology. **derivative** *n.* that which is derived or traceable back to something else; a word derived from another; *a.* obtained by derivation; secondary [L. *de,* down; *rivus,* a stream].

der•ma, der•mis (dur′•mą, dur′•mis) *n.* the true skin below epidermis. **dermal** *a.* **dermatic** *a.* consisting of skin. **-titis** *n.* inflammation of the skin. **-tology** *n.* branch of medical science concerned with the skin and skin diseases. **-tologist** *n.* skin specialist [Gk. *derma,* a skin].

der•o•gate (der′•ą•gāt) *v.i.* to lessen (as reputation). **derogation** *n.* **derogatory** *a.* tending to impair the value of; detracting. **derogatorily** *adv.* [L. *de,* from; *rogare,* to ask].

der•rick (der′•ik) *n.* an apparatus like a crane for hoisting heavy weights [fr. *Derrick,* a Tyburn hangman of 17th cent.].

der•rin•ger (der′•in•jęr) *n.* a short-barrelled pistol with a large bore [U.S. inventor].

der•vish (dur′•vish) *n.* a member of one of the mendicant orders among the Mohammedans [Pers. *darvish,* a poor man].

des•cant (des′•kant) *n.* a melody harmonizing with and sung or played as accompaniment to a musical theme; a discourse on a theme; *v.i.* to discourse fully; to sing. **-er** *n.* [L. *dis,* apart; *cantus,* song].

de•scend (di•send′) *v.t.* to go down; to traverse downwards; to flow down; *v.i.* to sink; to lower oneself or stoop to something; to fall (upon an enemy); to be derived by birth. **-ant** *n.* one descended from an ancestor; offspring. **-ent** *a.* descending. **descending** *a.* **descent** *n.* act of coming down; a slope or declivity; lineage [L. *de*, down; *scandere*, to climb].

de·scribe (di·skrīb′) *v.t.* to represent the features of; to portray in speech or writing. **describable** *a.* **description** (de·skrip′·shạn) *n.* act of describing; a representation, in words, of the qualities of a person or thing; sort; kind. **descriptive** *a.* **descriptively** *adv.* [L. *de*, down; *scribere*, to write].

de·scry (di·skrī′) *v.t.* to discover by the eye; to perceive from a distance; to make out. **descrier** *n.* [L. *de*, down; *scribere*, to write].

des·e·crate (des′·ạ·krāt) *v.t.* to violate the sanctity of; to profane. **-r, -or** *n.* **desecration** *n.* [L. *de*, away, *sacer*, holy].

de·sert (di·zŭrt′) *n.* that which is deserved; reward (for merit); punishment (for demerit) [L. *deservire*, to serve zealously].

des·ert (dez′·ẹrt) *n.* a wide, sandy waste region; *a.* uncultivated; solitary [L. *deserere*, to abandon].

de·sert (di·zŭrt′) *v.t.* to abandon; to leave; *v.i.* to quit the armed forces without authorization. **-ed** *a.* abandoned. **-er** *n.* **desertion** *n.* [L. *deserere*, to abandon].

de·serve (di·surv′) *v.t.* to earn by service; to merit; to be entitled to; to warrant; *v.i.* to be worthy of reward. **deservedly** *adv.* justly. **deserving** *a.* worthy; meritorious [L. *deservire*, to serve zealously].

des·ic·cate (des′·ạ·kāt) *v.t.* to extract all moisture from; to dry up; to dehydrate. **desiccant** *a.* drying; *n.* (*Chem.*) substance capable of absorbing moisture. **desiccation** *n.* [L. *desiccare*, to dry up].

de·sign (di·zīn′) *v.t.* to draw the outline of; to plan; *v.i.* to purpose; *n.* sketch in outline (esp. in architecture); a pattern (as in wallpaper, printed cloth, etc.); scheme or plan; purpose. **-able** *a.* **designate** (dez′·ig·nāt) *v.t.* to mark out and make known; to nominate or appoint. **designation** *n.* distinctive title. **designative** *a.* **-edly** *adv.* intentionally. **-er** *n.* one who designs or makes plans or patterns; a schemer or plotter. **-ful** *a.* **-ing** *a.* artful; selfishly interested [L. *de*, down; *signare*, to mark].

de·sire (di·zīr′) *v.t.* to yearn for the possession of; to request; to entreat; *n.* anything desired; a longing; object of longing; lust. **desirable** *a.* worth possessing. **desirably** *adv.* **desirableness, desirability** *n.* the state or quality of being desired. **desirous** *a.* full of desire; covetous [O.Fr. *desirer*, to want].

de·sist (di·zist′) *v.t.* to cease; to discontinue. **-ance, -ence** *n.* [L. *de*, from *sistere*, to stand].

desk (desk) *n.* a table for reading or writing; a lectern [L.L. *desca*, a table].

des·o·late (des′·ạ·lāt) *v.t.* to devastate; to depopulate; to make lonely or forlorn; *a.* (des′·a·lit) waste; deserted; unfrequented; dismal. **-ly** *adv.* **ness** *n.* **-r** *n.* **desolation** *n.* the act of laying waste; loneliness; misery. **desolatory** *a.* [L. *desolare*, to forsake].

de·spair (di·sper′) *v.i.* to be without hope; to lose heart; *n.* despondency; hopelessness. **-ing** *a.* full of despair. **-ingly** *adv.* [L. *desparare*].

des·patch See **dispatch.**

des·pi·ca·ble (des′·pik·ạ·bl) *a.* contemptible; vile; deserving to be despised. **despicably** *adv.* **despicability** *n.* [L. *despicere*, to despise].

de·spise (di·spīz′) *v.t.* to look down upon; to hold in contempt; to disdain; to scorn. **despisable** *a.* [L. *despicere*, to look down on].

de·spite (di·spīt′) *n.* contemptuous treatment; *prep* in spite of, notwithstanding. **-ful** *a.* **-fully** *adv.* [L. *despicere*, to look down on].

de·spoil (di·spoil′) *v.t.* to take away by force; to rob; to strip. **-er** *n.* a plunderer. **-ment, despoliation** *n.* [L. *de*, from; *spolium*, spoil].

de·spond (di·spand′) *v.i.* to be cast down in spirit. **-ence, -ency** *n.* dejection of mind; depression. **-ent** *a.* depressed. **-ently** *adv.* **-ingly** *adv.* [L. *de*, from; *spondere*, to promise].

des·pot (des′·pạt) *n.* one who rules with absolute power; a tyrant; one who enforces his will on others. **-ic** *a.* **-ically** *adv.* **-ism** *n.* the absolute power of one man unlimited by constitution [Gk. *despotēs*, a master].

des·sert (di·zurt′) *n.* a course served at end of a dinner [O.Fr. *desservir*, to clear the table].

des·tine (des′·tin) *v.t.* to predetermine (usu. passive). **destination** *n.* the purpose for which anything is destined; the place to which one is traveling. **destiny** *n.* state appointed; foreordained lot; fate [L. *destinare*, to establish].

des·ti·tute (des′·tạ·tūt) *a.* in want; needy; deprived of means of sustenance. **destitution** *n.* [L. *de*, from; *statuere*, to place].

de·stroy (di·stroi′) *v.t.* to pull down; to turn to rubble; to put an end to; to annihilate. *pa.p.* **-ed.** **-able** *a.* **-er** *n.* a type of fast warship armed with guns and torpedoes [L. *destruere*].

de·struc·tion (di·struk′·shạn) *n.* the act of destroying; state of being destroyed; ruin; death. **destructible** *a.* capable of being destroyed. **destructibleness, destructibility** *n.* **destructive** *a.* [L. *destruere*, to destroy].

des·ue·tude (des′·wi·tūd) *n.* discontinuance of a custom or practice [L. *desuetudo*].

de·sul·tor·y (des′·ạl·tōr·i·) *a.* leaping from one thing to another; unmethodical; aimless; rambling. **desultorily** *adv.* **desultoriness** *n.* [L. *desultor*, a circus rider].

de·tach (di·tach′) *v.t.* to separate; to disunite; to withdraw; to detail for special service (as troops). **-able** *a.* **-ed** *a.* standing alone (e.g. a house); impersonal; disinterested; unprejudiced. **-edly** *adv.* **-edness, -ment** *n.* process or state of being detached; that which is detached (as troops) [Fr. *détacher*, to unfasten].

de·tail (di·tāl′) *v.t.* to relate minutely; to record every item; to appoint for a special duty (e.g. troops); (dē′·tāl, di·tāl′) *n.* a minute part; item; (*Mil.*) special duty. **-ed** *a.* giving every particular fact [Fr. *tailler*, to cut].

de·tain (di·tān′) *v.t.* to keep back or from; to keep in custody. **-er** *n.* one who detains; (*Law*) illegal detention of another's possessions; a writ to keep in custody. **-ment, detention** *n.* [L. *detinere*, to keep back].

de·tect (di·tekt′) *v.t.* to uncover; to discover; to expose; to bring to light (esp. a crime); to perceive. **-able, -ible** *a.* **-or** *n.* one who or that which detects. **-ion** *n.* **-ive** *a.* employed in detecting; *n.* a member of the police force, not in uniform, who apprehends criminals and investigates cases [L. *detergere*, to uncover].

dé·tente (dā·tȧnt′) *n.* the easing of international tension [Fr.].

de·ter (di·tẹr′) *v.t.* to frighten from; to discourage; to restrain. *pr.p.* **-ring.** *pa.p.* **-red.** **-ment** *n.* hindrance. **-rent** *a.* having the power to deter; *n.* that which deters. **-rence** *n.* [L. *deterrere*, to frighten off].

de·terge (di·turj′) *v.t.* to cleanse (wound); to wipe off; to purge. **-nce, -ncy** *n.* **-nt** *a.* cleansing *n.* cleansing substance [L. *detergere*, to wipe off].

de·te·ri·o·rate (di·tir′·i·ạ·rāt) *v.t.* to make worse; to cause to depreciate; *v.i.* to become worse; to degenerate. **deterioration** *n.* [L. *deterior*, worse].

de·ter·mine (di·tur′·min) *v.t.* to fix the limits of; to define; to decide; to ascertain with precision; *v.i.* to make a decision or resolution; (*Law*) to terminate. **determinable** *a.* **determinant** *a.* serving to determine, fix, or limit; *n.* that which determines or causes determination. **determinate** *a.* having fixed limits; decisive; established. **determinately** *adv.* **determination** *n.* the act or process of determining fixed purpose; resolution; adherence to a definite line of action. **-d** *a.* resolute; unwavering; firm; purposeful. **-dly** *adv.* **determinism** *n.* the doctrine that man's actions and mental activity are governed by causes outside his own will [L. *determinare,* to limit].

de·test (di·test′) *v.t.* to dislike intensely; to hate; to abhor. **-able** *a.* **-ableness, -ability** *n.* **-ation** *n.* [L. *detestari,* to execrate].

de·throne (dē·thrōn′) *v.t.* to remove from a throne; to depose. **-ment** *n.*

de·to·nate (det′·ạ·nāt) *v.t.* to cause to explode; *v.i.* to explode with a loud report. **detonation** *n.* a sudden and violent explosion. **detonator** *n.* a detonating substance; device to make another substance explode [L. *detonare,* to thunder].

de·tour (dē′·toor) *n.* a roundabout way, a circuitous route; a digression [Fr. *détour*].

de·tract (di·trakt′) *v.t.* to take away a part from; to defame; *v.i.* (with *from*) to diminish. **-or** *n.* **-ingly** *adv.* **-ion** *n.* disparagement; slander [L. *detrahere,* to draw away].

de·tri·ment (det′·rạ·mạnt) *n.* injury; harm; loss. **-al** *a.* [L. *detrimentum,* a rubbing off].

de·trun·cate (di·trung′·kāt) *v.t.* to lop off from the trunk; to shorten. **detruncation** *n.*

de·tu·mes·cence (dē·tȯȯ·mes′·ạns) *n.* subsiding of a swelling, esp. lessening of the penis or the clitoris after orgasm. **detumescent** *a.* [L. *de,* down; *tumescere,* to swell up].

deuce (dūs) *n.* a card or die with two spots; (*Tennis*) score of 40 all [L. *duo,* two].

deuce (dūs) *n.* the devil (in mild imprecations); bad luck [prob. fr. L. *deus,* god].

deu·te·ri·um (dū·tir′·i·ạm) *n.* a form of hydrogen twice as heavy as the normal gas [Gk. *deutereion,* second place].

deu·ter·on·o·my (dū·tẹr·ȧn′·ạ·mi·) *n.* the fifth book of the Pentateuch [Gk. *deuteros,* second; *nomos,* law].

de·val·u·ate (dē·val′·yoo·āt), **devalue** *v.t.* to reduce the value of (esp. the currency). **devaluation** *n.* [L. *de,* down; *valere,* to be worth].

dev·as·tate (dev′·ạs·tāt) *v.t.* to lay waste. **devastation** *n.* act of laying waste; the state of being devastated; destruction; havoc [L. *devastare,* to lay waste].

de·vel·op (di·vel′·ạp) *v.t.* to cause to grow; to unfold gradually; to increase the resources of; (*Photog.*) to produce image on photographic plate or film by chemical application; *v.i.* to evolve by natural processes; to expand; to open out; to assume definite character. **-er** *n.* one who or that which develops; (*Photog.*) a chemical for producing image on plate or film. **-ment** *n.* a gradual unfolding or growth; unraveling of a plot; the result of previous causes [Fr. *développer,* to grow gradually].

de·vi·ate (dē′·vi·āt) *v.i.* to diverge; to turn away from the direct line; to swerve; *v.t.* to cause to swerve. **deviation** *n.* [L. *de,* from; *via,* a way].

de·vice (di·vīs′) *n.* that which is planned out or designed; contrivance; stratagem; (*Her.*) emblem on a shield [M.E. *devisen,* to contrive].

dev·il (dev′.l) *n.* the spirit of evil; (*Theol.*) tempter; Satan; fiend; any very wicked person; (*Colloq.*) a fellow; *v.t.* (*Colloq.*) to torment; (*Cookery*) to prepare with hot or savory seasoning. **-ish** *a.* **-ishly** *adv.* **—may-care** *a.* reckless. **-ment** *n.* mischief. **-ry, -try** *n* devilish conduct **-'s advocate,** one appointed to oppose a proposed canonization; (*Colloq.*) one who maintains an argument with which he really disagrees. **give the — his due,** give even the worst person credit for something [O.E. *deofol,* the devil; fr. Gk. *diabolos,* slandered].

de·vious (dē′·vi·ạs) *a.* not direct; circuitous; erring. **-ly, -ness** *n.* [L. *de,* from; *via,* a way].

de·vise (di·vīz′) *v.t.* to invent; to contrive; to scheme; to plan; (*Law*) to leave as a legacy; *v.i.* to consider; *n.* (*Law*) the act of bequeathing real estate by will; clause in will to this effect. **devisable** *a.* **devisal,** *n.* **-r** *n.* one who schemes or contrives. **devisor** *n.* one who bequeaths by will [M.E. *devisen,* to divide].

de·vi·tal·ize (dē·vī′·ta·līz) *v.t.* to deprive of life or vitality. **devitalization** *n.*

de·void (di·void′) *a.* empty; free from; without [L. *de,* from; *viduus,* deprived].

dev·o·lu·tion (dev·ạ·lȯȯ′·shạn) *n.* delegation of powers to subsidiary or local bodies; gradual retrogression (oppos. of *evolution*) (See *devolve*) [L. *devolutus,* rolled down].

de·volve (di·vȧlv′) *v.t.* to transmit; to transfer; to delegate; *v.i.* (foll. by *upon*) to fall to the lot of; (*Law*) to pass, by inheritance, from one to another [L. *devolvere,* to roll down].

de·vote (di·vōt′) *v.t.* to give oneself wholly to; to dedicate; to consecrate. **-d** *a.* **-dly** *adv.* **-dness** *n.* **devotee** (de·va·tē′) *n.* one who is devoted to a cause; a zealous supporter. **devotion** *n.* **devotions** *n.pl.* worship and prayer. **devotional** *a.* pert. to devotions; religious [L. *devovere,* to dedicate by vow].

de·vour (di·vour′) *v.t.* to swallow ravenously; to consume completely and wantonly; to destroy; (*Fig.*) to read avidly. **-ing** *a.* [L. *devorare,* to swallow up].

de·vout (di·vout′) *a.* pious; passionately religious; sincere. **-ly** *adv.* [L. *devovere,* to vow].

dew (dū) *n.* moisture in the atmosphere or in the soil itself, condensed on exposed surfaces, esp. at night; *v.t.* to moisten; to bedew. **-fall** *n.* the falling of dew, or the time when it falls. **-iness** *n.* **-y** *a.* [O.E. *deaw,* dew].

DEW (dū, dȯȯ) *n.* (*Mil.*) *d*istant *e*arly *w*arning system.

dex·ter (deks′·tẹr) *a.* pert. to the right hand; on the right hand side. **-ity** *n.* manual skill; mental adroitness; cleverness; right-handedness. **-ous, dextrous** *a.* **-ously** *adv.* **-ousness** *n.* **dextral** *a.* right as opposed to left. **dextrality** *n.* right-handedness. **dextrally** *adv.* [L. *dexter,* on the right hand].

dex·trin, dextrine (deks′·trin) *n.* a soluble gummy substance used for stiffening fabrics, sizing paper, mucilage, etc. [L. *dexter,* on the right].

di·a·be·tes (dī·ạ·bē′·tis, ·ēz) *n.* a disease marked by excessive flow of sugar-urine due to failure of pancreas to produce insulin [Gk. *diabetes,* fr. *dia,* through; *bainein,* to go].

di·a·bol·ic, diabolical (dī·ạ·bȧl′·ik, -i·kạl) *a.* devilish; fiendish; pert. to the devil. **-ally** *adv.* [Gk. *diabolos,* the devil].

di·ac·o·nal (dī·ak′·ạ·nạl) *a.* pert. to a deacon.

di·a·dem (dī′·ạ·dem) *n.* a fillet or head band worn as the symbol of royal power; a headdress or crown significant of royalty; (*Fig.*) sovereignty. **-ed** *a.* wearing a crown [Gk. *diadēma,* fr. *diadein,* to bind round].

di·ag·no·sis (dī·ạg·nō′·sis) *n.* a scientific discrimination of any kind; (*Med.*) the identification of a disease from its signs and symptoms. *pl.* **diagnoses. diagnose** *v.t.* (*Med.*) to ascertain from signs and symptoms the nature of a disease; to identify the root-cause of any social or other problems. **diagnostic** *a.* distinguishing; symptomatic; *n.* a symptom distinguishing one disease from another; a clue. **diagnostician** *n.* [Gk. *dia,* through; *gnosis,* an inquiry].

di·ag·o·nal (dī·ag′·ạ·nạl) *n.* (Geom.) a straight line joining two opposite angles in a rectilineal figure; a line, plane, part, etc. having an oblique direction or position; *a.* from corner to opposite corner; oblique. **-ly** *adv.* [Gk. *dia,* through; *gonia,* a corner].

di·a·gram (dī′·ạ·gram) *n.* a figure drawn to demonstrate a theorem; a drawing or plan in outline. **-matically** *adv.* [Gk. *dia,* through; *graphein;* to write].

di·al (dī′·ạl) *n.* an instrument for showing the time of day from the sun's shadow; the face of a sundial, clock, watch, etc.; any plate or face on which a pointer moves, as on a weighing machine; *v.t.* to measure on a dial; to call a number on automatic telephone. *pr.p.* **-ling.** *pa.p.* **-led** [L. *dies,* a day].

di·a·lect (dī′·ạ·lekt) *n.* a group variation of language; a mode of speech peculiar to a district or social group; vernacular [Gk. *dialektos*, manner of speech].

di·a·lec·tic, -al (dī·ạ·lek′·tik, ·ạl) *a.* pert. to dialectics; *n.* (usually *pl.*) the art of discussion, disputation, or debate; the science of reasoning. **-ally** *adv.* **dialectician** *n.* one skilled in debate; one who studies dialects [Gk. *dialektikē*, the art of debate].

di·a·logue (dī′·ạ·lawg) *n.* a conversation between two (or more) persons. **dialogistic** *a.* pert. to dialogue. **dialogize** *v.i.* to speak in dialogue [Gk. *dialogos*, a conversation].

di·al·y·sis (dī·al′·ạ·sis) *n.* (*Chem.*) separation of colloid (non-crystalline) from crystalline substances in solution, by filtration through a membrane; *pl.* **dialyses. dialytic** *a.* [Gk. *dia*, through; *luein*, to loosen].

di·am·e·ter (dī·am′·ạ·tẹr) *n.* (*Geom.*) a line passing through the center of a circle or other curvilinear figure, and terminated by the circumference; transverse measurement; unit of magnifying power of a lens. **diametric (-al)** *a.* pert. to the diameter; directly opposite [Gk. *dia*, through; *metron*, a measure].

di·a·mond (dī′·ạ·mạnd) *n.* one of the crystalline forms of carbon and the hardest substance known; a popular gem stone; a four-sided figure with two acute and two obtuse angles; a rhombus; one of the four suits of playing-cards; one of the smallest types of English printing (4½ point); playing field for baseball. *a.* resembling, set with, consisting of, shaped like diamonds. **— wedding,** the sixtieth anniversary of a marriage. **black diamonds** (*Colloq.*) coal. **rough diamond,** (*Colloq.*) a worthy but uncultured person [Fr. *diamant*, diamond].

di·a·pa·son (dī·ạ·pā′·zạn) *n.* correct pitch; harmony; the entire compass of a voice or instrument; the two foundation stops of an organ (*open* and *stopped diapason*) [Gk. *dia pason* = through all (the notes)].

di·a·per (dī′·ạ·pẹr) *n.* a linen or cotton cloth with diamond pattern; a baby's breechcloth; *v.t.* to change a baby's diaper; to ornament with a diaper pattern [O.Fr. *diapre*].

di·aph·a·nous (dī·af′·ạ·nạs) *a.* having the power to transmit light; transparent; translucent [Gk. *dia*, through; *phainein*, to show].

di·a·pho·ret·ic (dī·ạ·fạ·ret′·ik) *n.* (*Med.*) a medicine which induces perspiration; *a.* promoting perspiration [Gk. *dia*, through; *phorein*, to carry].

di·a·phragm (dī′·ạ·fram) *n.* (*Anat.*) a dividing membrane; a dome-shaped muscular partition between chest and abdomen; vibrating disc in telephone or microphone; a disc with a circular hole used in telescope or camera to cut off part of a ray of light. **-atic, -al** *a.* [Gk. *diaphragma*, a barrier].

di·ar·chy (dī′·ȧr·ki·) *n.* a system of government in which power is held jointly by two authorities [Gk. *dis*, twice; *archein*, to rule].

di·ar·rhe·a, diarrhoea (dī·ạ·rē′·ạ) *n.* an excessive and frequent looseness of the bowels. **diarrhetic** *a.* [Gk. *dia*, through; *rhein*, to flow].

di·a·ry (dī′·ạ·ri·) *n.* a daily record; a book in which a personal record of thoughts, action, etc. is kept. **diarist** *n.* [L. *dies*, a day].

di·a·stase (dī′·ạ·stās) *n.* an enzyme capable of converting starch into sugar. **diastasic** *a.* [Gk. *diastasis*, separation].

di·as·to·le (dī·as′·tạ·lē) *n.* (*Med.*) a rhythmical dilatation of the heart and arteries alternating with *systole* (contraction); the lengthening of a syllable usually short, before a pause [Gk. = a putting apart].

di·a·ther·mal (dī·ạ·thurm′·ạl) *a.* permeable by heat. **diathermanous, diathermous, diathermic** *a.* having the property of transmitting radiant heat. **diathermy** *n.* [Gk. *dia*, through; *thermē*, heat].

di·a·tom (dī′·ạ·tạm) *n.* one of an order of microscopic unicellular marine or vegetable organisms [Gk. *dia*, through; *tomē*, a cutting].

di·a·tom·ic (dī·ạ·tȧm′·ik) *a.* (*Chem.*) consisting of two atoms.

di·a·ton·ic (dī·ạ·tȧn′·ik) *a.* (*Mus.*) pert. to major or minor scales; proceeding by the tones, intervals, and harmonies of the natural scale [Gk. *dia*, through; *tonos*, tone].

di·a·tribe (dī′·ạ·trīb) *n.* a vituperative harangue; a wordy denunciation. **diatribist** *n.* [Gk. *diatribē*, a means of passing the time].

dib·ble (dib′·l) *n.* a pointed instrument used in gardening for making holes. Also **dibber.** *v.t.* to plant with a dibble; *v.i.* to make holes. **-r** *n.* [form of *dab*].

dice (dīs) *n.pl.* small cubes on each of the six faces of which are spots representing numbers 1-6; used from Egyptian times in games of chance; *Sing.* form **die;** *v.t.* to cut into small squares; *v.i.* to play with dice. **dicer** *n.* a gambler [O.Fr. *dez*, fr. L. *datus*, given, thrown].

di·ceph·a·lous (dī·sef′·ạ·lạs) *a.* having two heads [Gk. *dis*, twice; *kephalē*, the head].

di·chot·o·my (dī·kȧt′·ạm·i·) *n.* a cutting in two; (*Logic*) division of ideas into two classes. **dichotomize** *v.t.* and *v.i.* **dichotomous** *a.* [Gk. *dicha*, apart; *temnein*, to cut].

dick·er (dik′·ẹr) *v.t.* and *v.i.* to barter; to haggle; to quibble; *n.* a bargain; a deal [L. *decuria*, a group of ten (esp. hides)].

dick·ey, dicky (dik′·i·) *n.* a waist front for women; detachable shirt front; seat for servants at back of old-fashioned carriage.

Dic·ta·phone (dik′·tạ·fōn) *n.* a machine into which letters, etc. can be dictated and which re-dictates to the typist [Trademark].

dic·tate (dik·tāt′) *v.t.* to read aloud a passage for another to transcribe; to give orders; *v.i.* to speak with authority; to prescribe; to deliver commands; *n.* an order; command; direction that must be obeyed (usually *pl.*). **dictation** *n.* art or practice of dictating; that which is read aloud for another to write down. **dictator** *n.* one who holds absolute power. **dictatorial** *a.* pert. to or like a dictator; tending to force one's opinions on another. **dictatorially** *adv.* **dictatorship** *n.* [L. *dicere*, to say].

dic·tion (dik′·shạn) *n.* choice of words in speaking and writing; verbal style; enunciation [L. *dicere*, to say].

dic·tion·ar·y (dik′·shạn·er·i·) *n.* a book containing, alphabetically arranged, the words of a language, their meanings and etymology; a lexicon [L. *dicere*, to say].

Dic·to·graph (dik′·tạ·graf) *n.* sound-recording telephonic instrument [Trademark].

dic·tum (dik′·tạm) *n.* a positive assertion; an authoritative statement or opinion; a maxim; *pl.* **dicta** [L. = a thing said].

did (did) *pa.t.* of verb **do** [O.E. *dyde*].

di·dac·tic (dī·dak′·tik) *a.* designed to instruct; containing precepts or doctrines; (of people) opinionated. **-ally** *adv.* **-s** *n.* the science of teaching [Gk. *didaskein*, to teach].

did·y·mous (did′·ạ·mạs) *a.* twin [Gk. *didumos*].

die (dī) *n.* a small cube of wood, bone, or ivory used in games of chance; *pl.* **dice** (dīs). **the die is cast,** one's fate is irrevocably settled [O.Fr. *det*, fr. L. *datus*, given, thrown].

die (dī) *v.i.* to cease to live; to become extinct or extinguished; to wither; to decline. *pr.p.* **dying.** *pa.p.* **-d. dying** *a.* pert. to a person at the point of death; fading; languishing. **to die for** (*Colloq.*) to want desperately. **to die hard,** to resist stubbornly; to be long in dying [M.E. *deyan*, to die].

die (dī) *n.* a device for cutting in a press; an engraved metal block used for stamping a design as on a coin; the cubical part of a pedestal; a steel block used for cutting screws; *pl.* **dies. — casting** *n.* method of making castings in permanent molds [L. *dare*, to give].

di·e·lec·tric (dī·ạ·lek′·trik) *a.* non-conducting; *n.* name for a substance through or across which electric induction takes place [Gk. *dia*, through; *elektron*, amber].
di·er·e·sis, diaeresis (dī·er′·ạ·sis) *n.* a mark (..) placed over the second of two consecutive vowels to indicate that each is to be pronounced separately, as in coöperate. *pl.* **diereses, diaereses** (-ēz) [Gk. *diairesis*, division].
Die·sel en·gine (dē′·zl en′·jạn) *n.* an internal combustion engine [fr. R. *Diesel*, the inventor].
di·e·sis (dī′·ạ·sis) *n.* (*Print.*) a mark of reference, the double dagger (‡); *pl.* **dieses** [Gk. *diesis*, a quarter tone].
di·et (dī′·ạt) *n.* a system of food; what one habitually eats and drinks; food specially prescribed by a doctor; a regulated allowance of provisions; *v.i.* to prescribe a special course of foods; *v.i.* (*Colloq.*) to slim. **-ary** *n.* special course of feeding; daily allowance of food; *a.* pert. to diet. **-etic** *a.* pert. to diet. **-etics** *n.* the science and study of food values, and their effect on health. **-ician, -itian** *n.* [L. *diaeta*, a mode of living].
di·et (dī′·ạt) *n.* a legislative assembly in certain countries; an international conference [L. *dies*, a day].
dif·fer (dif′·ẹr) *v.i.* to be unlike; to have distinctive characteristics; to disagree (foll. by *from* or *with*); to be at variance. **-ence** *n.* unlikeness; dissimilarity; distinguishing characteristic; disagreement; contention; the amount by which one thing exceeds another in weight or number. **-ent** *a.* unlike; distinct; not the same (used with *from*). **-entia** *n.* (*Logic*) the essential quality or characteristic distinguishing any one species from another in a genus (e.g. rational power in *man*); *pl.* **-entiae. -ential** *a.* characteristic; special; discriminating; (*Math.*) pert. to infinitely small quantitative differences; proceeding by increments infinitely small. **-entially** *adv.* **-entiate** *v.t.* to make different; to distinguish; to classify as different; *v.i.* to acquire different characteristics. **-entiation** *n.* **-ently** *adv.* **-ential gear,** a mechanism by which two sets of wheels are made to rotate at different speeds, as wheels of a car [L. *dis-*, apart; *ferre*, to bear].
dif·fi·cult (dif′·ạ·kult) *a.* hard to do or understand; not easy; laborious; (of persons) hard to please; not amenable. **-ly** *adv.* **-y** *n.* laboriousness; a trouble; objection; demur; that which is not easy to do or understand. **-ies** *n.pl.* financial embarrassment [L. *dis-*, not; *facilis*, easy].
dif·fi·dent (dif′·ạ·dạnt) *a.* wanting confidence; timid; shy. **diffidence** *n.* lack of confidence; modesty. **-ly** *adv.* [L. *dis-*, not; *fidere*, to trust].
dif·fract (di·frakt′) *v.t.* to break or separate into parts, esp. of rays of light and sound waves. **diffraction** *n.* breaking up of wave motion (light, sound, etc); the phenomenon caused by light passing through a narrow slit [L. *dis*, apart; *frangere*, to break].
dif·fuse (dif·ūz′) *v.t.* to pour out in every direction; to spread; to scatter; to cause gases to mix by diffusion; *v.i.* to mix; to spread, as a liquid. **diffuse** (dif·ūs′) *a.* widely spread; wordy. **diffusely** (di·fūs′·li·) *adv.* **-ness** *n.* **diffusible** *a.* **diffusion** *n.* act or process of scattering abroad; (*Chem.*) term applied to the intermixture of two gases or fluids without chemical combination. **diffusive** *a.* spreading; expanding; prolix. **diffusively** *adv.* **diffusiveness** *n.* [L. *dis*, away; *fundere*, to pour].
dig (dig) *v.t.* to break and turn up earth, as with a spade; to excavate; to delve; (*Colloq.*) to poke or nudge someone; *v.i.* to till the soil; to use a spade, etc. *pr.p.* **-ging.** *pa.p., pa.t.* **dug.** *n.* a thrust; poke; jibe or taunt. **-ger** *n.* **-gings** *n.pl.* areas where mining or other digging is carried on [prob. O.Fr. *diguer*, to hallow out].
di·gest (dạ·jest′) *v.t.* to convert, as food in the stomach, into a substance which can be readily absorbed into the blood; to assimilate in the mind; to think over; *v.i.* to undergo digestion. **digest** (dī′·jest) *n.* a concise summary, or *the Digest*, an abridged version of the Roman laws compiled by order of Emperor Justinian; a magazine containing condensed version of articles already published elsewhere. **-er** *n.* **-ible** *a.* capable of being digested; easily assimilated. **-ibility** *n.* **digestion** *n.* the act of digesting. **digestive** *a.* promoting, or pert. to digestion; *n.* any medicine that aids digestion [L. *digerere*, to arrange].
dig·it (dij′·it) *n.* a finger; a finger's breadth, or three-quarters of an inch; (*Arith.*) integer under 10, so-called from counting on the fingers. **-al** *a.* pert. to the fingers; *n.* one of the keys of piano or organ. **-alin** *n.* the drug obtained from leaves of digitalis. **-alis** *n.* a genus of hardy plants including the foxglove; a strong drug obtained from foxglove, and used medicinally as sedative, narcotic and as cardiac stimulant. **-ate, -ated** *a.* having divisions like fingers. **-igrade** *n.* an animal which walks on its toes (e.g. dog); *a.* walking on the toes [L. *digitus*, a finger or toe].
di·glot (dī′·glȧt) *a.* speaking two languages [Gk. *dis*, twice; *glotta*, tongue].
dig·ni·fy (dig′·nạ·fī) *v.t.* to invest with dignity or honor; to exalt; to ennoble. **dignified** *a.* [L. *dignus*, worthy; *facere*, to make].
dig·ni·ty (dig′·nạ·ti·) *n.* state of being dignified in mind, character, or bearing; loftiness; high office or rank. **dignitary** *n.* one who holds a high position [L. *dignus*, worthy].
di·graph (dī′·graf) *n.* two vowels or two consonants combined to express one sound as *ea* in head [Gk. *dis*, twice; *graphein*, to write].
di·gress (dạ·gres′, dī·gres′) *v.i.* to wander from the main theme, topic, or argument; to be diffuse. **digression** *n.* **digressional, -ive** *a.* [L. *dis-*, aside; *gradus*, a step].
di·he·dral (dī·hē′·drạl) *a.* having two plane faces. **dihedron** *n.* a figure with two plane surfaces [Gk. *dis*, twice; *hedra*, base].
dike, dyke (dīk) *n.* an artificial embankment to prevent inundation of low lying ground, as in Holland; (*Geol.*) igneous rock, once molten, which has filled up fissures of stratified rocks [O.E. *dic*, a ditch].
di·lap·i·date (dạ·lap′·ạ·dāt) *v.t.* (*Lit.*) to pull stone from stone; to suffer to fall into ruin; to despoil; *v.i.* to be in a condition of disrepair. **-d** *a.* in ruins; decayed; tumbled down; (of persons) shabby; unkempt. **dilapidation** *n.* [L. *di-*, asunder; *lapis*, a stone].
di·late (dī·lāt′) *v.t.* to swell out; to expand in all directions; to distend; *v.i.* to widen; (*Fig.*) to expatiate; to speak at length. **dilatable** *a.* capable of dilation; elastic. **dilatancy, dilatation, dilation** *n.* expansion; a spreading or extending in all directions. **dilatant** *a.* **dilator, -r** *n.* [L. *di-*, apart; *latus*, borne].
dil·a·tory (dil′·ạ·tōr·i·) *a.* tardy; inclined to procrastination; loitering. **dilatorily** *adv.* **dilatoriness** *n.* [L. *dilatus*, postponed].
di·lem·ma (di·lem′·ạ) *n.* choice between alternatives equally undesirable; a predicament; (*Logic*) an argument which presents an antagonist with alternatives equally conclusive against him, whichever he chooses. **on the horns of a dilemma,** confronted with a perplexity [Gk. *dis*, twice; *lēmma*, an assumption].
dil·et·tante (dil·ạ·tan′·te·) *n.* a lover of the fine arts, esp. in a superficial way; a dabbler. *pl.* **dilettantes, -ti. dilettantish** *a.* **dilettantism, dilettanteism** *n.* [It.].
dil·i·gent (dil′·ạ·jạnt) *a.* steady and constant in application; industrious; assiduous. **diligence** *n.* **-ly** *adv.* [L. *diligere*, to choose].
dill (dil) *n.* a perennial yellow-flowered herb used in medicines and flavoring [O.E. *dile*].
dil·ly-dal·ly (dil′·i·-dal′·i·) *v.i.* (*Colloq.*) to

loiter; to delay [reduplication of *dally*].

di·lute (di·lo͞ot′) *v.t.* to make thinner or more liquid by admixture; to reduce the strength of by addition of something, esp. water; to weaken the force of; *v.i.* to become thin; *a.* reduced in strength; attenuated; thinned down; **diluent** *a.* diluting; making weaker; *n.* that which thins or weakens the strength, color, etc. **-ness** *n.* **dilution** *n.* [L. *diluere,* dissolve].

di·lu·vi·um (di·lo͞o′·vi·ạm) *n.* a surface deposit of sand, gravel, etc. regarded as glacial drift. **diluvial, diluvian** *a.* pert. to or produced by a flood, esp. the deluge in Noah's time [L. *diluvium,* flood].

dim (dim) *a.* not bright or distinct; faint; partially obscure; shadowy; (*Fig.*) dull of apprehension; vague; *v.t.* to cloud; to cause to grow dim; *v.i.* to become dull or indistinct. *pr.p.* **-ming.** *pa.p., pa.t.* **-med. -ly** *adv.* **-mer** *n.* in motoring, a device to diminish power of headlights. **-ness** *n.* [O.E. *dim*].

dime (dīm) *n.* U.S. silver coin equal to 10 cents [L. *decima,* a tenth].

di·men·sion (di·men′·shạn) *n.* a measurement of extent in a single direction (length, breadth, height, or thickness); usually *pl.* measurement in three directions (e.g. of a room); extent; capacity; (*Fig.*) importance. **-al** *a.* capable of being measured; pert. to a dimension [L. *dimensio,* a measuring].

dim·e·ter (dim′·ạ·tẹr) *n.* a verse with two measures or accents [Gk. *dis,* twice; *metron,* a measure].

di·min·ish (di·min′·ish) *v.t.* to cause to grow less; to weaken; to reduce; (*Mus.*) to lower a note by a semi-tone; *v.i.* to become smaller. **-ed** *a.* lessened; lowered; (*Mus.*) lowered by a semi-tone [L. *diminuere,* to break in small pieces].

di·min·u·en·do (di·min·yoo·en′·dō) *n.* (*Mus.*) a gradual decrease in volume of sound and marked >, the opposite of *crescendo* [It.].

dim·i·nu·tion (dim·ạ·nū′·shạn) *n.* the act or process of diminishing; state of being reduced in size, quality, or amount. **diminutive** *a.* of small size; minute; (*Gram.*) applied to a suffix expressing smallness, e.g. *-let, -ock; n.* a word formed from another by addition of such a suffix, as *hamlet, hillock* [L. *diminuere,* to break in small pieces].

dim·i·ty (dim′·i·ti·) *n.* a thin cotton cloth ribbed or figured [prob. Gk. *dimitos,* of double thread].

di·morph·ic (dī·mawr′·fik) *a.* existing in two forms; (*Chem.*) capable of crystallizing in two forms under different degrees of temperature. **dimorphism** *n.* **dimorphous** *a.* [Gk. *dis,* twice; *morphē,* shape].

dim·ple (dim′·pl) *n.* a slight natural depression or hollow on cheek, chin, arm, etc.; a slight indentation in any surface; *v.t.* to mark with dimples; *v.i.* to become dimpled [prob. dimin. of *dip*].

din (din) *n.* a loud, continuous noise; racket; clamor; *v.t.* to strike, stun with noise; to harass with insistent repetition. *pr.p.* **-ning.** *pa.p., pa.t.* **-ned** [O.E. *dyn,* noise].

dine (dīn) *v.t.* to entertain at dinner; to give facilities or accommodation for dining; *v.i.* to take dinner. **-r** *n.* one who dines; a compartment on a railway train for serving meals to passengers. Also **dining car. dinette** (dī·-net′) *n.* a small dining room. **dinner** (din′·ẹr) *n.* the principal meal of the day. **dinner jacket,** a black coat (without tails) worn as informal evening dress [Fr. *dîner,* to dine].

ding (ding) *v.t.* to ring, as a bell. **—dong** *n.* the sound of bells continuously rung; *a.* monotonous; strenuously contested as in *ding-dong* struggle [Scand.].

din·ghy, dingy, dingey (ding′·gi·) *n.* a small boat [Hind. *dengi,* a boat].

din·gy (din′·ji·) *a.* soiled; sullied; of a darkish color. **dinginess** *n.* [prob. conn. with *dung*].

di·no·saur (dī′·nạ·sawr) *n.* a gigantic extinct four-footed reptile of the Mesozoic age [Gk. *deinos,* terrible; *sauros,* a lizard].

dint (dint) *n.* a mark or depression made by a blow; force or energy exerted; *v.t.* to make a mark or dent by a blow. **by dint of,** by means of [O.E. *dynl,* a blow].

di·o·cese (dī′·ạ·sēs) *n.* the district in which a bishop exercises ecclesiastical jurisdiction. **diocesan** (dī·ȧs′·es·ạn or dī′·ạ·sē·zạn) *a.* pert. to a diocese; *n.* a bishop or holder of a diocese [Gk. *dioikēsis,* administration].

di·oe·cious, diecious (dī·ē′·shus) *a.* (*Bot.*) having the stamens (male) and pistils (female) borne by separate plants of the same species; (*Zool.*) having the male and female reproductive organs separate [Gk. *dis,* twice; *oikos,* a dwelling].

di·op·ter, dioptre (dī·ȧp′·tẹr) *n.* the unit for measuring power of a lens [Gk. *dioptron,* instrument for measuring angles].

di·o·ram·a (dī·ạ·ra′·mạ) *n.* a miniature, three-dimensional scene; a painting viewed through an opening, varied effects of reality being realized by manipulation of lights [Gk. *dia,* through; *horama,* a sight].

di·ox·ide (dī·ȧk′·sīd) *n.* a substance the molecules of which comprise one part metal, two parts oxygen [Gk. *dis,* twice; *oxus,* acid].

dip (dip) *v.t.* to immerse momentarily in a liquid; to dye; to lower and raise again, as a flag; to wash as a sheep; to baptize by immersion; *v.i.* to sink below at a certain level; to glance cursorily at; (*Geol.*) to incline downwards. *pr.p.* **-ping.** *pa.p., pa.t.* **-ped.** *n.* a liquid into which something is dipped; immersion; (*Geol.*) inclination downward of rock strata; a candle made by dipping wick in melted tallow. **-per** *n.* something used for dipping; a semi-aquatic diving bird; (*Astron.*) the Great Bear; the Little Bear. **-py** *a.* (*Slang*) crazy [O.E. *dyppan,* to plunge].

diph·the·ri·a (dif·thēr′·i·ạ) *n.* epidemic disease affecting mainly throat and air passages. **-l, diphtheric, diphtheritic,** *a.*

diph·thong (dif′·thawng) *n.* a union of two vowel sounds pronounced as one, as in p*oi*se, m*ou*th. **-al** *a.* **-ally** *adv.* **-ize** *v.t.* to develop a diphthong from a single vowel. **diphthongization** *n.* [Gk. *dis,* twice; *phthongos,* sound].

di·plex (dī′·pleks) *a.* (*Radio*) pert. to the reception or transmission of two messages simultaneously.

dip·lo·car·di·ac (dip′·lō·kȧr′·di·ak) *a.* (*Biol.*) having, as some birds, a double or divided heart [Gk. *diplous,* double; *kardia,* the heart].

di·plo·ma (di·plō′·mạ) *n.* a document or certificate conferring some honor, privilege, or degree, as that granted to graduates of a university; *v.t.* to furnish with a diploma [Gk. *diploma,* a folded letter].

di·plo·ma·cy (di·plō′·mạ·si·) *n.* the art of conducting international negotiations; political dexterity; tact in dealing with people. **diplomat, diplomatist** *n.* one skilled in the art of handling difficult international or personal relations; one engaged in administering international law. **diplomatic, -al** *a.* pert. to diplomacy. **diplomatically** *adv.* **diplomatic corps,** the body of accredited foreign diplomatists resident in any capital [Gk. *diploma,* a folded letter].

di·po·lar (dī·pō′·lẹr) *a.* having two poles, as a magnet. **dipolarize** *v.t.* to magnetize.

dip·so·ma·ni·a (dip·sạ·mā′·ni·ạ) *n.* an uncontrollable craving for alcoholic stimulants. **dipsomaniac** *n.* **dipsomaniacal** *a.* [Gk. *dipsa,* thirst; *mania,* madness].

Dip·ter·a (dip′·tẹr·ạ) *n.* an order of insects, including common housefly, gnat, mosquito, which have only two wings. **dipteral** *a.* **dipteran** *n.* a dipterous insect. **dipterous** *a.* of the order *Diptera* [Gk. *dis,* twice; *pteron,* a wing].

dip·tych (dip′·tik) *n.* an ancient writing tablet hinged in the middle and folding together like a book; a pair of carvings or pictures similarly hinged [Gk. *diptuchos,* folded double].

dire (dīr) *a.* dreadful; calamitous; disastrous. Also **-ful. -ly, -fully** *adv.* [L. *dirus,* terrible].

di·rect (di·rect′, dī′·rect) *a.* straight; straightforward; immediate; in line of descent; sincere; unambiguous; *v.t.* to aim at; to guide; to point out the way; to manage (a business); to prescribe a course or line of procedure; to write the name and address on a missive, etc.; *v.i.* to give direction; to act as a guide; *adv.* in a straight line. **direction** *n.* act of directing; instruction; guidance; management; order; superscription; prescription; address (on a letter); line taken by a moving body. **directional, -ing, -ive** *a.* tending to guide or to advise. **-ive** *n.* orders from a supreme authority. **-ly** *adv.* in a straight line; straightway; immediately after. **-ness** *n.* the quality of being direct, frank, or unimpeded by extraneous details. **-or** *n.* (*fem.* **-ress**) one who directs; a member of a board of managers in a large commercial firm, hospital, etc.; that which regulates a machine; in gunnery, an optical instrument for calculating line of firing. **-orate** *n.* a board of directors. **-orial** *a.* **-ory** *a.* containing directions; guiding; *n.* a book containing the alphabetically arranged names and addresses of the residents of a town or district; a collection of rules. **— current** (*abbrev.* D.C.) (*Elect.*) a current flowing in one direction (contrasting with *alternating current* (A.C.)). **direction finder** (*Radio*) an aerial which determines direction of incoming radio signals (*abbrev.* D/F) [L. *dirigere, directum,* to make straight].

dirge (durj) *n.* a funeral chant; a lament. **-ful** *a.* funereal [fr. L. *dirige* (lead thou), the opening word of Latin burial anthem].

dir·i·gi·ble (dir′·ạ·jạ·bl) *a.* capable of being directed or steered; *n.* a navigable balloon elongated in shape and propelled by engine-driven propellers [L. *dirigere,* to direct].

dirk (durk) *n.* a short dagger; *v.t.* to stab with a dirk.

dirn·dl (durn′·dl) *n.* a type of skirt [Ger. *Dirne,* a girl].

dirt (durt) *n.* any filthy substance, as mud, dust, excrement; loose soil; rubbish; squalor; obscenity. **—cheap** *a.* (*Colloq.*) uncommonly cheap. **-ily** *adv.* in a dirty manner; meanly. **-iness** *n.* **-y** *a.* foul; unclean; muddy; base; (of weather) stormy; rainy; *v.t.* to befoul [M.E. *drit,* excrement].

dis- *pref.* implying *separation,* as in *dis*miss; *negation,* as in*dis*band; *deprivation,* as in *dis*animate; *thoroughness,* as in *dis*annul.

dis·a·ble (dis·ā′·bl) *v.t.* to make incapable or physically unfit; to disqualify. **-ment** *n.* disability. **disability** *n.* the state of being disabled; incapacity.

dis·a·buse (dis·ạ·būz′) *v.t.* to free from misapprehension or error; to undeceive.

dis·ad·van·tage (dis·ạd·van′·tij) *n.* want of advantage; a drawback; a hindrance; a handicap; detriment; hurt. **disadvantageous** (dis·-ad·vạn·tā′·jạs) *a.* **disadvantageously** *adv.*

dis·af·fect (dis·ạ·fekt′) *v.t.* to alienate the affection of; to estrange; to fill with discontent. **-ed** *a.* discontented; disloyal (esp. to government). **-edly** *adv.* **-edness, disaffection** *n.*

dis·af·firm (dis·ạ·furm′) *v.t.* to annul; to invalidate; to reverse a decision. **disaffirmation** *n.*

dis·a·gree (dis′·ạ·grē) *v.i.* to be at variance; to differ in opinion; to be incompatible; to be detrimental to health (of food, climate, etc.). **-able** *a.* **-ably** *adv.* **-ment** *n.* difference of opinion; discord; discrepancy.

dis·al·low (dis·ạ·lou′) *v.t.* to refuse to allow; to reject as untrue or invalid. **-able** *a.* **-ance** *n.*

dis·ap·pear (dis·ạ·pir′) *v.i.* to vanish; to become invisible; to cease to exist. **disappearance** *n.*

dis·ap·point (dis·ạ·point′) *v.t.* to fail to realize the hopes of; to frustrate; to foil. **-ed** *a.* **-ing** *a.* causing disappointment. **-ment** *n.* state of being disappointed; the frustration of one's hopes; miscarriage which disappoints.

dis·ap·pro·bation (dis·ap·rạ·bā′·shạn) *n.* act of disapproving; censure; mental condemnation of what is considered wrong.

dis·ap·prove (dis·ạ·prȯȯv′) *v.t.* to form an unfavorable judgment of; to censure; to refuse to sanction; to dislike; *v.i.* (foll. by *of*). **disapproval** *n.* **disapprovingly** *adv.*

dis·arm (dis·ȧrm′) *v.t.* to deprive of arms; to render unable to attack; (*Fig.*) to conciliate; to allay; *v.i.* to lay down arms, esp. national armaments. **-ament** *n.* the act of reducing, in peacetime, the output of military and naval weapons as a prevention of war; the state of being disarmed. **-ing** *a.* ingenuous.

dis·ar·range (dis·ạ·rānj′) *v.t.* to disturb the order or arrangement of; to throw into confusion. **-ment** *n.*

dis·ar·ray (dis·ạ·rā′) *v.t.* to break the array of; to throw into disorder; to undress; *n.* disorder; confusion; state of undress.

dis·as·so·ci·ate (dis·ạ·sō′·shi·āt) *v.t.* to disunite; to dissociate.

dis·as·ter (diz·as′·tẹr) *n.* an adverse happening; sudden misfortune; catastrophe. **disastrous** *a.* [L. *dis*; *astrum,* a star].

dis·a·vow (dis·ạ·vou′) *v.t.* to refuse to acknowledge; to repudiate. **-al, -ment** *n.*

dis·band (dis·band′) *v.t.* to disperse (troops); to break up an organization; to dismiss; *v.i.* to break up; to disperse. **-ment** *n.*

dis·bar (dis·bȧr′) *v.t.* (*Law*) to expel a lawyer from the bar or from the legal profession. *pr.p.* **-ring.** *pa.p., pa.t.* **-red. -ment** *n.*

dis·be·lieve (dis·bạ·lēv′) *v.t.* to maintain to be untrue; to refuse to believe; *v.i.* to place no reliance or belief (foll. by *on* or *in*). **disbelief** *n.* **disbeliever** *n.*

dis·burse (dis·burs′) *v.t.* to pay out money; to expend. **-ment** *n.* expenditure. **-r** *n.* [L. *dis,* apart; Fr. *bourse,* purse].

disc See **disk.**

dis·card (dis·kȧrd′) *v.t.* and *v.i.* to put aside; to cast off; *n.* (dis′·kȧrd) the act of discarding; anything thrown out as useless.

dis·car·nate (dis·kȧr′·nit) *a.* bereft of flesh; having no physical body.

dis·cern (di·surn′) *v.t.* to distinguish clearly esp. by the sight; to perceive by the mind; to behold as separate. **-er** *n.* **-ible** *a.* **-ing** *a.* discriminating; judging with insight. **-ment** *n.* power or faculty of judging [L. *dis,* apart; *cernere,* to sift].

dis·charge (dis·chȧrj′) *v.t.* to free from a load or weight; to unload a cargo; to fire off the charge with which gun is loaded; to emit, as smoke; to perform, as a duty; to pay, as an account or a debt; to demobilize, as soldiers, etc.; to dismiss, as for failure in service or duty; *n.* act of discharging; performance; matter which exudes, as from an abscess; that which is discharged; the rate of flow of a liquid or waste matter through a pipe [Fr. *décharger,* to unload.]

dis·ci·ple (di·sī′·pl) *n.* one who receives instruction from another; one who adheres to a particular school of philosophy, religious thought, or art; a follower, esp. one of the twelve apostles of Christ. **-ship** *n.* [L. *discipulus,* a pupil].

dis·ci·pline (dis′·ạ·plin) *n.* instruction; training of the mind, or body, or the moral faculties; subjection to authority; self-control; *v.t.* to train; to improve behavior by judicious penal methods. **disciplinarian** *n.* one who enforces rigid discipline; a martinet. **disciplinary** *a.* **-r** *n.* [L. *disciplina,* training].

dis·claim (dis·klām′) *v.t.* to renounce claim to, or responsibility for; to disown; to repudiate; *v.i.* to give up all claim (foll. by *to*).

-ant *n.* **-er** *n.* denial; disavowal; repudiation.
dis·close (dis·klōz′) *v.t.* to unclose; to reveal; to divulge; to bring to light. **-r** *n.* **disclosure** *n.*
dis·col·or (dis·kul′·ẹr) *v.t.* to spoil the color of; to stain; *v..i* to become discolored or stained. **-ation, -ment** *n.* **-ed** *a.* stained.
dis·com·fit (dis·kum′·fit) *v.t.* to defeat; to disconcert; to foil; to baffle. **-ure** *n.* [O.Fr. *desconfit,* defeated].
dis·com·fort (dis·kum′·fẹrt) *n.* want of comfort; uneasiness; pain; *v.t.* to impair the comfort of; to make uneasy.
dis·com·mode (dis·kạ·mōd′) *v.t.* to put to inconvenience; to incommode; to disturb.
dis·com·pose (dis·kạm·pōz′) *v.t.* to upset the self-possession of; to disturb; to disarrange. **discomposure** *n.*
dis·con·cert (dis·kạn·surt′) *v.t.* to discompose; to embarrass. **-ment** *n.* state of disagreement.
dis·con·nect (dis·kạn·ekt′) *v.t.* to separate; to sever; to disjoint. **-ed** *a.* separated; incoherent.
dis·con·so·late (dis·kȧn′·sạ·lit) *a.* destitute of comfort or consolation; forlorn; utterly dejected. **-ly** *adv.* **-ness, disconsolation** *n.*
dis·con·tent (dis·kạn·tent′) *a.* not content; dissatisfied; *n.* want of contentment; dissatisfaction; state of being aggrieved; *v.t.* to cause to be ill-pleased; to dissatisfy. **-ed** *a.* **-edly** *adv.* **-edness, -ment** *n.*
dis·con·tin·ue (dis·kạn·tin′·ū) *v.t.* to interrupt; to break off; to stop; *v.i.* to cease. **discontinuance, discontinuation** *n.* interruption; cessation. **discontinuity** *n.* want of continuity. **discontinuous** *a.* intermittent.
dis·cord (dis′·kawrd) *n.* want of concord or agreement; lack of harmony; strife; (*Mus.*) a combination of inharmonious sounds. **discord** (dis·kawrd′) *v.i.* to disagree; to be out of tune. **discordance, discordancy** *n.* lack of spiritual (or musical) harmony. **discordant** *a.* out of harmony; jarring; dissonant. **discordantly** *adv.* [L. *discordia,* variance].
dis·count (dis·kount′) *v.t.* to pay in advance (a bill of exchange not yet due); to deduct a sum or rate per cent from; to disregard; *v.i.* to lend money with discount. **discount** (dis′·kount) *n.* a sum of money refunded on prompt payment of a bill; the allowance made on the retail price by a wholesaler to a retailer; a deduction [O.Fr. *descompter,* to count off].
dis·coun·te·nance (dis·koun′·tạn·ạns) *v.t.* to refuse to countenance or give approval to.
dis·cour·age (dis·kur′·ij) *v.t.* to deprive of courage; to dishearten; to deter. **-ment** *n.* act of discouraging; state of being discouraged; dissuasion; dejection. **discouraging** *a.*
dis·course (dis′·kōrs) *n.* a formal speech; a sermon; a dissertation; reasoning from premises; conversation. **discourse** (dis·kōrs′) *v.t.* to utter; *v.i.* to lecture; to converse; to hold forth (foll. usually by *upon*) [L. *discursus,* running to and fro].
dis·cour·te·ous (dis·kur′·ti·ạs) *a.* lacking in courtesy; rude. **-ly** *adv.* **discourtesy** *n.*
dis·cov·er (dis·kuv′·ẹr) *v.t.* to find out (esp. something hitherto unknown); to bring to light. **-able** *a.* **-er** *n.* **-y** *n.* the act of finding out; that which is discovered [Fr. *découvrir,* to reveal].
dis·cred·it (dis·kred′·it) *v.t.* to bring into disrepute; to disbelieve; *n.* loss of credit or of reputation. **-able** *a.* damaging; injurious to reputation.
dis·creet (dis·krēt′) *a.* prudent; circumspect; judicious; cautious (in action or speech). **-ly** *adv.* [L. *discretus,* separated, prudent].
dis·crep·an·cy (dis·krep′·ạn·si·) *n.* inconsistency; variance; difference. **discrepant** *a.* not tallying; inconsistent [L. *discrepare,* to jar].
dis·crete (dis·krēt′) *a.* separate; distinct. **-ly** *adv.* **-ness** *n.* [L. *discretus,* separated].
dis·cre·tion (dis·kresh′·ạn) *n.* the quality of being discreet; prudence; discernment; liberty to act according to one's judgment. **-al, -ary** *a.* **ally** *adv.* [L. *discretus,* separated, prudent].
dis·crim·i·nate (dis·krim′·ạ·nāt) *v.t.* to detect as different; to distinguish; to select; *v.i.* to make a distinction in. **-ly** *adv.* **discriminating** *a.* able to observe subtle differences; distinctive. **discriminatingly** *adv.* **discrimination** *n.* faculty of drawing nice distinctions; perception; a difference in treatment between persons, things, etc. **discriminative** *a.* marking a difference; characteristic [L. *discriminare,* to divide].
dis·cur·sive (dis·kur′·siv) *a.* passing from one topic to another; rambling; digressive; arguing from premises to conclusion. **-ly** *adv.* **-ness** *n.* **discursory** *a.* [L. *discursus*].
dis·cus (dis′·kạs) *n.* a circular plate of stone or metal, used in athletic contests [Gk. *diskos,* quoit].
dis·cuss (dis·kus′) *v.t.* to examine critically; to exchange ideas on; (*Colloq.*) to consume, as wine. **-able** (or **-ible**) *a.* **discussion** *n.* debate; act of exchanging opinions [L. *discutere,* to agitate].
dis·dain (dis·dān′) *v.t.* to look down upon, as unworthy or despicable; to scorn; *n.* scorn; arrogance; contempt. **-ful** *a.* **-fully** *adv.* **-fulness** *n.* [O.Fr. *desdeigner,* to scorn].
dis·ease (di·zēz′) *n.* an unhealthy condition of mind or body; malady; **-d** *a.* [O.Fr. *desaise,* discomfort].
dis·em·bark (dis·em·bȧrk′) *v.t.* to put on shore; to land passengers, goods, etc.; *v.i.* to land. **-ation, -ment** *n.*
dis·em·bod·y (dis·im·bạd′·i·) *v.t.* to free from the body or flesh. **disembodiment** *n.*
dis·em·bowel (dis·im·bou′·ạl) *v.t.* to take out the bowels; to gut; to eviscerate.
dis·en·chant (dis·in·chant′) *v.t.* to free from enchantment or glamor; to disillusion.
dis·en·fran·chise (dis·in·fran′·chīz) *v.t.* to deprive of the right to vote. **-ment** *n.*
dis·en·gage (dis·in·gāj′) *v.t.* to unfasten; to separate from an attachment; to release. **-d** *a.* unattached; available; at leisure. **-ment** *n.*
dis·en·tan·gle (dis·in·tang′·gl) *v.t.* to unravel; to untwist; to put in order.
dis·es·tab·lish (dis·ạs·tab′·lish) *v.t.* to deprive of established position; to deprive (a church) of state aid and recognition. **-ment** *n.*
dis·fa·vor (dis·fā′·vẹr) *n.* disapproval; dislike; state of being out of favor; *v.t.* to regard unfavorably.
dis·fig·ure (dis·fig′·yẹr) *v.t.* to mar the appearance of; to deface; to deform. **-ment** *n.* a defect; a blemish.
dis·fran·chise See **disenfranchise.**
dis·frock (dis·frȧk′) *v.t.* to unfrock; to deprive of the right to wear clerical garb.
dis·gorge (dis·gawrj′) *v.t.* to eject from the throat; to pour out (as a river into the sea); to hand over. **-ment** *n.*
dis·grace (dis·grās′) *n.* dishonor; discredit; shameful conduct; *v.t.* to bring dishonor to; to degrade. **-ful** *a.* shameful; discreditable.
dis·grun·tled (dis·grun′·tld) *a.* vexed; sulky.
dis·guise (dis·gīz′) *v.t.* to change the outward appearance of; to misrepresent; *n.* dress, manner, voice, etc. assumed to hide a person's real identity [O.Fr. *desguiser,* to change costume].
dis·gust (dis·gust′) *n.* loathing; nausea; aversion; repugnance; *v.t.* to provoke disgust in. **-edly** *adv.* **-ing** *a.* [L. *dis; gustus,* taste].
dish (dish) *n.* a plate or shallow concave vessel for serving food; the food in such a vessel; any concave object, like a dish; *v.t.* to put in a dish; [O.E. *disc,* a plate].
dis·ha·bille (dis·ạ·bēl′) *n.* partial undress; careless toilet for indoors. Also **deshabille** [Fr.].
dis·har·mo·ny (dis·har′·mạ·ni·) *n.* lack of harmony; discord.
dis·heart·en (dis·hȧr′·tn) *v.t.* to deprive of courage, confidence, or hope; to depress.
di·shev·el (di·shev′·ạl) *v.t.* to ruffle the hair;

to cause the hair or clothes to be untidy or unkempt; *v.i.* to spread in disorder. **-ment** *n.* [L. *dis*, in different directions; *capillus*, the hair].

dis·honest (dis·ȧn′·ist) *a.* lacking in honesty; inclined to cheat; unprincipled. **-ly** *adv.* **-ty** *n.*

dis·hon·or (dis·ȧn′·ẹr) *n.* loss of honor; disgrace; shame; indignity; *v.t.* to disgrace; to seduce; to refuse payment of. **-able** *a.* shameful; lacking integrity. **-ableness** *n.* **-ably** *adv.*

dis·il·lu·sion (dis·i·lòò′·zhạn) *v.t.* to free from illusion; to make the truth apparent; *n.* state of being disillusioned. **-ment** *n.*

dis·in·cline (dis·in·klīn′) *v.t.* to make unwilling; to excite dislike or aversion. **disinclination** *n.* unwillingness; reluctance; dislike.

dis·in·fect (dis·in·fekt′) *v.t.* to free from infection; to destroy disease germs. **-ant** *n.* a germicide. **disinfection** *n.* **-or** *n.*

dis·in·her·it (dis·in·her′·it) *v.t.* to deprive of rights and privileges of an heir.**-ance** *n.*

dis·in·te·grate (dis·in′·tạ·grāt) *v.t.* to break up; *v.i.* to crumble to pieces; to be resolved into elements. **disintegration** *n.* a gradual breaking up.

dis·in·ter (dis·in·tur′) *v.t.* to disentomb; to exhume; to unearth.

dis·in·ter·est·ed (dis·in′·tạ·res·tạd) *a.* free from self-interest; unprejudiced; (*Colloq.*) indifferent. **-ness** *n.*

dis·join (dis·join′) *v.t.* to sever; to disunite. **-t** *v.t.* to separate at the joints; to make incoherent; *v.i.* to fall to pieces. **-ted** *a.* unconnected; (of speech) rambling; incoherent.

dis·junct (dis·jungkt′) *a.* disjoined. **disjunction** *n.* disunion; severance; disconnection; (*Logic*) a statement of alternative possibilities. **-ive** *a.* [L. *dis*; *jugere, junctum*, to join].

disk, disc (disk) *n.* a at circular plate or surface; the face of sun or moon. **-al** *a.* **— jockey** *n.* (*Colloq.*) announcer of a radio program of recorded music [Gk. *diskos*, a round plate].

dis·like (dis·līk′) *v.t.* to have an aversion to; *n.* distaste; antipathy.

dis·lo·cate (dis·lō·kāt′) *v.t.* to put out of place or out of joint; to upset the normal working of. **dislocatedly** *adv.* **dislocation** *n.* (*Med.*) the displacement of a bone.

dis·lodge (dis·lȧj′) *v.t.* to remove from a position of rest, hiding, or defense; *v.i.* to depart. **dislodg(e)ment** *n.*

dis·loy·al (dis·loi′·ạl) *a.* failing in duty or allegiance; faithless; treacherous. **-ly** *adv.* **-ty** *n.*

dis·mal (diz′·mạl) *a.* gloomy; dreary; depressing; bleak. **-ly** *adv.* **-ness, -ity** *n.* [L. *dies mali*, ill-omened days].

dis·man·tle (dis·man′·tl) *v.t.* to strip of furnishings; to take apart [O.Fr. *desmanteler*, to strip].

dis·may (dis·mā′) *v.t.* to alarm; to deprive of courage; to fill with apprehension; *n.* consternation; loss of courage [L. *dis*, neg.; O.H. Ger. *magan*, to be strong].

dis·mem·ber (dis·mem′·bẹr) *v.t.* to tear limb from limb; to mutilate. **-ment** *n.*

dis·miss (dis·mis′) *v.t.* to send away; to disperse; to allow to go; to discharge from employment; to banish (from the mind). **-al** *n.*

dis·mount (dis·mount′) *v.i.* to alight from a horse, bicycle, etc.; *v.t.* to bring down from a place of elevation.

dis·o·bey (dis·ạ·bā′) *v.t.* to disregard orders or instructions; to refuse to do what is commanded. **disobedient** *a.* refusing to obey. **disobediently** *adv.* **disobedience** *n.*

dis·o·blige (dis·ạ·blīj′) *v.t.* to offend by an act of incivility; to refuse to grant a request to. **disobliging** *a.* ungracious; unwilling to accede to another's wishes.

dis·or·der (dis·awr′·dẹr) *n.* want of order; muddle; confusion; discomposure; ailment of body or mind; *v.t.* to throw out of order; to upset. **-ed** *a.* out of order; deranged. **-ly** *a.*

dis·or·gan·ize (dis·awr′·gạ·nīz) *v.t.* to upset the structure or regular system of; to throw into disorder. **disorganic** *a.* **disorganization**

dis·own (dis·ōn′) *v.t.* to repudiate ownership; to renounce.

dis·par·age (dis·par′·ij) *v.t.* to belittle; to lower in rank or reputation; to depreciate. **-ment** *n.* unjust comparison; act of undervaluing [O.Fr. *desparagier*, to marry unequally].

dis·pa·rate (dis′·pạ·rit) *a.* essentially different; dissimilar. **-ness** *n.* [L. *dis*, neg.; *par*, equal].

dis·par·i·ty (dis·par′·ạ·ti·) *n.* difference in form, character, or degree; incongruity.

dis·pas·sion (dis·pash′·ạn) *n.* lack of feeling; serenity. **-ate** *a.* free from passion; impartial.

dis·patch, despatch (des·pach′) *v.t.* to send away, esp. in haste; to execute promptly (as an order); to dispose of; to kill; *n.* something which is dispatched; speed; official message or document sent by special messenger; the sending out of mails, etc. **-er** *n.* [Fr. *dépêcher*, to expedite].

dis·pel (dis·pel′) *v.t.* to drive away; to scatter; to cause to disappear. *pr.p.* **-ling.** *pa.p., pa.t.* **-led** [L. *dis*, apart; *pellere*, to drive].

dis·pense (dis·pens′) *v.t.* to divide out in parts; to administer, as laws; to make up and distribute medicines; *v.i.* to excuse from; **dispensable** *a.* **dispensary** *n.* a place where medicines are made up and distributed. **dispensation** *n.* the act of distributing; the mode of God's dispensing mercies (e.g. *Mosaic, Christian*); a license to do what is normally prohibited. **-r** *n.* **to dispense with,** to do without [L. *dispensare*, to distribute by weight].

dis·perse (dis·purs′) *v.t.* to scatter here and there; to spread; to distribute; to place at intervals (as troops); *v.i.* to separate; to vanish; to be dispelled. **dispersal** *n.* **dispersedly** *adv.* **dispersedness** *n.* **dispersion** *n.* the act of dispersing; the state of being dispersed; (*Opt.*) the separation of light into its constituent rays by refraction through a prism. **dispersive** *a.* [L. *di-*, asunder; *spargere, sparsum*, to scatter].

dis·pir·it (dis·pir′·it) *v.t.* to deject; to depress; to discourage. **-ed** *a.*

dis·place (dis·plās′) *v.t.* to put out of position; to oust from situation or office. **-able** *a.* **Displaced Persons,** homeless war victims (*abbrev.* **D.P.**). **-ment** *n.* the act of putting out of place or removing from office; the weight of water, measured in tons, displaced by a floating ship.

dis·play (dis·plā′) *v.t.* to unfold; to exhibit; to set out conspicuously; *n.* exhibition; ostentation; exaggerated expression of feeling [L. *displicare*, to unfold].

dis·please (dis·plēs′) *v.t.* and *v.i.* to offend; to cause dissatisfaction to. **displeasure** (dis·-plezh′·ẹr) *n.* slight anger or irritation; dislike.

dis·pose (dis·pōs′) *v.t.* to arrange; to regulate; to adjust; to bestow for an object or purpose; to induce a tendency or inclination; *v.i.* to settle; to determine. **disposable** *a.* liable, free, to be disposed of or employed. **disposal** *n.* the the act of disposing or disposing of; control; regulation; management; transference (of property by a will). **disposed** *a.* inclined; minded; arranged. **disposedly** *adv.* **disposition** *n.* the act of disposing; arrangement; guidance; temperament. **to dispose of,** to get rid of; to refute (an argument); to finish (a task) [L. *dis*, apart; *ponere*, to place].

dis·pos·sess (dis·pạ·zes′) *v.t.* to put out of possession; to deprive of property; to eject. **-ion** *n.* **-or** *n.*

dis·proof (dis·pròòf′) *n.* the act of disproving; refutation; a proving to be erroneous.

dis·pro·por·tion (dis·prạ·pōr′·shạn) *n.* want of proportion, symmetry, proper quantity; *v.t.* to make unsuitable; to mismatch. **-able, -al, -ate, -ed** *a.*

dis·prove (dis·pròòv′) *v.t.* to prove to be false; to refute; to prove the opposite of.

dis·pute (dis·pūt′) *v.t.* to consider for and

against; to debate; to question the validity of; to argue; to discuss; to contend; *n.* an argument; a debate; a quarrel. **disputable** *a.* **disputably** *adv.* **disputability** *n.* the quality of being disputable. **disputant** *n.* one who takes part in a dispute; a controversialist. **disputation** *n.* a controversy in words; an academic discussion or argument. **disputatious, disputative** *a.* [L. *dis,* apart; *putare,* to think].

dis·qual·ify (dis·kwal′·a·fī) *v.t.* to make unfit for some special purpose; to incapacitate, to make ineligible; to deprive of legal power or right. **disqualification** *n.*

dis·qui·et (dis·kwī′·ạt) *v.t.* to render uneasy in mind; to disturb; to make restless; *n.* apprehensiveness; uneasiness **-ment, -ude** *n.* uneasiness; want of tranquility.

dis·qui·si·tion (dis·kwạ·zish′·ạn) *n.* a formal enquiry into a subject by argument or discussion; a systematic treatise. **-al, -ary** *a.* [L. *disquirere,* to investigate].

dis·re·gard (dis·ri·gȧrd′) *v.t.* to take no notice of; to ignore; *n.* indifference; lack of attention.

dis·re·pair (dis·ri·per′) *n.* state of being out of repair; delapidation.

dis·re·pute (dis·ri·pūt′) *n.* discredit; state of being unpopular. **disreputable** *a.* degraded; discreditable. **disreputableness** *n.*

dis·re·spect (dis·ri·spekt′) *n.* want of respect or deference; rudeness. **-ful** *a.* **-fully** *adv.*

dis·robe (dis·rōb′) *v.t.* to undress; to discard official dress.

dis·rupt (dis·rupt′) *v.t.* to break or burst asunder; to create a schism. **disruption** *n.* the act or process of disrupting; rent; breach. **disruptive** *a.* **disrupture** *n.* a bursting asunder [L. *dis,* apart; *rumpere,* to break].

dis·sat·is·fy (dis·sat′·is·fī) *v.t.* to fail to satisfy; to make discontented. **dissatisfaction** *n.*

dis·sect (dis·sekt′) *v.t.* to cut up; to divide a plant or a dead body of man or animal for minute examination of its parts; (*Fig.*) to criticize in detail. **dissection** *n.* the act or science of dissecting; the part dissected. **-or** *n.* [L. *dis,* apart; *secare,* cut].

dis·sem·ble (dis·sem′·bl) *v.t.* to hide under a false semblance; to disguise; to ignore; *v.i.* to give an erroneous impression; to assume a false appearance; to be hypocritical. **-r** *n.* [L. *dissimulare,* to conceal a fact].

dis·sem·i·nate (dis·sem′·ạ·nāt) *v.t.* to sow, as seed; to scatter abroad; (*Fig.*) to broadcast; to circulate. **dissemination** *n.* scattering; circulation. **disseminative** *a.* **disseminator** *n.* [L. *dis,* asunder; *seminare,* to sow].

dis·sent (dis·sent′) *v.i.* to differ in opinion; to disagree; to hold views differing from those of the established church; *n.* disagreement; difference of opinion; nonconformity. **dissension** *n.* open disagreement; quarrelling; discord. **-er** *n.* [L. *dis,* apart; *sentire,* to feel].

dis·ser·tate (dis′·ẹr·tāt) *v.i.* to discourse. **dissertation** *n.* a formal treatise or discourse, esp. a written thesis by a candidate for the Doctor's degree [L. *disserere,* to discuss].

dis·serve (dis·surv′) *v.i.* to serve badly another's interests. **disservice** *n.* injury; harm; a bad turn.

dis·sev·er (dis·sev′·ẹr) *v.t.* to separate; to disunite. **-ance, -ation, -ment** *n.*

dis·si·dent (dis′·ạ·dạnt) *a.* differing; disagreeing; *n.* a dissenter; a non-conformist. **dissidence** *n.* dissent [L. *dissidere,* to disagree].

dis·sim·i·lar (dis·sim′·ạ·lẹr) *a.* unlike; not similar. **dissimilarity, dissimilitude** *n.* unlikeness; difference. **-ly** *adv.*

dis·sim·u·late (dis·sim′·yạ·lāt) *v.t.* to dissemble; to feign; *v.i.* to conceal one's true feelings; to be hypocritical. **dissimulation** *n.* the act of pretending [L. *dissimulare*].

dis·si·pate (dis′·ạ·pāt) *v.t.* to scatter; to squander; to dispel; *v.i.* to disappear; to waste away; to lead a dissolute life. **-d** *a.* dissolute; debauched. **dissipation** *n.* **dissipative** *a.* [L. *dissipare,* to scatter].

dis·so·ci·ate (dis·sō′·shi·āt) *v.t.* to separate; to disunite; (*reflex.*) to disclaim connection with. **dissociability** *n.* **dissociable** *a.* capable of being dissociated; incongruous.**dissocial** *a.* anti-social. **dissociation** *n.* the act of dissociating or state of being dissociated; separation; (*Psych.*) term used to describe disunion of the mind, or split personality. **dissociative** *a.* [L. *dis,* asunder; *sociare,* to unite].

dis·sol·u·ble (di·sȧl′·yạ·bl) *a.* capable of being dissolved, liquefied, melted, or decomposed.

dis·so·lute (dis′·ạ·lòòt) *a.* lax in morals; dissipated. **-ly** *adv.* **-ness** *n.* **dissolution** *n.* act of dissolving or passing into solution; disintegration, esp. of body at death; dismissal of an assembly; termination (of marriage, partnership, etc.) [L. *dis,* asunder; *solvere,* to loosen].

dis·solve (di·zȧlv′) *v.t.* to break up, esp. a solid by the action of a liquid; to terminate (as a parliament); to annul (as a marriage); *v.i.* to melt; to waste away; to fade out; to be dismissed. **dissolvability, dissolvableness** *n.* **dissolvable** *a.* **dissolvent** *a.* having the power of dissolving substances [L. *dis,* asunder; *solvere,* to loosen].

dis·so·nant (dis′·ạ·nạnt) *a.* discordant; harsh; unharmonious. **dissonance** *n.* Also **dissonancy** [L. *dissonare,* to fail to harmonize].

dis·suade (di·swād′) *v.t.* to persuade not to; to advise against. **-r** *n.* **dissuasion** *n.* **dissuasive** *a.* [L. *dis,* apart; *suadere,* to advise].

dis·syl·la·ble. See **disyllable.**

dis·taff (dis′·taf) *n.* a cleft stick for holding the fiber (wool, flax, etc.) from which thread is made in the process of hand spinning. **the distaff side,** the female line [O.E. *distaef,* the staff holding flax for spinning].

dis·tance (dis′·tạns) *n.* the space between two objects; the interval between two events; remoteness; aloofness; reserve; *v.t.* to place at a distance; to outstrip; to surpass. **distant** *a.* far off; remote in time, place, or blood-relationship; aloof; reserved; faint. **distantly** *adv.* [L. *distantia,* remoteness].

dis·taste (dis·tāst′) *n.* dislike, esp. of food; aversion. **-ful** *a.* unpleasant.

dis·tem·per (dis·tem′·pẹr) *n.* a method of painting (also called *tempera*) with pigments, in powder form, mixed with any glutinous substance soluble in water; paint of this kind; *v.t.* to paint in distemper. [O.Fr. *destremper,* to moisten with water].

dis·tem·per (dis·tem′·pẹr) *n.* a disordered state of mind or body; disease, esp. a highly infectious inflammatory disease in young dogs [L. *dis,* apart; *temperare,* to control].

dis·tend (dis·tend′) *v.t.* to stretch out; to swell; to inflate. *v.i.* to become swollen or puffed out. **distensible** *a.* **distention, distension** *n.* [L. *dis,* apart; *tendere,* to stretch].

dis·till (dis·til′) *v.t.* to vaporize and recondense a liquid; to cause to fall in drops; to cause to trickle; (*Fig.*) to extract the essential quality of (as wisdom); *v.i.* to undergo distillation; to drop; to trickle; to ooze. **-ate** *n.* the essence produced by distilling. **-ation** *n.* act of distilling. **-atory** *a.* used in distilling. **-er** *n.* **-ery** *n.* a place where distilling is carried on, esp. of alcohol [L. *de,* down; *stillare,* to drip].

dis·tinct (dis·tingkt′) *a.* of marked difference; separate; clear; well-defined; obvious; precise. **distinction** *n.* separation; that which indicates individuality; eminence; repute; mark of honor bestowed for merit. **-ive** *a.* marking distinction or difference.**-ively** *adv.* **-iveness** *n.* **-ness** *n.* clarity [L. *distinctus,* separate].

dis·tin·guish (dis·ting′·gwish) *v.t.* to observe the difference between; to keep apart; to give individuality to; to discern; *v.i.* to make distinctions. **-ed** *a.* eminent; dignified. **-ing** *a.* peculiar; characteristic [L. *distinguere,* to separate].

dis·tort (dis·tawrt′) *v.t.* to twist out of shape; to misrepresent; to pervert. **-ed** *a.* **-edly** *adv.*

distortion *n.* a twisting awry; misrepresentation; *(Radio)* any deviation from the original wave-form of speech or sound during transmission [L. *dis*, asunder; *tortum*, to twist].

dis·tract (dis·trakt′) *v.t.* to draw away (the mind); to divert; to bewilder; to disturb mentally. **-ed** *a.* **-edly** *adv.* **-edness** *n.* **distraction** *n.* **-ive** *a.* **distraught** (dis·trawt′) *a.* perplexed; bewildered; frantic [L. *distractus*, drawn aside].

dis·train (dis·trān′) *v.t.* to seize goods, esp. to enforce payment of debt. **-ment, -t** *n.* seizure of goods. **-or, -er** *n.* [L. *dis*, asunder; *stringere*, to draw tight].

dis·tress (dis·tres′) *n.* extreme pain, mental or physical; misfortune; extreme poverty; *v.t.* to cause pain or anguish to; to harass; *(Law)* to distrain. **-ful** *a.* causing suffering. **-fully** *adv.* **distressed area,** a part of the country where unemployment is rife [L. *distringere*, to pull asunder].

dis·tri·bute (dis·trib′·ūt) *v.t.* to divide among several; to allot or hand out; to spread out; to classify. **distributable** *a.* **distribution** *n.* act of distributing; arrangement. **distributive** *a.* **distributor(-er)** *n.* [L. *dis*, asunder; *tribuere*, to allot].

dis·trict (dis′·trikt) *n.* a defined tract of land; an administrative division of a country; a region; *a.* local; regional; *v.t.* to divide into specified areas [L. *distringere*, tighten].

dis·trust (dis·trust′) *v.t.* to have no faith in; to suspect; to doubt; *n.* want of trust; doubt.

dis·turb (dis·turb′) *v.t.* to upset the normal condition of; to disquiet; to agitate; to ruffle. **-ance** *n.* uproar; confusion; derangement [L. *dis*, asunder; *turbare*, to agitate].

dis·un·ion (dis·ūn′·yạn) *n.* separation; discord; dissension. **disunite** *v.t.* to cause separation; to cause a breach between. **disunity** *n.*

dis·use (dis·ūs′) *n.* cessation of use or practice. **disuse** (dis·ūz′) *v.t.* to cease to use.

di·syl·la·ble (di·sil′·ạ·bl) *n.* a word of two syllables. Also **dissyllable** [Gk. *disyllabos*].

ditch (dich) *n.* a trench dug esp. for drainage or defense; a natural waterway; *v.t.* to cut a ditch in; *(Colloq.)* to get rid of; *v.i.* to make a forced 'landing' on the sea [O.E. *dic*, a ditch].

dith·er (diTH′·ẹr) *n.* *(Colloq.)* a state of nervous agitation or confusion [etym. uncertain].

dit·to (dit′·ō) *n.* that which has been said; the same; **— symbol:** ", placed below thing to be repeated; *adv.* as aforesaid; *v.t.* to copy [L. *dictus*, said].

dit·ty (dit′·i·) *n.* a song; a short poem to be sung [L. *dictare*, to dictate or compose].

dit·ty bag (dit′·i·bag) *n.* a small bag used by soldiers and sailors for holding needles, thread, etc. **ditty box** *n.* a box for the same purpose.

di·u·ret·ic (dī·yoo·ret′·ik) *a.* exciting the discharge of urine; *n.* a medicine which tends to increase the flow of urine. **diuresis** *n.* excessive urinary excretion [Gk. *dia*, through; *ourein*, to make water].

di·ur·nal (dī·ur′·nạl) *a.* belonging to the day (opp. of *nocturnal*); daily; *n.* a book containing the canonical hours of the R.C. breviary. **-ly** *adv.* [L. *dies*, a day].

di·va (dē′·vạ) *n.* a popular female singer; a prima donna [L. *diva*, fem. of *divus*, divine].

di·va·lent (dī·vā′·lent or div′·ạ·lent) *a.* *(Chem.)* capable of combining with two radicals; bivalent [Gk. *dis*, twice; L. *valere*, to be strong].

di·van (di·van′) *n.* a long cushioned seat; a Turkish council of state; a council room; a smoking room [Pers. *divan*, a long seat].

dive (dīv) *v.i.* to plunge into water head first; to remain under water, as a diver; to penetrate deeply into; to plunge the hand into; *n.* a plunge head-first; *(Slang)* a cheap restaurant of ill-repute. **diving bell** *n.* an apparatus by which deep-sea divers can work under water [O.E. *dufan*, to plunge].

di·verge (dạ·vurj′) *v.i.* to turn in different directions; to deviate from a course; to differ. **-ment, -nce, -ncy** *n.* deviation from a common center. **-nt** *a.* branching off; deviating. **-ntly** *adv.* [L. *dis*, asunder; *vergere*, to incline].

di·vers (dī′·vẹrz) *a.* several; sundry. **diverse** *a.* (modern var. of *divers*) of different kinds. **diversely** *adv.* **diversity** *n.* state of being unlike; variety [L. *diversus*, different].

di·ver·si·fy (dạ·vur′·sạ·fī) *v.t.* to make diverse or various; to give variety to [L. *diversus*, varied; *facere*, to make].

di·vert (dạ·vurt′) *v.t.* to turn aside; to alter the direction of; to draw off; to amuse or entertain. **diversion** *n.* **-ing** *a.* **divertissement** (dē·ver·tēs′·mong) *n.* a diversion; a short ballet or interlude between the acts of a play [L. *dis*, aside; *vertere*, to turn].

di·vest (dạ·vest′) *v.t.* to strip, as of clothes, equipment, etc.; to dispossess **-iture, -ment** *n.* [L. *dis*; *vestire*, to clothe].

di·vide (dạ·vīd′) *v.t.* to separate into parts; to share; to keep apart; to antagonize; *(Math.)* to find how many times one number is contained in another; *v.i.* to be separated; to part; *n.* act of dividing; a watershed. **-rs** *n.pl.* compasses for measuring or dividing lines. **the Great Divide,** death [L. *dividere*, to distribute].

div·i·dend (div′·ạ·dend) *n.* *(Arith.)* the sum to be divided by the divisor to obtain the quotient; interest payable on loans, invested money, etc.; the share of profits paid to holders of stocks, insurance, etc. [L. *dividere*, to share out].

di·vine (dạ·vīn′) *a.* belonging to or having the nature of God, or a god; devoted to the worship of God; holy; sacred; heavenly; superhuman; *n.* a priest; a clergyman; a theologian; *v.t.* and *v.i.* to forecast by supernatural means; to practice divination. **divination** *n.* the art or act of foretelling the future by non-rational methods; intuitive prevision; augury. **divinator, diviner** *n.* one who divines. **-ly** *adv.* **-ness** *n.* **divining rod,** a forked twig, usually of hazel, used to locate underground water. **divinity** *n.* state of being divine; God; a pagan deity; the study of theology [L. *divinus*, divine].

di·vi·sion (dạ·vizh′·ạn) *n.* the act of dividing; part of a whole; a section; a partition; difference in opinion; *(Mil.)* an army unit, the normal command of a *major-general*. **divisibility** *n.* **divisible** *a.* capable of being divided. **-al, divisionary** *a.* pert. to or belonging to a division; indicating a separation. **divisor** (dạ·vī′·zẹr) *n.* *(Math.)* the number by which another is divided [L. *divisus*, divided].

di·vorce (dạ·vōrs′) *n.* the legal dissolution of a marriage contract; separation; *v.t.* to obtain legal dissolution of a marriage; to separate; to sever; to disunite. **divorcee** *n.* a divorced person. **-ment** *n.* [L. *divortium*].

div·ot (div′·ạt) *n.* *(Golf)* a piece of turf cut out accidentally by golfer [etym. unknown].

di·vulge (dạ·vulj′) *v.t.* to disclose something secret or unknown; **divulgate** *v.t.* to publish. **-ment, -nce** *n.* [L. *dis*, asunder; *vulgus*, the common people].

Dixie (diks′·i·) *n.* the Southern States of the U.S.; a song [etym. unknown].

diz·zy (diz′·i·) *a.* giddy; light-headed; causing giddiness; *(Colloq.)* stupid; *v.t.* to make dizzy. **dizzily** *adv.* **dizziness** *n.* giddiness; vertigo [O.E. *dysig*, foolish].

do (dō) *(Mus.)* the first tone of the major diatonic scale. Also **doh.**

do (dòò) *v.t.* to perform; to execute; to affect; to finish; to prepare; to confer; *(Colloq.)* to swindle; *v.i.* to act; to be; as *auxil.* verb, used to give emphasis to principal verb as in *I do think you should go*; to avoid repetition of another verb, and in negative, emphatic and interrogative sentences. *pr.p.* **-ing.** *pa.t.* **did.** *pa.p.* **done.** *n.* **to do away with,** to destroy. **-er** *n.* an agent. **to do in,** to murder. **-ings** *n.pl.* things done; activities. **done-out** *a.* exhausted. [O.E. *don*, to do].

dob·bin (dob′·in) *n.* a name for patient, quiet

workhorse [nickname for *Robin*].

do·cent (dō′·sạnt) *n.* a teacher in a university below professorial rank [L. *docere*, to teach].

doc·ile (dȧs′·il) *a.* easily instructed or managed; tractable. **-ly** *adv.* [L. *docere*, to teach].

dock (dȧk) *v.t.* to cut short; to deduct; to clip (as an animal's tail); *n.* the part of tail left after clipping [M.E. *dok*, a tail].

dock (dȧk) *n.* wharf, or row of piers with buildings, etc. where ships are berthed, loaded, etc.; enclosed space in a law court where accused stands. **-age** *n.* space available in docks for ships; charge made for use of docks. **-er** *n.* one who works at the docks, esp. loading and unloading cargoes. **-yard,** *n.* an enclosed dock area where ships are built or repaired. **dry dock,** *n.* a dock from which water can be pumped out [O.Dut. *dokke*].

dock·et (dȧk′·it) *n.* (*Law*) a list of cases for trial; a summary of a written document; a memorandum; a bill or label affixed to goods giving instructions; *v.t.* to summarize; to mark the contents of papers on the back or outside sheet [prob. dim. of *dock*, to curtail].

dock·sid·ers (dȧk′·sīd·ers) *n.* trademark used for a type of boating shoe with non-skid soles.

doc·tor (dȧk′·tẹr) *n.* one who holds the highest degree granted by any faculty of a university; a medical practitioner; *v.t.* to treat medically; (*Colloq.*) to adulterate; to falsify; to repair temporarily; *v.i.* to practice medicine; to take medicine. **-ate** *n.* the degree or status of a university doctor. **-ship** *n.* **-ial** *a.* [L. = a teacher, fr. *docere*, to teach].

doc·trine (dạk′·trin) *n.* principle of belief; instruction; that which is taught. **doctrinal** *a.* pert. to doctrine, esp. Christian Church. **doctrinally** *adv.* **doctrinaire** (dȧk·tri·ner′) *n.* a theorist who tends to urge the application of a doctrine beyond all practical considerations; *a.* impracticable [Fr. fr. L. *doctrina*, teaching].

doc·u·ment (dȧk′·yạ·mạnt) *n.* an official paper containing information, giving instructions, or establishing facts; *v.t.* to furnish with written evidence of. **-al, documentary** *a.* pert. to, derived from, or in the form of a document. **-ation** *n.* the use of documentary evidence; the furnishing of such evidence. **-ed** *a.* [L. *documentum*, example].

dod·der (dȧd′·ẹr) *v.t.* or *v.i.* to totter or tremble, as with age. **-ing** *a.* [prob. dialect word].

do·dec·a·gon (dō·dek′·ạ·gȧn) *n.* a plane figure with twelve sides and twelve angles. **-al** *a.* [Gk. *dodeka*, twelve; *gonia*, an angle].

dodge (dȧj) *v.t.* to evade or escape by a sudden turning; to prevaricate; *v.i.* to twist aside (physically or morally); *n.* a quick, evasive movement; a trick; (*Colloq.*) **-r** *n.*

do·do (dō′·dō) *n.* an extinct flightless bird. *pl.* **-(e)s** [Port. *doudo*, silly].

doe (dō) *n.* the female of the fallow deer; also female of antelope, rabbit, hare, goat, rat, mouse, ferret. **-skin** *n.* the skin of a doe; a fine close-woven cloth [O.E. *da*, a doe].

does (duz) *3rd pers. sing. pr. ind.* of verb **do.**

dog (dawg) *n.* a common, carnivorous quadruped of the same genus as the wolf, mainly domesticated; a worthless fellow; (*Colloq.*) a young man-about-town; one of the two constellations of stars (*Canis Manjor, Canis Minor*); a metal bar for holding logs of wood or supporting fire-irons; *a.* male, as in *dog-wolf; v.t.* to follow closely, as a dog does; to keep at the heels of; to pursue relentlessly. *pr.p.* **-ging.** *pa.p.* **-ged.** **—collar. — days** *n.pl.* the hottest period of the northern summer, generally considered from July 3rd-August 11th. **—eared** *a.* (of a book) having the corners of the pages turned down. **-ged** *a.* stubborn; persistent. **-gedly** *adv.* **-gedness** *n.* **-gish** *a.* like a dog; surly. **-gy** *a.* pert. to dogs; fond of dogs (*Colloq.*) fashionable. **-house** *n.* a small hut for dogs. **dog Latin,** incorrect barbarous Latin. **-like** *a.* faithful. **— star** *n.* alternative name for Sirius, the principal star in the constellation *Canis Major*, and the brightest star in the heavens. **—tired,** *a.* dead-beat; completely exhausted. **-tooth,** *n.* a canine tooth; the eye-tooth (of a human being). **-watch** *n.* one of the two-hour watches on board ship from 4-6 or 6-8 p.m. **a dog in the manger,** a spoil-sport; one who refuses to let another enjoy what he himself has no use for. **a hot dog,** a hot sausage inside a roll. **in the doghouse,** in disfavor. **to go to the dogs,** to be ruined. **to let sleeping dogs lie,** not to stir up trouble unnecessarily [O.E. *docga*, a dog].

dog·ger·el (dog′·ẹr·ẹl) *n.* irregular, unpoetical burlesque verse; *a.* [etym. unknown].

dog·ma (dȧwg′·mạ) *n.* a philosophical tenet; theological doctrine authoritatively asserted; a principle or belief. **dogmatic, -al,** *a.* pert. to a dogma; opinionated; authoritative. **dogmatically** *adv.* **dogmatics** *n.* the science of systematized Christian doctrines; doctrinal theology. **-tize** *v.i.* to formulate a dogma; to express an opinion positively or arrogantly. **-tism** *n.* positive assertion; laying down the law. **-tist** *n.* [Gk. *dogma*, an opinion].

doi·ly (doi′·li·) *n.* a small table mat placed under dishes; a small, round, linen or paper mat put on plate holding cakes, etc. [fr. *Doily*, a haberdasher].

dol·ce (dōl′·chā) *a.* (*Mus.*) sweet; soft. [It. *dolce*, sweet].

dol·drums (dȧl′·drạmz) *n.pl.* a belt of calms at the Equator; (*Colloq.*) a state of depression.

dole (dōl) *v.t.* to distribute in small portions; *n.* something given or paid out; alms; a small portion [O.E. *dal*, a part].

dole·ful (dōl′·fạl) *a.* grievous; melancholic; dismal. **-ly** *adv.* **-ness** *n.* [O.Fr. *doel*, mourning].

doll (dȧl) *n.* a puppet; a toy baby as a child's plaything; (*Colloq.*) a pretty, rather brainless girl. **to doll up** (*Colloq.*) to dress up smartly [prob. fr. *Dolly*, abbrev. of Dorothy].

dol·lar (dȧl′·ẹr) *n.* a silver coin or paper note, the monetary unit of U.S.A. and Canada [Ger. *Taler*, short for *Joachimstaler*, the coin being first made at the silver mines of *Joachimstal*, Bohemia].

dol·lop (dȧl′·ạp) *n.* a lump, a shapeless mass [prob. Scand. *dolp*, a lump].

doll·y (dȧl′·i·) *n.* a wooden shaft attached to a disc with projecting arms, used in mining, pile-driving, etc.; a mobile platform; a small locomotive used in quarries, etc. **dollied** *a.* [prob. fr. *Dolly*].

dol·man (dȧl′·mạn) *n.* a long, loose Turkish garment; Hussar's coat worn like a cape; similar garment worn by women in Victorian days [Turk. *dolaman*, a cloak].

dol·men (dȧl′·men) *n.* a prehistoric tomb formed by a large unhewn stone resting on two or more unhewn uprights [Breton, *tol*, table; *men*, stone].

dol·or·ous (dō′·lẹr·ạs) *a.* full of, expressing, or causing grief. **-ly** *adv.* [L. *dolere*, to grieve].

dol·phin (dȧl′·fin) *n.* a sea mammal; a mooring buoy [Gk. *delphis*, a dolphin].

dolt (dōlt) *n.* a dull, stupid fellow; a blockhead. **-ish** *a.* **-ishly** *adv.* [M.E. *dold*, dulled].

do·main (dō·mān′) *n.* that which one has dominion over; property; (*Fig.*) the scope or sphere of any branch of human knowledge. **-al, dominial** *a.* [L. *dominus*, a lord].

dome (dōm) *n.* a hemispherical vault reared above the roof of a building; a large cupola. **-d, domical** *a.* possessing a dome [L. *domus*, a house].

Domes·day, Doomsday-book. See **doom.**

do·mes·tic (dạ·mes′·tik) *a.* pert. to a house or home; devoted to home and household affairs; tame (of animals); not foreign (of a country's policy); *n.* a household servant. **-ally** *adv.* **-ate** *v.t.* to make fond of domestic life; to tame animals. **domesticity** *n.* life in a household. **— science,** science of home management, etc.

[L. *domus*, a house].

dom·i·cile (dȧm′·ạ·sīl) *n.* an abode; a dwelling-house; (*Law*) a person's permanent residence; *v.t.* to establish in a fixed residence. **domiciliary** *a.* [L. *domicilium*, a dwelling].

dom·i·nant (dȧm′·ạ·nạnt) *a.* ruling; prevailing; (*Mus.*) having harmonic importance; *n.* (*Mus.*) the fifth note of the diatonic scale. **dominance** *n.* authority; ascendancy. **dominancy** *n.* **-ly** *adv.* **dominate** *v.t.* and *v.i.* to rule; to influence strongly; to sway; to tower over. **domination** *n.* authority. **dominative** *a.* ruling. **dominator** *n.* **domineer** *v.i.* to rule with arbitrary sway; to be overbearing. **domineering** *a.* arrogant. **dominion** *n.* lordship; sovereignty; territory under one government; a self-governing British colony [L. *dominari*, to be master].

do·min·i·cal (dạ·min′·i·kạl) *a.* belonging to Jesus as Lord, or the Lord's Day [L. *dominicus*, belonging to a lord].

Do·min·i·can (dạ·min′·i·kạn) *a.* belonging to *St. Dominic*, or to the order of preaching friars, founded by him (called also the *Black Friars*); *n.* a member of St. Dominic's order.

dom·i·no (dȧm′·ạn·ō) *n.* a long cloak of black silk with a hood, worn at masquerades; the person wearing such a cloak; a mask; one of the 28 oblong pieces marked each with a certain number of spots used in the game of *dominoes* [L. *dominus*, a master].

Don (dȧn) *n.* (*fem.* **Doña** (dawn′·yạ); **Donna** (Italian spelling) *n.* a Spanish title, the equivalent of the English *Sir* (formerly applied only to noblemen); a Spaniard. **don,** *n.* a fellow or tutor of Oxford or Cambridge University; a master at Winchester [Sp. fr. L. *dominus*, a master].

don (dȧn) *v.t.* to put on; to assume. *pr.p.* **-ning** *pa.p.*, *pa.t.* **-ned** [short fr. *do on*].

do·na·tion (dō·nā′·shạn) *n.* act of giving; a gift; a contribution. **donate** *v.t.* to present a gift. **donative** *n.* **donor** *n.* one who gives a donation; a benefactor [L. *donare*, to give].

done (dun) *pa.p.* of the verb **do. done!** agreed.

don·key (dȧng′·ki·) *n.* an ass; (*Colloq.*) a foolish person. **— engine** *n.* a small auxiliary steam engine.

don't (dōnt) contr. of **do not.**

doo·dle (dȯȯ′·dl) *v.i.* to scribble aimlessly [prob. form of *dawdle*].

doom (dȯȯm) *n.* fate; evil destiny; judgment; legal decree; ruin; *v.t.* to destine; to pass sentence on; to condemn. **-ed** *a.* under sentence. **-ful** *a.* **-sday** *n.* the Day of Judgment. **Doomsday or Domesday Book,** the census compiled by order of William the Conqueror, for purposes of taxation [O.E. *dom*, a judgment].

door (dōr) *n.* the wooden or metal structure, hinged or sliding, giving access to house, room, passage, or cupboard; the frame by which an entrance is closed; (*Fig.*) a means of approach. **dead as a door nail** (*Colloq.*) quite dead. **-post** *n.* the jamb. **-step** *n.* the step outside a door. **-way** *n.* the entrance to a house, room, etc. **to darken one's door,** to enter one's house [O.E. *duru*, a door].

dope (dōp) *n.* any thick liquid, or semi-liquid lubricant; a varnish; a preparation for coating the fabric surfaces of aircraft; a drug (orig. given to a horse before a race); any narcotic; (*Slang*) a stupid person; inside information (esp. about racehorses); *v.t.* to apply dope or varnish to; to administer dope to; (*Fig.*) to hoodwink. **dopey** *a.* stupefied with drugs; slow-witted [Dut. *doop*, a dipping].

Do·ri·an (dōr′·i·ạn) *a.* pert. to *Doris*, in ancient Greece, or to its inhabitants. **Doric,** *a.* pert. to Doris, the Dorians, or the simple style of architecture of the Dorians; (of dialect) unpolished; *n.* a mode of Greek music; the Doric dialect characterized by broad vowel sounds.

dor·mant (dōr′·mạnt) *a.* sleeping; hibernating; quiescent; not in action; unclaimed (as a title). **dormancy** *n.* state of being quiescent. **dormer-window** *n.* a small vertical window projecting from a roof slope. **dormitory** *n.* a building primarily containing sleeping rooms; a large sleeping apartment. **dormouse** *n.* a small, hibernating rodent [L. *dormire*, to sleep].

dor·sal (dawr′·sạl) *a.* pert. to, near, or belonging to, the back [L. *dorsum*, the back].

do·ry (dō′·ri·) *n.* a flat-bottomed boat.

dose (dōs) *n.* the prescribed quantity of medicine to be taken at one time; a portion; anything disagreeable that must be taken or done; *v.t.* to administer or order in doses; (*Colloq.*) to adulterate. **dosage** *n.* the practice of dosing; the amount of a dose. **dosimeter** *n.* an instrument for measuring minute doses accurately; (*Atomic Warfare*) a small instrument for recording the total dose of radioactivity accumulated up to the moment [Gk. *dosis*, a giving].

dos·si·er (dȧs′·i·ā) *n.* a set of documents [Fr.].

dot (dȧt) *n.* a small point or spot made with a pen, pencil, or sharp instrument; a speck; (*Mus.*) a point placed after a note or rest to lengthen the sound or pause by one-half; *v.t.* to mark with dots; to diversify as with small objects; *v.i.* to make dots. *pr.p.* **-ting.** *pa.p.* **-ted. -ty** *a.* marked with or consisting of dots. **dot and dash,** in Morse code, the short and long symbols [O.E. *dott*, a speck].

dot (dȧt) *n.* a dowry. **dotal** *a.* [Fr.].

dote (dōt) *v.i.* to be in one's dotage; to be foolishly sentimental; to be over-fond of. **dotage** *n.* childishness of old people; senility; excessive fondness. **dotard** *n.* one whose intellect is impaired by old age [O.Dut. *doten*, to be silly].

dou·ble (dub′·l) *a.* denoting two things of the same kind; existing in pairs; twice as much (quantity); twice as good (quality); serving for two; acting two parts; deceitful; ambiguous; *adv.* twice; two-fold; *v.t.* to multiply by two; to make twice as great; to fold in two; *v.i.* to increase to twice as much; to return upon one's track; to run (after marching); *n.* twice as much; that which is doubled over; a fold; a duplicate; an actor's substitute or understudy; a game with two on each side; two faults in succession; a running pace, twice as quick as marching. **— bass** *n.* the largest and lowest pitched of the stringed instruments, played with a bow. **—breasted** *a.* (of a coat) able to fasten over on either side. **— cross** *v.t.* (*Slang*) to cheat a swindler. **—dealing** *n.* duplicity. **—decker** *n.* a ship or bus with two decks. **—edged** *a.* having two edges; (*Fig.*) cutting both ways; effective for and against. **— entry** *n.* in bookkeeping, a system by which every entry is made both on debit and credit side of an account. **—faced** *a.* hypocritical. **-r** *n.* **doublet** *n.* one of a pair; a close-fitting garment for the upper part of body as worn by Elizabethan men; one of two words derived orig. from the same root but varying in spelling and meaning. **— time** *n.* the fastest marching pace next to a run. [L. *duo*, two].

doubt (dout) *v.t.* to disbelieve; to hold questionable; *v.i.* to be in a state of uncertainty; to hesitate; *n.* uncertainty of mind; misgiving; distrust of others. **-able** *a.* **-er** *n.* **-ful** *a.* dubious; uncertain in opinion. **-fully** *adv.* **-fulness** *n.* **-ing** *a.* undecided; hesitant. **-ingly** *adv.* **-less** *adv.* without doubt; probably. **-lessly** *adv.* [L. *dubitare*, to be uncertain].

douche (dȯȯsh) *n.* a jet of water directed upon or into the body; an apparatus for douching [It. *doccia*, a water-pipe].

dough (dō) *n.* a mass of flour moistened and kneaded, to be baked afterwards; (*Slang*) money. **-boy** *n.* (*Colloq.*) an infantryman. **-nuts** *n.* sweetened dough in shape of balls or rings, fried in fat and finally dipped in sugar. **-y** *a.* [O.E. *dah*].

dough·ty (dou′·ti·) *a.* (*Arch.*) brave; valiant. **doughtily** *adv.* [O.E. *dyhtig*, valiant].

dour (dour) *a.* sullen; gloomy; obstinate; forbidding in manner. **-ly** *adv.* [L. *durus*, hard].
douse, dowse (dous) *v.t.* to dip or plunge into water; (*Naut.*) to lower a sail; to put out.
dove (duv) *n.* a pigeon; a symbol of peace or of the Holy Ghost; (*Colloq.*) a person with a conciliatory attitude, esp. in international matters. **—colored** *a.* soft pinkish grey. **-cot(e)** *n.* nesting box of pigeons, usu. on top of a pole. **-tail** *n.* a joint made by fitting one piece toothed with tenons into corresponding mortises in another piece; *v.t.* to join together by this method; (*Fig.*) to link together [O.E. *dufedoppa*].
dow·a·ger (dou′.ạ.jẹr) *n.* (*Law*) widow with property or title left by her husband; (*Colloq.*) a dignified elderly lady [O.Fr. *douage*, a dower].
dow·dy (dou′.di.) *a.* untidy; lacking style; *n.* a dowdy woman. **dowdily** *adv.* **dowdiness** *n.*
dow·el (dou′.ạl) *n.* a wooden or iron pin for joining two adjacent boards or stones [M.E. *dowle*].
dow·er (dou′.ẹr) *n.* a widow's share of her husband's property; gift; talent. **-ed** *a.* **-less** *a.* **dowry** *n.* goods given to the husband by the bride or her family at marriage; a natural gift [L. *dotare*, to endow].
down (doun) *n.* the fine, soft feathers of birds. **-y** *a.* downlike; having down [Scand. *dunn*].
down (doun) *n.* a hillock of sand by the sea (same as *dune*); treeless land [O.E. *dun*, a hill].
down (doun) *prep.* along a descent; towards a lower place, situation, etc.; towards the mouth of a river; in the same direction as, as *down wind;* passing from the past to less remote times; as *down the ages; adv.* in a downward direction; on the ground; to the bottom; below the horizon. *v.t.* to knock down; *interj.* with verbs *get, kneel,* etc. understood; *n.* a reversal of fortune (as in the *ups and downs of life*). **-cast** *a* depressed; (of eyes) lowered; *n.* (in mining) a shaft for ventilation. **-fall** *n.* ruin; a heavy fall of rain, snow. **-fallen** *a.* **-hearted** *a.* despondent. **-hill** *a.* sloping; *adv.* on a slope. **-pour** *n.* a heavy fall of water, esp. rain. **-right** *adv.* completely; in plain terms; *a.* straightforward; unqualified. **-stairs** *adv.* in or to a lower floor of a house; *a.* pert. to the ground floor; *n.* the ground floor. **-stream** *adv.* with the current. **-trodden** *a.* trampled underfoot; oppressed. **-ward** *a.* **-wards** *adv.* **—town,** towards the center of the town [O.E. *of dune*, from the hill].
dowse (douz) *v.t., v.i.* to find subterranean water supply by means of a divining rod. **-r** *n.*
dox·ol·o·gy (dȧks.al′ạ.ji.) *n.* a short hymn of praise to God. [Gk. *daxa*, glory; *legein*, speak].
doze (dōz) *v.i.* to sleep lightly; to be half asleep; *n.* a nap [Scand. *dose*].
doz·en (duz′.n) *n.* a group of twelve things of the same kind; *a.* twelve. **baker's —, devil's —** *n.* thirteen [Fr. *douzaine*, twelve].
drab (drab) *n.* a dingy brownish-grey color; *a.* (*Fig.*) dull; monotonous [Fr. *drap*, cloth].
drach·ma (drak′.mạ) *n.* a Greek coin; an ancient Greek weight [Gk. *drachmē*, a handful].
draft (draft) *n.* a sketch or rough copy; a current of air; a selection for military service; an order directing payment of money by a bank; a drink; drawing of liquid from a cask. *v.t.* to draw the outline of; to compose and write; to take for military service. **-sman** *n.* one who draws plans for buildings, etc. **-smanship** *n.* **— treaty** *n.* a treaty drawn up in outline form. **-y** *a.* **-iness** *n.* [var. of *draught*].
drag (drag) *v.t.* to draw with main force; to trail slowly; to trawl with a drag; to harrow (the fields); *v.i.* to move heavily or slowly; *pr.p.* **-ging;** *pa.p.* **-ged;** *n.* a net or hook to bring up submerged things; a heavy harrow; a puff; a device acting as a brake on a wheel; anything that slows progress; (*Colloq.*) boring person or thing; (*Slang*) transvestite clothing. **-ger** *n.* **-net** *n.* a fishing net for dragging along the sea floor [O.E. *dragan*, to draw].
drag·gle (drag′.l) *v.t.* and *v.i.* to make or become wet and dirty by trailing on the ground.
dra·gon (drag′.ạn) *n.* a fabulous winged reptile represented as breathing out fire and smoke; (*Fig.*) an over-vigilant chaperon. **-et** *n.* a little dragon; a fish of the *Pegasus* genus. **-fly** *n.* an insect of brilliant coloring, with long slender body and two pairs of large, transparent wings. **-'s blood,** a carmine fruit resin used for coloring varnishes and lacquers; [Gk. *drakon*, a large serpent].
dra·goon (drạ.gòòn′) *n.* a cavalryman; *v.t.* to oppress; to enforce harsh disciplinary measures [Fr. *dragon*, a fire-spitting carbine].
drain (drān) *v.t.* to filter; to draw off by degrees; to make dry; to swallow down; to exhaust; to impoverish; *v.i.* to flow off or drip away gradually; *n.* a watercourse; a pipe, sewer or ditch; a gradual exhaustion of means, health, etc. **-able** *a.* **-age** *n.* act of draining; system of carrying away surplus water from an area by rivers, canals. **-er** *n.* a kitchen utensil like a rack, on which plates, etc. are placed to dry; a colander or sieve [O.E. *dragan*, to draw].
drake (drāk) *n.* the male of the duck.
dram (dram) *n.* (contr. of *drachma*) a unit of weight; (*apothecary*) ⅛ of an ounce [Gk. *drachmē*, a weight; orig. a handful].
dra·ma (drȧ′.mạ) *n.* a composition to be acted on the stage; the branch of literature dealing with plays; a series of real emotional events. **dramatic** *a.* pert. to the drama; striking; tense. **dramatically** *adv.* **dramatization** *n.* **dramatize** *v.t.* to adapt a novel, etc. for acting. **dramatist** *n.* a writer of plays. **-turge** *n.* **-turgy** *n.* the art of writing or producing plays. **dramatis personae** (dram′.ạ.tis pẹr.sōn′.ā) characters of a drama [Gk. *draein*, to do].
drank (drangk) *pa.t.* of **drink.**
drape (drāp) *v.t.* to hang something loosely in folds; to adorn with drapery. **drapery** *n.* cloth; hangings [Fr. *drap*, cloth].
dras·tic (dras′.tik) *a.* very powerful; harsh; thorough [Gk. *drastikos*, active].
drat (drat) *interj.* a mild expletive expressing annoyance [corrupt. of *God rot*].
draught (draft) *n.* **-s** *n.pl.* the game of checkers; *a.* drawn from a barrel, as beer. **-(s)man** *n.* checker. See **draft** [O.E. *dragan*, to draw].
draw (draw) *v.t.* to pull along; to haul towards oneself; to entice; to extract (as a tooth); to elicit an opinion from another; to deduce; to receive (as money, salary, etc.); to inhale; to sketch; to describe; to cast lots; to bring game, such as fox, out of hiding; to take out the entrails; *v.i.* to pull; to attract; to move towards; to pull out a weapon for action; to be equal in a match; to sketch; to cast lots; to have a free passage of air (as a chimney). *pr.p.* **-ing.** *pa.t.* **drew.** *pa.p.* **-n.** *n.* the act of drawing; a game ending with same score for both sides; an attraction. **-able** *a.* **-back** *n.* a disadvantage. **-bridge** *n.* a bridge that can be raised or let down. **-er** *n.* one who or that which draws; one who draws an order, draft, etc.; a lidless, sliding box in a table, chest, etc. **-ers** *n.pl.* close fitting undergarment for lower limbs. **-ing** *n.* the art of pulling; a lottery; the art of representing objects by line or color on paper, canvas, etc. **-ing-room** *n.* orig. a withdrawing room; a room in which guests are entertained; a private compartment on a train. **to draw a blank,** to fail to find what one is seeking. **to draw the line,** to stop. **drawn and quartered** quartered and disemboweled [O.E. *dragan*, to draw].
drawl (drawl) *v.i.* to speak with slow and lengthened tone; *v.t.* to utter (words) in this way; *n.* a manner of speech, slow and drawn out [Scand. *dralla*, to loiter].
dray (drā) *n.* a low cart for heavy goods. [O.E. *dragan*, to draw].

dread (dred) *n.* overwhelming apprehension; awe; terror; *a.* dreadful; awful; *v.t.* to regard with fear; *v.i.* to have fear of the future. **-ed** *a.* feared. **-ful** *a.* terrifying; terrible. **-fully** *adv.* **-fulness** *n.* **-nought** *n.* a large-sized battleship mounting heavy guns; a thick woolen overcoat [O.E. *ondraeden,* to fear].

dream (drēm) *n.* a series of images or thoughts in the mind of a person asleep; an idle fancy; a vision; an aspiration; *v.i.* to imagine things during sleep; to have yearnings; *v.t.* to see in a dream; *pa.t.* and *p.p.* **-ed** or **-t** (drēmd or dremt). **-er** *n.* **-ily** *adv.* **-iness** *n.* **-land** *n.* an imaginary land seen in dreams. **-less** *a.* **-like** *a.* visionary; unreal. **-y** *a.* [O.E. *dream*].

drear·y (drir′·i·) *a.* dismal; gloomy; bleak. **drearily** *adv.* **dreariness** *n.* (*Poetic*) **drear** *a.* [O.E. *dreorig,* mournful].

dredge (drej) *v.t.* to sprinkle. **-r** *n.* a flour can with perforated lid [O.Fr. *dragie,* a sweetmeat].

dredge (drej) *n.* a machine like a large scoop for taking up mud from a river bed, harbor, etc.; a dragnet for oysters or zoological specimens. Also **-r.** *v.t.* to scoop up or deepen with a dredge [conn. with *drag*].

dregs (dregz) *n.pl.* sediment in a liquid that falls to the bottom; lees; grounds; (*Fig.*) the most worthless class [Scand. *dreggjar,* dregs].

drench (drench) *v.t.* to wet thoroughly; to soak [O.E. *drencan,* to give to drink].

dress (dres) *v.t.* to put clothes on; to provide with clothes; to adorn; to treat (a sore); *v.i.* to put on one's clothes; *n.* clothes; a frock; adornment. **— circle** *n.* the lowest gallery in a theater, orig. for people in evening-dress. **-er** *n.* one who dresses; a dressing table or bureau. **-ing** *n.* clothes; a sterile substance for a wound; manure; substance used to stiffen fabrics; a sauce (as salad-dressing); stuffing for a fowl. **-ing-down** *n.* (*Colloq.*) a scolding. **-ing gown** *n.* a robe worn while dressing. **-ing table** *n.* a table with mirror used while dressing. **-maker** *n.* a person who makes women's dresses, etc. **-making** *n.* **-y** *a.* fond of dress; fashionable [O.Fr. *dresser,* to prepare].

drew (dròò) *pa.t.* of **draw.**

drib·ble (drib′·l) *v.i.* to trickle down, esp. of saliva of babies and idiots; (*Basketball*) to bounce the ball repeatedly; (*Other Sports*) to kick the ball forward by short kicks. **driblet** *n.* a small drop [dim. of *drip*].

dried (drīd) *pa.t.* and *pa.p.* of verb **dry.**

drift (drift) *n.* the state or process of being driven; that which is driven; the accumulation of substance driven by the wind, as snow; a slow surface current in the sea caused usually by the prevailing wind; deviation or tendency; *v.t.* to drive into heaps; to cause to float in a certain direction; *v.i.* to be floated along; to be piled in heaps; (*Fig.*) to follow unconsciously some trend in policy, thought or behavior. **-age** *n.* that which has drifted, as snow, seaweed, etc.; deviation of a ship from its course. **— anchor** *n.* an anchor for keeping a ship's head to the wind during a storm.**-er** *n.* an aimless wanderer. **-wood** *n.* wood cast on shore by tide [O.E. *drifan,* to drive].

drill (dril) *v.t.* to pierce; to bore a hole through; to sow, as seeds, in a row; to train in military tactics; to instruct thoroughly (in mental or physical exercises); *n.* revolving tool for boring holes in metal, stone, etc.; an implement for making holes for seed; a row of seeds or root crops; physical exercise or military training; instruction. **drilling** *n.* the process of making drills [prob. Dut. *drillen,* to bore].

drink (dringk) *v.t.* to swallow, as a liquid; to empty as a glass; to breathe in, as air; *v.i.* to swallow a liquid; to consume intoxicating liquor. *pa.t., pa.p.* **drunk.** *n.* liquid for drinking; intoxicating liquor. **-able** *a.* **-er** *n.* a tippler. **to drink in,** to absorb through the senses [O.E. *drincan,* to drink].

drip (drip) *v.t.* to let fall, drop by drop; *v.i.* to ooze; to trickle. *pr.p.* **-ping.** *pa.t., pa.p.* **-ped.** *n.* a drop; the sound made by water dripping; the projecting edge of a roof; (*Slang*) an insipid person. **-ping** *a.* thoroughly wet; *n.* that which falls in drops; *pl.* fat, from meat while roasting. **-stone** *n.* a projecting molding over doors to deflect rain water [O.E. *dryppan,* to fall in drops].

drive (drīv) *v.t.* to urge on; to keep in motion; to guide the course of; to cause (a machine) to work; to strike in, as a nail; to compel; to hurry; to conclude, as a bargain; to hit a ball with force, as in golf, tennis; to chase game towards sportsmen; *v.i.* to be forced along; to ride in a vehicle. *pr.p.* **driving.** *pa.t.* **drove.** *pa.p.* **driven.** *n.* an excursion in a vehicle; a private roadway; driving game towards sportsmen; the capacity for getting things done. **-r** *n.* one who or that which drives; a golf club for hitting ball from the tee; a drover. **to drive at,** to hint at [O.E. *drifan,* to drive].

driv·el (driv′·l) *v.i.* to dribble like a child; to talk nonsense; to be weak or foolish; *n.* nonsense. **-er** *n.* [O.E. *dreflian,* to slobber; conn. with *dribble*].

driz·zle (driz′·l) *v.t.* and *v.i.* to rain gently; *n.* fine rain [O.E. *dreosan,* to fall].

droit (drwȧ, droit) *n.* legal right [Fr. *droit*].

droll (drōl) *a.* laughable; funny; queer; *n.* a buffoon; a jester; an odd character. **-ery** *n.* [Fr. *drôle,* an amusing rascal].

drom·e·dar·y (drȧm′·e·der·i·) *n.* a one-humped Arabian camel [Gk. *dromas,* running].

drone (drōn) *n.* the male of the honey-bee; an idler who lives on the work of others; a deep, humming sound; the largest pipe of the bagpipes; its sound; *v.t.* and *v.i.* to hum; to speak or sing in a monotone [O.E. *dran,* a drone].

drool (dròòl) *v.i.* to slaver; to drivel; to speak foolishly [See **drivel**].

droop (dròòp) *v.i.* to hang down; to grow weak; to pine; to sag; to wilt (as flowers); *v.t.* to lower [Scand. *drupa,* to sink].

drop (drȧp) *n.* a globular particle of fluid that falls or is allowed to fall; a minute quantity of fluid in medical dose; anything hanging like a drop, or resembling a drop in size (as a jewel in a pendant, ear-ring, etc.); a fall; the trap door of a gallows; *v.t.* to let fall drop by drop; to let fall; to dismiss or break off (as an acquaintance); to set down from a vehicle; to write a letter or pass a remark, in a casual manner; (of animals) to give birth to prematurely; *v.i.* to fall in drops; to fall down suddenly; to sink to a lower level (as prices); to come to an end. *pr.p.* **-ping.** *pa.t.* and *pa.p.* **-ped. — curtain** *n.* a painted curtain lowered in front of theater stage between scenes in a play. **—kick** *n.* (*Football*) a kick effected by letting the ball fall from the hands to the ground to be kicked immediately on the rebound. **-let** *n.* a tiny drop of liquid. **-per** *n.* a small glass tube from which liquid is measured out in drops. **-pings** *n.pl.* dung. **to drop in,** to make an informal visit. **a drop in the bucket,** a small amount [O.E. *dropa,* a drop].

drop·sy (drȧp′·si·) *n.* a morbid collection of fluid in any part of body. **dropsical** *a.* [Gk. *hudrops,* fr. *hudor,* water].

dross (drȧs) *n.* the scum of metals thrown off in smelting; refuse [O.E. *dros,* dregs].

drought, drouth (drout, drouth) *n.* dryness; absence of rain over a prolonged period. **-iness** *n.* **-y** *a.* [O.E. *drugath,* dryness].

drove (drōv) *n.* a herd or flock, esp. on the move. **-r** *n.* one who drives cattle or sheep, esp. to market [O.E. *drifan,* to drive].

drown (droun) *v.t.* to suffocate by submerging in water; to deluge; to render inaudible; to overpower; *v.i.* to be suffocated in water [O.E. *druncnian,* to be drunk, to get drowned].

drowse (drouz) *v.t.* to make sleepy; *v.i.* to doze; be heavy with sleep; *n.* a half-sleep; a doze.

drowsy *a.* **drowsily** *adv.* **drowsiness** *n.* [O.E. *drusian,* to be sluggish].
drub (drub) *v.t.* to beat; to cudgel; *v.i.* to defeat. *pr.p.* **-bing.** *pa.p., pa.t.* **-bed. -bing** *n.* a thrashing [prob. Scand. *drabba,* to hit].
drudge (druj) *v.i.* to toil hard; to labor at menial tasks; *n.* one who must do menial work. **drudgery** *n.* hard, monotonous, toil. **drudgingly** *adv.* [O.E. *dreogan,* to perform].
drug (drug) *n.* any substance used in the composition of a medicine; a narcotic; (*Fig.*) a commodity unsaleable because of over-production; *v.t.* to mix with drugs; to administer a drug to someone; *v.i.* to take drugs habitually and in excess. *pr.p.* **-ging.** *pr.p.* **-ged. -gist** *n.* dealer in drugs; a pharmaceutical chemist.
Dru·id (drŏŏ′·id) *n.* a priest of the ancient Celtic peoples of Britain, Gaul, etc. who worshipped the oak tree. **-ism** *n.* [Celt.].
drum (drum) *n.* (*Mus.*) a percussion instrument comprising a hollow, parchment-covered cylinder beaten with a drumstick; anything drum-shaped; (*Anat.*) the middle portion of ear; *v.t.* to play on a drum; to teach by constant repetition; *v.i.* to beat on drum; to beat rhythmically. *pr.p.* **-ming.** *pa.p., pa.t.* **-med.** .. **— major** *n.* the leader of a marching drum corps or band. **-mer** *n.* one who plays a drum; a commercial traveler. **-stick** *n.* a padded stick for beating a drum; lower part of leg of cooked fowl [prob. imit. word].
drunk (drungk) *pa.p.* of **drink;** *a.* overcome by strong drink; intoxicated; *n.* a drunk person. **-ard** *n.* one who habitually drinks to excess. **-en** *a.* given to excessive drinking. **-enness** *n.* [O.E. *drincan,* to drink].
drupe (drŏŏp) *n.* a fleshy fruit, such as plum, cherry, or peach, with a stone or kernel containing the seed [L. *drupa,* an over-ripe olive].
dry (drī) *a.* free from moisture, rain, or mist; sear; not giving milk, as a cow; thirsty; unsweetened, as wines; uninteresting; sarcastic; plain, as facts; pert. to a district subject to prohibition laws; *v.t.* to free from moisture or wetness; to drain; *v.i.* to grow dry; to evaporate; (*Fig.*) to become void of ideas. **drier** *n.* **— battery** *n.* a battery composed of *dry cells* sealed in a container to prevent leakage. **to dry clean,** to clean garments with chemicals. **—fly** *n.* an artificial fly (in dry-fly fishing) played over surface of water. **— goods** *n.pl.* textile fabrics. **-ly, drily** *adv.* **— measure,** a measure of bulk, used for grain, etc. **-ness** *n.* **— rot** *n.* a decay caused by fungous disease. **—shod** *a.* with dry feet; without wetting one's feet [O.E. *dryge,* dry].
dry·ad (drī′·ad) *n.* in Greek mythology a spirit of the trees; a wood-nymph [Gk. *drus,* an oak tree].
du·al (dū′·ạl) *a.* consisting of two; twofold; (*Gram.*) of noun, etc. denoting two persons or things; *n.* (*Gram.*) the dual number. **duad** *n.* pair of things regarded as one. **-ism** *n.* a twofold division; the belief that two separate elements co-exist in the universe, namely spirit and matter; the belief in the existence of good and evil as separate entities. **-ist** *n.* **-ity** *n.* state of being double [L. *duo,* two].
dub (dub) *v.t.* to knight; to give a nickname to; to make smooth; to dress a fly for fishing; (*Film*) to provide a film with a sound track not in the original language. *pr.p.* **-bing.** *pa.p.* and *pa.t.* **-bed** [M.E. *dubben,* to adorn].
du·bi·ous (dū′·bi·ạs) *a.* doubtful; liable to turn out well or ill; (of a character) shady. **-ly** *adv.* **-ness** *n.* **dubiety** (dū·bī′·ạ·ti·) *n.* hesitancy; uncertainty. **dubitable** *a.* doubtful. **dubitancy, dubitation** *n.* [L. *dubius,* doubtful].
du·cal (dū′·kạl) *a.* pert. to a duke. **-ly** *adv.* in a ducal manner. **ducat** (duk′·ạt) *n.* a coin.
duce (dŏŏ′·chā) *n.* leader, esp. *'Il Duce,'*.
duchess (duch′·is) *n.* the wife or widow of a duke; a woman who holds a duchy in her own right. **duchy** *n.* dominions of dukes [L. *dux*].
duch·ess (duch′·es) *n.* See **ducal.**
duck (duk) *n.* a coarse cloth or light canvas used for small sails and clothing. **-s** *n.pl.* trousers made of this [Dut. *doeck,* linen cloth].
duck (duk) *n.* any broad-beaked, web-footed, short-legged water bird; female duck as distinct from male *drake;* (*Colloq.*) a darling; a sudden dip; a sudden lowering of head; (*World War* 2) an amphibious truck; *v.i.* to dip suddenly in water; to bend (head) suddenly; to cringe; *v.i.* to plunge into water; to dodge. **-bill** *n.* an Australian burrowing, egg-laying mammal. Also called **-billed platypus. -board** *n.* planking to cross swampy areas. **duckling** *n.* a young duck. **-pins,** small bowling pins. **-weed** *n.* minute, floating, green plants growing on all standing waters. [O.E. *ducan,* to dive].
duct (dukt) *n.* a canal or tube for conveying fluids, esp. in animal bodies, plants, etc. **-less glands** (*Anat.*) endocrine glands which discharge their secretions directly into the blood (e.g. thyroid, pituitary) [L. *ducere,* to lead].
duc·tile (duk′·tạl) *a.* (of metals) capable of being drawn out in fine threads or hammered thin; (*Fig.*) tractable; easily influenced. **ductility** *n.* [L. *ducere,* to lead].
dud (dud) *n.* anything defective or worthless; *n.pl.* clothes, esp. old and sloppy.
dude (dūd, dŏŏd) *n.* (*Slang*) a fop; a brainless dandy; an Easterner (a tenderfoot) who vacations on a ranch.
dudg·eon (duj′·ạn) *n.* anger; resentment, as in phrase *in high dudgeon* [etym. doubtful].
due (dū) *a.* owing; fitting to be paid or done to another; adequate; appointed to arrive (as a train); attributable; *adv.* exactly; duly; directly; *n.* that which is owed; right; (*pl.*) fee; tax. **duly** *adv.* properly; at the right time [O.Fr. *deu,* fr. L. *debere,* to owe].
du·el (dū′·ạl) *n.* a combat between two persons, generally an affair of honor; any two-sided contest; *v.i.* to fight a duel. **-ist** *n.* [It. from L. *duellum,* a fight between two].
du·en·na (dū·en′·ạ) *n.* a chaperon [Sp.].
du·et (dū·et′) *n.* a musical composition for two performers, vocal or instrumental. **-ist** *n.* [It. *duetto,* fr. L. *duo,* two].
duff (duf) *v.t.* to make old things look like new; to fake; (*Golf*) to make a bad stroke. **-er** *n.* (*Slang*) a poor player, an incompetent person [ẹtym. doubtful, prob. Scand. *dowf,* stupid].
duf·fel, duffle (duf′·l) *n.* a coarse woolen cloth with a thick nap; camping kit. **— bag** *n.* a canvas bag used for carrying clothes, etc. [fr. *Duffel* in Belgium].
dug (dug) *n.* a teat, esp. of an animal [Scand. *daegge,* to suckle].
dug (dug) *pa.t.* and *pa.p.* of **dig. -out** *n.* a canoe hollowed out of a tree trunk; a hole in the ground roughly roofed over to protect in trench warfare; (*Baseball*) covered shelter for players not on field [fr. *dig*].
duke (dūk) *n.* (*fem.* **duchess**) the highest order of nobility in the British peerage. **-dom** *n.* the status or possessions of a duke. See **ducal.**
dul·cet (dul′·sit) *a.* sweet to the ear; melodious [L. *dulcis,* sweet].
dul·ci·mer (dul′·sạ·mẹr) *n.* an old musical instrument probably like a small harp; a modern instrument related to the guitar [L. dulcis, sweet; Gk. *melos,* a song].
dull (dull) *a.* stupid; slow of hearing or seeing; tedious; uninspired; sleepy; dim or cloudy; obtuse; blunt; heavy; *v.t.* to stupefy; to blunt; to mitigate; *v.i.* to become dull. **-ard** *n.* a slow-witted person. **-ness** *n.* [O.E. *dol,* dull-witted].
dulse (duls) *n.* an edible reddish-brown seaweed [Gael. *duileasg*].
duly See **due.**
dumb (dum) *a.* lacking permanently the power of speech; mute; temporarily silent; inarticulate; (*Slang*) stupid; unresponsive; *v.t.* to silence. **-bell** *n.* two heavy iron balls connected

by a bar for a handle, used in gymnastic exercises; (*Slang*) a nitwit, moron. **-ly** *adv.* mutely; in silence. **-ness** *n.* **— show,** pantomime. **—waiter** *n.* a hand-operated elevator. **dum(b)found** *v.t.* to strike dumb; to nonplus; to amaze; **-ed** *a.* **dummy** *a.* dumb; sham; *n.* a dumb person; a tailor's mannequin; a sham package in a shop window; (*Cards*) the exposed hand in bridge or whist [O.E. *dumb,* mute].

dum-dum (dum′·dum) *n.* a soft nosed bullet [Bengal].

dump (dump) *v.t.* to throw down heavily; to deposit; to unload; to sell off surplus goods at a low price; *n.* refuse or scrap heap; a temporary store for munitions, etc.; (*Slang*) a poorly kept up place. **-ling** *n.* a ball of dough boiled in water, stock, etc.; a pudding, boiled or baked containing fruit. **-y** *a.* short; thick; squat. **-iness** *n.* **— truck** *n.* a truck whose body tilts and end opens for unloading.

dun (dun) *a.* greyish-brown color; dark; *n.* this color [O.E. *dunn,* dark brown].

dun (dun) *v.t.* to importune for payment of a debt. *pr.p.* **-ning.** *pa.p.* **-ned** [allied to *din*].

dunce (duns) *n.* one who is slow at learning; a dullard [fr. *Duns Scotus,* 13th cent.].

dun·der·head (dun′·dẹr·hed) *n.* a stupid person; a dunce. **-ed** *a.*

dune (dūn) *n.* a low hill of sand in desert areas or on the seacoast [O.Dut. *duna,* a hill].

dung (dung) *n.* the excrement of animals; manure; *v.t.* to treat with manure; *v.i.* to drop excrement. **-hill** *n.* a mound of dung; (*Fig.*) any mean condition [O.E. *dung,* muck].

dun·ga·ree (dung′·gạ·rē) *n.* a coarse hard-wearing cotton cloth. **-s** *n.pl.* trousers or overalls of this material [Hind.].

dun·geon (dun′·jạn) *n.* orig. the principal tower or 'keep' of a castle; a damp subterranean prison cell; *v.t.* to confine in a dungeon [Fr. *donjon,* fr. L. *dominus,* a master].

dunk (dungk) *v.t.* to dip (bread) into tea, coffee, soup, etc. [Ger. *Tunker,* a dipper].

du·o (dū′·ō) *n.* a duet; a pair of stage artistes.

du·o·de·cen·ni·al (dū·ạ·dạ·sen′·i·ạl) *a.* occurring every twelve years. **duodenary** *a.* pert. to 12 [L. *duodecim,* twelve; *annus,* a year].

du·o·dec·i·mo (dū·ạ·des′·ạ·mō) *n.* formed of sheets folded into twelve leaves (*abbrev.* 12 mo.); a 12 mo. book. **duodecimal** *a.* proceeding by twelves; *n.* a twelfth part. **duodecimals** *n.pl.* a method of computation by denominations of 12 instead of 10. **duodecimally** *adv.* [L. *duodecim,* twelve].

du·o·de·num (dū·ạ·dē′·nạm) *n.* upper part of intestines so called as it is about 12 finger-breadths long; *pl.* **duodena. duodenal** *a.* pert. to duodenum [L. *duodeni,* twelve each].

dupe (dūp) *n.* one who is easily cheated; *v.t.* to cheat; to mislead. **-ry** *n.* the art of cheating.

du·plex (dū′·pleks) *a.* twofold; double; *n.* a house consisting of two family units. **duple** *a.* double [L. *duplex,* double].

du·pli·cate (dū′·pli·kit) *a.* double; exactly resembling another; *n.* an exact copy; a replica, facsimile; a method of playing tournament bridge; *v.t.* (dū′·pli·kāte) to double; to make a copy. **duplication** *n.* **duplicator** *n.* a machine for making copies of written matter. **duplicity** *n.* double-dealing; deception [L. *duplicatus,* to double].

du·ra·ble (dyoor′·ạ·bl) *a.* lasting; able to resist wear and tear; not perishable; abiding. **-ness, durability** *n.* **durably** *adv.* **durance** *n.* confinement. **duration** *n.* continuance in time; period anything lasts [L. *durare,* to last].

du·ress (dyoo·res′) *n.* compulsion; imprisonment; coercion [O.Fr. *duresce,* hardship].

dur·ing (dyoor′·ing) *prep.* in the time of; in course of [*pr.p.* of obsolete *dure*].

dusk (dusk) *a.* tending to darkness; darkish; *n.* twilight; gloaming. **-y** *a.* partially dark; dim; dark-skinned [O.E. *dosc,* dark-colored].

dust (dust) *n.* very fine particles of matter deposited on the ground or suspended in the air; minute particles of gold in a river bed; powder; the ashes of the dead; *v.t.* to remove dust from; to sprinkle with powder. **— jacket** *n.* a book cover. **-er** *n.* one who dusts; a cloth for dusting; a tin with perforated lid for sprinkling flour, sugar, etc.; a light garment used as a robe. **-ily** *adv.* **-iness** *n.* **-ing** *n.* the act or process of removing dust from furniture, etc.; a sprinkling [O.E. *dust,* dust].

Dutch (duch) *a.* pert. to Holland, to its inhabitants, or to their language; *n.* the language, the people of Holland. **-man** *n.* **— treat,** an entertainment for which each person pays his own share. **like a Dutch uncle,** with frankness [M.Dut. *dutsch,* pert. to the Netherlands].

du·ty (dū′·ti·) *n.* that which is due; that which is demanded by law, morality, social conscience, etc.; military service; one's proper employment; a period of work set down for each person on a roster; customs or excise dues. **duteous** *a.* dutiful; obedient. **duteously** *adv.* **dutiable** *a.* subject to customs duties. Also **dutied. dutiful** *a.* attentive to duty; submissive; proceeding from a sense of duty. **dutifully** *adv.* **dutifulness** *n.* **—free** *a.* exempt from customs duty [O.Fr. *dueté,* what is owed].

dwarf (dwawrf) *n.* an animal, plant, or man abnormally small in size; *v.t.* to hinder the growth of; to make diminutive by comparison. **dwarf, -ish** *a.* undersized [O.E. *dweorg*].

dwell (dwel) *v.i.* to abide; to be domiciled; to deal with in detail, as in a speech. **-er** *n.* **-ing** *n.* habitation; abode [O.E. *dwellan,* to tarry].

dwin·dle (dwin′·dl) *v.i.* to grow less; to shrink; *v.t.* to lessen [O.E. *dwinan,* to fade].

dye (dī) *v.t.* to give a new color to; to stain; *v.i.* to undergo change of color. *pr.p.* **-ing.** *pa.p.* **-d** *n.* a coloring matter. **-r** *n.* one who is employed in dyeing. **-stuff** *n.* substance used for dyeing [O.E. *deagian,* to dye].

dying (dī′·ing) *pr.p.* of **die.**

dyke (dīk) *n.* See **dike.**

dy·nam·ic (dī·nam′·ik) *a.* pert. to force in motion; pert. to dynamics; (*Med.*) functional; (*Fig.*) possessing energy and forcefulness (of character). Also **-al. -s** *n.* branch of mechanics which deals with *force in motion.* **dynamism** *n.* a school of scientific thought which explains phenomena of universe as resulting from action of natural forces. **dynamist** *n.* **dynamite** *n.* a powerful high explosive, with great disruptive force; *v.t.* to blow up with dynamite. **dynamiter** *n.* one who uses dynamite, esp. for criminal purposes. **dynamo** *n.* a generator for transforming mechanical energy into electrical energy (short for *dynamo-electric machine*); *pl.* **dynamos. dynamograph** *n.* the recording registered on a dynamometer. **dynamometer** *n.* an instrument for measuring force [Gk. *dunamis,* power].

dy·nas·ty (dī′·nạs·ti·) *n.* a line of kings of the same family: the period of a family's rule. **dynast** *n.* a ruler. **dynastic** *a.* [Gk. *dunastēs,* a lord].

dyne (dīn′) *n.* a centimeter-gram-second unit of force, or system [Gk. *dunamis,* force].

dys- (dis) *prefix* fr. Gk. meaning bad, ill, difficult.

dys·en·ter·y (dis′·ạn·ter·i·) *n.* inflammation of the mucous membrane of the large intestine, accompanied by excessive discharge of the bowels, pain and fever. **dysenteric, -al** *a.* [*dus-,* ill; *entera,* the entrails].

dys·pep·sia (dis·pep′·si·ạ) *n.* indigestion. **dyspeptic** *a.* suffering from indigestion; morbid; *n.* one who suffers from dyspepsia [Gk. *dys-,* bad; *peptein,* to digest].

dys·pro·si·um (dis·prō′·zi·um) *n.* one of the rare earths, and the most magnetic metal known [Gk. *dusprositos,* hard to get at].

E

each (ēch) *a.* and *pron.* denoting every one of a number, separately considered. Abbrev. **ea.** [O.E. *aelc*].

ea·ger (ē′·gẹr) *a.* inflamed by desire; ardent; yearning; earnest. **-ly** *adv.* **-ness** *n.* [Fr. *aigre*, sour, keen].

ea·gle (ē′·gl) *n.* large bird of prey; a gold 10 dollar piece of the U.S.; a military standard; (*Golf*) a hole played in two under par. **—eyed** *a.* sharp-sighted. **eaglet** *n.* a young eagle.

ear (ēr) *n.* the fruiting spike of a cereal plant; *v.i.* to form ears [O.E. *ear*].

ear (ēr) *n.* the organ of hearing, esp. external part of it; sensitiveness to musical sounds; attention; ear-shaped projection. **-ache** *n.* acute pain in ear. **-drum** *n.* the middle ear or tympanum. **-ed** *a.* **-lobe** *n.* **-mark** *v.t.* to mark the ears for identification; to reserve for a particular purpose. **-shot** *n.* distance at which sounds can be heard. **-splitting** *a.* exceedingly loud and piercing. **-wax** *n.* cerumen, a waxy secretion of glands of ear. **-wig** *n.* an insect with a body terminating in a pair of horny forceps [O.E. *eare*].

earl (url) *n.* a nobleman ranking between a marquis and a viscount. **-dom** *n.* territory or dignity of an earl [O.E. *eorl*].

ear·ly (ur′·li·) *a.* and *adv.* in the beginning of a period of time; belonging far back in time; in the near future. **earliness** *n.* [O.E. *aerlice*].

earn (urn) *v.t.* to gain money by labor; to merit by service; to get. **-ings** *n.pl.* wages; savings [O.E. *earnian*].

ear·nest (ur′·nist) *a.* serious in intention; sincere; zealous; *n.* seriousness. **-ly** *adv.* **-ness** *n.* [O.E. *eornest*, zeal].

ear·nest (ur′·nist) *n.* a pledge; sum paid as binding [M.E. *ernes*].

earth (urth) *n.* the planet on which we live; the soil, dry land, on the surface of the earth; world matters, as opposed to spiritual. **-s** *n.pl.* term in chemistry for certain metallic oxides. **—bound** *a.* fixed firmly in the earth; worldly; **-en** *a.* made of earth. **-enware** *n.* crockery made of earth. **-iness** *n.* **-ling** *n.* a dweller on the earth. **-ly** *a.* belonging to the earth; terrestial; worldly. **-nut** *n.* a name of certain plants whose tubers are edible. **-quake** *n.* disturbance of the earth's surface due to contraction of a section of the crust of the earth. **-work** *n.* embankments. **-worm** *n.* the common worm. **-y** *a.* like or pertaining to earth; gross [O.E. *erothe*].

ease (ēz) *n.* leisure; quiet; freedom from anxiety, bodily effort, or pain; facility; natural grace of manner; *v.t.* to free from pain, disquiet, or oppression. **-ful** *a.* **-ment** *n.* something that comforts; (*Law*) a right in another's land, e.g. right of way. **easily** *adv.* **easiness** *n.* **easing** *n.* the act of alleviating or slackening. **easy** *a.* at ease; free from pain, care, anxiety; moderate; comfortable. **stand at ease!** military term to relax. **easy-chair** *n.* an armchair **easy-going** *a.* taking matters in an easy way [Fr. *aise*].

ea·sel (ē′·zl) *n.* a wooden frame to support pictures, etc. [Ger. *Esel*, an ass].

east (ēst) *n.* one of the four cardinal points; the part of the horizon where the sun rises; regions towards that; *a.* on, in, or near the east; *adv.* from or to the east. **-ern** *a.* toward, in, or from the east; oriental. **-ing** *n.* distance eastward from a given meridian. **-ward** *adv.* or *a.* toward the east. **-wards** *adv.* **Far East,** China, Japan, etc. **Middle East,** Iran, Iraq, etc. **Near East,** Turkey, Syria, Palestine, etc. [O.E. *east*].

East·er (ēs′·tẹr) *n.* a festival commemorating Christ's resurrection, falling on the Sunday after Good Friday [O.E. *Eastre*, spring festival of goddess of dawn].

eas·y. See **ease.**

eat (ēt) *v.t.* to chew and swallow, as food; to consume gradually; to destroy; gnaw; corrode; wear away; *v.i.* to take food. *pa.t.* **ate** (āt). *pa.p.* **-en.** **-able** *a.*, *n.* anything that may be eaten. **-s** *n.pl.* (*Slang*) food ready for consumption [O.E. *etan*].

eau (ō) *n.* French for *water*. *pl.* **eaux.** **— de Cologne** *n.* a perfume obtained by distillation.

eaves (ēvz) *n.pl.* the lower edges of a sloping roof overhanging the walls of a building. **-drop** *v.i.* to listen furtively to a conversation. **-dropper** *n.* [O.E. *efes*, an edge].

ebb (eb) *n.* the reflux of tide-water to the sea; diminution; *v.i.* to flow back; to sink. **— tide** *n.* the ebbing or retiring tide [O.E. *ebba*].

eb·on (eb′·ạn) *a.* black as ebony. **-y** *n.* a cabinet wood which is jet black. **-ite** *n.* hard rubber or form of a vulcanite [L. *ebenus*].

e·bul·lient (i·bul′·yạnt) *a.* boiling over; overflowing; exuberant; enthusiastic. **ebullience** *n.* **ebullition** *n.* act of boiling; outburst of feeling; agitation [L. *bullire*, to boil].

ec·cen·tric (ik·sen′·trik) *a.* departing from the center; not placed, or not having the axis placed, centrally; not circular (in orbit); irregular; odd; of a whimsical temperament; *n.* a disc mounted off center upon a shaft to change the rotary movement of a shaft into an up and down motion; a whimsical person; one who defies the social conventions. **-ally** *adv.* **-ity** *n.* the distance of a focus from the center of an ellipse; the deviation of two or more circles from a common center; departure from normal way of conducting oneself [Gk. *ek*, from; *kentron*, center].

ec·cle·si·a (i·klē′·zi·ạ) *n.* a church; a religious assembly. **-stic** *n.* a clergyman; a priest; *a.* **-stical** *a.* **-sticism** *n.* adherence to ecclesiastical principles. **ecclesiology** *n.* the science and study of church architecture and decoration. **ecclesiologist** *n.* [Gk. *ekklēsia*, church].

ech·e·lon (esh′·ạ·lán) *n.* a level of command; an arrangement of troops in parallel lines, each a little to left or right of another; a type of airplane formation [Fr. *échelle*, a ladder].

e·chi·nus (e·kī′·nạs) *n.* a sea-urchin; a rounded molding as that below the abacus of a Doric capital [Gk. *echinos*, a hedgehog].

ech·o (ek′·ō) *n.* repetition of sound produced by sound waves reflected from an obstructing object; close imitation of another's remarks or ideas; reverberation; repetition; answer; *pl.* **-es;** *v.t.* to send back the sound of; to repeat with approval; to imitate closely; *v.i.* **-ism** *n.* forming words to imitate natural sounds [Gk.].

é·clair (ā·klār′) *n.* a pastry filled with cream and frosted chocolate [Fr.].

é·clat (ā·klá′) *n.* splendor; approbation of success; renown; acclamation [Fr.].

ec·lec·tic (ik·lek′·tik) *a.* selecting at will; *n.* a thinker who selects and reconciles principles, opinions, belonging to different schools of thought. **-ally** *adv.* [Gk. *eklegein*, to pick out].

e·clipse (i·klips′) *n.* an interception of the light of one heavenly body by another; temporary effacement; *v.t.* to obscure or hide; to surpass [Gk. *ek*, out; *leipein*, to leave].

e·clip·tic (i·klip′·tik) *n.* the great circle on the celestial sphere which lies in the plane of the sun's apparent orbit round the Earth; *a.* **-al** *a.* [Gk. *ek*, out; *leipein*, to leave].

ec·logue (ek′·lawg) *n.* a short poem of a pastoral nature [Gk. *eklogē*, a selection].

ec·o·cide (ek′·ō·sīd) *n.* the destruction of the human environment or ecosystem, esp. through pollutants. **ecocidal** *a.* [fr. *ecology;* L. *-cida*, fr. *caedere*, to kill].

e·col·o·gy (e·kál′·ạ·ji·) *n.* a study of relations between animals, plants, people, and their environment [Gk. *aikos*, a house; *logos*, discourse].

e·con·o·my (e·kán′·ạ·mi·) *n.* wise expenditure of money; careful use of materials; management of the resources of a community; a saving harmonious organization. **economic, (al)** *a.* **economically** *adv.* **economics** *n.pl.* **political economy,** the science which deals with the production, distribution, and consumption of the world's resources and the management of state income and expenditure in terms of money. **economize** *v.i.* to expend with care and prudence; *v.t.* **economist** *n.* a student of economics; an economizer [Gk. *oikos*, a house; *nomos*, law].

éc·ru (ek′·ròò) *n.* beige [Fr. *écru*, unbleached].

ec·sta·sy (ek′·stạ·si·) *n.* abnormal emotional excitement when the mind is ruled by one idea, object, or emotion; a sense of uplift and joyfulness and increased well-being; excessive joy. **ecstatic** *a.* to be in a state of rapture; overjoyed. **ecstatically** *adv.* [Gk. *ekstasis*]

ec·to-, ect-, a prefix implying *outside, without* [Gk. *ektos*].

ec·to·plasm (ek′·tạ·plasm) *n.* (*Zool.*) exterior protoplasm of a cell; in spiritualism, an ethereal substance in which psychic phenomena may manifest themselves. **ectoplasmic** *a.* [Gk. *ektos*, outside; *plasma*, anything formed].

ec·u·men·ic, ecumenical (ek·yoo·men′·ik, ·i·kạl) *a.* universal; representative of the Church, universal or catholic. Also **oecumenic, -al** [Gk. *oikoumenē*, the inhabited world].

ec·ze·ma (ek′·sạ·mạ, eg·zē′·mạ) *n.* disease of the skin, characterized by itchiness and inflammatory eruption [Gk. *ekzema*].

ed·dy (ed′·i·) *n.* a current of air, smoke, or water, swirling back contrary to the main current; a vortex; *v.i.* to move in a circle [O.E. *ed* = black].

e·del·weiss (ā′·dl·vīs) *n.* a small white flowering plant found in the Swiss Alps [Ger. *edel*, noble; *weiss*, white].

E·den (ē′·dạn) *n.* the garden where Adam and Eve lived; a place of delight; a paradise.

e·den·tate (ē·din′·tāt) *a.* without front teeth; lacking teeth; *n.* an edentate animal [L. *e*, out of; *dens*, tooth].

edge (ej) *n.* the thin cutting side of the blade of an instrument; the part adjacent to the line of division; rim; keenness; *v.t.* to put an edge on; to sharpen; to fringe; to move almost imperceptibly; *v.i.* to move sideways. **-d** *a.* sharp; bordered. **-less** *a.* **-ways, -wise** *adv.* in the direction of the edge; sideways. **edging** *n.* border or fringe; narrow lace. **edgy** *a.* having an edge; irritable. **to be on edge,** to be irritable [O.E. *ecg*].

ed·i·ble (ed′·ạ·bl) *a.* fit for eating; *n.* an eatable. **edibility** *n.* [L. *edere*, to eat].

e·dict (ē′·dikt) *n.* a law or decree; order proclaimed by a government or king [L. *e*; *dicere*, to say].

ed·i·fy (ed′·ạ·fī) *v.t.* to build up, esp. in character or faith; to instruct in moral and religious knowledge. *pa.t.* and *pa.p.* **edified. edification** *n.* improvement of the mind or morals. **edifice** *n.* a fine building. **edifier** *n.* **edifying** *a.* [L. *aedificare*, to build].

ed·it (ed′·it) *v.t.* to prepare for publication; to compile; to direct a newspaper or periodical; to revise and alter or omit. **edition** *n.* the form in which a book is published; the number of copies of a book, newspaper, etc. printed at one time; an issue; copy or prototype. **-or** *n.* one who edits; **editorial** *n.* an article in a newspaper presenting the newspaper's point of view; *a.* pert. to or written by an editor [L. *edere*, to give out].

ed·u·cate (ej′·oo·kāt) *v.t.* to cultivate and discipline the mind and other faculties by teaching; send to school. **educable** *a.* able to absorb education. **educability** *n.* **education** *n.* process of training; knowledge. **educational** *a.* **educationally** *adv.* **educative** *a.* tending to educate. **educator** *n.* one who educates [L. *e*, out; *ducere*, to lead].

e·duce (i·dòòs′) *v.t.* to draw or bring out that which is latent; to elicit; to extract; to develop. **educible** *a.* **educt** *n.* that which is educed. **eduction** *n.* [L. *educere*, to lead out].

eel (ēl) *n.* a group of fishes with elongated bodies [O.E. *ael*].

e'en, e'er (ēn, er) *contr.* for *even, ever.*

ee·rie, eery (ē′·ri·) *a.* weird, superstitiously timid; frightening. **eerily** *adv.* **eeriness** *n.* [O.E. *earg*, timid].

ef·face (i·fās′) *v.t.* to erase or scratch out. **-ment** *n.* the act of effacing [Fr. *effacer*].

ef·fect (ạ·fekt′) *n.* that which is produced by an agent or cause; result; consequence; *v.t.* to bring about. **-s** *n.pl.* property. **-ive** *a.* in a condition to produce desired result; efficient; powerful. **-ively** *adv.* **-iveness** *n.* **-ual** *a.* producing the intended result; efficacious; successful. **-uality** *n.* **-ually** *adv.* **-uate** *v.t.* to bring to pass; to achieve; to effect. **in effect,** really; for practical purposes. **to take effect,** to become operative [L. *efficere*, to bring about].

ef·fem·i·nate (i·fem′·ạ·nit) *a.* unmanly; womanish [L. *effeminatus*, made womanish].

ef·fer·ent (ef′·ẹr·ạnt) *a.* conveying outward, or away from the center [L. *ex*, out; *ferre*, to carry].

ef·fer·vesce (ef·ẹr·ves′) *v.i.* to bubble, to seethe, as a liquid giving off gas; to be in a state of excitement; to froth up. **-nce** *n.* **-ent** *a.* bubbling; lively; sparkling [L. *effervescere*].

ef·fete (e·fēt′) *a.* no longer capable of bearing young; sterile; unfruitful; worn-out; spent [L. *effetus*, exhausted by breeding].

ef·fi·ca·cious (ef·ạ·kā′·shạs) *a.* productive of effects; producing the desired effect. **-ly** *adv.* **-ness, efficacity, efficacy** *n.* power to produce effects [L. *efficere*, to effect].

ef·fi·cient (ạ·fish′·ạnt) *a.* causing effects; producing results; capable; able; effective. **efficiency** *n.* power to produce the result required; competency. **-ly** *adv.* [L. *efficere*, to effect].

ef·fi·gy (ef′·ạ·ji·) *n.* an image or representation of a person. **hang in effigy,** to hang an image of a person as a public expression of hatred [L. *effigies*, fr. *fingere*, to form].

ef·flo·resce (ef·lō·res′) *v.i.* to burst into bloom; to blossom; (*Chem.*) to lose water of crystallization on exposure to air, so that crystals fall into powder. **-nce, -ncy** *n.* blooming; the time of flowering. **-ent** *a.* [L. *efflorescere*].

ef·flu·ent (ef′·loo·ạnt) *a.* flowing out; *n.* a stream which flows out from another river or lake. **effluence** *n.* a flowing out; issue; emanation [L. *efflorescens*].

ef·flu·vi·um (e·flòò′·vi·ạm) *n.* an exhalation with a disagreeable smell. *pl.* **effluvia. effluvial** *a.* [L. fr. *effluere*].

ef·flux (ef′·luks) *n.* the act of flowing out; that which flows out [L. *effluere*, flow out].

ef·fort (ef′·ẹrt) *n.* putting forth an exertion of strength or power, bodily or mental; attempt; achievement. **-less** *a.* [L. *ex*, out; *fortis*, strong]

ef·fron·ter·y (i·frun′·tẹr·i·) *n.* brazen impudence; audacity [Fr. *effronté* = without brow (for blushing)].

ef·fulge (e·fulj′) *v.i.* to shine brightly. **-nce** *n.* **-nt** *a.* diffusing a flood of light; radiant [L. *ex*, out, *fulgere*, to shine].

ef·fuse (e·fūz′) *v.t.* to pour out or forth; *a.* (*Bot.*) spread out; (of shells) slightly separated. **effusion** *n.* act of pouring out; that which is poured out. **effusive** *a.* gushing; demonstrative [L. *ex*, out; *fundere*, *fusum*, to pour].

e·gad (i·gad′) *interj.* a mild imprecation = by God.

egg (eg) *v.t.* to urge on; to encourage one to take action [O.N. *eggja*, fr. *egg*, edge].

egg (eg) *n.* an oval body laid by birds and a few animals in which the embryo continues development apart from parent body; matured female germ cell or ovum; anything egg-shaped. **— cell** *n.* the ovum, as distinct from any other cells associated with it. **-nog** *n.* a drink made of egg, milk, sugar, and wine. **-shell** *n.* **-plant** *n.* an edible plant with somewhat egg-shaped purple fruit [O.N. *egg*].

e·gis See **aegis.**

eg·lan·tine (eg′·lạn·tīn) *n.* the sweet brier; the honeysuckle [Fr. *églantine*].

e·go (ē′·gō, eg′·ō) *n.* I; the whole person; self; the personal identity. **-centric** *a.* self-centered. **-centricism, -centricity** *n.* **-ism** *n.* systematic selfishness; theory that bases morality on self-interest. **-ist** *n.* **-istic, -istical** *a.* **-mania,** *n.* abnormal self-esteem. **-tism** *n.* the habit of talking or writing incessantly of oneself; selfishness. **-tist** *n.* **-tistic, -tistical** *a.* **-tistically** *adv.* [L. *ego,* I].

e·gre·gious (i·grē′·jạs) *a.* remarkably flagrant. **-ly** *adv.* [L. *e,* out; *grex,* a flock].

e·gress (ē′·gres) *n.* act of leaving an enclosed place; exit; the right of departure. **egression** *n.* [L. *egressus*].

e·gret (ē′·grit) *n.* several species of heron [Fr. *aigrette*].

E·gyp·tian (ē·jip′·shạn) *a.* pert. to Egypt; *n.* a native of Egypt. **Egyptology** *n.* study of Egyptian history, antiques, and inscriptions. **Egyptologist** *n.*

ei·der (ī′·dẹr) *n.* **the eider duck,** a species of sea ducks. **— down** *n.* the breast down of the *eider duck*; a quilt stuffed with this down [O.N. *aethr*].

eight (āt) *n.* and *a.* one more than seven, written as 8 or VIII. **-een** *n.* and *a.* eight more than ten, written 18 or XVIII. **-eenth** *n.* and *a.* the eighth after the tenth, written 18th. **-fold** *a.* eight times any quantity. **eighth** *n.* and *a.* the first after the seventh; *n.* one of eight equal parts; 8th; (*Mus.*) the interval of an octave; the eighth note of the diatonic scale. **-ieth** *a.* ordinal corresponding to eighty, coming after the seventy-ninth; written 80th; *n.* one of eighty equal parts of a whole, written 1/80. **-y** *n.* and *a.* eight times ten; four-score [O.E. *eahla*].

ei·ther (ē′·, ī′·THẹr) *a.* or *pron.* one or the other; one of two; each; *adv.* or *conj.* bringing in the first of alternatives or strengthening an added negation [O.E. *aegther*].

e·jac·u·late (i·jak′·yạ·lāt) *v.t.* to utter suddenly and briefly; to eject; *v.i.* to utter ejaculations. **ejaculation** *n.* a short, sudden exclamation; a sudden emission. **ejaculatory** *a.* [L. *e,* out; *jacere,* to throw].

e·ject (i·jekt′) *v.t.* to throw out; to cast forth; to turn out; to dispossess of a house or estate. **-a** *n.* waste matter. **ejection** *n.* the act of casting out. **-ment** *n.* expulsion; dispossession; (*Law*) the forcible removal of a defaulting tenant by legal process from land or house. **-or** *n.* [L. *e,* out; *jacere,* to throw].

eke (ēk) *v.t.* to add or augment. **— out,** to supplement; to use makeshifts [O.E. *ecan*].

e·lab·o·rate (i·lab′·ạ·rāt) *v.t.* to put much work and skill on; to work out in detail; to take pains with; *v.i.* to give fuller treatment; *a.* (i·lab′·ạ·rit) worked out in details; highly finished; complicated. **-ly** *adv.* **-ness, elaboration** *n.* act of elaborating; progressive improvement [L. *e,* out; *labor,* labor].

é·lan (ā·làng′) *n.* dash; impetuosity [Fr.].

e·land (ē′·lạnd) *n.* the largest of the antelopes, found in Africa [Dut.].

e·lapse (i·laps′) *v.i.* of time, to pass by; to slip away [L. *e*; *labi, lapsus,* slide].

e·las·tic (i·las′·tik) *a.* possessing the property of recovering the original form when a distorting or constraining force has been removed; flexible; resilient; springy; *n.* a fabric whose threads are interwoven with strands of rubber; a rubber band. **elasticity** *n.* [Gk. *elaunein,* to drive].

e·late (i·lāt′) *v.t.* to raise or exalt the spirit of; make proud. **-d** *a.* **elation** *n.* exultation [L. *elatus,* lifted up].

el·bow (el′·bō) *n.* the joint between the arm and forearm; right angle bend for joining two pipes; any sharp bend or turn; *v.t.* and *v.i.* to push with the elbows; to jostle. **— grease** *n.* (*Colloq.*) hard work, as in rubbing vigorously. **— room** *n.* ample room for free movement [O.E. *elnboga*].

el·der (el′·dẹr) *a.* older; senior; prior; *n.* one who is older; a senior; an office bearer in certain Protestant churches. **-liness** *n.* **-ly** *a.* somewhat old; up in years. **eldest** *a.* the oldest of a family [O.E. *ẹldo*].

el·der (el′·dẹr) *n.* a flowering shrub which yields berries [O.E. *ellern*].

El Do·ra·do, Eldorado (el·dạ·rá′·dō) *n.* a fabulous city abounding in gold and precious stones; any similar place [Sp.=the gilded one].

e·lect (i·lekt′) *v.t.* to choose; to choose by vote; to appoint to office; to select; *v.i.* to determine on a course of action; *a.* chosen; selected from a number; (after a noun), appointed but not yet in office; *n.* those predestined to eternal life. **election** *n.* the act of electing or choosing; public voting for office. **electioneer** *v.i.* to work for the election of a candidate. **-ive** *a.* appointed by; dependent on choice. **-ively** *adv.* **-or** *n.* one with right to vote at election. **-oral** *a.* pertaining to electors or to elections. **-oral college** *n.* a body of electors chosen by voters in the states to elect the president and vice-president of the U.S. **-orate** *n.* the whole body of electors [L. *eligere*].

e·lec·tric (i·lek′·trik) *a.* pertaining to, charged with, worked by, producing electricity; thrilling. **— chair,** used for electrocuting criminals. **— eel,** a fresh water fish of S. America which is capable of inflicting powerful shocks. **-al** *a.*, **-ally** *adv.* **-ity** (tris′·ạ·ti·) *n.* a form of energy generated by friction, induction, or chemical change, and having magnetic and radiant effects; state of strong tension. **— unit,** of pressure = *volt*; of current = *ampere*; of power = *watt*; of resistance = *ohm* [Gk. *ēlektron,* amber].

e·lec·tri·cian (i·lek·trish′·ạn) *n.* a mechanic who makes or repairs electrical apparatus.

e·lec·tri·fy (i·lek′·trạ·fī) *v.t.* to charge with electricity; to thrill, startle, excite by an unexpected statement or action.

e·lec·tro- (i·lek′·trō) *prefix,* used in the construction of compound words referring to some phase of electricity. **-analysis** *n.* chemical analysis by electrolysis. **-cardiogram** *n.* a tracing of electrical changes of contractions of heart. **-cardiograph** *n.* machine which makes the tracing.

e·lec·tro·cute (i·lek′·trạ·kūt) *v.t.* to cause death by electric shock. **electrocution** *n.*

e·lec·trode (i·lek′·trōd) *n.* a metallic conductor of an open electric circuit in contact with some other kind of conductor [Gk. *ēlektron,* amber; *hodos,* way].

e·lec·tro·dy·nam·ics (i·lek·trō·dī·nam′·iks) *n.* a branch of the science of electricity which treats of the laws of electricity in motion or of electric currents and their effects.

e·lec·tro·ki·net·ics (i·lek′·trō·ki·net·iks) *n.* Same as **electrodynamics.**

e·lec·trol·y·sis (i·lek·tral′·ạ·sis) *n.* the resolution of dissolved or fused chemical compounds into elements by passing a current of electricity through them; (*Surg.*) destruction of hair roots, tumors, by an electric current. **electrolyze** *v.t.* to subject to electrolysis. **electrolyte** *n.* the liquid which carries the electric current between two electrodes [Gk. *ēlektron,* amber; *luein,* to loosen].

e·lec·tro·mag·net (i·lek·trō·mag′·nit) *n.* a mass of soft iron temporarily magnetized by being placed within a coil of insulated copper wire through which a current of electricity is passing. **-ic** *a.* **-ism** *n.* branch of electrical science which deals with the relation of magnetism and electricity.

e·lec·trom·e·ter (i·lek·tràm′·e·tẹr) *n.* an instrument for measuring electricity.

e·lec·tro·mo·tion (i·lek·trà·mō′·shạn) *n.* the flow of an electric current in a voltaic circuit. **electromotive** *a.* producing motion by means of electricity.

e·lec·tron (i·lek′·tràn) *n.* the lightest known particle, a constituent of all atoms around whose nuclei they revolve in orbits. **electronics** *n.* the branch of physics which deals with the behavior of free electrons. **— microscope,** an instrument of immense magnifying power in which controlled rays of electrons are used instead of light rays.

e·lec·tro·neg·a·tive (i·lek·trạ·neg′·ạ·tiv) *a.* carrying a negative charge of electricity.

e·lec·trop·a·thy (i·lek·tràp′·ạ·thi·) *n.* treatment of disease by means of electricity. Also **electrotherapy. electrotherapeutics** *n.*

e·lec·tro·plate (i·lek′·trạ·plāt) *v.t.* to cover with a coating of metal by means of electrolysis; *n.* an article so covered.

e·lec·tro·pos·i·tive (i·lek·trạ·pàs′·ạ·tiv) *a.* carrying a positive charge of electricity.

e·lec·tro·stat·ics (i·lek·trạ·stat′·iks) *n.* the branch of electrical science which treats of the behavior of electricity in equilibrium or at rest.

e·lec·tro·type (i·lek′·trạ·tīp) *n.* a facsimile printing plate of type or illustrations.

e·lec·trum (i·lek′·trạm) *n.* an alloy of gold and silver [Gk. *ēlektron*].

el·ee·mos·y·nar·y (el·ạ·mos′·ạ·nẹr·i·) *a.* by way of charity; given in charity [Gk. *eleēmosunē*, alms].

el·e·gant (el′·ạ·gạnt) *a.* graceful; tasteful; refined; luxurious. **-ly** *adv.* **elegance** *n.* grace; beauty; propriety; gentility; delicate taste [L. *elegans*].

el·e·gy (el′·ạ·ji·) *n.* a poem of mourning; a funeral song. **elegiac** *a.* pertaining to elegy; written in elegiacs. **elegiacs** *n.pl.* elegiac verse or couplets, each made up of a hexameter and a pentameter. **elegiacal** *a.* **elegiast, elegist** *n.* a writer of elegies [Gk. *elegos*, a lament].

e·lek·tron (i·lek′·tràn) *n.* a magnesium alloy of unusual lightness. See **elektrum** [Gk. = amber].

el·e·ment (el′·ạ·mạnt) *n.* the first principle or rule; a component part; ingredient; constituent; essential point; the habitation most suited to a person or animal; (*Chem.*) a substance which cannot be separated into two or more substances. **-s** *n.pl.* the bread and wine used in the Lord's Supper; fire, air, water and earth, supposed to be foundation of all things; the physical forces of nature which determine the state of the weather. **-al** *a.* of the powers of nature; not compounded; basic; fundamental. **-ary** *a.* pertaining to the elements or first principles of anything; rudimentary; simple [L. *elementum*].

el·e·phant (el′·ạ·fạnt) *n.* the largest four-footed animal, having a long flexible trunk, two ivory tusks, and exceedingly thick skin. **-ine** *a.* huge; unwieldy; ungainly. **-oid** *a.* like an elephant [Gk. *elephas*].

el·e·phan·ti·a·sis (el·ạ·fạn·tī′·ạ·sis) *n.* disease in which there is gross enlargement of the affected parts [Gk. *elephas*, an elephant].

el·e·vate (el′·ạ·vāt) *v.t.* to lift up; to raise to a higher rank or station; to elate. **elevated** *a.* raised; dignified; exhilarated; *n.* a railroad on elevated tracks. **elevation** *n.* the act of elevating or the state of being raised; elevated place, a hill, a height; (*Archit.*) geometrical projection, drawn to scale, of the vertical face of any part of a building or object. **elevator** *n.* the person or thing which lifts up; a lift or hoist; a silo where grain is stored; the rudder-like airfoil hinged to the tail of an aircraft. **elevatory** *a.* tending or having power to elevate [L. *levis*, light].

e·lev·en (i·lev′·n) *n.* and *a.* one more than ten, written as 11 or XI; a full team at football or hockey. **-th** *a.* the ordinal number corresponding to eleven, the next after tenth; *n.* one of 11 equal parts of a whole [O.E. *endlufan*].

elf (elf) *n.* a supernatural, diminutive being of folk-lore with mischievous traits; a hobgoblin; a dwarf; *pl.* **elves** (elvz). **-in** *n.* a little elf; **elfish** *a.* elf-like; rougish [O.E. *aelf*].

e·lic·it (i·lis′·it) *v.t.* to draw out; to extract; to bring to light facts by questioning or reasoning [L. *elicere*].

e·lide (i·līd′) *v.t.* to cut off or suppress a vowel or syllable. **elision** *n.* the suppression of a vowel or syllable [L. *elidere*, to strike out].

el·i·gi·ble (el′·i·jạ·bl) *a.* legally qualified; fit and worthy to be chosen; desirable. **eligibility** *n.* [L. *eligere*, to choose].

e·lim·i·nate (i·lim′·ạ·nāt) *v.t.* to remove; get rid of; set aside; separate; leave out of consideration; excrete; expel; obliterate. **elimination** *n.* **eliminator** *n.* [L. *eliminare*, to put out of doors].

e·li·sion See **elide.**

e·lite (i·lēt′) *n.* a choice or select body; the best part of society [Fr.].

e·lix·ir (i·lik′·ser) *n.* a cure-all; a medicine; the essence, vainly sought by the alchemists, which would have the power to transmute base metals into gold [Ar. *al-iksir*].

E·liz·a·be·than (i·liz·ạ·bē′·thạn) *a.* pert. to Queen Elizabeth I or her times; *n.* a writer or distinguished person of her reign.

elk (elk) *n.* the largest member of the deer family in the N. of Europe; in America, the wapiti; a leather used for shoes, etc. [O.E. *eolh*].

ell (el) *n.* an addition to a building, usually at right angles [from letter L].

el·lipse (i·lips′) *n.* a regular oval, formed by the line traced out by a point moving so that the sum of its distance from two fixed points always remains the same; the plane section across a cone not taken at right angles to the axis. **ellipsoid** *n.* a closed solid figure of which every plane section is an ellipse. **elliptic(al)** *a.* oval; pertaining to an ellipse [See **ellipsis**]. [Gk. *elleipsis*, a defect].

el·lip·sis (i·lip′·sis) *n.* in English syntax a term denoting the omission of a word or words from a sentence whereby the complete meaning is obtained by inference. **elliptic(al)** *a.* [Gk.].

elm (elm) a genus of trees [O.E.].

el·o·cu·tion (el·ạ·kū′·shạn) *n.* art of effective public speaking from the point of view of enunciation, voice-production, delivery. **-ary** *a.* **-ist** *n.* [L. *e*, out; *loqui*, to speak].

e·lon·gate (i′·lawng·gāt) *v.t.* to make longer; to lengthen; to extend; to draw out; *a.* (*Bot.*) tapering. **elongation** *n.* the act of stretching out; the part extended [L. *e*; *longus*, long].

e·lope (i·lōp′) *v.i.* to run away with a lover; to marry secretly; to bolt unexpectedly. **-ment** *n.* [O.Fr. *alouper*].

el·o·quence (el′·ạ·kwạns) *n.* the art or power of expressing thought in fluent, impressive and graceful language; oratory; rhetoric; fluency. **eloquent** *a.* **eloquently** *adv.* [L. *e*, out; *loqui*, to speak].

else (els) *adv.* besides; other; otherwise; instead. **-where** *adv.* in or to some other place [O.E. *elles*].

e·lu·ci·date (i·lòò′·sạ·dāt) *v.t.* to make clear or manifest; to throw light upon; to explain; illustrate. **elucidation** *n.* act of throwing light upon or explaining. **elucidative, elucidatory** *a.* **elucidator** *n.* [L. *e*; *lux*, light; *dare*, to give].

e·lude (i·lòòd′) *v.t.* to keep out of sight; to escape by stratagem, artifice, or dexterity; to evade; to baffle. **elusion** *n.* act of eluding; evasion. **elusive** *a.* **elusory** *a.* [L. *e*, out; *ludere*, to play].

el·van, elves, elvish See **elf.**

E·ly·si·um (e·lizh′·i·ạm) *n.* (*Myth.*) according

to the Greeks, the abode of the virtuous dead where the inhabitants lived a life of passive blessedness; any place of perfect happiness. **Elysian** *a.* like a paradise; blissful.

em- *prefix* in or with; or adding a transitive or casual force in the composition of verbs.

em (em) *n.* (*Print.*) Typographical unit of width, known as a pica or 12 pt. em (approx. ⅙th of an in.) used for measuring the length of a line of type.

e·ma·ci·ate (i·mā′·shi·āt) *v.t.* to make lean; to reduce one to flesh and bones; *v.i.* to waste away; to become extremely thin. **-d.** *a.* **emaciation** *n.* [L. *emaciare,* fr. *macies,* leanness].

em·a·nate (em′·ạ·nāt) *v.i.* to issue from; to originate; to proceed from; to arise (of intangible things). **emanant** *a.* flowing from. **emanation** *n.* a flowing out from; that which issues from a source; radioactive, chemically inert gas given off by radium, thorium and actinium. **emanative, emanatory** *a.* [L. *emanare,* to flow out].

e·man·ci·pate (i·man′·sạ·pāt) *v.t.* to set free from slavery or servitude; to set free from any restraint or restriction. **emancipation** *n.* **emancipator** *n.* [L. *emancipare*].

e·mas·cu·late (i·mas′·kạ·lāt) *v.t.* to castrate; to deprive of masculine qualities; to render effeminate. **emasculation** *n.* **emasculatory** *a.* [L. *e*; *masculus,* masculine].

em·balm (im·båm′) *v.t.* to preserve a corpse from decay by means of antiseptic agents, balm, aromatic oils and spices; to perfume; to cherish tenderly some memory of. **-er** *n.* **-ing, -ment** *n.* [Fr. *embaumer*].

em·bank (im·bangk′) *v.t.* to enclose or defend with a bank, mound, or earthwork. **-ment** *n.* the act of embarking; an earthwork built to prevent flooding or hold up a road, etc.

em·bar·go (im·bår′·gō) *n.* in international law, an order by which a government prevents a foreign ship from entering or leaving port; an order forbidding the despatch of a certain class of goods, usually munitions, to another country; a general prohibition. *pl.* **embargoes.** *v.t.* to lay an embargo upon [Sp. *embargar,* to impede].

em·bark (im·bårk′) *v.t.* to put on board a ship; to enter on some business or enterprise; *v.i.* to go on board a ship. **-ation** *n.* [Fr. *embarquer*].

em·bar·rass (im·bar′·ạs) *v.t.* to disconcert; to perplex; to abash; to impede; to involve one in difficulties, esp. regarding money matters. **-ed** *a.* **-ing** *a.* disconcerting. **-ment** *n.* [Fr. *embarrasser*].

em·bas·sy (em′·bạ·si·) *n.* the person sent abroad as an ambassador along with his staff; the residence of an ambassador [O.Fr. *ambasée*].

em·bat·tle (em·bat′·l) *v.t.* to furnish with battlements. **-ment** *n.*

em·bat·tle (em·bat′·l) *v.t.* to draw up in order of battle. **-d** *a.* [O.F. *embatailler*].

em·bed (im·bed′) *v.t.* to lay as in a bed; to bed in soil. Also **imbed.**

em·bel·lish (im·bel′·ish) *v.t.* to make beautiful or elegant with ornaments; to add fanciful details to a report or story. **-er** *n.* **-ingly** *adv.* **-ment** *n.* [Fr. *embellir,* to beautify].

em·ber (em′·bẹr) *n.* a live piece of coal or wood; *pl.* red-hot ashes [O.E. *aemerge*].

em·bez·zle (im·bez′·l) *v.t.* to misappropriate fraudulently. **-ment** *n.* **-r** *n.* [O.Fr. *enbesiler,* to damage, steal].

em·bit·ter (im·bit′·ẹr) *v.t.* to make bitter. **-ed** *a.*

em·bla·zon (em·blā′·zạn) *v.t.* to adorn with heraldic figures; to deck in blazing colors; to proclaim. **-ment** *n.* **-ry** *n.* emblazoning.

em·blem (em′·blạm) *n.* an object, or a representation of an object, symbolizing and suggesting to the mind something different from itself; sign; badge; symbol; device. **-atic, -al** *a.* **-atically** *adv.* **-atize** *v.t.* to represent by an emblem; to be an emblem of [Gk. *emblema,* a thing put in].

em·bod·y, imbody (im·bod′·i·) *v.t.* to form into a body; to incorporate; to give concrete expression to; to represent. **embodiment** *n.* an act of embodying; bodily representation.

em·bold·en (im·bōl′·d'n) *v.t.* to give boldness or courage to; to encourage.

em·bo·lism (em′·bạ·lizm) *n.* the insertion of days between other days to adjust the reckoning of time; (*Med.*) the result of the presence in the blood stream of a solid foreign substance, as a clot. **embolismal** *a.* [Gr. *embolē,* an insertion].

em·bos·om, imbosom (em·, im·booz′·ạm) *v.t.* to clasp or receive into the bosom; to enclose; to shelter; to foster.

em·boss (im·baws′) *v.t.* to raise or form a design above the surrounding surface. **-ed** *a.* **-ment** *n.* a boss or protuberance [O.Fr. *bosc*].

em·bow·el (em·bou′·ạl) *v.t.* to disembowel.

em·bow·er (em·bou′·ẹr) *v.t.* to lodge, or set in a bower; to surround (with flowers).

em·brace (em·brās′) *v.t.* to clasp in the arms; to press to the bosom; to avail oneself of; to accept; to encircle; *n.* a clasping in the arms; a hug [Fr. *embrasser,* fr. *bras,* arm].

em·bra·sure (em·brā′·zhẹr) *n.* the splay or bevel of a door or window where the sides slant on the inside; opening in a parapet of a fort to allow cannon-fire [Fr.].

em·bro·cate (em′·brō·kāt) *v.t.* to moisten and rub with lotion, etc. **embrocation** *n.* [Gk. *embrochē,* lotion].

em·broi·der (im·broi′·dẹr) *v.t.* to ornament fabrics with threads of silk, linen, etc. to form a design; to embellish, exaggerate a story. **-er** *n.* **-y** *n.* ornamental needlework [O.Fr. *broder*].

em·broil (em·broil′) *v.t.* to involve in a quarrel or strife; to entangle; to confound. **-ment** *n.* [Fr. *embrouiller,* to entangle].

em·bry·o (em′·bri·ō), **embryon** (em′·bri·ån) *n.* foetus during first months of gestation before quickening; a plant in rudimentary stage of development within seed; initial or rudimentary stage of anything; *a.* rudimentary; in the early stage. **-logic, -logical** *a.* pert. to embryology. **-logist** *n.* **-logy** *n.* science which deals with the growth and structure of the embryo. **-nic** *a.* rudimentary; at an early stage of development [Gk. *embruon*].

e·mend (i·mend′) *v.t.* to remove faults or blemishes from; to amend, esp. of correcting a literary text; to alter for the better. **emendate** *v.t.* **emendation** *n.* correction of errors or blemishes. **emendator** *n.* **-atory** *a.*

em·er·ald (em′·ẹr·ạld) *n.* precious stone of beryl species, transparent and bright green in color. **Emerald Isle,** Ireland [Fr. *émeraude*].

e·merge (i·mẹrj′) *v.i.* to rise out of a fluid; to come forth; to come into view; to come to notice. **-nce** *n.* coming into view; an outgrowth from a plant. **-ncy** *n.* state of pressing necessity; difficult situation; urgent need. **-nt** *a.* emerging; rising into view [L. *e,* out; *mergere,* to plunge].

e·mer·i·tus (i·mer′·ạ·tạs) *n.* and *a.* one who has honorably resigned or retired from a position of trust or responsibility but is retained on the rolls [L. = a veteran, fr. *e,* out; *merere,* to earn].

e·mer·sion (ē·mur′·shạn) *n.* an emerging.

em·er·y (em′·ẹr·i·) *n.* a naturally occurring mixture of corundum and iron oxide, used as an abrasive for polishing; *v.t.* to rub with emery [Gk. *smuris*].

e·met·ic (i·met′·ik) *a.* inducing vomiting; *n.* any agent which causes vomiting [Gk. *emetikos,* provoking sickness].

em·i·grate (em′·ạ·grāt) *v.i.* to leave one's country to settle in another. **emigrant** *a.* pert. to emigration; *n.* one who emigrates. **emigra-**

tion *n.* [L. *e,* out; *migrare,* to remove].

em·i·nent (em′·ạ·nạnt) *a.* exalted in rank, office, or public estimation; prominent. **eminence** *n.* elevation; rising ground; height; rank; official dignity; fame [L. *eminere,* to stand out].

e·mir (ạ·mēr′) *n.* a title bestowed on Moslem chiefs [Ar. *amir*].

em·is·sar·y (em′·ạ·ser·i·) *n.* agent charged with a secret mission; one sent on a mission [L. *e,* out; *mittere, missum,* to send].

e·mit (i·mit′) *v.t.* to send forth; to utter (a declaration). *pr.p.* **-ting.** *pa.p., pa.t.* **-ted. emission** *n.* **emissive** *a.* [L. *e,* out; *mittere,* to send].

e·mol·lient (i·mȧl′·i·ạnt) *a.* softening; relaxing; assuaging; a soothing agent or medicine [L. *mollis,* soft].

e·mol·u·ment (i·mȧl′·yoo·mạnt) *n.* profit arising from office or employment; gain; pay; salary; fee [L. *moliri,* to toil].

e·mo·tion (i·mō′·shạn) *n.* strong, generalized feeling; excitement or agitation. **-al** *a.* easily excited or upset. **-alism** *n.* tendency to emotional excitement. **-ally** *adv.* **-less** *a.* **emotive** *a.* causing emotion [L. *emotio,* fr. *emovere,* to stir].

em·pa·thy (em′·pạ·thi·) *n.* intellectual identification of oneself with another [Gk. *en,* in; *pathos,* feeling].

em·per·or (em′·pẹr·ẹr) *n.* the title assumed by the ruler of an empire [L. *imperare*].

em·pha·sis (em′·fạ·sis) *n.* stress on anything such as force of voice given to words or syllables. *pl.* **emphases, emphasize** *v.t.* to stress. **emphatic, emphatical** *a.* [Gk.].

em·pire (em′·pīr) *n.* imperial power; dominion; a country with its satellite states under the rule of an emperor or some other supreme control [L. *imperium,* command].

em·pir·ic, em·pir·i·cal (em·pir′·ik, -ạl) *a.* based on the results of experiment, observation, or experience, and not from mathematical or scientific reasoning; having reference to actual facts. **empiric** *n.* a quack; one who depends for his knowledge entirely on experience. **-ally** *adv.* **empiricism** *n.* the philosophical doctrine that sensory experience is the only source of knowledge; the formulation of scientific laws by the process of observation and experiment. **empiricist** *n.* [Gk. *en,* in; *peira,* trial].

em·place·ment (em·plās′·mạnt) *n.* the place or site of a building; a fortified position for a gun; placing in position.

em·ploy (em·ploi′) *v.t.* to give occupation to; to make use of; to hire or engage; to busy; to engross; to exercise; to occupy; (em′·ploi) *n.* paid service. **-able** *a.* **-ee** *n.* one who is employed at a wage or salary. **-er** *n.* **-ment** *n.* [Fr. *employer*].

em·po·ri·um (em·pō′·ri·ạm) *n.* a place of extensive commerce or trade; a mart; a big shop. *pls.* **emporia** [Gk. *emporos,* trader].

em·pow·er (im·pou′·ẹr) *v.t.* to give legal or moral power or authority to; to authorize.

em·press (em′·pris) *n.* the wife of an emperor; a female who exercises similar supreme power to that of an emperor.

emp·ty (emp′·ti·) *a.* containing nothing; wanting force or meaning; void; vacant; unoccupied; destitute; hollow; unreal; senseless; (*Colloq.*) hungry; *v.t.* to make empty; to pour out; to drain; *v.i.* to become empty; to discharge; **emptiness** *n.* [O.E. *aemtig*].

em·py·e·ma (em·pī·ē′·mạ) *n.* (*Med.*) a collection of pus in body cavity, esp. in pleura [Gk. *en; puon,* pus].

em·pyr·e·al (em·pir′·i·ạl) *a.* of pure fire or light; pert. to highest and purest regions of heaven. **empyrean** *a.* empyreal; *n.* highest heaven, or region of pure elemental fire; the firmament [Gk. *en,* in; *pur,* fire].

e·mu, emeu (ē′·mū) *n.* a large flightless bird, native of Australia [Port.].

em·u·late (em′·yoo·lāt) *v.t.* to strive to equal or surpass; to rival; to imitate. **emulation** *n.* act of attempting to equal or excel. **emulative** *a.* **emulator** *n.* **emulous** *a.* anxious to emulate or outdo another [L. *aemulari,* to rival].

e·mul·sion (i·mul′·shạn) *n.* a liquid mixture in which a fatty or oily substance is suspended in water and by aid of a mucilaginous medium forms a smooth milky white fluid; the coating of silver salts on a photographic film or plate. **emulsic** *a.* **emulsification** *n.* **emulsify** *v.t.* **emulsive** *a.* yielding a milk-like substance [L. *e,* out; *mulgere,* to milk].

en (en) *n.* a printer's unit of measurement equal to half an em [See **em**].

en- *prefix* in; with; or adding transitive or causal force in verb composition.

en·a·ble (in·ā′·bl) *v.t.* to make able; to authorize to empower; to fit; to qualify.

en·act (in·akt′) *v.t.* to make into a law; to act the part of. **-ing** *a.* **-ive** *a.* **-ment** *n.* the passing of a bill into law; a decree; a law.

e·nam·el (i·nam′·l) *n.* a vitreous compound fused into surface of metal, pottery, or glass for utility and ornament; the hard, glossy surface of teeth; paint with glossy finish; *v.t.* to enamel [Fr. *émail,* enamel].

en·am·or (in·am′·ẹr) *v.t.* to inflame with love; to captivate; to charm; to fascinate.

en·camp (in·kamp′) *v.t.* to form into a camp; *v.i.* to settle in or pitch a camp; to settle down temporarily. **-ment** *n.* an encamping; camp site.

en·case See **incase.**

en·caus·tic (en·kaws′·tik) *a.* pertaining to the fixing of colors by burning; *n.* an ancient style of decorative art, consisting in painting on heated wax [Gk. *en,* in; *kaustikos,* burnt].

en·ceinte (en·sānt′) *a.* pregnant; with child; *n.* the precincts within the walls of a fort [Fr.]

en·ceph·a·lon (en·sef′·ạ·lȧn) *n.* the brain. **encephalic** *a.* cerebral; relating to the brain. **encephalitis** *n.* inflammation of the brain. [Gk. *en,* in; *kephalē,* the head].

en·chain (en·chān′) *v.t.* to fasten with a chain; to hold fast. **-ment** *n.*

en·chant (in·chant′) *v.t.* to charm by sorcery; to hold, as by a spell. **-ed** *a.* delighted; held by a spell. **-er** *n.* (*fem.* **-ress**) one who enchants; a sorcerer. **-ingly** *adv.* **-ment** *n.* act of enchanting; incantation; magic; delight; fascination [Fr. *enchanter*].

en·chase (en·chās′) *v.t.* to adorn with chased work; to set with jewels. **-d** *a.*

en·cir·cle (in·sur′·kl) *v.t.* to enclose in a circle; to surround. **-ment** *n.*

en·clave (en′·klāv) *n.* a country, e.g. Switzerland, or an outlying province of a country, entirely surrounded by territories of another power; anything entirely enclosed into something else [L. *in; clavis,* a key].

en·clit·ic (en·klit′·ik) *n.* a word or particle united, for pronunciation, to another word so as to seem a part of it, e.g. *thee* in *prithee* [Gk. *en,* in; *klinein,* to lean].

en·close, inclose (in·klōz′) *v.t.* to shut in; to surround; to envelope; to contain. **enclosure** *n.*

en·co·mi·um (en·kō′·mi·ạm) *n.* high commendation; formal praise. *pl.* **-s, encomia. encomiast** *n.* eulogist. **encomiastic(al)** *a.* **encomiastically** *adv.* [Gk.].

en·com·pass (in·kum′·pạs) *v.t.* to include; to contain; to encircle. **-ment** *n.*

en·core (ang′·kōr) *interj.* again! once more! *n.* a recall awarded by an audience to a performer, artiste, etc.; the item repeated; *v.t.* to applaud with encore [Fr. = again].

en·coun·ter (in·koun′·tẹr) *v.t.* to meet face to face; to meet unexpectedly; to meet in a hostile manner; to contend against; to confront; *n.* an unexpected meeting; a fight or combat [Fr. *encontrer*].

en·cour·age (in·kur′·ij) *v.t.* to give courage to; to inspire with hope; to embolden. **-ment** *n.* that which gives courage; act of encouraging.

encouraging *a.* [Fr. *encourager*].

en·croach (in·krōch′) *v.i.* to invade the rights or possessions of another; to intrude on other's property. **-er** *n.* **-ingly** *adv.* **-ment** *n.* [Fr. *accrocher*, to hook on].

en·crust, encrustation See **incrust.**

en·cum·ber (in·kum′·bẹr) *v.t.* to load; to impede; to burden; to saddle with debts. **encumbrance** *n.* a burden; a dependent person; a legal claim on an estate [Fr. *encombrer*].

en·cyc·li·cal (en·sik′·li·kl) *a.* intended to circulate among many people and in many places; *n.* an encyclical letter, a letter addressed by the Pope to the bishops of the R.C. Church. Also **encyclic** [Gk. *en*, in; *kuklos*, a circle].

en·cy·clo·pe·di·a, encyclopaedia (en·sī·kla·pē′·di·ạ) *n.* works which give detailed account, in alphabetical order, of whole field of human knowledge, or of some particular section in it. **encyclopedian** *a.* embracing all forms of knowledge. **encyclopedic** *a.* having universal knowledge; full of information. **encyclopedist** *n.* a compiler of an encyclopedia [Gk. *enkuklios paideia*, all around education].

en·cyst (en·sist′) *v.t.* or *v.i.* to enclose or become enclosed in a sac or cyst.

end (end) *n.* the extreme point of a line; the last part in general; termination; conclusion; limit; extremity; final condition; issue; consequence; result; object; purpose; aim; death; a fragment; *v.t.* to bring to an end or conclusion; to destroy; to put to death; *v.i.* to come to the ultimate point; to finish; to be finished; to cease. **-ed** *a.* **-ing** *n.* termination; conclusion; the terminating syllable or letter of a word; suffix. **-less** *a.* **-lessly** *adv.* **-lessness** *n.* **at loose ends,** bored. **at one's wits' end,** perplexed; unable to proceed. **to make both ends meet,** to keep out of debt; to balance income and expenditure [O.E. *ende*].

en·dan·ger (in·dān′·jẹr) *v.t.* to place in jeopardy; to expose to loss or injury.

en·dear (in·dēr′) *v.t.* to render dear or more beloved. **-ed** *a.* **-ing** *a.* **-ingly** *adv.* **-ment** *n.* the state of being, or act of, endearing; tender affection; loving word; a caress.

en·deav·or (in·dev′·ẹr) *v.i.* to exert all strength for accomplishment of object; to attempt; to strive; *n.* attempt; effort; struggle [Fr. *devoir*, duty].

en·dem·ic, endemical (en·dem′·ik, -al) *a.* terms applied to recurring diseases confined to certain people or localities and which arise from local causes. **endemic** *n.* an endemic disease [Gk. *en*, in *dēmos*, a people].

en·dive (en′·dīv, ȧn·dēv′) *n.* an annual plant of the family *Compositae*, used for salads [Fr.].

en·do- (en′·dō) *prefix* indicating *within* [Gk. *endon*].

en·do·car·di·tis (en·dō·kȧr·dī′·tis) *n.* (*Med.*) inflammation of the lining membrane of the heart [Gk. *endon*, within; *kardia*, heart].

en·do·car·di·um (en·dạ·kȧr′·di·ạm) *n.* the lining membrane of the heart. **endocardiac** *a.* **endocardial** *a.*

en·do·crine (en′·dạ·krin) *a.* (*Zool.*) describing the tissues and organs giving rise to an internal secretion; *n.* any such secretion. **endocrinology** *n.* study of internal secretions of ductless glands [Gk. *endon*, within; *krinein*, to separate].

en·dog·a·my (en·dȧg′·ạ·mi·) *n.* the custom of compulsory marriage within the limits of a tribe or clan or between members of the same race. **endogamous** *a.* [Gk. *endon*, within; *gamos*, marriage].

en·do·plasm (en′·dạ·plazm) *n.* inner portion of cytoplasm of a cell [Gk. *endon*, within; *plasma*, a formation].

en·dorse, indorse (in·dors′) *v.t.* to write (esp. to sign one's name) on back of, as a check; to back (a bill, etc.); to sanction; to confirm; to vouch for; to ratify; **endorsable** *a.* **endorsee** *n.* the person to whom a bill of exchange, etc. is assigned by endorsement. **-ment** *n.* act of endorsing. **-r** *n.* [Fr. *endosser*, fr. *dos*, back; L. *dorsum*].

en·do·scope (en′·dạ·skōp) *n.* (*Med.*) an instrument for inspecting the cavities of internal parts of the body [Gk. *endon*, within; *skopein*, to see].

en·do·sperm (en′·dō·spurm) *n.* (*Bot.*) the nutritive starchy tissue which surrounds the embryo in many seeds. **-ic** *a.* [Gk. *endon*, within; *sperma*, seed].

en·dow (in·dou′) *v.t.* to settle, by deed or will, a permanent income on; to enrich or furnish. **-er** *n.* **-ment** *n.* the act of settling a fund or permanent provision for an institution or individual; grant; bequest; natural capacity [O Fr. *endouer*].

en·dure (in·door′) *v.t.* to remain firm under; to bear with patience; to put up with; to sustain; to suffer; to tolerate; *v.i.* to continue; to last. **endurable** *a.* can be endured, borne, or suffered. **endurableness** *n.* **endurably** *adv.* **endurance** *n.* power of enduring; act of bearing pain or distress; continuance; patience; fortitude; stamina. **-r** *n.* **enduring** *a.* and *n.* **enduringly** *adv.* [L. *indurare;* fr. *durus*, hard].

en·e·ma (en′·ạ·mạ) *n.* a liquid solution injected into intestine through rectum; device for this [Gk. fr. *en*, in; *hienai*, to send].

en·e·my (en′·ạ·mi·) *n.* one actuated by hostile feelings; an armed foe; opposing state; something harmful; *a.* of an enemy; due to an enemy [Fr. *ennemi*, fr. L. *inimicus*].

en·er·gy (en′·ẹr·ji·) *n.* vigor; force; activity; (*Mech.*) the power of doing mechanical work; **energetic(al)** *a.* exerting force; vigorous; active; forcible. **energetically** *adv.* **energize** *v.t.* to give energy to; *v.i.* to act energetically [Gk. *energeia*, activity].

en·er·vate (en′·ẹr·vāt) *v.t.* to deprive of nerve, strength, or courage; *a.* spiritless. **enervating, enervative** *a.* **enervation** *n.* [L. *enervare*, to deprive of sinew].

en·fee·ble (in·fē′·bl) *v.t.* to render feeble.

en·fi·lade (en·fạ·lād′) *n.* a line or straight passage; narrow line, as of troops in marching; fire from either flank along a line; *v.t.* to direct enfilading fire [Fr. *enfiler*, to string on a thread].

en·fold See **infold.**

en·force (in·fōrs′) *v.t.* to give strength to; to put in force; to impress on mind; to compel; to impose (action) upon; to urge on; to execute. **-able** *a.* **enforcedly** *adv.* under threat or compulsion. **-ment** *n.* [O.Fr. enforcer].

en·fran·chise (en·fran′·chīz) *v.t.* to set free from slavery; to extend political rights to; to grant the privilege of voting. **-ment** *n.*

en·gage (in·gāj′) *v.t.* to bind by contract, pledge, or promise; to hire; to order; to employ; to undertake; to occupy; to busy; to attract; to bring into conflict; to interlock; *v.i.* to begin to fight; to employ oneself (in); to promise. **-d** *a.* **-ment** *n.* act of engaging; state of being engaged; obligation by contract or agreement; pledge; betrothal; occupation; affair of business or pleasure; battle; encounter. **engaging** *a.* attractive; pleasing [Fr. *engager*].

en·gen·der (in·jen′·dẹr) *v.t.* to beget; to cause to exist; to sow the seeds of; to breed; to occasion or cause (strife) [Fr. *engendrer*].

en·gine (en′·jạn) *n.* any mechanical contrivance for producing and conveying motive power; a machine; *a.* **engineer** *n.* one who constructs, designs, or is in charge of engines, military works, or works of public utility (roads, docks, etc.); *v.t.* to direct or design work as a skilled engineer; to contrive; to bring about; to arrange. **engineering** *n.* the art of constructing and using machines or engines; the profession of an engineer. [Fr. *engin*, fr. L. *ingenium*, skill].

Eng·lish (ing′·glish) *a.* belonging to England

or its inhabitants; *n.* the people or the language of England; *v.t.* to anglicize. **-man** *n.* **Old English,** language to about 1150 A.D. **Middle English,** 1150-1500. **Modern English,** from 1500. **Basic English,** a skeleton form of the English language of less than a thousand words [O.E. *Englisc,* fr. *Engle,* Angle].

en·gorge (en·gawrj′) *v.t.* to swallow greedily and in large quantities; *v.i.* to feed with voracity; to devour. **-ment** *n.* [Fr. *engorger,* fr. *gorge,* the throat].

en·graft, ingraft (en·graft′) *v.t.* to graft on; to incorporate; to add to. **-ation** *n.* **-ment** *n.*

en·grain See **ingrain.**

en·grave (in·grāv′) *v.t.* to draw on a metal plate a design or picture by means of an incised line or on wood by leaving a raised surface; to imprint; to make a deep impression; *v.i.* to practice the art of engraving. **-r** *n.* **engraving** *n.* the art of cutting designs, etc. on wood, metal, or stone; an impression on art paper taken from an engraved block or plate; a print [See **grave**].

en·gross (in·grōs′) *v.t.* to occupy wholly; to absorb; to copy in a large fair hand or in legal form; to buy wholesale with a view to cornering the market; to monopolize. **-er** *n.* **-ing** *n.* **-ment** *n.* [Fr. *en gros,* in a large hand].

en·gulf, ingulf (in·gulf′) *v.t.* to swallow up or absorb as in a gulf; to encompass wholly.

en·hance (in·hans′) *v.t.* to intensify; to increase in value or worth; to add to the effect. **-ment** *n.* [Fr. *hausser,* to raise].

en·har·mon·ic, enharmonical (en·hȧr·mȧn′·ik, -al) *a.* (*Mus.*) having the same pitch but written in different notation, as G♯ and A♭; pert. to one of the three ancient Greek scales, the others being diatonic and chromatic [Gk, *en,* in; *harmonia,* harmony].

e·nig·ma (i·nig′·mạ) *n.* an obscure question or saying difficult of explanation; anything or anybody puzzling; a riddle. **-tic(al)** *a.* **-tically** *adv.* [Gk. *ainigma*].

en·jamb·ment (in·jam′·mạnt) *n.* in verse, continuation of a sentence from one line into the next [Fr. *en,* in; *jambe,* leg].

en·join (in·join′) *v.t.* to direct with authority; to order; to impose; to prescribe; (*Law*) to prohibit by judicial order; to put an injunction on. **-ment** *n.* [Fr. *enjoindre*].

en·joy (in·joi′) *v.t.* to delight in; to take pleasure in; to have the use or benefit of. **-able** *a.* pleasurable. **-ably** *adv.* **-ment** *n.* [Fr. *joie*].

en·large (in·lȧrj′) *v.t.* and *v.i.* to make or become larger; to broaden. **-d** *a.* **-ment** *n.* act of enlarging; expansion; an enlarged reproduction.

en·light·en (in·lit′·n) *v.t.* to give information to; to instruct; to make clear; to free from superstition, etc. **-ment** *n.* act of enlightening; state of being enlightened; intellectual revival in Europe during 18th cent.

en·list (in·list′) *v.t.* to enter on a list; to enroll; to secure support of; *v.i.* to engage in public service, as soldiers; to enter heartily into a cause. **-ment** *n.*

en·liv·en (in·līv′·ạn) *v.t.* to give life, action, or motion to; to quicken; to make gay. **-er** *n.*

en masse (en mas′, ȧn mȧs′) in a group [Fr.].

en·mesh, immesh, inmesh (en·mesh′) *v.t.* to catch in a mesh or net; to entangle; to trap.

en·mi·ty (en′·mạ·ti·) *n.* the quality of being an enemy; hostile or unfriendly disposition; hatred; rancour; hostility [Fr. *inimitié*].

en·noble (en·nō′·bl) *v.t.* to make noble; to raise to the peerage; to exalt; to dignify **-ment** *n.*

en·nui (ȧn′·wē) *n.* boredom; listlessness due to satiety or lack of interest.

e·nor·mous (i·nawr′·mạs) *a.* huge; vast; prodigious; immense; atrocious. **enormity** *n.* quality of being enormous; great wickedness; atrocity. **-ly** *adv.* **-ness** *n.* [L. *enormis,* abnormal].

e·nough (i·nuf′) *a.* as much or as many as need be; sufficient; adequate. *n.* a sufficiency; as much as satisfies conditions; *adv.* sufficiently; fully [O.E. *genog*].

e·nounce (ē·nouns′) *v.t.* to state; to declare; to pronounce; to proclaim. **-ment** *n.* [L. *enuntiare,* to declare].

en·quire, enquiry See **inquire, inquiry.**

en·rage (in·rāj′) *v.t.* to fill with rage; to provoke to frenzy or madness; to anger immoderately. **-d** *a.*

en·rapture (in·rap′·chẹr) *v.t.* to transport with pleasure, to delight excessively; to charm. **-d, enrapt** *a.*

en·rich (in·rich′) *v.t.* to make rich; to add to; to enhance; to embellish. **-ment** *n.*

en·robe (en·rōb′) *v.t.* to dress; to clothe.

en·roll (in·rōl′) *v.t.* to enter a name in a roll or register; to enlist; to record. *pa.t.* **-ment** *n.* the act of enrolling; number of persons enrolled [Fr. *enrôler*].

en·sconce (en·skȧns′) *v.t.* to shelter; to hide securely; to settle snugly [L. *in; condere,* to hide].

en·sem·ble (ȧn·sȧm′bl) *n.* all the parts taken together; general effect; an entire costume; (*Mus.*) concerted playing by a number of musicians; the group of players [Fr. = together].

en·shrine (in·shrīn′) *v.t.* to enclose in a shrine; to treasure with affection. **-ment** *n.*

en·shroud (en·shroud′) *v.t.* to shroud; to hide from view.

en·sign (en′·sīn) *n.* a badge of rank or insignia of office; a flag or banner; an emblem; (*U.S. Navy*) the lowest commissioned officer. **-cy, -ship** *n.* rank of an ensign [Fr. *enseigne.*]

en·sil·age (en′·sil·ij) *n.* a process of storing crops such as hay, etc. while green, to serve as winter food for cattle; fodder so stored [Fr.].

en·slave (in·slāv′) *v.t.* to reduce to slavery or bondage. **-ed** *a.* **-ment** *n.*

en·snare, insnare (en·snār′) *v.t.* to catch in a snare; to entrap; to entangle.

en·sue (en·so͝o′) *v.i.* to follow; to happen after; to be the consequence of. **ensuing** *a.* [Fr. *ensuivre,* fr. L. *insequi,* to follow up].

en·sure (in·shoor′) *v.t.* to make sure, safe, or certain; to bring about.

en·tail (in·tāl′) *n.* law restricting inheritance of land to a particular heir or line of heirs; a predetermined order of succession; an estate; *v.t.* to settle land on persons in succession, none of whom can then dispose of it; to involve as a result; to bring about or cause. **-ment** *n.* [Fr. *entailler,* to cut into].

en·tan·gle (in·tang′·gl) *v.t.* to twist or interweave so as not to be easily separated; to perplex; to ensnare. **-ment** *n.*

en·tente (ȧn·tȧnt′) *n.* cordial agreement or understanding; the nations or parties involved [Fr.].

en·ter (en′·tẹr) *v.t.* to go or come into; to pass within; to pierce; to penetrate; to invade; to join (a society, etc.); to put down one's name; *v.i.* to go or come in; to make a beginning; to take a part or interest in. **to enter on, upon,** to begin [Fr. *entrer*].

en·ter- (en′·tẹr) Gk. *prefix* used in the construction of compound words relating to the intestine. **-a** *n.pl.* **-ic** *a.* of or pertaining to the intestine; **-itis** *n.* inflammation of the intestines [Gk. *enteron,* intestine].

en·ter·prise (en′·tẹr·prīz) *n.* that which is undertaken or attempted; force of character in launching out; daring spirit; a bold attempt; **enterprising** *a.* adventurous; energetic. **enterprisingly** *adv.* [Fr.].

en·ter·tain (en·tẹr·tān′) *v.t.* to receive a guest; to show hospitality to; to lodge; to amuse; to divert; to consider favorably; to cherish; to hold in the mind. **-er** *n.* **-ing** *a.* **-ment** *n.* [Fr. *entretenir*].

en·thrall (en·thrawl′) *v.t.* to thrill; to captivate; to hold spellbound; to reduce to slavery.

en·throne (in·thrōn′) *v.t.* to place on a throne; to raise to sovereignty; to exalt. **-ment** *n.*

en·thu·si·asm (in·thū′·zi·azm) *n.* passionate zeal for a person, object or pursuit; keen interest. **enthusiast** *n.* one who is carried away by enthusiasm. **enthusiastic(al)** *a.* **enthusiastically** *adv.* [Gk. *enthousiasmos*, inspiration].

en·tice (in·tīs′) *v.t.* to draw on by exciting hope or desire; to lead astray. **-able** *a.* **-ment** *n.* act of enticing; that which incites to evil; allurement. **enticing** *a.* **enticingly** *adv.* [O.Fr. *enticier*, to provoke].

en·tire (in·tīr′) *a.* complete in all parts; whole; unimpaired; not castrated. **-ly** *adv.* **-ness, -ty** *n.* completeness [Fr. *entier*, fr. L. *integer*].

en·ti·tle (in·tī′·tl) *v.t.* to give a title to; to name; to qualify; to fit for; to give claim to; O.Fr. *entiteler*].

en·ti·ty (en′·tạ·ti·) *n.* a real being; reality; existence; a material substance [L.L. *entitas*, fr. *esse*, to be].

en·tomb (in·tòòm′) *v.t.* to deposit in a tomb; to inter; to bury. **-ment** *n.*

en·to·mol·o·gy (en·tạ·mál′·ạ·ji·) *n.* scientific study, classification, and collection of insects. **entomological** *a.* **entomologically** *adv.* **entomologize** *v.t.* to pursue the study of insects. **entomologist** *n.* [Gk. *entomon*, insect; *logos*, a discourse].

en·tou·rage (àn·tòò·ràzh′) *n.* surroundings; one's habitual associates; retinue [Fr.].

en·tr'acte (àn·trakt′) *n.* the interval or musical interlude between two acts of a play [Fr.].

en·trails (en′·trạlz) *n.pl.* the bowels; the intestines; the internal parts of anything [Fr.].

en·train (in·trān′) *v.t.* to enter or put into a railway train.

en·trance (en′·trans) *n.* the act of entering; right of access; a door, gateway, or passage to enter by; the beginning. **entrant** *n.* one who enters; a competitor.

en·trance (in·trạns′) *v.t.* to put into a trance; to ravish with delight and wonder. **-ment** *n.* **entrancing** *a.*

en·trap (in·trap′) *v.t.* to catch, as in a trap; to ensnare. **-ment** *n.*

en·treat (in·trēt′) *v.t.* to ask earnestly; to implore; *v.i.* to make an earnest request. **-y** *n.* act of entreating; supplication [O.Fr. *entraiter*].

en·tree (àn′·trā) *n.* right of access; a dish served before the main course, as a main course, or between main courses (used mostly now as a term for the main course); right of access [Fr.].

en·trench, intrench (in·trench′) *v.t.* to dig a trench; to surround, fortify as with a trench; *v.i.* to encroach. **-ment** *n.* a ditch or trench; any fortification or defense.

en·tre·pre·neur (àn·trạ·prạ·nur′) *n.* a contractor; an organizer of business, trade, or entertainment [Fr. *entreprendre*, to undertake].

en·trust, intrust (in·trust′) *v.t.* to charge with a responsibility; to confide to the care of.

en·try (en′·tri·) *n.* the act of entering; a place to enter by; an item noted down in a ledger, catalogue, or notebook; one entered in a contest [Fr. *entrer*].

en·twine, intwine (in·twīn′) *v.t.* to twist together; to plait; to encircle.

e·nu·mer·ate (i·nòò′·mạ·rāt) *v.t.* to count, one by one; to give in detail; to count. **enumeration** *n.* **enumerator** *n.* [L. *enumerare*, to number off].

e·nun·ci·ate (i·nun′·si·āt) *v.t.* to state clearly; to proclaim; to announce; to pronounce each syllable distinctly. **enunciable** *a.* **enunciation** *n.* the act of enunciating; articulation or pronunciation; a declaration or announcement. **enunciator** *n.* [L. *e*, out; *nuntiare*, to announce].

en·ure See **inure.**

en·vel·op (in·vel′·ạp) *v.t.* to cover by folding or wrapping; to surround. **envelope** (en′·vạ·lōp) *n.* a cover or wrapper, esp. the cover of a letter. **-ment** *n.* [Fr. *envelopper*].

en·ven·om (en·ven′·ạm) *v.t.* to impregnate with venom; to poison; to embitter.

en·vi·a·ble, envious See **envy.**

en·vi·ron (in·vī′·rạn) *v.t.* to surround; to encompass; to encircle; to envelop. **-ment** *n.* that which environs; external conditions which determine modifications in the development of organic life. **-s** *n.pl.* adjacent districts; neighborhood; suburbs [Fr. = about].

en·vis·age (en·viz′·ij) *v.t.* to look in the face of; to face; to imagine; to visualize [Fr. *envisager*].

en·voy (en′·voi) *n.* a diplomatic agent of a country below the rank of ambassador; messenger [Fr. *envoyer*, to send].

en·voy, envoi (en′·voi) *n.* an author's postscript, esp. in an additional stanza of a poem.

en·vy (en′·vi·) *v.t.* to grudge another person's good fortune; to feel jealous of; *pr.p.* **-ing;** *pa.p.* **envied.** *n.* pain or vexation excited by the sight of another's superiority or success; jealousy. **enviable** *a.* **envious** *a.* full of envy. **enviously** *adv.* [Fr. *envie*].

en·wrap, inwrap (en·rap′) *v.t.* to wrap up; to envelop; to engross.

en·wreathe, inwreathe (en·rēTH′) *v.t.* to encircle, as with a wreath.

en·zyme, enzym (en′·zīm) *n.* a complex organic substance which in solution produces fermentation and chemical change in other substances apparently without undergoing any change itself; a form of catalyst; digestive ferment. **enzymetic** *a.* [Gk. *en*, in; *zumē*, leaven].

E·o·li·an, Eolic See **Aeolian, Aeolic.**

e·o·lith (ē′·ạ·lith) *n.* the oldest known stone implement used by pre-historic men **-ic** *a.* pertaining to the earliest stage of human culture [Gk. *eos*, dawn; *lithos*, stone].

eon See **aeon.**

e·pact (ē′·pakt) *n.* the excess of a solar over a lunar month or year in number of days [Gk. *epagein*, to intercalate].

ep·au·let, epaulette (ep′·ạ·let) *n.* an ornamental shoulder-piece or badge of rank [Fr. *épaule*, shoulder].

é·pée (ā·pā′) *n.* a dueling sword with a sharp point but no cutting edge, used in fencing [Fr.].

e·pergne (i·purn′) *n.* an ornamental piece for center of table [Fr.].

ep·ex·a·ge·sis (ep·eks·ạ·jē′·sis) *n.* a further explanation of a previous statement. **epexegetic, epexegetical** *a.* [Gk. *epi*, further; and *exegesis*].

e·phed·rine (ef′·ạ·drēn) *n.* an alkaloid drug, derived from plants of the genus *Ephedra* [Gk. *ephedra*].

e·phem·er·a (i·fem′·ẹr·ạ) *n.* anything of temporary interest and value; a genus of insects, better known as May flies, which as adults, live only for one day; *pl.* **ephemerae. -l** *a.* lasting only a very short period of time; transitory. [Gk. *epi*, for; *hēmera*, a day].

e·phem·er·is (i·fem′·ẹr·is) *n.* (*Astron.*) a table or calendar giving for successive days the positions of heavenly bodies; *pl.* **ephemerides** [Gk. *epi*, for; *hēmera*, a day].

epi- Gk. *prefix* meaning upon, at, in addition to, etc., used in the construction of compound terms.

ep·ic (ep′·ik) *n.* a long narrative poem in the grand style, usually dealing with the adventures of great soldiers or heroes whose deeds are part of the history of a nation; a worthy subject for such a poem; *a.* in the grand style; lofty in conception; memorable; heroic [Gk. *epos*, a word].

ep·i·car·di·um (ep·i·kar′·di·ạm) *n.* (*Med.*) the serous membrane of the pericardium, the sac which envelops the heart. **epicardial** *a.* [Gk. *epi*, upon; *kardia*, the heart].

ep·i·cene (ep′·ạ·sēn) *a.* common to both sexes; (*Gram.*) of common gender, of nouns with but one form for both genders, e.g. sheep; *n.* a person having characteristics of both sexes; a hermaphrodite.

ep·i·cen·ter (ep′·ạ·sen·tẹr) *n.* the point on the upper crust of the earth below which an earthquake has originated.

ep·i·crit·ic (ep·a·krit′·ik) *a.* pert. to fine sensitivity, e.g. to the slightest sensation of heat or touch.

Ep·i·cu·rus (ep′·i·kyoor·ạs) *n.* a Greek philosopher (342-270 B.C.), the founder of the Epicurean school. **epicure** *n.* one with a refined taste in food and dring; one who applies himself to gross sensualism, esp. the delights of the table. **epicurean** *a.* *n.* a follower of Epicurus; a sensualist. **epicureanism** *n.* the doctrine that the chief end of man was physical and mental happiness.

ep·i·cy·cle (ep′·ạ·sī·kl) *n.* a circle whose center moves round in the circumference of a greater circle [Gk. *epi*, upon; *kuklos*, a wheel].

ep·i·dem·ic, epidemical (ep·ạ·dem′·ik, ·ạl) *a.* common to, or affecting a whole people or community; prevalent; general; prevailing for a time. **epidemic** *n.* the temporary appearance of infectious disease attacking whole communities [Gk. *epi*, among; *dēmos*, the people].

ep·i·der·mis (ep·ạ·dur′·mis) *n.* (*Anat.*) the outer protective layer of skin, otherwise the scarf skin, which covers the dermis or true skin underneath; (*Bot.*) a sheath, usually one cell in thickness, which forms a layer over surface of leaves. **epidermatoid, epidermic, epidermal, epidermidal** *a.* [Gk. *epi*, upon; *derma*, the skin].

ep·i·glot·tis (ep·ạ·glȧt′·is) *n.* a covering of elastic, cartilaginous tissue, which closes the opening leading into the larynx during the act of swallowing. **epiglottic** *a.* [Gk. *epi*, upon; *glotta*, the tongue].

ep·i·gram (ep′·ạ·gram) *n.* a neat, witty, pointed saying; originally an epitaph couched in verse form, and developed by the Latin epigrammatists into a short poem designed to display their wit. **-matic, -matical** *a.* **matically** *adv.* **-matize** *v.t.* **-matist** *n.* [Gk. *epi*, on; *gramma*, a writing].

ep·i·graph (ep′·ạ·graf) *n.* an inscription, esp. on a building, statue, etc.; an appropriate motto or saying at the beginning of a book or chapter [Gk. *epi*, upon; *graphein*, to write].

ep·i·lep·sy (ep′·ạ·lep·si·) *n.* a nervous disease characterized by sudden convulsions and unconsciousness, followed by temporary stoppage of breath and rigidity of the body. **epileptic** *n.* one subject to epilepsy [Gk. *epilēpsis*, seizure].

ep·i·logue (ep′·ạ·lawg) *n.* a short speech or poem recited at the end of a play; conclusion of a literary work [Gk. *epi*, upon; *logos*, speech].

E·piph·an·y (i·pif′·ạn·i·) *n.* a Church festival held on the twelfth day after Christmas; the manifestation of a god [Gk. *epi*, to; *phainein*, to show].

ep·i·phyte (ep′·i·fīt) *n.* a plant which grows on but does not draw nourishment from another plant [Gk. *epi*, upon; *phuton*, a plant].

e·pis·co·pa·cy (i·pis′·kạ·pạs·i·) *n.* the government of the church by bishops; the office of a bishop; prelacy; the body of bishops. **episcopal** *a.* belonging to or vested in bishops; governed by bishops. **episcopalian** *a.* of an episcopal system or church; *n.* a member or adherent of an episcopal church. **episcopalianism** *n.* the system of church government by bishops. **episcopally** *adv.* **episcopate** *n.* a bishopric; the office or order of bishop [Gk. *episkopos*, overseer].

ep·i·sode (ep′·ạ·sōd) *n.* an incident; an incidental narrative or series of events; a digression, only remotely relevant to the plot of a play or novel; (*Mus.*) an intermediate passage between various parts of a fugue. **episodal, episodic, episodical** *a.* **episodically** *adv.* [Gk. *epeisodion*, the part of a play between choral songs].

e·pis·tle (i·pis′·l) *n.* a letter, usually of the less spontaneous type, written for effect or for instruction, as the epistles of the New Testament. **epistolary** *a.* [Gk. *epistolē*].

ep·i·taph (ep′·ạ·taf) *n.* an inscription placed on a tombstone or cenotaph in commemoration of the dead [Gk. *epi*, upon; *taphos*, tomb].

ep·i·tha·la·mi·um (ep·i·thạ·lā′·mi·ạm) *n.* a nuptial song.

ep·i·the·li·um (ep·i·thē′·li·ạm) *n.* cellular tissue covering cutaneous, mucous, and serous surfaces [Gk. *epi*, upon; *thēlē*, a nipple].

ep·i·thet (ep′·ạ·thet) *n.* phrase or word used adjectivally to express some quality or attribute of its object; a designation; title; appellation. **epithetic, -al** *a.* [Gk. *epithetos*, added].

e·pit·o·me (i·pit′·ạ·mē) n. a brief summary; an abridgement of a book; abstract; synopsis; digest. **epitomize** *v.t.* to make or be a short abstract of [Gk. fr. *epitemnein*, to cut into].

e·poch (ep′·ạk) *n.* a fixed point or duration of time from which succeeding years are reckoned, as being specially marked by notable events; era; date; period; age. **-al** *a.* [Gk. *epochē*, a stop].

eq·ua·ble (ek′·wạ·bl) *a.* uniform in action or intensity; not variable; of unruffled temperament. **equability, -ness** *n.* **equably** *adv.* [L. *aequabilis*].

e·qual (ē′·kwạl) *a.* having the same magnitude, dimensions, value, degree, or the like; identical; equable; tantamount (to); not lop-sided; *n.* a person of the same rank, age, etc.; *v.t.* to be or make equal. **-ization** *n.* **-ize** *v.t.* to make or become equal. **-itarian** *n.* one who holds that all men are equal in status. **-ity** *n.* the state of being equal. **-ly** *adv.* [L. *aequus*, equal].

e·qua·nim·i·ty (ē·kwạ·nim′·ạ·ti·) *n.* evenness of mind or temper; composure; calmness [L. *aequus*, even; *animus*, mind].

e·quate (i·kwāt′) *v.t.* to make or treat as equal; to state or assume the equality of. **equation** *n.* the act of making equal; allowance for any inaccuracies; (*Math.*) an expression of the equality of two like algebraic magnitudes or functions by using the sign of equality (=) **equational** *a.* **equationally** *adv.* [L. *aequus*, equal].

e·qua·tor (i·kwā′·tẹr) *n.* a great circle supposed to be drawn round the earth 90° from each pole and dividing the globe into the N. & S. hemispheres; (*Astron.*) the celestial equator, another name for the equinoctial. **equatorial** *a.* of or pertaining to the equator; *n.* an astronomical telescope, so mounted that it automatically follows the diurnal course taken by the heavenly body under observation. **equatorially** *adv.* [L. *aequus*, equal].

eq·uer·ry (ek′·wẹr·i·) *n.* one charged with the care of horses; an officer whose duty it is to accompany the sovereign or royal prince when riding in state [Fr. *écurie*, stable].

e·ques·tri·an (i·kwes′·tri·ạn) *a.* pertaining to horses or horsemanship; mounted on a horse; *n.* (*fem.* **equestrienne**) a rider or circus-performer on a horse. **-ism** *n.* [L. *equus*, a horse].

e·qui- *prefix* fr. L. *aequus*, equal, used in the construction of compound words.

e·qui·an·gu·lar (ē·kwi·ang′·gyạ·lẹr) *a.* having equal angles.

e·qui·dis·tance (ē·kwạ·dis′·tạns) *n.* an equal distance from some point. **equidistant** *a.*

e·qui·lat·er·al (ē·kwạ·lat′·ẹr·ạl) *a.* having all the sides equal.

e·qui·li·brate (ē·kwạ·lī′·brāt) *v.t.* to balance exactly; to equipoise. **equilibrant** *n.* (*Phys.*) the single force which will balance any system of forces or produce equilibrium when used in conjunction with these forces. **equilibration** *n.* **equilibrator** *n.* in aviation the stabilizing fin which controls the balance of an airplane [L. *aequus*, equal; *libra*, a balance].

e·qui·lib·ri·um (ē·kwạ·lib′·ri·ạm) *n.* (*Mech.*) the state of rest of a body produced by action and reaction of a system of forces; equipoise;

a state of balance [L. *aequus*, equal; *libra*, a balance].

e·quine, equinal (e′·kwīn, ·ạl) *a.* pert. to a horse; *n.* a horse [L. *equis*, a horse].

e·qui·noc·tial (ē·kwạ·nȧk′·shạl) *a.* pert. to the equinoxes; *n.* (*Astron.*) a great circle in the heavens corresponding to the plane of the equator when extended (cf. **equinox**).

e·qui·nox (e′·kwạ·noks) *n.* the time at which the sun crosses the plane of the equator, approx. March 21 and Sept. 22, and day and night are equal; *pl.* [L. *aequus*, equal; *nox*, night].

e·quip (i·kwip′) *v.t.* to fit out; to supply with all requisites for service; to furnish; to array; to dress; *pr.p.* **-ping.** *pa.p., pa.t.* **-ped. equipage** (ek′·wi·pij) *n.* furniture, especially the furniture and supplies of a vessel or army; a carriage, horses and attendants; accoutrements. **-ment** *n.* act of equipping; the state of being equipped; outfit, especially a soldier's; apparatus [Fr. *équiper*].

e·qui·poise (e′·kwạ·poiz) *n.* the state of equality of weight or force; even balance.

eq·ui·ta·ble (ek′·wit·ạ·bl) *a.* giving, or disposed to give, each his due; just. **-ness** *n.* **equitably** *adv.* fairly; justly [L. *aequus*, equal].

eq·ui·ta·tion (ek·wi·tā′·shạn) *n.* skill in horsemanship; a ride on horseback [Fr. fr. L. *equus*, a horse].

eq·ui·ty (ek′·wạ·ti·) *n.* fairness; equal adjustment or distribution; giving to each his due according to the sense of natural right [L. *aequitas*].

e·quiv·a·lent (i·kwiv′·ạ·lạnt) *a.* and *n.* equal in value, power, import, etc.; (*Chem.*) of equal valency. **equivalence** *n.* identical value; state or condition of being equivalent. **equivalency** *n.* [L. *aequus*, equal; *valere*, to be worth].

e·quiv·o·cal (i·kwiv′·ạ·kạl) *a.* of double or doubtful meaning; questionable; ambiguous; doubtful; dubious. **-ly** *adv.* **-ness** *n.* **equivocate** *v.i.* to use words of doubtful signification to mislead; to prevaricate. **equivocation** *n.* **equivocator** *n.* [L. *aequus*, equal; *vox, vocis*, a voice].

e·ra (ēr′·ạ) *n.* a fixed point of time from which a series of years is reckoned; epoch; time; age; a memorable date or period [L. *aera*, counters, used in computation].

e·rad·i·cate (i·rad′·i·kāt) *v.t.* to pull up by the roots; to extirpate; to destroy. **eradicable** *a.* **eradication** *n.* [L. *e*, out; *radix*, a root].

e·rase (i·rās′) *v.t.* to rub or scrape out; to efface. **erasable** *a.* **-d** *a.* **-r** *n.* one who or that which erases. **-ment** *n.* **erasure** *n.* [L. *e*, out; *radere*, rasum, to scrape].

ere (ār) *adv.* before; sooner; *prep.* before; *conj.* sooner than [O.E. *aer*].

e·rect (i·rekt′) *v.t.* to set upright; to raise, as a building, etc.; to elevate; to construct; *a.* upright; pointing upwards. **-ion** *n.* **-or** *n.* [L. *erectus*, set upright].

erg (urg) *n.* the absolute unit of measurement of work and energy in the metric system; the work done by a force which produces a velocity of a centimeter per second in a mass of one gram [Gk. *ergon*, work].

er·go (ur′·gō) *adv.* therefore; consequently [L.].

er·got (ur′·gạt) *n.* a dried fungus used as a drug to stop bleeding and contract muscles [Fr. = bird's spur].

Er·in (ār′·in) *n.* Ireland.

er·mine (ur′·min) *n.* a member of weasel family the white winter coat of which is highly prized as a fur; the robe of a judge in England and so used as a synonym for *judge* [O.Fr.].

e·rode (i·rōd′) *v.t.* to eat into; to wear away; to corrode. **erodent** *n.* a caustic drug. **erose** *a.* appearing as if gnawed or worn irregularly. **erosion** *n.* act or operation of eating away; corrosion; denudation. **erosive** *a.* [L. *erodere*].

E·ros (ēr′·os, er′·os) *n.* (*Myth.*) the Greek god of love. **erotic** (i·rȧt·ik) *a.* pertaining to love; amatory; *n.* a love poem; **erotics** *n.pl.* science and art of love. **erotica** *n.* literature dealing with sexual love. **eroticism, erotism** *n.* in psycho-analysis, love in all its manifestations [Gk. *eros*, love].

err (ur) *v.i.* to commit a mistake; to be mistaken; to deviate; to go astray; to sin. **-atic(al)** (i·rat′·ik) *a.* roving; wandering; eccentric; changeable; capricious; not dependable. **-atic** *n.* a wanderer; a boulder transported by a glacier or other natural force. **-atically** *adv.* **-atum** *n.* an error in writing or printing. *pl.* **-ata** [L. *errare*, to wander].

er·rand (er′·ạnd) *n.* commission; message [O.E. *aerende*, a message].

er·rant (er′·ạnt) *a.* wandering; roving; wild; abandoned; *n.* a knight-errant. **-ly** *adv.* **-ry** *n.* a state of wandering about, esp. of a knight-errant in search of adventures [L. *errare*, to wander].

erratic, erratum etc. See **err.**

er·ror (er′·ẹr) *n.* a deviation from right or truth; a mistake; blunder; sin. **erroneous** *a.* wrong; incorrect; inaccurate; false. **erroneously** *adv.* **erroneousness** *n.* [L. errare, to wander].

er·satz (er′·zȧts′) *a.* substituted for articles in everyday use; artificial; makeshift [Ger.].

erst (urst) *adv.* (*Arch.*) formerly; of old; hitherto. **-while** *adv.* former [O.E. *aerest*].

e·ruct, e·ruc·tate (i·rukt′, ·tāt) *v.t.* to belch. **eructation** *n.* belching [L. *e*, out; *ructare*, to belch].

er·u·dite (er′·yoo·dīt) *a.* learned; deeply read; scholarly. **-ly** *adv.* **erudition** *n.* learning; scholarship [L. *eruditus*].

e·rupt (i·rupt′) *v.i.* to throw out; to break through; to break out in eruptions. **eruption** *n.* act of bursting forth; outburst of lava, ashes, gas, etc. from the crater of a volcano; a rash on the skin. **eruptive** *a.* breaking forth or out [L. *e*, out; *rumpere*, to burst].

er·y·sip·e·las (er·ạ·sip′·ạ·lạs) *n.* contagious disease causing acute inflammation of the skin [Gk. fr. *eruthos*, red; *pella*, skin].

es·ca·lade (es·kạ·lād′) *n.* mounting the walls of a fortress by means of ladders; *v.t.* to scale [Fr. fr. L. *scala*, a ladder].

es·ca·la·tor (es′·kạ·lā·tẹr) *n.* continuous, moving stairway [L. *scala*, a ladder].

es·cape (e·skāp′) *v.t.* to gain freedom; to evade; to elude; to pass unnoticed; *v.i.* to hasten away; to avoid capture; to become free from danger; *n.* flight from danger; evasion; leakage (of gas, etc.); an outlet for purposes of safety; a garden-plant growing wild and thriving; a conscious effort to forget mental troubles by taking up some other powerful interest. **escapable** *a.* **escapade** *n.* a wild prank or exploit. **-ment** *n.* the act or means of escaping; the contrivance in a time-piece which connects the wheel-work with the pendulum, allowing a tooth to escape at each vibration. **escapism** *n.* morbid desire to escape from the realities of life by concentrating on some other interest. **escapist** *n.* [Fr. *échapper*].

es·carp (es·kȧrp′) *v.t.* to make into a steep slope; *n.* **-ment** *n.* a steep, sloping bank [Fr. *escarper*].

es·cha·tol·o·gy (es·kạ·tȧl′·ạ·ji·) *n.* the department of theology which treats of the last things, such as death, the return of Christ, the resurrection, the end of the world, etc. [Gk. *eschatos*, last; *logos*, discourse].

es·cheat (es·chēt′) *n.* the legal process of property reverting to the crown or government on the tenant's death without heirs; an estate so lapsing; *v.t.* to forfeit; to confiscate; *v.i.* to revert to the crown or lord of the manor [O.Fr. *escheoir*, to fall due].

es·chew (es·chōō′) *v.t.* to shun; to avoid; to abstain from [O.Fr. *eschuer*].

es·cort (es′·kawrt) *n.* an armed guard for a traveller, etc.; a person or persons accompanying another on a journey for protection or as an act of courtesy. **escort** (i·skawrt′) *v.t.* to accompany; to convoy [Fr. *escorte*].

es·cri·toire (es·kri·twȧr′) *n.* a writing-desk provided with drawers [O.Fr. *escriptoire*].

Es·cu·la·pi·an (es·kū·lā′·pi·ạn) *a.* pertaining to the art of healing [*Aesculapius*, in classic mythology, the god of medicine].

es·cu·lent (es′·kyạ·lạnt) *a.* suitable as a food for man; edible; *n.* something which is eatable [L. *esculentus*].

es·cutch·eon (is·kuch′·ạn) *n.* in heraldry, a shield bearing armorial bearings; that part of a vessel's stern on which her name is inscribed; an ornamental plate or shield placed round a keyhole opening. **-ed** *a.* [L. *scutum*, a shield].

Es·ki·mo, Esquimau (es′·kạ·mō) *n.* and *a.* one of an aboriginal people thinly scattered along the northern seaboard of America and Asia and in many of the Arctic islands; *pl.* **Eskimos, Esquimaux** [etym. doubtful].

e·soph·a·gus (ē·sȧf′·ạ·gạs) *n.* the gullet [L. *oesophagus*].

es·o·ter·ic (es·ạ·ter′·ik) *a.* term applied to doctrines intended only for the inner circle of initiates; secret; profound [Gk. *esoterikos*, fr. *eso*, within].

es·pe·cial (ạs·pesh′·ạl) *a.* distinguished; preeminent; more than ordinary; particular. **-ly** *adv.* [O.Fr. *especiel*, fr. L. *species*].

Es·pe·ran·to (es·pạ·rȧn′·tō) *n.* a universal auxiliary language [coined word].

es·pi·o·nage (es′·pi·ȧ·nij or ·nȧzh) *n.* the practice of employing secret agents; spying [Fr. *espion*, a spy].

es·pla·nade (es·plạ·nād) *n.* a level space, esp. for a promenade as along the seafront of a town [Fr.].

es·pouse (ȧs·pouz′) *v.t.* to marry; to support, attach oneself to (a cause, etc.). **espousal** *n.* act of espousing. **espousals** *n.pl.* nuptials. **-r** *n.* [O.Fr. *espouser*].

es·prit (es·prē′) *n.* spirit; wit; liveliness. **esprit de corps** (es·prē·da·kōr′) loyalty and attachment to the group of which one is a member [Fr.].

es·py (ạs·pī′) *v.t.* to catch sight of [Fr. *espier*, to spy out].

-esque (esk) *suffix* in the manner or style of.

es·quire (es′·kwīr) *n.* originally, a squire or shield-bearer, one of two attendants on a knight; now a courtesy title [O.Fr. *escuyer*, fr. L. *scutarius*, a shield-bearer].

es·say (es′·ā) *n.* a literary composition, shorter than a treatise; a trial; an attempt. **essay** *v.t.* to try; to make experiment or trial of; to attempt. **-ist** *n.* a writer of essays [Fr. *essayer*, to try].

es·sence (es′·ạns) *n.* the very being or power of a thing; the formal cause of being; peculiar nature or quality; a being; essential part; a concentration of the active ingredients of a substance in a smaller mass; (*Med.*) a solution of essential oils in rectified alcohol; a perfume. **essential** *a.* belonging to the essence; necessary to the existence of a thing; inherent; *n.* something indispensable; a chief point; a leading principle. **essentiality** *n.* **essentially** *adv.* **essentialness** *n.* [Fr. from L. *esse*, to be].

es·tab·lish (ạs·tab′·lish) *v.t.* to make stable or firm; to set up; to found; to enact or decree by authority; to confirm; to prove; to verify; to substantiate; to set up and endow, as a state church by law. **-ed** *a.* fixed; settled; on the permanent staff; supported by the State. **-er** *n.* **-ment** *n.* act of establishing; that which is established; an institution; settlement; place of business, residence, etc.; the church established by the state. **-mentarian** *a.* and *n.* supporting church establishment [L. *stabilire*, fr. *stare*, to stand].

es·tate (ạs·tāt′) *n.* a piece of landed property; condition of life; rank; position; quality; property, real or personal; the total assets and liabilities of a bankrupt or of a deceased person. **the Three Estates** *n.pl.* in France, nobles, clergy, and middle class. **the Fourth Estate** *n.* (*Colloq.*) the press; journalism. **real —** *n.* property in land [O.Fr. *estat*].

es·teem (ạs·tēm′) *v.t.* to regard with respect or affection; to set a value on; to rate highly; *n.* high regard [L. *aestimare*, to estimate].

es·thet·ic. See **aesthetic.**

es·ti·ma·ble (es′·tạ·mạ·bl) *a.* able to be estimated or esteemed; worthy of regard. **estimably** *adv.* [L. *aestimare*].

es·ti·mate (es′·tạ·māt) *v.t.* to judge and form an opinion of the value, size, weight, etc. of; to compute; to calculate; *v.i.* to offer to complete certain work at a stated cost; *n.* appraisement; conjecture. **estimator** *n.* one who appraises [L. *aestimare*].

es·ti·va·tion, aes·ti·va·tion (es·tạ·vā′·shạn) *n.* a state of torpor, affecting some insects, during the dry summer months. **estival** *a.* pertaining to or continuing throughout the summer aestival. **estivate** *v.i.* (opp. of *hibernate*) [L. *aestus*, summer].

Es·to·ni·an (es·tō′·ni·ạn) *a.* pert. to *Estonia*, a country on the Baltic; the Finnish-Ugrian language.

es·top (es·tȧp′) *v.t.* (*Law*) to impede; to bar by one's own act [Fr. *étouper*, to stop up].

es·trange (ạs·trānj′) *v.t.* to alienate, as the affections; to divert from its original use, purpose, or possessor. **-d** *a.* **-ment** *n.* [O.Fr. *estrangier*, to make strange].

es·tro·gen (es′·trạ·jạn) *n.* any of several female sex hormones [Gk. *oistros*, frenzy; *genes*, born].

es·tu·ar·y (es′·choo·er·i·) *n.* a narrow arm of the sea at the mouth of a river, up which the tides penetrate twice daily. **estuarine** *a.* pert. to an estuary [L. *aestus*, tide].

e·su·ri·ent (ī·soor′·i·ạnt) *a.* hungry; voracious; gluttonous [L. *esuricus*, being hungry].

et cet·er·a (et set′·ęr·ạ) phrase meaning "and the others"; and so on (*abbrev.* **etc.**) [L.].

etch (ech) *v.t.* to make an engraving by eating away the surface of a metal plate with acid; *v.i.* to practice this art. **-er** *n.* one who etches. **-ing** *n.* the act or art of etching; the printed impression taken from an etched plate [Ger. *ätzen*, to eat into].

e·ter·nal (i·tur′·nạl) *a.* without beginning or end in relation to time; everlasting; timeless; immortal; imperishable. **-ize, eternize** *v.t.* to make eternal or immortal; to perpetuate. **-ly** *adv.* **eternity** *n.* the infinity of time; the future state after death [L. *aeternus*].

eth·ane (eth′·ān) *n.* a colorless, odorless, inflammable gas [fr. *ether*].

e·ther (ē′·thęr) *n.* the hypothetical non-material, imponderable medium supposed (in older theory) to permeate the whole of space and to transmit the waves of light, radiant heat, and electromagnetic radiation; the higher regions beyond the earth; (*Chem.*) a volatile liquid, prepared by the action of sulfuric acid on alcohol, used as a solvent and as an anesthetic. **-eal** *a.* pertaining to the ether; celestial; airy; delicate. **-ealization** *n.* **-alize** *v.t.* to render ethereal or spiritual. **-eality** *n.* the quality or state of being ethereal. **-eally** *adv.* [Gk. *aithēr*, the upper air].

eth·ic (eth′·ik), **eth·i·cal** (eth′·ik·ạl) *a.* relating to morals or moral principles. **-ally** *adv.* **-s** *n.pl.* philosophy which treats of human character and conduct, of distinction between right and wrong, and moral duty and obligations to the community [Gk. *ethos*, character].

E·thi·o·pi·a (ē·thi·ō′·pi·ạ) *n.* a country in E. Africa; formerly called Abyssinia. **-n** *n.* a native of Ethiopia; (*Arch.*) a black person; *a.* pertaining to Ethiopia.

eth·nic (eth′·nik), **eth·ni·cal** (-ạl) *a.* pert. to

races or peoples, esp. speech groups; ethnological; heathen; pagan. **ethnography** *n.* detailed study of the physical characteristics and social customs of racial groups. **ethnographer** *n.* **ethnographic** *a.* **ethnology** *n.* the science which traces the origin and distribution of races, their peculiarities and differences. **ethnological** *a.* **ethnologist** *n.* [Gk. *ethnos*, a people].

e·thos (ē'·thȧs) *n.* the character, customs, and habits which distinguish a people or community from another; in art, the inherent quality which conveys nobility, universality, etc. [Gk. *ethos*, custom].

eth·yl (eth'·ạl) *n.* (*Chem.*) the univalent radical C_2H_5; an antiknock fluid. **— alcohol** common alcohol [fr. *ether*, and Gk. *hulē*, material].

e·ti·o·late (ē'·ti·ạ·lāt) *v.t.* to render pale or unhealthy by denying light and fresh air; *v.i.* to become pale by being deprived of light, etc. **etiolation** *n.* [Fr. *étioler*, to become pale].

e·ti·ol·o·gy (ē·ti·ȧl'·ạ·ji·) *n.* the study of the causes of diseases. Also **aetiology** [Gk. *aitia*, cause; *logos*, discourse].

et·i·quette (et'·i·ket) *n.* the conventional code of good manners which governs behavior in society and in professional and business life decorum [Fr.].

E·ton·i·an (ē·tōn'·i·ạn) *n.* one educated at Eton College. **Eton collar,** white starched collar worn outside the jacket. **Eton jacket,** a boy's very short and tailless jacket.

E·tru·ri·an (i·troor'·i·ạn) *a.* of Etruria, the ancient Roman name of part of N.W. Italy. **Etruscan** n. a native of ancient Etruria; *a.* pert. to Etruria, its language, people and especially art and architecture.

e·tude (ā·tōōd') *n.* (*Mus.*) a study; a short musical composition [Fr.].

et·y·mol·o·gy (et·ạ·mȧl·'ạ·ji·) *n.* the investigation of the origins and meanings of words and word-forms. **etymological** *a.* **etymologically** *adv.* **etymologist** *n.* one versed in etymology [Gk. *etumon*, true meaning; *logos*, a discourse].

Eu·caine (ū·kān') *n.* a synthetic drug, resembling cocaine, used as a local anesthetic [Gk. *eu*, well; *(co)caine;* Trademark].

eu·ca·lypt (ū'·kạ·lipt) *n.* any member of the genus Eucalyptus. **eucalyptus** *n.* the gum tree of Australia with tough and durable wood. **eucalyptol** *n.* eucalyptus oil, a colorless, aromatic, oily liquid distilled from the leaves of the eucalyptus [Gk. *eu*, well; *kaluptos*, covered].

Eu·cha·rist (ū·kạ·rist) *n.* Holy Communion; the consecrated elements at the sacrament of the Lord's Supper. **-ic, -ical** *a.* [Gk. *eucharistia*, thanksgiving].

eu·chre (ū'·kẹr) *v.t.* (*Colloq.*) to outwit; to get the best of [game of *euchre*].

Eu·clid·e·an (ū·klid'·ȧ·ạn) *a.* pert. to Euclid of Alexandria who founded a school of mathematics about 300 B.C.; geometric; three dimensional.

eu·de·mon·ism, eudaemonism (ū·dē'·mạn·-izm) *n.* the doctrine that the attainment of personal happiness, power and honor is the chief end and good of man. **eudemonist** *n.* [Gk. *eu*, well; *daimon*, a spirit].

eu·gen·ic (ū·jen'·ik) *a.* pertaining to eugenics; relating to, or tending towards, the production of fine offspring. **-s** *n.pl.* the scientific application of the findings of the study of heredity to human beings with the object of perpetuating those inherent and hereditary qualities which aid in the development of the human race. **eugenist** *n.* [Gk. *eu*, well; *genes*, producing].

eu·gen·nol (ū'·jạ·nōl) *n.* an aromatic acid, obtained from the oil of cloves [Prince *Eugène* of Savoy, a patron of botany].

eu·lo·gy, eu·lo·gi·um (ū'·lạ·ji·, ū·lō'·ji·ạm) *n.* a speech or writing in praise, especially a speech praising a dead person. **eulogic, -al** *a.* commendatory; laudatory. **eulogize** *v.t.* to speak in flattering terms. **eulogist** *n.* **eulogistic** *a.* commendatory; laudatory. **eulogistically** *adv.* [Gk. *eulogia*, praise].

eu·nuch (ū'·nạk) *n.* a castrated male, especially in the Near East, in charge of the women of the harem [Gk. *eunē*, a bed; *echein*, to keep].

eu·pep·sia (ū·pep'·shạ) *n.* healthy normal digestion—opposed to *dyspepsia*. **eupeptic** *a.* [Gk. *eu*, well; *peptein*, to digest].

eu·phe·mism (ū·fạ·mizm) *n.* a figure of speech where a less disagreeable word or phrase is substituted for a more accurate but more offensive one. **euphemize** *v.t.* or *v.i.* to soften down an expression. **euphemistic** *a.* [Gk. *euphēmizein*, to use words of good omen].

eu·pho·ny (ū'·fạ·ni·) *n.* pleasantness or smoothness of sound; assonance; assimilation of the sounds of syllables to facilitate pronunciation and to please the ear. **euphonic, euphonious** *a.* **euphoniously** *adv.* [Gk. *eu*, well; *phonē*, sound].

eu·pho·ri·a (yoo·fōr'·i·ạ) *n.* a sense of health and well-being which may, however, be misleading; state of irrational happiness. **euphoric** *a.* [Gk.].

eu·phu·ism (ū'·fyoo·izm) *n.* an affected, elaborate, bombastic prose style of language, so called from *Euphues*, a work by John Lyly (1553-1606), in that style; a stilted expression. **euphuist** *n.* **euphuistic** *a.*

Eu·ra·sian (yoor·ā'·zhạn) *n.* offspring of mixed European and Asiatic parentage; *a.* pert. to Europe and Asia considered as one landmass or continent [fr. *Europe* and *Asia*].

eu·rhyth·mics (yoo·riTH'·miks) *n.pl.* an art of rhythmical free movement to music [Gk. *eu*, well; *rhuthmos*, rhythm].

Eu·rope (yoor'·ạp) *n.* the continent which extends from the Atlantic Ocean to Asia. **European** *a.* belonging to Europe; *n.* a native or inhabitant of Europe.

Eu·sta·chi·an (yoo·stā'·ki·ạn, ·shạn) *a.* derived from Bartolommeo *Eustachio* (c. 1500-1574), an Italian anatomist. **Eustachian tube,** open duct extending from throat near tonsils to middle ear.

eu·tec·tic (yoo·tek'·tik) *a.* easily melted or fused; *n.* in metallurgy, a particular mixture or alloy of metals whose melting point is lower than other mixtures of the same ingredients [Gk. *eu*, well; *tēktos*, molten].

eu·tha·na·sia (ū·thạ·nā'·zhạ) *n.* an easy, painless death; the putting of a person to death painlessly, esp. one in a hopeless condition. Also **euthanasy** [Gk. *eu*, well; *thanatos*, death].

e·vac·u·ate (i·vak'·yoo·āt) *v.t.* to make empty; to withdraw from; to excrete; *v.i.* to quit. **evacuant** *n.* a purgative. **evacuation** *n.* the act of evacuating, emptying out, withdrawing from; system by which noncombatants, in time of war, are sent to safe areas; (*Med.*) the discharge of fecal matter from the rectum. **evacuative** *a.* **evacuator** *n.* **evacuee** *n.* a person temporarily removed from dangerous area [L. *e*, out; *vacuus*, empty].

e·vade (i·vād') *v.t.* to avoid by dexterity, artifice, or stratagem; to elude; to escape; to avoid; to shun; to frustrate; to baffle. **evadable** *a.* [L. *e*, out; *vadere*, to go].

e·val·u·ate (i·val'·yoo·āt) *v.t.* to appraise or determine the value of. **evaluation** *n.* estimation of worth [Fr. *évaluer*].

ev·a·nesce (ev·ạ·nes') *v.i.* to vanish; to fade or melt away. **-nce** *n.* **-nt** *a.* vanishing; fleeting; transitory; scarcely perceptible. **-ntly** *adv.* [L. *evanescere*, to vanish].

e·van·gel (i·van'·jạl) *n.* good tidings; the Gospel; one of the first four books of the New Testament. **evangelic, evangelical** *a.* consonant with the Gospel; applied to those forms of Christianity which regard the atonement of Christ as the ground and central principle of the Christian faith; orthodox. **evangelical** *n.*

one who holds the views of the evangelical school. **evangelically** *adv.* **evangelicalness, evangelicism, evangelicalism, evangelism** *n.* a religious movement to spread actively the tenets of the Gospel. **-ization** *n.* the preaching of the Gospel; conversion. **-ize** *v.t.* and *v.i.* to convert, by preaching the Gospel. **-ist** *n.* **-istic** *a.* [Gk. *eu*, well; *angelia*, tidings].

e·vap·o·rate (i·vap′·ạ·rāt) *v.t.* and *v.i.* to pass off in vapor, as a fluid; to disperse; to disappear; to vaporize. **evaporable, evaporative** *a.* **evaporation** *n.* [L. *e*, out; *vapor*].

e·va·sion (i·vā′·zhạn) *n.* the act of evading or eluding; subterfuge to escape the force of an accusation, interrogation, or argument; excuse; dodge. **evasible** *a.* may be evaded. **evasive** *a.* tending to evade; marked by evasion; not straightforward. **evasively** *adv.*

eve (ēv) *n.* evening; the evening before some particular day; the period immediately preceding an event or important occasion. **even** *n.* evening (poetical). **even-song** *n.* evening prayer. **even-tide** *n.* evening [O.E. *aefen*].

e·ven (ēv′·n) *a.* level; equal in surface; uniform in rate of motion or mode of action; flat; smooth; uniform in quality; equal in amount; balanced; horizontal; equable; calm; unruffled; impartial; exactly divisible by two; *v.t.* to make even; to smooth; to equalize; *adv.* evenly; just; still; fully. **-handed** *a.* fair, impartial (of justice); just. **-ly** *adv.* **-ness** *n.* **—tempered** *a.* not irascible [O.E. *efen*].

eve·ning (ēv′·ning) *n.* the close of day; the decline or end of life. **evening dress,** formal dress worn at evening functions [O.E. *aefnung*].

e·vent (i·vent′) *n.* that which happens; a notable occurrence; affair; result; effect; item at a sports meeting. **-ful** *a.* full of exciting events; momentous. **-ual** *a.* happening as a consequence; resulting in the end; ultimate. **-uality** *n.* contingency; force of circumstances. **-ually** *adv.* **-uate** *v.i.* to happen [L. *evenire*, to come out].

ev·er (ev′·ẹr) *adv.* at any time; at all times; perpetually; constantly; unceasingly. **-glade** *n.* a swampy, grassy tract. **-green** *a.* always green; *n.* nondeciduous tree or shrub which remains green throughout the year. **-more** *adv.* unceasingly; eternally. **ever so** (*Colloq.*) extremely. **for ever and a day,** always.

ev·er·last·ing (ev·ẹr·last′·ing) *a.* enduring for ever; eternal; *n.* eternity; a flower which does not lose shape or color when dried.

e·vert (ē·vurt′) *v.t.* to turn inside out. **eversible** *a.* capable of being turned inside out. **eversion** *n.* [L. *e*, out; *vertere*, to turn].

ev·er·y (ev′·ri·) *a.* each of all; all possible. **-body** *n.* every person. **-day** *a.* ordinary. **-where** *adv.* in every place; universally. **—other,** every second; alternately [O.E. *aefre*, *yle*, ever each].

e·vict (i·vikt′) *v.t.* to dispossess by a judicial process; to expel; to eject; to turn out. **eviction** *n.* ejectment. **-or** *n.* [L. *evincere*, to conquer, to recover property by law].

ev·i·dent (ev′·ạ·dant) *a.* visible; clear to the vision; obvious. **evidence** *n.* that which makes evident; information in a law case; a witness; sign; indication; ground for belief; testimony; proof; attestation; corroboration; *v.t.* to render evident; to manifest. **evidential, evidentiary** *a.* furnishing evidence; proving conclusively. **-ly** *adv.* apparently; plainly. **to turn State's evidence,** to give evidence, on the part of one accused, against an accomplice [L. *e*, out; *videre*, to see].

e·vil (ē′·vl) *a.* having bad natural qualities; bad; harmful; disagreeable; vicious; corrupt; wicked; calamitous; unfortunate; *n.* harm; misfortune; wickedness; depravity; sinfulness; wrong; *adv.* in an evil manner. **— eye** *n.* the power of bewitching others by the glance of the eyes. **-ly** *adv.* **-ness** *n.* [O.E. *yfel*].

e·vince (i·vins′) *v.t.* to prove beyond any reasonable doubt; to show clearly; to make evident. **evincible** *a.* **evincibly** *adv.* **evincive** *a.* tending to prove [L. *evincere*, to prove].

e·vis·cer·ate (i·vis′·ẹr·āt) *v.t.* to disembowel; to take out the entrails or viscera. **evisceration** *n.* [L. *e*, out; *vicsera*, bowels].

e·voke (i·vōk′) *v.t.* to call up; to summon forth; to draw out; to bring to pass. **evocation** *n.* [L. *evocare*, to call out].

ev·o·lu·tion (ev·ạl·ōō′·shạn) *n.* gradual unfolding or growth; development; evolving; the scientific theory according to which the higher forms of life have gradually developed from simple and rudimentary forms; a movement to change position, order, and direction carried out by a body of troops. **-al, -ary** *a.* **-ism** *n.* **-ist** *n.* a biologist who accepts the scientific theory of evolution [L. *evolvere, evolutum*, to roll out].

e·volve (i·valv′) *v.t.* to develop gradually; to give off, as odors; to unfold; *v.i.* to develop, esp. by natural process; to open out [L. *evolvere*, to roll out].

ewe (ū) *n.* a female sheep [O.E. *eowy*].

ew·er (yoo′·ẹr) *n.* a large water jug with a wide spout [O.Fr. *euwier*, fr. *eau*, water].

ex- *prefix* fr. L. *ex*, out of, used in the construction of compound terms, signifying *out of, from, former* (as ex-M. P.)

ex·ac·er·bate (igz·, iks·as′·ẹr·bāt) *v.t.* to render more bitter; to increase the violence of; to exasperate; to irritate; to aggravate. **exacerbation** *n.* [L. *ex*, out of; *acerbus*, bitter].

ex·act (ig·zakt′) *a.* accurate; correct; precise; strict; *v.t.* to demand; to extort; to enforce; to insist upon. **-ing** *a.* making severe demands on; demanding extreme care or accuracy. **exaction** *n.* **-itude** *n.* extreme accuracy; correctness. **-ly** *adv.* precisely [L. *ex*, out; *agere, actum*, to drive].

ex·ag·ger·ate (ig·zaj′·ạ·rāt) *v.t.* to represent as greater than truth or justice will warrant; to magnify in the telling, describing, etc. **exaggeratedly** *adv.* **exaggeration** *n.* a statement going beyond the facts. **exaggerative** *a.* **exaggerator** *n.* **exaggeratory** *a.* [L. *exaggerare*, to heap up].

ex·alt (ig·zawlt′) *v.t.* to elevate as in rank; to praise; to elate with joy. **-ation** . **-ed** *a.* [L. *ex*, out; *altus*, high].

ex·am·ine (ig·zam′·in) *v.t.* to inquire into and determine; to try and assay by the appropriate tests; to inspect; to scrutinize; to explore; to investigate; to interrogate. **exam** *n.* (*Colloq.*) examination. **examinee** *n.* one who undergoes an examination test. **examination** *n.* the act of examining; interrogation; a scholastic test of knowledge, written or oral; judicial inquiry. **-r** *n.* [L. *examinare*, to weigh accurately].

ex·am·ple (ig·zam′·pl) *n.* a pattern; a thing illustrating a general rule; a specimen; sample [L. *exemplum*, a sample].

ex·as·per·ate (ig·zas′·pẹr·āt) *v.t.* to irritate in a high degree; to rouse angry feelings; to provoke beyond endurance. **exasperating** *a.* extremely trying; provoking. **exasperation** *n.* **-r** *n.* [L. *ex*, out; *asper*, rough].

ex·ca·vate (eks′·kạ·vāt) *v.t.* to hollow out; to form a cavity or hole in; to dig out. **excavation** *n.* **excavator** *n.* [L.].

ex·ceed (ik·sēd′) *v.t.* to pass or go beyond the limit of; *v.i.* to be greater; to surpass; to excel. **-ing** *a.* surpassing; excessive. **-ingly** *adv.* very; to a very high degree [L. *ex*, out; *cedere*, to go].

ex·cel (ik·sel′) *v.t.* to surpass, especially in good qualities; to be better than; to exceed; to outstrip; to outdo; *v.i.* to be very good; to be pre-eminent. *pr.p.* **-ling.** *pa.t.* and *pa.p.* **-led. -lence** *n.* **-lency** *n.* complimentary title borne by ambassadors, etc. **-lent** *a.* worthy; choice; remarkably good. **-lently** *adv.* [L. *excellere*, to rise above].

ex·cept (ik·sept′) *v.t.* to leave out; to exclude; *v.i.* to take exception to; to object; *prep.* with exclusion of; leaving out; excepting; all but; save; *conj.* with the exception (that). **-ing** *prep.* excluding. **exception** *n.* an excepting; that which is not included in a rule; objection. **exceptionable** *a.* objectionable. **exceptionably** *adv.* **exceptional** *a.* outstanding; superior. **exceptionally** *adv.* [L. *exceptus,* taken out].

ex·cerpt (ik·surpt′) *v.t.* to extract, to quote (a passage from a book, etc.). **excerpt** (ek′·surpt) *n.* a passage, quoted or culled from a book, speech, etc. [L. *excerpere,* to pluck out].

ex·cess (ik·ses′) *n.* that which surpasses or goes beyond a definite limit; extravagance; intemperance. **-ive** *a.* more than enough.

ex·cheq·uer (iks·chek′·ẹr) *n.* the public treasury [O.Fr. *eschequier*[.

ex·change (iks·chānj′) *v.t.* to give or take in return for; to barter; *n.* the act of giving or taking one thing in return for another; the transfer of goods between countries; a place for buying and selling stocks, securities, etc., or where other business of a special nature is carried on; the conversion of the currency of one country to that of another; the settling of debts by the transfer of credits or the interchange of drafts, etc. **-able** *a.*

ex·cheq·uer (iks·chek′·ẹr) *n.* the public treasury; (*Brit.*) the department in charge of public revenues; (*Colloq.*) funds [O.Fr. *eschequier*].

ex·cise (ek·sīz′) *n.* a tax or duty upon certain articles of home production and consumption; also includes licenses on certain employments, sports, etc.; *v.t.* to impose an excise duty on. **excisable** *a.* liable to excise duty [Dut. *accijns,* excise].

ex·cise (ik·sīz′) *v.t.* to cut out; to cut off; to expunge. **excision** (ik·sizh′·ạn) *n.* act of cutting; surgical operation [L. *ex,* out; *caedere,* to cut].

ex·cite (ik·sīt′) *v.t.* to rouse; to call into action; to stir up; to set in motion; to move to strong emotion; to stimulate. **excitability** *n.* **excitable** *a.* capable of being easily excited. **excitant** (ik′·si·tạnt) a stimulant. **excitation** *n.* the act of exciting; the excitement produced; the action of a stimulant on an organ of the body or of a plant. **excitative** *a.* **excitatory** *a.* tending to excite. **excited** *a.* **excitedly** *adv.* **-ment** *n.* abnormal activity; agitation; perturbation; commotion. **exciting** *a.* rousing to action; thrilling. **excitingly** *adv.* [L. *excitare*].

ex·claim (iks·klām′) *v.i.* and *v.t.* to utter loudly and vehemently; to declare suddenly. **exclamation** (eks·klạ·mā′·shạn) *n.* loud remark or cry, expressing joy, surprise, etc.; vehement utterance. **exclamation mark,** the mark (!) used to suggest sudden emotion. **exclamatory** *a.* [L. *ex,* out; *clamare,* to call].

ex·clude (eks·klòòd′) *v.t.* to thrust out; to shut out; to debar from; to eject. **exclusion** *n.* the act of excluding or debarring. **exclusive** *a.* excluding; debarring; limited to a special favored few. **exclusively** *adv.* **exclusiveness** *n.* [L. *ex,* out; *claudere,* to shut].

ex·cog·i·tate (eks·kȧj′·ạ·tāt) *v.t.* to find out by thinking; to think out. **excogitation** *n.* [L. *ex,* out; *cogitare,* to think].

ex·com·mu·ni·cate (eks·kạm·mūn′·ạ·kāt) *v.t.* to expel from the communion and membership of the church by an ecclesiastical sentence; to deprive of spiritual privileges. **excommunication** *n.* [L. *excommunicare,* to expel from a community].

ex·co·ri·ate (iks·kō′·ri·āt) *v.t.* to strip, wear, or rub the skin off; to flay. **excoriation** *n.* [L. *ex,* out; *corium,* the skin].

ex·cre·ment (eks′·kạ·mạnt) *n.* matter excreted; feces. **-al** *a.* **-itious** *a.* resembling feces [L. *excrementum*].

ex·cres·cence (iks·kres′·ạns) *n.* an abnormal protuberance which grows out of anything, as a wart or tumor; a normal outgrow, such as hair. **excrescent** *a.* growing out unnaturally; superfluous [L. *ex,* out; *crescere,* to grow].

ex·crete (iks·krēt′) *v.t.* to eject waste matter from the body; to expel. **excreta** *n.pl.* the normal discharges from the animal body as urine, feces, and sweat. **excretion** *n.* **excretive** *a.* **excretory** *a.* [L. *excernere,* to sift out].

ex·cru·ci·ate (iks·kròò′·shi·āt) *v.t.* to inflict the severest pain on; to torture, in body or mind. **excruciating** *a.* [L. *ex,* out; *cruciare,* to torture].

ex·cul·pate (iks·pạl′·pāt) *v.t.* to clear from a charge or imputation of fault or guilt. **exculpation** *n.* vindication. **exculpatory** *a.* [L. *ex,* out; *culpa,* fault].

ex·cur·sion (iks·kur′·zhạn) *n.* a short trip for a special purpose; deviation; digression. **-ist** *n.* one who makes a journey for pleasure. **excursive** *a.* prone to wander; rambling; digressive; diffusive. **excursus** *n.* a dissertation appended to a book and containing a fuller exposition of some relevant point [L. *ex,* out; *currere,* to run].

ex·cuse (iks·kūz′) *v.t.* to free from fault or blame; to free from obligation or duty; to pardon; to justify; to apologize; to exempt; to let off. **excuse** (iks·kūs′) *n.* a plea offered in extenuation of a fault, etc.; a pretext; an apology. **excusable** *a.* [L. *ex,* out; *causa,* a cause, accusation].

ex·e·crate (eks′·i· krāt) *v.t.* to feel or express hatred for; to curse; to abominate; to loathe; to detest utterly. **execrable** *a.* **execrably** *adv.* **execration** *n.* act of execrating; the object execrated; a curse; imprecation [L. *exsecrari,* to curse].

ex·e·cute (eks′·i·kūt) *v.t.* to carry out a task to the end, to accomplish; to give effect to; to perform; to complete; to enforce a judgment of a court of law; to sign a deed; to put to death by sentence of a court. **executable** *a.* **executant** *n.* a performer, esp. of music. **execution** *n.* the act of executing or performing; death penalty inflicted by law; performance; accomplishment; mode of performance; workmanship. **executioner** *n.* one who executes; a hangman. **executive** *a.* capable of executing or performing; administrative; *n.* a body appointed to administer the affairs of a corporation, a company, etc.; a high official of such a body; the administrative branch of a government. **executively** *adv.* **executor** *n.* (*fem.* **executrix, executress**) one who executes or performs; a person appointed under a will to fulfill its terms and administer the estate. **executorial** *a.* [L. *exsequi,* to follow out].

ex·e·ge·sis (eks·ạ·jē′·sis) *n.* literary commentary; interpretation and elucidation of Scripture. **exegete, exegetist** *n.* one versed in interpreting the text of the Scriptures. **exegetic, exegetical** *a.* [Gk. fr. *ex,* out; *hēgeesthai,* to lead].

ex·em·plar (ig·zem′·plẹr) *n.* a person or thing to be imitated; an original or pattern; model. **-ily** *adv.* in a manner to be imitated; by way of warning or example. **-iness** *n.* **-y** *a.* serving as a pattern or model; commendable [L. *exemplum,* sample].

ex·em·pli·fy (ig·zem′·pli·fī) *v.t.* to show by example; to illustrate; to make an attested copy of. *pr.p.* **-ing.** *pa.t., pa.p.* **exemplified. exemplification** *n.* [L. *exemplum,* an example; *facere,* to make].

ex·empt (ig·zempt′) *v.t.* to free from; to grant immunity from; *a.* not included; not liable for some duty; freed from; not affected by. **-ible** *a.* **exemption** *n.* act of exempting; state of being exempt; immunity [L. *exemptum,* taken out].

ex·er·cise (eks′·ẹr·sīz) *n.* the act of exercising; use (of limbs, faculty, etc.); use of limbs for health; practice for the sake of training; *pl.* military drill; a ceremony; *v.t.* to put in motion;

to use or employ; to exert; to apply; to engage; to practice; *v.i.* to take exercise [L. *exercere*, to keep at work].

ex·ert (ig·zurt′) *v.t.* to put forth, as strength, force, or ability; to exercise; to strive; to labor. **-ion** *n.* **-ive** *a.* [L. *exserere*, to put forth].

ex·hale (eks·hāl′) *v.t.* to breathe out; to give off as vapor or odor; to discharge; *v.i.* to rise or be given off as vapor. **exhalable** *a.* **exhalant** *a.* having the property of exhalation. **exhalation** *n.* [L. *ex*, out; *halare*, to breathe].

ex·haust (ig·zawst′) *v.t.* to draw out or drain off completely; to empty; to weaken; to tire; to use up; to squander; to discuss thoroughly; *n.* conduit through which steam, waste gases, and the like, after performing work, pass from the cylinders to the outer air; the steam or gases themselves. **-ed** *a.* tired out; fatigued; emptied; drawn out; consumed. **-ible** *a.* **-ion** *n.* act of exhausting or consuming; state of being completely deprived of strength or vitality. **-ive** *a.* tending to exhaust; comprehensive; thorough. **-ively** *adv.* [L. *ex*, out; *haurire, haustum*, to draw].

ex·hib·it (ig·zi′·bit) *v.t.* to hold forth or to expose to view; to show; to display; to manifest; to express; *n.* anything displayed at an exhibition. **-er, -or** *n.* one who sends articles to an exhibition for display. **-ion** (ek·sạ·bi′·shạn) *n.* the act of exhibiting; show; display; a public show (of works of art, etc.). **-ionism** *n.* a tendency to show off before people. **-ionist** *n.* **-ory** *a.* [L. *exhibere*, to hold forth].

ex·hil·a·rate (ig·zil′·ạ·rāt) *v.t.* to make cheerful; to animate. **exhilarant** *a.* exhilarating; exciting joy, mirth, or pleasure; *n.* anything which exhilarates. **exhilarating** *a.* **exhilaration** *n.* [L. *exhilarare*, fr. *hilaris*, happy].

ex·hort (ig·zawrt′) *v.t.* to incite by words of advice; to advise strongly; to admonish earnestly. **-ation** *n* **-ative, -atory** *a.* tending to exhort [L. *ex; hortari*, to encourage].

ex·hume (iks·hūm′) *v.t.* to dig up. **exhumation** *n.* **-r** *n.* [L. *ex*, out; *humus*, ground].

ex·i·gent (ek′·sạ·jạnt) *a.* calling for immediate action or aid; pressing; urgent. **exigence, exigency** *n.* urgent want; emergency. **exigible** *a.*

ex·i·gu·i·ty (ek·sạ·gū′·i·ti·) *n.* smallness; slenderness. **exiguous** *a.* [L. *exiguus*].

ex·ile (eg′·zil, ek′·s.l) *n.* separation or enforced banishment; a banished person; one living away from his native country; *v.t.* to banish or expel [L. *exsilium*, banishment].

ex·ist (eg·zist′) *v.t.* to be; to live; to subsist; to occur. **-ence** *n.* being; state of being actual; entity; life; **-ential** *a.* consisting in existence; ontological. **-entialism** *n.* (*Philos.*) a school which describes, analyzes, and classifies the experiences of an individual mind considered as *existences*. **-ibility** *n.* [L. *existere*, to come forth].

ex·it (eg′·zit, ek′·sit) *n.* a departure; a way out of a place; actor's departure from stage. **exeunt,** actors' departure from stage [L. = he goes out].

ex·o- *prefix* fr. Gk. *exo*, outside, without.

ex·o·bi·ol·o·gy (ek·sō·bī·ál′·ạ·ji·) *n.* the study of life beyond the atmosphere of the earth. **exobiologist** *n.* [Gk. *exo*, outside; *bios*, life; *logos*, a discourse].

ex·o·dus (ek′·sạ·dạs) *n.* a departure, esp. of a crowd. **Exodus** *n.* the second book of the Old Testament [Gk. *exodos*, way out].

ex·og·a·my (eks·ág′·ạ·mi·) *n.* a custom compelling a man to marry outside his tribe or social unit. **exogamous** *a.* [Gk. *exo*, outside; *gamos*, marriage].

ex·on·er·ate (eg·zán′·ẹr·āt) *v.i.* to declare free from blame or responsibility; to relieve of a charge or obligation. **exoneration** *n.* **exonerator** *n.* [L. *exonerare*, to unburden].

ex·o·ra·ble (ek′·sẹr·ạ·bl) *a.* capable of being moved by entreaty [L. *exorare*, to persuade by entreaty].

ex·or·bi·tant (ig·zạwr′·bạ·tạnt) *a.* very excessive; extravagant. **exorbitance, exorbitancy** *n.* **-ly** *adv.* [L. *ex*, out; *orbis*, a circle].

ex·or·cise (ek′·sawr·sīz) *v.t.* to cast out (evil spirits) by invocation; to free a person of evil spirits. **exorcism** *n.* [Gk. *exorkizein*].

ex·or·di·um (ig·zawr′·di·ạm) *n.* a beginning; the introduction part of a discourse or treatise. **exordial** *a.* [L. fr. *ex*, out; *ordiri*, to begin].

ex·o·skel·e·ton (ek·sō·skel′·ạ·tạn) *n.* (*Zool.*) external hard supporting structure such as scales, nails, feathers. **exoskeletal** *a.* [Gk. *exo*, outside].

ex·o·ter·ic, extrical (ek·sạ·tẹr′·ik, ·al) *a.* capable of being understood by, or suited for, the many; not secret; the opposite to *esoteric* [Gk. *exoterikos*, external].

ex·ot·ic (eg·zát′·ik) *a.* introduced from a foreign country; not indigenous; unusual or colorful. **-ism** (ig·zát′·i·cizm) *n.* [Gk. *exotikos*].

ex·pand (ik·spand′) *v.t.* to spread out; to enlarge; to increase in volume or bulk; to extend; to stretch; to develop. **expanse** *n.* a wide extent of surface. **-able, expansible** *a.* **expansibly** *adv.* **expansion** *n.* act of expanding; condition of being expanded; increase in one or more of the dimension of a body; spreading; distension; enlargement. **expansive** *a.* widely extended; effusive; communicative; diffusive. **expansively** *adv.* **expansiveness** *n.* [L. *ex*, out; *pandere*, to stretch].

ex·pa·ti·ate (ik·spā′·shi·āt) *v.i.* to speak or write at great length (on); **expatiation** *n.* **expatiative** *a.* [L. *exspatiari*, to wander].

ex·pa·tri·ate (eks·pā′·tri·āt) *v.t.* to banish from one's native land; to exile; (·it) *n.* **expatriation** *n.* [L. *ex*, out; *patria*, fatherland].

ex·pect (ek·spekt′) *v.t.* to look forward to; to look on as likely to happen; to look for as one's due; to anticipate; (*Colloq.*) to suppose. **-ance, -ancy** *n.* the act or state of expecting; that which is expected. **-ant** *a.* waiting; hopeful. **-antly** *adv.* **-ation** *n.* act or state of looking forward to an event. **-ations** *n.pl.* prospects in life; probable gain [L. *exspectare*, to look out for].

ex·pec·to·rate (ek·spek′·tạ·rāt) *v.t.* or *v.i.* to spit; to cough up. **expectorant** *a.* aiding expectoration; *n.* a drug or agent which promotes expectoration. **expectoration** *n.* the act of expectorating; sputum; spittle [L. *ex*, out; *pectus*, breast].

ex·pe·di·ent (ek·spē′·di·ạnt) *a.* suitable; fitting; advisable; politic; desirable; convenient; useful; *n.* suitable means to accomplish an end; means devised or employed in an exigency; shift; contrivance. **expediency** *n.* **-ly** *adv.* [L. *expedire*, to be fitting].

ex·pe·dite (ek′·spi·dit) *v.t.* to free from hindrance or obstacle; to hurry forward; *a.* quick; ready; unencumbered. **-ly** *adv.* **expedition** *n.* a journey for a specific purpose; the persons and equipment involved; efficient promptness; speed; **expeditionary** *a.* **expeditious** *a.* prompt; speedy [L. *ex*, out; *pes, pedis*, a foot].

ex·pel (ek·spel′) *v.t.* to drive or force out; to cast out; to eject; to exclude; *pr.p.* **-ling.** *pa.t.* and *pa.p.* **-led** [L. *ex*, out; *pellere*, to drive].

ex·pend (ek·spend′) *v.t.* to consume by use; to spend; to use up; to exhaust. **-able** *a.* **-iture** *n.* act of expending; that which is expended; expense; cost. **expense** *n.* big outlay; cost; expenditure. **expensive** *a.* costly; dear [L. *expendere*, to weigh out].

ex·pe·ri·ence (ek·spir′·i·ạns) *n.* practical knowledge gained by trial or practice; personal proof or trial; continuous practice; evidence; an event in one's life; *v.t.* to undergo; to feel; to endure; to encounter. **-d** *a.* skilled; expert; wise; capable; thoroughly conversant with. **experiential** *a.* relating to or having experience; empirical [L. *experiri*, to test].

ex·pe·ri·ment (ek·sper′·ạ·mant) *n.* the action of trying anything; putting to the proof or test; practical test; a trial to find out what happens; *v.i.* to make an experiment. **-al** *a.* founded on or known by experiment; pertaining to experiment. **-alist** *n.* **-ally** *adv.* **-ation** *n.* **-tative** *a.* **-er, -ist** *n.* [L. *experiri*, to try].

ex·pert (ek·spurt′) *a.* taught by use, practice, or experience; adroit; dexterous; skillful. (ex′·purt) *n.* an authority; a specialist. **-ly** *adv.* **-ness** *n.* [L. *expertus*, having tried].

ex·pi·ate (eks′·pi·āt) *v.t.* to make satisfaction or reparation for; to atone for; to make amends for. **expiable** *a.* **expiation** *n.* [L. *expiare*, to make amends for].

ex·pire (ek·spīr′) *v.t.* to breathe out; to emit; to exhale; *v.i.* to die; to die away; to come to an end. **expirant** *n.* one who is dying. **expiration** *n.* the exhalation of air from the lungs; end of a period of time; close; termination. **expiratory** *a.* **expiring** *a.* **expiry** *n.* conclusion [L. *ex*, out; *spirare*, to breathe].

ex·plain (eks·plān′) *v.t.* to make plain, manifest, or inteligible; to account for; to elucidate; to define. **-able** *a.* **explanation** *n.* act or method of explaining, expounding, or interpreting; the meaning of or reason given for anything. **explanative, explanatory** *a.* serving to explain [L. *explanare*, to make smooth].

ex·ple·tive (eks′·pli·tiv) *a.* serving only to fill out a sentence, etc.; added for ornamentation only; *n.* a word inserted to fill up or to add force to a phrase; an exclamation; an oath [L. *expletivus*, filling out].

ex·pli·cate (eks′·pli·kāt) *v.t.* to unfold the meaning of; to explain; to interpret; to elucidate. **explicable** *a.* **explication** *n.* **explicative, explicatory** *a.* [L. *explicare*, to unfold].

ex·plic·it (iks·plis′·it) *a.* stated in detail; stated, not merely implied; unambiguous; clear; unequivocal. **-ly** *adv.* **-ness** *n.* [L. *explicitus*].

ex·plode (ik·splōd′) *v.t.* to cause to blow up; to discredit; to expose (a theory, etc.); *v.i.* to burst with a loud report; to become furious with rage; to burst into unrestrained laughter. **-d** *a.* rejected; debunked. **explosion** *n.* the act of exploding; sudden release of gases, accompanied by noise and violence; a manifestation of rage. **explosive** *a.* liable to explode; *n.* a chemical intended to explode [L. *ex*, out; *plaudere*, to clap with the hands].

ex·ploit (eks·ploit′) *n.* a brilliant feat; a heroic deed; remarkable action, often in a bad sense; *v.t.* to make the most of; to utilize for personal gain. **-able** *a.* **-age, -ation** *n.* **-er** *n.* [Fr.].

ex·plore (ik·splōr′) *v.t.* to search through with the view of making discovery; to leave the beaten tracks; to investigate; to examine. **exploration** *n.* **exploratory** *a.* **-r** *n.* [L. *explorare*, to search out].

ex·plo·sive See **explode.**

ex·po·nent (ek·spō′·nạnt) *n.* one who expounds, demonstrates, or explains; a symbol; in algebra, index number or quantity, written to the right of and above another to show how often the latter is to be multiplied by itself, e.g. $a^3=a\times a\times a$. [L. *ex*, out; *ponere*, to place].

ex·port (eks·pōrt′) *v.t.* to send goods or produce out of a country. (ex′·port) *n.* act of exporting; that which is exported. **-able** *a.* **-ation** *n.* **-er** *n.* [L. *ex*, out; *portare*, to carry].

ex·pose (ik·spōz′) *v.t.* to lay open; to leave unprotected; to exhibit; to disclose; to submit a photographic plate or film to the light. **exposé** (eks·pō·zā′) *n.* an exposure or disclosure of discreditable facts. **exposition** *n.* act of exhibiting or expounding; exhibition; display; explanation. **expositor** *n.* **expository** *a.* **exposure** *n.* the act of exposing, laying bare, or disclosing shady or doubtful transactions; the state of being laid bare; aspect of a building relative to the cardinal points of the compass [L. *ex*, out, *ponere*, to place].

ex·pos·tu·late (ik·spȧs′·chạ·lāt) *v.i.* to remonstrate with; to reason earnestly. **expostulation** *n.* **expostulative, expostulatory** *a.* [L. *expostulare*, to demand urgently].

ex·pound (ek·spound′) *v.t.* to explain; to set forth; to interpret; [L. *exponere*].

ex·press (ik·spres′) *v.t.* to make known one's opinions or feelings; to put into words; to represent by pictorial art; to designate; to press or squeeze out; to send by express; *a.* definitely stated; closely resembling; specially designed; explicit; clear; plain; speedy; *adv.* post-haste; by express messenger or train; specially; on purpose; *n.* a messenger sent on a special errand; a fast train making few stops en route; a message. **-ible** *a.* **-ion** *n.* act of expressing; lively or vivid representation of meaning, sentiment, or feeling; the reflection of character or mood in the countenance; utterance; declaration; phrase; term; remark; aspect; look; (*Math.*) a quantity denoted by algebraic symbols. **-ionism** *n.* an antirealistic art theory that all art depends on the expression of the artist's creative self. **-ionist** *n.* **-ionless** *a.* **-ive** *a.* full of expression. **-ively** *adv.* **-iveness** *n.* **-ly** *adv.* plainly; explicitly; specially [L. *expressus*, squeezed out, clearly stated].

ex·pro·pri·ate (eks·prō′·pri·āt) *v.t.* to dispossess; to take out of the owner's hand. **expropriation** *n.* [L. *ex*, out; *proprius*, one's own].

ex·pul·sion (ik·spul′·shạn) *n.* the act of expelling or casting out; ejection; banishment. **expulsive** *a.* [L. *expulsus*, driven out].

ex·punge (ik·spunj′) *v.t.* to strike out; to erase; to obliterate; to cancel [L. *expungere*, to strike out].

ex·pur·gate (ek′·spẹr·gāt) *v.t.* to remove objectionable parts (from a book, etc.); to cleanse; to purify; to purge. **expurgation** *n.* **expurgator** *n.* [L. *expurgare*, to purge].

ex·qui·site (eks′·kwi·zit) *a.* of extreme beauty or delicacy; of surpassing excellence; extreme, as pleasure or pain. **-ly** [L. *exquisitus*, sought out].

ex·ser·vice (eks′·sur·vis) *a.* of or pertaining to one who has served in the armed forces.

ex·sic·cate (ek′·si·kāt) *v.t.* to dry up; to evaporate. **exsiccation** *n.* [L. *ex*, out; *siccus*, dry].

ex·tant (ik·stant′, ek′·stạnt) *a.* still existing [L. *ex*, out; *stare*, to stand].

ex·tem·po·re (ik·stem′·pạ·ri·) *a.* or *adv.* without previous study or meditation; offhand; on the spur of the moment. **extemporal, extemporaneous, extemporary** *a.* impromptu. **extemporization** *n.* act of speaking extempore. **extemporize** *v.i.* to speak extempore; to create music on the inspiration of the moment [L. *ex*, out of; *tempus, temporis*, time].

ex·tend (ik·stend′) *v.t.* to prolong in a single direction, as a line; to stretch out; to prolong in duration; to offer; to expand; to enlarge; *v.i.* to be continued in length or breadth; to stretch. **-ible, extensible, extensile** *a.* capable of being stretched, expanded, or enlarged. **extensibility** *n.* **extension** *n.* **extensional** *a.* **extensive** *a.* having wide extent; large; comprehensive; spacious. **extensively** *adv.* **extensiveness** *n.* **extensor** *n.* a muscle which straightens or extends a limb. **extent** *n.* space or degree to which a thing is extended; size; scope, a space; area; degree; volume; length; expanse [L. *extendere*, to stretch out].

ex·ten·u·ate (ek·sten′·yoo·āt) *v.t.* to palliate, as a crime; to mitigate; to make less blameworthy. **extenuating** *a.* **extenuation** *n.* [L. *ex*, out; *tenuare*, to make thin].

ex·te·ri·or (ek·stir′·i·ẹr) *a.* outer; outward; external; coming from without; *n.* the outside; outer surface; outward appearance.

ex·ter·mi·nate (ek·stur′·mạ·nāt) *v.t.* to root out; to destroy utterly. **extermination** *n.* **exterminator** *n.* [L. *ex*, out; *terminus*, boundary].

ex·ter·nal (ik·stur′·nạl) *a.* not inherent or essential; outward; exterior; superficial; extrinsic; apparent; **-s** *n.pl.* outward appearances; **-ly** *adv.* [L. *externus*, outside].

ex·tinct (eks·tingkt′) *a.* extinguished; put out; no longer existing; dead. **-ion** *n.* [L. *extinctus*].

ex·tin·guish (ek·sting′·gwish) *v.t.* to put out; to put an end to; to quench; to destroy; to obscure by superior splendor. **-able** *a.* **-er** *n.* [L. *extinguere*, to quench].

ex·tir·pate (ek′·stęr·pāt) *v.t.* to pull or pluck up by the roots; to destroy utterly. **extirpable** *a.* **extirpation** *n* **extirpator** *n.* [L. *exstirpare*, fr. *stirps*, stem].

ex·tol (ek·stōl′) *v.t.* to praise highly. *pr.p.* **-ling.** *pa.t.*, *pa.p.* **-led** [L. *extollere*, to lift up].

ex·tort (ek·stawrt′) *v.t.* to obtain by force or threats; to extract. **extorsive** *a.* serving or tending to extort. **-ion** *n.* act of extorting; illegal compulsion; unjust exaction. **-ionary, -ionate** *a.* **-ioner, -ionist** *n.* [L. *ex*, out; *torquere*, to wrench].

ex·tra- (eks′·trą) *prefix* fr. L. meaning *beyond, on the other side of, on the outside of;* used in many compound words denoting *beyond, without, more than, further than,* or generally, *excess.* **extra** *a.* extraordinary; additional; *adv.* unusually; especially; *n.* something extra; special edition of a newspaper; a person employed casually by film producers to play a minor role in a production. **-curricular** *a.* not included in a curriculum. **-galactic** *a.* beyond the Milky Way system. **-judicial** *a.* out of the proper court or the ordinary legal procedure. **-mural** *a.* beyond the walls, as outside a university. **-sensory** *a.* beyond the senses. **-sensory perception** *n.* an awareness of events not presented to the physical senses (*abbrev.* **E.S.P.**). **-territorial** *a.* outside the limits of a country or its jurisdiction. **-vehicular** *a.* (walk, work, etc.) performed outside a spacecraft while in outer space [L.].

ex·tract (ik·strakt′) *v.t.* to take out, esp. by force; to obtain against a person's will; to get by pressure, distillation, etc.; to copy out; to quote; to elicit; (*Math.*) to calculate; (eks′·trakt) *n.* matter obtained by distillation; concentrated drug, solution, syrup, etc.; a passage from a book, speech, etc. **-able, -ible** *a.* **-ion** *n.* act of extracting; that which is extracted; chemical operation of removing one or more substances from others by means of a solvent; parentage; ancestry; lineage; descent; (*Math.*) process of finding the root of a number. **-ive** *a.* **-or** *n.* [L. *ex*, out; *trahere, tractum*, to draw].

ex·tra·dite (eks′·trą·dīt) *v.t.* to deliver up a fugitive to another nation or authority. **extradition** *n.* [L. *ex*, out of; *tradere*, to deliver].

ex·tra·ne·ous (ek·strā′·ni·ąs) *a.* not naturally belonging to or dependent on a thing; not essential; foreign. **-ly** *adv.* [L. *extraneus*].

ex·tra·or·di·nar·y (eks·trawr′·dą·nęr·i·) *a.* beyond or out of the common order or method; exceeding the common degree or measure; employed on a special errand or duty. **extraordinarily** *adv.* **extraordinariness** *n.* [L. *extra*, beyond; *ordo, ordinis*, order].

ex·trav·a·gant (eks·trav′·ą·gąnt) *a.* profuse in expense; excessive; prodigal; wasteful; unrestrained. **extravagance** *n.* **extravagate** *v.i.* to wander beyond proper limits [L. *extra*, beyond; *vagari*, to wander].

ex·trav·a·gan·za (eks·trav·ą·gan′·zą) *n.* an extravagant, farcical, or fantastic composition, literary or musical [It.].

ex·tra·va·sate (eks·trav′·ą·sāt) *v.t.* to let out of the proper vessels, as blood; *a.* let out of its proper vessel [L. *extra*, beyond; *vas*, a vessel].

ex·tra·vert. See **extrovert.**

ex·treme (ek·strēm′) *a.* at the utmost point, edge, or border; outermost; of a high or highest degree; severe; excessive; last; most urgent; *n.* the utmost point or degree; a thing at one end or the other; the first and last of a series; great necessity. **-ly** *adv.* **extremism** *n.* holding extreme views or doctrines. **extremist** *n.* **extremity** *n.* the most distant point or side. **extremities** *n.pl.* hands and feet; arms and legs; extreme measures [L. *extremus*].

ex·tri·cate (eks′·trą·kāt) *v.t.* to free from difficulties or perplexities. **extricable** *a.* **extrication** *n.* [L. *extricare*].

ex·trin·sic, extrinsical (eks·trin′·sik, ·ąl) *a.* developing or having its origin from outside the body; not essential; not inherent [L. *extrinsecus*, on the outside].

ex·tro·vert (eks′·trō·vert) *n.* in psychology, a person whose emotions express themselves readily in external actions and events, as opposed to an *introvert.* **extroversion** *n.* [L. *extra*, outside of; *vertere*, to turn].

ex·trude (eks·trōōd′) *v.t.* to thrust out; to press out; to expel. **extrusion** *n.* [L. *ex*, out; *trudere*, to thrust].

ex·u·ber·ant (ek·zōō′·bęr·ant) *a.* effusive; vivacious; over abundant; prolific; **exuberance, exuberancy** *n.* state of being exuberant. **-ly** *adv.* [L. *ex*;*uber*, fertile].

ex·ude (eg·zōōd′) *v.t.* to discharge through the pores, as sweat; to discharge sap by incision, as a tree; *v.i.* to ooze out; to escape slowly, as a liquid [L. *ex*, out; *sudare*, to sweat].

ex·ult (eg·zult′) *v.i.* to rejoice exceedingly; to triumph; **-ance, -ancy** *n.* **-ant** *a.* **-tation** *n.* [L. *exultare*, to leap for joy].

ex·u·vi·ae (eg·zōō′·vi·ē) *n.pl.* (*Zool.*) cast off skin, teeth, shells, etc. of animals. **exuvial** *a.* **exuviate** *v.i.* [L. *exuere*, to strip off].

eye (ī) *n.* the organ of sight or vision; the power of seeing; sight; perforation; eyelet; bud; shoot; view; observation; judgment; keen sense of value; vigilance; anything resembling an eye; a small staple or ring to receive a door hook; an aperture for observing; *v.t.* to observe closely or fixedly; to look at; to view; *pr.p.* **eying** or **-ing.** *pa.t.* and *pa.p.* **-d** (īd). **-ball** *n.* the globe of the eye. **-brow** *n.* the arch of hairs. **-d** *a.* having eyes; spotted as if with eyes. **-glass** *n.* a glass to assist the sight; a monocle; the eyepiece of an optical instrument. *pl.* spectacles. **-lash** *n.* one of the hairs which edge the eyelid. **-let** *n.* a small eye or hole for a lace or cord, as in garments, sails, etc.; *v.i.* to make eyelets. **-lid** *n.* folds of skin which may be drawn at will over the eye. **— opener** *n.* surprising news; revealing statement. **-piece** *n.* lens in an optical instrument by means of which the observer views the image of the object formed in the focus of the other lenses. **-sight** *n.* power of vision; view; observation. **-sore** *n.* an object offensive to the eye. **-tooth** *n.* either of the two canine teeth of the upper jaw. **-wash** *n.* eye lotion. **-witness** *n.* one who gives testimony as to what he actually saw. **the green eye,** jealousy. **to see eye to eye,** to agree; to think alike [O.E. *eage*].

ey·rie (ār′·i·) *n.* the nest of a bird of prey.

F

fa·ble (fā′bl) *n.* a short tale or prolonged personification, often with animal characters, intended to convey a moral truth; a myth; a fiction; a falsehood; *v.t.* and *v.i.* to tell fables; to lie. *a.* mythical; legendary. **fabular fabulize** *v.i.* to compose fables. **fabulist** *n.* **fabulous** *a.* feigned or fabled; amazing; exaggerated [L. *fabula*, a story].

fab·ric (fab′·rik) *n.* structure; framework; woven, knitted or felted cloth; texture. **fabricate** *v.t.* to frame; to construct mechanically; to build according to standard specifications; to assemble from standardized components; to fake; to concoct. **-ation** *n.* **-ator** *n.* [L. *fabrica*, a workshop].

fa·cade (fa·sad′) *n.* the front view or elevation of a building [Fr. fr. It. *facciata,* the front of a building].

face (fās) *n.* the front of the head including forehead, eyes, nose, mouth, cheeks and chin; the outer appearance; cast of countenance; the outer or upper surface of any thing; the dial of a clock, etc.; the front; prestige; *v.t.* to confront; to stand opposite to; to admit the existence of (as facts); to oppose with courage; to put a layer of different material on to, or to trim an outer surface; *v.i.* to turn; **— card** *n.* a playing card, as king, queen and jack; **— cloth** *n.* a square of Turkish towelling for washing the face. **— lifting** *n.* an operation performed to remove wrinkles from the face. **— piece** *n.* the front part of a respirator. **— value** *n.* apparent worth. **facial** *a.* pert. to the face; *n.* (*Colloq.*) a beauty treatment for the face. **facies** (fā′·shi·ēz) *n.* the general appearance of anything. **facing** *n.* a covering in front for ornament or defense; material applied to the edge of a garment. [L. *facies,* a face].

facet (fas′·it) *n.* a small surface, as of a crystal or precious stone; aspect; *a.* having facets [Fr. *facette,* dim. of *face*].

fa·ce·tious (fa·sē′·shas) *a.* witty; jocular. **facetiae** (fa·sē′·shi·ē) *n.pl.* witty or humorous writings or sayings. *adv.* **-ness** *n.* [L. *facetus,* elegant].

fac·ile (fas′·l) *a.* easy; fluent; easily done; courteous; glib. **-ly** *adv.* **-ness** *n.* **facilitate** *v.t.* to make easy; to expedite. **facilitation** *n.* **facility** *n.* ease; deftness; aptitude; easiness of access [L. *facilis,* easy].

fac·sim·i·le (fak·sim′·a·li·) *n.* an exact copy; *a.* identical; *v.t.* to make a facsimile **facsimilist** *n.* **in facsimile,** accurately [L. *fac,* make (imper.); *simile,* like].

fact (fakt) *n.* anything done; anything actually true; that which has happened. **-ual** *a.* pert. to facts; actual. **matter-of-fact** *a.* prosaic; unimaginative [L. *factum,* thing done].

fac·tion (fak′·shạn) *n.* a group of people working together, esp. for subversive purposes; dissension; party clique. **factious** *a.* **factiously** *adv.* [Fr. fr. L. *factio,* a doing].

fac·ti·tious (fak·tish′·as) *a.* made or imitated by art, oppos. of *natural*; artificial; manufactured [L. *factitare,* to do frequently].

fac·tor (fak′·tẹr) *n.* (*Math.*) one of numbers which, multiplied together, give a given number; a contributory element or determining cause; *v.t.* (*Math.*) to express as a product of two or more quantities. **-ial** *a.* pert. to a factor. *v.t.* (*Math.*) to find the factors of a given number. **-ship** *n.* **-y** *n.* a building where things are manufactured [L. *facere,* to do].

fac·to·tum (fak·tō′·tạm) *n.* one who manages all kinds of work for an employer [L. *fac,* do (imper,); *totum,* all].

fac·ul·ty (fa′·kal·ti·) *n.* ability or power to act; mental aptitude; talent; natural physical function; a university department; the teaching body; the members of a profession, esp. medical; authorization. **facultative** a. optional [L. *facultas,* power].

fad (fad) n. a pet whim; a fancy or notion. **-dish** *a.* **-dy** *a.* **-dist** *n.* [etym. unknown].

fade (fād) *v.i.* to lose freshness, brightness, or strength gradually; to disappear slowly. **-less** *a.* not liable to fade; fast (of dye) [O.Fr. *fade,* dull].

fa·er·ie, faery (fē′·ri·) *n.* fairlyand; *a.* pert. to fairyland; fairy-like [var. of *fairy*].

fag (fag) *n.* toil; a tedious task; (Br. *Slang*) a cigarette; *v.t.* to exhaust; **-end** *n.* the tail end of anything; a remnant [etym. doubtful].

fag·ot, fag·got (fag′·ạt) *n.* a bundle of sticks for fuel; a bundle of steel rods cut for welding; *v.t.* to tie together; to embroider with a fagot stitch. **-ing, faggoting,** *n.* a kind of embroidery [Fr. *fagot,* a bundle of sticks].

Fahr·en·heit (far′·an·hīt) *n.* the term applied to a type of thermometer graduated so that freezing point of water is fixed at 32°, and boiling point at 212°. [German physicist, *Fahrenheit* (1686-1736)].

fail (fāl) *v.i.* to be lacking; to diminish; to deteriorate; to miss; to be unsuccessful in; to go bankrupt; *v.t.* to disappoint or desert; to omit; (*Colloq.*) to refuse to pass a candidate under examination. *pr.p.* **-ing.** *pa.p.* **-ed.** **-ing** *n.* a fault; a weakness; a shortcoming; *prep.* in default of. **-ure** *n.* bankruptcy; lack of success [O.Fr. *faillir,* to deceive].

fain (fān) *adv.* (*Poetic*) gladly. [O.E. *faegen,* joyful].

faint (fānt) *a.* lacking strength; indistinct; giddy; timorous; *v.i.* to become weak; to grow discouraged; to swoon; *n.* a swoon. **—heart** *n.* and *a.* **—hearted** *a.* cowardly; timorous. *adv.* indistinctly [O.Fr. *feint, pa.p.* of *feindre,* to feign].

fair (fer) *a.* clear; free from fault or stain; light-colored; blond; beautiful; not cloudy; hopeful; just; plausible; middling; *adv.* in a fair or courteous manner; according to what is just. **— copy** *n.* a rewritten, corrected copy. **— game,** open to banter. **-ish** a. rather fair. **-ly** *adv.* justly; tolerably; wholly. **-ness** *n.* **— play** *n.* straightforward justice. **— spoken** *n.* polite; plausible. **-way** *n.* a navigable channel on a river; (*Golf*) the stretch of ground between the tee and the green, which is freed from rough grass. **fair and square,** honest; honestly [O.E. *faeger,* pleasant].

fair (fer) *n.* periodic competitive exhibition for showing produce of a district; a sale of fancy articles to raise money for charitable purposes [O.Fr. *feire,* L. *feria,* a holiday].

fair·y (fer′·i·) *n.* an imaginary creature in the form of a diminutive human being, supposed to meddle, for good or for ill, with the affairs of men; *a.* fairy-like; dainty. **-land** *n.* land of the fairies; wonderland. **— tale** *n.* a story about fairies and magic; (*Colloq.*) improbable tale [O.Fr. *faerie,* enchantment].

faith (fāth) *n.* belief, esp. in a revealed religion; trust or reliance; a system of religious doctrines believed in; loyalty; pledged word. **-ful** a. loyal; reliable; honorable; exact. **-fully** *adv.* **-fulness** *n.* [O.Fr. *fei,* faith].

fake (fāk) *v.t.* to conceal the defects of, by artifice; to copy, as an antique, and pass it off as genuine; *v.i.* to pretend; *n.* a fraud; a deception; a forgery; a faker. **-r** *n.* [prob. Dut. *feague,* to touch up].

fa·kir (fạ·kir′, fā′·ker) *n.* a member of a sect of religious mendicants in India [Ar. *faqir,* a poor man].

Fa·lan·gists (fạ·lanj′·ists) *n.pl.* Spanish military Fascists, who co-operated with Franco during Spanish Civil War (1936-39).

fal·cate (fal′·kāt) *a.* (*Bot.* and *Zool.*) sickle shaped; crescent [L. *falx.* a sickle].

fal·con (faw′·kn, fȧl′·kạn) *n.* a sub-family of birds of prey, allied to the hawk, with strong curved beak and long sickle-shaped claws; one of these birds, trained to hunt game; **-er** *n.* one who breeds and trains falcons or hawks for hunting wild-fowl. **-ry** *n.* the sport of flying hawks in pursuit of game [O.Fr. *faucon,* a falcon].

fal·de·ral (fal·der·al′) *n.* the refrain to a song; anything trifling; a gew-gaw. Also

fald·stool (fawld′·stŏŏl) *n.* a portable, folding stool; stool before which kings kneel at their coronation; a litany-desk [O.H. Ger. *faldstuol*, a folding stool].

fall (fawl) *v.i.* to descend from a higher to a lower position; to drop; to collapse; to abate; to decline in value; to become degraded; to happen; to be captured. *pr.p.* **-ing.** *pa.t.* **fell.** *pa.p.* **-en.** *n.* the act of falling; a drop; capitulation; the amount (of rain, snow, etc.) deposited in a specified time; a cascade; a wrestling bout; a moral lapse, esp. that of Adam and Eve; diminution in value, amount, or volume; the autumn. **-en** *a.* prostrate; degraded; of loose morals. **-ing-star** *n.* a meteor. **—out** *n.* radioactive particles which descend to earth after a nuclear explosion. [O.E. *feallan*, to fall].

fal·la·cy (fal′·a·si·) *n.* deceptive appearance; a delusion; an apparently forcible argument which is really illogical; sophistry. **fallacious** a. misleading; illogical. **fallaciously** *adv.* [L. *fallax*, deceitful].

fal·li·ble (fal′·a·bl) *a.* liable to error; not reliable. **fallibility** *n.* the quality of being fallible. **fallibly** *adv.* [L. *fallere*, to fail].

fal·low (fal′·ō) *a.* left untilled for a season; (*Fig.*) untrained (of the mind); *n.* land which has lain untilled and unsown for a year or more; *v.t.* to plough without sowing [etym. doubtful, prob. O.E. *fealh*, a harrow].

fallow (fal′·ō) *a.* a pale yellow or light brown color. [O.E. *fealwes*, of a brown color].

false (fawls) *a.* untrue; inaccurate; dishonest; deceptive; artificial. **— face** *n.* a mask. **-hood** *n.* an untruth; a lie. **-ly** *adv.* **-ness** *n.* **falsifiable** *a.* capable of being falsified. **falsification** *n.* **falsifier** *n.* one who falsifies. **falsify** *v.t.* to distort the truth; to forge; to tamper with; to prove to be untrue. **falsity** *n.* an untrue statement; deception [L. *falsus*, mistaken].

fal·set·to (fawl·set′·ō) *n.* forced high notes esp. of a male voice [It. dim. of *falso*, false].

fal·ter (fawl′·tẹr) *v.i* to stumble; to hesitate; to lack resolution; to stammer.

fame (fām) *n.* public report or rumor, esp. good repute. **-d** *a.* celebrated. **famous** *a.* celebrated; noted; (*colloq.*) excellent. **famously** *adv.* [L. *fama*, a report].

fa·mil·iar (fạ·mil′·yẹr) *a.* intimate; informal; free; unconstrained; well-known; current; conversant with; *n.* a close acquaintance. **-ize** *v.t.* to make familiar; (*Reflex.*) to get to know thoroughly (foll. by *with*). **familiarity** *n.* intimacy; forwardness. **-ly** *adv.* [L. *familiaris*, pert. to a household].

fam·i·ly (fam′·a·li.) *n.* parents and their children; the children of the same parents; descendants of one common ancestor; (*Biol.*) group of individuals within an order or subdivision of an order; a group of languages derived from a common parent tongue. **— tree,** a diagram representing the genealogy of a family. **— way,** pregnancy [L. *familia*].

fam·ine (fam′·in) *n.* large-scale scarcity of food; extreme shortage; starvation. **famish** *v.t.* to starve; *v.i.* to feel acute hunger, famished *a.* [L. *fames*, hunger].

fan (fan) *n.* an instrument to produce currents of air or assist ventilation; a decorative folding object, made of paper, silk, etc. used to cool face; a winnowing-implement; a small sail on a windmill to keep large sails to the wind; *v.t.* to cool with a fan; to ventilate; to winnow; to cause to flame (as a fire); to excite; to spread out like a fan. *pr.p.* **-ning.** *pa.p.* **-ned. -light** *n.* a window, usually semicircular, over a doorway. **-ner** *n.* [O.E. *fann*, a winnowing-fan].

fan (fan) *n.* (*Slang*) a devoted admirer [*abbrev. of fanatic*].

fa·nat·ic (fạ·nat′·ik) *n.* a person inspired with excessive and bigoted enthusiasm, esp. a religious zealot; devotee; *a.* over-enthusiastic; immoderately zealous. **-al** *a.* **-ally** *adv.* **fanaticism** *n.* violent enthusiasm [L. *fanum*, a temple].

fan·cy (fan′·si·) *n.* the faculty of creating within the mind images of outward things; an image thus conceived; a whim; a notion; partiality; *a.* pleasing to the taste; guided by whim; elaborate; *v.t.* to imagine; to have a liking for; to desire; to breed (as dogs); **fancier** *n.* one who has a specialized knowledge, esp. of the breeding of animals. **fanciful** *a.* capricious; unreal; fantastic; **fancifully** *adv.* **fancifulness** *n.* **— ball** *n.* a ball at which the dancers wear costumes. **-free** *a.* heart-free [contr. fr. *fantasy*].

fan·fare (fan′·fār) *n.* a flourish of trumpets; a showy display. [Fr. *fanfarer*, to blow trumpets].

fang (fang) *n.* the canine tooth of a carnivorous animal; the long perforated tooth of a poisonous serpent [O.E. = a seizing].

fan·gled (fang′·gld) *a.* orig. meant fashionable, now exists only in the epithet *new-fangled*, new fashioned, hence unfamiliar,

fan·tan (fan′·tan) *n.* a Chinese gambling game [Chin.].

fan·ta·sy (fan′·ta·si) *n.* fancy; mental image; caprice; hallucination. Also **phantasy. fantasia** (fan·tā′·zha) *n.* (*Mus.*) a composition not conforming to the usual rules of music. **fantasied** *a.* fanciful. **fantasm** *n.* same as **phantasm. fantastic, -al** *a.* fanciful; wild; irregular; capricious. **fantastically** *adv.* [Gk. *phantasia*, appearance].

far (fȧr) *a.* distant; remote; more distant of two; *adv.* to a great extent or distance; to a great height; considerably; very much; *n.* a distant place. **-ther** *a.* (*comp.*). **-thest** *a.* (superl.) *adv.* **— East,** that part of Asia including India, China, Japan. **-fetched** *a.* (*Fig.*) incredible; strained. **-seeing,** or **-sighted** *a.* seeing to a great distance; (*Fig.*) taking a long view; prudent [O.E. *feor*, far].

far·ad (far′·ad) *n.* the unit of electrostatic capacity—the capacity of a condenser which requires one coulomb to raise its potential by one volt. **faraday,** *n.* the quantity of electricity required to liberate 1 gram-equivalent of an ion. **faradaic, faradic** *a.* pert. to induced electrical currents [fr. M. *Faraday*, scientist].

farce (fȧrs) *n.* orig. a dramatic interlude; a style of comedy marked by boisterous humor and extravagant gesture; absurd or empty show; a pretense. **farceur** (fạr·sur′) *n.* a joker; a wag. **farcical** *a.* pert. to a farce; absurdly ludicrous; sham. **farcically** *adv.* [O.Fr. *farce*, stuffing].

fare (fer) *v.i.* to be in any state, bad or good; to get on; to happen; to be entertained at table; *n.* the sum paid by a passenger on a vehicle; a passenger; food and drink at table. **-well** *interj.* (*Lit.*) may it go well with you; good-bye; *n.* a parting wish for someone's welfare; the act of taking leave; *a.* parting; last [O.E. *faran*, to go].

fa·ri·na (fa·rē′·na, fa·rī′·na) *n.* flour or meal of cereal grains, used for cereal and puddings; starch [L. *farina*, ground corn].

farm (fȧrm) *n.* a tract of land set apart for cultivation or for other industries, as dairy farm, etc.; the buildings on this land; *v.t.* cultivate land for agricultural purposes; to collect (taxes, etc.) on condition of receiving a percentage of what is yielded; *v.i.* and *t.* to cultivate; to operate a farm. **-er** *n.* **-ing**

n. the occupation of cultivating the soil. **-stead** *n.* a farm with all the outbuildings attached to it. **-yard** *n.* enclosure surrounded by farm buildings [M.E. *ferme*, payment].

far·o (fer'.ō) *n.* a gambling game of cards [fr. *Pharaoh*, one of the cards].

far·ra·go (fạr.ā'.gō, fạr.á'.gō) *n.* a medley; a miscellaneous collection. **farraginous** *a.* confusedly mixed [L. *farrago*, mixed fodder].

far·ri·er (far'.i.ẹr) *n.* Br. a veterinarian. **-y** *n.* [L. *ferrum*, iron].

far·row (far'.ō) *n.* a litter of pigs; *v.t.* to give birth to (pigs); *v.i.* to bring forth pigs [O.E. *fearh*, a pig].

far·ther (fár'.THẹr) *a.* more far; more remote; *adv.* to a greater distance. **-most** *a.*

far·thing (fár'.THing) *n.* (*Brit.*) the fourth of a penny [O.E. *feorthing*, a fourth part].

fas·ci·a (fash'.i.a) *n.* a band, fillet, or bandage; (*Archit.*) a strip of flat stone between two moldings; [L. *fascia*, a band].

fas·ci·cle (fas'.i.kl) *n.* (*Bot.*) a close cluster of leaves or flowers as in the sweet william; a small bundle of nerve fibers; a serial divisoin of a book. **fasicular, fasiculate** *a.* [L. *fasciculus*, a small bundle].

fas·ci·nate (fas'.ạ.nāt) *v.t.* to enchant; to deprive of the power of movement, by a look. **fascinating** *a.* **fascination** *n.* the act of fascinating; enchantment; irresistible attraction. **fascinator** *n.* [L. *fascinare*].

fas·cism (fash'.ism) *n.* a centralized autocratic national regime with extremely nationalistic policies with an economic system based on state-controlled capitalism. **Fascist** *n.* [It. *fascio*, a bundle].

fash·ion (fash'ạn) *n.* the style in which a thing is made or done; pattern; the mode or cut, esp. of a dress; custom; appearance; *v.t.* to form; to shape. **-able** *a.* **-ably** *adv.* [O.Fr. *facon*, a manner].

fast (fast) *v.i.* to abstain from food; to deny oneself certain foods as a form of religious discipline; *n.* abstinence from food; a day of fasting [O.E. *faestan*, to fast].

fast (fast) *a.* rapid; securely fixed; firm; tight shut; profound; immovable; permanent, as a dye; stable; in advance of the correct time, as a clock; loyal, as friends; dissipated, as *a fast life; adv.* firmly; soundly; securely; dissipatedly; rapidly. **-ness** *n.* security; a stronghold [O.E. *faest*, firm].

fas·ten (fas'.n) *v.t.* to fix firmly; to hold together; *v.i.* to fix itself; to catch (of a lock). **-er** *n.* a contrivance for fixing things firmly together. **-ing** *n.* that by which anything fastens, as a lock, bolt, nut, screw [O.E. *faest*, firm].

fas·tid·i·ous (fas.tid'.i.ạs) *a.* difficult to please; discriminating. **-ly** *adv.* **-ness** *n.* [L. *fastidium*, loathing].

fat (fat) *a.* (*comp.*) **-ter.** (*superl.*) **-test.** fleshy; plump; oily; yielding a rich supply; productive; profitable; *n.* an oily substance found in animal bodies; solid animal or vegetable oil; the best or richest part of anything; *v.t.* to make fat; *v.i.* to grow fat. *pr.p.* **-ting.** *pa.p.* **-ted. -head** *n.* (*Slang*) a stupid person. **-headed** *a.* **-ling** *n.* a young fattened animal. **-ness** *n.* the quality or state of being fat; corpulence; fertility. **-ted** *a.* fattened. **-ten** *v.t.* to make fat; to make fertile; *v.i.* to grow fat. **-tener** *n.* **-tiness** *n.* **-ty** *a.* resembling or containing fat; greasy [O.E. *faet*, fat].

fate (fāt) *n.* an inevitable and irresistible power supposedly controlling human destiny; appointed lot; death; doom. **the Fates,** the three goddesses supposed to preside over the course of human life. **fatal** *a.* causing death; appointed by fate; calamitous. **fatalism** *n.* the doctrine that all events are predetermined and unavoidable. **fatalist** *n.* **fatalistic** *a.* **fatality** *n.* accident causing death; the state of being fatal; inevitable necessity. **-d** *a.* destined; pre-ordained; doomed. **-ful** *a.* momentous; irrevocable. **-fully** *adv.* **-fulness** *n.* [L. *fatum*].

fa·ther (fá'.THẹr) *n.* a male parent; a male ancestor more remote than a parent; a title of respect paid to one of seniority or rank, esp. to church dignitaries, priests, etc.; the first person of the Trinity; oldest member of a community; a producer, author or contriver; *v.t.* to make oneself the father of; to adopt; to assume or admit responsibility for. **-hood** *n.* the state of being a father; paternity. **—in-law** *n.* (*pl.* **-s-in-law**) the father of one's wife or husband. **-land** *n.* the land of one's fathers. **-less** *a.* without a father living. **-liness** *n.* **-ly** *a.* and *adv.* like a father in affection and care; paternal; benevolent. **-ship** *n.* [O.E. *faeder*, a father].

fath·om (faTH'.ạm) *n.* a nautical measure of depth, 6 ft. *v.t.* to ascertain the depth of; to sound; (*Fig.*) to get to the bottom of; to understand. **-able** *n.* **-less** *a.* incapable of being fathomed; unplumbed. **-lessly** *adv.* [O.E. *faethm*, the outstretched arms].

fa·tigue (fạ.tēg') *n.* weariness from bodily or mental exertion; toil; non-military routine work of soldiers; *v.t.* to weary by toil; to exhaust the strength of; to tire out. *pr.p.* **-ing.** *pa.p.* **-d** [Fr. *fatiguer*, to weary].

fat·u·ous (fa'.choo.ạs) *a.* silly. **fatuity** *n.* unconsciously foolish; inanity; foolishness. **-ness** *n.* [L. *fatuus*, silly].

fau·cet (faw'.sit) *n.* a fixture for controlling the flow of liquid from a pipe, etc.; a tap [O.Fr. *fausset*].

faugh (faw) *interj.* an exclamation of contempt or disgust [imit.].

fault (fawlt) *n.* a failing; blunder; mistake; defect; flaw; responsibility for error; (*Geol.*) a dislocation of rock strata; in hunting, the loss of the scent trail; (*Elect.*) a defect in electrical apparatus. **-ed** *a.* (*Geol.*) broken by one or more faults. **-ily** *adv.* **-iness** *n.* **-less** *a.* without flaws; perfect. **-lessly** *adv.* **-lessness** *n.* perfection. **-y** *a.* imperfect. [O. Fr. *faute*, error].

fau·na (fawn'.a) *n.* a collective term for the animals of any given geographical region or geological epoch [L. *Fauna*, sister of *Faunus*, a god of agriculture].

fa·ve·o·late (fav.ē'.ō.lāt) *a.* pitted; cellular; resembling a honeycomb. [L. *faveolus*, a little honeycomb].

fa·vor (fā'.vẹr) *n.* a gracious act; kind regard; goodwill; partiality; token of generosity or esteem; a gift; *v.t.* to regard with kindness; to show bias towards; to tend to promote; (*Colloq.*) to resemble in feature. **-able** *a.* friendly; propitious; advantageous; suitable; satisfactory. **-ableness** *n.* **-ably** *adv.* **-ed** *a.* fortunate; lucky featured, as in *ill-favored.* **-ite** *n.* a person or thing regarded with special favor; the likely winner; *a.* regarded with particular affection; most esteemed. **-itism** *n.* undue partiality [L. *favor*, partiality].

fawn (fawn) *n.* a young deer; its color; *a.* delicate yellowish-brown; *v.i.* to give birth to a fawn [O.Fr. *faon*, fr. L. *fetus*, offspring].

fawn (fawn) *v.i.* to flatter unctuously; to curry favor. **-er** *n.* **-ing** *n.* servile flattery; *a.* over-demonstrative. **-ingly** *adv.* **-ingness** *n.* [M.E. *faunen*, to rejoice].

fay (fā) *n.* a fairy; an elf [O.Fr. *fae*].

fe·al·ty (fē'.ạl.ti.) *n.* fidelity; obligations binding a vassal to his lord [O.Fr. *fealte*, fidelity].

fear (fir) *n.* alarm; dread; solicitude; anxiety; reverence towards God; *v.t.* to regard with dread or apprehension; to anticipate (as a disaster); to hold in awe; *v.i.* to be afraid;

to be anxious. **-ful** *adv.* **-fulness** *n.* **-less** *a.* without fear; intrepid; dauntless. **-lessly** *adv.* **lessness** *n.* courage; intrepidity.**-some** *a.* causing fear; terrifying [O.E. *faer,* danger].

fea·si·ble (fē′.zạ.bl) *a.* capable of being done; suitable. **-ness, feasibility** *n.* **feasibly** *adv.* [Fr. *faisible,* that can be done].

feast (fēst) *n.* a day of joyful or solemn commemoration; a banquet; something very enjoyable; *v.t.* to feed sumptuously; to regale; *v.i.* to eat sumptuously; to be highly gratified or delighted. **-er** *n.* [L. *festum,* a holiday].

feat (fēt) *n.* an exploit or action of extraordinary strength, courage, skill, or endurance [Fr. *fait,* fr. L. *factum,* a deed].

feath·er (feTH′.ẹr) *n.* one of the epidermal growths forming the body-covering of a bird; a plume; the feathered end or an arrow; feathers, as a cap or arrow. **-bed** *n.* a mattress stuffed with feathers; *v.t.* (*Colloq.*) to pamper; to keep supernumeraries on a job. **-brained, -headed, -pated** *a.* weak-minded; inane. **-stitch** *n.* an embroidery stitch resembling a feather. **-weight,** the lightest weight that may be carried by a race-horse; a boxer weighing not more than 126 lbs.; any very light or insignificant person or thing. **-y** *a.* pert. to, covered with, or resembling feathers [O.E. *fether,* feather].

fea·ture (fē′.cher) *n.* any part of the face; distinctive characteristic; main attraction; *pl.* the face; *v.t.* to portray; to outline; to present as the leading attraction. **-less** *a.* void of striking features. [O.Fr. *faiture,* something made].

feb·ri·fuge (feb′.rạ.fūj) *n.* a drug taken to allay fever. **febrifugal** *a.* **febrile** (fē′.bril, feb′.ril) *a.* feverish; accompanied by fever. **febrility** *n.* [L. *febris,* fever].

Feb·ru·ar·y (feb′.ròò.e.ri.) *n.* the second month of the year [L. *Februaris,* fr. *Februa,* the Roman festival of purification].

fe·ces, faeces (fē′sēz) *n.pl.* dregs; the solid waste matter from the bowels. **fecal** (.kạl) *a.* [L. *faeces,* grounds].

fe·cund (fe′.kạnd) *a.* prolific; fruitful; fertile. **-ate** (fē′.kun′.dāt, fek′.un.dāt) *v.t.* to make fruitful; to impregnate. **-ation** *n.* **-ity** *n.* the quality or power of reproduction; fertility; productiveness [L. *fecundus,* fruitful].

fed (fed) *pa.t.* and *pa.p.* of the verb **feed.**

fed·er·al (fed′.er.al) *a.* pert. to a league or treaty, esp. between states; of an association of states which, autonomous in home affairs, combine for matters of wider national and international policy; pert. to such a central government; pert. to the Union in the Civil War. **federacy** *n.* **-ize** *v.t.* to form a union under a federal government. **-ism** *n.* **-ist** *n.* a supporter of such a union. **federate** *v.t.* to unite states into a federation. *a.* united; allied. **federation** *n.* a federal union. **federative** *a.* [L. *foedus,* a compact].

fee (fē) *n.* orig. land held from a lord on condition of certain feudal services; remuneration for professional services; payment for special privilege; *v.t.* to pay a fee to. **fee-simple,** unrestricted ownership or inheritance [O.E. *feoh,* cattle or property].

fee·ble (fē′.bl) *a.* weak; deficient in strength; frail; faint. **—minded** *a.* mentally subnormal. **-ness** *n.* **feebly** *adv.* [Fr. *faible,* weak].

feed (fēd) *v.t.* to give food to; to supply with nourishment; to supply with material (as a machine); *v.i.* to eat; to subsist. *pa.p.* and *pa.t.* **fed.** *n.* that which is consumed, esp. by animals; the material supplied to a machine or the channel by which it is fed. **-er** *n.* one who feeds; a device for supplying a machine with material; a channel taking water to a reservoir; a branch railway-line. **-ing** *n.* act of eating; that which is consumed; grazing. [O.E. *fedan,* to feed].

feel (fēl) *v.t.* to perceive by the touch; to handle; to be sensitive to; to experience emotionally; to have an intuitive awareness of; *v.i.* to know by the touch; to be conscious of being; to give rise to a definite sensation; to be moved emotionally. *pa.p. pa.t.* **felt** *n.* the sensation of touch; the quality of anything touched. **-er** *n.* (*Zool.*) one of the tactile organs (antennae, tentacles, etc.) of certain insects and animals; a tentative remark, proposal, etc. to sound the opinions or attitude of others. **-ing** *n.* sense of touch; awareness by touch; intuition; sensibility; sympathy. **-ings** *n.pl.* emotions; *a.* kindly; responsive; possessing great sensibility. **-ingly** *adv.* [O.E. *felan,* to feel].

feet (fēt) *n.pl.* of **foot.**

feign (fān) *v.t.* to invent; to pretend; to counterfeit. **-ed** *a.* pretended; disguised. **-edly** *adv.* **-edness** *n.* **-ing** *n.* pretense; invention. **feint** *n.* an assumed appearance; a misleading move in boxing, military operations, etc. *v.i.* to make a deceptive move [Fr. *feindre,* to feign].

feld·spar (feld′.spàr) *n.* a constituent of granite and other igneous rocks; a crystalline mineral comprising silicates of aluminium with varying proportions of potassium, calcium and sodium. *a.* [Ger. *Feld,* field; *Spath,* a spar].

fe·lic·i·ty (fi.lis′.ạ.ti.) *n.* happiness; bliss; skill. **felicitate** *v.t.* to express joy or pleasure to; to congratulate. **felicitation** *n.* congratulation; the act of expressing good wishes. **felicitous** *a.* happy; appropriate; aptly expressed [L. *felix,* happy].

fe·line (fē′.līn) *a.* pert. to cats; cat-like; (*Fig.*) treacherous [L. *feles,* a cat].

fell (fel) *a.* cruel; ruthless; deadly [O.Fr. *fel.* cruel].

fell (fel) *n.* an animal's skin or hide [O.E. *fel,* a skin].

fell (fel) *pa.t.* of the verb **fall.**

fell (fel) *v.t.* to cause to fall; to cut down; to sew an overlapping flax seam. **-er** *n.* [O.E. *fellan,* to cause to fall].

fell (fel) *n.* a tract of high moorland, as in the English Lake District [Scand. *fiall,* rock].

fel·low (fel′.ō) *n.* a man; boy; (*Colloq.*) suitor; an associate; an equal; a person; a worthless person; a graduate student on a grant for special study; member of a literary or scientific society. **— traveller** *n.* sympathizer with the Communist Party, but not a member of it. **-ship** *n.* the state of being a fellow; companionship; community of feeling, interest, etc.; a foundation for the maintenance of a resident university graduate; the grant made by such a foundation [M.E. *felawe,* a partner].

fel·on (fel′.ạn) *n.* one who has committed felony; (*Med.*) inflammation of top joint of the finger; a whitlow; *a.* fierce; traitorous. **-ious** *a.* **-iously** *adv.* **-iousness** *n.* **-y** *n.* (*Law*) a crime more serious than a *misdemeanor* (as murder, manslaughter, etc.) [O.Fr. *felon,* a traitor].

felt (felt) *pa.t.* and *pa.p.* of **feel.**

felt (felt) *n.* a closely matted fabric of wool, hair, etc.; *v.t.* to make into felt; to cover with felt; *v.i.* to become matted like felt. **-ing** *n.* the art or process of making felt; the felt itself [O.E. *felt,* something compact]

fe·male (fē′.māl) *n.* one of the sex that bears young; (*Bot.*) a plant which produces fruit; *a.* pert. to the child-bearing sex; feminine. **femineity** (fe.mạ.nē′.ạ.ti.) *n.* the quality of being a woman. **feminine** *a.* pert. to or associated with women; womanly;

tender; (of males) effeminate. **femininely** *adv.* **feminineness, femininity** *n.* the nature of the female sex; womanliness. **feminism** *n.* the doctrine that maintains the equality of the sexes; advocacy of women's rights.

fe·mi·nist (fe′·mi·nist) *n.* one who advocates women's rights and interests [L. *femina*].

fe·mur (fē′·mẹr) *n.* the thigh-bone. **femoral** *a.* [L. *femur*, the thigh].

fen (fen) *n.* (*Brit.*) low-lying marshy land [O.E. *fenn*, a bog].

fence (fens) *n.* a wall or hedge for enclosing; the art of fencing; a receiver of stolen goods; *v.t.* to enclose with a fence; to guard; *v.i.* to practise the art of sword-play; to evade a direct answer to an opponent's challenge; to equivocate. **-r** *n.* one who is skilled in fencing. **fencing** *n.* the art or practice of self-defense with the sword, foil, etc.; the act of enclosing by a fence; the materials of which a fence is made [abbrev. of *defence*].

fend (fend) *v.t.* to ward off; *v.i.* to resist; to parry; (*Colloq.*) to provide. **-er** *n.* that which acts as a protection; the metal part over wheels of an automobile; a metal guard to prevent coals falling beyond hearth; a device, usually a bundle of rope, to break the impact of a ship drawing alongside a wharf or other vessel [abbrev. of *defend*].

fenestra (fi·nes′·trạ) *n.* a hole; an opening. Also **fenester. fenestral** *a.* **fenestrate, fenestrated** *a.* (*Bot.*) having transparent spots; (*Archit.*) having windows. **fenestration** *n.* the state of being perforated; arrangement of windows in a building [L. *fenestra*, a window].

fen·nel (fen′·el) *n.* a perennial umbelliferous plant with yellow flowers [O.E. *finul*, fr. L. *faenum*, hay].

fer·ment (fur′·ment) *n.* a substance which causes fermentation, as yeast; fermentation; (*Fig.*) tumult; agitation. (fẹr·ment′) *v.t.* to induce fermentation in; to arouse a commotion; *v.i.* to undergo fermentation; to work (of wine); to become excited; to be in a state of agitation. **-ability** *n.* **-able** *a.* **-ation** *n.* the decomposition of organic substances produced by the action of a living organism, or of certain chemical agents. **-ative** *a.* [L. *fermentum*, leaven].

fern (furn) *n.* plant characterized by fibrous roots, and leaves called fronds. **-y** *a.* [O.E.].

fe·roc·ity (fạ·ràs′·à·ti·) *n.* cruelty; savage fierceness of disposition. **ferocious** *a.* fierce; violent; wild. **ferociously** *adv.* **ferociousness** *n.* [L. *ferox*, wild].

fer·ret (fer′·it) *n.* a small, partially domesticated variety of polecat; *v.t.* to hunt out to search out [O.Fr. *furet*, a ferret].

fer·ric (fer′·ik) *a.* pert. to or extracted from iron; applied to compounds of trivalent iron, **— acid,** an acid containing iron and oxygen. [L. *ferrum*, iron].

fer·ro- (fer′·ō) *prefix* fr. L. *ferrum*, containing or made of iron, occurring in compound words **-concerte** *n.* reinforced concrete; concrete with inner skeleton of iron or steel. **-magnetic** *a.* reacting like iron in a magnetic field. **ferrous** *a.* pert. to iron.

fer·rule (fer′·ạl, fer′·ȯȯl) *n.* a metal tip or ring on a cane, etc. to prevent splitting. Also **ferule** [O.Fr. *virelle*, a bracelet].

fer·ry (fer′·i·) *v.t.* to transport over stretch of water by boat. *n.* a place where one is conveyed across a river, etc. by boat; the ferry-boat; the right of transporting passengers and goods by this means. **ferriage** *n.* transport by ferry; the fare paid for such transport [O.E. *faran*, to go].

fer·tile (fur′·til) *a.* producing or bearing abundantly; prolific; fruitful; (*Fig.*) inventive. **-ly** *adv.* **-ness, fertilization** *n.* the act of fertilizing; enrichment of soil, by natural or artificial means; (*Biol.*) union of the female and male cells. **fertilize** *v.t.* to make fruitful; (*Biol.*) to fecundate; (*Bot.*) to pollinate. **fertilizer** *n.* one who, or that which, fertilizes; material (e.g. manure, nitrates) to enrich soil. **fertility** *n.* [L. *fertilis*, fruitful].

fer·ule (fer·ạl, fer′·ȯȯl) *n.* a rod or ruler for punishing children [L. *ferula*, rod].

fer·vent (fur′·vạnt) *a.* glowing; ardent; zealous; enthusiastic. **fervency** *n.* ardor; intensity of devotion. **-ly** *adv.* **fervid** *a.* burning; vehement; intense. **fervidity** *n.* **fervidly** *adv.* **fervidness** *n.* zeal; enthusiasm. **fervor** *n.* heat; ardor; passion [L. *fervere*, to boil].

fes·cue (fes′·kū) *n.* a kind of tough grass; a teacher's small pointer [M.E. *festu*, a bit of straw].

fes·tal (fes′·tạl) *a.* pert. to feast or festival; joyous; gay. **-ly** *adv.* [O.Fr. *feste*, a feast].

fes·ter (fes′·tẹr) *v.t.* to cause to putrefy; *v.i.* to become inflamed; to suppurate; to rot; to become embittered; *n.* an ulcer; a sore [O.Fr. *festre*, an ulcer].

fes·tive (fes′·tiv) *a.* festal; joyous; convivial. **festival** *n.* a feast or celebration; an annual competition or periodic gathering of musical or dramatic societies. **-ly** *adv.* **festivity** *n.* merriment; merrymaking; festival [L. *festivus*, festive].

fes·toon (fes·tȯȯn′) *n.* garland hanging in a curve; *v.t.* [Fr. fr. L.L. *festo*, a garland].

fetch (fech) *v.t.* to go for and bring; to summon; to bring or yield (a price); *v.i.* to go and bring things; *n.* the act of bringing; a trick or artifice; an apparition; a person's double. **-ing** *a.* attractive; alluring [O.E. *feccan*, to bring].

fete (fāt) *n.* a festival; a holiday; *v.t.* to honor with celebrations. **feted** *a.* honored [L. *festum*, a feast].

fet·id (fet′·id) *a* having a strong, offensive smell. Also **foetid** [L. *fetidus*, stinking].

fe·tish, fetich, fetiche (fet′·ish) *n.* an object or image superstitiously invested with divine or demoniac power, and, as such, reverenced devoutly; anything regarded with exaggerated reverence. **-ism,** *n.* fetish worship. **-istic,** *a.* [Port. *feitico*, magic].

fet·lock (fet′·làk) *n.* the tuft of hair on a horse's leg.

fet·ter (fet′·ẹr) *n.* a chain or shackle for the feet (usually pl.); an impediment or restriction; *v.t.* to shackle; to restrain [O.E. *fetor*, fr. *fet*, the feet].

fet·tle (fet′·l) *n.* condition [O.E. *fetel*, a girdle].

fe·tus, foetus (fē′·tạs) *n.* the young of vertebrate animals between the embryonic and independent states. **fetal, foetal** *a.* **fetation, foetation** *n.* pregnancy. **feticide, foeticide** *n.* destroying of the fetus; abortion [L. *fetus*, a bringing forth].

feud (fūd) *n.* a lasting, hereditary strife between families or clans; deadly hatred [M.E. *fede*, enmity].

feud (fūd) *n.* an estate or land held on condition of service; a fief. **-al** *a.* pert. to feuds or to feudalism. **-alism** *n.* a system which prevailed in Europe in the Middle Ages, by which vassals held land from the King and the tenants-in-chief in return for military service. Also **feudal system. -ary, -atory** *a.* holding land by feudal tenure; *n.* a vassal holding land in fee [L. L. *feudum*, a fief].

fe·ver (fē′·vẹr) *n.* bodily disease marked by unusual rise of temperature and usually a quickening of pulse; violent mental or emotional excitement; *v.t.* to put into a fever. *v.i.* to become fevered. **-ed** *a.* affected with fever; frenzied. **ish** *a.* slightly fevered;

agitated. **-ishly** *adv.* [O.E. *fefor*, forever].
few (fū) *a.* not many; *n.* and *pron.* a small number. **-ness** *n.* [O.E. *feawe*, few].
fez (fez) *n.* a red, brimless felt hat with tassel worn in Egypt, Turkey, etc. [prob. fr. *Fez* in Morocco].
fi·a·cre (fi·á′·kr) *n.* a hackney coach [fr. *Hotel St. Fiacre* [Paris].
fi·an·ce (fē·ạn·sā′) *n.* (*fem.* **fiancee**) a betrothed man [Fr. *fiancer*, to betroth].
fi·as·co (fē·as′·kō) *n.* any spectacular failure [It. *fiasco*, a bottle].
fi·at (fī′·at) *n.* a formal command; an authoritative order [L. *fiat*, let it be done].
fib (fib) *n.* a falsehood; a mild lie; *v.i.* to tell a petty lie *pr.p.* **-bing.** *pa.p.*; *pa.t.* **-bed.**
fi·ber (fī′·bẹr) *n.* one of the bundles of thread-like tissue constituting muscles, etc.; any thread-like substance used for weaving fabric; character, as in *moral fiber*. **-ed** *a.* **-less** *a.* **fibriform** *a.* **fibril** *n.* a very small fiber. **fibrillose** *a.* (*Bot.*) covered with fibers. **fibrillous** *a.* composed of small fibers. **fibrin** *n.* a proteid formed in coagulation of blood. **fibroid** *a.* of a fibrous nature; *n.* a fibrous tumor. **fibrous** *a.* composed of fibers. **fibrousness** *n.* [L. *fibra*, a fiber].
fib·u·la (fib′·yạ·la) *n.* (*Archeal.*); (*Med.*) the slender outer bone of the leg between knee and ankle. **-r** *a.* [L.*fibula*, a clasp].
fich·u (fi′·shòò) *n.* a triangular cape worn over the shoulders and tying in front; a ruffle of lace, etc. worn at the neck [Fr.].
fick·le (fik′·l) *a.* inconstant; capricious; unreliable. **-ness** *n.* [O.E. *ficol*, cunning].
fic·tile (fik′·til) *a.* capable of being molded; plastic; used of all objects shaped in clay by a potter [L. *fictilis*].
fic·tion (fik′·shạn) *n.* literature dealing with imaginary characters and situations; something invented, or imagined. **-al** *a.* **fictitious** *a.* imaginary; feigned; false; **fictitiously** *adv.* [L. *fictus*, invented].
fid·dle (fid′·l) *n.* a stringed musical instrument; a violin; wooden framework around dining-tables on board a ship; *v.t.* and *v.i.* to play on a fiddle; to trifle. **— bow** *n.* the bow used in playing a violin. **—de-dee** *n.* nonsense. **—faddle** *v.i.* to trifle; to dawdle; *n.* triviality; *interj.* rubbish′ **-sticks** (*interj.*) nonsense. **fiddling** *a.* trifling [O.E. *fithele*].
fi·del·i·ty (fī·del′·ạ·ti·) *n.* faithfulness; loyalty; devotion to duty; adherence to marriage vows; accuracy [L. *fidelis*, faithful].
fidg·et (fij′·it) *v.i.* to move restlessly; to be uneasy; *n.* uneasiness. **-s** *n.pl.* nervous restlessness. **-y** *a.* [fr. Scand. *fikja*].
fi·du·ci·ar·y (fi·dòò′·shi·er·i·) *a.* holding or held in trust; (of paper currency) depending for its value on public confidence; *n.* a trustee. **fiducial** *a.* having faith or confidence [L. *fiducia*, confidence].
field (fēld) *n.* cleared land; a division of farm land; scene of a battle; the battle itself; any wide expanse; areas of observation; locality of operations, as in surveying; sphere of influence within which magnetic, electrostatic, or gravitational forces are perceptible; the surface of an escutcheon; the background of a flag, coin, etc. on which a design is drawn; the people following a hunt; (sports) area of ground used for sports; (*Cricket*) the side which is not batting; a collective term for all the competitors in an athletic contest or all the horses in a race; an area rich in some natural product (e.g. coal-field, oil-field); *v.t.* (*Baseball*) to catch the ball; *v.i.* to act as fielder. **— artillery** *n.* light guns for active operations. **— battery** *n.* battery of field guns. **— book** *n.* book used for notes by land surveyor or naturalist. **— day** *n.* a day for athletic contests; a gala day. **-er** *n.* one who fields at cricket, baseball, etc. **— glass** *n.* a binocular telescope. **— gun** *n.* a small cannon on a carriage. **— marshal** *n.* the highest rank in the British and several other armies. **— officer** *n.* a commissioned officer in rank between a captain and a general. **-piece** *n.* a field-gun. **—sports** *n.pl.* out-of-door sports as hunting, racing, etc. [O.E. *feld*, a field].
fiend (fēnd) *n.* a demon; the devil; a malicious foe; (*Colloq.*) one who is crazy about something, as, *a fresh-air fiend*. **-ish** *a.* [O.E. *feond*, an enemy].
fierce (fērs) *a.* ferocious; violent; savage; intense. **-ly** *adv.* **-ness** *n.* ferocity; rage [O.Fr. *fers*, bold].
fi·er·y (fi′·er·i·) *a.* flaming; hot; (*Fig.*) ardent; fierce; vehement; irritable. **fierily** *adv.* **fieriness** *n.* [fr. *fire*].
fife (fif) *n.* a high-pitched flute. **-r** *n.* one who plays the fife [O.Fr. *fifre*, a fife].
fif·teen (fif′·tēn) *a.* and *n.* five and ten; the symbol, 15 or XV. *a.* the fifth after the tenth; making one of fifteen equal parts. [O.E. *fif*, five; *tene*, ten].
fifth (fifth) *a.* next after the fourth; *n.* one of five equal parts of a whole. **— column,** any organization within a country deliberately assisting the enemy by acts of sabotage, etc. **— columnist** *n.* **-ly** *adv.*
fif·ty (fif′·ti·) *a.* and *n.* five times ten; the symbol 50 or L. **fiftieth** *a.* next in a series of forty-nine others; making one of fifty equal parts of a whole; *n.* a fiftieth part. **to go fifty-fifty** (*Colloq.*) share and share alike [O.E. *fiftig*, fifty].
fig (fig) *n.* a Mediterranean tree or its fruit (*Colloq.*) something insignificant [Fr. *figue*].
fight (fit) *v.t.* to wage war against; to contend against; to oppose; *v.i.* to take part in single combat or battle; to resist. *pa.p.* **fought** (fawt). *n.* a combat; a battle; a struggle; pugnacity. **-er** *n.* one who fights; an aircraft designed for fighting. **-ing** *a.* able to, or inclined to, fight; pert. to a fight [O.E. *feohtan*].
fig·ment (fig′·mạnt) *n.* an invention, fiction, or fabrication [L. *figmentum*, an image].
fig·ure (fig′·yer) *n.* outward form of anything; the form of a person; a diagram, drawing, etc.; a design; an appearance; steps in a dance; the sign of a numeral, as 1, 2, 3; *v.t.* to cover with patterns; to note by numeral characters; to calculate; to symbolize; to image in the mind; *v.i.* to make a figure. **-d** *a.* esp. adorned with patterns, as *figured muslin*. **figurative** *a.* representing by a figure; not literal; abounding in figures of speech. **figuratively** adv. **figurativeness** *n.* **-head** *n.* the norminal head of an organization, without real authority; ornamental figure under the bowsprit of a ship. **figurine** *n.* a statuette. **figure of speech,** an unusual use of words to produce a desired effect, such as metaphor, simile, etc. [L. *figura*, fr. *fingere*, to form].
fil·a·ment (fil′·ạ·ment) *n.* a slender thread; a fiber, (*Bot.*) the stalk of a stamen; (*Elect.*) a fine wire, usually of tungsten, which glows to incandescence by the passage of an electric current. *a.* like a filament. **-ous** *a.* thread-like [L. *filum, thread*].
filbert (fil′·bert) *n.* the nut of the hazel-tree
filch (filch) *v.t.* to steal; to pilfer. **-er** *n.*
file (fīl) *n.* an orderly line; a cabinet, wire, or portfolio for keeping papers in order; the papers or cards thus kept; *v.t.* to set in order in a public record office; *v.i.* to march in a file; to make application. **Indian** or **single file,** a single line of men marching one behind the other. **rank and file,** non-commissioned soldiers; the general mass of people as

distinct from well-known figures [L. *filum*, a thread].

file (fīl) *n.* a steel instrument for smoothing rough surfaces or cutting through metal. *v.t.* to cut or abrade with a file. *pr.p.* **filing.** *pa.p.* **-d. filing** *n.* a particle of metal rubbed off by a file; the action of abrading stone or cutting metal [O.E. *feol*, a file].

fil·i·al (fil′.i.al) *a.* pert. to or befitting a son or daughter. **-ly** *adv.* **filiation** *n.* being a child of a certain parent; derivation [L. *filius*, a son].

fil·i·bus·ter (fil′.a.bus.ter) *n.* one who deliberately obstructs legislation, esp. by making long speeches; a lawless adventurer; a buccaneer. *v.i.* to act as a filibuster [Fr. *filibustier*, a freebooter].

fil·i·form (fil′.a.form) *a.* thread-like [L. *filum*, a thread].

fil·i·gree (fil′.i.grē) *n.* ornamental openwork of gold or silver wire; anything highly ornamental but fragile. **-d** *a.* [L. *filum*, thread; *granum*, grain].

Fil·i·pi·no (fil.a.pēn′.ō) *n.* a native of the Philippine Islands.

fill (fil) *v.t.* to make full; to replenish; to occupy as a position; to supply as a vacant office; to pervade; to stop up (a tooth); *v.i.* to become full; *n.* a full supply. **-er** *n.* one who, or that which, fills; a funnel-shaped vessel for filling bottles; **-ing** *n.* that which fills up a space, as gold, etc. used by dentists; a mixture put into sandwiches, cakes, etc.; *a.* satisfying; ample. **filling station,** a roadside depot for supplying gasoline, oil etc., to motorists [O.E. *fyllan*, to make full].

fil·let (fil′.it) *n.* a narrow band, esp. round the head; (fi.lā′) piece of meat cut from the thigh; a piece of meat boned and rolled; fish after bones are removed; *v.t.* to bind with a fillet; to bone (meat or fish, etc.); [Fr. *filet*, a thread].

fil·lip (fil′.ap) *v.t.* to strike with the nail of the finger, first placed against the ball of the thumb then released with a sudden jerk; to incite; to spur on; a jerk of the finger; an incentive; a stimulus [form of *flip*].

fil·ly (fil′.i.) *n.* a young mare; a lively or wanton young woman [dim. of *foal*].

film (film) *n.* a thin coating or membrane; a delicate filament; dimness over the eyes; (*Photog.*) a roll of flexible, sensitized material used for photography; pictures taken on this roll; *pl.* (*Colloq.*) a movie show; *v.t.* to cover with a film; to take a moving picture of; to reproduce on a film. **-iness** *n.* **-y** *a.* composed of or covered with film; membranous; sheer [O.E. *filmen*, membrance].

fi·lose (fī′.lōs) *a.* having a thread-like ending [L. *filum*, thread].

fil·ter (fil′.ter) *n.* a device for separating liquids from solids, or for straining impurities from liquids; any porous material such as filter paper, charcoal, etc.; a device for removing dust from the air; (*Photog.*) a piece of colored glass placed in front of the lens, passing certain rays only; *v.t.* to purify by passing through a filter; to filtrate; *v.i.* to pass through a filter; **filtrate** *v.t.* to filter; *n.* the liquid which has been strained through a filter. **filtration** *n.* **— bed** *n.* a layer of sand or gravel at bottom of a reservoir for purifying the water. [O.Fr. *filtre*, a strainer].

filth (filth) *n.* foul matter; dirt; pollution; (*Fig.*) immorality; obscenity. **-ily** *adv.* **-iness** *n.* **-y** *a.* [O.E. *fylth*, foulness].

fim·bri·a (fim′.bri.a) *n.* (*Zool.*) a fringe or fringe-like structure. **fimbriate, fimbriated** *a.* fringed [L. *fimbria*, thread].

fin (fin) *n.* a paddle-like organ of fishes and other aquatic forms serving to balance and propel; (*Aero.*) a vertical surface, fixed usually on the tail of an aircraft to aid lateral and directional stability. [O.E. *finn*, a fin].

fi·nal (fī′.nal) *a.* pert. to the end; last; decisive; conclusive; ultimate; *n.* the last stage of anything; *pl.* the last examination or contest in a series. **-ist** *n.* a competitor who reaches the finals of a contest. **-ity** *n.* the state of being final; conclusiveness. **-ize** *v.t.* to give a final form to. **-ly** *adv.* [L. *finis*, the end].

fi·na·le (fi.ná′.li.) *n.* the end; (*Mus.*) the last movement of a musical composition; final scene; a conclusion [It. *finale*, the end].

fi·nance (fa.nans′ or fī′.nans) *n.* the science of controlling public revenue and expenditure; the management of money affairs; *pl.* the income of a state or person; resources; funds; *v.t.* to provide funds for; to supply capital. **financial** *a.* pert. to finance; fiscal. **financially** *adv.* **financier** (fin.an.sēr′) *n.* one who deals in large-scale money transactions [Fr. fr. L.L. *finare*, to pay a fine].

finch (finch) *n.* the name applied to various species of small, seed-eating birds including the *chaffinch, bullfinch* [O.E. *finc*, finch].

find (fīnd) *v.t.* to come to by searching; to meet with; to discover; to perceive; to experience; (*Law*) to give a verdict; *pa.t., pa.p.* **found.** *n.* a discovery, esp. of unexpected value. **-er** *n.* **-ing** *n.* the act of one who finds; a legal decision arrived at by a jury after deliberation; a discovery [O.E. *findan*, to find].

fine (fīn) *a.* excellent; thin; slender; minute; delicate; noble; polished; showy; striking; refined (as *fine gold*); keen; appealing aesthetically (as the *Fine Arts*); perceptive; *v.t.* to make fine; to refine or purify; *v.i.* to become fine, pure, or slender; *adv.* **—drawn** *a.* invisibly mended (of cloth); delicately thin (of wire); subtly conceived (of an argument); **-ly** *adv.* **-ness** *n.* the state of being fine; the amount of gold in an alloy. **-r** *n.* refiner. **-ry** *n.* ornament; gay clothes; a furnace for making wrought iron. **—spun,** *a.* drawn out to a gossamer thread; (*Fig.*) subtle; ingenious. **finessé** (fa.nes′) *n.* subtlety of contrivance to gain a point; stratagem; (*Whist, Bridge, etc.*) the attempt to take a trick with a low card while holding a higher card; *v.i.* and *v.t.* to use artifice; to try to take a trick by finesse [Fr. *fin*, exact].

fine (fīn) *n.* a sum of money imposed as a penalty for an offense; conclusion, as in phrase *in fine; v.t.* to impose a fine on [L.L. *finis*, a payment].

fi·nesse See **fine.**

fin·ger (fing′.ger) *n.* a digit; any one of the extremities of the hand, excluding thumb; the width or length of a finger; something like a finger; *v.t.* to touch with fingers; to handle; to perform with fingers; to purloin; to meddle with; *v.i.* to use the fingers. **— alphabet** *n.* the finger-language of the deaf and dumb. **— board** *n.* that part of a violin, etc. on which fingers are placed; the keyboard of a piano. **— bowl** *n.* a small bowl of water to cleanse fingers at dinner. **-ing** *n.* the act of touching or handling lightly with fingers; the manner of manipulating the fingers in playing an instrument. [O.E. *finger*, a finger].

fin·i·al (fin′.i.al) *a.* ornamental topping of lamp, gable, etc. [L. *finire*, to finish].

fin·i·cal (fin′.i.kal) *a.* affectedly fine; overfastidious. **-ly** *adv.* **finicking, finicky,** *a.* over-particular [prob. fr. *fine*].

fi·nis (fī′.nis) *n.* an end; conclusion [L.].

fin·ish (fin′.ish) *v.t.* to bring to an end; to terminate; to destroy; to complete; *v.i.* to conclude; *n.* that which finishes, or perfects; last stage; the final coat of paint, etc. **-ed** *a.* terminated; perfect; polished; talented; **-er** *n.* one who or that which finishes or gives the final touches. **-ing school,** a school for completing the education of young women [Fr. *finir,* to finish].

fi·nite (fī′·nīt) *a.* limited in quantity, degree, or capacity; bounded; countable; measurable (*Gram.*) used of a *predicating* verb (limited by number and person), oppos. of *infinitive* of verb. **-ly** *adv.* **-ness, finitude** *n.* [L. *finire,* to finish].

Finn (fin) *n.* a native of Finland. **Finnic, Finnish** *a.* **Finlander** *n.* a Finn.

fin·nan-had·dock (fin′·ạn-ha′·dạk) *n.* smoked haddock, esp. that cured at Findon, Scotland. Also **finnan haddie.**

fir (fur) *n.* cone-bearing, evergreen tree, yielding valuable timber. **—cone** *n.* fruit of the fir. [O.E. *furh-* (*wudu*), fir-(wood)].

fire (fīr) *n.* heat and light caused by combustion; burning; conflagration; ignited fuel; flame; discharge of firearms; ardor; spiritual or mental energy; impassioned eloquence; *v.t.* to set on fire; to kindle; to supply with fuel; to discharge (firearms, etc.); to inflame; to incite; (*Colloq.*) to dismiss; *v.i.* to be ignited; to be stimulated; to discharge firearms. **— alarm** *n.* an alarm giving warning of an discharges by fire exploding gunpowder. outbreak of fire. **-arm** *n.* a weapon which discharges by fire exploding gunpowder. **-ball** *n.* a meteor; (*Mil.*) a ball filled with combustibles. **—bomb** an incendiary bomb. **-box** *n.* the fire chamber of a locomotive. **-brand** *n.* a piece of flaming wood; a torch; (*Fig.*) one who incites others to strife. **— brigade** *n.* men specially trained to deal with fire. **-bug** *n.* an incendiary; (*Colloq.*) one quilty of arson. **-damp** *n.* gas generated in coal mines, which mixed with air, explodes violently in contact with a naked light. **-dog** *n.* (Same as andirons). **— escape** *n.* iron stair used as emergency exist from burning building. **-fly** *n.* a type of beetle which has light-producing organs. **-man** *n.* a member of a fire-fighting unit; a man who tends a furnace; a stoker. **-place** *n.* hearth or grate. **-plug** *n.* a hydrant for drawing water by hose to extinguish a fire. **-proof** *a.* **-r** *n.* **— screen** *n.* a movable protective screen in front of a fire. **-side** *n.* the hearth; (*Fig.*) home. **-water** *n.* term used by Am. Indians for whisky, brandy, etc. **-wood** *n.* wood for fuel; kindling. **-work** *n.* a preparation containing gunpowder, sulfur, etc. for making spectacular explosions. **firing line** *n.* the area of a battle zone within firing range of the enemy. **firing party** or **squad,** soldiers detailed to fire the final salute at a military funeral, or to shoot a condemned person [O.E. *fyr,* a fire].

fir·kin (fur′·kin) *n.* a small cask [O.Dut. *vierde,* four; and dim. suffix kin].

firm (furm) *a.* fixed; solid; compact; rigid; steady; unwavering; stern; inflexible. **-ly** *adv.* **-ness** *n.* [L. *firmus,* steadfast].

firm (furm) *n.* the name, title, or style under which a company transacts business [It. *firma,* a signature].

fir·ma·ment (fur′·ma·mạnt) *n.* the expanse of the sky; the heavens [L. *firmamentum,* a support, the sky].

first (furst) *a.* preceding all others in a series or in kind; foremost (in place); earliest (in time); most eminent; most excellent; highest; chief; *adv.* before anything else in time, place, degree, or preference; *n.* beginning; a first-class honors degree at a university. **— aid** *n.* preliminary treatment given to injured person before the arrival of a doctor. **—born** *n.* eldest child. **—class** *a.* first-rate; of highest worth; of superior accommodation; *adv.* in the first-class (of a train, boat, etc.). **—fruits** *n.pl.* earliest gathered fruits, orig. dedicated to God; (*Fig.*) earliest results or profits. **—hand** *a.* obtained direct from the source. **-ly** *adv.* **—rate** *a.* of highest excellence [O.E. *fyrst,* first].

firth (furth) *n.* (*Scot.*) a long narrow inlet of the sea or estuary of a river [O.N. *fird*].

fisc (fisk) *n.* the State treasury; public revenue. **fiscal** *a.* pert. to the public treasury or revenue; pert. to financial matters generally.

fish (fish) *n.* a cold-blooded, aquatic vertebrate animal, with limbs represented by fins, and breathing through its gills; the flesh of fish; *pl.* **fish, fishes.** *v.t.* to catch by fishing; *v.i.* to follow the occupation of a fisherman, for business or pleasure; to extract information, etc. by indirect, subtle questions (foll. by *for*). **-er** *n.* one who fishes; a marten. **-erman** *n.* one whose employment is to catch fish; one who fishes for pleasure; an angler. **-ery** *n.* the business of fishing; a fishing-ground; the legal right to fish in a certain area. **-hook** *n.* a barbed hook for catching fish by line. **-ily** *adv.* **-iness** *n.* **-ing** *n.* the act of fishing. **-ing rod** *n.* a long supple rod with line attached, used by anglers. **-ing tackle** *n.* an angler's gear comprising, rod, lines, hooks, etc. **— meal** *n.* dried fish ground into meal. **— story** (*Colloq.*) *n.* an unbelievable story. **-tail** *a.* shaped like the tail of a fish. **-wife** *n.* a woman selling fish in the streets; a shrill, nagging woman. **-y** *a.* abounding in fish; pert. to fish (of smell); expressionless; glazed (of eye); dubious (of a story). [O.E. *fisc,* fish].

fish (fish) *n.* a strip of wood fixed longitudinally to strengthen a mast, or clamp two pieces together; *v.t.* to splice; to join together. **-plate, — joint** *n.* a metal clamp used to join lengths of train rails together [Fr. *fiche,* a pin or peg].

fis·sile (fis′·il) *a.* capable of being split or cleft in the direction of the grain [L. *findere, fissum,* to cleave].

fis·sion (fish′·ạn) *n.* the process of splitting or breaking up into parts; (*Biol.*) cell-cleavage; in nuclear physics, the splitting of an atomic nucleus into two approx. equal fragments and a number of neutrons, with the liberation of a large amount of energy; *v.t.* and *i.* to split into two parts. **-able** *a.* [L. *findere, fissum,* to cleave].

fis·sure (fish′·ȧr) *n.* a cleft, crack, or slit [L. *findere, fissum,* to cleave].

fist (fist) *n.* the hand clenched with fingers doubled into the palm; (*Colloq.*) handwriting. **-ic** *a.* pugilistic. **-icuff** *n.* a blow with the fist; **-icuffs** *n.pl.* boxing; a brawl. **-y** *a.* [O.E. *fust,* the fist].

fis·tu·la (fis′·choo·lạ) *n.* (*Med.*) a narrow duct; an infected channel in the body leading from an internal abscess to the surface. **-r, fistulous** *a.* (*Bot.*) hollowed like a pipe [L. *fistula,* a pipe].

fit (fit) *a.* (*comp.*) **-ter.** (*superl.*) **-test.** adapted to an end or purpose; becoming; suitable; qualified; proper; vigorous (of bodily health); *v.t.* to make suitable; to qualify; to adapt; to adjust; to fashion to the appropriate size; *v.i.* to be proper or becoming. *pr.p.* **-ting.** *pa.p., p.t.* **-ted. -ly** *adv.* **-ness** *n.* the state of being fit; appropriateness; sound bodily health. **-ter** *n.* one who or that which makes fit; a tailor or dressmaker who fits clothes on a person; a mechanic who assembles separate parts of a machine. **-ting** *a.* appropriate; suitable; *n.* anything used in fitting up; a trial of a garment to see that it fits. **-tings** *n.pl.* fixtures; equipment. **-tingly** *adv.*

fit (fit) *n.* a sudden and violent attack of a disorder; a paroxysm; a seizure; a spasmodic attack (as of sneezing); a momentary impulse. **-ful** *a.* spasmodic; intermittent. **-fully** *adv.* [O.E. *fitt*, a struggle].

fit (fit) *n.* a song, or division of a poem; a canto [M.E. *fitte*, a stanza].

five (fīv) *n.* four and one; the symbol 5, or V; *a.* one more than four. **-fold** *a.* five times repeated; quintuple. **-r** *n.* (*Colloq.*) a five-dollar bill [O.E. *fif*].

fix (fiks) *v.t.* to make firm; to establish; to secure; to make permanent, as a photograph; to make fast, as a dye; to immobilize; to determine; to gaze at; to repair; to put in order; *v.i.* to settle permanently; to become hard; *n.* (*Colloq.*) dilemma; predicament; determination of the position of a ship or airplane by observations or radio signals. **-ation** *n.* the act of fixing; steadiness; (*Med.*) in psycho-analysis, an emotional arrest of part of the psycho-sexual development. **-ative** *n.* a fixing agent; a chemical which preserves specimens in a life-like condition; *a.* capable of fixing colors or structure of specimens. **-ed** *a.* settled, permanent, not apt to change; steady. **-edly** *adv.* **-edness** *n.* **-er** *n.* one who, or that which, fixes. **-ity** *n.* fixedness; immobility. **-ings** *n.pl.* (*Colloq.*) apparatus; trimmings. **-ture** *n.* that which is fixed or attached; (house) anything of an accessory nature considered a part of the real property [L. *fixus*, fixed].

fizz (fiz) *v.i.* to make a hissing sound; to splutter; to effervesce; *n.* a hissing sound; any effervescent liquid. **fizzle** *v.i.* to fizz or splutter. *n.* (*Colloq.*) a fiasco. **-y** *a.* [imit.].

fjord See **fiord.**

flab·ber·gast (flab′·er·gast) *v.t.* (*Colloq.*) to overcome with amazement; to confound [prob. conn. with *flabby*].

flab·by (flab′·i·) *a.* soft; yielding to the touch; drooping; weak; lacking in moral fiber. **flabbily** *adv.* **flabbiness** *n.* [fr.*flap*].

flac·cid (flak′·sid) *a.* soft; flabby; limp. **-ly** *adv.* **-ness, -ity** *n.* [L. *flaccidus*, flabby].

flag (flag) *v.i.* to hang loosely; to grow spiritless or dejected; to become languid; to lose vigor, *pr.p.* **-ging.** *pa.p.* **-ged.**

flag (flag) *n.* a flat paving stone; a type of sandstone which splits easily into large slabs. Also **-stone** [Ice. *flaga*, a slab].

flag (flag) *n.* (*Bot.*) a popular name of certain species of plants belonging to the genus *Iris*, with long sword-shaped leaves.

flag (flag) *n.* an ensign or colors; a standard; a banner as a mark of distinction, rank, or nationality; the bushy tail of a setter dog; *v.t.* to decorate with flags or bunting; to convey a message by flag signals. **— officer** *n.* an admiral, entitled to display a flag indicating his rank; the commander of a fleet or squadron. **-ship** *n.* the ship flying the admiral's flag. **white flag,** the symbol of truce or surrender. **yellow flag,** a flag indicating that a ship is in quarantine. **to dip the flag,** to lower, then hoist, flag as a mark of respect.**to fly a flag half-mast,** to hoist flag half-way as token of mourning [etym. doubtful, prob. Scand.].

flag·el·late (flaj′·ạ·lāt) *v.t.* to whip; to scourge; to flog; *a.* (*Biol.*) having a long thread-like appendage, like a lash. **flagellantism, flagellation** *n.* **flagellant** *n.* an ascetic who voluntarily scourges himself as punishment for sin [L. *flagellare, to scourge*].

flag·eo·let (flaj·ạ·let′) *n.* a small non-reed wind instrument [dim. of O.Fr. *flageol*, a pipe].

fla·gi·tious (flạ·jish′·ạs) *a.* shamefully criminal [L. *flagitiosus* disgraceful].

flag·on (flag′·ạn) *n.* a vessel for holding liquids, usually with handle, spout and lid [Fr. *flacon*, a flask].

fla·grant (flā′·grạnt) *a.* glaring; notorious; scandalous. **flagrance, flagrancy** *n.* **-ly** *adv.* [L. *flagrare*, to burn].

flail (flāl) *n.* an implement for threshing grain by hand, consisting of a stout stick attached to a handle [L. *flagellum*, a whip].

flair (fler) *n.* instinctive discernment; a keen scent [Fr. *flairer*, to scent out].

flak (flak) *n.* anti-aircraft fire (*World War* 2) [Ger. (*abbrev.*) *Flugabwehrkanone*, anti-aircraft gun].

flake (flāk) *n.* a scale-like particle; a piece of a thin layer; *v.t.* to form into flakes; to cover with flakes; *v.i.* to scale; to fall in flakes. **flaky** *a.* consisting of flakes [Scand. *flaki*, flake].

flam·beau (flam′·bō) *n.* a flaming torch; an ornamental candlestick; *pl.* **flambeaux** [Fr. fr. L. *flamma*, a flame].

flam·boy·ant (flam·boi′·ạnt) *a.* (*Archit.*) characterized by flame-like tracery and florid ornamentation of windows, panels, etc.; florid; showy; ornate. **flamboyance, flamboyancy** *n.* [Fr. *flamboyer*, to flame].

flame (flām) *n.* a mass of burning vapor or gas; a blaze of light; fire in general; ardor; vehemence of mind or imagination; (*Slang*) a sweetheart; *v.i.* to blaze; to blush; to become violently excited, fervent, or angry. **—colored** *a.* of the color of a flame; bright red or yellow. **— thrower** *n.* a short range trench weapon throwing ignited fuel into the enemy's lines. **flaming** *a.* blazing; gaudy; fervent. **flamingly** *adv.* **flammability** *n.* **flammable** *a.* [L. *flamma*, a flame].

fla·min·go (flạ·ming′.gō) *n.* tropical wading bird [L. *flamma*, a flame].

flan (flan) *n.* a pastry shell or cake filled with fruit filling [O.Fr. *flaon*, a flat cake].

flange (flanj) *n.* a projecting edge, as of a railway-car wheel to keep it on the rails, or of castings to fasten them together; *v.t.* [O.Fr. *flanche*, fr. *flanc*, a side].

flank (flangk) *n.* the fleshy part of side of animal between ribs and hip; the right or left side of an army; part of a bastion; the side of a building; *v.t.* to stand at the side of; to protect the flank of an army, etc.; to border *v.i.* [O.Fr. *flanc*, the side].

flan·nel (flan′·ạl) *n.* a soft-textured, loosely woven woolen cloth. **-s** *n.pl.* clothes made of this, esp. sports garments; woolen undergarments; *a.* made of flannel; *v.t.* to cover or rub with flannel. **-ette** *n.* a cotton material like flannel [W. *gwlanen*, fr. *gwlan*, wool].

flap (flap) *n.* the motion or noise of anything broad and hanging loose; a piece of flexible material attached on one side only and usually covering an opening, as of envelope; anything hinged and hanging loose; *v.t.* to cause to sway or flutter; to strike with something broad and flexible, such as a duster; to move rapidly up and down; *v.i.* to flutter; to fall like a flap; to move, as wings. *pr.p.* **-ping.** *pa.p.* **-ped.** **-jack** *n.* a broad, flat pancake. **-per** *n.* one who or that which flaps; (*Slang*) the hand; (*Colloq.*) an adolescent girl; a flighty, young woman [imit.].

flare (fler) *v.i.* to burn with a glaring, unsteady or fitful flame; to burst out with flame, anger, etc.; to curve out; *n.* an unsteady, blazing light; a brilliant, often colored, light used as a signal; a spreading or curving out, as the hull of a ship; a sudden burst of flame, passion, etc. **flared** *a.* (of a skirt) spreading gradually out toward the bottom. **flaring** a. [Scand. *flara*, to blaze].

flash (flash) *n.* a sudden brief burst of light; an instant or moment; a fleeting emotional outburst; (*Colloq.*) thieves' language; rush of water; a news story; *a.* showy; tawdry; pert. to thieves; *v.i.* to blaze suddenly and die out; to give out a bright but fitful gleam; to shine out, as a stroke of wit or sudden idea; to pass swiftly; *v.t.* to cause to flash; to transmit instantaneously, as news by radio, telephone, etc. **— back** *n.* momentary turning back to an episode in a story. **— bulb** *n.* (*Photog.*) an electric bulb giving brilliant flash for night picture. **-ily** *adv.* **-iness** *n.* **-light** *n.* a portable light powered by batteries or a small generator. **-y** *a.* showy; tawdry; cheap. [M.E. *flarihe(n)*, rise and dash].

flask (flask) *n.* a narrow-necked, usually flat bottle easily carried in the pocket; a wicker-covered bottle; a powder-horn. **-et** *n.* a small flask; a long, shallow basket [It. *fiasco*].

flat (flat) *a.* (*comp.*) **-ter.** (*superl.*) **-test.** level; even; tasteless; monotonous; dull; unqualified; without point or spirit; uniform; spread out; downright; (*Mus.*) below the true pitch (opp. of *sharp*); *n.* a level surface; low-lying sometimes flooded, tract of land; a shoal; (*Mus.*) a note, a semitone below the natural; the symbol for this; a piece of canvas or board mounted on a frame used as stage scenery. *adv.* prone; exactly. (*Mus.*) in a manner below true pitch. **—finish** *n.* a flat surface in paint work. **—footed** *a.* having fallen arches in the feet. **-iron** *n.* an iron for smoothing linen, etc. **-ly** *adv.* peremptorily. **-ness** *n.* **— rate,** uniform rate. **-ten** *v.t.* to make flat; to lower the true musical pitch of; **-top** *n.* an aircraft carrier. **-ware** *n.* silver knives, forks, etc. [Scand. *flatr*, flat].

flat·ter (flat′·ẹr) *v.t.* to praise unduly and insincerely; to pay fulsome compliments to; to depict as being an improvement on the original. **-er** *n.* **-ing** *a.* **-ingly** *adv.* **-y** *n.* the act of flattering; undue praise [O.Fr. *flater*, to smooth].

flat·u·lent (fla′·chạ·lạnt) *a.* pert. to or affected with wind or gas in stomach and intestines; (*Fig.*) empty; vapid. **flatulence, flatulency** *n.* distension of stomach or intestines by excessive accumulation of wind or gas. **-ly** *adv.* **flatus** *n.* air or gas in stomach, etc. [L. *flare*, to blow].

flaunt (flawnt) *v.t.* to display ostentatiously or impudently; *v.i.* to wave or move in the wind; to parade showily; *n.* a vulgar display.

fla·vor (flā′·vẹr) *n.* savor; quality affecting taste or smell; distinctive quality of a thing. *v.t.* to season; (*Fig.*) to give zest to. **-ous** *a.* **-ing** *n.* substance to add flavor to a dish, e.g. spice, essence [O.Fr. *flaur*, smell].

flaw (flaw) *n.* a crack; a defect; a weak point as in an argument; *v.t.* to break; to crack; **-less** *a.* perfect [Scand. *flaga*, a slab].

flaw (flaw) *n.* a sudden gust of wind; a squall [Dut. *vlaag*, a gust of wind].

flax (flaks) *n.* the fibers of an annual blue-flowered plant, *Linum*, used for making linen; the plant itself. **-en** *a.* pert. to or resembling flax; loose or flowing; of the color of unbleached flax, hence yellowish or golden (esp. of hair) [O.E. *flaex*, flax].

flay (flā) *v.t.* to skin; (*Fig.*) to criticize bitterly [O.E. *flean*, to strike].

flea (flē) *n.* a small, wingless, very agile insect with irritating bite. **—bitten** *a.* bitten by a flea; (*Fig.*) mean; worthless [O.E. *fleah*, a flea].

fleck (flek) *n.* a spot; a streak; *v.t.* to spot; to dapple [Scand. *flekka*, to spot].

fled (fled) *pa.t.* and *pa.p.* of **flee.**

fledge (flej) *v.t.* to supply with feathers for flight, as an arrow; to rear a young bird; *v.i.* to acquire feathers; to become able to fly (of birds). **-ling** *n.* a young bird just fledged; (*Fig.*) a young untried person [O.E. *flycge*, feathered].

flee (flē) *v.i.* to fly or retreat from danger; *v.t.* to hasten from; *pr.p.* **-ing.** *pa.p., p.t.* **fled** [O.E. *fleon*, to fly].

fleece (flēs) *n.* the coat of wool covering a sheep or shorn from it; anything resembling wool; *v.t.* to shear wool (from sheep); (*Fig.*) to rob; to swindle. **fleecy** *a.* woolly; resembling wool [O.E. *fleos*, fleece].

fleet (flēt) *n.* a group of ships; a force of naval vessels under one command; (*Fig.*) a number of motor vehicles, etc. organized as a unit [O.E. *fleot*, a ship].

fleet (flēt) *n.* a creek, inlet, or small stream [O.E. *fleot*, an inlet].

fleet (flēt) *a.* swift; nimble. *v.i.* to pass swiftly; *v.t.* to make to pass quickly. **-ing** *a.* transient; ephemeral; passing. **-ingly** *adv.* **-ness** *n.* swiftness. **—footed** *a.* swift of foot [O.E. *fleotan*, to swim].

Flem·ing (flem′·ing) *n.* a native of Flanders, **Flemish** *a.* pert. to Flanders [Dut. *Vlaamsch*].

flense (flens) *v.t.* to cut up the blubber of, as a whale [Dan. *flense*].

flesh (flesh) *n.* the body tissue; the muscles, fat, etc. covering the bones of an animal; the body as distinct from the soul; mankind; kindred; sensuality; the pulpy part of fruit; *v.t.* to incite to hunt, as a hound, by feeding it on flesh; to glut; to thrust into flesh, as a sword; to remove flesh from the under side of hides preparatory to tanning process. **-color** *n.* the pale pink color of the human skin (of white races). **-iness** *n.* state of being fleshy; plumpness. **-ings** *n.pl.* flesh-colored tights worn by dancers, acrobats, etc. **-less** *a.* **-liness** *n.* **-ly** *a.* corporeal; worldly; sensual. **-pot** *n.* a vessel in which meat is cooked; (*Fig.*) luxurious living. **— wound** *n.* **-y** *a.* pert. to flesh; corpulent; gross; (*Bot.*) thick and soft. **proud flesh** (*Med.*) a growth of granular tissue over a wound [O.E. *flaesc*, flesh].

fletch (flech) *v.t.* to feather (as an arrow). *n.pl.* feathers on an arrow [Fr. *flèche*, an arrow].

fleur·de·lis (flur·dạ·lē′) *n.* a design based on the shape of an iris; the royal insignia of France [Fr. *fleur-de-lis*, flower of the lily].

flew (flòò) *pa.t.* of verb **fly.**

flex (fleks) *v.t.* and *v.i.* to bend (as the joints of the body). **-ibility** *n.* quality of being pliable; (*Fig.*) adaptability; versatility. **-ible** a. **-ibly** *adv.* **-ile** *a.* bendable. **-ion, flection** *n.* a bend; a fold; an inflection. **-or** *n.* a muscle. **-uose, -uous** *a.* bending; tortuous. **-ure** *n.* act of bending; a bend [L. *flexus*, bent].

flick (flik) *v.t.* to strike lightly, as with whip; *n.* light, smart stroke.

flick·er (flik′·ẹr) *v.i.* to flutter; to waver; to quiver; to burn unsteadily. *n.* act of wavering; quivering [O.E. *flicorian*, to flutter].

flight (flīt) *n.* the act or power of flying; the distance covered in flying; a journey by airplane; a formation of planes forming a unit; a flock of birds; a soaring, as of the imagination; a discharge of arrows; a volley; a series of steps between successive landings. **— deck,** *n.* the deck of an aircraft carrier for planes to land or take off. **-y** *a.* capricious; giddy; volatile [O.E. *flyht*, flight].

flight (flīt) *n.* the act of fleeing; retreat. **to put to flight,** to rout [O.E. *fleon*, to flee].

flim·sy (flim′·zi·) *a.* thin; fragile; unsubstantial; *n.* thin, transfer-paper; (*Slang*) a banknote. **flimsily** *adv.* **flimsiness.**

flinch (flinch) *v.i.* to shrink from pain or difficulty; to wince. **-ing** *n.* the act of flinching [O.Fr. *flenchir*, to turn aside].

fling (fling) *v.t.* to throw from the hand; to hurl; to send out; to plunge; *v.i.* to flounce; to throw oneself violently. *pa.t., pa.p.* **flung.**

n. a cast or throw; a gibe; abandonment to pleasure; lively dance. **-er** *n.* [Scand. *flanga*, to move violently].

flint (flint) *n.* quartz, which readily produces fire when struck with steel; anything hard; a prehistoric stone weapon; *a.* made of flint. **-lock** *n.* a gunlock with a flint fixed on the hammer for firing the priming. **-y** *a.* made of, or resembling, flint; (*Fig.*) hard-hearted; cruel [O.E. *flint*].

flip (flip) *n.* a drink composed of eggs, sugar and liquor [prob. fr. verb *flip*].

flip (flip) *v.t.* to flick; to jerk. *pr.p.* **-ping.** *pa.t., pa.p.* **-ped,** *n.* a flick; a snap. **-per** *n.* the limb of an animal which facilitates swimming; (*Slang*) the human hand [var. of *flap*].

flip·pant (flip′·ạnt) *a.* pert. to shallow; smart or pert in speech. **flippancy** *n.* **-ly** *adv.*

flirt (flurt) *v.t.* to jerk, as a bird's tail; to move playfully to and fro, as a fan; *v.i.* to move about briskly; to play the coquette; to dally; *n.* a jerk; a philanderer; a flighty girl. **-ation** *n.* **-atious** *a.* [etym. doubtful].

flit (flit) *v.i.* to fly away; to dart along; to flutter. *pr.p.* **-ting.** *pa.t., pa.p.* **-ted** [Scand. *flytja*, to cause to float].

flit·ter (flit′·ẹr) *v.i.* to flutter.

float (flōt) *v.i.* to rest or drift on the surface of a liquid; to be buoyed up; to be suspended in air; to wander aimlessly; *v.t.* to cause to stay on the surface of a liquid; to cover a surface with water; to set going, as a business company; to put into circulation; *n.* anything which is buoyant; a raft; cork or quill on a fishing line, or net; a hollow floating ball of metal indicating depth of liquid in tank or cistern; a plasterer's trowel; (*Aero.*) a streamlined attachment to a seaplane enabling it to float; theater footlights. **-able** *a.* **-age** *n.* See **flotage. -ation** *n.* See **flotation. -er** *n.* **-ing** *a.* buoyant on surface of the water or in air; movable; fluctuating; in circulation. **-ing dock,** a floating dry dock. **-ingly** *adv.* **-ing population,** shifting population. **-ing ribs,** lower ribs not connected to breastbone [O.E. *flotian*, to float].

flo·cus (flȧk′·ạs) *n.* a long tuft of wool or hair; *pl.* **flocci** (flok′·sī). **floccose** (flȧk′·ōs) **flocculent,** *a.* woolly; having tufts; flaky [L. *floccus*, flock of wood].

flock (flȧk) *n.* a small tuft of wool; refuse of wool in cloth making, used for stuffing cushions, etc.; small wool fibers used in making wall paper [L. *floccus*, flock of wool].

flock (flȧk) *n.* a collection of animals a crowd of people; a Christian congregation; *v.i.* to come together in crowds [O.E. *flocc*, a band].

floe (flō) *n.* an extensive field of ice floating in the sea [Scand. *flo*, a layer].

flog (flȧg) *v.t.* to beat or strike, as with a rod or whip; to thrash; *pr.p.* **-ging.** *pa.t., pa.p.* **-ged** [L. *flagellare*, to whip].

flood (flud) *n.* an overflow of water; an inundation; a deluge; the flowing in of the tide; (*Lit.* and *Fig.*) a torrent. *v.t.* to overflow; to drench; (*Fig.*) to overwhelm; *v.i* to spill over; to rise (as the tide). **-lighting** *n.* artificial lighting by lamps fitted with special reflectors.— **tide** *n.* the rising tide; (*Fig.*) peak of prosperity [O.E. *flod*, a stream].

floor (flōr) *n.* the horizontal surface of a room upon which one walks; a story; any level area; inside bottom surface of anything (room, sea, etc.); minimum level, esp. of prices. *v.t.* to cover with a floor; to strike down; (*Colloq.*) to perplex; to stump (in argument). **-age** *n.* floor space. **-cloth** *n.* a heavy material used for covering floors. **-er** *n.* a knock-out blow; (*Colloq.*) a baffling examination question or situation. **-ing** *n.* materials for floors. **— show** *n.* a show at a nightclub. **— walker** *n.* a person employed by a store to supervise one floor [O.E. *flor*].

flop (flop) *v.t.* to flap; to set down heavily. *v.i.* to drop down suddenly or clumsily. *pr.p.* **-ping,** *pa.t. pa.p.* **-ped.** *n.* a fall, as of a soft, outspread body; (*Slang*) a fiasco. **-py** *a.* slack; (of a hat brim) wide and soft [var. of *flap*].

flo·ra (flō′·rạ) *n.* the plants native to a certain geographical region or geological period; a classified list of such plants. **floral** *a.* **florally** *adv.* adorned with flowers. **floriated,** *a.* **floret** *n.* a single flower in a cluster of flowers; a small compact flower head. **florist** *n.* a grower or seller of flowers [L. *Flora*, the goddess of flowers].

flo·res·cence (flō·res′·ạns) *n.* a bursting into flower. **florescent** *a.* [L. *florescere*, to burst into flower].

flor·id (flawr′·id) *a.* bright in color; overelaborate; ornate; (of complexion) highly colored; (*Archit.*) overly decorative. **-ly** *adv.* **-ity** *n.* [L. *floridus*, flowery].

floss (flȧs) *n.* untwisted threads of very fine silk; the outer fibers of a silkworm's cocoon. **-silk** *n.* very soft silk thread. **-y** *a.* [It. *floscio*, soft].

flo·tage (flō′·tij) *n.* state or act of floating; the floating capacity of anything; (*Colloq.*) flotsam [O.E. *flotian*, to float].

flo·ta·tion (flō·tā′·shạn) *n.* the act of floating; science of floating bodies; act of launching, esp. a business venture, loan, etc. Also **floatation** [O.E. *fltian*, to float].

flo·til·la (flō-til′·ạ) *n.* a fleet of small vessels [Sp. *flotilla*, a little fleet].

flot·sam (flȧt′·sạm) *n.* goods lost by shipwreck and found floating on the sea [O.Fr. *flotaison*, a floating].

flounce (flouns) *v.i.* to turn abruptly; to flounder about; *n.* a sudden, jerky movement [Scand. *flunsa*, to plunge].

flounce (flouns) *n.* a plaited border or frill on hem of a dress; *v.t.* to trim with a flounce. **flouncing** *n.* material used for flounces [M.E. *frounce*, a plait].

floun·der (floun′·dẹr) *n.* a small, edible flatfish [Scand. *flundra*, a flounder].

floun·der (floun′·dẹr) *v.i.* to struggle helplessly, as in marshy ground; to tumble about; (*Fig.*) to stumble hesitatingly, as in a speech.

flour (flour) *n.* the finely ground meal of wheat, etc.; any finely powdered substance; *v.t.* to turn into flour; to sprinkle with flour. **-y** *a.* [Fr. *fleur de farine*, the flower (i.e. the best) of meal].

flour·ish (flur′·ish) *v.t.* to decorate with flowery ornament or with florid diction; to brandish; *v.i.* to grow luxuriantly; to prosper; to execute ostentatiously a passage of music; *n.* ornament; a fanciful stroke of the pen; rhetorical display; (*Mus.*) florid improvisation either as prelude or addition to a composition; a fanfare; brandishing (of a weapon); **-ing** *a.* thriving; vigorous [M.E. *florisshen*, to blossom].

flout (flout) *v.t.* to mock; to disregard with contempt; *v.i.* to jeer; *n.* an expression of contempt; a gibe; an insult [prob. fr. M.E. *flouten*, to play the flute].

flow (flō) *v.i.* to run, as a liquid; to rise, as the tide; to circulate, as the blood; to issue forth; to glide along; to proceed from; to fall in waves, as the hair; *v.t.* to overflow; *n.* a stream; a current; the rise of the tide; any easy expression of thought, diction, etc.; copiousness; output. **-ing** *a.* moving; running; fluent; curving gracefully, as lines; falling in folds, as drapery. **-ingly** *adv.* [O.E. *flowan*, to flow].

flow·er (flou′·ẹr) *n.* (*Bot.*) the reproductive

organ in plants; a blossom; the choicest part of anything; the finest type; a figure of speech; an ornament in shape of a flower; *v.t.* to adorn with flowers or flower-like shapes; *v.i.* to produce flowers; to bloom; to come to prime condition. **-ed** *a.* decorated with a flower pattern, as fabric. **-et** *n.* a small flower; a floret. **-ing** *a.* having flowers. **-s** *n.pl.* a substance in the form of a powder, as *flowers of sulphur*. **-y** *a.* abounding in, or decorated with, flowers; (of style) highly ornate; euphuistic [L. *flos*, a flower].

flown (flōn) *pa.p.* of **fly.**

flu (flòò) *n.* (*Colloq.*) influenza.

fluc·tu·ate (fluk′·chòò·āt) *v.i.* to move up and down, as a wave; to be unstable; to be irresolute. **fluctuant** *a.* **fluctuation** *n.* a vacillation [L. *fluctus*, a wave].

flue (flòò) *n.* a shaft or duct in a chimney; a pipe for conveying air through a boiler; the opening in the pipe of an organ.

flu·ent (flòò·ạnt) *a.* flowing; ready in the use of words; (of lines) gracefully curved. **fluency** *n. adv.* [L. *fluere*, to flow].

fluff (fluf) *n.* light, floating down; downy growth of hair on skin; *v.t.* to give a fluffy surface to; *v.i.* to become downy; (*Slang*) to make errors in the speaking of a stage part. **-y** *a.* [prob. var. of *flue*].

fluid (flòò′·id) *n.* a substance which flows (liquid, gas, etc.); a non-solid; *a.* capable of flowing; liquid; gaseous; shifting. **-ify** *v.t.* to make fluid. **-ity, -ness** *n.* the state or quality of being a non-solid; (*Fig.*) the state of being alterable. **-ly** *adv.* [L. *fluidus*, flowing].

fluke (flòòk) *n.* the flounder; a parasitic worm; the flattened barb at the extremity of either arm of an anchor [O.E. *floc*, a flat-fish].

fluke (flòòk) *n.* (*Colloq.*) any lucky chance.

flung (flung) *pa.t., pa.p.* of **fling.**

flunk (flungk) (*Colloq.*) *v.i.* to fail as in an examination or course; *v.t.* to fail in; to disqualify a student for low achivement; to give a student a failing grade; *n.* a failure.

flun·ky (flung′·ki·) *n.* a liveried manservant; a toady; an obsequious person. **-ism** *n.* [Fr. *flanquer*, to run at the side of].

flu·or (flòò′·ẹr) *n.* a mineral, fluoride of source of fluorine. **-esce** *v.i.* to exhibit calcium, usually called *fluorite*. **-escence** *n.* the property of a substance of producing light when exposed to radiation. **-escent** *a.* **-escent lamp** *n.* a glass tube coated on the inside with a fluorescent substance that emits light when acted upon by an electric current. **-ide** *n.* a compound of fluorine with another element. **-idation** *n.* the addition of fluorides to a public water supply to reduce tooth decay. **-ine** *n.* a pale yellow very active gaseous element [L. *fluere*, to flow].

flur·ry (flur′·i·) *n.* a sudden, brief gust of wind; bustle; commotion; *v.t.* to agitate; to fluster [prob. imit. *flutter* and *hurry*].

flush (flush) *v.i.* to turn red in the face; to blush; to flow with a rush; *v.t.* to cause to blush or turn red; to animate with high spirits; to cleanse with a rush of water; *n.* a flow of water; a rush of blood to the face; elation; freshness [origin uncertain].

flush (flush) *v.t.* to cause to start, as a hunter, a bird; *v.i.* to fly up quickly and suddenly from concealment; *n.* the act of starting up; a flock of birds flying up suddenly [M.E. *fluschen*, to fly up].

flush (flush) *n.* a run of cards of the same suit [L. *fluxus*, a flowing].

flush (flush) *v.t.* to level up; *a.* being in the same plane; well-supplied, as with money; full; (*Print.*) even with margins.

flus·ter (flus′·tẹr) *v.t.* to make agitated; to flurry; *v.i.* to be confused and flurried; *n.* confusion; nervous agitation. **-ed** *a.* [Scand. *flaustr*, hurry].

flute (flòòt) *n.* a musical tubular wind-instrument; a stop in the pipe-organ; (*Archit.*) a vertical groove in the shaft of a column; a similar groove as in a lady's ruffle; *v.i.* to play the flute; to sing or recite in flute-like tones; *v.t.* to play (tune) on the flute; to make flutes or grooves in. **fluted** *a.* ornamented with grooves, channels, etc. **fluting** *n.* action of playing a flute; the ornamental vertical grooving on a pillar, on glass, or in a lady's ruffle. **flutist** *n.* one who plays a flute. Also **flautist. fluty** *a.* [L.L.*flauta*].

flut·ter (flut′·ẹr) *v.t.* to cause to flap; to throw into confusion; to move quickly; *v.i.* to flap the wings; to move with quick vibrations; (of heart) to palpitate; *n.* quick and irregular motion; nervous hurry; confusion [O.E. *flotorian*, to float about].

flu·vi·al (flòò′·vi·ạl) *a.* pert. to, or produced by, a river. [L. *fluvius*, a river].

flux (fluks) *n.* the act of flowing; fluidity; (*Phys.*) the rate of flow; (*Med.*) morbid discharge of body-fluid, esp. blood; dysentery; (*Chem.*) a substance added to another to promote fusibility; continuous process of change; *v.t.* to fuse; to melt; *v.i.* to flow. **-ion** *n.* a flow or flux [L. *fluere*, to flow].

fly (flī) *v.t.* to cause to fly; to direct the flight of; to flee from; *v.i.* to move through the air, as a bird or an aircraft; to become airborne; to travel by airplane; to move rapidly; to flee; *pr.p.* **-ing** *pa.t.* **flew** (flòò). *pa.p.* **flown.** *n.* a winged insect, esp. of the order *Diptera;* a housefly; a fishhook in imitation of a fly; a flap on a garment covering a row of buttons or other fastener; (*Sports*) a ball sent high in the air (*pa.t., pa.p.* in baseball, **flied**). **flies** *n.pl.* the space above a theater stage where scenery is moved. **-ing** *n.* moving through the air; air navigation; *a.* capable of flight; streaming; swift. **-ing-boat** *n.* a seaplane. **-ing-buttress** (*Archit.*) an arched prop attached only at one point to the mass of masonry whose outward thrust it is designed to counteract. **-ing-saucer** *n.* name given to a saucer-like object reputedly seen flying at tremendous speeds and high altitudes. **-ing squirrel,** squirrel-like rodent with expanding fold of skin between front and hind legs. **-ing visit,** a hasty, unexpected visit. **-leaf** *n.* the blank page at the beginning or end of a book. **-man** *n.* a scene-shifter in the theater. **-paper** *n.* a paper smeared with sticky substance to trap flies. **-wheel** *n.* a heavy-rimmed wheel attached to the crankshaft of an engine to regulate its speed or accumulate power [O.E. *fleogan*, to fly].

foal (fōl) *n.* the young of a mare or she-ass; a colt or a filly; *v.t.* and *v.i.* to bring forth a foal [O.E. *fola*, a young animal].

foam (fōm) *n.* froth; spume; the bubbles of air on surface of effervescent liquid; *v.i.* to froth; to bubble; to gather foam; **-ing** *a.* **-ingly** *adv.* **— rubber** *n.* latex made into a soft, elastic, and porous substance, resembling a sponge. **-y** *a.* frothy [O.E. *fam*, foam].

fob (fȧb) *n.* a small pocket in the waistband for holding a watch; a chain with seals, etc. dangling from the pocket [Dial H. Ger. *fuppe*, a pocket].

fo'c's'le See **forecastle.**

fo·cus (fō′·kus) *n.* the point at which rays of light meet after reflection or refraction; (*Geom.*) one of two points connected linearly to any point on a curve; any point of concentration; *pl.* **-es, foci** (fō′·sī); *v.t.* to bring to a focus; to adjust; to concentrate; *v.i.* to converge. *pr.p.* **-ing.** *pa.p.* **-ed. focal**

a. pert. to a focus. **focalize** *v.t.* to bring into focus; to cause to converge; to concentrate. **focalization** *n.* **in focus,** clearly outlined; well defined. **out of focus,** distorted [L. *focus*, a fireplace].

foe (fō) *n.* an enemy; an adversary; a hostile army [O.E. *fah*, hostile].

foe·tus See **fetus.**

fog (fȧg) *n.* thick mist; watery vapor in the lower atmosphere; a cloud of dust or smoke obscuring visibility; (*Fig.*) mental confusion; *v.t.* to shroud in fog; to perplex the mind. *v.i.* to become cloudy or obscured. **— bank** *n.* a mass of fog. **-bound** *a.* hindered by fog from reaching destination, as a ship, train, etc. **-gily** *adv.* **-giness** *n.* **-gy** *a.* **-horn** *n.* a loud siren used during fog for warnings.

fo·gy, fogey (fō'·gi·) *n.* dull, old fellow; an elderly person whose ideas are behind the times.

foi·ble (foi'·bl) *n.* weakness of character; a failing [O.Fr. *foible*, weak].

foil (foil) *v.t.* to frustrate; to baffle; to put off the scent *n.* a blunt sword, with button on point, for fencing practice [O.Fr. *fuler*, to trample on].

foil (foil) *n.* a thin leaf of metal, as *tinfoil*; a thin leaf of metal placed under gems to increase their brilliancy or color; a thin coating of quicksilver amalgam on the back of a mirror; (*Archit.*) a leaf-like ornament in windows, niches, etc. (*trefoil*, *quatrefoil*, *cinquefoil*, etc.); (*Fig.*) anything serving to set off something else [L. *folium*, a leaf].

foist (foist) *v.t.* to palm off; to insert surreptitiously or unwarrantably. **-er** *n.* [prob. Dut. *vuisten*, to take in the hand].

fold (fōld) *n.* a doubling over of a flexible material; a pleat; a coil (or rope); a crease or a line made by folding; (*Geol.*) a dip in rock strata caused originally by pressure; *v.t.* to double over; to enclose within folds or layers; to embrace; *v.i.* to be pleated or doubled. **-er** *n.* the one who or that which folds; a folded, printed paper; a file for holding papers, etc. [O.E. *fealdan*, to fold].

fold (fōld) *n.* an enclosure for sheep; a flock of sheep; the church; a congregation; *v.t.* to confine in a fold [O.E. *fald*, a stall].

fol·der·al See **falderal.**

fo·li·age (fō'·li·ij) *n.* leaves of a plant in general; leafage. **-d** *a.* having leaves. **foliate** *v.t.* to hammer (metal) into laminae or foil; (*Archit.*) to ornament with leaf design; to number the leaves (not pages) of a book; *a.* resembling a leaf; having leaves. **foliated** *a.* **foliation** *n.* **foliolate** *a.* pert. to leaflets or the separate parts of a compound leaf [L. *folium*, a leaf].

fo·li·o (fō'·li·ō) *n.* a sheet of paper once folded; a book of such folded sheets; the two opposite pages of a ledger used for one account and numbered the same; (*Print*) page number in a book; *a.* pert. to or formed of sheets folded so as to make two leaves; *v.t.* to number the pages of a book on one side only [L. *folium*, a leaf].

folk (fōk) *n.* people in general, or as a specified class. **-s** *n.pl.* (*Colloq.*) one's own family and near relations; *a.* originating among the common people. **— dance** *n.* a traditional country dance. **-lore** *n.* popular superstitions or legends; the study of traditional beliefs [O.E. *folc*, the people].

fol·li·cle (fȧl'·i·kl) *n.* (*Bot.*) a one-celled seed vessel; (*Zool.*) a small sac; (*Anat.*) a gland, as in *hair-follicle*. **follicular** *a.* pert. to a follicle [L. *folliculus*, a little bag].

fol·low (fȧl'·ō) *v.t.* to go after; to move behind; to succeed (in a post); to adhere to (a belief); to practice (as a trade or profession); to comprehend; to watch carefully; to keep in touch with; *v.i.* to come after; to pursue; to occur as a consequence; *n.* the act of following. **-er** *n.* one who comes after; adherents; vocation; *a.* coming next after [O.E. *folgian*, to accompany].

fol·ly (fȧl'·i·) *n.* want of sense; weakness of mind; a foolish action; (*pl.*) a theatrical revue [O.Fr. *fol*, a fool].

fo·ment (fō·ment') *v.t.* to encourage or instigate; to bathe with warm water to relieve pain. **-ation** *n.* instigation, of discord, etc.; the action of applying warm lotions; the lotion applied. **-er** *n.* [L. *fomentum*, a poultice].

fond (fȧnd) *a.* loving; doting; very affectionate. **fond of,** much attached to; **-le** *v.t.* to caress; to stroke tenderly. **-ly** *adv.* **-ness** *n.* [M.E. *fonned*, infatuated].

fon·dant (fȧn'·dant) *n.* a thick, creamy sugar candy [Fr. *fondre*, to melt].

font (fȧnt) *n.* a stone basin for holding baptismal water; a receptable for holy water [L. *fons*, a fountain].

food (fóód) *n.* matter which one feeds on; solid nourishment as contrasted with liquids; that which, absorbed by any organism, promotes growth; (*Fig.*) mental or spiritual nourishment. **-stuff** *n.* edible commodity with nutritional value [O.E. *foda*, food].

fool (fóól) *n.* one who behaves stupidly; one devoid of common sense; a simpleton, a clown; a dupe; *v.t.* to make a fool of, to impose on; to trick *v.i.* to behave like a fool; to trifle. **-ery** *n.* silly behavior; foolish act. **-hardily** *adv.* **-hardiness** *n.* **-hardy** *a.* recklessly daring; venturesome. **-ish** *a.* weak in intellect; ill-considered; stupid. **-ishly** *adv.* **-ishness** *n.* **-ing** *n.* foolery. **-proof** *a.* (of machines) so devised that mishandling cannot cause damage to machine or personnel; **-scap** *n.* any of various sizes of writing paper. [L. *folis*, a windbag].

foot (foot) *n.* the extreme end of the lower limbs, below the ankle; a base or support, like a foot; the end of a bed, couch, etc. where the feet would normally lie; foot-soldiers; a measure of length = 12 inches; (*Prosody*) a combination of syllables measured according to quantity or stress-accent; the bottom of a page, ladder, etc.; the total of an account; *pl.* **feet.** *v.t.* to traverse by walking; (*Colloq.*) to add (an account); (*Colloq.*) to pay (a bill); to put a new foot on; *v.i.* to dance; to walk. **-age** *n.* the length expressed in feet. **-ball** *n.* a game played by two teams of eleven each trying to carry or pass the ball over the opponents' goal line; the elongated inflated leather ball used in the game; the round ball used in soccer. **-ed** *a.* having feet or a foot (usually in compounds as *two-footed*, *sure-footed*). **-fall** *n.* a step; sound of a step. **-gear** *n.* boots and shoes; stockings, socks.**-hold** *n.* a support for the foot; space to stand on. **-ing** *n.* ground to stand on; the part of a construction contacting the ground; status (in society) **-lights** *n.pl.* a row of screened lights along the front of the stage; (*Fig.*), the theater; the profession of acting. **—loose** *a.* free to do as one likes.**-man** *n.* liveried man-servant; a trivet. **-note** *n.* a note of reference or explanation at foot of a page. **foot and mouth disease,** a highly contagious disease of sheep, swine, and esp. horned cattle. [O.E. *fot*. foot].

fop (fȧp) *n.* a conceited, effeminate man; a dandy. **-pery** *n.* affection in dress and manners. **-pish** *a.* vain. **-pishly** *adv.* **-pishness** *n.* [M.E. *foppe*, a fool].

for (fawr) *prep.* in place of; instead of; because of: during; as being; considering; in return for; on behalf of; in spite of; in respect to; intended to belong to; suited to; with the purpose of. *conj.* because. **as for,**

regarding [O.E. *for*, for].
for- *prefix*. survives in a few words of O.E. origin, with various meanings; utterly, as in *for*lorn; prohibition, as in *for*bid; neglect, as in *for*sake; away, as in *for*get.
for·age (fawr'·ij) *n*. food for horses and cattle; the search for this or any provisions; *v.t.* to supply with provender; to plunder; *v.i.* to rove in search of food; (*Fig.*) to rummage. [O.Fr. *fourage*, forage].
fo·ra·men (fō·rā'·mạn) *n*. a small aperture, esp. in a bone; *pl.* **foramina** [L. a hole].
for·as·much (fawr·az·much') *conj.* seeing that; because; since.
for·ay (fawr'·ā) *n*. a raid to get plunder; *v.t.* to pillage.
for·bade (fẹr·bad') *pa.t.* of **forbid.**
for·bear (fawr·bār') *v.t.* to abstain from; to avoid; to bear with; *v.i.* to refrain from; to control one's feelings. *pa.t.* **forbore.** *pa.p.* **forborne. -ing.** *a.* long-suffering [O.E. *forberan*, to suffer, endure].
for·bid (fẹr·bid') *v.t.* to prohibit; to order to desist; to exclude. *pa.t.* **forbade** (fẹr·bad') or **forbad.** *pa.p.* **-den. -den** *a.* prohibited. **-ding** *a.* repellent; menacing; sinister. **-dingly** *adv.* [O.E. *forbeodan*, to prohibit].
force (fōrs) *n*. strength; energy; efficacy; coercion; power; operation; body of soldiers, police, etc.; (*Mech.*) that which produces a change in a body's state of rest or motion; (*Law*) unlawful violence to person or property. **Forces** *n.pl.* Army, Navy and Air Force; *v.t.* to compel (physically or morally); to strain; to ravish; to overpower (*Hort.*) to cause plants to bloom, or ripen before normal time. **-d** a. achieved by great effort, or under compulsion; lacking spontaneity, as *forced laugh*. **-ful** *a.* full of energy; vigorous. **-fully** *adv.* **-less** *a.* weak; inert. **-r** *n.* **forcible** *a.* having force; compelling; cogent; effective. **forcibly** *adv.* **forcing** *n.* the action of using force or applying pressure; the art of ripening plants, fruits, etc. before their season. [O.E. *force*, strength].
for·ceps (fawr'·seps) *n*. a surgical instrument like tongs. [L.].
ford (fōrd) *n*. a shallow part of a stream, etc. where a crossing can be made on foot; *v.t.* to cross by a ford. **-able** *a.* [O.E. *faran*, to go].
fore (fōr) *a.* in front; forward; prior; *adv.* in front, as opp. to *aft; n.* the front. *interj.* (*Golf*) a warning cry to person in the way [O.E. *fore*, before].
fore- *prefix* meaning in front or beforehand.
fore·arm (fōr'·ȧrm) *n*. the part of the arm between the elbow and the wrist.
fore·arm (fōr·ȧrm') *v.t.* to take defensive precautions.
fore·bear, forbear (fōr'·bār) *n*. an ancestor.
fore·bode (fōr·bōd') *v.t.* to predict (esp. something unpleasant); to prognosticate; to presage. **-ment** *n.* **foreboding** *n.* an intuitive sense of impending evil or danger.
fore·cast (fōr'·kast) *n*. a prediction; (*Meteor.*) a general inference as to the probable weather to come; *v.t.* and *v.i.* to conjecture beforehand; to predict.
fore·cas·tle, fo'c'sle (fōk'·sl) *n*. (*Naut.*) the upper deck forward of the foremast; forepart under deck, forming crew's quarters.
fore·close (fōr·klōz') *v.t.* (*Law*) to prevent; to exclude; to deprive of the right to redeem a mortgage or property. **foreclosure** *n.*
fore·date (fōr·dāt') *v.t.* to antedate.
fore·doom (fōr·dòòm') *v.t.* to judge in advance; to predestine to failure, etc.
fore·fa·ther (fōr'·fȧ·THẹr) *n*. an ancestor.
fore·fin·ger (fōr'·fing·gẹr) *n*. the finger next to the thumb; the index finger.
fore·foot (fōr'·foot) *n*. one of the front feet of a quadruped.
fore·front (fōr'·frunt) *n*. the foremost place; the center of interest.
fore·go (fōr·gō') *v.t.* to precede. **-ing** *a.* preceding; just mentioned. **-ne** *a.* predetermined or inevitable, as in a *foregone conclusion.*
fore·ground (fōr'·ground) *n*. the part of the ground nearest the spectator; the part of a picture which seems nearest the observer.
fore·hand (fōr'·hand) *n*. the part of a horse in front of the rider; *a.* done beforehand; (*Tennis*) used of a stroke played *forward* on the right or natural side, as opp. to *backhand.* **-ed** *a.*
fore·head (fawr'·id, fawr'·hed) *n*. the upper part of the face above the eyes; the brow.
for·eign (fawr'·in) *a.* situated outside a place or country; alien; irrelevant; introduced from outside. **-er** *n.* a native of another country; an alien. **-ism** *n.* [O.Fr. *forain*, fr. L. *foris*, outside].
fore·know (fōr·nō') *v.t.* to know or sense beforehand. **foreknowledge** *n.*
fore·land (fōr'·lạnd) *n*. a promontory; a cape; shore area round a port.
fore·lock (fōr'·lȧk) *n*. a lock of hair on the forehead.
fore·man (fōr'·mạn) *n*. the principal member and spokesman of a jury; the overseer of a group of workmen.
fore·mast (fōr'·mast) *n*. the mast in the forepart of a vessel, nearest the bow.
fore·most (fōr'·mōst) *a.* first in place or time; first in dignity or rank.
fore·named (fōr'·nāmd) *a.* already mentioned.
fore·noon (fōr'·nòòn) *n*. the part of the day before noon; morning.
fo·ren·sic (fạ·ren'·sik) *a.* pert. to the law courts, public discussion, or debate. **-ally** *adv.* [*L. forensis*, pert. to the forum].
fore·or·dain (fōr·awr·dān') *v.t.* to predetermine; to decree beforehand.
fore·part (fōr'·pȧrt) *n*. the part before the rest; the beginning.
fore·run (fōr·run') *v.t.* to run before; to precede; to outrun. **-ner** *n.* a messenger sent in advance; a harbinger; a precursor.
fore·said (fōr'·sed) *a.* mentioned before.
fore·sail (fōr'·sāl or fō'sl) *n*. the lowest square sail on the foremast.
fore·see (fōr·sē') *v.t.* to see beforehand; to foreknow *pa.t.* **foresaw,** *pa.p.* **foreseen. foresight** *n.* wise forethought; prudence; (*Mil.*) front sight on gun [O.E. *foreseon*].
fore·sha·dow (fōr·shad'·ō) *v.t.* to shadow or indicate beforehand; to suggest in advance.
fore·shore (fōr'·shōr) *n*. the part of the shore between the level of high tide and low tide.
fore·short·en (fōr·shōr'·ten) *v.t.* to represent (in art) according to perspective; to depict to the eye, as seen obliquely.
fore·show (fōr·shō') *v.t.* to prognosticate.
fore·skin (fōr'·skin) *n*. the skin covering the glans penis; prepuce.
for·est (fawr'·ist) *n*. a tract of wooded, uncultivated land; the trees alone; *a.* sylvan; *v.t.* to cover with trees. **-er** *n.* one who practices forestry; one who has forest land, game, etc. under supervision. **-ry** *n.* the science of growing timber [L. *foris*, outside].
fore·stall (fōr·stawl') *v.t.* to thwart by advance action; to buy up goods before they reach the market, so as to resell at maximum price; to get in ahead of someone else. **-er** *n.* **-ment** *n.* [O.E. *foresteall* intervention].
fore·taste (fōr'·tāst) *n*. a taste beforehand; anticipation; *v.t.* to taste before full possession.
fore·tell (fōr·teḷ') *v.t.* to predict; to prophesy. *pr.p.* **-ing** *pa.t., pa.p.* **foretold.**
fore·thought (fōr'·thawt) *n*. anticipation; provident care; a thinking beforehand.
fore·to·ken (fōr'·tō·kạn) *n*. a token or sign received beforehand; a prophetic sign; *v.t.* to indicate beforehand [O.E. *foretacn*].
fore·top (fōr'·tȧp) *n*. (*Naut.*) platform at the

head of the foremast; an animal's forelock.
for·ev·er (fer·ev′·ẹr) *adv.* always; eternally; *n.* eternity. **-more** *adv.*
fore·warn (fōr·wawrn′) *v.t.* to warn or caution in advance.
fore·word (fōr′·wurd) *n.* a preface; an introductory note to a book.
for·feit (fōr′·fit) *v.t.* to be deprived of, as a punishment; *n.* that which is forfeited; a fine or penalty. **-able** *a.* **-ure** *n.* the act of forfeiting; the state of being deprived of something as a punishment; the thing confiscated [O.Fr. *forfaire,* to transgress].
for·gather, foregather (fōr·gaTH′·ẹr) *v.i.* to meet with friends; to come together socially.
for·gave (fẹr·gāv′) *pa.t.* of verb **forgive.**
forge (fōrj) *v.t.* a furnace for heating iron red hot so that it can be hammered into shape; to fabricate; to counterfeit; *v.i.* to work with metals; to commit forgery. **-r** *n.* **forgery** *n.* the making of an imitation of money, work of art, etc., and representing it as genuine; the act of falsifying a document, or illegally using another's signature; that which is forged [L. *fabrica,* a workshop].
forge (fōrj) *v.i.* to move forward steadily.
for·get (fẹr·get′) *v.t.* to lose remembrance of; to neglect inadvertently; to disregard. *pr.p.* **-ting.** *pa.t.* **forgot.** *pa.p.* **forgot** or **forgotten. -table** *a.* **-ful** *a.* apt to forget; heedless; oblivious. **-fully** *adv.* **-fulness** *n.* [O.E. *forgietan,* to forget].
for·give (for·giv′) *v.t.* to pardon; to cease to bear resentment against; to cancel (as a debt); *v.t.* to exercise clemency; to grant pardon. *pa.t.* **forgave.** *pa.p.* **forgiven. forgivable** *a.* **-ness** *n.* **forgiving** *a.* ready to pardon [O.E. *forgiefan,* to give up].
for·go (fōr·gō′) *v.t. pa.t.* **forwent,** *pa.p.* **foregone.** to renounce; to abstain from possession or enjoyment.
fork (fōrk) *n.* an implement with two or more prongs at the end; a table utensil of silver, etc. usually with four prongs; anything shaped like a fork; a pronged instrument which when struck gives forth a fixed musical note (tuning-fork); the bifurcation of a road, etc.; each part into which anything divides, as a road, river, etc.; *v.i.* to divide into branches; *v.t.* to pitch with a fork, as hay; to lift with a fork (as food); to form a fork. **-ed, -y** *a.* shaped like a fork; cleft. [O.E. *forca,* a fork].
for·lorn (faur·lōrn′) *a.* deserted; forsaken; *adv.* **-ness** *n.* [O.E. *forleosan,* to lose].
form (fōrm) *n.* shape or appearance; configuration; the human body; a mold; state of health; model; style; method of arrangement of details; etiquette; an official document or questionnaire with details to be filled in by applicant; *v.t.* to give shape to; to construct; to devise; to be an element of; to arrange to conceive; to build up (as a sentence); *v.i.* to assume position; to develop. **-al** *a.* according to form; regular; methodical; conventional; ceremonious. **-alization** *n.* **-alize** *v.t.* and *v.i.* to give form to; to make formal. **-alism** *n.* the quality of being formal; undue insistence on conventional forms, esp. in religion or the arts. **-alist** *n.* **-ality** *n.* quality of being conventional or pedantically precise; propriety. **-ally** *adv.* **-ation** *n.* the act of forming; structure; an arrangement, of troops, aircraft, etc. **-ative** *a.* giving form; conducive to growth. **-less** *a.* [L. *forma,* shape].
-form *suff.* in the shape of, as *cruciform* in the shape of a cross.
form·al·de·hyde (fōr·mal′·dạ·hīd) *n.* a colorless, pungent gas, soluble in water, used as a disinfectant and preservative.
for·mat (fōr′·mat) *n.* the general make-up of a book, its size, shape, style of binding, quality of paper, etc. [L. *forma,* a shape].
for·mer (fōr′·mẹr) *a.* preceding in time; long past; first mentioned. **-ly** *adv.*
for·mic (fōr′·mik) *a.* pertaining to ants [L. *formica,* an ant].
for·mi·da·ble (fōr′·mi·dạ·bl) *a.* exciting fear or apprehension; overwhelming. **formidability, -ness** *n.* **formidably** *adv.* [L. *formidare,* to fear].
for·mu·la (fōr′·myạ·lạ) *n.* a prescribed form; a conventional phrase; a confession of faith; (*Math.*) a general rule or principle expressed in algebraic symbols; (*Chem.*) the series of symbols denoting the component parts of a substance; (*Med.*) *a.* prescription; *pl.* **-s, formulae** (.lē). **formularization, formulation** *n.* **formulary** *n.* a book containing formulas, or prescribed ritual; *a.* prescribed. **formulate, formulize** *v.t.* to reduce to a formula; to express in definite form [L. dim. of *forma,* a shapel].
for·ni·cate (fōr′·ni·kāt) *v.i.* to indulge in unlawful sexual intercourse. **fornication** *n.* sexual intercourse between unmarried persons. **fornicator** *n.* [L. *fornix,* a brothel].
for·sake (fẹr·sāk′) *v.t.* to abandon; to leave or give up entirely. *pr.p.* **forsaking.** *pa.t.* **forsook** *pa.p.* **forsaken. forsaken** *a.* deserted [O.E. *forsacan,* to relinquish].
for·sooth (fẹr·sòòth′) *adv.* in truth; indeed.
for·swear (fōr·swār) *v.t.* to renounce on oath; to deny; *v.i.* to swear falsely; to commit perjury. *pa.t.* **forswore.** *pa.p.* **forsworn** [O.E. *forswerian,* to renounce].
for·syth·i·a (fẹr·sith′·i·ạ) *n.* a spring-flowering shrub with bright yellow blossoms [Eng. 18th cent. botanist William *Forsyth*].
fort (fōrt) *n.* a stronghold; a small fortress; outpost [L. *fortis,* strong].
forte (fōrt) *n.* a strong point; that in which one excels [Fr. *fort,* strong].
forte (fōr′·te) *a.* and *adv.* (*Mus.*) loud; loudly; *n.* a loud passage. **fortissimo** *adv.* very loudly [It. fr. L. fortis, *strong*].
forth (fōrth) *adv.* forwards, in place or time; out from concealment; into view; away. **-coming** *a.* ready to come forth or appear; available. **-right** *a.* straightforward; frank. **-with** *adv.* immediately [O.E. *fore,* before].
for·ti·fy (fōr′·tạ·fī) *v.t.* to strengthen, as by forts, batteries, etc.; to invigorate; to corroborate. *pr.p.* **-ing.** *pa.t., pa.p.* **fortified, fortification** *n.* the art or act of strengthening; a defensive wall; a fortress [L. *forotis,* strong; *facere,* to make].
for·ti·tude (fōr′·tạ·tūd) *n.* power to endure pain or confront danger; resolute endurance; **fortitudinous** *a.* courageous [L. *fortitudo*].
fort·night (fōrt′· nīt) *n.* the space of fourteen days; two weeks. **-ly** *a.* and *adv.* at intervals of a fortnight [contr. of O.E. *feowertyne niht,* fourteen nights].
for·tress (fōr′·tris) *n.* a fortified place; a stronghold [O.Fr. *forteresse,* a stronghold].
for·tu·i·tous (fōr·tū′·ạ·tạs) *a.* happening by chance; accidental. **-ness, fortuity** *n.* [L. *fortuitus,* casual].
for·tune (fōr′·chạn) *n.* chance; that which befalls one; good luck or ill luck; possessions, esp. money or property. **fortunate** *a.* lucky; propitious. **fortunately** *adv.* **fortunateness** *n.* **-teller** *n.* one who reveals the future by palmistry, crystal-gazing, etc. [L. *fortuna*].
for·ty (fōr′·ti.) *a.* and *n.* four times ten; a symbol expressing this, as 40, XL. **fortieth** *a.* fortieth part. [O.E. *feowertig,* forty].
fo·rum (fō′·rạm) *n.* the market place of ancient Rome where legal as well as commercial business was conducted; a public discussion of questions of common interest; tribunal [L. *forum,* the market-place].
for·ward (fōr′·wẹrd) *adv.* towards a place in front; onwards in time; in a progressive or conspicuous way; *a.* toward or at the

forepart, as in a ship; eager; progressive; bold; *n.* (*Sports*) a player in the front line; *v.t.* to promote; to redirect (letter, parcel) to new address; to send out or dispatch. **-ness** *n.* the state of being advanced; precocity; presumption [O.E. *fore*, before; *weard*, in the direction of].

fos·sil (fås′·il) *n.* any portion of an animal or vegetable organism or imprint of such, which has undergone a process of petrifaction and lies embedded in the rock strata; (*Colloq.*) an antiquated person or thing; *a.* pert. to or resembling a fossil. **-iferous** *a.* bearing or containing fossils. **-ize** *v.t.* to turn into a fossil; to petrify; *v.t.* to become a fossil [L. *fodere*, *fossum*, to dig].

fos·ter (faws′·tẹr) *v.t.* to rear; to promote; to cherish. **— brother** *n.* a boy fostered with another child of different parents. **— child** *n.* a child reared by one who is not the parent. **— daughter, — son** *n.* a child brought up as a daughter or son, but not so by birth. **— father, — mother, — parent** *n.* [O.E. *fostrian*, to nourish].

fought (fawt) *pa.t.* and *pa.p.* of verb **fight.**

foul (foul) *a.* filthy; containing offensive or putrescent matter; obscene; wicked; stormy of weather; contrary (of wind); full of weeds; entangled (of ropes); unfair; *n.* the breaking of a rule (in sports); *v.t.* to make foul; to obstruct deliberately; to clog or jam; *v.i.* to become foul, clogged, or jammed; to come into collision. **-ly** *adv.* **-mouthed** *a.* using language scurrilous, obscene, or profane. **— play,** cheating; (*Law*) criminal violence; murder [O.E. *ful*, filthy].

found (found) *pa.t.* and *pa.p.* of verb **find.** **-ling** *n.* a small child who has been found abandoned.

found (found) *v.t.* to lay the basis or foundation of; to establish; to endow; *v.i.* to rely; to depend. **-ation** *n.* the act of founding; the base or substructure of a building; groundwork; underlying principle; an endowment; an endowed institution. **-er** *n.* [Fr. *fonder*, to establish].

found (found) *v.t.* to melt (metal, or materials for glassmaking) and pour into a mold; to cast. **-er** *n.* **-ing** *n.* metal casting. **-ry** *n.* works for casting metals; the process of metal casting [Fr. *fondre*, to melt].

foun·der (foun′·dẹr) *v.t* to cause inflammation in the feet (of a horse) so as to lame; to cause to sink (as a ship); *v.i.* to collapse; to fill with water and sink; to fail; to stumble and become lame [O.Fr. *fondrer*, to fall in].

foun·tain (foun′·tạn) *n.* a natural spring; an artificial jet of water. **fount** *n.* a spring of water; a source. **-head** *n.* source of a stream; (*Fig.*) the origin. [L. *fons*, a spring].

four (fōr) *a.* one more than three; twice two; *n.* the sum of four units; the symbol representing this sum—4, IV. **-flusher** *n.* (*Slang*) one who bluffs. **-fold** *a.* quadruple; folded or multiplied four times. **—in-hand** *n.* a necktie; a team of four horses drawing a carriage; the carriage itself. **—poster** *n.* a bed with four posts. **-some** *n.* a group of four persons. **—square** *a.* having four equal sides and angles. **-teen** *n.* the sum of four and ten; the symbol representing this—14, XIV; *a.* four and ten. **-teenth** *a.* making one of fourteen equal parts. **-th** *a.* next after third; *n.* one of four equal parts. **-thly** *adv.* [O.E. *feower*, four].

fowl (foul) *n.* barnyard cock or hen; the flesh of a fowl; a similar game bird; *pl.* **-s, fowl.** *v.i.* to catch or kill wild fowl. **-er** *n.* one who traps wild fowl. **-ing-piece** *n.* a light shotgun for shooting wild fowl [O.E. *fugol*, a bird].

fox (fåks) *n.* (*fem.* **vixen**) an animal of the canine family, genus *Vulpes*, reddish-brown or gray in color, with large, bushy tail and erect ears; a wily person; *v.t.* to trick; to make sour, in fermenting; to mislead. **— brush** *n.* the bushy tail of a fox. **-glove** *n.* a tall plant with white or purple-pink bell-shaped flowers and leaves which yield digitalis used medicinally as heart stimulant. **-hole** *n.* (*Mil.*) a small trench; a dugout for one or more men. **— hunt** *n.* the pursuit of a fox by huntsmen and hounds.**-iness** *n.* the quality of being foxy; discoloration (in paper); the state of being sour (of beer). **— terrier** *n.* a popular breed of dog sometimes trained for unearthing foxes. **— trot** *n.* a social dance. **-y** *a.* pert. to foxes; cunning; reddish-brown in color. **-ily** *adv.* slyly [O.E. *fox*, a fox].

foy·er (foi′·ẹr) *n.* a theater or hotel lobby; an entrance hall [Fr.].

fra·cas (frā′·kạs) *n.* a noisy quarrel; a disturbance; a brawl [Fr.].

frac·tion (frak′·shạn) *n.* a small portion; a fragment; (*Arith.*) a division of a unit. **decimal fraction,** a fraction expressed with numerator above, and denominator below the line. **-al** *a.* **fractious** *a.* quarrelsome; peevish. **fractiously** *adv.* **fracture** *n.* the act of breaking; a breach or rupture; the breaking of a bone; *v.t.* to break; to crack; *v.i.* to become broken. **compound fracture,** a fracture of a bone, the jagged edge of which protrudes through the skin. **simple fracture,** a fracture where the bone is broken, but surrounding tissues and skin are undamaged [L. *frangere*, *fractum*, to break].

frag·ile (fraj′·ạl) *a.* easily broken; frail; brittle. **fragility** *n.* [L. *fragilis*, breakable].

frag·ment (frag′·mạnt) *n.* a portion broken off; a part; an unfinished portion, as of a literary composition. **-al** *a.* (*Geol.*) composed of fragments of different rocks. **-ary** *a.* broken [L. *frangere*, to break].

fra·grant (frā′·grạnt) *a.* sweet smelling. **fragrance, fragrancy** *n.* sweet scent; perfume; pleasant odor. **-ly** *adv.* [L. *fragrare*].

frail (frāl) *a.* fragile; easily destroyed; infirm; morally weak. **-ly** *adv.* **-ness, -ty** *n.* quality of being weak [O.Fr. *fraile*, weak].

frame (frām) *v.t.* to construct; to contrive; to provide with a frame; to put together, as a sentence; (*Colloq.*) to bring a false charge against; *v.i.* to take shape; *n.* anything made of parts fitted together; the skeleton of anything; a structure; the case or border around a picture; a mood of the mind; a glazed structure in which plants are protected from frost; a structure upon which anything is stretched. **-work** *n.* the fabric which supports anything. **framing** *n.* [O.E. *framian*, to be helpful].

franc (frangk) *n.* a coin (100 centimes) and monetary unit of France, Belgium and Switzerland [O.Fr. *franc*].

fran·chise (fran′·chīz) *n.* the right to vote; a privilege conferred by a government; permission by a manufacturer to sell his products [O.Fr. *franc*, free].

Fran·cis·can (fran·sis′·kan) *n.* one of the order of friars founded by Francis of Assisi.

Fran·co- (frangk′·ō) *prefix*, French, in combinations. **Francophile** *n.* one who admires France and all things French. **Francophobe** *n.* one who hates things French.

fran·gi·ble (fran′·ji·bl) *a.* breakable; fragile. **frangibility** *n.* [L. *frangere*, to break].

frank (frangk) *a.* open; candid; unreserved; *v.t.* to exempt from charge, esp. postage; *n.* a signature on outside of a letter authorizing its free delivery. **-ly** *adv.* candidly. **-ness** *n.* openness; honesty; candor [Fr. *franc*; free].

Frank (frangk) *n.* a member of one of the

Germanic tribes which settled in Gaul giving France its name.

Frank·en·stein (frangk′·ạn·stīn) *n.* any creation which brings disaster or torment to its author [from Mary Shelley's novel].

frank·furter (frangk′·fẹr·ter) *n.* a smoked sausage [G. City of Frankfurt].

frank·in·cense (frangk′·in·sens) *n.* a dry, perfumed resin, burned as incense [Fr. *franc*, pure; *encens*, incense].

Frank·lin (frangk′·lin) *n.* a type of open iron stove [fr. Benj. *Franklin*].

fran·tic (fran′·tik) *a.* frenzied; wild. **-ally** *adv.* [O.Fr. *frenetique*, mad].

fra·ter·nal (fra·tur′·nạl) *a.* pert. to a brother or brethren; brotherly. *adv.* **fraternization** *n.* **fraternize** *v.i.* to associate with others in a friendly way. **fraternizer** *n.* **fraternity** *n.* a student society, designated by letters of the Greek alphabet; brotherhood; a group of men associated for a common purpose [L. *frater*, a brother].

frat·ri·cide (frat′·ri·sīd) *n.* the crime of killing a brother; one who commits this crime. **fratricidal** *a.* [L. *frater*, a brother; *caedere*, to kill].

fraud (frawd) *n.* deception deliberately practiced; trickery; (*Colloq.*) a cheat; imposter. **-ulence, -ulency** *n.* trickery, deceitfulness. **-ulent** *a.* pert. to or practicing fraud; dishonest. **-ulently** *adv.* [L. *fraus*, a fraud].

fraught (frawt) *a.* loaded; charged [Dut. *vracht*, a load].

fray (frā) *n.* an affray; a brawl; a contest [contr. of *affray*].

fray (frā) *v.t.* to wear through by friction; to ravel the edge of cloth; (*Fig.*) to irritate, as the nerves, or temper; *v.i.* to become frayed [Fr. *frayer*, to rub].

fraz·zle (fraz′·l) *v.t.* to fray; to exhaust; *n.* exhaustion [etym. unknown].

freak (frēk) *n.* a sudden whim; a prank; capricious conduct; something or someone abnormal; *a.* odd; unusual. **-ish** *a.* **-ishly** *adv.* **-ishness** *n.* [prob. O.E. *frec*, bold].

freak (frēk) *v.t.* to spot or streak or dapple; *n.* a streak [prob. from *freckle*].

freck·le (frek′·l) *n.* a small brownish spot on the skin; any small spot; *v.t.* to color with freckles; *v.i.* to become covered with freckles. **freckly,** *a.* [M.E. *frakin*, a freckle].

free (frē) *a.* having political liberty; unrestricted; loose; independent; open; liberal; spontaneous; irregular; licentious; exempt from impositions, duties, or fees (as trade, education); *adv.* without hindrance; gratis; *v.t.* to set at liberty; to emancipate; to clear; to disentangle. *pr.p.* **-ing.** *pa.p.* **-d. -booter** *n.* one who wanders about for plunder; a pillager. **-man** *n.* one who has been freed from slavery. **-dom** *n.* liberty; immunity; indecorous familiarity; **-hand,** unrestricted authority; drawn by hand without instruments, etc. **-handed** *a.* generous; liberal. **-hold** *n.* the tenure of property in fee simple, or fee tail, or for life; *a.* held by freehold. **freeholder** *n.* **—lance** *n.* orig. a mercenary soldier who sold his services to any country, esp. said of a journalist, not attached to a particular staff. **— love** *n.* doctrine that sexual relations should be unhampered by marriage, etc. **-ly** *adv.* **-man** *n.* a man who is not a slave; one who enjoys the full privileges of a corporate body. **-mason** *n.* orig. a member of an organization of skilled masons; now, a member of a fraternal association for mutual assistance and social enjoyment. **-masonic** *a.* **-masonry** *n.* **-ness** *n.* **—spoken** *a.* accustomed to speak without reserve. **-stone** *n.* a building-stone easily quarried, cut, and carved; peach, plum, etc. in which the pit does not cling. **-thinker** *n.* one who professes to be independent of all religious authority; a rationalist. **-thinking, — thought** *n.* **— trade,** the policy of unrestricted, international trade. **-trader** *n.* **— verse** *n.* a form of verse unrestricted in length of line, meter, stanza form, and generally without rhyme. **— will** *n.* the power of the human will to choose without restraint; *a.* voluntary [G.E. *freo*, free].

freeze (frēz) *v.t.* to harden into ice; to congeal; to preserve by refrigeration; to paralyze with cold or terror; to render credits unrealizable; become congealed or stiff with cold. *pr.p.* **freezing.** *pa.t.* **froze.** *pa.p.* **frozen** *n.* frost. **freezing point** *n.* the temperature at which a liquid turns solid, esp. that at which water freezes, marked 32° F. or 0° C. [O.E. *freosan*, to freeze].

freight (frāt) *n.* the cargo of a ship, etc.; a load; charge for conveyance of goods; *v.t.* to load a ship, etc. **-age** *n.* charge for transport of goods; freight. **-er** *n.* one who receives and forwards freight; a cargo boat [late form of *fraught*].

French (french) *a.* pert. to France or its inhabitants; *n.* the inhabitants or the language of France. **French chalk,** a variety of talc. **— horn** *n.* a musical wind instrument with mellow note like a hunting horn. **-man** (*fem.* **Frenchwoman**) *n.* a native of France. **— window,** one functioning as door and window.

fren·zy (fren′·zi·) *n.* violent agitation of the mind; madness; *v.t.* to render frantic. **frenzied** *a.* **frenetic** (also **phrenetic**) *a.* mad; frenzied [Gk. *phrenitis*, inflammation of the brain].

Fre·on (frē′·ȧn) *n.* gas used in refrigeration and for air-conditioning [Trademark].

fre·quent (frē′·kwạnt) *a.* happening at short intervals; constantly recurring; repeated. **frequent** (fri·kwent′) *v.t.* to visit often. **frequency** *n.* the state of occurring repeatedly; periodicity; (*Phys.*) number of vibrations per second of a recurring phenomenon. **-ation** *n.* the practice of visiting repeatedly. **-ative** *a.* (*Gram.*) denoting the repetition of an action; *n.* (*Gram.*) a word, usually a verb, expressing frequency of an action. **-er** *n.* **-ly** *adv.* **-ness** *n.* [L. *frequens*].

fres·co (fres′·kō) *n.* a method of mural decoration on walls of fresh, still damp, plaster. *v.t.* to paint in fresco [It. *fresco*, fresh].

fresh (fresh) *a.* vigorous; unimpaired; new; not stale; brisk; original; unsalted; (*Slang*) impudent; *n.* a stream of fresh water; a freshet. **-en** *v.t.* to make fresh; *v.i.* to grow fresh; to become vigorous. **-ener** *n.* **-et** *n.* an inundation caused by rains or melting snows; a fresh-water stream. **-man** *n.* a first-year University or high school student. **-ness** *n.* **—water** *a.* pert. to or living in water which is not salt [M.E. *fresch*, fresh].

fret (fret) *v.t.* to wear away by friction; to eat away; to ruffle; to irritate; *v.i.* to wear away; to be corroded; to be vexed or peevish; *pr.p.* **-ting.** *pa.t., pa.p.* **-ted.** *n.* irritation; erosion. **-ful** *a.* querulous. **-fully** *adv.* **-fulness** *n.* [O.E. *fretan*, to devour].

fret (fret) *n.* ornamental work, consisting usually of strips, interlaced at right angles. **-ted, -ty** *a.* ornamented with frets. **-work** *n.* decorative, perforated work on wood or metal [O.Fr. *frete*, interlaced work].

fret (fret) *n.* a small piece of wood or wire fixed on the fingerboard, as of a guitar, under the strings [prob. O.Fr. *frete*, ferrule].

Freud·i·an (froi′·di·an) *a.* pert. to *Sigmund Freud*, (1856-1939) the Austrian psychoanalyst, or to his theories.

fri·a·ble (frī·a·bl) *a.* easily crumbled or reduced to powder. **-ness, friability** *n.* [L. *friabilis*, crumbling].

fri·ar (frī′·ẹr) *n.* a member of one of the orders (*R.C.*) of mendicant monks. **-y** *n.* a monastery [L. *frater*, a brother].

frib·ble (frib'·l) *n.* a frivolous person or thing; *v.i.* to fritter away time.

fri·cas·see (frik·ą·sē') *n.* a dish of fowl, rabbit, etc. stewed with rich gravy sauce; *v.t.* to make a fricassee [Fr.].

fric·tion (frik'·shąn) *n.* the act of rubbing one thing against another; (*Phys.*) the resistance which a body encounters in moving across the surface of another with which it is in contact; unpleasantness. **fricative** *a.* produced by friction. **-al** *a.* caused by friction. **-ally** *adv.* [L. *fricare*, to rub].

Fri·day (frī'·di·) *n.* the sixth day of the week [O.E. *Frig*, wife of Odin; *daeg*, a day].

fried (frīd) *pa.t.* and *pa.p.* of verb **fry.**

friend (frend) *n.* one attached to another by esteem and affection; an intimate associate; a supporter. **Friend** *n.* a member of the Quakers. **-less** *a.* without friends. **-liness** *n.* **-ly** *a.* having the disposition of a friend; kind; propitious. **-ship** *n.* attachment; comradeship. **Society of Friends,** the Quaker sect [O.E. *freond*, a friend].

frieze (frēz) *n.* a heavy woolen cloth with nap on one side [Fr. *frise*, a curl].

frieze (frēz) *n.* decoration on the upper part of the wall, around a mantel, etc. [Fr. *frise*, a fringe].

fri·gate (frig'·it) *n.* a fast 2-decked sailing ship of war of the 18th and 19th centuries. [It. *fregata*, a frigate].

fright (frīt) *n.* sudden and violent fear; extreme terror; alarm; (*Colloq.*) an ugly or grotesque person or object; *v.t.* to make afraid. **-en** *v.t.* to terrify; to scare. **-ened** *a.* **-ful** *a.* terrible; calamitous; shocking. **-fully** *adv.* terribly; (*Colloq.*) very. **-fulness** *n.* **-some** *a.* frightful [O.E. *fyrhto*, fear].

frig·id (frij'·id) *a.* very cold (esp. of climate); passionless; stiff. **-ity** *n.* coldness. **-ly** *adv.* **-ness** *n.* **Frigidaire** *n.* (Trademark) a refrigerator [L. *frigidus*, cold].

frill (fril) *n.* a gathered cloth or paper edging; a ruffle; (*Fig.*) excessive ornament (as in style); *v.t.* to ornament with a frill; *v.i.* to become crinkled like a frill [etym. doubtful].

fringe (frinj) *n.* loose threads as ornamental edging of cloth; anything suggesting this, as a fringe of hair; the outside edge of anything; *v.t.* to adorn with fringe; to border [O.Fr. *fringe, a border*].

frip·per·y (frip'·ęr·i·) *n.* tawdry finery; ostentation [Fr. *fripperie*, old clothes].

frisk (frisk) *v.i.* to leap; to gambol; to skip; *v.t.* (*slang*) to feel a person's clothing for concealed weapons; (*Slang*) to steal in this way; *n.* a frolic. **-ily** *adv.* playfully. **-iness** *n.* **-y** *a.* lively [O.Fr. *frisque*, lively].

frit·ter (frit'·ęr) *n.* a slice of fruit or meat dipped in batter and fried to form a cake [O.Fr. *friture*, something fried].

frit·ter (frit'·ęr) *v.t.* to waste (time, energy, etc.) in a futile way. **-er** *n.* [prob. conn. with L. *frangere*, to break].

friv·ol (friv'·ąl) *v.t.* and *v.i.* to squander, esp. time or energy; to fritter away. **frivolity** *n.* the act or habit of idly wasting time; lack of seriousness. **-ous** *a.* **-ously** *adv.* **-ousness** *n.* [L. *frivolus*, paltry].

frizz (friz) *v.t.* to curl; to crisp; *n.* a row of small curls. **-zle** *v.t.* to curl; in cooking, to crisp by frying; *n.* curled hair [O.Fr. *friser*].

fro (frō) *adv.* from; back, as in *to and fro.*

frock (fråk) *n.* a woman's dress; a monk's long, wide sleeved garment. **— coat** *n.* a double-breasted, full skirted coat worn by men [O.Fr. *froc*, a monk's frock].

frog (fråg) *n.* an amphibious, tailless animal, (developed from a tadpole); hoarseness caused by mucus in the throat; a V-shaped horny pad on the sole of a horse's foot; a V-shaped section of track where two sets of rails cross; ornamental braiding on uniform, or ornamental fastening of loop and button; *v.t.* to ornament with frogs. **-men** *n.* the nickname given to underwater swimming men [O.E. *frogga*, a frog].

frol·ic (frål'·ik) *n.* a merry-making; gaiety; *a.* full of pranks; merry; *v.i.* to play merry pranks; to have fun. *pr.p.* **-king.** *pa.t., pa.p.* **-ked.** **-some** *a.* [Dut. *vroolijk*, merry].

from (frum) *prep.* away; forth; out of; on account of; at a distance [O.E. *fram*, from].

frond (frånd) *n.* (*Bot.*) an organ of certain flowerless plants, such as ferns, in which leaf and stem are combined and bear reproductive cells [L. *frons*, a leaf].

front (frunt) *n.* the forepart, the forehead; the human countenance; (*Mil.*) firing line; battle zone; (*Colloq.*) outward appearance *a.* pert. to, or at the front of, anything; *adv.* to the front; *v.t.* and *v.i.* to have the face or front towards any point. **-age** *n.* the front part of general exposure of a building; land abutting on street, river, or sea. **-al** *a.* pert. to the forehead or foremost part; (*Mil.*) direct, as an attack, without flanking movement; *n.* a bone of the forehead; an ornamental cloth for altar front [L. *frons*, the forehead].

fron·tier (frun'·tir) *n.* border of a country; the undeveloped areas of a country, knowledge, etc.; *a.* bordering; pioneering. **-sman** *n.* one who settles on a frontier [Fr.].

fron·tis·piece (frun'·tis·pēs) *n.* (*Archit.*) the main face of a building; an engraving or decorated page fronting the title page of a book [L. *frons*, the front; *specere*, to see].

frost (frawst) *n.* condition when water turns to ice, i.e. when temperature falls below 32° F.; severe cold; frozen dew; (*Slang*) a failure; a disappointment; *v.t.* to cover with hoar-frost; to nip (as plants); to ice a cake **-bite** *n.* freezing of the skin and tissues due to exposure to extreme cold. **-bitten** *a.* **-ed** *a.* covered with frost or anything resembling it. **-ily** *adv.* **-iness** *n.* **-y** *a.* accompanied with frost; chilly; white; grey-haired; frigid (in manner or feeling) [O.E. *forst*, fr. *freosan*, to freeze].

froth (frawth) *n.* spume; foam; trivial things or ideas; *v.t.* to cause to froth; *v.i.* to bubble. **-iness** *n.* **-y** *a.* [Scand. *frotha*, froth].

fro·ward (frō'·ęrd) *a.* perverse; refractory. **-ly** *adv.* **-ness** *n.* [O.E. *fra*, away, and *ward*].

frown (froun) *v.i.* to wrinkle the brow; to scowl; *v.t.* to rebuke by a stern look; *n.* a wrinkling of the brow to express disapproval [O.Fr. *froignier*, to look sullen].

frow·zy (frou'·zi·) *a.* musty; unkempt.

fro·zen (frō'·ząn) *pa.p.* of the verb **freeze.**

fruc·ti·fy (fruk'·ti·fī) *v.t.* to make fruitful; to fertilize; *v.i.* to bear fruit. **fructiferous** *a.* fruitbearing. **fructose** *n.* fruit sugar; levulose [L. *fructus*, fruit].

fruc·tose (frook'·tōs) *n.* a sweet form of sugar that occurs naturally esp. in fruits and honey.

fru·gal (fròò'·gąl) *a.* sparing; thrifty; economical. **-ly** *adv.* **-ity** *n.* [L. *frugalis*, thrifty].

fruit (fròòt) *n.* the produce of the earth used for man's needs; the edible produce or seed of a plant; offspring; the consequence or outcome; *v.i.* to produce fruit. **-age** *n.* fruit collectively. **fruitarian** *n.* one who lives almost wholly on fruit. **-er** *n.* fruit grower; fruit-carrying ship. **-ful** *a.* producing fruit; abundant; profitable. **-fully** *adv.* **-fulness** *n.* **-ing** *n.* the process of bearing fruit. **-less** *a.* having no fruit; (*Fig.*) profitless; vain; empty. **-lessly** *adv.* **-lessness** *n.* **— sugar** *n.* glucose; levulose. **-y** *a.* resembling fruit; mellow [O.Fr. *fruit*, fruit].

fru·i·tion (fròò·ish'·ąn) *n.* fulfillment of hopes and desires [L. *fruitio*, enjoyment].

frump (frump) *n.* a dowdy, cross woman.

frus·trate (frus'·trāt) *v.t.* to bring to nothing; to balk; to thwart; to circumvent. **frus-**

tration *n.* disappointment; defeat. **frustrative** *a.* [L. *frustrari,* to deceive].
frus·tum (frus'·təm) *n.* (Geom.) the remaining part of a solid figure when the top has been cut off by a plane parallel to the base. *pl.* **-s, frusta** [L. *frustrum,* a piece].
fry (frī) *v.t.* to cook with fat in a pan over the fire; *v.i.* to be cooked in a frying pan; to sizzle. *pr.p.* **-ing** *pa.t., pa.p.* **fried. -er, frier** *n.* [O.Fr. *frire,* to roast].
fry (frī) *n.* young fish just spawned; young children [M.E. *fri,* offspring].
fuch·sia (fū'·shə) *n.* a genus of flowering plants, with drooping bright purplish red flowers [fr. *Fuchs,* German botanist].
fud·dle (fud'·l) *v.t.* to make confused.
fudge (fuj) *interj.* stuff; nonsense; *n.* a soft chocolate candy; space reserved in a newspaper for last minute news.
fu·el (fū'·əl) *n.* anything combustible to feed a fire, as wood, coal; *v.t.* to provide with fuel [O.Fr. *fouaille,* fr. L. *focus,* a health].
fu·gi·tive (fū'·jə·tiv) *a.* escaping; fleeing; fleeting; wandering; *n.* a refugee; one who flees from justice. [L. *fugere,* to flee].
fugue (fūg) *n.* (*Mus.*) a musical composition for voices and or instruments based on chief and subsidiary themes [L. *fuga,* flight].
ful·crum (ful'·krəm) *n.* (*Mech.*) the pivot of a lever; (*Fig.*) means used to achieve a purpose. *pl.* **-s, fulcra** [L. *fulcrum,* a bedpost].
ful·fill (fool·fil') *v.t.* to carry into effect; to execute; to discharge; to satisfy (as hopes). **-er** *n.* **-ment** *n.* accomplishment; completion [O.E. *full,* full; *fyllan,* to fill].
ful·gent (ful'·jənt) *a.* shining; dazzling. **fulgency** *n.* **-ly** *adv.* [L. *fulgere,* to shine].
fu·lig·i·nous (fū·lij'·ən·əs) *a.* sooty; dusky [L. *fuligo,* soot].
full (fool) *a.* filled to capacity; replete; crowded; complete; plump; abundant; showing the whole surface (as the moon); ample (of garments, etc.); clear and resonant (of sounds); *n.* the utmost extent; highest degree. *adv.* quite; completely; exactly. **—blooded** *a.* of pure race; vigorous. **—blown** *a.* fully developed, as a flower. **— dress** *n.* dress worn on ceremonial occasions; *a.* formal. **-y** *adv.* completely [O.E. *full,* full].
full (fool) *v.t.* to cleanse, shrink and thicken cloth in a mill; *v.i.* to become thick or felted. **-er** *n.* one who fulls cloth [O.E. *fullian,* to whiten cloth].
ful·mi·nate (ful'·mi·nāt) *v.t.* to flash; to explode; to thunder forth official censure; *n.* a compound of fulminic acid exploding by percussion, friction, or heat, as *fulminate of mercury.* **fulminant** *a.* fulminating. **fulmination** *n.* the act of fulminating; an explosion; a biting denunciation. **fulminatory, fulmineous, fulminous** *a.* pert. to or like thunder and lightening [L. *fulmen,* lightning].
ful·some (fool'·səm) *a.* excessive; insincere, **-ly** *adv.* **-ness** *n.* [O.E. *full*].
ful·vous (ful'·vəs) *a.* tawny; dull yellow. [L. *fulvus,* tawny].
fu·ma·role (fū'·mə·rōl) *n.* a small fissure in volcano [Fr. *fumerole,* a smoke-hole].
fum·ble (fum'·bl) *v.i.* to grope blindly or awkwardly; *v.t.* to handle clumsily [Scand. *fumla,* to grope].
fume (fūm) *n.* pungent vapor from combustion or exhalation; (*Fig.*) excitement; rage; *v.i.* to smoke; to be in a rage; *v.t.* to send forth as fumes [L. *fumus,* smoke].
fu·mi·gate (fū'·mi·gāt) *v.t.* to expose to poisonous gas or smoke, esp. for the purpose of destroying germs; to perfume or deodorize. **fumigator** *n.* apparatus or substance used in fumigation [L. *fumigare,* to smoke].
fun (fun) *n.* merriment; hilarity; sport. **-nies** *n.pl.* (*Colloq.*) comic strips. **-nily** *adv.* **-niness** *n.* **-ny** *a.* full of fun [M.E. *fonnen*].
fu·nam·bu·late (fū·nam'·byə·lāt) *v.i.* to balance and walk on a tight-rope. **funambulist** *n.* [L. *funis,* a rope; *ambulare,* to walk].
func·tion (fungk'·shən) *n.* performance; the special work done by an organ or structure; office; ceremony; (*Math.*) a quantity the value of which varies with that of another quantity; a social entertainment; *v.i.* to operate; to fulfil a set task. **-al** *a.* having a special purpose; pert. to a duty or office. **-ally** *adv.* **-ary** *n.* an official [L. *functus,* to perform].
fund (fund) *n.* permanent stock or capital; an invested sum, the income of which is used for a set purpose; a store; ample supply; *pl.* money in hand; *v.t.* to establish a fund for the payment of interest or principal. **-ed** *a.* [L. *fundus,* the bottom].
fun·da·men·tal (fun·də·men'·təl) *a.* pert. to the foundations; basic; essential; original; *n.* a primary principle; (*Mus.*) the bottom note of a chord. **-ism** *n.* belief in literal truth of the Bible. **-ist** *n.* **-ly** *adv.* [L. *fundamentum,* the foundation].
fu·ne·ral (fū'·nə·ral) *n.* the ceremony of burying the dead; obsequies; *a.* pert. to or used at burial. **funerary, funereal** *a.* gloomy [L. *funus,* burial rites].
fun·gus (fung'·gəs) *n.* any of a group of thallophytes (molds, mushrooms, mildews, puffballs, etc.) (*Path.*) a spongy, morbid growth; proud flesh. *pl.* **fungi** (fun'·ji), **-es, fungiform** *a.* fungus or mushroom-shaped. **fungicide** *n.* any preparation which destroys molds or fungoid growths. **fungoid, fungous** *a.* pert. to or caused by fungus [L. *fungus,* a mushroom].
fu·ni·cle (fū'·ni·kl) *n.* (*Bot.*) the stalk of a seed. **funicular** *a.* pert. to, or worked by rope. **funicular railway,** a cable railway [L. *funiculus,* dim. of *funis,* a cord].
funk (fungk) *n.* (*Colloq.*) abject terror; panic; *v.i.* and *v.t.* to be terrified of or by.
fun·nel (fun'·əl) *n.* an inverted hollow metal cone with tube, used for filling vessels with narrow inlet; the smokestack of a steamship [L. *fundere,* to pour].
fur (fur) *n.* the short, fine, soft hair of certain animals; animal pelts used for coats, etc.; coating on the tongue; deposit on inside of kettles, etc. *v.t.* to line, face, or cover with fur; to coat with morbid matter. *pr.p.* **-ring.** *pa.p.* **-red. -rier** *n.* a dealer in furs. **-ry** *a.* [M.E. *forre,* fur].
fur·be·low (fur'·bə·lō) *n.* an ornament; a ruffle [Sp. *falbala,* a flounce].
fur·bish (fur'·bish) *v.t.* to polish; to burnish; to renovate [O.Fr. *fourbir,* to polish].
fur·cate (fur'·kāt) *a.* forked; branched like a fork; *v.i.* to branch out [L. *furca,* a fork].
fu·ri·ous (fyoo'·ri·əs) *a.* raging; violent; savage. **-ly** *adv.* [L. *furiosus,* raging].
furl (furl) *v.t.* to roll, as a sail [contr. of O.Fr. *fardel,* a bundle].
fur·long (fur'·lawng) *n.* eighth of mile; 220 yards [O.E. *furh,* a furrow; *lang,* long].
fur·lough (fur'·lō) *n.* leave of absence; *v.t.* to grant leave [Dut. *verlof,* permission].
fur·nace (fur'·nəs) *n.* an enclosed structure for the generating of heat required for smelting ores, warming houses, etc.; a place of severe trial [L. *fornus,* an oven].
fur·nish (fur'·nish) *v.t.* to supply; to equip; to fit out. **-er** *n.* **-ings** *n.pl.* fittings, of a house, esp. furniture, curtains, carpets, etc.
fur·ni·ture (fur'·ni·cher) *n.* equipment; that which is put into a house, office, etc. for use or ornament [Fr. *fournir,* to provide].
fu·ror (fū'·rawr) *n.* wild excitement; enthusiasm [L. *furor,* rage].
fur·row (fur'·ō) *n.* a trench made by a plough; channel; groove; deep wrinkle; *v.t.* to plough; to mark with wrinkles. **-y** *a.* [O.E. *furh,* a furrow].
fur·ther (fur'·THər) *a.* more remote; addi-

tional; *adv.* to a greater distance; moreover. **-more** *adv.* moreover; besides. **-most** *a.* most remote. **furthest** *adv.* and *a.* most remote. (**farther, farthest** are preferred as *comp.* and *superl.* of **far**) [O.E. *furthor,* comp. of *forth,* forwards].

fur·ther (fur′·THẹr) *v.t.* to help forward; to promote. **-ance** *n.* the act of furthering [O.E. *fyrthia,* to promote].

fur·tive (fur′·tiv) *a.* done stealthily; covert; sly. **-ly** *adv.* [L. *fur,* a thief].

fu·ry (fyoo′·ri·) *n.* rage; passion; frenzy [L. *furia,* rage].

fus·cous (fus′·kạs) *a.* of a dark greyish-brown color [L. *fuscus,* dark].

fuse (fūz) *v.t.* to melt (as metal) by heat; to amalgamate; *v.i.* to become liquid; *n.* a tube filled with combustible matter, used in blasting or discharge of bombs, etc.; a device used as a safety measure in electric lighting and heating systems. **fusibility** *n.* **fusible** *a.* **fusion** *n.* the act or process of melting; the state of being melted or blended; coalition [L. *fundere, fusum,* to melt].

fu·see (fū-zē′) *n.* the spindle-shaped wheel in a clock or watch, round which the chain is wound; a match; a red signal flare. Also **fuzee** [Fr. *fuseé,* a spindleful].

fu·se·lage (fū′·sa.lij or fū·zạ·lazh′) *n.* the body of an airplane [O.Fr. *fusel,* a spindel].

fu·sil (fū′·sil) *n.* a light flintlock musket. **-lade** *n.* the simultaneous discharge of firearms [O.Fr. *fuisil,* a flintmusket].

fuss (fus) *n.* bustle; unnecessary ado; needless activity; *v.i.* to become nervously agitated; *v.t.* to bother another with excessive attentions. **—budget** *n.* (*Colloq.*) a fussy person. **-ily** *adv.* **-iness** *n.* **-y** *a.*

fus·tian (fust′·chạn) *n.* a coarse cotton twilled fabric, corduroy, velveteen; (*Fig.*) bombast [M.E. *fustyane,* fr. *Fustat* (*Egypt*)].

fus·ti·ga·tion (fus·tạ·gā′·shạn) *n.* a thrashing with a stick. **fustigate** *v.t.* to cudgel [L. *fustigare,* to cudgel].

fu·tile (fū′·til) *a.* ineffectual, unavailing, useless. **-ly** *adv.* **futility** *n.* uselessness; fruitlessness [L. *futilis,* worthless].

fu·ture (fūt′·cher) *a.* about to happen; that is to come hereafter; *n.* time to come. **futurism** *n.* a modern aesthetic movement marked by complete departure from tradition. **futurist** *n.* **futuristic** *a.* **futurity** *n.* time to come [L. *futurus,* about to be].

fuzz (fuz) *n.* fine, light particles; fluff; **-iness** *n.* **-y** *a.*

G

gab (gab) *n.* (*Colloq.*) trifling talk; chatter; *v.i.* to chatter. *pr.p.* **-bing.** *pa.t.* **-bed.** **-by** *a.* **-ble** *n., v.i.* **the gift of gab,** a talent for talking.

gab·ar·dine (gab′·ẹr·dēn) *n.* a firm, woven twilled fabric of cotton, rayon or wool. Also **gaberdine** [Sp. *gabardina*].

ga·ble (gā′·bl) *n.* the end of a house, esp. the vertical triangular ends of a building from the eaves to the top; a similar construction projecting from a roof [O.N. *gafl*].

gad (gad) *v.i.* to go about idly; to ramble. *pr.p.* **-ding.** *pa.p.* and *pa.t.* **-ded.** **-about** *v.i.* to wander idly; *n.* a pleasure seeker [O.E. *gaedeling,* a comrade].

gad·fly (gad′·flı) *n.* a cattle biting fly; (*Fig.*) a tormentor [fr. *gad,* a goad].

gadg·et (gaj′·it) *n.* (*Colloq.*) a general term for any small mechanical contrivance or device.

Gael (gāl) *n.* a Scottish Highlander of Celtic origin. **-ic** *a. n.* the language of the Gaels.

gaff (gaf) *n.* a barbed fishing spear; a stick with an iron hook for landing fish; *v.t.* to seize (a fish) with a gaff [Fr. *gaffe*].

gaf·fer (gaf′·ẹr) *n.* (*Brit.*) an old man, esp. a country man [contr. of *grandfather*].

gag (gag) *n.* something thrust into or over the mouth to prevent speech; *v.t.* to apply a gag to; to silence by force; *v.i.* to heave with nausea. *pr.p.* **-ging.** *pa.t., pa.p.* **-ged.** [imit.].

gag (gag) *n.* (*Colloq.*) words inserted by an actor which are not in his part; a joke.

gage (gāj) *n.* a pledge or pawn; a glove, gauntlet, cast down as challenge; a challenge; [O.Fr. *guage*]. [Sir William *Gage*].

gage (gāj) *n.* a kind of plum; a greengage [fr.

gage (gāj) *v.t.* See **gauge.**

gag·gle (gag′·l) *v.i.* to cackle like geese; *n.* a flock of geese [imit.].

gai·e·ty (gā′·ạ·ti·) *n.* mirth; merriment; glee; jollity. **gaily** *adv.* merrily [Fr. *gai*].

gain (gān) *v.t.* to attain to, or reach; to get by effort; to get profit; to earn; to win; *v.i.* to have advantage or profit; to increase; to improve; to make an advance; *n.* profit; advantage; increase. **-ful** *a.* profitable; lucrative. **-fully** *adv.* **-fulness** *n.* [Fr. *gagner,* to earn].

gain·say (gān·sā′) *v.t.* to contradict; to deny. *pa.p.* and *pa.t.* **-said** [O.E. *gean,* against, and *say*].

gait (gāt) *n.* manner of walking or running; pace [var. of *gate*].

gai·ter (gā′·tẹr) *n.* covering for instep and ankle fitting over the shoe; a spat [Fr. *guétre*].

gal (gal) *n.* (*Slang*) a girl.

ga·la (gā′·lạ) *n.* a show or festivity; *a.* festive [It. *gala,* finery].

gal·ax·y (gal′·ạk·si·) *n.* a band of stars encircling the heavens; a brilliant assembly of persons. (G) the Milky Way. **galactic** *a.* [Gk. *gala, galaktos,* milk].

gale (gāl) *n.* a wind between a stiff breeze and a hurricane; (*Colloq.*) an outburst of noise.

gale (gāl) *n.* a shrub found in marshes, giving off a pleasant fragrance [O.E. *gagel*].

ga·le·na (gạ·lē′·nạ) *n.* sulfide of lead, the principal ore from which lead is extracted [L. *galena,* lead ore].

gall (gawl) *n.* bile secreted in the liver; anything bitter; bitterness; rancor; (*Slang*) effrontery; impudence. **— bladder** *n.* a small sac on the under side of the liver, in which the bile is stored. **-stone** *n.* a concretion formed in the gall bladder [O.E. *gealla*].

gall (gawl) *v.t.* to fret and wear away by rubbing; to vex, irritate, or harass; *n.* a skin wound caused by rubbing. **-ing** *a.* irritating [O.E. *gealla*].

gal·lant (gal′·ạnt) *a.* splendid or magnificent; noble in bearing or spirit; brave; chivalrous; courteous to women; amorous. (ga·lant′) *n.* a brave, high-spirited man; a courtly or fashionable man; a lover or paramour. **-ly** *adv.* **-ry** *n.* bravery; chivalry [Fr. *galant*].

gal·leon (gal′·i·ạn) *n.* a large, clumsy sailing ship built up high at bow and stern [Sp.].

gal·ler·y (gal′·ẹr·i·) *n.* a long corridor, hall, or room; a room or series of rooms in which works of art are exhibited; a balcony; the uppermost tier of seats, esp. in theater; audience or spectators; a passage in a mine; a tunnel [Fr. *galerie*].

gal·ley (gal′·i·) *n.* a low, one-decked vessel, navigated both with oars and sails; a large rowboat; the kitchen of a ship; (*Print.*) an oblong tray on which type is placed when set up. **— proof** *n.* (*Print.*) a proof taken from the galley on a long strip of paper, before it is made up in pages. **— slave** *n.* one who was condemned for some criminal offence to row in the galleys [L.L. *galea*].

gal·liard (gal′·yẹrd) *n.* a lively dance [Fr.].

Gal·lic (gal′·ik) *a.* pert. to ancient Gaul, or France; French. **gallicize** *v.t.* to make French in opinions, manners [L. *Gallia,* Gaul].
gal·li·mau·fry (gal·ạ·maw′·fri·) *n.* a hash of various meats; a hodgepodge [O.Fr. *galimafree*].
gal·li·na·ceous (gal·ạ·nā′·shạs) *a.* belonging to the order of birds which includes domestic fowls, pheasants, etc. [L. *galling,* a hen].
gal·li·pot (gal′·i·pȧt) *n.* a small earthenware pot, for medicines [*galley,* and *pot*].
gal·li·um (gal′·i·ạm) *n.* a soft grey metal of extreme fusibility [L. *gallus,* a cock. *Lecoq* the discoverer].
gal·li·vant (gal·ạ·vant′) *v.i.* to gad about.
gal·lon (gal′·ạn) *n.* a measure of capacity both for liquid and dry commodities, containing four quarts [O.Fr. *jalon*].
gal·lop (gal′·ạp) *n.* fastest gait of horse, when it lifts forefeet together, and hind feet together; a ride at a gallop; *v.i.* to ride at a gallop; to go at full speed; *v.t.* to cause to gallop. **-ing** *a.* speedy; swift [Fr. *galoper*].
gal·lows (gal′·ōz) *n.* a frame from which criminals are hanged [O.E. *galga*].
gal·lus·es (gal′·ạs·iz) *n.pl.* suspenders [fr. *gallows*].
ga·loot (ga·lȯȯt′) *n.* (*Colloq.*) an uncouth or awkward fellow.
gal·op (gal′·ạp) *n.* a lively dance [Fr.].
ga·lore (gạ·lōr′) *adv.* abundantly; in plenty [Gael. *gu leor,* enough].
ga·losh, golosh (gạ·lȧsh′) *n.* (usually pl.) a rubber overshoe [Fr. *galoche*].
gal·va·nism (gal′·vạ·nizm) *n.* the branch of science which treats of the production of electricity by chemical action. **galvanic** *a.* **galvanize** *v.t.* to apply galvanic action to; to stimulate by an electric current; (*Fig.*) to stimulate by words or deeds; to coat metal with zinc. **galvanization** *n.* **galvanizing** *n.* coating with zinc (by galvanic action). **galvanometer** *n.* an instrument for detecting and measuring the strength and direction of electric currents. **galvanoscope** *n.* an instrument for detecting the existence and direction of an electric current. **galvanic battery,** an apparatus for generating electricity by chemical action on a series of zinc or copper plates. **galvanized iron,** iron coated with zinc to prevent rust [fr. Luigi *Galvani,* inventor].
gamb (gam) *n.* an animal's leg. **gam** *n.* (Slang) a woman's leg [L. *gamba,* leg].
gam·bit (gam′·bit) *n.* in chess, opening move involving sacrifice of pawn [It. *gambetto,* wrestler's trip, fr. *gamba,* leg].
gam·ble (gam′·bl) *v.i.* to play for money; to risk esp. by financial speculation; *v.t.* to lose or squander in speculative ventures; *n.* a risky undertaking; a reckless speculation. **-r** *n.* [O.E. *gamen,* a game].
gam·bol (gam′·bạl) *v.i.* to leap about playfully; to skip and dance about. *n.* a dancing or skipping about; a frolic [Fr. *gambade*].
game (gām) *n.* any sport; a pastime; a contest for amusement; a trial of strength, skill, or chance; an exercise or play for stakes; victory in a game; frolic; mockery; hence, an object of ridicule; animals and birds protected by law and hunted by sportsmen; *a.* pert. to animals hunted as game; brave; plucky; *v.i.* to gamble. *n.pl.* athletic contests. **-ly** *adv.* **-ness** *n.* **-ster** *n.* a gambler. **gaming** *a.* playing cards, dice, etc. for money; gambling. **gamy** *a.* having the flavor of dead game which has been kept uncooked for a long time. **— cock** *n.* breed of cock trained for cockfighting. **— preserve,** land stocked with game for hunting or shooting. **— warden** *n.* an official who enforces game laws. **big game,** all large animals hunted for sport. **fair game** (*Fig.*) a person considered easy subject for jest. **to play the game,** to act in a sportsmanlike way [O.E. *gamen*].
game (gām) *a.* (*Colloq.*) of an arm or leg, lame; injured [O.Fr. *gambi,* bent].
gam·ete (gam·ēt′) *n.* a protoplasmic body, ovum, or sperm, which unites with one of opposite sex for conception [Gk. *gamos,* marriage].
gam·in (gam′·in) *n.* a street-urchin [Fr.].
gam·ma (gam′·ạ) *n.* the third letter of the Greek alphabet. **— rays,** electro-magnetic radiations, of great penetrative powers, given off by radioactive substances, e.g. radium.
gam·mon (gam′·ạn) *n.* the thigh of a pig, smoked or cured [Fr. *jambon,* ham].
gam·ut (gam′·ạt) *n.* the whole series of musical notes; a scale; the compass of a voice; the entire range [L. *gamma,* and *ut,* names of notes]
gan·der (gan′·dẹr) *n.* a male goose; (*Slang*) a look [O.E. *gandra*].
gang (gang) *n.* people banded together for some purpose, usually bad; body of laborers working together. *v.i.* (*Colloq.*) to act as a gang (followed by *up*) **-ster** *n.* one of a gang of criminals [O.E. *gangan,* to go].
gan·gling (gang′·gling) *a.* lanky and loosely knit in build [O.E. *gangan,* to go].
gan·gli·on (gang′·gli·ạn) *n.* a globular, hard tumor, situated on a tendon. *pl.* **-s, ganglia. gangliate** *a.* furnished with ganglia. **-ic** *a.* [Gk. *ganglion,* an encysted tumor].
gang plank (gang′ plangk′) *n.* a moveable plank bridge between a ship and the shore.
gan·grene (gang′·grēn) *n.* the first stage of mortification or death of tissue in the body; *v.t.* and *v.i.* to affect with, or be affected with, gangrene. **gangrenous** *a.* mortified; putrefying [Gk. *gangraina*].
gang·way (gang′·wā) *n.* a passageway; a platform and ladder slung over the side of a ship; *interj.* make way, please! [O.E. *gangweg*].
gan·net (gan′·it) *n.* the solan goose, a seafowl of the pelican tribe [O.E. *ganot*].
gant·let (gȧnt′·lit) *n.* a former military or naval punishment in which the offender was made to run between files of men who struck him as he passed. **to run the gantlet** (erroneously, **gauntlet**), to undergo this ordeal; to face any unpleasant ordeal [Scand.].
gan·try (gan′·tri·) *n.* a structure to support a crane, railway-signal, etc.
gaol (jāl) *n.* (*Brit.*) a jail. **-er** *n.* [form of *jail*].
gap (gap) *n.* an opening; a breach; a mountain pass [O.N. = chasm].
gape (gāp) *v.i.* to open wide, esp. the mouth; to stare with open mouth; to yawn. *n.* a wide opening; the act of gaping. **the gapes,** a fit of yawning; a disease of poultry and other birds, characterized by gaping [O.N. *gapa*].
gar (gȧr) *n.* a fish of the pike family. Also **garfish** [O.E. *gar,* a dart, spear].
ga·rage (gạ·rȧzh′, gạ·raj′) *n.* a covered enclosure for motor vehicles; a fuel and repair station for motor vehicles; *v.t.* to place in a garage [Fr. *gare,* a station].
garb (gȧrb) *n.* clothing; mode or style of dress; *v.t.* to dress [O.Fr. *garbe,* dress].
gar·bage (gȧr′·bij) *n.* kitchen refuse; anything worthless.
gar·ble (gȧr′·bl) *v.t.* to pervert or mutilate, as a story, a quotation, an account, etc. by picking out only certain parts [Ar. *ghirbal,* a sieve].
gar·den (gȧr′·dn) *n.* ground for cultivation of flowers, vegetables, etc. generally attached to a house; pleasure grounds; *v.i.* to cultivate, or work in, a garden. **-er** *n.* **-ing** *n.* the act of tending a garden [Fr. *jardin*].
gar·de·nia (gȧr·dē′·ni·ạ) *n.* a genus of tropical trees and shrubs with sweet-scented, beautiful white flowers [fr. A. *Garden,* Amer. botanist].
gar·gan·tu·an (gȧr·gan′·choo·ạn) *a.* immense, enormous, esp. of appetite [fr. *Gargantua,* hero of Rabelais' book].
gar·gle (gȧr′·gl) *v.t.* to rinse (mouth or throat),

preventing water from going down throat by expulsion of air from lungs; *v.i.* to make a sound of gargling; to use a gargle; *n.* a throat wash [O.Fr. *gargouille*, throat].

gar·goyle (gȧr′·goil(*n.* a projecting spout, often in the form of a grotesque carving [O.Fr. *gargouille*, the throat].

gar·ish (gar′·ish) *a.* gaudy; showy; glaring; dazzling. **-ly** *adv.* [M.E. *gauren*, to stare].

gar·land (gȧr′·lạnd) *n.* a wreath of flowers, branches, feathers, etc.; an anthology; *v.t.* to ornament with a garland [O.Gr. *garlande*].

gar·lic (gȧr′·lik) *n.* a plant having a bulbous root, a strong smell like onion, and a pungent taste. **-ky** *a.* [O.E. *garleac*].

gar·ment (gȧr′·mạnt) *n.* any article of clothing [Fr. *garnement*, equipment].

gar·ner (gȧr′·nẹr) *n.* a granary; *v.t.* to store in a granary; to gather up [L. *granarium*].

gar·net (gȧr′·nit) *n.* a semi-precious stone, usually of a dark-red color and resembling a ruby; a dark-red color [Fr. *grenat*].

gar·nish (gȧr′·nish) *v.t.* to adorn; to embellish; to ornament; (*Cookery*) to make food attractive or appetizing; *n.* ornament; decoration; **-ment** *n.* **garniture** *n.* that which garnishes [Fr. *garnir*, to furnish].

ga·rotte. See **garrote.**

gar·ret (gar′·it) *n.* upper floor of a house; an attic [O.Fr. *garite*, a place of safety].

gar·ri·son (gar′·ạ·sn) *n.* a body of troops stationed in a fort, town, etc.; the fort or town itself; *v.t.* to occupy with a garrison [O.Fr. *garison*, fr. *garir*, to protect].

gar·rote (ga·rȧt′, -rōt′) *n.* a Spanish mode of execution by strangling; apparatus for this punishment; *v.t.* to execute by strangulation; to seize by the throat, in order to throttle and rob [Sp. *garrote*, a cudgel].

gar·ru·lous (gar′·ạ·lạs) *a.* talkative; loquacious. **-ly** *adv.* **-ness** *n.* **garrulity** *n.* [L. *garrire*, to chatter].

gar·ter (gȧr′·tẹr) *n.* a string or band worn near the knee to keep a stocking up; the badge of the highest order of knighthood in Great Britain; *v.t.* to support with a garter [O.Fr. *gartier*, fr. *garet*, the bend of the knee].

gas (gas) *n.* an elastic fluid such as air, esp. one not liquid or solid at ordinary temperatures; mixture of gases, used for heating or lighting; an anesthetic; (*Mil.*) a chemical substance used to poison or incapacitate the enemy; (*Slang*) empty talk; (*Colloq.*) gasoline; *v.t.* to poison with gas; *v.i.* (*Slang*) to talk emptily; to talk unceasingly. *pr.p.* **-sing.** *pa.p.*, *pa.t.* **-sed.** **-eous** *a.* like, or in the form of gas. **-ification** *n.* **-ify** *v.t.* to convert into gas, as by the action of heat, or by chemical processes. **-sy** *a.* full of gas. **-bag** *n.* (*Slang*) a very talkative person. **— burner** *n.* a gas jet or stove. **—guzzler** *n.* (*Slang*) a large car that uses a wasteful amount of gas. **— jet** *n.* a nozzle or burner of a gas burner; the burner itself. **— mask** *n.* a respirator worn to protect against poisonous gases. **— meter** *n.* a metal box used to measure the amount of gas consumed. **-ohol** *n.* a combustible liquid consisting of 90% unleaded gasoline and 10% alcohol. **-ometer** *n.* an apparatus for measuring or storing gas. **— range** *n.* a gas cooking stove [coined by Flemish chemist, Van Helmont, fr. Gk. *chaos*, chaos].

Gas·con (gas′·kạn) *n.* a native of *Gascony*, in S.W. France. **gascon** *n.* a boaster.

gash (gash) *v.t.* to make a long, deep cut in; *n.* a deep cut [O.Fr. *garser*, to slash].

gas·ket (gas′·kit) *n.* (*Naut.*) a flat, plaited cord, used to furl the sail or tie it to the yard; a washer between parts such as the cylinder head and cylinder block [Fr. *garcette*].

gas·o·line, gas·o·lene (gas′·ạ·lēn) *n.* a volatile, inflammable, liquid mixture produced by the distillation of petroleum, used as a fuel, solvent, etc. [*gas;* L. *oleum*, oil; *-ine*].

gasp (gasp) *v.i.* to struggle for breath with open mouth; to pant; *v.t.* to utter with gasps; *n.* the act of gasping; a painful catching of the breath [O.N. *geispa*, to yawn].

gas·tric (gas′·trik) *a.* pert. to the stomach. **gastritis** (gas·trī′·tis) *n.* inflammation of the stomach. **gastro-enteritis** *n.* inflammation of the stomach and intestines. **gastrology** *n.* [Gk. *gastēr*].

gas·tron·o·my (gas·trȧn′·ạ·mi·) *n.* the art of good eating; epicurism. **gastronome, gastronomer, gastronomist** *n.* one fond of good living. **gastronomic(al)** *a.* [Gk. *gastēr*, the stomach; *nemein*, regulate].

gas·tro·pod (gas′·trạ·pȧd) *n.* a class of molluscs, e.g. snails and whelks, having a fleshy ventral disk, which takes the place of feet [Gk. *gaster*, the stomach; *pous*, *podos*, the foot].

gat (gat) *n.* (*Slang*) a pistol [fr. *Gat*ling gun].

gate (gāt) *n.* an opening into an enclosure, through a fence, wall, etc.; a mountain pass or defile; an entrance; a device for stopping passage of water through a dam or lock; the number of people paying to watch a game; also the money taken. **—crasher** *n.* one attending a social function uninvited. **-way** *n.* an entrance [O.E. *geat*, a way].

gath·er (gaTH′·ẹr) *v.t.* to bring together; to collect; to pick; in sewing, to draw into puckers; to infer or deduce; to harvest; *v.i.* to come together; to congregate; to increase; to wrinkle, as the brow; to swell up and become full of pus (of a sore or boil); *n.* a pucker or fold in cloth. **-ing** *n.* an assemblage; a crowd; an abscess [O.E. *gaderian*, fr. *gador*, together].

Gat·ling-gun (gat′·ling gun) *n.* an early machine gun [invented by R. J. *Gatling*].

gauche (gōsh) *a.* awkward; clumsy; tactless. **-rie** (gō·shạ·rē′) *n.* [Fr.].

gau·cho (gou′·chō) *n.* a cowboy of the S. American pampas [Sp.].

gaud (gawd) *n.* a piece of worthless finery; a trinket. **-ily** adv. **-y** *a.* [L. *gaudium*, joy].

gauge (gāj) *v.t.* to ascertain the capacity of; to measure the ability of; to estimate; *n.* an instrument for determining dimensions or capacity; a standard of measure; test; criterion; the distance between the rails of a railway. **-r** *n.* one who gauges, esp. an exciseman who measures the contents of casks [O.Fr. *gauge*].

Gaul (gawl) *n.* an old name for France; a Frenchman [L. *Gallia*].

gaunt (gawnt) *a.* lean and haggard; pinched and grim; desolate. **-ly** *adv.* **-ness** *n.*

gaunt·let (gawnt′·lit) *n.* a glove with metal plates on the back, worn formerly as armor; a glove with a long cuff. **to run the —** (See *gantlet*). **to throw down, to take up, the —,** to give, accept, a challenge [Fr. *gant*, a glove].

gauss (gous) *n.* (*Elect.*) the unit of density of a magnetic field [fr. Karl F. *Gauss*, a German scientist, 1777-1855].

gauze (gawz) *n.* a thin, transparent fabric. **gauziness** *n.* **gauzy** *a.* [Fr. *gaze*].

gave (gāv) *pa.t.* of **give.**

gav·el (gav′·ạl) *n.* a mallet; a small wooden hammer used by a judge, chairman, or auctioneer.

ga·votte (gạ·vȧt′) *n.* an old dance after the style of the minuet but not so stately; the music for it [Fr. *gavotte*].

gawk (gawk) *n.* an awkward person; a simpleton; a booby; *v.i.* to stare stupidly. **-y** *a.*

gay (gā) *a.* lively; merry; light-hearted; showy; dissipated; **-ly, gaily** *adv.* **-ety, gaiety** *n.* [Fr. *gai*].

gay (gā) *a.* homosexual; n. a homosexual.

gaze (gāz) *v.i.* to look fixedly; to stare; *n.* a fixed, earnest look; a long, intent look. **-r** *n.* one who gazes.

ga·ze·bo (gạ·zē′·bō) *n.* a summerhouse commanding a wide view; a belvedere.

ga·zelle (gą·zel′) *n.* a small, swift, graceful antelope [Ar. *ghazal*].

ga·zette (gą·zet′) *n.* a newspaper (now used in newspaper titles). **gazetteer** (gaz·ę·tēr′) *n.* formerly a writer for a gazette; now, a geographical dictionary [It. *gazetta*].

gear (gir) *n.* apparatus; equipment; tackle; a set of tools; harness; rigging; clothing; goods; utensils; a set of toothed wheels working together, esp. by engaging cogs, to transmit power or to change timing; *v.t.* to provide with gear; to put in gear; *v.i.* to be in gear. **-ing** *n.* the series of toothed wheels for transmitting power, changing speed, etc. **—wheel** *n.* a wheel having teeth or cogs [M.E. *gere*].

gee (jē) *interj.* a command to a horse to turn to the right; exclamation of surprise.

geese (gēs) *n.* plural of **goose.**

gee·zer (gē′·zęr) *n.* (*Slang*) an old fellow; a queer old chap [corrupt. of *guiser*].

Gei·ger counter (gī′·gęr) *n.* a hypersensitive instrument for detecting radio-activity, cosmic radiation, etc. [H. *Geiger*, Ger. physicist].

gei·sha (gā′·shą) *n.* a Japanese dancing girl.

gel (jel) *n.* (*Chem.*) a colloidal solution which has set into a jelly; *v.i.* to become a gel. **-ling.** *pa.t., pa.p.* **-led. -ation** *n.* a solidifying by means of cold [L. *gelare*, tc freeze].

gel·a·tin, gelatine (jel′·ą·tin) *n.* a glutinous substance gotten by boiling parts of animals (bones, hoofs, etc.) which is soluble in hot water and sets into a tremulous jelly. **-ous** (ją·lat′·-i·nąs) *a.* of the nature or consistency of gelatin; like jelly. **-ate, -ize** *v.t.* to convert into gelatine. **-ation** *n.* [It. *gelata*, jelly].

geld (geld) *v.t.* to castrate. **-ing** *n.* a castrated animal, esp. a horse [O.N. *geldr*, barren].

gel·id (jel′·id) *a.* cold as ice. **-ly** *adv.* **-ness, gelidity** *n.* [L. *gelidus*, fr. *gelu*, frost].

gem (jem) *n.* a precious stone of any kind; a jewel; anything of great value; *v.t.* to adorn with gems. *pr.p.* **-ming.** *pa.p., pa.t.* **-med** [L. *gemma*].

gem·i·nate (jem′·ą·nāt) *a.* doubled; existing in pairs; *v.i.* and *t.* to make or become paired or doubled. **gemination** *n.* [L. *geminare*, to double].

Gem·i·ni (jem′·ą·nī) *n.pl.* the third sign of the Zodiac; a constellation containing the two bright stars Castor and Pollux, twin heroes of Greek legend [L. *geminus*, twin-born].

gem·ma (jem′·ą) *n.* (*Bot.*) a bud; (*Zool.*) a bud-like outgrowth which becomes a separate individual. *pl.* **gemmae. gemmate** *a.* having buds; *v.i.* to propagate by buds, as coral. **gemmation** *n.* budding; (*Zool.*) reproduction by gemmae. **gemmiparous** *a.* producing buds; (*Zool.*) propagating by buds [L. *gemma*, a bud].

gen·darme (zhȧn·dȧrm′) *n.* an armed military policeman in France. **gendarmeria** (zhȧn·-dȧrm′·rē) *n.* the corps of armed police [Fr. fr. *gens d'armes*, men-at-arms].

gen·der (jen′·dęr) *n.* (*Colloq.*) sex, male or female; (*Gram.*) the classification of nouns according to sex (actual or attributed) or animateness [L. *genus, generis*, a kind].

gene (jēn) *n.* the hereditary factor which is transmitted by each parent to offspring and which determines hereditary characteristics [Gk. *genos*, origin].

ge·ne·al·o·gy (jēn·i·ȧl′·ą·ji·) *n.* a record of the descent of a person or family from an ancestor; the pedigree of a person or family; lineage. **genealogist** *n.* one who traces the descent of persons or families. **genealogical** *a.* [Gk. *genea*, birth; *logos*, discourse].

gen·er·a (jen′·ą·rą) *n.* See **genus.**

gen·er·al (jen′·ą·rąl) *a.* relating to a genus or kind; pert. to a whole class or order; not precise, particular, or detailed; usual, ordinary, or prevalent; embracing the whole, not local or partial; *n.* (*U.S. Army*) brigadier general, lieutenant general, major general, general, general of the Army, or general of the Armies. **-ly** *adv.* as a whole; for the most part; commonly; extensively. **-ity** *n.* indefiniteness; vagueness; a vague statement; the main body. **-ship** *n.* military skill in a commander; leadership. **-issimo** *n.* the chief commander (in certain countries). **in —,** in most respects. **— practitioner** *n.* a doctor whose work embraces all types of cases [L. *generalis*].

gen·er·al·ize (jen′·ęr·ąl·īz) *v.t.* to reduce to general laws; to make universal in application; *v.i.* to draw general conclusions from particular instances; to speak vaguely. **generalization** *n.* a general conclusion from particular instances [fr. *general*].

gen·er·ate (jen′·ę·rāt) *v.t.* to bring into being; to produce; (*Math.*) to trace out. **generation** *n.* a bringing into being; the act of begetting; the act of producing; that which is generated; a step in a pedigree; all persons born about the same time; the average time in which children are ready to replace their parents (about 25 years); family. **generative** (jen′·ą·rą·tiv) *a.* having the power of generating or producing; prolific. **generator** *n.* one who, or that which, generates; a begetter; a machine for converting mechanical into electrical energy [L. *generare*, to procreate].

ge·ner·ic (ją·ner′·ik) *a.* pert. to a genus; of a general nature in regard to all members of a genus. **-ally** *adv.* [L. *generus*, kind].

gen·er·ous (jen′·ęr·ąs) *a.* liberal, free in giving; abundant; copious; rich (wine). **-ly** *adv.* **generosity** *n.* magnanimity; liberality in giving [L. *generosus*, of noble birth].

gen·e·sis (jen′·ą·sis) *n.* origin; creation; birth. *pl.* **geneses** (jen′·s·sēs). **Genesis** *n.* the first book of the Old Testament [Gk.].

gen·et (jen′·it). See **jennet.**

ge·net·ic (ją·net′·ik) *a.* pert. to origin, creation, or reproduction. **-s** *n.* the scientific study of the heredity of individuals, esp. of inherited characteristics. **— engineering** *n.* the work on biological improvements in a species (human, animal, or plant) through manipulation of the genetic code. **-ist** *n.* [Gk. *gignesthai*, to be born].

Ge·ne·van (ją·nē′·vąn) *a.* pert. to *Geneva*, in Switzerland. **Geneva Conventions** *n.pl.* international agreements, signed at Geneva in 1864, 1868, 1906, and 1949, to lessen sufferings of the wounded in war by providing for the neutrality of hospitals, ambulances, etc.

gen·ial (jēn′·yąl) *a.* kindly; sympathetic; cordial; sociable; of a climate, mild and conducive to growth. **-ity** (jē·ni·al′·ą·ti·) *n.* the quality of being genial; friendliness; sympathetic cheerfulness. **-ly** *adv.* [L. *genialis*].

ge·ni·e (jē′·ni·) *n.* a jinni. *pl.* **genii** (jē′·ni·ī) [Ar. *jinnee*].

gen·i·tal (jen′·ą·tąl) *a.* pert. to generation, or to the organs of generation. **-s** *n.pl.* the external sexual organs. Also **-ia** (jen·ą·tā′·li·ą) [L. *genitalis*, fr. *gignere*, to beget].

gen·i·tive (jen′·ą·tiv) *a.* pert. to, or indicating, source, origin, possession, etc.; *n.* (*Gram.*) the case used to indicate source, origin, possession and the like [L. *genitivus*].

gen·ius (jēn′·yąs) *n.* one's mental endowment or individual talent; the animating spirit of a people, generation, or locality; uncommon intellectual powers; a person endowed with the highest mental gifts [L.].

gen·o·cide (jen′·ą·sīd) *n.* race murder. **genocidal** *a.* [Gk. *genos*, race; L. *caedere*, to kill].

gen·re (zhȧn′·rą) *n.* a kind; sort; style. **— painting** *n.* painting which portrays scenes in everyday life [Fr. = style, kind].

gent (jent) *n.* (*Colloq.*) a gentleman; a would-be gentleman [fr. *gent*leman].

gen·teel (jen.tēl′) *a.* possessing the qaulities belonging to high birth and breeding; well-bred; stylish; refined. **-y** *adv.* **-ness** *n.* **gentility** (jen.til′.i.ti) *n.* [Fr. *gentil*].

gen·tian (jen′.shạn) *n.* the common name of Gentiana, plants whose root is used medicinally as a tonic and stomachic; its flower is usually of a deep, bright blue [L. *gentiana*].

gen·tile (jen′.tīl) *n.* one who is not a Jew; *a.* formerly (among Christians), heathen [L. *gens*, a nation].

gen·tle (jen′.tl) *a.* kind and amiable; mild and refined in manner; quiet and sensitive of disposition; meek; moderate; gradual; of good family; *v.t.* (*Colloq.*) to tame; to make docile. **gently** *adv.* **-folk** *n.pl.* persons of good breeding and family. **-ness** *n.* **gentry** (jen′.tri.) *n.* people of birth and good breeding; the class of people between the nobility and the middle class [L. *gentilis*].

gen·tle·man (jen′.tl.mạn) *n.* a man of good breeding and refined manners; a man of good family; a polite term for a man. *pl.* **gentlemen. -ly** *a.* **-like** *a.* **gentlewoman** *n.* a woman of good family or of good breeding; a woman who waits upon a person of high rank. **-'s gentleman,** a valet. **-'s agreement,** one binding in honor but not legally [L. *gentilis*].

gen·u·flect (jen′.yoo.flekt) *v.i.* to bend the knee, esp. in worship. **genuflection, genuflexion** *n.* **-or** *n.* **-ory** *a.* [L. *genu*, the knee; *flectere*, to bend].

gen·u·ine (jen′.yoo.in) *a.* real; true; pure; authentic; sincere. **-ly** *adv.* [L. *genuinus*].

ge·nus (jē′.nạs) *n.* a class; an order; a kind; (*Nat. Hist.*) a subdivision ranking next above species, and containing a number of species having like characteristics. *pl.* **genera** (jen′.ạ.rạ) [L. *genus, generis*, a kind].

ge·o-, ge- combining forms fr. Gk. *gē*, meaning earth, ground, soil. **geocentric** *a.* (*Astron.*) having reference to the earth as center [Gk. *kentron*, the center].

ge·ode (jē′.ōd) *n.* in mineralogy, a rounded nodule of stone, containing a cavity, usually lined with crystals [Gk. *geodēs*, earth-like].

ge·od·e·sy (jē.ȧd′.ạ.si.) *n.* the mathematical survey and measurement of the earth's surface, involving allowance for curvature. **geodetic, geodetical** *a.* [Gk. *gē*; *daiein*, to divide].

ge·og·ra·phy (jē.ȧg′.rạ.fi.) *n.* the science of the earth's form, its physical divisions into seas, rivers, mountains, plains, etc.; a book on this. **geographer** *n.* one versed in geography. **geographic, geographical** *a.* pert. to geography. **geographically** *adv.* [Gk. *gē*, the earth; *graphein*, to write].

ge·ol·o·gy (jē.ȧl′.ạ.ji.) *n.* the science of the earth's crust, the rocks, their strata, etc. **geological** *a.* **geologically** *adv.* **geologist** *n.* [Gk. *gē*, the earth; *logos*, discourse].

ge·om·e·try (jē.ȧm′.ạ.tri.) *n.* the mathematical study of the properties of lines, angles, surfaces, and solids. **geometric(al)** *a.* pert. to geometry. **geometrically** *adv.* **geometrician** *n.* one skilled in geometry. **geometric progression** (*Math.*) a series of quantities in which each quantity is obtained by multiplying the preceding term by a constant factor, e.g. 2, 6, 18, 54, etc. (3 being the constant factor) [Gk. *gē*, the earth; *metron*, a measure].

ge·oph·a·gy (jē.ȧf′.a.ji.) *n.* the practice of eating earth, dirt, clay, etc. Also **geophagism** *n.* [Gk. *gē*, earth; *phagein*, to eat].

ge·o·pol·i·tics (jē.ō.pȧl′.ạ.tiks) *n.pl.* the study of the influence of geographical situation upon the politics of a nation. **geopolitical** *a.* [Gk. *gē*, the earth; *politēs*, a citizen].

geor·gette (jawr.jet′) *n.* a fine semi-transparent silk fabric [fr. *Georgette*, Fr. modiste].

geor·gic (jawr′.jik) *n.* a pastoral poem [Gk. *gē*, the earth; *ergon*, a work].

ge·ot·ro·pism (jē.ȧt′.rạ.pizm) *n.* (*Bot.*) the tendency of a growing plant to direct its roots downwards. **geotropic** *a.* [Gk. *gē*, the earth; *tropos*, a turning].

ge·ra·ni·um (jạ.rā′.ni.ạm) *n.* plant having showy flowers [Gk. *geranos*, a crane].

ger·i·at·rics (jer.i.at′.riks) *n.* science of the diseases and care of the old [Gk. *geras*, old age].

germ (jurm) *n.* the rudimentary form of a living thing, whether animal or plant; a microscopic organism; a microbe; a bud; that from which anything springs. **-icide** *n.* a substance for destroying disease-germs. **germicidal** *a.* **— warfare** waged with bacteria for weapons [L. *germen*, a bud].

ger·man (jur′.mạn) *a.* closely related. **germane** (jer.mān′) *a.* appropriate; relevant; allied; akin [L. *germanus*, fully akin].

Ger·man (jur′.mạn) *a.* belonging to *Germany;* *n.* a native of Germany; the German language. **Germanic** *a.* pert. to Germany; Teutonic. **Germanize** *v.t.* to make German. **German measles,** a disease like measles, but less severe [L. *Germanus*].

ger·man·der (jẹr.man′.dẹr) *a.* genus of herb-like plants having medicinal properties [Gk. *chamai*, on the ground; *drus*, a tree].

ger·ma·ni·um (jur.mā′.ni.ạm) *n.* a rare metallic element [L. *Germanus*, German].

ger·mi·nal (jur′.mạ.nal) *a.* pert. to a germ or seed-bud [L. *germen*, bud].

ger·mi·nate (jur′.mạ.nāt) *v.i.* to sprout; to bud; to shoot; to begin to grow; *v.t.* to cause to grow. **germinative** *a.* pert. to germination. **germination** *n.* [L. *germen*, a bud].

ger·on·tol·o·gy (jẹr.ạn.tȧl′.ạ.ji.) *n.* the science that studies the decline of life, esp. of man [Gk. *geron*, an old man].

ger·ry·man·der (ger., jer.i.man′.dẹr) *v.t.* to arrange or redistribute electoral districts to private advantage [fr. Gov. *Gerry* of Mass.].

ger·und (jer′.ạnd) *n.* part of the Latin verb used as a verbal noun; the dative of the O.E. or modern English infinitive, used to express purpose. **gerundial** *a.* of the nature of a gerund. **gerundive** *n.* the future passive participle of a Latin verb expressing the action of having to be done [L. *gerere*, to do].

ge·stalt (ge.shtawlt′) *n.* pattern; a whole which is more than the sum of its parts [Ger.].

Ge·sta·po (gạ.stȧp′.ō) *n.* the secret police of the German Nazi party [contr. of *Ge*heime *Sta*ats*po*lizei = secret state-police].

ges·ta·tion (jes.tā′.shạn) *n.* carrying young in womb; pregnancy [L. *gestare*, to bear].

ges·tic·u·late (jes.tik′.yạ.lāt) *v.i.* to make violent gestures or motions, esp. with hands and arms, when speaking. **gesticulation** *n.* a gesture [L. *gestus*, gesture].

ges·ture (jes′.chẹr) *n.* a motion of the head, hands, etc. as a mode of expression; an act indicating attitude of mind; *v.i.* to make gestures [L. *gerere*, to do].

get (get) *v.t.* to procure; to obtain; to gain possession of; to come by; to win, by almost any means; to receive; to earn; to induce or persuade; (*Colloq.*) to understand; (*Arch.*) to beget; *v.i.* to become; to reach or attain; to bring one's self into a condition. *pr.p.* **-ting.** *pa.t.* **got.** *pa.p.* **got, gotten. -away** (get′.a.wā) *n.* (*Colloq.*) escape. **get-up** *n.* (*Colloq.*) equipment; dress; energy [O.E. *gitan*].

gew·gaw (gū′.gaw) *n.* a showy trifle; a bauble [O.E. *gifu*, a gift].

gey·ser (gī′.zẹr) *n.* a hot spring which spouts water intermittently [O.N. *geysa*, to gush].

ghast·ly (gast′.li.) *a.* horrible; shocking. Also *adv.* **ghastliness** *n.* [O.E. *gaestlic*, terrible].

gher·kin (gur′.kin) *n.* a small species of cucumber used for pickling [Dut. *agurkje*].

ghet·to (get′.ō) *n.* a section to which Jews were restricted; a section of a city in which members of a national or racial group live or are restricted [It.].

ghost (gōst) *n.* the apparition of a dead person; a specter; a disembodied spirit; semblance or shadow; (*Colloq.*) a person who does literary or artistic work for another, who takes the credit for it. **-ly** *a.* **-liness** *n.* **-like** *a.* **Holy Ghost,** the Holy Spirit; the third element in the Trinity [O.E. *gast*].

ghoul (gōōl) *n.* imaginary evil being. **-ish** *a.* [Ar. *ghul*].

gi·ant (jī′·ạnt) *n.* (*fem.* **giantess**) a man of extraordinary bulk and stature; a person of unusual powers, bodily or intellectual; *a.* like a giant. **-ism** *n.* (*Med.*) abnormal development [Fr. *géant*].

gib·ber (jib′·ẹr) *v.i.* and *t.* to speak rapidly and inarticulately; to chatter. **-ish** *n.* meaningless speech; nonsense [imit. origin].

gib·bet (jib′·it) *n.* a gallows; *v.t.* to hang on a gallows [O.Fr. *gibet*, a stick].

gib·bon (gib′·ạn) *n.* a tailless, long-armed ape of S.E. Asia [Fr.].

gib·bous (gib′·ạs) *a.* rounded and bulging [L. *gibbus*, a hump].

gibe, jibe (jīb) *v.i.* to taunt; to sneer at; to scoff at; *n.* an expression of contempt; a taunt.

gib·lets (jib′·lits) *n. pl.* the internal edible parts of poultry, e.g. heart, liver, gizzard, etc. [O.Fr. *gibelet*].

gid·dy (gid′·i·) *a.* dizzy; feeling a swimming sensation in the head; liable to cause this sensation; whirling; flighty; frivolous. **giddily** *adv.* **giddiness** *n.* [O.E. *gydig*, insane].

gift (gift) *n.* a present; a thing given; a donation; natural talent; faculty; power; *v.t.* to endow; to present with; to bestow. **-ed** *a.* possessing natural talent. **-edness** *n.* [fr. *give*].

gig (gig) *n.* a light carriage with one pair of wheels, drawn by a horse; a ship's boat.

gi·gan·tic (jī·gan′·tik) *a.* like a giant; of extraordinary size; huge. **-ally** *adv.* [Gk. *gigas*].

gig·gle (gig′·l) *v.i.* to laugh in a silly way, with half-suppressed catches of the breath; *n.* such a laugh. **-r** *n.* **giggling** *n.* [imit. origin].

gig·o·lo (jig′·ạ·lō) *n.* a professional male dancing-partner [Sp.].

gild (gild) *v.t.* to overlay with gold-leaf or gold-dust; to make gold in color; to brighten; to give a fair appearance to; to embellish [O.E. *gyldan*].

gill (jil) *n.* a measure of capacity containing one fourth of a pint [O.Fr. *gelle*].

gill (gil) *n.* the organ of respiration in fishes and other water animals (usually *pl.*) [Scand.].

gill (gil) *n.* a ravine or narrow valley, with a stream running through it. Also **ghyll** [O.N. *gil*, a fissure].

gilt (gilt) *n.* a thin layer of gold, or something resembling gold; *a.* yellow like gold; gilded. **-edged** *a.* having the edges gilded; of the best quality [O.E. *fyldan*].

gim·bals (jim′·bạlz, gim′·bạlz) *n.pl.* a contrivance of rings and pivots for keeping a ship's compass, etc. always in a horizontal position [L. *gemelli*, twins].

gim·crack (jim′·krak) *n.* a showy or fanciful trifle; *a.* showy but worthless [E. *jim*, neat; *crack*, a lad, a boaster].

gim·let (gim′·lit) *n.* a small implement with a screw point and a cross handle, for boring holes in woods; *v.t.* [O.Fr. *guimbelet*].

gim·mick (gim′·ik) *n.* (*Slang*) any device by which a magician works a trick; a gadget.

gimp (gimp) *n.* a narrow fabric or braid used as an edging or trimming [Fr. *guimpe*].

gin (jin) *n.* a distilled alcoholic beverage, flavored with juniper berries, orange peel, etc. [Fr. *genièvre* fr. L. *juniperus*, juniper].

gin (jin) *n.* a snare or trap; a machine for separating the seeds from cotton; *v.t.* to clear cotton of seeds by a gin; to catch in a snare. *pr.p.* **-ning.** *pa.p.* and *pa.t.* **-ned** [fr. *engine*].

gin·ger (jin′·jẹr) *n.* a plant of the Indies with a hot-tasting spicy root; (*Slang*) spirit; a light reddish-yellow color; *v.t.* to flavor with ginger. **— ale** *n.* an effervescent beverage. **-bread** *n.* a cake, flavored with ginger and molasses; showy ornamentation. **-y** *a.* hot and spicy [L. *zingiber*].

gin·ger·ly (jin′·jẹr·li·) *adv.* cautiously; carefully.

ging·ham (ging′·ạm) *n.* a kind of cotton cloth, usually checked or striped [Jav. *ginggang*, striped].

gin·gi·vi·tis (jin·ji·vī′·tis) *n.* inflammation of the gums [L. *gingiva*, the gum; *-itis*, inflammation].

gin rum·my (jin·rum′·i·) *n.* a card game for two or more players.

gin·seng (jin′·seng) *n.* a plant, the root valued as medicine [Chin. *jin-tsan*].

gip·sy See **Gypsy.**

gi·raffe (jạ·raf′) *n.* an African animal with spotted coat and very long neck and legs [Fr. fr. Ar. *zaraf*].

gird (gurd) *v.t.* to encircle with any flexible band; to put a belt around; to equip with, or belt on, a sword. *pa.p.* and *pa.t.* **-ed** or **girt. -er** *n.* an iron or steel beam used as a support in constructional engineering [O.E. *gyrdan*].

gir·dle (gur′·dl) *n.* that which girds or encircles, esp. the waist; a tight-fitting undergarment worn for support of the lower part of the body; *v.t.* [O.E. *gyrdel.*]

girl (gurl) *n.* a female child; a young unmarried woman. **-hood** *n.* the state, or time, of being a girl. **-ish** *a.* like a girl. **-ishly** *adv.* **-ishness** *n.* [M.E. *gurle*].

girt (gurt) alternate *pa.p.* and *pa.t.* of **gird.**

girth (gurth) *n.* band to hold a saddle, blanket, etc. in place on a horse; a girdle; the measurement around a thing [fr. *gird*].

gist (jist) *n.* the main point of a question; the substance or essential point of any matter [O.Fr. *gist*, it lies].

give (giv) *v.t.* to bestow; to make a present of; to grant; to deliver; to impart; to assign; to yield; to supply; to make over; to cause to have; to pronounce, as an opinion, etc.; to pledge, as one's word; *v.i.* to yield; to give away; to move; *n.* elasticity; a yielding to pressure. *pr.p.* **giving.** *pa.p.* **given.** *pa.t.* **gave. -n** *a.* granted; admitted; supposed; certain; particular; addicted to; inclined to. **-r** *n.* **to give away,** to bestow; (*Colloq.*) to betray [O.E. *giefan*].

giz·zard (giz′·ẹrd) *n.* a bird's strong muscular second stomach [O.Fr. *gezier*].

gla·cé (gla·sā′) *a.* of a cake, iced; of a kind of leather, polished or glossy; of fruits, candied [Fr. *glace*, ice].

gla·cier (glā′·shẹr) *n.* a mass of ice, formed by accumulated snow in high cold regions, which moves very slowly down a mountain. **glacial** (glā′·shạl) pert. to ice or its action; pert. to glaciers; icy; frozen; crystallized. **glaciate** *v.t.* to cover with ice; to turn to ice. **glaciology** *n.* the scientific study of the formation and action of glaciers [Fr. *glace*, ice].

glad (glad) *a.* pleased; happy; joyous; giving joy. **-den** *v.t.* to make glad; to cheer; to please. **-ly** *adv.* with pleasure; joyfully; cheerfully. **-ness** *n.* **-some** *a.* giving joy; cheerful; gay. **glad rags** (*Slang*) dressy clothes [O.E. *glaed*].

glade (glād) *n.* a grassy open space in a wood

glad·i·a·tor (glad′·i·ā·tẹr) *n.* literally, a swordsman; a combatant who fought in the arena; one involved in a fight [L. *gladius*, a sword].

glad·i·o·lus (glad·i·ō′·lạs) *n.* a plant of the iris family, with long sword-shaped leaves [L. *gladius*, a sword].

Glad·stone (glad′·stōn) *n.* a leather traveling-bag hinged along the bottom to open out flat [fr. Brit. statesman, W. E. *Gladstone*].

glair (gler) *n.* white of egg; size or gloss made

from it; any substance resembling it; *v.t.* to smear with glair. **-eous, -y** *a.* [Fr. *glaire*].

glam·our (glam′·ęr) *n.* deceptive or alluring charm; witchery. **-ous** *a.* Also **glamor** [corrupt. of *gramarye*, magic].

glance (glans) *n.* a quick look; a glimpse; a flash or sudden gleam of light; an allusion or hint; an oblique hit; *v.t.* to cast a glance; *v.i.* to give a swift, cursory look; to allude; to fly off in an oblique direction; to flash or gleam. **glancing** *a.* [Ger. *Glanz*, luster].

gland (gland) *n.* an organ or collection of cells secreting and abstracting certain substances from the blood and transforming them into new compounds. **-ers** *n.* a disease of horses. **-ular, -ulous** *a.* consisting of or pert. to glands [L. *glans*, an acorn].

glare (glār) *n.* a strong, dazzling light; an overwhelming glitter; showiness; a fierce, hostile look or stare; *v.i.* to shine with a strong dazzling light; to be too showy; to stare in a fierce and hostile manner. **glaring, glary** *a.* brilliant; open and bold [O.E. *glaer*, amber].

glass (glas) *n.* a hard, brittle, generally transparent substance formed by fusing silica with fixed alkalis; articles made of glass, e.g. a drinking-glass or tumbler, a looking-glass or mirror, a telescope, a weather glass or barometer; the quantity contained in a drinking glass; *a.* made of glass; *v.t.* to cover with glass; to glaze. **-es** *n.pl.* spectacles. **-y** *a.* made of glass; vitreous; like glass; dull or lifeless. **-ily** *adv.* **-iness** *n.* **-ful** *n.* the contents of a glass. **— blowing** *n.* the art of shaping and fashioning glass by inflating it through a tube, after heating. **— blower** *n.* **-ware** *n.* articles made of glass [O.E. *glaes*].

glau·co·ma (glaw·kō′·mą) *n.* (*Med.*) a serious eye disease causing tension and hardening of the eyeball with progressive loss of vision [Gk.].

glau·cous (glaw′·kąs) *a.* sea-green; covered with a fine bloom, as a plum [Gk. *glaukos*, blue-gray].

glaze (glāz) *n.* the vitreous, transparent coating of pottery or porcelain; any glossy coating; *v.t.* to furnish with glass, as a window; to overlay with a thin, transparent surface, as earthenware; to make glossy. **-r** *n.* a workman who glazes pottery, cloth, etc. **glazier** (glā′·zhęr) *n.* one who sets glass in windows, etc. [O.E. *glaes*, glass].

gleam (glēm) *n.* a faint or transient ray of light; brightness; glow; *v.i.* to shoot or dart, as rays of light; to flash; to shine faintly [O.E.].

glean (glēn) *v.t.* to gather after a reaper, as grain; to collect with patient labor; to cull the fairest portion of; to pick up (information); *v.i.* to gather. **-er** *n.* **-ings** *n.pl.* what is collected by gleaning [O.Fr. *glener*].

glebe (glēb) *n.* soil; ground; land belonging to a parish church [L. *gleba*, a clod].

glede (glēd) *n.* a bird of prey [O.E. *glida*].

glee (glē) *n.* mirth; merriment; joy; a part song for three or more voices. **-ful** *a.* **-fully** *adv.* **-fulness** *n.* **— club** *n.* a group of singers [O.E. *gleo*, mirth].

gleet (glēt) *n.* thin watery discharge from a sore [O.Fr. *glete*, a flux].

glen (glen) *n.* a valley, usually wooded and with a stream [Gael. *gleann*].

glen·gar·ry (glen·gar′·i·) *n.* a Highlander's cap, boat-shaped, with two ribbons hanging down behind [fr. *Glengarry*, Scotland].

glib (glib) *a.* smooth; fluent. **-ly** *adv.* **-ness** *n.*

glide (glīd) *v.i.* to move gently or smoothly; to go stealthily or gradually; of an airplane, to move, or descend, usually with engines shut off; *n.* a sliding movement. **-r** *n.* one who or that which, glides; a plane capable of flight without motive power, by utilizing air currents [O.E. *glidan*].

glim·mer (glim′·ęr) *v.i.* to shine faintly and unsteadily; to flicker; *n.* a faint, unsteady light; a faint glimpse; an inkling. Also **-ing** *n.* and *a.* [M.E. *glimeren*].

glimpse (glimps) *n.* a momentary view; a passing appearance; a faint notion; *v.t.* to catch a glimpse of; *v.i.* to look briefly [M.E. *glimsen*, to shine faintly].

glint (glint) *n.* glitter; a faint gleam; a flash; *v.i.* to glitter [M.E. *glent*].

glis·sade (gli·sād′, ·sȧd′) *n.* the act of sliding down a slope of ice or snow; in dancing, a gliding step sideways; *v.i.* to perform a glissade [Fr. *glisser*, to slide].

glis·ten (glis′·n) *v.i.* to glitter; to sparkle; to shine; *n.* [O.E. *glisnian*].

glit·ter (glit′·ęr) *v.i.* to shine with a bright, quivering light; to sparkle; to be showy and attractive; *n.* a bright, sparkling light; brilliance [O.N. *glitra*].

gloam·ing (glō·ming) *n.* twilight; dusk [O.E.].

gloat (glōt) *v.i.* to gaze with adulation; to think about with evil satisfaction. **-ing** *a.*

globe (glōb) *n.* a round body; a sphere; a heavenly sphere, esp. the earth; a sphere with a map of the earth or the stars; anything approximately of this shape, e.g. a fish bowl, a lamp shade, etc. **global** *a.* taking in the whole world. **globate, globated** *a.* spherical. **globoid** *a.* globe-shaped. **globose, globous** *a.* round, spherical (or nearly so). **globosity** *n.* **globular** *a.* globe-shaped (or nearly so). **globularity** *n.* **globularly** *adv.* **globule** (glȧb′·yool) *n.* a small particle of matter of a spherical form; a tiny pill. **globulous** *a.* **-trotter** *n.* traveler; tourist [L. *globus*, a round mass].

glob·u·lin (glȧb′·yą·lin) *n.* one of the proteins of the blood [fr. *globule*].

glock·en·spiel (glȧk′·ąn·spēl) *n.* a musical instrument consisting of a row of bells suspended from a rod, or of a series of flat bars, which when struck with a mallet give forth a bell-like sound; a carillon [Ger. *Glocke*, a bell; *Spiel*, play].

glom·er·ate (glȧm′·ą·rit) *a.* gathered into a cluster. **glomeration** *n.* [L. *glomus*, a ball].

gloom (glòòm) *n.* thick shade; partial or almost total darkness; melancholy; *v.i.*to become dark or threatening; to be dejected. **-y** *a.* dark and dreary; melancholy. **-ily** *adv.* **-iness** *n.* [O.E. *glom*].

glo·ry (glō′·ri·) *n.* renown; whatever brings honor; praise and adoration; divine happiness; height of excellence or prosperity; splendor or brilliance; a halo; *v.i.* to be proud; boast; to exult triumphantly. **gloriole** (glō′·ri·ōl) *n.* a halo. **glorious** *a.* illustrious; conferring renown; splendid; noble. **gloriously** *adv.* **gloriousness** *n.* **glorify** *v.t.* to exalt; to praise esp. in worship; to make eternally blessed; to shed radiance on; to magnify. **glorifier** *n.* **glorification** *n.* [L. *gloria*].

gloss (glaws) *n.* luster from a smooth surface; polish; a deceptively fine exterior; *v.t.* to make smooth and shining; to render plausible; (with *over*) to mitigate or excuse something harsh or unpleasant. **-y** *a.* smooth and shining [O.N. *glossi*, a blaze].

gloss (glaws) *n.* an explanatory note upon some word or passage in a text, written in the margin or between the lines; *v.t.* and *i.* to annotate [Gk. *glōssa*, the tongue].

glos·sal (glȧs·ąl) *a.* (*Anat.*) pert. to the tongue [Gk. *glossa*, the tongue].

glos·sa·ry (glȧs′·ą·ri·) *n.* a vocabulary of obscure or technical words; vocabulary to a book. **glossarial** *a.* **glossarist** *n.* a compiler of a glossary [Gk. *glōssa*, the tongue].

glot·tis (glȧt′·is) *n.* (*Anat.*) the narrow opening at the top of the larynx or windpipe, between the vocal chords. **glottal** *a.* [Gk. fr. *glōssa*, *glotta*, the tongue].

glove (gluv) *n.* a cover for the hand and wrist

with a sheath for each finger; *v.t.* to cover with a glove. **-r** *n.* one who makes or sells gloves [O.E. *glof*].

glow (glō) *v.i.* to shine with intense heat; to be bright or red; to feel hot, as the skin; to rage; *n.* incandescence; warmth or redness; sensation of warmth; ardor. **-ing** *a.* bright; warm; enthusiastic. **-ingly** *adv.* [O.E. *glowan*].

glow·er (glou′·ęr) *v.i.* to stare sullenly or with anger; *n.* a scowl.

gloze (glōz) *v.t.* to smooth over; to explain away; to flatter [M.E. *glosen*].

glu·cose (glòò′·kōs) *n.* a white crystalline sugar obtained from fruits and honey [Gk. *glukus*, sweet].

glue (glòò) *n.* an adhesive, gelatinous substance; *v.t.* to join with glue; to cause to stick as with glue. **-y** *a.* [O.Fr. *glu*].

glum (glum) *a.* sullen; moody; morose. **-ness** *n.* **-ly** *adv.* [M.E. *glommen*, to frown].

glu·on (glòò′·ȧn) *n.* (*Nuclear Phys.*) a particle that holds together the nuclei of atoms, binding quarks to form protons, etc. [fr. *glue;* suffix *-on*].

glut (glut) *v.t.* overindulge; to fill to excess; *pr.p.* **-ting;** *pa.p., pa.t.* **-ted;** *n.* an oversupply [L. *gluttire*, to swallow].

glu·ten (glòò′·tęn) *n.* the protein of wheat and other cereals. **-ous** *a.* [L.].

glut·ton (glut′·n) *n.* one who eats too much; (*Fig.*) one eager for anything in excess, e.g. work, books, etc.; carnivore of weasel family, wolverine. **-ize** *v.i.* to eat to excess. **-ous** *a.* **ously** *adv.* **-y** *n.* [Fr. *glouton*].

glyc·er·ine (glis′·ęr·in) *n.* a sweet, colorless, odorless, syrupy liquid. Also **glycerol** [Gk. *glukeros*, sweet].

gly·co·gen (glī′·kạ·jin) *n.* the form in which the body stores carbohydrates (starch); animal starch [Gk. *glukus*, sweet].

gly·col (glī′·kōl) *n.* an artificial compound linking glycerine and alcohol, used as an anti-freeze.

glyph (glif) *n.* a shallow vertical channel or carved fluting [Gk. *gluphein*, to carve].

glyp·tic (glip′·tik) *a.* pert. to carving, esp. on gems. **-s** *n.* the art of engraving on precious stones. **glyptograph** *n.* the engraving. **glyptography** *n.* [Gk. *glyptos*, carved].

gnar (nȧr) *v.i.* to growl; to snarl.

gnarl (nȧrl) *n.* a knot in wood. **-ed** (nȧrld), **-y** *a.* knotty; knobby [M.E. *knurre*].

gnash (nash) *v.t.* to grind the teeth together, as in anger or pain; *n.* a grinding of the teeth. **-ing** *n.* [imit. origin].

gnat (nat) *n.* a kind of small biting insect [O.E.].

gnaw (naw) *v.t.* to wear away with the teeth; to bite steadily, as a dog a bone; to fret; to corrode; *v.i.* to use the teeth in biting; to cause steady pain. **-er** *n.* **-ing** *a., n.* [O.E. *gnagan*].

gneiss (nīs) *n.* a metamorphic rock similar to granite [Ger.].

gnome (nōm) *n.* (*Myth.*) a dwarflike guardian of precious metals hidden in the earth; a goblin [Gk. *gnōmē*, intelligence].

gnome (nōm) *n.* a wise saying; a maxim. **gnomic(al)** *a.* [Gk. *gnōmē*, thought].

gno·mon (nō′·mȧn) *n.* the pin, rod, or plate which casts the shadow on a sundial; an indicator; (*Geom.*) the part of a rectangular figure which remains when a similar rectangle is taken from one corner of it. **-ic(al)** *a.* [Gk. *gnōmōn*, pin of a sundial.]

gno·sis (nō′·sis) *n.* mystical knowledge. **gnostic** (nȧs′·tik) *a.* pert. to knowledge; having special knowledge [Gk. *gignoskein*, to know].

GNP (jē·en·pē′) *n.* *g*ross *n*ational *p*roduct.

gnu (nòò) *n.* antelope resembling an ox; the wildebeest [Kaffir, *ngu*].

go (gō) *v.i.* to pass from one place or condition to another; to move along; to be in motion; to proceed; to depart; to elapse; to be kept; to put; to be able to be put; to result; to contribute to a result; to tend to; to pass away; to become; to fare. *pr.p.* **-ing** *pa.p.* **gone** (gawn). *pa.t.* **went.** *n.* a going; (*Colloq.*) vigor; (*Colloq.*) an attempt; (*Colloq.*) a success. **-er** *n.* **-ing** *n.* the state of the ground or roads; working conditions. *a.* moving; successful. **-ings-on** (*Colloq.*) usually in a bad sense, behavior; conduct. **gone** *a.* lost; beyond recovery; weak and faint. **-between** *n.* an intermediary. **-cart** *n.* wooden framework on casters, for teaching infants to walk. **to go in for,** to indulge in. **to go off,** to depart; to explode; to disappear; to become less efficient, popular, fashionable, etc. [O.E. *gan*].

goad (gōd) *n.* a sharp, pointed stick for driving cattle; anything that urges to action; *v.t.* to drive with a goad; to urge on; to irritate. [O.E. *gad*].

goal (gōl) *n.* an object of effort; an end or aim; in a race, the winning post; in football, hockey, etc., the space marked by two upright posts and a cross-bar; the act of kicking or driving the ball between these posts [Fr. *gaule*, a pole].

goat (gōt) *n.* a long-haired, ruminant quadruped with cloven hoofs and curving horns; the 10th sign of the Zodiac, Capricorn; (*Slang*) one who must take the blame for another. **-ee** (gō·tē′) *n.* a small tuft of beard on the chin. **—herd** *n.* one who tends goats. **-ish** *a.* like a goat; lecherous. **to get one's goat** (*Colloq.*) to annoy or irritate one [[O.E. *gat*].

gob (gȧb) *n.* a lump or mass. **gobbet** *n.* a small mass; a mouthful [O.Fr. *gobe*, a mouthful].

gob (gȧb) *n.* (*Slang*) a nickname for U.S. sailor.

gob·ble (gȧb′·l) *v.t.* to eat hurriedly or greedily. **-r** *n.* a greedy eater O.Fr. *gober*, to devour].

gob·ble (gȧb′·l) *n.* the throaty, gurgling cry of the turkey cock; *v.i.* to make such a noise. **-r** *n.* a turkey [imit.].

gob·ble·dy·gook (gȧb′·l·di·gook) *n.* (*Slang*) pompous, wordy talk or writing [fr. **gobble**].

Gob·e·lin (gȧb′·ạ·lin) *n.* rich French tapestry [fr. *Gobelin*, tapestry makers in Paris].

gob·let (gȧb′·lit) *n.* a drinking glass with a stem and foot [O.Fr. *gobelet*].

gob·lin (gȧb′·lin) *n.* an evil or mischievous sprite or elf; a gnome [Gk. *kobalos*, a mischievous spirit].

god (gȧd) *n.* a being of more than human powers; a divinity; an idol; any person honored unduly; any object esteemed as the chief good; *n.pl.* false deities; (G) the Supreme Being; Jehovah. **-dess** *n.* a female god or idol. **godly** *a.* reverencing God; pious; devout. **godliness** *n.* holiness; righteousness. **-less** *a.* wicked; impious; acknowledging no God. **godsend** *n.* an unexpected piece of good fortune. **-speed** *n.* a prosperous journey; a wish for success given at parting. **-forsaken** *a.* dreary; dismal [O.E. *god*, cf. Ger. *Gott*].

god·child (gȧd′·chīld) *n.* one for whom a person becomes sponsor, guaranteeing his religious education. Also. **-daughter, -son, -parent, -mother, -father,** the sponsor.

god·wit (gȧd′·wit) *n.* a long-billed wading bird [O.E. *god*, good; *wiht*, a creature].

gog·gle (gȧg′·l) *v.i.* to roll the eyes; to stare; *n.* a rolling of the eyes; *a.* rolling; bulging; protruding (of the eyes). **-s** *n.pl.* spectacles to protect the eyes [Gael. *gog*, a nod].

goi·ter (goi′·tęr) *n.* a swelling on the front of the neck, the enlargement of the thyroid gland. **goitrous** *a.* [L. *guttur*, the throat].

gold (gōld) *n.* a precious metal of a bright yellow color; money; riches; a bright yellow color; *a.* made of gold; of color of gold. **-en** *a.* made of gold; having the color of gold; precious. **-finch** *n.* a beautiful bird, so named from its color. **-fish** *n.* a small fish of the carp family named from its color. **-smith** *n.* one who manufactures vessels and ornaments of gold. **-beater** *n.* one who beats gold into gold leaf. **-digger** *n.* one who digs or mines gold; (*Slang*) an unscrupulous flirt, expert at obtaining money from male friends. **-dust** *n.* gold in very fine particles. **-leaf** *n.* gold beaten into an extremely thin leaf or foil, used for gilding. **-mine** *n.* a mine from which gold is due; a source of wealth. **-plate** *n.* vessels or utensils made of gold (collectively). **-rush** *n.* the mad scramble to reach a new goldfield. **— standard,** a currency system under which banknotes are exchanged for gold at any time. **-en age,** the most flourishing period in the history of a nation. **-enrod,** a plant with branching clusters of small yellow flowers. **-en rule,** the rule of doing as you would be done by. **-en wedding,** the fiftieth wedding anniversary [O.E.].

golf (gȧlf) *n.* out door game played with set of clubs and a ball, in which the ball is driven with the fewest possible strokes, into a succession of holes. *v.i.* to play this game. **-er** *n.* **— course, — links** tract of land for playing golf [Dut. *kolf*, a club].

gol•ly (gȧl′.i.) *interj.* to express joy, sorrow, surprise, etc. [fr. *God*].

go•losh See **galosh.**

gon•ad (gōn′.ad) *n.* (*Biol.*) a gland that produces reproductive cells; ovary or testis. **-al** *a.* [Gk. *gonos*, seed].

gon•do•la (gȧn′.dạ.lạ) *n.* a long, narrow, flat-bottomed boat, used in the canals of Venice. **gondolier** (gon.dạ.lēr′) *n.* the boatman [It.].

gone (gawn) *pa.p.* of the verb **go. -r** *n.* (*Slang*) one who is in a hopeless state; *a.* beyond recovery [O.E. *gan*].

gong (gȧng) *n.* a circular metal plate which gives out a deep note when struck with a soft mallet; anything used in this way; as a call to meals [Malay].

gon•o•coc•cus (gȧn.ạ.kȧk′.ạs) *n.* (*Med.*) microbe of gonorrhea. **gonorrhea** (gȧn.ạ.rē′.ạ) *n.* [Gk. *gonos*, seed; *kokkos*, a berry; *rhoia*, a flowing].

good (good) *a.* commendable; right; proper; suitable; excellent; virtuous; honest; just; kind; affectionate; safe; sound; valid; solvent; adequate; full, as weight, measure, etc.; skillful. *comp.* **better.** *superl.* **best.** *n.* that which is good; welfare; well-being; profit; advantage; *n.pl.* property; wares; commodities; merchandise; (*Colloq.*) evidence of guilt; textiles; *interj.* well! right! so be it! **-ish** *a.* (of quality) pretty good; (of quantity) fairly plentiful. **-ly** *a.* handsome; pleasant; of considerable size. **-liness** *n.* **-ness** *n.* the quality of being good; *interj.* used for emphasis; *pl.* **-ies** candy; sweets. **—by** *interj.* contraction of God be with you!; farewell! *n.* a farewell. **— day** *interj.* greeting at meeting or parting. **—for-nothing** *a.* worthless; shiftless; *n.* a shiftless person; a loafer. **— humor** *n.* a happy or cheerful state of mind. **—humored** *a.* **— nature** *n.* natural kindness of disposition; **—natured** *a.* **—naturedly** *adv.* **— turn,** a kindly action. **— will** *n.* benevolence; kindly disposition; (*Commerce*) the right, on transfer or sale of a business, to the reputation, trade, and custom of that business. **to be to the good,** to show a profit [O.E. *god*].

goof (gȯȯf) *n.* (*Slang*) a silly person; a mistake. *v.*

goose (gȯȯs) *n.* a web-footed bird like a duck but larger; the flesh of the bird; a simpleton; a tailor's smoothing iron; *pl.* **geese** (gēs). **gosling** (gȧz′.ling) *n.* a young goose. **— flesh** *n.* a bristling state of the skin due to cold or fright. **— step** *n.* (*Mil.*) a marching step with legs kept stiff and lifted high at each step; *v.i.* to use the goose step [O.E. *gos*].

goose•ber•ry (gȯȯs′.ber.i.) *n.* a thorny shrub cultivated for its fruit; fruit of the shrub.

go•pher (gō′.fer) *n.* in N. America, the ground-squirrel; a kind of rat with pouched cheeks [Fr. *gaufre*, a honeycomb].

gore (gōr) *n.* thick or clotted blood; blood. **gory** *a.* bloody [O.E. *gor*, dirt].

gore (gōr) *v.t.* to pierce with a spear, horns, or tusks [O.E. *gar*, a spear].

gore (gōr) *n.* a tapering piece of material inserted in a garment or a sail, to widen it; *v.t.* to cut into a wedge shape; to supply with a gore [O.E. *gara*, a pointed piece of land].

gorge (gawrj) *n.* a narrow pass between mountains; a full meal; *v.t.* to swallow with greediness; *v.i.* to feed greedily and to excess [L. *gurges*, a whirlpool].

gor•geous (gawr′.jis) *a.* splendid; showy; magnificent; richly colored. **-ly** *adv.* [O.Fr. *gorgias*].

Gor•gon (gawr′.gạn) *n.* (*Myth.*) one of three sisters of terrifying aspect; (*l.c.*) any one, esp. a woman, who is terrifying or repulsive looking. **-esque** *a.* repulsive [Gk. *gorgos*].

Gor•gon•zo•la (gawr.gạn.zō′.lạ) *n.* a milk cheese made in Italy [fr. *Gorgonzola*, Italy].

go•ril•la (gạ.ril′.ạ) *n.* an ape inhabiting W. Africa, of great size and strength [Afr.].

gor•mand See **gourmand.**

gorse (gawrs) *n.* (*Brit.*) a prickly shrub, bearing yellow flowers [O.E. *gorst*].

gosh (gȧsh) *interj.* (*Colloq.*) a minced and very mild oath [corrupt. of *God*].

gor•y See **gore.**

gosh (gȧsh) *interj.* (*Colloq.*) a minced and very mild oath [corrupt. of *God*].

gos•hawk (gȧs′.hawk) *n.* a large powerful hawk [O.E. *gos*, a goose; *hafoc*, a hawk].

gos•ling See **goose.**

gos•pel (gȧs′.pạl) *n.* glad tidings; the revelation of the Christian faith; story of Christ's life as found in first four books of New Testament; doctrine; belief accepted as infallibly true; *a.* pert. to, or in accordance with, the gospel [O.E. *god*, good; *spell*, a story].

gos•sa•mer (gȧs′.ạ.mẹr) *n.* a filmy substance, like cobwebs; thin, gauzy material; *a.* light, thin and filmy [M.E. *gossomer*].

gos•sip (gȧs′.ạp) *n.* idle talk about others, regardless of fact; idle talk or writing; one who talks thus; *v.i.* to talk gossip; to chat [M.E *god*, God; *sib*, related].

got (gȧt) *pa.p.* and *pa.t. of* **get.**

Goth (gȧth) *n.* a member of ancient Teutonic tribe; a barbarian. **-ic** *a.* pert. to Goths; barbarous; pert. to pointed-arch style of architecture; *n.* the language of Goths; (*l.c.*) a printing type Gothic [L. *Gothicus*].

got•ten *pa.p.* of **get.**

gouache (gwȧsh) *n.* water-color painting with opaque colors mixed with water and gum; a picture painted thus [It. *guazzo*, a wash].

Gou•da (gou′.dạ) *n.* a well-known Dutch cheese [fr. *Gouda*, Holland].

gouge (gouj) *n.* a chisel with a curved cutting edge, for cutting grooves or holes; *v.t.* to cut or scoop out with a gouge; to hollow out; to force out, as the eye of a person, with the thumb or finger [Fr.].

gou•lash (gȯȯ′.lȧsh) *n.* a Hungarian stew.

gourd (gawrd) *n.* trailing or climbing plant: pumpkin, squash, etc.; large, fleshy fruit of this plant; its dried rind used as bottle, drinking vessel, etc.; a small-necked bottle or flask [L. *cucurbita*, a gourd].

gour•mand (goor′.mạnd) *n.* one fond of eating; a judge of fine foods. Also **gormand, gourmet** (goor′.mā) [Fr.].

gout (gout) *n.* a disease characterized by acute inflammation and swelling of the smaller joints. **-iness** *n.* **-y** *a.* [Fr. *goutte*, a drop].

gov•ern (guv′.ẹrn) *v.t.* to rule; to direct; to guide; to control; to regulate by authority; to keep in subjection; (*Gram.*) to be followed by a case, etc.; *v.i.* to exercise authority; to administer the laws. **-able** *a.* **-ance** *n.* directions; control; management. **-ess** *n.* woman with authority to control and direct; a lady, usually resident in a family, in charge of children's education. **-ment** *n.* act of governing; exercise of authority; the system of governing in a state or community; the ruling power in a state; territory over which rule is exercised; the administrative council or body; the executive power; control; rule. **-mental** *a.* **-or** *n.* the executive head of a state; a ruler; regulating mechanical device for velocity, pressure, etc. [L. *gubernare*, to steer].

gown (goun) *n.* a loose, flowing garment; outer dress of a woman; official robe of professional men and scholars, as in a university; *v.t.* to dress in a gown; *v.i.* to put on a gown [O.Fr. *gonne*, loose robe].

grab (grab) *v.t.* to grasp suddenly; to snatch; to clutch; to seize. *pr.p.* **-bing.** *pa.p.* and *pa.t.* **-bed.** *n.* a sudden clutch; unscrupulous seizure.

grace (grās) *n.* charm; attractiveness; easy and refined motion, manners, etc.; favor; divine favor; a short prayer of thanksgiving before or after a meal; a period of delay granted as a favor; the ceremonious title used when addressing a duke, or archbishop; *v.t.* to adorn; to honor; to add grace to. **-ful** *a.* displaying grace or charm in form or action; elegant; easy. **-fully** *adv.* **-fulness** *n.* **-less** *a.* lacking grace. **gracious** (grā′·shạs) *a.* favorable; kind; friendly; merciful; pleasing; proceeding from divine grace; **graciously** *adv.* **graciousness** *n.* **— note** *n.* (*Mus.*) a note that is an embellishment, not essential to the melody [L. *gratia*, favor].

grac·ile (gras′·il) *a.* slender; gracefully slight. **gracility** *n.* [L. *gracilis*, slender].

gra·da·tion (gra·dā′·shạn) *n.* successive stage in progress; degree; a step, or series of steps; the state of being graded or arranged in ranks. **gradate** (grā′·dāt) *v.t.* to cause to change by imperceptable degrees, as from one color to another [L. *gradatio*].

grade (grād) *n.* a step or degree in rank, merit, quality, etc.; a class or category; a mark or rating of a student's work; degree of rise of a slope; a gradient; *v.t.* to arrange in order, degree, or class; to gradate [L. *gradus*, a step].

gra·di·ent (grā′·di·ạnt) *a.* moving by steps; rising or descending by regular degrees; *n.* the degree of slope of a road or railway; an incline [L. *gradiens*, going, stepping].

grad·u·al (gra′·joo·ạl) *a.* proceeding by steps or degrees; progressive; changing imperceptibly; *n.* (*Eccl.*) book of music sung by the choir. **-ly** *adv.* [L. *gradus*, a step].

grad·u·ate (graj′·oo·āt) *v.t.* to grant a diploma or university degree; to mark with degrees; to divide into regular steps; *v.i.* to receive a diploma or university degree; (graj′·oo·it) *n.* one who has received a diploma or degree upon completing a course of study. **graduator** *n.* an instrument for dividing a line into regular intervals. **graduation** *n.* [L. *gradus*, a step].

graft, graff (graft, graf) *v.t.* to insert a bud or small branch of a tree into another; to transplant living tissue, e.g. skin, bone, etc. from one part of the body to another; *n.* a bud, etc. so inserted, or a piece of tissue so transplanted [Fr. fr. Gk. *grapheion*, a pencil].

graft (graft) *v.i.* to exercise political privilige; to use influence unfairly for self-advancement or profit; *n.* self-advancement or profit by unfair means. **-er** *n.*

gra·ham (grā′·ạm) *a.* made of whole-wheat flour [S. *Graham*, Amer. physician].

grail (gral) *n.* a cup. **The Holy Grail,** in medieval legend, the cup or vessel used by Jesus at the Last Supper [O.Fr. *graal*, a flat dish].

grain (grān) *n.* a kernel, esp. of corn, wheat, etc.; fruit of certain kindred plants, viz. corn, wheat, rye, barley, oats, etc. (used collectively); any small, hard particle; slightest amount; the smallest unit of weight; that arrangement of the particles of any body which determines its roughness, markings or texture; (*Fig.*) natural temperament or disposition; *v.t.* to paint in imitation of the grain of wood; to form into grains, as sugar, powder, etc. **-ed** (grānd) *a.* **against the grain,** *i.e.* against the fiber of the wood; hence (*Fig.*) against a natural inclination [L. *granum*, seed].

gram (gram) *n.* unit of weight in metric system = 15.432 grains. Also **gramme** [Fr. fr. Gk. *gramma*, small weight].

gram·mar (gram′·ẹr) *n.* the science of language; a system of general principles for speaking and writing according to the forms and usage of a language; a textbook for teaching the elements of language. **-ian** (gra·me′·ri·ạn) *n.* a philologist; **grammatical** (grạ·mat′·i·kạl) *a.* pert to grammar; according to the rules of grammar [Gk. *gramma*, a letter].

gramme See **gram.**

gram·o·phone (gram′·ạ·fōn) *n.* a phonograph [Gk. *gramma*, a letter; *phonē*, sound].

gram·pus (gram′·pạs) *n.* a blowing and spouting sea creature of the dolphin family [L. *crassus piscis*, a fat fish].

gran·a·ry (gran′·ạ·ri·) *n.* a storehouse for threshed grain; a barn [L. *granum*, grain].

grand (grand) *a.* great; high in power and dignity; illustrious; eminent; distinguished; imposing; superior; splendid; lofty; noble; sublime; dignified; majestic; chief; final; indicating family relationship of the second degree; *n.* (*Mus.*) a grand piano; (*Slang*) a thousand dollars. **-child** *n.* a son's or daughter's child. **-daughter, -son** *n.* a son's or daughter's daughter. **-ee** (gran·dē′) *n.* a Spanish or Portuguese nobleman; a great personage. **-eur** (gran′·jẹr) *n.* nobility of action; majesty; splendor; magnificence. **-father (-mother)** *n.* a father's or mother's father (mother). **-father('s)-clock,** *n.* a tall, old-fashioned clock, standing on the floor. **-iloquence** (gran·dil′·ạ·kwens) *n.* lofty words or phrases; pomposity of speech. **-iloquent** *a.* **-iose** (gran′·di·os) *a.* imposing; striking; bombastic. **-iosely** *adv.* **-iosity** *n.* **-ly** *adv.* in a grand manner, splendidly. **-ma** *n.* grandmother. **-mother-clock** *n.* similar to a grandfather-clock but smaller. **-ness** *n.* greatness; magnificence. **-pa** *n.* a grandfather. **-parent** *n.* grandfather or grandmother. **— piano,** a large harp-shaped piano, with a horizontal frame. **— slam** (*Cards*) the winning of all the tricks at Bridge. **-stand** *n.* main seating structure for spectators at a sporting event [L. *grandis*, great].

grange (grānj) *n.* a farm; (*Cap.*) an association of farmers [L. *granum*, grain].

gran·ite (gran′·it) *n.* a hard igneous rock, consisting of quartz, feldspar, and mica; gray or pink in color [It. *granito*, grained].

gran·ny (gran′·i·) *n.* (*Colloq.*) grandmother; an old woman [abbrev. of *grandmother*].

grant (grant) *v.t.* to allow; to yield; to concede; to bestow; to confer; to admit as true; *n.* a bestowing; a gift; an allowance. **-er, -or** *n.* (*Law*) the person who transfers property [O.Fr. *garanter*, to promise].

gran·ule (gran′·yool) *n.* a little grain; a small particle. **granular** *a.* consisting of grains or granules. **granulate** *v.t.* to form into grains; to make rough on the surface; *v.i.* to be formed into grains. **granulated** *a.* **granulation** *n.* the process of forming into grains; (*Med.*) the development of new tissue in a wound, characterized by the formation of grain-like cells [L. *granulum*, dim. of *granum*, a grain].

grape (grāp) *n.* the fruit of the vine. **-ry** *n.* a place for the cultivation of grapes. **— fruit** *n.* a large round citrus fruit with yellow rind. **— sugar** *n.* a simple sugar, found abundantly in grapes; dextrose. **-vine** *n.* the grape-bearing vine plant; (*Colloq.*) a person-to-person means of secret communication. **sour grapes** (*Fig.*) things falsely despised merely because unattainable [Fr. *grappe*, a bunch of grapes].

graph (graf) *n.* a diagram or curve representing the variation in value of some phenomenon or relationship of two or more things, according to stated conditions; *v.t.* to show variation by means of a diagram. **-ic(al)** *a.* pert. to writing or delineating; truly descriptive; vivid. **-ically** *adv.* **-ic arts,** drawing, engraving, and painting. **-ics** *n.* the art of drawing, esp. mechanical drawing. **-ite** *n.* a natural form of carbon used in the making of the 'lead' of pencils; plumbago; blacklead. **-ology** *n.* the study of handwriting as an index of character [Gk. *graphein*, to write].

grap·nel (grap'·nạl) *n.* an iron instrument with hooks or claws for clutching an object; a small anchor with several claws [O.Fr. *grape*, a hook].

grap·ple (grap'·l) *v.t.* to seize firmly; to seize with a grapnel; *v.i.* to come to grips; to contend; *n.* a grapnel; a grip; a contest at close quarters. **grappling-iron** *n.* a large grapnel [O.Fr. *grape*, a hook].

grasp (grasp) *v.t.* to seize firmly; to clutch; to take possession of; to understand. *v.i.* to endeavor to seize; to catch at; *n.* a firm grip of the hand; the power of seizing and holding; reach of the arms; mental power or capacity. **-ing** *a.* seizing; greedy of gain [O.E. *graspen*].

grass (gras) *n.* herbage; pasture for cattle; ground covered with grass; *v.t.* to cover with grass; to feed with grass. **-y** *a.* **-hopper** *n.* a jumping, chirping insect, allied to the locust family. **-land** *n.* permanent pasture-land. **—roots** (*Colloq.*) *a.* close to, or from, the people. **— widow** *n.* a woman separated or divorced from her husband [O.E. *gaers*].

grate (grāt) *n.* a frame of bars for holding fuel while burning; a framework of crossed bars. **grating** *n.* a partition of parallel or cross bars [L. *cratis*, a hurdle].

grate (grāt) *v.t* .to rub or scrape into small bits; to rub together with a harsh sound; *v.i.* sound harshly; to irritate. **-r** *n.* an instrument with a rough surface for rubbing off small particles [Fr. *gratter*, to scratch].

grate·ful (grāt'·fạl) *a.* thankful; pleasant; [L. *gratus*, pleasing].

gra·ti·fy (grat'·ạ·fī) *v.t.* to give pleasure to; to satisfy. **-ing** *a.* **gratifier** *n.* one who gratifies. **gratification** *n.* the act of pleasing; satisfaction [L. *gratus*, pleasing].

grat·in (grȧ'·tạn) *n.* (*Cookery*) a dish prepared with a covering of bread crumbs or cheese. **au gratin** (ō grȧ'·tạn) *a.* food so cooked [Fr. *gratin*, fr. *gratin*, fr. *gratter*, to grate].

gra·tis (gra'·tis) *adv.* free [L. *gratia*, a favor].

grat·i·tude (grat'·ạ·tūd) *n.* thankfulness [L. *gratus*, pleasing, thankful].

gra·tu·i·ty (grạ·tū'·ạ·ti·) *n.* a gift of money for services rendered; a tip; something given freely. **gratuitous** *a.* free; voluntary; granted without obligation; asserted without cause or proof. **gratuitously** *adv.* [L. *gratuitus*, done without profit].

gra·va·men (grạ·vā'·mạn) *n.* stress laid on a part; substantial ground or reason for a charge; a grievance [L. *gravis*, heavy].

grave (grāv) *n.* a hole dug for a dead body; a place of burial; (*Fig.*) death. **-stone** *n.* a memorial stone set at a grave. **-yard** *n.* a burial ground [O.E. *braef*].

grave (grāv) *a.* solemn; serious; weighty; important. **grave** (grȧv) *n.* the 'grave' accent in French or its sign (\`). **-ly** *adv.* [L. *gravis*, heavy].

grave (grāv) *v.t.* to engrave; to impress deeply. **-n image,** an idol [O.E. *grafan*, to dig].

grave (grāv) *v.t.* to clean a ship's bottom [Fr. *grève*, a beach].

grav·el (grav'·ạl) *n.* small stones; coarse sand; small pebbles; (*Med.*) an aggregation of minute crystals in the urine; *v.t.* to cover with gravel; to puzzle. (*Colloq.*) to irritate. **-ly** *a.* [O.Fr. *grave*, the beach].

grav·id (grav'·id) *a.* pregnant [L. *gravis*, heavy].

grav·i·tate (grav'·ạ·tāt) *v.i.* to obey the law of gravitation; to tend towards a center of attraction; to be naturally attracted to. **gravitation** *n.* the act of gravitating; the tendency of all bodies to attract each other. **gravitational, gravitative** *a.* [L. *gravis*, heavy].

grav·i·ty (grav'·ạ·ti·) *n.* weight; heaviness; seriousness; the force of attraction of one body for another, esp. of objects to the earth. **specific gravity,** the relative weight of any substance as compared with the weight of an equal volume of water [L. *gravitas*, fr. *gravis*, heavy].

gra·vy (grā'·vi·) *n.* the juices from meat in cooking; sauce made with this. (*Slang*) easy profit. **— boat** *n.* a dish for holding gravy.

gray, grey (grā) *a.* between black and white in color, as ashes or lead; clouded; dismal; turning white; hoary; aged; *n.* a gray color; a gray horse; *v.t.* to cause to become gray; *v.i.* to become gray. **-ish** *a.* somewhat gray. **— matter** the gray nerve tissue of the brain and spinal cord; (*Colloq.*) brains, intellect. **-ness** *n.* **-lag** *n.* wild goose [O.E. *graeg*].

graze (grāz) *v.t.* to touch lightly in passing; to abrade the skin thus; *n.* a light touch in passing; a grazing.

graze (grāz) *v.t.* to feed, as cattle, with grass; *v.i.* to eat grass or herbage [O.E. *grasian*].

grease (grēs) *n.* soft melted fat of animals; thick oil as a lubricant; (grēz, grēs) *v.t.* to apply grease to; (*Slang*) to bribe. **greasy** *a.* like grease; oily; fat; (*Fig.*) slippery. **— monkey** (*Slang*) a mechanic. **— paint** actors' make-up. **-r** *n.* **greasiness** *n.* [Fr. *graisse*, fr. *gras*, fat].

great (grāt) *a.* large in size or number; long in time or duration; admirable; eminent; uncommonly gifted; of high rank; mighty; pregnant; denoting relationship, either in the ascending or descending line; (*Slang*) splendid. **-ly** *adv.* **-ness** *n.* **-coat** *n.* an overcoat. **great-grandchild** *n.* the child of a grandchild. **Great Britain** England, Wales and Scotland. **Great Dane,** a large dog with short, smooth hair [O.E.].

greaves (grēvz) *n.pl.* the dregs of melted tallow [O.N.].

Gre·cian (grē'·shạn) *a.* Greek; pert. to Greece; *n.* a native of Greece; a Greek scholar [L. *Graecus*].

greed (grēd) *n.* an eager and selfish desire; covetousness; avarice. **-y** *a.* having a keen desire for food, drink, wealth, etc.; ravenous. **-ily** *adv.* **-iness** *n.* [O.E. *graedig*, hungry].

Greek (grēk) *a.* pert. to Greece; Grecian; *n.* a native of Greece; the language of Greece [L. *Graecus*].

green (grēn) *a.* of color between blue and yellow; grass-colored; emerald-colored; containing its natural sap; unripe; inexperienced; easily deceived; sickly; wan. *n.* the color; a communal piece of grass-covered land; (*Golf*) the putting-green. *n.pl.* fresh leaves or branches; wreaths; green leafy vegetables. **-ery** *n.* a place where plants are cultivated; vegetation. **-ish** a somewhat green. **-ness** *n.* the quality of being green; freshness. **—eyed** *a.* having green eyes; (*Fig.*) jealous. **—eyed monster,** jealousy. **-gage** *n.* a small, green plum. **-heart** *n.* a very hard wood. **-horn** *n.* an inexperienced person. **-house** *n.* a glass building for keepihg or growing plants. **— light** traffic signal to go; (*Colloq.*) authorization. **— thumb** apparent skill in growing plants. **-sward** *n.* turf [O.E.].

Greenwich time, (grin'·ij, gren·ich) the basis

for calculating standard time everywhere.

greet (grēt) *v.t.* to salute; to welcome; to accost; to receive. **-ing** *n.* a salutation; expression of good wishes [O.E. *gretan*].

gre·gar·i·ous (gri·gar′·i·ạs) *a.* living in flocks or herds; fond of company. **-ly** *adv.* **-ness** *n.* [L. *gregarius*, fr. *grex*, a flock].

Gre·go·ri·an (gre·gō′·ri·ạn) *a.* pert. to the Popes Gregory I through XIII. **— calendar,** the present day calendar, introduced in 1582. **— chants,** unaccompanied music used in R.C. worship.

grem·lin (grem′·lin) *n.* (*World War* 2) a mischievous pixy haunting aircraft and causing engine trouble [Fr. dial. *grimelin*, brat].

gre·nade (gri·nād′) *n.* an explosive shell or bomb, thrown by hand or shot from a rifle; a glass projectile containing chemicals. **grenadier** (gren·ạ·dir′) *n.* formerly, a soldier trained to throw grenades; a soldier in the Grenadier Guards of Brit. Army [Fr. *grenade*, a pomegranate].

gren·a·dine (gren′·ạ·dēn) *n.* a syrup for flavoring drinks [Fr. fr. *grenade*].

grew *pa.t.* of **grow.**

grey See **gray.**

grey·hound (grā′·hound) *n.* a swift, slender dog, used in racing [O.E. *grighund*].

grid (grid) *n.* a frame of bars; a grating; a grid-iron; (*Elect.*) a lead or zinc plate in a storage battery; (*Electronics*) an electrode of wire mesh in an electron tube [O.Fr. *gredil*].

grid·dle (grid′·l) *n.* flat utensil for cooking over direct heat; *v.t.* to cook on a griddle. [O.Fr. *gredil*, fr. L. *cratis*, hurdle].

grid·i·ron (grid′·ī·ẹrn) *n.* a framework of metal bars, for broiling meats, fish, etc.; a football field [O.Fr. *gredire, gredil*, a griddle].

grief (grēf) *n.* deep sorrow; pain; the cause of sorrow or distress [Fr. fr. L. *gravis*, heavy].

grieve (grēv) *v.t.* to cause grief; to afflict; to vex; to offend; *v.i.* to feel grief; to be distressed; to lament. **grievance** *n.* a real or imaginary complaint; a cause of grief or uneasiness. **-r** *n.* **grievous** *a.* causing sadness; atrocious. **grievously** *adv.* [O.Fr. *grever*, to afflict].

grill (gril) *v.t.* to broil on a gridiron; to question relentlessly; *n.* a cooking utensil for broiling meat, fish, etc.; the food cooked on one [Fr. *gril*, a gridiron].

grille (gril) *n.* a metal grating screening a window, doorway, etc. **grillwork** *n.* [O.Fr. *gredil*, a griddle].

grim (grim) *a.* stern; severe; of forbidding aspect; fierce; surly. **-ly** *adv.* **-ness** *n.* [O.E. *grimm*, fierce].

gri·mace (gri·mās′) *n.* a distortion of the face to express contempt, dislike, etc.; a wry face; *v.i.* to make a grimace [Fr.].

gri·mal·kin (gri·mawl′·kin) *n.* an old cat, esp. a she-cat; a spiteful old woman.

grime (grīm) *n.* ingrained dirt; soot; *v.t.* to soil deeply; to dirty. **grimy** *a.* dirty.

grin (grin) *v.i.* to show the teeth as in laughter derision, or pain. *pr.p.* **-ning.** *pa.t., pa.p.* **-ned.** *n.* a wide smile [O.E. *grennian*].

grind (grīnd) *v.t.* to crush to powder between hard surfaces; to sharpen by friction; to rub harshly; to turn a crank to operate; to grate; *v.i.* to grind; (*Colloq.*) to work hard. *pa.p.* and *pa.t.* **ground.** *n.* the action of grinding; (*Colloq.*) a laborious task; (*Colloq.*) a hard-working student. **-ers** *n.pl.* (*Colloq.*) the teeth [O.E. *grindan*].

grin·go (gring′·gō) *n.* in Spanish-speaking America, a contemptuous name for a foreigner.

grip (grip) *n.* a firm hold; a grasp or pressure of the hand; a clutch; mastery of a subject, etc · a handle; a suitcase; *v.t.* to grasp or hold tightly; (*Fig.*) to hold the attention of. *pr.p.* **-ping.** *pa.p., pa.t.* **-ped. -per** *n.* [O.E. *gripa*].

gripe (grīp) *v.t.* to grip; to oppress; to afflict with sharp pains; *v.i.* to grasp at gain; to suffer griping pains; (*Colloq.*) to complain constantly; *n.* grasp; clutch; severe intestinal pain. **griping** *a.* [O.E. *gripan*].

grippe (grip) *n.* influenza [Fr.].

gris·ly (griz′·li·) *a.* grim; horrible. **grisliness** *n.* [O.E. *grislic*, terrible].

grist (grist) *n.* a supply of grain to be ground; the meal ground; (*Fig.*) profit; gain [O.E.].

gris·tle (gris′·l) *n.* a smooth, solid, elastic substance in animal bodies; cartilage [O.E.].

grit (grit) *n.* the coarse part of meal; particles of sand; coarse sandstone; (*Fig.*) courage; spirit; resolution; *pl.* grain coarsely ground; *v.t.* to grind (the teeth); to grate; *v.i.* to cover with grit. *pr.p.* **-ting.** *pa.t., pa.p.* **-ted. -ty** *a.* [O.E. *greot*, sand].

griz·zle (griz′·l) *n.* gray hair. **-d** *a.* gray; gray-haired. **grizzly** *a.* gray; *n.* a grizzly bear, a large ferocious bear of N. Amer. [Fr. *gris*, gray].

groan (grōn) *v.i.* to make a low deep sound of grief or pain; to be overburdened; *n.* the sound. **-er** *n.* **-ing** *n.* [O.E. *granian*, to weep].

groats (grōts) *n.pl.* hulled grain, esp. oats [O.E. *greot*, a particle].

gro·cer (grō′·sẹr) *n.* storekeeper. **-y***n.* a store. **groceries** *n.pl.* goods sold by a grocer [O.Fr. *grossier*, wholesale].

grog (grȧg) *n.* a mixture of spirits, esp. rum and cold water. **-gy** *a.* drunk; unsteady; shaky [fr. Admiral Vernon (*Brit.*) who wore *grogram* breeches].

grog·ram (grȧg′·rạm) *n.* a coarse material of silk and mohair [O.Fr. *grosgrain*].

groin (groin) *n.* the depression where the abdomen joins the thigh.

grom·met (grȧm′·it) *n.* a metal eyelet used for fastening [Fr. *gourmette*, a curb-chain].

groom (grōōm) *n.* a servant in charge of horses; a bridegroom; an officer in the English royal household; *v.t.* to dress with neatness and care; to tend a horse.

groove (grōōv) *n.* a channel or hollow, esp. one cut by a tool; a rut; a routine; *v.t.* to cut a groove in [Dut. *groefe*, a trench].

grope (grōp) *v.t.* to feel about; to search blindly as if in the dark [O.E. *grapian*].

gros·beak (grōs′·bēk) *n.* a bird of the Finch family [Fr. *gros*, big; *bec*, a beak].

gros·grain (grō′·grān) *n.* corded ribbon or cloth [Fr. *gros grain*, large grain].

gross (grōs) *a.* coarse; indecent; crude; thick; rank; glaring; total, not net; *n.* twelve dozen; mass; bulk; *v.t.* to earn a total of. **-ly** *adv.* **-ness** *n.* [Fr. *gos*, big].

gro·tesque (grō·tesk′) *a.* wildly formed; irregular in design or form; *n.* a whimsical figure; a caricature. **-ness** [Fr. fr. It. *grotta*, a grotto].

grot·to (grȧt′·ō) *n.* a natural cave; an artificial structure in gardens, etc. in imitation of such a cave. [It. *grotta*].

grouch (grouch) *n.* (*Colloq.*) a complaint; a a grumbler; *v.i.* to grumble. **-y** *a.* **-iness** *n.* [fr. *grudge*].

ground (ground) *pa.p.* and *pa.t.* of **grind.**

ground (ground) *n.* the surface of the earth; dry land; territory; a special area of land; soil; the sea bottom; reason; motive; basis; (*Elect.*) a conducting line between electrical equipment and the ground; (*Art*) the surface or coating to work on; *v.t.* to establish; to instruct in elementary principles; to place on the ground; (*Naut.*) to run ashore; *v.i.* to come to the ground. **-s** *n.pl.* dregs; sediment; lands around a house. **-less** *a.* without reason. **-ed** *a.* (*Aviat.*) of aircraft, unable to fly because of weather conditions. **-ing** *n.* the background; thorough knowledge of the essentials of a subject. **-work** *n.* foundation; basis; the essential part; first principles. **— rent** *n.* rent paid to a landlord for the privilege of building on his ground.

— swell *n.* a broad, deep swell of the ocean felt some distance from a storm [O.E. *grund*].
group (gro͝op) *n.* a number of persons or things near, placed, or classified together; a class; a cluster, crowd, or throng; a military unit; (*Art*) two or more figures forming one artistic design; *v.t.* to arrange in groups; *v.i.* to fall into groups. **-ing** *n.* [Fr. *groupe*].
grouse (grous) *n.* a round, plump game-bird.
grouse (grous) *v.i.* (*Colloq.*) to grumble; to complain; *n.* a complaint.
grout (grout) *n.* coarse meal; thin mortar to fill cracks; plaster; *v.t.* to fill with grout [O.E. *gaut*, coarse meal].
grove (grōv) *n.* a group of trees [O.E. *graf*].
grov·el (gräv′·l, gruv′·l) *v.i.* to lie face downward, from fear or humility; to crawl thus; to abase oneself. **-er** *n.* **-ing** *a.* servile [O.N. *a grufa*, face downwards].
grow (grō) *v.t.* to produce by cultivation; to raise; *v.i.* to develop naturally; to increase in size, height, etc.; to become by degrees. *pa.p.* **-n.** *pa.t.* **grew** (gro͝o). **-er** *n.* **-th** (grōth) *n.* the process of growing; something already grown; (*Med.*) a morbid formation; a tumor. **grown-up** *n.* an adult [O.E. *growan*].
growl (groul) *v.i.* to make a low guttural sound, of anger or menacing like an animal; to grumble; *n.* such a sound. **-er** *n.* [imit. origin].
grub (grub) *v.t.* to dig superficially; to root up; *v.i.* to dig; to rummage; (*Fig.*) to plod; *n.* the larva of a beetle; that which is dug up for food; (*Slang*) food. *pr.p.* **-bing.** *pa.p., pa.t.* **-bed. -ber** *n.* **-biness** *n.* the state of being grubby. **-by** *a.* unclean; dirty, grimy [M.E. *grobben*, to dig].
grudge (gruj) *v.t.* to be reluctant to give or allow; to envy; *n.* a feeling of ill will; resentment. **grudging** *a.* [O.Fr. *groucer*].
gru·el (gro͝o′·ạl) *n.* a food made by boiling oatmeal in water; a thin porridge; *v.t.* to subject to great strain. **-ing** *a.* exhausting [O.E. = crushed meal].
grue·some (gro͝o′·sạm) *a.* causing horror, fear or loathing [M.E. *grue*, to shudder].
grum·ble (grum′·bl) *v.i.* to murmur with discontent; to complain; to make growling sounds; *n.* grumbling; a complaint [imit. origin].
grump·y (grum′·pi·) *a.* surly; irritable; gruff. **grumpily** *adv.* **grumpiness** *n.* [imit. origin].
grunt (grunt) *v.i.* of a pig, to make its characteristic sound; to utter a sound like this; *n.* a deep, guttural sound; a pig's sound. **-er** *n.* **-ing** *a.* [O.E. *grunnettan*].
Gru·yère (gro͝o·yer′) *n.* a whole-milk cheese [fr. *Gruyère*, Switzerland].
guar·an·tee (gar·ạn·tē′) *n.* formal assurance given by way of security; an assurance of the truth, genuineness, permanence, etc. of something, the one who receives such promise or assurance; guaranty; security; an assurance; *v.t.* to promise; to answer for. **guaranty** (gar′·ạn·ti·) *n.* a pledge of commitment; security; basis of security. **guarantor** *n.* [Fr. *garantir*, to protect].
guard (gárd) *v.t.* to protect from danger; to accompany for protection; to watch by way of caution or defense; *v.i.* to keep watch; to take precautions; *n.* he who, or that which, guards; a sentry; a watch, as over prisoners; a protective device. **-ed** *a.* cautious; wary. **-edly** *adv.* **-house** *n.* a place for the detention of military prisoners. **-ian** *n.* a keeper; a protector; (*Law*) one who has custody of a minor. **-ianship** *n.* [Fr. *garde*].
gua·va (gwá′·vạ) *n.* a genus of tropical American trees and shrubs, bearing pear-shaped fruit used for jelly [Sp. *guayaba*].
gu·ber·na·to·ri·al (go͝o·bẹr·nạ·tōr′·i·ạl) *a.* pert. to a governor [L. *gubernare*, to govern].
gudg·eon (guj′·un) *n.* a metal pin at the end of an axle on which the wheel turns; the socket of a hinge into which the pin fits [O.Fr. *goujon*, pivot].
guer·don (gur′·dạn) *n.* (*Poetic*) a reward [O.Fr. *gueredon*].
Guern·sey (gurn′·zi) *n.* breed of dairy cattle. **guernsey** *n.* knitted woolen shirt.
guer·ril·la guerilla (gạ·ril′·ạ) *n.* a member of a band of irregular troops taking part in a war independently of the principal combatants; *a.* pert. to this kind of warfare [Sp. *guerrilla*, dim. of *guerra*, war].
guess (ges) *v.t.* and *i.* to estimate without calculation or measurement; to judge at random; to conjecture; to suppose; *n.* a rough estimate; a random judgment [M.E. *gessen*].
guest (gest) *n.* a visitor received or entertained; one living in a hotel, boarding-house, etc. [O.E. *gest*].
guf·faw (guf·aw′) *n.* a burst of boisterous laughter; *v.i.* to laugh boisterously [imit.].
guide (gīd) *n.* one who shows the way; an adviser; an official accompanying tourists; a sign, mark, or device to indicate direction; a book of instruction or information; *v.t.* to lead; to direct; to influence; to act as a guide to. **guidance** *n.* direction. **-book** *n.* a descriptive handbook for tourists, travelers, etc. **guided missile,** powered rocket or other projectile which can be directed by remote control. **-post** *n.* a sign-post [Fr. *guider*, to guide].
guild (gild) *n.* a society for mutual help, or with a common object [O.E. *gild*, money].
guile (gīl) *n.* craft; cunning. **-ful** *a.* **-less** *a.* honest; innocent; sincere [O.Fr. *guile*, deceit].
guil·lo·tine (gil′·ạ·tēn) *n.* a machine for beheading by the descending stroke of a heavy blade; a paper cutting machine; *v.t.* to use a guillotine upon [fr. Joseph *Guillotin*].
guilt (gilt) *n.* the fact or state of having offended; criminality and consequent liability to punishment. **-y** *a.* judged to have committed a crime. **-ily** *adv.* **-iness** *n.* **-less** *a.* innocent [O.E. *gylt*, crime, fr. *gildan*, to pay].
guimpe (gimp) *n.* a short-sleeved blouse [Fr.].
guin·ea (gin′·i·) *n.* a former Brit. gold coin. **— fowl** *n.* a fowl allied to the pheasant. **— pig** *n.* (corrupt. of *Guiana* pig) a small rodent, used frequently in scientific experiments; (*Fig.*) a person used as a subject for experimentation [fr. *Guinea*, in W. Africa].
guise (gīz) *n.* external appearance, semblance; pretense [Fr. *guise*, manner].
gui·tar (gi·tár′) *n.* a six-stringed musical instrument resembling the lute. **-ist** *n.* a player of the guitar [Fr. *guitare*].
gulch (gulch) *n.* a ravine; a deep-walled valley.
gulf (gulf) *n.* a large bay; a sea extending into the land; a deep chasm; any wide separation; *v.t.* to swallow up [Gk. *kolpos*, a bay].
gull (gul) *n.* a long-winged, web-footed seabird [Bret. *gwelan*, to weep].
gull (gul) *n.* a dupe; a food; *v.t.* to deceive; to trick; to defraud. **-ible** *a.* easily imposed on; credulous. **-ibility** *n* [fr. *gull*, the sea-bird considered to be stupid].
gul·let (gul′·it) *n.* the tube from mouth to stomach; the throat [L. *gula*, the throat].
gul·ly (gul′·i·) *n.* a channel or ravine worn by water; a ravine; a ditch [fr. *gullet*].
gulp (gulp) *v.t.* to swallow eagerly; to swallow in large amounts; *v.t.* to gasp; to choke; *n.* an act of gulping; an effort to swallow; a large mouthful [imit.].
gum (gum) *n.* the firm flesh in which the teeth are set [O.E. *goma*, the jaws].
gum (gum) *n.* a sticky substance issuing from certain trees; this substance used for stiffening or adhesive purposes; resin; an adhesive; chewing gum; *v.t.* to coat with gum; *v.i.* to exude gum; to become clogged. *pr.p.* **-ming.** *pa.p., pa.t.* **-med. -miness** *n.* **-my** *a.* consisting of gum; sticky. **— elastic** *n.* rubber. **-drop** *n.* small jelly-like candy. **— tree** *n.* any species of gum yielding tree: the eucalyptus,

sour gum, sweet gum, etc. **chewing gum** *n.* a sticky preparation for chewing [Fr. *gomme*].

gum·bo (gum′·bō) *n.* okra; soup thickened with this.

gump·tion (gump′·shąn) *n.* (*Colloq.*) resourcefulness; courage; common sense; courage.

gun (gun) *n.* a weapon consisting of a metal tube from which missiles are thrown by explosion; a firearm, cannon, rifle, pistol, etc.; a gun-like device; *v.i.* to shoot with a gun. *pr.p.* **-ning.** *pa.p., pa.t.* **-ned. -ner** *n.* one who works a gun. **-nery** *n.* the firing of guns; the science of artillery. **-ning** *n.* the shooting of game. **-boat** *n.* a small armed patrol ship. **— metal** *n.* dark gray. **-powder** *n.* an explosive. **-runner** *n.* a gun smuggler. **-shot** *n.* the range of a gun; a shot fired from a gun. **-smith** *n.* one who makes, repairs, deals in guns. **a son of a gun** (*Colloq.*) a rascal [M.E. *gunne*].

gun·ny (gun′·i·) *n.* strong, coarse sacking made from jute [Hind.].

gun·nel See **gunwale.**

gun·wale (gun′·l) *n.* upper edge of the side of a boat or ship. Also **gunnel** [fr. *Gunhilda*, a medieval war engine].

gup·py (gup′·i·) *n.* tiny fresh-water fish [fr. R. T. L. *Guppy* of Trinidad].

gur·gi·ta·tion (gur·ją·tā′·shąn) *n.* a surging rise and fail [L. *gurgitare*, to flood].

gur·gle (gur′·gl) *n.* a bubbling noise; *v.i.* to make a gurgle [imit.].

gush (gush) *v.i.* to flow out suddenly and copiously; (*Colloq.*) to display exaggerated and effusive affection; *n.* a sudden copious flow; (*Colloq.*) effusive talk. **-er** *n.* a gushing person; an oil-well with a natural flow. **-iness** *n.* **-ing, -y** *a.* effusive.

gus·set (gus′·it) *n.* a triangular piece of material inserted in a garment to strengthen or enlarge it [Fr. *gousset*, the arm-pit].

gust (gust) *n.* a sudden blast of wind; a burst of rain, etc.; an outburst of passion. **-y** *a.* [O.N. *gustr*].

gus·to (gus′·tō) *n.* keen enjoyment; zest; artistic style [L. *gustus*, taste].

gut (gut) *n.* a material made from animal intestines, as violin strings, etc.; tennis rackets; a narrow passage; a strait; *n.pl.* entrails; intestines; (*Colloq.*) courage; pluck; determination; *v.t.* to remove the entrails from; to destroy the interior as by fire.*pr.p.* **-ting.** *pa.p.* and *pa.t.* **-ted** [O.E. *guttas*, (pl.)].

gut·ter (gut′·ęr) *n.* a passage for water; a trough or pipe for conveying rain from the eaves of a building; a channel at the side of a road for carrying water; *v.t.* to make channels in; *v.i.* to flow in streams; of a candle to melt away so that wax runs off in channels. **-snipe** *n.* the common snipe; a child homeless or living in the streets [L. *gutta*, a drop].

gut·tur·al (gut′·ęr·ął) *a.* pert. to or produced in the throat; *n.* a guttural sound [L. *guttur*, throat].

guy (gī) *n.* a rope or chain to steady a thing: boat, tent, etc.; *v.t.* to guide with a guy. Also **-rope** [O.Fr. *guier*, to guide].

guy (gī) *n.* (*Slang*) a fellow; *v.t.* (*Slang*) to ridicule; to make fun of [fr. *Guy* Fawkes].

guz·zle (guz′·l) *v.t.* and *i.* to drink greedily. **-r** *n.* [Fr. *gosier*, the gullet].

gym·kha·na (jim·ká′·ną) *n.* a place for athletic games; a sports meet [Urdu *gend-khana*, a racket court, *lit.* a ball house].

gym·na·sium (jim·nā′·zi·ąm) *n.* a building or room equipped for physical training or sports; (gim·ná′·zi·ąm) in Germany, a High School. *pl.* **gymnasia** or **-s. gymnast** (jim′·nást) *n.* an expert in gymnastics. **gymnastic** *a.* **gymnastics** *n.pl.* muscular and bodily exercises. **gym** *n.* a gymnasium; a school athletic course [Gk. *gymnasion* fr. *gumnos*, naked].

gy·ne·col·o·gy (ji· (or gī)·ną·kál′·ą·ji·) *n.* (*Med.*) the science which deals with the diseases and disorders of women, esp. the organs of generation. **gynecologist** *n.* Also **gynaecology,** etc. [Gk. *gunē*, a woman; *logos*, discourse].

gyp·sum (jip′·sąm) *n.* a mineral, consisting mostly of sulfate of lime, used for making plaster of Paris [Gk. *gupsos*, chalk].

Gyp·sy (jip′·si·) *n.* one of a nomadic tribe of Indian origin (*l.c.*) a person who resembles or lives like a Gypsy; *a.* of or like a Gypsy [corrupt. fr. *Egyptian*].

gy·rate (jī′·rāt) *v.i.* to revolve around a central point; to move in a circle; to move spirally. **gyratory** *a.* **gyration** *n.* a circular or spiral motion [L. *gyrare*, to turn, whirl].

gy·ro·man·cy (jī′·rō·man·si·) *n.* divination performed by drawing a circle, and walking in it till dizziness causes a fall [Gk. *guros*, a circle; *manteia*, divination].

gy·ro·scope (jī′·rą·skōp) *n.* a wheel so mounted that its axis can turn freely in any direction when set rotating and left undisturbed, it will maintain the same direction in space, independently of its relation to the earth Gk. *guros*, a circle; *skopein*, to view].

H

ha (há) *interj.* denoting surprise, joy, or grief [imit. origin].

ha·be·as cor·pus (hā′·bi·ąs kawr′·pąs) *n.* writ requiring that a prisoner be brought to court to determine legality of confinement [L. = that you have the body].

ha·ber·dash·er (hab′·ęr·dash·ęr) *n.* a dealer in men's furnishings. **-y** *n.* [etym. uncertain].

ha·bil·i·ment (hą·bil′·ą·mąnt) *n.* (usually in *pl.*) dress [Fr. *habiller*, to clothe].

hab·it (hab′·it) *n.* custom; usage; tendency to repeat an action in the same way; mental condition acquired by practice; dress, esp. a *riding-habit; v.t.* to dress; to clothe. **-ual** *a.* formed by habit. **-ually** *adv.* **habituate** *v.t.* to accustom to a practice or usage; to familiarize; (*Colloq.*) to frequent. **-uation** *n.* **-ude** *n.* customary manner of action; repetition of an act, thought, or feeling; confirmed practice. **-ué** (hą·bich′·ą·wā) *n.* a frequenter (of a place) [L. *habitus*, attire, state, fr. *habere*, to have].

hab·it·a·ble (hab′·it·ą·bl) *n.* fit to live in. **-ness, habitability** *n.* **habitably** *adv.* **habitant** *n.* an inhabitant. **habitat** *n.* the natural home of an animal or plant; place of residence. **habitation** *n.* the act of inhabiting; a place of abode [L. *habitare*, to dwell].

ha·chure (hash′·oor) *n.* shading on a map to show mountains; *v.t.* to mark with this [Fr.].

ha·cien·da (há·si·en′·dą) *n.* a ranch; an estate in S. America [Sp.].

hack (hak) *v.t.* to cut irregularly; to notch; *v.i.* to make cuts or notches; to give harsh dry coughs; *n.* a cut; a notch; an ax, a pick; a short cough [O.E. *haccian*].

hack (hak) *n.* a horse for ordinary riding; a horse worn out by over work; a drudge, esp. literary; *a.* hackneyed; hired; a hired carriage; (*Colloq.*) a taxi; *v.t.* to let out for hire; to hackney; *v.i.* (*Colloq.*) to drive a taxi [short for *hackney*].

hack (hak) *n.* one who enjoys working with computers; v. to work with computers as a sport.

hack·ney (hak′·ni·) *n.* a horse for riding or driving; a horse (and carriage) kept for hire; *a.* to let out for hire; *v.i.* to use often; to make trite or commonplace. **-ed** *a.* commonplace [Fr. *haquenée*, a pacing horse].

had (had) *pa.p.* and *pa.t.* of **have.**

had·dock (had′·ạk) *n.* a fish of the cod family.

Ha·des (hā′·dēz) (*Myth.*) the underworld; (*l.c.*) (*Colloq.*) hell [Gk. = the unseen].

haft (haft) *n.* a handle, esp. of a knife; a hilt; *v.t.* to set in a handle [O.E. *haeft*].

hag (hag) *n.* an ugly old woman; a witch. **-gish** *a.* like a hag. **-gishly** *adv.* **-ridden** *a.* troubled with nightmares [O.E. *haegtesse*, a witch].

hag·gard (hag′·ẹrd) *a.* wild-looking; lean and gaunt; *n.* untrained hawk. **-ly** *adv.* [O.Fr. *hagard*].

hag·gle (hag′·l) *v.t.* to hack; to mangle; *v.i.* to dispute terms; to be difficult in bargaining; *n.* act of haggling. **-r** *n.* [O.N. *hoggva*, to chop]

Hag·i·og·ra·pha (hag·i·, hā·ji·ág′·rạ·fạ) *n.pl.* the last of the three divisions of the Old Testament [Gk. *haigos*, holy; *graphein*, to write].

hag·i·ol·o·gy (hag·i·, hā·ji·ál′·ạ·ji·) *n.* a history of the lives of saints. **hagiologist** *n.* **hagiography** *n.* the branch of literature which treats of the lives of saints [Gk. *hagios*, holy; *logos*, discourse; *graphein*, to write].

ha-ha (hȧ·hȧ′) *n.* a sunken fence [Fr.].

hail (hāl) *n.* frozen rain falling in pellets; *v.i.* to rain hail; *v.t.* to pour down like hail. **-stone** *n.* frozen raindrops [O.E. *hagol*].

hail (hāl) *v.t.* to greet, salute or call; *n.* an exclamation of respectful salutation. **— fellow** *n.* (often **hail-fellow well met**) an intimate companion; *a.* on intimate terms. **to hail from,** to come from [O.N. *heill*, healthy].

hair (hār) *n.* a filament growing from the skin of an animal; such filaments collectively, esp. covering the head; bristles; anything small or fine. **-ed** *a.* having hair. **-iness** *n.* **-y** *a.* covered with, made of, resembling hair. **-breadth** (hār′·bredth). **-s-breadth** *n.* the breadth of a hair; a very small distance; *a.* very narrow. **-brush** *n.* a brush for the hair. **-cloth** *n.* cloth made wholly or partly of hair. **-dresser** *n.* one who dresses or cuts hair; (*Brit.*) a barber. **-pin** *n.* a special two-legged pin for controlling hair. **-pin bend,** a bend of the road in the form of a U. **—raising** *a.* terrifying; alarming. **— shirt** *n.* a shirt made of haircloth, worn by penitents, ascetics, etc. **-splitting** *n.* and *n.* minute distinctions in reasoning. **-spring** *n.* a fine spring in a watch. **— trigger** *n.* a secondary trigger releasing the main one by very slight pressure [O.E. *haer*].

hal·cy·on (hal′·si·ạn) *n.* the kingfisher; *a.* calm. **— days,** peaceful, tranquil days; calm weather just before and after the winter solstice [Gk. *halkuon*, kingfisher, associated with calm sea].

hale (hāl) *a.* robust; sound; healthy, esp. in old age. **-ness** *n.* [O.E. *hal*, whole].

hale (hāl) *v.t.* to haul [O.Fr. *haler*, to pull].

half (haf) *n.* either of two equal parts of a thing. *pl.* **halves** (havz); (*Golf*) a hole neither won nor lost; *a.* forming a half; *adv.* to the extent of half. **—and-half** *n.* a mixture of two things in equal proportions; *adv.* in two equal portions. **-back** *n.* (*Football*) a player, or position, behind the forward line. **—baked** *a.* underdone; immature; silly. **—breed** *n.* one whose parents are of different races. **— brother** *n.* a brother by one parent only. **—caste** *n.* a half-breed. **— dozen** *n.* six. **— hearted** *a.* lukewarm. **— mast** *n.* the position of a flag lowered halfway down the staff, as a signal of distress, or as a sign of mourning. **— measure** *n.* inadequate means to achieve an end. **— moon** *n.* the moon when half its disk appears illuminated; a semicircle. **— nelson** *n.* a hold in wrestling. **— title** *n.* the name of a book, or subdivision of a book, occupying a full page. **—tone** *n.* an illustration printed from a relief plate, showing light and shade by minute dots, made by photographing the subject through a closely ruled screen. **—wit** *n.* an imbecile; a blockhead. **—witted** *a.* **halve** (hav) *v.t.* to divide into two equal portions; to reduce to half the previous amount [O.E. *haelf*].

hal·i·but (hal′·ạ·bạt) *n.* a large, flat sea fish [M.E. *haly*, holy; *butt*, a flatfish].

hal·i·to·sis (hal·ạ·tō′·sis) *n.* foul or offensive breath [L. *halitus*, breath].

hall (hawl) *n.* a corridor in a building; a place of public assembly; a room at the entrance of a house; a building belonging to a collegiate institution, guild, etc. **-mark** *n.* the mark used to indicate the standard of tested gold and silver; any mark of quality [O.E. *heal*].

Hal·le·lu·jah, Halleluiah (hal·ạ·lòò′·yạ) *n.* and *interj.* used in songs of praise to God [Heb. *hallelu*, praise ye; *Jah*, Jehovah].

hal·liard See **halyard.**

hal·loo (hạ·lòò′) *n.* a hunting cry; a shout or call to draw attention; *v.t.* to encourage with shouts, esp. dogs in hunting [imit.].

hal·low (hal′·ō) *v.t.* to make holy; to consecrate; to treat as sacred; to reverence. **-ed** *a.* **Hallowe'en** *n.* the evening before All Hallows' or All Saints' day (Oct. 31st).

hal·lu·ci·nate (hạ·lòò′·sạ·nāt) *v.t.* to produce illusion in the mind of. **hallucination** *n.* illusion; seeing something that is not present; delusion. **hallucinative, hallucinatory** *a.* [L. *hallucinari*, to wander in mind].

ha·lo (hā′·lō) *n.* a circle of light around the moon, sun, etc.; a ring of light around a saint's head in a picture. *pl.* **-s, -es** [Gk. *halōs*, a threshing-floor; a disk].

hal·o·gen (hal′·ạ·jạn) *n.* (*Chem.*) one of the elements chlorine, bromine, iodine, and fluorine [Gk. *hals*, salt; root *gen-*, producing].

halt (hawlt) *n.* a stoppage on a march or journey; *v.t.* to cause to stop; *v.i.* to make a stop [Ger. *Halt*, stoppage].

halt (hawlt) *v.i.* to falter in speech or walk; to hesitate; *n.* cripple. **-ing** *a.* [O.E. *healt*].

hal·ter (hawl′·tẹr) *n.* a rope or strap with headstall to fasten or lead horses or cattle; a noose for hanging a person; *v.t.* to fasten with a rope or strap [O.E. *haelftre*].

halve (hav) *v.t.* to divide into two equal parts.

hal·yard, halliard (hal′·yẹrd) *n.* (*Naut.*) a rope for hoisting or lowering yards or sails [corrupt. of *halier*, fr. *hale* = to haul].

ham (ham) *n.* the thigh of any animal, esp. a hog's thigh cured by salting and smoking; the region behind the knee; (*Slang*) an actor who overacts; an amateur transmitter and receiver of radio messages. **-string** *n.* a tendon at the back of the knee; *v.t.* to cripple by cutting this [O.E. *hamm*].

ham·burg·er (ham′·bur·gẹr) *n.* ground beef, seasoned and formed into cakes, frequently served in a bun [Ger. *Hamburg*].

ham·let (ham′·lit) *n.* a small village [O.E. *ham*, a dwelling].

ham·mer (ham′·ẹr) *n.* a tool, usually with a heavy head at the end of a handle, for beating metal, driving nails, etc.; a contrivance for exploding the charge of a gun; *v.t.* and *i.* to beat with, or as with, a hammer; to work hard at. **-head** *n.* a rapacious kind of shark. **-headed** *a.* having a head shaped like a hammer. **to hammer out** (*Fig.*) to find a solution by full investigation of all difficulties. **to come under the hammer,** to be sold by auction. [O.E. *hamor*].

ham·mock (ham′·ạk) *n.* a kind of hanging bed, consisting of a piece of canvas, and suspended by cords from hooks [Sp. *hamaca*].

ham·per (ham′·pẹr) *n.* a large covered basket for conveying goods [O.Fr. *hanapier*, a case for *hanaps*, goblets].

ham·per (ham′·pẹr) *n.* (*Naut.*) cumbrous

equipment; *v.t.* to impede; to obstruct the movements of [etym. uncertain].

ham·shack·le (ham′·shak·l) *v.t.* to fasten the head of an animal to one of the forelegs [fr. *hamper* and *shackle*].

ham·ster (ham′·stẹr) *n.* a species of rodent, remarkable for having cheek pouches [Gk.].

ham·string See **ham.**

hand (hand) *n.* the extremity of the arm beyond the wrist; a pointer on a dial, e.g. on a watch; a measure of the hand's breadth, four inches; a style of handwriting; cards dealt to a player; a manual worker; a sailor; side; direction; agency; service; aid; skill; *a.* belonging to, worn on, carried in, the hand; made or operated by hand; *v.t.* to give with the hand; to deliver; to pass; to hold out. **-y** *a.* convenient; close at hand; clever with the hands. **-y man** *n.* one hired for odd jobs. **-ily** *adv.* **-iness** *n.* **-bag** *n.* a bag for carrying in the hand. **-bill** *n.* printed sheet for circulation by hand. **-book** *n.* a short treatise; a manual. **-breath** *n.* the breadth of a hand (about four inches). **-cart** *n.* a small cart drawn or pushed by hand. **-cuff** *n.* shackle around wrist connected by a chain with one on other wrist; a manacle; *v.t.* to manacle. **-ful** *n.* as much as the hand will grasp or contain. **-maid(en)** *n.* a female servant. **— out** (*Slang*) food or money given to a beggar. **-rail** *n.* the rail of a staircase. **— to hand** *a.* in personal encounter; at close quarters. **— to mouth** *a.* precarious; without thought of the future. **-writing** *n.* the way a person writes. **at first hand,** direct from the original source. **in hand,** under control. **off-hand** *adv.* without attentive consideration; immediately. **on hand,** ready for distribution; available for disposal. **with a heavy hand,** sternly; severely. **with a high hand,** arrogantly. **an old hand,** a person with experience; a veteran. **second hand,** not new; having already been used. **to change hands,** to become the property of another. **to show one's hand,** to reveal one's intentions. [O.E. *hand*].

hand·i·cap (han′·di·kap) *n.* a race or contest in which competitors' chances are equalized by starts given, weights carried, etc.; a condition so imposed; (*Fig.*) a disability; *v.t.* to hinder or impede [fr. *hand in cap;* orig. a lottery game].

hand·i·craft (han′·di·kraft) *n.* manual occupation or skill; work performed by the hand [O.E. *handcraeft*].

hand·ker·chief (hang′·kẹr·chif) *n.* a small square of fabric carried in the pocket for wiping the nose, etc.; a kerchief for head or neck.

han·dle (hand′·d'l) *v.t.* to touch or feel with the hand; to manage; to wield; to deal with; to deal in; *n.* the part of a thing by which it is held; (*Fig.*) a fact that may be taken advantage of [O.E. *handlian*].

hand·some (han′·sạm) *a.* of fine appearance; generous. **-ly** *adv.* **-ness** *n.* [orig. = pleasant to handle].

hang (hang) *v.t.* to suspend; to put to death by suspending from gallows; to cover with, as wallpaper, curtains, pictures, etc.; to fix on hinges, as a door; to display; *v.i.* to be suspended; to incline; to be in suspense; to linger; to cling to. *pa.p.* and *p.t.* **-ed** or **hung.** *n.* the way in which a thing hangs; (*Colloq.*) meaning; manner of doing. **-dog** *n.* a degraded fellow; *a.* having a sneaking look. **-er** *n.* that by which a thing is suspended, e.g. a *coat-hanger.* **-ing** *n.* death by suspension; that which is hung, as curtains, etc. for a room (used chiefly in *pl.*); *a.* punishable by death; suspended. **-man** *n.* one who hangs another; a public executioner. **-nail** *n.* piece of skin hanging from root of fingernail. **-over** *n.* depressing after-effects of drinking. **to hang in the balance,** to be in doubt or suspense. **hang! hang it! hang it all!** mild oaths [O.E. *hangian*].

han·gar (hang′·ẹr) *n.* a shed for aircraft [Fr. = *a shed*].

hank (hangk) *n.* a coil, esp. as a measure of yarn (of cotton = 840 yards; of worsted = 560 yards); (*Naut.*) a ring at the corner of a sail [O.N. *hanki*].

han·ker (hang′·kẹr) *v.i.* to long for; to crave. **-ering** *n.* an uneasy longing for; a craving

han·som (han′·sạm) *n.* a light two-wheeled cab with the driver's seat at the back [fr. the inventor, Joseph A. *Hansom,* 1803-1882].

hap·haz·ard (hap·haz′·ẹrd) *n.* chance; accident; *a.* ransom; without design. **-ly** *adv.* **-ness** *n.* [O.N. *happ,* luck].

hap·less (hap′·lis) *a.* unlucky. **-ly** *adv.* [O.N. *happ,* luck].

hap·pen (hap′·in) *v.i.* to come by chance; to occur; to take place. **-ing** *n.* occurrence; event [O.N. *happ,* luck].

hap·py (hap′·i·) *a.* glad; content; lucky; fortunate; apt; fitting. **happily** *adv.* **happiness** *n.* [O.N. *happ,* luck].

ha·ra·ki·ri (hȧ·rạ·kēr′·i·) *n.* a method of suicide by disembowelment. Also **hari-kari** [Jap. *hara,* the belly; *kiri,* to cut].

ha·rangue (hạ·rang′) *n.* a loud, passionate speech; *v.i.* to deliver a harangue; *v.t.* to speak vehemently to. **-r** *n.* [O.H. Ger. = a ring of hearers].

har·ass (har′·ạs, hạ·ras′) *v.t.* to attack repeatedly; to worry; to trouble. **-ed** *a.* **-er** *n.* **-ing** *a.* **-ment** *n.* [Fr. *harasser*].

nounces another's approach; a forerunner

har·bin·ger (hạr′·bin·jẹr) *n.* one who announces another's approach; a forerunner [M.E. *herbergeour,* provider of lodging].

har·bor (hȧr·bẹr) *n.* shelter for ships; a port; any shelter; *v.t.* to give shelter to; to protect *v.i.* to take shelter [M.E. *herberwe*].

hard (hȧrd) *a.* firm; solid; resisting pressure; difficult; harsh; unfeeling; difficult to bear; strenuous; bitter, as winter; keen, as frost; strong, said of alcoholic liquors; *adv.* vigorously; intently; solidly. **-en** *v.t.* to make hard or more hard; to strengthen; to confirm in wickedness or obstinacy; to make less sympathetic; *v.i.* to become hard. **-ly** *adv.* with difficulty; not quite; scarcely; severely. **-core** *a.* intransigent; unchanging; (*Colloq.*) pruriently explicit. **-ness** *n.* **-ship** *n.* severe toil or suffering; ill-luck; privation; suffering. **— and fast,** strict; rigid. **—bitten** *a.* tough; stubborn. **—boiled** *a.* boiled till hard, e.g. of an egg; (*Slang*) tough; unfeeling. **— by,** near; close at hand. **— cash,** coins, as opposed to paper money. **-headed** *a.* shrewd; intelligent; practical. **-hearted** *a.* cruel; merciless; unsympathetic. **-tack,** a large coarse unsalted biscuit. **— up,** (*Colloq.*) very short of money; poor. **-ware** *n.* articles made of metal, e.g. tools, locks, fixtures, etc.; the electronic equipment and machinery used in computer operations (See *software*). **to die —,** to die after a fierce struggle. **a die—** (*Fig.*) one who clings desperately to long-held opinions [O.E. *heard*].

har·dy (hȧr′·di·) *a.* robust; bold; brave; daring; able to bear exposure. **hardily** *adv.* **hardihood** *n.* extreme boldness. **hardiness** *n.* vigor; robustness [Fr. *hardi,* bold].

hare (hār) *n.* a rodent with long hind legs, long ears, short tail, and divided upper lip, noted for its speed. **-brained** *a.* wild; heedless. **-lip** *n.* (*Med.*) a congenital fissure in the upper lip. **-lipped** *a.* [O.E. *hara*].

har·em (hār′·ạm) *n.* apartment for females in a Mohammedan household; the occupants [Ar. *haram,* forbidden].

ha·ri-ka·ri. See **hara-kiri.**

hark (hȧrk) *v.i.* to listen; *interj.* listen! hear! **to — back** (*Fig.*) to return to some previous point in an argument [M.E. *herkien;* cf. E. *hearken*].

har·lot (hȧr′·lạt) *n.* a prostitute. **-ry** *n.* prostitution [O.Fr. = a vagabond].

harm (hȧrm) *n.* injury; hurt; damage; misfortune; *v.t.* to hurt; to injure. **-ful** *a.* hurtful; injurious. **-fully** *adv.* **-fulness** *n.* **-less** *a.* **-lessly** *adv.* **-lessness** *n.* [O.E. *hearm*].

har·mo·ny (hȧr·mạ·ni·) *n.* agreement; concord; friendliness; peace; a melodious sound; a combination of musical notes to make chords; the science that treats of musical sounds in their combination and progression. **harmonic** (hȧr·mȧn′·ik), **harmonical** *a.* **harmonically** *adv.* **harmonica** *n.* a mouth organ. **harmonicon** *n.* a mouth organ; an orchestration. **harmonics** *n.* the science of harmony, of musical sounds. **harmonious** (hȧr·mō′·ni·ạs) *a.* vocally or musically concordant; symmetrical; living in peace and friendship. **harmoniously** *adv.* **harmoniousness** *n.* **harmonize** *v.t.* to bring into harmony; to cause to agree; to reconcile; (*Mus.*) to arrange into parts for the voice, or with instrumental accompaniments; *v.i.* to be in harmony; to agree; (*Colloq.*) to sing in harmony. **harmonizer** *n.* **harmonist** *n.* a harmonizer; a musical composer. **harmonium** *n.* a small reed organ. **harmonic progression,** a series of numbers whose reciprocals are in arithmetical progression, e.g. ½, ⅓, ¼, etc. or 10, 12, 15 [Gk. *harmonia,* fr. *harmozein,* to fit together].

har·ness (hȧr′·nis) *n.* the working gear, straps, bands, etc. of a draft animal, esp. a horse; *v.t.* to put harness on [Fr. *harneis*].

harp (hȧrp) *n.* a stringed musical instrument played by hand; *v.i.* to play on the harp; to dwell persistently upon a particular subject. **-ist** *n.* a player on the harp. **-sichord** (hȧrp′·si·kawrd) *n.* an old-fashioned musical instrument, a forerunner of the piano [O.E. *hearpe*].

har·poon (hȧr·pòòn′) *n.* a barbed spear with a rope attached for catching whales, etc.; *v.t.* to strike with a harpoon. **-er** *n.* [Fr. *harpon*].

Har·py (hȧr′·pi·) *n.* (*Myth.*) ravenous monster, with head and breast of woman and wings and claws of vulture; (*l.c.*) a rapacious woman [Gk. *harpazein,* to seize].

har·ri·dan (har′·i·dạn) *n.* a haggard old woman; a shrew [corrupt. of Fr. *haridelle,* a worn-out horse].

har·row (har′·ō) *n.* a toothed agricultural implement to level, break clods, or cover seed when sown; *v.t.* to draw harrow over; (*Fig.*) to distress greatly. **-er** *n.* **-ing** *a.* [M.E. *harwe*].

har·ry (har′·i·) *v.t.* to ravage; to pillage; to torment [O.E. *hergian,* to make war].

harsh (hȧrsh) *a.* rough; unpleasing to the touch or taste; severe; unfeeling. **-ly** *adv.* **-ness** *n.* [M.E. *harsk*].

hart (hȧrt) *n.* a male deer or stag, esp. over five years old [O.E. *heort*].

harte·beest (hȧrt′·bēst) *n.* a large S. African antelope [Dut.].

har·um-scar·um (hār′·ạm-skār′·ạm) *a.* reckless; wild; *n.* a rash person [perh. *hare,* and *scare*].

har·vest (hȧr′·vist) *n.* (season for) gathering crops; the crop itself; *v.t.* to gather in. **-er** *n.* one who harvests; a reaping-machine. **— moon** *n.* the full moon nearest the autumn equinox [O.E. *haerfest,* autumn].

has (haz) 3rd sing. pres. indic. of the verb **have. —been** *n.* (*Colloq.*) a person long past his best.

hash (hash) *v.t.* to chop into small pieces; to mince; *n.* that which is hashed; a dish of hashed meat and potatoes; (*Slang*) a mess [Fr. *hacher,* to chop].

hasp (hasp) *n.* a clasp passing over a staple for fastening a door, etc.; *v.t.* to fasten with a hasp [O.E. *haepse*].

has·sock (has′·ạk) *n.* a padded cushion for kneeling or for a footstool; a tuft of grass [O.E. *hassuc,* coarse grass].

haste (hāst) *n.* speed; quickness; hurry; *v.i.* (*Poet.*) to hasten. **-n** (hās′·n) *v.t.* to urge forward; to accelerate; *v.i.* to hurry. **-er** *n.* **hasty** *a.* speedy; quick; over-eager; rash; passionate. **hastily** *adv.* [O.Fr. *haste*].

hat (hat) *n.* covering for head, usually with brim. **-ter** *n.* one who makes, or sells hats. **top —** *n.* a silk hat with a high crown. **to pass (round) the —,** to make a collection, esp. to pay expenses [O.E. *haett*].

hatch (hach) *v.t.* to bring forth young birds from the shell; to incubate; to plot; *v.i.* to come forth from the shell; *n.* the act of hatching; the brood hatched. **-er** *n.* **-ery** *n.* a place for hatching eggs, esp. of fish [M.E. *hacchen*].

hatch (hach) *n.* the lower half of a divided door; an opening in a floor or roof; the boards, etc. covering a hatchway; the hatchway itself. **-back** *n.* a car with a rear that opens upward, above additional storage space or a folding seat. **-way** *n.* a square opening in a ship's deck through which cargo, etc. is lowered [O.E. *haec,* a gate].

hatch (hach) *v.t.* to shade with lines [Fr. *hacher,* to chop].

hatch·et (hach′·ạt) *n.* a small ax with a short handle. **— faced** *a.* having a face with sharp features. **to bury the —,** to make peace [Fr. *hache,* an axe].

hate (hāt) *v.t.* to dislike strongly; to bear malice to; to detest; *n.* strong dislike; aversion; hatred. **-ful** *a.* detestable. **-fully** *adv.* **-fulness** *n.* **-r** *n.* **hatred** *n.* aversion; active ill-will; enmity [O.E. *hatian,* to hate; *hete,* hatred].

haugh·ty (haw′·ti·) *a.* proud. **haughtily** *adv.* **haughtiness** *n.* [Fr. *haut,* high, fr. L. *altus*].

haul (hawl) *v.t.* to pull with force; to drag; to steer a ship closer to the wind; *v.i.* to pull; of wind, to shift, to veer; *n.* a hauling; a catch; good profit, gain, or acquisition. **-age** *n.* the act of pulling; the charge for hauling; the carrying of goods, material, etc. by road. **-er** *n.* one who hauls. **close-hauled** *a.* (*Naut.*) of a ship, with the sails trimmed to keep her close to the wind [Fr. *haler*].

haunch (hawnch) *n.* the part of the body between ribs and thighs; the hip [Fr. *hanche*].

haunt (hawnt) *v.t.* to frequent; of ghosts, to visit regularly; *v.i.* to loiter about a place; *n.* a place of frequent resort. **-ed** *a.* frequently visited by ghosts [Fr. *hanter,* to frequent].

haut·boy (hō′·boi) *n.* an older form of the oboe [Fr. *haut,* high; *bois,* wood].

hau·teur (hō·tur′) *n.* haughtiness; haughty manner or spirit; arrogance [Fr.]

have (hav) *v.t.* to hold or possess; to be possessed or affected with; to seize; to bring forth; to enjoy; to be obliged (to do); (as an auxiliary verb, forms the perfect and other tenses). *pr.p.* **having.** *pa.p., pa.t.* **had** [O.E. *habban*].

ha·ven (hā′·vn) *n.* a bay or inlet giving shelter for ships; any place of shelter [O.E. *haefen*].

hav·er·sack (hav′·ẹr·sak) *n.* a soldier's canvas ration-bag; a similar bag for travelers [Ger. *Habersack,* an oat sack].

hav·oc (hav′·ạk) *n.* pillage; devastation; ruin [fr. to 'cry havoc,' to give the signal for pillage; O.Fr. *havot,* plunder].

haw (haw) *n.* a hesitation in speech; *v.i.* to speak hesitatingly [imit.]

haw (haw) *interj.* a command to horses, usu. to turn left; *v.t., v.i.* to turn left.

hawk (hawk) *n.* a bird of prey of the falcon family; (*Colloq.*) a person with a warlike stance, esp. in international matters; *v.t., v.i.* to hunt with hawks, as in falconry. **-er** *n.* a falconer. **-ing** *n.* falconry [O.E. *hafoc*].

hawk (hawk) *v.i.* to clear the throat noisily;

n. an audible clearing of the throat.
hawk (hawk) *v.i.* to carry about wares for sale; to peddle. **-er** *n.* an itinerant dealer; a peddler [Dut. *heuker*, a huckster].
hawk (hawk) *n.* a plasterer's tool for holding plaster.
hawse (hawz) *n.* the part of a ship's bows with holes for cables [O.E. *heals*, the prow].
haw·ser (haw′·zẹr) *n.* a large rope or small cable [O.Fr. *haucier*, to raise].
hay (hā) *n.* grass mown and dried for fodder. **— fever** *n.* irritation of the mucous membrane of the nose. **-maker** *n.* one who cuts and dries grass for hay. **-rick, -stack** *n.* a large pile of hay with ridged or pointed top. **-seed** *n.* grass seed; (*Colloq.*) a rustic; a country bumpkin [O.E. *hieg*].
haz·ard (haz′·ẹrd) *n.* chance; a chance; risk; danger; (*Golf*) an inclusive term for all obstacles on the golf course; a game played with dice; *v.t.* to expose to risk; to run the risk of. **-ous** *a.* dangerous; risky [Fr. *hasard*].
haze (hāz) *n.* a misty appearance in the air; mental obscurity. **hazy** *a.* **hazily** *adv.*
haze (hāz) *v.t.* to torment or punish by the imposition of disagreeable task; to play tricks on [O.Fr. *haser*, to annoy].
ha·zel (hā′·zl) *n.* a nut-bearing bush or small tree; the reddish-brown color of the nuts; *a.* of this color. **-nut** *n.* the nut of the hazel tree [O.E. *haesel*].
H-bomb (āch′·bȧm) *n.* a *h*ydrogen *bomb*, a bomb more destructive than an atom bomb, deriving its energy from the thermonuclear fusion of hydrogen isotopes.
he (hē) *pron.* the 3rd pers. sing. masc. pronoun. **—man** *n.* (*Colloq.*) a very virile man [O.E.].
head (hed) *n.* the upper part of a man's or animal's body; the brain; intellectual capacity; upper part of anything; the top; the chief part, a chief; something the shape of a head; progress; a section of a chapter; the source of a stream, a cape or headland; a crisis; freedom to go on; *a.* chief; principal; of wind, contrary; *v.t.* to lead; to be at the head of; to direct; to go in front, so as to hinder; *v.i.* to originate; to form a head; to make for. **-y** *a.* impetuous; apt to intoxicate. **-ily** *adv.* **-iness** *n.* **-ache** (hed′·āk) *n.* a nerve-pain in the head. **-achy** *a.* **-er** *n.* (*Colloq.*) a plunge, head foremost into water; in building, a brick laid so that its end forms part of the surface of the wall. **-gear** *n.* a hat; the harness about an animal's head. **—hunting** *n.* raiding to procure human heads as trophies. **-ing** *n.* the act of providing with a head; a title. **-land** *n.* a cape; a promontory. **-light** *n.* a strong light carried on the front of a locomotive, motor vehicle, etc. **—line** *n.* a summary of news in large print in a newspaper; a caption. **-long** *adv.* with the head foremost; rashly; *a.* steep; rash; reckless. **-man** *n.* the chief, esp. of a tribe. **-master, -mistress** *n.* the person in charge of a school; the principal. **-most** *a.* most advanced; foremost. **—on** *a.* meeting head to head; head first. **-phone** *n.* a telephone-receiver to clip on head (usu. *pl.*). **-piece** *n.* a helmet; the head; brainpower. **-quarters** *n.pl.* (*Mil.*) a center of operations. **-sail** *n.* any sail forward of the mast. **-sman** *n.* an executioner. **-stall** *n.* the part of the bridle that fits round the head. **-stone** *n.* a memorial stone placed at the head of a grave. **-strong** *a.* obstinate; self-willed. **-way** *n.* progress. **— over heels,** completely; deeply. **to keep one's —,** to keep calm [O.E. *heafod*].
heal (hēl) *v.t.* to make whole; to restore to health; to make well; *v.i.* to become sound. **-er** *n.* **-ing** *a.* [O.E. *haelan*, fr. *hal*, whole].
health (helth) *n.* soundness of body; general condition of the body. **-y** *a.* having, or tending to give, health; sound; wholesome. **-ily** *adv.* **-iness** *n.* **-ful** *a.* [O.E. *haelth*, fr. *hal*, whole].
heap (hēp) *n.* a number of things lying one on another; a pile; a mass; (*Colloq.*) a great quantity; *v.t.* to throw or lay in a heap; to amass [O.E. *heap*].
hear (hēr) *v.t.* to perceive with the ear; to listen to, to heed, (*Law*) to try (a case); *v.i.* to perceive sound; to learn by report. *pr.p.* **-ing.** *pa.p., pa.t.* **-d** (*hurd*). **-er** *n.* **-ing** *n.* the act of perceiving sound; the sense by which sound is perceived; audience; earshot. **-say** *n.* rumor; common talk. **hear! hear!** *interj.* indicating approval of a speaker's words or opinions [O.E. *hieran*].
hearse (hurs) *n.* a vehicle to carry a coffin to the place of burial [Fr. *herce*, a harrow].
heart (hȧrt) *n.* the hollow, muscular organ which makes the blood circulate; the seat or source of life; the seat of emotions and affections; the inner part of anything; courage; warmth or affection; a playing-card marked with a figure of a heart. **-y** *a.* cordial; friendly; vigorous; in good health; of a meal, satisfying the appetite. **-ily** *adv.* **-iness** *n.* **-less** *a.* without heart; unfeeling. **-en** *v.t.* to encourage; to stimulate. **-ache** *n.* sorrow; anguish. **-blood** *n.* life; essence. **-break** *n.* overpowering sorrow. **-broken** *a.* overwhelmed with grief. **-burn** *n.* a form of dyspepsia. **-strings** *n.pl.* (*Fig.*) affections; emotions. **at —,** at bottom, inwardly. **by —,** by rote; by memory. **to wear one's — on one's sleeve,** to show one's feelings openly [O.E. *heorte*].
hearth (hȧrth) *n.* the fireside; the house itself; home [O.E. *heorth*].
heat (hēt) *n.* hotness; a sensation of this; hot weather or climate; warmth of feeling; anger; excitement; sexual excitement in animals, esp. female; *v.t.* to make hot; to excite; *v.i.* to become hot. **-ed** *a.* (*Fig.*) of argument, etc., passionate; intense. **-edly** *adv.* **-er** *n.* **— shield** *n.* the coating or device on the nose of a spacecraft, to absorb heat during reentry. **— wave** *n.* a spell of abnormally hot weather [O.E. *haetu*].
heath (hēth) *n.* waste land; moor; shrub of genus Erica. **-y** *a.* [O.E. *haeth*].
hea·then (hē′·THẹn) *n.* one who is not an adherent of a religious system; an infidel; a pagan; an irreligious person; *a.* **-ish** *a.* **-ism** *n.* pagan worship; the condition of being heathen [O.E. *haethen*].
heath·er (heTH′·ẹr) *n.* a small plant of the genus Erica, bearing purple, and sometimes white, bell-shaped flowers; heath [fr. *heath*].
heave (hēv) *v.t.* to lift with effort; to throw (something heavy); to utter (a sigh); to pull on a rope, etc.; to haul; (*Geol.*) to displace; *v.i.* to rise and fall in alternate motions, e.g. of heavy breathing, of waves, etc.; to try to vomit; *n.* a heaving; an effort to lift something; a rise and fall; an attempt to vomit. *pr.p.* **heaving.** *pa.p., pa.t.* **-d, hove. to — to,** to bring a ship to a standstill [O.E. *hebban*].
heav·en (hev′·n) *n.* the sky; the upper air; the abode of God; God himself; a place of bliss; supreme happiness. **-ly** *a.* pert. to, or like, heaven; pure; divine; *adv.* in a heavenly manner. **-liness** *n.* **-ward, -wards** *adv.* toward heaven. **in seventh —,** in a state of supreme bliss [O.E. *heofon*].
Heav·i·side lay·er (hev′·i·sīd lā′·ẹr) *n.* the upper part of the atmosphere, which reflects radio waves [fr. Oliver *Heaviside*, English physicist, 1850-1925].
heav·y (hev′·i·) *a.* weighty; striking or falling with force; large in amount, as a debt; rough, as the sea; abundant, as rain; clayey, as soil; sad; hard to bear; difficult; dull; sluggish, serious; over compact; indigestible. **heavily** *adv.* **heaviness** *n.* **—handed** *a.* awkward; severe; oppressive. **— headed** *a.* drowsy. **—hearted** *a.* sad. **—weight** *n.* (*Boxing*) a boxer exceeding 175 lbs. in weight [O.E. *hefig*,

fr. *hebban*, to heave].

heb·do·mad (heb·dạ·mad′) *n.* a group of seven things; a week [Gk. *hebdomas*, seventh].

He·brew (hē′·bròò) *n.* one of the ancient inhabitants of Palestine; an Israelite; a Jew; the language. **Hebraic** (hē·brā′·ik) *a.* pert. to the Hebrews, or to their language [Heb. *'ibhri,'* one from across the river Euphrates].

hec·a·tomb (hek′·ạ·tōm) *n.* any large number of victims [Gk. *hekaton*, a hundred; *bous*, an ox].

heck·le (hek′·l) *n.* a comb for cleaning flax; *v.t.* to comb flax; to ask awkward questions of a speaker at a public meeting.

hec·to- *prefix* combining to form derivatives used in the metric system. **-gram, -gramme** hek′·tạ·gram) *n.* a weight of 100 grammes = 3.527 ounces. **-liter** (hek′·tạ·lēt·ẹr) *n.* a unit of capacity, containing 100 liters = 26.418 U.S. gallons. **-meter** (hek·tạ·mē·tẹr) *n.* a unit of length = 100 meets = 109.363 yards [fr. Gk. *hekaton*, one hundred].

hec·tic (hek′·tik) *a.* exciting; wild; consumptive affected with hectic fever [Gk. *hektikos*, habitual].

hec·to·graph (hek′·tạ·graf) *n.* an apparatus for multiplying copies of writings [Gk. *hekaton*, a hundred; *graphein*, to write].

Hec·tor (hek′·tẹr) *n.* the chief hero of Troy in war with Greeks. (*l.c.*) *n.* a bully; a brawler; a blusterer; *v.t.* and *i.* to bully; to bluster.

hedge (hej) *n.* a fence of bushes; a protecting barrier; *v.t.* to enclose with a hedge; to fence, as fields; to obstruct; to hem in; *v.i.* to bet on both sides so as to guard against loss; to shift; to shuffle; to skulk. **hedging** *n.* **hedgy** *a.* **-hog** *n.* a small quadruped, covered on the upper part of its body with prickles or spines. **-hopping** *n.* in aviation, flying very low. **-row** *n.* a row of bushes forming a hedge [O.E. *hecg*].

he·don·ism (hē′·d'n·izm) *n.* the doctrine that pleasure is the chief good. **hedonist** *n.* [Gk. *hēdonē*, pleasure].

heed (hēd) *v.t.* to take notice of; to care for; to mind; to observe; *n.* attention; notice; care; caution. **-ful** *a.* watchful; attentive. **-fully** *adv.* **-fulness** *n.* **-less** *a.* [O.E. *hedan*].

hee·haw (hē′·haw) *v.i.* to bray, of an ass [imit. origin].

heel (hēl) *n.* back part of foot, shoe, boot, or stocking; back part of anything; (*Slang*) an undesirable person; *v.t.* to add a heel to, as in knitting; to touch ground, or a ball, with the heel. **— of Achilles** (*Fig.*) a vulnerable part. **down at the heels,** slovenly; seedy; ill-shod [O.E. *hela*].

heel (hēl) *v.i.* of a ship; to lean to one side; to incline; *v.t.* to cause to do this [O.E. *hieldan*, to incline].

heft (heft) *v.t.* to try the weight by lifting; (*Colloq.*) to heave up or lift; *n.* weight. **-y** *a.* heavy; vigorous [fr. *heave*].

he·gem·o·ny (hi·jem′·ạ·nē, hej′·ạ·mōn·i·) *n.* leadership; predominance. **hegemonic** *a.* Gk. *hēgemōn*, a leader].

He·gi·ra, hejira (hi·jī′·rạ) *n.* Mohammed's flight from Mecca to Medina, A.D. 622 [Ar. *hijrah*, flight].

heif·er (hef′·ẹr) *n.* a young cow that has not had a calf [O.E. *heahfore*].

height (hīt) *n.* measurement from base to top; quality of being high; a high position; a hill; eminence. **-en** *v.t.* to make high or higher; to intensify [O.E. *hiehthu*].

hei·nous (hā′·nạs) *a.* extremely wicked; atrocious; odious [Fr. *haineux*, hateful].

heir (ār) *n.* (*fem.* **-ess**) a person legally entitled to succeed to property or rank. **— apparent** *n.* the person who is first in the line of succession to an estate, crown, etc. **-loom** *n.* article of personal property which descends to heir along with inheritance; a thing that has been in a family for generations [L. *heres*].

he·ji·ra See **hegira.**

held (held) *pa.p.* and *pa.t.* of **hold.**

hel·i·cal (hel′·i·kạl) *a.* pert. to a helix; spiral. **helicopter** *n.* an airplane which can rise or descend vertically; an autogiro [Gk. *hēlix*, spiral; *pteron*, a wing].

he·li·o·gram (hē′·li·a·gram) *n.* a message transmitted by heliograph [Gk. *hēlios*, the sun; *gramma*, a writing].

he·li·o·graph (hē′·li·ạ·graf) *n.* signaling apparatus employing a mirror to reflect the sun's rays; an instrument for photographing the sun; *v.t.* to signal by means of a heliograph. **-ic** *a.* **heliography** *n.* [Gk. *hēlios*, the sun; *graphein*, to write].

he·li·o·trope (hē′·li·ạ·trōp) *n.* a plant with fragrant purple flowers; the color of the flowers, or their scent; a bloodstone. **heliotropism** *n.* (*Bot.*) the tendency of plants to direct their growth towards light [Gk. *hēlios*, the sun; *tropos*, a turn].

he·li·um (hē′·li·ạm) *n.* (*Chem.*) an inert noninflammable,light gas [Gk. *hēlios*, the sun].

he·lix (hē′·liks) *n.* a spiral, e.g. wire in a coil, or a corkscrew; (*Zool.*) a genus including the snail; (*Anat.*) the outer rim of the ear. **helical** *a.* spiral [Gk. *helix*, a spiral].

hell (hel) *n.* the abode of the damned; the lower regions; a place or state of vice, misery, or torture. **-ish** *a.* infernal. **-ishly** *adv.* **-ishness** *n.* **-ion** *n.* troublemaker [O.E. *hel*].

Hel·lene (hel′·ēn) *n.* an ancient Greek; a subject of modern Greece. **Hellenic** *a.* **Hellen-ism** *n.* Grecian culture; a Greek idiom. **Hellenist** *n.* a Greek scholar. **Hellenistic** *a.* [Gk. *Hellēn*].

hel·lo (hạ·lō′, he·lō′) *interj.* a greeting or call to attract attention.

helm (helm) *n.* (*Naut.*) a tiller or wheel for turning the rudder of a ship; (*Fig.*) control; guidance; *v.t.* to steer; to control [O.E. *helma*].

helm (helm) *n.* (*Arch.*) a helmet. **helmet** *n.* a defensive covering for the head; anything similar in shape or position [O.E. *helm*].

hel·minth (hel′·minth) *n.* an intestinal worm. [Gk. *helmins*, a worm].

hel·ot (hēl′·ạt, hē′·lạt) *n.* a serf in ancient Sparta; a slave; serfdom [Gk. *Heilōtēs*].

help (help) *v.t.* to aid; to assist; to support; to succor; to relieve; to prevent; *v.i.* to lend aid; to be useful; *n.* the act of helping; one who, or that which, helps; aid; assistance; support; a domestic servant. **-er** *n.* **-ful** *a.* **-fulness** *n.* **-ing** *n.* a portion of food. **-less** *a.* not able to take care of oneself; weak; dependent. **-lessly** *adv.* **-lessness** *n.* **-mate** *n.* an assistant; a partner; a wife or husband. Also **-meet** [O.E. *helpna*].

hel·ter-skel·ter (hel·tẹr-skel′·tẹr) *adv.* in disorder; in hurry and confusion.

Hel·ve·tia (hel·vē′·shạ) *n.* the Latin, and political, name for Switzerland.

hem (hem) *n.* border, esp. one made by sewing; *v.t.* to fold over and sew down; to edge; to enclose (followed by *in*). *pr.p.* **-ming.** *pa.p.* and *pa.t.* **-med** [O.E.].

hem (hem) *interj.* and *n.* a kind of suppressed cough, calling attention or expressing doubt; *v.i.* to make the sound.

he·ma-, hemo- (hē′·mạ) a word element meaning "blood" [Gk. *haima*].

he·mal, haemal (hē′·mạl) *a.* of the blood; on same side of body as the heart and great bloodvessels [Gk. *haima*, blood].

hem·a·tin, haematin (hem′·ạ·tin, hē′·mạ·tin) *n.* the constituent of hemoglobin containing iron [Gk. *haima*, blood].

hem·i-, *prefix* from Greek *hēmi*, half, combining to form derivatives.

hem·i·sphere (hem′·ạ·sfēr) *n.* a half sphere; half of the celestial sphere; half of the earth. **hemispheric, hemispherical** *a.*

hem·i·stich (hem′·ạ·stik) *n.* half a line of verse.

hem·lock (hem′·lȧk) *n.* a poisonous umbelliferous plant; a coniferous spruce [O.E. *hemlic*].

he·mo·glo·bin, haemoglobin (hē·mạ·glō′·-bin) *n.* the coloring matter of the red blood corpuscles [Gk. *haima*, blood; L. *globus*, a ball].

he·mo·phil·i·a, haemophilia (hē·mạ·fil′·i·ạ) *n.* (*Med.*) tendency to excessive bleeding due to a deficiency in clotting power of blood; *n.* a bleeder [Gk. *haima*, blood; *philein*, to love].

hem·or·rhage, haemorrhage (hem′·ạr·ij) *n.* (*Med.*) a flow of blood; a discharge of blood from the blood vessels; bleeding. **hemorrhagic** *a.* [Gk. *haima*, blood; *rhēgnunai*, to burst].

hem·or·rhoids, haemorrhoids (hem′·ạ·-roidz) *n.pl.* dilated veins around anus; piles. [Gk. *haima*, blood; *rhein*, to flood].

he·mo·stat·ic, haemostatic (hē·mạ·stat′·ik) *n.* an agent which stops bleeding; a styptic. Also *a.* [Gk. *haima*, blood; *stasis*, a standing].

hemp (hemp) *n.* a plant whose fiber is used in the manufacture of coarse cloth, ropes, cables, etc. **-en** *a.* [O.E. *henep*].

hen (hen) *n.* the female of any bird, esp. the domestic fowl; (*Colloq.*) the female of certain crustaceans, e.g. the lobster, crab, etc. **-coop** *n.* a large cage for poultry. **— party** *n.* (*Slang*) a social gathering of women only. **-peck** *v.t.* to domineer over a husband [O.E. *henn*].

hence (hens) *adv.* from this point; for this reason; *interj.* go away! begone! **-forth, -forward** *adv.* from now [M.E. *hennes*].

hench·man (hench′·mạn) *n.* a servant; a loyal supporter [M.E. *henxi-man*, a groom].

hen·dec·a·gon (hen·dek′·ạ·gȧn) *n.* a plane figure having eleven sides [Gk. *hendeka*, eleven; *gōnia*, an angle; *sullabē*, a syllable].

hen·na (hen′·ạ) *n.* a shrub or small tree of the Near East; a dye made from it [Ar. *hinna*].

hep (hep) *a.* (*Slang*) informed; smart.

he·pat·ic (hi·pat′·ik) *a.* pert. to the liver. **hepatitis** *n.* [Gk. *hēpar*, the liver].

hep·ta- (hep′·tạ) *prefix* from Greek, *hepta*, seven, combining to form derivatives. **-l** *n.* a group of seven. **-gon** *n.* a plane figure with seven sides. **-gonal** *a.* **-meter** *n.* a line of verse of seven feet.

hep·tar·chy (hep′·tȧr·ki·) *n.* government by seven persons; the country governed by them; a group of seven kingdoms [Gk. *hepta*, seven; *archein*, to rule].

her (hur) *pron.* the objective case of the pronoun **she;** also, the possessive case used adjectivally. **hers** *pron.* the absolute possessive case. **herself** *pron.* emphatic and reflexive form [O.E. fr. *hire*, gen. and dat. of *heo*, she].

her·ald (her′·ạld) *n.* an officer who makes royal proclamations, arranges ceremonies, keeps records of those entitled to armorial bearings, etc.; a messenger; an envoy; a forerunner. **heraldic** (he·ral′·dik) *a.* **-ry** *n.* the art or office of a herald; the science of recording genealogies and blazoning armorial bearings [O.Fr. *herault*].

herb (urb, hurb) *n.* a plant with a soft stem which dies down after flowering; a plant of which parts are used for medicine, food, or scent. **-aceous** (hur·bā′·shạs) *a.* pert. to herbs. **-age** *n.* herbs; nonwoody vegetation; (*Brit.*) green food for cattle. **-al** *a.* pert. to herbs; *n.* a book on herbs. **-alist** *n.* dealer in herbs [L. *herba*, grass].

Her·cu·les (hur′·kyạ·lēz) *n.* (*Myth.*) Latin name of Greek hero Heracles distinguished for his prodigious strength; hence any person of extraordinary strength and size. **Herculean** *a.*

herd (hurd) *n.* a number of animals feeding or traveling together; a drove of cattle; a large number of people; *v.i.* to go in a herd; *v.t.* to tend (a herd); to drive together. **-er** *n.* **-sman** *n.* one who tends cattle [O.E. *hirde*].

here (hēr) *adv.* in this place; at or to this point (opposed to *there*). **-about, -abouts** *adv.* about this place. **-after** *adv.* after this; *n.* a future existence. **-by** *adv.* by means of this; by this. **-in** *adv.* in this. **-on** *adv.* hereupon. **-to** *adv.* to this. **-tofore** *adv.* up to the present; formerly. **-with** *adv.* with this [O.E. *her*].

he·red·i·ty (hạ·red′·ạ·ti·) *n.* the transmission of characteristic traits and qualities from parents to offspring. **hereditable** *a.* heritable **hereditament** *n.* (*Law*) property that may be inherited. **hereditary** *a.* descending by inheritance [L. *heres*, an heir].

her·e·sy (her′·ạ·si·) *n.* opinion contrary to orthodox opinion, teaching, or belief. **heresiarch** (hạ·rē′·zi·ȧrk) *n.* the originator or leader of a heresy. **heretic** *n.* one holding opinions contrary to orthodox faith. **heretical** *a.* [Gk. *hairesis*, a choice, a school of thought].

her·it·a·ble (her′·ạ·tạ·bl) *a.* that can be inherited; attached to the property or house, as opposed to movable. **heritage** *n.* that which may be or is inherited. **heritor** *n.* one who inherits [L. *heres*, an heir].

her·maph·ro·dite (hur·maf′·rạ·dit) *n.* and *a.* animal or flower with the characteristics of both sexes; having normally both sexual organs. **hermaphroditic, hermaphroditical** *a.* **hermaphrodism, hermaphroditism** *n.* [Gk. *Hermaphroditos*, the son of *Hermes* and *Aphrodite* who became joined in one body with a nymph called Salmacis].

her·met·ic (hur·met′·ik) *a.* pert. to alchemy; magical; sealed. **— sealing,** the airtight closing of a vessel by fusion [Gk. *Hermes*].

her·mit (hur′·mit) *n.* a person living in seclusion, esp. from religious motives; a recluse. **-age** *n.* the abode of a hermit [Gk. *erēmitēs*, fr. *erēmos*, solitary].

her·ni·a (hur′·ni·ạ) *n.* (*Med.*) the external protrusion of any internal part through the enclosing membrane; rupture [L.].

he·ro (hē′·rō) *n.* (*fem.* **heroine** (her′·ō·in)) one greatly regarded for his achievements or qualities; the chief man in a poem, play, or story; an illustrious warrior. *pl.* **-es. heroic** *a.* pert. to a hero; bold; courageous; illustrious; narrating the exploits of heroes, as a poem; denoting the verse or measure in such poems. **heroical** *a.* **heroically** *adv.* **heroics** *n.pl.* high-flown language; bombastic talk. **heroism** (her′·ō·izm) *n.* courage; valor; bravery [Gk. *hērōs*, a demigod, a hero].

her·o·in (her′·ō·in) *n.* (*Med.*) habit-forming drug used as a sedative [Ger. trade name].

her·on (her′·ạn) *n.* a long-legged wading bird. [O.Fr. *hairon*; Fr. *héron*].

her·pes (hur′·pēz) *n.* a skin disease. **herpetic** *a.* [Gk. fr. *herpein*, to creep].

her·pe·tol·o·gy (hẹr·pạ·tȧl′·ạ·ji·) *n.* the study of reptiles [Gk. *herpein*, to creep].

Herr (her) *n.* the German equivalent of Mr. *pl.* **Herren** [Ger. *Herrenvolk*, master race].

her·ring (her′·ing) *n.* a familiar sea-fish, moving in shoals, much used as a food. **-bone** *n.* a zig-zag pattern. **red herring,** herring cured and dried by a special process; (*Fig.*) subject deliberately introduced into a discussion to divert criticism from main issue [O.E. *haering*].

hers See **her.**

hes·i·tate (hez′·ạ·tāt) *v.i.* to feel or show indecision; to hold back; to stammer. **hesitant** *a.* pausing; slow to decide. **hesitance, hesitancy** *n.* **hesitation** *n.* doubt; indecision. **hesitantly, hesitatingly** *adv.* [L. *haesitare*, fr. *haerere*, to stick fast].

Hes·per·us (hes′·pẹr·ạs) *n.* the planet Venus as the evening star. **Hesperian** (hes·pē′·ri·-ạn) *a.* western [Gk. *hesperos*, evening].

Hes·sian (he′·shạn) *a.* pert. to *Hesse*, in Germany; *n.* a native of Hesse. **— boots,** high, tasseled boots first worn by Hessian troops.

he·ter·o·dox (het′·ạ·rạ·dȧks) *a.* contrary to

accepted opinion, esp. in theology; not orthodox; heretical. **-y** *n.* [Gk. *heteros*, different; *doxa*, an opinion].

he·ter·o·ge·ne·ous (het·ẹr·ạ·jē′·ni·ạs) *a.* composed of diverse elements; differing in kind; dissimilar. **heterogeneity, -ness** *n.* [Gk. *heteros*, different; *genos*, kind].

het·er·o·gen·e·sis (het·ẹr·ō·jen′·ạ·sis) *n.* (*Biol.*) spontaneous generation. **heterogenetic** *a.* [Gk. *heteros*, different; *genesis*, generation].

he·ter·o·sex·u·al (het·ẹr·ō·sek′·shoo·ạl) *a.* directed towards the opposite sex [Gk. *heteros*, different; L. *sexus*].

hew (hū) *v.t.* to chop or cut with an ax or sword; to cut in pieces; to shape or form. *pa.p.* **-ed** *or* **-n. -er** *n.* [O.E. *heawan*].

hex (hex) *n.* a witch; (*Colloq.*) a jinx.

hex·a- *prefix* from Gk. *hex*, six, combining to form derivatixes, e.g. **-gon** *n.* a plane figure having six sides and six angles. **-gonal** *a.* **-hedron** *n.* solid figures having six faces, e.g. a cube. [Gk. *gōnia*, an angle; *hedra*, a base; L. *angulus*, a corner].

hex·ad (hek′·sad) *n.* a group of six [Gk. *hex*, six].

hex·am·e·ter (hek·sam′·ạ·tẹr) *n.* a verse of six feet [Gk. *hex*, six; *metron*, a measure].

hex·a·pod (hek′·sạ·pȧd) *n.* a six-footed insect [Gk. *hex*, six; *pous*, a foot].

hey (hā) *interj.* used to call attention, or to express joy, wonder, or interrogation. **-day** *n.* the time of fullest strength and greatest vigor.

hi·a·tus (hī·ā′·tạs) *n.* a gap in a series; an opening; a lacuna; the pronunciation without elision of two adjacent vowels in successive syllables [L. fr. *hiare*, to gape].

hi·ber·nate (hī′·bẹr·nāt) *v.i.* to winter; to pass the winter, esp. in a torpid state. **hibernation** *n.* [L. *hibernare*, fr. *hiems*, winter].

Hi·ber·ni·a (hī·bur′·ni·ạ) the Latin name for Ireland. **Hibernian** *a., n.*

Hi·bis·cus (hī·bis′·kạs) *n.* (*Bot.*) a genus of shrubs or tree with large flowers [Gk. *hibiskos*].

hic·cup (hik′·up) *n.* a spasm of the breathing organs with an abrupt cough-like sound; the sound itself; *v.i.* to have this. *pr.p.* **-ping.** *pa.p.* and *pa.t.* **-ped** [of imit. origin].

hick (hik) *n.* (*Slang*) a farmer.

hick·ory (hik′·ạr·i·) *n.* a nut-bearing tree; its tough wood [*pohickery*, native name].

hi·dal·go (hi·dal′·gō) *n.* a Spanish nobleman [Sp. *hijo de algo* = son of something].

hide (hīd) *v.t.* to put or keep out of sight; to keep secret; *v.i.* to lie concealed. *pa.p.* **hidden, hid.** *pa.t.* **hid. hidden** *a.* concealed; secret; unknown. **hiddenly** *adv.* **hiding** *n.* concealment; a place of concealment [O.E. *hydan*].

hide (hīd) *n.* skin of an animal; the dressed skin of an animal; (*Slang*) human skin; *v.t.* (*Colloq.*) to flog. **-bound** *a.* of animals, having the skin too close to the flesh; bigoted; narrow-minded. **hiding** *n.* (*Colloq.*) a flogging [O.E. *hyd*].

hid·e·ous (hid′·ē·ạs) *a.* repulsive; revolting; horrible; frightful. **-ly** *adv.* [Fr. *hideux*].

hie (hī) *v.i.* and *refl.* to go quickly; to hurry on; to urge on [O.E. *higian*, to strive].

hi·er·arch (hī′·ẹr·ȧrk) *n.* one who has authority in sacred things; a chief priest. **-al, -ical** *a.* **-ically** *adv.* **-y** *n.* a graded system of people or things; government by priests; the organization of the priesthood according to different grades; each of the three orders of angels. [Gk. *hieros*, holy; *archein*, to rule].

hi·er·at·ic (hī·ẹr·at′·ik) *a.* priestly; pert. to a cursive style of ancient Egyptian writing, used by the priests [Gk. *hieratikos*, priestly].

hi·er·o- *prefix* from Gk. *hieros*, holy, combining to form derivatives, e.g. **hierograph** *n.* a sacred inscription. **hierology** *n.* the science or study of sacred things, esp. of the writings of the ancient Egyptians.

hi·er·o·glyph·ic (hī·ẹr·ạ·glif′·ik) (usually *pl.*) *n.* ancient Egyptian characters or symbols used in place of letters; picture-writing. Also **hieroglyph. hieroglyphic, hieroglyphical** *a.* [Gk. *hieros*, holy; *gluphein*, to carve].

hig·gle (hig′·l) *v.i.* to dispute about terms, esp. in bargaining [fr. E. *haggle*].

high (hī) *a.* elevated; tall; towering; far up; elevated in rank, etc.; chief; eminent; proud; loud; angry, as words; strongly marked, as color; dear; costly; extreme; sharp, as tone or voice; tainted, as meat; remote from equator, as latitude; (*Colloq.*) drunk; *adv.* far up; strongly; to a great extent. **-ly** *adv.* **-ball** *n.* mixed whisky and soda. **—born** *a.* of noble birth. **-bred** *a.* of superior breeding, thoroughbred. **-brow** *a.* and *n.* (*Colloq.*) intellectual, esp. in a snobbish manner. **—falutin′, —faluting** *a.* pretentious. **—frequency** *n.* (*Radio*) any frequency above the audible range. **—flown** *a.* elevated; extravagant. **-flyer, -flier** *n.* (*Fig.*) an ambitious person. **-lands** *n.pl.* a mountainous region. **Highlander** *n.* an inhabitant of a mountainous region, esp. highlands of Scotland. **-lights** *n.pl* (*Art.*) the brightest parts of a painting; (*Fig.*) moments of crisis; persons of importance. **-ness** *n.* the quality of being high; a title of honor to princes and princesses. **-pitched** *a.* of a shrill sound. **-road** *n.* a main road. **— school, a** school (grades 9 through 12), following grammar school; a school (grades 10 through 12), following junior high school (grades 7 through 9); **— seas,** the sea or ocean beyond the three-mile belt of coastal waters. **-spirited** *a.* bold; daring. **—strung** *a.* in a state of tension. **— treason,** any breach of allegiance due from a citizen to the government. **— water** *n.* a high tide at which the tide reaches its highest elevation. **-way** *n.* a main road; a public road; an ordinary route. **-wayman** *n.* a robber on a public road, esp. a mounted one [O.E. *heah*].

hi·jack·er (hī′·jak·ẹr) *n.* (*Slang*) one who robs; a smuggler or a bootlegger.

hike (hīk) *v.i.* to walk; to tramp; *v.t.* to hoist or carry on one's back; *n.* a journey on foot. **-r** *n.*

hi·lar·i·ous (hi·la′·ri·ạs) *a.* mirthful; joyous. **-ly** *adv.* **hilarity** *n.* merriment; boisterous joy [Gk. *hilaros*, cheerful].

hill (hil) *n.* a natural elevation of land; a small mountain; a mound; *v.t.* to heap up. **-y** *a.* full of hills. **-iness** *n.* **-ock** *n.* a small hill [O.E. *hyll*].

hilt (hilt) *n.* the handle of a sword, dagger, etc. [O.E. *hilt*].

him (him) *pron.* the objective case of the pronoun **he. -self** *pron.* emphatic and reflexive form of **he** and **him** [O.E.].

hind (hīnd) *n.* the female of the deer.

hind, hind·er (hīnd, hīnd′·ẹr) *a.* at the back; placed at the back; a combining form in such words as **-leg. -most** *a.* the furtherest behind; the last [O.E. *hinder*].

hin·der (hin′·dẹr) *v.t.* to prevent from progressing; to stop. **-er** *n.* **hindrance** *n.* the act of impeding progress; obstruction; obstacle [O.E. *hindrian*, to keep back].

Hin·du·stan (hind′·doo·stan) *n.* (*Geog.*) the name applied to the country of the upper valley of the R. Ganges, India. **Hindi, Hindes** (hin′·dē) *n.* an Indo-Germanic language spoken in N. India. **Hindu, Hindoo** (hin′·dȯȯ) *n.* a native of Hindustan. **Hindustani, Hindoostanee** *n.* chief language of Hindu India; also known as 'Urdu' [Urdu, *Hind*, India].

hinge (hinj) *n.* a movable joint, as that on which a door, lid, etc. hangs; point on which thing depends; *v.t.* to attach with, or as with a hinge; *v.i.* to turn on; to depend on [M.E. *heng*].

hint (hint) *n.* a slight allusion; an indirect suggestion; an indication; *v.t.* and *i.* to allude to indirectly [O.E. *hentan*, to seize].

hin·ter·land (hint′·ẹr·land) *n.* the district inland from the coast or a river [Ger.].
hip (hip) *n.* the upper part of the thigh; the haunch; the angle of 2 sloping sides of a roof; *interj.* a cheer [O.E. *hype*].
hip (hip) *n.* the fruit of the rose, esp. of the wild-rose [O.E. *heope*].
hip·ped (hipt) *a.* (*Slang*) obsessed (with *on*) [corrupt. of *hypochondria*].
Hip·poc·ra·tes (hi·pȧk′·rạ·tēz) *n.* a Greek physician, the 'Father of Medicine,' born about 460 B.C. **Hippocratic** *a.* pert. to him.
hip·po·drome (hip′·ạ·drōm) *n.* in ancient Greece and Rome, a stadium for horse and chariot races; an arena [Gk. *hippos*, a horse; *dromos*, a course].
hip·po·pot·a·mus (hip·ạ·pȧt′·ạ·mạs) *n.* a very large pachydermatous African quadruped frequenting rivers. *pl.* **-es** or **hippopotami** (hip·ạ·pȧt′·ạ·mī) [Gk. *hippos*, a horse; *potamos*, a river].
hir·cine (hur′·sīn) *a.* pert. to a goat; strong-smelling (like a goat) [L. *hircus*, a goat].
hire (hīr) *n.* payment for the use of a thing; wages; a hiring or being hired; *v.t.* to pay for the use of a thing; to contract with for wages; to take care or give on hire. **-r** *n.* **-ling** *n.* one who serves for wages (generally used in contempt) [O.E. *hur*, wages].
hir·sute (hur′·so͝ot) *a.* hairy; (*Bot.*) set with bristles [L. *hirsutus*, hairy].
his (hiz) *pron.* and *a.* the possessive case of the pronoun **he,** belonging to him [O.E.].
his·pid (his′·pid) *a.* (*Bot.*) bristly; having rough hairs [L. *hispidus*, rough].
hiss (his) *v.i.* to make a sound like that of *ss* as in 'ass,' esp. to express strong dislike or disapproval; *n.* the sound. **-ing** *n.* [imit.].
hist (hist) *interj.* a word used to command attention or silence.
his·ta·mine (his′·ta·mēn) *n.* substance released by the tissues in allergic reactions [*histidine* + *amine*].
his·to- *prefix* from Gk. *histos*, a web or tissue, combining to form derivatives, e.g.—**histology** (his·tȧl′·ạ·ji·) *n.* the science that treats of the minute structure of the tissues of animals, plants, etc. [Gk. *histos*, tissue; *logos*, a discourse].
his·to·ry (his′·tạ·ri·) *n.* the study of past events; a record of events in the life of a nation, state, institution, epoch, etc.; a description of animals, plants, minerals, etc. existing on the earth, called **natural history. historian** (his·tō′·ri·ạn) *n.* a writer of history. **historic** *a.* pert. to, or noted in, history. **historical** *a.* of, or based on, history; belonging to the past. **historically** *adv.* **historicity** *n.* the historical character of an event; the genuineness of it [Gk. *historia*, an inquiry].
his·tri·on·ic (his·trē·ȧn′·ik) *a.* theatrical; affected. **-al** *a.* **-ally** *adv.* **-s** *n.pl.* theatrical representation [L. *histrio*, an actor].
hit (hit) *v.t.* to strike with a blow or missile; to affect severely; to find; *v.i.* to strike; to light (upon). *pr.p.* **-ting.** *pa.p.* and *pa.t.* **hit.** *n.* a blow; a stroke; a success [O.E. *hyttan*].
hitch (hich) *v.t.* to raise or move with a jerk; to fasten with a loop; etc.; to harness; *v.i.* to be caught or fastened; *n.* a jerk; a fastening, loop, or knot; a difficulty; (*Slang*) to marry. **-er** *n.* **to -hike,** to travel by begging rides from motorists, etc. [etym. uncertain].
hith·er (hiTH′·ẹr) *adv.* to or toward this place; *a.* situated on this side. **-most** *a.* nearest in this direction. **-to** *adv.* up to now [O.E. *hider*].
hive (hīv) *n.* a place where bees live; place of great activity; *v.t.* to gather or place bees in a hive; *v.i.* to enter a hive; to take shelter together; to live in company [O.E. *hyf*].
hives (hīvz) *n.* an eruptive skin disease.
hoar (hōr) *a.* gray with age; grayish-white. **-y** *a.* white or gray with age; venerable; of great antiquity. **-frost** *n.* white frost; frozen dew [O.E. *har*].
hoard (hōrd) *n.* a stock or store, esp. if hidden away; a treasure; *v.t.* to store secretly; *v.i.* to lay up a store. **-er** *n.* [O.E. *hord*, treasure].
hoarse (hōrs) *a.* rough and harsh sounding; husky; having a hoarse voice. **-ly** *adv.* **-ness** *n.* [O.E. *has*].
hoax (hōks) *v.t.* to deceive by an amusing or mischievous story; to play a trick upon for sport; *n.* a practical joke. **-er** *n.* [contr. fr. *hocus*].
hob (hȧb) *n.* the flat-topped casing of a fireplace where things are placed to be kept warm. **-nail** *n.* a large-headed nail for boot soles.
hob (hȧb) *n.* an elf; (*Colloq.*) mischief. **-goblin** *n.* a mischievous elf; a bogy [corrupt. of *Robin* or *Robert*].
hob·ble (hȧb′·l) *v.i.* to walk lamely; to limp; *v.t.* to tie the legs together of a horse, etc.; to impede; *n.* a limping gait; a fetter; a rope for hobbling [etym. uncertain].
hob·ble·de·hoy (hȧb′·l·di·hoi) *n.* a clumsy youth [etym. uncertain, perh. fr. *hobble*].
hob·by (hȧb′·i·) *n.* formerly a small horse; a favorite pursuit or pastime. **-horse** *n.* a stick with a horse's head, or a rocking horse used as a child's toy; at fairs, etc. a wooden horse on a merry-go-round [*Hob*, for *Robert*].
hob·nail See **hob.**
hob·nob (hȧb′·nȧb) *v.i.* to drink together; to be very friendly with [etym. uncertain].
ho·bo (hō′·bō) *n.* a vagrant; a tramp.
hock (hȧk) *n.* the joint of a quadruped's hind leg between the knee and the fetlock [O.E. *hoh*, the heel].
hock (hȧk) *v.t.*, *n.* pawn [D. *hok*, debt].
hock·ey (hȧk′·i·) *n.* a game played with a ball or disk and curved sticks [perh. fr. O.Fr. *hoquet*, a crook].
ho·cus (hō′·kạs) *v.i.* to hoax; to stupefy with drugs. **hocus-pocus** *n.* an incantation; a juggler's trick; trickery [a sham L. formula used by jugglers].
hod (hȧd) *n.* a small trough on a staff used by builders for carrying mortar, bricks, etc. [Fr. *hotte*, a basket].
hodge-podge (hȧj′·pȧj) *n.* a medley or mixture. Also **hotchpotch** [fr. *hocher*, to shake; *pot*, a pot].
hoe (hō) *n.* a tool for breaking ground, scraping out weeds, etc.; *v.t.* to break up or weed with a hoe. **-r** *n.* [O.Fr. *houe*].
hoe·down (hō′·doun) *n.* lively square dance.
hog (hawg, hȧg) *n.* a swine; a pig, esp. if reared for fattening; (*Colloq.*) a greedy or dirty fellow; *v.t.* (*Slang*) to take more than one's share of; to cut (horse's mane short); *v.i.* to arch the back. **-gish** *a.* like a hog. **-back, -s-back** *n.* a crested hill-ridge. **-tie** *v.* (*Colloq.*) to make incapable as if by tying up. **-wash** *n.* kitchen swill etc. used for feeding pigs; anything worthless [O.E. *hogg*].
hogs·head (hawgz′·, hȧgz′·hed; hawgz′·ạd) *n.* a large cask; a liquid measure [etym uncertain].
hoi pol·loi (hoi′·pạ·loi′) *n.pl.* the masses [Obs.].
hoist (hoist) *v.t.* to raise aloft, esp. of flags; to raise with tackle, etc.; *n.* a hoisting; an elevator; a lift [Dut. *hijschen*, to hoist].
hold (hōld) *v.t.* to keep fast; to grasp; to support in or with the hands, etc.; to own; to occupy; to detain; to celebrate; to believe; to contain; *v.i.* to cling; not to give way; to abide (by); to keep (to); to proceed; to be in force. *pa.p.* and *pa.t.* **held.** *n.* a grasp; grip; handle; binding power and influence; a prison. **-er** *n.* **-ing** *n.* land, farm, etc. rented from another; stocks held. **to hold up,** to support; to cause delay; to obstruct; to commit robbery with threats of violence [O.E. *healdan*].

hold (hōld) *n.* the space below the deck of a ship, for cargo [earlier *hole*].

hole (hōl) *n.* a hollow; cavity; pit; den; lair; burrow; opening; a perforation; mean habitation; (*Colloq.*) awkward situation; *v.t.* to make a hole in; to perforate; to put into a hole; *v.i.* to go into a hole [O.E. *hol*, a hollow].

hol·i·day (hȧl′·ą·dā) *n.* a day of rest from work esp. in memory of an event or a person [fr. *holy day*].

Hol·land·er (hȧl′·ąn·dẹr) *n.* a native of Holland, the Netherlands.

hol·ler (hȧl′·ẹr) *v.* (*Dial.*) shout; yell.

hol·low (hȧl′·ō) *n.* a cavity; a hole; a depression; a valley; *a.* having a cavity; not solid; empty; *v.t.* to make a hollow in. **—eyed** *a.* with sunken eyes. **—toned** *a.* deep toned. **-ware** *n.* silver serving dishes [O.E. *holh*].

hol·ly (hȧl′·i·) *n.* an evergreen shrub with prickly leaves and red berries [O.E. *holegn*].

hol·ly·hock (hȧl′·ē·hȧk) *n.* a tall garden plant [A.S. = *holy hock*, O.E. *hoc*, mallow].

hol·o- a combining form, fr. Gk. *holos*, whole, used in many derivatives. **-caust** (hȧl′·ą·kawst) *n.* a burnt offering; destruction, or slaughter. **-graph** *n.* and *a.* any writing, as a letter, deed, will, etc. wholly in the handwriting of the signer of it. **-graphic** *a.* [Gk. *kaustos*, burnt; *graphein*, to write]. [tol. **-ed** *a.* [Dut.].

hol·ster (hōl′·stẹr) *n.* a leather case for a pis-

ho·ly (hō′·li·) *a.* belonging to, or devoted to, God; morally perfect; divine; sacred; pious; religious. **holily** *adv.* **holiness** *n.* the quality of being holy. **— day** *n.* a religious festival. **Holy Ghost, Holy Spirit,** the third person of the Godhead or Trinity. **Holy Land,** Palestine. **— orders** *n.* the office of a clergyman; the Christian ministry [O.E. *halig*].

hom·age (hȧm′·ij, ȧm′·ij) *n.* in feudal times, service due by a vassal to his over-lord; tribute; respect paid; reverence; deference [Fr. *hommage*, fr. *homme*, a man].

hom·burg (hȧm′·burg) *n.* a type of men's soft, felt hat [fr. *Homburg*, in Germany].

home (hōm) *n.* one's fixed residence; a dwelling-place; a native place or country; an institution for the infirm, sick, poor, etc.; *a.* pert. to, or connected with, home; not foreign; domestic; *adv.* to or at one's home; to the point aimed at; close. **— economics** *n.pl.*, theory and practice of homemaking. **-lessness** *n.* the state of being without a home. **-ly** *a.* belonging to home; plain; ugly. **-liness** *n.* **—grown** *a.* grown in one's own garden, locality, etc. **-land** *n.* one's native land. **—made** *a.* made at home. **— rule** *n.* self-government. **— run** *n.* (*Baseball*) a safe hit that allows a batter to touch all bases to score a run. **-sick** *a.* depressed in spirits through absence from home. **-sickness** *n.* **-spun** *a.* spun or made at home; anything plain or homely. **-stead** *n.* a house with land and buildings. **— stretch** *n.* on a race-course, the part between the last curve and the finish line; the final stage. **-work** *n.* schoolwork to be done outside of class. [O.E. *ham*].

home (hōm) *v.i.* of a pigeon, to fly home; *v.t.* in naval warfare, to guide (another ship or aircraft) by radio to the attack of a target.

ho·me·op·a·thy (hō·mē·ȧp′·ą·thi·) *n.* the treatment of disease by the administration of very small doses of drugs which would produce in a healthy person effects similar to the symptoms of the disease. Also **homeotherapy. homeopath, homeopathist** *n.* **homeopathic** *a.* [Gk. *homoios*, like; *pathos*, feeling].

hom·i·cide (hȧm′·ą·sīd) *n.* manslaughter; the one who kills. **homicidal** *a.* [L. *homo*, a man; *caedere*, to kill].

hom·i·ly (hȧm′·ą·li·) *n.* a discourse on a religious or moral subject; a sermon. **homilist** *n.* [Gk. *homilia*, converse].

hom·i·ny (hȧm′·ą·ni·) *n.* maize porridge [Amer.-Ind.].

ho·mo- a combining form fr. Gk. *homos*, the same. **-centric** *a.* having the same center.

ho·moe·o·path. See **homeopathy.**

ho·mog·e·ne·ous (hō·mą·jē′·ni·ąs) *a.* of the same kind or nature; similar; uniform. **-ness, homogeneity** (hō·mą·ją·nē′·ą·ti·) *n.* sameness; uniformity. **homogenize** *v.* to make uniform [Gk. *homo*, the same; *genos*, a kind].

hom·o·graph (hȧm′·ą·graf) *n.* a word having the same spelling as another, but different meaning, origin, and/or pronunciation [Gk. *homos*, the same; *graphein*, to write].

ho·mol·o·gate (hō·mȧl′·ą·gāt) *v.t.* to approve; to confirm. **homologous** *a.* having the same relative value, position, etc. **homologation** *n.* [Gk. *homos*, the same; *legein*, to say].

hom·o·nym (hȧm′·ą·nim) *n.* a word having the same pronunciation as another but a different meaning, e.g. *air* and *heir*. Also **homophone** [Gk. *homos*, the same; *onoma*, a name].

ho·mo sa·pi·ens (hō′·mō·sā′·pi·ąns) *n.* scientific term for human being, man.

ho·mo·sex·u·al·i·ty (hō·mą·sek·shoo·al′·ą·ti·) *n.* sexual attraction to persons of the same sex. **homosexual** *n., a.* [Gk. *homos*, the same; and *sex*].

hone (hōn) *n.* a stone for sharpening knives, etc.; *v.t.* to sharpen on one [O.E. *han*, a stone].

hon·est (ȧn′·ist) *a.* upright; dealing fairly; just; faithful; free from fraud; unadulterated. **-ly** *adv.* **-y** *n.* upright conduct or disposition; (*Bot.*) a small flowering plant with semi-transparent, silvery pods [L. *homestus*, honorable].

hon·ey (hun′·i·) *n.* the sweet, thick fluid collected by bees from flowers; anything very sweet; sweetness; (*Colloq.*) sweetheart; darling; *a.* sweet; luscious; *v.t.* to sweeten. *pa.p., a.* **-ed** (hun′·id). **honied** *a.* sweet; (*Fig.*) flattering. **-bee** *n.* the common hive-bee. **-comb** *n.* the structure of wax in hexagonal cells in which bees place honey, eggs, etc.; anything resembling this; *v.t.* to fill with cells or perforations. **-combed** *a.* **-dew** (hun′·i·dū) *n.* a sweet sticky substance found on plants; a melon. **-moon** *n.* the holiday taken by a newly-wed couple; *v.i.* **-suckle** *n.* a climbing plant with yellow flowers [O.E. *hunig*].

honk (hawngk) *n.* the cry of the wild goose; any sound resembling this [imit.].

honk·y-tonk (hȧng′·ki·tȧngk) *n.* (*Slang*) a cheap saloon [echoic].

hon·or (ȧn′·ẹr) *n.* high respect; renown; glory; reputation; sense of what is right or due; a source or cause of honor; high rank or position; a title of respect given to a judge, etc.; chastity; *v.t.* to respect highly; to confer a mark of distinction on; to accept or pay (a bill, etc.) when due. **-s** *n.pl.* public marks of respect or distinction; distinction given a student for outstanding work. **-able** *a.* worthy of honor; upright; a title of distinction or respect. **-ably** *adv.* **-ableness** *n.* **an affair of —** *n.* a duel. **maid of —** *n.* a lady in the service of a queen or princess; chief attendant of a bride [Fr. *honneur*, fr. L. *honor*].

hon·or·ary (ȧn′·ą·rer·i·) *a.* conferred for the sake of honor only; holding a position without pay or usual requirements. **honorarium** (ȧn·ą·re′·ri·ąm) *n.* a sum of money granted voluntarily to a person for services rendered. **honorific** *a.* conferring honor; *n.* term of respect [L. *honorarius*].

hooch (hȯȯch) *n.* (*Slang*) alcoholic liquor [fr. Amer. Ind. *hoochinoo*].

hood (hood) *n.* a covering for the head and neck, often part of a cloak or gown; an appendage to a graduate's gown designating his university and degree; the cover of an automobile engine; a hoodlum; *v.t.* to cover with a hood. **-wink** *v.t.* to blindfold; to deceive [O.E. *hod*].

hood·lum (hȯȯd′·ląm) *n.* a holligan.

hoo·doo (hòò′·dòò) (*Colloq.*) *n.* uncanny, bad luck; a cause of such luck [same as voodoo].

hoo·ey (hòò′·i·) *interj., n.* (*Slang*) nonsense.

hoof (hoof, hòòf) *n.* the horny casing of the foot of a horse, ox, sheep, etc.; *pl.* **-s, hooves** [O.E.]

hook (hook) *n.* a bent piece of metal, etc. for catching hold, hanging up, etc.; a bent piece of barbed steel for catching fish; anything curved or bent like a hook; *v.t.* and *i.* to fasten, draw, catch, etc. with a hook; to catch a fish with a hook; (*Golf*) to drive a ball in a curve to the left; (*Boxing*) to deliver a blow with bent elbow. **hooks and eyes,** bent metallic clips and catches used for fastening. **-up** *n.* the interconnection of broadcasting stations for relaying program; a connection [O.E. *hoc*].

hook·ah, hoo·ka (hoo′·ką) *n.* a tobacco pipe in which the smoke is drawn through water and a long tube [Ar. *huqqah*, a vessel].

hook·worm (hook′·wurm) *n.* (*Med.*) a parasitic worm, infesting the intestines.

hoo·li·gan (hòòl′·i·gąn) *n.* one of a gang of street roughs; a rowdy [name of a person].

hoop (hoop, hòòp) *n.* a band for holding together the staves of casks, etc.; a circle of wood or metal for rolling as a toy; a stiff circular band to hold out a woman's skirt; *v.t.* to bind with a hoop. [O.E. *hop*].

hoot (hòòt) *n.* the cry of an owl; a cry of disapproval; *v.t.* to assail with hoots; *v.i.* to cry as an owl; to cry out in disapproval. **-er** *n.* [imit.].

hooves (hoovz, hòòvz) *pl.* of **hoof.**

hop (hȧp) *v.i.* of persons, to spring on one foot; of animals or birds, to leap or skip on all feet at once. *pr.p.* **-ping.** *pa.p.* and *pa.t.* **-ped.** *n.* an act or the action of hopping; (*Slang*) a dance; (*Aviation*) one stage in a flight. **-per** *n.* one who hops; a device for feeding material into a mill or machine; a railroad car with dumping device for coal, sand, etc. **hop-o-my-thumb** *n.* a dwarf [O.E. *hoppian*].

hop (hȧp) *n.* a climbing plant with bitter cones used to flavor beer, etc.; *v.t.* to flavor with hops. **-s** *n.pl.* the cones of the hop plant [Dut.].

hope (hōp) *n.* a desire combined with expectation gives grounds for hoping; thing desired; *v.t.* to desire, with belief in possibility of obtaining; *v.i.* to feel hope. **-ful** *a.* **-fully** *adv.* **-fulness** *n.* **-less** *a.* **-lessly** *adv.* [O.E. *hopian*].

hop·scotch (hȧp′·skȧch) *n.* a child's game, played on an arrangement of squares [E. *hop; scotch,* a slight cut or score].

ho·ral (hō′·rąl) *a.* of or pert. to an hour; hourly [L. *hora*, an hour].

horde (hōrd) *n.* a great multitude; a troop of nomads or tent-dwellers [Turk. *ordu*, a camp].

hore·hound (hōr′·hound) *n.* a plant with bitter juice, used for coughs or as a tonic; a candy flavored with the herb. Also **hoarhound** [O.E. *harehune*].

ho·ri·zon (hą·rī′·ząn) *n.* the boundary of the part of the earth seen from any given point; the line where earth (or sea) and sky seem to meet. **horizontal** (hąr·ą·zȧn′·tąl) *a.* parallel to the horizon; level. **horizontally** *adv.* [Gk. *horizein*, to bound].

hor·mone (hawr′·mōn) *n.* a substance secreted by certain glands which passes into the blood and stimulates the action of various organs [Gk. *hormaein*, to set moving].

horn (hawrn) *n.* a hard projecting organ growing from heads of cows, deer, etc.; substance forming this organ; tentacle of a snail, etc.; a wind instrument of music; a drinking cup; a utensil for holding gunpowder; a sounding contrivance on motors as warning; either of the extremities of the crescent moon; *v.t.* to furnish with horns; to gore. **-y** *a.* of, or made of, horn; hard or callous. **-beam** *n.* a small tree or shrub. **-book** *n.* a primer for children, formerly covered with horn to protect it. **-pipe** *n.* an old musical instrument; a vigorous dance; the lively tune for such a dance. **horn of plenty,** or cornucopia; a representation of a horn, filled with flowers, fruit and grain [O.E.].

hor·net (hawr′·nąt) *n.* a large insect of the wasp family [O.E. *hyrnet*, dim. of *horn*].

ho·ro- from Gk. *hōra*, time; used as a combining form, e.g.—**horologe** (hawr′·ą·lōj) *n.* an instrument of any kind for telling the time. **horologer, horologist** *n.* **horology** *n.* the science of measuring time; the art of making timepieces [Gk. *hōra*, time; *legein*, to tell; *metron*, a measure].

hor·o·scope (hȧr′, hawr′·ą·skōp) *n.* a chart of of the heavens which predicts the character and potential abilities of the individual as well as future events. **horoscopic** *a.* [Gk. *hōra*, time; *skopein*, to observe].

hor·rent (hawr′·ąnt) *a.* (*Poet.*) standing erect, as bristles; bristling [L. *horrere*, to bristle].

hor·ri·ble (hȧr′, hawr′·ą·bl) *a.* tending to excite horror, fear, dread. **horribly** *adv.* **-ness** *n.* **horrid** *a.* frightful; shocking; abominable. **horrify** *v.t.* to strike with horror, dread, repulsion; to shock. **horrific** (hȧ, haw·rif′·ik) *a.* causing horror [L. *horrere*, to bristle].

hor·ror (hȧ′, haw′·ręr) *n.* a painful emotion of fear, dread and repulsion; that which excites dread and abhorrence [L. from *horrere*, to bristle].

horse (hawrs) *n.* a large hoofed quadruped used for riding, drawing vehicles, etc.; the male of the horse species, as distinct from the female (the mare); mounted soldiers; in gymnastics, a vaulting-block; a frame for drying clothes; *v.t.* to provide with a horse, or horses; to carry or support on the back; *v.i.* to mount on a horse. **horsy** *a.* pert. to horses; fond of, or interested in, horses. **horsiness** *n.* **-back** *n.* the back of a horse. **-fly** *n.* a stinging fly troublesome to horses. **-hair** *n.* hair from the tail or mane of a horse; haircloth. **-laugh** *n.* a loud boisterous laugh. **-leech** *n.* a large kind of leech.**-man** *n.* a man on horseback; a skilled rider. **-manship** *n.* the art of riding or of training horses. **— opera** (*Film Slang*) a thriller film with a Wild West setting. **-pistol** *n.* an old kind of large pistol. **-play** *n.* rough and boisterous play. **-power** *n.* (abbrev. **h.p.**), the power a horse is capable of exerting; estimated (in *Mechanics*) to be the power of lifting 33,000 lb. one foot high in one minute. **-radish** *n.* a cultivated plant used for sauces, salads, etc. **-sense** *n.* (*Colloq.*) common sense. **-shoe** *n.* a curved, narrow band of iron for nailing to the underpart of the hoof [O.E. *hors*].

hor·ta·tive, hor·ta·tory (hawr′·tą·tiv, hawr′·tą·tō·ri·) *a.* tending or serving to exhort; advisory [L. *hortari*, to exhort].

hor·ti·cul·ture (hawr′·ti·kul·chęr) *n.* gardening; the art of cultivating a garden [L. *hortus, garden; colere,* to cultivate].

ho·san·na (hō·zan′·ą) *n.* a cry of praise to God; an exclamation of adoration [Gk.].

hose (hōz) *n.* stockings; socks; a covering for the legs and feet; tight-fitting breeches or pants; a flexible tube or pipe for conveying water; *v.t.* to water with a hose. **hosier** (hō′·zhęr) *n.* dealer in hosiery. **hosiery** *n.* a collective word for stockings and similar garments [O.E. *hosa*].

hos·pice (hȧs′·pis) *n.* a traveler's house of rest kept by a religious order [L. *hospitium*, fr. *hospes*, a guest].

hos·pi·ta·ble (hȧs′·pi·tą·bl) *a.* receiving and entertaining guests in a friendly and liberal fashion. **hospitality** *n.* generous reception of strangers and guests [L. *hospes*, a guest].

hos·pi·tal (hȧs′·pi·tal) *n.* an institution for the care of the sick. **-ization** *n.* being in the hospital. **-ize** *v.t.* [L. *hospes*, a guest].

host (hōst) *n.* one who lodges or entertains another; an innkeeper; an animal or plant which has parasites living on it. **-ess** *n.* a woman who entertains guests. **hostel** (hás′·-tạl) *n.* a lodging place for young people who are hiking or traveling by bicycle; (*Arch.*) an inn. **hostelry** *n.* (*Arch.*) an inn [L. *hospes,* a host or guest].

host (hōst) *n.* a large number; a multitude; a crowd; (*Arch.*) an army. **the heavenly host,** the angels and archangels; the stars and planets [L. *hostis,* an enemy].

Host (hōst) *n.* the bread consecrated in the Eucharist [L. *hostia,* a sacrificial victim].

hos·tage (hás′·tij) *n.* one handed over to the enemy as security [O.Fr. *hostage,* fr. L. *hospes,* a guest].

hos·tel See **host.**

hos·tile (hás′·tạl) *a.* of, or pert. to, an enemy; unfriendly; opposed. **-ly** *adv.* **hostility** *n.* opposition; *pl.* state or acts of warfare [L. *hostis,* an enemy].

hos·tler, ostler (hás′·lẹr, ás′·lẹr) *n.* (*Arch.*) a groom at an inn [O.Fr. *hostel*].

hot (hát) *a.* of high temperature; very warm; of quick temper; ardent or passionate; (of dance music) florid and intricate. **-ly** *adv.* **-ness** *n.* **-bed** *n.* in gardening, a glass-covered bed for bringing on plants quickly; hence (*Fig.*) any place conducive to quick growth (e.g. of scandal, vice, etc.). **—blooded** *a.* high-spirited; quick to anger. **— dog** *n.* (*Colloq.*) a sandwich roll with hot sausage inside. **-foot** *adv.* swiftly; in great haste. **-head** *n.* an impetuous person. **-house** *n.* heated house, usually of glass for rearing of plants [O.E. *hat*].

ho·tel (hō·tel′) *n.* a large and superior kind of inn. **-keeper** *n.* [Fr. *hotel*].

Hot·ten·tot (hát′·n·tát) *n.* a member of a native race of S. Africa [Dut. imit.].

hound (hound) *n.* a dog used in hunting, esp. in hunting by scent; (*Slang*) despicable man; (*Slang*) an addict or fan; *v.t.* to chase with, or as with, hounds; (with 'on') to urge or incite; to pursue, to nag [O.E. *hund*].

hour (our) *n.* the twenty-fourth part of a day, or 60 minutes; the time of day; an appointed time or occasion; *pl.* the fixed times of work, prayers, etc. **-glass** *n.* a sand-glass running for an hour. **— hand** *n.* the index which shows the hour on the face of a watch, clock, or chronometer. **-ly** *adv.* happening every hour; frequently [L. *hora*].

hou·ri (hòò′·ri; hou′·ri·) *n.* a nymph of the Mohammedan paradise [Pers. *huri*].

house (hous) *n.* a dwelling-place; a legislative or other assembly; a family; a business firm; audience at theater, etc.; dynasty; a school residence hall. *pl.* **houses** (houz′·ạs). **house** (houz) *v.t.* to shelter; to receive; to store; *v..i* to dwell. **housing** (hou′·zing) *n.* shelter; the providing of houses; a support for part of a machine, etc. **-ful** *n.* **-less** *a.* **-hold** *n.* the inmates of a house; *a.* domestic. **-keeper** *n.* the woman who attends to the care of the household. **-wife** *n.* the mistress of a family; a little case or bag for materials used in sewing. **-wifery** (hous′·wīf·ri·) *n.* housekeeping. **-boat** *n.* a flat-bottomed barge, with a houselike superstructure. **—fly** *n.* the common fly or *musca domestica.* **— physician, — surgeon** *n.* the resident medical officer of a hospital, etc. **-warming** *n.* a merrymaking to celebrate entry into a new house. **the House,** the House of Representatives [O.E. *hus*].

hous·ing (hou′·zing) *n.* a saddle-cloth; *pl.* the trappings of a horse [Fr. *housse*].

hove (hōv) *pa.p.* and *pa.t.* of **heave.**

hov·el (huv′·ạl, háv′·ạl) *n.* a small, mean house; *v.t.* to put in a hovel [dim. of O.E. *hof,* a dwelling].

hov·er (huv′·ẹr, háv′·ẹr) *v.i.* to hang fluttering in the air, or on the wing; to loiter; to waver.

how (hou) *adv.* in what manner; by what means; to what degree or extent; in what condition. **-beit** (hou·bē′·it) *adv.* nevertheless. **-ever** (hou·ev′·ẹr) *adv.* in whatever manner or degree; *conj.* in spite of how. **-soever** *adv.* however [O.E. *hu*].

how·itz·er (hou′·it·sẹr) *n.* a form of gun, with a high trajectory [Bohemian *houfnice,* an engine for hurling stones].

howl (houl) *v.i.* to utter a prolonged, wailing cry such as that of a wolf or dog; to cry; (*Colloq.*) to laugh heartily; *v.i.* to utter with howling; *n.* a wail or cry. **-er** *n.* one who howls; (*Colloq.*) a ridiculous blunder [imit. origin].

hoy·den, hoiden (hoi′·dn) *n.* a rude, bold girl; a tomboy. **-ish** *a.* romping; bold; boisterous.

hub (hub) *n.* the central part, or nave, of a wheel; center of activity [var. of *hob*].

hub·bub (hub′·ub) *n.* a commotion [imit.].

hub·by (hub′·i·) *n.* (*Colloq.*) husband.

huck·a·back (huk′·ạ·bak) *n.* a kind of coarse linen with an uneven surface, much used for towels. Also **huck** [L. Ger. *hukkebak*].

huck·le·ber·ry (huk′·l·ber·i·) *n.* an American shrub which bears small black or dark blue berries [O.E. *heorot-berge*].

huck·le·bone (huk′·l·bōn) *n.* the hipbone; the anklebone [dim. of *huck,* hook].

huck·ster (huk′·stẹr) *n.* retailer of small articles; a street peddler; a mean, mercenary fellow; (*Colloq.*) an advertising man; *v.i.* to peddle [O.Dut. *hoekster*].

hud·dle (hud′·l) *v.t.* to crowd together; to heap together confusedly; *v.i.* to press together. **to go into a huddle with** (*Slang*) to meet in conference with [etym. uncertain].

hue (hū) *n.* color; tint.**-d** *a.* having a color (generally in compounds) [O.Fr. *hiw*].

hue (hū) *n.* an outcry; now only used in **hue and cry,** a loud outcry [Fr. *huer,* to hoot].

huff (huf) *n.* a fit of petulance or anger; *v.t.* to bully; *v.i.* to take offense. **-y** *a.*

hug (hug) *v.t.* to clasp tightly in the arms; to embrace; to cling to. *pr.p.* **-ging.** *pa.t., pa.p.* **-ged.** *n.* a close embrace [etym. uncertain].

huge (hūj) *a.* very large; immense; enormous. **-ly** *adv.* **-ness** *n.* [O.Fr. *ahuge*].

Hu·gue·not (hū′·gạ·nát) *n.* a 16th cent. French Protestant [etym. uncertain].

huh (hu) *interj.* expressing contempt, surprise or to ask a question.

hu·la (hoo′·lạ) *n.* native Hawaiian dance.

hulk (hulk) *n.* the body of a ship, esp. dismantled ship; anything big and unwieldy; *v.i.* to be bulky; (*Dial.*) to slouch. **-ing, -y** *a.* unwieldy; clumsy [O.E. *hulc,* ship].

hull (hul) *n.* husk of any fruit, seed, or grain; frame or body of a vessel; *v.t.* to remove shell or husk; to pierce hull of, as of a ship [O.E. *hulu,* husk].

hul·la·ba·loo (hul′·ạ·bạ·lòò) *n.* uproar; outcry [imit. origin].

hul·lo, hul·loa (hạ·lō′) *niterj.* hello.

hum (hum) *v.t.* to sing with the lips closed; *v.i.* to make droning sound, as bee. *n.* the noise of bees or the like; a low droning; (*Colloq.*) to be very busy. *pr.p.* **-ming.** *pa.p.* and *pa.t.* **-med** [imit. origin].

hu·man (hū′·mạn) *a.* belonging to, or having the qualities of, man or mankind. **-ly** *adv.* **-ness** *n.* **humane** (hū·mān′) *a.* having the moral qualities of man; kind; benevolent. **-ness** *n.* **-ism** *n.* a philosophic mode of thought devoted to human interests; literary culture. **-ist** *n.* one who pursues the study of human nature or the humanities. **-istic** *a.* pert. to humanity; pert. to humanism or humanists. **-ize** *v.t.* to render human or humane. **humanity** *n.* the quality of being human; human nature; the human race; kindness or benevolence. **humanities** *n.pl.* language, literature, art, philosophy, etc. **humanitarian** *n.* one who denies the divinity of Jesus; a philanthropist. **-kind** *n.* the whole race of man [L. *humanus*].

hum·ble (hum′·bl) *a.* lowly; meek; not proud, arrogant, or assuming; modest; *v.t.* to bring low; to make meek. **humbly** *adv.* **-ness** *n.* [L. *humilis*, fr. *humus*, the ground].

hum·bug (hum′·bug) *n.* a hoax; sham; nonsense; an impostor; *v.t.* to hoax; to deceive.

hum·drum (hum′·drum) *a.* commonplace; dull [redupl. of *hum*, imit. of monotony].

hu·mer·al (hū′·mẹr·ạl) *a.* belonging to the shoulder. **humerus** *n.* the long bone of the upper arm [L. *humerus*, the shoulder].

hu·mid (hū′·mid) *a.* damp; moist. **-ly** *adv.* **humidify** *v.t.* to make humid. **humidity, -ness** *n.* dampness; moisture. **humidor** *n.* a device for keeping the air moist in a jar, case, etc., such a case. [L. *humidus*, moist].

hu·mil·i·ate (hū·mil′·i·āt) *v.t.* to humble; to lower the dignity of. **humiliating** *a.* painfully humbling. **humiliation** *n.* **humility** *n.* the state of being humble and free from pride [L. *humiliare*, fr. *humilis*, low].

hum·mock (hum′·ạk) *n.* a hillock; a ridge on an ice field [dim. of *hump*].

hu·mor (hū′·, ū′·mẹr) *n.* quality of imagination quick to perceive the ludicrous or to express itself in an amusing way; fun; caprice; disposition; mood; state of mind; the fluids of animal bodies; *v.t.* to indulge; to comply with mood or whim of. **-esque** (hū·mẹr·esk′) *n.* musical composition of fanciful character. **-ist** *n.* one who shows humor in speaking or writing. **-ous** *a.* full of humor. **-ously** *adv.* [L. *humor*, moisture].

hump (hump) *n.* the protuberance or hunch formed by a crooked back; a hillock; *v.t.* to bend into a hump shape. **-back** *n.* a person with a crooked back. **—backed** *a.* [etym. uncertain].

hu·mus (hū′·mạs) *n.* a brown or black constituent of the soil, composed of decayed vegetable or animal matter [L. *humus*, the ground].

Hun (hun) *n.* a barbarian.

hunch (hunch) *n.* a hump; (*Slang*) an intuition or presentiment; *v.t.* to bend or arch into a hump; *v.i.* to move forward in jerks.

hun·dred (hun′·drạd) *n.* a cardinal number, the product of ten times ten; the symbol 100 or C; *a.* ten times ten. **-fold** *a.* a hundred times as much. **-th** *a.* last, or one, of a hundred; *n.* one of a hundred equal parts. **-weight** *n.* an avoirdupois weight of 100 lb. written *cwt.* [O.E. *hund*, hundred, with *raed*, reckoning].

hung (hung) *pa.p.* and *pa.t.* of **hang.**

hun·ger (hung′·gẹr) *n.* discomfort or exhaustion caused by lack of food; a craving for food; any strong desire; *v.i.* to feel hunger; to long for; *v.t.* to starve. **hungry** *a.* feeling hunger. **hungrily** *adv.* **— strike** *n.* refusal of all food as a protest [O.E. *hungor*].

hunk (hungk) *n.* a lump [Prov. E.].

hunt (hunt) *v.t.* to pursue and prey on (as animals on other animals); to pursue animals or game for food or sport; to search diligently after; to drive away; to use in hunting (as a pack of hounds); *v.i.* to go out in pursuit of game; to search; *n.* the act of hunting; chase; search; an association of huntsmen. **-er** *n.* one who hunts; a horse or dog used in hunting [O.E. *huntian*].

hur·dle (hur′·dl) *n.* a barrier in a race course; an obstacle; *v.t.* to enclose with hurdles; to jump over; to master a problem, etc. [O.E. *hyrdle*].

hur·dy-gur·dy (hur′·di·gur′·di·) *n.* an old-fashioned musical instrument played by turning a handle; a street-organ [imit. origin].

hurl (hurl) *v.t.* to send whirling; to throw with violence; *n.* a violent throw [etym. uncertain].

hur·ly-bur·ly (hur′·li·bur′·li·) *n.* tumult; bustle; confusion [etym. uncertain].

hur·rah, hurra (hạ·rá′) *interj.* used as a shout of joy. Also **hurray** [Ger.].

hur·ri·cane (hur′·i·kān) *n.* a wind of 60 m.p.h. or over; a violent cyclonic storm of wind and rain. **— deck** *n.* the upper deck of steamboats. **— lamp** *n.* a candlestick or lamp with a chimney [Sp. *huracán*].

hur·ry (hur′·i·) *v.t.* to hasten; to impel to greater speed; to urge on; *v.i.* to move or act with haste; *n.* the act of pressing forward in haste; quick motion. **hurried** *a.* done in haste; working at speed. **hurriedly** *adv.*

hurt (hurt) *v.i.* to cause pain; to wound or bruise; to impair or damage; to wound feelings; *v.i.* to give pain; *n.* wound, injury, or harm. **-ful** *a.* [Fr. *heurter*, to run against].

hur·tle (hur′·tl) *v.t.* to fling, to dash against; *v.i.* to move rapidly; to rush violently; to dash (against) [See *hurt*].

hus·band (huz′·bạnd) *n.* a married man; *v.t.* to manage with economy; (*Obs.*) to till the soil. **-man** *n.* a farmer. **-ry** *n.* farming; thrift [O.E. *husbonda*, the master of the house].

hush (hush) *interj.* or *imper.* be quiet! silence! *n.* silence or stillness; *v.t.* to make quiet; (with *up*) to keep secret; *v.i.* to be silent [imit].

husk (husk) *n.* the dry, external covering of certain seeds and fruits; the chaff of grain; *pl.* waste matter; refuse; *v.t.* to remove the outer covering. **-y** *a.* full of husks; dry, esp. of the throat, hence, rough in tone; hoarse; (*Colloq.*) big and strong. **-ily** *adv.* **-iness** *n.*

husk·y (hus′·ki·) *n.* an Eskimo sled-dog.

hus·sar (hu·zár′) *n.* one of the light cavalry of European armies [Hung. *huszar*, a freebooter].

hus·sy (hus′·, huz′·i·) *n.* an ill-behaved woman; a saucy girl [contr. fr. *housewife*].

hus·tings (hus′·tingz) *n.* any platform from which political campaign speeches are made; election proceedings [O.E. *hus*, a house; *thing*, an assembly].

hus·tle (hus′·l) *v.t.* to push about; to jostle; *v.i.* to hurry; to bustle; *n.* speed; jostling. **-r** *n.* [Dut. *hutselen*, to shake up].

hut (hut) *n.* a small house or cabin [Fr. *hutte*].

hutch (huch) *n.* a chest or box; a grain-bin; a pen for rabbits, etc. [Fr. *huche*, a coffer].

huz·za, huzzah (hu·zá′) *n.* a shout of joy or approval [Ger.].

hy·a·cinth (hī′·ạ·sinth) *n.* a bulbous plant; a purplish-blue color; a red variety of zircon. [Gk. *huakinthos*, doublet of *jacinth*].

hy·a·line (hī′·ạ·līn) *a.* glassy; transparent; crystalline [Gk. *hualos*, glass].

hy·brid (hī′·brid) *n.* the offspring of two animals or plants of different species; a mongrel; a word compounded from different languages; *a.* cross-bred [L. *hibrida*].

hy·dra (hī′·drạ) *n.* (*Myth.*) a monstrous water-serpent with many heads, slain by Hercules; (*Zool.*) a small fresh-water polyp [Gk. *hudra*, a water-snake].

hy·dran·gea (hī·drān′·jạ) *n.* a genus of shrubs producing large flower clusters [Gk. *hudor*, water; *angeion*, a vessel].

hy·drant (hī′·drạnt) *n.* a water-pipe with a nozzle to which a hose can be attached; a fire-plug [Gk. *hudor*, water].

hy·drate (hī′·drāt) *n.* (*Chem.*) a compound of water with another compound or an element; *v.t.* to combine with water. **hydrated** *a.* **hydration** *n.* [Gk. *hudor*, water].

hy·drau·lic (hī·draw′·lik) *a.* pert. to hydraulics; relating to the conveyance of water; worked by water power [Gk. *hudor*, water; *aulos*, a pipe].

hy·dro- *prefix* fr. Gk. *hudor*, water, combining to form derivatives; in many compounds used to indicate hydrogen. **-carbon** *n.* a compound of hydrogen and carbon. **-cephalus** (hī·drō·sef′·ạ·lạs) *n.* (*Med.*) an excess of cerebrospinal fluid in the brain; water on the brain. **-cephalic, -cephalous** *a.* **-chloric** *a.* containing hydrogen and chlorine. **-chloric acid,** a strong acid [Gk. *kelē*, a tumor; *kephale*, the head; *chloros*, green].

hy·dro·dy·nam·ics (hī·drō·dī·nam′·iks) *n.pl.* the branch of physics which deals with the flow of fluids, whether liquid or gases [Gk. *hudor*, water; *dunamis*, power; *kinein*, to move].

hy·dro·e·lec·tric (hī·drō·i·lek′·trik) *a.* pert. to the generation of electricity by utilizing water power [Gk. *hudor*, water].

hy·dro·gen (hī′·drą·jąn) *n.* an inflammable, colorless, and odorless gas, the lightest of all known substances. **hydrogenous** (hī·drȧ′·je·nąs) *a.* — **bomb** *n.* atom bomb of enormous power [Gk. *hudor*, water; *gennaein*, to produce].

hy·drol·o·gy (hī·drȧl′·ą·ji·) *n.* the science of the properties, laws, etc. of water. **hydrolysis** (hī·drȧl′·ą·sis) *n.* a chemical process by which the oxygen or hydrogen in water combines with an element, or some element of a compound, to form a new compound. **hydrolytic** *a.* [Gk. *hudor*, water; *logos*, a discourse; *luein*, to loosen].

hy·drom·e·ter (hī·drȧm′·ą·tęr) *n.* a graduated instrument for finding the specific gravity, and thence the strength of liquids [Gk. *hudor*, water; *merton*, a measure].

hy·drop·a·thy (hī·drȧp′·ą·thi·) *n.* the treatment of diseases with water, including the use of cold or warm baths. Also **hydrotherapy.** [Gk. *hudor*, water; *pathos*, suffering].

hy·dro·pho·bi·a (hī·drą·fō′·bi·ą) *n.* an acute infectious disease in man caused by the bite of a mad dog; rabies; an extreme dread of water, esp. as a supposed symptom of the disease [Gk. *hudor*, water; *phobos*, fear].

hy·dro·plane (hī′·drą·plān) *n.* an airplane designed to land on and take off from water; a kind of flat-bottomed boat designed to skim over the surface of the water [Gk. *hudor*, water; *sphaira*, a sphere].

hy·drous (hī′·drąs) *a.* containing water; containing hydrogen [Gk. *hudor*, water].

hy·e·na (hī·ē′·ną) *n.* a carnivorous mammal of Asia and Africa, allied to the dog. **laughing hyena**, the striped hyena [Gk. *huaina*, sow-like].

hy·giene (hī·jēn) *n.* medical science which deals with the preservation of health. **hygienic** (hī·gē·en′·ik, hī·jen′·ik) *a.* pert. to hygiene; sanitary. **hygienist** *n.* [Gk. *hugiēs*, healthy].

hy·gro- *prefix* fr. Gk. *hugros*, moist, combining to form derivatives.

hy·gro·scope (hī′·grą·skōp) *n.* an instrument which indicates variations of humidity in the atmosphere, without showing its exact amount [Gk. *hugros*, moist; *skopein*, to view].

Hy·men (hī′·mąn) *n.* (*Myth.*) the god of marriage; (*l.c.*) membrane fold at entrance to female sex organs. **hymeneal** (hī·mą·nē′·ąl) *a.* pert. to marriage [Gk. *humēn*].

hy·me·nop·ter·ous (hī·mą·nȧp′·tęr·ąs) *a.* belonging or pert. to an order of insects (Hymenoptera) as the bee, the wasp, etc. [Gk. *humēn*, membrane; *pteron*, a wing].

hymn (him) *n.* an ode or song of praise, esp. a religious one; a sacred lyric; *v.t.* to praise in song; *v.i.* to sing in worship. **-al** (him′·nąl) *n.* a hymn book [Gk. *humnos*, a festive song].

hy·per·bo·la (hī·pur′·bą·lą) *n.* (*Geom.*) a curve formed by a section of a cone when the cutting plane makes a greater angle with the base than the side of the cone makes. **hyperbolic** *a.* [Gk. *huyer*, over; *bolē*, a throw].

hy·per·bo·le (hī·pur′·bą·lē) *n.* (*Gram.*) a figure of speech which expresses much more or much less than the truth, for the sake of effect; exaggeration. **hyperbolic, hyperbolical** *a.* **hyperbolically** *adv.* **hyperbolize** *v.t.* and *i.* to state with hyperbole [Gk. *huper*, beyond; *bolē*, a throw].

hy·per·crit·ic (hī·pęr·krit′·ik) *n.* one who is critical beyond measure or reason. **-al** *a.* **-ally** *adv.* [Gk. *huper*, over; *kritikos*, critical].

hy·per·phys·i·cal (hī·pęr·fiz′·i·kal) *a.* supernatural [Gk. *huper*, beyond; *phusis*, nature].

hy·per·sen·si·tive (hī·pęr·sen′·są·tiv) *a.* abnormally sensitive. **-ness, hypersensitivity** *n.* [Gk. *huper*, beyond; L. *sentire*, to feel].

hy·per·tro·phy (hī·pur′·trą·fi·) *n.* (*Med.*) abnormal enlargement of organ or part of body [Gk. *huper*, over; *trophē*, nourishment].

hy·phen (hī′·fąn) *n.* a mark (-) used to connect syllables or compound words; *v.t.* to connect with a hyphen. **-ated** *a.* [Gk. *hupo*, under; *hen*, one].

hyp·no·sis (hip·nō′·sąs) *n.* the state of being hypnotized; abnormal sleep. **hypnotic** *a.* tending to produce sleep; pert. to hypnotism; *n.* a drug that induces sleep; a hypnotized person. **hypnotize** *v.t.* to produce a mental state resembling sleep. **hypnotism** *n.* an abnormal mental state resembling sleep. **hypnotist** *n.* [Gk. *hupnos*, sleep].

hy·po- (hī′·pō) *prefix* fr. Gk. meaning under, beneath, below.

hy·po·chon·dri·a (hīp·ą·kȧn′·dri·ą) *n.* a mental disorder, in which one is tormented by melancholy and gloomy views, especially about one's own health. **hypochondriac** *a.* affected by hypochondria; *n.* a person so affected [Gk. *hupo*, under; *chondros*, a cartilage].

hy·poc·ri·sy (hi·pȧk′·rą·si·) *n.* stimulation or pretense of goodness; feigning to be what one is not; insincerity. **hypocrite** (hip′·ą·krit) *n.* one who dissembles his real nature; a pretender to virtue or piety; a deceiver. **hypocritical** *a.* [Gk. *hupowritēs*, an actor].

hy·po·der·mic (hī·pą·dur′·mik) *a.* pert. to parts underlying the skin; *n.* the injection of a drug beneath the skin by means of a needle and small syringe. **-ally** *adv.* [Gk. *hupo*, under; *derma*, the skin].

hy·pos·ta·sis (hī·pȧs′·tą·sąs) *n.* essential nature of anything; the substance of each of the three divisions of the Godhead; (*Med.*) a deposit of blood in an organ; *pl.* **hypostases** [Gk. *hupo*, under; *stasis*, state].

hy·pot·e·nuse (hī·pȧt′·e·nȯȯs) *n.* (*Geom.*) the side of a right-angled triangle which is opposite the right angle [Gk. *hupoteinousa*, extending under].

hy·poth·e·cate (hī·pȧ′·thą·kāt) *v.t.* to give in security; to mortgage [Gk. *hupothēkē*, a pledge].

hy·poth·e·sis (hī·pȧth′·ą·sis) *n.* *pl.* **hypotheses**, a supposition used as a basis from which to draw conclusions; a theory. **hypothesize** *v.i.* and *v.t.* to form and to assume by a hypothesis. **hypothetic, hypothetical** *a.* [Gk. *hupothesis*, a proposal].

hys·te·ri·a, hysterics (his·ti′·ri·ą, his·ter′·iks) *n.* an affection of the nervous system, characterized by excitability and lack of emotional control. **hysteric, hysterical.** *a.* **hysterically** *adv.* [Gk. *hustera*, womb].

I

I (ī) *pron.* the pronoun of the first person singular, the word by which a speaker or writer denotes himself [O.E. *ic*; cf. Ger. *ich*; L. *ego*; Gk. *egō*].

i·am·bus (ī·am′·bąs) *n.* a metrical foot of two syllables, the first short or unaccented, and the second long or accented. **iamb** *n.* shorter form of *iambus*, **iambic** *a.* [Gk.].

i·at·ric, iatrical (ī·at′·rik, ·ąl) *a.* pert. to physicians, medicine [Gk. *iatros*, physician].

I·ber·ri·an (ī·bi′·ri·an) *a.* pert. to Iberia, viz. Spain and Portugal; *n.* early inhabitant of ancient Iberia [L. *Iberia*, Spain].

i·bex (ī′·beks) *n.* variety of wild goat [L.].

i·bis, *n.* a stork-like wading bird, allied to the

spoonbills [Gk.].

I·car·i·an (ī·ker′·i·an) *a.* adventurous in flight; rash [fr. *Icarus*].

ice (īs) *n.* frozen water; a frozen dessert made with fruit juices and water; (*Slang*) diamonds; *v.t.* to cover with ice; to freeze; to chill with ice; to frost a cake; *pr.p.* **icing.** **— age** (*Geol.*) Pleistocene period, the series of glacial epochs. **—belt** *n.* the belt of ice fringing land in Arctic and Antarctic regions. **-berg** *n.* a detached portion of a glacier floating in the sea. **-blink** *n.* a whitish light due to reflection from a field of ice. **-boat** *n.* a boat adapted for being pulled over ice. **-bound** *a.* surrounded by or jammed in ice. **-breaker** *n.* a vessel designed to open passage through ice-bound waters; social start. **-cap** *n.* a glacier formed by the accumulation of snow and ice on a plateau and moving out from the center in every direction. **— cream** *n.* a frozen food made esp. of cream or milk sweetened and flavored. **—fall** *n.* a glacier as it flows over a precipice. **— field** *n.* a vast expanse of sea either frozen or covered with floating masses of ice. **— floe** *n.* a large mass of floating ice. **— hockey** *n.* game played by skaters on ice with a hard rubber disk (the puck). **— pack** *n.* drifting field of ice, closely packed together. **— pick** *n.* an implement for cutting ice. **— skate** *n.* a shoe fitted with a metal runner for skating on ice. **— sheet** *n.* an enormous glacier covering a huge area, valleys and hills alike. **icily** *adv.* coldly. **iciness** *n.* **icing** *n.* a covering of sugar on cakes, etc.; formation of ice on part of an airplane. **icy** *a.* pert. to ice; ice-like; frigid [O.E. *is*; Ger. *Eis*].

Ice·land·er (īs′·lan·dẹr) *n.* a native of Iceland. **Icelandic** *a.*

ich·nol·o·gy (ik·nál′·a·ji·) *n.* the classification of fossil footprints [Gk. *ichnos*, track; *logos*, a discourse].

i·chor (ī′·kawr, ·kẹr) *n.* (*Gk. Myth*) the fluid which flowed in the veins of the Gods; the colorless, watery discharge from ulcers. **-ous** *a.* [Gk. *ichor*].

ich·thy·ol·o·gy (ik·thi·ál′·ạ·ji·) *n.* the branch of zoology which treats of fishes. **ichthyological** *a.* **ichthyologist** *n.* **ichthyic** *a.* pert. to fish. **ichthyoid** *a.* fish-like [Gk. *ichthus*, fish; *logos*, discourse].

i·ci·cle (ī′·si·kl) *n.* a pendent conical mass of ice, slowly built up by freezing of drops of water [O.E. *isgicel*].

i·con (ī′·kán) *n.* any sign which resembles the thing it represents; a venerated representation of Christ, an angel, or a saint, found in Greek and Orthodox Eastern Churches. **-ic, -ical** *a.* pert. to icons. **-oclasm** *n.* act of breaking images; an attack on the cherished beliefs or enthusiasms of others. **-oclast** *n.* a breaker of images; one who exposes or destroys shams of any kind. **-ography** *n.* the making of an icon; the subject matter, or the analysis of an icon. **-olater** *n.* an image worshipper. **-olatry** *n.* image worship [Gk. *eikōn*, an image].

ic·ter·us (ik′·tạ·rạs) *n.* jaundice. **icteric, icterical** *a.* [Gk. *ikteros*, jaundice].

id (id) *n.* in psycho-analysis, the primary source in individuals of instinctive energy and impulses [L. = it).

i·de·a (ī·dē′·ạ) *n.* a product of intellectual action; way of thinking; a thought; belief; plan; aim; principle at the back of one's mind. **ideal** *a.* existing in fancy only; perfect; satisfying desires; *n.* an imaginary type or norm of perfection to be aimed at. **idealization** *n.* **idealize** *v.t.* to represent or look upon as ideal; to make or render ideal; to refine. **idealizer** *n.* an idealist. **idealism** *n.* tendency to seek the highest spiritual perfection; imaginative treatment in comparative disregard of the real; the doctrine that appearances are purely the perceptions, the ideas, of subjects, that the world is to be regarded as consisting of mind; **-list** *n.* **-listic** *a.* pert. to idealism or idealists; perfect; consummate. **-lity** *n.* ideal state or quality; capacity to form ideals of beauty and perfection; condition of being mental. **-lly** *adv.* **-tion** *n.* the process of forming an idea. **-tional** *a.* [Gk. *idea*, fr. *idein*, to see].

i·den·ti·cal (ī·den′·ti·kal) *a.* the very same; not different. **-ly** *adv.* **-ness** *n.* exact sameness [L. *idem*, the same].

i·den·ti·fy (ī·den′·tạ·fī) *v.t.* to establish the identity of; to ascertain or prove to be the same; to recognize; to associate (oneself) in interest, purpose, use, etc. **identifiable** *a.* **identification** *n.*

i·den·ti·ty (ī·den′·tạ·ti·) *n.* state of having the same nature or character with; absolute sameness, as opposed to mere similarity; individuality [L. *idem*, the same].

id·e·o·graph (id′·ē·ạ·graf) *n.* a picture, symbol, diagram, etc., suggesting an idea or object without specifically naming it; a character in Chinese and kindred languages. **ideogram** *n.* an ideograph. **-ic, -ical** *a.* **ideography** *n.* [Gk. *idea*, an idea; *graphein*, to write].

i·de·ol·o·gy (ī·dē·ál′ạ·ji·) *n.* the body of beliefs of any group; (*Philos.*) science of origin of ideas; visionary theorizing. **ideologic, ideological** *a.* **ideologist** *n.* a theorist. [Gk. *idea*; *logos*, discourse].

ides (īdz) *n.pl.* in the Roman calendar, the 15th day of March, May, July, and October, and the 13th day of the other months [Fr. fr. L. *Idus*].

id·i·o·cy *n.* See **idiot.**

id·i·om (id′·i·ạm) *n.* a peculiar mode of expression; the genius or peculiar cast of a language; colloquial speech; dialect. **-atic, -atical** *a.* **-atically** *adv.* [Gk. *idios*, one's own].

id·i·o·syn·cra·sy (id·i·ạ·sin′·krạ·si·) *n.* a peculiarity in a person; fad; peculiar view. **idiosyncratic, idiosyncratical** *a.* [Gk. *idios*, peculiar; *sunkrasis*, mixing together].

id·i·ot (id′·i·ạt) *n.* one mentally deficient; a born fool. **idiocy** *n.* state of being an idiot; extreme and permanent mental deficiency. **-ic, -ical** *a.* utterly senseless or stupid. **-ically** *adv.* **-ism** *n.* natural imbecility [Gk. *idiōtes*, a private person].

i·dle (ī′·dl) *a.* doing nothing; inactive; lazy; unused; frivolous; *v.t.* to spend in idleness; *v.i.* to be idle or unoccupied. **-ness** *n.* **-r** *n.* **idly** *adv.* [O.E. *idel*].

i·dol (ī′·dạl) *n.* an image of a diety as an object of worship; a false god; object of excessive devotion. **-ater** *n.* (*fem.* **idolatress**) a worshipper of idols. **-atrize** *v.t.* to worship as an idol. **-atrous** *a.* **-atrously** *adv.* **-atry** *n.* worship of idols or false gods; excessive and devoted admiration. **-ization** *n.* **-ize** *v.t.* to make an idol of; to love or venerate to excess. **-izer** *n.* [Gk. *eidōlon*, image].

i·dyl, idyll (ī′·dạl) *n.* a short pastoral poem; a picture of simple perfection and loveliness. **-lic** *a.* pert. to idyls; of a perfect setting; blissful [Gk. *eidullion*, dim. of *eidos*, a picture].

if (if) *conj.* on the condition or supposition that; whether; in case that [O.E. *gif*].

ig·loo (ig′·lòò) *n.* a dome-shaped house built of blocks of hard snow by Eskimos [Eskimo].

ig·ne·ous (ig′·ni·ạs) *a.* resembling fire; (*Geol.*) resulting from the action of intense heat [L. *ignis*, fire].

ig·nite (ig·nīt′) *v.t.* to set on fire; to kindle;

v.i. to catch fire; to begin to burn. **ignitible** *a.* **ignition** *n.* act of kindling or setting on fire; (internal-combustion engine) the process or device which ignites the fuel [L. *ignis,* fire].

ig·no·ble (ig·nō′·bl) *a.* of humble birth or family; mean; base; inferior. **ignobility, -ness** *n.* **ignobly** *adv.* [L. *in,* not; *nobilis,* noble].

ig·no·min·y (ig′·nạ·min·i·) *n.* public disgrace or dishonor; infamous conduct. **ignominious** *a.* humiliating; dishonorable. **ignominiously** *adv.* **ignominiousness** *n.* [L. *ignominia*].

ig·no·ra·mus (ig·nạ·ra′·mạs) *n.* an ignorant person [L. = we are ignorant].

ig·no·rant (ig′·nạ·rạnt) *a.* uninstructed; uninformed; unlearned. **ignorance** *n.* **-ly** *adv.* [L. *ignorare,* not to know].

ig·nore (ig·nōr′) *v.t.* to refuse to take notice of; not to recognize [L. *ignorare,* not to know].

i·gua·na (i·gwa′·nạ) *n.* a family of lizards, found in tropical America [Sp.].

i·lex (ī′·leks) *n.* the common holly of Europe; a genus of evergreen trees and shrubs, including the holm oak [L.].

ilk (ilk) *a.* the same. **of that ilk,** family or kind [O.E. *ilc*].

ill (il) *a.* bad or evil in any respect; sick; unwell; wicked; faulty; ugly; disastrous; unfavorable; *n.* evil of any kind; misfortune; misery; pain; *adv.* not well; faultily; unfavorably; not rightly (*compar.* **worse;** *superl.* **worst**). **-ness** *n.* sickness [O.N. *illr*].

ill- (il) *prefix,* used in the construction of compound words, implying badness in some form or other. **—advised** *a.* badly advised. **—disposed** *a.* not friendly; hostile; maliciously inclined. **—fated** *a.* destined to bring misfortune. **—favored** *a.* ugly. **—gotten** *a.* not honestly obtained. **—humor** *n.* bad temper. **—natured** *a.* surly; cross; peevish. **—omened** *a.* inauspicious; attended by evil omens. **—starred** *a.* born under the influence of an unlucky star; unlucky. **—tempered** *a.* quarrelsome. **—will** *n.* malevolence; bad feeling; enmity [O.N. *illr.*].

il·le·gal (i·lē′·gạl) *a.* contrary to law; unlawful. **-ize** *v.t.* to render unlawful. **-ity** *n.* unlawful act. **-ly** *adv.* [L.*il* + *legalis,* law].

il·leg·i·ble (i·lej′·ạ·bl) *a.* incapable of being read or deciphered; unreadable; indistinct. **-ness, illegibility** *n.* **illegibly** *adv.*

il·le·git·i·mate (i·li·jit′·ạ·mit) *a.* unlawful; not authorized by good usage; born out of wedlock. **illegitimacy** *n.* bastardly; illegality. **-ly** *adv.* [L. *in-,* not; *legitimate*].

il·lib·er·al (i·lib′·ẹr·ạl) *a.* not liberal; not free or generous; niggardly; narrow-minded; intolerant. **illiberality** *n.*

il·lic·it (i·lis′·it) *a.* not permitted; unlawful; unlicensed. **-ly** *adv.* **-ness** *n.*

il·lim·it·a·ble (i·lim′·it·ạ·bl) *a.* incapable of being limited or bounded; immeasurable; infinite.

il·lit·er·ate (i·lit′·ẹr·it) *a.* unable to read or write; unlettered; *n.* a person unable to read or write. *adv.* **-ness, illiteracy** *n.*

il·log·i·cal (i·lȧj′·i·kạl) *a.* not according to the rules of logic; unsound; fallacious. **-ly** *adv.* **-ness, illogicality** *n.*

il·lu·mi·nate (i·lòò′·mạ·nāt) *v.t.* to enlighten, literally and figuratively; to light up; to throw light upon; to embellish, as a book or manuscript with gold and colors. **illuminable** *a.* **illuminant** *a.* and *n.* a source of light. **illumination** *n.* act of giving light; that which supplies light; instruction; enlightenment; decoration on manuscripts and books. **illuminative** *a.* giving light; instructive; explanatory. **illuminator** *n.* **illumine** *v.t.* and *v.i.* [L. *illuminare,* to light].

il·lu·sion (i·lòò′·zhạn) *n.* an erroneous interpretation or unreal image presented to the bodily or mental vision; a false perception; deceptive appearance, esp. as a conjuring trick; fallacy. **illusionist** *n.* a professional entertainer who produces illusions. **illusive, illusory** *a.* deceiving by false appearances. **illusively** *adv.* **illusiveness** *n.* [L. *illusio,* mocking].

il·lus·trate (il′·ạs·trāt, il·us′·trāt) *v.t.* to make clear or bright; to exemplify, esp. by means of figures, diagrams, etc.; to adorn with pictures. **illustration** *n.* act of making clear or bright; explanation; a pictorial representation accompanying a printed description. **illustrative, illustratory** *a.* serving to illustrate. **illustratively** *adv.* **illustrator,** *n.* [L. *illustrare,* to light up].

il·lus·tri·ous (i·lus′·tri·ạs) *a.* conferring honor; possessing honor or dignity. **-ness** *n.* [L. *illustris,* clear].

im·age (im′·ij) *n.* a mental picture of any object; a representation of a person or object; a copy; a symbol; idol; figure of speech; (*Optics*) the representation of an object formed at the focus of a lens or mirror by rays of light refracted or reflected to it from all parts of the object; *v.t.* to form an image of; to reflect; to imagine. *n.* images regarded collectively; figures of speech; imagination. **imagism** *n.* clear-cut presentation of a subject. **imagist** *n.* one of a modern poetical group who concentrates on extreme clarity by the use of precise images. [L. *imago,* an image].

im·ag·ine (i·maj′·in) *v.t.* to form in the mind an idea or image; to conjecture; to picture; to believe; to suppose; *v.i.* to form an image of; to picture in the mind. **imaginable** *a.* **imaginableness** *n.* **imaginably** *adv.* **imaginary** *a.* existing only in imagination or fancy; fanciful; unreal. **imaginative** *a.* proceeding from the imagination; gifted with the creative faculty; fanciful. **imagination** *n.* the mental faculty which apprehends and forms ideas of external objects; the poetical faculty. **imaginatively** *adv.* **imaginativeness** *n.* [L. *imago,* an image].

i·mam, imaum (i·mȧm′, i·mawm′) *n.* a Moslem priest [Ar. *imam,* a chief].

im·be·cile (im′·bạ·sil) *a.* mentally feeble; silly; idiotic; *n.* one of feeble mentality. **imbecility** *n.* [*L. imbecillus,* weak in mind or body].

im·bed (im·bed′) *v.t.* See **embed.**

im·bibe (im·bīb′) *v.t.* to drink in; to absorb; to receive into the mind; *v.t.* to drink. **imbiber** *n.* [L. *in; bibere,* to drink].

im·brue (im·bròò′) *v.t.* to wet; to drench as in blood [O.Fr. *embuer,* to drink in].

im·bro·glio (im·brōl′·yō) *n.* an intricate, complicated plot; confusion [It.].

im·bue (im·bū′) *v.t.* to inspire; to tinge deeply; to saturate [L. *imbuere,* to wet].

im·i·tate (im′·ạ·tāt) *v.t.* to follow, as a pattern, model, or example; to copy. **imitable** *a.* capable or worthy of being copied. **imitation** *n.* a servile reproduction of an original; a copy; mimicry. **imitative** *a.* inclined to imitate; not original. **imitatively** *adv.* **imitativeness** *n.* **imitator** *n.* [*L. imitari*].

im·mac·u·late (i·mak′·yoo·lạt) *a.* without blemish; spotless; unsullied; pure; undefiled. **-ly** *adv.* **-ness** *n.* **Immaculate Conception,** the dogma that the Blessed Virgin Mary was conceived and born without taint of sin.

im·ma·nent (im′·ạ·nạnt) *a.* abiding in; inherent; intrinsic; innate. **immanence, immanency** *n.* [L. *in; manere,* to dwell].

im·ma·te·ri·al (im·ạ·ti′·ri·ạl) *a.* not consisting of matter; incorporeal; of no essential consequence; unimportant. **-ize** *v.t.* to separate from matter. **-ism** *n.* doctrine that matter only exists as a process of the mind; pure idealism. **-ist** *n.*

im·ma·ture (im·ạ·toor′) *a.* not mature or ripe; raw; unformed; undeveloped; untimely. **-ness, immaturity** *n.*

im·meas·ur·a·ble (i·mezh′·ẹr·ạ·bl) *a.* incapable of being measured; illimitable; infinite; boundless. **immeasurably** *adv.*

im·me·di·ate (i·mē′·di·ạt) *a.* occurring at once; without delay; present; not separated by others. **immediacy** *n.* immediateness. **-ly** *adv.* **-ness** *n.* [L.L. *immediatus*].

im·me·mo·ri·al (i·mạ·mōr′·i·ạl) *a.* beyond the range of memory; of great antiquity. **immemorable** *a.* **-ly** *adv.*

im·mense (i·mens′) *a.* unlimited; immeasureable; very great; vast; huge; prodigious; enormous. **-ly** *adv.* **-ness, immensity** *n.* vastness; boundlessness [L. *immensus*, unmeasured].

im·merge (i·murj′) *v.t.* to plunge into [L. *in; mergere*, to plunge].

im·merse (i·murs′) *v.t.* to plunge into anything, esp. a fluid; to dip; to baptize by dipping the whole body; to absorb. **immersable, immersible** *a.* **-d** *a.* doused; submerged; engrossed. **immersion** *n.* [L. *in; mergere, mersum*, to plunge].

im·mi·grate (im′·ạ·grāt) *v.i.* to migrate into a country. **immigrant** *n.* **immigration** *n.* [L. *in*: *migrare*, to remove].

im·mi·nent (im′·ạ·nạnt) *a.* threatening immediately to fall or occur. **imminence** *n.* **-ly** *adv.* [L. *imminere*, to overhang].

im·mis·ci·ble (i·mis′·i·bl) *a.* not capable of being mixed. **immiscibility** *n.*

im·mit·i·ga·ble (i·mit′·i·gạ·bl) *a.* incapable of being mitigated or appeased; relentless.

im·mo·bile (i·mō′·bạl) *a.* incapable of being moved; fixed; immovable. **immobilize** *v.t.* to render immobile.

im·mod·er·ate (i·måd′·ẹr·ạt) *a.* exceeding just bounds; excessive. **-ness** *n.* extravagance. **-ly** *adv.* **immoderation** *n.*

im·mod·est (i·måd′·ist) *a.* wanting in modesty or delicacy; indecent; shameless; impudent. **-ly** *adv.* **-y** *n.* shamelessness.

im·mo·late (im′·ạ·lāt) *v.t.* to sacrifice; to offer as a sacrifice; to kill as a religious rite. **immolation** *n.* **immolator** *n.* [L. *immolare*, to sprinkle with sacrificial meal].

im·mor·al (i·mår′·, i·mawr′·al) *a.* uninfluenced by moral principle; wicked. **-ity** *n.* vice; profligacy; injustice. **-ly** *adv.*

im·mor·tal (i·mawr′·tạl) *a.* not mortal; having an eternal existence; undying; deathless; *n.* one exempt from death or decay; a divine being. **immortalize** *v.t.* to make famous for all time; to save from oblivion. **immortality** *n.* perpetual life. flower [Fr.].

im·mov·a·ble (i·mòòv′·a·bl) *a.* incapable of being moved; firmly fixed; fast; resolute. **-ness, immovability** *n.* **immovably** *adv.*

im·mune (i·mūn′) *a.* exempt; free from infection; protected against any particular infection; *n.* one who is so protected. **immunization** *n.* the process of rendering a person or animal immune. **immunize** *v.t.* **immunity** *n.* [L. *in-*, not; *munis*, serving].

im·mure (i·myoor′) *v.t.* to enclose within walls; to imprison [L. *in; murus*, a wall].

im·mu·ta·ble (i·mū′·tạ·bl) *a.* not susceptible to any alteration; invariable; unalterable. **immutability, immutableness** *n.*

imp (imp) *n.* a little demon; a mischievous child. **-ish** *a.* like an imp; mischievous [O.E. *impa*, fr. Gk. *emphytos*, grafted on].

im·pact (im·pakt′) *v.t.* to press or drive forcibly together. **impact** (im′·pact) *n.* impulse communicated by one object striking another; collision [L. *in*, into; *pingere*, to strike].

im·pair (im·per′) *v.t.* to diminish in quantity, value, excellence, or strength; to injure; to weaken [Fr. *empirer*, to grow worse].

im·pale (im·pāl′) *v.t.* to fix on a sharpened stake; inclose with stakes; to put to death by fixing on an upright, sharp stake. **-ment** *n.* [L. *in*. into; *palus*, a stake].

im·pal·pa·ble (im·pal′·pạ·bl) *a.* not capable of being felt or perceived by the senses, esp. by touch; exceedingly fine in texture; not readily understood or grasped. **impalpability** *n.* **impalpably** *adv.*

im·pan·el (im·pan′·ạl) *v.t.* to place a name on a panel or list; to enter the names of a jury on a panel; to form a jury by roll-call. **-ment** *n.*

im·part (im·pårt′) *v.t.* to bestow a share or portion of; to grant; to divulge; to disclose.

im·par·tial (im·pår′·shạl) *a.* not partial; without prejudice; not taking sides; unbiased. **impartiality, impartialness** *n.*

im·part·i·ble (im·pårt′·i·bl) *a.* not divisible (of landed property).

im·pas·sa·ble (im·pas′·ạ·bl) *a.* incapable of being passed; impervious; impenetrable; pathless. **impassability, impassableness** *n.*

im·passe (im·pas′, im′·pas) *n.* deadlock; dilemma; fix [Fr.].

im·pas·sion (im·pash′·ạn) *v.t.* to move or affect strongly with passion. **-ed** *a.*

im·pas·sive (im·pas′·iv) *a.* not susceptible of pain or suffering; insensible; showing no emotion; calm. **-ly** *adv.* **-ness, impassivity** *n.*

im·pa·tient (im·pā′·shạnt) *a.* uneasy or fretful under trial or suffering; averse to waiting; restless. **impatience** *n.* **-ly** *adv.*

im·pav·id (im·pav′·id) *a.* fearless [L. *in* + *pavidus*, fearing].

im·peach (im·pēch′) *v.t.* to charge with a crime or misdemeanor; to call to account; to denounce; to challenge. **-able** *a.* **-er** *n.* **-ment** *n.* the trial of a public official, by the upper house of the legislature, the lower house having made the charge [orig. to hinder, Fr. *empêcher*, to prevent].

im·pec·ca·ble (im·pek′·ạ·bl) *a.* not liable to sin or error; perfect. **impeccability, impeccancy** *n.* [L. *in-*, not; *peccare*, to sin].

im·pe·cu·ni·ous (im·pi·kū′·ni·ạs) *a.* having no money; poor; hard up. **impecuniosity** *n.* dire poverty [L. *in-*, not; *pecunia*, money].

im·pede (im·pēd′) *v.t.* to stop the progress of; to hinder; to obstruct. **impedance** *n.* hindrance; (*Elect.*) opposition offered to an alternating current by resistance, inductance, or capacity, or by combined effect of all three. **impedible** *a.* **impediment** *n.* that which hinders; stammer. **impedimenta** *n.pl.* baggage, esp. military; encumbrances. **impedimental** *a.* [L. *impedire*, to shackle].

im·pel (im·pel′) *v.t.* to drive or urge forward; to induce; to incite. *pr.p.* **-ling.** *pa.t.* and *pa.p.* **-led.** **-lent** *a.* impelling; *n.* a force which impels. **-ler** *n.* [L. *in*, into; *pellere*, to drive].

im·pend (im·pend′) *v.i.* to hang over; to threaten; to be imminent. **-ence, -ency** *n.* **-ent** *a.* impending; threatening [L. *impendere*, to hang over].

im·pen·e·tra·ble (im·pen′·ạ·trạ·bl) *a.* incapable of being penetrated or pierced; obscure. **impenetrability** *n.* quality of being impenetrable; that property of matter by which it excludes all other matter from the space it occupies.

im·pen·i·tent (im·pen′·ạ·tạnt) *a.* not repenting of sin; not contrite; obdurate.

im·per·a·tive (im·per′·ạ·tiv) *a.* expressive of command; authoritative; obligatory; absolutely necessary; peremptory. **-ly** *adv.* [L. *imperare*, to command].

im·per·cep·ti·ble (im·pẹr·sep′·tạ·bl) *a.* not discernible by the senses; minute. **-ness, imperceptibility** *n.* **imperceptibly** *adv.* **imperceptive** *a.* not having power to perceive.

im·per·fect (im·pur′·fikt) *a.* wanting some part or parts; defective; faulty; *n.* (*Gram.*) tense denoting an action in the past but incomplete, or continuous action in the past. **-ly** *adv.* **imperfection** *n.*
im·per·fo·rate, imperforated (im·pur′·fą·rąt) *a.* not perforated or pierced.
im·pe·ri·al (im·pi′·ri·ąl) *a.* pertaining to an empire or to an emperor; royal; sovereign; majestic. **-ism** *n.* the system of government in an empire; policy of national territorial expansion. **-ist** *n.* **-istic** *a.* [L. *imperium*].
im·per·il (im·per′·il) *v.t.* to bring into peril; to endanger; to hazard; to risk.
im·pe·ri·ous (im·pi′·ri·ąs) *a.* commanding; domineering; dictatorial. **-ly** *adv.* **-ness** *n.* [L. *imperiosus*, full of command].
im·per·ish·a·ble (im·per′·ish·ą·bl) *a.* not liable to decay or oblivion; indestructible. **-ness** *n.* **imperishability** *n.*
im·per·ma·nence (im·pur′·ma·nąns) *n.* want of permanence or stability.
im·per·me·a·ble (im·pur′·mē·ą·bl) *a.* not permitting passage, as of fluid or gas, through its substance; impervious. **impermeability** *n.* **-ness** *n.* **impermeably** *adv.*
im·per·son·al (im·pur′·sąn·ąl) *a.* having no personal reference; objective; (*Gram.*) form of verb used only in 3rd person singular with nominative *it.* e.g. *it hails.* **-ly** *adv.*
im·per·son·ate (im·pur′·sąn·āt) *v.t.* to invest with a real form, body or character; to represent in character or form; to act a part on the stage; to imitate. **impersonation** *n.* **impersonator** *n.*
im·per·ti·nent (im·pur′·tą·nąnt) *a.* having no bearing on the subject; irrelevant; impudent; saucy. **impertinence** *n.*
im·per·turb·a·ble (im·pęr·tur′·bą·bl) *a.* incapable of being disturbed or agitated; unmoved; composed. **imperturbability** *n.* **imperturbably** *adv.* **imperturbation** *n.*
im·per·vi·a·ble, im·per·vi·ous (im·pur′·vi·ąbl, ·vi·us) *a.* not admitting of entrance or passage through; impenetrable; impassable; not to be moved by argument or importunity. **-ness, imperviability** *n.* **imperviously** *adv.*
im·pe·ti·go (im·pą·tī′·gō) *n.* (*Med.*) a pustulous skin disease [L. *impetere*, to rush upon].
im·pet·u·ous (im·pech′·choo·ąs) *a.* rushing with force and violence; vehement; hasty. **-ly** *adv.* **-ness, impetuosity** *n.* precipitancy; fury [L. *impetus*, attack].
im·pe·tus (im′·pą·tąs) *n.* the force with which a body moves; momentum; boost [L.].
im·pi·e·ty (im·pī′·ą·ti·) *n.* lack of reverence.
im·pinge (im·pinj′) *v.i.* (foll. by *on, upon, against*) to fall or dash against; to touch on; to infringe [L. *impingere*, to strike].
im·pi·ous (im′·pi·ąs) *a.* not pious; proceeding from or manifesting a want of reverence. **-ly** *adv.* **-ness, impiety** *n.*
im·pla·ca·ble (im·plak′·, im·plāk′·ą·bl) *a.* inexorable; not to be appeased; unrelenting. **-ness, implacability** *n.*
im·plant (im·plant′) *v.i.* to set in; to insert; to sow (seed); to plant (shoots); to instill, or settle in the mind or heart.
im·plead (im·plēd′) *v.t.* to sue at law.
im·ple·ment (im′·plą·mąnt) *n.* a weapon, tool, or instrument; a utensil; *v.t.* (im′·plą·ment) to fulfill an obligation or contract which has been entered into; to give effect to; to carry out; to supplement. **-al** *a.* **-ation** *n.* [L *implere*, to fill up].
im·pli·cate (im′·pli·kāt) *v.t.* to involve; to include; to entangle; to imply. **implication** *n.* the implied meaning; a logical deduction; entanglement.**implicative** *a.* tending to implicate. **implicatively** *adv.* **implicit** *a.* implied; without questioning. **implicitly** *adv.* [L. *implicare* to entangle].
im·plore (im·plōr′) *v.t.* to entreat earnestly; to beseech. **imploration** *n.* **-r** *n.* **imploringly** *adv.* [L. *in*, in; *plorare*, to weep].
im·ply (im·plī′) *v.t.* to contain by implication; to involve as necessary; to signify; to insinuate; to suggest [L. *implicare*, to entangle].
im·po·lite (im·pą·līt′) *a.* uncivil; rude; discourteous. **-ly** *adv.* **-ness** *n.*
im·pol·i·tic (im·pál′·ą·tik) *a.* ill-advised; not in the best interests of; inexpedient. **impolicy** *n.* injudicious action. **-ly** *adv.*
im·pon·der·a·ble (im·pan′·dęr·ą·bl) *a.* without perceptible weight; not able to be weighed; *n.pl.* natural phenomena such as heat, electricity, etc., which do not alter the weight of substances; the unknown factors which may influence human activities. **-ness, imponderability** *n.*
im·port (im·pōrt′) *v.t.* to bring in from abroad; to convey a meaning; to be of consequence. **-ance** *n.* consequence; moment. *a.* **-antly** *adv.* **-ation** *n.* act of bringing from another country [L. *in*, into; *portare*, to carry].
im·por·tune (im·per·tūn′) *v.t.* to request with urgency; to pester with requests; to entreat; to solicit. **importunacy, importunateness** *n.* **importunate** *a.* earnestly solicitous; persistent in urging a claim; troublesome. **importunately** *adv.* [L. *importunus*, troublesome].
im·pose (im·pōz′) *v.t.* to lay on; to levy; to lay, as a charge or tax; to force oneself upon others; to lay on hands in ordination; *v.i.* (with *upon*) to deceive; to take undue advantage of a person's good-nature; to impress. **imposable** *a.* **imposing** *a.* adapted to impress considerably; commanding; grand. **imposition** *n.* act of imposing, laying on, enjoining, indicting, etc.; that which is imposed; a tax; a burden [Fr. *imposer*].
im·pos·si·ble (im·pás′·ą·bl) *a.* that which cannot be done; incapable of existing in conception or in fact; unfeasible; unattainable. *interj.* absurd! **impossibility** *n.*
im·post (im′·pōst) *n.* tax duty [Fr. *impôt*].
im·pos·tor (im·pás′·tęr) *n.* one who assumes a false character; one who deceives others; a cheat. **imposture** *n.* deception [L. *imponere*, to place upon].
im·po·tent (im′·pą·tąnt) *a.* powerless; wanting natural strength; without sexual power (of a male). **impotence, impotency** *n.*
im·pound (im·pound′) *v.t.* to confine cattle in a pound or pen; to restrain within limits; (*Law*) to retain documents in a civil case with a view to criminal proceedings.
im·pov·er·ish (im·páv′·ęr·ish) *v.t.* to reduce to poverty; to exhaust the strength, richness, or fertility of land. **-ed** *a.* **-ment** *n.* [O. Fr. *empovrir*].
im·prac·ti·ca·ble (im·prak′·ti·ką·bl) *a.* not able to be accomplished; unfeasible. **impracticability, impracticableness** *n.* **impractical** *a.* not practical.
im·pre·cate (im′·pri·kāt) *v.t.* to invoke by prayer (evil) upon; to curse. **imprecation** *n.* **imprecatory** *a.* [L. *imprecari*, to invoke by prayer].
im·preg·na·ble (im·preg′·ną·bl) *a.* not to be stormed or taken by assault; not to be moved, impressed, or shaken. **impregnability** *n.* **impregnably** *adv.* [Fr. *imprenable*, fr. L. *in-*, not; *prehendere*, to take].
im·preg·nate (im·preg′·nāt) *v.t.* to make pregnant; to render fertile; to saturate; to imbue. **impregnable** *a.* **impregnation** *n.* [L. *impregnare*].
im·pre·sa·ri·o (im·prą·sá′·ri·ō) *n.* an organizer of public entertainments, a teacher or manager of concert artists [It].
im·press (im·pres′) *v.t.* to take forcibly, per-

sons or goods, for public service; to commandeer. **-ment** *n.* [L. *in,* in, into; *praestare,* to furnish].

im·press (im·pres′) *v.t.* to press in or upon; to make a mark or figure upon; to fix deeply in the mind; to stamp. (im′·pres) *n.* a mark made by pressure; stamp; impression wrought on the mind. **-ibility** *n.* susceptibility. **-ible** *a.* capable of being impressed. **-ibly** *adv.* **impression** *n.* act of impressing; a mark or stamp made by pressure; psychological effect or influence on the mind; opinion; idea. **impressionable** *a.* susceptible to external influences. **-ive** *a.* making or fitted to make a deep impression on the mind. **-ively** *adv.* **-iveness** *n.* [L. *imprimere,* fr. *premere,* to press].

im·pres·sion·ism (im·presh′·ạn·izm) *n.* a revolutionary modern movement, originating in France, in art, literature and music, aiming at reproducing the *impression* which eye and mind gather, rather than representing actual fact. **impressionist** *n.*

im·pri·ma·tur (im·prạ·mā′·tẹr) *n.* a license to print a book; official approval [L. = 'let it be printed'].

im·print (im·print′) *v.t.* to mark by pressure; to fix indelibly, as on the mind; to print. (im′·print) *n.* an impression; name of printer or publisher on title page or at the end of a book.

im·prob·a·ble (im·prȧb′·ạ·bl) *a.* unlikely. **improbability** *n.* **improbably** *adv.*

im·pro·bi·ty (im·prō′·bi·ti·) *n.* want of integrity or rectitude; dishonesty.

im·promp·tu (im·prȧmp′·tōō) *adv.* or *a.* offhand [Fr. fr. L. *promptus,* ready].

im·prop·er (im·prȧp′·ẹr) *a.* unsuitable to the end or design; unfit; indecent; inaccurate. **-ly** *adv.* **impropriety** *n.* offense against rules of conduct; the use of a word in its wrong sense.

im·prove (im·prōōv′) *v.t.* to make better; to employ to good purpose; to make progress; *v.i.* to grow better; to become more prosperous. **improvability, improvableness** *n.* **improvable** *a.* **improvably** *adv.* **-ment** *n.* the act of improving; state of being improved; progress. **improvingly** *adv.*

im·prov·i·dent (im·prȧv′·ạ·dạnt) *a.* not prudent or foreseeing; neglecting to provide for the future. **improvidence** *n.*

im·pro·vise (im·prẹ·vīz′) *v.t.* to extemporize; to make the best of materials at hand; to compose, speak or perform without preparation. **improvisation** (im·prȧv·i·zā′·shạn) *n.* **-r** *n.* [L. *in-,* not; *provisus,* foreseen].

im·pru·dent (im·prōō′·dạnt), *a.* lacking in discretion, **imprudence** *n.* **-ly** *adv.*

im·pu·dent (im′·pyạ·dạnt) *a.* brazen; boldfaced; rude. **impudence** *n.* **-ly** *adv.* [L. *impudens,* shameless].

im·pugn (im·pūn′) *v.t.* to call in question; to contradict; to challenge the accuracy of a statement. **-able** *a.* **-er** *n.* **-ment** *n.* [L. *impugnare,* to assail].

im·pulse (im′·puls) *n.* the motion or effect produced by a sudden action or applied force; push; thrust; momentum; sudden thought. **impulsion** *n.* impelling force; incitement. **impulsive** *a.* having the power of impelling; acting momentarily without due thought. **impulsively** *adv.* **impulsiveness** *n.* [L. *impellere, impulsion,* to urge on. Cf. *impel*].

im·pu·ni·ty (im·pūn′·ạ·ti·) *n.* exemption from punishment, injury, or loss [L. *impunitas,* without punishment].

im·pure (im·pyoor′) *a.* not pure; mixed; adulterated; foul; unchaste. **-ly** *adv.* **impurity, impureness** *n.*

im·pute (im·pūt′) *v.t.* to ascribe to (in a bad sense); to attribute to. **imputable** *a.* **imputableness, imputability** *n.* **imputation** *n.* act of imputing; suggestion of evil. **imputative** *a.* **imputatively** *adv.* [L. *in; putare,* to reckon, to think].

in (in) *prep.* within; inside of; indicating a present relation to time, space, or condition; *adv.* inside; closely; with privilege or possession; immediately. **in so far as,** to the extent that. **inasmuch as,** considering that [O.E.].

in·a·bil·i·ty (in·ạ·bil′·ạ·ti·) *n.* want of strength, means, or power; impotence.

in·ac·cu·rate (in·ak′·yạr·ạt) *a.* not correct; not according to truth or reality; erroneous. **inaccuracy** *n.* **-ly** *adv.*

in·ac·tive (in·ak′·tiv) *a.* not disposed to action or effort; idle; inert; lazy; (*Chem.*) showing no tendency to combine with other elements. **inaction** *n.* **inactivate** *v.t.* to make inactive. **inactivation** *n.* **-ly** *adv.* **inactivity** *n.* want of action or energy.

in·ad·e·quate (in·ad′·ạ·kwạt) *a.* insufficient; too cramped; incapable. **inadequacy** *n.* **-ly** *adv.* **-ness** *n.*

in·ad·mis·si·ble (in·ạd·mis′·ạ·bl) *a.* not allowable; improper. **inadmissibly** *adv.*

in·ad·vert·ent (in·ad·vur′·tạnt) *a.* not turning the mind to a matter; inattentive; thoughtless; careless. **inadvertence, inadvertency** *n.* **-ly** *adv.*

in·ad·vis·a·ble (in·ạd·vī′·zạ·bạl) *a.* not recommended; inexpedient. **inadvisability** *n.* **inadvisably** *adv.*

in·al·ien·a·ble (in·āl′·yạn·ạ·bl) *a.* incapable of being separated or transferred.

in·ane (in·ān′) *a.* empty; void; foolish; silly. **inanition** *n.* state of being empty; exhaustion; starvation. **inanity** *n.* vacuity; silly remark [L. *inanis*].

in·an·i·mate (in·an′·ạ·mạt) *a.* destitute of life or spirit. **inanimation** *n.* **-ness** *n.*

in·ap·pli·ca·ble (in·ap′·lik ạ·bl) *a.* not applicable; unsuitable; irrelevant; inappropriate.

in·ap·pre·ci·a·ble (in·ạ·prē′·shi·ạ·bl) *a.* not worth reckoning; not able to be valued.

in·ap·pro·pri·ate (in·ạ·prō′·pri·ạt) *a.* unsuitable; at the wrong time. **-ly** *adv.* **-ness** *n.*

in·apt (in·apt′) *a.* inappropriate; unsuitable; awkward; clumsy. **-itude** *n.* unfitness; awkwardness. **-ly** *adv.*

in·ar·tic·u·late (in·ȧr·tik′·ya·lạt) *a.* unable to put one's ideas in words; not uttered distinctly; not jointed. **-ly** *adv.* **-ness** *n.* **inarticulation** *n.*

in·as·much *adv.* See **in.**

in·au·di·ble (in·aw′·di·bl) *a.* not able to be heard; noiseless; silent. **inaudibility, inaudibleness** *n.* **inaudibly** *adv.*

in·au·gu·rate (in·aw′·gyạ·rāt) *v.t.* to induct into an office in a formal manner; to install; to set in motion or action; to begin. **inaugural, inauguratory** *a.* **inauguration** *n.* opening ceremony. **inaugurator** *n.* [L. *inaugurare,* to take auguries before action].

in·aus·pi·cious (in·aw·spish′·ạs) *a.* not auspicious; ill-omened. **-ly** *adv.* **-ness** *n.*

in·born (in′·bawrn) *a.* born in or with; innate; natural; inherent.

in·bred (in′·bred) *a.* bred within; innate; inherent. **inbreed** *v.t.* to mate animals of the same blood stock; to marry within the family or tribe. **inbreeding** *n.*

in·cal·cu·la·ble (in·kal′·kyạ·la·bl) *a.* countless; beyond calculation; uncertain. **incalculability, -ness** *n.*

in·can·des·cent (in·kạn·des′·ạnt) *a.* glowing with white heat and providing light. **incandescense** *n.* white heat [L. *in,* in; *candescere,* to begin to glow].

in·can·ta·tion (in·kan·tā′·shạn) *n.* a formula or charm-words used to produce magical or supernatural effect. **incantatory** *a.* [L. *incantare,* to sing spells. Cf. *enchant*].

in·ca·pa·ble (in·kā′·pạ-bl) *a.* wanting ability or capacity; not admitting of; not susceptible of. **incapability** *n.*

in·ca·pa·ci·tate (in·kạ·pas′·ạ·tāt) *v.t.* to render incapable. **incapacitation** *n.* act of disqualifying. **incapacity** *n.* want of capacity; lack of normal intellectual power; inability; incapability; legal disqualification.

in·car·cer·ate (in·kår′·sẹr·āt) *v.t.* to confine; to imprison. **incarcerator, incarceration,** *n.* [L. *in; carcer,* prison].

in·car·na·dine (in·kår′·nạ·dīn) *a.* flesh-colored; of a carnation color; crimson; *v.t.* to dye crimson [Fr. fr. L. *caro,* flesh].

in·car·nate (in·kår′·nāt) *v.t.* to put into concrete form; to embody in flesh, esp. in human form; *a.* (in·kår′·nạt) embodied in flesh; typified. **incarnation** *n.* embodiment; that which embodies and typifies an abstraction [L. *in; caro, carnis,* flesh].

in·cen·di·ar·y (in·sen′·di·er·i·) *n.* one who maliciously sets fire to property; an agitator who inflames passions; a fire bomb; *a.* pert. to malicious burning of property; tending to inflame dissension. **incendiarism** *n.* arson [L. *incendere,* to set on fire].

in·cense (in-sens′) *v.t.* to inflame to violent anger [L. *incendere,* to set on fire].

in·cense (in′·sens) *n.* a mixture of aromatic gums and spices which, when burned, produces a sweet-smelling smoke, used for religious purposes; flattery; adulation; *v.t.* to perfume with incense [L. *incendere,* to burn].

in·cen·tive (in·sen′·tiv) *a.* inciting; provoking; *n.* motive; spur; stimulus; encouragement [L. *incentivus,* setting the tune].

in·cep·tion (in·sep′·shạn) *n.* beginning; start; origin. **inceptive** *a.* **inceptively** *adv.* [L. *incipere, inceptum,* to begin].

in·ces·sant (in·ses′·ạnt) *a.* continuing or following without interruption. **incessancy** *n.* **-ly** *adv.* [L. *in-,* not; *cessare,* to cease].

in·cest (in′·sest) *n.* sexual intercourse of kindred within the forbidden degrees.**-uous** *a.* [L. *in-,* not; *castus,* chaste].

inch (inch) *n.* twelfth part of a linear foot; a small degree or quantity; *v.i.* to push forward by slow degrees; to edge forward [L. *uncia,* twelfth part of anything].

in·cho·ate (in′·kō·at) *a.* just begun; rudimentary; incipient. **-ly** *adv.* **inchoation** *n.* early stage or state. **inchoative** *a.* [L. *in, choare,* to begin].

in·ci·dent (in′·sạ·dạnt) *a.* liable to happen; subordinate to; falling upon, as a ray of light upon a reflecting surface; naturally attaching to; *n.* that which takes place; event; occurrence; episode; subordinate action. **incidence** *n.* range of influence; the manner of falling upon. **-al** *a.* and *n.* **-ally** *adv.* **-alness** *n.* [L. *incidere,* to fall in].

in·cin·er·ate (in·sin′·ẹr·āt) *v.t.* to consume by fire; to burn to ashes. **incineration** *n.* **incinerator** *n.* furnace for consuming refuse [L. *incinerare,* to reduce to ashes].

in·cip·i·ent (in·sip′·i·ạnt) *a.* beginning; originating. **incipience, incipiency** *n.* [L. *incipere,* to begin].

in·cise (in·sīz′) *v.t.* to cut into; to carve; to engrave. **incision** (in·sizh′·ạn) *n.* the act of cutting with a sharp instrument; a cut; gash. **incisive** *a.* having the quality of cutting or penetrating; sharp; biting; trenchant; **incisively** *adv.* **incisiveness** *n.* **incisor** *n.* one of the eight front cutting teeth[L. *incidere,* to cut into].

in·cite (in·sīt′) *v.t.* to move the mind to action; to spur on. **incitant** *n.* a stimulant; *a.* exciting. **incitation** (in·sī·tā′·shun) *n.* **-ment** *n.* act of inciting; motive; incentive. *n.* [L. *incitare,* to rouse].

in·clem·ent (in·klem′·ạnt) *a.* not clement; severe; harsh; stormy. **inclemency** *n.*

in·cline (in·klīn′) *v.t.* to cause to deviate from a line or direction; to give a tendency to, as to the will or affections; to bend; to turn from the vertical. *v.i.* to deviate from the vertical; to be disposed. (in′·klīn) *n.* an ascent or descent; a slope. **inclination** *n.* act of inclining; bent of the mind or will; leaning; tendency towards; favor for one thing more than another. **-d** *a.* [L. *in; clinare,* to lean].

in·clude (in·klòòd′) *v.t.* to confine within; to comprise. **inclusion** *n.* act of including; state of being included or confined. **inclusive** *a.* taking in the stated limit, number, or extremes; enclosing; embracing. **inclusively** *adv.* [L. *includere,* to shut in].

in·cog·ni·to (in·kåg′·ni·tō) *a.* and *adv.* in a disguise; in an assumed character and under an assumed name; *n.* (*fem.* **incognita**) the state of being unknown; a person who conceals his identity under a false name [L. *incognitus,* unknown].

in·co·her·ent (in·kō·hir′·ạnt) *a.* not connected or clear; confused. **incoherence** *n.* **-ly** *adv.* **incoherency** *n.*

in·com·bus·ti·ble (in·kạm·bust′·ạ·bl) *a.* not capable of being burned. **incombustibility, incombustibleness** *n.* **incombustibly** *adv.*

in·come (in′·kum) *n.* the gain or reward from one's labors or investments; annual receipts; rent; profit; interest. **-r** *n.* a newcomer. **incoming** *n.* a coming in; revenue; *a.* coming in; entering; **— tax,** tax levied on income.

in·com·men·su·ra·ble (in·kạ·men′·sạ·ra·bl) *a.* having no common measure or standard of comparison. **-ness** *n.* **incommensurably** *adv.* **incommensurate** *a.* not admitting of a common measure; unequal; out of proportion. **incommensurately** *adv.*

in·com·mode (in·kạ·mōd′) *v.t.* to put to inconvenience or discomfort; to hinder. **incommodious** *a.* inconvenient; too small. **incommodiously** *adv.* **incommodity** *n.* [L. *in-,* not; *commodus,* convenient].

in·com·mu·ni·ca·ble (in·kạ·mū′·ni·kạ·bl) *a.* incapable of being communicated or shared. **incommunicability** *n.* **-ness** *n.* **incommunicably** *adv.* **incommunicative** *a.* reserved; not ready to impart information.

in·com·mu·ni·ca·do (in·kạ·mū·ni·kà′·dō) *a.* of a prisoner, deprived of communication with other people [Sp.].

in·com·pa·ra·ble (in′·kåm′·per·ạ·bl) *a.* not admitting any degree of comparison; unequaled; unrivaled. **incomparability** *n.* **-ness** *n.* **incomparably** *adv.*

in·com·pat·i·ble (in·kạm·pat′·ạ·bl) *a.* incapable of existing side by side; unable to live together in harmony. **incompatibility, incompatibleness** *n.* **incompatibly** *adv.*

in·com·pe·tent (in·kåm′·pạ·tạnt) *a.* not efficient in the performance of function; inadequate; incapable. **incompetence** *n.* **incom-**

in·com·plete (in·kam·plēt′) *a.* defective; unfinished; imperfect. **-ly** *adv.*

in·com·pre·hen·si·ble (in·kåm·pri·hen′·sa·bl) *a.* incapable of being comprehended or understood. **-ness, incomprehensibility, incomprehension** *n.* difficulty of understanding; quality or state of being incomprehensible. **incomprehensibly** *adv.* **incomprehensive** *a.* limited; not extensive.

in·com·pres·si·ble (in·kạm·pres′·ạ·bl) *a.* cannot be compressed or reduced in bulk.

in·con·ceiv·a·ble (in·kạn·sēv′·ạ·bl) *a.* not capable of being conceived in the mind; unthinkable. **inconceivability, inconceivableness** *n.* **inconceivably** *adv.*

in·con·clu·sive (in·kạn·klòò′·siv) *a.* not decisive or conclusive; not settling a point in debate or a doubtful question. **-ly** *adv.*

in·con·gru·ous (in·kång′·groo.ạs) *a.* inappropriate; not reciprocally agreeing;

(*Math.*) not coinciding. **incongruent** *a.* **incongruity, incongruousness** *n.*

in·con·se·quent (in·kán′·sạ·kwent) *a.* not following from the premises; illogical; irrelevant. **inconsequence** *n.* **inconsequential** *a.* not to the point; illogical; of no import; trivial. **inconsequentially** *adv.*

in·con·sid·er·a·ble (in·kạn·sid′·ẹr·ạ·bl) *a.* unworthy of consideration; unimportant.

in·con·sid·er·ate (in·kạn·sid′·ẹr·ạt) *a.* thoughtless; careless of others' feelings.

in·con·sis·tent (in·kạn·sis′·tạnt) *a.* liable to sudden and unexpected change; changeable; not agreeing. **inconsistency** *n.* **-ly** *adv.*

in·con·spic·u·ous (in·kạn spik′·yoo·ạs) *a.* scarcely noticeable; hardly discernible.

in·con·stant (in·kán′·stạnt) *a.* not constant or consistent; subject to change. **inconstancy** *n.* **-ly** *adv.*

in·con·ti·nent (in·kán′·tạ·nạnt) *a.* morally incapable of restraint. **incontinence, incontinency** *n.* **-ly** *adv.*

in·con·tro·vert·i·ble (in·kán·trạ·vur′·tạ·bl) *a.* too clear or certain to admit of dispute; unquestionable. **incontrovertibly** *adv.*

in·con·ven·ient (in·kạn·vēn′·yạnt) *a.* awkward; unsuitable. **inconvenience** *v.t.* to put to trouble or annoyance. **inconvenience, inconveniency** *n.* **-ly** *adv.*

in·con·vert·i·ble (in·kạn·vur′·tạ·bl) *a.* cannot be changed or exchanged; of paper money, notes which cannot be converted into gold on demand. **inconvertibility** *n.*

in·co·or·di·nate (in·kō·awr′·dạ·nạt) *a.* not in orderly relation with one another.

in·cor·po·rate (in·kawr′·pạ·rāt) *v.t.* and *v.i.* to combine, as different ingredients, into one body or mass; to give a material form to; to constitute into a corporation; *a.* formed into an incorporation. **incorporation** *n.* act of incorporating; state of being incorporated; the formation or embodying of an association or society. **incorporative** *a.* **incorporeal** *a.* not possessed of a body; immaterial; unsubstantial; spiritual. **incorporeality** *n.*

in·cor·rect (in·kạ·rekt′) *a.* not in accordance with the truth; improper.**-ly** *adv.* **-ness** *n.*

in·cor·ri·gi·ble (in·kawr′·i·jạ·bl) *a.* beyond any hope of reform or improvement in conduct; *n.* such a person.

in·cor·rupt (in·kạr·upt′) *a.* morally pure; not open to bribery; free from decay. **-ible** *a.* **-ibility** *n.* **-ly** *adv.* **-ness** *n.*

in·crease (in·krēs′) *v.t.* to make greater; to extend; to lengthen; *v.t.* to become greater; to multiply by the production of young. (**in′·**krēs) *n.* growth; produce; profit; interest; progeny; offspring; enlargement; addition. **increasable** *a.* **increasingly** *adv.* [L. *increscere,* fr. *crescere,* to grow].

in·cred·i·ble (in·kred′·ạ·bl) *a.* impossible to be believed; surpassing belief; amazing. **incredibility, -ness** *n.* **incredibly** *adv.*

in·cred·u·lous (in·krej′·ạ.lạs) *a.* not disposed to believe; showing unbelief. **incredulity** *n.* disbelief. **-ness** *n.* **-ly** *adv.*

in·cre·ment (in′·krạ·mạnt) *n.* increase; matter added; growth; annual augmentation of a fixed amount to a salary. **-al** *a.* [L. *incrementum,* fr. *increscere,* to increase].

in·crim·i·nate (in·krim′·ạ·nāt) *v.t.* to charge with a crime; to involve one in a criminal action. **incriminatory** *a.* [L. *in; crimen,* a charge].

in·crust, encrust (in·, en·krust′) *v.t.* to cover with a crust; *v.i.* to form a hard covering or crust on the surface. **-ation** *n.*

in·cu·bate (ing·, in′·kyạ·bāt) *v.i.* to sit, as on eggs, for hatching; to brood; of disease germs, to pass through the stage between infection and appearance of symptoms; *v.t.* to hatch; to ponder over. **incubation** *n.* **incubative, incubatory** *a.* **incubator** *n.* a cabinet, in which the heat is automatically regulated, used to hatch eggs; similar devices for premature infants or bacterial cultures. [L. *in; cubare,* to lie].

in·cu·bus (ing′·, in′·kyạ·bạs) *n.* a nightmare; any burdensome or depressing influence [L. *in,* upon; *cubare,* to lie].

in·cul·cate (in·kul′·kāt) *v.t.* (foll. by *in* or *on*) to urge forcibly and repeatedly; to impress by admonition. **inculcation** *n.* **inculcator** *n.* [L. *inculcare,* to stamp in].

in·cum·bent (in·kum′·bạnt) *a.* lying or resting upon; resting on, as duty; *n.* holder of an office. **incumbency** *n.* [L. *incumbere,* to lie upon].

in·cur (in·kur′) *v.t.* to become liable to; to bring upon oneself. *pr.p.* **-ring.** *pa.t.* and *pa.p.* **-red** [L. *in,* into; *currere,* to run].

in·cur·a·ble (in·kyoor′·ạ·bl) *a.* not able to be cured; *n.* one beyond cure. **incurability** *n.*

in·cu·ri·ous (in·kyoo′·ri·ạs) *a.* not inquisitive or curious; indifferent. **-ly** *adv.*

in·cur·sion (in·kur′·zhạn) *n.* a raid into a territory with hostile intention. **incursive** *a.* [L. *in,* into; *currere,* to run].

in·curve (in·kurv′) *v.t.* to bend into a curve; *v.i.* to bend inward. **incurvate** *v.t.* to bend inward or upward; *a.* curved in.

in·debt·ed (in·det′·ạd) *a.* placed under an obligation; owing; beholden. **-ness** *n.*

in·de·cent (in·dē′·sạnt) *a.* unbecoming; immodest; obscene. **indecency** *n.* lack of decency. **-ly** *adv.*

in·de·ci·pher·a·ble (in·di·sī′·fer·a·bl) *a.* incapable of being deciphered; illegible.

in·de·ci·sion (in·di·sizh′·ạn) *n.* want of decision; irresoluteness; shilly-shallying. **indecisive** *a.* inconslusive; doubtful; wavering. **indecisively** *adv.* **indecisiveness** *n.*

in·de·clin·a·ble (in·di·klīn′·ạ·bl) *a.* (*Gram.*) having no inflections or cases.

in·dec·o·rous (in·dek′·ạ·rạs, in·di·kōr′·ạs) *a.* contrary to good manners. **-ly** *adv.* **-ness, indecorum** *n.* impropriety.

in·deed (in·dēd′) *adv.* in reality; in truth; in fact; certainly. *interj.* denotes surprise.

in·de·fat·i·ga·ble (in·di·fat′·i·gạ·bl) *a.* incapable of being fatigued; unwearied; untiring. **-ness, indefatigability** *n.* **indefatigably** *adv.* [L. *in-; defatigare,* to tire].

in·de·fea·si·ble (in·di·fēz′·ạ·bl) *a.* not to be defeated; incapable of being made void; irrevocable. **indefeasibility** *n.* **indefeasibly** *adv.* [O.Fr. *defaire,* to undo].

in·de·fen·si·ble (in·di·fen′·sạ·bl) *a.* incapable of being maintained, vindicated, or justified; untenable; unjustifiable; unexcusable.

in·de·fin·a·ble (in·di·fīn′·ạ·bl) *a.* not able to be defined. **indefinably** *adv.*

in·def i·nite (in·def′·ạ·nit) *a.* having no known limits; (*Gram.*) not pointing out with precision the person, thing, or time to which a part of speech refers. **-ly** *adv.* **-ness, indefinitude** *n.* want of precision. **— article,** a, an.

in·del·i·ble (in·del′·ạ·bl) *a.* not to be blotted out or erased; ineffaceable; ingrained. **indelibility, -ness** *n.* **indelibly** *adv.* [L. *in-,* not; *delere,* to destroy, blot out].

in·del·i·cate (in·del′·ạ·kạt) *a.* offensive to good manners or to purity of mind; indecorous. **indelicacy** *n.* **-ly** *adv.*

in·dem·ni·fy (in·dem′·nạ·fī) *v.t.* to reimburse; to give security against; to free one from the consequences of a technically illegal act. **indemnification** *n.* **indemnitor** *n.* **indemnity** *n.* an agreement to render a person immune from a contingent liability; compensation [L. *indemnis,* unharmed].

in·de·mon·stra·ble (in·de·mán′·strạ.bl) *a.* cannot be demonstrated or proved.

in·dent (in·dent′) *v.t.* to cut into points or inequalities; to make notches or holes in; to make an order (*upon* some one *for*); to indenture; (*Print.*) to begin the first line of a paragraph farther away from the margin than the remaining lines; *v.i.* to wind back and forth; to make an agreement; to make out an order in duplicate. (in′•dent) *n.* a cut or notch; a dent; a mark, as of a tooth; an order for goods. **-ation** *n.* a notch; a depression. **-ure** *n.* a contract of apprenticeship; [L. *in*, in; *dens*, a tooth].

in•de•pen•dent (in•di•pen′•dạnt) *a.* not dependent; not subject to the control of others; unrelated; free; self-supporting. **independence, independency** *n.* **-ly** *adv.*

in•de•scrib•a•ble (in•di•skrīb′•ạ•bl) *a.* incapable of being described.

in•de•struct•i•ble (in•di•struk′•tạ•bl) *a.* not able to be destroyed; imperishable. **indestructibility** *n.* **indestructibly** *adv.*

in•de•ter•mi•na•ble (in•di•tur′•min•ạ•bl) *a.* cannot be determined, classified, or fixed. **-ness** *n.* **indeterminably** *adv.* **indeterminate** *a.* not settled or fixed in detail; indefinite. **indeterminately** *adv.* **indeterminateness, indetermination** *n.* an unsettled or wavering state of the mind.

in•dex (in′•deks) *n.* any table for facilitating reference in a book; a directing sign; that which points out, shows, indicates, or manifests; a pointer or hand which directs to anything; the forefinger or pointing finger; the ratio between the measurement of a given substance and that of a fixed standard; (*Math.*) the figure or letter showing the power of a quantity; the exponent of a power. *pl.* **-es, indices.** *v.t.* to provide with an index or table references; to place in alphabetical order in an index. **-er** *n.* one who compiles an index [L. = an indicator].

In•di•a (in′•di•ạ) *n.* a country in Asia, named from river *Indus.* **— ink,** ink composed of lamp-black mixed into a paste with gum. **— paper,** a very thin tough and opaque paper made from fibers. **— rubber** *n.* natural rubber obtained from latex [Sans. *sindhu,* a river].

In•di•an (in′•di•ạn) *a.* pert. to India in Asia, to the East Indies, or to the aborigines of America; *n.* a native of India in Asia, of the East Indies, or one of the aboriginal inhabitants of America. **— club,** bottle-shaped wooden club, used in physical exercise. **— corn,** maize. **— file,** single file. **— giver** *n.* (*Colloq.*) one who takes back a gift. **— red** an earthy pigment with a purple-russet color, due to the presence of peroxide of iron. **— summer** mild, warm, hazy weather of autumn [Cans. *sindhu,* a river].

in•di•cate (in′•dạ•kāt) v.t. to point out; to be a sign of; to denote; to show; to signify. **indication** *n.* act of indicating; mark; token; sign. **indicative** *a.* pointing out; denoting; (*Gram.*) applied to that mood of the verb which affirms or denies; *n.* the direct mood of a verb. **indicatively** *adv.* **indicator** *n.* one who indicates; a pointer; an instrument used to gauge and record varying conditions. **indicatory** *a.* [L. *indicare,* to show].

in•dict (in•dīt′) *v.t.* to charge with a crime; to accuse; to arraign. **-able** *a.* **-ment** *n.* the act of indicting; a formal charge of crime. [L. *in; dicere,* to declare].

in•dif•fer•ent (in•dif′•er•ạnt) *a.* uninterested; without concern; not making a difference; having no influence or weight; of no account; neither good nor bad. **indifference** *n.* **-ly** adv.

in•di•gene (in′•dạ•jēn) *n.* an aborigine; a native animal or plant. Also **indigen. indigenous** *a.* born or originating in a country; native. **indigenously** *adv.* [L. *indigena,* a native].

in•di•gent (in′•dạ•jent) *a.* destitute of property or means of subsistence; needy; poor. **indigence** *n.* [L. *indigere,* to lack].

in•di•gest•ed (in•dạ•jest′•ạd) *a.* not digested; lacking order or system. **indigestibility** *n.* **indigestible** *a.* incapable of being digested. **indigestibly** *adv.* **indigestion** *n.* inability to digest food or difficulty and discomfort in doing so; dyspepsia. **indigestive** *a.*

in•dig•nant (in•dig′•nạnt) *a.* moved by a feeling of wrath, mingled with scorn or contempt; roused. **-ly** *adv.* **indignation** *n.* righteous wrath. **indignity** *n.* affront; contemptuous treatment [L. *in-,* not; *dignari,* to deem worthy].

in•di•go (in′•di•gō) *n.* a blue dye-stuff derived from many leguminous plants; *a.* of a deep-blue color [L. *indicum,* fr. *Indicus,* of India].

in•di•rect (in•dạ•rekt′) *a.* not direct or straight; crooked; dishonest. **-ion** *n.* roundabout way; deliberate attempt to mislead; trickery. **-ly** *adv.* **-ness** *n.*

in•dis•creet (in•dis•krēt′) *a.* not discreet; imprudent; injudicious; reckless. **-ly** *adv.* **indiscretion** (in•dis•kresh′•ạn) *n.* an indiscreet act; the quality of being indiscreet.

in•dis•crim•i•nate (in•dis•krim′•ạ•nạt) *a.* wanting discrimination; not making any distinction. **-ly** *adv.* **indiscriminating, indiscriminative** *a.* **indiscrimination** *n.*

in•dis•pen•sa•ble (in•dis•pen′•sạ•bl) *a.* absolutely necessary; not to be set aside. **indispensability, -ness** *n.* **indispensably** *adv.*

in•dis•pose (in•di•spōz′) *v.t.* to render unfit or unsuited; to make somewhat ill; to render averse or disinclined (toward). **-d** *a.* averse; ill. **indisposition** *n.*

in•dis•put•a•ble (in•dis•pū′•tạ•bl, in•dis′•pyoo•tạ•bl) *a.* too obvious to be disputed.

in•dis•sol•u•ble (in•dis•al′•yạ•bl) *a.* not capable of being dissolved; perpetually binding or obligatory; inviolable. **-ness, indissolubility** *n.* **indissolubly** *adv.*

in•dis•tinct (in•dis•tingkt′) *a.* not distinct or distinguishable; not clearly defined or uttered; obscure; dim. **-ive** *a.* not capable of making distinctions; not distinctive. **-ly** *adv.*

in•dis•tin•guish•a•ble (in•dis•ting′•gwish•ạ bl) *a.* may not be distinguished. **-ness** *n.* **indistinguishably** *adv.*

in•dite (in•dīt′) *v.t.* to compose; to write. **-ment** *n.* [O. Fr. *enditer*].

in•di•vid•u•al (in•dạ•vij′•o̤o̤•ạl) *a.* not divided; single; peculiar to single person or thing; distinctive; *n.* a single being, or thing. **-ization** *n.* **-ize, individuate** *v.t.* to distinguish individually; to particularize. **-ism** *n.* quality of being individual; a political or economic theory which asserts the rights of the individual as against those of the community. **-ist** *n.* **-istic** *a.* **-ity** *n.* separate or distinct existence; personality. **-ly** *adv.* [L. *individuus,* undivided].

in•di•vis•i•ble (in•dạ•viz′•ạ•bl) *a.* not divisible; not separate. **indivisibility, -ness** *n.* **indivisibly** *adv.*

in•doc•tri•nate (in•dak′•tri•nāt) *v.t.* to instruct; to imbue with political or religious principles and dogmas. **indoctrination** *n.*

in•do•lent (in′•dạ•lạnt) *a.* habitually idle or lazy; indisposed to exertion. **indolence, indolency** *n.* **-ly** *adv.* [L. *in-,* not; *dolere,* to feel pain].

in•dom•i•ta•ble (in•dam′•ạt•ạ•bl) *a.* not to be subdued; that cannot be overcome. **indomitably** *adv.* [L. *in-,* not; *domitare,* to tame].

In•do•ne•sia (in•dạ•nē′•zhạ) *n.* Republic of S.E. Asia (since 1945). **-n** *a.* [*Indo,* and Gk. *nēsos,* an island].

in•door (in′•dōr) *a.* being within doors; under cover. **indoors** *adv.*

in•dorse, in•dorse•ment See **en•dorse.**

in•du•bi•ta•ble (in•dū′•bit•ạ•bl) *a.* too obvious to admit of doubt; unquestionable; quite certain. **indubitably** *adv.*

in•duce (in•dūs′) *v.t.* to overcome by persuasion or argument; to persuade; to produce or cause (as electricity) **-ment** *n.* that which induces or persuades to action. **-r** *n.* **inducible** *a.* [L. *inducere,* to lead in].

in·duct (in·dukt′) *v.t.* to bring in or introduce; to install or put formally into office; to bring into military service. **-ile** *a.* of a metal not capable of being drawn out into wires or threads. **-ility** *n.* **-ion** *n.* installation of a person in an office; an introduction to a poem or play; (*Elect.*) the transfer of a magnetic or electric state from an electrified to a non-electrified body, by proximity; (*Logic*) a process of finding explanations. **-ional** *a.* **-ive** *a.* **-ively** *adv.* **-or** *n.* [L. *in,* into; *ducere,* to lead].

in·dulge (in·dulj′) *v.t.* to give freedom or scope to; to allow one his own way; to gratify; *v.i.* (usu. followed by *in*) to give oneself to the habit or practice of. **-nce** *n.* **-nt** *a.* yielding; compliant; very forbearing. **-ntly** *adv.* [L. *indulgere,* to be indulgent].

in·du·rate (in′·dyą·rāt) *v.t.* to make hard; to deprive of sensibility; *v.i.* grow hard; to harden. [L. *in,* in; *durus,* hard].

in·dus·try (in′·dąs·tri·) *n.* habitual diligence in any employment, bodily or mental; steady application to work; a particular branch of trade or manufacture. **industrial** *a.* pert. to industry or manufacture. **industrialism** *n.* system of industry or manufacture on a large scale. **industrially** adv. **industrious** *a.* diligent in business or study. **industriously** *adv.* **industriousness** *n.* [L. *industria*].

in·e·bri·ate (in·ē′·bri·āt) *v.t.* to make drunk; to intoxicate; to exhilarate; *a.* intoxicated; *n.* a habitual drunkard. **inebriation, inebriety** *n.* drunkenness. **inebrious** *a.* stupidly drunk [L. *in; ebrius,* drunk].

in·ed·i·ble (in·ed′·ą·bl) *a.* not eatable; unfit for food. **inedibility** *n.*

in·ef·fa·ble (in·ef′·ą·bl) *a.* incapable of being expressed in words; indescribable; unutterable. **-ness, ineffability** *n.* **ineffably** *adv.* [L. *in-,* not; *effabilis,* speakable].

in·ef·face·a·ble (in·ą·fās′·ą·bl) *a.* incapable of being rubbed out. **ineffaceably** *adv.*

in·ef·fec·tive (in·ą·fek′·tiv) *a.* incapable of producing any effect or the effect intended; useless; inefficient. **-ly** *adv.* **ineffectual** *a.* not producing the proper effect; vain; fruitless; futile. **ineffectuality, ineffectualness** *n.* **ineffectually** *adv.*

in·ef·fi·ca·cy (in·ef′·ą·ką·si·) *n.* want of power to produce the proper effect. **inefficacious** *a.* **inefficaciously** *adv.*

in·ef·fi·ci·ent (in·ą·fish′·ąnt) *a.* not fitted to perform the work in a capable, economical way. **inefficiency** *n.* **-ly** *adv.*

in·e·las·tic (in·i·las′·tik) *a.* not elastic; rigid; unyielding. **inelasticity** *n.*

in·el·e·gant (in·el′·ą·gąnt) *a.* lacking in form or beauty; wanting grace or ornament. **inelegance, inelegancy** *n.* **-ly** *adv.*

in·el·i·gi·ble (in·el′·i·ją·bl) *a.* unsuitable; legally disqualified. **ineligibility** *n.*

in·e·luc·ta·ble (in·i·luk′·tą·bl) *a.* inevitable. **ineluctability** *n.* [L. *in-; eluctari,* to struggle out].

in·ept (in·ept′) *a.* not apt or fit; inexpert; unsuitable; foolish. **-itude, -ness** *n.* **-ly** *adv.* [L. *in,* not; *aptus,* fit].

in·e·qual·i·ty (in·i·kwal′·ą·ti·) *n.* want of equality; disparity; inadequacy; unevenness.

in·eq·ui·ta·ble (in·ek′·wi·tą·bl) *a.* not fair or just; not according to equity.

in·e·rad·i·ca·ble (in·i·rad′·i·ką·bl) *a.* incapable of being rooted out; deep-seated.

in·ert (in·urt′) *a.* without the power of action or resistance; sluggish; without active chemical properties. **inertia** (in·ur′·shą) *n.* inactivity; that property of matter by which it tends when at rest to remain so, and when in motion to continue moving in a straight line. **-ly** *adv.* **-ness** *n.* [L. *iners,* sluggish].

in·es·cap·a·ble (in·ą·skāp′·ą·bl) *a.* inevitable; incapable of escape or of being evaded.

in·es·sen·tial (in·ą·sen′·shąl) *a.* not necessary; immaterial; of little consequence.

in·es·ti·ma·ble (in·es′·ti·mą·bl) *a.* not possible to be estimated; of untold value; incalculable; **inestimably** *adv.*

in·ev·i·ta·ble (in·ev′·i·tą·bl) *a.* unavoidable; certain to take place or appear. **-ness, inevitability** *n.* **inevitably** *adv.* [L. *in-; evitare,* to avoid].

in·ex·act (in·ig·zakt′) *a.* not exact; not strictly true. **-itude, -ness** *n.*

in·ex·cus·a·ble (in·ik·skūz′·ą·bl) *a.* not admitting excuse or justification; unpardonable.

in·ex·haust·i·ble (in·ig·zaws′·tą·bl) *a.* incapable of being exhausted, emptied, or spent; unfailing. **inexhaustibility** *n.* **inexhaustibly** *adv.* **inexhaustive** *a.*

in·ex·o·ra·ble (in·ek′·sęr·ą·bl, in·egz′·er·ą·bl) *a.* not to be persuaded or moved by entreaty; unyielding. **-ness, inexorability** *n.* **inexorably** *adv.* [L. *in-; exorare,* to entreat].

in·ex·pe·di·ent (in·ik·spē′·di·ąnt) *a.* not advisable; impolitic; undesirable at the moment. **inexpedience, inexpediency** *n.*

in·ex·pen·sive (in·ik·spen′·siv) *a.* cheap.

in·ex·pe·ri·ence (in·ik·spēr′·i·ąns) *n.* absence or want of experience. **-d** *a.*

in·ex·pert (in·ek′·spurt) *a.* unskilled; clumsy; awkward. **-ness** *n.*

in·ex·pi·a·ble (in·ek′·spi·ę·bl) *a.* admitting of no atonement; implacable; inexorable.

in·ex·pli·ca·ble (in·eks′·pli·ką·bl) *a.* incapable of being explained. **inexplicability,** *n.* **inexplicably** *adv.*

in·ex·plic·it (in·iks·plis′·it) *a.* not explicit; not clearly stated; ambiguous; equivocal.

in·ex·press·i·ble (in·iks·pres′·ą·bl) *a.* cannot be expressed; indescribable. **inexpressibly** *adv.*

in·ex·pres·sive (in·iks·pres′·iv) *a.* not expressive; lacking emphasis; insignificant.

in·ex·ten·si·ble (in.ik·sten′·są·bl) *a.* not capable of extension. **inextensibility** *n.*

in·ex·tin·guish·a·ble (in·ik·sting′·gwish·ą·bl) *a.* cannot be extinguished; unquenchable.

in·ex·tri·ca·ble (in·eks′·tri·ką·bl, in·iks·tri′·ką·bl) *a.* not to be extricated or disentangled, as a knot or coil; incapable of being cleared up or explained. **inextricably** adv.

in·fal·li·ble (in·fal′·ą·bl) *a.* incapable of error; certain; unerring; sure. **infallibilism, infallibility** *n.* **infallibly** *adv.*

in·fa·my (in′·fą·mi·) *n.* total loss of reputation; public disgrace; ill-fame. **infamous** *a.* (in′·fą·mąs) of evil fame or reputation. **infamously** *adv.* [L. *in-; fama,* report].

in·fant (in′·fąnt) *n.* a young baby; (*Law*) a person under 21; *a.* pert. to infants or infancy. **infancy** *n.* the early stage of life preceding childhood; (*Law*) life to the age of twenty-one; the first stage of anything. **infanticide** (in·fan′·tą·sīd) *n.* the killing of a newly-born child. **-ile** *a.* pert. to infants; extremely childish. **infantilism** *n.* arrested development, carrying childish characteristics into adult life. **infantile paralysis,** an infectious disease, poliomyelitis, which leads to paralysis [L. *infans,* unable to speak].

in·fan·try (in′·fąn·tri·) *n.* foot-soldiers [It. *infanteria*].

in·fat·u·ate (in·fach′·òò·wāt) *v.t.* to render foolish; to inspire with a foolish passion. **-d** *a.* greatly enamored. **infatuation** *n.* excessive and foolish love [L. *in; fatuus,* foolish].

in·fea·si·ble (in·fē′·zą·bl) *a.* not capable of being done or accomplished; impracticable.

in·fect (in·fekt′) *v.t.* to affect (with disease); to make noxious; to corrupt; to influence the mood or emotions of people. **-ion** *n.* **-ious.**

-ive *a.* causing infection; catching. **-iously** *adv.* [L. *inficere,* to dip into].

in·fe·lic·i·ty (in·fạ.lis′·ạ·ti·) *n.* unhappiness; anything not appropriate. **infelicitous** *a.*

in·fer (in·fur′) *v.t.* to draw as a conclusion; to deduce; to conclude; to imply. *pr.p.* **-ring.** *pa.t.* and *pa.p.* **-red. -able** *a.* **-ence** *n.* deduction. **-ential** *a.* deduced or deducible by inference. **-entially** *adv.* [L. *inferre,* to bring in].

in·fe·ri·or (in·fi′·ri·ẹr) *a.* lower in rank, order, place, or excellence; of less value; poorer in quality; *n.* a person of a lower rank or station. **-ity** *n.* a lower state of condition. **-ly** *adv.* **-ity complex,** subconscious sense of inferiority [L. comp. of *inferus,* low].

in·fer·nal (in·fur′·nạl) *a.* pert. to the lower regions; hellish. **-ity** *n.* **-ly** *adv.* **inferno** *n.* hell; any place resembling hell; furnace. [L. *infernus,* fr. *inferus,* low].

in·fest (in·fest′) *v.t.* to inhabit; to swarm in such numbers as to be a source of annoyance. **-ed** *a.* covered with body parasites as lice, etc.; plagued **-ation** *n.* [L. *infestare,* fr. *infestus,* unsafe].

in·fi·del (in′·fạ·dạl) *a.* unbelieving; skeptical; *n.* one who is without religious faith; unbeliever; **-ity** *n.* unfaithfulness to the marriage contract; treachery; lack of religious faith [L. *infidelis,* unfaithful].

in·field (in′·fēld) *n.* *(Baseball)* the three basemen and the short stop, or the diamond; a field in close proximity to a farmhouse. **-er** *n.*

in·fil·trate (in·fil′·trāt) *v.t.* to filter into; to enter gradually; to pass through enemy's lines, one by one; *v.i.* to pass in or through by filtering, or as by filtering. *n.* that which infiltrates. **infiltration** *n.*

in·fi·nite (in′·fạ·nit) *a.* unlimited in time or space; without end, limits, or bounds; *(Math.)* greater than any assignable quantity; numberless; immeasurable; *n.* the boundlessness and immeasurableness of the universe; the Almighty, the Infinite Being. **-ly** *adv.* exceedingly. **-ness** *n.* **infinitesimal** *a.* infinitely small. **infinitesimality** *n.* **infinitesimally** *adv.* **infinitude** *n.* boundlessness (of space and time). **infinity** *n.* unlimited and endless extent. [L. *infinitus,* unbounded].

in·fin·i·tive (in·fin′·ạ·tiv) *n.* the simple form of the verb which can be preceded by *to* (*to be*); *a.* not defined or limited. [L. *infinitus,* unbounded].

in·firm (in·furm′) *a.* not strong; feeble; weak; sickly; irresolute. **-ary** *n.* a hospital for the weak and infirm. **-ity,** disease; failing. **-ly** *adv.* [L. *in-; firmus,* strong].

in·flame (in·flām′) *v.t.* to set on fire; to arouse, as desire; to provoke; to be affected with inflammation. **inflammable** *a.* combustible; easily aroused. **inflammability, inflammableness** *n.* **inflammably** *adv.* **inflammation** *n.* inflaming; diseased condition of a part of the body characterized by heat, redness and pain. **inflammatory** *a.* tending to arouse passions; pert. to inflammation [L. *inflammare,* to set on fire].

in·flate (in·flāt′) *v.t.* to swell with air or gas; to raise (price) artificially; to increase (currency) abnormally. **-d** *a.* swollen; bloated; bombastic; pumped up. **inflatable** *a.* **inflation** *n.* swelling; increase in the amount of fiduciary (paper or token) money issued, beyond what is justified by the country's tangible resources; a rise in prices. **inflationary** *a.* [L. *in; flare,* to bowl].

in·flect (in·flekt′) *v.t.* to bend; to modulate the voice; to modify (words) to show grammatical relationships. **-ion,** *n.* a bending inwards or deviation; a variation in the tone of the voice; variation in the terminations of words to express grammatical relations. **-ional** *a.* **-ive** *a.* subject to inflection. **inflexibility** *n.* **inflexible** *a.* incapable of being bent; unyielding to influence or entreaty; unbending. **inflexibly** *adv.* [L. *in,* in; *flectere,* to bend].

in·flict (in·flikt′) *v.t.* to lay on; to impose (a penalty, etc.); to afflict with something painful. **-ion** *n.* pain; burden. **-ive** *a.* [L. *in,* in; *fligere,* to strike].

in·flu·ence (in′·flòò·ạns) *n.* power over men or things; effect on the mind; *(Electrostatics)* induction of a charge by a charged conductor; *v.t.* to act on the mind; to sway; to bias; to induce. **influential** *a.* exerting influence or power; possessing great authority. **influentially** *adv.* [L. *in,* in; *fluere,* to flow].

in·flu·en·za (in·flòò·en′·zạ) *n.* *(Med.)* an acute, infectious epidemic catarrhal fever [It. = influence].

in·flux (in′·fluks) *n.* act of flowing in; the mouth of a stream; the place where one stream flows into another.

in·fold, enfold (in-, en·fōld′) *v.t.* to wrap up; to enclose; to encircle.

in·form (in·fawrm′) *v.t.* to tell; to accumulate knowledge; to inspire; *v.i.* to give information.

in·form (in·fawrm′) *a.* without form. **-al** *a.* without formality, unceremonious. **-ality** *n.* **-ant** *n.* one who imparts news. **-ation** *n.* knowledge; intelligence; news. **-ative, -atory** *a.* educational. **-ed** *a.* educated. **-er** *n.* one who gives information about a violation of the law [L. *informare,* to give form to].

in·frac·tion (in·frak′·shạn) *n.* breach; violation.

in·fran·gi·ble (in·fran′·jạ·bl) *a.* not capable of being broken; not to be violated. **infrangibility** *n.* [L. *in-,* not; *frangere,* to break].

in·fra·red (in·frạ·red′) *a.* of the longer invisible heat rays below the red end of the visible spectrum.

in·fre·quent (in·frē′·kwạnt) *a.* seldom happening; rare; uncommon. **infrequence, infrequency** *n.* **-ly** *adv.*

in·fringe (in·frinj′) *v.t.* to violate; to transgress. **-ment** *n.* breach; breaking (of a law) [L. *in; frangere,* to break].

in·fu·ri·ate (in.fyoor′·i·āt) *v.t.* to make furious, to enrage; to madden. **infueriation** *n.* [L. *in; furia,* rage].

in·fuse (in·fūz′) *v.t.* to pour into; to instill; to inspire; to steep in order to extract soluble properties. **infusible** *a.* capable of being infused; not capable of fusion. **infusibility** *n.* **infusion** *n.* act of infusing, instilling, or inspiring; aqueous solution containing the soluble parts of a substance, made by pouring boiling water over it, cooling and straining [L. *in,* in; *fundere, fusum,* to pour].

in·gen·ious (in·jēn′·yạs) *a.* skilled in inventing or thinking out new ideas; curious or clever in design; skillfully contrived. **-ly** *adv.* **-ness, ingenuity** (in·jạ·nòò′·i·ti·) *n.* [L. *ingenium,* natural ability].

in·ge·nue (ạn·zhạ·nòò′) *n.* an artless, naive, girl; an actress who plays such a part [Fr.].

in·gen·u·ous (in·jen′·yoo·ạs) *a.* frank; artless; innocent. **-ly** *adv.* **-ness** *n.* [L. *ingenuus* free-born, frank].

in·got (ing′·gạt) *n.* a metal casting, esp. of unwrought silver or gold [O.E. *in; geotan,* to pour].

in·grain, engrain (in-, en·grān′) *v.t.* to fix firmly in the mind. (in′·grain) *a.* firmly fixed; dyed, before manufacture into articles. **-ed** *a.*

in·grate (in′·grāt) *n.* an ungrateful person. **ingratitude** *n.* want of gratitude; unthankfulness.

in·gra·ti·ate (in·grā′·shi·āt) *v.t.* to work oneself into favor with another **ingratiation** *n.* [L. *in; gratia,* favor].

in·gre·di·ent (in·grē′·di·ạnt) *n.* a component part of any mixture; one part or element of a compound [L. *ingredi,* to go in].

in·gress (in′·gres) *n.* entrance; power, right, or means of entrance [L. *ingredi, ingressum,* to go in].

in·grow·ing (in′·grō·ing) *a.* growing inwards, esp. of a toenail. **ingrowth** *n.* **ingrown** *a.*

in·gur·gi·tate (in·gur′·ją·tāt) *v.t.* to swallow up greedily or hastily; to engulf. **ingurgitation** *n.* [L. *in,* in; *gurges,* a whirlpool].

in·hab·it (in·hab′·it) *v.t.* to live or dwell in; to occupy. **-able** *a.* possible to be dwelt in. **-ant** *n.* one who inhabits; a resident. **-ation** *n.* [L. *in,* in; *habitare,* to dwell].

in·hale (in·hāl′) *v.t.* to breathe in, as air, tobacco smoke, etc.; to draw in the breath. **inhalant** *n.* a volatile medicinal remedy to be inhaled. *a.* **inhalation** *n.* act of drawing air into the lungs. **inhalator** *n.* apparatus to help one inhale [L. *in,* in; *halare,* to breathe].

in·here (in·hir′) *v.i.* (usu. followed by *in*) to exist in; to belong naturally to; to be a quality of; to be vested in, as legal rights. **-nce, -ncy** *n.* **-nt** *a.* existing in something so as to be inseparable. **-ntly** *adv.* [L. *in,* in; *haerere,* to stick].

in·her·it (in·her′·ąt) *v.t.* to receive by descent, or by will; to fall heir to; to derive (traits, etc.) from parents; *v.i.* to succeed as heir. **-able** *a.* **-ance** *n.* what is inherited. **-or** *n.* (*fem.* **-ress, -rix**) [L. *in,* in; *heres,* an heir].

in·hib·it (in·hib′·it) *v.t.* to hold back; to forbid; to restrain. **inhibition** (in·i·bi′·shąn) *n.* a subconscious repressed emotion which controls or colors a person's attitude or behavior. **-ory** *a.* prohibiting; forbidding; restraining [L. *inhibere,* to hold in].

in·hos·pi·ta·ble (in·hàs′·pi·tą·bl) *a.* averse to showing kindness to strangers or guests; discourteous. **-ness, inhospitality** *n.* **inhospitably** *adv.* [L. *hospes,* a guest].

in·hu·man (in·hū′·mąn) *a.* not human or humane; without feeling or pity. **inhumane** (in·hū·mān′) *a.* cruel. **-ity** *n.*

in·hume (in·hūm′) *v.t.* to put into the ground; to bury. **inhumation** *n.* [L. *humus,* ground].

in·im·i·cal (in·im′·i·kąl) *a.* like an enemy; unfriendly. **-ly** *adv.* [L. *inimicus,* an enemy].

in·im·i·ta·ble (in·im′·i·tą·bl) *a.* defying imitation; incomparable. **inimitably** *adv.*

in·iq·ui·ty (in·ik′·wą·ti·) *n.* gross injustice; want of moral principle; wickedness; a crime. **iniquitous** *a.* **iniquitously** *adv.* [L. *iniquitas* fr. *in-,* not; *aequus,* fair, even].

in·i·tial (i·nish′·ąl) *a.* occurring at the beginning; commencing; early; *v.t.* to put one's initials to, in the way of acknowledgment. *n.* the first letter of a word, esp. a name. **initiate,** *v.t.* to begin; to start (a movement, etc.); to instruct in the rudiments of; to admit into a society, etc., with formal rites; *n.* one who is initiated. **initiation** *n.* **initiative** *a.* serving to initiate; *n.* the first step; the quality of being able to set things going for the first time. **initiator** *n.* **initiatory** *a.* introductory [L. *initialis,* fr. *initium,* a beginning].

in·ject (in·jekt′) *v.t.* to throw in; to force in; to introduce (a fluid) under the skin by means of a hollow needle. **-ion** *n.* the act of injecting or throwing into; fluid so injected. **-or** *n.* [L. *injicere,* fr. *jacere,* to throw].

in·ju·di·cious (in·jòò·dish′·ąs) *a.* ill-advised; imprudent; lacking in judgment **injudicial** *a.* not according to the form of law. **-ly** *adv.*

in·junc·tion (in·jungk′·shąn) *n.* an order or command; an exhortation; a precept [L. *in,* in; *jungere, junctum,* to join].

in·jure (in′·jęr) *v.t.* to do wrong, injury, damage, or injustice to. **injurious** *a.* causing injury or damage. **injuriously** *adv.* **injury** *n.* wrong; damage; harm [L. *injuria,* fr. *jus,* law].

in·jus·tice (in·jus′·tis) *n.* an unjust act; want of justice; wrong.

ink (ingk) *n.* a fluid, black or colored, used for writing, printing and sketching; *v.t.* to cover or smear with ink. **-well** *n.* container for ink. **-iness** *n.* **-y** *a.* resembling ink [O.Fr. *enque* = Fr. *encre*].

ink·ling (ingk′·ling) *n.* a hint or whisper; slight knowledge [etym. doubtful].

in·land (in′·ląnd) *a.* remote from the sea; interior; carried on within a country; *n.* (in·land′) the interior part of a country. **-er** *n.*

in·laws (in′·lawz) *n.pl.* (*Colloq.*) one's relations by marriage.

in·lay (in·lā′) *v.t.* to ornament, by cutting out part of a surface and inserting pieces of pearl, ivory, wood, etc., to form a pattern. *pa.p.* **inlaid.** *n.* inlaid pattern.

in·let (in′·let) *n.* an entrance; a small bay or creek; an insertion.

in·mate (in′·māt) *n.* a dweller in a house or institution; a fellow-lodger.

inn (in) *n.* a house which provides lodging accommodation for travelers; a hotel; restaurant or tavern. **-keeper** *n.* one who keeps an inn. [O.E.].

in·nate (i·nāt′) *a.* inborn; native; natural; inherent; congenital. **-ly** *adv.* [L. *innatus*].

in·ner (in′·ęr) *a.* farther in; interior; private; not obvious; **-most, inmost.** *a.* farthest in. [O.E. *innera,* comp. fr. *inne,* within].

in·ner·vate (in′·ęr·vāt). Also **innerve,** *v.t.* to give nervous strength to; to stimulate. **innervation** *n.* [L. *in; nervus,* sinew].

in·ning (in′·ing) *n.* in games, a side's turn of batting; the ingathering of grain; reclaiming of land [O.E. *inn,* in, within].

in·no·cent (in′·ą·sąnt) *a.* free from guilt; blameless; harmless, sinless; simple; *n.* an innocent person, esp. a child; a guileless, unsuspecting person. **innocence, innocency** *n.* **-ly** *adv.* [L. *in-,* not; *nocere,* to harm].

in·noc·u·ous (in·àk′·yoo·ąs) *a.* producing no ill effects; harmless. **-ly** *adv.* **-ness** [L. *in-,* not; *nocere,* to harm].

in·no·vate (in′·ą·vāt) *v.t.* to make changes by introducing something new. **innovation** *n.* a new idea [L. *innovare,* fr. *novus,* new].

in·nox·ious (in·àk′·shąs) *a.* innocuous; harmless in effects [L. *innoxius*].

in·nu·en·do (in·ū·en′·dō) *n.* an allusive remark (usually deprecatory); an indirect hint [L. = by nodding to, fr. *nuere,* to nod].

in·nu·mer·a·ble (i·nū′·męr·ą·bl) *a.* not able to be numbered; countless; very numerous. **innumerability** *n.* **innumerably** *adv.*

in·nu·tri·tion (in·nòò·trish′·ąn) *n.* want of nutrition. **innutritious** *a.*

in·ob·serv·ant (in·ąb·zer′·vąnt) *a.* not observant; heedless. **inobservance** *n.* failure to observe (the law, church-going, etc.).

in·oc·u·late (in·àk′·yą·lāt) *v.t.* (*Med.*) to introduce into the body pathogenic bacteria (e.g. typhoid inoculation) or living virus (e.g. smallpox vaccination) to secure immunity; to imbue strongly with opinions. **inoculation** *n.* [L. *inoculare,* fr. *oculus,* eye, bud].

in·op·er·a·ble (in·àp′·ęr·a·bl) *a.* (*Surgery*) not in a condition for operating on. **inoperative** *a.* not operating; without effect.

in·op·por·tune (in·àp·ęr·tūn′) *a.* unseasonable in time; not convenient; untimely. **-ly** *adv.* **inopportunity** *n.*

in·or·di·nate (in·awr′·dą·nąt) *a.* not limited; disordered. **-ness** *n.* **-ly** *adv.* excessively.

in·or·gan·ic (in·awr·gan′·ik) *a.* devoid of an organized structure; not derived from animal or vegetable life. **-ally** *adv.*

in·os·cu·late (in·as′·kyą·lāt) *v.t.* and *v.i.* to join by openings (arteries, etc.).

in·pa·tient (in′·pā·shąnt) *n.* a patient who is lodged and fed while receiving medical attention in a hospital.

in·put (in′·poot) *n.* (*Elect.*) the power supplied to battery, condenser, etc.

in·quest (in′·kwest) *n.* a judicial inquiry, esp. one presided over by a coroner, with or without a jury, into the cause of a person's death.

in·qui·e·tude (in·kwī′·ą·tūd) *n.* uneasiness either of body or of mind; restlessness.

in·quire, enquire (in-, en·kwir′) *v.i.* to ask questions; to make investigation; to seek information; *v.t.* to ask about. **-r** *n.* **inquiring** *a.* given to inquiring; prying. **inquiringly** *adv.* **inquiry** *n.* investigation; a question [L. *inquirere,* fr. *quaerere,* to seek].

in·qui·si·tion (in·kwą·zish′·ąn) *n.* a strict investigation; official inquiry; an ecclesiastical tribunal, 'the Holy Office,' established by the R.C. Church in the Middle Ages for the trial and punishment of heretics. **-al** *a.* **inquisitive** *a.* apt to ask questions; prying; curious to know. **inquisitively** *adv.* **inquisitiveness** *n.* **inquisitor** *n.* one whose official duty it is to make inquiries; a member of the Court of Inquisition. **inquisitorial** *a.* **inquisitorially** *adv.* [L. *inquisitio,* fr. *inquirere,* to search out].

in·re (in·rē′, ·rā′) *prep.* in the matter of; concerning (often abbreviated to **re**) [L.]

in·road (in′·rōd) *n.* a sudden incursion into enemy territory; a sudden invasion; raid.

in·sane (in·sān′) *a.* unsound in mind; mentally diseased; lunatic. **-ly** *adv.* **-ness, insanity** *n.* lunacy; madness.

in·sa·tia·ble (in·sā′·shą·bl) *a.* incapable of being satisfied; voracious; rapacious. **-ness, insatiability** *n.* **insatiably** *adv.*

in·sa·ti·ate (in·sā′·shi·ąt) *a.* not to be satisfied. **-ly** *adv.* **-ness** *n.*

in·scribe (in·skrīb′) *v.t.* to write upon; to engrave; to address or dedicate; to draw a geometrical figure inside another so as to touch but not intersect. **inscribable** *a.* **-r** *n.* **inscription** *n.* act of inscribing; words inscribed on a monument, coin, etc.; dedication of a book, etc.; **inscriptional, inscriptive** *a.* [L. *in; scribere,* to write].

in·scru·ta·ble (in·skróó′·tą·bl) *a.* incapable of being searched into and understood by inquiry or study; mysterious. **inscrutability, -ness** *n.* **inscrutably** *adv.* [L. *in-,* not; *scrutari,* to search].

in·sect (in′·sekt) *n.* one of a class of invertebrate animals called the *Insecta. a.* pert. to insects; small; insignificant. **insecta** *n.* the insect or hexapod (six-legged) class of arthropods. **insecticide** *n.* killing insect pests; chemical preparation for the destruction of noxious insects. **-ivorous** *a.* living on insects [L. *in,* in; *secare,* to cut].

in·se·cure (in·si·kyoor′) *a.* not securely fixed; dangerous to life or limb; unsafe; unguarded; having doubts and fears. **insecurity** *n.*

in·sem·i·nate (in·sem′·ȧ·nāt) *v.t.* to sow; to impregnate. **insemination** *n.* conception [L. *in,* into; *semen,* seed].

in·sen·sate (in·sen′·sāt) *a.* destitute of sense; without power of feeling. **-ly** *adv.*

in·sen·si·ble (in·sen′·są·bl) *a.* without bodily sensation; not perceived by the senses; unconscious; callous; imperceptible **-ness** *n.* **insensibility, insensibly** *adv.*

in·sen·si·tive (in·sen′·są·tiv) *a.* not sensitive; callous. **-ness, insensitivity** *n.*

in·sen·ti·ent (in·sen′·shi·ąnt) *a.* not having perception; inanimate.

in·sep·a·ra·ble (in·sep′·ą·rą·bl) *a.* not divisible or separable; always in close association; *n.pl.* persons or things that are seldom seen apart. **inseparably** *adv.*

in·sert (in·surt′) *vt.* to put in; to place among; to introduce. (in′·surt) *n.* anything inserted. **-ion** *n.* the act of inserting; that which is inserted [L. *in.* in; *serere,* to join].

in·side (in′·sīd) *prep.* or *adv.* within the sides of; in the interior; *a.* internal; interior; *n.* the part within; *pl.* (*Colloq.*) inward parts; guts. **-r** *n.* (*Colloq.*) one who is within a certain group or has special advantages.

in·sid·i·ous (in·sid′·i·ąs) *a.* lying in wait; treacherous; advancing imperceptibly. **-ly** *adv.* **-ness** *n.* [L. *insidiosus,* fr. *insidere,* to lie in wait.].

in·sight (in′·sīt) *n.* view of the interior of anything; mental penetration; clear understanding; power of discernment.

in·sig·ni·a (in·sig′·ni·ą) *n.pl.* symbols of authority, dignity, or office; badges; emblems [L. fr. *signum,* sign].

in·sig·ni·fi·cant (in·sig·nif′·ą·kąnt) *a.* signifying very little; having little importance, use, or value; trifling. **insignificance, insignificancy** *n.* **-ly** *adv.*

in·sin·cere (in·sin·sir′) *a.* not sincere; dissembling; hypocritical; not to be trusted. **-ly** *adv.* **insincerity** *n.* hypocrisy.

in·sin·u·ate (in·sin′·yą·wāt) *v.t.* to introduce gently and adroitly; to suggest by remote allusion; to work oneself into favor; *v.i.* to ingratiate oneself. **insinuating** *a.* **insinuatingly** *adv.* **insinuation** *n.* act of gaining favor by artful means; hint; suggestion. **insinuative** *a.* **insinuator** *n.* **insinuatory** *a.* [L. *insinuare,* to introduce tortuously].

in·sip·id (in·sip′·id) *a.* destitute of taste; deficient in spirit, life, or animation. **-ly** *adv.* **-ness, -ity** *n.* [L. *insipidus,* tasty].

in·sip·i·ent (in·sip′·i·ąnt) *a.* not wise; foolish. **insipience** *n.* [L. *insipiens*].

in·sist (in·sist′) *v.i.* to dwell upon as a matter of special moment; to be urgent or pressing; (foll. by *on* or *upon*) to hold firmly to. **-ence** *n.* persistent demand or refusal to give way. **-ency** *n.* pertinacity. **-ent** *a.* [L. *insistere,* fr. *sistere,* to stand].

in·so·bri·e·ty (in·są·brī·ąt·i·) *n.* drunkeness.

in·so·lent (in′·są·ląnt) *a.* proud and haughty; overbearing. **insolence** *n.* contemptuous rudeness or arrogance. **-ly** *adv.* [L. *in-,* not; *solere,* to be accustomed].

in·sol·u·ble (in·sál′·yą·bl) *a.* incapable of being dissolved; inexplicable; not to be explained. **insolubility, -ness** *n.* **insolvable** *a.*

in·sol·vent (in·sál′·vąnt) *a.* not able to pay one's debts; bankrupt; *n.* one who is bankrupt. **insolvency** *n.*

in·som·ni·a (in·sám′·ni·ą) *n.* chronic sleeplessness from any cause [L.].

in·so·much (in·są·much′) *adv.* so that; to such a degree; in such wise that.

in·sou·ci·ance (in·sóó′·si·ąns) *n.* carelessness of feeling or manner; an air of indifference. **insouciant** *a.* carefree; indifferent [Fr.].

in·spect (in·spekt′) *v.t.* to view narrowly and critically; to examine officially as troops, arms, or goods offered for sale, etc. **-ingly** *adv.* **inspection** *n.* careful survey; official examination. **inspectional, -ive** *a.* **-or** *n.* official examiner; a police officer ranking below a superintendent; anyone who inspects. **-orate** *n.* a district under an inspector; a body of inspectors generally. **-orial** *a.* [L. *inspicere,* to look into].

in·spire (in·spīr′) *v.t.* to breathe in; to infuse thought or feeling into; to affect as with a supernatural influence; to arouse; *v.i.* to give inspiration; to inhale. **inspirable** *a.* **inspiration** *n.* act of drawing in the breath; communication of ideas from a supernatural source; a bright idea. **inspirational** *a.* **inspiratory** *a.* tending to inspire; encouraging. **inspired** *a.* inhaled; actuated by Divine influence [L. *in; spirare,* to breathe].

in·sta·bil·i·ty (in·stą·bil′·ą·ti·) *n.* want of stability or firmness.

in·stall (in·stawl′) *v.t.* to place in position; to have something put in; to induct, with ceremony, a person into an office. **installation** *n.* complete equipment of a building for heating, lighting, etc.; generally, placing in position for use. **-ment** *n.* act of installing; a periodical payment of the part cost of something; a portion.

in·stance (in′·stạns) *n.* case in point; example; *v.t.* to mention as an example; to cite. **instant** *a.* urgent; pressing; immediate; current (usu. abbreviated to inst.); *n.* a particular point of time; moment. **instantaneity** *n.* **instantaneous** *a.* done in an instant; happening in a moment. **instantaneously** *adv.* **instantaneousness** *n.* **instantly** *adv.* at once [L. *in; stare,* to stand].

in·stead (in·sted′) *adv.* in the stead, place, or room; in one's stead [*stead*].

in·step (in′·step) *n.* the arched upper part of the human foot, near the ankle, which gives spring to the step; that part of a shoe, etc., which covers the instep; the hind-leg of a horse from the hock to the pastern joint.

in·sti·gate (in′·stạ·gāt) *v.t.* to goad or urge forward; to incite, esp. to evil; to bring about. **instigation** *n.* **instigator** *n.* [L. *instigare,* to incite].

in·still (in·stil′) *v.t.* to put in by drops; to infuse slowly; to introduce by degrees (into the mind). **-ed. -ation, -ment** *n.* [L. *in; stillare,* to drip].

in·stinct (in′·stingkt) *n.* intuition (in *neurology*) compound reflex action; (in *psychology*) an innate train of reflexes; inborn impulse or propensity; unconscious skill; intuition. (in·stingkt′) *a.* charged; full; urged from within; animated. **instinctively, instinctly** *adv.* **instinctivity** *n.* [L. *instinctus,* fr. *instinguere,* to urge].

in·sti·tute (in′·stạ·tūt) *v.t.* to establish; to found; to appoint; to set going; to originate; to lay down as a law; *n.* a society or organization established for promoting some particular work, scientific, educational, etc. **institutes** *n.pl.* a book of precepts, principles or rules; a text-book on legal principles. **institution** *n.* the act of instituting or establishing; an established law, custom, or public occasion; an institute; (*sociol.*) an organized pattern of group behavior established and generally accepted as a fundamental part of a culture, such as slavery. **institutional** *a.* **institutionally** *adv.* **institutive** *a.* tending or intended to instigate or establish; endowed with the power to ordain. **institutively** *adv.* **institutor, -r** *n.* [L. *instituere,* to set up].

in·struct (in·strukt′) *v.t.* to teach; to inform; to prepare someone for (e.g., an examination); to order or command; to give directions to. **-ible** *a.* **-ion** *n.* the act of instructing or teaching; education; order. **-ional** *a.* **-ive** *a.* fitted to instruct; containing edifying matter; conveying knowledge or information. **-ively** *adv.* **-iveness** *n.* **-or** *n.* [L. *instructus*].

in·stru·ment (in′·strạ·mạnt) *n.* a tool or implement; a person or thing made use of; a means of producing musical sounds; (*Law*) a formal or written document. **-al** (in·strạ·ment′·al) *a.* serving as an instrument or means; helpful; pert. to musical, surgical, or other instruments; performed with or composed for a musical instrument or instruments; (*Gram.*) in some inflected languages, denoting a case, having as chief function the indication of means or agency. **-alist** *n.* one skilled in playing upon a musical instrument. **-ality** *n.* the quality of being instrumental, of serving some purpose; agency or means; good offices. **-ally** *adv.* **-ation** *n.* the art of writing and arranging musical compositions for the individual instruments of a band or orchestra; orchestration. [L. *instruere,* to build].

in·sub·or·di·nate (in·sạ·bawr′·dạ·nit) *a.* disobedient; unruly. **insubordination** *n.*

in·suf·fer·a·ble (in·suf′·ẹr·ạ·bl) *a.* not able to be endured; intolerable. **insufferably** *adv.*

in·suf·fi·cient (in·sạ·fish′·ạnt) *a.* not enough; deficient. **insufficiency** *n.* **-ly** *adv.*

in·su·lar (in′·syoo·lẹr) *a.* pert. to or like an island; isolated; narrow-minded or prejudiced. **-ism, -ity** *n.* **-ly** *adv.* [L. *insula,* an island].

in·su·late (in′·sạ·lāt) *v.t.* to keep rigidly apart from contact with other people; to bar the passage of electricity, heat, sound, light, dampness, or vibration by the use of non-conducting materials. **insulation** *n.* [L. *insula,* an island].

in·su·lin (in′·sạ·lin) *n.* a hormone secreted in the pancreas; organic drug for the treatment of diabetes [L. *insula,* island].

in·sult (in·sult′) *v.t.* to treat with insolence or contempt by words or action; to abuse; to affront. (in′·sult) *n.* gross abuse offered to another [L. *insultare,* to leap upon].

in·su·per·a·ble (in·sōō′·pẹr·a·bl) *a.* not able to be overcome or surmounted; invincible. **insuperability,** *n.* **insuperably** *adv.*

in·sup·port·a·ble (in·sạ·pōr′·tạ·bl) *a.* incapable of being borne or endured. **-ness** *n.* *insupportably adv.*

in·sure (in·shoor′) *v.t.* to make sure or certain; to make safe (against); to ensure; to secure the payment of a sum in event of loss, death, etc., by a contract and payment of sums called premiums. **insurable** *a.* **insurance** *n.* contract between two parties whereby the insurer agrees to indemnify the insured upon the occurrence of a stipulated contingency [L. *in; securus,* secure].

in·sur·gent (in·sur′·jạnt) *a.* rising in opposition to lawful authority; rebellious; *n.* one in revolt; a rebel. **insurgency** *n.* incipient stage of revolt. Also **insurgence.**

in·sur·mount·a·ble (in·sẹr·moun′·tạ·bl) *a.* not able to be surmounted or overcome. **insurmountability** *n.* **insurmountably** *adv.*

in·sur·rec·tion (in·sạ·rek′·shạn) *n.* a rising against civil or political authority. **-al, -ary** *a.* **-ist** *n.* [L. *insurgere,* to rise upon].

in·sus·cep·ti·ble (in·sạ·sep′·tạ·bl) *a.* not susceptible; not to be moved, affected, or impressed. **insusceptibility** *n.*

in·take (in′·tāk) *n.* that which is taken in; quantity taken in; inlet of a tube or cylinder; a point of narrowing or contraction.

in·tan·gi·ble (in·tan′·jạ·bl) *a.* not perceptible to the touch; not clear to the mind. **-ness, intangibility** *n.* **intangibly** *adv.*

in·te·ger (in′·tạ·jẹr) *n.* the whole of anything; whole number (as opposed to a fraction or a mixed number). **integral** (in′·tạ·grạl) *a.* denoting a whole number or quantity; constituting an essential part of a whole; *n.* a whole number; (*Math.*) a sum of differentials. **integrally** *adv.* **integrate** *v.t.* to make entire; to give the sum or total. **integration** *n.* act of making a whole out of parts. **integrator** *n.* **integrity** *n.* the state of being entire; wholeness; probity; honesty; uprightness [L. *integer,* entire].

in·teg·u·ment (in·teg′·yạ·mạnt) *n.* the outer protective layer of tissue which covers a plant or animal; the skin. **integumentary** *a.* [L. *integumentum,* fr. *integere,* to cover].

in·tel·lect (in′·tạ·lekt) *n.* the faculty of reasoning and thinking; mental power; mind; understanding; *pl.* the senses. **-ive** *a.* pert. to intellect as distinguished from the senses.

in·tel·lect·u·al (in·tạ·lek′·choo·ạl) *a.* of high mental capacity; having the power of understanding; *n.* one well endowed with intellect. **-ism** *n.* the doctrine that knowledge is derived from pure reason; emphasis on the value of the rational faculties. **-ity** *n.* intellectual powers. **-ly** *adv.* [L. *intelligere,* to understand].

in·tel·li·gent (in·tel′·ạ·jạnt) *a.* having or showing good intellect; quick at understanding. **intelligence** *n.* inborn quickness of understanding an dadaptability to relatively new situations; information. **-ly** *adv.* **-sia** *n.* the intellectual or cultured classes. **intelligible** *a.* that can be readily understood; rational. **intelligibleness, intelligibility** *n.* **intelligibly** *adv.* **intelligence quotient** (abbrev. I.Q.) the numerical rating of general intelligence by use of psychological tests [L. *intelligere,* to understand].

in·tem·per·ate (in·tem′·pęr·ąt) *a.* immoderate; indulging to excess any appetite or passion; addicted to an excessive use of liquor; extreme in climate. **intemperance** *n.* excess of any kind. **-ly** *adv.* [L. *intemperatus*].

in·tend (in·tend′) *v.t.* and *v.i.* to design; to purpose; to mean; to have in mind.**-ant** *n.* one who has the charge of some public business. **-ancy** *n.* the office of an intendant. **-ed** *a.* and *n.* (*Colloq.*) betrothed [L. *intendere,* to bend the mind on].

in·tense (in·tens′) *a.* to an extreme degree; very strong or acute; emotional. **-ly** *adv.* **-ness, intensity** *n.* severity; ardor; earnestness; the strength of an electric current. **intensification** *n.* **intensify** *v.t.* to render more intense; to increase or augment; *v.i.* to become more intense. *pa.t.* and *pa.p.* **intensified. intensive** *a.* giving emphasis; unrelaxed; increasing in force. **intensively** *adv.* [L. *intendere, intensum,* to stretch].

in·tent (in·tent′) *a.* having the mind bent on an object; eager in pursuit of; firmly resolved; preoccupied; absorbed; *n.* intention; aim; purpose; view; object. **-ion** *n.* design; aim; purpose. **-ional, -ioned** *a.* done purposely. **-ionally** *adv.* **-ly** *adv.* **-ness** *n.* [L. *intendere,* to turn the mind to].

in·ter- (in′·tęr) *prefix* fr. L. *inter,* between, among, with, amid.

in·ter (in·tur′) *v.t.* to bury. *pr.p.* **-ring.** *pa.t.* and *pa.p.* **-red. -ment** *n.* burial [Fr. *enterrer,* fr. L. *in; terra,* earth].

in·ter·act (in·tęr·akt′) *v.i.* to act mutually on each other. **-ion** *n.*

in·ter·cede (in·tęr·sēd′) *v.i.* to act as peacemaker; to plead in favor of one; to mediate. **-r** *n.* **intercession** *n.* the act of interceding. **intercessor** *n.* a mediator; a pleader. **intercessorial, intercessory** *a.* [L. *inter,* between; *cedere,* to go].

in·ter·cept (in·ter·sept′) *v.t.* to stop or obstruct passage; to seize in transit; (*Math.*) to cut off a part of a line at two points; *n.* the part of a line between any two points. **-er, -or** *n.* **-ion** *n.* **-ive** *a.* [L. *inter,* between; *capere, captum,* to seize].

in·ter·ces·sion, intercessor See **intercede.**

in·ter·change (in·ter·chānj′) *v.t.* to exchange; to reciprocate; *v.i.* to succeed alternately; to exchange places; *n.* (in′·tęr·chānj) access to a freeway; a mutual exchange. **-able** *a.* **-ability, -ableness** *n.*

in·ter·com (in′·tęr·kȧm) (*Slang*) *n.* internal telephonic system. **-municate** (in·tęr·ką·mū′·ni·kāt) *v.t.* to exchange conversations or messages. **-munication** *a.,n.* **-municative** *a.*

in·ter·con·nect (in·tęr·ką·nekt′) *v.t.* and *v.i.* to connect mutually and intimately.

in·ter·cos·tal (in·tęr·kȧs′·tąl) *a.*(*Anat.*) between the rigs [L. *inter,* between; *costa,* a rib].

in·ter·course (in′·tęr·kōrs) *n.* communication between individuals; exchange of goods; correspondence by letter; coition [O.Fr. *entrecours,* fr. L. *inter,* between; *currere,* to run].

in·ter·cur·rent (in·tęr·kur′·ąnt) *a.* running between or among; occurring during the course of another (disease); intervening.

in·ter·de·pend (in·tęr·di·pend′) *v.i.* to depend mutually. **-ence** *n.* **-ent** *a.* **-ently** *adv.*

in·ter·dict (in·tęr·dikt′) *v.t.* to forbid; to prohibit; to restrain; to debar from communion with a church; to lay under an interdict. (in′·tęr·dikt) *n.* prohibition; (*Law*) a prohibitory act or decree; a papal ordinance by which certain persons are debarred from participating in the sacraments, church offices or ecclesiastical burial. **-ion** *n.* **-ive, -ory** *a.* [L. *interdicere,* to prohibit].

in·ter·est (in′·tęr·ąst, in′·trist) *v.t.* to engage and keep the attention of; to arouse the curiosity of; to cause to feel interest; *n.* special attention; concern; regard to personal profit or advantage; curiosity; the profit per cent derived from money lent. **-ed** *a.* having a share in; feeling an interest in. **-edly** *adv.* **-edness** *n.* **-ing** *a.* appealing to or exciting one's interest or curiosity. **-ingly** *adv.* **compound —,** interest on the principal and also on the added interest as it falls due. **simple interest,** interest only on the principal during the time of loan. [L. *interesse,* to be of concern to].

in·ter·fere (in·tęr·fir′) *v.i.* to be in or come into, opposition; to enter into or take part in the concerns of others; to intervene. **-nce** *n.* meddling with other people's business; uncalled-for intervention; (*Radio*) anything generally which prevents the proper reception of radio waves. **-r** *n.* **interferingly** *adv.* [L. *inter,* between; *ferire,* to strike].

in·ter·im (in′·tęr·im) *n.* the time between; the meantime; *a.* for the time being; temporary; provisional [L.].

in·te·ri·or (in·tī′·ri·ęr) *a.* inner; internal; inland, away from coast or frontiers; *n.* the inside part or portion; the inland part of a country. **-ly** *adv.* [L. compar. of *interus,* fr L. *intra,* within].

in·ter·ject (in·tęr·jekt′) *v.t.* to throw between; to insert; to exclaim abruptly. **-ion** *n.* act of throwing between; a word which expresses strong emotion or passion when suddenly uttered. **-ional, -ionary, .-ory** *a.* **-ionally** *adv.* [L. *inter,* between; *jacere, jactum,* to throw].

in·ter·lace (in·tęr·lās′) *v.t.* to lace together; to entwine; to unite; to interweave.

in·ter·lard (in·tęr·lȧrd′) *v.t.* to diversify by mixture (of words, etc.).

in·ter·line (in·tęr·līn′) *v.t.* to write or mark between the lines of a book, document, etc.; to put an inner lining in a garment between the outer material and the regular lining. **-al, -ar** *a.* between lines. **-ate** *v.t.* to mark between the lines. **interlining** *n.* inner lining of a garment; interlineation [L. *interlineare*].

in·ter·lock (in·tęr·lak′) *v.t.* to unite by locking together; to fasten together so that one part cannot move without the other; *v.i.* to be locked or jammed together.

in·ter·lo·cu·tion (in·tęr·lō·kū′·shąn) *n.* dialogue; a conference; speaking in turn. (in·tęr·lȧk′·yą·ter) *n.* one who speaks in his turn; one who questions another [L. *interloqui,* to speak between].

in·ter·lope (in·tęr·lōp′) *v.i.* to traffic without a proper license; to intrude into other people's affairs. **-r** *n.* [L. *inter,* between; Dut. *loopen,* to run].

in·ter·lude (in′·tęr·lòòd) *n.* a dramatic or musical performance given between parts of an independent play; an interval; an incident during a pause in the proceedings [L. *inter,* between; *ludus,* play].

in·ter·mar·ry (in·tęr·mar′·i·) *v.i.* to connect families or races by a marriage between two of their members; to marry within close relationship. **intermarriage** *n.*

in·ter·me·di·ate (in·tęr·mē′·di·ąt) *a.* lying or being between two extremes; in a middle position; intervening; *n.* anything in between; *v.i.* to mediate; to intervene. **intermediacy** *n.* state of being intermediate; mediation. **intermediary** *a.* acting between; interposed; intermediate; *n.* one who acts as a go-between or mediator. **intermedium** *n.* intervening person or instrument. **intermedi-**

ation *n.* [L. *inter*, between; *medius*, middle].
in·ter·ment See **inter.**
in·ter·mez·zo (in·tẹr·met′·sō, med′·zō) *n.* a light dramatic entertainment between the acts of a tragedy, grand opera, etc.; an interlude; (*Mus.*) a short movement connecting more important ones in a symphony, sonata, opera, etc. [It. = in between].
in·ter·mi·na·ble (in·tur′·mi·nạ·bl) *a.* endless; unlimited. **-ness** *n.* **interminably** *adv.*
in·ter·min·gle (in·tẹr·ming′·gl) *v.t.* to mingle or mix together.
in·ter·mit (in·tẹr·mit′) *v.t.* to give up or forbear for a time; to interrupt; *v.i.* to cease for a time. *pr.p.* **-ting.** *pa.t., pa.p.* **-ted. intermission** *n.* intervening period of time; suspension; interval. **intermissive.** *a.* coming after temporary cessations. **-tence, -tency** *n.* **-tent** *a.* occurring at intervals; ceasing at intervals; coming and going. **-tently** *adv.* [L. *inter*, between; *mittere, missum*, to send].
in·ter·mix (in·tẹr·miks′) *v.t.* and *v.i.* to mix together. **-ture** *n.*
in·tern (in·turn′) *v.t.* to confine (in a place), esp. aliens or suspects in time of war; (in′·turn) *n.* a resident doctor in a hospital. Also **interne. internee** *n.* one who is confined to a certain place. **-ment** *n.* **-ship** *n.* [L. *internus*, internal].
in·ter·nal (in·tur′·nạl) *a.* interior; inner; inward; domestic, as opposed to foreign. **-ly** *adv.* **— combustion**, the process occurring by exploding in one or more piston-fitted cylinders a mixture of air and fuel [L. *internus*, inward].
in·ter·na·tion·al (in·tẹr·nash′·ạn·al) *a.* pert. to the relations between nations; *n.* a game or match between teams representing their respective countries; a player who participates in such. **-ism** *n.* a political theory which aims at breaking down the artificial barriers which separate nations. **-ist** *n.* **-ly** *adv.*
in·ter·ne·cine (in·tẹr·nē′·sin) *a.* mutually destructive; deadly [L. *inter*; *necare*, to kill].
in·ter·nee See **intern.**
in·ter·nist *n.* (in·tur′·nist) a specialist in internal medicine.
in·ter·nun·ci·o (in·tẹr·nun′·shi·ō) *n.* the pope's representative; an envoy. **internuncial** *a.* [L. *internuntius*, a messenger].
in·ter·pel·late (in·tẹr·pel′·āt) *v.t.* to interrupt a speaker in a legislative assembly by demanding an explanation. **interpellation** *n.* **interpellator** *n.* [L. *inter; pellere*, to drive].
in·ter·pen·e·trate (in·tẹr·pen′·ạ·trāt) *v.t.* to grow through one another; to penetrate thoroughly. **interpenetration** *n.*
in·ter·plan·e·tar·y (in·tẹr·plan′·ạ·ter·i·) *a.* situated between the planets.
in·ter·play (in′·tẹr·plā) *n.* reciprocal action of two things; interchange of action and reaction; give and take.
in·ter·po·late (in·tur′·pạ·lāt) *v.t.* to insert new (esp. misleading) matter into a text; to interpose with some remark; (*Math.*) to infer the missing terms in a known series of numbers. **interpolation** *n.* **interpolator** *n.* [L. *interpolare*, to furbish up].
in·ter·pose (in·tẹr·pōz′) *v.t.* and *i.* to place or come between; to thrust in the way; to offer, as aid or service; to interrupt. **interposal** *n.* **-r** *n.* **interposition** *n.* [L. *inter; ponere*, to place].
in·ter·pret (in·tur′·prạt) *v.t.* to explain the meaning of; to put a construction on; to translate orally for the benefit of others. **-able** *a.* **-ation** *n.* act of interpreting; translation; meaning; artist's version of a dramatic part or musical composition. **-ative** *a.* explanatory. **-er** *n.* [L. *interpres*, an interpreter].
in·ter·reg·num (in·tẹr·reg′·nạm) *a.* the time a throne is vacant between the death or abdication of a king and the accession of his successor; any interruption in continuity. [L. *inter; regnum*, rule].
in·ter·re·la·tion (in·tẹr·ri·lā′·shạn) *n.* reciprocal or mutual relation.**-ship** *n.*
in·ter·ro·gate (in·ter′·ạ·gāt) *v.t.* to question; to examine by questioning, esp. officially. **interrogation** *n.* close questioning; a question. **interrogation mark,** the mark (?) placed after a question. **interrogative** *a.* **interrogatory** *a.* [L. *inter; rogare*, to ask].
in·ter·rupt (in·tạ·rupt′) *v.t.* to break in upon; to stop course of; to break continuity of. **-edly** *adv.* **-er** *n.* **-ion** *n.* intervention; suspension; hindrance. **-ive** *a.* [L. *interruptus*, broken apart].
in·ter·sect (in·tẹr·sekt′) *v.t.* to cut into or between; to divide into parts; to cross one another. **-ion** *n.* an intersecting; the point where lines, roads, etc., cut or cross one another. **-ional** *a.* [L. *intersectus*, cut off].
in·ter·sperse (in·tẹr·spurs′) *v.t.* to scatter or place here and there, in no fixed order; to mingle. **interspersion** *n.* [L. *inter*, among; *spargere, sparsum*, to scatter].
in·ter·stel·lar (in·tẹr·stel′·ẹr) *a.* passing between, or situated among, the stars. Also**-y.**
in·ter·stice (in·tur′·stis) *n.* a small gap or chink in the body of an object or between two things; a crevice. **interstitial** (in·tẹr·stish′·ạl) *a.* [L. *interstitium*].
in·ter·twine (in·tẹr·twīn′) *v.t.* to twine or twist together.
in·ter·val (in′·tẹr·vạl) *n.* time or distance between; a pause; a break; (*Mus.*) difference in pitch between any two tones [L. *intervallum*, fr. *inter*; *vallum*, a wall].
in·ter·vene (in·tẹr·vēn′) *v.i.* to come or be between; to happen in the meantime; to interfere; to interrupt; to interpose.**-r** *n.* **intervention** *n.* **interventionist** *n.* or *a.* [L. *inter*; *venire*, to come].
in·ter·view (in′·tẹr·vū) *n.* a meeting or conference; a meeting of a journalist and a person whose views he wishes to publish; *v.t.* to have an interview with. **-er** *n.* [Fr. *entrevue*].
in·tes·tate (in·tes′·tāt) *a.* not having made a valid will; not disposed of by will; *n.* a person who dies intestate. **intestacy** *n.* [L. *in-*, not; *testari*, to make a will].
in·tes·tine (in·tes′·tin) *a.* internal; domestic; civil (of war, etc.); *n.pl.* the bowels; the entrails. **intestinal** *a.* [L. *intestinus*].
in·ti·mate (in′·tạ·mạt) *a.* innermost; familiar; closely-related; close; *n.* an intimate friend; *v.t.* **intimate** (in′·tạ·māt) to hint; to imply. **intimacy** *n.* the state of being intimate; sexual relations. **-ly** *adv.* **intimation** *n.* a notice; a hint [L. *intimus*, inmost].
in·tim·i·date (in·tim′·ạ·dāt) *v.t.* to force or deter by threats; to inspire with fear; to frighten into action; to cow. **intimidation** *n.* **intimidator** *n.* [L. *in*; *timidus*, fearful].
in·to (in′·too) *prep.* expresses motion to a point within, or a change from one state to another.
in·tol·er·a·ble (in·tål′·ạ·rạ·bl) *a.* insufferable; unbearable.**-ness** *n.* **intolerably** *adv.* **intolerance** *n.* **intolerant** *a.* **intolerantly** *adv.*
in·tone (in·tōn′) *v.t.* to utter or recite with a long drawn out musical note or tone; to chant; *v.i.* to modulate the voice; to give forth a deep protracted sound. **intonate** *v.t.* to intone. **intonation** *n.*
in·tox·i·cate (in·tåk′·sạ·kāt) *v.t.* to make drunk; to excite beyond self-control. **intoxicating** *a.* producing intoxication; heady. **intoxicant** *n.* an intoxicating liquor. **intoxication** *n.* [Gk. *toxikon*, poison].
in·tra- (in′·tra) *prefix* fr. L. *intra*, within, inside of, used in the construction of many compound terms. **-cellular** *a.* within a cell.

-muscular *a.* inside a muscle. **-venous** *a.* within a vein.

in·trac·ta·ble (in·trak′·tạ·bl) *a.* not to be managed or governed; unmanageable; stubborn. **intractability, intractably** *adv.*

in·tra·mu·ral (in·trạ·myoo′·ral) *a.* pert. to a single college or its students; within the walls or limits.

in·tran·si·gent (in·tran′·sạ·jạnt) *a.* refusing in any way to compromise or to make a settlement (esp. in political matters); irreconcilable; *n.* one who adopts this attitude. **intransigence,** *n.* **-ly** *adv.* [Fr. *intransigeant*].

in·tran·si·tive (in·tran′·sạ·tiv) *a.* (*Gram.*) denoting such verbs as express an action or state which is limited to the agent, or which does not pass over to, or operate upon, an object.

in·trep·id (in·trep′·id) *a.* free from fear or trepidation. **-ity** *n.* undaunted courage. **-ly** *adv.* [L. *in-*, not; *trepidus*, alarmed].

in·tri·cate (in′·tri·kạt) *a.* involved; entangled; complicated; difficult. **intricacy, -ness** *n.* **-ly** *adv.* [L. *intricare*, to entangle].

in·trigue (in′·trig) *n.* a plot to effect some purpose by secret artifices; illicit love; (in·trēg′) *v.i.* to scheme secretly; to plot; to carry on illicit love; *v.t.* to fascinate; to arouse interest in; to puzzle. *pr.p.* **intriguing. intrigant, -r** *n.* **intriguing** *a.* **intriguingly** *adv.* [Fr. fr. L. *intricare*, to entangle].

in·trin·sic (in·trin′·sik) *a.* from within; having internal value; inherent. **-ality** *n.* **-ally** *adv.* [L. *intrinsecus*, inwardly].

in·tro- (in′·trō) *prefix*, a variation of intra, *inwards*, used in compound terms.

in·tro·duce (in·trạ·dūs′) *v.t.* to lead or bring in; to bring forward; to insert; to make known formally (one person to another); to import; to begin. **introduction** (in·trạ·duk′·shạn) *n.* act of introducing or bringing into notice; the act of making persons formally acquainted with one another; the preliminary section of a speech or discourse; prologue; the preface to a book; an elementary treatise on some branch of knowledge. **introductory, introductive** *a.* **introductively, inductorily** *adv.* [L. *introducere*, to lead in].

in·tro·spect (in·trạ·spekt′) *v.t.* to look within; to inspect; *v.i.* to pre-occupy oneself with one's own thoughts, emotions and feelings. **-ion** *n.* close (often morbid) examination of one's thoughts and feelings. **-ive** *a.* **-ively** *adv.* [L. *intro*, within; *specere*, to look].

in·tro·vert (in·trạ·vurt′) *v.t.* to turn inward; (in′·trạ·vurt) *n.* a self-centered, introspective individual. Cf. *extrovert.* **introversion** *n.* **introversive, -ive** *a.* [L. *intro*, within; *vertere*, to turn].

in·trude (in·trōōd′) *v.i.* to thrust oneself in; to enter unwelcome or uninvited into company; to trespass; *v.t.* to force in.**-r** *n.* **intrusion** *n.* **intrusive** *a.* **intrusively** *adv.* **intrusiveness** *n.* [L. *in*; *trudere*, to thrust].

in·trust See **entrust.**

in·tu·i·tion (in·tōō·ish′·ạn) *n.* immediate and instinctive perception of a truth; direct understanding without reasoning. **intuit** *v.t.* and *v.i.* to know intuitively. **-al** *a.* **-alism, -ism** *n.* the doctrine that the perception of good and evil is by intuition. **-alist** *n.* **intuitive** *a.* having instinctively immediate knowledge or perception of something. **intuitively** *adv.* [L. *intueri*, to look upon].

in·tu·mesce (in·tōō·mes′) *v.i.* to swell; to enlarge or expand, owing to heat. **-nce** *n.*

in·twine See **entwine.**

in·un·date (in′·ạn·dāt, in·un′·dāt) *v.t.* to overflow; to flood; to overwhelm. **inundation** *n.* [L. *inundare*, to flood, fr. *unda*, a wavel.

in·ure (in·yoor′) *v.t.* to accustom (to); to habituate by use; to harden (the body) by toil, etc. **-ment** *n.* [*in*, into + obs. *ure*, to work, fr. Fr. *œuvre*, work].

in·vade (in·vād′) *v.t.* to attack; to enter with hostile intentions; to violate; to encroach upon. **-r** *n.* **invasion** *n.* **invasive** *a.* [L. *invadere*, to go in].

in·val·id (in·val′·id) *a.* not valid; void; of no legal force; weak. *v.t.* to render invalid. **-ate** *v.* **-ation** *n.* **-ity, -ness** *n.*

in·va·lid (in′·va·lid) *n.* a person enfeebled by sickness or injury; *a.* ill; sickly; weak; *v.t.* and *v.i.* to make invalid; to send away as an invalid. [L. *invalidus*, infirm].

in·val·u·a·ble (in-val′·yạ·bl) *a.* incapable of being valued; priceless; of very great value.

in·var·i·able (in·ve′·ri·ạ·bl) *a.* not displaying change; always uniform; (*Math.*) constant. **-ness, invariability** *n.* **invariably** *adv.* **invariant** *n.* a constant quantity.

in·va·sion (in·vā′·zhạn) *n.* See **invade.**

in·vec·tive (in·vek′·tiv) *n.* violent outburst of censure; abuse; vituperation. *a.* abusive [L. *invectio*, fr. *invehere*, to bring against].

in·veigh (in·vā′) *v.i.* to exclaim or rail against. **-er** *n.* [L. *invehere*, to bring against].

in·vei·gle (in·vā′·gl) *v.t.* to entice by deception or flattery; to allure; to mislead into something evil; to seduce. **-ment** *n.* **-r** *n.* [Fr. *aveugler*, to blind].

in·vent (in·vent′) *v.t.* to devise something new or an improvement; to contrive; to originate; to think out something untrue. **-ion** *n.* act of producing something new; an original contrivance; a deceit, fiction, or forgery. **-ive** *a.* able to invent; of an ingenious turn of mind; resourceful. **-ively** *adv.* **-or** *n.* [L. *invenire*, to come upon, to discover].

in·ven·to·ry (in′·vạn·tōr·i·) *n.* a detailed list of articles comprising the effects of a house, etc.; a catalog of moveables; *v.t.* to make a list or enter on a list [L. *inventarium*, a list of things found].

in·verse (in′·vurs) *a.* inverted; opposite in order or relation. **-ly** *adv.* **inversion** *n.* the act of inverting; the state of being inverted; change of order or time; (*Gram.*) a change of the natural arrangement of words. **inversive** *a.* [L. *in*, *vertere*, *versum*, to turn].

in·vert (in·vurt′) *v.t.* to turn over; to put upside down; to place in a contrary order. **-edly** *adv.* [L. *in*; *vertere*, to turn].

in·ver·te·brate (in·vur′·tạ·brạt, -brāt) *a.* not having a vertebral column or backbone; spineless, weak-willed; *n.* animal, such as an insect, snail, etc., with no spinal column.

in·vest (in·vest′) *v.t.* to lay out capital with a view to profit; to clothe, as with office or authority; to dress; to lay siege to; *v.t.* to make a purchase or an investment. **-iture** *n.* ceremony of installing anyone in office. **-ment** *n.* the act of investing; the capital invested to produce interest or profit; blockade. **-or** *n.* [L. *investire*, to clothe].

in·ves·ti·gate (in·ves′·tạ·gāt) *v.t.* to inquire into; to examine thoroughly. **investigable** *a.* **investigation** *n.* **investigator** *n.* **investigatory** *a.* [L. *vestigare*, to track].

in·vet·er·ate (in·vet′·ẹr·it) a. firmly established by long continuance; obstinate; deep-rooted **-ly** *adv.* **-ness, inveteracy,** *n.* [L. *inveterare*, to grow old].

in·vid·i·ous (in·vid′·i·ạs) *a.* likely to provoke envy, ill-will or hatred; offensive. **-ly** *adv.* **-ness** *n.* [L. *invidia*, envy].

in·vig·or·ate (in·vig′·ẹr·āt) *v.t.* to give vigor to; to animate with life and energy; to strengthen. **invigoration** *n.* **-d** *a.* [L. *in*; *vigor*, force].

in·vin·ci·ble (in·vin′·sạ·bl) *a.* unconquerable; insuperable. **-ness, invincibility** *n.* **invincibly** [L. *in-*, not; *vincere*, to conquer].

in·vi·o·la·ble (in·vī′·ạl·ạ·bl) *n.* not to be violated; sacred. **inviolably** *adv.* **inviolate** *a.* unprofaned; uninjured. **inviolately** *adv.* **in-**

violateness *n.* [L. *in; violare,* to violate].

in·vis·i·ble (in·viz'·ạ·bl) *a.* incapable of being seen; unseen; indiscernible. **invisibility, -ness** *n.* **invisibly** *adv.*

in·vite (in·vīt') *v.t.* to ask by invitation; to attract. **invitation** (in·vi·tā'·shạn) *n.* act of inviting; the spoken or written form with which a request for a person's company is extended. **-r** *n.* **inviting** *a.* alluring, attractive. **invitingly** *adv.* [L. *invitare*].

in·vo·ca·tion (in·vạ·kā'·shạn) *n.* act of addressing in prayer; a petition for divine help and guidance. **invocatory** *a.* [See **invoke.**]

in·voice (in'·vois) *n.* a detailed list of goods, with prices, sold or consigned to a purchaser; *v.t.* to make such a list. [pl. of obs. *invoy,* fr. Fr. *envoi,* a sending].

in·voke (in·vōk') *v.t.* to address (esp. God) earnestly or solemnly in prayer; to beg for protection or assistance; to implore; to summon [L. *in; vocare,* to call].

in·vol·un·ta·ry (in·vál'·ạn·te·ri·) *a.* outside the control of the will; not proceeding from choice; unintentional; instinctive. **involuntarily** *adv.* **involuntariness** *n.*

in·vo·lute (in'·vạ·lòót) *a.* (*Bot.*) rolled inwardly or spirally; *n.* the locus of the far end of a perfectly flexible thread unwound from a circle and kept constantly taut. **involution** *n.* that in which anything is involved; the process of raising a quantity to any power; entanglement; complication. [See **involve**].

in·volve (in·válv') *v.t.* to envelop; to wrap up; to include; to comprise; to embrace; to implicate (a person); to complicate (a thing); to entail; to include; to twine; to interlace; to overwhelm; to multiply a number any number of times by itself. **-ment** *n.* [L. *in; volvere, volutum,* to roll].

in·vul·ner·a·ble (in·vul'·nẹr·ȧ·bl) *a.* incapable of being wounded or injured. **invulnerability,** *n.* **invulnerably** *adv.*

in·ward (in'·wẹrd) *a.* placed within; towards the inside; interior; internal; seated in the mind or soul; *n.* that which is within. esp. in *pl.,* the viscera; *adv.* toward the inside; into the mind. Also **inwards; -ly** *adv.* in the parts within, secretly; in the mind or soul [O.E. *inneward*].

i·o·dine (ī'·ạ·dīn, dēn) *n.* a non-metallic chemical element belonging to the halogen group. **iodiferous** *a.* yielding iodine. **iodize,** to treat with compounds of iodine, e.g. common salt. **iodoform** *n.* a powdered crystalline compound of iodine [Gk. *ioeidēs,* violet-like, from the color of its fumes].

i·on (ī'·ạn, ·ȧn) *n.* electrically charged atom or radical which has gained, or lost, one or more electrons and which facilitates the transport of electricity through an electrolyte or the gas in a gas-discharge tube. **ionic** *a.* pert. to ions. **-ization** *n.* splitting up of a liquid during electrolysis or of a gas during a glow discharge, into ions. **-ize** *v.t.* **ionosphere** *n.* the layer of ionized molecules in the upper atmosphere beyond the stratosphere [Gr. *ion*].

I·on·ic (ī·ȧn'·ik) *a.* pert. to section of Greece; (*Archit.*) denoting type of column with fluted molding and ram's horn design.

i·o·ta (ī·ō'·tạ) *n.* a very small quantity or degree; a jot [Gk. the name of the smallest letter of the Greek alphabet = I. i.].

ir- (ir) *prefix* for *in;* not, before 'r.'

IRA (ī·ȧr·ā') *n.* individual retirement account.

i·ras·ci·ble (i·ras'·ạ·bl) *a.* easily provoked; hot-tempered, **irascibility** *n.* **irascibly** *adv.* [L. *irasci,* to be angry].

i·rate (ī·rāt') *a.* angry; incensed; enraged [L. *iratus,* fr. *irasci,* to be angry].

ire (īr) *n.* anger; wrath. **-ful** *a.* **-fully** *adv.* **-fully** *adv.* **-fulness** *n.* [L. *ira,* anger].

irid-, irido-, *prefix* fr. Gk. *iris,* rainbow, used in the construction of compound terms, pertaining to the iris of the eye or to the genus of plants, as **iridescence** (i·rạ·des'·ạns) *n.* rainbow-like display of colors. **iridescent** *a.*

iris (ī·ris) *n.* (*Anat.*) the thin contractile, colored membrane between the cornea and the lens of the eye, perforated in the center by an opening called the pupil; (*Bot.*) a genus of flowering plants of the natural order *Iridaceae,* the rainbow; an appearance resembling the rainbow [Gk. *iris,* rainbow].

I·rish (ī'·rish) *a.* pert. to Ireland; *n.* the early language spoken in Ireland—now known as *Erse.* **-ism** *n.* a mode of speaking, phrase, or idiom of Ireland. **-man, -woman** *n.* **— moss,** carageen, a form of edible seaweed.

irk (urk) *v.t.* to weary; to trouble; to distress (used impersonally as, **it irks me**). **-some** *a.* wearisome; annoying. **-somely** *adv.* [M.E.]

i·ron (ī'·ẹrn) *n.* the most common and useful of the metallic elements; something hard and unyielding; an instrument or utensil made of iron; an instrument used, when heated, to press and smooth cloth; in golf, an iron-headed club. **-s** *n.pl.* fetters; manacles; *a.* made of iron; resembling some aspect of iron; robust; inflexible; unyielding; *v.t.* to smooth with a heated flat iron; *v.i.* to furnish or arm with iron; to fetter. **-clad** *a.* covered or protected with sheets of iron; *n.* a vessel prepared for naval warfare by having the parts above water plated with iron. **-er** *n.* **— gray** *a.* of a dark color. **— horse** *n.* a locomotive. **— lung** *n.* an apparatus which maintains artificial respiration continuously. **— ore** *n.* a rock containing iron-rich compounds from which commercial iron is obtained. **-smith** *n.* a worker in iron. **-stone** *n.* any ore of iron mixed with clay, etc. **-y** *a.* made of or resembling iron. **cast iron, pig iron** *n.* the iron obtained by smelting iron ore with charcoal, coke, or raw coal in a blast furnace. **corrugated iron,** plate of galvanized iron, corrugated to give it stiffness, used for temporary roofing, fencing, etc. **galvanized iron,** sheet iron coated with zinc to minimize the effects of rusting. **— age,** period following Bronze age, when iron was substituted for bronze in the making of tools, weapons, and ornaments. **— Curtain,** the ban placed by the U.S.S.R. on free exchange of information, news, etc., between Eastern and Western Europe. **to have too many irons in the fire,** to attempt to do too many things at the same time [O.E. *iren*].

i·ro·ny (ī'·rạ·ni·) *n.* a mode of speech in which the meaning is the opposite of that actually expressed; sarcasm; satire. **ironic, ironical** (i·rȧn'·ik, ·al) *a.* **ironically** *adv.* [Gk. *eirōneia,* dissimulation in speech].

ir·ra·di·ate (i·rā'·di·āt) *v.t.* to shine upon, throw light upon; to illuminate; *v.i.* to emit rays; to give forth light; *a.* illumined with beams of light. **irradiance, irradiancy** *n.* effulgence; emission of rays of light; splendor. **irradiant** *a.* **irradiation** *n.* exposure to X-rays, ultra-violet rays, solar rays, etc.; illumination; brightness; enlightenment. **irradiative** *a.* **irradiator** *n.*

ir·ra·tion·al (i·rash'·ạn·ạl) *a.* incompatible with or contrary to reason. **-ity** *n.* **-ly** *adv.*

ir·re·claim·a·ble (ir·i·klā·ma·bl) *a.* incapable of being reclaimed. **irreclaimably** *adv.*

ir·rec·on·cil·a·ble (i·rek·ạn·sīl'·ạ·bl) *a.* incapable of being reconciled; inconsistent. **-ness, irreconcilability** *n.* **irreconcilably** *adv.*

ir·re·cov·er·a·ble (ir·i·kuv'·ẹr·ạ·bl) *a.* cannot be recovered; irreparable; irretrievable. **-ness** *n.* **irrecoverably** *adv.*

ir·re·deem·a·ble (ir·i·dēm'·ạ·bl) *a.* not redeemable; incorrigible; hopelessly lost; not convertible (as paper money into specie). **-ness, irredeemability** *n.* **irredeemably** *adv.*

ir·re·duc·i·ble (ir.i.dūs′.ą.bl) *a.* that which cannot be reduced or lessened. **-ness, irreducibility** *n.* **irreducibly** *adv.*

ir·ref·u·ta·ble (i.ri.fū′.tą.bl, ir.ref′.yą.tą.bl) *a.* that cannot be refuted. **irrefutability** *n.* **irrefutably** *adv.*

ir·reg·u·lar (i.reg′.yą.lęr) *a.* not regular; not according to rule; deviating from the moral standard; (*Gram.*) not inflected according to normal rules; *n.* a member of an armed force outside government control. **-ity** *n.* **-ly** *adv.*

ir·rel·a·tive (i.rel′.ą.tiv) *a.* not relative; unconnected. **-ly** *adv.*

ir·rel·e·vant (i.rel′.ą.vant) *a.* not logically pertinent. **irrelevancy** *n.* **-ly** *adv.*

ir·re·li·gion (ir.i.lij′.ąn) *n.* state of indifference or opposition to religious beliefs. **irreligious** *a.* **irreligiously** *adv.* profanely; impiously. **irreligiousness** *n.* ungodliness.

ir·re·me·di·a·ble (ir.i.mē′.di.a.bl) *a.* not to be remedied or redressed. **-ness** *n.* **irremediably** *adv.*

ir·re·place·able (ir.i.plā′.są.bl) a. that cannot be passed by or forgiven; unpardonable.

ir·rep·a·ra·ble (i.rep′.ąr.ą.bl) *a.* that cannot be repaired or rectified. **-ness** *n.* **irreparability** *n.* **irreparably** *adv.*

ir·re·place·able (ir.i.plā′.są.bl) *a.* that cannot be replaced; indispensable; unique.

ir·re·press·i·ble (ir.i.pres′.ą.bl) *a.* not able to be kept under control. **irrepressibility** *n.* **-ness** *n.* **irrepressibly** *adv.*

ir·re·proach·a·ble (ir.i.prō′.chą.bl) *a.* free from blame; faultless. **irreproachably** *adv.*

ir·re·sist·i·ble (ir.i.zis′.tą.bl) *a.* incapable of being resisted; too strong, fascinating, charming, etc., to be resisted. **-ness, irresistibility** *n.* **irresistibly** *adv.*

ir·res·o·lute (i.rez′.a.lòòt) *a.* infirm or inconstant in purpose; vacillating. **-ly** *adv.* **-ness, irresolution** *n.*

ir·re·spec·tive (ir.i.spek′.tiv) *a.* and *adv.* without regard to; apart from. **-ly** *adv.*

ir·re·spon·si·ble (ir.i.spąn′.są.bl) *a.* not liable to answer (for consequences); carefree; without a due sense of responsibility. **irresponsibility** *n.* **irresponsibly** *adv.*

ir·re·spon·sive (ir.i.spán′.siv) *a.* not responsive (to); unanswering; taciturn. **-ness** *n.*

ir·re·triev·a·ble (ir.i.trē′.vą.bl) *a.* incapable of recovery or repair. **-ness** *n.* **irretrievability** *n.* **irretrievably** *adv.*

ir·rev·er·ent (i.rev′.ą.rant) *a.* not reverent; disrespectful. **irreverence** *n.* **-ly** *adv.*

ir·re·vers·i·ble (ir.i.vur′.są.bl) *a.* that cannot be reversed, turned back, recalled, or annulled. **irreversibly** *adv.*

ir·rev·o·ca·ble (i.rev′.ą.ką.bl) *a.* incapable of being recalled or revoked. **-ness, irrevocability** *n.* **irrevocably** *adv.*

ir·ri·gate (ir′.ą.gāt) *v.t.* to water (by artificial channels). **irrigable, irrigative** *a.* **irrigation** *n.* the artificial application of water to the land for the purpose of increasing its fertility; (*Med.*) the washing out of a wound, etc. to keep it moist. **irrigator** *n.* [L. *irrigare*, fr. *rigare*, to moisten].

ir·ri·tate (ir′.ą.tāt) *v.t.* to excite to anger; to annoy; to excite heat and redness in the skin by friction. **irritability** *n.* **irritable** *a.* easily provoked or annoyed; fretful; able to be acted upon by stimuli. **irritableness** *n.* **irritably** *adv.* **irritant** *a.* irritating; *n.* that which irritates or causes irritation.**irritation** *n.* exasperation: anger; the act of exciting heat, redness, or action in the skin or flesh by external stimulus. **irritative** *a.* tending to irritate [L. *irritare*].

ir·rup·tion (i.rup′.shan) *n.* a sudden invasion; a violent incursion into a place; a breaking or bursting in. **irruptive** *a.* **irruptively** *adv.* [L. *irruptio*].

is (iz) *v.* the *third pers. sing. pres. indic.* of the verb **to be** [O.E.].

is·land (ī′.ląnd) *n.* a piece of land surrounded by water; anything resembling this, e.g. a street-refuge. **-er** *n.* an inhabitant of an island [earlier *iland*, O.E. *iegland*].

isle (īl) *n.* an island. **islet** (ī′.let) *n.* a tiny island [O.Fr. *isle*. L. *insula*].

-ism (izm) *n.* a jocular reference to any distinctive doctrine, theory, or practice [English suffix, *-ism*].

i·so- (i′.so) *prefix* fr. Gk. *isos*, equal, used in the construction of compound terms.

i·so·bar (ī′.są.bár) *n.* a line on a map joining up all those points where the mean height of the barometer is the same; *pl.* species of atoms having the same atomic weight but different atomic numbers. **-ic** *a.* consisting of isobars. **-ometric** *a.* showing equal barometric pressure (Gk. *isos*, equal; *baros*, weight].

i·so·dy·nam·ic (ī.są.dī.nam′.ik) *a.* having equal force or power.

i·so·gon (ī′.są.gán) *n.* a plane figure having equal angles. **isogonal** (ī.ság′.ą.nąl) *a.* **-ic** *a.* [Gk. *isos*, equal; *gonia*, angle].

i·so·late (ī′.są.lāt) *v.t.* to place in a detached position; to place apart or alone; to insulate; (*Chem.*) to obtain a substance in a pure state. **isolation** *n.* state of being isolated. **isolation hospital,** a hospital for infectious diseases. **isolationist** *n.* one who advocates non-participation in world-politics [It. *isolato*, detached, fr. L. *insula*, an island].

i·so·met·ric (ī.są.met′.rik) *a.* of equal measurement.

i·so·mor·phism (ī.są.mawr′.fizm) *n.* similarity of structure, esp. between the crystals of different chemical substances. **isomorphic** *a.* **isomorphous** *a.* [Gk. *isos*, equal; *morphē*, shape].

i·sos·ce·les (ī.sás′.ą.lēz) *a.* having two sides which are equal (said of a triangle) [Gk. *isos*, equal; *skelos*, a leg].

i·so·topes (ī′.są.tōps) *n.pl.* (*physics*) of most of the elements, atoms with nuclei of slightly different weights [Gk. *isos*, equal; *topos*, place].

Is·ra·el (iz′.ri.ąl) *n.* since 1948, the name of the Jewish State in Palestine; (*Bib.*) the Jewish people **Israeli** (iz.rāl′.i.) *n.* an inhabitant of Israel. **-ite** *n.* (*Bib.*) a descendant of Israel or Jacob; a Jew. **-itic, -itish,** *a.* [Heb. *Israel*, he who striveth with God].

is·sue (ish′.òò) *n.* act of passing or flowing out; the act of sending out; that which is issued; a topic of discussion or controversy; a morbid discharge from the body; outlet; edition; consequence; result; progeny; offspring; (*Law*) the specific point in a suit between two parties requiring to be determined; *v.t.* to send out (a book, etc.); to put into circulation; to proclaim or set forth with authority; to supply with equipment, etc.; *v.i.* to pass or flow out; to come out; to proceed; to be born or spring from. **-less** *a.* **-er** *n.* **at issue** (point) to be debated or settled. **to join issue,** to take opposite views on a point in debate [O.Fr. *issir*, to go out].

isth·mus (is′.mąs) *n.* a narrow neck of land connecting two larger portions. **isthmian** *a.* [Gk. *isthmos*].

it (it) *pron.* the neuter pronoun of the third person; *n.* (*Colloq.*) sexual attractiveness; sex appeal; perfection [O.E. *hit*].

I·tal·ian (i.tal′.yąn) *a.* pert. to Italy, its inhabitants or their language.

i·tal·ics (i.tal′.iks) *n.pl.* a printing type having the type sloping from the right downwards. *as these letters.* **italicization** *n.* **italicize** *v.t.* to print thus.

itch (ich) *n.* an irritation in the skin; scabies; an irrepressible desire; *v.i.* to feel uneasiness or irritation in the skin; to be inordinately anxious or desirous to; to be hankering after. **-iness** *n.* **-y** *a.* **an itching palm,** a grasping disposition; greed [O.E. *giccan*, to itch].

i·tem (ī′·tạm) *n.* a piece of news, as in a newspaper; an entry in an account or list; a detail. **itemize** *v.t.* to list by items; to give particulars [L.].

it·er·ate (it′·ạ·rāt) *v.t.* to repeat; to do again. **iteration** *n.* **iterative, iterant** *a.* repeating [L. *iterare*, fr. *iterum*, again].

i·tin·er·ant (ī·tin′·ạ·rạnt) *a.* traveling from place to place; traveling on circuit; of no settled abode. *n.* one who goes from place to place, esp. on business. **itineracy, itinerancy** *n.* **-ly** *adv.* **itinerary** *n.* a record of travel; a route, line of travel; a guide-book for travelers. **itinerate** *v.i.* to travel up and down a country, esp. in a regular circuit. **itineration** *n.* [L. *iter, itineris*, a journey].

its (its) the *possessive case* of *pron. it.* **itself** *pron.* the neuter reciprocal pronoun applied to things; the reflexive form of it.

i·vo·ry (ī′·vạ·ri.) *n.* the hard, white, opaque, dentine constituting tusks of elephant, walrus, etc.; as carving of ivory; creamy white color. *n.pl.* (*Colloq.*) keys of a piano; the teeth. *a.* made of or like ivory [Fr. *ivoire*, fr. L. *ebur*, ivory].

i·vy (ī′·vi·) *n.* a climbing evergreen plant. **ivied** *a.* covered with ivy [O.E. *ifig*].

J

jab (jab) *v.t.* to poke sharply; to stab; *pr.p.* **-bing.** *pa.t., pa.p.* **-bed.** *n.* a sharp poke, stab, or thrust [prob. imit.].

jab·ber (jab′·ẹr) *v.i.* to chatter; to speak quickly and indistinctly; *v.t.* to utter indistinctly; *n.* rapid, incoherent talk. **-er** *n.* **-ingly** *adv.* [prob. imit.].

ja·bot (zha·bō′) *n.* a frill or fall of lace on a woman's dress; orig. a ruffle on a man's shirt.

ja·cinth (jā′·sinth) *n.* the hyacinth [contr. of L. *hyacinthus*, a precious stone].

Jack (jak) *n.* a popular nickname and diminutive of *John;* (*l.c.*) a fellow; a laborer, as *steeple-jack;* a sailor; the knave in a pack of cards; a device to facilitate removal of boots, as a *boot-jack;* a mechanical device for turning a roasting-spit; a portable apparatus for raising heavy weights, esp. for raising a motor vehicle to change a tire; a flag or ensign; the male of certain animals, as *jackass; v.t.* to raise with a jack. Also **jack up. -boot** *n.* a long boot reaching above the knee formerly worn by cavalry. **—in-the-box** *n.* a child's toy comprising a small figure which springs out of a box when the lid is lifted. **-knife** *n.* a strong clasp knife. **— o' lantern,** a lantern made from hollowed-out pumpkin, with holes cut to make a face. **—of-all-trades** *n.* one who can turn his hand to anything. **-pot** *n.* a pool, in poker, which cannot be opened except by player holding two jacks or better; (*Slang*) the pay-off. **-rabbit** *n.* a hare with very long ears. **-tar,** a sailor. **Union Jack,** the national flag of Gt. Britain. **yellowjack** *n.* yellow fever [fr. *John*, infl. by Fr. *Jacques*].

jack·al (jack′·ạl, ·awl) *n.* a bashy-tailed carnivorous animal of Asia and Africa; wild dog; (*Fig.*) a servile creature [Pers. *shaghal*].

jack·ass (jak′·as) *n.* a male ass; a stupid fellow; a blockhead [*Jack*, the male; and *ass*].

jack-daw (jak′·daw) *n.* a glossy, black bird of the crow family [fr. *Jack; daw*].

jack·et (jak′·it) *n.* a short, sleeved coat; outer covering or skin (as of potatoes); an outer casing, as for a boiler to keep in heat; a loose dust-cover for a book; *v.t.* to cover with a jacket [O.Fr. *jaquet*, dim. of *jaque*, a coat of mail].

Jac·o·be·an (jak·a·bē′·ạn) *a.* pert. to reign of James I; used mainly of architecture, indoor decoration, and furniture (dark oak) of Stuart period; *n.* person of this period [L. *Jacobus*, James].

Jac·o·bin (jak′·ạ·bin) *n.* a French Dominican friar, so called from monastery of *St. Jacques*, Paris; a member of society of French Revolutionists [Fr. fr. L. *Jacobus*, James].

Ja·cob's lad·der (jā′·kạbz·lad′·ẹr) *n.* (*Naut.*) a rope ladder with wooden rungs [Heb. *ya'aqob*, Jacob].

jac·quard (ja·kȧrd′) *n., a.* pattern woven into fabrics [fr. Fr. inventor of loom, *Jacquard*].

jade (jād) *n.* an over-worked, worn-out horse; a mean woman; a saucy wench; *v.t.* to tire; to wear out. *pr.p.* **jading.** *pa.p.* **jaded. jaded** *a.* tired; weary; sated [Scand. *jalda*, a mare].

jade (jād) *n.* a very hard, compact silicate of lime and magnesia, of various colors, carved for ornaments [Span. (*piedra de*) *ijada*, a stone for curing a pain in the side].

jag (jag) *n.* a notch; a ragged protuberance; (*Bot.*) cleft or division; *v.t.* to notch; to slash. *pr.p.* **-ging.** *pa.p.* **-ged. -ged, -gy** *a.* notched; rough-edged; sharp. **-gedness** *n.* (*Slang*) a spree, as **a talking jag** [etym. doubtful].

jag·uar (jag′·wȧr) *n.* a large spotted yellowish beast of prey [Braz.].

jail (jāl) *n.* a prison; *v.t.* to take into custody. (*Br.*) **goal. — bird** *n.* a prisoner; a criminal. **-er, -or** *n.* one who has charge of prisoners in the cells [O.Fr. *gaole*, a prison].

jal·ap (jal′·ạp) *n.* a drug used as a purgative esp. in dropsy [fr. *Xalapa*, in Mexico]. [car.

ja·lop·y (ja·lȧp′·i·) *n.* (*Slang*) an old, decrepit

jal·ou·sie (jal′·ạ·sē) *n.* a blind or shutter with slats at an angle. **-d** *a.* [Fr. *jalousie*, suspicion].

jam (jam) *n.* preserve made from fruit, boiled with sugar. **-my** *a.* [etym. doubtful].

jam (jam) *v.t.* to squeeze tight; to wedge in; to block up; to stall (a machine); *v.i.* to cease to function because of obstruction. *pr.p.* **-ming.** *pa.p.* **-med.** *n.* a crush; a hold-up (as of traffic); (*Colloq.*) a tight corner. **-ming** *n.* (*Radio*) to interfere with signals by sending out others of like frequency [prob. var. of *champ*].

jamb (jam) *n.* the side piece of a door, fireplace, etc. [Fr. *jambe*, a leg].

jam·bo·ree (jam·bạ·rē′) *n.* a large, usually international, rally of Boy Scouts; (*Slang*) a noisy gathering [etym. unknown].

jan·gle (jang′·gl) *v.t.* to ring with a discordant sound; *v.i.* to sound out of tune; to wrangle; *n.* a discordant sound; a dispute. **jangling** *n.* [imit. O.Fr. *jangler*].

jan·i·tor (jan′·i·tẹr) *n.* (*fem.* **janitress**) a caretaker of a building; a doorkeeper; a porter [L. *janitor*].

Jan·i·zar·y (jan′·ạ·zạr·i·) *n.* a soldier of the Turkish Sultan [Turk. *yenitsheri*, the new soldiers].

Jan·u·ar·y (jan′·yạ·wer·i·) *n.* the first month, dedicated by Romans to *Janus*, the god with two faces. **janus-faced** *a.* untrustworthy [L. *Janus*, a Roman deity].

Ja·pan (jạ·pan′) *n.* a N.E. Asiatic insular country. **-ese** (ja·pạ·nēz′) *n.* a native of Japan; *a.* pert. to Japan, the people or language. **japan** *v.t.* to make black and glossy; to lacquer with black varnish. *pr.p.* **-ning.** *pa.p.* **-ned.** *n.* the black laquer japanned [Jap.].

jape (jāp) *n.* a jest [O.Fr. *japer*, to jest].

jar (jȧr) *n.* vessel narrower at top than at base, with or without handles [Fr. *jarre*].

jar (jär) *v.i.* to give forth a discordant sound; to vibrate discordantly; to affect the nerves, feelings, etc. unpleasantly; to conflict; *v.t.* to cause to vibrate by sudden impact; to shake physically or mentally. *pr.p.* **-ring.** *pa.p.* **-red.** *n.* a harsh, grating sound; a jolting movement; conflict. **-ringly** *adv.* [prob. imit.].

jar·gon (jar′·gạn) *n.* confused speech; gibberish; slang; technical phraseology.

jas·mine (jas′·min) *n.* a shrub with fragrant white, yellow or pink flowers. Also **jessamine** [Pers. *yasmin*, jasmine].

jas·per (jas′·pẹr) *n.* an opaque form of quartz, often highly colored [Gk. *iaspis*, chalcedony].

ja·to (jā′·tō) *n.* kind of rocket to assist the take-off of heavily loaded aircraft [*J*et *A*ssisted *T*ake *O*ff].

jaun·dice (jawn′·dis, jän′·dis) *n.* a disease, characterized by yellowness of skin and eyes; *v.t.* to affect with jaundice. **-d** *a.* affected with jaundice; (*Fig.*) jealous; prejudiced [Fr. *jaune*, yellow].

jaunt (jawnt, jänt) *v.i.* to make an excursion; *n.* an outing; a ramble. **-ing** *a.* rambling.

jaun·ty (jawn′·ti·, jän′·ti·) *a.* sprightly; airy; trim. **jauntily** *adv.* [Fr. gentil, genteel].

jave·lin (jav′·lin) *n.* a light hand-thrown spear [Fr.].

jaw (jaw) *n.* one of the two bones forming framework of mouth and containing the teeth; the mouth; part of any device which grips or crushes object held by it, as a vice; (*Slang*) loquacity; *pl.* narrow entrance to a gorge; *v.t.* (*Slang*) to scold; (*Slang*) to gossip. **-bone** *n.* bone of the mouth in which teeth are set. **-breaker** (*Colloq.*) a word hard to pronounce; (*Colloq.*) a large piece of hard candy.

jay (jā) *n.* a chattering, perching bird with gay plumage; (*Fig.*) a foolish person. **-walker** *n.* (*Colloq.*) a careless or absent-minded pedestrian who disregards traffic rules [etym. doubtful].

jazz (jaz) *n.* syncopated, noisy music played as accompaniment to dancing; *a.* like or pert. to jazz; *v.t.* and *v.i.* to dance to or play jazz music; (*Slang*) to put vigor and liveliness into. **-y** *a.* [Negro word].

jeal·ous (jel′·ạs) *a.* envious; suspicious; apprehensively watchful; solicitous; zealously careful. **-y** *n.* [O.Fr. fr. Gk. *zelos*, emulation].

jean (jēn) *n.* a strong, twilled cotton cloth; *n.pl.* overalls; trousers [prob. fr. L. *Genua*, Genoa].

jeep (jēp) *n.* light motor utility truck designed in *World War* 2 [G.P., of general purposes].

jeer (jir) *v.i.* to mock; to deride; *v.t.* to treat scoffingly; *n.* a gibe; a railing remark. **-er** *n.*

Je·ho·vah (ji·hō′·vạ) *n.* (*Bib.*) Hebrew name of the supreme God [Heb. *Yahweh*].

je·june (ji·jòòn′) *a.* empty; barren; uninteresting; dry. **-ly** *adv.* [L. *jejunus*, hungry].

jel·ly (jel′·i·) *n.* any gelatinous substance; the juice of fruit boiled with sugar. **jell** *v.i.* to stiffen. **jellied** *a.* of the consistency of jelly. **jellify** *v.t.* to make into jelly; *v.i.* to become set like a jelly. **-fish** *n.* popular name given certain marine animals of soft gelatinous structure [Fr. *gelée*, frost].

jen·ny (jen′·i·) *n.* a spinning machine; a female ass; a female bird, the wren (usually *jenny-wren*) [dim. of *Jane*].

jeo·par·dy (jep′·ẹr·di·) *n.* danger; risk. **jeopardize** *v.t.* to endanger; to imperil [Fr. *jeu parti*, a divided game].

Jer·e·mi·ah (jer·ạ·mi′·ạ) *n.* (*Bib.*) a Hebrew prophet and author of the Book of Lamentations; any doleful prophet. **jeremiad** *n.* a tale of grief or complaint.

jerk (jurk) *v.t.* to throw with a quick motion; to twitch; to give a sudden pull, twist, or push; *n.* a short, sudden thrust, pull, start, etc.; a spasmodic twitching. **-er** *n.* **-ily** *adv.* **-iness** *n.* **-water** *a.* (*Colloq.*) insignificant. **-y** *a.* fitful; spasmodic; lacking rhythm [imit. word].

jerk (jurk) *v.t.* to cure (meat) by cutting in long slices and drying in the sun. **-ed** *a.* [Peruv. *charqui*, dried beef].

jer·kin (jur′·kin) *n.* a close-fitting jacket or waistcoat [prob. *Dut.* jurk, a frock].

jer·o·bo·am (jer·ạ·bō′·ạm) *n.* a large bowl; a huge bottle, in capacity eight times the ordinary size [1 Kings, 11].

Jer·sey (jur′·zi·) *n.* the largest of the Channel Islands; a cow of Jersey breed; *a.* pert. to State of New Jersey. **jersey** *n.* a close-fitting, knitted, woolen jacket, vest, or pullover; a knitted cloth [fr. *Jersey*].

jess (jes) *n.* a strap of leather or silk tied round the legs of a hawk; *v.t.* to put jesses on [O.Fr. *ges*, a throw].

jest (jest) *n.* a joke; a quip; banter; an object of ridicule; *v.i.* to joke; to scoff. **-er** *n.* one who jests; a professional fool, originally attached to the court or lord's manor. **-ful** *a.* **-ingly** *adv.* [M.E. *jeste*, an exploit].

Jes·u·it (jezh′·ū·it) *n.* one of a religious order founded by Ignatius Loyola in 1534 under the title of The Society of Jesus; a crafty person; a prevaricator [fr. *Jesus*].

jet (jet) *n.* a variety of very hard, black lignite, capable of a brilliant polish and much used for ornaments; *a.* made of, or having the glossy blackness of, jet. **—black** *a.* black like jet. **-tiness** *n.* **-ty** *a.* [O.Fr. *jet*].

jet (jet) *n.* a sudden rush, as of water or flame, from a pipe; the spout or nozzle emitting water, gas, etc.; a jet airplane; *v.t.* to spout; *v.i.* to shoot forth; to travel by jet. *pr.p.* **-ting.** *pa.t.* **-ted.** **— airplane** *n.* a plane with jet propulsion. **— propulsion** *n.* propulsion of a machine by the force of a jet of fluid or of heated gases, expelled backwards from the machine. **— set** *n.* wealthy people who jet between fashionable international resorts [Fr. *jeter*, to throw].

jet·sam (jet′·sạm) *n.* goods thrown overboard to lighten a ship in distress; goods washed ashore from a wrecked ship. **jettison** *n.* act of throwing overboard; jetsam; *v.t.* to throw overboard, as cargo; (*Fig.*) to abandon, as a scheme [O.Fr. *jetée*, thrown out].

jet·ty (jet′·i·) *n.* a structure of piles, stones, etc. built to protect a harbor; a landing pier [O.Fr. *jetée*, thrown out].

Jew (jòò) *n.* an adherent of Judaism; a person descended, or regarded as descended, from the ancient Hebrews. **-ish** *a.* of or pert. to Jews or Judaism; *n.* (*Colloq.*) Yiddish. **-ishness** *n.* **-ry** *n.* the Jewish people; a ghetto [Heb. *Yehudah*, Judah].

jew·el (jòò′·ạl) *n.* a precious stone; an ornament set with gem(s); a highly valued person or thing; *v.t.* to adorn with jewels; to fit (as a watch) with a jewel for pivot-bearings. **-er** *n.* one who makes or deals in jewels. **-ery** *n.* jewels collectively [O.Fr. *joel*, jewel].

Jez·e·bel (jez′·ạ·bel) *n.* a wicked, wanton woman [*Jezebel*, wife of Ahab].

jib (jib) *n.* (*Naut.*) a triangular stay-sail in front of forward mast; the projecting beam of a crane or derrick; *v.t., v.i.* to jibe; also **gybe;** (*Colloq.*) to agree; *n.* a jeer; also **gibe.**

jibe (jīb) *v.t.* to swing (the sail) from one side of the ship to the other; *v.i.* to swing round (of the sail) when running before the wind; to alter the course so that the sail shifts; (*Colloq.*) to agree; *n.* a jeer; also **gibe.**

jif·fy (jif′·i·) *n.* (*Colloq.*) a moment; an instant.

jig (jig) *n.* a lively dance; music for this; (*Slang*) a trick; a tool or fixture used to guide cutting tools in the making of duplicate parts; *v.t.* to jerk up and down; *v.i.* to dance; to bob up and down. *pr.p.* **-ging.** *pa.p.* **-ged.** **-saw** *n.* a narrow saw in a frame for cutting curves, etc. **-saw puzzle** *n.* a picture cut into irregular pieces for putting together again.

jig·ger (jig′·ẹr) *n.* one who or that which jigs; any mechanical device which operates with jerky movement esp. an apparatus for washing and separating ores by shaking in sieves under water; an iron-headed golf club for approach shots; a bridge for a billiard cue; (*Naut.*) light tackle; (*Naut.*) a sail nearest the stern; (*Colloq.*) any gadget; a 1½ oz. measure for liquor.

jig·ger (jig′·ẹr) *n.* Also **chigger.** a flea, the female of which burrows under the human flesh to lay its eggs [var. of *chigoe*].

jig·gle (jig′·l) *v.i.* and *v.t.* to move with repeated short, quick jerks; *n.* a short, quick movement [etym. uncertain].

ji·had (ji·had′) *n.* a holy war to the death proclaimed by Mohammedans against the foes of Islam; (*Fig.*) a campaign launched against any doctrine. Also **jehad** [Ar.].

jilt (jilt) *n.* one, esp. a woman, who capriciously disappoints a lover; *v.t.* to deceive or disappoint in love; to break an engagement to marry [prob. fr. *jillet,* dim. of *Jill*].

Jim Crow (jim-krō) *a.* discriminating against or segregating Negroes [*Jim* and *crow*].

jim·my (jim·i·) *n.* a small crowbar, as used by burglars; *v.t.* to force open [var. of *James*].

jin·gle (jing′·gl) *v.t.* to cause to give a sharp, tinkling sound; *v.i.* to tinkle; to give this effect in poetry; *n.* a tinkling sound, as of bells; correspondence of sounds, rhymes, etc., in verse to catch the ear [imit].

jin·go (jing′·gō) *n.* a mild oath, as in *By Jingo;* one who expresses vehement patriotism (from the popular songs of the late 1870's, 'We don't want to fight, but *by Jingo* if we do...'). **jingo, -ish** *a.* **-ism** *n.*

jinks (jingks) *n.pl.* lively pranks [Scot.]. spirits of Mohammedan mythology [Ar. *jinni*].

jinn (jin) *n.pl.* (*sing.* **jinnee, jinni, genie**) spirits of Mohammedan mythology, supposedly able to assume the forms of men and animals [Ar. *jinni*].

jin·rik·i·sha (jin·rik′·shạ) *n.* a small, two-wheeled hooded carriage pulled by one or more men, commonly used in Japan (*abbrev.* **rickshaw**) [Jap. *jin,* a man; *riki,* power; *sha,* a carriage].

jinx (jingks) *n.* a person or thing of ill-omen.

jit·ney (jit′·ni·) *n.* public bus or car traveling a regular route.

jit·ters (jit′·ẹrs) *n.pl.* (*Slang*) a state of nervous agitation. **jitterbug** *n.* a jazzdancer. **jittery** *a.* [prob. imit.].

jiu·jit·su See **jujutsu.**

jive (jiv) *n.* and *v.i.* (*Slang*) exuberant variation on modern swing-time dance steps.

job (jab) *n.* a piece of work; labor undertaken at a stated price or paid for by the hour; position; habitual employment or profession; *a.* lumped together (of miscellaneous articles); *v.i.* to do odd jobs; to act as a jobber; to use influence unscrupulously; *v.t.* to buy and sell as a jobber; to let out work in portions. *pr.p.* **-bing.** *pa.p.* **-bed. -ber** *n.* a wholesale dealer who sells to retailers; one who transacts public business to his own advantage; one who does odd jobs. **-bery** *n.* underhand means to gain private profit at the expense of public money; fraudulent dealings. **-bing** *a.* **— lot,** a large amount of goods as handled by a jobber; a lot of inferior quality. **— printing, — work,** the printing of handbills, circulars, etc.

Job (jōb) *n.* (*Bib.*) a Hebrew patriarch of the Old Testament regarded as a monument of patience; any person accepting continued disaster with infinite patience. **a Job's comforter,** one who aggravates the distress of another while pretending to console him.

jock·ey (jak′·i·) *n.* a professional rider in horse-races; *v.t.* to ride as a jockey; to maneuver for one's own advantage; to trick; *v..i* to cheat. **-ism, -ship** *n.* [dim. of *Jock*].

jo·cose (jō·kōs′) *a.* given to jesting; waggish. **-ly** *adv.* **-ness, jocosity** (jō·kas′·ạ·ti·) *n.* the quality or state of being jocose. **jocular** (jak′·yạ·lẹr) *a.* given to jesting; facetious. [L. *jocus,* a jest].

joc·und (jak′·ạnd) *a.* merry; gay; genial. **-ity, -ness** *n.* **-ly** *adv.* [L. *jucundus,* gay].

jodh·purs (jad′·poorz) *n.pl.* long riding breeches, close-fitting from knee to ankle [fr. *Jodhpur,* a native Indian State].

jog (jag) *v.t.* to push with the elbow or hand; to nudge; to stimulate (as the memory); *v.i.* to move on at a slow jolting pace; to plod on. *pr.p.* **-ging.** *pa.p.* **-ged;** *n.* a nudge; a reminder; a slow walk, trot, etc.

jog (jag) *n.* a projecting part [var. of **jag**].

jog·gle (jag′·l) *v.t.* to shake slightly; to join by notches to prevent sliding apart; *v.i.* to shake; to totter; *n.* a jolt; a joint of two bodies so constructed by means of notches, that sliding apart is prevented; a metal pin joining two pieces of stone [dim. of **jog**].

John (jan) *n.* a proper name; a familiar appellation. **— Barleycorn,** whisky. **— Bull,** the typical Englishman. **— Doe,** fictitious plaintiff in a law-case. **— Hancock** (*Colloq.*) one's signature. **johnny cake** corn bread; *l.c.* (*Slang*) a toilet [L. *Johannes,* John].

John·so·ni·an (jan·sō′·ni·ạn) *a.* pert. to *Dr. Samuel Johnson* (1709-84), or to his literary style.

join (join) *v.t.* to bring together; to fasten; to unite; to act in concert with; to become a member of; to return to (as one's ship); to unite in marriage; *v.i.* to meet; to become united in marriage, partnership, league, etc.; to be in contact; *n.* a junction; a fastening. **joinder** *n.* (*Law*) a union. **-er** *n.* one who or that which joins; a carpenter. **-ery** *n.* the trade of a joiner. **to join battle,** to begin fighting. **to join issue,** to take different sides on a point in debate [Fr. *joindre,* to join].

joint (joint) *n.* the place where two things are joined; the articulation of two or more bones in the body; a hinge; (*Bot.*) the point where a leaf joins the stem; a cut of meat with bone prepared by butcher for the table; (*Slang*) a low-class public house; *v.t.* to unite; to provide with joints; to cut at a joint, as meat; *v.i.* to fit like joints; *a.* jointed; held in common. **-ed** *a.* having joints. **-ly** *adv.* together; co-operatively. **—stock company,** a mercantile, banking, or co-operative association with capital made up of transferable shares. **-ure** *n.* property settled on a woman at marriage to be hers on the decease of her husband. **out of joint,** dislocated; (*Fig.*) disordered [Fr. *joindre,* to join].

joist (joist) *n.* a beam to which the boards of a floor or the laths of a ceiling are nailed [O.Fr. *giste,* fr. *gésir,* to lie].

joke (jōk) *n.* something said or done to provoke laughter; a witticism; a prank; *v.t.* to make merry with; to banter; *v.i.* to make sport; to be merry. **-r** *n.* one who makes jokes or plays pranks; (*Slang*) a fellow; (*Cards*) an extra card in the pack, used in some games, such as poker; a hidden clause which changes the original intent of a bill, document, etc. **jokingly** *adv.* [L. *jocus,* a joke].

jol·ly (jal′·i·) *a.* jovial; gay; enjoyable; *v.t.* (*Colloq.*) to humor a person with pleasant talk; (*Colloq.*) to tease. **jollification** *n.* a celebration; a noisy party. **jolliness, jollity** *n.* mirth; boisterous fun [O.Fr. *joli,* gay].

jol·ly·boat (jal′·i·bōt) *n.* a ship's small boat [prob. Dut. *jolle,* a boat].

jolt (jōlt) *v.t.* to shake with a sudden jerk; *v.i.* to shake, as a vehicle on rough ground; *n.* a sudden jerk [etym. unknown].

Jo·nah (jō′·nạ) *n.* (*Bib.*) a Hebrew prophet; (*Colloq.*) a person who brings bad luck.

Jon·a·than (jàn′·ạ·thạn) *n.* a variety of eating apple. [Fr. fr. L. *juncus,* a rush].
jon·quil (jàn′·kwil) *n.* a variety of narcissus
jo·rum (jō′·rạm) *n.* a large drinking vessel; a large quantity of liquid. [to banter.
josh (jàsh) *v.t.* and *v.i.* to make fun of, to tease,
joss (jàs) *n.* a Chinese idol [corrupt of Port. *deos,* a god].
jos·tle (jàs′·l) *v.t.* to push against, esp. with the elbow; *v.i.* to push; to strive for position; *n.* a pushing against [fr. *joust*].
jot (jàt) *n.* an iota; something negligible; *v.t.* to scribble down; to make a memorandum of. *pr.p.* **-ting.** *pa.p.* **-ted. -ter** *n.* **not to care a jot,** not to care at all [Gk. *iota,* the letter i].
joule (jòòl, joul) *n.* (*Elect.*) a unit of work; the energy expended in 1 sec. by 1 ampere flowing through a resistance of 1 ohm [fr. *J. P. Joule,* English physicist, 1818-89].
jour·nal (jur′·nạl) *n.* a diary; a book recording daily transactions of a business firm; a daily newspaper; a periodical. **-ese** *n.* a term of contempt for the second-rate literary style of journalists. **-ize** *v.i.* to write for a journal; to keep a daily record of events. **-ism** *n.* **-ist** *n.* one who writes professionally for a newspaper or periodical. **-istic** *a.* [Fr. fr. L. *diurnalis,* daily].
jour·ney (jur′·ni·) *n.* travel from one place to another; distance covered in a specified time; *v.i.* to travel. *pr.p.* **-ing.** *pa.p.* **-ed. -man** *n.* orig. one hired to work by the day; a skilled mechanic or artisan who has completed his apprenticeship [O.Fr. *jornée,* a day].
joust (joust, just) *n.* a mock encounter on horseback; a tournament; *v.i.* to tilt [O.Fr. *juster,* to approach].
Jove (jōv) *n.* Jupiter. **jovial** *a.* orig. born under the influence of the planet Jupiter; gay; convivial. **joviality, jovialness** *n.* **jovially** *adv.* [L. *jovialis,* of Jupiter] .
jowl (joul) *n.* the jaw; the cheek; the dewlap, of cattle [O.E. *ceafl,* a jaw].
joy (joi) *n.* gladness; exhilaration of spirits; *v.i.* to rejoice; to exult. *pr.p.* **-ing.** *pa.p.* **-ed. -ful** *a.* **-fully** *adv.* **-fulness** *n.* **-less** *a.* dismal. **-lessly** *adv.* **-lessness** *n.* **-ous** *a.* full of joy. **-ously** *adv.* **-ousness** *n.* **-ride** *n.* (*Slang*) a pleasure ride or stolen ride. **-stick** *n.* (*Colloq.*) the control stick of an aircraft [O.Fr. *joie,* joy].
ju·bi·lant (jòò′·bạ·lạnt) *a.* exulting; rejoicing. **-ly** *adv.* **jubilate** *v.i.* to rejoice; to exult. **jubilate** (jòò·bạ·là′·tē) *n.* the hundredth psalm as a canticle in the Anglican church service. **jubilation** *n.* rejoicing; exultation [L. *jubilare,* to shout for joy].
ju·bi·lee (jòò′·bi·lē) *n.* the fiftieth anniversary of any outstanding event; a festival or time of rejoicing. **silver jubilee,** the twenty-fifth anniversary. **diamond jubilee,** the sixtieth anniversary [Heb. *yobel* ,a ram, or ram's horn trumpet].
Ju·da·ism (jòò′·dē·izm) *n.* the religious doctrines and rites of the Jewish people. **Judaic, -al** *a.* pert. to the Jews. **Judaically** *adv.* [L. *Judacus,* a Jew].
Ju·das (jòò′·dạs) *n.* (*Bib.*) the disciple of Christ who betrayed him; a traitor. **—kiss** *n.* a treacherous act disguised as kindness.
judge (juj) *n.* one who judges; an officer authorized to hear and determine civil or criminal cases, and to administer justice; an arbitrator; *pl.* a book of the Old Testament; *v.t.* to decide; to hear and try a case in a court of law; to give a final opinion or decision (as in a performance); to criticize; *v.i.* to act as a judge; to form an opinion; to come to a conclusion. **-ship** *n.* the office of a judge. **judgment** *n.* the act of judging; a legal decision arrived at by a judge in a court of law; discernment; an opinion. **Judgment Day,** doomsday [L. *judex,* a judge].
ju·di·ca·ture (jòòd′·i·kạ·chẹr) *n.* the power of of justice; a judge's period of office. **judicable** dispensing justice; judges collectively; a court *a.* capable of being tried or judged. **judicative** *a.* having the power to judge. **judicatory** *a.* dispensing justice. **judicial** *a.* pert to a court of justice or to a judge; impartial. **judicially** *adv.* **judiciary** *n.* judicial branch of government; the judicial system; judges collectively; *a.* pert. to the courts of law; passing judgment or sentence. **judicious** *a.* wise; prudent; showing discrimination [L. *judicare,* to judge].
ju·do (jòò′·dō) *n.* a form of jujitsu [Jap.].
jug (jug) *n.* a vessel of earthenware, glass, etc., with handle and narrow neck; other vessels for holding liquids; (*Slang*) jail; *v.t.* to put in a jug; (*Slang*) to put in jail. *pr.p.* **-ging.** *pa.p.* **-ged** [etym. uncertain].
jug·ger·naut (jug′·ẹr·nawt) *n.* any fanatical idea for which people are prepared to sacrifice their lives; any irresistible, tyrannical force which crushes all that obstructs its path [Hind. *Jagannath,* the lord of the universe].
jug·gle (jug′·l) *v.t.* to toss up and keep in motion a number of balls, plates, etc.; to defraud; *v.i.* to perform tricks with the hands; to use trickery; *n.* a trick by sleight of hand; verbal trickery. **juggler** *n.* one who juggles; a twister; a cheat. **jugglery** *n.* [O.Fr. *jogler,* to jest].
jug·u·lar (jug′·yạ·lẹr) *a.* pert. to the neck or throat; *n.* one of the large veins of the neck [L. *jugulum,* the throat].
juice (jòòs) *n.* sap; the liquid constituent of fruits or vegetables; (*Slang*) gasoline or electricity. **juiciness** *n.* **juicy** *a.* [L. *jus,* broth].
ju·jit·su (jòò·jit′·sòò) *n.* a form of wrestling, originating in Japan. Also **jujutsu** [Jap.].
juke box (jòòk′·bàks) *n.* (*Colloq.*) a coin operated phonograph.
ju·lep (jòò′·lạp) *n.* a sweet drink, esp. one in which medicine is taken. **mint julep** [Pers. *gul,* rose; *ab,* water].
Jul·ian (jòòl′·yạn) *a.* pert. to Julius Caesar. **Julian Calendar,** the calendar as adjusted by Julius Caesar in 46 B.C. in which the year was made to consist of 365 days, 6 hours.
ju·li·enne (jòò·li·en′) *n.* a clear soup containing vegetables finely shredded; *a.* of vegetables in thin strips [Fr.].
Ju·ly (joo·lī′) *n.* the seventh month of the year [fr. *mensis Julius,* month of Julius Caesar].
jum·ble (jum′·bl) *v.t.* to mix in a confused mass; *v.i.* to be in a muddle; *n.* a miscellaneous collection; a chaotic muddle [prob. from *jump* and *tumble*].
jum·ble (jum′·bl) *n.* a thin, sweet, sticky cake.
jum·bo (jum′·bō) *n.* a huge person, animal, or thing, esp. the famous elephant in the 1880's.
jump (jump) *v.t.* to spring over; to spring off; to skip (as page of a book); *v.i.* to lift feet from ground and alight again; to spring; *n.* a leap; a bound; a sudden, nervous start; *pl.* (*Colloq.*) nervousness. **-er** *n.* **-iness** *n.* nervous twitching. **-y** *a.* **-ing-bean** *n.* the seed of a Mexican plant containing larva which make it appear to jump [prob. imit.].
jum·per (jump′·ẹr) *n.* a one-piece sleeveless dress [prob. fr. Fr. *jupe,* a petticoat].
junc·tion (jungk′·shạn) *n.* the act of joining; the place or point of joining; a connection. **juncture** *n.* a joint; an exigency; a particular moment in the trend of affairs [L. *jungere,* to join].
June (jòòn) *n.* the sixth month of the year [L. *Junius,* the month of Juno].
jun·gle (jung′·gl) *n.* land covered with forest trees, tangled undergrowth, esp. the dense forests of equatorial latitudes. **— fever** *n.* a severe form of malaria [Hind. *jungal,* forest].
jun·ior (jòòn′·yẹr) *a.* younger, esp. of a son with the same name as his father; of lower

status; *n.* a young person; the younger of two; a minor; one in a subordinate position; a student in the next to last year of study [L. compar. of *juvneis*, young].

ju·ni·per (jȯȯ′·nạ·pẹr) *n.* a genus of evergreen coniferous shrub [L. *juniperus*].

junk (jungk) *n.* a flat-bottomed Chinese vessel [Port. *junco*, a boat].

junk (jungk) *n.* useless, discarded articles; pieces of old cordage used for oakum; (*Naut.*) hard, dry salted meat; *v.t.* to turn into junk. **—dealer, -man** *n.* one who buys and sells junk [L. *juncus*, a rush].

Jun·ker (yoong′·kẹr) *n.* a young German noble; a member of that reactionary political party in Prussia which stood for the landed interests of the aristocracy. **-ism** *n.* [Ger. *Junker*, a young noble].

jun·ket (jung′·kit) *n.* a dessert of milk curded with flavored rennet; a pleasure excursion; *v.i.* to feast; to picnic; to go on a pleasure trip; *v.t.* to entertain [L. *juncus*, a rush].

jun·ta (hoon′·tạ, jun′·tạ) *n.* a meeting; a council of state in Spain or Italy [Sp. *junta*, a committee].

jun·to (jun′·tō) *n.* a group of conspirators; a cabal [Sp. *junta*, a committee].

Ju·pi·ter (jȯȯ′·pạ·tẹr) *n.* in Roman mythology, the supreme god and ruler of heaven. Also **Jove;** the largest and brightest of the outer planets [L. fr. *Jovis*, *pater*, father Jove].

ju·rid·i·cal (joo·rid′·ik·ạl) *a.* pert. to law, or the administration of justice. **-ly** *adv.* [L. *juridicus*, judicial].

ju·ris·dic·tion (joor·is·dik′·shạn) *n.* the administration of justice; legal authority; the limit or extent within which this authority may be exercised. **-al, jurisdictive** *a.* [L. *jus*, law; *dicere*, to say].

ju·ris·pru·dence (joor·is·prȯȯ′·dans) *n.* the science of law; the study of the fundamental principles underlying any legal system; a body of laws. **medical jurisprudence,** forensic medicine, study of medicine as it concerns criminal law [L. *jus*, law; *prudentia*, knowledge].

ju·rist (joor′·ist) *n.* one versed in the law [L. *jus*, law].

ju·ry (joor′·i·) *n.* a body of citizens selected and sworn to give a verdict from the evidence produced in court; a committee chosen to decide the winners in a competition. **juror** *n.* one who serves on a jury. **-man, -woman** [O.Fr. *jurée*, an oath].

jus·sive (jus′·iv) *a.* (*Gram.*) expressing a command; *n.* a grammatical form expressing a command [L. *jubere*, to command].

just (just) *a.* equitable; true; founded on fact; proper; fair; well-deserved; *adv.* exactly; closely; scarcely. **-ly** *adv.* in a just manner; deservedly; uprightly. **-ness** *n.* equity; fairness [L. *justus*, upright].

jus·tice (jus′·tis) *n.* the quality of being just; equity; merited reward or punishment; the administration of the law; a judge; a magistrate. **-ship** *n.* the office of a judge. **justiciary** *a.* pert. to the administration of the law. **Justice of the Peace** (J.P.), a local officer authorized to try minor cases, administer oaths, perform marriages, etc. [L. *justitia*, justice].

jus·ti·fy (jus′·tạ·fī) *v.t.* to prove the justice of; to vindicate; to excuse; to adjust. *pr.p.* **justifying.** *pa.p.* **justified. justifiable** *a.* defensible; excusable. **justifiableness** *n.* **justifiably** *adv.* **justification** *n.* vindication; (*Theol.*) absolution [L. *justificare*, to justify].

jut (jut) *v.i.* to project. *pr.p.* **-ting.** *pa.t., pa.p.* **-ted** [a form of *jet*].

jute (jȯȯt) *n.* fiber of an Indian plant [Bengali fr. Sans. *juta*, a tress of hair].

Jutes (jȯȯts) *n.pl.* a Teutonic tribe [O.E. *Jote*].

ju·ve·nes·cent (jȯȯ·vạn·es′·ạnt) *a.* becoming young. **juvenescence** *n.* [L. *juvenis*, young].

ju·ve·nile (jȯȯ′·vạ·nīl, -nạl) *a.* young; youthful; puerile; *n.* a young person; a book written for children. **-ness, juvenility** *n.* **juvenilia** *n.pl.* works of author produced in childhood and early youth [L. *juvenilis*, youthful].

jux·ta·pose (juks·tạ·pōs′) *v.t.* to place side by side. **juxtaposition** *n.* the act of placing side by side; contiguity [L. *juxta*, near; *ponere*, to place].

K

ka·i·nite (kā′·nīt) *n.* hydrated compound of the chlorides and sulphates of magnesium and potassium [Gk. *kainos*, new].

Kai·ser (kī′·zẹr) *n.* the name derived from the Latin *Caesar*, given to the emperors of the Old Holy Roman Empire, and of the rulers of the German Empire. **-ship** *n.* [Ger.].

kale (kāl) *n.* colewort; a hardy member of the mustard family with curled leaves; [O.E. *cawel*, fr. L. *caulis*, a stalk].

ka·lei·do·scope (ka·lī′·da·skōp) *n.* an optical instrument, varying symmetrical, colorful patterns being displayed on rotation. **kaleidoscopic** *a.* ever-changing in beauty and form; variegated [Gk. *kalos*, beautiful; *eidos*, form; *skopein*, to view].

kame (kāme) *n.* a high narrow ridge of gravel and sand left by a glacier.

ka·mi·ka·ze (kȧ·ma·kȧ′·zi·) *n.* a suicide attack by Jap. pilot [Jap.].

kam·pong (kam·pawng′) *n.* a native Hawaiian; a native of any South Sea island [Hawaiian = a man].

kan·ga·roo (kang·gạ·rȯȯ′) *n.* a ruminating marsupial found in Australia.

Kant·i·an (kan′·ti·ạn) *a.* pert. to the German philosopher, Immanuel Kant, or his school of philosophy.

ka·o·lin (kā′·ạ·lin) *n.* China clay; fine porcelain clay chiefly produced from feldspar in China, U.S.A. and Cornwall by weathering [Chin. *kaoling*, high hill].

ka·pok (kā·pȧk′) *n.* a silky white vegetable fiber used for stuffing and for sound insulation; W. Indian evergreen tree [Malay].

ka·put (kạ·poot′) *n.* (*Slang*) finished; no good; all over; done for [Ger.].

kar·at (kar′·ạt) *n.* in fineness of gold, a twenty-fourth part (pure gold being 24 karats fine) (Gk. *Keras*, horn].

kath·ode See **cathode.**

kat·i·on, cation (kat′·i·ạn) *n.* an electro-positive ion which, in electrolysis, travels towards the cathode; a neutral atom which in consequence of losing an electron, has a positive charge [Gk. *kata*, down; *ienai*, to go].

ka·ty·did (kā′·ti·did) *n.* a green insect of the grasshopper family [Imit.]

ka·va (kȧ′·vạ) *n.* an intoxicating Polynesian beverage [Hawaiian].

kay·ak (kī′·ak) *n.* the Eskimo seal-skin canoe, long, narrow and covered over.

keck (kek) *v.i.* to retch, as if about to vomit; to show disgust [imit. of the sound].

keck·le (kek′·l) *v.t.* to protect a cable or hawser from damage by fraying, by wrapping old rope, etc., round the length likely to be affected [etym. doubtful].

kedge (kej) *n.* a small anchor *v.t.* to warp, as a ship; to move a ship by means of small anchors and hawsers [Fr.].

keel (kēl) *n.* the length-wise beam of a ship on which the frames of the ship rest; hence, a ship; a similar part on some other structure; *v.i.* to turn up the keel; to provide with a keel **-haul** *v.t.* to haul under the keel of a ship by ropes attached to the yard-arms

to keel over, (*Collog.*) to fall over; to capsize [O.E. *ceol*, a ship].

keen (kēn) *a.* having a fine cutting edge; sharp; penetrating; piercing (of wind); eager; intense; acrimonious; caustic (tongue); shrewd; discerning. **-ly** *adv.* [O.E. *cene*].

keen (kēn) *n.* Irish dirge; *v.i.* to wail over the dead before burial [Ir. *caoine*].

keep (kēp) *v.t.* to retain possession of; to detain; to observe; to carry out; to have the care of; to maintain; to cause to continue; to reserve; to manage; to commemorate; *v.i.* to remain (in good condition); to continue; *pa.p., pa.t.* **kept** *n.* guardianship; maintenance; the chief tower or dungeon (donjon) of a castle; a stronghold. **-er** *n.* one who keeps or guards; an attendant; a gamekeeper; a finger-ring to prevent another from slipping off. **-ing** *n.* care; custody; support; harmony. **-sake** *n.* anything given to recall the memory of the giver [O.E. *cepan*].

keg (keg) *n.* a small barrel [O.N. *kaggi*, cask].

kelp [kelp] *n.* the calcined ash of certain seaweeds, used as a source of iodine; a general name for large sea-weeds [etym. unknown].

Kelt, Keltic Same as **Celt, Celtic.**

kelt (kelt) *n.* a salmon which has just spawned.

kemps (kemps) *n.pl.* coarse rough hairs in wool.

ken (ken) *n.* view; range of sight or knowledge [O.E. *cennan*, to know].

ken·nel (ken'·ạl) *n.* a house or shelter for dogs; an establishment where dogs are bred or lodged; the hole of a fox or other animal; a small hovel of a house; *v.t.* to confine in a kennel; *v.i.* to live in a kennel. *pr.p.* **-ling.** *pa.p.* **-led** [Fr. *chenil*, fr. L. *canis*, a dog].

ken·ning (ken'·ing) *n.* a descriptive, poetical name used in place of the usual name of a thing or person [Ice.].

kent·ledge (kent'·lij) *n.* pig iron placed in a ship's hold for permanent ballast.

kep·i (kep'·i·) *n.* a light military cap, flat-topped with a straight peak [Fr.].

kept (kept) *pa.t.* and *pa.p.* of **keep.**

ker·a·sine (ker'·ạ·sin) *a.* horny; [Gk. *keros*, a horn].

ker·at'(o)-, ker·ạt(ạ)) *prefix*, fr. Gk. *keras*, a horn, used in the formation of compound terms. **keratin** (ker'·ạ·tin) *n.* an essential constituent of horny tissue. **keratoid** *a.* horny. **keratosis** *n.* (*Med.*) a skin disease characterized by abnormal thickening.

ker·chief (kur'·chif) *n.* any cloth used in dress, esp. on the head or round the neck.**-ed** *a.* [Fr. *couvre-chef*, cover-head].

ker·mis, kermess (kur'·mis) *n.* a festival or fair in the Low Countries; (*U.S.*) a similar affair, usually for charitable purposes; originally a dedication service at the opening of a new church [Dut. *kerk*, church; *mis*, mass].

kern (kurn) *n.* (*Print.*) a part of the face of a type projecting beyond the body, as an italic *f* [L. *cardo*, hinge].

ker·nel (kur'·nạl) *n.* the inner portion, the seed, of the stony endocarp of a drupe; the edible part of a nut; the body of a seed; central or essential part; the nucleus [O.E. *cyrnel*, dim. of *corn*].

ker·o·sene (ker'·ạ·sēn) *n.* an illuminating or burning oil [Gk. *kēros*, wax].

ker·sey (kur'·zi·) *n.* coarse woolen cloth, usually ribbed [*Kersey*, England].

ketch (ketch) *n.* a small two-masted vessel.

ketch·up, catch·up, cat·sup (kech'·ạp) *n.* a sauce made from mushrooms, tomatoes or walnuts [Malay *kechap*].

ket·tle (ket'·l) *n.* a metal vessel, with spout and handle, used for heating and boiling water or other liquids; a cooking pot. **-drum** *n.* a musical percussion instrument made of a hemispherical copper shell covered with vellum. **-drummer** *n.* **a pretty kettle of fish,** an awkward affair [O.N. *ketilla*].

key (kē) *n.* a low-lying island or reef near the coast, used esp. of Spain's former possessions off the coast of Florida [Sp. *cayo*, a reef].

key (kē) *n.* an instrument which shuts or opens a lock; an instrument by which anything is turned or opened; a spanner; the highest central stone of an arch; a lever in a musical instrument, depressed by the fingers in playing; a lever on a typewriter for actuating the mechanism; in engineering, a hand tool for valve control; a switch adapted for making and breaking contact in an electric circuit; in carpentry, a small piece of hardwood inserted in joints to prevent sliding; (*Mus.*) the keynote of a scale, or tonality; the pitch of a voice; solution or explanation; a translation of a book, esp. the classics, or solutions to questions set. *a.* critical; of vital importance; controlling. **-board** *n.* the whole range of keys on a keyed instrument. **-hole** *n.* a hole in a door or lock for receiving a key. **— industry,** an industry on which vital interests of the country or other industries depend. **— man** *n.* an indispensable employee. **-note** *n.* (*Mus.*) the first tone of the scale in which a passage is written; the essential spirit of speech, thought, etc.; the policy to be followed by a political party, etc., as set forth in an initial address. **— ring** *n.* a ring for keeping a number of keys together. **— signature** *n.* (*Mus.*) the essential sharps and flats placed at the beginning of a piece after the clef to indicate the tonality. **-stone** *n.* the wedge-shaped central stone at the crown of an arch; something on which other things depend. **all keyed up,** agog with excitement and expectation [O.E. *caeg*].

khak·i (ka'·ki·) *a.* dust-colored or buff; *n.* a cloth of this color, used for the uniforms of soldiers [Urdu = *dusty*].

khan (kȧn) *n.* a title of respect in various Mohammedan countries among Mongol races, a king, prince, or chief. **-ate** *n.* the dominion of a Khan [Pers. = a lord or prince].

khe·dive (kạ·dēv') *n.* the title of the Turkish ruler of Egypt [Fr. fr. Pers. = prince].

kib·itz (kib'·its) *v.i.* (*Colloq.*) to act as a kibitzer. **-er** *n.* (*Colloq.*) a spectator of a game, esp. cards, who looks at a player's hand over his shoulder; someone who gives unwanted advice [G. *kiebitz*].

kib·lah, keb·lah (kib'·lạ, keb'·lạ) *n.* the point towards which Mohammedans turn their faces in prayer [Ar. *qiblah*].

ki·bosh (kī'·bȧsh, ki·bȧsh') *n.* (*Colloq.*) nonsense; rubbish. **to put the kibosh on,** to silence; to defeat; to make impossible.

kick (kik) *v.t.* to strike or hit with the foot; *v.i.* to strike out with the foot; (*Colloq.*) to resist; to recoil violently (of a rifle, etc.); *n.* a blow with the foot; the recoil of a gun; (*slang*) stimulation; (*Colloq.*) thrill (*Colloq.*) complaint. **-er** *n.* **-back** *n.* (*Colloq.*) a vigorous response; a portion of a worker's wages taken out by his supervisor. **-off** *n.* the commencement of a game of football. **to kick over the traces,** to throw off all restraint; to rebel openly. **to kick the bucket** (*Slang*) to die. **drop kick** *n.* (*football*) a kick made as the ball, just dropped from the hand, rebounds from the ground. **place kick** *n.* kicking a football placed or held on the ground [M.E. *kiken*, of unknown origin].

kid (kid) *n.* a young goat; leather made from the skin of a goat; (*Slang*) a child; *pl.* gloves of smooth kid leather; *a.* made of kid leather [O.N. *kith*].

kid (kid) *vt.* and *i.* (*Slang*) to tease; to fool. *pr.p.* **-ding.** *pa.p., pa.t.* **-ded.** *n.* teasing. **-der** *n.*

kid·nap (kid'·nap) *v.t.* to carry off, abduct, or forcibly secrete a person (esp. a child). **-er** *n.*

-ing *n.* [E.*kid*, a child; *nap*, to nab].
kid·ney (kid′·ni·) *n.* one of two glandular organs in the lumbar region of the abdominal cavity which excrete urine; animal kidney used as food; kind; temperament. **— bean,** the kidney-shaped seed of a bean plant.
kill (kil) *v.t.* to deprive of life; to slay; to put to death; to destroy; to neutralize; to weaken or dilute; to render inactive; to pass (time); *n.* the act or time of killing; the animal killed. **-er** *n.* **-er whale** *n.* the grampus, a whale capable of swallowing seals, porpoises, etc., whole. **-ing** *a.* depriving of life; very exhausting; fascinating; (*Colloq.*) exceedingly funny. *n.* the act of destroying life; game killed on a hunt; (*Colloq.*) a profitable business deal. **-ingly** *adv.*
kiln (kil, kiln) *n.* furnace or oven for burning, baking or drying something. **—dry** *v.t.* to dry in a kiln [L. *culina*, an oven].
ki·lo- *prefix* fr. Gk. *chilioi*, one thousand, in the metric system denoting a thousand. **-cycle** *n.* the unit for measuring vibrations, esp. the frequency of electromagnetic waves, 1000 complete cycles or oscillations per second. **-gram** *n.* 1000 grams, equal to 2.2046 lbs. avoirdupois. **-liter** *n.* 1000 liters. **-meter** *n.* 1000 meters, 3280.899 feet or nearly $\frac{5}{8}$ of a mile. **-watt** *n.* an electric unit of power equal to 1000 watts. **-watt-hour,** *n.* one kilowatt expended for one hour, approximately 1.34 hp.
kilt (kilt) *n.* a short skirt usually of tartan cloth, deeply pleated, reaching from waist to knees [Dan. *kille*, to tuck up].
kim·bo (kim′·bō) *a.* crooked; bent; **akimbo.**
ki·mo·no (kạ·mō′·nạ) *n.* a striped or flowered overgarment with short wide sleeves, worn in Japan by both men and women; a dressing-gown in imitation of this style [Jap.].
kin (kin) *n.* family relations; relationship; affinity; *a.* of the same nature or kind; kindred; akin. **next of kin,** the person or persons closest in relationship to a deceased person [O.E. *cynn*].
-kin (kin) *noun suffix*, used as a diminutive, e.g. *lambkin*, a little lamb.
kind (kīnd) *n.* genus; sort; variety; class; particular nature; *a.* having a sympathetic nature; considerate; good; benevolent; obliging. **-hearted** *a.* **-heartedness** *n.* **-liness** *n.* benevolence. **-ly** *a.* and *adv.* **-ness** *n.* kind feeling or action. [O.E. *gecynde*, nature].
kin·der·gar·ten (kin′·dẹr·gar′·tn) *n.* a school for young children where they are taught by the organizing of their natural tendency to play [Ger. = children's garden].
kin·dle (kin′·dl) *v.t.* to set on fire; to light; to excite (the passions); to inflame; *v.i.* to catch fire; to become bright or glowing; to grow warm or animated. **kindling** *n.* the act of starting a fire; the material for starting a fire [O.N. *kynda*].
kin·dred (kin′·drạd) *n.* relation by birth; affinity; relatives by blood or marriage; *a.* related; cognate; of like nature; congenial; similar [M.E. *kinrede*].
kine (kīn) *n.pl.* a plural form of **cows.**
kin·e·mat·ic, kin·e·mat·i·cal (kin·ạ·mat′·ik, ·i·kal) *a.* relating to pure motion. **-s** *n.pl.* the branch of mechanics dealing with problems of motion [Gk. *kinēma*, movement].
kin·es·the·si·a (kin·ạs·thē′·zhạ) *n.* muscle sense; the perception of muscular effort. **kinesthetic** *a.* Also **kinaesthesia, kinesthesis** [Gk. *kinein*, to move; *aisthēsia*, perception].
ki·net·ic, kinetical (kạ·net′·ik, ·i·kạl) *a.* relating to motion; imparting or growing out of motion. **-s** *n.* the science which treats of changes in movements of matter produced by forces [Gk. *kinein*, to move].
king (king) *n.* (*fem.* **queen**) supreme ruler of a country; a sovereign; a monarch; one who is distinguished above all others of his compeers; a playing card in each suit with a picture of a king; the chief piece in the game of chess; in checkers, a man which is crowned. **-craft. -dom** *n.* realm; sphere; domain; one of the great divisions (animal, vegetable, and mineral) of Natural History. **-fisher** *n.* a stout-billed bird, with brilliant plumage. **-hood** *n.* kingship. **-let** *n.* a petty king; small bird **-like, -ly** *a.* **-pin** *n.* (*Fig.*) in bowling, the pin at the front apex when the pins are set up (*Fig.*) the most important person in a group. **-'s English,** correct English usage. [O.E. *cyning*].
kink (kingk) *n.* a short twist, accidentally formed, in a rope, wire, chain, etc.; in the neck, a cramp or crick; a mental twist; a whim; *v.i.* and *v.t.* to twist spontaneously; to form a kink (in).
kins·folk (kinz′·fōk) *n.* blood relations; kin; members of the same family; also **kinfolk. kinship** *n.* state or condition of being related by birth. **kinsman, kinswoman** *n.* [*kin*].
ki·osk (kē·ȧsk′) *n.* an open pavilion or summerhouse, supported by pillars; an erection, resembling a sentry box, for the sale of periodicals, candy, tobacco, etc.; a bandstand [Turk. *kioshk*].
kip (kip) *n.* the untanned hide of young cattle; a bundle of a definite number of hides.
kip·per (kip′·ẹr) *n.* herring, salmon, etc. split, then smoked; *v.t.* to cure fish by splitting, salting, smoking, or drying.
kirk (kurk) *n.* (*Scot.*) a church building; the (Established) Church of Scotland [Scand.].
kis·met (kis′·met) *n.* fate or destiny [Ar.].
kiss (kis) *v.t.* and *v.i.* to touch with the lips, in affection or reverence; to touch gently; *n.* a salute by touching with lips. **-able** *a.* **-er** *n.* one who kisses; (*Slang*) the mouth. [O.E. *cyssan*].
kit (kit) *n.* a soldier's outfit, excluding his uniform; a set of tools or implements; personal effects; a wooden tub.
kitch·en (kich′·ạn) *n.* a room in which food is prepared and cooked. **-ette** *n.* a small kitchen. **— garden** *n.* a garden for raising vegetables for the table. **— police** (abbrev. (**K.P.**) soldiers on kitchen duty. **-ware** *n.* cooking utensils [L. *coquing*, a kitchen].
kite (kīt) *n.* bird of prey of Falcon family; a sheet of paper, silk, etc., stretched over a light frame and flown by means of a cord attached and held from ground [O.E. *cyta*].
kith (kith) *n.* in phrase **kith and kin,** friends and acquaintances [O.E. *cuththu*].
kit·ten (kit′·n) *n.* a young cat; *v.i.* to bring forth young cats. **-ish** *a.* like a kitten; playful. **kitty** *n.* a pet name for a cat [dim. of *cat*].
kit·ty (kit′·i·) *n.* the pool in card games; cards left over after a deal to be used as part of the game.
ki·wi (kē′·wē) *n.* a New Zealand flightless bird; the apteryx [imit. fr. its cry].
klang (klang) *n.* the sound of metal striking metal; a complex musical tone, consisting of a fundamental with its harmonics [Ger.].
klax·on (klak′·san) *n.* electric horn on motor cars. [Trade Name].
klep·to·ma·ni·a (klep·tạ·mā′·ni·ạ) *n.* an uncontrollable impulse to steal or secrete things. **-c** *n.* [Gk. *kleptein*, to steal; *mania*, madness].
klick See **click.**
klieg eyes (klēg īz) *n.pl.* eye strain due to the excessive brilliancy of incandescent floodlighting lamps. **klieg light** *n.* a powerful incandescent lamp used in film studios for floodlighting [proper name].
knack (nak) *n.* inborn dexterity; adroitness; mannerism; habit [etym. uncertain].
knag (nag) *n.* a knot in wood; *a.* knotty;

rough [M.E. *knagge,* a knot in wood].

knap·sack (nap′·sak) *n.* a bag for food and clothing, borne on the back; a rucksack [Dut. *knapzak*].

knar (nȧr) *n.* a knot in a tree or in timber. [Dut. *knorf.* knot].

knave (nāv) *n.* a dishonest person; a rascal; (*Cards*) a jack. **-ry** *n.* roguery; trickery; sharp practice. **knavish** *a.* fraudulent; mischievous; roguish. **knavishly** *adv.* [O.E. *cnafa,* a boy. Cf. Ger. *Knabe,* a boy].

knead (nēd) *v.t.* to work dough by pressing with the heel of the hands, and folding over; to work or shape anything by pressure; to massage. **-er** *n.* [O.E. *cnedan*].

knee (nē) *n.* the joint formed by the articulation of the femur and the tibia, the two principal bones of the leg; a similar joint or region in other vertebrates; part of a garment covering the knee; *v.t.* to touch with the knees. **— breeches** *n.pl.* breeches reaching and fastened just below the knee. **-cap** *n.* the patella, a flattened bone in front of knee joint; a covering to protect the knees, esp. of horses. [O.E. *cneow*].

kneel (nēl) *v.i.* to bend a knee to the floor; to fall on the knees; to rest on the knees as in prayer. *pa.t.* and *pa.p.* **-ed** or **knelt. -ing** *n.* [fr. *knee*].

knell (nel) *n.* the stroke of a bell rung at a funeral or death; a death signal; a portent of doom; *v.i.* to toll; *v.t.* to summon by tolling bell [E. *cnyll*].

knew (nū) *pa.t.* of **know.**

knick·er·bock·ers (nik′·ẹr·bak′·ẹrz) *n.pl.* loose breeches gathered in at the knees. Also **knickers** [fr. the pseudonym of Washington Irving].

knick-knack (nik′·nak) *n.* a trifle, toy, or trinket. **-ery** *n.* knick-knacks collectively [reduplication of *knack*].

knife (nīf) *n.pl.* **knives** (nīvz) a cutting instrument; *v.t.* to stab with a knife. **— edge** *n.* the sharp edge of a knife; anything with a thin, sharp edge [O.E. *cnif*].

knight (nīt) *n.* orig. in feudal times, a young man admitted to the privilege of bearing arms; a minor piece in chess bearing a horse's head; *v.t.* to dub or create a knight. **—errant** *n.* a knight who wandered about in search of adventures. **—errantry** *n.* **-hood** *n.* the dignity or order of knights. **-liness** *n.* **-ly** *a.* and *adv.* [O.E. *cniht,* youth].

knit (nit) *v.t.* to form fabric by the interlooping of yarn or thread by means of needles or a machine; to cause to grow together, as a fractured bone; to contract (the brows); to unite closely; *v.i.* to be united closely. *pr.p.* **-ting.** *pa.t.* and *pa.p.* **-ted. -ter** *n.* **-ting** *n.* **-wear** *n.* knitted garments [O.E. *cynttan*].

knives (nīvz) pl. of **knife.**

knob (nȧb) *n.* a rounded lump; a hard protuberance or swelling; a boss or stud; small round handle of a door, etc.; a rounded hill. **-bed** *a.* set with or containing knobs. **-biness** *n.* **-by** *a.* full of knobs; lumpy. [M.E. *knop*].

knock (nȧk) *v.t.* and *v.i.* to strike or beat with something hard or heavy; to strike against; to rap; to make a periodic noise, due to a faulty bearing in a reciprocating engine or to pinking in a gasoline engine; (*Colloq.*) to disparage, to criticize adversely; *n.* a stroke with something heavy; a rap on a door; a blow; the noise of a faulty engine. **-er** *n.* one who knocks; an ornamental metal attachment on a door. **—kneed** *a.* having the knees bent inward. **-out** *n.* (*Slang*) something or someone overwhelmingly attractive; a blow in a boxing match which knocks out an adversary [O.E. *cnocian*].

knoll (nōl) *n.* a small rounded hill; the top of a hill; a hillock; a mound [O.E. *cnoll*].

knoll Same as **knell.**

knot (nȧt) *n.* a complication of threads, cords, or ropes, formed by tying or entangling; in cordage, a method of fastening a rope to an object or to another rope; an epaulet; ribbon folded in different ways; a bond of union; a small group (of people or things); a difficulty; a hard lump, esp. of wood where a branch has sprung from the stem; (*Bot.*) a node in a grass stem; (*Naut.*) a measure of speed of ships, equal to one nautical mile (6,080 ft.) per hour; *v.t.* to form a knot in; *v.i.* to form knots. *pr.p.* **-ting.** *pa.t.* *pa.p.* **-ted. -hole** *n* a hole in a board where a piece of a knob has fallen out. **-tiness** *n.* **-ty** *a.* full of knots; difficult; puzzling [O.E. *cnotta*].

knout (nout) *n.* a whip consisting of leather, thongs, [Russ. *knut,* a whip].

know (nō) *v.t.* to be aware of; to have information about; to have fixed in the mind; to be acquainted with; to recognize; to have experience; to understand; to have sexual intercourse with; *v.i.* to have information or understanding. *pa.t.* **knew** (nū). *pa.p.* **-n. -ing** *a.* professing to know; shrewd; deliberate; clever. **-ingly** *adv.* **to know the ropes,** to know from experience what to do [O.F. *cnawan*].

know·ledge (nȧl′·ij) *n.* direct perception; understanding; acquaintance with; practical skill; information; learning. **-able** *a.* well informed [E. *know*].

knuck·le (nuk′·l) *n.* the joint of a finger; the knee-joint of a calf or pig; *v.t.* to strike with the knuckles; *v.i.* to hold the knuckles close to the ground in the game of marbles. **brass knuckle** *n.pl.* iron or brass rings fitting across the knuckles, used to deliver murderous blows. **to knuckle down,** to tackle a job vigorously. **to knuckle down** or **under,** to yield or submit [M.E. *knokel*].

knurl (nurl) *n.* a series of ridges or rough indentations on the edge of a thumbscrew, coin, etc.; *v.t.* to roughen edges of a circular object; to mill; to indent. **-ed.** *a.*

ko·a·la (kō·ȧ′·lạ) *n.* a small marsupial of arboreal habit, native to Australia [Aborig].

Ko·dak (ko•dak) *n.* (an arbitrarily coined word) a trademark for photographic film, apparatus and supplies (orig. a small hand camera).

kohl (kōl) *n.* powdered antimony or lead sulfide used in the East for darkening eyebrows and eyelashes [Ar.]

kohl·ra·bi (kōl′·rȧ·bi·) *n.* a variety of cabbage with an edible turnip-shaped stem [Ger.].

ko·la (kō′·lạ) *n.* an African tree whose seeds or nuts contain a large quantity of caffeine and are used as a stimulant [Native].

ko·lin·sky (kạ·lin′·ski·) *n.* Siberian polecat or mink; its fur [*Kola Peninsula*].

kood·doo (ko̍o̍′·do̍o̍) *n.* the striped antelope of Africa. Also **kudu** [S. Afr.].

kook·a·bur·ra (kook′·ạ·bẹr′·ạ) *n.* the great kingfisher with a laugh-like cry [Austral.].

Koran (kạ·rȧn′, kō′·ran) *n.* sacred book of Islam, containing revelations received by Mohammed. [Ar. *quaran,* reading].

ko·sher (kō′·shẹr) *a.* (of food) pure, clean, esp. meat, made ceremonially clean according to Jewish ordinances [Heb. *kasher,* proper].

kow·tow, kotow (kou′·tou) *v.i.* to perform the Chinese ceremony of prostration; to abase oneself; to fawn on someone [Chin.].

kraal (krȧl) *n.* a Hottentot or Kaffir village consisting of a group of huts encircled by a stockade [Dut. fr. Port. *curral,* a cattlepen].

kra·sis (krā′·sis) *n.* mixture of wine and water used for the Eucharist [Gk.].

krem·lin (krem′·lin) *n.* the citadel of a Russian town or city; (*cap.*) the citadel of Moscow, the seat of Soviet government [Russ.].

kreut·zer (kroit′·zer) *n.* an old German coin: a modern Austrian monetary unit.

Krish·na (krish′·nạ) *n.* in Hinduism, the last incarnation of Vishnu [Sans.].
kro·ne (krōn′·e) *n.* a silver coin of Denmark and Norway; *pl.* **-r.** Also an old coin of Austria and Germany; *pl.* **-n.**
kryp·ton (krip′·tȧn) *n.* a non-metallic chemical element belonging to the group of rare gases, present in the proportion of about one part in twenty million in the atmosphere [Gk. *kruptein,* to conceal].
ku·dos (kū′·dȧs) *n.* fame; glory; credit [Gk.].
ku·du. Same as **koodoo.**
Ku Klux Klan (kū′·kluks-klan) *n.* a lawless secret society founded c. 1865, terrorizing blacks and advocating white supremacy [Gk. *kuklos,* a circle].
ku·lak (kȯȯ′·lȧk) *n.* a prosperous land holder in Russia who resisted the efforts of the Soviet to nationalize agriculture [Russ. = a fist, a forestaller].
kum·mel (kim′·ạl) *n.* a liqueur flavored with cumin and caraway seeds [Ger. = caraway].
kum·quat (kum′·kwȧt) *n.* a shrub, native to China and Japan, producing a small orange-like fruit [Chinese = a golden orange].
Kuo·min·tang (kwō′·min·tȧng) *n.* former political party in China.
ky·pho·sis (kī·fō′·sis) *n.* humpback, angular deformity of the spine [Gk.].
kyr·i·e (kir′·i·ē) *n.* the words and music of part of the service in the R.C. Church; the response in the Anglican communion service after each of the Ten Commandments [Gk.].

L

la (lȧ) *n.* (*Mus.*) syllable for sixth tone of scale in tonic sol-fa notation.
lab·da·num (lab′·dạ·nạm) *n.* a fragrant resin used in perfumes, etc. Also **ladanum** [Gk. *ladanon*].
la·bel (lā′·bạl) *n.* paper, card, etc., affixed to anything, denoting its contents, nature, ownership, destination, etc.; (*Fig.*) a classifying phrase or word applied to persons, etc.; (*Archit.*) a dripstone; *v.t.* to affix a label to; to identify by a label [O.Fr. *label,* a strip].
la·bel·lum (lạ·bel′·ạm) *n.* the posterior petal of a flower of the orchid type [L. *labellum,* a small lip].
la·bi·al (lā′·bi·ạl) *a.* pert. to the lips; formed by the lips, as certain speech sounds such as *p, b, w,* or *o; n.* a sound formed by the lips. **-ize** *v.t.* to give a labial character to a sound. **labiate, labiated** *a.* (*Bot.*) with calyx or corolla formed in two parts, resembling lips [L. *labium,* lip].
la·bi·o·den·tal (lā′·bi·ō·den′·tạl) *a.* pert. to the lips and teeth; *n.* a sound made with the lips and teeth, as *f* and *v.* **labium** *n.* a lip or lip-like structure; *pl.* **labia** [L. *labium,* a lip].
la·bor (lā′·bẹr) *n.* exertion of body or mind; toil; work demanding patience and endurance; manual workers collectively or politically; (*Med.*) the pains of childbirth; *v.i.* to work strenuously; to take pains; to move with difficulty; (*Med.*) to suffer the pains of childbirth; (*Naut.*) to pitch and roll. **-ious** *a.* toilsome; industrious. **-iously** *adv.* **-iousness** *n.* **-ed** *a.* **-er** *n.* **— union** *n.* an organization of workers for mutual aid and protection and for collective bargaining [L. *labor,* work].
lab·o·ra·to·ry (lab′·rạ·tōr·i·) *n.* a placed used for experiments or research in science, pharmacy, etc., or for manufacture of chemicals in industry (*abbrev.* **lab**) [L. *laborare,* to work].
la·bret (lā′·bret) *n.* an ornament inserted into a hole pierced in the lip, worn by some primitive tribes. **labral** *a.* **labrose** *a.* having thick lips. **labrum** *n.* a liplike structure. *pl.* **labra** [L. *labrum,* a lip].
la·bur·num (lạ·bur′·nạm) *n.* a small, hardy deciduous tree [L.].
lab·y·rinth (lab′·ạ·rinth) *n.* a system of intricate winding passages; a maze; (*Med.*) the intricate passages of the internal ear. **-ian, -ine** *a.* [Gk. *laburinthos,* a maze].
lac, lakh (lak) *n.* one hundred thousand, as a *lac of rupees* [Hind. *lakh,* 100,000].
lac (lak) *n.* a deep-red resinous substance, the excretion of an insect, found specially on trees in southern Asia, and used as a dye, in varnishes, sealing wax, etc. **seed-lac** *n.* the resinous substance cleared from twigs, etc. **shell-lac, shellac** *n.* the resin melted and cleared of impurities [Hind. *lakh,* 100,000].
lace (lās) *n.* a string or cord used for fastening dress, shoes, etc.; a net-like fabric of linen, cotton or silk with ornamental design interwoven by hand or machine; a tissue of silver or gold threads used as trimming; *v.t.* to fasten with a lace; to ornament with lace; to mix, as coffee, with a dash of brandy; *v..i* to be fastened with a lace. **lacing** *n.* a fastening formed by a lace threaded through eyeholes; a trimming of lace; (*Colloq.*) a thrashing. **lacy** *a.* [O.Fr. *las,* a noose].
lac·er·ate (las′·ẹ·rāt) *v.t.* to tear; to rend; to injure; to afflict sorely. **-d** *a.* torn; mangled. **laceration** *n.* [L. *lacerare,* to tear].
lach·ry·mal (lak′·rạ·mạl) *a.* pert. to or producing tears, as *lachrymal* duct, the tear duct; *n.* one of the tear glands; a small vessel, in ancient graves, supposed to contain tears of the bereaved [L. *lacrima,* a tear].
lack (lak) *v.t.* and *v.i.* to be destitute of; to want; *n.* deficiency; shortage; need; want. **-luster** *a.* dim; wanting in brightness; *n.* dimness [M.Dut. *lak,* deficiency].
lack·a·dai·si·cal *a.* affectedly pensive or languid [abbrev. of *Alack-a-day*].
lack·ey (lak′·i·) *n.* a liveried manservant; a footman; a follower; *v.t.* or *v.i.* to attend or serve as a lackey. Also **lacquey** [O.Fr. *laquais*].
la·con·ic (lạ·kȧn′·ik) *a.* brief; concise; expressing maximum meaning in the minimum of words. Also **-al. -ally** *adv.* **laconism** *n.* a brief, pithy style of speech; terse, sententious saying [Gk. *lakōn,* Spartan].
lac·quer, lacker (lak′·ẹr) *n.* a varnish consisting of a solution of shellac in alcohol; *v.t.* to cover with a film of lacquer; to varnish [Fr. *lacre,* a kind of sealing-wax].
la·crosse (lạ·kraws′) *n.* an outdoor ball game played with a *crosse* or stick which has a net at the end [Fr. *la crosse,* the crook].
lac·te·al (lak·ti·ạl) *a.* pert. to milk; milky; resembling chyle; *n.* an absorbent vessel conveying chyle from the intestines to the thoracic duct. **lactate** *n.* (*Chem.*) a salt of lactic acid; *v.i.* to produce milk. **lactation** *n.* the act of giving or secreting milk; the period during which a mother suckles her child. **lacteous** *a.* resembling milk. **lactic** *a.* pert. to milk; procured from milk or whey, as *lactic acid.* **lactose** *n.* milk-sugar [L. *lacteus,* milky].
la·cu·na (la·kū′·nạ) *n.* a hollow; a hiatus; an omission. *pl.* **lacunae** [L. *lacuna,* a pit].
lad (lad) *n.* (*fem.* **lass**) a young man; a boy [M.E. *ladde,* a serving-man].
lad·der (lad′·ẹr) *n.* a frame of wood, steel, ropes, etc., consisting of two sides connected by rungs for climbing; anything resembling a ladder; a means of ascent [O.E. *hlaeder*].
lade (lād) *v.t.* to load; to burden; to draw (fluid) by means of a ladle. *pa.t.* **-d.** *pa.p.* **-n.** **lading** *n.* the act of loading; freight [O.E. *hladan,* to load].

la·dle (lā′·dl) *n.* a long-handled spoon; *v.t.* to draw off with a ladle [O.E. *hladan*, to lade].

la·dy (lā′·di·) *n.* a well-bred woman; orig. a woman having authority over a household or estate; a woman of social distinction, position; a polite term for any woman. *pl.* **ladies. Lady** *n.* (*Brit.*) the title given to the wife of any nobleman ranking below a duke; the title of the daughter of a duke, marquis, or earl; the courtesy title of the wife of a knight or baronet. **-bird** *n.* a small spotted beetle. **-finger** *n.* a finger-shaped cake. **— in waiting** *n.* a lady appointed to attend a queen or princess. **-ish** *a.* affecting the airs of a lady. **—killer** *n.* (*Slang*) a man who imagines he has a fascination to women. **-like** *a.* **-love** *n.* a sweetheart. **-ship** *n.* the title of a lady [O.E. *hlaefdige*, a kneader of bread].

lag (lag) *v.t.* to bind round, as pipes, boiler, etc., with non-conducting material to prevent loss of heat; *n.* piece of lagging material [Scand. *lög*, a barrel stave].

lag (lag) *n.* time lapse; retardation; *v.i.* to move slowly; to fall behind. *pr.p.* **-ging.** *pa.p.* **-ged. -gard** *n.* a listless person. **-ger** *n.* **-ging** *a.* loitering. **-gingly** *adv.* [Celt].

lag (lag) *n.* (*Colloq.*) a convict [etym. unknown]

la·goon (lạ·gòòn′) *n.* a shallow pond or lake; a lake in a coral atoll [It. *laguna*].

la·ic (lā′·ik) *a.* lay; secular; *n.* a layman. **-ally** *adv.* **-ize** (lā·ạ·sīz) *v.t.* to secularize; to render lay or laic [Gk. *laos*, the people].

laid (lād) *pa.t.* and *pa.p.* of the verb **lay;** *a.* put down; (of paper) having a slightly ribbed surface showing the marks of the close parallel wires on which pulp was laid. **— up,** indisposed; (*Naut.*) dismantled; temporarily out of service, for repairs [Fr. verb *lay*].

lain (lān) *pa.p.* of verb **lie.**

lair (lār) *n.* a den or bed of a wild animal; a place to rest. *v.t.* and *v.i.* to place or lie in a lair [O.E. *leger*, a bed].

lais·sez-faire (les′·ā·fār′) *n.* a policy of non-interference. Also **laisser-faire** [Fr. *laissez-faire*, 'let do.'].

la·i·ty (lā′·ạ·ti·) *n.* the people, as distinct from the clergy [See **lay**].

lake (lāk) *n.* a large sheet of water within land. [O.E. *lac*, a lake].

lakh Same as **lac.** [100,000].

lam (lam) *v.t.* (*Slang*) to beat; to flog [Scand. *lama*, to beat].

lam (lam) *n.* (*Slang*) hasty escape; *v.i.* to run off quickly.

la·ma (là′·mạ) *n.* a Buddhist priest in Tibet. **Lamaism** *n.* form of Buddhist religion practiced in Tibet. **Dalai-Lama** *n.* or **Grand Lama,** the chief of the lamas [Tib. *blama*, a spiritual teacher]

La·maze (lạ·màz′) *a.* relating to a method of childbirth involving preparation by the mother, in order to suppress pain and eliminate the use of drugs [Ferdinand Lamaze Fr. obstetrician].

lamb (lam) *n.* the young of a sheep; the flesh of lamb as food; a young and innocent person; *v.i.* to bring forth lambs. **-kin** *n.* a little lamb. **-like** *a.* gentle. **-skin** *n.* [O.E. *lamb*, a lamb].

lam·baste (lam·bāst′) *v.t.* (*Slang*) to beat or scold severely.

lam·bent (lam′·bạnt) *a.* playing on the surface; gleaming; flickering; playing lightly and gracefully over a subject; said of wit. **lambency** *n.* [L. *lambere*, to lick].

lame (lām) *a.* crippled in a limb; hobbling; (*Fig.*) unsatisfactory, as an excuse; imperfect; *v.t.* to cripple. **— duck** *n.* (*Colloq.*) formerly, a Congressman serving at the last session of his term; temporarily disabled. **-ly** *adv.* **-ness** *n.* **-ish** *a.* rather lame [O.E. *lama*].

lamé (la·mā′) *n.* a textile containing metal threads giving a gold or silver effect [Fr.].

la·mel·la (lạ·mel′·ạ) *n.* a thin plate-like structure or scale. *pl.* **lamellae. lamellar, lamellate** *a.* composed of thin plates or scales. [L. *lamella*, a thin plate].

la·ment (lạ·ment′) *v.i.* to utter cries of sorrow; to bemoan; to mourn for; *v.t.* to deplore; *n.* a heartfelt expression of sorrow; an elegy or dirge. **lamentable** (lam′·ạn·tạ·bl) *a.* grievous; sad. **lamentably** *adv.* **-ation** *n.* the act of lamenting; audible expression of grief. **Book of Lamentations** (*Bib.*) one of the poetical books of the Old Testament. **-ed** *a.* mourned. **-ing** *a.* grieving. **-ingly** *adv.* [L. *lamentari*, to wail].

lam·i·na (lam′·ạ·nạ) *n.* a thin plate or scale lying over another; (*Bot.*) the blade of a leaf. *pl.* **laminae. laminable, laminar, laminary** *a.* consisting of, or resembling, thin plates. **laminate** *v.t.* to cause to split into thin plates; to make into thin layers (as metal); to cover with one layer or build up with many layers; *v.i.* to split into layers. **laminate, -d** *a.* formed of thin plates; stratified. **lamination** *n.* [L. *lamina*, a thin plate].

lamp (lamp) *n.* a vessel containing combustible oil to be burned by a wick, or inflammable gas from a jet; any light-giving contrivance. **-black** *n.* a fine soot formed by the smoke of burning gas, oil, etc.; the pigment from this soot [Gk. *lampas*, a torch].

lam·poon (lam·pòòn′) *n.* a bitter personal satire, usually in verse; abusive or scurrilous publication; *v.t.* to abuse in written satire. **-er** *n.* **-ery** *n.* [O.Fr. *lampon*, a drinking song].

la·nate (lā′·nāt) *a.* wooly; (*Bot.*) covered with fine hairs resembling wool [L. *lama*, wool].

lance (lans) *n.* a former war weapon consisting of a spearhead on a long wooden shaft; the soldier armed with a lance; a lancet; *v.t.* to pierce with a lance; to open with a lancet. **-r** *n.* a cavalry soldier armed with a lance; *pl.* a square dance, like quadrilles. **lancet** *n.* a small two-edged surgical knife. **lancet arch** *n.* narrow, pointed arch. **a free lance,** one who acts on his own initiative; a journalist not attached to the staff of any particular newspaper [O.Fr. *lance*, a light spear].

lan·ci·nate (lan′·sạ·nāt) *v.t.* to tear; to lacerate [L. *lancinare*, to tear].

land (land) *n.* earth; the solid matter of surface of globe; any area of the earth; ground; soil; the inhabitants of a country; real estate; *v.t.* to set on shore; to bring to land; (*Colloq.*) to gain; to catch; *v.i.* to go on shore; to disembark; (*Aero.*) to bring an aircraft to rest on land or water. **— breeze** *n.* an off-shore current or air. **-ed** *a.* pert. to, or possessing, real estate. **-fall** *n.* sighting of land by a ship at sea. **— grant** *n.* a grant of land from the government esp. for colleges, railroads, etc. **—grant college** *n.* a college supported with the aid of such grants according to the Morrill Acts (1862, 1890). **-holder** *n.* a proprietor of land. **-ing** *n.* the act of coming to land; disembarkation; the level part of a staircase between two flights of steps; the place where passengers land. **-ing gear** *n.* the wheeled under-carriage of an airplane on which it rests when landing or taking off. **-ing net** *n.* a net used by anglers for landing a fish already caught by rod. **-lady** *n.* the owner of property who leases land, buildings, etc. to tenants; one who lets rooms in a house; the proprietress of an inn. **-locked** *a.* enclosed by land. **-lord** *n.* the owner of houses rented to tenants; the proprietor of an inn, etc. **-lubber** *n.* a landsman (term used by sailors); one who knows little or nothing about boats. **-mark** *n.* a mark to indicate a boundary; any outstanding or elevated object indicating general direction or distinguishing a particular locality. **— mine** *n.* military high-explosive bomb. **— office** *n.* a government office for business concerning public lands. **-scape** *n.* that portion of land which the eye can comprehend in a single view; a pictorial representation of an actual or imagined inland scene. **-scape architecture** *n.* art of aesthetically arranging or changing features of the landscape. **-scape gardener,** one who is employed professionally to lay out gardens, etc. **-scapist** *n.* a painter of landscape. **-slide** *n.* a fall of rock from a hillside or cliff; (*Fig.*) a sudden overwhelming victory [O.E. *land,* land].

lan·dau (lan′·daw) *n.* a carriage, the top of which may be opened and thrown back. **landaulet, landaulette** *n.* an automobile with folding hood [fr. *Landau* (in Germany)].

land·grave (land′·grāv) *n.* a German nobleman [Ger. *Land,* land; *Graf,* a count].

lane (lān) *n.* a narrow track between hedges or across fields; a narrow street or road; a specified route followed by ships or airplanes; part of a street or highway for one line of traffic [O.E. *lane,* an alley].

lan·guage (lang′·gwij) *n.* speech; expression of ideas by words or written symbols; mode of speech peculiar to a nation, a class, profession, etc.; communication of animals, etc. or by any means. **dead language,** a language not spoken now, as opposed to *living language* [Fr. *langue,* language].

lan·guid (lang′·gwid) *a.* indifferent; listless; flagging from exhaustion. **-ly** *adv.* **-ness** *n.* **languish** *v.i.* to become languid; to droop with weariness; to pine or suffer; to become wistful. **-ing** *a.* drooping; sentimental. **-ingly** *adv.* **-ment** *n.* **languor** *n.* lassitude; sentimental softness [L. *languere,* to be weary].

lan·gur (lung′·go͝or) *n.* a long-tailed Indian monkey [Hind.].

lank (langk) *a.* drooping; gaunt and thin; long and straight, as hair. **-y** *a.* tall and slender. **-ly** *adv.* **-ness, -iness** *n.* [O.E. *hlanc,* lean].

lon·o·lin, lanoline (lan′·a̤·lin) *n.* an oily substance obtained from wool [L. *lana,* wool; *oleum,* oil].

lan·tern (lan′·te̤rn) *n.* something portable or fixed, enclosing a light and protecting it from wind, rain, etc.; a little dome over a roof to give light; a square turret placed over the junction of the cross in a cathedral, with windows in each side of it; the light chamber of a lighthouse. **— jaws** *n.* hollow cheeks. **Chinese lantern,** a colored, collapsible paper lantern. **magic lantern,** an instrument by means of which magnified images of small objects or pictures are thrown on a screen in a dark room [Fr. *lanterne,* a lamp].

lan·yard, laniard (lan′·ye̤rd) *n.* a short rope or line for fastening; a cord, with knife attached, worn round the neck [Fr. *lanière,* a rope].

La·od·i·ce·an (lā·a̤·da̤·sē′·a̤n) *a.* like the Christians of *Laodicea;* lukewarm in religion; lacking strong feeling on any subject; (Rev. 3) ([fr. *Laodicea*].

lap (lap) *n.* that part of the clothing between waist and knees of a person who is sitting; the part of the body thus covered; an overlying part of any substance or fixture; a course or circuit, as in bicycle-racing, etc.; that in which anything rests or is fostered as the *lap of luxury;* *v.t.* to lay over or on; *v.i.* to be spread or laid on or partly over; to be turned over or on; to lie upon and extend beyond. **-el** *n.* that part of a coat or dress which laps over the facing. **-ped** *a.* **-ful** *n.* that which fills a lap. **-pet** *n.* a part of a garment which hangs loose; a fold of flesh. **-peted** *a.* [O.E. *laeppa,* loosely].

lap (lap) *v.i.* to take up food or drink by licking; to make a sound like an animal lapping its food; *v.t.* to lick up; to wash or flow against. *pr.p.* **-ping.** *pa.p.* **-ped.** *n.* the act or sound of lapping; something lapped up [O.E. *lapian,* to drink].

la·pel See **lap.**

lap·i·dar·y (lap′·a̤·der·i·) *a.* pert. to stones or to the art of cutting stones; pert. to inscriptions and monuments; *n.* one who is skilled in the cutting, polishing and engraving of precious stones. **lapidate** *v.t.* to stone (to death). **lapillus** *n.* a small rounded fragment of lava. *pl.* **lapilli, lapis lazuli** *n.* an opaque mineral, sapphire-blue in color, much used in jewelry, ornaments, mosaics, etc. [L. *lapis,* a stone].

Lapp (lap) *n.* a native of Lapland. Also **Laplander. Laplandish, Lappish** *a.*

lapse (laps) *v.i.* to slip or fall; to fail to maintain a standard of conduct; to pass from one proprietor to another because of negligence; to pass slowly or by degrees; *n.* a slip or fall; a gliding; a passing of time; an error of omission; failure to do one's duty; (*Law*) termination of legal possession through negligence. **lapsable** *a.* **-d** *a.* no longer valid or operative; [L. *lapsus,* a fall].

lar·ce·ny (lȧr′·sa̤n·i·) *n.* theft. **larcenist** *n.* a thief. **larcenous** *a.* thieving; pilfering [O.Fr. *larrecin,* theft].

larch (lȧrch) *n.* a genus of cone-bearing deciduous tree [L. *larix*].

lard (lȧrd) *n.* the clarified fat of swine; *v.t.* to smear with fat; to stuff, as meat or fowl, with bacon or pork; (*Fig.*) to embellish, as to *lard one's speech with metaphors.* **-aceous** *a.* fatty. **-y** *a.* [L. *lardum,* the fat of bacon].

lard·er (lȧr′·de̤r) *n.* a pantry where meat and food stuffs are kept; supply of provisions [O.Fr. *lardier,* a bacon tub].

large (lȧrj) *a.* of great size; spacious; extensive; liberal; numerous; extravagant; *adv.* in a large way. **-hearted** *a.* generous; liberal. **-ly** *adv.* **-ness** *n.* bigness [L. *largus,* abundant].

lar·gess (lȧr′·jes) *n.* a generous gift; a donation. Also **largesse** [L. *larqiri,* to give freely].

lar·ghet·to (lȧr·get′·ō) *a.* (*Mus.*) rather slow; less slow than *largo.* **largo** (*Mus.*) *a.* and *adv.* slow and stately [It. *largo,* slow].

lar·i·at (lar′·i·a̤t) *n.* a lasso; a rope or thong of leather, with a noose for catching wild horses, etc. [Sp. *la reata,* the rope].

lark (lȧrk) *n.* a frolic; a prank; *v.i.* to play practical jokes [O.E. *lac,* play].

lark (lȧrk) *n.* a small songbird. **-spur** *n.* the delphinium [M.E. *laverock,* a lark].

lar·rup (lar′·a̤p) *v.t.* (*Colloq.*) to thrash. **-er** *n.* [Dut. *larpen,* to beat].

lar·va (lȧr·va̤) *n.* an insect in the caterpillar, grub, or maggot stage. *pl.* **larvae. -l** *a.* [L. *larva,* a ghost].

lar·ynx (lar′·ingks) *n.* the upper part of the trachea or windpipe; a cartilaginous cavity containing the vocal cords. *pl.* **-es, larynges** (·in·jēz). **laryngeal, laryngal** *a.* pert. to the larynx. **laryngitis** *n.* inflammation of the larynx. **laryngoscope** *n.* a special mirror for examining the larynx [Gk. *larunx,* the throat].

las·civ·i·ous (la̤·siv′·i·a̤s) *a.* loose; lustful; wanton. **-ly** *adv.* **-ness** *n.* [L. *lascivus,* wanton].

lash (lash) *n.* the thong of a whip; a cord; a stroke with a whip; a satirical or sarcastic reproof; an eyelash; *v.t.* to strike with a lash; to dash against, as waves; to bind with a rope; to scourge with bitter criticism; *v.i.* to ply the whip. **-ing** *n.* the act of whipping; the ropes fastening anything securely [etym. doubtful].

lass (las) *n.* a young woman; a girl; a sweetheart. **lassie** *n.* a little girl [prob. Scand.].

las·si·tude (las′·a̤·tūd) *n.* exhaustion of body or mind; languor [L. *lassus,* faint].

las·so (las′·ō) *n.* a long rope with a noose, used for catching wild horses; a lariat. *pl.* **-s, es** *v.t.* to catch with the lasso [Sp. fr. L. *laqueus,* a noose].

last (last) *a.* following all the rest; most recent; most unlikely; final; supreme; *adv.* finally; immediately before in time; in conclusion; *n.* the end. **-ly** *adv.* **the Last Supper,** the memorial supper celebrated by Jesus on the eve of his betrayal. **at last,** finally [contr. of *latest.*]

last (last) *n.* a model of the human foot in wood on which shoes are made or repaired; *v.t.* to fit with a last [O.E. *last,* a trace or track]

last (last) *v.i.* to continue in time; to endure; to remain unimpaired in strength or quality; to suffice. **-ing** *a.* durable; permanent [O.E. *laestan,* to continue on a track].

Las·tex (las′·teks) *n.* a fine rubber thread wound with cotton, rayon, or silk and woven or knitted into fabrics [Trademark].

lat·a·ki·a (lat·ạ·kē′·ạ) *n.* a superior quality of Turkish tobacco from *Latakia* in Syria.

latch (lach) *n.* a small piece of iron or wood used to fasten a door; a catch; *v.t.* to fasten with a latch. **-key** *n.* a key used for raising the latch of a door; a pass-key [O.E. *laeccan,* to catch].

late (lāt) *a.* behindhand; coming after; delayed; earlier than the present time; occurring at the close of a period of time; no longer in office; deceased; *adv.* after the usual time; not long ago; far into the night, day, week, etc. **-ly** *adv.* **-ness** *n.* tardiness. **-r** *a.* (comp. of *late*) subsequent; posterior. **-st** *a.* (superl. of *late*) longest after the usual time; most recent or up-to-date, as news. **latter** (lat′·ẹr) *a.* (var. of *later*) later or more recent; the second of two just mentioned; modern. **latterly** *adv.* **of late,** recently [O.E. *laet,* slow].

la·tent (lā′·tạnt) *a.* not visible or apparent; dormant; hid; concealed. **latency** *n.* **-ly** *adv.* **— heat,** heat which is absorbed in changing a body from solid to liquid, or liquid to gas, without increasing its temperature [L. *latere,* to lie hid].

lat·er·al (lat′·ẹr·ạl) *a.* relating to the side. **-ly** *adv.* **— pass** (*Football*) a short pass parallel to the goal line [L. *latus, lateris,* side].

Lat·er·an (lat′·ẹr·ạn) *n.* the Pope's cathedral Church in Rome; *a.* pert. to church councils [fr. *Lateranus,* orig. owner of land].

la·tex (lā′·teks) *n.* the milky sap of trees, plants, the milky juice of the rubber tree. *pl.* **latices** [L. *Latex,* a liquid].

lath (lath) *n.* a thin, narrow slip of wood to support plaster, slates, etc. *pl.* **laths** (laTHz); *v.t.* to line with laths. **-er** *n.* **-ing** *n.* the process of constructing with laths; the work done [O E. *laettu,* a thin strip].

lathe (lāTH) *n.* a machine-tool for turning articles of wood, metal, etc.; *v.t.* to shape on a lathe [Scand.].

lath·er (laTH′·ẹr) *n.* foam or froth made with soap and water; froth from sweat; *v.t.* to spread over with lather; *v.i.* to form a lather [O.E. *leathor,* lather].

Lat·in (lat′·in) *a.* pert. to *Latium,* a part of ancient Italy with Rome as its chief center, or its inhabitants; written or spoken in Latin; pert. to the Roman Catholic Church (as distinct from the Greek Church); *n.* language or person descended linguistically from the ancient Latins. **-ize** *v.t.* to give a Latin form to; to translate into Latin; *v.i.* to use Latin words. **-ism** *n.* a Latin idiom. **-ist** *n.* a Latin scholar or expert. **-ity** *n.* the Latin language and its idiom. **— America,** parts of Central and South America where Romance languages are spoken. **— Church,** the Roman Catholic Church using Latin as its official language. **— languages,** those languages derived mainly from Latin as French, Italian, Spanish, Rumanian.

lat·i·tude (lat ·ạ·tūd) *n.* distance, measured in degrees, north or south of the equator; any region defined according to latitude; the angular distance of a heavenly body from the ecliptic; (*Fig.*) breadth of signification; deviation from a standard, esp. religious or ethical; scope; range. **latitudinal** *a.* pert. to latitude. **latitudinarian** *a.* broad; liberal, esp. in religious principles; *n.* one who departs from, or is indifferent to, strictly orthodox religious principles. **latitudinal** *a.* [L. *latitudo,* breadth].

la·trine (lạ·trēn′) *n.* a toilet, esp. in barracks, hospitals, etc. [L. *latrina,* bath].

lat·ten (lat′·ạn) *n.* a metallic alloy of copper and zinc, with appearance of brass; metal in thin sheets [Ger. *Latte,* a thin plate].

lat·ter See **late.**

lat·tice (lat′·is) *n.* framework of wood, metal, etc., formed by strips, laths, or bars crossing each other; a gate, trellis, or window thus formed; *v.t.* to furnish with a lattice. **-work** *n.* a trellis, etc. [Fr. *latte,* a lath].

Lat·vi·an (lat′·vi·ạn) *a.* pert. to the Baltic state of Latvia; Lettish.

laud (lawd) *v.t.* to praise in words or singing; to extol; *n.* a eulogy; praise; *pl.* in R.C. services, the prayers immediately after matins. **-ability** *n.* praiseworthiness. **-able** *a.* commendable. **-ableness** *n.* **-ably** *adv.* **-ation** *n.* praise; eulogy; the act of praising highly. **-atory** *a.* expressing praise [L. *laudare,* to praise].

laugh (laf) *v.i.* to express mirth spontaneously; to make an involuntary explosive sound of amusement; to be merry or gay; *n.* mirth peculiar to human species; laughter. **-able** *a.* droll; ludicrous; comical. **-ableness** *n.* **-ably** *adv.* **-er** *n.* **-ing** *a.* happy; merry. **-ing gas** *n.* nitrous oxide gas used as anesthetic in dental operations. **-ing hyena** *n.* the spotted hyena with a peculiar cry like a human laugh. **-ing jackass** *n.* the great kingfisher of Australia. **-ingly** *adv.* **-ing stock** *n.* object of ridicule. **-ter** *n.* merriment; audible expression of amusement. **to laugh up one's sleeve,** to laugh inwardly [O.E. *hlihan,* to laugh].

launch, lanch (lawnch, lạnch) *v.t.* to throw as a lance; to let fly; to cause to slide into the water for the first time, as a ship; to initiate, as an attack; to start a new activity; *v.i.* to go into the water; to push out to sea; to go forth; to expatiate, as in talk; to embark upon; *n.* the sliding of a ship into the water for the first time. **— vehicle** *n.* a rocket used to place a satellite or space vehicle in orbit. **-ing pad** *n.* platform from which a missile is fired by remote control [M.E. *lanchen,* to drop].

launch (lawnch, lȧnch) *n.* the largest boat carried on a warship; an open boat driven by steam, gasoline, or electricity [Sp. *lancha,* a pinnace].

laun·dry (lawn′·dri·, lȧn′·dri·) *n.* a place where clothes are washed, dried, and ironed; the process of washing clothes, etc.; clothes thus washed, etc. **launder** *v.t.* to wash clothes; *n.* (*Mining*) a long hollow trough for conveying powdered ore from the box where it is bruised. **launderer** *n.* **laundress** *n.* a woman who washes and irons clothes. **-man** *n.* a man who collects and delivers laundry or who works in a laundry [L. *lavandus,* to be washed].

lau·rel (law′·rạl) *n.* evergreen shrub, much used formerly to make wreaths symbolic of honor; *pl.* (*Fig.*) honors; *a.* consisting of laurel. **laureate** *a.* crowned with laurel; *n.* esp. in *Poet Laureate.* **laureateship** *n.* **-ed** *a.* [L. *laurus,* a bay-tree].

la·va (lȧ′·vạ) *n.* the molten rock, ejected by a volcano, hardening as it cools [It. fr. L. *lavare,* to wash].

la·va·bo (la·vā′·bō) *n.* ceremonial washing of a celebrant's hands after the offertory and before the eucharist, esp. in R.C. service; the towel or basin used in this ceremony [L.].

lave (lāv) *v.t.* (*Poetic*) to wash; to bathe; *v.i.* to bathe; to wash oneself. **lavatory** *n.* a place for washing [L. *lavare,* to wash].

lav·en·der (lac′·ạn·dẹr) *n.* an aromatic plant of mint family, yielding an essential oil; pale-lilac color of lavender flowers; dried flowers used as a sachet; *v.t.* to sprinkle or perfume with lavender [Fr. *lavande*, fr. L. *lavare*, to wash].

lav·ish (lav′·ish) *a.* over-generous; extravagant; ample; *v.t* to expend or bestow extravagantly. **-ly** *adv.*, *n.* [O. E. *lafian*, to pour out].

law (law) *n.* a rule established by authority; a body of rules the practice of which is authorized by a community or state; legal science; established usage; a rule, principle, or maxim of science, art, etc.; the legal profession; legal procedure; (*Theol.*) the Jewish or Mosaic code, as distinct from the Gospel. **—abiding** *a.* well-behaved; conforming to the law. **— court** *n.* a court in which lawcases are heard and judged. **-ful** *a.* allowed by law; legitimate. **-fully** *adv.* **-fulness** *n.* **-giver** *n.* a legislator. **-less** *a.* not conforming to the law; violent. **-lessly** *adv.* **-lessness** *n.* **— officer** *n.* a policeman. **-suit** *n.* a process in law for recovery of a supposed right. **-yer** *n.* a practitioner of law. **common law,** body of laws established more by custom than by definite legislation. **written law,** statute law, codified and written down, as distinct from *Common law* [O.E. *lagu*, a thing laid down].

lawn (lawn) *n.* a stretch of closely-cut, carefully-tended grass. **— mower** *n.* a machine for cutting grass [O.Fr. *launde*, a plain].

lawn (lawn) *n.* a fine linen or cambric; a. made of lawn [fr. *Laon*, a town in France].

lax (laks) *a.* slack; flabby; loose, esp. in moral sense; careless; not constipated. **-ative** *a.* having purgative effect; *n.* an aperient. **-ity, -ness** *n.* slackness; looseness of moral standards; want of exactness [L. *laxus*, loose].

lay (lā) *v.t.* to place or put down; to apply; to beat down, as corn; to cause to subside; to exorcise, as an evil spirit; to spread on a surface; to wager; to produce, to prepare; to station, as an ambush; to form, as a plot; to set out dishes, etc. (on a table); to charge, as with a responsibility; *v.i.* to produce eggs. *pr.p.* **-ing.** *pa.t.*, *pa.p.* **laid.** *n.* a situation; disposition. **-er** *n.* a person who or that which lays, as a bricklayer, hen, etc.; a thickness or coating laid down; a stratum of rock or vegetation; the shoot of a plant partly covered with earth, thus laid to encourage propagation. **-erage** *n.* the artificial propagation of plants by layers. **— off** *n.* a slack time in industry. **— out** *n.* that which is laid out; the design or plans, as of a garden. **— over** *n.* stop, or break, in a trip. [O.E. *lecgan*, to lay].

lay (lā) past tense of **lie** (to recline).

lay (lā) *n.* a song; a narrative poem such as was recited by minstrels [O.Fr. *lai*, a song].

lay (lā) *a.* pert. to the laity, as distinct from the clergy; unprofessional. **laicize** *v.t.* to deprive of clerical character. **laity** *n.* **— brother** *n.* a servant in a monastery. **-figure** *n.* a jointed figure used by artists in imitation of the human form; a person of rather negative character. **-man** *n.* one of the laity, or people; one who is not an expert in a branch of knowledge. **— sister** *n.* a woman who serves the nuns in a convent [Gk. *laos*, the people].

lay·ette (lā·et′) *n.* a complete outfit for a new-born baby [Fr.].

laz·ar (laz′·ęr) *n.* a person afflicted with a loathsome disease, like *Lazarus*, the beggar [fr. *Lazarus*, the beggar, Luke 16].

laze (lāz) *v.i.* (*Colloq.*) to be lazy; to lounge [fr. *lazy*].

la·zy (lā′·zi·) *a.* disinclined to exertion; slothful; *v.i.* to be lazy. **lazily** *adv.* **laziness** *n.* **-bones** *n.* (*Colloq.*) a lazy fellow; an idler [O.Fr. *lasche*, weak].

lea (lē) *n.* (*Poetic*) a meadow; land left untilled; pasturage [O.E. *leah*, a field].

leach (lēch) *v.t.* to wash by causing water to pass through; (*Bot.*) to remove salts from soil by percolation; *v.i.* to pass through by percolation; *n.* act of leaching; material leached; a vessel used for leaching. Also **letch. -y** *a.* porous [O.E. *leccan*, to moisten].

lead (led) *n.* a well-known malleable bluish-grey metal, ductile and heavy, used for roofing, pipes, etc.; a plummet for sounding ocean depths; a thin strip of type metal to separate lines of print; graphite for pencils; bullets; *pl.* sheets of lead for roof coverings; *a.* made of, or containing lead. **-ed** *a.* fitted with lead; set in lead, as panes of glass. **-en** *a.* made of lead; heavy; dull. **-ing** *n.* frame or cover of lead. **— pencil** *n.* a pencil containing graphite. **— poisoning** *n.* a form of poisoning called plumbism caused by lead being absorbed into the blood and tissues. **-y** *a.* [O.E. *lead*, lead].

lead (lēd) *v.t.* to show the way; to guide; to direct; to persuade; to precede; (*Cards*) to play the first card of a round; *v.i.* to go in front and show the way; to outstrip; to conduct; to tend to; *n.* front position; precedence; guidance; direction; priority; principal part in a play or film; an electric wire or cable; the first card played in a card-game; a dog's chain or leash. **-er** *n.* a guide; a conductor; a commander; (chiefly *Brit.*) the leading editorial in a newspaper; the foremost horse in a team; (*Mus.*) a performer who leads an orchestra or choir; (*Print.*) a series of dots (. . .) to guide the eye across the page. **-ership** *n.* the state or function of a leader. **-ing** *n.* direction; the act of guiding. **-ing-article** *n.* a leader or editorial in a newspaper. **-ing-lady, -man** *n.* the actress (or actor) playing the principal role. **-ing-question** *n.* (*Law*) a question so phrased as to suggest the answer expected. **to lead astray,** to tempt from virtue [O.E. *laedan*, to lead].

leaf (lēf) *n.* thin deciduous shoot from the stem or branch of a plant; anything resembling a leaf in shape or thinness; a sheet of paper, esp. as part of a book, with a page on each side; side of a double door or a shutter; one of the sections of a dropleaf or extension table; a hinged flap; a very thinly beaten plate, as of gold. *pl.* **leaves.** *v.i.* to shoot out leaves. **-age** *n.* leaves collectively; foliage. **-iness** *n.* **-less** *a.* devoid of leaves. **-let** *n.* a tiny leaf; a printed sheet advertisement, notice of meeting, etc. **— mold** *n.* leaves decayed and reduced to mold, used as manure. **-y** *a.* full of leaves. **to turn over a new leaf,** to reform [O.E. *leaf*, leaf].

league (lēg) *n.* an old nautical measure equal to three geographical miles [O.Fr. *legue*, fr. (L.L.) *leuca*, a Gallic mile of 1500 paces].

league (lēg) *n.* a compact made between nations or individuals for mutual aid and the promoting of common interests; an association, as of football clubs, for match games to be played during a season; *v.i.* to combine in an association [Fr. *ligue*, a conspiracy].

lea·guer (lē′·gęr) *n.* a military camp, esp. a siege camp [Dut. *leger*, a camp].

leak (lēk) *n.* a crack, crevice, fissure, or hole in a vessel; the oozing of liquid from such; (*Elect.*) an escape of electrical current from a faulty conductor; *v.i.* to let fluid into, or out of, a defective vessel. **-age** *n.* an oozing or quantity of liquid which passes through a defect in a vessel; (*Fig.*) the giving away of secrets, news, etc., through unauthorized channels. **-iness** *n.* **-y** *a.* having leaks. **spring a leak,** to develop a crack or flaw [Scand. *leka*, a drip].

lean (lēn) *v.t.* to incline; to cause to rest against; *v.i.* to deviate from the perpendicular; to incline. *pa.t.* and *pa.p.* **leaned** or **leant** (lent). *n.* a slope; a rest against. **-ing** *n.* inclination (of body or mind). **—to** *n.* a shed built against a wall or side of a house or supported at one end by posts or trees [O.E. *hlaenan*, to cause to incline].

lean (lēn) *a.* thin; wanting in flesh or fat; (*Fig.*) empty; impoverished; *n.* that part of meat consisting of flesh without fat. **-ly** *adv.* **-ness** *n.* [O.E. *hlaene,* thin].

leap (lēp) *v.i.* to spring; to jump up or forward; to vault; *v.t.* to pass over by leaping. *pr.p.* **-ing** *pa.t.* and *pa.p.* **-ed** or **leapt** (lept). *n.* jumping up or forward; a sudden rise (as of book-sales). **-frog** *n.* a game, in which one stoops down, and another vaults over his head. **— year** *n.* a year of 366 days [O.E. *hleapan,* to leap].

learn (lurn) *v.t.* to acquire knowledge; to get to know; to gain skill by practice; *v.i.* to gain knowledge; to take example from. *pa.t.* and *pa.p.* **-ed** (lurnd) or **-t. -ed** (lurn′·ạd) *a.* having knowledge; erudite. **-edly** *adv.* **-edness** *n.* **-er** *n.* **-ing** *n.* that which is learned; letters; science; literature, erudition [O.E. *leornian*].

lease (lēs) *n.* a contract renting lands, houses, farms, etc., for a specified time; time covered by lease; any tenure; *v.t.* to grant possession of lands, etc., to another for rent; to hold a lease. **— hold** *a.* held on lease [O.Fr. *laissier,* to transmit].

leash (lēsh) *n.* a line by which a hawk, dog, or other animal is held; a set of three hounds, or hares or foxes held in leash; *v.t.* to hold by a leash; to bind [O.Fr. *lesse,* a thong].

least (lēst) *a.* (superl. of **little**) smallest; faintest; most minute; *adv.* in the smallest degree; *n.* the smallest amount. **-ways, -wise** (*Colloq.*) *adv.* at least; however. **at least,** at any rate [O.E. *laest,* smallest].

leath·er (leTH′·ẹr) *n.* the skin of an animal dressed and prepared for use; anything made of leather; *v.t.* to apply leather to; (*Colloq.*) to thrash with a strap. **-back** *n.* a large sea turtle. **— bound** *a.* (of a book) bound in calf, morocco, or other leather. **-ing** *n.* (*Colloq.*) a thrashing. **-n** *a.* made of leather. **-neck** *n.* (*Slang*) a U.S. marine. **-y** *a.* like leather; tough. **patent leather,** leather with shiny, varnished surface [O.E. *lether,* leather].

leave (lēv) *n.* liberty granted; formal good-bye; furlough; permission to be temporarily absent from duty. **French leave,** absence without permission [O.E. *leaf,* permission].

leave (lēv) *v.t.* to quit; to forsake; to omit; to remove; to allow to remain unaltered; to bequeath; to permit; to entrust; to refer; *v.i.* to depart from; to withdraw. *pr.p.* **leaving.** *pa.p.* **left. leavings** *n.pl.* things left; relics; refuse [O.E. *laefan,* to bequeath].

leav·en (lev′·n) *n.* a substance due to fermentation which causes bread dough to rise; (*Fig.*) anything which causes a general change in the mass; *v.t.* to raise with leaven; to create a spiritual change [L. *levare,* to raise].

lech·er (lech′·ẹr) *n.* a man given to lewdness; a fornicator. **-ous** *a.* lascivious; lustful. **-ously** *adv.* **-ousness, -y** *n.* [O.Fr. *lechier,* to lick].

lec·tern (lek′·tẹrn) *n.* a reading desk in a church [L.L. *lectrum,* a reading-desk].

lec·tion (lek′·shạn) *n.* a variation in copies of a manuscript; a portion of scripture read during a church service. **-ary** *n.* a book containing portions of the Scripture to be read on particular days. **lector** *n.* a reader; a minor ecclesiastic in the early church; a lecturer in a college or university [L. *legere,* to read].

lec·ture (lek′·chẹr) *n.* a discourse on any subject; a formal reproof; *v.t.* to instruct by discourses; to reprove; *v.i.* to deliver a formal discourse. **-r** *n.* one who lectures; an assistant to a professor in a university department. **-ship** *n.* [L. *legere, lectum,* to read].

led (led) *pa.t.* and *pa.p.* of verb **lead.**

ledge (lej) *n.* a projection, as from a wall or cliff; a shelf; a ridge of rock near the surface of the sea [M.E. *legge,* a bar].

ledg·er (lej′·ẹr) *n.* a book in which a business firm enters all debit and credit items in summary form; a cash book; a flat stone lying horizontally as on a grave; one of the pieces of timber used in a scaffolding; *a.* stationary (only in compound words). **— line** *n.* a line with hook and sinker to keep it stationary; (*Mus.*) an additional line above or below the staff for notes outside the normal range. Also **leger** [prob. M.E. *leggan,* to lie].

lee (lē) *n.* a place protected from the wind; shelter; *a.* pert. to the part or side farthest from the wind. **-board** *n.* a plank lowered on the side of a boat to diminish its drifting to leeward. **-gage** *n.* the sheltered side. **— shore** *n.* the shore on the lee-side of a vessel. **—side** *n.* the side of a vessel opposite to the direction from which the wind is blowing. **— tide** *n.* a current running in the direction the wind is blowing. **-ward** (lē′·wẹrd, lòò′·wẹrd) *a.* pert. to, or in, the direction towards which the wind is blowing. **-way** *n.* the side movement of a vessel to the leeward of her course; loss of progress; (*Colloq.*) extra time, space, etc. [O.E. *hleo,* a shelter].

leech (lēch) *n.* a blood-sucking worm used for bloodletting; (*Archaic*) physician; *v.t.* to bleed by application of leeches [O.E. *laece,* one who heals].

leek (lēk) *n.* a biennial bulbous plant allied to the onion; also, the national emblem of Wales [O.E. *leac,* leek].

leer (lēr) *n.* a sly or furtive look expressive of malignity, lasciviousness, or triumph; *v.i.* to look with a leer [O.E. *hleor,* cheek].

leer·y (lēr′·i·) *a.* wary; suspicious.

lees (lēz) *n.pl.* the sediment which settles at the bottom of a wine-cask; dregs [Fr. *lie*].

left (left) *a.* on the side of the body which is westward when one is facing north. Also **left-hand.** *n.* the side opposite to the right; in some legislative assemblies, the left side of the speaker's chair where the opposition members sit, hence an extreme or radical party; *adv.* to or on the left. **—hand** *n.* the left side; *a.* situated on the left side; executed with the left hand. **—handed** *a.* using the left hand more easily than the right; awkward. **—handedness** *n.* **— wing** *n.* a political group with extremist views [M.E. *lift,* weak].

left (left) *pa.t.* and *pa.p.* of the verb **leave.**

leg (leg) *n.* the limb of an animal used in supporting the body and in walking, esp. that part of the limb between the knee and the foot; any support, as leg of a table; one of the two divisions of a forked object, as compasses; part of a garment covering the leg; (*Naut.*) a ship's course covered on one tack; *v.i.* (*Colloq.*) to walk briskly; to run. *pr.p.* **-ging.** *pa.t.* and *pa.p.* **-ged. -ged.** *a.* having legs, as *three-legged stool.* **-ging** *n.* a garment to cover the legs. **-gy** *a.* having disproportionately long legs, as a very young animal. **-less** *a.* without legs. **—of-mutton** *a.* shaped like a leg of mutton, as of a sleeve; triangular, as a sail [Scand. *legar,* a leg].

leg·a·cy (leg′·ạ·si·) *n.* a bequest; a gift of personal property by will. **legatee** *n.* one who receives a legacy [L. *legare,* to bequeath].

le·gal (lē′·gạl) *a.* pert. to, or according to, the law; defined by law; statutory; binding; constitutional. **-ization** *n.* **-ize** *v.t.* to make lawful; to sanction. **-ity** *n.* conformity to law. **-ly** *adv.* **— tender,** the form of money, coin, or notes, which may be lawfully used in paying a debt [L. *lex, legis,* a law].

leg·ate (leg′·ạt) *n.* Pope's highest diplomatic envoy; a diplomatic minister below ambassadorial rank. **-ship** *n.* **legatine** *a.* of a legate. **legation** (li·gā′·shạn) *n.* a minister and his staff; the official residence or offices of a diplomatic minister [L. *legatus,* an envoy].

le·ga·to (li·gá′·tō) *adv.* (*Mus.*) in a smooth, gliding manner [L. *ligare,* to tie].

leg·end (lej′·ạnd) *n.* orig. a chronicle of the

lives of the saints; any traditional story of ancient times; an inscription on a coin, medal, etc. **-ary** *n.* book of, relater of, legends; *a.* comprising legends; fabulous; strange. **-ry** *n.* legends collectively [L. *legendus*, to be read].

le·ger·de·main (lej·ẹr·dạ·män′) *n.* a sleight of hand; trickery [Fr. *léger de main*, light of hand].

leg·er·line (lej′·ẹr·lin). See **ledger.**

leg·horn (leg′·hawrn) *n.* a plaited straw, from Leghorn in Italy; a hat made of this straw; a breed of domestic fowl.

leg·i·ble (lej′·ạ·bl) *a.* capable of being read. **legibly** *adv.* **-ness, legibility** *n.* [L. *legere*, to read].

le·gion (lē′·jạn) *n.* in ancient Rome, a body of infantry of from 3,000 to 6,000; a military force; a great number. **-ary** *a.* relating to, or consisting of, a legion or legions; containing a great number; *n.* a soldier of a legion. **-naire** *n.* a legionary. **Legionnaire** *n.* member of the American Legion [L. *legio, legionis*].

le·gion·el·lo·sis (lē·jạn·ạ·lō′·sis) *n.* a disease similar to pneumonia, often called Legionnaires' disease [fr. its occurrence at a convention of the American *Legion*].

leg·is·late (lej′·is·lāt) *v.i.* to make or enact laws. **legislation** *n.* act of legislating; laws made. **legislative** *a.* having power to make laws; constitutional. **legislatively** *adv.* **legislator** *n.* one who enacts laws; a member of the legislature. **legislature** *n.* the body empowered to make and repeal laws [L. *lex*, a law; *ferre, latum*, to carry].

le·git·i·mate (li·jit′·ạ·mit) *a.* lawful; born in lawful wedlock; justifiable; genuine; *v.t.* (li·jit′·ạ·māt) to make lawful; to render legitimate; to pronounce lawful or proper. **legitimacy** *n.* the state of being legitimate. **-ly** *adv.* **-ness** *n.* **legitimation** *n.* the act of investing with the rights and privileges of lawful birth. **legitimize** *v.t.* to legitimate. **legitimism** *n.* **legitimist** *n.* one who upholds legitimate authority [L. *legitimus*, lawful].

leg·ume (leg′·ūm) *n.* a seed pod with two valves and having the seeds attached at one suture, as the pea; a plant bearing seed-pods. **leguminous** *a.* [Fr. *légume*, a vegetable].

lei (lā) *n.* a garland of flowers worn around the neck [Haw.].

lei·sure (lē′·zhẹr) *n.* freedom from occupation; spare time; *a.* unoccupied. **leisurable** *a.* **-d.** *a.* free from business duties. **-ly** *a.* unhurried; slow; *adv.* slowly [O.Fr. *leisir*, to be lawful].

leit·mo·tif (līt′·mō·tēf) *n.* (*Mus.*) a theme associated with a person or idea, constantly recurring in a composition [Ger. *leiten*, to lead; Fr. *motif*, motive].

lem·ma (lem′·ạ) *n.* (*Math.*) a subsidiary proposition; (*Logic*) a premise taken for granted; a theme; a heading of an entry. *pl.* **-s, -ta** [Gk. *lemma*, something taken for granted].

lem·on (lem′·ạn) *n.* an oval-shaped fruit with rind pale yellow in color and containing very acid pulp and juice; the tree which provides this fruit; (*Colloq.*) an inferior product; *a.* of the color of lemon rind. **-ade** *n.* a cooling drink made of lemon juice, sugar, and water [Fr. *limon*, the lemon fruit].

le·mur (lē′·mẹr) *n.* one of a family of nocturnal monkey-like mammals found in Madagascar [L. *lemur*, a ghost].

lend (lend) *v.t.* to grant the temporary use of; to give in general; to let out money at interest; to serve for; *v.i.* to make a loan. *pr.p.* **-ing.** *pa.p.* **lent. -er** *n.* [O.E. *laen*, a loan].

lend-lease *n.* the pooling of material resources of Allied nations in the struggle against Germany and Japan (W.W. II); *v.t.* to grant (material aid) to a foreign country in accordance with the Lend-Lease Act of March 11, 1941.

length (length) *n.* the measurement of anything from end to end; extension; duration of time; extent; intervening distance, as in a race; the quantity of a syllable or vowel in prosody. **-en** *v.t.* to extend in length; to protract; *v.i.* to grow longer. **-ily** *adv.* **-iness** *n.* **-wise** *a.* in the direction of the length. **-y** *a.* [O.E. *lang*, long].

le·ni·ent (lē′·ni·ẹnt) *a.* clement; acting without severity. **lenience, leniency** *n.* the quality of being lenient; clemency. **-ly** *adv.* **lenitive** *n.* a medicine which eases pain; *a.* soothing; emollient. **lenity** *n.* [L. *lenis*, soft].

lens (lenz) *n.* (*Optics*) a piece of glass or other transparent substance ground with one or both sides curved so as to refract rays of light, and thereby modify vision; the crystalline biconvex tissue between the cornea and retina of the eye. *pl.* **lenses** [L. *lens*, a lentil].

Lent (lent) *n.* the season of 40 days from Ash Wednesday until Easter Day. **-en** *a.* pert. to Lent [O.E. *lencten*, spring].

len·tic·u·lar (len·tik′·yoo·lẹr) *a.* shaped like a lens or lentil; resembling a double-convex lens. Also **lentiform. lentoid** *a.* lens-shaped [L. *lenticula*, a small lentil].

len·til (len′·til) *n.* a Mediterranean plant allied to the bean [L. *lens*, a lentil].

len·to (len′·tō) *adv.* (*Mus.*) slowly [It.].

l'en·voi (len·voi′ or lawng′·vwȧ) *n.* a kind of postscript to a poem; a short, final stanza [O.Fr. *l'envoi*, the sending].

Le·o (lē′·ō) *n.* the lion, the fifth sign of the Zodiac which the sun enters about July 22nd. **leonine** *a.* of or like a lion [L. *leo*, a lion].

leo·pard (lep′·ẹrd) *n.* a large carnivorous member of the cat family, of a yellow or fawn color with black spots [Gk. *leōn*, lion; *pardos*, pard].

le·o·tard (lē′·ạ·tȧrd) *n.* a one-piece tight-fitting garment worn by dancers [after *Léotard*, 19th cent. Fr. aerial performer].

lep·er (lep′·ẹr) *n.* a person afflicted with leprosy; (*Fig.*) an outcast. **leprosy** *n.* a chronic contagious disease affecting skin, tissues and nerves. **leprous** *a.* [Gk. *lepros*, scaly].

Lep·i·dop·ter·a (lep·ạ·dȧp′·tẹr·ạ) *n.pl.* an order of insects having four wings covered with gossamer scales, as moths, butterflies, etc. **-l, lepidopterous** *a.* [Gk. *lepis*, a scale; *pteron*, a wing].

lep·re·chaun (lep′·rạ·kawn) *n.* a sprite; a brownie commonly referred to in Irish folk-stories [Ir.].

lep·ro·sy (lep′·rạ·si·) *n.* See **leper.**

Les·bi·an (lez′·bi·ạn) *a.* pert. to the island of *Lesbos* (Mytilene) in the Aegean Sea, or to the ancient school of lyric poets there; amatory; *n.* a woman who is sexually attracted to another woman; a homosexual woman [Gk. *lesbōs*].

lese maj·es·ty (lēz′·maj·is·ti·) *n.* (*Law*) a crime committed against the sovereign, or sovereign power of a state; high treason [Fr. fr. L. *laesa majesta*, injured majesty].

le·sion (lē′·zhạn) *n.*(*Med.*) any morbid change in the structure or functioning of the living tissues of the body; injury; (*Law*) loss or injury [L. *laedere, laesum*, to hurt].

less (les) *a.* smaller in size; not equal to in number; lower; inferior; *adv.* in a smaller or lower degree; *n.* a smaller portion; the inferior. **-en** *v.t.* to make less; to diminish; *v.i.* to contract; to decrease. **-er** *a.* smaller; inferior [O.E. *laes*, less].

les·see (les·ē′) *n.* one to whom a lease is granted [fr. *lease*].

les·son (les′·n) *n.* a reading; a piece of instruction; something to be learned by pupils; a Scripture passage read aloud as part of church service; instruction gained by experience; reproof; *v.t.* to teach [Fr. fr. L. *legere*, to read].

lest (lest) *conj.* for fear that [O.E.].

let (let) *v.t.* to allow; to give permission; to cause to do (foll. by *infin.* without *to*); to grant the temporary use of, for hire; *v.i.* to be rented; (*Colloq.*) to be dismissed (foll. by *out*). *pr.p.* **-ting.** *pa.t.* and *pa.p.* **let.** [O.E. *laeten,* to permit].

le·thal (lē′·thạl) *a.* deadly; mortal. **lethiferous** *a.* deadly [L. *letum,* death].

leth·ar·gy (leth′·ẹr·ji·) *n.* unnaturally heavy drowsiness; overpowering lassitude; inertia. **lethargic, lethargical** *a.* drowsy; apathetic. **lethargically** *adv.* [Gk. *lēthargōs,* forgetful].

le·the (lē′·thē) *n.* oblivion. **-an** [Gk. *lēthē,* a forgetting].

let·ter (let′·ẹr) *n.* a mark or symbol used to represent an articulate, elementary sound; a written or printed communication; an epistle; the literal statement; printing-type; *pl.* learning; erudition; *v.t.* to impress or form letters on. **— box** *n.* a box for receiving letters, as on inside of house door. **— carrier** *n.* a postman. **-ed** *a.* literate; educated; versed in literature, science, etc.; inscribed with lettering. **-er** *n.* **— file** *n.* a device for holding letters for reference. **-head** *n.* printed heading on business stationery. **-ing** *n.* the act of impressing letters; the letters impressed. **-press** *n.* printed matter as distinct from illustrations, diagrams, etc.; print. **letter of credit,** a letter authorizing money to be paid by a bank to the bearer. **letters patent,** a document under seal of the state, granting some property privileges or authority, or conferring the exclusive right to use an invention or design [L. *littera,* a letter].

Let·tic (let′·ik) *a.* pert. to the Letts or to their language; *n.* the language of the Letts. Also **Lettish. Letts** *n.pl.* the inhabitants of Lithuania and Latvia.

let·tuce (let′·is) *n.* a common garden plant, used in salads [L. *lactuca,* lettuce].

leu·co·cyte (lȯȯ′·kạ·sīt) *n.* one of the white corpuscles of the blood, destroying bacteria [Gk. *leukos,* white; *kutos,* a cell].

leu·ke·mi·a, leukaemia (lȯȯ·kē′·mē·ạ) *n.* a disease characterized by an excessive number of white corpuscles in the blood [Gk. *leukos,* white].

Le·vant (lạ·vant′) *n.* Eastern Mediterranean countries; (*l.c.*) a superior grade of morocco leather. **-er** *n.* wind blowing from E. Spain towards Levant. **-ine** *a.* pert. to Levant; *n.* native of the Levant [L. *levare,* to raise].

le·va·tor (lạ·vā′·tẹr) *n.* a muscle in the body which raises any part, as the eyelid, lips, etc. [L. *levare,* to raise].

lev·ee (lev′·ē, lạ·vē′) *n.* a reception; orig. a reception held by royal personage on rising from bed [Fr. *lever,* to rise].

lev·ee (lev′·ē) *n.* a river embankment to prevent flooding; a quay [Fr. *levée,* raised].

lev·el (lev′·ạl) *n.* a line or plane which is everywhere parallel to the horizon; the horizontal plane on which a thing rests; a state of equality; an instrument for finding or drawing a true horizontal line; *a.* not having one part higher than another; even; horizontal; equal in rank or degree; *v.t.* to make horizontal; to reduce to the same height with something else; to raze; to make equal in rank, etc.; to point a gun or arrow at the mark. **—headed** *a.* balanced; prudent. **-er** *n.* **-ing** *n.* the act of making a surface even with another; the process of ascertaining the difference of elevation between two points, by the use of a *leveling* instrument. **-ing rod** *n.* a graduated rod used in surveying [L. *libella,* a water-level].

lev·er (lev′·ẹr, lē′·vẹr) *n.* a bar used to exert pressure or sustain a weight at one point of its length by receiving a force or power at a second, and turning at a third on a fixed point called a fulcrum; a crowbar for forcing open; *v.t.* to raise up; to force open. **-age** *n.* the action of a lever; mechanical advantage gained by use of the lever [L. *levare,* to raise].

le·vi·a·than (lạ·vī′·ạ·thạn) *n.* a huge aquatic animal; a whale; a sea-monster; anything of colossal size [Heb. *livyathan,* a sea-monster].

Le·vi's (lē′·vīz) *n.* blue denim jeans [*Trademark*].

lev·i·ta·tion (lev·ạ·tā′·shạn) *n.* the act of making buoyant or light; the phenomenon of heavy bodies being made to float in air by spiritual agencies. **levitate** *v.t.* [L. *levis,* light].

Le·vite (lē′·vīt) *n.* one of the tribe of Levi; lesser priest in ancient Jewish synagogue. **Levitic, -al** (le·vit′·ik, ·al) *a.* **Leviticus** *n.* (*Bib.*) third book of Old Testament [fr. *Levi*].

lev·i·ty (lev′·ạ·ti·) *n.* lightness; buoyancy; lack of seriousness [L. *levis,* light].

le·vo·ro·ta·tion (lē·vạ·rō·tā′·shạn) *n.* counterclockwise or left-hand rotation. **levorotatory** *a.* [L. *laevus,* left].

lev·u·lose (lev′·yoo·lōs) *n.* fruit sugar found in honey and certain fruits [L. *laevus,* left].

lev·y (lev′·i·) *v.t.* to raise by assessment, as taxes; to enlist or collect, as troops; to impose, as a fine; *v.i.* to make a levy; *n.* collection of assessment by authority or compulsion, for public services; the money or troops thus collected [L. *levare,* to raise].

lewd (lȯȯd) *a.* obscene; indecent; given to unlawful indulgence. **-ly** *adv.* **-ness** *n.* [O.E. *laewede,* lay].

lex·i·con (lek′·si·kȧn) *n.* a dictionary, esp. of Greek, Latin, or Hebrew; a vocabulary list relating to a particular subject, class, etc. **lexical** *a.* pert. to a lexicon. **lexicographer** *n.* one who compiles a dictionary. **lexicographic, -al** *a.* **lexicologist** *n.* an expert in lexicology. **lexicography** *n.* the art or process of compiling a dictionary. **lexicology** *n.* the science which deals with the exact significance and use of vocabulary [Gk. *lexis,* speech; *graphein,* to write; *logos,* a discourse].

li·a·ble (lī′·ạ·bl) *a.* obliged in law or equity; subject; answerable; responsible. **liability** *n.* the state of being liable; responsibility; obligation; *pl.* debts [Fr. *lier,* to bind].

li·ai·son (lē·ā·zȧn′) *n.* a union; connection; illicit intimacy between a man and a woman; (*Mil.*) contact maintained between one unit or command and another; the sounding, as in French, of the final consonant of a word before the initial vowel or mute *h* of the next word [Fr. fr. L. *ligare,* to bind].

li·a·na (li·ȧn′·ạ) *n.* a climbing tropical plant [Fr. *liane*].

li·ar (lī′·ẹr) *n.* one who tells lies [fr. *lie*].

li·ba·tion (lī·bā′·shạn) *n.* the ceremonial pouring of wine in honor of some deity; the liquid itself; (*Colloq.*) a drink [L. *libare,* to pour].

li·bel (lī′·bạl) *n.* a defamatory writing or printed picture; (*Law*) a written statement by the plaintiff of his allegations in a law case; (*Colloq.*) a statement injurious to a person's character; *v.t.* to defame by a writing, picture, etc.; to proceed against, by filing a libel. **-er** *n.* **-ous, -lous** *a.* defamatory; containing a libel. **-ously** *adv.* [L. *libellus,* a little book].

lib·er·al (lib′·ẹr·ạl) *a.* open-minded; generous; catholic; unbiased; (in politics) favoring democratic or progressive ideals, and freedom of religion; *n.* one who favors greater political and religious freedom from tradition; supporter of a liberal political party. **-iaztion** *n.* the process of gaining greater freedom. **-ize** *v.t.* to cause to be freer or more enlightened. **-ism** *n.* liberal principles. **-ist** *n.* **liberality** *n.* generosity; munificence; catholicity of mind. **-ly** *adv.* **liberate** *v.t.* to set free. **liberation** *n.* the act of setting free; the state of being free from bondage. **liberator** *n.* one who sets others free, esp. from tyranny [L. *liberalis,* befitting a freeman].

lib·er·ty (lib′·ẹr·ti·) *n.* freedom from bondage or restraint; power to act according to one's natural rights as an individual; privilege; undue freedom of act or speech; *pl.* rights, privileges, etc., conferred by grant or prescription. **libertarian** *n.* one who upholds the doctrine of freewill. **libertarianism** *n.* **libertine** (lib'.ęr.tēn) *n.* one who leads a dissolute life; *a.* dissolute [L. *libertas,* liberty].

li·bi·do (li.bē'.dō, li.bi'.dō) *n.* in psychology, the emotional craving behind all human impulse; esp. used by Freud to denote the sex-urge. **libidinous** (li.bid'.ą.nąs) *a.* lewd; obscene; lustful. **libidinously** *adv.* [L. *libido,* desire].

Li·bra (lī'.brą) *n.* the balance, the 7th sign of the Zodiac [L. *libra,* a balance].

li·brar·y (lī'.bre.ri.) *n.* a collection of books; the room or building which contains it. **librarian** *n.* the person in charge of a library; one trained and engaged in library work. **librarianship** *n.* **— science** *n.* the knowledge and skills required for library service [L. *liber,* a book].

li·brate (lī'.brāt) *v.i* to be poised; to oscillate. **libration** *n.* balancing; a quivering motion. **libratory** *a.* [L. *libra,* a balance].

li·bret·to (li.bret'.ō) *n.* the words of an opera or oratorio. **librettist** *n.* the writer of librettos [It. = a little book].

Lib·y·an (lib'.i.ąn) *a.* pert. to *Libya* in N. Africa or to the language of the district.

lice (līs) *pl.* of **louse.**

li·cense (lī'.sans) *n.* authority granted to do any act; a legal permit; excess of liberty; *v.t.* to permit by grant of authority. **licensable** *a.* **-d** *a.* privileged; holding a license. **licensee** *n.* one who is given a license. **-r** *n.* one legally entitled to grant a license. **licentiate** *n.* one who has a license to practice a profession. **licentious** *a.* using excessive license; absence of moral or legal restraints. **licentiously** *adv.* **licentiousness** *n.* [L. *licentia,* freedom].

li·chen (lī'.kąn) *n.* one of an order of cellular flowerless plants; (*Med.*) a skin eruption [L. fr. Gk. *leichēn,* moss].

lic·it (lis'.it) *a.* lawful; allowable. **-ly** *adv.* [L. *licitus,* lawful].

lick (lik) *v.t.* to pass or draw the tongue over; to lap; to take in by the tongue; to touch lightly (as flames); (*Colloq.*) to thrash; to be superior over; *n.* a lap with the tongue; a small portion; (*Colloq.*) a brief attempt; *pl.* a beating. **-er** *n.* **-ing** *n.* a lapping with tongue; a flogging; a beating (in a competition) [O.E. *liccian*].

lic·o·rice, liquorice (lik'.ą.ris) *n.* a Mediterranean plant, the root of which contains a sweet juice; the brittle, black substance extracted from the roots of this plant, and used medicinally and in candy [Gk. *glukus,* sweet; *rhiza,* a root].

lic·tor (lik'.tęr) *n.* an officer who attended a Roman magistrate, bearing the fasces [L. fr. *ligare,* to bind].

lid (lid) *n.* a cover of a vessel or box; the covering of the eye [O.E. *hlid,* a cover].

lie (lī) *v.i.* to utter untruth; to misrepresent; to deceive; to make false statement. *pr.p.* **lying.** *pa.t.* and *pa.p.* **-d.** *n.* a deliberate falsehood. **liar** *n.* one who utters a falsehood. **lying** *a.* addicted to telling lies [O.E. *leogan,* to lie].

lie (lī) *v.i.* to be recumbent; to be in a horizontal position or nearly so; to be situated; to lean; to be at rest; to press upon; (*Law*) to be admissible. *pr.p.* **lying.** *pa.t.* **lay.** *pa.p.* **lain.** *n.* manner of lying [O.E. *licgan,* to lie].

lie·der (lē'.dęr) *n.pl.* German lyrics set to music; *sing.* **lied** [Ger. *Lied,* a song].

lief (lēf) *adv.* gladly; willingly [O.E. *leof,* loved].

liege (lēj) *a.* bound by feudal tenure; (of a lord) entitled to receive homage; *n.* a vassal; a feudal lord to whom allegiance is owed [O.Fr. *liege,* an overlord].

li·en (lēn, lē'.ąn) *n.* (Law) a legal claim upon real or personal property for the satisfaction of some debt or duty [Fr., fr. L. *ligare,* to bind].

lieu (lòò) *n.* place; stead, as in phrase *in lieu of* [Fr.].

lieu·ten·ant (lòò.ten'.ąnt) *n.* a deputy; an officer who takes the place of a superior in his absence; rank below a captain (*Army*) or below a lieutenant commander (*Navy*). **— colonel** *n.* the rank below a colonel. **— commander** *n.* (*Navy*) the rank intermediate between that of lieutenant and commander corresponding to that of major (*Army*). **— general** *n.* military rank intermediate between that of major general and general [Fr. *lieu,* place; *tenant,* holding].

life (līf) *n.* existence; vitality; condition of plants, animals, etc. in which they exercise functional powers; the span between birth and death; mode of living; narrative of a person's history; animation. *pl.* **lives. — and death** *a.* desperate. **— assurance** or **insurance** *n.* insurance of a person's life. **— belt** *n.* a belt either inflated, or made buoyant with cork. **-boat** *n.* a special type of boat, designed for stability in stormy seas. **— expectancy** *n.* probable life span. **-guard** *n.* someone employed at a swimming pool, etc. to prevent accidents. **— history** *n.* the cycle of life of a person, organism, etc. **— interest** *n.* interest in an estate or business which continues during one's life, but which cannot be bequeathed by will. **—jacket** *n.* a life belt. **-less** *a.* inanimate; dead; inert. **-lessly** *adv.* **-lessness** *n.* **-like** *a.* like a living creature; resembling closely. **-line** *n.* a line attached to a lifebuoy or lifeboat; the line which lowers and raises a deep-sea diver; (*Fig.*) that which keeps a nation alive. **-long** *a.* lasting a lifetime. **— preserver** *n.* any apparatus (as life belt, -buoy -line) for preserving or rescuing life. **-r** *n.* (*Colloq.*) a criminal who has received a life sentence. **-saver** *n.* someone who rescues a person, esp. from drowning; (*Slang*) a person or thing which spares one embarrassment, difficulty, etc. **-size** *a.* resembling in proportions the living model. **-time** *n.* the duration of person's life. **-work** *n.* any task, usually creative, demanding a lifetime's work [O.E. *lif,* life].

LIFO (lī'.fō) *n.* abbrev. of *l*ast-*i*n, *f*irst-*o*ut, a method of inventory valuation.

lift (lift) *v.t.* to raise; to take up and remove; to elevate socially; to exalt spiritually; (*Colloq.*) to steal; to take passengers on a bus, etc.; *v.i.* to rise; to be dispersed; *n.* the act of lifting; assistance; the helping of a person on his way by offering conveyance in one's car; (*Brit.*) an elevator; a rise in the ground; (*Aero.*) an air force acting at right angles on aircraft's wing, thereby lifting it. **—off** *n.* the vertical take-off of spacecraft or aircraft; *v.i.* [Scand. *lypta,* to raise].

lig·a·ment (lig'.ą.mąnt) *n.* anything which binds one thing to another; (*Anat.*) strong fibrous tissue bands connecting the bones of the body; a bond. **-al, -ary, -ous** *a.* **ligate** (lī'.gāt) *v.t.* to bind; to bandage. **ligation** *n.* the act of binding; the state of being bound with a ligature. **ligature** *n.* anything which binds; a bandage ;(*Mus.*) a line connecting two notes; (*Print.*) type consisting of two or more letters joined [L. *ligare,* to bind].

light (līt) *v.i.* to come to by chance; to alight; to settle. *pr.p.* **-ing.** *pa.p.* **-ed, lit** [O.E. *lihtan,* to dismount].

light (līt) *a.* having little weight; not heavy; easy; active; nimble; loose or sandy, as soil; moderate, as wind; spongy, as cake; not heavily armed, as a cruiser; unsettled; volatile; trivial; wanton; easily disturbed, as sleep; *adv.* **-en** *v.t.* to make less heavy; to jettison; to enliven; *v.i.* to become less heavy or gloomy. **-ly** *adv.* **-er** *n.* a barge used in loading and unloading ships anchored out from the dock. **-erage** *n.*

the price paid for loading and unloading ships. **-erman** *n.* **—fingered** *a.* dexterous, esp. in picking pockets. **—footed** *a.* agile. **—handed** *a.* delicate of touch; empty-handed. **—headed** *a.* delirious; frivolous. **—hearted** *a.* carefree; gay. **—minded** *a.* frivolous. **—s** *n.pl.* the lungs of a slaughtered animal. **-some** *a.* lively; cheerful. **-weight** *a.* (of a boxer) weighing less than 135 lbs.; *n.* (*Colloq.*) a person of little importance; **-ness** *n.* quality of being light [O.E. *leoht,* light].

light (līt) *n.* that form of radiant energy which stimulates visual perception; anything which has luminosity; day; illumination; a source of illumination; the illuminated part of a scene or picture; point of view; aspect; spiritual or mental enlightenment; any opening admitting light into a building; *a.* bright; not dark; whitish; pale (of color); *v.t.* to give light or fire to; *v.i.* to begin to burn; to become bright; to express joy (as in the face). *pr.p.* **-ing.** *pa.t.* and *pa.p.* **-ed** or **lit. -en** *v.t.* to illuminate. **-er** *n.* a mechanical device for producing a flame, as a cigarette-lighter; one who lights street lamps, etc. **-house** *n.* a tower-like structure built at danger points on seacoast and provided with very powerful light to serve as warning to ships. **-ing** *n.* illumination; the arrangement of lights in a building; the effect of light, esp. in a picture. **-ish** *a.* rather light or pale in color. **-ness** *n.* **-ship** *n.* a floating lighthouse. **— year** *n.* (*Astron.*) the distance in a year (calculated at 5,878,000,000,000 miles) light travels. **to see the light,** to be born; to comprehend. **footlights** *n.pl.* the row of electric lights along the edge of the stage in a theater. **Northern Lights,** aurora borealis. **lit** (*Slang*) drunk [O.E. *leoht,* light].

light·ning (līt′·ning) *n.* a flash produced by an electrical discharge between two clouds, or between cloud and ground. **— bug** *n.* a firefly. **— rod** *n.* a rod serving, by a connected wire called a **lightning-conductor,** to carry electric current into the earth or water, thereby preventing building from being struck by lightning [M.E. *lihtnen,* to flash].

lig·ne·ous (lig′·ni·ạs) *a.* woody; resembling wood. **lignify** *v.t.* to convert into wood. **lignin** *n.* an organic substance formed in the woody tissues of plants. **lignite** *n.* coal of recent origin still showing ligneous texture; brown coal [L. *lignum,* wood].

lig·ure (lig′·yoor) *n.* a precious stone [fr. *Liguria,* a district of Italy].

like (līk) *a.* equal; similar; *n.* an equal; a person or thing resembling another; an exact resemblance; *prep.* similarly to; *conj.* (*Colloq.*) as; as if. **-lihood** *n.* probability. **-ly** *a.* probable; credible; of excellent qualities; *adv.* probably. **liken** *v.t.* to represent as similar; to compare. **-ness** *n.* resemblance; an image, picture, or statue. **-wise** *adv.* in like manner; also; moreover [O.E. *gelic,* similar].

like (līk) *v.t.* to be pleased with or attracted by; to enjoy; to approve; *v.i.* to be pleased; *n.* a liking, as in phrase, *'likes and dislikes.'* **lik(e)able** *a.* pleasing; congenial; attractive. **lik(e)ableness** *n.* **-ly** *a.* pleasing. **liking** *n.* [O.E. *lician,* to please].

li·lac (lī′·lạk) *n.* a shrub, with delicately perfumed flower clusters, purple, pale mauve, or white in color; a pale mauve color; *a.* of lilac color [Pers. *lilak,* the indigo flower].

li·li·pu·tian (lil·i·pū′·shạn) *n.* an inhabitant of *Lilliput* described by Jonathan Swift in his *Gulliver's Travels;* a person of diminutive size; *a.* diminutive; dwarfed.

lilt (lilt) *n.* a light or rhythmic tune; *v.t.* and [*v.i.* to sing.

li·ly (lil′·i·) *n.* a bulbous plant, with fragrant and showy bell-shaped flowers; *a.* resembling a lily; pure; pale; delicate. **liliaceous** *a.* pert. to lilies. **—livered** *a.* cowardly. **—white** *a.* pure white; unsullied [O.E. *lilie,* a lily].

limb (lim) *n.* an extremity of the human body, as an arm or leg; a branch of a tree [O.E.].

limb (lim) *n.* an edge or border; (*Astron.*) the rim of a heavenly body; (*Bot.*) the expanded part of a petal [L. *limbus,* a hem].

lim·ber (lim′·bẹr) *n.* the detachable front part of a gun-carriage; *v.t.* to attach to a gun-carriage [Fr. *limonière,* a cart with shafts].

lim·ber (lim′·bẹr) *a.* easily bent; pliant; supple.

lim·bo (lim′·bō) *n.* a region intermediate between heaven and hell in which the souls of unbaptized children etc., are confined after death; a region of forgotten things; neglect; oblivion; jail [L. *limbus,* the edge].

lime (līm) *n.* the linden tree; *a.* pert to the linden tree [corrupt. of O.E. *lind,* the linden tree].

lime (līm) *n.* a tree which produces a small sour kind of lemon; the fruit of this tree [Fr. fr. Span. *lima*].

lime (līm) *n.* birdlime; oxide of calcium; white, caustic substance obtained from limestone, shells, marble, etc.; a calcium compound to enrich soil; *v.t.* to smear with lime; to ensnare; to cement; to manure with lime. **-kiln** *n.* a furnace in which limestone is heated to produce lime. **-light** *n.* a powerful light, as on a stage; the public view. **-stone** *n.* a rock consisting chiefly of carbonate of lime. **limy** *a.* covered with or impregnated with lime; sticky; resembling lime [O.E. *lim,* cement].

li·men (lī′·mạn) *n.* the threshold of consciousness. **liminal** *a.* [L. *limen,* threshold].

lim·er·ick (lim′·ẹr·ik) *n.* a five-lined nonsense verse [said to be from a song introducing the place name *Limerick*].

lim·ey (lī·mi·) *n.* (*Slang*) a British person, [esp. a sailor.

lim·it (lim′·it) *n.* boundary; edge; utmost extent; (*Slang*) an outrageous or intolerable person or thing; *v.t.* to confine within certain bounds; to curb; to restrict the signification of. **-able** *a.* that may be bounded or restricted. **-ary** *a.* of, pert. to, or serving as a limit; restricted. **limitation** *n.* **-ative, -ed** *a.* circumscribed; narrow. **-edly** *adv.* **-edness** *n.* **-less** *a.* boundless; immeasurable; infinite. **limited liability,** said of a joint stock company in which liability of the shareholder is in proportion to the amount of his stock [L. *limes,* a boundary].

limn (lim) *v.t.* to draw or paint; to illuminate a manuscript. **limner** *n.* painter; one who decorates books with pictures [M.E. *limnen,* to decorate].

lim·ou·sine (lim′·ạ·zēn) *a.* pert. to a type of closed automobile with roof over the driver's head; *n.* a closed car [fr. *Limousin,* a French province].

limp (limp) *v.i.* to walk lamely; *n.* lameness [O.E. *lemp-healt,* lame].

limp (limp) *a.* wanting in stiffness, as covers of a book; flaccid; flexible; (*Fig.*) lethargic; exhausted [Scand. *limpa,* weakness].

lim·pet (lim′·pạt) *n.* a small, univalve conical shaped shellfish which clings firmly to rocks. **—mine** *n.* (*World War* 2) a small suction mine attached by hand to the hull of a ship [O.E. *lempedu,* a lamprey].

lim·pid (lim′·pạd) *a.* clear; translucent; crystal. **-ness, -ity** *n.* **-ly** *adv.* [L. *limpidus,* clear].

linch·pin (linch′·pin) *n.* a pin used to prevent a wheel from sliding off the axle tree [O.E. *lynis,* axletree; and *pin*].

lin·den (lin′·dạn) *n.* a tree with yellowish flowers and heart-shaped leaves [O.E. *lind,* the lime-tree].

line (līn) *n.* a rope, wire or string; a slender cord; a thread-like mark; an extended stroke; (*Math.*) that which has one dimension, length, but no breadth or thickness; a curve connecting points which have a common significance (as the Equator, isotherms, isobars, contours, etc.); a boundary; a row or continued series; progeny; a verse; a short letter or note; a course of conduct, thought, or policy; a trend;

a department; a trade, business or profession; a system of buses, trains, or passenger aircraft under one management; a railway track; a formation of naval vessels; the regular infantry of an army; harmony; graceful cut (as of a costume, dress); a path; a thin crease; parts of a play memorized by an actor or actress; military fieldworks; *v.t.* to mark out with lines; to form in a line; to border. **linage** *n.* number of lines on a page; payment according to the number of lines. **lineage** *n.* descendants in a line from common progenitor; pedigree. **lineal** *a.* composed of lines; pert. to, or in the direction of, a line; directly descended from a common ancestor. **lineality** *n.* **lineally** *adv.* **lineament** *n.* feature; form; characteristic; outline of a body or figure. **linear** *a.* pert. to, or consisting of, a line; drawn in lines. **linearly** *adv.* **lineate(d)** *a.* marked by lines. **lineation** *n.* the act of marking with lines; the lines marked or engraved. **-d** *a.* marked with lines; ruled. **— engraving** *n.* a process of engraving lines on a copper plate. **-r** *n.* a steamship or passenger aircraft belonging to a regular transport line. **linesman** *n.* one who installs and repairs telephone and electric lines, etc.; an official (at football or tennis match) who determines whether ball has crossed the outside line or not. **—up** *n.* a marshaling of forces, or resources. **the line,** the Equator [L. *linea*, a string of flax].

line (līn) *v.t.* to cover on the inside, as a garment, pan, etc. **lining** *n.* the material used; contents [M.E. *linen*, to cover].

lin·en (lin′·ạn) *n.* thread or cloth made from flax; underclothing; napery; *a.* made of flax or linen [O.E. *lin*, flax].

lin·ger (ling′·gẹr) *v.i.* to delay; to dally; to loiter. **-er** *n.* **-ing** *a.* protracted [O.E. *lengan*, to protract].

lin·ge·rie (lȧn′·jạ·rā, lȧn′·zhạ·rē) *n.* orig. linen goods; women's underclothing [Fr. *linge*, linen].

lin·go (ling′·gō) *n.* language; a dialect; jargon corrupt. of L. *lingua*, language].

lin·gual (ling′·gwạl) *a.* pert. to the tongue; *n.* a sound or letter made by the tongue, as *d, l, n.* **-ly** *adv.* **linguiform** *a.* shaped like a tongue. **linguist** *n.* fluent speaker of several languages; an expert in linguistics. **linguistic** *a.* **linguistically** *adv.* **linguistics** *n.* study of human speech including its sounds, history, nature, structure, etc.; comparative philology. **lingulate, lingular** *a.* (*Bot.*) shaped like a tongue [L. *lingua*, a tongue].

lin·i·ment (lin′·ạ·mạnt) *n.* a lotion or soft ointment [L. *linere*, to besmear].

link (lingk) *n.* a single ring of a chain; anything doubled and closed like a link; a connection; the 1/100 part of a chain (7.92 inches). *v.t.* to connect by a link; (*Fig.*) to combine for a common purpose; *v.i.* to be coupled. **-age** *n.* a system of connections. **missing link,** a connection without which a chain of argument is incomplete; (*Zool.*) that form of animal life the scientific knowledge of which is required to complete the chain of evolution of man from the ape [O.E. *hlence*, a ring].

links (lingks) *n.pl.* a golf course [O.E. *hlinc*, a ridge].

lin·net (lin′·ạt) *n.* a small song bird of the finch family [O.Fr. *linette*, fr. L. *linum*, flax].

li·no·le·um (li·nō′·li·ạm) *n.* a hard floor covering of burlap impregnated with a cement of linseed oil, cork, etc. [L. *linum*, flax; *oleum*, oil].

Lin·o·type (līn′·ạ·tīp) *n.* a type-setting machine in which the matter is cast in solid lines of type [Trademark].

lin·seed (lin′·sēd) *n.* flaxseed. **— cake,** compressed mass of husks of linseed, after oil has been pressed out, much used for cattle feeding. **— oil,** the oil pressed out of linseed [O.E. *linsaed*, flaxseed].

lin·sey-wool·sey (lin′·zi·-wool′·zi·) *a.* made of wool and linen mixed; (*Fig.*) shoddy; *n.* inferior stuff [O.Fr. *linsel*, and *wool*].

lint (lint) *n.* a linen material, one side with a soft, wooly surface formerly used for dressing wounds; scraps of thread; fluff from cloth [L. *linteum*, a linen cloth].

lin·tel (lin′·tạl) *n.* a horizontal beam or stone over a doorway or window [L.L. *lintellus*].

li·on (lī′·ạn) *n.* (*fem.* **-ess**) the largest of the cat tribe, tawny-colored, with powerful, tufted tail, the male having a shaggy mane; (*Fig.*) a person of fierce courage; a celebrity; (*Astron.*) a sign of the Zodiac (Leo). **—hearted** *a.* courageous. **-ize** *v.t.* to treat as a celebrity [L. *leo*, a lion].

lip (lip) *n.* one of the two fleshy, outer edges of the mouth; a liplike part; the edge of anything; brim; (*Slang*) impertinent talk; *pl.* the organs of speech as represented by the lips; *v.t.* to touch with the lips; to speak; *a.* pert. to or made by the lips. **-ped** *a.* having a lip or lips. **— reading** *n.* the art of 'hearing' by reading the motions of a speaker's lips; this system as taught to the deaf. **— service** *n.* superficial devotion to a person or cause. **-stick,** a salve, in the form of a small stick, used by women to redden the lips [O.E. *lippa*].

li·quate (li′·kwāt) *v.t.* to melt; to separate or purify solids or gases by liquefying. **liquation** *n.* [L. *liquare*, to be fluid].

liq·ue·fy (lik′·wạ·fī) *v.t.* to transform a liquid; to melt; *v.i.* to become liquid. **liquefaction** *n.* the act of liquefying; the state of being liquefied. **liquefiable** *a.* [L. *liquefacere*, to melt].

li·queur (li·kur′) *n.* a preparation of distilled liquors flavored with fruits or aromatic substances [Fr.].

liq·uid (lik′·wid) *a.* fluid; in a state intermediate between a solid and a gas; flowing smoothly; (of sounds) pleasing to the ear; *n.* a substance intermediate between a solid and a gas which assumes the shape of the vessel which contains it; the name popularly applied to a consonant which has a smooth flowing sound (*l, r*). **-ate** *v.t.* to settle a debt; to wind up the affairs of business, etc.; to convert into cash; to destroy; *v.i.* (of business) to be wound up. **-ation** *n.* **-ator** *n.* **-ity** *n.* [L. *liquidus*, fluid].

liq·uor (lik′·ẹr) *n.* any liquid or fluid, esp. alcoholic [Fr. fr. L. *liquere*, to be fluid].

li·ra (lī′·rạ, lē′·rạ) *n.* the monetary unit and a silver coin of Italy; a monetary unit and gold coin of Turkey [It.].

lisle (līl) *n.* a fine hard-twisted cotton or linen thread [formerly made at *Lille*, France].

lisp (lisp) *v.i.* to speak imperfectly, esp. to substitute the sound *th* for *s*; *v.t.* to pronounce with a lisp; *n.* the habit of lisping. **-ing** *n.* [O.E. *wlisp*, stammering].

lis·some (lis′·um) *a.* supple; flexible; lithe. **-ness** *n.* [fr. *lithesome*].

list (list) *n.* the outer edge or selvage of woven cloth; a row or stripe; a roll; a catalogue; a register; a boundary line enclosing a field of combat at a tournament, esp. in *pl.* **lists;** the field thus enclosed; *v.t.* to sew together strips of cloth; to enter in a catalogue or inventory; *v.i.* to enlist [O.E. *liste*, a border].

list (list) *v.i.* (*Naut.*) to lean or incline (of a ship); *v.t.* to cause to lean; *n.* an inclination to one side [O.E. *lystan*, to desire].

lis·ten (lis′·n) *v.i.* to attend closely; to yield to advice. **list** *v.t.* and *v.i.* to listen (*Poet*). **-er** *n.* **to listen in,** to listen without taking part; to eavesdrop [O.E. *hlyst*, hearing].

list·less (list′·lạs) *a.* indifferent; languid; apathetic. **-ly** *adv.* **-ness** *n.* [O.E. *lust*, pleasure].

lit (lit) *pa.t.* and *pa.p.* of verb **light.**

lit·a·ny (lit′·ạ·ni·) *n.* an earnest prayer of supplication [Gk. *litaneia*, supplication].

li·ter (lē′·tẹr) *n.* a unit of volume in the

metric system, equal to 1.0567 quarts. Also **litre** [Gr. *litra,* pound].

li·te·ral (lit′·ạ·rạl) *a.* according to the letter; real; not figurative; word for word, as a translation. **-ism** *n.* keeping to the literal sense; exact representation in art or literature. **-ist** *n.* **-istic** *a.* **-ize** *v.t.* **-ly** *adv.* [L. *litera,* a letter].

lit·er·ar·y (lit′·ẹr·er·i·) *a.* pert. to letters or literature; versed in literature. **literacy** *n.* state of being literate, opp. of *illiteracy.* **literate** *a.* versed in learning and science; educated; *n.* one who is able to read and write. **literati** *n.pl.* men of letters; educated people. [L. *litera,* a letter].

lit·er·a·ture (lit′·ạ·rạ·choor, ·chẹr) *n.* the body of writings of a language, period, subject, etc.; (*Colloq.*) any printed matter, as advertisements, brochures [L. *litteratura,* learning].

lithe (līth) *a.* capable of being easily bent; supple; pliant. **-ly** *adv.* **-ness** *n.* **-some** *a.* [O.E. *lithe,* gentle].

li·thog·e·nous (li·tháj′·ạ·nạs) *a.* rock-producing, as certain corals [Gk. *lithos,* a stone; *genesthai,* to be born].

lith·o·glyph (lith′·ō·glif) *n.* an engraving on a precious stone [Gk. *lithos; gluphein,* to carve].

lith·o·graph (lith′·ạ·graf) *v.t.* to trace on stone, zinc, or aluminium, and transfer to paper by special printing process; *n.* a print from stone, etc. **lithographer** (li·thág′·rạ·fẹr) *n.* **lithographic, -al** *a.* **lithographically** *adv.* **lithography** *n.* the art of tracing designs on stone or other media, and taking impressions of these designs [Gk. *lithos,* a stone; *graphein,* to write].

lith·oid, -al (lith′·oid, ·ạl) *a.* resembling a stone [Gk. *lithos,* a stone].

li·thol·o·gy (li·thál′·a·ji·) *n.* the science which treats of the characteristics of rocks; (*Med.*) the study of calculi in the body [Gk. *lithos,* a stone; *logos,* a discourse].

lith·o·tint (lith′·ạ·tint) *n.* the lithographic production of a tinted picture; the picture itself [Gk. *lithos,* a stone; and *tint*].

lith·o·tome (lith′·ạ·tōm) *n.* a stone resembling an artificially cut gem; (*Surg.*) an instrument for performing a lithotomy. **lithotomic** *a.* **lithotomist** *n.* **lithotomy** (li·thát′·ạ·mi·) *n.* (*Surg.*) the operation by which stones are removed from the bladder [Gk. *lithos,* a stone; *tomē,* a cutting].

lith·o·type (lith′·ạ·tīp) *n.* a stereotype plate; print from this plate. **lithotypy** *n.* [Gk. *lithos,* a stone; *tupos,* type].

Lith·u·a·ni·an (lith·oo·ā′·ni·ạn) *n.* a native of Lithuania; the language. Also **Lett.**

lit·i·gate (lit′·ạ·gāt) *v.t.* to contest in law; *v.i.* to carry on a lawsuit. **litigable** *a.* **litigant** *n.* a person engaged in a lawsuit; *a.* engaged in a lawsuit. **litigation** *n.* judicial proceedings. **litigator** *n.* one who litigates. **litigiosity** (lạ·tij·i·ás′·ạ·ti·) *n.* **litigious** *a.* given to engaging in lawsuits [L. *litigare,* to dispute].

lit·mus (lit′·mạs) *n.* a bluish purple vegetable dye (obtained from lichens) which turns red with an acid, and blue with an alkali. **— paper,** used to test solutions.

li·to·tes (lī′·tạ·tēz) *n.* a figure of speech which expresses a strong affirmative, by using the negative of its contrary, as in phrase, *not a few* [Gk. *litos,* simple].

lit·ter (lit′·ẹr) *n.* a heap of straw as bedding for animals; a vehicle containing bed carried on men's shoulders; a stretcher; odds and ands left lying about; state of disorder; a family of young pigs, puppies, etc., brought forth at one birth; *v.t.* to bring forth young; to scatter indiscriminately about; to make untidy with odds and ends [Fr. *litière,* a bed].

lit·tle (lit′·l) *a.* small in size, extent, or quantity; brief; slight; mean; *n.* a small quantity or space; *adv.* in a small quantity or degree (*comp.* **less;** *superl.* **least**). **-ness** *n.* [O.E. *lytel*].

lit·to·ral (lit′·ẹr·ạl) *a.* pert. to a lake or seashore [L. *litoralis,* pert. to the seashore].

lit·ur·gy (lit′·ẹr·ji·) *n.* the established ritual for public worship in a church, esp. the Mass. **liturge** *n.* a leader in public worship. **liturgic, -al** *a.* **liturgically** *adv.* **liturgics** *n.* the study of church worship and its ritual. **liturgist** *n.* [Gk. *leitourgia,* a public service].

live (liv) *v.i.* to have life; to subsist; to be conscious; to dwell; to enjoy life; to keep oneself (as on one's income); *v.t.* to spend; to pass. **livable** *a.* habitable [O.E. *lifian,* to live].

live (līv) *a.* having life; quick; active; vital; unexploded, as a mine; burning, as coal; full of zest; dynamite. **lived** (līvd) *a.* used in compounds as *long-lived, short-lived.* **—circuit** *n.* a circuit through which an electric current is passing. **liven** *v.t.* to enliven. **-stock** *n.* the general term for horses, cattle, pigs, etc., on a farm. **— wire** *n.* a wire carrying an electric current; an energetic person [O.E. *lif,* life].

live·li·hood (līv′·li·hood) *n.* a means of living; sustenance [O.E. *lif,* life; *lad,* a way].

live·long (liv′·lawng) *a.* the entire [O.E. *leof,* dear].

live·ly (līv′·li·) *a.* animated; active; gay; exciting; light; *adv.* briskly. **livelily** *adv.* **liveliness** *n.* [O.E. *liflic,* life-like].

liv·er (liv′·ẹr) *n.* (*Anat.*) glandular organ in body secreting bile; the flesh of this organ in animals or fowls used as food. **-ish** *n.* off-color because of a disordered liver. **-wort** *n.* a moss-like plant with liver-shaped leaves. **-wurst** *n.* a sausage with a large amount of liver. **lily-livered** *a.* cowardly [O.E. *lifer,* liver].

liv·er·y (liv′·ẹr·i·) *n.* orig. the special dress or food *delivered* by a lord to his household retinue; a dress peculiar to a certain group, as members of a medieval guild or trade; any characteristic uniform of an employee, as of a chauffeur; a livery stable; the body of liverymen. **liveried** *a.* clothed in a livery. **-man** *n.* one who works in a livery stable. **— stable** *n.* a stable where horses and vehicles are kept for hire [O.Fr. *livrée,* an allowance].

liv·id (liv′·id) *a.* black and blue; discolored, as flesh, by bruising. **-ness, lividity** *n.* [L. *lividus,* bluish].

liv·ing (liv′·ing) *a.* having life; active; flowing (of water); resembling closely; contemporary; *n.* livelihood; maintenance; mode of life. **— language,** a language still in use. **— room** *n.* *n.* a sitting-room [O.E. *lif,* life].

liz·ard [liz′·ẹrd] *n.* an order of four-footed scale-clad reptiles [L. *lacerta*].

lla·ma (lȧ′·mạ) *n.* a S. America two-toed ruminant, used as a beast of burden [Peruv.].

lo (lō) *interj.* look! behold! [O.E. *la,* (imit.)].

loach (lōch) a small river fish [Fr. *loche*].

load (lōd) *n.* a burden; the amount normally carried at one time; any heavy weight; a cargo; (*Elect.*) amount of electrical energy drawn from a source; (*Fig.*) burden of anxiety; *pl.* (*Colloq.*) plenty; heaps; *v.t.* to burden; to put on, for conveyance; to freight; to overweight; to overwhelm (with gifts, adulation, etc); to charge (a gun); to weight (as dice); to insert a spool into (as a camera); *v.i.* to take on a load or cargo; to charge a firearm; to become loaded. **-ed** *a.* weighted; (*Slang*) drunk. **-ing** *n.* the act of loading; freight. **— line** *n.* a line painted on the side of a vessel to indicate maximum immersion when loaded. **-stone** *n.* a metal which attracts other metals [O.E. *lad*].

loaf (lōf) *n.* shaped portion of dough baked in the oven; a lump of sugar. *pl.* **loaves. meatloaf** *n.* meat cooked in a loaf tin or shaped in a mass [O.E. *hlaf,* a loaf].

loaf (lōf) *v.i.* to spend (time) idly; to lounge. **-er** *n.* one who loafs; a moccasin style of shoe.

loam (lōm) *n.* a rich, fertile soil of clay, sand,

oxide of iron, and carbonate of lime; a mixture of clay, sand, and chopped straw used in making molds for founding [O.E. *lam*, clay].

loan (lōn) *n.* the act of lending; that which is lent, esp. money for interest; *v.t.* to lend; to lend at interest. **-ee, -er** *n.* **— office** *n.* a pawnbroker's shop [O.N. *lan*, loan].

loath, loth (lōth) *a.* unwilling; reluctant; disinclined [O.E. *lath*, hateful].

loathe (lōTH) *v.t.* to detest; to abominate; to be nauseated by. **loathing** *n.* disgust; repulsion. **loathly** *a.* **loathsome** *a.* detestable; repugnant. **loathsomely** *adv.* **loathsomeness** *n.* [O.E. *lath*, hateful].

lob (lȧb) *n.* (*Tennis*) a ball rising high in air over opponent's head; *v.t.* to bowl underhand; to hit (tennis ball, shuttle-cock) high into air; *v.i.* to deliver a lob. *pr.p.* **-bing.** *pa.p.* **-bed.** [Scand. *lobbe*, a lump of fat].

lob·by (lȧb′·i·) *n.* a passage, or hall, forming the entrance to a public building or private dwelling; a waiting-room; a pressure group seeking to influence members of a legislature; *v.i.* to solicit votes of members of a legislature; *v.t.* to secure the passage of a bill, to influence a legislator by lobbying. **-ing** *n.* **-ism** *n.* **-ist** *n.* [L.L. *lobia*, a portico].

lobe (lōb) *n.* a rounded division of an organ; the lower, fleshy, rounded part of human ear; a division of the lung; (*Bot.*) rounded division of a leaf. **lobar** *a.* **lobate, lobed, lobose** *a.* having a lobe or lobes [Gk. *lobos*].

lo·bel·ia (lō·bē′·li·ạ) *n.* a genus of herbaceous plants (including the blue dwarf variety) [fr. *Lobel*, botanist to James I].

lob·lol·ly (lȧb′·lȧl·i·) *n.* a pine tree of the southern U.S.

lob·ster (lȧb′·stẹr) *n.* an edible, marine, long-tailed crustacean, with pincer-claws. **— pot,** a trap in which lobsters are caught [corrupt. of L. *locusta*, a lobster].

lo·cal (lō′·kạl) *a.* pert. to a particular place; confined to a definite spot, district, or part; circumscribed; *n.* some person or thing belonging to a district; a suburban train. **locale** *n.* the scene of an occurrence; the scene of a film-shot. **localization** *n.* the act of localizing. **localize** *v.t.* to assign to a definite place; to decentralize. **locality** *n.* position of a thing; site; neighborhood. **-ly** *adv.* **locate** *v.t.* to set in a particular place; to find the exact position of. **location** *n.* act of locating; situation; geographical position; the out-of-doors site of a film production. **locative** (lȧk′·ạ·tiv) *n.* (*Gram.*) the case form denoting the 'place where.' [L. *locus*, a place].

loch (lȧk) *n.* a lake, esp. in Scotland; an arm of the sea (as Loch Fyne) [Gael.].

lock (lȧk) *n.* a strand or tress of hair; *pl.* hair of the head [O.E. *locc*, a tress].

lock (lȧk) *n.* a device for fastening a door, box, case, etc.; a mechanism on a gun to keep it from firing; an appliance to check the revolution of a wheel; an accidental stoppage of any mechanism; an enclosure in a canal with gate at each end for allowing vessels to pass from one level to another; the grappling hold, in wrestling; *v.t.* to fasten with a lock and key; to furnish with locks, as a canal; to hold tightly; *v.i.* to become fastened; to jam. **-er** *n.* a drawer, small chest, etc. where valuables may be locked. **-et** *n.* a small case containing portrait, lock of hair, worn on a chain. **-jaw** *n.* a contraction of the muscles of the jaw; tetanus. **-nut** *n.* a second nut screwed on top of the first nut to prevent loosening. **-out** *n.* a refusal by an employer to admit employees until a dispute has been amicably settled. **-smith** *n.* one who makes and repairs locks. **-up** *n.* a prison [O.E. *loc*, a fastening].

lo·co·mo·tion (lō·kạ·mō′·shạn) *n.* the act or process of moving from place to place. **locomotive** *a.* capable of moving from one place to another; *n.* an engine which moves by its own power, as a railway engine. **locomotivity** *n.* **locomotor** *n.* person or thing with power to move; *a.* pert. to locomotion [L. *locus*, a place; *movere, motum*, to move].

lo·cus (lō′·kạs) *n.* the exact position of anything; (*Math.*) the path traced out by a point moving in accordance with some mathematical law; *pl.* **loci** (lō′·sī) [L. *locus*, a place].

lo·cust (lō′·kạst) *n.* a winged insect, allied to the grasshopper and found in N. Africa, Asia, and the U.S.; a thorny-branched N. American tree with very durable wood [L. *locusta*].

lo·cu·tion (lō·kū′·shạn) *n.* speech; mode or style of speaking [L. *loqui*, to speak].

lode (lōd) *n.* a metallic vein; a body of ore. **-star, loadstar** *n.* a star by which one steers, esp. the Pole-star. **lodestone** see **loadstone** [O.E. *lad*, a course].

lodge (lȧj) *n.* a small country-house; a cottage at the entrance to an estate; a branch of a society, as of Freemasons, or the building where such a society meets; *v.i.* to dwell in temporarily; to reside; to become embedded in; *v.t.* to deposit for preservation; to infix; to rent out rooms; to lay flat; to harbor; to put (as money) in a bank; to allege, as an accusation. **lodg(e)ment** *n.* lodgings; accumulation of something deposited; (*Mil.*) occupation of a position by a besieging party. **-r** *n.* one who occupies rooms for rent. **lodging(s)** *n.* room(s) let temporarily [O.Fr. *loge*, an apartment].

loft (lawft) *n.* an upper room; an attic in space between top story and roof; the gallery in a church, as the *organ-loft; v.t.* (*Golf*) to strike a ball high. **-ily** *adv.* **-iness** *n.* **-y** *a.* elevated; towering; haughty [Scand. *lopt*, air].

log (lawg, lȧg) *n.* an unhewn piece of timber; an apparatus to measure the speed of a ship and distance covered; the tabulated record of a ship's voyage; a logbook; *a.* made of logs; *v.t.* to fell and trim trees; to clear woodland; to keep records of. *pr.p.* **-ging.** *pa.t., pa.p.* **-ged.** **-book** *n.* a daily record of events on a ship's voyage. **— cabin** *n.* a hut made of lopped tree trunks. **-ger** *n.* a lumberjack. **-ging** *n.* the process of cutting trees and getting the logs to a sawmill to be cut for lumber. **-rolling** *n.* act of clearing logs, esp. from a neighbor's land, hence mutual help esp. in politics [M.E. *logge*].

lo·gan·ber·ry (lō′·gạn·ber·i·) *n.* a shrub, a cross between raspberry and blackberry [hybridized by *Logan*, 1881].

log·a·rithm (lawg′·, lȧg′·ạ·riTHm) *n.* the index of the power to which a fixed number or base must be raised to produce the number; a method of reducing arithmetical calculations to a minimum by substituting addition and subtraction for multiplication and division. [Gk. *logos*, ratio; *arithmos*, a number].

log·ger·head (lawg′·, lȧg′·ẹr·hed) *n.* a blockhead; a dunce; a kind of turtle. **at loggerheads,** quarrelling; at cross-purposes [fr. *log* and *head*].

log·gia (lȧj′·i·ạ, law′·jȧ) *n.* a kind of open elevated gallery with pillars, common in Italian buildings [Cf. **lodge**].

log·ic (lȧj′·ik) *n.* the science of reasoning; the science of pure and formal thought; (*Colloq.*) commonsense. **-al** *a.* pert. to formal thought; skilled in logic; reasonable. **logicality, -alness** *n.* **-ally** *adv.* **logician** *n.* one skilled in logic [Gk. *logos*, speech].

lo·gis·tic, -al (lạj·is′·tik, -ạl) *a.* pert. to calculating. **-s** *n.pl.* (used as *sing.*); (*Mil.*) branch of military science which deals with the moving of and providing for troops [Gk. *logizesthai*, to compute].

log·o·gram (lawg′·, lȧg′·ạ·gram) *n.* a symbol representing a whole word or phrase [Gk. *logos*, a word; *gramma*, a letter].

lo·go·gra·pher (lō·gág′·rạ·fẹr) *n.* a speech-writer in ancient Greek times. **logography** *n.* a method of printing in which words cast in a single type are used instead of single letters [Gk. *logos*, a word; *graphein*, to write].

loin (loin) *n.* part of animal or man above hips and on either side of spinal column; a cut of meat from this part of an animal. **-cloth** *n.* [L. *lumbus*, loin].

loi·ter (loi′·tẹr) *v.i.* to linger; to be slow in moving; to spend time idly. **-er** *n.* **-ingly** *adv.* [Dut. *leuteren*, to delay].

loll (lál) *v.i.* to lounge about lazily; to hang out, as the tongue; *v.t.* to permit to hang out [Scand. *lolla*, to be lazy].

lol·li·pop lollipop (lál′·i·páp) *n.* a piece of flavored toffee or hard candy on a stick [etym. doubtful].

lone (lōn) *a.* solitary; standing by itself. **-liness, -ness** *n.* **-ly** *a.* alone; unfrequented. **-some** *a.* solitary. **-somely** *adv.* **-someness** *n.* [abbrev. fr. *alone*].

long (lawng) *a.* extended in distance or time; drawn out in a line; protracted; slow in coming; continued at great length; *adv.* to a great extent; at a point of duration far distant; *v.i.* to be filled with a yearning to desire. **— ago** *adv.* in the remote past. **-boat** *n.* the largest boat carried by a sailing ship. **-bow** *n.* a bow drawn by hand, and usually 5½-6 feet long—so called to distinguish it from the *Cross*-bow. **—drawn** *a.* protracted. **longeron** (lán′·jẹr·-án) *n.* (*Aero.*) a main longitudinal strength member of a fuselage. **longevity** (lawng·-jev′·ạ·ti·) *n.* length of life; uncommonly prolonged duration of life. **longevous** *a.* long-lived. **-hand** *n.* ordinary handwriting (opp. *shorthand*). **—headed** *a.* far-seeing; prudent. **-horn** *n.* a kind of cattle of Mexico and U.S. **— house** *n.* a long communal dwelling of the Iroquois Indians. **— hundred** *n.* Br. hundredweight, 120 pounds. **-ing** a yearning; a craving. **-ingly** *adv.* **-ish** *a.* rather long. **longitude** (lán′·jạ·tūd) *n.* angular distance east or west of a given meridian, measured in degrees; (*Astron.*) angular distance from vernal equinox on the ecliptic. **longitudinal** *a.* pert. to length or longitude; lengthwise; *n.* a girder running lengthwise in a ship or airship. **longitudinally** *adv.* **— measure** *n.* linear measure. **—range** *a.* having the power to fire a great distance, as a gun; able to fly or sail great distances without refueling, as aircraft, submarine, etc. **-shore** *a.* existing or employed on the shore. **-shoreman** *n.* a dock laborer. **-sightedness** *n.* (*Med.*) hypermetropia, an abnormal eye condition whereby the rays of light are focused *beyond* and not on the retina. **—standing** *a.* having existed for some time. **—suffering** *a.* patiently enduring. **—winded** *a.* able to run a great distance without becoming short of breath; tedious; loquacious. **-wise, -ways** *a.* lengthwise. **before long,** soon [O.E. *lang*, long].

loo (lòò) *n.* a card-game; *v.t.* to win in a game of loo [abbrev. fr. *lanterloo*].

look (look) *v.i.* to turn one's eyes upon; to seem to be; to consider; to seem; to face, as a dwelling; *v.i* to express by a look; *n.* the act of directing one's gaze upon; facial expression generally; aspect; view. **-er** *n.* one who looks. **-er-on** *n.* a spectator. **-ing** *n.* a search. **-ing glass** *n.* a mirror. **-out** *n.* a watch; a place from which a careful watch is kept; person stationed to keep watch [O.E. *locian*, to look].

loom (lòòm) *n.* a machine for weaving cloth from thread by interlacing threads called the *woof* through threads called the *warp*; part of the shaft of an oar inside the rowlock [O.E. *geloma*, a tool].

loom (lòòm) *v.i.* to emerge indistinctly and larger than the real dimensions; to appear over the horizon; (*Fig.*) to assume great importance.

loom (lòòm) *n.* a kind of guillemot; a puffin; a loon [Scand. *lomr*, a sea bird].

loon (lòòn) *n.* a large fish-eating diving bird of the northern regions [same as *loom*].

loon·y (lòòn′·i·) *n.* (*Colloq.*) a crazy person; *a.* (*Slang*) very foolish [fr. *lunatic*].

loop (lòòp) *n.* a doubling of string or rope, through which another string may run; anything with a similar shape; (*Aero.*) an aerial maneuver in which plane describes a complete circle; *v.t.* to fasten by a loop; to form into a loop. **-ed** *a.* [prob. Ir. *lub*, a bend].

loop·hole (lòòp′·hōl) *n.* a narrow slit or opening as in the walls of a fortification; (*Fig.*) a way out of a difficult situation.

loose (lòòs) *v.t.* to free from constraint; to untie; to disconnect; to relax; to discharge; *v.i.* to set sail; to let go; *a.* free; slack; unsewed; unbound; flowing; diffuse; incoherent; careless; inaccurate; lax; inclined to diarrhea. **—jointed** *a.* loosely built. **—leaf** *a.* having sheets of paper which can be removed and rearranged. **-ly** *adv.* **loosen** *v.t.* to make loose; to unfasten; *v.i.* to become loose; to become relaxed. **loosener** *n.* **-ness** *n.* **—tongued** *a.* prating; indiscreet [O.E. *leas*, loose].

loot (lòòt) *n.* plunder; the act of plundering; *v.t.* and *v.i.* to plunder; to appropriate illegally [Sans. *lut*, booty].

lop (láp) *v.t.* to cut off, esp. top of anything; to cut away superfluous parts. *pr.p.* **-ping.** *pa.t., pa.p.* **-ped.** *n.* twig from tree; act of lopping. **-per** *n.* **-ping** *n.* [Dut. *lubben*, to cut].

lop (láp) *v.i.* to hang down loosely. *pr.p.* **-ping.** *pa.t., pa.p.* **-ped. —eared** *a.* having drooping ears. **—sided** *a.* heavier on one side than the other; askew [prob. imit.].

lope (lōp) *v.i.* to run with a long, leisurely gait; *n.* an easy gait [O.N. *hlaupa*, to leap].

lo·qua·cious (lō·kwā′·shạs) *a.* talkative; babbling; garrulous. **-ly** *adv.* **-ness, loquacity** *n.* talkativeness [L. *loquax*, talkative].

lo·quat (lō′·kwát) *n.* a low-growing Japanese plum tree; the fruit itself [Chinese].

lo·ran (lō′·rạn) *n.* (*Flying*) a navigational device which locates the position of an airplane [From *long* + *range* + *navigation*].

lord (lawrd) *n.* a master; a ruler; a king; (*Brit.*) a proprietor of a manor; any peer of the realm; courtesy title; the holder of certain high government offices; (*Cap.*) the Supreme Being; Jehovah; God; Christ; *v.i.* to play the lord; to domineer. **-liness** *n.* **-ling** *n.* a petty or unimportant lord. **-ly** *a.* pert. to, or like, a lord; imperious; proud; magnificent. **-ship** *n.* the state of being a lord; authority; estate owned by a lord; (*Brit.*) (with *his, your*) a formal mode of address in speaking to a lord, bishop [O.E. *hlaford*, the keeper of the bread].

lore (lōr) *n.* learning; erudition; traditional knowledge [O.E. *lar*, lore].

lor·gnette (lawr·nyet′) *n.* a pair of eyeglasses attached to a long handle; an opera glass [Fr. *lorgner*, to stare at].

lo·ri·ca (lạ·rī′·kạ) *n.* a cuirass; (*Zool.*) a protective covering of bony plates, scales, etc., like a cuirass. **loricate** *v.t.* to clothe in mail; to cover with a coating; *a.* (*Zool.*) having protective covering of bony plates, as crocodiles [L. *lorica*, a breastplate].

lorn (lawrn) *a.* (*Arch.*) lost; forsaken; desolate [O.E. *loren*, *pa.p.* of *leosan*, to lose].

lor·ry (lawr′·i·) *n.* (*esp. Brit.*) a wagon for transporting heavy loads; a car on rails, used in factories, mines, etc.; (*Brit.*) a truck.

lose (looz) *v.t.* to be deprived of; to mislay; to forfeit; to fail to win; to miss; to waste, as time; to destroy; *v.i.* to fail; to suffer loss; to become bewildered. *pr.p.* **losing.** *pa.t.* and *pa.p.* **lost. losable** *a.* **-r** *n.* **losing** *a.* producing loss. **loss** *n.* the act of losing; that which is lost; defeat; diminution; bereavement; harm; waste by escape or leakage; number of casualties suffered in war. **lost** *a.* mislaid; bewildered; bereft [O.E. *leosan*, to lose].

lot (lȧt) *n.* what happens by chance; destiny; object used to determine something by chance; the choice thus determined; a separate part; a large number of articles such as at an auction sale; (*Motion Pictures*) the area covered by film studio and its subsidiary buildings; (*Colloq.*) a great many; *v.t.* to allot; to separate into lots. **-tery** *n.* a scheme by which prizes are given to people, not on merit, but by drawing lots. **a job-lot,** a miscellaneous collection of articles, sold as one item [O.E. *hlot*, a share].

loth (lōth) *a.* Same as **loath.**

Lo·thar·i·o (lō·thar′·i·ō) *n.* libertine, rake [fr. *Lothario*, in Rowe's *The Fair Penitent*].

lo·tion (lō′·shạn) *n.* a fluid with healing, antiseptic properties esp. for the skin [L. *lavare*, *lotum*, to wash].

lot·to (lȧt′·ō) *n.* a game of chance [fr. *lot*].

lo·tus (lō′·tạs) *n.* the Egyptian water lily; a decorative representation, as in Egyptian and Hindu art; a genus of plants including the British bird'sfoot trefoil; a N. African shrub, the fruit of which was reputed, in Greek legend, to induce in those who consumed it an overpowering lethargy. Also **lotos.** **—eater** *n.* (*Fig.*) one who gives up an active life for one of slothful ease [Gk. *lōtus*].

loud (loud) *a.* making a great sound; noisy; flashy; obtrusive; vulgar. **loud, -ly** *adv.* **-ness** *n.* **-speaker** *n.* a device which makes speech, music, etc. audible at a distance [O.E. *hlud*].

lou·is (lòò′·i·) *n.* an obsolete French gold coin worth 20 francs. Also **— d'or. — quatorze, — quinze, — seize,** applied to architecture, furniture, style of interior decoration characteristic of the reigns of the French Kings Louis XIV, VX, XVI [Fr.].

lounge (lounj) *v.i.* to recline at ease; to loll; to spend time idly; *n.* the act of lounging; a room in which people may relax; a kind of sofa.

louse (lous) *n.* a small wingless parasitic insect infesting hair and skin of human beings; a sucking parasite found on mammals or plants. *pl.* **lice. lousily** (louz′·ạ·li·) *adv.* **lousiness** *n.* **lousy** *a.* infested with lice; (*Slang*) mean; despicable [O.E. *lus*, a louse].

lout (lout) *n.* a clumsy fellow; a bumpkin; *v.i.* to bend. **-ish** *a.* **-ishly** *adv.* [etym. uncertain].

lou·ver (lòò′·vẹr) *n.* an opening in the roof of ancient buildings for the escape of smoke or for ventilation; a slot for ventilation [O.Fr. *louvert* for *l'ouvert*, the open space].

love (luv) *n.* affection; strong liking; goodwill; benevolence; charity; devoted attachment to one of the opposite sex; passion; the object of affection; the personification of love: Cupid; (*Tennis*) no score; *v.t.* to show affection for; to be delighted with; to admire passionately; *v.i.* to be in love; to delight. **lovable** *a.* worthy of affection; engaging. **lovableness** *n.* **— affair** *n.* a passionate attachment between two members of the opposite sex. **— apple** *n.* the tomato. **—bird** *n.* a small parrot with bright-colored plumage. **-charm** *n.* a philter. **—child** *n.* an illegitimate child. **— feast** *n.* a religious festival among the early Christians during which collections were made for the poor. **—in-a-mist** *n.* fennel. **—in-idleness** *n.* the pansy. **—knot** *n.* a bow of ribbon tied in a special way, as a token of love. **-less** *a.* lacking love; not founded on love. **— letter** *n.* a letter written to a sweetheart. **—lies-bleeding** *n.* a garden flower with reddish-purple spike flowers. **-liness** *n.* **—lock** *n.* a curl worn on the forehead or over the temple. **-lorn** *a.* forsaken. **-ly** *a.* very beautiful; **-making** *n.* courtship. **— match** *n.* a marriage founded on true love. **— philter** *or* **— potion** *n.* a drink supposed to induce the emotion of love towards a chosen person. **-r** *n.* one who loves, esp. one of the opposite sex; an admirer, as of the arts. **loverlike** *a.* **loverly** *adv.* **— seat** *n.* a seat for two. **-sick** *a.* pining because of love. **—song** *n.* lyric inspired by love. **—token** *n.* an object, as a ring, given as a symbol of love. **loving** *a.* affectionate; loyal. **loving-cup** *n.* large drinking-vessel with two handles, given as a prize or trophy. **lovingly** *adv.* **lovingness** *n.* [O.E. *lufu*, love].

low (lō) *a.* not high; lying near the ground; depressed below the adjacent surface; near the horizon; shallow; not loud, as a voice; moderate, as prices; dejected; lewd; weak; cold, as a temperature; humble; (of dress) décolleté; *adv.* not high; in a low voice; cheaply. **-born** *a.* of humble birth. **-boy** *n.* a chest about three feet high usu. with two tiers of drawers and on slender legs. **-brow** *n.* a non-intellectual. **Low Countries,** the Netherlands, Belgium, and Luxemburg. **-down** *a.* mean; underhand; *n.* (*Slang*) full information. **-er** *v.t.* to cause to descend; to take down; to humble; to diminish resistance; to make cheap; to reduce pitch; *a.* (*compar.* of *low*) less exalted. **-er case** *n.* abbrev. *l.c.*) small letters as opposed to capitals. **-land** *n.* country which is relatively flat in comparison with surrounding hilly district. **-lander** *n.* an inhabitant of flat land, esp. in Scotland. **-liness** *n.* **-ly** *a.* humble; meek; **—pressure,** having only a small expansive force (less than 50 lbs. to the square inch) said of steam and steam engines [O.N. *lagr*].

low (lō) *v.i.* to bellow as an ox or cow; *n.* the noise made [O.E. *hlowan*, to low].

low·er (lou′·ẹr) *v.i.* to frown; to look gloomy or threatening, as the sky; *n.* a scowl; sullenness. **-ing** *a.* **-ingly** *adv.* Also **lour** [M.E. *louren*, to frown].

lox (lȧks) *n.* liquid oxygen [from *l*iquid *ox*ygen]. *n.* salty smoked salmon [Yid. *lachs*, salmon].

loy·al (loi′·ạl) *a.* faithful to the lawful government, the sovereign, a cause, or a friend. **-ist** *n.* a faithful follower of a cause. **-ly** *adv.* **-ty** *n.* fidelity [Fr. fr. L. *lex*, a law].

loz·enge (lȧz′·inj) *n.* a figure with two acute and two obtuse angles; small (often medicated) confection orig. lozenge-shaped.

lub·ber (lub′·ẹr) *n.* a heavy, clumsy fellow.

lu·bri·cate (lòò′·bri·kāt) *v.t.* to make smooth or slippery; to smear with oil, grease, etc., to reduce friction. **lubricant** *n.* any oily substance used to reduce friction; *a.* having the property of reducing friction. **lubrication** *n.* **lubricative** *a.* **lubricator** *n.* **lubricity** *n.* slipperiness [L. *lubricare*, to make slippery].

luce (lòòs) *n.* a fresh-water fish, the pike when full grown [O.Fr. *lus*, a pike].

lu·cent (lòò′·sạnt) *a.* shining; bright. **lucency** *n.* **lucernal** *a.* pert. to a lamp [L. *lucere*].

lu·cid (lòò′·sid) *a.* shining; clear; easily understood, as of style; normally sane. **-ness, -ity** *n.* **-ly** *adv.* [L. *lux*, light].

Lu·ci·fer (lòò′·sạ·fẹr) *n.* the planet Venus, when appearing as the morning star; Satan. [L. *lucifer*. light-bearing].

Lu·cite (lòò′·sīt) *n.* a very clear plastic compound [Trademark].

luck (luk) *n.* accidental fortune, good or bad; fate; chance. **-ily** *adv.* **-iness** *n.* **-less** *n.* unfortunate. **-lessly** *adv.* **-lessness** *n.* **-y** *a.* fortunate; fortuitous [Dut. *luk*, fate].

lu·cre (lòò′·kẹr) *n.* material gain; profit, esp. ill-gotten. **lucrative** *a.* profitable. **lucratively** *adv.* **filthy lucre** (*Slang*) money [L. *lucrum*].

lu·cu·brate (lòò′·kyạ·brāt) *v.i.* to study by lamp or candlelight, or at night. **lucubration** *n.* nocturnal study; the product of such study. **lucubrator** *n.* **lucubratory** *a.* [L. *lucubrare*, to work by candlelight].

lu·cu·lent (lòò′·kyạ·lạnt) *a.* clear; self-evident.

-ly *adv.* [L. *lux,* light].

lu·di·crous (lòò'.di.kras) *a.* provoking laughter; ridiculous; droll. **-ly** *adv.* **-ness** *n.* [L. *ludus,* sport].

luff (luf) *v.i.* to turn the head of a ship towards the wind; to sail nearer the wind; *n.* the windward side of a ship [M.E. *lof,* a paddle].

Luft·waf·fe (looft'.vȧ.fa) *n.* the German Air Force [Ger. *Luft,* the air; *Waffe,* a weapon].

lug (lug) *v.t.* to pull with force; to tug; to haul; to drag. *pr.p.* **-ging.** *pa.t.* and *pa.p.* **-ged. -gage** *n.* a traveler's trunks, baggage, etc. [Scand. *lugga,* to pull the hair].

lug (lug) *n.* a projecting piece by which an object may be grasped, supported, etc. [Scand. *lugga,* a forelock].

lu·gu·bri·ous (lòò.gū'.bri.as) *a.* mournful; woeful; dismal. **-ly** *adv.* [L. *lugere,* to mourn].

lug·worm (lug'.wurm) a large earthworm.

luke·warm (lòòk'.wawrm) *a.* moderately warm; tepid; indifferent. **-ly** *adv.* **-ness** *n.* [M.E. *leuk,* tepid; *warm*].

lull (lul) *v.t.* to soothe to sleep; to quiet; *v.i.* to become quiet gradually; *n.* a period of quiet in storm or noise. **-aby** (.a.bī) *n.* a song sung to a child to soothe it to sleep [Scand. *lulla*].

lum·ba·go (lum.bā'.gō) *n.* a painful rheumatic affection of the lumbar muscles. **lumbaginous, lumbar, lumbral** *a.* pert. to the lower part of the back [L. *lumbus,* the loin].

lum·ber (lum'.bər) *n.* anything useless and cumbersome; odds and ends hoarded; timber cut and split for market; *v.i.* to prepare timber for market; *v.t.* to heap in disorder. **-er, -jack, -man,** *n.* **-ing** *n.* **-yard** *n.* [fr. *Lombard,* a pawnbroker's shop].

lum·ber (lum'.bər) *v.i.* to move heavily. **-er** *n.* **-ing** *a.* [Scand. *lomra,* to resound].

lu·mi·nar·y (lòò'.ma.ner.i.) *n.* any body which gives light, esp. one of the heavenly bodies; (*Fig.*) a person of outstanding qualities. **luminant** *a.* giving out light. **lumination** *n.* **luminescence** *n.* the quality of being luminescent; phosphorescence. **luminescent** *a.* **lumeniferous** *a.* yielding light. **luminous** *a.* shining; brilliant; glowing; brilliant in mind; lucid; comprehensible. **luminously** *adv.* [L. *lumen,* a light].

lump (lump) *n.* a small mass of matter of indefinite shape; a swelling; the gross; (*Colloq.*) a stupid, clumsy person; *a.* in a mass; *v.t.* to throw into a mass; to take in the gross. **lumpy** *a.* full of lumps; uneven. **in the lump,** taken as an aggregate [Scand. *lump,* a block].

lu·nar (lòò'.nər) *a.* pert. to the moon; measured by revolutions of the moon. Also **lunary. lunacy** *n.* madness, formerly supposed to be influenced by changes of moon. **lunatic** *a.* insane; *n.* a mad person. **lunation** *n.* the period from one new moon to the next. **lunar month,** period of the moon's revolution, about 29½ days. **lunar year,** period of twelve synodic lunar months (354⅓ days). **lunate** *a.* crescent-shaped [L. *luna,* the moon].

lunch (lunch) *n.* a light meal taken between breakfast and dinner. Also **-eon.** *v.i.* to take lunch. **-eonette** *n.* [dial. *lunsh,* a lump].

lune (lòòn) *n.* anything in the shape of a half-moon. **lunette** *n.* a crescent-shaped opening in a vault to let in light [L. *luna,* the moon].

lung (lung) *n.* one of the two main organs of respiration in a breathing animal. **-ed** *a.* [O.E. *lungen,* lungs].

lunge (lunj) *n.* in fencing, a sudden thrust; *v.i.* to thrust [Fr. *allonger,* to stretch].

lu·pine (lòò'.pīn) *a.* wolflike [L. *lupus,* a wolf].

lu·pine (lòò'.pan) *n.* a genus of leguminous plants, some cultivated for their flowers, others for cattle fodder [L. *lupinus,* pert. to a wolf].

lu·pus (lòò'.pas) *n.* a spreading tubercular condition affecting the skin [L. *lupus,* a wolf].

lurch (lurch) *n.* a sudden roll of a ship to one side; a staggering movement; *v.i.* to stagger.

lurch (lurch) *n.* a critical move in the game of cribbage. **to leave in the lurch,** to desert in a moment of need [Fr. *lourche,* a game].

lure (loor) *n.* a decoy used by the falconer to recall the hawk; an artificial bait; *v.t.* to entice; to decoy [Fr. *leurre,* a bait].

lu·rid (loo'.rid) *a.* extravagantly colored; (*Fig.*) startling; ghastly pale. **-ly** *adv.* [L. *luridus,* pale yellow].

lurk (lurk) *v.i.* to lie hidden; to lie in wait. **-er** *n.* [Scand. *lurka,* to go slowly].

lus·cious (lush'.as) *a.* excessively sweet; cloying. **-ly** *adv.* **-ness** *n.* [etym. doubtful].

lush (lush) *a.* luxuriant; juicy [*luscious*].

lush (lush) *n.* (*Slang*) a habitually drunken person.

lust (lust) *n.* longing desire; sexual appetite; craving; *v.i.* to desire passionately; to have sexual appetites. **-ful** *a.* having inordinate carnal desires; sensual. **-fully** *adv.* **-fulness** *n.* **-iness** *n.* **-ily** *adv.* **lusty** *a.* vigorous; robust [O.E. *lust,* pleasure].

lus·ter (lus'.tər) *n.* clearness; glitter; gloss; renown; radiance; chandelier with drops or pendants of cut glass; a cotton dress fabric with glossy, silky surface; a pottery glaze. **lustrous** *a.* gleaming; bright. **lustrously** *adv.* [L. *lustrare,* to make bright]. [Fr.].

lus·trine (lus'.trin) *n.* a glossy silk fabric.

lus·trum (lus'.tram) *n.* a period of five years; purification, (Rom. times) every five years. **lustral** *a.* pert. to, or used in, purification. **lustration** *n.* the act of purifying; the sacrifice or ceremony by which cities, fields, armies, or people were purified [L. *lustrare,* to purify].

lute (lòòt) *n.* a stringed instrument with a pear-shaped body. **lutanist, luter, lutist** *n.* a lute-player. **—string** *n.* [O.Fr. *lut*].

Lu·ther·an (lòò'.thər.an) *a.* pert. to *Luther* the German reformer, or to his doctrines; *n.* a follower of Martin Luther; a member of the Lutheran Church. **-ism, Lutherism.**

lu·thern (lòò'.thərn) *n.* a dormer-window.

lux·ate (luk'.sāt) *v.t.* to put out of joint; to dislocate. **luxation** *n.* [L. *luxare,* to dislocate].

luxe See **de luxe.**

lux·u·ry (luk'.sha.ri.) *n.* indulgence in the pleasures which wealth can procure; that which is not a necessity of life. **luxuriance, luxuriancy, luxuriety** *n.* **luxuriant** *a.* in great abundance; dense or prolific, as vegetation. **luxuriantly** *adv.* **luxuriate** *v.i.* to grow luxuriantly; to live luxuriously. **luxurious** *a.* self-indulgent in appetite, etc.; sumptuous. **luxuriously** *adv.* **luxuriousness** *n.* [L. *luxus,* excess].

Ly·ce·um (lī.sē'.am) *n.* orig. a place in Athens where Aristotle taught his pupils; (*l.c.*) a lecture hall [Gk. *Lukeion*].

lydd·ite (lid'.it) *n.* picric acid; a powerful explosive used in shells [fr. *Ludd* in Kent].

lye (lī) *n.* alkaline solution of wood ashes and water; used in soap making [O.E. *leah*].

ly·ing (lī'.ing) *a.* recumbent. **lying-in** *n.* the confinement of a pregnant woman [fr. *lie*].

ly·ing (lī'.ing) *a.* untruthful; *n.* habit of being untruthful. **-ly** *adv.* [fr. *lie*].

lymph (limf) *n.* an alkaline fluid, watery in appearance, contained in the tissues and organs of the body. **-atic** *a.* pert. to lymph; sluggish. **-atics** *n.pl.* small vessels in the body containing lymph. **-oid** *a.* like, composed of, lymph [L. *lympha,* water].

lynch (linch) *v.t.* to inflict capital punishment (on an accused) illegally [fr. *Charles Lynch,* Virginia planter (18th cent.)].

lynx (lingks) *n.* an animal of the cat tribe with abnormally keen sight [Gk. *lunx*].

ly·on·naise (lī'.a.nāz) *a.* prepared with onions [Fr.].

lyre (līr) *n.* a stringed, musical instrument in

use among ancient Greeks, esp. to accompany minstrels. **lyrate** *a.* shaped like a lyre. **-bird** *n.* an Australian bird with tail feathers which curve upward in the shape of a lyre. **lyric** (lir'·ik) *n.* orig. a poem sung to music; a short, subjective poem expressing emotions of poet. **lyric(al)** *a.* pert. to the lyre; suitable to be sung to a musical accompaniment; used of poetry expressing emotion. **lyricism** *n.* lyrical quality of a poem; emotional expression. **lyrist** *n.* **lyricist** *n.* [Gk. *lura*, a lyre].

M

ma·am (mam) *n.* contr. of **madam.**

ma·ca·bre (mą·kà'·bęr) *a.* gruesome; ghastly; grim. **macaberesque** *a.* [O.Fr. *macabre*].

mac·a·dam (mą·kad'·ąm) *n.* a road-surface material of crushed stones. **-ize** *v.t.* [fr. J. L. *MacAdam*, the inventor (d. 1836)].

ma·caque (mą·kàk·') *n.* a genus of Asian monkeys. **macaco** *n.* Braz. monkey [Port. *macaco*, a monkey].

mac·a·ro·ni (mak·ą·rō'·ni·) *n.* a paste of wheat flour made in long slender tubes; a dandy of the 18th cent. **-c** *a.* affected; *n.* burlesque verse with Latinized endings [It.].

mac·a·roon (mak'·ą·ròòn) *n.* a small cooky made of white of egg, ground almonds, and sugar [Fr. *macaroon*].

ma·caw (mą·kaw') *n.* a long-tailed S. Amer. parrot [Brazil. *macao*].

mace (mās) *n.* a heavy club of metal; a staff carried as an emblem of authority; a billiard cue [O.Fr. *mace*, a mallet].

mace (mās) *n.* a spice made from nutmeg.

Mace (mās) *n.* a liquid that disables temporarily, mainly when sprayed in the face causing eye and skin irritations and other discomforts [Trademark].

mac·er·ate (mas'·ą·rāt) *v.t.* to soften by soaking; to cause to grow thin; *v.i.* to become soft; to waste away. **maceration** *n.* [L. *macerare*, to steep].

ma·che·te (mą·che'·ti·) *n.* a heavy knife or cleaver used to cut down sugar canes, and as a weapon [Sp.].

Mach·i·a·vel·lian (mak·i·ą·vel'·i·ąn) *a.* pert. to Machiavelli; unscrupulous; crafty; *n.* an unprincipled ruthless ruler. **-ism** *n.* [fr. *Machiavelli*, Florentine statesman].

mach·i·nate (mak'·ą·nāt) *v.t.* to contrive, usually with evil or ulterior motive; *v.i.* to conspire. **machination** *n.* the act of contriving or plotting, with evil intent; an intrigue [L. *machinari*, to plot].

ma·chine (mą·shēn') *n.* (*Mech.*) any contrivance for the conversion and direction of motion; an engine; a vehicle; a person who acts like an automaton; a politically controlled organization; *v.t.* to use a machine. **— gun** *n.* an automatic small-arms weapon capable of continuous firing. **-ry** *n.* machines collectively; the parts of a machine; any combination of means to an end. **— tool** *n.* a tool for cutting, shaping, and turning operated by machinery. **machinist** *n.* [L. *machina*].

mack·er·el (mak'·ęr·ąl) *n.* an edible sea fish with blue and black stripes above and silver color below [O.Fr. *mackerel*].

mack·i·naw (mak'·ą·naw) *n.* a short woolen coat, usually plaid [Ojibwa Indian = turtle].

mack·in·tosh (mak'·in·tàsh) *n.* a waterproof coat [fr. *Charles MacIntosh*, the inventor].

mac·ra·mé (mak'·rą·mā) *n.* a fringe, thread, or cord knotted into a coarse fabric, usu. in decorative designs [Fr., fr. Ar. *miqramah*, a veil].

mac·ro·bi·ot·ic (mak·rō·bī·àt'·ik) *a.* long lived. **macrobiosis** *n.* long life. **macrobiotics** *n.* study of longevity [Gk. *makros*, long; *bios* life].

mac·ro·cosm (mak'·rą·kàzm) *n.* the great universe. **-ic** *a.* [Gk. *makros*, long; *cosmos*, the world].

ma·cron (mā'·kràn) *n.* short line put over vowel to show it is long in quantity or quality, as *fāte* [Gk. *makros*, long].

mac·ro·scop·ic (mak·rą·skàp'·ik) *a.* visible to the naked eye; opp. of *microscopic*. **-ally** *adv.* [Gk. *makros*, long; *skopein*, to see].

mac·u·la (mak'·yą·lą) *n.* a spot. *pl.* **maculae. maculate** *v.t.* to spot. **maculation** *n.* the act of spotting; a spot. **maculose** *a.* spotted [L.].

mad (mad) *a.* (*comp.* **-der;** *superl.* **-dest**) deranged in mind; insane; crazy; frenzied; angry; infatuated; irrational, as a scheme. **-cap** *n.* a rash person; *a.* uncontrolled. **-den** *v.t.* to enrage; to drive mad; to annoy; *v.i.* to behave as a madman. **-dening** *a.* **-ly** *adv.* **-house** *n.* an asylum for patients with mental disorders; a place of confusion. **-man** *n.* a lunatic. **-ness** *n.* insanity; anger [O.E. *gemaed*, foolish].

mad·am (mad'·ąm) *n.* a formal mode of address in speaking to a married or elderly woman. **madame** (mą·dam') *n.* French form. *pl.* **mesdames** (mā·dàm') [O.Fr. *ma dame*, my lady].

Ma·dei·ra (mą·dir'·ą) *n.* a rich amber-colored wine from *Madeira*, Port.

ma·de·moi·selle (mad·ą·mą·zel') *n.* French mode of addressing unmarried lady [Fr.].

Ma·don·na (mą·dàn'·ą) *n.* the Virgin Mary; a statue of the Virgin [It. *mia*, my; *donna*, a lady].

mad·ras (mad'·rąs) *n.* a fine cotton cloth,usu. striped or plaid [fr. *Madras*, India].

mad·re·pore (mad'·rą·pōr) *n.* white perforate coral [It. *madre*, a mother; L. *porus*, a pore].

mad·ri·gal (mad·ri·gąl) *n.* a short love poem; an unaccompanied part-song, usually syncopated in rhythm, popular in 16th and 17th cents.

mael·strom (māl'·strąm) *n.* a whirlpool; (*Fig.*) menacing state of affairs [Dut. = a whirlpool].

ma·es·to·so (mī·stō'·sō) *a.* and *adv.* (*Mus.*) with dignity [It.].

maes·tro (mīs'·trō) *n.* master, esp. an eminent composer, conductor, or teacher of music [It.].

Mae West (mā·west) *n.* an inflatable life-jacket [fr. *Mae West*, film star].

ma·fi·a (mà'·fi·a) *n.* a criminal Sicilian secret society; hostility to the law. Also **maffia** [It.].

mag·a·zine (mag'·ą·zēn) *n* a military storehouse; part of a ship where ammunition is stored; compartment in a rifle holding the cartridges; a periodical containing miscellaneous articles [Fr. *magasin*, a warehouse].

ma·gen·ta (mą·jen'·tą) *n.* a purplish dye from coal tar [discovery in *Magenta*, It.].

mag·got (mag'·ąt) *n.* a grub; larva of a house-fly; (*Fig.*) a whim [M.E. *maddok*, a flesh worm].

Ma·gi (mā'·jī) *n.pl.* a class of priests among the ancient Persians; in the N.T. the Wise Men who came to visit the infant Jesus [Gk. *magos*, a magician].

mag·ic (maj'·ik) *n.* the feigned art of influencing nature or future events by occult means; sorcery; charm. **-al** *a.* **-ally** *adv.* **-ian** (mą·jish'·ąn) *n.* one skilled in magic; a conjurer. **— lantern,** early form of projector using slides. **black magic,** magic by aid of evil spirits [Gk. *magikos*].

mag·is·te·ri·al (maj·ąs·tir'·i·ąl) *a.* pert. to or conducted by a magistrate; authoritative; judicial; overbearing. **-ly** *adv.* [L. *magister*].

mag·is·trate (maj'·ąs·trāt) *n.* a person vested with public judicial authority; a justice of the peace. **magistracy** *n.* the position of a magistrate; the body of magistrates [L. *magistratus*].

mag·ma (mag'·mą) *n.* a paste of mineral or organic matter; (*Geol.*) the molten rock beneath the earth's crust; (*Pharm.*) a salve [Gk. to knead].

Mag·na Car·ta (Charta) (mag′·nạ kȧr′·tạ) *n.* Great Charter of English public and private liberties signed by King John, 1215 (L.)].

mag·na·nim·i·ty (mag·nạ·nim′·ạ·ti·) *n.* greatness of mind; generosity of heart esp. in forgiveness. **magnanimous** *a.* **magnanimously** *adv.* [L. *magnus*, great; *animus*, the mind].

mag·nate (mag′·nāt, -net) *n.* an eminent person, esp. a wealthy business man [L. *magnus*, great].

mag·ne·si·um (mag·nē′·zē·ạm, -zhạm) *n.* the silvery-white metallic base of magnesia, burning with an intensely brilliant white light and used for fireworks, flash bulbs, etc. [Gk. *Magnesia* (lithos), magnesian stone].

mag·net (mag′·nạt) *n.* the loadstone; a bar of iron having property of attracting iron or steel and, when suspended, of pointing N. and S.; a person or thing with powers of attraction. **-ic, (al)** *a.* pert. to a magnet; attractive. **-ically** *adv.* **-ist** *n.* an expert in magnetism. **-izable** *a.* **-ization** *n.* **-ize** *v.t.* to give magnetic properties to; to attract; *v.i.* to become magnetic. **-ism** *n.* the natural cause of magnetic force; the science of the phenomena of magnetic force; attraction. **magneto** *n.* a magnetoelectric machine, esp. used to generate ignition spark in internal-combustion engine. **magnetic field,** the sphere of influence of magnetic forces. **magnetic needle,** a small magnetized pivoted steel bar of a compass which always points approximately north. **magnetic north,** the north as indicated by the pivoted bar of the mariner's compass. **magnetic poles,** two nearly opposite points on the earth's surface [Gk. *magnētis* (lithos), a magnet].

mag·ni·fy (mag′·nạ·fī) *v.t.* to make greater; to cause to appear greater. **Magnificat** *n.* the song of the Virgin Mary. **magnification** *n.* the act of magnifying. **magnificent** *a.* splendid; brilliant;. **magnificence** *n.* **magnificently** *adv.* **magnifico** *n.* a Venetian nobleman; person of importance. **magnified** *n.* one who or the instrument which magnifies [L. *magnus*, great; *facere*, to make].

mag·nil·o·quent (mag·nil′·ạ·kwạnt) *a.* speaking pompously; boastful. **magniloquence** *n.* [L. *magnus*, great; *loqui*, to speak].

mag·ni·tude (mag′·nạ·tūd) *n.* greatness; size; importance [L. *magnitudo*, greatness].

mag·no·li·a (mag·nō′·li·ạ) *n.* a species of tree bearing large perfumed flowers [fr. *Magnol*, French botanist].

mag·num (mag′·nạm) *n.* a wine-bottle holding two quarts. **— opus** *n.* one's best artistic or literary work [L. *magnus*, great].

mag·pie (mȧg′·pī) *n.* a bird of the crow family, with a harsh chattering cry; an idle chatterer [contr. of *Margaret* and *pie*].

Mag·yar (mag′·yȧr) *n.* dominant people of Hungary; the language of Hungary.

ma·ha·ra·jah (mȧ·hạ·rȧ′·jạ) *n.* (*fem.* **maharani** or **maharanee**) the title of an Indian prince [Sans. *maha*, great; *raja*, a prince].

ma·hat·ma (mạ·hȧt′·mạ) *n.* a man of saintly life with supernatural powers derived from purity of soul [Sans. *mahatma*, high-souled].

mah·jong (mȧ·jȧng′) *n.* old Chinese game for four played with small tiles [Chin.].

ma·hog·a·ny (mạ·hȧg′·a·ni·) *n.* a tree of hard, reddish wood used for furniture; the red-brown color of mahogany [W. Ind.].

maid (mād) *n.* a girl or unmarried woman; a female domestic servant. **old maid,** a spinster; a game of cards. **-en,** *n.* a maid; *a.* pert. to a maid; unmarried; unused; first. **-enhair** *n.* a kind of fern with delicate fronds. **-enhood,** *n.* virginity; purity. **-enliness** *n.* **-enly** *a.* gentle; modest. **-en name,** surname of a woman before marriage [O.E. *maegden*, a maid].

mail (māl) *n.* defensive armor composed of steel rings or plates; *v.t.* to clothe in armor [O.Fr. *maille*, mail].

mail (māl) *n.* letters, packages, etc., carried by post; the person or means of conveyance for transit of letters, parcels, etc.; *v.t.* to post; to send by mail. **-bag** *n.* the sack in which letters are put for transit. **-boat, -car, -plane, -train, -man** *n.* means of conveyance of letters [O.Fr. *male*, a trunk or mail].

maim (mām) *v.t.* to deprive of the use of a limb; to disable; to disfigure. **-er** *n.* [O.Fr. *mahaing*, a bruise].

main (mān) *a.* principal; first in size, importance, etc.; sheer; *n.* the chief part; strength, as in *might and main*; (*Poet.*) the open sea or ocean or the mainland; the principal pipe or line in water, gas, or electricity system. **-land** *n.* a continent as distinct from islands. **-ly** *adv.* **-spring** *n.* the principal spring in a watch or other mechanism; motive power. **-stay** *n.* the chief support [O.E. *maegen*, main].

main·tain (mān·tān′) *v.t.* and *v.i.* to hold or keep in any state; to sustain; to preserve; to defend, as an argument; to support. **-able** *a.* **-er** *n.* **maintenance** *n.* the act of maintaining; means of support [Fr. *maintenir*, to hold].

maize (māz) *n.* Indian corn, a cereal; yellow [Sp. *maiz*].

maj·es·ty (maj′·ạs·ti·) *n.* grandeur; exalted dignity; royal state; the title of a sovereign. **majestic, -al** *a.* [L. *majestas*, dignity].

ma·jol·i·ca (mạ′·jạl′·i·kạ) *n.* a decorative, enameled pottery [fr. *Majorca*].

ma·jor (mā′·jẹr) *a.* greater in number, quality, quantity, or extent; (*Mus.*) greater by a semitone; pert. to a field of study; *n.* a person who has reached the age of 21; an officer in the army ranking below a lieutenant-colonel; a principal field of study. *v.i.* to specialize. **—domo** *n.* a steward; (*Colloq.*) an organizer. **— general** *n.* an army officer in rank below a lieutenant-general. **majority** *n.* the greater part; more than half; full legal age (21) [L. *major*, greater].

make (māk) *v.t.* to cause to be or do; to create; to constitute; to compel; to appoint; to secure; to arrive at; to reckon; to perform; *v.i.* to go; to start; *pa.t.* and *pa.p.* **made.** *n.* structure; texture; form; style; brand. **—believe** *n.* pretense; *v.i.* to pretend. **-r** *n.* **Maker** *n.* God. **-shift** *n.* a temporary expedient. **-up** *n.* arrangement or layout of a printed page, magazine, etc.; cosmetics; nature; a making up for [O.E. *macian*, to make].

mal·a·chite (mal′·ạ·kīt) *n.* a green carbonate of copper, used for inlaid work [Gk. *malachē*, mallow].

mal·ad·just·ment (mal·ạ·just′·mạnt) *n.* faulty adjustment; inability to adjust to one's environment.

mal·ad·min·is·tra·tion (mal·ạd·min·ạ·strā′·shạn) *n.* faulty administration, esp. of public affairs.

mal·a·droit (mal·ạ·droit′) *a.* clumsy; awkward. **-ness** *n.*

mal·a·dy (mal′·ạ·di·) *n.* a disease; ailment.

mal de mer, seasickness [Fr. *malade*, sick].

Mal·a·gas·y (mal·ạ·gas′·i·) *n.* a native of, or the language of, Madagascar; *a.*

ma·laise (ma·lāz′) *n.* a physical discomfort [[Fr.].

mal·a·prop(ism) (mal′·ạ·prȧp·(izm) *n.* the ludicrous misuse of a word [Fr. *mal à propos*, ill-suited].

ma·lar·i·a (mạ·lar′·i·ạ) *n.* a febrile disease transmitted by the bite of mosquito; **malarious** *a.* [It. *malaria*, bad air].

Ma·lay (mā′·lā) *n.* a native of the Malay Peninsula; *a.* Also **Malayan.**

mal·con·tent (mal′·kạn·tent) *a.* discontented; rebellious. **-ed** *a.* **-edly** *adv.* **-edness** *n.*

male (māl) *a.* pert. to the sex which begets young; masculine; (*Bot.*) having stamens; *n.* a male animal [L. *masculus*, male].
mal·e·dic·tion (mal·ạ·dik′·shàn) *n.* evil-speaking; a curse. **maledictory** *a.* slander [L. *male*, badly; *dicere*, to speak].
mal·e·fac·tor (mal′·ạ·faktẹr) *n.* an evil-doer; a criminal. **malefaction** *n.* a crime [L. *male*, badly; *facere*, to do].
ma·lev·o·lent (ma·lev′·ạ·lạnt) *a.* evilly disposed; malicious. **malevolence** *n.* ill will; malice. **-ly** *adv.* [L. *male*, badly; *velle*, to wish].
mal·fea·sance (mal·fē′·zans) *n.* misconduct, esp. in public affairs [Fr.].
mal·for·ma·tion (mal·fawr·mā′·shạn) *n.* irregular formation. **malformed** *a.* deformed.
mal·func·tion (mal·fungk′·shạn) *v.i.* to fail to operate correctly or normally [L. *male*, badly; L. *functio*].
mal·ic (mā′·lik) *a.* from the apple [L. *malum*, apple].
mal·ice (mal′·is) *n.* ill will; spite; desire to injure others; (*Law*) criminal intention. **malicious** *a.* spiteful; showing malice. **maliciously** *adv.* **maliciousness** *n.* **with malice aforethought** (*Law*) with deliberate criminal intention [L. *malitia*, ill-will].
ma·lign (mạ·lin′) *a.* malicious; evil; spiteful; *v.t.* to slander; to vilify. **malignance, malignancy** *n.* **malignant** *a.* being evilly disposed; harmful; (of disease) virulent; likely to prove fatal. **malignantly** *adv.* **-er** *n.* **malignity** *n.* [L. *malignus*, ill-disposed].
ma·lin·ger (mạ·ling′·gẹr) *v.i.* to feign illness in order to avoid duty. **-er** *n.* a shirker [Fr. *malingre*, ailing].
mall (mawl) *n.* a level, shaded walk; a heavy mallet used in game of pall-mall (var. of *maul*) L. *malleus*, a hammer].
mal·lard (mal′·ẹrd) *n.* a wild drake or duck.
mal·le·a·ble (mal′·i·ạ·bl) *a.* capable of being hammered or extended by beating; amenable; tractable. **malleability** *n.* **malleate** *v.t.* to hammer; to draw into a plate or leaf by beating. **malleation** *n.* [L. *malleus*, a hammer].
mal·let (mal′·ạt) *n.* any of various types of wooden hammer [Fr. *maillet*, a small hammer].
mal·low (mal′·ō) *n.* plant with downy leaves, and having emollent properties [L. *malva*].
mal·nu·tri·tion (mal·nū·tri′·shạn) *n.* the state of being undernourished.
mal·o·dor·ous (mal·ō′·dẹr·ạs) *a.* having an offensive odor. **malodor** *n.*
mal·prac·tice (mal·prak′·tis) *n.* professional impropriety or negligence.
malt (mawlt) *n.* barley or other grain steeped in water till it germinates, then dried in a kiln for use in brewing; *v.t.* to make into malt; *v.i.* to become malt. **-ed milk** *n.* a powder of malted grains and dried milk; a drink made by mixing this with milk and ice cream. **— extract** *n.* a medicinal body-building food. **— liquor,** a liquor made from malt by fermentation and not by distillation, as beer, stout, ale. **-ose** *n.* a sugar produced by the action of malt on starch [O.E.].
Mal·tese (mawl′·tēz) *n.* a native of *Malta*; its dialect and people.
mal·treat (mal·trēt′) *v.t.* to ill-treat; to abuse; to handle roughly. **-ment** *n.*
mal·ver·sa·tion (mal·vẹr·sā′·shạn) *n.* corruption in office; fraudulent handling of public funds [L. *male*, ill; *versari*, to be engaged in].
mam·bo (mȧm′·bō) *n.* rhythmic music and dance of Sp. Amer. origin.
mam·ba (mȧm′·bạ) *n.* a poisonous snake of Africa [Kaffir].
mam·ma (mam′·a) *n.* child's name for mother [imit.].
mam·ma (mam′·ạ·) *n.* milk-secreting gland in females. *pl.* **mammae. mammary** *a.* [L. the breast].
Mam·ma·li·a (ma·ma′·li·ạ) *n.pl.* (*Zool.*) the class of mammals or animals which suckle their young. **mammal** *n.* one of the *Mammalia*. **-n** *a.* [L. *mamma*, the breast].
mam·mon (mam′·ạn) *n.* wealth personified and worshipped [Syrian *mamon*, wealth].
mam·moth (mam′·ạth) *n.* a huge extinct elephant; *a.* colossal [Russ. *mammant*].
mam·my (mam′·i·) *n.* a Negro woman who took care of white children in the South; Mother: a child's word [Dial.].
man (man) *n.* a human being; an adult male; a manly person; a male servant; a husband; the human race; a piece used in such games as chess, checkers, etc. *pl.* **men.** *v.t.* to furnish with men; to fortify; *pr.p.* **-ning.** *pa.t.* and *pa.p.* **-ned. —eater,** a cannibal; a tiger, etc.; a shark. **-ful** *a.* vigorous; sturdy. **-fully** *adv.* **-fulness** *n.* **-hole** *n.* an opening large enough to admit a man leading to a drain, sewer, etc. **-hood** *n.* the state of being a man; courage. **—hour** *n.* work performed by one man in one hour. **-kind** *n.* human beings. **-liness** *n.* **-ly** *a.* bold; resolute; dignified; not effeminate; masculine. **-nish** *a.* like a man. **-nishly** *adv.* **-nishness** *n.* **—of-war,** a warship. **—power** *n.* a unit of power equal to one-eighth of a horsepower; the total number of people in industry, the armed forces, etc. **-servant** *n.* a male servant. **-slaughter** *n.* culpable homicide without malice aforethought. **man in the street,** average man [O.E. *mann*].
man·a·cle (man′·ạ·kl) *n.* a handcuff; *v.t.* to fetter with handcuffs [O.Fr. *manicle*].
man·age (man′·ij) *v.t.* to direct; to control; to carry on; to cope with; *v.i.* to direct affairs; to succeed. **-ability** *n.* **-able** *a.* capable of being managed. **-ment** *n.* the act of managing; administration; body of directors controlling a business. **-r** *n.* one who manages: one in charge. **managerial** *a.* [L. *manus*, the hand].
Man·chu (man′·chȯȯ) *n.* one of the original inhabitants of Manchuria; *a.* of Manchuria [Chin.].
man·ci·ple (man′·si·pl) *n.* a steward; a caterer [L. *manceps*, a purchaser].
man·da·mus (man·dā′·mus) *n.* a written order [L., we command].
man·da·rin (man′·dạ·rin) *n.* a European name for a Chinese provincial governor; the language used in Chinese official circles; a small orange; a long brocade coat with loose sleeves [Port. *mandarin*].
man·date (man′·dāt) *n.* an official order; a precept; a prescript of the Pope; a commission to act as representative of a body of people. **mandatary** *n.* one to whom a mandate is given by a **mandator. -d** *a.* committed to a mandate, as *mandated territories.* **mandatory** *a.* containing a mandate; obligatory [L. *mandatum*, an order].
man·di·ble (man′·di·bl) *n.* a jaw; in vertebrates, the lower jaw; in birds, the upper or lower beak. **mandibular** *a.* [L. *mandibula*].
man·do·lin (man′·dạ·lin) *n.* a musical instrument with a rounded pear-shaped body [It. *mandola*, a lute].
man·drake (man′·drāk) *n.* a narcotic plant, the root thought to resemble human form [M.E. *mandragge*].
man·drel (man′·drel) *n.* a shaft on which objects may be fixed for turning, milling, etc.; the spindle of a lathe. Also **mandril.**
man·drill (man′·dril) *n.* a large African baboon [Fr.].
mane (mān) *n.* long hair on the neck of an animal [O.E. *manu*, neck].
ma·nège (ma·nezh′) *n.* the art of horsemanship; a riding-school [Fr.].
ma·neu·ver (mạ·nȯȯ′·vẹr) *n.* a controlled strategic movement; scheme; artiface. *pl.* peacetime exercises of troops; *v.t.* to direct skillfully; **-able** *a.* **-ability** *n.* **-er** *n.* [Fr. fr. L. to work by hand].
man·ga·nese (mang′·gạ·nēz) *n.* a greyish, hard, brittle metal which oxidizes rapidly in

humid atmosphere [O.Fr. *manganese*].

mange (mānj) *n.* a parasitic disease affecting the skin of animals causing hair to fall out. **manginess** *n.* **mangy** *a.* [O.Fr. *manjue*, itch].

man·ger (mān′·jẹr) *n.* a trough for holding fodder for cattle [Fr. *manger*, to eat].

man·gle (mang′·gl) *n.* a machine for pressing linen between rollers; *v.t.* to smooth with a mangle. **-r** *n.* [Dut. *mangel*].

man·gle (mang′·gl) *v.t.* to hack; to mutilate; to spoil the beauty of [prob. O.Fr. *mahaigner*, to maim].

man·go (mang′·gō) *n.* a tropical tree, the unripe fruit used in making chutney [Malay, *mangga*].

man·grove (man′·grōv) *n.* a tropical tree the bark of which is used in tanning [Malay, *mangri* + *grove*].

man·han·dle (man′·han·dl) *v.* to handle roughly.

man·hat·tan (man·hat′·n) *n.* a cocktail containing whisky, vermouth, bitters [Amer].

ma·ni·a (mā′·ni·a) *n.* madness; a violent excitement; extravagant enthusiasm; an obsession. **maniac** *n.* a madman; *a.* raving; frenzied. **maniacal** *a.* [Gk.].

man·i·cure (man′·ạ·kyoor) *n.* the care of the hands and nails. **manicurist** *n.* one who gives this treatment; *v.t.* to file, and polish the nails [L. *manus*, the hand; *cura*, care].

man·i·fest (man′·ạ·fest) *a.* clearly visible; apparent to the mind or senses; *v.t.* to make clear; to reveal; *n.* a detailed list of goods transported. **-able, -ible** *a.* capable of being clearly revealed. **-ation** *n.* the act of revealing; the state of being revealed; display; disclosure. **-ly** *adv.* obviously. **manifesto** *n.* a public declaration of the principles or policy of a leader or party; *pl.* **manifestoes** [L. *manifestus*, clear].

man·i·fold (man′·ạ·fōld) *a.* many and varied; numerous; *v.t.* to make many copies of, as letters, by a machine, such as a duplicator; *n.* something with many parts; (*Mech.*) a pipe fitted with several lateral outlets [fr. *many* and *fold*].

man·i·kin (man′·ạ·kin) *n.* a little man; a dwarf; a model of the human body used in medical schools; a mannequin. Also **manakin** [Dut. *mannekin*, a double dim. of **man**].

ma·nil·a (mạ·nil′·ạ) *n.* a cigar made in *Manila*, capital of the Philippine Islands. **— hemp,** a fiber used for making ropes, twine, sails, etc. **— paper,** a stout buff-coolred paper

man·i·ple (man′·ạ·pl) *n.* part of a Roman legion; a scarf worn by celebrant at mass. **manipular** *a.* [L. *manipulus*, a handful].

ma·nip·u·late (mạ·nip′·yoo·lāt) *v.t.* to operate with the hands; to manage (a person) in a skillful, esp. unscrupulous way; to falsify; *v.i.* to use the hands. **manipulation** *n.* **manipular, manipulative, manipulatory** *a.* **manipulator** *n.* [L. *manipulus*, a handful].

man·na (man′·ạ) *n.* the food supplied miraculously to the Israelites in the wilderness; sweetish juice of the ash; spiritual nourishment; [Heb. *man*, a gift].

man·ne·quin (man′·ạ·kin) *n.* one employed to model new fashions; figure for a similar purpose. Also **manequin, manikin** [Fr. *mannequin*, a puppet].

man·ner (man′·ẹr) *n.* way of doing anything; custom; style; a person's habitual bearing; *pl.* social behavior; customs. **-ed** *a.* having manners (in compound *well-mannered*). **-ism** *n.* a personal peculiarity of bearing, speech, or style of expression; affection. **-liness** *n.* politeness; decorum. **-ly** *a.* having good manners; courteous; civil; respectful; *adv.* civilly; respectfully. **to the manner born,** having natural talent for special work or position [Fr. *manière*, manner].

man·or (man′·ẹr) *n.* (*Brit.*) the land belonging to a lord; a unit of land in feudal times over which the owner had full jurisdiction [O.Fr. *manoir*, a dwelling].

man·sard roof (man′·sȧrd ro͝of) *n.* roof in which lower slope is nearly vertical and upper much inclined (fr. F. *Mansard*, Fr. arcritect].

manse (mans) *n.* a minister's residence [L.L. *mansa*, a dwelling].

man·sion (man′·shạn) *n.* a large, imposing house; a manor house [L. *manere*, to remain].

man·sue·tude (man′·swạ·to͝od) *n.* gentleness; tameness [L. *manus*, a hand; *suescere*, to accustom].

man·tel (man′·tl) *n.* the shelf above a fireplace; the framework around a fireplace. **-piece** *n.* the shelf [form of *mantle*].

man·til·la (man·til′·ạ) *n.* a veil covering head and shoulders, worn by Spanish women; a short cape [dim. of Sp. *mante*, a cloak].

man·tis (man′·tis) *n.* a genus of insects holding the forelegs folded as if praying [Gk. *mantis*, a prophet].

man·tis·sa (man·tis′·ạ) *n.* the decimal part of a logarithm [L. *mantissa*, a makeweight].

man·tle (man′·tl) *n.* a loose outer garment; a cloak; a covering; *v.t.* to cover; to hide; *v.i.* to form a covering; to suffuse; to flush. **mantlet** *n.* (*Mil.*) a bullet-proof shelter [L. *mantellum*, a cloak].

man·tu·a (man′·choo·ạ) *n.* a woman's loose gown [Fr. *manteau*].

man·u·al (man′·yoo·ạl) *a.* pert. to, made by or done with the hand; *n.* a handbook or small textbook; a keyboard of a pipe-organ. **-ly** *adv.* [L. *manus*, the hand].

man·u·fac·ture (man·yạ·fak·chẹr) *n.* making goods either by hand or by machine (esp. mass-production; anything produced from raw materials; *v.t.* to make from raw materials; to fabricate; *v.i.* to be engaged in manufacture. **manufactory** *n.* a factory. **-r** *n.* [L. *manus*, the hand; *facere*, to make].

man·u·mit (man·yạ·mit′) *v.t.* to give freedom to a slave; to emancipate. *pr.p.* **-ting.** *pa.p., pa.t.* **-ted. manumission** *n.* [L. *manumittere*, to send from one's hand].

ma·nure (mạ·noor′) *v.t.* to enrich soil with fertilizer; *n.* animal excrement used as fertilizer [contr. of Fr. *manoeuvrer*, to work with the hands].

man·u·script (man′·yạ·skript) *a.* written, or typed, by hand; *n.* a book written by hand; an author's script or typewritten copy for perusal by publisher [L. *manus*, hand; *scribere, scriptum*, to write].

man·y (men′·i·) *a.* comprising a great number (*comp.* **more;** *superl.* **most**); *n. pro.* a number of people or things. **-sided** *a.* talented [O.E. *manig*, many].

map (map) *n.* a representation, esp. on a plane surface, of the features of the earth, or of part of it; a chart of the heavens; a plan or delineation; *v.t.* to draw a map of; to fill in details in a blank map; to plan; *pr.p.* **-ping.** *pa.t.* and *pa.p.* **-ped** [L. *mappa*, a napkin].

ma·ple (mā′·pl) *n.* a deciduous tree, valuable for its timber and the sap from which sugar is extracted [O.E. *mapultreow*, the maple tree].

mar (mȧr) *v.t.* to injure; to impair; to disfigure. *pr.p.* **-ring.** *pa.p.* **-red** [O.E. *merran*, to hinder].

mar·a·bou (mar′·ạ·bo͝o) *n.* a kind of stork; the feathers of this bird used as trimming.

ma·ra·ca (ma·rȧ′·kạ) *n.* gourd shaped rattle [Braz.].

mar·a·schi·no (mar·ạ·skē′·nō) *n.* a sweet liqueur distilled from cherries [It. *amarasca*, a sour cherry].

mar·a·thon (mar′·ạ·thȧn) *n.* a foot race (approx. 26 miles); endurance contest [Gk. Myth. runner, *Marathon to Athens*}].

ma·raud (mạ·rawd′) *v.i.* to rove in quest of plunder; to loot. **-er** *n.* **-ing** *n.* and *a.* [O.Fr. *marauder*, to play the rogue].

mar·ble (mȧr′·bl) *n.* hard limestone which takes on a brilliant polish and is used for ornaments, statuary, etc.; a little ball of marble, glass, etc., used in games; *a.* made of marble; cold; insensible; *v.t.* to color like streaked marble. **-ed** *a.* veined like marble. **marbly** *a.* **-ize,** *v.t.* make like marble [Gk. *marmairein*, to sparkle].

mar·ca·site (mȧr′·kạ·sīt) *n.* white iron pyrite used in jewelry because of its brilliance [Fr.].

mar·cel (mȧr·sel′) *n.* an artificial hair wave. **-led** *a.* [fr. *Marcel*, the inventor].

March (mȧrch) *n.* third month of year, named after *Mars*, Roman god of war.

march (mȧrch) *n.* a border; a frontier; *pl.* [O.E. *mearc*, mark].

march (mȧrch) *v.i.* to move in order, as soldiers; to proceed at a steady pace; *v.t.* to cause to move in military array; *n.* distance marched; a musical composition to accompany a march; steady advance, as the *march of time*. **-er** *n.* [Fr. *marcher*, to walk].

mar·chion·ess (mȧr′·shạn·is) *n.* the wife of a marquis; lady, holding in her own right, the rank of marquis [L.L. *marchionissa*, fem. of *marchio*, ruler of the march].

march·pane See **marzipan.**

mare (mer) *n.* the female of the horse, mule, donkey, etc. [O.E. *merc*, fem. of *mearh*, a horse].

mar·ga·rine (mȧr′·jạ·rạn) *n.* pearly wax-like substance obtained from animal fat; a fatty extract of certain vegetable oils; a butter substitute made from vegetable oils or animal fats [Gk. *margaron*, a pearl].

mar·gin (mar′·jạn) *n.* a border; a blank space at top, bottom and sides, of a written or printed page; allowance made for contingencies; *v.t.* to provide with margin; to enter in the margin. **-al** *a.* pert. to a margin; entered in the margin. **-alia** *n.pl.* notes jotted in the margin. **-al** *a.* **-ally** *adv.* **-ate, -d** *a.* [L. *margo*, the edge].

mar·gue·rite (mȧr′·gạ·rēt) *n.* a large ox-eye daisy [L. *margarita*, a pearl].

mar·i·gold (mar′·ạ·gōld) *n.* name applied to a plant bearing yellow or orange flowers [prob. fr. Virgin *Mary* and *gold*].

ma·ri·jua·na (mạr·ạ·hwȧ′·nạ) *n.* a type of hemp dried and used as tobacco, having a narcotic effect [Sp.].

ma·rim·ba (mạ·rim′·bạ) *n.* a jazz-band instrument resembling the xylophone [Afr.].

ma·ri·na (mạ·rē′·nạ) *n.* a small harbor or boat basin [L. *marinus*, the sea]

mar·i·nade (mar·ạ·nād′) *n.* a seasoned vinegar or wine used for steeping meat, fish, vegetables. *v.t.* to marinate. **marinate** *v.t.* to let food stand in a marinade [Fr. *mariner*, pickle in brine].

ma·rine (mạ·rēn′) *a.* pert. to the sea; found in, or near, the sea; pert. to shipping or overseas trade. **-r** (mar′·i·nẹr) *n.* a sailor or seaman [L. *mare*, the sea].

mar·i·o·nette (mar·i·ạ·net′) *n.* a puppet worked by strings [Fr. dim. of *Marion*].

mar·i·tal (mar′·ạ·tạl) *a.* pert. to a husband or to marriage [L. *maritus*, married].

mar·i·time (mar′·ạ·tīm) *a.* pert. to the sea; bordering on the sea; living near the sea; pert. to overseas trade or navigation [L. *maritimus*, fr. *mare*, the sea].

mar·jo·ram (mȧr′·jạ·rạm) *n.* an aromatic plant of the mint family used in cookery.

mark (mȧrk) *n.* a visible sign; a cross; a character made by one who cannot write; a stamp; a proof; a target; a point; an attainable standard; a numerical assessment of proficiency, as in an examination; a flaw or disfigurement; a peculiarity or distinguishing feature; (*Running*) starting post; indication of position, depth, etc. *v.t.* to make a sign upon; to stamp or engrave; to notice; to assess, as an examination paper; *v.i.* to observe particularly. **-ed** *a.* outstanding; notorious. **-edly** *adv.* noticeably. **-er** *n.* **-ing** *n.* design of marks. **-sman** *n.* one who is expert at hitting a target. **-smanship** *n.* shooting skill. **-up** *n.* the amount added to the cost of an article in determining the selling price. **beside the —,** irrelevant. **easy —** *n.* (*Colloq.*) a dupe; a gull. **to make one's —,** to achieve success [O.E. *mearc*, a boundary].

mark (mȧrk) *n.* unit of exchange of various countries [O.E. *marc*].

mar·ket (mȧr′·kit) *n.* a public meeting place for the purchase and sale of commodities; a trading-center; demand; country or geographical area regarded as a buyer of goods; price or value at a stated time; *v.i.* to buy or sell; *v.t.* to produce for sale in a market. **-able** *a.* suitable for selling. **-ably** *adv.* **— place** *n.* **— price** *n.* the current price of a commodity [L. *mercatus*, trade].

marl (mȧrl) *n.* a crumbly soil used for fertilizer and in brick making; *v.t.* to manure with marl. **-y** *a.* [O.Fr. *marle*, marl].

mar·lin (mȧr′·lin) *n.* a large slender deep-sea fish [fr. *marlin*, spike (snout)].

mar·line (mȧr′·lin) *n.* a small rope used to secure a splicing. **-spike** *n.* a pointed tool used to separate strands of a rope in splicing [Dut. *marren*, to bind; *lijn*, a line].

mar·ma·lade (mȧr′·mạ·lād) *n.* a preserve made of the pulp and peel of fruit [Port. *marmelo*, a quince].

mar·mo·set (mȧr′·mạ·set, ·zet) *n.* a small monkey of S. America [Fr. *marmouset*, a small grotesque figure (on fountains)].

mar·mot (mȧr′·mạt) *n.* a bushy-tailed rodent; the prairie dog [Fr. *marmot*, a mountain rat].

ma·roon (mạ·ròòn′) *n.* orig. a fugitive slave of the W. Indies; a marooned person; *v.t.* to put ashore on a desolate island; to isolate, cut off; *v.i.* to live as if marooned [Sp. (*ci*)*marron*, a runaway slave].

ma·roon (mạ·ròòn′) *a.* brownish-crimson; *n.* [Fr. *marron*, a chestnut].

marque (mȧrk) *n.* seizure by way of retaliation. usually **letter of marque** [Fr. fr. Prov. *marcar*, to seize as a pledge].

mar·quee (mȧr·kē′) *n.* a roof-like structure or awning outside a public building [orig. *marquees*, fr. Fr. *marquise*, the tent of a marquis].

mar·que·try (mȧr′·kạ·tri) *n.* decorative, inlaid wood; the process of inlaying wood with designs. Also **marqueterie** [Fr. *marqueter*, to variegate].

mar·quis (mȧr′·kwis, ·kē) *n.* noble ranking next below a duke. Also **marquess** (*fem.* **marchioness**). **marquise** (mȧr·kēz′) *n.* in France, the wife of a marquis; pointed oval diamond [O.Fr. *marchis*, ruler of the marches].

mar·que·sette (mȧr·kwi·zet′, ·ki·zet′) *n.* thin, lightweight fabric.

mar·riage See **marry.**

mar·row (mar′·ō) *n.* the soft substance in the cavities of bones; the essence of anything. **-bone** *n.* a bone containing marrow; *pl.* the knees [O.E. *meary*, marrow].

mar·ry (mar′·i·) *v.t.* to unite, take, or give in wedlock; *v.i.* to enter into matrimony. **marriage** (mar′·ij) *n.* the legal union of husband and wife; the ceremony, civil or religious, by which two people of opposite sex become husband and wife. **-able** *a.* [L. *maritare*, to marry].

Mars (mȧrz) *n.* the Roman god of war; the planet nearest to the earth. **Martian** *n.* an imaginary inhabitant of Mars [L.].

Mar·seil·laise (mȧr·sạ·yez′ or mȧr·sạ·lāz′) *n.* the French national anthem.

marsh (mȧrsh) *n.* a tract of low, swampy land; *a.* pert. to swampy areas. **-fever** *n.* malaria. **-gas** *n.* a gaseous product of decomposing organic matter. **-mallow** *n.* a red flowered plant growing in marshes; a confection made from the root of this, or from gelatin. **-y** *a.* boggy; swampy [O.E. *merisc*, full of meres].

mar·shal (màr′·shạl) *n.* a civil officer of a district with powers of a sheriff; a person in charge of arrangements for ceremonies, etc.; military rank in Fr. and Brit. armed forces. *v.t.* to dispose in order, as troops; (*Fig.*) to arrange, as ideas [O.Fr. *mareschal*, a horse servant].

mar·su·pi·al (màr·sòò′·pi·ạl) *a.* having an external pouch, to carry the young; *n.* a marsupial or pouched animal (opossum, kangaroo) [L. *marsupium*, a pouch].

mart (màrt) *n.* a market [contr. of *market*].

mar·ten (màr′·tạn) *n.* a kind of weasel, valued for its fur [O.Fr. *martre*].

mar·tial (màr′·shạl) *a.* pert. to war or to the armed services; warlike; military. (*Cap.*) *a.* pertaining to Mars. **-ly** *adv.* **— law,** law enforced by military authorities and superseding civil law [L. *Mars*, the god of war].

mar·tin (màr′·tin) *n.* a bird of the swallow family [fr. *Martin*].

mar·ti·net (màr′·tạ·net) *n.* a strict disciplinarian [fr. Fr. officer, *Martinet*].

mar·tin·gale (màr′·tạn·gāl) *n.* a strap fastened to a horse's girth to keep its head down; (*Naut.*) a stay for a jib boom. Also **martingal.**

mar·ti·ni (màr·tē′·ni·) *n.* a cocktail of vermouth, gin and bitters.

mar·tyr (màr′·tẹr) *n.* one who suffers punishment or the sacrifice of his life for adherence to principles or beliefs; a constant sufferer; *v.t.* to put to death for refusal to abandon principles. **-dom** *n.* the suffering and sacrifice of a martyr. **-ology** *n.* a history of martyrs [L. Gk. *martus*, a witness].

mar·vel (màr′·vạl) *n.* anything wonderful; *v.i.* to wonder exceedingly. **-ous** *a.* wonderful; astonishing. **-ously** *adv.* **-ousness** *n.* [O.Fr. *merveille*, a wonder].

Marx·ism (màrk′·sizm) *n.* the doctrines of *Karl Marx*, which profoundly influenced Socialists and communists of Europe in later part of 19th cent. **Marxian, Marxist** *a.* **Marxist** *n.*

mar·zi·pan (màr′·zạ·pan) *n.* a paste of ground almonds, sugar and egg white made into confections. Also **marchpane.**

mas·car·a (mas·ka′·rạ) *n.* a cosmetic preparation for eyelashes.

mas·cot (mas′·kàt) *n.* a person or thing reputed to bring good luck.

mas·cu·line (mas′·kyạ·lin) *a.* male; strong; virile; (of a woman) mannish; (*Gram.*) of male gender. **-ness, masculinity** *n.* [L. *masculus*, male].

mash (mash) *v.t.* to beat to a pulp or soft mass; to mix malt with hot water; *n.* a thick mixture of malt and hot water for brewing; a mixture of bran meal, etc. given to horses and cattle; a pulpy mass [O.E. *masc*, mash].

mash (mash) *v.t.* (*Slang*) to pay court to; to flirt. **-er** *n.* a lady-killer.

mash·ie (mash′·i·) *n.* a golf club with short iron head [prob. corrupt. of Fr. *massue*, a club].

mask (mask) *n.* a covering for the face; an impression of a human face, as a *deathmask;* a respirator to be worn as protection against poison gas; a false face, as worn by children at Hallowe'en; a disguise; a masquerade; (*Fig.*) a pretext; *v.t.* to hide, as with a mask; *v.i.* to assume a disguise [Fr. *masque*].

mas·och·ism (mas′·ạ·kizm) *n.* a form of sex gratification by endurance of physical or mental pain. **masochist** *n.* [fr. *von Sascher-Masoch*, Austrian novelist].

ma·son (mā′·sn) *n.* a builder in stone, brick, etc.; a Freemason. **-ic** *a.* pert. to freemasonry. **-ry** *n.* the work of a mason; stonework; freemasonry [Fr. *maçon*, a mason].

Ma·son·ite (mā·sạn·it) *n.* a fiberboard made from pressed wood fibers used in building [fr. W. H. *Mason*, Amer. engineer; Trademark].

mas·quer·ade (mas·kạ·rād′) *n.* an assembly of masked persons; disguise; *v.i.* to take part in a masquerade; to disguise [Fr. *mascarade*].

mass (mas) *n.* the quantity of matter in a body; a shapeless lump; magnitude; crowd; chief portion; *v.t.* to collect in a mass; *v.i.* to assemble in large numbers. **-ive** *a.* forming a mass; bulky; weighty. **-ively** *adv.* **-iveness** *n.* **— meeting** *n.* a large public meeting or demonstration. **— production** *n.* cheap production in great quantities. **the masses,** the common people [L. *massa*, a lump].

Mass (mas) *n.* the communion service in the R.C. Church; the music to accompany High Mass. **High Mass,** Mass celebrated with music. **Low Mass,** a simple celebration of Mass without music. Also **mass** [O.E. *maesse*, fr. L. *missa*, mass].

mas·sa·cre (mas′·ạ·kẹr) *n.* general, ruthless slaughter; carnage; *v.t.* to slaughter indiscriminately [O.Fr. *maçacre*, slaughter].

mas·sage (mạ·sàzh′) *n.* a treatment of physical disorders by kneading, rubbing, carried out by specialists; *v.t.* to treat by massage. **massagist, masseur** *n.* (*fem.* **masseuse**) a specialist in massage [Fr. fr. Gk. *massein*, to knead].

mas·sive See **mass.**

mast (mast) *n.* upright pole supporting rigging and sails of a ship; *v.t.* to furnish with mast or masts. **-ed** *a.* **-head** *n.* top portion of a ship's mast; newspaper or magazine trademark or business information [O.E. *maest*, the stem of a tree].

mast (mast) *n.* fruit of oak, beech, esp. as food for swine [O.E. *maest*, fodder].

mas·ter (mas′·tẹr) *n.* one who directs and controls; an employer of labor; male head of a household; a ship captain; a graduate degree in arts, or science (*abbrevs.* M.A., M.Sc.); courtesy title given the sons of a family, esp. by servants; an expert; a famous artist, esp. an *old master;* one who organizes and leads a fox hunt, as *master of foxhounds; a.* chief; dominant; skilled; *v.t.* to become the master of; to become expert at; to overcome. **-ful** *a.* compelling; domineering. **-fully** *adv.* **-fulness** *n.* **— key** *n.* a key which opens several locks. **-ly** *a.* highly competent; supremely proficient; *adv.* with the skill of an expert. **-mind** *n.* a first-class mind; chief controlling power behind a scheme. **— of ceremonies** *n.* one who presides over entertainment. **-piece** *n.* a brilliantly executed work. **-stroke** *n.* a masterly action. **— switch** *n.* an electric switch which must be turned on before other switches will function. **-y** *n.* supremacy; action of mastering; consumate skill; victory [L. *magister*, a master].

mas·ti·cate (mas′·tạ·kāt) *v.t.* to chew; to reduce to a pulp. **masticable** *a.* capable of being chewed. **mastication** *n.* the process of chewing. **masticator** *n.* crushing machine [L. *masticare*, to chew].

mas·tiff (mas′·tif) *n.* a powerful breed of dog [O.Fr. *mastin* confused with *mestif*, mongrel].

mas·ti·tis (mas·tī′·tis) *n.* (*Med.*) inflammation of the breast [Gk. *mastos*, the breast].

mas·to·don (mas′·tạ·dàn) *n.* an extinct mammal resembling an elephant. **mastodontic** *a.* [Gk. *mastos*, the breast; *odous*, the tooth].

mas·toid (mas′·toid) *a.* nipple-shaped; *n.* the prominence on the temporal bone behind the human ear. **-itis** *n.* inflammation of the mastoid area [Gk. *mastos*, the breast].

mas·tur·bate (mas′·tẹr·bāt) *v.i.* to practice self-excitation; auto-eroticism. **masturbation** *n.* **masturbator** *n.* [L. *masturbari*].

mat (mat) *n.* a coarse fabric of twin, rope, or rushes for wiping the shoes on; a rug; a heat-resisting covering of cork, plastic, etc., for protecting surface of a table; a border or frame for a picture; a tangled mass of hair; *v.t.* to lay or cover with mats; *v.i.* to become a tangled mass. *pr.p.* **-ting.** *pa.t.* and *pa.p.* **-ted** [L. *matta*, a mat].

mat, matte (mat) *a.* having a dull finish; not shiny [Fr. *mate*].

mat·a·dor, matadore (mat′·ạ·dawr) *n.* the man who kills the bull in a Sp. bullfight [Sp. fr. L. *mactare*, to kill].

match (mach) *n.* splint of wood or taper tipped with a substance capable of ignition by friction with a rough surface; a piece of rope for firing a gun; a fuse [Fr. *mèche*, a wick].

match (mach) *n.* a person or thing equal to or resembling another; a sporting contest; a marriage; a mate; *v.i.* to correspond in quality, quantity, color, etc.; *v.t.* to compete with; to unite in marriage; to be the same as. **-less** *a.* having no match; peerless; unique. **-maker** *n.* one who schemes to bring about a marriage [O.E. *gemaecca*, a mate].

mate (māt) *n.* a companion; a spouse; one of a pair; an assistant; *v.t.* to match; to mar; *v.i.* to pair [O.Dut. *maet*, a companion].

mate (māt) *v.t.* to checkmate (chess); *n.* checkmate [abbrev. of *checkmate*].

ma·té, mate (mȧ′·tā) *n.* an evergreen tree of Brazil and Paraguay, the leaves of which are dried and used as tea [Native *mati*, the vessel for infusing tea].

ma·te·ri·al (ma·ti′·ri·ạl) *a.* consisting of matter corporeal; (of persons) not spiritually minded; essential; appreciable; worthy of consideration; *n.* the substance out of which something is fashioned; fabric; the accumulated data out of which a writer creates a work of literary, historical, or scientific value; materials collective. **-ization** *n.* **ize** *v.t.* to render material; to give bodily form to; *v.i.* to become fact. **-ism** *n.* the theory that matter, and matter only, exists in the universe; an attitude which ignores spiritual values. **-istic, -al** *a.* **-ly** *adv.* appreciably [L. *materia*, matter].

ma·té·ri·el (mạ·tir·i·el′) *n.* weapons, equipment, tools, supplies necessary [Fr. = material].

ma·te·ri·a med·i·ca (mạt·tir′·i·ạ med′·i·kạ) *n.* (*Med.*) the substances used in the making of medicines, drugs, etc.; the science relating to medicines and their curative properties [L.].

ma·ter·nal (mạ·tur′·nạl) *a.* pert. to a mother; motherly; related on the mother's side. **-ly** *adv.* **maternity** *n.* motherhood; childbirth [L. *mater*, a mother].

math·e·mat·ics (math·ạ·mat′·iks) *n.* the science of quantity and space, including arithmetic, algebra, trigonometry, geometry. **mathematical** *a.* pert. to mathematics; accurate. **mathematician** *n.* [Gk. *mathēma*, learning].

mat·in (mat′·in) *n.* a morning song; a morning service [Fr. *matin*, morning].

ma·tri·arch (mā′·tri·ȧrk) *n.* a woman in a position analagous to that of a patriarch. **-al** *a.* **-alism** *n.* government exercised by a mother [L. *mater*, a mother; Gk. *archein*, to rule].

ma·tri·cide (mat′·rạ·sīd) *n.* the murder of a mother; one who kill his own mother [L. *mater*, a mother; *caedere*, to kill].

ma·tric·u·late (mạ·trik′·yạ·lāt) *v.t.* and *i.* to enroll as a student, esp. of a college; to enter, by matriculation. **matriculation** *n.* [L. *matricula*, a register].

mat·ri·mo·ny (mat′·rạ·mō·ni·) *n.* marriage; wedlock. **matrimonial** *a.* [L. *matrimonium*].

ma·trix (mā′·triks or mat′·riks) *n.* the womb; the cavity where anything is formed; a mold, esp. for casting printer's type; rock where minerals are embedded. *pl.* **matrices, -es** [L. *matrix*, the womb].

ma·tron (mā′·trạn) *n.* a married woman; a woman in charge of domestic affairs of an institution. **-like, -ly** *adv.* like a matron; mature; staid [L. *matrona*, a married lady].

matte See **mat.**

mat·ter (mat′·ẹr) *n.* that which occupies space and is the object of the senses; substance; cause of a difficulty; subject of a book, speech, sermon; occasion; (*Med.*) pus; *v.i.* to be of importance; to signify; (*Med.*) to discharge pus. **—of-fact** *a.* prosaic; unimaginative [L. *materia*, matter].

mat·ting (mat′·ing) *n.* mat work; coarse material used as floor covering [fr. *mat*].

mat·tock (mat′·ạk) *n.* a kind of pickaxe with only one end pointed, used for loosening soil [O.E. *mattuc*].

mat·tress (mat′·rạs) *n.* a casing of strong fabric filled with hair, foam rubber, cotton, etc. used on or as a bed [O.E. fr. Ar. *natrah*, a place where anything is thrown].

mat·u·rate (mach′·ạ·rāt) *v.i.* to mature. **maturation** *n.* [L. *maturus*, ripe].

ma·ture (mạ·toor′) *a.* ripe; fully developed; (*Med.*) come to suppuration; resulting from adult experience; due for payment, as a bill; *v.t.* to ripen; to perfect; *v.i.* to become ripe; to become due, as a bill. **maturable** *a.* **-ly** *adv.* **-ness, maturity** *n.* ripeness; the state or quality of being fully developed [L. *maturus*, ripe].

ma·tu·ti·nal (mạ·tòò′·tẹ·nạl) *a.* morning; early. **-ly** *adv.* [L. *matutinus*, of the morning].

maud·lin (mawd′·lin) *a.* over-sentimental; tearful [contr. of O.Fr. *Maudeleine*, Mary Magdalen, painted as weeping].

maul (mawl) *n.* a heavy wooden hammer; *v.t.* to maltreat; to handle roughly. **-er** *n.* [L. *malleus*, a hammer].

Mau Mau (mou′·mou′) *n.* a secret, terrorist society in Kenya.

maun·der (mawn′·dẹr) *v.i.* to mutter; to talk or to wander aimlessly.

mau·so·le·um (maw·sạ·lē′·ạm) *n.* a large imposing tomb. **mausolean** *a.* [orig. the tomb of *Mausolus*, King of Caria, 350 B.C.].

mauve (mōv, mawv) *n.* a delicate purple color; *a.* of this color [Fr. fr. L. *malva*, the mallow].

mav·er·ick (mav′·ẹr·ik) *n.* an unbranded calf; an independent [fr. S. *Maverick*, Texas rancher].

maw (maw) *n.* the stomach of an animal; in birds, the craw [O.E. *maga*, maw].

mawk·ish (mawk′·ish) *a.* loathsome; sickly sweet; maudlin. **-ly** *adv.* [M.E. *mathek*, a maggot]

max·il·lar·y (mak′·sạ·ler·i·) *a.* pert. to the upper jawbone or jaw; *n.* a jawbone. **maxilla** *n.* the upper jaw; *pl.* **maxillae** [L. *maxilla*, a jawbone].

max·im (mak′·sim) *n.* an accepted principle; an axiom; a proverb or precept [L. *maximus*].

max·i·mum (mak′·sạ·mạm) *a.* greatest; *n.* the greatest number, quantity or degree; the highest point; peak; opp. *minimum.* **maximal** *a.* of the greatest value [L. superl. of *magnus*, great].

may (mā) *v.i.* expressing possibility, permission, contingency; uncertainty; hope. *pa.t.* **might** (mīt). **maybe, (mayhap,** *Arch.*) *adv.* perhaps; possibly [O.E. *maeg*, may].

May (mā) *n.* the fifth month of the year; (*Fig.*) youthful prime. **-day** *n.* the first day of May. (*l.c.*)**-flower** *n.* trailing arbutus; any flower blooming in May. **-flower** *n.* the ship in which the Pilgrims sailed to Plymouth, Mass. in 1620. **-fly** *n.* an ephemeral insect; an artificial fly for fishing. **-pole** *n.* a pole with streamers, around which people danced on May Day [L. *Maius*, the month of May].

may·hem (mā′·hem) *n.* (*Law*) the offense of maiming by violence [O.Fr. *mahaigne*, injury].

may·on·naise (mā·a·nāz′) *n.* a sauce or dressing for salads [Fr.].

may·or (mā′·ẹr) *n.* the chief official of a city or town. **-al** *a.* **-alty, -ship** *n.* the office of mayor [Fr. *maire*, mayor].

maze (māz) *n.* a network of intricate paths; a labyrinth; confused condition; mental perplexity [M.E. *masen*, to confuse].

ma·zur·ka, ma·zour·ka (mạ·zur′·kạ) *n.* a Polish dance; the music for this [Pol.].

me (mē) *pron.* the objective case of first pers. pronoun, '*I*'.

mead (mēd) *n.* a fermented drink made of honey, yeast and water [O.E. *meodu*].

mead·ow (med′·ō) *n.* a low, level tract of grassland; pasture. **— lark** *n.* a yellow-breasted Amer. songbird. **-y** *a.* [O.E. *mawan*, to mow].

mea·ger (mē′·gẹr) *a.* scanty; having little flesh; gaunt. **-ly** *adv.* **-ness** *n.* [Fr. *maigre*, thin].

meal (mēl) *n.* the food served at one time; a repast [O.E. *mael*, time].

meal (mēl) *n.* edible grain coarsely ground. **-iness** *n.* **— worm** *n.* an insect found in meal. **-y** *a* like meal; powdery; spotty. **-y-mouthed** *a.* apt to mince words; not blunt [O.E. *melo*, meal].

mean (mēn) *a.* humble in rank or birth; sordid; lacking dingity; stingy; malicious; (*Colloq.*) disagreeable; selfish; (*Slang*) skillful. **-ly** *adv.* **-ness** *n.* [O.E. *gemaene*, common].

mean (mēn) *a.* in a middle position; average; *n.* the middlepoint of quantity, rate, position, or degree; *pl.* resources; wealth; agency. **-time,** the interval between two given times. **-time, -while** *adv.* in the intervening time [L. *medius*, the middle].

mean (mēn) *v.t.* to have in view; to intend; to signify; *v.i.* to form in the mind; to be disposed. *pa.t.* and *pa.p.* **meant** (ment). **-ing** *n.* that which is meant; sense; signification; *a.* expressive. **-ingful** *a.* **-ingless** *a.* [O.E. *maenan*, to signify].

me·an·der (mē·an′·dẹr) *v.i.* to flow with a winding course; to saunter aimlessly; *n.* a circuitous stroll; the winding course of a river (usu. *pl.*). **-ing** *a.* winding. **meandrous** *a.* [Gk. *Maiandros*, a winding river of Asia Minor].

mea·sles (mē′·zạlz) *n.* (*Med.*) a highly contagious disease, charatcerized by rash of bright red spots; a disease affecting cattle and pigs caused by tapeworms. **measly** *a.* having measles; (*Fig.*) worthless; skimpy. **German measles,** a disease resembling measles but less severe [Dut. *mazelen*, measles].

meas·ure (mezh′·ẹr) *n.* dimension reckoned by some standard; an instrument for measuring; a vessel of predetermined capacity; a course of action; an act of the legislature; means to an end; (*Mus.*) tempo; the notes between two bars in staff notation; *pl.* (*Geol.*) layers of rock; strata; *v.t.* to ascertain the quantity or dimensions of; to assess; to distribute by measure; *v.i.* to have an ascertained value or extent; to compare favorably with. **measurable** *a.* capable of being measured. **measurably** *adv.* **-d** *a.* of specified measure; uniform; calculated. **-less** *a.* boundless; infinite. **-ment** *n.* dimension, quantity, etc., ascertained by measuring with fixed unit. **-r** *n.* [L. *mensura*, a measure].

meat (mēt) *n.* flesh used as food; food of any kind. **-iness** *n.* **-y** *a.* full of meat; (*Fig.*) pithy; compact with ideas [O.E. *mete*, food].

Mec·ca (mek′·a) *n.* the reputed birthplace of Mohammed; a holy city; (*l.c.*) the focal point for people drawn by common interest.

me·chan·i·cal (mạ·kan′·i·kạl) *a.* pert. to machines, mechanism, or mechanics; produced or operated by machinery; automatic. **mechanic** *n.* one who works with or repairs machines or instruments. **-ly** *adv.* **mechanician** *n.* a machine-maker or repairer. **mechanics** *n.* that branch of applied mathematics which deals with force and motion; the science of machines. **mechanization** *n.* the change to mechanical power. **mechanize** *v.t.* to make mechanical; to equip with machines. **mechanized** *a.* **mechanism** *n.* the structure of a machine; machinery; a piece of machinery; (*Fig.*) technique; the philosophical doctrine that all phenomena of life admit of physiochemical proof. **mechanist** *n.* **mechanistic** *a.* [Gk. *mēchanē*, a contrivance].

med·al (med′·l) *n.* a piece of metal, struck like a coin, as a memento or reward; *v.t.* to decorate with a medal. **-ic** (mạ·dal′·ik) *a.* pert. to medals. **-lion** *n.* a large medal; a metal disk, usually round, with portrait in bas-relief. **-ist** *n.* a maker of medals; one who has been awarded a medal [Fr. *médaille*, a metal disc].

med·dle (med′·l) *v.i.* to interfere officiously; to tamper with. **-r** *n.* **-some** *a.* interfering [L. *miscere*, to mix].

me·di·a (mē′·di·a) *n.* the various agencies of mass communication [L. *medius*, the middle].

me·di·al (mē′·di·ạl) *a.* in, or through, the middle; pert. to a mean or average. **median** *a.* situated in the middle; *n.* (*Geom.*) a line drawn from vertex of a triangle to the middle point of the opposite side [L. *medius*, the middle].

me·di·ate (mē′·di·ạt) *a.* being between two extremes; intervening; depending on an intermediary; not direct; (mē′·di·āte) *v.i.* to interpose between contending parties to effect a reconciliation; *v.t.* to settle by mediation. **mediacy** *n.* **-ly** *adv.* **mediation** *n.* the act of mediating; the steps taken to effect a reconciliation. **mediatize** *v.t.* to annex a small state, still leaving the ruler his title. **mediator** *n.* [L. *medius*, the middle].

med·ic (med′·ik) *n.* a leguminous plant with leaves like clover, used as fodder; (*Colloq.*) a doctor [Gk. *mēdikē* (*poa*), 'Median' grass].

med·i·cal (med′·i·kạl) *a.* pert. to medicine or the art of healing; medicinal. **medicable** *a.* capable of being cured; **-ly** *adv.* **medicament** *n.* any healing remedy. **medicate** *v.t.* to treat with medicine. **medicated** *a.* **medication** *n.* **medicative** *a.* [L. *medicus*, a physician].

Med·i·care, med·i·care (med′·i·ker) *n.* a national program of medical and health insurance for the aged and the needy [fr. *medi*cal and *care*].

med·i·cine (med′·ạ·sin) *n.* any substance used in the treatment of disease; the science of healing and prevention of disease; charm or magic; *v.t.* to administer medicine to. **medicinal** *a.* pert. to medicine; remedial. **medicinally** *adv.* **— man** *n.* a priest of local religions. **medico** *n.* (*Colloq.*) a doctor or medical student [L. *medicus*, a physician].

me·di·e·val, me·di·ae·val (med·i·ē′·vạl) *a.* pert. to or characteristic of the Middle Ages. **medi(a)evalist** *n.* one who makes a special study of the Middle Ages [L. *medius*, middle; *aevum*, an age].

me·di·o·cre (mē′·di·ō·kẹr) *a.* middling; neither good nor bad; second-rate. **mediocrity** *n.* [L. *mediocris*].

med·i·tate (med′·ạ·tāt) *v.t.* to consider thoughtfully; to intend; *v.i.* to ponder, esp. on religious matters. **-d** *a.* planned. **meditation** *n.* the act of meditating; deep thought. **meditative** *a.* given to reflection. **meditatively** *adv.* [L. *meditari*, to consider].

med·i·ter·ran·e·an (med·ạ·tẹr·rā′·ni·ạn) *a.* (of water) encircled by land. **Mediterranean** *a.* pert. to the sea between Europe and Africa, so called because it was regarded as being in the *middle* of the Old World [L. *medius*, the middle; *terra*, the earth].

me·di·um (mē′·di·ạm) *n.* that which is in the middle; a means; an agency; in spiritualism, an intermediary professing to give messages from the dead; in bacteriology, a substance used for cultivation of bacteria; *pl.* **-s, media;** *a.* middle; average; middling [L. *medius*, the middle].

med·ley (med′·li·) *n.* a miscellaneous collection of things; a miscellany [O.Fr. *medler,* to mix].
me·dul·la (mą·dul′·á) *n.* marrow in a bone; inner tissue of a gland; pith of hair or plants. *pl.* **-e.** *a.* comprising or resembling marrow, covered with medullary substance, etc. **medullate(d)** *a.* **medullose** *a.* like pith [L. *medulla,* marrow].
me·du·sa (mę·dòò′·są) *n.* a kind of jellyfish, with tentacles [Gk. *Medousa*].
meed (mēd) *n.* reward; recompense [O.E. *med*].
meek (mēk) *a.* submissive; humble; mild. **-ly** *adv.* **-ness** *n.* [O.E. *meoc,* meek].
meer·schaum (mir′·shąm, ·shawm) *n.* a fine, white clay used for the bowl of tobacco pipes; a pipe of this [Ger. *Meer,* the sea; *Schaum,* foam].
meet (mēt) *a.* fit; suitable. **-ly** *adv.* **-ness** *n.* [O.E. *(ge)maele,* suitable].
meet (mēt) *v.t.* to encounter; to join; to find; to satisfy; to pay, as a debt; to await arrival, as of a train; *v.i.* to converge at a specified point; to combine; to assemble in company. *pa.t.* and *pa.p.* **met.** *n.* an assembly of people, as at a fox-hunt. **-ing** *n.* a coming together, as of roads, rivers; encounter; people gathered together for worship, entertainment, discussion, sport, etc. [O.E. *metan,* to meet].
me·ga- Gr. *prefix* meaning great, mighty.
meg·a·cycle (meg′·ą·sī·kl) *n.* (*Elect.*) one million cycles [Gk. *megas,* great; *kuklos,* a circle].
meg·a·lith (meg′·ą·lith) *n.* a huge stone. **-ic** *a.* pert. to huge ancient stone monuments or circles [Gk. *megas,* great; *lithos,* a stone].
meg·a·lo·ma·ni·a (meg·ą·lą·mā′·ni·ą) *n.* a form of insanity in which the patient has grandiose ideas of his own importance; lust for power. **-c** *n.* [Gk. *megas,* great; *mania,* madness].
meg·a·phone (meg′·ą·fōn) *n.* a large funnel-shaped device to increase the volume of sounds [Gk. *megas,* great; *phōnē,* a sound].
meg·a·ton (meg′·ą·tàn) *n.* a unit for measuring the power of thermonuclear weapons.
meg·ohm (meg′·ōm) *n.* one million ohms [Gk. *megas,* great; and *ohm*].
me·grim (mē′·grim) *n.* a severe headache usu. on one side; *pl.* depression [Gk. *hemi-,* half; *kranion,* the skull].
mei·o·sis (mī·ō′·sis) *n.* (*Rhet.*) a figure of speech which makes a deliberate understatement to achieve emphasis; a form of litotes [Gk. *meiosis,* lessening].
mel·an·chol·y (mel′·ąn·kàl·i·) *n.* depression of spirits; morbidity; *a.* gloomy; depressed; pensive. **melancholia** *n.* morbid state of depression; abnormal introspectiveness bordering on insanity [Gk. *melas,* black; *cholē,* bile].
Mel·a·ne·sian (mel·ą·nē′·shąn) *a.* pert to *Melanesia,* a S. Pacific dark-skinned island group; *n.* a native; the language of Melanesia [Gk. *melas,* black; *nēsos,* island].
mé·lange (mā·lànzh′) *n.* a mixture; a medley [Fr. *mêler,* to mix].
mel·a·nin (mel′·ą·nin) *n.* a black pigment found in the eye, hair and skin. **melanic** *a.* black. **melanism** *n.* an excess of coloring matter in the skin [Gk. *melas,* black].
Mel·ba toast (mel′·bą tōst′) *n.* thin slice of toast.
meld (meld) *v.t.* and *i.* to blend; merge; a combination of cards melded [fr. *melt, weld*].
mê·lée (mā′·lā) *n.* a confused, hand-to-hand fight [Fr. *mêler,* to mix].
mel·io·rate (mēl′·yą·rāt) *v.t.* to improve; *v.i.* to become better. **melioration** *n.* **meliorator** *n.* **meliorism** *n.* the doctrine that the world is capable of improvement [L. *melior,* better].
mel·lif·er·ous (mą·lif′·ęr·ąs) *a.* producing honey. **mellifluence** *n.* a flowing sweetly or smoothly. **mellifluent, mellifluous** *a.* **mellifluently, mellifluously** *adv.* [L. *mel,* honey; *ferre,* to bear].
mel·low (mel′·ō) *a.* soft and ripe; well-matured; genial; jovial; resonant, as a voice; (*Slang*) somewhat intoxicated; *v.t.* to soften; to ripen; *v.i.* to become soft or ripe; to become maturely wise. **-ly** *adv.* **-ness** *n.* [O.E. *meary,* soft].
me·lo·de·on (mą·lō′·di·ąn) *n.* a small hand keyboard organ; a kind of accordion [Gk.].
me·lod·ic. See **melody.**
mel·o·dra·ma (mel·ą·dràm′·a) *n.* a dramatic entertainment, sensational and emotional; a play of romantic sentiment and situation. **-tic** *a.* [Gk. *melos,* a song; *drama,* a play].
mel·o·dy (mel′·ą·di·) *n.* a rhythmical succession of single sounds forming an agreeable musical air; a tune. **melodic** *a.* pert. to melody; melodious. **melodious** *a.* tuneful; pleasing to the ear. **melodiously** *adv.* **melodiousness** *n.* **melodist** *n.* a musical composer or singer [Gk. *melōidia,* a song].
mel·on (mel′·ąn) *n.* a kind of gourd with a sweet, juicy pulp, and a center full of seeds [Gk. *mēlon,* an apple].
melt (melt) *v.t.* to reduce to a liquid state; to dissolve; to soften; to make tender; *v.i.* to become liquid or molten; to blend; to vanish; to become tender. **-down** *n.* (*Nuclear Phys.*) the accidental melting of uranium pellets and/or the rods that contain them, with the risk of releasing immense amounts of radiation. **-ing** *a.* softening; languishing, as looks; tender [O.E. *meltan,* to melt].
mem·ber (mem′·bęr) *n.* a limb, esp. of an animal body; a constituent part of a complex whole; one of a society, group, etc. **-ed** *a.* having limbs. **-ship** *n.* the state of being a member, or one of a group; members collectively [L. *membrum,* a limb].
mem·brane (mem′·brān) *n.* (*Anat.*) a thin, flexible tissue forming or lining an organ of the body; a sheet of parchment. **membranous** *a.* [L. *membrana,* parchment].
me·men·to (mi·men′·tō) *n.* anything which serves as a reminder of a person or event; a souvenir [L. *meminisse,* to remember].
mem·o (mem′·ō) *n.* (*Colloq.*) memorandum.
mem·oir (mem′·wàr) *n.* a short, biographical sketch; a scientific record of personal investigations on a subject. **-s** *n.pl.* reminiscences. **-ist** *n.* [L. *memoria,* memory].
mem·o·ry (mem′·ą·ri·) *n.* the faculty of retaining and recalling knowledge; recollection. **memorabilia** *n.pl.* things worthy of note. **memorable** *a.* noteworthy. **memorably** *adv.* **memorandum** *n.* a note or reminder; (*Law*) a summary of a transaction; in diplomacy, an outline of the state of a question; *pl.* **memorandums, memoranda. memorial** *a.* serving as a reminder; contained in the memory; *n.* anything intended to commemorate a person or an event. **memoralize** *v.t.* to commemorate; to present a memorial. **memorize** *v.t.* to commit to memory. **memorization** *n.* [L. *memoria,* memory].
men (men) *pl.* of **man.**
men·ace (men′·ąs) *n.* a threat or threatening; potential danger; *v.t.* to threaten. **menacing** *a.* **menacingly** *adv.* [L. *minari,* to threaten].
mé·nage (mą·nàzh′) *n.* a household; housekeeping [Fr., fr. L. *mansio,* a dwelling].
me·nag·er·ie (mą·naj′·ęr·i·) *n.* a collection of caged wild animals for exhibition [Fr. *ménage,* a household].
mend (mend) *v.t.* to repair; to set right; to improve; *v.i.* to improve; *n.* a mended place; improvement. **-er** *n.* **-ing** *n.* [fr. *amend*].
men·da·cious (mem·dā′·shąs) *a.* given to telling lies; untruthful. **-ly** *adv.* **mendacity** *n.* prevarication; a tendency to lying [L. *mendax*].
men·di·cant (men′·di·kąnt) *a.* begging; living as a beggar; *n.* a beggar. **mendicancy, mendicity** *n.* the practice of living by alms. [L. *mendicare,* to beg].

me·ni·al (mē′·ni·ạl) *a.* pert. to domestic service; servile; *n.* a servant; a servile person. **-ly** *adv.* [O.Fr. *mesnee,* a household].
me·nin·ges (mạ·nin′·jēz) *n.pl.* the three membranes enveloping the brain and spinal cord. *sing.* **meninx, meningitis** (·jī′·tis) *n.* (*Med.*) inflammation of these membranes [Gk. *mēninx,* a membrane].
me·nis·cus (mạ·nis′·kạs) *n.* a lens convex on one side and concave on the other; the curved surface of a liquid in a vessel; (*Math.*) a crescent. **meniscal, meniscate** *a.* **menisciform** *a.* crescent-shaped [Gk. *mēniskos,* a crescent].
Men·non·ite (men′·ạn·īt) *n.* a member of or pert. to a Prot. sect favoring plain dress and plain living [fr. *Menno* Simons, leader].
men·o·pause (men′·ạ·pawz) *n.* female change of life [Gk. *mēn,* a month; *pausis,* cessation].
men·sal (men′·sạl) *a.* monthly [L. *mensis*].
men·ses (men′·sēz) *n.pl.* the monthly discharge from the uterus of the female. **menstrual** *a.* monthly; pert. to the menses. **menstruate** *v.i.* to discharge the menses. **menstruation** *n.* **menstruous** *a.* [*pl.* of L. *mensis,* a month].
men·stru·um (men′·stroo·ạm) *n.* a solvent [L. *menstrua,* the menses].
men·sur·a·ble (men′·sher·a·bl) *a.* capable of being measured. **mensurability** *n.* **mensural** *a.* pert. to measure. **mensuration** *n.* the act, process, or art of measuring; (*Math.*) the determination of length, area, and volume. **mensurative** [L. *mensura,* measure].
men·tal (men′·tạl) *a.* pert. to, or of, the mind; performed in the mind; (*Colloq.*) mentally ill. **-ity** (men·tal′·ạ·ti·) *n.* intellectual power; mental attitude. **-ly** *adv.* **— deficiency** subnormal intelligence [L. *mens,* the mind].
men·thol (men′·thawl) *n.* a camphor obtained from oil of peppermint. **-ated** *a.* treated or flavored with menthol [L. *mentha,* mint].
men·tion (men′·shạn) *n.* a brief notice; a casual comment; *v.t.* to notice; to name. **-able** *a.* fit to be remarked on [L. *mentio*].
men·tor (men′·tẹr) *n.* an experienced and prudent adviser. **-ial** *a.* [Gk. *Mentōr,* the adviser of Telemachus].
men·u (men′·ū) *n.* a bill of fare; the food served [Fr. *menu,* a list].
Meph·i·stoph·e·les (mef·is·tȧf′·ạ·lēz) *n.* (*Myth.*) the devil. **Mephistophelean** *a.* sinister.
me·phi·tis (me·fī′·tis) *n.* noxious exhalation, esp. from the ground or from decaying matter. **mephitic** *a.* [L.].
mer·can·tile (mur′·kạn·til, ·tīl) *a.* pert. to commerce. **mercantilism** *n.* the mercantile system. **mercantilist** *n.* **— system,** the economic theory that money alone is wealth and that a nation's exports should far exceed its imports [L. *mercari,* to traffic].
mer·ce·nar·y (mur′·se·ner·i·) *a.* working merely for money or gain; hired; greedy.*n.* a hired soldier. **mercenarily** *adv.* **mercenariness** *n.* [L. *merces,* wages].
mer·cer·ize (mur′·sạ·rīz) *v.t.* to treat cotton fabrics with caustic lye to impart a silky finish. **-d** *a.* [fr. J. *Mercer,* inventor of the process].
mer·chant (mur′·chant) *n.* one who engages in trade; a storekeeper. *a.* pert. to trade or merchandise. **merchandise** *n.* commodities bought and sold. **-man** *n.* a ship carrying goods. **— marine,** the ships and men engaged in commerce [L. *mercari,* to traffic].
Mer·cu·ry (mur′·kyạ·ri·) *n.* the planet of the solar system nearest to the sun. **(m)** *n.* a metallic chemical element, silvery white in color, with very low melting point (also called *quicksilver*), used in barometers, thermometers, etc. **mercurial** *a.* pert to, or consisting of, mercury; sprightly; agile; erratic. **mercurialize** *v.t.* to make mercurial; to treat with mercury. **mercurous, mercuric** *a.* (*Chem.*) pert. to compounds of mercury [L. *Mercurius,* prob. fr. *merx,* goods; also Gk. *Myth*].
mer·cy (mur′·si·) *n.* forbearance; clemency; leniency shown to a guilty person; compassion. **merciful** *a.* full of mercy; compassionate. **mercifully** *adv.* **mercifulness** *n.* **merciless** *a.* void of pity; callous; cruel. **mercilessly** *adv.* **mercilessness** *n.* [L. *merces,* reward].
mere (mēr) *n.* (*Poetic*) a pool or lake [O.E. *mere,* a stretch of water].
mere (mēr) *a.* nothing but; simple. **-ly** *adv.* simply; solely [L. *merus,* undiluted].
mer·e·tri·cious (mer·ạ·trish′·ạs) *a.* tawdry; cheap (as of style). **-ly** *adv.* **-ness** *n.* [L. *meretrix,* a harlot].
mer·gan·ser (mẹr·gan′·sẹr) *n.* a diving fish-eating bird [L. *mergus,* a diving bird; *anser,* a goose].
merge (murj) *v.t.* to cause to be swallowed up; to plunge or sink; *v.i.* to lose identity by being absorbed in something else; to be swallowed up or lost. **-r** *n.* a combine of commercial or industrial firms [L. *mergere,* to dip].
me·rid·i·an (mạ·rid′·i·ạn) *n.* an imaginary line passing through the poles at right angles to the equator; (*Astron.*) a circle passing through the poles of the heavens and the zenith of the observer; the highest attitude of sun or star; midday; *a.* pert. to midday; supreme. **meridional** *a.* pert. to the meridian; southerly. **meridionally** *n.* [L. *meridianus,* pert. to noon].
me·ringue (mạ·rang′) *n.* a mixture of sugar and white of egg whipped till stiff, and baked in a cool oven; a small cake or pie topping of this [Fr.].
me·ri·no (mạ·rē′·nō) *n.* a breed of sheep with very fine, thick fleece, orig. from Spain; a dress fabric of this wool; *a.* pert. to the merino [Sp. *merino,* an inspector of sheepwalks].
mer·it (mer′·it) *n.* quality of deserving reward; excellence; worth; *pl.* the rights and wrongs, as of a law case; *v.t.* to earn; to deserve. **-orious** *a.* deserving reward. **-oriously** *adv.* [L. *meritum,* desert].
mer·lin (mur′·lin) *n.* a species of falcon [O.Fr. *esmerillon,* a falcon].
mer·lon (mur′·lạn) *n.* solid part of a parapet between two openings [Fr. fr. L. *murus,* a wall].
mer·maid (mur′·mād) *n.* an imaginary sea-creature with the upper body and head of a woman, and the tail of a fish. **merman** *n.* the male equivalent [O.E. *mere,* a lake; and *maid*].
mer·ry (mer′·i·) *a.* gay; hilarious; lively. **merrily** *adv.* **merriment, merriness** *n.* gaiety with noise and laughter; hilarity. **—go-round** *n.* a revolving platform with horses, cars, etc. **—making** *n.* festivity [O.E. *myrge,* pleasant].
mer·thi·o·late (mẹr·thī′·ạ·lāt) *n.* an antiseptic and germicide [fr. *mercuri-thiosalicylate*].
me·sa (mā′·sạ) *n.* a high plateau [Sp. = table].
mes·dames (mā·dạm′) *n.pl.* of madam, Mrs. [Fr.].
mes·en·te·ry (mes′·ạn·ter·i·) *n.* a fold of abdominal tissue keeping the intestines in place. **mesenteric** *a.* [Gk. *mesos,* middle; *enteron,* intestine].
mesh (mesh) *n.* the space between the threads of a net; network; *v.t.* to net; to ensnare; *v.i.* to become interlocked, as gears of a machine [O.E. *max,* net].
mes·mer·ism (mez′·mẹr·izm) *n.* exercising an influence over will and actions of another; hypnotism. **mesmeric, -al** *a.* of or pert. to mesmerism. **mesmerization** *n.* **mesmerize** *v.t.* to hypnotize. **mesmerizer, mesmerist** *n.* [fr. F. A. *Mesmer,* a Ger. physician].
mesne (mēn) *a.* middle; (*Law*) intermediate [O.Fr. *mesne,* middle].
mes·o·lith·ic (mez·ạ·lith′·ic) *a.* of period between paleolithic and neolithic ages [Gk.

mesos, middle; *lithos*, a stone].

me·son (mez′·ȧn) *n.* a particle equal in charge to, but having greater mass than, an electron or positron, and less mass than a neutron or proton [Gk. *meson*, neut. of *mesos*, middle].

Mes·o·po·ta·mi·a (mes·ạ·pạ·tā′·mi·ạ) *n.* the land between Euphrates and Tigris; now Iraq [Gk. *mesos*, middle; *potamos*, a river].

Mes·o·zo·ic (mes·ạ·zō′·ik) *a.* pert. to the second geological period [Gk. *mesos*, middle; *zōe*, life].

mess (mes) *n.* unpleasant mixture; disorder; a muddle; *v.t.* to dirty; to muddle. **-y** *a.* dirty; untidy; chaotic [form of *mash*].

mess (mes) *n.* a dish of food served at one time; the meal; a number of people who eat together, esp. in army, navy, etc.; *v.t.* to supply meals to; *v.i.* to eat in company. **-kit** *n.* a soldier's portable eating equipment [O.Fr. *mes*, a dish].

mes·sage (mes′·ij) *n.* a communication, verbal or written, sent by one person to another; an inspired utterance. **messenger** *n.* one who delivers a communication; one employed to deliver goods [L. *mittere*, to send].

mes·si·ah (mạ·sī′·ạ) *n.* an expected savior or liberator. **messianic** *a.* [Heb. *mashiah*, anointed].

mes·suage (mes′·wij) *n.* (*Law*) a dwelling-house with lands and outbuildings [O.Fr. *mesuage*, a holding of land].

mes·ti·zo (mes·tē′·zō) *n.* a half-caste, esp. the offspring of a Spaniard and an Amer. Indian [Sp. fr. L. *miscere*, to mix].

met (met) *pa.t.* and *pa.p.* of the verb **meet.**

me·ta·bo·lism (mạ·tab′·ạl·izm) *n.* the name given to the chemical changes continually going on in the cells of living matter. **metabolic** *a.* **metabolize** *v.t.* [Gk. *metabolē*, change].

me·ta·car·pus (met·ạ·kȧr′·pạs) *n.* the hand between the wrist and fingers; the bones of this part. **metacarpal** *a.* [Gk. *meta*, after; *karpos*, the wrist].

met·age (mēt′·ij) *n.* official weighing, as of coal; the price paid for this [fr. *mete*].

met·al (met′·ạl) *n.* a mineral substance, opaque, fusible and malleable, capable of conducting heat and electricity; molten glass; (*Fig.*) courage; mettle; *v.t.* to furnish or cover with metal. **-lic** (mạ·tal′·ik) *a.* pert. to, like, or consisting of, metal. **-lically** *adv.* **-ize** *v.t.* to make metallic. **-loid** *n.* an element with both metallic and non-metallic properties, as arsenic; *a.* pert. to a metal. **base metals,** copper, lead, zinc, tin as distinct from precious metals, gold and silver [Gk. *metallon*, a mine].

met·al·lur·gy (met′·ạl·ur·ji·) *n.* the art of working metals or of obtaining metals from ores. **metallurgic** *a.* **metallurgist** *n.* [Gk. *metallon*, a metal; *ergon*, a work].

met·a·mor·pho·sis (met·ạ·mawr′·fạ·sis) *n.* a change of form or structure; evolution; *pl.* **metamorphoses. metamorphic** *a.* subject to change of form. **metamorphism** *n.* the state of being metamorphic. **metamorphose** *v.t.* to transform in form or nature [Gk. *meta*, over; *morphē*, shape].

met·a·phor (met′·ạ·fawr, fẹr) *n.* a figure of speech which makes an *implied* comparison between things which are not *literally* alike. **-ically** *adv.* **-ist** *n.* **mixed metaphor,** a combination of metaphors drawn from different sources [Gk. *metapherein*, to transfer].

met·a·phrase (met′·ạ·frāz) *n.* literal, word for word translation from foreign language (opp. of *paraphrase*); *v.t.* to translate literally. **metaphrast** *n.* one who makes a literal translation. **metaphrastic** *a.* literal [Gk. *meta*, over; *phrasis*, a saying].

met·a·phys·ics (met·ạ·fiz′·iks) *n.* the science which investigates first causes of all existence and knowledge; speculative philosophy. **metaphysical** *a.* **metaphysically** *adv.* **metaphysician** *n.* [Gk. *meta*, after; *phusis*, nature].

me·tas·ta·sis (mạ·tas′·tạ·sis) *n.* change of position, state, or form; shift of malignant cells from one part of the body to another. *pl.* **metastases. metasticize** *v.i.* [Gk. = removal].

met·a·tar·sus (met·ạ·tȧr′·sạs) *n.* the front part of the foot excluding the toes. **metatarsal** *a.* [Gk. *meta*, beyond; *tarsos*, the flat of the foot].

met·a··zo·a (met·ạ·zō′·ạ) *n.pl.* multi-cellular organisms. **metazoan** *n. sing.*, *a.* **metazoic** *a.* [Gk. *meta*, after; *zōon*, an animal].

mete (mēt) *v.t.* to distribute by measure; to allot, as punishment [O.E. *metan*, to measure].

me·te·or (mē′·ti·ẹr) *n.* any rapidly passing, luminous body seen in the atmosphere; a shooting star. **-ic** *a.* pert. to a meteor; influenced by atmospheric conditions; swift; dazzling. **-ite** *n.* a mass of stone or metal from outer space which lands on earth. **-ograph** *n.* an instrument for automatically recording weather conditions. **-ography** *n.* **-oid** *n.* a body in space which becomes a meteor on passing through the atmosphere of the earth. **-ological** *a.* **ologist** *n.* **-ology** *n.* the science which treats of atmospheric phenomena, esp. in relation to weather forecasts [Gk. *meteōros*, lofty].

me·ter (mē′·tẹr) *n.* a unit of length in the metric system, 39.37 U.S. inches (See *metric*) [Gk. *metron*, a measure].

me·ter (mē′·tẹr) *n.* an instrument for recording the consumption of gas, electricity, water, etc. [Gk. *metron*, a measure].

me·ter (mē′·tr) *n.* in poetry, the rhythmical arrangement of syllables, these groups being termed *feet*; verse; stanza-form; (*Music*) rhythmical structure indicated by measures; time or beat. **metronome** *n.* (*Mus.*) an instrument like an inverted pendulum for beating out time in music [Gk. *metron*].

meth·a·done (meth′·ạ·dōn) *n.* a narcotic drug used for treating heroin addiction and for relieving pain [I.S.V., *meth*yl; *a*mino; *di*phenyl; heptan*one*].

meth·ane (meth′·ān) *n.* an inflammable, hydrocarbon gas. **methanol** *n.* methyl or wood alcohol [fr. *methyl*].

meth·od (meth′·ạd) *n.* manner of proceeding esp. in scientific research; orderliness; system; technique. **-ic(al)** *a.* arranged systematically; orderly. **-ically** *adv.* **-ology** *n.* [Gk. *meta*, after; *hodos*, a way].

Meth·o·dist (meth′·ạ·dist) *n.* a member of Protestant sect founded in 18th cent. by Charles and John Wesley [fr. *method*].

meth·yl (meth′·ạl) *n.* the chemical basis of wood [Gk. *methu*, wine; *hulē*, wood].

me·tic·u·lous (mạ·tik′·yạ·lạs) *a.* over-scrupulous as to detail. **-ly** *adv.* [L. *metus*, fear].

mé·tier (māt′·yā) *n.* profession or vocation; the occupation for which one is best suited [Fr.].

me·ton·y·my (me·tȧn′·ạ·mi·) *n.* (*Rhet.*) a figure of speech in which the name of one thing is put for another associated with it. **metonym** *n.* **metonymic(al)** *a.* **metonymically** *adv.* [Gk. *meta*, expressing change; *onoma*, a name].

met·ric (met′·rik), **met·ri·cal** (met′·ri·kạl) *a.* pertaining to measurement, esp. to the metric system. **metric system** *n.* decimal system of weights and measures based on meter, kilogram, and liter. **metrication** *n.* the changing over to the metric system. **metrology** *n.* the science of weights and measures [Gk. *metron*, a measure].

me·trop·o·lis (mạ·trȧp′·ạ·lis) *n.* the chief city of an area; a large city; a diocese. **metropolitan** *a.* pert. to a metropolis; pert. to the see of a metropolitan bishop; *n.* one who lives in a metropolis or has the manners, etc. of one who does [Gk. *mētēr*, a mother; *polis*, a city].

met·tle (met′·l) *n.* spirit; courage. **-some** *a.* **to be on one's —,** to be roused to do one's best [fr. *metal*].

mew (mū) *n.* a seagull [O.E. *maew*, a gull].
mew (mū) *v.t.* to shed or cast; to confine, as in a cage; *v.i.* to molt; *n.* a cage for hawks; a den. *n.pl.* stables around a court or alley [O.Fr. *muer*, to change; *mew*, a cage].
mewl (mūl) *v.i.* to whimper or whine [fr. *mew*].
Mex·i·can (mek′·sạ·kạn) *n.* a native or inhabitant of Mexico; *a.*
mez·za·nine (mez′·ạ·nēn) *n.* (*Archit.*) a low story between two main ones; in a theater usu. the first few rows in the balcony [It. *mezzo*, middle].
mez·zo (met′·sō) *a.* middle; moderately. **—soprano** *n.* voice between soprano and contralto. **-tint** *n.* a method of copperplate engraving in which a roughened surface is scraped according to degrees of light and shade required. [It. *mezzo*, half].
mi·as·ma (mī·az′·mạ) *n.* noxious exhalations from decomposing matter. **-l, -tic, miasmic** *a.* [Gk. *miasma*, a stain].
mi·ca (mī′·kạ) *n.* a group of mineral silicates capable of cleavage into very thin, flexible, and often transparent laminae. *a.* [L. *mica*, a crumb].
mice (mīs) *pl.* of **mouse.**
Mich·ael·mas (mik′·l·mạs) *n.* the feast of the archangel Michael, Sept. 29.
mi·crobe (mī′·krōb) *n.* a minute organism; a bacterium or disease germ. **microbial, microbian, microbic** *a.* **microbiology** *n.* the science of microbes. **microbiological** *a.* [Gk. *mikros*, small; *bios*, life].
mi·cro·ceph·a·lous (mī·krō·sef′·ạ·lạs) *a.* (*Med.*) having a very small head [Gk. *mikros*, small; *kēphalả*, the head].
mi·cro·coc·cus (mī·krō·kảk′·ạs) *n.* a spherical or oval organism or bacterium [Gk. *mikros*, small; *kokkos*, a berry].
mi·cro·cosm (mī′·krạ·kảzm) *n.* miniature universe; man, regarded as the epitome of the universe; a community symbolical of humanity as a whole. **microcosmic,** *a.* [Gk. *mikros*, small; *kosmos*, the universe].
mi·cro·film (mī′·krạ·film) *n.* film used to make reduced photographic copies of books, etc. [Gk. *mikros*, small; and *film*].
mi·cro·graph (mī′·krạ·graf) *n.* an instrument for producing microscopic engraving; a microphotograph. **micrographer** *n.* **micrography** *n.* the study of microscopic objects; the art of writing or engraving on a minute scale [Gk. *mikros*, small; *graphein*, to write].
mi·crol·o·gy (mī·krảl′·ạ·ji·) *n.* the science which deals with microscopic objects; (*Fig.*) overscrupulous attention to small details [Gk. *mikros*, small; *logos*, a discourse].
mi·crom·e·ter (mī·krảm′·ạ·tẹr) *n.* an instrument for measuring very small distances or angles. **micrometric, -al** *a.* [Gk. *mikros*, small; *metron*, a measure].
mi·cron (mī′·krản) *n.* the millionth part of a meter [Gk. *mikros*, small].
mi·cro·or·gan·ism (mī·krō·awr′·gạn·izm) *n.* a microscopic organism [Gk. *mikros*, small; *organon*, an instrument].
mi·cro·phone (mī′·krạ·fōn) *n.* an instrument for turning sound waves into electrical waves so enabling them to be transmitted; mouthpiece for broadcasting (*Colloq.* abbrev. **mike**); an instrument for making faint sounds louder. [Gk. *mikros*, small; *phōne*, a sound].
mi·cro·pho·tog·ra·phy (mī·krạ·fạ·tảg′·rạ·fi·) *n.* the art of producing minute photographs. **microphotograph** *n.* [Gk. *mikros*, small; *phos*, light; *graphein*, to write].
mi·cro·scope (mī′·krạ·skōp) *n.* an optical instrument for magnifying minute objects. **microscopic, -al** *a.* visible only with a microscope; very minute. **microscopically** *adv.* **microscopy** *n.* [Gk. *mikros*, small; *skopein*, to see].
mi·cro·zo·a (mī·krạ·zō′·ạ) *n.pl.* microscopic animals. **-n** *a.* and *n. sing.* [Gk. *mikros*, small; *zōon*, an animal; *zumē*, leaven].
mic·tu·ri·tion (mik·chạ·rish′·ạn) *n.* (*Med.*) the passing of urine. **micturate** *v.i.* [L. *micturire*, to pass urine].
mid (mid) *a.* situated between extremes; middle, as in *mid-air, mid-Atlantic*. **-day** *n.* and *a.* noon; pert. to noon. **-night** *n.* twelve o'clock at night. **-shipman** *n.* rank in U.S. Navy and Coast Guard held by young men attending service academies; **-ships** *adv.* amidships. **-summer** *n.* the middle of summer. **-way** *adv.* halfway. **-winter** *n.* middle of the winter [O.E.].
mid (mid) *prep.* amidst (in poetry).
mid·dle (mid′·l) *a.* equidistant from the extremes; intermediate; *n.* middle point. **-aged** *a.* pert. to the period of life between 40 and 60. **-man** *n.* an agent acting between producer and consumer; a go-between. **-weight** *n.* (*Boxing*) a boxer of a weight not more than 160 lbs. **middling** *a.* of medium size, quality; *adv.* moderately. **Middle Ages,** the period of European history from the Fall of the Roman Empire (about A.D. 476) to the Fall of Constantinople (1453). **— class,** that section of the community between the very wealthy higher social classes and the laboring classes; the bourgeoisie. **Middle East,** that part of the world between the *Near East* and the *Far East;* Egypt, Syria, Palestine, Arabia, Iraq and Iran. **Middle English,** the English language as written and spoken between 1150-1500 (approx.) [O.E. *middel*].
mid·dy (mid′·i·) *n.* (*Colloq.*) a midshipman; a loose blouse with a sailor collar.
midge (mij) *n.* a gnat; a very small person. **midget** *n.* a dwarf; *a.* miniature [O.E. *mycge*, a gnat].
mid·riff (mid′·rif) *n.* the diaphragm; body part between chest and abdomen [O.E. *mid*, middle; *hrif*, the belly].
midst (midst) *n.* the middle; *prep.* amidst [M.E.].
mid·wife (mid′·wīf) *n.* a woman who assists another at childbirth. *pl.* **midwives** [O.E. *mid*, with; *wif*, a woman].
mien (mēn) *n.* manner; bearing; general appearance.
miff (mif) *v.t.* and *i.* to offend or take offense [Ger. *muffen*, to sulk].
might (mīt) *pa.t.* of verb **may.**
might (mīt) *n.* power; strength; energy. **-iness** n. the state of being powerful; greatness. **-y** *a.* having great strength or power; exalted [O.E. *meaht*, might].
mi·gnon·ette (min′·yạ·net) *n.* a sweet-scented, greenish-gray flowered plant [dim. Fr. *mignon*, a darling].
mi·graine (mī′·grān) *n.* severe headache often accompanied by nausea. cf. **megrim.**
mi·grate (mī′·grāt) *v.i.* to remove one's residence from one place to another; (of birds) to fly to another place in search of warmer climate. **migrant** *n.* a person or creature who migrates. **migration** *n.* the act of migrating; a mass removal. **migratory** *a.* [L. *migrare*, to go].
Mi·ka·do (mạ·kả′·dō) *n.* the Emperor of Japan [Jap. *mi*, august; *kado*, the door].
mike (mīk) *n.* (*Colloq. abbrev.*) a microphone.
mil (mil) *n.* .001 in., a unit of measurement in calculating the diameter of wire [L. *mille*, a thousand].
milch (milch) *a.* giving milk [M.E. *milch*, milk].
mild (mīld) *a.* gentle; kind; placid; calm, or temperate, as weather. **-ly** *adv.* **-ness** [O.E. *milde*, gentle].
mil·dew (mil′·dòò) *n.* whitish coating of minute fungi on plants; a mold on paper, cloth, leather caused by dampness; *v.t.* and *v.i.* to taint or be tainted with mildew. **-y** *a.* [O.E. *mele*, honey; *deaw*, dew].

mile (mīl) *n.* a measure of length equal to 5280 ft. **geographical** or **nautical mile,** 1/60 of 1 degree of the earth's equator, 6,080.2 ft. **-age** *n.* distance in miles; rate of travel calculated in miles; traveling expenses calculated on the number of miles traveled. **-r** *n.* a man or horse trained to run a mile. **-stone** *n.* roadside marker; a stage or crisis in one's life [O.E. *mil,* fr. L. *mille passus,* 1000 paces].

mil·i·ar·y (mil′·i·er·i·) *a.* like millet seeds. **miliaria,** *n.* (*Med.*) a fever, accompanied by a rash resembling millet seeds (heat rash) [L. *milium,* millet].

mi·lieu (mēl·yoo′) *n.* environment [Fr. = middle].

mil·i·tant (mil′·i·tạnt) *a.* aggressive; serving as a soldier. **militancy** *n.* war-like, fighting spirit. **-ly** *adv.* **militarism** *n.* military spirit; excessive emphasis on military power; opp. of *pacifism.* **militarist** *n.* one who upholds the doctrine of militarism; a student of military science. **military** *a.* pert. to soldiers, arms, or war; warlike; *n.* the army. **military police,** soldiers performing duties of police in the army. **militate** *v.i.* to be combative; to work against (or for); to have an adverse effect on [L. *miles,* a soldier].

mi·li·tia (mạ·lish′·ạ) *n.* a citizen army, liable to be called out in an emergency [L. *miles,* a soldier].

milk (milk) *n.* a white fluid secreted by female mammals for nourishment of their young and in some cases used for humans; the juice of certain plants; *v.t.* to draw milk from; (*Colloq.*) to fleece or exploit a person; *v.i.* to give milk. **— and water** *a.* insipid. **—bar** *n.* a counter where milk drinks, etc. are sold. **-er** *n.* a milking-machine; a cow which yields milk. **— fever,** a fever sometimes contracted after childbirth **-iness** *n.* **-ing** *n.* the quantity of milk yielded at one time; the drawing of milk. **-like** *a.* **-maid** *n.* a dairymaid or woman who milks cows. **-man** *n.* a man who milks cows; a man who delivers milk. **-sop** *n.* a weak, effeminate man. **-tooth** *n.* one of the temporary baby teeth. **-weed** *n.* wild plant with milky sap. **-wood** *n.* kind of tropical trees yielding latex. **-y** *a.* like, full of, or yielding milk. **Milky Way,** the Galaxy, an irregular, luminous belt in the heavens, from the light of innumerable stars. **condensed milk,** milk with sugar added and evaporated to the consistency of syrup. **evaporated milk,** unsweetened condensed milk [O.E. *meolc,* milk].

mill (mil) *n.* a building equipped with machinery to grind grain into flour; an apparatus for grinding, as *coffee-mill;* a factory or machinery used in manufacture, as *cotton-mill, paper-mill;* (*Slang*) a boxing match. *v.t.* to grind; to cut fine grooves on the edges of (coins); to full (cloth); to dress or puify (ore); (*Slang*) to box; *v.i.* to go round in circles, as cattle, or crowds of people. **-board** *n.* stout pasteboard used in bookbinding. **-dam** *n.* a dam built to provide water for turning a mill wheel. **-ed** *a.* having the edges raised and grooved, as coins; rolled into sheets, as metal. **-er** *n.* **-ing** *n.* grinding in a mill; fulling cloth, or grooving raised edges of a coin, or pressing crude rubber under rollers; *a.* (*Slang*) confused; without direction, as *milling crowds.* **-pond** *n.* milldam. **-race** *n.* the current of water which turns millwheel. **-stone** *n.* one of the flat stones used in grinding grain; a burden. **— wheel** *n.* a water wheel for driving mill machinery. **-wright** *n.* one who sets up machinery in a mill [O.E. *myln,* to grind].

mill (mil) *n.* one thousandth of a dollar; one tenth of a cent [L. *mille,* thousand].

mil·len·ni·um (mil·en′·i·ạm) *n.* a thousand years; a future time or perfect peace on earth. **millennarian** *n.* one who believes in the millennium. **millennary** *a.* comprising a thousand; *n.* a period of a thousand years. **millennial** *a.* [L. *mille,* a thousand; *annus,* a year].

mil·li·pede (mil′·i·pēd) *n.* an insect with many legs [L. *mille,* thousand; *pes,* a foot].

mil·li- *prefix* one thousandth of. **-gram** *n.* one thousandth of a gram. **-meter** *n.* one thousandth of a meter [L. *mille,* a thousand].

mil·liard (mil′·yẹrd) *n.* a thousand millions; a billion [Fr.].

mil·li·ner (mil′·ạn·ẹr) *n.* one who makes or sells ladies' hats. **-y** *n.* [fr. *Milan*].

mil·lion (mil′·yạn) *n.* a thousand thousands (1,000,000); **-aire** *n.* one whose wealth amounts to a million (or more) dollars. **-fold** *a.* **-th** *n. a.* one of a million parts; **the millions,** the masses [Fr.].

milque·toast (milk·tōst) *n.* a timid shrinking person [fr. H. T. Webster's comic strip character].

milt (milt) *n.* the spleen; the reproductive glands or secretion of the male fish; *v.t.* to impregnate the female roe. **-er** *n.* [O.E. *milte*].

mime (mīm) *n.* a farce in which scenes of real life are expressed by gesture only; an actor in such a farce; *v.i.* to act in a mime; to express by gesture. **mimetic(al)** *a.* imitative. **mimic** (mi′·mik) *v.t.* to imitate; to burlesque; to ridicule by imitating another. *pr.p.* **-king** *pa.p., pa.t.* **-ked.** *n.* one who mimics or caricatures; *a.* mock, as in *mimic battle;* feigned. **mimicry** *n.* the art or act of mimicking [Gk. *mimos,* an actor].

mim·e·o·graph (mim′·i·ạ·grạf) *n.* a form of duplicating-machine [Gk. *mimeisthai,* to imitate; *graphein,* to write].

Mi·mo·sa (mi·mō′·sạ) *n.* a genus of leguminous plants, shrubs, or trees, with small, fluffy flowers [Gk. *mimos,* an imitator].

min·a·ret (min·ạ·ret′) *n.* a turret on a Mohammedan mosque [Ar. *manarat,* a lighthouse].

min·a·to·ry (min′·ạ·tōr·i·) *a.* threatening; menacing. **minacious** *a.* **minacity** *n.* [L. *minari,* to threaten].

mince (mins) *v.t.* to cut or chop into very small pieces; (*Fig.*) to tone down; *v.i.* to speak or walk with affected elegance. **-meat** *n.* currants, raisins, spices, apple, suet and sugar, chopped and mixed together, used as pie filling (*Fig.*) anything chopped up. **mincing** *a.* speaking or walking with affected elegance. **mincingly** *adv.* [O.E. *minsian,* to make small].

mind (mīnd) *n.* the intellectual faculty; the understanding; memory; opinion; inclination; purpose; a person regarded as an intellect; *v.t.* to obey; to attend to; to heed; to object to; to take care of; *v.i.* to be careful; to care. **-ed** *a.* disposed; inclined. **-edness** *n.* **-ful** *a.* attentive; observant; aware. **-fully** *adv.* **-fulness** *n.* **-less** *a.* stupid; careless. **— reader** *n.* one who can sense another's thoughts. **absent minded,** forgetful [O.E. *gemynd,* the mind].

mine (mīn) *n.* a pit in the earth from which minerals are excavated; a hidden explosive to blow up a wall, vessel, etc.; a profitable source; *pl.* the mining industry; *v.i.* and *v.t.* to place mines; to dig a mine or in a mine; to burrow; to undermine; to sap. **— field** *n.* an area of land or stretch of the sea where mines have been placed. **— layer** *n.* a vessel which places submarine or floating mines. **— sweeper** *n.* a vessel with nets for clearing a mine field [Fr. *miner,* to mine].

mine (mīn) *poss. pron.* belonging to me; [O.E. *min*].

min·er·al (min′·ẹr·ạl) *n.* any substance, generally inorganic, taken from the earth by mining; a chemical element or compound occurring in nature; *a.* pert. to or containing minerals; inorganic. **-ization** *n.* **-ize** *v.t.* to convert into or impregnate with minerals. **-ogy** (min·ẹr·ál′·ạ·ji·) *n.* the science of minerals and their classification. **mineralogist** *n.* **— water,**

water, impregnated with mineral substance, used medicinally [Fr. *miner,* to mine].
mi·ne·stro·ne (min·ạ·strō′·ni·) *n.* thick vegetable soup [It.].
min·gle (ming′·gl) *v.t.* to mix; to blend; to join in; *v.i.* to become mixed. **-r** *n.* **mingling** *n.* blend [O.E. *mengan,* to mix].
min·i·a·ture (min′·i·ạ·chẹr) *n.* a small-sized painting done on ivory, vellum, etc.; anything on a small scale; *a.* minute. **miniaturize** *v.t.* to make on a small scale [L. *miniare,* to paint red].
min·i·fy (min′·i·fī) *v.t.* to lessen; to minimize [L. *minor,* less; *facere,* to make].
min·im (min′·im) *n.* anything very minute; (*Med.*) 1/60 of a fluid dram; a drop; (*Mus.*) a half note. **minimal** *a.* smallest possible. **minimize** *v.t.* to reduce; to depreciate. **minimization** *n.* **minimum** *n.* the least to which anything may be reduced [L. *minimus,* least].
min·ion (min′·yạn) *n.* a favorite; a servile flatterer; (*Print.*) a small type [Fr. *mignon,* a darling].
min·is·ter (min′·is·tẹr) *n.* an agent or instrument; a clergyman; (*Brit.*) one entrusted with a govt. department; to serve; *v.i.* to supply things needed. **-ial** *a.* executive; pert. to the work of a minister. **-ially** *adv.* **-ing** *a.* serving. **ministrant** *n.* one who ministers; a helper. **ministration** *n.* the act of performing a service. **ministrative** *a.* **ministry** *n.* the act of ministering; the office or functions of a minister; the clergy [L. *minister,* a servant].
min·i·ver (min′·ạ·vẹr) *n.* fine white fur [O.Fr. *menu,* small; *vair,* fur].
mink (mingk) *n.* a semiaquatic animal of the weasel tribe; its fur [Scand.].
min·now (min′·ō) *n.* a small freshwater fish [O.E. *myne,* a small fish].
mi·nor (mī′·nẹr) *a.* lesser; inferior in bulk, degree, importance, etc.; subordinate; (*Mus.*) lower by a semi-tone; *n.* a person under 21. **-ity** (mī·nȧr′·i·ti·) *n.* the state of being under age; the lesser number, oppos. of *majority.* **— key** (*Mus.*) a key characterized by a minor third, sixth, or seventh [L. *minor,* less].
Mi·nor·ca (min·awr′·kạ) *n.* a breed of fowl [Sp. fr. *Minorca* island].
min·ster (min′·stẹr) *n.* church cathedral [O.E. *mynster,* a monastery].
min·strel (min′·strạl) *n.* a medieval poet or wandering singer; an entertainer in a minstrel show (a comic variety show with performers in blackface) [O.Fr. *menestrel,* a jester].
mint (mint) *n.* the place where money is coined; a great amount of money; *a.* as issued (before use); *v.t.* to make by stamping, as coins; to invent. **-age** *n.* process of minting money [O.E. *mynet,* money].
mint (mint) *n.* an aromatic plant used for medicinal and culinary purposes; a candy flavored with it. **— julep,** an iced drink of whiskey and sugar flavored with mint [O.E. *minte*].
min·u·end (min′·ū·end) *n.* the number from which another is to be subtracted [L. *minuendus,* to be made less].
min·u·et (min·ū·et′) *n.* a slow, stately dance; music, to which the minuet is danced [Fr. *menuet,* fr. *menu,* small].
mi·nus (mī′·nạs) *prep.* less by; *a.* showing subtraction; negative *n.* the sign (—) of subtraction; an amount less than nothing. **-cule** (mi·nus′·kūl) *a.* small; *n.* a lower-case letter, oppos. of *majuscule* [L. *minor,* less].
mi·nute (mī·nòòt′) *a.* very small; slight; particular; exact. **-ly** *adv.* **-ness** *n.* **minutiae** (min·ū′·shi·ē) *n.pl.* minute details [L. *minuere, minutum,* to lessen].
min·ute (min′·it) *n.* the 60th part of an hour or degree; a moment. *pl.* the official record of a meeting; *v.t.* to make a note of.**— hand** *n.* longer of two hands on clock or watch indicating minutes. **-ly** *adv.* occurring every minute [L. *minuere minutum,* to lessen].
minx (mingks) *n.* a pert, saucy girl.
mir·a·cle (mir′·ạ·kl) *n.* a wonder; a supernatural happening; a prodigy. **— play** *n.* a popular medieval form of drama based on the lives of the saints, or on Biblical history. **miraculous** *a.* supernatural; extraordinary. **miraculously** *adv.* [L. *miraculum,* wonder].
mi·rage (mi·rȧzh′) *n.* an optical illusion; a delusion [L. *mirare,* to wonder at].
mire (mīr) *n.* slimy soil; mud; defilement; *v.t.* to plunge into or cover with mud; *v.i.* to sink in mud. **miriness** *n.* **miry** *a.* [O.N. *myrr,* marsh].
mir·ror (mir′·ẹr) *n.* a looking glass; a pattern or model; a reflection, as a *mirror of the times; v.t.* to reflect [L. *mirare,* to look at] .
mirth (murth) *n.* gaiety; merriment; joyousness; laughter. **-ful** *a.* **-fulness** *n.* **-less** *a.* grim. **-lessly** *adv.* [O.E. *myrgth,* merry].
MIRV (murv) *n.* a missile with separable warheads for different targets [fr. *m*ultiple *i*ndependently targeted *r*eentry *v*ehicle].
mis- (mis) *prefix* meaning *wrong, bad,* or *not.*
mis·ad·ven·ture (mis·ạd·ven′·chẹr) *n.* an unlucky adventure; a mishap.
mis·ad·vise (mis·ạd·vīz′) *v.t.* to advise wrongly. **-d** *a.* ill-advised.
mis·al·li·ance (mis·ạ·lī′·ạns) *n.* an unfortunate alliance, esp. in marriage.
mis·an·thrope (mis′·ạn·thrōp) *n.* a hater of mankind. **misanthropically** *adv* **misanthropy** *n.* hatred of mankind [Gk. *misein,* to hate; *anthrōpos,* a man].
mis·ap·ply (mis·ạ·plī′) *v.t.* to apply wrongly or dishonestly. **misapplication** *n.*
mis·ap·pre·hend (mis·ap·ri·hend′) *v.t.* to apprehend wrongly; to misconceive. **misapprehension** *n.* **misapprehensive** *a.*
mis·ap·pro·pri·ate (mis·ạ·prō′·pri·āt) *v.t.* to use wrongly, esp. to embezzle money. **misappropriation** *n.*
mis·be·got·ten (mis·bi·gȧt′·n) *a.* unlawfully conceived; illegitimate.
mis·be·have (mis·bi·hāv′) *v.i.* to behave badly, improperly or dishonestly. **misbehavior** *n.*
mis·be·lieve (mis·bi·lēv′) *v.t.* to believe wrongly. **misbelief** *n.* belief in false ideas.
mis·cal·cu·late (mis·kal′·kyạ·lāt) *v.t.* to calculate wrongly. **miscalculation** *n.*
mis·car·riage (mis·kar′·ij) *n.* failure; premature birth. **miscarry** *v.i.* to fail to fulfill the intended effect; to give birth prematurely.
mis·ce·ge·na·tion (mis·i·jạ·nā′·shạn) *n.* marriage or sexual relations between persons considered to be of different races [L. *miscere,* to mix; *genus,* a race].
mis·cel·la·ne·ous (mis·ạl·ā′·ni·ạs) *a.* mixed; heterogeneous. **-ly** *adv.* **miscellanist** *n.* a writer of miscellanies. **miscellany** *n.* a medley, esp. a collection. **miscellanea** *n.pl.* odds and ends [L. *miscellaneus,* fr. *miscere,* to mix].
mis·chance (mis·chans′) *n.* a mishap; ill-luck.
mis·chief (mis′·chif) *n.* harm; damage; conduct intended to annoy; the cause of such trouble. **—maker** *n.* one who stirs up trouble. **mischievous** *a.* tending to stir up trouble; playfully annoying. **mischievously** *adv.* **mischievousness** *n.* [O.Fr. *meschever,* to come to grief].
mis·ci·ble (mis′·i·bl) *a.* capable of being mixed. **miscibility** *n.* [L. *miscere,* to mix].
mis·con·ceive (mis·kạn·sēv′) *v.t.* to misunderstand. **misconception** *n.*
mis·con·duct (mis·kȧn′·dukt) *n.* bad management; dishonest conduct; (mis·kạn·dukt′) *v.t.* to mismanage.
mis·con·strue (mis·kạn·stròò′) *v.i.* to interpret wrongly; misunderstand. **misconstruction** *n.*
mis·count (mis·kount′) *v.t.* to count wrongly; to miscalculate; (mis′·kount) *n.* a wrong count.

mis·cre·ant (mis′·krē·ant) *n.* unprincipled person [O.Fr. *mescreant,* unbeliever].
mis·cue (mis·kū′) *n.* (*Billiards*) a stroke spoiled by the cue slipping; a mistake; *v.t.*
mis·date (mis·dāt′) *v.t.* to put a wrong date on; *n.* a wrong date.
mis·deal (mis·dēl′) *v.t.* and *i.* to deal cards wrong. *pa.t.* **misdealt** *n.* wrong deal.
mis·deed (mis·dēd′) *n.* an evil deed, a crime.
mis·de·mean·or (mis·dạ·mēn′·ẹr) *n.* dishonest conduct; (*Law*) a crime less than felony. **misdemean** *v.i.* to misbehave.
mis·di·rect (mis·dạ·rekt′) *v.t.* to direct or advise wrongly. **-tion** *n.*
mi·ser (mī′·zẹr) *n.* one who hoards money and lives in wretched surroundings. **-ly** *a.* greedy; stingy. **-liness** *n.* [L. = wretched].
mis·er·a·ble (miz′·ẹr·ạ·bl) *a.* unhappy; causing misery; worthless; deplorable. **miserably** *adv.* [L. *miser,* wretched].
mis·e·re·re (miz·ạ·re′·ri·) *n.* Psalm 51, a cry for mercy [L. = take pity].
mis·er·y (miz′·ẹ·ri·) *n.* great unhappiness; extreme pain of body or mind [L. *miser*].
mis·fea·sance (mis·fē′·zạns) *n.* (*Law*) wrongdoing; a misuse of lawful authority [O.Fr. *mesfaire,* to do wrong].
mis·fire (mis·fīr′) *n.* (of internal combustion engine, gun, etc.) failure to start or go off; *v.i.* to fail to start or fire.
mis·fit (mis′·fit) *n.* a bad fit; *v.t.* and *i.*
mis·for·tune (mis·fawr′·chạn) *n.* ill luck; a calamity.
mis·give (mis·giv′) *v.t.* to fill with doubt; to cause to hesitate; *v.i.* to fail *pa.t.* **misgave.** *pa.p.* **misgiven. misgiving** *n.* distrust; suspicion. [ly. **-ment** *n.*
mis·gov·ern (mis·guv′·ẹrn) *v.t.* to govern bad-
mis·guide (mis·gīd′) *v.t.* to lead astray; to advise wrongly. **misguidance** *n.*
mis·han·dle (mis·hand′·dl) *v.t.* to maltreat; to bungle.
mis·hap (mis′·hap) *n.* accident.
mish·mash (mish′·mȧsh) *n.* a jumble [fr. *mash*].
mis·in·form (mis·in·fawrm′) *v.t.* to give wrong information to. **-ant, -ation** *n.*
mis·in·ter·pret (mis·in·tur′·prit) *v.t.* to interpret or explain wrongly. **-ation** *n.* **-er** *n.*
mis·join·der (mis·join′·dẹr) *n.* (*Law*) introduction into court of parties or causes not belonging.
mis·judge (mis·juj′) *v.t.* to judge wrongly; to miscalculate. **-ment** *n.*
mis·lay (mis·lā′) to lay down something in a place which cannot later be recollected. *pa.t., pa.p.* **mislaid.**
mis·lead (mis·lēd′) *v.t.* to lead astray; to delude. *pa.p.* **misled. -ing** *a.*
mis·man·age (mis·man′·ij) *v.t.* to manage incompentently. **-ment** *n.*
mis-name (mis·nām′) *v.t.* to call by the wrong name.
mis·no·mer (mis·nō′·mẹr) *n.* a wrong name; incorrect designation [O.Fr. *mesnommer,* to name wrongly].
mi·so·ga·my (mi·sȧg′·ạ·mi·) *n.* hatred of marriage. **misogamist** *n.* [Gk. *miseein,* to hate; *gamos,* marriage].
mi·sog·y·ny (mi·sȧj′·ạ·ni·) *n.* hatred of women. **misogynist** *n.* **misogynous** *a.* [Gk. *miseein,* to hate; *gunē,* a woman].
mis·place (mis·plās′) *v.t.* to place wrongly; to mislay.
mis·print (mis·print′) *v.t.* to make an error in printing; (mis′·print) *a.* a printing error.
mis·pro·nounce (mis·prạ·nouns′) *v.t.* to pronounce incorrectly. **mispronunciation** *n.*
mis·quote (mis·kwōt′) *v.t.* to quote incorrectly.
mis·reck·on (mis·rek′·n) *v.t.* to estimate or reckon incorrectly. **-ing** *n.*
mis·rep·re·sent (mis·rep·ri·zent′) *v.i.* to represent falsely; to report inaccurately. **-ation** *n.*
mis·rule (mis·ròòl′) *n.* disorder; misgovernment.
Miss (mis) *n.* title of unmarried women; girl [contr. of *mistress*]..
miss (mis) *v.t.* to fail to hit, reach, find, catch, notice; to be without; to feel the want of; to avoid; to omit; *v.i.* to fail to hit; to fall short of one's objective; *n.* failure to hit, reach, find, etc.; escape, as in *a lucky miss.* **-ing** *a.* lost; failing [O.E. *missan,* to fail].
mis·sal (mis′·ạl) *n.* a book containing the R.C. service of the mass for a year [L. *missa,* mass].
mis·sel (mis′·l) *n.* the large European thrush, supposed to eat *mistletoe berries* [O.E. *mistel,* mistletoe].
mis·shape (mis·shāp′) *v.t.* to shape badly; to deform. **-en** *a.*
mis·sile (mis′·l) *n.* that which is thrown or shot. **guided missile** *n.* a projected unmanned object which travels above the earth and performs some specific function, such as communication; *a.* capable of being thrown or shot [L. *mittere, missum,* to send].
mis·sion (mish′·ạn) *n.* the act of sending; the duty on which one is sent; a group of people sent to a foreign country for religious work; a delegation sent to a foreign country; vocation. **-ary** *a.* pert. to missions or missionaries; *n.* one sent to preach religion, esp. in a foreign country; one who does social service among the poor. [L. *mittere, missum,* to send].
mis·sive (mis′·iv) *n.* a letter or message [L. *missum,* to send].
mis·spell (mis·spel′) *v.t.* to spell incorrectly. **-ing** *n.* an error in spelling.
mis·spend (mis·spend′) *v.t.* to spend foolishly; to squander. *pa.t.* and *pa.p.* **misspent.**
mist (mist) *n.* visible vapor in the lower atmosphere; droplets of rain; a cloudiness or film; *v.t.* or *v.i.* to dim or be dimmed, as by a mist. **-y** *a.* dim; obscured. **-ily** *adv.* **-iness** *n.* [O.E. *mist,* darkness].
mis·take (mis·tāk′) *v.t.* to misunderstand; to take one person for another; *v.i.* to err; *n.* an error. *pa.t.* **mistook.** *pa.p.* **mistaken. mistakable** *a.* **mistaken** *a.* wrong; misunderstood. **mistakenly** *adv.* [M.E. *mistaken,* to take wrongly].
mis·ter (mis′·tẹr) *n.* sir; title of courtesy to a man (*abbrev.* **Mr.**) [form of *master*].
mis·time (mis·tīm′) *v.t.* to time wrongly. **-d** *a.*
mis·tle·toe (mis′·l·tō) *n.* a parasitic, evergreen plant with white berries [O.E. *mistel,* mistletoe; *tan,* a twig].
mis·tral (mis′·trạl) *n.* a cold, often violent, N.W. wind which blows over S. France [Fr. *mistral,* a master (wind)].
mis·tress (mis′·tris) *n.* (*fem.* of **master**) a woman in authority (as over a household, animal, institution); a kept woman; formerly, a title of address [O.Fr. *maistresse,* fem.]
mis·tri·al (mis·trī′·ạl) *n.* a trial made invalid by an error in proceedings.
mis·trust (mis·trust′) *n.* lack of confidence; *v.t.* to suspect; to lack faith in. **-ful** *a.*
mis·un·der·stand (mis·un·dẹr·stand′) *v.t.* to interpret incorrectly; to form a wrong judgment. **-ing** *n.* a misconception; a slight quarrel.
mis·use (mis·ūz′) *v.t.* to use improperly; to maltreat. (mis·ūs′) *n.* improper use. **misusage** *n.* abuse.
mite (mīt) *n.* any very small thing or person; a kind of arachnid, as *cheese-mite;* a very small coin [O.Dut. *mijt,* a small coin].
mi·ter (mī′·tẹr) *n.* a bishop's headdress, a tall cap; in carpentry, a joint made by two pieces of wood fitting into each other at an angle of 45°; *v.t.* to confer a miter on; to join at an angle. **mitral, mitriform** *a.* shaped like a miter; (*Bot.*) conical. **— block, — board,** or **— box** *n.* a piece of wood acting as a guide in sawing a *miter-joint.* **-d** *a.* wearing a miter; cut like a miter [Gk. *mitra,* a headboard].
mit·i·gate (mit′·ạ·gāt) *v.t.* to relieve; to alle-

viate; to temper. **mitigable** *a.* capable of being lessened. **mitigation** *n.* alleviation. **mitigative, mitigatory** *a.* **mitigator** *n.* [L. *mitigare*, to lessen].

mi·to·sis (mī·tō′·sis) *n.* (*Biol.*) method of cell division in which chromatin divides into chromosomes [Gk. *mitos*, thread; *osis*, action].

mitt (mit) *n.* a covering for wrist and hand leaving fingers exposed; a baseball glove, with palm heavily padded; (usu. *pl.*) padded mitten worn by boxers. **-ten** *n.* a glove with thumb, but palm and fingers all in one [L. *medius*, middle].

mix (miks) *v.t.* to unite into a mass; to blend; to combine a mixture; to associate; *v.i.* to become mingled; to associate; *n.* a muddle; a mixture. **-able** *a.* **-ed** *a.* mingled; blended; **-er** *n.* one who or that which mixes; one who is sociable, as a *good mixer.* (*Slang*) a social gathering. **-ture** *n.* the act of mixing; that which is mixed; (*Chem.*) a combination of substances which retain their individual properties, as contrasted with a *compound.* **-up** *n.* (*Colloq.*) confusion. **-ed marriage,** a marriage between two people of different religions [L. *miscere*].

miz·zen, mizen (miz′·n) *n.* fore-and-aft sail of a vessel. **-mast** *n.* the mast bearing the mizzen [Fr. *misaine*, a fore-sail].

mne·mon·ic, -al (ni·mȧn′·ik, ·al) *a.* assisting the memory. **-s** *n.pl.* the art of assisting the memory; artificial aids to memory [Gk. *mnēmōn*, mindful].

mo·a (mō′·ạ) *n.* an extinct N. Z. flightless bird of very large size [Maori].

moan (mōn) *n.* a low cry of grief or pain; *v.i.* to utter a low, wailing cry; *v.t.* to lament [O.E. *maenan*, to lament].

moat (mōt) *n.* a deep trench around a castle, usu. filled with water [O.Fr. *mote*, a trench].

mob (mȧb) *n.* a disorderly crowd of people; a rabble; the populace; *v.t.* to attack in a disorderly crowd; to jostle. *pr.p.* **-bing.** *pa.p., pa.t.* **-bed. -ocracy** *n.* the rule of the mob. **-ocrat** mob leader. **-ster** *n.* (*Slang*) gangster [L. *mobile vulgus*, the fickle masses].

mob·cap (mȧb′·kap) *n.* a frilled cap, tied under the chin, worn by women in the 18th cent. [Dut. *mop*, a coif].

mo·bile (mō′·bl) *a.* easily moved; changing; facile; (of troops) mechanized; capable of moving rapidly from place to place; *n.* (mō′·bēl) an artistic arrangement of wires, etc., easily set in motion. **mobilization** *n.* the wartime act of calling up men and women for active service. **mobilize** *v.t.* to gather together available resources. **mobility** *n.* the state of being mobile [L. *mobilis*, movable].

moc·ca·sin (mȧk′·ạ·sin) *a.* shoe of soft leather worn by N. American Indians, trappers, etc.; a bedroom slipper of similar shape; a poisonous water snake [N. Amer. Ind.].

mo·cha (mō′·kạ) *n.* a coffee orig. from *Mocha* in Yemen; *a.* flavored with coffee.

mock (mȧk) *v.t.* to laugh at; to ridicule; to make a fool of; to defy; to mimic; substitute. **-er** *n.* **-ery, -ing** *n.* the act of mocking; derision; travesty; false show. **-heroic** *a.* burlesquing the serious or heroic style. **-ing.** *a.* scornful; derisive. **-ing bird,** a N. American bird which imitates other birds. **— orange,** shrub with fragrant white flowers. **— turtle,** a soup made of calf's head and spices to imitate turtle soup [Fr. *moquer*].

mode (mōd) *n.* manner, form, or method; custom; fashion; (*Mus.*) one of the two classes of keys (major or minor); (*Gram.*) the *mood* of the verb. **modal** *a.* relating to mode or form. **modality** *n.* **modish** *a.* fashionable. **modishly** *adv.* **modishness** *n.* **modiste** (mōd·ēst′) *n.* a dealer in the latest fashions [L. *modus*, manner].

mod·el (mȧd′·l) *n.* an exact, three-dimensional representation of an object, in miniature; a pattern or standard to copy; one who poses for an artist; a mannequin; *a.* serving as a model or criterion; *v.t.* to make in model; to copy from a pattern or standard to shape, as clay, wax, etc.; *v.i.* to practice modeling. **-er** *n.* **-ing** *n.* the art of working in plastic materials or of making models; shaping [O.Fr. *modelle*, a pattern].

mod·er·ate (mȧd′·ẹr·it) *a.* restrained; temperate; average; not extreme; (mȧd′·ẹr·āt) *v.t.* to restrain; to control; to decrease the intensity or pressure of; *v.i.* to become less violent or intense; to act as moderator; *n.* a person of moderate opinions in politics, etc. **-ly** *adv.* **-ness** *n.* **moderation** *n.* moderating; freedom from excess. **moderatism** *n.* non-extremist views. **moderator** *n.* arbitrator [L. *moderare*, to limit].

mod·ern (mȧd′·ẹrn) *a.* pert. to present or recent time; up-to-date; *n.* a person living in modern times; one up-to-date in outlook and ideas. **-ization** *n.* **-ize** *v.t.* to bring up-to-date. **-ism** *n.* sympathy with modern ideas. **-ist** *n.* one who upholds modern ideas. **modernity** *n.* the state or quality of being modern [L. *modernus*, fr. *modo*, just now].

mod·est (mȧd′·ist) *a.* unassuming; restrained; decent; retiring in manner; not excessive, as *modest* means. **-ly** *adv.* **-ty** *n.* the quality of being modest [L. *modestus*, moderate].

mod·i·cum (mạd′·i·kạm) *n.* a small amount [L. *modicus*, moderate].

mod·i·fy (mȧd′·ạ·fī) *v.t.* to moderate; to alter the form or intensity of; (*Philol.*) to change the sound of a vowel by the influence of a following vowel; (*Gram.*) to qualify the meaning of, as of a verb by an adverb. **modifiable** *a.* **modification** *n.* the act of modifying; the state of being modified; a change of form, manner, or intensity. **modifier** *n.* [L. *modificare*].

mod·u·late (mȧj′·oo·lāt) *v.t.* to regulate, esp. the pitch of the voice; to adapt; (*Mus.*) to change the key of; *v.i.* (*Mus.*) to pass from one key to another. **modular** *a.* of a mode, modulation, or module. **modulation** *n.* the act of modulating; the changing of the pitch or key; (*Elect.*) the variation of the amplitude or frequency of continuous waves, usu. by a lower frequency. **modulator** *n.* one who, or that which modulates. **module** *n.* a unit of measurement; (*Archit.*) the radius of a shaft at its base. **modulus** *n.* (*Math.*) a constant number, coefficient, or quantity which measures a force, function, or effect. (*pl.* **moduli**) [L. *modulari*, to measure].

mo·gul (mō′·gul) *n.* a powerful or important person [Pers. *Mughul*, Mongolian conqueror].

mo·hair (mō′·hār) *n.* the silky hair of the Angora goat; fabric from this or similar hair. *a.* [Ar. *mukhayyar*, hair-cloth].

Moslem religion

Mo·ham·me·dan (mo·ham′·ạ·dạn) *a.* of Mohammed or the Moslem religion; *n.* a Moslem. **-ism** *n.* Moslem religion; Islam [fr. *Mohammed*, Ar. prophet, 570?-632].

Mo·ha·ve (mō·hȧ′·vi·) *n.* a tribe of Amer. Indians. Also **Mojave** [Native].

Mo·hawk (mō′·hawk) *n.* the name of a N. Amer. Indian tribe [Native].

Mo·hi·can (mō·hē′·kạn) *n.* a N. Amer. Indian tribe of Algonquin stock. Also **Mahican, Mohegan** [Native].

moi·e·ty (moi′·ạ·ti·) *n.* half [Fr. *moitié*, half].

moire (mwȧ·rā′) *n.* watered fabric; *a.* having a wavy pattern [var. of *mohair*].

moist (moist) *a.* damp; humid; rather wet. **-en** (mois′·n) *v.t.* to make moist; to dampen. **moistness, moisture** (mois′·chẹr) *n.* that which causes dampness; condensed vapor. **-ureless** [O.Fr. *moiste*, fresh].

mo·lar (mō′·lẹr) *a.* grinding or able to grind,

as back teeth; *n.* a back double-tooth [L. *molere,* to grind].

mo·las·ses (mą·las′·ąz) *n. sing.* a dark-colored syrup obtained from sugar; treacle [L. *mellaceus,* honey-like].

mold (mōld) *n.* a pattern, form or matrix for giving shape to something in a plastic or molten state; a shape to form a model;character; *v.t.* to shape; to influence. **-er** *n.* one who molds or makes molds. **-ing** *n.* anything molded, esp. anything molded, esp. ornamentation of wood. Also **mould** [L. *modulus,* a small measure].

mold (mōld) *n.* fine, soft soil; the upper layer of the earth. **-er** *v.i.* to decay; to crumble away; to turn to dust. Also **mould** [O.E. *molde*].

mold (mōld) *n.* a downy fungus which grows on leather, cheese, bread, etc. if exposed to dampness; mildew. **-iness** *n.* **-y** *a.* affected by mold; musty; (*Fig.*) antiquated. Also **mould.**

mole (mōl) *n.* a slightly raised, dark spot on the skin [O.E. *mal,* a spot].

mole (mōl) *n.* a small burrowing animal; *v.t.* to burrow. **-hill** *n.* a small mound of earth. **-skin** *n.* the fur of a mole; a fabric with soft surface [M.E. *molle,* a mole].

mole (mōl) *n.* a breakwater [L. *moles,* a mass].

mol·e·cule (mȧl′·ą·kūl) *n.* the smallest portion of a substance which can retain the characteristics of that substance. **molecular** *a.* **molecular weight,** the weight of a molecule of a substance in relation to the weight of a hydrogen atom [dim. fr. L. *moles,* a mass].

mo·lest (mą·lest′) *v.t.* to trouble; to accost with sinister intention. **-ation** *n.* [L. *molestus,* troublesome].

mol·li·fy (mȧl′·ą·fī) *v.t.* to appease; to placate; to soften. **mollifiable** *a.* **mollification** *n.* **mollifier** *n.* [L. *mollificare,* to make soft].

mol·lusk, mol·lusc (mȧl′·ąsk) *n.* an invertebrate animal with soft, pulpy body and a hard outer shell (oyster, snail, etc.) **molluscan** *a.* **molluscoid, -cous** *a.* like a mollusk [L. *mollusca,* a soft nut].

mol·ly·cod·dle (mȧl′·i·kȧd·l) *n.* a milksop; *v.t.* or *v.i.* to coddle or be coddled or pampered [dim. of *Mary; coddle*].

molt (mōlt) *v.t.* and *i.* to shed feathers, as of birds, or skins, as of snakes; *n.* the act of shedding. Also **moult** [L. *mutare,* to change].

mol·ten (mōl′·tąn) *a.* melted; of metals, liquified [*Arch. pa.p.* of *melt*].

mo·lyb·de·num (mą.ib′·dą·nąm) *n.* a rare metal, used in alloys [Gk. *molubdos,* lead].

mom (mȧm) *n.* (*Colloq.*) mother. Also **mommy.**

mo·ment (mō′·mąnt) *n.* a short space of time; interval; importance; the measure of a force by its effect in causing rotation. **-arily** *adv.* **-ariness** *n.* **-ary** *a.* very brief. **-ous** (mō·men′·tas) very important. **-tum** (mō·men′·tąm) *n.* the impetus in a body; increasing force [L. *momentum,* movement].

mon·a·chism (mȧn′·ą·kizm) *n.* monasticism. **monachal** *a.* of monks [L. *monachus,* a monk].

mon·ad (mȧn′·ąd) *n.* (*Biol.*) a single-celled organism; (*Chem.*) an atom with the valence of one; (*Philos.*) an individual thought of as a microcosm. **-ism, -ology** *n.* the theory of monads [Gk. *monos,* alone].

mon·arch (mȧn′·ęrk) *n.* a hereditary sovereign; the supreme ruler of a state; *a.* supreme. **-ial, -ic, -al** *a.* pert. to a monarch or a monarchy. **-ically** *adv.* **-ism** *n.* the principles of monarchy; devotion to a royalist acuse. **-ist** *n.* advocate of monarchy; a royalist. **-y** *n.* government by a single ruler; a kingdom or empire [Gk. *monos,* alone; *archein,* to rule].

mon·as·ter·y (mȧn′·ąs·ter·i·) *n.* a settlement of monks. **monasterial, monastic** *a.* pert. to monasteries, monks or nuns. **monastic** *n.* a monk. **monasticism** (mąn·as′·ti·sizm) *n.* the monastic way of life [Gk. *monasterion*].

mon·au·ral (mȧn·aw′·rąl) *a.* of sound reproduction from one source only.

Mon·day (mun′·di·) *n.* the second day of the week [O.E. *mona,* the moon].

mon·e·tary (mȧn′·ą·ter·i) *a.* concerning money or coinage [L. *moneta,* a mint].

mon·ey (mun′·i·) *n.* any form of token, as coin, banknote, used as medium of exchange, and stamped by state authority; currency; wealth. *pl.* **monies. — bags** *n.pl.* a wealthy person. **-ed** *a.* wealthy. **— lender** *n.* one who lends money and charges interest. **—making** *a.* profitable. **— order,** an order for money, issued at one post office and payable at another [L. *moneta,* a mint].

mon·ger (mung′·gęr) *n.* (*Brit.*) a dealer, usu. in compound words, as *fishmonger, ironmonger, rumormonger* [O.E. *mangere,* a merchant].

Mon·gol (mȧng′·gąl) *n.* a native of Mongolia (Asia); *a.* Also **Mongolian. -ism** *n.* arrest of physical and mental development with Asiatic features. **-oid** *a.* resembling the Mongols.

mon·goose (mȧn′·gȯȯs) *n.* a small weasel-like animal, a snake-killer. *pl.* **mongooses** [Tamil]

mon·grel (mȧng′·grąl) *a. n.* impure; hybrid of mixed breed [O.E. *mang,* a mixture].

mon·ism (mōn′·izm) *n.* the philosophical doctrine which seeks to explain varied phenomena by a single principle. **monist** *n.* **monistic** *a.* [Gk. *manos,* single].

mo·ni·tion (mō·nish′·ąn) *n.* cautionary advice; admonition; notice; (*Law*) a summons. **monitive** *a.* expressing warning [L. *monitio,* warning].

mon·i·tor (mȧn′·i·tęr) *n.* one who cautions; one appointed to help keep order; a large lizard; (*Arch.*) armed warship for coastal service; *v.t.* to watch or check on a person or thing, radio or TV. **-ial** (mȧn·i·tōr′·i·ąl) *a.* **-ially** *adv.* **-y** *a.* warning [L. *monere, monitum,* to warn].

monk (mungk) *n.* a hermit; a member of a religious community living in a monastery. **-hood** *n.* **-ish** *a.* monastic. **-hood** *n.* a herbaceous poisonous plant [Gk. *monachos*].

mon·key (mung′·ki·) *n.* a long-tailed mammal of the order of Primates resembling man in organization; mischievous child; the weighted head of a pile driver; a hammer for driving home bolts; *v.i.* to imitate as a monkey; (*Colloq.*) to meddle with, as to *monkey with.* **-shine** (*Slang*) *n.* a prank. **— wrench** *n.* wrench with movable jaw.

mo·no- *prefix* meaning sole, single [Gk. *monos,* alone, single].

mon·o·bloc (mȧn′·ą·blȧk) *n.* the cylinders of the internal-combustion engine in one casting [Gk. *monos,* single; and *block*].

mon·o·car·pous (mȧn·ą·kȧrp′·ąs) *a.* bearing fruit only once. **monocarp** *n.* [Gk. *monos,* single; *karpos,* fruit].

mon·o·chord (mȧn′·ą·kawrd) *n.* a one-stringed instrument; a one-stringed device for measuring musical intervals.

mon·o·chrome (mȧn′·ą·krōm) *n.* a painting in different tones of the same color. **monochromatic, monochromic** *a.* **monochromatism** *n.* color-blindness [Gk. *monos,* single; *chrōma,* color].

mon·o·cle (mȧn′·ą·kl) *n.* a single eyeglass [Gk. *monos,* single; L. *oculus,* the eye].

mon·o·cot·y·le·don (mȧn·ą·kȧt·ą·lē′·dąn) *n.* a plant with only one seed lobe. **-ous** *a.* [Gk. *monos,* single; *kotulē,* a cup].

mo·noc·ra·cy (mą·nȧk′·rą·si·) *n.* government by a single person. **monocrat** *n.* [Gk. *monos,* single; *kratein,* to rule].

mon·o·dy (mȧn′·ą·di·) *n.* an elegy expressive of mourning; a monotonous tone. **monodic, -al** *a.* **monodist** *n.* [Gk. *monos,* single; *ōdē,* song].

mo·nog·a·my (mą·nȧg′·ą·mi·) *n.* the state of being married to one person at a time. **monogamist** *n.* **monogamous** *a.* [Gk. *monos,* single; *gamos,* marriage].

mon·o·gen·e·sis (mán·ạ·jen′·ạ·sis) *n.* the descent of an organism or all living things, from a single cell. **monogenetic** *a.* **monogenism** *n.* the theory of the descent of all human beings from an original single pair. Also **monogeny** [Gk. *mnoos*, single; *gignesthai*, to be born].

mon·o·gram (mán′·ạ·gram) *n.* two or more letters, as initials of a person's name, interwoven. **monogrammatic** *a.* [Gk. *manos*, alone; *gramma*, a letter].

mon·o·graph (mán′·ạ·graf) *n.* a specialized treatise on a single subject or branch of a subject. **-er** (mạ·nág′·rạ·fẹr) **-ist** *n.* **monographic, -al** *a.* [Gk. *monos*, single; *graphein*, to write].

mo·nog·y·nous (mạ·náj′·a·nus) *a.* (*Bot.*) having single pistil; (*Zool.*) mating with a single female. **monogyny** *n.* the custom of having only one female mate [Gk. *monos*, single; *gunē*, a female].

mon·o·lith (mán′·ạ·lith) *n.* a monument or column fashioned from a single block of stone. **-al, -ic** *a.* [Gk. *monos*, alone; *lithos*, a stone].

mon·o·logue (mán′·ạ·lawg) *n.* a dramatic scene in which an actor soliloquizes; a dramatic entertainment by a solo performer. **-ist** *n.* Also **monolog. monologist** *n.* [Gk. *monos*, single; *logos*, a speech].

mon·o·ma·ni·a (mán·ạ·mā′·ni·ạ) *n.* a form of mental derangement in which sufferer is irrational on one subject only, or is obsessed by one idea. **monomaniac** *n.* **monomaniacal** *a.* [Gk. *monos*, single; *mania*, madness].

mo·no·mi·al (mán·ō′·mi·ạl) *a.* (*Math.*) comprising a single term or expression; *n.* an algebraic expression containing a single term [Gk. *monos*, single; *onoma*, a name].

mon·o·nym (mán′·ạ·nim) *n.* a name comprising a single term. **mononymic** *a.* [Gk. *monos*, single; *onoma*, a name].

mon·o·pho·bia (mán·ạ·fō′·bi·ạ) *n.* (*Path.*) a morbid fear of being alone [Gk. *monos*, single; *phobos*, fear].

mon·o·plane (mán′·ạ·plān) *n.* an aircraft with only one set of wings.

mo·nop·o·ly (mạ·náp′·ạ·li·) *n.* the sole right to trade in certain commodities; exclusive possession or control; a commodity so controlled; a controlling company. **monopolize** *v.t.* to have a monopoly; to take possession to exclusion of others. **monopolizer, monopolist** *n.* **monopolistic** *a.* [Gk. *manos*, single; *pōlein*, to sell].

mon·o·syl·la·ble (mán·ạ·sil′·ạ·bl) *n.* a word of one syllable. **monosyllabic** *a.* having one syllable; speaking in words of one syllable. **monosyllabism** *n.*

mon·o·the·ism (mán′·ạ·thē·izm) *n.* the doctrine which admits of one God only. **monotheist** *n.* **monotheistic** *a.*

mon·o·tint (mán′·ạ·tint) *n.* a sketch or painting in one tint.

mon·o·tone (mán′·ạ·tōn) *n.* a single, unvaried tone or sound; a series of sounds of uniform pitch; sameness of any kind. **monotonic, monotonous** (mạ·nát′·ạ·nạs) uttered or recited in one tone; dull; unvaried. **monotony** (mạ·nát′·ạ·ni·) *n.* tedious uniformity of tone; lack of variety or variation; sameness [Gk. *monos*, single; *tonos*, a tone].

mon·o·type (mán′·ạ·tīp) *n.* (*Biol.*) a genus with one species. **Monotype** (*Print.*) (Trademark) a two-part machine for setting and casting type in individual letters, as distinct from *Linotype*. **monotypic** *a.* [Gk. *monos*, single; and *type*].

mon·o·va·lent (mán·a·vā′·lant) *a.* (*Chem.*) having a valency of one; univalent. **monovalence, monovalency** *n.*

mon·ox·ide (ma·nak′·sid) *n.* oxide containing one oxygen atom in a molecule.

Mon·sei·gneur (mawn·se′·nyẹr) *n.* my lord; a title given in France to princes, bishops, etc. (*abbrev.* **Mgr.**); *pl.* **Messeigneurs** (me·sen·-yurz′). **Monsignor** (mán·sēn·yẹr) an Italian title given to prelates (*abbrev.* **Mgr.** or **Monsig.**); also **monsignore;** *pl.* **monsignori** [L. *meus*, my; *senior*, older].

mon·soon (mán·sòòn′) *n.* a seasonal wind of S. Asia which blows on-shore from the S.W. in summer, and off-shore from the N.E. in winter; the very heavy rainfall season in summer, esp. in India. **-al** *a.* [Ar. *mausin*, a season].

mon·ster (mán′stẹr) *n.* a creature of unnatural shape; a person of abnormal callousness, cruelty, or wickedness. **monstrosity** *n.* an unnatural production; an abnormal creature; a freak. **monstrous** *n.* abnormal; enormous; horrible; shocking. **monstrously** *adv.* [L. *monstrum*, a marvel].

mon·strance (mán′·strạns) *n.* a shrine for the consecrated host in R.C. services [L. *monstrare*, to show].

mon·tage (mán·tázh′) *n.* (*Motion pictures*) assembling various shots of a film into one well-arranged series; a picture made by superimposing various elements from several sources [Fr. *monter*, to mount].

month (munth) *n.* one of the twelve divisions of the year. **calendar —** *n.* 31, 30, or 28 (29) days; the period of the complete revolution of the moon. **lunar —** *n.* about 29 days; a period of 28 days, or four complete weeks. **-ly** *a.* lasting, performed in, a month; *n.* a publication produced once each month; *adv.* once a month. **monthlies** *n.pl.* the menses [O.E. *monath*, a month].

mon·u·ment (mán′·yạ·mạnt) *n.* any structure, as a tombstone, building tablet, erected to the memory of person, or event; an ancient record; an achievement of lasting value. **-al** *a.* like, or worthy of, a monument; massive; colossal. **-ally** *adv.* [L. *monumentum*, fr. *monere*, to remind].

moo (mòò) *v.i.* to make the noise of a cow; to low; *n.* the lowing of a cow [imit.].

mooch (mòòch) *v.t.*, *v.i.* (*Colloq.*) to loiter; to sponge from another [O.Fr. *muchier*, to hang about].

mood (mòòd) *n.* (*Gram.*) the inflection of a verb expressing its function, as *indicative, imperative, subjunctive, infinitive;* (*Logic*) a form of syllogism; (*Mus.*) mode; the arrangement of intervals in the scale, as *major, minor* [var. of *mode*].

mood (mòòd) *n.* disposition; frame of mind; temper. **-ily** *adv.* **-iness** *n.* temporary depression of spirits; captiousness. **-y** *a.* peevish; sulky; depressed; angry [O.E. *mod*, mind].

moon (mòòn) *n.* the satellite which revolves around the earth in the period of a lunar month; any secondary planet; a month; anything crescent-shaped or shining like the moon; *v.i.* to behave or wander about aimlessly. **-beam** *n.* a ray of moonlight. **-calf** *n.* a fool. **-faced** *a.* having a round, expressionless face. **-light** *v.i.* (*Colloq.*) to work at an additional job after one's regular work. **-shine** *n.* light of the moon; nonsense; (*Colloq.*) smuggled liquor. **-shot** *n.* the launching of a missile to the moon. **-stone** *n.* an almost pellucid form of feldspar. **-struck** *a.* dazed [O.E. *mona*].

Moor (moor) *n.* a native of the Barbary States; one of the conquerors of Spain in the 8th cent. **-ish** *a.* [L. *Maurus*, *Mauretania*].

moor (moor) *n.* (*Brit.*) marshy wasteland. **-ish, -y** *a.* **-land** *n.* a heath [O.E. *mor*, marshland].

moor (moor) *v.t.* to secure by cables and anchors, as a vessel. **-age** *n.* place where vessel or airship is moored; charge for mooring. **-ing** *n.* the act of securing a ship; the place where a ship is moored (prob. Dut. *marren*, to tie].

moose (mòòs) *n.* largest species of deer; elk [Amer. Ind.].

moot (mòòt) *v.t.* to debate; to discuss; *a.* debatable; *n.* a discussion; in olden times, a council. **— court** *n.* a mock court [O.E. *gemot*, an assembly].

mop (māp) *n.* a bunch of soft cotton yarn or rags attached to handle for washing or polishing; a bushy head of hair; *v.t.* to wipe or polish. *pr.p.* **-ping.** *pa.p.* **-ped** [L. *mappa*, a napkin].

mope (mōp) *v.i.* to be dull or depressed; to sulk. **moping** *a.* listless; gloomy. **mopishly** *adv.* dispiritedly [Dut. *moppen*, to sulk].

mo·ped (mō′·ped) *n.* a heavy bicycle with a small motor; *v.i.* **-ing** *n.* **-er** *n.* [fr. *mo*tor and *ped*al].

mop·pet (map′·ạt) *n.* (*Colloq.*) a doll; a child [fr. *mop*].

mo·raine (mạ·rān′) *n.* rock debris which accumulates along the sides or at the end of a glacier [Fr.].

mor·al (mar′·ạl, mawr′·ạl) *a.* pert. to right conduct or duties; ethical; virtuous; chaste; discriminating between right and wrong; didactic; verified by reason or probability; *n.* the underlying meaning implied in a fable, allegory, etc. **-s** *n.pl.* ethics; conduct, esp. concerning sex-relations; habits. **-ization** *n.* **-ize** *v.t.* to explain in a moral sense; to draw a moral from; *v.i.* to reflect on ethical values of. **-izer, -ist** *n.* one who moralizes; one who studies or teaches ethics; one who accepts ethics instead of religion as an adequate guide to good living. **-istic** *a.* **-ity** (mạ·ral′·i·ti·) *n.* the practice of moral duties; virtue; ethics. **-ly** *adv.* **— victory** *n.* a defeat which in a deeper sense is a victory [L. *moralis*, of manners or customs].

mo·rale (mạ·ral′) *n.* the disposition or mental state which causes a man or body of people to face an emergency with spirit, fortitude, and unflagging zeal [Fr.].

mo·rass (mạ·ras′) *n.* marshy ground; difficult state of affairs [Dut. *moeras*, a marsh].

mor·a·to·ri·um (mawr·ạ·tō′·ri·ạm) *n.* a law to delay payment of debts for a given period of time; the period of suspension of payments; **moratory** *a.* delaying [L. *mora*, delay].

mo·ray (maw′·rā) *n.* a sharp-toothed marine eel [Gk. *muraina*].

mor·bid (mawr′·bid) *a.* diseased; unhealthy; (of the mind) excessively gloomy. **-ity** *n.* **-ly** *adv.* **-ness** *n.* **morbific** *a.* causing unhealthiness of body or mind [L. *morbus*, disease].

mor·dant (mawr′·dạnt) *n.* any substance, metallic or vegetable, which fixes dyes; a corrosive acid used in etching; *a.* biting; corrosive; sarcastic. **mordacious** *a.* acrid; sarcastic. **mordaciously** *adv.* **mordacity** *n.* **-ly** *adv.* [L. *mordere*, to bite].

mor·dent (mōr′·dạnt) *n.* (*Mus.*) a trill [L. *mordere*, to bite].

more (mōr) *a.* (*comp.* of **much, many;** *superl.* **most**) greater in amount, degree, quality, etc.; in greater number; additional; *adv.* in a greater quantity, extent, etc.; besides; *n.* something additional [O.E. *mara*].

mor·el (mạ·rel′) *n.* an edible mushroom [Fr. *morille*].

mo·rel (mạ·rel′) *n.* the common and deadly nightshade [O.Fr. *morel*, black].

mo·rel·lo (mạ·rel′·ō) *n.* a variety of dark red cherry used in manufacture of brandy. Also **morel** [It. *morello*, dark-skinned].

more·o·ver (mōr·ō′·vẹr) *adv.* besides; also; further [fr. *more*].

mor·ga·nat·ic (mawr·gạ·nat′·ik) *a.* applied to a marriage betweeen a man of high, esp. royal rank, and a woman of lower station, the issue having no claim to his rank or property. **-ally** *adv.* [Ger. *Morgengabe*, a morning gift].

mo·res (maw′·rāz) *n.pl.* customs [L.].

morgue (mawrg) *n.* a place where bodies of people killed in accidents, etc., are taken to await identification; a library of clippings, etc. kept by a newspaper or publication [Fr.].

mor·i·bund (mawr′·i·bund) *a.* at the point of death [L. *moribundus*, dying].

Mor·mon (mawr′·man) *n.* alleged 4th cent. prophet & author, writings published 1830 by Joseph Smith, founder of the Church of Jesus Christ of Latter-Day Saints; member of The Church professing Theocracy &, formerly, polygamy. **-ism** *n.*

morn (mawrn) *n.* (*Poetic*) the early part of the day [O.E. *morgen*, morning].

morn·ing (mawr′·ning) *n.* the first part of the day between dawn and midday; (*Fig.*) the first part of anything; *a.* pert. to or happening at this time. **—glory** *n.* a twining vine with flowers. **—coat** *n.* a tail-coat with cutaway front. **— star** *n.* a planet visible before sunrise [M.E. *morwening*, the coming of the day].

mo·ron (mōr′·ȧn) *n.* an adult with the mental development of an 8-12 yr. old child. **moronic** *a.* [Gk. *moros*, stupid].

mo·rose (mạ·rōs′) *a.* sullen; gloomy; soured in nature. **-ly** *adv.* **-ness** *n.* [L. *morosus*, fretful].

mor·pheme (mawr′·fēm) *n.* (*Gram.*) the smallest meaningful linguistic unit: *free form* as **boy,** or *bound form* as **ish** in **boyish.**

mor·phine (mawr′·fēn) *n.* an alkaloid of opium; a drug used to induce sleep and to deaden pain. [fr. *Morpheus*, Gk. god of sleep].

mor·ph-, morphic, morphous word elements meaning form or shape [Gk.].

mor·row (mar′·ō) *n.* next day; (*Poet.*) morning [O.E. *morgen*, the morning].

Morse (mawrs) *n.* a system of telegraphic signals in which the alphabet is represented by combinations of dots and dashes [fr. Amer. inventor S. F. B. *Morse*].

mor·sel (mawr′·sạl) *n.* a mouthful; a small piece [O.Fr. dim fr. L. *morsus*, a bite].

mor·tal (mawr′·tạl) *a.* subject to death; fatal; meriting damnation, as sin; implacable, as a foe; *n.* a human being. **-ity** (mawr·tal′·i·ti·) *n.* death; death-rate; the human race. **-ly** *adv.* [L. *mortalis*, fr. *mors*, death].

mor·tar (mawr·tẹr) *n.* a thick bowl of porcelain, glass, etc., in which substances are pounded with a pestle; a mill for pulverizing ores; (*Mil.*) a short-barreled cannon for short-distance firing of heavy shells; a cement made of lime, sand and water, used in building; *v.t.* to pound in a mortar; to cement, with mortar. **-board** *n.* a square board used when mixing mortar; an academic cap [L. *mortarium*].

mort·gage (mawr′·gij) *n.* (*Law*) a conveyance of property in security of a loan; the deed effecting this; *v.t.* to pledge as security. **mortgagee** *n.* one to whom a mortgage is given. **mortgagor** *n.* one who gives a mortgage to a mortgagee [O.Fr. *mort*, dead; *gage*, a pledge].

mor·ti·cian (mawr·tish′·ạn) *n.* an undertaker [L. *mors*, death].

mor·ti·fy (mawr′·tạ·fī) *v.t.* to discipline the flesh; to humiliate; to vex; *v.i.* (*Med.*) to become gangrenous. **mortification** *n.* the act of mortifying or the state of being mortified; humiliation; (*Med.*) gangrene; the death of one part of a living body L. *mors*, death; *facere*, to make].

mor·tise (mawr′·tis) *n.* a hole in a piece of wood to receive the projection or tenon of another piece, made to fit it. Also **mortice.** *v.t.* to cut or make a mortise in; to join with a mortise.

mort·main (mawrt′·mān) *n.* an inalienable bequest; the holding of land by a corporation, which cannot be transferred [O.Fr. *mortmain*, dead hand].

mor·tu·ar·y (mawr′·choo·er·i·) *n.* a place for the temporary reception of dead bodies; *a.* pert. to burial [L. *mortus*, dead].

mo·sa·ic (mō·zā′·ik) *a.* pert. to or made of mosaic; *n.* inlaid work of colored glass or marble [Gk. *mousa*, a muse].

Mo·sa·ic (mō·zā′·ik) *a.* (*Bib.*) pert. to *Moses*, or to the laws and writing attributed to him.

Mo•selle (mō·zel′) *n.* a light wine (fr. *Moselle*, Fr.].

Mos•lem (mȧz′·lạm) *n.* a Mohammedan; *a.* pert. to the Mohammedans or their religion. Also **Muslim** [Ar. *muslim*, true believer].

mosque (mȧsk) *n.* a Mohammedan temple [Ar. *masjid*, temple].

mos•qui•to (mạ·skē′·tō) *n.* an insect which draws blood, leaving a raised, itchy spot. **— net** *n.* a net covering to ward off mosquitos [L. *musca*, a fly].

moss (maws) *n.* a small, thickly growing plant which thrives on moist surfaces; lichen. **— agate** *n.* an agate with moss-like markings. **-back** *n.* (*Colloq.*) an extreme conservative. **-iness** *n.* **-y** *a.* covered with moss [O.E. *mos*, bog-land].

most (mōst) *a.* (*superl.* of **much, many;** *comp.* **more**) the greatest number or quantity; greatest; *adv.* in the greatest degree; *n.* the greatest quantity, number, etc. **-ly** *adv.* for the most part [O.E. *maest*, most].

mot (mō) *n.* pithy, witty saying [Fr. = word].

mote (mōt) *n.* a small particle; a speck of dust [O.E. *mot*, a particle].

mo•tel (mō·tel′) *n.* lodging for travelers [*mot*or and hot*el*].

mo•tet (mō·tet′) *n.* a musical composition for (unaccompanied) voices, to words from Scripture [Fr. dim. of *mot*, a word].

moth (mawth) *n.* a nocturnal winged insect; larva of this insect which feeds on cloth, esp. woolens. **— balls** *n.pl.* balls of moth repellent. **—eaten** *a.* eaten into holes by moth larva; decrepit [O.E. *moththe*].

moth•er (muTH′·ẹr) *n.* a female parent; the head of a convent; the origin of anything; *a.* characteristic of a mother; native; original; *v.t.* to be the mother or author of; to adopt as one's own; to cherish, as a mother her child. **-hood** *n.* the state of being a mother. **—in-law** *n.* the mother of one's wife or husband. **-liness** *n.* **-ly** *a.* having attributes of a mother. **— of pearl** *n.* the iridescent lining of several kinds of shells. **Mother Superior,** the head of a convent. **— tongue** *n.* one's native language [O.E. *modor*, a mother].

mo•tif (mō·tēf′) *n.* the dominant theme in a literary or musical composition [O.Fr.].

mo•tion (mō′·shạn) *n.* the act of moving; movement; a gesture; a proposal made in an assembly; *v.t.* to guide by gesture; *v.i.* to gesture. **-less** *a.* still; immobile. **— picture** *n.* a series of photographs projected on a screen rapidly, as to approximate lifelike movement [L. *movere, motum*, to move].

mo•tive (mō′·tiv) *n.* that which incites to action; motif; *a.* causing movement or motion; *v.t.* to impel; to motivate. **motivate** *v.t.* to incite. **motivation** *n.* **-less** *a.* without purpose or direction. **motivity** *n.* capacity to produce motion [L. *movere, motum*, to move].

mot•ley (mȧt′·li·) *a.* vari-colored; diversified; *n.* a jester's dress; a diversified mixture.

mo•tor (mō′·tẹr) *n.* that which imparts motion; a machine which imparts motive power, esp. the internal-combustion engine; *a.* causing motion; (*Anat.*) producing muscular activity, as *motor nerves; v.t., v.i.* to travel by, or convey in, a motor driven vehicle. **-cade** *n.* procession of automobiles. **— home** *n.* a truck-size motor vehicle outfitted as a self-contained traveling home. **-ize** *v.t.* to mechanize (the transport of the army). **-ist** *n.* one who drives or travels in an automobile. **-man** *n.* one who drives a streetcar [L. *motor*, a mover].

mot•tle (mȧt′·l) *v.t.* to mark with spots of different colors; to dapple. **-d** *a.* variegated.

mot•to (mȧt′·ō) *n.* a maxim or principle of behavior [L. *muttum*, a murmur].

moue (mȯȯ) *n.* a pout [Fr.].

mou•lage (mȯȯ′ī·lȧzh) *n.* moldmaking [Fr.].

mound (mound) *n.* an artificial elevation of earth; a knoll; an earthwork for defensive purposes; a heap; (*Baseball*) point from which pitcher delivers the ball; *v.t.* to fortify with a mound; to heap [O.E. *mund*, a defense].

mount (mount) *n.* (*poet.*, except in proper names) a mountain or hill; that on which anything is mounted for exhibition; a horse for riding; *v.t.* to raise up; to ascend; to get on a horse or bicycle; to frame (a picture); to set (gem-stones); to put on a slide for microscope examination; to stage a play with costumes, scenery, etc.; to raise guns into position; *v.i.* to rise up; to get up; to increase. **-ed** *a.* **-ing** *n.* **to mount guard,** to be on sentry duty; to keep watch over [L. *mons*, a mountain].

moun•tain (mount′·n) *n.* a high hill; *a.* pert. to a mountain; growing or living on a mountain. **— ash** *n.* any of a variety of small trees. **— dew** *n.* (*Slang*) whisky. **-eer** *n.* one who lives on or climbs high mountains. **— goat** *n.* the Rocky Mountain goat. **— laurel** *n.* American laurel. **-ous** *a.* very steep; full of mountains; colossal. **— range** *n.* a series or system of mountains [L. *mons*, a mountain].

moun•te•bank (moun′·tạ·bangk) *n.* a quack doctor; a charlatan [It. *montambanco*, mount on bench or platform].

Mount•ie (moun′·ti·) *n.* a member of the Canadian N.W. Mounted Police.

mourn (mōrn, mawrn) *v.t.* to grieve over; to lament; *v.i.* to express grief; to wear mourning. **-er** *n.* **-ful** *a.* sad; dismal. **-fully** *adv.* **-fulness** *n.* **-ing** *n.* the act of grieving; lamentation; wearing of black as a sign of grief; the period during which such clothes are worn [O.E. *murnan*, to grieve].

mouse (mous) *n.* a small rodent found in fields, or houses; a timid person. *pl.* **mice. mouse** (mouz) *v.t.* and *v.i.* to catch mice; to search for patiently or slyly; to prowl. **—color** *a.* dark greyish brown. **-r** *n.* an animal which catches mice. **—trap** *n.* **mousy** *a.* resembling a mouse in color; timid; quiet drab [O.E. *mus*, a mouse].

mousse (mȯȯs) *n.* a light-frozen dessert [Fr. *mousse*, froth]; a foam used in hairstyling.

mouth (mouth) *n.* an opening between lips of men and animals through which food is taken; lips, as a feature; the cavity behind the lips containing teeth, tongue, palate, and vocal organs; an opening as of a bottle, cave, etc.; the estuary of a river; a wry face. *pl.* **mouths** (mouTHz); *v.t.* (mouTH) to speak, with noticeable use of the mouth; to put or take into the mouth; to mumble; *v.i.* to make grimaces. **-ful** as much as the mouth conveniently holds; a small amount. **— organ** *n.* harmonica. **-piece** *n.* the part of a musical instrument, pipe, etc., held in mouth; (*Fig.*) a spokesman; a newspaper (as expressing public opinion) [O.E. *muth*, the mouth].

move (mȯȯv) *v.t.* to set in motion; to stir emotions of; to prevail on; to incite; to propose for consideration; *v.i.* to change one's position, posture, residence, etc.; to march; to make a proposal or recommendation; *n.* the act of moving; a change of residence; a movement, as in game of checkers. **movable, moveable** *a.*; *n.pl.* (*Law*) the furnishings of a house which are not permanent fixtures; **-ment** *n.* the act of moving; the part of a machine which moves; organized activity of a society; a division of a musical composition; evacuation of the bowels. **-r** *n.* **movies** *n.pl.* (*Colloq.*) motion pictures. **moving** *a.* causing motion; affecting the emotions; pathetic. **moving picture** *n.* motion picture. **moving staircase,** an escalator [L. *movere*, to move].

mow (mō) *v.t.* to cut down with a scythe or machine; to cut down in great numbers, as enemy. **-er** *n.* one who or that which mows [O.E. *mawan*, to mow].

mow (mou) *n.* a heap of hay, or corn, in a barn;

v.t. to put in a mow as a *haymow* [O.E. *muga*, a heap].

much (much) *a.* (*comp.* **more;** *superl.* **most**) great in quantity or amount; abundant; *n.* a great quantity; *adv.* to a great degree or extent; almost. **-ness** *n.* greatness. **-ly** *adv.* (*Colloq.*) much. **to make much of,** to treat as of great importance [M.E. *muchel*].

mu·cid (mū′·sid) *a.* moldy, musty. Also **-ous. -ness** *n.* [L. *mucidus*, moldy].

mu·ci·lage (mū′·sạ·lig) *n.* a gummy substance extracted from plants and animals; an adhesive. **mucilaginous** *a.* slimy; sticky [L. *mucus*, mucus].

muck (muk) *n.* moist manure; anything vile or filthy; *v.t.* to manure; to make filthy. **-iness** *n.* **-y** *a.* filthy [O.N. *myki*, dung].

muck·rake (muk′·rāk) *n.* one esp. a reporter, who searches for corruption, scandal [fr. a *muck raker*, coined by T. Roosevelt].

mu·cus (mū′·kạs) *n.* a viscid fluid secreted by the mucous membranes; slimy. **mucoid** *a.* like mucus. **mucous** *a.* of mucus; slimy [L.].

mud (mud) *n.* soft, wet dirt; aspersions, as in *to throw mud at a person* **-dily** *adv.* **-diness** *n.* **-dy** *a.* consisting of mire or mud; dull; cloudy, as liquid; *v.t.* to soil with mud; to confuse. *pr.p.* **-ding.** *pa.p., pa.t.* **-ded. -flat** *n.* a stretch of mud below high-water. **-guard** *n.* a shield to protect from mud splashes [O.L. Ger. *mudde*, mud].

mud·dle (mud′·l) *v.t.* to make muddy; to confuse; to bewilder; to mix up; *v.i.* to be confused; *n.* confusion; jumble [fr.*mud*].

muff (muf) *n.* a warm covering for both hands, usu. of fur, shaped like a cylinder and open at both ends; (*Baseball*) failure to hold a ball one has caught; *v.t.* to bungle [fr. Dut. *mof*, mitten]

muf·fin (muf′·in) *n.* a small cup-shaped bread, usu. eaten hot.

muf·fle (muf′·l) *v.t.* to wrap up for warmth or to hide something; to deaden (sound of); *n.* something used to deaden sound or provide warmth. **-d** *a.* **-r** *n.* a scarf; a silencer [O.Fr. *moufle*, a thick glove].

muf·ti (muf′·ti·) *n.* a Mohammedan advisor in regard to religious law; civilian dress worn by soldiers when off duty [Ar.].

mug (mug) *n.* a straight-sided earthenware or metal cup with or without a handle; the contents of this; (*Slang*) the face or mouth, a grimace, a rough person; *v.t.* (*Slang*) to attack from behind, by strangling, with intent to rob. *v.i.* (*Slang*) to grimace or overact. *pr.p.* **-ging.** *pa.p., pa.t.* **-ged. -ger** *n.*

mug·gins (mug′·inz) *n.* (*Brit.*) a simpleton; a game of dominoes.

mug·gy (mug′·i·) *a.* warm and humid, as weather; close; enervating. **mugginess** *n.* [O.N. *mugga*, a mist].

mug·wump (mug′·wump) *n.* one who holds independent political views [N. Amer. Ind. *mugquomp*, big chief].

mu·lat·to (mạ·lat′·ō) *n.* offspring of white person and Negro. *pl.* **-es** [Port. *mulato*, of mixed breed].

mul·ber·ry (mul′·ber·i·) *n.* a deciduous tree on the leaves of which the silkworm feeds; the fruit of this tree; a purplish-brown color [L. *morum*; A.S. *herie*].

mulch (mulch) *n.* a protective covering of straw, manure, etc., for plants; *v.t.* to treat with mulch [M.E. *molsh*, soft].

mulct (mulkt) *n.* a fine imposed as a penalty; *v.t.* to punish with a fine; to deprive of [L. *mulcia*, a fine].

mule (mūl) *n.* the hybrid offspring of a donkey or horse; a small tractor for hauling, in mines, along canals, etc.; a heelless bedroom slipper; an obstinate person. **-teer** *n.* a mule driver. **mulish** *a.* obstinate; pig-headed. **mulishly** *adv.* **mulishness** *n.* [O.E. *mul*, a he-ass].

mull (mul) *v.t.* to heat, sweeten and spice (wine, ale, etc.). **-ed** *a.*

mull (mul) *v.i.* to muse upon; to cogitate.

mul·let (mul′·ạt) *n.* an edible fish [L. *mullus*].

mul·li·gan (mul′·i·gạn) *n.* a stew made from left-over meat and vegetables.

mul·li·ga·taw·ny (mul·i·gạ·taw′·ni·) *n.* a rich soup flavored with curry, thickened with rice [Tamil].

mul·lion (mul′·yạn) *n.* a dividing upright between the lights of windows, panels, etc. *v.t.* to divide by millions. **-ed** *a.* [L. *mancus*, maimed].

mul·ti- *prefix*, fr. L. *multus*, many.

mul·ti·col·or (mul′·ti·kul·ẹr) *a.* having many colors. **-ed** *a.*

mul·ti·far·i·ous (mul·tạ·far′·i·ạs) *a.* manifold; made up of many parts [L. manifold].

mul·ti·form (mul′·ti·fawrm) *a.* having many forms. **-ity** *n.*

mul·ti·lat·e·ral (mul·ti·lat′·ẹr·ạl) *a.* having many sides. **-ly** *adv.* [L. *multus*, many; *latus*, a side].

mul·ti-mil·lion·aire (mul′·ti·mil′·yạn·er) *n.* a person who is worth several million dollars.

mul·ti·par·tite (mul·ti·pȧr′·tīt) *a.* having many parts; (*Govt.*) pert. to an agreement among three or more states; multilateral.

mul·ti·ped (mul′·ti·ped) *n.* and *a.* (animal) with many feet. Also **multipede.**

mul·ti·ple (mul′·tạ·pl) *a.* manifold; of many parts; repeated many times; *n.* (*Math.*) a quantity containing another an exact number of times. **— fission** *n.* repeated division [L. *multiplex*, manifold].

mul·ti·ply (mul′·tạ·plī) *v.t.* to increase in number; to add a number to itself a given number of times; *v.i.* to increase; to grow in number. **multiplex** *a.* multiple; (of telegraph) capable of transmitting numerous messages over the same wire. **multipliable, multiplicable** *a.* **multiplicand** *n.* the number to be multiplied. **multiplication** *n.* the act of multiplying; a rule or operation by which any given number may be added to itself any specified number of times (the symbol ×). **multiplicative** *a.* **multiplicator** *n.* a multiplier. **multiplicity** *n.* the state of being multiplied; great number. **multiplier** *n.* a number by which another, the **multiplicand,** is multiplied [L. *multus*, many; *plicare*, to fold].

mul·ti·tude (mul′·tạ·tūd) *n.* a great number; numerousness; a crowd; an assemblage. **multitudinous** *a.* made up of a great number [L. *multitudo*].

mul·ti·va·lent (mul·tạ·vā′·lạnt) *a.* (*Chem.*) having a valency of more than two. **multivalence, multivalency** *n.*

mul·ti·valve (mul′·ti·valv) *a.* having many valves; *n.* a mollusk with a shell of many valves.

mum (mum) *a.* silent; *n.* silence. **mum's the word,** keep it a secret [imit.].

mum (mum) *v.t.* to perform in dumb show; to act in a mask. **-mer** *n.* one who performs. **-mery** *n.* exaggerated ceremony. *pr.p.* **-ming.** *pa.p., pa.t.* **-med** [Dut. *mommen*, to mask].

mum·ble (mum′·bl) *v.t., i.* to utter, speak indistinctly; *n.* an indistinct utterance [fr. *mum*].

mum·bo jum·bo (mum′·bō jum′·bō) *n.* meaningless ritual [fr. Afr. idol worship].

mum·my (mum′·i·) *n.* a dead body preserved by embalming. **mummified** *a.* **mummification** *n.* **mummify** *v.t.* to embalm and dry as a mummy; *v.i.* to become dried up like a mummy [Pers. *mum*, wax].

mumps (mumps) *n.* a highly infectious disease causing painful swelling of face and neck glands (form of *mum*).

munch (munch) *v.t.* and *v.i.* to chew noisily and steadily [M.E. imit.].

mun·dane (mun′·dān) *a.* pert. to this world; worldly [L. *mundus*, the world].

mu·nic·i·pal (mū·nis′·ạ·pạl) *a.* pert. to local

government or to internal affairs (not international). **-ity** (mū·nis·ạ·pal′·i·ti·) *a* town or district with its own local self-government. **-ly** *adv.* [L. *municipium*, a free town].

mu·nif·i·cence (mū·nif′·ạ·sạns) *n.* liberality; generosity. **munificent** *a.* very generous. **munificently** *adv.* [L. *munus*, a gift; *facere*, to make].

mu·ni·ment (mū′·nạ·mạnt) *n.* means of protection. *pl.* title deeds; charter [L. *munire*, to fortify].

mu·ni·tion (mū·nish′·ạn) *v.t.* to equip with the weapons of war; *n.* (usually *pl.*) military stores or weapons [L. *munifus*, fortified].

mu·ral (mūr′·ạl) *a.* pert. to a wall; on a wall; *n.* a wall painting [L. *muralis*].

mur·der (mur′·dẹr) *n.* homicide with premeditated and malicious intent; *v.t.* to commit a murder; to kill; to mar by incompetence. **-er** *n.* (*fem.* **-ess**). **-ous** *a.* bloody; homicidal. **-ously** *adv.* [O.E. *morthor*, murder].

mu·ri·ate (myoo′·ri·āt) *n.* a chloride. **muriated** briny. **muriatic acid,** hydrochloric acid [L. *muria*, brine].

murk (murk) *a.* dark; *n.* darkness; gloom. **-y** *a.* dark; misty. **-ily** *adv.* **-iness** *n.* [O.E. *mirce*, dark].

mur·mur (mur′·mẹr) *n.* a low, unbroken sound, as of wind, water, etc.; a complaint expressed in subdued tones; softly uttered speech; *v.i.* to make a low sound; to speak in subdued tones; to complain. **-er** *n.* [L. *murmur*, a low sound].

mur·rain (mur′·in) *n.* a disease affecting cattle, foot-and-mouth disease [O.Fr. *morine*, a plague].

mus·cat (mus′·kat) *n.* a sweet grape; **-el** (mus·kạ·tel′) *n.* a wine made from this grape [It. *moscato*, musk-flavored].

mus·cle (mus′·l) *n.* a band of contractile fibrous tissue which produces movement in an animal body; strength. **—bound** *a.* with muscles enlarged and stiffened from too much exercise. **-d** *a.* having muscle; muscular. **muscular** *a.* pert. to muscle; brawny; strong. **muscularity** *n.* **muscularly** *adv.* **to muscle in** (*Slang*) to break in by force [L. *musculus*, a muscle].

mus·coid (mus′·koid) *a.* (*Bot.*) like moss. **muscology** *n.* the study of mosses [L. *muscus*, moss].

Mus·co·vite (mus′·kạ·vīt) *n.* a native or inhabitant of Moscow or of Russia. **muscovite** *n.* white mica; *a.* pert. to Moscow or to Russia.

Muse (mūz) *n.* (*Gk. myth.*) one of the nine daughters of Zeus and Mnemosyne, who each presided over one of the liberal arts. *n.* inspiration. **the muse,** poetry [Gk. *Mousa*].

muse (mūs) *v.i.* to think over dreamily; to ponder; to consider meditatively; *n.* reverie; contemplation. **musingly** *adv.* reflectively [O.Fr. *muser*, to loiter].

mu·settte (mū·zet′) *n.* a small bagpipe; a melody for this instrument; a reed stop on an organ; a country dance [O.Fr. a small bagpipe].

mu·se·um (mū·zē′·ạm) *n.* a building or room housing a collection of works of art, antiques, objects of natural history, the sciences, etc. [Gk. *Mouseion*, a temple of the Muses].

mush (mush) *n.* a pulp; (*U.S.*) porridge of corn meal; a soft mass; (*Slang*) sentimentality. **-y** *a.* **-iness n.** [form of *mash*].

mush (mush) *v.t.* to journey on foot with dogs over snowy wastes; *interj.* command to dogs to start or speed up.

mush·room (mush′·room) *n.* an edible fungus of very quick growth; (*Fig.*) an upstart; *a.* of rapid growth; shaped like a mushroom; *v.i.* to gather mushrooms; to grow quickly [prob. fr. Fr. *mousse*, moss].

mu·sic (mū′·zik) *n.* the art of combining sounds or sequences of notes into harmonious patterns pleasing to the ear and satisfying to the emotions; melody; musical composition or score. **-al** *a. pert.* to music; set to music; appreciative of music; trained or skilled in the art of music. **-ally** *adv.* **— box** *n.* a box which when wound up plays a tune. **-al comedy,** a form of light entertainment in which songs, dialogue, dancing, humor are combined with a not too serious plot. **-ale** (mū·zi·kal′) *n.* a private party with music. **— hall** *n.* a hall for musical programs. **-ian** (mū·zi′·shạn) *n.* a composer or skilled performer of musical compositions. **-ology** *n.* the scientific study of music [Gk. *mousikos*, pert. to the Muses].

musk (musk) *n.* a fragrant substance obtained from a gland of the musk deer; the perfume of this; any plant with a musky perfume. **-cat** *n.* civet. **— deer** *n.* a small, hornless deer. Also **Muscovy-duck. -melon** *n.* common melon. **— ox** *n.* a sheep-like ox with brown, long-haired shaggy coat. **-rat** *n.* a large N. Amer. water rat with musk-gland, valued for its fur. **— rose** *n.* a climbing rose with white blossoms faintly perfumed with musk. **-y** *a.* having the smell of musk [L. *muscus*, musk].

mus·ket (mus′·kit) *n.* (formerly) a hand gun or matchlock. **-eer** *n.* a soldier armed with a musket [O.Fr. *mousquet*, a sparrow hawk].

Mus·lim (muz′·lạm) *n.* See **Moslem.**

mus·lin (muz′·lin) *n.* a thin cotton cloth of open weave; *a.* made of muslin [fr. *Mosul*, in Iraq].

mus·quash (mus′·kwȧsh) *n.* the muskrat, or its fur [Amer. Ind.].

muss (mus) *v.t.* (*Colloq.*) to disorganize; to make messy. **-y** *a.*

mus·sel (mus′·l) *n.* a class of marine bivalve shellfish [L. *musculus*, mussel].

must (must) *v.i.* to be obliged, by physical or moral necessity; *v.aux.* to express compulsion, obligation, probability, certainty, dependent on verb used with it; *n.* a necessity [O.E. *moste*, pret. of verb, *not*, may].

must (must) *n.* wine newly pressed from grapes but not fermented [L. *mustus*, new].

mus·tache (mạs·tash′) *n.* the hair on the upper lip [Fr. *moustache*].

mus·tang (mus′·tang) *n.* a wild horse of the Amer. prairies; a bronco [Sp. *mestengo*, belonging to graziers].

mus·tard (mus′·tẹrd) *n.* a plant with yellow flowers and pungent seeds; a powder or paste made from the seeds, used as a condiment. **— gas,** dichlorodiethyl sulphide, an oily liquid, irritant war-gas [O.Fr. *moustarde*].

mus·ter (mus′·tẹr) *v.t.* to assemble, as troops for a parade; to gather together, as one's resources; *v.i.* to be assembled together; *n.* an assembling of troops, etc. **to pass muster,** to be up to standard [O.Fr. *mostre*, show].

mus·ty (mus′·ti·) *a.* moldy; stale. **mustily** *adv.* **-iness** *n.* [L. *mustum*, new wine].

mu·ta·ble (mū′·tạ·bl) *a.* subject to change; inconstant. **-ness, mutability,** *n.* **mutably** *adv.* **mutate** *v.t.* to change, as a vowel by the influence of another in a subsequent syllable. **mutation** *n.* change; the process of vowel change; (*Biol.*) a complete divergence from racial type which may ultimately give rise to a new species. **mutative, mutatory** *a.* [L. *mutare*, to change].

mute (mūt) *a.* dumb; silent; unexpressed in words; not sounded, as *e* of *cave;* *n.* a person who cannot speak; (*Mus.*) a device to soften or muffle tone; *v.t.* to muffle the sound of. **-ly** *adv.* **-ness** *n.* [L. *mutus*, dumb].

mu·ti·late (mū′·tạ·lāt) *v.t.* to maim; to cut off; to impair by removing an essential part. **mutilation** *n.* **mutilator** *n.* [L. *mutilus*, maimed].

mu·ti·ny (mū′·ti·ni·) *n.* insurrection against lawful authority, esp. military or naval; *v.i.* to rise in mutiny. **mutineer** *n.* **mutinous** *a.* rebellious; seditious [Fr. *mutin*, mutinous].

mutt (mut) *n.* (*Slang*) a fool; a dog, a mongrel.

mut·ter (mut′·ẹr) *v.t.* to speak indistinctly or in a low voice; to grumble. **-er** *n.* **-ing** *n.*
mut·ton (mut′·n) *n.* the flesh of sheep, esp. mature sheep, as food. **—chop whiskers,** side whiskers [Fr. *mouton*, a sheep].
mu·tu·al (mū′·choo·ạl) *a.* reciprocally acting or related; interchanged; done by each to the other; common to several, as a *mutual friend.* **-ity** *n.* the quality of being reciprocal. **-ly** *adv.* [L. *mutuus*, borrowed].
mu·zhik (mȯȯ·zhēk′) *n.* a Russian peasant.
muz·zle (muz′·l) *v.t.* the snout; the mouth and nose of an animal; a cage-like fastening for the mouth to prevent biting; the open end of a gun; *v.t.* to put a muzzle on; to gag; to enforce silence [L. *musus*, a snout].
muz·zy (muz′·i·) *a.* (*Colloq.*) dazed; bewildered.
my (mī) *poss. a.* belonging to **me** [contr. of *mine;* O.E. *min*, of me].
my·col·o·gy (mī·kȧl′·ạ·ji·) *n.* the science of fungi. **mycologist** *n.* **mycophagy** *n.* the eating of fungi [Gk. *mukēs*, a mushroom].
my·e·lin (mī′·ạ·lạn) *n.* (*Zool.*) the fatty substance forming the sheath of nerve fibers. **myelitis** *n.* inflammation of the spinal cord or bone marrow [Gk. *muelos*, marrow].
my·na(h) (mī′·nạ) *n.* a tropical starling, one variety mimics human speech [Hind.].
my·o- *prefix* from Gk. **mys, myos** meaning muscle.
my·o·car·di·tis (mī·ạ·kȧr·dīt′·ạs) *n.* (*Med.*) inflammation of the heart muscle.
my·o·ma (mī·ō′·mạ) *n.* tumor of muscle tissue.
my·o·pi·a (mī·ō′·pi·ạ) *n.* near-sightedness. **myopic** *a.* [Gk. *muein*, to close; *ōps*, the eye].
my·o·sis (mī·ō′·sis) *n.* prolonged contraction of the pupil of the eye [Gk. *myein*, to close; *-osis*].
my·o·so·tis (mī·ạ·sō′·tis) *n.* a genus of herbs including the forget-me-not [Gk. = mouse-ear].
myr·i·ad (mir′·i·ạd) *n.* an indefinitely large number; *a.* countless [Gk. *murias*, ten thousand].
myr·i·a·pod (mir′·i·ạ·pȧd) *n.* (*Zool.*) an animal with great number of legs, as centipede [Gk. *murias*, ten thousand; *pous*, a foot].
myr·me·col·o·gy (mur·mạ·kȧl′·ạ·ji·) *n.* the scientific study of ants and ant life [Gk. *murmēx*, an ant].
myrrh (mur) *n.* a transparent yellow-brown aromatic gum resin formerly used as incense, now used in antiseptics [Gk. *murrha*, myrrh].
myr·tle (mur′·tl) *n.* an evergreen plant with fragrant flowers and glossy leaves; (*U.S.*) the periwinkle [O.Fr. *myrtille*, the myrtle-berry].
my·self (mī·self′) *pron.* I or me, used emphatically, or reflexively.
mys·ter·y (mis′·tẹr·i·) *n.* anything strange and inexplicable; a puzzle; a religious truth beyond human understanding; secrecy; a medieval drama based on Scripture; *pl.* rites known to and practiced by initiated only. **mysterious** *a.* strange; occult; incomprehensible. **mysteriously** *adv.* [Gk. *mystēria*, secret religious rites].
mys·tic (mis′·tik) *a.* pert. to a mystery, to secret religious rites, or to mysticism; symbolical of spiritual truth; strange; *n.* one who believes in mysticism; one who seeks to have direct contact with the Divine by way of spiritual ecstasy and contemplation. **-al** *a.* **-ally** *adv.* **-ism** (mis′·ti·sizm) *n.* the doctrine of the mystics; study of spiritual experience; obscurity of doctrine. **mystification** *n.* **mystify** *v.t.* to perplex; to puzzle [Gk. *mustikos*, pert. to one initiated in the mysteries].
myth (mith) *n.* a fable; a legend embodying primitive faith in the supernatural; an invented story; an imaginary person or thing. **-ic, -ical** *a.* pert. to myths; fabulous; non-existent. **-ically** *adv.* **-ologic, (-al)** *a.* pert. to mythology; legendary. **-ologically** *adv.* **-ologist** *n.* one who has studied myths of various countries; a writer of fables. **-ology** *n.* a collection of myths; the science of myths; a treatise on myths [Gk. *muthos*, a story].
myx·e·de·ma (mik·sạ·dē′·mạ) *n.* (*Med.*) a disease caused by deficiency of secretion from thyroid gland [Gk. *muxa*, mucus; *oidēma*, swelling].

N

nab (nab) *v.t.* to catch hold of; to seize suddenly. *pr.p.* **-bing.** *pa.t., pa.p.* **-bed** [Dan. *nappe*, to catch].
na·bob (nā′·bȧb) *n.* a Mohammedan chief in India; any man of great wealth [Hind. *nawwab*].
na·celle (nạ·sel′) *n.* the part fixed to the wing of any aircraft serving to enclose engine, crew, passengers, and goods [Fr. fr. L. *navicella*, a little ship].
na·cre (nā′·kẹr) *n.* mother-of-pearl. **nacreous** *a.* [Fr. fr. Sp. *nacar*].
na·dir (nā′·dẹr) *n.* point of the heavens directly opposite the zenith; the lowest or most depressed stage [Ar. *nazir*, opposite].
nag (nag) *n.* a small horse; an old horse; (*Colloq.*) any horse [etym. uncertain].
nag (nag) *v.t.* and *v.i.* to worry by constant faultfinding; to scold. *pr.p.* **-ging.** *pa.t.* and *pa.p.* **-ged. -ger** *n.* [Sw. *nagga*, to peck].
nai·ad (nā′·ad, or nī′·ad) *n.* (*Class. Myth.*) a nymph of the streams. [Gk. *naias*].
nail (nāl) *n.* the horny shield covering the ends of the fingers or toes; a claw; a strip of pointed metal provided with a head, for fastening wood, etc.; *v.t.* to fasten with a nail; to fix or secure; to confirm or pin down; (*Colloq.*) to seize hold of. **— brush** *n.* a small brush for cleaning the fingernails. **-er** *n.* **-ery** *n.* a factory where nails are made. [O.E. *naegel*].
na·ïve (nȧ·ēv′) *a.* having native or unaffected simplicity; childishly frank; artless. **-ly** *adv.* **naïveté** (nȧ·ēv·tā′) *n.* childlike ingenuousness. Also **naivety** [Fr.].
na·ked (nā′·kid) *a.* having no clothes; exposed; bare; nude; uncovered; unarmed; manifest; evident; undisguised; simple; sheer. **-ly** *adv.* **-ness** *n.* [O.E. *nacod*].
nam·by-pam·by (nam′·bi·pam′·bi·) *a.* insipid, lacking strength of character; weakly sentimental [a nickname for *Ambrose Philips*, a poet who wrote childishly affected verse].
name (nām) *n.* the term by which any person or thing is known; appellation; designation; title; fame; reputation; family; *v.t.* to give a name to; to call or mention by name; to nominate; to specify; to christen; **-less** *a.* without a name; dishonored; obscure; unspeakable. **-lessly** *adv.* **-ly** *adv.* by name; that is to say. **-sake** *n.* a person who bears the same name as another [O.E. *nama*].
nan·keen (nan·kēn′) *n.* a cotton fabric dyed buff [*Nanking*, China, where first woven].
nan·ny (nan′·i·) *n.* (*Brit.*) a child's nurse. **— goat** *n.* a she-goat.
nap (nap) *n.* a short sleep; a doze; *v.i.* to indulge in a short sleep; to be unprepared. *pr.p.* **-ping** *pa.t., pa.p.* **-ped** [O.E. *knappian*].
nap (nap) *n.* fine hairy surface of cloth; the pile of velvet [Dut. *nop*].
na·palm (nā′·pȧm) *n.* jellied gasoline used in flame throwers.
nape (nāp) *n.* the back part of the neck [O.E. *hnaepp*, bowl].
na·per·y (nā′·per·i·) *n.* household linen, esp. for the table [O.Fr. *naperie*].
naph·tha (nap′·tha, naf′·thạ) *n.* a clear,

volatile, inflammable liquid distilled from petroleum, wood, etc. **-lene** *n.* a white, solid crystalline hydrocarbon distilled from coal tar and familiar in the form of moth balls [Gk.].

nap·kin (nap'·kin) *n.* a cloth used for wiping the hands or lips at table [Fr. *nappe*, cloth].

na·po·le·on (na·pōl'·yan) *n.* a pastry of several cream-filled layers; a French gold coin; a card game. **-ic** *a.* pert. to Napoleon I or III.

Nar·cis·sus (nȧr·sis'·as) *n.* bulbous plant genus including the daffodil, jonquil, narcissus. **narcissism** *n.* in psychoanalysis, an abnormal love and admiration for oneself. **narcissist** *n.* [fr. *Gk. Myth.*].

nar·cot·ic (nȧr·kȧt'·ik) *a.* producing stupor or inducing sleep; *n.* a substance which relieves pain and induces sleep and, in large doses, insensibility and stupor; one addicted to the habitual use of narcotics. **narcosis** *n.* a state of unconsciousness or stupor with deadening of sensibility to pain, produced by narcotics. **narc, nark, narko** *n.* (*Slang*) a local or federal *narc*otics detective [Gk. *narkōtikos*, benumbed].

nard (nȧrd) *n.* the spikenard, a plant which yields an odorous unguent. **-ine** *a.* [Pers.].

nar·rate (na·rāt', nar'·āt) *v.t.* to relate; to tell (story) in detail; to give an account of; to describe. **narration** *n.* an account. **narrative** *n.* a tale; a detailed account of events; *a.* pert. to, containing, narration. **narratively** *adv.* **narrator** *n.* [L. *narrare*].

nar·row (nar'·ō) *a.* of little breadth; not wide or broad; limited; bigoted; illiberal; *v.t.* to make narrow; *v.i.* to become narrow **-s** *n.* straits. **-ly** *adv.* **—minded** *a.* bigoted; illiberal; prejudiced [O.E. *nearu*].

nar·whal (nȧr'·whȧl) *n.* a cetaceous mammal, closely related to the white whale, with one large protruding tusk [Dan. *narhval*].

NASA (nas'·a) *n.* *N*ational *A*eronautics and *S*pace *A*dministration.

na·sal (nā'·zal) *a.* pert. to the nose; *n.* a nasal sound or letter, such as *m* or *n*. **-ize** *v.i.* to render (a sound) nasally. **-ity** *n.* the quality of being nasal. **-ly** *adv.* [L. *nasus*, the nose].

nas·cent (nas'-, nās'·ant) *a.* at the moment of being born; just beginning to exist. **nascence, nascency** *n.* [L. *nasci*, to be born].

na·stur·tium (na·stur'·sham) *n.* (*Bot.*) a common trailing garden plant of the genus Tropaeolum [L. = twisting the nose].

nas·ty (nas'·ti·) *a.* very dirty; filthy; disgusting; offensive; repulsive; unpropitious (of the weather, etc.); ill-natured; indecent. **nastily** *adv.* **nastiness** *n.* [etym. uncertain].

na·tal (nā'·tal) *a.* pert. to one's place of birth or date of birth; **-ity** *n.* birth rate. **— day** *n.* birthday [L. *natus*, born].

na·tant (nā'·tant) *a.* (*Bot.*) floating on the surface. **natation** *n.* swimming. **natatorium** *n.* a swimming pool. **natatory, natatorial** *a.* used or adapted for swimming [L. *nature*, to swim].

na·tion (nā'·shan) *n.* a people inhabiting a country under the same government; an aggregation of persons of the same origin and language [L. *natio*, a tribe].

na·tion·al (nash'·an·al) *a.* belonging to or pertaining to a nation; public; general; *n.* member of a nation. **-ization** *n.* **-ize** *v.t.* to make national; to acquire and manage by the state; to make a nation of. **-ism** *n.* devotion to the interests of one's nation. **-ist** *n.* one who advocates a policy of national independence. **-ity** *n.* the quality of being a nation or belonging to a nation; one's nation; patriotism. **-ly** *adv.* **— anthem** *n.* a hymn or song expressive of patriotism, praise, or thanksgiving. **National Guard** *n.* State military force which can be called to active duty [L. *natio*].

na·tive (nā'·tiv) *a.* pert. to one's birth; belonging by birth; innate; indigenous; natural; of metals, occurring in a natural state; pert. to natives; *n.* a person born in a place; **-ly** *adv.* **Native American** *n.*, *a.* American Indian. **nativity** *n.* the time or circumstances of birth; in astrology, the position of the stars at a person's birth [L. *nativus*, inborn].

NATO (nā'·tō) *n.* *N*orth *A*tlantic *T*reaty *O*rganization.

nat·ty (nat'·i·) *a.* neat; trim; tidy; spruce. **nattily** *adv.* [etym. unknown].

nat·u·ral (nach'·a·ral) *a.* in accordance with, belonging to, or derived from, nature; inborn; unconstrained; normal; in a state of nature; unaffected; unassuming; true to life; illegitimate; (*Mus.*) not modified by a flat or sharp; *n.* an idiot; (*Colloq.*) a person or thing naturally suitable; (*Mus.*) a character used to remove the effect of an accidental sharp or flat which has preceded it. **-ization** *n.* **-ize** *v.t.* to give to an alien the rights of a native subject; to adopt a foreign word etc., as native; to accustom, as to a climate. **-ism** *n.* natural condition or quality; the system of those who deny miracles, prophecies, etc. **-ist** *n.* one versed or interested in natural history. **-istic** *a.* in accordance with nature. **-istically** *adv.* **-ly** *adv.* **-ness** *n.* **— gas** *n.* an inflammable product occurring in association with mineral oil deposits. **— history** *n.* the science which deals with the earth's crust and its productions, but applies more especially to biology or zoology. **— philosophy** *n.* the science of nature and of the physical properties of bodies; physics. **— religion** *n.* religion which is derived from nature and reason without resource to revelation. **— science** *n.* the science of nature as distinguished from mental and moral science and mathematics [fr. *nature*].

na·ture (nā'·cher) *n.* the world, the universe, known and unknown; the power underlying all phenomena in the material world; the innate or essential qualities of a thing; the environment of man; the sum total of inheritance; natural disposition; innate character; of a material, the average excellence of its qualities when unaffected by deteriorating influences; sort; kind; vital functions of organs of the body; state of nakedness. **-d** *a.* in compounds, showing one's innate disposition, as *good-, bad-natured* [L. *natura*].

naught (nawt) *n.* (*Arch.*) nothing; figure 0; zero. Also **nought. -y** *a.* wayward; not behaving well; mischievous; bad. **-ily** *adv.* **-iness** *n.* [O.E. *nawiht*].

nau·se·a (naw'·zē·a, naw'·s(h)ē·a, naw'·zha) *n.* any sickness of the stomach accompanied with a propensity to vomit; a feeling of disgust; sea-sickness. **-te** *v.i.* to feel nausea; *v.t.* to loathe; to fill with disgust; to affect with nausea. **nauseous** *a.* loathsome; disgusting; producing nausea. **nauseously** *adv.* [Gk. = seasickness, fr. *naus*, a ship].

nau·ti·cal (naw'·ti·kal) *a.* pert. to ships, seamen, or navigation. **-ly** *adv.* **— mile** *n.* 6,080.2 ft. [Gk. *nautēs*, a sailor].

nau·ti·lus (naw'·ta·las) *n.* a genus of cephalopod mollusc with many-chambered spiral shells. **nautiloid** *a.* [Gk. *nautilos*, a sailor].

na·val (nā'·val) *a.* pert. to ships, esp. warships; belonging to or serving with the navy [L. *navis*, a ship].

nave (nāv) *n.* the middle or body, of a church [L. *navis*, a ship].

na·vel (nā'·vl) *n.* the umbilicus, place of attachment of the umbilical cord to the body of the embryo, marked by a rounded depression in the center of the lower part of the abdomen; the central part [O.E. *nafela*].

na·vic·u·lar (na·vik'·ya·ler) *a.* shaped like a boat; relating to small ships or boats; *n.* one of the bones of the wrist and ankle [L. *navic-*

ularis; fr. *navis,* a ship].

nav·i·gate (nav′·i·gāt) *v.t.* and *v.i.* to steer or manage a ship or aircraft; to sail upon or through; **navigable** *a.* may be sailed over or upon; seaworthy; steerable (of balloons). **navigability, navigableness** *n.* **navigably** *adv.* **navigation** *n.* the science of directing course of seagoing vessel and of ascertaining its position at any given time; the control and direction of aircraft in flight; **navigator** *n.* [L. *navigare,* to sail].

na·vy (nā′·vi·) *n.* a fleet; the warships of a country with their crews and organization. **— blue** *n.* and *a.* dark blue [L. *navis,* a ship].

nay (nā) *adv.* no; not only this, but; *n.* denial; refusal [O.N. *nei,* never].

Naz·a·rene (naz′·a·rēn) *n.* a native of *Nazareth;* name given to Jesus; *pl.* an early Christian sect.

Na·zi (nat′·zi·) *n.* and *a.* a member of the National Socialist Party of Germany (1922-1945). **-sm, -ism** *n.* [Ger. *nazional,* national].

Ne·an·der·thal (nē·an′·der·tal) *a.* denoting a man of the earliest long-headed race in Europe which became extinct at least 20,000 years ago [fr. a cave in *Neanderthal,* Ger.].

neap (nēp) *a.* low; *n.* neap tide. **— tide** *n.* the tide whose rise and fall is least marked [O.E. *nep.*].

Ne·a·pol·i·tan (nē·ạ·pal′·ạ·tạn) *a.* and *n.* pert. to Naples or its inhabitants [Gk. *Neapolis,* fr. *neos,* news; *polis,* a city].

near (nir) *adv.* at or to a short distance; *prep.* close to; *a.* close; closely related; stingy; *v.t.* and *v.i.* to approach. **-by** *a.* in close proximity; adjacent. **— East,** part of Asia nearest Europe, from Asia Minor to Persia. **-ly** *adv.* closely; intimately; almost. **-ness** *n.* **-side** *n.* of horses, vehicles, etc., the left side. **-sighted** *a.* myopic; short-sighted. **-sighted-ness** *n.* [O.E. *near,* nigher].

neat (nēt) *a.* orderly; clean; trim; well-fitting; undiluted; clever; in good taste; dexterous; precise; net. **-ly** *adv.* **-ness** *n.* [Fr. *net,* clean, pure].

neb (neb) *n.* the bill or beak of a bird; the nose [O.E. *nebb* the face].

neb·u·la (neb′·yạ·lạ) *n.* a slight greyish speck on the cornea of the eye; a cloudlike celestial phenomenon consisting of vastly diffused gas or of tenuous material throughout which fine lust in an incandescent state is distributed. *pl.* **-e. -r** *a.* **nebulosity** *n.* cloudiness; vagueness. **nebulous** *a.* cloudy, hazy, indistinct; vague; formless; pert. to nebula. **nebulousness** *n.* [L. = mist].

nec·es·sar·y (nes′·ạ·ser·i·) *a.* needful; requsite indispensable; that must be done; *n.* a needful thing; essential need. **necessarily** *adv.* [L. *necessarius*].

ne·ces·si·ty (nạ·ses′·ạ·ti·) *n.* pressing need; indispensability; compulsion; needfulness; urgency; poverty; a requisite; an essential. **necessitate** *v.t.* to make necessary or indispensable; to force; to oblige. **necessitous** *a.* needy; destitute [L. *necessitas*].

neck (nek) *n.* the part of the body joining the head to the trunk; the narrower part of a bottle, etc.; a narrow piece of anything between wider parts; *v.t.* (*Slang*) to hug; to cuddle. **-erchief** *n.* a band of cloth or kerchief worn round the neck. **-lace** *n.* a string of beads or precious stones worn round neck. **-piece** *n.* a scarf, usually of fur, **-tie** *n.* a tie for the neck. **neck and neck,** just even [O.E. *hnecca,* nape of neck].

ne·cro- *prefix,* fr. Gk. *nekros,* a dead body, used in the construction of compound terms, signifying death in some form. **-logy** *n.* a register of deaths; a collection of obituary notices. **-mancy** *n.* the art of predicting future events by conjuring up the spirits of the dead; black magic; enchantment. **-mancer** *n.* a sorcerer; a magician. **-mantic** *a.* pert. to magic. **-polis** *n.* a cemetery. **-psy, -scopy** *n.* a postmortem; autopsy. **-sis** *n.* gangrene, mortification. **-tic** *a.*

nec·tar (nek′·tẹr) *n.* the fabled drink of the gods; any delicious beverage; honey-like secretion of the nectary gland of flowers. **-eal, -ean, -eous, -ous** *a.* sweet as nectar; resembling nectar; delicious. **-ed** *a.* flavored with nectar; very sweet. **-ine** *a.* sweet as nectar; *n.* a smooth-skinned variety of peach [Gk. *nektar*].

need (nēd) *n.* a constitutional or acquired craving or want, appeased by recurrent satisfactions; want; necessity; requirement; urgency; poverty; destitution; extremity; urgency; *v.t.* to be in want of; to require; *v.i.* to be under a necessity. **-ful** *a.* necessary; requisite **-fully** *adv.* **-fulness** *n.* **-ily** *adv.* **-iness** *n.* condition of need. **-less** *a.* unnecessary; not needed. **-lessly** *adv.* **-lessness** *n.* **-y** *a.* in need; indigent [O.E. *nied*].

nee·dle (nēd′·l) *n.* a slender pointed instrument with an eye, for passing thread through cloth, etc.; a slender rod for knitting; anything like a needle, as the magnet of a compass, a hypodermic syringe, an etcher's burin, an obelisk, a sharp-pointed rock, leaf of the pine, etc.; the reproducing needle of a phonograph. **-point** *n.* a hand-made lace; canvas with a design worked in yarn. **-work** *n.* [O.E. *naedl*].

ne'er (ner) *adv.* poetical form of never. **—do-well** *a., n.* good-for-nothing; worthless.

ne·far·i·ous (ni·fa′·ri·ạs) *a.* wicked in the extreme; iniquitous. **-ly** *adv.* **-ness** *n.* [fr. L.].

ne·gate (ni·gāt′) *v.t.* to deny; to prove the contrary. **negation** *n.* the act of denying; negative statement; disavowal; contradiction [L. *negare,* to deny].

neg·a·tive (neg′·ạ·tiv) *a.* expressing denial, prohibition, or refusal; lacking positive qualities; not positive; stopping or withholding; (*Elect.*) at a lower electric potential; (*Algebra*) minus; *n.* a proposition in which something is denied; a negative word; a photographic plate in which lights and shades are reversed; *v.t.* to refuse to sanction; to reject. **-ly** *adv.* **-ness** *n.* [L. *negare,* to deny].

neg·lect (ni·glekt′) *v.t.* to disregard; to take no care of; to fail to do; to omit through carelessness; to slight; *n.* omission; disregard; careless treatment; slight. **-edness** *n.* **-er** *n.* **-ful** *a.* careless; inclined to be heedless. **-fully** *adv.* [L. *neglegere,* to neglect].

neg·li·gee (neg·lạ.zhā′) *n.* a woman's loose dressing gown [Fr.].

neg·li·gence (neg′·lạ·jạns) *n.* want of due care; carelessness; habitual neglect. **negligent** *a.* careless; inattentive; untidy. **negligently** *adv.* **negligible** *a.* hardly worth noticing [L. *neglegere,* to neglect].

ne·go·ti·ate (ni·gō′·shi·āt) *v.t.* to settle by bargaining; to arrange; to transfer (a bill, etc.); (*Colloq.*) to surmount; *v.i.* to discuss with a view to finding terms of agreement; to bargain. **negotiable** *a.* capable of being negotiated; transferable. **negotiability** *n.* **negotiation** *n.* **negotiant, negotiator** *n.* [L. *negotiari,* fr. *negotium,* business].

Ne·gro (nē′·grō) *n.* (*often offensive*) a member of the dominant ethnic group of Africa; a black (male or female); *a.* **-id** *a.* resembling this group [Sp. and Port., fr. L. *niger,* black].

neigh (nā) *v.i.* to whinny, like a horse; *n.* cry of a horse [O.E. *hnaegan*].

neigh·bor (nā′·bẹr) *n.* a person who lives, works, near another; *a.* neighboring; *v.t.* to adjoin; to be near. **-hood** *n.* adjoining district and its people; proximity; vicinity. **-ing** *a.*

close by. **-ly** *a.* friendly; sociable; helpful. **-liness** *n.* [O.E. *neahgebur*].

nei·ther (nē′·THẹr, nī′·THẹr) *a.* and *pron.* not the one or the other; *adv.* not on the one hand; not either; *conj.* nor yet; not either [O.E. *nahwaether*, not whether].

nem·a·tode, nematoid (nem′·ạ·tōd, ·toid) *a.* thread-like. **nematoidea** *n.pl.* roundworms, threadworms [Gk. *nēma*, thread; *eidos*, form].

nem·e·sis (nem′·ạ·sis) *n.* inevitable retributive justice [Gk. *nemein*, to distribute, deal out].

ne·o- (nē′·ō) *prefix* used in the construction of compound terms, signifying *new, recent* [Gk.].

ne·o·dym·i·um (nē·ō·dim′·i·ạm) *n.* a metallic element belonging to the group of rare earth metals [Gk. *neos*, new; and *didymium* (a once supposed element)].

ne·o·lith·ic (nē·ō·lith′·ik) *a.* (*Geol.*) pert. to the late Stone Age.

ne·ol·o·gy (nē·ál′·ạ·ji·) *n.* the introduction of new words into a language; new doctrines, esp. rationalistic, in theology. **neologian, neologist** *n.* one who coins new words or holds novel doctrines in religion. **neologic, neological** *a.* **neologize** *v.i.* to coin new words. **neologism** *n.* a newly-coined word or phrase; a new doctrine [Gk. *neos*, new; *logos*, word].

ne·on (nē′·ȧn) *n.* a non-metallic chemical element belonging to the group of the rare gases. **— light, — sign,** or **— tube,** one containing neon gas and glowing with a characteristic reddish-orange light [Gk. *neos*, new].

ne·o·pho·bi·a (nē·ō·fō′·bi·ạ) *n.* a dread of the unknown [Gk. *neos*, new; *phobos*, fear].

ne·o·phyte (nē′·ạ·fīt) *n.* a novice; a convert [Gk. *neos*, new; *phutos*, grown].

ne·pen·the, nepenthes (ni·pen′·thē, ·thēz) *n.* in Greek mythology, a drug with power of banishing grief; any narcotic drug to relieve pain; genus of Asiatic plants [Gk. *nē-*, not; *phenthos*, grief].

neph·ew (nef′·ū) *n.* a brother's or sister's son; son of one's husband's or wife's brother or sister [Fr. *neveu*, fr. L. *nepos*, a nephew].

nephr- (or nephro-) prefix used in the construction of compound terms, from Greek *nephros*, a kidney. **-algia, -algy** *n.* pain in the kidney. **-ic** *a.* pert. to the kidneys. **-itic(al)** *a.* pert. to (diseases of) the kidneys. **-itis** *n.* Bright's disease, non-infective inflammation of the kidney.

nep·o·tism (nep′·ạ·tizm) *n.* undue favoritism in awarding public appointments to one's relations [L. *nepos*, a nephew].

Nep·tune (nep′·to͝on) *n.* (*Myth.*) the Roman god of the sea; second most remote planet of solar system [L.].

nerve (nurv) *n.* one of the bundles of fibers which convey impulses either *from* brain (motor nerves) to muscles, etc., producing motion, or *to* brain (sensory nerves) from skin eyes, nose, etc., producing sensation; mid-rib or vein of a leaf; sinew; tendon; fortitude; courage; cool assurance; (*Slang*) impudence. *pl.* irritability; unusual sensitivity to fear, annoyance, etc.; *v.t.* to give courage or strength to. **-d** *a.* **-less** *a.* lacking in strength or will; incapable of effort. **-lessness** n. **nervine** *a.* acting on the nerves; *n.* a nerve-tonic. **nervy** *a.* *(Slang)* bold; showing courage [L. *nervus*, sinew].

nerv·ous (nurv′·ạs) *a.* pert. to, containing, or affecting nerves; uneasy; apprehensive. **-ly** *adv.* **-ness** *n.* **— breakdown** *n.* a condition of mental depression [L. *nervus*, a sinew].

nes·cience (nesh′·ạns) *n.* the condition of complete ignorance; lack of knowledge; agnosticism. **nescient** *a.* ignorant; agnostic [L. *nescier*, not to know].

nest (nest) *n.* the place in which a bird or other animal lays and hatches its eggs; any snug retreat; a set of boxes, tables, etc., which fit into one another; *v.t.* to form to place in a nest; *v.i.* to occupy or build a nest. **-ling** *n.* a bird too young to leave the nest. **— egg** *n.* an egg left in a nest to induce a bird to lay; a small sum of money put aside for some later purpose [O.E.].

nes·tle (nes′·l) *v.i.* to settle comfortably and close to one another; to lie snugly, as in a nest; (of a house) to be situated in a sheltered spot [O.E. *nestlian*].

net (net) *n.* an open-work fabric of meshes of cord, etc.; sections of this used to catch fish, protect fruit, etc.; lace formed by netting; a snare. *a.* made of netting; reticulate; caught in a net; *v.t.* to cover with, or catch in, a net; to veil; *v.t.* to make net or network. *pr.p.* **-ting.** *pa.t.* and *pa.p.* **-ted. -ted** *a.* **-ting** *n.* the act or process of forming network; net-like fabric; snaring by means of a net. **-work** *n.* anything made like, or resembling, a net; (*Radio*) a group of transmitting stations producing programs carried by long-distance telephone wires to affiliated stations for broadcasting [O.E. *nett.*].

net (net) *a.* left after all deductions; free from deduction; *v.t.* to gain or produce as clear profit; *pr.p.* **-ting.** *pa.p.* **-ted. — price,** net price without discount [Fr. = clean].

neth·er (neTH′·ẹr) *a.* lower; low-lying; lying below; belonging to the lower regions.**-most** *a.* lowest. **-ward(s)** *adv.* in a downward direction [O.E. *neothera*].

net·tle (net′·l) *n.* a common weed covered with fine stinging hairs; *v.t.* to irritate; to provoke; to make angry; to rouse to action. **— rash** *n.* an irritating eruption in the skin [O.E. *netele*].

neur-, neuro- *prefix* from Gk. *neuron*, a nerve.

neu·ral (nyoo′·rạl) *a.* pert. to the nerves or nervous system [Gk. *neuron*, a nerve].

neu·ral·gia (nyoo·ral′·jạ) *n.* a spasmodic or continuous pain occurring along the course of one or more distinct nerves. **neuralgic** *a.* [Gk. *neuron*, a nerve; *algos*, pain].

neu·ras·the·ni·a (nyoor·ạs·thē′·ni·ạ) *n.* a condition of nervous debility characterized by lack of energy, restlessness, headache and insomnia. **neurasthenic** *a.* [Gk. *neuron*, a nerve; *astheneia*, weakness].

neu·rax·is (nyoo·rak′·sis) *n.* the cerebrospinal axis, or central nervous system, including the brain and spinal cord.

neu·ri·tis (nyoo·rī′·tis) *n.* an inflammatory condition of a nerve [Gk. *nueron*, a nerve].

neu·rol·o·gy (nyoo·rál′·ạ·ji·) *n.* the study of the structure, function and diseases of the nervous system. **neurological** *a.* **neurologist** *n.* [Gk. *neuron*; *logos*, discourse].

neu·ron (nyoor′·ȧn) *n.* a nerve cell and all its processes [Gk. = nerve].

neu·ro·path (nyoo′·rạ·path) *n.* a person subject to a nervous disorder. **-ic, -ical** *a.* pert. to nervous diseases. **-ist** (nyoo·ráp′·ạ·thist) *n.* an abnormal or diseased condition of the nervous system [Gk. *neuron*, nerve; *pathos*, suffering].

neu·ro·sis (nyoo·rō′·sis) *n.* a psychic or mental disorder resulting in partial personality disorganization. *pl.* **neuroses. neurotic** (nyoo·rát′·ik) *a.* pert. to the nerves; *n.* a highly strung person [Gk. *neuron*, a nerve].

neu·ter (nū′·tẹr) *a.* neither masculine nor feminine; (*Bot.*) possessing neither stamens nor carpels; *n.* the neuter gender; an imperfectly developed female, as the worker-bee [L. = neither].

neu·tral (nū′·trạl) *a.* taking neither side in

a war, dispute, etc.; indifferent; without bias; grey; intermediate (shade of color); neither acid nor alkaline; asexual; *n.* nation, person, not taking sides in a dispute; the position in a gear-mechanism when no power is transmitted. **-ize** *v.t.* to render neutral; to make ineffective; to counterbalance. **-ity** *n.* non-intervention by a state or third-party in a dispute; the state of being neutral. **-ly** *adv.* [L. *neuter*, neither].

neu·tron (nū′·tran) *n.* one of the minute particles composing the nucleus of an atom. **— bomb** *n.* a small nuclear warhead that releases radiation lethal to humans but does not destroy buildings, etc. [L. *neuter*, neither].

nev·er (nev′·ẹr) *adv.* at no time; not ever; in no degree; (*Colloq.*) surely not. **-more** *adv.* **-theless** *conj.* none the less; in spite of that; notwithstanding [O.E. *naefre*].

new (nū) *a.* not existing before; lately discovered or invented; not ancient; *adv.* (usu. *new-*) recently; freshly. **-ly** *adv.* **-ish** *a.* somewhat new. **-ness** *n.* **-born** *a.* recently born; born anew. **-comer** *n.* one who has just settled down in a strange place or taken up a new post. **-fangled** *a.* lately devised; novel (in a depreciatory sense). **— fashioned** *a.* just come into fashion; the latest in style. **New Style** *n.* a term to denote dates reckoned by the Gregorian calendar. **New Deal** *n.* a campaign initiated in 1933 by President Franklin Roosevelt involving social reforms. **New Englander** *n.* a native or resident of any of the six N. E. states of the U.S.A. **— moon** *n.* the period when the first faint crescent of the moon becomes visible. **New Testament** *n.* later of the two main divisions of Bible. **New World** *n.* N. and S. America [O.E. *niwe*].

new·el (nū′·ạl) *n.* the post supporting the balustrade to a flight of stairs [L. *nodus*, a knot].

news (nōōz) *n.pl.* used as *n.sing.* report of recent happenings; fresh information; tidings; intelligence. **-boy** *n.* a boy who sells or distributes newspapers. **— bulletin** *n.* the latest news, esp. as disseminated by radio or television. **-monger** *n.* busy-body; *gossip*. **-paper** *n.* a regular publication giving latest news. **-print** *n.* cheap paper for newspapers. **-reel** *n.* a short film depicting items of news and topical features. **-stand** *n.* a stand where newspapers, magazines, etc. are sold. **-y** *a.* gossipy; full of news.

newt (nūt) *n.* a salamander; an eft [M.E. *an ewte*]. fr. O.E. *efeta*. an *eft*].

next (nekst) *a.* nearest; immediately following in place or time; *adv.* nearest or immediately after; on the first future occasion; *prep.* nearest to. **-ly** *adv.* in the next place. **— of kin** *n.* nearest blood relative. **-door** *a.* [O.E. *niehst*, superl. of *neah*, nigh].

nex·us (nek′·sạs) *n.* a tie, connection, or bond [L. *nectere*, to bind].

nib (nib) *n.* something small and pointed; beak of a bird; point of a pen. **-bed** *a.* having a nib [form of *neb*].

nib·ble (nib′·l) *v.t.* to bite a little at a time; *v.i.* to catch at (as a fish); to bite gently; to dally with; *n.* a tiny bite [L.G. *nubbelen*].

nib·lick (nib′·lik) *n.* a golf-club with an iron-head, well laid back, designed for lofting.

nice (nīs) agreeable; attractive; kind; exact; delicate; dainty. **-ly** *adv.* **-ness** *n.* **-ty** (nī′·sạ·ti·) *n.* precision; delicacy; exactness; refinement [O.Fr. *nice*, foolish].

niche (nich) *n.* a recess in a wall for a statue, bust, etc.; one's ordained position in life or public estimation; *v.t.* to place in a niche. **-d** *a.* [Fr., fr. It. *nicchia*].

nick (nik) *v.t.* to make a notch in; to indent; to catch exactly; *n.* a notch; a slit; the opportune moment as *in the nick of time*.

nick·el (nik′·ạl) *n.* a silver white metallic element, malleable and ductile, and much used in alloys and plating; a five-cent piece; *v.t.* to plate with nickel. **— plating** *n.* plating of metals with nickel to provide a bright surface and to keep down rust. **— silver** *n.* an alloy of copper, nickel, and zinc; German silver [fr. Ger. *Kupfernickel*, copper demon].

nick·el·o·de·an (nik·ạl·ō′·di·ạn) *n.* a player phonograph operated by the insertion of a nickel [Fr.].

nick·nack. See **knickknack.**

nick·name (nik′·nām) *n.* a name given in contempt, derision, or familiarity to some person, nation, or object [orig. *an eke name*, an added name, fr. *eke*, to increase].

nic·o·tine (nik′·ạ·tēn) *n.* a colorless, highly poisonous alkaloid present in the tobacco plant [Jean *Nicot*, who introduced the plant into France].

nid·i·fi·ca·tion (nid·ạ·fạ·kā′·shạn) *n.* the act of building a nest. **nidify** *v.i.* to build a nest. **nidus** (ī) *n.* a nest; (*Med.*) a nucleus of infection [L. *nidus*, a nest; *facere*, to make].

nidus. See **nidification.**

niece (nēs) *n.* the daughter of a brother or sister or of one's husband's or wife's brother or sister [Fr. *nièce*, fr. L. *neptis*].

nif·ty (nif′·ti·) *a.* (*Colloq.*) fine; smart.

nig·gard (nig′·ẹrd) *n.* a very miserly person; *a.* stingy. **-ly** *a.* **-liness** *n.* meanness [M.E. *negarde*].

nig·gle (nig′·l) *v.i.* to trifle; to be too particular about details. **-r** *n.* **niggling, niggly** *a., n.* [prob. fr. Norw. dial. *nigla*].

nigh (nī) *a.* near; direct; *adv.* near [O.E. *neah*].

night (nīt) *n.* the time of darkness from sunset to sunrise; end of daylight; intellectual or spiritual darkness; ignorance; death. **-ly** *a.* happening or done every night; of the night; *adv.* every night; by night. **-cap** *n.* a cap worn in bed; (*Colloq.*) an alcoholic drink at bedtime. **— club** *n.* establishment for dancing and entertainment remaining open until early morning. **-dress, -gown** *n.* a loose gown worn in bed. **-fall** *n.* the close of day. **-hawk** *n.* a nocturnal bird; (*Colloq.*) one who is up late habitually. **-light** *n.* bulb of low wattage kept burning all night. **-long** *a.* persisting all night. **-mare** *n.* a terrifying feeling of oppression or suffocation arising during sleep; a frightening dream. **— owl** *n.* (*Colloq.*) one who habitually keeps late hours. **— school** *n.* a school for the continuation of studies after working hours. **— shift** *n.* employees who work regularly during night; duration of this work. **-shirt** *n.* a loose shirt used for sleeping in. **-time** *n.* period of night. **-ward** *a.* towards night. **— watchman** *n.* [O.E. *niht*].

night·in·gale (nīt′·ạn·gāl) *n.* a bird of the thrush family, the male being renowned for its beautiful song at night [O.E. *niht*, night; *galan*, to sing].

ni·hil (nī′·hil), **nil** (nil) *n.* nothing; zero. **nihilism** *n.* the rejection of all religious and moral principles as the only means of obtaining social progress; the denial of all reality in phenomena; in 19th cent. the opposition in Russia to all constituted authority or government. **nihilist** *n.* **nihilistic** *a.* [L.].

Ni·ke (nī′·kē) *n.* a U.S. Army supersonic guided missile [*Gk. Myth.*, goddess of victory].

nim·ble (nim′·bl) *a.* light and quick in motion. **-ness** *n.* **—witted** *a.* quick-witted. **nimbly** *adv.* [O.E. *niman*, to take].

nim·bus (nim′·bạs) *n.* a cloud or atmosphere

around a person or thing; in representation of saints, angels, etc., the circle of light surrounding the head; a halo; an aureole. *pl.* **-es** *or* **nimbi** [L. = cloud].

nin·com·poop (nin'·kạm·pòóp) *n.* a foolish person; a simpleton [origin uncertain].

nine (nīn) *a.* and *n.* one more than eight; the symbol 9 or IX; a baseball team; **-fold** *a.* nine times repeated. **-teen** *a.* and *n.* nine and ten. **-teenth** *a.* and *n.* **ninetieth** *a.* the tenth after the eightieth. **-ty** *a.* and *n.* **ninth** *a.* the first after the eighth; *n.* **ninthly** *adv.* **-pins** *n.* a game in which nine erect wooden pegs are to be knocked down by a ball. **the Nine,** the Muses [O.E. *nigon*].

nin·ny (nin'·i·) *n.* a fool; a dolt [It. *ninno,* a child].

ni·non (nē'·nàn) *n.* a glossy lightweight dress fabric of silk [Fr. proper name].

nip (nip) *v.t.* to pinch sharply; to detach by pinching; to check growth (as by frost); to smart. *pr.p.* **-ping.** *pa.t.* and *pa.p.* **-ped.** *n.* a pinch; sharp touch of frost; a sip. **-per** *n.* one who or that which nips; the great claw (as of a crab); *pl.* small pincers. **-piness** *n.* **-pingly** *adv.* **-py** *a.* sharp in taste; curt; smarting [etym. uncertain, cf. Dut. *nijpen*].

nip·ple (nip'·l) *n.* the protuberance in the center of a breast by which milk is obtained from the female during breast-feeding; a teat; the mouthpiece of a nursing bottle; a small metal projection pierced so that oil or grease may be forced into a bearing surface by means of a grease gun [etym. uncertain, cf. *nib*].

Nip·pon (nip'·àn) *n.* Japan. **-ese** *n., a.* [Jap. = rising of the sun].

Nir·va·na (nir·vá'·nạ) *n.* in Buddhism, that state of blissful repose or absolute existence reached by one in whom all craving is extinguished [Sans].

ni·sei (nē'·sā') *n.* Am. citizen born of Japanese parents.

ni·si (nī'·sī) *conj.* unless. **decree nisi** (*Law*) a decree to take effect after a certain period of time has elapsed unless some valid objection arises [L.].

nit (nit) *n.* the egg of an insect parasite, esp. of a louse [O.E. *hnitu*].

ni·ter (nī'·ter) *n.* potassium nitrate; saltpeter, a white crystalline solid used in the manufacture of gunpowder, acids, etc. **nitrate** *n.* a salt of nitric acid; a fertilizer. **nitrated** *a.* combined with nitric acid. **nitration** *n.* the conversion of nitrites into nitrates by the action of bacteria; the introduction of a nitro-group (NO_2) into an organic substance. **nitric** *a.* containing nitrogen. **nitric acid,** a powerful, corrosive acid. **nitride** *n.* a compound of a metal with nitrogen. **nitrify** *v.t.* to treat a metal with nitric acid; to oxidize to nitrates or nitrites, esp. by action of bacteria. **nitrite** *n.* a salt of nitrous acid. **nitrous oxide,** laughing gas, used as an anaesthetic in dentistry [Gk. *nitron*].

ni·tro- (nī·trạ) *prefix* used in the formation of compound terms, signifying, formed by, or containing, *niter*. **-glycerine** *n.* a powerful oily liquid explosive [Gk. *nitron,* native soda].

ni·tro·gen (nī'·trạ·jạn) *n.* a non-metallic gaseous chemical element, colorless, odorless and tasteless, forming nearly four-fifths of the atmosphere. **nitrogenous** *a.*

nit·wit (nit'·wit) *n.* (*Colloq.*) a fool. **-ted** *a.* [Dut. *niets,* nothing; O.E. *witan,* to know].

nix (niks) *n.* (*Slang*) nothing [Dut. *niets*].

no (nō) *a.* not any; *adv.* expresses a negative reply to a question or request; not at all; *n.* a refusal; a denial; a negative vote. **-es** *n.pl.* term used in parliamentary proceedings, *the noes have it.* **no man's land,** the terrain between the front lines of opposing forces [O.E. *na*].

nob (nàb) *n.* (*Slang*) the head [fr. *knob*].

No·bel Prize (nō·bel' prīz) *n.* one of six prizes awarded annually to persons who have distinguished themselves in physics, chemistry, medicine or physiology, literature, economics, or the promotion of peace [Alfred *Nobel,* Swedish inventor (1833-96)].

no·bil·i·ty (nō·bil'·ạ·ti·) *n.* the class holding special rank, usually hereditary, in a state; the quality of being noble; grandeur; loftiness and sincerity of mind or character [L. *nobilis,* noble].

no·ble (nō'·bl) *a.* distinguished by deeds, character, rank, or birth; of lofty character; titled; *n.* a nobleman; a peer; an old English gold coin. **-man** *n.* (*fem.* **-woman**). **-ness** *n.* **nobly** *adv.* [L. *nobilis*].

no·bod·y (nō'·bàd·i·) *n.* no one; a person of no importance.

nock (nak) *n.* notch, esp. of bow or arrow; upper end of fore-and-aft sail [*notch*].

noc·turn (nàk'·turn) *n.* a service held during the night. **-e** *n.* a painting of a night scene; a musical composition of a gentle and simple character. **-al** *a.* pertaining to night; happening or active by night. **-ally** *adv.* [L. *nocturnus,* of the night].

noc·u·ous (nàk'·yoo·ạs) *a.* hurtful; noxious. **-ly** *adv.* [L. *nocere,* to hurt].

nod (nàd) *v.t., v.i.* to incline the head forward by a quick motion, signifying assent or drowsiness; to droop the head; to be sleepy; to sway; to bow by way of recognition; *pr.p.* **-ding**; *pa.t., pa.p.* **-ded**; *n.* an act of nodding. **-der** *n.* [M.E. *nodden*].

nod·al. See **node.**

nod·dy (nàd'·i·) *n.* a simpleton; a fool; a seabird [fr. *nod*].

node (nōd) *n.* a knot or knob; (*Geom.*) a point at which a curve crosses itself to form a loop; (*Elect.*) a point in a circuit carrying alternating currents at which the amplitude of current or voltage is a minimum; (*Astron.*) one of two points at which the orbit of a planet intersects the plane of the ecliptic; (*Med.*) a small protuberance or hard swelling; (*Bot.*) the part of a stem to which a leaf is attached; an articulation. **nodal, nodical** *a.* pert. to nodes. **nodated** *a.* knotted. **nodation** *n.* the knots. **nodular** *a.* like a nodule. **nodulated** *a.* having nodules. **nodule** *n.* a small node or act of making knots. **nodiferous** *a.* (*Bot.*) having nodes. **nodose, nodous** *a.* full of swelling [L. *nodus,* a knot].

no·ël (nō·el') *n.* Christmas; a carol [Fr., fr. L. *natalis,* birthday].

no-fault (nō'fawlt) *a.* designating a form of (automobile) insurance that pays the victim promptly without first establishing who is to blame; designating a form of divorce granted without seeking or establishing blame. **— divorce** *n.* **— insurance** *n.*

nog (nàg) *n.* a wooden peg or block [Scand.].

nog (nàg) *n.* a beverage made with eggs and usually liquor; eggnog; a kind of strong ale. **-gin** *n.* a small mug; a very small drink; (*Slang*) the head [Ir. *noigin*].

no·how (nō'·hou) *adv.* (*Colloq.*) in no way; not at all.

noise (noiz) *n.* sound; din; loud outcry; *v.t.* to spread by rumor; *v.i.* to sound loud. **-less** *a.* making no noise; silent. **-lessly** *adv.* **-lessness** *n.* **noisy** *a.* making much noise; clamorous. **noisily** *adv.* **noisiness** *n.* [M.E.].

noi·some (noi'·sạm) *a.* injurious to health; noxious; offensive; disgusting; evil smelling. **-ly** *adv.* **-ness** *n.* [obs. *noy,* for *annoy*].

no·mad (nō'·mad) *a.* roaming from pasture to pasture; *n.* a wanderer; a member of a wandering tribe. **-ic** *a.* pert. to nomads; having no fixed dwelling place. **-ism** *n.* [Gk. *nomas,* pasturing].

nom de plume (nàm' dạ plòóm') *n.* a pen name [Fr.].

no·men·cla·tor (nō′·mạn·klā·tẹr) *n.* one who gives names to things. **nomenclatural** a. **nomenclature** (nō′·mạn·klā·chẹr) *n.* a system of naming; the vocabulary of a science, etc. [L. *nomen*, a name; *calare*, to call].

nom·i·nal (nạm′·ạ·nạl) *a.* pert. to a name; existing only in name, ostensible; titular; (*Gram.*) pert. to a noun. **-ism** *n.* the doctrine that the universal, or general, has no objective existence or validity, being merely a name expressing the qualities of various objects resembling one another in certain respects. **-ist** *n.* one who holds these views, the opposite of a *realist*. **-istic** *a.* **-ly** *adv.* in name only; not really [L. *nominalis*, fr. *nomen*, a name].

nom·i·nate (nȧm′·ạ·nāt) *v.t.* to put forward the name of, as a candidate; to propose; to designate. **nomination** *n.* act of nominating; power or privilege of nominating. **nominative** *a.* (*Gram.*) denoting the subject; *n.* a noun or pronoun which is the subject of a verb. **nominator** *n.* one who nominates. **nominee** *n.* one who is nominated [L. *nominare*, to name].

non- *prefix* from L. *non* = not, used in the formation of compound terms signifying absence or omission. **-combatant** *n.* a member of the armed forces whose duties do not entail an active part in military operations, e.g., chaplain, surgeon, etc.; an unarmed civilian. **-commissioned** *a.* of ranks between a private and warrant officer; (*abbrev.* **noncom**) **-commital** *a.* deliberately avoiding any direct statement as to one's opinions or course of future action. **-conductor** *n.* a substance which will not conduct electricity, heat, or sound; insulator. **-ferrous** *a.* of an alloy or metal containing no, or only the merest trace of, iron. **-intervention** *n.* not intervening or interfering in the affairs or policies of another, esp. in international affairs, **-stop** *a.* not stopping.

non·age (nȧn′·ij) *n.* minority (under 21 years of age); a period of immaturity [L. *non*, not; and *age*].

non·a·ge·nar·i·an (nȧn·ạ·jạ·ner′·i·ạn) *n.* one who is ninety years old or upwards; *a.* relating to ninety [L. *nonaginta*, ninety].

nonce (nȧns) *n.* **for the nonce,** for the occasion only; for the present [earlier *the(n) -anes*, the once].

non·cha·lance (nȧn′·shạ·lȧns) *n.* unconcern; coolness; indifference; **nonchalant** *a.* **nonchalantly** *adv.* [Fr. *non*, not; *chaleur*, heat].

non·con·form·ist (nȧn·kạn·fawr′·mist) *n.* one who refuses to comply with the usages and rites of an established church, etc. **nonconforming** *a.* **nonconformity** *n.*

non·de·script (nȧn′·dạ·skript) *a.* lacking in distinction; hard to classify; *n.* [*nom*, not; *descriptus*, described].

none (nun) *a.* and *pron.* no one; not anything. **-such, nonsuch** *n.* a person or thing without a rival or equal. **nonetheless,** nevertheless; all the same [O.E. *nan*].

nones (nōnz) *n. pl.* one of the canonical hours of the R.C. Breviary, the *ninth* hour after sunrise at the equinox, viz. 3 p.m., or the appropriate mass celebrated at this time [L. *nonus*, ninth].

non·en·ti·ty (nȧn·ẹn′·tạ·ti·) *n.* a thing not existing; nonexistence; a person of no importance; a mere nobody [L. *non*, not; *ens, entis*, a being].

non·ju·ror (nȧn·joor′·ẹr) *n.* one who refuses to swear allegiance or take an oath. **nonjuring** *a.*

non·pa·reil (nȧn·pạ·rel′) *n.* a person or thing without an equal; a printing type, between ruby and emerald, counting 6 points; *a.* unrivalled; peerless; matchless [Fr. *non*, not; *pareil*, equal].

non·plus (nȧn′·plus) *n.* perplexity; puzzle; inability to say or do more; quandary; *v.t.* to confound or bewilder completely [L. *non*, not; *plus*, more].

non·sense (nȧn′·sens) *n.* lack of sense; language without meaning; absurdity; silly conduct. **nonsensical** *a.* **nonsensically** *adv.* [L. *non*, not].

non·such See **none.**

noo·dle (nòò′·dl) *n.* a simpleton; (*Slang*) the head [conn. with *noddy*].

noo·dle (nòò′·dl) *n.* a strip of dough, made of flour and eggs, baked and served in soups [Ger. *nudel*].

nook (nook) *n.* a corner; a recess; a secluded retreat [ME. *nok*].

noon (nòòn) *n.* midday; twelve o'clock by day; the exact instant when, at any given place, the sun crosses the meridian. **-day, -tide** *n.* and *a.* midday [L. *nona (hora)*, ninth hour; See **nones.**

noose (nòòs) *n.* a running loop with a slip knot which binds closer the more it is drawn; snare; tight knot; *v.t.* to tie, catch in noose [L. *nodus*, knot].

nor (nawr) a particle introducing the second clause of a negative proposition; and not [M.E. *nother*].

Nor·dic (nawr′·dik) *a.* of or pert. to peoples of Germanic, esp. Scandinavian, stock.

norm (nawrm) *n.* a rule or authoritative standard; a unit for comparison; a standard type or pattern; a model; a class-average test score. **-a** *n.* a rule, pattern, or standard; a pattern or templet; a mason's square for testing. **-al** *a.* conforming to type or natural law; (*Math.*) perpendicular; *n.* (*Math.*) a perpendicular to a line, surface, or tangent at point of contact; the standard; the average. **-alcy** (nawr′·mal·si·) *n.* normality. **normality** *n.* normal state or quality. **-ly** *adv.* **-ative** *a.* setting up a norm; regulative. **-al school,** a training college for teachers [L. *norma*, a rule].

Nor·man (nawr′·mạn) *n.* a native of Normandy; *a.* pert. to Normandy or the Normans. **— architecture,** a style of medieval architecture characterized by rounded arch and massive simplicity. [O.Fr. *Normant*, fr. Scand. = Northmen].

Norse (nawrs) *a.* pert. to ancient Scandinavia, esp. Norway, its language, or its people; *n.* Norwegians or ancient Scandinavians; the old Scandinavian language [Scand. *norsk*, north].

north (nawrth) *n.* the region or cardinal point in the plane of the meridian to the left of a person facing the rising sun; the part of the world, of a country, etc., towards this point; *adv.* towards or in the north; *a.* to, from, or in the north. **northerly** (nawr′·THẹr·li·) *a.* towards the north; of winds, coming from the north. **northern** *a.* pert. to the north; in or of the north. **northerner** *n.* an inhabitant of the northern parts of a country. **northernly** *adv.* in a northern direction. **northernmost** *a.* situated at the most northerly point. **-ward, -wardly** *a.* situated towards the north; *adv.* in a northerly direction. **-wards** *adv.* **-east (-west)** *n.* the point between the north and the east (west); *a.* pert. to, or from, the northeast (-west) **-easter (-wester)** *n.* a wind from the northeast (-west). **-easterly (-westerly)** *a.* towards or coming from the northeast (-west). **-eastern (-western)** *a.* belonging to the northeast (-west). **-eastward (-westward)** *a.* towards the northeast (-west). **northern lights,** aurora borealis. **North Pole,** northern extremity of earth's axis. **North Star** *n.* polar star, the only star which does not change its apparent position [O.E.].

Nor·we·gian (nawr·wē′·jạn) *a.* pert. to Norway; *n.* a native or language of Norway.

nose (nōz) *n.* the organ for breathing and smelling; power of smelling or detecting; any projection resembling a nose, as prow of a ship; *v.t.* to detect by smell; to nuzzle; to sniff; to move forward; *v.i.* to smell; to pry; to push forward. **— bag** *n.* a bag containing provender fastened to a horse's head. **— dive** *n.* in aviation, a sudden steep plunge directly towards an objective, usually from a great height; *v.i.* to perform this evolution. **-gay** *n.* a bunch of sweet-smelling flowers; a bouquet. **nosing** *n.* the molded projecting edge of the tread of a step. **nosy** *a.* (*Colloq.*) inquisitive [O.E. *nosu*].

nose- *prefix* fr. Greek, *nosos,* disease, used in formation of compound words. **nosology** (nō-sȧl′·ạ·ji·) *n.* branch of medicine treating generally of diseases; systematic classification of phases of disease. **nosological** *a.* **nosologist** *n.*

nos·tal·gia (nȧs·tal′·jạ) *n.* homesickness; a phase of melancholia due to the unsatisfied desire to return home. **nostalgic** *a.* [Gk. *nostos,* return; *algos,* pain].

nos·tril (nȧs′·tril) *n.* one of the external openings of the nose [O.E. *nosy,* nose; *thyrel,* opening].

nos·trum (nȧs′·trạm) *n.* a quack remedy; a patent medicine of doubtful efficacy; a pet scheme, pushed by some visionary [L. = our].

not (nȧt) *adv.* a word expressing denial, negation, or refusal [*nought*].

no·ta·ble (nō′·tạ·bl) *a.* worthy of notice; remarkable; *n.* a person of distinction. **notabilia** *n.pl.* things worth noting; famous remarks. **notability** *n.* an eminent person. **-ness** *n.* **notably** *adv.* [L. *nota,* note].

no·ta·ry (nō′·tạ·ri·) *n.* a *notary-public,* a person authorized to record statements, to certify deeds, to take affidavits, etc., on oath [L. *notarius,* a secretary].

no·ta·tion (nō·tā′·shạn) *n.* any system of figures, signs and symbols which conveys information; the act or process of noting; a note [L. *nota,* a mark].

notch (nȧch) *n.* a V-shaped cut or indentation; nick; a groove formed in a piece of timber to receive another piece; (*U.S.*) a pass between mountains; *v.t.* to make notches in; to indent; to secure by a notch; to score (a run) [O.F. *osche,* a notch].

note (nōt) *n.* a mark; a brief comment; *pl.* a record of a lecture, speech, etc.; a memorandum; a short letter; a diplomatic paper; a written or printed promise of payment; a musical tone; a character to indicate a musical tone; notice; distinction; fame; *v.t.* to observe; to set down in writing; to attend to; to heed. **-book** *n.* a book for jotting down notes, memoranda, etc. **-d** *a.* well-known by reputation or report; celebrated; **-dly** *adv.* **-dness** *n.* **— paper** *n.* a small size of writing paper. **-worthy** *a.* worthy of notice; remarkable. **— of hand,** a promissory note [L. *notare,* to mark].

noth·ing (nuth′·ing) *n.* not anything of account, value, note, or the like; non-existence; nonentity; nought; zero; trifle; *adv.* in no degree; not at all. **-ness** *n.* [fr. no thing].

no·tice (nō′·tis) *n.* act of noting; remarking, or observing; cognizance; regard; note; heed; consideration; news; a review; a notification; *v.t.* to observe; to remark upon; to treat with regard. **-able** *a.* **-ably** *adv.* **to give notice,** to warn beforehand. **to receive one's notice,** to be informed that one's services are about to be terminated [L. *notus,* known].

no·ti·fy (nō′·ta·fī) *v.t.* to report; to give notice of or to; to announce; to inform. **notifiable** *n.* **notification** *n.* act of making known or giving notice; official notice or announcement [L. *notus,* known; *facere,* to make].

no·tion (nō′·shạn) *n.* apprehension; idea; conception; opinion; belief; sentiment; fancy; inclination; *pl.* small articles such as sewing supplies, etc. [L. *notio*].

no·to·ri·e·ty (nō·tạ·rī′·ạt·i·) *n.* the state of being generally known, esp. in a disreputable way; discreditable publicity. **notorious** *a.* generally known (usually in a bad sense); infamous. **notoriously** *adv.* **notoriousness** *n.* [L. *notus,* known].

not·with·stand·ing (not·with·stand′·ing) *adv.* nevertheless; however; yet; *prep.* in spite of; despite; *conj.* although.

nou·gat (nȯȯ′·gạt) *n.* a confection of almonds, pistachio-nuts, or other nuts, in a sugar and honey paste [Fr.].

nought See **naught.**

noun (noun) *n.* (*Gram.*) a word used as a name of a person, quality, or thing; a substantive [L. *nomen,* a name].

nour·ish (nur′·ish) *v.t.* to supply with food; to feed and cause to grow; to nurture; to encourage. **-ing** *a.* nutritious. **-ment** *n.* food; nutriment; the act or state of nourishing [Fr. *nourrir,* fr. L. *nutrire,* to feed].

no·va (nō′·vạ) *n.* a new star. *pl.* **novae** [L. = new].

nov·el (nȧv′·ạl) *a.* of recent origin or introduction; new; unusual; *n.* a fictitious prose tale dealing with the adventures or feelings of imaginary persons so as to portray, by the description of action and thought, the varieties of human life and character. **-ette** *n.* a shorter form of novel. **-ist** *n.* a writer of novels. **-ty** *n.* newness; something new or unusual [L. *novus,* new].

No·vem·ber (nō·vem·bẹr) *n.* the eleventh month of the year [L. *novem,* nine].

no·vena (nō·vē′·nạ) *n.* (*R.C.*) devotions on nine consecutive days; lasting nine days [L. *novem,* nine].

nov·ice (nȧv′·is) *n.* a candidate for admission to a religious order; one new to anything; an inexperienced person; a beginner. **novicate, novitiate** *n.* the state or time or being a novice; a novice [L. *novus,* new].

No·vo·cain (nō′·vạ·kān) *n.* a nonirritant drug which has replaced cocaine as a local anesthetic [Trademark].

now (nou) *adv.* at the present time; *conj.* this being the case; *n.* the present time. **-adays** *adv.* in these days. **now! now!** a form of admonition. **now and then,** occasionally [O.E. *nu*].

no·where (nō′·hwer) *adv.* not in any place. **nowise** *adv.* not in any manner or degree.

nox·a (nȧk′·sạ) *n.* (*Med.*) anything harmful to the body; *pl.* **-e. noxal** *a.* **noxious** *a.* hurtful; pernicious; unwholesome. **noxiously** *adv.* **noxiousness** *n.* [L. *noxa,* injury].

noz·zle (nȧz′·l) *n.* a projecting spout or vent; the outlet end of a pipe, hose, etc.; (*Colloq.*) the nose [dim. of *nose*].

nu·ance (nȯȯ·ȧns′) *n.* a shade or subtle variation in color, tone of voice, etc.; (*Mus.*) a delicate gradation of tone and expression in performance on an instrument [Fr. = a shade].

nub (nub) *n.* a knob; lump; protuberance; (*Colloq.*) point; gist.

nu·cle·us (nū′·kli·ạs) *n.* a central part of anything; the starting point of some project or idea; (*Astron.*) the dark center of a sunspot; the denser core or head of a comet; (*Biol.*) the inner essential part of a living cell; (*Physics*) the core of the atom, composed of protons and neutrons. *pl.* **nuclei** (nū′·kli·ī). **nuclear** *a.* **nuclear energy,** a more exact term for atomic energy; energy freed or absorbed during reactions taking place in atomic nuclei. **nuclear fission,** a process of disintegration which breaks up into chemically different atoms. **nucleate** *v.t.* to gather into or round a nucleus. **nucleolus** *n.* a minute body of condensed chromatin inside a nucleus [L. = kernel].

nude (nūd) *a.* bare; naked; undraped; uncovered; *n.* a picture or piece of sculpture in the nude. **-ly** *adv.* **-ness, nudity,** *n.* nakedness. **nudism** *n.* cult emphasizing practice of nudity for health. **nudist** *n.* [L. *nudus,* naked].

nudge (nuj) *v.t.* to touch slightly with the elbow; *n.* a gentle push [etym. uncertain].

nug·get (nug′·it) *n.* rough lump or mass, esp. of native gold [etym. uncertain].

nui·sance (nū′·sạns) *n.* something harmful, offensive, or annoying; a troublesome person; a pest; an inconvenience [Fr. *nuisant,* harming; fr. L. *nocere,* to harm].

null (nul) *a.* of no legal validity; void; nonexistent; of no importance; *v.t.* to annul; to render void. **-ify** *v.t.* to make null; to render useless; to invalidate; **-fication** *n.* **ifier** *n.* **-ity** *n.* state of being null and void [L. *nullus,* none].

numb (num) *a.* insensible; insensitive; chilled; *v.t.* to benumb; to paralyze. **-ness** *n.* [O.E. *numen,* taken].

num·ber (num′·bẹr) *n.* a word used to indicate how great any quantity is when compared with the unit quantity, one; a sum or aggregate of quantities; a collection of things; an assembly; a single issue of a publication; a piece of music; (*Gram.*) classification of words as to singular or plural; *pl.* metrical feet or verse; rhythm; *v.t.* to give a number to; to count; to reckon; to estimate; *v.i.* to amount to.**-s** *n.pl.* (*Bib.*) fourth book of Pentateuch. **-er** *n.* **-less** *a.* innumerable. **numerability, numerableness** *n.* **numerable** *a.* may be numbered or counted [Fr. *nombre,* fr. L. *numerus*].

nu·mer·al (nū′·mẹr·ạl) *a.* designating a number; *n.* a sign or word denoting a number. **numerable** *a.* able to be counted. numerably *adv.* **-ly** *adv.* according to number. **numerary** *a.* belonging to, or an integral part of, a certain number, as opposed to *supernumerary.* **numerate** *v.t.* to count; to read figures according to their notation. **numeration** *n.* **numerator** *n.* top part of a fraction, figure showing how many of the fractional units are taken. **numeric(al)** *a.* of, or in respect of, numbers. **numerically** *adv.* **numerous** *a.* many. **numerously** *adv.* **numerousness** *n.* [L. *numerus,* a number].

nu·mis·mat·ic (nū·mis·mat′·ik) *a.* pert. to coins and medals, esp. as an aid to study of archaeology. **numismatist** *n.* **numismatography, numismatology** *n.* science of coins and medals in relation to archaeology and history. **numismatologist** *n.* [L. *numisma,* current coin].

num·skull (num′·skul) *n.* (*Colloq.*) dolt; dunce; a stupid person [*numb, skull*].

nun (nun) *n.* a female member of a religious order, vowed to celibacy, and dedicated to active or contemplative life. **-nery** *n.* convent of nuns [L.L. *nonna*].

nun·ci·o (nun′·shi·ō) *n.* a diplomatic representative of the Pope abroad. **nunciature** *n.* [It. fr. L. *nuntius,* a messenger].

nun·cu·pate (nung′·kyoo·pāt) *v.t.* and *v.i.* to vow publicly; to dedicate; to declare orally, as a will. **nuncupation** *n.* **nuncupative** *a.* oral; not written. **nuncupator** *n.* **nuncupatory** *a.* oral; verbal [L. *nuncupare,* to name].

nup·tial (nup′·shạl, ·chạl) *a.* pert. to or constituting ceremony of marriage; *pl.* wedding ceremony; marriage [L. *nuptiae,* wedding].

nurse (nurs) *n.* a person trained for the care of the sick or injured; a woman tending another's child; *v.t.* to tend, as a nurse; to suckle; to foster; to husband; to harbor (a grievance); to manage skillfully (the early stages of some project). **-maid, nurserymaid** *n.* a girl in charge of young children. **-r** *n.* **nursery** *n.* a room set aside for children; a place for the rearing of plants. **nurseryman** *n.* one who raises plants for sale. **nursery rhymes,** jingling rhymes written to amuse young children. **nursery school,** a school for children of 2-5 years of age. **nursling** *n.* an infant; anything which is carefully tended at inception. **wet-nurse** *n.* woman who suckles infant of another [Fr. *nourrice,* fr. L. *nutrix,* a nurse].

nur·ture (nur′·chẹr) *n.* nurturing; education; rearing; breeding; nourishment; (*Biol.*) the various environmental forces, which combined, act on an organism and further its existence; *v.t.* to nourish; to cherish; to tend; to train; to rear; to bring up. **-r** *n.* [Fr. *nourriture,* nourishment].

nut (nut) *n.* a fruit consisting of a hard shell enclosing a kernel; a hollow metal collar, the internal surface of which carries a groove or thread into which the thread of a screw fits; (*Slang*) the head; blockhead; *v.i.* to gather nuts; *pr.p.* **-ting.** *pa.t.* and *pa.p.* **-ted. -brown** *a.* of the color of a nut. **— butter,** a butter substitute made from nut oil. **-cracker** *n.* an instrument for cracking nuts; bird of crow family. **-hatch** *n.* a climbing bird, allied to titmice. **-shell** *n.* the hard shell enclosing the kernel of a nut. **-ter** *n.* one who gathers nuts. **-tiness** *n.* taste of nuts. **-ting** *n.* **-ty** *a.* abounding in nuts; having a nut-flavor; (*Slang*) silly; imbecile. **a hard nut to crack,** a difficult problem to solve; a person difficult to deal with [O.E. *hnutu*].

nu·tant (nū′·tạnt) *a.* (*Bot.*) hanging with the apex of the flower downwards; nodding. **nutation** *n.* nodding; (*Astron.*) slight periodic wobbling of direction of Earth's axis [L. *nutare,* to nod].

nut·meg (nut′·meg) *n.* an aromatic flavoring spice [E. *nut;* O.Fr. *mugue,* musk].

nu·tri·ent (nū′·tri·ant) *a.* nourishing; *n.* something nutritious. **nutriment** *n.* that which nourishes; food; sustenance. **nutrition** *n.* the act of nourishing. **nutritional, nutritious, nutritive, nutritory** *a.* nourishing; promoting growth [L. *nutrire,* to nourish].

nuz·zle (nuz′·l) *v.t.* and *v.i.* to rub with the nose; to nestle; to burrow or press with the nose [*nose*].

nyc·ta·lo·pi·a (nik·tạ·lō′·pi·ạ) *n.* night blindness [Gk. *nux,* night; *alaos,* blind; *ēps,* eye].

ny·lon (nī′·lån) *n.* an artificial fabric the yarn of which is produced synthetically; *n.pl.* stockings made of nylon yarn [fr. *N* (ew) *Y*(ork), *Lon*(don)].

nymph (nimf) *n.* a lesser goddess inhabiting a mountain, grove, fountain, river, etc.; a girl distinguished by her grace and charm. **-al, -ean, -ic, -ical** *a.* **-like** *a.* **-omania** *n.* a morbid and uncontrollable sexual desire in women. **-omaniac** *n.* [Gk. *nymphē,* a bride].

nymph (nimf) *n.* the pupa or chrysalis of an insect [Gk. *nymphē,* a nymph].

nys·tag·mus (nis·tag′·mạs) *n.* eye disease with involuntary twitching oscillation of eyes [Gk. *nustazein,* to nod].

O

O, oh (ō) *interj.* an exclamation of address, surprise, sorrow, wonder, entreaty [O.E. *ea*].
oaf (ōf) *n.* a changeling; dolt; lout; simpleton. *pl.* **oafs** or **oaves. -ish** *a.* loutish; awkward [O.N. *alfr*, an elf].
oak (ōk) *n.* a familiar forest tree yielding a hard, durable timber and acorns as fruit. **-en** *a.* made of oak. **— apple** *n.* a gall or swelling on oak leaves caused by the gallfly [O.E. *ac*].
oar (ōr) *n.* a wooden lever with a broad blade worked by the hands to propel a boat; an oarsman; *v.t.* and *v.i.* to row. **-ed** *a.* having oars. **-man** *n.* a rower. **-manship** *n.* art of rowing. **to put in one's oar** (*Slang*) to meddle; to interfere [O.E. *ar*].
o·a·sis (ō·ā′·sis) *n.* a fertile spot in the desert. *pl.* **oases** (ō·ā′·sēz) [Gk.].
oat (ōt) *n.* but usually in *pl.* **oats,** the grain of a common cereal plant, used as food; the plant; (*Poet.*) a shepherd's musical pipe; a pastoral song. **-en** *a.* made of oat-straw or oatmeal. **-cake** *n.* a thin cake of oatmeal. **-meal** *n.* meal made from oats. **to sow wild oats,** to indulge in youthful follies before settling down [O.E. *ate*].
oath (ōth) *n.* confirmation of the truth by naming something sacred, esp. God; a statement or promise confirmed by an appeal to God; a blasphemous use of the name of God; any imprecation. *pl.* **oaths** (ōTHz) [O.E. *ath*].
ob·bli·ga·to (ȧb·li·gȧ′·tō) *n.* (*Mus.*) a part in a musical composition for a particular instrument, of such importance that it is indispensable to the proper rendering of the piece; —also *a.* Also **obligato** [It.].
ob·du·rate (ȧb′·dyoo·rạt) *a.* hard-hearted; stubborn; unyielding. **-ly** *adv.* **obduracy** *n.* [L. *obduratus*, hardened].
o·be·di·ent (ō·bē′·di·ạnt) *a.* subject to authority; willing to obey. **-ly** *adv.* **obedience** *n.* submission to authority; doing what one is told [L. *obedire*].
o·bei·sance (ō·bā′·sạns) *n.* a bow, curtsy or gesture of deference [Fr. *obéissance*, obedience].
ob·e·lisk (ȧb′·ạ·lisk) *n.* a tall, four-sided, tapering pillar, ending in a small pyramid; in printing, a reference mark (†) also called 'dagger'; an **obelus** (*pl.* **obeli**), the marks — or ÷ [Gk. *obeliskos*].
o·bese (ō·bēs′) *a.* fat; fleshy. **obesity** *n.* excessive fatness [L. *obesus*].
o·bey (ō·bā′) *v.i.* to be obedient; *v.t.* to comply with the orders of; to yield submission to; to be ruled by [L. *obedire*].
ob·fus·cate (ȧb·fus′·kāt) *v.t.* to darken; to confuse or bewilder. **obfuscation** *n.* obscurity; confusion [L. *obfuscare*, to darken].
o·bit (ō′·bit) *n.* (*Slang*) abbrev. of **obituary. obituary** *a.* pert. to death of person; *n.* a notice, often with a biographical sketch, of the death of a person [L. *obitus*, approach, fr. *obire*, to go to meet].
ob·ject (ȧb′·jekt) *n.* anything presented to the mind or senses; a material thing; an end or aim; (*Gram.*) a noun, pronoun, or clause governed by, and dependent on, a transitive verb or a preposition. **-less** *a.* having no aim or purpose [L. *objetus*, thrown in the way].
ob·ject (ạb·jekt′) *v.t.* to offer in opposition; to put forward as reason against; *v.i.* to make verbal opposition; to protest against; to feel dislike or reluctance. **objection** (ạb·jek′·shạn) *n.* act of objecting; adverse reason; difficulty or drawback; argument against. **objectionable** *a.* **objectionably** *adv.* **-or** *n.* [L. *ob*, in the way of; *jacere*, to throw].
ob·jec·tive (ạb·jek′·tiv) *a.* pert. to the object; relating to that which is external to the mind; unbiased; (*Gram.*) denoting the case of the object. **-ly** *adv.* **objectivity** *n.* the quality of being objective [Fr. *objectif*].
ob·jur·gate (ȧb′·jẹr·gāt) *v.t.* to reprove; to blame; to berate. **objurgation** *n.* **objurgatory** *a.* [L. *objurgare*, to blame].
ob·late (ȧb·lāt′) *a.* (*Geom.*) flattened at the poles (said of a spheroid, like the earth). **-ness** *n.* [L. *oblatus*, brought forward].
ob·late (ȧb′·lāt) *n.* a person dedicated to religious work, esp. the monastic service. **oblation** *n.* something offered to God, or a god; a gift to the church [L. *oblatus*, brought forward, offered].
ob·li·gate (ȧb′·li·gāt) *v.t.* to bind, esp. by legal contract; to put under obligation. **obligation** *n.* the binding power of a promise or contract; indebtedness for a favor of kindness; a duty; a legal bond. **obligatory** (ạ·blig′·ạ·tōr·i·) *a.* binding legally or morally; compulsory. **obligatorily** *adv.* [L. *obligare*, fr. *ligare*, to bind].
o·blige (ạ·blīj′) *v.t.* to constrain by physical, moral, or legal force; to lay under an obligation; to do a favor to; to compel. **-d** *a.* grateful; indebted. **-ment** *n.* a favor. **obliging** *a.* helpful; courteous. **obligingly** *adv.* **obligingness** *n.* [L. *obligare*, fr. *ligare*, to bind].
ob·lique (ō·blēk′) *a.* slanting; inclined; indirect; obscure; not straightforward; underhand. **-ly** *adv*, **-ness, obliguity** (ạ·blik′·wi·ti·) *n.* slant or inclination; deviation from moral uprightness; dishonesty [L. *obliquus.*].
ob·lit·er·ate (ạ·blit′·ạ·rāt) *v.t.* to blot out; to efface or destroy. **obliteration** *n.* the act of blotting out; destruction; extinction. **obliterative** *a.* [L. *obliterare*, fr. *litera*, a letter].
ob·liv·i·on (ȧ·bliv′·i·ạn) *n.* a forgetting, or being forgotten; forgetfulness; heedlessness. **oblivious** *a.* forgetful; causing to forget; heedless. **obliviously** *adv.* **obliviousness** *n.* [L. *oblivisci*, to forget].
ob·long (ȧb′·lawng) *a.* longer than broad; *n.* (*Geom.*) a rectangular figure with adjacent sides unequal [L. *oblongus*].
ob·lo·quy (ȧb′·lạ·kwi·) *n.* abusive speech; disgrace [L. *obloquium*, a speaking against].
ob·nox·ious (ȧb·nȧk′·shạs) *a.* offensive; objectionable. **-ly** *adv.* **-ness** *n.* [L. *obnoxius*, exposed to harm].
o·boe (ō′·bō) *n.* (*Mus.*) a woodwind instrument, long and slender, with tone produced by a double reed; an organ reed stop. **oboist** *n.* [Fr. *hautbois*, high, wood].
ob·scene (ȧb·sēn) *a.* offensive to modesty; indecent; filthy. **-ly** *adv.* **-ness** *n.* **obscenity** (ob·sen′·i·ti·) *n.* lewdness; indecency [L.].
ob·scure (ȧb·skūr′) *a.* dark; hidden; dim; uncertain; humble; *v.t.* to dim; to conceal; to make less intelligible; to make doubtful. **-ly** *adv.* **-ness** *n.* **obscurity** *n.* absence of light; a state of retirement; lack of clear expression or meaning [L. *obscurus*, covered over].
ob·se·quy (ȧb′·sạ·kwi·) *n.* funeral rite; a funeral. **obsequial** *a.* [L.L. *obsequiae*].
ob·se·qui·ous (ạb·sē′·kwi·ạs) *a.* servile; fawning. **-ly** *adv.* **-ness** *n.* [L. *obsequi*, to comply with].
ob·serve (ạb·zurv′) *v.t.* to watch; to note systematically; to perform or keep religiously; to remark; *v.i.* to take notice; to make a remark; to comment. **observable** *a.* **observance** *n.* the act of observing; a paying attention; the keeping of a law, custom, religious rite; a religious rite; a rule or practice. **observant** *a.* quick to notice; alert; carefully attentive; obedient to. **observantly** *adv.* **observation** *n.* the action or habit of observing; the result of watching, examining, and noting; attentive watchfulness; a comment; a remark. **observatory** *n.* a building for the observation and study of astronomical, meteorological, etc.,

phenomena. **-r** *n.* [L. *observare,* to watch].

ob·sess (ạb·ses′) *v.t.* to haunt; to fill the mind completely; to preoccupy. **-ion** *n.* complete domination of the mind by one idea; a fixed idea [L. *obsidere, obsessum,* to besiege].

ob·sid·i·an (ạb·sid′·i·an) *n.* vitreous lava or glassy volcanic rock [fr. *Obsius,* the discoverer].

ob·so·lete (ȧb·sạ·lēt) *a.* no longer in use; out of date. **-ly** *adv.* **-ness** *n.* **obsolescent** *a.* becoming obsolete; going out of use. **obsolescence** *n.* [L. *obsolescere,* to grow out of use].

ob·sta·cle (ȧb′·stạ·kl) *n.* anything that stands in the way; an obstruction; a hindrance [L. *ob,* in the way of; *stare,* to stand].

ob·stet·rics (ạb·stet′·riks) *n.* (*Med.*) the science dealing with the care of pregnant women; midwifery. **obstetric, obstetrical** *a.* **obstetrician** *n.* [L. *obstetrix,* a midwife].

ob·sti·nate (ȧb′·stạ·nạt) *a.* stubborn; not easily moved by argument; unyielding. **-ly** *adv.* **-ness** *n.* **obstinacy** *n.* unreasonable firmness; stubbornness [L. *obstinatus*].

ob·strep·er·ous (ab·strep′·ạ·rạs) *a.* noisy; clamorous; vociferous; unruly; *adv.* **-ness** *n.* [L. *ob,* against; *strepere,* to make a noise].

ob·struct (ạb·strukt′) *v.t.* to block up; to impede; to hinder the passage of; to retard; to oppose; to block out. **-er, -or** *n.* **-ion** *n.* the act of obstructing; that which obstructs or hinders. **-ive** *a.* **-ively** *adv.* [L. *ob,* against; *struere,* to build up].

ob·tain (ạb·tān′) *v.t.* to gain; to acquire; to procure; *v.i.* to be customary or prevalent; to hold good. **-able** *a.* procurable. **-ment** *n.* Also **obtention** [L. *obtinere*].

ob·trude (ạb·tro̤o̤d′) *v.t.* to thrust forward unsolicited; to push out; *v.i.* to intrude. **-r** *n.* **obtrusion** *n.* the act of obtruding. **obtrusive** *a.* **obtrusively** *adv.* [L. *ob; trudere,* to thrust].

ob·tuse (ạb·to̤o̤s′) *a.* blunt; dull of perception; stupid; (*Geom.*) greater than a right angle, but less than 180°. **-ly** *adv.* **-ness** *n.* [L. *obtundere, obtusum,* to blunt].

ob·verse (ȧb′·vurs, ạb·vurs′) *a.* having the base narrower than the apex; being a counterpart; facing the observer; of a coin, bearing the head; *n.* face of a coin, medal, etc. (opp. of 'reverse'); the front or principal aspect. **-ly** *adv.* [L. *ob,* toward; *versum,* to turn].

ob·vi·ate (ȧb′·vi·āt) *v.t.* to intercept and remove (as difficulties); to make unnecessary [L. *ob; viare,* to go].

ob·vi·ous (ȧb′·vi·ạs) *a.* easily seen or understood; evident; apparent. **-ly** *adv.* **-ness** *n.* [L. *obvius,* in the way].

oc·a·ri·na (ȧk·ạ·rē′·nạ) *n.* a small musical wind-instrument with finger holes [It. *oca,* a goose, from its shape].

oc·ca·sion (ạ·kā′·zhạn) *n.* opportunity; a juncture favorable for something; reason or justification; a time of important occurrence; *v.t.* to cause; to bring about. **-al** *a.* occurring now and then; incidental; meant for a special occasion. **-ally** *adv.* from time to time [L. *occasio,* fr. *cadere,* to fall].

oc·ci·dent (ȧk′·sạ·dạnt) *n.* part of the horizon where the sun sets, the west. **occidental** *a.* western; *n.* (*Cap.*) native of Europe or America [L. *occidere,* to go down].

oc·ci·put (ȧk′·si·put) *n.* the back part of the head. **occipital** (ȧk·sip′·i·tạl) *a.* [L. *ob,* over against; *caput,* the head].

oc·clude (ạ·klo̤o̤d′) *v.t.* to shut in or out; (*Chem.*) to absorb gas. **occlusion** *n.* **occlusive** *a.* [L. *ob; claudere, clausum,* to shut].

oc·cult (ạ·kult′) *a.* secret; mysterious; magical; supernatural; *v.t.* to conceal; to hide from view; to eclipse. **-ly** *adv.* **occultation** *n.* the eclipse of a heavenly body by another. **-ism** *n.* the doctrine or study of the supernatural, magical, etc. [L. *occulere,* to hide].

oc·cu·py (ȧk′·yạ·pī) *v.t.* to take possession of; to inhabit; to fill; to employ. **occupancy** *n.* the act of having or holding possession; tenure. **occupant** *n.* one who occupies or is in possession. **occupation** *n.* occupancy; possession; temporary possession of enemy country by the victor; employment; trade; calling; business, profession. **occupational** *a.* **occupier** *n.* [L. *occupare,* to take possession of].

oc·cur (ạ·kur′) *v.i.* to come to the mind; to happen; to be met with. *pr.p.* **-ring.** *pa.p.* and *pa.t.* **-red.** **-rence** *n.* a happening; an event. [L. *occurrere,* to run against].

o·cean (ō′·shạn) *n.* great body of salt water surrounding land of globe; one of the large divisions of this; the sea; *a.* pert. to the great sea. **-ic** (ō·shi·an′·ik) *a.* pert. to, found, or formed in the ocean. **-ography** *n.* the scientific description of ocean phenomena. **-ographer** *n.* **-ographic, -ographical** *a.* **-ology** *n.* science which relates to the ocean [Gk. *ōkeanos,* a stream encircling the world].

o·ce·lot (ō′·sạ·lȧt) *n.* a S. Amer. quadruped of the leopard family [Mex. *ocelotl*].

o·cher (ō′·kẹr) *n.* various natural earths used as yellow, brown, or red pigments. **-ous, -y** *a.* [Gk. *ōchra,* yellow ocher].

o'clock (ạ·klạk′) *adv.* by the clock.

oct- *prefix* fr. Gk. *oktō,* eight. Also **octa-, octo-.** **-agon** (ȧk′·tạ·gȧn) *n.* a plane figure with 8 sides and 8 angles. **-agonal** *a.* **-ahedron** *n.* a solid figure with 8 plane faces. **-ahedral** *a.* **-ane** *n.* (*Chem.*) a hydrocarbon of the paraffin series, used as a fuel. **-angular** *a.* having 8 angles. **-ant** *n.* the eighth part of a circle; an instrument for measuring angles, having an arc of 45°.

oc·tave (ȧk′·tāv) *n.* the week following the celebration of a principal Church festival; a stanza of 8 lines; (*Mus.*) an interval of 8 diatonic notes comprising a complete scale; a note 8 tones above or below another note; a group of 8 [L. *octavus,* eighth].

oc·ten·ni·al (ȧk·ten′·i·ạl) *a.* happening every eighth year; lasting for 8 years [L. *octo,* eight; *annus,* a year].

oc·tet (ȧk·tet′) *n.* (*Mus.*) a group of 8 musicians or singers; a composition for such a group; a group of 8 lines, esp. the first 8 lines of a sonnect. Also **-te** [L. *octo,* eight].

Oc·to·ber (ȧk·tō′·bẹr) *n.* tenth month [eighth month of ancient Roman year].

oc·to·ge·nar·i·an (ȧk·tạ·jạ·ne′·ri·ạn) *a., n.* a person between 80 and 90 years of age. [L. *octogenarius,* of eighty].

oc·to·pus (ȧk′·tạ·pạs) *n.* a mollusk with 8 arms or tentacles covered with suckers [Gk. *okto,* eight; *pous,* a foot].

oc·u·lar (ȧk′·yạ·ler) *a.* pert. to the eye, or to sight; visual; *n.* the eyepiece of an optical instrument. **oculist** *n.* a specialist in the defects and diseases of the eye [L. *oculus,* the eye].

OD (ō·dē′) *n.* (*Slang*) an *overdose,* esp. of a narcotic; *v.i.* to take an overdose, esp. a fatal one. *pr.p.* **OD'ing.** *pa.t., pa.p.* **OD'd, ODed.**

o·da·lisque (ō′·dạ·lisk) *n.* a female slave or concubine in an Oriental harem. Also **odalisk** [Fr., fr. Turk.].

odd (ȧd) *a.* not even; not divisible by two; left over after a round number has been taken away; extra, surplus; casual or outside the reckoning; occasional; out-of-the-way; eccentric; strange. **-ity** *n.* quality of being odd; peculiarity; queer person or thing. **-ly** *adv.* **-ness** *n.* **odds** *n.pl.* the difference in favor of one as against another; advantage or superiority; the ratio by which one person's bet exceeds another's; likelihood or probability [O.N. *odda-* (*tala*), odd- (number)].

ode (ōd) *n.* a lyric poem of exalted tone [Gk. *ōdē,* a song].

o·di·um (ō′·di·ạm) *n.* hatred; the state of being hated; general abhorrence incurred by a person or action; stigma. **odious** *a.* **odiously** *adv.* **odiousness** *n.* [L. = hatred].

o·dont- (ō·dạnt′) *prefix* from the Gk. *odous, odontos,* a tooth. **odontalgia** (ō.dȧn.tȧl′.ji.ạ) *n.* toothache. **odontology** *n.* the science of the teeth [Gk. *algos,* pain; *logos,* discourse].

o·dor (ō′·dẹr) *n.* smell; fragrance; perfume; repute or estimation. **-iferous** (ō·dạ·rif′·ạ·rạs) a sweet-scented; having a strong smell. **-iferously** *adv.* **-iferousness** *n.* **-less** *a.* **-ous** *a.* fragrant; scented. [L. *odor*].

O·dys·seus (ō·dis′·ūs, ō·dis′·ē·ạs) *n.* (*Myth.*) (L. Ulysses) hero of Homer's **Odyssey** (od′·i·si·) *n.* a Greek epic poem glorifying the adventures and wanderings of Odysseus; hence, any long, adventurous journey.

Oed·i·pus (ē·dạ·pạs) *n.* (*Myth.*) a king of Thebes who unwittingly slew his father and married Jocasta, his mother. **Oedipus complex,** in psychoanalysis, a complex involving an abnormal love by a person for the parent of opposite sex.

o'er (ōr) *prep.* (*Poet.*) a contr. for **over.**

oe·soph·a·gus See **esophagus.**

of (ȧv, uv) *prep.* belonging to; from; proceeding from; relating to; concerning [O.E.].

off (awf) *adv.* away; in general, denotes removal or separation, also completion, as in *to finish off; prep.* not on; away from; *a.* distant; on the farther side; less than satisfactory; discontinued; free; *interj.* begone! depart! **-ing** *n.* the more distant part of the sea visible to an observer; **-ish,** *a.* inclined to stand aloof; **-ishly** *adv.* **-ishness** *n.* in the offing, not very distant. **—chance** *n.* a slight chance. **—color** *a.* poor in color; of doubtful propriety. **-hand** *a.* without preparation; free and easy; curt; *adv.* without hesitation; impromptu. **-set** *n.* a shoot or side-branch; a sum set off against another as an equivalent; compensation; (*Print.*) the smudging of a clean sheet; a process in lithography; *v.t.* to counterbalance or compensate. **-shoot** *n.* that which shoots off or separates from a main branch or channel; a descendant. **— side** *a.* (*Football, etc.*) of a player, being illegally ahead of the ball, etc. **-spring** *n.* children; progeny; issue. **off and on,** intermittently [form of *of*].

of·fal (awf′·ạl) *n.* waste meat; entrails of animals; refuse [fr. *off* and *fall*].

of·fend (ạ·fend′) *v.t.* to displease; to make angry; to wound the feelings of; *v.i.* to cause displeasure; to do wrong; to sin. **-er** *n.* [L. *offendere,* to strike against].

of·fense (ạ·fens′) *n.* transgression; sin; insult; wrong; resentment; displeasure; a cause of displeasure. **offensive** *a.* causing or giving offense; used in attack; insulting; unpleasant; *n.* attack; onset; aggressive action. **offensively** *adv.* **offensiveness** *n.* [L. *offendere,* to strike against].

of·fer (awf′·ẹr) *v.t.* to present for acceptance or refusal; to tender; to bid, as a price; to propose; to attempt; to express readiness to do; *v.i.* to present itself or to occur; *n.* an act of offering; a presentation; a price bid; a proposal, esp. of marriage. **-ing** *n.* that which is offered, as a contribution through the church; a sacrifice; a gift. **-er** *n.* [L. *offerre*].

of·fer·to·ry (awf′·ẹr·tor·i·) *n.* (*R.C.*) a part of the mass during which the elements are offered up; the collection of money during the church service; the part of the service, or the music, when offerings are made [L. *offertorium*].

of·fice (awf′·is) *n.* a place for doing business; a duty; a service; a function; an official position; a form of worship; a religious service; **-s** *n.pl.* acts of kindness; help. **-r** *n.* a person who holds an official position; one who holds commissioned rank in the navy, army, air force, etc. [L. *officium,* duty].

of·fi·cial (ạf.ish′.ạl) *a.* pert. to an office; vouched for by one holding office; authorized; *n.* one holding an office, esp. in a public body. **-ly** *adv.* **-dom** *n.* officials collectively; their work, usually in contemptuous sense [L. *officium,* a duty].

of·fi·ci·ate (ạ·fish′·i·āt) *v.i.* to perform the duties of an officer; to perform a divine service [L. *officium,* duty].

of·fi·cious (ạ·fish′·ạs) *a.* given to exaggerate the duties of an office; importunate in offering service; meddlesome. **-ly** *adv.* **-ness** *n.* [L. *officium,* a duty].

of·ten (awf′·n) *adv.* frequently; many times. **oft, -times, ofttimes,** *adv.* archaic forms of 'often' [O.E. *oft.*].

o·gle (ō′·gl, ȧ′·gl) *v.i.* to make eyes: *v.t.* to make eyes at; to cast amorous glances at; *n.* an amorous glance. **-r** *n.* [L.Ger. *oegeln,* fr. *oegen,* to eye].

o·gre (ō·gẹr) *n.* (*fem.* **ogress**) a fabulous man-eating giant. **-ish, ogrish** *a.* [Fr.]

oh (ō) *interj.* an exclamation of surprise, sorrow, pain, etc. Also **oho!**

ohm (ōm) *n.* the standard unit of electrical resistance. **-meter** *n.* an instrument for measuring electrical current and resistance [fr. George S. *Ohm* (1787-1854)].

oil (oil) *n.* one of several kinds of light viscous liquids, obtained from various plants, animal substances, and minerals, used as lubricants, illuminants, fuel, medicines, etc.; *v.t.* to apply oil to; *v.i.* to take oil aboard as fuel. **-er** *n.* one who, or that which, oils; an oilcan. **-y** *a.* consisting of, or resembling, oil; greasy; fawning; subservient. **-ily** *adv.* **-iness** *n.* **-s** *n.pl.* (*Paint.*) short for 'oil-colors' **-cloth** *n.* coarse canvas cloth coated with oil and pigment to make waterproof, used for table coverings, etc. **— colors** *n.pl.* (*Paint.*) colors made by grinding pigments in oil. **— field** *n.* a region rich in mineral oil. **— painting** *n.* one done in oil colors. **-skin** *n.* cloth made waterproof with oil; *pl.* rain clothes of this material. **— well** *n.* boring made in district yielding petroleum [L. *oleum*].

oint·ment (oint′·mạnt) *n.* an unguent; [O.Fr. *oignement*].

o·kay (ō·kā′) *a.* and *adv.* abbrev. to **O.K.,** an expression signifying approval.

old (ōld) *a.* advanced in age; having lived or existed long; belonging to an earlier period; not new or fresh; stale; out of date. **-en** *a.* old; ancient; pert. to the past. **-ish** *a.* somewhat old. **-ness** *n.* **—fashioned** *a.* out of date; not modern. **Old Harry,** the devil; Satan. **— maid,** a spinster; (*Cards*) a round game. **— master,** a painting by a famous artist, esp. of 15th and 16th cents. **Old Nick,** the devil. **— school.** *a.* old-fashioned. **Old Testament,** the first division of Bible. **Old World,** the Eastern hemisphere [O.E. *eald*].

o·le·ag·i·nous (ō·lē·aj′·ạ·nạs) *a.* oily; greasy; (*Fig.*) fawning; unctuous [L. *oleum,* oil].

o·le·an·der (ō·lē·an′·dẹr) *n.* a beautiful, evergreen shrub with red and white flowers [Fr.].

o·le·as·ter (ō·lē·as′·tẹr) *n.* the wild olive [L. fr. *olea,* an olive].

o·le·o (ō′·lē·ō) *prefix* fr. L. *oleum,* oil. **-graph** *n.* a lithograph in oil colors [Gk. *graphein,* to write].

o·le·o·mar·ga·rine (ō·lē·ō·mȧrj′·ạ·rạn) *n.* a butter substitute. *Abbrev.* oleo.

ol·fac·tion (ȧl·fak′·shạn) *n.* smelling; sense of smell. **olfactory** *a.* pert. to smelling [L. *olere,* to smell; *facere,* to make].

ol·i·gar·chy (ȧl′·i·gȧr·ki·) *n.* government in which supreme power rests with a few; those who constitute the ruling few. **oligarch** *n.* a member of an oligarchy. **oligarchal** *a.* **oligarchic(al)** *a.* [Gk. *oligos*, few; *archein*, to rule].

ol·i·go·cene (ȧl′.o.gō.sēn) *a.* (*Geol.*) pert. to a geological period between the eocene and miocene [Gk. *oligos*, little; *kainos*, recent].

o·li·o (ō′.li.ō) *n.* a highly-spiced stew of meat and vegetables; a medley [Sp. *olla*, fr. L. *olla*, a pot].

ol·ive (ȧl′.iv) *n.* an evergreen tree, long cultivated in the Mediterranean countries for its fruit; its oval, oil-yielding fruit; a color, of a greyish, ashy green; *a.* of the color of an unripe olive, or of the foliage. **—branch** *n.* an emblem or offer of peace. **— oil** *n.* oil expressed from olives [L. *oliva*].

O·lym·pi·a (ō.lim′.pi.ạ) (*Class. Hist.*) a plain in ancient Greece, the scene of the Olympic Games. **-d** *n.* the name given to period of four years between each celebration of Olympic Games. **Olympic** *a.* pert. to Olympia, or to the games. **Olympics** *n.pl.* the Olympic Games. **-n** pert. to Mount *Olympus*.

o·me·ga (ō.meg′.ạ) *n.* the last letter of the Greek alphabet; hence, the end. **the alpha and —,** the beginning and the end [Gk.].

om·e·let, omelette (ȧm′.let) *n.* a dish of eggs beaten with milk and seasonings and cooked in a frying pan [Fr.].

o·men (ō′.mạn) *n.* a sign of future events; a foreboding; *v.t.* to foreshadow by means of signs; to augur [L.].

om·i·nous (ȧm′.ạ.nạs) *a.* foreboding evil; threatening; inauspicious. **-ly** *adv.* **-ness** *n.* [L. *ominosus*, fr. *omen*].

o·mit (ō.mit′) *v.t.* to leave out; to neglect; to fail to perform. *pr.p.* **-ting.** *pa.p., pa.t.* **-ted. omission** *n.* neglect; failure to do; that which is omitted or left undone. **omissible** *a.* **omissive** *a.* [L. *omittere*].

om·ni- (ȧm′.ni.) *prefix* fr. L. *omnis*, all.

om·ni·bus (ȧm′.nạ.bus) *n.* a bus; *a.* being 'several in one,' e.g. *omnibus volume;* a kind of anthology [L. *omnibus* = for all].

om·ni·far·i·ous (ȧm′.ni.fár′.i.ạs) *a.* consisting of all varieties [fr. L.].

om·ni·po·tent (ȧm.nip′.ạ.tạnt) *a.* all-powerful, esp. of God; almighty. **-ly** *adv.* **omnipotence** *n.* unlimited power.

om·ni·pres·ent (ȧm.ni.prez′.ạnt) *a.* present in all places at the same time. **omnipresence** *n.* [L. *omnis*, all; and *present*].

om·nis·cience (ȧm.nish′.ạns) *n.* infinite knowledge. **omniscient** *a.* all-knowing.

om·niv·o·rous (ȧm.niv′.ạ.rạs) *a.* all-devouring; eating every kind of food. **-ly** *adv.* [L. *omnis*, all; *vorare*, to devour].

on (awn, ȧn) *prep.* above and touching; in addition to; following from; referring to; at; near; towards, etc.; *adv.* so as to be on; forwards; continuously [O.E.].

once (wuns) *adv.* at one time; on one occasion; formerly; ever; *n.* one time. **at —,** immediately [fr. *one*].

on·col·o·gy (ȧng.kȧl′.ạ.ji.) *n.* the study and treatment of tumors. **oncologic** *a.* **oncologist** *n.* [Gk. *onkos*, a mass; *logos*, a discourse].

on·com·ing (awn′-, ȧn′.kum.ing) *a.* approaching; *n.* approach [fr. *on* and *coming*].

one (wun) *a.* single; undivided; only; without others; identical; *n.* the number or figure 1, I; the lowest cardinal number; unity; a single specimen; *pron.* a particular but not stated person; any person. **-ness** *n.* unity; uniformity; singleness. **-self** *pron.* one's own self or person. **—horse** *a.* drawn by one horse; (*Colloq.*) of no importance; insignificant; paltry. **—sided** *a.* esp. of a contest, game, etc., limited to one side; considering one side only; partial; unfair. **—way** *a.* denoting a system of traffic circulation in one direction only [O.E. *an*].

on·er·ous (ȧn′.ẹr.ạs) *a.* burdensome; oppressive. **-ly** *adv.* **-ness** *n.* [L. *oneris*, a load].

on·go·ing (awn′-, ȧn′.go.ing) *n.* a going on; advance; procedure; *a.* continuing.

on·ion (un′.yạn) *n.* an edible, bulbous plant with pungent odor. **— skin** *n.* thin, glazed paper [L. *unio.*].

on·look·er (awn′-, ȧn′.look.ẹr) *n.* a spectator; an observer [fr. *on* and *look*].

on·ly (ōn′.li.) *a.* being the one specimen; single; sole; *adv.* solely; singly; merely; exclusively; *conj.* but then; except that; with this reservation [O.E. *anlic*, one like].

on·o·mat·o·poe·ia (ȧn.ạ.mat.ạ.pē′.yạ) *n.* the formation of a word by using sounds that resemble or suggest the object or process to be named, e.g. *hiss, ping-pong.* **onomatopoeic, onomatopoetic** *a.* [Gk. *onoma*, a name; *poiein*, to make].

on·set (awn′-, ȧn′.set) *n.* a violent attack; an assault [fr. *on* and *set*].

on·shore (awn′-, ȧn′.shōr) *a.* towards the land, esp. of a wind [fr. *on* and *shore*].

on·slaught (awn′-, ȧn′.slawt) *n.* attack; an onset; an assault [Dut. *aanslag*].

on·to (awn′-, ȧn′.tȯȯ) *prep.* upon; on the top; to.

on·tol·o·gy (ȧn.tȧl′.ạ.ji.) *n.* the science that treats of reality of being; metaphysics. **ontological** *a.* **ontologist** *n.* [Gk. *ōn, ontos*, being; *logos*, discourse].

o·nus (ō′.nạs) *n.* burden; responsibility [L.].

on·ward (awn′-, ȧn′.wẹrd) *a., adv.* advancing; going on; forward. **-s** *adv.* in a forward direction; ahead [E. *on;* O.E. *weard*, in the direction of].

on·yx (ȧn′.iks) *n.* a variety of quartz [Gk. *onux*, a fingernail].

oo·dles (ȯȯ′.dlz) *n.pl.* (*Slang*) superabundance.

ooze (ȯȯz) *n.* soft mud or slime; a gentle flow; a kind of deposit on the bottom of the sea; *v.i.* to flow gently as if through pores; to leak or percolate; *v.t.* to exude or give out slowly. **oozy** *a.* [M.E. *wose*, fr. O.E. *wase*, mud].

o·pac·i·ty. See **opaque.**

o·pal (ō′.pạl) *n.* a mineral with varying hues of green, yellow, and red. **-escent** (ō.pạl.es′.ạnt) *a.* of changing iridescent color, like an opal. **-escence** *n.* **-ine** (ō′.pạl.in) *a.* like opal [L. *opalus*].

o·paque (ō.pāk′) *a.* not transparent; impenetrable to light; not lucid; dull-witted. **-ly** *adv.* **-ness** *n.* **opacity** *n.* [L. *opacus*].

ope (ōp) *v.t., v.i.* (*Poet.*) to open.

OPEC (ō′pek) *n.* *O*rganization of *P*etroleum *E*xporting *C*ountries.

o·pen (ō′.pn) *a.* not shut or blocked up; allowing passage in or out; not covered (with trees); not fenced; without restrictions; available; exposed; frank and sincere; *n.* clear, unobstructed space; *v.t.* to set open; to uncover; to give access to; to begin; to cut or break into; *v.i.* to become open; to begin; (*Theat.*) to have a first performance. **-er** *n.* one who or that which opens. **-ing** *a.* first in order; initial; *n.* a hole or gap; an open or cleared space; an opportunity; a beginning. **-ly** *adv.* publicly; frankly. **-ness** *n.* **-cast** *a.* (*Mining*) excavated from the surface, instead of from underground. **—handed** *a.* generous; liberal. **—hearted** *a.* frank. **—minded** *a.* free from prejudices [O.E.].

op·er·a (ȧp′.ạ.rạ) *n.* a musical drama; the theater where opera is performed. **-tic** *a.* pert. to opera. **operetta** *n.* a short light opera. **grand —** *n.* opera in which no spoken dialogue is permitted. **— bouffe** (bȯȯf) a farcical play set to music. **— glass, — glasses** *n.* a small binocular used in theaters. **—hat** *n.* a man's collapsible tall hat [It., fr. L. *opera*, work].

op·er·ate (ȧp′.ạ.rāt) *v.t.* to cause to function; to effect; *v.i.* to work; to produce an effect; to exert power; to perform an act of surgery;

to deal in stocks and shares, esp. speculatively. **operation** *n.* the act of operating; a method or mode of action; treatment involving surgical skill; movement of an army or fleet (usu. in *pl.*). **operational** *a.* **operative** *a.* having the power of acting; exerting force; producing the desired effect; efficacious; *n.* artisan or workman; factory hand. **operator** *n.* [L. *operari,* to work].

o·per·cu·lum (ō·pur′·kyạ·lạm) *n.* a lid or cover, in plants; a lid-like structure in mollusks [L. fr. *operire,* to cover].

op·er·ose (ȧp′·ạ·rōs) *a.* laborious; industrious. **-ly** *adv.* **-ness** *n.* [L. *opus,* work].

oph·i·(o)- *prefix* fr. Gk. *ophis,* a snake. **ophidian** (ō·fid′·i·ạn) *n.* a snake; *a.* snake-like.

oph·thal·mi·a (ȧf·thal′·mi·ạ) *n.* (*Med.*) inflammation of the eye. **ophthalmic** *a.* of the eye.**ophthalmologist** *n.* a physician skilled in the study and treatment of the eye. **ophthalmology** *n.* the science dealing with the structure, functions, and diseases of the eye. **ophthalmoscope** *n.* an instrument for viewing the interior of the eye [Gk. *ophthalmos,* the eye; *logos,* discourse; *skopein,* to view].

o·pi·ate (ō′·pi·ạt) *n.* any preparation of opium; a narcotic; anything that dulls or stupefies; *a.* containing opium; inducing sleep. **opiatic** *a.* [fr. *opium*].

o·pine (ō·pīn′) *v.t.* and *i.* to think or suppose; to hold or express an opinion [L. *opinari*].

o·pin·ion (ạ·pin′·yạn) *n.* judgment or belief; estimation; formal statement by an expert. **-ated** *a.* dogmatic [L. *opinio*].

o·pi·um (ō′·pi·ạm) *n.* narcotic used to induce sleep or allay pain [Gk. *opion,* poppy-juice].

o·pos·sum (ạ·pȧs′·ạm) *n.* a small marsupial animal. Also **possum** [N. Amer. Ind.].

op·po·nent (ạ·pō′·nạnt) *a.* opposite; opposing; antagonistic; *n.* one who opposes [L. *opponere,* to place against].

op·por·tune (ȧp·ẹr·tūn′) *a.* well-timed; convenient. **-ly** *adv.* **-ness** *n.* **opportunism** *n.* the policy of doing what is expedient at the time regardless of principle. **opportunist** *n.* **opportunity** *n.* a fit or convenient time; a good chance [L. *opportunus*].

op·pose (ạ·pōz′) *v.t.* to set against; to resist; to compete with. **opposable** *a.* **-r** *n.* [L. *opponere,* to place against].

op·po·site (ȧp′·ạ·zit) *a.* contrary facing; contrary; diametrically different; *n.* the contrary; *prep.* and *adv.* in front of; on the other side; across from; **-ly** *adv.* facing each other. **-ness** *n.* **opposition** (ȧp·ạ·zish′·ạn) *n.* the state of being opposite; resistance; contradiction; an obstacle; a party opposed to that in power [L. *opponere, oppositum,* to place against].

op·press (ạ·pres′) *v.t.* to govern with tyranny; to treat severely; to lie heavily on. **-ion** (ạ·presh′·ạn) *n.* harshness; tyranny; dejection. **-ive** *a.* unreasonably burdensome; hard to bear. **-ively** *adv.* **-iveness** *n.* **-or** *n.* [L. *opprimere, oppressum,* to press down].

op·pro·bri·um (ạ·prō′·bri·ạm) *n.* reproach; disgrace; infamy. **opprobrious** *a.* reproachful and contemptuous; shameful. [L.].

op·pugn (ạ·pūn′) *v.t.* to dispute; to oppose. **-er** *n.* **oppugnant** (ạ·pug′·nạnt) *a.* opposing. **-ancy** *n.* opposition [L. *oppugnare,* to fight against].

opt (ȧpt) *v.i.* to make a choice; to choose. **-ative** (ȧp′·tạ·tiv) *a.* expressing wish or desire; *n.* (*Gram.*) a mood of the verb expressing wish. [L. *optare,* to wish].

op·tic (ȧp′·tic) *a.* pert. to the eye or to sight; pert. to optics; *n.* the eye. **-s** *n.* the science which deals with light and its relation to sight. **-al** *a.* pert. to vision; visual. **-ally** *adv.* **optician** (ȧp·tish′·ạn) *n.* a maker of, or dealer in, optical instruments, esp. spectacles [Gk. *optikos*].

op·ti·mism (ȧp′·tạ·mizm) *n.* belief that everything is ordered for the best; disposition to look on bright side. **optimist** *n.* believer in optimism; one who takes hopeful view. **optimistical** *a.* [L. *optimus,* best].

op·tion (ȧp′·shạn) *n.* the power or right of choosing; choice. *a.* left to one's free choice. **-ally** *adv.* [L. *optare,* to choose].

op·u·lent (ȧp′·yạ·lạnt) *a.* wealthy; abundantly rich. **-ly** *adv.* **opulence, opulency** *n.* wealth; riches [L. *opulentus*].

o·pus (ō′·pạs) *n.* a work; a musical composition; *pl.* **opera** (ȧp′·ạ·rạ). **magnum opus,** a writer's most important work [L. *opusculum* dim. of *opus,* work].

or (awr) *conj.* introducing an alternative; if not; (*Arch.*) before [M.E. *other*].

or·a·cle (awr′·ạ·kl) *n.* shrine where ancient Greeks consulted deity; response given, often obscure; a person of outstanding wisdom. **o·rac·u·lar** (aw·rak′·yạ·lẹr) *a.* **oracularly** *adv.* [L. *oraculum*].

o·ral (ō′·rạl) *a.* spoken; pert. to the mouth. **-ly** *adv.* [L. *os, oris,* the mouth].

or·ange (awr′·inj) *n.* a juicy, gold-colored citrus fruit; tree bearing it; reddish yellow color like an orange; *a.* reddish yellow in color. **-ade** (or·anj·ād′) *n.* drink of orange juice, sugar, and water [Arab. *naranj*].

o·rang-u·tan, o·rang-ou·tang (ō·rang′·oo·tang) *n.* a large long-armed ape [Malayan = man of the woods].

o·rate (ō·rāt′) *v.i.* to talk loftily; to harangue. **oration** (ō·rā′·shạn) *n.* a formal and dignified public speech. **orator** *n.* one who delivers an oration; one distinguished for gift of public speaking. **oratorical** *a.* pert. to orator(y); rhetorical. **oratorically** *adv.* **oratorio** (or·ạ·tō′·ri·ō) *n.* a religious musical composition for voices and orchestra. **oratory** *n.* the art or exercise of speaking in public; eloquence; a chapel or small room for private devotions [L. *orare,* to speak].

orb (awrb) *n.* a sphere or globe; (*Poet.*) a heavenly body; the globe surmounted by a cross, which forms part of the regalia in England; (*Poet.*) the eye. **-it** *n.* (*Astron.*) path traced by one heavenly body in its revolution round another; range of influence or action; the eye socket. **-ital** *a.* [L. *orbis,* a circle].

or·chard (awr′·chẹrd) *n.* a garden or enclosure containing fruit trees [O.E. *ortgeard*].

or·ches·tra (awr′·kis·trạ) *n.* the space in a theater occupied by musicians; the main floor of a theater; a group of performers on various musical instruments. **orchestral** *a.* **orchestrate** *v.t.* to arrange music for performance by an orchestra. **-tion** *n.* [Gk. *orcheisthai,* to dance].

or·chid, orchis (awr′·kid, awr′·kis) *n.* a genus of plants with fantastically-shaped flowers of varied and brilliant colors. **-aceous** *a.* pert. to the orchid [Gk. *orchis,* a testicle].

or·dain (awr·dān′) *v.t.* to decree; to destine; to appoint; to admit to the Christian ministry; to confer holy orders upon. **-ment** *n.* (rare). **ordination** *n.* the act of ordaining admission to the ministry [L. *ordo,* order].

or·deal (awr′·dēl, awr′·dē·ạl) *n.* an ancient method of trial by requiring the accused to undergo a dangerous physical test; a trying experience; a test of endurance [O.E. *ordal,* a judicial test].

or·der (awr′·dẹr) *n.* rank; class; group; regular arrangement; sequence; succession; method; regulation; a command or direction; mode of procedure; an instruction; a monastic society; one of the five styles of architecture (Doric, Ionic, Corinthian, Tuscan, and Composite); a subdivision of a class of plants or animals, made up of genera; an honor conferred for distinguished civil or military services; in trade, detailed instructions, by a customer, of goods to be supplied. *v.t.* to arrange; to command; to require; to regulate; to systematize; to give an order for. **-ly** *a.* methodical; tidy; well regulated; peaceable; *n.* a soldier following an officer to carry orders; in a hospital, an attendant; *adv.* in right order. **-liness** *n.* **holy orders,** generally, ordination to the Christian ministry. **to take orders,** to accept instructions; (*Church*) to be ordained. **by order,** by command. **in order to,** for the purpose of [L. *ordo,* order].

or·di·nal (awr′·dạ·nạl) *a.* and *n.* showing order or position in a series, e.g. *first, second,* etc.; pert. to an order, of plants, animals, etc. a church service book for use at ordinations [L. *ordo,* order].

or·di·nance (awr′·dạ·nạns) *n.* an established rule, religious rite, or ceremony; a decree [O. Fr. *ordenance*].

or·di·nar·y (awr′·dạ·nẹr·i·) *a.* usual; regular; habitual; normal, commonplace; plain; *n.* something customary; a church service book. **ordinarily** *adv.* [L. *ordo,* order].

or·di·na·tion See **ordain.**

ord·nance (awrd′·nạns) *n.* collective term for heavy mounted guns; military weapons of all kinds, ammunition, etc. [var. of *ordinance*].

or·dure (awr′·jẹr) *n.* dung; filth [O.Fr. *ord.* vile].

ore (ōr) *n.* a native mineral from which metal is extracted [O.E. *ora*].

or·gan (awr′·gạn) *n.* a musical instrument of pipes worked by bellows and played by keys; a member of an animal or plant exercising a special function; a medium of information. **organic** *a.* pert. to or affecting bodily organs; having either animal or vegetable life; derived from living organisms; systematic; organized. **organically** *adv.* **-ism** *n.* an organized body or system; a living body. **-ist** *n.* a player on the organ. **— grinder** *n.* a player of a barrel organ. **— loft** *n.* gallery for an organ. **— stop** *n.* a series of pipes of uniform tone or quality; one of a series of knobs for manipulating and controlling them. **organic chemistry,** the branch of chemistry dealing with the compounds of carbon [Gk. *organon,* an instrument].

or·gan·dy (awr′·gạn·di·) *n.* a muslin of great transparency and lightness. Also **organdie** [Fr. *organdi*].

or·gan·ize (awr·′gạ·nīz) *v.t.* to give a definite structure; to prepare for transaction of business; to get up, arrange, or put into working order; to unite in a society. **organizable** *a.* **organization** *n.* act of organizing; the manner in which the branches of a service, etc., are arranged; individuals systematically united for some work; a society. **-r** *n.* [Gk. *organon,* an instrument].

or·gasm (awr′·gazm) *n.* immoderate action or excitement, esp. sexual. **orgastic** *a.* [Gk. *orgaein,* to be lustful].

or·gy (awr′·ji·) *n.* a drunken or licentious revel; a debauch. **orgiastic** *a.* [Gk. *orgia* (*pl.*) Bacchic rites].

o·ri·el (ō′·ri·ạl) *n.* a projecting window; the recess in a room formed by such a window [O.Fr. *oriol,* a porch].

o·ri·ent (ō′·ri·ạnt) *a.* rising, as the sun; lustrous (applied to pearls); *n.* the east; Eastern countries; *v.t.* to place so as to face the east; to determine the position of, with respect to the east; to take one's bearings. **oriental** *a.* eastern; pert. to, coming from, of, the east; *n.* (*Cap.*) an Asiatic. **orientate** *v.t.* and *i.* to orient; to bring into clearly understood relations. **orientation** *n.* the act of turning to, or determining, the east; sense of direction; determining one's position [L. *oriens,* rising, fr. *oriri,* to rise].

or·i·fice (awr′·ạ·fis) *n.* a mouth or opening; perforation; vent [L. *orificium,* fr. *os,* the mouth; *facere,* to make].

or·i·gin (awr′·ạ·jin) *n.* beginning; starting point; a source; parentage; birth; nationality. **original** (ạ·rij′·ạ·nȧl) *a.* earliest; first; new, not copied or derived; thinking or acting for oneself; *n.* origin; model; a pattern. **originally** *adv.* **originality** *n.* the quality of being original; initiative. **originate** *v.t.* to bring into being; to initiate; *v.i.* to begin; to arise. **originative** *a.* **origination** *n.* **originator** *n.* [L. *origo,* fr. *oriri,* to rise].

o·ri·ole (ō′·ri·ōl) *n.* bird of the thrush family [O.Fr. *oriol,* fr. L. *aurum,* gold.]

or·i·son (awr′·i·zȧn) *n.* a prayer [L.*orare,* to pray].

or·mo·lu (awr·mạ·lòò) *n.* an alloy of copper, zinc and tin [Fr. *or,* gold; *moulu* ground, fr. *moudre,* to grind].

or·na·ment (awr′·nạ·mạnt) *n.* decoration; any object to adorn or decorate; *v.t.* to adorn; to beautify; to embellish. **ornamental** *a.* serving to decorate. **ornamentally** *adv.* **ornamentation** *n.* decoration. **ornate** *a.* richly decorated. **ornately** *adv.* **ornateness** *n.* [L. *ornamentum*].

or·ni·tho- *prefix* fr. Gk. *ornis, ornithos,* a bird, used in derivatives. **ornothology** (awr·na·thȧl′·ạ·ji·) the scientific study of birds. **ornithological** *a.* **ornithologist** *n.* [Gk. *logos,* discourse; *rhunchos,* the beak].

o·ro·tund (ō′·rạ·tund) *a.* of voice or speech, full, clear, and musical; of style, pompous [L. *os, oris,* the mouth; *rotundus,* round].

or·phan (awr′·fan) *n.* and *a.* a child bereft of one or both parents; *v.t.* to make an orphan. **-age** *n.* a home or institution for ophans. **-hood, -ism** *n.* [Gk. *orphanos,* bereaved].

or·pi·ment (awr′·pi·mạnt) *n.* a yellow mineral of the arensic group, used as a dye [L. *aurum,* gold; *pigmentum,* a pigment].

or·rer·y (awr′·ạ·ri·) *n.* a mechanical model of the solar system, showing the revolutions of the planets, etc. [fr. the Earl of *Orrery,* for whom one was made in 1715].

or·ris (awr′·is) *n.* a kind of iris. **-root** *n.* the dried root, used as a powdėr in perfumery and medicine [form of *iris*].

or·tho·dox (awr′·thạ·dȧks) *a.* having the correct faith; sound in opinions or doctrine; conventional. **-ly** *adv.* **-y** *n.* soundness of faith, esp. in religion. **-ness** *n.* [Gk. *orthos,* right; *doxa,* opinion].

or·thog·ra·phy (awr·thȧg′·rạ·fi·) *n.* correct spelling. **orthographer** *n.* **orthographic, orthographical** *a.* **orthographically** *adv.* [Gk. *orthos,* correct; *graphein,* to write].

or·tho·pe·dics, orthopaedics (awr·thạ·pēd′·iks) *n.* treatment and cure of bodily deformities, esp. in children. Also **orthop(a)edia, orthop(a)edy. orthopedic** *a.* **orthopedist** *n.* [Gk. *orthos,* straight; *pais,* paidos, a child].

os·cil·late (ȧs′·ạ·lāt) *v.i.* to swing to and fro; to vibrate; to vary between extremes; (*Radio*) to set up wave motion in a receiving set. **oscillation** *n.* a pendulum-like motion; variation between extremes. **oscillator** *n.* **oscillatory** *n.* [L. *oscillare,* to swing].

os·cu·late (ȧs′·kyạ·lāt) *v.t.* and *i.* to kiss; (*Math.*) to touch, as curves; *a.* of species sharing characteristics. **osculant, osculation** *n.* kissing; contact. **osculatory** *a.* [L. *osculum,* a kiss].

os·mi·um (ȧz′·mi·ạm) *n.* (*Chem.*) a hard, bluish-white metal [fr. Gk. *osmē,* smell].

os·mo·sis (ȧs·mō′·sis) *n.* (*Chem.*) the tendency of fluid substances, if separated by a porous membrane, to filter through it and become equally diffused. **osmotic** (ȧs·mȧt′·ik) *a.* [Gk. *ōsmos,* fr. *ōthein,* to push].

os·prey (ȧs′·prē, ·prā) *n.* the fish hawk or sea eagle; erroneously applied to an egret plume used in millinery [corrupt. of *ossifrage*, the sea eagle].

oss- (ȧs-) *prefix* fr. L. *os, ossis*, bone, used in many derivatives. **-eous** (ȧs′·ē·ạs) *a.* pert. to or resembling bone; bony. **-icle** *n.* a small bone, esp. of the middle ear. **-iferous** *a.* containing, or yielding, bones. **-ification** *n.* hardening into bone. **-ify** *v.t.* to harden into bone; *v.i.* to become bone, of cartilage, etc. **-uary** (ȧs′·ū·er·i·) *n.* a memorial place for holding the bones of the dead.

os·si·frage (ȧs′·ạ·frij) *n.* the osprey [L. *ossifraga*, the bonebreaker].

os·te·al (ȧs′·ti·ạl) *a.* (*Med.*) pert. to, or like, bone. **osteitis** *n.* inflammation of the bone [Gk. *osteon*, bone].

os·ten·si·ble (ȧs·ten′·sạ·bl) *a.* professed; used as a blind; apparent. **ostensibly** *adv.* **ostensibility** *n.* [L.*ostendere*, to show].

os·ten·ta·tion (ȧs·tạn·tā′·shạn) *n.* vainglorious display; showing off. **ostentatious** *a.* fond of display; characterized by display **ostentatiously** *adv.* **ostentatiousness** *n.* [L. *ostendere*, to show].

os·te·o- (ȧs′·ti·ō) *prefix* fr. Gk. *osteon*, bone, used in derivatives mainly medical. **-arthritis** (ȧr·thrī′·tis) *n.* chronic inflammation of a joint. **osteoid** *a.* resembling bone. **osteology** *n.* that branch of anatomy dealing with bones, their structure, etc. **osteologist** *n.*

os·te·op·a·thy (ȧs·ti·ȧ′·path·i·) *n.* a system of healing, based on the belief that the human body can effect its own cure with the aid of manipulative treatment of the spinal column, joints, etc.; manipulative surgery. **osteopath** *n.* a practitioner of this system. **osteopathic** *a.* [Gk. *osteon*, bone; *pathos*, feeling].

os·tra·cise (ȧs′·trạ·sīz) *v.t.* to exclude from society; to exile; to boycott. **ostracism** *n.* exclusion from society; social boycotting [Gk. *ostrakon*, a shell].

os·trich (ȧs′·trich) *n.* a large flightless bird, native of Africa [Gk. *strouthos*].

oth·er (uTH′·ẹr) *a.* and *pron.* not this; not the same; different; opposite; additional; *adv.* otherwise. **-wise** *adv.* differently; in another way; *conj.* else; if not. **every other,** every second (one); each alternate. **-worldly** *a.* spiritual [O.E. *other*].

o·ti·ose (ō′·shi·ōs, ō′·ti·ōs) *a.* at ease; at leisure; superfluous; futile [L. *otium*, easel].

o·ti·tis (ō·tī′·tis) *n.* (*Med.*) inflammation of the ear. **otology** *n.* [Gk. *ous, ōtos*, the ear].

ot·ta·va ri·ma (a·tȧ·vạ·rē′·mạ) *n.* a stanza of eight lines [It. *ottava*, octave + *rhyme*].

ot·ter (ȧt′·ẹr) *n.* an aquatic, fish-eating animal of the weasel family [O.E.*otor*].

Ot·to·man (ȧt′·ạ·mạn) *a.* pert. to the Turks; *n.* a cushioned seat without back or arms [fr. Turkish Sultan *Othman*, or *Osman*].

ought (awt) *auxil. v.* to be bound by moral obligation or duty [O.E. *ahte*, owed].

ought (awt) *n.* a form of 'nought'; nothing.

Oui·ja (wē′·jạ, ·jē) *n.* board with letters, used at seances to answer questions [Trademark, coined fr. Fr. *oui*, yes; Ger. *ja*, yes].

ounce (ouns) *n.* a unit of weight, abbrev. oz.; in avoirdupois weight = 1/16 of a pound; in troy weight 1/12 of a pound; a fluid measurement [L. *uncia*, a twelfth part].

ounce (ouns) *n.* snow leopard [O.Fr. *once*].

our (our) *n.* belonging to us. **-s** *poss. pron.* used with a noun. **-self** *pron.* myself (in regal or formal style). **-selves** *pron. pl.* we, i.e. not others [O.E. *ure*].

oust (oust) *v.t.* to put out; to expel; to dispossess, esp. by unfair means [O.Fr. *oster*; Fr. *ôter*, to remove].

out (out) *adv.* on, at, or to, the outside; from within; from among; away; not in the usual or right place; not at home; in bloom; disclosed; exhausted; destitute; in error; at a loss; on strike; unemployed; *a.* outlying; remote; *prep.* outside; out of; *interj.* away! begone! *v.t.* to put out; to knock out; **-er** *a.* being on the outside; away from the inside. **-ermost, -most** *a.* [O.E. *ut*].

out·bal·ance (out·bal′·ans) *v.t.* to exceed in weight; to be heavier than.

out·bid (out·bid′) *v.t.* to bid more than; to offer a higher price.

out·board (out′·bōrd) *a.* projecting beyond and outside the hull of a ship, e.g. of a ladder; also, of a detachable motor.

out·break (out′·brāk) *n.* a sudden breaking out; a burst, esp. of anger; the beginning, esp. of an epidemic of disease, of war, etc.

out·build·ing (out′·bild·ing) *n.* an outhouse; a building detached from the main building.

out·burst (out′·burst) *n.* a bursting out, esp. of anger, laughter, cheering, etc.

out·cast (out′·kast) *a.* cast out as useless; *n.* one rejected by society.

out·class (out·klas′) *v.t.* to exceed in skill or quality; to surpass.

out·come (out′·kum) *n.* issue; result.

out·crop (out′·krȧp) *n.* the coming out of a stratum of rock, coal, etc.

out·cry (out′·krī) *n.* a loud cry; a cry of distress, complaint, disapproval, etc.

out·dis·tance (out·dis′·tạns) *v.t.* to surpass in speed; to get ahead of.

out·do (out·do̊o̊′) *v.t.* to excel; surpass.

out·door (out′·dōr) *a.* out of doors; in the open air. **-s** *adv.* outside.

out·field (out′·fēld) *n.* the field or fields farthest from the farm buildings; (*Baseball*) the part of the field beyond the diamond or infield; the players there.

out·fit (out′·fit) *n.* a supply of things, esp. clothes, tools, etc., required for any purpose; equipment; kit; (*Slang*) a company of people; a crowd; *v.t.* to supply with equipment, etc. **-ter** *n.* one who supplies equipment.

out·flank (out·flangk′) *v.t.* (*Mil.*) to succeed in getting beyond the flank of the enemy.

out·go (out·gō′) *v.t.* to go beyond; *n.* (out′·gō) expenditure; outlay. **-ing** *a.* sociable; departing; going out.

out·grow (out·grō′) *v.t.* to surpass in growth; to become too large or old for; to grow out of. **-th** *n.* what growth out of anything.

out·house (out′·hous) *n.* a building, separate from main building; a privy.

out·ing (out′·ing) *n.* a going out; an excursion; a trip; an airing.

out·land·ish (out·lan′·dish) *a.* remote; barbarous; not according to custom; queer.

out·law (out′·law) *n.* one placed beyond the protection of the law; a bandit; *v.t.* to declare to be an outlaw. **-ry** *n.* defiance of the law.

out·lay (out′·lā) *n.* expenditure; expenses.

out·let (out′·let) *n.* a passage or way out; an exit; a vent; an opening.

out·line (out′·līn) *n.* the lines that bound a figure; a boundary; a sketch without details; a rough draft; a general plan; *v.t.* to draw in outline; to give a general plan of.

out·live (out·liv′) *v.t.* to live longer than.

out·look (out′·look) *n.* a looking out; a prospect; a person's point of view; prospects.

out·ly·ing (out′·lī·ing) *a.* lying at a distance; remote; isolated; detached.

out·mod·ed (out·mō′·dạd) *a.* out of fashion.

out·num·ber (out·num′·bẹr) *v.t.* to exceed in number.

out·pa·tient (out′·pā′·shạnt) *n.* a patient who comes to a hospital, infirmary, etc., for treatment but is non-resident.

out·post (out′·pōst) *n.* (*Mil.*) a small detachment posted some distance from the main body.

out·pour (out·pōr′) *v.t.* to pour out; to flow

over. **-pour, -ing** *n.* an overflow.

out·put (out′·poot)*n.* production; the amount of goods produced in a given time.

out·rage (out′·rāj) *n.* excessive violence; violation of others' rights; gross insult or indignity; *v.t.* to do grievous wrong or violence to; to insult grossly. **outrageous** (out·rā′·jąs) *a.* violent; atrocious. **outrageously** *adv.*

out·ride (out·rīd′) *v.t.* to ride faster than; to ride farther than; (*Naut.*) of a ship, to live through a storm. **-r** *n.* a servant on horseback who rides beside a carriage.

out·rig·ger (out′·rig·ęr) *n.* (*Naut.*) a projecting spar for extending sails, ropes, etc.; a frame on the side of a rowing-boat with a rowlock at the outer edge; projecting framework, with a float attached to it, to prevent a canoe from upsetting [earlier *outligger;* Dut. *uitlegger*, outlyer].

out·run (out·run′) *v.t.* to exceed in speed; to run farther or faster than; to leave behind.

out·set (out′·set) *n.* a setting out; commencement; beginning; start.

out·side (out·sīd′) *n.* the outer surface; the exterior; the farthest limit; *a.* pert. to the outer part; exterior; external; outdoor; *adv.* not inside: out of doors; in the open air; *prep.* on the outer part of.**-r** *n.* one not belonging to a particular party, set, circle, etc.

out·size (out′·sīz) *a.* and *n.* larger than the normal size, esp. of garments.

out·skirt (out′·skurt) *n.* generally in *pl.* the border; the suburbs of a town.

out·spo·ken (out·spō′·kn) *a.* not afraid to speak aloud one's opinions; bold of speech.

out·stand·ing (out·stand′·ing) *a.* standing out; prominent; conspicuous; of debts, unpaid; of work, etc., still to be done.

out·strip (out·strip′) *v.t.* to surpass; to outrun; to leave behind.

out·vote (out·vōt′) *v.t.* to defeat by a greater number of votes.

out·ward (out′·węrd) *a.* pert. to the ouside; external; exterior; *adv.* towards the outside. **-s** *adv.* outward; toward the outside. **-ly** *adv.*

out·weigh (out·wā′) *v.t.* to exceed in weight, value, influence, etc.

out·wit (out·wit′) *v.t.* to defeat by cunning, stratagem, etc.; to get the better of.

o·va (ō′·vą) *n.pl.* eggs; the female germ cells; *sing.* **ovum** (ō′·vum) **ovary** *n.* one of two reproductive organs in female animal in which the ova are formed and developed; (*Bot.*) the part of the pistil containing the seed. **ovarial, ovarian** (ō·ver′·i·al, -ąn) *a.* pert. to the ovary [L. *ovum*, an egg].

o·val (ō′·vąl) *a.* egg-shaped; elliptical; *n.* an oval figure. **-ly** *adv.* [L. *ovum*, and egg].

o·va·tion (ō·vā′·shąn) *n.* an enthusiastic burst of applause; a triumphant reception [L. *ovatio*, to celebrate a triumph].

ov·en (uv′·n) *n.* an enclosed chamber in a stove, for baking or heating [O.E. *ofēn*].

o·ver (ō′·vęr) *prep.* above; on; upon; more than; in excess of; across; from side to side of; throughout; etc.; *adv.* above; above and beyond; going beyond; in excess; too much; past; finished; across; *a.* upper; outer; covering; *n.* **-all** *a.* inclusive [O.E. *afer*].

o·ver·act (ō·vęr·akt′) *v.t.* and *i.* to play a part (in a play) in an exaggerated manner.

o·ver·all (ō′·vęr·awl) *n.* loose trousers worn over the ordinary clothing as a protection against dirt, etc. Also *n.pl.*

o·ver·arm (ō′·vęr·ȧrm) *a.* and *adv.* in swimming, ball, etc., with the hand and arm raised.

o·ver·awe (ō·vęr·aw′) *v.t.* to restain by awe.

o·ver·bal·ance (ō·vęr·bal′·ąns) *v.t.* to exceed in weight, value, etc.; *v.i.* to lose balance.

o·ver·bear (ō·vęr·ber′) *v.t.* to bear down; to repress; to overpower. **-ing** *a.* domineering.

o·ver·board (ō′·vęr·bōrd) *adv.* over the side of a ship; out of a ship into the water.

o·ver·cast (ō·vęr·kast′) *v.t.* to cast over; to cloud; to darken; to stitch over roughly. **overcast** *a.* cloudy; dull.

o·ver·charge (ō·vęr·chȧrj′) *v.t.* and *i,* to load too heavily; to charge too high a price.

o·ver·coat (ō′·vęr·kōt) *n.* an outdoor garment for men worn over ordinary clothing.

o·ver·come (ō·vęr·kum′) *v.t.* and *i.* to conquer; to overpower; to get the better of.

o·ver·do (ō·vęr·dóó′) *v.t.* to do to much; to fatigue; to exaggerate. *pa.t.* **overdid.** *pa.p.* **overdone** *a.* exaggerated; over-acted; overcooked.

o·ver·dose (ō·vęr·dōs′) *v.t.* to give an excessive dose; *n.* to take too great a dose.

o·ver·draw (ō·vęr·draw′) *v.t.* and *i.* to exaggerate; to draw money in excess of one's credit. **overdraft** *n.* act of overdrawing; amount drawn from bank in excess of credit.

o·ver·dress (ō·vęr·dres′) *v.t.* and *i.* to dress too showily for good taste.

o·ver·due (ō·vęr·dū′) *a.* unpaid at right time; not having arrived at right time.

o·ver·es·ti·mate (ō·vęr·es′·tą·māt) *v.t.* to estimate too highly.

o·ver·flow (ō·vęr·flō) *v.t.* to flow over; to flood; to fill too full; *v.i.* to flow over the edge, bank, etc.; to abound. *n.* what flows over; flood; excess; superabundance; surplus.

o·ver·grow (ō·vęr·grō′) *v.t.* to grow beyond; to cover with growth; *v.i.* to grow beyond normal size. **overgrown** *a.* covered with grass, weeds, etc. **overgrowth** *n.*

o·ver·hand (ō′·vęr·hand) *a.* and *adv.* (*Ball, Swimming, etc.*) with the hand raised.

o·ver·hang (ō·vęr·hang′) *v.t.* and *i.* to hang over; to jut over; to threaten.

o·ver·haul (ō·vęr·hawl′) *v.t.* to examine thoroughly and set in order; to overtake in pursuit. **overhaul** *n.* a thorough examination, esp. for repairs; repair.

o·ver·head (ō′·vęr·hed) *a.* and *adv.* over the head; above; aloft; in the sky; the permanent expenses of running a business.

o·ver·hear (ō·vęr·hir′) *v.t.* to hear by accident. *pa.p.* and *pa.t.* **overheard.**

o·ver·joy (ō·vęr·joi′) *v.t.* to fill with great joy.

o·ver·land (ō′·vęr·land) *a.* and *adv.* wholly by land, esp. of a journey.

o·ver·lap (ō·vęr·lap′) *v.t.* and *i.* to lap over; to rest upon and extend beyond.

o·ver·lay (ō·vęr·lā′) *v.t.* to spread over, to cover completely; to span. *n.* a covering, as a transparent sheet, superimposed on another.

o·ver·lie (ō·vęr·lī′) *v.t.* to lie on the top of; to smother a baby by lying on it in bed.

o·ver·load (ō·vęr·lōd′) *v.t.* to place too heavy a load on. *n.* an excessive load.

o·ver·look (ō·vęr·look′) *v.t.* to look over; to inspect; to superintend; to fail to notice by carelessness; to excuse; to pardon.

o·ver·lord (ō′·vęr·lawrd) *n.* one who is lord over another; a feudal superior.

o·ver·much (ō·vęr·much′) *a.* and *adv.* too much.

o·ver·night (ō·vęr·nīt′) *adv.* through and during the night; on the previous evening.

o·ver·pow·er (ō·vęr·pou′·ęr) *v.t.* to conquer by superior strength; to subdue; to crush.

o·ver·rate (ō·vęr·rāt′) *v.t.* to put too high a value on; to assess too highly.

o·ver·reach (ō·vęr·rēch′) *v.t.* to reach beyond; to cheat.

o·ver·ride (ō·vęr·rīd′) *v.t.* to ride over; to ride too much; to set aside; to cancel. *n.* a gear; larger than usual payment.

o·ver·rule (ō·vęr·róól′) *v.t.* to rule against or over; to set aside by superior authority.

o·ver·run (ō·vęr·run′) *v.t.* to run over; to grow over, e.g. as weeds; to take possession by spreading over, e.g. as an invading army.

o·ver·seas (ō′·vęr·sēz) *a.* and *adv.* from or to a country of place over the sea; foreign.

o·ver·see (ō·vęr·sē′) *v.t.* to superintend; to

supervise. **overseer** *n.* a supervisor.
o·ver·shad·ow (ō·vẹr·shad'·ō) *v.t.* to cast a shadow over; to outshine (a person).
o·ver·shoe (ō'·vẹr·shòò) *n.* a shoe made of rubber, felt, etc., worn over the ordinary shoe.
o·ver·shoot (ō·vẹr·shòòt') *v.t.* to shoot beyond or over; to send too far; to go too far.
o·ver·sight (ō·vẹr·sīt) *n.* failure to notice; unintentional neglect; management.
o·ver·state (ō·vẹr·stāt') *v.t.* to exaggerate, **-ment** *n.* exaggeration.
o·ver·strain (ō·vẹr·strān') *v.t.* and *i.* to strain too much; (*Fig.*) to work too hard; *n.* overwork. **-ed** a.
o·ver·strung (ō·vẹr·strung') *a.* too highly strung; in a state of nervous tension.
o·vert (ō'·vurt) *a.* open to view. **-ly** *adv.* [Fr. *ouvert*, open].
o·ver·take (ō·vẹr·tāk') *v.t.* to come up with; to catch; to take by surprise.
o·ver·throw (ō·vẹr·thrō') *v.t.* to throw over or down; to upset; to defeat. *pa.t.* **overthrew;** *pa.p.* **overthrown. overthrow** *n.* the act of throwing over; defeat; ruin; fall.
o·ver·time (ō'·vẹr·tīm) *n.* time at work beyond the regular hours; the extra wages paid for such work.
o·ver·ture (ō·vẹr·cher) *n.* an opening of negotiations; a proposal; an offer; (*Mus.*) an orchestral introduction [Fr. *ouvrir*, to open].
o·ver·turn (ō·vẹr.turn') *v.t.* and *i.* to throw down or over; to upset; to turn over.
o·ver·ween·ing (ō·vẹr·wē'·ning) *a.* conceited; arrogant [O.E. *oferwenian*, to become insolent].
o·ver·weight (ō·vẹr·wāt') *n.* excess weight; extra weight beyond the just weight.
o·ver·whelm (ō·vẹr·hwelm') *v.t.* to crush; to submerge; to overpower. **-ing** *a.* decisive; irresistible. **-ingly** *adv.* [M.E. *whelmen*, to overturn].
o·ver·work (ō·vẹr·wurk') *v.t.* and *i.* to work too hard. **overwork** *n.* **overwrought** (ō·vẹr-rawt') *a.* tired out; highly excited.
o·vi- (ō'·vi) *prefix* fr. L. *ovum*, an egg, used in derivatives. **oviduct** *n.* a passage for the egg, from the ovary. **oviferous** *a.* egg-bearing. **oviform** *a.* egg-shaped. **oviparous** *a.* producing eggs.
o·vine (ō'·vīn) *a.* pert. to sheep; like a sheep [L. *ovis*, a sheep].
o·vo- *prefix* fr. L. *ovum*, an egg, used in derivatives. **ovoid** (ō'·void) *a.* egg-shaped; oval.
o·vum See **ova.**
owe (ō) *v.t.* to be bound to repay; to be indebted for. **owing** (ō'·ing) *a.* requiring to be paid [O.E. *agan*].
owl (oul) *n.* a night bird of prey; a solemn person. **-et** *n.* a young owl; a small owl. **-ish** *a.* owllike in appearance [O.E.*ule*].
own (ōn) *a.* is used to emphasize possession, e.g. my *own* money; *v.t.* to possess; to acknowledge; to admit; *v.i.* to confess. **-er** *n.* the rightful possessor. **-ership** *n.* right of possession [O.E. *agen* (*a.*), *agnian* (*v.*)].
ox (àks) *n.* a large cloven-footed and usually horned farm animal; a male cow. *pl.* **-en. -eye** *n.* daisylike plant. **-bow** *n.* U-shaped part of ox yoke [O.E. *oxa*].
ox·al·ic ac·id (àk·sal'·ik as'·ạd) *n.* a poisonous acid found as an acid salt in wood sorrel. [Gk. *oxus*, sharp bitter].
ox·blood (àks'·blud) *n.* deep red color.
ox·ford (àks'·ferd) *n.* a low shoe laced over the instep [Oxford (England)].
ox·ide (àk'·sīd) *n.* a compound of oxygen and one other element. **oxidize, oxidate** *v.t.* and *i.* to combine with oxygen to form an oxide; of metals, to rust, to become rusty. **oxidization** *n.* [Gk. *oxus*, acid].
ox·y- *prefix* fr. Gk. *oxus* sharp, used in derivatives. **-acetylene** (àk'·si·ạ·set'·ạ·lēn) *a.* denoting a very hot blowpipe flame, produced by a mixture of oxygen and acetylene, and used in cutting steel plates, etc.
ox·y·gen (àk'·si·jạn) *n.* a colorless, odorless, and tasteless gas, forming about ½ by volume of the atmosphere, and essential to life, combustion, etc. **-ate, -ize** *v.t.* to combine or treat with oxygen. **-ation** *n.* **-ous** (àk·sij'·ạ·nạs) *a.* pert. to or obtained from, oxygen [Gk. *oxas*, acid; *gignesthai*, to be born].
ox·y·mo·ron (àk·si·mō'·ràn) *n.* a figure of speech in which two words or phrases of opposite meaning are set together for emphasis or effect, e.g. 'falsely true' [Gk. *oxus*, sharp; *mōros*, dull, stupid].
oys·ter (ois'·tẹr) *n.* an edible, bivalve shellfish; something from which one may get an advantage [Gk. *ostreon*].
o·zone (ō'·zōn) *n.* a condensed and very active form of oxygen with a peculiar, pungent odor; (*Colloq.*) invigorating air. **ozonic** *a.* [Gk. *ozein*, to smell.]

P

pab·u·lum (pab'·yạ·lạm) *n.* food; nourishment (for body and mind). **pabular** *a.* [L.].
pace (pās) *n.* a step; the length of a step in walking (about 30 inches); gait; rate of movement; *v.t.* to measure by steps; to set the speed for; *v.t.* to walk with measured fashion. **-d** *a.* having a certain gait. **-r** *n.* one who sets the pace for another [L. *passus*, a step].
pach·y (pak'·i·) *prefix* from Gk. *pachus*, thick, **-derm** (pak'·i·durm) *n.* a thick-skinned, nonruminant quadruped, e.g. the elephant. **-dermatous** *a.* thick-skinned; insensitive.
pac·i·fy (pas'·ạ·fī) *v.t.* to appease; to tranquilize. **pacifism** *n.* a doctrine which advocates abolition of war; antimilitarism. **pacifist** *n.* **pacific** *a.* peaceful; calm or tranquil; peaceable; not warlike. **pacification.** *n.* **pacificatory** *a.* tending to make peace; conciliatory. **pacifier** *n.* [L. *pacificus*, peacemaking, fr. *pax*, peace].
pack (pak) *n.* bundle for carrying, esp. on back; a lot or set; a band (of animals); a set of playing cards; mass of floating ice; treatment of a fevered patient by enveloping in moist wrapping; army rucksack; *v.t.* to arrange closely in a bundle, box or bag; to stow away within; to fill, press together; to carry; to load; (with *off*) to dismiss summarily; *v.i.* to collect in packs, bales, or bundles. **-age** *n.* a bundle or parcel. **-er** *n.* **-et** *n.* a small package; a packet boat or mail boat. **-et boat** *n.* a ship that sails regularly for the conveyance of mail and passengers. **— horse** *n.* a horse for carrying burdens, in panniers or in packs. **-ing** *n.* any material used to pack, fill up, or make close. **-ing case** *n.* a box in which to pack goods. **-man** *n.* a pedlar. **-saddle** *n.* a saddle for supporting loads on animal's back [Fr. *paquet*].
pact (pakt) *n.* an agreement; a compact [L. *pactum*, a thing covenanted].
pad (pad) *n.* anything stuffed with soft material, to fill out or protect; a cushion; sheets of paper fastened together in a block; the foot or sole of certain animals; *v.t.* to furnish with a pad; to stuff; to expand. *pr.p.* **-ding.** *pa.p.* and *pa.t.* **-ded. -ding** *n.* the material used in stuffing; unnecessary matter inserted in a book, speech, etc., to expand it [etym. uncertain].
pad (pad) *n.* an easy-paced horse; a highway

robber; *v.i.* to trudge along; to travel on foot [Dut. *pad*, a path].

pad·dle (pad′·l) *n.* a short oar with a broad blade at one or each end; a balance or float of a paddle wheel, a flipper; *v.t.* and *i.* to propel by paddles [etym. uncertain].

pad·dle (pad′·l) *v.i.* to walk with bare feet in shallow water; to dabble [etym. uncertain].

pad·dock (pad′·ạk) *n.* a small grass field or enclosure where horses are saddled before race [earlier *parrock*, fr. O.E. *pearroc*, a park].

pad·dy (pad′·i·) *n.* rice in the husk; rice in general [Malay *padi*].

pad·lock (pad′·lȧk) *n.* a detachable lock with a hinged hoop to go through a staple or ring; *v.t.* to fasten with a padlock [etym. uncertain].

pa·dre (pȧ′·drā, drē) *n.* priest; chaplain [It. and Sp. = father, fr. L. *pater*].

pae·an (pē′·ạn) *n.* orig. a joyful song in honor of Apollo; hence, any shout, song, or hymn of triumph or praise [Gk. *Paian*, the physician of the Gods, epithet of Apollo].

pa·gan (pā′·gan) *n.* a heathen; *a.* heathenish; idolatrous, **-ish** *a.* **-ize** *v.t.* to render pagan. **-ism** *n.* [L. *paganus*, a peasant].

page (pāj) *n.* one side of a leaf of a book or manuscript; *v.t.* to number the pages of. [Fr. *page*, fr. L. *pagina*, a leaf].

page (pāj) *n.* formerly a boy in service of a person of rank; a uniformed boy attendant esp. in a hotel; *v.t.* to summon by sending a page to call [Fr. *page*].

pag·eant (paj′·ạnt) *n.* a show of persons in costume in procession, dramatic scenes, etc. a spectacle. **-ry** *n.* a brilliant display; pomp [L. *pagina*, a stage].

pa·go·da (pạ·gō′·dạ) *n.* a temple or sacred tower in India, Burma, etc. [Port. *pagode*].

paid (pād) *pa.p.* and *pa.t.* of the verb **pay.**

pail (pāl) *n.* a round, open vessel of wood, tin, etc., for carrying liquids; a bucket.

pain (pān) *n.* bodily or mental suffering; distress; *pl.* trouble; exertion; *v.t.* to inflict bodily or mental suffering upon. **-ful** *a.* full of pain; causing pain; difficult; **-fully** *adv.* **-fulnes** *n.* **-less** *a.* **-lessly** *adv.* **-lessness** *n.* **-staking** *a.* carefully laborious [L.*poema*, punishment].

paint (pānt) *n.* coloring matter for putting on surface with brush, etc.; *v.t.* to cover or besmear with paint; to make a picture with paint; to adorn with, or as with, paint; *v.i.* to practice the art of painting. **-er** *n.* **-ing** *n.* laying on colors; the art of representing natural objects in colors; a picture in paint [L. *pingere*, to paint].

paint·er (pān′·tẹr) *n.* a rope at the bow of a boat used to fasten it to any other object [Gk. *panthera*, hunting net].

pair (par) *n.* two things of a kind; a single article composed of two similar pieces, e.g. a pair of scissors; a courting, engaged, or married couple; a mated couple of animals or birds; *v.t.* to unite in couples; *v.i.* to be joined in couples; to mate [L. *par*, equal].

pa·ja·mas (pạ·jȧ′·maz) *n.pl.* loose trousers, worn by Mohammedans; a sleeping suit. Also **pyjamas** [Pers. *pāejāmas*, a leg garment].

pal (pal) *n.* (*Colloq.*) a close friend [Gipsy].

pal·ace (pal′·is, ȧs) *n.* the house in which a great personage, resides; any magnificent house. **palatial** (pạ·lā′·shạl) *a.* [L. *palatium*].

pal·a·din (pal′·ạ·din) *n.* a knight-errant; one of the twelve peers of Charlemagne [L. *palatinus*, an officer of the palace].

pal·an·quin, palankeen (pal·ạn.kēn′) *n.* a light, covered litter suspended from poles and borne on the shoulders of men—used in India and the East. [Hind. = a bed].

pal·ate (pal′·ạt) *n.* the roof of the mouth; sense of taste; relish; liking. **palatable** *a.* agreeable to the taste or mind; savory. **palatably** *adv.* **palatal** *a.* pert. to palate; of a sound, produced by placing tongue against palate [L. *palatum*].

pa·la·tial See **palace.**

pal·a·tine (pal′·ạ·tīn) *a.* pert. to a palace; having royal privileges; *n.* one who possesses royal privileges; a count palatine. **palatinate** *n.* the office or dignity of a palatine; the territory under his jurisdiction [L. *Mons Palatinus*, the Palatine hill].

pa·lav·er (pạ·lȧ′·vẹr) *n.* idle talk; empty conversation [Port. *palavra*, a word].

pale-, palae-, paleo-, palaeo- *prefix* from Gk. *palaios*, ancient. **-ography** (pāl·ē·ȧg′·rạ·fi·) *n.* ancient writings; act of deciphering ancient writings. **-ographic** *a.* **-ographer** *n.* **-olith** (päl′·ē·ạ·lith) *n.* an unpolished stone implement of the earlier stone age. **-olithic** *a.* **-ology** (pāl·ē·ȧl′·ạ·ji·) *n.* study of antiquities; archaeology. **-ologist** *n.* **-ontology** (pāl·ē·an·tȧl·ạ·ji) *n.* study of fossils. **-ontologist** *n.* **-ontological** *a.* **-ozoic** (pāl·ē·ạ·zō′·ik) *a.* denoting the lowest fossiliferous strata and the earliest forms of life.

pale (pāl) *a.* faint in color; not ruddy or fresh; whitish; dim; wan; *v.t.* to make pale; *v.i.* to become pale. **-ly** *adv.* **-ness** *n.* **palish** *a.* somewhat pale. **-face** *n.* name given to a white person by Red Indians [Fr. *pâle*, fr. L. *pallidus*, pale].

pale (pāl) *n.* a pointed wooden stake; a narrow board used for making a fence; a boundary; *v.t.* to enclose with stakes; to encompass. [Fr. L. *palus*, a stake].

pal·ette (pal′·it) *n.* a thin oval board on which a painter mixes his colors [L. *pala*, a spade].

pal·frey (pawl′·fri·) *n.* a small saddle horse, esp. for a lady [O. Fr. *palefrei*, fr. L. *paraveredus*, an extra post horse].

Pa·li (pȧ′·lē) *n.* the sacred language of the Buddhists [Sans. *pāli*, canon].

pal·in·drome (pal′·in·drōm) *n.* a word or sentence that is the same when read backward or forward, e.g. *level* [Gk. *palin*, back; *dromos*, running].

pal·i·sade (pal·ạ·sād′) *n.* fence of pales or stakes; (*pl.*) an expanse of high cliffs; *v.t.* to enclose with palisades [L. *palus*, stake].

pall (pawl) *n.* a large, usually black cloth laid over the coffin at a funeral; an ecclesiastical mantle; something that spreads gloom [L. *pallium*, a cloak].

pall (pawl) *v.t.* to make tedious or insipid; *v.i.* to become tedious or insipid [prob. shortened fr. *appal*].

Pal·la·di·an (pạ·lā′·di·ạn) *a.* denoting a classical style of architecture [fr. Andria *Palladio*, a 16th cent. Italian architect].

pal·la·di·um (pạ·lā′·di·ạm) *n.* a rare metal of the platinum group [fr. Gk. *Pallas*].

pal·la·di·um (pạ·lā′·di·ạm) *n.* a safeguard; *pl.* **paladia.** [Gk. *Palladion*].

pal·let (pal′·it) *n.* a palette; a tool with a flat blade used by potters, etc. [form of *palette*].

pal·li·ate (pal′·i·āt) *v.t.* to lessen or abate without curing; to excuse or extenuate. **palliation** *n.* **palliative** (pal′·i·ā·tiv) *a.* serving to extenuate, to mitigate. *n.* that which mitigates, alleviates [L. *palliatus*, dressed in a cloak].

pal·lid (pal′·id) *a.* deficient in color; pale; wan, **-ly** *adv.* **-ness** *n.* **pallor** *n.* paleness [L. *pallidus*, pale].

palm (pȧm) *n.* the inner, slightly concave surface of hand, between wrist and fingers; lineal measure, reckoned as 3 or 4 inches; flat, expanding end of any arm-like projection, esp. blade of oar; that part of glove that covers palm; *v.t.* to conceal in the palm; to impose by fraud (with 'off'). **palmar** (pȧl′·

mẹr) *a.* pert. to the palm. **palmate** *a.* having shape of hand; (*Zool.*) web-footed. **-ist** *n.* one who claims to tell fortunes by the lines on the palm of the hand. **-istry** *n.* [L. *palma*, the palm].

palm (pȧm) *n.* a branchless, tropical tree; a branch or leaf of this tree used as a symbol of victory; prize or honor. **-er** (pȧ′.mẹr) *n.* in the Middle Ages, one who visited the Holy Land, and bore a branch of palm in token thereof; an itinerant monk. **-etto** *n.* a species of palm tree. **-y** *a.* bearing palms; (*Fig.*) prosperous; flourishing. (*Cap.*) — **Sunday,** Sunday before Easter [L. *palma*, a palm].

pal·my·ra (pal·mī′.rạ) *n.* a tall E. Indian palm [Port. *palmeira*].

pal·pa·ble (pal′.pạ.bl) *a.* capable of being touched or felt; certain; obvious. **palpably** *adv.* **-ness** *n.* **palpate** *v.t.* (*Med.*) to examine with the hand. **palpation** *n.* [L. *palpare*, to feel].

pal·pi·tate (pal′.pạ.tāt) *v.i.* to beat rapidly, as heart; to throb; to pulsate. **palpitation** *n.* [L. *palpitare*, fr. *palpare*, to feel].

pal·sy (pawl′.zi.) *n.* paralysis; *v.t.* to paralyze. **palsied** *a.* [fr. *paralysis*].

pal·ter (pawl′.tẹr) *v.i.* to trifle with; to deal evasively; to use trickery; to dodge. **-er** *n.* **paltry** *a.* mean; worthless. **paltriness** *n.*

pam·pas (pam′.pạz) *n.pl.* vast grassy, treeless plains in S. America [Sp. *pampas*, fr. Peruv. *bamba*, a plain].

pam·per (pam′.pẹr) *v.t.* to gratify unduly; to over-indulge; to coddle. **-er** *n.* [perh. L. Ger. *pampen*, to cram].

pam·phlet (pam′·flit) *n.* a thin, paper-covered, unbound book; a short treatise or essay on a current topic. **-eer** *n.* a writer of pamphlets [O.Fr. *Pamphilus*, the title of a medieval poem].

pan (pan) *n.* a broad, shallow metal vessel for house hold use; anything resembling this; of an old type of gun, part of the flintlock that held the priming; abbrev. of brainpan, the upper part of the skull; *v.t.* and *i.* to wash gold-bearing soil in a pan in order to separate earth and gold; (*Colloq.*) to criticize; to turn out (fr. *panorama*) [O.E. *panne*].

pan- (pan) *prefix* fr. Gk. *pas, pantos*, all, used in such words as **Pan-American** *a.* pert. to movement of the American republics to foster collaboration between N. and S. America.

pan·a·ce·a (pan·ạ·sē′.ạ) *n.* a cure for all diseases; a universal remedy [Gk. *panakeia*, a universal remedy].

pa·nache (pa·nash′) *n.* plume of feathers used as an ornament on a cap, etc. [Fr.].

Pan·a·ma (pan.ạ.mȧ′) *n.* a hat made of fine, pliant strawlike material [made in S. America, but not in *Panama*].

pan·cake (pan′·kāk) *n.* a thin cake of batter fried in a pan; *v.i.* to land an airplane almost vertically and in a level position.

pan·chro·mat·ic (pan·krō·mat′.ik) *a.* (*Phot.*) pert. to plates or films which, although reproduced in monochrome, give to all colors their proper values [Gk. *pan*, all; *chrōma*, color].

pan·cre·as (pan′.krē.ạs) *n.* (*Anat.*) digestive gland behind stomach; in animals, the sweetbread. **pancreatic** *a.* [Gk. *pan*, all; *kreas*, flesh].

pan·da (pan′.dạ) *n.* a raccoon-like animal; the bearcat [Native word].

pan·dect (pan′·dekt) *n.* usually a treatise that contains the whole of any science; *pl.* any code of laws [Gk. *pandektēs*, all receiving, comprehensive].

pan·dem·ic (pan·dem′.ik) *a.* of a disease, universal; widely distributed; affecting a nation [Gk. *pan*, all; *dēmos*, people].

pan·de·mo·ni·um (pan·dạ·mō′·ni·ạm) *n.* the abode of evil spirits; any disorderly, noisy place or gathering; a riotous uproar [Gk. *pan*, all; *daimōn*, a demon].

pan·der (pan′.dẹr) *n.* a go-between in base love intrigues; *v.i.* to act as a pander; to help to satisfy any unworthy desires [fr. *Pandarus*, in Chaucer's *Troilus and Cressida*].

pane (pān) *n.* a sheet of glass in a window; a square in a pattern. **-d** (pānd) *a.* [Fr. *pan*, a flat section].

pan·e·gyr·ic (pan.ạ.jir′.ik) *n.* a speech or writing of praise; a eulogy. **-al** *a.* **panegyrist** *n.* one who writes or pronounces a eulogy. **panegyrize** *v.t.* to praise highly [Gk. *pan*, all; *agora*, an assembly].

pan·el (pan′.ạl) *n.* a rectangular piece of cloth, parchment, or wood; a sunken portion of a door, etc.; a list of jurors; a jury; a group of speakers, etc. *v.t.* to divide into, or decorate with panels. **-ing** *n.* paneled work. **-ist** *n.* member of a panel [O.Fr. = a small panel].

pang (pang) *n.* a sudden pain, physical or mental [etym. doubtful].

pan·ic (pan′.ik) *n.* sudden terror, often unreasoning; infectious fear; *a.* extreme and illogical (of fear); *v.i.* to be seized with sudden, uncontrollable fright. *pr.p.* **panicking.** *pa.p. and pa.t.* **panicked. panicky** *a.* affected by panic. — **stricken,** — **struck** *a.* seized with paralyzing fear [Gk. = fear excited by *Pan*].

pan·ier (pan′.yẹr) *n.* one of a pair of baskets carried on each side of a pack animal; a puffing-out round hips of a lady's skirt; framework to achieve this [L. *panarium*, a breadbasket].

pan·o·ply (pan′.ạ.pli.) *n.* a complete suit of armor; anything that covers or envelops completely. **panoplied** *a.* fully armed [Gk. *pan*, all; *hopla*, arms].

pan·o·ram·a (pan.ạ.rȧ′.mạ) *n.* a complete view in every direction; a picture exhibited by being unrolled and made to pass continuously before the spectator. **panoramic** *a.* [Gk. *pan*. all; *horama*, a view].

pan·sy (pan′.zi.) *n.* a cultivated species of violet with richly colored flowers; (*Slang*) an effeminate man [Fr. *pensée*, thought].

pant (pant) *v.i.* to breathe quickly and in a labored manner; to gasp for breath; to yearn (with 'for' or 'after'); *v.t.* to utter gaspingly; *n.* a gasp [O.Fr.].

pan·ta·loon (pan·tạ.lòòn′) *n.(pl.)* tight trousers [It. *pantalone*, buffoon].

pan·the·ism (pan′.thē.izm) *n.* the doctrine that identifies God with the universe, everything being considered as part of or a manifestation of Him. **pantheist** *n.* **pantheistic (al)** *a.* **pantheology** *n.* a system which embraces all religions and all gods [Gk. *pan*, all; *theos*, god].

pan·ther (pan′.thẹr) *n.* (*fem.* **-ess**) a variety of leopard [Gk. *panthēr*].

pan·to- (pan′.tạ) *prefix* fr. Gk. *pas, pantos*, all, used in derivatives. **-graph** (pant′.ạ. graf) *n.* an instrument for copying drawings, maps, etc., on an enlarged, a reduced, or the same scale [Gk. *graphein*, to write].

pan·to·mime (pant′.ȧ.mīm) *n.* a dramatic entertainment in dumb show; a gesture without speech; *v.t.* and *i.* to act or express by gestures only. **pantomimic** *a.* **pantomimist** *n.* [Gk. *pas, pantos*, all; *mimos*, mimic].

pan·try (pan′.tri.) *n.* a small room for storing food or kitchen utensils [L. *panis*, bread].

pants (pants) *n.pl.* (*Colloq.*) trousers [abbrev. of *pantaloons*].

pap (pap) *n.* soft food for infants, etc. [fr. baby language].

pap (pap) *n.* a nipple; a teat; something resembling a nipple [M.E. *pappe*].

pa·pa·cy (pā′.pạ.si.) *n.* the office and dignity of the Pope; Popes collectively. **papal** (pā′. pȧl) *a.* [It. *papa*, father].

pa·pav·er·ous (pạ.pav′.ẹr.ạs) *a.* pert. to or resembling the poppy. Also **papaveraceous** *a.* [L. *papaver*, the poppy].

pa·paw, pawpaw (pa̤·paw′) *n.* a N. American tree with purple flowers and edible yellow fruit [Sp. *papayo*].

pa·per (pā′·pe̤r) *n.* a material made by pressing pulp of rags, straw, wood, etc., into thin flat sheets; a sheet of paper written or printed on; a newspaper; an article or essay; a document; wall covering; a set of examination questions; *n.pl.* document(s) establishing one's identity; ship's official documents; *a.* consisting of paper; *v.t.* to cover with paper. **-y** *a.* resembling paper. **— clip** *n.* a device for holding together sheets of paper. **— hanger** *n.* one who hangs paper on walls. **— knife** *n.* a knife with a blunt blade for opening envelopes, etc. **— money** *n.* official pieces of paper issued by a government or bank for circulation. **-weight** *n.* small, heavy object to prevent loose sheets of paper from being displaced [O.F. *papier*, fr. L. *papyrus*, paper].

pa·pier-mâ·ché (pā·pe̤r·ma̤·shā′) *n.* paper pulp, mixed with glue, etc., shaped or molded into articles [Fr. *papier*, paper; *mâché*, chewed].

pa·pil·la (pa̤·pil′·a̤) *n.* a small nipple-shaped protuberance in a part of the body, e.g. on surface of tongue [L. *papilla*, the nipple].

pa·pist (pā′·pist) *n.* a supporter of the papal system; a Roman Catholic. **papistic(al)** *a.* **-ry** *n.* [Fr. *papiste*, fr. *pape*, the Pope].

pa·poose (pa·pōōs′) *n.* a N. Amer. Indian baby.

pap·pus (pap′·a̤s) *n.* down, as on the seeds of the thistle, dandelion, etc. **pappose** (pap·ōs′) *a.* downy [Gk. *pappos*, down].

pap·ule (pap′·ūl) *n.* a pimple [L.].

pa·py·rus (pa̤·pī′·ra̤s) *n.* a species of reed, the pith of which was used by the ancients for making paper; a manuscript on papyrus. *pl.* **papyri** [Gk. *papyros*, an Egyptian rush].

par (pȧr) *n.* equality of value or circumstances; face value (of stocks and shares); (*Golf*) the number of strokes for hole or course in perfect play [L. *par*, equal].

par·a·ble (par′·a̤.bl) *n.* story or allegory with a moral. **parabolical** *a.* **parabolically** *adv.* [Gk. *parabolē*, a comparison].

pa·rab·o·la (pa̤·rab′·a̤·la) *n.* (*Geom.*) a conic section made by a plane parallel to side of cone. **parabolic** *a.* **paraboloid** *n.* solid formed when parabola is revolved round its axis [Gk. *para*, beside; *bole*, a throw].

par·a·chute (par′·a̤·shōōt) *n.* a collapsible umbrellalike device used to retard the descent of a falling body. **parachutist** *n.* **— troops** *n.pl.* *See* **paratroops** [Fr. *parer*, to make ready; *chute*, a fall].

par·a·clete (par′·a̤·klēt) *n.* (*Bib.*) the name given to the Holy Spirit; one called to aid or support; an advocate [Gk. *paraklētos*, called to help].

pa·rade (pa̤·rād′) *n.* a public procession; a muster of troops for drill or inspection; the ground on which such a muster takes place; display; show; *v.t.* to make a display or spectacle of; to marshal in military order; *v.i.* to march in military array; to march in procession with display [L. *parare*, to prepare].

par·a·digm (par′·a̤·dim) *n.* an example; a model; (*Gram.*) a word, esp. a noun, verb, etc., given as an example of grammatical inflexions. **-atic** (par·a̤·dig·mat′·ik) *a.* **-atically** *adv.* [Gk. *paradeigma*, a model].

par·a·dise (par′·a̤·dīs) *n.* the garden of Eden; Heaven; a state of bliss. **paradisaic** (par·a̤·di·sā′·ik), **paradisaical** *a.* pert. to or like paradise [Gk. *paradeisos*, a pleasure-ground].

par·a·dox (par′·a̤·dȧks) *n.* a statement seemingly absurd or self-contradictory, but really founded on truth. **-ical** *a.* **-ically** *adv.* [Gk. *para*, against; *doxa*, an opinion].

par·af·fin (par′·a̤·fin) *n.* a white wax-like substance obtained from crude petroleum, shale, coal tar, wood, etc. [L. *parum*, little; *affinis*, related].

par·a·gon (par′·a̤·ga̤n) *n.* a pattern of excellence [It. *paragone*].

par·a·graph (par′·a̤·graf) *n.* a distinct part of a writing; a section or subdivision of a passage, indicated by the sign ¶, or begun on a new line; *v.t.* to arrange in paragraphs. **-ic** *a.* [Gk. *paragraphos*, a marginal stroke].

par·a·keet (par′·a̤·kēt) *n.* a small long-tailed parrot. Also **parrakeet, paroquet** [Fr. *perroquet*, a parrot].

par·al·de·hyde (pa̤·ral′·da̤·hīd) *n.* a powerful hypnotic [Gk. *para* and *aldehyde*].

par·al·lel (par′·a̤·lel) *a.* continuously at equal distance apart; precisely corresponding; similar; *n.* a line equidistant from another at all points; a thing exactly like another; a comparison; a line of latitude; *v.t.* to make parallel; to represent as similar; to compare. **-ism** *n.* the state of being parallel; comparison, resemblance. **— bars,** horizontal bars for gymnastic exercises [Gk. *parallēlos*, beside one another].

par·al·lel·o·gram (par·a̤·lel′·a̤·gram) *n.* a four-sided plane figure with both pairs of opposite sides parallel [Gk. *parallēlos*, beside one another; *gramma*, a line].

pa·ral·y·sis (pa̤·ral′·a̤·sis) *n.* (*Med.*) loss of power of movement or sensation. **paralyze** (par′·a̤·līz) *v.t.* to affect with paralysis; to make useless; to cripple. **paralytic** *a.* pert. to, affected with, paralysis; *n.* one affected with paralysis. **infantile paralysis,** inflammation of grey matter in spinal cord, usually in children; poliomyelitis [L., fr. Gr. *paralysis*, to loosen at the side].

par·a·mount (par′·a̤·mount) *a.* superior; of highest importance; chief. **-cy** *n.* **-ly** *adv.* [Fr. *par amont*, upwards].

par·a·mour (par′·a̤·moor) *n.* a partner in an illicit love intrigue [Fr. *par amour*, through love].

par·a·noi·a, paranoea (par·a̤·noi′·a̤, ·nē′·a̤) *n.* (*Med.*) a form of chronic insanity, often characterized by delusions of grandeur, persecution, etc. **paranoiac** *a.* and *n.* [Gk. *para*, beside; *noein*, to think].

par·a·pet (par′·a̤·pet) *n.* a low wall or railing at the edge of a bridge, quay, balcony, etc.; a breastwork to protect soldiers [It. *parare*, to ward off; *petto*, the breast].

par·a·pher·na·li·a (par·a̤·fe̤(r)·nā′·li·a̤, ·nāl′·ya̤) *n.pl.* personal belongings; furnishings or accessories; (*Law*) goods of wife beyond dowry [Gk. *para*, beyond; *phernē*, a dower].

par·a·phrase (par′·a̤·frāz) *n.* a restatement of a passage; a free translation into the same or another language; an interpretation; *v.t.* to express in other words; to interpret freely. [Gk. *para; phrazein*, to speak].

par·a·site (par′·a·sīt) *n.* formerly, one who habitually ate at the table of another, repaying with flattery; a hanger-on; a plant or animal that lives on another. **parasitic** *a.* **parasitically** *adv.* **parasitology** *n.* the study of parasites, esp. as causes of disease. **parasitological** *a.* **parasitologist** *n.* [Gk. *parasitos*; fr. *para*, beside; *sitos*, food].

par·a·sol (par′·a̤·sawl) *n.* a small, light sun umbrella [It. *parare*, to ward offi; *sole*, the sun].

par·a·troops (par′·a̤·trōōps) *n.pl.* (*World War 2*) troops organized to descend by parachute with their equipment from airplanes and gliders. **paratrooper** *n.*

par·boil (pȧr′·boil) *v.t.* to boil partially; to precook [L. *per*, thoroughly, confused with 'part'; *boil*].

par·cel (pȧr′·sa̤l) *n.* (*Arch.*) a part or portion, a bundle or package (wrapped in paper);

a number of things forming a group or lot; a piece of land; *v.t.* to divide into portions; to distribute; to wrap up. [Fr. *parcelle*, a little part].

parch (pȧrch) *v.t.* to scorch; to shrivel with heat; to dry to an extreme degree; *v.i.* to be dry from heat [M.E. *parchen*].

parch·ment (pȧrch′·mạnt) *n.* the skin of a sheep or goat, etc., prepared for writing on; a document written on this [fr. *Pergamum* in Asia Minor, here first used].

par·don (pȧr′·dạn) *v.t.* to forgive; to free from punishment; to excuse; *n.* forgiveness; remission of a penalty. **-able** *a.* excusable. [Fr. *pardonner*].

pare (par) *v.t.* to cut or shave off; to remove the outer skin; to peel. **-er** *n.* **paring** *n.* the action of peeling; that which is pared off [Fr. *parer*, to make ready].

par·e·gor·ic (par·ạ·gawr′·ik) *a.* soothing; assuaging pain; *n.* a soothing medicine [Gk. *parēgorikos*, comforting].

par·ent (par·ạnt) *n.* a father or mother; one who, or that which, brings forth or produces. **-age** *n.* descent from parents; birth; extraction. **parental** (pạ.ren′.tạl) *a.* pert. to, or becoming, parents; tender; affectionate. **parentally** *adv.* [L. *parere*, to bring forth].

pa·ren·the·sis (pạ·ren′·thạ·sis) *n.* a word or sentence inserted in a passage independently of the grammatical sequence and usually marked off by brackets, dashes, or commas; **parentheses** (-sēz) *n.pl.* round brackets ( ), used for this. **parenthetic, parenthetical** *a.* expressed as a parenthesis; interposed. [Gk. *para*, beside; *en*, in; *thesis*, a placing].

pa·ri·ah (pạ·rī′·ạ) *n.* in S. India, one deprived of all religious or social rights; a member of the lowest or no caste; an outcast from society [Tamil, *paraiyar*, a drummer].

pa·ri·e·tal (pạ·rī′·ạ·tạl) *a.* pert. to a wall; pert. to the wall of the body or its cavities [L. *paries* a wall].

par·ish (par′·ish) *n.* an ecclesiastical district under a priest or clergyman; a local church and its area of activity; *a.* pert. to a parish. **parishioner** (pạ·rish′·ạn·ẹr) *n.* an inhabitant of a parish; a member of a parish church [Gk. *para*, beside; *oikos*, a dwelling].

par·i·ty (par′·ạ·ti·) *n.* equality; analogy; close correspondence [L. *par, paris*, equal].

park (pȧrk) *n.* a large piece of ground, usually with grass and trees for public use and recreation; a sports' ground; grounds around a country house; *v.t.* to enclose in a park; to leave an automobile in a certain place [O.E. *pearroc;* Fr. *parc*].

par·ka (pȧr′·kạ) *n.* an Eskimo garment of undressed skin; a hooded outer garment [Aleutian].

par·lance (pȧr′·lạns) *n.* a way of speaking; **parley** (pȧr′·li·) *n.* a meeting between leaders of opposing forces to discuss terms; *v.i.* to hold a discussion about terms [Fr. *parler*, to speak].

par·lia·ment (pȧr′·lạ·mạnt) *n.* (*usually cap.*) the supreme legislature of the United Kingdom, composed of the House of Lords and House of Commons; any similar assembly. **-ary** *a.* pert. to, enacted by, or according to, the established rules of parliament; of language, admissible in parliamentary debate, hence, decorous and non-abusive. **-arian** *n.* a skilled debater in parliament [Fr. *parlement*, fr. *parler*, to speak].

par·lor, parlour (pȧr′·lẹr) *n.* living room; a semi-private room in an inn [Fr. *parloir*, fr. *parler*, to speak].

par·lous (pȧr′·lạs) *a.* (*Arch.*) perilous; critical [fr. *perilous*].

Par·nas·sus (pȧr·nas′·ạs) *n.* a mountain in ancient Greece, sacred to Apollo and the Muses; (*Fig.*) poetry; an anthology of poetry.

pa·ro·chi·al (pạ·rō′·ki·ạl) *a.* pert. to a parish; provincial; narrow-minded **-ly** *adv.* **-ism** *n.* [L. *parochia*, a parish, fr. Gk. *paroikein* to dwell near].

par·o·dy (par′·ạ·di·) *n.* an imitation of a poem, song, etc., where the style is the same but the theme ludicrously different; a feeble imitation; *v.t.* to write a parody of; to burlesque in verse. **parodist** *n.* [Gk. *para*, beside (i.e. imitating); *ōdē*, a song].

pa·role (pạ·rōl′) *n.* release of a prisoner on condition of good behavior; word of honor, esp. a promise given by a prisoner of war not to attempt to escape [Fr. *parole*, a word].

par·o·no·ma·si·a (par·ạ·nō·mā′·zhi·ạ, ·zi·ạ) *n.* a play on words; a pun. **paronym** *n.* a word similar to another in having the same derivation or root. **paronymous** *a.* [Gk. *para*, beside; *anoma*, a name].

pa·rot·id (pạ·rȧt′·id) *a.* near the ear; *n.* a large salivary gland, in front of and below the ear [Gk. *para*, beside; *ous, ōtos*, the ear].

par·ox·ysm (par′·ȧk·sizm) *n.* sudden, violent attack of pain, rage, laughter; fit; convulsion [Gk. *para*, beyond; *oxus*, sharp].

par·quet (pȧr′·kā, -ket) *n.* flooring of wooden blocks; *v.t.* to lay such a floor. **-ry** *n.* [Fr. flooring].

parr (pȧr) *n.* a young salmon.

par·ri·cide (par′·ạ·sīd) *n.* one who murders his parent, a near relative, or a person who is venerated; the crime itself [L. *pater*, a father; *caedere*, to kill].

par·rot (par′·ạt) *n.* tropical bird; one who repeats words, actions, ideas, etc. of another [Fr. *perroquet*, a parrot].

par·ry (par′·i·) *v.t.* to ward off; to turn aside; to avoid [L. *parare*, to prepare].

parse (pȧrs) *v.t.* to classify a word or analyze a sentence in terms of grammar. **parsing** *n.* [L. *pars*, part, *pars orationis*, part of speech].

Par·see, parsi (pȧr′·sē) *n.* a follower of the disciples of Zoroaster; a fire worshipper. **-ism** *n.* [Pers. *Parsi*, a Persian].

par·si·mo·ny (pȧr′·sạ·mō·ni·) *n.* stinginess; undue economy. **parsimonious** *a.* **parsimoniously** *adv.* **parsimoniousness** *n.* [L. *parcere*, to spare].

pars·ley (pȧrs′·li·) *n.* a garden herb, used as a flavoring or garnish in cookery [Gk. *petroselinon*, rock parsley].

pars·nip (pȧrs′·nip) *n.* a root vegetable, carrot-like in shape [L. fr. *pastinare*, to dig up].

par·son (pȧr′·sn) *n.* a clergyman; the incumbent of a parish. **-age** *n.* the residence of a parson. (*Colloq.*) **-'s nose,** the rump of a fowl [*person*].

part (pȧrt) *n.* a portion, fragment, or section of a whole; a share or lot; a division; an actor's role; duty; interest; a melody in a harmonic piece; *pl.* accomplishments or talents; region; *v.t.* to divide; to separate; to share; *v.i.* to separate; to take leave; to part with or give up. **-ing** *n.* the act of separating; leave-taking; division; dividing line; *a.* given on taking leave. **-ly** *adv.* in part; in some measure or degree. **-ible** *a.* divisible. **-ibility** *n.* [L. *pars*, a part].

par·take (pȧr·tāk′) *v.t.* and *i.* to have or take a share in; to take food or drink. *pr.p.* **partaking.** *pa.p.* **-n.** *pa.t.* **partook.** **-r** *n.* [fr. *part* and *take*].

par·terre (pȧr·ter′) *n.* an ornamental arrangement of flower beds; the rear section of the main floor of a theater [Fr. *par terre*, on the earth].

par·the·no·gen·e·sis (pȧr·thạ·nō·jen′·ạ·sis) *n.* reproduction without sexual union [Gk. *parthenos*, virgin; *genesis*, birth].

Par·the·non (par′·thạ·nȧn) *n.* famous Doric temple of Athena [Gr. *parthenos*, virgin].

par·tial (pàr′·shạl) *a.* affecting only a part; not total; inclined to favor unreasonably. **-ly** *adv.* **partiality** *n.* quality of being partial; favoritism; fondness for [L. *pars,* part].

par·tic·i·pate (pàr·tis′·ạ·pāt) *v.t.* and *i.* to share in; to partake (foll. by 'in'). **participant** *n.* a partaker; *a.* sharing. **participator** *n.* **participation** (pàr·tis·ạ·pā′·shạn) *n.* [L. *pars,* part; *capere,* to take].

par·ti·ci·ple (pàr′·tạ·si·pl) *n.* (*Gram.*) an adjective formed by inflection from a verb. **participial** *a.* [L. *particeps,* sharing].

par·ti·cle (pàr·′tạ·kl) *n.* a minute portion of matter; (*Gram.*) a part of speech which is uninflected and of subordinate importance [L. *particula,* a little part].

par·ti-col·ored, party-colored (pàr′·ti·kul·ẹrd) *a.* having different colors; variegated.

par·tic·u·lar (pàr·tik′·yạ·lẹr) *a.* relating to a single person or thing, not general; considered apart from others; minute in details; fastidious in taste; *n.* a single point or circumstance; a detail or item. **-ly** *adv.* especially; in a high degree; with great attention. **particularity** *n.* quality or state of being particular; individual characteristic. **-ize** *v.t.* and *i.* to mention one by one; to give in detail; to specify. **-ization** *n.* [L. *particularis*].

par·ti·san, partizan (pàr′·tạ.zạn) *n.* adherent, often prejudiced, of a party or cause; a member of irregular troops engaged in risky enterprises; *a.* adhering to a faction. **-ship** *n.* [Fr.].

par·ti·san (pạr′·tạ.zạn) *n.* a long-handled pike [O.Fr. *pertuisane*].

par·ti·tion (pàr·tish′·ạn) *n.* division or separation; any of the parts into which a thing is divided; that which divides or separates, as a wall, etc.; *v.t.* to divide into shares; to divide by walls. **partitive** *n.* a word expressing partition; a distributive; *a.* denoting a part. **partitively** *adv.* [L. *partitio*].

part·ner (pàrt′·nẹr) *n.* a partaker; a sharer; an associate, esp. in business; a husband or wife; one who dances with another; in golf, tennis, etc., one who plays with another; *v.t.* in games, to play with another against opponents. **-ship** *n.* the state of being a partner; the association of two or more persons for business [L. *pars,* a part].

par·tridge (pàr′·trij) *n.* a small game bird of the grouse family [Gk. *perdix*].

par·tu·ri·ent (pàr·tyoo′·ri·ạnt) *a.* bringing forth or about to bring forth young. **parturition** *n.* the act of bringing forth young [L. *parturire,* to be in labor].

par·ty (pàr′·ti·) *n.* a number of persons united in opinion; a political group; a social assembly; a participator; an accessory; a litigant; *a.* pert. to a party or faction. **—colored** *a.* parti-colored [O.Fr. *partir,* to divide].

par·ve·nu (pàr′·vạ.nū) *n.* an upstart; one who has risen socially, esp. by the influence of money [Fr. fr. *parvenir,* to arrive at].

Pasch (pask) *n.* Passover; Easter. **-al** *a.* **— lamb,** lamb eaten at Passover; (P-L, in *Christ.*) Christ [Heb. *pesach,* to pass over].

pas·quin (pas′·kwin) *n.* a writer of lampoons or satires; a lampoon or satire; *v.t.* and *i.* to lampoon. **-ade** *n.* a lampoon [fr. It. *Pasquino,* Roman statue on which political lampoons were posted].

pass (pas) *v.t.* to go by, beyond, through etc.; to spend; to exceed; to approve; to disregard; to circulate; to send through; to move; *v.i.* to go; to elapse; to undergo examination successfully; to happen; to die; to circulate. *pa.p.* **-ed, past.** *pa.t.* **-ed.** *n.* a passage or way, esp. a narrow and difficult one; a passport; a permit; success in an examination, test, etc.; in football, hockey, etc., the passing of the ball from one player to another. **-able** *a.* that may be passed or crossed; fairly good; admissible; current. **-ably** *adv.* **-book** *n.* a bankbook. **-key** *n.* a latchkey; a master-key. **-port** *n.* an official document, issued by a State Department, granting permission to travel abroad. **-word** *n.* (*Mil.*) a selected word given to sentries, soldiers, etc. used to distinguish friend from enemy. **to pass the buck** (*Slang*) to shift responsibility to another [L. *passus,* a step].

pas·sage (pas′·ij) *n.* the act, time, or right of passing; movement from one place to another; a voyage across the sea; fare for a voyage; an entrance or exit; part of a book, etc.; the passing of a law. **passage of arms,** a feat of arms. **bird of passage,** a migratory bird [Fr. fr. L. *passus,* a step, a pace].

pas·sé (pa·sā′) *a.* past one's best; faded; rather out of date; antiquated [Fr.].

pas·sen·ger (pas′·ạn.jẹr) *n.* a traveller, esp. by some conveyance; *a.* adapted for carrying passengers [O.Fr. *passager*].

Pas·ser·i·for·mes (pas′·ẹr·i·fawr·mēz) *n.* the largest order of birds [L. *passer,* a sparrow].

pas·sim (pas′·im) *a.* here and there [L.].

pas·sion (pash′·ạn) *n.* intense emotion, as of grief, rage, love; eager desire; (*Cap.*) the story of Christ's suffering and last agony. **-ate** *a.* easily moved to anger; moved by strong emotions; vehement. **-ately** *adv.* **-ateness** *n.* **-less** *a.* **— play** *n.* a theatrical representation of Christ's passion. **— week** *n.* the week immediately preceding Easter [L. *passio,* fr. *pati,* to suffer].

pas·sive (pas′·iv) *a.* inactive; submissive; acted upon, not acting; *n.* (*Gram.*) (or passive voice) the form of the verb which expresses that the subject is acted upon. **-ly** *adv.* **-ness** *n.* [L. *pati, passus,* to suffer].

Pass·o·ver (pas′·ō.vẹr) *n.* a feast of the Jews to commemorate the time when God, smiting the first-born of the Egyptians, passed over the houses of Israelites [*pass* and *over*].

past *pa.p.* of **pass.**

past (past) *a.* pert. to former time; gone by; elapsed; ended; *n.* former state; bygone times; one's earlier life; *prep.* beyond; after; exceeding; beyond the scope of; *adv.* by; beyond. **— master,** a former master of a guild, freemasons, etc.; one adept or proficient [fr. *pass*].

paste (pāst) *n.* a soft composition, as of flour and water; dough prepared for pies, etc.; any soft plastic mixture or adhesive; a fine glass for making artificial gems; *v.t.* to fasten with paste; (*Slang*) to strike. **pasty** *a.* (pās′·ti·) like paste. **pastry** (pās′·tri·) *n.* the crust of pies and tarts; articles of food made of paste or dough. **pastry-cook** *n.* who makes and sells pastry. **-board** (pāst′·bōrd) *n.* a stiff, thick paper; *a.* made of pasteboard; flimsy or unsubstantial [O.Fr.].

pas·tel (pas′·tel) *n.* a colored chalky crayon; a drawing made with such crayons. **— shades,** delicate and subdued colors [F., fr. It. *pastello,* dim. fr. L. *pasta,* paste].

pas·tern (pas′·tern) *n.* part of horse's leg between fetlock and hoof [O.Fr. *pasturon,* shackle of horse at pasture].

Pas·teur (pas.tur′) *n.* a French chemist and biologist. **pasteurization** *n.* the sterilization of milk, etc. by heating to 140° F. or over and then cooling. **pasteurize** *v.t.*

pas·tic·cio, pastiche (pas·tēch′·ō, pas·tēsh′) *n.* a medley made up from various sources; a picture or literary composition in the style of a recognized author or artist [It.].

pas·tille, pastil (pas·tēl′, pas′·til) *n.* an aromatic substance burned for cleansing or scenting a room; a small lozenge, aromatic or medicated [Fr. fr. L. *pastillus,* a little loaf].

pas·time (pàs′·tīm) *n.* that which amuses and

makes time pass agreeably; recreation; diversion [fr. *pass* and *time*].
pas·tor (pas'·tẹr) *n.* a minister of the gospel. **-al** *a.* pert. to shepherds or rural life; relating to a pastor and his duties. *n.* a poem describing rural life; an idyll. **-ally** *adv.* **-ate** *n.* the office or jurisdiction of a spiritual pastor. **-ship** *n.* [L. *pastor*, a herdsman].
pas·ture (pas'·chẹr) *n.* grass for food of cattle; ground on which cattle graze; *v.t.* to feed on grass; *v.i.* to graze. **pasturable** *a.* **pasturage** *n.* pasture land; the business of grazing cattle [L. *pascere*, to feed].
past·y See **paste.**
pat (pat) *n.* a light, quick blow, esp. with hand or fingers; a small lump, esp. of butter; *v.t.* to strike gently. *pr.p.* **-ting.** *pa.p.* and *pa.t.* **-ted** [imit. origin].
pat (pat)*a.* ready; apt; at right moment; *adv.* opportunely; exactly. **-ness** *n.* [fr. *pat*].
patch (pach) *n.* a piece of material used to mend a hole, rent, etc.; a covering for a wound; small spot of black silk formerly worn on cheek by ladies; *v.t.* to mend with a patch; to repair clumsily. **-y** *a.* full of patches; unequal. **-work** *n.* work made by sewing together pieces of cloth of different material and color [O.Fr. *pieche*, a piece].
pate (pāt) *n.* the top of the head; the head.
pâ·té de foie gras (pȧt·ā' dạ fwȧ·grȧ) a paste of goose liver [Fr.].
pa·tel·la (pạ·tel'·ạ) *n.* the kneecap [L. = small pan].
pat·en (pat'·ạn) *n.* the plate on which the bread of the Eucharist is placed [L. *patina*, a plate].
pat·ent (pā'·tạnt, pat'·ạnt) *a.* open; evident; protected by a patent; *n.* short for *letters patent*, an official document granting a right or privilege, or securing the exclusive right to invention; the invention itself. *v.t.* to secure or protect by a patent. **-ly** *adv.* openly; evidently. **-ee** (pat·ạn·tē') *n.* one who has secured a patent. **— leather,** leather with a varnished or lacquered surface [L. *patens*, open].
pa·ter·nal (pạ·tur'·nạl) *a.* pert. to a father; fatherly; hereditary. **-ly** *adv.* **paternity** *n.* the relation of a father to his offspring; authorship [L. *pater*, a father].
pa·ter·nos·ter (pat·ẹr·nȧs'·tẹr) *n.* the Lord's Prayer [L. *pater*, father; *noster*, our].
path (path) *n.* a way, course, or track of action, conduct, or procedure. **-finder** *n.* a pioneer. **-way** *n.* a narrow footway [O.E. *paeth*].
pa·thet·ic (pạ·thet'·ik) *a.* affecting or moving the tender emotions; causing pity; touching. Also **-al. -ally** *adv.*
path·o- *prefix* fr. Gk. *pathos*, suffering, feeling, used in derivatives. **-genesis, pathogeny** (path·ạ·jen'·ạ·sis, pạ·thȧj'·ȧ·ni·) *n.* the origin and development of disease. **-genetic, -genic** *a.* causing disease. **-logy** *n.* the science and study of diseases, their causes, nature, cures, etc.**-logic, -logical** *a.* **-logically** *adv.* **-logist** *n.* [Gk. *genesis*, birth; *logos*, discourse].
pa·thos (pā'·thȧs) *n.* the power of exciting tender emotions; deep feeling [Gk. *pathos* fr. *paschein*, to suffer].
pa·tient (pā'·shạnt) *a.* bearing trials without murmuring; not easily made angry; calm; not hasty; *n.* a person under medical treatment. **-ly** *adv.* **patience** *n.* the quality of enduring with calmness; quiet perseverance [L. *pati*, to suffer].
pa·ti·o (pa'·ti·ō) *n.* the inner court of a Spanish house [Sp.].
pat·ois (pat'·wȧ) *n.* a dialect; illiterate or provincial form of speech; jargon [Fr.].
pa·tri·arch (pā'·tri·ark) *n.* the father and ruler of a family, esp. in Biblical history; the highest dignitary in the Eastern church; a venerable old man. **-al** *a.* **-ate** *n.* dignity or jurisdiction of a patriarch. **-y** *n.* government by the head or father of a tribe [Gk. *pater*, father; *archein*, to rule].
pa·tri·cian (pạ·trish'·ạn) *a.* pert, to the senators of ancient Rome and their descendants; of high birth; noble or aristocratic; *n.* [L. *patricius*, fr. *pater*, father, senator].
pat·ri·cide (pat'·rạ·sīd) *n.* murder of one's father [L. *pater*, father; *caedere*, to kill].
pat·ri·mo·ny (pat'·rạ·mō·ni·) *n.* a right or estate inherited from one's father or ancestors; heritage; a church estate or revenue. **patrimonial** *a.* **patrimonially** *adv.* [L. *patrimonium* fr. *pater*, father].
pa·tri·ot (pā'·tri·ạt) *n.* one who loves his country and upholds its interests. **-ic** *a.* filled with patriotism. **-ically** *adv.* **-ism** *n.* love for, and loyalty to, one's country [L. *patria*, fatherland].
pa·trol (pạ·trōl') *v.t.* and *i.* to go or walk around a camp, garrison, etc. in order to protect it. *pr.p.* **-ling.** *pa.p.* and *pa.t.* **-led.** *n.* a going of the rounds by a guard; the man or men who go to the rounds [O.Fr. *patrouiller*].
pa·tron (pā'·trạn) *n.* (*fem.* **-ness**) a man who protects or supports a person, cause, entertainment, artistic production, etc.; a guardian saint; (*Eccles.*) one who has the right of appointment to a benefice; a regular customer. **-age** *n.* countenance, support, or encouragement given to a person or cause; condescending manner; in trade, regular customer. **-ize** *v.t.* to act as a patron to; to assume the air of a superior towards; to frequent, as a customer. **patronizing** *a.* **patronizingly** *adv.* **— saint,** a saint who is regarded as the special protector of a person, city, trade, etc. [L. *patronus*, fr. *pater*, father].
pat·ro·nym·ic (pat·rạ·nim'·ik) *n.* a name derived from parent or ancestor; a surname [Gk.*patōr*, father; *onoma*, a name].
pat·ten (pat'·ạn) *n.* a wooden sandal worn in wet weather [Fr. *patin*].
pat·ter (pat'·ẹr) *v.i.* to make a quick succession of small taps or sounds, like those of rain falling [frequentative of *pat*].
pat·ter (pat'·ẹr) *v.t.* to speak rapidly and indistinctly; to mutter; *v.i.* to talk glibly or mechanically; to say prayers; *n.* chatter; prattle; lingo of a professoin or class; jargon [fr. *paternoster*].
pat·tern (pat'·ẹrn) *n.* a model, example, or guide; a decorative design; *v.t.* to design from a pattern; to imitate [M.E. *patron*, a model].
pat·ty (pat'·i·) *n.* a little pie [Fr. *pâté*].
pau·ci·ty (paw'·sạ·ti·) *n.* fewness; scarcity; smallness of quantity [L. *paucus*, few].
paunch (pawnch, pȧnch) *n.* the belly **-iness** *n.* **-y** *a.* [L. *pantex*].
pau·per (paw'·pẹr) *n.* (*fem.* **-ess**) a very poor person, esp. one supported by the public. **-ize** *v.t.* to reduce to pauperism [L., poor].
pause (pawsz) *n.* a temporary stop or rest; cessation; hesitation; a break in speaking, reading, or writing; in music, a sign · or · placed under or over a note to indicate the prolongation of a note or rest; *v.i.* to make a short stop; to cease for a time [Gk. *pausis*].
pave (pāv) *v.t.* to form a level surface with stone, brick, etc.; to make smooth and even; (*Fig.*) to prepare. **-ment** *n.* a paved floor, road, or sidewalk; material used [L. *pavire*, to ram down].
pav·id (pav'·id) *a.* timid; shy [L. *pavidus*].
pa·vil·ion (pạ·vil'·yạn) *n.* orig. a tent; hence, anything like a tent, e.g. a garden summerhouse [Fr. fr. L. *papilio*, a butterfly, a tent].
paw (paw) *n.* the foot of an animal having claws; (*Slang*) the hand; *v.t.* and *i.* to scrape

with the paws; (*Colloq.*) to stroke or fondle with hands clumsily, rudely [O.Fr. *poe*].

pawn (pawn) *n.* something deposited as security for money borrowed; a pledge; the state of being pledged; *v.t.* to deposit as security for a loan; to pledge. **-broker** *n.* one who lends money on something deposited with him. [L. *pannus*, cloth].

pawn (pawn) *n.* a piece of the lowest rank in the game of chess; (*Fig.*) a person who is a mere tool in the hands of another [L.L. *pedo*, a foot soldier].

pay (pā) *v.t.* to discharge one's obligations to; to give money, etc., for goods received or services rendered; *v.i.* to recompense; to be remunerative; to be worth the trouble. *pa.p.* and *pa.t.* **paid** (pād). *n.* reward; compensation; wages; salary. **-able** *a.* justly due; profitable. **-ee** (pā·ē′) *n.* one to whom money is paid. **-er** *n.* one who pays. **-ment** *n.* the act of paying; discharge of a debt; recompense [L. *pacare*, to appease].

pay (pā) *v.t.* (*Naut.*) to cover with pitch; to make waterproof [L. *picare*, to pitch].

pea (pē) *n.* the fruit, growing in pods, of a leguminous plant; the plant itself. **-nut** *n.* the earth nut. **— soup** *n.* soup made of dried peas. **sweet pea,** a climbing garden annual, bearing sweet-scented flowers [Gk. *piscos*].

peace (pēs) *n.* calm; repose; freedom from disturbance, war, or hostilities. **-able** *a.* in a state of peace; disposed to peace; not quarrelsome. **-ably** *adv.* **-ableness** *n.* **-ful** *a.* free from war, tumult, or commotion; mild; undisturbed. **-fully** *adv.* **-fulness** *n.* **-maker** *n.* one who makes peace [L. *pax, pacis*].

peach (pēch) *n.* a juicy fruit with light orange flesh, and a velvety skin; the tree which bears this fruit; a pale orange-pink color. **-y** *a.* peach-like; (*Slang*) excellent [Fr. *pêche*].

peach (pēch) *v.i.* (*Slang*) to inform against; to tell tales [*abbrev.* fr. *impeach*].

pea·cock (pē′·ka̤k) *n.* (*fem.* **peahen**) *a.* bird remarkable for the beauty of its plumage, and for its large tail; a person vain of his appearance. **peafowl** *n.* the peacock or peahen. **— blue,** lustrous greenish blue [L. *pavo*, a peacock; and *cock*].

peak (pēk) *v.i.* to waste or pine away. **-y** *a.* thin, sickly. **-ed** *a.* [etym. unknown].

peak (pēk) *n.* the sharp top of a hill; the pointed top of anything; the projecting part of a cap brim; the maximum point of a curve or record. [Fr. *pic;* conn. with *pike*].

peal (pēl) *n.* a loud sound, or succession of loud sounds, as of thunder, bells, laughter, etc.; a set of bells attuned to each other; *v.t.* and *i.* to sound loudly [*abbrev.* fr. *appeal*].

pear (pār, per) *n.* a sweet, juicy fruit of oval shape; tree on which it grows [L. *pirum*].

pearl (purl) *n.* a hard, smooth, lustrous substance, found in several mollusks, particularly pearl oyster, and used as a gem; something very precious; a small size of printing type, a creamy grey; *a.* made of pearls; pert. to pearls; *v.t.* to adorn with pearls; to take a round form like pearls. **-y** *a.* of the color of pearls; like pearls; abounding in pearls; clear; pure. **-iness** *n.* [Fr. *perle*].

peas·ant (pez′·a̤nt) *n.* a rural laborer; a rustic; *a.* rural. **-ry** *n.* peasants collectively [Fr. *paysan*].

peat (pēt) *n.* a brown, fibrous turf, formed of decayed vegetable matter, which is used as fuel. **-y** *a.* like peat, in texture or color. **—bog, —moss** *n.* marshland of which the foundation is peat [etym. uncertain].

peb·ble (peb′·l) *n.* a small, roundish stone; transparent and colorless rock crystal used for spectacle lenses. **-d, pebbly** *a.* full of pebbles [O.E. *papol*].

pe·can (pi·kán′, ·kan′) *n.* a smooth-shelled oval nut with edible kernel; the tree on which it grows [Amer. Indian].

pec·ca·ble (pek′·a̤·bl) *a.* liable to sin. **peccability** *n.* liability to sin. **peccant** *a.* sinful; offensive; causing trouble; (*Med.*) morbid. **peccancy** *n.* [L. *peccare*, to sin].

pec·ca·dil·lo (pek·a̤·dil′·ō) *n.* a trifling offense; an indiscreet action. [Sp. *pecadillo*, fr. *pecado*, a sin; L. *peccare*, to sin].

peck (pek) *n.* a measure of capacity for dry goods = 2 gallons, or the fourth part of a bushel; a great deal [O.Fr. *pek*].

peck (pek) *v.t.* and *i.* to strike with the beak; to pick up with the beak; to dab; to eat little quantities at a time; *n.* (*Colloq.*) a kiss. **-er** *n.* [form of *pick*].

pec·tin (pek′·tin) *n.* a carbohydrate from fruits which yields a gel [Gr. *pektos*, congealed].

pec·to·ral (pek′·te̤r·a̤l) *a.* pert. to the breast or chest [L. *pectus*, the breast].

pec·u·late (pek′·ya̤·lāt) *v.t.* and *i.* to embezzle. **peculation** *n.* **peculator** *n.* [L. *peculari*].

pe·cul·iar (pi·kūl′·ye̤r) *a.* belonging solely to; appropriate; particular; singular; strange. **-ly** *adv.* **peculiarity** (pi·kū·li·ar′·a·ti·) *n.* something that belongs to only one person, thing, class, people; a distinguishing feature; characteristic [L. *peculium*, property].

pe·cu·ni·ar·y (pe·kū′·ni·e·ri·) *a.* pert. to, or consisting of, money. **pecunniarily** *adv.* [L. *pecunia*, money, fr. *pecus*, cattle].

ped·a·gogue (ped′·a̤·gȯg) *n.* a schoolteacher; a pedantic person. **pedagogic** (ped·a̤·gáj′·ik), **pedagogical** *a.* **pedagogy** (ped′·a̤·gō·ji·), **pedagogics** *n.* science of teaching [Gk. *pais*, a boy; *agogos*, leading].

pe·dal (ped′·a̤l) *a.* pert. to the foot; *n.* a mechanical contrivance to transmit power by using foot as a lever, e.g. on bicycle, sewing-machine. *v.t.* and *i.* to use the pedals of an organ, piano, etc.; to propel a bicycle by pedaling. [L. *pes, pedis*, the foot].

ped·ant (ped′·a̤nt) *n.* one who insists unnecessarily on petty details of book learning, grammatical rules, etc.; one who shows off his learning. **-ic, -ical** *a.* **pedantically** *adv.* **-ry** *n.* [perh. conn. with *pedagogue*].

ped·dle (ped′·l) *v.t.* to travel from place to place selling small articles; *v.t.* to sell or hawk goods thus. **-r; pedlar** *n.* one who peddles goods; [O.E. *ped*, a basket].

ped·es·tal (ped′·is·ta̤l) *n.* anything that serves as a support or foundation; the base of a column, statue, etc. [Fr. *piédestal*].

pe·des·tri·an (pa̤·des′·tri·a̤n) *a.* going on, performed on, foot; of walking; commonplace; *n.* a walker; one who journeys on foot [L. *pedester*, fr. *pes*, a foot].

pe·di·at·rics (pēd·i·at′·riks) *n.* (*Med.*) the branch dealing with the diseases and disorders of children. **pediatric** *a.* **pediatrician** *n.* [Gk. *paidos*, a child; *iatrikos*, healing].

pe·dic·u·lar (pi·dik′·ya̤·le̤r) *pert.* to lice [L. *pediculus*, a louse].

ped·i·cure (ped′·i·kūr) *n.* treatment of the feet [L. *pes, pedis*, the foot; *cura*, care].

ped·i·gree (ped′·a̤·grē) *n.* a line of ancestors; genealogy; *a.* having a line of ancestors [M.E. *pedegru* fr. Fr. *pied de grue*, crane's foot].

ped·i·ment (ped′·a̤·ma̤nt) *n.* (*Archit.*) the triangular ornamental facing of a portico door, or window, etc. **pedimental** *a.* [earlier *periment*, perh. fr. *pyramid*].

pe·dom·e·ter (pi·dám′·a̤·te̤r) *n.* an instrument which measures the distance walked by recording the number of steps [L. *pes, pedis*, the foot; Gk. *metrom*, a measure].

pe·dun·cle (pi·dung′·kl) *n.* a flower stalk; (*Zool.*) a stalk or stalklike process in an animal body, **peduncular** *a.* [dim. of L. *pes, pedis*, a foot].

peek (pēk) *v.i.* to peep; to peer; *n.* a glance [etym. uncertain].

peel (pēl) *v.t.* to strip off the skin, bark, or rind; to free from a covering; *v.i.* to come off, as the skin or rind; *n.* the outside skin of a fruit; rind or bark [L. *pilare*, to deprive of hair].

peel (pēl) *n.* wooden shovel used by bakers [L. *pala*, a spade].

peep (pēp) *v.i.* to look through a crevice; to look furtively or slyly; to emerge slowly; *n.* a furtive or sly glance. **— show** *n.* a small exhibit, viewed through an aperture containing a magnifying glass [etym. uncertain].

peep (pēp) *v.i.* to cry, as a chick [imit].

peer (pir) *n.* (*fem.* **-ess**) an equal in any respect; a nobleman; a member of the House of Lords; an associate. **-age** *n.* the rank of a peer; the body of peers. **-less** *a.* having no equal. **-lessly** *adv.* **-lessness** *n.* [L. *par*, equal].

peer (pir) *v.i.* to look closely and intently; to peer; to appear [etym. doubtful].

pee·vish (pē′·vish) *a.* fretful; irritable; hard to please; childish. **-ly** *adv.* **-ness** *n.* **peeve** *v.t.* to annoy.

peg (peg) *n.* a nail or pin of wood or other material; (*Colloq.*) a step or degree; *v.t.* to fix or mark with a peg; *v.i.* to persevere. *pr.p.* **-ging** *pa.t.*, *pa.p.* **-ged** [etym. uncertain].

Pe·king·ese′ (Pē·kạn·ēz′) *n.* a breed of Chinese lap-dog. *abbrev.* **peke.**

pe·koe (pē′·kō) *n.* a black tea of superior quality [Chin. *pek*, white; *ho*, down (i.e. with 'down' on the leaves)].

pel·i·can (pel′·i·kan) *n.* a large water fowl [Gk. *pelekan*].

pe·lisse (pạ·lēs′) *n.* formerly, a robe of silk or other material, worn by ladies; a fur-lined coat [L. *pellis*, skin].

pel·let (pel′·it) *n.* a little ball; a pill; small shot [Fr. *pelote*, a ball].

pell-mell (pel-mel′) *adv.* in utter confusion; helter-skelter [Fr. *mêler*, to mix; *pêle*, being a rhyme with *mêle*].

pel·lu·cid (pạ·lòò′·sid) *a.* perfectly clear; translucent. **-ly** *adv.* **-ness** *n.* [L. *per*, very; *lucidus*, clear].

pelt (pelt) *n.* raw hide; undressed skin of furbearing animal [L. *pellis*, skin].

pelt (pelt) *v.t.* to strike with missiles; *v.i.* of rain, etc. to fall heavily; to throw missiles; to run fast [etym. uncertain].

pel·vis (pel′·vis) *n.* (*Anat.*) the bony basin-shaped cavity at the base of the human trunk. **pelvic** *a.* [L. = a basin].

pen (pen) *n.* an instrument for writing with ink; a large wing feather (a quill) used for writing; *v.t.* to write; to compose and set down. *pr.p.* **-ning.** *pa.p.* and *pa.t.* **-ned.** **-knife** *n.* a pocketknife. **-man** *n.* one who writes a good hand; an author. **-manship** *n.* **— name** *n.* an assumed name of author. [L. *penna*, a feather].

pen (pen) *n.* a small enclosure, as for sheep; a coop. *v.t.* to confine in a pen: to shut in. *pr.p.* **-ning** *pa.p.*, *pa.t.* **-ned** [O.E. *penn*].

pe·nal (pē′·nạl) *a.* pert. to, prescribing, incurring, inflicting, punishment. **-ize** *v.t.* to make penal; to impose a penalty upon; to handicap. **-ly** *adv.* **penalty** (pen′·ạl·ti·) *n.* punishment for a crime or offense; in games, a handicap imposed for infringement of rule, etc.; **penology** *n.* study and arrangement of prisons and prisoners [L. *poena*, punishment].

pen·ance (pen′·ạns) *n.* suffering submitted to in penitence; act of atonement [L. *penitentia*].

pence (pens) *n.pl.* See **penny.**

pen·chant (pen′·chạnt) *n.* a strong mental inclination [Fr. *pencher*, to lean].

pen·cil (pen′·sil) *n.* a stick of graphite encased in wood, used for writing or drawing; (*Math.*) a system of rays which converge to, or diverge from, a point; *v.t.* to draw, write with pencil. **-ed** *a.* marked, as with pencil; having pencils or rays. **-ing** *n.* the work of a pencil [L. *penicillum*, a little tail].

pend·ant (pen′·dant) *n.* a hanging ornament, esp. a locket or earring; a lamp or chandelier hanging from the ceiling; a complement or parallel. **pendent** *a.* suspended; hanging; projecting. **pendently** *adv.* **pending** *a.* awaiting settlement; in suspense; undebted; *prep.* during; until [L. *pendere*, to hang].

pen·du·lous (pen′·jạ·lạs) *a.* hanging loosely; swinging. **-ly** *adv.* **-ness** *n.* **pendulum** *n.* a body suspended from a fixed point, and swinging freely; the swinging rod with weighted end which regulates movements of a clock, etc. [L. *pendulus*, hanging].

pen·e·trate (pen′·ạ·trāt) *v.t.* to enter into; to pierce; to pervade or spread through; to touch with feeling; to arrive at the meaning of; *v.i.* to make a way to, or through. **penetrating** *a.* **penetrable** *a.* capable of being entered or pierced; susceptible. **penetrably** *adv.* **penetrability** *n.* **penetration** *n.* [L. *penetrare*].

pen·guin (pen′·gwin) *n.* a flightless sea bird inhabiting the S. temperate and Antarctic regions [W. *pen*, head; *gwyn*, white].

pen·i·cil·lin (pen·i·sil′·in) *n.* an antibacterial agent produced from the fungus *penicillium.*

pen·in·su·la (pạ·nin′·sa·lạ) *n.* a portion of land nearly surrounded by water, and connected with the mainland by an isthmus **-r** *a.* [L. *paene*, almost; *insula*, an island].

pe·nis (pē′·nis) *n.* the male organ of generation. **penial** *a.* [L.].

pen·i·tent (pen′·ạ·tạnt) *a.* deeply affected by sense of guilt; contrite; repentant; *n.* one who repents of sin. **-ly** adv. **penitence** *n.* sorrow for having sinned; repentance. **penitential** (pen·ạ·ten′·shạl) *a.* pert. to or expressing penitence; *n.* among R.C.s, a book containing rules of penance. **penitentially** *adv.* **penitentiary** (pen·ạ·ten′·shạ·ri·) *a.* pert. to punish by confinement; *n.* a prison; (*R.C.*) an officer who prescribes penance; [L. *paenitere*, to repent].

pen·nant (pen′·ạnt) *n.* a very long, narrow flag tapering to a point. Also **pennon** [Fr. *pennon*, fr. L. *penna*, a feather].

pen·nate (pen′·āt) *a.* winged; feathered. Also **pennated. penniform** *a.* feather-shaped [L. *penna*, a feather].

pen·ny (pen′·i·) *n.* the U.S. and Canadian cent; an English coin (about 2 U.S. cents); a small sum. *pl.* **pennies. penniless** *a.* without money; poor. **-weight** (pen′·i·wāt) *n.* a troy weight of 24 grains (*abbrev.* **pwt.**).

pen·sile (pen′·sl) *a.* hanging; suspended; pendulous [L. *pensilis*].

pen·sion (pen′·shạn) *n.* an annual grant of money for past services; an annuity paid to retired officers, soldiers, etc.; *v.t.* to grant a pension to. **-er** *n.* one who receives a pension [L. *pensio*, payment].

pen·sive (pen′·siv) *a.* thoughtful; deep in thought; somewhat melancholy **-ly** *adv.* **-ness** *n.* [Fr. *pensif*, fr. *penser*, to think].

pent (pent) *a.* closely confined; shut up [fr. *pen* = an enclosure].

pen·ta- (pen′·tạ) *prefix* fr. Gk. *pente*, five, used in derivatives. **-gon, -gram** *n.* (*Geom.*) a plane figure having five angles and five sides. **-gonal** *a.* **-cle** *n.* a five-pointed star, formerly a magic symbol. **-meter** *n.* verse of five feet.

pen·tane (pen′·tān) *n.* a paraffin hydrocarbon, a very inflammable liquid [Gk. *pente*, five].

Pen·ta·teuch (pen′·tạ·tūk) *n.* the first five books of the Old Testament [Gk. *pente*, five; *teuchos*, a book].

Pen·te·cost (pen′·tạ·kawst) *n.* a Jewish festival, celebrated on the 50th day after the Passover; a Christian festival (Whitsunday) commemorating the descent of the Holy Ghost on the Apostles.**Pentecostal** *a.* [Gk. *pentōkostos*, fiftieth].

pent·house (pent′·hous) *n.* an apartment, or structure, on the roof of a building; a shed attached to a main building, its roof sloping down from the wall [Fr. *appentis*, fr. L. *pendere*, to hang].

pen·to·thal (pen′·ta·thawl) *n.* sometimes called the 'truth' drug; an anesthetic [Trade Name].

pe·nult (pē·nult′) *n.* the next to last syllable of a word. **penultimate** (pi·nul′·ti·mạt) *a.* next to last [L. *paene*, almost; *ultimus*, last].

pe·num·bra (pin·um′·brạ) *n.* in an eclipse, the partially shadowed region which surrounds the full shadow [L. *paene*, almost; *umbra*, shade].

pen·u·ry (pen′·yạ·ri·) *n.* extreme poverty; want or indigence; scarcity. **penurious** (pạ·noo′·ri·ạs) *a.* miserly. **penuriously** *adv.* **penuriousness** *n.* [L. *penuria*].

pe·on (pē′·ȧn, ·ạn) *n.* in Mexico, a day laborer or serf; in India, a foot soldier, or messenger. **-age** *n.* [Sp., L. *pes*, a foot].

pe·o·ny (pē′·ạ·ni·) *n.* plant having beautiful, showy flowers [Gk. *paiōnia*, healing, fr. *Paiōn*, the physican of the gods].

peo·ple (pē′·pl) *n.* the body of persons that compose a community, tribe, nation, or race; the populace as distinct from rulers; *v.t.* to populate [L. *populus*].

pep (pep) *n.* (*Slang*) vigor; energy. **-py** *a.* **-piness** *n.* [short for *pepper*].

pep·per (pep′·ẹr) *n.* a pungent, spicy condiment obtained from an E. Indian plant; *v.t.* to sprinkle with pepper; to pelt with missiles. **-y** *a.* having the qualities of pepper; pungent; irritable. **-iness** *n.* **—corn** *n.* the berry or fruit of the pepper-plant; something of insignificant value. **-mint** *n.* a pungent plant which yields a volatile oil; essence gotten from this oil; a lozenge flavored with this essence [Gk.*peperi*].

pep·sin, pepsine (pep′·sin) *n.* a ferment formed in gastric juice of man and animals, and serving as an aid to digestion. **peptic** *a.* pert. to pepsin and to digestion; *n.pl.* medicines that promote digestion. **peptone** (pep′·tōn) *n.* one of the soluble compounds due to the action of pepsin, etc. on proteins. **peptonize** *v.t.* to convert food into peptones [Gk. *pepsis*, digestion].

per·ad·ven·ture (pur·ạd·ven′·chẹr) *adv.* by chance; perhaps; possibly; *n.* doubt; question [O.Fr. *par aventure*].

per·am·bu·late (pẹr·am′·byạ·lāt) *v.t.* to walk through or over; formerly to survey the boundaries of; *v.i.* to walk about; to stroll. **perambulation** *n.* **perambulator** *n.* one who perambulates; a small carriage for a child. **perambulatory** *a.* [L. *per; ambulare*, to walk].

per an·num (pẹr·an′·nạm) L. by the year; annually.

per·cale (pẹr·kal′) *n.* closely woven cotton cloth [Per. *pargal*].

per cap·i·ta (pẹr·kap′·ạ·tạ) L. for each person.

per·ceive (pẹr·sēv′) *v.t.* to obtain knowledge of through the senses; to see, hear, or feel; to understand. **perceivable** *a.* **perceivably** *adv.* **-r** *n.* **perceptible** (pẹr·sep′·ti·bl) *a.* capable of being perceived; discernible. **perceptibly** *adv.* **perceptibility** *n.* **perception** (pẹr·sep′·shạn) *n.* the faculty of perceiving; intuitive judgment. **perceptive** *a.* having perception; used in perception.**perceptual** *a.* involving perception [L. *percipere*].

per·cent·age (pẹr·sen′·tij) *n.* proportion or rate per hundred. **per centum** (*abbrev.* **per cent**) by, in, or for, each hundred; portion [L. *per*, through; *centum*, a hundred].

perch (purch) *n.* an edible fresh-water fish [Gk. *perkē*].

perch (purch) *n.* roosting bar for birds; high place; lineal measure (also 'pole' or 'rod') = 5½ yards; a measure of area = 30¼ square yards; *v.t.* to place on a perch; *v.i.* to alight or settle on a perch [L. *pertica*, a pole].

per·chance (pẹr·chans′) *adv.* perhaps; by chance [L. *per*, through; and *chance*].

per·cip·i·ent (pẹr·sip′·i·ạnt) *a.* having the faculty of perception; perceiving; *n.* one who has the power of perceiving. **percipience, percipiency** *n.* [L. *percipere*, to perceive].

per·co·late (pẹr′·kạ·lāt) *v.t.* and *i.* to pass slowly through small openings, as a liquid; to filter. **percolation** *n.* **percolator** *n.* a coffee pot fitted with a filter [L. *per*, through; *colare*, to strain].

per·cuss (pẹr·kus′) *v.t.* to strike sharply. **percussion** (pẹr·kush′·ạn) *n.* a collision; an impact; (*Med.*) tapping the body to determine condition of internal organ. **-ive** *a.* [L. *percutere*, to strike].

per di·em (pẹr·dī′·ạm) L. daily.

per·di·tion (pẹr·dish′·ạn) *n.* utter loss; ruin; damnation [L. *perdere*, to lose].

per·e·gri·nate (pẹr′·ạ·gri·nāt) *v.i.* to travel from place to place; to journey. **peregrination** *n.* a wandering about. **peregrinator** *n.* [L. *peregrinus*, foreign].

per·emp·to·ry (pạ·remp′·tạ·ri·) *a.* authoritative; dictatorial; non-debatable; decsive; absolute. **peremptorily** *adv.* **peremptoriness** *n.* [L. *perimere, peremptum*, to destroy].

per·en·ni·al (pạ·ren′·i·ạl) *a.* lasting through the year; lasting; everlasting; lasting more than two years; *n.* a plant lasting for such a time.**-ly** *adv.* [L. *per*, through; *annus*, a year].

per·fect (pur′·fikt) *a.* complete; faultless; correct; excellent; of the highest quality; (*Gram.*) a tense denoting completed action; **perfect** (pur′·fekt or pẹr·fekt′) *v.t.* to finish or complete; to make perfect; to improve; to make skillful. **-ly** *adv.* **perfectible** *a.* capable of becoming perfect. **perfectibility** *n.* **perfection** *n.* state of being perfect. **perfectionist** *n.* one who believes that moral perfection is attainable, or that he has attained it [L. *perfectus*, done thoroughly].

per·fer·vid (pẹr·fur′·vid) *a.* very eager [L.].

per·fi·dy (pur′·fạ·di·) *n.* treachery; breach of faith; violation of trust. **perfidious** *a.* treacherous. **perfidiously** *adv.* **perfidiousness** *n.* [L. *perfidia*, faithlessness].

per·fo·rate (pur′·fạ·rāt) *v.t.* to pierce; to make a hole or holes in. **perforation** *n.* act of perforating; a hole, or series of holes [L. *per*. through; *forare*, to bore].

per·force (pẹr·fōrs′) *adv.* by force; of necessity [L. *per;* and *force*].

per·form (pẹr·fawrm′) *v.t.* to do; to accomplish; to fulfill; to represent on the stage; *v.i.* to do; to play, as on a musical instrument. **-ing** *a.* trained to act a part or do tricks. **-er** *n.* **-ance** *n.* act of performing; execution or carrying out; the thing done [L. *per*, thoroughly; Fr. *fournir;* to furnish or complete].

per·fume (pur′·fūm) *n.* a sweet scent or fragrance; a substance which emits an agreeable scent. (pẹr·fūm′) *v.t.* to fill or imbue with an agreeable odor; to scent. **-r** *n.* a maker or seller of perfumes. **perfumery** *n.* perfumes in general; the art of making perfumes [L. *per*, through; *fumare*, to smoke].

per·func·to·ry (pẹr·fungk′·tạ·ri.) *a.* done as a duty, carelessly and without interest; indifferent; superficial. **perfunctorily** *adv.* [L. *perfungi*, to perform].

per·go·la (pur′· gạ·lạ) *n.* an arbor or covered

walk formed of growing plants trained over trelliswork. [It.].

per·haps (pẹr·haps′) *adv.* it may be; possibly; perchance [L. *per*, through; E. *hap*, chance].

per·i·car·di·um (pẹr·i·kär′·di·ạm) *n.* (Anat.) the double membranous sac which encloses the heart. **pericardiac, pericardial** *a.* [Gk. *peri*, round; *kardia*, the heart].

per·i·gee (per′·ạ·jē) *n.* that point in the moon's orbit nearest to the earth. opp. to *apogee* [Gk. *peri*, round; *gē*, the earth].

per·il (per′·ạl) *n.* danger; hazard; exposure to injury or loss; *v.t.* to expose to dangers, etc. **-ous** *a.* full of peril. **-ously** *adv.* **-ousness** n. [L. *periculum*, danger].

per·im·e·ter (pạ·rim′·ạ·tẹr) *n.* (*Geom.*) the outer boundary of a plane figure; the sum of all its sides; circumference. **perimetrical** *a.* [Gk. *peri*, around; *metron*, a measure].

pe·ri·od (pi′·ri·ạd) *n.* a particular portion of time; the time in which a heavenly body makes a revolution; a series of years; a cycle; conclusion; a punctuation mark (.), at the end of a sentence; menstruation; *a.* of furniture, dress, a play, etc., belonging to a particular period in history. **periodic** *a.* recurring at regular intervals. **periodical** *a.* periodic; pert. to a periodical; *n.* a publication, esp. a magazine issued at regular intervals. [Gk. *peri*, around; *hodos*, a way].

per·i·pa·tet·ic (per·ạ·pạ·tet′·ik) *a.* walking about; pert. to the philosophy of Aristotle. **-ism** *n.* [Gk. *peri*, around, about; *patein*, to walk].

pe·riph·er·y (pạ·rif′·ạ·ri·) *n.* circumference; perimeter; the outside. **peripheral** *a.* [Gk. *peri*, around; *pherein*, to bear].

pe·riph·ra·sis (pạ·rif′·rạ·sis) *n.* a roundaway of speaking or writing; circumlocution. *pl.* **periphrases. periphrastic** *a.* circumlocutory. **periphrastically** *adv.* [Gk. *peri*, around; *phrasis*, speaking].

per·i·scope (per′·ạ·skōp) *n.* an optical instrument which enables an observer to view surrounding objects from a lower level [Gk. *peri*, around; *skopein*, to see].

per·ish (per′·ish *v.t.* and *i.* to die; to waste away; to decay; to be destroyed. **-able** *a.* liable to perish, decay, etc., e.g. fish, fruit, etc. [L. *perire; per*, completely; *ire*, to go].

per·i·to·ne·um (per·ạ·tạ·nē′·ạm) *n.* membrane which lines abdominal cavity, and surrounds intestines, etc. **peritonitis** *n.* inflammation of peritoneum [Gk. *peritonaion*, stretch over].

per·i·wig (per′·i·wig) *n.* a wig; a peruke. **-ged** *a.* [Fr. *perrugue*, a wig].

per·i·win·kle (per′·i·wing·kl) *n.* an edible shellfish [O.E. *pinewincle*, a whelk].

per·i·win·kle (per′·i·wing·kl) *n.* a trailing shrub with blue flowers; myrtle [L. *pervinca*].

per·jure (pur′·jẹr) *v.t.* to violate one's oath (used reflex.). **-d** *a.* guilty of perjury. **perjury** *n.* false testimony; the crime of violating one's oath. **-r** *n.* [L. *per; jurare* to swear].

perk (purk) *v.t.* to make spruce or trim; *v.i.* to become brisk and lively again (with 'up'). **-y** *a.* jaunty; pert; trim [Celt].

per·ma·nent (pur′·ma·nạnt) *a.* remaining unaltered; lasting. *n.* a wave put into the hair to last several months. **-ly** *adv.* **permanence** *n.* [L. *per*, through; *manere*, to remain].

per·man·ga·nate (pur·mang′·gạ·nāt) *n.* a salt of an acid of manganese, which, dissolved in water, forms a disinfectant and antiseptic.

per·me·ate (pur′·mi·āt) *v.t.* to penetrate and pass through; to diffuse itself through; to saturate. **permeable** *a.* admitting of passage of fluids. **permeably** *adv.* **permeability** (pur·mē·ā·bil′·ạ·ti·) *a.* capable of permeating [L. *per*, through; *meare*, to pass].

per·mit (pẹr·mit′) *v.t.* to allow; to give leave or liberty to; *v.t.* to give leave. **permit** (pur′·mit) *n.* written permission. *pr.p.* **-ting.** *pa.p.* and *pa.t.* **-ted. permission** *n.* authorization; leave or license granted. **permissible** *a.* allowable. **permissibly** *adv.* **permissive** *a.* allowing. **permissively** *adv.* [L. *permittere*].

per·mute (pẹr·mūt′) *v.t.* to change the order of **permutable** *a.* **permutably** *adv.* **permutableness, permutability** *n.* **permutation** *n.* (*Math.*) the arrangement of a number of quantities in every possible order [L. *per*, thoroughly; *mutare*, to change].

per·ni·cious (pẹr·nish′·ạs) *a.* having the quality of destroying or injuring; wicked. **-ly** *adv.* **-ness** *n.* [L. *per* thoroughly; *nex*, death by violence].

per·nick·et·y (pẹr·nik′·ạ·ti·) *a.* (*Colloq.*) unduly fastidious about trifles [Scot.].

per·o·ra·tion (per·ạ·rā′·shạn) *n.* the concluding part of an oration. **perorate** *v.i.* to deliver a speech [L. *perorare*, to speak to the end].

per·ox·ide (pạ·rȧk′·sīd) *n.* (*Chem.*) oxide containing more oxygen than the normal oxide of an element; *v.t.* (*Colloq.*) to bleach the hair with peroxide of hydrogen.

per·pen·dic·u·lar (pur·pạn·dik′·yạ·lẹr) *a.* exactly upright or vertical; at right angles to the plane of the horizon; at right angles to a given line or surface; *n.* a line at right angles to the plane of the horizon or to any line or plane; the latest of the styles of English Gothic architecture, marked by stiff, straight lines; upright position. **-ly** *adv.* [L. *perpendiculum*, a plumb-line].

per·pe·trate (pur′·pạ·trāt) *v.t.* to commit (something bad, esp. a crime). **perpetration** *n.* **perpetrator** *n.* [L. *perpetrare*, to accomplish].

per·pet·u·al (pẹr·petch′·oo·wạl) *a.* continuing indefinitely; everlasting. **-ly** *adv.* **perpetuate** *v.t.* to make perpetual; not to allow to be forgotten. **perpetuation** *n.* **perpetuity** (pur·pạ·tū′·ạ·ti·) *n.* the state or quality of being perpetual [L. *perpetualis*].

per·plex (pẹr·pleks′) *v.t.* to make intricate, or difficult; to puzzle; to bewilder. **-ed** *a.* puzzled; bewildered. **-ing** *a.* **-ity** *n.* bewilderment; a confused state of mind [L. *per*, thoroughly; *plectere*, to weave].

per·qui·site (pur′·kwạ·zit) *n.* a casual payment in addition to salary, etc.; a tip [L. *perquisitum*, a thing eagerly sought].

per·se·cute (pur′·si·kūt) *v.t.* to oppress unjustly for the holding of an opinion; to subject to persistent ill-treatment; to harass. **persecution** *n.* **persecutor** *n.* [L. *persequi*, to pursue].

per·se·vere (pur·sạ·vēr) *v.i.* to persist; to maintain an effort; not to give in. **persevering** *a.* **perseveringly** *adv.* **perseverance** *n.* [L. *per*, thoroughly; *severus*, strict].

per·sian (pur′·zhạn) *a.* pert. to Persia (now Iran) its people, or the language. **— cat,** a breed of cat with long, silky fur.

per·si·flage (pur′·si·flȧzh) *n.* idle banter [Fr. fr. L. *per*, through; *sifilare, sibilare*, to hiss].

per·sim·mon (pẹr·sim′·ạn) *n.* an American tree with plumlike fruit [Amer.-Ind.].

per·sist (pẹr·sist′) *v.i.* to continue firmly in a state or action in spite of obstacles or objections. **-ent** *a.* persisting; steady; persevering; lasting. **-ently** *adv.* **-ence, -ency** *a.* [L. *persistere*, fr. *sistere*, to stand].

per·son (pur′·sạn) *n.* a human being; an individual; the body of a human being; a character in a play; (*Gram.*) one of the three classes of personal pronouns (first, second, or third) showing the relation of the subject to a verb, as speaking, spoken to, or spoken of. **-able** *a.* attractive in appearance. **-age** *n.* a person, esp. of rank or social position. **-al** *a.*

pert. to, peculiar to, or done by, a person; pert. to bodily appearance; directed against a person; (*Gram.*) denoting the pronouns, I, you, he, she, it, we, you, and they. **-ally** *adv.* in person; individually. **-ality** *n.* individuality; distinctive personal qualities. **personalty** (pur′.sạn.ạl.ti.) *n.* (*Law*) personal effects; movable possessions. **-ate** *v.t.* to assume character of; to pretend to be. **-ator** *n.* **-ation** *n.* [L. *persona*].

per·son·i·fy (pẹr.sán′.ạ.fī) *v.t.* to endow inanimate objects or abstract ideas with human attributes; to be an outstanding example of. **personification** *n.* [L. *persona*, a person; *facere*, to make].

per·son·nel (pur.sạn.el′) *n.* the persons employed in a public service, business, office, etc.; staff [Fr. fr. L. *persona*, person].

per·spec·tive (pẹr.spek′.tiv) *n.* the art of drawing objects on a plane surface to give impression of the relative distance of objects, indicated by the convergence of their receding lines; relation of parts of a problem, etc. in the mind [L. *per*, through; *specere*, to look].

per·spi·ca·cious (pur.spi.kā′.shạs) *a.* of acute discernment; of keen understanding. **-ly** *adv.* **perspicacity** (pur.spi.kas′.ạ.ti.) *n.* quick mental insight or discernment. **perspicuous** (pẹr.spik′.ū.ạs) *a.* clear to the understanding; lucid. **perspicuously** *adv.* **perspicuousness** *n.* **perspicuity** (pur.spi.kū′.ạ.ti.) *n.* clearness [L. *perspicax*, keen of sight].

per·spire (pẹr.spīr′) *v.t.* to emit through the pores of the skin; *v.i.* to evacuate the moisture of the body through the pores of the skin; to sweat. **perspiration** *n.* the process of perspiring; the moisture emitted [L. *per*, through; *spirare*, to breathe].

per·suade (pẹr.swād′) *v.t.* to influence by argument, entreaty, etc.; to win over. **persuasive** (pẹr.swā′.siv) *a.* having the power of persuading. **persuasively** *adv.* **persuasiveness** *n.* **persuasion** (pẹr.swā′.zhạn) *n.* the act of persuading; the quality of persuading; conviction; belief; sect. **persuasible** *a.* [L. *per*, thoroughly; *suadere*, to advise].

pert (purt) *a.* bold; forward; saucy. **-ly** *adv.* **-ness** *n.* [O.Fr. *apert*].

per·tain (pẹr.tān′) *v.i.* to belong; to concern [L. *pertinere*, to belong].

per·ti·na·cious (pur.tạ.nā′.shạs) *a.* adhering to an opinion, etc. with obstinacy; persevering; resolute. **-ly** *adv.* **-ness** *n.* **pertinacity** (pẹr.ti.nas′.i.ti.) *n.* [L. *pertinax*, tenacious].

per·ti·nent (pur′.tạ.nạnt) *a.* related to the subject or matter in hand. **-ly** *adv.* **pertinence, pertinency** *n.* [L. *pertinere*, to belong].

per·turb (pẹr.turb′) *v.t.* to disturb; to trouble greatly. **-ation** (pur.tẹr.bā′.shạn) *n.* mental uneasiness or disquiet; disorder [L. *per*, thoroughly; *turbare*, to disturb].

Pe·ru (pạ.ròò′) *n.* a republic on the west coast of S. America. **-vian** *n.* a native of Peru; *a.* pert. to Peru.

pe·ruse (pạ.ròòz′) *v.t.* to read through, esp. with care. **perusal** *n.* the act of perusing [*per*, thoroughly; and *use*].

per·vade (pẹr.vād′) *v.t.* to spread through the whole of; to be diffused through all parts of. **pervasion** (pẹr.vā′.zhun) *n.* **pervasive** *a.* [L. *per*, through; *vadere*, to go].

per·verse (pẹr.vurs′) *a.* obstinately or unreasonably wrong; refusing to do the right, or to admit error; self-willed. **-ness, perversity** *n.* [L. *per*, thoroughly; *vertere*, to turn].

per·ver·sion (pẹr.vur′.zhan) *n.* a turning from the true purpose, use, or meaning; corruption; unnatural manifestation of sexual desire. **perversive** *a.* tending to pervert [L. *per*, thoroughly; *vertere*, to turn].

per·vert (pẹr.vurt′) *v.t.* to turn from its proper purpose; to misinterpret; to lead astray; to corrupt. **pervert** (pur′.vẹrt) *n.* one who has deviated from the normal, esp. from right to wrong [L. *per*, thoroughly; *vertere*, to turn].

per·vi·ous (pur′.vi.ạs) *a.* giving passage to; penetrable. **-ness** *n.* [L. *per*, through, *via*, way].

pes·si·mism (pes′.ạ.mizm) *n.* the doctrine that the world is fundamentally evil; the tendency to look on the dark side of things (opp. of *optimism*); melancholy. **pessimist** *n.* **pessimistic** *a.* **pessimistically** *adv.* [L. *pessimus*, worst].

pest (pest) *n.* a plague or pestilence; a troublesome or harmful thing or person; nuisance. **-iferous** *a.* pestilential; carrying disease; (*Colloq.*) annoying [L. *pestis*, a plaque].

pes·ter (pes′.tẹr) *v.t.* to trouble or vex persistently; to annoy [O.Fr. *empestrer*, fr. L.L. *pastorium*, a foot shackle].

pest·i·cide (pes′.tạ.sīd) *n.* a pest killer.

pes·ti·lence (pes′.ti.lens) *n.* any infectious or contagious, deadly disease. **pestilent** *a.* producing disease; noxious; harmful to morals. **pestilential** (pes.tạ.len′.shạl) *a.* pert. to, or producing, pestilence; destructive; wicked [L. *pestis*, plague].

pes·tle (pes′.l, pes′.tl) *n.* an instrument for pounding substances in a mortar [L. *pistillum*, fr. *pinsere*, to pound].

pet (pet) *n.* an animal or person kept or regarded with affection; a favorite; *a.* favorite; *v.t.* to make a pet of; to indulge. *pr.p.* **-ting.** *pa.p.* and *pa.t.* **-ted** [etym. uncertain].

pet (pet) *n.* a sudden fit of peevishness [etym. uncertain].

pet·al (pet′.ạl) *n.* a colored flower-leaf. **-ed, -led** *a.* having petals. **-ine** *a.* pert. to, resembling, a petal [Gk. *petalon*, a thin plate].

pe·ter (pē′.tẹr) *v.i.* (*Colloq.*) to become exhausted, gradually smaller, weaker, etc. (with *out*) [fr. name *Peter*].

pet·it (pet′.i., pe.tē′) (*Law*) small; minor. *fem.* **petite** (pạ.tēt′) small, dainty, trim of figure. **— point** *a.* slanting stitch used in embroidery and tapestry [Fr.].

pe·ti·tion (pạ.tish′.ạn) *n.* a formal request or earnest prayer; *v.t.* and *i.* to present a petition to; to entreat. **-ary** *a.* **-er** *n.* [L. *petere*, to ask].

pet·ri·fy (pet′.rạ.fī) *v.t.* to turn into stone; to make hard like stone; to make motionless with fear; *v.i.* to become like stone. *pr.p.* **petrified, pertifactive** *a.* [L. and Gk. *petra*, rock, stone; *facere*, to make].

pe·tro *prefix* fr. L. and Gk. *petra*, rock, stone, used in derivatives. **petrography** (pạ.trág′.rạ.fi.) *n.* the science of describing and classifying rocks. **petrographic(al)** *a.* **petrology** *n.* a branch of geology dealing with the composition, structure, and classification of rocks, their origin and sequence of formation. **petrologic(al)** *a.* **petrous** (pe′.trạs) *a.* pert. to, or like, rock; rocky; hard [Gk. *graphein*, to write; *logos*, discourse].

pe·tro·le·um (pạ.trō′.lī.ạm) *n.* a mineral oil drawn from the earth by means of wells. **petrol** *n.* (*Brit.*) gasoline. **petrolic** *a.* [L. *petra*, rock; *oleum*, oil].

pet·ti·coat (pet′.i.kōt) *n.* a woman's underskirt; (*Colloq.*) a woman; *a.* feminine [orig. *petty coat*, a small coat].

pet·ti·fog·ger (pet′.i.fág.ẹr) *n.* a low class person given to mean dealing in small matters. **pettifog** *v.i.* **-y** *n.* low trickery. **pettifogging** *a.* [etym. uncertain].

pet·tish (pet′.ish) *a.* petulant; easily annoyed. **-ly** *adv.* **-ness** *n.* [fr. *pet*, a fit of temper].

pet·ty (pet′.i.) *a.* small; unimportant; trivial; small-minded; of lower rank. **pettily** *adv.* **pettiness** *n.* **— cash,** small items of expenditure, esp. in an office. — **officer,** a non-commissioned officer in the Navy [Fr. *petit,* small].

pet·u·lant (pech′·ạ·lạnt) *a.* given to small fits of temper; irritable. **-ly** *adv.* **petulance, petulancy** *n.* peevishness; crossness; fretfulness [L. *petulans,* wanton].

pe·tu·ni·a (pạ·tū′·ni·ạ) *n.* a common garden plant with showy flowers [Braz. *petun,* tobacco].

pew (pū) *n.* a long, fixed bench in a church [O.Fr. *puie,* a platform].

pe·wee (pē′·wē) *n.* a small bird, the phoebe. Also **pewit** [imit. of its note].

pew·ter (pū′·tẹr) *n.* an alloy of tin and lead or some other metal, esp. copper; ware made of this; *a.* made of pewter [O.Fr. *peutre*].

phae·ton (fā′·tạn) *n.* a light, four-wheeled, open carriage.

phal·ange See **phalanx.**

pha·lan·ger (fạ·lan′·jẹr) *n.* genus of furry marsupial, some winged; flying squirrel [Gk. *phalangion,* a spider's web].

pha·lanx (fā′·langks) *n.* in ancient Greece, a company of soldiers in close array; hence, any compact body of people; (*Anat.*) a small bone of a toe or finger. *pl.* **-es, phalanges** [Gk.].

phal·lus (fal′·ạs) *n.* sexual organs. *pl.* **phalli. phallic** *a.* [Gk. *phallos*].

phan·tasm (fan′·tazm) *n.* an imaginary vision; a phantom; a specter. **-al, -ic** *a.* **phantasmagoria** (fan·taz·mạ·gō′·ri·ạ) *n.* an exhibition of optical illusions; a shifting scene of dim or unreal figures. **phantasmagoric** *a.* **phantasy** *n.* See **fantasy. phantom** (fan′·tạm) *n.* an apparition; a specter; a ghost; *a.* spectral [Gk. *phainein,* to show].

Phar·aoh (fā′·rō) *n.* 'The Great House' a title of the kings of ancient Egypt.

Phar·i·see (far′·i·sē) *n.* (*Bib.*) one of a Jewish sect noted for their strict observance of the forms of the Law. **Pharisaic** (far·ạ·sā′·ik), **Pharisaical** *a.* **Pharisaically** *adv.* **-ism, Pharisaism,** *n.* [Heb. *parash,* to separate].

phar·ma·ceu·ti·cal (fȧr·mạ·sū′·tik·ạl) *a.* pert. to pharmacy. **pharmaceutics** *n.pl.* the science of pharmacy. **pharmaceutist** *n.* [Gk. *pharmakon,* a drug].

phar·ma·cy (fȧr′·mạ·si·) *n.* the science of preparing, compounding, and dispensing drugs and medicines; a drugstore. **pharmacist** *n.* one skilled in pharmacy. **pharmacology** *n.* the study of drugs and their action. **pharmacologist** *n.* one skilled in pharmacy. **pharmacopoeia** (fȧr·mạ·kạ·pē′·yạ) *n.* an authoritative book containing information on medicinal drugs [Gk. *pharmakon,* a drug].

phar·ynx (far′·ingks) *n.* the cavity at back of mouth, opening into the gullet. *pl.* **pharynges. pharyngeal** (fạ·rin′·jạl) *a.* Also **pharyngal. pharyngitis** (far·in·jī′·tis) *n.* (*Med.*) inflammation of pharynx. **pharyngoscope** *n.* instrument for examining throat [Gk. *pharunx,* the pharynx].

phase (fāz) *n.* (*Astron.*) an aspect of moon or a planet; a stage in development; an aspect of a subject or question. **phasic** *a.* [Gk. *phasis,* an appearance].

pheas·ant (fez′·ạnt) *n.* a gamebird with brilliant plumage [Gk. *Phasis,* a river in Colchis, whence the bird first came].

phe·nom·e·non (fạ·nȧm′·ạ·nȧn) *n.* anything appearing or observed, esp. if having scientific interest; a remarkable person or thing; (*Philos.*) sense appearance as opposed to real existence. *pl.* **phenomena. phenomenal** *a.* pert. to a phenomenon; remarkable; extraordinary. **phenomenally** *adv.* [Gk. *phainomenon,* a thing appearing].

phew (fū) *interj.* expressing disgust, impatience, relief, etc.

phi·al (fī′·ạl) *n.* a small glass bottle; a vial [Gk. *phialē,* a flat vessel].

phi·lan·der (fạ·lan′·dẹr) *v.i.* to flirt. **-er** *n.* [Gk. *philos,* loving; *anēr,* a man].

phi·lan·thro·py (fi·lan′·thrạ·pi·) *n.* love of mankind, esp. as shown in acts of charity; an act of charity. **philanthropic** (fil·an·throp′·ik), **philanthropical** *a.* **philanthropically** *adv.* **philanthropist** *n.* one who loves and seeks to do good to his fellowmen. Also **philanthrope** [Gk. *philos,* loving; *anthrōpos,* man].

phi·lat·e·ly (fạ·lat′·ạ·li·) *n.* stamp collecting. **philatelic** *a.* **philatelist** *n.* [Gk. *philos,* loving; *atelēs,* franked].

phil·har·mon·ic (fil·ẹr·mȧn′·ik, fil·har·mȧn′·ik) *a.* loving harmony or music; musical [Gk. *philos,* loving; *harmonia,* harmony].

Phi·lis·tine (fil′·ạs·tīn, ·tin) *n.* one with no love of music, painting, etc.; an uncultured person [*Bib.* Phillistine].

phi·lol·o·gy (fi·lȧl′·ạ·ji·) *n.* scientific study of origin, development, etc. of languages. **philological** *a.* **philologian** (fi·lạ·lō′·ji·ạn) **philologist** *n.* one versed in philology [Gk. *philos,* loving; *logos,* word, speech].

phi·los·o·phy (fạ·lȧs′·ạ·fi·) *n.* originally, any branch of investigation of natural phenomena; now, the study of beliefs regarding God, existence, conduct, etc. and of man's relation with the universe; a calmness of mind; composure. **philosopher** *n.* a student of philosophy. **philosophic** (fil·ạ·sȧf′·ik) **philosophical** *a.* pert. to philosophy; wise; calm. **philosophically** *adv.* **philosophize** *v.i.* to reason like a philosopher; to theorize; to moralize. **philosophism** *n.* a pretended system of philosophy; sophism [Gk. *philos,* loving; *sophia,* wisdom].

phil·ter (fil′·tẹr) *n.* a drink supposed to excite love; any magic potion. Also **philtre** [Gk. *philtron,* fr. *philos,* loving].

phle·bi·tis (flạ·bi′·tis) *n.* (*Med.*) inflammation of a vein. **phlebitic** *a.* **phlebotomy** *n.* (*Surg.*) blood-letting [Gk. *phleps,* a vein].

phlegm (flem) *n.* a secretion of thick mucous substance discharged from throat by expectoration; calmness; apathy; sluggishness. **phlegmatic** (fleg·mat′·ik) *a.* cool and collected; unemotional. [Gk. *phlegma*].

phlox (flȧks) *n.* a genus of garden plants [Gk. = a flame].

phoe·be (fē·bi·) *n.* a small American flycatcher [imit.]

pho·bi·a (fō′·bi·ạ) *n.* a morbid dread of anything; used esp. as a suffix, e.g. claustro*phobia,* hydro*phobia,* etc. [Gk. *phobos,* fear].

Phoe·nix, Phenix (fē′·niks) *n.* (*Myth.*) a fabulous Arabian bird, symbol of immortality; a paragon [Gk. *phoinix*].

phone (fōn) *n., v.t.* and *i.* (*Colloq.*) *abbrev.* of **telephone** [Gk. *phōnē,* sound].

phone (fōn) *n.* a sound made in speaking. **phonic** *a.* pert. to sound, esp. to speech sounds. **phonics** *n.* method of teaching reading, etc. on basis of speech sounds [Gk. *phone*].

pho·neme (fō′·nēm) *n.* a member of the set of smallest units of speech sounds that serve to distinguish utterances. **phonemic** *a.* **phonemically** *adv.* **phonemics** *n.* branch of linguistics which deals with phonemes. [F.]

pho·net·ic (fō·net′·ik) *a.* pert. to the voice; pert. to, or representing, vocal sounds. Also **-al** *a.* **-ally** *adv.* **-s** *n.* the branch of the study of language which deals with speech sounds, and their production. **-ize** *v.t.* to represent phonetically. — **spelling,** a simplified system of spelling in which same letter or symbol is always used for same sound, e.g. cat = kat [Gk. *phōnē,* sound].

pho·no- (fō′·nō) *prefix* fr. Gk. *phōnē,* sound, used in many derivatives. **-gram** *n.* a character or symbol, esp. in shorthand, used to represent a speech sound. **-graph** *n.* an instrument for reproducing sounds from records. **phonography** *n.* a system of shorthand. **phonology** (fō·nàl′·ạ·ji·) *n.* study of speech sounds; phonetics. **-logic(al)** *a.*

pho·ny, phoney (fō′·ni·) *a.* (*Slang*) sham; counterfeit.

phos·phate (fàs′·fāt) *n.* a salt of phosphoric acid. **phosphatic** *a.* **— of lime,** commercially, bone-ash. **phosphide** *n.* a compound of phosphorus with another element, e.g. copper [fr. *phosphorus*].

phos·pho·rus (fàs′·fẹr·ạs) *n.* a non-metallic element, a yellowish waxlike substance giving out a pale light in the dark. **phosphorous** *a.* pert. to phosphorus. **phosphorescence** (fàs·fẹr·es′·ạns) *n.* the giving out of light without heat, as phosphorus, the glow-worm, decaying fish, etc. **phosphorescent** *a.* **phosphoric** *a.* pert. to, or obtained from, phosphorus; phosphorous. **phosphureted** *a.* combined with phosphorus [Gk. *phōs,* light; *phoros,* bearing].

pho·to (fō′·tō) *n.* (*Colloq.*) *abbrev.* of photograph; *v.t.* to photograph.

pho·to (fō′·tō) *prefix* fr. Gk. *phōs, phōtos,* light, used in derivatives. **-chemistry** (fō·tō·kem′·is·tri·) *n.* the branch of chemistry which treats of the chemical action of light. **-electron** *n.* an electron liberated from a metallic surface by the action of a beam of ultraviolet light. **— finish,** in racing, a photo taken at the finish to show correct placing of contestants. **-genic** *a.* producing light; of a person, having features, etc. that photograph well.

pho·tog·ra·phy (fạ·tàg′·rạ·fi·) *n.* the art of producing pictures by the chemical action of light on a sensitive plate or film. **photograph** *n.* a picture so made; *v.t.* to take a photograph of. **photographer** *n.* **photographic(al)** *a.* pert. to, resembling, or produced by, photography. **photographically** *adv.* [Gk. *phōs,* light; *graphein,* to write; Fr. *gravure,* an engraving; Gk. *lithos,* a stone].

pho·tol·o·gy (fō·tàl′·ạ·ji·) *n.* the science of light. **photometer** *n.* an instrument for measuring the intensity of light [Gk. *phōs,* light; *logos,* discourse; *metron,* a measure].

pho·ton (fō′·tàn) *n.* the unit of measurement of light intensity [Gk. *phōs, phōtos,* light].

pho·to·stat (fō′·tō·stat) *n.* a photographic apparatus for making copies of documents, etc. directly on paper; *v.t.* to copy thus. **photostatic** *a.* [Trade Name].

pho·to·syn·the·sis (fō·tō·sin′·thạ·sis) *n.* the process by which a plant, under the influence of sunlight, can build up, in its chlorophyll-containing cells, carbohydrates from the carbon dioxide of the atmosphere and from the hydrogen of the water in the soil [Gk. *phōs, phōtos,* light; *sun,* together; *thesis,* a placing].

phrase (frāz) *n.* a small group of words forming part of a sentence; a short pithy expression; a characteristic mode of expression; (*Mus.*) a short, distinct part of a longer passage; *v.t.* to express suitably in words. **phraseogram** (frā′·zi·ạ·gram) *n.* in shorthand, a symbol used to represent a phrase. **-ology** *n.* a mode of expression; the choice of words used in speaking or writing [Gk. *phrazein,* to speak].

phre·net·ic (fri·net′·ik) *a.* having the mind disordered; frenzied; frantic [Gk. *phrēn,* the diaphragm, the mind].

phre·nol·o·gy (fri·nal′·ạ·ji·) *n.* character reading from the shape of the head. **phrenologic(al)** *a.* **phrenologically** *adv.* **phrenologist** *n.* [Gk. *phrēn,* mind; *logos,* discourse].

phthi·sis (thī′·sis) *n.* (*Med.*) a wasting away of the lungs; consumption. **phthisic** (tiz′·ik), **phthisical** (tiz′·ik·ạl) *a.* [Gk. fr. *phthiein,* to waste away].

phy·lac·ter·y (fạ·lak′·tạ·ri·) *n.* a charm or amulet; a small leather case containing strips of vellum, inscribed with certain verses of the Law and worn on the forehead or left arm by male Jews during morning prayer [Gk. *phylassein,* to guard].

phy·log·e·ny (fī·làj′·ạ·ni·) *n.* (*Bot.*) the evolution of an animal or plant type. **phylum** (fī′·lạm) *n.* one of the primary divisions of the animal or plant kingdoms. *pl.* **phyla** [Gk. *phylon,* a race; *genesis,* origin].

phys·ic (fiz′·ik) *n.* (*Arch.*) a cathartic; medicine; *v.t.* to give a dose of physic to. *pr.p.* **physicking.** *pa.p.* and *pa.t.* **physicked.** **physician** (fạ·zish′·ạn) *n.* one skilled in the art of healing; a medical doctor [Gk. *physis,* nature].

phys·i·cal (fiz′·ik·ạl) *a.* pert. to physics; pert. to nature; bodily, as opposed to mental or moral; material. **-ly** *adv.* [Gk. *physis,* nature].

phys·ics (fiz′·iks) *n.* sciences (excluding chemistry and biology) which deal with natural phenomena, e.g. motion, force, light, sound, electricity, etc. **physicist** (fiz′·i·sist) *n.* [Gk. *physis,* nature].

phys·i·og·no·my (fiz·i·àg′·nạ·mi·, fiz·i·àn′·ạ·mi·) *n.* art of judging character from contours of face; face itself; expression of the face. **physiognomic, physiognomical** *a.* **physiognomist** *n.* [Gk. *physis,* nature; *gnōmōn,* a judge].

phys·i·og·ra·phy (fiz·i·àg′·rạ·fi·) *n.* the study and description of natural phenomena; physical geography. **physiographer** *n.* [Gk. *physis,* nature; *graphein,* to write].

phys·i·ol·o·gy (fiz·i·àl′·ạ·ji·) *n.* science which deals with functions and life processes of plants, animals, and human beings. **physiological** *a.* **physiologist** *n.* [Gk. *physis,* nature; *logos,* discourse].

phys·i·o·ther·a·py (fiz·i·ō·ther′·ạ·pi·) *n.* the application of massage, manipulation, light, heat, electricity, etc., for treatment of certain disabilities [Gk. *physis,* nature; *therapeuein,* to cure].

phy·sique (fi·zēk′) *n.* bodily structure and development [Fr. fr. Gk. *physis,* nature].

phy·to (fī′·to) *prefix* fr. Gk. *phyton,* a plant. **phytogenesis** (fī·tō·jen′·ạ·sis), **phytogeny** (fī·tàj′·ạ·ni·) *n.* the evolution of plants.

pi (pī) *n.* the Greek letter π, esp. as a mathematical symbol for the ratio of the circumference of a circle to its diameter, approx. $3\frac{1}{7}$, or 3.14159.

pi·a·no (pē·à′·nō) *adv.* (*Mus.*) softly. **pianissimo** *adv.* very softly [It.].

pi·a·no (pē·a′·nō) *n. abbrev.* of **pianoforte** (pē·à·nō·fōr′·te) *n.* a musical instrument having wires of graduated tension, struck by hammers moved by notes on a keyboard. **pianist** (pē′·ạ·nist, pē·an′·ist) *n.* one who plays the piano [It. *piano e forte* = soft and strong].

pi·as·ter (pi·as′·tẹr) *n.* a monetary unit of several Eastern countries [It. *piastra*].

pi·az·za (pē·az′·ạ, pē·at′·sạ) *n.* a porch of a house; a public square [It.].

pi·ca (pī′·kạ) *n.* (*Print.*) a size of type, having 6 lines to the inch [L. *pica,* a magpie].

pic·a·dor (pik·ạ·dawr′) *n.* a mounted bullfighter armed with a lance to prod the bull [Sp. *pica,* a pike].

pic·a·roon (pik′·ạ·ròòn) *n.* an adventurer; a pirate. **picaresque** (pik·ạ·resk′) *a.* of a novel, dealing with the lives and adventures of rogues [Sp. *picaro,* a rogue].

pic·ca·lil·li (pik·ạ·lil′·i·) *n.* a pickle of vegetables [etym. uncertain].

pic·co·lo (pik′·ą·lō) *n.* (*Mus.*) a small flute, sounding an octave higher than the ordinary flute [It.].

pick (pik) *v.t.* to peck at, like birds with their bills; to pierce with a pointed instrument; to open with a pointed instrument, as a lock; to pluck, or cull, as flowers, etc.; to raise or lift (with *up*); to choose or select; to rob; to pluck the strings of a musical instrument; (*Colloq.*) to eat; *v.i.* to eat daintily or without appetite; *n.* a sharp-pointed tool; the choicest or best of anything. **-ax** *n.* an instrument for digging. **-ing** *n.* the act of one who picks; stealing. **-ings** *n.pl.* gleanings; perquisites, often obtained by slightly underhand methods. **— on** (*Colloq.*) to nag; to find fault. **— pocket** *n.* one who steals from pockets. **—me-up** *n.* a drink that acts as a stimulant or restorative [M.E.].

pick·er·el (pik′·ą·rąl) *n.* a young pike; a kind of pike [dim. of *pike*].

pick·et (pik′·it) *n.* a sharpened stake (used in fortifications, etc.); a peg or pale; a guard posted in front of an army; a party sent out by trade unions to dissuade men from working during a strike; *v.t.* to fence with pickets. **— line** *n.* a line of demonstrators or strikers walking up and down [Fr. *piquet*, fr. *pic*, a pike].

pick·le (pik′·l) *n.* brine or vinegar in which fish, meat, or vegetables are preserved; any food preserved in brine or vinegar; (*Colloq.*) a difficult situation; *v.t.* to preserve with salt or vinegar. **-d** *a.* (*Slang*) drunk. **-s** *n.pl.* vegetables in vinegar and spices [M.E. *pykyl*, *pikille*].

pic·nic (pik′·nik) *n.* pleasure excursion with meal out of doors; agreeable situation; *v.i.* to go on a picnic. *pr.p.* **-king.** *pa.p.*, *pa.t.* **-ked** [etym. uncertain].

pi·cot (pē′·kō) *n.* a small projecting loop of thread forming part of an ornamental edging to ribbon, lace, etc. [Fr.].

pic·ric ac·id (pik′·rik as′·id) *n.* a poisonous, crystalline substance used in solution as a dressing for burns, for dyes, explosives, etc. [Gk. *pikros*, bitter].

pic·to·graph (pik′·tą·graf) *n.* a picture representing an idea [L. *pingere*, *pictum*, to paint; Gk. *graphein*, to write].

pic·to·ri·al (pik·tō′·ri·ąl) *a.* pert. to pictures; expressed by pictures; illustrated. **-ly** *adv.* [L. *pictor*, a painter].

pic·ture (pik′·chęr) *n.* a representation of objects or scenes on paper, canvas, etc., by drawing, painting, photography, etc.; a mental image; a likeness or copy; an illustration; picturesque object; a graphic or vivid description in words; *v.t.* to draw or paint an image or representation of; to describe graphically; to recall vividly. **-sque** (pik·-chęr·esk′) *a.* making effective picture; vivid in description. **-squely** *adv.* **-squeness** *n.* **— gallery** *n.* a hall containing a collection of pictures for exhibition. [L. *pingere*, *pictum*, to paint].

pid·dle (pid′·l) *v.i.* to trifle. **piddling** *a.* trifling [etym. uncertain].

pidg·in (pij′·in) *n.* an auxiliary language developed for trade and other exchange between peoples, mixing words and grammars of their languages, as *pidgin English* [supposedly a Chin. corruption of *business*].

pie (pī) *n.* (*Cookery*) a dish of meat or fruit covered with upper or lower pastry crust or both; (*Print.*) a confused mass of type [etym. uncertain].

pie (pī) *n.* a magpie. **-bald** (pī′.bawld) *a.* irregularly marked; streaked with any two colors. **-d** *a.* piebald; variegated [L. *pica*, a magpie; *bald* = *balled*, streaked].

piece (pēs) *n.* a part of anything; a bit; a portion; a single object; a separate example; a coin; a counter in chess, checkers, etc.; a literary work; a musical composition; a gun; a plot of land; *v.t.* to mend; to put together. **— goods** *n.pl.* textile fabrics sold by measured lengths of the material. **— meal** *adv.* little by little; gradually. **— work** *n.* work paid for by the amount done, and not by the hour, day, etc. **— of eight,** an old Spanish dollar = eight reals [Fr. *pièce*].

pier (pir) *n.* a piece of solid, upright masonry, as a support or pillar for an arch, bridge, or beam; a structure built out over the water as a landing. **— glass** *n.* a tall mirror, esp. a wall mirror between two windows [Fr. *pierre*, stone, fr. L. *Petra*].

pierce (pirs) *v.t.* to thrust into, esp. with a pointed instrument; to make a hole in; to penetrate; *v.i.* to enter; to penetrate. **piercing** *a.* penetrating; sharp; keen. **piercingly** *adv.* [Fr. *percer*].

pi·e·ty (pī′·ą·ti·) *n.* the quality of being pious; devotion to religion; affectionate respect for one's parents. **pietist** *n.* an ultra-pious person; a sanctimonious person. **pietistic** *a.* **pietism** *n.* [L. *pietas*, fr. *pius*, pious].

pig (pig) *n.* a hoofed domestic animal, reared for its flesh; oblong mass of smelted metal, as pig iron; *v.i.* to bring forth pigs. **-gish** *a.* pert. to, or like, pigs; dirty; greedy; stubborn. **-tail** *n.* the tail of a pig; a braid of hair hanging from the back of the head; a roll of twisted tobacco. **—eyed** *a.* having small, sly eyes. **-headed** *a.* obstinate; stupidly perverse. **— iron, — lead,** iron, lead, cast in rough oblong bars. **-nut** *n.* the nut of the brown hickory. **-skin** *n.* strong leather made from the pig's skin, and used for saddles, etc. (*Colloq.*) a football. **-sticking** *n.* hunting wild boar with a spear, popular in India. **-sty** *n.* a covered enclosure for keeping pigs; a dirty house or room [M.E. *pigge*].

pi·geon (pij′·ąn) *n.* any bird of the dove family, both wild and domesticated; a simpleton or dupe. **— English** *n.* See **pidgin English.** **—hearted** *a.* timid. **-hole** *n.* a little division in a desk or case, for holding papers, etc.; *v.t.* to place in the pigeonhole of a desk, etc.; to shelve for future reference; to classify. **—toed** *a.* having turned-in toes [Fr. fr. L. *pipio*, *pipionis*, a young piping bird].

pig·ment (pig′·mant) *n.* paint; coloring matter; coloring matter in animal tissues and cells. **-ation** *n.* (*Biol.*) coloring matter [L. *pigmentum*].

pigmy. See **pygmy.**

pike (pīk) *n.* a sharp point; an old weapon consisting of a long, wooden shaft with a flat-pointed steel head; a voracious freshwater fish; a turnpike or tollgate. **-staff** *n.* a staff with a sharp metal spike [O.E. *pic*, a point].

pi·las·ter (pi′·las·tęr, pi·las′·tęr) *n.* a square column, usually set in a wall [It. *pilastro*, fr. L. *pila*, a pillar].

pil·chard (pil′·chęrd) *n.* a sea fish resembling the herring, but smaller [etym. uncertain].

pile (pīl) *n.* a mass or collection of things; a heap; a large building or mass of buildings; in atomic energy research, the nuclear energy furnace, made by accumulation of uranium and graphite. (*Colloq.*) a large fortune; *v.t.* to throw into a pile or heap; to accumulate [*L. pila*, a pillar].

pile (pīl) *n.* a beam driven vertically into the ground to support a building, a bridge etc.; *v.t.* to drive piles into; to support with piles. **-driver** *n.* a machine for driving in piles [O.E. *pil*, a dart].

pile (pīl) *n.* fur or hair; nap of a fabric, esp.

if thick and close-set, as in velvet [L. *pilus*, a hair].

piles (pīlz) *n.pl.* a disease of the rectum; hemorrhoids [L. *pila*, a ball].

pil·fer (pil′·fẹr) *v.t.* and *i.* to steal in small quantities [O.Fr. *pelfrer*].

pil·grim (pil′·grim) *n.* a traveler, esp. one who journeys to visit a holy place. **-age** *n.* journey to a holy place; any long journey [O.Fr. *pelegrin*, fr. L. *peregrinus*, a stranger].

pill (pil) *n.* a small ball of medicine, to be swallowed whole; anything disagreeable that has to be endured; (*Slang*) an unpopular person. **-box** *n.* (*Mil.*) a small concrete fort [L. *pilula*, dim. fr. *pila*, a ball].

pil·lage (pil′·ij) *n.* the act of plundering; plunder or spoil; *v.t.* to plunder [Fr. *piller*, fr. L. *pilare*, to plunder].

pil·lar (pil′·ẹr) *n.* a slender upright structure of stone, iron, etc.; a column; a support. **-ed** *a.* [L. *pila*, a column].

pil·lion (pil′·yạn) *n.* a cushioned pad put behind the saddle on a horse as a seat for a second person [Gael. *pillean*, a pack-saddle].

pil·lo·ry (pil′·ạ·ri·) *n.* an old instrument used to punish offenders, consisting of a frame with holes for head and hands in which the person was confined and exposed to pelting and ridicule; *v.t.* to punish by putting into a pillory; to expose to ridicule and abuse. [Fr. *pilori*]

pil·low (pil′·ō) *n.* a cushion, esp. for the head of a person in bed; *v.t.* to place on a pillow. **-case, -slip** *n.* a removable covering for a pillow [O.E. *pyle*].

pi·lose (pī′·lōs) *a.* hairy; covered with hair. Also **pilous pilosity** *n.* [L. *pilosus*, hair].

pi·lot (pī′·lạt) *n.* a person qualified to take charge of a ship entering or leaving a harbor, or where knowledge of local waters is needed; one qualified to operate an aircraft; a steersman; a guide; a small jet of gas kept burning in order to light a stove, etc.; *v.t.* to direct the course of; to guide through dangers or difficulties. **— engine** *n.* a locomotive sent on ahead to clear the way for a train [Fr. *pilote*].

pi·men·to (pi·men′·tō) *n.* allspice; pimiento, a reddish pepper [Sp. fr. L. *pigmentum*, spice].

pimp (pimp) *n.* a procurer; a pander; *v.i.* to pander [Fr. *pimper*, to dress up].

pim·per·nel (pim′·pẹr·nel) *n.* an annual plant of the primrose family [Fr. *pimprenelle*].

pim·ple (pim·′pl) *n.* a small, red, pustular spot on the skin. **-d, pimply** *a.*

pin (pin) *n.* a short, thin piece of stiff wire with a point and head for fastening soft materials together; a wooden or metal peg or rivet; an ornament that fastens on cloth; (*Golf*) a thin metal or wooden stick (with a flag) to mark the position of the hole; a rolling pin; a clothespin; a trifle; *pl.* (*Slang*) the legs; *v.t.* to fasten with pins; to seize and hold fast. *pr.p.* **-ning.** *pa.p.* and *pa.t.* **-ned. -cushion** *n.* a small pad in which pins are stuck. **— money** *n.* an allowance for incidental or personal expenses. **-point** *v.t.* to locate (a target) with great accuracy.**-up girl** (*Colloq.*) one whose photograph is pinned up on the wall; hence, any good-looking girl [O.E. *pinn*, a peg].

pin·a·fore (pin′·ạ·fōr) *n.* an apron for a child or young girl [E. *pin* and *afore*].

pince·nez (pans′·nā) *n.* a pair of eyeglasses fixed to the nose by a spring clip [Fr. *pincer*, to pinch; *nez*, the nose].

pin·cers (pin′·sẹrz) *n.pl.* a tool for gripping, composed of two limbs crossed and pivoted; nippers; pliers; the claw of a lobster, crab, etc. [Fr. *pincer*, to pinch)].

pinch (pinch) *v.t.* to nip or squeeze, e.g. between the thumb and finger; to stint; to make thin, e.g. by hunger; (*Slang*) to steal; to arrest; *v.i.* to press hard; to be miserly; *n.* as much as can be taken up between the thumb and finger; a nip; an emergency. **-ed** *a.* (*Fig.*) thin and hungry looking [Fr. *pincer*].

Pin·dar (pin′·dẹr) *n.* great lyric poet of ancient Greece (522-443 B.C.). **Pindaric** (pin·dar′·ik) *a.* pert. to the poet or his poetry; *n.* an imitation of one of his odes.

pine (pīn) *n.* a coniferous tree with evergreen, needlelike leaves; wood of this tree; (*Colloq.*) a pineapple. **-y, piny** *a.* **-apple** *n.* tropical plant and its fruit resembling a pine cone; the ananas; (*Mil. Slang*) a hand grenade. **— cone** *n.* fruit of the pine [*L. pinus*].

pine (pīn) *v.t.* to waste away from grief, anxiety, want, etc.; to languish; to wither; to desire eagerly [O.E. *pinian*, fr. *pin*, pain].

pin·fold (pin′·fōld) *n.* a pound; enclosure for stray cattle [for *pindfold* = pound-fold].

ping (ping) *n.* the sound that a bullet makes **—pong** *n.* table tennis [imit.].

pin·ion (pin′·yạn) *n.* the outermost joint of a bird's wing; wing; feather; a small wheel with teeth working into the teeth of a larger wheel; *v.t.* to cut off the pinion; to restrain by binding arms to body; to shackle [O.Fr. *pignon*].

pink (pingk) *n.* a carnation, a garden flower of various colors; a light crimson color; that which is supremely excellent; *a.* of a pale crimson color [etym. uncertain].

pink (pingk) *v.t.* to pierce with small holes; to pierce with a sword, etc.; to ornament the edge with notches, etc. [M.E. *pinken*, to prick].

pink (pingk) *v.t.* of a motor engine, to make a metallic, knocking sound [imit.].

pin·na (pin′·ạ) *n.* a feather; the fin of a fish. **-te, -ted** *a.* feather-shaped; having wings or fins [L.*pinna*, for *penna*, a feather].

pin·na·cle (pin′·ạ·kl) *n.* a slender turret elevated above the main building; a rocky mountain peak; a summit; (*Fig.*) the climax [L. *pinna*, a feather, a battlement].

pint (pīnt) *n.* a liquid and a dry measure equal to ½ quart [Fr. *pinte*].

pin·to (pin′·tō) *n.* a piebald horse [Sp.].

pi·o·neer (pī·ạ·nēr′) *n.* one who originates anything or prepares the way for others; *v.i.* to open a way or originate; an explorer; (*Mil.*) one of an advance body clearing or repairing a road for troops [Fr. *pionnier*, fr. *pion*, a foot-soldier].

pi·ous (pī′·ạs) *a.* having reverence and love for God; marked by pretended or mistaken devotion;**-ly** *adv.* [L. pius].

pip (pip)*n.* the seed of an apple, orange, etc. **-less** *a.* [*abbrev.* fr. *pippin*].

pip (pip) *n.* a disease in the mouth of fowls [L.L. *pipita*, fr. *pituita*, phlegm].

pip (pip) *n.* a rootstock of a plant; (*Radio*) each of the six shrill notes broadcast as a time signal.

pipe (pīp) *n.* a tubular instrument of music; any long tube; a tube of clay, wood, etc. with a bowl for smoking; a bird's note; a pipeful of tobacco; a pipe-like vein of ore; *pl.* bagpipes; *v.t.* to perform on a pipe; to utter in a shrill tone; to convey by means of pipes; to ornament with a piping or fancy edging; *v.i.* to play on a pipe, esp. the bagpipes; to whistle. **piped** (pīpt) *a.* furnished with a pipe; tubular; conveyed by pipes. **piping** *a.* giving forth a shrill sound; *n.* the act of playing on a pipe; a system of pipes (for gas, water, etc.); a kind of cord trimming for ladies' dresses; ornamentation made on cakes **— clay** *n.* a fine, whitish clay used in the manufacture of tobacco pipes; *v.t.* to whiten with pipe clay. **— line** *n.* a long line of piping for conveying water, oil, etc. [O.E. *pipe*, fr. L. *pipa*].

pi·pette (pi·pet′) *n.* a thin, glass tube used for withdrawing small quantities of a liquid from a vessel [Fr. dim. of *pipe*].

pip·it (pĭp′·it) *n.* small bird resembling the lark [imit.].

pip·pin (pip′·in) *a.* one of several kinds of apple [O.Fr. *pepin*, a seed].

pi·quant (pē′·kạnt) *a.* agreeably pungent to the taste; arousing interest. **-ly** *adv.* **piquancy** (pē′·kạn·si·) *n.* [Fr. *piquer*, to prick].

pique (pēk) *v.t.* to irritate; to hurt the pride of; to displease; to stimulate; to pride oneself. *pr.p.* **piquing.** *pa.p.* and *pa.t.* **piqued** (pēkt); *n.* annoyance from a slight; vexation [Fr. *piquer*, to prick].

pi·qué (pi·kā′) *n.* a ribbed cotton fabric [Fr.].

pi·rate (pī′·rạt) *n.* a sea robber; a vessel manned by sea robbers; a publisher, etc. who infringes copyright; *v.t.* and *v.i.* to act as a pirate; to plunder; to publish or reproduce regardless of copyright. **piratical** *a.* **piratically** *adv.* **piracy** *n.* [Gk. *peirates*, fr. *peiraein*, to attempt].

pir·ou·ette (pir·o͝o·et′) *n.* a spinning round on the toes of one foot; *v.i.* to do this [Fr.].

pis·ca·tol·o·gy (pis·kạ·tál′·ạ·ji·) *n.* the study of fishing. **piscator** (pis·kā′·tor) *n.* an angler; a fisherman. **piscatorial, piscatory** *a.* pert. to fishermen or fishing. [L. *piscis*, a fish].

Pis·ces (pis′·ēz) *n.pl.* (*Astron.*) the Fishes, the twelfth sign of the zodiac [L. *piscis*, a fish].

pis·ci·na (pis·ī·na) *n.* a stone basin near the altar. **-l** *a.* [L. *piscis*, a fish].

pis·cine (pis′·īn) *a.* pert. to fishes [L.].

pis·ta·chi·o (pis·ta′(tā′)·shi·ō) *n.* the nut of an Asiatic tree, whose kernel is used for flavoring [Sp. fr. Gk. *pistakion*].

pis·til (pis′·tl) *n.* the seed-bearing organ of a flower, consisting of the stigma, style, and ovary. **-late** *a.* having a pistil but sometimes no stamen [L. *pistillum*, a pestle].

pis·tol (pis′·tl) *n.* a small handgun; *v.t.* to shoot with a pistol [Fr. *pistole*].

pis·ton (pis′·tạn) *n.* a closely fitting metal disk moving to and fro in a hollow cylinder, e.g. as in a steam engine, automobile, etc. **— rod** *n.* a rod which connects the piston with another part of the machinery [It. *pistone*, fr. L. *pinsere*, *pistum*, to pound].

pit (pit) *n.* a deep hole in the ground, esp. one from which coal etc. is dug or quarried; the abyss of hell; a hollow or depression; an area for cock-fighting, etc.; in the theater, the section for musicians in front of stage; in motor racing, the base where cars are refilled, etc.; *v.t.* to mark with little hollows, as by pustules; to place in a pit; to put forward as an antagonist in a contest. *pr.p.* **-ting.** *pa.p.* and *pa.t.* **-ted;** *a.* marked with small hollows. **-fall** *n.* a pit lightly covered, intended to entrap animals; any hidden danger [O.E. *pytt*, fr. L. *puteus*, a well].

pit·a·pat (pit′·ạ·pat) *adv.* in a flutter; with palpitation; *n.* a light, quick step; *v.i.* to go pitapat. *pr.p.* **-ting.** *pa.p.*, *pa.t.* **-ted** [reduplication of *pat*].

pitch (pich) *n.* a thick, black, sticky substance obtained by boiling down tar; *v.t.* to cover over, smear with pitch. **-iness** *n.* **—black, —dark** *a.* very dark [L. *pix*].

pitch (pich) *v.t.* to throw, toss, fling; to set up (a tent, camp, wickets, etc.); (*Music*) to set the keynote of; *v.i.* to alight; to fix one's choice on (with 'on'); to plunge or fall forward; to slope down; of a ship, to plunge. *n.* the act of tossing or throwing; a throw or toss; steepness of a roof; downward slope; the highest point; the plunging motion of a vessel lengthwise; degree of acuteness of musical note; the distance between consecutive threads of a screw, or between successive teeth of a gear. **-ed** (picht) *a.* **-er** *n.* **-fork** *n.* a fork for tossing hay, etc.; *v.t.* to lift with a pitchfork [form of *pick*].

pitch·er (pich′·er) *n.* a jug; a vessel for pouring liquids, usually with a handle and a lip or spout [L.L. *picarium*, a goblet].

pith (pith) *n.* the soft, spongy substance in the center of plant stems; the essential substance; force or vigor. **-y** *a.* consisting of pith; terse and forceful; energetic. **-ily** *adv.* **-iness** *n.* **-less** *a.* [O.E. *pitha*].

pit·tance (pit′·ạns) *n.* an allowance for living expenses; a very small income [Fr. *pitance*, allowance of food in a monastery].

pi·tu·i·tar·y (pi·tū′·ạ·ter·i·) *a.* pert. to the pituitary gland. **— gland,** a ductless gland at base of the brain, secreting an endocrine influencing growth [L. *pituita*, mucus].

pit·y (pit′·i·) *n.* sympathy or sorrow for others' suffering; a cause of grief or regret; *v.t.* to feel grief or sympathy for. **-ing** *a.* expressing pity. **-ingly** *adv.* **pitiable** *a.* deserving pity. **pitiably** *adv.* **pitiful** *a.* full of pity; tender; woeful; exciting pity. **pitifully** *adv.* **pitifulness** *n.* **pitiless** *a.* feeling no pity; hardhearted. **pitilessly** *adv.* **pitilessness** *n.* **piteous** (pit′·i·ạs) *a.* fitted to excite pity; sad or sorrowful [L. *pietas*, piety].

piv·ot (piv′·ạt) *n.* a pin or shaft on which a wheel or other body turns; that on which important results depend; *v.t.* to turn as on a pivot. **-al** *a.* **-ally** *adv.* [Fr.].

pix·y, pixie (pik′·si·) *n.* a fairy or elf. **pixilated** *a.* amusingly accentric [etym uncert.].

piz·zi·ca·to (pit·si·kȧ′·to) *a.* (*Mus.*) a direction for stringed instruments denoting that the strings be plucked with the fingers [It.].

pla·ca·ble (plak′·ȧ·bl, plā′·kạ·bl) *a.* readily appeased or pacified; willing to forgive. **-ness, placability** *n.* **placate** (plȧk′·āt) *v.t.* to appease, conciliate. **placatory** *a.* [L. *placare*, to appease].

plac·ard (plak′ẹrd) *n.* a written or printed paper posted in a public place. **placard** (plạ·kard′) *v.t.* to post placards [Fr.].

place (plās) *n.* a particular part of space; a spot; a locality; a building; rank; position; priority of position; stead; duty; office or employment; (*Sport*) a position among the first three competitors to finish; *v.t.* to put in a particular spot; to find a position for; to appoint; to fix; to put; to identify. **-d** *a.* in a race, etc., to be first, second, or third at the finish. **— kick** *n.* (*Football*) one made by kicking the ball after it has been placed on the ground for the purpose. **to give place,** to make room for [*L. platea*, a broad street; fr. Gk. *platus*, broad].

pla·cen·ta (plạ·sen′·tạ) *n.* (*Med.*) the soft, spongy substance (expelled from the womb after birth) through which the mother's blood nourishes the fetus; (*Bot.*) the part of the plant to which the seeds are attached. **-l** *a.* [L. = a flat cake].

plac·id (plas′·id) *a.* calm; peaceful. **-ly** *adv.* **-ity** *n.* mildness; sweetness; serenity [L. *placidus*, fr. *placere*, to please].

plack·et (plak′·it) *n.* a slit at the top of a woman's skirt [Fr. *plaquet*].

pla·gi·a·rize (plā′·ji·ạ·rīz) *v.t.* to steal the words, ideas, etc. of another and use them as one's own. **plagiarism** *n.* the act of plagiarizing; literary theft. **plagiarist** *n.* **plagiary** *n.* [L. *plagiarius*, a kidnapper].

plague (plāg) *n.* a deadly, epidemic, and infectious disease; a pestilence; a nuisance; *v.t.* to vex; to trouble or annoy. *pr.p.* **plaguing.** *pa.p.* and *pa.t.* **-d. plaguy** (plā′·gi·) *a.* [L. *plaga*, a blow].

plaid (plad) *n.* a long, woolen garment, usually with a tartan pattern, worn as a wrap by Scottish Highlanders; *a.* marked with stripes. **-ed** *a.* [Gael. *plaide*].

plain (plān) *a.* evident; clear; unobstructed; not intricate; simple; ordinary; without decoration; not beautiful; level; flat; even; *adv.* clearly; *n.* a tract of level country.**-ly** *adv.* **-ness** *n.* **— sailing** *n.* an unobstructed course of action. **— song** *n.* the traditional chants of the Christian church, sung in unison [L. *planus*, smooth].

plaint (plānt) *n.* (*Poet.*) a lamentation; (*Law*) a statement in writing of the complaint, accusation, etc. **-iff** *n.* the one who sues in a court of law. **-ive** *a.* expressing grief; sad; mournful. **-ively** *adv.* [L. *plungere, planctum*, to lament].

plait (plāt, plat) *n.* a fold; a braid of hair, straw, etc., *v.t.* to interweave strands of hair, straw, etc. Also **pleat** [L. *plicatus*, folded].

plan (plan) *n.* a drawing representing a thing's horizontal section; a diagram; a map; a project; a design; a scheme; *v.t.* to make a plan of; to arrange beforehand. *pr.p.* **-ning** *pa.p.* and *pa.t.* **-ned** [L. planus, flat].

plane (plān) *n.* a flat, level surface; (*Geom.*) a surface such that, if any two points on it be joined by a straight line, that line will lie wholly on the surface; *a.* perfectly level; pert. to, or lying in, a plane. **— geometry,** branch of geometry which deals with plane, not solid, figures [L. *planus*, level].

plane (plān) *n.* abbrev. of 'airplane'; the wing of an airplane or glider; *v.i.* to glide [Fr. *planer*, to hover].

plan·et (plan'·ạt) *n.* a celestial body revolving round the sun (e.g. Venus, Mars, etc.) as distinct from the fixed stars. **-arium** (plan·ạ·te'·ri·ạm) *n.* a working model of the planetary system; a projected representation of the heavens on a dome. **-ary** *a.* pert. to planets; of the nature of a planet; erratic; wandering; (*Astrol.*) under the influence of a planet. **-oid** *n.* a minor planet [Gk. *planētēs*, wanderer].

plan·gent (plan'·jạnt) *a.* of sound, vibrating; resounding. **plangency** *n.* [L. *plangere*, to beat].

plan·ish (plan'·ish) *v.t.* to make smooth or flat by light hammering; to flatten between rollers. **-er** *n.* [L. *planus*, level].

plank (plangk) *n.* a thick, heavy board; an article of policy in a political program; *v.t.* to lay with planks. **-ing** *n.* planks collectively [L. *planca*].

plank·ton (plangk'·tạn) *n.* (*Biol.*) the minute animal and vegetable organisms floating in the ocean [Gk. *planktos*, wandering].

plant (plant) *n.* a living organism belonging to the vegetable kingdom, generally excluding trees and shrubs; a slip or cutting; machinery, tools, etc., used in an industrial undertaking; (*Slang*) a swindle, hoax, trick; *v.t.* to set in ground for growth; to implant (ideas, etc.). **-ation** (plan·tā'·shạn) *n.* large estate for growing a certain crop. **-er** *n.* one who plants; the owner of a plantation [O.E.].

plaque (plak) *n.* a thin, flat, ornamental tablet hung on a wall or inserted into a wall or furniture [Fr.].

plash (plash) *n.* a puddle; a splashing sound; *v.i.* to dabble in water. **-y** *a.* [Dut. *plassen*, to splash].

plas·ma (plaz'·mạ) *n.* (*Biol.*) protoplasm; the fluid part of the blood, as opposed to the corpuscles. Also **plasm. -tic, plasmic** *a.* [Gk. *plasma*, fr. *plassein*, to form or mold].

plas·ter (pas'·tẹr) *n.* a composition of lime, water, and sand, for coating walls; gypsum, for making ornaments, molds, etc.; (*Med.*) an adhesive, curative application; (*Surg.*) a composition used to hold a limb, etc. rigid; *v.t.* to cover with plaster; to smooth over or conceal. **-er** *n.* [Gk. *plassein*, to mold].

plas·tic (plas'·tik) *a.* capable of molding or of being molded; pliable; capable of change; *n.* a substance capable of being molded; a group of synthetic products derived from casein, cellulose, etc. which may be molded into any form. **plasticity** (plas·tis'·ạ·ti·) *n.* quality of being plastic. **— art,** the art of representing figures in sculpture or by modeling in clay. **— surgery,** the art of restoring lost or damaged parts of the body by grafting on sound tissue [Gk. *plassein*, to mold].

Plas·ti·cine (plas'·ti·sēn) *n.* modeling material easily manipulated [Trademark].

plat (plat) *n.* map [fr. *plot*].

plate (plāt) *n.* a shallow, round dish from which food is eaten; a plateful; a flat, thin sheet of metal, glass, etc.; (*Dentistry*) a thin sheet of vulcanic, or metal, to hold artificial teeth; (*Photog.*) short for 'photographic plate'; a separate page of illustrations in a book; *v.t.* to cover with a thin coating of gold, silver, or other metal; to protect with steel plates, *e.g.* as a ship. **-r** *n.* **— armor** *n.* very heavy, protective armor for warships. **— glass** *n.* thick glass, rolled in sheets and used for windows, mirrors, etc. [Gk. *platus*, broad].

pla·teau (pla·tō') *n.* a tract of level, high ground. *pl.* **plateaus, plateaux** (pla·tōz') [Fr. fr. Gk. *platus*, flat].

plat·en (plat'·ạn) *n.* (*Print.*) the plate which presses the paper against the type; the roller of a typewriter [O.Fr. *platine*, a flat piece].

plat·form (plat'·fawrm) *n.* a wooden structure raised above the level of the floor, as a stand for speakers; a landing area at a railway-station; (*Mil.*) a stage on which a gun is mounted; policy of a political party [Fr. *plate-forme* = flat form].

plat·i·num (plat'·ạ·nạm) *n.* a hard, silvery-white, malleable metal. **platinic, platinous** *a.* **platinoid** *n.* a metal found associated with platinum, e.g. iridium; an alloy of copper, zinc, nickel, and tungsten [Sp. *platina*, fr. *plata*, silver].

plat·i·tude (plat'·ạ·tūd) *n.* a commonplace remark; dullness of writing or speaking. **platitudinous** *a.* [Fr. fr. Gk. *platus*, flat].

Pla·to (plā'·tō) *n.* a famous Greek philosopher (427-347 B.C.). **Platonic** (plạ·tàn'·ik), **-nical** *a.* pert. to Plato or to his philosophy. **-nism** *n.* the doctrines of Plato. **-nist** *n.* **Platonic love,** spiritual affection between man and woman without sexual desire.

pla·toon (plạ·to͝on') *n.* (*Mil.*) a small body of soldiers employed as a unit [Fr. *peloton*, a knot, a ball].

plat·ter (plat'·ẹr) *n.* a large, shallow plate or dish [Fr. *plat*, a dish].

plat·y·pus (plat'·a·pas) *n.* a small, aquatic, furred animal of Australia; the duckbill [Gk. *platus*, flat; *pous*, a foot].

plau·dit (plaw'·dit) *n.* enthusiastic applause. **-ory** *a.* expressing approval [L. *plaudere*, to clap the hands].

plau·si·ble (plaw'·zạ·bl) *a.* having the appearance of being true; apparently right; fair-spoken. **plausibly** *adv.* **plausibility** *n.* [L. *plaudere*, to praise].

play (plā) *v.t.* and *i.* to move with light or irregular motion; to frolic; to flutter; to amuse oneself; to take part in a game; to gamble; to act a part on the stage; to perform on a musical instrument; to operate; to trifle with; *n.* a brisk or free movement; activity; action; amusement; fun; frolic; sport gambling; a dramatic piece or performance. **-er** *n.* **-able** *a.* **-ful** *a.* fond of play or fun; lively. **-fully** *adv.* **-bill** *n.* a bill or poster to advertise a play. **-boy** *n.* a habitual pleasure-seeker. **-fellow** *n.* a playmate. **-ground** *n.* an open space or courtyard for recreation. **-house** *n.* a theater. **-mate** *n.* a companion in play.**-pen** *n.* a portable enclosure for small children to play in. **-thing**

n. a toy. **playwright** (plā′•rīt) *n.* a writer of plays; a dramatist. **-ing card** *n.* one of a set of cards, usually 52 in number, used in card games [O.E. *plegan,* to play].

plea (plē) *n.* (*Law*) the defendant's answer to the plaintiff's declaration; an excuse; entreaty [Fr. *plaider,* to plead].

plead (plēd) *v.t.* to allege in proof or vindication; (*Law*) to argue at the bar; *v.i.* to carry on a lawsuit; to present an answer to the declaration of a plaintiff; to urge reasons in support of or against; to beg or implore. *pa.p.* and *pa.t.* **-ed.** Also (*Colloq.*) **pled. -er** *n.* **-ing** *a.* entreating; *n.* the art of conducting a cause as an advocate; entreaty; supplication [Fr. *plaider*].

pleas•ance (plez′•ạns) *n.* a pleasure garden [L. *placere,* to please].

please (plēz) *v.t.* to excite agreeable sensations or emotions in; to gratify; to delight; to satisfy; *v.i.* to give pleasure; used as *abbrev.* of 'if you please,' in a polite request. **pleasant** (plez′•ạnt) *a.* fitted to please; cheerful; lively; merry; agreeable. **pleasantly** *adv.* **pleasantness** *n.* **pleasantry** (plez′•ạnt•ri•) *n.* playfulness in conversation; a joke; a humorous act; *pl.* **pleasantries. pleasing** (plē′•zing) *a.* agreeable; gratifying. **pleasingly** *adv.* **pleasingness** *n.* **pleasure** (plezh′•ẹr) *n.* agreeable sensation or emotion; gratification of the senses or mind; amusement, diversion, or self-indulgence; choice; a source of gratification. **pleasurable** *a.* **pleasurably** *adv.* [L. *placere,* to please].

pleat (plēt) *n.* a flattened fold fastened in position; *v.t.* to make pleats [var. of *plait*].

ple•be•ian (pli•bē′•an) *a.* pert. or belonging to the common people; vulgar; uncultured; *n.* a common person [L. *plebs,* common people].

pleb•i•scite (pleb′•i•sīt, pleb′•i•sit) *n.* a vote of the whole community or nation [L. *plebis citum,* a decree of the plebs].

plec•trum (plek′•trạm) *n.* a small device used for plucking the strings of a mandalin, etc. Gk. *plēktron,* fr. *plēssein,* to strike].

pledge (plej) *n.* something deposited as a security; a sign or token of anything; a drinking to the health of; a solemn promise; *v.t.* to deposit in pawn; to leave as security; to engage for, by promise or declaration; to drink the health of [O.Fr. *plege*].

ple•na•ry (plē′•nạ•ri•, ple′•nạ•ri•) *a.* full, entire, complete; unqualified; (for an assembly) fully attended.**plenarily** *adv.* **plenariness** *n.* **plenipotentiary** (plen•ạ•pạ•ten′•shạ•ri•) *n.* an ambassador with full powers; *a.* possessing full powers.**plenitude** (plen′•ạ•tūd) *n.* fullness; abundance [L. *plenus,* full; *potens,* potent].

plen•ty (plen′•ti•) *n.* a full supply; abundance; quite enough; sufficiency. **plenteous** (plen′•ti•ạs) *a.* copious; abundant; rich. **plenteously** *adv.* **plentiful** *a.* abundant; ample. **plentifully** *adv.* [L. *plenus,* full].

ple•num (plē′•nạm) *n.* space as considered to be full of matter (opposed to *vacuum*); a condition of fullness [L. *plenus,* full].

pleth•o•ra (pleth′•ạ•ra) *n.* an excess of red corpuscles in the blood; superabundance. **plethoric** *a.* [Gk. *plethōra,* fullness].

pleu•ra (ploo′•rạ) *n.* (*Med.*) the membrane lining the chest and covering the lungs. *pl.* **-e. -l** *a.* **pleurisy** *n.* (*Med.*) inflammation of the pleura [Gk. *pleura,* the side].

plex•us (pleks′• ạs) *n.* a network, esp. of nerves, blood vessels, fibers, etc. **plexal** *a.* [L. = a twining].

pli•a•ble (plī′•ạ•bl) *a.* easily bent; easily influenced. Also **pliant** (plī′•ạnt). **pliably, pliantly** *adv.* **pliability, pliancy** *n.* [L. *plicare,* to fold].

pli•ca (plī′•kạ) *n.* a fold. **-te, -ted** *a.* (*Bot.*) folded; pleated [L. *plicare,* to fold].

pli•ers (plī′•ẹrz) *n.pl.* small pincers with a flat grip [fr. *ply,* to bend].

plight (plīt) *n.* a state or condition of a distressing kind; predicament [L. *plicare,* to fold; O.E. *plit,* a fold or plait].

plight (plīt) *v.t.* to pledge, as one's word of honor; to betroth [O.E. *pliht,* risk].

plinth (plinth) *n.* a square slab, forming the base of a column; the projecting band running along the foot of a wall [Gk. *plinthos,* a brick].

plod (plȧd) *v.t.* to tread with a heavy step; *v.i.* to walk or work laboriously; to toil or drudge *pr.p.* **-ding** *pa.t., pa.p.* **-ded** [imit].

plot (plȧt) *n.* a small patch of ground; a plan of a field, farm, etc. drawn to scale; the plan of a play, novel, etc.; a secret scheme; a conspiracy. *v.t.* to draw a graph or plan of; to plan or scheme. *v.i.* to conspire. *pr.p.* **-ting** *pa.t., pa.p.* **-ted** [O.Fr. *pelote* clod; *Fr.* complot].

plov•er (pluv′•ẹr) *n.* one of various kinds of wading birds [L. *pluvia,* rain].

plow (plou) *n.* an implement with a heavy cutting blade for turning up the soil; *v.t.* to turn up with the plow; to furrow; to advance laboriously; *v.i.* to till the soil with a plow. **-share** *n.* the heavy iron blade of a plow [O.E. *ploh*].

pluck (pluk) *v.t.* to pull off; to pick, as flowers; to strip off feathers, as a fowl; to snatch, or pull with sudden force; *n.* a pull or jerk; the act of plucking; courage or spirit. **-y** *a.* brave; spirited. **-iness** *n.* [O.E. *pluccian*].

plug (plug) *n.* anything used to stop a hole; a cake of compressed tobacco; (*Elect.*) a device for connecting and disconnecting of a circuit; *abbrev.* for spark plug; *v.t.* to stop with a plug; to insert a plug in; (*Slang*) to shoot; (*Slang*) to advertise a song or tune by having it played constantly; *v.i.* (*Colloq.*) to keep doggedly at work (with 'at'). *pr.p.* **-ging.** *pa.p.* and *pa.t.* **-ged** [Dut].

plum (plum) *n.* a round or oval fruit; the tree that bears it; a particularly good appointment or position; a dark purplish color [O.E. *plume*].

plum•age (plȯȯ′•mij) *n.* a bird's feathers, collectively [Fr. fr. L. *pluma,* a feather].

plumb (plum) *n.* a weight of lead attached to a line, and used to determine perpendicularity; the perpendicular position; *a.* perpendicular; *adv.* perpendicularly; (*Colloq.*) utterly, absolutely; *v.t.* to adjust by a plumb line; to sound or take the depth of water with a plummet. **-er** (plum′•ẹr) *n.* one who installs or repairs water and sewage systems. **-ic** *a.* (*Chem.*) containing lead. **-ing** (plum′•ing) *n.* the trade of a plumber; the system of water and sewage pipes in a building. **— line** *n.* a weighted string for testing the perpendicular. **— bob** *n.* the weight at the end of this line [L. *plumbum,* lead].

plum•ba•go (plum•bā′•gō) *n.* black lead; graphite [L. *plumbum,* lead].

plume (plȯȯm) *n.* a feather or tuft of feathers; a crest on a helmet; a token of honor; *v.t.* to furnish with plumes; (*Fig.*) to boast of [L. *pluma,* a feather].

plum•met (plum′•it) *n.* a plumb bob; a weight; *v.i.* to fall like a dead weight [L. *plumbum,* lead].

plump (plump) *a.* of rounded form; moderately fat. **-ness** *n.* [Dut. *plomp,* blunt].

plump (plump) *v.i.* to fall or sit down heavily and suddenly; to vote for one candidate; *v.t.* to drop or throw abruptly; *a.* direct; abrupt; downright; *adv.* heavily; abruptly; bluntly; *n.* a sudden fall [perh. imit. origin].

plu•mule (plȯȯ′•mūl) *n.* a small, downy feather; [L. *pluma,* a feather].

plun•der (plun′•dẹr) *v.t.* to rob systematically;

to take by force; *n.* the act of robbing by force; property so obtained. [Ger. *plündern*].

plunge (plunj) *v.t.* to thrust forcibly into; to immerse suddenly in a liquid; *v.i.* to throw oneself headlong into; (*Colloq.*) to gamble recklessly; *n.* the act of plunging; a dive; a sudden rush. **-r** *n.* one who plunges; a solid, cylindrical rod used as a piston in pumps [Fr. *plonger*, fr. L. *plumbum*, lead].

plu·per·fect (plòò′·pur·fikt) *a.* (*Gram.*) of a tense, expressing action completed before another action in the past [L. *plus quam perfectum*, more than perfect].

plu·ral (ploo′·rạl) *a.* more than one; (*Gram.*) denoting more than one person or thing; *n.* (*Gram.*) a word in its plural form. **-ly** *adv.* **-ism** *n.* (*Philos.*) doctrine that existence has more than one ultimate principle. **-ist** *n.* **-istic** *a.* **-ity** *n.* large number; a majority of votes; state of being plural [L. *plus*, more].

plus (plus) *n.* symbol of addition (+); positive quantity; extra quantity; *a.* to be added; (*Math.*, *Elect.*, etc.) positive; *prep.* with the addition of. **— fours** *n.pl.* wide knickers worn by golfers [L. *plus*, more].

plush (plush) *n.* a fabric with a long, velvet-like nap [Fr. *peluche*, fr. L. *pilus*, hair].

Plu·to (plòò′·tō) *n.* (*Myth.*) god of the lower world; the planet farthest from the sun. **-nic rocks** (*Geol.*) name given to igneous rocks formed by action of intense subterranean heat. **-nium** *n.* a metal of high atomic weight made by bombarding atoms of uranium with neutrons.

plu·toc·ra·cy (plòò·tȧk′·rạ·si·) *n.* government by the wealthy class. **plutocrat** *n.* a wealthy person. **plutocratic** *a.* [Gk. *ploutos*; wealth; *kratein*, to rule].

plu·vi·al (plòò′·vi·ạl) *a.* pert. to rain; rainy. Also **pluvious** [L. *pluvia*, rain].

ply (plī) *v.t.* to wield; to work at steadily; to use or practice with diligence; to urge; *v.i.* to work steadily; of a boat, etc. to run regularly between fixed places [fr. *apply*].

ply (plī) *n.* a fold; a strand of yarn; thickness. *pl.* **plies. -wood** *n.* board made of two or more thin layers of wood cemented together [Fr. *plier*, to fold, fr. L. *plicare*].

pneu·mat·ic (nū·mat′·ik) *a.* pert. to air or gas; inflated with wind or air; operated by compressed air. **-s** *n.pl.* the branch of physics dealing with the mechanical properties of gases [Gk. *pneuma*, breath].

pneu·ma·tol·o·gy (nū·mạ·tȧl′·ạ·ji·) *n.* the doctrine of spiritual existences [Gk. *pneuma*, spirit; *logos*, a discourse].

pneu·mo·nia (nū·mō′·ni·ạ) *n.* acute inflammation of a lung [Gk. *pneuma*, breath].

poach (pōch) *v.t.* to cook eggs, by breaking them into a pan of boiling water [Fr. *pocher*].

poach (pōch) *v.t.* and *i.* (*chiefly Brit.*) to take game or fish from another's property without permission. **-er** *n.* [Fr. *poche*, a pocket].

pock (pȧk) *n.* pustule on skin, as in smallpox. **— mark** *n.* pit left in skin by pock [O.E. *poc*, a pustule].

pock·et (pȧk′·it) *n.* a small pouch or bag inserted into a garment; a cavity or hollow; (*Mil.*) isolated area held by the enemy; *v.t.* to put in the pocket; to take surreptitiously, esp. money; to accept without resentment, as an insult. **— battleship** *n.* a heavily armored, high-powered, German battleship, of not more than 10,000 tons. **-book** *n.* a small bag or case for holding money or papers. **— money** *n.* money for small, personal expenses, e.g. allowance to child. **in pocket,** having funds [Fr. *pochette*, dim, of *poche*, pouch].

pod (pȧd) *n.* a seed vessel of a plant, esp. a legume, as peas, beans, etc.

po·em (pō′·ạm) *n.* a composition in verse; any composition written in elevated and imaginative language; opp. to 'prose.' **poesy** *n.* poetry. **poetically** *adv.* **poetics** *n.* principles of art of poetry; criticism of poetry. **poetry** (pō′·it·ri·) *n.* language of imagination expressed in verse; metrical composition. **poetaster** (pō′·it·as·tẹr) *n.* a would-be poet; a petty rhymster. **poeticize, poetize** *v.t.* and *i.* to treat poetically; to write poetry. **poetic justice,** ideal justice, in which crime is punished and virtue rewarded. **poetic license,** latitude in grammar or facts, allowed to poets. **poet laureate,** official poet [Gk. *poiēma*, fr. *poiein*, to make].

poign·ant (poin′·ạnt, poin′·yạnt) *a.* acutely painful; strongly appealing; pungent. **-ly** *adv.* **poignancy** *n.* [L. *pungere*, to prick].

point (point) *n.* sharp or tapering end of anything; dot or mark; dot in decimal system; punctuation mark; full stop; (*Geom.*) that which has position but no magnitude; item or detail; gist of argument; striking or effective part of a speech, story, etc.; moment of time; purpose; physical quality in animals, esp. for judging purposes; (*Geog.*) headland; one of the 32 direction marks of a compass; unit of scoring in certain games; (*Print.*) unit of measurement of size of type (72 points = 1 inch); a fine lace made with a needle; *v.t.* to sharpen; to give value, force, etc. to words, etc.; to aim or direct; to fill up joints with mortar; to punctuate; *v.i.* to show direction or position by extending a finger, stick, etc.; of a dog, to indicate the position of game by standing facing it. **-ed** *a.* having a sharp point; direct; telling; aimed; (*Archit.*) pert. to the style having pointed arches, i.e. Gothic. **-edly** *adv.* **-edness** *n.* **-less** *a.* having no point; blunt; irrelevant; insipid. **-er** *n.* **-ing** *n.* punctuation; filling the crevices of walls with mortar. **—blank** *a.* aimed horizontally; straightforward; *adv.* at short range [L. *punctum*, fr. *pungere*, to prick].

poise (poiz) *v.t.* to place or hold in a balanced or steady position; *v.i.* to be so held; to hover; to balance; *n.* equilibrium; carriage of the head, body, etc.; self-possession [L. *pendere*, to weigh].

poi·son (poi′·zn) *n.* any substance which kills or injures when introduced into a living organism; that which has an evil influence on health or moral purity; *v.t.* to give poison to; to infect; to corrupt. **-er** *n.* **-ous** *a.* having a deadly or injurious quality; corrupting. **-ously** *adv.* **— ivy** *n.* a vine which, if touched, causes a skin rash. **—pen** *n.* writer of malicious, anonymous letters [L. *potio*, potion].

poke (pōk) *v.t.* to push or thrust against with a pointed object, e.g. with a finger, stick, etc.; to thrust in; to tease; *v.i.* to make thrusts; to pry; to dawdle; a thrust or push; a woman's bonnet with a projecting brim. **-r** *n.* a metal rod for stirring the fire. **poky** *a.* small; slow [M.E. *poken*].

poke (pōk) *n.* (*Dial.*) a sack; a small bag [Fr. *poche*, a pocket].

pok·er (pō′·kẹr) *n.* a card game in which the players bet on the value of their hands. **—faced** *a.* having an expressionless face.

po·lar (pō′·lẹr) *a.* pert. to, or situated near, the North or South Poles; pert. to the magnetic poles (points on the earth's surface where a magnetic needle dips vertically); pert. to either pole of a magnet; directly opposed; having polarity. **-ity** (pō·lar′·ạ·ti·) *n.* the state of being polar; the condition of having opposite poles; the power of being attracted to one pole, and repelled from the other. **— bear**, a large, white bear, found in the Arctic regions [Gk. *polos*, a pivot].

po·lar·ize (pō′·lạ·rīz) *v.t.* to give polarity to; (*Elect.*) to reduce the electromotive force (E.M.F.) of a primary cell by the accumulation of certain electrolytic products on the plates; (*Chem.*) to separate the positive and negative charges on a molecule; (*Light*) to confine the vibrations of light waves to certain directions, e.g. to a plane. **polarization** *n.* **polaroid** *n.* [fr. *polar*].

pole (pōl) *n.* a long, rounded piece of wood or metal; a measure of length = 5½ yards; a measure of area = 30¼ square yards; *v.t.* to propel with a pole. **— jump** *n.* in athletics, a jump over a high bar with the help of a long pole [L. *palus*, a stake].

pole (pōl) *n.* either of the ends of the axis of a sphere, esp. of the earth (in the latter case called the North Pole and South Pole); either of the opposite ends or terminals of a magnet, electric battery, etc. **-star** *n.* the North Star; a guide; an indicator [Gk. *polos*, a pivot].

Pole (pōl) *n.* a native of Poland. **Polish** *a.* pert. to Poland or the Poles.

pole·axe (pōl′·aks) *n.* a battle axe with a long handle. [E. *poll*, the head, and *axe*].

pole·cat (pol′·kat) *n.* a small, carnivorous animal, resembling the weasel; a skunk [O.Fr. *pole*, a hen (fr. its preying on poultry)].

po·lem·ic (pō·lem′·ik) *a.* controversial; disputatious; *n.* controversy; controversialist. **-s** *n.pl.* art of controversy; controversial writings or discussions, esp. religious. Also **polemical** *a.* **polemically** *adv.* [Gk. *polemos*, war].

po·lice (pạ·lēs′) *n.* the civil force which maintains public order; the members of the force; *v.t.* to control with police; to keep in order. **-man, — officer** *n.* (*fem.* **-woman**) member of a police force. **— court** *n.* a court for the trial of minor offenses. **— station** *n.* the headquarters of the police [Gk. *polis*, a city].

pol·i·cy (pál′·ạ·si·) *n.* a course of action adopted, esp. in state affairs; prudent procedure [Gk. *polis*, a city].

pol·i·cy (pál′·ạ·si·) *n.* a document containing a contract of insurance [Gk. *apodeixis*, proof].

pol·i·o·my·e·li·tis (pōl·i·ō·mī·ạ.li′·tis) *n.* (*Med.*) inflammation of the grey matter of the spinal cord; infantile paralysis. *abbrev.* **polio** [Gk. *polios*, grey; *muelos*, marrow].

pol·ish (pál′·ish) *v.t.* to make smooth and glossy; to make polite and cultured; *v.i.* to become polished; *n.* the act of polishing; a smooth, glassy surface; a substance used in polishing; refinement; elegance of manners. **-er** *n.* [Fr. *polir*, fr. L. *polire*].

Pol·ish See **Pole.**

po·lite (pạ·līt′) *a.* elegant in manners; well-bred; courteous; refined. **-ly** *adv.* **-ness** *n.* [L. *politus*, polished].

pol·i·tic (pál′·ạ·tik) *a.* prudent; wise; shrewd; cunning; advisable. **-s** *n.pl.* the art of government; political affairs, life, or principles. **-ly** *adv.* **-al** *a.* pert. to the state or its affairs; pert. to politics. **-ally** *adv.* **politician** (pál·ạ·tish′·ạn) *n.* a holder of a political position; a statesman; a member of a political party. **polity** *n.* civil government; the form or constitution of government. **political economy,** the science dealing with the nature, production, distribution, and consumption of wealth [Fr. *politique*, fr. Gk. *polis*, a city].

pol·ka (pōl′·kạ) *n.* a lively dance of Bohemian origin; music for it [fr. *Polish*].

poll (pōl) *n.* (top of) the head; a register of persons; a list of persons entitled to vote; (the place) of voting; number of votes recorded; *v.t.* to cut off the top of, e.g. tree; to cut short horns of cattle; to canvass; to receive (votes); to cast a vote; *v.i.* to vote. **— tax** *n.* a tax on each person who votes. [Low Ger. *polle*, the head].

pol·lack (pál·ạk) *n.* fresh water fish.

pol·lard (pál′·ẹrd) *n.* a tree on which a close head of young branches has been made by polling; a hornless animal of a normally horned variety. See **poll.**

pol·len (pál′·ạn) *n.* the fertilizing dust of a flower. **pollinate** *v.t.* to fertilize a flower by conveying pollen to the pistil [L. = fine flour].

pol·lute (pạ·lòòt′) *v.t.* to make foul or unclean; to defile; to desecrate. **pollution** *n.* [L. *polluere*].

po·lo (pō′·lō) *n.* a game like hockey played on *horseback;* also **water polo.**

pol·o·naise (pōl·ạ·nāz) *n.* a slow stately dance, of Polish origin; the music for it [Fr. = Polish].

po·lo·ni·um (pạ·lō′·ni·ạm) *n.* a metallic, radio active chemical [fr. *Poland*].

pol·ter·geist (pōl′·tẹr·gīst) *n.* a mysterious spirit believed to create noise and disturbance [Ger. *Polter*, uproar; *Geist*, a ghost].

pol·troon (pál·tròòn′) *n.* a coward. **-ery** *n.* [Fr. *poltron*, fr. It. *poltro*, lazy].

pol·y- *prefix* fr. Gk. *polus*, many words used in derivatives. **polyandry** (pál′·i.an.dri.) *n.* a custom by which a wife has more than one husband. **-androus** *a.* (*Bot.*) having more than 20 stamens. **-chrome** *n.* a picture, statue, etc. in several colors. **-chromatic, -chromic, -chromous** *a.* many-colored.

po·lyg·a·my (pạl·ig′·ạ·mi·) *n.* the practice of having more than one wife at the same time. **polygamous** *a.* **polygamist** *n.* [Gk. *polus*, many; *gamos*, marriage].

pol·y·glot (pál′·i·glát) *a.* pert. to, or speaking, several languages; *n.* a person who speaks several languages; a book, esp. the Bible, in which the text is printed side by side in different languages [Gk. *polus*, many; *glōtta*, the tongue].

pol·y·gon (pál′·i·gán) *n.* a plane figure with more than four sides or angles. **polygonal** *a.* [Gk. *polus*, many; *gōnia*, an angle].

po·lyg·y·ny (pa·lij′·a·ny) *n.* practice of polygamy [See *polygamy*].

pol·y·he·dron (pál·i·hē′·drạn) *n.* (*Geom.*) a solid figure with many faces, usually more than six [Gk. *polus*, many; *hedra*, a base].

pol·y·mor·phous (pál·i·mawr′·fạs) *a.* assuming many forms. Also **polymorphic. polymorphism** *n.* [Gk. *polus*, many; *morphē*, form].

Pol·y·ne·sia (pál·ạ·nē′·zhạ) *n.* (*Geog.*) a group of islands in the S. Pacific, east of Australia. **-n** *a.* [Gk. *polus*, many; *nēsos*, an island].

pol·y·no·mi·al (pál·i·nō′·mi·ạl) *n.* (*Alg.*) a quantity having many terms [Gk. *polus*, many; L. *nomen*, a name].

pol·y·phon·ic (pạl·i·fạn′·ik) *a.* pert. to polyphony. **polyphony** (pạl·if′·ạn·i·) *n.* (*Mus.*) a kind of composition in which melodic strains are simultaneously developed without being subordinate to each other [Gk. *polus*, many; *phonē*, a voice].

pol·y·syl·a·ble (pál·i·sil′·ạ·bl) *n.* a word of three or more syllables. **polysyllabic** *a.* [Gk. *polus*, many, and *syllable*].

pol·y·tech·nic (pál·i·tek′·nik) *a.* pert. to many arts and sciences; *n.* a school or college of applied arts and sciences [Gk. *polus*, many; *technē*, art]

pol·y·the·ism (pál′·i·thē·izm) *n.* belief in the existence of many gods, or in more than one. **polytheist** *n.* **polytheistic** *a.* [Gk. *polus*, many; *theos*, a god].

po·made (pō·mad′) *n.* scented ointment for the hair. Also **pomatum. pomander** *n.* ball of or case for mixture of perfumes [L. Fr. *pommade*].

pome (pōm) *n.* any fruit having a fleshy body, core, etc. like the apple, pear, pomegranate, etc. [L. *pomum*, an apple].

pome·gran·ate (pám′·gra·nit) *n.* a large fruit containing many seeds in a red pulp [L. *pomum*, an apple, *granatum*, having seeds].

pom·er·a·ni·an (pám·ạ·rā′·ni·ạn) *n.* a small

breed of dog with bushy tail, sharp pointed muzzle, pointed ears and long silky hair [fr. *Pomerania*, in Germany].

pom·mel (pum′·ạl) *n.* the knob of a sword hilt; the front part of a saddle; *v.t.* to strike repeatedly, as with the fists [O. Fr. *pomel*, a little apple].

pomp (pȧmp) *n.* splendid display or ceremony; magnificence. **-ous** *n.* showy with grandeur; of a person, self-important; of language, inflated. **-ously** *adv.* **-ousness** *n.* **-osity** *n.* [Gk. *pompē*, a solemn procession].

pom·pa·dour (pȧm′·pạ.dōr) *n.* woman's high swept hairstyle; man's hair style with hair brushed up from forehead [Fr. Marquese de *Pompadour*].

pom·pa·no (pȧm′·pạ·nō) *n.* food fish [Sp.].

pom·pon (pȧm′·pȧn) *n.* the ball of colored wool worn in front of the shako, etc.; small, compact chrysanthemum [Fr.].

pond (pȧnd) *n.* a pool of water, either naturally or artificially enclosed [same as *pound*].

pon·der (pȧn′·dẹr) *v.t.* to weigh in the mind; to consider attentively; *v.i.* to mediate. **-er** *n.* **-ing** *a.* [L. *pondus*, weight].

pon·der·ous (pȧn′·dẹr·ạs) *a.* very heavy; weighty; massive; unwieldy; dull or lacking in spirit. **-ly** *adv.* **-ness** *n.* **ponderosity** *n.*

pon·iard (pȧn′·yẹrd) *n.* a slender dagger [Fr. *poignard*, fr. *poing*, the fist].

pon·tiff (pȧn′·tif) *n.* the Pope; a bishop; a high priest. **pontifical** *a.* belonging to a high priest; popish; pompous and dogmatic; *n.pl.* the garb of a priest, bishop, or pope. **pontifically** *adv.* **pontificate** *n.* the state, dignity, or term of office of a priest, bishop, or pope. [L. *pontifex*, a high priest].

pon·toon (pȧn·to̤on′) *n.* a low, flat-bottomed boat; a support in building a temporary bridge [Fr. fr. L. *pons*, a bridge].

po·ny (pō′·ni.) *n.* a small breed of horse; [O.Fr. *poulenet*, fr. *poulain*, a colt].

poo·dle (po̤o̤′·dl) *n.* one of a breed of dogs with thick, curly hair, often clipped into ornamental tufts [Ger. *Pudel*].

pooh (po̤o̤) *interj.* an exclamation of scorn or contempt. **pooh-pooh** *v.t.* to express contempt.

pool (po̤o̤l) *n.* a small body of still water; a deep place in a river [O.E. *pol*].

pool (po̤o̤l) *n.* the collective stakes in various games; the place where the stakes are put; a variety of billiards; a combination of capitalists to fix prices and divide into a common fund; *v.i.* to form a pool [Fr. *poule*, a hen].

poop (po̤o̤p) *n.* the stern of a ship; raised deck at the stern [L. *puppis*, the stern].

poor (poor) *a.* having little or no money; without means; needy; miserable; wretched; unfortunate; feeble; deserving of pity; unproductive; of inferior quality. **-ly** *adv.* inadequately; with little or no success; without spirit; *a.* (*Colloq.*) somewhat ill; out of sorts. **-ness** *n.* **—spirited** *a.* cowardly; mean. **-house** *n.* an institution for lodging the poor at public expense [L. *pauper*, poor].

pop (pȧp) *n.* an abrupt, small explosive sound; a shot; an effervescing drink; *v.i.* to make a sharp, quick sound; to go or come unexpectedly or suddenly; to dart; *v.t.* to put or place suddenly; *adv.* suddenly. *pr.p.* **-ping** *pa.p.* and *pa.t.* **-ped.** **-corn** *n.* Indian corn exposed to heat causing it to burst open. **-gun** *n.* a child's toy gun for shooting pellets, etc. by the expansion of compressed air [imit. origin].

Pope (pōp) *n.* the Bishop of Rome and head of the R.C. Church. **popish** (pō′·pish) *a.* pert. to the Pope or the papacy. **-dom** *n.* the office, dignity, or jurisdiction of the Pope. [L. *papa*, father].

pop·in·jay (pȧp′·in.jā) *n.* a vain, conceited fellow [O.Fr. *papegai*, a parrot].

pop·lar (pȧp′·ler) *n.* a tree noted for its slender tallness [L. *populus*].

pop·lin (pȧp′·lin) *n.* a corded fabric of silk, cotton, or worsted [etym. uncertain].

pop·py (pȧp′·i·) *n.* a bright flowered plant, one species of which yields opium [L. *papaver*, a poppy].

pop·py·cock (pȧp′·i·kȧk) *n.* nonsense.

pop·u·lace (pȧp′·yạ·lis) *n.* the common people; the masses. **populate** *v.t.* to people. **population** *n.* the total number of people in a country, town, etc. **populous** *a.* thickly inhabited [L. *populus*, the people].

pop·u·lar (pȧp′·yạ·lẹr) *a.* pert. to the common people; liked by the people; finding general favor; easily understood. **-ly** *adv.* **-ize** *v.t.* to make popular; to make familiar, plain, easy, etc. to all. **-ization** *n.* **-ity** *n.* public favor [L. *populus*, the people].

por·ce·lain (pōrs′·lin, pōr′·sạ·lin) *n.* the finest kind of earthenware—white, glazed and semi-transparent; china; *a.* made of porcelain [It. *porcellana*, a delicate shellfish].

porch (pōrch) *n.* a covered entrance to a doorway; a veranda [L. *porticus*, a colonnade].

por·cine (pawr′·sīn) *a.* pert. to, or like, swine; swinish [L. *porcus*, a pig].

por·cu·pine (pawr′·kyạ·pīn) *n.* a large quadruped of the rodent family, covered with spines [L. *porcus*, a pig; *spina*, a spine].

pore (pōr) *n.* a minute opening in the skin for the passage of perspiration. **porous** *a.* full of pores [Gk. *poros*, a passage].

pore (pōr) *v.i.* to look at with steady attention, esp. in reading or studying (with 'over').

pork (pōrk) *n.* the flesh of swine used for food. **-y** *a.* like pork; fat; greasy. **-er** *n.* a hog, fattened for eating. [L. *porcus*, a pig].

por·nog·ra·phy (pawr·nȧg′·rạ·fi·) *n.* obscene literature or pictures. **pornographer** *n.* **pornographic** *a.* [Gk. *pornē*, a harlot; *graphein*, to write].

por·poise (pạr′·pạs) *n.* a blunt-nosed cetacean mammal 5 to 8 feet long, frequenting the northern seas; a dolphin [L. *porcus*, a hog; *piscis*, a fish].

por·ridge (pawr′·ij) *n.* (*Brit.*) a soft breakfast food [form of *pottage*].

por·rin·ger (pawr′·in·jẹr) *n.* a small bowl for porridge [Fr. *potager*, a soup-basin].

port (pōrt) *n.* a harbor; a town with a harbor; a haven; a refuge [L. *portus*].

port (pōrt) *n.* the way in which a person carries himself; *v.t.* (*Mil.*) to carry (a rifle) slanting upwards in front of the body. **-ly** *a.* dignified in appearance; corpulent [L. *portare*, to carry].

port (pōrt) *n.* a strong, sweet, dark-red wine [fr. *Oporto*, Portugal].

port (pōrt) *n.* the left side of a ship, looking towards the bow.

port·a·ble (pōr′·tạ.bl)) *a.* capable of being easily carried. **portability** *n.* [L. *portare*, to carry].

por·tage (pōr′·tij) *n.* the act of carrying or transporting goods; the charge for transport; [L. *portare*, to carry].

por·tal (pōrt′·ạl) *n.* a gate or entrance. [Fr. *portail*, fr. L. *porta*, a gate].

por·tend (pōr·tend′) *v.t.* to foretell; to give warning in advance; to be an omen of. **portent** *n.* an omen, esp. of evil. **portentous** *a.* serving to portend; omnious [L. *portendere*, to foretell].

por·ter (pōr′·tẹr) *n.* a door- or gatekeeper; railway sleeping-car attendant [L. *porta*, gate].

por·ter (pōr′·tẹr) *n.* one employed to carry baggage, esp. at stations or hotels. **-age** *n.* fee for hire of a porter.

por·ter·house (pōr′·tẹr·house) *n.* place where beer (porter) was served. **— steak** choice cut of beef next to the sirloin [L. *portare*, to carry].

port·fo·li·o (pōrt·fō′·li·ō) *n.* case for holding loose documents, drawings, etc.; office of a minister of state [L. *portare,* to carry; *folium,* a leaf].

port·hole (pōrt′·hōl) *n.* window in side of ship [L. *porta,* gate].

por·ti·co (pōr′·ti·kō) *n.* (*Archit.*) a row of columns in front of the entrance to a building; a covered walk [L. *porticus*].

por·tion (pōr′·shạn) *n.* a piece; a part; a share; a helping of food; destiny; lot; a dowry; *v.t.* to divide into shares; to give a dowry to. **-less** *a.* [L. *portio*].

por·tray (pōr·trā′) *v.t.* to represent by drawing, painting, acting, or imitating; to describe vividly in words. **-al** *n.* the act of portraying; the representation. **-er** *n.* **portrait** (pōr′·trāt) *n.* picture of a person, esp. of the face; a graphic description of a person in words. **portraiture** *n.* the art of portrait painting [L. *protrahere,* to draw forth].

Por·tu·guese (pōr′·chạ·gēz′) *a.* pert. to Portugal, its inhabitants, or language.

pose (pōz) *n.* attitude or posture of a person, natural or assumed; a mental attitude or affectation; *v.t.* to place in a position for the sake of effect; to lay down or assert; *v.i.* to assume an attitude; to affect or pretend to be of a certain character [Fr. *poser,* to place].

pose (pōz) *v.t.* to puzzle; to embarrass by a difficult question. **-r** *n.* [short fr. *oppose*].

pos·it (pȧz′·it) *v.t.* to place or set in position; to lay down as a fact or principle [L. *ponere, positum,* to place].

po·si·tion (pạ·zish′·ạn) *n.* place; situation; the manner in which anything is arranged; posture; social rank or standing; employment [L. *ponere positum,* to place].

pos·i·tive (pȧz′·ạ·tiv) *a.* formally laid down; clearly stated; absolute; dogmatic; of real value; confident; not negative; plus; (*Math.*) pert. to a quantity greater than zero; (*Gram.*) denoting the simplest value of an adjective or adverb; (*Colloq.*) utter; downright; *n.* the positive degree of an adjective or adverb, i.e. without comparison; in photography, a print in which the lights and shadows are not reversed (as in the negative). **-ly** *adv.* **-ness** *n.* **positivism** *n.* the philosophical system which recognizes only matters of fact and experience. **positivist** *n.* a believer in this doctrine. **— pole,** of a magnet, the north-seeking-pole. **— sign,** the sign (+ read *plus*) of addition [L. *ponere, positum,* to place].

pos·i·tron (pȧz′·ạ·trān) *n.* particle differing from an electron in that it has positive electrical charge; a **posi**tive elec**tron.**

pos·se (pȧs′·i·) *n.* a company or force, usually with legal authority; men under orders of the sheriff, maintaining law and order [L. *posse,* to be able].

pos·sess (pạ·zes′) *v.t.* to own or hold as property; to have as an attribute; to enter into and influence, as an evil spirit or passions. **-ed** *a.* influenced, as by an evil spirit; demented. **-ion** *n.* the act of possessing; ownership; actual occupancy; the state of being possessed; the thing possessed. **-ive** *a.* denoting possession; *n.* (*Gram.*) the possessive case or pronoun. **-ively** *adv.* **-or** *n.* [L. *possidere, possessum,* to possess].

pos·si·ble (pȧs′·ạ·bl) *a.* capable of being or of coming into, being; feasible. **possibly** *adv.* **possibility** *n.* [L. *possibilis*].

pos·sum (pȧs′·sạm) *n.* (*Colloq.*) an opossum. **to play possum,** to feign; to pretend; to deceive [fr. *opossum*].

post (pōst) *n.* a piece of timber or metal, set upright as a support; a prop or pillar; *v.t.* to attach to a post or wall, as a notice or advertisement. **-er** *n.* one who posts bills; a large placard for posting [L. *postis*].

post (pōst) *n.* a fixed place; a military station or the soldiers occupying it; an office or position of trust, service, or emolument; a trading settlement; formerly, a stage on the road for riders carrying mail; *v.t.* to station or place; *v.i.* to inform; to travel with speed. **-age** *n.* the cost of conveyance by mail. **-al** *a.* pert. to the post office or mail service. **-man** *n.* one who delivers mail. **-mark** *n.* a post office mark which cancels the postage stamp and gives place and time of mailing. **-master** *n.* the manager of a post office. **-master general** *n.* the chief of the post office department of a government. **— card** *n.* a stamped card on which a message may be sent through the mail. **-haste** *adv.* with great speed. **— office** *n.* an office where letters and parcels are received for distribution; the government postal department. **-age stamp** *n.* an adhesive stamp, affixed to mail to indicate payment [L. *ponere,* to place].

post- (pōst) *adv.* and *prefix* fr. L. *post,* after, behind, used in many compound words. **-date** *v.t.* to put on a document, letter, etc., a date later than the actual one. **-diluvian** *a.* living or happening after the Flood. **-graduate** *a.* of academic study, research, etc., undertaken after taking a university degree. **-impressionism** *n.* a movement in painting, sculpture, etc. which aims at artistic self-expression, or subjective as opposed to objective representation of things. **—mortem** *a.* after death; *n.* the dissection of a body after death; an autopsy. **-natal** *a.* after birth. **-primary** *a.* of education, beyond the elementary school.

pos·te·ri·or (pȧs·ti′·ri·ẹr) *a.* coming after; situated behind; later; hinder; *n.* the rump. **-ly** *adv.* **-ity** *n.* the state of being later or subsequent. **posterity** (pȧs·ter′·ạt·i·) *n.* future generations [L. *posterus,* behind].

pos·tern (pōs′·tẹrn) *n.* a back door or gate; *a.* rear; private [L. *posterus,* behind].

post·hu·mous (pȧs′·chạ·mạs) *a.* born after the death of the father; published after the death of the author; occurring after death. **-ly** *adv.* [L. *postumus,* last, but confused with L. *humus,* the ground].

pos·til·ion, postillion (pōs·til′·yạn) *n.* the rider mounted on the near horse of a team drawing a carriage [Fr. *postillon*].

post·pone (pōst·pōn′) *v.t.* to put off till a future time; to defer; to delay. **-ment** *n.* **-r** *n.* [L. *post,* after; *ponere,* to place].

post·pran·di·al (pōst·pran′·di·ạl) *a.* after-dinner [L. *post,* after; *prandium,* repast].

post·script (pōst′·skript) *n.* something added to a letter after the signature; *abbrev.* **P.S.** [L. *post,* after; *scribere, scriptum,* to write].

pos·tu·late (pȧs′·chạ·lāt) *v.t.* to assume without proof; to lay down as self-evident; to stipulate; *n.* a prerequisite; a proposition assumed without proof. **postulant** *n.* one who makes a request or petition; a candidate, esp. for admission to a religious order. **postulation** *n.* [L. *postulare,* to demand].

pos·ture (pȧs′·chẹr) *n.* the position of a body, figure, etc. or of its several members; attitude; *v.i.* to assume an artificial or affected attitude. **postural** *a.* [L. *ponere, positum,* to place].

po·sy (pō′·zi·) *n.* a bouquet; a flower [*poesy*].

pot (pȧt) *n.* a rounded vessel of metal, earthenware, etc., used for cooking, holding fluids. plants, etc.; the contents of a pot; (*Slang*) a large sum of money; *v.t.* to plant in pots; to preserve (as jam, chutney, etc.). *pr.p.* **-ting.** *pa.p.* and *pa.t.* **-ted. -bellied** *a.* corpulent.**-hole** *n.* cavity formed in rock by action of stones in the eddy of a stream; a hole in the roadway. **-luck** *n.* whatever may happen to have been provided for a meal. **-shot** *n.* a shot at random [O.E. *pott*].

po·ta·ble (pō′·tạ·bl) *a.* drinkable. **potation**

n. a drinking; a draft [L.*potare,* to drink].

pot·ash (pȧt′·ash) *n.* a powerful alkali obtained from wood ashes. **potassium** *n.* metallic base of potash [*pot* and *ash*].

po·ta·to (pạ.tā′.tō) *n.* an edible tuber widely grown for food. *pl.* **-es** [Sp. *patata*].

po·tent (pō′·tnt) *a.* having great authority or influence; powerful; mighty; procreative. **-ly** *adv.* **potency** *n.* moral or physical power; influence; energy; efficacy. **-ate** *n.* one who possesses power; a monarch. **-ial** (pạ.ten′. shạl) *a.* latent; existing in possibility but not in actuality; *n.* inherent capability of doing anything; (*Elect.*) the level of electric pressure. **-ially** *adv.* **-iality** (pạ.ten.shi.al′.ạ. ti.) *n.* possibility as distinct from actuality. **-ial difference** (*Elect.*) the difference of pressure between two points; voltage [L. *potens,* powerful, fr. *posse,* to be able].

poth·er (pȧTH′·ẹr) *n.* disturbance; fuss; *v.i.* and *v.t.* to harass; to worry [etym. uncertain].

po·tion (pō′·shạn) *n.* a dose, esp. of liquid, medicine, or poison [fr. L. *potare,* to drink].

pot·pour·ri (pō·poo·rē′) *n.* a mixture of dried rose petals, spices, etc.; a musical or literary medley [Fr. *pot,* a pot; *pourri,* rotten].

pot·tage (pȧt′·ij) *n.* soup or stew; (*Bib.*) a dish of lentils [Fr. *potage,* soup].

pot·ter (pạt′.ẹr) *n.* a maker of earthenware vessels. **-y** *n.* pots, vessels, etc. made of earthenware; the place where it is made; the art of making it [fr. *pot*].

pouch (pouch) *n.* a small bag or sack; a bag-like receptacle in which certain animals, e.g. the kangaroo, carry their young; *v.t.* to pocket; to cause to hang like a pouch [Fr. *poche,* a pocket].

poult (pōlt) *n.* a young fowl. **poultry** (pōl′. tri.) *n.* domestic fowls. **-erer** *n.* a dealer in poultry [Fr. *opulet,* a chicken].

poul·tice (pōl′.tis) *n.* a hot, moist mixture applied to a sore, etc.; *v.t.* to apply a poultice to [L. *puls,* porridge].

pounce (pouns) *v.i.* to spring upon suddenly; to swoop; *n.* a swoop or sudden descent.

pounce (pouns) *n.* a fine powder used to prevent ink from spreading on unsized paper; a powder used for dusting over perforations in order to trace a pattern; *v.t.* to sprinkle with pounce [L. *pumex,* pumice].

pound (pound) *n.* a measure of weight (*abbrev.* **lb.**), 16 ounces avoirdupois, or 12 ounces troy; a unit of British money (*abbrev.* **£**), **-age** *n.* charge of so much per pound. **-al** *n.* a unit of force [L. *pondus,* weight].

pound (pound) *v.t.* and *i.* to beat or strike; to crush to pieces or to powder; to walk, run, etc., heavily [O.E. *punian*].

pound (pound) *n.* an enclosure for animals; *v.t.* to shut up in one [O.E. *pund*].

pour (pōr) *v.i.* to come out in a stream, crowd, etc.; to flow freely; to rain heavily; *v.t.* to cause to flow, as a liquid from a vessel; to shed; to utter [etym. unknown].

pout (pout) *v.i.* to thrust out the lips, as in displeasure, etc.; to look sullen or sulky; *n.* the act of pouting; a protrusion of the lips. **-er** *n.* one who pouts; a pigeon with the power of inflating its crop [etym. uncertain].

pov·er·ty (pȧv′.ẹr.ti.) *n.* the state of being poor; poorness; lack of means [L. *pauperlas,* fr. *pauper,* poor].

pow·der (pou′.dẹr) *n.* dust; a solid matter in fine dry particles; a medicine in this form; short for gunpowder, face powder, etc.; *v.t.* to reduce to powder; to pulverize; to sprinkle with powder; *v.i.* to fall into powder; to crumble. **-y** *a.* like powder. **— magazine** *n.* a place where ammunition is stored. [Fr. *poudre,* fr. L. *pulvis,* dust].

pow·er (pou′.ẹr) *n.* a capacity for action, physical, mental, or moral; energy; might; agency or motive force; authority; one in authority; influence or ascendancy; a nation; mechanical energy; (*Math.*) the product arising from the continued multiplication of a number by itself. **-ful** *a.* having great power; capable of producing great effect. **-fully** *adv.* **-fulness** *n.* **-less** *a.* **-lessly** *adv.* **-lessness** *n.* **-house, — station** *n.* a building where electric power is generated [O.Fr. *poer*].

pow·wow (pou′.wou) *n.* orig. a feast, dance, or conference among N. American Indians; hence, any conference [N. Amer. Ind.].

pox (pȧks) *n.* a disease attended with pustules on the skin, as smallpox, chickenpox, etc.; syphilis [orig. pl. of *pock*].

prac·tice (prak′.tis) *n.* performance or execution, as opposed to theory; custom or habit; systematic exercise for instruction; training; exercise of a profession. **practice** or **practise** *v.t.* to put into action; to do frequently or habitually; to exercise a profession; to exercise in; to train; *v.i.* to perform certain acts customerily; to exercise a profession. **practicable** (prak′.ti.kạ.bl) *a.* capable of being accomplished or put into practice; capable of being used, e.g. a weapon, a road, etc. **practicably** *adv.* **practicableness** *n.* **practicability** *n.* **practical** *a.* pert. to practice or action; capable of being turned to account; useful; virtual. **practically** *adv.* **practicalness** *n.* **practicality** *n.* **practitioner** (prak.tish′.ạn.ẹr) *n.* one engaged in a profession, esp. law or medicine [Gk. *praktikos,* concerned with action].

prag·mat·ic, pragmatical (prag.mat′.ik, .i.kạl) *a.* pert. to state affairs; concerned with practical consequences; matter-of-fact; officious or meddlesome. **-ally** *adv.* **-alness** *n.* **pragmatize** *v.t.* to represent an imaginary thing as real. **pragmatism** *n.* a philosophy based on the conception that the truth of a doctrine is to be judged by its practical consequences. **pragmatist** *n.* [Gk. *pragmatikos,* pert. to business].

prai·rie (pre′.ri.) *n.* a large tract of grassland, destitute of trees. **— chicken** *n.* grouse. **— dog** *n.* a small burrowing rodent. **— schooner** *n.* a covered wagon. **— wolf** *n.* the coyote [Fr. fr. L. *pratum,* a meadow].

praise (prās) *v.t.* to express approval or admiration; to glorify; *n.* approval of merit; commendation; worship. **—worthy** *a.* deserving of praise [O.Fr. *preiser*].

pra·line (prȧ′.lēn) *n.* a candy made by roasting almonds in boiling sugar [Fr. fr. *Duplessis-Praslin,* who first made it].

prance (prans) *v.i.* to spring or bound like a high-spirited horse; to swagger; to caper, esp. of children; *n.* a prancing movement. *n.*

pran·di·al (pran′.di.ạl) *a.* pert. to dinner [L. *prandium,* lunch].

prank (prangk) *n.* a mischievous trick; a practical joke.

prate (prāt) *v.t.* and *i.* to talk idly; to utter foolishly; *n.* chatter. **prattle** *n.* [M.E. *praten*].

prawn (prawn) *n.* an edible crustacean of the shrimp family [etym. unknown].

prax·is (prak′.sis) *n.* practice; a set of examples for practice [Gk. fr. *prassein,* to do].

pray (prā) *v.i.* to ask earnestly; to entreat; to petition; *v.i.* to make a request or confession, esp. to God; to commune with God. **-er** *n.* one who prays; the act of praying; an earnest entreaty; the words used; the thing asked for; a petition **-erful** *a.* devout [L. *precari*].

pre- *prefix* fr. L. *prae,* before, beforehand, used with many nouns and verbs.

preach (prēch) *v.i.* and *t.* to deliver a sermon; to speak publicly on a religious subject, esp. as a clergyman; to advocate. **-er** *n.* **-ment** *n.* a sermon, esp. one of exaggerated solemnity [L. *praedicare,* to proclaim].

pre·am·ble (prē′.am.bl) *n.* the introductory

part of a discourse, story, document, etc.; a preface [L. *praeambulus*, walking before].

pre·ar·range (prē·ạ·rānj′) *v.t.* to arrange beforehand. **-ment** *n.*

pre·car·i·ous (pri·ka′·ri·ạs) *a.* depending on the will or pleasure of another; depending on circumstances; uncertain; dangerous; perilous. **-ly** *adv.* **-ness** *n.* [L. *precarius*, obtained by entreaty].

pre·cau·tion (pri·kaw′·shạn) *n.* care taken beforehand; *v.t.* to forewarn. **-ary** *a.* characterized by precaution.

pre·cede (prē·sed′) *v.t.* to go before in place, time, rank, or importance. **-nt** *a.* preceding; **-nt** (pre′·sạ·dạnt) *n.* something done, or said, that may serve as an example in similar cases. **-ntly** *adv.* **-nce** (prē·sē′·dạns) *n.* the act of preceding; priority in position, rank, or time. **preceding** *a.* [L. *prae*, before; *cedere*, to go].

pre·cen·tor (prē·sen′·tẹr) *n.* one who leads a church choir [L. *prae*, before; *cantor*, a singer].

pre·cept (prē′·sept) *n.* an instruction intended as a rule of conduct, esp. moral conduct; a maxim; a commandment or exhortation; (*Law*) a written warrant or mandate given to an administrative officer. **-ive** *a.* [L. *praecipere, praeceptum*, to order].

pre·ces·sion (prē·sesh′·ạn) *n.* a going before. **-al** *a.* [L. *praecedere*, to go before].

pre·cinct (prē′·singt) *n.* a division of a city for police protection, voting, etc.; a boundary or limit; a minor territorial division. [L. *prae*, before; *cigere*, to gird].

pre·cious (presh′·ạs) *a.* of great value or price; costly; highly esteemed; over-refined; fastidious; *adv.* (*Colloq.*) extremely. **-ly** *adv.* [Fr. *précieux*, fr. L. *pretium*, price].

prec·i·pice (pres′·ạ·pis) *n.* a very steep or perpendicular place, as a cliff-face. **precipitous** *a.* very steep. **precipitously** *adv.* **precipitousness** *n.* [L. *praeceps*, headlong].

pre·cip·i·tate (pri·sip′·ạ·tāt) *v.i.* to throw headlong; to urge on eagerly; to hasten the occurrence of; (*Chem.*) to cause to separate and fall to the bottom, as a substance in solution; of vapor, to condense; *v.i.* (*Chem.*) to fall to the bottom of a vessel, as a sediment; *n.* (*Chem.*) that which is precipitated in a liquid; sediment; *a.* headlong; rash or over-hasty. **-ly** *adv.* **precipitable** *a.* **precipitance, precipitancy** *n.* headlong hurry; rash haste. **precipitant** *a.* falling headlong; too hasty; unexpectedly hastened; *n.* (*Chem.*) a substance which, added to a liquid, decomposes it and precipitates a sediment. **precipitantly** *adv.* **precipitation** (pre·sip·i·tā′·shun) *n.* the act of precipitating; rash haste; a falling headlong; condensation of vapor, rain, snow, etc. [L. *praeceps*, headlong].

pré·cis (prā·sē′) *n.* a concise statement; an abstract or summary [Fr.].

pre·cise (pri·sīs′) *a.* exact; definite; distinct; prim. **-ly** *adv.* **-ness** *n.* **precision** (pre·sizh′·un) *n.* accuracy; definiteness; *a.* done with great accuracy [Fr. *précis*, exact].

pre·clude (pri·klòòd′) *v.t.* to shut out; to hinder; to prevent from happening **preclusion** *n.* **preclusive** *a.* [L. *prae*, before; *claudere*, to shut].

pre·co·cious (pri·kō′·shạs) *a.* (*Bot.*) ripe or developed too soon; having the mental powers or bodily growth developed at an early age; premature; forward. **-ly** *adv.* **-ness, precocity** *n.* [L. *praecox;* early ripe].

pre·con·ceive (prē·kạn·sēv′) *v.t.* to form an opinion or idea of beforehand. **preconception** *n.* a prejudice.

pre·con·cert (prē·kạn·surt′) *v.t.* to settle beforehand.

pre·cur·sor (prē·kur′·sẹr) *n.* a person or thing going before; a forerunner; a harbinger. **-y, precursive** *a.* [L. *prae*, before; *currere*, to run].

pre·da·cious (pri·dā′·shus)*a.* living on prey; predatory. **predatory** (pred′·ạ·tōr·i·) *a.* living by preying on others; plundering; pillaging. Also **predaceous** [L. *praeda*, booty].

pre·date (prē·dāt′) *v.t.* to date earlier than the true date; to antedate [*pre* and *date*].

pred·e·ces·sor (pre·dạ·ses′·ẹr) *n.* one who has preceded another in an office, position, etc. [L. *prae*, before; *decedere*, to withdraw].

pre·des·tine (prē·des′·tin) *v.t.* to destine beforehand; to foreordain. **predestinate** *v.t.* to determine beforehand; to foreordain. **predestination** *n.* (*Theol.*) the doctrine that the salvation or damnation of individuals has been foreordained by God; the determination beforehand of future events; destiny; fate. **predestinarian** *n.* a believer in this doctrine.

pre·de·ter·mine (prē·di·tur′·min) *v.t.* to determine beforehand. **predeterminate** *a.* determined beforehand. **predetermination** *n.*

pred·i·ca·ble (pred′·i·kạ·bl) *a.* able to be predicated or affirmed; *n.* anything that can be affirmed of something. **predicability** *n.* [L. *praedicare*, to proclaim].

pre·dic·a·ment (pri·dik′·ạ·mạnt) *n.* an awkward plight; a trying situation [L. *praedicare*, to proclaim].

pred·i·cate (pred′·i·kāt) *v.t.* to affirm; to assert; to declare; (pred′·i·kạt) *n.* that which is predicated; (*Gram.*) a statement made about the subject of the sentence. **predication** *n.* **predicative** *a.* **predicatively** *adv.* [L. *praedicare*, to proclaim].

pre·dict (prē·dikt′) *v.t.* to tell beforehand; to foretell; to prophesy. **-able** *a.* **-ion** *n.* the act of foretelling; prophecy. **-ive** *a.* **-or** *r.* [L. *praedicere*, to say before].

pre·di·gest (prē·di·jest′) *v.t.* to subject food to artificial digestion before eating.

pre·di·lec·tion (prē·di·lek′·shạn) *n.* a prepossession of mind in favor of something; partiality [L. *prae*, before; *dilectus*, chosen].

pre·dis·pose (prē·dis·pōz′) *v.t.* to incline beforehand; to give a tendency or bias to; to render susceptible to. **predisposition** *n.*

pre·dom·i·nate (pri·dám′·ạ·nāt) *v.i.* to surpass in strength, influence, or authority; to rule; to have ascendancy; to prevail. **predominance, predominancy** *n.* ascendancy; superiority. **predominant** *a.* superior in influence, authority, etc.; having ascendancy. **predominantly** *adv.* [*pre* and *dominate*].

pre·em·i·nent (prē·em′·ạ·nạnt) *a.* distinguished above others; outstanding. **-ly** *adv.* **preeminence** *n.*

pre-emp·tion (prē·em(p)′·shạn) *n.* the act or right of purchasing before others. **pre-empt** (prē·em(p)t′) *v.t.* to appropriate beforehand. [L. *prae*, before; *emptio*, a buying].

preen (prēn) *v.t.* to trim or dress with the beak, as birds do their feathers; to primp [form of *prune*].

pre·ex·ist (prē·ig·zist′) *v.i.* to exist beforehand, or before something else. **-ence** *n.* **-ent** *a.*

pre·fab (prē·fab′) *n.* a prefabricated house.

pre·fab·ri·cate (prē·fab′·rạ·kāt) *v.t.* to build houses and ships in standardized units in factories for rapid assembly. **prefabrication** *n.*

pref·ace (pref′·ạs) *n.* introductory remarks at beginning of book, or spoken before a discourse; foreword; *v.t.* to furnish with a preface. **prefatory** (pref′·ạ·tō·ri·) *a.* introductory [L. *prae*, before; *fari*, to speak].

pre·fect (prē′·fekt) *n.* an ancient Roman magistrate; head of a department. **-orial** *a.* **-ship** *n.* [L. *praefectus*, set before].

pre·fer (pri·fur′) *v.t.* to like better; to choose rather; to promote to an office or dignity. **-able** (pref′·ẹr·ạ·bl) *a.* worthy of preference; more desirable. **-ably** *adv.* **-ence** *n.*

what is preferred; choice. **-ential** (pref.ạ.ren′.shạl) *a.* giving or receiving a preference. **-ment** *n.* advancement or promotion; a position of honor [L. *prae,* before; *ferre,* to bear].

pre·fix (prē′.fiks) *n.* a letter, syllable, or word put at the beginning of another word to modify its meaning, e.g. *pre*digest, *under*ground. **prefix** (prē.fiks′) *v.t.*

preg·na·ble (preg′.nạ.bl) *a.* able to be taken by assault or force [L. *prehendere,* to take].

preg·nant (preg′.nạnt) *a.* being with child; fruitful; full of meaning. **-ly** *adv.* **pregnancy** *n.* [L. *praegnans*].

pre·hen·sile (prē.hen′.sil) *a.* (*Zool.*) capable of grasping [L. *prehendere,* to seize].

pre·his·to·ry (prē.hist′.ẹr.i.) *n.* the period before written records were kept; the study of this period. **prehistoric** *a.*

prej·u·dice (prej′.oo.dis) *n.* an opinion, favorable or unfavorable (more often the latter), formed without fair examination of facts; bias; *v.t.* to bias; to influence; to injure. **prejudicial** (prej.oo.dish′.ạl) *a.* injurious. [L. *prae,* before; *judicium,* judgment].

prel·ate (prel′.ạt) *n.* a bishop, or other church dignitary of equal or higher rank. **prelatic, prelatical** *a.* **prelacy** *n.* the office or dignity of a prelate; government by prelates; episcopacy; bishops collectively. [L. *praelatus,* put before].

pre·lect (prē.lekt′.) *v.i.* to deliver a lecture or discourse in public. **prelection** *n.* a lecture. [L. *prae,* before; *legere, lectum,* to read].

pre·lim·i·nary (pri.lim′.ạ.ner.i.) *a.* introductory; preparatory; *n.* an introduction; a preparatory measure; (often used in *pl.*) [L. *prae,* before; *limen,* a threshold].

prel·ude (prel′.ūd) *n.* an introductory performance or event; a musical introduction; a preliminary; *v.t.* to serve as a prelude or forerunner to. **prelusive, prelusory** *a.* introductory [L. *prae,* before; *ludere,* to play].

pre·ma·ture (prē′.mạ.tūr) *a.* ripe before the natural or proper time; untimely; overhasty. **-ly** *adv.* **-ness, prematurity** *n.*

pre·med·i·tate (prē.med′.ạ.tāt) *v.t.* to consider, or revolve in the mind beforehand.

pre·mier (prē′.myẹr) *a.* first; chief or principal; most ancient; *n.* (*Great Britain, France*) the prime minister. **-ship** *n.* [Fr. fr. *primarius,* of the first rank].

pre·miere (pri.myir′) *n.* a first public performance of a play, etc. [Fr. = first].

prem·ise (pri.mīz′) *v.t.* to set forth beforehand, or as introductory to the main subject; to lay down general propositions on which the subsequent reasonings rest. **premise** (prem′.is) *n.* Also **premiss,** a proposition previously supposed or proved; a proposition from which an inference or conclusion is drawn. *n.pl.* a building with its adjuncts [L. *prae,* before; *mittere, missum,* to send].

pre·mi·um (prē′.mi.ạm) *n.* a prize; a fee paid to learn a trade or profession; money paid for insurance; the amount exceeding the par value of shares of stock. **at a premium,** in great demand [L. *praemium,* reward].

pre·mo·ni·tion (prē.mạ.nish′.ạn) *n.* previous warning; an instinctive foreboding; presentment. **premonitory** *a.* **premonitorily** *adv.* [L. *prae,* before; *monere,* to warn].

pre·na·tal (prē.nā′.tal) *a.* previous to birth.

pre·oc·cu·py (prē.ák′.yạ.pī) *v.t.* to take possession of before another; to engage the attention of. **preoccupied** *a.* occupied previously; engrossed in thought; absorbed in mediation. **preoccupancy** *n.* **preoccupation** *n.*

pre·or·dain (prē.awr.dān′) *v.t.* to ordain beforehand; to foreordain. **preordination** *n.*

prep (prep) *n.* (*Colloq.*) preparatory school.

pre·paid (prē.pād′) *a.* paid in advance.

pre·pare (pri.par′) *v.t.* to make ready for use; to fit for a particular purpose; to provide; to fit out; *v.i.* to make things ready; to make oneself ready. **preparation** (prep.ạ.rā′.shạn) *n.* the act of making ready for use; readiness; a substance, esp. medicine or food, made up for use. **preparative** *a.* tending to prepare for; *n.* anything which serves to prepare. **preparatively** *adv.* **preparatory** *a.* preparing the way; preliminary; introductory. **preparedness** (prạ.par′.ạd.nạs) *n.* [L. *prae,* before; *parare,* to make ready].

pre·pay (prē.pā′) *v.t.* to pay beforehand [*pre* and *pay*].

pre·pon·der·ate (pri.pán′.dẹr.āt) *v.i.* to exceed in power, influence, numbers, etc.; to outweigh. **preponderance** *n.* superiority of power, numbers, etc. **preponderant** *a.* **preponderantly** *adv.* [L. *prae,* before; *pondus, ponderis,* a weight].

prep·o·si·tion (prep.ạ.zish′.ȧn) *n.* (*Gram.*) a word, e.g. *with, by, for,* etc., used before a noun or pronoun to show the relation to some other word in the sentence. **-al** *a.* [L. *prae,* before; *ponere, positum,* to place].

pre·pos·sess (prē.pạ.zes′) *v.t.* to possess beforehand; to influence a person's mind, heart, etc. beforehand; to prejudice favorably. **-ing** *a.* tending to win a favorable opinion; attractive. **-ingly** *adv.* **prepossession** *n.*

pre·pos·ter·ous (pri.pás′.tẹr.ạs) *a.* contrary to nature, truth, reason, or common sense; utterly absurd. **-ly** *adv.* **-ness** *n.* [L. = before, behind, fr. *prae,* before; *posterus,* after].

prep·py (prep′.ē) *n.* a student at a preparatory school; a person who behaves like a preppy; *a.* a neat classic style of dress. **preppily** *adv.* [L. *parare,* to make ready].

pre·rog·a·tive (pri.rág′.ạ.tiv) *n.* an exclusive right or privilege by reason of rank, position, etc. [L. *prae,* before; *rogare,* to ask].

pres·age (pres′.ij) *n.* an indication of what is going to happen; an omen. **presage** (pri.sāj′) *v.t.* to foretell; to forebode; to have a presentiment of. **-ful** *a.* warning [L. *prae,* before; *sagire,* to perceive acutely].

pres·by·o·pi·a (prez.bi.ō′.pi.ạ) *n.* farsightedness (occurring in advancing age) [Gk. *presbutēs,* an old man; *ops.* an eye].

Pres·by·te·ri·an (prez.bi.tir′.i.ạn) *n.* one belonging to Presbyterian Church. **-ism** *n.* **presbytery** *n.* a body of elders; court of pastors [Gk. *presbuteros,* elder, fr. *presbuteros,* elder, fr. *presbus,* old].

pre·sci·ence (pre′.shi.ạns) *n.* knowledge of events before they take place. **prescient** *a.* [O.Fr. fr. L. *praescientia,* foreknowledge].

pre·scribe (pri.skrīb′) *v.t.* to lay down authoritatively for direction; to set out rules for; (*Med.*) to order or advise the use of. **-r** *n.* **prescript** *n.* direction; ordinance. **prescription** (pri.skrip′.shạn) *n.* the act of prescribing or directing; a doctor's direction for use of medicine. **prescriptive** *a.* [L. *praescribere,* to write before].

pres·ent (prez′.ạnt) *a.* being in a certain place; here or at hand; now existing; (*Gram.*) pert. to time that now is; *n.* present time; (*Gram.*) the present tense. **presence** *n.* the state of being present; nearness or proximity; the person of a superior; mien or appearance; apparition. **-ly** *adv.* at once; soon; by and by [L. *praesens,* being present].

pre·sent (pri.zent′) *v.t.* to introduce into the presence of; to exhibit or offer to the notice; to offer as a gift; to bestow; to aim, as a weapon; *n.* (prez′.ạnt) a gift. **-able** *a.* fit to be presented. **-ation** (prez.ạn.tā′.shạn) *n.* the act of presenting; the state of being presented; that which is presented. **-ment** *n.* the act or state of presenting; representation; the laying of a formal statement [L. *praesentare,* to place before].

pre·sen·ti·ment (pri.zen′.tạ.mạnt) *n.* a

previous notion or opinion; anticipation of evil; foreboding.

pre·serve (pri·zurv′) *v.t.* to keep from injury or destruction; to keep in a sound state; *n.* that which is preserved, as fruit, etc.; any medium used in preserving; a place for the preservation of game, fish, etc. **-r** *n.* **preservable** *a.* **preservation** (prez·ẹr·va′·shạn) *n.* the act of preserving or keeping safe; the state of being preserved; safety. **preservative** *n.* that which preserves; *a.* having the power of preserving. **preservatory** *a.* [L. *prae,* before; *servare,* to protect].

pre·side (pri·zīd′) *v.i.* to be chairman of a meeting; to direct; to control; to superintend. **president** (prez′·ạ·dạnt) *n.* the head of a society, company, association, etc.; the elected head of a republic. **presidency** *n.* the office, or term of office, of a president. **presidential** *a.* pert. to a president, his office, dignity, etc. [L. *prae,* before; *sedere,* to sit].

press (pres) *v.t.* to push or squeeze; to crush; to hug; to embrace closely; to drive with violence; to hurry; to urge steadily; to force; to solicit with importunity; to constrain; to smooth by pressure; *v.i.* to exert pressure; to strive eagerly; to crowd; to throng; to hasten; *n.* an instrument or machine for squeezing, compressing, etc.; a printing machine; printing and publishing; newspapers collectively; a crowd; a throng; urgent demands; stress; a cupboard for clothes, etc. **-ing** *a.* urgent; persistent. **— agent** *n.* one employed to advertise and secure publicity for any person or organization. **to go to press,** of a newspaper, to start printing [L. *pressare,* fr. *premere,* to squeeze].

press (pres) *v.t.* to force to serve in the navy or army [L. *praestare,* to furnish].

pres·sure (presh′·ẹr) *n.* the act of pressing; state of being pressed; influence; urgency.

pres·su·ri·za·tion (presh·ẹr·ạ·zā′·shạn) *n.* maintenance of pressure inside aircraft at great altitudes. **pressurize** (presh′·ẹr·īz) *v.t.*

pres·ti·dig·i·ta·tion (pres·tạ·dij·ạ·tā·shạn) *n.* conjuring; sleight of hand. **prestidigitator** *n.* a conjurer (conjuror); a magician [L. *praesto,* ready; *digitus.* a finger].

pres·tige (pres·tēzh′, pres′·tēj) *n.* influence resulting from past achievement, character, reputation, etc. [Fr. = marvel].

pres·to (pres′·tō) *adv.* (*Mus.*) quickly [It. fr. L. *praesto,* ready].

pre·sume (pri·zōōm′) *v.t.* to take for granted; to suppose to be true without proof; to venture; *v.i.* to act in a forward manner; to take liberties. **presumable** *a.* probable. **presumably** *adv.* **presumption** (pri·zum(p)′·shạn) *n.* the act of, or grounds for, presuming; strong probability; that which is taken for granted; arrogance of opinion or conduct; boldness. **presumptive** (pri·zum(p)′·tiv) *a.* presuming; based on probability; that may be assumed as true or valid until the contrary is proved. **presumptively** *adv.* **presumptuous** *a.* forward; taking liberties. *n.* [L. *prae,* before; *sumere,* to take].

pre·sup·pose (prē·sạ·pōz′) *v.t.* to assume or take for granted beforehand.

pre·tend (pri·tend′) *v.t.* to assert falsely; to counterfeit; to make believe; *v.i.* to lay claim (to); to make pretense; to aspire (to) **-er** *n.* one who simulates or feigns; a claimant, esp. to the throne. **pretense** *n.* simulation; the act of laying claim; assumption; pretext. **pretentious** (pri·ten′·shạs) *a.* given to outward show; presumptuous and arrogant. **pretentiously** *adv.* **pretentiousness** *n.* [L. *prae,* before; *tendere,* to stretch].

pre·ter- *prefix* fr. L. *praeter,* meaning beyond, above, more than, etc., used in combining forms. **-natural** (pre·tẹr·nach′·ẹr·ạl) *a.* beyond or different from what is natural.

pret·er·it, preterite (pret′·ẹr·it) *a.* (*Gram.*) past (applied to the tense that expresses past action or state); *n.* (*Gram.*) the preterit or past definite tense [L. *praeter,* beyond; *ire, itum,* to go].

pre·text (prē′·tekst) *n.* ostensible reason or motive which cloaks the real reason; pretense [L. *prae,* before; *texere,* to weave].

pret·ty (prit′·i·) *a.* of a beauty that is charming and attractive, but not striking or imposing; neat and tasteful; pleasing; fine or excellent in an ironical sense; *adv.* in some degree; moderately; fairly; rather. **prettily** *adv.* **prettiness** *n.* [O.E. *praettig,* crafty].

pre·vail (pri·vāl′) *v.i.* to gain the upper hand or mastery; to succeed; to be current; to be in force; to persuade or induce (with 'on' or 'upon'). **-ing** *a.* **prevalent** (prev′·ạ·lạnt) *a.* most generally; extensively existing; rife. **prevalently** *adv.* **prevalence** *n.* [L. *prae,* before; *valere,* to be strong].

pre·var·i·cate (pri·var′·ạ·kāt) *v.i.* to evade the truth. **prevarication** *n.* **prevaricator** *n.* [L. *prae,* before; *varus,* crooked].

pre·vent (pri·vent′) *v.t.* to keep from happening; to stop. **-able** *a.* **-ion** *n.* obstruction; hinderance; preventive. **-ive** *a.* tending to prevent or ward off; *n.* that which prevents; antidote to keep off disease [L. *prae,* before; *venire, ventum,* to come].

pre·view (prē′·vū) *n.* a private showing of works of art, films, etc. before being exhibited in public [*pre* and *view*].

pre·vi·ous (prē′·vi·ạs) *a.* preceding; happening before; (*Slang*) hasty. **-ly** *adv.* **-ness** *n.* [L. *prae,* before; *via,* a way].

pre·vise (pri·viz′) *v.t.* to foresee; to forewarn. **prevision** *n.* foresight; foreknowledge [L. *prae,* before; *videre, visum,* to see].

prey (prā) *n.* any animal hunted and killed for food by another animal; a victim; *v.i.* (with 'on' or 'upon') to seize and devour; to weigh heavily; to pillage [Fr. *proie,* fr. L. *praeda*].

price (prīs) *n.* the amount at which a thing is valued, bought, or sold; value; cost; *v.t.* to fix the price of; to ask the cost of. **-less** *a.* beyond any price. [L. *pretium,* price].

prick (prik) *n.* a sharp-pointed instrument; a puncture made by a sharp point; the act of pricking; a sharp, stinging pain; hence, (*Fig.*) remorse; a spur; *v.t.* to pierce slightly with a sharp point; to incite; to affect with sharp pain; to sting; to erect (the ears). **-er** *n.* [O.E. *prica,* a point].

prick·le (prik′·l) *n.* a small sharp point; a thorn; a spike; a bristle; (*Colloq.*) a pricking feeling; *v.t.* to prick slightly; *v.i.* to feel a tingling sensation. **prickly** *a.* full of prickles; stinging; tingling [O.E. *prica,* a point].

pride (prīd) *n.* the state or quality of being proud; too high an opinion of oneself; worthy self-esteem. **-ful** *a.* **to pride oneself on (upon)**, to be proud of; to take credit for [O.E. *pryte,* fr. *prut,* proud].

priest (prēst) *n.* (*fem.* **-ess**) a clergyman; in R.C. and Episcopal churches; in pagan times, one who officiated at the altar, or performed the rites of sacrifice. **-like, -ly** *a.* **-liness** *n.* **-hood** *n.* [O.E. *preost,* fr. Gk. *presbuteros,* elder].

prig (prig) *n.* a conceited person who professes superiority. **-gish** *a.*

prim (prim) *a.* formal and precise; affectedly nice; prudish. **-ly** *adv.* **-ness** *n.* [O.Fr. fr. L. *primus,* first]

pri·ma (prē′·mạ) *a* first. **— donna,** the principal female singer in an opera. **— facie** (fā′·shi·) at first view. **— facie case,** a case based on sufficient evidence to go to a jury [It. *prima,* first; *donna,* a woman; L. *facies,* appearance].

pri·ma·cy See **primate.**

pri·mal (prī·′mạl) *a.* first, original; chief.

primary *a.* first in order of time, development, importance; preparatory; elementary; *n.* that which stands highest in rank or importance; a preliminary election (often *pl.*); **primarily** *adv.* in the first place. **primary colors,** red, yellow and blue from which other colors may be made [L. *primus,* first].

pri·mate (prī′.māt) *n.* (*Brit.*) the chief dignitary in a church; an archbishop. **primacy** (prī′.mạ.si.) *n.* the chief dignity in a national church; the office or dignity of an archbishop [L.L. *primas,* a chief, fr. *primus,* first].

prime (prīm) *a.* first in time; original; first in degree or importance; foremost; of highest quality; (*Math.*) that cannot be separated into factors; *n.* the earliest stage or beginning; spring; youth; full health or strength; the best portion; *v.t.* to prepare a firearm by charging with powder; to prepare wood with a protective coating before painting it; to fill with water, etc., as a pump, to make it start working; to instruct beforehand. **-r** *n.* one who, or that which, primes, esp. a percussion cap, etc. used to ignite the powder of cartridges, etc.; (prim′.ẹr) a small elementary book used in teaching. **-ly** *adv.* **-ness** *n.* **priming** *n.* the powder, etc. used to fire the charge in firearms. **— minister,** the first minister of state in some countries. **— number,** a number divisible without remainder only by itself or one [L. *primus,* first].

pri·me·val (prī.mē′.vạl) *a.* original; primitive;**-ly** *adv.* [L. *primus,* first; *aevum,* age].

prim·i·tive (prim′.ạ.tiv) *a.* pert. to the beginning or origin; being the earliest of its kind; old-fashioned; plain and rude; (*Biol.*) rudimentary; undeveloped; **-ly** *adv.* **-ness** *n.* [L. *primitivus,* fr. *primus,* first].

pri·mo·gen·i·ture (prī.mạ.jen′.ạ.chẹr) *n.* the state of being the first-born child; the right of the eldest son to inherit his parents' property. **primogenital, primogenitary** *a.* **primogenitor** *n.* the earliest ancestor [L. *primus,* first; *genitor,* a father, fr. *gignere,* to beget].

pri·mor·di·al (prī.mawr′.di.ạl) *a.* existing from the beginning; first in order; primeval [L. *primus,* first; *ordiri,* to begin].

prim·rose (prim′.rōz) *n.* a plant bearing pale-yellow and other colored flowers in spring [M.E. *primerole,* fr. L. *primus,* first].

prince (prins) *n.* (*fem.* **princess**) a ruler or chief; the son of a king or emperor; a title of nobility. **-dom** *n.* the jurisdiction, rank, or estate of a prince. **-ly** *a.* stately; august; dignified. **-liness** *n.* **Prince Consort,** the husband of a reigning queen [L. *princeps,* a prince].

prin·ci·pal (prin′.sạ.pạl) *a.* chief in importance; first in rank, character, etc.; *n.* the chief person in authority; a leader; the head of certain institutions, esp. a school; the chief actor in a crime; a chief debtor; a person for whom another is agent; a sum of money lent and yielding interest. **-ly** *adv.* **-ship** *n.* the office or dignity of a principal. **principality** *n.* the territory or dignity of a prince; sovereignty [L. *principalis*].

prin·cip·i·a (prin.sip′.i.a, pring.kip′.i.ạ) *n.pl.* first principles; beginnings [L. *principium,* a beginning].

prin·ci·ple (prin′.sạ.pl) *n.* a fundamental truth or law; a moral rule or settled reason of action; uprightness; honesty; an element.**-d** *a.* guided by certain rules of conduct [L. *principium,* a beginning].

print (print) *v.t.* to impress; to reproduce words, pictures, etc. by pressing inked types on paper, etc.; to produce in this way; to write in imitation of this; to publish; *n.* an impression or mark left on a surface by something pressed against it; printed fabric; printed lettering; an engraving; a photograph. **-er** *n.* one engaged in the setting of type for, and the printing of books, newspapers, etc. **-ing press** *n.* a machine for reproducing on paper, etc. impressions made by inked type [L. *premere,* to press].

pri·or (prī′.ẹr) *a.* previous; former; earlier; preceding in time; *n.* (*fem.* **-ess**) the superior of a priory; one next in dignity to an abbot. **-ity** (prī.awr′.ạ.ti.) *n.* the state of being antecedent in time; precedence; preference in regard to privilege. **-y** *n.* a religious house, [L. *prior,* former].

prism (prizm) *n.* (*Geom.*) a solid whose bases or ends are any similar, equal, and parallel plane figures, and whose sides are parallelograms; (*Optics*) a transparent figure of this nature, usually with triangular ends. **-atic(al)** *a.* **-atically** *adv.* **prismatic colors,** the seven colors, red, orange, yellow, green, blue indigo, violet, into which a ray of light is separated by a prism [Gk. *prisma; eidos,* form].

pris·on (priz′.n) *n.* building for confinement of criminals; jail; any place of confinement or restraint. **-er** (priz′.nẹr) *n.* one confined in prison; one captured in war [L. *prensio,* fr. *praehendere,* to seize].

pris·tine (pris′.tēn) *a.* belonging to the earliest time; original; pure [L. *pristinus,* fr. *priscus,* of old].

private (prī′.vat) *a.* not public; belonging to or concerning an individual; peculiar to oneself; personal; secluded; secret; of a soldier, not holding any rank; *n.* a common soldier. **-ly** *adv.* **-ness** *n.* **privacy** (prī′.vạ.si.) *n.* the state of being in retirement from company; solitude; seclusion; secrecy [L. *privatus,* fr. *privus,* single].

pri·va·teer (prī.vạ.tir′) *n.* an armed private vessel commissioned by a government to attack enemy ships.

pri·va·tion (prī.vā′.shạn) *n.* the state of being deprived, esp. of something required; destitution; want. **privative** (priv′.ạ.tiv) *a.* causing privation; consisting in the absence of something; denoting negation.

priv·et (priv′.it) *n.* an evergreen shrub.

priv·i·lege (priv′.i.lij) *n.* a special right or advantage; *v.t.* to grant some special favor to. **-d** *a.* enjoying a special right or immunity [L. *privilegium,* private law, fr. *lex,* a law].

priv·y (priv′.i.) *a.* private; admitted to knowledge of a secret; *n.* a person having an interest in a law suit; a latrine. **privily** *adv.* **privity** *n.* private knowledge; connivance. **— to,** secretly informed of. **Privy Council,** (*Brit.*) the council which advises the sovereign on matters of government [Fr. *privé,* fr. L. *privatus,* private].

prize (prīz) *n.* a reward given for success in competition; a reward given for merit; a thing striven for; a thing won by chance, e.g. in a lottery. *v.t.* to value highly; to esteem. **— fight** *n.* a professional boxing match. **— fighter** *n.* [O.Fr. *pris*].

prize (prīz) *n.* an enemy ship or property captured in naval warfare. **— court** *n.* court to adjudicate on prizes captured in naval warfare [Fr. *prise,* a seizing].

pro- (prō) *prefix* fr. L. or Gk. meaning for; instead of; on behalf of; in front of; before; forward; according to.

prob·a·ble (pråb′.ạ.bl) *a.* likely; to be expected; having more evidence for than against. **probably** *adv.* **probability** *n.* likelihood; anything that has appearance of truth [L. *probare,* to prove].

pro·bate (prō′.bāt) *n.* the process by which a last will and testament is legally authenticated after the testator's death; an official copy of a will; *v.t.* to establish the validity of a will [L. *probare,* to prove].

pro·ba·tion (prō.bā′.shạn) *n.* a trial or test of a person's character, conduct, ability, etc.; the testing ,of a candidate before admission to full membership of a body, esp. a religious sect or order; a system of releasing offenders, esp. juveniles, and placing them under supervision of.-**al** *a.* -**ary** *a.* -**er** *n.* a person undergoing probation. **probative** (prō′.bạ.tiv) *a.* pert. to, serving for, or offering, trial or proof [L. *probare*, to prove].

probe (prōb) *n.* (*Med.*) instrument for examining a wound, ulcer, cavity, etc.; an investigation; *v.t.* to explore a wound, etc. with a probe; to examine thoroughly [L. *probare*, to prove].

pro·bi·ty (prō′.bạ.ti.) *n.* integrity; rectitude; honesty [L. *probus*, good].

prob·lem (prȧb′.lẹm) *n.* a matter proposed for solution; a question difficult of solution; a puzzle. -**atical** *a.* questionable; uncertain; disputable; doubtful. -**atically** *adv.* [Gk. *problēma*, a thing thrown before].

pro·bos·cis (prō.bȧs′.is) *n.* an elephant's trunk; the snout of other animals [Gk. fr. *pro*, before; *boskein*, to feed].

pro·ceed (prō.sēd′) *v.i.* to move onward; to advance; to renew progress; to pass from one point or topic to another; to come forth; to carry on a series of acts; to take legal proceedings. -**ing** *n.* going forward; movement or process; *pl.* (*Law*) the several steps of prosecuting a charge, claim, etc.; a record of business done by a society. **proceeds** (prō′.sēdz) *n.pl.* yield; sum realized by a sale. **procedure** (prạ.sē′.jẹr) *n.* act, method of proceeding [L. *procedere*, to go forward].

pro·cess (prȧ′.ses) *n.* continued forward movement; lapse of time; a series of actions or measures; a method of operation; (*Anat.*) a projecting part or growth; (*Law*) procedure; *v.t.* to subject to some process, as food or material. **procession** (prạ., prō.sesh′.ạn) *n.* a moving line of people, cars, animals, etc.; regular progress. -**ional** *a.* pert. to a procession; *n.* a hymn sung during a church procession — **server** *n.* one who serves notices to appear in court [L. *processus*].

pro·claim (prō.klām′) *v.t.* to make known by public announcement; to declare.-**ant**, -**er** *n.* one who proclaims. **proclamation** (prạk.lạ.mā′.shạn) *n.* the act of announcing publicly; an official public announcement [L. *pro*, before; *clamare*, to cry out].

pro·cliv·i·ty (prō.kliv′.ạ.ti.) *n.* inclination; propensity; proneness; aptitude [L. *pro*, forward; *clivus*, a slope].

pro·cras·ti·nate (prō.kras′.tạ.nāt) *v.i.* to put off till some future time. **procrastination** *n.* **procrastinator** *n.* [L. *procrastinare*, fr. *cras*, tomorrow].

pro·cre·ate (prō′.krē.āt) *v.t.* to bring into being; to beget; to generate. **procreation** *n.* **procreative** *a.* having the power to beget; productive. **procreativeness** *n.* **procreator** *n.* [L. *pro*, forth; *creare*, to produce].

proc·tor (prȧk′.tẹr) *n.* (*Law*) one who manages the affairs of another in a court; one who supervises students in an examination; *v.t.* to supervise in an examination. -**ial** *a.* -**ship** *n.* [*abbrev.* of *procurator*].

pro·cum·bent (prō.kum′.bạnt) *a.* lying face down; (*Bot.*) growing along the ground [L. *pro*, forward; *cumbere*, to lie down].

proc·u·ra·tion (prȧk.yạ.rā′.shạn) *n.* management of another's affairs; power of attorney. [L. *pro*, for; *curare*, to see to].

pro·cure (prō.kyoor′)*v.t.* to acquire; to obtain; to get; to bring about; *v.i.* to act as a procurer. **procurable** *a.* obtainable. -**ment** *n.* -**r** *n.* (*fem.* **procuress**) one who procures; one who supplies women for immoral purposes [L. *pro*, for; *curare*, to see to].

prod (prȧd) *v.t.* to poke with something pointed; to goad; *n.* a pointed instrument; a poke, *pr.p.* -**ding.** *pa.p.* and *pa.t.* -**ded.**

prod·i·gal (prȧd′.i.gạl) *a.* wasteful; spending recklessly; *n.* one who spends recklessly; a spendthrift. -**ly** *adv.* -**ity** *n.* reckless extravagance [L. *prodigere*, to squander].

prod·i·gy (prȧd′.i.ji.) *n.* a person or thing causing wonder; a marvel; a very gifted person; a monster; a portent. **prodigious** (prạ.dij′.ạs) *a.* like a prodigy; marvelous; enormous; extraordinary. **prodigiously** *adv.* [L. *prodigium*, a portent or sign].

pro·duce (prạ.dòòs′) *v.t.* to bring forth; to exhibit; to give birth to; to yield; to make; to cause; of a play, to present it on the stage. **produce** (prȧd′.òòs) *n.* that which is produced; product; agricultural products; crops. -**r** *n.* [L. *pro*, forward; *ducere*, to lead].

prod·uct (prȧd′.ạkt) *n.* that which is produced; (*Arith.*) a number resulting from the multiplying of two or more numbers. **production** (prạ.duk′.shạn) *n.* the act of producing; the things produced. -**ive** *a.* having the power to produce; creative; fertile; efficient. -**ively** *adv.* -**iveness**, -**ivity** *n.* [L. *pro*, forward; *ducere*, to lead].

pro·em (prō′.em) *n.* a preface; an introduction. -**ial** *a.* [Gk. *pro*, before; *oimos*, a path].

pro·fane (prō.fān′) *a.* not sacred; irreverent; blasphemous; vulgar; *v.t.* to treat with irreverence; to put to a wrong or unworthy use; to desecrate. -**ly** *adv.* -**ness** *n.* -**r** *n.* **profanation** (prȧf.ạ.nā′.shạn) *n.* the act of violating sacred things. **profanity** (pro.fan′.i.ti.) *n.* profaneness; irreverence; the use of bad language [L. *pro*, before; *fanum*, a temple].

pro·fess (prạ.fes′) *v.t.* to make open declaration of; to confess publicly; to affirm belief in; to pretend to knowledge or skill in. -**ed** *a.* openly acknowledged. -**ion** (prȧ.fesh′.ạn) *n.* the act of professing; that which one professes; occupation or calling, esp. one requiring learning. -**ional** *a.* pert. to a profession or calling; engaged in for money, as opposed to *amateur*; *n.* one who makes a livelihood in sport or games (*abbrev.* **pro**). -**ionally** *adv.* [L. *profiteri*, *professus*, to acknowledge].

pro·fes·sor (prạ.fes′.ẹr) *n.* one who makes profession; a teacher of the highest rank in a university. **professorial** (prō.fạ.sō′.ri.ạl) *a.* -**ially** *adv.* **professoriate** (prō.fạ.sō′.ri.it) *n.* the office of a professor; his period of office; body of professors. -**ship** *n.* [L. *profiteri*, *professus*, *to acknowledge*].

prof·fer (prȧf′.ẹr) *v.t.* to offer for acceptance; -**er** *n.* [L. *proferre*, to bring forward].

pro·fi·cient (prạ.fish′.ạnt) *a.* thoroughly versed or qualified in any art or occupation; skilled; *n.* an expert. -**ly** *adv.* **proficience**, **proficiency** *n.* [L. *proficere*, to be useful].

pro·file (prō′.fil) *n.* an outline or contour; a portrait in a side view; the side face; short biographical sketch; *v.t.* to draw the outline of [L. *pro*, before; *filum*, thread].

prof·it (prȧf′.it) *n.* advantage or benefit; the excess of returns over expenditure; pecuniary gain in any transaction or occupation; *v.t.* to be of service to; *v.i.* to gain advantage; to grow richer. -**able** *a.* yielding profit or gain; advantageous; helpful. -**ably** *adv.* -**ableness** *n.* **profiteer** (prȧf.ạ.tēr′)*n.* one who makes excessive profits; *v.i.* to make such profits [L. *profectus*, fr. *proficere*, to make progress].

prof·li·gate (prȧf′.lạ.gat, .gāt) *a.* abandoned to vice; dissolute; extravagant; *n.* a depraved person. -**ly** *adv.* -**ness** *n.* **profligacy** (prȧf′.li.gạ.si.) *n.* a vicious and dissolute manner of living [L. *profligatus*, ruined].

pro·found (prạ.found′) *a.* deep; intellectually deep; learned; deeply felt. -**ly** *adv.* **profundity** *n.* depth of place, knowledge, skill, feeling [L. *profundus*, deep].

pro·fuse (prạ.fūs′) *a.* giving or given generously; lavish; extravagant. -**ly** *adv.* -**ness**, **profusion** (prạ.fū′.shạn) *n.* great abundance [L. *pro*, forth; *fusum*, to pour].

prog·e·ny (pràj′·ạ.ni.) *n.* descendants; offspring; children. **progenitive** *a.* pert. to the production of offspring. **progenitor** (prō. jen′.i.tẹr) *n.* ancestor; forefather [L. *pro.* before; *gignere,* to beget].

prog·no·sis (pràg.nō′.sis) *n.* a forecast; (*Med.*) foretelling the course of a disease. *pl.* **prognoses. prognostic** (pràg.nàs′.tik) *a.* foretelling; forecasting; predicting; *n.* a forecast; a prediction. **prognosticate** *v.t.* to foretell; to predict; to prophesy. **prognostication** *n.* **prognosticator** *n.* [Gk. *pro,* before; *gnōsis,* knowledge].

pro·gram, programme (prō′.gram) *n.* a plan or detailed notes of intended proceedings at a public entertainment, ceremony, etc.; a party policy at election time [Gk. *pro,* before; *gramma,* a writing].

prog·ress (pràg′.res) *n.* a moving forward; advancement; development. **progress** (prạ. gres′) *v.i.* to move forward; to advance; to develop; to improve. **-ion** (prạ.gresh′.ạn) *n.* the act of moving forward; onward movement; progress. **-ional** *a.* **-ive** *a.* moving forward gradually; advancing; improving; favoring progress or reform. **-ively** *adv.* **-iveness** *n.* **arithmetical progression,** a series of numbers increasing or decreasing by the same amount, e.g. 3, 6, 9, 12, 15, etc. **geometrical progression,** a series of numbers increasing or decreasing by a common ratio, e.g. 3, 9, 27, 81, etc. [L. *progredi, progressus,* to go forward].

pro·hib·it (prō.hib′.it) *v.t.* to forbid; to prevent; to hinder. **-er, -or** *n.* **-ion** (prō.(h)ạ. bish′.ạn) *n.* the act of forbidding; interdict; the forbidding by law of manufacture, importation, sale, or purchase of alcoholic liquors. **-ionist** *n.* one in favor of prohibition. **-ive, -ory** *a.* tending to forbid, prevent, or exclude; exclusive. **-ively** *adv.* [L. *prohibere*].

pro·ject (prạ.jekt′) *v.t.* to throw or cast forward; to plan; to contrive; to throw a photographic image on a screen; *v.i.* to jut out; to protrude. **project** (pràj′.ekt) *n.* a plan; a scheme; a task. **-ile** (prạ.jek′.til) *a.* capable of being thrown; *n.* a heavy missile, esp. a shell or cannon ball. **-ion** *n.* the act of projecting; something that juts out; a plan; delineation; the representation on a plane of a curved surface or sphere; in psychology, mistaking for reality something which is only an image in the mind. **-ive** *a.* **-or** *n.* an apparatus for throwing photographic images, esp. films, on a screen [L. *projicere, propectum,* to throw forward].

pro·lapse (prō′.laps) *n.* (*Med.*) the falling down of a part of the body from its normal position, esp. womb or rectum [L. *prolapsus,* fr. *prolabi,* to fall or slide forward].

pro·lep·sis (prō.lep′.sis) *n.* a figure of speech by which objections are anticipated and answered; an error in chronology, consisting in antedating an event; *pl.* **prolepses. proleptical** *a.* [Gk. *pro,* before; *lēpsis,* a taking].

pro·le·tar·i·an (prō.lạ.te′.ri.ạn) *a.* pert. to the proletariat; belonging to the working class; *n.* one of the proletariat. **proletariat** (prō.lạ.te′.ri.ạt) *n.* propertyless wage-earners who live by sale of their labor [L. *proles,* offspring].

pro·lif·er·ous (prō.lif′.ẹr.ạs) *a.* (*Biol.*) reproducing freely by cell division; developing anthers. **-ly** *adv.* **proliferate** *v.t.* to bear; *v.i.* to reproduce by repeated cell division. **proliferation** *n.* increase [*L. proles,* offspring; *ferre,* to bear].

pro·lif·ic (prạ.lif′.ik) *a.* bringing forth offspring; fruitful, abundantly productive; bringing about results. **-ally** *adv.* [L. *proles,* offspring; *facere,* to make].

pro·lix (prō′.liks) *a.* long drawn out; diffuse; wordy. **-ly** *adv.* **-ity** *n.* [L. *prolixus*].

pro·loc·u·tor (prō.làk′.yạ.tẹr) *n.* a chairman of an assembly [L. *pro; locutus,* to speak].

pro·logue (prō′.lawg) *n.* the preface or introduction to a discourse, poem, book, or performance, esp. the address spoken before a dramatic performance; *v.t.* to preface [Gk. *pro,* before; *logos,* discourse].

pro·long (prō.lawng′) *v.t.* to lengthen out; to extend the duration of. **-ation** *n.* the act of lengthening out; a part prolonged; extension [L. *pro*; *longus,* long].

prom (pràm) *n.* (*Colloq.*) a formal ball [*Abbrev.* of *promenade*].

prom·e·nade (pràm.ạ.nād′, nàd) *n.* a leisurely walk, generally in a public place; a place adapted for such a walk; a march of dancers, as at the opening of a ball or in a square dance; *v.i.* to walk for pleasure, display, or exercise. **-r** *n.* [Fr.].

prom·i·nent (pràm′.ạ.nạnt) *a.* sticking out; projecting; conspicuous; distinguished. **-ly** *adv.* **prominence, prominency** *n.* [L. *prominere,* to jut out].

pro·mis·cu·ous (prạ.mis′.kyoo.ạs) *a.* mixed without order or distinction; indiscriminate. **-ly** *adv.* **-ness, promiscuity** (pràm.is.kū′. ạ.ti.) *n.* [L. *promiscuus,* fr. *miscere,* to mix].

prom·ise (pràm′.is) *n.* an undertaking to do or not to do something; cause or grounds for hope; *v.t.* to give one's word to do or not to do something; to give cause for expectation; to agree to give; *v.i.* to assure by a promise; to give grounds for hope. **-r** *n.* **promisor** *n.* (*Law*) the person by whom a promise is made. **promising** *a.* likely to turn out well or to succeed; hopeful [L. *promittere, promissum,* to promise].

prom·is·so·ry (pràm′.ạ.sōr.i.) *a.* containing a promise. **— note,** written agreement to pay sum to named person at specified date [L. *promittere,* to promise].

prom·on·to·ry (pràm′.ạn.tōr.i.) *n.* a point of high land jutting out into the sea [L. *promontorium,* fr. *mons,* a mountain].

pro·mote (prạ.mōt′) *v.t.* to move forward; to move up to a higher rank or position; to encourage the growth or development of; to help organize a new business venture or company. **-r** *n.* a supporter; an initiator, esp. of a new business venture, etc. **promotion** *n.* advancement; preferment; a higher rank, station, or position. **promotive** *a.* [L. *promovere, promotum,* to move forward].

prompt (pràmpt) *a.* ready and quick to act; done at once; punctual; *v.t.* to excite to action; to suggest; to help out (actor or speaker) by reading, suggesting next words. **-ly** *adv.* **-er** *n.* one who reminds or helps out an actor, speaker, etc. **-itude, -ness** *n.* readiness; quickness of decision and action. [L. *promptus,* fr. *promere,* to put forth].

pro·mul·gate (pràm′.ạl.gāt) *v.t.* to proclaim; to publish; to make known officially. **promulgation** *n.* [L. *promulgare*].

prone (prōn) *a.* lying face downward; sloping; inclined; naturally disposed. **-ly** *adv.* **-ness** *n.* inclination; tendency [L. *pronus*].

prong (pràng) *n.* one of the pointed ends of a fork; a spike [etym. uncertain].

pro·noun (prō.′noun) *n.* (*Gram.*) a word used instead of a noun [*pro* and *noun*].

pro·nounce (prạ.nouns′) *v.t.* to speak with the correct sound and accent; to speak distinctly; to utter formally or officially; to declare or affirm. **-d** *a.* strongly marked; very definite or decided. **-able** *a.* **-ment** *n.* a formal declaration. **-r** *n.* **pronouncing** *a.* teaching or indicating pronounciation. **pronunciation** (prạ.nun.si.ā′.shạn) *n.* the act of uttering with the proper sound and accent; [L. *pronuntiare,* to proclaim].

pron·to (pràn′.tō) *adv.* (*Colloq.*) promptly; quickly [Sp.].

proof (próóf) *n.* something which proves; a test or trial; any process to ascertain correctness, truth, or facts; demonstration; evidence that convinces the mind and produces belief; argument; standard strength of alcoholic spirits; (*Print.*) a trial impression from type, on which corrections may be made; *a.* firm in resisting; impenetrable; serving as proof or designating a certain standard or quality; *v.t.* to render proof against. **-reader** *n.* one who corrects printer's proofs [L. *probare,* to prove].

prop (pråp) *v.t.* to support by placing something under or against; to sustain. *pr.p.* **-ping.** *pa.t., pa.p.* **-ped.** *n.* that which supports; a stay [M.E. *proppe*].

prop·a·gan·da (pråp·a·gan′·dą) *n.* the propagating of doctrines or principles; the opinions or beliefs thus spread; (*R.C.*) a society in Rome charged with the management of missions. **propagandize** *v.t.* and *i.* to spread propaganda. **propagandist** *n.* [fr. L. *de propaganda fide,* concerning the spreading of the faith].

prop·a·gate (pråp′·ą·gāt) *v.t.* to cause to multiply or reproduce by generation; to breed; to spread the knowledge of; to transmit or carry forward; *v.i.* to have young; to breed. **propagator** *n.* **propagation** *n.* [L. *propagare,* to propagate plants by slips].

pro·pel (prą·pel′) *v.t.* to drive forward; to press onward by force; to push. *pr.p.* **-ling.** *pa.p.* **-led. -ler** *n.* one who, or that which, propels; a revolving shaft with blades for driving a ship or airplane [L. *pro,* forward; *pellere,* to drive].

pro·pen·si·ty (prą·pen′·są·ti·) *n.* bent of mind; leaning or inclination [L. *pro,* forward; *pendere, pensum,* to hang].

prop·er (pråp′·ęr) *a.* fit; suitable; correct or according to usage.**-ly** *adv.* **— fraction** (*Arith.*) one in which the numerator is less than the denominator [L. *proprius,* own].

prop·er·ty (pråp′·ęr·ti·) *n.* an inherent or esential quality or peculiarity; ownership; the thing owned; possessions; land; *pl.* theatrical requisites, as scenery, costumes, etc. [L. *proprietas,* fr. *proprius,* own].

proph·e·cy (pråf′·ą·si·) *n.* the foretelling of future events; prediction; revelation of God's will. **prophesy** (pråf′·ą·sī) *v.t.* to foretell; to predict; to utter by divine inspiration; *v.i.* to utter predictions. **prophet** (pråf′·it) *n.* (*fem.* **prophetess**) one who foretells future events; an inspired teacher or revealer of the Divine Will. **prophetic(al)** *a.* [Gk. *prophētēs,* aforespeaker].

pro·phy·lac·tic (prō·fą·lak′·tik) *a.* (*Med.*) tending to prevent disease, preventive; *n.* medicine or treatment tending to prevent disease. **prophylaxis** *n.* preventive treatment of disease [Gk. *phulassein,* to guard].

pro·pin·qui·ty (prō·ping′·kwą·ti·) *n.* nearness in time or place; nearness in blood relationship [L. *propinquitas,* fr. *prope,* near].

pro·pi·ti·ate (pra·pish′·i·āt) *v.t.* to appease; to conciliate; to gain the favor of. **propitiation** *n.* appeasement; conciliation; atonement. **propitiator** *n.* **propitiatory** *a.* serving, or intended, to propitiate. **propitious** (prą·pish′·ąs) *a.* favorable; favorably inclined. **propitiously** *adv.* [L. *propitiare*].

pro·po·nent (prą·pō′·nąnt) *n.* one who supports or makes a proposal [see **propound**].

pro·por·tion (prą·pōr′·shąn) *n.* relative size, number, or degree; comparison; relation; relation between connected things or parts; symmetrical arrangement, distribution, or adjustment; (*Arith.*) equality of ratios; the rule of three; *n.pl.* dimensions; *v.t.* to arrange the proportions of. **-al** *a. n.* a number of quantity in arithmetical or mathematical proportion. **-ally** *adv.* **-ality** *n.* **-ate** *a.* **-ed** *a.* **-ment** *n.* [L. *proportio,* fr. *portio,* a share].

pro·pose (prą·pōz′) *v.t.* to offer for consideration; to suggest; to nominate; *v.i.* to form a plan; to intend; to offer oneself in marriage. **proposal** *n.* the act of proposing; what is offered for consideration; an offer, esp. of marriage. **-r** *n.* **proposition** (pråp·ą·zish′·ąn) *n.* a proposal; a statement or assertion. **propositional** *a.* [L. *proponere,* to put forward].

pro·pound (prą·pound′) *v.i.* to offer for consideration; to propose; to set (a problem) [L. *pro,* forth; *ponere,* to place].

pro·pri·e·tor (prą·prī′·ą·tęr) *n.* (*fem.* **proprietress, proprietrix**) one who is the owner of property, a business, restaurant, etc. **proprietary** *a.* pert. to an owner; made and sold by an individual or firm having the exclusive rights of manufacture and sale. **-ship** *n.* [L. *proprius,* one's own].

pro·pri·e·ty (prą·prī′·ą·ti·) *n.* properness; correct conduct [L. *proprius,* one's own].

pro·pul·sion (prą·pul′·shąn) *n.* the act of driving forward. **propulsive, propulsory** *a.* tending, or having power, to propel [L. *pro,* forward; *pellere, pulsum,* to drive].

pro·rate (prō′·rāt) *v.t.* and *i.* to divide or distribute proportionally. **proratable** *a.* **pro rata** in proportion [fr. L].

pro·sa·ic (prō·zā′·ik) *a.* dull and unimaginative; commonplace. Also **-al, -ally** *adv.* [L. *prosus,* straight-forward].

pro·sce·ni·um (prō·sē′·ni·ąm) *n.* the part of the stage in front of the curtain [Gk. *pro,* before; *skēnē,* the stage].

pro·scribe (prō·skrīb′) *v.t.* to put outside the protection of the law; to outlaw; to prohibit. **-r** *n.* **proscription** *n.* **proscriptive** *a.* [L. *proscribere,* to publish].

prose (prōz) *n.* ordinary language in speech and writing; language not in verse; *a.* pert. to prose; not poetical; *v.i.* to write prose; to speak or write in a dull, tedious manner. **prosy** *a.* dull and tedious. **prosily** *adv.* [L. *prosa* (*oratio*), direct (speech)].

pros·e·cute (pràs′·i·kūt) *v.t.* to follow or pursue with a view to reaching or accomplishing something; (*Law*) to proceed against judicially; *v.i.* to carry on a legal suit. **prosecution** *n.* (*Law*) the institution and carrying on of a suit in a court of law; the party by which legal proceedings are instituted, as opposed to the *defense.* **prosecutor** *n.* (*fem.* **prosecutrix**) [L. *prosequi,* to follow].

pros·e·lyte (pràs′·ą·līt) *n.* a convert to some party or religion; *v.t.* to convert. **proselytize** *v.t.* to make converts. **proselytism** *n.* [Gk. *prosēlutos,* a newcomer].

pros·o·dy (pràs′·ą·di·) *n.* the science of versification. **prosodic** (prą·sàd′·ik) *a.* **prosodist** *n.* one skilled in prosody [Gk. *pros,* to, *ōdē,* a song].

pros·pect (pràs′·pekt) *n.* a wide view; anticipation; reasonable hope; promise of future good. *v.t.* and *i.* to search or explore (a region), esp. for precious metals, oil, etc. **-ive** *a.* looking forward; relating to the future. **-ively** *adv.* **-or** *n.* **-us** *n.* a preliminary statement of an enterprise [L. *prospicere,* to look forward].

pros·per (pràs′·pęr) *v.t.* to cause to succeed; *v.i.* to succeed; to do well. **-ity** *n.* **-ous** *a.* **-ously** *adv.* [L. *prosper,* fortunate].

pros·tate (pràs′·tāt) *n.* a small gland at the neck of the bladder in males. Also **— gland** [Gk. *pro,* before; *statos,* placed].

pros·ti·tute (pràs′·tą·tūt) *n.* a harlot; *v.t.* to make a prostitue of; to put to base, infamous, or unworthy use. **prostitution** *n.* [L. *prostituere,* to offer for sale].

pros·trate (pràs′·trāt) *a.* lying on the

ground, esp. face downwards; mentally or physically exhausted; *v.t.* to lay flat, as on the ground; to bow down in adoration; to overcome. **prostration** *n.* [L. *pro*, forward; *sternere, stratum*, to lay flat].

pro·tag·o·nist (prō·tag′·ạn·ist) *n.* the principal actor in a drama; a leading character [Gk. *prōtos*, first; *agōnistēs*, an actor].

pro·tect (prạ·tekt′) *v.t.* to defend; to guard; to put a tariff on imports to encourage home industry. **-ion** *n.* defending from injury or harm; state of being defended; that which defends. **-ionism** *n.* the doctrine of protecting industries by taxing competing imports. **-ive** *a.* affording protection; sheltering. **-ively** *adv.* **-or** *n.* one who or that which, defends, **-orate** *n.* (period of) office of a protector of a state; political administration of a state or territory by another country [L. *pro.* in front of; *tegere*, to cover].

pro·té·gé (prō′·tạ.zhā) *n.* (*fem.* **protégée**) one under the care, protection, or patronage of another (Fr. *protéger*, to protect].

pro·te·in (prō′·tēn) *n.* a nitrogenous compound required for all animal life processes. Also **proteid** [Gk. *prōtos*, first].

pro·test (prạ·test′) *v.i.* to assert formally; to make a declaration against; *v.t.* to affirm solemnly; to object to. **protest** (prō′·test) *n.* a declaration of objection. **-ant** (prạ·tes′·tant) *n.* one who holds an opposite opinion. **Protestant** (prát′·ạs·tạnt) *a.* pert. or belonging to any branch of the Western Church outside the Roman communion; *n.* a member of such a church. **Protestantism** *n.* **protestation** *n.* a solemn declaration, esp. of dissent [L. *pro*, before; *testari*, to witness].

pro·tha·la·mi·on (prō·thạ.lā′·mi·ạn) *n.* a song written in honor of a marriage. Also **prothalamium** [Gk. *pro*, before; *thalamọs*, the bridal chamber].

pro·to- (prō′·tō) *prefix* fr. Gk. *prōtos*, first; hence, original; primitive. **-plasm** *n.* a semi-fluid substance forming the basis of the primitive tissue of animal and vegetable life; living matter. **-plasmatic, -plasmic** *a.* **-type** (prō′·tạ·tīp) *n.* original or model from which anything is copied; a pattern, **-typal, -typic(al)** *a.* **Protozoa** (prō·tạ·zō′·ạ) *n.pl.* first or lowest division of animal kingdom, consisting of microscopic, unicellular organisms. **-zoon** (prō·tạ.zō′·ạn) *n.* a member of this division. **-zoal, -zoan, -zoic** *a.*

pro·to·col (prō′·tạ·kál) *n.* an original copy; a rough draft, esp. a draft of terms signed by negotiating parties as the basis of a formal treaty or agreement; rules of diplomatic etiquette [Gk. *prōtokollon*, a flyleaf glued on to a book].

pro·ton (prō′·tán) *n.* in physics, the unit of positive electricity, found in the nuclei of all atoms [Gk. *prōtos*, first].

pro·tract (prō·trakt′) *v.t.* to lengthen; to draw out; to prolong; to draw to scale. **-ed** *a.* prolonged; long drawn out; tedious. **-ion** *n.* **-ive** *a.* **-or** *n.* a mathematical instrument for measuring angles; (*Anat.*) a muscle which draws forward or extends a limb [L. *pro*, forward; *trahere, tractum*, to draw].

pro·trude (prō·tròòd′) *v.t.* and *i.* to stick out; to project; to thrust forward. **protrusion** *n.* the act of thrusting forward; the state of being protruded or thrust forward; that which protrudes. **protrusive** *a.* [L. *pro*, forward; *trudere, trusum*, to thrust].

pro·tu·ber·ant (prō·tū′·ber·ạnt) *a.* bulging; swelling out; prominent. **-ly** *adv.* **protuberance** *n.* [L. *protuberare*, to swell].

proud (proud) *a.* haughty; self-respecting. **-ly** *adv.* **— flesh,** excessive granulation in tissue of healing wound [O.E. *prut*, proud].

prove (pròòv) *v.t.* to try by experiment; to ascertain as fact, by evidence; to demonstrate; to show; to establish the validity of (a will, etc.) *v.i.* to turn out (to be, etc.); to be found by trial. *pr.p.* **proving.** *pa.p.* **-d** or **-n.** *pa.t.* **provable** *a.* able to be proved. [L. *probare*, to test].

prov·e·nance (práv′·ạ·nạns) *n.* source or place of origin. Also **provenience** (prō.vē′·ni·ạns [L. *pro*, forth; *venire*, to come].

prov·en·der (práv′·ạn·dẹr) *n.* a dry food for beasts; fodder; hence provisions; food [O.Fr. *provendre*].

proverb (prạv′·ẹrb) *n.* a short pithy saying to express a truth or point a moral; an adage. **Proverbs** *n.pl.* (*Bib.*) book of Old Testament. **-ial** *a.* pert. to or resembling a proverb; well-known. **-ially** *adv.* [L. *proverbium*, fr. *verbum*, a word].

pro·vide (prạ·vīd′) *v.t.* to supply; to furnish; to get or make ready for future use; *v.i.* to make preparation; to furnish support (for). **providence** (prov′·i·dẹns) *n.* prudence; wise economy; God's care; an event regarded as an act of God. **Providence** *n.* God Himself. **provident** *a.* prudent; thrifty. **providently** *adv.* **providential** (práv·ạ·den′·shạl) *a.* effected by divine foresight; fortunate; lucky. **-r** *n.* [L. *pro*, before; *videre*, to see].

prov·ince (práv′·ins) *n.* a division of a country or empire; an administrative district; a district under the jurisdiction of an archbishop; a sphere of action; a department of knowledge; one's special duty. **provincial** prạ·vin′·shạl) *a.* pert. to a province or the provinces; countrified; narrow; *n.* an inhabitant of a province. **provincially** *adv.* [L. *provincia*].

pro·vi·sion (prạ·vizh′·ạn) *n.* the act of providing; measures taken beforehand; store esp. of food (generally in *pl.*); a condition or proviso; *v.t.* to supply with provisions. **-al** *a.* temporary; adopted for the time being. **-ally** *adv.* [L. *pro*, before; *videre, visum*, to see].

pro·vi·so (prạ·vī′·zō) *n.* a condition or stipulation in a deed or contract. *pl.* **-s** or **-es.** **-ry** *a.* containing a proviso or condition; temporary [L. *proviso quod*, it being provided that].

pro·voke (prạ·vōk′) *v.t.* to excite or stimulate to action, esp. to arouse to anger or passion; to bring about or call forth. **provoking** *a.* **provocation** (práv·ạ·kā′·shạn) *n.* the act of provoking; that which provokes. **provocative** (prạ·vák′·ạ·tiv) *a.* serving or tending to provoke. **provocatively** *adv.* **provocativeness** *n.* [L. *provocare*, to call forth].

prov·ost (práv′·ạst) *n.* in certain colleges on administrative assistant to the president. **— marshal** (prō′·vō·már′·shạl) *n.* an officer in charge of the military police (army), or of prisoners (navy) [L. *praepositus*, placed before].

prow (prou) *n.* the forepart or bow of a ship; (*Poetic*) a ship [L. *prora*].

prow·ess (prou′·is) *n.* bravery, esp. in war; valor; achievement [Fr. *prouesse*].

prowl (proul) *v.i.* to roam about stealthily; *n.* the act of prowling [M.E. *prollen*].

prox·i·mate (prák′·si·mit) *a.* next or nearest; closest; immediately following or preceding. **-ly** *adv.* **proximity** *n.* being next in time, place, etc.; immediate nearness. **proximo** *adv.* in or of the coming month [L. *proximus*, nearest].

prox·y (prák′·si.) *n.* an authorized agent or substitute; one deputed to act for another; a writing empowering one person to vote for another [short fr. *procuracy*].

prude (pròòd) *n.* a woman of affected or over-sensitive modesty or reserve. **prudish** *a.* **-ry** *n.* affected modesty; primness; stiffness [O.Fr. *prode*, discreet].

pru·dent (pròò·dạnt) *a.* cautious and judicious; careful; not extravagant. **-ly** *adv.* **prudence** *n.* **-ial** (proo.den'.shal) *a.* **-ially** *adv.* [L. *prudens,* foreseeing].

prune (proon) *n.* a dried plum [Fr., fr. L. *prunum,* a plum].

prune (proon) *v.t.* to cut off dead parts, excessive branches, etc. [O.Fr. *proignier*].

pru·ri·ent (proor.i.ant) *a.* given to, or springing from, unclean or lewd thoughts. **-ly** *adv.* **prurience, pruriency** *n.* [L. *prurire,* to itch].

Prus·sia (prush'.a) *n.* formerly the leading state of Germany, and the recognized home of German militarism. **-n** *n., a.* **-n blue** *n.* a deep blue salt of potassium and iron, used as a pigment. **prussic acid** *n.* hydrocyanic acid.

pry (prī) *v.i.* to look curiously; to peer; to nose about. *pr.p.* **-ing.** *pa.p., pa.t.* **pried** (prīd). **prier, -er** *n.* [M.E. *prien,* to peer].

psalm (sàm) *n.* a sacred song or hymn. **the Psalms** a book of the Old Testament. **-ist** (sàm'.ist, sal'.mist) *n.* a writer of psalms. **-ody** (sà'.ma.di., sal'.ma.di.) *n.* the art or practice of singing sacred music; psalms collectively. **-odist** *n.* a singer of psalms. **Psalter** (sawl'.ter) *n.* the Book of Psalms. **psaltery** *n.* an obsolete stringed instrument like the zither [Gk. *psalmos,* a twanging of strings].

pseu·do- (sū'.dō) *prefix* fr. Gk. *pseudes,* false; pretended; sham; not real; wrongly held to be, etc. Also **pseud-. -nym** (sū'.da.nim) *n.* a fictitious name; a pen name. **-nymous** *a.*

pshaw (shaw) *interj.* expressing contempt, impatience, etc. [imit.].

psit·ta·co·sis (sit.a.kō'.sis) *n.* a fatal disease found in parrots and communicable to man [L. *psittacus,* a parrot].

pso·ri·a·sis (sa.rī.à.sis) *n.* chronic skin disease.

psy·che (sī.kē) *n.* the soul personified; the principle of life [Gk. *psychē,* soul, mind].

psych·e·del·ic (sīk.a.del'.ik) *a.* causing or experiencing a state of euphoria with heightened perception or hallucination; *n.* a psychedelic drug. **-ally** *adv* [Gk. *psyche,* soul, mind; *delein,* to make manifest].

psy·chi·a·try (sī.ki'.a.tri.) *n.* study and treatment of mental disorders. **psychiater, psychiatrist** *n.* a specialist in mental disorders. **psychiatric(al)** *a.* [Gk. *psuchē,* mind; *iatros,* a physician].

psy·chic (sī'.kik) *a.* pert. to soul, spirit, or mind; spiritualistic; *n.* one sensitive to spiritualistic forces; medium. **-al** *a.* **-ally** *adv.* **-ist** *n.*

psy·cho·a·nal·y·sis (sī'.kō.an.al'.a.sis) *n.* process of studying the unconscious mind. **psychoanalyze** *v.t.* **psychoanalyst** *n.* **psychoanalytic(al)** *a.*

psy·chol·o·gy (sī.kàl'.a.ji.) *n.* the scientific study of the mind, its activities, and human and animal behavior. **psychological** *a.* **psychologically** *adv.* **psychologist** *n.*

psy·cho·pa·thol·o·gy (sī.kō.pa.thàl'.a.ji.) *n.* the science or study of mental diseases. **psychopathy** (sī.kàp'.a.thi.) *n.* mental affliction. **psychopath** *n.* one so afflicted. **psychopathic** *a.*

psy·cho·sis (sī.kō'.sis) *n.* a general term for any disorder of the mind. *pl.* **psychoses.**

psy·cho·so·mat·ic (sī.kō.sa.mat'.ik) *a.* of mind and body as a unit; treatment of physical diseases as having a mental origin [Gk. *soma,* body].

psy·cho·ther·a·py (sī.kō.ther'.a.pi.) *n.* the treatment of disease through the mind, e.g. by hypnotism, auto-suggestion, etc. **psychotherapeutic(-al)** *a.*

ptar·mi·gan (tàr'.ma.gan) *n.* a bird of the grouse family [Gael. *tārmachan*].

pter·o- (ter'.ō) *prefix* fr. Gk. *pteron,* a wing. **-dactyl** (ter.a.dak'.til) *n.* extinct flying reptile with bat-like wings [Gk. *dactylos,* a finger].

pto·maine (tō'.mān, tō.mān') *n.* substance, usually poisonous, found in putrefying organic matter [Gk. *ptōma,* a corpse].

pu·ber·ty (pū'.ber.ti.) *n.* the earliest age at which an individual is capable of reproduction. **pubescence** (pū.bes'.ans) *n.* the period of sexual development; puberty. **pubescent** *a.* [L. *pubertas,* fr. *pubes,* adult].

pub·lic (pub'.lik) *a.* of, or pert. to, the people; not private or secret; open to general use; accessible to all; serving the people; *n.* community or its members; a section of community. **-ly** *adv.* **-ation** *n.* making known to the public; proclamation; printing a book, etc. for sale or distribution; a book, periodical, magazine, etc. **publicize** *v.t.* to make widely known; to advertize. **publicist** *n.* one versed in, or who writes on, international law, or matters of political or economic interest. **publicity** (pub.lis'.a.ti.) *n.* the state of being generally known; notoriety; advertisement. **— prosecutor,** the legal officer appointed to prosecute criminals in serious cases on behalf of the state. **— school,** one of a system of schools maintained at public expense [L. *publicus,* fr. *populus,* the people].

pub·lish (pub'.lish) *v.t.* to make generally known; to proclaim; to print and issue for sale (books, music, etc.); to put into circulation. **-er** *n.* [L. *publicus*].

puce (pūs) *a.* brownish purple; *n.* the color [Fr. = a flea].

puck (puk) *n.* a rubber disk used in ice hockey; a mischievous sprite.

puck·er (puk.er) *v.t.* and *i.* to gather into small folds or wrinkles; to wrinkle; *n.* a wrinkle; a fold; **-y** *a.* [fr. *poke,* a bag].

pud·ding (pood'.ing) *n.* name of various forms of cooked foods, usually in a soft mass, served as a dessert.

pud·dle (pud'.l) *n.* a small pool of dirty water; a mixture of clay and water used as rough cement; *v.t.* to make muddy; to line embankments, etc. with puddle; to stir molten pig iron; *v.i.* to make muddy. **puddling** *n.* **-r** *n.* [O.E. *pudd,* a ditch].

pu·er·ile (pū'.er.il) *a.* childish; foolish; trivial. **-ly** *adv.* **puerility** *n.* childishness; triviality [L. *puer,* a boy].

pu·er·per·al (pū.ur'.per.al) *a.* pert. to, or caused by childbirth. **— fever** (*Med.*) a fever developing after childbirth [L. *puer,* a child; *parere,* to bear].

puff (puf) *n.* a short blast of breath or wind; its sound; a small quantity of smoke, etc.; a swelling; a light pastry; a soft pad for applying powder; exaggerated praise, esp. in a newspaper; a quilt; *v.i.* to send out smoke, etc. in puffs; to breathe hard; to pant; to swell up; *v.t.* to send out in a puff; to blow out; to smoke hard; to cause to swell; to praise unduly. **-er** *n.* **-ing** *n.* **-ingly** *adv.* **-y** *a.* inflated; swollen; breathing hard. **-iness** *n.* **— paste** *n.* a short, flaky paste for making light pastry [imit. origin].

puf·fin (puf'.in) *n.* a sea bird of the auk family with a parrot-like beak [M.E. *pofin*].

pug (pug) *n.* a small, snub-nosed dog; *a.* **— nose** *n.* a turned-up nose.

pug (pug) *v.t.* to make clay plastic by grinding with water; to fill in spaces with mortar in order to deaden sound [etym. uncertain].

pu·gil·ism (pū'.ja.lizm) *n.* the art of fighting with the fists; boxing. **pugilist** *n.* a boxer. **pugilistic** *a.* [L. *pugil,* a boxer, fr. *pugnus,* the fist].

pug·na·cious (pug.nā'.shas) *a.* given to fighting; quarrelsome. **-ly** *adv.* **pugnacity** (pug.nas'.a.ti.) *n.* [L. *pugnare,* to fight].

pu·is·sant (pū'.i·sạnt, pwis'.ạnt) *a.* powerful; mighty. **-ly** *adv.* **puissance** *n.* power [Fr. fr. L. *potens*, powerful].
puke (pūk) *v.t.* and *i.* to vomit.
pul·chri·tude (pul'.kri·tūd) *n.* beauty; comeliness [L. *pulcher*, beautiful].
pule (pūl) *v.i.* to chirp; to cry weakly; to whimper; to whine [imit. origin].
pull (pool) *v.t.* to draw towards one; to drag; to haul; to tug at; to pluck; to row a boat; *v.i.* to draw with force; to tug; *n.* act of pulling; force exerted by it; a tug; a means of pulling; effort; (*Slang*) influence, unfair advantage; (*Print.*) a rough proof; (*Golf*) a curving shot to the left. **-er** *n.* **—over** *n.* sweater put on by pulling over head [O.E. *pullian*].
pul·let (pool'.it) *n.* a young hen [Fr. *poulet*].
pul·ley (pool'.i·) *n.* a small wheel with a grooved rim on which runs a rope, used for hauling or lifting weights [Fr. *poulie*].
Pull·man·car (pool'.man.kȧr) *n.* a railway car. *Also* **Pullman** [fr. G. M. *Pullman* (1831-97), the inventor].
pul·mo- (pul'.mạ) *prefix* from L. *pulmo*, the lung. **-nary** (pul'.mạ.ner·i·) *a.* pert. to or affecting the lungs. **-nic** *a.* pert. to, or affecting, the lungs.
pulp (pulp) *n.* a soft, moist, cohering mass of animal or vegetable matter; the soft, succulent part of fruit; the material of which paper is made; *v.t.* to reduce to pulp; to remove the pulp from. **-y** *a.* like pulp. **-iness** *n.* [L. *pulpa*, flesh, pith].
pul·pit (pool'.pit) *n.* elevated place in a church for preacher [L. *pulpitum*, a stage].
pul·sate (pul'.sāt) *v.t.* to beat or throb, as the heart; to vibrate; to quiver. **pulsation** *n.* **pulsatile** *a.* pulsating; producing sounds by being struck, as a drum. **pulsative, pulsatory** *a.* capable of pulsating; throbbing [L. *pulsare*, to throb].
pulse (puls) *n.* the beating or throbbing of the heart or blood vessels, esp. of the arteries; the place, esp. on the wrist, where this rhythmical beat is felt; any measured or regular beat. *v.i.* to throb or pulsate [L. *pulsus*, beating].
pulse (puls) *n.* leguminous plants or their seeds, as beans, peas, etc. [L. *puls*, porridge].
pul·ver·i·ze (pul'.vẹr.īz) *v.t.* to reduce to a fine powder; to smash or demolish; *v.i.* to fall down into dust. **pulverization** *n.* **-r** *n.* [L. *pulvis*, dust].
pu·ma (pū'·mạ) *n.* a large American carnivorous animal of the cat family; cougar [Peruv.].
pum·ice (pum'·is) *n.* Also **— stone,** a light, porous variety of lava, used for cleaning, polishing, etc. [L. *pumex*].
pum·mel See **pommel.**
pump (pump) *n.* an appliance used for raising water, putting in or taking out air or liquid, etc.; *v.t.* to raise with a pump, as water; to free from water by means of a pump; to extract information by artful questioning; *v.i.* to work a pump; to raise water with a pump [Fr. *pompe*].
pump (pump) *n.* a low, thin-soled shoe [Dut.].
pump·kin (pump'·kin) *n.* a plant of the gourd family; its fruit, used as food [O.Fr. *pompon*, fr. Gk. *pepon*, ripe].
pun (pun) *n.* a play on words similar in sound but different in sense; *v.i.* to use puns. *pr..p.* **-ning.** *pa.p.* and *pa.t.* **-ned.** **-ster** *n.* one who makes puns.
punch (punch) *n.* a drink made of fruit juices, sugar, and water, sometimes carbonated or with liquor [Hind. *panch*, five (ingredients)].
punch (punch) *n.* a tool used for making holes or dents; a machine for perforating or stamping; *v.t.* to perforate, dent, or stamp with a punch [Fr. *poinçon*, an awl, fr. L. *pungere*, to pierce].
punch (punch) *v.t.* to strike with the fist; to beat; to bruise; of cattle, to drive; *n.* a blow with the fist; (*Slang*) energy [fr. *punish*].
punc·tate (pungk'·tāt) *a.* having many points; having dots scattered over the surface. Also **punctated** [L. *pungere*, to pierce].
punc·til·i·o (pungk·til'·i·ō) *n.* a fine point of etiquette; formality. *a.* attentive to punctilio; strict in the observance of rules of conduct, etc.; scrupulously correct. **-usly** *adv.* **-usness** *n.* [L. *punctum*, a point].
punc·tu·al (pungk'·choo·ạl) *a.* arriving at the proper or fixed time; prompt; not late; (*Geom.*) pert. to a point. **-ly** *adv.* **-ity** *n.* [L. *punctum*, a point].
punc·tu·ate (pungk'·choo·āt) *v.t.* to separate into sentences, clauses, etc. by periods, commas, colons, etc.; to emphasize in some significant manner; to interrupt at intervals. **punctuation** *n.* the act or system separating by the use of **punctuation marks** (the period, comma, colon, semi-colon, etc.) [L. *punctum*, a point].
punc·ture (pungk'·chẹr) *n.* an act of pricking; a small hole made by a sharp point; a perforation; *v.t.* to make a hole with a sharp point [L. *pungere*, to prick].
pun·dit (pun'·dit) *n.* a title given to a Hindu scholar; any learned person [Hind. *pandit*].
pun·gent (pun'·jạnt) *a.* sharply affecting the taste or smell; stinging; sarcastic; caustic. **-ly** *adv.* **pungency** *n.* [L. *pungere*, to prick].
pun·ish (pun'·ish) *v.t.* to inflict a penalty for an offense; to chastise. **-able** *a.* **-ment** *n.* **punitive** (pū'·ni·tiv) *a.* pert. to or inflicting punishment [L. *punire*, to punish].
punk (pungk) *n.* crumbly, decayed wood; *a.* (*Slang*) worthless [etym. uncertain].
punt (punt) *v.t.* and *i.* to kick a football, when dropped from the hands, before it touches the ground; *n.* such a kick
pu·ny (pu'·ni·) *a.* small and feeble; petty. **puniness** *n.* [O.Fr. *puisne*].
pup (pup) *n.* a puppy or young dog; a young seal; *v.i.* to bring forth puppies or whelps. *pr.p.* **-ping.** *pa.p., pa.t.* **-ped** [short fr. *puppy*, fr. Fr. *poupée*, a doll or puppet].
pu·pa (pū'·pạ) *n.* the third stage in the metamorphosis of an insect, when it is in a cocoon; a chrysalis. *pl.* **pupae** (pū'·pē). **-l** *a.* **-te** *v.i.* to become a pupa [L. *pupa*, a girl].
pu·pil (pū'·pil) *n.* a student; a boy or girl under the care of a guardian; the small circular opening in the center of the iris of the eye. **-age** *n.* the state of being a pupil; the period of time during which one is a pupil. **-lary** *a. pert.* to a pupil or ward; pert to the pupil of the eye [L. *pupillus*, an orphan boy].
pup·pet (pup'·it) *n.* a marionette; a person whose actions are completely controlled by another. **-ry** *n.* a puppet show [Fr. *popuée*, a doll; L. *puppa*].
pup·py See **pup.**
pur·blind (pur'·blīnd) *a.* almost blind; dull in understanding. **-ly** *adv.* **-ness** *n.* [fr. *pure* and *blind*].
pur·chase (pur'·chas) *v.t.* to buy; to obtain by any outlay of labor, time, sacrifice, etc.; (*Law*) to obtain by any means other than inheritance; *n.* acquisition of anything for a price or equivalent; a thing bought; **purchasable** *a.* **-r** *n.* [Fr. *pourchasser*, to obtain by pursuit].
pure (pyoor) *a.* free from all extraneous matter; untainted; spotless; blameless; unsullied; chaste; innocent; absolute; theoretical, not applied. **-ly** *adv.* entirely; solely. **-ness** *n.* **purity** *n.* freedom from all extraneous matter; freedom from sin or evil [L. *purus*].
pu·rée (pyoo·rā') *n.* a thick soup [Fr.].
purge (purj) *v.t.* to purify; to cleanse; to clear out; to clear from guilt, accusation, or

the charge of a crime, etc.; to remove from an organization, political party, army, etc. undesirable or suspect members; to cleanse the bowels by taking a cathartic medicine; *n.* a cleansing, esp. of the bowels; a purgative. **purgation** (pur.gā′.shạn) *n.* act of cleansing or purifying; act of freeing from imputatiaon of guilt; purging. **purgative** (pur′.gạ.tiv) *a.* having the power of purging; *n.* any medicine which will cause evacuation of bowels. **purgatory** (pur′.gạ.tōr.i.) *a.* tending to cleanse; purifying; expiatory; *n.* in R.C. faith, place where souls of dead are purified by suffering; (*Fig.*) a place or state of torment. **purgatorial** *a.* [L. *purgare*, fr. *purus*, pure].

pu·ri·fy (pyoor′.ạ.fi) *v.t.* to make pure, clear, or clean; to free from impurities; to free from guilt or defilement; *v.i.* to become pure. **purification** (pyoor.ạ.fạ.kā′.shạn) *n.* **purificative** *a.* **purifier** *n.* [L. *purus*, pure; *facere*, to make].

pur·ist (pyoor′.ist) *n.* an advocate of extreme care or precision in choice of words, etc.; a stickler for correctness [L. *purus*, pure].

Pu·ri·tan (pyoor′.a.tạn) *n.* a member of the extreme Protestant party, who desired further *purification* of the Church after the Elizabethan reformation; (*l.c.*) a person of extreme strictness in morals or religion; *a.* pert. to Puritans or to puritan. **-ic(al)** *a.* pert. to Puritans, their doctrine and practice; over-scrupulous. **-ically** *adv.* **-ism** *n.* doctrine and practice of Puritans; narrow-mindedness [L. *puritas*, purity, fr. *purus*].

purl (purl) *n.* an embroidered border; a knitting stitch that is reverse of plain stitch; *v.t.* to ornament with purls; *v.i.* to knit in purl. Also **pearl** [fr. *purfle*].

purl (purl) *v.i.* to flow with a burbling sound or gentle murmur [imit. origin].

pur·lieu (pur′.lòò) *n.* ground bordering on something; *pl.* outlying districts; outskirts [O. Fr. *purallee*, a survey].

pur·loin (pur.loin′) *v.i.* to steal; to pilfer [O.Fr. *purloigner*, to put far away].

pur·ple (pur′.pl) *n.* a color between crimson and violet; robe of this color, formerly reserved for royalty; royal dignity; *a.* purple-colored; dark red; *v.i.* to make or dye a purple color; *v.i.* to become purple. **born to the purple,** of princely rank [Gk. *porphura*, shellfish that gave Tyrian purple].

pur·port (pur′.pōrt) *n.* meaning; apparent meaning; import; aim. **purport** (pẹr.pōrt′) *v.t.* to mean; to be intended to seem [O. Fr. *porporter*, to embody].

pur·pose (pur′.pạs) *n.* object in view; aim; end; plan; intention; effect; purport; *v.t.* to intend; to mean to. **-ly** *adv.* intentionally; expressly. **-ful** *a.* determined resolute. **-fully** *adv.* **-less** *a.* aimless. **-lessly** *adv.* **purposive** *a.* done with a purpose [O.Fr. *porpos*, fr. *porposer*, to propose].

pur·pu·ra (pur′.pyạ.rạ) *n.* (*Med.*) the appearance of purple patches under the skin, caused by hemorrhage; shellfish, yielding purplish fluid. **purpureal** (per.pū′.rē.ạl) *a.* purple. **purpuric** *a.* pert. to purpura [Gk. porphura]. See **purple.**

purr (pur) *n.* a low, murmuring sound made by a cat; *v.i.* to utter such a sound.

purse (purs) *n.* a small bag or pouch to carry money in; money offered as a prize, or collected as a present; money; *v.t.* to wrinkle up; to pucker. **-r** *n.* (*Naut.*) officer in charge of accounts, etc. on board a ship. **-ful** *a.* enough to fill a purse. **— strings** *n.pl.* power to control expenditure [Fr. *bourse*, a purse, fr. Gk. *bursa*, a hide].

pur·sue (pẹr.sū′) *v.t.* to follow with the aim of overtaking; to run after; to chase; to aim at; to seek; to continue; *v.i.* to go on; to proceed; **-r** *n.* **pursuance** *n.* the act of pursuing. **pursuant** *a.* done in consequence, or performance, of anything. **pursuit** (pẹr.sūt′) *n.* the act of pursuing; a running after; chase; profession; occupation. **pursuivant** (pur′.swi.vạnt) *n.* an attendant [Fr. *poursuivre*, fr. L. *prosequi*, to follow].

pu·ru·lent (pyoor′.ạ.lạnt) *a.* pert. to, containing, or discharging pus, or matter; septic; suppurating. **purulence, purulency** *n.* [L. *pus, puris*, matter].

pur·vey (pẹr.vā′) *v.t.* (*Brit.*) to furnish or provide; to supply, esp. provisions. **-ance** *n.* act of purveying; supplies; former royal prerogative of requisitioning supplies, or enforcing personal service. **-or** *n.* [L. *providere*, to provide].

pur·view (pur′.vū) *n.* the enacting clauses of a statute; scope; range. [Fr. *pourvu*, provided].

pus (pus) *n.* the yellowish-white matter produced by suppuration [L. *pus*, matter].

push (poosh) *v.t.* to move or try to move away by pressure; to drive or impel; to press hard; to press or urge forward; to shove; *v.i.* to make a thrust; to press hard in order to move; *n.* a thrust; any pressure or force applied; emergency; enterprise; (*Mil.*) an advance or attack on a large scale. **-er** *n.* **-ing** *a.* given to pushing oneself or one's claims; self-assertive. **-ingly** *adv.* [Fr. *pousser*, fr. L. *pellere*, to drive].

pu·sil·lan·i·mous (pū.sạ.lan′.ạ.mạs) *a.* cowardly; faint-hearted; mean-spirited. **-ly** *adv.* **pusillanimity** *n.* [L. *pusillus*, very small; *animus*, spirit].

a young girl. **-y** *n.* dim. of puss; a cat.

pus·tule (pus′.chool) *n.* a small swelling or pimple containing pus. **pustular, pustulous** *a.* [L. *pustula*, a blister].

put (poot) *v.t.* to place; to set; to lay; to apply; to state; to propose; to throw; *v.i.* to go. *pr.p.* **-ting.** *pa.p.* and *pa.t.* **put.** *n.* a throw, esp. of a heavy weight. **to put about** (*Naut.*) to alter a ship's course [Late O.E. *putian*].

pu·ta·tive (pū′.tạ.tiv) *a.* commonly thought; supposed; reputed. **-ly** *adv.* **putation** *n.* [L. *putare*, to think].

pu·tre·fy (pū′.trạ.fi) *v.t.* and *i.* to make or become rotten; to decompose; to rot. **putrefaction** *n.* the rotting of animal or vegetable matter; rottenness; decomposition. **putrefactive** *a.* **putrescence** *n.* tendency to decay; rottenness. **putrescent** *a.* **putrid** (pū′.trid) *a.* in a state of decay; (*Colloq.*) very bad. **putridity, putridness** *n.* [L. *putere*, to rot; *facere*, to make].

putt (put) *v.t.* and *i.* (Golf) to hit a ball in the direction of the hole; (*Scot.*) to throw (a weight or iron ball) from the shoulder; *n.* the stroke so made in golf; the throw of the weight. **-er** *n.* one who putts; a short golf club [var. of *put*].

put·ter (put′.ẹr) *v.i.* to work or act in a feeble, unsystematic way; to dawdle. Also **potter.** [var. of *potter*, O.E. *potian*, to poke].

put·ty (put′.i.) *n.* a kind of paste or cement, used by plasterers; *v.t.* to fix, fill up, etc. with putty. **puttier** *n.* [Fr. *potée*, the contents of a pot].

puz·zle (puz′.l) *n.* a bewildering or perplexing question; a problem, etc. requiring clever thinking to solve it; a conundrum; *v.t.* to perplex; to bewilder; (with 'out') to solve after hard thinking; (with 'over') to think hard over; *v.i.* to be bewildered. **-r** *n.* **puzzling** *a.* bewildering, perplexing [fr. M.E. *opposal*, a question, interrogation].

py·e·mi·a, pyaemia (pī.ē′.mi.ạ) *n.* (*Med.*) blood-poisoning [Gk. *pyon*, pus; *haima*, blood].

Pyg·my, Pigmy (pig′.mi.) *n.* one of a race

of dwarf Negroes of C. Africa. (*l.c.*) a very small person or thing; a dwarf; *a.* diminutive [Gk. *pygmē*, a measure of length from elbow to knuckles].

py·lon (pī′·lạn) *n.* a post or tower marking an entrance, a course for air races, etc.; the gateway of an ancient support; power-transmission cables [Gk. *pylōn*, a gateway].

py·or·rhe·a (pī·ạ·rē′·ạ) *n.* (*Med.*) a dental discharge of pus from the gums. Also **pyorrhoea** [Gk. *pyon*, pus; *rhoia*, a flowing].

pyr·a·mid (pir′·ạ·mid) *n.* a solid figure on a triangular, square, or polygonal base, and with sloping sides meeting at an apex; a structure of this shape. **-al** *a.* pert. to, or having the form of a pyramid. **-ally** *adv.* [Gk. *pyramis*].

pyre (pīr) *n.* a pile of wood for burning a dead body; funeral pile [Gk. *pyra*, fire].

py·ret·ic (pī·ret′·ik) *a.* (*Med.*) pert. to, producing, or relieving, fever; feverish. **pyrexia** *n.* fever [Gk. *pyretos*, fever, fr. *pur*, fire].

py·rite (pī′·rīt) *n.* a yellow mineral formed of sulphur and iron; iron pyrites. **pyrites** (pī·rī′·tēz, pī′·rīt) *n.pl.* a name for many compounds of metals with sulphur, esp. iron pyrites, or copper pyrites. **pyritic, pyritiferous, pyritous** *a.* pert. to, or yielding, pyrites [Gk. *pyra*, fire].

py·ro- (pī′·rạ) *prefix* fr. Gk. *pur*, fire, used in many derivatives. **— electricity** *n.* the property possessed by some crystals, of becoming electrically polar when they are heated.

py·ro·ma·ni·a (pī·rạ·mā′·ni·ạ) *n.* a mania for setting things on fire. **pyromaniac** *n.* [Gk. *pyr*, fire; and *mania*].

py·ro·tech·nics (pī·rạ·tek′·niks) *n.pl.* the art of making fireworks; the art of displaying them. Also **pyrotechny. pyrotechnic, pyrotechnical** *a.* [Gk. *pyr*, fire; *technē*, art].

Py·thag·o·ras (pi·thag′·a·ras) *n.* a Greek philosopher and mathematician (582-507 B.C.).

py·thon (pī′·thȧn) *n.* a large, non-poisonous snake that kills its prey by crushing it; a spirit; [Gk. *Pythōn*, the serpent slain by Apollo near Delphi].

pyx (piks) *n.* the vessel in which the consecrated bread or Host is kept; a box at a Brit. mint in which specimen coins are kept for trial and assay; *v.t.* to test by assay. **-is** *n.* a small pyx; a casket [Gk. *pyxis*, fr. *pyxos*, a box tree].

Q

quack (kwak) *v.i.* to cry like a duck; to act as a quack; *n.* cry of duck or like sound; one who pretends to skill in an art, esp. in medicine; a charlatan; *a.* pert. to quackery. **-ery** *n.* **-salver** *n.* a quack doctor [imit.].

Quad·ra·ges·i·ma (kwod·ra·jes′·i·mạ) *n.* (*Church*) the first Sunday of Lent. **-l** *a.* pert. to Lent [L. *quadragesimus*, fortieth].

quad·ran·gle (kwȧd′·rang.gl) *n.* in geometry, a plane figure having four sides and angles; a square or court surrounded by buildings (*abbrev.* **quad**) **quadrangular** *a.* [L. *quattuor*, four and *angle*].

quad·rant (kwȧd′·rạnt) *n.* the fourth part of the area of a circle; an arc of 90°; an instrument for taking altitude of heavenly bodies; in gunnery, an instrument to mark the degrees of a gun's elevation [L. *quadrans*, a fourth part].

quad·rate (kwȧd′·rāt) *a.* having four sides and four right angles; square; divisible by four (used chiefly in anatomical names); *n.* square; **quadrate** *v.i.* to agree; to suit.

quadratic (kwȧd·rat′·ik) *a.* pert. to, or resembling, a square; square; (*Alg.*) involving the second but no higher power of the unknown quantity, esp. in **quadratic equation.** **quadrature** (kwȧd′·rạ·chẹr) *n.* the act of squaring or reducing to a square; the position of one heavenly body with respect to another 90° away [L. *quadratus*, squared].

quad·ri- (kwod′·ri·) *comb. form*, four [L. *quattuor*, four].

quad·ri·cen·ten·ni·al (kwȧd·rạ·sen·ten′·i·ạl) *a.* pert. to a period of four hundred years; *n.* the four hundredth anniversary [L. *quattuor*, four; *centum*, hundred; *annus*, a year].

quad·ri·lat·er·al .. (kwȧd·rẹ·lat′·ẹr·ạl) *a.* having four sides; *n.* (*Geom.*) a plane figure having four sides [L. *quattuor*, four; *latus*, side].

qua·drille (kwạ·dril′, kạ·dril′) *n.* an 18th cent. card game; a square dance; also, the music played to such a dance [L. *quadrus*, square].

quad·ril·lion (kwȧd·ril′·yon) *n.* a number represented in the Fr. and U.S. notation by one with 15 ciphers annexed; in Great Britain and Ger. by one followed by 24 ciphers [L. *quattuor*, four and *million*].

quad·ri·no·mi·al (kwȧd·rạ·nō′·mi·ạl) *a.* (*Alg.*) consisting of four terms.

quad·ri·par·tite (kwȧd·rạ·pȧr′·tīt) *a.* divided into four parts.

quad·roon (kwȧd·ro͝on·) *n.* offspring of mulatto and white; one who is one-fourth Negro [Sp. *cuarteró*, fr. L. *quartus*, fourth].

quad·ru·mane (kwȧd′·roo·mān) *n.* an animal which has all four feet formed like hands. **quadrumanous** *a.* four-handed [L.*quatiuor*, four; *manus*, the hand].

quad·ru·ped (kwȧd′·roo·ped) *n.* an animal having four feet; *a.* having four feet [L. *quattuor*, four; *pes, pedis*, a foot].

quad·ru·ple (kwȧd′·ro͝o·pl) *a.* fourfold; *n.* a four fold amount; a sum four times as great as another; *v.t.* to multiply by four; *v.i.* to be multiplied by four. **-t** *n.* one of four children born at a birth. **quadruplicate** *v.t.* to multiply by four; *n.* one of four things corresponding exactly; *a.* fourfold. **quadruplication** *n.* [L. *quadru-plus*, fourfold].

quaff (kwȧf) *v.t.* and *i.* to swallow in large drafts; *n.* a drink.

quag·mire (kwag′·mīr) *n.* soft, wet land, yielding under the feet; a bog; (*Fig.*) a difficult position. **quaggy** *a.* spongy; boggy; like quagmire. [fr. *quake*].

quail (kwāl) *v.i.* to lose spirit; to shrink or cower; to flinch [Fr. *cailler*, to curdle].

quail (kwāl) *n.* a game bird [Fr. *caille*].

quaint (kwānt) *a.* interestingly old-fashioned or odd; curious and fanciful; whimsical. **-ly** *adv.* **-ness** *n.* [O.Fr. *cointe*, prudent].

quake (kwāk) *v.i.* to tremble or shake with fear, cold, or emotion; to quiver or vibrate; *n.* a shaking or trembling; *abbrev.* of 'earthquake' [O.E. *cwacian*].

Quak·er (kwāk′·ẹr) *n.* (*fem.* **-ess**) a member of the Society of Friends, a religious sect founded in the 17th cent. by George Fox. **-ism** *n.*

qual·i·fy (kwȧl′·ạ·fī) *v.t.* to ascribe a quality to; to describe (as); to fit for active service or office; to prepare by requisite training for special duty; to furnish with the legal title to; to limit; to diminish; *v.i.* to make oneself competent; to show oneself fit for. **qualifier** *n.* **qualifiable** *a.* **qualification** *n.* the act of qualifying or condition of being qualified; any endowment or acquirement that fits a person for an office or employment; modification; restriction [L. *qualis*, of what kind; *facere*, to make].

qual·i·ty (kwȧl′·ạ·ti·) *n.* a particular property inherent in a body or substance; an essential attribute or characteristic; character or nature; degree of excellence. **qualitative** *a.* [L. *qualitas*, of what kind.]

qualm (kwåm) *n.* a sudden attack of illness, faintness, nausea, distress; a scruple of conscience [M.E. *qualme*].

quan·da·ry (kwạn′·dri·, -dạ·ri·) *n.* a state of perplexity; a predicament; a dilemma.

quan·ti·fy (kwån′·tạ·fī) *v.t.* to fix or express the quantity of; to measure. **quantification** *n.* [*L. quantus*, how much; *facere*, to make].

quan·ti·ty (kwån·tạ·ti·) *n.* property of things ascertained by measuring; amount; bulk; a certain part; a considerable amount; number; (*Pros.*) the length or shortness of vowels, sounds, or syllables. **quantities** *n.pl.* abundance; profusion. **quantitative** *a.* relating to quantity [L. *quantus*, how much].

quan·tum (kwån′·tạm) *n.* quantity or amount; (*Phys.*) smallest amount of radiant energy. *pl.* **quanta** [L. *quantus*, how much].

quar·an·tine (kwawr′·ạn·tēn) *n.* isolation of infected persons to prevent spread of disease; the period during which a ship, with infectious disease aboard, is isolated; *v.t.* to put under quarantine [Fr. *quarantaine*, forty days].

quar·rel (kwawr′·ạl) *n.* rupture of friendly relations; an angry altercation; a dispute; *v.i.* to dispute; to wrangle; to disagree. **-er** *n.* **-some** *a.* apt to quarrel; irascible; contentious [L. *queri*, to complain].

quar·ry (kwawr′·i·) *n.* an excavation whence stone is dug for building; any source from which material may be extracted; *v.t.* to dig from a quarry. *pa.p.*, *pa.t.* **quarried** [L. *quadrare*, to square, hew (stones)].

quar·ry (kwawr′·i·) *n.* prey; victim [O.Fr. *cuiree*, fr. L. *corium*, skin].

quart (kwawrt) *n.* the fourth part of a gallon; one eighth of a peck [L. *quartus*, fourth].

quart·er (kwawr′·tẹr) *n.* fourth part; (*U.S. and Canada*) one fourth of a dollar, or the coin valued at this amount; one of the four cardinal points of the compass; one limb of a quadruped with the adjacent parts; a term in a school, etc.; part of a ship's side aft of mainmast; a region; a territory; a division of a town, or county; clemency. **-s** *n.pl.* assigned position; lodgings, esp. for soldiers; shelter; *v.t.* to divide into four equal parts; to divide up a traitor's body; to furnish with shelter; *v.i.* to have temporary residence. **-ing** *n.* an assignment of quarters for soldiers. **-ly** *a.* consisting of a fourth part; occurring every quarter of a year; *n.* a review or magazine published four times a year; *adv.* by quarters; once in a quarter of a year. **—deck** *n.* a part of deck of a ship which extends from stern to mainmast. **-master** *n.* (*Mil.*) an officer in charge of quarters, clothing, stores, etc.; (*Naut.*) a petty officer who attends to steering, signals, stowage, etc. **-master-sergeant** *n.* the N.C.O. assistant to the quartermaster [L. *quartarius*, fr. *quartus*, fourth].

quar·tet, quartette (kwawr·tet′) *n.* (*Mus.*) a composition of four parts, each performed by a single voice or instrument; set of four who perform this; a group of four [Fr.].

quar·to (kwawr′·tō) *a.* denoting the size of a book in which the paper is folded to give four leaves to the sheet (*abbrev.* **4to**); *n.* a book of the size of the fourth of a sheet [L. *in quarto*, in a fourth part].

quartz (kwawrts) *n.* minerals consisting of silica or silicon dioxide [Ger. *quarz*].

qua·sar (kwā′·sår, -zẹr) *n.* one of a number of very distant starlike objects that emit immense quantities of light and/or radio waves [fr. *quasi* and stell*ar*].

quash (kwåsh) *v.t.* to crush; to quell; (*Law*) to annul, overthrow, or make void [L. *quassare*, to shake].

qua·si (kwā′·sī, kwå′·sē) as if; as it were; in a certain sense or degree; seeming; apparently; it is used as adj. or adv. and as prefix to noun, adj., or adv. [L.].

quat·rain (kwåt′·rān) *n.* (*Pros.*) a stanza of four lines [L. *quattaor*, four].

qua·ver (kwā′·vẹr) *v.i.* to shake, tremble, or vibrate; to sing or play with tremulous modulations; *v.t.* to utter or sing with quavers or trills; *n.* a trembling, esp. of the voice.

quay (kē, kwā) *n.* a landing place used for the loading and unloading of ships; a wharf. **-age** *n.* payment for use of a quay; space occupied by quays [Fr. *quai*].

quea·sy (kwē′·zi·) *a.* affected with nausea; squeamish; fastidious. **queasily** *adv.* **queasiness** *n.* [etym. uncertain].

queen (kwēn) *n.* the consort of a king; a woman who is the sovereign of a kingdom; the sovereign of a swarm of bees, ants, etc.; any woman who is pre-eminent; one of the chief pieces in a game of chess. *v.i.* to act the part of a queen (usu. 'to queen it'). **-ly** *a.* like, appropriate to a queen; majestic. **-liness** *n.* **-hood** *n.* state or position of a queen. **— consort** *n.* the wife of a king. **— dowager** *n.* the widow of a king. **— mother** *n.* a queen dowager who is also mother of reigning monarch. **— regent** *n.* a queen reigning in her own right. [O.E. *cwen*, a woman].

queer (kwir) *a.* odd; singular; quaint; (*Colloq.*) of a questionable character; faint or out of sorts; *v.t.* (*Slang*) to spoil. **-ly** *adv.* **-ish** *a.* somewhat queer. **-ness** *n.* [Ger. *quer*, oblique, crosswise].

quell (kwel) *v.t.* to subdue; to put down; to suppress forcibly. **-er** *n.* [O.E. *cwellan*, to kill].

quench (kwench) *v.t.* to extinguish; to put out, as fire or light; to cool or allay; to stifle; to slake (thirst). **-able** *a.* **-less** *a.* **-er** *n.* [O.E. *cwencan*].

quer·u·lous (kwer′·ạ·lạs) *a.* peevish; fretful. **-ly** *adv.* **-ness** *n.* [L. *queri*, to complain].

que·ry (kwir′·i·) *n.* a question; an inquiry; a mark of interrogation; *v.t.* to inquire into; to call in question; to mark as of doubtful accuracy [L. *quaerere* to seek or inquire].

quest (kwest) *n.* search; the act of seeking; the thing sought; *v.i.* to search; to seek [L. *quaerere*, *quaestum*, to seek].

ques·tion (kwes′·chạn) *n.* interrogation; inquiry; that which is asked; subject of inquiry or debate; (subject of) dispute; a matter of doubt or difficulty; a problem; *v.t.* to inquire of by asking questions; to be uncertain of; to challenge; to take objection to; to interrogate; **-able** *a.* doubtful; suspicious. **-ably** *adv.* **-ableness** *n.* **-er** *n.* **— mark** *n.* a mark of interrogation (?). **out of the question,** not to be thought of. **to beg the question,** to assume as fact something which is to be proved [L. *quaestio*, fr. *quaerere*, to seek, ask].

ques·tion·naire (kwes·chạ·ner′) *n.* a list of questions. [Fr.].

queue (kū) *n.* a pigtail [Fr. fr. L. *cauda*, a tail].

quib·ble (kwib′·l) *n.* an evasion of the point in question by a play upon words, or by stressing unimportant aspect of it; equivocation; *v.i.* to use quibbles. **-r** *n.* [dim. of obs. *quib*].

quick (kwik) *a.* animated; sprightly; ready or prompt; sensitive; rapid; hasty; impatient; fresh and invigorating; pregnant; *n.* living persons; sensitive flesh under nails; (*Fig.*) one's tenderest susceptibilities; *adv.* also **-ly,** rapidly; promptly. **-ness** *n.* **-en** *v.t.* to make alive; to make active or sprightly; to hasten; to sharpen or stimulate; *v.i.* to become alive; to move with greater rapidity. **-ener** *n.* **-ening** *n.* a making or becoming quick; first movement of fetus in womb. **-sand** *n.* sand, readily yielding to pressure, esp. if loose and mixed with water. **-silver** *n.* mercury. **-step** *n.* a march; a lively dance step [O.E. *cwic*, alive].

quid (kwid) *n.* a portion suitable for chewing, esp. of tobacco; a cud [form of *cud*].

quid (kwid) *n.* (*Brit. Slang*) a pound sterling.

quid·di·ty (kwid'·ą·ti·) *n.* a trifling nicety; a quibble; the essence of anything [L. *quidditas* fr. *quid*, what?].

qui·es·cent (kwī·es'·ąnt) *a.* still; inert; motionless; at rest. **-ly** *adv.* **quiescence, quiescency** *n.* [L. *quiescere*, to rest].

qui·et (kwī'·ąt) *a.* still; peaceful; not agitated; placid; of gentle disposition; not showy; *n.* calm; peace; tranquillity; *v.t.* to reduce to a state of rest; to calm; to allay or appease; to silence; *v.i.* to become quiet. **-en** (*Dial.*) *v.t.* and *i* to quiet. **-ly** *adv.* **-ness** *n.* **-ude** *n.* freedom from noise, disturbance, alarm; tranquillity; repose. **quietus** (kwī·ē'·tąs) *n.* final acquittance, of debt, etc.; (*Fig.*) extinction [L. *quietus*].

quill (kwil) *n.* a large, strong, hollow feather used as a pen; a spine or prickle, as of a porcupine; a piece of small reed on which weavers wind thread; an implement for striking the strings of certain instruments; *v.t.* to plait or form into small ridges [M.E. *quil*].

quilt (kwilt) *n.* any thick, warm coverlet; *v.t.* to stitch together, like a quilt, with a soft filling; to pad. **-ed.** *a.* [L. *culcita*, a cushion].

qui·na·ry (kwī'·ną·ri·) *a.* consisting of, or arranged in, fives [L. *quinque*, five].

quince (kwins) *n.* a hard, yellow, acid fruit, somewhat like an apple [Fr. *coing;* L. *cydonium;* fr. *Cydonia*, a city in Crete].

qui·nine (kwī·nīn) *n.* a bitter alkaloid obtained from various species of cinchona bark; it is used as a tonic and febrifuge. **quinic** *a.* [Peruv. *kina*, bark].

quin·qu(e)- (kwin'·kw(a)), *prefix* fr. L. *quinque*, five.

Quin·qua·ges·i·ma (kwing·kwą·jes'·ą·mą) *n.* the Sunday before Ash Wednesday, so called because fifty days before Easter [L. *quinquagesimus*, fiftieth].

quin·sy (kwin'·zi·) *n.* a severe inflammation of the throat and tonsils [Gk. *kunanchē*, fr. *kuōn*, a dog; *anchein*, to choke].

quin·tes·sence (kwin·tes'·ąns) *n.* the pure essence of anything; the perfect embodiment of a thing. **quintessential** *a.* [L. *quinta essentia*, fifth essence].

quin·tet, quintette (kwin·tet') *n.* (*Mus.*) a composition for five voices or instruments; a company of five singers or players; a set of five [L. *quintus*, fifth].

quin·til·lion (kwin·til'·yąn) *n.* (*U.S. and France*) a number represented by one with 18 ciphers following; *(Great Britain and Germany)* one with 30 ciphers following [fr. L. *quintus*, fifth, and million].

quin·tu·ple (kwin'·tòò·pl) *a.* multiplied by five; fivefold; *v.t.* to make fivefold; to multiply by five. **-ts** *n.pl.* five children at a birth (*Colloq.* **quints**) [fr. L. *quintus*, fifth, by imit. of quadruple].

quip (kwip) *n.* a smart, sarcastic turn of phrase; a gibe; a witty saying. **-ster** *n.* [L. *quippe*, indeed (ironical)].

quire (kwīr) *n.* 24 sheets of paper of the same size, the twentieth part of a ream [O.Fr. *quaier*, fr. L. *quattuor*, four].

quirk (kwurk) *n.* sudden turn or twist; a quibble; a peculiarity. **-y** *a.* [etym. uncertain].

quit (kwit) *v.t.* to depart from; to leave; to cease from; to give up; to let go; *v.i.* to depart; to stop doing a thing; *a.* released from obligation; free. *pr.p.* **-ting** *pa.p., pa.t.,* **quit** or **-ted. -tance** *n.* discharge from a debt of obligation; receipt. **-ter** *n.* (*Colloq.*) a person easily discouraged. **to be quits,** to be equal with another person by repayment (of money, of good, or evil) [O.Fr. *quiter*, fr. L. *quietare*, to calm].

quite (kwīt) *adv.* completely; wholly; entirely; positively [M.E. *quite*, free].

quiv·er (kwiv'·ęr) *n.* a case or sheath for holding arrows [O.Fr. *cuivre*, fr. Ger.].

quiv·er (kwiv'·ęr) *v.i.* to shake with a tremulous motion; to tremble; to shiver; *n.* the act of quivering; a tremor [O.E. *cwifer*, to risk].

Qui·xo·te (kē·hōt'·i·, kwik'·sȧt) *n.* the hero of the great romance of Miguel Cervantes. **quixotic** (kwik·sȧt'·ik) *a.* like Don Quixote; ideally and extravagantly romantic. **quixotically** *adv.* **quixotism. quixotry** *n.*

quiz (kwiz) *n.* a test or examination; a hoax or jest. *v.t.* to question. *pr.p.* **-zing.** *pa.p. pa.t.* **zed, -zer** *n.* **-zical** *a.* odd; amusing; teasing [etym. unknown].

quoin (koin) *n.* (*Archit.*) the external angle, esp. of a building; a cornerstone; (*Gun.*) a metalic wedge inserted under the breech of a gun to raise it; (*Print.*) a small wooden wedge used to lock the types in the galley etc. [Fr. *coin*, a corner].

quoit (kwoit) *n.* a flat, iron ring to be pitched at a fixed object in play; *pl.* game of throwing these on to a peg; *v.i.* to play at quoits.

quon·dam (kwȧn'·dąm) *a.* former; that was once; sometime [L. = formerly].

quo·rum (kwō'·rąm) *n.* the number of members that must be present at a meeting to make its transactions valid [L.]

quo·ta (kwō'·tą) *n.* a proportional part or share [L. *quot*, how many?].

quote (kwōt) *v.t.* to copy or repeat a passage from; to cite; to state a price for; *n.* a quotation; *pl.* quotation marks. **quotation** (kwō·tā'·shąn) *n.* **— marks** *n.pl.* marks ("—") used to indicate beginning and end of a quotation [Late L. *quotare*, to distinguish by numbers, fr. L. *quot*, how many?].

quoth (kwōth) *v.t.* (*Arch.*) said; spoke (used only in the 1st and 3rd persons) [O.E. *cwethan*, to say].

quo·tid·i·an (kwō·tid'·i·ąn) *a.* daily; *n.* thing returning daily, esp. fever [L. *quotidie*, daily].

quo·tient (kwō'·shąnt) *n.* number resulting from division of one number by another [L. *quotients*, how many times?].

R

rab·bet (rab'·it) *n.* a groove made so as to form, with a corresponding edge, a close joint; *v.t.* to cut such an edge [O.Fr. *raboter*, to plane].

rab·bi (rab'·ī), **rab·bin** (rab'·in) *n.* a Jewish teacher of the Law. **-nic(al)** [*Heb.* = my master].

rab·bit (rab'·it) *n.* a small, burrowing rodent mammal, like the hare, but smaller. **— hutch** *n.* an enclosure for rearing tame rabbits. **-ry, — warren** *n.* the breeding place of wild rabbits [etym. uncertain].

rab·ble (rab'·l) *n.* a noisy, disorderly crowd; the common herd; *v.t.* to mob.

rab·id (rab'·id) *a.* furious; fanatical; affected with rabies. **-ly** *adv.* **-ness, -ity** *n.* [L. *rabidus*].

ra·bies (rā'·bēz) *n.* canine madness; hydrophobia [L. fr. *rabere*, to be mad].

rac·coon, racoon (ra·kòòn') *n.* one of a genus of plantigrade carnivorous mammals of N. America [Algonquin].

race (rās) *n.* the descendants of a common ancestor; distinct variety of human species; a peculiar breed, as of horses, etc.; lineage;

descent. **racial** *a.* pert. to race or lineage. **racially** *adv.* **racialism, racism** *n.* animosity shown to peoples of different race [It. *razza*].

race (rās) *n.* swift progress; rapid motion; a contest involving speed; a strong current of water; the steel rings of an antifriction ball bearing; *v.t.* to cause to run rapidly; *v.i.* to run swiftly; of an engine, pedal, etc., to move rapidly without control. **-r** *n.* one who races; a racehorse, yacht, car, etc., used for racing. **— horse** *n.* a horse bred to run for a stake or prize. **— track** *n.* a track used for horse racing, etc. **racing** *n.* [O.E. *ras*, a swift course].

ra·chis (rā′·kis) *n.* an axial structure, such as vertebral column in animals, the stem of a plant, a quill, etc. *pl.* **rachides. rachitic** *a.* having rickets. **rachitis** (rạ·kī′·tis) *n.* rickets [Gk. *rhachis*, the spine].

rack (rak) *n.* an instrument for stretching; an instrument of torture by which the limbs were racked to point of dislocating; hence, torture; an open framework for displaying books, bottles, hats, baggage, etc.; a framework in which hay is placed; a straight cogged bar to gear with a toothed wheel to produce linear motion from rotary motion, or vice-versa; *v.t.* to stretch almost to breaking point; to overstrain; to torture; to place in a rack. **-ed** *a.* **-ing** *a.* agonizing (pain). **— and ruin** destruction [Dut. *rak*, fr. *reckken*, to stretch].

rack·et, racquet (rak′·it) *n.* bat used in tennis, etc.; a snowshoe. **-s** *n.pl.* a ball game played in a paved court with walls [Fr. *raquette*].

rack·et (rak′·it) *n.* a confused, clattering noise; din; (*Slang*) an occupation by which much money is made illegally; *v.i.* to make noise or clatter. **-eer** *n.* a gangster.

rac·on·teur (rak·ȧn·tur′) *n.* one skilled in telling anecdotes [Fr. *raconter*, to recount].

rac·y (rā′·si·) *a.* lively; having a strong flavor; spicy; pungent. **racily** *adv.* **raciness** *n.*

rad (rad) *n.* a standard unit of *rad*iation absorbed by the body.

ra·dar (rā′·dȧr) *n.* radiolocation or apparatus used in it [fr. *ra*dio *d*etecting *a*nd *r*anging].

ra·di·al (rā′·di·ạl) *a.* pert. to a ray, radius, or radium; branching out like spokes of a wheel [L. *radius*, a ray].

ra·di·an (rā′·di·ạn) *n.* (*Math.*) the angle subtended by an arc of a circle equal in length to the radius of a circle.

ra·di·ant (rā′·di·ạnt) *a.* emitting rays; beaming; radiating; *n.* (*Astron.*) point in sky from which a shower of meteors appears to come; (*Opt.*) luminous point from which rays of light emanate. **radiance, radiancy** *n.* brilliancy; splendor. **-ly** *adv.* [L. *radius*, a ray].

ra·di·ate (rā′·di·āt) *v.i.* to branch out like the spokes of a wheel; to emit rays; to shine, *v.t.* to emit rays, as heat, etc. *a.* with rays diverging from a center. **radiation** *n.* emission and diffusion of rays from central point; (*Phys.*) energy propagated in the form of waves or particles. **radiator** *n.* any device which radiates or emits rays of heat or light; apparatus for heating rooms; in motoring, apparatus to split up and cool circulating water in water-cooling system [L. *radius*, a ray].

rad·i·cal (rad′·i·kạl) *a. pert.* to the root; original; basic; complete; thorough; of extreme or advanced liberal views; *n.* (*Gram.*) a root; a primitive word; a politician who advocates thorough reforms; (*Chem.*) a basal atomic group of elements which passes unchanged through a series of reactions of the compound of which it is a part; (*Bot.*) a radicle; a rootlet; (*Math.*) a quantity expressed as the root of another. **-ism** *n.* root and branch political reform. **-ly** *adv.* **-ness** *n.* [L. *radix*, a root].

rad·i·cle (rad′·i·kạl) *n.* (*Med.*) the initial fibril of a nerve; (*Bot.*) the primary root of an embryo plant; rootlet [L. *radix*, a root].

ra·di·o- (rā′·di·ō) *prefix* meaning *of rays, radiation,* or *radium.* **— active** (rād·ē·ō·-ak′·tiv) *a.* emitting from an atomic nucleus invisible rays which penetrate matter. **-activity** *n.* **-element** *n.* metallic chemical element having radioactive properties. **-graph** *n.* an instrument for measuring and recording the intensity of the heat given off by the sun; a photograph taken by means of X-ray or other rays. **-grapher** *n.* **-graphy** *n.* **-logy** *n.* the science of radioactivity in medicine. **-logist** *n.* **-scopy** *n.* examination by X-rays. **-therapy, -therapeutics** *n.* treatment of disease by radium or X-rays [L. *radius*, a ray].

ra·di·o (rā·di·ō) *n.* wireless telephony or telegraphy; apparatus for reception of broadcast; a radio telegram. **— astronomy** *n.* the branch of astronomy that deals primarily with radio waves rather than visible light. **-gram** *n.* a telegram transmitted by radio. **— telescope** *n.* a large concave antenna for detecting radio waves from outer space [L. *radius*, a ray].

rad·ish (rad′·ish) *n.* an annual herb with pungent edible root [L. *radix*, a root].

ra·di·um rā′·di·ạm) *n.* a metallic, radioactive element [L. *radius*, a ray].

ra·di·us (rā′·di·ạs) *n.* a straight line from center of circle to circumference; the spoke of a wheel; distance from any one place; the bone on the thumb side of forearm; movable arm of a sextant. *pl.* **-es, radii** [L. = a ray].

ra·dix (rā′·diks) *n.* a root; source; origin; a radical; (*Anat.*) the point of origin of a structure, as the root of a tooth; (*Math.*) fundamental base of system of logarithms or numbers. *pl.* **-es, radices** [L. = root].

ra·don (rā′·dȧn) *n.* a gaseous, radioactive element; radium emanation.

raff (raf) *n.* the mob; a worthless fellow (See *riff-raff*). **-ish** *a.* [O.Fr. *raffer*, to snatch].

raf·fi·a (raf′·i·a) *n.* the fiber from a cultivated palm used for mats, baskets, etc. [fr. Malagasy].

raf·fle (raf′·l) *n.* a lottery; *v.t.* to sell by raffle. **-r** *n.* [orig. a dicing game, Fr. *rafle*].

raft (raft) *n.* an improvised float of planks or logs fastened together; *v.i.* to proceed by raft [O.N. *raptr*].

raft (raft) *n.* (*Colloq.*) a great quantity.

raft·er (raf·tẹr) *n.* a sloping beam, from the ridge to the eaves, to which the roof covering is attached; *v.t.* to provide with rafters [O.E. *raefter*].

rag (rag) *n.* a fragment of cloth; a remnant; a scrap; (*Slang*) a newspaper; *a.* made of rags. **-amuffin** *n.* a ragged, dirty and disreputable person. **-man, -picker** *n.* one who collects rags. **-tag** *n.* the rabble; riffraff. **-time** *n.* popular dance music, marked by strong syncopation. **-weed** *n.* a widespread weed, common cause of hay fever. [O.E. *ragg*].

rag (rag) *v.t.* to tease; to nag; *pr.p.* **-ging** *pa.t.* and *pa.p.* **-ged** [etym. uncertain].

rage (rāj) *n.* violent excitement or anger; craze; fashion; *v.i.* to be furious with anger; to rave. **raging** *a.* [Fr., fr. L. *rabies*, madness].

rag·ged (rag′·ạd) *a.* worn to tatters; dressed in rags; jagged; slip-shod; imperfectly performed; not rhythmical. **-ly** *adv.* **-ness** *n.*

rag·lan (rag′·lạn) *n.* an overcoat with wide sleeves running up to the neck, not to the shoulders [fr. Lord *Raglan*, 1788-1855].

ra·gout (ra·gȯȯ′) *n.* fragments of meat, stewed and highly seasoned; a hash [Fr.].

raid (rād) *n.* a hostile incursion depending on surprise and rapidity; surprise visit by police to suspected premises; an attack on a town by hostile aircraft; *v.t.* to make a sudden attack upon. **-er** *n.* [var. of *road*].

rail (rāl) *n.* a piece of timber or metal extending from one post to another, as of a fence or balustrade; bars of steel on which the flanged wheels of vehicles run; a track for locomotives; a railway; a horizontal bar for support; top of ship's bulwarks; *v.t.* to enclose with rails; to send by railway. **-ing** *n.* material for rails; a construction of rails. **-road** *n.* a road on which steel rails are laid for wheels to run on; a system of such rails and all equipment; the company that runs it. **-way** *n.* a line of tracks, for wheeled vehicles [O.Fr. *reille,* fr. L. *regula,* a rule].

rail (rāl) *n.* wading birds [Fr. *râle*].

rail (rāl) *v.i.* to use insolent and reproachful language; to utter abuse. **-er** *n.* **-lery** *n.* good-humored banter; ridicule [Fr. *railler*].

rai·ment (rā′·mant) *n.* (*Poetic*) clothing dress; apparel [for *arraiment,* fr. *array*].

rain (rān) *n.* condensed moisture, falling in drops from clouds; a shower; *v.t.* and *v.i.* to fall as rain; to pour down like rain. **-bow** *n.* arch showing seven prismatic colors and formed by refraction and reflection of sun's rays in falling rain. **— check** *n.* a ticket for a future performance, game, etc. when one is stopped by rain. **-coat** *n.* a light, rainproof overcoat. **-fall** *n.* a fall of rain; the amount of rain, in inches, which falls in a particular place in a given time. **-iness** *n.* **-less** *a.* **-proof** *a.* impervious to rain. **-y** *a.* [O.E. *regn*].

raise (rāz) *v.t.* to cause to rise; to elevate; to promote; to build up; to collect; to produce by cultivation; to rear; to increase; to enliven; to give up (seige); to heighten (voice); *a.* **-d** *a.* elevated. **raising** *n.* [O.N. *reisa*].

rai·sin (rā′·zn) *n.* a dried grape [O.Fr. *raizin* fr. L. *racemus,* a bunch of grapes].

raj (ráj) *n.* sovereignty; rule; dominion. **raja, rajah** *n.* king, prince, or noble of the Hindus [Hind. *raja*].

rake (rāk) *n.* a long-handled garden implement; an agricultural machine used in haymaking; *v.t.* and *v.i.* to scrape with a toothed implement; to draw together, as mown hay; to sweep or search over; to ransack; to scour; to fire shot lengthwise into a ship, etc. **a rake-off** (*Slang*) a monetary commission esp. if illegal [O.E. *raca*].

rake (rāk) *n.* a dissolute man of fashion; a libertine **rakish** *a.* **rakishly** *adv.* [M.E. *rakel;* corrupt, of *rake-hell*].

rake (rāk) *n.* an angle of inclination; the inclination of masts from the perpendicular; the projection of the upper parts of the stem and stern beyond the keel of a ship; *v.i.* to incline from perpendicular. **rakish** *a.* having a backward inclination of the masts; speedy-looking. **rakishly** *adv.* [Scand. *raka,* to reach].

ral·ly (ral′·i·) *v.t.* and *v.i.* to reassemble; to collect and restore order, as troops in confusion; to recover (strength; health); to return a ball (in tennis). *n.* act of rallying; assembly; outdoor demonstration; lively exchange of strokes in tennis [Fr. *rallier*].

ram (ram) *n.* male sheep; a swinging beam with a metal head for battering; a hydraulic engine; a beak projecting from bow of warship; (*Astron.*) Aries, one of the signs of zodiac; *v.t.* to consolidate loose material with a rammer; to drive against with violence; to butt; to cram; *pr.p.* **-ming.** *pa.t.* and *pa.p.* **-med, -er** *n.* [O.E. *ram*].

ram·ble (ram′·bl) *v.i.* to walk without definite route; to talk or write incoherently; *n.* a short stroll or walk. **-r** *n.* one who rambles; a climbing rose. **rambling** *a.* wandering.

ram·bunc·tious (ram.bung(k)′·shas) *a.* boisterous; noisy (*Slang*).

ram·e·kin (ram′·a·kin) *n.* a cheese preparation or other food mixture baked in a small dish; the dish itself [F. *ramequin*].

ram·i·fy (ram′·a·fī) *v.t.* and *v.i.* to branch out in various directions. **ramification** *n.* a branch; any subdivision proceeding from a main structure [L. *ramus,* a branch; *facere,* to make].

ramp (ramp) *v.i.* to rear up on hind legs; *n.* a gradual slope; [Fr. *ramper,* to climb].

ram·page (ram′·pāj) *n.* a state of excitement or passion, as **on the rampage;** *v.i.* (ram·pāj′) to rush about, in a rage; to act violently. **-ous** *a.* [fr. *ramp*].

ramp·ant (ramp′·ant) *a.* rearing; violent; in full sway; rank. **rampancy** *n.* [Fr. *ramper,* to climb].

ram·part (ram′·párt) *n.* mound of earth around fortified place; that which provides security; *v.t.* to strengthen with ramparts [Fr. *rempart*].

ram·rod (ram′·rád) *n.* rod used in ramming down charge of a gun; a rod for cleaning barrel of a rifle, etc. [fr. *ram.*].

ram·shack·le (ram′·shak.l) *a.* tumble-down; rickety; beyond repair [fr. *shake*].

ran (ran) *pa.t.* of run.

ranch (ranch) *n.* prairie land for sheep and cattle rearing; a farm; *v.i.* to keep a ranch. **-er** *n.* man who owns or works on a ranch [Sp. Amer. *rancho,* a grazing farm].

ran·cid (ran′·sid) *a.* having a rank smell; smelling or tasting like stale fat. **-ly** *adv.* **-ness, -ity** *n.* [L. *rancidus*].

ran·cor (rang′·ker) *n.* bitter and inveterate ill-feeling. **-ous** *a.* evincing intense and bitter hatred; malignant. **-ously** *adv.* [L. *rancor*].

rand (rand) *n.* thin inner sole of shoe; high land above river valley [O.E. *rand,* a border].

ran·dom (ran′·dam) *a.* done haphazardly; aimless; fortuitous; *n.* in phrase, **at random,** haphazard [O.Fr. *random,* headlong rush].

ra·nee, rani (rán′·ē) *n.* in India, a queen or wife of a prince.

rang (rang) *pa.t.* of ring.

range (rānj) *v.t.* to set in a row; to rank; to rove over; *v.i.* to extend; to roam; to be in line with; to pass from one point to another; to fluctuate between, as prices, etc.; *n.* limits, or distance within which something is possible; a row; a large kitchen stove; line of mountains; compass or register of voice or instrument; distance to a target; place for practice shooting; pasture land. **-er** *n.* keeper of park or forest. **rangy** *a.* roaming; long-limbed; slender [Fr. *ranger,* fr. *rang,* a rank].

rank (rangk) *n.* row or line; soldiers standing side by side; grade in armed services; status; a class; social position; eminence; relative position; *pl.* enlisted soldiers; *v.t.* to arrange in class, order, or division; to place in line or abreast; to take rank over; *v.i.* to be placed in a rank or class; to possess social or official distinction. **-er** *n.* **-ing** *n.* arrangement; disposition [Fr. *rang*].

rank (rangk) *a.* growing too thickly; exuberant; offensively strong of smell; rancid; gross; vile; excessive. **-le** *v.i.* to be inflamed; to become more violent; to remain a sore point with. **-ly** *adv.* **-ness** *n.* [O.E. *ranc,* strong, proud].

ran·sack (ran′·sak) *v.t.* to search thoroughly; to plunder [O.N. *rannsaka*].

ran·som (ran′·sam) *n.* a price paid for release of prisoner; immense sum of money; *v.t.* to redeem from captivity [O.Fr. fr. L. *redemptio,* buying back].

rant (rant) *v.i.* to rave; to talk wildly and noisily; *n.* noisy and meaningless declamation; boisterous talk. **-er** *n.* [O.Dut. *ranten,* to rave].

rap (rap) *n.* a smart, light blow; a knock on door, etc.; a tap; *v.t.* and *v.i.* to deliver a smart blow; to knock; *pr.p.* **-ping.** *pa.t.* and *pa.p.* **-ped** [prob. imit.].

ra·pa·cious (ra·pā′·shas) *a.* subsisting on prey; greedy; grasping. **-ly** *adv.* **-ness, rapacity** *n.* [L. *rapere,* to seize].

rape (rāp) *n.* carnal knowledge of a female against her will; the act of snatching or carrying off by force; *v.t.* to ravish or violate [L. *rapere,* to seize].

rape (rāp) *n.* an annual of the cabbage family, the seeds of which yield vegetable oils [L. *rapum*, turnip].

rap·id (rap′·id) *a.* very quick; fast; speedy; hurried; descending steeply. **-s** *n.pl.* part of a river where current rushes over rocks. **-ity** *n.* **-ly** *adv.* **-ness** *n.* [L. *rapidus*].

ra·pi·er (rā′·pi·ęr) *n.* a light, slender, pointed sword, for thrusting only [Fr. *rapière*].

rap·ine (rap′·in) *n.* act of plundering; pillage; plunder [L. *rapina*, fr. *rapere*, to snatch].

rap·port (ra·pōr′) *n.* harmony; agreement. **en rapport,** in relation to; in harmony with [Fr.].

rap·proche·ment (ra·prōsh·máng′) *n.* reconciliation; restoration of friendly relations [Fr.].

rap·scal·lion (rap·skal′·yąn) *n.* a scamp; a rascal. See **rascal.**

rapt (rapt) *a.* intent; transported; in a state of rapture. **-ure** *n.* extreme joy; ecstasy; bliss; exultation. **-urous** *a.* ecstatic; exulting. **-urously** *adv.* [L. *rapere, raptum*, to snatch away].

rare (rer) *a.* underdone (of meat) [O.E. *hrere*, boiled gently].

rare (rer) *a.* uncommon, few and far between; thin, not dense, as air; extremely valuable; of the highest excellence. **-faction** *n.* act of rarefying; decrease of quantity of a gas in fixed volume. **rarefy** (rer′·ą·fī) *v.t.* to make rare or less dense; *v.i.* to become less dense. **-ly** *adv.* **-ness** *n.* **rarity** *n.* state of being rare; thinness; something rare or seldom seen [L. *rarus*].

rare·bit (rer′·bit) *n.* (*Cookery*) Welsh rabbit; cheese sauce on toast, etc. [corrupt. of *rabbit*].

ras·cal (ras′·kąl) *n.* a rogue; a scoundrel; a scamp; *a.* dishonest; low. **-ity** *n.* knavery; base villainy. **-ly** *a.* [O.Fr. *rascaille*, the rabble].

rash (rash) *a.* without reflection; precipitate. **-ly** *adv.* **-ness** *n.* [Dut. *rasch*, quick].

rash (rash) *n.* a temporary, superficial eruption of the skin [O.Fr. *rasche*, itch].

rash·er (rash′·ęr) *n.* a thin slice of bacon [Fr. *arracher*, to tear up].

rasp (rasp) *v.t.* to rub or file; to scrape (skin) roughly; to speak in grating manner; to irritate; *n.* a form of file with one side flat and the other rounded; a rough, grating sound. **-ing** *a.* emitting a harsh, grating sound; irritating. **-ingly** *adv.* [O.Fr. *rasper*].

rasp·ber·ry (raz′·ber·i·) *n.* a plant, cultivated for its fruit; a small drupe, the fruit of the plant; (*Slang*) derisory applause [E. *rasp*, rough, like a file].

rat (rat) *n.* large rodent; (*Slang*) one who deserts his party; (*Colloq.*) padding to puff out women's hair; *v.i.* to hunt rats; to abandon party or associates in times of difficulty. *pr.p.* **-ting** *pa.t.* and *pa.p.* **-ted.** **-ter** *n.* a rat-catcher; a terrier which kills rats. **-ting** *n.* [O.E. *raet*].

rat·a·fi·a (rat·a·fē′·a) *n.* a liquer, such as curaçoa; a cordial [Fr.].

ratch·et (rach′·it) *n.* a bar or piece of mechanism turning at one end upon a pivot, while the other end falls into teeth of wheel, allowing the latter to move in one direction only [Fr. *rochet*, ratchet of a clock].

rate (rāt) *n.* established measure; degree; standard; proportion; ratio; value; price; movement, as fast or slow; *v.t.* to estimate value; to settle relative scale, rank, price or position of; *v.i.* to be set in a class; to have rank. **-able, ratable** *a.* **ratability** *n.* **rating** *n.* assessment; (*Naut.*) classification of a ship; amount set as a rate [O.Fr. fr. L. *rata* (*pars*), fixed portion].

rate (rāt) *v.i.* to take to task; to chide.

rather (raTH′·ęr) *adv.* preferably; on the other hand; somewhat [O.E. *hrathe*, quickly].

rat·i·fy (rat′·ą·fī) *v.t.* to confirm or sanction officially; to make valid. **ratification** *n.* [L. *ratus*, fixed; *facere*, to make].

rat·ing See **rate.**

ra·tio (rā′·shō) *n.* relation one quantity has to another, as expressed by number of times one can be divided by the other; proportion [L.].

ra·ti·oc·i·nate (rash·i·ás′·à·nāt) *v.i.* to reason logically. **ratiocination** *n.* deductive reasoning. **ratiocinative** *a.* [L.*ratiocinari*, to reckon].

ra·tion (ra′·shąn, rā′·shąn) *n.* fixed allotted portion; daily allowance of food, drink, etc., to armed forces; *pl.* provisions; *v.t.* to limit to fixed amount [Fr. fr. L. *ratio*].

ra·tion·al (rash′·ąn·ąl) *a.* sane; sensible; reasonable; (*Math.*) a quantity expressed in finite terms or whose root is a whole number. **-e** (rash·ą·nal′) *n.* logical basis; exposition of principles. **-ization** *n.* in psychology, the attempt to square one's conscience by inventing reasons for one's own conduct; **-ize** *v.t.* **-ism** *n.* philosophy which makes reason the sole guide; system opposed to supernatural or divine revelation. **-ist** *a.* **istic(al)** *a.* **-istically** *adv.* **-ity** *n.* the power or faculty of reasoning; soundness of mind. **-ly** *adv.* [L. *rationalis*, fr. *ratio*, reason].

rats·bane (ratz′·bān) *n.* rat poison.

rat·tan, ratan (ra·tan′) *n.* a species of palm found in India and the Malay Peninsula; the stems used for wickerwork, etc.; a walking-stick made from a rattan cane [Malay, *rotan*].

rat·tle (rat′·l) *v.i.* to clatter; to speak (on) eagerly and noisily; to move along, quickly and noisily; *v.t.* to shake briskly, causing sharp noises; (*Colloq.*) to disconcert, or ruffle; *n.* a rapid succession of clattering sounds; a toy for making a noise; rings at the end of a rattlesnake's tail. **-brained, -headed, -pated** *a.* empty-headed; giddy; lacking stability. **-snake** *n.* an American poisonous snake. **rattling** *n.* clattering; *a.* brisk; lively; first-rate; *adv.* extremely; very [M.E. *ratelen*].

rat·ty (rat′·i·) *a.* full of rats; (*Slang*) shabby.

rau·cous (raw′·kąs) *a.* hoarse; harsh; rough. **-ly** *adv.* [L.*racus*].

rav·age (rav′·ij) *v.t.* to lay waste; to despoil; to plunder; *n.* ruin; destruction [Fr.].

rave (rāv) *v.i.* to talk in delirium or with great enthusiasm. **-r** *n.* **raving** *n.* delirium; incoherent or wild talk; *a.* delirious; (*Colloq.*) exceptional. **ravingly** *adv.* [O.Fr. *raver*].

rav·el (rav′·ąl) *v.t.* to entangle; to make intricate; to fray out; *v.i.* to become twisted and involved; to fall into confusion. *n.* complication; unraveled thread [Dut. *ravelen*].

ra·ven (rā′·vąn) *n.* crow with glossy black plumage, predatory in habit; *a.* glossy black, esp. of hair [O.F. *hraefn*].

rav·en, ravin (rav′·n) *v.t.* and *v.i.* to devour; to prowl for prey; to be ravenous; *n.* rapine; plunder; spoil. **-er** *n.* a plunderer. **-ous** *a.* famished; voracious; eager for prey. **-ously** *adv.* [Fr. *ravir*, fr. *L. rapere*, to seize].

ra·vine (ra·vēn′) *n.* a deep, narrow gorge; a gully [O.Fr. fr. L. *rapere*, to carry off].

rav·ish (rav′·ish) *v.t.* to seize and carry away by violence; to rape; to enrapture; to charm eye or ear. **-er** *n.* **-ing** *a.* entrancing; captivating. **-ingly** *adv.* **-ment** *n.* [Fr. *ravir*, fr. L. *rapere*, to carry off].

raw (raw) *a.* not cooked; not covered with skin; chilly and damp; untrained; not manufactured. *n.* a sore; naked state. **-boned** *a.* having little flesh; gaunt. **-hide** *n.* compressed untanned leather; a riding whip of untanned leather. **-ly** *adv.* **-ness** *n.* **— deal,** unfair and undeserved treatment [O.E. *hreaw*].

ray (rā) *n.* a narrow beam of light; the path along which light and electro-magnetic waves travel in space; a heat radiation; one of a number of lines diverging from a common point or center; a gleam or suggestion (of hope, truth, etc.); *v.t.* and *v.i.* to radiate; to send forth rays. **-ed** *a.* having rays [O.Fr. *raye,* fr. L. *radus,* a beam].

ray (rā) *n.* a flat fish allied to skate, shark, and dogfish [O.Fr. *raye*].

ray·on (rā′·ȧn) *n.* a synthetic fibrous material in imitation of silk [Fr.].

raze, rase (rāz) *v.t.* to level to the ground; to destroy completely; to demolish [Fr. *raser,* fr. L. *radere, rasum,* to scrape].

ra·zor (rā′·zẹr) *n.* a keen-edged cutting appliance for shaving. **-back** *n.* kind of hog; rorqual or finbacked whale [Fr. *rasoir,* fr. L. *radere, rasum,* to scrape].

razz (raz) *v.t.* to ridicule [fr. *raspberry*].

re-, *prefix* used in the formation of compound words,usually to signify *back* or *again* [L.]

re (rē) *prep.* in reference to; concerning. **in re,** in the case (of) [L. *res,* thing].

reach (rēch) *v.t.* to extend; to stretch; to touch by extending hand; to attain to or arrive at; to come to; to obtain; to gain; *v.i.* to stretch out the hand; to strain after; to be extended; to arrive; *n.* reaching; easy distance; mental range; scope; grasp; straight stretch of water, etc. **-able** *a.* [O.E. *raecan,* to stretch out].

re·act (rē·akt′) *v.i.* to respond to stimulus; to exercise a reciprocal effect on each other; to resist the action of another body by an opposite effect; (*Chem.*) to cause or undergo a chemical or physical change when brought in contact with another substance or exposed to light, heat, etc. **-ance** *n.* (*Elect.*) resistance in a coil to an alternating current due to capacity or inductance in the circuit. **-ion** *n.* action in opposite direction to another; the response to stimulus, influence, events, etc. **-ionary** *a.* tendency to reaction. *n.* one opposed to progressive ideas in politics, religion, thought, etc. **-ionist** *n.* **-ivation** *n.* restoration to an activated state. **-ive** *a.*

re·act (rē′·akt) *v.t.* to act again; to repeat.

re·ac·tor (rē·act′·ẹr) *n.* apparatus for generating heat by nuclear fission.

read (rēd) *v.t.* to peruse and understand written or printed matter; to interpret mentally; to read and utter; to understand any indicating instrument (as a gas meter); *v.i.* to perform the act of reading; to find mentioned in writing or print; to surmise. *pa.t.* and *pa.p.* **read** (red). **read** (red). *a.* versed in books; learned. **-able** (rēd) *a.* well written; informative; interesting; legible. **-ably** (rēd) *adv.* **-er** (rēd) *n.* one who reads; one whose office is to read prayers; one who determines suitability for publication of manuscripts offered to publisher; corrector of printer's proofs; a reading book. **-ing** (rēd) *a.* pert. to reading; *n.* act of reading; a public recital of passages from books; interpretation of a passage from a book [O.E. *raedan,* to make out].

read·i·ly, readiness See **ready.**

re·ad·just (rē·ạ·just′) *v.t.* to adjust or put in order again. **-ment** *n.*

read·y (red′·i·) *a.* prepared; fitted for use; handy; prompt; quick; willing; apt; *v.t.* to prepare. *n.* position of a fighting unit or their weapons, as *at the ready.* **readily** *adv.* **readiness** *n.* **—made** *a.* not made to measure. **— money,** cash in hand [O.E. *raede*].

re·a·gent (rē·ā·′jạnt) *n.* any substance employed to bring about a characteristic reaction in chemical analysis. **reagency** *n.*

re·al (rē′·ạl) *a.* actual; not sham; not fictitious or imaginary; not assumed; unaffected; (*Law*) heritable; denoting property not movable or personal, as lands and tenements. **reality** (ri·al′·a·ti·) *n.* actuality; fact; truth. **-ly** *adv.* actually; indeed; *interj.* is that so? **-ty** *n.* real estate. **— estate, — property,** immovable property [L.L. *realis,* fr. L. *res,* a thing].

re·al (rē′·ȧl) *n.* an obsolete Spanish coin [Sp. fr. L. *regalis,* royal].

re·al·ize (rē′·ạl·īz) *v.t.* to make real; to yield (profit); to convert into money; to apprehend or grasp the significance of. **realization** *n.* **realism** *n.* interest in things as they are; practical outlook on life; representation in art or letters of real life, even if sordid and repellent; (*Philos.*) doctrine that matter has a separate existence apart from conceptions of it in the mind; doctrine that general terms and ideas have objective existence and are not mere names. **realist** *n.* **realistic** *a.* pert. to realism; factual; practical; true to life. **realistically** *adv.* [Fr. *réaliser*].

reality, realtor, realty See **real** (1).

realm (relm) *n.* kingdom; province; region [O.Fr. *realme,* fr. L. *regalis,* royal].

ream (rēm) *n.* a paper measure containing from 472 to 516 sheets, usually 500 sheets (20 quires) [Ar. *rizmah,* bundle].

ream (rēm) *v.t.* to enlarge or make a tapered or conical hole with a reamer. **-er** *n.* a machine tool for enlarging a hole [O.E. *rum,* room].

reap (rēp) *v.t.* to cut down ripe grain for harvesting; to harvest; to receive as fruits of one's labor. **-er** *n.* a harvester; a reaping machine [O.E. *ripan*].

rear (rir) *n.* back of hindmost part; part of army or fleet behind the others. **-most** *a.* last of all; at the very back [L. *retro,* behind].

rear (rir) *v.t.* to raise; to bring to maturity, as young; to erect or build; *v.i.* to rise up on the hindlegs, as a horse [O.E. *raeran*].

re·arm (rē·ȧrm′) *v.t.* to equip the fighting services with new weapons. **-ament** *n.*

re·ar·range (rē·ạ·rānj′) *v.t.* to arrange anew; to set in a different order. **-ment** *n.*

rea·son (rē′·zn) *n.* a faculty of thinking; power of understanding; intelligence; the logical premise of an argument; cause; motive; purpose; excuse; *v.i.* to exercise rational faculty; to deduce from facts or premises; to argue with; *v.t.* to discuss by arguments. **-able** *a.* rational; just; fair. **-ableness** *n.* **-ably** *adv.* **-er** *n.* **-ing** *n.* [Fr. *raison,* fr. L. *ratio,* reason].

re·as·sure (rē·ạ·shoor′) *v.t.* to free from fear; to allay anxiety; to restore confidence, or spirit to **reassurance** *n.* **reassuring** *a.*

re·bate (rē′·bāt) *v.t.* to allow as discount; *n.* deduction [Fr. *rabattre,* to beat down].

re·bate. See **rabbet.**

reb·el (reb′·ạl) *n.* one who resists the lawful authority of a government; revolter; revolutionist; one who is defiant;*a.* rebellious. **rebel** (ri·bel′) *v.i.* to take up arms against state or government; to revolt. *pr.p.* **-ling.** *pa.t.* and *pa.p.* **-led. -lion** *n.* organized resistance to authority; insurrection; mutiny. **-lious** *a.* [L. *rebellare,* fr. *bellum,* war].

re·birth (rē·burth′) *n.* state of being born again, spiritually; renaissance, as in the Rebirth of Learning.

re·bound (rē·bound′) *v.i.* to leap back; to recoil; to bound repeatedly; *v.t.* to cause to fly back; (rē′·bound) *n.* rebounding; recoil..

re·buff (ri·buf′) *n.* a blunt, contemptuous refusal; a snub; a repulse; *v.t.* to beat back; to check; to snub [It. *rebuffo,* reproof].

re·buke (ri·būk′) *v.t.* to censure; to reprove; to reprimand; *n.* reprimand; reproof [O.Fr. *revuchier*, repulse].

re·bus (rē′·bạs) *n.* an enigmatical representation of a name, word, or phrase by pictures suggesting syllables [L. = by things].

re·but (ri·but′) *v.t.* to refute, to disprove; *pr.p.* **-ting.** *pa.t.* and *pa.p.* **-ted. -table** *a.* **-tal** *n.* refutation of an argument [Fr. *re-voutier*, to repulse].

re·cal·ci·trate (ri·kal′·si·trāt) *v.i.* to kick back; to be refractory. **recalcitrant** *n.* one who defies authority; *a.* refractory; willfully disobedient. **recalcitrance, recalcitration** *n.* [L. *recalcitrare*, to kick back].

re·call (ri·kawl′) *v.t.* to call back; to take back (a gift, etc.); to annul or revoke; to call to mind; to remember; *n.* (rē′·kawl) act of recalling; a summons to return.

re·cant (ri·kant′) *v.t.* to take back, words or opinions; to retract; *v.i.* to unsay. **-ation** *n.* [L. *recantare*, fr. *re-*, back; *contare*, to sing].

re·ca·pit·u·late (rē·kạ·pich′·ạ·lāt) *v.t.* to relate in brief the matter or substance of a previous discourse; *v.i.* to sum up what has been previously said. **recapitulation** *n.* [L. *capitulum*, a small head].

re·cap·ture (rē·kap′·chẹr) *v.t.* to capture back; to regain; *n.* act of retaking.

re·cast (rē·kast′) *v.t.* to cast or mold again; to remodel; to throw back; to add up figures in a column a second time.

re·cede (ri·sēd′) *v.i.* to move or fall back; to retreat; to withdraw; to ebb. **receding** *a.*

re·ceipt (ri·sēt′) *n.* the act of receiving; a written acknoweldgment of money received; a recipe in cookery; *pl.* money received; *v.t.* to give a receipt for [L. *recipere, receptum*, to receive].

re·ceive (ri·sēv′) *v.t.* to take; to accept; to get (an offer, etc.); to acquire; to welcome or entertain; to hold; to take or buy stolen goods. **receivable** *a.* **-r** *n.* one who receives; receptacle, place of storage, etc.; one who receives goods knowing them to have been stolen; appointed by court to receive profits of business being wound up by that court; (*Chem.*) a vessel into which spirits are emitted in distillation; a radio receiving set; earpiece of a telephone. **receiving** *n.* [O.Fr. fr. L. *recipere*, to take back].

re·cent (rē′·sạnt) *a.* that has lately happened; new; **-ly** *adv.* **-ness** *n.* [L. *recens*].

re·cep·ta·cle (ri·sep′·tạ·kạl) *n.* a vessel—that which receives, or into which anything is ıeceived and held [L. *recipere, receptum*, to receive].

re·cep·tion (ri·sep′·shạn) *n.* receiving; welcome; ceremonial occasion when guests are personally announced; the quality of signals received in broadcasting. **receptible** *a.* receivable. **-ist** *n.* person in hotel, office, etc., who receives guests or clients. **receptive** *a.* able to grasp ideas or impressions quickly. **receptiveness, receptivity** *n.* [L. *recipere, receptum*, to receive].

re·cess (rē′·ses) *n.* a withdrawing from usual activity; suspension of business; vacation, as of legislative body or school; a secluded place; a niche or cavity in a wall; (*Zool.*) a small cleft or indentation in an organ; *v.t.* to make, or place in, a recess; *v.i.* to go on a recess. **-ed** *a.* fitted with recess. **-ion** *n.* act of receding or withdrawing; a period of reduced trade or business; a procession at the close of a service. **-ional** *a.* pert. to recession; *n.* hymn sung as clergyman leaves chancel. **-ive** *a.* **-iveness** *n.* [L. *recessus*, fr. *recedere* to recede].

re·cher·che (rẹ·shur′·shā) *a.* of studied elegance; choice; exquisite; exclusion [Fr].

rec·i·pe (res′·ạ·pē) *n.* a prescription; a cookery receipt [L. imper. of *recipere*, to take].

re·cip·i·ent (ri·sip′·i·ạnt) *a.* receptive; *n.* one who receives [L. *recipere*, to receive].

re·cip·ro·cal (ri·sip′·rạ·kạl) *a.* moving backwards and forwards; alternating; mutual; complementary; (*Gram.*) reflexive; *n.* idea or term alternating with, or corresponding to, another by contrast or opposition; quantity arising from dividing unity by any quantity. **-s** *n.pl.* two numbers which multiplied give unity, e.g. $\frac{9}{5} \times \frac{5}{9} = 1$. **-ly** *adv.* **-ness** *n.* **reciprocate** *v.t.* to make return for; to interchange; *v.i.* to move backwards and forwards; to act interchangeably; to alternate. **reciprocating, reciprocatory** *a.* **reciprocation** *n.* mutual giving and receiving. **reciprocative** *a.* **reciprocity** (res·ạ·prȧs′·ạ·ti·) *n.* action and reaction; the discharge of mutual duties or obligations [L. *reciprocus*, turning back].

re·ci·sion (ri·sizh′·ạn) *n.* the act of cutting, annulling [L. *rescindere, rescissus*, to cut off].

re·cite (ri·sīt′) *v.t., v.i.* to repeat aloud esp. before an audience. **recital** *n.* act of reciting; what is recited; detailed narration; a musical or dramatic performance by one person or by one composer or author. **recitation** *n.* reciting; repetition of something from memory. **recitative** (res·ạ·tȧ·tēv′) *n.* declamation to musical accompaniment, as in opera; *a.* in the style of recitative. **-r** *n.* [L. *recitare*, to read aloud].

reck (rek) *v.t., v.i.* (*Arch.*) to heed. **-less** *a.* rashly negligent. **-lessly** *adv.* **-lessness** *n.* [O.E. *reccan*, to care for].

reck·on (rek′·n) *v.t., v.i.* to count; to calculate; to estimate; to value; (*Colloq.*) to think; to be of opinion. **-er** *n.* one who reckons; table of calculations. **-ing** *n.* computing; calculation; a bill [M.E. *rekkenen*].

re·claim (ri·klām′) *v.t.* to bring into a state of productiveness, as waste land, etc.; to win back from error or sin. **-able** *a.* able to be reclaimed or reformed. **reclamation** (rek·-lạ·mā′·shạn) *n.*

re·claim (rē·klām′) *v.t.* to demand the return of.

re·cline (ri·klīn′) *v.t.* to lean back; *v.i.* to assume a recumbent position; to rest. **-r** *n.* [L. *reclinare*].

rec·luse (rek′·lòòs) *a.* secluded from the world; solitary; *n.* a hermit. [L. *reclusus*, shut away.]

rec·og·nize (rek′·ạg·nīz) *v.t.* to know again; to identify; to acknowledge; to treat as valid; to realize; to salute. **recognizable** *a.* **recognizably** *adv.* **recognizance** *n.* acknowledgment of a person or thing; an obligation, under penalty, entered into before some court or magistrate to do, or to refrain from doing, some particular act; sum pledged as surety. **recognition** *n.* recognizing; acknowledgment. **recognitive, recognitory** *a.* [L. *recognoscere*].

re·coil (ri·koil′) *v.i.* to start, roll, bound, fall back; to draw back; to rebound; (rē′·koil) *n.* return motion; a starting or falling back [Fr. *reculer*, to spring back].

rec·ol·lect (rek·ạ·lekt′) *v.t.* to recall; to remember. **-ion** *n.* power of recalling ideas to the mind; remembrance; things remembered [L. *recolligere*, to collect again].

re·com·bi·nant (rē·kȧm′·bi·nạnt) *n.* (*Genetics*) an organism in which a new combination has occurred; *a.* **recombination** *n.*

rec·om·mend (rek·ạ·mend′) *v.t.* to speak well of; to commend; to advise. **-able** *a.* worthy of recommendation. **-ation** *n.* recommending; a statement that one is worthy of favor or trial.

rec·om·pense (rek′·ạm·pens) *v.t.* to repay; to reward, to make an equivalent return for service, loss, etc.; to make up for; *n.* repay-

ment; requital [Fr. *récompenser*].
rec·on·cile (rek′·ạn·sīl) *v.t.* to conciliate; to restore to friendship; to make agree; to become resigned (to); to adjust or compose. **reconcilable** *a.* **-ment, reconciliation** *n.* renewal of friendship; harmonizing of apparently opposed ideas, etc.; (*Bib.*) expiation; **reconciliatory** *a.* [L. *reconciliare*].
rec·on·dite (rek′·ạn·dīt) *a.* hidden from view or mental perception; obscure; little known. **-ness** *n.* [L. *reconditus*, hidden away].
re·con·di·tion (rē·kạn·dish′·ạn) *v.t.* to restore to sound condition, either person or thing; to renovate; to repair.
re·con·nais·sance (ri·kȧn′·ạ·sạns) *n.* an examination or survey, by land or air, for engineering or military operations [Fr.].
re·con·noi·ter (rē·kạ·noi′·tẹr) *v.t.* to make a preliminary survey of, esp. with a view to military operations; *v.i.* to make reconnaissance; to scout; *n.* a preliminary survey [Fr. *reconnoître, reconnaître*, to recognize].
re·con·sid·er (rē·kạn·sid′·ẹr)*v.t.* to consider again; to take up for renewed discussion.
re·con·sti·tute (rē·kȧn′·stạ·to͝ot) *v.t.* to constitute anew; to reconstruct; to restore a dehydrated substance to original form.
re·con·struct (rē·kạn·strukt′) *v.t.* to rebuild; to enact (*crime*) on actual spot, in course of judicial proceedings. **reconstruction** *n.*
re·cord (ri·kawrd′) *v.t.* to commit to writing; to make a note of; to register (a vote); to inscribe; to make a sound record; *v.i.* to speak, sing, etc. for reproduction on a record. **record** (rek′·ẹrd) *n.* register; authentic copy of any writing; personal history; list; finest performance or highest amount ever known; a disk, cylinder, roll, etc. for mechanical reproduction of sound; *pl.* public documents. **-er** *n.* one who registers writings or transactions; apparatus for registering data, by some form of symbol or line; instrument which transforms sounds into disk impressions; an instrument which registers sounds on wire tape; an ancient, flute-like musical instrument. **-ing** *n.* the making, or reproduction of, sound by mechanical means. **off the record,** unofficial [L. *recordari*, to remember].
re·count (rē·kount′, ri·kount′) *v.t.* to count again; to relate; to recite; to enumerate; *n.* a second enumeration [O.Fr. *reconter*].
re·coup (ri·ko͝op′) *v.t.* to recover equivalent for what has been lost or damaged; to compensate [Fr. *recouper*, to cut again].
re·course (rē′·kōrs) *n.* application made to another in difficulty or distress; person or thing resorted to [L. *recurrere*, to run back].
re·cov·er (ri·kuv′·ẹr) *v.t.* to get back; to revive; to reclaim; to rescue; (*Law*) to obtain (damages) as compensation for loss, etc.; *v.i.* to regain health or a former state; **-able** *a.* **-y** *n.* regaining, retaking, or obtaining possession; restoration to health; amends for a bad start in business, sport, etc. [O.Fr. *recuvrer*, fr. L. *recuperare*].
re·cov·er (rē·kuv′·ẹr) *v.t.* to put a fresh cover on; to cover again.
rec·re·ant (rek′·ri·ạnt) *a.* cowardly; craven; false; *n.* a craven; an apostate. **recreancy** *n.* [O.Fr. *recroire*, to take back one's pledge].
re·cre·ate (rek′·ri·āt) *v.t.* to give fresh life to; to restore; to reanimate; to refresh from weariness. **recreation** *n.* recreating; any pleasurable interest; amusement. **recreational** *a.* [L. *recreare*, to make again].
re·crim·i·nate (ri·krim′·ạ·nāt) *v.t.* and *v.i.* to charge an accuser with a similar crime. **recrimination** *n.* a counter-charge brought by the accused against the accuser; mutual abuse and blame. **recriminative, recriminatory** *a.* [L. *re-*, back; *crimen*, charge].
re·cru·desce (rē·kro͝o·des′) *v.i.* to break out again; to revive; **-nce, -ncy** *n.* **-nt** *a.* [L. *recrudescere*, to become raw again].
re·cruit (ri·kro͝ot′) *v.t.* to enlist persons for army, navy, etc.; to repair by fresh supplies; to renew in strength; *v.i.* to obtain new adherents; to gain health, spirits, etc.; *n.* a newly enlisted soldier; a fresh adherent. **-al, -ing, -ment** *n.* [O.Fr. *recruter*, fr. L. *recrescere*, to grow again].
rec·tan·gle (rek′·tang·gl) *n.* a four-sided figure with four right angles. **rectangular** *a.* [L. *rectus*, right, straight; *angulus*, an angle].
rec·ti·fy (rek′·tạ·fī) *v.t.* to set right; to correct; to purify; to convert an alternating current of electricity into a direct current; **rectifiable** *a.* **rectification** *n.* **rectifier** *n.* one who corrects; a device which rectifies; a transformer; one who refines spirits by repeated distillations [L. *rectus*, straight; *facere*, to make].
rec·ti·lin·e·al, rectilinear (rek·tạ·lin′·i·ạl, -ạr) *a.* consisting of, or bounded by straight lines [L. *rectus*, straight; *linea*, a line].
rec·ti·tude (rek′·tạ·tūd) *n.* moral uprightness; honesty of purpose [L. fr. *rectus*, right].
rec·to (rek′·tō) *n.* the right-hand page of an open book—opp. to *verso* [L. = on the right].
rec·tor (rek′·tẹr) *n.* clergyman of Episcopal Church who has charge of a parish; (*R.C.*) head of a religious house, college. **-y** *n.* house of a rector [L. fr. *regere, rectum*, to rule].
rec·tum (rek′·tạm) *n.* lower end of the large intestine. *pl.* **recta. rectal** *a.* [L. *rectus*, straight].
re·cum·bent (ri·kum′·bạnt) *a.* reclining; lying on back [L. *recumbere*, to lie down].
re·cu·per·ate (ri·kū′·pẹr·āt) *v.i.* to win back health and strength; to recover from financial loss. **recuperation** *n.* convalescence. **recuperative** *a.* [L. *recuperare*, to recover].
re·cur (ri·kur′) *v.i.* to happen again; to return periodically; *pr.p.* **-ring.** *pa.t.* and *pa.p.* **-red. -rence, -rency** *n.* **-rent** *a.* returning periodically [L. *re-*, again; *currere*, to run].
re·curve (ri·kurv′) *v.t.* to bend backwards.
rec·u·sant (rek′·ū·zạnt) *a.* obstinate in refusal; *n.* dissenter or nonconformist who refuses to conform to authority, esp. in religious matters. [L. *recusare*, to refuse].
red (red) *a.* (*comp.* **-der;** *superl.* **-dest**) of the color of aterial blood, rubies, glowing fire, etc.; of color, including shades, as scarlet, crimson, vermilion, orange-red and the like; of or connected with bloodshed, revolution, left-wing politics, etc.; *n.* color of blood; a socialist; communist, bolshevist; a Russian soldier; a danger signal. **-den** *v.t.* to make red; *v.i.* to become red; to blush; **-ness** *n.* state or quality of being red. **—blooded** *a.* vigorous; manly. **-breast** *n.* the robin. **-cap** *n.* a porter at a transportation terminal. **-coat** *n.* a British soldier, because of the bright scarlet tunic. **— corpuscle,** a colored blood corpuscle, containing hemoglobin and carrying oxygen. **Red Cross,** international emblem of organization for relief of sick and wounded in war time and for helping distressed persons in emergencies, as floods. **—handed** *a.* having red hands—hence, in the very act, orig. of a murderer. **— hat,** a cardinal's hat. **— heat** *n.* temperature of a body emitting red rays, about 700°-800° C. **— herring,** the common herring, cured by drying, smoking and salting; (*Colloq.*) any topic introduced to divert attention from main issue. **—hot** *a.* heated to redness; eager; enthusiastic. **Red Indian** *n.* a copper-colored aboriginal native of N. America. **—letter** *a.* applied to principal holy days, —hence, any memorable (day). **— pepper,** seasoning, such as cayenne. **-skin** *n.* a N. American Indian. **— tape,** slavish adherence

to official regulations, fr. red tape used for tying up government documents. **-wing** *n.* a blackbird with a red patch on wings. **-wood** *n.* any wood yielding a red dye; the sequoia tree of California, a gigantic evergreen coniferous tree. **to paint the town —,** to have a noisy good time. **to see —,** to become infuriated [O.E. *read*].

re·dact (ri·dakt′) *v.t.* to digest or reduce to order, literary, or scientific materials. **-ion** *n.* **or** *n.* an editor [L. *redactum,* to drive back].

re·deem (ri·dēm′) *v.t.* to regain; to take out of pawn; to ransom; to deliver from sin; to make good; to recover. **-able** *a.* **-ableness** *n.* **-er** *n.* [L. *redimere,* to buy back].

re·demp·tion (ri·demp′·shạn) *n.* redeeming or buying back; deliverance from sin; salvation. **-er** *n.* one who has redeemed himself. **redemptive** *a.* redeeming. **redemptory** *a.* [L. *redimmere, redemptum,* to buy back].

red·in·te·grate (ri·din′·tạ·grāt) *v.t.* to make whole again; to renew. **redintegration** *n.* L. *redintegrare,* to make whole again].

re·di·rect (rē·di·rekt′) *v.t.* to direct again; to readdress a communication. **-ion** *n.*

re·dis·trib·ute (rē·dis·trib′·ūt) *v.t.* to deal out or apportion again. **redistribution** *n.*

red·lin·ing (red′·lī·ning) *n.* the practice on the part of banks to refuse mortgage loans in what banks consider blighted areas [fr. marking such areas in red on a map].

red·o·lent (red′·ạ·lạnt) *a.* diffusing a strong or fragrant odor; scented; reminiscent (of). **redolence** *n.* [L. *redolere,* to smell strongly].

re·doubt (ri·dout′) *n.* a central part within fortifications for a final stand by the defenders [Fr. *redoute,* fr. L. *re-,* back; *ducere,* to lead].

re·doubt·able (ri·dou′·tạ·bl) *a.* dreaded; formidable; valiant. [O.Fr. *redouter,* to fear].

re·dound (ri·dound′) *v.i.* to contribute or turn to; to conduce (to); to recoil; to react (upon) [L. *re-,* back; *undare,* to surge].

re·draft (rē·draft′) *v.t.* to draft a second time; *n.* a second copy; a new bill of exchange.

re·dress (ri·dres′) *v.t.* to make amends for; to set right; to compensate; to adjust; (rē′·dres) *n.* reparation; amendment; relief; remedy. **-er** *n.* **-ible** *a.* [Fr. *redresser*].

re·duce (ri·dūs′) *v.t.* to diminish in number, length, quantity, value, price, etc.; to lower; to degrade; (*Chem.*) to remove oxygen or add hydrogen; to decrease valency number; to separate metal from its ore by heat and chemical affinities; to add electrons to an ion; (*Arith.*) to change, as numbers, from one denomination into another without altering value; to slim; to impoverish; to subdue. **-d.** *a.* **reducible** *a.* **reduction** *n.* reducing; subjugation; diminution; curtailment; amount by which something is reduced. **reductive** *a.* having the power of reducing. **reductively** *adv.* **reducing agent** *n.* a reagent for abstracting oxygen or adding hydrogen [L. *re-*; *ducere,* to lead].

re·dun·dant (ri·dun′·dạnt) *a.* superfluous; serving no useful purpose; using more words than necessary for complete meaning **redundance, redundancy** *n.* **-ly** *adv.* [L. *redundare,* to overflow].

re·ech·o (rē·ek′·ō) *v.t.* to echo back.

reed (rēd) *n.* a tall hollow-stemmed grass growing in water or marshes; in certain wind-instruments, a thin strip of cane or metal which vibrates and produces a musical sound; a musical instrument made of the hollow joint of some plant; a pastoral pipe; thatching straw; an arrow; a molding; *v.t.* to thatch; to fit with a reed. **-ed** *a.* covered with reeds; molded like reeds. **-er** *n.* a thatcher. **-iness** *n.* **—instrument** *n.* (*Mus.*) a wind-instrument played by means of a reed, as the oboe, English horn, bassoon, clarinet, saxophone, etc. **— pipe** *n.* organ pipe whose tone is produced by vibration of metal tongue. **— stop** *n.* organ stop owing its tone to vibration of little metal tongues. **-y** *a.* [O.E. *hreod*].

reef (rēf) *n.* a portion of a square sail which can be rolled up and made fast to the yard or boom; *v.t.* to reduce the area of sail by taking in a reef. **-er** *n.* one who reefs; a sailor's close-fitting jacket. **— knot** *n.* (*Naut.*) a square knot [O.N. *rif,* reef, rib].

reef (rēf) *n.* a ridge of rock near the surface of the sea; a lode of auriferous rock [O.N. *rif*].

reek (rēk) *n.* smoke; vapor; fume; *v.i.* to emit smoke; to steam; to smell strongly unpleasant. **-ing** *a.* **-y** *a.* [O.E. *rec*].

reel (rēl) *n.* frame or bobbin on which yarn or cloth is wound; cylinder turning on an axis for winding log or fishing lines; a flanged spool on which film is wound; *v.t.* to wind upon a reel; to draw (in) by means of a reel. **to — off,** to recite rapidly [O.E. *hreol*].

reel (rēl) *v.i.* to stagger; to sway from side to side; to whirl; to be dizzy [O.E. *hreol*].

reel (rēl) *n.* a sprightly dance tune; a Scottish dance for two or more couples [Gael. *righil*].

re·en·try (rē·en′·tri·) *n.* the return of a spacecraft into the earth's atmosphere; a second or repeated entry.

reeve (rēv) *v.t.* to pass line through any hole in a block, cleat, ring, etc., for pulling a larger rope after it [Dut. *reef,* a reef].

reeve (rēv) *n.* official in early English times as shire reeve (sheriff) [O.E. *gerefa*].

re·fec·tion (ri·fek′·shạn) *n.* refreshment; a simple repast; a lunch. **refectory** *n.* a hall in a monastery, convent, school, or college where meals are served [L. *reficere, refectum,* to remake].

re·fer (ri·fur′) *v.t.* to direct to; to assign to; *v.i.* to have reference or relation to; to offer, as testimony in evidence of character, qualification, etc.; to allude (to). *pr.p.* **-ring.** *pa.t., pa.p.* **-red. -able, -rable** *a.* may be referred to or assigned to. **-ee** *n.* an arbitrator; an umpire; a neutral judge in various sports. **-ence** *n.* appeal to the judgment of another; relation; one of whom inquiries can be made; a passage in a book to which reader is referred; a quotation; a testimonial. **-endum** *n.* a popular vote for ascertaining the public will on a single definite issue. **-ential** *a.* containing a reference; used for reference [L. *re-,* back; *ferre,* to carry].

re·fine (ri·fīn′) *v.t.* to purify; to reduce crude metals to a finer state; to clarify; to polish or improve; to free from coarseness, vulgarity, etc.; *v.i.* to become pure; to improve in accuracy, excellence, or good taste. **-d** *a.* purified or clarified; polished; well-bred. **-dly** *adv.* **-ment** *n.* **-ry** *n.* place where process of refining sugar, oil, metals, etc. is effected [Fr. *raffiner*].

re·flect (ri·flekt′) *v.t.* to throw back, esp. rays of light, heat, or sound, from surfaces; to mirror; *v.i.* to throw back light, heat, etc.; to meditate; to consider attentively; to cast discredit on; to disparage. **-ed** *a.* **-ing** *a.* thoughtful; throwing back rays of light, etc. **-ingly** *adv.* **-ion** *n.* reflecting; return of rays of heat or light, or waves of sound, from a surface; image given back from mirror or other reflecting surface; meditation; contemplation. **-ive** *a.* reflecting; meditative; (*Gram.*). reflective; reciprocal. **-ively** *adv.* **-iveness** *n.* a reflecting surface [L. *reflectere,* to bend back].

re·flex (rē′·fleks) *a.* turned, bent, or directed backwards; reflected; (*Mech.*) produced by reaction; (*Anat.*) denoting the involuntary action of the motor nerves under a stimulus from the sensory nerves; involuntary; automatic; *n.* reflection; a reflected image; a reflex action; *v.t.* (ri·fleks′) to bend back; to reflect. **-ible** *a.* **-ibility** *n.* **-ive** *a.* bending or turned backwards; reflective; of certain verbs, whose subject and object are the same person or thing; of pronouns which serve as objects to reflexive verbs; as *myself*, etc. **-ively** *adv.* **-ly** *adv.* **conditioned reflex,** reflex action due to power of association and suggestion [L. *re-*, back; *flectere*, to bend].

re·flux (rē′·fluks) *n.* a flowing back; ebbing.

re·form (ri·fawrm′) *v.t.* to restore; to reclaim; to amend; to improve; to eliminate (abuse, malpractice); *v.i.* to amend one's ways; to improve; *n.* amendment; improvement; rectification; correction. **-able** *a.* **reformation** (ref′·ẹr·mā·shạn) *n.* reforming; change for the better; religious movement of 16th cent. in which a large section of the church broke away from Rome. **-ative** *a.* aiming at reform. **-atory** *a.* tending to reform; *n.* institution for reforming young law-breakers. **-ed** *a.* amended; reclaimed **-er** *n.* one who reforms; an advocate of reform.

re·fract (ri·frakt′) *v.t.* to bend sharply; to cause to deviate from a direct course, as rays of light on passing from one medium to another. **-able** *a.* **-ed** *a.* **-ing** *a.* serving to refract; refractive. **-ion** *n.* **-tive** *a.* **-or** *n.* [L. *re-*, back; *frangere, fractum*, to break].

re·frac·to·ry (ri·frak′·tạ·ri.) *a.* sullen or perverse in opposition or disobedience; suitable for lining furnaces because of resistance to fusion at very high temperatures; (*Med.*) resistent to treatment. **refractorily** *adv.* [L. *re-*, back; *frangere*, to break].

re·frain (ri·frān′) *v.i.* to abstain. **-ment** *n.* [L. *refrenare*, to bridle].

re·frain (ri·frān′) *n.* chorus recurring at end of each verse of song; constant theme [Fr. fr. L. *refringere*, to break off].

re·fran·gi·ble (ri·fran′·jạ·bl) *a.* able to be refracted [L. *re-*, back; *frangere*, to break].

re·fresh (ri·fresh′) *v.t.* to make fresh again; to revive; to renew; to enliven; to provide with refreshment; to freshen up. **-er** *n.* one who, or that which, refreshes; (*Slang*) a refreshing drink. **-ing** *a.* invigorating; reviving. **-ment** *n.* restoration of strength; that which adds fresh vigor, as rest, drink, or food—hence, *pl.* food and drink [O.Fr. *refrescher*].

re·frig·e·rate (ri·frij′·ẹr·āt) *v.t.* to make cold or frozen; to preserve food, etc., by cooling; *v.i.* to become cold. **refrigerant** *a.* **refrigeration,** *n.* **refrigerative, refrigeratory** *a.* cooling. **refrigerator** *n.* apparatus and plant for the manufacture of ice; chamber for preserving food by mechanical production of low temperatures [L. *re-*, again; *frigus*, cold].

ref·uge (ref′·ūj) *n.* shelter; asylum; retreat; harbor. **refugee** *n.* one who flees to a place of safety [L. *re*, back; *fugere*, to flee].

re·ful·gent (ri·ful′·jạnt) *a.* shining; splendid. **refulgence** *n.* splendor. Also **refulgency** [L. *re-*, again; *fulgere*, to shine].

re·fund (ri·fund′) *v.t.* to return in payment or compensation for; to repay. **refund** (rē′·fund) *n.* repayment [L. *re-*, back; *fundere*, to pour].

re·fur·bish (rē·fur′·bish) *v.t.* to furbish up again; to retouch; to renovate; to polish up.

re·fuse (rē·fūz′) *v.t.* to deny or reject; to decline; *v.i.* to decline something offered; not to comply. **refusal** *n.* act of refusing; the first chance of accepting or declining an offer; an option [Fr. *refuser*, fr. L. recusare, to refuse].

ref·use (ref′·ūs) *a.* rejected; worthless; *n.* waste matter; trash [Fr. *refuser*, to refuse].

re-fuse (rē·fūz′) *v.t.* of metals, to fuse or melt again. **refusion** *n.*

re·fute (ri·fūt′) *v.t.* to overthrow by argument; to prove to be false. **refutable** *a.* capable of being refuted. **refutably** *adv.* **refutation** *n.* [L. *refutare*, to repel].

re·gain (ri·gān) *v.t.* to recover; to retrieve; to get back; to reach again.

re·gal (rē′·gạl) *a.* pert. to a king; kingly; royal. **regalia** (re·gā′·li·a) *n.pl.* insignia of royalty, as crown, scepters, orbs, etc. **regality** *n.* royalty; sovereignty; an ensign of royalty. **-ly** *adv.* [L. *regalis*, royal].

re·gale (ri·gāl′) *v.t.* to entertain in sumptuous manner; *v.i.* to feast [Fr. *régaler*].

re·gard (ri·gȧrd′) *v.t.* to observe; to gaze; to consider; to pay respect to; *n.* aspect; esteem; account; gaze; heed; concern; *pl.* compliments; good wishes. **-able** *a.* **-ful** *a.* heedful. **-fully** *adv.* **-ing** *prep.* concerning—also **in, with, regard to, as regards. -less** *a.* without regard; careless; neglectful. **-lessly** *adv.* [Fr. *regarder*].

re·gat·ta (ri·gat′·ạ) *n.* boat races [*It.* orig. a gondola race in Venice].

re·gen·cy See **regent.**

re·gen·er·ate (ri·jen′·ēr·āt) *v.t.* and *v.i.* to give fresh life or vigor to; to reorganize; to recreate the moral nature; to cause to be born again; *a.* born anew; changed from a natural to a spiritual state; regenerated. **regeneracy, regeneration** *n.* **regenerative** *a.*

re·gent (rē′·jạnt) *a.* holding the office of regent; exercising vicarious authority; *n.* one who governs a kingdom during the minority, absence, or disability of sovereign. **regency** *n.* office and jurisdiction of a regent [L. *regere*, to rule].

reg·i·cide (rej′·ạ·sīd) *n.* one who kills, or the killing of, a king. **regicidal** *a.* [L. *rex, regis*, a king; *caedere*, to slay].

re·gime (rā·zhēm′) *n.* style or tenure of rule or management; administration; an ordered mode of dieting [Fr.].

reg·i·men (rej′·ạ·mạn) *n.* orderly government; systematic method of dieting, exercising, etc. [L. = rule, government].

reg·i·ment (rej′·ạ·mạnt) *n.* a body of soldiers commanded by a senior officer and consisting of companies, batteries, battalions, or squadrons, according to branch of service; *v.t.* to form into a regiment: to systematize. **-al** *a.* **-ation** *n.* thorough systemization and control [L. *regimentum*, government].

re·gion (rē′·jạn) *n.* territory of indefinite extent; district; part of body; sphere or realm. **-al** *a.* **-ally** *adv.* [L. *regio*, a district].

reg·is·ter (rej′·is·tẹr) *n.* a written account; an official record; a list; the book in which a record is kept; an alphabetical index; an archive; a catalog; a registration; a metal damper to close a heating duct; any mechanical contrivance which registers or records; (*Mus.*) row of organ pipes with same tone color; organ stop; compass of a voice or instrument; *v.t.* to record; to enroll; to indicate, by cash register, scales, etc., by facial expression. **registrable** *a.* **-ed** *a.* **registrant** *n.* one who registers. **registrar** *n.* an official who keeps a register or record. **registration** *n.* entry or record; total entries registered. **registry** *n.* office for registering births, deaths and marriages. **-ed mail,** a method of postal delivery by which mail is insured against loss or damage in transit [O.Fr. *registre*].

reg·nal (reg′·nạl) *a.* pert. to reign of monarch. **regnancy** *n.* rule; reign [L. *regnare*, to reign].

re·gress (rē′·gres) *n.* passage back; the power of passing back; re-entry; *v.i.* (ri·gres′) to go or fall back; to return to a former state; (*Astron.*) to move from east to west. **-ion** *n.* returning; retrogression; (*Psych.*) diversion of psychic energy, owing to obstacles encountered, into channels of fantasy instead of reality. **-ive** *a.* [L. *regressus*, fr. *rẹgredi*, to go back].

re·gret (ri·gret′) *v.t.* to grieve over; to lament; to deplore; *pr.p.* **-ting.** *pa.t.* and *pa.p.*

-ted. *n.* grief; sorrow; remorse. **-ful** *a.* **-fully** *adv.* **-table** *a.* deserving regret; lamentable. **-tably** *adv.* **-ter** *n.* [Fr. *regretter*].

reg·u·lar (reg′·yạ.lẹr) *a.* conforming to, governed by rule; periodical; symmetrical; orderly; strict; habitual; straight; level; natural; standing (army); (*Colloq.*) out and out; belonging to a monastic order (opp. to *secular*); *n.* a member of any religious order who professes to follow a certain rule (*regula*) of life; a soldier belonging to a permanent, standing army. **-ization** *n.* **-ity** *n.* conformity to rule; uniformity. **-ly** *adv.* [L. *regula*, a rule].

reg·u·late (reg′·yạ.lāt) *v.t.* to adjust by rule, method, etc.; to arrange; to control. **regulation** *n.* regulating or controlling; state of being reduced to order; a law; an order. **regulator** *n.* [L. *regula*, a rule].

re·gur·gi·tate (rē.gur′.jạ.tāt) *v.t.* to throw, flow, or pour back in great quantity; *v.i.* to be thrown or poured back. **regurgitation** *n.* [L. *re-*, back; *gurges*, a gulf].

re·ha·bil·i·tate (rē.(h)ạ.bil′.ạ.tāt) *v.t.* to restore to reputation or former position; to recondition. **rehabilitation** *n.* [L. *re-*, again; *habitare*, to make *fit*].

re·hash (rē.hash′) *v.t.* to mix together and use or serve up a second time.

re·hearse (ri.hẹrs′) *v.t.* and *v.i.* to repeat aloud; to practice (play, etc.); to recite; to recapitulate; to narrate. **rehearsal** *n.* trial performance of a play, opera, etc. [O.Fr. *rehercer*, to repeat (lit. rake over again)].

Reich (rīk) *n.* German Confederation of States. **-stag** *n.* the German parliament. [Ger.].

re·i·fy (rē′.i.fī) *v.t.* to make concrete or real. **reification** *n.* [L. *res*, a thing; *facere*, to make].

reign (rān) *n.* royal authority; the period during which a sovereign occupies throne; influence; *v.i.* to possess sovereign power [O.Fr. *regne*, fr. L. *regnare*, to rule].

re·im·burse (rē.im.burs′) *v.t.* to refund; to pay back; to give the equivalent of. **-ment** *n.* **-r** *n.* [Fr. *rembourser*, fr. *bourse*, a purse].

rein (rān) *n.* strap of bridle to govern a horse, etc.; means of controlling, curbing; restraint; *pl.* power, or means of exercising power [O.Fr. *reine*, fr. L. *retinere*, to hold back].

re·in·car·nate (rē.in.kȧr′.nāt) *v.t.* to embody again in the flesh. **reincarnation** *n.*

rein·deer (rān′.dir) *n.* large deer of colder regions. **— moss** *n.* lichen, the winter food of reindeer [O.N. *hreinndyri*].

re·in·force (rē.in.fōrs′) *v.t.* to strengthen with new force, esp. of troops or ships; to increase. **-ment** *n.* **reinforced concrete** *n.* concrete strengthened by the inclusion in it of steel nets, rods, girders, etc. [Fr. *renforcer*].

re·in·state (rē.in.stāt′) *v.t.* to restore to former position. **-ment** *n.*

re·is·sue (rē.ish′.oo) *v.t.* to issue again; to republish; *n.* a new issue; a reprint.

re·it·er·ate (rē.it′.ẹr.āt) *v.t.* to repeat again and again. **reiterant** *a.* **reiteration** *n.*

re·ject (ri.jekt′) *v.t.* to cast from one; to throw away; to refuse; to put aside; (rē′jekt) *n.* a person or thing rejected as not up to standard. **-ion** *n.* [L. *re-*, back; *jacere*, to throw].

re·joice (ri.jois′) *v.t.* to give joy to; to cheer; to gladden; *v.i.* to exult; to triumph. **rejoicing** *n.* act of expressing joy; *pl.* public expression of joy; festivities. [Fr. *réjouir*].

re·join (rē.join′) *v.t.* to unite again; to meet again; to enter again, as society, etc.; *v.i.* to become united again; to reply. **-der** *n.* an answer to a reply [Fr. *rejoindre*].

re·ju·ve·nate (ri.jòò′.vạ.nāt) *v.t.* to make young again. **rejuvenation** *n.* **rejuvenator** *n.* **rejuvenesce** *v.i.* to grow young again. **rejuvenescence** *n.* **rejuvenescent** *a.* [L. *re-*, again; *juvenis*, young].

re·lapse (ri.laps′) *v.i.* to slide back, esp. into state of ill health, error, evil ways; *n.* a falling back [L. *relapsus*, to slip back].

re·late (ri.lāt′) *v.t.* to tell; to establish relation between; *v.i.* to have relation (to); to refer (to). **-d** *a.* connected by blood or marriage; allied; akin. **relation** *n.* telling; *pl.* dealings between persons or nations; connection between things; kindred; connection by consanguinity or affinity; a relative. **relational** *a.* indicating some relation. **relationship** *n.* [L. *referre*, *relatum*, to bring back].

rel·a·tive (rel′.ạ.tiv) *a.* dependent on relation to something else, not absolute; comparative; respecting; connected; related; (*Gram.*) noting a relation or reference to antecedent word or sentence; *n.* a person connected by blood or affinity; a word relating to an antecedent word, clause, or sentence. **-ly** *adv.* comparatively. **-ness** *n.* **relativity** *n.* being relative; doctrine that measurement is conditioned by the choice of co-ordinate axes e.g., all observable motion, and time, are relative [fr. *relate*].

re·lax (ri.laks′) *v.t.* to make less severe or stern; to loosen; *v.i.* to become loosened or feeble; to unbend; to become less severe; to ease up. **-ation** *n.* act of relaxing; recreation; mitigation. **-ing** *a.* [L. *re-*, again; *laxus*, loose].

re·lay (rē.lā′, ri.lā′) *n.* supplies conveniently stored at successive stages of a route; a gang of men, a fresh set of horses, etc., ready to relieve others; a device for making or breaking a local electrical circuit; an electro-magnetic device for allowing a weak signal from a distance to control a more powerful local electrical circuit; a low-powered broadcasting station which broadcasts programs originating in another station; *v.t.* to pass on, as a message, broadcast, etc. **— race,** a race between teams of which each runner does a part of the distance [Fr. *relais*, a rest].

re·lease (ri.lēs′) *v.t.* to set free; to allow to quit; to exempt from obligation; (*Law*) to remit a claim; *n.* liberation; exemption; discharge; acquittance; a catch for controlling mechanical parts of a machine; (*Law*) a surrender of a right or claim. **releasable** *a.* [O.Fr. *relaissier*].

rel·e·gate (rel′.ạ.gāt) *v.t.* to send away; to banish; to consign; to demote. **relegation** *n.* [L. *re-* back; *legare*, to send].

re·lent (ri.lent′) *v.i.* to give up harsh intention; to yield. **-less** *a.* showing no pity or sympathy. **-lessly** *adv.* **-lessness** *n.* [Fr. *ralentir*, to slacken].

rel·e·vant (rel′.ạ.vạnt) *a.* bearing upon the case in hand; pertinent. **relevance, relevancy** *n.* **-ly** *adv.* [L. *relevare*, to raise up].

re·li·a·ble (ri.lī.ạ.bl) *a.* trustworthy; honest; creditable. **-ness, reliability** *n.* **reliably** *adv.* **reliance** *n.* trust; confidence; dependence. **reliant** *a.* [fr. *rely*].

rel·ic (rel′.ik) *n.* something surviving from the past [L. *reliquus*, remaining].

re·lief (ri.lēf′) *n.* removal or alleviation of pain, distress, or other evil; help; remedy; one who relieves another at his post; prominence; a sculptured figure standing out from a plane surface. **— map** *n.* a map showing the elevations and depressions of a country in relief [L. *re-*, again; *levare*, to raise].

re·lieve (ri-lēv′) *v.t.* to alleviate; to free from trial, evil, or distress; to release from a post by substitution of another; to remedy; to lighten (gloom, etc.). **relieving** *a.* serving to relieve. [L. *re-*, again; *levare*, to raise].

re·li·gion (ri.lij′.ạn) *n.* belief in supernatural power which governs universe; recognition of God as object of worship; practical piety; any system of faith and worship. **-ist -ary, -er** *n.* one who makes inordinate professions of religion. **religiosity** *n.* sense of, or tendency towards, religiousness. **religious** *a.* **religiously** *adv.* [L. *religio*].

re·lin·quish (ri·ling′·kwish) *v.t.* to give up; to yield. **-er** *n.* **-ment** *n.* [L. *relinquere*].

rel·i·quar'y (rel′·ạ·kwer·i·) *n.* a depository or casket in which relics of saints or martyrs are preserved; a shrine [Fr. *reliquaire*].

rel·ish (rel′·ish) *v.t.* to taste with pleasure; to like immensely; *v.t.* to have a pleasing taste; to savor; *n.* savor; flavor; what is used to make food more palatable, as sauce, seasoning, etc.; liking [O.Fr. *reles*, aftertaste].

re·luc·tant (ri·luk′·tạnt) *a.* unwilling; disinclined. **reluctance, reluctancy** *n.* **-ly** *adv.* [L. *reluctari*, to struggle against].

re·ly (ri·lī′) *v.i.* to trust; to depend; **relier** *n.* [L. *religare*, to bind fast].

rem (rem) *n.* the dosage of radiation that produces the same biological effect as the exposure to one roentgen of X-rays [fr. *r*oentgen *e*quivalent, *m*an].

REM (rem) *n.* the *r*apid *e*ye *m*ovement(s) during the dream stages of sleep.

re·main (ri·mān′) *v.i.* to stay; to continue or endure; to be left. **-s** *n.pl.* a corpse; unpublished literary works of deceased. **-der** *n.* what remains; remnant; in real property law, an interest in an estate which only operates after the termination of a prior interest [L. *re-*, back; *manere*, to stay].

re·mand (ri·mand′) *v.t.* to send back, as an accused person sent back to prison while further inquiries are made; *n.* such a recommittal [*re-*, back; *mandare*, to commit].

re·mark (ri·màrk′) *v.t.* to take notice of; to express in words or writing; to comment; notice; heed; regard. **-able** *a.* extraordinary. **-ableness** *n.* **-ably** *adv.* [Fr. *remarquer*].

rem·e·dy (rem′·ạ·di·) *n.* a means of curing or relieving a disease, trouble, fault, etc.; legal means to recover a right, or to obtain redress; cure; antidote; *v.t.* to restore to health; to heal; to cure; to put right. *a.* curable. **remedial** *a.* [L. *remedium*].

re·mem·ber (ri·mem′·bẹr) *v.t.* to retain in the memory; to recollect; to reward for services rendered; *v.i.* to have in mind. **-able** *a.* **remembrance** *n.* act or power of remembering; state of being remembered; memory; token; keepsake [L. *re-*; *memor*, mindful].

re·mind (ri·mīnd′) *v.t.* to cause to remember. **-er** *n.* one who, or that which, reminds.

rem·i·nis·cence (rem·ạ·nis′·ạns) *n.* state of calling to mind; a recollection of past events; a remembrance. **-s** *n.pl.* memoirs. **reminiscent** *a.* [L. *reminisci*, to remember].

re·mise (ri·mīz′) *v.t.* to send back or remit, esp. in law; to resign or surrender (property, etc.) by deed; *n.* (*Law*) a surrender [O.Fr.].

re·miss (ri·mis′) *a.* not prompt or exact in duty; careless. **-ful** *a.* **-ible** *a.* able to be pardoned or remitted. **-ion** *n.* act of remitting; abatement; diminution; pardon; forgiveness of sin. **-ive** *a.* **-ly** *adv.* **-ness** *n.* [L. *remissus*, sent back].

re·mit (ri·mit′) *v.t.* to send back; to transfer; to send accused for trial back to a lower court; to restore; to slacken (efforts); to forgive; to refrain from exacting debt, etc.); *v.i.* to abate in force; to slacken off. *pa.p.* **-ting.** *pa.t., pa.p.* **-ted.** *n.* **-tal** *n.* act of remitting to another court. **-tance** *n.* **-tent** *a.* increasing and decreasing at periodic intervals [L. *remittere*, to send back].

rem·nant (rem′·nạnt) *n.* fragment of cloth; scrap; residue; remainder [O.Fr. *remanant*].

re·mon·strate (ri·màn′·strāt) *v.t.* to make evident by strong protestations *v.i.* to present strong reasons against; to speak strongly against. **remonstrance** *n.* expostulation; protest. **remonstrant** *n.* one who remonstrates; *a.* expostulatory. **remonstration** *n.* **remonstrative, remonstratory** *a.* [L. *re-*, again; *monstrare*, to point out].

re·morse (ri·mawrs) *n.* self-reproach excited by sense of guilt; repentance. **-ful** *a.* penitent; repentant. **-fully** *adv.* **-less** *a.* relentless; pitiless [L. *remordere*, to bite back].

re·mote (ri·mōt′) *a.* far back in time or space; not near; slight; **-ly** *adv.* **-ness** *n.* **— control,** control of apparatus from a distance [L. *re-*, back; *movere*, *motum*, to move].

re·move (ri·mȯȯv′) *v.t.* to take or put away; to dislodge; to transfer; to withdraw; to extract; to banish; to dismiss from a post; *v.i.* to change place or residence; *n.* removal; change of place; a step in any scale of gradation. **removable** *a.* not permanently fixed. **removal** *n.* removing; transferring to another house; dismissal from a post. **-d** *a.* denoting distance of relationship. **-r** *n.* [L. *re-*, back; *movere*, to move].

re·mu·ner·ate (ri·mū′·nạ·rāt) *v.t.* to reward for services; to recompense; to conpensate. **remunerable** *a.* that may, or should be, remunerated. **remuneration** *n.* reward; recompense; salary **remunerative** *a.* [L. *re-*, again; *munerare*, to give].

ren·ais·sance (ren·ạ·sàn(t)s′, ·zàn(t)′s) (*Cap.*) *n.* a rebirth; a period of intellectual revival, esp. of learning in fourteenth to sixteenth, cents.; *a.* pert. to renaissance. Also **renascence** [Fr.].

re·nal (rē′·nạl) *a.* pert. to kidneys [L. *renes*].

re·nas·cent (ri·nas′·ạnt) *a.* springing into being again; regaining lost vigor. **renascence** *n.* See **renaissance** [L. *re-*, again; *nasci*, to be born].

rend (rend) *v.t.* to tear asunder; to pull to pieces; to split; to lacerate. *pa.t.* and *pa.p.* **rent** [O.E. *rendan*, to cut].

ren·der (ren′·dẹr) *v.t.* to give in return; to deliver up; to supply; to present; to make or cause to be; to translate from one language into another; to interpret music; to portray; to extract animal fats by heating. **-able** *a.* **-er** *n.* **-ing** *n.* **rendition** *n.* rendering [Fr. *rendre*].

ren·dez·vous (ràn′·dạ·vȯȯ) *n.* an appointed place for meeting; *v.i.* to assemble at a prearranged place [Fr. = betake yourselves].

ren·di·tion See **render.**

ren·e·gade (ren′·ạ·gād) *n.* one faithless to principle or party; a deserter; *a.* apostate; false. **renege** (ri·nig′) *v.t.* and *v.i.* to deny; to desert; to break a promise; to revoke at cards [L. *re-*, again; *negare*, to deny].

re·new (ri·nū′) *v.t.* and *v.i.* to restore; to renovate; to revive; to begin again; to recommence.**-able** *a.* **-al** *n.* revival; restoration; regeneration.

ren·net (ren′·it) *n.* any preparation used for curdling milk and in preparation of cheese; junket, etc. [M.E. *rennen*, to run, congeal].

re·nounce (ri·nouns′) *v.t.* to disavow; to give up; to reject; *v.i.* to fail in following suit when a card of the suit is in the player's hand. **-ment, renunciation** *n.* [L. *renuntiare*, to protest against].

ren·o·vate (ren′·ạ·vāt) *v.t.* to make as good as new; to overhaul and repair. **renovation** *n.* [L. *renovare*, fr. *novus*, new].

re·nown (ri·noun′) *n.* great reputation; fame. **-ed** *a.* famous; noted; eminent [O.Fr. *renoun*, fr. *renomer*, to make famous].

rent (rent) *pa.t.* and *pa.p.* of **rend;** *n.* an opening made by rending; a tear; a fissure; a split; a breach; a rupture; a rift.

rent (rent) *n.* a periodical payment at an agreed rate for use and enjoyment of something, esp. land, houses; rental; hiring charge; *v.t.* to lease; to hold by lease; to hire; *v.i.* to be leased or let for rent. **-able** *a.* **-al** *n.* the amount of rent; a rent roll; *a.* pert.

to rent.**-er** *n.* one who rents [Fr. *rente,* income].

re·nun·ci·a·tion (ri·nun·si·ā′·shạn) *n.* a surrender of claim or interest; rejection; repudiation. Also **renunciance. renunciative, renunciatory** *a.* See **renounce.**

re·or·gan·ize (rē·awr′·ga·nīz) *v.t.* to organize anew.

rep, repp (rep) *n.* a thick corded worsted, cotton, or silk fabric.

re·pair (ri·per′) *v.t.* to restore to a sound or good state after injury; to mend; to redress; *n.* restoration; mending. **-able** *a.* **-er** *n.* [O. Fr. *reparer*].

re·pair (ri·pār′) *v.i.* to go; to betake oneself [L. *repatriare,* to return to one's country].

rep·a·ra·ble (rep′·ạ·rạ·bl) *a.* that can be made good. **reparably** *adv.* **reparation** *n.* repairing or making amends; redress; compensation. **reparative** *a.* [O.Fr. *reparer*].

rep·ar·tee (rep·ẹr·tē′) *n.* apt, witty reply; gift of making such replies [Fr. *repartie,* orig. answering thrust in fencing].

re·past (ri·past′) *n.* a meal [Fr. *repas,* a meal].

re·pa·tri·ate (rē·pā′·tri·āt) *v.t.* to restore to one's own country; to bring back prisoners of war and refugees from abroad. **repatriation** *n.* [L.L. *repatriare*].

re·pay (rē·pā′) *v.t.* to pay back; to make return or requital for; to require. *pa.t.* and *pa.p.* **repaid. -able** *a.* **-ment** *n.*

re·peal (ri·pēl′) *v.t.* to revoke, rescind, annul, as a deed, will, law, or statute; to abrogate; to cancel; *n.* revocation; abrogation.**-able** *a.* [O.Fr. *rapeler,* fr. *appeler,* to appeal].

re·peat (ri·pēt′) *v.t.* to say or do again; to reiterate; to echo; to tell; *n.* repetition; encore; (*Mus.*) sign that a movement is to be performed twice, indicated by inclusion within dots of part to be repeated. **-able** *a.* **-ed** *a.* frequent; recurring **-edly** *adv.* **-er** *n.* one who, or that which, repeats; firealarm which may be discharged many times in quick succession; a person who repeats a course of study.**-ing** *n.* **-ing decimal** (*Arith.*) a decimal in which same figure(s) repeat ad infinitum. [L. *repetere,* to try or seek again].

re·pel (ri·pel′) *v.t.* to drive back; to repulse; to oppose; to excite revulsion in; *v.i.* to have power to drive away; to cause repugnance. *pr.p.* **-ling.** *pa.t.* and *pa.p.* **-led. -lence, -lency** *n.* **-lent** *a.* driving back; tending to repel; *n.* that which repels. **-ler** *n.* [L. *re-,* back; *pellere,* to drive].

re·pent (ri·pent′) *v.t.* and *v.i.* to feel regret for a deed or omission; to desire to change one's life as a result of sorrow for one's sins. **-ance** *n.* sorrow for a deed or regret; contrition; penitence **-ant** *a.* [Fr. *se repentir*].

re·per·cus·sion (rē·pẹr·kush′·ạn) *n.* act of driving back; reverberation; rebound; recoil; echo; indirect effect. [fr. *percussion*].

rep·er·toire (rep·ẹr·twår′) *n.* list of plays, operas, musical works, dramatic rôles, within sphere of operations of a company or of an individual.**repertory** *n.* a repertoire; a place in which things are disposed in an orderly manner; *a.* pert. to the stock plays of a resident company [Fr. fr. L. *repertorium*].

rep·e·ti·tion (rep·ạ·tish′·ạn) *n.* act of repeating; the thing repeated; a copy. **repetitious** *a.* full of repetitions. **repetitive** *a.* involving much repetition [fr. *repeat*].

re·pine (ri·pīn′) *v.i.* to fret. **repining** *n.*

re·place (ri·plās) *v.t.* to put back into place; to supply an equivalent for; to substitute for. **-able** *a.* **-ment** *n.* restoration; substitution.

re·plen·ish (ri·plen′·ish) *v.t.* to fill up again; to restock; to refill; to furnish; to supply. **-ment** *n.* [L. *re-,* again; *plenus,* full].

re·plete (ri·plēt′) *a.* full; completely filled; surfeited. **-ness, repletion** *n.* satiety; surfeit; (*Med.*) fullness of blood; plethora [L. *re-,* again; *plere, pletum,* to fill].

rep·li·ca (rep′·li·kạ) *n.* exact copy of work of art by the artist of the original; facsimile. **-te** *v.t.* to fold or bend back; to duplicate. **-tion** *n.* an answer; reply; (*Law*) reply of a plaintiff to defendant's plea; a copy [L. *replicare,* to fold back].

re·ply (ri·plī′) *v.t.* and *v.i.* to return an answer; to respond; to rejoin. *n.* answer; response [O.Fr. *replier,* fr. L. *replicare,* to fold back].

re·port (ri·pōrt′) *v.t.* to relate; to take down in writing; to give an account of; to name as an offender; to narrate; *v.i.* to make official statement; to furnish in writing an account of a speech, or the proceedings of a public assembly; to present oneself as to superior officer; *n.* an official statement of facts; rumor; reverberation, as of gun; account of proceedings, debates, etc. of public bodies; repute; reputation. **-er** *n.* one who reports, esp. for newspapers. [L. *reportare,* to bring back].

re·pose (ri·pōz′) *v.t.* to rely on; to put trust (in). **reposit** *v.t.* to lay up, to lodge, in a place of safety. **repository** *n.* place where valuables are deposited for safety; a burial vault; a storehouse [Fr. *reposer,* fr. L. *reponere,* to place back].

re·pose (ri·pōz′) *v.i.* to rest; to sleep; to recline; to depend on; *v.t.* to lay at rest; *n.* sleep; relaxation. **-al** *n.* **-ful** *a.* **-fully** *adv.* [L. *repausare,* to pause again].

re·pous·sé (rạ·pòò·sā′) *a.* embossed; hammered into relief from reverse side; *n.* a style of raised ornamentation in metal [Fr.].

rep·re·hend (rep·ri·hend′) *v.t.* to find fault with; to blame; to rebuke. **reprehensible** *a.* blameworthy. **reprehensibly** *adv.* **reprehension** *n.* act of reprehending; reproof. [L. *reprehendere,* lit. to take hold again].

rep·re·sent (rep·ri·zent′) *v.t.* to be or express the counterpart or image of; to recall by description or portrait; to pretend to be; to be the agent for; to act or play the part of; to personate; to be the member (of the House of Representatives, etc.) for. **-able** *a.* **-ation** *n.* describing, or showing; that which represents, as a picture; description; account; a dramatic performance; the act of representing (in parliament, etc.). **-ational** *a.* **-ative** *a.* typical; representing; exhibiting a likeness; *n.* an agent, deputy, delegate, or substitute; local member of a legislative body. [Fr. *représenter*].

re·press (ri·pres′) *v.t.* to keep under control; to put down; to reduce to subjection; to quell; to check. **-er, -or** *n.* **-ible** *a.* **-ibly** *adv.* **-ion** *n.* check; restraint; in psychoanalysis, the rejection from consciousness of anything unpleasant. **-ive** *a.* [L.*reprimere, repressum,* to repress].

re·prieve (ri·prēv′) *v.t.* to remit or commute a sentence; to grant temporary relief; *n.* temporary suspension of execution of sentence; rest or relief [fr. Fr. *reprendre,* to take back].

rep·ri·mand (rep′·rạ·mand) *v.t.* to reprove severely; to chide. *n.* a sharp rebuke; a severe admonition [Fr. *réprimande*].

re·print (rē·print′) *v.t.* to print again. (rē′·print) *n.* a second or a new impression or edition of any printed work.

re·pris·al (ri·prī′·zạl) *n.* an act of retaliation or retribution [Fr. *représaille*].

re·proach (ri·prōch′) *v.t.* to censure; to upbraid; to rebuke; *n.* reproof; rebuke; discredit; an object of scorn. **-ful** *a.* expressing censure. **-fully** *adv.* **-fulness** *n.* [Fr. *reprocher*].

rep·ro·bate (rep′·rạ·bāt) *v.t.* to disapprove with signs of extreme dislike; to exclude from hopes of salvation; *a.* depraved; cast off by

God; *n.* profligate; hardened sinner; scoundrel. **reprobation** *n.* condemnation; censure; rejection [L. *reprobare,* to reprove].

re·pro·duce (rē·prạ·dūs′) *v.t.* to produce over again; to produce likeness or copy of; to imitate; *v.i.* to propagate; to generate. **reproducible** *a.* **reproduction** *n.* a repeat; a facsimile, as of a painting, photograph, etc.; process of multiplication of living individuals or units whereby the species is perpetuated, either sexual or asexual. **reproductive** *a.* pert. to reproduction; yielding a return or profits.

re·proof (ri·proȯf′) *n.* reprimand; rebuke; censure; admonition. **reprove** *v.t.* to charge with a fault; to rebuke. **reprovable** *a.* deserving or calling for censure. **reproval** *n.* [O.Fr. *reprover,* fr. L. *reprobare,* to reprove].

rep·tile (rep′·tīl) *n.* animal of class **Reptilia,** cold-blooded, air-breathing vertebrates which move on their bellies or by means of small, short legs; a groveling or contemptible person [L. *reptilis,* creeping].

re·pub·lic (ri·pub′·lik) *n.* a state, without a hereditary head, in which supremacy of the people or its elected representatives is formally acknowledged; commonwealth. **-an** *a.* pert. to republic; *(Cap.)* one of the two traditional political parties of the U.S.A. **-anism** *n.* [L. *res publica,* common weal].

re·pu·di·ate (ri·pū′·di·āt) *v.t.* to cast off; to reject; to disclaim; to disown. **repudiation** *n.* [L. *re-,* away; *pudere,* to be ashamed].

re·pug·nance (ri·pug′·nạns) *n.* state or condition of being repugnant. **repugnancy** *n.* a settled or habitual feeling of aversion. **repugnant** *a.* contrary; distasteful in a high degree; offensive; adverse [L. *repugnare,* to fight back].

re·pulse (ri·puls′) *v.t.* to beat or drive back; to repel decisively; to reject; *n.* state of being repulsed; act of driving off; rebuff; rejection. *n.* **repulsion** *n.* act of driving back; state of being repelled; feeling of aversion; repugnance. **repulsive** *a.* loathsome. **repulsively** *adv.* [L. *repulsum,* to drive back].

re·pute (ri·pūt′) *v.t.* to account or consider; to reckon; *n.* good character; reputation; credit; esteem. **reputation** (rep·yạ·tā′·shạn) *n.* estimation in which a person is held; repute; known or reported character; general credit; good name; fame; renown. **reputable** *a.* held in esteem; respectable; creditable. **reputably** *adv.* **reputedly** *adv.* generally understood or believed [L. *reputare,* to reckon].

re·quest (ri·kwest′) *v.t.* to ask for earnestly; to petition; to beg; *n.* expression of desire for; petition; suit; demand **-er** *n.* [O.Fr. *requeste*].

Re·qui·em (rek′·wi·ạm) *n.* (*R.C.*) celebration of the mass for soul of a dead person; dirge; music for such a mass [L.].

re·quire (ri·kwīr′) *v.t.* to claim as by right; to make necessary; to demand; to need. **-ment** *n.* act of requiring; what is required; need; an essential condition [L. *requirere,* to seek]

req·ui·site (rek′·wạ·zit) *a.* necessary; needful; indispensable; essential; *n.* something necessary or indispensable. **requisition** *n.* a demand made on a community by a military force; formal demand made by one state to another; a written order for materials or supplies; a formal demand; *v.t.* to demand certain supplies or materials, esp. for troops; to request formally; to seize. **requisitionist** *n.* one who makes a requisition [L. *requirere, requisitum,* to seek].

re·quite (ri·kwīt′) *v.t.* to return an equivalent in good or evil; to repay; to make retaliation. **requital** *n.* that which requires or repays; compensation [*re-,* and *quit*].

re·scind (ri·sind′) *v.t.* to annul; to cancel; to revoke; to repeal; to reverse; to abrogate. **-able** *a.* **recission** *n.* act of rescinding. **rescissory** *a.* [L. *rescindere,* to cut off].

re·script (rē′·skript) an edict or decree [L. *rescriptum,* written back].

res·cue (res′·kū) *v.t.* to free from danger, evil, or restraint; to set at liberty; to deliver. *n.* rescuing; deliverance. **-r** *n.* [O.Fr. *rescourre*].

re·search (ri·surch′, rē′·surch) *n.* diligent search or inquiry; scientific investigation and study to discover facts; *v.i.* to make research; to examine with care. **-er** *n.*

re·seat (rē·sēt′) *v.t.* to provide with a new seat or set of seats; to patch (trousers, etc.).

re·sem·ble (ri·zem′·bl) *v.t.* to be like or similar to; **resemblance** *n.* likeness; similarity. **resembling** *a.* [Fr. *ressembler*].

re·sent (ri·zent′) *v.t.* to consider as an injury or affront; to take ill; to be angry at. **-er** *n.* **-ful** *a.* full of, or readily given to, resentment. **-fully** *adv.* **-ment** *n.* deep sense of affront; indignation [L. *re-,* again; *sentire,* to feel].

re·serve (ri·zurv′) *v.t.* to hold back; to set apart; to keep for future use; to retain; to keep for some person; *n.* keeping back; what is reserved; supply of stores for future use; body of men discharged from armed forces but liable to be recalled in an emergency; funds set aside for possible contingencies; reticence; an area of land for a particular purpose. **reservation** *n.* reserving or keeping back; what is kept back; booking of a hotel room, etc.; a proviso or condition; a tract of land reserved for some public use. **-d** *a.* kept back; retained or booked; self-restrained; uncommunicative. **-dly** *adv.* **-dness** *n.* **reservist** *n.* a member of the armed forces belonging to reserves [L. *reservare,* to keep back].

res·er·voir (rez′·ẹr·vwår) *n.* area for storage and filtering of water; a large supply [Fr.].

re·set (rē·set′) *v.t.* to set again. *pr.p.* **-ting.** *pa.p., pa.t.* **reset.**

re·side (ri·zīd′) *v.i.* to dwell permanently; to abide; to live; to be vested in; to be inherent in. **-nce** *n.* act, or time, of dwelling in a place; place where one resides; house. **-ncy** *n.* a residence. **-nt** *a.* dwelling; residing; *n.* one who resides in a place. **-ntial** *a.* pert. to a residence; pert. to a part of a town consisting mainly of dwelling houses. **-ntiary** *a.* having residence; *n.* a resident, esp. clergyman required to reside for a certain time within precincts of cathedral [L. *residere,* fr. *sedere,* to sit].

res·i·due (rez′·ạ·dū) *n.* balance or remainder. **residual** *a.* remaining after a part is taken away. **residuals** *n.pl.* the continued payment to a performer for each rerun of a film, television commercial, etc. **residuary** *a.* pert. to residue or part remaining. **residuum** *n.* what is left after any process of separation or purification; balance or remainder [L. *residuum*].

re·sign (ri·zīn′) *v.t., v.i.* to relinquish formally (office, etc.); to yield to; to give up; to submit to. **resignation** (rez·ig·nā′·shạn) *n.* giving up, as a claim, possession, office, or place; relinquishment; patience and endurance. **-ed** *a.* relinquished; surrendered; acquiescent; submissive; patient. **-edly** *adv.* [L. *resignare,* to unseal].

re·sile (ri·zīl′) *v.i.* to draw back from a previous offer, decision, etc.; to retreat; to recoil; to rebound. **resilience** (ri·zil′·yạns), **resiliency** *n.* springing back or rebounding; elasticity, esp. of mind. **resilient** *a.* springing back; rebounding; elastic; buoyant; possessing power of quick recovery [L. *resilire,* to jump back].

res·in (rez′·in) *n.* general term for brittle, glassy, thickened juices exuded by certain plants; a resinous substance left after distillation of crude turpentine; fossilized remains, as amber, copal, kauri gum, etc.; *v.t.* to dress or coat with resin. **-ous** *a.* [L. *resina*].

re·sist (ri·zist′) *v.t.* and *v.i.* to oppose; to withstand; to strive against. **-ance** *n.* opposition; hindrance; (*Elect.*) opposition offered by a circuit to passage of a current through it; power possessed by an individual to resist disease; in physics, forces tending to arrest movements. **-ant** *n.* one who, or that which, resists. *a.* offering or making resistance. **-er** *n.* **-ibility, -ibleness** *n.* the quality or state of being resistible. **-ible** *a.* **-ibly, -ingly** *adv.* **-less** *a.* irresistible; unable to resist. **-lessly** *adv.* **-lessness** *n.* **-or** *n.* a resistance coil or similar apparatus possessing resistance to electrical current. **-ance coil,** a coil of insulated wire whose resistance has been adjusted to a stated value. **-ance movement,** the organized, underground movement [L. *resistere*, to oppose].

res·o·lute (rez′·ạ·lūt) *a.* having a decided purpose; determined; *n.* a determined person; **-ly** *adv.* **-ness** *n.* determination. **resolution** *n.* act, purpose, or process of resolving; intention; firmness; solution; decision of court or vote of assembly; motion or declaration [L. *resolvere, resolutum*, to unite].

re·solve (ri·zȧlv′) *v.t.* to separate the component parts of; to solve and reduce to a different form; to make clear; to unravel; (*Math.*) to solve; (*Med.*) to clear of inflammation; *v.i.* to determine; to decide; to purpose; to melt; to dissolve; to determine unanimously or by vote; *n.* act of resolving; that which is resolved on; firm determination. **resolvable** *a.* **-d** *a.* determined; resolute. **-dly** *adv.* **-dness** *n.* [L. *resolvere*, to untie].

res·o·nant (rez′·ạ·nạnt) *a.* resounding; echoing; sonorous; ringing. **resonance** *n.* [L. *re-*, again; *sonare*, to sound].

re·sort (ri·zawrt′) *v.i.* to go; to have recourse; to frequent; *n.* a frequented place; vacation spot; recourse; aid. **last resort,** the last resource [Fr. *ressortir*, to rebound, to go back].

re·sound (ri·zound′) *v.i.* to sound back; to send back sound; *v.i.* to echo; to reverberate.

re·source (ri·sōrs′, rē·sōrs′) *n.* that to which one resorts, or on which one depends, for supply or support; skill in improvising; means; contrivance; *pl.* pecuniary means; funds; wealth. **-ful** *a.* clever in devising fresh expedients. **-fully** *adv.* **-fulness** *n.* [Fr. *ressource*].

re·spect (ri·spekt′) *v.t.* to esteem; to honor; to refer to; to relate to; *n.* consideration; deference; *pl.* expression of esteem; good wishes. **-able** *a.* worthy of respect; reputable; decent; moderate. **-ability, -ableness** *n.* **-ably** *adv.* **-ful** *a.* deferential; polite. **-fully** *adv.* **-fulness** *n.* **-ing** *prep.* regarding; concerning. **-ive** *a.* relative; not absolute. **-ively** *adv.* each [L.*respiecere*, to look back].

re·spire (ri·spīr′) *v.t.* and *v.i.* to breathe. **respirable** *a.* fit to be breathed. **respiration** *n.* process of breathing. **respirational** *a.* respiratory. **respirator** *n.* a device to produce artificial respiration. **respiratory** (res′. or res·pī′) *a.* serving for, pert. to, respiration [L. *respirare*].

res·pite (res′·pit) *n.* a temporary intermission; suspension of execution of a capital sentence; *v.t.* to grant a respite to; to reprieve; to relieve by interval of rest [O.Fr. *respit*].

re·splend·ent (ri·splen′·dạnt) *a.* shining with brilliant luster; very bright; dazzling. **resplendence, resplendency** *n.* **-ly** *adv.* [L. *resplendere*, to shine].

re·spond (ri·spȧnd′) *v.i.* to answer; to reply; to correspond to; to react **-ent** *a.* answering; giving response; *n.* (*Law*); defendant; one who refutes in a debate [L. *respondere*, to reply].

re·sponse (ri·spȧns′) *n.* answer or reply; part of liturgy said or sung by choir and congregation in answer to versicles of priest; in R.C. church, anthem after morning lessons, etc. **responsibility** *n.* state of being responsible; that for which any one is responsible; a duty; a charge; an obligation **responsible** *a.* accountable; trustworthy; rational. **responsibly** *adv.* **responsive** *a.* able, ready, or inclined, to respond. **responsively** *adv.* **responsiveness** *n.* [L. *respondere, responsum*, to reply].

rest (rest) *n.* repose; a cessation from motion or labor; that on which anything rests or leans; a place where one may rest; a pause; *v.t.* to lay at rest; *v.i.* to cease from action; to repose; to stand or be fixed (on); to sleep; to be dead; to remain (with), for decision, etc.; to be undisturbed. **-ful** *a.* soothing; peaceful; quiet. **-fully** *adv.* **-fulness** *n.* **-less** *a.* continually on the move; unsettled in mind; uneasy. **-lessly** *adv.* **-lessness** *n.* **to lay to rest,** to bury [O.E.].

rest (rest) *v.i.* to remain; to continue to be; *n.* that which is left over or remainder [L. *restare*, to remain].

res·tau·rant (res′·tạ·rȧnt) *n.* a place where customers are provided with meals on payment. **restaurateur** (res·to′·rạ·tẹr) *n.* proprietor of a restaurant [Fr.].

res·ti·tu·tion (res·tạ·tòò′·shạn) *n.* the act of restoring, esp. to the rightful owner; reparation; indemnification; compensation. **restitutive** *a.* **restitutor** *n.* [L. *restituere, restitutum*, to replace].

res·tive (res′·tiv) *a.* impatient; fidgety; uneasy; obstinate; stubborn. **-ly** *adv.* **-ness** *n.* [O.Fr. *restif*, stubborn].

re·store (ri·stōr′) *v.t.* to give back or return; to recover from ruin or decay; to repair; to renew; to replace; to reinstate; to heal; to revive; to cure. **restorable** *a.* **restoration** *n.* replacement; recovery; reconstruction; reestablishment; (*Cap.*) establishment of monarchy by return of Charles II in 1660. **restorative** *a.* having power to renew strength, vigor, etc.; *n.* a remedy for restoring health and vigor [L. *restaurare*, to repair].

re·strain (ri·strān′) *v.t.* to hold back; to hinder; to check. **-able** *a.* **-edly** *adv.* with restraint. **-ment** *n.* **-t** *n.* curb; repression; hinderance; imprisonment [O.Fr. *restraindre*, fr. L. *re-*, back; *stringere*, to bind].

re·strict (ri·strikt′) *v.t.* to restrain within bounds; to limit **-ed** *a.* limited. **-edly** *adv.* **-ion** *n.* act of restricting; state of being restricted; limitation, confinement; restraint. **-ive** *a.* **-ively** *adv.* [L. *restringere*, to bind fast].

re·sult (ri·zult′) *v.i.* to follow, as a consequence; to issue (in); to terminate; *n.* issue; effect; outcome; answer to a calculation. *a.* following as a result [L. *resultare*, to leap back].

re·sume (ri·zūm)′) *v.t.* to renew; to recommence; to take again. **résumé** (rā·zū·mā′) *n.* a summing up; an abstract. **resumable** *a.* **resumption** *n.* act of taking back or taking again; a fresh start. **resumptive** *a.* resuming [L. *re-*, again; *sumere*, to take].

re·surge (ri·surj′) *v.i.* to rise again. **-nce** *n.* **-nt** *a.* rising again (from the dead) [L. *re-*, again; *surgere*, to rise].

res·ur·rect (rez′·ạ·rekt) *v.t.* to restore to life; to use again. **-ion** *n.* rising of the body after death; (*Cap.*) Christ's arising from the grave after Crucifixion; a revival. **-ion, -ionary** *a.* **-ionist** *n.* one who resurrects, revives, etc.; a believer in resurrection; one who stealthily exhumed bodies from the grave to sell for anatomical purposes [L. *re-*, again; *surgere*, to rise].

re·sus·ci·tate (ri·sus′·ạ·tāt) *v.t.* to restore to

life one apparently dead; to revive; *v.i.* to come to life again. **resuscitable** *a.* **resuscitation** *n.* **resuscitative** *a.* tending to revive or reanimate. **resuscitator** *n.* [L. *resuscitare*, to raise up again].

re·tail (rē.tāl′) *v.t.* to sell to consumer, esp. in small quantities; to tell. **retail** *a.* denoting sale to consumer, as opposed to wholesale; *n.* sale in small quantities. **-er** *n.* **-ment** *n.* [O.F. *retailler*, to cut up].

re·tain (ri.tān′) *v.t.* to continue to keep in possession; to hold; to reserve; to engage services of. **-able** *a.* **-er** *n.* one who retains; adherent or follower; a fee paid to secure services of, esp. lawyer. **-ment** *n.* [L. *retinere*, to hold back].

re·tal·i·ate (ri.tal′.i.āt) *v.t.* and *v.i.* to repay in kind; to return like for like; to requite. **retaliation** *n.* **retaliative, retaliatory** *a.* **retaliator** *n.* [L. *retaliare*, fr. *talis*, like].

re·tard (ri.tạrd′) *v.t.* to hinder progress; to make slow or late; to impede. **-ation** *n.* delaying; hindrance; diminishing velocity of a moving body; rate of loss of velocity; delayed mental development in children. **-ment** *n.* [L. *retardare*, fr. *tardus*, slow].

retch (rech) *v.i.* to strain at vomiting. **-ing** *n.* [O.E. *hraecan*].

re·ten·tion (ri.ten′.shan) *n.* act or power of retaining; memory. **retentive** *a.* **retentively** *adv.* **retentiveness** *n.* [fr. *retain*].

ret·i·cent (ret′.ạ.sạnt) *a.* reserved; uncommunicative. **reticence** *n.* also **reticency. -ly** *adv.* [L. *reticere*, fr. *tacere*, to be silent].

ret·i·cle (ret′.ạ.kl) *n.* a group of lines or wires in the focus of an optical instrument. **reticule** *n.* a little bag; a reticle. **reticular, reticulary** *a.* having the form of a net; intricate. **reticulate** *v.t.* to cover with netlike lines; to make like a net; *a.* Also **reticulated. reticulation** *n.* [Fr. *reticule*, fr. L. *rete*, a net].

re·ti·form (rē′.tạ.fawrm) *a.* having form of a net; reticulated [L. *rete*, a net; *forma*, form].

ret·i·na (ret′.i.nạ) *n.* innermost, semi-transparent, sensory layer of the eye from which sense impressions are passed to the brain. **-l** *a.* [L. *rete*, a net].

ret·i·nue (ret′.i.nū) *n.* a body of hired servants or followers; a train of attendants; suite [Fr. *retenir*, to retain].

re·tire (ri.tīr′) *v.t.* to compel one to retire from office; to withdraw from circulation notes or bills; *v.i.* to go back; to withdraw; to retreat; to give up formally one's work or office; to go to bed. **retiral** *n.* act of retiring; occasion when one retires from office, etc. **-d** *a.* secluded; private; sequestered; withdrawn permanently from one's daily work. **-dly** *adv.* **-ment, -dness** *n.* act of retiring; state of being retired. **retiring** *a.* reserved; modest [Fr. *retirer*, to pull back].

re·tort (ri.tawrt′) *v.t.* to repay in kind; to hurl back (chare, etc.); *v.i.* to make a smart reply; *n.* vigorous reply or repartee; a vessel in which substances are distilled [L. *retorquere, retortum*, to twist back].

re·trace (rē.trās′) *v.t.* to trace back or over again; to go back the same way. **-able** *a.*

re·tract (ri.trakt′) *v.t.* and *v.i.* to draw back; to take back, as a statement; to go back on one's word. **-able** *a.* **-ation** *n.* recalling of a statement or opinion; recantation. **-ile** *a.* (*Zool.*) capable of being drawn back or inwards, as claws, etc. **-ion** *n.* the act of drawing back; disavowal; recantation; retractile power. **-ive** *a.* **-ively** *adv.* [L. *re-*, back; *trahere, tractum*, to draw].

re·tread (rē.tred′) *v.t.* to tread again; to replace a worn tread on the outer cover of a rubber tire with a new tread.

re·treat (ri.trēt′) *n.* retiring or withdrawing; a military signal for retiring; a military call at sunset, on a bugle; place of seclusion; period of retirement for prayer and meditation; *v.i.* to move back; to betake oneself to a place of security; to retire before an enemy. **-ing** *a.* sloping backward, as forehead or chin [Fr. *retraite*, fr. *retraire*, to draw back].

re·trench (ri.trench′) *v.t.* to cut down (expense, etc.); to curtail; to remove; *v.i.* to economize. **-ment** *n.* diminution of expenditure; economy; (*Fort.*) extra parapet and ditch within a rampart to prolong defense [Fr. *retrancher*, to cut off].

ret·ri·bu·tion (ret.rạ.bū′.shạn) *n.* just or suitable return; esp. for evil deeds; requital; repayment. **retributive, retributory** *a.* [L. *retributio*].

re·trieve (ri.trēv′) *v.t.* to gain back; to recover; to reestablish (former position, fortune, etc.); to repair; (of a dog) to find and bring back shot game. **retrievable** *a.* **retrievably** *adv.* **-ment, retrieval** *n.* **-r** *n.* dog trained to find and bring back game [Fr. *retrouver*, to find again].

ret·ro- (ret′.rō) *prefix* fr. L. *retro*, back, backward, used in the formation of compound words.

ret·ro·act (ret.rō.akt′) *v.i.* to act backwards; to react **-ion** *n.* **-ive** *a.* acting in regard to past events; retrospective. **-ively** *adv.* [L. *retro*, backward; *agere, actum*, to act].

ret·ro·cede (ret.rō.sēd′) *v.t.* to go or move back. **retrocession** *n.* going back [L. *retro*, backward; *cedere*, to go].

ret·ro·grade (ret′.rō.grād) *v.i.* to move backward; to deteriorate; to decline; *a.* tending to a backward direction; deteriorating; reactionary; retrogressive. **retrogradation** *n.* *n.* **retrogress** *v.i.* to move backwards; to deteriorate. **retrogression** *n.* act of going backward; a decline into an inferior state of development. **retrogressive** *a.* moving backward; reactionary; degenerating; assuming baser characteristics. **retrogressively** *adv.* [L. *retro*, backward; *gradi*, to go].

re·trorse (rē.trawrs′) *a.* bending or pointing backwards, as feathers of birds. Also **retroverse. -ly** *adv.* [L. *retro*, backwards; *vertere, versum*, to turn].

ret·ro·spect (ret′.rō.spekt) *n.* a looking back; survey of past events; a review. **-ion** *n.* **-ive** *a.* tending to look back; applicable to past events; of laws, rules, etc., having force as if enacted or authorized at earlier date. **-ively** *adv.* [L. *retro*, backward; *specere*, to look].

ret·ro·verse (ret′.rō.vers) *a.* bent backwards; retrorse. **retroversion** *n.* **retrovert** (rē′., ret.′) *v.t.* to turn back [L. *retro*, backward; *vertere, versum*, to turn].

re·turn (ri.turn′) *v.t.* to bring, give, or send back; to restore; to report officially; to elect; to yield (a profit); to reciprocate; *v.i.* to go or come back; to recur; to reply; *n.* coming back to the same place; what is returned, as a payment; profit; an official report, esp. as to numbers; repayment; restitution. **-able** *a.* **— match** *n.* second game played by same opponents. **— ticket** *n.* ticket for journey, there and back [Fr. *retourner*].

re·un·ion (rē.ūn′.yạn) *n.* union formed anew after separation; a social gathering. **reunite** *v.t.* and *v.i.* to unite again; to join after separation.

rev (rev) *n.* (*Colloq.*) revolution of an engine; *v.t.* and *v.i.* to run (an engine). *pr.p.* **-ving.** *pa.t.* and *pa.p.* **-ved.**

re·veal (ri.vēl′) *v.t.* to disclose; to show. **-able** *a.* **-er** *n.* **-ment** *n.* disclosure; revelation. **-ed law,** divine law. **-ed religion,** founded on revelation. Opposite of *natural religion* [L.

revelare, to draw back the veil].

rev•eil•le (rev′.ạ.li.) *n.* the bugle call or roll of drums sounded in military establishments at daybreak to rouse inmates [Fr. *réveillez (-vous)* wake up!].

rev•el (rev′.ạl) *v.i.* to make merry; to carouse; to delight in. *pr.p., pa.t., pa.p. and n.* festivity; noisy celebration; *pl.* entertainment, with music and dancing. **-er** *n.* **-ment, -ry** *n.* [O.Fr. *reveler,* to make tumult].

rev•e•la•tion (rev.ạ.lā′.shạn) *n.* act of revealing; God's disclosure of himself to man; *(Cap.)* last book of New Testament. **-al, revelatory** *a.* [L. *revelare,* to draw back the veil].

rev•e•nant (rev′.ạ.nạnt) *n.* one returned from long absence or apparently from the dead; a specter; a ghostly visitant [Fr.].

re•venge (ri.venj′) *v.t.* to make retaliation for; to return injury for injury; to avenge; *n.* revenging; infliction of injury in return for injury; passion for vengeance. **-ful** *a.* **-fully** *adv.* **-fulness** *n.* [O.Fr. *revenger,* fr. L. *re-,* again; *vindicare,* to claim].

rev•e•nue (rev′.ạ.nū) *n.* income derived from any source, esp. annual income of a state or institution; proceeds; receipts; profits. [Fr. *revenue,* return, fr. L. *revenire,* to come back].

re•ver•ber•ate (ri.vur′.bẹr.āt) *v.t.* and *v.i.* to send back, as sound; to reflect, as light or heat; to re-echo; to resound. **reverberant** *a.* resounding; beating back. **reverberation** *n.* **reverberative** *a.* tending to reverberate. **reverberator** *n.* **reverberatory** *a.* producing reverberation [L. *reverberare,* to beat back].

re•vere (ri.vir′) *v.t.* to regard with mingled fear, respect and affection; to reverence. **-nce** *n.* awe mingled with respect and esteem; veneration; a bow, curtsy, or genuflection; (*Cap.*) a title applied to a clergyman; *v.t.* to revere; to venerate. **-nd** *a.* worthy of reverence; venerable; a title of respect given to clergy (*abbrev.* **Rev.**) **-nt** *a.* feeling, showing, behaving with, reverence. **-ntial** *a.* respectful. **-ntially, -ntly** *adv.* [O.Fr. *reverer,* fr. L. *vereri,* to feel awe].

rev•er•ie, revery (rev′.ẹr.i.) *n.* state of mind, akin to dreaming; rhapsody; musing [Fr. *rêverie,* fr. *rêver,* to dream].

re•vers (rạ.vir′) *n.* part of garment turned for ornamentation, as lapel [O.Fr. = reverse].

re•verse (ri.vurs′) *v.t.* to change completely; to turn in an opposite direction; to give a contrary decision; to annul; to overturn; to transpose; to invert; *v.i.* to change direction; *n.* side which appears when object is turned round; opposite or contrary; crest side of coin or medal, as distinguished from *obverse;* check; defeat; misfortune; gear to drive a car backward; *a.* turned backward; opposite. **reversal** *n.* reversing, changing, overthrowing, annulling.**-d** *a.* turned in opposite direction; inverted; annulled. **-ly** *adv.* **reversibility** *n.* property of being reversible. **reversible** *a.* capable of being used on both sides or in either direction. **reversibly** *adv.* **reversion** *n.* returning or reverting; a deferred annuity; right or hope of future possession; (*Law*) return of estate to grantor or his next-of-kin, after death of grantee or legatee; interest which reverts to a landlord after expiry of lease; *(Biol.)* a tendency to revert to long-concealed characters of previous generations; atavism. **reversional, reversionary** *a.* involving a reversion. **reversive** *a.* [L. *re-,* back; *vertere, vérsum,* to turn].

re•vert (ri.vurt′) *v.i.* to return to former state or rank; to come back to subject; to turn backwards; (*Law*) to return by reversion to donor; *v.t.* to turn back or reverse. **-ible** *a.* [L. *re-,* again; *vertere,* to turn].

re•view (ri.vū′) *v.t.* to re-examine; to consider critically (book); to inspect troops, etc. *n.* revision; survey; inspection, esp. of massed military forces; a critical notice of a book, etc.; periodical devoted to critical articles, current events, etc. **-er** *n.* one who writes critical reviews; examiner; inspector [Fr. *revoir,* to see again].

re•vile (ri.vīl′) *v.t.* to abuse with opprobrious language; to vilify; to defame. **-ment** *n.* **-r** *n.* [O.Fr. *reviler*].

re•vise (ri.vīz′) *v.t.* to look over and correct; to review, alter and amend; *n.* a revised form; a further printer's proof to ensure all corrections have been made. **revisal** *n.* review; reexamination. **revision** *n.* revisal; revised copy of book or document. **-r** *n.* **revisional, revisionary** *a.* pert. to revision. **revisory** *a.* having power to revise (*Cap.*). **-d Version,** new translation of Bible in 1881 (New Testament) and 1884 (Old Testament) [L. *revisere*].

re•vive (ri.vīv′) *v.i.* to come back to life, vigor, etc.; to awaken; *v.t.* to resuscitate; to re-animate; to renew; to recover from neglect; to refresh (memory). **revivability** *n.* **revivable** *a.* capable of being revived. **revivably** *adv.* **revival** *n.* reviving or being revived; renewed activity, of trade, etc.; a wave of religious enthusiasm worked up by powerful preachers; awakening; reappearance of old, neglected play, etc. **revivalism** *n.* religious fervor of a revival. **revivalist** *n.* one who promotes religious revivals. **-r** *n.* one who, or that which, revives; a stimulant. **revivification** *n.* renewal of life and energy. **revivify** *v.t.* to reanimate; to reinvigorate [L. *re-,* again; *vivere,* to live].

re•voke (ri.vōk′) *v.t.* to annul; to repeal; to reverse (a decision); *v.i.* at cards, to fail to follow suit. *n.* neglect to follow suit at cards. **-r** *n.* **revocable** *a.* able to be revoked. **revocableness, revocability** *n.* **revocably** *adv.* **revocation** *n.* repeal; reversal. **revocatory** *a.* [L. *revocare,* to recall].

re•volt (ri.vōlt′) *v.i.* to renounce allegiance; to rise in rebellion; to feel disgust; *v.t.* to shock; to repel; *n.* act of revolting; rebellion; mutiny; disgust; loathing. **-er** *n.* **-ing** *a.* disgusting. **-ingly** *adv.* [Fr. *révolter*].

rev•o•lu•tion (rev.ạ.lū′.shạn) *n.* motion of body round its orbit or focus; turning round on axis, time marked by a regular recurrence (as seasons); a radical change in constitution of a country after revolt. **-ary** *a.* pert. to revolution; marked by great and violent changes; *n.* one who participates in a revolution. **-ize** *v.t.* to change completely [L. *revolvere, revolutum,* to turn round].

re•volve (ri.vȧlv′) *v.i.* to turn round on an axis; to rotate; to meditate; *v.t.* to cause to turn; to rotate; to reflect upon. **revolvable** *a.* **-r** *n.* pistol [L. *revolvere,* to turn round].

re•vue (ri.vū′) *n.* theatrical entertainment, partly musical comedy, with little continuity of structure or connected plot [Fr.].

re•vul•sion (ri.vul′.shạn) *n.* sudden, violent change of feeling; repugnance or abhorrence; reaction; (*Med.*) counterirritation. **revulsive** *a.* [L. *revellere, revulsum,* to tear away].

re•ward (ri.wawrd′) *v.t.* to give in return for; to recompense; to remunerate; *n.* what is given in return; return for voluntary act; assistance in any form. **-er** *n.* **-ing** *a.* [O.Fr. *rewarder* = Fr. *regarder,* to look upon].

rhab•do- (rab.dạ) *prefix* used in formation of scientific compound terms, signifying *a rod* or *rod-like.* **rhaboid** *a.* rod-shaped. **-mancy** *n.* divination by rod or wand, to trace presence of ores or water underground [Gk. *rhabdos,* a rod].

rhap•so•dy (rap′.sạ.di.) *n.* collection of verses; an intense, rambling composition or discourse; (*Mus.*) an irregular composition in a free style. **rhapsodic(al)** *a.* in extravagant, irregular style. **rhapsodically** *adv.* **rhapsodize** *v.t.* and *v.i.* to sing or recite, as a rhapsody; to be ecstatic over. **rhapsodist** *n.* one who recites or composes a rhapsody [Gk. *rhapsōdia*].

Rhen·ish (ren'·ish) *a.* of or pert. to River Rhine; *n.* wine from grapes grown in Rhineland [L. *Rhenus*].

rhe·o- *prefix* used in the formation of scientific compound terms, signifying *flowing* from Gk. *rhein,* to flow. **rheometer** (rē·àm'·ạ·tẹr) *n.* instrument for measuring force of flow of fluids. **-stat** *n.* instrument for controlling and varying within limits value of resistance in electrical circuit. **rheostatic** *a.*

rhe·sus (rē'·sạs) *n.* small Indian monkey. **rhesian** *a.* **rhesus factor** (*Med.*) Rh factor; a peculiarity of red cells of blood of most individuals, the so-called **rhesus positive,** rendering transfusion of their blood unsuitable for rhesus negative minority of patients. [L.]

rhet·o·ric (ret'·ạ·rik) *n.* art of persuasive or effective speech or writing; declamation; artificial eloquence or sophistry; exaggerated oratory. **rhetorical** *a.* concerning style or effect; of the nature of rhetoric. **rhetorical question,** statement in the form of question to which no answer is expected. **rhetorically** *adv.* **rhetorician** *n.* a teacher of or one versed in principles of rhetoric [Gk. *rhētorikos,* fr. *rhētōr,* a public speaker].

rheum (ròòm) *n.* thin, serous fluid secreted by mucous glands and discharged from nostrils or eyes during catarrh or a common cold. **-atic, -atical** *a.* pert. to or suffering from rheumatism. **-atism** *n.* a disease with symptoms of sharp pains and swelling in muscles and larger joints. **-atoid** *a.* resembling rheumatism. **-y** *a.* (*Literary*) full of rheum (esp. eyes); damp. **rheumatoid arthritis,** severe chronic inflammation of joints, esp. knees and fingers [Gk. *rheuma,* flow].

rhi·nal (rī'·nạl) *a* pert. to the nose [Gk. *rhis, rhinos,* nose].

rhine·stone (rīn'·stōn) *n.* paste imitation of diamonds [fr. the *Rhine*].

rhi·noc·er·os (rī·nàs'·ạ·rạs) *n.* thick-skinned mammal allied to elephant, hippopotamus, etc. with strong horn (sometimes two) on nose [Gk. *rhis, rhinos,* the nose; *keras,* a horn].

rhi·zo- (rī·zō) *prefix* used in construction of compound terms, from Greek, *rhiza,* a root. **rhizome** (rī'·zōm) *n.* subterranean shoot, often bearing scales which are membranous, and usually giving off adventurous roots. **-matous** *a.* of the nature of a rhizome.

rhod-, rhodo- *prefix* used in the formation of compound terms, signifying rose-colored from Greek, *rhodon,* a rose. **-ocyte** *n.* red blood corpuscle. **rhododendron** *n.* evergreen flowering shrub with magnificent red or white blossoms.

rhom·bus (ràm'·bạs) *n.* (*Geom.*) parallelogram whose sides are all equal but whose angles are not right angles. **rhomb** *n.* a lozenge or diamond-shaped figure; rhombus. **rhombic, rhombiform, rhomboid, rhomboidal** *a.* **rhomboid** *n.* parallelogram like rhombus, but having only opposite sides and angles equal [Gk. *rhombos*].

rhu·barb (ròò'·bàrb) *n.* two species of cultivated plants, familiar rhubarb of kitchen garden, and an eastern variety whose roots are used as a purgative. (*Slang*) heated discussion [Gk. *rha,* rhubarb; *barbaron,* foreign].

rhumb, rumb (rum, rumb) *n.* any of 32 cardinal points on compass [Gk. *rhombos,* a rhomb].

rhyme (rīm) *n.* identity of sound in word endings of verses; verses in rhyme with each other; word answering in sound to another word; *v.t.* to put into rhyme; *v.i.* to make verses. **-r, rhymster** *n.* one who makes rhymes; a minor poet; a poetaster. **— scheme,** pattern or arrangement of rhymes in stanza [O.E. *rim,* number].

rhythm (rithm) *n.* regular or measured flow of sound, as in music and poetry, or of action, as in dancing; measured, periodic movement, as in heart pulsations; regular recurrence; symmetry. **-ic(al)** *a.* **-ically** *adv.* **-ics** *n.* science of rhythm [Gk. *rhuthmos,* fr. *rhein,* to flow].

ri·ant (rī'·ạnt) *a.* laughing; merry; genial. **-ly** *adv.* [Fr. *rire,* to laugh].

rib (rib) *n.* one of arched and very elastic bones springing from vertebral column; anything resembling a rib, as a bar of a firegrate, wire support of umbrella. *v.t.* to furnish with ribs. *pr.p.* **-bing.** *pa.t.* and *pa.p.* **-bed. -bing** *n.* an arrangement of ribs [O.E. *ribb*].

rib·ald (rib·ạld) *a.* low; vulgar; indecent. **-ry** *n.* vulgar language or conduct; obscenity. **-ish** *a.* [Fr. *ribaud*].

rib·bon (rib'·ạn) *n.* woven strip of material such as silk or satin, as trimming or fastening for a dress; colored piece of silk as war medal; part of insignia of order of knighthood; anything in strips resembling ribbon; inked tape in a typewriter. **Blue Ribbon,** first prize award [O.Fr. *riban*].

ri·bo·fla·vin (rī·bạ·flā'·vin) *n.* chemical substance present in vitamin B2 complex, with marked growth promoting properties [L.L. *ribus,* currant; *flavus,* yellow].

rice (rīs) *n.* annual grass plant, cultivated in Asia, the principal food of one-third of world. **— paper** *n.* very thin and delicate paper used in China and Japan for drawing and painting [Gk. *oruza*].

rich (rich) *a.* wealthy; abounding in possessions; well supplied; fertile; abounding in nutritive qualities; of food, highly seasoned or flavored; mellow and harmonious (voice); *n.* the wealthy classes. **-es** *n.pl.* wealth. **-ly** *adv.* **-ness** *n.* [O.E. *rice,* rich].

rick·ets (rik'·its) *n.* rachitis, infantile disease marked by defective development of bones. **rickety** *a.* affected with rickets; shaky; unstable; insecure [etym. uncertain].

rick-shaw. See **jinrickisha.**

ric·o·chet (rik'·ạ·shā) *n.* glancing rebound of object after striking flat surface at oblique angle; *v.t.* and *v.i.* to rebound [Fr.].

rid (rid) *vt.* to free of; to relieve of; to remove by violence; to disencumber. *pr.p.* **-ding.** *pa.t.* and *pa.p.* **rid** or **-ded. -dance** *n.* deliverance; removal. **a good riddance,** a welcome relief [O.E. *hreddan,* to snatch away].

rid·den (rid'·n) *pa.p.* of **ride.**

rid·dle (rid'·l) *n.* large sieve for sifting or screening gravel, etc.; *v.t.* to separate, as grain from chaff, with a riddle; to pierce with holes as in a sieve; to pull (theory, etc.) to pieces. **riddlings** *n.pl.* coarse material left in sieve [O.E. *hridder*].

rid·dle (rid'·l) *n.* enigma; puzzling fact, thing, person; *v.i.* to speak in, make, riddles [O.E. *raedelse. fr. raedan,* to read, to guess]

ride (rīd) *v.t.* to be mounted on horse, bicycle, etc.; to traverse or cover distance; *v.i.* to be carried on back of an animal; to be borne along in a vehicle; to lie securely at anchor; to float lightly. *pr.p.* **riding.** *pa.t.* **rode;** *pa.p.* **ridden.** *n.* act of riding; journey on horseback, in a vehicle, etc.; roadway, etc. **-r** *n.* one who rides; addition to a document; supplement to original motion or verdict. **riding** *a.* used for riding on; used by a rider; *n.* act of riding. **riding habit** *n.* outfit worn by ladies on horseback. **to ride over,** to tyrannize. **to ride rough-shod,** to show no

consideration for others [O.E. *ridan*].
ridge (rij) *n.* line of meeting of two sloping surfaces; long narrow hill; strip of upturned soil between furrows; highest part of roof; horizontal beam to which tops of rafters are fixed; tongue of high pressure on meteorological map; *v.t.* to form into ridges; *v.i.* to rise in ridges; to wrinkle. **-d** *a.* having ridges on its surface. **— pole** *n.* horizontal beam at peak of roof, tent, etc. [O.E. *hrycg*, the back].
rid·i·cule (rid′·ạ·kūl) *n.* mockery; raillery; derision; *v.t.* to deride; to mock; to make fun of. **-r** *n.* **ridiculous** *a.* exciting ridicule; ludicrous, laughable. [L. *ridere*, to laugh].
rife (rīf) *a.* prevailing; prevalent; abundant; plentiful. **-ly** *adv.* **-ness** *n.* [O.E.].
riff·raff (rif′·raf) *n.* the rabble (*Dial*) trash [M.E. *rif* and *raf*].
ri·fle (rī·fl) *v.t.* to search and rob; to strip; to plunder. **-r** *n.* **rifling** *n.* pillaging [O.Fr. *rifler*, fr. Ice. *hrifa*, to seize].
ri·fle (rī′·fl) *v.t.* to make spiral grooves in (gun barrel, etc.), *n.* a shoulder weapon or artillery piece whose barrel is grooved. **rifling** *n.* the arrangement of grooves in a gun barrel or rifle tube. **-man.** *n.* a man armed with rifle [Dan. *rifle*, to groove].
rift (rift) *n.* cleft; fissure; *v.t.* and *v.i.* to crack [fr. *rive*, to rend].
rig (rig) *v.t.* to provide (ship) with spars, ropes, etc.; to equip; (*Colloq.*) to arrange fraudulently; to clothe. *pr.p.* **-ging.** *pa.t.* and *pa.p.* **-ged** *n.* manner in which masts and sails of vessel are rigged; equipment used in erecting or installing machinery, etc.; (*Colloq.*) dress; a horse and trap. **-ger** *n.* **ging** *n.* system of ropes and tackle, esp. for supporting mast or controlling sails; adjustment of different components of an aircraft [Scand.].
right (rīt) *a.* straight; proper; upright; in accordance with truth and duty; being on same side of person toward the east when facing north; in politics, implying preservation of existing, established order or of restoring former institutions; (*Geom.*) applied to regular figures rising perpendicularly; correct; true; *adv.* in a right manner; according to standard of truth and justice; very; correctly; properly; exactly; to the right hand; *n.* that which is correct; uprightness; a just claim; legal title; that which is on right side, or opposite to left; political party inclined towards conservatism and preservation of status quo; *v.t.* to set upright; to do justice to; to make right; *v.i.* to recover proper or natural position; to become upright. **-ful** *a.* legitimate; lawful; true; honest; reasonable; fair. **-fully** *adv.* **-fulness** *n.* **-ly** *adv.* in accordance with justice; correctly. **-ness** *n.* correctness; justice. **-about** *adv.* in or to the opposite direction. **—angled** *a.* having a **right angle,** one of ninety degrees. **—hand** *a.* belonging to the right hand; pert. to most reliable assistant. **— of way** *n.* right of passage [O.E. *riht*].
right·eous (rī′·chạs) *a.* doing what is right; just; upright; godly. **-ly** *adv.* **-ness** *n.* [O.E. *riht*, right; *wis*, wise].
rig·id (rij′·id) *a.* stiff; not easily bent; strict; rigorous. **-ness, -ity** *n.* **-ly** *adv.* [L. *rigidus*].
rig·ma·role (rig′·mạ·rōl) *n.* a succession of meaningless, rambling statements; foolish talk [corrupt. of *ragman roll*, a list of names].
rig·or (rig′·ẹr) *n.* strictness, severity, stiffness, (*Med.*) a chill with fever; insensitive state of plants or animals. **-ism** *n.* strictness; austerity. **-ist** *n.* a person of strict principles. **-ous** *a.* **-ously** *adv.* **-ousness** *n.* **— mortis,** stiffening of body after death [L.].
rile (rīl) *v.t.* (*Colloq.* or *Dial.*) to anger; to exasperate; to irritate [a form of *roil*].
rill (ril) *n.* a small brook; rivulet; a streamlet. **-et** *n.* a tiny stream [Ger. *Rille*, a furrow].
rim (rim) *n.* margin; brim; border; metal ring forming outer part of a car wheel and carrying the tire; *v.t.* to furnish with a rim; *pr.p.* **-ming.** *pa.t.* and *pa.p.* **-med. -less** *a.* [O.E. *rima*].
rime Same as **rhyme.**
rime (rīm) *n.* white or hoarfrost; frozen dew or vapor. **rimy** *a.* [O.E. *hrim*].
ri·mose (rī′·mōs) *a.* having surface covered with fissures or cracks. Also **rimous** [L. *rimosus*].
rind (rīnd) *n.* the external covering or coating of trees, fruits, cheese, bacon, etc.; skin; peel, etc. *v.t.* to strip off rind [O.E. *rindle*].
ring (ring) *n.* small circle of gold, etc. esp. on finger; band, coil, rim; circle formed for dance or sports; round enclosure, as in circus, auction mart, etc.; area within roped square for boxing, etc.; a combination of persons to control prices within a trade; *v.t.* to encircle; to put ring through an animal's nose; to cut a ring around trunk of a tree. **-ed** *a.* wearing, marked with, formed of, or surrounded by, a ring or rings. **-ing** *n.* **-leader** *n.* the leader of people associated together for a common object, usually in defiance of law and order. **-less** *a.* **-let** *n.* small ring; long curl of hair. **-mail** *n.* chain armor. **-master** *n.* one who directs performance in circus ring. **-worm** *n.* contagious disease of skin, esp. of scalp, leaving circular bare patches [O.E. *hring*].
ring (ring) *v.t.* to cause to sound, esp. by striking; to produce, by ringing; *v.i.* to give out a clear resonant sound, as a bell; to chime; to resound; to be filled, as with praise, tidings, etc.; to continue sounding, as ears. *pa.t.* **rang,** *rarely* **rung.** *pa.p.* **rung.** *n.* a resonant note; chime (of church bells); act of ringing; a telephone call. **to ring down,** to cause theater curtain to be lowered. **to ring false,** to sound insincere [O.E. *hringan*].
rink (ringk) *n.* place for skating or curling; members of a side at bowling or curling; floor for roller skating, etc.; broad strip of a bowling-green [etym. doubtful].
rinse (rins) *v.t.* to wash out, by filling with water, etc., and emptying; to wash without the use of soap; **rinsing** *n.* [Fr. *rincer*].
ri·ot (rī′·ạt) *n.* tumultuous disturbance of peace; wanton behavior; noisy festivity; tumult; uproar; profusion, as of color. *v.i.* to make, or engage in, riot; to revel; to disturb peace. **-er** *n.* **-ing** *n.* **-ous** *a.* engaging in riot; unruly; boisterous. **-ously** *adv.* **-ousness** *n.* **-ry** *n.* riotous conduct. **to read the riot act** (*Colloq.*) to scold and threaten punishment. **to run riot,** to behave wildly, without restraint [O.Fr. *riotte*].
rip (rip) *v.t.* to rend; to slash; to tear off or out; to slit; to saw wood along direction of grain; *v.i.* to tear; to move quickly and freely. *pr.p.* **-ping.** *pa.t.* and *pa.p.* **-ped.** *n.* rent; tear. **-per** *n.* **-ping** *a.* **-cord** *n.* cord to withdraw parachute from pack so that ascending air forces it open. **— roaring** (*Slang*) *a.* hilarious. **-saw** *n.* saw with large teeth for cutting timber in direction of grain [O.N. *rippa*, to scratch].
rip (rip) *n.* a stretch of broken water in sea or river. **— current, — tide** [etym. doubtful].
ri·par·i·an (rạ·, rī·pār·i·ạn) *a.* pert. to, or situated on, banks of a river [L. *ripa*, a river bank].
ripe (rīp) *a.* ready for reaping; mature; fully developed; sound (judgment, etc.); ready (for) **-ly** *adv.* **-n** *v.t.* to hasten process of riping; to mature; *v.i.* to grow ripe; to come to perfection. **-ness** *n.* [O.E.].
ri·poste (ri·pōst′) *n.* quick return thrust in fencing; smart reply; repartee [Fr.].
rip·ple (rip′·l) *n.* fretting or dimpling of sur-

face of water; a little wave; subdued murmur or sound; *v.t.* to cause ripple in; *v.i.* to flow or form into little waves. [var. of *rimple*, for O.E. *hrimpan*, to wrinkle].

rise (rīz) *v.i.* to ascend; to get up; to get out of bed; to appear above horizon; to originate; to swell; to increase in value, price, power; to revolt; to reach a higher rank; to revive. *pr.p.* **rising**. *pa.t.* **rose**. *pa.p.* **-n.** *n.* act of rising; that which rises or seems to rise; increase, as of price, wages, etc.; source; elevation. **-r** *n.* one who, or that which, rises; vertical part of a step. **rising** *n.* getting up; revolt; insurrection; *a.* mounting; advancing. **to get a rise out of,** to tease someone to the point of anger [O.E. *risan*].

ris·i·ble (riz′·ạ·bl) *a.* very prone to laugh; capable of exciting laughter; mirth provoking. **-ness, risibility** *n.* **risibly** *adv.* [L. *risibilis*, fr. *ridere*, to laugh].

risk (risk) *n.* danger; peril; hazard; amount covered by insurance; person or object insured; *v.t.* to expose to danger or possible loss. **-er** *n.* **-y** *a.* [Fr. *risque*].

ris·qué (ris·kā) *a.* daringly close to impropriety [F. *risquer*].

ri·sot·to (ri·zawt′·tō) *n.* Italian dish of shredded onions, meat, and rice [It.].

ris·sole (ris′·ōl) *n.* fish or meat minced and fried with bread crumbs and eggs [Fr.].

rite (rīt) *n.* formal practice or custom, esp. religious; form; ceremonial. **ritual** *a.* pert. to rites; ceremonial; *n.* manner of performing divine service; prescribed book of rites. **ritualism** *n.* adherence to and fondness for decorous ceremonial customs in public worship. **ritualist** *n.* **ritualistic** *a.* **ritually** *adv.* [L. *ritus*].

ri·val (rī′·vạl) *n.* competitor; opponent; *a.* having same pretensions or claims; competing; *v.t.* to vie with; to strive to equal or excel. **-ry** *n.* keen competition; emulation [L. *rivalis*].

rive (rīv) *v.t.* to rend asunder; to split; to cleave; *v.i.* to be split or rent asunder. **-d.** *pa.p.* **-d, -n** [O.N. *rifa*].

riv·er (riv′·ẹr) *n.* natural stream of water flowing in a channel; a copious flow; abundance. **-ine** *a.* situated near or on river. **— basin** *n.* area drained by a river and its tributaries. **-bed** *n.* channel of a river. **— horse** *n.* the hippopotamus. **-side** *n.* the bank of a river [Fr. *rivière*].

riv·et (riv′·it) *n.* cylindrical iron or steel pin with strong flat head at one end, used for uniting two overlapping plates, etc. by hammering down the stub end; *v.t.* to fasten with rivets; to clinch; to fasten firmly [Fr.].

riv·u·let (riv′·yạ·lit) *n.* a little river.

roach (rōch) *n.* fresh-water fish [O. Fr. *roche*].

roach. See **cockroach.**

road (rōd) *n.* a track or way prepared for passengers, vehicles, etc., direction; way; route; a place where vessels may ride at anchor. **-block** *n.* an obstruction placed across a road to stop someone. **-house** *n.* a restaurant, hotel, etc., at the roadside. **— show,** traveling company of actors. **-side** *n.* strip of ground along edge of road. **-way** *n.* a road. **to take to the road,** to adopt life of a tramp [O.E. *rad*, riding].

roam (rōm) *v.t.* and *v.i.* to wander; to ramble; to rove; *n.* a ramble; a walk. **-er** *n.*

roan (rōn) *a.* having coat in which the main color is thickly interspersed with another, esp. bay or sorrel or chestnut mixed with white or grey; *n.* a roan horse; smooth-grained sheepskin, dyed and finished [Fr. *rouan*].

roar (rōr) *v.t.* and *v.i.* to shout; to bawl; to make loud, confused sound, as winds, waves, traffic, etc.; to laugh loudly; *n.* sound of roaring, deep cry. **-ing** *n.* act or sound of roaring. **-ingly** adv. **-ing trade,** brisk, profitable business [O.E. *rarian*].

roast (rōst) *v.t.* to cook by exposure to open fire or in oven; to expose to heat (as coffee, etc.); (*Slang*) to reprimand; *v.i.* to become over-heated; *n.* what is roasted, as joint of meat; *a.* roasted. **-ing** *n.* **-er** *n.* [O.Fr. *rostir*].

rob (ràb) *v.t.* to take by force or stealth; to plunder; to steal. *pr.p.* **-bing**. *pa.t.* and *pa.p.* **-bed. -ber** *n.* **-bery** *n.* forcibly depriving a person of money or of goods [O.Fr. *rober*].

robe (rōb) *n.* a long outer garment, esp. of flowing style; ceremonial dress denoting state, rank, or office; gown; large covering, as lap robe; *v.t.* to invest with a robe; to array; to dress. **robing** *n.* [Fr.].

rob·in (ràb′·in) *n.* brown red-breasted bird of thrush family; Also **— redbreast** [O.Fr. *Robin*, for *Robert*].

ro·bot (rō′·bàt) *n.* automaton; mechanical man; person of machine-like efficiency [fr. play, R.U.R. (Rossum's Universal Robots, by Karel Capek). Pol. *robotnik*, workman].

ro·bust (rō·bust′) *a.* strong; muscular, sound; vigorous. **-ly** *adv.* **-ness** *n.* [L. *Robustus*, fr. *robur*, an oak, strength].

Ro·chelle salt (rō·shel′·sawlt) *n.* tartrate of sodium and potassium, used as aperient [*La Rochelle*, a town in France.]

roch·et (ràch′·it) *n.* garment like a surplice, of white lawn, usually with tight sleeves, worn by bishops [O.Fr.].

rock (ràk) *n.* large mass of stone; (*Geol.*) any natural deposit of sand, earth, or clay when in natural beds; firm foundation. **-ery** *n.* small artificial mound of stones planted with flowers, ferns, etc. **-iness** *n.* **-y** *a.* full of rocks; resembling rocks; unfeeling. **— bottom** *a.* lowest possible; *n.* lowest level. **— crystal** *n.* transparent quartz used in making certain lenses. **— garden** *n.* a garden laid out with rocks and plants. **— salt** *n.* unrefined sodium chloride found in great natural deposits. **the Rock,** Gibraltar. **on the rocks** (*Colloq.*) having no money or resources [Fr. *roche*].

rock (ràk) *v.t.* to sway to and fro; to put to sleep by rocking; to lull; to sway, with anger, etc.; *v.i.* to be moved, backward and forward; to reel; to totter. **-er** *n.* curving piece of wood on which cradle or chair rocks; rocking horse or chair; pivoted lever having a rocking motion. **-y** *a.* disposed to rock; shaky. **-ing** *n.* **-ing chair** *n.* chair mounted on rockers. **-ing horse** *n.* wooden horse mounted on rockers; a hobbyhorse. **off one's rocker** (*Slang*) eccentric [O.E. *roccian*].

rock·et (ràk′·it) *n.* cylindrical tube filled with a mixture of sulfur, niter, and charcoal, which, on ignition, hurls the tube forward by action of liberated gases; a similar tube which draws a life-line towards ship in distress; firework; *v.i.* to soar up; to increase rapidly in price, etc. [It. *rochetta*, dim. of *rocca*, a distaff].

ro·co·co (rō·kō′·kō) *n.* style of architecture, overlaid with profusion of delicate ornamentation [Fr.].

rod (ràd) *n.* slender, straight, round bar, wand, stick, or switch; birch rod for punishment; cane; emblem of authority; fishing-rod; lightning conductor; linear measure equal to 5½ yards or 16½ feet [O.E. *rodd*].

rode (rōd) *pa.t.* of **ride.**

ro·dent (rō′·dạnt) *a.* gnawing; *n.* gnawing animal, as rabbit, rat [L. *rodere*, to gnaw].

ro·de·o (rō′·di·ō) *n.* roundup of cattle to be branded or marked; exhibition and contest in steer wrestling and bronco busting by cowboys [Sp.].

rod·o·mont (ràd′·ạ·mànt) *n.* a braggart; *a.*

boasting; bragging. **rodomontade** *n.* vain boasting; bluster; rant; *v.i.* to boast; to brag; to bluster [*Rodomonte,* the blustering opponent of Charlemagne, depicted in Ariosto's *Orlando Furioso*].

roe (rō) *n.* small deer; female hart. **-buck** *n.* male of roe [O.E. *rah*].

roe (rō) *n.* the eggs or spawn of fish [Scand.].

roent·gen (rent′·gen) *n.* (*Nuclear Physics*) measuring unit of radiation dose. **— rays** *n.pl.* X-rays. **-ize** *v.t.* to submit to action of X-rays. Also **Röntgen** [Wilhelm von Roentgen (1845-1923), German physicist].

ro·ga·tion (rō·gā′·shạn) *n.* in ancient Rome demand, by consuls or tribunes, of a law to be passed by people; supplication. **Rogation Days,** three days preceding Ascension Day, on which special litanies are sung or recited by R.C. clergy and people in public procession, invoking a blessing on crops. **rogatory** *a.* commissioned to gather information [L. *rogare,* to ask].

rogue (rōg) *n.* vagrant; rascal; knave; mischievous person. **roguery** *n.* knavish tricks; cheating; waggery. **roguishly** *adv.* **roguishness** *n.* **rogues' gallery,** a collection of photographs of convicted criminals [O.Fr. *rogue,* proud].

rogue (rōg) *v.t.* and *v.i.* to remove plant from crop (potatoes, cereals, etc.) when that plant falls short of standard or is of another variety from the crop, in order to keep strain pure; *n.* plant so removed; plant that falls short of a standard or has reverted to original type.

rois·ter (rois·tẹr) *v.i.* to bluster; to bully; to swagger. **-er** *n.* **-ous** *a.* [O.Fr. *ruster,* a rough, rude fellow, fr. L. *rusticus,* rustic].

role (rōl) *n.* a part played by an actor in a drama—hence, any conspicuous part or task in public life [Fr.].

roll (rōl) *v.t.* to turn over and over; to move by turning on an axis; to form into a spherical body; to drive forward with a swift and easy motion; to level with a roller; to beat with rapid strokes, as a drum; to utter vowels, letter *r*) with a full, long-drawn sound; *v.i.* to move forward by turning; to revolve upon an axis; to keep falling over and over; to sway; to reel; to rock from side to side, as ship; of aircraft, to turn about the axis, *i.e.* a line from nose to tail, in flight; *n.* rolling; a piece of paper, etc. rolled up; any object thus shaped; bread baked into small oval or rounded shapes; official list of members; register; catalog; continuous sound, as thunder; a full corkscrew revolution of an airplane about its longitudinal fore and aft axis during flight. **-able** *a.* **— call** *n.* calling over list of names to check absentees. **-er** *n.* cylinder of wood, stone, metal, etc. used in husbandry and the arts; a cylinder which distributes ink over type in printing; long, swelling wave; long, broad bandage; small, insectivorous bird which tumbles about in the air. **-er skate** *n.* skate with wheels or rollers instead of steel runner. **-ing** *a.* moving on wheels; turning over and over; undulating, as a plain; *n.* (*Naut.*) reeling of a ship from side to side. **-ing pin** *n.* cylindrical device for rolling out dough. **-ing stone,** person incapable of settling down in any one place [Fr. *rouler,* fr. L. *rotula,* a little wheel].

rol·lick (rȧl′·ik) *v.i.* to move about in a boisterous, careless manner; *n.* frolicsome gaiety. **-ing** *a.* jovial; high-spirited [etym. unknown].

ro·ly-po·ly (rō′·li-pō′·li·) *a.* plump and rounded. [redupl. of *roll*].

Ro·ma·ic (rō·mā′·ik) *n.* modern Greek [Fr. *romaïque,* fr. Mod. Gk. *Rhōmaikos* fr. *Rhōmē,* Rome].

Ro·man (rō′·mạn) *a.* pert. to Rome or Roman people; pert. to R.C. religion; in printing, upright letters as distinguished from *Italic* characters; expressed in letters, not in figures, as I., IV., i., iv., etc. (as distinguished from Arabic numerals, 1, 4, etc.). **-ic** *a.* **-ize** *v.t.* to introduce many words and idioms derived from Latin; to convert to Roman Catholicism; *v.i.* to use Latin expressions; to conform to R.C. opinions or practices. **-ism** *n.* tenets of Church of Rome. **-ist** *n.* **Romish** *a.* relating to Rome or to R.C. church. **Romist** *n.* Roman Catholic. **— candle,** a firework which throws out differently colored stars. **— Catholic,** a member or adherent of section of Christian Church which acknowledges supremacy of Pope; *a.* pert. to Church of Rome. **— Catholicism** [L. *Romanus,* fr. *Roma,* Rome].

Ro·mance (rō·mans′) *n.* languages; *a.* pert. to these languages. **romance** *n.* narrative of knight-errantry in Middle Ages; ballad of adventures in love and war; any fictitious narrative treating of olden times; historical novel; story depending mainly on love interest; romantic spirit or quality; (*Mus.*) composition sentimental and expressive in character; *v.i.* to write or tell romances; embroider one's account or description with extravagances. **-r,** *n.* **romansque,** *a.* pert. to the portrayal of fabulous or fanciful subjects in literature (*Cap.*) pert. to any form of architecture derived from Roman, as Lombard, Saxon, etc., devleoped in the 10th to 13th centuries in southern western Europe. **romantic** *a.* pert. to romance; fictitious; fanciful; sentimental; imaginative. **romantically** *adv.* **romanticism** *n.* the reactionary movement in literature and art against formalism and classicism; state of being romantic. **romanticist** *n.* [O.Fr. *romans,* It. *romanza.*

Rom·a·ny, Rommany (rȧm′·ạ·ni·) *n.* a Gypsy; the language of the Gypsies [Gypsy *rom,* a man].

romp (rȧmp) *v.i.* to leap and frisk about in play; to frolic; *n.* a tomboy; a boisterous form of play. **-ers** *n.pl.* a child's overall, with leg openings. **-ish** *a.* [earlier, *ramp*].

ron·deau (ron′·dō) *n.* poem, usually of thirteen lines with only two rhymes, the opening words recurring additionally, after eighth and thirteenth lines;. (*Mus.*) rondo. **rondel** *n.* poem of thirteen or fourteen iambic lines, first two lines of which are repeated in middle and at close. **rondo** *n.* musical setting of a rondeau; sanota movement in music in which a principal theme is repeated two or three times [Fr.].

Rönt·gen. See **roentgen.**

rood (rood) *n.* a length of 5½ to 8 yards; fourth part of acre, equal to 40 square rods or 1,210 square yards; a cross or crucifix, esp. one placed in a church over entrance to choir. **— loft** *n.* a small gallery over rood screen of church. [O.E. *rōd,* a rod, a cross].

roof (roof, roof) *n.* outside structure covering building; framework suppporting this covering; stratum immediately above seam in mine; upper part of any hollow structure or object, as roof of cave, mouth, etc.; ceiling; *v.t.* to cover with a roof; to shelter. **— garden** *n.* miniature garden on flat roof. **-tree** *n.* the ridgepole or roof itself. [O.E. *hrof*].

rook (rook) *n.* in chess, one of the four pieces placed on corner squares of the board; also known as a castle [Pers. *rukh*].

rook (rook) *n.* blueblack,hoarse-voiced bird of crow family; swindler; a card-sharp; *v.t.* to cheat; to swindle. **-ery** *n.* colony of rooks and their nests **-ie** *n.* Army slang for a recruit [O.E. *hroc*].

room (room, room) *n.* (enough) space; apartment or chamber; scope; opportunity; occasion; *pl.* lodgings; *v.i.* to lodge. **-ful** *a.* **-ily** *adv.* **-iness** *n.* spaciousness. **-y** *a.*

spacious; wide [O.E. *rum*].

roost (ro͝ost) *n.* pole on which birds rest at night; perch; collection of fowls roosting together; *v.i.* to settle down to sleep, as birds on a perch; to perch. **-er** *n.* a cock [O.E. *hrost*].

root (ro͝ot, root) *n.* part of plant which grows down into soil seeking nourishment for whole plant; plant whose root is edible, as beetroot; part of anything which grows like root, as of tooth, cancer, etc.; source; origin; vital part; basis; bottom; primitive word from which other words are derived; (*Math.*) factor of quantity which, when multiplied by itself the number of times indicated by the index number, will produce that quantity, e.g. 4 is third (or cube) root of 64 (symbol $\sqrt{}$), for $4 \times 4 \times 4 = 64$; *v.t.* to plant and fix in earth; to impress deeply in mind; to establish firmly; to pull out by roots (followed by *out*) *v.i.* to enter earth, as roots; to be firmly fixed or established. **-ed** *a.* firmly established. **-stock** *n.* a rhizome. **root and branch,** entirely; completely [O.E. *wyrt*].

root (ro͝ot) *v.t.* and *v.i.* to turn up with the snout, as swine; to rummage; to uncover (with *up)* [O.E. *wrot*, a snout].

root (ro͝ot) *v.i.* to cheer [*Slang*].

rope (rōp) *v.t.* stout cord of several twisted strands of fiber or metal wire; row of objects strung together, as onions, pearls, etc.; *v.t.* to fasten with a rope; to mark off a race track, etc., with ropes; to lasso. **-ladder, -bridge,** etc. *n.* one made of ropes [O.E. *rap*].

Roque·fort (rōk′·fẹrt) *n.* a cheese of ewe's milk [*Roquefort*, in France].

ror·qual (rawr′·kwạl) *n.* a genus of whale [Scand. *röd*, red; *hval*, *whale*].

Ro·sa·ceae (rō·zā′·sē·ī) *n.pl.* order of plants including rose, strawberry, blackberry, spiraea. **rosaceous** *a.* roselike; belonging to rose family. **rosarium** *n.* rose garden [L. *rosa*, rose].

ro·sa·ry (rō′·zạ·ri·) *n.* rose garden; string of prayer beads [L. *rosa*, a rose].

rose (rōz) *pa.t.* of **rise.**

rose (rōz) *n.* typical genus (*Rosa*) of plant family of Rosaceae; shade of pink; rosette; perforated nozzle of tube or pipe, as on watering can. **-ate** *a.* rosy; full of roses; blooming; optimistic. **-bud** *n.* the bud of the rose; **—colored** *a.* having color of a rose; unwarrantably optimistic. **— water** *n.* water tinctured with roses by distillation **— window** *n.* circular window with a series of mullions diverging from center. **-wood** *n.* rich, dark red hardwood from S. America, used for furniture making. **rosily** *adv.* **rosiness** *n.* **rosy** *a.* like a rose; blooming; red; blushing; bright; favorable [L. *rosa*, a rose].

rose·mar·y (rōz′·me·ri·) *n.* a small fragrant evergreen shrub, emblem of fidelity [L. *ros*, dew; *marinus*, marine].

ro·sette (rō·zet′) *n.* something fashioned to resemble a rose, as ribbon; a rose-shaped architectural ornament. [Fr. dim. of *rose*].

ros·in (ràz′·in) *n.* resin in solid state; *v.t.* to rub or cover with rosin. **-y** *a.* [Fr. *résine*].

ros·ter (ràs′·tẹr) *n.* a list or plan showing turns of duty; register of names [Dut. *rooster*, a corrupt. of L. *register*].

ros·trum (rạs′·trạm) *n.* snout or pointed organ; beak of a ship; raised platform; pulpit. **rostral** *a.* pert. to a rostrum. **rostrate, rostrated** *a.* beaked [L. = a beak].

ros·y, See **rose.**

rot (ràt) *v.t.* and *v.i.* to decompose naturally; to become morally corrupt; to putrefy; to molder away. *pr.p.* **-ting.** *pa.t.* and *pa.p.* **-ted** *n.* rotting; decomposition; decay; disease of sheep, as **foot-rot;** form of decay which attacks timber, usually **dry rot** (*Slang*) nonsense [O.E. *rotian*].

ro·ta (rō′·tạ) *n.* roster, list, or roll; an ecclesiastical tribunal in the R.C. church which acts as court of appeal [L. = wheel].

ro·ta·ry (rō′·tẹr·i·) *a.* turning, as a wheel; rotatory; *n.* (*Cap.*) international association of business men's clubs. **Rotarian** *n.* member of Rotary Club. **— engine** (*Aero.*) engine in which cylinder and crankcase rotate with propeller [L. *rota*, a wheel].

ro·tate (rō′·tāt) *v.t.* to cause to revolve; *v.i.* to move around pivot; to go in rotation; to revolve; *a.* (*Bot.*) wheel-shaped, as a calyx. **rotation** *n.* turning, as a wheel or solid body on its axis; (*Astron.*) period of rotation of planet about its imaginary axis; serial change, as **rotation of crops. rotational** *a.* **rotator** *n.* **rotatory** *a.* turning on an axis, as a wheel; going in a circle; following in succession [L. *rota*, a wheel].

rote (rōt) *n.* mechanical repetition [O.Fr. *rote*, track].

ro·tis·ser·ie (rō·tis′·ẹr·i·) *n.* grill with a turning spit [Fr. *rotir*, to roast].

ro·tor (rō′·tẹr) *n.* revolving portion of dynamo, motor, or turbine [short for *rotator*].

rot·ten (ràt′·n) *a.* putrefied; decayed; unsound; corrupt; (*Slang*) bad; worthless. **-ly** *adv.* **-ness** *n.* **rotter** *n.* (*Slang*) a worthless, unprincipled person [fr. *rot*].

ro·tund (rō·tund′) *a.* round; globular; plump. **-a** *n.* circular building or hall, covered by dome. **-ity, -ness** *n.* globular form; roundness [L. *rotundus*, fr. *rota*, a wheel].

rou·é (ro͝o′·ā) *n.* a libertine; a profligate; a rake [Fr. = one broken on the wheel].

rouge (ro͝ozh) *n.* fine red powder used by jewelers; cosmetic for tinting cheeks; *v.t.* and *v.i.* to tint (face) with rouge [Fr. = red].

rough (ruf) *a.* not smooth; rugged; uneven; unhewn; shapeless; uncut; unpolished; rude; harsh; boisterous; stormy; approximate; having aspirated sound of *h; adv.* in rough manner; *n.* crude, unfashioned state; parts of golf course adjoining fairway and greens; *v.t.* to make rough; to roughen; to rough-hew; to shape out in rough and ready way. **-age** *n.* fibrous, unassimilated portions of food which promote intestinal movement. **— diamond,** uncut diamond; a person of ability and worth, but uncouth. **-en** *v.t.* to make rough; *v.i.* to become rough. **—hew** *v.t.* to hew coarsely; to give first form to a thing. **-house** *n.* rowdy, boisterous play. **-ly** *adv.* **-neck** *n.* (*Slang*) ill-mannered fellow; a tough. **-ness** *n.* **to rough it,** to put up with hardship and discomfort [O.E.*ruh*].

rou·lade (ro͝o·làd′) *n.* (*Mus.*) embellishment; trill [Fr. *rouler*, to roll].

rou·leau (ro͝o·lō′) *n.* little roll; roll of coins in paper; little roll or chain of red corpuscles; *pl.* **-x, -s** [Fr. dim. of O.Fr. *role*, a roll].

rou·lette (ro͝o·let′) *n.* game of chance, played with a revolving disk and a ball [Fr. dim. of O.Fr. *roule*, wheel].

round (round) *a.* circular; spherical; curved; whole; total; not fractional, as a number; plump; smooth; flowing, as style or diction; plain; (of vowel) pronounced with rounded lips; *n.* circle; ring, globe; circuit; cycle; series; a course of action performed by persons in turn; toasts; a certain amount (of applause); walk by guard to visit posts, sentries, etc.; beat of policeman, milkman, etc.; a game (of golf); one of successive stages in competition; 3-minute period in boxing match; step of a ladder; ammunition unit; circular dance; short, vocal piece, in which singers start at regular intervals after each other; *adv.* on all sides; circularly; back to the starting point; about; *v.t.* to make circular, spherical, or cylindrical; to go around; to smooth; to finish; *v.i.* to grow or become round or full in form. **-about** *a.* indirect; circuitous. **-el** *n.* round window or panel; kind of dance; rondel; small circular shield. **-elay** *n.* round or country dance; an air or tune in three parts, in which the first strain is repeated in the others. **-er** *n.* a tool for rounding off objects; one who makes rounds; habitual drunkard or criminal. **Roundhead** *n.* a Puritan (so called from practice of cropping hair close); republican in time of Commonwealth. **-house** *n.* (*Naut.*) a cabin built on after part of quarterdeck; circular building for locomotives. **-ly** *adv.* vigorously; fully; open. **-ness** *n.* **— robin** *n.* petition, etc. having signatures arranged in a circular form so as to give no clue to order of signing. **-table conference,** one where all participants are on equal footing. **-up,** *n.* collecting cattle into herds; throwing cordon around area by police or military for interrogating all found within; *v.t.* to collect and bring into confined space. **to round off,** to [Fr. *rond*].

roup (roop) *n.* a contagious disease of domestic poultry [O.E. *hropan,* to cry].

rouse (rouz) *v.t.* to wake from sleep; to excite to action; to startle or surprise; *v.i.* to awake from sleep or repose. **-r** *n.* **rousing** *a.*

rout (rout) *n.* tumultuous crowd; rabble; defeat of army or confusion of troops in flight; *v.t.* to defeat and throw into confusion [L. *ruptus,* broken].

rout (rout) *v.i.* to roar; to snore [O.E. *hrutan*].

rout (rout) *v.t.* to turn up with the snout; to cut grooves by scooping or gouging; to turn out of bed; *v.i.* to poke about [fr. *root,* dig.].

route (ròòt) *n.* course or way which is traveled or to be followed. **en route,** on the way [Fr.].

rou·tine (ròò·tēn′) *n.* regular course of action adhered to by order or habit; *a.* in ordinary way of business; according to rule [Fr.].

rove (rōv) *v.t.* to wander or ramble over; to plough into ridges; *v.i.* to wander about; to ramble. **-r** *n.* wanderer; pirate ship; roving machine. **roving** *n.* and *a.* [Dut. *roofer,* a robber].

row (rō)*n.* persons or things in straight line; a rank; a file; a line [O.E. *raw*].

row (rō) *v.t.* to impel (a boat) with oars; to transport, by rowing; *v.t.* to labor with oars; *n.* spell of rowing; a trip in a rowboat. **-boat** *n.* boat impelled solely by oars [O.E. *rowan*].

row (rou) *n.* riotous, noisy disturbance; a dispute. **-dy** *a.* noisy and rough; *n.* hooligan. **-dyism, -diness** *n.* [etym. uncertain].

row·an (rō′·ạn) *n.* mountain ash producing clusters of red berries. [Scand.].

row·el (rou′·ạl) *n.* wheel of a spur, furnished with sharp points [Fr. *roue,* a wheel].

roy·al (roi′·ạl) *a.* pert. to the crown; worthy of, befitting, patronized by, a king or queen; kingly; *n.* a size of paper; small sail above topgallant-sail; third shoot of stag's horn. **-ism** *n.* principles of government by king. **-ist** *n.* adherent to sovereign, or one attached to kingly government. **-ly** *adv.* **-ty** *n.* kingship; kingly office; person of king or sovereign; members of royal family; royal prerogative; royal domain; payment to owner of land for right to work minerals, or to inventor for use of his invention, or to author depending on sales of his book [Fr. fr. L. *regalis,* fr. *rex,* a king].

rub (rub) *v.t.* to subject to friction; to abrade; to chafe; to remove by friction; to wipe; to scour; to touch slightly; *v.i.* to come into contact accompanied by friction; to become frayed or worn with friction. *pr.p.* **-bing.** *pa.t.* and *pa.p.* **-bed.** *n.* rubbing; difficulty, impediment; a sore spot from rubbing; **-ber** *n.* **-bing** *n.* impression of coin, lettering on book, etc. obtained by rubbing thin paper placed on object with pencil or similar article; applying friction to a surface. **to rub in,** to emphasize by constant reiteration [etym. obscure].

rub·ber (rub′·ẹr) *n.* coagulated sap of certain tropical trees; caoutchouc; gum elastic; India rubber for erasing pencil marks, etc. a series of an odd number, usually three, of games; the winning game in the series; *pl.* overshoes; galoshes: *a.* made of rubber. **-ized** *a.* impregnated or mixed with rubber, as rubberized fabrics. **-neck** *n.* (*Slang*) a tourist eager to see every important building, sight, or spectacle [fr. *rub*].

rub·bish (rub′·ish) *n.* waste or rejected matter; anything worthless: refuse; nonsense [etym. uncertain].

rub·ble (rub′·l) *n.* upper fragmentary decomposed mass of stone overlying a solid stratum of rock; masonry built of rough stone, of all sizes and shapes; rough stones used to fill up spaces between walls, etc. **-rubbly** *a.* [O.Fr. *robel,* dim. of *robe, robbe,* trash].

rube (ròòb) *n.* (*Slang*) a farmer; a rustic [*abbrev.* fr. *Reuben*].

Ru·bi·con (ròò·bi·kȧn) *n.* stream in Italy, between Roman Italy and Cisalpine Gaul. **to cross the Rubicon,** to take a decisive, irrevocable step.

ru·bi·cund (ròò′·bạ·kund) *a.* ruddy; florid; reddish. **-ity** *n.* [L. *rubicundus,* fr. *ruber, red*].

ru·bid·i·um (ròò·bid′·i·ạm) *n.* rare silvery metallic element, one of the alkali metals [L. *rubidus,* red].

ru·ble (ròò′·ble) *n.* Russian monetary unit. Also **rouble** [Russ. *rubl*].

ru·bric (ròò′·brik) *n.* medieval manuscript or printed book in which initial letter was illumined in red; heading or portion of such a work, printed in red—hence, the title of a chapter, statute, etc. originally in red; an ecclesiastical injunction or rule; *v.t.* to illumine with or print in red. **-al** *a.* colored in red; to formulate as a rubric. **-ian** *n.* one versed in the rubrics. **rubricist** *n.* a strict adherent to rubrics; a formalist [L. *rubrica,* red earth, fr. *ruber,* red].

ru·by (ròò′·bi·) *n.* a red variety of corundum valued as a gem; purple-tinged red color; *a.* having the dark-red color of a ruby [L. *ruber,* red].

ruche (ròòsh) *n.* pleated trimming for dresses, sewn down the middle and not at top, as in box pleatings. **ruching** *n.* material for ruches; ruches collectively [Fr.].

ruck (ruk) *v.t.* to wrinkle; to crease; *v.i.* to be drawn into folds; *n.* fold; crease; wrinkle [O.N. *hrukka*].

ruck (ruk) *n.* rank and file; common herd [etym. doubtful].

ruck·sack (ruk′·sak) *n.* pack carried on back by climbers, etc. [Ger. = 'back-pack'].

ruc·tion (ruk′·shạn) *n.* (*Colloq.*) disturbance; row; rumpus [perh. fr. *eruption*].

rudd (rud) *n.* British fresh-water fish allied to the roach [O.E. *rudu,* redness].

rud·der (rud′·ẹr) *n.* flat frame fastened vertically to stern of ship, which controls direction; in plane, flat plane surface hinged to tail unit and used to provide directional control and stability; anything which guides, as a bird's tail-feathers [O.E. *rothor*].

rud·dle (rud′·l) red ocher, used for marking sheep; *v.t.* to mark (sheep) with ruddle [O.E. *rudu,* redness].

rud·dock (rud′·ok) *n.* European robin [O.E. *rudig,* reddish].

rud·dy (rud′·i·) *a.* of a red color; of healthy flesh color; rosy; **ruddiness** *n.* [O.E. *rudig,* reddish].

rude (ròòd) *a.* uncivil; primitive; roughly made. **-ly** *adv.* **-ness** *n.* [L. *rudis,* rough].

ru·di·ment (ròò′·dạ·mạnt) *n.* beginning; germ; vestige; (*Biol.*) imperfectly developed or formed organ; *pl.* elements, first principles, beginning (of knowledge, etc.) **-al, -ary** *a.* **-arily** *adv.* [L. *rudimentum,* fr. *rudis,* rude].

rue (ròò) *v.t.* and *v.i.* to grieve for; to regret;

to repent of. *pr.p.* **-ing.** **-ful** *a.* woeful; mournful; sorrowful. **-fully** *adv.* [O.E. *hreowan*, to be sorry for].

rue (ròò) *n.* aromatic, bushy, evergreen shrub; any bitter infusion [L. *ruta*].

ruff (ruf) *n.* broad, circular collar, plaited, crimped, or fluted; something similar; light-brown mottled bird, the male being ringed with ruff or frill of long, black, red-barred feathers during breeding season; (*fem.*) **reeve**; neck fringe of long hair or feathers on animal or bird. **-ed** *a.* [etym. uncertain].

ruff (ruf) *n.* trumping at cards when one cannot follow suit; *v.t.* to trump instead of following suit [O.Fr. *roffle*].

ruf·fi·an (ruf′·i·ạn) *n.* a rough, lawless fellow; desperado; *a.* brutal. **-ism** *n.* conduct of a ruffian. **-ly** [O.Fr. fr. It. *ruffiano*].

ruf·fle (ruf′·l) *v.t.* to make into a ruff; to draw into wrinkles, open plaits, or folds; to furnish with ruffles; to roughen surface of; to annoy; to put out (of temper); *v.i.* to flutter; to jar; to be at variance; to grow rough; *n.* a strip of gathered cloth, attached to a garment, a frill; agitation; commotion [Dut. *ruifelen*, to rumple].

ru·fous (ròò′·fạs) *a.* (*Bot.*) brownish red [L. *rufus*, red].

rug (rug) *n.* piece of carpeting [*Scand.*].

rug·by (rug′·bi·) *n.* English form of football, played with teams of 15 players each [fr. *Rugby*, public school].

rug·ged (rug′·id) *a.* rough; uneven; jagged; wrinkled; harsh; inharmonious; homely; unpolished; sturdy, vigorous. **-ly** *adv.* **-ness** *n.* [rug].

ru·gose (ròò′·gōs) *a.* wrinkled; ridged. **-ly** *adv.* **rugosity** *n.* [L. *ruga*, a wrinkle].

ru·in (ròò′·in) *n.* downfall; remains of demolished or decayed city, fortress, castle, work of art, etc.; state of being decayed; *v.t.* to bring to ruin; to injure; to spoil; to mar; to cause loss of fortune or livelihood to. **-s** *n.pl.* ruined buildings, etc. **-ation** *n.* state of being ruined; act or cause of ruining. **-er** *n.* **-ous** *a.* fallen to ruin; dilapidated; injurious; destructive. **-ously** *adv.* [L. *ruina*, fr. *ruere*, to rush down].

rule (*ròòl*) *n.* act, power, or mode of directing; government; sway; control; authority; precept; prescribed law; established principle or mode of action; regulation; habitual practice; standard; an instrument to draw straight lines; (*Print.*) thin strip of brass or type metal, type high, to print a line or lines; *v.t.* to govern; to control; to determine; to decide authoritatively; to mark with straight lines, using ruler; *v.i.* to have command; to order by rule; to prevail. **-r** *n.* one who rules; sovereign; instrument with straight edges for drawing lines. **ruling** *a.* governing; managing; predominant; *n.* an authoritative decision; a point of law settled by a court of law [L. *regula*, fr. *regere*, to govern].

rum (rum) *n.* spirit distilled from sugar-cane skimmings or molasses. **-runner** *n.* smuggler. **-my** *n.* (*Slang*) a drunkard [etym. uncertain].

rum-ba (rum′·bạ) *n.* Cuban dance [Sp.].

rum·ble (rum′·bl) *v.i.* to make a low, vibrant, continuous sound; to reverberate; *v.t.* to cause to roll along or utter with a low heavy sound; to polish in a tumbling box *n.* dull, vibrant, confused noise, as of thunder; seat for footmen at back of carriage; a tumbling box; (*Slang*) fight. **-r** *n.* [imit.].

ru·mi·nant (ròò′·mạ·nạnt) *n.* animal which chews cud, as sheep, cow;*a.* chewing cud. **ruminate** *v.t.* to chew over again; to ponder over; to muse on; *v.i.* to chew cud; to meditate. **ruminatingly** *adv.* **rumination** *n.* **ruminative** *a.* **ruminator** *n.* [L. *ruminare*, to chew cud].

rum·mage (rum′·ij) *v.t.* to search thoroughly into or through; to ransack; *v.i.* to make a search; *n.* careful search; odds and ends. **-r** *n.* [orig. stowage of casks, O.Fr. *arrumage*].

rum·my (rum′·i·) *n.* a simple card game for any number of players.

ru·mor (ròò′·mẹr) *n.* current but unproved report; common talk; *v.t.* to spread as a rumor [L. *rumor*, noise].

rump (rump) *n.* end of backbone of animal with the parts adjacent; buttocks; hinder part; remnant of anything [Scand.].

rum·ple (rum′·pl) *v.t.* to muss; to crease; to crumple; *n.* an irregular fold [O.E. *hrimpan*, to wrinkle].

rum·pus (rum′·pạs) *n.* (*Colloq.*) an uproar; a noisy disturbance [etym. doubtful].

run (run) *v.i.* to move rapidly on legs; to hurry; to contend in a race; to stand as candidate for; to travel or sail regularly; to extend; to retreat; to flee; to flow; to continue in operation; to continue without falling due, as a promissory note or bill; to have legal force; to fuse; to melt; to average; to turn or rotate; to be worded; *v.t.* to cause to run; to drive, push, or thrust; to manage; to maintain regularly, as bus service; to operate; to evade (a blockade); to smuggle; to incur (risk). *pr.p.* **-ning.** *pa.t.* **ran.** *pa.p.* **run.** *n.* flow; channel; act of running; course run; regular, scheduled journey; pleasure trip by car, cycle, etc.; unconstrained liberty; range of ground for grazing cattle, feeding poultry, etc.; trend; kind or variety; vogue; point gained in cricket or baseball; a great demand; period play holds the stage; (*Mus.*) rapid scale passage, roulade. **-about** *n.* motorboat or a small open car; a gadabout.**-away** *n.* fugitive; horse which has bolted.**-ner** *n.* one taking part in a race; messenger; a long, slender prostrate stem which runs along the ground; one of curved pieces on which sleigh, skate, etc slides; device for facilitating movement of sliding doors, etc.; narrow strip of carpet; smuggler. **-ner-up** *n.* one who gains second place. **-ning** *a.* flowing; entered for a race, as a horse; successive (numbers); continuous (as an order, account); discharging (pus); cursive; easy in style; effortless; *n.* moving or flowing quickly; chance of winning; operation of machine, business, etc. **-ning board** *n.* narrow, horizontal platform running along locomotive, carriage, car, etc., to provide step for entering or leaving. **-ning commentary,** broadcast description of event by eye-witness. **-ning knot,** knot made so as to tighten when rope is pulled. **-way** *n.* prepared track on airfields for landing and taking off. **also ran,** an unsuccessful competitor. **in the long run,** in the end; ultimately. **to run amok,** to go mad. **to run riot,** to give way to excess. **to run to earth,** to capture after a long pursuit [O.E. *rinnan*].

run·dle (run′·dl) *n.* a rung or step of a ladder; something which rotates like a wheel [fr. *round*].

rune (ròòm) *n.* letter or character of old Teutonic and Scandinavian alphabets; magic; mystery. **runic** *a.* [O.N. *run*, a mystery].

rung (rung) *pa.p.* of **ring.**

rung (rung) *n.* rounded step of a ladder; crossbar or spoke [O.E. *hrung*, a beam].

run·nel (run′·ạl) *n.* small brook or rivulet; a gutter [O.E. *rinnelle*, a brook].

runt (runt) *n.* small, weak specimen of any animal, person or thing [etym. doubtful].

ru·pee (ròò·pē′) *n.* standard Indian monetary unit, silver coin [Urdu, *rupiyah*].

rup·ture (rup′·chẹr) *n.* breaking or bursting; state of being violently parted; breach of concord between individuals or nations; hernia; forcible bursting, breaking, or tearing of a bodily organ or structure; *v.t.* to part by violence; to burst (a blood-vessel, etc.) [L.

ruptura, fr. *rumpere*, to break].

ru·ral (roo′·ral) *a.* pert. to the country; pert. to farming or agriculture; rustic; pastoral. **-ize** *v.t.* to make rural; *v.i.* to live in the country; to become rural. **-ism** *n.* **-ly** *adv.* [L. *ruralis*, fr. *rus*, the country].

ruse (ro͝oz) *n.* artifice; trick; strategem [Fr.].

rush (rush) *v.t.* to carry along violently and rapidly; to take by sudden assault; to hasten forward; *v.i.* to move violently or rapidly; to speed; *n.* heavy current of water, air, etc.; haste; eager demand (for an article); **-er** *n.* [M.E. *ruschen*].

rush (rush) *n.* name of plants of genus Juncus, found in marshy places; stem as a material for baskets, etc.; thing of little worth; taper; straw. **—bottomed** *a.* of chair with seat made of rushes. **-y** *a.* [O.E. *rysc*].

rusk (rusk) *n.* biscuit or light, hard bread [Sp. *rosca*, roll of bread].

rus·set (rus′·it) *a.* of reddish-brown color; *n.* homespun cloth dyed this color; apple of russet color [Fr. *roux*, red].

Rus·sian (rush′·an) *a.* pert. to Russia; *n.* general name for Slav races in Russia; native or inhabitant of Russia; Russian language. **Russo-** *prefix* Russian. **— dressing** *n.* mayonnaise mixed with catchup or chili sauce.

rust (rust) *n.* coating formed on iron or various other metals by corrosion; reddish fungus disease on plants; *v.t.* to corrode with rust; to impair by inactivity; *v.i.* to become rusty; to dissipate one's potential powers by inaction. **-ily** *adv.* **-iness** *n.* **— proof** *a.* not liable to rust. **-y** *a.* [O.E.].

rus·tic (rus′·tik) *a.* pert. to the country; rural; awkward; *n.* a simple country person. **-ally** *adv.* **-ate** *v.t.* to compel to reside in country; to make rustic; *v.i.* to live in the country. **-ation** *n.* **-ity** *n.* [L. *ruslicus*, fr. *rus*, the country].

rus·tle (rus′·l) *v.i.* to make soft, swishing sounds, like rubbing of silk cloth or dry leaves; (*Slang*) to be active and on the move; *v.t.* (*U.S.*) to steal, esp. cattle; *n.* a soft whispering sound. **-r** *n.* one who, or that which, rustles; (*Slang*) hustler; cattle thief. **rustling** *n.* [imit. origin].

rut (rut) *n.* furrow made by wheel; settled habit or way of living; groove; *v.t.* to form ruts in; *pr.p.* **-ting**. *pa.t.* and *pa.p.* **-ted** [Fr. *route*, a way, track, etc.].

rut (rut) *n.* time of sexual excitement and urge among animals, esp. of deer; *v.i.* to be in heat [O.Fr. fr. L. *rugire*, to roar].

ruth·less (ro͝oth′·las) *a.* pitiless; cruel. **-ly** *adv.* **-ness** *n.* [*rue*].

rye (rī) *n.* a kind of grass allied to wheat, whiskey made from rye [O.E. *ryge*].

S

Sab·bath (sab′·ath) *n.* seventh day of week; Sunday; Lord's Day. **Sabbatarian** *n.* member of certain Christian sects, e.g. Seventh-day Adventists, who observe seventh day Saturday, as the Sabbath; strict observer of Sabbath. **Sabbatarianism** *n.* **Sabbatic, -al** *a.* pert. to Sabbath; (*l.c.*) rest-bringing. *n.* (*l.c.*) a period of leave from a job. **Sabbatical year,** in the Jewish ritual, every seventh, in which the lands were left untilled, etc.; (*l.c.*) a year periodically interrupting one's normal course of work, wholly devoted to further intensive study or one's special subject [Heb. *shabbath*].

saber (sā′·ber) *n.* sword with broad and heavy blade, slightly curved toward the point; cavalry sword; *v.t.* to wound or cut down with saber. Also **sabre** [Fr.]

Sa·bine (sā′·bīn) *n.* one of an ancient tribe of Italy who became merged with the Romans; *a.* pert. to the Sabines.

sa·ble (sā′·bl) *n.* small carnivorous mammal of weasel tribe; sable fur; (*Her.*) tincture or color black; *pl.* mourning garments; *a.* black; made of sable [O.Fr.].

sab·ot (sab′·ō) *n.* a wooden shoe worn by the peasantry of France and Belgium [Fr.].

sab·o·tage (sa.ba.tázh′) *n.* willful damage or destruction of property perpetrated for political or economic reasons. **saboteur** *n.* one who commits sabotage [Fr. *sabot*].

sac (sak) *n.* pouch-like structure or receptacle in animal or plant; cyst-like cavity [Fr. = sack].

saccharin, saccharine (sak′·a·rin) *n.* a white crystalline solid substance, with an intensely sweet taste. **saccharine** *a.* pert. to sugar; over-sweet; cloying; sickly sentimental. **saccharify** *v.t.* to convert into sugar. **saccharinity** *n.* **saccharize** *v.t.* to convert into sugar. **saccharoid, -al** *a.* having granular texture resembling that of loaf sugar. **saccharose** *n.* cane sugar [Gk. *sakchari*, sugar].

sac·cule (sak′·ūl) *n.* a small sac. **saccular** *a.* like a sac [dim. of L. *saccus*, a bag].

sac·er·do·tal (sas.er.dō′.tal) *a.* pert. to priests, or to the order of priests. **-ism** *n.* the system, spirit, or character of priesthood; **-ist** *n.* **-ly** *adv.* [L. *sacerdos*, a priest].

sa·chem (sā′·cham) *n.* a Red Indian chief; a political boss, esp. a Tammany leader [Amer.-Ind.].

sa·chet (sa·shā′) *n.* a small scent-bag or perfume cushion [Fr.].

sack (sak) *n.* a large bag, usually of coarse material; contents of sack; also **sacque,** loose garment or cloak; any bag; *v.t.* to put into sacks. **-cloth** *n.* coarse fabric of great strength used for making sacks; in Scripture, garment worn in mourning or as penance. **-ful** *n.* quantity which fills sack. **-ing** *n.* coarse cloth or canvas. **— race** *n.* race in which legs of contestants are encased in sacks [Heb. *saq*. a coarse cloth].

sack (sak) *n.* old name for various kinds of dry wines, esp. Spanish sherry [Fr. *sec*, dry].

sack (sak) *v.t.* to plunder or pillage; to lay waste; *n.* pillage of town. **-ing** *n.* [Fr. *sac*, plunder].

sac·ra·ment (sak′·ra·mant) *n.* one of the ceremonial observances in Christian Church. Lord's Supper; solemn oath; materials used in a sacrament. **-al** *n.* any observance, ceremony, or act of the nature of a sacrament instituted by R.C. Church; *a.* belonging to, or of nature of, sacrament; sacred. **-ally** *adv.* **-arian** *n.* one who believes in efficacy of sacraments. **-arianism** *n.* [L. *sacer*, sacred].

sac·ri·fice (sak′·ra·fīs, ·fīz) *v.t.* to consecrate ceremonially offering of victim by way of expiation or propitiation to deity; to surrender for sake of obtaining some other advantage; to offer up; to immolate; *v.i.* to make offerings to God of things consumed on the altar; *n.* anything consecrated and offered to divinity; anything given up for sake of others. **-r** *n.* **sacrificial** *a.* relating to, performing, sacrifice. **sacrificially** *adv.* [L. *sacrificium*].

sac·ri·lege (sak′·ra·lij) *n.* profanation of sacred place or thing; church robbery. **sacrilegious** *a.* violating sacred things; profane; desecrating. **sacrilegiously** *adv.* **sacrilegiousness** *n.* [L. *sacer*, sacred; *legere*, to gather].

sac·ris·tan (sak′·ris·tan) *n.* officer in church

entrusted with care of sacristy or vestry. sexton. **sacristy** *n.* vestry [L. *sacer*, sacred].

sac·ro·sanct (sak′·rō·sangkt) *a.* inviolable and sacred in the highest degree. **-ity** *n.* [L. *sacrosanctus*, consecrated].

sa·crum (sā′·kram) *n.* a composite bone, triangular in shape, at the base of the spinal column. *pl.* **sacra** [L. = the sacred (bone)].

sad (sad) *a.* sorrowful; affected with grief; deplorably bad; somber-colored. **-den** *v.t.* to make sad or sorrowful; *v.i.* to become sorrowful and downcast. **-ly** *adv.* **-ness** *n.* [O.E. *saed*, sated].

sad·dle (sad′·l) *n.* rider's seat to fasten on horse, or form part of a cycle, etc.; part of a shaft; joint of mutton or venison containing part of backbone with ribs on each side; ridge of hill between higher hills; *v.t.* to put a saddle upon; to burden with; to encumber. **-bag** *n.* one of two bags united by strap and hanging on either side of horse. **-bow** *n.* bow or arch in front of saddle. **-cloth** *n.* housing or cloth placed upon saddle. **-girth** *n.* band passing under belly of horse to hold saddle in place. **— horse** *n.* horse for riding, as distinguished from one for driving. **-r** *n.* one who makes saddles and harness for horses. **saddlery** *n.* materials for making saddles and harness; occupation of saddler; room for storing saddles. **—shaped** *a.* **-tree** *n.* frame of saddle [O.E. *sadol*].

sad-ism (sā′·dizm, sad′·izm) *n.* insatiate love of inflicting pain for its own sake. **sadist** *n.* one who practices this; a consistently inhumane person. **sadistic** *a.* [Marquis de *Sade* (1740-1814) whose writings exemplify it].

sa·fa·ri (sa·fá′·ri.) *n.* hunting expedition [Swahili, **safar,** a journey].

safe (sāf) *a.* free from harm; unharmed; unhurt; sound; protected; sure; *n.* a fireproof chest for protection of money and valuables; case with wire gauze panels to keep meat, etc. fresh. **—conduct** *n.* passport to pass through a dangerous zone. **— deposit** *a.* pert. to box or vault where valuables are stored and protected. **-guard** *n.* protection; precaution; convoy; escort; passport; *v.t.* to make safe; to protect. **-ly** *adv.* **-ness** *n.* **-ty** *n.* **-ty belt** *n.* belt to keep person afloat in water, to prevent injury in automobile, aircraft, etc. **-ty-catch** *n.* contrivance to prevent accidental discharge of gun. **-ty razor** *n.* one in which blade fits into holder with guard to ensure safety for rapid shaving. **-ty valve** *n.* automatic valve fitted to boiler, to permit escape of steam when pressure reaches danger point; outlet for pent-up emotion [Fr. *sauf*, fr. L. *salvus*].

saf·fron (saf′·ran) *n.* plant of iris family, used in medicine and as a flavoring and coloring in cookery; *a.* deep yellow [Fr. *safran*].

sag (sag) *v.i.* to sink in middle; to hang sideways or curve downwards under pressure; to give way; to tire. *pr.p.* **-ging.** *pa.p.* **-ged.** *n.* a droop [M.E. *saggen*].

sa·ga (sá′·ga) *n.* a prose narrative, written in Iceland in the 12th and 13th centuries, concerning legendary and historic people and actions of Iceland and Norway; novels describing life of a family [O.N. = a tale].

sa·ga·cious (sa·gā′·shas) *a.* quick of thought; acute; shrewd. **-ly** *adv.* **-ness, sagacity** *n.* shrewdness; discernment; wisdom [L. *sagax*].

sage (sāj) *n.* dwarf shrub of mint family, used for flavoring [Fr. *sauge*, fr. L. *salvia*].

sage (sāj) *a.* wise; discerning; solemn; *n.* wise man. **-ly** *adv.* **-ness** *n.* [Fr. fr. L. *sapere*, to be wise].

sage-brush (sāj′·brush) *n.* a shrub smelling like sage and found chiefly on western plains of U.S.

Sa·git·ta (saj′·it·a) *n.* a constellation north of Aquila—the Arrow. **sagittal, sagittate** *a.* shaped like an arrow or arrowhead. **sagittally** *adv.* **Saggitarius** n. the Archer, 9th sign of zodiac; constellation in Milky Way [L. = arrow].

sa·go (sā′·gō) *n.* dry, granulated starch [Malay, *sagu*].

sa·hib (sá′·ib) *n.* (fem. **sahiba** or **mem sahib**) courtesy title in India for European or high-born Indian [Ar. = lord, master].

said (sed) *pa.t.* and *pa.p.* of **say;** the before-mentioned; already specified; aforesaid.

sail (sāl) *n.* sheet of canvas to catch wind for propelling ship; sailing vessel; a journey upon the water; arm of windmill; *v.t.* to navigate; to pass in a ship; to fly through; *v.i.* to travel by water; to begin a voyage; to glide in stately fashion. **-able** *a.* navigable. **-boat** *n.* a boat propelled by sails. **-cloth** *n.* canvas used in making sails. **-ing** *n.* art of navigating. **-less** *a.* **-or** *n.* mariner; seaman; tar. **-or-hat** *n.* straw hat. **full sail,** with all sails set. **under sail,** to have sails spread. **to sail close to the wind,** to sail with sails of ship barely full; to run great risks. **to sail under false colors,** to act under false pretenses [O.E. *segel*].

saint (sānt) *n.* outstandingly devout and virtuous person; one of the blessed in heaven; one formally canonized by R.C. Church; *v.t.* to canonize. **-ed** *a.* pious; hallowed; sacred; dead. **-hood** *n.* **—like, -ly** *a.* devout; godly; pious. **-liness** *n.* **-'s day,** day on which falls celebration of particular saint. **All-Saints' Day,** 1st November. **St. Bernard,** dog famous for guiding and rescuing travelers lost in snow. **St. Patrick's Day,** 17th March. **St. Valentine's Day,** 14th February. **St. Vitus's dance,** chorea. **Latter-day Saints**, the Mormons. **patron saint,** saint held to be a protector [Fr. fr. L. *sanctus*, consecreated].

sake (sāk) *n.* cause; behalf; purpose; account; regard. **for the sake of,** on behalf of [O.E. *sacu*, dispute at law].

sa·ke (sá′·ki) *n.* national beverage of Japan, fermented from rice [Jap.].

sal (sal) *n.* salt (much used in compound words pert. esp. to pharmacy).**— ammoniac** *n.* ammonium chloride, used in composition of electric batteries and in medicine as expectorant and stomachic. **— volatile** *n.* mixture of ammonium carbonate with oil of nutmeg, oil of lemon and alcohol, used as a stimulant, antacid, or expectorant [L.].

sa·laam (sa·lám′) *n.* salutation, a low bow, of ceremony or respect in the East; *v.t.* to salute; to greet [Ar. = peace].

sa·la·cious (sa·lā′·shas) *a*. lustful; lewd; lecherous. **-ly** *adv.* **-ness, salacity** *n.* [L. *salax*, fr. *salire*, to leap].

sal·ad (sal′·ad) *n.* green vegetables raw or cooked, meat, fish, fruit, dressed with various seasonings or dressings. **—dressing** *n.* a sauce for salads. **— days,** early years of youthful inexperience [Fr. *salade*, fr. L. *sal*, salt].

sal·a·man·der (sal′·a·man.der) *n.* small, tailed amphibian, allied to newt. **salamandriform, salamandrine** *a.* pert. to or shaped like a salamander; fire-resisting [Gk. *salamandra*].

sa·la·mi (sa.lá′·mi.) *n.* Italian salted sausage.

sal·a·ry (sal′·a·ri.) *n.* fixed remuneration, usually monthly, for services rendered; stipend. **salaried** *a.* [L. *salarilum*, saltmoney, soldier's pay].

sale (sāl) *n.* exchange of anything for money; demand (for article); public exposition of goods; a special disposal of stock at reduced prices. **-able, salable** *a.* capable of being sold. **-ableness** *n.* **-ably** *adv.* **— price** *n.*

special, low price. **-sman** *n.* man who sells. **-smanship** *n.* art of selling goods. **-swoman** *n.* [O.E. *sala*].

sal·i·cin (sal′·ą·sin) *n.* a bitter white crystalline glucocide obtained from bark of aspen and used as drug. **salicylate** *n.* any salt of salicylic acid. **salicylic** *a.* derived from salicin. **salicylic acid,** white crystalline solid obtained from aspen bark or synthetically from phenol [L. *salix*, a willow].

sa·li·ent (sā′·li·ąnt) *a.* moving by leaps; pro-angle formed by intersection of adjacent surfaces; projecting angle in line of fortifications, etc. **-ly** *adv.* [L. *salire*, to leap].

sa·lif·er·ous (są·lif′·ęr·ąs) *a.* bearing or producing salt [L. *sal*, salt; *ferre*, to bear].

sal·i·fy (sal′·a·fī) *v.t.* to form a salt by combining an acid with a base; to combine with a salt. **salifiable** *a.*

sa·line (sā′·līn) *a.* of or containing salt; salty; *n.* a saline medicine. **salina** *n.* salt marsh; saltworks. **saliniferous** *a.* producing salt. **salinity** *n.* [L. *salinus*].

sa·li·va (są·lī′·vą) *n.* digestive fluid or spittle, secreted in mouth by salivary glands. **-ry** *a.* pert. to, producing saliva. **-te** *v.t.* to produce abnormal secretion of saliva [L.].

sal·low (sal′·ō) *a.* of sickly yellow color; of pale, unhealthy complexion. **-ish** *a.* **-ness** *n.* [O.E. *salo*].

sal·ly (sal′·i·) *n.* sudden eruption; issuing of troops from besieged place to attack enemy; sortie; witticism; *v.i.* to issue suddenly. [L. *satire*, to leap].

salm·on (sam′·ąn) *n.* silver-scaled fish with orange-pink flesh. **—pink** *n.* orange pink. **— trout** *n.* sea or white-trout, fish resembling salmon in color but smaller [L. *salmo*].

sa·lon (są·làn′) *n.* spacious apartment for reception of company; hall for exhibition of art [Fr.]

sa·loon (są·lòòn′) *n.* public dining room; principal cabin in steamer; a place where liquor is sold and drunk. [Fr. *salon*].

sal·si·fy, salsafy (sal′·są·fi·) *n.* hardy, biennial, composite herb with edible root; oyster plant [Fr. fr. It. *sassefrica*, goat's beard].

salt (sawlt) *n.* sodium chloride or common salt, substance used for seasoning food and for preservation of meat, etc; compound resulting from reaction between acid and a base; savor; piquancy; wit; (*Colloq.*) an old sailor; *pl.* (*Chem.*) combinations of acids with alkaline or salifiable bases; (*Med.*) saline cathartics, as Epsom, Rochelle, etc.; *a.* containing or tasting of salt; preserved with salt; pungent; *v.t.* to season or treat with salt. **-er** *n.* **-ern** *n.* saltworks. **-ing** *n.* land covered regularly by tide. **-less** *a.* **— lick** *n.* salt for animals to lick. **— marsh** *n.* land with low growth liable to be overflowed by sea. **-ness** *n.* salt taste; state of being salt. **—water** *n.* water impregnated with salt; sea water. **-y** *a.* **salt of the earth,** persons of the highest reputation or worth. **to take with a grain of salt,** to be sceptical of [O.E. *sealt*].

sal·tant (sal′·tąnt) *a.* leaping; jumping; dancing. **saltation** *n.* [L. *salire*, to leap].

sal·tire, saltier (sal′·tir) *n.* cross in the shape of an X, or St. Andrew's cross [O.Fr. *saulloir*].

salt·pe·ter (sawlt′·pē′·tęr) *n.* common name for niter or potassium nitrate, used in manufacture of glass, nitric acid, etc. [L. *sal petrae*, salt of the rock].

sa·lu·bri·ous (są·lū′·bri·ąs) *a.* wholesome; healthy. **-ly** *adv.* **-ness, salubrity** *n.* [L. *salus*, health].

sal·u·tar·y (sal′·yą·ter·i.) *a.* wholesome; resulting in good; healthful; beneficial. **salutarily** *adv.* **salutariness** *n.* [L. *salus*, health].

sa·lute (są·lūt′) *v.t.* to address with expressions of kind wishes; to recognize one of superior rank by a sign; to honor by a discharge of cannon or small arms, by striking colors, etc.; to greet; *n.* greeting showing respect. **salutation** *n.* saluting; words uttered in welcome; opening words of a letter. **salutatory** *a.* welcoming; *n.* opening address of welcome at commencement exercises of school or college. **salutatorian** *n.* student of graduating class who delivers such an address [L. *salutare*, to wish health to].

salvage. See **salve.**

sal·va·tion (sal·vā′·shąn) *n.* preservation from destruction; redemption; deliverance. **Salvation Army** *n.* international religious organization for revival of religion among the masses. **Salvationist** *n.* active member of Salvation Army [L. *salvare*, to save].

salve (salv) *v.t.* to save or retrieve property from danger or destruction. **salvability** *n.* **salvable** *a.* capable of being used or reconstructed in spite of damage. **salvage** *n.* compensation allowed to persons who assist in saving ship or cargo, or property in general, from destruction; property, so saved; *v.t.* to save from ruins, shipwreck, etc. **-r, salvor** *n.* [L. *salvare*, to save].

salve (sav) *n.* healing ointment applied to wounds or sores; *v.t.* to anoint with such; to heal; to soothe (conscience) [O.E. *sealf*].

sal·ver (sal′·vęr) *n.* a tray for visiting cards [Sp. *salva*, a foretasting].

sal·vo (sal′·vō) *n.* guns fired simultaneously, or in succession, as salute; sustained applause or welcome from large crowd. *pl.* **salvo(e)s** [It. *salva*, a volley].

sal volatile. See **sal.**

SAM (sam) *n.* surface-to-*a*ir *m*issile.

Sa·mar·i·tan (są·mar′·ą·tan) *a.* pert. to Samaria in Palestine; *n.* native or inhabitant of Samaria; kind-hearted, charitable person (fr. parable of good Samaritan, Luke 10).

sam·ba (sam′·bą) *n.* a dance of S. American origin; the music for such a dance; *v.i.* [Port., fr. Afr.].

Sam Browne (sam broun) *n.* military belt with a strap across the right shoulder.

same (sām) *a.* identical; of like kind; unchanged; uniform; aforesaid. **-ly** *adv.* **-ness** *n.* near resemblance; uniformity [O.N. *samr*).

sam·ite (sam′·īt) *n.* rich silk material; any lustrous silk stuff [Fr. *samit*, fr. Gk. *hexamitos*, woven with six threads].

sam·o·var (sam′·ą·vàr) *n.* Russian tea urn.

Sam·o·yed (sam′·ą·yed) *n.* Mongolian people inhabiting N. shores of Russia and Siberia; their language; breed of dog, orig. a sledge dog.

sam·pan (sam′·pan) *n.* a Chinese light river vessel. Also **sanpan** [Malay, fr. Chin. *san*, three; *pan*, a board].

sam·phire (sam′·fīr) *n.* European herb found on rocks and cliffs, St. Peter's wort [corrupt. of Fr. *Saint Pierre*].

sam·ple (sam′·pl) *n.* specimen; example; *v.t.* to take or give a sample of; to try; to test; to taste. **-r** *n.* one who samples; beginner's exercise in embroidery [M.E. *essample; fr.* L. *exemplum*, example].

sam·u·rai (sam′·oo·rī) *n.* member of hereditary military caste in Japan from 12th to mid-19th cent. *pl.* **samurai** [Jap.].

san·a·tive (san′·ą·tiv) *a.* having power to cure or heal. **-ness** *n.* **sanatorium** *n.* institution for open-air treatment of tuberculosis; institution for convalescent patients; *pl.* **sanatoria;** also **sanitarium;** *pl.* **sanitaria** (See *sanitary*). **sanatory** *a.* healing [L. *sanare*, to heal].

sanc·ti·fy (sangk′·tą·fī) *v.t.* to set apart as sacred or holy; to hallow; to consecrate; to purify. **sanctification** *n.* purification and freedom from sin. **sanctified** *a.* hallowed; sanctimonious. **sanctifiedly** *adv.* **sanctimonious** *a.* hypocritically pious. **sanctimoniously** *adv.* **sanctimoniousness, sanctimony** *n.* affected piety. **sanctitude** *n.* saintliness; holiness. **sanctity** *n.* quality of being sacred; state of being pure and devout; state of being solemnly binding on one; inviolability [L. *sanctus*, holy].

sanc·tion (sangk′·shạn) *n.* solemn ratification; express permission; authorization; approval; legal use of force to secure obedience to law; anything which serves to secure obedience to law; anything which serves to move a person to observe or refrain from given mode of conduct; *v.t.* and *v.i.* to confirm; to authorize; to countenance. **sanctions** *n.pl.* measures to enforce fulfillment of international treaty obligations [L. *sanctus*, holy].

sanc·tu·ar·y (sangk′·choo·er·i·) *n.* holy place; shrine; the chancel; a church or other place of protection for fugitives. **sanctum** *n.* sacred place; private room or study. **sanctum sanctorum,** holy of holies in Jewish temple; exclusive private place [L. *sanctus*, holy].

sand (sand) *n.* fine, loose grains of quartz or other mineral matter formed by disintegration of rocks; *n.pl.* sandy beach; desert region; moments of time; *v.t.* to sprinkle or cover with sand; to smooth with sandpaper. **-bag** *n.* bag filled with sand or earth, for repairing breaches in fortification, etc. **-bank** *n.* shoal of sand thrown up by sea. **— bar** *n.* barrier of sand facing entrance of river estuary. **-blast** *n.* jet of sand driven by a blast of air or steam, for roughening, cleaning, cutting. **— dune** *n.* ridge of loose sand. **-ed** *a.* sprinkled with sand. **— glass** *n.* hourglass, instrument for measuring time by running of sand. **-iness** *n.* state of being sandy; a sandy color. **-ing** *n.* cleaning up wood by rubbing with sandpaper. **-paper** *n.* stout paper or cloth coated with glue and then sprinkled over with sand, used as an abrading agent for smoothing wood, etc. *v.t.* to smooth with sandpaper. **-piper** *n.* small wading bird of plover family. **-stone** *n.* rock employed for building and making grindstones. **-storm** *n.* a storm of wind carrying dust. **-y** *a.* like or covered with sand; not firm or stable; yellowish brown [O.E.].

san·dal (san′·dạl) *n.* a shoe consisting of flat sole, bound to foot by straps or thongs. **-led** *a.* [Gk. *sandalon*].

san·dal·wood (san′·dạl·wood) *n.* fragrant heartwood of santalum [Ar. *sandal*].

sand·er·ling (san′·dẹr·ling) *n.* a wading bird of the plover family.

sand·wich (sand′·wich) *n.* two thin pieces of bread with slice of meat, etc., between them (said to have been a favorite dish of Earl of *Sandwich*); *v.t.* to make into sandwich; to form of alternating layers of different nature; to insert or squeeze in between, making a tight fit. **— man** *n.* man carrying two advertising boards, one slung before and one behind him.

sane (sān) *a.* of sound mind; not deranged; rational; reasonable; lucid. **-ly** *adv.* **-ness** *n.* [L. *sanus*, healthy].

sang (sang) *pa.t.* of **sing.**

sang-froid (sȧn·frwȧ′) *n.* composure of mind; imperturbability [Fr. *sang*, blood; *froid*, cold].

san·guine (sang′·gwin) *a.* hopeful; confident; cheerful; deep red; florid; *n.* a crayon; blood-red color. **sanguinarily** *adv.* **sanguinariness** *n.* **sanguinary** *a.* bloody; bloodthirsty; murderous. **-ly** *adv.* **-ness** *n.* **-ous** *a.* bloody; blood-red; blood-stained; containing blood. [L. *sanguis*, blood].

San·he·drin (san′·hē·drin) *n.* supreme court of Ancient Jerusalem; any similar Jewish assembly. Also **Sanhedrim.** [Heb. fr. Gk. *sun*, together; *hedra*, seat].

san·i·tar·y (san′·ạ·te·ri·) *a.* pert. to health; hygienic; clean; free from dirt, germs, etc. **sanitarian** *n.* one interested in the promotion of hygienic reforms. **sanitarily** *adv.* **sanitation** *n.* the measures taken to promote health and to prevent disease; hygiene. **sanitarium,** *n.* private hospital for treatment of special or chronic diseases; health retreat; sanitorium. **sanitary napkin,** pad or absorbent material for use during menstruation [L. *sanitas*, health].

san·i·ty (san′·ạ·ti·) *n.* state of being sane; soundness of mind [L. *sanus*, sane].

sank (sangk) *pa.t.* of the verb **sink.**

sans·cu·lotte (sanz·kū·lȧt′) *n.* ragged fellow; a name given in the first French Revolution to extreme republican party [Fr. = without knee breeches].

San·skrit, Sanscrit (san′·skrit) *n.* classic literary language of ancient India, member of Indo-European family of languages [Sans. *samskrita*, perfected, finished].

San·ta Claus (san′·tạ klawz) *n.* traditional 'Father Christmas' of children [corrupt. of *St. Nicholas*, patron saint of children].

sap (sap) *n.* watery juice of plants, containing mineral salts, proteins and carbohydrates; (*Slang*) a stupid person. **-head** *n.* (*Slang*) dolt. **-less** *a.* **-ling** *n.* young tree; youth. doltishness. **-py** *a.* juicy; (*Slang*) silly. **-wood** *n.* alburnum, exterior part of wood of tree next to bark [O.E. *saep*].

sap (sap) *n.* tunnel driven under enemy positions for purpose of attack; *v.t.* and *v.i.* to undermine; to impair insidiously; to exhaust gradually. *pr.p.* **-ping.** *pa.t.* and *pa.p.* **-ped** [It. *zappa*, a spade].

sap·id (sap′·id) *a.* savory; palatable; tasty. **-ity** *n.* [L. *sapere*, to taste].

sa·pi·ent (sā′·pi·ạnt) *a.* discerning; wise; sage. **sapience** *n.* **-ly** *adv.* [L. *sapiens*, wise].

sap·o·na·ceous (sap·ạ·nā′·shạs) *a.* resembling soap; slippery, as if soaped. **saponify** *v.t.* to convert into soap. **saponin** *n.* glucoside obtained from many plants used for foam baths, fire extinguishers, detergents, etc. due to frothy qualities [L. *sapo*, soap].

sa·por (sā′·pẹr) *n.* taste; savor; flavor. **-oific** *a.* producing taste or flavor. **-osity** *n.* [L. = taste].

Sap·phic (saf′·ik) *a.* pert. to Sappho, lyric poetess of Greece of 7th cent. B.C.; denoting verse in which three lines of five feet each are followed by line of two feet; *n.* Sapphic verse. **sapphism** *n.* unnatural sexual relations between women.

sap·phire (saf′·īr) *n.* translucent precious stone of various shades of blue; *a.* deep, pure blue [Gk. *sapheiros*].

sar·a·band (sar′·ạ·band) *n.* slow, stately dance, introduced by Moors into Spain in 16th cent.; in England, country dance [Pers. *sarband*, a fillet].

Sar·a·cen (sar′·ạ·sạn) *n.* Arab or Mohammedan who invaded Europe and Africa; an infidel. **-ic, -ical** *a.* [L. *Saracenus*].

Sar·a·to·ga trunk (sar·ạ·tō′·gạ·trungk) *n.* a large trunk for ladies' dresses.

sar·casm (sȧr·kazm) *n.* taunt; scoffing gibe; veiled sneer; irony; use of such expressions. **sarcastic, -al** *a.* bitterly satirical and cutting; taunting. **sarcastically** *adv.* [Gk. *sarkasmos*].

sar·coph·a·gus (sȧr·kȧf′·ạ·gạs) *n.* kind of limestone used by Greeks for coffins and believed to consume flesh of bodies deposited in it; stone coffin; monumental chest or case of stone, erected over graves. *pl.* **sarcophagi** [Gk. *sarx*, flesh; *phagein*, to eat].

sar·dine (sȧr·dēn′) *n.* small fish of herring family in young stage salted and preserved in oil [It. *sardina*, fr. the island of Sardinia].

sar·don·ic (sȧr·dȧn′·ik) *a.* (of laugh, smile) bitter, scornful, derisive, mocking. **-ally** adv. [L. *sardonicus*].

sar·do·nyx (sȧr′·dȧ·niks) *n.* semi-precious stone [Gk. = Sardinian onyx].

sar·gas·sum (sȧr·gas′·ạm) *n.* genus of seaweeds. **sargasso** *n.* gulfweed. **Sargasso Sea,** part of Atlantic covered with seaweed [Sp. *sargazo*].

sa·ri (sȧ′·rē) *n.* long outer garment of Hindu women. Also **saree** [Hind.].

sa·rong (sạ·rawng′) *n.* garment draped round waist by Malayans [Malay].

sar·sa·pa·ril·la (sȧrs·(a)·pạ·ril′·ạ) *n.* several plants of genus Smilax, with roots yielding medicinal sarsaparilla, a mild diuretic; a soft drink flavored with the extract [Sp. *zarzaparilla*].

sar·to·ri·al (sȧr·tō·′·ri·ạl) *a.* pert. to tailor, tailoring [L. *sartor*, a tailor].

sash (sash) *n.* silken band; belt or band, usually decorative, worn round body [Arab. *shash*].

sash (sash) *n.* frame of window which carries panes of glass [Fr. *chassis*].

sas·sa·fras (sas′·ạ·fras) *n.* a tree of the laurel family; the dried bark of the root, used for flavoring beverages, etc.

sat (sat) *pa.t.* and *pa.p.* of **sit.**

Sa·tan (sā′·tạn) *n.* the devil. **-ic, -al** *a.* devilish; infernal; diabolical. **-ically** *adv.* [Heb. = enemy].

satch·el (sach′·ạl) *n.* small bag for books, etc. [L. *saccellus*, small sack].

sate (sāt) *v.t.* to satisfy appetite of; to glut [earlier *sade*, to make sad].

sa·teen (sa·tēn′) *n.* glossy cloth for linings, made of cotton in imitation of satin [fr. satin].

sat·el·lite (sat′·a·līt) *n.* one constantly in attendance upon important personage; an obsequious follower; (*Astron.*) a secondary body which revolves round planets of solar system; a moon. **satellite** (earth) *n.* an object launched into space by man to orbit the earth for scientific purposes. **satellitic** *a.* [L. *satelles*].

sa·ti·ate (sā′·shi·āt) *v.t.* to satisfy appetite of; to surfeit; to sate. **satiability** *n.* **satiable** *a.* capable of being satisfied. **satiation** *n.* state of being satiated. **satiety** (sạ·tī′·ạ·ti·) *n.* state of being satiated; feeling of having had too much [L. *satiare*, fr. *satis*, enough].

sat·in (sat′·n) *n.* soft, rich, usually silk fabric with smooth, lustrous surface; *a.* made of satin; smooth; glossy. **-et** *n.* thin kind of satin; glossy cloth of cotton warp and woolen weft, to imitate satin. **-wood** *n.* beautiful hard yellow wood, valued in cabinet work for veneers. **-y** *a.* [Fr. fr. It. *seta*, silk].

sat·ire (sat·īre) *n.* literary composition holding up to ridicule vice or folly of the times; use of irony, sarcasm, invective, or wit. **satiric, -al** *a.* **satirically** *adv.* **satiricalness** *n.* **satirize** *v.t.* to make object of satire. **satirist** *n.* [L. *satira*, a literary medley].

sat·is·fy (sat′·is·fī) *v.t.* to gratify fully; to pay, fulfill, supply, recompense, adequately; to convince; to content; to answer; to free from doubt; *v.i.* to give content; to supply to the full; to make payment. **satisfaction** *n.* **satisfactorily** *adv.* **satisfactoriness** *n.* **satisfactory** *a.* **-ing** *a.* affording satisfaction, esp. of food. **-ingly** *adv.* [L. *satisfacere*].

sa·trap (sā′·trap) *n.* governor of province under ancient Persian monarchy; petty, despotic governor. **-al** *a.* **-y** *n.* government, jurisdiction of satrap [Gk. *satrapēs*].

sat·u·rate (sach′·ạ·rāt) *v.t.* to soak thoroughly; to steep; to drench. **-d** *a.* **saturation** *n.* act of saturating; complete penetration; condition of being saturated; solution of a body in a solvent, until solvent can absorb no more; in magnetism, state when increase of magnetizing force produces no further increase of flux-density in magnet; purity of color, free from white **saturator** *n.* contrivance for saturating air of factory, etc. with water-vapor [L. *saturare*].

Sat·ur·day (sat′·ẹr·di) *n.* seventh day of week [O.E. *Saeterdaeg*, day of Saturn].

Sat·urn (sat′·ẹrn) *n.* old deity, father of Jupiter; sixth of major planets in order of distance from sun. **Saturnalia** *n.pl.* festival in ancient Rome in honor of Saturn; time of carnival and unrestrained license; orgy. **saturnalian** *a.* **Saturnian** *a.* pert. to epoch of Saturn; golden; distinguished for prosperity and peacefulness. **saturnine** *a.* gloomy, sluggish in temperament [L. *Saturnus*, god of agriculture].

sat·yr (sā′·tẹr, sat′·ẹr) *n.* woodland deity in Greek mythology, part human and part goat, fond of sensual enjoyment; lecherous person. **satyriasis** *n.* excessive and morbid desire for sexual intercourse exhibited by men. **-omaniac** *n.* **-ical** *a.* pert. to satyrs [Gk. *saturos*].

sauce (saws) *n.* liquid or soft seasoning for food to render it more palatable or to whet appetite; condiment; relish; (*Colloq.*) impudence; cheek; *v.t.* to season with sauce; to give flavor or interest to; (*Colloq.*) to be rude in speech or manner.**-pan** *n.* meal pot with lid and long handle used for cooking. **saucy** *a.* bold; pert; cheeky. **saucily** *adv.* **sauciness** *n.* [Fr. fr. L. *sal*. salt].

sau·cer (saw′·sẹr) *n.* orig. vessel for sauce; small plate put under cup [Fr. *saucière*].

sauer·kraut (sour′·krout) *n.* cabbage cut fine and allowed to ferment in brine [Ger.].

saun·ter (sawn′·tẹr) *v.i.* to stroll. *n.* leisurely walk or stroll. **-er** *n.* **-ing** *n.*

sau·ri·an (saw′·ri·an) *n.* lizard-like reptile [Gk. *sauros*, a lizard].

sau·sage (saw′·sij) *n.* meat minced and seasoned and enclosed in thin membranous casing obtained from small entrails of pig or sheep [Fr. *saucisse*].

sau·té (sō·tā) *a.* cooked in little fat [Fr.].

sau·terne (sō·turn′) *n.* a well-known white wine, from *Sauternes*, S. W. France.

sav·age (sav′·ij) *a.* remote from human habitation; wild; uncivilized; primitive; cruel; *n.* man in native state of primitiveness; a barbarian. **-ly** *adv.* **-ry** *n.* ferocity; barbarism [L. *silvaticus*, fr. *silva*, a wood].

sa·vant (sa·vȧnt′, sav′·ạnt) *n.* a man of learning [Fr. fr. *savoir*, to know].

save (sāv) *v.t.* to rescue, preserve from danger, evil, etc.; to redeem; to protect; to secure; to maintain (face, etc.); to keep for future; to lay by; to hoard; to obviate need of; to spare; to except; *v.i.* to lay by money; to economize; *prep.* except; *conj.* but. **savable** *a.* capable of being saved; retrievable. **-r** *n.* **saving** *a.* frugal; thrifty; delivering from sin; implying reservation, as *saving clause; prep.* excepting; with apology to; *n.* economy; *pl.* earnings or gains put by for future. **savingly** *adv.* **savings bank** *n.* bank for receipt and accumulation of savings [Fr. *sauver*, fr. L. *salvare*, to save].

sav·ior (sāv′·yẹr) *n.* one who saves or delivers from destruction or danger; (*Cap.*) the Redeemer, Jesus Christ. Also **saviour** [L. *salvare*, to save].

sa·voir-faire (sav·wȧr·fer′) *n.* the knack of knowing the right thing to do at the right time; tact [Fr.].

sa·vor (sā′·vẹr) *n.* taste; flavor; relish; odor; smack; distinctive quality; *v.t.* to like; to taste or smell with pleasure; to relish; *v.i.* to have a particular smell or taste; to resemble; to indicate the presence of. **-ily** *adv.* **-less** *a.* **-y** *a.* having savor; tasty. Also *savour* [L. *sapor*, taste].

sa·vor·y (sā′·vẹr·i·) *n.* genus of aromatic plants, often grown as pot-herbs, the leaves being used in cooking as flavoring [fr. *savour*].

sav·vy (sav′·i·) *v.t.* *(Slang)* to understand; *n.* intelligence [Sp. *saber*; Fr. *savoir*, to know].

saw (saw) *pa.t.* of the verb **see.**

saw (saw) *n.* old saying; maxim; proverb; aphorism; adage [O.E. *sagu*].

saw (saw) *n.* hand or mechanical tool with thin blade, band, or circular disk with serrated edge, used for cutting; *v.t.* and *v.i.* to cut with a saw; *pa.t.* **sawed.** *pa.p.* **sawed** or **sawn. -bones** *n.* (*Slang*) surgeon. **-dust** *n.* small particles of wood, etc. made by action of a saw. **-er** *n.* **-mill** *n.* place where logs are sawn by mechanical power. **—toothed** *a.* having serrations like a saw. **-yer** *n.* one who saws timber; wood-boring larva of longicorn beetle [O.E. *saga*].

sax·horn (saks′·hawrn) *n.* brass wind instrument [Adolphe *Sax*, inventor, c. 1842].

sax·i·frage (sak′·sạ·frij) *n.* popular name of various plants, most of them true rock plants [L. *saxum*, a stone; *frangere*, to break].

Sax·on (sak′·sạn) *n.* one of the people who formerly dwelt in N. Germany and who invaded England in the 5th and 6th cents.; a person of English race; native of Saxony; language of Saxons; *a.* pert. to Saxons, their country, their language; Anglo-Saxon [O.E. *Seaxa, Seaxan*, fr. *seax*, a knife].

Sax·o·ny (sak′·sạ·ni·) *n.* very fine quality of wool; flannel [*Saxony*, where first produced].

sax·o·phone (sak′·sạ·fōn) *n.* brass wind-instrument, with a reed and clarinet mouthpiece, fingered like an oboe [A. J. *Sax*, the inventor; Gk. *phōnē*, a sound].

say (sā)*v.t.* to utter with speaking voice; to state; to express; to allege; to repeat (lesson, etc.); to recite; to take as near enough. *pa.t.* and *pa.p.* **said** (sed). *n.* something said; what one has to say; share in a decision. **-er** *n.* **-ing** *n.* a verbal utterance; spoken or written expression of thought; proverbial expression; adage [O.E. *secgan*].

scab (skab) *n.* crust forming over open wound or sore; contagious skin disease, resembling mange, which attacks horses, cattle and sheep; disease of apple and pear; non-union worker; (*Slang*) despicable person; *v.i.* to heal over; to form a scab. *pa.t.* and *pa.p.* **-bed.** *pr.p.* **-bing. -bed** *a.* covered with scabs. **-bedness** *n.* **-by** *a.* [O.N. *skabbi*].

scab·bard (skab′·ẹrd) *n.* sheath for sword or dagger; *v.t.* [O.Fr. *escalberc*].

sca·bies (skā′·bēz) *n.* skin disease caused by parasite; the itch; the scab [L.].

sca·bi·ous (skā′·bi·ạs) *a.* consisting of scabs; scabby; itchy [L. *scabies*, the itch].

sca·brous (skā′·brạs) *a.* rough; scaly; harsh; full of difficulties; indelicate. **-ly** *adv.* **-ness** *n.* [L. *scaber* rough].

scad (skad) *n.* *a* species of mackerel; *pl.* (*Slang*) a great quantity [form of *shad*].

scaf·fold (skaf′·ạld) *n.* temporary structure for support of workmen, used in erecting, altering, or repairing buildings; framework; stage; platform, esp. for execution of criminal; *v.t.* to furnish with a scaffold; to prop up. **-ing** *n.* scaffold [O.Fr. *eschafault*].

scal·a·wag, scallawag (skal′·ạ·wag) *n.* (*Colloq.*) scamp; worthless fellow.

scald (skawld) *v.t.* to burn with moist heat or hot liquid; to cleanse by rinsing with boiling water; to heat to point approaching boiling point; *n.* injury by scalding [L. *ex*, out of; *calidus*, hot].

scald See **skald.**

scale (skāl) *n.* dish of a balance; balance itself; machine for weighing, chiefly in *pl.;* Libra, one of signs of zodiac; *v.t.* to weigh, as in scales [O.N. *skal*, bowl].

scale (skāl) *n.* horny or bony plate-like outgrowth from skin of certain mammals, reptiles, and fishes; any thin layer or flake on surface; *v.t.* to deprive of scales; *v.i.* to come off or peel in thin layers. **-d** *a.* having scales. **-less** *a.* **scaliness** *n.* being scaly. **scaling** *n.* removing of scales. **scaly** *a.* covered with scales; resembling scales [O.Fr. *escale*, husk].

scale (skāl) *n.* series of steps or gradations; comparative rank in society; ratio between dimensions as shown on map, etc. to actual distance, or length; scope; basis for a numerical system, as *binary scale*; instrument for measuring, weighing, etc. (*Mus.*) succession of notes arranged in order of pitch between given note and its octave; gamut; *v.t.* to climb as by a ladder; to clamber up; to measure; *v.i.* to mount [L. *scala*, a ladder].

sca·lene (skā·lēn) *a.* uneven; *(Geom.)* having all three sides unequal; *n.* a scalene triangle [Gk. *skalēnos*, uneven].

scal·lion (skal′·yạn) *n.* a variety of shallot [L. (*cepa*) *Ascalonia*, onion of Ascalon].

scal·lop, scollop (skal′·ạp) *n.* bivale mollusk with ribbed, fan-shaped shell and beautiful coloring; ornamental edge of rounded projections; dish resembling scallop shell to serve oysters, etc.; *v.t.* to cut edge of material into scallops [O.Fr. *escalope*, a shell].

scalp (skalp) *n.* covering dome of cranium consisting of skin and hair; skin and hair torn off by Indian warriors as token of victory; *v.t.* to deprive of integument of head; to make quick profits in buying and prompt reselling [contr. of *scallop*].

scal·pel (skal′·pel) *n.* small, straight surgical knife with convex edge [L. *scalpere*, to cut].

scamp (skamp) *n.* scoundrel; rascal; rogue; *v.t.* to execute work carelessly [O.Fr. *escamper*, to decamp].

scam·per (skam′·pẹr) *v.i.* to run about; to run away in haste and trepidation; *n.* a hasty, impulsive flight [fr. *scamp*].

scan (skan) *v.t.* to examine closely; to scrutinize; to measure or read (verse) by its metrical feet (*Radar*) to traverse an area with electronic beams. *v.i.* to be metrically correct. *pr.p.* **-ning.** *pa.t.* and *pa.p.* **-ned. -ning** *n.* (*Television*) process of dissecting a picture to be transmitted. **-sion** *n.* act or mode of scanning poetry [L. *scandere*, to climb].

scan·dal (skan′·dạl) *n.* malicious gossip; disgraceful action; disgrace; injury to a person's character; **-bearer, -monger** *n.* one who delights in spreading malicious scandal and gossip. **-ize** *v.t.* to shock by disgraceful actions **-ous** *a.* bringing shame; disgraceful. **-ously** *adv.* **-ousness** *n.* [Gk. *skandalon*, a cause of stumbling].

Scan·di·na·vi·a (skan·dạ·nā′·vi·ạ) *n.* peninsula of Norway, Sweden, and Finland, but historically and linguistically includes Denmark and Iceland. **-n** *a.* pert. to Scandinavia [L. *Scandinavia* or *Scandia*].

scansion. See **scan.**

scant (skant) *a.* barely sufficient; inadequate; *v.t.* to put on short allowance; to fail to give full measure; **-ily** *adv.* **-iness** *n.* **-ly** *adv.* sparingly; scarcely; barely. **-ness** *n.* scantiness; insufficiency. **-y** *a.* [O.N. *skamt*, short].

scant·ling (skant′·ling) *n.* a small amount; a small piece of timber; a stud [Fr. *échantillon*, a sample].

scape·goat (skāp′·gōt) *n.* in Mosaic ritual, goat upon whose head were symbolically placed sins of people; one who has to shoulder blame due to another. **scapegrace** *n.* graceless, good-for-nothing fellow [fr. *escape*].

scaph·oid (skaf′·oid) *a.* boat-shaped [Gk. *skaphē*, a boat; *eidos*, form].

scap·u·la (skap′·ya̤·la̤) *n.* shoulder blade. *pl.* **scapulae.** **-r** *a.* pert. to scapula; *n.* bandage for shoulder blade; part of habit of certain religious orders in R.C. church; sleeveless monastic garment. Also **-ry** [L. *scapulae*, the shoulder blades].

scar (skȧr) *n.* permanent mark left on skin after healing of a wound, burn; a cicatrix; any blemish; *v.t.* to mark with scar; *v.i.* to heal with a scar [O.Fr. *escare*].

scar·ab (skar′·a̤b) *n.* bettle regarded by ancient Egyptians as emblematic of solar power; gem cut in shape of this bettle, as amulet [L. *scarabaeus*].

scarce (skers) *a.* not plentiful; deficient; wanting; rare; infrequent; uncommon; scanty; **-ly** *adv.* hardly; not quite. **-ness, scarcity** *n.* being scarce; lack; deficiency [O.Fr. *escars*].

scare (sker) *v.t.* to terrify suddenly; to alarm; to drive away by frightening; *n.* sudden alarm (esp. causeless); panic; fright. **-crow** *n.* figure set up to frighten away birds from crops; a miserable-looking person in rags. **-monger** *n.* alarmist [O.N. *skirra*].

scarf (skȧrf) *n.* long, narrow, light article of dress worn loosely over shoulders or about neck; a muffler. *pl.* **-s, scarves** [O.Fr. *escrepe*, a purse hanging from the neck].

scarf (skȧrf) *v.t.* to unite lengthways to pieces of timber by letting notched end of one into a similar end of the other, then securing them with bolt or strap. *n.* joint for connecting timbers lengthways, the two pieces overlapping [Scand. = *skarf*, a joint].

scar·i·fy (skar′·a̤·fī) *v.t.* to scratch or slightly cut the skin; to stir the surface soil of; to lacerate; to criticize unmercifully. **scarification** *n.* **scarifier** *n.* [L. *scarificare*].

scar·la·ti·na (skar·la̤·tē′·na̤) *n.* scarlet fever [It.].

scar·let (skȧr′·lit) *n.* bright red color of many shades; cloth of scarlet color; *a.* of this color **— fever** *n.* childhood disease characterized by a scarlet rash. **-hat** *n.* a cardinal's hat. **— pimpernel,** small annual herb with red flowers. **— runner** *n.* bean plant with twining stem and scarlet flowers [O.Fr. *escarlate*].

scarp (skȧrp) *n.* steep inside slope of ditch in fortifications; *v.t.* to make steep. **-ed** *a.* steeply sloping [It. *scarpa*].

scar·y (sker′·i·) *a.* (*Colloq.*) producing fright or alarm; exceedingly timid [fr. *scare*].

scat (skat) *v.i.* to hurry off; *v.t.* to order off with "scat!"

scathe (skāth) *v.t.* to criticize harshly. **scathing** *a.* damaging; cutting; biting. **scathingly** *adv.* [O.N. *skatha*].

sca·tol·o·gy (ska̤·tȧl′·a̤·ji·) *n.* scientific study of fossilized excrement of animals; interest in obscene literature. **scatological** *a.* [Gk. *skor, skatos*, dung].

scat·ter (skat′·e̤r) *v.t.* to strew about; to sprinkle around; to put to rout; to disperse; *v.i.* to take to flight; to disperse. **-brain** *n.* a giddy, thoughtless person. **-brained** *a.* **-ed** *a.* widely separated or distributed; distracted. **-er** *n.* **-ing** *n.* act of dispersing; effect of irregularly reflected light; (*Radio*) general re-radiation of wave-energy when a ray meets an obstacle in its path; *a.* dispersing; sporadic; diversified. **-ingly** *adv.*

scav·en·ger (skav′·in·je̤r) *n.* one employed in cleaning streets, removing refuse, etc.; animal which feeds on carrion; *v.i.* to scavenge. **scavenge** *v.t.* to cleanse streets, etc. [orig. *scavager*, inspector of goods for sale, later, of street cleansing, fr. O.E. *sceawian*, to inspect].

sce·nar·i·o (sa̤·ner′·i·ō) *n.* script or written version of play to be produced by motion picture; plot of a play. **scenarist** *n.* [It.].

scene (sēn) *n.* place, time of action of novel, play, etc.; a division of a play; spectacle, show, or view; episode; unseemly display of temper; minor disturbance. **-ry** *n.* stage settings; natural features of landscape which please eye. **— shifter** *n.* one who manages the scenery in theatrical representation. **scenic** *a.* pert. to scenery; theatrical; picturesque. **scenographic, -al** *a.* drawn in perspective. **scenographically** *adv.* **scenography** *n.* [L. *scena*].

scent (sent) *v.t.* to discern or track by sense of smell; to give a perfume to; to detect; to become suspicious of; *v.i.* to smell; *n.* odor or perfume; fragrance; aroma; trail left by odor. **-ed** *a.* perfumed. **to put off the scent,** to mislead wilfully [Fr. *sentir*, to smell].

sceptic. See **skeptic.**

scepter (sep′·te̤r) *n.* ornamental staff or baton, as symbol of royal power; royal or imperial dignity. **-ed** *a.* invested with a scepter, regal. Also **sceptre** [Gk. *skēptron*, a staff].

sched·ule (skej′·ool) *n.* document containing list of details forming part of principal document, deed, etc.; tabulated list; order of events; timetable; *v.t.* to note and enter in a schedule [L. a small scroll].

sche·ma (skē′·ma̤) *n.* plan or diagram; outline; scheme; *pl.* **-ta.** **-tic** *a.* **-tically** *adv.* **-tize** *v.t.* to form a scheme [Gk.].

scheme (skēm) *n.* plan; design; system; plot; draft; outline; a syllabus; tabulated statement; diagram; *v.t.* to plan; to contrive; to frame; *v.i.* to intrigue; to plot. *pr.p.* **scheming.** **-r** *n.* **scheming** *n.* and *a.* planning; plotting. **schemist** *n.* schemer [Gk. *schēma*, form].

scher·zo (sker′·tsō) *n.* (*Mus.*) composition of a lively, playful character [It. = a jest].

schil·ling (shil′·ing) *n.* orig. a German coin, re-introduced into Austrian monetary system in 1925 [Ger.].

schism (sizm) *n.* split of a community into factions; division of a church or religious denomination; crime of promoting this. **schismatic** *a.—n.* one who separates from a church. **-atical** *a.* schismatic. **-atically** *adv.* [Gk. *schisma*, a cleft].

schiz·o- (skiz′·ō) *prefix* fr. Greek, *schizein*, to cleave, used in the construction of compound terms. **schizoid** *a.* exhibiting slight symptoms of schizophrenia. **-phrenia** (skiz·a̤·frē′·ni·a̤) *n.* mental disorder known as 'split personality,' characterized by a social behavior, introversion, and loss of touch with one's environment. **-phrenic** *a.*

schnapps, schnaps (shnaps) *n.* kind of Holland gin [Ger.].

schol·ar (skȧl′·e̤r) *n.* learned person; holder of scholarship. **-ly** *a.* learned. **-ship** *n.* learning; erudition; a grant to aid a student. **scholastic** *a.* pert. to schools, scholars, or education; pert. to schools or scholars of philosophy of Middle Ages; pedantic; *n.* schoolman who expounded medieval philosophy; Jesuit student who has not yet taken Holy Orders. **scholastically** *adv.* **Scholasticism** *n.* system of philosophy during Middle Ages [Gk. *scholē*, a school].

scho·li·ast (skō′·li·ast) *n.* ancient commentator or annotator of classical texts. **scholiastic** *a.* **scholium** *n.—pl.* **scholia,** marginal note or comments [Gk. *scholiastēs*, commentator].

school (skȯȯl) *n.* a shoal (of fish, whales, etc.) [Dut. *school*, crowd]

school (skȯȯl) *n.* institution for teaching or giving instruction in any subject; pupils of a school; sessions of instruction; group of writers, artists, thinkers, etc. with principles or methods in common; branch of study, in a university; *v.t.* to educate; to discipline; to instruct; to train. **-boy** *n.* boy attending school or of school age. **-mate** *n.* contemporary at school. **-man** *n.* learned doctor of Middle Ages, versed in scholasticism. **-master** *n.* master in charge of school; male teacher in school. **-room** *n.* **-teacher** *n.* **boarding school,** residential school for boys or girls. **preparatory school,** private school which prepares young people for college. **public school,** *see* **public** [Gk. *scholē*, leisure; place for discussion].

schoon·er (skȯȯ′.nẹr) *n.* small sharp-built vessel, having two masts, fore-and-aft rigged; (*Colloq.*) extra large glass for holding beer; [orig. *scooner*, fr. Prov. E. *scoon*, to make flat stone skip along surface of water. O.E. *scunian*].

schot·tische, shottish (shȧt′.ish) *n.* round dance resembling polka; music in 2⁄4 time for this dance. **Highland schottische,** lively dance to strathspey tunes, Highland fling [Ger. = Scottish].

sci·at·i·ca (sī.at′.i.kạ) *n.* neuralgia of sciatic nerve, with pains in region of hip. **sciatic, -al** *a.* situated in, or pert. to, hip region. **-lly** *adv.* [Late L. fr. Gk. *ischion*, hip-joint].

sci·ence (sī′.ạns) *n.* systematic knowledge of natural or physical phenomena; truth ascertained by observation, experiment, and induction; ordered arrangement of facts known under classes or heads; theoretical knowledge as distinguished from practical; knowledge of principles and rules of invention, construction, mechanism, etc. as distinguished from art. **scientific, -al** *a.* **scientifically** *adv.* **scientism** *n.* outlook and practice of scientist. **scientist** *n.* a person versed in science, esp. natural science. **Christian Science,** religious doctrine of faith healing, bodily diseases being due to errors of mortal mind and therefore curable by faith and prayer. **domestic science,** study of good housekeeping. **natural science, physical science,** science which investigates nature and properties of material bodies and natural phenomena. **pure science,** science based on self-evident truths, as mathematics, logic, etc. [L. *scientia*, knowledge].

scim·i·tar (sim′.ạ.tẹr) *n.* short saber with curved, sharp-edged blade broadening from handle [Pers. *shimshir*].

scin·til·la (sin.til′.ạ) *n.* spark; least particle. **-nt** *a.* emitting sparks; sparkling. **-te** *v.i.* to emit sparks; to sparkle; to glisten. **-tion** *n.* [L. = a park].

sci·o·lism (sī′.ạ.lizm) *n.* superficial knowledge used to impress other. **sciolist** *n.* one possessed of superficial knowledge; charlatan. **sciolistic** *a.* [L. *scire*, to know].

sci·on (sī′.ạn) *n.* slip for grafting; offshoot; a descendant; heir [Fr.].

scis·sile (sis′.ạl) *a.* (*Bot.*) capable of being cut, split, or divided. **scission** *n.* act of cutting; division [L. *scindere, scissum*, to cut].

scis·sors (siz′.ẹrz) *n.pl.* instrument of two sharp-edged blades pivoted together for cutting; small shears. **scissor** *v.t.* to cut with scissors [Fr. *ciseaux*].

scle·ro- (sklēr′.ạ) *prefix* fr. Gk. *skléros*, hard, used in the construction of compound terms, implying hardness or dryness. **sclera** (sklir′.ạ) *n.* strong, opaque fibrous membrane forming outer coat of eyeball, the white of the eye. **scleral** *a.* hard, bony. **scleritis** *n.* inflammation of sclera of eye. **scleroderma, sclerodermia** *n.* chronic skin disease characterized by hardness and rigidity. **sclerodermatous** *a.* (*Zool.*) possessing a hard, bony, external structure for protection. **sclerodermatous, sclerodermic, sclerodermous** *a.* pert. to scleroderma; having a hard outer skin. **scleroid** *a.* of hard texture. **scleroma** *n.* hardening of tissues. **sclerosal** *a.* pert. to sclerosis. **sclerosis** *n.* hardening of organ as a result of excessive growth of connective tissue; induration.

scoff (skȧf, skawf) *v.i.* to treat with derision; to mock; to jeer; *n.* expression of scorn; an object of derision. **-er** *n.* **-ingly** *adv.* [Scand.].

scold (skōld) *v.t.* and *v.i.* to find fault (with); to chide; to reprove angrily; to rebuke; *n.* one who scolds; a nagging, brawling woman. **-er** *n.* **-ing** *n.* rebuke.**-ingly** *adv.* [Ger. *schelten*, to brawl].

sconce (skȧns) *n.* ornamental bracket fixed to wall, for carrying a light; small fort or breastwork; [O.Fr. *esconce*, fr. L. *abscondere*, to bide].

scone (skōn) *n.* a thin, flat cake.

scoop (skȯȯp) *n.* article for ladling; kind of shovel; hollow place; (*Colloq.*) lucrative speculation; (*Slang*) publication of exclusive news in newspaper; *v.t.* to ladle out, shovel, lift, dig or hollow out with scoop; (*Slang*) to publish exclusive news; [prob. fr. Sw. *skopa*, a scoop].

scoot (skȯȯt) *v.i.* to move off quickly; to dart away suddenly; to scamper off. **-er** *n.* a toy consisting of flat board mounted on two wheels, on which one foot rests, propelled by other foot and guided by handle attached to front wheel [fr. *shoot*].

scope (skōp) *n.* range of activity or application; space for action; room; play; outlet; opportunity [It. *scopo*, a target].

scor·bu·tic (skawr.bū′.tik) *a.* affected with, or relating to, scurvy.

scorch (skawrch) *v.t.* to burn the surface of; to parch; to shrivel; to char; to singe; to wither; to blast; *v.i.* to be burnt on surface; to dry up; to parch; (*Colloq.*) to drive at excessive speed. **scorched-earth policy,** destroying everything of value in path of hostile army. **-er** *n.* anything which scorches; a biting,, sarcastic remark; (*Colloq.*) one who drives furiously; hot, sultry day. **-ing** *a.* burning superficially; oppressively hot.

score (skōr) *n.* a cut, notch, line, stroke; tally-mark, reckoning, bill, account; number twenty; reason; sake; number of points, runs, goals, etc. made in a game; arrangement of different parts of a musical composition on the page so that each bar may be read in all parts simultaneously; *v.t.* to mark with lines, scratches, furrows; to cut; to write down in proper order; to orchestrate; to enter in account book, to record; to make (points, etc.) in game; *v.i.* to add a point, run, goal, etc. in a game; to make a telling remark; to achieve a success. **-r** *n.* one who keeps official record of points, runs, etc. made in the course of a game; one who makes the point, run, etc. in a game. **scoring** *n.* **-book, -card, -sheet,** *n.* [O.N. *skor*, notch].

sco·ri·a (skō′.ri.ạ) *n.* dross or slag resulting from smelting of metal ores; rough, angular material sent out by volcano. *pl.* **scoriae.** **scorify** *v.t.* to reduce to dross or slag [Gk. *skoria*, dross].

scorn (skawrn) *n.* extreme disdain or contempt; object of derision; *v.t.* to contemn; to despise; to spurn. **-ful** *a.* **-fully** *adv.* [O.Fr. *escarnir*].

Scor·pi·o (skawr′.pi.ō) *n.* Scorpion, 8th sign of zodiac; scorpion. **-n** *n.* insect allied to spiders having slender tail which ends in very acute sting; whip armed with points like scorpion's tail; vindicative person with virulent tongue [L.].

scot (skȧt) *n.* formerly, tax, contribution, fine. **—free** *a.* unhurt; exempt from payment [O.N. *skot*, a tax].

Scot (skȧt) *n.* native of Scotland [O.E. *Scottas* (*pl.*) Irishmen].

Scotch (skȧch) *a.* pert. to Scotland or its inhabitants; Scots (adj. form usually preferred in Scotland); Scottish; *n.* Scots; Scots dialect; Scotch whiskey. **— broth,** broth made of pearl barley, various vegetables and beef for seasoning. **— pine,** Northern pine and Baltic fir or pine. **-man** *n.* a Scotsman. **— terrier,** small short-legged, rough-coated dog.

scotch (skȧch) *v.t.* to support, as a wheel, by placing some object to prevent its rolling; to prevent progress being made; to kill project in its initial stages; *n.* prop., wedge, strut.

scotch (skȧch) *v.* to wound slightly; to cut; *n.* scratch; mark or score.

Scots (skȧts) *n.* dialect of English spoken in lowland Scotland; *a.* pert. to Scotland; Scottish. **-man, -woman** *n.* [O.E. *Scottas*].

Scot·tish (skȧt′·ish) *a.* pert. to Scotland or its people; Scots; Scotch [O.E. *Scottas*].

scoun·drel (skoun′dral) *n.* rascal; villain. **-ly** *a.* [etym. uncertain].

scour (skour) *v.t.* to clean or polish the surface of, by hard rubbing; to purge violently; to flush out; *v.i.* to clean by rubbing; *n.* act or material used in scouring. **-er** *n.* [O.Fr. *escurer*].

scour (skour) *v.t.* to pass rapidly along or over in search of something; to range; *v.i.* to scamper; to rove over; to scurry along. **-er** *n.* [etym. uncertain].

scourge (skurj) *n.* whip made of leather thongs; lash; punishment; a grievous affliction; one who or that which inflicts pain or devastates country; *v.t.* to flog; to lash; to chastise; to torment [L. *excoriare*].

scout (skout) *n.* one sent out to reconnoiter; lookout; a Boy Scout or Girl Scout; reconnaissance airplane; *v.t.* to reconnoiter; to spy out. **-master** *n.* adult instructor and organizer in the Boy Scouts [O.Fr. *escoute,* fr. *escouter,* to listen].

scout (skout) *v.t.* to reject with contempt; to sneer at [O.N. *skuta,* a taunt].

scow (skou) *n.* large flat-bottomed barge, with square ends; lighter [Dut. *schouw*].

scowl (skoul) *v.i.* to wrinkle brows in displeasure; to frown gloomily or sullenly; to look sullen, or annoyed; *n.* an angry frown [Scand.].

scrab·ble (skrab′·l) *v.t.* to scribble; to scrawl; *v.i.* to scratch with hands; [var. of *scrapple,* frequentative of *scrape*].

scrag (skrag) *n.* anything thin, lean, gaunt, or shrivelled; (*Slang*) long, thin neck; lean end of neck of mutton; *v.t.* (*Slang*) to wring neck of; to hang; to execute. **-ged** *a.* lean; thin. **-gedness, -giness** *n.* **-gily** *adv.* **-gly** *a.* rough and unkempt. **-gy** *a.* lean; jagged [earlier *crag*].

scram (skram) *interj.* (*Slang*) clear out′

scramble (skram′·bl) *v.t.* to move by crawling, climbing, etc. on all fours; to clamber; to struggle with others for; *v.t.* to collect together hurriedly and confusedly; to cook eggs by stirring when broken, in frying pan; *n.* scrambling; disorderly proceeding. **scrambling** *a.*

scrap (skrap) *n.* small detached piece or fragment; material left over which can be used as raw material again; *pl.* odds and ends; *v.t.* to make into scraps; to discard; *pa.t.* and *pa.p.* **-ped.** *pr.p.* **-ping. -book** *n.* a blank book in which to put clippings, pictures, etc. **-heap** *n.* a rubbish heap; pile of old iron, etc. **-py** *a.* consisting of scraps; fragmentary [O.N. *skrap*].

scrap (skrap) *n.* and *v.i.* (*Slang*) fight; quarrel. **-pily** *adv.* **-piness** *n.* [var. of *scrape*].

scrape (skrāp) *v.t.* to abrade; to grate; to scratch; to remove by rubbing; to clean or smooth thus; *v.i.* to produce grating noise; to live parsimoniously; to bow awkwardly with drawing back of foot; to scratch in earth, as fowls; *n.* act or sound of scraping; scratch; predicament; embarrassing situation. **-r** *n.* one who, or that which, scrapes; tool with thin blade for scraping [O.E. *scrapian*].

scratch (skrach) *v.t.* to score or mark a narrow surface wound with claws, nails, or anything pointed; to abrade skin; to erase; to scrape; to withdraw name of entrant for race or competition; to write in a hasty, careless manner; to rub an itchy spot; *v.i.* to use claws or nails in tearing, abrading, or shallow digging; to strike out one's name from list of competitors; *n.* slight wound, mark, or sound made by sharp instrument; mark indicating the starting point in a handicap race; one who concedes a start in distance, time, etc. to other competitors; *a.* taken at random, brought together in a hurry, as *a scratch team;* denoting competitor without handicap. **-er** *n.* **-y** *a.* [mixture of earlier *scrat* and *cratch,* both of Teut. origin].

scrawl (skrawl) *v.t.* to write or draw untidily; to scribble; *v.i.* to write unskillfully; *n.* hasty, careless writing; **-er** *n.* [perh. fr. *scrabble*].

scraw·ny (skraw′·ni·) *a.* lean; scraggy; rawboned. **scrawniness** *n.* [var. of *scranny*].

scream (skrēm) *v.t.* and *v.i.* to utter a piercing cry; to shriek; to laugh immoderately; *n.* a shrill, piercing cry; a person who excites much laughter; laughter-provoking incident. **-ing** *a.* [imit. origin].

scree (skrē) *n.* pile of débris at base of cliff or hill; a talus [etym. uncertain].

screech (skrēch) *v.i.* to utter a harsh, shrill cry; *n.* a shrill and sudden, harsh cry. **— owl** *n.* owl with persistent harsh call [earlier *scritch,* of imit. origin].

screed (skrēd) *n.* long letter or passage; long boring speech [O.E. *screade,* a shred].

screen (skrēn) *n.* covered frame to shelter from heat, light, draft, or observation; partition of stone, metal, or wood, cutting off one part of ecclesiastical building from the rest; coarse, rectangular sieve for grading coal, pulverized material, etc.; white surface on which image is projected by optical means; troops thrown out towards enemy to protect main body; *v.t.* to provide with shelter or concealment; to protect from blame or censure; to sift; to film; to project film, latern slide, etc. on a screen; to subject a person to political scrutiny. **-ing** *n.* employing a metal sheath to screen a magnetic field from the outside surroundings; (*Nuclear Physics*) reduction in intensity of radiations on passing through matter. **the screen,** the movies. **smoke screen** *n.* dense smoke artificially disseminated to conceal movements [O. Fr. *escran*].

screw (skrȯȯ) *n.* in mechanics, a machine consisting of an inclined plane wound round a cylinder; cylinder with a spiral ridge running round it, used as holding agent or as mechanical power; turn of screw; twist to one side; a screw propeller; *v.t.* to fasten with screw; to press or stretch with screw; to work by turning; to twist round; to obtain by pressure; to extort; *v.i.* to assume a spiral motion; to move like a screw. **-driver** *n.* tool for turning screws. **-ed** *a.* **-er** *n.* **-ing** *a.* **— propeller** *n.* revolving shaft carrying two or more symmetrically arranged fan-like blades or flanges to create forward thrust of a ship. **— thread** *n.* spiral ridge, triangular or rectangular in section, on a screw cylinder. **-y** *a.* tortuous, like the thread or motion of a screw; (*Slang*) crazy; daft [O.Fr. *escroue*].

scrib·ble (skrib′·l) *v.t.* and *v.i.* to write carelessly; to draw meaningless lines; to scrawl; *n.* something scribbled. **-r** *n.* bad or careless writer; a writer of unimportant trifles; **scribbling** *a.* used for scribbling; *n.* careless writing [L. *scribere,* to write].

scribe (skrīb) *n.* a writer; official or public

writer; clerk; copyist; official copyist and expounder of Mosaic and traditional Jewish law; *v.t.* to incise wood, metal, etc. with a sharp point as a guide to cutting; **scribal** *a.* pert. to a scribe. **-r** *n.* sharp-pointed instrument used to mark off work [L. *scribere*, to write].

scrim·mage (skrim′·ij) *n.* a confused struggle; a tussle for the ball in football [Cf. *skirmish*].

scrimp (skrimp) *v.t.* to make too short or small; to stint.**-ed** *a.* **-ily** *adv.* **-iness** *n.* **-y** *a.* [O.E. *scrimman*, to shrink].

scrim·shaw (skrim′·shaw) (*Naut.*) *v.t.* and *v.i.* to make decorative article out of bone, whale's tooth, shell, etc.; *n.* such work.

scrip (skrip) *n.* a writing; interim certificate of holding bonds, stock, or shares [var. of *script*].

script (skript) *n.* kind of type, used in printing and typewriting, to imitate handwriting; handwriting; text of words of play, or of scenes and word of film; text of spoken part in broadcast; (*Law*) original or principal document [L. *scribere, scriptum*, to write].

scrip·ture (skrip′·chẹr) *n.* anything written; sacred writing; passage from Bible. **the Scriptures,** Old and New Testaments. **scriptural, scripture** *a.* according to Scriptures; biblical [L. *scribere, scriptum*, to write].

scrive·ner (skriv′·ạn·ẹr) *n.* rotary [L. *scribere*, to write].

scrof·u·la (skráf′·yạ·lạ) *n.* a tuberculous condition most common in childhood. **scrofulitic, scrofulous** *a.* [L. = a little sow]

scroll (skrōl) *n.* roll of paper or parchment; a list; flourish at end of signature; ornament consisting of spiral volutes; (*Her.*) motto-bearing ribbon or inscription. **-ed** *a.* formed like, or contained in, a scroll [O.Fr. *escrou*].

scro·tum (skrō′· tạm) *n.* external muscular sac which lodges testicles of the male.

scrounge (skrounj) *v.t.* and *v.i.* (*Slang*) to pilfer. **-r** *n.* **scrounging** *n.*

scrub (skrub) *v.t.* to clean with a hard brush, etc. and water; to scour; to rub; *v.i.* to clean by rubbing; to work hard for a living; *pa.t.* and *pa.p.* **-bed.** *pr.p.* **-bing.** *n.* act of scrubbing [D. *schrubben*].

scrub (skrub) *n.* stunted growth of trees and shrubs; an animal of unknown or inferior breeding; *a.* stunted; inferior; (*Sports*) pert. to a substitute team without training. **-by** *a.* mean and small; stunted; covered with scrub; unshaved [var. of *shrub*].

scruff (skruf) *n.* the back of the neck; nape. Also **skruff** (etym. uncertain].

scrump·tious (skrump′·shạs) *a.* (*Slang*) delicious; delightful; nice.

scrunch (skrunch) *v.t.* to crush with the teeth; to crush [fr. *crunch*].

scru·ple (skrò͝ò′·pl) *n.* very small quantity; feeling of doubt; conscientious objection; qualm; *v.i.* to hesitate from doubt; to have compunction. **scrupulous** *a.* extremely conscientious; attentive to small points. **scrupulously** *adv.* **scrupulousness, scrupulosity** *n.* [L. *scrupulus*].

scru·ti·ny (skrò͝ò′·tạ·ni·) *n.* close search; critical examination; searching look or gaze. **scrutator** *n.* one who examines closely. **scrutinate, scrutinize** *v.t.* to examine into critically [L. *scrutari*, to examine closely].

scud (skud) *v.i.* to move quickly; to run before a gale; *pr.p.* **-ding.** *pa.t.* and *pa.p.* **-ded.** *n.* act of moving quickly; ragged cloud drifting rapidly in strong wind [Scand.].

scuff (skuff) *v.t.* to graze against; *v.i.* to shuffle along without raising the feet. *n.* a mark left by scuffing; a flat slipper with covering only over toes [Sw. *skuffa*, to push].

scuf·fle (skuf′·l) *v.i.* to struggle at close quarters; to fight confusedly; to shuffle along; *n.* confused fight, or struggle; a shuffling. **-r** *n.* [Sw. *skuffa*, to push].

scull (skul) *n.* short light oar pulled with the one hand; light racing boat of a long, narrow build; *v.t.* to propel boat by two sculls; to propel boat by means of oar placed over stern and worked alternately, first one way and then the other [O.Fr. *escuelerie*, fr. *escuele*, a dish].

scul·lion (skul′·yạn) *n.* (*Arch.*) male underservant who performed menial work; low, mean, dirty fellow [O.Fr. *escouillon*, a dishcloth].

sculp·ture (skulp′·cher) *n.* art of reproducing objects in relief or in the round out of hard material by means of chisel; carved work; art of modeling in clay or other plastic material, figures or objects to be later cast in bronze or other metals; *v.t.* to represent by sculpture. **sculptor** *n.* (*fem.* **sculptress**) one who carves or molds figures. **sculptural** *a.* [L. *sculpere, sculptum*, to carve].

scum (skum) *n.* impurities which rise to surface of liquids; foam or froth of dirty appearance; vile person or thing, riffraff; *v.t.* to take scum off; to skim; *v.i.* to form scum. *pr.p.* **-ming.** *pa.t.* and *pa.p.* **-med, -my** *a.* covered with scum; low-bred [Dan. *skum*, froth].

scup·per (skup′·ẹr) *n.* channel alongside bulwarks of ship to drain away water from deck; [O.Fr. *escopir*, to spit out].

scurf (skurf) *n.* dry scales or flakes formed on skin; anything scaly adhering to surface. **-y** *a.* covered with scurf [O.E. *sceorf*].

scur·ril·ous (skur′·i·lạs) *a.* indecent; abusive; vile. **-ness, scurrility** *n.* vulgar language; vile abuse. **-ly** *adv.* [L. *scurrilis*].

scur·ry (skur′·i·) *v.i.* to hurry along; to run hastily. **-ing** *n.* [fr. *scour*].

scur·vy (skur′·vi·) *n.* deficiency disease due to lack of vitamin C; (*Med.*) scorbutus; *a.* afflicted with the disease; mean; low; vile. **scurvily** *adv.* in a scurvy manner. **scurviness** *n.* [fr. *scurf*].

scut (skut) *n.* a short tail, as that of a hare [O.N. *skjota*, to jut out].

scu·tate (skū′·tāt) *a.* (*Bot.*) shield-shaped; (*Zool.*) protected by scales or shieldlike processes [L. *scutum*, a shield].

scutch·eon. See **escutcheon.**

scu·tel·lum (skū·tel′·ạm) *n.* horny plate or scale. **scutellate, -d** *a.* (*Bot.*) rounded and nearly flat, like a saucer. **scutelliform** *a.* scutellate. **scutiform** *a.* (*Bot.*) shield-shaped [L. = a *salver*].

scut·tle (skut′·l) *n.* wide-mouthed vessel for holding coal [O.E. *scutel*].

scut·tle (skut′·l) *n.* hole with a cover, for light and air, cut in ship's deck or hatchway; hinged cover of glass to close a port-hole; *v.t.* to make holes in ship, esp. to sink it. **-butt** *n.* (*Naut.*) a water cask; (*Slang*) rumor [O.Fr. *escoutille*, a hatchway].

scut·tle (skut′·l) *v.i.* to rush away; to run hurriedly [freq. of *scud*].

scythe (sīTH) *n.* mowing implement; *v.t.* to cut with scythe; to mow [O.E. *sithe*].

sea (sē) *n.* mass of salt water covering greater part of earth's surface; named broad tract of this; certain large expanses of inland water, when salt; billow, or surge; swell of ocean; vast expanse; flood; large quantity. **— anemone** *n.* beautifully colored radiate marine animal, found on rocks on seacoast. **-board** *n.* coastline and its neighborhood; seashore. **—borne** *a.* carried on the sea or on a seagoing vessel. **— breeze** *n.* one which blows from sea toward land. **-coast** *n.* shore or border of land adjacent to sea. **— dog** *n.* dogfish; seal; pirate; old, experienced sailor. **-faring** *a.* **-girt** *a.* encircled by the sea. **-going**

a. pert. to vessels which make long voyages by sea. — **green** *a.* having color of sea water; being of faint green color, with a slightly bluish tinge. — **gull** *n.* any gull. — **horse** *n.* a small fish, allied to pipedish, with horselike head; the walrus; fabulous animal, part horse, part fish. — **legs** *n.pl.* ability to walk on ship's deck in spite of rough seas. — **level** *n.* level of the sea taken at mean tide. — **lion** *n.* lion-headed, eared type of seal, eared seal. **-man** *n.* a sailor. **-manlike, -manly** *a.* **-manship** *n.* art of managing and navigating properly ship at sea. **-plane** *n.* airplane which can take off from and alight on sea. **-port** *n.* town with harbor. — **power,** command of the seas; nation with powerful fleet. **-scape** *n.* a picture representing maritime scene or view. — **serpent** *n.* enormous marine animal of serpenting form said to inhabit ocean. — **shell** *n.* a marine shell. **-shore** *n.* land adjacent to sea; (*Law*) ground between ordinary high-water mark and low-water mark. **-sick** *a.* suffering from seasickness. **-sickness** *n.* a disturbance of the nervous system with nausea and vomiting, produced by rolling and pitching of vessel at sea. **-side** *n.* and *a.* land adjacent to the sea. — **wall** *n.* embankment to prevent erosion or flooding. **-ward** *a.* and *adv.* towards the sea. **-weed** *n.* collective name for large group of marine plants (Algae). **-worthy** *n.* fit for proceeding to sea; able to stand up to buffetings of waves. **-worthiness** *n.* **at sea,** on the ocean; away from land; bewildered. **high seas,** the open sea [O.E. *sae*].

seal (sēl) *n.* an aquatic carnivorous animal with flippers as limbs, of which the eared variety furnishes rich fur pelt as well as oil; *v.i.* to hunt for seals. **-er** *n.* ship, or person, engaged in seal fishing. **-ery** *n.* seal-fishing station. **-skin** *n.* dressed skin or fur of eared seal; *a.* made of sealskin [O.E. *seolh*].

seal (sēl) *n.* piece of metal or stone engraved with a device, cipher, or motto for impression on wax, lead, etc.; impression made by this (on letters, documents, etc.); that which closes or secures; symbol, token, or indication; arrangement for making drainpipe joints airtight; *v.t.* to affix a seal to; to confirm; to ratify; to settle, as doom; to shut up; to close up joints, cracks, etc. **-ed** *a.* having a seal affixed; enclosed; ratified. **-ing wax** *n.* wax composed of shellac or other resinous substances and turpentine tinted with coloring matter. — **ring** *n.* a signet ring. [O.Fr. *seel*, fr. L. *sigillum*, a seal].

seam (sēm) *n.* line of junction of two edges, e.g. of two pieces of cloth, or of two planks; thin layer or stratum, esp. of coal; *v.t.* to join by sewing together; to mark with furrows or wrinkles; to scar. **-less** *a.* having no seams; woven in the piece. **-ster** *n.* (*fem.* **-stress, sempstress**) one who sews by profession. **-y** *a.* showing seams; sordid [O.E. fr. *siwian*, to sew].

sé·ance (sā′·àns) *n.* essembly; meeting of spiritualists for consulting spirits and communicating with 'the other world' [Fr.].

sear (sir) *v.t.* to scorch or brand with a hot iron; to dry up; to wither; to render callous; to brown meat quickly *a.* (*Poetic.*) dry; withered [O.E. *searian*].

search (surch) *v.t.* to look over or through in order to find; to probe into; *v.i.* to look for; to seek; to explore; *n.* searching; quest; inquiry; investigation. **-ing** *a.* thorough; penetrating; keen; minute. **-ingly** *adv.* **-ingness** *n.* **-light** *n.* electric arc-light which sends concentrated beam in any desired direction. — **warrant** *n.* warrant to enable police to search premises of suspected person [Fr. *chercher*, to look for].

sea·son (sē′·zn) *n.* one of four divisions of year—spring, summer, autumn, winter; in tropical regions, the wet or dry period of year; busy holiday period; time of the year for certain activities, foods, etc.; convenient time; period; time; *v.t.* to render suitable; to habituate; to give relish to; to spice; to mature; *v.i.* to grow fit for use; to become adapted. **-able** *a.* suitable or appropriate for the season; opportune; timely; fit. **-ableness** *n.* **-ably** *adv.* **-al** *a.* depending on, or varying with, seasons. **-ally** *adv.* **-ing** *n.* flavoring. — **ticket** *n*, one valid for definite period. **open season,** time when something is permitted [L. *satio*, sowing].

seat (sēt) *n.* thing made or used for sitting; manner of sitting (of riding, etc.); right to sit (e.g. in council, etc.); sitting part of body; part of trousers which covers buttocks; locality of disease, trouble, etc.; country house; place from which a country is governed; *v.t.* to place on a seat; to cause to sit down; assign a seat to; to fit up with seats; to establish. **-ed** *a.* fixed; confirmed; settled. [O.N. *saeti*].

se·ba·ceous (si·bā′·shạs) *a.* made of, or pert. to tallow or fat; secreting oily matter [L. *sebum*, tallow].

se·cant (sē′·kant, kạnt) *a.* cutting; dividing into two parts; *n.* any straight line which cuts another line, curve, or figure; a straight line drawn from center of circle through one end of an arc, and terminated by a tangent drawn through other end; in trigonometry, ratio of hypotenuse to another side of a right-angled triangle is secant of angle between these two sides. [L. *secare*, to cut].

se·cede (si·sēd′) *v.i.* to withdraw formally from federation, alliance, etc. **-er** *n.* **secession** *n.* seceding from fellowship, alliance, etc.; withdrawal; departure [L. *secedere*, to go apart].

se·clude (si·klòòd′) *v.t.* to shut up apart; to guard from or to remove from sight or resort. **-d** *a.* shut off; remote; sequestered. **-dly** *adv.* **seclusion** *n.* **seclusive** *a.* tending to seclude; retiring [L. *secludere*, to shut away].

sec·ond (sek′·ạnd) *a.* next to first; other; another; inferior; subordinate; *n.* one who, or that which, follows the first; one next and inferior; one assisting, esp. principal in duel or boxing-match; sixtieth part of a minute; (*Mus.*) interval contained between two notes on adjacent degrees of the staff; moment; *n.pl.* inferior quality of commodity or article; *v.t.* to support, esp. a motion before a meeting or council; to back; to encourage.**Second Advent,** belief that Christ will return to earth in visible form. —**best** *n.* and *a.* best except one. — **childhood,** dotage, senility. —**class** *a.* of an inferior order; mediocre. —**hand** *a.* not new; having been used or worn; indirect. — **lieutenant** *n.* lowest commissioned rank in Army. **-ly** *adv.* in the second place. — **nature,** acquired habit. —**rate** *a.* of inferior quality, value, etc. — **sight** *n.* prophetic vision. **to play second fiddle,** to play or act subordinate part [L. *secundus*].

sec·ond·ar·y (sek′·ạn·der·i·) *a.* succeeding next in order to the first; of second place, origin, rank; second-rate; inferior; unimportant; pert. to education and schools intermediate between elementary schools and university; (*Geol.*) relating to Mesozoic period; *n.* one who occupies a subordinate place. — **color,** color obtained by combination of primary colors, blue, red, and yellow. **secondarily** *adv.* in a secondary or subordinate manner; not primarily. [fr. *second*].

se·cret (sē′·krit) *a.* kept or meant to be kept from general knowledge; concealed; unseen; private; *n.* something kept secret or concealed; a mystery; governing principle known only to initiated. **secrecy** *n.* keeping or being kept secret; fidelity in keeping a secret; retirement; privacy; concealment. **-ly** *adv.* **-ness** *n.* secrecy. **secretive** (or ·krē′·) *a.* uncommunicative; reticent; underhand. **-ively** *adv.* **-iveness** *n.* [L. *secretus*, separated].

sec·re·tar·y (sek′·ra̤·ter·i·) *n.* one employed to deal with papers and correspondence, keep records, prepare business, etc.; confidential clerk; official in charge of a particular department of government; a desk with bookshelves on top. **secretarial** *a.* pert. to duties of a secretary. **secretariat** *n.* administrative office or officials controlled by secretary; the secretarial force of an office. **-ship** *n.* office or post of a secretary [L. *secretum* (something) secret].

se·crete (si·krēt) to hide or conceal; of gland, etc. to collect and supply particular substance in body; *a.* separate; distinct. **secreta** *n.pl.* products of secretion. **secretion** *n.* substance elaborated by gland out of blood or body fluids; process of so secreting or elaborating. **secretional** *a.* **secretive** *a.* promoting or causing secretion. **secretor** *n.* a secreting organ or gland. **secretory** *a.* [L. *secernere, secretum*, to set apart].

sect (sekt) *n.* religious denomination; followers of philosopher or religious leader; faction. **-arian** *a.* pert. to a sect; *n.* one of a sect; a bigot; a partisan. **-arianism** *n.* devotion to the interests of a sect. **-ary** *n.* one of a sect; a dissenter [L. *secta*, fr. *sequi*, to follow].

sec·tion (sek′·sha̤n) *n.* cutting or separating by cutting; part separated from the rest; division; portion; a piece; a subdivision of subject matter of book, chapter, statute; printer's reference mark (§) used for footnotes; representation of portion of building or object exposed when cut by imaginary vertical plane so as to show its construction and interior; surveyor's scaled drawing showing variations in surface level of ground along base-line; *(Geom.)* plane figure formed by cutting a solid by another plane; line formed by intersection of two surfaces; distinct part of a city, country, people, etc.; small military unit; (*Bot.* and *Zool.*) thin, translucent slice of organic or inorganic matter mounted on slide for detailed microscopic examination. **-al** *a.* pert. to, made up of sections; partial; local; (of paper) ruled in small squares. **-alism** *n.* partial regard for limited interests of one particular class at expense of others. **-ally** *adv.* **-ize** *v.t.* to divide out in sections [L. *secare, sectum*, to cut].

sec·tor (sek′·te̤r) *n.* portion of circle enclosed by two radii and the arc which they intercept; mathematical instrument; *(Mil.)* a subdivision of the combat area. **-al** *a.* [L. *secare, sectum*, to cut].

sec·u·lar (sek′·ya̤·le̤r) *a.* worldly; temporal, as opposed to spiritual; lay; pert. to anything not religious; lasting for, occurring once in, a century or age; *n.* layman; clergyman, not bound by vow of poverty and not belonging to religious order. **-ization** *n.* **secularize** *v.t.* to convert from spiritual to secular use; to make worldly. **secularism** *n.* ethical doctrine which advocates a moral code independent of all religious considerations or practices. **-ist** *n.* **-ity** *n.* worldliness; secularism. **-ly** *adv.* [L. *saecularis*, fr. *saeculum*, an age, a century].

se·cure (si·kūr′) *a.* free from care, anxiety, fear; safe; fixed; stable; in close custody; certain; confident; *v.t.* to make safe, certain, fast; to close, or confine, effectually; to gain possession of; to obtain; to assure. **securable** *a.* **securance** *n.* assurance; act of securing. **-ly** *adv.* **-ness** *n.* free from anxiety; feeling of security. **-r** *n.* **security** *n.* being secure; what secures; protection; assurance; anything given as bond, caution, or pledge. **Security Council** *n.* branch of United Nations Organization, set up in 1945, to settle international disputes and to prevent aggression. **securities** *n.pl.* general term for shares, bonds, stocks, debentures, etc.; documents giving to holder right to possess certain property [L. *securus*, fr. *se-*, without; *cura*, care].

se·dan (si·dan′) *n.* old-time closed conveyance with a chair inside for one, carried on two poles; a sedan chair; a closed automobile with two full seats [orig. made at *Sedan*, France].

se·date (si·dāt′) *a.* staid; not excitable, composed; calm. **-ly** *adv.* **-ness** *n.* **sedative** *a.* tending to calm; soothing; *n.* agent, external or internal, which soothes [L. *sedare*, to calm].

sed·en·tar·y (sed′·a̤n·ter·ī·) *a.* sitting much; requiring sitting posture, as certain forms of employment; inactive. **sedentariness** *n.* [L. *sedere*, to sit].

sedge (sej) *n.* any marshgrass. **sedgy** *a.* [O.E. *secg*].

sed·i·ment (sed′·a̤·ma̤nt) *n.* matter which settles to bottom of liquid; lees; dregs. **-ary** *a.* composed of sediment, esp. of rock laid down as deposits by water action. **-ation** *n.* [L. *sedere*, to settle].

se·di·tion (si·dish′·a̤n) *n.* any act aimed at disturbing peace of realm or producing insurrection. **-ary** *n.* one who incites sedition. **seditious** *a.* pert. to, tending to excite sedition. **seditiously** *adv.* **seditiousness** *n.* [L. *seditio*, a going apart].

se·duce (si′·dūs′) *v.t.* to lead astray; to draw aside from path of rectitude and duty; to induce woman to surrender chastity; to allure. **-ment** *n.* seduction. **-r** *n.* **seducible** *a.* liable to be led astray; corruptible. **seduction** *n.* act of seducing. **seductive** *a.* **seductively** *adv.* **seductiveness** *n.* [L. *seducere*, to lead aside].

sed·u·lous (sej′·a̤·la̤s) *a.* diligent; steady; industrious; persevering. **sedulity** *n.* **-ness** *n.* **-ly** *adv.* [L. *sedulus*].

see (sē) *n.* diocese or jurisdiction of bishop; province of archbishop. **the Holy See,** the papal court [O.Fr. *siet*, fr. L. *sedere*, to sit].

see (sē) *v.t.* to perceive by eye; to behold; to observe; to form an idea; to understand; to have interview with; to visit; to meet with; *v.i.* to have the power of sight; to pay regard; to consider; to give heed; to understand; to apprehend. *pa.t.* **saw.** *pa.p.* **seen.** **-r** *n.* one who sees; one who foresees events, has second-sight; a prophet. **-ing** *conj.* considering; since; *n.* act of perceiving; sight [O.E. *seon*].

seed (sēd) *n.* ovule, which gives origin to new plant; one grain of this; such grains saved or used for sowing; that from which anything springs; origin; source; progeny; offspring; sperm; first principle; *v.t.* to sow with seed; to remove seeds from; to arrange draw for sports tournament, so that best players, etc. should not be drawn against each other in earlier rounds; *v.i.* to produce seed; to shed seed. **-ed** *a.* sown. **-ily** *adv.* in seedy manner. **-iness** *n.* being seedy; shabbiness. **-less** *a.* **-ling** *n.* young plant or tree, grown from seed. **-y** *a.* abounding with seeds; run to seed; shabby; worn out; miserable looking. **to run to seed,** to produce flowers and seed at expense of leaves or roots; to go to waste or ruin [O.E. *saed*].

seek (sēk) *v.t.* to make search or enquiry for; to look for; to ask for; to strive after; *v.i.* to make search. *pa.t.* and *pa.p.* **sought.** **-er** *n.* [O.E. *secan*].

seem (sēm) *v.i.* to appear (to be or to do); to look; to appear to one's judgment. **-ing** *a.* appearing like; apparent; *n.* appearance; apparent likeness; **-ingly** *adv.* **-liness** *n.* **-ly**

a. fit; becoming; *adv.* in a decent or proper manner [O.N. *söma*].
seen (sēn) *pa.p.* of **see.**
seep (sēp) *v.i.* to ooze; to trickle; to leak away. **-age** *n.* [O.E. *sipian,* to soak].
se·er (sē′·ęr) *n.* a prophet [fr. *see*].
seer·suck·er (sir′.suk·ęr) *n.* a cotton fabric of alternating plain and crinkled stripes [fr. Pers. *shir o shakkar* = milk and sugar].
see·saw (sē′.saw) *n.* game in which two children sit at opposite ends of plank supported in middle and swing up and down; plank for this; up-and-down motion; *a.* moving up and down or to and fro; reciprocal; *v.i.* to move up and down [imit.].
seethe (sēTH) *v.t.* to soak; *v.i.* to be in a state of ebullition; to be violently agitated; [O.E. *seothan,* to boil].
seg·ment (seg′.mąnt) *n.* part cut off from a figure by a line; part of circle contained between chord and arc of that circle; section; portion; part; *v.t.* and *v.i.* to separate into segments. **-al** *a.* relating to a segment. **-ary, -ate** *a.* **-ation** *n.* **-ed** *a.* [L. *segmentum*].
seg·re·gate (seg′.rą.gāt) *v.t.* and *v.i.* to set or go apart from the rest; to isolate; to separate; *a.* set apart; separate from the others. **segregation** *n.* [L. *segregare,* to remove from the flock (*grex*)].
se·gui·dil·la (se.gē.dē′.lyą) *n.* graceful, lively Spanish dance; music for it [Sp.].
seign·ior (sēn′.yawr), **sei·gneur** (sēn.yur′) *n.* a feudal lord of a manor; title of honor or respectful address. **-age, seignorage** *n.* anything claimed by sovereign or feudal superior as prerogative. **-ality** *n.* authority or domains of a seignior. **-ial, -ial, signorial** *a.* manorial. **grand seignor,** Sultan of Turkey [Fr. fr. L. *senior,* elder].
seine (sān) *n.* open net for sea fishing. *v.t.* to catch fish by dragging a seine through water [Fr. fr. L. *sagena,* a fishing net].
seism (sīzm) *n.* earthquake. **-al, -ic** *a.* pert. to or produced by earthquake. **-ogram** *n.* record of earthquake made by seismograph. **-ograph** *n.* instrument which records distance and intensity of slightest earth tremors. **-ologic, -al** *a.* **-ologist** *n.* one versed in seismology. **-ology** *n.* the study of earthquakes and their causes and effects [Gk. *seismos,* an earthquake].
seize (sēz) *v.t.* to grasp; to take hold of; to take possession of by force or legal authority; to arrest; to capture; to comprehend; *v.i.* to take hold. **seizable** *a.* **seizure** *n.* act of seizing; thing or property seized; sudden attack, as apoplectic stroke [Fr. *saisir*].
sel·dom (sel′.dąm) *adv.* rarely [O.E. *seldum*].
se·lect (są.lekt′) *v.t.* to choose; to cull; to prefer; *a.* of choice quality; of special excellence; chosen; picked; exclusive; *n.* the best people. **-ed** *a.* **-edly** *adv.* **-ion** *n.* selecting; things selected; variety of articles from which to select; (*Mus.*) medley; (*Biol.*) process, according to the evolutionary theory, by which certain members of species survive and others, unfit, are gradually eliminated. **-ive** *a.* having power of selection; discriminating. **-ively** *adv.* **-ivity** *n.* **-or** *n.* [L. *seligere, selectum*].
sel·e·nite (sel′ąn·īt) *n.* a colorless and translucent crystalline form of gypsum (calcium sulphate) [Gk. *selēnē,* the moon].
self (self) *n.* one's individual person; one's personal interest; ego; subject of individual consciousness; selfishness. *pl.* **selves** (selvz). *pron. affix* used to express emphasis or a reflexive usage; *a.* of color, uniform, same throughout; of same material, etc.; *prefix* used in innumerable compounds. **—abandonment** *n.* disregard of self. **—abnegation** *n.* self-denial. **—abuse** *n.* masturbation; abuse of one's own powers. **—assurance** *n.* self-confidence. **—centered** *a.* egoistic. **—confidence** *n.* whole-hearted reliance on one's own powers and resources. **—confident** *a.* **—consciousness** *n.* an embarrassed state of mind leading to confusion due to belief that one is object of critical judgment by others present. **—conscious** *a.* **—contained** *a.* of a reserved nature; complete in itself; (of a house) having a separate entrance, detached. **—control** *n.* control over oneself, temper, emotions, and desires. **—defense** *n.* the act of defending one's person or justifying one's actions. **—denial** *n.* refraining from gratifying one's desires or appetites; unselffishness, to the point of deprivation. **—determination** *n.* free will; right of a people or nation to work out its own problems and destiny, free from intereference from without. **—governing** *a.* autonomous; having a legislature elected by, and responsible to, those governed. **—government** *n.* **—indulgence** *n.* undue gratification of one's appetites or desires. **—interest** *n.* selfishness. **-ish** *a.* concerned unduly over personal profit or pleasure; lacking consideration for others; mercenary; greedy. **-less** *a.* unselfish. **—pity** *n.* morbid pleasure in nursing one's own woes. **—possessed** *a.* calm and collected; able to control one's feelings and emotions; composed; undisturbed. **—preservation** *n.* instinctive impulse to avoid injury or death. **—respect** *n.* a proper regard for one's own person, character, or reputation. **—respecting** *a.* **—respectful** *a.* **—righteous** *a.* thinking oneself faultless; esteeming oneself as better than others; pharisaical; sanctimonious. **—sacrifice** *n.* foregoing personal advantage or comfort for the sake of others. **-same** *a.* the very same; identical. **—satisfaction** *n.* personal reassurance; (in a bad sense) smug conceit. **—satisfied** *a.* **—seeker** *n.* one who seeks only his own own profit or pleasure. **—seeking** *a.* seeking one's own interest or happiness. **—starter** *n.* an automatic contrivance used for starting internal-combustion engine of automobile. **—styled** *a.* so-called, without any real warrant or authority; self-assumed. **—sufficient** *a.* sufficient in itself; relying on one's own powers. **—supporting** *a.* not dependent on others for a living [O.E.].
sell (sel) *v.i.* to dispose of for an equivalent, usually money; to deal in; to betray for money or a consideration; to delude; (*Slang*) to trick; to have for sale; to promote sale of; *v.t.* to fetch a price; to be in demand; *pa.t.* and *pa.p.* **sold.** *n.* deception; hoax. **-er** *n.* one who sells; vendor [O.E. *sellan*].
Selt·zer (selt′.sęr) *n.* a carbonated mineral water; artificial mineral water; aerated with carbon dioxide [corrupt. of *Selters*].
sel·vage, selvedge (sel′.vij) *n.* edge of cloth finished to prevent raveling; strong edging of web [for *self-edge*].
selves (selvz) *n.pl.* of **self.**
se·man·tic (są.man′.tik) *a.* pert. to meaning of words. **-s** *n.pl.* branch of linguistic research concerned with studying meaning and changes in meaning of words [Gk. *sēmainein,* to mean].
sem·a·phore (sem′.ą.fōr) *n.* a post with movable arm or arms used for signaling; a system of signaling by human or mechanical arms [Gk. *sēma,* sign; *pherein,* to bear].
se·ma·si·ol·o·gy (są.mā.si.ȧl′.ą.ji.) *n.* the science of the development of the meanings of words, semantics. **semasiological** *a.* [Gk. *sēmasia,* meaning; *logos* a discourse].
sem·blance (sem′.bląn(t)s) *n.* real or seeming likeness; appearance; image; form; figure [Fr. *sembler,* to seem].
se·men (sē′.mąn) *n.* male secretion containing sperm [L. = seed].

se·mes·ter (sạ.mes′.tẹr) *n.* one of two or three divisions of the school year [Fr. *semestre*, fr. L. *sex*, six; *mensis*, a month].

sem·i- (sem′.i) *prefix* with the meaning of half, partly, imperfectly, etc., used in the construction of compound terms, the meaning being usually obvious. **-annual** *a.* half-yearly. **-breve** *n.* (*Mus.*) a whole note. **-circle** *n.* plane figure bounded by diameter and portion of circumference of a circle which it cuts off. **-circled, -circular** *a.* **-colon** *n.* punctuation mark (;) used to separate clauses of a sentence requiring a more marked separation than is indicated by a comma. **-final** *n.* a match, round, etc. qualifying winner to contest the final. **-tone** *n.* (*Mus.*) half a tone; smallest interval used in music [L. = half].

semi·con·duc·tor (sem′•i•kȧn•dukt′•er) *n.* a solid material such as silicon which conducts electricity at high temperatures and insulates at low temperatures.

sem·i·nal (sem′.ạ.nạl) *a.* pert. to seed of plants or semen of animals; reproductive. **semination** *n.* act of sowing or disseminating; seeding. **seminiferous, seminific** *a.* seedbearing [L. *semen*, seed].

sem·i·nar (sem′.ạ.nȧr) *n.* group of advanced students pursuing research in a specific subject under supervision [L. *semen*, seed].

sem·i·nar·y (sem′.ạ.ner.i.) *n.* academy; secondary school for girls; a training college for priesthood or ministry; *a.* trained in seminary. **seminarist** *n.* [L. *seminarium*, nursery].

se·mi·ol·o·gy (sē.mi.al.a.ji.) *n.* (*Med.*) study of signs and symptoms of disease; symptomatology. **semiotics** *n.* science or language of signs. [Gk. *sēmeion*, a mark].

Sem·ite (sem′.īt) *n.* member of a speech family comprising Hebrews, Arabs, Assyrians, etc.; descendant of Shem (Genesis x). **Semitic** *a.*

sem·o·li·na (sem.ạ.lē′.nạ) *n.* hard grains of wheat used in production of spaghetti, macaroni, etc. Also **semola** [L. *simila*, wheatmeal].

sen (sen) *n.* Japanese copper coin.

sen·ate (sen′.it) *n.* supreme legislative and administrative assembly in ancient Rome; upper house of legislature, e.g. U.S., France, Canada, and others; governing or advisory body in many universities. **senator** *n.* a member of a senate. **senatorial** *a.* [L. *senatus*, council of old men, fr. *senex*, old man].

send (send) *v.t.* to cause to go; to transmit; to forward; to despatch; to throw; *v.i.* to despatch messenger; to transmit message. *pa.t.* and *pa.p.* **sent** [O.E. *sendan*].

se·nes·cence (sạ.nes′.ạns) *n.* the state of growing old; decay; old age. **senescent** *a.* growing old [L. *senescere*, to grow old].

sen·es·chal (sen′.ạ.shạl) *n.* functionary who superintended household affairs of feudal lord in Middle Ages; steward [O.Fr.].

se·nile (sē′.nīl) *a.* pert. to old age; aged; doting. **senility** *n.* degenerative physical or mental conditions accompanying old age; old age [L. *senex*, old man].

sen·ior (sēn′.yẹr) *a.* older; superior in rank or standing; pert. to highest class of school or college; *n.* a person older, or of higher rank, or of longer service, than another; an aged person; a member of a senior class. **-ity** *n.* state of being older; precedence in rank, or longer in service; priority [L. = older].

sen·na (sen′.ạ) *n.* a valuable purgative drug [Ar. *sana*].

se·ñor (sān.yawr′) *n.* Spanish form of address; sir; gentleman; equivalent to Mr.; **-a** *n.* lady; madam; Mrs. **-ita** *n.* young lady; Miss.

sen·sa·tion (sen.sā′.shạn) *n.* what we learn through senses; state of physical consciousness; effect produced on a sense organ by external stimulus; excited feeling or state of excitement; exciting event; strong impression. **sensate** *a.* perceived by the senses. **-al** *a.* pert. to perception by senses; producing great excitement and surprise; melodramatic. **-alist** *n.* **-ally** *adv.* [L. *sensus*, feeling].

sen·sa·tion·al·ism (sen.sā′.shạn.ạ.liz.ạm) *n.* matter, language or style designed to excite and please vulgar taste; sensualism. (*philos.*) doctrine that all knowledge originates in sense perception [L. *sensus*, feeling].

sense (sens) *n.* any of the bodily faculties of perception or feeling; sensitiveness of any or all of these faculties; ability to perceive; mental alertness; consciousness; significance; meaning; coherence; wisdom; good judgment; prudence. *pl.* wits; faculties; *v.t.* to perceive; to suspect; (*Colloq.*) to understand. **-less** *a.* destitute of sense; insensible; unfeeling; silly; foolish; stupid; absurd. **-lessly** *adv.* **-lessness** *n.* [L. *sentire, sensum*, to feel].

sen·si·ble (sen′.sạ.bl) *a.* capable of being perceived by the senses; characterized by good sense; perceptible; aware; conscious; appreciable; reasonable. **sensibility** *n.* power of experiencing sensation; faculty by which mind receives intuitions; capacity of feeling. **sensibly** *adv.* [fr. *sense*].

sen·si·tive (sen′.sạ.tiv) *a.* open to, or acutely affected by, external stimuli or impressions; easily affected or altered; responsive to slight changes; easily upset by criticism. **-ly** *adv.* **-ness** *n.* quality or state of being sensitive. **sensitivity** *n.* sensitiveness; keen sensibility; capacity to receive and respond to external stimuli [Fr. *sensitif*, fr. L. *sentire*, to feel].

sen·si·tize (sen′.sạ.tīz) *v.t.* to render sensitive; in photography, to render film, paper, etc. sensitive to the chemical action of light. **sensitizer** *n.* [L. *sensus*, feeling].

sen·so·ry (sen′.sạ.ri.) *a.* pert. to, or serving, senses; conveying sensations, as the nerve-fibers [L. *sensus*, feeling].

sen·su·al (sen′.shoo′.al) *a.* pert. to the senses; given to pursuit of pleasures of sense; self-indulgent; voluptuous; lewd. **-ization** *n.* **-ize** *v.t.* to make or render sensual. **-ism** *n.* fleshly indulgence. **-ist** *n.* one given to lewd or loose mode of life; **-istic** *a.* **-ity** *n.* **-ly** *adv.* **sensuous** *a.* stimulating, or apprehended by, senses. **sensuously** *adv.* **sensuousness** *n.* [L. *sensus*, feeling].

sent (sent) *pa.t.* and *pa.p.* of **send.**

sen·tence (sen′.tạns) *n.* combination of words, which is complete as expressing a thought; opinion; judgment passed on criminal by court or judge; decision; *v.t.* to pass sentence upon; to condemn. **sententious** (sen.ten′.chạs) *a.* abounding with axioms and maxims; short and energetic; pithy; moralizing [L. *sententia*, an opinion].

sen·tient (sen′.shi.ạnt) *a.* feeling or capable of feeling; perceiving by senses; sensitive. **sentience, sentiency** *n.* consciousness at a sensory level. **-ly** *adv.* [L. *sentire*, to feel].

sen·ti·ment (sen′.tạ.mạnt) *n.* abstract emotion; tendency to be moved by feeling rather than idea; opinion. **sentimental** (sen.tạ.men′.tạl) *a.* abounding with sentiment; romantic; emotional; foolishly tender. **-alism, -ality** *n.* affected and distorted expression of sentiment revealing a superficiality of feeling. **-alist** *n.* one given to sentimental talk; one swayed by emotions rather than by reason. [O.Fr. *sentement*, fr. L. *sentire*, to feel].

sen·ti·nel (sen′.tạ.nạl) *n.* guard; sentry; *a.* acting as sentinel; watching [Fr. *sentinelle*].

sen·try (sen′.tri.) *n.* soldier on guard; sentinel; duty of sentry. **— box** *n.* small shelter used by sentry [fr. *sanctuary*, a place of safety].

se·pal (sē′.pạl) *n.* (*Bot.*) leaf-like member of outer covering, or calyx, of flower. **-ous** *a.*

having sepals [Fr. *sépale*].

sep·a·rate (sep′·ạ·rāt) *v.t.* to part in any manner; to divide; to disconnect; to detach; to withdraw; to become disunited; *a.* divided; disconnected; apart; distinct; individual. **separability** *n.* **separable** *a.* **-ly** *adv.* **-ness** *n.* **separation** *n.* act of separating; state of being separate. **separationist** *n.* one who supports policy of breaking away from a union of states or countries; a separatist. **separatism** *n.* act or policy of separating or withdrawing from any union, esp. religious or political. **separatist** *n.* [L. *separare*].

se·pi·a (sē′·pi·ạ) *n.* brown pigment obtained from ink bags of cuttlefish, uased as watercolor [Gk. = cuttlefish].

sep·sis (sep′·sis) *n.* (*Med.*) state of having bodily tissue infected by bacteria. **septic** *a.* [Gk. = putrefaction].

sept (sept) *n.* clan, race, or family, proceeding from common progenitor.

Sep·tem·ber (sep·tem′·bẹr) *n.* ninth month of year (L. *septem*, seven, as being 7th month of Roman year].

sep·te·nar·y (sep′·tạ′·nẹr·i·) a. crossing of seven; lasting seven years; occurring once in seven years. [L. *septem*, seven].

sep·tet, septette (sep·tet′) *n.* (*Mus.*) composition for seven voices or instruments [L. *septem*, seven].

sep·tic (sep′·tik) *a.* pert. to sepsis; infected. **-emia, -aemia** (sep·tạ·sē·mi·ạ) *n.* blood poisoning. **-ally** *adv.* [Gk.].

sep·tu·a·ge·nar·i·an (sep·t(y)oo·ạ·jạ·ner′·i·ạn) *n.* person between seventy and eighty years of age. **septuagenary** *a.* consisting of seventy; seventy years old; *n.* a septuagenarian [L. *septuaginta*, seventy].

Sep·tu·a·ges·i·ma (sep·t(y)oo·ạ·jes′·ạ·mạ) *n.* third Sunday before Lent, seventy days before Easter. [L. *septuagesimus*, seventieth].

Sep·tu·a·gint (sep′·too·ạ·jint) *n.* the first and only complete version in Greek of the Old Testament. **-al** *a.* [L. *septuaginta*, seventy (compilers)].

sep·tu·ple (sep′·too·pl) *a.* sevenfold; *v.t.* to multiply by seven [L. *septem*, seven].

sep·ul·cher (sep′·al·kẹr) *n.* tomb; grave; burial vault; *v.t.* to place in a sepulcher. **sepulchral** (sạ·pul′·krạl) *a.* pert. to burial, the grave, or monuments erected to dead; funereal; mournful. **sepulture** *n.* act of burying dead [L. *Sepulcrum*].

se·qua·cious (sạ·kwā′·shạs) *a.* following; attendant; easily led. **-ness, sequacity** *n.* [L. *sequi*, to follow].

se·quel (sē′·kwạl) *n.* that which follows; consequence; issue; end; continuation, complete in itself, of a novel or narrative previously published [L. *sequi*, to follow].

se·quence (sē′·kwạns) *n.* connected series; succession; run of three or more cards of same suit in numerical order; part of scenario of film; (*Mus.*) repetition of musical figure, either melodic or harmonic, on different degrees of sale. **sequent** *a.* following; succeeding; *n.* sequence. **sequential** *a.* in succession. **sequentially** *adv.* [L. *sequi*, to follow].

se·ques·ter (si·kwes′·tẹr) *v.t.* to put aside; to separate; to seclude; to cause to retire into

se·quin (sē′·kwin) *n.* small, ornamental metal disk on dresses, etc. [It. *zecchino*, fr. *zecca*, mint].

Se·quoi·a (si·kwoi′·ạ) *n.* genus of gigantic coniferous evergreen trees native to California [fr. *Sequoiah*, a Cherokee Indian chief].

se·ragl·io (si·ral′·yō) *n.* harem or women's quarters in royal household [It. *serraglio*, an enclosure, fr. L. *sera*, a bolt].

ser·aph (ser′·af) *n.* member of the highest order of angels. **-s, -im** *n.pl.* **-ic, -ical** *a.* [Heb.].

Serb, Serbian (surb, sur′·bi·ạn) *a.* pert. to Serbia; *n.* native or inhabitant of Serbia, the chief constituent state of Yugoslavia.

sere (sir) *a.* dry; withered [fr. *sear*].

ser·e·nade (ser·ạ·nād′) *n.* music of quiet, simple, melodious character sung or played at night below person's window, esp. by lover; *v.t.* to entertain with serenade. **-r** *n.* **serenata** *n.* instrumental work, between suite and symphony [It. *serenata*, fr. *sereno*, the open air].

ser·en·dip·ity (ser·ạn·dip′·ạ·ti·) *n.* knack of stumbling upon interesting discoveries in a casual manner ['The Three Princes of Serendip' by Horace Walpole].

se·rene (sạ·rēn′) *a.* clear and calm; unclouded; fair; unruffled; quiet; placid; composed. **-ly** *adv.* **-ness, serenity** *n.* condition or quality of being serene [L. *serenus*, clear].

serf (surf) *n.* under feudalism; a bondman; vassal. **-age, -dom, -hood** *n.* [L. *servus*, a slave].

serge (surj) *n.* hard-wearing worsted fabric [L. *serica*, silk].

ser·geant, sergeant (sàr′·jạnt) *n.* noncommissioned officer in army, ranking above corporal; police officer ranking above constable; officer of a law court. **-ship, sergeancy** *n.* **— at arms** *n.* officer attendant on legislative body, charged with preservation of order. **— major** *n.* highest noncommissioned officer [Fr. *sergent*, fr. L. *serviens*, serving].

se·ri·al (sir′·i·ạl) *a.* consisting of a series; appearing in successive parts or installments; *n.* a periodical publication; a tale or writing published or broadcast, etc., in successive numbers or programs. **-ize** *v.t.* to publish as a serial. **-ly, seriately** *adv.* in a regular series or order. **seriatim** (sir·ē·āt′·am) *adv.* point by point; one after another [fr. *series*].

se·ries (sir′·ēz) *n.* *s.* and *pl.* succession of related objects or matters; sequence; order; related objects or matters; sequence; set; books, bound and printed in same style, usually on kindred subjects; (*Elect.*) end-to-end arrangement of batteries or circuits which are traversed by the same current [L.].

ser·if (ser′·if) *n.* (*Printing*) a fine line at the end of the stems and arms of unconnected Roman type letters, as M, y, etc.

se·ri·ous (sir′·i·ạs) *a.* grave in manner or disposition; earnest; important; attended with danger; in earnest. **-ly** *adv.* **-ness** *n.* [L. *serius*].

ser·jeant. See **sergeant.**

ser·mon (sur′·mạn) *n.* discourse for purpose of religious instruction usually based on Scripture; serious and admonitory address. **-ic, -al** *a.* of the nature of a sermon. **-ize** *v.t.* to preach earnestly; to compose a sermon. **-izer** n. [L. *sermo*, a discourse].

se·rous (sir′·ạs) *a.* pert. to, containing, or producing serum; watery; thin. **serosity** *n.* state of being serous [L. *serum*].

ser·pent (sur′·pạnt) *n.* snake; reptile without feet; treacherous or malicious person; kind of firework; (*Cap.*) constellation in northern hemisphere (*Mus.*) bass wooden wind instrument bent in a serpentine form; *a.* deceitful treacherous. **-ine** *a.* relating to, or like, serpent; winding; spiral; meandering; crafty; treacherous; *n.* skin; *v.i.* to wind in and out like a serpent. **-inely** *adv.* [L. *serpere*, to creep].

ser·rate, serrated (ser′·āt, ·ed) *a.* notched or cut like saw, as a leaf edge. **serration** *n.* formation in shape of saw. **serrature** *n.* series of notches, like that of saw. **serriform** *a.* toothed like a saw. [L. *serra*, a saw].

ser·ried (ser′·id) *a.* in close order; pressed shoulder to shoulder [Fr. *serrer*, to lock].

se·rum (sir′·ạm) *n.* watery secretion; whey; thin straw-colored fluid, residue of plasma or liquid part of the blood; such fluid used for inoculation or vaccination [L. = whey].

serv·ant (sur′·vạnt) *n.* personal or domestic attendant; one who serves another. **civil servant,** member of the civil service; government employee [L. *servire,* to serve].

serve (surv) *v.t.* to work for; to be a servant to; to minister to; to wait on; to attend; to help; to distribute, as rations, stores, etc.; to promote; to advance; to forward; to satisfy; to deliver formally; *v.i.* to work under another; to carry out duties; to be a member of a military, naval, etc. unit; to be useful, or suitable, or enough; in tennis, to resume play by striking the ball diagonally across court; *n.* in tennis, act of serving a ball. **servable** *a.* capable of being served. **-r** *n.* one who serves; a salver or small tray [L. *servire,* to serve].

serv·ice (sur′·vis) *n.* state of being a servant; work done for and benefit conferred on another; act of kindness; department of public employment; employment of persons engaged in this; military, naval, or air-force duty; advantage; use; form of divine worship; regular supply, as water, bus, electricity, etc.; (*Law*) serving of a process or summons; turn for serving ball at tennis, etc.; a set of dishes, etc.; *v.t.* to perform service for, e.g., automobiles, etc. **-able** *a.* useful; helpful; convenient; in fair working order. **— station** *n.* a place for buying gasoline, oil, etc. and making minor repairs on automobiles. **active service,** military, naval, or air force service against an enemy. **dinner-service, table-service, tea-service,** complete set of the appropriate dishes. **the Services,** the armed forces [L. *servire,* to serve].

serv·ice (sur′·vis) *n.* a small fruit tree; the shadbush [corrupt. of L. *sorbus*].

ser·vi·ette (sur·vi·et′) *n.* a table napkin [Fr.].

ser·vile (sur′·vạl) *a.* pert. to or befitting a servant or slave; submissive; dependent; menial. **-ly** *adv.* **servility** *n.* [L. *servilis,* slavish].

ser·vi·tor (sur′·vạ.tẹr) *n.* attendant; follower or adherent. **servitude** *n.* slavery; bondage [L. *servire,* to serve].

ses·a·me (ses′·ạ·mē) *n.* annual berbaceous plant cultivated in India and Asia Minor for seeds from which oil is extracted. [Gk.].

ses·qui- (ses′·kwi) *prefix* denoting a proportion of 3:2. **-alteral, -alterate, -alterous** *a.* one and a half more. **-centennial** *a.* pert. to a century and a half; *n.* the 150th anniversary. **-pedalian** *a.* measuring a foot and a half long; applied humorously to any long cumbersome technical word or to one given to using unnecessarily long words. **-pedalianism** *n.* [L. *sesqui,* one half more].

ses·sile (ses′·ạl) *a.* attached by the base, as a leaf; fixed and stationary [L. *sessilis,* low, fr. *sedere, sessum,* to sit].

ses·sion (sesh′·ạn) *n.* actual sitting of a court, council, etc. for transaction of business; term during which a court, council, and the like, meet for business; a period of time at school or college when a definite course of instruction is given. **-al** *a.* [L. *sessio,* fr. *sedere,* to sit].

ses·tet, seste (ses′·tet) *n.* (*Mus.*) composition for six instruments or voices; last six lines of a sonnet [L. *sextus,* sixth].

set (set) *v.t.* to put; to cause to sit; to seat; to place; to plant; to make ready; to adjust; to arrange (of hair) while wet; to fix, as precious stone in metal; to convert into curd; to extend (sail); to reduce from dislocated or fractured state, as limb; to adapt, as words to music; to compose type; to place a brooding fowl on nest of eggs; to crouch or point, as dog, to game; to clench (teeth); to stake; *v.i.* to pass below horizon; to go down; to strike root; to become fixed or rigid; to congeal or solidify; to put forth an effort; to begin. *pr.p.* **-ting.** *pa.t.* and *pa.p.* **set.** [O.E. *settan*].

set (set) *n.* a number of things or persons associated as being similar or complementary or used together, etc.; the manner in which a thing is set, hangs, or fits, as a dress; permanent change of shape or figure in consequence of pressure or cooling; an attitude or posture; young plant, cutting, or slip for planting out; direction, tendency, drift; figure of square dance; group or clique; setting of sun; equipment to form the ensemble of a scene for stage or film representation; (*Radio*) complete apparatus for reception (or transmission) of radio signals and broadcasts; (*Tennis*) series of games forming unit for match-scoring purposes; (*print.*) width of type character; a wooden or granite block or set; *a.* fixed; firm; prescribed; regular; established; arranged; appointed; obstinate; determined. **-back** *n.* check to progress [O.Fr. *sette,* sect or O.E. *settan*].

se·ta (sē′·tạ) *n.* bristle or bristlelike structure. **setaceous, setose** *a.* bristly [L. = a bristle].

set·tee (se·tē′) *n.* couch or sofa [Cf. *settle*].

set·ter (set′·ẹr) *n.* hunting, formerly dog trained to crouch or set when game was perceived [fr. *set*].

set·ting (set′·ing) *n.* fixing, adjusting, or putting in place; descending below horizon, as of sun; bezel which holds a precious stone, etc. in position; mounting of scene in play or film; background or surroundings [fr. *set*].

set·tle (set′·l) *v.t.* to put in place, order, arrangement, etc.; to fix; to establish; to make secure or quiet; to decide upon; to bring (dispute) to an end; to reconcile; to calm; to pay; to liquidate; to secure by legal deed, as a pension, annuity, etc.; to take up residence in; to colonize; *v.i.* to become fixed or stationary; to arrange; to come to rest; to (cause to) sink to bottom; to subside; to take up residence in; to dwell; to become calm; to become clear (of liquid). **-d** *a.* fixed; permanent; deeprooted; decided; quiet; methodical; adjusted by agreement. **-ment** *n.* act of settling; state of being settled; colonization; a colony; (*Law*) transfer of real or personal property to a person; sum secured to a person. **-r** *n.* one who makes his home in a new country; colonist. **settling** *n.* the act of making a settlement; act of subsiding; adjusting of matters in dispute; *pl.* sediment [O.E. *setl,* a seat].

set·tle (set′·l) *n.* long high-backed bench; settee [O.E. *setl,* a seat].

sev·en (sev′·ạn) *a.* one more than six; *n.* number greater by one than six, symbol 7 or VII; **-fold** *a.* repeated seven times; increased to seven times the size; *adv.* seven times as much or as often. [O.E. *seoton*].

sev·en·teen (sev′·ȧn·tēn) *a.* one more than sixteen; *n.* sum of ten and seven; symbol 17, or *XVII* a. and n. the seventh after the tenth [O.E. *seofontiene*].

sev·enth (sev′·ạnth) *a.* constituting one of seven equal parts; *n.* one of seven equal parts. **Seventh-day Adventists,** Christian sect observing seventh day as Sabbath. **Seventh heaven,** supreme ecstasy or beatitude. [fr. *seven*].

sev·en·ty (sev′·ạn·ti·) *a.* seven times ten; *n.* sum of seven times ten; the symbol 70 or LXX. **seventieth** *a.* constituting one of seventy equal parts [O.E. *seofontig*].

sev·er (sev′·ẹr) *v.t.* to part or divide by violence; to sunder; to cut or break off; *v.i.* to divide; to make a separation. **-able**

a. **-ance** *n.* separation; partition [Fr. fr. L. *separare*].

sev·er·al (sev′.ẹr.ạl) *a.* more than two; some; separate; distinct; various; diffierent; *pron.* several persons or things. **-ly** *adv.* apart from others [O.Fr. fr. L. *separare*].

se·vere (sạ.vir′) *a.* serious; rigidly methodical; harsh; not flowery, as style. **-ly** *adv.* **-ness, severity** *n.* sternness; harshness; rigor; austerity; intensity [L. *severus*].

Sè·vres (se′.vr) *n.* and *a.* name of a fine porcelain made at *Sèvres*, France.

sew (sō) *v.t.* to fasten together with needle and thread; to join with stitches; *v.i.* to practice sewing. **-er** *n.* one who sews. **-ing** *n.* and *a.* **-ing-machine** *n.* automatic machine adapted for all kinds of sewing operations [O.E. *seowian*].

sew·age (sòò′.ij) *n.* drainage; organic refuse carried off by a regular system of underground pipes [fr. *sewer*].

sew·er (sòò′.ẹr) *n.* underground drain or conduit to remove waste water and organic refuse. **-age** *n.* underground system of pipes and conduits to carry off surface water and organic refuse [O.Fr. *esseveur*].

sex (seks) *n.* state of being male or female; sum total of characteristics which distinguish male and female organisms; function by which most animal and plant species are perpetuated; males or females collectively. **— appeal,** what makes person sexually desirable or attractive. **-ual** *a.* pert. to sex or sexes; pert. to genital organs. **-ual intercourse,** coition. **-uality** *n.* **-ually** *adv.* [L. *sexus*].

sex-, comb. form, six.

sex·ag·e·nar·y (seks.aj.ạ.ner.i.) *a.* pert. to the number sixty; proceeding by sixties. **sexagenarian** *n.* person of age of sixty [L. *sexaginta*, sixty].

Sex·a·ges·i·ma (seks.ạ.jas′.ạ.mạ) *n.* second Sunday before Lent, sixty days before Easter **sexagesimal** *a.* *sexagesimus*, sixtieth].

sex·en·ni·al (seks.en′.i.ạl) *a.* continuing for six years; happening once every six years. Also **sextennial. -ly , sextennially** *adv.* [L. *sex*, six; *annus*, a year].

sex·tant (seks′.tant) *n.* an astronomical instrument used in measuring angular distances [L. *sextus*, sixth].

sex·ten·nial. See **sexennial.**

sex·tet, sex·tette (seks.tet′) *n.* musical composition for six voices or instruments; company of six singers or instrumentalists [L. *sex*, six].

sex·ton (seks′.tạn) *n.* church lay officer acting as caretaker and may also be grave digger [corrupt, of *sacristan*].

sex·tu·ple (seks′.yoo.pl) *a.* sixfold; six times as many; *v.t.* to multiply by six [L. *sex*, six; *plicare*, to fold].

sfor·zan·do (sfawr.tsàn′.dō) *a.* (*Mus.*) forced or pressed; strongly accented. Usually *abbrev.* to **sf., sfz.,** or denoted by symbols ∧, >. [It.].

shab·by (shab′.i.) *a.* torn or worn to rags; poorly dressed; faded; worn; mean. **shabbily** *adv.* **shabbiness** *n.* [O.E. *sceabb*, scab].

shack (shak) *n.* roughly built wooden hut; shanty [fr. *ramshackle*].

shack·le (shak′.l) *n.* metal loop or staple; U-shaped steel link with a pin closing the free ends; *pl.* fetters; manacles; anything which hampers; restraints; *v.t.* to fetter; to hamper [O.E. *sceacul*, a bond].

shad (shad) *n.* name of several species of herring family [O.E. *sceadd*].

shade (shād) *n.* partial darkness, due to interception of light; place sheltered from light, heat, etc.; screen; darker part of anything; depth of color; tint; hue; a very minte difference; *pl.* invisible world or region of the dead; Hades; *v.t.* to shelter or screen, from light or a source of heat; to darken; to dim; to represent shades in a drawing; to pass almost imperceptibly from one form or color to another. **-d** *a.* **shadily** *adv.* in shady manner. **shadiness** *n.* quality of being shady. **shading** *n.* interception of light; slight variation; light and color values in a painting or drawing. **shady** *a.* providing shade; in shade; (*Colloq.*) disreputable; not respectable; doubtful; suspicious [O.E. *sceadu*].

shad·ow (shad′.ō) *n.* patch of shade; dark figure projected by anything which intercepts rays of light; darker or less illuminated part of picture; inseparable companion; ghost; phantom; gloom; slight trace; *v.t.* to cast a shadow over; to follow and watch closely. **— boxing** *n.* boxing practice, without opponent. **-er** *n.* one who dogs the footsteps of another. **-iness** *n.* **-ing** *n.* gradation of light and color; shading. **-y** *a.* full of shadow; serving to shade; faint; unsubstantial; obscure; unreal [O.E. *sceadu*].

shaft (shaft) *n.* straight rod, stem, or handle; shank; stem of arrow; arrow; anything long and slender, as a tall chimney, the well of an elevator, vertical passage leading down to mine or excavation, etc.; part of column between base and capital; revolving rod for transmitting power; stem of feather; pole of carriage. **-ing** *n.* system of long rods and pulleys used to transmit power to machinery [O.E. *sceaft*].

shag (shag) *n.* coarse, matted wool or hair; long and coarse nap on some types of woolen fabrics; strong mixture of tobacco leaves cut and shredded for smoking; *a.* rough; shaggy. **-gedness, -giness** *n.* **-gy** *a.* covered with rough hair or wool; rough; unkempt [O.E. *sceacga*, a head of hair].

shah (shạ) *n.* *abbrev.* of Shah-in-Shah (King of Kings), the title given to the monarchs of Iran, Persia [Pers.].

shake (shāk) *v.t.* to cause to move with quick vibrations; to weaken stability of; to impair resolution of; to trill, as note in music; to agitate; *v.i.* to tremble; to shiver; to totter. *pa.t.* **shook.** *pa.p.* **-n.** *n.* shaking; vibration; jolt; severe shock to system; friendly grasping of hands by two individuals; (*Mus.*) trill; (*Colloq.*) moment. **-down** *n.* (*Colloq.*) extortion of money. **-n** *a.* weakened; agitated; cracked. **shakily** *adv.* **shakiness** *n.* **shaky** *a.* easily moved; unsteady; weak; tottering; unreliable. **to shake off,** to get rid of [O.E. *sceacan*].

shak·o (shak′.ō) *n.* military peaked headdress, shaped like truncated cone and usually plumed in front [Hung. *csako*].

shale (shāl) *n.* (*Geol.*) clay or mud become hardened and which splits into thin plates, parallel to stratification [O.E. *scealu*, scale].

shall (shall) *v.i.* and *aux.* used to make compound tenses or moods to express futurity, obligation, command, condition or intention [O.E. *sceal*].

shal·low (shal′.ō) *a.* having little depth of water; having little knowledge; superficial; *n.* place where water is of little depth; shoal, flat, or sandbank. **-ly** *adv.* **-ness** *n.*

sham (sham) *n.* any trick, fraud, or device which deludes; pretense; counterfeit; imitation; *a.* counterfeit; false; pretended; *v.t.* to counterfeit; to feign, to pretend; *v.i.* to make false pretenses. *pr.p.* **-ming.** *pa.t.* and *pa.p.* **-med** [etym. uncertain].

sham·ble (sham′.bl) *v.i.* to walk unsteadily with shuffling gait [etym. uncertain].

shame (shām) *n.* emotion caused by consciousness of something wrong or dishonoring in one's conduct or state; cause of disgrace; dishonor; ignominy; *v.t.* to cause to feel shame; to disgrace; to degrade; to force by shame (into), **-faced** *a.* bashful; modest. **-facedly** *adv.* **-facedness** *n.* **-ful** *a.* disgraceful. **-fully**

adv. **-fulness** *n.* **-less** *a.* destitute of shame; brazen-faced; immodest. **-lessly** *adv.* **-lessness** *n.* [O.E. *sceamu*].

sham·my. See **chamois.**

sham·poo (sham·pòò′) *v.t.* to wash (scalp); to massage; *n.* act of shampooing; preparation used. **-er** *n.* [Hind. *champna*, to knead].

sham·rock (sham′·ràk) *n.* small trefoil plant; national emblem of Ireland [Ir. *seamrog*, trefoil].

shang·hai (shang·hī′) *v.t.* to drug or render a man unconscious by violence so that he may be shipped as member of a crew; to bring by deceit and force; *pa.t.* and *pa.p.* **shanghaied** [*Shanghai*, China].

Shan·gri·la (shang′·gri·là) *n.* a peaceful, untroubled place to which one may escape [From the name of the hidden retreat in James Hilton's *Lost Horizon*].

shank (shangk) *n.* lower part of leg, from knee to ankle; shin-bone; stem of anchor, pipe, etc.; shaft of a column; long connecting part of an appliance. **-'s mare,** one's own legs [O.E. *sceanca*, leg].

shan·tung (shan·tung′) *n.* silk cloth with rough, knotted surface made from the wild silkworm [Chinese province].

shan·ty (shant′·i·) *n.* shabby dwelling; crude wooden building [Fr. *chantier*, a workshop].

shan·ty (shant′·i·) *n.* sailor's song. Also **chanty, chantey** [Fr. *chanter*, to sing].

shape (shāp) *v.t.* to mold or make into a particular form; to give shape to; to figure; to devise; *v.i.* to assume a form or definite pattern; *n.* form; figure; appearance; outline; pattern; mold; condition; **-able, shapable** *a.* capable of being shaped; shapely.**-less** *a.* without regular shape or form; deformed; ugly. **-lessness** *n.* **-liness** *n.* beauty of shape or outline. **-ly** *a.* [O.E. scieppan].

shard (shàrd) *n.* broken fragment, esp. of earthenware; hard wing-case of bettle. Also **sherd** [O.E. *sceard*, a fragment].

share (sher) *n.* pointed, wedge-shaped, cutting blade of plough [O.E. *scear*].

share (sher) *n.* part allotted; portion; unit of ownership in public company entitling one to share in profits; *v.t.* to give or allot a share; to enjoy with others; to apportion; *v.i.* to take a share; to partake; to participate. **-cropper** *n.* a tenant farmer, esp. in the South. **-r** *n.* [O.E. *scearu*, a cutting or division].

shark (shàrk) *n.* general name applied to certain voracious marine fishes; swindler; rapacious fellow; (*Slang*) an expert. **-skin** *n.* stiff, smooth-finished rayon fabric [etym. unknown].

sharp (shàrp) *a.* having keen, cutting edge or fine point; abrupt; having ready perception; quick; shrewd; acid; acrid; pungent; sarcastic; harsh; painful intense dealing cleverly but unfairly artful; strongly marked, esp. in outline; shrill; (*Mus.*) raised a semi-tone in pitch; *n.* acute sound, esp. note raised semitone above its proper pitch; (*Mus.*) sign indicating this; (*Colloq.*) an expert; *v.t.* and *v.i.* to raise or sound a half tone above a given tone; *adv.* punctually. **-en** *v.t.* to give a keen edge or fine point to; to make more eager or intelligent; to make more tart or acid; (*Mus.*) to raise a semi-tone. **-ener** *n.* one who, or that which, sharpens; instrument for putting fine point on lead-pencil, etc. **-er** *n.* swindler; cheat; **—eyed** *a.* very observant. **-ly** *adv.* **-ness** *n.* **-shooter** *n.* skilled, long-range marksman. **-shooting** *n.* **-sighted** *a.* **-witted** *a.* having acute mind [O.E. *scearp*].

shat·ter (shat′·ẹr) *v.t.* to break into many pieces; to smash; to disorder; *v.i.* to fly in pieces [doublet of *scatter*].

shave (shāv) *v.t.* to pare away; to cut close, esp. hair of face or head with razor; to cut off thin slices; to miss narrowly; to graze; *v.i.* to shave oneself; *pa.p.* **-d** or **-n.** *n.* act of shaving; thin slice or shaving; tool for shaving; narrow escape; close miss. **-r** *n.* one who shaves; (*Colloq.*) a young lad. **shaving** *n.* act of shaving; what is shaved off. **close** or **near shave,** very narrow escape from danger [O.E. *sceafan*, to scrape].

Sha·vi·an (shā′·vi·an) *n.* of or pertaining to George Bernard Shaw.

shawl (shawl) *n.* cloth used by women as loose covering for neck and shoulders; *v.t.* to wrap in a shawl [Pers. *shal*].

shay (shā) *n.* an obsolete one-horse carriage [var. of *chaise*].

she (shē) *pron.* this or that female; feminine pronoun of the third person; a female (used humorously as a noun); also, in compound words, as *she-bear* [O.E. *seo*].

sheaf (shēf) *n.* bundle of stalks of wheat, rye, oats, or other grain; any similar bundle; a sheave; *pl.* **sheaves.** *v.t.* to make sheaves; *v.i.* to collect and bind corn, etc. into sheaves [O.E. *sceaf*].

shear (shir) *v.t.* to clip or cut through with shears or scissors; to clip wool (from sheep); to fleece; to deprive. *v.i.* to divide by action of shears; to reap with a sickle. *pa.t.* **-ed.** *pa.p.* **-ed, shorn** *n.* (*Engineering*) stress in a body in a state of tension due to a force acting parallel with its section; shearing; curve; *pl.* a cutting instrument, consisting of two blades movable on a pin; large pair of scissors. **-er** *n.* **-ing** *n.* operation of clipping or cutting with shears; wool, etc. cut off with shears [O.E. *sceran*].

sheath (shēth) *n.* close-fitting cover, esp. for knife or sword; scabbard; thin protective covering. **-e** *v.t.* to put into a sheath; to envelop; to encase. **-ing** *n.* that which sheathes; metal covering for underwater structures as a protection against sea organisms, etc. [O.E. *scaeth*].

sheave (shēv) *n.* grooved wheel in block, etc. on which a rope works [doublet of *shive*].

sheave (shēv) *v.t.* to bind into sheaves; to sheaf [fr. *sheaf*].

shed (shed) *n.* shelter used for storage or workshop; [doublet of *shade*].

shed (shed) *v.t.* to cause to emanate, proceed, or flow out; to spill; to let fall; to cast off, as hair, feathers, shell; to spread; to radiate; *v.i.* to come off. *pr.p.* **-ding.** *pa.t.* and *pa.p.* **shed.** [O.E. *sceadan*, to divide].

sheen (shēn) *n.* gloss; glitter; brightness; light reflected by a bright surface. **-y** *a.* [O.E. *sciene*, beautiful].

sheep (shēp) *n. sing.* and *pl.* ruminant mammal, valued for its flesh and its solf fleecy wool; simple, bashful person; *pl.* pastor's church congregation. **-cote** *n.* enclosure affording shelter for sheep. **-dip** *n.* tank containing insecticide through which sheep are passed to free them from ticks; anti-parasitic solution or sheep-wash so used. **-dog** *n.* any breed of dog trained to tend and round up sheep. **-fold** *n.* sheepcote. **-ish** *a.* like a sheep; bashful; shy and embarrassed; awkwardly timid and diffident. **-ishly** *adv.* **-ishness** *n.* **-'s eyes,** fond, languishing glances. **-shank** *n.* knot or hitch for temporarily shortening rope, halyard, etc. **-shearer** *n.* one who clips wool from sheep. **-shearing** *n.* **-skin** *n.* skin of sheep; leather, parchment, or rug made from this; (*Colloq.*) diploma; **black sheep,** disreputable member of family; rogue [O.E. *sceap*].

sheer (shir) *a.* pure; unmixed; absolute; downright; perpendicular; of linen or silk, very thin; *adv.* quite; completely [O.E. *scir*, pure, bright].

sheer (shir) *v.i.* to deviate from the right course; to swerve; *n.* longitudinal, upward curvature of ship's deck towards bow or stern; a swerve [Dut. *scheren*].

sheet (shēt) *n.* any broad expanse; a broad piece of cloth spread on bed; broad piece of paper; newspaper; broad expanse of water, or the like; broad, thinly expanded portion of metal or other substance; *v.t.* to cover, as with a sheet. **— metal,** etc. *n.* metal in broad, thin sheets. **-ing** *a.* process of forming into sheets; cloths used for bed coverings; **— lightning** *n.* sudden glow appearing on horizon due to reflection of forked lightning. **—music** *n.* music printed on unbound sheets of paper [O.E. *scete*].

sheik, sheikh (shēk, shāk) *n.* Arab chief; a title of respect to Moslem ecclesiasts [Ar.].

shek·el (shek'·l)*n.* among ancient Hebrews, orig. weight, and later name of a gold or silver coin. *pl.* *(Colloq.)* money; coins; cash [Heb. *sheqel*].

shel·drake (shel'·drāk) *n.* (*fem.* **shelduck**) genus of wild duck [O.E. *sheld, variegated*; and *drake*].

shelf (shelf) *n.* board fixed horizontally on frame, or to wall, for holding things; ledge of rocks; sandbank in sea, rendering water shallow. *pl.* **shelves** (shelvz). *a.* [O.E. *scelf*].

shell (shel) *n.* hard, rigid, outer, protective covering of many animals, particularly mollusks; outer covering of eggs of birds; protective covering of certain seeds; hollow steel container, filled with high explosive, for discharging from mortar or gun; outer part of structure left when interior is removed; frail racing boat or skiff; group of electrons in atom all having same energy. **-back** *n.* old sailor. **-ed** *a.* having shell; stripped of shell; damaged by shellfire. **-fish** *n.* aquatic animal with external covering of shell, as oysters, lobster, crustacean, mollusk. **-proof** *a.* capable of withstanding bombs or high-explosives. **-shock** *n.* war neurosis, disturbance of mind and nervous system due to war conditions [O.E. *sciell*].

shel·lac (shạ·lak') *n.* refined, melted form of seed lac, obtained from resinous deposit secreted by insects on certain Eastern trees, used as varnish. *v.t.* to cover with shellac [*shel(l)* and *lac*].

shel·ter (shel'·tẹr) *n.* place or structure giving protection; that which covers or defends; a place of refuge; asylum; *v.t.* to give protection to; to screen from wind or rain; *v.i.* to take shelter. **-er** *n.* [etym. uncertain].

shelve (shelv) *v.t.* to furnish with shelves; to place on a shelf; to put aside, as unfit for use; to defer consideration of; *v.i.* to slope gradually; to incline. **shelving** *n.* [fr. *shelf*].

she·nan·i·gan (shạ·nan'·ạ·gạn) *n.* (*Slang*) nonsense. *usu. pl.* foolishness.

shep·herd (shep'·ẹrd) *n.* (*fem.* **shepherdess**) one who tends sheep; pastor of church; *v.t.* to tend sheep; to watch over and guide. **-'s-crook** *n.* long staff, with end curved to form large hook. [O.E. *sceaphirde*].

Sher·a·ton (sher'·ạ·tạn) *n.* style of furniture design distinguished for grace and beauty [Thomas *Sheraton* (1751-1806), the designer].

sher·bet (shẹr'·bạt) *n.* a frozen dessert made with fruit juices, milk, egg white or gelatin [Ar. *sharbat*, a drink].

sherd. *See* **shard.**

she·rif, shereef (shạ·rēf') *n.* a descendant of Mohammed [Ar. *sharif*, noble].

sher·iff (sher'·if) *n.* orig. governor of a shire, a 'shire-reeve' in England; chief law enforcement officer [O.E. *scirgerefa*, a shire-reeve].

Sher·pa (shẹr'·pạ) *n.* one of Nepal tribe, employed as porter or guide on Himalayan mountaineering expeditions.

sher·ry (sher'·i·) *n.* Spanish wine of deep amber color [fr. *Jerez*, near Cadiz].

Shet·land (shet'·lạnd) (*Geog.*) group of islands off N. coast of Scotland. **-er** *n.* **— pony** small breed of pony.

shib·bo·leth (shib'·bạ·leth) *n.* testword or password; a distinctive custom [Heb.].

shield (shēld) *n.* broad piece of armor carried on arm; buckler; anything which protects or defends; escutcheon or field on which are placed bearings in coats of arms; *v.t.* to protect; to defend; to screen; to ward off; to forfend [O.E. *scield*].

shift (shift) *v.t.* to change position (of); to transfer from one place to another; to move; to change gears in an automobile; *v.i.* to move; to change place, course; to change in opinion; *n.* change; evasion; expedient; squad or relay of workmen; time of their working. **-er** *n.* **-iness** *n.* trickiness of character or behavior. **-ing** *a.* changing place or position; displacing; fickle; unreliable. **-less** *a.* lacking in resource or character; aimless; not to be depended upon. **-lessness** *n.* **-y** *a.* not to be trusted; unreliable. **make-—,** to manage or contrive somehow [O.E. *sciftan*, to arrange].

Shi·ite (shē'·it) *n.* a member of the branch of Islam (mainly in Iran) that considers Mohammed's son-in-law, Ali, as his legitimate successor (See *Sunnite*). **Shiism** *n.* **Shiitic** (shē·it'·ik) *a.* [Ar. *shi'i*, follower].

shil·ling (shil'·ing) *n.* British silver coin of the value of twelve pence [O.E. *scilling*].

shil·ly-shal·ly (shil'·i·shal'·i·) *n.* vacillation; indecision; *v.i.* to hesitate or trifle; to waver. **shilly-shallier** *n.* [redupl. of *shall I*].

shim·mer (shim'·ẹr) *v.i.* to shine with faint, tremulous light; to glisten; *n.* faint, quivering light or gleam. **-ing** *n.* **-y** *a.* [O.E. *scimian*].

shim·my (shim'·i·) *n.* dance characterized by exaggerated wriggling; wobbling, as in wheel of a car; *v.i.* to wobble [fr. *chemise*].

shin (shin) *n.* forepart of leg, between ankle and knee; shank; *v.i.* to climb (up) with aid of one's arms and legs. **-bone** *n.* tibia, larger of two bones of leg [O.E. *scinu*].

shin·dig (shin'·dig) *n.* (*Colloq.*) social affair [var. of *shindy*].

shine (shīn) *v.i.* to give out or reflect light; to radiate; to sparkle; to perform in brilliant fashion; *pa.t., pa.p.* **shone;** *v.t.* to cause to shine; to polish, shoes, etc.; *pa.t., pa.p.* **-d;** *n.* brightness; gloss; (*Colloq.*) liking. **-r** (*Slang*) a black eye. **shining** *a.* glistening; splendid. **shininess** *n.* **shiny** *a.* bright; glossy; unclouded [O.E. *scinan*].

shin·gle (shing'·gl) *n.* rounded water-worn pebbles. **shingly** *a.* [Norw. *singel*].

shin·gle (shing'·gl) *n.* thin, rectangular slat for roofing and house siding; a short haircut; small signboard (esp. of physician, lawyer); *v.t.* to cover with shingles; to crop women's hair close [L. *scindula*].

shin·gles (shing'·glz) *n.pl.* (*Med.*) *herpes zoster*, viral infection of nerve ganglia, accompanied by severe pain [L. *cingulum*, a belt].

Shin·to (shin'·tō) *n.* native religion of Japan. **-ism** *n.* [Chin. *shin*, god; *tao*, the way].

ship (ship) *n.* a vessel for carriage of passengers and goods by sea; *v.t.* to engage for service on board a ship; to place object in position, as oar; to take in water (over the side); *v.i.* to transport. *pr.p.* **-ping.** *pa.t., pa.p.* **-ped. -board** *n.* deck or side of ship. **-builder** *n.* one who constructs ships; naval architect. **-building** *n.* **-master** *n.* captain **-mate** *n.* fellow sailor. **-ment** *n.* process of shipping; cargo. **-owner** *n.* **-per** *n.* one who forwards commodities. **-ping** *n.* collective body of ships in one place; mercantile vessels generally; tonnage; the business of transporting goods. **-shape** *a.* orderly, trim; *adv.* properly. **-wreck** *n.* loss of ship by accident; total destruction; ruin. **-wright** *n.* one engaged in building or repairing ships. **-yard** *n.* place where ships are built or repaired [O.E. *scip*].

shire (shīr) *n.* territorial division in Great Britain; county [O.E. *scir.* district].

shirk (shurk) *v.t.* to evade; to try to avoid (duty, etc.) **-er** *n.* one who seeks to avoid duty.

shirr (shur) *n.* in needlework, row of puckering or gathering; *v.t.* to gather with parallel threads; to bake eggs.

shirt (shurt) *n.* garment for upper part of body. **-sleeve** *a.* simple; plain. **-waist** *n.* woman's blouse. **to keep one's shirt on** (*Slang*) to be patient [O.E. *scyrfe*].

shiv·er (shiv′·er) *v.t.* to quiver or shake from cold or fear; to tremble; to shudder; *v.t.* to cause to shake; *n.* shaking or shuddering; a vibration. **-y** *a.* inclined to shiver; tremulous.

shiv·er (shiv′·ẹr) *n.* small piece or splinter; *v.t.* and *v.i.* to break into many small pieces or splinters; to shatter [M.E. *scifre*].

shoal (shōl) *n.* large number of fish swimming together; a crowd; *v.i.* to crowd together [O.E. *scolu,* company, fr. L. *schola,* a school].

shoal (shōl) *n.* a sandbank or bar; shallow water; *a.* shallow; *v.i.* to become shallow. **-y** *a.* full of shoals [O.E. *sceald,* shallow].

shoat (shōt) *n.* a young pig [M.E. *schote*].

shock (shȧk) *n.* violent impact or concussion when bodies collide; clash; percussion; conflict; emotional disturbance produced by anything unexpected, offensive, or displeasing; sudden depression of the system due to violent injury or strong mental emotion; paralytic stroke; effect of electric discharge through body; *v.t.* to strike against suddenly; to strike with surprise, horror, or disgust. **—absorber** *n.* anything to lighten a blow, shock, or ordeal. **-er** *n.* **-ing** *a.* appalling; terrifying; frightful; repulsive; offensive. **-ingly** *adv.* **—proof** *a.* able to withstand shocks [Fr. *choquer*].

shock (shȧk) *n.* disordered mass of hair; *a.* shaggy; bushy. [O.E. *scucca,* a demon].

shock (shȧk) *n.* group of sheaves of grain; *v.t.* to make into shocks [Dut. *schocke*].

shod (shȧd) *pa.t.* and *pa.p.* of verb **shoe.**

shod·dy (shȧd′·i·) *n.* inferior textile material; *a.* inferior; of poor quality.

shoe (shòò) *n.* covering for foot, but not enclosing ankle; metal rim or curved bar nailed to horse's hoof; various protective plates or under-coverings; apparatus which bears on the live rail in an electric railways in order to collect current to actuate the motor; *v.t.* to furnish with shoes; to put shoes on. *pr.p.* **-ing.** *pa.t., pa.p.* **-horn** *n.* curved piece of horn, metal, etc. used to help foot into shoe. **lace** *n.* for fastening shoe on foot. **-less** *a.* **-maker** *n.* **-r** *n.* one who makes or repairs shoes. **-string** *n.* a shoelace; (*Colloq.*) small amount of money [O.E. *scoh*].

shone (shōn) *pa.t.* and *pa.p.* of **shine.**

shoo (shòò) *interj.* begone (used esp. in scaring away fowls and other animals); *v.t.* to scare or drive away [imit.].

shook (shook) *pa.t.* of **shake.**

shoot (shòòt) *v.t.* to discharge missile from gun, etc.; to kill or wound with such a missile; to propel quickly; to thrust out; to pass swiftly over (rapids) or through (arch of bridge); to photograph episode or sequence of motion picture; *v.i.* to move swiftly and suddenly; to let off a gun, etc.; to go after game with gun; to just out; to sprout; to bud; to dart through (as severe pain); to advance; to kick towards goal. *pa.t.* and *pa.p.* **shot.** *n.* shooting; young branch or stem. **-er** *n.* **-ing** *n.* act of discharging firearms, etc.; the act of killing game. **-ing-gallery** *n.* long room for practice with rifles. **-ing-star** *n.* incandescent meteor. [O.E. *sceotan*].

shop (shȧp) *n.* building where goods are made, or sold; workshop; store *v.i.* to visit shops to purchase articles. *pr.p.* **-ping** *pa.t.* and *pa.p.* **-ped.** **-keeper** *n.* one who keeps retail shop. **-keeping** *n.* **-lifter** *n.* one who makes petty thefts from shop counters. **-ping** *n.* visiting shops with view to purchasing. **-ping-bag,** or **-basket** *n.* receptacle for holding articles purchased. **-worn** *a.* soiled or tarnished by long exposure in shop. [Fr. *échoppe,* a booth].

shore (shōr, shawr) *n.* land adjoining sea or large lake; *v.t.* to put ashore [Dut. *schor*].

shore (shōr, shawr) *n.* strong beam set obliquely against wall of building or ship to prevent movement during alterations; *v.t.* to support by post or buttress; to prop. **shoring** *n.* props for support [etym. uncertain].

shorn (shawrn) *pa.p.* of **shear;** *a.* cut off; having the hair or wool cut off [fr. *shear*].

short (shawrt) *a.* having little length; not long in space; low; not extended in time; limited or lacking in quantity; hasty of temper; crumbling in the mouth; pronounced with less prolonged accent; brief; near; concise; pithy; abrupt; destitute; crisp; *adv.* suddenly; abruptly; without reaching the end; *n.* short film to support feature film; short circuit; *pl.* short trousers reaching down to above knees. **-age** *n.* insufficient supply; deficiency. **-bread** *n.* rich cake or butter cooky. **-cake** *n.* sweetened biscuit or cake filled and topped with fruit and whipped cream. **— circuit** *n.* passage of electric current by a shorter route than that designed for it; *v.t.* to cause short circuit; to by-pass. **-coming** *n.* failing; fault; defect. **-cut** *n.* quicker but unorthodox way of reaching a place or of accomplishing a task, etc. **-en** *v.t.* to make shorter; to render friable, as shortbread, with butter or lard; to abridge; to lessen; *v.t.* to contract; to lessen. **-ening** *n.* lard, butter, or other fat used when baking pastry, etc. **-hand** *n.* system of rapid reporting by means of signs or symbols. **—handed** *a.* not having the full complement or sta ffon duty. **-horn** *n.* a breed of English cattle with short horns. **-ly** *adv.* in a brief time; soon; in a few words; curtly. **-ness** *n.* **— shrift,** summary treatment. **-sighted** *a.* not able to see distinctly objects some distance away; lacking in foresight.**—sightedly** *adv.* **-sightedness** *n.* **—tempered** *a.* easily roused to anger. **— waves** (*Radio*) electromagnetic waves whose wave length is, by international definition, between 10 and 50 meters. **—winded** *a.* affected with shortness of breath; easily made out of breath. **in short,** briefly. [O.E. *schort*].

shot (shȧt) *pa.t.* and*pa.p.* of **shoot.**

shot (shȧt) *a.* pert. to fabrics woven with warp and weft of contrasting tints or colors, so that shade changes according to angle of light [fr. *shoot*].

shot (shȧt) *n.* act of shooting; skilled marksman; one of small pellets, contained in cartridge fired from sporting rifle; heavy, solid, round missile, formerly fired from cannon; range of such missiles; charge of blasting powder; stroke in billiards, tennis, etc.; a photograph; a try to attempt; (*Slang*) injection of a drug; *v.t.* to load or weight with shot. *pr.p.* **-ting.** *pa.t.* and *pa.p.* **-ted.** **-gun** *n.* smoothbore gun for shooting small game or birds. [O.E. *sceot*].

should (shood) *v.* and *aux.* used in Future-in-the-Past tenses of verbs with pronouns I or we; auxiliary used after words expressing opinion, intention, desire, probability, obligation, etc. (Cf. *shall*).

shoul·der (shōl′·dẹr) *n.* ball and socket joint formed by humerus (bone of the upper arm) with scapula (shoulder-blade); upper joint of foreleg of animal; anything resembling human shoulder, as prominent part of hill; graded strip along edge of road; *v.t.* to push forward with shoulders; to bear (burden, etc.); to accept (responsibility); *v.i.* to push forward through crowd. **— blade** *n.* flat bone of shoulder; scapula. [O.E. *sculdor*].

shout (shout) *n.* loud, piercing cry; call for help; *v.t.* and *v.i.* to utter loud sudden cry.

shove (shuv) *v.t.* to push; to press against; to jostle; *v.i.* to push forward; to push off from shore in a boat, using oar; *n.* act of pushing; push [O.E. *scufan*].

shov·el (shuv′·l) *n.* spade wtih broad blade slightly hollowed; scoop; machine for scooping and lifting; *v.t.* to lift or move with a shovel; *v.i.* to use shovel. **-ler** *n.* [O.E. *scofl*].

show (shō) *v.t.* to present to view; to point out; to display; to exhibit; to disclose; to explain; to demonstrate; to prove; to conduct; to guide; *v.i.* to appear; to be visible; to come into sight. *pa.p.* **-n** *or* **-ed.** *n.* act of showing; that which is shown; spectacle; exhibition; display; *(Colloq.)* theatrical performance or movie. **-bill** *n.* broad sheet containing advertisement. **-bread** *n.* Same as **shewbread. -case** *n.* glass case for display of goods, museum exhibits, etc. **-down** *n.* laying down of cards, face upwards, at poker or other card games; open disclosure of truth, clarification. **-er** (shō′·ẹr) *n.* one who shows or exhibits. **-ily** *n.* **-man** *n.* one who presents a show; one who is skilled at presenting things. **-manship** *n.* **— place** *n.* place of local interest made especially attractive to draw tourists. **-room** *n.* room where goods are laid out for inspection. **-y** *a.* gaudy; attracting attention; ostentatious. **to show off,** to make an ostentatious display. **to show up,** to stand out prominently; to hold up to ridicule; to appear [O.E. *sceawian*, to look at].

show·er (shou′·ẹr) *n.* a brief fall of rain or hail; anything coming down like rain; great number; *v.t.* to wet with rain; to give abundantly; *v.i.* to rain; to pour down. **— bath** *n.* bath equipped with fine-spraying apparatus. **— proof** *a.* impervoius to rain. **-y** *a.* raining intermittently [O.E. *scur*].

shrank (shrangk) *pa.t.* of **shrink.**

shrap·nel (shrap′·nạl) *n.* shell timed to explode over, and shower bullets and splinters on, personnel; shell splinters [Gen. *Shrapnel*].

shred (shred) *n.* long, narrow piece cut or torn off; strip; fragment; scrap; *v.t.* to cut or tear to shreds; to tear into strips. *pr.p.* **-ding.** *pa.t.* and *pa.p.* **-ded** [O.E. *screade*].

shrew (shròò) *n.* noisy, quarrelsome woman; a termagant; diminutive mammal, resembling, but unrelated to, mouse. **-ish** *a.* having manners of a shrew. **-ishly** *adv.* **-ishness** *n.* [O.E. *screawa*, shrew mouse].

shrewd (shròòd) *a.* intelligent; discerning; sagacious; knowing; cunning. **-ly** *adv.* **-ness** *n.* [fr. *shrew*].

shriek (shrēk) *v.t.* and *v.i.* to scream, from fright, anguish, or bad temper; to screech; *n.* a loud, shrill cry [imit. origin].

shrift (shrift) *n.* confession made to a priest; absolution. **short shrift,** summary treatment [O.E. *scrifan*, to prescribe (penance)].

shrike (shrīk) *n.* bird which preys on birds, frogs, and insects, and impales victims on thorns; butcherbird [imit. of cry O.E. *scric*].

shrill (shril) *a.* uttering an acute sound; piercing; high-pitched; *v.i.* to sound in a shrill tone. **-y** *adv.* piercingly [M.E. *shrille*].

shrimp (shrimp) *n.* small edible crustacean allied to prawns; small person; *v.i.* to catch shrimps with net. **-er** *n.* [M.E. *shrimpe*].

shrine (shrīn) *n.* case in which sacred relics are deposited; tomb of saint; place of worship; any sacred place [L. *scrinium*, chest, box].

shrink (shringk) *v.i.* to contract; to dwindle; to recoil; to draw back; *v.t.* to cause to contract. *pa.t.* **shrank, shrunk.** *pa.p.* **shrunk. -age** *n.* act or amount of shrinking. **shrunken** *a.* narrowed in size [O.E. *scrincan*].

shrive (shrīv) *v.t.* to give absolution to; to confess (used reflexively); *v.i.* to receive or make confession *pa.t.* **-d** or **shrove.** *pa.p.* **shriven** [O.E. *scrifan*, to prescribe].

shriv·el (shriv′·l) *v.t.* and *v.i.* to cause to contract and wrinkle; to wither.

shroud (shroud) *n.* that which clothes or covers; sheet for a corpse; winding sheet; *pl.* strongest of the wire-rope stays which support mast athwartships; *v.t.* to enclose in winding sheet; to cover wtih shroud; to screen; to wrap up; to conceal [O.E. *scrud*, a garment].

shrove (shrōv) *pa.t.* of the verb **shrive. Shrovetide** *n.* period immediately before Lent, ending on Shrove Tuesday [fr. *shrive*].

shrub (shrub) *n.* any hard-wooded plant of smaller and thicker growth than tree; bush; low, dwarf tree. **-bery** *a.* collection of shrubs. **-by** *a.* of nature of shrub; full of shrubs [O.E. *scrybb*].

shrug (shrug) *v.i.* to raise and narrow shoulders in disdain, etc. *v.t.* to move (shoulders) thus. *pr.p.* **-ging.** *pa.t.* and *pa.p.* **-ged.** *n.* drawing up of shoulders [ME *schruggen*].

shrunk, shrunken See **shrink.**

shuck (shuk) *n.* husk or pod; shell of nut; *v.t.* to remove husk, pod, or shell from [Cf. *chuck*, to throw].

shud·der (shud′·ẹr) *v.i.* to tremble violently, esp. with horror or fear; to shiver; to quake; *n.* trembling or shaking. **-ing** *n.* and *a.* trembling; shivering [M.E. Cf. Ger. *schaudern*].

shuf·fle (shuf′·l) *v.t.* to shove one way and the other; to throw into disorder; to mix (cards); to scrape (feet) along ground; *v.i.* to change position of cards in pack; to prevaricate; to move in a slovenly manner; to scrape floor with foot in dancing or walking; *n.* act of throwing into confusion by change of places; artifice or pretext; scraping movement of foot in dancing. **—board** *n.* a game in which disks are shoved into numbered divisions at the end of a long playing area.

shun (shun) *v.t.* to keep clear of; to avoid. *pr.p.* **-ning.** *pa.t.* and *pa.p.* **-ned** [O.E. *scunian*].

shunt (shunt) *v.t.* to move or turn off to one side; to move (train) from one line to another; to divert (electric current); *v.i.* to go aside; to turn off. *n.* act of shunting.**-er** *n.* railway employee who shunts rolling-stock.

shut (shut) *v.t.* to close to hinder ingress or egress; to forbid entrance to; *v.i.* to close itself; to become closed. *pr.p.* **-ting.** *pa.t.* and *pa.p.* **shut.** *a.* closed; made fast. **-down** *n.* stoppage of work or activity. **-ter** *n.* one who, or that which,shuts; movable protective screen for window; automatic device in camera which allows light from lens to act on film or plate for a predetermined period. **to shut down,** to stop working; to close (business, etc.). **to shut up**, to close; to fasten securely; (*Colloq.*) to stop talking [O.E. *scyttan*].

shut·tle (shut′·l) *n.* instrument used in weaving for shooting thread of woof between threads of warp; similar appliance in sewing machine to form a lock stitch; *v.t.* and *v.i.* to move backwards and forwards. **-cock** *n.* cork with fan of feathers for use with battledore or in badminton; game itself. [O.E. *scytel*, a missile].

shy (shī) *a.* sensitively timid; reserved; easily frightened; bashful; cautious; falling short; *v.i.* to start suddenly aside. *pa.t.* and *pa.p.* **shied. -ly** *adv.* **-ness** *n.* **-ster** *n.* unscrupulous lawyer or person. [*eschif*].

shy (shī) *v.t.* to throw; to fling. *pa.t.* and *pa.p.* **shied.** *n.* throw; cast.

Si·a·mese (sī·a·mēz′) *a.* pert. to Siam, the people, or language; *n.* native of Siam; the language. **— twins,** joined twins.

sib (sib) *a.* having kinship; related by blood; akin; *n.* a blood relation [O.E. Cf. Ger. *sippe*].

Si·be·ri·an (sī·bi′·ri·ạn) *a.* pert. to Siberia, part of the Soviet Union.

sib·i·lance (sib′·ạ·lạns) *n.* hissing sound; quality of being sibilant. Also **sibilancy. sibilant** *a. n.* letter uttered with hissing of voice, as *s, x,* etc. **sibilate** *v.t.* to pronounce with hissing sound [L. *sibilare,* to whistle].

sib·yl (sib′·il) *n.* a name applied to certain votaresses of Apollo, endowed with visionary, prophetic power; prophetess; witch. **-lic, -line** *a.* [Gk. *Sibulla*].

sic (sik) *adv.* abbreviated form of *sic in originail* (Lat. = so it stands in the original) printed in brackets as guarantee that passage has been quoted correctly; so; thus[L.].

sic·ca·tion (si·kā′·shạn) *n.* act or process of drying. **siccative** *a.* drying; causing or tending to dry; *n.* a drier [L. *siccus,* dry].

Si·cil·i·an (si·sil′·yạn) *a.* pert. to island of Sicily; *n.* native of Sicily.

sick (sik) *a.* affected with physical or mental disorder; diseased; ill; ailing; tired of. **— bay** *n.* place set aside on ship for treating the sick. **— benefit** *n.* allowance made to insured person while ill and off duty. **-en** *v.t.* to make sick; to disgust; *v.i.* to become sick; to be filled with abhorrence. **-ening** *a.* causing sickness or disgust; nauseating. **-eningly** *adv.* **— headache** *n.* migraine. **-ly** *a.* somewhat sick; ailing; weak; pale; arising from ill health. **-ness** *n.* state of being sick; illness; disordered state of stomach [O.E. *seoc*].

sick·le (sik′·l) *n.* reaping hook with semi-circular blade and a short handle [L. *secula,* fr. *secare,* to cut].

side (sīd) *n.* one of surfaces of object, esp. upright inner or outer surface; one of the edges of plane figure; margin; border; any part viewed as opposite to another; part of body from hip to shoulder; slope, as of a hill; one of two parties, teams, or sets of opponents; body of partisans; sect or faction; line of descent traced through one parent; *a.* being on the side; lateral; indirect; incidental; *v.i.* (with) to hold or embrace the opinions of another; to give support to one of two or more contending parties. **— arms** *pl.* weapons carried on side of body. **-board** *n.* piece of furniture designed to hold dining utensils, etc. in dining room. **-car** *n.* small box-shaped body attached to motorcycle. **—issue** *n.* subsidiary to main argument or business. **— light** *n.* any source of light situated at side of room, door, etc.; lantern, showing red or green, on side of a vessel; incidental information or illustration. **— line** *n.* any form of profitable work which is ancillary to one's main business or profession; (*Sports*) line marking the side boundaries of playing field. **—long** *a.* lateral; oblique; not directly forward; *adv.* obliquely; on the side. **-r** *n.* **-saddle,** saddle for woman on horseback, not astride, but with both feet on one side of horse. **-show** *n.* minor entertainment or attraction; subordinate affair. **-slip** *n.* involuntary skid or slide sideways; *v.i.* to skid. **-splitting** *a.* exceedingly ludicrous and laughter-provoking. **—step** *n.* to step to one side; *v.i.* to step to one side. **-stroke** *n.* style of swimming where body is turned on one side. **-swipe** (*U.S.*) *n.* a blow with or on the side; *v.t.* to strike such a blow. **-track** *v.t.* to shunt into siding; to postpone indefinitely; to shelve; *n.* a railway siding. **siding** *n.* short line of rails on which trains are shunted from main line. **sidle** *v.i.* to move sideways; to edge

si·de·re·al (sī·di′·rē·ạl) *a.* relating to constellations and fixed stars; measured or determined by apparent motion of stars [L. *sidus, sideris,* a star].

sid·er·ite (sid′·ẹr·īt) *n.* brown ironstone [Gk. *sidēritis,* the lodestone].

siege (sēj) *n.* the surrounding of a town or fortified place by hostile troops in order to induce it to surrender either by starvation or by attack at suitable juncture; continuous effort to gain (affection, influence, etc.); *v.t.* to besiege [Fr. *siège,* seat, siege].

si·en·na (sē·en′·ạ) *n.* natural yellow earth which provides pigment. **burnt sienna,** pigment giving reddish-brown tint. **raw sienna,** pigment giving a yellowish-brown tint [fr. *Sienna,* Italy].

si·er·ra (sē·er′·ạ) *n.* chain of mountains with saw-like ridge [Sp. fr. L. *serra,* a saw].

si·es·ta (sē·es′·tạ) *n.* rest or sleep in afternoon esp. in hot countries; afternoon nap [Sp. = the sixth (hour) i.e. moon].

sieve (siv) *n.* utensil with wire netting or small holes for separating fine part of any pulverized substance from the coarse; *v.t.* to sift [O.E. *sife*].

sift (sift) *v.t.* to separate coarser portion from finer; to sieve; to bolt; to scrutinize; to examine closely [O.E. *sife,* a sieve].

sigh (sī) *v.i.* to make a deep, single respiration, as expression of exhaustion or sorrow; *v.t.* to utter sighs over; *n.* long, deep breath, expression of sorrow, fatigue, regret, or relief [O.E. *sican*].

sight (sīt) *n.* one of the five senses; act of seeing; faculty of seeing; that which is seen; view; glimpse; anything novel or remarkable; exhibition; spectacle; (*Colloq.*) pitiful object; a piece of metal near breech of firearm to assist the eye in correct aiming; any guide for eye to assist direction; *v.t.* to catch sight of; to see; to give proper elevation and direction to instrument by means of a sight; *v.i.* to take aim by means of a sight. **-less** *a.* blind; invisible. **-lessly** *adv.* **-lessness** *n.* **-liness** *n.* comeliness. **-ly** *a.* pleasing to the eye; graceful; handsome. **second-sight** *n.* gift of prophetic vision [O.E. *sihth,* fr. *seon,* to see].

sig·il (sij′·il) *n.* seal; signet; occult sign. **sigillary** *a.* [L. *sigillum,* a seal].

sig·ma (sig′·mạ) *n.* the Greek letter (Σ, σ, s) corresponding to letter *s;* symbol indicating, in mathematics, etc., summation; 200; millesecond or $\frac{1}{1000}$ second. **sigmate, sigmoid** *a.* curved like letter S. [Gk.].

sign (sīn) *n.* movement, mark, or indication to convey some meaning; token; symbol; omen; signboard; password; (*Math.*) character indicating relation of quantities, or operation to be performed, as $+$, $\times$, $\div$, $=$ etc.; (*Mus.*) any character, as flat, sharp, dot, etc.; (*Astron.*) the twelfth part of the ecliptic or zodiac; *v.t.* to represent by sign; to affix signature to; to ratify; *v.i.* to make a signal, sign, or gesture; to append one's signature. **-board** *n.* board displaying, advertising, name of business firm, etc. **-manual** *n.* an autograph signature appended [L. *signum*].

sig·nal (sig′·nạl) *n.* sign to give notice of some occurrence, command, or danger to persons at a distance; that which in the first place impels any action; sign; token; semaphore, esp. on railway; (*Radio*) any communication made by emission of radio waves from a transmitter; *v.t.* to communicate by signals; *v.i.* to make signals. *pr.p.* **-ing.** *pa.t.* and *pa.p.* **-ed.** *a.* pert. to a signal; remarkable; conspicuous. **-ize** *v.t.* to make notable, distinguished, or remarkable; to point out. **-er** *n.* **-ly** *adv.* eminently; remarkably [L. *signum*, a sign].

sig·na·to·ry (sig′·nạ·tō·i·) *a.* and *n.* (one) bound by signature to terms of agreement. [L. *signare*, to sign].

sig·na·ture (sig·′nạ·chẹr) *n.* a sign, stamp, or mark impressed; a person's name written by himself; act of writing it; letter or number printed at bottom of first page of section of book to facilitate arrangement when binding; (*Mus.*) the flats or sharps after clef which indicate key (**key signature**), followed by appropriate signs giving value of the measures contained in each bar (**time signature**). [L. *signare*, to sign].

sig·net (sig′·nit) *n.* seal used for authenticating documents. **— ring** *n.* finger ring on which is engraved monogram or seal of owner [L. *signum*, a mark].

sig·ni·fy (sig′·nạ·fī) *v.t.* to make known by a sign; to convey notion of; to denote; to indicate; to mean; *v.i.* to express meaning; to be of consequence. *pa.t.* and *pa.p.* **signified. significance** *n.* importance; weight; meaning; import. **significant** *a.* fitted or designed to signify or make known something; important. **significantly** *adv.* **signification** *n.* act of signifying that which is expressed by signs or words; meaning; sense. **significative** *a.* **significatory** *a.* having meaning [L. *significare*, fr. *signum*, a sign; *facere*, to make].

si·gnor (sē′·nyōr) *n.* Italian lord or gentleman; ttile of respect or address equivalent to *Mr.* **signora** (sē·nyō′·rạ) *n. fem.* [It.].

si·lage (sī′·lij) *n.* compressed, acid-fermented fodder, orig. packed green in a silo for preservation [fr. *ensilage*].

si·lence (sī′·lạns) *n.* stillness; quietness; calm; refraining from speed; muteness; secrecy; oblivion; *interj.* be quiet!; *v.t.* to cause to be still; to forbid to speak; to hush; to calm; to refute; to gag; to kill. **-r** *n.* **silent** *a.* **silently** *adv.* **silentness** *n.* [L. *silentium*].

si·lex (sī′·leks) *n.* silica; trade name for coffee maker made of heat-resistant glass [L. = flint].

sil·hou·ette (sil·ȯȯ·et′) *n.* portrait or picture cut from black paper or done in solid black upon a light ground; outline of object seen against the light; *v.t.* to represent in outline; to cause to stand out in dark shadow against a light background [Fr.].

sil·i·ca (sil′·i·kạ) *n.* silicon dioxide, main component of most rocks, occurring in nature as sand, flint, quartz, etc. **silicate** *n.* salt of silicic acid. **silicated** *a.* combined or coated with silica. **silicate of soda,** waterglass. **siliceous** (sạl·ish′·ạs) *a.* pert. to silica in a finely divided state. Also **silicious. silicic** (sạl·is′·ik) *a.* derived from or containing silica [L. *silex*].

sil·i·cones (sil′·ạ·kōnz) *n.pl.* new family of materials—petroleum, brine, ordinary sand [L. *silex*, flint].

silk (silk) *n.* fine, soft, lustrous thread obtained from cocoons made by larvae of certain moths, esp. silkworm; thread or fabric made from this; *a.* made of silk. **-en** *a.* made of, or resembling, silk; soft; smooth; silky. **-iness** *n.* **-screen** *a.* and *n.* (pert. to) the reproduction of a design by means of a pattern made on a screen of nylon or silk. **-worm** *n.* caterpillar of any moth which produces silk, esp. Bombyx mori. **-y** *a.* [O.E. *seoloc*].

sill (sil) *n.* base or foundation; horizontal member of stone, brick, or wood at the bottom of window frame, door, or opening [O.E. *syll*].

sil·ly (sil′·i.) *a.* weak in intellect; foolish; senseless; stupid; (*Arch.*) simple; *n.* silly person. **sillily** *adv.* **silliness** *n.* foolishness [O.E. *saelig*, happy, fortunate].

si·lo (sī′·lō) *n.* large, airtight tower, elevator, or pit in which green crops are preserved for future use as fodder; *v.t.* to preserve in a silo. Cf. [Sp.].

silt (silt) *n.* fine, alluvial, soil, particles; mud; sediment; *v.t.* to choke or obstruct with silt (generally with up); *v.i.* to become filled up with silt [etym. uncertain].

sil·ver (sil′·vẹr) *n.* soft, white, metallic element, very malleable and ductile; silverware; silver coins; anything resembling silver; *a.* made of, or resembling, silver; white or gray, as hair; having a pale luster, as moon; soft and melodious, as voice or sound; bright, silvery; *v.t.* to coat or plate with silver; to apply amalgam of tinfoil and quicksilver to back of a mirror; to tinge with white or gray; to render smooth and bright; *v.i.* to become gradually white, as hair. **-ize** *v.t.* to coat or cover thinly with a film of silver. *n.* **— lining,** prospect of better times to come. **-plate** *n.* metallic articles coated with silver. **-plated** *a.* **-plating** *n.* deposition of silver on another metal by electrolysis. **-ware** *n.* articles made of silver. **— wedding,** 25th anniversary of marriage. **-ry** *a.* like silver; lustrous; (of sound) soft and clear [O.E. *siolfor*].

sim·i·an (sim′·i·ạn) *a.* pert. to or like an ape generally; *n.* a monkey or ape [L. = ape].

sim·i·lar (sim′·ạ·lẹr) *a.* like; resembling; exactly corresponding; (*Geom.*) of plane figures, differing in size but having all corcesponding angles and side ratios uniform. **-ity** *n.* quality or state of being similar. **-ly** *adv.* [L. *similis*, like].

sim·i·le (sim′·ạ·lē) *n.* figure of speech using some point of resemblance observed to exist between two things which differ in other respects [L. *similis*, like].

si·mil·i·tude (sạ·mil′·ạ·tūd) *n.* state of being similar or like; resemblance; likeness; parable [L. *similis*, like].

sim·mer (sim′·er) *v.t.* to cause to boil gently; *v.i.* to be just bubbling or just below boiling-point; to be in a state of suppressed anger or laughter; *n.* gentle, gradual heating [imit.].

si·mo·ni·ac (sạ·mō′·ni·ak) *n.* one guilty of simony. **-al** *a.* **-ally** *adv.* **simonist** *n.* one who practices simony [Cf. *simony*].

si·mo·ny (sī′·mạ.ni·, sim′·a·ni·) *n.* the offense of offering or accepting money or other reward for nomination or appointment to an ecclesiastical office or other benefit [See *Acts* 8].

sim·per (sim′·pẹr) *v.i.* to smile in a silly, affected manner; *n.* smile with air of silliness or affectation. **-er** *n.* [etym. uncertain].

sim·ple (sim′·pl) *a.* single; not complex; entire; mere; plain, sincere; clear; intelligible; simple-minded; (*Chem.*) composed of a single element; *n.* something not compounded. **— interest,** money paid on principal borrowed but not on accrued interest as in compound interest. **—minded** *a.* ingenuous; open; frank; mentally weak. **-ness** *n.* **-ton** *n.* foolish person; person of weak intellect. **simplicity** *n.* artlessness; sincerity; clearness; simpleness. **simplification** *n.* act of making simple or clear; thing simplified. **simplificative** *a.* tending to simplify. **simplify** *v.t.* to make or render simple, plain, or easy. *pa.t.* and *pa.p.* **simplified. simply** *adv.* in a simple manner; plainly; unostentatiously; without affectation [L. *simplus*].

sim·u·la·crum (sim·yạ·lā′·krạm) *n.* image; representation. *pl.* **simulacra** [L.].

sim·u·lant (sim′·yạ·lạnt) *a.* simulating; having the appearance of; *n.* one simulating something. **simular** *a.* simulated; counterfeit; feigned; *n.* one who pretends to be what he is not; a simulator.

sim·u·late (sim′·yạ·lāt) *v.t.* to assume the mere appearance of, without the reality; to feign. **simulation** *n.* **simulator** *n.* [L. *simulare*, to make like].

si·mul·ta·ne·ous (sim·ạl·tā′·nē·ạs) *a.* existing or occurring at same time. **-ness, simultaneity** *n.* **-ly** *adv.* [L. *simul*].

sin (sin) *n.* transgression against divine or moral law, esp. when committed consciously; conduct or state of mind of a habitual or unrepentant sinner; iniquity; evil; *v.i.* to depart from path of duty prescribed by God; to violate any rule of duty; to do wrong. *pr.p.* **-ning.** *pa.t.* and *pa.p.* **-ned.** **-ful** *a.* iniquitous; wicked; unholy. **-fully** *adv.* **-fulness** *n.* **-ner** *n.* [O.E. *synn*].

since (sins) *adv.* from then till now; subsequently; ago; *prep.* at some time subsequent to; after; *conj.* from the time that; seeing that; because; inasmuch as [earlier *sithens*, O.E. *siththan*].

sin·cere (sin·sir′) *a.* not assumed or merely professed; straightforward. **-ly** *adv.* **-ness, sincerity** (sin·ser′·ạ·ti·) *n.* state or quality of being sincere; honesty of mind or intention; truthfulness [L. *sincerus*, pure].

sine (sīn) *n.* (*abbrev.* **sin**) (*Math*) perpendicular drawn from one extremity of an arc to diameter drawn through other extremtiy; function of one of the two acute angles in a right-angle triangle, ratio of line subtending this angle to hypotenuse [L. *sinus*, a curve].

si·ne·cure (sī′·ni·kūr, sin′·ạ·kūr) *n.* office, position, etc. with salary but with few duties. **sinecurist** *n.* one who holds, or seeks sinecure [L. *sine cura*, without care].

sin·ew (sin′·ū) *n.* ligament or tendon which joins muscle to bone; strength; source of strength or vigor. **-ed** *a.* having sinews; strong; firm. **-y** *a.* well braced; muscular; strong [O.E. *sinu*].

sing (sing) *v.t.* to utter with musical modulations of voice; to celebrate in song; to praise in verse; *v.i.* to utter sounds with melodious modulations of voice; to pipe, twitter, chirp, as birds; to hum; to reverberate. *pa.t.* **sang** or **sung.** *pa.p.* **sung.** **-er** *n.* one who sings; vocalist. **-ing** *n.* art of singing; vocal music; a humming noise (in the ear, on a telephone circuit, etc.) [O.E. *singan*].

singe (sinj) *v.t.* to burn the surface slightly; to burn loose fluff from yarns, etc. *pr.p.* **-ing.** *n.* superficial burn [O.E. *sencgan*, to make hiss].

Sin·gha·lese (sing·gạ·lēz′) *a.* pert. to Ceylon, its people, or language. *n.* a native of Ceylon [Sans. *Sinhala*].

sin·gle (sing′·gl) *a.* sole; alone; separate; individual; not double; unmarried; sincere; whole-hearted; straightforward; upright; *n.* unit; (*Cricket*) one run; (*Tennis*) game confined to two opponents; *v.t.* (with *out*) to select from a number; to pick; to choose. **—breasted** *a.* of a garment, buttoning on one side only. **— entry** *n.* in bookkeeping, entry of each transaction on one side only of an account. **—handed** *a.* and *adv.* without help; unassisted. **-hearted** *a.* sincere. **—minded** *a.* having but one purpose or aim; sincere. **-ness** *n.* state of being single; honesty of purpose; freedom from deceit or guile; sincerity. **singly** *adv.* one by one; by oneself [L. *singuli*, one at a time].

sin·gle·ton (sing′·gl·tạn) *n.* (*Cards*) hand containing only one card of some suit, or the card itself [dim. of *single*].

sing·song (sing′·sawng) *n.* rhythmical, monotonous fashion of uttering. *a.* monotonous; droning [redup. of *sing*].

sin·gu·lar (sing′·gyạ·lẹr) *a.* existing by itself; denoting one person or thing; individual; unique; outstanding; *n.* single instance; word in the singular number. **-ize** *v.t.* to make singular or unique. **-ity** *n.* state of being singular; anything unusual or remarkable; oddity. **-ly** *adv.* [L. *singularis*].

Sin·ic (sin′·ik) *a.* Chinese. **Sinicise** (sin′·ạ·sīz) *v.t.* to give a Chinese character to. **-ism** *n.* mode of thought or customs peculiar to the Chinese [Gk. *Sinai*, the Chinese].

sin·is·ter (sin′·is·tẹr) *a.* on left hand; evil-looking; unlucky (left being regarded as unlucky side). **sinistral** *a.* to the left; reversed; (*Bot.*) having whorls not turning normally [L. = on the left hand].

sink (singk) *v.t.* to cause to descend; to submerge; to lower out of sight; to dig; to excavate; to ruin; to suppress; to invest; *v.i.* to subside; to descend; to penetrate (into); to decline in value, health, or social status; to be dying; to droop; to decay; to become submerged. *pa.t.* **sank** or **sunk.** *pa.p.* **sunk.** *n.* a receptacle for washing up, with pipe for carrying away waste water; marsh or area in which river water percolates through surface and diasppears; place notoriously associated with evildoing. **-er** *n.* weight fixed to anything to make it sink, as on net, fishing-line, etc. **-ing** *n.* operation of excavating; subsidence; settling; abatement; ebb; part sunk below surrounding surface. **-ing fund,** fund set aside at regular intervals to provide replacement of wasting asset or repayment of particular liability [O.E. *sincan*].

Si·no-, in compounds, meaning Chinese [Gk. *Sinai*, Chinese].

Si·nol·o·gy (sī·nȧl′·ạ·ji·) *n.* that branch of knowledge which deals with the Chinese language, culture, history, religion and art. [Gk. *Sinai*, the Chinese; *logos*, a discourse].

sin·u·ate (sin′·yoo·āt) *v.i.* to bend in and out; to wind; to turn; *a.* (sin′·yoo·it) (*Bot.*) wavy; tortuous; curved on the margin, as a leaf. Also **-d.** **sinuation** *n.* **sinuose, sinuous** *a.* bending in and out; of serpentine or undulating form; morally crooked; supple. **sinuously** *adv.* [L. *sinus*, a fold].

si·nus (sī′·nạs) *n.* (*Anat.*) opening; hollow; cavity; (*Path.*) groove or passage in tissues leading to a deep-seated abscess, usually in nose or ear. **-itis** *n.* inflammation of sinus [L. *sinus*, a curve].

Sioux (sȯȯ) *n.* member of great Siouan division of N. American aborigines; their language. *pl.* **Sioux** (sȯȯ, sȯȯz).

sip (sip) *v.t.* and *v.i.* to drink or imbibe in very small quantities; to taste. *pr.p.* **-ping.** *pa.t.* and *pa.p.* **-ped.** *n.* a small portion of liquid sipped with the lips [O.E. *sypian*, to soak].

si·phon, syphon (sī′·fạn) *n.* a bent tube or pipe by which a liquid can be transferred by atmospheric pressure from one receptacle to another; bottle provided with internal tube and lever top, for holding and delivering aerated water; projecting tube in mantle of shell of bivalve; *v.t.* to draw off by means of a siphon. *n.* action of a siphon [Gk. = tube].

sir (sur) *n.* a title of respect to any man of position; title of knight or baronet [var. of *sire*].

sire (sīr) *n.* title of respect to a king or emperor; male parent of an animal (applied esp. to horses); *pl.* (*Poetic*) ancestors; *v.t.* to beget (of animals) [Fr. fr. L. *senior*, elder].

si·ren (sī′·rạn) *n.* (*Myth.*) one of several nymphs said to sing with such sweetness that sailors were lured to death; seductive alluring woman; form of horn which emits series of loud, piercing notes used as warning signal;

steam whistle; the mud-eel; *a.* pert. to, or resembling a siren; alluring; seductive [Gk. *Seirēn*].

Sir·i·us (sir′·i·as) *n.* (*Astron.*) a star of the first magnitude known as the Dog Star [L.].

sir·loin (sur′·lion) *n.* the upper part of a loin of beef [O.Fr. *surloigne*].

si·roc·co (si·rák′·ō) *n.* a hot, southerly, dust-laden wind from Africa, chiefly experienced in Italy, Malta and Sicily [It.].

si·sal (sis′·al, sī′·sal) *n.* fiber plant, native to Florida and Yucatan providing **sisal-grass** (**sisal-hemp**) [*Sisal*, a seaport in *Yucatan*].

sis·sy (sis′·i·) *n.* (*Colloq.*) ineffective effeminate man or boy; *a.* effeminate.

sis·ter sis′·ter) *n.* female whose parents are same as those of another person; correlative of brother; woman of the same faith; female of the same society, convent, abbey; nun; *a.* standing in relation of sister; related; of a similar nature to, as institute, college, etc. **-hood** *n.* state of being a sister; society of women united in one faith or order. **—in-law** *n.* husband's or wife's sister; brother's wife. *pl.* **-s-in-law, -like, -ly** *a.* [O.N. *systir*].

Sis·tine (sis′·tēn) *a.* pert. to any Pope named Sixtus. **— Chapel,** the Pope's private chapel in the Vatican at Rome.

sit (sit) *v.i.* to rest upon haunches, a seat, etc.; to remain; to rest; to perch, as birds; (of hen) to cover and warm eggs for hatching; to be officially engaged in transacting business, as court, council, etc.; to be in session; to be representative in legislative for constituency; to pose for portrait; to press or weigh (upon); to fit (of clothes); *v.t.* to keep good seat, upon, as on horseback; to place upon seat; *pr.p.* **-ting.** *pa.t.* and *pa.p.* **sat.** *n.* position assumed by an object after being placed. **-ter** *n.* one who sits; one who poses for artist; bird sitting on its eggs; one who stays with children while parents are out. **-ting** *n.* state of resting on a seat, etc.; act of placing oneself on a seat; session; business meeting; time given up to posing for artist; clutch of eggs for incubation; *a.* resting on haunches; perched. **-ting-room** *n.* [O.E. *sittan*].

site (sīt) *n.* situation; plot of ground for, or with, building; locality; place where anything is fixed; *v.t.* to place in position; to locate [L. *situs*, a site].

si·tol·o·gy (sī·tál′·a·ji·) *n.* dietetics [Gk. *silos*, food; *logos*, a discourse].

sit·u·ate (sich′·oo·āt) *v.t.* to give a site to; to place in a particular state or set of circumstances; to locate; **-d** *a.* located; placed with reference to other affairs, etc. **situation** *n.* location; place or position; site; condition; job; post; plight [L. *situs*, a site].

six (siks) *a.* one more than five; *n.* sum of three and three; symbol 6 or VI. **-fold** *a.* six times as much or as many. **-footer** *n.* person six feet in height. **-pence** *n.* silver coin in British currency of value of six pennies. **-penny** *a.* worth sixpence; paltry; of small value. **-shooter** *n.* a six-chambered revolver. **-teen** *n.* and *a.* six and ten, symbol 16 or XVI. **-teenth** *a.* sixth after the tenth; being one of sixteen equal parts into which anything is divided; *n.* one of sixteen equal parts; a division of the inch; (*Mus.*) semiquaver. **-th** *a.* next in order after the fifth; one of six equal parts; *n.* (*Mus.*) an interval comprising six degrees of the staff, as A to F. **-ty** *a.* six times ten; three score; *n.* symbol 60 or LX. **-tieth** *a.* next in order after the fifty-ninth; one of sixty equal parts; *n.* **at sixes and sevens,** in disorder and confusion [O.E. *siex*].

size (sīz) *n.* bulk; bigness; comparative magnitude; dimensions; extent; conventional measure of dimension; *v.t.* to arrange according to size. **-able, sizable** *a.* of considerate size or bulk. **to size up,** to estimate possibilities of; to take measure of [contr. of *assize*].

size (sīz) *n.* substance of a gelatinous nature, like weak glue; *v.t.* to treat or cover with size [Fr. *assise*, a layer (e.g. of paint, etc.)].

siz·zle (siz′·l) *v.i.* to make hissing or sputtering noise; (*Colloq.*) to suffer from heat. *n.* hissing, sputtering noise. **sizzling** *n.* [imit.].

skald (skáld) *n.* ancient Scandinavian poet **-ic** *a.* Also **scald** [O.N. *skald*].

skate (skāt) *n.* steel blade attached to boot, used for gliding over ice; *v.i.* to travel over ice on skates. **-r** *n.* **skating** *n.* **skating-rink** *n.* stretch of ice or flat expanse for skating; ice-rink. **roller skate** *n.* skate with wheels in place of steel blade [Dut. *schaats*].

skate (skāt) *n.* a large, edible, flat fish of the ray family [O.N. *skata*].

skean (skēn) *n.* Highland dagger or dirk; long knife [Gael. *sgian*, knife].

ske·dad·dle (ski·dad′·l) *v.i.* (*Colloq.*) to scamper off; *n.* hasty, disorderly flight.

skeet (skēt) *n.* trapshooting with clay targets thrown into the air.

skein (skān) *n.* small hank, of fixed length, of thread, silk, or yarn, doubled and secured by loose knot [O.Fr. *escaigne*].

skel·e·ton (skel′·a·tan) *n.* body framework providing support for human or animal body; any framework, as of building, plant, etc.; general outline; *a.* pert. to skeleton; containing mere outlines. Also **skeletal. — crew, staff, etc.,** minimum number of men employed on some essential duty [Gk. *skeletos*, dried up].

skel·ter. See **helter-skelter.**

skep (skep) *n.* beehive made of straw; light basket [O.N. *skeppa*, a basket].

skep·tic (skep′·tik) *n.* one who doubts, esp. existence of God, or accepted doctrines; rationalist; agnostic; unbeliever; **-al** *a.* doubtful; doubting; disbelieving. **-ally** *adv.* **-alness** *n.* **skepticize** *v.i.* to doubt everything. **skepticism** *n.* doubt in absence of conclusive evidence; theory that positive truth is unattainable by human intellect [Gk. *skeptesthai*, to investigate].

sker·ry (sker′·i·) *n.* rocky isle; reef [O.N.].

sketch (skech) *n.* first rough draft or plan of any design; outline; drawing in pen, pencil, or similar medium; descriptive essay or account, in light vein; a short, humorous one-act play; *v.t.* to draw outline of; to make rough draft of; *v.i.* to draw; to make sketches. **-er** *n.* **-ily** *adv.* **-iness** *n.* lack of detail. **-y** *a.* containing outline or rough form; inadequate; incomplete [Dut. *schets*].

skew (skū) *a.* awry; oblique; askew; turned aside; *n.* anything set obliquely or at an angle to some other object; a deviation; *v.t.* to put askew; to skid. **—bald** *a.* of horse, bay and white in patches. [O.Fr. *escuer*].

skew·er (skū′·er) *n.* pointed rod for fastening meat to a spit, or for keeping it in form while roasting; *v.t.* to fasten with skewers.

ski (skē, in Norway, shē) *n.* long wooden runner strapped to foot, for running, sliding and jumping over snow; *v.i.* to run, slide, or jump on skis. **-er** *n.* [Norw.].

ski·a·graph (ski′·a·graf) *n.* an X-ray photograph. Also **skiagram. -er** *n.* one who takes X-ray photographs. **-ic** *a.* [Gk. *skia*, a shadow; *graphein*, to write].

skid (skid) *n.* a piece of timber to protect side of vessel from injury; drag placed under wheel to check speed of vehicle descending steep gradient; inclined plane down which logs, etc. slide; low, wooden platform for holding and moving loads; *v.i.* to slide or slip sideways; *v.t.* to slide a log down a skid; to place on skids. *pr.p.* **-ding** *pa.p., pa.t.* **-ded** [O.N. *skidh*].

skiff (skif) *n.* a small rowboat or sailboat [Fr. *esquif*].

skill (skil) *n.* practical ability and dexterity; knowledge; expertness; aptitude. **-ful** *a.* expert; skilled; dexterous. **-fully** *adv.* **-fulness** *n.* **-ed** *a.* [O.N. *skil*, distinction].

skil·let (skil'·it) *n.* a frying pan [O.Fr. *escuellete*].

skim (skim) *v.t.* to remove from surface of liquid; to glide over lightly and rapidly; to glance over in superficial way; to graze; *v.i.* to pass lightly over; to glide along; to hasten over superficially. *pr.p* **-ming.** *pa.t.* and *pa.p.* **-med.** *n.* skimming; matter skimmed off. **-mer** *n.* **— milk** *n.* milk from which cream has been removed [O.Fr. *escumer*].

skimp (skimp) *v.t.* to stint; *v.i.* to be mean or parsimonious; to economize in petty fashion. **-y** *a.* scant; meager; stingy.

skin (skin) *n.* external protective covering of animal bodies; epidermis; a hide; a pelt; coat of fruits and plants; husk or bark; thick scum; *v.t.* to strip off skin or hide of; to flay; to graze; to peel; (*Slang*) to cheat; to swindle. **—deep** *a.* superficial. **—flint** *n.* miser. **— game** *n.* cheating and swindling. **— grafting** *n.* transplanting healthy skin to wound to form new skin. **-ner** *n.* dealer in hides; furrier.**-niness** *n.* leanness. **-ny** *a.* of skin; very lean or thin. **—tight** *a.* fitting close to skin. [O.N. *skinn*].

skip (skip) *v.t.* to leap over lightly; to omit without noticing; *v.i.* to leap lightly, esp. in frolic; to frisk; to pass from one thing to another; to clear repeatedly a rope swung in play under one's feet; (*Colloq.*) to run away hastily. *pr.p.* **-ping.** *pa.t.* and *pa.p.* **-ped.** *n.* light leap, spring, or bound; an omission. **-ping** *a.* characterized by skips.

skip·per (skip'·ẹr) *n.* captain of ship or team [Dut. *schipper*].

skirl (skurl) *v.i.* to sound shrilly. *n.* shrill, high-pitched sound of bagpipe [var. of *shrill*].

skir·mish (skur'·mish) *n.* irregular, minor engagement between two parties of soldiers; *v.i.* [Fr. *escarmouche*].

skirt (skurt) *n.* lower part of coat, gown; outer garment of a woman fitted to and hanging from waist; petticoat; flap; border; margin; edge; rim; *v.t.* to be on border; to go around. **-ing** *n.* material for women's skirts; border [O.N. *skyria*].

skit (skit) *n.* satirical gibe; lampoon; short, usually humorous, play; *v.i.* to leap aside. **-tish** *a.* frisky; frivolous; fickle; apt to shy, of a horse. **-tishly** *adv.* **-tishness** *n.*

skit·tle (skit'·l) *n.* game of ninepins.

skive (skīv) *v.t.* in shoe-making, to pare away edges of leather [Ice, *skifa*, to split].

skiv·vy (skiv'·i·) *n.* (*Slang*) undershirt.

skoal (skōl) *interj.* salutation, hail! in toasting [Dan. *skaal*, bowl; a toast].

skulk (skulk) *v.i.* to sneak out of the way; to lurk or keep out of sight in a furtive manner; to act sullenly; *n.* one who skulks.

skull (skul) *n.* bony framework which encloses brain; cranium along with bones of face. **— cap** *n.* brimless cap fitting close to head. **— and crossbones,** a symbol for poison, formerly used on pirate flags [M.E. *skulle*].

skunk (skungk) *n.* small N. American burrowing animal, allied to weasel, which defends itself by emitting evil-smelling fluid; (*Colloq.*) a base, mean person [Amer.-Ind. *seganku*].

sky (skī) *n.* the apparent vault of heaven; heavens; firmament; climate. *v.t.* **—blue** *n.* and *a.* azure; cerulean. **-ey** *a.* (*Poetic*) like the sky. **—gazer** *n.* visionary.**—high** *a.* and *adv.* at a great elevation; carried away with excitement or anticipation. **-lark** *n.* bird which sings as it soars; *v.i.* (*Colloq.*) to indulge in boisterous byplay. **—larking** *n.* **-light** *n.* glazed opening in roof or ceiling. **-line** *n.* horizon; silhouette of buildings, etc. on horizon. **-scraper** *n.* lofty building with numerous stories. **-writing** *n.* writing in air for advertising or propaganda purposes by smoke from an airplane [O.N. *sky*, a cloud].

Skye (skī) *n.* or **Skyeterrier,** breed of Scotch terrier, with long hair. [Isle of *Skye*].

slab (slab) *n.* thickish, flat, rectangular piece of anything; concrete paving-block; thick slice of cake, etc.

slack (slak) *a.* not taut; not closely drawn together; not holding fast; remiss about one's duties; easy-going; *n.* part of a rope which hangs loose; quiet time. **-en** *v.t.* to loosen; to moderate; to relax; to leave undone; to slake; *v.i.* to become slack; to lose cohesion; to relax; to dodge work; to languish; to flag. **-er** *n.* one who shirks work. **-ly** *adv.* **-ness** *n.* **-s** *n.pl.* loose trousers worn by men or women. [O.E. *slaec*].

slack (slak) *n.* the finer screenings of coal which pass through a half-inch mesh; coal-dust; dross. **-heap** *n.* [Ger. *Schlacke*, dross].

slag (slag) *n.* silicate formed during smelting of ores; scoria of a volcano; *v.i.* to form slag [Ger. *Schlacke*, dross].

slain (slān) *pa.p.* of the verb **slay.**

slake (slāk) *v.t.* to quench; to extinguish; to combine quicklime with water; to slacken; *v.i.* to become mixed with water [O.E. *slacian*].

slam (slam) *v.t.* to shut violently and noisily; to bang; to hit; to dash down; to win all, or all but one, of the tricks at cards. *pr.p.* **-ming.** *pa.t.* and *pa.p.* **-med.** *n.* act of slamming; bang; **slam** (**grand** or small) thirteen or twelve tricks taken in one deal in cards.

slan·der (slan'·dẹr) *n.* false or malicious statement about person; defamation of character by spoken word; calumny; *v.t.* to injure by maliciously uttering false report; to defame. **-er** *n.* **-ous** *a.* [Fr. *esclandre*].

slang (slang) *n.* word or expression in common colloquial use but not regarded as standard English; jargon peculiar to certain sections of public, trades, etc.; argot; *a.* pert. to slang; *v.t.* to vituperate; to revile; to scold.

slant (slant) *v.t.* to turn from a direct line; to give a sloping direction to; *v.i.* to lie obliquely; to slope; to incline; *n.* slanting direction or position; slope; point of view or illuminating remark (on); *a.* sloping; oblique. **-ingly** *adv.* **-ly, -wise** *adv.* [Swed. *slinta*, to slide].

slap (slap) *n.* blow with open hand or flat instrument; insulting remark; *v.t.* to strike with open hand or something flat. *pr.p.* **-ping.** *pa.t.* and *pa.p.* **-ped.** *adv.* with a sudden blow; (*Colloq.*) instantly; directly. **-stick** *n.* boisterous farce of pantomine or low comedy. [imit. origin].

slash (slash) *v.t.* to cut by striking violently and haphazardly; to make gashes in; to slit; *v.i.* to strike violently and at random with edged weapon; *n.* long cut; gash; cutting stroke; large slit in garment. **-er** *n.* [O.Fr. *esclachier*, to sever].

slat (slat) *n.* narrow strip of wood, metal, etc. a lath *pl.* (*Slang*) ribs. **-ted** *a.* covered with slats [O.Fr. *esclat*, fragment].

slate (slāt) *n.* a form of shale, composed mainly of aluminium silicate, which splits readily into thin leaves; prepared piece of such stone, esp. thin piece for roofing houses, etc.; dark blue-gray color; list of candidates for offices; *a.* made of slate; bluish-gray; *v.t.* to cover with slates; to put on a list for nomination, etc. **slating** *n.* act of covering with slates; roof-covering thus put on. **slaty** *n.* [O.Fr. *esclat*, a splinted].

slat·tern (slat'·ẹrn) *n.* slut; slovenly woman or girl. **-liness** *n.* **-ly** *a.* like a slattern; *adv.* in slovenly manner [Scand. *slat*, to strike].

slaugh·ter (slaw'·tẹr) *n.* act of slaughtering; carnage; massacre; butchery; killing of animals to provide food; *v.t.* to kill; to slay in battle; to butcher, **-er** *n.* **-house** *n.* place where cattle are slaughtered. **-ous** *a.* bent on slaughter; destructive. **-ously** *adv.* [O.N. *slatr*, butcher's meat].

Slav (slàv) *n.* a member of a group of peoples in E. and S.E. Europe, comprising Russians, Ukrainians, White Russians, Poles, Czechs, Slovaks, Serbians, Croats, Slovenes and Bulgarians; *a.* relating to the Slavs; Slavic; Slavonic. **-ic** *a.* **-onic** *a.* [etym. unknown].

slave (slāv) *n.* person held legally in bondage to another; bondman; one who has lost all powers of resistance to some pernicious habit or vice; *v.i.* to work like a slave, to toil unremittingly. **-driver** *n.* an overseer in charge of slaves at work; exacting taskmaster. **-r** *n.* person or ship engaged in slave traffic. **-ry** *n.* condition of slave compelled to perform compulsory work for another; bondage; servitude. **— trade** *n.* traffic in human beings. **— trader** *n.* **slavish** *a.* pert. to slaves; menial; drudging; servile; base; mean; imitative. **slavishly** *adv.* **slavishness** *n.* **white slavery,** traffic in women and girls for immoral purposes [Fr.*esclave*, fr. *Slav*].

slav·er (slàv′·ẹr) *n.* saliva running from mouth; sentimental nonsense; *v.t.* to smear with saliva issuing from mouth; *v.i.* to slobber; to talk in a weakly sentimental fashion. **-er** *n.* [O.N. *slafra*, to slaver].

slaw (slaw) *n.* sliced cabbage served cooked, or uncooked, as a salad [Dut. *sla*, salad].

slay (slā) *v.t.* to kill; to murder; to slaughter. *pa.t.* **slew.** *pa.p.* **slain.** **-er** *n* [O.E. *slean*, to smite].

sleave (slēv) *n.* knotted or entangled part of silk or thread; a fine wisp of silk made by separating a thread; *v.t.* to separate and divide as into threads [etym. uncertain].

slea·zy (slē′·zi) *a.* thin or poor in texture.

sled, sledge (sled, slej) *n.* a vehicle on runners, for conveying loads over hard snow or ice; a sleigh; a small flat sled for coasting; *v.t.* to convey on a sled; *v.i.* to ride on a sled [Dut. *slede*].

sledge (slej) *n.* large, heavy hammer. [O.E. *slecg*].

sleek (slēk) *a.* having a smooth surface; glossy; not rough; ingratiating; *v.t.* to make smooth; to calm; to soothe; *adv.* **-ly** *adv.* **-ness** *n.* [O.N. *slikr*, smooth].

sleep (slēp) *v.i.* to rest by suspension of exercise of powers of body and mind; to become numb (of limb); to slumber; to doze; to repose; to rest; to be dead. *pa.t.* and *pa.p.* **slept.** *n.* slumber; repose; rest; death. **-er** *n.* one who sleeps; railway sleeping car; **-ily** *adv.* in drowsy manner. **-iness** *n.* **-ing** *a.* resting in sleep; inducing sleep; adapted for sleeping; *n.* state of resting in sleep; state of not being raised or discussed. **-ing-bag** *n.* bag of thick material, waterproofed on outside, for sleeping in the open. **-ing-car** *n.* railway car with berths, compartments, etc. **-ing sickness** *n.* brain infection causing increased drowsiness. **-less** *a.* wakeful; restless; alert; vigilant; unremitting. **-lessly** *adv.* **-lessness** *n.* **-walker** *n.* one who walks in his sleep or in trance; somnambulist. **-walking** *n.* **-y** *a.* inclined to sleep; drowsy [O.E. *slaepan*].

sleet (slēt) *n.* rain that is partly frozen; *v.i.* to fall as fine pellets of ice. **-iness** *n.* **-y** *a.* [M.E. *slete*].

sleeve (slēv) *n.* part of garment which covers arm; casing surrounding shaft of engine; wind-sock used on airfields as wind-indicator; *v.t.* to furnish with sleeves. [O.E. *sliefe*].

sleigh (slā) *n.* a sled; an open carriage on runners, usually horse-drawn; *v.i.* to drive in a sleigh [Dut. *slee*].

sleight (slīt) *n.* artful trick; skill. **— of hand** *n.* legerdemain; juggling [O.N. *slaegth*].

slen·der (slen′·dẹr) *a.* thin or narrow; weak; feeble; not strong. **-ly** *adv.* **-ness** *n.* [M.E. *slendre*].

slept (slept) *pa.t.* and *pa.p.* of **sleep.**

sleuth (slōōth) *n.* bloodhound; a relentless tracker; (*Colloq.*) detective. **-hound** *n.* bloodhound [O.N. *sloth*, a track].

slew (slòò) *pa.t.* of **slay.**

slew, slue (slòò) *v.t.* and *v.i.* to turn about; to swing round [etym. unknown].

slice (slīs) *v.t.* and *v.i.* to cut off thin flat pieces; to strike a ball so that its line of flight diverges well to the right; to part like the cut of a knife; *n.* thin, flat piece cut off; broad, flat, thin knife for serving fish; spatula; share or portion; stroke at golf, etc. in which ball curls away to the right. **-r** *n.* [O. Fr. *esclice*].

slick (slik) *a.* smooth; sleek; smooth-tongued; smart; clever; slippery; *adv.* deftly; cleverly; *v.t.* to sleek; to make glossy. *n.* a smooth spot, as one covered with oil. See **sleek.**

slick·er (slik′·ẹr) *n.* waterproof coat.

slid, slidden See **slide.**

slide (slīd) *v.i.* to slip smoothly along; to slip, to glide, esp. over ice; to pass imperceptibly; to deteriorate morally; *v.t.* to move something into position by pushing along the surface of another body; to thrust along; to pass imperceptibly. *pr.p.* **sliding.** *pa.t.* **slid.** *pa.p.* **slid** or **slidden.** *n.* sliding; track on ice made by sliding; sliding part of mechanism; anything which moves freely in or out; photographic film holder for projecting; smooth and easy passage; chute; a narrow piece of glass to carry small object to be examined under microscope; moving part of trombone or trumpet. **-r** *n.* **— rule** *n.* mathematical instrument for rapid calculations. **sliding-scale** *n.* schedule of wages, prices, duties, etc. showing automatic variations [O.E. *slidan*].

slight (slīt) *a.* trifling; inconsiderable; not substantial; slim; slender; *n.* contempt by ignoring another; disdain; insult; *v.t.* to ignore; to disdain; to insult. **-ing** *n.* act or instance of disrespect; *a.* disparaging. **-ingly** *adv.* **-ly** *adv.* to slight extent; not seriously. **-ness** *n.* [O.N. *slettr*].

slim (slim) *a.* of small diameter or thickness; slender; thin; slight; unsubstantial; *comp.* **-mer,** *superl.* **-mest.** *v.t.* and *v.i.* to make or become slim; *pa.t., pa.p.* **-med.** *pr.p.* **-ming.** **-ly** *adv.* frail [Dut. = crafty].

slime (slīm) *n.* soft, sticky, moist earth or clay; greasy, viscous mud; mire; viscous secretion of snails, etc.; **slimily** *adv.* **sliminess** *n.* **slimy** *a.* [O.E. *slim*].

sling (sling) *n.* pocket of leather, etc., with a string attached at each end for hurling a stone; catapult; swinging throw; strap attached to rifle; hanging bandage, for supporting an arm or hand; rope, chain, belt, etc. for hoisting weights; *v.t.* to throw by means of sling or swinging motion of arm; to hoist or lower by means of slings; to suspend. *pa.t.* and *pa.p.* **slung.** **-er** *n.* [O.N. *slyngva*].

sling (sling) *n.* American iced drink of sweetened gin (or rum) with water, fruit juice [Ger. *schlingen*, to swallow].

slink (slingk) *v.i.* to move in a stealthy, furtive manner. *pa.t.* and *pa.p.* **slunk** [O.E. *slincan*, to creep].

slip (slip) *v.t.* to move an object smoothly, secretly, or furtively into another position; to put on, or off easily; to loosen; to release (dog); to omit; to miss; to overlook; to escape (memory); to escape from; of animals, to give premature birth to; *v.i.* to lose one's foothold; to move smoothly along surface of; to withdraw quietly; to slide; to make a mistake; to lose one's chance; to pass without notice. *pr.p.* **-ping.** *pa.t.* and *pa.p.* **-ped.** *n.* act of slipping; unintentional error; false step; twig for grafting separated from main stock; leash for dog; long, narrow, piece; loose garment worn under woman's dress; covering for a pillow; skid; inclined plane from which ships are launched. **— cover** *n.* a removable covering for upholstered furniture. **-knot** *n.* running knot which slips along rope around which it is made, forming loop. **-per** *n.* light shoe for indoor use; dancing-shoe.**-perily** *adv.* **-periness** *n.* condition of being slippery. *a.* so smooth as to cause slipping or to be difficult to hold or catch; not affording a firm footing; unstable; untrustworthy; changeable; artful; wily. **-shod** *a.* having shoes down at heel; untidy; slovenly; inaccurate. **-up** *n.* (*Colloq.*) a mistake [O.E. *slipan*].

slit (slit) *v.t.* to cut lengthwise; to cut open; to sever; to rend; to split; *v.i.* to be slit. *pr.p.* **-ting.** *pa.t.* and *pa.p.* **slit.** *n.* straight, narrow cut or incision; narrow opening. **-ter** *n.* [O.E. *slitan*].

slith·er (sliTH′·ẹr) *v.i.* to slide and bump (down a slope, etc.); to move in a sliding, snakelike fashion; *n.* act of slithering; rubble [var. of *slidder*].

sliv·er (sliv′·ẹr) *v.t.* to divide into long, thin strips; *v.i.* to split; to become split off; *n.* thin piece cut lengthwise; splinter [O.E. *slifan*, to split].

slob·ber (slȧb′·ẹr) *v.i.* to let saliva drool from mouth; dribble; *v.t.* to cover with saliva. *n.* saliva coming from mouth; sentimental drivel. Also **slabber. -er** *n.* [var. of *slaver*].

sloe (slō) *n.* blackthorn; small dark fruit of blackthorn. **— gin** *n.* liqueur from gin and sloes [O.E. *sla*].

slog (slȧg) *v.t.* to hit wildly and vigorously; *v.i.* to work or study with dogged determination; to trudge along; *pr.p.* **-ging.** *pa.t.* and *pa.p.* **-ged, -ger** *n.* [O.E. *slean*, to strike].

slo·gan (slō′·gan) *n.* war cry of Highland clan in Scotland; distinctive phrase used by a political party; catchword for focusing public interest, etc. [Gael. *sluagh-ghairm*].

sloop (sló͝op) *n.* one-masted sailing vessel [Dut. *sloep*].

slop (slȧp) *n.* liquid carelessly spilled; puddle; *pl.* water in which anything has been washed; liquid refuse; *v.t.* to spill; to soil by spilling over; *v.i.* to overthrow or be spilled. *pr.p.* **-ping.** *pa.t.* and *pa.p.* **-ped. —basin, —bowl** *n.* basin or bowl for holding dregs from teacups. **-pily** *adv.* **-piness** *n.* **-py** *a.* wet; muddy; slovenly; untidy; (*Colloq.*) mawkishly sentimental [O.E. *sloppe*].

slope (slōp) *n.* upward or downward inclination; slant; side of hill; *v.t.* to form with slope; to place slanting; *v.i.* to assume oblique direction; to be inclined. **sloping** *a.* [O.E. *slupan*, to slip away].

slosh (slȧsh) *n.* soft mud; *v.t.* to stir in liquid; *v.i.* to splash, stir about, in mud, water, etc. [fr. *slush*].

slot (slȧt) *n.* slit cut out for reception of object or part of machine; slit where coins are inserted into automatic machines; *v.t.* to make a slot in. *pr.p.* **-ting.** *pa.t.* and *pa.p.* **-ted. — machine** *n.* automatic machine worked by insertion of coin [O.Fr. *esclot*].

sloth (slawth) *n.* lethargy; indolence. **-ful** *a.* inactive; sluggish; lazy. **-fully** *adv.* **-fulness** *n.* [O.E. slaewth, *fr. slaw*, slow].

sloth (slōth, slawth) *n.* group of edentate mammals of S. America which cling mostly to branches of trees [fr. *slow*].

slouch (slouch) *n.* ungraceful, stooping manner of walking or standing; shambling gait; *v.i.* to shamble; to sit or stand in a drooping position; *v.t.* to depress; to cause to hang down loosely. **— hat** *n.* soft hat with a broad, flexible brim. **-y** *a.* inclined to slouch.

slough (slou) *n.* bog; swamp [O.E. *sloh*].

slough (sluf) *n.* cast-off outer skin, esp. of snake; dead mass of soft tissues which separates from healthy tissues in gangrene or ulcers; *v.t.* to cast off, or shed, as a slough; *v.i.* to separate as dead matter which forms over sore; to drop off [etym. uncertain].

Slo·vak (slō·vak′) *n.* member of Slav people in northern Carpathians, closely related to Czechs; language spoken in Slovakia; *a.* pert. to Slovaks. Also **Slovakian.**

slov·en (sluv′·n) *n.* person careless of dress, or negligent of cleanliness. **-liness** *n.* **-ly** *a.* *adv.* in slipshod manner [etym. uncertain].

slow (slō) *a.* not swift; not quick in motion; gradual; indicating time earlier than true time; mentally sluggish; dull; wearisome; *adv.* slowly; *v.t.* to render slow; to retard; to reduce speed of: *v.i.* to slacken speed. **-ly** *adv.* **— match** *n.* fuse made so as to burn slowly, for firing mines, etc. **— motion** *n.* and *a.* in motion pictures, motion shown in exaggeratedly slow time. **-ness** *n.* **-witted** *a.* mentally slow, dull; apathetic. [O.E. *slaw*, sluggish].

sludge (sluj) *n.* mud which settles at bottom of waterways, of vessel containing water, or a shaft when drilling; semi-solid; slimy matter precipitated from sewage in sedimentation tank. **sludgy** *a.* [var. *of slush*].

slug (slug) *n.* one of land snails without a shell, a common pest in gardens. **-gard** *n.* person habitually lazy and idle; *a.* disinclined to exert oneself; habitually indolent; slothful; slow-moving. **-gishly** *adv.* **-ishness** *n.* [Scand.].

slug (slug) *n.* small thick disk of metal; a piece of metal fired from gun; solid line of type cast by linotype process.

slug (slug) (*Colloq.*) *v.i.* to strike heavily; to slog; *n.* heavy blow [O.E. *slean*, to strike].

sluice (slóós) *n.* valve or shutter for regulating flow; a natural channel for drainage; artificial channel along which stream flows; sluicing; *v.t.* to drain through a sluice; to wash out, or pour over with water; *v.i.* to run through a sluice or other stream of water. **— box** *n.* trough used in goldmining [O.Fr. *escluse*].

slum (slum) *n.* squalid street, or quarter of town, characterized by gross over-crowding, dilapidation, poverty, vice and dirt; *v.i.* to visit slums. *pr.p.* **-ming** *pa.t.* and *pa.p.* **-med.**

slum·ber (slum′·bẹr) *v.i.* to sleep lightly; to be in a state of negligence, sloth, or inactivity; *n.* light sleep; doze. **-er** *n.* **-ous, slumbrous** *a.* inducing slumber; drowsy [O.E. *sluma*].

slump (slump) *n.* act of slumping; sudden, sharp fall in prices or volume of business done; industrial or financial depression; *v.i.* to drop suddenly; to droop; to decline suddenly in value, volume, or esteem; to sink suddenly when crossing snow, ice, boggy ground, etc.

slung (slung) *pa.t.* and *pa.p.* of **sling.**

slunk (slungk) *pa.t.* and *pa.p.* of **slink.**

slur (slur) *v.t.* to pass over lightly; to depreciate; to insult; to pronounce indistinctly; (*Mus.*) to sing or play in a smooth, gliding style; to run one into the other, as notes. *pr.p.* **-ring.** *pa.t.* and *pa.p.* **-red.** *n.* slight blur in print; stigma; reproach; implied insult; (*Mus.*) mark, thus (‿ or ⁀) connecting notes that are to be sung to same syllable, or made in one continued breath; indistinct sound [O. Dut. *slooren*, to trail (in mud)].

slush (slush) *n.* half-melted snow; soft mud; any greasy, pasty mass; overly sentimental talk or writings;*v.t.* to splash or cover with slush; to flush a place with water. **-y** *a.* [var. of *sludge*].

slut (slut) *n.* dirty, untidy woman; slattern. **-tish** *a.* untidy and dirty. [M.E. *slutte*].

sly (slī) *a.* artfully cunning; mischievous. **-ly** *adv.* **-ness** *n.* [O.N. *slaegr*].

smack (smak) *v.t.* to make a loud, quick noise

(with lips) as in kissing or after tasting; to slap loudly; to strike; *v.i.* to make sharp, quick noise with lips; *n.* quick, sharp noise, esp. with lips; a loud kiss; a slap [imit.].
smack (smak) *v.i.* to have a taste or flavor; to give a suggestion (of); *n.* a slight taste [O.E. *smaec*, taste].
smack (smak) *n.* small sailing vessel, usually for fishing [Dut. *smak*].
small (smawl) *a.* little in size, number, degree, etc.; not large; unimportant; short; weak; slender; mean; *n.* small or slender part, esp. of back. **-ish** *a.* rather small. **-ness** *n.* **— arms** *n.pl.* hand firearms, e.g. rifles, pistols, etc. **— change,** coins of small value, e.g. pennies, nickels, dimes, etc. **— fry** *n.* young fish; children. **— talk** *n.* gossip; light conversation [O.E. *smael*].
small·pox (smawl′·pȧks) *n.* infectious disease, characterized into pustules [E. *small;* O.E. *poc.* a pustule].
smart (smȧrt) *n.* sharp, stinging pain; pang of grief; hurt feelings, etc. *v.i.* to feel such a pain; to be punished (with 'for'); *a.* causing a sharp, stinging pain; clever; active; shrewd; trim; neat; well-dressed; fashionable. **-ly** *adv.* **-ness** *n.* **smarten** (smȧr′·tn) *v.t.* and *v.i.* to make more spruce [O.E. *smeortan*, to feel pain].
smash (smash) *v.t.* to break into pieces to shatter; to hit hard; to ruin; *v.i.* to break into pieces; to dash violently against; of a business firm, to fail; *n.* crash; heavy blow; accident, wrecking vehicles; utter ruin; of business firm, bankruptcy. **-ing** *a.* [fr. E. *mash*, to mix up].
smat·ter (smat′·ẹr) *v.i.* to talk superficially; **-ing** *n.* slight, superficial knowledge.
smear (smēr) *v.t.* to rub over with a greasy, oily, or sticky substance; to daub; to impute disgrace to; (*U.S. Slang*) to defeat thoro-oughly; *n.* mark, stain. **-iness** *n.* **-y** *a.* [O.E. *smeru*, fat].
smell (smel) *n.* sense of perceiving odors by nose; act of smelling; (unpleasant) odor; scent; perfume; *v.t.* to perceive by nose; to detect; *v.i.* to use nose; to give out odor. *pr.p.* **-ing.** *pa.p.* and *pa.t.* **-ed** or **smelt. -ing** *n.* **-y** *a.* having unpleasant smell. **-ing salts** *n.pl.* scented ammonium carbonate used to relieve faintness, headache, etc. [M.E. *smel*].
smelt (smelt) *n.* small, silvery fish of salmon family [O.E. *smelt*].
smelt (smelt) *v.t.* to melt or fuse ore in order to extract metal. **-ing** *n.* [Sw. *smalla*, to melt].
smi·lax (smī′·laks) *n.* genus of evergreen climbing shrubs [Gk. = bindweed].
smile (smīl) *v.i.* to express pleasure, approval, amusement, contempt, irony, etc. by curving lips; to look happy; *v.t.* to express by smile; *n.* act of smiling; pleasant facial expression. **smiling** *a.* cheerful; gay joyous. [Sw. *smila*].
smirch (smurch) *v.t.* to dirty; to soil; to stain; to bring disgrace upon; *n.* stain [M.E. *smeren*, to smear].
smirk (smurk) *v.i.* to smile in an affected or conceited manner; *n.* [O.E. *smercian*, to smile].
smite (smīt) *v.t.* to hit hard; to strike with hand, fist, weapon, etc.; to defeat; to afflict; *v.i.* to strike. *pa.p.* **smitten** (smit′·n). *pa.t.* **smote** (smōt). **-r** *n.* [O.E. *smitan*, to smear].
smith (smith) *n.* one who shapes metal, esp. with hammer and anvil; blacksmith. **-y** *n.* smith's workship; forge [O.E. *smith*].
smith·er·eens (smiTH·ẹr·ēnz′) *n.pl.* (*Colloq.*) small bits. Also **smithers** [fr. *smite*].
smit·ten (smit′·n) *pa.p.* of **smite.**
smock (smȧk) *n.* a loose garment worn over other clothing as a protection while working. **-ing** *n.* embroidered gathering of dress, blouse, etc. into honeycomb pattern [O.E. *smoc*].
smog (smȧg, smawg) *n.* mixture of smoke and fog in atmosphere [from *smoke* and *fog*].
smoke (smōk) *n.* cloudy mass of suspended particles that rises from fire or anything burning; spell of tobacco smoking; cigar or cigarette; *v.t.* to consume (tobacco opium, etc.) by smoking; to expose to smoke (esp. in curing fish, etc.); *v.i.* to inhale and expel smoke of burning tobacco; to give off smoke. **-r** *n.* one who smokes tobacco; railroad car or section in which smoking is permitted; social gathering for men at which smoking is allowed. **smoking** *n.* **smokiness** *n.* **smoky** *a.* emitting smoke; filled with smoke; having color, taste of smoke [O.E. *smoca*].
smol·der (smōl′·der) *v.i.* to burn slowly without flame; of feelings, esp. anger, resentment, etc., to exist inwardly [M.E. *smolder*].
smolt (smōlt) *n.* young salmon.
smooth (smòòTH) *a.* not rough; level; polished; gently flowing; calm; steady in motion; pleasant; easy; *v.t.* to make smooth; to polish; to calm; to soothe; to make easy; *adv.* in a smooth manner. **-ly** *adv.* [O.E. *smoth*].
smor·gas·bord (smōr′·gạs·bōrd) *n.* meal of appetizers served buffet style [Sw.].
smote (smōt) *pa.p.* and *pa.t.* of **smite.**
smoth·er (smuTH′·ẹr) *v.t.* to destroy by depriving of air; to suffocate; to conceal; *v.i.* to be stifled; to be without air; *n.* thick smoke or dust [O.E. *smorian*, to choke].
smudge (smuj) *n.* smear; stain; dirty mark; blot; smoky fire to drive off insects or protect fruit trees from pests; *v.t.* to smear; to make a dirty mark; *v.i.* to become dirty or blurred.
smug (smug) *a.* very neat and prim; self-satisfied; complacent. **-ly** *adv.* **-ness** *n.* [L. Ger. *smuk*, neat].
smug·gle (smug′·l) *v.t.* to import or export goods secretly to evade customs duties. **-r** *n.* **smuggling** *n.* [L. Ger. *smuggeln*].
smut (smut) *n.* black particle of dirt; spot caused by this; fungoid disease of cereals, characterized by blackening of ears of oats, barley, etc.; lewd or obscene talk or writing; *v.t.* to blacken; to smudge. *pr.p.* **-ting.** *pa.p.* and *pa.t.* **-ted. -ty** *a.* soiled with smut; obscene; lewd. **-tily** *adv.* **-tiness** *n.*
smutch (smuch) *v.t.* to blacken, as with soot, etc.; *n.* dirty spot; stain; smudge.
snack (snak) *n.* share; slight, hasty meal. **— bar** *n.* place for service of light, hurried meals [fr. *snatch*].
snaf·fle (snaf′·l) *n.* horse's bridle bit jointed in middle but without curb; *v.t.* to put one on a horse [Dut. *snavel*, nose of animal].
snag (snag) *n.* stump projecting from tree-trunk; stump or tree-trunk sticking up in a river impeding passage of boats; any obstacle, drawback, or catch; *v.t.* to catch on a snag. *pr.p.* **-ging.** *pa.p.*, *pa.t.* [O.T. *snagi*, a point].
snail (snāl) *n.* slow-moving mollusk with spiral shell; slow person [O.E. *snaegel*].
snake (snāk) *n.* long, scaly, limbless reptile; serpent; treacherous person; *v.t.* (*U.S.*) to drag along, e.g. log; *v.i.* to move like a snail. **snaky** *a.* pert. to, or resembling, snake; full of snakes [O.E. *snaca*].
snap (snap) *v.t.* to break abruptly; to crack; to seize suddenly; to snatch; to bite; to shut with click; (*Photog.*) to take snapshot of; *v.i.* to break short; to try to bite; to utter sharp, cross words; to make a quick, sharp sound; to sparkle. *pr.p.* **-ping.** *pa.p.* and *pa.t.* **-ped.** *n.* act of seizing suddenly, esp. with teeth; bite; sudden breaking; quick, sharp sound; small spring catch, as of a bracelet; crisp cooky; short spell of frosty weather; (*Photog.*) short for snapshot; (*Slang*) an easy job; *a.* sudden; unprepared; without warning. **-per** *n.* one who snaps; kind of fresh-water

turtle. **-py** *a.* lively; brisk; (*Colloq.*) smartly dressed; quick. **-dragon** *n.* (*Bot.*) a flowering plant. **-shot** *n.* photograph [Dut. *snappen*].

snare (snār) *n.* running noose of cord or wire, used to trap animals or birds; a trap; anything by which one is deceived; *n.pl.* (*Mus.*) catgut strings across lower head of snare drum to produce rattling sound; *v.t.* to catch with snare; to entangle. **— drum** *n.* small drum carried at the side [O.N. *snara*].

snarl (snárl) *v.i.* to growl like an angry dog; to speak in a surly manner; *n.* growling sound; surly tone of voice. **-er** *n.* [imit.].

snarl (snárl) *n.* tangle or knot of hair, wool, etc.; complication; *v.t.* and *v.i.* to entangle or become entangled [fr. *snare*].

snatch (snach) *v.t.* to seize hastily or without permission; to grasp; *v.i.* to make quick grab or bite (at); *n.* quick grab; small bit or fragment [M.E. *snacchen*].

sneak (snēk) *v.i.* to creep or steal away; to slink; *v.t.* (*Slang*) to steal; *n.* furtive, cowardly fellow. **-er** *n.* **-ers** *n.pl.* (*U.S.*) light, soft-soled shoes. **-ing** *a.* mean; contemptible; secret. **-ingly** *adv.* **-iness, -ingness** *n.* quality of being sneaky; slyness. **-y** *a.* sneaking; mean; underhand [O.E. *snican*, to creep].

sneer (snēr) *v.i.* to show contempt by facial expression, as by curling lips; to smile, speak, or write scornfully; *n.* look of contempt or ridicule; scornful utterance. **-er** *n.* **-ing** *a.*

sneeze (snēze) *v.i.* to expel air through nose and mouth with sudden convulsive spasm and noise; *n.* a sneezing [O.E. *fneosan*].

snick (snik) *n.* small cut; notch; nick; *v.t.* to cut; to notch; to clip; [Scand. *snikka*, to cut].

snicker (snik′·ẹr) *v.i.* to laugh with small, audible catches of voice; to giggle; *n.* half-suppressed laugh [imit. origin].

sniff (snif) *v.i.* to draw in breath through nose with sharp hiss; to express disapproval, etc. by sniffing; to snuff; *v.t.* to take up through nose; to smell; *n.* act of sniffing; that which is sniffed. **-le** *v.i.* to sniff noisily through nose; to snuffle. **-ler** *n.* **snifter** (*Slang*) small drink of liquor [imit. origin].

snip (snip) *v.t.* to clip off with scissors; to cut; *n.* a single, quick stroke, as with scissors; a bit cut off; small piece of anything; *pl.* strong hand shears for cutting sheet metal. *pr.p.* **-ping.** *pa.p.* and *pa.t.* **-ped. -per** *n.* **-pet** *n.* a fragment [Dut. *snippen*].

snipe (snīp) *n.* long-billed gamebird, frequenting marshy places; a shot; *v.i.* to shoot snipe; (*Mil.*) to shoot from cover; *v.t.* to hit by so shooting. **-r** *n.* [O.N. *snipa*].

sniv·el (sniv′·l) *n.* running at the nose; sham emotion; whining, as a child. *v.i.* to run at the nose; to show real or sham sorrow; to cry or whine, as children [O.E. *snyflan*].

snob (snȧb) *n.* one who judges by social rank or wealth rather than merit; one who ignores those whom he considers his social inferiors. **-bery** *n.* **-bish** *a.* **-bishly** *adv.* **-bishness** *n.* [etym. uncertain].

snood (snòòd) *n.* ribbon formerly worn to hold back hair; fillet; netlike covering for head or part of hat [O.E. *snod*].

snoop (snòòp) *v.i.* (*Colloq.*) to investigate slyly; to pry into; *n.* one who acts thus.

snoot (snòòt) *n.* snout; nose; contemptuous; **-ily** *adv.* arrogantly; **-iness** *n.*; **-y,** *a.* (*Colloq.*) snobbish [ME *snute*].

snooze (snòòz) *n.* (*Colloq.*) short sleep; nap; *v.i.* to take a snooze [perh. fr. *snore*].

snore (snōr) *v.i.* to breathe heavily and noisily during sleep; *n.* such noisy breathing. **-r** *n.* [O.E. *snora*, a snore].

snor·kel (snōr′·kạl) *n.* device for submarines and divers for air intake [Gr. *Schnorkel*, spiral].

snort (snawrt) *v.i.* to force air with violence through nose, as horses; to express feeling by such a sound; *v.t.* to express by snort; *n.* snorting sound [imit. origin].

snout (snout) *n.* projecting nose and jaws of animal, esp. of pig; any projection like a snout [O.E. *snut*].

snow (snō) *n.* frozen vapor which falls in flakes; snowfall; mass of flakes on the ground; (*Slang*) narcotic drug, in powdered form; *v.t.* to let fall like snow; to cover with snow; *v.i.* to fall as or like snow.**-y** *a.* covered with, full of snow; white. **-ily** *adv.* **-iness** *n.* **-ball** *n.* round mass of snow pressed or rolled together; shrub bearing balllike clusters of white flowers; anything increasing like snowball; *i.t.* to pelt with snowballs; *v.i.* to grow rapidly; like a rolling snowball. **— blindness** *n.* temporary blindness caused by glare of sun from snow. **—bound** *a.* shut in by heavy snowfall. **-drift** *n.* mass of snow driven into a heap by wind. **-drop** *n.* bulbous plant bearing white flowers in early spring. **-fall** *n.* falling of snow; amount of snow falling in given time or place. **-flake** *n.* small, thin, feathery mass of snow. **— line** *n.* line on mountain above which snow never melts. **-plow** *n.* machine for clearing snow from roads, etc. **-shoe** *n.* light, wooden framework with interwoven leather thongs for traveling over deep snow [O.E. *snaw*].

snub (snub) *v.t.* to check or rebuke with rudeness or indifference; to repress intentionally; *pr.p.* **-bing.** *pa.p.* and *pa.t.* **-bed.** *n.* intentional slight; rebuff; check; *a.* of nose, short and slightly turned up [O.N. *snubba*, to rebuke].

snuff (snuf) *n.* charred part of wick of candle or lamp; *v.t.* to nip this off; to extinguish. **-ers** *n.pl.* instrument resembling scissors, for snuffing candles [M.E. *snoffe*].

snuff (snuf) *v.t.* to draw up or through nostrils; to sniff; to smell; to inhale; *v.i.* to draw air or snuff into nose; to take snuff; *n.* powdered tobacco for inhaling through nose; sniff. **-er** *n.* **-box** *n.* a small box for snuff [Dut. *snuffen*].

snuf·fle (snuf′·l) *v.i.* to breathe noisily through nose, esp. when obstructed; to sniff continually; to speak through nose; *n.* act of snuffling; a nasal twang. **-r** *n.* [fr. *snuff*].

snug (snug) *a.* cosy; trim; comfortable; sheltered; close fitting. **-ly** *adv.* **-ness** *n.* cosiness. **-gery** *n.* a cosy room. **-gle** *v.i.* to lie close to, for warmth or from affection; to nestle [Scand.].

so (sō) *adv.* in this manner or degree; in such manner; very; to such degree (with *as* or *that* coming after); the case being such; accordingly; *conj.* therefore; in case that; *interj.* well! **— long** (*Colloq.*) good-bye. **so-so** *a.* (*Colloq.*) fair; middling; tolerable; *adv.* fairly; tolerably [O.E. *swa*].

soak (sōk) *v.t.* to steep; to wet thoroughly; to permeate; *v.i.* to lie steeped in water or other fluid; (*Colloq.*) to drink to excess; *n.* a soaking; the act of soaking; heavy rain; (*Colloq.*) a hard drinker. **-er** *n.* **-ing** *a.* wetting thoroughly; drenched; *n.* [O.E. *socian*].

soap (sōp) *n.* compound of oil or fat with alkali, used in washing; *v.t.* and *v.i.* to apply soap to. **-y** *a.* pert. to soap; covered with soap; like soap. **-iness** *n.* **— bubble** *n.* iridescent bubble from soapsuds. **— opera** n. (*Colloq.*) highly dramatized radio serial. **-stone** *n.* soft, smooth stone, with soapy feel; talc. **-suds** *n.pl.* foamy mixture of soap and water [O.E. *sape*].

soar (sōr) *v.i.* to fly high; to mount into air; to glide; to rise far above normal or to a great height [L. *ex*, out of; *aura*, the air].

sob (sȧb) *v.i.* to catch breath, esp. in weeping;

to sigh with convulsive motion. *pr.p.* **-bing.** *pa.p.* and *pa.t.* **-bed.** *n.* convulsive catching of breath, esp. in weeping or sighing [imit.].

so·ber (sō'·ber) *a.* temperate; not intoxicated; exercising cool reason; subdued; *v.t.* and *v.i.* to make or become sober. **-ly** *adv.* **-ness** *n.* **sobriety** (sō·brī'·e·ti·) *n.* habit of being sober; habitual temperance; moderation; seriousness [L. *sobrius*].

so·bri·quet (sō'·bri·kā) *n.* nickname, an assumed name. Also **soubriquet** (sòò-) [Fr.].

soc·cer (sak'·ẹr) *n.* association football [fr. *soc* in association].

so·cia·ble (sō'·shạ·bl) *a.* inclined to be friendly; fond of company. **sociably** *adv.* **-ness** *n.* **sociability** *n.* friendliness; geniality [L. *socius*, a companion].

so·cial (sō'·shạl) *a.* pert. to society; affecting public interest; pert. to world of fashion, etc.; living in communities, as ants; sociable; companionable; convivial; *n.* social meeting. **sociably** *adv.* **-ite** (sō'·shạl·īt) *n.* member of fashionable society [L. *socius*, a companion].

so·cial·ism (sō'·shạl·izm) *n.* economic and political system, aiming at public or government ownership of means of production, etc. **socialize** *v.t.* to make social; to transfer industry, etc. from private to public or government ownership. **socialization** *n.* **socialist** *a.* pert. to socialism. **socialistic** *a.* **socialistically** *adv.* [L. *socius*, a companion].

so·ci·e·ty (sạ·sī'·ạ·ti·) *n.* people in general; community; people of culture and good breeding in any community; the wealthy classes; the world of fashion; fellowship; wealthy; a company; an association; a club [L. *socius*, a companion].

so·ci·ol·o·gy (sō·shi·ál'·ạ·ji·) *n.* science of origin, development, and nature of problems confronting society; social science. **sociological** *a.* **sociologist** *n.* [L. *socius*, a companion; Gk. *logos*, a discourse].

sock (sák) *n.* orig. a low-heeled shoe; a short stocking [L. *soccus*, a light shoe].

sock (sák) *v.t.* (*Slang*) to hit hard; *n.* a blow.

sock·et (sák'·ạt) *n.* opening or hollow into which anything is fitted; cavity of eye, tooth, etc.; *v.t.* to provide with, or place in, socket.

sock·eye (sák'·ī) *n.* a red salmon.

sod (sád) *n.* flat piece of earth with grass; turf; *v.t.* to cover with turf. *pr.p.* **-ding.** *pa.p., pa.t.* **-ded.**

so·da (sō'·dạ) *n.* name applied to various compounds of sodium, e.g. *baking soda, caustic soda, washing soda.* (See **sodium**); (*Colloq.*) soda water. **— fountain** *n.* case for holding soda water; shop selling soft drinks, ices, etc. **— water** *n.* drink made by charging water with carbon dioxide [It. fr. L. *solidus*, firm].

so·dal·i·ty (sō·dal'·ạ·ti·) *n.* fellowship; an association [L. *sodalis*, a comrade].

sod·den (sád'·n) *a.* soaked; soft with moisture; dull and heavy; stupid.

so·di·um (sō'·di'ạm) *n.* silvery-white metallic alkaline element, the base of soda (symbol, **Na.** fr. L. *natrium*). **— bicarbonate,** compound of sodium and carbon, used in cooking, medicine, etc.; baking soda. **— carbonate,** washing soda. **— chloride,** common household salt [fr. *soda*].

sod·o·my (sád'·ạm·i·) *n.* unnatural sexual intercourse, esp. between males or with an animal [fr. *Sodom*, Bib. city].

so·fa (sō'·fà) *n.* an upholstered couch [Ar. *Suffah*, cushion].

soft (sawft) *a.* yielding easily to pressure; not hard; easily shaped or molded; smooth; gentle; melodious; quiet; susceptible; sentimental; weak; weak in intellect; not astringent; containing no alcohol; in phonetics, esp. of consonants 'c' and 'g,' pronounced with a sibilant sound; *adv.* softly; quietly. **-ish** *a.* somewhat soft. **-ly** *adv.* **-ness** *n.* **-ball** *n.* a game similar to baseball. **-headed** *a.* weak in intellect. **-hearted** *a.* kind; gentle; merciful. **— landing** *n.* the safe landing of a spacecraft at reduced speed. **-ware** *n.* the written or printed material used in computer programming (See *hardware*) [O.E. *softe*].

soft·en (sawf'·n) *v.t.* to make soft or softer; to lighten; to mitigate; to tone down; to make less loud; *v.t.* to become soft or softer. **-ing** *n.* [O.E. *softe*].

sog·gy (ság'·i·) *a.* soaked with water; sodden [Icel. *soggr*, damp].

soi·gné (swán'·yā) *a.* well finished; exquisitely groomed [Fr.].

soil (soil) *v.t.* to make dirty; to defile; filth; manure; top layer of earth's surface; earth, as food for plants [O.Fr. *soile*].

soi·rée (swà·rā') *n.* a social evening, a reception [Fr. = evening].

so·journ (sō'·jurn) *to* dwell for a time; (sō·jurn') *n.* short stay [L. *sub*, under; *diurnus*, of a day].

sol·ace (sál'·ạs) *n.* comfort in grief; consolation; *v.t.* to console [L. *solari*, to comfort].

so·lan (sō'·lạn) *n.* large sea bird like a goose; a gannet. Also **— goose** [O.N. *sula*].

so·lar (sō'·lẹr) *a.* pert. to, caused by, measured by, sun. **-ize** *v.t., v.i.* to expose to sun's rays. **-ium** (sō·lar'·i·um) *n.* a sun room or porch; *pl.* **-ia. — plexus** (*Med.*) network of nerve tissue and fibers at back of stomach; (*Colloq.*) the pit of the stomach. **— system** *n.* sun and all the heavenly bodies revolving around it [L. *sol*, the sun].

sold (sōld) *pa.p., pa.t.* of **sell.**

sol·der (sád'·ẹr) *n.* easily melted alloy for joining metals; *v.t.* to join or mend with solder [L. *solidare*, to make solid].

sol·dier (sōl'·jẹr) *n.* man engaged in military service; enlisted man as distinguished from commissioned officer. **-y** *n.* soldiers collectively; troops. **— of fortune** *n.* military adventurer [L. *solidus*, a coin].

sole (sōl) *n.* flat of the foot; under part of boot or shoe; lower part of anything, or that on which anything rests; small flatfish, used for food; *v.t.* to supply with a sole [L. *solea*].

sole (sōl) *a.* being, or acting, without another; alone; only. **-ly** *adv.* alone; only [L. *solus*].

sol·e·cism (sál'·ạ·sizm) *n.* breach of grammar; a breach of etiquette. **solecist** *n.* one guilty of solecism [Gk. *soloikos*, speaking incorrectly].

sol·emn (sál'·ạm) *a.* marked, or performed, with religious ceremony; impressive; grave; inspiring awe or dread. **-ly** *adv.* **-ness** *n.* **-ize** (sál'·ạm·nīz) *v.t.* to perform with ceremony or legal form. **-ity** (sạl·em'·ni·ti·) *n.* sacred rite or formal celebration; gravity; seriousness [L. *sollemnis*, yearly, solemn].

so·len (sō·lạn) *n.* genus of bivalve molluscs having a long, slender shell; razor-shell. **-oid** *n.* (*Elect.*) cylindrical coil of wire (without fixed iron core) forming electromagnet when carrying current [Gk. *sōlēn*, a channel pipe; *eidos*, form].

sol·fa (sōl·fà') *v.i.* to sing notes of scale [It. *sol* and *fa*].

so·lic·it (sạ·lis'·it) *v.t.* to ask with earnestness; to petition; *v.i.* to try to obtain, as trade, etc.; to accost. **-ant** *n.* one who solicits; petitioner. **-ation** *n.* earnest request; invitation; petition. **-or** *n.* one who solicits; official in charge of legal matters of city, department of government, etc. **-ous** *a.* anxious; eager; earnest. **-ously** *adv.* **-ousness, -ude** *n.* state of being solicitous; uneasiness; anxiety [L. *sollicitare*, to stir up].

sol·id (sál'·id) *a.* not in a liquid or gaseous state; hard; compact; firm; not hollow; dependable; sound; unanimous; (*Geom.*) having length, breadth, and thickness; whole; complete; *n.* a firm, compact body; (*Geom.*) that which has length, breadth and thickness; (*Physics*) substance which is not liquid nor gaseous. **-ly** *adv.* **-arity** *n.* state of being solidly united in support of common interests, rights, etc. **-ity** *n.* state of being solid; compactness; hardness [L. *solidus*, firm].

so·lid·i·fy (sạ.lid′.ȧ.fī) *v.t.* to make solid or firm; to harden; *v.i.* to become solid [L. *solidus*, firm; *facere*, to make].

sol·i·dus (sȧl′.i.dạs) *n.* oblique stroke (/) in fractions, dates, etc. *pl.* **solidi** [L.].

so·lil·o·quy (sạ.lil′.ạ.kwi.) *n.* talking to oneself; monologue, esp. by actor alone on stage. **soliloquize** *v.i.* to recite a soliloquy; to talk to oneself [L. *solus*, alone; *logui*, to speak].

sol·i·taire (sȧl′.ạ.ter) *a.* living alone; done or spent alone; lonely; secluded; single; sole; *n.* hermit; recluse; a single gem set by itself. **solitarily** *adv.* **solitariness** *n.* **solitude** *n.* being alone; seclusion; lonely place or life [L. *solus*, alone].

so·lo (sō′.lō) *n.* musical composition played or sung by one person; in aviation, flight by single person; *pl.* (sō′.lōz) or **soli** (sō′.lē); *a.* done or performed by one person; unaccompanied; alone. **soloist** (sō′.lō.ist) *n.* (*Mus.*) performer of solos [It. fr. L. *solus*, alone].

sol·tice (sȧl′.stis) *n.* either of two points in sun's path at which sun is farthest N. or S. from equator, about June 21 and December 22 respectively. **solstitial** (sȧl.sti′.shạl) *a.* [L. *sol*, the sun; *sistere*, to cause to stand].

sol·u·ble (sȧl′.yạ.bl) *a.* capable of being dissolved in a liquid; able to be solved or explained. **solubility** *n.* [L. *solubilis*, fr. *solvere*, to loosen].

so·lus (sō′.lạs) *a.* as a stage direction, alone. *fem.* **sola**]L. = alone[.

so·lu·tion (sạ.lòò′.shạn) *n.* process of finding answer to problem; answer itself; dissolving gas, liquid, or solid, esp. in liquid; mixture so obtained; commonly, a mixture of a solid in a liquid; *v.t.* to coat with solution, as a puncture. **solute** *n.* substance dissolved in a solution [L. *solvere*, *solutum*, to loosen].

solve (sȧlv) *v.t.* to work out; to find the answer to; to explain; to make clear. **solvable** *a.* capable of explanation; able to be worked out. **-r** *n.* **solvent** *a.* having the power to dissolve another substance; able to pay all one's debts; *n.* substance, able to dissolve another substance. **-ncy** *n.* state of being able to pay one's debts [L. *solvere*, to loosen].

so·mat·ic (sō.mat′.ik) *a.* pert. to the body; corporeal; physical. Also **-al** [Gk. *sōma*, a body].

som·ber (sȧm′.bẹr) *a.* dark; gloomy; melancholy. **-ly** *adv.* **-ness** *n.* **sombrous** *a.* (*Poet.*) somber **sombrously** *adv.* [Fr. fr. L. *sub umbra*, under shade].

som·bre·ro (sȧm.bre′.rō) *n.* broad-brimmed felt hat [Sp. *sombre*, shade].

some (sum) *a.* denoting an indefinite number, amount, or extent; amount of; one or other; a certain; particular; approximately; (*Colloq.*) remarkable; (*pron.*) portion; particular persons not named; *adv.* approximately. **-body** *n.* person not definitely known; person of importance. **-how** *adv.* in one way or another; by any means. **-one** *pron.* somebody; person not named. **-such** *a.* denoting person or thing of the kind specified. **-thing** *n.* thing not clearly defined; an indefinite quantity or degree; *adv.* in some degree. **-time** *adv.* at a time not definitely stated; at one time or other; at a future time; *a.* former. **-times** *adv.* at times; now and then; occasionally. **-what** *n.* indefinite amount or degree; *adv.* to some extent; rather. **-where** *adv.* in an unnamed or unknown place [O.E. *sum*].

som·er·sault (sum′.ẹr.sawlt) *n.* a movement in which one turns heels over head; *v.i.* [L. *supra*, above; *saltus*, a leap].

som·nam·bu·late (sȧm.nam′.byạ.lāt) *v.i.* to walk in one's sleep. **somnambulation** *n.* **somnambulism** *n.* habit of walking in one's sleep; sleepwalking. **somnambulist** *n.* a sleepwalker. **somnambulistic** *a.* [L. *somnus*, sleep; *ambulare*, to walk].

som·ni·fa·cient (sȧm.ni.fā′.shạnt) *a.* inducing sleep; *n.* soporific. **somniferous** *a.* inducing sleep. **somnific** *a.* causing sleep [L. *somnus*, sleep; *facere*, to make; *ferre*, to bring].

som·no·lent (sȧm′.nạ.lȧnt) *a.* sleepy; drowsy. **-ly** *adv.* drowsily. **somnolence** *n.* sleepiness; drowsiness. Also **somnolency.** **somnolescent** *a.* half asleep [L. *somnus*].

son (sun) *n.* male child; male descendant, however distant; term of affection; native of a place; disciple. **—in-law** *n.* the husband of one's daughter [O.E. *sunu*].

so·nant (sō′.nant) *a.* pert. to sound; (*Phonetics*) of certain alphabetic sounds, voiced; *n.* a syllabic sound. **sonance** *n.* [L. *sonare*].

so·na·ta (sạ.nȧ′.tạ) *n.* a musical composition in three or four movements. **sonatina** (sȧ.nạ.tē′.nạ) *n.* a short sonata [It. fr. L. *sonare*, to sound].

song (sawng) *n.* singing; poem, or piece of poetry, esp. if set to music; piece of music to be sung; musical sounds made by birds; (*Colloq.*) a mere trifle. **— bird** *n.* a singing bird. **-ster** *n.* (*fem.* **songstress**) one who sings; a song bird [O.E. *sang*, fr. *singan*, to sing].

son·ic (sȧn′.ik) *a.* pertaining to sound; devoting speed approximate to that of sound.

son·net (sȧn′.ạt) *n.* poem of fourteen lines of iambic pentameter, with a definite rhyme scheme. **soneteer** *n.* a writer of sonnets [It. *sonetto*, fr. L. *sonus*, a sound].

so·no·rous (sạ.nōr′.as) *a.* giving out a deep, loud sound when struck; resonant; high-sounding. *adv.* **-ness, sonority** *n.* [L. *sonorus*, noisy].

soon (sòòn) *adv.* in a short time; shortly; without delay; willingly [O.E. *sona*, at once].

soot (soot) *n.* a black powdery substance formed by burning coal, etc.; *v.t.* to cover with soot. **-y** *a.* pert. to, or like, soot; covered with soot; black; dingy; dirty [O.E. *set*].

sooth (sòòth) *n.* (*Arch.*) truth; reality. **-sayer** *n.* one who claims to be able to foretell future. **-saying** *n.* [O.E. *soth*, true].

soothe (sòòTH) *v.t.* to please with soft words or kind actions; to calm; to comfort; to allay, as pain. **soothing** *a.* **soothingly** *adv.* [O.E. *sothian*, to show to be true].

sop (sȧp) *n.* piece of bread, etc., dipped in a liquid; anything given to pacify or quieten; bribe; *v.t.* to steep in liquid. *pr.p.* **-ping.** *pa.p.* and *pa.t.* **-ped.** **-ping** *a.* soaked; wet through. **-py** *a.* soaked; rainy [O.E. *sopp*, fr. *supan*, to sip].

soph·ism (sȧf′.izm) *n.* specious argument; clever but fallacious reasoning. **sophist** *n.* orig. in ancient Greece, teacher of logic, rhetoric, philosophy; one who uses fallacoius or specious arguments. **sophistry** *n.* practice of sophists. **sophistic, sophistical** *a.* **sophistically** *adv.* **sophisticate** *v.t.* to deceive by using sophisms; to make artificial; to make wise in the ways of the world. **sophisticated** *a.* **sophistication** *n.* [Gk. *sophisma*, wise].

soph·o·more (sȧf′.ạ.mōr) *n.* second-year student of university, college, or high school [Gk. *sophos*, wise].

so·por (sō′·pẹr) *n.* unnaturally deep sleep. **-ific** *a.* causing or inducing sleep; *n.* drug, which induces deep sleep. **-iferous, soporose** *a.* causing sleep; sleepy. [L. *sopor*, deep sleep].
so·pran·o (sạ·pra′·nō) *n.* highest type of female or boy's voice; soprano singer; *pl.* **-s, soprani** (sō·prȧ′·nī) [It. fr. *sopra*, above].
sor·cer·y (sawr′·sạ·ri·) *n.* witchcraft; magic; enchantment. **sorcerer** *n.* a magician. *fem.* **sorceress,** a witch [L. *sortiri*, to cast lots].
sor·did (sawr′·did) *a.* filthy; squalid; meanly avaricious. **-ly** *adv.* **-ness** *n.* [L. *sordidus*].
sore (sōr) *a.* painful when touched; causing pain; tender; distressed; grieved; (*Colloq.*) angry; *n.* diseased, injured, or bruised spot on body; **-ly** *adv.* **-ness** *n.* [O.E. *sar*].
sor·ghum (sawr·′gạm) *n.* cereal grasses of several varieties, used for making molasses, forage, hay, brooms, etc.; the syrup from sweet sorghums [etym. uncertain].
so·ror·i·ty (sạ·rawr′·i·ti·) *n.* a girls' or women's society [L. *soror*, a sister].
so·ro·sis (sạ·rō′·sis) *n.* compound fleshy fruit, e.g. pineapple; women's club [Gk. *sōros*, heap].
sor·rel (sawr′·ạl) *n.* meadow plant with sour taste [O.Fr. *surelle*].
sor·rel (sawr′·ạl) *a.* reddish-brown; *n.* (horse of) reddish-brown color [O.Fr. *sorel*].
sor·row (sȧr′·ō, sawr′·ō) *n.* pain of mind; grief; sadness; distress; cause of grief, etc.; *v.i.* to feel pain of mind; to grieve. **-er** *n.* **-ful** *a.* causing sorrow; sad; unhappy. **-fully** *adv.* **-fulness** *n.* [O.E. *sorh*].
sor·ry (sȧr′·i; sawr′·i·) *a.* feeling regret; pained in mind; mean; shabby; wretched; worthless. **sorriness** *n.* [O.E. *sarig*].
sort (sawrt) *n.* kind or class; persons or things having same qualities; quality; character; order or rank; *v.t.* to classify; to put in order. **-er** *n.* [L. *sors*, a share, a lot].
sor·tie (sawr′·tē) *n.* sally by besieged forces to attack besiegers; flight by warplane [Fr. *sortir*, to go out].
S.O.S. (es·ō·es) *n.* international code signal call of distress, esp., by radio telegraph (· · · — — — · · ·); any appeal for help.
sot (sȧt) *n.* confirmed drunkard. **-tish** *a.* stupid through drink [Fr. *sot*, foolish].
sot·to vo·ce (sȧt′·tō vō′·chā) *adv.* under one's breath [It. *sotto*, under; *voce*, the voice].
sou (sȯȯ) *n.* former French coin of various values [Fr. fr. L. *solidus*, a coin].
soubriquet See **sobriquet.**
souf·flé (sȯȯ·flā′) *n.* a delicate dish made of eggs and baked [Fr. *scuffler*, to blow].
sough (suf, sou) *n.* low murmuring, sighing sound; *v.i.* [O.E. *swogan*, to resound].
sought (sawt) *pa.p.* and *pa.t.* of **seek.**
soul (sōl) *n.* spiritual and immortal part of human being; seat of emotion, sentiment, and aspiration; the center of moral powers; spirit; the essence; the moving spirit; a human being. **-ful** *a.* full of soul, emotion, or sentiment. **-fully** *adv.* **-less** *a.* without a soul; not inspired; prosaic [O.E. *sawol*].
sound (sound) *a.* healthy; in good condition; solid; entire; profound; free from error; reliable; solvent, as a business firm; *adv.* soundly; completely. **-ly** *adv.* thoroughly. **-ness** *n.* [O.E. *gesund*, healthy].
sound (sound) *n.* long, narrow stretch of water; channel; strait [O.E. *sund*].
sound (sound) *v.t.* to find depth of water, by means of line and lead; (*Fig.*) to try to discover the opinions of; *v.i.* to find depth of water; of a whale, to dive suddenly. **-ing** *n.* measuring the depth of water, esp. with a weighed line; measurement obtained [Fr. *sonder*].
sound (sound) *n.* that which is heard; auditory effect; the distance within which a sound is heard; noise; *v.t.* to cause to make a sound; to utter; to play on; to signal; to examine with stethoscope; *v.i.* to make a noise; to be conveyed by sound; to appear; to seem. **-ing** *a.* making a sound; resonant. **— barrier** (*Aero.*) colloq. term for phenomena occurring when an aircraft reaches speed in excess of that of sound. **— track** *n.* strip on one side of motion-picture film which records sound vibrations. **—waves** *n.pl.* vibrations of the air producing sound. **-board, -ing box** *n.* board or box which reinforces sound from musical instrument; canopy over pulpit for directing voice towards the congregation [L. *sonus*].
soup (sȯȯp) *n.* liquid food made by boiling meat, vegetables, etc. [Fr. *souper*, to sup].
soup·çon (sȯȯp·sȧn′) *n.* suspicion; hence, very small quantity; a taste [Fr.].
sour (sour) *a.* acid; having a sharp taste; pungent; rancid; cross; *v.t., v.i.* to make or become sour. **-ed** *a.* embittered; aggrieved. **-ly** *adv.* **-ness** *n.* [O.E. *sur*].
source (sōrs) *n.* spring; fountain; origin (of stream, information, etc. [L. *surgere*, to rise].
sour·dough (sour′·dō) *n.* fermented batter of flour and water used to leaven fresh dough; prospector; pioneer [*sour* and *dough*].
souse (sous) *v.t.* to steep in brine; to pickle; to plunge into a liquid; to soak; *n.* a pickle made with salt; brine; anything steeped in it; a drenching [form of *sauce*, fr. L. *sal*, salt].
sou·tane (sȯȯ·tȧn′) *n.* gown worn by R.C. priests; cassock [L. *subtus*, beneath].
south (south) *n.* cardinal point of compass opposite north; region lying to that side; *a.* pert. to, or coming from, the south; *adv.* toward or in the south; *v.i.* to move towards the south. **-erly** *a.* (suTH′·ẹr·li·) *a.* pert. to south. **-ern** *a.* in, from, or towards, the south. **-erner** *n.* native of south of a country, etc. **-ernly** *adv.* towards the south. **-ernmost** *a.* lying farthest towards the south. **-ward** *a.* and *adv.* towards south; *n.* southern direction. **-wardly** *a., adv.* **-wards** *adv.* **-wester** *n.* a strong wind from southwest; waterproof hat [O.E. *suth*].
sou·ve·nir (sȯȯ·vạ·nir′, sȯȯ′·vạ·nir) *n.* a keepsake; a memento [Fr. *souvenir*, to remind].
sov·er·eign (sạv′·rạn) *n.* ruler; British gold coin = one pound sterling = 20 shillings; *a.* supreme in power; chief; efficacious in highest degree. **-ty** *n.* supreme power [O.Fr. *sovrain*, fr. L. *supra*, above].
so·vi·et (sō′·vi·et) *n.* council. **Soviet** *n.* political body, consisting of representatives of workers and peasants, elected to local municipalities, regional councils, etc. and sending delegates to higher congresses. **Soviet Union** *n.* the Union of Soviet Socialist Republics; Russia (*abbrev.* **U.S.S.R.**) [Russ.].
sow (sou) *n.* female pig; in smelting, bar of cast iron [O.E. *su*].
sow (sō) *v.t.* to scatter or deposit (seed); to spread abroad; to disseminate; *v.i.* to scatter seed. *pa.p.* **sown** (sōn), **sowed** (sōd). *pa.t.* **-ed -er** *n.* [O.E. *sawan*].
soy (soi) *n.* sauce made from soybean **-bean** *n.* seed of leguminous plant [Jap. *shoyu*].
Spa (spa) *n.* inland watering place in Belgium. **spa** *n.* any place with mineral spring.
space (spās) *n.* expanse of universe; area; room; period of time; extent; empty place; *v.t.* to place at intervals. **-craft, -ship** *n.* a vehicle capable of traveling in outer space. **-walk** *n.* the activity of an astronaut outside a spacecraft while in outer space. **spacious** (spā′·shạs) *a.* roomy; capacious; extensive. **spaciously** *adv.* [Fr. *espace*, fr. L. *spatium*].

spade (spād) *n.* digging tool, with flat blade and long handle; *v.t.* to dig with spade. **-work** *n.* preliminary tasks [O.E. *spadu*].

spade (spād) *n.* (*Cards*) one of two black suits, marked by figure like a pointed spade [Sp. *espada*, a sword].

spa·ghet·ti (spạ·get′·ti·) *n.* footstuff resembling macaroni but thinner [It. *spago*, cord].

spake (spāk) *pa.t.* (*Arch.*) of **speak.**

span (span) *pa.t.* of **spin.**

span (span) *n.* distance between thumb and little finger, when fingers are fully extended; this distance as measure = 9 in; short distance or period of time; distance between supports of arch. roof, etc.; of airplane, distance from wing-tip to wing-tip; pair, of horses or oxen harnessed together; *v.t.* to reach from one side of to the other; to extend across. *pr.p.* **-ning.** *pa.p.* and *pa.t.* **-ned.** **-ner** *n.* one who spans; tool for tightening screw nuts [O.E. *spann*].

span·drel (span′·drạl) *n.* (*Archit.*) the space between outer curves of arch and square head over it; ornamental design in corner of postage stamp [etym. uncertain].

span·gle (spang′·gl) *n.* a small piece of glittering metal, used to ornament dresses; *v.t.* to adorn with spangles; *v.i.* to glitter [O.E. *spang*, a buckle].

Span·iard (span′·yerd) *n.* native of Spain. **Spanish** *a.* of, or pert. to, Spain; *n.* language of Spain.

span·iel (span′·yạl) *n.* breed of dogs, with long, drooping ears; fawning person [O.Fr. *espagneul*, Sangish].

spank (spangk) *v.i.* to move with vigor or spirit. **-ing** *a.* moving with quick, lively step; dashing. **-er** *n.* fast-going horse, ship, etc.; (*Naut.*) fore-and-aft sail attached to the mast nearest the stern [Dan. *spanke*, to strut].

spank (spangk) *v.t.* to strike with flat of hand, esp. on buttocks as punishment; *n.* slap [imit. origin].

spar (spȧr) *v.i.* to fight with the fists, in fun or in earnest; to fight with spurs, as in cock fighting; to dispute, bandy words. *pr.p.* **-ring.** *pa.p.* and *pa.t.* **-red** [etym. uncertain].

spar (spȧr) *n.* pole or beam, esp. as part of ship's rigging [O.N. *sparri*].

spar (spȧr) *n.* crystalline mineral which has luster [O.E. *spaerstan*, gypsum].

spare (sper) *v.t.* and *v.i.* to use frugally; to do without; to save; to omit; to leave unhurt; to give away; *a.* frugal; scanty; scarce; parsimonious; thin; lean; additional; in reserve; not in use; *n.* that which is held in reserve; a duplicate part. **-ly** *adv.* **-ness** *n.* thinness; leanness. **sparing** *a.* **sparingly** *adv.* [O.E. *sparian*].

spark (spȧrk) *n.* small glowing or burning particle; flash of light; trace or particle of anything; in internal-combustion engines, electric flash which ignites explosive mixture in cylinder; (*Colloq.*) gay, dashing young fellow; *v.i.* to send out sparks. **— plug** *n.* in internal-combustion engines, device for igniting explosive gases; (*Colloq.*) one who animates a group [O.E. *spearca*].

spar·kle (spȧrk′.l) *n.* small spark; a glitter; a gleam; vivacity; *v.i.* to emit small flashes of light; to gleam; to glitter; to effervesce. **-r** *n.* one who, or that which, sparkles; (*Slang*) a diamond. **sparkling** *a.* [O.E. *spearca*].

spar·row (spar′·ō) *n.* small brown bird of finch family. **—grass** *n.* (*Colloq.*) asparagus. [O.E. *spearwa*].

sparse (spȧrs) *a.* thinly scattered; scanty; rare. **-ly** *adv.* **-ness** *n.* scantiness [L. *spargere, sparsum*, to scatter].

Spar·ta (spȧr′·tạ) *n.* ancient Greek city-state. **Spartan** *n.* citizen of this town; one who is frugal and faces danger, etc. without flinching; *a.* pert. to Sparta; dauntless.

spasm (spaz′·ạm) *n.* sudden, involuntary contraction of muscle(s); sudden, convulsive movement, effort, emotion, etc.; fitful effort. **spasmodic(al)** *a.* pert. to spasms; convulsive; fitful. **spasmodically** *adv.* by fits and starts. **spastic** *a.* (*Med.*) pert. to spasms; in a rigid condition, due to spasm; applied to people suffering from cerebral palsy. *n.* such a person [Gk. *spasmos*, fr. *spaein*, to draw].

spat (spat) *pa.t.* of **spit.**

spat (spat) *n.* kind of cloth gaiter, reaching a little above ankle. Usually in *pl.* **spats** [*abbrev.* of *spatterdash*].

spat (spat) *n.* spawn of shellfish or oyster; *v.i.* to spawn, of oysters [fr. *spit*].

spate (spāt) *n.* flood in a river, esp. after heavy rain; inundation [Gael. *speid*].

spathe (spāTH) *n.* leaflike sheath enveloping flower cluster. **spathed, spathose** *a.* [Gk. *spathē*, a broad blade].

spa·tial (spā′·shạl) *a.* pert. to space. **-ly** *adv.* [L. *spatium*].

spat·ter (spat′·ẹr) *v.t.* to cast drops of water, mud, etc. over; to splash; *v.i.* to fall in drops; *n.* the act of spattering; a slight splash [Dut. *spatten*, to burst].

spat·u·la (spach′·ạ·lạ) *n.* broad-bladed implement for spreading paints, turning foods in frying pan, etc. **spatular, spatulate** *a.* [Gk. *spathē*, a broad blade].

spav·in (spav′·in) *n.* swelling on horse's leg, causing lameness. **-ed** *a.* [O.Fr. *esparvain*].

spawn (spawn) *n.* eggs of fish, frogs; offspring; *v.t.* and *v.i.* of fish, frogs, to cast eggs; to produce offspring [O.Fr. *espandre*, fr. L. *expandere*, to spread out].

speak (spēk) *v.i.* to utter words; to tell; to deliver a discourse; *v.t.* to utter; to pronounce; to express in words; to express silently or by signs; *pr.p.* **-ing.** *pa.p.* **spoken.** *pa.t.* **spoke.** **-er** *n.* one who speaks; orator. **the Speaker,** presiding officer of the House of Representatives and of similar legislative bodies. **-ing** *n.* *a.* having power to utter words; eloquent; lifelike, e.g. of picture. **-easy** *n.* (*Slang*) illegal saloon, esp. during prohibition [O.E. *sprecan*].

spear (sper) *n.* long, pointed weapon, used in fighting, hunting, etc.; sharp-pointed instrument for catching fish; lance; pike; *v.t.* to pierce or kill with spear. **-head** *n.* iron point, barb, or prong of a spear; leader of an advance; **— side** *n.* male branch of a family [O.E. *spere*].

spe·cial (spesh′·ạl) *a.* pert. to a species or sort; particular; beyond the usual; distinct; intimate; designed for a particular person or purpose. **-ly** *adv.* **-ize** *v.t.* to make special or distinct; to adapt for a particular purpose; *v.i.* to devote oneself to a particular branch of study. **-ization** *n.* act of specializing. **-ist** *n.* one trained and skilled in a special branch. **-istic** *a.* **-ty** *n.* a special characteristic of a person or thing; a special product; that in which a person is highly skilled. [L. *species*, a kind].

spe·cie (spē′·shē) *n.* coined money [L. *species*, a kind].

spe·cies (spē′·shēz) *n.* kind; variety; sort; class; subdivision of a more general class or genus [L. *species*, a kind].

spe·cif·ic (spi·sif′·ik) *a.* pert. to, or characteristic of, a species; peculiar to; well defined; precise; *n.* a specific statement, etc. **-ally** *adv.* **— gravity,** weight of substance expressed in relation to weight of equal volume of water [L. *species*, a kind; *facere*, to make].

spec·i·fi·ca·tion (spes·ạ·fạ·kā′·shạn) *n.* act

of specifying; statement of details, requirements, etc. **specify** *v.t.* to state definitely; to give details of; to indicate precisely. **specifiable** *a.* [L. *species*, a kind; *facere*, to make].

spec·i·men (spes′·a̦·ma̦n) *n.* part of anything, or one of a number of things, used to show nature and quality of the whole; sample [L. *specere*, to look].

spe·cious (spē′·sha̦s) *a.* having a fair appearance; superficially fair or just; apparently acceptable, esp. at first sight. **-ly** *adv.* **-ness speciosity** *n.* [L. *speciosus*, fair to see].

speck (spek) *n.* small spot; particle; very small thing; *v.t.* to mark with specks. **-le** *n.* a small speck or spot; *v.t.* to mark with small spots. **speckled** *a.* **-less** *a.* [O.E. *specca*].

spec·ta·cle (spek′·ta̦·kl) *n.* sight; show; thing exhibited; a pageant. **spectacles** *n.pl.* eyeglasses. **-ed** *a.* wearing spectacles. **spectacular** *a.* showy; making great display. **spectacularly** *adv.* [L. *spectare*, to look at].

spec·ta·tor (spek′·tā·te̦r) *n.* an onlooker; ghost; apparition. **spectral** *a.* pert. to a specter; ghostly; pert. to spectrum. **spectrally** *adv.* **spectrum** *n.* the colored band into which a ray of light can be separated as in the rainbow; *pl.* **spectra** [L. *spectrum*, an image].

spec·tro- (spek′·trō) *prefix* fr. L. *spectrum*, an image, used in many derivatives. **-graph** *n.* scientific instrument for photographing spectra. **-scope** *n.* instrument for production and examination of spectra. **-scopic, -scopical** *a.* [Gk. *graphein*, to write; *skopein*, to view].

spec·u·late (spek′·ya̦·lāt) *v.i.* to make theories or guesses; to meditate; to engage in risky commercial transactions. **speculation** *n.* act of speculating; theorizing; guess; practice of buying shares, etc. in the hope of selling at a high profit. **speculative** *a.* given to speculation. **speculatively** *adv.* **speculator** *n.* **speculatory** *a.* [L. *speculari*, to observe].

spec·u·lum (spek′·ya̦·la̦m) *n.* mirror; reflector of polished metals, esp. as used in reflecting telescopes; (*Surg.*) instrument for examining interior cavity of body. *pl.* **specula** [L. fr. *specere*, to observe].

sped (sped) *pa.p.* and *pa.t.* of **speed.**

speech (spēch) *n.* power of speaking; what is spoken; faculty of expressing thoughts in words; enunciation; remarks; conversation; language; formal address; an oration. **-less** *a.* without power of speech; dumb; silent. **-lessly** *adv.* **-lessness** *n.* **-ify** *v.i.* to make speech, esp. long and tedious one. **-ifier** *n.* [O.E. *spraec*].

speed (spēd) *n.* swiftness of motion; rate of progress; velocity; *v.t.* to cause to move faster; to aid; to bid farewell to; *v.i.* to move quickly or at speed beyond legal limit; to increase speed. *pa.p.* and *pa.t.* **sped. -y** *a.* quick; rapid; prompt. **-ily** *adv.* **-boat** *n.* very fast motor boat. **-ometer** *n.* instrument indicating speed, usually in miles per hour. **-way** *n.* track for racing [O.E. *sped*].

spell (spel) *n* word or words supposed to have magical power; magic formula; fascination. **-bind** *v.t.* to hold as if by spell; to enchant; to fascinate. *pa.p., pa.t.* **-bound** *a.* [O.E. *spell*, a narrative].

spell (spel) *n.* a turn of work or duty; a brief period of time [O.E. *spelian*, to act for].

spell (spel) *v.t.* to read letter by letter; to mean; *v.i.* to form words with proper letters. *pa.p.* and *pa.t.* **-ed** or **spelt** [O.E. *spell*, a narrative].

spe·lun·ker (spē′·lungk·er) one who explores caves.

spend (spend) *v.t.* and *v.i.* to pay out; to disburse; to pass, as time; to employ; to waste; to exhaust. *pa.p., pa.t.,* **spent** *a.* exhausted; worn out; of a fish, having deposited spawn. **-er** *n.* **-thrift** *n.* one who spends money foolishly or extravagantly; *a.* extravagant [O.E. *spenden*].

sperm (spurm) *n.* fertilizing fluid of male animals; the male cell. **—oil** *n.* oil obtained from sperm whale. **— whale** *n.* cachalot, large whale, valuable for its oil and for spermaceti. **spermaceti** (spur·ma̦·sē′·ti·, spur·ma̦·set′·i·) *n.* waxlike substance obtained from head of sperm whale. **-atic** *a.* pert. to sperm [Gk. *sperma*, seed].

sperm·a·to- *prefix* fr. Gk. *sperma*, seed. **spermatoid** *a.* resembling sperm. **spermatozoon** (spur·ma̦·ta̦·zō′·a̦n) *n.* male generative cell, found in semen. *pl.* **-zoa, -zoal, -zoan** *a.*

spew, spue (spū) *v.t.* and *v.i.* to eject from the stomach; to vomit [O.E. *spiwan*].

sphere (sfir) *n.* round, solid body, ball; globe; celestial body; range of knowledge, influence, etc.; field of action; social status; position; *v.t.* to put in a sphere; to encircle, **spheral** (sfi′·ra̦l) *a.* formed like a sphere. **spheric** (sfer′·ik) *a.* pert. to heavenly bodies. **spherical** *a.* sphere-shaped. **spherically** *adv.* **sphericity** *n.* roundness. **spheroid** (sfi′·roid) *n.* body almost, but not quite, spherical, e.g. orange, earth, etc. **spheroidal** *a.* having form of spheroid. Also **spheroidic. spherule** (sfir′·ūl) *n.* a small sphere. **spherular, spherulate** *a.* [Gk. *sphaira*, a globe].

sphinc·ter (sfingk′·te̦r) *n.* (*Anat.*) circular muscle which contracts or expands orifice of an organ, e.g. round anus [Gk. *sphingein*, to bind tight].

sphinx (sfingks) *n.* (*Myth.*) fabulous monster, with winged body of lion and head of woman, which proposed riddles; statue of this; (*Fig.*) one whose thoughts are difficult to guess; enigmatic person. (*Cap.*) huge statue of recumbent lion with man's head in Egypt [Gk. *sphinx*, literally, the strangler].

sphyg·mus (sfig′·ma̦s) *n.* (*Med.*) pulse. **sphygmic** *a.* [Gk. *sphugmos*, the pulse].

spice (spīs) *n.* aromatic substance, used for seasoning; spices collectively (*Fig.*) anything that adds flavor, zest, etc. *v.t.* to season with spice. **spicery** *n.* spices collectively. **spicy** *a.* **spicily** *adv.* [O.Fr. *espice*].

spi·der (spī′·de̦r) *n.* small, eight-legged insect-like animal that spins web to catch flies, etc.; a frying pan; a trivet; an evil person. *a.* like a spider; full of spiders; very thin. **—monkey** *n.* monkey with long, thin legs and tail [O.E. *spinnan*, to spin].

spied (spīd) *pa.p.* and *pa.t.* of **spy.**

spig·ot (spig′·a̦t) *n.* peg for stopping hole in cask; a faucet which controls flow [L. *spica*, an ear of corn].

spike (spīk) *n.* sharp-pointed piece of metal or wood; large nail; ear of corn, etc.; (*Bot.*) flower-cluster growing from central stem; *v.t.* furnished with spikes; pointed (*Slang*) to add liquor to a drink. **spiky** *a.* to supply, set, fasten, or pierce with spikes; pointed [O.N. *spik, a nail*].

spill (spil) *v.t.* to cause to flow out; to pour out; to shed (blood); to throw off, as from horse, etc.; to upset; *v.i.* to flow over; to be shed; to be lost or wasted; *n.* a spilling; fall or tumble, as from vehicle, horse, etc. *pa.p.* and *pa.t.* **-ed** or **spilt. -er** *n.* **-way** *n.* channel for overflow water from dam [O.E. *spillian*, to destroy].

spill (spil) *n.* thin strip of wood or twist of paper, for lighting a fire, pipe, etc.; a peg [Dut. *speld*, a splinter].

spin (spin) *v.t.* to twist into threads; to cause to revolve rapidly; to whirl; to twirl; to draw out tediously, as a story; to prolong; *v.i.* to make thread, as a spider, etc.; to revolve rapidly; to move swiftly; *n.* rapid whirling motion; short, quick run or drive. *pr.p.* **-ning.** *pa.p.* and *pa.t.* **spun** or (*Arch.*)

span. -ner *n.* **-ning jenny** *n.* machine for spinning several threads simultaneously. **-ning wheel** *n.* outdated device for spinning cotton, wool, flax, etc. into thread or yarn [O.E. *spinnan*].

spin·ach (spin′·ich) *n.* leafy vegetable used for food. **spinaceous** *a.* [O.Fr. *espinage*].

spin·dle (spin′·dl) *n.* long, slender rod, used in spinning, for twisting and winding the thread; measure of yarn, thread, or silk; shaft; axis; *v.i.* to grow long and slender. **spindly** *a.* long and slender. **spindling** *a.* [O.E. *spinel*, fr. *spinnan*, to spin].

spine (spīn) *n.* thorn; quill; backbone; back of book. **spinal** *a.* pert. to spine or backbon. **-less** *a.* having no spine; weak of character. **spiny** *a.* full of spines; like a spine; thorny; prickly; perplexing. **spinule** *n.* small spine. **spinal column,** the backbone [L. *spina*, a thorn].

spin·et (spin′·it) *n.* musical instrument like a harpsichord [O.Fr. *espinette*, fr. L. *spina*].

spin·na·ker (spin′·a·kẹr) *n.* a large triangular sail [etym. uncertain].

spin·ster (spin′·stẹr) *n.* orig. one who spins; unmarried woman. **-hood** *n.* **spinstress** *n.* woman who spins [O.E. *spinnan*, to spin].

spi·ra·cle (spī′·ra·kl, spir′·a·kl) *n.* breathing-hole; blowhole of whale. **spiracular, spiraculate** *a.* [L. *spirare*, to breathe].

Spi·rae·a (spī·rē′·a) *n.* a genus of herbaceous plants, including meadowsweet, bearing white or pink flowers [Gk. *speira*, a coil].

spi·rant (spī′·rant) *n.* consonant pronounced with perceptible emission of breath [L. *spirare*, to breathe].

spire (spīr) *n.* winding line like threads of screw; curl; coil. **spiral** *a.* winding; coiled; *n.* spiral curve; coil; whorl; *v.i.* to follow spiral line; to coil; to curve [Gk. *speira*, coil].

spire (spīr) *n.* blade of grass; stalk; slender shoot; anything tall and tapering to point; (tapering part of) steeple; peak; *v.i.* to rise high, like spire. **spiral** *a.* like a spire. **spiry** *a.* having spires; tapering [O.E. *spir*, a stalk].

spir·it (spir′·it) *n.* vital force; immortal part of man; soul; specter; ghost; frame of mind; disposition; temper; eager desire; mental vigor; courage; essential character; (*Cap.*) Holy Spirit; liquid got by distillation, esp. alcoholic; *v.t.* to carry away mysteriously; to put energy into. **spirits** *n.pl.* a state of mind; mood; distilled alcoholic liquor. **-ed** *a.* full of spirit and vigor; lively; animated. **-edly** *adv.* **-edness** *n.* **-ism** *n.* See **spiritualism. -less** *a.* without spirit or life; lacking energy; listless. **-essly** *adv.* **-uous** *a.* containing alcohol; distilled [L. *spiritus*, fr *spirare*, to breathe].

spir·it·u·al (spir′·it·choo·al) *a.* pert. to spirit or soul; not material; unworldly; pert. to sacred things; holy; *n.* Negro sacred song or hymn. **-ly** *adv.* **-ize** *v.t.* to make spiritual; to make pure in heart. **-ism, spiritism** *n.* belief that spirits of dead can communicate with living people. **-ist** *n.* [L. *spiritus*, breath].

spit (spit)) *n.* pointed rod put through meat for roasting; narrow point of land projecting into sea; *v.t.* to thrust spit through; to impale *pr.p.* **-ting.** *pa.p. pa.t.* **-ted.** [O.E. *spitu*].

spit (spit) *v.t.* to eject from mouth; to expel; *v.i.* to eject saliva from mouth; to expectorate; to hiss, esp. of cats; *pr.p.* **-ting**.*pa.p. pa.t.* **spat.** *n.* saliva; act of spitting; like fall of fine rain; (*Colloq.*) an exact likeness. **-ter** *n.* **-tle** *n.* saliva ejected from mouth; frothy secretion of certain insects. **-toon** *n.* a vessel for spittle; cuspidor [O.E. *spittan*].

spite (spīt) *n.* malice; ill will; *v.t.* to treat maliciously; to try to injure or thwart; to annoy. **-ful** *a.* **-fully** *adv.* **-fulness** *n.* **in spite of,** in defiance of [fr. *despite*].

spit·fire (spit′·fīr) *n.* hot tempered person [*spit* and *fire*].

spitz (spitz) *n.* a kind of Pomeranian dog [Ger. = pointed].

splash (splash) *v.t.* to spatter water, mud, etc. over; to soil thus; to print in bold headlines; *v.i.* to dash or scatter, of liquids; to dabble in water; to fall in drops; *n.* sound of object falling into liquid, mud, etc.; spot; daub. **-y** *a.* wet and muddy. **-board** *n.* mud guard. **-down** *n.* the landing of a spacecraft on water [imit. origin].

splat·ter (splat′·ẹr) *v.t., v.i.* to splash; to spatter [fr. *spatter*].

splay (splā) *v.t.* to slope; to slant; to spread outwards; *a.* turned outwards; at and broad; *n.* slanting surface of opening, as at window. **-foot** *n.* flat foot [fr. *display*].

spleen (splēn) *n.* ductless organ lying to left of stomach; ill humor; spite; melancholy; irritability [Gk. *splēn*].

splen·did (splen′·did) *a.* magnificent; gorgeous; (*Colloq.*) excellent. **-ly** *adv.* **splendor** (splen′·dẹr) *n.* brilliant luster; pomp. **splendorous** *a.* [L. *splendere*, to shine].

sple·net·ic (spli·net′·ik) *a.* pert. to spleen; morose; irritable. *n.* one suffering from disease of spleen; irritable person [Gk. *splēn*].

splice (splīs) *v.t.* to join together; to join, as wood, etc. by overlapping and binding; (*Colloq.*) to marry; *n.* union [Dut. *splissen*].

splint (splint) *n.* rigid piece of material for holding broken limb in position; bony excrescene on inside of horse's leg; *v.t.* to bind with splints. **-er** *n.* thin piece of wood, metal, etc. split off; *v.t., v.i.* to make or break into thin pieces. **-ery** *a.* [Swed.].

split (split) *v.t.* to cut lengthwise; to cleave; to tear apart; to separate; to divide; *v.i.* to break asunder; to part lengthwise; to dash to pieces; to separate; *pr.p.* **-ting;** *pa.p., pa.t.* **split;** *n.* crack; fissure; breach; share. **-ing** *n.* cleaving or rending; *a.* severe; distressing. **— infinitive** *n.* insertion of adverb or adverbial phrase between *to* and verb of infinitive. **—level** *a.* describing a home that has several levels separated by steps. **to — hairs,** to make fine distinctions [Dut. *splitten*].

splut·ter (splut′·ẹr) *v.t.* to utter incoherently with spitting sounds; *v.t.* to emit such sounds; to speak hastily and confusedly; *n.* such sounds or speech; a confused noise. **-er** *n.* [imit. origin].

Spode (spōd) *n.* highly decorated porcelain [Josiah *Spode*, pottery manufacturer].

spoil (spoil) *v.t.* to damage; to injure; to cause to decay; to harm character by indulgence; *v.i.* to go bad; to decay. *pa.p., pa.t.* **-ed, spoilt. -er** *n.* one who takes a delight in interfering with enjoyment of others. **-s** *n.pl.* booty; prey; plunder [L. *spoliare*].

spoke (spōk) *pa.t.* of **speak. -s-man** *n.* one deputed to speak for others.

spoke (spōk) *n.* one of small bars connecting hub of wheel with rim; rung of ladder. **-shave** *n.* planning tool [O.E. *spaca*].

spo·li·ate (spō′·li·āt) *v.t.* to rob; to plunder; *v.i.* to practice plundering. **spoliative** *a.* **spoliation** *n.* the act of despoiling; robbery; destruction. **spoliator** *n.* [L. *spoliare*].

spon·dee (spȧn′·dē) *n.* in poetry, a foot of two long syllables (— —). **spondaic** (spȧn·dā′·ik) *a.* [Gk. *spondē*, drink offering].

sponge (spunj) *n.* marine animal of cellular structure, outer coating of whose body is perforated to allow entrance of water; skeleton of this animal, used to absorb water; act of cleaning with sponge; (*Colloq.*) parasite; sponger; hanger-on; (*Colloq.*) habitual drinker; *v.t.* to wipe, cleanse, with sponge; *v.i.* to live at expense of others. **-r** *n.* **spongy**

(spun′.ji.) *a.* sponge-like; of open texture; full of small holes; absorbent; wet and soft, esp. of ground. **sponginess** *n.* **-cake** *n.* light, sweet cake. **to throw in the sponge,** to acknowledge defeat [Gk., L. *spongia*].

spon·sor (spån′.sẹr) *n.* one who is responsible for another; surety; godfather or godmother; guarantor; a patron; *v.t.* to support; to act as guarantor or patron of; to pay for a radio or television program including advertisements of one's own goods. **-ial** *a.* **-ship** *n.* [L. *spondere, sponsum,* to promise].

spon·ta·ne·ous (spån.tā′.nē.ạs) *a.* of one's own free will; voluntary; natural; produced by some internal cause, said of physical effects, as combustion, growth, etc. **-ly** *adv.* **-ness, spontaneity** (spån.tạ.nē′.ạ.ti.) *n.* [L. *sponte,* of one's own free will].

spoof (spòòf) *n.* (*Slang, chiefly Brit.*) hoax; swindle; *v.t.* to fool; to hoax.

spook (spòòk) *n.* (*Colloq.*) ghost; apparition. **-ish, -y** *a.* [Dut.].

spool (spòòl) *n.* small cylinder for winding thread, wire, etc.; *v.t.* to wind on spool [O.Fr. *espole*].

spoon (spòòn) *n.* implement, with bowl at end of handle, for carrying food to the mouth. etc.; golf club with wooden head; *v.t.* and *v.i.* to use, hit with spoon; (*Golf*) to scoop ball high in air; (*Colloq.*) to make love. **-ful** *n.* quantity spoon can hold; small quantity; (*Med.*) half an ounce. **-bill** *n.* long-legged wading bird with spoon-shaped bill **—feed** *v.t.* to feed with a spoon; (*Fig.*) to do overmuch for a person, thus weakening his self-reliance *pa.p., pa.t.* **-fed** *a.* [O.E. *spon*].

spoon·er·ism (spòòn′.ẹr.ism) *n.* transposition of letters of spoken words, causing a humorous effect, e.g. a *half-warmed fish* for a 'half-formed wish' [fr. Dr. A. W. *Spooner*].

spoor (spoor) *n.* track or trail of wild animal [Dut. = a track].

spo·rad·ic (spạ.rad′.ik) *a.* occurring singly here and there; occasional. Also **-al. -ally** *adv.* [Gk. *sporadikos,* fr. *speirein,* to sow].

spore (spōr) *n.* in flowerless plants, e.g. in ferns, minute cell with reproductive powers; germ; seed. **sporangium** *n.* spore case. *pl.* **sporangia. sporangial** *a.* **sporoid** *a.* spore-like [Gk. *spora,* seed].

spor·ran (spawr′.ạn) *n.* large pouch worn in front of the kilt [Gael. *sporan*].

sport (spōrt) *n.* that which amuses; diversion; pastime; merriment; object of jest; mockery; outdoor game or recreation esp. of athletic nature; freak of nature; (*Colloq.*) a dandy; good loser; one willing to take a chance; *v.t.* (*Colloq.*) to display in public; to show off; *v.i.* to play; to take part in out-door recreation. **-s** *n.pl.* games; athletic meetings. **-ing** *a.* pert. to sport or sportsmen; (*Colloq.*) willing to take a chance. **-ive** *a.* pert. to sport; playful. **-s-man, -s-woman** *n.* **-s-manship** *n.* practice or skill of a sportsman; fairmindedness. **-s-manlike** *a.* [fr. *disport*].

spot (spåt) *n.* speck; blemish, esp. on reputation; place; locality; *v.t.* to cover with spots; to stain; to place billiard ball on marked point; (*Colloq.*) to detect; to recognize; *v.i.* to become marked. *pr.p.* **-ting.** *pa.p.* and *pa.t.* **-ted. -less** *a.* without spot or stain; scrupulously clean; pure; innocent. **-lessly** *adv.* **-lessness** *n.* **-ted, -ty** *a.* marked with spots or stains; irregular. **-tedness, tiness** *n.* **-ter** *n.* **— cash,** immediate payment; ready money. **-light** *n.* apparatus used to throw concentrated beam of light on performer on stage; light thrown; the public eye.**on the spot,** immediately; (*Slang*) in a dangerous or embarrassing position [O.N. *spotti*].

spouse (spous) *n.* married person, husband or wife. **spousal** *a.* pert. to spouse, marriage [L. *sponsus,* promise].

spout (spout) *v.t.* to shoot out, as liquid through a pipe; (*Colloq.*) to utter in a pompous manner; to recite; *v.i.* to gush out in jet; (*Colloq.*) to speak volubly; *n.* projecting tube, pipe, etc., for pouring liquid; a pipe or tube for leading off rain from roof. **-er** *n.*

sprag (sprag) *n.* piece of wood or metal used to lock wheel of vehicle; device to prevent vehicle running backwards on hill [Dan.].

sprain (sprān) *v.t.* to wrench or twist muscles or ligaments of a joint; to overstrain; *n.* such an injury.

sprang (sprang) *pa.t.* of the verb **spring.**

sprat (sprat) *n.* small sea fish, allied to herring and pilchard [O.E. *sprot*].

sprawl (sprawl) *v.i.* to sit or lie with legs outstretched or in ungainly position; to move about awkwardly; to spread out irregularly; to write carelessly and irregularly; *n.* act of sprawling [O.E. *spreawlian*].

spray (sprā) *n.* twigs; small, graceful branch with leaves and blossoms; sprig.

spray (sprā) *n.* fine droplets of water driven by wind from tops of waves, etc.; shower of fine droplets of any liquid, e.g. medicine, perfume, etc.; spraying machine; atomizer; *v.t.* to sprinkle. **-er** *n.* [L. Ger. *Sprci*].

spread (spred) *v.t.* to stretch out; to extend; to cover surface with; to scatter; to unfold, as wings; to circulate, as news, etc.; to convey from one to another, as disease; to set and lay food on table; *v.i.* to extend in all directions; to become spread, scattered, circulated, etc.; *n.* extension; expanse; covering for bed, etc.; (*Colloq.*) feast. *pa.p.* and *pa.t.* **spread. -ing** *n.* act of extending. **—eagle** *n.* eagle with wings stretched out; *a.* with arms and legs stretched out; bombastic; *v.t.* to lie with outstretched limbs [O.E. *spraedan*].

spree (sprē) *n.* lively frolic; drinking bout [Ir. *spre,* a spark].

sprig (sprig) *n.* small shoot or twig; ornament in form of spray; scion; youth; small, headless nail; *v.t.* to mark, adorn, with figures of sprigs or sprays. *pr.p.* **-ging.** *pa.p., pa.t.* **-ged** [O.E. *spraec,* a twig].

spright·ly (sprīt′.li.) *a.* lively; airy; vivacious. **sprightliness** *n.* [old form of *sprite*].

spring (spring) *v.i.* to leap; to jump; to shoot up, out, or forth; to appear; to recoil; to result, as from a cause; to issue, as from parent or ancestor; to appear above ground; to grow; to thrive; *v.t.* to cause to spring up; to produce unexpectedly; to start, as game; to cause to explode, as a mine; to develop leak; to bend so as to weaken; to release, as catch of trap; *n.* a leap; a bound; a jump; recoil; a contrivance of coiled or bent metal with much resilience; resilience; flow of water from earth; fountain; any source; origin; a crack; season of year; upward curve of arch. *pa.p.* **sprung.** *pa.t.* **sprang** or **sprung. -er** *n.* one who springs; breed of spaniel. **-y** *a.* elastic; light in tread or gait. **-iness** *n.* **-board** *n.* springy board used in jumping and diving. **-time** *n.* season of spring [O.E. *springan*].

springe (sprinj) *n.* snare with a spring noose; *v.t.* to catch in a springe [fr. *spring*].

sprin·kle (spring′.kl) *v.t.* to scatter small drops of water, sand, etc.; to scatter on; to baptize with drops of water; *v.i.* to scatter (a liquid or any fine substance); *n.* small quantity scattered; occasional drops of rain. **-d** *a.* marked by small spots. **-r** *n.* one who sprinkles. **sprinkling** *n.* act of scattering; small quantity falling in drops [O.E. *sprengan*].

sprint (sprint) *v.i./n.* short run at full speed. **-er** *n.* [Cf. *spurt*].

sprit (sprit) *n.* (*Naut.*) small spar set diagonally across fore-and-aft sail to extend it [O.E. *spreot,* a pole].

sprite (sprīt) *n.* elf; a fairy; a goblin [L. *spiritus*, spirit].
sprock·et (spràk′·it) *n.* toothlike projection on outer rim of wheel, e.g. of bicycle, for engaging links of chain [etym. uncertain].
sprout (sprout) *v.i.* to begin to grow; to put forth shoots; to spring up; *n.* shoot; bud. [O.E. *sprutan*].
spruce (spròòs) *a.* neat in dress; smart; dapper; trim; *v.t., v.i.* to dress smartly. **-ly** *adv.* **-ness** *n.* [M.E., fr. O.Fr. *Pruce*, Prussia].
spruce (spròòs) *n.* common name of some coniferous trees [M.E., fr. O.Fr. *Pruce*, Prussia].
sprung (sprung) *pa.p., pa.t.* of **spring.**
spry (sprī) *a.* nimble; agile [Scand.].
spud (spud) *n.* small spadelike implement; (*Colloq.*) potato [etym. uncertain].
spue. See **spew.**
spume (spūm) *n., v.i.* froth; foam; scum. **spumous** *a.* **spumy** *a.* [L. *spuma*].
spun (spun) *pa.p., pa.t.* **spin.**
spunk (spungk) *n.* wood that readily takes fire; (*Colloq.*) spirit. **-y** *a.* (*Colloq.*) plucky [L. *spongia*, a sponge].
spur (spur) *n.* pricking instrument worn on horseman's heels, used as goad; anything that incites to action; projection on the leg of a cock; mountain projecting from range; projection; *v.t.* to apply spurs to; to urge to action; *v.i.* to ride hard; to press forward. *pr.p.* **-ring.** **-red** *a.* wearing spurs; (*Bot.*) having spur-like shoots; incited [O.E. *spora*].
spurge (spurj) *n.* plant of several species, having milky juice [L. *expurgare*, to purge].
spu·ri·ous (spyoo′·ri·ạs) *a.* not genuine or authentic; false. **-ly** *adv.* [L. *spurius*].
spurn (spurn) *v.t.* to reject with disdain; to scorn; *n.* disdainful rejection [O.E. *spornan*].
spurt (spurt) *v.t.* to force out suddenly in a stream; to squirt; *v.i.* to gush out with force; to make a short, sudden, and strong effort, esp. in a race; *n.* a sudden, strong flow or effort. Also **spirt** [O.E. *spryttan*].
sput·nik (spoot′·nik) *n.* a satellite launched into orbit by Russia [Russ. = fellow traveler].
sput·ter (sput′·ẹr) *v.t.* to throw out in small particles with haste and noise; to utter excitedly and indistinctly; *v.t.* to scatter drops of saliva; to speak rapidly; to fly off with crackling noise; *n.* act of sputtering; sound made. **-er** *n.* [fr. *spout*].
spu·tum (spū′·tạm) *n.* spittle; saliva. *pl.* **sputa** [L. *spuere*, *sputum*, to spit].
spy (spī) *n.* one who enters enemy territory secretly, to gain information; secret agent; one who keep watch on others. *v.t.* to catch sight of; to notice; to discern; *v.i.* to act as a spy. **-glass** *n.* small telescope [Fr. *espion*, fr. L. *specere*, to look].
squab (skwȧb) *a.* fat and short; *n.* nestling pigeon used for food [etym. uncertain].
squab·ble (skwȧb′·l) *v.i.* to wrangle; to dispute noisily; *n.* petty, noisy quarrel [imit.].
squad (skwȧd) *n.* (*Mil.*) smallest unit of soldiers, etc.; small party of men at work; gang [Fr. *escouade*].
squad·ron (skwȧd′·rạn) *n.* a military tactical unit; an athletic team [It. *squadra*, a square].
squal·id (skwȧl′id) *a.* mean and dirty, esp. through neglect; filthy; foul. *adv.* **-ity, -ness, squalor** *n.* filth; foulness [L. *squalidus*].
squall (skwawl) *v.t., v.i.* to scream or cry out violently; *n.* loud scream; sudden gust of wind. **-y** *a.* [imit. origin].
squa·ma (skwā′·mạ) *n.* scale; scalelike part. *pl.* **squamae** (skwā′·mē) [L. = a scale].
squan·der (skwȧn′·dẹr) *v.t.* to waste; to dissipate. **-er** *n.* spendthrift [Scand.].
square (skwer) *n.* plane figure with four equal sides and four right angles; anything shaped like this; in town, open space of this shape; carpenter's instrument for testing or drawing right angles; body of soldiers drawn up in form of square; (*Math.*) product of a number or quantity multiplied by itself; *a.* square shaped; rectangular; at right angles; giving equal justice; fair; balanced or settled, as account or bill; *adv.* squarely; directly; *v.t.* to make like a square; to place at right angles; (*Math.*) to multiply by itself; to balance; to settle; to put right; (*Colloq.*) to win over by bribery; *v.i.* to agree exactly; **-ly** *adv.* **-ness** *n.* **squarish** *a.* nearly square. **— dance,** old-fashioned dance for four couples. **— inch, foot, yard,** etc., area equal to surface of square with sides one inch, foot, yard, etc. long. **—rigged** *a.* (*Naut.*) of a ship, fitted with square sails. **— root,** number or quantity which, when multiplied by itself, produces the number of which it is the square root. **-shooter** *a.* (*Colloq.*) person who is honest [L. *quadrare*, to square, fr. *quattuor*, four].
squash (skwȧsh) *v.t.* to beat or crush flat; to squeeze to pulp; to suppress; *v.i.* to fall into a soft, flat mass; *n.* anything soft and easily crushed; packed crowd; game played with rackets. **-iness** *n.* **-y** *a.* [L. *ex*, out; *quassus*, to shake].
squash (skwȧsh) *n.* gourdlike fruit [Amer.-Ind. *asquash*, raw, green].
squat (skwȧt) *v.i.* to sit on heels; to crouch, as animal; to settle on land without having title to it, or in order to acquire title; *a.* short and thick; sitting close to ground. *pr.p.* **-ting.** *pa.p.* and *pa.t.* **-ted.** **-ter** *n.* [O.Fr. *esquatir*].
squaw (skwaw) *n.* N. American Indian woman, esp. wife [N. Amer. Ind. *eskaw*].
squeak (skwēk) *n.* short, sharp, shrill sound; sharp, unpleasant, grating sound; (*Colloq.*) a narrow escape; *v.i.* to utter, or make, such sound; (*Slang*) to give away secret. **-y** *a.*
squeal (skwēl) *n.* long, shrill cry; *v.i.* to utter long, shrill cry; (*Slang*) to turn informer. **-er** *n.* [imit. origin].
squeam·ish (skwēm′·ish) *a.* easily made sick; easily shocked; over-scrupulous; fussy. **-ly** *adv.* **-ness** *n.* [O.Fr. *escoymous*].
squee·gee (skwē′·jē) *n.* implement with rubber edge on head, for clearing water from deck of ship, floor, pavement, etc. Also **squilgee** [fr. *squeeze*].
squeeze (skwēz) *v.t.* to press or crush; to compress; to extract by pressure; to force into; (*Colloq.*) to subject to extortion; *v.i.* to force one's way; to press; *n.* pressure; compression; close hug or embrace; (*Colloq.*) difficult situation. **squeezable** *a.* [O.E. *cwisan*].
squelch (skwelch) *n.* crushing blow; suppression; sound made when withdrawing feet from sodden ground; *v.t.* to crush down; (*Colloq.*) to silence with a crushing remark; *v.i.* to make sound of a squelch [etym. uncertain].
squid (skwid) *n.* a kind of sea mollusc.
squil·gee (skwil·′·jē) *n.* Same as **squeegee.**
squill (skwil) *n.* plant of lily family whose bulb has emetic properties. **-s** *n.pl.* drug from bulb of squill [Gk. *skilla*].
squint (skwint) *a.* looking obliquely; having eyes turned in; *v.t.* to cause to squint; *v.i.* to be cross-eyed; to glance sideways; to look with eyes partly closed; *n.* act, habit of squinting; (*Med.*) strabismus; hasty glance; peep. **-eyed** *a.* squinting; cross-eyed; spiteful.
squire (skwīr) *n.* formerly, knight's attendant; (*Brit.*) rural landowner; lady's escort; *v.t.* to escort [fr. *esquire*].
squirm (skwurm) *v.i.* to move like a snake, eel, worm, etc.; to wriggle. **-iness** *n.* **-y** *a.*
squir·rel (skwur′·ạl) *n.* small graceful animal with bushy tail, living in trees and feeding on nuts; its fur [O.Fr. *escureul*].
squirt (skwurt) *v.t.* and *v.i.* to eject, or be ejected, in a jet; to spurt; *n.* instrument for squirting; syringe; thin jet of liquid. **-er** *n.*

stab (stab) *v.t.* to pierce or wound with pointed instrument; to hurt feelings of; *v.i.* to strike with pointed weapon; *n.* blow or wound so inflicted; sudden pain. *pr.p.* **-bing.** *pa.p.* and *pa.t.* **-bed. -ber** *n.* [fr. Gael. *stob*, stake].

sta·bi·lize (stā′.bạ.līz) *v.t.* to make stable, fixed, etc.; to fix exchange value of currency of a country. **stabilization** *n.* **stabilizer** *n.* that which stabilizes; horizontal tailplane of aircraft. **stability** (stạ.bil′.ạ.ti.) *n.* steadiness [L. *stabilis*, fr. *stare*, to stand].

sta·ble (stā′.bl) *a.* firmly fixed, established; steady; lasting; resolute; **stably** *adv.* Also **stabile.** [L. *stabilis*, fr. *stare*, to stand].

sta·ble (stā′.bl) *n.* building for horses, usually divided into stalls; racehorse trainer's establishment; *v.t.* to put into, or keep in, stable; *v.i.* to be in stable [L. *stabulum*, a stall, fr. *stare*, to stand].

stac·ca·to (stạ.kȧ′.tō) *a.* and *adv.* (*Mus.*) short, sharp, and distinct [It. fr. L. *staccare*, to separate].

stack (stak) *n.* large heap or pile, esp. of hay, straw, or wood; number of chimneys standing together; a chimney; (*Colloq.*) a great number; *pl.* book shelves. *v.t.* to heap or pile up; to arrange cards for cheating [O.N. *stakkr*].

sta·di·um (stā.di.ạm) *n.* arena for sports events, entertainments, etc., with seats for spectators [L. fr. Gk. *stadion*].

staff (staf) *n. pl.* **-s** or **staves** (stāvz): pole or stick used in walking, climbing, etc. or for support or defense; prop; stick, as emblem of office or authority; flagpole; (*Mus.*) five lines and four spaces on which music is written; (*Arch.*) stanza. (with *pl.* **-s**): body of persons working in office, school, etc.; *v.t.* to provide with staff. [O.E. *staef*].

stag (stag) *n.* male of red or other large deer; man who attends party without a woman. (*Slang*) party for men only [O.E. *stagga*].

stage (stāj) *n.* raised floor or platform esp. of theater, etc.; theatrical profession; dramatic art of literature; scene of action; degree of progress; point of development; distance between two stopping places on a journey; *v.t.* to put (a play) on stage. **staging** *n.* scaffolding. **-coach** *n.* four-wheeled passenger vehicle, horse drawn. **-fright** *n.* extreme nervousness felt when facing audience.**-struck** *a* smitten with love for stage as career. **-whisper** *n.* loud whisper intended to be heard [O.Fr. *estage*, fr. L. *stare*, to stand].

stagger (stag′.ẹr) *v.i.* to walk or stand unsteadily; to reel; to totter; to hestitate; *v.t.* to cause to reel; to cause to hesitate; to shock; to distribute in overlapping periods; to arrange in zigzag fashion; *n.* act of staggering; unsteady movement. **-ing** *a.* amazing; astounding [O.N. *stakra*, to push].

stag·nate (stag′.nāt) *v.i.* to cease to flow; to be motionless; to be dull. **stagnant** *a.* of water, not flowing; hence, foul; impure; not brisk; dull. **stagnantly** *adv.* **stagnation** *n.* [L. *stagnum*, pool].

staid (stād) *a.* of sober and quiet character; steady; sedate; **-ly** *adv.* **-ness** *n.* [fr. *stay*].

stain (stān) *v.t.* and *v.i.* to discolor; to spot; to blot; to dye; to color, as wood, glass, etc.; to mark with guilt; *n.* discoloration; spot; dye; taint of guilt; disgrace. **-less** *a.* without a stain; not liable to stain or rust, esp. of a kind of steel. **-ed-glass,** glass with colors fused into it [L. *tingere*, to color].

stair (stār) *n.* steps one above the other for connecting different levels. **-s** *n.pl.* flight of steps. **-case** *n.* flight of steps with railings, etc. Also **-way** [M.E. *steire*, climb].

stake (stāk) *n.* sharpened stick or post; post to which one condemned to be burned, was tied; death by burning; money laid down as wager; interest in result of enterprise; *pl.* money in contention; *v.t.* to mark out with stakes; to wager; to risk; to pledge. **at stake,** risked; involved [O.E. *staca*].

sta·lac·tite (stạ.lak′.tīt) *n.* deposit of carbonate of lime, hanging like icicle from roof of cave. **stalactic, stalactitic** *a.* **stalactical** *a.* [Gk. *stalaktos*, droppings].

sta·lag (stạ′.lȧg) *n.* (*World War 2*) prisoner-of-war camp [Ger. *Stammlager*].

sta·lag·mite (stạ.lag′.mīt) *n.* deposit of carbonate of lime from floor of cave. **stalagmitic(al)** [Gk. *stalagma*, that which drops].

stale (stāl) *a.* not fresh; kept too long, as bread; tasteless; musty; having lost originality;trite; common; *v.t.* to make tasteless; *v.i.* to lose freshness.**-ly** *adv.* **-ness** *n.* [O.Fr. *estale*, spread out].

stale (stāl) *v.i.* of horses, to make water; *n.*

stale·mate (stāl′.māt) *n.* (*Chess*) position, resulting in drawn game; deadlock; standstill; *v.t.* to bring to a standstill [*stale* and *mate*].

stalk (stawk) *n.* stem of plant, leaf, etc., [M.E.].

stalk (stawk) *v.i., t.* to steal up to game cautiously; to walk in stiff and stately manner; *n.* act of stealing up to game; stiff and stately gait. **-er** *n.* **-ing-horse** *n.* horse or figure of one, behind which a sportsman takes cover when stalking game; pretense; feint; pretext [O.E. *stealcian*, to walk cautionsly].

stall (stawl) *n.* compartment for animal in stable; erection for display and sale of goods; a pew or enclosed seat in cathedral or church; protective sheath for injured finger; *v.t.* and *v.i.* to place or keep in stall; to come to a standstill; of engine or automobile, to stop running unintentionally; of aircraft, to lose flying speed and controllability [O.E. *steall*, a standing place, esp. for cattle].

stall (stawl) (*Slang*) pretense, trick; *v.i.* to evade question [O.E. *stelan*, to *steal*].

stal·lion (stal′.yạn) *n.* an uncastrated male horse kept for breeding [fr. *stall*].

stal·wart (stawl′.wẹrt) *a.* sturdy; strong; brave; steadfast; *n.* strong, muscular person; staunch supporter. **-ly** *adv.* [O.E. *staelworthe*].

sta·men (stā′.mạn) *n.* (*Bot.*) male organ of flowering plant, pollen-bearing part. **staminal** *a.* pert. to stamens, or to stamina. L. = fiber, thread].

stam·i·na (stam′.ạ.nạ) *n.* power of endurance; staying power; vigor.

stam·mer (stam′.ẹr) *v.i.* to speak with repetition of syllables or hesitatingly; to stutter; *n.* halting enunciation; stutter. **-er** *n.* **-ing** *n.* stammer; stutter [O.E. *stamerian*].

stamp (stamp) *v.i.* to put down a foot with force; *v.t.* to set down (a foot) heavily or with force; to make an official mark on; to affix postage stamp; to distinguish by a mark; to brand; to fix deeply; *n.* act of stamping; instrument for making imprinted mark; mark imprinted; die; piece of gummed paper printed with device, as evidence of postage, etc.; character; form. **-er** *n.* [O.E. *stempan*].

stam·pede (stam.pēd′) *n.* sudden, frightened rush, esp. of herd of cattle, crowd, etc.; *v.t.* to put into a state of panic; *v.i.* to take part in a stampede; to rush off in a general panic [Sp. *estampido*, a crash].

stance (stans) *n.* position of feet in certain games, e.g. golf [L. *stare*, to stand].

stanch (stȧnch) *v.t.* to stop or check flow (of blood). *a.* firm; loyal; trustworthy. **-ly** *adv.* **-ness** *n.* Also **staunch** [O.F. estancher].

stan·chion (stan′.chạn) *n.* upright support; iron bar, used as prop [O.Fr. *estance*, fr. L. *stare*, to stand].

stand (stand) *v.i.* to remain at rest in upright position; to be situated; to become or remain stationary; to stop; to endure; to adhere to principles; to have a position, order, or rank; to consist; to place oneself; to adhere to; to persist; to insist; to be of certain height; (*Naut.*) to hold course or direction; to continue in force; (*Colloq.*) to treat; *v.t.* to endure; to sustain; to withstand; to set; *pa.p.* and *pa.t.* **stood.** *n.* place where one stands; place for taxicabs; structure for spectators; piece of furniture on which things may be placed; stall for display of goods; position on some question. **-by** *n.* something in reserve. **-in** *n.* (*Film*) actor or actress who stands in the place of principal player until scene is ready to be shot. **-off, -offish** *a.* haughty; reserved; aloof. **-offishness** *n.* **-point** *n.* a point of view. **to stand-down** (*Law*) to leave the witness stand. **to stand out,** to be conspicuous [O.E. *standan*].

stand·ard (stan′·dẹrd) *n.* weight, measure, model, quality, etc. to which others must conform; criterion; pole with a flag; flag esp. ensign of war; royal banner; upright support; *a.* serving as established rule, model, etc.; having fixed value; uniform; standing upright. **-ize** *v.t.* to make of, or bring to, uniform level of weight, measure, quality, etc. **-ization** *n.* [O.Fr. *estendard,* a royal banner].

stand·ing (stan′·ding) *a.* established by law, custom, etc.; settled; permanent; not flowing; erect; *n.* duration; existence; continuance; reputation. **— army,** force maintained in peacetime. **— orders,** permanent rules [O.E. *standan*].

stank (stangk) *pa.t.* of the verb **stink.**

stan·za (stan′·zạ) *n.* group of lines or verses of poetry having definite pattern; loosely, division of poem.. **stanzaic** (stan·zā′·ik) *a.* [It. stanza, fr. L. *stare,* to stand].

sta·ple (stā′·pl) *n.* settled market; chief product of a country or district; unmanufactured material; fiber of wool, cotton, flax, etc.; *a.* established in commerce; settled; regularly produced or made for market; principal; chief; *v.t.* of textiles, to grade according to length and quality of fiber. **-r** *n.* [O.Fr. *estaple,* a general market].

sta·ple (stā′·pl) *n.* U-shaped piece of metal with pointed ends to drive into wood used with hook, as locking device for a door, etc.; piece of wire to hold sheets of paper together **-r** *n.* mechanical device for fastening papers together [O.E. *stapel,* a prop].

star (stȧr) *n.* shining celestial body, seen as twinkling point of light; five or six-pointed figure asterisk; leading actor or actress; *v.t.* to set or adorn with stars; to cast (in play) as leading actor; *v.i.* to shine, as star; to play principal part. *pr.p.* **-ring**; *pa.p., pa.t.* **-red. -let** *n.* small star; beginning actress. **-light** *n.* light from stars. **-lit** *a.* **-red** *a.* **-ry** *a.* **-riness** *n.* **-fish** *n.* marine animal shaped like a star. **-gazing** *n.* practice of observing stars; astrology [O.E. *steorra*].

star·board (stȧr′·bẹrd) *n.* right-hand side of a ship, looking forward; *a.* pert. to, or on this side; *v.t.* to put (the helm) to starboard [O.E. *steorbord,* the steer side].

starch (stȧrch) *n.* substance forming main food element in bread, potatoes, etc. and used, mixed with water, for stiffening linen, etc.; formality; primness; *v.t.* to stiffen with starch. **-y** *a.* pert. to, containing, starch; (*Colloq.*) stiff; formal. **-ily** *adv.* **-iness** *n.* [O.E. *stearc,* rigid].

stare (ster) *v.i.* to look fixedly; to gaze; *v.t.* to abash by staring at; *n.* fixed, steady look. **-r** *n.* **staring** *n. a.* [O.E. *starian*].

stark (stȧrk) *a.* stiff; rigid; desolate; naked; downright; utter; *adv.* completely. **-ly** *adv.* [O.E. *steare,* rigid].

star·ling (stȧr′·ling) *n.* bird, bluish-black and speckled [O.E. *staer,* starling].

start (stȧrt) *v.i.* to make sudden movement; to spring; to wince; to begin, esp. journey; to become loosened or displaced; *v.t.* to cause to move suddenly; to set going; to, begin; to loosen; to displace; *n.* sudden involuntary movement, spring or leap; act of setting out; beginning; in sports, advantage of lead in race. **-er** *n.* [O.E. *sturtan*].

star·tle (stȧr′·tl) *v.t.* to cause to start; to excite by sudden alarm; to give a fright to; *v.i.* to move abruptly, esp. from fright, apprehension, etc. **startling** *a.* alarming; astonishing; surprising. **startlingly** *adv.* [fr. *start*].

starve (stȧrv) *v.i.* to suffer from hunger; to die of hunger; to be short of something necessary; *v.t.* to cause to suffer or die from lack of food, etc. **starvation** *n.* the suffering from lack of food, warmth, etc. [O.E. *steorfan,* to die].

state (stāt) *n.* condition of person or thing; place or situation; temporary aspect of affairs; rank; high position; formal dignity; politically organized community; civil powers of such; *a.* pert. to state; governmental; ceremonial; *v.t.* to set forth; to express in words; to specify. **-d** *a.* fixed; regular; settled. **-ly** *a.* dignified; imposing; majestic. **-liness** *n.* **-ment** *n.* act of expressing in words; what is expressed; formal account of indebtedness. **-craft** *n.* political sagacity; statesmanship. **-less** *a.* without nationality. **-room** *n.* a private cabin in a ship, train, etc. **-sman** *n.* one skilled in art of government; able politician. **-sman-like** *a.* **-smanship** *n.* [L. *status,* fr. *stare,* to stand].

stat·ic (stat′·ik) *a.* pert. to bodies at rest, or in equilibrium; motionless; *n.* (*Radio*) crackling noises during reception due to atmospheric electricity. **-al** *a.* static. **-s** *n.pl.* branch of mechanics dealing with bodies at rest [Gk. *statikos,* causing to stand].

sta·tion (stā′·shạn) *n.* place where thing or person stands; position; situation; condition of life; rank; regular stopping place for trains, etc.; local or district office for police force, fire-brigade, etc.; *v.t.* to put in a position; to appoint to place of duty. **-ary** *a.* not moving; fixed; regular; stable [L. *stare,* to stand].

sta·tion·er (stā′·shạn·ẹr) *n.* one who deals in writing materials. **-ery** *n.* wares sold by stationer [L. *statiōnāries,* stationary].

sta·tis·tics (stạ·tis′·tiks) *n.pl.* numerical data collected systematically, summarized, and tabulated; science of collecting and interpreting such information. **statistic(al)** *a.* **statistically** *adv.* **statistician** (stạt·ạs·tish′·ạn) *n.* one skilled in statistics. **statist** (stā′·tist) *n.* statistician [Gk. *statizein,* to set up].

sta·tor (stā′·tẹr) *n.* (*Elect.*) the stationary part of a generator [L. *stare,* to stand].

stat·ue (stach′·o̤o̤) *n.* image of person or animal, carved out of solid substance or cast in metal. **statuary** *n.* collection of statutes. **statuesque** (stach·oo·esk′) *a.* like a statue; imposing. **statuette** (stach·oo·et′) *n.* small statute [L. *statua,* a standing image].

stat·ure (stach′·er) *n.* the heights of a person or animal [L. *statura,* fr. *stare,* to stand].

sta·tus (stā′·tạs) *n.* position; rank; position of affairs [L. fr. *stare,* to stand].

stat·ute (stach′·o̤o̤) *n.* law passed by legislature; established rule or law. **statutory** *a.* enacted, defined, or authorized by statute [L. *statutum,* that which is set up].

staunch. See **stanch.**

stave (stāv) *n.* one of curved strips of wood forming cask; rung of ladder; staff; five lines and spaces on which musical notes are written; verse or stanza; *v.t.* to fit with staves; to break stave(s) of (cask); to knock hole in side of; to ward off; to deter. *pa.p.* and *pa.t.* **-d** or **stove** [fr. *staff*].

staves (stāvz) *n.pl.* See **staff** and **stave.**
stay (stā) *v.t.* to restrain; to check; to stop; to support; to satisfy; to last; *v.i.* to remain; to continue in a place; to dwell; to pause; *n.* remaining or continuing in a place; halt; support; postponement, esp. of a legal proceeding. **-s** *n.pl.* laced corset [O.E. *staeg*].
stay (stā) *n.* (*Naut.*) strong rope or wire to support a mast or spar; *v.t.* to support or incline to one side with stays; to put on the other track; *v.t.* to change tack; to go about [O.E. *staeg*].
stead (sted) *n.* place which another had; place; use; benefit; advantage; service; frame of bed. [O.E. *stede*, position, place].
stead·fast (sted′·fast) *a.* firmly fixed; steady; constant. **-ly** *adv.* **-ness** *n.* [O.E. *stede*, place; *faest*, firm].
stead·y (sted′·i·) *a.* firm; constant; uniform; temperate; industrious; reliable; *v.t.* to make steady; to support; *v.i.* to become steady; **steadily** *adv.* **steadiness** *n.* [O.E. *stede*, position, place].
steak (stāk) *n.* slice of meat, esp. beef; also, slice of fish [O.N. *steik*].
steal (stēl) *v.t.* to take by theft; to get by cunning or surprise; to win gradually by skill, affection, etc.; *v.i.* to take what is not one's own; to move silently, or secretly. *pa.p.* **stolen** (stōlạn). *pa.t.* **stole** (stōl). **stealth** (stelth) *n.* secret means used to accomplish anything; concealed act. **stealthy** (stel′·thi·) *a.* done by stealth. **stealthiness** *n.* [O.E. *stelan*].
steam (stēm) *n.* vapor rising from boiling water; water in gaseous state; any exhalation of heated bodies; *a.* worked by steam; *v.t.* to apply steam; to; to cook or treat with steam; *v.i.* to give off steam; to rise in vapor; to move under power of steam. **-y** *a.* pert. to, or like, steam; full of steam; misty. **-iness** *n.* **-er** *n.* steamship; vessel for cooking or washing by steam; something operated by steam. **-roller** *n.* heavy roller, driven by steam, used in road making [O.E. *steam*].
ste·a·rin (stē·ạ·rin) *n.* solid substance occurring in natural fats; hard, waxy solid used in manufacture of candles. Also **stearine.** **stearic** *a.* [Gk. *stear*, suet].
steed (stēd) *n.* horse [O.E. *steda*, stallion].
steel (stēl) *n.* hard and malleable metal, made by mixing carbon in iron; tool or weapon of steel; *a.* made of steel; hard; inflexible; unfeeling; *v.t.* to overlay, point, or edge, with steel; to harden; to make obdurate. **-y** *a.* made of, or like, steel; hard; obdurate; relentless. **-iness** *n.* **— engraving** *n.* method of incising on steel; the print [O.E. *style*].
steel·yard (stēl′·yȧrd) *n.* balance with unequal arms and movable weight [etym. uncertain].
steep (stēp) *a.* having abrupt or decided slope; precipitous; (*Colloq.*) very high or exorbitant, esp. of prices; *n.* steep place; precipice. **-ly** *adv.* **-en** *v.t.* and *v.i.* to make, or become, steep [O.E. *steap*].
steep (stēp) *v.t.* to soak in a liquid; to drench; to saturate; *v.i.* to be soaked; *n.* act or process of steeping; liquid used [O.N. *steypa*, to pour out].
stee·ple (stē′·pl) *n.* a church tower with a spire. **-chase** *n.* a cross-country horse race; horse race on a course specially set with artificial obstacles; a cross-country footrace. **-jack** *n.* a skilled workman who climbs steeples, tall chimneys, etc. [O.E. *steap*, lofty].
steer (stir) *n.* a young male ox; a bullock [O.E. *steor*, a bullock].
steer (stir) *v.t.* to guide or direct the course of (a ship, car, etc.) by means of a rudder, wheel, etc.; *v.i.* to guide a ship, automobile, etc.; to direct one's course. **-age** *n.* the part of a ship allotted to passengers paying the lowest fare. **-er, -sman** *n.* the man who steers; the helmsman of a ship.**-ing gear** *n.* the mechanism for steering a vessel, vehicle, etc. [O.E. *stieran*].
stel·lar (stel′·ẹr) *a.* pert. to, or like, stars; starry. **stellate, stellated** *a.* arranged in the form of a star; star-shaped; radiating. **stelliform** *a.* **stellular** *a.* [L. *stella*, a star].
stem (stem) *n.* the principal stalk of a tree or plant; any slender stalk of a plant; any slender shaft resembling a stalk; branch of family; curved or upright piece of timber or metal to which two sides of ship are joined; part of word to which inflectional endings are added; *v.t.* to remove the stem of; *v.i.* to originate. *pr.p.* **-ming** *pa.p.* and *pa.t.* **-med** [O.E. *stefn*]
stem (stem) *v.t.* to check; to stop; to dam up. *pr.p.* **-ming.** *pa.p.* and *pa.t.* **-med** [O.N. *stemma*].
stench (stench) *n.* strong, offensive odor [O.E. *stenc*].
sten·cil (sten′·sil) *n.* thin sheet of metal, paper, etc. pierced with pattern or letters, so that when placed on any surface and brushed over with paint, ink, etc., the design is reproduced; design so reproduced; *v.t.* to mark or paint thus. *pr.p.* **-ing.** *pa.p.* and *pa.t.* **-ed**
ste·nog·ra·phy (ste·nȧg′·rạ·fi·) *n.* shorthand writing. **stenograph** *n.* character used in stenography; the script; stenographic machine; *v.i.* to write in shorthand. **stenographer, stenographist** *n.* **stenotype** *n.* a machine for writing shorthand; **stenographic, stenographical** *a.* [Gk. *stenos*, narrow; *graphein*, to write].
step (step) *v.i.* to move and set down the foot; to walk, esp. short distance; to press with the foot; *v.t.* to set or place, as foot; to measure in paces; (*Naut.*) to set up (mast); *n.* act of stepping; complete movement of foot in walking, dancing, etc.; distance so covered; manner of walking; footprint; footfall; tread of stair; degree of progress; measure; grade; (*Naut.*) socket for mast; *pr.p.* **-ping.** *pa.p.* and *pa.t.* **-ped.** **-per** *n.* **-ping stone** *n.* stone for stepping on when crossing stream, etc.; (*Fig.*) aid to success [O.E. *staeppan*].
step- (step) *prefix*, showing relationship acquired by remarriage. **-father** *n.* second, or later, husband of one's mother. Similarly **-mother, -brother, -sister.**
steppe (step) *n.* vast, treeless plain, as in Siberia [Russ. = a heath].
ster·e·o- (ster′·i·ō, stir′·i·ō·) fr. Gk. *stereos*, solid, used in referring to hardness solidity, three-dimensionality. **-phonic** *a.*, of or denoting a system of placing microphone to impart greater realism of sound.
ster·e·o·scope (stir′·i·, ster′·i·ạ·skōp) *n.* optical instrument in which two pictures taken at different viewpoints are combined into one image, with effect of depth and solidity. **-scopic(al)** *a.* **-scopically** *adv.* **-scopy** *n.* [Gk. *stereos*, solid; *skopein*, to view].
ster·e·otype (stir′·i·, ster′·i·ạ·tīp) *n.* in printing, plate made by pouring metal into mold of plaster or papier-maché made from original type; fixed form. *a.* pert. to stereotypes; *v.t.* to make a stereotype from; to print from stereotypes; to fix unalterably; to reduce to empty formula; to make always the same. **-d** *a.* **-r, stereotypist** *n.* [Gk. *stereos*, solid; and *type*].
ster·ile (ster′·il) *a.* barren; not fertile; unable to have offspring; producing no fruit, seed, or crops; (*Med.*) entirely free from germs of all kinds. **sterilize** *v.t.* to make steril; to deprive of power of having offspring; to destroy germs, esp. by heat or antiseptics. **sterlization** *n.* **sterlizer** *n.* **sterility** *n.* barrenness [L. *sterilis*, barren].
ster·ling (stur′·ling) *a.* pert. to standard

value, weight, or purity of silver 92½% pure); of solid worth; genuine; pure; denoting British money.

stern (sturn) *a.* severe; strict; rigorous.**-ly** *adv.* **-ness** *n.* [O.E. *styrne*].

stern (sturn) *n.* after part of ship; rump or tail of animal [O.N. *stjorn*, steering].

ster·num (stur′·nạm) *n.* breastbone. *pl.* **sterna. sternal** *a.* [Gk. *sternon*, the chest].

ster·nu·ta·tion (stẹr·nyạ·tā′·shạn) *n.* act of sneezing; sneeze [L. *sternutare*].

ster·tor (stur′·tẹr) *n.* heavy, sonorous breathing. **-ous** *a.* **-ously** *adv.* [L. *stertere*, to snore]

stet (stet) *v.i.* word used by proofreaders as instruction to printer to cancel previous correaction. *pr.p.* **-ting.** *pa.p., pa.t.* **-ted.** [L. = let it stand]

steth·o·scope (steth′·ạ·skōp) *n.* instrument for listening to action of lungs or heart. [Gk. *stēthos*, chest; *skopein*, to see].

ste·ve·dore (stēv′·ạ·dōr) *n.* one who loads and unloads ships [Sp. *estivador*, a wool packer, fr. L. *stipare*, to press together].

stew (stū) *v.t.* to cook slowly in a closed vessel; to simmer; *v.i.* to be cooked slowly; to feel uncomfortably warm; (*Slang*) to fuss or worry; *n.* stewed meat, etc. (*Colloq.*) nervous anxiety; **-ed** *a.* [O.Fr. *estuve*, a stove].

stew·ard (stū′·ẹrd) *n.* one who manages another's property; on ship, attendant on passengers; catering-manager of club. **-ess** *n. fem.* female steward. **-ship** *n.* office of steward; management [O.E. *stigweard*, fr. *stig*, a house; *weard*, a ward].

stib·i·um (stib′·i·ạm) *n.* antimony **stibial** *a.* [L.].

stich (stik) *n.* verse or line of poetry, of whatever measure or number of feet **-ic** *a.* pert. to stich. **-ometry** *n.* measurement of manuscript by number of lines it contains. **-ometric, ometrical** *a.* [Gk. *stichos*, row].

stick (stik) *n.* small branch cut off tree or shrub; staff; rod; (*Print.*) instrument in which types are arranged in words and lines; set of bombs dropped one after the other; (*Colloq.*) stiff or dull person [O.E. *sticca*].

stick (stik) *v.t.* to stab; to pierce; to jab; to puncture; to fasten; to cause to adhere; to fix; to thrust; (*Colloq.*) to endure; *v.i.* to pierce; to adhere closely; to remain fixed; to hesitate; to be unable to proceed; to be puzzled, e.g. by a problem. *pa.p.* and *pa.t.* **stuck. -er** *n.* **-y** *a.* adhesive; viscous; tenacious; (*Colloq.*) embarrassing. **-iness** *n.* **-ing plaster** *n.* adhesive bandage for small wounds, cuts, etc. **stuck up,** conceited [O.E. *stician*, to pierce].

stick·le (stik′·l) *v.i.* to hold out stubbornly. **-r** *n.* one who insists on trifles of procedure, etc. [O.E. *stihlan*, to control].

stick·pin (stik′·pin) *n.* necktie pin.

stiff (stif) *a.* not easily bent; not flexible or pliant; moved with difficulty; firm; hard; stubborn; formal in manner; high in price; *n.* (*Slang*) corpse. **-ly** *adv.* **-ness** *n.* **-en** *v.t.* and *v.i.* to make or become stiff or stiffer. **-ener** *n.* one who, or that which, stiffens. **—necked** *a.* stubborn; obstinate [O.E. *stif*].

sti·fle (stī′·fl) *v.t.* and *v.i.* to smother; to suppress; to repress. **stifling** *a.* airless; close.

stig·ma (stig′·mạ) *n.* brand; mark of disgrace; stain on character; blemish on skin; (*Bot.*) top of pistil of a flower. *pl.* **-s** or **-ta. stigmata** (stig′·ma·tạ) *n.pl.* marks resembling five wounds of Christ, said to have been miraculously impressed on bodies of certain saints. **-tic(al)** *a.* pert. to, or marked with stigma; giving reproach or disgrace; **-tization** *n.* **-tizer** *n.* [Gk. *stigma*, a tattoo mark].

stile (stīl) *n.* arrangement of steps for climbing fence or wall; a turnstile; in paneling or framing, upright sidepiece [O.E. *stigel*].

sti·let·to (sti·let′·ō) *n.* small dagger; pointed instrument used in needlework [It. fr. L. *stilus*, a pointed instrument].

still (stil) *a.* motionless; silent; quiet; peaceful; of wine, not sparkling; *n.* stillness; (*Photog.*) enlargement of one unit of film; *v.t.* to quiet; to silence; to calm; *adv.* to this time; yet; even; *conj.* yet; however. **-ness** *n.* **-birth** *n.* state of being dead at time of birth. **-born** *a.* **— life** (*Art*) inanimated objects as subject of painting [O.E. *stille*].

still (stil) *n.* apparatus for distilling [L. *stillare*, to drip].

stilt (stilt) *n.* pole with foot-rest, for walking raised from ground; *v.i.* to walk on stilts. **-ed** *a.* formal; stiff; pretentious [Dut. *stelt*].

stim·u·lus (stim′·yạ·lạs) *n.* goad; incentive; stimulant; (*Bot.*) sting; prickle. *pl.* **stimuli. stimulate** *v.t.* to rouse to activity; to excite; to increase vital energy of. **stimulater** *n.* **stimulant** *a.* serving to stimulate; *n.* that which spurs on; (*Med.*) any agent or drug which temporarily increases action of any organ of body. **stimulation** *n.* **stimulative** *a., n.* [L. *stimulus*, a goad].

sting (sting) *n.* pointed organ often poisonous, of certain animals, insects, or plants; thrust, wound, or pain of one; any acute physical or mental pain; *v.t.* to thrust sting into; to cause sharp pain to; to hurt feelings; to incite to action; (*Slang*) to overcharge; *v.i.* to use a sting. *pa.p.* and *pa.t.* **stung. -er** *n.* **-ing** *a.* **-ingly** *adv.* [O.E. *stingan*].

stin·gy (stin′·ji·) *a.* meanly avaricious; miserly. **stinginess** *n.* [fr. *sting*].

stink (stingk) *v.i.* to give out strongly offensive smell; *pa.p.* **stunk** (stungk) *pa.t.* **stank** (stangk) or **stunk.** *n.* stench. **-er** *n.* one who, or that which, stinks; (*Slang*) objectionable person or thing. **-ing** *a.* [O.E. *stincan*].

stint (stint) *v.t.* to limit; to keep on short allowance; to skimp; *v.i.* to be frugal; *n.* limitation of supply or effort; allotted task. **-ed** *a.* [O.E. *styntan*, to blunt].

sti·pend (stī′·pend) *n.* money paid for a person's services; regular payment.**-iary** *a.* receiving salary; *n.* one who performs services for fixed salary [L. *stipendium*, wages].

stip·ple (stip′·l) *v.t.* and *v.i.* to engrave, draw, or paint by using dots instead of lines; *n.* this process. **-r** *n.* **stippling** *n.* [Dut. *slip*, a point].

stip·u·late (stip′·yạ·lāt) *v.i.* to arrange; to settle definitely; to insist on in making a bargain or agreement. **stipulation** *n.* specified condition. **stipulator** *n.* [L. *stipulari*].

stir (stur) *v.t.* to set or keep in motion; to move; to mix up ingredients, materials, etc. by circular motion of utensil; to rouse; to incite; *v.i.* to begin to move; to be in motion; to be emotionally moved; *pr.p.* **-ring.** *pa.p.* and *pa.t.* **-red.** *n.* act of stirring; commotion. **-rer** *n.* **-ring** *a.* active; energetic; exciting; rousing; *n.* act of stirring [O.E. *styrian*].

stir·rup (stur′·ạp) *n.* metal loop hung from strap, for foot of rider on horse. [O.E. *stigrap*, mount rope].

stitch (stich) *n.* in sewing, a single pass of needle; loop or turn of thread thus made; in knitting, crocheting, etc., single turn of yarn or thread around needle or hook; bit of clothing; sharp, sudden pain in the side; *v.t.* and *v.i.* to form stitches; to sew. **-er** *n.* **-ing** *n.* work done by sewing [O.E. *stician*, to pierce].

stith·y (stith′·i·) *n.* anvil; forge [O.N. *stethi*, anvil].

stoat (stōt) *n.* ermine or weasel, esp. in its summer fur of reddish-brown color.

stock (stȧk) *n.* stump or post; stem or trunk of tree or plant; upright block of wood; piece of wood to which the barrel, lock, etc. of firearm are secured; crossbar of anchor; ancestry; family; domestic animals on farm; supply of goods merchant has on hand; government securities; capital of company or corporation; quantity; supply; juices of meat, etc. to form a liquid used as foundation of soup; close-fitting band of cloth worn round neck; garden plant bearing fragrant flowers; gillyflower; *pl.* frame of timber supporting a ship while building; old instrument of punishment in form of wooden frame with holes in it, to confine hands and feet of offenders; *v.t.* to lay in supply for future use; to provide with cattle, etc. *a.* used, or available, for constant supply; commonplace; pert. to stock. **-breeder** *n.* one who raises cattle, horses, etc. **-broker** *n.* one who buys and sells stocks or shares for others. **-broking** *n.* **— exchange,** building in which stockbrokers meet to buy and sell stocks and shares. **-in-trade** *n.* goods merchant, shopkeeper, etc. has on hand for supply to public. **-market,** stock exchange. **-still** *a.* still as stock or post; motionless. **—taking** *n.* act of preparing inventory of goods on hand; sizing up of a situation. **— yard** *n.* large yard with pens for cattle, sheep, pigs, etc., esp. for those to be slaughtered [O.E. *stocc,* a stick].

stock·ade (stȧ·kād′) *n.* enclosure or pen made with posts and stakes; *v.t.* to surround, enclose, or defend by erecting line of stakes [Sp. *estacada,* a stake].

stock·fish (stȧk′·fish) *n.* codfish, hake, etc., split and dried in open air [fr. *stock*].

stock·ing (stȧk′·ing) *n.* woven or knitted covering for foot and leg [fr. *stock*].

stock·y (stȧk′·i.) *a.* short and stout; thickset. **stockily** *adv.* [fr. *stock*].

stodge (stȧj) *v.i.* to stuff; to cram. **stodgy** *a.* heavy; lumpy; indigestible; *(Fig.)* dull and uninteresting. **stodginess** *n.*

sto·ic (stō′·ik) *n.* disciple of Greek philosopher Zeno; one who suffers without complaint; person of great self-control; one indifferent to pleasure or pain. **-al** *a.* suffering without complaint; being indifferent to pleasure or pain. **-ally** *adv.* **-ism** *n.* endurance of pain, hardship, etc. without complaint [Gk. *stoa,* porch (where Zeno taught his philosophy)].

stoke (stōk) *v.t.* and *v.i.* to stir up, feed, or tend (fire). **-r** *n.* [Dut. *stoken,* to kindle a fire].

stole (stōl) *pa.t.* of **steal.**

stole *(stōl), n.* long, narrow scarf worn by bishops, priests, etc. during mass; woman's long, narrow scarf [Gk. *stole,* a robe].

stol·en (stōl′·n) *pa.p.* of **steal.**

stol·id (stȧl′·id) *a.* dull or stupid; not easily excited. **-ly** *adv.* **-ness, -ity** *n.* [L. *stolidus*].

stomach (stum′·ak) *n.* chief digestive organ in any animal; appetite; desire; *v.t.* to put up with; to endure. **-er** *n.* formerly part of a woman's dress. **-ic** *n.* *(Med.)* any medicine for aiding digestion [Gk. *stomachos,* the gullet, fr. *stoma,* a mouth].

stone (stōn) *n.* hard, earthy matter of which rock is made; piece of rock; *(chiefly Brit.)* a measure of weight equal to 14 lb.; hard center of certain fruits; gem; concretion in kidneys or bladder; *a.* made of stone, stoneware, earthenware; *v.t.* to pelt with stones; to remove stones from, as from fruits. **stony** *a.* like stone; full of stones; pitiless. **stonily** *adv.* **stoniness** *n.* **Stone Age,** primitive stage of human development when man used stone for tools and weapons. **-blind** *a.* entirely blind. **-crop** *n.* creeping plant found on old walls, etc. **-deaf** *a.* completely deaf. **-mason** *n.* worker or builder in stone. **-'s throw** *n.* as far as one can throw a stone; hence, not far away [O.E. *stan*].

stood (stood) *pa.p.* and *pa.t.* of **stand.**

stooge (stòòj) *n.* *(Slang)* one who bears blame for others; *(Colloq.)* actor serving as butt of another's jokes; *v.t.* to act as stooge.

stool (stòòl) *n.* chair with no back; low backless seat for resting feet on; seat for evacuating bowels; discharge from bowels. **-pigeon** *n.* pigeon used to trap other pigeons; *(Slang)* person used as decoy. [O.E. *stol*].

stoop (stòòp) *v.i.* to bend body; to lean forward; to have shoulders bowed forward, as from age; to bow one's head; to condescend; to lean forward; *n.* act of stooping; stooping carriage of head and shoulders [O.E. *stupian*].

stoop (stòòp) *n.* raised entrance landing or porch in front of doorway [D. *stoep*].

stop (stȧp) *v.t.* to fill up opening; to keep from opening; to keep from going forward; to bring to a halt; to obstruct; to check; to impede; to hinder; to suspend; to withhold; to desist from; to bring to an end; *v.i.* to cease; to halt; *pr.p.* **-ping.** *pa.p.* and *pa.t.* **-ped;** *n.* act of stopping; state of being stopped; halt; halting place; pause; delay; hindrance; any device for checking movement, e.g. peg, pin, plug, etc.; *(Mus.)* any device for altering or regulating pitch, e.g. vent hole in wind instrument; set of organ pipes; lever for putting it in action; consonant (p, t, etc.) produced by checking escape of breath from mouth by closure of lips, teeth, etc. **-page** *n.* state of being stopped; act of stopping; obstruction; cessation. **-per** *n.* one who, or that which, stops; plug for closing mouth of bottle, etc.; *v.t.* to close with a stopper. **-cock** *n.* valve for regulating flow of liquid. **—gap** *n.* a temporary substitute. **— watch** *n.* special watch whose hands can be started or stopped instantly [O.E. *stoppian,* to plug].

store (stōr) *n.* great quantity; abundance; reserve supply; stock; shop; *pl.* supplies; *v.t.* to collect; to accumulate; to hoard; to place in a warehouse. **storage** *n.* act of placing goods in a warehouse; space occupied by them; price paid. [L. *instaurare,* to restore].

stork (stawrk) *n.* large wading bird allied to heron and ibis [O.E. *storc*].

storm (stawrm) *n.* violent wind or disturbance of atmosphere with rain, snow, etc.; tempest; gale; assault on fortified place; commotion; outburst of emotion; *v.t.* to take by storm; to assault; *v.i.* to raise tempest; to rage; to fume; to scold violently. **-y** *a.* tempestuous; boisterous; violent; passionate. **-ily** *adv.* **-iness** *n.* **—bound** *a.* delayed by storms. [O.E. *storm*].

sto·ry (stō′·ri·) *n.* history or narrative of facts or events; account; tale; legend; anecdote; plot; rumor; *(Colloq.)* falsehood; a lie. **storied** (stō′·rid) *a.* told in a story; having a history. **-teller** *n.* one who tells stories [Gk. *historia*].

story (stō′·ri·) *n.* horizontal division of building; set of rooms on one floor. **storied** *a.*

stoup (stòòp) *n.* holy-water basin [O.N.].

stout (stout) *a.* strong; robust; vigorous; bold; resolute; thickset; bulky; *n.* strong, dark-colored beer; porter. **-ly** *adv.* **-ness** *n.* **-hearted** *a.* brave; courageous; intrepid [O.F. *estoul,* proud, fierce].

stove (stōv) *n.* apparatus heated by gas, electricity, etc. for cooking, warming room, etc.; oven of blast furnace; **-pipe** *n.* metal pipe for carrying off smoke from stove [O.E. *stofa,* a heated room].

stove (stōv) *pa.p.* and *pa.t.* of **stave.**

stow (stō) *v.t.* to fill by packing closely; to arrange compactly, as cargo in ship; *(Slang)* to cease; to conceal. **-age** *n.* act of packing closely; space for stowing goods; charge made for stowing goods. **-away** *n.* one who hides on ship to obtain free passage [O.E. *stow,* a place].

strad·dle (strad′·l) *v.i.* to spread legs wide; to stand or walk with legs apart; *v.t.* to bestride something; *(Colloq.)* to seem to favor both sides of an issue; *n.* act of straddling;

astraddle *adv.* astride [fr.*stride*].
Strad·i·var·i·us (strad·ạ·va′·ri·ạs) *n.* a violin, usually of great value, made at Cremona, Italy, by Antonio *Stradivari* (1649-1737).
strafe (strāf) *v.t.* (*Mil. Slang*) to bombard heavily; to attack with machine-gun fire from airplanes [Ger. *strafen*, to punish].
strag·gle (strag′·l) *v.i.* to wander from direct course; to stray; to get dispersed; to lag behind; to stretch beyond proper limits; as branches of plant. **-r** *n.* one who, or that which, straggles. **straggling** *a.*
straight (strāt) *a.* passing from one point to another by nearest course; without a bend; direct; honest; upright; frank; (*U.S.*) of whisky, etc. undiluted; *n.* straightness; straight part, e.g. of racing-track; *adv.* in a direct line or manner; directly; without ambiguity; at once. **-ly** *adv.* **-en** *v.t.* to make straight. **-ener** *n.* **-away** *a.* straight forward. **-forward** *a.* proceeding in a straight course; honest; frank; simple [O.E. *streht*].
strain (strān) *n.* race; breed; stock; inherited quality [O.E. *streon*].
strain (strān) *v.t.* to stretch tight; to stretch to the full or to excess; to exert to the utmost; to injure by over-exertion, as muscle; to wrench; to force; to stress; to pass through sieve; to filter; *v.i.* to make great effort; to filter; *n.* act of straining; stretching force; violent effort; injury caused by over-exertion; wrench, esp. of muscle; sound; tune; style; manner; tone of speaking or writing. **-ed** *a.* done with effort; forced; unnatural; **-er** *n.* filter; sieve [L. *stringere*, to make tight].
strait (strāt) *n.* narrow channel of water connecting two larger areas; difficulty; financial embarrassment. **-en** *v.t.* to narrow; to put into position of difficulty or distress. **— jacket** *n.* garment for restraint of violently insane. **—laced** *a.* laced tightly in stays; puritanical; austere [L. *stringere, strictum*, to draw tight].
strand (strand) *n.* (*Poetic*) edge of sea or lake; the shore; *v.t.* to cause to run aground; to drive ashore; to leave in helpless position; *v.i.* to run aground. **-ed** *a.* [O.E. *strand*].
strand (strand) *n.* single string or wire of rope; any string, e.g. of hair, pearls, etc.; *v.t.* to make rope by twisting strands together [O.Fr. *estran*, a rope].
strange (strānj) *a.* unaccustomed; not familiar; uncommon; odd; extraordinary. **-ly** *adv.* **-ness** *n.* **-r** *n.* one from another country, town, place, etc.; unknown person; newcomer; one unaccustomed (to) [O.Fr. *estrange*].
stran·gle (strang′·gl) *v.t.* to kill by squeezing throat; to choke; to stifle; to suppress. **-r** *n.* **strangulate** *v.t.* to constrict so that circulation of blood is impeded; to compress; to strangle. **strangulation** *n.* [L. *strangulare*].
strap (strap) *n.* long, narrow strip of leather, cloth, or metal; strop; strip of any material for binding together or keeping in place; *v.t.* to fasten, bind, chastize with strap; to sharpen (a razor). *pr.p.* **-ping.** *pa.p.* and *pa.t.* **-ped. -ping** *n.* act of fastening with strap; material used; punishment with strap; *a.* (*Colloq.*) tall; robust [O.E. *strop*].
stra·ta (strā′·ta) *n.pl.* See **stratum.**
strat·a·gem (strat′·ạ·jạm) *n.* artifice in war; scheme for deceiving enemy; ruse [Gk. *stratēgein*, to lead an army].
strat·e·gy (strat′·ạ·ji·) *n.* art of conducting military or naval operations; generalship; skillful management in getting the better of an adversary.
strategic (strạ·tē′·jik) *a.* pert. to, based on, strategy. **strategics** *n.pl.* strategy. **strategical** *a.* **strategically** *adv.* **strategist** *n.* [Gk. *stratēgein*, to lead army].
strat·i·fy (strat′·ạ·fī) *v.t.* to form or deposit in strata or layers. **stratification** *n.* [L. *stratum*, a layer].
strat·o·sphere (strat′·ạ·sfir) *n* upper part of atmosphere, six miles or more above earth [L. *stratum*, layer, and *sphere*].
stra·tum (strā′·tạm, strat′·ạm) *n.* bed of earth, rock, coal, etc. in series of layers; any bed or layer; class in society. *pl.* **strata. stratus** *n.* cloud form, in low, horizontal layers or bands. *pl.* **strati** [L. *stratum*, fr. *sternere*, to spread out].
straw (straw) *n.* stalk of wheat, rye, etc. after grain has been thrashed out; collection of such dry stalks, used for fodder, etc.; hollow tube for sipping beverage; thing of very little value; *a.* made of straw [O.E. *streaw*].
straw·ber·ry (straw′·be·ri·) *n.* a red berry with delicious taste [O.E. *steaw*, straw; *berige*, a berry].
stray (strā) *v.i.* to wander from path; to digress; *a.* wandering; strayed; lost; occasional; *n.* stray animal; lost child [O.Fr. *estraier*].
streak (strēk) *n.* line, or long band, of different color from the background; stripe; flash of lightning; trait; strain; *v.t.* to mark with streaks. **-ed, -y** *a.* [O.E. *strica*, a stroke].
stream (strēm) *n.* flowing body of water, or other liquid; river, brook, etc.; current; course; trend; steady flow of air or light, or people; *v.i.* to issue in stream; to flow or move freely; to stretch in long line; to float or wave in air; *v.t.* to send out in a stream; to send forth rays of light. **-y** *a.* **-er** *n.* long, narrow flag; pennant; auroral beam of light shooting up from horizon. **-let** *n.* little stream. **-line** *n.* line of current of air; shape of a body (e.g. car, ship, etc.) calculated to offer least resistance to air or water when passing through it; *v.t.* to design body of this shape [O.E.].
street (strēt) *n.* road in town or village, usually with houses or buildings at the side. **-walker** *n.* one who walks the streets; prostitute [L. *strata* (*via*), a paved (way)].
strength (strength) *n.* quality of being strong; capacity for exertion; ability to endure; power or vigor; physical, mental, or moral force; potency of liquid, esp. of distilled or malted liquors; intensity; force of expression; vigor of style; support; security; force in numbers, e.g. of army. **-en** *v.t.* to make strong or stronger; to reinforce; *v.i.* to become or grow strong or stronger. **-ener** *n.* [O.E. *strengthu*].
stren·u·ous (stren′·yoo·ạs) *a.* eagerly pressing; energetic; full of, requiring effort. **-ly** *adv.* **-ness** *n.* **strenuosity** *n.* [L. *strenuus*].
strep·to·coc·cus (strep·tạ·kȧk′·ạs) *n.* (*Med.*) bacterium of chain formation, the organism responsible for serious infections. *pl.* **streptococci** (·kȧk′·ī) [Gk. *streptos*, bent; *kokkos*, grain].
strep·to·my·cin (strep·tō·mī′·sạn) *n.* (*Med.*) antibiotic drug related to penicillin [Gk. *streptos*, bent; *mukēs*, fungus].
stress (stres) *n.* force; pressure; strain; emphasis; weight or importance; accent; (*Mech.*) force producing change in shape of body; *v.t.* to lay stress on [O.Fr. *estrecier*]...
stretch (strech) *v.t.* to pull out; to tighten; to reach out; to strain; to exaggerate; *v.i.* to be drawn out; to be extended; to spread; *n.* extension; strain; effort; extent; expanse; long line or surface; unbroken period of time. **-er** *n.* one who, or that which, stretches; a frame or litter for carrying sick or wounded; brick or stone laid lengthwise along line of wall [O.E. *streccan*].
strew (strōō) *v.t.* to scatter over surface; to spread loosely. *pa.p.* **-ed** or **-n,** *pa.t.* **-ed** [O.E. *streowian*].
stri·a (strī′·ạ) *n.* line or small groove. *pl.* **-e**

(strī′·ē) thread-like lines, as on surface of shells, rocks, crystals, etc. **-te, -ted** *a.* marked with striae. **-tion** *n.* [L. *stria*, a furrow].

strick·en (strik′·n) *a.* struck; smitten; afflicted; worn out [fr. *strike*].

strict (strikt) *a.* stern; severe; exacting; rigid; unswerving; without exception; accurate. **-ly** *adv.* **-ness** *n.* **-ure** *n.* severe criticism; (*Med.*) morbid contraction of any passage of body, esp. urethra [L. *stringere, strictum*, to tighten].

stride (strīd) *n.* long step, or its length; *v.t.* to pass over with one long step; *v.i.* to walk, with long steps. *pa.p.* **stridden** (strid′·n). *pa.t.* **strode** [O.E. *stridan*].

stri·dent (strī′·dạnt) *a.* harsh in tone; grating; jarring.**stridence, stridency** *n.* **-ly** *adv.* [L. *stridere*, to creak].

strife (strīf) *n.* conflict; struggle [O.Fr. *estrif*].

strike (strīk) *v.t.* to hit; to smite; to dash against; to collide; to sound; to cause to sound; to occur to; to impress; to afflict; to stamp; to cause to light, as match; to lower, as flag or sail; to take down, as tent; to ratify; to conclude; to come upon unexpectedly, as gold; to cancel; *v.i.* to hit; to deliver blow; to dash; to clash; to run aground; to stop work for increase of wages, etc.; to take root, of a plant; *n.* a stoppage of work to enforce demand; find, esp. in prospecting for gold; stroke of luck. *pa.p.* **struck,** or **-n** *pa.t.* **struck. striking** *a.* affecting with strong emotions; impressive. **strikingly** *adv.* [O.E. *strican*, to move, to wipe].

string (string) *n.* cord; twine; ribbon; thick thread; cord or thread on which things are arranged, e.g. *string of pearls*; chain; succession; series; stretched cord of gut or wire for musical instrument; vegetable fiber, as *string beans;* all race horses from certain stable; *pl.* stringed musical instruments collectively; *v.t.* to furnish with strings; to put on string, as beads, pearls, etc.; *v.i.* to stretch out into a long line; to form strings; to become fibrous. *pa.p.* and *pa.t.* **strung. -ed** *a.* **-y** *a.* fibrous; of person, long and thin. **-iness** *n.* [O.E. *streng*].

strin·gent (strin′·jạnt) *a.* binding strongly; strict; rigid; severe. **-ly** *adv.* **-ness, stringency** *n.* [L. *stringere*, to tighten].

strip (strip) *v.t.* to pull or tear off; to peel; to skin; to lay bare; to divest; to rob; *v.i.* to take off one's clothes; *n.* long, narrow piece of anything. *pr.p.* **-ping.** *pa.p.* and *pa.t.* **-ped** (stript). **-ling** *n.* youth [O.S. *strypan*, to plunder].

stripe (strīp) *n.* narrow line, band, or mark; strip of material of a different color from the rest; (*Mil.*) V-shaped strip of material worn on sleeve as badge of rank; chevron; stroke made with lash, whip, scourge, etc.; *v.t.* to mark with stripes; to lash. **-d** (strīpt) *a.* [*Dut.* streep].

strive (strīv) *v.i.* to try hard; to make an effort; to struggle; to contend. *pa.p.* **-n.** *pa.t.* **strove.** *n.* [O.Fr. *estriver*].

strode (strōd) *pa.t.* of **stride.**

stroke (strōk) *n.* blow; paralytic fit; apoplexy; any sudden seizure of illness, misfortune, etc.; sound of bell or clock; mark made by pen, pencil, brush, etc.; completed movement of club, stick, racquet, etc.; in swimming, completed movement of arm; in rowing, sweep of an oar; rower nearest stern who sets the time and pace; entire movement of piston from one end to other of cylinder; single, sudden effort, esp. if successful, in business, diplomacy, etc.; piece of luck; *v.t.* to set time and pace for rowers [O.E. *stracian*, to strike].

stroke (strōk) *v.t.* to pass hand gently over; to caress; to soothe; *n.* act of stroking [O.E. *stracian*, to strike].

stroll (strōl) *v.i.* to walk leisurely from place to place; to saunter; to ramble; *n.* a leisurely walk. **-er** *n.* [etym. uncertain].

strong (strawng) *a.* having physical force; powerful; muscular; able to resist attack; healthy; firm; solid; steadfast; well-established; violent; forcible; intense; determined; not easily broken; positive. **-ly** *adv.* [O.E. *strang*].

stron·ti·um (strán′·shi·ạm) *n.* (*Chem.*) a yellowish, reactive, metallic element [*Strontian*, Scotland].

strop (stráp) *n.* strip of leather for sharpening razor; *v.t.* to sharpen on strop. *pr.p.* **-ping.** *pa.p.* and *pa.t.* **-ped** *(stropt)* [L. *struppus*].

stro·phe (strō′·fē) *n.* in ancient Greek drama, song sung by chorus while dancing from right to left of orchestra; stanza. **strophic** *a.* [Gk. *strophē*, a turning].

strove (strōv) *pa.t.* of **strive.**

struck (struk) *pa.p.* and *pa.t.* of **strike.**

struc·ture (struk′·chẹr) *n.* that which is built; building; manner of building; arrangement of parts or elements; organization. **structural** *a.* **structurally** *adv.* [L. *struere, structum*, to build].

stru·del (stroo′·dl) *n.* type of Ger. pastry.

strug·gle (strug′·l) *v.i.* to put forth great efforts, esp. accompanied by violent twistings of body; to contend; to strive; *n.* violent physical effort; any kind of work in face of difficulties; strife. *n.* [etym. uncertain].

strum (strum) *v.t.* and *v.i.* to play badly and noisily on (stringed instrument). *pr.p.* **-ming.** *pa.p.* and *pa.t.* **-med** [imit. origin].

strum·pet (strum′·pit) *n.* prostitute; harlot.

strung (strung) *pa.p.* and *pa.t.* of **string.**

strut (strut) *v.i.* to walk pompously; to walk with affected dignity; *n.* stiff, proud and affected walk; pompous gait. *pa.p.* **-ting.** *pa.p. and pa.t.* **-ted** [O.E. *strutian*, to stick out stiffly].

strut (strut) *n.* rigid support, usually set obliquely; support for rafter; *v.t.* to brace.

strych·nine (strik′·nīn) *n.* highly poisonous alkaloid; stimulant. Also **strychnin** [Gk. nightshade].

stub (stub) *n.* stump of a tree; short, remaining part of pencil, cigarette, etc.; *v.t.* to clear (ground) by rooting up stumps of trees; to strike toe against fixed object. *pr.p.* **-bing.** *pa.p.* and *pa.t.* **-bed. -bed** *a.* short and blunt like stump; obtuse. **-by** *a.* abounding in stubs; short and thickset. **-biness** *n.* [O.E. *stybb*].

stub·ble (stub′·l) *n.* short ends of cornstalks left after reaping; short growth of beard. **-d** *a.* **stubbly** *a.* [L. *stipula*, fr. *stipes*, stalk].

stub·born (stub′·ẹrn) *a.* fixed in opinion; obstinate. *adv.* **-ness** *n.* [M.E. *stoburn*].

stuc·co (stuk′·ō) *n.* plaster of lime, sand, etc. used on walls, and in decorative work; *v.t.* to make stucco [It.].

stuck (stuk) *pa.p.* and *pa.t.* of **stick. -up** *a.* (*Colloq.*) conceited.

stud (stud) *n.* a movable, double-headed flat-headed nail; boss; upright wooden support, as in wall; *v.t.* to furnish with studs; to set thickly in, or scatter over. *pr.p.* **-ding.** *pa.p.* and *pa.t.* **-ded** [O.E. *studu*, a post].

stud (stud) *n.* collection of horses, kept for breeding, or racing; place where they are kept. **-book** *n.* official book for recording pedigrees of thoroughbred animals [O.E. *stod*].

stu·dent (stū′·d(ạ)nt) *n.* one who studies; scholar at university or other institutions for higher education. [L. *studere*, to be zealous].

stu·di·o (stū′·di·ō) *n.* workroom of artist, sculptor, or professional photographer; where film plays are produced; a room equipped for broadcasting of radio and television programs [It.].

stu·di·ous (stū′·di·ạs) *a.* given to, or fond of, study; thoughtful; contemplative; painstaking; careful (of); deliberate. **-ly** *adv.* [L. *studium,* zeal].

stud·y (stud′·i·) *n.* application of the mind to books, etc. to gain knowledge; subject of such application; branch of learning; thoughtful attention; meditation; room for study; preliminary sketch by an artist; *v.t.* to set the mind to; to examine carefully; to scrutinize; to ponder over; *v.i.* to read books closely in order to gain knowledge. **studied** (stud′·id) also *a.* examined closely; carefully considered and planned [L. *studium,* zeal].

stuff (stuf) *n.* essential part; material; (*Brit.*) cloth not yet made into garments; goods; belongings; useless matter; worthless things, trash, esp. in *stuff and nonsense; v.t.* to fill by pressing closely; to cram; in cookery, to fill, e.g. chicken with seasoning; to fill skin, e.g. of animal, bird, etc. to preserve it as specimen; *v.i.* to eat greedily. **-ing** *n.* material used to stuff or fill anything [O.Fr. *estoffe,* fr. L. *stupa,* tow].

stuff·y (stuf′·i·) *a.* badly ventilated; airless; dull; conceited **stuffiness** *n.* [Fr. *étouffer,* to choke, stifle].

stul·ti·fy (stul′·ta·fī) *v.t.* to make to look ridiculous; to make ineffectual; to destroy the force of [L. *stultus,* foolish].

stum·ble (stum′·bl) *v.i.* to trip in walking and nearly fall; to walk in unsteady manner; to fall into error; to speak hesitatingly; *v.t.* to cause to trip; to mislead; *n.* act of stumbling; wrong step; error. **stumblingly** *adv.* **stumbling block** *n.* obstacle; hindrance [M.E. akin to *stammer*].

stump (stump) *n.* part of tree left after trunk is cut down; part of limb, tooth, etc. after main part has been removed; remnant; *pl.* (*Colloq.*) legs; *v.t.* to reduce to a stump; to cut off main part; to puzzle or perplex; (*Colloq.*) to tour (district) making political speeches; *v.i.* to walk noisily or heavily. **-y** *a.* full of stumps; short and thick [ME *stumpe*].

stun (stun) *v.t.* to knock senseless; to daze; to stupefy; to amaze. *pr.p.* **-ning.** *pa.p.* and *pa.t.* **-ned** (stund). **-ner** *n.* **-ning** *a.* rendering senseless (*Slang*) striking; excellent [O.Fr. *estoner*].

stung (stung) *pa.p.* and *pa.t.* of **sting.**

stunk (stungk) *pa.p.* and *pa.t.* of **stink.**

stunt (stunt) *v.t.* to check the growth of; to dwarf. **-ed** *a.* [O.E. *stunt,* dull].

stunt (stunt) *n.* (*Colloq.*) any spectacular feat of skill or daring, esp. if for display, or to gain publicity [etym. uncertain].

stu·pe·fy (stū′·pạ·fī) *v.t.* to deprive of full consciousness; to dull the senses; to stun; to amaze. **stupefier** *n.* **stupefaction** *n.* act of making stupid; dazed condition; utter amazement. **stupefactive** *a.* **stupefacient** *a.* and *n.* [L. *stupere,* to be amazed; *facere,* to make].

stu·pen·dous (stū·pen′·das) *a.* astonishing, esp. because of size, power, etc.; amazing. **-ly** *adv.* **-ness** *n.* [L. *stupere,* to be amazed].

stu·pid (stū′·pid) *a.* slow-witted; unintelligent; foolish; dull. **-ly** *adv.* **-ness, -ity** *n.* [L.].

stu·por (stū′·pẹr) *n.* complete or partial loss of consciousness; dazed state; lethargy. **-ous** *a.* [L. *stupere,* to be struck senseless].

stur·dy (stur′·di.) *a.* hard; robust; vigorous; strongly built; firm. **sturdily** *adv.* **sturdiness** *n.* [O.Fr. *estourdi,* stunned, amazed].

stur·geon (stur′·jạn) *n.* large fish, whose roe is made into caviar [Fr. *esturgeon*].

stut·ter (stut′·ẹr) *v.i.* and *v.t.* to speak with difficulty; to stammer; *n.* the act or habit of stuttering, **-er** *n.* **-ing** *a.* [M.E. *stoten*].

sty (stī) *n.* place to keep pigs; hence, any filthy place [O.E. *stig*].

sty, stye (stī) *n.* small abscess on edge of eyelid [O.E. *stigend*].

styg·i·an (stij′·i·ạn) *a.* pert. to river *Styx* in Hades; infernal; gloomy; dismal [L. *Stygius*].

style (stīl) *n.* pointed instrument used by the ancients for writing on waxed tablets; engraving-tool; etching-needle; manner of expressing thought in writing, speaking, acting, painting, etc.; in the arts, mode of acting, painting, etc.; in the arts, mode of expression or performance peculiar to individual, group, or period; in games, manner of play and bodily action; mode of dress; fashion; fine appearance; mode of address; title; mode of reckoning time; sort, kind, make, shape, etc. of anything; (*Bot.*) stem-like part of pistil of flower, supporting stigma; pin of a sundial; *v.t.* to give title, official or particular, in addressing or speaking of (person); to term; to name; to call. **-t** *n.* stiletto; probe.**stylize** *v.t.* to make conform to convention. **stylish** *a.* fashionable; elegant. **stylishly** *adv.* **stylishness** *n.* **stylist** *n.* writer, who is attentive to form and style; one who is master of style. **stylistic** *a.* **stylistically** *adv.* **stylus** *n.* style [L. *stilus*].

sty·mie (stī′·mi·) *n.* (*Golf*) position on putting-green resulting from one player's ball coming to rest between hole and opponent's ball; (*Fig.*) to thwart [etym. unknown].

styp·tic (stip′·tik) *a.* contracting; astringent; *n.* (*Med.*) any substance used to arrest bleeding [Gk. *stuphein,* to contract].

sua·sion (swā′·zhạn) *n.* persuasion; advisory influence [L. *suadere,* to advise].

suave (swȧv, swāv) *a.* pleasant; agreeable; smoothly polite; bland. **-ly** *adv.* **suavity** *n.* [L. *suavis,* sweet].

sub (sub) *n.* (*Colloq.*) shortened form of subaltern, sub-lieutenant, subscription, substitute, submarine, etc.

sub- (sub) *prefix,* meaning under, below, from below, lower, inferior, nearly, about, somewhat, slightly, moderately, used in many words, e.g. **-acute** *a.* moderately acute or severe [L.].

sub·al·tern (sạ·bawl′·tẹn) (*Mil.*) *a.* of lower rank [L. *sub,* under; *alternus,* in turn].

sub·a·que·ous (sub·ā′·kwi·ạs) *a.* living, lying, or formed under water. **subaquatic** *a.*

sub·arc·tic (sub·ȧrk′·tik) *a.* pert. to region or climate immediately next to the Arctic.

sub·con·scious (sub·kȧn′·shạs) *a.* pert. to unconscious activities which go on in mind; partially conscious; *n.* subconscious mind.**-ly** *adv.*

sub·cu·ta·ne·ous (sub·kū·tā′·ni·ạs) *a.* under the skin. **-ly** *adv.*

sub·di·vide (sub·da·vīd′) *v.t.* to divide a part, or parts of, into other parts; to divide again; *v.i.* to be subdivided. **subdivision** *n.* act of subdividing; result of subdividing.

sub·duc·tion (sub·duk′·shan) *n.* withdrawal; deduction [L. *subducere,* to withdraw].

sub·due (sub·dū′) *v.t.* to bring under one's power; to conquer; to bring under control; to reduce force or strength of; to soften. **-d** *a.* **-r** *n.* **subdual** *n.* act of subduing; state of being subdued [L. *subducere,* to withdraw]. to withdraw].

sub·ed·it (sub·ed′·it) *v.t.* to act under an editor; to be assistant editor. **-or** *n.*

sub·head·ing (sub·hed′·ing) *n.* division of main heading.

sub·hu·man (sub·hū′·man) *a.* less than human.

sub·ject (sub′·jikt) *a.* under power or control of another; owing allegiance; subordinate; dependent; liable to; prone; exposed; *n.* one under the power or control of another; one owing allegiance to a sovereign, state, government, etc.; a person, animal, etc. as an object of experiment, treatment, operation, etc.; matter under consideration or discussion, written or spoken; topic; theme; (*Mus.*) principal theme or melody of movement; (*Gram.*) a word or words in sentence of which something is affirmed; (*Philos.*) conscious self; thinking mind. **subject** (sub·jekt′) *v.t.* to bring under power or control of; to subdue; to cause to undergo; to submit. **-ion** *n.* act of bringing under power or control; state of being under control. **-ive** *a.* pert. to subject; existing in the mind; arising from senses; relating to, or reflecting, thoughts and feelings of person; (*Gram.*) pert. to subject of sentence. **-ively** *adv.* **-iveness** *n.* **-ivity** *n.* [L. *sub*, under; *jacere*, to throw].

sub·join (sub·join′) *v.t.* to append; to annex. **-der** *n.* something added at end.

sub·ju·gate (sub′·jòò·gāt) *v.t.* literally, to bring under the yoke; to force to submit; to conquer. **subjugation** *n.* **subjugator** *n.* [L. *sub*, and *jugum*, yoke].

sub·junc·tive (sạb·jungk′·tiv) *a.* denoting subjunctive mood; mood of verb implying condition, doubt, or wish [L. *sub; jungere*, to join].

sub·lease (sub′·lēs) *n.* lease granted to another tenant by one who is himself a tenant; (sub·lēs′) *v.t.* to grant or hold a sublease.

sub·let (sub·let′) *v.t.* to let to another tenant property of which one is a tenant; *pr.p.* **-ting.** *pa.t. pa.p.* **sublet.**

sub·li·mate (sub′·li·māt) *v.t.* (Chem.) to convert solid directly into vapor and then allow it to solidify again; to purify thus; to direct repressed impulses, esp. sexual, towards new aims and activities. *n.* (*Chem.*) substance that has been sublimated. **sublimation** *n.* [L. *sublimare*, to lift up].

sub·lime (sạ·blīm′) *a.* exalted; eminent; inspiring awe, adoration, etc.; majestic; grandiose; *n.* that which is sublime; *v.t.* to sublimate; to purify; to exalt; to ennoble. **-ly** *adv.* **-ness, sublimity** (sạ·blim′·ạ·ti·) *n.* [L. *sublimis*, high].

sub·lim·i·nal (sub·lim′·ạn·ạl) *a.* in psychology, below level of consciousness.

sub-ma·chine gun (sub·mạ·shēn′·gun) *n.* (*Mil.*) light, portable machine gun.

sub·ma·rine (sub·mạ·rēn′) *a.* situated, living, or able to travel under surface of sea; *n.* submersible boat, esp. one armed with torpedoes.

sub·merge (sạb·murj′) *v.t.* to put under water; to cover with water; to flood; (*Fig.*) to overwhelm; *v.i.* to go under water. **-nce** *n.* [L. *sub; mergere*, to dip].

sub·merse (sạb·murs′) *v.t.* to submerge; to put under water. **submersible** *a.* **submersion** *n.* [L. *submergere*].

submit (sạb·mit′) *v.t.* to put forward for consideration; to surrender; *v.i.* to yield oneself to another; to surrender. *pr.p.* **-ting.** *pa.p.* and *pa.t.* **-ted. submission** *n.* act of submitting; humility; meekness. **submissive** *a.* ready to submit; obedient; docile; humble. **submissively** *adv.* **submissiveness** *n.* resignation [L. *sub*; *mittere*, to put].

sub·mul·ti·ple (sub·mul′·tạ·pl) *n.* number or quantity that divides into another exactly.

sub·nor·mal (sub·nawr′·mạl) *a.* below normal.

sub·or·di·nate (sạ·bawr′·dạ·nit) *a.* lower in rank, importance, power, etc.; *n.* one of lower rank, importance, etc. than another; one under the orders of another; *v.t.* (sạ·bawr′·dạ·nāt) to make or treat as subordinate; to make subject. **-ly** *adv.* **-ness, subordinacy** *n.* **subordination** *n.* [L. *sub*, under; *ordinare*, to set in order].

sub·orn (sạ·bawrn′) *v.t.* to induce (person) to commit perjury; to bribe to do evil. **-ation** *n.* **-er** *n.* [L. *sub*, under; *ornare*, to furnish].

sub·poe·na (su(b)·pē′·nạ) *n.* (*Law*) writ summoning person to appear in court (under penalty for non-appearance); *v.t.* to issue such an order [L. under penalty].

sub·rep·tion (sub·rep′·shạn) *n.* concealment or misrepresentation of truth. **subreptitious** *a.* [L. *sub*, under; *rapere*, to seize].

sub·scribe (sạb·skrīb′) *v.t.* to write underneath; to sign at end of paper or document; to give, or promise to give, (money) on behalf of cause; to contribute; *v.i.* to promise in writing to give a sum of money to a cause; (with *to*) to pay in advance for regular supply of issues of newspaper, magazine, etc.; to agree with or support. **-r** *n.* **subscript** *a.* written underneath. **subscription** *n.* act of subscribing; name or signature of subscriber; money subscribed or gifted; receipt of periodical for fee paid.

sub·se·quent (sub′·si·kwạnt) *a.* following or coming after in time; happening later. **-ly** *adv.* [L. *sub*; sequi, to follow].

sub·serve (sạb·surv′) *v.t.* to serve in small way; to help forward; to promote. **subservient** *a.* serving to promote some purpose; submissive; servile. **subserviently** *adv.* **subservience, subserviency** *n.* state of being subservient.

sub·side (sạb·sīd′) *v.i.* to sink or fall to the bottom; to settle; to sink to lower level; to abate. **subsidence, subsidency** *n.* act of subsiding [L. *sub*, under; *sidere*, to settle].

sub·sid·i·ar·y (sạb·sid′·e·ri·) *a.* pert. to subsidy; aiding, helping, supplementary, secondary; auxiliary; *n.* one who, or that which, helps; auxiliary [L. *subsidium*, a reserve].

sub·si·dy (sub′·si·di·) *n.* financial aid; government grant for varoius purposes, e.g. to encourage certain industries, to keep cost of living steady, etc.; also in return for help in time of war. **subsidize** *v.t.* to pay subsidy to [L. *subsidium*].

sub·sist (sạb·sist′) *v.i.* to continue to be; to exist; to live (on); *v.t.* to support with food; to feed. **-ent** *a.* having real being; existing. **-ence** *n.* act of subsisting; things or means by which one supports life; livelihood [L. *subsistere*, fr. *sistere*, to stand].

sub·soil (sub′·soil) *n.* the layer of earth lying just below the top layer.

sub·son·ic (sub·sán′·ik) *a.* pert. to speeds less than that of sound; below 700-750 m.p.h.

sub·stance (sub′·stạns) *n.* essence; material, etc. of which anything is made; matter; essential matter of book, speech, discussion, etc.; real point; property. **substantial** (sạb·stan′·shi·āt) *v.t.* to make substantial; to give substance to; to bring evidence for; to establish truth of. **substantiation** *n.* **substantive** *a.* having independent existence; real; fixed; (*Gram.*) expressing existence; pert. to noun, or used as noun; *n.* (*Gram.*) noun. **substantively** *adv.* [L. *substart*, to be present].

sub·sti·tute (sub′·sti·tūt) *v.t.* to put in place of another; to exchange. *v.i.* to take place of another; *n.* one who, that which, is put in place of another. **substitution** *n.* **substitutional, substitutionary** *a.* **subsitutionally** *adv.* [L. *sub*, under; *statuere*, to appoint].

sub·sra·tum (sub·strā′·tạm) *n.* underlying stratum or layer of soil, rock, etc.; a basic element. *pl.* **substrata. substrative** *a.*

sub·sume (sạb·sóòm′) *v.t.* to include under a class as belonging to it, e.g. 'all sparrows are birds.' **subsumption** *n.* **subsumptive** *a.*

sub·ten·ant (sub·ten′·ạnt) *n.* tenant who rents house, farm, etc. from one who is himself a tenant. **subtenancy** *n.*

sub·tend (sạb·tend′) *v.t.* (*Geom.*) of line, to

extend under or be opposite to, e.g. angle.
sub·ter·fuge (sub′·tẹr·fūj) *n.* that to which a person resorts in order to escape from a difficult situation, to conceal real motives, to avoid censure, etc.; an underhand trick; evasion [L. *subter*, under; *fugere*, to flee].
sub·ter·ra·ne·an (sub-tạ·rā′·nē·ạn) *a.* being or lying under surface of earth. Also **subterraneous, subterrene** (sub·tạ·rēn′), **subterrestrial** [L. *sub*, under; *terra*, the earth].
sub·ti·tle (sub′·tī·tl) *n.* additional title of book; half-title; film caption.
sub·tle (sut′·l) *a.* delicate; acute; discerning; clever; ingenious; intricate; making fine distinctions. **subtly** *adv.* **-ness, -ty** (sutl′·ti·) *n.* quality of being subtle; artfulness; a fine distinction [L. *subtilis*, fine woven].
sub·tract (sub·trakt′) *v.t.* to take away (part) from rest; to deduct one number from another to find difference. **-ion** *n.* act or operation of subtracting. **-ive** *a.* **subtrahend** *n.* quantity or number to be subtracted from another [L. *sub; trahere*, to draw].
sub·trop·i·cal (sub·tráp′·i·kạl) *a.* designating zone just outside region of the tropics.
sub·urb (sub′·urb) *n.* residential district on outskirts of town; *pl.* outskirts. **suburban** *a.* and *n.* **-ia** *n.* suburbs and their inhabitants [L. *sub*, under; *urbs*, city].
sub·ven·tion (sub·ven′·shạn) *n.* act of coming to the help of; government grant; subsidy [L. *sub*, under; *venire*, to come].
sub·vert (sạb·vurt′) *v.t.* to overthrow, esp. government; to destroy; to ruin utterly; **-er** *n.* **subversion** *n.* the act of subverting; overthrow; ruin. **subversive** *a.* [L. *sub*, under; *vertere*, to turn].
sub·way (sub′·wā) *n.* underground passage; underground railway.
suc·ceed (sạk·sēd′) *v.t.* to come immediately after; to follow in order; to take place of, esp. of one who has left or died; *v.i.* to come next in order; to become heir (to); to achieve one's aim to prosper. **-er** *n.* **success** *n.* favorable accomplishment; prosperity; one who has achieved success. **successful** *a.* **successfully** *adv.* **successfulness** *n.* **succession** (sạk·sesh′·ạn) *n.* act of following in order; sequence; series of persons or things according to some established rule; line of descendants; act or right of entering into possession of property, place, office, title, etc., of another, esp. of one near of kin. **successional** *a.* **successionally** *adv.* **successive** *a.* following in order; consecutive. **successively** *adv.* **successor** *n.* one who succeeds or takes place of another [L. *succedere*].
suc·cinct (sạk·singkt′) *a.* closely compressed; expressed in few words; terse; concise. **-ly** *adv.* **-ness** *n.* [L. *succingere*, to gird up].
suc·cor (suk′·ẹr) *v.t.* to help esp. in great difficulty or distress; to relieve; to comfort; *n.* aid; support. **-er** *n.* [L. *succurrere*].
suc·cu·lent (suk′·yạ·lant) *a.* full of juice; juicy. **-ly** *adv.* **succulence** *n.* juiciness [*L. succus*, juice].
suc·cumb (sạ·kum′) *v.i.* to yield; to submit; to die [L. *sub*, under; *cumbere*, to lie down].
such (such) *a.* of like kind; of that kind; of same kind; similar; of degree, quality, etc. mentioned; certain or particular; *pron.* used to denote a certain person or thing; these or those. **-like** *a.* similar; *pron.* similar things (but not defined); this or that [O.E. *swylc*].
suck (suk) *v.t.* to draw into mouth (by using lips and tongue); to draw liquid from (by using mouth; to roll (candy) in mouth; to absorb; *v.i.* to draw in with mouth; to drink from mother's breast; *n.* act of drawing with the mouth; milk drawn from mother's breast. **-er** *n.* one who, or that which, sucks; organ by which animal adheres by suction to any object; fresh water fish; shoot of plant from roots or lower part of stem; (*Slang*) person easily deceived. **-ing** *a.* **-le** *v.t.* to give suck to; to feed at mother's breast. **-ling** *n.* young child or animal not yet weaned [O.E. *sucan*].
su·crose (sòò′·krōs) *n.* white, sweet, crystalline substance; cane sugar, beet sugar, etc. [Fr. *sucre*, sugar].
suc·tion (suk′·shạn) *n.* act of sucking or drawing in; act of drawing liquids, gases, dust, etc. into vessel by exhausting air in it; 'force' that causes one object to adhere to another when air between them is exhausted. **— pump** *n.* pump in which water or other liquid is raised by atmospheric pressure [L. *sugere*, to suck].
sud·den (sud′·n) *a.* happening without notice or warning; coming unexpectedly; done with haste; abrupt. **-ly** *adv.* **-ness** *n.* [Fr. *soudain*, fr. L. *subitus*, unexpected].
suds (sudz) *n.pl.* water in which soap has been dissolved; froth and bubbles on it [O.E. *seothan*, to seethe].
sue (sòò) *v.t.* (*Law*) to seek justice by taking legal proceedings; to prosecute; *v.i.* to begin legal proceedings; to petition [L. *sequi*, follow].
suède (swād) *n.* soft, undressed kid leather; *a.* made of undressed kid [Fr. *Suède*, Sweden].
su·et (sū′·it) *n.* hard animal fat around kidneys and loins, used in cooking. **-y** *a.* [L. *sebum, fat*].
suf·fer (suf′·ẹr) *v.t.* to endure; to undergo; to allow; to tolerate; *v.i.* to undergo pain, punishment, etc.; to sustain a loss. **-able** *a.* **-ableness** *n.* **-ably** *adv.* **-ance** *n.* the state of suffering; toleration [L. *sub*, under; *ferre*, to bear].
suf·fice (sạ·fīs′·) *v.t.* to satisfy; *v.i.* to be enough; to meet the needs of. **sufficient** (sạ·fish′·ạnt) *a.* enough; satisfying the needs of. **sufficiently** *adv.* **sufficiency** *n.* [L. *sufficere*, to satisfy].
suf·fix (suf′·iks) *n.* letter or syllable added to end of word; affix. *v.t.* to add to end of. **-al** *a.* **-ion** *n.* [L. *sub; figere*, to fix].
suf·fo·cate (suf′·ạ·kāt) *v.t.* to kill by choking; to smother; to stifle; *v.i.* to be choked, stifled, or smothered. **suffocating** *a.* **suffocatingly** *adv.* **suffocation** *n.* [L. *suffocare*].
suf·frage (suf′·rij) *n.* vote; right to vote. **-tte** *n.* woman who agitated for women's right to vote [L. *suffragium*, a vote].
suf·fuse (sạ·fūz′) *v.t.* to spread over, as fluid; to well up; to cover. **suffusion** *n.* **suffusive** *a.* [L. *sub*, under; *fundere*, to pour].
sug·ar (shoog′·ẹr) *n.* sweet, crystalline substance; any substance like sugar; (*Fig.*) sweet words; flattery; *v.t.* to sweeten with sugar; *v.i.* to turn into sugar. *a.* made of, tasting of, or containing sugar; sweet; flattering. **-iness** *n.* **— cane,** tall grass whose sap yields sugar. **— loaf** *n.* a cone-shaped mass of hard, refined sugar. **— plum** *n.* sweetmeat; bonbon [Fr. *sucre*].
sug·gest (sạg·jest′) *v.t.* to bring forward; to propose; to hint; to insinuate. **-er** *n.* **-ion** *n.* proposal; hint; in psychiatry, influence exercised over subconscious mind of a person, resulting in a passive acceptance by him of impulses, beliefs, etc. **-ive** *a.* tending to call up an idea to the mind; hinting at; tending to bring to the mind indecent thoughts; improper. **-ively** *adv.* **-iveness** *n.* [L. *suggerere*, to carry up].
su·i·cide (sòò′·ạ·sīd) *n.* one who kills himself intentionally; act of doing this. **suicidal** (sòò·ạ·sī′·dạl) *a.* pert. to, tending to suicide; (*Fig.*) disastrous; ruinous. **suicidally** *adv.* [L. *sui*, of oneself; *caedere*, to kill].
suit (sòòt) *n.* act of suing; petition; request;

action in court of law; courtship; series or set of things of same kind or material; set of clothes; any of four sets in pack of cards; *v.t.* to fit; to go with; to appropriate; to be adapted to; to meet desires of; *v.i.* to agree; to be convenient. **-able** *a.* proper; appropriate; becoming. **-ably** *adv.* **-ability, -ableness** *n.* **-ing** *n.* material for making suits. **-or** *n.* one who sues; a wooer; a lover. [Fr. *suivre*, to follow, fr. L. *sequi*].

suite (swēt) *n.* train of followers or attendants; retinue; a number of things used together, e.g. set of apartments, furniture; (*Mus.*) series of dances or other pieces [Fr. fr. *suivre*, to follow].

su·ki·ya·ki (sòò·kē·ya'·kē) *n.* Jap. dish of fried meat, vegetables, etc.

sul·cus (sul'·kạs) *n.* groove; a furrow. **sulcate, sulcated** *a.* **sulcation** *n.* [L.].

sul·fa (sul'·fạ) *n.* abbrev. for *sulfa drugs*, a group of antibacterial compounds used in the treatment of disease, injury, etc.

sul·fate (sul'·fāt) *n.* salt of sulfuric acid. **sulfide** *n.* compound of sulfur with metal or other element. **sulfite** *n.* salt of sulfurous acid [L. *sulphur*].

sul·fur (sul'·fẹr) *n.* yellow, nonmetallic element, burning with blue flame and giving off suffocating odor. **-ous** *a.* **-y** *a.* **-ic acid,** colorless acid, having strong corrosive action [L. *sulphur*].

sulk (sulk) *v.i.* to be silent owing to ill humor, etc.; to be sullen; *n.* sullen fit or mood. **-y** *a.* silent and sullen; morose; *n.* light two-wheeled carriage for one person. **-ily** *adv.* **-iness** *n.*

sul·len (sul'·ạn) *a.* gloomily ill-humored; silently morose. **-ly** *adv.* **-ness** *n.* the state of being sullen [L. *solus*, alone].

sul·ly (sul'·i·) *v.t.* to soil; to stain; to disgrace; *v.i.* to be sullied [Fr. *souiller*, to soil].

sul·tan (sul'·tạn) *n.* Mohammedan prince or ruler. **-a** *n.* wife, mother, or daughter of sultan; kind of raisin [Fr. fr. Ar. *sultan*, victorious].

sul·try (sul'·tri·) *a.* hot, close, and oppressive; sweltering. **sultrily** *adv.* **sultriness** *n.* [form of *sweltry*, fr. *swelter*].

sum (sum) *n.* result obtained by adding together two or more things, quantities, etc.; total; aggregate; summary; quantity of money; *v.t.* (generally with *up*) to add up; to find total amount; to make summary of main parts. *pr.p.* **-ming.** *pa.p.* and *pa.t.* **-med. -mation** *n.* act of summing up; total reckoning [L. *summa*, total amount].

sum·ma·ry (sum'·ạ·ri·) *a.* expressed in few words; concise; done quickly and without formality; *n.* abridgment or statement of chief points of longer document, speech; etc.; epitome. **summarily** *adv.* **summarize** *v.t.* **summarist** *n.* **summarization** *n.* **summarizer** *n.* [Fr. *sommaire*].

sum·mer (sum'·ẹr) *n.* warmest of four seasons of year, season between spring and autumn; commonly, months of June, July, and August; *a.* pert. to period of summer; *v.i.* to pass the summer. *a.* like summer. **-y** *a.* [O.E. *sumor*].

sum·mer·sault *n.* See **somersault.**

sum·mit (sum'·it) *n.* highest point; top, esp. of mountain [L. *summus*, highest].

sum·mon (sum'·ạn) *v.t.* to demand appearance of, esp. in court of law; to send for; to gather up (energy, etc.). **-er** *n.* **-s** *n.* (*Law*) document ordering person to appear in court; any authoritative demand; *v.t.* to serve with summons [L. *summonere*, to hint].

sump (sump) *n.* lowest part of excavation, esp. of mine, in which water collects; well in crankcase of motor vehicle for oil [Dut. *somp*].

sump·tu·ar·y (sump'·chòò·er·i·) *a.* pert. to or regulating, expenditure. **sumptuous** *a.* costly; lavish; magnificent. **sumptuously** *adv.* **sumptuousness** *n.* [L. *sumptus*, cost].

sun (sun) *n.* luminous body round which earth and other planets revolve; its rays; any other heavenly body forming the center of system of planets; anything resembling sun, esp. in brightness; *v.t.* to expose to sun's rays; to warm (oneself) in sunshine. *pr.p.* **-ning.** *pa.p.*, *pa.t.* **-ned. -ny** *a.* pert. to, like, sun; exposed to sun; warmed by sun; cheerful. **-niness** *n.* **-bathe** *v.i.* to expose body to sun. **-beam** *n.* ray of sunlight. **-burn** *n.* darkening of skin, acompanied often by burning sensation, due to exposure to sun; *v.t., v.i.* to darken by exposure to sun. **-burned, burnt** *a.* **— dial** *n.* device for showing time by shadow cast by a raised pin. **-down** *n.* sunset. **-flower** *n.* tall plant with large, round, yellow-rayed flowers. **-light** *n.* light of sun. **-lit** *a.* lighted by sun. **-rise** *n.* first appearance of sun above horizon in morning; dawn; east. **-set** *n.* descent of sun below horizon; west. **-shade** *n.* parasol. **-shine** *n.* light of sun; cheerfulness. **-shiny** *a.* **-spot** *n.* dark, irregular patches seen periodically on surface of sun. **-stroke** *n.* feverish and sudden prostration caused by undue exposure to very strong sunlight [O.E. *sunne*].

Sun·belt, Sun Belt (sun'·belt) *n.* (*Colloq.*) most of the rapidly developing southwest region of the U.S.

sun·dae (sun'·di) *n.* ice-cream served with topping [perh. fr. *Sunday*].

Sun·day (sun'·di) *n.* first day of week; [O.E. *sunnan*, sun; *daeg*. day].

sun·der (sun'·dẹr) *v.t.* to separate; to divide; to sever; *v.i.* to come apart. **sundry** *a.* separate; several; various. **sundries** *n.pl.* sundry things; odd items [O.E. *syndrian*, separate].

sung (sung) *pa.p.* of **sing.**

sunk (sungk) *pa.p.*, alt. *pa.t.* of **sink.**

sunk·en (sungk'·ạn) alt. *pa.p.* of **sink.**

Sun·nite (soon'·īt) *n.* a member of the main branch of Islam that accepts the Sunna, a book of traditional teachings, as a supplement to the Koran (See *Shiite*); *a.* Also **Sunni, Sunnism** *n.* [Ar. *sunnah*, form, tradition].

sup (sup) *v.t.* to take in sips; to sip; to eat with spoon, as soup; *v.i.* to have supper; to sip; *pr.p.* **-ping;** *pa.p.*, *pa.t.* **-ped;** *n.* small mouthful; sip [O.E. *supan*].

su·per (sòò'·pẹr) *n.* supernumerary (actor); superintendent; short for superfine, superexcellent, etc. [L. = above].

su·per- (sòò'·pẹr) *prefix* fr. L. *super*, above, over, higher, superior, extra, etc.

su·per·a·ble (sòò'·pẹr·ạ·bl) *a.* capable of being overcome [L. *superare*, to overcome].

su·per·a·bound (sòò'·pẹr·ạ·bound') *v.i.* to be exceedingly abundant. **superabundant** *a.* much more than enough; excessive. **superabundantly** *adv.* **superabundance** *n.*

su·per·an·nu·ate (sòò·pẹr·an'·yoo·āt) *v.t.* to pension off because of age or infirmity. **superannuation** *n.* pension [L. *super*, above; *annus*, year].

su·perb (soo·purb') *a.* grand; splendid; magnificent; stately; elegant. **-ly** *adv.* **-ness** *n.* [L. *superbus*, proud].

su·per·car·go (sòò·pẹr·kàr'·gō) *n.* ship's officer who takes charge of cargo.

su·per·charge (sòò'·pẹr·chạrj) *v.t.* to charge or fill to excess.

su·per·cil·i·ar·y (sòò·pẹr·sil'·i·er·i·) *a.* pert. to eyebrow. **supercilious** *a.* lofty with pride; haughty and indifferent. **superciliously** *adv.* [L. *supercilium*, the eyebrow].

su·per·e·go (sòò·pẹr·ē'·gō) *n.* in psychoanalysis, that unconscious morality which directs action of censor.

su·per·er·o·ga·tion (sòò·pẹr·er·ạ·gā'·shạn) *n.* doing more than duty or necessity requires.

[L. *super*, above; *erogare*, to expend].

su·per·fi·cial (sòò·pẹr·fish′·ạl) *a.* on surface; not deep; shallow; understanding only what is obvious. **-ly** *adv.* **-ity** (fish·i·al′·ạ·ti·) [L. *super*, above; *facies*, the face].

su·per·fine (sòò′·pẹr·fīn) *a.* fine above others; of first class quality; very fine.

su·per·flu·ous (soo·pur′·floo·ạs) *a.* more than is required or desired; useless. **-ly** *adv.* **superfluity** *n.* state of being superfluous; quantity beyond what is required; a superabundance. **-ness** *n.* [L. *super*, over; *fluere*, to flow].

su·per·heat (sòò·pẹr·hēt′) *v.t.* to heat (steam) above boiling point of water, done under a pressure greater than atmospheric; to heat (liquid) above its boiling point.

su·per·het·er·o·dyne (sòò·pẹr·het′·ạr·ạ·dīn) *n.* (*Radio*) receiving set of great power and selectivity. *abbrev.* **superhet.**

su·per·hu·man (sòò·pẹr·hū′·mạn) *a.* more than human; divine; excessively powerful.

su·per·im·pose (sòò·pẹr·im·pōz′) *v.t.* to lay upon another thing. **superimposition** *n.*

su·per·in·tend (sòò·pẹr·in·tend′) *v.t.* to manage; to supervise; to direct; to control; *v.i.* to supervise. **-ence, -ency** *n.* **-ent** *a.* superintending; *n.* one who superintends [L. *superintendere*].

su·pe·ri·or (sạ·pi′·ri·ẹr) *a.* upper; higher in place, position, rank, quality, etc.; surpassing others; being above, or beyond, power or influence of; too dignified to be affected by; supercilious; snobbish; *n.* one who is above another, esp. in rank or office; head of monastery or other religious house. **superiority** (sạ·per·i·àr′·i·ti·) *n.* [L. *superior*, higher].

su·per·la·tive (sạ·pur′·lạ·tiv) *a.* of or in the highest degree; surpassing all others; supreme; (*Gram.*) denoting, as form of adjective or adverb, highest degree of quality; *n.* superlative degree of adjective or adverb. **-ly** *adv.* [fr. L. *super*, above; *ferre, latum*, to carry].

su·per·man (soo′·pẹr·man) *n.* ideal man; one endowed with powers beyond those of the ordinary man.

su·per·nal (sòò·pur′·nạl) *a.* pert. to things above; celestial; heavenly; exalted.

su·per·nat·u·ral (sòò·pẹr·nach′·ạ·rạl) *a.* beyond powers or laws of nature; miraculous.

su·per·nu·mer·ar·y (sòò·pẹr·nū′·mẹr·er·i·) over and above; extra; *n.* person or thing in excess of what is necessary or usual; actor with no speaking part [L. *super*, above; *numerus*, a number].

su·per·scribe (sòò·pẹr·skrīb′) *v.t.* to write or engrave on outside or top of. **superscription** *n.* act of superscribing; words written or engraved on top or outside of anything.

su·per·sede (sòò·pẹr·sēd) *v.t.* to set aside; to replace by another person or thing; to take the place of. **supersession** *n.* [L. *super*, above; *sedere*, to sit].

su·per·son·ic (sòò·pẹr·sàn′·ik) *a.* pert. to soundwaves of too high a frequency to be audible; denoting a speed greater than that of sound, i.e. more than 750 miles per hour.

su·per·sti·tion (sòò·pẹr·stish′·ạn) *n.* belief in, or fear of, what is unknown, mysterious, or supernatural; religion, opinion, or practice based on belief in divination, magic, omens, etc. **superstitious** *a.* pert. to, believing in, or based on, superstition. **superstitiously** *adv.* [L. *superstitio*, excessive fear of the gods].

su·per·struc·ture (sòò·pẹr·struk′·chẹr) *n.* structure built on top of another; the part of building above foundation. **superstructive, superstructural** *a.*

su·per·vene (sòò·pẹr·vēn′) *v.i.* to happen in addition, or unexpectedly; to follow closely upon. **supervenient** *a.* **supervenience, supervention** *n.* act of supervening [L. *super*, above; *venire*, to come].

su·per·vise (sòò·pẹr·vīz′) *v.t.* to oversee; to superintend; to inspect; to direct and control. **supervision** (vizh′·ạn) *n.* act of supervising; superintendence; inspection. Also **supervisal** *n.* **supervisor** (vī′·zẹr) *n.* **supervisory** *a.* [L. *super*, over; *videre, visum*, to see].

su·pine (sòò′·pīn) *a.* lying on one's back; indolent; inactive [L. *supinus*, fr. *sub*, under].

sup·per (sup′·pẹr) *n.* the last meal of the day [Fr. *souper*, to sup].

sup·plant (sạ·plant′) *v.t.* to displace (person) esp. by unfair means; to take the place of. **-er** *n.* [L. *supplantare*, to trip up, fr. *planta*, the sole of the foot].

sup·ple (sup′·l) *a.* easily bent; flexible; limber; obsequious; *v.t.* and *v.i.* to make or become supple. **-ly** *adv.* **-ness** *n.* [L. *supplex*, suppliant].

sup·ple·ment (sup′·lạ·mạnt) *n.* something added to fill up or supply deficiency; appendix; special number of newspaper; extra charge; (*Geom.*) number of degrees which must be added to angle or arc to make 180° or two right angles. **supplement** (sup′·lạ·ment) *v.t.* to fill up or supply deficiency; to add to; to complete. **-al** *a.* **-ary** *a.* added to additional [L. *supplementum*, fr. *supplere*, to fill up].

sup·pli·ant (sup′li·ạnt) *a.* supplicating; asking humbly and submissively; beseeching; *n.* one who supplicates. **-ly** *adv.* **supplicant** *a.* supplicating; *n.* one who supplicates; suppliant. **supplicate** *v.t.* and *v.i.* to ask humbly; to beg earnestly; to petition. **supplication** *n.* [L. *supplicare*, to kneel down, fr. *plicare*, to fold].

sup·ply (sạ·plī′) *v.t.* to provide what is needed; to furnish; to fill the place of; *n.* act of supplying; what is supplied; stock; store; **supplies** *n.pl.* food or money. **supplier** *n.* [L.*supplere*, to fill up].

sup·port (sạ·pōrt′) *v.t.* to keep from falling; to bear weight of; to sustain; to bear or tolerate; to encourage; to furnish with means of living; *n.* act of sustaining; advocacy; maintenance or subsistence; one who, or that which, supports. **-er** *n.* [L. *sub*, under; *portare*, to carry].

sup·pose (sạ·pōz′) *v.t.* to assume as true without proof; to advance or accept as a possible or probable fact, condition, etc.; to imagine. **-d** *a.* imagined; accepted; put forward as authentic. **supposedly** (sạ·pōz′·id·li·) *adv.* **supposable** *a.* [Fr. *supposer*].

sup·po·si·tion (sup·ạ·zish′·ạn) *n.* act of supposing; assumption; that which is supposed; **-ally** *adv.* **supposititious** (sạ·pàz·ạ·tish′·ạs) [L. *sub*, under; *ponere, positum*, to place].

sup·pos·i·to·ry (sạ·pàz′·ạ·tōr·i·) *n.* medicinal substance, cone-shaped, introduced into a body canal [L. *sub*, under; *ponere, positum*, to place].

sup·press (sạ·pres′) *v.t.* to put down or subdue; to overpower and crush; to quell; to stop. **suppression** (sạ·presh′·ạn) *n.* **-ive** *a.* **-or** *n.* [L. *sub*, under; *premere, pressum*, to press].

sup·pu·rate (sup′·yạ·rāt) *v.i.* to form pus; to fester. **suppurative** *a.* tending to suppurate. **suppuration** *n.* [L. *sub*, under; *pus*, matter].

su·pra- (sòò′·prạ) L. *prefix*, meaning above.

su·preme (sạ·prēm′) *a.* holding highest authority; highest or most exciting; greatest possible; uttermost. **-ly** *adv.* **-ness** *n.* **supremacy** (sạ·prem′·ạ·si·) *n.* state of being highest in power and authority; utmost excellence [L. *supremus*].

sur- *prefix*, meaning over, above, upon, in addition [Fr. fr. L. *super*, over].

sur·cease (sur·sēs′) *v.t.* (*Arch.*) to cause to cease; *v.i.* to cease; *n.* cessation [L. *supersedere*, to refrain from].

sur·charge (sur·chàrj′) *v.t.* to make additional

charge; to overload or overburden. **surcharge** (sur′·chårj) *n.* excessive charge, load, or burden; additional words or marks superimposed on postage stamp.

sur·cin·gle (sur′·sing·gl) *n.* belt, band, or girth for holding something on a horse's back [L. *super,* over; *cingulum,* a belt].

sur·coat (sur′·kōt) *n.* long and flowing cloak worn by knights over armor [O.Fr. *surcote*].

surd (surd) *a.* (*Math.*) not capable of being expressed in rational numbers; radical; (*Phon.*) uttered with breath alone, not voice, as *f, p, k,* etc.; *n.* (*Math.*) quantity that cannot be expressed by rational numbers, or which has no root [L. *surdus,* deaf].

sure (shoor) *a.* certain; positive; admitting of no doubt; firmly established; strong or secure. **-ly** *adv.* certainly; undoubtedly; securely. **-ness** *n.* **-ty** (shoor′·ạ·ti·) *n.* certainty; that which makes sure; security against loss or damage; one who makes himself responsible for obligations of another [L. *securus,* sure].

surf (surf) *n.* foam or water of sea breaking on shore or reefs, etc.

sur·face (sur′·fis) *n.* external layer or outer face of anything; outside; exterior; *a.* involving the surface only; *v.t.* to cover with special surface; to smooth; *v.i.* to come to the surface [L. *super,* over; *facies,* the face]

sur·feit (sur′·fit) *v.t.* to overfeed; to fill to satiety; *n.* excess in eating and drinking; oppression caused by such excess. **-er** *n.* **-ing** *n.* [Fr. *surfaire,* to overdo].

surge (surj) *n.* rolling swell of water, smoke, people; large wave or billow; *v.i.* to swell; to rise high and roll, as waves. **surging** *a.* [L. *surgere,* to rise].

sur·geon (sur′·jạn) *n.* medical man qualified to perform operations; one who practices surgery. **surgery** *n.* branch of medicine dealing with cure of disease or injury by manual operation; operating room. **surgical** *a.* **surgically** *adv.* [Fr. *chirurgien*].

sur·ly (sur′·li·) *a.* of unfriendly temper; rude; uncivil; sullen. **surlily** *adv.* **surliness** *n.*

sur·mise (sẹr·mīz′) *v.t.* to imagine or infer something without proper grounds; to make a guess; to conjecture; *n.* supposition; a guess or conjecture [O.Fr. *surmise,* accusation].

sur·mount (sẹr·mount′) *v.t.* to rise above; to overtop; to conquer or overcome. **-able** *a.* [Fr. *sur,* over; *monter,* to mount].

sur·name (sur′·nām) *n.* family name [Fr. *surnam*].

sur·pass (sẹr·pas′) *v.t.* to go beyond; to excel; to outstrip. **-ing** *a.* excellent; in an eminent degree; exceeding others [Fr. *sur,* beyond; *passer,* to pass].

sur·plice (sur′·plis) *n.* white linen vestment worn over cassock by clergy [L.L. *superpellicium,* overgarment].

sur·plus (sur′·plus) *n.* excess beyond what is wanted; excess of income over expenditure; *a.* more than enough [L. *super,* over; *plus,* more].

sur·prise (sẹ(r)·prīz′) *v.t.* to fall or come upon unawares; to capture by unexpected attack; to strike with astonishment; *n.* act of coming upon unawares; astonishment; unexpected event, piece of news, gift, etc. **surprisal** *n.* act of surprising or state of being surprised. **surprising** *a.* **surprisingly** *adv.* [L. *super,* over; *prehendere,* to catch].

sur·re·al·ism (sạ·rē′·al·iz·ạm) *n.* 20th cent. phase in art and literature of expressing subconscious in images without order or coherence, as in dream. **surrealist** *n.* **surrealistic** *a.* [Fr. *sur,* over; *realism*].

sur·ren·der (sạ·ren′·dẹr) *v.t.* to yield or hand over to power of another; to resign; to yield to emotion, etc.; *v.i.* to cease resistance; to give oneself up into power of another; to capitulate; *n.* act of surrendering. **-er** *n.* [L. *super,* over; *reddere,* to restore].

sur·rep·ti·tious (sur·ạp·tish′·ạs) *a.* done by stealth; furtive; clandestine. **-ly** *adv.* [L. *surripere,* fr. *sub,* under; *rapere,* to seize].

sur·rey (sur′·i.) *n.* lightly-built, four-wheeled carriage [prob. fr. proper name].

sur·ro·gate (sur′·ạ·gāt) *n.* deputy or delegate; deputy who acts for bishop or chancellor of diocese. **-ship** *n.* [L. *sub,* under; *rogare,* to ask].

sur·round (sạ·round′) *v.t.* to be on all sides of; to encircle; (*Mil.*) to cut off from communication or retreat; **-ings** *n.* that which surrounds; *pl.* things which environ; neighborhood [L. *superundare,* to overflow].

sur·tax (sur′·taks) *n.* additional tax; *v.t.* to impose extra tax on.

sur-veil·lance (sẹr·vā′·lạns) *n.* close watch; supervision [Fr. fr. *surveiller,* to watch over].

sur·vey (sẹr·vā′) *v.t.* to look over; to view as from high place; to take broad, general view; to determine shape, extent, position, contour, etc. of tract of land by measurement. **survey** (sur′·vā) *n.* general view, as from high place; attentive scrutiny; measured plan or chart of any tract of country. **-or** *n.* one who surveys [L. *super,* over; *videre,* to see].

sur·vive (sẹr·vīv′) *v.t.* to live longer than; to outlive or outlast; *v.i.* to remain alive. **survival** *n.* living longer than, or beyond life of another person, thing, or event; any rite, habit, belief, etc. remaining in existence after what justified it has passed away. **survivor** *n.* **surviving** *a.* [L. *super,* over; *vivere,* to live].

sus·cep·ti·ble (sa·sep′·tạ·bl) *a.* capable of; readily impressed; sensitive **susceptibly** *adv.* **-ness** *n.* **susceptibility** *n.* capacity for catching disease, for feeling, or emotional excitment; sensitiveness; *pl.* sensitive spots in person's nature. **susceptive** *a.* receptive **susceptivity, susceptiveness** *n.* [L. *suscipere,* to take up, receive].

suspect (sạ·spekt′) *v.t.* to imagine existence or presence of; to imagine to be guilty; to conjecture; to mistrust. **suspect** (sus′·pekt) *n.* suspected person; *a.* inspiring distrust. **-er** *n.* [L. *suspicere,* to look at secretly].

sus·pend (sạ·spend′) *v.t.* to cause to hang; to bring to a stop temporarily; to debar from an office or privilege; to defer or keep undecided. **er** *n.* one who suspends; *pl.* pair of straps for holding up trousers, skirt, etc. **suspense** *n.* state of being suspended; state of uncertainty or anxiety; indecision. **suspension** *n.* act of suspending or state of being suspended; delay or deferment; temporary withdrawal from office, function or privilege.**suspensive** *a.* **suspensively** *adv.* **suspensor** *n.* **suspensory** *a.* [L. *sub,* under; *pendere,* to hang].

sus·pi·cion (sạ·spish′·ạn) *n.* act of suspecting; imagining of something being wrong, on little evidence; doubt; mistrust; slight trace or hint. **suspicious** *a.* feeling suspicion; mistrustful; arousing suspicion. **suspiciously** *adv.* [L. *suspicere,* to look at secretly].

sus·tain (sạ·stān′) *v.t.* to keep from falling or sinking; to nourish or keep alive; to endure or undergo; (Law) to allow the validity of. **-able** *a.* **-er** *n.* **sustenance** (sus′·tạ·nạns) *n.* that which sustains (life); food, nourishment. **sustentation** *n.* **sustentative** *a.* **sustention** *n.* [L. *sustinere,* to support].

sut·ler (sut′·lẹr) *n.* formerly person who followed army and sold provisions, liquors, etc., to troops [Dut. *zoetelaar,* a small tradesman].

su·ture (sòò′·chẹr) *n.* sewing up of wound; a stitch; connection or seam, between bones of skull; *v.t.* to join by stitching. **sutural** *a.* united by sutures [L. *suere, sutum,* to sew].

su·ze·rain (sòò′·zạ·rạn, ·rān) *n.* feudal lord;

paramount ruler. **-ty** *n.* authority or dominion of **suzerain** [Fr. *suzerain*, paramount].

svelte (svelt) *a.* supple; lithe; slender [Fr.].

swab (swȧb) *n.* mop for rubbing over floors, decks, etc.; bit of cotton on stick for applying medicine, cleaning parts of body, etc. *v.t.* to clean with mop or swab. *pr.p.* **-bing.** *pa.t.* and *pa.p.* **-bed. -ber** *n.* [Dut. *zwabber*, ship's drudge].

swad·dle (swȧd′.l) *v.t.* to bind or wrap as with bandages; *n.* the cloth wrapping [O.E. *swathy* a bandage].

swag (swag) *n.* (*Colloq.*) bundle; stolen goods or booty; [O.N. *swagga*, to walk unsteadily].

swage (swāj) *n.* tool for bending, marking, or shaping metal. *v.t.* [L.L. *soca*, a rope].

swag·ger (swag′.ẹr) *v.i.* to walk with a conceited or defiant strut; to boast or brag; *n.* defiant or conceited bearing; boastfulness. **-er** *n.* **-ing** *a.* [perh. fr. *swag*].

Swa·hi·li (swȧ.hē′.li.) *n.* people of mixed Bantu and Arab stock, occupying Zanzibar and adjoining territory; their language. (Poetic) **-an** *a.* [Ar. = coast-man].

swain (swān) *n.* (*Poetic*) country lad; rustic lover; suitor [O.N. *sveinn*, a boy, a servant].

swal·low (swȧl′.ō) *n.* small migratory, passerine, insectivorous bird. **-tail** *n.* forked tail; kind of butterfly [O.E. *swealwe*].

swal·low (swȧl′.ō) *v.t.* to receive into stomach through mouth and throat; to absorb; (*Colloq.*) to accept without criticism or scruple; *v.i.* to perform act of swallowing; *n.* act of swallowing; amount taken down at one gulp. **-er** *n.* [O.E. *swelgan*].

swam (swam) *pa.t.* of **swim**.

swamp (swȧmp, swawmp) *n.* tract of wet, spongy, low-lying ground; marsh; *v.t.* to cause to fill with water, as boat; *v.i.* to overwhelm; to sink. **-y** *a.* [Scand.].

swan (swȧn) *n.* large, web-footed bird of goose family, having very long, gracefully curving neck. **-nery** *n.* place where swans are bred. **-'s-down** *n.* fine, soft feathers on swan, used for powder puffs, etc.; thick cotton or woolen cloth with soft nap on one side.. **-song.** song which, according to myth, swan sings before dying; [O.E.].

swank (swangk) *v.i.* (*Slang*) to show off; to swagger; *n.* (*Slang*) style; swagger; *a.* (*Slang*) ostentations; showy. **-y** *a.*

swap (swȧp) *v.t.* and *v.i.* to exchange; to barter; *n.* exchange. *pr.p.* **-ping.** *pa.p.* and *pa.t.* **-ped.** Also **swop** [M.E. *swappe*, strike].

sward (swawrd) *n.* land covered with short green grass; turf; *v.t.* to cover with sward. **-ed** *a.* [O.E. *sweard*, skin of bacon].

swarm (swawrm) *n.* large number of insects esp. in motion; crowd; throng; great multitude or throng; *v.i.* to collect in large numbers [O.E. *swearm*].

swarm (swawrm) *v.i.* to climb with arms and legs [etym. uncertain].

swarth·y (swawr′.THi.) *a.* dark in hue; of dark complexion [O.E. *sweart*].

swash·buck·ler (swȧsh′.buk.lẹr) *n.* swaggering bully. **swashbuckling** *a.* [imit.].

swas·ti·ka (swȧs′.ti.kạ) *n.* symbol in form of Greek cross with ends of arms bent at right angles, all in same direction, thus 卐, used as badge of Nazi party [Sans. *svasti*, well being].

swat (swȧt) *v.t.* (*Colloq.*) to hit smartly; to kill, esp. insects. *pr.p.* **-ting.** *pa.t., pa.p.* **-ted.**

swatch (swȧch) *n.* piece of cloth, cut as a sample of quality [var. of *swath*].

swath (swȧth, swawth) *n.* line of hay or grain cut by scythe or mowing machine; Also **swathe** (swāTH) [O.E. *swaeth*, a track].

swathe (swāTH) *v.t.* to bind with bandage; to envelop in wraps; *n.* bandage; folded or draped band [O.E. *swathian*].

sway (swā) *v.t.* to cause to incline to one side or the other; to influence or direct; *v.i.* to incline or be drawn to one side or the other; to swing unsteadily; to totter; *n.* swaying or swinging movement; control. **-er** *n.* **-back** *a.* having inward curve of the spine [M.E. *sweyen*].

swear (swār) *v.t.* to utter, affirm or declare on oath; *v.i.* to utter solemn declaration with appeal to God for truth of what is affirmed; (*Law*) to give evidence on oath; to use name of God or sacred things profanely; to curse. *pa.p.* **sworn.** *pa.t.* **swore. -er** *n.* **-ing** *n.* **to swear by,** (*Colloq.*) to have great confidence in [O.E. *swerian*].

sweat (swet) *n.* moisture excreted from skin; perspiration; moisture exuding from any substance; state of sweating; (*Colloq.*) state of anxiety; *v.t.* to cause to excrete moisture from skin; to employ at wrongfully low wages; *v.i.* to excrete moisture; (*Colloq.*) to toil or drudge at. **-er** *n.* warm knitted jersey or jacket. **-y** *a.* damp with sweat; causing sweat; like sweat. **-ily** *adv.* **-iness** *n.* [O.E. *swat*].

Swede (swēd) *n.* native of Sweden. **Swedish** *a.* pert. to Sweden; *n.* language of Swedes.

sweep (swēp) *v.t.* to pass brush or broom over to remove loose dirt; to pass rapidly over, with brushing motion; to scan rapidly; *v.i.* to pass with swiftness or violence; to move with dignity; to extend in a curve; to effect cleaning with a broom; *n.* act of sweeping; reach of a stroke; curving or wide-flung gesture, movement, or line; powerful drive forward, covering large area; long, heavy oar, used either to steer or to propel. *pa.p.* and *pa.t.* **swept. -er** *n.* **-ing** *a.* moving swiftly; of great scope; comprehensive. **-ingly** *adv.* **— stake(s)** *n.* gambling on race or contest, in which participators' stakes are pooled, and apportioned to drawers of winning horses [O.E. *swapan*].

sweet (swēt) *a.* tasting like sugar; having agreeable taste; fragrant; melodious; pleasing to eye; gentle; affectionate; dear or beloved; likeable; *n.* sweetness; darling; *pl.* confections. **-en** *v.t.* to make sweet, pleasing, or kind. **-ening** *n.* act of making sweet; ingredient which sweetens. **-ly** *adv.* **-ness** *n.* **-bread** *n.* pancreas or thymus of animal, as food. **-heart** *n.* lover or beloved person; darling. **meat** *n.* confection; candy. **-pea** *n.* climbing plant with fragrant flowers. **-potato** *n.* sweet, starchy tuber [O.E. *swete*].

swell (swel) *v.t.* to increase size, sound, etc.; to dilate; to augment; *v.i.* to grow larger; to expand; to rise in waves; to grow louder; to be filled to bursting point with some emotion. n. act of swelling; increase in bulk, intensity, importance, etc.; slight rise in ground level; slow heaving and sinking of sea after storm; *pa.p.* **swollen** or **swelled.** *pa.t.* **-ed. -ing** *n.* act of swelling; state of being swollen; prominence or protuberance; (*Med.*) enlargement [O.E. *swellan*].

swel·ter (swel′.tẹr) *v.i.* to be oppressive, or oppressed, with heat; to perspire profusely; *n.* heated or sweaty state. **-ing** *a.* **sweltry** *a.* [O.E. *sweltan*, to swoon or perish].

swept (swept) *pa.t.* and *pa.p.* of **sweep.**

swerve (swurv) *v.i.* to depart from straight line; to deviate; *v.t.* to cause to bend or turn aside; *n.* act of swerving [O.E. *sweorfan*, to rub, file].

swift (swift) *a.* quick; rapid; prompt; moving quickly. **-ly** *adv.* **-ness** *n.* speed; *a* quick-flying migratory bird, resembling swallow; common newt [O.E. *swifan*, to move quickly].

swig (swig) *v.t.* and *v.i.* (*Colloq.*) to gulp down; to drink in long drafts; *n.* long draft *pr.p.* **-ging.** *pa.p., pa.t.* **-ged** [O.E. *swelgan*, to swallow].

swill (swill) *v.t.* and *v.i.* to drink greedily;

n. act of swilling; pig food; hogwash slops. **-er** *n.* [O.E. *swilian*, to wash].

swim (swim) *v.i.* to propel oneself in water by means of hands, feet, or fins, etc.; to float on surface; to move with gliding motion, resembling swimming; *v.t.* to cross or pass over by swimming; to cause to swim; *n.* act of swimming; spell of swimming. *pr.p.* **-ming.** *pa.p.* **swum.** *pa.t.* **swam. -mer** *n.* **-mingly** *adv.* easily, successfully [O.E. *swimmen*, to be in motion].

swim (swim) *v.i.* to be dizzy or giddy; *n.* dizziness or unconsciousness *pr.p.* **-ming.** *pa.p.* **swum;** *pa.t.* **swam.** [O.E. *swima*, to faint].

swin·dle (swin'·dl) *v.t.* and *v.i.* to cheat or defraud; to obtain by fraud; *n.* act of defrauding [Ger. *schwindeln*, to cheat].

swine (swīn) *n. sing.* and *pl.* thick-skinned domestic animal, fed for its flesh; pig; hog. **—herd** *n.* one who tends swine. **swinish** *a.* like swine; gross, brutal [O.E. *swin*].

swing (swing) *v.i.* to move to and fro, esp. as suspended body; to sway; to turn on pivot; to progress with easy, swaying gait; (*Colloq.*) to be executed by hanging; to wheel around; *v.t.* to attach so as to hang freely; to move to and fro; to cause to wheel about a point; to brandish; *n.* act of swinging or causing to swing; extent, sweep, or power of anything that is swung; motion to and fro; seat suspended by ropes, on which one may swing. *pa.p.* and *pa.t.* **swung. -er** *n.* **-ing** *a.* moving to and fro; moving with vigor and rhythm. **-ingly** *adv.* [O.E. *swingan*, to swing, whirl].

swing (swing) *n.* (*Mus.*) kind of jazz music [O.E. *swingan*].

swipe (swīp) *v.t.* and *v.i.* to strike with a wide, sweeping blow, as with a bat, racket, etc.; (*Slang*) to steal; *n.* sweeping stroke [O.E. *swipian*, to beat].

swirl (swurl) *n.* eddy of wind or water; whirling motion; a twist of something; *v.i.* to whirl; *v.t.* to carry along with whirling motion [O.N. *svirla*, to whirl round].

swish (swish) *n.* whistling or hissing sound; *v.i.* to move with hissing or rustling sound.

Swiss (swis) *n. sing.* and *pl.* native of Switzerland; people of Switzerland; *a.* pert. to Switzerland or the Swiss [O. Ger. *Swiz*].

switch (swich) *n.* flexible twig or rod; tress of false hair; on railway, movable rail for transferring train from one set of tracks to another; (*Elect.*) device for making, breaking, or transferring, electric current; act of switching; *v.t.* to strike with switch; to wisk; to shift or shunt (train) to another track; (*Elect*) to turn electric current off or on with switch; to transfer one's thoughts to another subject; to transfer. **-er** *n.* **—like** *a.* **-back** *n.* zigzag method of ascending slopes, **-board** *n.* set of switches at telephone exchange [Old Dut. *swick*, a whip].

swiv·el (swiv'·l) *n.* ring turning on pivot, forming connection between two pieces of mechanism and enabling one to rotate independently of the other; *v.i.* to swing on pivot; *v.t.* to turn as on pivot [O.E. *swifan*, to revolve].

swol·len (swōl'·ạn) *a.* swelled. *pa.p.* of **swell.**

swoon (swòòn) *v.i.* to faint; *n.* fainting fit [O.E. *swogan*, to sigh deeply].

swoop (swòòp) *v.t.* to catch up with sweeping motion (with 'up'); *v.i.* to sweep down swiftly upon prey, as hawk or eagle; *n.* sweeping downward flight [O.E. *swapan*, to rush].

swop. See **swap.**

sword (sōrd, sawrd) *n.* weapon for cutting or thrusting, having long blade; emblem of judicial punishment or of authority. **-fish** *n.* large fish with sword-like upper jaw. **-play** *n.* fencing. **-sman** *n.* one skillful with sword. **—smanship** *n.* [O.E. *sweord*].

swore (swōr) *pa.t.* of **swear.**

sworn *pa.p. of* **swear.**

swum (swum) *pa.p.* of **swim.**

swung (swung) *pa.p.* and *pa.t.* of **swing.**

syb·a·rite (sib'·ạ·rīt) *n.* person devoted to luxury and pleasure. **sybaritic, sybaritical** *a.* [L. *Sybaris*, Greek city].

syc·a·more (sik'·ạ·mōr) *n.* tree with broad leaves, allied to plane tree and maple; kind of fig tree of Egypt and Asia Minor [Gk. *sukon*, fig; *moron*, black mulberry].

syc·o·phant (sik'·ạ.fạnt) *n.* flatterer, or one who fawns on rich or famous; parasite; *a.* servile; obsequious. **sychophancy, -ism** *n.* **-ic, -ical, -ically** *adv.* **-ish** *a.* [Gk. *sukophantēs*, to show].

syl·la·ble (sil'·ạ·bl) *n.* sound uttered at single effort of voice, and constituting word, or part of word; *v.t.* to utter in syllables; to articulate. **syllabic, syllabical** *a.* pert. to, or consisting of, a syllable(s). **syllabically** *adv.* **syllabicate, syllabify, syllabize,** *v.t.* to divide into syllables [Gk. *sullabē*, that which is held together].

syl·la·bus (sil'·ạ·bạs) *n.* outline or program of main points in a course of lectures, etc. [Gk. *sun*, together; *lambanein*, to take].

syl·lo·gism (sil'·ạ·jizm) *n.* formal statement of argument, consisting of three parts, major premise, minor premise, and conclusion, conclusion following naturally from premises. **syllogize** *v.t.* and *v.i.* to reason by means of syllogisms. **syllogization** *n.* **syllogizer** *n.* **syllogistic, syllogistical** *a.* [Gk. *sullogismos*, a reckoning together].

sylph (silf) *n.* elemental spirit of the air; fairy or sprite; graceful girl. **-id** *n.* little sylph. **-like** *a.* graceful [Fr. *sylphe*].

syl·van (sil'·vạn) *a.* forest-like; abounding in forests; pert. to or inhabiting the woods [L. *silva*, a wood].

sym·bi·o·sis (sim·bī·ō'·sis) *n.* (*Biol.*) living together of different organisms for mutual benefit, as in the lichens. **symbiotic** *a.* **symbiont** *n.* organism living in symbiosis [Gk. *sun*, together; *bios*, life].

sym·bol (sim'·bạl) *n.* something that represents something else, esp. concrete representation of moral or intellectual quality; emblem; type character or sign used to indicate relation or operation in mathematics; in chemistry, letter or letters standing for atom of element. **-ic, -ical** *a.* **-ically** *adv.* **-ize** *v.t.* to stand for, or represent; to represent by a symbol or symbols. **-ism** *n.* representation by symbols; system of symbols; in art and literature, tendency to represent emotions by means of symbols, and to invest ordinary objects with imaginative meanings. **-ist** *n.* one who uses symbols; adherent of symbolism in art and literature [Gk. *sumbolon*, a token].

sym·me·try (sim'·ạ·tri·) *n.* due proportion between several parts of object; exact correspondence of opposite sides of an object to each other. **symmetric, symmetrical** *a.* **symmetricalness** *n.* **symmetrize** *v.t.* [Gk. *sun*, together; *metron*, measure].

sym·pa·thy (sim'·pạ·thi·) *n.* fellow feeling, esp. feeling for another person in pain or grief; sharing of emotion, interest, desire, etc.; compassion or pity. **sympathetic(al)** *a.* exhibiting or expressing sympathy; compassionate; congenial; (*Med.*) denoting a portion of the nerve system in body. **sympathetically** *adv.* **sympathize** *v.i.* **sympathizer** *n.* [Gk. *sun*, together; *pathos*, feeling].

sym·pho·ny (sim'·fạ·ni·) *n.* (*Mus.*) composition for full orchestra, consisting of four contrasted sections or movements. **symphonic** *a.* **symphonist** *n.* composer of symphonies. [Gk. *sun*, together; *phōnē*, sound].

sym·po·si·um (sim·pō′·zi·ạm) *n.* gathering, esp. one at which interchange or discussion of ideas takes place; series of short articles by several writers dealing with common topic. *pl.* **symposia** [Gk. *sun*, together; *posis*, a drinking].

symp·tom (simp′·tạm) *n.* (*Med.*) perceptible change in body or its functions, which indicates disease; sign of the existence of something. **-atic(al)** *a.* [Gk. *sun*, together; *ptōma*, a fall].

syn- (sin) *prefix* from Gk. *sun*, meaning with, together, at the same time; becomes *sym-* before *p*, *b*, and *m*, and *syl-* before *l*.

syn·a·gogue (sin′·ạ·gȧg) *n.* congregation of Jews met for worship; Jewish place of worship. **synagogical** (sin·ạ·gȧj′·ạ·kạl) *a.* [Gk. *sun*, together; *agein*, to lead].

syn·chro·nize (sing′·krạ·nīz) *v.i.* to agree in time; to be simultaneous; *v.t.* to cause to occur at the same time. **synchronization** *n.* **synchronism** *n.* concurrence of events; simultaneousness. **synchronal** *a.* **synchronous** *a.* [Gk. *sun*, together; *chronos*, time].

syn·chro·tron (sing′·krạ·trȧn) *n.* scientific machine, used in atom research, for accelerating electrons to very high speeds [Gk. *sun*, together; *chronos*, time].

syn·co·pate (sing′·kạ·pāt) *v.t.* (*Gram.*) to contract, as a word, by taking one or more sounds or syllables from middle; in music, to alter rhythm by accenting a usually unaccented note, or causing the accent to fall on a rest, or silent beat. **syncopation** *n.* [Gk. *sun*, together; *kopē*, a cutting].

syn·cope (sing′·kạ·pē) *n.* the omission of one or more letters from the middle of a word; *(Med.)* a fainting or swooning. **syncopal, syncopic** *a.* [same origin as *syncopate*].

syn·dic (sin′·dik) *n.* legal representative chosen to act as agent for corporation or company. **-ate** *n.* council of syndics; body of persons associated to carry out enterprise; association of industrialists or financiers formed to carry out industrial project, or to acquire monopoly in certain goods; *v.t.* to control by a syndicate; to publish news, etc. simultaneously in several periodicals owned by one syndicate [Gk. *sundikos*, an advocate].

syn·ec·do·che (si·nek′·dạ·kē) *n.* (*Rhet.*) figure of speech by which the whole is put for the part, or a part for the whole. **synecdochic(al)** *a.* [Gk.].

syn·fu·el (sin′·fū·ạl) *n.* any man-made liquid *syn*thetic *fuel*, esp. fuel resulting from coal-to-oil conversion.

syn·od (sin′ạd) *n.* an assembly of ecclesiastics; convention or council. **-al, -ic(al)** *a.* **-ically** *adv.* [Gk. *sunodos*, assembly].

syn·o·nym (sin′·ạ·nim) *n.* word which has approximately the same meaning as another. **-ous** *a.* **-ously** *adv.* [Gk. *sun*, together; *onoma*, name].

syn·op·sis (si·nȧp′·sis) *n.* general outlook, view; summary. *pl.* **synopses** (-sēz). **synoptic(al)** *a.* **synoptically** *adv.* [Gk. *sun*, together; *opsis*, view].

syn·tax (sin′·taks) *n.* rules governing sentence construction. **syntactic(al)** *a.* **syntactically** *adv.* [Gk. *sun*, together; *tassein*, to put in order].

syn·the·sis (sin′·thạ·sis) *n.* combination or putting together; combining of parts into whole (opp. of *analysis*); (*Chem.*) uniting of elements to form compound; (*Gram.*) building up of words into sentences, and of sentences into more complex forms. *pl.* **syntheses** (-sēz). **synthetic -(al)** *a.* pert. to, consisting in, synthesis; not derived from nature; artificial; spurious. **synthetically** *adv.* **synthesize, synthetize** *v.t.* **-t, synthetist** *n.* [Gk. *sun*, together; *thesis*, a placing].

syph·i·lis (sif′·ạ·lis) *n.* contagious venereal disease. **syphilitic** *a.* [fr. *Syphilus*, shepherd in Latin poem (1530)].

sy·phon. See **siphon.**

Syr·i·a (sir′·i·ạ) *n.* country in W. Asia. **-c** *n.* language of Syria. **-n** *n.* native of Syria; *a.* pert. to Syria.

syr·inge (sạ·rinj′ sir′·inj) *n.* tube and piston serving to draw in and then expel fluid; *v.t.* to inject by means of syringe [Gk. *surinx*, a pipe or reed].

syr·inx (sir′·ingks) *n.* (*Mus.*) Pan-pipe; (*Anat.*) the Eustachian tube; vocal organ of birds. *pl.* **-es, syringes** (gēz). **syringeal** (si·rin′·je·ạl) *a.* [Gk.*surinx*, a reed or pipe].

syr·up, sirup (sir′·ạp) *n.* fluid separated from sugar in process of refining. **-y** *a.* [O.Fr. *syrop*, fr. Ar. *sharab*, a beverage].

sys·tem (sis′·tạm) *n.* assemblage of objects arranged after some distinct method, usually logical or scientific; whole scheme of created things regarded as forming one complete whole; universe; organization; classification; set of doctrines or principles; the body as functional unity. **-atic, -atical** *a.* **-atically** *adv.* **-atize, -ize** *v.t.* to reduce to system; to arrange methodically. **-atization, -ization** *n.* [L.L. *systema*, organized whole].

sys·to·le (sis′·tạ·lē) *n.* contraction of heart and arteries for expelling blood and carrying on circulation. opp. to *diastole;* (*Gram.*) shortening of long syllable. **systolic** *a.* contracting [Gk. fr. *sun*, together, *stellein*, to place].

T

tab (tab) *n.* small tag or flap; a label [fr. *tape*].

tab·ard (tab′·ẹrd) *n.* sleeveless tunic worn over armor by knights; tunic emblazoned with royal arms, worn by heralds. Also **taberd.**

tab·by (tab′·i·) *n.* stout kind of watered silk; striped cat, esp. female; old maid; a malicious gossip; *a.* striped; *v.t.* to give watered finish to, as silk [Ar. *attabi*, a watered silk].

tab·er·nac·le (tab′·ẹr·nak·l) *n.* movable shelter esp. for religious worship by Israelites; place for worship; human body [L. *tabernaculum*, a small tent].

tab·la·ture (tab′·lạ·chẹr) *n.* painting on ceiling or wall; mental picture [fr. *table*].

ta·ble (tā′·bl) *n.* smooth flat surface of wood, etc. supported by legs, as article of furniture for working at, or serving meals; any flat surface, esp. slab bearing inscription; food served on table; systematic arrangement of figures, facts, etc. as *multiplication table;* index, scheme, or schedule; synopsis; one of the divisions of decalogue; upper, flat surface of gemstone; *a.* pert. to or shaped like a table; *v.t.* to form into a table or catalogue; to lay down, as money in payment of a bill; to postpone for subsequent consideratioon. **-spoon** *n.* a large spoon for serving, measuring, etc., holding ½ fluid ounce. **— tennis** *n.* game of indoor tennis played on a table; ping-pong; **-ware** *n.* utensils (incl. china, glass and silver) for table use [L. *tabula*, a board].

tab·leau (tab′·lō) *n.* vivid representation of scene in history, literature, art, etc. by group of persons appropriately dressed and posed. *pl.* **tableaux** (tab′·lōz). **— vivant** (tab′·lō·vē′·vȧnt) *n.* living picture; tableau [Fr. *tableau*, a picture].

tab·let (tab′·lit) *n.* anything flat on which to write; pad; slab of stone with inscription;

small, compressed solid piece of medication, detergent, etc. [dim. of *table*].

tab·loid (tab′·loid) *n.* illustrated newspaper, giving topical and usually sensational events in compressed form; compressed lozenge.

ta·boo (tạ·bòò) *n.* system among natives of the Pacific islands by which certain objects and persons are set aside as sacred or accursed; political, social, or religious prohibition; *a.* prohibited; proscribed; *v.t.* to forbid the use of; to ostracize [Polynesian *tapu*, consecrated].

ta·bor (tā′·bẹr) *n.* small drum like a tambourine. **-et** *n.* small tabor; embroidery frame; low cushioned stool [O.Fr. *tabour*, a drum].

tab·u·lar (tab′·yạ·lẹr) *a.* pert. to, or resembling, a table in shape; having a broad, flat top; arranged systematically in rows or columns. **-ize** *v.t.* to tabulate. **-ly** *adv.* **tabulate** *v.t.* to put or form into a table, scheme or synopsis [L. *tabula*, a table].

ta·chom·e·ter (tạ·kȧm′·ạ·tẹr) *n.* instrument for measurement of speed [Gk. *tachus*, swift; *metron*, a measure].

tac·it (tas′·it) *a.* implied, but not expressed; silent; **-ly** *adv.* **-urn** *a.* silent; reserved of speech. **-urnity** *n.* **-urnly** *adv.* [L. *tacitus*].

tack (tak) *n.* small sharp-pointed nail; long stitch; ship's course in relation to position of her sails; course of action; *v.t.* to fasten with long, loose stitches; to append; to nail with; *v.t.* to change ship's course by moving position of sails; to change policy. **-er** *n.* **-iness** *n.* stickiness. **-y** *a.* sticky; viscous [O.Fr. *tache*, nail].

tack (tak) *n.* food; fore.

tack·le (tak′·l) *n.* mechanism of ropes and pulleys for raising heavy weights; rigging, etc. of ship; equipment or gear; (*Football*) move by player to grasp and stop opponent; *v.t.* to harness; to lay hold of; to undertake; (*Football*) to seize and stop. **tackling** *n.* gear; rigging of a ship. **— block** *n.* pulley [Scand. *taka*, to grasp].

tact (takt) *n.* intuitive understanding of people; awareness of right thing to do or say to avoid giving offense. **-ful** *a.* **-fully** *adv.* **-ile** *a.* pert. to sense of touch; capable of being touched or felt; tangible. **-less** *a.* wanting in tact. **-ual** *a.* pert. to sense of touch [L. *tangere, tactum*, to touch].

tac·tics (tak′·tiks) *n. sing.* science of disposing of military, naval, and air units to the best advantage; adroit management of situation. **tactic, -al** *a.* **tactically** *adv.* **tactician** *n.* [Gk. *taktika*, tactics].

tad·pole (tad′·pōl) *n.* young of frog in its first state before gills and tail are absorbed [O.E. *tad*, a toad; and *poll*].

taf·fe·ta (taf′·ạ·tạ) *n.* light-weight glossy silk of plain weave. Also **taffety** [Pers. *taftah*, woven].

tag (tag) *n.* metal point at end of a shoelace, etc.; tab on back of boot; tie-on label; appendage; catchword; hackneyed phrase; ragged end; refrain; game in which one player chases and tries to touch another; *v.t.* to fit with tags; to add on; (*Colloq.*) to follow behind. *pr.p.* **-ging.** *pa.t.* and *pa.p.* **ged.** [Scand. *tagg*, a spike].

Ta·hi·tian (tạ·hē′·ti·ạn, shạn) *a.* pert. to island of Tahiti or its inhabitants.

Ta·ic (tȧ′·ik) *a.* pert. to inhabitants of Indo-China or their language; *n.* [Chin.].

tail (tāl) *n.* (*Law*) a limitation of ownership; entail; *a.* being entailed. **-age** *n.* [Fr. *taille*, cutting].

tail (tāl) *n.* flexible prolongation of animal's spine; back, lower, or inferior part of anything; (*Colloq.*) *pl.* reverse side of coin; queue; train of attendants; (*Aero.*) group of stabilizing planes or fins at rear of airplane; *pl.* tail-coat; *v.t.* to furnish with tail; to extend in line; to trail. **-board** *n.* movable board at back of cart. **-coat** *n.* man's evening dress coat with tails. **-ed** *a.* **-less** *a.* **-light** *n.* usu. red rear light of vehicle. **-piece** *n.* ebony strip below bridge of violin to which strings are attached; ornamental design marking close of chapter in book. **-plane** *n.* (*Aero.*) stabilizing surface at rear of aircraft [O.E. *taegl*, a tail].

tai·lor (tāl′·ẹr) *n.* one who makes clothes; *v.t.* and *v.i.* to make men's suits, women's costumes, etc. **-ing** *n.* work of a tailor. **-less** *a.* **-made** *a.* made by tailor; plain in style and fitting perfectly [O.Fr. *taillier*, to cut].

taint (tānt) *v.t.* to impregnate with something poisonous; to contaminate; *v.i.* to be infected with incipient putrefaction; *n.* touch of corruption; (*Fig.*) moral blemish [L. *tingere, tinctum*, to dye].

take (tāk) *v.t.* to grasp; to capture; to receive; to remove; to win; to inhale; to choose; to assume; to suppose; to photograph; *v.i.* to be effective; to catch; to please; to go; to direct course of; to resort to; *pr.p.* **taking.** *pa.t.* **took.** *pa.p.* **-n.** *n.* quantity of fish caught at one time; one of several movie shots of same scene; act of taking; receipts *n.* (*Slang*) fraud; hoax. **—off** *n.* (*Colloq.*) mimicry; caricature; (*Aero.*) moment when aircraft leaves ground. *n.* **taking** *n.* act of taking or gaining possession; agitation; *pl.* cash receipts of shop, theater, etc.; *a.* attractive; infectious. **takingly** *adv.* **takingness** *n.* quality of being attractive [Scand. *taka*, to seize].

talc (talk) *n.* hydrated silica of magnesia; fine, slightly perfumed powder; mineral with soapy feel. **-ose** *a.* pert. to or composed of talc. **-um** *n.* powdered talc, as toilet powder [Ar. *talq*.]

tale (tāl) *n.* narrative; story; what is told; false report; gossip; **-bearer** *n.* one who spitefully informs against another [O.E. *talu*, a reckoning].

tal·ent (tal′·ạnt) *n.* ancient weight and denomination of money; faculty; special or outstanding ability. **-ed** *a.* gifted [Gk. *talanton*].

tal·is·man (tal′·is·mạn) *n.* object endowed with magical power of protecting the wearer from harm; lucky charm. **-ic, -al** *a.* [Gk. *telesma*, payment].

talk (tawk) *v.t.* and *v.i.* to converse; to speak; to discuss; to persuade; *n.* conversation; short dissertation; rumor; gossip. **-ative** *a.* loquacious; chatty. **-atively** *adv.* **-ativeness** *n.* **-er** *n.* **-ie** *n.* (*Colloq.*) a sound film. **-ing** *a.* capable of speaking [M.E. *talken*, to speak].

tall (tawl) *a.* high in stature; lofty; (*Slang*) excessive; exaggerated. **-ness** *n.*

tal·low (tal′·ō) *n.* animal fat melted down and used in manufacture of candles, etc.; *v.t.* to smear with tallow. **-ish** *a.* pasty; greasy. **-like, -y,** *a.* [M.E. *talgh*, tallow].

tal·ly (tal′·i·) *n.* something on which a score is kept; the score; business account; match; identity label; *v.t.* to score; to furnish with a label; *v.i.* to correspond; to agree. *pa.t.* and *pa.p.* **tallied. tallier** [L. *talea*, a slip of wood].

Tal·mud (tal′·mud) *n.* standard collection of texts and commentaries on Jewish religious law. **-ic(al)** *a.* **-ist** *n.* student of the Talmud. **-istic** *a.* [Aramaic *talmud*, instruction].

tal·on (tal′·ạn) *n.* hooked claw of bird of prey. **-ed** *a.* having talons [L. *talus*, the heel].

tam·a·risk (tam′·ạ·risk) *n.* evergreen shrub with pink and white flowers [L. *tamarix*].

tam·bour (tam′·boor) *n.* small flat drum; circular embroidery-frame; piece of embroidery worked in metal threads on tambour [Fr. = a drum].

tam·bour·ine (tam·bạ·rēn′) *n.* round, shallow, single-sided drum with jingling metal disks, used to accompany Spanish dances [Fr.].

tame (tām) *a.* domesticated; subdued; insipid; dull; cultivated; *v.t.* to domesticate; to discipline; to curb; to reclaim. **-ability, tamability, -ableness** *n.* **-able** *a.* **-ly** *adv.* **-ness** *n.* **-r** *n.* [O.E. *tam*, tame].

tam o' shan·ter (tam'·ạ·shan'·tẹr) *n.* round flat cap, *abbrev.* **tam** [fr. Burns's poem].

tamp (tamp) *v.t.* to ram down; to plug a shot-hole with clay during blasting operations.

tam·per (tam'·pẹr) *v.i.* to meddle; to interfere with; to alter or influence with malicious intent. **-er** *n.* [var. of *temper*].

tam·pon (tam'·pȧn) *n.* *(surg.)* a plug of cotton, etc. to close a wound, retard bleeding [Fr.].

tan (tan) *n.* bark of oak, etc. bruised to extract tannic acid for tanning leather; yellowish brown color; sunburn; *v.t.* to convert skins into leather by soaking in tannic acid; to make bronze-colored; (*Colloq.*) to thrash; *v.i.* to become sunburned. *pr.p.* **-ning.** *pa.t.* and *pa.p.* **-ned. -nate** *n.* (*Chem.*) salt of tannic acid. **-ner** *n.* one who works in tannery. **-nery** *n.* place where leather is made. **-nic** *a.* pert. to tannin. **-nin** *n.* now called **tannic acid. -ning** *n.* [Fr. *tannique* fr. *tannin*, tan].

tan·dem (tan'·dạm) *adv.* one behind the other; *n.* pair of horses so harnessed; a bicycle for two people [L. *tandem*, at length].

tang (tang) *n.* a projection or prong (of a tool) which connects with the handle; a pungent smell or taste; a distinctive flavor; *v.t.* to furnish (a tool) with a tang. **-ed, -y** *a.* [Scand. *tange*, a point].

tan·gent (tan'·jạnt) *n.* *(Geom.)* line which touches curve but, when produced, does not cut it; *a.* touching but not intersecting. **tangency, tangence** *n.* state of touching. **tangential** *a.* pert. to, or in direction of, a tangent; digressing. **tangentially** *adv.* [L. *tangere*, to touch].

tan·ge·rine (tan·jạ·rēn') *n.* small sweet orange originally grown near Tangiers.

tan·gi·ble (tan'·ji·bl) *a.* perceptible by the touch; palpable; concrete. **tangibility** *n.* **tangibility** *adv.* [L. *tangere*, to touch].

tan·gle (tang'·gl) *n.* knot of raveled threads, hair, etc.; confusion; *v.t.* to form into a confused mass; to muddle.

tan·go (tang'·gō) *n.* S. American dance of Spanish origin in two-four time [Sp.].

tank (tangk) *n.* large basin, cistern, or reservoir for storing liquids or gas; part of a railway engine, car, etc. where water, gas, etc. is stored; a mechanically propelled bullet-proof heavily armored vehicle with caterpillar treads; *v.t.* to store or immerse in a tank. **-age** *n.* storage of water, oil, gas, etc. in a tank; cost of this; liquid capacity of tank; fertilizing agent from refuse. **-er** *n.* vessel designed to carry liquid cargo [L. *stagnum*, a pool].

tank·ard (tang'·kẹrd) *n.* large drinking vessel, with lid and handle [O.Fr. *tancquard*, drinking-vessel].

tan·nin See **tan.**

tan·sy (tan'·si·) *n.* common perennial plant used in medicine [*athanasia*, immortality].

tan·ta·lize (tan'·tạ·līz) *v.t.* to torment by keeping just out of reach something ardently desired; to tease. **tantalizing** *a.* provocative; teasing [fr. *Tantalus*, Gr. Myth.].

tan·ta·lum (tan'·tạ·lạm) *n.* (*Chem.*) rare metallic element, symbol **Ta,** used for filaments of electric lamps, chemical apparatus, and surgical instruments [fr. *Tantalus*].

tan·ta·mount (tan'·tạ·mount) a. equivalent in value or significance [L. *tantus*, so much].

tan·trum (tan'·trạm) *n.* fit of bad temper.

Tao·ism (tou·izm) *n.* a Chinese philosophical and religious system founded on the doctrines of *Lao-tsze.* **Taoist** *n.* **Taoistic** *a.* [Chin. *tao*, a way].

tap (tap) *v.t.* to strike lightly; to fix patch of leather or metal on shoe; *v.i.* to strike gentle blow. *pr.p.* **-ping.** *pa.p.* **-ped.** *n.* a rap; *pl.* military signal for lights out; leather patch or piece of metal on shoe sole. **— dance** *n.* a dance step audibly tapped out with the feet. **-dance** *v.i.* [imit].

tap (tap) *n.* hole, pipe, or screw device with valve, through which liquid is drawn; liquor of particular brewing in a cask; instrument of hardened steel for cutting internal screw-heads; (*Elect.*) connection made at intermediate point on circuit; *v.t.* to pierce to let fluid flow out, as from a cask, tree, etc.; to furnish (cask) with tap; (*Surg.*) to draw off fluid from body, as from lung, abdomen, etc.; to listen in deliberately on telephone conversation; *pr.p.* **-ping.** *pa.p.* **-ped. -per** *n.* one who taps. **-room** *n.* bar, of inn or hotel, for sale of liquor. **-root** *n.* the root of a plant which goes straight down into earth without dividing. **on tap,** of liquor, drawn from cask, not bottled; (*Fig.*) at hand [O.E. *taeppa*].

tape (tāp) *n.* narrow piece of woven material used for tying, fastening clothes, etc.; strip of this marking finish line on racetrack; strip of paper used in a printing telegraph instrument, etc., strip of paper or linen marked off in inches used for measuring; *v.t.* to tie or fasten with tape; to measure. **— measure** *n.* strip marked in inches. **-worm** *n.* parasite found in alimentary canal of vertebrates [O.E. *taeppe*, a band].

ta·per (tā'·pẹr) *n.* long wick for lighting candles; a slender candle; *v.i.* to narrow gradually toward one end; *v.t.* to cause to narrow. **-ing** *a.* narrowing gradually [O.E. *tapor*].

tap·es·try (tap'·ạs·tri·) *n.* fabric covering for furniture, walls, etc. woven by needles, not in shuttles [Fr. *tapis*, carpet].

tap·i·o·ca (tap·i·ō'·kạ) *n.* starchy gramular substance used for desserts, thickening, etc. [Braz. *tipi*, residue; *ok*, to press out].

ta·pir (tā'·pẹr) *n.* ungulate mammal with pig-like body and flexible proboscis [Braz.].

tap·is (tap'·ē, tap'·is) *n.* carpeting; tapestry [Fr. *tapis*, carpet].

tap·pet (tap'·it) *n.* small lever [O.Fr. *tapper*, to rap].

tar (tạr) *n.* (*Colloq.*) sailor [fr. *tarpaulin*].

tar (tȧr) *n.* dark-brown or black viscid liquid, a by-product in destructive distillation of wood (esp. pine), coal, etc., used for waterproofing, road-laying, and as antiseptic and preservative; *v.t.* to smear, cover, or treat with tar. *pr.p.* **-ring.** *pa.t.* and *pa.p.* **-red. -ry** *a.* pert. to, smeared with, or smelling of, tar [O.E. *teru*, pitch].

tar·an·tel·la (tar'·ạn·tel'·ạ) *n.* Italian dance with rapid, whirling movements; music for it [fr. *Taranto*, in S. Italy].

ta·ran·tu·la (tạ·ranch'·ạ·la) *n.* large, hairy, venomous spider [fr. *Taranto*].

tar·boosh (tȧr'·bòósh) *n.* cap resembling a fez, usually red with dark blue tassel [Ar.].

tar·dy (tȧr'·di·) *a.* slow; dilatory; late. **tardily** *adv.* **tardiness** *n.* [L. *tardus*].

tare (ter) *n.* plant grown for fodder; a weed.

tare (ter) *n.* allowance made for weight of container, such as cask, crate, etc. in reckoning price of goods [Ar. *tarhah*, to reject].

tar·get (tȧr'·git) *n.* mark to aim at in shooting, esp. flat circular board with series of concentric circles; circular railway signal near switches; butt; object of attack [fr. *targe*].

tar·iff (ta'·rif) *n.* list of goods (imports and exports) on which duty is payable; the duty imposed. [Ar. *ta'rif*, giving information].

tarn (tȧrn) *n.* (*Literary*) small lake among

mountains [Scand.].

tar·nish (tȧrnish) *v.t.* to lessen luster of; to sully, as one's reputation; *v.i.* to become dull, dim, or sullied [Fr. *ternir*, to tarnish].

ta·ro (tȧ'·rō) *n.* plant of Pacific islands, cultivated for edible leaves and root [Native].

tar·pau·lin (tȧr·paw'·lin) *n.* canvas sheet treated with tar to make it waterproof; oilskin coat, hat, etc. [fr. *tar* and *pauling*, a covering].

tar·pon (tȧr'·pạn) *n.* large edible fish of herring family.

tar·ra·gon (tar'·ạ·gȧn) *n.* perennial herb cultivated for its aromatic leaves [Gk. *drakon*, a dragon].

tar·ry (tar'·i·) *v.i.* to stay; to linger; to delay; to stay behind [L. *tardus*, slow].

tar·sus (tȧr'·sạs) *n.* ankle. *pl.* **tarsi. tarsal** *a.* [Gk. *tarsos*, the sole of the foot].

tart (tȧrt) *a.* sour to taste; acid; (*Fig.*) caustic; severe. **-ish** *a.* rather sour. **-ly** *adv.* **-ness** *n.* [O.E. *teart*, acid].

tart (tȧrt) *n.* small pastry cup containing fruit or jam; (*Slang*) girl; prostitute [O.Fr. *tarte*].

tar·tan (tȧr'·tạn) *n.* woolen cloth of colored plaids, each genuine Scottish clan possessing its own pattern; *a.* made of tartan.

Tar·tar (tȧr'·tẹr) *n.* native of Tartary. Also **Tatar. tartar** *n.* irritable, quick-tempered person [fr. *Tatar*, a Mongol tribe].

tar·tar (tȧr'·tẹr) *n.* crude potassium tartrate; crust deposited in wine cask during fermentation (purified, it is called **cream of tartar;** in crude form, **argol);** acid incrustation on teeth. **-ous** *a.* consisting of tartar; containing tartar. **-ic** *a.* pert. to, or obtained from, tartar. **tartrate** *n.* a salt of tartaric acid. **-ic acid,** organic hydroxy-acid found in many fruits; in powder form used in manufacture of cooling drinks. **cream of tartar,** purified form of tartar used medicinally and as raising agent in baking [Fr. *tartre*].

task (task) *n.* specific amount of work apportioned and imposed by another; set lesson; duty; *v.t.* to impose task on; to exact. **-er** *n.* **— force** *n.* body of soldiers sent to do specific operation. **-master** (*fem.* **-mistress**) *n.* overseer [L. *taxare*, to rate].

Tas·ma·ni·an (taz·mā'·ni·ạn) *a.* pert. to or belonging to Tasmania, island south of Australia; *n.* native of Tasmania. [fr. *Tasman*, discoverer].

Tass (tȧs) *n.* official news agency of the U.S.S.R. [Russ. *Telegrafnoje Agentstvo Sovjetskovo Sojuza* = *Soviet Telegraphic Agency*].

tas·sel (tas'·l) *n.* ornamental fringed knot of silk, wool, etc.; pendent flower of some plants. **-ed** *a.* [L. *taxillus*, a small die].

taste (tāst) *v.t.* to perceive or test by tongue or palate; to appraise flavor of by sipping; to experience; *v.i.* to try food with mouth; to eat or drink very small quantity; to have specific flavor; *n.* act of tasting; one of five senses; flavor; predilection; aesthetic appreciation; judgment; small amount. **-ful** *a.* having or showing good taste. **-fully** *adv.* **-fulness** *n.* **-less** *a.* insipid. **-lessly** *adv.* **-lessness** *n.* **-r** *n.* one whose palate is trained to discern subtle differences in flavor, as *teataster.* **tastily** *adv.* with good taste. **tasty** *a.* savory [L. *taxare*, to estimate].

tat (tat) *v.i.* to make tatting. *pr.p.* **-ting.** *pa.t., pa.p.* **-ted. -ting** *n.* lace-like edging made from fine crochet or sewing thread [prob. Scand. *taeta*, shreds].

tat·ter (tat'·ẹr) *n.* rag; shred of cloth or paper hanging loosely; *v.t.* and *v.i.* to tear or hang in tatters. **-demalion** *n.* ragged fellow. **-ed** *a.* **-y** *a.* [Scand. *toturr*, rag].

tat·tle (tat'·l) *v.i.* to prattle; to gossip; to tell a secret; *n.* chatter. **-r** *n.* [imit.].

tat·too (ta·tòó') *n.* beat of drum or bugle as signal to return to quarters; a rapping sound; *v.i.* to beat tattoo [Dut. *taptoe*].

tat·too (ta·tòó') *v.t.* to prick colored designs, initials, etc. into skin with indelible colored inks; *n.* such design.**-er** *n.* [Tahitian *tatau*].

tau (tou, taw) *n.* Greek letter T.

taught (tawt) *pa.t.* and *pa.p.* of verb teach.

taunt (tawnt) *v.t.* to reproach with insulting words; to gibe at; to sneer at; *n.* gibe; sarcastic remark. **-er** *n.* **-ing** *a.* [O.Fr. *tanter*, to provoke].

tau·rus (tawr'·ạs) *n.* Bull, 2nd sign of Zodiac, which sun enters about April 21st. **taurian** *a.* pert. to a bull. **taurine** *a.* bovine. [Gk.].

taut (tawt) *a.* tight; fully stretched; (of a ship) trim. **-en** *v.t.* to make tight or tense. **-ness** *n.* [a form of tight].

tau·tol·o·gy (taw·tȧl'·ạ·ji·) *n.* needless repetition of same idea in different words in same sentence. **tautologic, -al** *a.* **tautologically** *adv.* **tautologism** *n.* superfluous use of words [Gk. *tauto*, the same; *logos*, a word].

tav·ern (tav'·ẹrn) *n.* licensed house for sale of liquor; inn [L. *taberna*, booth].

taw (taw) *n.* large marble for children's, game; the line from which the marble is shot; a game of marbles [Gk. letter T.].

taw·dry (taw'·dri·) *a.* showy but cheap; gaudy. **tawdrily** *adv.* **tawdriness** *n.* [fr. *St. Audrey*, cheap laces sold at her fair].

taw·ny (taw'·ni·) *a.* of yellow-brown color. **tawniness** *n.* [O.Fr. *tanné*, tanned].

tax (taks) *n.* levy imposed by state on income, property, etc.; burden; severe test; *v.t.* to impose tax on; to subject to severe strain; to challenge or accuse; (*Law*) to assess cost of actions in court. **-able** *a.* **-ness, -ability** *n.* **-ably** *adv.* **-ation** *n.* act of levying taxes; assessing of bill of costs; aggregate of particular taxes. [L. *taxure*, to rate].

tax·i (tak'·si·) *n.* (*abbrev.* of **taximeter cab)** an automobile for hire, fitted with a taximeter; any car plying for hire; *v.i.* to travel by taxi; of aircraft, to travel on ground (or surface of water) under its own power. *pr.p.* **-ing.** *pa.p.* **-ed, -cab** *n.* automobile for public hire. **— driver, — man** *n.* **-meter** *n.* instrument which automatically registers mileage and corresponding fare of journey by taxi.

tax·i·der·my (tak'·sạ·dur·mi·) *n.* art of preparing and preserving pelts of animals and stuffing them for exhibition. **taxidermist** *n.* **taxidermal, taxidermic** *a.* [Gk. *taxis*, an arrangement].

tea (tē) *n.* dried and prepared leaf of tea plant, native to China and Japan, and grown in India, Ceylon, etc.; infusion of dry tea in boiling water; any infusion of plant leaves, etc. or of chopped meat; reception at which tea is drunk. **— service** *n.* **— set** *n.* cups, saucers, plates, etc. for use at tea. **-spoon** *n.* small-sized spoon used with the teacup. **-spoonful** *n.* ⅓ tablespoon. **black tea,** tea allowed to ferment between two processes of rolling and firing. **green tea,** tea left exposed to air for only short time before firing. **Russian tea,** tea served in glasses with slice of lemon and sugar [Chin.].

teach (tēch) *v.t.* to instruct; to educate; to discipline; to impart knowledge of; *v.i.* to follow profession of a teacher. *pa.t.* and *pa.p.* **taught** (tawt). **-ability** *n.* **-able** *a.* capable of being taught; willing to learn. **-ableness** *n.* **-er** *n.* one who instructs [O.E. *taecan*].

teak (tēk) *n.* tree of E. Indies yielding very hard, durable timber [Malay].

team (tēm) *n.* two or more oxen, horses, or other beasts of burden harnessed together; group of people working together for common purpose; side of players in game, as *football team.* **-ster** *n.* one who drives team or a truck, as an occupation. **-work** *n.* co-operation among members of a group [O.E. *team*, offspring].

tear (tir) *n.* small drop of fluid secreted by lachrymal gland, appearing in and flowing from eyes, chiefly due to emotion; any transparent drop; *pl.* grief; sorrow. **drop** *n.* tear. **-ful** *a.* weeping. **-fully** *adv.* **-fulness** *n.* **— gas** *n.* irritant gas causing abnormal watering of eyes and temporary blindness. **-less** *a.* dryeyed [O.E. *tear*, a tear]

tear (ter) *v.t.* to pull apart forcibly; to rend; *v.i.* to become ripped or ragged; *(Colloq.)* to move violently; to rush; to rage. *pr.p.* **-ing.** *pa.t.* **tore.** *pa.p.* **torn.** *n.* rent; fissure. **-er** *n.* [O.E. *teran*, to tear].

tease (tēz) *v.t.* to comb or card wool, hair, etc.; to raise pile of cloth; to harass; to annoy in fun; to chaff. **-r** *n.* **-teasing** *a.* [O.E. *taesan*, to pluck].

teat (tit) *n.* nipple of female breast; dug of animal; rubber nipple of baby's feeding bottle [O.E. *tit*].

tech·ni·cal (tek′·ni·kal) *a.* pert. to any of the arts, esp. to useful or mechanical arts; connected with particular art or science; accurately defined; involving legal point. **-ity** *n.* state of being technical; term peculiar to specific art; point of procedure. **-ly** *adv.* **-ness** *n.* **technician** *n.* expert in particular art or branch of knowledge. **technics** *n.pl.* arts in general; industrial arts. **technique** (tek·nēk′) *n.* skill acquired by thorough mastery of subject; method of handling materials of an art. **technologic, -al** *a.* pert. to technology. **technologically** *adv.* **technologist** *n.* **technology** *n.* science of mechanical and industrial arts, as contrasted with fine arts; technical terminology [Gk. *technē*, art].

Tech·ni·col·or (tek′·ni·kul·ẹr) *n.* trade name for color movie photography.

tec·ton·ic (tek·tȧn′·ik) *a.* pert. to building; *(Geol.)* pert. to earth's crust [Gk. *tekton*, builder].

te·di·ous (tē′·di·ạs) *a.* wearisome; protracted; irksome. **-ness** *n.* **-ly** *adv.* **tedium** *n.* wearisomeness [L. *taedium*, weariness].

tee (tē) *n.* tiny cone of sand, wooden peg, etc. on which golf ball is placed for first drive of each hole; teeing ground which marks beginning of each hole on golf course. *v.t.* to place (ball) on tee [etym. uncertain].

tee (tē) *n.* the letter T; anything shaped like a T; *a.* having the form of a T.

teem (tēm) *v.i.* to bring forth, as animal; to be prolific; to be stocked to overflowing. **-ing** *a.* prolific [O.E. *team*, offspring].

teens (tēnz) *n.pl.* the years of one's age, thir*teen* through nine*teen*. **teen-ager** *n.* a young person of this age.

tee·ny (tēn′·i·) *(Colloq.)* very small [*tiny*].

tee·ter (tē′·tẹr) *v.i. (Colloq.)* to seesaw; vacillate; *n.* a seesaw or motion of seesaw [fr. *titter*].

teeth. See **tooth.**

teeth·ing (tēTH′·ing) *n.* the process, in babyhood, of cutting the first teeth. **teethe** *v.i.* to cut the first teeth [fr. *tooth*].

tee·to·tal (tē·tō′·tạl) *a.* pert. to teetotalism; abstemious. **-er** *n.* one who abstains from intoxicating liquors. **-ism** *n.* [redupl. of initial letter of *total*].

teg·u·ment (teg′·yạ·mạnt) *n.* covering, esp. of living body; skin; integument. **-al, -ary** *a.* [L. *tegere*, to cover].

tel·e·cast (tel′·ạ·kast) *v.i.* to transmit program by television [Gk. *tēle*, far; and *cast*].

tel·e·gram (tel′·ạ·gram) *n.* message sent by telegraph. **-mic** *a.*

tel·e·graph (tel′·ạ·graf) *n.* electrical apparatus for transmitting messages by code to a distance; a message so sent; *v.i.* to send a message by telegraph. **-er** (or tạ·leg′·rạ.fẹr) **-ist** (or tạ·leg′·) *n.* one who operates telegraph, **-ic(al)** *a.* **-ically** *adv.* **telegraphy** *n.* electrical transmission of messages to a distance. [Gk. *tēle*, far; *graphein*, to write].

tel·e·ol·o·gy (tel·i·ȧl′·ạ·ji·) *n.* science or doctrine of final causes. **teleologic, -al** *a.* **teleologically** *adv.* **teleologist** *n.* [Gk. *telos*, end; *logos*, discourse].

te·lep·a·thy (tạ·lep′·ạ·thi·) *n.* occult communication of facts, feelings, impressions between mind and mind at a distance; thought-transference. **telepathic** *a.* [Gk. *tēle*, far; *pathos*, feeling].

tel·e·phone (tel′·ạ·fōn) *n.* electrical instrument by which sound is transmitted and reproduced at a distance; *v.t.* and *v.i.* to communicate by telephone. **telephonic** *a.* **telephonically** *adv.* **telephonist** *n.* telephone operator, esp. at switchboard of exchange. **telephony** *n.* art or process of operating telephone [Gk. *tēle*, far; *phonē*, a sound].

tel·e·pho·to (tel·ạ·fō′·tō) *a.* pert. to a camera lens which makes distant objects appear close.

Tel·e·Promp·Ter (tel′·ạ·prȧmp·tẹr) *n.* in television, a device to enable the speaker to refer to his script out of sight of the cameras, thus giving viewers the impression of a talk without script [Trademark].

tel·e·scope (tel′·ạ·skōp) *n.* optical instrument for magnifying distant objects; *v.t.* to slide or drive together, as parts of telescope; *v.i.* to be impacted violently, as cars in railway collision. **telescopic, -al** *a.* pert. to or like a telescope. [Gk. *tēle*. afar; *skopein*, to see].

Tel·e·type (tel′·ạ·tip) *n.* automatically printed telegram; the apparatus by which this is done [Gk. *tēle*, far; and *type*; Trademark.]

tel·e·vi·sion (tel′·ạ·vizh′·ạn) *n.* transmission of scenes, persons, etc. at a distance by means of electro-magnetic radio waves. **televise** *v.t.* [Gk. *tēle*, far, and *vision*].

tell (tel) *v.t.* to recount or narrate; to divulge; to inform; to count; *v.i.* to produce marked effect; to betray (as secret); to report. *pa.t.* and *pa.p.* **told.** **-er** *n.* narrator; bank clerk who pays out money; one who counts votes; enumerator. **-ing** *a.* effective; striking. **-ingly** *adv.* **-tale** *n.* one who betrays confidence; an informer; *a.* warning; tending to betray [O.E. *tellan*, to count].

te·mer·i·ty (tạ·mer′·ạ·ti·) *n.* rashness; audacity [L. *temere*, rashly].

tem·per (tem′·pẹr) *v.t.* to mingle in due proportion; to soften, as clay, by moistening; to bring (metal) to desired degree of hardness and elasticity by heating, cooling, and reheating; to regulate; to moderate; *n.* consistency required and achieved by tempering; attitude of mind; composure; anger; irritation. **-ed** *a.* having a certain consistency, as clay, or degree of toughness, as steel; having a certain disposition, as *good-tempered, bad-tempered.* **-edly** *adv.* **-ing** *n.* **-er** *n.* [L. *temperare*, to combine in due proportion].

tem·per·a (tem′·pẹr·ạ) *n.* process of painting using pigments mixed with size, casein, or egg instead of oil. also **tempora** [It. = to temper].

tem·per·a·ment (tem′·pẹr(a)mạnt) *n.* natural disposition; physical, moral and mental constitution peculiar to individuals; *(Mus.)* system of adjusting tones of keyboard instrument, such as a piano, so as to adapt the scale for all keys. **-al** *a.* liable to moods; passionate **-ally** *adv.* [L. *temperamentum*, disposition].

tem·per·ance (tem′·pẹr·ạns) *n.* moderation; self-discipline, esp. of natural appetites; total abstinence from, or modification in, consumption of intoxicating liquors; sobriety [L. *temperantia*, moderation].

tem·per·ate (tem′·pẹr·it) *a.* moderate; abstemious; (of climate) equable; not extreme. **-ly** *adv.* **-ness** *n.* **temperative** *a.* **tempera-**

ture *n.* degree of heat or cold of atmosphere or of a human or living body; fevered condition. **— zones,** areas of earth between polar circles and tropics. [L. *temperare,* to moderate].

tem·pest (tem′·pist) *n.* wind storm of great violence; any violent commotion. **-uous** *a.* pert. to tempest; violent. **-uously** *adv.* **-uousness** *n.* [L. *tempestas,* weather, storm].

tem·ple (tem′·pl) *n.* place of worship; place dedicated to pagan deity; a building devoted to some public use. [L. *templum,* a sacred place].

tem·ple (tem′·pl) *n.* part of forehead between outer end of eye and hair. **temporal** *a.* [L. *tempora,* the temples].

tem·plet, tem·plate (tem′·plit) *n.* pattern of wood or metal cut to shape required for finished flat object [prob. fr. L. *templum,* small rafter].

tem·po (tem′·po) *n.* (*Mus.*) time; degree of speed or slowness at which passage should be played or sung; the degree of movement, as in the plot of a drama [It.].

tem·po·ral (tem′·pạ·rạl) *a.* pert. to time or to this life; transient; secular; **temporality** *n.* concept of time; state of being temporal or temporary; *pl.* material possessions, esp. ecclesiastical revenues. **-ly** *adv.* **temporariness** *n.* **temporarily** *adv.* only for a time. **temporariness** *n.* **temporary** *a.* lasting only for a time; fleeting. **temporization** *n.* **temporize** *v.i.* to act so as to gain time; to hedge; to compromise. **temporizer** *n.* **temporizing** *n.* [L. *tempus,* time].

tempt (tem(p)t) *v.t.* to induce to do something; to entice. **-ation** *n.* act of tempting; that which tempts; inducement to do evil; **-er** *n.* (*fem.* **-ress**) one who tempts, esp. Satan. **-ing** *a.* attractive; seductive. **-ingly** *adv.* **-ingness** *n.* [O.Fr. *tempter,* to entice].

ten (ten) *a.* twice five; one more than nine; *n.* the number nine and one; the figure or symbol representing this, as 10, X. **-fold** *a.* ten times repeated; *adv.* ten times as much. **-th** *a.* next after the ninth; being one of ten equal divisions of anything; *n.* one of ten equal parts; tenth part of anything; tithe. **-thly** *adv.* [O.E. *ten,* ten].

ten·a·ble (ten′·ạ·bl) *a.* capable of being held, defended, or logically maintained. **-ness, tenability** *n.* [L. *tenere,* to hold].

te·na·cious (tạ·nā′·shạs) *a.* holding fast; adhesive; retentive; pertinacious. **-ly** *adv.* **-ness, tenacity** *n.* [L. *tenax,* holding fast].

ten·ant (ten′·ạnt) *n.* (Law) one who has legal possession of real estate; one who occupies property for which he pays rent; *v.i.* to hold or occupy as tenant. **tenancy** *n.* act and period of holding land or property as tenant; property held by tenant. **-able** *a.* fit for occupation. **-ry** *n.* tenants or employees collectively on estate [L. *tenere,* to hold].

tend (tend) *v.i.* to hold a course; to have a bias or inclination. **-ency** *n.* inclination; bent. **-entious** *a.* (of writings) having a biased outlook [L. *tendere,* to stretch].

tend (tend) *v.t.* to look after; to minister to. **-er** *n.* one who tends; small vessel supplying larger one with stores, etc., or landing passengers; car attached to locomotive, carrying water and fuel [contr. of *attend*].

ten·der (ten′·dẹr) *v.t.* to offer in payment or for acceptance; *n.* an offer, esp. contract to undertake specific work, or to supply goods at fixed rate. **legal tender,** currency recognized as legally acceptable in payment of a debt [L. *tendere,* to stretch out].

ten·der (ten′·dẹr) *a.* soft; delicate; expressive of gentler passions; considerate; immature; sore; not tough (of meat). **-foot** *n.* one not yet hardened to ranching or mining life; novice. **-ly** *adv.* **-ness** *n.* [L. *tener,* delicate].

ten·der·loin (ten′·dẹr·loin) choice cut of beef between loin and ribs; (*Cap.*) district in a city noted for vice and police corruption.

ten·don (ten′·dạn) *n.* a tough fibrous cord attaching muscle to bone. **tendinous** *a.* [L. *tendere,* to stretch].

ten·dril (ten′·dril) *n.* spiral shoot of climbing plant by which it clings to another body for support; curl, as of hair. **-lar, -ous** *a.* [Fr. *tendrille*].

ten·e·brous (ten′·ạ·brạs) *a.* dark; obscure; **tenebrosity** *n.* [L. *tenebrae,* darkness].

ten·e·ment (ten′·ạ·mant) *n.* building divided into separate apartments, usu. of very poor quality, and let to different tenants. **-al, tenementary** *a.* [L. *tenere,* to hold].

ten·et (ten′·it) *n.* any opinion, dogma, or principle which a person holds as true [L. *tenere,* to hold].

ten·nis (ten′·is) *n.* game for two or four players, played on a court by striking a ball with rackets, across a net; a version of this played on a grass called *lawn tennis.* **— court** *n.* specially marked enclosed court for tennis.

ten·on (ten′ ạn) *n.* end of piece of wood shaped for insertion into cavity (*mortise*) in another piece to form a joint; *v.t.* to join with tenons. [L. *tenere,* to hold].

ten·or (ten′·ẹr) *n.* general drift, course, or direction, of thought; purport; (*Mus.*) highest male adult voice; one who sings tenor; *a.* pert. to tenor voice [L. *tenere,* to hold]

tense (tens) *n.* (*Gram.*) form of verb which indicates *time* of action, as *present, past* or *future tense* [L. *tempus,* time].

tense (tens) *a.* stretched; strained almost to breaking point; unrelaxed; (of vowel) made by tongue tensed, as ē. **-ly** *adv.* **-ness** *n.* **tensibility, -ness** *n.* the quality of being **tensile. tensible, tensile** *a.* capable of being stretched or subjected to stress, as metals; capable of being made taut, as violin strings. **tension** *n.* act of stretching; strain; a state of being nervously excited or overwrought; (of metals) *pulling* stress as opposed to *compressive* stress; (*Elect.*) potential. **tensor** *n.* body muscle which stretches [L. *tendere,* to *stretch*].

tent (tent) *n.* portable canvas shelter stretched and supported by poles and firmly pegged ropes; small plug of compressed absorbent gauze, or lint, which swells when moistened, used to keep open a wound, etc.; *v.i.* to live in tent; to pitch tent; *v.t.* to keep open, as wound, with tent. **-ed** *a.* covered with tents. [L. *tendere,* to stretch].

ten·ta·cle (ten′·ta·kl) *n.* long flexible appendage of head or mouth in many lower animals for exploring, touching, grasping, and sometimes moving; feeler. **tentacular** *a.* **—like** *a.* [L. *tentare,* to feel].

ten·ta·tive (ten′·tạ·tiv) *a.* experimental; done or suggested as a feeler or trial. **-ly** *adv.* [L. *tentare,* to try].

ten·ter (ten′·tẹr) *n.* machine for stretching cloth by means of hooks; *v.t.* to stretch on hooks. **-hook** *n.* one of the sharp hooks by which cloth is stretched on a tenter. **on tenterhooks,** state of anxiety [L. *tendere,* to stretch].

ten·u·i·ty (ten.ū·i·ti·) *n.* smallness of diameter; thinness. **tenuous** *a.* slender; gossamer-like; unsubstantial. **tenuously** *adv.* **tenuousness** *n.* [L. *tenuis,* thin].

ten·ure (ten′ yẹr) *n.* holding of office, property, etc.; condition of occupancy [L. *tenere,* to hold].

te·pee (tē′·pē) *n.* Indian wigwam or conical tent. Also **teepee.**

tep·e·fy (tep′·ạ·fī) *v.t.* to make moderately warm. **tepefaction** *n.* [L. *tepere,* to be warm; *facere,* to make].

tep·id (tep′·id) *a.* moderately warm; lukewarm. **-ity, -ness** *n.* [L. *tepidus,* warm].
ter·cel (tur′·sạl) *n.* a young male falcon [dim. of L. *tertius,* third].
ter·cen·te·nar·y (tur.sen′.tạ.ne.ri. or tur′. sen.ten.ạ.ri.) *n.* the 300th anniversary of an event; *a.* pert. to a period of 300 years [L. *ter,* thrice; *centum,* a hundred].
ter·cet (tur′·set) *n.* (*Mus.*) triplet; (*Pros.*) group of three lines or verses [L. *ter,* thrice].
ter·gi·ver·sate (tur′.ji.vẹr.sāt) *v.i.* to make use of subterfuges; to be shifty or vacillating; to apostatize. **tergiversation** *n.* **tergiversator** *n.* [L. *tergum,* the back; *vertere,* to turn].
term (turm) *n.* limit, esp. of time; period during which law courts are sitting, schools, universities, etc. are open; fixed day when rent is due; word or expression with specific meaning; (*Math.*) member of compound quantity; *pl.* stipulation; relationship, as *on friendly terms*; charge as for accommodation, etc. as *hotel terms; v.t.* to give name to; to call. **-inological** *a.* pert. to terminology. **-inologically** *adv.* **-inologist** *n.* **-inology** *n.* technical words; nomenclature [L. *terminus,* end].
ter·ma·gant (tur′.mạ.gạnt) *n.* quarrelsome, shrewish woman; *a.* scolding; quarrelsome. [*Tervagan,* Mohammedan diety].
ter·mi·nate (tur′.mạ.nāt) *v.t.* to set limit to; to end; to conclude; *v.i.* to come to an end; to finish. **terminable** *a.* capable of being terminated; liable to cease. **terminal** *n.* extremity; large railroad station with yards, shops, etc. (*Elect.*) metal attachment such as screw, block, clamp for connecting end of circuit; *a.* pert. to end; belonging to terminus or terminal; occurring in, or, at end of, a term; (*Bot.*) growing at tip. **terminally** *adv.* **termination** *n.* act of terminating; finish; conclusion; ending of word. **terminational** *a.* **terminative** *a.* **terminatively** *adv.* **terminus** *n.* end; farthest limit; railway station, airport, etc., at end of line; *pl.* **termini, terminuses** [L. *terminus,* the end].
ter·mite (tur′.mīt) *n.* insect, very destructive to wood [L. *termes,* a wood worm].
tern (turn) *n.* sea bird allied to gull [Scand.].
tern (turn) *n.* that which consists of three; *a.* threefold. **-al, -ary** *a.* consisting of three; proceeding by threes; (*Chem.*) comprising three elements, etc. **-ate** *a.* arranged in threes; (*Bot.*) having three leaflets. **-ion** *n.* group of three [L. *terni,* three each].
Terp·sich·o·re (turp.sik′.ạ.rē) *n.* (*Myth.*) Muse of choral song and dancing. **-an** *a.* pert. to Terpsichore or to dancing [Gk. *Terpsichorē,* fond of dancing].
ter·ra (ter′.ạ) *n.* earth as in various Latin phrases. **— cotta** *n.* reddish, brick-like earthenware, porous and unglazed. **— firma** *n.* dry land. **— incognita** *n.* unexplored territory, **terranean** *a.* belonging to surface of earth. **-neous** *a.* growing on land. **terraqueous** (ter.ā′.kwe.ạs) *a.* comprising both land and water, as the globe [L. *terra,* the earth].
ter·race (ter′.ạs) *n.* level shelf of earth, natural or artificial; flat roof used for open-air activities; *v.t.* to form into terraces [L. *terra,* the earth].
ter·rain (ter′.ān, tạ.rān′) *n.* tract of land, esp. as considered for suitability for various purposes [L. *terra,* the earth].
ter·ra·pin (ter′.ạ.pin) *n.* edible tortoise found in eastern U.S. [Amer.-Ind.].
ter·raz·zo-pav·ing (tạ.rat′.tsō.pāv′.ing) *n.* kind of mosaic paving in concrete chips [It.].
ter·rene (te.rēn′) *a.* pert. to earth; earthy; terrestrial [L. *terra,* the earth].
ter·res·tri·al (tạ.res′.tri.ạl) *a.* pert. to earth; existing on earth; earthly, as opp. to *celestial; n.* inhabitant of earth [L. *terra,* the earth].
ter·ri·ble (ter′.ạ.bl) *a.* calculated to inspire fear or awe; frightful; dreadful; formidable; (*Colloq.*) very bad. **-ness** *n.* **terribly** *adv.* [L. *terrere,* to frighten].
ter·ri·er (ter′.i.ẹr) *n.* breed of small or meddium-sized dog, originally trained for hunting foxes, badgers, etc. [M.E. *terrere,* a burrowing dog].
ter·ri·fy (ter′.ạ.fī) *v.t.* to frighten greatly; to inspire with terror. *pa.t.* **terrific** *a.* causing terror or alarm; (*Colloq.*) tremendous. **terrifically** *adv.* [L. *terrere,* to terrify; *facere,* to make].
ter·ri·to·ry (ter′.ạ.tōr.i.) *n.* large tract of land, esp. under one governmental administration; part of country which has not yet attained political independence. **territorial** *a.* pert. to territory; limited to certain district. **territoriality** *n.* [L. *terra,* the earth].
ter·ror (ter′.ẹr) *n.* extreme fear; violent dread; one who or that which causes terror. **-ization** *n.* **-ize** *v.t.* to fill with terror; to rule by intimidation. **-izer** *n.* **-ism** *n.* mass-organized ruthlessness. **-ist** *n.* one who rules by terror [L. *terrere,* to frighten].
ter·ry cloth (ter′.i.klȧth) *n.* cotton fabric with pile of uncut loops on both sides.
terse (turs) *a.* (of speech, writing, etc.) concise; succinct; brief. **-ly** *adv.* **-ness** *n.* [L. *terpere, tersum,* to smooth].
ter·tian (tur′.shạn) *a.* (*Med.*) occurring every other day; *n.* fever, such as malaria, with paroxysms occurring at intervals of forty-eight hours [L. *textius,* third].
ter·ti·ar·y (tur′.she.ri.) *a.* of third formation or rank; (*Geol.*) (*Cap.*) pert. to era of rock formation following Mezozoic; *n.* (*Geol.*) (*Cap.*) the tertiary era [L. *tertius,* third].
ter·za·ri·ma (ter′.tsạrē′.mạ) *n.* form of stanza arrangement of iambic pentamenter lines in groups of three, rhyming aba, bcb, cdc [It. *terza,* third; *rima,* rhyme].
tes·sel·late (tes′.ạ.lāt) *v.t.* to pave with tesserae; to make mosaic paving with square-cut stones. **tessella, tessera** *n.* (*pl.* **tessellae, tesserae**) one of the square stones etc. used in tessellated paving. **tessellation** *n.* [L. *tessera,* a square block].
test (test) *n.* critical examination; grounds for admission or exclusion; (*Chem.*) reagent; substance used to analyze compound into its several constituents; a touchstone; vessel in which metals are refined; *v.i.* to make critical examination of; to put to proof; (*Chem.*) to analyze nature and properties of a compound. **— case** *n.* (*Law*) case tried for purpose of establishing a precedent. **-er** *n.* **-ing** *n. a.* demanding endurance. **— paper** *n.* examination paper; litmus or other impregnated paper used to test acid or alkaline content of chemical solution. **— pilot** *n.* experienced pilot engaged in testing flying qualities of new types of aircraft. **— tube** *n.* glass tube rounded and closed at one end, used in chemical tests [L. *testa,* earthen pot].
tes·ta·ment (tes′.tạ.mạnt) *n.* solemn declaration of one's will; one of the two great divisions of the Bible, as the *Old Testament,* or the *New Testament.* **testamental, testamentary** *a.* pert. to testament or will; bestowed by will [L. *testari,* to witness].
tes·tate (tes′.tāt) *a.* having left a valid will. **testacy** *n.* state of being testate. **testator** *n.* (*fem.* **testatrix**) one who leaves a will [L.*testari,* to witness].
tes·ter (tes′.tẹr) *n.* flat canopy, esp. over a bed [O.Fr. *teste,* the head].
tes·ti·cle (tes′.ti.kl) *n.* one of the two male reproductive glands. **testicular** *a.* **testic-**

ulate, -d *a.* having testicles; resembling testicle in shape. **testis** *n.* a testicle. *pl.* **testes** [L. *testis* testicle].

tes·ti·fy (tes'·tạ·fī) *v.i.* to bear witness; to affirm or declare solemnly; to give evidence upon oath. *v.t.* to bear witness to; to manifest. **testifier** *n.* [L. *testis,* a witness; *facere,* to make].

tes·ti·mo·ny (tes'·tạ·mō·ni·) *n.* solemn declaration or affirmation; proof of some fact; in Scripture, the two tables of the law; divine revelation as a whole. **testimonial** *a.* containing testimony; *n.* written declaration testifying to character and qualities of person, esp. of applicant for a position; a tribute to person's outstanding worth [L. *testimonium*].

tes·ty (tes'·ti·) *a.* fretful; irascible [O.Fr. *teste,* head].

tet·a·nus (tet'·ạ·nạs) *n.* a disease in which a virus causes spasms of violent muscular contraction; lockjaw; spasmodic muscular contraction or rigidity caused by intake of drugs. **tetanic** *a.* [Gk. *tetanos,* stretched].

tetch·y (tech'·i·) *a.* peevish; fretful. **tetchily** *adv.* Also **techy** [Fr. *tache,* blemish].

teth·er (teTH'ẹr) *n.* rope or chain fastened to grazing animal to keep it from straying; *v.t.* to confine with tether; to restrict movements of [Scand.].

te·tre- (tet'·rạ) *prefix* meaning *four* [Gk.].

tet·rad (tet'·rad) *n.* the number four; group of four things [Gk. *tetras*].

tet·ra·gon (tet'·rạ·gȧn) *n.* a plane figure, having four angles. **tetragonal** *a.*

tet·ra·gram (tet'·rạ·gram) *n.* word of four letters; (*Geom.*) figure formed by four right angles.

tet·ra·he·dron (tet·rạ·hē'·drạn) *n.* solid figure enclosed by four triangles; triangular-based pyramid. **tetrahedral** *a.* [Gk. *tetra-,* four; *hedra,* a base].

te·tral·o·gy (te·tral'·ạ·ji·)*n.* group of four dramas or operas connected by some central event or character [Gk. *tetra-,* four; *logos,* a discourse]. [four measures.

te·tram·e·ter (te·tram'·ạ·tẹr) *n.* verse of

te·trarch (tet'·rȧrk) *n.* Roman governor of fourth part of a province. **-ate, -y** *n.* office of tetrarch; province ruled by tetrarch. **-ic, -al** *a.* [Gk. *tetra-,* four; *archos,* ruler].

tet·ter (tet'·ẹr) *n.* skin disease; ringworm; *v.t.* to affect with this. **-ous** *a.* [O.E. *teter,* ringworm].

Teu·ton (tū'·tạn) *n.* member of one of Germanic tribes; (*Colloq.*) a German. **Teutonic** (tū·tȧn'·ik) *a.* pert. to Teutons or their lan- (tū·tȧn'·ik) *a.* pert. to Teutons or their language. [L. *Teutones*].

text (tekst) *n.* original words of author, orator, etc. as distinct from paraphrase or commentary; verse or passage of Scripture chosen as theme of sermon. **-book** *n.* manual of instruction. **-ual** *a.* pert. to text or subject matter; based on actual text or wording; literal. **-ually** *adv.* [L. *texere,* to weave].

tex·tile (teks'·tīl, tạl) *a.* pert. to weaving; capable of being woven; *n.* fabric made on loom [L.*texere,* to weave].

tex·ture (teks'·chẹr) *n.* quality of surface of a woven material; disposition of several parts of anything in relation to whole; surface quality; that which is woven [L. *texere*].

Thai·land (tī'·land) *n.* Siam.

tha·las·sic (tha·las'·ik) *a.* pert. to the sea; living in the sea [Gk. *thalassa,* the sea].

thal·lus (thal'·ạs) *n.* simple plant organism which shows little or no differentiation into leaves, stem, or root as in *fungi, algae,* etc. *pl.* **thalli** [Gk. *thallos,* green shoot].

than (THan) *conj.* introducing adverbial clause of comparison and occurring after comparative form of an adjective or adverb [O.E. *thonne,* than].

than·a·tol·o·gy (than·ạ·tȧl'·ạ·ji·) *n.* the study of death and of problems related to dying. **thanatologist** *n.* [Gk. *thanatos,* death; *logos,* a discourse].

thane (thān) *n.* in Anglo-Saxon community, member of class between freemen and nobility [O.E. *thegn,* soldier].

thank (thangk) *v.t.* to express gratitude to; *n.* expression of gratitude (usu. *pl.*). **-fulness** *n.* **-less** *a.* ungrateful; unappreciated by others. **-lessly** *adv.* **-lessness** *n.* **-sgiving** *n.* act of rendering thanks; service held as expression of thanks for Divine goodness. **Thanksgiving Day** *n.* fourth Thursday in November set apart for rendering thanks to God for blessings granted to nation [O.E. *thanc,* thanks].

that (THat) *demons. pron., a.* pointing out a person or thing, or referring to something already mentioned; not this but the other; *pl.* **those;** *rel. pron.* who or which; *conj.* introducing a noun clause, adjective clause, or adverbial clause of purpose, result, degree, or reason [O.E. *thaet*].

thatch (thach) *n.* straw, rushes, heather, etc. use to roof cottage, or cover stacks of grain; (*Colloq.*) hair; *v.t.* to roof with thatch. **-er** *n.* **-ing** *n.* [O.E. *thaec,* a roof, thatch].

thaw (thaw) *v.t.* to cause to melt by increasing temperature; to liquefy; *v.i.* to melt, as ice, snow, etc.; to become warmer; (*Fig.*) to become genial; *n.* [O.E. *thawian,* to melt].

the (THạ, emphatic THē) *a., def. art.* placed before nouns, and used to specify general conception, or to denote particular person or thing; *adv.* by so much; by that amount, as *the more the merrier* [O.E.].

the·ar·chy (thē·ȧr·ki·) *n.* theocracy; government by gods. **thearchic** *a.* [Gk. *theos,* a god; *archē,* rule].

the·a·ter (thē'·ạ·tẹr) *n.* in Ancient Greece, a large, open-air structure used for public assemblies, staging of dramas, etc.; building for plays or motion pictures; lecture or demonstration room for anatomy studies; field of military, naval, or air operations. Also **theatre. theatric(al)** *a.* **theatrically** *adv.* **theatricals** *n.pl.* dramatic performances, esp. by amateurs [Gk. *theatron*].

thee (THē) (*Arch.*) *pron.* objective case of **thou.**

theft (theft) *n.* act of stealing [O.E. *theof,* a thief].

their (THer) *a., pron.* of them; possessive case of **they. theirs** *poss. pron.*; form of **their** used absolutely [Scan. *theira,* their].

the·ism (thē'·izm) *n.* belief in existence of personal God who actively manifests himself in world. **theist** *n.* **theistic(al)** *a.* [Gk. *theos,* a god].

them (THem) *pron.* objective and dative case of **they** [O.E. *thaem*].

theme (thēm) *n.* subject of writing or discussion; brief essay; (*Mus.*) groundwork melody recurring at intervals and with variations. **thema** *n.* subject. **thematic** *a.* **thematically** *adv.* **— song** *n.* recurring melody in play, film [Gk. *thema,* something laid down].

them·selves (THem·selvz') *pron. pl.* of **himself, herself,** and **itself;** emphatic form of **them** or **they;** reflexive form of **them.**

then (THen) *adv.* at that time; immediately afterwards; thereupon; that being so; for this reason; *conj.* moreover; therefore; *a.* existing or acting at particular time. **now and —,** occasionally [doublet of *than*].

thence (THens) *adv.* from that place; from that time; for that reason. **-forth** *adv.* from that time on [M.E. *thennes*].

the·oc·ra·cy (thē·ȧk'·rạ·si·) *n.* government of state professedly in the name, and under direction, of God; government by priests.

theocrat, theocratist *n.* ruler under this system. **theocratic, -al** *a.* **theocratically** *adv.* [Gk. *theos*, a god; *kratos*, power].
the·od·o·lite (thē.ȧd′.ạ.līt) *n.* instrument for measuring angles, used in surveying.
the·ol·o·gy (thē.al′.ạ.ji.) *n.* science which treats of facts and phenomena of religion, and relations between God and man. **theologian** *n.* one learned in theology. **theologic, -al** *a.* pert. to theology. **theologically** *adv.* **theologize** *v.t.* to render theological; to theorize upon theological matters. **theologist** *n.* [Gk. *theos*, god; *logos*, discourse].
the·oph·a·ny (thē.ȧf′.ạ.ni.) *n.* manifestation of God to men, in human form. **theophanic** *a.* [Gk. *theos*, a god; *phainesthai*, to appear].
the·o·rem (thē′.ạ.rạm) *n.* established principle; (*Math.*) proposition to be proved by logical reasoning; algebraical formula. **-atic, -al** *a.* [Gk. *theorēma*, speculation].
the·o·ry (thē′.ạ.ri.) *n.* supposition put forward to explain something; speculation; exposition of general principles as distinct from practice and execution; (*Colloq.*) general idea; notion. **theoretic, -al** *a.* pert. to or based on theory; speculative as opp. to *practical*. **theoretics** *n.pl.* speculative side of science. **theorize** *v.t.* to form a theory; to speculate. **theorizer, theorist** *n.* **theorization** *n.* [Gk. *theoria*, speculation].
ther·a·peu·tic (ther.ạ.pū′.tik) *a.* pert. to healing. **-ally** *adv.* **-s** *n.* branch of medicine concerned with treatment and cure of diseases. **therapeutist** *n.* [Gk. *therapeuein*, to attend (medically)].
ther·a·py (ther′.ạ.pi.) *n.* remedial treatment, as *radio-therapy* for cure of disease by radium [Gk. *therapeia*, (medical) attendance].
there (THer) *adv.* in that place; farther off opp. to *here;* as an introductory adverb it adds little to the meaning of the sentence as *'There is someone at the door'*; *interj.* expressing surprise, consolation, etc. **-about, -abouts** *adv.* near that place, number or quantity. **-after** *adv.* after that time. **-by** *adv.* by that means; in consequence. **-fore** *conj.* and *adv.* consequently; accordingly. **-in** *adv.* in that, or this place, time, or thing; in that particular. **-inafter** *adv.* afterwards in same document. **-of** *adv.* of that or this. **-to** *adv.* to that or this. **-upon** *adv.* upon that or this; consequently; immediately. **-with** *adv.* with that or this; straightway. [O.E. *thaer*, there].
therm (thurm) *n.* a unit of heat; the large calorie, also small calorie; unit of 1.000 large calories. **-ae** *n.pl.* hot springs; Roman baths. **-al** *a.* pert. to heat. **-ic** *a.* caused by heat. [Gk. *thermē*, heat].
therm·i·on (thur′.mi.ạn) *n.* positively or negatively charged particle emitted from incandescent substance. **thermionic** *a.* pert to thermions. **thermionic current** (*radio*) flow of electrons from filmament to plate of thermionic valve. **thermionics** *n.* branch of science dealing with thermions [Gk. *thermē*, heat; *ion*, going].
ther·mo·chem·is·try (thur.mō.kem′.is.tri.) *n.* branch of science which deals with heat in relation to chemical processes.
ther·mo·dy·nam·ics (thur.mō.dī.nam′.iks) *n.* branch of science which deals with the conversion of heat into mechanical engery.
ther·mo·e·lec·tric·i·ty (thur.mō.i.lek.tris′.ạ.ti.) *n.* electricity developed by action of heat alone on two different metals. **thermoelectric, -al** *a.* [Gk. *thermē*, heat; and *electricity*].
ther·mo·gen·e·sis (thur.mō.jen′.ạ.sis) *n.* production of heat, esp. in body. **thermogenetic, thermogenic** *a.*
ther·mom·e·ter (thẹr.mȧm′.ạ.tẹr) *n.* instrument for measuring temperature, usually consisting of graduated and sealed glass tube with bulb containing mercury. **thermometric, -al** *a.* **thermometrically** *adv.* **thermometry** *n.* [Gk. *thermē*, heat; *metron*, measure].
ther·mo·mo·tor (thur.mạ.mō′.tẹr *n.* engine worked by heat or hot air.
ther·mo·pile (thur′.mạ.pīl) *n.* instrument for measuring minute variations in temperature.
ther·mo·scope (thur′.mạ.skōp) *n.* instrument for detecting fluctuations in temperature without actual measurement.
Ther·mos (thur′.mạs) *n.* double-walled bottle or the like which substantially retains temperature of liquids by the device of surrounding interior vessel with a vacuum jacket [Trade Name].
ther·mo·stat (thur′.mạ.stat) *n.* instrument which controls temperature automatically. **thermostatic** *a.* **thermostatics** *n.* science dealing with equilibrium of heat [Gk. *thermē*, heat; and *static*].
ther·mot·ic (thẹr.mȧt′.ik) *a.* pert. to heat, Also **-al** *n.* the science of heat [Gk. *thermotēs*, heat].
the·sau·rus (thi.sawr′.ạs) *n.* treasury of knowledge, etc.; lexicon; encyclopedia [Gk. *thēsauros*, treasure-house].
these (THēz) *demons. a.* and *pron. pl.* of this.
the·sis (THē′sis) *n.* what is laid down as a proposition; dissertation *pl.* **theses. thetic** *a.* dogmatic [Gk. *thesis*, placing].
Thes·pis (thes′.pis) an Athenian of 6th cent. B.C. supposed inventor of trageday. **Thespian** *a.* pert. to drama; *n.* an actor; a tragedian.
the·ur·gy (thē′.ur′.ji.) *n.* art of working so-called miracles by supernatural agency. **theurgic, -al** *a.* **theurgically** *adv.* **theurgist** *n.* [Gk. *theos*, god; *ergon*, a work].
thew (thū) *n.* muscle; sinew; brawn (usually *pl.* [O.E. *theaw*, manner, or strength].
they (THā) *pron. pers. pl.* of **he, she, it**; indefinitely, for a number of persons.
thi·a·mine (thī′.ạ.mēn, mạn) *n.* Vitamin B, complex compound, deficiency of which causes beriberi also **thiamin** [Gk. *theion*, sulphur, and *amine*].
thick (thik) *a.* dense; foggy; not thin; abundant; packed; muffled, as *thick voice*; mentally dull; (*Slang*) intimate; *n.* thickest part; *adv.* thickly; to a considerable depth. **-en** *v.t.* to make thick; *v.i.* to become thick. **-ening** *n.* something added to thicken. **-et** *n.* dense growth of shrubs, trees, etc. **-headed** *a.* dull mentally. **-ly** *adv.* **-ness** *n.* quality of being thick; measurement of depth between opposite surfaces; layer. **—set** *a.* closely planted; sturdily built [O.E. *thicce*, thick].
thief (thēf) *n.* (*pl.* **thieves**) one who steals the goods and property of another. **thieve** *v.t.* to take by theft; *v.i.* to steal. **thievery** *n.* **thievish** *a.* addicted to stealing. **thievishness** *n.* [O.E. *theof*].
thigh (thī) *n.* fleshy part of leg between knee and trunk [O.E. *theoh*, thigh].
thim·ble (thim′.bl) *n.* metal or bone cap for tip of middle finger, in sewing; anything shaped like a thimble. **-ful** *n.* the quantity contained in a thimble; very small amount [O.E. *thymel*, thumb].
thin (thin) *a. comp.* **-ner.** *superl.* **-nest.** having little depth or thickness; slim; lean; flimsy; sparse; fine; *adv.* sparsely; not closely packed *v.t.* to make thin; to rarefy; *v.i.* to grow or become thin. *pr.p.* **-ning.** *pa.p., pa.t.* **-ned. -ly** *adv.* **-ness** *n.* **-ning** *n.* [O.E. *thynne*, thin].
thine (THīn) *pron. poss.* form of **thou** (*Arch.*) belonging to thee; thy [O.E. *thin*].
thing (thing) *n.* material or inanimate object;

entity; specimen; commodity; event; action; person (in pity or contempt); *pl.* belongings; clothes, furniture [O.E. *thing*, an object].

think (thingk) *v.t.* to conceive; to surmise; to believe; to consider; to esteem; *v.i.* to reason; to form judgment; to deliberate; to imagine; to recollect. *pa.t.* and *pa.p.* **thought** (thawt). **-able** *a.* **-ing** *a.* reflective; rational [O.E. *thencan*].

thi·o (thī′.ō) word element used in chemistry to illustrate the replacement by sulfur of part or all of the oxygen atoms in a compound. Also **thi-**.

third (thurd) *a.* next after the second; forming one of three equal divisions; *n.* one of three equal parts; (*Mus.*) interval of three diatonic degrees of the scale. **-class** *a.* pert. to accommodation for passengers not traveling first or second class; inferior. **— estate,** the commons. **-ly** *adv.* **—rate** *a.* of third-class quality; inferior [O.E. *thridda*, third].

thirst (thurst) *n.* desire to drink; suffering endured by too long abstinence from drinking; craving; *v.i.* to crave for something to drink; to wish for earnestly. **-er** *n.* **-ily** *adv.* **-iness** *n.* **-y** *a.* having a desire to drink; dry; parched; eager for [O.E. *thurst*, thirst].

thir·teen (thur′.tēn) *a.* ten and three; *n.* sum of ten and three; symbol representing thirteen units, as 13, XIII. **-th** *a.* next in order after twelfth; being one of thirteen equal parts; *n.* one of these parts [O.E. *threo*, three; *tyn*, ten].

thir·ty (thur′.ti.) *a.* three times ten; *n.* sum of three times ten; symbol representing this, as 30, XXX. **thirtieth** *a.* next in order after twenty-ninth; being one of thirty equal parts; *n.* thirtieth part [O.E. *thritig*, thirty].

this (THis) *demons. pron.* and *a.* denoting a person or thing near at hand, just mentioned, or about to be mentioned [O.E.].

this·tle (this′.l) *n.* one of the numerous prickly plants of the genus *Carduus*, with yellow or purple flowers; national emblem of Scotland. **—down** *n.* feathery down of thistle seeds. **thistly** *a.* [O.E. *thistel*, a thistle].

thith·er (thiTH′.ẹr) *adv.* to that place; to that point, end, or result. **-ward** *adv.* toward that place [O.E. *thider*].

thole (thōl) *v.t.* pin in gunwale of boat to keep oar in rowlock. Also **-pin** [O.E. *thol*, a rowlock].

Tho·mism (tō′.mizm) *n.* doctrines expounded in theology of *Thomas Aquinas* (1226-74). **Thomist** *n.* adherent of Thomism.

thong (thawng) *n.* narrow strap of leather used for reins, whiplash, etc.; long narrow strip of leather used in leathercraft [O.E. *thwang*, a thong].

tho·rax (thōr′.aks) *n.* part of body between neck and abdomen; chest cavity containing heart, lungs, etc. **thoracic** *a.* [Gk. *thorax*].

thorn (thawrn) *n.* sharp, woody shoot on stem of tree or shrub; prickle; hawthorn; (*Fig.*) anything which causes trouble or annoyance; name in O.E. of the rune for *th*. **-y** *a.* full of thorns; prickly; beset with difficulties [O.E. *thorn*, a prickle].

thor·ough (thur′.ō) *a.* complete; absolute. **-bred** *a.* (of animals) pure bred from pedigree stock; (of people) aristocratic hence, high-spirited; mettlesome; *n.* animal (esp. horse) of pure breed. **-fare** *n.* passage through; highway. **-ly** *adv.* **-ness** *n.* [form of *through*].

those (THōz) *a.* and *pron. pl.* of **that.**

thou (THou) *pron. pres., 2nd sing.* denoting the person addressed (used now only in solemn address, and by the Quakers).

though (THō) *conj.* granting; admitting; even if; notwithstanding; however [O.E. *theah*].

thought (thwat) *pa.t.* and *pa.p.* of **think.**

thought (thawt) *n.* act of thinking; that which one thinks; reflection; opinion; serious consideration. **-ful** *a.* contemplative; attentive; considerate. **-fully** *adv.* **-fulness** *n.* **-less** *a.* without thought; heedless; impulsive; inconsiderate. **-lessly** *adv.* **-lessness** *n.* [O.E. *gethoht*, thought].

thou·sand (thou′.zạnd) *a.* consisting of ten hundred; used indefinitely to express large number; *n.* the number ten hundred; symbol for this, 1,000 or M; any large number. **-fold** *a.* multiplied by a thousand. **-th** *a.* constituting one of thousand equal parts; next in order after nine hundred and ninety-nine; *n.* thousandths part [O.E. *thusend*].

thrall (thrawl) *n.* slave; bondsman; servitude. **-dom, thraldom** *n.* bondage [O.N. *thrael*, bondage].

thrash (thrash) *v.t.* to thresh; to flog; to defeat soundly. **-er** *n.* **thrashing** *n.* act of thrashing; corporal punishment; flogging. [var. of *thresh*].

thra·son·i·cal (thrā.sȧn′.i.kạl) *a.* boastful; bragging. **-ly** *adv.* [fr. *Thraso*, a braggart].

thread (thred) *n.* very thin twist of wool, cotton, linen, silk, etc.; filament as of gold, silver; prominent spiral part of screw; consecutive train of thought; *v.t.* to pass thread through eye of needle; to string together, as beads; to pick one's way with careful deliberation. **-bare** *a.* worn away with wear; shabby; hackneyed; trite. **-worm** *n.* thread-like parasitic worm often found in intestines of children. **-y** *a.* [O.E. *thrawan*, to twist].

threat (thret) *n.* declaration of determination to harm another; menace. **-en** *v.t.* to menace; to declare intention to do harm to; to portend. **-ener** *n.* **-ening** *a.* menacing; portending something undesirable; (of clouds or sky) lowering [O.E. *threatnian*, to urge].

three (thrē) *a.* two and one; *n.* sum of two and one; symbol of this sum, 3 or iii. **-fold** *a.* triple. **—ply** *a.* having three layers or thicknesses; having three strands twisted together, as wool. **-score** *a.* and *n.* sixty. **-some** *n.* game (as golf) played by three players; group of three people. **the three R's,** reading, riting, rithmetic [O.E. *threo*, three].

thren·o·dy (thren′.ạ.di.) *n.* song of lamentation; dirge. Also **threnode. threnodial, threnodic** *a.* pert. to threnody; funereal. [Gk. *thrēnos*, lament; *odē*, song].

thresh *v.t.* to separate grain from chaff by use of flail or machine; to beat. **-er** *n.* [O.E. *therscan*, to beat].

thresh·old (thresh′.ōld) *n.* door sill; point of beginning [O.E. *therscan*, to thresh; *wald*, wood].

threw (thròò) *pa.t.* of **throw.**

thrice (thrīs) *adv.* three times; repeatedly; much, as in *thrice blessed* [O.E. *thriwa*].

thrift (thrift) *n.* economical management; frugality; plant, the sea pink. **-ily** *adv.* **-iness** *n.* frugality. **-less** *a.* extravagant; wasteful. **-lessly** *adv.* **-y** *a.* [fr. *thrive*].

thrill (thril) *n.* emotional excitement; quivering sensation running through nerves and body; *v.t.* to stir deeply; to arouse tingling emotional response; *v.i.* to feel a glow of excitement, enthusiasm, etc. **-er** *n.* (*Colloq.*) sensational novel, play, or film, etc. **-ing** *a.* **-ingly** *adv.* [O.E. *thyrlian*, to bore a hole].

thrive (thrīv) *v.i.* to prosper; to grow abundantly; to develop healthily. *pa.t.* **throve** and **-d.** *pa.p.* **thriven** (thriv′.n) **-d. thriving** *a.* **thrivingly** *adv.* [O.N. *thrifa*, to grasp].

throat (thrōt) *n.* forepart of neck; passage connecting back of mouth with lungs, stomach, etc.; narrow entrance. **-iness** *n.* quality of having throaty or muffled voice. **-y** *a.* guttural; muffled [O.E. *throte*, the throat].

throb (thrȧb) *v.i.* to pulsate; to beat. as heart,

with more than usual force. *pr.p.* **-bing.** *pa.t.* and *pa.p.* **-bed.** *n.* pulsation; palpitation (of heart, etc.); beat [etym. doubtful].

throe (thrō) *n.* suffering; pain; *pl.* pains of childbirth [O.E. *thrawa*, suffering].

throm·bo·sis (thrȧm·bō′·sis) *n.* formation of blood clot in vein or artery [Gk. *thrombos*].

throne (thrōn) *n.* chair of state; royal seat; bishop's seat in his cathedral; sovereign power and dignity; *v.t.* to place on royal seat; to exalt. *pr.p.* **throning.** *pa.p.* **-d** [Gk. *thronos*, a seat].

throng (thrawng) *n.* multitude; crowd; *v.t.* to mass together; to press in crowds [O.E. *thringan*, to press].

throt·tle (thrȧt′·l) *n.* windpipe; valve controlling amount of vaporized fuel delivered to cylinders in internal-combustion engine, or pressure of steam in steam engine; *v.i.* to choke by external pressure on windpipe; to obstruct steam in steam engine; (*Fig.*) to suppress; to silence; *v.i.* to pant for breath, as if suffocated [dim. of *throat*].

through (thròò) *prep.* from end to end of; going in at one side and out the other; by passing between; across; along; by means of; as consequence of; *adv.* from one end or side to the other; from beginning to end. *a.* (of railway train) passing from one main station to another without intermediate stops; unobstructed, as *through-road.* **through and through,** completely. **-ly** (*Arch.*) *adv.* thoroughly. **-out** *adv.* and *prep.* wholly; completely; during entire time of [O.E. *thurh*, through].

throv (thrōv) *pa.t.* of **thrive.**

throw (thrō) *v.t.* to fling, cast, or hurl; to propel; to send; to twist into thread, as silk; to mold on potter's wheel; to unseat, as of a horseman; to shed, as snake's skin; to produce offspring, as animal; to spread carelessly; *v.i.* to cast, to hurl. *pr.p.* **-ing.** *pa.t.* **threw.** *pa.p.* **-n.** *n.* the act of throwing; distance something can be thrown; light blanket. **-er** *n.* **-n** *a.* [O.E.thrawan].

thrum (thrum) *n.* fringe of threads left on loom after web is cut off [O.N. *thromr*, edge].

thrum (thrum) *v.t.* to strum on instrument; to play carelessly; to drum with fingers *pr.p.* **-ming.** *pa.p.*, *pa.t.* **-med.** [O.N. *thruma*, rattle].

thrush (thrush) *n.* song bird [O.E. thrysce].

thrush (thrush) *n.* (*Med.*) inflammatory disease affecting mouth, tongue and lips, commonly found in young children; a disease affecting the feet of horses, etc. [O.E. *thyrre*, dry].

thrust (thrust) *v.t.* to push or drive with sudden force; to pierce; *v.i.* to make a push; to attack with a pointed weapon; to intrude; to push way through. *pa.t.* and *pa.p.* **thrust.** *n.* push; stab; assault; horizontal outward pressure as of arch against its abutments; stress acting horizontally, as in machinery; (*Geol.*) upward bulge of layer of rock due to lateral pressure. **-er** *n.* [Scand. *thrysia*, to press].

thud (thud) *n.* dull sound made by blow or heavy fall; *v.i.* to make sound of thud; [O.E. *thoden*, noise].

thug (thug) cutthroat; ruffian; gangster. **-gery** *n.* [Hind. *thag*].

Thule (thū′·lē) *n.* name in ancient times for most northerly part of world. Orkneys, Shetlands, Iceland, etc. [Gk. *Thoulē*].

thumb (thum) *n.* short, thick finger of human hand; part of glove which covers this; *v.t.* to manipulate awkwardly; to soil with thumb marks; (*Slang*) to hold up thumb, to solicit lift in automobile. **-ed** *a.* having thumbs; soiled with thumb marks. **-less** *a.* **-like** *a.* **-nail** *n.* nail on human thumb. **-nail sketch,** miniature; succinct description. **-screw** *n.* old instrument of torture by which thumb was compressed till the joint broke. **by rule of thumb,** by rough estimate [O.E. *thuma*, a thumb].

thump (thump) *n.* blow of fist; sudden fall of heavy body or weight; thud; *v.t.* to beat with something heavy; *v.i.* to strike or fall with a thud. **-er** *n.* **-ing** *a.* very large; much exaggerated [imit.].

thun·der (thun′·dẹr) *n.* rumbling sound which follows lightning flash; any very loud noise; *v.t.* to declaim or rage with loud voice; *v.i.* to rumble with thunder; to roar. **-bolt** *n.* flash of lightning followed by peal of thunder; anything totally unexpected and unpleasant. **-clap** *n.* a peal of thunder. **the thundered,** the god Jupiter; **-ing** *n.* thunder; booming, as of guns. *a.* making a loud noise; (*Colloq.*) outstanding; excessive. **-ous** *a.* **-ously** *adv.* **-storm** *n.* storm of thunder and lightning with torrential rain **-struck** *a.* speechless with amazement. **-y** *a.* **to steal someone's thunder,** to win applause expected by someone else; to expose or use first someone else's chief point(s) [O.E. *thunian*, to rattle].

thu·ri·ble (thyoo′·rạ·bl) *n.* a metal censer. **thurifer** *n.* one who carries and swings a thurible [L. *thus, thuris*, frankincense].

Thurs·day (thurz′·dē) *n.* fifth day of week, after *Thor*, Scandinavian god of thunder.

thus (THus) *adv.* in this or that manner; to this degree or extent; so; in this wise. **thus far,** so far [O.E. *thus*, by this].

thwack (thwak) *v.t.* to beat; to flog; *n.* heavy blow; a hard slap [O.E. *thaccian*, to stroke].

thwart (thwawrt) *a.* lying across; transverse; athwart; *v.t.* to hinder; to frustrate; to stop; *n.* seat across or athwart a row boat; *adv.* and *prep.* across. **-er** *n.* **-ing** *a.* [O.N. *thvert*, across].

thy (THī) *poss. a.* of thee; belonging to thee [contr. fr. *thine*].

thyme (tīm) *n.* small flowering shrub cultivated for its aromatic leaves for use as flavoring in cookery [Gk. *thumon*].

thy·mus (thī′·mạs) *n.* small ductless gland in upper part of the chest [Gk.].

thy·roid (thī′·roid) *a.* signifying cartilage of larynx or a gland of trachea. **— gland,** ductless gland situated in neck on either side of trachea, secreting hormone which profoundly affects physique and temperament of human beings [Gk. *thureos*, a shield; *eidos*, a form].

thy·self (THī·self′) *pron. reflex.* or *emphatic*, of a person, thou or thee.

ti·ar·a (tī·or′·a, ti·ȧr′·a) *n.* lofty turban worn by ancient Persian kings and dignitaries; triple, gem-studded crown worn by Pope on ceremonial occasions; gem-studded coronet worn by ladies [Gk. *tiara*, headdress].

tib·i·a (tib′·i·ạ) *n.* shinbone; inner and usually larger of two bones of leg, between knee and ankle. *pl.* **-s, tibiae. -l** *a.* [L. *tibial*].

tic (tik) *n.* spasmodic twitching of muscle, esp. of face [Fr. *tic*, twitching].

tick (tik) *n.* a parasitic bloodsucking insect [M.E. *teke*].

tick (tik) *n.* cover of mattress, pillow, etc. **-ing** *n.* specially strong material used for mattress covers, etc. [Gk. *thēkē*, a case].

tick (tik) *v.i.* to make small, recurring, clicking sound, as watch; *n.* sound made by watch. **-er** *n.* anything which ticks regularly; machine which records on tape; (*Colloq.*) watch or clock; the heart [imit.].

tick (tik) *v.t.* to mark or dot lightly; *n.* small mark placed after word, entry, etc., esp. in checking; [M.E. *tek*, a touch].

tick·et (tik′·it) *n.* piece of cardboard or paper entitling admission to anything, to travel by public transport, to participate in function, etc.; price tag; label; (*U.S.*) list of candidates in an election; *v.t.* to mark with ticket. **season ticket,** ticket entitling holder to attend a series of concerts, lectures, etc. or to travel daily between certain specified stations over a certain period of time [O.Fr. *etiquet*, label].

tick·le (tik′.l) *v.t.* to touch skin lightly so as to excite nerves and cause laughter; to titillate; to amuse; *v.i.* to feel sensation of tickling; to be gratified. **-r** *n.* **ticklish** *a.* easily tickled; requiring skillful handling. **ticklishly** *adv.* **ticklishness** *n.* [freq. of *tick*, to touch lightly].

tid·bit (tid′.bit) *n.* choice morsel. Also **titbit** [Scand. *titto*, small bird].

tid·dly·winks (tid′.li.wingks) *n.pl.* game in which players try to snap small disks into cup.

tide (tīd) *n.* time; season, as in *eventide, Eastertide;* periodical rise and fall of ocean due to attraction of moon and sun; (*Fig.*) trend. **to tide over,** to manage temporarily; to surmount meantime. **tidal** *a.* pert. to tide. **tidal basin,** harbor which is affected by tides. **tidal wave,** mountainous wave as caused by earthquake, atom bomb explosion, etc. **-less** *a.* having no tides. **ebb,** or **low, tide,** the falling level of the sea. **flood,** or **high, tide,** the rising level of the sea. **neap tide,** minimum tide. **spring tide,** maximum tide [O.E. *tid*, time].

ti·dings (tī′.dingz) *n.pl.* news; information [O.N. *tithindi*, to happen].

ti·dy (tī′.dy.) *a.* neat; orderly; (*Colloq.*) comfortable; of fair size; *n.* chair-back cover; *v.t.* to put in order [M.E. tidy, timely].

tie (tī) *v.t.* to fasten by rope, string, etc.; to fashion into knot; to bind together, as rafters, by connecting piece of wood or metal; to hamper; (*Mus.*) to connect two notes with tie; *v.t.* (*Sport*) to make equal score, etc. *pr.p.* **tying.** *pa.t.* and *pa.p.* **tied.** *n.* knot; necktie; fastening; connecting link; equality of score; (*Mus.*) curved line connecting two notes indicating that sound is sustained for length of both notes; traverse supports for railroad tracks. **— beam** *n.* horizontal timber connecting two rafters. **-r** *n.* [O.E. *teah*, a rope].

tier (tir) *n.* row or rank, esp. when two or more rows are arranged behind and above the other [Fr. *tirer*, to draw].

tierce (tirs) *n.* cask containing third of pipe or 42 wine gallons; third of canonical hours, or service at 9 a.m.; in fencing, particular thrust (third position) [Fr. *tiers*, third].

tiff (tif) *n.* slight quarrel; *v.i.* to quarrel

ti·ger (tī′.gər) *n.* (fem. **tigress**) fierce carnivorous quadruped of cat tribe, with tawny black-striped coat. **-cat** *n.* wild cat; ocelot or margay. **— lily** *n.* tall Chinese lily with flaming orange flowers spotted with black [Gk. *tigris*].

tight (tīt) *a.* firm; compact; compressed; not leaky; fitting close or too close to body; tense; (*Colloq.*) restricted for want of money; (*Slang*) drunk; *adv.* firmly. **-en** *v.t.* to make tight or tighter; to make taut; *v.i.* to become tight or tighter. **-ener** *n.* **-ly** *adv.* **-ness** *n.* **-rope** *n.* a strong, taut rope, or steel wire on which acrobats perform. *n.pl.* close-fitting woven hose and trunks worn by acrobats, dancers, etc. [O.N. *thettr*, watertight].

til·de (til′.də) *n.* the mark (~) placed over the letter *n* in Spanish, to indicate a following *y* sound, as in cañon (canyon).

tile (tīl) *n.* a thin piece of slate, baked clay, plastic, asphalt, etc. used for roofs, walls, floors, drains, etc.; (*Slang*) a silk top-hat; *v.t.* to cover with tiles. **-r** *n.* **tiling** *n.* [L. *tegula*].

till (til) *n.* a money box or drawer in a shop counter; a cash register [etym. doubtful].

till (til) *prep.* as late as; until; *conj.* to the time when [M.E. *til*, up to].

till (til) *v.t.* to cultivate; to plow the soil, sow seeds, etc. **-age** *n.* the act of preparing the soil for cultivation; the cultivated land. **-er** *n.* [O.E. *tilian*, to till].

till (til) *n.* boulder clay or glacial drift.

til·ler (til′.ər) *n.* a bar used as a lever, esp. for turning a rudder [O.Fr. *tellier*, weaver's beam].

tilt (tilt) *v.t.* to raise one end of; to tip up; to thrust, as a lance; to forge with a tilt hammer; *v.i.* to charge on horseback with a lance, as in a tournament; to slant; *n.* a thrust, as with a lance; a medieval sport in which competitors armed with lances charged each other; inclination. **-er** *n.* **— hammer** *n.* a heavy hammer used in iron works and tilted by a lever [O.E. *tealt*, tottering].

tilt (tilt) *n.* canvas covering of a cart; a small canvas awning; *v.t.* to cover with a tilt [O.E. *teld*, a tent].

tim·bal (tim′.bəl) *n.* kettledrum [Sp. *timbal*, a kettledrum].

tim·ber (tim′.bər) *n.* trees or wood suitable for building purposes; trees collectively; single unit of wooden framework of house; rib of ship; *v.t.* to furnish with timber. **-ed** *a.* **— line** *n.* tree line, above which altitude trees will not grow [O.E.].

tim·bre (tim′.bər, tàn′.br) *n.* special tone quality in sound of human voice or instrument [Fr. *timbre*].

tim·brel (tim′.brəl) *n.* kind of drum, or tambourine [O.Fr. *timbre*].

time (tīm) *n.* particular moment; period of duration; conception of past, present, and future, as sequence; epoch; opportunity; occasion; (*Mus.*) rhythmical arrangement of beats within measures or bars; *v.t.* to ascertain time taken, as by racing competitor; to select precise moment for; (*Mus.*) to measure; *v.i.* to keep or beat time. **-s** *n.pl.* period, as *Victorian times;* term indicating multiplication, as *four times four.* **— bomb** *n.* delayed-action bomb. **—honored** *a.* revered because of age; venerable. **-keeper** *n.* one who keeps a record of men's hours of work; clock or watch. **-less** *a.* eternal; unending. **-lessly** *adv.* **-liness** *n.* **-ly** *a.* opportune. **-piece** *n.* clock. **-r** *n.* a stop watch. **-server** *n.* **-serving** *n.* selfish opportunism. **— sharing** *n.* the simultaneous employment of a computer by many users at different locations. **-table** *n.* booklet containing times of departure and arrival of trains, buses, steamers, etc. **-worn** *a.* aged; decayed. **timing** *n.* control of speed of an action or actions for greatest effect. **Greenwich —** *n.* standard time as settled by passage of sun over meridian at Greenwich [O.E. *tima*, time].

tim·id (tim′.id) *a.* lacking courage or self-confidence; shy. **-ness, -ity** *n.* **-ly** *adv.* **timorous** *a.* frightened; very timid. **timorously** *adv.* **timorousnes** *n.* [L. *timidus*].

ti·moc·ra·cy (tī.màk′.rə.si.) *n.* government in which possession of property is necessary qualification for holders of offices [Gk. *timē*, honor; *kratos*, power].

tim·o·thy (tim′.ə.thi.) *n.* grass grown for hay, and valued as fodder.

tim·pa·no (tim′.pə.nō) *n.* kettledrum, esp. as part of percussion section of orchestra. *pl.* **timpani. timpanist, tympanist** *n.* [Gk. *tumpanon*, a kettledrum].

tin (tin) *n.* soft, whitish-gray metal, very malleable and ductile, used for plating, as constituent of alloys (e.g., pewter, bronze) and for food containers in canning industry; tin can; (*Slang*) money; *a.* made of tin or plated with tin; *v.t.* to plate with tin. *pr.p.* **-ning.** *pa.p., pa.t.* **-ned. — foil** *n.* wafer-thin sheets of tin; **-ned** *a.* preserved in a tin; plated with tin. **-ner, -man** *n.* a tin miner; one who makes tin plate. **-ning** *n.* **-ny** *a.* like tin; making a sound like tin when struck

-type *n.* (*Photog.*) ferrotype; positive on varnished tin plate. **-ware** *n.* utensils, etc. made of tin plate [O.E. *tin*, tin].

Tin Pan Alley (tin′.pan.a′.li.) (*Slang*) the world of the composers of popular music.

tinc·ture (tingk′.cher) *n.* tinge or shade of color; faint trace; (*Pharm.*) solution of a substance in alcohol; *v.t.* to tinge; to imbue; to affect to a small degree [L. *tinctura*, dyeing].

tin·der (tin′.der) *n.* anything inflammable used for kindling fire from a spark [O.E. *tynder*, tinder].

tine (tīn) *n.* tooth or prong of fork; spike of harrow; branch of deer's antler. *a.* [O.E. *tind*, point].

ting (ting) *n.* sharp, ringing sound, as of bell; tinkle; *v.t.* and *v.i.* to tinkle. [imit.].

tinge (tinj) *v.t.* to color or flavor slightly; to temper. *n.* a faint touch [L. *tingere*].

tin·gle (ting′.gl) *v.i.* to feel faint thrill or pricking sensation; *n.* pricking sensation [prob. freq. of *ting*].

tink·er (tingk′.er) *n.* mender of pots, kettles, etc., esp. one who travels round countryside; jack of all trades; *v.i.* to do the work of a tinker; to attempt to mend [M.E. *tinker*, one who makes a sharp sound].

tin·kle (tingk′.l) *v.t.* to cause to make small, quick, metallic sounds; *v.i.* to make series of quick, sharp sounds; to jingle; *n.* small, sharp, ringing sound. **tinkling** *n. a.* [M.E. *tinken*, to chink].

tin·sel (tin′.sal) *n.* very thin, glittering, metallic strips for decorations, etc.; (*Fig.*) anything showy or flashy; *a.* gaudy; showy and cheap; *v.t.* to decorate with tinsel; to make gaudy. **—like** *a.* [Fr. *étincelle*, a spark].

tint (tint) *n.* hue or dye; faint tinge; color with admixture of white; *v.t.* to give faint coloring to; to tinge **-er** *n.* [L. *tinctus*, dyed].

tin·tin·nab·u·la·tion (tin.ti.nab.ya.lā′.shan) *n.* tinkling sound of bells pealing. **tintinnabular, tintinnabulary, tintinnabulous** *a.* [L. *tintinnare*, to jingle].

ti·ny (tī′.ni.) *a.* very small; diminutive. Also **teeny.**

tip (tip) *n.* point of anything slender; end; top; *v.t.* to form a point on; to cover tip of. *pr.p.* **-ping.** *pa.p.* **-ped. -toe** *adv.* on tips of toes; *v.t.* to walk on tips of toes; to walk stealthily. [var. of *top*].

tip (tip) *v.t.* to touch lightly; to tap; to tilt; to overturn; to weigh down, as scales; (*Slang*) to give useful hint to, esp. about betting odds; to recompense with small gratuity; *v.i.* to fall to one side; to give gratuity; *n.* light stroke; private information; advice; gratuity; *n.* **-ping** *n.* **-ster** *n.* one who sells tips regarding horse-racing, etc. [M.E. *tipen*, to overthrow].

tip·pet (tip′.it) *n.* scarf or cloth of fur [L. *tapete*, tapestry].

tip·ple (tip′.l) *v.i.* to drink small quantities of intoxicating liquor frequently; *v.t.* to drink excessively. *n.* strong drink. **-r** *n.* [Scand. *tipla*, to drink little and often].

tip·sy (tip′.si.) *a.* intoxicated; staggering. **tipsily** *adv.* **tipsiness** *n.* [fr. *tipple*].

ti·rade (tī.rād′) *n.* long denunciatory speech; volley of abuse [It. *tirata*, a drawing out].

tire (tīr) *v.t.* to weary or fatigue; *v.i.* to become wearied, bored, or impatient. **-d** *a.* wearied; bored. **-dness** *n.* **-less** *a.* **-lessly** *adv.* **-some** *a.* [O.E. *tiorian*, to be tired].

tire (tīr) *n.* hoop of iron, rubber, or rubber tube, etc. placed around a wheel [form of *attire*].

tir·o See **tyro.**

tis·sue (tish′.òò) *n.* (*Biol.*) any of cellular structures which make up various organs of plant or animal body; unbroken series; web; fine cloth interwoven with gold or silver; *a.* made of tissue. **-d** *a.* made of or resembling tissue. **— paper** *n.* very thin, white or colored semi-transparent paper [Fr. *tissu*, fr. L.*texere*, to weave].

tit (tit) *n.* small bird, e.g. titmouse [O.N. *tittr*, a little bird.

tit (tit) *n.* teat [O.E. *tit*, a nipple].

Ti·tan (tī′.tan) *n.* (*Gk. Myth.*) one of sons of Uranus and Gaea (Heaven) and Earth); (*l.c.*) person of magnificent physique or of brilliant intellectual capacity; *a.* pert. to Titans; (*l.c.*) colossal; mighty. **Titanic** *a.* pert. to Titans; colossal.

tithe (tīTH) *n.* tenth part; orig. tenth part of produce of land and cattle given to the church, later paid in form of tax; small portion; *v.t.* to levy a tithe; *v.i.* to give a tithe. **-r** *n.* **-less** *a.* [O.E. *teotha*, tenth].

tit·ian (tish′.an) *a.* rich auburn; from color of hair in many portraits by Titian, Italian painter.

tit·il·late (tit′.a.lāt) *v.t.* to tickle, usually in sense of stimulating mind, palate, etc.—**titillation** *n.* process of titillating; any pleasurable sensation. **titillative** *a.* [L. *titillare*, to tickle].

tit·i·vate (tit′.a.vāt) *v.i.* and *v.t.* (*Slang*) to put finishing touches to one's general appearance **titivator** *n.* [perh. fr. *tidy*].

ti·tle (tī′.tl) *n.* inscription put over, or under, or at beginning of, anything; designation; appellation denoting rank or office; that which constitutes just claim or right; (*Law*) legal proof of right of possession; title deed. **-d** *a.* having title, esp. aristicratic title. **— deed** *n.* document giving proof of legal ownership of property. **— page** *n.* page of book on which is inscribed name of book, author and publication data. **— role** *n.* part in play from which it takes its name [L. *titulus*, title].

tit·mouse (tit′.mous) *n.* small bird which builds in holes of trees; tit; tomtit. *pl.* **titmice** [M.E. *tit*, small; *mase*, name for several small birds].

ti·trate (tī′.trāt) *v.t.* to determine amount of ingredient in solution by adding quantities of standard solution until required chemical reaction is observed. **titration** *n.* [Fr. *titre*, title].

tit·ter (tit′.er) *v.i.* to give smothered laugh; to giggle; *n.* **-er** *n.* [imit.].

tit·tle (tit′.l) *n.* minute particle; whit; jot [L. *titulus*, superscription, small stroke to indicate contraction].

tit·u·lar (tich′.(y)a.ler) *a.* pert. to or having a title; nominal; ruling in name but not in deed. **titularity** *n.* **-y** *a.* titular; *n.* nominal holder of title [L. *titulus*, a title].

tme·sis (mē′.sis) *n.* separation of two parts of compound word by one or more interpolated words, as 'from *what* direction *soever*' [Gk. fr. *temnein*, to cut].

to (tòò) *prep.* expressing motion towards; as far as; regarding; unto; upon; besides; compared with; as to; expressing purpose, as in gerundial infinitive indicating dative case or indirect object; preceding infinitive mood of the verb: *adv.* forward; into customary position [O.E. *to*, to].

toad (tōd) *n.* amphibian resembling frog, but brownish with dry warty skin and short legs; mean, detestable person. **-stool** *n.* fungus resembling mushroom, but poisonous. **-y** *n.* obsequious flatterer; social parasite; *v.i.* to flatter excessively; to fawn on. *pr.p.* **-ying.** *pa.t.* and *pa.p.* **-ied. -yish** *a.* **-yism** *n.* sycophancy [O.E. *tadige*, a toad].

toast (tōst) *v.t.* to dry or warm by exposure to fire; to crisp and brown (as bread) before fire, under grill, etc.; to drink to health of, or in honor of; *v.i.* to drink a toast; *n.* slice of bread crisped and browned on both sides by heat; person in whose honor toast is drunk; the drink itself. **-er** *n.* **-master** *n.* one who presides at luncheon or dinner, proposes toasts, introduces speakers, etc. [L. *tostus*, roasted].

to·bac·co (tạ·bak′·ō) *n.* plant, dried leaves of which are used for chewing, smoking, or as snuff. *pl.* **-s, -es** [Sp. *tabaco*].

to·bog·gan (tạ·bȧg′·ạn) *n.* flat-bottomed sled used for coasting down snow-clad hill slopes; *v.i.* to slide down hills on toboggan. **-ing** *n.* [Amer.-Ind.].

to·by (tō′·bi·) *n.* small jug in shape of an old man wearing a three-cornered hat [fr. *Toby*, personal name].

toc·ca·ta (tạ·kȧ′·ta) *n.* (*Mus.*) composition for organ or piano which tests player's technique and touch [It.].

toc·sin (tȧk′·sin) *n.* alarm bell or its ringing sound [Fr.

to·day, to-day (tạ·dā′) *n.* this day; present time; *adv.* on this day; at the present time [O.E. *to-daege*, today].

tod·dle (tȧd′·l) *v.i.* to walk with short, hesitating steps. *n.* unsteady gait. **-r** *n.* child just learning to walk [prob. form of *totter*].

tod·dy (tȧd′·i·) *n.* fermented juice of certain E. Indian palm trees; drink of whisky, sugar, and hot water [Hind. *tari*, juice of palm tree].

to-do (tạ·dòò′) *n.* a commotion; a fuss [fr. *to* and *do*].

toe (tō) *n.* one of five small digits of foot; forepart of hoof; part of boot, shoe, or stocking covering toes; outer end of head of golf club; *v.t.* to touch or reach with toe; *v.i.* to tap with toes. **-d** *a.* having toes [O.E. *ta*, the toe].

tof·fee, tof·fy (tȧf′·i·) *n.* hard candy made of sugar, butter, flavoring, etc. boiled together. Also **taffy** [etym. uncertain].

tog (tȧg) *n.* (*Slang*) clothes. usu. in *pl.* *v.i.* to dress *pr.p.* **-ging.** *pa.p., pa.t.* **-get** [prob. fr. L. *toga*, a robe].

to·ga (tō′·gạ) *n.* loose outer garment worn by Roman citizens. **-ed, togated** *a.* wearing a toga [L. fr. *tegere*, to cover].

to·geth·er (tạ·geTH′·ẹr) *adv* in company; in or into union; simultaneously; in same place [O.E. *to*, to; *geador*, together].

toil (toil) *v.i.* to labor; to move with difficulty; *n.* exhausting labor; drudgery; task. **-er** *n.* **-ful, -some** *a.* laborious. **-somely** *adv.* **-someness** *n.* **-worn** *a.* weary with toil; (of hands) hard and lined with toil [O.Fr. *touiller*, to entangle].

toil (toil) *n.* a net or snare; mesh. usu. *pl.* [Fr. *toile, cloth*].

toi·let (toi′·lit) *n.* process of dressing; mode of dressing; a lavatory. Also **toilette** (twạ·let′). **— articles** *n.pl.* objects used in dressing, as comb, brush, mirror, toothbrush, etc. **— paper** *n.* thin paper for lavatory use. **— powder** *n.* talcum powder [Fr. *toilette*, dim. of *toile*, cloth].

to·ken (tō′·kạn) *n.* sign; symbol; concrete expression of esteem; coin-like piece of metal for special use, as *bus token, etc.* **— payment** *n.* deposit paid as token of later payment of full debt [O.E. *tacen*, symbol].

told (tōld) *pa.t.* and *pa.p.* of verb **tell.**

tol·er·ate (tȧl′·ạ·rāt) *v.t.* to permit to be done; to put up with. **tolerable** *a.* endurable; supportable; passably good. **tolerability, tolerableness** *n.* **tolerably** *adv.* **tolerance** *n.* forbearance. **tolerant** *a.* forbearing; broad-minded. **tolerantly** *adv.* **toleration** *n.* act of tolerating; practice of allowing people to worship as they please; granting to minorities political liberty. **tolerationist** *n.* **tolerator** *n.* [L. *tolerare*, to bear].

toll (tōl) *n.* tax, esp. for right to use bridge, ferry, public road, etc.; charge for long-distance telephone call. *v.i.* to exact toll. **— bar** *n.* formerly bar which could be swung across road to stop travelers to pay toll. [O.E. *toll*, tax].

toll (tōl) *v.t.* to cause to ring slowly, as bell, esp. to signify death; *v.i.* to peal with slow, sonorous sounds; *n.* [M.E. *tollen*, to pull].

tom (tȧm) *n.* used to denote male animal as tomcat. **-boy** *n.* girl of boyish behavior; hoyden, romping, mischievous girl. **-fool** *n.* complete fool. **-foolery** *n.* nonsensical behavior. [fr. *Thomas*].

tom·a·hawk (tȧm′·ạ·hawk) *n.* war hatchet used by N. American Indians; *v.t.* to wound or kill with tomahawk [Amer.-Ind.].

to·ma·to (tạ·mā′·tō) *n. pl.* **-es.** plant with red or yellow fruit much used in salads. [Sp. *tomate*].

tomb (tòòm) *n.* a grave; underground vault; any structure for a dead body. **-stone** *n.* stone erected over grave [Gk. *tumbos*, a sepulchral mound].

tome (tōm) *n.* a book; a large, heavy volume [Gk. *tomos*, a piece cut off].

to·mor·row (tạ·mawr′·ō) *n.* day after today; *adv.* on the following day [O.E. *to*, and *morgen*, morning].

tom·tit (tȧm′·tit) *n.* a small bird [fr. *tit* as in *titmouse*].

tom-tom (tȧm′·tȧm) *n.* small drum used by Indian and African natives. Also **tam-tam** [Hind.]

ton (tun) *n.* weight consisting of 20 cwt. or 2000 lb.; measure of capacity varying according to article being measured; *pl.* (*Colloq.*) great amount or number. **-nage** *n.* cubical content (100 cub. ft.) or burden (40 cub. ft.) of ship in tons; duty on ships estimated per ton; shipping collectively assessed in tons. Also **tonnage** [O.E. *tunne*, vat].

ton (tȧn) *n.* fashion; latest mode [Fr.].

tone (tōn) *n.* quality or pitch of musical sound; modulation of speaking or singing voice; color values of picture; (*Mus.*) one of larger intervals of diatonic scale, smaller intervals being called *semitones;* (*Med.*) natural healthy functioning of bodily organs; general character, as of manners, morals, or sentiment; (*Gram*). pitch on one syllable of word; *v.t.* to give tone or quality to; to modify color or general effect of, as in photograph; to tune (instrument); *v.i.* to blend (with). **tonal** *a.* **tonality** *n.* quality of tone or pitch; system of variation of keys in musical composition; color scheme of picture. **tonally** *adv.* **— deaf** *a.* unable to distinguish musical intervals. *a.* having tone etc. [Gk. *tonos*, tension].

ton·ga (tȧng′·ga) *n.* a light, two-wheeled vehicle used in India [Hind.].

tong (tȧng, tawng) *n.* (in *U.S.*) an association exclusively for Chinese people [Chin. *t'ang*, meeting-place].

tongs (tȧngz, tawngz) *n.pl.* implement consisting of pair of pivoted levers, for grasping e.g. pieces of coal [O.E. *tange*, tongs].

tongue (tung) *n.* flexible muscular organ in mouth used in tasting, swallowing, and for speech; facility of utterance; language; anything shaped like a tongue; clapper of bell; narrow spit of land; slip of wood fitting into groove; *v.t.* to modulate with tongue as notes of flute; to chide; *v.i.* to use tongue as in playing staccato passage on flute; to chatter. **-d** *a.* having a tongue. **—tied** *n.* having tongue defect causing speech impediment; speechless through shyness [O.E. *tunge*].

ton·ic (tȧn′·ik) *a.* pert. to tones or sounds; having an invigorating effect bodily or mentally; *n.* a medicine which tones up the system; anything invigorating; (*Mus.*) a key note **-ally** *adv.* **tonicity** (tō·nis′·ạ·ti·) *n.* **— sol-fa,** a system of musical notation in which sounds are represented by syllables as do, ray, me, fah, etc. [Gk. *tonos*, act of stretching].

to·night, to-night (tạ·nīt′) this night; night

following this present day; *adv.* on this night [fr. *to* and *night*].
ton·nage *n.* See **ton.**
ton·sil (tȧn′·sil) *n.* one of two oval-shaped lymphoid organs on either side of pharynx. **-(l)itis** *n.* inflammation of the tonsils [L. *tonsillae*, tonsils].
ton·sure (tȧn′·shẹr) *n.* act of shaving part of head as token of religious dedication; shaved crown of priest's head. **tonsor** *n.* barber. **tonsorial** *a.* pert. to a barber or his work (usu. humorous) [L. *tonsura*, clipping].
ton·tine (tȧn′·tēn) *n.* shared annuity [fr. *Lorenzo Tonti*, the originator].
too (tòò) *adv.* in addition; more than enough; moreover [stressed form of *to*].
took (took) *pa.t.* of **take.**
tool (tòòl) *n.* implement or utensil operated by hand, or by machinery; cutting or shaping part of a machine; means to an end; *v.t.* to cut, shape, or mark with a tool; to indent a design on leather book cover, etc. with pointed tool. **-ing** *n.* [O.E. *tol*, a tool].
toot (tòòt) *v.t.* to cause to sound, as an automobile horn or wind instrument; *n.* sound of horn, etc.; hoot. [imit.].
tooth (tòòth) *n.* hard projection in gums of upper and lower jaws of vertebrates, used in mastication; prong as of comb, saw, rake; cog of wheel. *pl.* **teeth.** *v.t.* to provide with teeth; to indent; *v.i.* to interlock. **-ache** *n.* pain in tooth. **-brush** *n.* small brush for cleaning teeth. **-ed** *a.* **-some** *a.* palatable; pleasant to taste. **-y** *a.* having prominent teeth; toothed [O.E. *toth*, a tooth].
top (tȧp) *n.* highest part of anything; upper side; highest rank; first in merit; green part of plants above ground; (*Naut.*) platform surrounding head of lower mast. *a.* highest; most eminent; best; *v.t.* to cover on the top; to rise above; to cut off top of; to hit, as golf ball, above center; to surpass; *v.i.* to be outstanding. **-coat** *n.* overcoat. **— hat** *n.* tall silk hat. **—heavy** *a.* unbalanced; having top too heavy for base. **-most** *a.* supreme; highest. **-notch** *a.* describing persons of high ability or anything which is super-excellent. **-per** something placed on the top; (*Slang*) top hat; topcoat. **-ping** *n.* act of lopping off top of something, as highest branches of tree; what is cut off; something put on top of a thing as decoration, to complete it, etc. *a.* **-pingly** *adv.* **-sail** *n.* square sail on top-mast. **-soil** *n.* surface layer of soil [O.E. *top*, summit]. [pointed end.
top (tȧp) *n.* child's toy made to spin on its
to·paz (tō′·paz) *n.* gem stone, translucent and of varied colors [etym. uncertain].
tope (tōp) *v.i.* to drink hard or to excess. **-r** *n.* [Fr. *toper*, to clinch bargain].
to·pee (tō·pē′) *n.* pith helmet worn by Europeans in tropical climates. Also **topi** [Hind. *topi*, hat].
to·pi·a (tō′·pi·ạ) *n.* mural decoration comprising landscapes, popular in Roman houses. **topiary** *a.* cut into ornamental shapes, as trees, hedges, etc. *n.* topiary work or art; a garden or single shrub so trimmed. **topiarist** *n.* [L. *topia*, ornamental gardening].
top·ic (tȧp′·ik) *n.* subject of essay, discourse, or conversation; branch of general subject. **-al** *a.* pert. to a place; up-to-date; concerning local matters. **-ally** *adv.* [Gk. *topos*, a place].
to·pog·ra·phy (tạ·pȧg′·rạ·fi·) *n.* description of a place; scientific or physical features of region. **topographer** *n.* **topographic, -al** *a.* [Gk. *topos*, a place; *graphein*, to write].
top·ple (tȧp′·l) *v.t.* to throw down; to overturn; *v.i.* to overbalance [freq. of *top*].
top·sy-tur·vy (tȧp′·si·tur′·vi·) *adv.* upside down; *a.* turned upside down; *n.* disorder; chaos [prob. O.E. *top*, and *tearflian*, to roll].
toque (tōk) *n.* brimless woman's hat [Fr.].
To·rah (tōr′·ạ) *n.* the Pentateuch; (l.c.) whole scripture of Judaism [Heb. law].
torch (tawrch) *n.* piece of wood with some substance at the end soaked in inflammable liquid, and used as portable light. **-bearer** *n.* [L. *torquere*, to twist].
tore (tōr) *pa.t.* of **tear.**
tor·e·a·dor (tawr′·i·a·dawr) *n.* bull fighter [Sp. fr. L. *taurus*, a bull].
tor·ment (tawr′·ment) *n.* extreme pain of body; anguish of mind; misery; cause of anguish. **torment** *v.t.* to inflict pain upon; to torture; to vex; to tease. **tormenting** *a.* **tormentingly** *adv.* **tormentor, tormenter** *n.* [L. *tormentum*, instrument of torture].
torn (tōrn) *pa.p.* of **tear.**
tor·na·do (tawr·nā′·dō) *n.* whirling progressive windstorm causing wide-spread devestation. [Sp. *tronada*, thunderstorm].
tor·pe·do (tawr·pē′·dō) *n.* cigar-shaped underwater projectile with high explosive charge; type of explosive mine; electric ray fish which electrocutes its prey. *pl.* **-es.** *v.t.* to attack, hit, or sink with torpedoes. **-ist** *n.* expert in handling and firing torpedoes [L. *torpere*, to be numb].
tor·pid (tawr′·pid) *a.* dormant, as hibernating animal; lethargic; physically or mentally inert. **-ity** *n.* inactivity; lethargy. **-ly** *adv.* **-ness** *n.* **torpor** *n.* sluggishness; inertia. **torporific** *a.* [L. *torpere*, to be numb].
torque (tawrk) *n.* collar of gold wires twisted together, worn by ancient Britons, Gauls, etc. Also **torc;** (*Mech.*) rotating power in mechanism. **-d** *a.* [L. *torquere*, to twist].
tor·re·fy (tawr′·ạ·fī) *v.t.* to scorch; to parch; to roast, as metals. **torrefaction** *n.* [L. *torrere*, to burn; *facere*, to make].
tor·rent (tawr′·ạnt) *n.* swift-flowing stream; downpour, as of rain; rapid flow, as of words. **-ial** *a.* pert. to, resembling torrent; overwhelming [L. *torrens*, a boiling stream].
tor·rid (tawr′·id) *a.* extremely hot, dry or burning; passionate. **-ness, torridity** *n.* **-ly** *adv.* **— zone,** broad belt lying between Tropics of Cancer and Capricorn [L. *torrere*, to burn].
tor·sion (tawr′·shạn) *n.* act of turning or twisting; (*Mech.*) force with which twisted wire or similar body tends to return to original position. *a.* **— balance,** delecate scientific instrument for measuring minute forces by means of small bar suspended horizontally at end of very fine wire [L. *torquere*, to twist].
tor·so (tawr′·sō) *n.* trunk of human body; statue with head and limbs cut off [It.].
tort (tawrt) *n.* (*Law*) private injury to person or property for which damages may be claimed in court of law. **-ious** *a.* **-iously** *adv.* [L. *torquere*, to twist].
tor·til·la (tawr·tē′·(y)ạ) *n.* round, thin cake of corn meal [Sp. dim. of *torta*, a tart].
tor·toise (tawr′·tạs) *n.* land reptile or turtle; a very low person or thing; **-shell** *n.* horny mottled brown outer shell of tortoise used commercially for combs, etc.; *a.* mottled like tortoise shell [L. *tortus*, twisted].
tor·tu·ous (tawr′·choo·ạs) *a.* full of twists; crooked; devious; circuitous; deceitful. **-ity** *n.* **-ly** *adv.* **-ness** [L. *tortuosus*].
tor·ture (tawr′·chẹr) *n.* act of deliberately inflicting extreme pain as punishment or repraisal; anguish; torment; *v.t.* to put to torture; to inflict agony. *n.* **torturing** *a.* **torturous** *a.* [L. *tortura*, twisting].
to·ry (tōr′·i·) *a.* supporter of Britain in the American Revolution; (*Brit.*) a member of the Conservative party. **-ism** *n.* [Ir. *toruighe*, a pursuer].
toss (taws) *v.t.* to throw upwards with a jerk; to cause to rise and fall; to agitate violently; *v.i.* to be tossed; to roll and tumble; to be restless; *n.* fling; sudden fall from

horseback; distance anything is tossed. **-er** *n.* **-ing** *n.* **-up,** tossing of coin to decide issue; (*Colloq.*) even chance [W. *tosio,* to jerk].

tot (tȧt) *n.* anything small, esp. a child; [Scand. *tottr,* dwarf].

to·tal (tō·tạl) *a.* full; complete; utter; absolute; *n.* the whole; sum; aggregate; *v.t.* to sum; to add; *v.i.* to amount to. **-izator,** *n.* machine which registers totals. **-ity** *n.* whole sum; entirety. **-ly** *adv.* **-ness** *n.* [L. *totus* whole].

to·tal·i·tar·i·an (tō·tạl·ȧ·tar′·i·ạn) *a.* relating to open-party dictorial form of government. **totalitarianism** *n.*

tote (tōt) *v.t.* (*Colloq.*) to carry; to bear; to transport.

to·tem (tō′·tạm) *n.* natural object, such as animal or plant, taken by primitive tribe as emblem of hereditary relationship with that object; image of this. **-ic** *a.* **-ism** *n.* **-ist** *n.* member of tribe. **-istic** *a.* **— pole** *n.* pole with totems carved on it, one above the other [Amer.-Ind.].

tot·ter (tȧt′·ẹr) *v.i.* to walk with faltering steps; to sway; to shake; to reel. **-er** *n.* **-ing** *a.* **-ingly** *adv.* **-y** *a.* unsteady [O.E. *tealt,* unsteady].

tou·can (to͝o′·kan, too·kȧn′) *n.* bird of tropical Am. [Braz.].

touch (tuch) *v.t.* to come in contact with; to finger; to reach; to attain; to treat of, superficially; to move deeply; to equal in merit; to play on; (*Slang*) to borrow from; *v.i.* to be in contact; to take effect on; *n.* contact; sense of feeling; quality of response in handling of instrument or color; individual style of execution; unique quality; trace or tinge; test; mild attack. **-able** *a.* **-ableness** *n.* **— and go,** precarious situation. **— down** (*Football*) scoring by having ball behind goal line. **-ed** *a.* (*Slang*) crazy. **-er** *n.* **-ily** *adv.* **-iness** *n.* **-ing** *a.* emotionally moving; pathetic; *prep.* concerning; referring to. **-ingly** *adv.* **-ingness** *n.* **-stone** *n.* variety of compact, siliceous stone, used for testing purity of gold and silver; criterion; standard of judgment. **-y** *a.* easily offended; hypersensitive. [Fr. *toucher*].

tough (tuf) *a.* flexible but not brittle; not easily broken; firm; difficult to chew; stouthearted; vigorous; hardy; difficult to solve; (*Slang*) vicious; *n.* a bully; a ruffian. **-en** *v.t.* to make tough, or hardy; *v.i.* to become tough. **-ly** *adv.* **-ness** *n.* [O.E. *toh,* tough].

tou·pee (to͝o·pā′) *n.* wig or artificial lock of hair [Fr. *toupet,* a tuft of hair].

tour (toor) *n.* journey from place to place in a country; excursion; spell of duty; *v.t.* to travel round; to visit as part of tour. **-ism** *n.* **-ist** *n.* one who makes a tour; sightseer [Fr. *tour,* a turn].

tour·ma·lin(e) (toor′·mạ·lin) *n.* crystalline mineral [fr. Singh. *toramalli,* cornelian].

tour·na·ment (tur., toor′·nạ·mạnt) *n.* mock fight, common form of contest and entertainment in medieval times; any sports competition or championship. **tourney** *n.* a tournament [O.Fr. *tournoiement,* a turning].

tour·ni·quet (toor′·ni·ket) *n.* surgical device for arresting hemorrhage by compression of a blood vessel, as a bandage tightened by twisting [Fr. fr. *tourner,* to turn].

tous·le (tou′·zạl) *v.t.* to make untidy by pulling, as hair; to dishevel. *a.* untidy [conn. with *tussle*].

tout (tout) *v.i.* and *v.t.* to solicit business, etc.; to give a tip on a race horse; to praise highly *n.* one who pesters people to be customers; hanger-on at racing stables. **-er** *n.* [O.E. *totian,* to peep out].

tow (tō) *v.t.* to drag through water by rope or chain; to pull along; *n.* act of pulling; rope or chain used for towing; course fiber of hemp used in rope making. **-age** *n.* act of or charge for towing. **-(ing)-path** *n.* path alongside canal used by horses towing canal barge. **to take in tow,** to pull along; (*Fig.*) to take charge of [O.E. *togian,* to pull].

to·ward(s) (tōrd(z), tawrd(s)) *prep.* in direction of; near (of time); with respect to; regarding [O.E. *toweard,* future].

tow·el (tou′·ạl) *n.* cloth or paper for drying skin, or for domestic purposes.**-ing** *n.* soft fabric for making towels. [O.H. Ger. *twahan,* to wash].

tow·er (tou′·ẹr) *n.* lofty, round or square structure; *v.i.* to be lofty or very high; to soar; to excel. **-ed** *a.* having towers. **-ing** *a.* lofty; violent [L. *turris,* tower].

town (toun) *n.* collection of houses etc., larger than village; inhabitants of town; *a.* pert. to town. **— clerk** n. official in charge of administrative side of a town's affairs. **-ship** *n.* a division of a county **-speople** *n.* inhabitants of town [O.E. *tun,* an enclosure].

town·house (town·hous) *n.* a single-family house of two or three stories connected to a similar house by a common sidewall; a row house.

tox·i·col·o·gy (tȧk·sạ·kȧl′·ạ·ji·) *n.* science of poisons, their effects, nature, etc. **toxemia,** *n.* bloodpoisoning. **toxemic** *a.* **toxic, -al** *a.* poisonous. **toxically** *adv.* **toxicant** *a.* poisonous; *n.* poison. **toxicological** *a.* **toxicologist** *n.* **toxin** *n.* poison usually of bacterial origin [Gk. *toxikon,* poison].

toy (toi) *n.* child's plaything; bauble; trifle; *v.i.* to daily; to trifle [Dut. *tuig,* tool].

trace (trās) *n.* mark; footprint; vestige; minute quantity; remains; outline; barely perceptible sign; *v.t.* to copy or draw exactly on a superimposed sheet; to follow track or traces of; to work out step by step; *v.i.* to move. **-able** *a.* capable of being traced or detected; attributable. **-ableness** *n.* **-ably** *adv.* **-er** *n.* **tracing** *n.* traced copy of drawing. **tracing-paper** *n.* specially prepared, transparent paper for tracing design, etc. [L. *trahre,* to draw].

trace (trās) *n.* strap, rope, chain, by which horse pulls vehicle [L. *trahere,* draw].

tra·che·a (trā′·ki·a, trạ·kē′·ạ) *n.* windpipe between lungs and back of throat. *pl.* **tracheae, -l** *a.* **tracheotomy** *n.* (*Surg.*) operation by which opening is made in windpipe [Gk. *tracheia* (*artēria*), windpipe, and *trachēlos,* neck].

track (trak) *n.* mark left by something; footprint; pathway trodden out by usage; laid-out course for racing; (or railway) metal rails forming a permanent way; (of motor vehicles) distance between wheels on one axle; (of aircraft) actual direction along which airplane is passing over ground; wheelband of tank or tractor; (*Fig.*) evidence; trace; *v.t.* to follow trail or traces of; to make a track of footprints on; *v.i.* to follow a trail; to run in the same track (of wheels); to be in alignment. **-er** *n.* **— meet,** athletic contest in sports held on a track, racing, jumping, etc. [O.Fr. *trac,* track of horse].

tract (trakt) *n.* region of indefinite extent; continuous period of time; short treatise, esp. on practical religion. **-ability** *n.* quality or state of being tractable. **-able** *a.* docile; amenable to reason. **-ableness** *n.* **-ably** *adv.* **-ile** *a.* capable of being drawn out; (of metals) ductile. **-ility** *n.* **traction** (trak′·shạn) *n.* act of drawing or pulling; gripping power, as of a wheel on a road.**tractional** *a.* **traction-engine** *n.* locomotive, steam-driven, for haulage. **-ive** *a.* having power to haul heavy loads; pulling. **-or** *n.* motor vehicle for drawing agricultural machinery [L. *trahere, tractum,* to draw].

trade (trād) *n.* the business of buying and selling; commerce; barter; occupation, esp. in industry, shopkeeping, etc.; employees collectively in a particular trade; vocation; *v.t.* to carry on a trade; to engage in commerce; *v.t.* to exchange. **-mark** *n.* registered name or device on maker's goods, protected by law. **— name** *n.* name generally used for a manufactured article; official name of a firm. **-r** *n.* merchant; trading vessel. **— union** *n.* association of workmen; labor union. **— unionist** *n.* member of trade union. **— wind** *n.* a steadily blowing wind between the tropics and the equator. **trading** *n.* [O.E. *tredan*, to tread].

tra·di·tion (trạ.dish'·ạn) *n.* belief, custom, narrative, etc. transmitted by word of mouth from age to age; religious doctrine preserved orally from generation to generation. **-al, -ary** *a.* **-alism** *n.* **-alist** *n.* **-alistic** *a.* [L. *tradere*, to hand over].

tra·duce (trạ.dūs') *v.t.* to defame the character of; to calumniate. **-r** *n.* a slanderer [L. *traducere*, to lead along].

traf·fic (traf'·ik) *n.* commerce; business dealings; illegal buying and selling, as *drug traffic*; movement of people, vehicles, etc. to and fro, in streets; coming and going of ships, trains, aircraft, etc.; people, vehicles, etc. collectively in any given area; *v.i.* to carry on trade; to do business, esp. illegally; *pr.p.* **—king.** *pa.t.* and *pa.p.* **-ked. -ker** *n.* [Fr. *trafiquer*, to traffic].

trag·e·dy (traj'·ạ.di·) *n.* serious and dignified dramatic composition in prose or verse with unhappy ending; sad or calamitous event. **tragedian** (trạ.jēd'·i.an) *n.* actor in or writer of tragedy. **tragedienne** *n. fem.* **tragic, -al** *a.* pert. to tragedy; distressing; calamitous. **tragically** *adv.* **tragicalness** *n.* **tragic irony,** use in tragedy of words which convey a deeper meaning to audience than to speaker—form of *dramatic irony*. **tragicomedy** *n.* drama combining tragedy and comedy [Gk. *trafōidia*, goat-song (reason for name variously explained)].

trail (trāl) *v.t.* to draw along ground or through water; to follow track of; (*Colloq.*) to follow behind; to carry rifle in hand at an angle, with butt close to the ground; to make a track by treading the ground; *v.i.* to dangle loosely, touching ground; to grow to great length as plant; to drag one foot wearily after other; *n.* track followed by hunter; visible trace left by anything; scent of hunted animal; something drawn behind; part of guncarriage which rests on ground during firing. **-er** *n.* vehicle towed by another. **-less** *a.* [O.Fr. *trailer*, to tow a boat].

train (trān) *v.t.* to discipline; to instruct or educate; to submit person to arduous physical exercise, etc. for athletics; to teach animal to be obedient, to perform tricks, or compete in races; to cause plant to grow in certain way; to aim, as gun, before firing; *v.i.* to exercise body or mind to achieve high standard of efficiency; *n.* retinue; procession of people; line of cars drawn by locomotive on railway track; trailing folds of lady's evening dress; strong of pack animals; sequence of events, ideas, etc.; trail of gunpowder to lead fire to explosive charge. **-ed** *a.* **-ee** *n.* one who is training. **-er** *n.* **-ing** *n.* [O.Fr. *trahiner*, to drag].

trail oil (trā'·oil) *n.* oil extracted from blubber of whales [O.Dut. *traen*, whale oil].

traipse (trāps) *v.i.* (*Colloq.*) to walk aimlessly.

trait (trāt) *n.* distinguishing feature, esp. in character [Fr. *trait*, a feature].

trai·tor (trā'·tẹr) *n.* (*fem.* **traitress**) one who betrays person, country, or cause. **-ous** *a.* guilty of treachery; pert. to treason or to traitors. **-ously** *adv.* [L. *tradere*,, to hand over].

tra·jec·to·ry (trạ.jek'·tạ.ri·) *n.* curve of projectile in its flight through space [L. *trans*, across; *facere*, to throw].

tram·mel (tram'·ạl) *n.* long net for catching birds or fish; shackle for training horse to walk slowly; anything which impedes movement; *v.t.* to impede; to hinder; to confine. **-er,** *n.* [O.Fr. *tramail*, a net].

tramp (tramp) *v.t.* to tread heavily; to hike over or through; *v.i.* to go on a walking tour; to plod; to wander as vagrant; *n.* homeless vagrant; a long walk; cargo boat with no regular route. **-er** *n.* [M.E. *trampen*].

tram·ple (tram'·pl) *v.t.* to tread heavily underfoot; to oppress; to treat with contempt; *v.i.* to tread heavily; *n.* act of trampling. **-r** *n.* [freq. of *tramp*].

tram·po·line (tram'·pạ.lēn) *n.* can.. as springboard. **trampolinist** *n.* [It. *trampolino*, a springboard].

trance (trans) *n.* state of insensibility; a fit of complete mental absorption; (*Spiritualism*) condition in which medium is supposedly controlled by outside agency; semi-conscious condition [O.Fr. *transe*, a swoon].

tran·quil (trang'·kwil) *a.* calm; serene; undisturbed. **-ly** *adv.* **tranquillity** *n.* **-ness** [L. *tranquillus*].

trans- (tranz, trans) *pref.* meaning across, beyond, on the other side of [L. *trans*, across].

trans·act (tranz·, trans·akt') *v.t.* to carry through; to negotiate; *v.i.* to do (business). **-or** *n.* **-ion** *n.* act of transacting business; *pl.* records of, or lectures delivered to, a society. **-ional** *a.*

trans·al·pine (tranz·, trans·al'·pīn) *a.* north of Alps (as from Rome).

trans·at·lan·tic (trans·at·lan'·tik) *a.* across the Atlantic.

tran·scend (tran·send') *v.t.* to go beyond; to excel; to surpass. **-ence, -ency** *n.* quality of being transcendent; (*Theol.*) supremacy of God above all human limitations. **-ent** *a.* supreme in excellence; surpassing all; beyond all human knowledge. **-ently** *adv.* **-entness** *n.* **-ental** *a.* abstruse; supernatural; intuitive. **-entalism** *n.* **-entalist** *n.* **-entally** *adv.* [L. *trans*, across; *scandere*, to climb].

trans·con·ti·nen·tal (trans·kȧn·tạ.nen'·tạl) *a.* crossing a continent.

tran·scribe (tran·skrīb') *v.t.* to copy out; to write over again; to reproduce in longhand or typescript notes taken in shorthand; (*Mus.*) to rearrange composition for another instrument or voice. **-r** *n.* **transcript** *n.* that which is transcribed; written copy. **transcription** *n.* act of copying; transcript.

tran·sect (tran·sekt') *v.t.* to cut transversely.

tran·sept (tran'·sept) *n.* transverse portion of church at right angles to nave. **-al** *a.* **-ally** *adv.* [L. *septum*, enclosure].

trans·fer (trans·fur') *v.t.* to move from one place to another; to transport; to remove; to pass an impression from one surface to another, as in lithography, photography, etc.; to convey, as property, legally to another. *pr.p.* **-ring.** *pa.t.* and *pa.p.* **-red. transfer** (trans'·fẹr) *n.* removal from one place to another; ticket allowing change of vehicle during single trip without further charge; design to be, or which has been transferred. **-ability** *n.* **-able** *a.* capable of being transferred; valid for use by another. **-ence** *n.* the act of transferring; in psychoanalysis, redirection of emotion, when under, analytical examination, towards someone else. **thought transference** *n.* telepathy. **-or, -rer** *n.* [L. *trans*, across; *ferre*, to bear].

trans·fig·ure (trans·fig'·yẹr) *v.t.* to change outward appearance of; to make more beautiful or radiant. **-ment** *n.* **transfiguration** *n.* change of appearance.

trans·fix (trans·fiks′) *v.t.* to pierce through; to impale; to astound; to stun. **-ion** *n.*

trans·form (trans·fawrm′) *v.t.* to change form, nature, character, or disposition of; to transmute; *v.i.* to be changed. **-able** *a.* **-ation** *n.* change of outward appearance or inner nature. **-ative** *a.* **-er** *n.* one who or that which transforms; an electrical device for changing voltage up or down. **-ing** *a.* [L. *transformare,* to change].

trans·fuse (trans·fūz′) *v.t.* to pour, as liquid, from one receptacle into another; (*Med.*) to transfer blood from one person to vein of another. **-r** *n.* **transfusible** *a.* **transfusive** *a.* **transfusion** *n.* [L. *trans,* across; *fundere, fusum,* to pour].

trans·gress (tranz·, trans·gres′) *v.t.* to overstep a limit; to violate law or commandment; *v.i.* to offend by violating a law; to sin. **transgression** *n.* act of violating civil or moral law; offense. **-ive** *a.* **-ively** *adv.* **-or** *n.* [L. *transgressus,* to step across].

tran·sient (tran′·shạnt) *a.* fleeting; ephemeral; momentary; not permanent; **transience, transiency** *n.* **-ly** *adv.* **-ness** *n.* [L. *trans,* across; *ire,* to go].

trans·it (tran′·sit, ·zit) *n.* the act of conveying; conveyance; (*Astron.*) apparent passage of celestial body across meridian of a place, or of a smaller planet across disc of larger; a surveyor's instrument for measuring angles. **transition** *n.* passage from one place to another; change from one state or condition to another; (*Mus.*) passing directly from one key to another. **transitional, transitionary** *a.* **transitionally** *adv.* **transitive** *a.* having power of passing across; (*Gram.*) denoting verb, the action of which passes on to direct object, as *he broke his leg.* **-ively** *adv.* **-iveness** *n.* **-orily** *adv.* **-oriness** *n.* state of being transitory. **-ory** *a.* [L. *transitus,* a passing across].

trans·late (tranz·, trans·lāt′) *v.t.* to turn from one language into another; to change from one medium to another; to remove from one place to another; to appoint bishop to different see; to convey to heaven without death; *v.i.* to be capable of translation. **translatable** *a.* **translation** *n.* **translator** *n.* [L. *transferre, translatum,* to carry over].

trans·lit·er·ate (tranz·, trans·lit′·ạ·rāt) *v.t.* to write words of language in alphabetic symbols of another. **transliteration** *n.* **transliterator** *n.*

trans·lu·cent (tranz·, trans·lòò′·sạnt) *a.* semitransparent; diffusing light but not revealing definite contours of object, as *frosted* glass. **translucence, translucency** *n.* **-ly** *adv.* **translucid** *a.* translucent [L. *trans,* across; *lucere,* to shine].

trans·mi·grate (tranz·, trans·mī′·grāt) *v.i.* to pass from one country to another as permanent residence; (of soul) to pass at death into another body or state. **transmigration** *n.* **transmigrator** *n.* **transmigratory** *a.*

trans·mit (trans·mit′) *v.t.* to send from one person or place to another; to communicate; to pass on, as by heredity. *pr.p.* **-ting.** *pa.t.* and *pa.p.* **-ted. transmissibility** *n.* **transmissible, transmittible** *a.* capable of being transmitted. **transmission** *n.* act of transmitting; in motoring, gear by which power is transmitted from engine to axle; (*Radio.*) radiation of electromagnetic waves by transmitting station. **-tal** *n.* transmission. **-tance** *n.* **-ter** *n.* one who or that which transmits; apparatus for transmitting radio waves through space [L. *trans,* across; *mittere,* to send].

trans·mute (tranz·, trans·mūt′) *v.t.* to change from one nature, species, form, or substance into another. **transmutable** *a.* **transmutableness** *n.* **transmutability** *n.* **transmutably** *adv.* **transmutant** *a.* **transmutation** *n.* act or process of transforming; alteration, esp. biological transformation of one species into another; in alchemy, supposed change of baser metals into gold. **transmutative** *a.* **-r** *n.* [L. *trans,* across; *mutare,* to change].

tran·som (tran′·sạm) *n.* window over a doorway; lintel separating it from door; horizontal crossbar in window; transverse beam across sternpost of ship [L. *transtrum,* crossbeam].

trans·par·ent (trans·par′·ạnt) *a.* that may be distinctly seen through; pervious to light; clear; ingenuous; obvious. **transparence, transparency** *n.* **-ly** *adv.* **-ness** *n.* [L. *trans,* across; *parere,* to appear].

tran·spire (tran·spīr′) *v.t.* to emit through pores of skin; *v.i.* to exhale; (*Bot.*) to lose water by evaporation; to come out by degrees; to become known; loosely used as a synonym for *to happen.* **transpiration** *n.* **transpiratory** *a.* [L. *trans,* across; *spirare,* to breathe].

trans·plant (tranz·plant′) *v.t.* to remove and plant elsewhere; (*Surg.*) to graft live tissue from one part of body to another. **-able** *a.* **-ation** *n.* **-er** *n.*

trans·port (trans·pōrt′) *v.t.* to convey from one place to another; to banish, as criminal, to penal colony; to overwhelm emotionally. **transport** *n.* vehicles collectively used in conveyance of passengers; a troopship; passion; ecstasy. **-able** *a.* **-ability** *n.* **-er** *n.* **-ation** *n.* act or means of transporting from place to place; banishment, for felony. **-ted** *a.* [L. *trans,* across; *portare,* to carry].

trans·pose (trans·pōz′) *v.t.* to change respective place or order of two things; to alter order of words; (*Mus.*) to change key of a composition. **transposable** *a.* **transposal** *n.* change of order. **transposition** *n.* **transpositional** *a.* [L. *trans,* across; *ponere, positum,* to place].

tran·sub·stan·ti·ate (tran·sạb·stan′·shi′·āt) *v.t.* to change into another substance. **transubstantiation** *n.* doctrine held by R.C. Church that the 'whole substance' of the bread and wine in the Eucharist is, by reason of its consecration, changed into flesh and blood of Christ, the appearance only of the bread and wine remaining the same [L. *trans,* across; *substantia,* substance].

tran·sude (tran·sūd′) *v.i.* to pass through pores of substance [L. *trans,* across; *sudare,* to sweat].

trans·verse (trans·vurs′) *a.* lying in crosswise direction. **transversal** *n.* line which cuts across, two or more parallel lines. **-ly** *adv.* [L. *trans,* across; *vertere, versum,* to turn].

trap (trap) *n.* device, mechanical or otherwise, for catching animals, vermin, etc.; snare; U-shaped bend in pipe which, by being always full of water, prevents foul air or gas from escaping; stratagem; plot to catch person unawares; *v.t.* to catch in a trap, or by stratagem. *pr.p.* **-ping.** *pa.p., pa.t.* **-ped. -door** *n.* hinged door in floor or ceiling. **-per** *n.* [O.E. *traeppe*].

trap (trap) *n.* one of several dark-colored igneous rocks. **-pean, -pose, -py** *a.* [Scand. *trappa,* stairs].

trap (trap) *pl.* (*Colloq.*) one's belongings, luggage, etc.; *v.t.* to adorn. *pr.p.* **-ping.** *pa.p., pa.t.* **-ped. -pings** *n.pl.* ornaments, gay coverings [Fr. *drap,* cloth].

tra·pe·zi·um (trạ·pē′·zi·ạm) *n.* quadrilateral with no parallel sides; (*Anat.*) one of wrist bones *pl.s.* **trapezia. trapeze** *n.* apparatus comprising horizontal crossbar swing for gymnastics, acrobatic exhibitions, etc. **trapezoid** *n.* quadrilateral with only two of its sides parallel. **trapezoidal** *a.* [Gk. *trapezion,* a little table].

trash (trash) *v.t.* to lop off, as branches, leaves, etc.; *n.* worthless refuse; rubbish; loppings of trees, bruised sugar canes, etc. **-ily** *adv.* **-iness** *n.* **-y** *a.* worthless; cheap; shoddy [prob. Scand. *tros.* twigs for fuel].

trass (tras) *n.* volcanic material used in making cement [Dut. *tras*].

trau·ma (traw′·mạ) *n.* (*Med.*) bodily injury caused by violence; emotional shock (psychic trauma) with a lasting effect. *pl.* **-ta. -tic** *a.* [Gk. *trauma,* a wound].

trav·ail (trav′·āl) *n.* painful, arduous labor; pains of childbirth; *v.i.* (*Arch.*) to labor with difficulty; to suffer pangs of childbirth [Fr. *travail,* labor].

trave (trāv) *n.* beam; frame in blacksmith's shop to keep horse steady [L. *trabs,* beam].

trav·el (trav′·ạl) *v.t.* to journey over; to pass; *v.i.* to move; to journey on foot or in a vehicle; to tour, esp. abroad. *n.* act of traveling; journey; touring, esp. abroad; (*Mach.*) distance a component is permitted to move; *pl.* prolonged journey, esp. abroad; book describing traveler's experiences and observations. **-ed** *a.* **-er** *n.* **-er's check,** check issued by bank, express company, etc. which may be cashed by anyone in whose presence it is endorsed. **-ing** *a.* **-ogue** *n.* travel lecture illustrated by slides, film, etc.; geographical film [a form of *travail*].

tra·verse (trav′·ẹrs) *a.* lying across; built crosswise; anything set across; a partition; (*Archit.*) barrier, movable screen, or curtain; gallery across church; zigzag course of a ship; lateral movement; *v.t.* to cross; to thwart; to obstruct; to survey across a plot of ground; to rake with gun fire from end to end; to pivot laterally; to discuss, as topic, from every angle; to deny formally, in pleading at law; *v.i.* to turn, as on pivot; to move sideways. **traversable** *a.* **-r** *n.* [L. *trans,* across; *vertere, versum,* to turn].

trav·es·ty (trav′·is·ti·) *n.* burlesque imitation of a work; parody; *v.t.* to make a burlesque of; to caricature [Fr. *travestir,* to disguise].

trawl (trawl) *v.t.* to catch fish with a trawl; *v.i.* to drag with a trawl; *n.* a strong fishing net, shaped like a large bag with one end open. **-er** *n.* who fishes with a trawl; fishing vessel. **-ing** *n.* [O.Fr. *trauler,* to drag].

tray (trā) *n.* flat, shallow, rimmed vessel used for carrying dishes, food, etc. [O.E. *trog,* a trough].

treach·er·y (trech′·ẹr·i·) *n.* violation of allegiance or faith; treason; perfidy. **treacherous** *a.* **treacherously** *adv.* [O.Fr. *trechier,* to deceive].

tread (tred) *v.i.* to walk; to move with stately or measured step; (of fowls) to copulate; to crush; *v.t.* to step or walk one; to crush with foot; to oppress; to operate with foot, as treadle. *pa.t.* **trod.** *pa.p.* **trod** or **trodden.** *n.* act of stepping; pace; that which one steps on, as surface of horizontal step of flight of stairs; sole of boot or shoe; part of a rubber tire in contact with ground. **-ing** *n.* **-le,** *n.* part of machine operated by foot pressure as sewing machine, etc.; pedal; *v.i.* to work treadle. **-ler** *n.* **-mill** *n.* mill worked by persons or animals treading upon steps on periphery of a wheel; drudgery [O.E. *tredan,* to tread].

trea·son (trē′·zn) *n.* disloyalty to country; act of betrayal. **-able** *a.* treason. **-ableness** *n.* **-ably** *adv.* **-ous** *a.* [O.Fr. *traison,* betrayal].

treas·ure (trezh′·ẹr) *n.* accumulated wealth; hoard of valuables; that which has great worth; *v.t.* to hoard; to value; to cherish, as friendship. **— chest** *n.* box for storing valuables. **-r** *n.* person appointed to take charge of funds of society, church, club, etc. **-ship** *n.* **—trove** *n.* any money, bullion, treasure, etc., of unknown ownership, which one finds. **treasury** *n.* place where treasure, hoarded wealth, or public funds are deposited; storehouse of facts and information; anthology. **Treasury** *n.* government department which controls management of public revenues. **treasury note** *n.* currency note isued by the United States Treasury [Fr. *trésor,* treasure].

treat (trēt) *v.t.* to entertain with food or drink; to pay for another's entertainment or refreshment; to behave towards; to apply a remedy to; to subject, as a substance, to chemical experiment; to consider as a topic for discussion; to discourse on; *v.i.* to discourse; to come to terms of agreement, as between nations; to give entertainment; *n.* entertainment given as a celebration or expression of regard; (*Colloq.*) something that gives special pleasure; one's turn to pay for another's entertainment. **-er** *n.* **-ing** *n.* act of standing treat. **-ise** *n.* dissertation on particular theme. **-ment** *n.* act or mode of treating person, subject, artistic work, etc.; method of counteracting disease or of applying remedy for injury. **-y** *n.* a negotiated agreement betwen states; a pact [L. *tracture,* to handle].

tre·ble (treb′·l) *a.* threefold; triple; (*Mus.*) playing or singing highest part; *n.* highest part; *n.* highest of four principal parts in music; soprano part or voice; *v.t.* to multiply by three; *v.i.* to become three times as much. **trebly** *adv.* [L. *triplus*].

tree (trē) perennial plant, having trunk, bole, or woody stem with branches; any plant resembling form of tree; (*Arch.*) cross of Christ; *v.t.* to chase up a tree; to corner. **-less** *a.* **-lessness** *n.* **-top** *n.* uppermost branches of tree. **family tree,** genealogical table of ancestry [O.E. *treow,* tree].

tre·foil (trē′·foil) *n.* plant of genus *Trifolium,* with leaves comprising three leaflets; clover; (*Archit.*) ornament of three cusps in circle resembling three-leaved clover [L. *tres,* three; *folium,* leaf].

trek (trek) *v.i.* to migrate; *pr.p.* **-king.** *pa.p., pa.t.* **-ked.** *n.* journey by wagon; mass-migration. **-ker** *n.* [Dut. *trekken,* to draw].

trel·lis (trel′·is) *n.* light-weight lattice structure esp. as frame for climbing plants. **-ed** *a.* **-work** *n.* lattice work [L. *trilix,* three-ply].

trem·ble (trem′·bl) *v.i.* to shake involuntarily to quivẹr; to quake; *n.* involuntary shaking; quiver; tremor. **-r** *n.* **trembling** *n.* **trembling** *adv.* **trembly** *a.* shaky; **tremulant, tremulous** *a.* quivering; quaking; fearful. **tremulously** *adv.* **tremulousness** *n.* [L. *tremere,* to shake].

tre·men·dous (tri·men′·dạs) *a.* awe-inspiring; formidable; (*Colloq.*) great. **-ly** *adv.* **-ness** *n.* [L. *tremere,* to tremble].

tre·mo·lan·do (trem·ạ·lán′·dō) *a.* (*Mus.*) tremulous. **tremolo** *n.* quivering of singing voice; device on organ to produce similar sound. [It.].

trem·or (trem′·ẹr) *n.* involuntary quiver; a nervous thrill; shaking, as caused by earthquake. **-less** *a.* steady [L.].

trem·u·lous See **tremble.**

trench (trench) *v.t.* to cut or dig, as a ditch; to turn over soil by digging deeply; to fortify with ditch using earth dug out for rampart; *v.i.* to encroach; n. ditch; deep ditch to protect soldiers from enemy fire. **-ancy** *n.* quality of being trenchant. **-ant** *a.* penetrating; keen; clear-cut; **— coat** *n.* waterproof coat. **-ing** *n.* [O.Fr. *trenchier,* to cut].

trench·er (tren′·chẹr) *n.* (*Arch.*) wooden plate

for holding food [O.Fr. *trenchoir*, platter].

trend (trend) *v.i.* to stretch in a certain direction; *n.* inclination; tendency; general direction [O.E. *trendln*, to make round].

tre·pan (tri·pan′) *n.* heavy tool for boring shafts; (*Surg.*) obsolete cylindrical saw (improved version called **trephine** (tri·fin′) *v.t.* to cut disks out of metal plates, etc.; to operate with trepan. *pr.p.* **-ning.** *pa.p., pa.t.* **-ned. -ation, -ning** *n.* [Gk. *trupanon*, borer].

trep·id (trep′·id) *a.* quaking. **-ation** *n.* involuntary trembling; alarm; fluster [L. *trepidus*].

tres·pass (tres′·pas, pas) *v.i.* to cross boundary line of another's property unlawfully; to intrude; to encroach; to violate moral law; *n.* **-er** *n.* [L. *trans*, across; *passus*, a step]

tress (tres) *n.* long lock, curl, braid or strand of hair; ringlet. **-ed** *a.* [O.Fr. *tresse*].

tres·tle (tres′·l) *n.* frame consisting of two pairs of braced legs fixed underneath horizontal bar, used as support; similar construction supporting a bridge [O.Fr. *trested*, a crossbeam].

tri- (trī) *prefix* meaning three, thrice, threefold [L. *tres*, Gk. *treis*, *tria*, three].

tri·ad (trī′·ad) *n.* union of three; (*Chem.*) trivalent atom; (*Mus.*) the common chord, one of three notes; poem with triple grouping, common in Celtic literature. **-ic** *a.* **-ist** *n.* writer of triads [Gk. *trias*, group of three].

tri·al (trīal) *n.* act of trying, testing, or proving properties of anything; experimental examination; affliction; judicial examination in law court of accused person [fr. *try*].

tri·an·gle (trī′·ang·gl) *n.* (*Math.*) figure bounded by three lines and containing three angles; anything shaped like a triangle; (*Mus.*) small percussion instrument consisting of a bar of steel bent in shape of triangle and struck with small steel rod. **-d** *a.* **triangular** *a.* **triangularity** *n.* **triangularly** *adv.*

tri·ar·chy (trī′·ár·ki·) *n.* government by three persons; a state so governed.

tri·a·tom·ic (trī·a·tám′·ik) *a.* consisting of three atoms; having valency of three.

tribe (trīb) *n.* family, race, or succession of generations descending from same progenitor; nation of barbarian clans each under one leader; group of plants or animals within which members reveal common characteristics; (*Colloq.*) very large family. **tribal** *a.* **tribalism** *n.* tribal feeling; tribal life. **tribally** *adv.* **-sman** *n.* one of a tribe [L. *tribus*, one of *three* divisions of Roman people].

trib·u·la·tion (trib·ya·lā′·shan) *n.* severe affliction; prolonged suffering, esp. of mind [L. *tribulum*, instrument for threshing corn].

trib·une (trib′·ūn) *n.* in ancient Rome, magistrate chosen by the people to defend their rights; champion of the masses; a raised platform or pulpit. **tribunal** *n.* bench on which judge or magistrates sit; court of justice. **tribunate, tribuneship** *n;* office or functions of tribune [L. *tribus*, a tribe].

tri·bute (trib′·ūt) *n.* personal testimony to achievements or qualities of another; prearranged payment made at stated times by one state to another as price of peace and protection; tax. **tributarily** *adv.* **tributary** *a.* paying tribute; subordinate; contributory; (of river) flowing into main river; *n.* one who pays tribute; stream flowing into larger river [L. *tribuere*, to assign].

trice (trīs) *n.* moment; a very short time [O.Dut. *trisen*, to hoist].

tri·ceps (trī′·seps) *a.* three-headed; *n.* three-headed muscle as at back of upper arm [L. *tres*, three; *caput*, the head].

trich·i·no·sis (trik·a·nō′·sis) *n.* disease due to the presence of the nematode worm **trichina** in the intestines and muscular tissue [Gk. *trichinos*, hair].

tri·cho- *pref.* fr. Gk. *thrix*, *trichos*, hair.

tri·chol·o·gy (tri·kál′·a·ji·) *n.* study of hair and diseases affecting it.

tri·cho·sis (tri·kō′·sis) *n.* any disease affecting the hair.

tri·chot·o·mous (trī·kát′·a·mas) *a.* divided into three or threes. **trichotomy** *n.* [Gk. *tricha*, in three; *tomē*, a cutting].

trick (trik) *n.* artifice or stratagem designed to deceive; conjurer's sleight of hand; prank for mischief, or to annoy; mannerism; dexterity; cards played out in one round, and taken by player with winning card; spell at the helm of ship; *v.t.* to deceive; to hoax; to mystify; to dress, trim, or decorate. **-er** *n.* **-ery** *n.* practice of playing tricks; fraud. **-ily** *adv.* **-iness** *n.* **-sy** *a.* tricky; ingenious; neat. **-ster,** *n.* cheat; swindler. **-y** *a.* full of tricks; crafty; requiring great dexterity; intricate [O.Fr. *tricher*, to beguile].

trick·le (trik′·l) *v.i.* to flow gently in a slow, thin stream; to move slowly, one by one; *n.* thin flow of liquid; slow movement of anything.

tri·col·or (trī′·kul·er) *n.* national flag of three colors, esp. French national flag. **-ed** *a.*

tri·corn (trī′·kawrn) *a.* having three horns, or points; *n.* three-cornered hat [L. *tricornis*].

tri·cot (trē·cot) *n.* fabric of wool; machine-made knitwear fabric. **-tine** *n.* a ribbed, fine woolen fabric, machine-made [Fr. *tricot*, knitting].

tri·cus·pid (trī·kus′·pid) *a.* having three cusps or points, as certain teeth, or a valve of the right ventricle of the heart.

tri·cy·cle (trī′·si·kl) *n.* three-wheeled cycle, esp. for children's use; *v.t.* to ride a tricycle. **tricyclist** *n.* [Gk. *treis*, three; *kuklos*, a circle].

tri·dent (trī′·dant) *n.* three-pronged scepter, symbol of Neptune; any three-pronged instrument, such as fish-spear. **-ate,** *a.* having three prongs [L. *tres*, three; *dens*, a tooth].

tried See **try.**

tri·en·ni·al (trī·en′·i·al) *a.* lasting for three years; happening once every three years. **-ly** *adv.* [L. *tres*, three; *annus*, a year].

tri·fle (trī′·fl) *n.* anything of little value or importance; paltry amount; pewter; *v.i.* to speak or act lightly; to be facetious; to toy, or waste time. **-r** *n.* **trifling** *a.* trivial.**trifling, -ly** *adv.* [O.Fr. *trufle*, mockery].

tri·form (trī′·fawm) *a.* having a triple form. Also**-ed. -ity** *n.*

tri·fur·cate (trī·fer′·kāt) *a.* having three branches **trifurcation** *n.* [L. *tres*, three; *furca*, a fork].

trig (trig) *a.* trim; neat; strong [O.N. *tryggr*, firm].

trig·ger (trig′·er) *n.* catch of firearm which, when pulled, releases hammer of lock [Dut. *trkken*, to pull].

tri·glyph (trī′·glif) *n.* grooved rectangular block in Doric frieze, repeated at equal intervals. **-ic, -al** *a.* [Gk. *treis*, three; *gluphein*, to carve].

trig·o·nom·e·try (trig·a·nam′·at·ri·) *n.* branch of mathematics which deals with relations between sides and angles of triangle. **trigonometer** *n.* instrument for solving plane right-angled triangles by inspection. **trigonometric, -al** *a.* **trigonometrically** *adv.* [Gk. *trigonon*, a triangle; *metron*, a measure].

tri·he·dral (trī·hē′·dral) *a.* (*Math.*) having three sides or faces. **trihedron** *n.* [Gk. *treis*, three; *hedra*, seat].

tri·lat·er·al (trī·lat′·er·al) *a.* having three sides; arranged by three parties, as *trilateral pact.* **-ly** *adv.*

tri·lin·e·ar (trī·lin′·ē·er) *a.* consisting of three lines [L. *tres*, three; *linea*, a line].

tri·lin·gual (trī·ling′·gwal) *a.* expressed in three languages; speaking three languages.

trill (tril) *v.t.* and *v.i.* to sing or play (instrument) with vibratory quality; to pronounce, as letter 'r'; *n.* shake or vibration of voice, in singing; consonant, such as 'r' pronounced with trill [It. *trillare*, to shake].

tril·lion (tril′·yạn) *n.* million million million (British) i.e. 1 with 18 ciphers; a million million (U.S.) i.e. 1 with 12 ciphers.

tril·o·gy (tril′·ạ·ji·) *n.* group of three plays, novels, etc. with common theme, or common central character [Gk. *treis*, three; *logos*, a speech or discourse].

trim (trim) *a.* (*compar.*) **-mer.** (*superl.*) neat; in good order; to dress; to decorate, as hat; to clip shorter; to supply with oil and adjust wick, as lamp; (*Naut.*) to arrange sails according to wind direction; *v.i.* to balance; to fluctuate between two parties, so as to appear to favor each. *pr.p.* **-ming.** *pa.t.* and *pa.p.* **-med.** *n.* dress; decoration; order; anything trimmed off; **-ly** *adv.* **-mer** *n.* one who trims; instrument for clipping; **-ming** *n.* that which trims, edges, or decorates; a beating; **-ness** *n.* neatness; compactness; readiness for use [O.E. *trymian*, to strengthen].

trim·e·ter (trim′·ạ·tẹr) *n.* verse containing three measures; *a.* **trimetric, -al** *a.*

tri·nal (trī′·nạl) *a.* threefold; of three, as *trinal unity*, three in one. **trinary** *a.* consisting of three parts; ternary. **trine** *a.* threefold; *n.* group of three; aspect of two planets distant from each other 120°, or one-third of the zodiac [L. *trinus*]...

tri·ni·tro·tol·u·ene (trī·nī·trō·tál′·yoo·ēn) *n.* (*abbrev.* **T.N.T.**) high explosive.

Trin·i·ty (trin′·ạ·ti·) *n.* union of one Godhead of Father, Son, and Holy Ghost; (*l.c.*) any combination of three people or things as one. **Trinitarian** *a.* pert. to doctrine of the Trinity; *n.* one who believes in this doctrine. **Trinitarianism** *n.* [L. *trinitas*, three].

trin·ket (tring′·kit) *n.* small ornament worn as ring, brooch, etc.; ornament of little value. **-ry** *n.* [prob. fr. M.E. *trenket*, small knife].

tri·no·mi·al (trī·nō′·mi·ạl) *a.* (*Bot. Zool.*) having three names as of *order, species* and *subspecies;* (*Math.*) consisting of three terms connected by sign + or —; *n.* a trinomial quantity [L. *tres*, three; *omen*, a name].

tri·o (trē′·ō) *n.* group of three persons or things; (*Mus.*) composition arranged for three voices, or instruments. [It. fr. L. *tres*, three].

tri·ode (trī′·ōd) *n.* (*Radio*) three-electrode thermionic valve [Gk. *treis*, three; *hodos*, a way].

tri·o·let (trī′·ō·lit) *n.* a short poem of eight lines with rhyme pattern abaaabab [Fr. *triolet*, a little trio].

tri·ox·ide (trī·ạk′·sīd) *n.* (*Chem.*) compound comprising three atoms of oxygen with some other element [*tri-*, and *oxide*].

trip (trip) *v.t.* to cause to stumble; to frustrate; to loose, as ship's anchor; to start up, as machine, by releasing clutch; *v.i.* to walk or dance lightly; to stumble over an obstacle; to make a false step; (with *up*) to detect an error in another's statement. *pr.p.* **-ping.** *pa.p.* **-ped.** *n.* quick, light step; a journey; false step; indiscretion in speech or conduct. **-per** *n.* one who trips; device to start a mechanism. **-ping** *a.* light-footed. **-pingly** *adv.* [M.E. *trippen*, to tread on].

tri·par·tite (trī·pár′·tīt) *a.* divided into three parts; having three corresponding parts; arranged or agreed to, by three parties or nations, as *tripartite pact.* **tripartition** *n.*

tripe (trīp) *n.* large stomach of ruminating animal, prepared for food; (*Slang*) rubbish.

triph·thong (trif′·thawng) *n.* a syllable containing three vowels together as in *beauty* [Gk. *treis*, three; *phthongos*, a sound].

tri·ple (trip′·l) *a.* consisting of three united; three times repeated; *v.t.* to make three times as much or as many; *v.i.* to become trebled. **-crown** *n.* papal tira. **triplet** *n.* three of a kind; three consecutive verses rhyming together; (*Mus.*) three notes played in the time of two; one of three children born at a birth. **triplex** *a.* threefold; *n.* (*Mus.*) triple time. **triplicate** *a.* threefold; made three times as much; *n.* third copy corresponding exactly to two others; *v.t.* to treble; to make three copies of. **triplication** *n.* [L. *triplex*, threefold].

tri·pod (trī′·pȧd) *n.* stool, vessel, etc. on three-legged support; three-legged, folding stand for for a camera, etc.; *a.* having three legs. **tri-tripodal, tripodic** *a.* [Gk. *treis*, three; *pous*, a foot].

trip·o·li (trip′·ạ·li·) *n.* mineral substance used for polishing metals, stones, etc.; originally brought from *Tripoli.*

trip·tych (trip′·tik) *n.* writing tablet in three parts; altarpiece or picture in three panels, [Gk. *treis*, three; *plux*, *pluchos*, a fold].

tri·sect (trī·sekt′) *v.t.* to divide into three equal parts, as a line or angle. **-ion** *n.*

triste (trēst) *a.* sad; melancholy [Fr.].

tri·sul·fide (trī·sul′·fīd) *n.* (*Chem.*) chemical compound containing three sulfur atoms.

tri·syl·la·ble (tri·sil′·ạ·bl) *n.* word of three syllables. **trisyllabic, -al** *a.* **trisyllabically** *adv.* [Gk. *treis*, three; *sullabē*, syllable].

trite (trīt) *a.* made stale by use; hackneyed; banal. **-ly** *adv.* **-ness** *n.*[L.*tritus*, rubbed away].

Tri·ton (trī′·tạn) *n.* (*Gk. Myth.*) god of the sea. **triton** *n.* (*Zool.*) marine mollusk with spiral shell.

trit·u·rate (trich′·ạ·rāt) *v.t.* to rub or grind to a very fine powder. **triturable** *a.* **trituration** *n.* [L. *triturare*, to pulverize].

tri·umph (trī′·ạmf) *n.* victory; conquest; rejoicing; great achievement; *v.i.* to celebrate victory with great pomp and ceremony; to achieve success; to prevail; to exult. **-al** *a.* pert. to triumph; expressing joy for success. **-antly** *adv.* [L. *triumphus*, a solemn procession].

tri·um·vir (trī·um′·vẹr) *n.* one of three men sharing governing power in ancient Rome. *pl.* **-i, -s. -al** *a.* **-ate** *n.* coalition of three men in office or authority [L. *tres*, three; *vir*, a man].

tri·une (trī′·ūn) *a.* three in one. **triunity** *n.* [L. *tres*, three; *unus*, one].

tri·va·lent (trī′·vā·lạnt) *a.* (*Chem.*) having valency of three; capable of combining with or replacing three atoms of hydrogen. **trivalence** *n.*

triv·et (triv′·it) *n.* three-legged stool or support; iron tripod for standing a pot or kettle over fire; short-legged metal rack to put under a hot platter, etc. [L. *tres*, three; *pes*, foot].

triv·i·al (triv′·i·ạl) *a.* paltry; of little consequence. **-ism** *n.* **triviality** *n.pl.* trifles; insignificant matters. **-ly** *adv.* **-ness** *n.* [L. *trivalis*, pert. to crossroads, hence commonplace].

tro·che (trō′·kē) *n.* medicinal lozenge [Gk. *trochos*, pill].

tro·chee (trō′·kē) *n.* in English prosody, metrical foot of two syllables, first one accented, as *ho′·ly.* **trochaic** *n.* trochaic foot or verse. **trochaic, -al** *a.* [Gk. *trochaios*, running].

trod, trodden *pa.t., pa.p.* of **tread.**

trog·lo·dyte (trág′·lạ·dīt) *n.* cave dweller; a hermit. [Gk. *troglē*, a cave; *duein*, to enter].

troi·ka (troi′·kạ) *n.* Russian carriage or sledge drawn by three horses abreast; triunal.

Tro·jan (trō′·jạn) *a.* pert. to ancient Troy; *n.* inhabitant of Troy.

troll (trōl) *n.* (*Scand. Myth*) a giant; mischievous hump-backed cave-dwelling dwarf.

troll (trōl) *v.t.* and *v.i.* to roll; to sing in a rich, rolling voice; to sing in succession the parts of a round; to fish with baited line trailing behind boat; *n.* a round or catch; act of trolling. **-er** *n.*

trol·ley (trál′·i·) *n.* form of truck, body of

which can be tilted over; device to connect electric streetcar with wires. **— bus,** passenger bus not operating on rails but drawing powers from overhead wires. **— car** *n.* electric streetcar.

trol·lop (tràl′·ạp) *n.* a slattern; a prostitute; **-y** *a.* slovenly; tawdry [prob. fr. *troll*].

trom·bone (tràm′·bōn) *n.* deep-toned brass musical instrument. **trombonist** *n.* [It. *tromba*, a trumpet].

troop (tròòp) *n.* large assembly of people; body of cavalry; *pl.* soldiers collectively; an army; *v.i.* to flock; to gather in a crowd. **-er** *n.* mounted policeman; state policeman; horse cavalryman. **-ship** *n.* vessel for transporting soldiers [Fr. *troupe*].

trope (trōp) *n.* word or phrase used metaphorically. **tropical** *a.* figurative. **tropically** *adv.* **tropist** *n.* one who uses figurative language. **tropological, -al** *a.* containing figures of speech. **tropology** *n.* figurative language; study of such language; a metaphorical interpretation of the Bible [Gk. *tropos*, a turn].

troph·ic, -al (tràf′·ik, -ạl) *a.* pert. to nutrition. **trophi** *n.pl.* masticating organs of insect.. **trophology** *n.* the scientific study of nutrition [Gk. *trophē*, feeding].

tro·phy (trō′·fi·) *n.* orig. pile of arms taken from vanquished enemy; memorial of victory; memento; mural decoration, as stag's antlers; prize, esp. for sports, etc. [Gk. *tropaion*].

trop·ic (tràp′·ik) *n.* one of the two circles of celestial sphere, situated 23½° N. (*Tropic of Cancer*) and 23½° S. (*Tropic of Capricorn*) of equator, and marking the point reached by the sun at its greatest declination north and south; one of the two corresponding parallels of latitude on terrestrial globe. *pl.* region (*torrid zone*) between tropics of Cancer and Capricorn. **tropic, -al** *a.* pert. to or within tropics; (of climate) very hot. **-ally** *adv.* [Gk. *tropos*, a turn].

trop·o·sphere (trpōp′·ạ·sfir) *n.* lower layer of atmosphere below stratosphere [Gk. *tropos*, a turn; *sphaira*, sphere].

trop·po (tràp′·ō) *adv.* (*Mus.*) too much. **non troppo,** moderately [It.].

trot (tràt) *v.i.* (of horse) to move at sharp pace; (of person) to move along fast; *v.t.* to cause to trot. *pr.p.* **-ting.** *pa.p.*, *pa.t.* **-ted.** *n.* brisk pace of horse; quick walk. **-ter** *n.* one who trots; horse which trots; foot of an animal [O.Fr. *troter*].

troth (trawth, tràth, trōth) *n.* (*Arch*). truth; fidelity. **to plight one's troth,** to become engaged to be married [O.E. *treowth*, truth].

trou·ba·dour (tròò′·bạ·dōr) *n.* one of school of Provençal poets between 11th and 13th cents., whose poems were devoted to lyrical and amatory subjects [Prov. *trobador*, poet].

trou·ble (trub′·l) *v.t.* to stir up; to vex; to distress; to bother; *v.i.* to take pains; to feel anxiety; *n.* disturbance; agitation of mind; unrest; ailment; inconvenience. **-r** *n.* **-some** *a.* difficult; vexatious; irksome. **-somely** *adv.* **-someness** *n.* **—shooter** *n.*, expert in discovering and eliminating trouble [L. *turbulare*, to disturb].

trough (trawf) *n.* long, open vessel for water or fodder for animals; channel; depression, as between waves; part of cyclone where atmospheric pressure is lowest [O.E. *trog*, hollow vessel of wood].

trounce (trouns) *v.t.* to punish or beat severely; (*Colloq.*) to defeat completely [Fr. *tronce*, a stump].

troupe (tròòp) *n.* company or troop, esp. of actors, acrobats, etc. **-r** *n.* member of a theatrical troupe [Fr.].

trou·sers (trou′·zẹrz) *n.pl.* a man's two-legged outer garment extending from waist to ankles; slacks. **trousered** *a.* wearing trousers. **trouserless** *a.* [O.Fr. *trousses*, breeches].

trous·seau (tròò′·sō) *n.* bride's outfit of clothes, etc. *pl.* **trousseaux** or **trousseaus** [Fr.]

trout (trout) *n.* fish resembling salmon [O.E. *truht*, trout].

trow·el (trou′·ạl) *n.* mason's tool for spreading and dressing mortar; garden tool for scooping out earth, plants, etc.; *v.t.* to smooth or lift with trowel [L. *trulla*, a small ladle].

troy weight (troi′·wāt) *n.* system of weight for precious metals and gems [fr. *Troyes*, in France].

tru·ant (tròò′·ạnt) *n.* one who shirks his duty; pupil who absents himself from school; *a.* wandering from duty; idle; *v.i.* to play truant. **truancy** *n.* [O.Fr. *truant*, vagrant].

truce (tròòs) *n.* temporary cessation of hostilities; armistice; lull [O.E. *treow*, faith].

truck (truk) *v.t.* to exchange; to barter; *v.i.* to deal with by exchange; *n.* exchange of commodities; (*Colloq.*) dealings; (*Colloq.*) rubbish; junk; (*U.S.*) garden produce. **-er** *n.* **— farm** *n.* a small farm on which vegetables are grown for market [Fr. *troquer*, to truck].

truck (truk) *n.* horsedrawn or automotive vehicle for hauling. small wooden wheel; porter's barrow for heavy luggage. **-age** *n.* transport by trucks; cost of such transport. **-le** *n.* small wheel or castor; truckle bed; *v.i.* to fawn on. **— bed** *n.* low bed on castors which may be pushed beneath another [Gk. *trochos*, a wheel].

truc·u·lent (truk′·yạ·lạnt) *a.* fierce; aggressive; ruthless. **truculence, truculency** *n.* **-ly** *adv.* [L. *trux*, fierce].

trudge (truj) *v.t.* to go on foot; to plod along; *n.* wearisome walk.

trudg·en (truj′·ạn) *n.* fast racing stroke in swimming. [fr. *J. Trudgen*, English swimmer].

true (tròò) *a.* conformable with fact; genuine; exact; loyal; trustworthy; *v.t.* to adjust accurately, as machine; to straighten; *adv.* truly conforming to type (of plants, etc.). **—blue** *a.* unchanging; stanch; true.**-ness** *n.* **truism** *n.* self-evident truth. **truly** *adv.* [O.E. *treowe*, true].

truf·fle (truf′·l) *n.* tuber-shaped edible underground fungus with unique flavor [prob. L. *tuber*, swelling, truffle].

tru·ism See **true.**

trull (trul) *n.* a trollop [var. of *troll*].

trump (trump) *n.* (*Arch.*) trumpet; its sound. **-et** *n.* wind instrument of brass, consisting of long tube bent twice on itself, ending in wide bell-shaped mouth, and having finger stops; powerful reed stop of pipe organ with full trumpet-like sound; call of the elephant; *v.t.* to proclaim by trumpet; to bellow; (*Fig.*) to praise loudly; *v.i.* to play on trumpet; (of elephant) to utter characteristic cry through trunk. **-eter** *n.* one who plays on trumpet; kind of domestic pigeon; long-necked S. American bird, resembling crane; wild swan of N. America. **-eting** *n.* [Fr. *trompe*].

trump (trump) *n.* one of the suit of cards, declared by cutting, dealing, or bidding which takes any card of another suit; (*Colloq.*) excellent fellow; *v.t.* and *v.i.* to play trump card; to take a trick with trump. [Fr. *triomphe*, triumph, game of cards].

trump (trump) *v.t.* to fabricate; to deceive. **-ery** *n.* anything showy but of little value; rubbish [Fr. *tromper*, to deceive].

trun·cate (trung′·kāt) *v.t.* to cut off; to lop; to maim. **truncate, -d, truncation** *a.* appearing as if cut off at tip; blunt [L. *truncare*].

trun·dle (trun′·dl) *n.* anything round or capable of being rolled; a small wheel or castor; act of rolilng; *v.t.* to roll on little wheels; to bowl, as child's hoop, barrel, etc. *v.i.* to roll. **— bed** *n.* a truckle bed [O.E. *trendel*, a wheel].

trunk (trungk) *n.* stem of tree, as distinct

from branches and roots; body minus head and limbs; torso; shaft of column; main part of anything; main lines of railway, bus, or telephone system; large box of metal, hide, etc., with hinged lid, for storage or as luggage; proboscis of elephant; *pl.* short, tight-fitting pants, esp. for swimming.

truss (trus) *n.* bundle; as hay or straw; tuft of flowers on top of a long stem; framework of beams or girders constructed to bear heavy loads; (*Med.*) appliance to keep hernia in place; (*Naut.*) iron clamp fixing lower yards to masts; *v.t.* to bind or pack close; to support, as a roof, or bridge span, with truss; to skewer, as fowl, before cooking [Fr. *trousse*].

trust (trust) *n.* confidence; reliance; implicit faith; moral responsibility; property used for benefit of another; combine of business firms in which shareholders turn over stock to board of trustees; *v.t.* to rely upon; to have implicit faith in; to give credit; to entrust; to hope; to believe; *v.i.* to be confident or to confide in; *a.* held in trust. **-ee** *n.* person or group which manages the business affairs of another; **-eeship** *n.* **-er** *n.* **-ful** *a.* **-fully** *adv.* **-fulness** *n.* **-ily** *adv.* **-iness** *n.* quality of being trusty. **-ing** *a.* confiding. **-ingly** *adv.* **-worthiness** *n.* **-worthy** *a.* **-y** *a.* reliable; *n.* reliable prisoner given special privileges [O.N. *traust*, confidence].

truth (trȯȯth) *n.* honesty; conformity to fact or reality; veracity; constancy; true statement; undisputed fact. **-ful** *a.* **-fully** *adv.* **-fulness** *n.* **-less** *a.* [O.E. *treowe*, true].

try (trī) *v.t.* to test; to attempt; (*Law*) to examine judicially; to purify or refine, as metals; *v.i.* to endeavor; to make effort. *pa.t.* and *pa.p.* **tried.** *n.* trial; effort; (*Colloq.*) attempt. **tried** *a.* **trier** *n.* [O.Fr. *trier*, to pick out].

tryst (trist) *n.* appointment to meet; place appointed for meeting.**-er** *n.* [var. of *trust*].

Tsar (tsȧr) *n.* same as **Czar.**

tset·se (tset'·sē) *n.* African fly, its bite causing sleeping sickness [S. Afr.].

T square (tē·skwer) *n.* ruler with crossbar at one end for drawing parallel lines.

tub (tub) *n.* vessel to bathe in; open, wooden vessel formed of staves, heading and hoops, as used for washing clothes, etc.; small cask; (*Colloq.*) slow, cumbersome boat. **-by** *a.* shaped like a tub; (of persons) squat and portly. [M.E. *tubbe*, a tub].

tu·ba (tū'·bạ) *n.* (*Mus.*) largest brass instrument of orchestra; organ stop. *pl.* **-s, tubae** [L. *tuba*, trumpet].

tube (tūb) *n.* long hollow cylinder for conveyance of liquids, gas, etc.; pipe; siphon; *abbrev.* for tube-railway where rails are laid through immense steel tubes; (*Anat.*) cylindrical-shaped organ; small container with screw cap; stem of plant; inner rubber tire of bicycle or automobile wheel; **tubing** *n.* **tubular** *a.* **tubulate, -d, tubulous, tubulose** *a.* **tubule** *n.* a small tube [L. *tubus*, a tube].

tub·er (tū'·ber) *n.* fleshy, rounded underground stem or root, containing buds for new plant; (*Med.*) a swelling. **-ous, -ose** *a.* [L. *tuber*, a swelling].

tu·ber·cle (tū'·bẹr·kl) *n.* small swelling; nodule; (*Med.*) morbid growth, esp. on lung causing *tuberculosis*. *a.* having tubercles. **tubercular, tuberculate, -d, tuberculose, tuberculous** *a.* pert. to tubercles; nodular; affected with tuberculosis. **tuberculin** *n.* liquid extract from tubercle bacillus used as injection in testing for, or in treatment of, tuberculosis. **tuberculosis** *n.* (*Colloq. abbrev.* **T.B.**) consumption; phthisis, disease caused by infection with the tubercle bacillus. **tuberculum** *n.* tubercle [L. *tuberculum*, a small tuber].

tuck (tuk) *v.t.* to make fold(s) in cloth before stitching down; to roll up, as sleeves; to make compact; to enclose snugly in bed clothes; *n.* flat fold in garment to shorten it, or as ornament; **-er** *n.* tucked linen or lace front worn by women; *v.t.* (*slang*) to exhaust [M.E. *tukken*, to pull].

Tu·dor (tū'·dẹr) *a.* pert. to period of Tudors (1485-1603) or to style of architecture in that period.

Tues·day (tūz'·di·) *n.* third day of week [O.E. *Tiwesdaeg*, day of *Tiw*, god of war].

tuft (tuft) *n.* cluster; bunch of something soft, as hair, feathers, threads, etc.; *v.t.* to adorn with, arrange in tufts. **-ed, -y** *a.*

tug (tug) *v.t.* to pull with effort; to haul along; *v.i.* to pull with great effort; to comb, as hair, with difficulty. *pr.p.* **-ging.** *pa.t.* and *pa.p.* **-ged.** *n.* strong pull; tussle; tugboat. **-boat** *n.* a small but powerful boat used for towing larger vessel. **tug of war** *n.* sports contest, in which two teams pull at either end of rope, until losing team is drawn over center line [O.N. *toga*, to pull].

tu·i·tion (tū·ish'·ạn) *n.* the price for instruction; teaching. **-al, -ary** *a.* [L. *tueri*, to watch].

tu·lip (tū'·lạp) *n.* bulbous plant popular in Holland [Turk. *tulbend*, turban].

tulle (tȯȯl) *n.* fine silk net used for dresses, hats, etc. [fr. *Tulle*, France].

tum·ble (tum'·bl) *v.i.* to fall heavily; to trip over; to toss from side to side; to turn head over heels; to perform acrobatic tricks; to slump, as prices; *v.t.* to overturn; to rumple, as bedclothes; to toss about, as contents of drawer; *n.* act of tumbling; fall; confusion. **—down** *a.* ramshackle; derelict. **-er** *n.* one who tumbles; acrobat; kind of pigeon; glass drinking vessel; spring catch of a lock. **tumbling** *n.* act of falling or turning somersault [O.E. *tumbian*, to dance].

tum·brel, tumbril (tum'·brạl) *n.* cart used for carrying dung; low open cart in which victims of French Revolutionists were conveyed to guillotine [Fr. *tomber*, to fall].

tu·me·fy (tū'·mạ·fī) *v.t.* to cause to swell; *v.i.* to swell; to develop into a tumor. **tumefaction** *n.* a swelling; a tumor [L. *tumere*, to swell; *facere*, to make].

tu·mid (tū'·mid) *a.* swollen; turgid; pompous. **tumescence** *n.* **tumescent** *a.* **-ness, tumidity** *n.* **-ly** *adv.* [L. *tumere*].

tu·mor (tū'·mẹr) *n.* (*Med.*) morbid overgrowth of tissue, sometimes accompanied by swelling. **-ous** *a.* Also **tumour** [L. *tumere*, to swell].

tu·mult (tū'·mult) *n.* commotion as of a crowd; violent uproar; mental disturbance. **-uary, -uous** *a.* confused; uproarious; disturbing. **-uously** *adv.* **-uousness** *n.* [L. *tumultus*, uproar].

tu·mu·lus (tū'·myạ·lạs) *n.* artificial burial mound, erected by primitive peoples; barrow. *pl.* **-es, tumuli. tumulous** *a.* [L. fr. *tumere*, to swell].

tun (tun) *n.* large cask; measure of liquid, as for wine, usually equivalent to 252 gallons; *v.t.* to store in casks [O.E. *tunne*, a cask].

tu·na (tȯȯ'·nạ) *n.* large oceanic food and game fish. [Sp.].

tun·dra (tun'·drạ) *n.* one of vast treeless plains of Arctic Circle [Russ. *tundra*, a marsh].

tune (tūn) *n.* melody; rhythmical arrangement of notes and chords in particular key; quality of being in pitch; mood; unison; harmony; *v.t.* to adjust to proper pitch; to harmonize; to adapt or make efficient, esp. part of machine; (*Radio*) to adjust circuit to give resonance at desired frequency. **tunable** *a.* **tunableness** *n.* **tunably** *adv.* **-ful** *a.* melodious; harmonious. **-fully** *adv.* **-fulness** *n.* **-less** *a.* without melody; discordant; silent. **-r** *n.* **tuning fork** *n.* steel two-pronged instrument giving specified note when struck. **in tune** (*Fig.*) mentally and emotionally adjusted, as to one's company or environment. **out of tune,** at variance with. **to tune in** (*Radio*) to adjust radio set to desired wavelength [O.Fr. *ton*, a tone].

tung·sten (tung'.stạn) *n.* hard grey metallic element used in alloys, special forms of steel, and for filaments in electric lamps [Scand. *tung*, heavy; *sten*, a stone].

tu·nic (tū'.nik) *n.* short-sleeved knee-length garment worn by women and boys in ancient Greece and Rome; short-sleeved eccles. vestment; blouselike outer garment extending to hips [L. *tunica*, undergarment of both sexes].

tun·nel (tun'.ạl) *n.* subterranean passage; burrow of an animal; *v.t.* and *v.i.* to cut tunnel through; to excavate. **-er** n. [O.Fr. *tonne*, tun or cask].

tun·ny (tun'.i.) *n.* edible fish of mackerel family; tuna fish [Gk. *thunnos*].

tur·ban (tur'.bạn) *n.* Oriental male headdress comprising long strip of cloth swathed round head or cap; close-fitting cap or scarf headdress worn by women. **-ed** *a.* **-like** *a.* [Turk. *tulbend*].

tur·bid (tur'.bid) *a.* having dregs disturbed; muddy; thick; dense. **-ly** *adv.* **-ness, -ity** *n.* [L. *turbidus*, fr. *turbare*, to disturb].

tur·bine (tur'.bin or .bīn) *n.* rotary engine driven by steam, hot air, or water striking on curved vanes of wheel, or drum; high speed prime mover used for generating electrical energy. **turbinal, turbinate** *a.* coiled like a spiral. **turbojet** *n.* jet propelled gas turbine. **turboprop,** jet engine in which turbine is coupled to propeller [L. *turbo*, whirl].

tur·bot (tur'.bạt) *n.* large flat sea fish [L. *turbo*, a top].

tur·bu·lent (tur'.byạ.lạnt) *a.* disturbed; in violent commotion; refractory. **-ly** *adv.* **turbulence, turbulency** *n.* [L. *turbare*, to disturb].

tu·reen (tòò.rēn' or tyoo.rēn') *n.* large, deep dish with removable cover, for serving soup [Fr. *terrine*, an earthen vessel].

turf (turf) *n.* surface soil containing matted roots, grass, etc.; sod; peat; a race-course. *v.t.* to cover with turf, as lawn. **-like** *a.* **the turf,** track over which horse races are run. **-man** *n.* one interested in horse racing. **-y** *a.* covered with turf [O.E. *turf*, turf].

turgent (tur'.jạnt) *a.* (*obs.*) swelling; puffing up like a tumor; pompous; bombastic. **-ly** *adv.* **turgescence, turgescency** *n.* swelling caused by congestion; empty bombast. **turgid** *a.* swollen; distended abnormally; bombastic. **turgidity, turgidness** *n.* **-ly** *adv.* [L. *turgere*, to swell].

Turk (turk) *n.* native of *Turkey;* Ottoman; a fierce person; a Mohammedan. **-ish** *a.* pert. to Turks or Turkey. **-ish bath,** steam or hot air bath after which person is rubbed down, massaged, etc. **-ish towel,** an absorbent towel.

tur·key (tur'.ki.) *n.* large bird, bred for food; guinea fowl. **— trot** *n.* an eccentric ragtime dance [fr. *Turkey*].

tur·mer·ic (tur'.mẹr.ik) *n.* E. Indian plant; powder prepared from it used as a condiment, dye, medicine [L. *terra merita*, deserving earth].

tur·moil (tur'.moil) *n.* commotion; tumult.

turn (turn) *v.t.* to move round; to cause to revolve; to deflect; to form on lathe; to change direction of; to convert; to upset or nauseate; to blunt; *v.i.* to rotate; to move as on a hinge; to depend; to become giddy, nauseated, or upset; (of tides) to change from ebb to flow or the reverse; to become sour, as milk; *n.* act of turning; change of bend; an action, as *good turn*; action done in rotation with others; short walk; a subtle quality of expression, as *turn of phrase;* crisis. **-about** *n.* merry-go-round; reversal of position, opinion. **-coat** *n.* renegade; one who betrays party or other principles. **-ing** *n.* act of turning; deflection; winding; juncing and two roads or streets; process of shaping and rounding articles with lathe. **-ing point** *n.* decisive moment; crisis. **-key** *n.* one in charge of prison keys; warder. **—out** *n.* act of coming forth; production, as of factory; number of people at any gathering. **-over** *n.* total sales made by a business in certain period; rate at which employees are replaced; tart of pastry folded over a filling of jam, or fruit. **-pike** *n.* **-pike road** *n.* main highway with tollgate. **-spit** *n.* one who turns a spit. **-stile** *n.* revolving gate for controlling admission of people. **-stile justice** *n.* a court system that supposedly acquits criminals easily or imposes minimum sentences, with the offenders soon caught in a similar misdeed and processed in like manner. **-table** *n.* revolving circular platform for turning locomotives on to another line or in opposite direction; revolving disk of a phonograph. **to turn —,** to decline; to reject. **to — in,** to bend inwards; to hand in; to go to bed [O.E. *tyrnan*, to turn].

tur·nip (tur'.nip) *n.* plant of mustard family.

tur·pen·tine (tur'.pạn.tīn) *n.* oily liquid extracted by distillation of resin exuded by pine and other coniferous trees [Gk. *terebinthos*].

tur·pi·tude (tur'.pạ.tūd) *n.* revolting baseness; lewdness; infamy [L. *turpis*, base].

tur·quoise (tur'.kwoiz, -koiz) *n.* bluish-green gem stone [*Turkish* (stone)].

tur·ret (tur'.it) *n.* small tower on building; revolving gun tower on ship, tank, or aircraft. **-ed** *a.* having turrets [O.Fr. *tourete*, a little tower].

tur·tle (tur'.tl) *n.* a tortoise, esp. a marine tortoise [Fr. *tortue*, tortoise].

tur·tle·dove (tur'.tl.duv) kind of pigeon, noted for its soft cooing [L. *turtur*, a dove].

Tus·can (tus'.kạn) *a.* pert. to Tuscany in Italy; (*Archit.*) denoting the simplest of the five classical styles in architecture.

tusk (tusk) *n.* the long, protruding side tooth of certain animals such as elephant, wild boar, walrus. **-ed** *a.* **-er** *n.* animal with fully developed tusks. **-y** *a.* **-less** *a.* **-like** *a.* [O.E. *tusc*, tooth].

tus·sle (tus'.l) *n.*, *v.t.* struggle; scuffle.

tus·sock (tus'.ạk) *n.* (*Poet.*) clump, tuft, or hillock of growing grass [etym. doubtful].

tut (tut) *interj.* exclamation of irritation.

tu·te·lage (tū.tạ.lij) *n.* guardianship; instruction state or period of being under this. **tutelar, tutelary** *a.* having protection over a person or place; protective [L. *tutela*].

tu·tor (tū'.tẹr) *n.* (*Law*) one in charge of minor; private teacher; (*Brit.*) university lecturer who directs and supervises studies of undergraduates; *v.t.* to teach; to prepare another for special examination by private coaching; to have guardianship of. **-ial** *a.* pert. to tutor. **-ially** *adv.* **-ing** *n.* **-ship** *n.* [L. *tutor*, a guardian].

tut·ti-frut·ti (tòò'.ti.fròò'.ti.) *n.* preserve of fruits; ice cream sundae with fruit, nuts, etc.; ice cream made with mixed fruits [It. = all fruits].

tux·e·do (tuk.sē'.dō) *n.* semiformal dinner jacket [fr. *Tuxedo Park*, a country club].

twad·dle (twȧd'.l) *n.* inane conversation; non-sensical writing; *v.i.* to talk inanely. **-r** *n.* **twaddling** *n.* twaddle. **twaddly** *a.* silly.

twain (twān) *a.*, *n.* (*Arch.*) two [O.E. *twegin*].

twang (twang) *n.* sharp, rather harsh sound made by tense string sharply plucked; nasalized speech; *v.t.* to pluck tense string of instrument; *v.i.* to speak with a twang [limit.].

tweak (twēk) *v.t.* to twist and pull with sudden jerk; *n.* sharp pinch or jerk [var. of *twitch*].

'twas (twȯz) *contr.* of *it was.*

tweed (twēd) *n.* heavy woolen fabric esp. for costumes, coats, suits; *a.* of tweed [fr. mistaken reading of '*tweel*'].

'tween (twēn) *contr.* of **between. 'tween deck,** between upper and lower decks.

tweez·ers (twē'.zẹrz) *n. sing.* small pair of pincers, esp. for pulling superfluous hairs.

twelve (twelv)*a.* one more than eleven; two and ten; dozen; *n.* sum of ten and two; symbol representing twelve units, as 12, xii. **twelfth** *a.* next after eleventh; constituting one of twelve equal parts; *n.* one of twelve equal parts. **Twelfth Day,** January 6th, twelfth day after Christmas; Feast of Epiphany. **twelfthly** *adv.* **Twelfth Night,** evening of, or before, Twelfth Day, when special festivities were held. **the Twelve,** twelve Apostles [O.E. *twelf,* twelve].

twen·ty (twen'.ti.) *a.* twice ten; nineteen and one; *n.* number next after nineteen; score; symbol representing twenty units, as 20, xx. **twentieth** *a.* next after nineteenth; *n.* one of twenty equal parts. **—fold** *adv.* twenty times as many [O.E. *twentig*].

'twere (twur) *cont.* of *it were.*

twice (twīs) *adv.* two times; doubly [O.E. *twa,* two].

twid·dle (twid'.l) *v.t.* to play with; to twirl idly; *v.i.* to spin round; to trifle with. **-r** *n.* **to twiddle one's thumbs,** to have nothing to do [etym. doubtful].

twig (twig) *n.* small shoot or branch of tree. **-gy** *a.* covered with twigs [O.E. *twig,* branch].

twi·light (twī'.līt) *n.* half-light preceding sunrise or, esp., immediately after sunset; faint, indeterminate light; *a.* pert. to or like twilight. **— sleep,** in obstetrics, modern method of inducing state of partial insensibility in woman in childbirth by use of drug, scopolamine-morphine [lit, 'between-light'; O.E. *twa,* two; *leoht,* light].

twill (twil) *n.* fabric woven with diagonal ribbing; *v.t.* to weave with twill [O.E. *twilic,* two-threaded].

twin (twin) *n.* one of two born at birth; exact counterpart; *a.* being one of two born at birth; consisting of two identical parts; growing in pairs. **-ned** *a.* **— beds** *n.pl.* two single beds of identical size. **—born** *a.* born at the same birth. **— brother, sister** *n.* **—screw** *a.* of a vesel having two propellers on separate shafts [O.E. *twinn,* double].

twine (twīn) *n.* cord composed of two or more strangs twisted together; spring; tangle; *v.t.* to twist together; to entwine; to encircle; *v.i.* to wind; to coil spirally, as tendrils of plant; to follow circuitous route. **twining** *a.* winding; coiling [O.E. twin, double-thread].

twinge (twinj) *n.* sudden, acute spasm of pain; pang; *v.t.* (*Dial*) to tweak; to effect momentarily with sudden pain [O.E. *twengan,* to pinch].

twin·kle (twing'.kl) *v.i.* to sparkle; (of eyes) to light up; of feet to move quickly and neatly; *n.* act of twinkling; gleam of amusement in eyes; flicker; quick movement of feet, esp. in dancing; : sparkle. *n.* **twinkling** *n.* twinkle; an instant [O.E. *twinclian,* to sparkle].

twirl (turl) *v.t.* to whirl around; to flourish; to twiddle; *v.i.* to turn round rapidly; *n.* a rapid, rotary motion; a flourish; curl; convolution. **-er** *n.* one who or that which twirls; (*Colloq.*) baseball pitcher. [O.E. *thwiri,* a whisk for beating milk].

twist (twist) *v.t.* to contort; to coil spirally; to wind; to encircle; to distort; to form, as cord, from several fibers wound together; *v.i.* to become tangled or distorted; to wriggle; to be united by winding around each other; to coil; to follow a roundabout course; *n.* turning movement; curve; bend; act of entwining; a turn in meaning; a heavy silk thread; small roll of tobacco; **-ed** *a.* **-er** *n.* one who, or that which, twists; swindler. **-ability** *n.* **-able** *a.* **-ingly** *adv.* [O.E. *twist,* rope].

twit (twit) *v.t.* to taunt; to reproach; to tease. *pr.p.* **-ting.** *pa.t.* and *pa.p.* **-ted.** *n.* taunt [O.E. *twiccian,* to pluck].

twitch (twich) *v.t.* to pull suddenly with a slight jerk; to snatch; *v.i.* to be suddenly jerked; to contract with sudden spasm, as a muscle; to quiver; *n.* sudden spasmodic contraction of fiber or muscle. **-ing** *n.* [O.E. *twiccian,* to pluck].

twitch-grass (twich'.gras) *n.* prolific weed, couch grass or quitch grass.

twit·ter (twit'.ẹr) *n.* chirping sound; slight trembling of nerves; half-suppressed laugh; *v.i.* to make succession of small light sounds; to chirp; to talk rapidly and nerviously; to titter. **-ing** *n.* **-y** *a.* [imit.].

'twixt (twikst) *prep.* contr. of **between.**

Two (tòò) *a.* one and one; *n.* sum of one and one; symbol representing two units, as 2, ii; a pair. **—edged** *a.* having two sharp edges, as a sword; (*Fig.*) ambiguous. **—faced** *a.* having two faces; hypocritical; double-dealing. **-fold** *a.* double; doubly. **—handed** *a.* requiring two hands or two players; ambidextrous. **-penny** (tup'.ạn.i.) (*Brit.*) *a.* costing two pennies; (*Colloq.*) worthless; *n.* kind of ale. **—ply** *a.* having two strands twisted together, two layers, etc. **—seater** *n.* small automobile designed for two people only. **—sided** *a.* having two surfaces or aspects; (of cloth) reversible; (*Fig.*) double-dealing.

ty·coon (tī.kòòn') *n.* former title of a Japanese official; head of great business combine; a magnate [Jap. *taikun,* great prince].

tyke (tīk) *n.* a cur; boor; (*Colloq.*) small child [Sc. *tīk,* bitch)].

tym·pa·num (tim'.pạ.nạm) *n.* a drum (*Anat.*) cavity of the middle ear; ear drum; (*Archit.*) flat, triangular space between sides of pediment; similar space over door between lintel and arch. *pl.* **-s, tympana. tympanal, tympanic** *a.* like a drum; pert. to middle ear. **tympanist** *n.* one who plays drum or any percussion instrument [Gk. *tumpanon,* a kettle-drum].

type (tīp) *n.* model; pattern; class or group; person or thing representative of group or of certain quality; stamp on either side of a coin; (*Chem.*) compound which has basic composition of other more complex compounds; (*Biol.*) individual specimen representative of species; (*Print.*) metal block on one end of which is raised letter, etc.; such blocks collectively; similar block in typewriter; style or form of printing; *v.t.* to typify; to represent in type; to reproduce by means of typewriter; to classify; *v.i.* to use a typewriter. **typal** *a.* **— cutter** *n.* one who engraves blocks for printing types. **— founder** *n.* one who casts type for printing. **— metal** *n.* alloy of lead, antimony,and tin used for casting type. **-script** *n.* a typewritten document. **-setting** *n.* process or occupation of preparing type for printing. **-writer** *n.* machine with keyboard operated by fingers, which produces printed characters on paper; typist **-writing** *n.* **-written** *a.* **typical** (tip′.ą.kąl) *a. pert.* to type; symbolic; true bolize; to exemplify. **typing** *n.* act of typing; script typed. **typist** *n.* one who operates typewriter. **typographer** *n.* printer. **typographic, -al** *a.* pert. to printing. **typography** *n.* art of printing; style or mode of printing [Gk. *tupos,* mark of a bowl].

ty·phoid (tī′.foid) *a.* resembling typhus; pert. to typhoid fever; **— fever** *n.* infectious disease characterized by severe diarrhea, profound weakness, and rash. **-al** *a.* [Gk. *tuphos,* fever; *eidos,* form].

ty·phoon (tī.fòòn′) *n.* cyclonic hurricane occurring in China seas. **typhonic** *a.* [Ar. *tufan*].

ty·phus (tī′.fąs) *n.* highly contagious disease caused by virus conveyed by body lice and characterized by purplish rash, prostration, and abnormally high temperature. **typhous** *a.* [Gk. *tuphos,* fever].

ty·rant (tī′.rąnt) *n.* in ancient Greece, usurper; harsh, despotic ruler; any person enforcing his will on others, cruelly and arbitrarily. **tyrannic, -al, tyrannous** (tir′.ąn.ąs) *a.* **tyrannically** *adv.* **tyrannously** *adv.* **tyrannicalness** *n.* **tyrannize** *v.i.* to rule tyrannically; to exert authority ruthlessly; *v.t.* to subject to tyrannical authority. **tyrannizer** *n.* **tyrannizingly** *adv.* **tyranny** (tir′.ą.nē) *n.* despotic government; cruelly harsh enforcement of authority [Gk. *turannos,* an unconstitutional ruler].

ty·ro (tī′.rō) *n.* beginner; novice. Also **tiro** [L. *tiro,* recruit].

Tzar, Tzarina Same as **Czar, Czarina.**

U

u·biq·ui·ty (ū.bik′.wą.ti.) *n.* existing in all places at same time; omnipresence. **ubiquitous, ubiquitary** *a.* existing or being everywhere. **ubiquitously** *adv.* **ubiquitousness** *n.* omnipresence [L. *ubique,* everywhere].

U-boat (ū′.bōt) *n.* German submarine [Ger. *untersee,* under the sea, and *boat*].

ud·der (ud′.ęr) *n.* milk gland of certain animals, as cow [O.E. *uder,* udder].

u·dom·e·ter (ū.dàm′.ą.tęr) *n.* instrument for measuring rainfall. **udometry** *n.* **udometric** *a.* [L.*udus,* moist; *metron,* measure].

ug·ly (ug′.li.) *a.* offensive to the sight; of disagreeable aspect; dangerous, of situation. **uglify** *v.t.* to make ugly. **uglification** *n.* **ugliness** *n.* **uglily** *adv.* [O.N. *uggr,* fear].

u·kase (ū′.kās) *n.* official Russian decree [Russ. *ukaz,* edict].

U·krain·i·an (ū.krā′.ni.ąn) *n.* citizen of Ukraine in S.W. Russia; Slavic language related to Russian. *a.* pert. to Ukraine.

u·ku·le·le (ū.ką.lā′.li.) *n.* small four-stringed instrument like guitar [Hawaiian].

ul·cer (ul′.sęr) *n.* superficial sore discharging pus; (*Fig.*) source of corruption. **-ate** *v.i.* to become ulcerous. **-ated, -ative** *a.* **-ation** *n.* **-ed** *a.* having ulcers. **-ous** *a.* having ulcers; like an ulcer. **-ously** *adv.* **-ousness** *n.* [L. *ulcus*].

ul·lage (ul′.ij) *n.* amount which cask lacks of being full; loss of wine, grain, etc. by leakage [O.Fr. *eullage,* the filling up of a cask].

ul·na (ul′.ną) *n.* the larger of two bones of forearm. *pl.* **-s, ulnae. -r** *a.* [L. *ulna,* elbow].

ul·ster (ul′.stęr) *n.* long loose overcoat originally made in *Ulster,* Ireland. **-ed** *a.*

ul·te·ri·or (ul.tir′.i.ęr) *a.* situated on the farther side; beyond; (of motives) undisclosed; not frankly stated. **-ly** *adv.* [L. *ulterior,* farther].

ul·ti·mate (ul′.tą.mit) *a.* farthest; final; primary; conclusive. **-ly** *adv.* **-ness** *n.* **ultimatum** (ul.tą.mā′.tąm) *n.* final proposition; final terms offered as basis of treaty; *pl.* **ultimatums, ultimata. ultima** *n.* last syllable of a word. **ultimo** *a.* in the month preceding current one (*abbrev.* **ult.**) [L. *ultimus,* last].

ul·tra (ul′.trą) *a.* beyond; extreme; in combination words with or without hyphen, as *ultra modern* [L. *ultra,* beyond].

ul·tra·ma·rine (ul.trą.mą.rēn′) *a.* situated beyond the sea; *n.* bright blue pigment obtained from powdered lapis lazuli, or synthetically [L. *ultra,* beyond; *mare,* the sea].

ul·tra·mon·tane (ul.trą.màn′.tān) *a.* being beyond the mountains, esp. the Alps; used of Italians by those on northern side of Alps, and vice versa; pert. to absolute temporal and spiritual power of Papacy or to party upholding this claim; *n.* advocate of extreme or ultra-papal views. **ultramontanism** *n.* **ultramontanist** *n.*

ul·tra·vi·o·let (ul.trą.vī.ą.lit) *a.* beyond limit of visibility at violet end of the spectrum.

ul·u·lant (ūl′.yą.ląnt) *a.* howling. **ululate** *v.i.* to howl; to lament. **ululation** *n.* [L.].

um·bel (um′.bąl) *n.* (*Bot.*) flower clusters, the stalks of which rise from a common center on main stem, forming a convexed surface above, as in carrot, parsley, etc. **-lar, -late, -d** *a.* having umbels. **-liferous** *a.* bearing umbels. **-liform** *a.* having shape of umbel [L. *umbella,* little shade].

um·ber (um′.bęr) *n.* natural earth pigment, yellowish-brown in color when raw, reddish-brown when calcined or burnt [fr. *Umbria,* in Italy].

um·bil·i·cal (um.bil′.ą.kąl) *a.* pert. to umbilicus or umbilical cord. **— cord** (*Anat.*) fibrous cord joining fetus to placenta. **-umbilicus** *n.* the navel. **umbiliform** *a.* [L. *umbilicus*].

um·bra (um′.brą) *n.* shadow; (*Astron.*) complete shadow cast by earth or moon in eclipse, as opposed to *penumbra,* partial shadow in eclipse. **-l** *a.* [L. *umbra,* shadow].

um·brage (um′.brij) *n.* (*Poet.*) shadow; feeling of resentment. **-ous** *a.* shady. **-ously** *adv.* **to take —,** to feel resentful [L. *umbra, shadow*].

um·brel·la (um.brel′.ą) *n.* light-weight circular covering of silk or other material on folding framework of spokes, carried as protection against rain (or sun). **-less** *a.* **-like** *a.* **— stand** *n.* stand for holding umbrellas [It. *ombrella,* dim. of *ombra,* shade].

um·laut (òòm′.lout) *n.* term used to denote mutation, e.g., caused by influence of vowel *i* (earlier *j*) on preceeding vowel such as a, o, u; in Modern German this vowel mutation is indicated by diaeresis over vowel, as in Führer (Fuehrer); in English it is seen in plural forms of man (*men*), mouse (*mice*), foot (*feet*). Also called **mutation** [Ger. = changed sound].

um·pire (um′.pīr) *n.* person chosen to arbitrate in dispute; impartial person chosen to see that rules of game are properly enforced; referee; *v.t., v.i.* to act as umpire [orig. *numpire,* fr. O.Fr. *nomper,* peerless].

un- *prefix* before nouns, adjectives, and adverbs adding negative force; before verbs, expressing reversal of the action, separation, etc.

UN, U.N. (ū.en′) *n.* *U*nited *N*ations.

un·a·bashed *a.* **(abash)**
un·a·bat·ed *a.* **(abate)**
un·a·ble *a.* **(able)**
un·a·bridged *a.* **(abridge)**
un·ac·cent·ed *a.* **(accent)**
un·ac·cept·a·ble *a.* **(accept)**
un·ac·com·mo·dat·ing *a.* **(accommodate)**
un·ac·com·pa·nied (un.ạ.kum′.pạ.nēd) *a.* not accompanied; sung or played on instrument without piano, organ, or orchestral accompaniment.
un·ac·count·a·ble *a.* **(account)**
un·ac·cus·tomed *a.* **(accustom)**
un·ac·quaint·ed *a.* **(acquaint)**
un·a·dorned *a.* **(adorn)**
un·a·dul·ter·at·ed *a.* **(adulterate)**
un·ad·vised *a.* **(advise)**
un·af·fect·ed (un.ạ.fek′.tid) *a.* not affected unmoved; straightforward; sincere. **-ly** *adv.* simply; void of affection.
un·a·fraid *a.* **(afraid)**
un·aid·ed *a.* **(aid)**
un·al·loyed *a.* **(alloy)**
un·al·ter·a·ble (un.awl′.tẹr.ạ.bl) *a.* not capable of alteration; fixed; permanent. **-ness unalterability** *n.* **unalterably** *adv.* **unaltered** *a.* unchanged.
un·am·bi·tious *a.* **(ambition)**
u·nan·i·mous (yòò.nan′.ạ.mạs) *a.* all of one mind; agreed to by all parties. **unanimity** (ū′.nạ.nim.ạ.ti.) *n.* **-ly** *adv.* **-ness** *n.* [L. *unus*, one; *animus*, mind].
un·an·nealed *a.* **(anneal)**
un·an·nounced *a.* **(announce)**
un·an·swer·a·ble *a.* **unanswerability, -ness** *n.* **(answer)**
un·ap·pre·ci·at·ed *a.* **unapprecaitive** *a.* **(appreciate)**
un·ap·proach·a·ble *a.* **-ness** *n.* **unapproachably** *adv.* **(approach)**
un·arm (un.ȧrm′) *v.t.* to disarm; to render harmless; *v.i.* to lay down arms. **-ed** *a.* defenseless. **-ored** *a.* without weapons; (of ships, etc.) not protected by armor plating.
un·a·shamed *a.* **(ashamed)**
un·asked *a.* **(ask)**
un·as·sail·a·ble (un.a.sāl′.ạ.bl) *a.* not assailable; irrefutable; invincible. **unassailed** *a.*
un·as·sim·i·la·ted *a.* **unassimilable** *a.* **unassimilating** *a.* **(assimilate)**
un·as·sist·ed *a.* **(assist)**
un·as·sum·ing (un.ạ.sòòm′.ing) *a.* not assuming; modest; not overbearing.
un·at·tached (un.ạ.tacht′) *a.* not attached; dangling; not posted to a particular regiment; not married or engaged.
un·at·tain·a·ble *a.* **unattainably** *adv.* **(attain)**
un·at·tend·ed *a.* **unattending** *a.* **unattentive** *a.* **(attend)**
un·at·test·ed *a.* **(attest)**
un·at·trac·tive (un.ạ.trak′.tiv) *a.* not attractive; repellent; plain; not prepossessing. **-ly** *adv.* **-ness** *n.*
un·au·thor·ized *a.* **unauthoritative** *a.* **(authorize)**
un·a·vail·ing (un.ạ.vāl′.ing) *a.* not availing; fruitless; having no result. **unavailability** *n.* **unavailable** *a.* not procurable; not at one's disposal. **-ly** *adv.* fruitlessly.
un·a·void·a·ble *a.* **-ness, unavoidability** *n.* **unavoidably** *adv.* **unavoided** *a.* **(avoid)**
un·a·ware (un.ạ.wār′) *a.* having no knowledge of; *adv.* unawares. **-s** *adv.* unexpectedly; without previous warning.
un·baked *a.* **(bake)**
un·bal·ance (un.bal′.ạns) *v.t.* to upset. **-d** *a.* not balanced; lacking equipoise, or mental stability; not adjusted or equal on credit and debit sides (of ledger). **unbalance** *n.*
un·bar *v.t.* and *i.* **(bar)**
un·bear·able (un.ber′.ạ.bl) *a.* not bearable; intolerable; (of pain) excruciating. **-ness** *n.* **unbearably** *adv.*
un·beat·en *a.* **(beat)**
un·be·com·ing (un.bi.kum′.ing) *a.* not becoming; not suited to the wearer; (of behavior) immodest; indecorous. **-ly** *adv.*
un·be·fit·ting *a.* **(befit)**
un·be·known (un.bi.nōn′) *a.* not known. **-st** *adv.* without the knowledge of.
un·be·lief *n.* **unbelievability** *n.* **unbelievable** *a.* **unbelieving** *a.* **unbelievingly** *adv.* **(believe)**
un·belt *v.t.* **(belt)**
un·bend (un.bend′) *v.t.* to free from bend position; to straighten; to relax; to loose, as anchor; *v.i.* to become relaxed; to become more friendly. *pa.t., pa.p.* **bent** *or* **-ed. ing** *a.* not pliable; rigid; (*Fig.*) coldly aloof; resolute. **-ingly** *adv.* **unbent** *a.* straight.
un·bi·ased *v.t.* **(bias)**
un·bid·den *a.* **(bid)**
un·bind *v.t.* **(bind)**
un·bit·ten *a.* **(bite)**
un·blamed *a.* **(blame)**
un·bleached *a.* **(bleach)**
un·blem·ished (un.blem′.isht) *a.* not blemished; faultness; (of character) pure; perfect. **unblemishable** *a.*
un·blessed or **unblessed** *a.* **(Bless)**
un·blink·ing *a.* **(blink)**
un·blush·ing·ly *adv.* **(blush)**
un·bod·ied (un.bȧd′.id) *a.* free from the body; incorporeal.
un·bolt *v.t.* **-ed** *a.* **(bolt)**
un·bolt·ed (un.bōl′.tid) *a.* (of grain) unsifted; not fastened with a bolt. **unbolt** *v.t.*
un·born (un.bawrn′) *a.* not yet born; future, as *unborn generations.*
un·bos·om (un.booz′.ạm) *v.t.* to disclose freely; to reveal one's intimate longings.
un·bound (un.bound′) *a.* not bound; free; without outer binding, as a book; *pa.p., pa.t.* of **unbind. -ed** *a.* illimitable; abundant; irrepressible. **-edly** *adv.*
un·bowed *a.* **(bow)**
un·break·a·ble *a.* **(break)**
un·bri·dle (un.brī′.dl) *v.t.* to remove the bridle from, as a horse. **-d** *a.* unrestrained; voilently passionate.
un·bro·ken (un.brō′.kn) *a.* complete; whole; (of horse) untamed; inviolate; continuous.**-ly** *adv.* **-ness** *n.*
un·buck·le *v.* **-d** *a.* **(buckle)**
un·bur·den (un.bur′.dn) *v.t.* to relieve of a burden; (*Fig.*) to relieve the mind of anxiety. **-ed** *a.* **-ing** *n.a.*
un·bur·ied *a.* **(bury)**
un·burned *a.* **(burn)**
un·busi·ness·like *a.* **(business)**
un·but·ton *v.t.* **(button)**
un·cage *v.t.* **(cage)**
un·cal·cu·la·ted *v.t.* **(calculate)**
un·called (un.kawld′) *a.* not summoned. **uncalled for,** unnecessary or without cause.
un·can·ny (un.kan′.i.) *a.* weird; unearthly. **uncannily** *adv.* **uncanniness** *n.*
un·caused *a.* **(cause)**
un·ceas·ing *a.* **-ly** *adv.* **(cease)**
un·cer·e·mo·ni·ous (un.ser.ạ.mō′.ni.ạs) *a.* not ceremonious; informal; abrupt. **-ly** *adv.* **-ness** *n.*
un·cer·tain (un.sur′.t(i)n) *a.* not certain; not positively known; unreliable; insecure. **-ly** *adv.* **-ness** *n.* **-ty** *n.* state of being or that which is uncertain; lack of assurance.
un·chain *v.t.* **(chain)**
un·change·a·ble *a.* **unchangeability, -ness** *n.* **unchangeably** *adv.* **unchanged** *a.* **unchanging** *a.* **unchangingly** *adv.* **(change)**
un·char·i·ta·ble *a.* **-ness** *n.* **uncharitably** *adv.* **(charity)**
un·chart·ed (un.chȧr′.tid) *a.* not shown on a map; unexplored.
un·checked *a.* **(check)**
un·chris·tian *a.* **-ly** *adv.* **(christian)**
un·church (un.church′) *v.t.* to excommuni-

cate; to deprive of name and status of a church.

un·ci·al (un′·shal) *a.* pert. to a type of rounded script, found in ancient MSS from 4th-9th cents.; *n.* uncial letter or manuscript. **-ly** *adv.* [L. *uncia,* inch; (*lit.*) letters, an inch high].

un·ci·form (un′·si·fawrm) *a.* shaped like a hook. **uncinal, uncinate** *a.* hooked; having hook-like prickles. [L. *uncus,* a hook].

un·cir·cum·cised (un·sur′·kam·sīzd) *a.* not circumcised; Gentile. **uncircumcision** *n.*

un·civ·il *a.* **-ity, ness** *n.* **-ized** *a.* **-ly** *adv.* **(civil, civilize)**

un·claimed *a.* **(claim)**

un·clasped *a.* **(clasp)**

un·clear *a.* **(clear)**

un·cloud·ed *a.* **(cloud)**

un·cle (ung′·kl) *n.* brother of one's father or mother; any elderly man; (*Slang*) pawnbroker. [L. *avunculus,* mother's brother].

un·clean (un·klēn′) *a.* not clean; filthy; ceremonially unsanctified; obscene. **uncleanliness** *n.* (un·klen′·li·nas). **-ly** (un·klēn′·li·, or un·klen·li··) *a. adv.* **-ness** *n.*

un·clench *v.t.* **(clench)**

un·clothe *v.t.* **-d** *a.* **(clothe)**

un·cock (un·kȧk′) *v.t.* to let down hammer of gun without exploding charge.

un·coil *v.t.* **(coil)**

un·come·ly (un·kum′·li·) *a.* not comely; unprepossessing; ugly; obscene.

un·com·fort·a·ble *a.* **-ness** *n.* **uncomfortably** *adv.* **uncomforted** *a.* **(comfort)**

un·com·mer·cial *a.* **(commerce)**

un·com·mit·ted *a.* **(commit)**

un·com·mon *a.* **-ly** *adv.* **-ness** *n.* **(common)**

un·com·mu·ni·ca·tive (un·ka·mū′·na·kā′·tiv) *a.* not communicative; discreet; taciturn. **-ly** *adv.* **-ness** *n.* **uncommunicable** *a.* not capable of being shared or communicated. **uncommunicableness** *n.* **uncommunicated** *a.*

un·com·plain·ing (un·kam·plān′·ing) *a.* not complaining; resigned. **-ly** *adv.* without complaint.

un·com·plet·ed *a.* **(complete)**

un·com·pli·men·ta·ry *a.* **(compliment)**

un·com·pro·mis·ing (un·kȧm·pra·mī′·zing) *a.* not compromising; making no concession; rigid. **-ly** *adv.*

un·con·cealed *a.* **(conceal)**

un·con·cern (un·kan·surn′) *n.* lack of concern; apathy. **-ed** *a.* not concerned; disinterested; apathetic; not involved. **-edly** *adv.* **-edness** *n.*

un·con·di·tioned (un·kan·dish′·and) *a.* not subject to conditions; absolute; instinctive. **unconditional** *a.* complete; absolute; without reservation. **unconditionally** *adv.* **— reflexes,** the instinctive responses of an animal to external stimuli.

un·con·firmed *a.* **(confirm)**

un·con·gen·i·al *a.* **(congenial)**

un·con·nect·ed *a.* **(connect)**

un·con′quer·a·ble *a.* **unconquerably** *adv.* **(conquer)**

un·con·scion·a·ble (un·kȧn′·shan·a·bl) *a.* beyond reason; unscrupulous; excessive. **-ness** *n.* **unconscionably** *adv.*

un·con·scious (un·kȧn′·shas) *a.* not conscious; unaware; deprived of consciousness; involuntary. **-ly** *adv.* **-ness** *n.* state of being insensible. **the unconscious,** in psychoanalysis, part of mind which appears to act without a conscious effort of will.

un·con·sti·tu·tion·al (un·kȧn·sti·tū′·shan·al) *a.* not constitutional; contrary to the constitution, as of a society or state. **constitutionality** *n.* **-ly** *adv.*

un·con·strained *a.* **-ly** *adv.* **unconstraint** *n.* **(constrain)**

un·con·trol·la·ble (un·kan·trōl′·a·bl) *a.* not capable of being controlled; unmanageable; irrepressible. **-ness** *n.* **uncontrollably** *adv.*

uncontrolled *a.* not controlled; (of prices) not restricted by government regulations. **uncontrolledly** *adv.*

uncon·ven·tion·al (un·kan·ven′·shan·al) *a.* **-ity** *n.* **-ly** *adv.* not conforming to convention, rule or precedent.

un·con·ver·sant *a.* **(converse** *v.***)**

un·con·vert·ed (un·kan·vur′·tid) *a.* not converted; unchanged in heart; heathen; not changed in opinion; **unconversion** *n.* **unconvertible** *a.* not convertible.

un·con·vinced *a.* **unconvincing** *a.* **(convince)**

un·cooked *a.* **(cook)**

un·cork *v.t.* **(cork)**

un·cor·rupt·ed *a.* **(corrupt)**

un·count·ed *a.* not counted; innumerable.

un·cou·ple (un·kup′·l) *v.t.* to loose, as a dog from a leash; to disjoin, as railway carriages. **-d** *a.* not mated; not joined.

un·couth (un·kòòth′) *a.* awkward in manner; strange; unpolished; unseemly. **-ly** *adv.* **-ness** *n.* [O.E. *cuth,* known].

un·cov·a·nant·ed (un·kuv′·a·nan·tid) *a,* not agreed to by covenant.

un·cov·er *v.t.* **(cover)**

un·crowned *a.* **(crown)**

unc·tion (ungk′·shan) *n.* act of anointing with oil, as in ceremony of consecration or coronation; (*Med.*) ointment; act of applying ointment; that which soothes; insincere fervor. **unctuosity** *n.* **unctuous** *a.* oily; excessively suave. **unctuously** *adv.* **unctuousness** *n.* **extreme unction,** R.C. rite of anointing the dying [L. *unguere, unctum,* to anoint].

un·cul·ti·va·ble (un·kul′·ti·va·bl) *a.* not capable of being cultivated; waste. **uncultivated** *a.* not cultivated; not tilled; (*Fig.*) undeveloped. **uncultured** *a.* not cultured; not educated; crude.

un·cured *a.* **(cure)**

un·cut *a.* **(cut)**

un·damped (un·dampt′) *a.* not damped; dry; (*Fig.*) not downhearted or dispirited.

un·dat·ed *a.* **(date)**

un·daunt·ed *a.* **-ly** *adv.* **(daunt)**

un·de·ceive (un·di·sēv′) *v.t.* to free from deception. **-d** *a.*

un·de·cid·ed (un·di·sī′·did) *a.* not settled; irresolute; vacillating. **undecidable** *a.* not capable of being settled. **-ly** *adv.*

un·de·ci·pher·a·ble *a.* **(decipher)**

un·de·clared (un·di·klārd′) *a.* not declared; (of taxable goods at customs) not admitted as being in one's possession during customs' examination.

un·de·fen·ded *a.* **(defend)**

un·de·filed *a.* **(defile** *v.***)**

un·de·fined *a.* **undefinable** *a.* **(define)**

un·dem·o·crat·ic (un·dem·a·krat′·ik) *a.* not according to the principlesa of democracy. **undemocratize** *v.t.* to make undemocratic.

un·de·mon·stra·tive *a.* **-ly** *adv.* **-ness** *n.* **(demonstrate)**

un·de·ni·a·ble *a.* **undeniably** *adv.* **(deny)**

un·de·nom·i·na·tion·al *a.* **(denomination)**

un·de·pend·a·ble *a.* **(depend)**

un·der (un′·der) *prep.* below; beneath; subjected to; less than; liable to; included in; in the care of; during the period of; bound by; *adv.* in a lower degree or position; less; *a.* subordinate; lower in rank or degree. **under age,** younger than 21 years [O.E. *under*].

un·der·act (un·der·akt′) *v.t.* or *v.i.* to act a part in a play in a colorless, ineffective way.

un·der·arm (un′·der·ȧrm) *a.n.* under the arm; armpit; *adv.* from below the shoulder (as a throw); *v.t.* to arm insufficiently. **-ed** *a.*

un·der·bid (un·der·bid′) *v.t.* to bid lower than another for a contract, etc.; to make lower bid at bridge than one's cards justify.

pr.p. **-ding.** *pa.p., pa.t.* **underbid. -der** *n.*

un·der·bred (un.dẹr.bred′) *a.* of inferior manners; not thoroughbred.

un·der·brush (un′.dẹr.brush) *n.* undergrowth of shrubs and bushes.

un·der·car·riage (un′.dẹr.kar.ij) *n.* (*Aero.*) landing gear of aircraft.

un·der·charge (un.dẹr.chárj.) *v.t.* to charge less than true price; *n.* price below the real value.

un·der·clothes (un′.dẹr.klō(TH)z) *n.pl.* garments worn below the outer clothing, esp. next the skin; underclothing; lingerie. **underclothed** *a.* **underclothing** *n.*

un·der·cov·er (un′.dẹr.kuv′.ẹr) *a.* (*Colloq.*) secret; used esp. of secret service agents.

un·der·cur·rent (un′.dẹr.kur.ạnt) *n.* current under surface of main stream, sometimes flowing in a contrary direction; hidden tendency.

un·der·cut (un.dẹr.kut′) *v.t.* to cut away from below, as coal seam; to strike from beneath; to sell goods cheaply in order to capture a market or monopoly; (*Golf*) to hit ball so it backspins. *pr.p.* **-ting.** *pa.p., pa.t.* **undercut.** *a.* produced by cutting away from below. (un′.dẹr.cut) *n.* act of cutting away from below; (*Boxing*) punch from underneath.

un·der·de·vel·op (un.dẹr.di.vel′.ạp) *v.t.* (*Photog.*) to develop insufficiently so that the photographic print is indistinct. **-ed** *a.* not developed physically; (of film) not sufficiently developed.

un·der·dog (un′.dẹr.dawg) *n.* (*Colloq.*) dog which is beaten in fight; person who fares badly in any struggle.

un·der·dose (un.dẹr.dōs′) *v.t.* to give an insufficient dose (of medicine) to; (un′.dẹr.dōs) *n.* an insufficient dose.

un·der·es·ti·mate (un.dẹr.es′.tạ.māt) *v.t.* to miscalculate the value of; to rate at too low a figure; *n.* an inadequate valuation.

un·der·ex·posed (un.dẹr.iks.pōzd′) *a.* (*Photog.*) insufficiently exposed to the light to impress details on a sensitive surface with clarity of outline. **underexposure** *n.*

un·der·feed (un.dẹr.fēd′) *v.t.* to feel insufficiently; to undernourish. **underfed** *a.*

un·der·foot (un.dēr.foot′) *adv.* beneath the feet; *a.* lying under the foot; in subjection.

un·der·gar·ment (un′.dẹr.gár.mạnt) *n.* a garment worn underneath the outer clothes.

un·der·go (un.dẹr.gō′) *v.t.* to bear; to suffer; to sustain; to participate in. *pr.p.* **-ing.** *pa.t.* **underwent.** *pa.p.* **undergone.**

un·der·grad·u·ate (un.dẹr.graj′.òò.it) *n.* student attending classes for his first degree at a university or college; *a.* pert. to such student or university course.

un·der·ground (un′.dẹr.ground) *a.* under the ground; subterranean; secret; *n.* (*chiefly Brit.*) a subway; (*Fig.*) secret organization or resistance movement; *adv.* below surface of earth; secretly.

un·der·growth (un′.dẹr.grōth) *n.* small trees, shrubs, or plants growing beside taller trees.

un·der·hand (un′.dẹr.hand) *adv.* by secret means; fraudulently; *a.* (*Sports*) served or thrown, as a ball, with hand underneath and an upward swing of the arm from below the waist; sly and dishonorable. **-ed** *a.* **-edly** *adv.* **-edness** *n.*

un·der·hung (un.dẹr.hung′) *a.* projecting beyond upper jaw, as lower jaw.

un·der·lay (un.dẹr.lā) *v.t.* to lay underneath; to support by something put below; *n.* something placed under another thing; piece of paper, cardboard, etc. used by printers to raise type plate; floor covering laid underneath a carpet. *pa.p., pa.t.* **underlaid.**

un·der·lie (un.dẹr.lī′) *v.t.* to lie underneath; to be the basis of. *pr.p.* **underlying.** *pa.p.* **underlain** or **underlaid.** *pa.t.* **underlay.** **underlying** *a.* basic; placed beneath; obscure.

un·der·line (un.dẹr.līn′) *v.t.* to mark with line below, for emphasis; to emphasize. (un′.dẹr.līn) *n.* **-d** *a.*

un·der·ling (un′.dẹr.ling) *n.* one who holds inferior position; subordinate member of a staff; a weakling.

un·der·manned (un.dẹr.mand′) *a.* supplied (as a ship) with too small a crew; having too small a staff.

un·der·mine (un.dẹr.mīn) *v.t.* to excavate for the purpose of mining, blasting, etc.; to erode; to sap, as one's energy; to weaken insidiously.

un·der·neath (un.dẹr.nēth′) *adv.* and *prep.* beneath; below; in a lower place.

un·der·nour·ished (un.dẹr.nur′.isht) *a.* insufficiently nourished. **undernourishment** *n.*

un·der·pass (un′.dẹr.pas) *n.* road or passage (for cars, pedestrians) under a highway or railroad.

un·der·pay (un.dẹr.pā′) *v.t.* to pay inadequately for the work done; to exploit. *pa.p., pa.t.* **underpaid. -ment** *n.*

un·der·pin·ning (un.dẹr.pin′.ing) *n.* a support; *pl.* the legs.

un·der·priv·i·leged (un.dẹr.priv′.ạ.lijd) *a.* deficient in the necessities of life because of poverty, discrimination, etc.

un·der·proof (un′.dẹr.pròòf) *a.* containing less alcohol than proof spirit.

un·der·rate (un.dẹr.rāt′) *v.t.* to rate too low; to underestimate.

un·der·score (un.dẹr.skōr) *v.t.* to underline for emphasis. **-d** *a.*

un·der·sec·re·tar·y (un′.dẹr.sek′.rạ.ter.i.) *n.* secretary who ranks below the principal secretary., esp. of government department.

un·der·sell (un.dẹr.sel′) *v.t.* to sell more cheaply than another. *pa.p., pa.t.* **undersold. -er** *n.*

un·der·set (un′.dẹr.set) *n.* (*Naut.*) an ocean undercurrent.

un·der·shot (un′.dẹr.shát) *a.* (of mill-wheel) turned by water flowing under; having a protruding lower jaw.

un·der·side (un.dẹr.sīd) *n.* the surface underneath.

un·der·sign (un.dẹr.sin′) *v.t.* to write one's name at the foot of or underneath. **-ed** *a.*

un·der·sized (un′.dẹr.sīzd) *a.* smaller than normal size; dwarf. Also **undersize.**

un·der·skirt (un′.dẹr.skurt) *n.* petticoat; skirt worn or placed under another.

un·der·stand (un.dẹr.stand′) *v.t.* to comprehend; to grasp the significance of. *pàp., pa.t.* **understood. -able** *a.* **-ably** *adv.* **-ing** *n.* **-ingly** *adv.* [O.E. *understandan*].

un·der·state (un.dẹr.stāt′) *v.t.* to state less strongly than truth warrants; to minimize deliberately. **-ment** *n.*

un·der·stud·y (un′.dẹr.stud.i.) *n.* one ready to substitute for principal actor (or actress) at a moment's notice; *v.t.* to study theatrical part for this purpose.

un·der·take (un.dẹr.tāk′) *v.t.* to take upon oneself as a special duty; to agree (to do); to warrant; *v.i.* to be under obligation to do something; (*Colloq.*) to make arrangements for burial. *pa.t.* **undertook.** *pa.p.* **-n. -r** *n.* one who undertakes; one who manages a burial. **undertaking** *n.* project; guarantee.

un·der·tone (un′.dẹr.tōn) *n.* low, subdued tone of voice or color.

un·der·tow (un′.dẹr.tō) *n.* undercurrent or backwash of a wave after it has reached the shore.

un·der·val·ue (un.dẹr.val′.ū) *v.t.* to set too low a price on; to esteem lightly; to underestimate; *n.* an underestimate. **undervaluation** *n.*

un·der·wear (un′.dẹr.wer) *n.* underclothes.
un·der·went (un.dẹr.went′) *pa.t.* of **undergo.**
un·der·wood (un′.dẹr.wood) *n.* small trees growing among larger trees.
un·der·world (un′.dẽr.wurld) *n.* the nether regions; Hades; the antipodes; section of community which lives by vice and crime.
un·der·write (un.dẹr.rīt′) *v.t.* to write under something else; to subscribe; to append one's signature, as to insurance policy; to undertake to buy shares not bought by the public, and thereby guarantee success of issue of business capital. *pa.t.* **underwrote.** *pa.p.* **underwritten.** *n.*
un·der·wrought (un.dẹr.rawt′) *pa.t.* and *pa.p.* of **underwork.**
un·de·served *a.* **undeserving** *a.* **undeservingly** *adv.* **(deserve)**
un·de·sir·a·ble (un.di.zīr′.ạ.bl) *a.* not desirable; having no appreciable virtues; *n.* person of ill-repute. **undesirability. undesirably** *adv.* **undesiring, undesirous** *a.* not desirous.
un·de·ter·mined *a.* **undeterminable** *a.* **undeterminate** *a.* **(determine)**
un·de·terred *a.* **(deter)**
un·de·vel·oped *a.* **(develop)**
un·de·vi·at·ing (un.dē′.vi.ā.ting) *a.* not deviating; resolute in pursuing a straight course; (*Fig.*) resolute of purpose.
un·did (un.did′) *pa.t.* of **undo.**
un·dies (un′.dēz) *n.pl.* (*Colloq. abbrev.*) women's underwear.
un·dif·fer·en·ti·at·ed *a.* **(differ)**
un·di·gest·ed *a.* **(digest)**
un·di·lut·ed *a.* **(dilute)**
un·di·min·ished *a.* **(diminish)**
un·dine (un.dēn′) *n.* water sprite; [L. *unda,* a wave].
un·di·rect·ed *a.*
un·dis·ci·plined *a.* **(discipline)**
un·dis·crim·i·nat·ing *a.* **(discriminate)**
un·dis·guised *a.* **(disguise)**
un·dis·mayed *a.* **(dismay)**
un·dis·posed *a.* **(dispose)**
un·dis·put·ed *a.* **undisputable** *a.* **undisputableness** *n.* **-ly** *adv.* **(dispute)**
un·dis·solved *a.* **(dissolve)**
un·dis·tin·guished *a.* **distinguishable** *a.* **undistinguishableness** *n.* **(distinguished)**
un·dis·turb·ed *a.* **(disturb)**
un·di·vid·ed *a.* **(divide)**
un·do (un.dȯȯ′) *v.t.* to reverse what has been done; to annul; to loose; to unfasten; to damage character of. *pa.t.* **undid.** *pa.p.* **undone. undoer** *n.* **-ing** *n.* act of reversing what has been done; ruin, esp. of reputation. **undone** *a.* ruined; not done; not completed.
un·do·mes·tic *a.* **-ated** *a.* **(domestic)**
un·doubt·ed *a.* **-ly** *adv.* **undoubtably** *adv.* **undoubtful** *a.* **(doubt)**
un·dress (un′.dres) *n.* informal dress; off-duty military uniform. (un.dress′) *v.t.* and *i.* **-ed** *a.*
un·due (un.dū′) *a.* not yet payable; unjust; immoderate; not befitting the occasion. **-ness** *n.*
un·du·late (un′.dyạ.lāt) *v.t.* to move up and down like waves; to cause to vibrate; *v.i.* to move up and down; to vibrate; to have wavy edge; *a.* (un′.dyạ.lit) wavy. **undulant** *a.* undulating; wavy. **-ly** *adv.* **undulating** *a.* wavy; having series of rounded ridges and depressions, as surface of landscape. **undulatingly** *adv.* **undulation** *n.* wave; fluctuating motion, as of waves; wave-like contour of stretch of land; series of wavy lines; vibratory motion. **undulatory** *a.* pert. to undulation; moving like a wave; pert. to theory of light which argues that light is transmitted through ether by wave motions. [L. *unda,* a wave].
un·du·ly (un.dȯȯ′.li.) *adv.* unjustly; improperly; excessively.
un·dy·ing *a.* not dying; immortal; everlasting. **-ly** *adv.* **-ness** *n.*
un·earned (un.urnd′) *a.* not earned by personal labor. **— income,** income derived from sources other than salary, fees, etc. **— increment,** increased value of property, land, etc. due to circumstances other than owner's expenditure on its upkeep.
un·earth (un.urth′) *v.t.* to dig up; to drive as a fox, rabbit, etc. from its burrow; to bring to light. **-liness** *n.* **-ly** *a.* not of this world; supernatural.
un·eas·y (un.ē′.zi.) *a.* anxious; awkward; uncomfortable. **uneasiness** *n.* **uneasily** *adv.* **(ease)**
un·e·co·nom·ic *a.* **(economy)**
un·ed·i·fy·ing *a.* **(edify)**
un·ed·u·cat·ed *a.* **(education)**
un·em·ploy·ment (un.im.ploi′.mạnt) *n.* state of being unemployed. **— benefit,** money received by unemployed workers according to conditions laid down by insurance regulations. **— insurance,** insurance against periods of unemployment contributed to by workers, employers, etc. **unemployed** *n.a.*
un·end·ing *a.* **unended** *a.* **-ly** *adv.* **(end)**
un·en·dur·a·ble *a.* **(endure)**
un·en·light·ened *a.* **(enlighten)**
un·e·qual *a.* **-led** *a.* **-ly** *adv.* **-ness** *n.* **(equal)**
un·e·quiv·o·cal *a.* **-ly** *adv.* **(equivocal)**
un·er·ring (-ly). *a.* and *adv.* **(err)**
U·nes·co (ū.nes′.kō) *n.* coined word from initial letters of *U*nited *N*ations *E*ducational, *Scientific and Cultural Organization,* established in November, 1945.
un·es·sen·tial *a.* **(essential)**
un·e·ven *a.* **-ly** *adv.* **(even)**
un·e·vent·ful *a.* **(event)**
un·ex·cep·tion·a·ble *a.* **unexceptional** *a.* **(except)**
un·ex·e·cut·ed *a.* **(execute)**
un·ex·pect·ed (un.iks.pek′.tid) *a.* not expected; sudden; without warning. **-ly** *adv.* **-ness** *n.*
un·ex·pired *a.* **(expire)**
un·ex·plained *a.* **(explain)**
un·ex·plored *a.* **(explore)**
un·ex·pressed *a.* **(express)**
un·ex·tin·guished *a.* **(extinguish)**
un·ex·tir·pat·ed *a.* **(extirpate)**
un·fad·a·ble *a.* **unfaded** *a.* **unfading** *a.* **(fade)**
un·fail·ing (un.fāl′.ing) *a.* not liable to fall; ever loyal; inexhaustible. **-ly** *adv.* **-ness** *n.*
un·fair (un.fār′) *a.* not fair; unjust; prejudiced; contrary to the rules of the game. **-ly** *adv.* **-ness** *n.*
un·faith·ful *a.* **-ly** *adv.* **-ness** *n.* **(faith)**
un·fal·ter·ing *a.* **(falter)**
un·fa·mil·iar *a.* **-ity** *n.* **-ly** *adv.* **(familiar)**
un·fash·ion·a·ble *a.* **-ness** *n.* **unfashionably** *adv.* **(fashion)**
un·fas·ten *v.t.* **-ed** *a.* **(fasten)**
un·fath·om·a·ble *a.* **-ness** *n.* **unfathomably** *adv.* **unfathomed** *a.* **(fathom)**
un·fa·vor·a·ble *a.* **(favor)**
un·feel·ing (un.fēl′.ing) *a.* void of feeling; callous; unsympathetic. **-ly** *adv.*
un·feigned *a.* **-ly** *adv.* **-ness** *n.* **(feign)**
un·fet·ter *v.t.* **-ed** *a.* **(fetter)**
un·fil·i·al *a.* **(filial)**
un·fin·ished (un.fin′.isht) *a.* not finished; roughly executed; not published. **unfinish** *n.* **unfinishable** *a.*
un·fit *a.* **-ly** *adv.* **-ness** *n.* **-ting** *a.* **-tingly** *adv.* **(fit)**
un·fledged (un.flejd′) *a.* not yet covered with feathers; immature.
un·fleshed (un.flesht′) *a.* (of sword) not yet used in fighting; not having tasted blood.

unfleshly *a.* uncorporeal. **unfleshy** *a.* having no flesh.
un·flinch·ing *a.* **-ly** *adv.* **(flinch)**
un·fold (un·fōld′) *v.t.* to open the folds of; to spread out; to disclose; *v.i.* to expand. **-er** *n.* **-ing** *n.* **-ment** *n.* **-ed** *a.*
un·fore·seen (un·fōr·sēn′) *a.* unexpected. **unforeseeable** *a.* not capable of being foreseen; unpredictable. **-unforeseeing** *n.*
un·for·get·ta·ble *a.* **unforgettably** *adv.* **(forget)**
un·for·giv·a·ble *a.* **unforgiving** *a.* **unforgivingness** *n.* **unforgotten** *a.* **(forgive)**
un·formed (un·fawrmd′) *a.* not formed; amorphous; immature.
un·for·tu·nate *a.* **-ly** *adv.* **-ness** *n.* **(fortune)**
un·found·ed (un·foun′·did) *a.* not based on truth; not established. **-ly** *adv.* **-ness** *n.* **(found)**
un·fre·quent·ed *a.* **unfrequent** *a.* **(frequent)**
un·friend·ly *a.* **unfriended** *a.* **unfriendedness** *n.* **unfriendliness** *n.* **(friend)**
un·frock (un·frák) *v.t.* to deprive of a frock, esp. to deprive of the status of a monk or priest. **-ed** *a.*
un·fruit·ful (un·frȯȯt′·fạl) *a.* not productive; not profitable.
un·furl (un·furl′) *v.t.* and *i.* to open or spread out.
un·fur·nished *a.* **unfurnish** *v.t.* **(furnish)**
un·gain·ly (un·gān′·li·) *a.* clumsy; awkward; *adv.* in a clumsy manner. **ungainliness** *n.* [M.E. *ungein*, awkward].
un·gar·nished *a.* **(garnish)**
un·gen·er·ous *a.* **(generous)**
un·gen·tle *a.* **-manly** *adv.* **(gentle)**
un·glaze *v.t.* **-d** *a.* **(glaze)**
un·god·ly (un·gȧd′·li·) *a.* not religious; sinful; (*Colloq.*) *outrageous(ly)*. **ungodliness** *n.*
un·gov·ern·a·ble *a.* **-ness** *n.* **ungovernably** *adv.* **ungoverned** *a.* **(govern)**
un·grace·ful *a.* **-ly** *adv.* **-ness** *n.* (graceful).
un·gra·cious *a.* **-ly** *adv.* **(grace)**
un·gram·mat·i·cal *a.* **-ly** *adv.* **(grammar)**
un·grate·ful *a.* **-ly** *adv.* **-ness** *n.* **(grateful)**
un·ground·ed (un·groun′·did) *a.* having no foundation; false.
un·grudg·ing *a.* **ungrudged** *a.* **-ly** *adv.* **(grudge)**
un·gual (ung·gwạl) *a.* having nails, hooves, or or claws. **ungulate** (ung′·gvạ·lit) *a.* having hoofs, *n.* one of the hoofed mammals [L. *unguis*, a nail].
un·guard·ed *a.* **-ly** *adv.* **-ness** *n.* **(guard)**
un·guent (ung′·gwạnt) *n.* ointment. **-ary** *a.* pert. to unguents. **unguinous** *a.* oily [L. *unguere*, to anoint].
un·hal·lowed (un·hal′·ōd) *n.* unholy; not consecrated; wicked. **unhallowing** *n.*
un·hamp·ered *a.* **(hamper)**
un·hand (un·hand′) *v.t.* to let go. **-ily** *adv.* awkwardly. **-iness** *n.* **-led** *a.* not handled. **-y** *a.* not handy; inconvenient; lacking skill.
un·hap·py *a.* **unhappily** *adv.* **unhappiness** *n.* **(happy)**
un·harmed *a.* **(harm)**
un·har·ness *a.* **(harness)**
un·health·y *a.* **unhealthful** *a.* **unhealthfully** *adv.* **unhealthfulness** *n.* **unhealthily** *adv.* **unhealthiness** *n.* **(health)**
un·heard (un·hurd′) *a.* not heard; not given hearing. **unheard of,** unprecedented.
un·heed·ed *a.* **(heed)**
un·hes·i·tat·ing (un·hez′·ạ·tā·ting) *a.* not hesitating; spontaneous; resolute. **-ly** *adv.* without hesitation.
un·hinge (un·hinj′) *v.t.* to take from the hinges; (*Fig.*) to cause mental instability. **-d** *a.* (of the mind) unstable; distraught.
un·hitch *v.* **(hitch)**
un·ho·ly (un·hō′·li·) *a.* not sacred; (*Colloq.*) dreadful. **unholily** *adv.* **unholiness** *n.* **(holy)**
un·hon·ored *a.* **(honor)**
un·hook *v.t.* **(hook)**
un·horse (un·hawrs′) *v.t.* to throw from a horse; to cause to fall from a horse.
un·hur·ried *a.* **(hurry)**
un·hurt *a.* **-ful** *a.* **(hurt)**
un·hy·gi·en·ic (un·hī·ji·en′·ik) *a.* not hygienic; unsanitary; unhealthy.
u·ni-, (ūni) *prefix* denoting one or single [fr. L. *unus*, one].
u·ni·ax·i·al (ū·ni·ak′·si·ạl) *a.* having a single axis; having one direction along which ray of light can travel without bifurcation. **-ly** *adv.*
u·ni·cam·er·al having one legislative chamber.
u·ni·cel·lu·lar (ū·ni·sel′·yạ·lẹr) *a.* having a single cell; monocellular.
u·ni·corn (ū′·ni·kawrn) *n.* (*Myth.*) horselike animal with a single horn protruding from forehead [L. *unus*, one; *cornu*, horn].
un·i·de·al (un·ī·dē′·ạl) *a.* realistic; prosaic. **-ism** *n.*
u·ni·form (ū′·nạ·fawrm *a.* having always same form; conforming to one pattern; regular; consistent; not varying, as temperature; *n.* official dress, as a livery, etc. **-ed** *a.* wearing uniform. **-ity** *n.* conformity to pattern or standard. **-ly** *adv.* **-ness** *n.* [L. *unus*, one; *forma*, form].
u·ni·fy (ū′·nạ·fī) *v.t.* to make into one; to make uniform. **unifiable** *a.* capable of being made one. **unification** *n.* act of unifying; state of being made one; welding together of separate parts. **unifier** *n.* [L. *unus*, one; *facere*, to make].
u·ni·lat·er·al (ū·ni·lat′·ẹr·ạl) *a.* one-sided; binding one side only, as in party agreement. **-ity** *n.* **-ly** *adv.*
u·ni·loc·u·lar (ū·ni·lạk′·ū·lạr) *a.* having single chamber or cavity.
un·im·ag·i·na·ble (un·i·maj′·i·nạ·bl) *a.* not imaginable; inconceivable. **-ness** *n.* **unimaginably** *adv.* **unimaginative** *a.* not imaginative; dull; uninspired. **unimaginatively** *adv.* **unimaginativeness** *n.* **unimagined** *a.* not imagined.
un·im·paired *a.* **(impair)**
un·im·peach·a·ble (un·im·pēch′·ạ·bl) *a.* not impeachable; irreproachable; blameless. **-ness, unimpeachability** *n.* **unimpeachably** *adv.* **unimpeached** *a.*
un·im·por·tant *a.* **unimportance** *n.* **(import)**
un·im·proved *a.* **(improve)**
un·in·flect·ed *a.* **(inflect)**
un·in·formed (un·in·fawrmd′) *a.* having no accurate information; ignorant; not expert.
un·in·hab·it·able *a.* **uninhabitability** *n.* **uninhabited** *a.* **(inhabit)**
un·in·jured *a.* **(injure)**
un·in·spired **(inspire)**
un·in·sured *a.* **(insure)**
un·in·tel·li·gent *a.* **unintelligence** *n.* **unintelligently** *adv.* **unintelligibility** *n.* **unintelligible** *a.* **unintelligibleness** *n.* **unintelligibly** *adv.* **(intelligent)**
un·in·ten·tion·al *a.* **-ly** *adv.* **(intent)**
un·in·ter·est·ed *a.* **-ly** *adv.* **-ness** *n.* **uninteresting** *a.* **uninterestingly** *adv.* **(interest)**
un·in·ter·rupt·ed *a.* **-ly** *adv.* **(interrupt)**
un·in·vit·ed *a.* **uninviting** *a.* **uninvitingly** *adv.* **(invite)**
un·ion (ūn′·yạn) *n.* act of joining two or more things into one; federation; marriage; harmony; combination of administrative bodies for a common purpose; trade union; **-ed** *a.* joined. **-ist** *n.* one who supports union. **Union Jack,** national flag of United Kingdom [Fr. *union*, fr.L. *unus*, one].

u·nip·a·rous (ū·nip′·ạ·rạs) *a.* producing normally just one at a birth; (*Bot.*) having single stem [L. *unus*, one; *parere*, to bring forth].
u·nique (ū·nēk′) *a.* single in kind; having no like or equal; unusual; different. **-ly** *adv.* **-ness** *n.* [L. *unicus*, one].
u·ni·sex·u·al (ū·ni·sek′·shoo·ạl) *a.* of one sex only, as a plant; not hermaphrodite or bisexual. **-ity** *n.* **-ly** *adv.*
u·ni·son (ū′·nạ·sạn) *n.* harmony; concord; (*Mus.*) identity of pitch. **in unison,** with all voices singing the same note at the same time; sounding together; in agreement.
u·nit (ū′·nit) *n.* single thing or person; group regarded as one; standard of measurement; (*Math.*) the least whole number. **-ary** *a.* pert. to unit(s); whole [L. *unus*, one].
U·ni·tar·i·an (ū·ni·ter′·i·ạn) *n.* one who rejects doctrine of the Trinity and asserts the oneness of God and the teachings of Jesus. **-ism** *n.* [L. *unus*, one].
u·nite (ū·nīt′) *v.t.* to join; to make into one; to form a whole; to associate; to cause to adhere; *v.i.* to be joined together; to grow together; to act as one; to harmonize. **united** *a.* joined together; harmonious; unanimous. **unitedly** *adv.* **-r** *n.* **unity** *n.* state of oneness; agreement; coherence; combination of separate parts into connected whole, or of different people with common aim; (*Math.*) any quantity taken as one. **unitive** *a.* **United Nations,** international organization, formed 1942. **United Nations Organization,** international organization set up after *World War* 2 with Security Council as chief executive body. *Abbrev.* **UN. United States,** N. Amer. country; federal union of 50 states U.S.A. [L. *unus*, one].
u·ni·va·lent (u·ni·vā′·lạnt) *a.* (*chem.*) having a valence of one; (*Bot.*) unpaired. **univalence, univalency** *n.*
u·ni·valve (ū′·ni·valv) *a.* having only one valve; *n.* a single-shelled mollusk. Also **univalvular** *a.*
u·ni·verse (ū′·ni·vurs) *n.* all created things regarded as a system or whole; the world. **universal** *a.* pert. to universe; embracing all created things; world-wide; general (as opp. of *particular*); *n.* universal proposition; general concept; (in motoring) universal joint. **-ize** *v.t.* to make universal. **-ization** *n.* **Universalism** *n.* theological doctrine of the ultimate salvation of all mankind. **Universalist** *n.* **universalistic** *a.* **-ity** *n.* **— joint** (in motoring device whereby one part of machine has perfect freedom of motion in relation to another. **-ly** *adv.* **-ness** *n.* [L. *unus*, one; *vertere, versum*, to turn].
u·ni·ver·si·ty (ū·ni·vur′·sạ·ti·) *n.* institution for educating students in higher branches of learning, and having authority to confer degrees [L. *universitas*, a corporation].
un·just *a.* **-ifiable** *a.* **-ifiably** *adv.* **-ly** *adv.* **-ness** *n.* **(just)**
un·kempt (un·kempt′) *a.* dishevelled; rough [O.E. *un-*, not; *cemban*, to comb].
un·kind (un·kīnd) *a.* not kind, considerate, or sympathetic; cruel. **-liness** *n.* **-ly** *a.* **-ness** *n.* **(kind)**
un·know·a·ble (un·nō′·ạ·bl) *a.* not capable of being known; *n.* that which is beyond man's power to understand; the absolute. **-ness** *n.* **unknowably** *adv.* **unknowing** *a.* ignorant. **unknowingly** *adv.* **unknown** *a.* not known; incalculable; *n.* unknown quantity; unexplored regions of mind; part of globe as yet unvisited by man.
un·lace *n.* **(lace)**
un·lament·ed *a.* **(lament)**
un·latch *v.* **(latch)**
un·law·ful *a.* **-ly** *adv.* **-ness** *n.* **(law)**
un·learn *v.t.* **-ed** *a.* **(learn)**
un·leash *v.t.* **-ed** *a.* **(leash)**
un·leav·ened (un·lev′·and) *a.* not leavened; made without yeast, as *unleavened bread.*
un·less (un·les′) *conj.* except; if not; supposing that; *prep.* except.
un·let·tered (un·let′·ẹrd) *a.* illiterate.
un·li·censed *a.* **(license)**
un·like (un·lik′) *a.* not like; dissimilar; *prep.* different from; *adv.* in a different way from. **-lihood, -ness** *n.* **-ly** *a.* improbable; unpromising; *adv.* improbably. **-liness** *n.*
un·lim·it·ed *a.* **-ly** *adv.* **(limit)**
un·load (un·lōd′) *v.t.* to remove load from; to remove charge from, as gun; to sell out quickly, as stocks, shares, etc. before slump; (*Fig.*) to unburden, as one's mind; *v.i.* to discharge cargo. **-ed** *a.* not containing a charge, as gun; not containing a plate or film, as camera.
un·lock *v.t.* **(lock)**
un·looked-for (un·lookt′·fawr) a. unexpected, unforeseen.
un·loose (un·lòòs′) *v.t.* to set free. **-n** *v.t.*
un·lov·a·ble *a.* **unloved** *a.* **unloving** *a.* **(love)**
un·love·ly *a.* **unloveliness** *n.* **(lovely)**
un·luck·y *a.* **unluckily** *adv.* **unluckiness** *n.* **(lucky)**
un·make (un·māk′) *v.t.* to destroy what has been made; to annul; to ruin, destroy; to depose. *pa.p., pa.t.* **unmade. -r** *n.* **unmade** *a.* not made. **unmakable** *a.* **unmaking** *n.*
un·man *v.t.* **—like** *a.* **-liness** *n.* **-ly** *a.* **-ned** *a.* **(man)**
un·man·age·a·ble *a.* **-ness** *n.* **unmanageably** *adv.* **unmanaged** *a.* **(manage)**
un·man·ner·ly *a.* **unmannered** *a.* **unmannerliness** *n.* **(manner)**
un·marked (un·markt′) *a.* without a mark.
un·mar·ried *a.* **unmarriageable** *a.* **unmarriageableness** *n.* **(marry)**
un·mask *v.t.* **-ed** *a.* **(mask)**
un·mean·ing (un·mēn′·ing) *a.* without meaning; unintentional; insignificant. **-ly** *adv.* **unmeant** (un·ment′) *a.* not intended; accidental.
un·meas·ured *a.* **unmeasurable** *a.* **unmeasurably** *adv.* **(measure)**
un·men·tion·a·ble (un·men′·shạn·ạ·bl) *a.* not worthy of mention; not fit to be mentioned. **-ness** *n.* **-s** *n.pl.* facetious synonym for undergarments.
un·mer·ci·ful (un·mur′·si·fạl) *a.* having or showing no mercy; cruel. **-ly** *adv.*
un·mind·ed (un·mīn′·did) *a.* not remembered **unmindful** *a.* forgetful; regardless. **unmindfully** *adv.* **unmindfulness** *n.*
un·mis·tak·a·ble (un·mis·tāk′·ạ·bl) *a.* clear; plain; evident. **unmistakably** *adv.*
un·mit·i·gat·ed (un·mit′·i·gāt·id) *a.* not softened or lessened; absolute; unmodified.
un·mixed *a.* **(mix)**
un·mo·lest·ed *a.* **(molest)**
un·moor *v.t.* **(moor)**
un·mor·al (un·màr′., un·mawr′·ạl) *a.* not concerned with morality or ethics. **-izing** *a.* not given to reflecting on ethical values.**-ity** *n.* **-ly** *adv.*
un·mount·ed *a.* **(mount)**
un·moved *a.* **unmovable, unmoveable** *a.* **unmoving** *a.* **(move).**
un·mu·si·cal *a.* **-ity** *n.* **-ly** *adv.* **(music)**
un·named *a.* **(name)**
un·nat·u·ral *a.* **-ize** *v.t.* **-ized** *a.* **-ly** *adv.* **(natural)**
un·nav·i·ga·ble *a.* **unnavigability** *n.* **unnavigated** *a.* **(navigate)**
un·nec·es·sar·y *a.* **unnecessarily** *adv.* **unnecessariness** *n.* **(necessary)**
un·nerve (un·nurv′) to deprive of courage, strength; cause to feel weak. *v.t.* **-d** *a.*
un·no·ticed *a.* **(notice)**

un·num·bered (un·num′·bẹrd) *a.* not counted; innumerable.
un·ob·served *a.* **(observe)**
un·ob·struct·ed *a.* **(obstruct)**
un·ob·tru·sive *a.* **-ly** *adv.* **-ness** *n.* **(obtrude)**
un·oc·cu·pied (un·ȧk′·yȧ·pīd) *a.* not occupied; untenanted; not engaged in work; not under control of troops.
un·of·fi·cial *a.* **(official)**
un·o·pened *a.* **(open)**
un·or·gan·ized (un·ōr′·gạ·nīzd) *a.* without organic structure; having no system or order; not belonging to a labor union.
un·op·posed *a.* **(oppose)**
un·or·tho·dox *a.* **(orthodox)**
un·os·ten·ta·tious *a.* **-ly** *adv.* **(ostentation)**
un·pack (un·pak′) *v.t.* to remove from a pack or trunk; to open by removing packing; *v.i.* to empty contents of. **-ed** *a.* **-er** *n.*
un·paid *a.* **(pay)**
un·pal·at·a·ble *a.* **(palate)**
un·par·al·leled (un·par′·ạ·leld) *a.* having no equal; unprecedented.
un·par·don·a·ble *a.* **unpardonably** *adv.* **unpardoned** *a.* **(pardon)**
un·par·lia·men·ta·ry (*un·pạr·lạ·men′·tạ·*ri·) *a.* contrary to parliamentary law or usage.
un·peo·ple *v.t.* **(people)**
un·per·turbed *a.* **-ness** *n.* **(perturb)**
un·pick *v.t.* **-ed** *a.* **(pick)**
un·placed *a.* **unplace** *v.t.* **(place)**
un·pleas·ant *a.* **-ly** *adv.* **-ness** *n.* **unpleasing** *a.* **unpleasingly** *adv.* **unpleasurable** *a.* **(please)**
un·pol·ished *a.* **(polish)**
un·pop·u·lar *a.* **unpopularity** *n.* **(popular)**
un·prec·e·dent·ed (un·pres·ạ·den′·tid) *a.* without precedent; having no earlier example; novel. **-ly** *adv.*
un·pol·lut·ed *a.* **(pollute)**
un·pre·dict·a·ble *a.* **(predict)**
un·pre·med·i·tat·ed *a.* **unpremeditable** *a.* **-ly** *adv.* **-ness, unpremeditation** *n.* **(premeditate)**
un·pre·pared *a.* **-ly** *adv.* **-ness** *n.* **(prepare)**
un·pre·pos·sess·ing *a.* **unprepossessed** *a.* **(prepossess)**
un·pre·ten·tious *a.* **(pretend)**
un·prin·ci·pled *a.* **(principle)**
un·print·a·ble (un·print′·ạ·bl) *a.* not printable; too shocking to be set down in print.
un·pro·duc·tive *a.* **-ly** *adv.* **-ness** *n.* **(product)**
un·pro·fes·sion·al (un·prạ·fesh′·ạn·l) *a.* not professional; contrary to professional ethics. **-ly** *adv.* **(profess)**
un·prof·it·a·ble *a.* **-ness** *n.* **unprofitably** *adv.* **(profit)**
un·prom·is·ing *a.* **(promise)**
un·pro·nounce·a·ble *a.* **(pronounce)**
un·pro·tect·ed *a.* **(protect)**
un·pro·vid·ed *a.* **(provide)**
un·pro·voked *a.* **(provoke)**
un·pruned *a.* **(prune** *v.***)**
un·pub·lished *a.* **(publish)**
un·pun·ished *a.* **unpunishable** *a.* **(punish)**
un·qual·i·fied (un·kwạl′·ạ·fīd) *a.* not qualified; not having proper qualifications; not modified; absolute. **unqualifying** *a.*
un·quench·a·ble *a.* **(quench)**
un·ques·tion·a·ble *a.* **unquestionability, -ness** *n.* **unquestionably** *adv.* **unquestioned** *a.* **unquestioning** *a.* **(question)**
un·qui·et *a.* **(quiet)**
un·quote (un·kwọ̄t) *v.t.* and *i.* to end a quotation.
un·rav·el *v.t.* **-ed** *a.* **(ravel)**
un·read (un·red′) *a.* (of a book) not read; not having gained knowledge by reading. **-able** (un·rēd′·ạ·bl) *a.* not readable—illegible, uninteresting or unsuitable.
un·ready *a.* **unreadily** *adv.* **(ready)**
un·re·al (un·rēl′) *a.* not real; insubstantial; illusive. **-izable** *a.* not realizable.**-izableness** *n.* **-ized** *a.* not realized; unfulfilled. **unreality** *n.* want of reality. **-ly** *adv.* **-ity** *n.*
un·rea·son (un·rē′·zn) *n.* lack of reason; irrationality. **-able** *a.* immoderate; impulsive; exorbitant (of prices). **-ableness** *n.* **-ably** *adv.* **-ed** *a.* not logical. **-ing** *a.* irrational.
un·rec·og·nized *a.* **unrecognizable** *a.* **-izably** *adv.* **(recognize)**
un·re·cord·ed *a.* **(record)**
un·rec·ti·fied *a.* **(rectify)**
un·reeve *v.t.* **(reeve** *v.***)**
un·re·fined *a.* **(refine)**
un·re·gen·er·ate *a.* **unregeneracy, unregeneration** *n.* **-ly** *adv.* **(regenerate)**
un·re·lat·ed (un·ri·lāt′·id) *a.* not related; having no apparent connection; diverse.
un·re·lent·ing *a.* **-ly** *adv.* **(relent)**
un·re·li·a·ble *a.* **unreliability, -ness** *n.* **(reliable)**
un·re·lieved *a.* **(relieve)**
un·re·mem·bered *a.* **(remember)**
un·re·mit·ting (un·ri·mit′·ing) *a.* not relaxing; incessant; persistent. **unremitted** *a.* not remitted. **unremittedly, -ly** *adv.*
un·re·proved *a.* **(reproof)**
un·re·quit·ed *a.* **unrequitable** *a.* **-ly** *adv.* **(requite)**
un·rest (un·rest′) *n.* want of rest; disquiet; political or social agitation. **-ful** *a.* **-fulness** *n.* **-ing** *a. not resting.* **-ingly** *adv.*
un·re·strained *a.* **(restrain)**
un·re·strict·ed *a.* **-ly** *adv.* **(restrict)**
un·right·eous *a.* **-ly** *adv.* **-ness** *n.* **unrightful** *a.* **unrightfully** *adv.* **-fulness** *n.* **(righteous, right)**
un·ripe *a.* **-ned** *a.* **-ness** *n.* **(ripe)**
un·robe *v.t.* and *v.i.* **(robe)**
un·ri·valed *a.* **(rival)**
un·roll *v.* **(roll)**
un·ruf·fled (un·ruf′·ld) *a.* not ruffled; placid. **unruffle** *v.i.* to become placid.
un·ruled (un·rȯȯld′) *a.* not ruled; ungoverned; (of paper) blank; unrestrained. **unruliness** *n.* state of being unruly. **unruly** *a.* lawless; disobedient.
un·sad·dle *v.* **(saddle)**
un·safe *a.* **-ly** *adv.* **-ness** *n.* **-ty** *n.* **(safe)**
un·sale·a·ble *a.* **unsalability** *n.* **(sale)**
un·san·i·tar·y *a.* **(sanitary)**
un·sat·is·fac·to·ry *a.* **unsatisfactorily** *adv.* **unsatisfactoriness** *n.* **unsatisfied** *a.* **unsatisfying** *a.* **(satisfy)**
un·sa·vo·r·y *a.* **unsavorily** *adv.* **unsavoriness** *n.* **(savory)**
un·say (un·sā′) *v.t.* to retract (what has been said). *p.pa., pa.t.* **unsaid.**
un·scathed (un·skāTHd′) *a.* unharmed; without injury.
un·schooled *a.* **(school)**
un·sci·entif·ic *a* **-ally** *adv.*
un·scram·ble (un·skram′·bl) *v.t.* to decode a secret message; to straighten out.
un·scru·pu·lous (un·skrȯȯ′·pyạ·lạs) *a.* not scrupulous; ruthless; having no moral principles. **-ly** *adv.* **-ness** *n.*
un·seal *v.t.* **-ed** *a.* **(seal** *n., v.t.***)**
un·sea·son·a·ble (un·sē′·zạn·ạ·bl) *a.* untimely; out of season. **-ness** *n.* **unseasonably** *adv.* **unseasoned** *a.*
un·seat (un·sēt′) *v.t.* to throw from a horse; to deprive of official seat.
un·seem·li·ness *n.* **unseemly** *a.* and *adv.* **(seem)**
un·seen *a.* **(see)**
un·self·con·scious (un·self·kȧn′·shạs) *a.* not self-conscious; natural. **-ly** *adv.* **-ness** *n.*
un·self·ish *a.* **-ly** *adv.* **-ness** *n.* **(self)**
un·set·tle (un·set′·l) *v.t.* to move or loosen

from a fixed position; to disturb mind; to make restless or discontented. **-d** *a.* not settled; changeable, as weather; unpaid, as bills; not allocated; not inhabited. **-dly** *adv.* **-dness, -ment** *n.* **unsettling** *a.* disturbing.
un·shack·le *v.t.* **-d** *a.* **(shackle)**
un·shad·ed *a.* **(shade)**
un·shak·en *a.* **(shake)**
un·shav·en *a.* **(shave)**
un·sheathe *n.* **(sheath)**
un·shed *a.* **(shed)**
un·shod (un·shȧd′) *a.* barefoot.
un·sight·ed (un·sī′·tid) *a.* not sighted; not observed; (of gun) without sights; (of shot) aimed blindly. **unsightable** *a.* invisible. **unsightliness** *n.* ugliness. **unsightly** *a.* ugly; revolting to the sight.
un·skill·ful *a.* **-ly** *adv.* **-ness** *n.* **unskilled** *a.* **(skill)**
un·sling (un·sling′) *v.t.* (*Naut.*) to remove slings from, as from cargo; to take down something which is hanging by sling, as a rifle. *pa.p., pa.t.* **unslung.**
un·smil·ing *a.* **-ly** *adv.* **(smile)**
un·so·cia·ble *a.* **unsociability, -ness** *n.* **unsociably** *adv.* **(sociable)**
un·smirched *a.* **(smirch)**
un·so·lic·i·ted (un·sạ·lis′·i·tid) *a.* not solicited; gratuitous. **unsolicitous** *a.* unconcerned.
un·so·phis·ti·cat·ed (un·sạ·fis′·ti·kāt·id) *a.* not sophisticated; ingenuous; simple. **-ly** *adv.* **-ness, unsophistication** *n.*
un·sound (un·sound′) *a.* imperfect; damaged: decayed; (of the mind) insane; not based on reasoning; fallacious. **-ly** *adv.* **-ness** *n.*
un·speak·a·ble (un·spēk′·ạ·bl) *a.* beyond utterance or description (in good or bad sense); ineffable. **unspeakably** *adv.* **unspeaking** *a.* dumb.
un·spoiled *a.* Also **unspoilt (spoil)**
un·sport·ing (un·spōr′·ting) *a.* (*Colloq.*) not like sportsman; unfair. **unsportsmanlike** *a.* not in accordance with the rules of fair play.
un·spot·ted *a.* **(spot)**
un·sprung (un·sprung′) *a.* not fitted with springs, as a vehicle, chair, etc.
un·sta·ble (un·stā′·bl) *a.* unsteady; wavering; not firm; unreliable; (*Chem.*) applied to compounds which readily decompose or change into other compounds. **unstability, -ness** *n.* **unstably** *adv.* **(stable** *a.***)**
un·stained *a.* **(stain)**
un·stead·y *a.* **unsteadily** *adv.* **unsteadiness** *n.* **(steady)**
un·stead·fast *a.* **unsteadfastly** *adv.* **unsteadfastness** *n.* **(steadfast)**
un·stop (un·stȧp′) *v.t.* to open by removing a stopper, as a bottle; to clear away an obstruction; to open organ stops. *pr.p.* **-ping.** *pa.p., pa.t.* **-ped.** *a.* not stopped; having no cork or stopper.
un·strained (un·strānd′) *a.* not strained, as through a filter; (*Fig.*) relaxed; friendly.
un·stuck (un·stuk′) *a.* not glued together.
un·sub·dued *a.* **(subdue)**
un·sub·stan·tial *a.* **(substantial)**
un·suc·cess·ful (un·sạk·ses′·fạl) *a.* not succeeding; unfortunate; incomplete. **-ly** *adv.* **-ness** *n.*
un·suit·a·ble *a.* **unsuitability** *n.* **unsuited** *a.*
un·sul·lied *a.* **(sully)**
un·sung (un·sung′) *a.* not sung or spoken; not celebrated.
un·sup·port·ed (un·sạ·pōr′·tạd) *a.* not supported; without backing. **unsupportable** *a.* not supportable; intolerable.
un·sure *a.* **-ness** *n.* **(sure)**
un·sur·passed *a.* **(surpass)**
un·sus·pect·ed *a.* **(suspect)**
un·sus·pi·cious *a.* **(suspicious)**
un·sweet·ened *a.* **(sweeten)**
un·swept *a.* **(sweep)**
un·swerv·ing *a.* **-ly** *adv.* **(swerve)**
un·sym·pa·thet·ic *a.* **-ally** *adv.* **unsympathizable** *a.* **unsympathizing** *a.* **(sympathy)**
un·taint·ed *a.* **(taint)**
un·tan·gle *v.* **(tangle)**
un·tar·nished *a.* **(tarnish)**
un·taught (un·tawt′) *a.* *pa.p., pa.t.* of **unteach**; uneducated; ignorant; natural, without teaching.
un·ten·a·ble *a.* **(tenable)**
un·thank·ful (un·thangk′·fạl) *a.* ungrateful.
un·tamed *a.* **untamable** *a.* **(tame)**
un·think·ing (un·thingk′·ing) *a.* thoughtless; heedless. **-ly** *adv.* **unthinkable** *a.* **(think)**
un·ti·dy *a.* **untidily** *adv.* **untidiness** *n.*
un·tie *v.t.* **-d** *a.* **(tie)**
un·til (un·til′) *prep.* till; to; as far as; as late as; *conj.* up to the time that; to the degree that.
un·time·ly (un·tīm′·li·) *a.* not timely; premature; inopportune. **untimeliness** *n.*
un·tir·ing *a.* **untirable** *a.* **untired** *a.* **-ly** *adv.* **(tire** *v.***)**
un·to (un′·tȯȯ) *prep.* (*Poet.*) to; until [M.E. *und to*, up to, as far as].
un·touch·a·ble (un·tuch′·ạ·bl) *a.* incapable of being touched; unfit to be touched; out of reach; belonging to non-caste masses of India; *n.* non-caste Indian whose touch or even shadow was regarded as defiling. **-untouchability** *n.* **untouched** *a.*
un·to·ward (un·tōrd′) *a.* unlucky; inconvenient; hard to manage.
untrained *a.* **(train)**
un·trav·eled (un·trav′·eld) *a.* not having traveled; unexplored.
un·tried (un·trīd′) *pa.p., pa.t.* of **try**; not proven, attempted or tested, not tried in court.
un·trimmed *a.* **(trim)**
un·true (un·trȯȯ′) *a.* not true; false; disloyal; not conforming to a requisite standard. **-ness** *n.* **untruly** *adv.* falsely. **untruth** *n.* **untruthful** *a.* dishonest; lying. **untruthfully** *adv.* **untruthfulness** *n.*
un·turned *a.* **(turn)**
un·twist *v.* **(twist)**
un·tu·tored *a.* **(tutor)**
un·used (un·ūzd′) *a.* not used; not accustomed. **unusual** *a.* not usual; uncommon; strange. **unusually** *adv.* **unusualness** *n.*
un·ut·ter·a·ble (un·ut′·ẹr·ạ·bl) *a.* unspeakable beyond utterance; **unutterability** *n.* **unutterably** *adv.* **unuttered** *a.* unspoken.
un·var·nished *a.* **(varnish)**
un·vary·ing *a.* **(vary)**
un·veil *v.t.* **(veil)**
un·ver·i·fied *a.* **(verify)**
un·vexed *a.* **(vex)**
un·vis·it·ed *a.* **(visit)**
un·want·ed *a.* **(want)**
un·war·rant·a·ble (un·war′·ạnt·ạ·bl) *a.* justifiable; improper. **-ness** *n.* **unwarrantably** *adv.* **unwarranted** *a.* **unwarrantedly** *adv.* **(warrant)**
un·war·y *a.* **unwarily** *adv.* **unwariness** *n.* **(wary)**
un·washed (un·wȧsht′) *a.* not washed; dirty; not reached by the sea.
un·well (un·wel′) *a.* ill; ailing.
un·wept (un·wept′) *a.* not mourned or regretted.
un·whole·some *a.* **-ly** *adv.* **-ness** *n.* **(wholesome)**
un·wield·y *a.***unwieldily** *adv.* **unwieldiness** *n.* **(wield)**
un·will·ing (un·wil′·ing) *a.* loathe; reluctant. **-ly** *adv.* **-ness** *n.* **(will)**
un·wind (un·wīnd′) *v.t.* to wind off; to loose what has been wound; to roll into a ball from a skein, as wool, silk, etc.; *v.i.* to become un-

wound. *pa.p., pa.t.* **unwound.**
un·wit·ting (un·wit'·ing) *a.* unawares; not knowing. **-ly** *adv.*
un·wont·ed (un·wunt'·ạd, un·wōnt'ạd) *a.* unaccustomed; unusual. **-ly** *adv.* **-ness** *n.*
un·work·a·ble *a.* **(work)**
un·world·ly *a.* **unworldliness** *n.* **(worldly)**
un·wor·thy *a.* **unworthily** *adv.* **unworthiness** *n.* **(worthy)**
un·writ·ten (un·rit'·n) *a.* not written; oral. **— law** *n.* law originating in custom, usage, or court rather than books.
un·yield·ing (un·yēl'·ding) *a.* not yielding; stubborn; not flexible. *adv.* **-ness** *n.*
un·yoke *vt.* **(yoke)**
up (up) *adv. prep.* to or toward a higher place or degree; on high; on one's legs; out of bed; above horizon; in progress; in revolt; as far as; of equal merit or degree; competent; *a.* advanced; standing; reaching; tending toward; higher; even with; finished; *v.t., i.* to put or take up; to raise; to bet more. *pr.p.* **-ping.** *pa.p., pa.t.* **-ped. —-and-coming,** alert; enterprising.
u·pas (ū'·pạs) *n.* tree of E. Indian islands, yielding sap of deadly poison [Malay = poison].
up·braid (up·brād') *v.t.* to reprove severely; to chide; *v.i.* to voice a reproach. **-ing** *n.* reproach; *a.* reproachful [O.E. *up,* on; *bregdan,* to braid].
up·bring·ing (up'·bring·ing) *n.* the process of rearing and training a child; education.
UPC (ū·pē·sē') *U*niversal *P*roduct *C*ode, consisting of a series of black bars and numbers on packages, book covers, etc., for electronic scanning at the checkout counter.
up·coun·try (up'·kun·tri·) *adv.* inland; *a.* away from the sea.
up·date (up'·dāt) *v.t.* bring up-to-date.
up·end (up·end') *v.t.* to stand on end.
up·grade (up'·grād) *a., adv.* uphill; *n.* incline; *v.t.* to raise to a higher level.
up·heave (up·hēv') *v.t.* to lift up, as heavy weight. **upheaval** *n.* raising up, as of earth's surface, by volcanic force; (*Fig.*) any revolutionary change in ideas, etc.
up·held (up·held') *pa.t., pa.p.* of **uphold.**
up·hill (up'·hil) *a.* going up; laborious; difficult; (up·hil') *adv.* towards higher level.
up·hold (up·hōld') *v.t.* to hold up; to sustain; to approve; to maintain, as verdict in law court. *pa.p., pa.t.* **upheld. -er** *n.*
up·hol·ster (up·hōl'·ster) *v.t.* to stuff and cover furniture. **-y** *n.* craft of stuffing and covering furniture, etc.; material used. **-er** *n.*
up·keep (up'·kēp) *n.* maintenance; money required for maintenance, as of a home.
up·land (up'·land) *n.* high land or region. *a.* pert. to or situated in higher elevations.
up·lift (up·lift') *v.t.* to lift up; to improve conditions of, morally, socially etc.; to exalt; (up'·lift) *n.* emotional or religious stimulus; moral and social improvement; a brassiere. **-er** *n.* **-ment** *n.*
up·on (ạ·pȧn') *prep.* on [O.E. *uppon,* on].
up·per (up'·ẹr) *a.* higher in place, rank, or dignity; superior; more recent; *n.* the part above; (*Colloq.*) upper berth. **-s** *n.pl.* (*Colloq.*) upper teeth. **—case** *n.* (*Print.*) (case containing) capital letters. **-cut** *n.* (*Boxing*) blow struck upwards inside opponent's guard; *v.t.* to deliver such blow. **—hand** *n.* superiority; advantage over another. **uppish, uppity** (*Colloq.*) *a.* arrogant; affectedly superior in manner or attitude. **uppishly** *adv.* **uppishness** *n.* **-most** *a., adv.*
up·right (up'·rīt) *a.* standing up; honest; *adv.* in such a position; *n.* a vertical part.
up·rise (up·rīz') *v.i.* to rise up; to revolt. *pa.p.* **-n** (up·ri'·zạn). *pa.t.* **uprose. uprising** *n.* insurrection; revolt; a slope.
up·roar (up'·rōr) *n.* tumult; violent, noisy disturbance. **-ious** *a.* **-iously** *adv.* **-iousness** *n.* [Dut. *oproer*].
up·root (up·ro͝ot') *v.t.* to tear up by the roots; to eradicate. **-al** *n.* **-er** *n.*
up·set (up·set') *v.t.* to turn upside down; to knock over; to defeat; to disturb or distress. *pr.p.* **-ting** *pa.p., pa.t.* **upset;** (up'·set) *n.* an overturn; overthrow; confusion; *a.* disordered; worried; overturned. **— price,** lowest price at which goods will be sold by auction.
up·shot (up'·shȧt) *n.* final issue; conclusion.
up·side (up'·sīd) *n.* the upper side. **—down** *adv.* with the upper side underneath; inverted; in disorder.
up·stage (up'·stāj') *a.,* adv. of or toward rear of stage; *v.t.* to act on stage so as to minimize another actor.
up·stairs (up·sterz') *adv.* in the upper story; on the stairs; *a.* pert. to upper story; *n.* upper story.
up·stand·ing (up·stan'·ding) *a.* erect; honorable.
up·start (up'·stȧrt) *n.* one who has suddenly risen to wealth, power, or honor; parvenu; *v.i.* to rise suddenly.
up·stream (up'·strēm) *adv.* in direction of source (of stream).
up·stroke (up'·strōk) *n.* the upward line in handwriting; upward stroke.
up·surge (up·surj') *v.t.* to surge upwards. (up'·surj) *n.* welling, as of emotion.
up·sweep (up'·swēp) *n.* a curve upward; an upswept hair-do.
up·swing (up'·swing) *n.* a trend upward.
up·thrust (up'thrust) *n.* upward thrust.
up·to·date (up'·tạ·dāt') *a.* modern; most recent; extending up to, pert. to, the present time.
up·town (up'·toun) *a.* pert. to, or in upper part of, town; *adv.*
up·turn (up·turn') *v.t.* to turn up. (up'·turn) *n.* an upward turn for the better. **-ing** *n.*
up·ward (up'·wẹrd) *a.* directed towards a higher place; *adv.* upwards. **-s, -ly** *adv.* towards higher elevation or number [O.E. *upweard,* upward].
u·ran·i·nite (yoo·rān'·ạ·nīt) *n.* pitchblende, in which uranium was first found in 1789.
u·ra·nite (yoor'·ạ·nīt) *n.* an almost transparent ore of uranium. **uranitic** *a.*
u·ra·ni·um (yoo·rā'·ni·ạm) *n.* radio-active metallic element (symbol U), used as an alloy in steel manufacture and in the production of atom bomb. **uranic, uranous** *a.* [fr. *Uranus,* the planet].
u·ra·nog·ra·phy (yoor·ạ·nȧg'·rạ·fi·) *n.* descriptive astronomy. **uranographer, uranographist** *n.* **uranographic, uranographical** *a.* **uranometry** *n.* measurement of heavens; chart of heavens [Gk. *ouranos,* heaven].
ur·ban (ur'·bạn) *a.* pert, to, or living in, city or town. **urbane** *a.* refined; suave; courteous. **urbanely** *adv.* **urbanity** *n.* **-ize** *v.t.* to make urban; to bring town conditions and advantages to rural areas. [L. *urbs,* a city].
ur·chin (ur'·chin) *n.* sea urchin; (*Arch.*) hedgehog (*Arch.*) goblin; mischievous child; a child [L. *ericius,* hedgehog].
Ur·du (oor·do͞o') *n.* a language form of Hindustani, mixture of Persian, Arabic, and Hindi [Hind. *urdu,* camp].
u·re·a (ū'·rē·ạ) *n.* crystalline solid, the principle organic constituent of urine [Gk. *ouron,* urine].
u·re·ter (ū·rē'·tẹr) *n.* one of two ducts of kidney conveying urine to bladder. **urethra** *n.* duct by which urine passes from bladder. *pl.* **urethrae. urethral** *a.* [Gk. *ouron,* urine].
urge (urj) *v.t.* to press; to drive; to exhort;

to simulate; to solicit earnestly; *v.i.* to press onward; to make allegations, entreaties, etc. *n.* act of urging; incentive; irresistible impulse. **-ncy** *n.* quality of being urgent; compelling necessity; importunity. **-nt** *a.* calling for immediate attention; clamant; importunate. **-ntly** *adv.* **-r** *n.* [L.*urgere*, to press].

u·rine (ū′·rin) *n.* yellowish fluid secreted by kidneys, passed through ureters to bladder from which it is discharged through urethra. **uremia** *n.* toxic condition of the blood caused by insufficient secretion of urine. **uremic** *a.* **uric** *a.* pert. to or produced from urine. **urinal** *n.* vessel into which urine may be discharged; a place for urinating. **urinary** *a.* pert. to urine. **urinate** *v.i.* to pass urine. **urination** *n.* **urinogenital** *a.* pert. to urinary and genital organs. **urology** *n.* branch of Med. dealing with urinogenital system. **urologist** *n.* [Gk. *euron*, urine].

urn (urn) *n.* vase-shaped vessel of pottery or metal with pedestal, and narrow neck, as used for ashes of dead after cremation; vessel of various forms usually fitted with tap, for liquid in bulk, as *tea urn*. **-al** *a.* [L. *urna*].

ur·sine (ur′·sin) *a.* pert. to or resembling a bear. **ursiform** *a.* resembling bear in shape [L. *ursus*, a bear].

us (us) *pron. pl.* the objective form of **we.**

use (ūz) *v.t.* to make use of; to employ; to consume or expend (as in material); to practice habitually; to accustom; to treat; *v.i.* to be accustomed (only in past tense). **use** (ūs) *n.* act of using or employing for specific purpose; utility; custom; (*Law*) profit derived from trust. **usable** *a.* fit for use. **usability** *n.* **usage** *n.* mode of using; treatment; long-established custom. **usance** *n.* usual time allowed for payment of foreign bills of exchange. **-ful** *a.* of use; handy; profitable; serviceable; **-fully** *adv.* **-fulness** *n.* **-less** *a.* of no use; inefficient; futile. **-lessly** *adv.* **-lessness** *n.* **-r** *n.* [L. *uti, usus*, to use].

ush·er (ush′·ẹr) *n.* doorkeeper; one who conducts people to seats in church, theater, etc.; official who introduces strangers or walks before person of high rank; *v.t.* to act as usher. **-ette** *n.* girl employed, as in theater to show patrons to seats. **to usher in,** to precede [O. Fr. *ussier*, fr. L. *ostiarius*, a doorkeeper].

us·que·baugh (us′·kwi·baw) *n.* whiskey [Gael. *uisge*, water, *beatha*, life].

u·su·al (ū′·zhoo·ạl) *a.* customary; ordinary. **-ly** *adv.* **-ness** *n.* [L. *usus*, to use].

u·su·fruct (ū′·zạ·frạkt) *n.* right of using and enjoying produce benefit, or profits of another's property provided that the property remains undamaged. **-uary** *a.* pert. to usufruct; *n.* one who has the use of another's property by usufruct [L. *usus*, use; *fructus*, fruit].

u·surp (ū·surp′, zurp′) *v.t.* to take possession of unlawfully or by force. **-ation** *n.* act of usurping; violent or unlawful seizing of power [L. *usurpare*, to seize].

u·su·ry (ū′·zhạ·ri·) *n.* charging of exorbitant interest on money lent. **usurer** *n.* money lender who charges exorbitant rates of interest **usurious** *a.* **usuriously** *adv.* **usuriousness** *n.* [L. *usura*, use].

u·ten·sil (ū·ten′·sạl) *n.* vessel of any kind which forms part of domestic, esp. kitchen, equipment [L. *utensilis*, fit for use].

u·ter·ine (ū′·tẹr·in) *a.* pert. to uterus or womb; born of the same mother but by a different father. **uterus** *n.* womb [L. *uterus*].

u·til·i·tar·i·an (ū·til·ạ·ter′·i·ạn) *a.* pert. to utility or utilitarianism; of practical use. *n.* one who accepts doctrines of utilitarianism. **-ism** *n.* ethical doctrine, the ultimate aim and criterion of all human actions must be 'the greatest happiness for the greatest number' [L. *utilis*, useful].

u·ti·lize (ū·tạ·līz) *v.t.* to put to use; to turn to profit. **utilizable** *a.* **utilization** *n.* **-r** *n.* **utility** *n.* usefulness; quality of being advantageous; *pl.* public services, as gas, electricity, telephone, etc. [L. *utilis*, useful].

ut·most (ut′·mōst) *a.* situated at farthest point or extremity; to highest degree; *n.* most that can be; greatest possible effort [O.E. *utemest*, superb. of *ut*, out].

u·to·pi·a (ū·tō′·pi·ạ) *n.* any ideal state, constitution, system, or way of life. **-n** *a.* ideally perfect but impracticable; visionary [=nowhere; Gk. *ou*, not; *topos*, place].

u·tri·cle (ū′·tri·kl) *n.* (*Bot.*) little bag or bladder, esp. of aquatic plant; (*Anat.*) a sac in inner ear influencing equilibrium. **utricular, utriculate** *a.* [L. *utriculus*, small bag].

ut·ter (ut′·ẹr) *a.* total; unconditional. **-ly** *adv.* **-ness** *n.* [O.E. *utor, outer*].

ut·ter (ut′·ẹr) *vt.* to speak; to disclose; to put into circulation. **-able** *a.* **-ableness** *n.* **-ance** *n.* act of speaking; manner of delivering speech; something said; a cry. **-er** *n.* [O.E. *utian*, to put out].

ut·ter·most (ut′·ẹr·mōst) *a.* farthest out; utmost; *n.* the highest degree.

u·vu·la (ū′·vyạ·lạ) *n.* fleshy tag suspended from middle of lower border of soft palate. **-r** *a.* [L. *uva*, grape].

ux·o·ri·ous (uk·sōr′·i·ạs) *a.* foolishly or excessively fond of one's wife. **uxorial** *a.* pert. to wife. **-ly** *adv.* **-ness** *n.* [L. *uxor*].

V

va·cant (vā′·kạnt) *a.* empty; void; not occupied; unintelligent. **-ly** *adv.* **vacancy** *n.* emptiness; opening; lack of thought; place or post, unfilled. **vacate** (vā′·kāt) *v.t.* to leave empty or unoccupied; to quit possession of; to make void. **vacation** *n.* act of vacating; intermission of stated employment; recess; holidays. **vacational** *a.* **vacationist** *n.* [L. *vacare*, to be empty].

vac·cine (vak·sēn′., vak′·sēn) *a.* pert. to, or obtained from cows; *n.* virus of cowpox, used in vaccination; any substance used for inoculation against disease. **vaccinate** *v.t.* to inoculate with cowpox, to ward off smallpox or lessen severity of its attack. **vaccination** *n.* act or practice of vaccinating; the inoculation. **vaccinator** *n.* [L. *vacca*, cow].

vac·il·late (vas′·ạ·lāt) *v.i.* to move to and fro; to waver; to be unsteady; to fluctuate in opinion. **vacillating, vacillatory** *a.* **vacillation** *n.* [L. *vacillare*].

vac·u·um (vak′·yoom) *n.* space devoid of all matter; space from which air, or other gas, has been almost wholly removed, as by air pump. **vacuous** *a.* empty; vacant; expressionless; unintelligent. **-ly** *adv.* **-ness** *n.* **vacuity** (vạ·kū′·ạ·ti·) *n.* emptiness; empty space; lack of intelligence. **— cleaner** *n.* apparatus for removing dust from carpets, etc. by suction. **— bottle** *n.* double-walled flask with vacuum between walls, for keeping contents at temperature at which they were inserted. **— tube** used in Radio, TV, and electronic equipment; a sealed tube containing metallic electrodes but (almost) no air or gas. [L. *vacuus*, empty].

va·de·me·cum (vā′·dē·mē′·kạm) *n.* small handbook or manual for ready reference [L. =go with me].

vag·a·bond (vag′·ạ·bȧnd) *a.* moving from place to place without settled habitation; wandering; *n.* wanderer or vagrant, having no settled habitation; idle scamp; rascal. **-age ism,** *n.* [L. *vagari,* to wander].

va·gar·y (vā'.gą.ri., vą.ger'.i.) *n.* whimsical or freakish notion; unexpected action; caprice. **vagarious** *a.* [L. *vagari,* to wander].

va·gi·na (vą.jī'.ną) *n.* (*Anat.*) canal which leads from uterus to external orifice; (*Bot.*) sheath as of leaf **-l** *a.* [L.].

va·grant (vā'.grąnt) *a.* wandering from place to place; moving without certain direction; roving; *n.* idle wanderer; vagabond; disorderly person; beggar. **-ly** *adv.* **vagrancy** *n.* [L. *vagari,* to wander].

vague (vāg) *a.* uncertain; indefinite; indistinct; not clearly expressed. **-ly** *adv.* **-ness** *n.* [L. *vagus,* wandering].

vain (vān) *a.* useless; unavailing; fruitless; empty; worthless; conceited; **-ly** *adv.* **-ness** *n.* **vanity** (van'.ą.ti.) *n.* conceit; something one is conceited about; worthlessness; dressing table. **vanity case** *n.* lady's small handbag or case, fitted with powder puff, mirror, lipstick, etc. [L. *vanus,* empty].

vain·glo·ry (vān.glō'.ri.) *n.* excessive vanity; boastfulness. **vainglorious** *a.* **vaingloriously** *adv.* **vaingloriousness** *n.* [*vain* and *glory*].

val·ance (val'.ąns) *n.* short drapery across the top of a window, bed, etc.; similar facing of wood or metal. **-d** *a.* [O.Fr. *avalant* to hang].

vale (vāl) *n.* valley [L. *vallis,* valley].

val·e·dic·tion (val.ą.dik'.shąn) *n.* farewell; a bidding farewell. **valedictory** *a.* bidding farewell; suitable for leave-taking; *n.* a valedictory address, esp. by a school valedictiorian. **valedictorian** *n.* student in a graduating class with the highest scholastic standing who gives the valedictory at graduation exercises. [L. *valedicere,* to say farewell].

va·lence, va·len·cy (vā'.ląns, vā'.ląn.si.) *n.* (*Chem.*) the combining power of an element or atom as compared with a hydrogen atom [L. *valere,* to be strong].

Va·len·ci·ennes (vą.len(t).sē.enz') *n.* rich lace, made orig. at *Valenciennes,* in France.

va·len·tine (val'.ąn.tīn) *n.* sweetheart chosen on *St. Valentine's* day; card containing profession of love, sent on *St. Valentine's* day, Feb. 14th [L. proper name *Valentinus*].

va·le·ri·an (vą.lir'.i.ąn) *n.* flowering herb with strong odor; its root, used as sedative drug [O.Fr. *valeriance*].

val·et (val'.it, val'.ā) *n.* manservant who cares for clothing, etc. of his employer [Fr. *valet,* a groom, Doublet of *varlet*].

val·e·tu·di·nar·i·an (val.ą.tū.dą.ner'.i.ąn) *a.* sickly; infirm; solicitous about one's own health; *n.* person of sickly constitution; person disposed to live life of an invalid. **-ism** *n.* **valetudinary** *a.* [L. *valetudo,* health].

Va·hal·la (val.hal'.ą) *n.* (*Norse myth.*) hall of immortality where Odin received souls of heroes slain in battle [O.N. *valr,* slain; *holl,* hall].

val·iant (val'.yąnt) *a.* brave; heroic; courageous; intrepid. **-ly** *adv.* **-ness** *n.* **valiance, valiancy** *n.* valor; courage [L. *valere,* to be strong].

val·id (val'.id) *a.* sound or well-grounded; capable of being justified; (*Law*) legally sound; executed with proper formalities. **-ly** *adv.* **-ate** *v.t.* to make valid; to ratify. **-ation** *n.* **-ness, -ity** *n.* [L. *validus,* strong].

va·lise (vą.lēs') *n.* suitcase [Fr.].

Val·kyr (val'.kir) *n.* (*Norse myth.*) one of Odin's nine handmaidens. who conduct the souls of slain heroes to Valhalla. Also **Valkyrie** (val.wir'.i.) **Valkyria** (val.kir'.yą). **Valkyrian** *a.*

val·ley (val'.i.) *n.* low ground between hills; river basin [L. *vallis,* vale].

val·or (val'.ęr) *n.* bravery; prowess in war; courage. **-ous** *a.* brave; fearless. **-ously** *adv.* **-ousness** *n.* [L. *valere,* to be strong].

valse (vàls) *n.* waltz, esp. one played as concert piece [Fr.].

val·ue (val'.ū) *n.* worth; utility; importance; estimated worth or valuation; precise significance; equivalent; (*Mus.*) duration of note; *v.t.* to estimate worth of; to hold in respect and admiration; to prize. **-r** *n.* **-less** *a.* **valuable** *a.* precious; worth a good price; worthy; *n.* thing of value (generally *pl.*) **valuableness** *n.* **valuably** *adv.* **valuate** *v.t.* to set value on; to appraise. **valuation** *n.* value estimated or set upon a thing; appraisal. **-d** *a.* **valuator** *n.* [L. *valere,* to be worth].

valve (valv) *n.* device for closing aperture (as in pipe) in order to control flow of fluid, gas, etc. (*Anat.*) structure (as in blood-vessel) which allows flow of fluid in one direction only; (*Zool.*) either of two sections of shell of mollusk; (*Mus.*) device in certain instruments (as horn, trumpet, etc.) for changing tone. **-less, -like** *a.* **valvular** *a.* **-let, valvule** *n.* small valve [L. *valva,* leaf of folding door].

va·moose (va.mòòs') *v.i., t.* (*Slang*) to depart quickly; to leave; to decamp [Sp. *vamos,* let us go].

vamp (vamp) *n.* upper leather of shoe or boot; new patch put on old article; (*Mus.*) improvised accompaniment; *v.t.* to provide (shoe, etc.) with new upper leather; to patch; (*Mus.*) to improvise accompaniment to [Fr. *avant-pied,* front of foot].

vamp (vamp) *n.* (*Slang*) woman who allures and exploits men; adventuress; *v.t.* and *v.i.* (*Slang*) to allure and exploit; to flirt unscrupulously [contr. of *vampire*].

vam·pire (vam'.pīr) *n.* reanimated body of dead person who cannot rest quietly in grave, but arises from it at night and sucks blood of sleepers; one who lives by preying on others; extortioner; a vamp. **— bat** *n.* of several species of bat of S. America which sucks blood of animals. **vampiric, vampirish** *a.* **vampirism** *n.* [Fr fr. Serbian *vampir*].

van (van) *n.* covered wagon or motor truck for goods [contr. of *caravan*].

van (van) *n.* leaders of a movement. **-guard** *n.* detachment of troops who march ahead of army [Fr. *avant,* before; *garde,* a guard].

va·na·di·um (vą.nā'.di.ąm) *n.* a metallic element (the hardest known) used in manufacture of hard steel [fr. *Vanadis,* Scand. goddess].

van·dal (van'.dąl) *n.* one who wantonly damages or destroys property of beauty or value; **-ic** *a.* **-ism** *n.* [L. *Vandalus,* Vandau, tribe which ravaged Europe in 5th cent.].

van·dyke (van.dīk') *n.* one of the points forming an edge, as of lace, ribbon, etc.; broad collar with deep points of lace as worn in portraits by *Van Dyck;* painting by Van Dyck. **— beard,** pointed beard. **— brown,** dark brown [*Van Dyck,* Flemish painter].

vane (vān) *n.* a device on a windmill, spire, etc. to show the direction of the wind; a weathercock; the blade of a propeller, of a windmill, etc.; a fin on a bomb to prevent swerving **-d** *a.* **-less** *a.* [O.E. *fana,* a banner].

van·guard (van'.gàrd) *n.* See **van** (2).

va·nil·la (vą.nil'.ą) *n.* tropical American plant of orchid family; long pod of plant, used as flavoring. **vanillic** *a.* **vanillin** *n.* [dim. fr. Sp. *vaina,* sheath].

van·ish (van'.ish) *v.i.* to pass away; to be lost to view; to disappear; (*Math.*) to become zero. **-er** *n.* **-ing** *a.* disappearing. **-ingly** *adv.* [L. *evanescere,* fr. *vanus,* empty].

van·i·ty. See **vain.**

van·quish (vang'.kwish) *v.t.* to conquer in battle; to defeat in any contest; to get the better of; **-able** *a.* **-er** *n.* [Fr. *vaincre,* fr. L. *vincere*].

van·tage (van'.tij) *n.* better situation or opportunity; advantage; in tennis, same as 'advantage.' Used esp. in — **ground,** position of advantage [M.E. *avantage*, advantage].

vap·id (vap'·id) *a.* having lost its life and spirit; flat; inspid; dull. **-ly** *adv.* **-ness, vapidity** *n.* [L. *vapidus*, state].

va·por (vā'·pẹr) *n.* any light, cloudy substance which impairs clearness of atmosphere, as mist, fog, smoke, etc.; a substance converted into gaseous state; anything unsubstantial; *pl.* (*Arch.*) disease of nervous debility; depression; melancholy; *v.i.* to pass off in vapor; (*Fig.*) to talk idly; to brag. **-ize** *v.t.* to convert into vapor; *v.i.* to pass off in vapor. **-izable** *a.* **-ization** *n.* **-izer** *n.* mechanism for splitting liquid into fine particles. **-ish** *a.* full of vapor; prone to depression. **-ishness** *n.* **-ous** *a.* like vapor; unsubstantial; full of fanciful talk. **-ously** *adv.* **-ousness** *n.* **-ings** *n.pl.* boastful talk. **-y** *a.* full of vapor; depressed [L. *vapor*].

var·i·a·ble (ver'·i·ạ·bl) *a.* changeable; capable of being adapted; unsteady or fickle; *n.* that which is subject to change; symbol that may have infinite number of values; indeterminate quantity; shifting wind. **variably** *adv.* **-ness** *n.* **variability** *n.* (*Biol.*) tendency to vary from average characteristics of species. **variant** *a.* different; diverse; *n.* different form or reading. **variance** *n.* difference that produces controversy; state of discord or disagreement. **variation** (ver'·i·ā'·shạn) *n.* act of varying; alteration; modification; extent to which thing varies; (*Gram.*) change of termination; in magnetism, deviation of magnetic needle from true north; (*Mus.*) repetition of theme or melody with various embellishments and elaborations. **at variance,** not in harmony or agreement [L. *variare*, to change, vary].

var·i·col·ored (ver'·i·kul·ẹrd) *a.* having various colors.

var·i·cose (var'·i·kōs) *a.* enlarged or dilated, as veins, esp. in legs [L. *varix*, a dilated vein; fr. *varus*, crooked].

var·ied *a.* See **vary.**

var·i·e·gate (ver'·i·ạ·gāt, ver'·i·gāt) *v.t.* to diversify by patches of different colors; to streak, spot, dapple, etc. **variegation** *n.* **-d** *a.* [L. *varius*, various; *agere*, to make].

va·ri·e·ty (vạ·rī'·ạ·ti·) *n.* state of being varied; diversity; collection of different things; many-sidedness; different form of something; subdivision of a species. — **show** *n.* mixed entertainment, consisting of songs, dances, short sketches, juggling, etc. [L. *varietas*, variety, fr. *varius*, various].

var·i·o·rum (ver·i·ō'·rạm, var·i·ō'·rạm) *n.* an edition of a work with notes by various commentators [L. = of various men].

var·i·ous (ver'·i·ạs, var'·i·ạs) *a.* different; diverse; manifold; separate; diversified. **-ly** *adv.* **-ness** *n.* [L. *varius*].

var·let (vȧr'·lit) *n.* (*Arch.*) page or attendant; scoundrel. **-ry** *n.* [O.Fr. *varlet*, var. of *vaslet*, fr. L.L. *vassalus*, vassal].

var·nish (vȧr'·nish) *n.* clear, resinous liquid laid on work to give it gloss and protection; glossy appearance; outward show; *v.t.* to lay varnish on; to conceal something with fair appearance **-ed** *a.* [Fr. *vernis*, varnish].

var·si·ty (vȧr'·sạ·ti·) *n.* team, usu. athletic, representing a university, school, etc. in competition; *a.* designating such a team [contr. of *university*].

var·y (ver'·i·, var'·i·) *v.t.* to change; to make different or modify; to diversify; *v.i.* to alter, or be altered; to be different; **varied** *a.* various; diverse; diversified. **varier** *n.* **-ingly** *adv.* [L. *variare*, to vary].

vas (vas) *n.* (*Anat.*) vessel or duct. **-cular** (vas'·kyạ·lạr) *a.* pert. to vessels or ducts for conveying blood, lymph, sap, etc. **-culum** *n.* botanist's collecting box. **-omotor** *a.* pert. to nerves controlling tension of blood vessels and thus the flow of blood. *n.pl.* **vasa** [L.].

vase (vās, vāz) *n.* vessel for flowers or merely for decoration; large sculptured vessel, used as ornament, in gardens, on gateposts, etc. [L. *vas*, vessel].

Vas·e·line (vas'·ạ·lēn) *n.* petrolatum, a petroleum-derivative used in ointments, pomades, as lubricant, etc. [Trademark].

vas·sal (vas'·ạl) *n.* one who holds land from superior, and vows fealty and homage to him; dependant; retainer. **-age** *n.* state of being a vassal [Fr. fr Celt. *gwaz*, servant].

vast (vast) *a.* of great extent; very spacious; very great in numbers or quantity; *n.* (*Poet.*) boundless space. **-ly** *adv.* **-ness** *n.* **-itude** *n.* [L. *vastus*, very great].

vat (vat) *n.* large vessel, tub, for holding liquids [O.E. *foel*, a vessel, cask].

vat·ic (vat'·ik) *a.* prophetic; oracular. Also **-al** *a.* **-inal** (vạ·tis'·i·nạl) *a.* **-inate** (vạ·tis'·i·nāte) *v.t.* and *i.* to prophesy. **-ination** (vat·ạ·si·nā'·shan) *n.* [L. *vates*, a prophet].

Vat·i·can (vat'·i·kạn) *n.* palace and official residence of Pope on Vatican Hill (L. *Mons Vaticanus*), in Rome; papal authority.

vaude·ville (vawd'·(ạ)vil, vōd'·vil) *n.* stage show with mixed specialty acts; variety show [fr. *Vau de Vire* in Normandy].

vault (vawlt) *n.* arched roof; room or passage covered with vault, esp. subterranean; cellar; sky; anything resembling a vault; *v.t.* to cover with arched roof; to form like vault. **-ed** *a.* arched [L. *volutus*, turned].

vault (vawlt) *v.i.* to spring or jump with hands resting on something; to leap or spring, as horse; *v.t.* to spring or jump over; *n.* such a spring [Fr. *volte*, turn; fr. L. *volutus*].

vaunt (vawnt, vȧnt) *v.t.* to boast of; to make vain display of; *n.* boast; vainglorious display. **-er** *n.* **-ingly** *adv.* [O.Fr. *vanter;* fr. L. *vanitas*, vanity].

VCR (vē·sē·ȧr') *n.* videocassette recorder; a videotape recorder which uses videocassettes.

veal (vēl) *n.* flesh of a calf killed for the table [O.Fr. *veel*, fr. L. *vitellus*, calf].

vec·tor (vek'·tẹr) *n.* (*Math.*) any quantity requiring direction to be stated as well as magnitude in order to define it properly; disease-carrying insect. **vectorial** *a.* [L. *vehere*, *vectum*, to convey].

Ve·da (vē'·dạ) *n.* most ancient sacred literature of Hindus. **Vedic** *a.* pert. to the Vedas [Sans. *veda*, knowledge].

ve·dette (vạ·det') *n.* mounted sentinel placed in advance of outposts to give notice of danger

veer (vēr) *v.t.* and *v.i.* to turn; of wind, to change direction, esp. clockwise; (*Naut.*) to change ship's course; (*Fig.*) to change one's opinion or point of view [Fr. *virer*].

veg·e·ta·ble (vej'·(ạ)·tạ·bl) *a.* belonging to plants; having nature of plants; *n.* plant, esp. plant used as food, e.g. potato, carrot, cabbage, bean. **vegetal** *a.* **vegetarian** (vej·ạ·ter'·i·ạn) *n.* one who abstrains from animal flesh and lives on vegetables, eggs, milk, etc.; *a.* pert. to vegetarianism; consisting of vegetables. **vegetarianism** *n.* **vegetate** *v.i.* to grow as plant does; to lead idle, unthinking life. **vegetation** *n.* process of vegetating; vegetable growth; plants in general. **vegetational** *a.* **vegetative** *a.* **vegetatively** *adv.* **vegetativeness** *n.* [L. *vegetare*, to enliven].

ve·he·ment (vē'·ạ·mạnt) *a.* acting with great force; impetuous; vigorous; passionate. **-ly** *adv.* **vehemence, vehemency** *n.* impetuosity; fury; violence; fervor [L. *vehemens*, eager].

ve·hi·cle (vē'·(h)ạ·kl) *n.* any means of conveyance (esp. on land) as carriage, etc.; liquid medium in which drugs are taken, or pigments applied; means or medium of expression or communication. **vehicular** (vē·hik′·yạ·lẹr) *a.* Also **vehiculatory** (L. *vehiculum,* fr. *vehere,* to carry].

veil (vāl) *n.* piece of thin, gauzy material worn by women to hide or protect face; covering; curtain; disguise; *v.t.* to cover with veil; to conceal. **-ed** *a.* **-less** *a.* **-like** *a.* **-ing** *n.* act of covering with veil; material from which veil is made. **to take the veil,** to become a nun [L. *velum*].

vein (vān) *n.* each of the vessels or tubes which receive blood from capillaries and return it to heart; (loosely) any blood vessel; (*Biol.*) one of the small branching ribs of leaf or of insect's wing; layer of mineral intersecting a stratum of rock; streak or wave of different color appearing in wood, marble, etc.; distinctive tendency; mood or cast of mind; *v.t.* to mark with veins. **-ed** *a.* **-less** *a.* surface. **-ous, -y** *a.* **venation** *n.* [L. *vena*].

veld, veldt (felt, velt) *n.* in S. Africa, open grass country [Dut. *veld,* a field].

vel·lum (vel′·ạm) *n.* fine parchment made of skin; paper of similar texture; *a.* [O.Fr. *velin,* fr. L. *vitulus,* calf].

ve·loc·i·pede (vạ·làs′·ạ·pēd) *n.* a vehicle propelled by the rider, early form of bicycle or tricycle [L. *velox,* swift; *pes,* the foot].

ve·loc·i·ty (vạ·làs′·ạ·ti·) *n.* rate of motion; swiftness; speed; distance traversed in unit time in a given direction [L. *velox,* swift].

ve·lours (vạ·loor′) *n. sing.* and *pl.* fabric resembling velvet or plush. Also **velour** [Fr.].

vel·vet (vel′·vit) *n.* soft material of silk with thick short pile on one side; *a.* made of velvet; soft and delicate. **-y** *a.* soft as velvet. **-een** *n.* a pile fabric made of cotton, or of silk and cotton mixed [L.L. *vellutum,* fr. L. *villus,* shaggy hair].

ve·nal (vē′·nạl) *a.* to be obtained for money; prepared to take bribes; mercenary. **-ly** *adv.* **venality** *n.* quality of being purchaseable [L. *venalis,* fr. *venus,* sale].

ve·nat·ic, ve·nat·i·cal (vi·nat′·ik, ·i·kạl) *a.* relating to hunting. **-ally** *adv.* [L. *venari,* to hunt].

vend (vend) *v.t.* to sell; to dispose of by sale. **-ible** *a.* **-ibly** *adv.* **-ibility, -ibleness** *n.* the quality of being saleable. **-or** *n.* person who sells. **-ue** *n.* public auction [L. *vendere*].

ven·det·ta (ven·det′·ạ) *n.* blood feud, in which it was the duty of the relative of murdered man to avenge his death by killing murderer or relative of murderer; any bitter feud [It. fr. L. *vindicta,* revenge].

ve·neer (vạ·nēr′) *n.* thin layer of valuable wood glued to surface of inferior wood; thin coating of finer substance; superficial charm or polish of manner; *v.t.* to coat or overlay with substance giving superior surface; to disguise with superficial charm. **-ing** *n.* act of treating with veneer; thin layer used in this process [Fr. *fournir,* to furnish].

ven·er·ate (ven′·ạ·rāt) *v.t.* to regard with respect and reverence. **venerator** *n.* **veneration** *n.* respect mingled with awe; worship. **venerable** *a.* worthy of veneration; deserving respect by reason of age, character, etc.; sacred by reason of religious or historical associations, aged. **venerability, venerableness** *n.* **venerably** *adv.* [L. *venerari,* to worship].

ve·ne·re·al (vạ·nir′·i·ạl) *a.* pert. to sexual intercourse; arising from sexual intercourse with infected persons [L. *Venus, Veneris,* goddess of Love].

ven·er·y (ven′·ạ·ri·) *n.* (*Arch.*) hunting; sports of the chase [L. *venari,* to hunt].

Ve·ne·tian (vạ·nē′·shạn) *a.* pert. to city of Venice, Italy; *n.* native, inhabitant of Venice. **— blind,** blind made of thin, horizontal slats, so hung as to overlap each other when closed.

venge·ance (ven′·jạns) *n.* infliction of pain or loss on another in return for injury or offense. **vengeful** *a.* disposed to revenge; vindictive. **vengefully** *adv.* **vengefulness** *n.* [L. *vindicare,* to avenge].

ve·ni·al (vē′·ni·ạl) *a.* capable of being forgiven; excusable. **-ly** *adv.* **-ness, -ity** *n.* [L. *venialis,* pardonable, fr. *venia,* forgiveness].

ven·i·son (ven′·ạ·zn) *n.* flesh of the deer [Fr. *vendison,* fr. L. *venari,* to hunt].

ven·om (ven′·ạm) *n.* poison, esp. that secreted by serpents, bees, etc.; spite; malice. **-ous** *a.* poisonous; spiteful; malicious. **-ously** *adv.* **-ousness** *n.* [L. *veneum,* poison].

ve·nous, ve·nose (vē′·nạs) *a.* pert. to veins or the blood in veins. **venosity** *n.* [L. *venosus,* fr. *vena,* vein].

vent (vent) *n.* small opening; outlet; flue or funnel of fireplace; touch hole of gun; utterance; emission; voice; escape; anus of certain lower animals; slit in back of coat; *v.t.* to give opening or outlet to; to let escape; to utter or voice; to publish. **-age, -er** *n.* **-less** *a.* **to give vent to,** to pour forth [Fr. *fendre,* fr. L. *findere,* to cleave].

ven·ti·late (ven′·tạ·lāt) *v.t.* to remove foul air from and supply with fresh air; to expose to discussion; to make public. **ventilation** *n.* replacement of stale air by fresh air; free exposure to air; open discussion. **ventilator** *n.* contrivance for keeping air fresh [L. *ventilare,* fr. *ventus,* wind].

ven·tral (ven′·trạl) *a.* belonging to belly; abdominal; opp. of *dorsal;* *n.* one of the pair of fins on belloy of fish. **ventricle** *n.* (*Anat.* or *Zool.*) small cavity in certain organs, esp. one of chambers of heart. **ventricular** *a.* [L. *ventralis,* fr. *venter,* belly].

ven·tril·o·quism (ven·tril′·ạ·kwizm) *n.* art of speaking in such a way that words or sounds seem to come from some source other than speaker. Also **ventriloquy. ventriloquist** *n.* **ventriloquistic** *a.* **ventriloquize** *v.i.* to practice ventriloquism [L. *venter,* belly; *loqui,* to speak].

ven·ture (ven′·chẹr) *n.* undertaking of chance or danger; business speculation; *v.t.* to expose to hazard; to risk; *v.i.* to run risk; to dare; to have presumption to. **-r** *n.* **venturous** *a.* daring; risky. **venturously** *adv.* **venturousness** *n.* **-some** *a.* bold; dangerous. **-someness** *n.* [contr. of *adventure*].

ven·ue (ven′·ū) *n.* (*Law*) district in which case is tried; scene of an event [L. *venire,* to come].

ven·ule (ven′·ūl) *n.* small vein.

Ve·nus (vē′·nạs) *n.* (*Myth.*) Roman goddess of love and beauty; brightest planet of solar system; beautiful woman [L.].

ve·ra·cious (vạ·rā′·shạs) *a.* truthful; true. **-ly** *adv.* **-ness** *n.* **veracity** (vạ·ras′·ạ·ti·) *n.* quality of being truthful; truth; correctness [L. *verax, veracis,* fr. *verus,* true].

ve·ran·da, verandah (vạ·ran′·dạ) *n.* open porch or gallery, along side of house, often with roof [Sp. *veranda,* balcony].

verb (vurb) *n.* (*Gram.*) part of speech which expresses action or state of being. **-less** *a.* **-al** *a.* pert. to words; expressed in words, esp. spoken words; literal or word for word; pert. to verb; derived from verb. **-ally** *adv.* **-alize** *v.t.* and *v.i.* to put into words; to turn into verb. **-alization** *n.* **-alism** *n.* something expressed orally; over-attention to use of words; empty words. **-alist, -alizer** *n.* **-atim** (vẹr·bā′·tim) *a.* and *adv.* word for word [L. *verbum,* a word].

ver·be·na (vẹr·bē′·nạ) *n.* genus of plants of

family Verbenaceae, used in ornamental flower beds. Also called **vervain** [L.].

ver·bi·age (vur′.bi.ij) *n.* excess of words; use of many more words than are necessary; wordiness. **verbose** (vẹr.bōs′) *a.* prolix; tedious because of excess of words. **verbosely** *adv.* **verboseness, verbosity** (vẹr.bȧs′.ạ.ti.) *n.* [L. *verbum*, a word].

ver·bo·ten (fẹr.bō′.tan) *a.* forbidden [Ger].

ver·dant (vur′.dant) *a.* green or fresh; flourishing; ignorant or unsophisticated. **-ly** *adv.* **verdancy** *n.* **verdure** (vur′.jẹr) *n.* greenness or freshness; green vegetation. **-less** *a.* [O.Fr. *verd*, fr. L. *viridis*, green].

ver·dict (vur′.dikt) *n.* decision of jury in a trial; decision or judgment [O.Fr. *verdit*, fr. L. *vere dictum*, truly said].

ver·di·gris (vur′.di.grēs) *n.* green rust on copper, bronze, etc.; basic acetate of copper, used as pigment, etc. [O.Fr. *verd de Gris*, Greek green].

verge (vurj) *n.* border, or edge; brink; a rod of office; mace of bishop, etc. **-r** *n.* one who carries verge or emblem of authority; caretaker of church [L. *virga*, slender twig].

verge (vurj) *v.i.* to tend; to slope; to border upon [L. *vergere*, to tend towards].

ver·i·fy (ver′.ạ.fi) *v.t.* to prove to be true; to confirm truth of; **verifier** *n.* **verifiable** *a.* **verifiability** *n.* **verification** *n.* act of verifying or state of being verified; confirmation [L. *versus*, true; *facere*, to make].

ver·i·ly (ver′.i.li.) *adv.* (*Arch.*) truly; certainly.

ver·i·sim·i·lar (ver.ạ.sim′.ạ.lẹr) *a.* having the appearance of truth; probable; likely. **-ly** *adv.* **verisimilitude** *n.* appearance of truth; probability; likelihood [L. *verus*, true; *similis*, like].

ver·i·ta·ble (ver′.ạ.tạ.bl) *a.* actual; genuine. **-ness** *n.* **veritably** *adv.* [L. *veritas*, truth].

ver·i·ty (ver′.ạ.ti.) *n.* quality of being true; truth; reality [L. *veritas*].

ver·juice (vur′.jóós) *n.* sour juice of crab-apples, unripe grapes, etc. used in cooking; sourness of disposition [Fr. *verjus*, fr. L. *viridis*, green; *jus*, juice].

ver·mi- (vur′.mi) *prefix.* fr. L. *vermis*, worm. **-an** *a.* worm-like; pert. to worms, **-celli** (.sel′.i., .chel′.i.) *n.* paste made from same ingredients as macaroni, and formed into slender worm-like threads. **-cide** *n.* any substance that destroys worms. **-icidal** *a.* **-icular** *a.* pert. to worm; like a worm in shape or movement; vermiculate. **-cularly** *adv.* **-culate** *a.* *v.t.* to ornament in pattern like worm tracks. **-culation** *n.* **-form** *a.* having shape of a worm.

ver·mil·ion (ver.mil′.yạn) *n.* prepared red sulfide of mercury; brilliant red color; *v.t.* to color with red. Also **vermeil** [L. *vermiculus*, little worm].

ver·min (vur′.min) *n.* collectively noxious or troublesome small animals or insects, e.g. squirrels, rats, worms, lice, etc.; low contemptible persons. **-ous** *a.* infested by vermin; caused by vermin; tending to breed vermin. **-ously** *adv.* **-ousness** *n.* [L. *vermis*, worm].

ver·mouth, vermuth (vẹr.móóth′, vur′.móóth) *n.* cordial of white wine flavored with wormwood, used as aperitif [Ger.].

ver·nac·u·lar (vẹr.nak′.yạ.lẹr) *a.* belonging to country of one's birth; native (usu. applied only to language or idiom); *n.* native idiom of place; mother tongue; common name for a plant, animal, etc. [L. *vernaculus*, native, fr. *verna*, home-born slave].

ver·nal (vur′.nạl) *a.* belonging to, or appearing on, spring; youthful. **-ly** *adv.* — **equinox,** equinox occurring about March 21 [L. *ver*, spring].

ver·ni·er (vur′.ni.ẹr) *n.* short, graduated-scale instrument, for measuring fractional parts [fr. P. *Vernier*, inventor].

Ver·o·nal (ver′.ạ.nal) *n.* hypnotic or sedative drug; barbital [Trademark].

ve·ron·i·ca (vạ.rȧn′.i.kạ) *n.* genus of plants, including speedwell [L. *vettonica*, betony].

ver·ru·ca (vạ.róó′.kạ) *n.* wart or wart-like elevation. *pl.* **verrucae** (.sē), **verrucose, verrucous** *a.* **verrucosity** *n.* [L.].

ver·sa·tile (vur′.sạ.til) *a.* having aptitude in many subjects; liable to change; capable of moving freely in all directions. **-ly** *adv.* **-ness, versatility** *n.* [L. *versatilis*, fr. *versare*, fr. *vertere*, to turn].

verse (vurs) *n.* metrical line containing certain number of feet; metrical arrangement of language; short division of any literary composition; stanza; piece of poetry. **-d** (vurst) *a.* skilled; experienced (foll. by 'in'); practiced. **versicle** *n.* little verse. **versify** (vur′.sạ.fi) *v.t.* to turn prose into verse; to express in verse. *v.i.* to make verses. **versification** *n.* **versifier** *n.* [L. *vertere*, *versum*, to turn].

ver·sion (vur′.zhạn) *n.* translation; account from particular point of view **-al** *a.* [L. *versio*, fr. *vertere*, to turn].

vers li·bre (ver′ lē′.br) *n.* free verse [Fr.].

ver·so (vur′.sō) *n.* left-hand page; reverse side of coin or medal [L.].

ver·sus (vur′.sạs) *prep.* (*Law, Games*) against; contrasted with [L.].

ver·te·bra (vur′.tạ.brạ) *n.* one of the small bony segments of spinal column. *pl.* **-e. -l** *a.* pert. to vertebrae or spine. **vertebrate** *a.* having backbone; *n.* vertebrate animal [L.].

ver·tex (vur′.teks) *n.* highest point; summit; top of head; (*Astron.*) zenith; (*Geom.*) angular point of triangle etc. *pl.* **-es, vertices** (vur′.tạ.sēz). **vertical** *a.* situated at vertex; directly overhead or in the zenith; upright or perpendicular; *n.* vertical line. **vertically** *adv.* **verticalness** *n.* **verticality** *n.* [L.].

ver·ti·go (vur′.ti.gō) *n.* sensation of whirling or swimming of head, with loss of equilibrium; dizziness. **vertiginous** (vẹr.tij′.ạ.nạs) *a.* revolving; giddy; causing giddiness. **vertiginously** *adv.* **vertiginousness** *n.* [L. *vertigo*, whirling, *fr. vertere*, to turn].

ver·tu. See **virtu.**

ver·vain (vur′.vān) *n.* plant of genus *Verbena* [L. *verbena*].

verve (vurv) *n.* enthusiasm or vigor; energy; spirit [Fr.].

ver·y (ver′.i.) *a.* true; real; actual; genuine; now used chiefly to emphasize word following. *adv.* in a high degree; extremely. **verily** *adv.* truly [L. *versus*, true].

ves·i·cal (ves′.i.kạl) *a.* (*Med.*) pert. to bladder. **vesicant** *a.* tending to raise blisters; *n.* blistering application. **vesicate** *v.t.* to raise blisters on. **vesication** *n.* process of blistering. **vesicle** *n.* small bladder-like structure; blister; cyst. **vesicular** (vạ.sik′.yạ.lẹr) *a.* pert. to vesicles. **vesiculate, vesiculose, vesiculous** *a.* vesicular **vesiculation** *n.* [L. *vesica*, bladder].

Ves·per (ves′. pẹr) *n.* the evening star, Venus; (*l.c.*) evening; *a.* (*l.c.*) pert. to evening or vespers. **-s** *n.pl.* an evening prayer; evensong; late afternoon or evening service.

ves·pi·ar·y (ves.pi.er′.i.) *n.* paperlike wasps' nest. **vespid** *n.* social wasp or bee [L. *vespa*, wasp].

ves·sel (ves′.ạl) *n.* utensil for holding either liquids or solids; large ship; (*Anat.*) tube or canal; recipient or means of conveying something [L. *vas*].

vest (vest) *n.* short, sleeveless garment worn under a man's suit coat; undergarment; *v.t.* to clothe; to cover; to put in possession; to endow; to furnish with authority. **-ed** *a.* that cannot be transferred or taken away; robed.

-ment *n.* ceremonial or official garment. -ure *n.* (*Arch.*) clothing. -ee *n.* a vest. —pocket *a.* relatively small (as a book) [L. *vestis,* garment].

ves·tal (ves′·tạl) *a.* chaste; pure. *n.* nun; chaste woman [fr. Rom. Myth. *Vesta,* goddess of the hearth].

ves·ti·bule (ves′·tạ.būl) *n.* small room or hall between outer and inner doors at entrance to house or building [L. *vectibulum,* entrance].

ves·tige (ves′·tij) *n.* trace or sign; mark of something that has been; remains; (*Biol.*) trace of some part or organ formerly present in body. **vestigial** *a.* **vestigially** *adv.* [L. *vestigium,* a footprint].

ves·try (ves′·tri·) *n.* room attached to church for holding ecclesiastical vestments, prayer meetings, etc.; committee of parishioners to deal with parochial affairs. **-man** *n.* [L. *vestiarium,* fr. *vestis,* garment].

vet (vet) *n.* (*Colloq. abbrev.*) veterinary surgeon or a veteran.

vetch (vech) *n.* plant of bean family used for fodder [L. *vicia*].

vet·er·an (vet′·ẹr·ạn) *n.* person who has served a long time; *a.* long practiced [L. *veteranus,* fr. *vetus,* old].

vet·er·i·nar·y (vet′·ẹr·ạ.ner·i·) *a.* pert. to healing diseases and surgical treatment of domestic animals. **veterinarian** *n.* one skilled in medical and surgical treatment of animals [L. *veterinarius,* pert. to beasts of burden].

ve·to (vē′·tō) *n.* power or right of forbidding. *pl.* **-es.** *v.t.* to withhold assent to; to reject. **-er** *n.* **-less** *a.* [L. *veto,* I forbid].

vex (veks) *v.t.* to make angry; to irritate; to distress. **-ation** *n.* **-atious** *a.* causing vexation; distressing. **-atiously** *adv.* **-atiousness** *n.* **-ed** *a.* [L. *vexare,* to harass].

vi·a (vī·ạ, vē′·ạ) *prep.* by way of [L.].

vi·a·ble (vī′·ạ.bl) *a.* born alive and sufficiently developed to be able to live; capable of living or growth. **viability** *n.* [L. *vita,* life].

vi·a·duct (vī′·ạ.dukt) *n.* high bridge or series of arches for carrying road or railway over valley etc. [L. *via,* way; *ducere,* to lead].

vi·al (vī′·ạl) *n.* small glass bottle; phial; *v.t.* to put into a vial [Gk. *phialē,* shallow bowl].

vi·and (vī′·ạnd) *n.* article of food; chiefly *pl.* food, victuals, provisions [L. *vivenda,* provisions, fr. *vivere,* to live].

vi·at·i·cum (vī·at′·i·kạm) *n.* supplies for a journey; Communion or Eucharist given to dying person. *pl.* **-s, viatica** [L. *via,* a way].

vi·brate (vī′·brāt) *v.t.* to move to and fro; to cause to quiver; to measure by vibrations or oscillations; *v.i.* to swing or oscillate; to quiver; to thrill or throb; of sound, to produce quivering effect; to sound tremulous. **vibration** *n.* **vibrator** *n.* **vibratory** *a.* vibrating; causing vibration. **vibrant** *a.* vibrating; thrilling or throbbing; powerful. **vibrancy** *n.* **vibrantly** *adv.* [L. *vibrare,* to swing or shake].

vi·bur·num (vī·bur′·nạm) *n.* any of a group of shrubs of honeysuckle family [L.].

vic·ar (vik′·ẹr) *n.* a deputy; clergyman. **-age** *n.* residence of vicar. **-ial** (vī·ker′·i·ạl) *a.* pert. to, acting as, vicar. **-ship** *n.*

vi·car·i·ous (vī·kar′·i·ạs) *a.* delegated; substituted; done or suffered for another. **-ly** *adv.* **-ness** *n.* [L. *vicarius,* deputy].

vice (vīs) *n.* depravity or immortal conduct; blemish or defect in character, etc.; failing or bad habit. **vicious** (vish′·ạs) *a.* depraved; wicked; spiteful; not well broken, as horse. **viciously** *adv.* **viciousness** *n.* **vicious circle,** describes state in which remedy for evil produces second evil, which when remedied in its turn leads back to first [L. *vitium,* blemish, fault].

vice See **vise.**

vice- (vīs) *prefix* in words signifying persons, denoting one who acts in place of another, or one who is second in authority, as **vice-admiral, vice-chairman, vice-president, vice-principal,** *etc.* [L. *vice,* in place of].

vice·ge·rent (vīs.jir′·ạnt) *a.* exercising delegated power; *n.* holder of delegated authority [L. *vice,* in place of; *gerere,* to act].

vice·roy (vīs′·roi) *n.* governor of country or province who rules as representative of his king; red and black butterfly [L. *vice,* in place of; *roi,* king].

vi·ce ver·sa (vī′·si·vẹr′·sạ) *adv.* the order being reversed; the other way round [L.].

vi·chy·ssoise (vē·shē·swȧz′) *n.* thick cream soup of potatoes [Fr.].

vi·cin·i·ty (vạ.sin·ạ.ti·) *n.* neighborhood; nearness or proximity. **vicinage** (vis′·n·ij) *n.* neighborhood [L. *vicinus,* near].

vi·sious See **vice.**

vi·cis·si·tude (vạ.sis′·ạ.tūd) *n.* regular change or succession; alteration; *pl.* ups and downs of fortune. **vicissitudinary, vicissitudinous** *a.* [L. *vicissitudo,* alteration].

vic·tim (vik′·tim) *n.* living creature sacrificed in performance of religious ceremony; person, or thing, destroyed or sacrified; person who suffers; dupe or prey. **-ize** *v.t.* to make victim of. **-ization** *n.* **-izer** *n.* [L. *victima*].

vic·tor (vik′·tẹr) *n.* one who defeats enemy in battle; conqueror; winner in contest. **-y** *n.* defeat of enemy in battle, or of antagonist in contest; conquest; triumph. **-ious** (vik·tōr′·i·ạs) *a.* having conquered; indicating victory; triumphant; winning. **-iously** *adv.* **-iousness** *n.* [L. *victor,* fr. *vincere* to conquer].

vic·to·ri·a (vik·tōr′·i·ạ) *n.* low four-wheeled carriage with folding top; early touring car with folding top [fr. Queen *Victoria*].

Vic·to·ri·an (vik·tōr′·i·ạn) *a.* of or characteristic of time of Queen *Victoria;* prudish; easily shocked; (of style) ornate, flowery.

vic·tro·la (vik·trō′·lạ) *n.* a phonograph [Trade Mark].

vict·ual (vit′·l) *v.t.* to supply with provisions; *v.i.* to take in provisions. **-s** *n.pl.* (*Colloq.*) food. **-er** (vit′·lẹr) *n.* one who supplies provisions. **-ess** *a.* [L. *victualis,* of food].

vi·cu·na (vi·kū′·nạ) *n.* S. Amer. animal; soft shaggy wool or fabric made from it [Sp.].

vid·e·o (vid′·i·ō *n.* television; *a.* of picture phase of television (opp. to *audio*) [L. = I see].

vi·dette. See **vedette.**

vie (vī) *v.i.* to strive for superiority; to contend. *pr.p.* **vying.** *pa.p.* and *pa.t.* **-d** (vīd) [O.Fr. *envier,* to challenge].

view (vū) *n.* sight; inspection by eye or mind; power of seeing; range of sight; what is seen; pictured representation of scene; manner of looking at anything, esp. mental survey; opinion; aim or intention. *v.t.* to see; to look at; to survey mentally; to consider. **-er** *n.* **-less** *a.* **— finder** *n.* device in camera for showing limits of picture. **-point** *n.* attitude or standpoint. **on view,** displayed. **in view of,** taking into consideration [L. *videre,* to see].

vig·il (vij′·il) *n.* staying awake at night, either for religious exercises, or to keep watch; a watch or watching; *pl.* nocturnal devotions. **-ant** *a.* watchful; alert; corcumspect. **-ante** (an′·ti·) *n.* a member of an unlawful group which sets itself up to control and punish crime. **-antly** *adv.* **-ance** *n.* wakefulness; watchfulness [L. *vigilia,* a watch].

vigilia, a watch].

vi·gnette (vin·yet′) *n.* orig. running ornament of leaves or tendrils; small designs used as headings or tail pieces in books; any engraving, woodcut, etc. not enclosed within border; photograph or portrait showing only head or quarter-length likeness against shaded background; short, neat description in words [Fr. dim. of *vigne*, vine].

vig·or (vig′·ẹr) *n.* active strength; capacity for exertion; energy; vitality; forcefulness of style, in writing. **-ous** *a.* full of physical or mental strength; powerful. **-ously** *adv.* **-ousness** *n.* **-oso** *a. Mus. direction.* (*Brit.*) **vigour** [L.]

vi·king (vī′·king) *n.* Scand. sea rover or pirate who ravaged the northwest coast of Europe (8th 10th cent.) [O.N. *vikingr*].

vile (vīl) *a.* mean; worthless; base; depraved; repulsive; shockingly bad. **-ly** *adv.* **-ness** *n.* **vilify** (vil′·ạ·fī) *v.t.* to speak ill of; to try to degrade by slander; to defame or traduce. **vilifier** *n.* **vilification** *n.* [L. *vilis*, base].

vil·la (vil′·ạ) *n.* country seat; large suburban residence [L. = a farm-house].

vil·lage (vil′·ij) *n.* assemblage of houses, smaller than town and larger than hamlet; *a.* pert. to village; rustic. **-r** *n.* an inhabitant of a village [L. *villaticus*, of a villa].

vil·lain (vil′·ạn) *n.* wicked, depraved or criminal person. **-ous** *a.* wicked; vile. **-ously** *adv.* **-ousness** *n.* **-y** *n.* extreme wickedness; an act of great depravity [L.L. *villanus*, farm servant].

vil·la·nelle (vil·ạ·nel′) *n.* poem of 19 lines on 2 rhymes having 5 three-lined stanzas, followed by one of four lines [It. *villanella*].

vil·lein (vil′·in) *n.* serf who was slave to his lord but free with respect to others. **-age** *n. serfdom* [fr. *villain*].

vil·lus (vil′·ạs) *n.* one of the small, fine, hair-like processes which cover certain membranes; any of the fine soft hairs covering certain fruits, flowers, or plants. *pl.* **villi** (vil′·ī) **villous** *a.* [L. *villus*, shaggy hair].

vim (vim) *n.* force; energy; vigor [L. *vis*, force].

vin·ai·grette (vin·ạ·gret′) *n.* small box, containing sponge saturated with aromatic vinegar salts, etc.; a savory sauce [Fr. dim. fr. *vinaigre*, vinegar].

vin·ci·ble (vin′·sạ·bl) *a.* that may be conquered. **vincibility** *n.* [L. *vincere*].

vin·cu·lum (ving′·kyạ·lạm) *n.* bond of union; (*Alg.*) straight, horizontal mark placed over several members of compound quantity to be treated as one quantity. *pl.* **vincula** [L. = bond, fr. *vincire*, to bind].

vin·di·cate (vin′·dạ·kāt) *v.t.* to justify; to maintain as true and correct; to clear of suspicion, dishonor, etc. **vindicable** *a.* **vindicability** *n.* **vindication** *n.* justification; defense of statement against denial or doubt. **vindicator** *n.* **vindicatory** *a.* [L. *vindicare*, to claim].

vin·dic·tive (vin·dik′·tiv) *a.* given to revenge; revengeful. **-ly** *adv.* **-ness** *n.* [L. *vindicta*, vengeance].

vine (vīn) *n.* woody, climbing plant that produces grapes; any plant which trails or climbs. **vinery** *n.* greenhouse for rearing vines. **-yard** (vin′·yẹrd) *n.* plantation of grapevines. **vinic** *a.* pert. to, or obtained from, wine; alcoholic. **viniculture** *n.* cultivation of vines. **vinicultural** *a.* **viniculturist** *n.* **vinaceous, vinous** *a. pert.* to, or like, wine [L. *vinea*, vine; *vinum*, wine].

vin·e·gar (vin′·ạ·gẹr) *n.* acid liquor obtained from malt, wine, cider, etc. by fermentation, and used as condiment or in pickling. *a.* like vinegar; sour. **-y** *a.* [Fr. *vinaigre*, fr. L. *vinum*, wine; *acer*, sour].

vin·tage (vin′·tij) *n.* gathering of grapes; season's yield of grapes or wine; wine of particular year (*Colloq.*) any output of a season — **wine,** wine made from grapes of particularly good year [L. *vindermia*, vintage].

vi·nyl (vī′·nil, vin′·il) *n.* man-made plastic material.

vi·ol (vī′·ạl) *n.* medieval stringed musical instrument like violin but larger. **bass-viol** *n.* predecessor of violoncello. **-ist** *n.* one who plays viol [Fr. *viole*].

vi·o·la (vī·ō′·lạ) *n.* instrument larger than violin, but smaller than violoncello; alto or tenor violin [It.].

vi·o·la (vī′·ō·lạ) *n.* (*Bot.*) genus of plants including violet and pansy [L.].

vi·o·late (vī′·ạ·lāt) *v.t.* to infringe or break a promise; to treat with disrespect; to outrage or rape. **violation** *n.* transgression; profanation; ravishment; infringement. **violative** *a.* **violator** *n.* **violability** *n.* **violable** *a.* [L. *violare*].

vi·o·lence (vī′·ạ·lạns) *n.* force; vehemence; intensity; assault or outrage. **violent** *a.* characterized by physical force, esp. improper force; forcible; furious; passionate. **violently** *adv.* [L. *violare*, fr. *vis*. force].

vi·o·let (vī′·ạ·lit) *n.* flower of genus Viola, generally of bluish-purple color; color produced by combining blue and red; *a.* bluish or purple [Fr. fr. L. *viola*].

vi·o·lin (vī·ạ·lin′) *n.* modern musical instrument of viol family, with four strings, played with bow; fiddle. **-ist** *n.* [It. *violino*].

vi·o·lon·cel·lo (vī·ạ·lạu·chel′·ō) *n.* bass violin, much larger than violin, held between player's knees; usually *abbrev.* **cello. violoncellist** *n.* [It. dim of *violone*].

vi·per (vī′·pẹr) *n.* a venomous snake; malicious person.**-ish** *a.* like a viper. **-ine, -ous** *a. venomous* [L. *vipera*].

vi·ra·go (vi·rā′·gō) *n.* turbulent or scolding woman [L.].

vi·res·cent (vi·res′·ạnt) *a.* turning green. **virescense** *n.* **viredescent** *a.* **viredity** *n.* greeness, freshness [L. *virescere* fr. *viridis*, green].

vir·gin (vur′·jin) *n.* girl or woman who has not had sexual intercourse; maiden; *a.* without experience of sexual intercourse; unsullied; chaste; fresh; untilled (of land). **-al** *a.* pert. to virgin; maidenly; fresh and pure; *n.* old musical instrument like spinet. **-ity** *n.* **the Vigin,** mother of Christ [L. *virgo*, *virginis*, maiden].

Vir·gin·ia creep·er (vẹr·jin′·yạ krēp′·ẹr) climbing vine whose leaves turn bright red in autumn. **Virginia reel,** a country dance.

Vir·go (vur′·gō) *n.* (*Astron.*) the Virgin, one of the signs of Zodiac [L. *virgo*, virgin].

vir·gule (vur′·gūl) *n.* short diagonal line (/) between 2 words indicating either may be used [L. *verga*, slender twig].

vir·i·des·cent, viridity See **virescent.**

vir·ile (vir′·il) *a.* pert. to man; masculine; strong; having vigor. **virility** *n.* manliness; power of procreation [L. *vir*. man].

vir·tu (vur·tòò′) *n.* objects of art or antiquity, collectively; taste for objects of art [It. fr. L. *virtus*, excellence].

vir·tu·al (vur′·choo·ạl) *a.* being in essence or effect, though not in fact; potential. **-ly** *adv.* to all intents and purposes. **-ity** *n.* [L. *virtus*, excellence].

vir·tue (vur′·chòò) *n.* moral excellence; merit; good quality; female chastity; power or efficacy. **virtuous** *a.* upright; dutiful; chaste. **virtuously** *adv.* **virtuousness** *n.* [L. *virtus*, manly excellence].

vir·tu·o·so (vur·chòò·ō′·sō) *n.* one with great knowledge of fine arts; highly skilled musician, painter, etc. *pl.* **-s, virtuosi. virtuosity** (vur·chòò·ás′·ạ·ti·) *n.* great technical skill in fine arts, esp. music [It.].

vir·u·lent (vir′·ya̧·la̧nt) *a.* extremely poisonous; bitter in enmity; malignant; deadly. **-ly** *adv.* **virulence** *n.* acrimony; rancor; malignity; bitterness. **virulency** *n.* **virus** (vī′·ra̧s) *n.* organism causing disease; corrupting influence [L. *virus,* poison].

vi·sa (vē′·za̧) *n.* official endorsement, as on passport, in proof that document has been examined and found correct, granting entry into that country [Fr. fr. L. *videre, to see*].

vis·age (viz′·ij) *n.* face; countenance; look or appearance. **-d** *a.* [Fr.].

vis·a·vis (vē′·za̧·vē) *adv.* face to face; *n.* person facing another [Fr. = face to face].

vis·cer·a (vis′·a̧·ra̧) *n.pl.* internal organs of body; intestines; entrails. **-l** *a.* [pl. of L. *viscus*].

vis·cid (vis′·id) *a.* glutinous; sticky; tenacious.**-ity** *n.* **viscose** (vis′·kōs) *n.* viscid solution of cellulose, drawn into fibers and used in making rayon, cellophane. **viscous** (vis′·ka̧s) *a.* glutinous; tenacious; thick. **viscosity** *n.* [L. *viscidus,* sticky, fr. *viscum,* birdlime].

vis·count (vī′·kount) *n.* (*fem.* **-ess**) a degree or title of nobility next in rank below earl [L. *vice,* in place of; *comes,* companion].

vise (vīs) *n.* device with two jaws that can be brought together with screw, for holding steady anything which needs filing, etc. Also **vice** [Fr. *vis,* a screw].

vis·i·ble (viz′·a̧·bl) *a.* that can be seen; perceptible; in view. **visibly** *adv.* **visibility** *n.* degree of clarity of atmosphere, esp. for flying [L. *visibilis,* fr. *videre,* to see].

vi·sion (vizh′·a̧n) *n.* act or faculty of seeing external objects; sight; thing seen; imaginary sight; phantom; imaginative insight or foresight. **-ary** *a.* apt to see visions; indulging in fancy or reverie; impractical; existing only in the imagination; *n.* one prone to see visions. **-al** *a.* [L. *visio,* sight, fr. *videre,* to see].

vis·it (viz′·it) *v.t.* to go, or come, to see; to punish; *v.i.* to be a guest; *n.* act of visiting or going to see; stay or sojourn; official or formal inspection. **-ant** *a.* visiting. *n.* one who visits; migratory bird. **-ation** *n.* act of visiting; formal or official inspection; visit of inordinate length; dispensation of divine favor or anger. **-or** *n.* one who visits. **-orial, -atorial** *a.* pert. to official visit or visitor **-ing** *n.a.* [L. *visitare,* fr. *videre,* to see].

vi·sor (vī′·zȩr) *n.* front part of helmet which can be lifted to show face; propecting from brim of cap; similar protective device on car windshield. **-ed** *a.* **-less** *a.* [Fr. *visière,* fr. O.Fr. *vis,* face].

vis·ta (vis′·ta̧) *n.* view, esp. distant view, as through avenue of trees; mental view [It. fr. L. *videre,* to see].

vis·u·al (viz′., vizh′·oo·a̧l) *a.* relating to sight; used in seeing; visible. **-ly** *adv.* by sight; with reference to vision. **-ize** *v.t.* to make visual; to call up mental picture of. **-ization** *n.* **-izer** *n.* [L. *visualis*].

vi·tal (vī′·ta̧l) *a.* necessary to or containing life; very necessary. **-s** *n.pl.* essential internal organs, as lungs, heart, brain. **-ly** *adv.* **-ize** *v.t.* to give life to; to lend vigor to. **-ization** *n.* **-ity** *n.* the principle of life; vital force; vigor. **— statistics** data concerning births, deaths, etc. [L. *vitalis,* belonging to life].

vi·ta·min (vī′·ta̧·min) *n.* any of a group of chemical substances present in various foods and indispensable to health and growth [L. *vita,* life].

vi·ti·ate (vish′·i·āt) *v.t.* to make faulty or impure; to corrupt; to impair; to invalidate. **vitiation** *n.* **vitiator** *n.* [L. *vitium,* vice].

vit·i·cul·ture (vit′·a̧·kul′·chȩr) *n.* cultivation of grapevines [L. *vitis,* vine].

vit·re·ous (vit′·ri·a̧s) *a.* pert. to, or resembling, glass; glassy; derived from glass. **-ness** *n.* **vitrescent** *a.* tending to become like glass; capable of being formed into glass. **vitrescence** *n.* **vitric** *a.* [L. *vitrum,* glass].

vit·ri·fy (vit′·ra̧·fī) *v.t.* to convert into glass or glassy substance; *v.i.* to be converted into glass. **vitrifiable** *a.* **vitrifiability** *n.* **vitrifaction, vitrification** *n.* [L. *vitrum,* glass; *facere,* to make].

vit·ri·ol (vit′·ri·a̧l) *n.* sulfuric acid. **-ic** *a.* pert. to, resembling, derived from, vitriol; sarcastic, caustic; bitter. **-ize** *v.* **-ization** *n.* [L. *vitreolus,* of glass].

vi·tu·per·ate (vī·to͝o′·pa̧·rāt) *v.t.* to abuse in words; to revile; to berate. **vituperative** *a.* abusive; scolding. **vituperatively** *adv.* **vituperator** *n.* **vituperation** *n.* [L. *vituperare,* to blame].

vi·va (vē′·va̧) *interj.* long live [It.].

vi·va·ce (vē·va′·chi) *adv.* (*Mus.*) with spirit [It.].

vi·va·cious (vī·vā′·sha̧s) *a.* lively; sprightly; animated; having great vitality. **-ly** *adv.* **vivacity** (vī·vas′·a̧·ti) *n.* liveliness [L. *vivax,* fr. *virere,* to live].

vi·var·i·um (vī·ver′·i·a̧m) *n.* place for keeping or raising living animals or plants [L.].

vi·va vo·ce (vī′·va̧ vō′·si·) *adv.* orally; *a.* oral [L. = with the living voice].

viv·id (viv′·id) *a.* animated; lively; clear; evoking brilliant images; (of color) bright; glaring. **-ly** *adv.* **-ness** *n.* [L. *vividus,* lively, fr. *vivere,* to live].

viv·i·fy (viv′·a̧·fī) *v.t.* to endue with life; to animate; to make vivid. **vivification** *n.* **vivifier** *n.* [L. *vivus,* living; *facere,* to make].

vi·vip·a·rous (vī·vip′·a̧·ra̧s) *a.* producing young in living state, instead of eggs. **-ly** *adv.* **-ness, viviparity** *n.* [L *vivus,* living; *parere,* to give birth].

viv·i·sec·tion (viv·a̧·sek′·sha̧n) *n.* dissection of, or experimenting on, living animals for purpose of physiological investigations **-al** *a.* **-ist** *n.* [L. *vivus,* alive; *secare,* to cut].

vix·en vik′·en) *n.* she-fox; cross bad-tempered woman. **-ish** *a.* [O.E. *fyxen,* a she-fox].

vi·zier, vi·zir (vi·zir′) *n.* high executive officer in Turkey and other Oriental countries. **-ate, -ship** *n.* **-ial** *a.* [Ar. *wazir*].

vo·ca·ble (vō′·ka̧·bl) *n.* a word esp. with ref. to sound rather than meaning; term [L. *vocabulum,* an appellation].

vo·cab·u·lar·y (vō·kab′·ya̧·ler·i·) *n.* list of words, usu. arranged in alphabetical order and explained; wordbook; stock of words used by language, class, or individual [L. *vocabulum,* a word].

vo·cal (vō′·ka̧l) *a.* pert. to voice or speech; having voice; uttered by voice; (*Phon.*) sounded; having character of vowel. **-ly** *adv.* **-ize** *v.t.* to make vocal; to utter with voice, and not merely with breath; *v.i.* to make vocal sounds. **-ist** *n.* [L. *vox,* the voice].

vo·ca·tion (vō·kā′·sha̧n) *n.* divine call to religious career; profession, or occupation. **-al** *a.* **-ally** *adv.* [L. *vocare,* to call].

voc·a·tive (vȧk′·a̧·tiv) *a.* relating to, used in, calling or address; *n.* (*Gram.*) case used in direct address. [L. *vocare,* to call].

vo·cif·er·ate (vō·sif′·a̧·rāt) *v.t.* to utter noisily or violently; to bawl; *v.i.* to cry with loud voice. **vociferation** *n.* **vociferator** *n.* **vociferous** *a.* making loud outcry; noisy or clamorous. **vociferously** *adv.* **vociferousness** *n.* [L. *vox, vocis,* the voice; *ferre,* to carry].

vod·ka (vȧd′·kȧ) *n.* in Russia and Poland alcoholic liquor distilled from cereals or potatoes [Russ. = little water].

vogue (vōg) *n.* prevailing fashion; mode; style; current usage [Fr.].

voice (vois) *n.* faculty of uttering audible sounds; utterance; quality of utterance; expression of feeling or opinion; vote; (*Gram.*) mode of inflecting verbs, as *active, passive voice; v.t.* to give expression to; to announce. **-d** (voist) *a.* furnished with voice or with expression; (*Phon.*) uttered with vocal tone. **-ful** *a.* **-less** *a.* **-lessly** *adv.* **-lessness** *n.* **-print** *n.* an electronically produced graphic representation of a person's speech pattern, used for identification; *v.i.* **-printing** *n.* [L. *vox,* voice].

void (void) *a.* empty; being without; not legally binding; *n.* an empty space; *v.t.* to make vacant; to empty out; to make ineffectual or invalid. **-er** *n.* **-ness** *n.* **-able** *a.* **-ance** *n.* act of voiding; state of being void; (*Eccles.*) ejction from benefice [O.Fr. *voit*].

voile (voil, vwål) *n.* thin cotton, woolen, or silk material [Fr. = veil].

vo•lant (vō'.lạnt) *a.* borne through the air; capable of flying [L. *volare,* to fly].

Vo•la•pük (vō.lạ.pēk') *n.* artificial language invented in 1879 [= world's speech].

vol•a•tile (vål'.ạ.tạl) *a.* evaporating quickly; easily passing into a vapor state; fickle. **volatilize** *v.t., v.i.* to render or become volatile; to cause to pass off in vapor. **volatilizable** *a.* **volatilization** *n.* **volatizer** *n.* **volatility** *n.* [L. *volatilis,* flying].

vol•ca•no (vål.kā'.nō) *n.* opening in crust of earth, from which heated solid, liquid, and gaseous matters are ejected. **volcanic** (vål.-kan'.ik) *a.* **volcanically** *adv.* **volcanicity** [It., fr. L. *Vulcanus,* god of fire, whose forge was supposed to be below Mt. Etna].

vole (vōl) *n.* mouse-like rodent living out-of-doors [Scan. *voll,* field].

vol•i•tant (vål'.ạ.tạnt) *a.* volant; flying; having power of flight; **volitation** *n.* flight. **volitational** *a.* [L. *volare,* to fly].

vo•li•tion (vō.lish'.ạn) *n.* act of willing or choosing; exercise of will. **-al** *a.* **-ally** *adv.* **volitive** *a.* [L. *volo, velle,* to be willing].

vol•ley (vål'.i.) *n.* discharge of many shots or missiles at one time; missiles so discharged; rapid utterance; (*Tennis*) return of ball before it touches ground; *v.t.* to discharge in a volley; *v.i.* to fly in a volley; to sound together; (*Tennis*) to return ball before it touches ground. **-er** *n.* **-ball** *n.* team game played with ball and net [L. *volare,* to fly].

volt (vōlt) *n.* practical unit of electro-motive force, being the pressure which causes current of one ampere to flow through resistance of one ohm. **-age** *n.* electro-motive force reckoned in volts. **-aic** *a.* **-meter** *n.* instrument used for measuring electro-motive force in volts [*Volta,* Italian scientist].

volt, volte (vōlt) *n.* in fencing, sudden turn or movement to avoid thrust; gait, or track, made by horse going sideways round center; circle so made [Fr., fr. L. *volvere,* to roll].

volte-face (vawlt.fás') *n.* turning round; sudden reversal of opinion or direction [Fr.].

vol•u•ble vål'.yạ.bl) *a.* having flowing and rapid utterance; fluent in speech; glib. **volubly** *adv.* **-ness, volubility** *n.* [L. *volubilis,* fr. *volvere,* to roll].

vol•ume (vål'.yạm) *n.* formerly, roll or scroll; book; part of a work which is bound; bulk or compass; cubical content; power, fullness of voice or musical tone. **volumetric** *a.* pert. to measurement by volume. **volumetrically** *adv.* **voluminal** *a.* pert. to cubical content. **voluminous** *a.* consisting of many volumes; bulky. **voluminousness** *n.* **voluminosity** *n.* [L. *volumen,* roll or scroll, fr. *volvere,* to roll].

vol•un•tar•y (vål'.ạn.ter.i.) *a.* proceeding from choice or free will; unconstrained; spontaneous; subject to the will; *n.* organ solo played during, or after, church service. **voluntarily** *adv.* **voluntariness** *n.* [L. *voluntas,* will].

vol•un•teer (val.ạn.tēr') *n.* one who enters service, esp. military, of his own free will; *a.* serving as a volunteer; composed; pert. to volunteers; *v.t.* to offer or bestow voluntarily; *v.i.* to enter into of or of one's own free will [L. *voluntas,* free will].

vo•lup•tu•ar•y (vạ.lup'.chòò.er.i.) *n.* one addicted to luxurious living or sensual gratification; sensualist; *a.* concerned with, or promoting, sensual pleasure. **voluptuous** *a.* **voluptuously** *adv.* **voluptuousness** *n.* [L. *voluptas,* pleasure].

vo•lute (vạ.lòòt') *n.* (*Archit.*) spiral scroll used in Ionic, Corinthian, and Composite capitals; (*Zool.*) tropical spiral shell; *a.* rolled up spiraled. **-d** *a.* **volution** *n.* [L. *volvere, volutum,* to roll].

vom•it (våm'.it) *v.t.* to eject from stomach by mouth; to spew or disgorge; *v.i.* to eject contents of stomach by mouth; *n.* matter ejected from stomach. **-er** *n.* **-ive** *a.* **-ory** *a.* provoking vomiting; *n.* emetic; an opening through which matter is discharged [L. *vomere,* to throw up].

voo•doo (vòò'.dòò) *n.* body of primitive rites and practices; one who practices such rites; evil spirit; *a.* belonging to, or connected with, system of voodoo. **-ism** *n.* [Creole Fr. *vaudoux,* a sorcerer].

vo•ra•cious (vō.rā'.shạs) *a.* greedy in eating; eager to devour; ravenous. **-ly** *adv.* **-ness, voracity** (vō.ras'.i.ti.) *n.* [L. *vorax,* greedy to devour].

vor•tex (vawr'.teks) *n.* whirling motion of any fluid, forming depression in center of circle; whirlpool; whirling mass of air, fire, etc. which draws with irresistable power. *pl.* **-es, vortices** (vawr'.ti.sēz) **vortical, vorticose** *a.* **vortically** *adv.* [L.].

vo•ta•ry (vō'.tạ.ri.) *a.* consecrated by vow devoted to any service, study, etc. **votaress** or promise; *n.* one engaged by vow; one *n.(fem.)* [L. *votum,* vow].

vote (vōt) *n.* formal expression of wish, choice, or opinion, of individual, or a body of persons; expression of will by a majority; right to vote; suffrage; what is given or allowed by vote; *v.t.* to declare by general consent; *v.i.* to express one's choice, will, or preference. **-r** *n.* [L. *votum,* vow].

vo•tive (vō'.tiv) *a.* offered or consecrated by vow; given in fulfillment of vow. **-ly** *adv.* **-ness** *n.* [L. *votivus,* promised by vow].

vouch (vouch) *v.t.* to warrant; to attest; to affirm; *v.i.* to bear witness; to be guarantee (for). **-er** *n.* one who bears witness or attests to anything; paper or document that serves to vouch truth of accounts, or to establish facts; receipt [L. *vocare,* to call].

vouch•safe (vouch.sāf') *v.t.* to condescend to grant or do something; *v.i.* to deign. **-ment** *n.*

vow (vou) *n.* solemn promise made esp. to deity; *v.t.* to consecrate or dedicate by solemn promise; to devote; *v.i.* to make vow or solemn promise [L. *votum,* vow].

vow•el (vou'.ạl) *n.* any vocal sound (such as *a, e, i, o, u*) produced with least possible friction or hindrance from any organ of speech; letter or character that represents such sound; *a.* pert. to vowel. **-less** *a.* **-ize** *n.* **-ization** *n.* [L. *vocalis,* fr. *vox,* voice].

voy•age (voi'.ij) *n.* journey esp. by sea; *v.i.* to sail or traverse by water. **-r** *n.* one who makes voyage [Fr. fr. L. *viaticum,* traveling money, fr. *via,* way].

Vul·can (vul′.kạn) *n.* (*Myth.*) Roman god of fire and of metal working. **vulcanize** *v.t.* to treat rubber with sulfur at high temperature to increase durability and elasticity. **vulcanization** *n.* **vulcanite** *n.* rubber hardened by vulcanizing. **vulcanizable** *a.* **vulcanizer** *n.* [L. *Vulcanus*, god of fire].

vul·gar (vul′.gẹr) *a.* of common people; in common use; coarse or offensive; rude; boorish. **-ly** *adv.* **-ian** *n.* vulgar person, esp. rich and unrefined. **-ize** *v.t.* to make vulgar. **-izer** *n.* **-ization** *n.* **-ism** *n.* vulgar expression; grossness of manners. **-ness, vulgarity** *n.* commonness; lack of refinement in manners; coarseness of ideas or language [L. *vulgaris*, fr. *vulgus*, the common people].

vul·ner·a·ble (vul′.nẹr.(ạ).bl) *a.* capable of being wounded; offering open to criticism; assailable; in contract bridge, denoting side which has won first game in rubber and is subject to increased honors and penalties. **-ness, vulnerability** *n.* **vulnerably** *adv.* [L. *vulnus*, wound].

vul·pine (vul′.pīn) *a.* pert. to fox; cunning; crafty [L. *vulpes*, fox].

vul·ture (vul′.chẹr) *n.* large, rapacious bird of prey; rapacious person. **vulturine, vulturish, vulturious** *a.* characteristic of vulture; rapacious [L. *vultur*].

vul·va (vul′.vạ) *n.* fissure in external organ of generation in female [L.].

vy·ing (vī′.ing) *pr.p.* of **vie.**

W

wad (wȧd) *n.* little tuft or bundle; soft mass of loose, fibrous substance, for stuffing, etc., roll of bank notes; *v.t.* to form into wad; to line with wadding; to pad; *pr.p.* **-ding.** *pa.t.* and *pa.p.* **-ded. -ding** *n.* soft material for wads [Scand.].

wad·dle (wȧd′.l) *v.i.* to walk like duck, with short swaying steps; *n.* slow, rocking gait [freq. of *wade*].

wade (wād) *v.i.* to walk through something which hampers movement, as water, mud, etc.; to cope with, as accumulation or work; *v.t.* to cross (stream) by wading; *n.* a wading. **-r** *n.* one who wades; long-legged bird, e.g. stork, heron. **-rs** *n.pl.* high waterproof boots [O.E. *wadan*].

wa·di, wa·dy (wạd′.i.) *n.* channel or stream which is dry except during rainy season [Ar. *wadi*, ravine].

wa·fer (wā′.fẹr) *n.* very thin biscuit; thin disk of unleavened bread, used in Eucharist service of R.C. Church; thin, adhesive disk for sealing letters; *v.t.* to seal or close with wafer. **-y** *a.* [O.Fr. *waufre*].

waf·fle (wȧf′.l) *n.* a thin cake of batter with criss-cross pattern. **— iron** *n.* hinged metal utensil for baking both sides of waffle at once [Dut. *wafel*, a wafer].

waft (wȧft, waft) *v.t.* to impel lightly through water or air; *v.i.* to float gently; *n.* breath or slight current of air or odor; puff. **-ure** *n.* [O.E. *wafian*, to wave].

wag (wag) *v.t.* to cause to move to and fro; *v.i.* to shake; to swing; to vibrate. *pr.p.* **-ging.** *pa.p., pa.t.* **-ged.** *n.* swinging motion, to and fro [O.E. *wagian*].

wag (wag) *n.* droll, witty person; humorist. **-gery** *n.* pleasantry; prank; jocularity. **-gish** *a.* frolicsome; droll. **-gishly** *adv.* **-gishness** *n.* [orig. E. *wag-halter*, one who deserves hanging—jocularly].

wage (wāj) *v.t.* to carry on; *n.* (usu. *pl.*) payment paid for labor or work done; hire; reward; pay [O.Fr. *wagier*].

wa·ger (wā′.jẹr) *n.* something staked on issue of future event or of some disputed point; bet; stake; *v.t.* to bet; to lay wager. **-er** *n.* [O.Fr. *wageure*, fr. Gothic, *wadi*, pledge].

wag·gle (wag′.l) *v.t.* and *v.i.* to move one way and the other; to wag [freq. of *wag*].

wag·on (wag′.ạn) *n.* four-wheeled vehicle or truck, for carrying heavy freight; (*Brit.*) railway freight car. (*Colloq.*) station wagon; police wagon. **-er,** *n.* one who drives wagon. **-ette** *n.* four-wheeled open carriage with two lengthwise seats facing one another behind driver's seat. **-less** *a.* **-load** *n.* [Dut. *wagen*].

wag·tail (wag′.tāl) *n.* bird distinguished by long tail almost constantly in motion.

waif (wāf) *n.* homeless person, esp. neglected child; stray article or animal [Ice. *veif*].

wail (wāl) *v.t.* and *v.i.* to lament (over); to express sorrow audibly; to weep; to bewail; to bemoan; to cry loudly; *n.* loud weeping; great mourning; doleful cry. **-er** *n.* **ing** *n.* **-ingly** *adv.* [O.N. *vaela*].

wain (wān) *n.* (*Poetic*) wagon, esp. in farm use. **wainwright** *n.* wagon maker [O.E. *waegen*].

wain·scot (wān′.skạt) *n.* paneling of wood or other material used as lining for inner walls of building; lower part of a wall; *v.t.* to line with wainscoting. **-ing** *n.* wall paneling material [Low, Ger. *wagenschot*, oak wood].

waist (wāst) *n.* part of human body immediately below ribs and above hips; garment or part of woman's dress covering from neck to waist; middle part of anything; part of upper deck of ship which lies between quarter-leck and forecastle. **-band** *n.* part of dress or trousers which fits round waist [M.E. *waste*, growth, fr. *wax*, to grow].

wait (wāt) *v.t.* to stay for; *v.i.* to stop until arrival of some person or event; to be temporarily postponed; to be expecting; to serve at table; to attend (on); *n.* act, period of waiting. **-er** *n.* one who waits; a man who waits on table; tray. **-ing** *n.* and *a.* **-ing-list** *n.* list of names of those wishing some article, etc. in short supply. **-ing room** *n.* room set aside for use of people waiting in public place, office, etc. **-ress** *n.* female waiter [O.Fr. *waiter*, to lurk]

waive (wāv) *v.t.* to give up claim to; to forgo; (*Law*) to relinquish a right, etc. **-r** *n.* (*Law*) relinquishment, or statement of such [O.N.Fr. *weyver*, to renounce].

wake (wāk) *v.t.* to rouse from sleep; to waken; to excite; to kindle; to provoke; *v.i.* to awaken; to be stirred up or roused to action. *pa.t.* and *pa.p.* **-d** or **woke.** *pr.p.* **waking.** *n.* vigil; act of sitting up overnight with corpse. **-ful** *a.* indisposed to sleep; sleepless; watchful; wary. **-fully** *adv.* **-n** *vt., i.* **-ner** *n.* **waking** *a.* as in *waking hours*, period when one is not asleep [O.E. *wacian*].

wake (wāk) *n.* that part of track immediately astern of ship; air disturbance caused in rear of airplane in flight. **in the wake of,** following behind; in rear of [Dut. *wak*].

wale (wāl) *n.* mark left on flesh by rod or whip; ridge in the weave of a fabric; *v.t.* to mark with wales. **waling** *n.* wale, piece of heavy timber fastened horizontally to tie together boards supporting sides of trench or vertical pieces of jetty [O.E. *walu*].

walk (wawk) *v.t.* to pass through, along, upon; to cause to step slowly; to lead, drive, or ride (horse) at a slow pace; *v.i.* to go on foot; to appear as specter; to conduct oneself; *n.* act of walking; slowest pace of quadruped; characteristic gait or style of walking; path for pedestrians; avenue set with trees; stroll; distance walked over; sphere of life; conduct. **-er** *n.* **-ie-talkie** *n.* portable wireless combined transmitting and receiving set. **-out** *n.* a strike. **—over** *n.* in sporting contests, easy victory. **—on** minor role in a play. **—up** apartment house without an elevator. [O.E. *wealcan*, to roll].

wall (wawl) *n.* structure of brick, stone, etc. serving as fence, side of building, etc.; surface or side; anything resembling a wall; *pl.* fortifications; works for defense; *v.t.* to enclose with wall; to block up with wall. **—board** *n.* lining of various materials for applying to or making walls. **-ed** *a.* provided with walls; fortified. **-flower** *n.* garden plant, with sweet-scented flowers; lady left sitting at dance for lack of partners. **-less** *a.* **-like** *a.* [L. *vallum*].

wal·la·by (wȧ′·ạ·bi·) *n.* a small kangaroo [Austral. native name].

wal·la·roo (wȧl·ạ·ròò′) *n.* large kangaroo [Austral.].

wal·let (wȧl′·it) *n.* folding pocketbook for paper money identification, cards, etc.

wall-eye (wawl′·ī) *n.* variety of fish having large eyes. affection of the eye due to opacity of cornea; an eye turned outward. **-d** *a.* glary-eyed [Scand.].

Wal·loon (wȧ·lòòn′) *n.* descendant of ancient Belgae, race of mixed Celtic and Roman stock, now French speaking population of Belgium; their dialect; *a.* of, or pert, to, Walloons [O.Fr. *Wallon*, fr. L. *Gallus*, a Gaul].

wal·lop (wȧl′·ạp) *v.t.* (*Colloq.*) to beat soundly; to strike hard; *n.* stroke or blow. **-ing** *n.* a thrashing; *a.* tremendous; big.

wal·low (wȧl′·ō) *v.i.* to roll about (in mud, etc.); to thrive or revel in filth, vice, luxury, etc. [O.E. *wealwian*, to roll round].

wal·nut (wawl′·nut) *n.* large tree producing rich, dark-brown wood of fine texture; fruit of tree, large nut with crinkled shell [O.E. *wealh*, foreign; *knutu*, nut].

wal·rus (wawl′·rạs) *n.* mammal closely related to seal but with down-turned tusks [Dan. *hvalros* = whale-horse].

waltz (wawlts) *n.* ballroom dance in three-four time; music for this dance; *v.i.* to dance a waltz; to skip about, from joy, etc. **-er** *n.* **-ing** *n.* [Ger. *walzer*, fr. *walzen*, to roll].

wamp·pum (wȧm′·pạm) *n.* strings of shells, strung like beads, used as money and for ornament by N. American Indians [Native, *wanpanpiak*, string of white shell beads].

wan (wȧn) *a.* having a sickly hue; pale; pallid; ashy; gloomy. **-ly** *adv.* **-ness** *n.* [O.E.].

wand (wȧnd) *n.* long, slender, straight rod; rod used by conjurers or as sign of authority [O.N. *vondr*, switch].

wan·der (wȧn′·dẹr) *v.i.* to ramble; to go astray; to be delirious; to depart from subject. **-er** *n.* **-ing** *a.* rambling; unsettled; *n.* journeying here and there, usually in *pl.* **-ingly** *adv.* **-lust** (wȧn′·dẹr·lust) *n.* urge to wander or travel [O.E. *wandrian*].

wane (wān) *v.i.* to decrease; to fail; *n.* decrease of illuminated part of moon; decline; diminution [O.E. *wanian*, fr. *wan*, wanting].

wan·gle (wang′·gl) *v.t.* (*Colloq.*) to obtain by deception or trickery; *v.i.* to manage with difficulty. **-r** *n.* (*Colloq.*) trickery; artifice.

want (wawnt) *n.* scarcity of what is needed; poverty; *v.t.* to be without; lack; *v.t.* to be without; to lack; to need; to crave; *v.i.* to be lacking; to have need. **-ed** *a.* desired; required; sought after; searched for (by police). **-er** *n.* **-less** *a.* **-ing** *a.* lacking; deficient. *prep.* without; minus. **-s** *n.pl.* requirements [O.N. *vant*].

wan·ton (wawn′·tạn) *a.* dissolute; unrestrained; recklessly arrogant, malicious; *n.*; *v.i.* **-ly** *adv.* **-ness** *n.* [M.E. *wantowen*].

wap·i·ti (wȧp′·ạ·ti·) *n.* N. American elk related to red deer [Amer.-Ind.].

war (wawr) *n.* armed conflict between two (groups of) states; state of opposition or hostility; profession of arms; art of war; *v.i.* to make war; to carry on hostilities; to contend. *pr.p.* **-ring.** *pa.t.* and *pa.p.* **-red. — cry** *n.* wild whoop or battle cry uttered by attacking troops; slogan. **— dance** *n.* wild dance, among savages, preliminary to entering battle. **-fare** *n.* hostilities. **—head** *n.* explosive cap on missile. **—horse** *n.* charger. **-like** *a.* disposed for war; martial; hostile; **-monger** *n.* advocator of war. **—paint** *n.* special adornment of Indians when on warpath; (*Slang*) full dress or regalia. **-path** *n.* military foray, esp. among Amer. Indians on scalping expedition. **-ship** *n.* vessel equipped for war. Also **man·of·war. civil war,** war between citizens of same country. **cold war,** state of international hostility short of actual warfare [O.N.Fr. *werre*, Fr. *guerre*].

war·ble (wawr′·bl) *v.t.* to sing in quavering manner; to trill; to carol; *v.i.* to sound melodiously; *n.* soft, sweet flow of melody; carol; song. **-r** *n.* one that warbles; bird with pleasant trilling song [O. Fr. *werbler*].

war·ble (wawr′·bl) *n.* hard tumor on back of horse. **— fly,** fly which lays its eggs in skin of cattle, horses, etc.

ward (wawrd) *v.t.* to repel; to turn aside; *n.* division of city; room for patients in hospital; guardianship; minor legally in the care of a guardian; divisions of a prison; custody; district of city or town for purposes of administration, voting, etc. slot in key; defensive movement in fencing, parry. **-en** *n.* civil defense officer; keeper; supervisor of prison. **-er** *n.* watchman; staff of authority. **-robe** *n.* cupboard for holding clothes; wearing apparel in general. **-room** *n.* mess room on liner or battleship for senior officers. **-ship** *n.* office of guardian; state of being under guardian [O.E. *weard*, protection].

ware (wer) *n.* article of merchandise; pottery; usually in combinations as, *earthenware, hardware*, etc.; *pl.* goods for sale; commodities; merchandise. **-house** *n.* storehouse for goods; *v.t.* to store in warehouse [O.E.*waru*].

ware (wer) *a.* aware; cautious; *v.t.* to beware of [A.S. *warian*]

war·i·ly, war·i·ness See **wary.**

warm (wawrm) *a.* having heat in moderate degree; not cold; hearty; lively; of colors, suggesting heat, as red, orange, yellow; excited; passionate; affectionate; *v.t.* to communicate moderate degree of heat to; to excite interest or zeal in; *v.i.* to become moderately heated; to become animated. **—blooded** *a.* of animals with fairly high and constant body-temperature; passionate; generous. **—hearted** *a.* affectionate; kindly disposed; sympathetic. **-ly** *adv.* **-ness, -th** *n.* slight heat; cordiality; heartiness; enthusiasm [O.E.*wearm*].

warn (wawrn) *v.t.* to notify by authority; to caution; to admonish; to put on guard. **-ing** *n.* advance notice of anything; admonition; caution; notice to leave premises, situation, etc.; *a.* cautioning [O.E.*warnian*].

warp (wawrp) *v.t.* to twist permanently out of shape; to bend; to pervert; to draw vessel or heavy object along by means of cable coiled on windlass; *v.i.* to turn, twist, or be twisted; *n.* distortion of wood due to unequal shrinkage in drying; system of spun threads extended lengthwise in loom on which woof is woven; a towing line. **-ed** *a.* twisted by unequal shrinkage; perverted; depraved. **-er** *n.* one who, or that which, warps. **-ing** *n.* [O.E. *weorpan*, to throw, to cast].

war·rant (wår′., wawr′.ạnt) *v.t.* to give justification for; to authorize or sanction with assurance of safety; to guarantee to be as represented; to vouch for; to assure; to indemnify against loss; *n.* (*Law*) instrument which warrants or justifies act otherwise not permissible or legal; instrument giving power to arrest offender; authorization; guarantee; naval or military writ inferior to commission. **-able** *a.* **-ably** *adv.* **-ableness** *n.* **-ed** *a.* guaranteed. **-er, -or** *n.* **-y** *n.* security; guarantee. **— officer,** officer in Navy and Army intermediate between non-commissioned and commissioned officer [O.Fr. *warantir*].

war·ren (wawr′.ạn) *n.* enclosure for breeding rabbits and other game; overcrowded slum [O.Fr. *warenne,* Fr. *garenne*].

war·ri·or (wawr′.i.ẹr) *n.* soldier; fighting man; brave fighter [*war*].

wart (wawrt) *n.* small hard conical excrescence on skin; (*Bot.*) hard, glandular protuberance on plants and trees. **— hog** *n.* African mammal of pig family with large warty protuberances on face. **-y** *a.* [O.E. *wearte*].

war·y (war′.i., wer′.i.) *a.* cautious; heedful; careful; prudent. **warily** *adv.* **wariness** *n.* [*ware*].

was (wuz) *pa.t.* of verb **to be** [O.E. *waes*].

wash (wåsh, wawsh) *v.t.* to free from dirt with water and soap; to tint lightly and thinly; to separate, as gold, by action of water; *v.i.* to perform act of ablution; to cleanse clothes in water; to be washable; *n.* clothes, etc. washed at one time; liquid applied to surface as lotion or coat of paint; flow of body of water; rough water left behind by vessel in motion; marsh or fen; shallow bay or inlet **-able** *a.* **-board** *n.* baseboard; board with a corrugated surface for washing clothes on; board above gunwale of boat to keep waves from washing over. **-er** *n.* one who washes; flat ring of metal, rubber, etc to make a tight joint, distribute pressure from nut or head of bolt, prevent leakage, etc. **-erman, -erwoman** *n.* **-basin, -bowl, -tub** *n.* for washing purposes. **-iness** *n.* state of being washy, weak, or watery. **-ing** *n.* act of one who washes; ablution; clothes washed at one time; *a.* used in, or intended for, washing. **-ing soda,** form of sodium carbonate used in washing. **-out** *n.* cavity in road, etc. caused by action of flood water; (*Colloq.*) failure or fiasco. **-y** *a.* watery; weak; thin; insipid. **-ed out,** exhausted; faded [O.E. *wascan*].

wasp (wåsp, wawsp) *n.* stinging insect like bee with longer body and narrow waist; an ill-natured, irritable person. **-ish** *a.* like wasp; irritable; snappy. **-ishly** *adv.* **-ishness** *n.* **—waisted** *a.* having slender waist [O.E. *waesp, waeps*].

was·sail (wås′.ạl) *n.* ancient salutation in drinking of health; celebration or festivity; spiced ale; *v.i.* to carouse; to drink wassail; **-er** *n.* [O.E. *wes hal,* be hale = 'your health'].

waste (wāst) *v.t.* to expend uselessly; to use extravagantly; to squander; to neglect; to lay waste; to spoil; *v.i.* to wear away by degrees; to become worn and emaciated; to decrease; to wither; *a.* lying unused; of no worth; desolate; unproductive; *n.* act of wasting; that which is wasted; refuse; uncultivated country; loss; squandering. **wastage** *n.* loss by use, leakage, or decay. **-basket** *n.* container for waste materials. **-ful** *a.* full of waste; destructive; prodigal; extravagant. **-fully** *adv.* **-fulness** *n.* **-land** *n.* barrenland. **— pipe** *n.* discharge pipe for drainage water. **-r** *n.* **wastrel** *n.* waster; profligate; spendthrift. **to waste away,** to be in state of decline. **to lay waste,** to devastate [O.Fr. *waster;* L. *vastare,* to lay waste].

watch (wach) *n.* state of being on the lookout; close observation; vigil; one who watches; watchman; sentry; city night patrol of earlier times; portable timekeeper for pocket, wrist, etc.; one of the divisions of working day on ship; sailors on duty at the same time; division of the night; *v.t.* to give heed to; to keep in view; to guard; to observe closely; *v.i.* to be vigilant; to be on watch; to keep guard; to be wakeful; to look out (for); to wait (for). **-dog** *n.* guard dog; any watchful guardian. **-er** *n.* **-ful** *a.* vigilant; attentive; cautious. **-fully** *adv.* **-fulness** *n.* **-maker, -making** *n.* **—man** *n.* man who guards property. **—night,** New Year's Eve. **—word** *n.* password; a slogan; rallying cry [O.E. *waecce*].

wa·ter (waw′.tẹr, wå′.tẹr) *n.* transparent, tasteless liquid, substance of rain, rivers, etc.; body of water; river; lake; sea; saliva; tear; urine; serum; transparency of gem; *v.t.* to wet or soak with water; to put water into; to cause animal to drink; to irrigate; to give cloth wavy appearance; *v.i.* to shed water; to issue as tears; to gather saliva in mouth as symptom of appetite; to take in or obtain water. **— closet** *n.* sanitary convenience flushed by water. **—color** *n.* artist's color ground up with water; painting in this medium. **—colorist** *n.* **-course** *n.* channel worn by running water; canal. **—cress** *n.* aquatic plant with succulent leaves. **-ed** *a.* diluted with water; of silk fabrics upon which wavy pattern has been produced. **-fall** *n.* fall or perpendicular descent of water of river; cascade; cataract. **-fowl** *n.* any aquatic bird with webbed feet and coat of closely packed feathers or down. **— gauge** *n.* instrument for measuring height of water in boiler, etc. **—glass** *n.* mixture of soluable silicates of potash and soda, used in storing eggs or for preserving stone work; glass for drinking water. **-iness** *n.* state of being watery. **-ing place** *n.* a place where water may be obtained. **-ish** *a.* containing too much water; watery; thin. **-less** *a.* **— level** *n.* level formed by surface of still water; leveling instrument in which water is employed. **-lily** *n.* aquatic plant with fragrant flowers and large floating leaves. **—line** *n.* line on hull of ship to which water reaches. **—logged** *a.* saturated or full of water. **— main** *n.* large pipe running under streets, for conveying water. **—man** *n.* man who manages water craft; ferryman. **— mark** *n.* in paper making, faint translucent design stamped in substance of sheet of paper and serving as trademark. **-melon** *n.* large fruit with smooth, dark-green rind and red pulp. **— moccasin** *n.* poisonous semiaquatic pit viper of southern U.S., related to copperhead. **— polo** *n.* ball game played in water. **— power** *n.* power of water used as prime mover. **-proof** *a.* impervious to water; *v.t.* to make impervious to water. **-shed** *n.* area drained by a river. **-spout** *n.* whirlwind over water, producing vortex connecting sea and cloud, resulting in moving gyrating pillar of water; drain carrying rain water down side of building. **-tight** *a.* so fitted as to prevent water escaping or entering. **— tower** *n.* raised tank for water storage. **-way** *n.* fairway for vessels; navigable channel. **— wings** *n.pl.* small rubber floats filled with air to support learners at swimming. **-works** *n.pl.* reservoirs, etc. for the purification, supply and distribution of water; (*Slang*) tears. **-y** *a.* resembling water; thin or transparent, as a liquid. **above water,** financially sound; solvent. **heavy water,** deuterium oxide, differing from ordinary water in its density, boiling-point, and physiological actions. **high (low) water,**

highest (lowest) elevation of tide; maximum (minimum) point of success, etc. **mineral water,** water impregnated with mineral matter and possessing specific medicinal properties; artificially aerated water. **in hot water,** involved in trouble. **in low water,** financially embarrassed. **of the first water,** of finest quality. **to hold water,** of statement, to be tenable or correct. **to water down,** to moderate [O.E. *waeter*].

watt (wȧt) *n.* unit of power represented by current of one ampere produced by electromotive force of one volt (746 watts = 1 horsepower) [fr. James *Watt*, 1736-1819].

wat·tle (wȧt′·l) *n.* fleshy excrescence, usually red, under throat of cock or turkey; one of numerous species of Australian acacia; woven work made of sticks and twigs for roofs, fences, etc. **-d** *a.* [O.E. *watel, watul*, hurdle].

wave (wāv) *n.* waving movement or gesture of hand; advancing ridge or swell on surface of liquid; surge; undulation; unevenness; extended group of attacking troops or planes; rise of enthusiasm, heat, etc.; wavelike style of hair dressing; spatial form of electrical oscillation propagated along conductor or through space; passage of sound or light through space; *pl.* (*Poet.*) the sea; *v.t.* to raise into inequalities of surface; to move to and fro; to give the shape of waves; to brandish; to beckon; *v.i.* to wave one way and the other; to flap; to undulate; to signal. **—band** *n.* range of wave lengths allotted for broadcasting, morse signals, etc. **-d** *a.* undulating. **wavily** *adv.* **— length** *n.* distance between maximum positive points of two successive waves; velocity of wave divided by frequency of oscillations. **—let** *n.* ripple. **—like** *a.* **waviness** *n.* **waving** *a.* moving to and fro. **wavy** *a.* [O.E. *wafian*, to brandish].

wa·ver (wā′·vẹr) *v.i.* to move to and fro; to fluctuate; to vacillate; to tremble; to totter. **-er** *n.* **-ing** *n.* and *a.* **-ingly** *adv.* [M.E. *waveren*, to wander about].

wax (waks) *n.* a fatty acid ester of a monohydric alcohol; an amorphous, yellowish, sticky substance derived from animal and vegetable substances; beeswax; sealing wax, cerumen, waxy secretion of ear; *v.t.* to smear, rub, or polish with wax. **-bill** *n.* name given to several small, seed-eating cage birds. **-en** *a.* made of or resembling wax; plastic; impressionable. **-er** *n.* **-iness** *n.* **-ing** *n.* **—paper** *n.* paper coated with wax, used for airtight packing. **-wing** *n.* hook-billed bird of chatterer family with quills tipped with red hornlike appendages resembling sealing wax. **-work** *n.* figure modeled in wax. *pl.* exhibition of wax figures. **-y** a. made of or like wax [O.E. *weax*, beeswax].

wax (waks) *v.i.* to increase in size; to grow; opposite of *wane* [O.E. *weaxan*].

way (wā) *n.* street; highway; passage; path; lane; route; progress; distance; method; mode; custom; usage; habit; means; plan; desire; momentum; movement of ship through water; state or condition. **-bill** *n.* list of passengers or articles carried by vehicle. **-farer** *n.* wanderer on foot. **-faring** *a.* and *n.* **-lay** *v.t.* to lie or wait in ambush for; *pa.t.* and *pa.p.* **-laid. -layer** *n.* **-side** *n.* border of road or path; *a.* adjoining side of road. **-ward** *a.* liking one's way; perverse; refractory. **-wardly** *adv.* **—wardness** *n.* **ways and means,** methods; resources. **by the way,** as we proceed; incidentally. **right-of-way** *n.* right to use path through private property; such a path. **under way,** of vessel when moving. **to make way,** to step aside [O.E. *weg*].

we (wē) *pron.* plural form of **I;** another person, or others, and I [O.E.].

weak (wēk) *a.* feeble; frail; delicate; fragile; easily influenced; simple; low; faint; thin; watery; diluted; inconclusive; (*Gram.*) of verb, forming past by addition of *d* or *t.* **-en** *v.t.* to make weak; *v.i.* to become weak or less resolute. **—minded** *a.* indecisive. **—kneed** *a.* irresolute. **-liness** *n.* **-ling** *n.* feeble person, physically or mentally. **-ly** *adv.* **-ness** *n.* **-er sex,** women [O.N. *veikr*].

weal (wēl) *n.* streak left on flesh by blow of stick or whip; wale [fr. *wale*].

weal (wēl) *n.* (*Arch.*) prosperity; welfare. **the common weal,** well-being and general welfare of state or community [O.E. *wela*].

weald (wēld) *n.* (*Poetic*) woodland; open country. [O.E. *weald*, forest].

wealth (welth) *n.* riches; affluence; opulence; abundance. **-iness** *n.* **-y** *a.* [O.E. *wela*, well-being].

wean (wēn) *v.t.* to discontinue breast-feeding of infant gradually; to detach or alienate. **-ling** *n.* newly-weaned infant [O.E. *wenian*, to accustom].

weap·on (wep′·ạn, wep′·n) *n.* instrument to fight with [O.E. *waepen*].

wear (wer) *v.t.* to carry clothes, decorations and the like, upon the person; to consume or impair by use; to deteriorate by rubbing; *v.i.* to last or hold out; to be impaired gradually by use or exposure. *pa.t.* **wore.** *pa.p.* **worn.** *n.* act of wearing; impairment from use; style of dress; fashion; article worn. **-able** *a.* **-er** *n.* **-ing** *a.* intended for wearing; exhausting; exhausting to mind and body. **-ing-apparel** *n.* dress in general. **wear and tear,** loss or deterioration due to usage. **to wear off,** to disappear slowly. **wear out,** become useless [O.E. *werian*].

wear (wer) *v.t., i.* to bring ship on the other tack by presenting stern to wind; opposite to *tack.* *pa.t.* **wore.** *pa.p.* **worn** [var. of *veer*].

wear·y (wir′·i·) *a.* fatigued; tired; bored; exhausted; tiresome; *v.t.* to exhaust one's strength or patience; to make weary; *v.i.* to become weary; to become dissatisfied with. **wearily** *adv.* **weariless** *a.* tireless. **weariness** *n.* **wearisome** *a.* tedious; causing annoyance or fatigue. **wearisomely** *adv.* **wearisomeness** *n.* [O.E. *werig*].

wea·sel (wē′·zl) *n.* small, long-bodied, short-legged, bloodthirsty carnivor [O.E. *wesle*].

weath·er (weTH′·ẹr) *n.* combination of all atmospheric phenomena existing at one time in any particular place; *v.t.* to expose to the air; to season by exposure to air; to sail to windward of; to endure; *v.i.* to decompose or disintegrate, owing to atmospheric conditions. **—beaten** *a.* seasoned, marked, or roughened by continual exposure to rough weather. **Weather Bureau** (bū·rō′) *n.* meteorological office directed by U.S. Department of Commerce. **— chart** *n.* synoptic chart, an outline map on which lines are plotted to indicate areas of similar atmospheric pressure along with other meteorological conditions. **—cock** *n.* pivoted vane, commonly in shape of cock, to indicate direction of wind; one who changes his mind repeatedly. **— forecast** *n.* prediction of probable future weather conditions based on scientific data collected by meteorological office. **— gauge** *n.* bearing of ship to windward of another. **—glass** *n.* instrument to indicate changes in atmospheric pressure; barometer. **-ing** *n.* process of decomposing of rocks, wood, etc. exposed to elements. **— report,** daily report of meteorological conditions. **—strip** *v.t.* to fit with weather stripping (strips used to keep out draft around doors, windows). **—vane** *n.* weather cock. **under the weather,** (*Colloq.*) ill; drunk [O.E. *weder*].

weave (wēv) *v.t.* to cross the warp by the woof on loom; to interlace threads, etc.; to construct, to fabricate, as a tale; *v.i.* to practice weaving; to move from side to side; *pa.t.* **wove;** *pa.p.* **woven;** *n.* style of weaving. **-r** *n.* [O.E. *wefan*].

web (web) *n.* that which is woven; whole piece of cloth woven in loom; weaver's warp; membrane which unites toes of water fowls; network spun by spider; anything as plot, intrigue, cunningly woven. **-bed** *a.* having toes united by membrane of skin. **-bing** *n.* strong, hemp fabric woven in narrow strips, used for chairs, etc. **—footed** *a.* [O.E.].

wed (wed) *v.t.* to take for husband or wife; to marry; to join closely; *v.i.* to contract matrimony. *pr.p.* **-ding.** *pa.t., pa.p.* **-ded, wed. -ded** *a.* married; wholly devoted (to art, etc.). **-ding** *n.* nuptial ceremony; nuptials; marriage [O.E. *weddian*].

wedge (wej) *n.* piece of wood or metal, tapering to thin edge at fore end, used for splitting, lifting heavy weights, etc.; anything shaped like a wedge; something used for dividing; *v.t.* to jam; to compress; to force (in); to squeeze (in); to fasten with a wedge. **-d** *a.* cuneiform or wedge-shaped; jammed tight [O.E. *wecg*].

Wedg·wood (wej′·wood) *n., a.* fine Eng. pottery [fr. Josiah *Wedgwood*].

wed·lock (wed′·lȧk) *n.* marriage; married state [O.E. *wed,* a pledge; *lac,* a gift].

Wednes·day (wenz′·di·) *n.* fourth day of week [O.E. *Wodnesdaeg,* day of Woden].

wee (wē) *n.* small; tiny [M.E. *we, wei,* bit].

weed (wēd) *n.* plant growing where it is not desired; sorry, worthless person or animal; (*Colloq.*) cigar; tobacco; *v.t.* to free from weeds; to remove (something undesirable). **—killer** *n.* preparation for killing weeds. **-y** *a.* full of weeds; lanky and weakly. **to — out,** to eliminate [O.E. *weed*].

weed (wēd) *n.* (*Arch.*) garment; mourning garb, as of widow (usu. *pl.*) [O.E. *waed*].

week (wēk) *n.* seven successive days, usually Sunday to Sunday. **—day** *n.* any day of week except Sunday. **—end** *n.* Friday or Saturday to Monday; holiday for this period. **-ly** *a.* pert. to a week; happening once a week. *n.* publication issued weekly; *adv.* once a week. **Holy Week, Passion Week** *n.* week preceding Easter Sunday [O.E. *wicu*].

weep (wēp) *v.i.* to grieve for by shedding tears; to cry; to drip; to exude water; *v.t.* to lament; to bewail. *pa.t., pa.p.* **wept. -er** *n.* one who weeps; crepe band worn by men at funerals; male professional mourner; mourning sleeve, sash, or veil. **-ing** *a.* of trees whose branches droop, as *weeping* willow. **-y** *a.* [O.E. *wepan*].

wee·vil (wē′·val) *n.* common name given to thousands of different kinds of small beetles, all distinguished by heads lengthened out to resemble beaks—larvae attack plants and stored grain [O.E. *wifed*].

weft (weft) *n.* filling thread carried by shuttle under and over the warp in a weaving loom. Also **woof** [O.E. *wefta*].

weigh (wā) *v.t.* to find weight of; to deliberate or consider carefully; to oppress; to raise (anchor, etc.); *v.i.* to have weight; to be considered as important; to bear heavily (on). **-er** *n.* **-t** *n.* gravity as property of bodies; heavy mass; object of known mass for weighing; importance; power and influence; *v.t.* to make more heavy. **-tily** *adv.* **-tiness** *n.* **-tless** *a.* having little or no weight, esp. if there is no gravitational pull. **-tlessly** *adv.* **-tlessness** *n.* **-ty** *a.* having great weight; important; momentous; forcible. **dead weight** *n.* heavy burden [O.E. *wegan*].

weir (wir) *n.* fence of stakes set in stream for taking fish; a dam [O.E. *wer*].

weird (wird) *a.* unearthly; uncanny; (*Colloq.*) odd. **-ly** *adv.* **-ness** *n.* [O.E. *wyrd,* fate].

welch (welch) *v.t., i.* (*Slang*) to welsh. **-er** *n.*

wel·come (wel′·kạm) *a.* received gladly; causing gladness; free to enjoy or use; *n.* kind or hearty reception; *v.t.* to greet with kindness and pleasure.

weld (weld) *v.t.* to join pieces of heated, plastic metal by fusion without soldering materials, etc.; to unite closely; *n.* homogeneous joint between two metals. **-er** *n.* [var. of *well,* to boil up].

wel·fare (wel′·fār) *n.* well-doing or well-being; prosperity.

well (wel) *n.* shaft or tube sunk deep in ground to obtain water, oil, etc.; spring; fountain; source; bottom of elevator shaft; cavity or pit below ground level; chamber for catching surplus water or oil; enclosure in hold of fishing vessel, for preservation of fish; *v.i.* to issue forth in volume, as water [O.E. *wella*].

well (wel) *a. comp.* **better.** *superl.* **best.** in good health; fortunate; comfortable; satisfactory; *adv.* agreeably; favorably; skillfully; intimately; satisfactorily; soundly; *interj.* exclamation of surprise, interrogation, resignation, etc. **—advised** *a.* prudent; sensible. **—appointed** *a.* handsomely furnished or equipped. **—balanced** *a.* eminently sane. **—being** *n.* welfare. **-born** *a.* of good family. **—bred** *a.* courteous and refined in manners; of good stock. **—favored** *a.* good-looking; pleasing to the eye. **—informed** *a.* knowing inner facts; possessing wide range of general knowledge; having considerable knowledge. **—meaning** *a.* having good intentions. **—nigh** *adv.* nearly; almost. **—spoken** *a.* cultured in speech; favorably commented on; speaking easily, fluently, graciously. **—timed** *a.* opportune. **—to-do** *a.* wealthy. **as well as,** in addition to; besides; **-spring,** source of stream, knowledge [O.E. *wel*].

Welsh, Welch (welsh, welch) *a.* relating to Wales or its inhabitants; *n.* language or people of Wales. **—man, —woman** *n.* **— rabbit,** or **rarebit,** savory dish consisting of melted cheese on toast [O.E. *waelisc,* foreign].

welsh, welch (welsh, welch) *v.t.* and *v.i.* (*Slang*) to cheat by failing to pay a debt or meeting an obligation. **-er** *n.* [perh. fr. Ger. *welken,* to fade].

welt (welt) *n.* cord around border or seamline of upholstery, etc.; a flat, overlapping seam; narrow strip of leather between upper and sole of shoe; weal; (*Colloq.*) ridge on flesh from whiplash, etc. *v.t.* to furnish with welt; (*Colloq.*) beat soundly. **-ed** *a.* **-ing** *n.*

wel·ter (wel′·ter) *v.i.* to roll about; to wallow in slime, blood, etc.; *n.* confusion; turmoil. **-ing** *a.* [O.E. *wealt,* unsteady].

wel·ter·weight (wel′·ter·wāt) *n.* in boxing or wrestling, class of contestants weighing between 135lb. and 147lb.; boxer or wrestler of this weight.

wen (wen) *n.* small superficial tumor or cyst, esp. on scalp. **-nish** *a.* [O.E. *wenn*].

wench (wench) *n.* girl; maid; (*Arch.*) lewd woman; *v.i.* (*Arch.*) to associate with wenches. (*Arch.*) **-ing** *n.* fornication [O.E. *wencel*].

wend (wend) *v.t.* (*Arch.*) to direct; to betake (one's way); *v.i.* to go [O.E. *wendan,* to turn].

went (went) *pa.t.* of **wend;** *pa.t.* of **go.**

wept (wept) *pa.t.* and *pa.p.* of **weep.**

were (wur) *pa.t.* plural, and subjunctive singular and plural, of **be** [O.E. *waeron*].

were·wolf, wer·wolf (wir′·woolf) *n.* human being who, at will, could take form of wolf while retaining human intelligence [O.E. *wer,* a man; *wulf*, a wolf].

Wes·ley·an (wes′.li.an) *n.* pert. to Wesley or Wesleyanism. **-ism** *n.* Wesleyan Methodism, i.e. religion practiced in methodical manner [John *Wesley*, (1703-1791)].

west (west) *n.* point in heavens where sun sets; one of four cardinal points of compass; region of country lying to the west; *a.* situated in, facing, coming from the west; *adv.* to the west. **-erly** *a.* situated in west; of wind, blowing from west; *adv.* in west direction; *n.* wind blowing from west. **-ern** *a.* situated in west; coming from west; *n.* inhabitant of western country or district; film featuring cowboys in western states of U.S. **-erner** *n.* native of the west.**-ernmost, -most** *a.* farthest to west. **-ward** *a.* and *adv.* toward west. **-ward(s)** *adv.* **-bound** *a.* going west [O.E.].

wet (wet) *a.* *comp.* **-ter.** *superl.* **-test.** containing water; full of moisture; humid; dank; damp; rainy; *n.* water; moisture; rain; *v.t.* to make wet; to moisten; *pr.p.* **-ting.** *pa.p.* **wet** or **ted. -blanket** *n.* a kill-joy. **-ness** *n.* **—nurse** *n.* woman who suckles child of another. **-tish** *a.* humid; damp [O.E. *waet*].

weth·er (weTH′.er) *n.* castrated ram [O.E.].

whack (hwak) *v.t.* to hit, esp. with stick; to beat; (*Slang*) to share; *v.i.* to strike with smart blow; *n.* blow; (*Slang*) chance; good condition; share. **-y** *a.* [fr. *thwack*].

whale (hwāl) *n.* large fishlike mammal; (*Slang*) something huge; *v.i.* to hunt for whales. **-back** *n.* type of freight vessel on Great Lakes in N. America with covered, rounded deck. **-boat** *n.* long boat with sharp bow at each end. **-bone** *n.* baleen, an elastic, flexible, horny product of jaws of baleen whale. **— oil** *n.* lubricating oil extracted from blubber of sperm whale. **-r** *n.* man or ship engaged in whaling industry. [O.E. *hwael*].

whale (hwāl) *v.t.* (*Slang*) to thrash. **whaling** *n.* a thrashing.

wharf (hwawrf) *n.* structure on bank of navigable waters at which vessels can be loaded or unloaded; quay. *pl.* **-s, wharves.** *v.t.* to moor at, or place on, wharf. **-age** *n.* charge for use of wharf; wharf accommodation. **-inger** (hwawr′.fin.jer) *n.* one who owns or has charge of wharf [O.E. *hwearf*].

what (hwát, hwut) *pron.* interrogative pronoun (used elliptically, in exclamation, or adjectively); relative pronoun, meaning that which (used adjectively); *a.* which; which kind; *conj.* that; *interj.* denoting surprise, anger, confusion, etc.; *adv.* to what degree? **-ever** *pron.* anything that; all that. **-soever** *pron.* whatever [O.E. *hwaet*].

what·not (hwut′.nát) *n.* piece of furniture, having shelves for books, bric-a-brac, etc.; indescribable thing.

wheal (hwēl) *n.* raised spot or ridge on skin due to mosquito bite, hives, etc. [O.E. *hwele*].

wheat (hwēt) *n.* edible portion of annual cereal grass providing most important bread food of the world. **-en** *a.* made of wheat or whole flour [O.E. *hwgete*].

whee·dle (hwē′.dl) *v.t.* to cajole; to coax.

wheel (hwēl) *n.* solid disk or circular frame with spokes. *pl.* controlling forces; circular frame used for punishing criminals; (*Colloq.*) bicycle; steering wheel; wheeling movement; *v.t.* to convey on wheels; to furnish with wheels; *v.i.* to turn on, or as on, axis; to change direction by pivoting about an end unit, as in marching; to roll forward; to revolve. **-barrow** *n.* conveyance with a single wheel and two shafts for pushing. **-er** *n.* one who wheels; maker of wheels; hindmost horse, nearest wheels of carriage. **-house** *n.* (*Naut.*) a deckhouse to shelter steersman. **-ing** *n.* **-wright** *n.* one who makes and repairs wheels [O.E. *hweol*].

wheeze (hwēz) *v.i.* to breathe audibly and with difficulty; *n.* the sound or act of wheezing; (*Colloq.*) joke. **-r** *n.* **wheezingly** *adv.* **wheezy** *a.* **wheezily** *adv.* **wheeziness** *n.* [O.N. *hvaesa*, to hiss].

whelk (hwelk) *n.* spiral-shelled sea snail used as bait and food [O.E. *weoloc*].

whelm (hwelm) *v.t.* to cover completely; to submerge; to overpower.

whelp (hwelp) *n.* young dog, lion, seal, wolf, etc.; a youth (contemptuously); *v.i.* and *v.t.* to bring forth young [O. E. *hwelp*].

when (hwen) *adv.* and *conj.* at what time? at the time that; whereas; at which time. **-ce** *adv.* and *conj.* from what place; from what, or which, cause, etc. **-cesoever** *adv.* and *conj.* from whatsoever place, source, or cause.**-e'er** or **-ever** *adv.* and *conj.* at whatever time. **-soever** *adv.* and *conj.* whenever [O.E. *hwaenne*].

where (hwer) *adv.* and *conj.* at what place?; in what circumstances? at or to the place in which. **-abouts** *adv.* and *conj.* about where; near what or which place? *n.* place where one is. **-as** *conj.* considering that; when in fact. **-at** *adv.* and *conj.* at which; at what. **-by** *adv.* and *conj.* by which; how. **-fore** *adv.* for which reason? why? *conj.* accordingly; in consequence of which; *n.* the cause. **-in** *adv.* in which; in which, or what, respect, etc.; in what. **-of** *adv.* of which; of what. **-on** *adv.* on which; on what. **-soever** *adv.* in, or to, whatever place. **-to** *adv.* to which; to what; to what end. **-upon** *adv.* upon which; in consequence of which. **-'er, -ver** *adv.* at whatever place. **-with** *adv.* with what. **the wherewithal,** the money; the means [O.E. *hwaer*].

wher·ry (hwer′.i.) *n.* a light rowboat; skiff. (*Brit.*) vessel used in fishing; light barge.

whet (hwet) *v.t.* to sharpen by rubbing; to make sharp, keen, or eager; to stir up; *n.* act of sharpening. *pr.p.* **-ting.** *pa.t.* and *pa.p.* **-ted. -stone** *n.* fine-grained stone used for sharpening cutlery and tools; sharpener. **-ter** *n.* [O.E. *hwettan*].

wheth·er (hweTH′.er) *conj.* used to introduce the first of two or more alternative clauses, the other(s) being connected by *or* [O.E.*hwaether*].

whew (hwū) *n.* or *interj.* whistling sound, expressing astonishment, dismay, or pain.

whey (hwā) *n.* clear liquid left as residue of milk after separation of fat and casein (curd). **—face** *n.* palefaced person. **—faced** *a.* **-ey** *a.* [O.E. *hwaeg*].

which (hwich) *pron.* as interrogative, signifying *who*, or *what one*, of a number; as relative, used of things; a thing or fact that; whatever. **-ever, -soever** *pron., a.* whether one or the other [O.E. *hwilc*].

whiff (hwif) *n.* puff of air, smoke, etc.; an odor; *v.t.* to throw out in whiffs; to blow; *v.i.* to emit whiffs, as of smoke [imit.].

whif·fle (hwif′.l) *v.t.* to disperse, as by a puff; *v.i.* to veer, as wind; to be fickle[fr. *whiff*].

Whig (hwig) *n.* (*U.S.*) supporter of American Revolution; member of early political party (1834-1955); (*Brit.*) political party supporting Hanoverian succession but after 1832 replaced by term, 'Liberal'; *a.* pert. to Whigs.**-gish** *a.* **-gism** *n.* [contr. fr. Scots *whiggamore*].

while (hwīl) *n.* space of time; *conj.* during time when; as long as; whereas; *adv.* during which. **whilom** (hwīl′.am) *adv.* (*Arch.*) formerly; *a.* former. **to while away,** to pass time (usually idly) [O.E. *hwil*, time].

whim (hwim) *n.* passing fancy; caprice; fad. **-sical** *a.* capricious; freakish; fanciful; quaint. **-sicality** *n.* fanciful idea; whim. **-sically** *adv.* **-sicalness** *n.* **-sy** *n.* caprice; fancy [O.N. *hvima*, to have straying eyes].

whim·brel (hwim′·brạl) *n.* bird resembling, but small than, curlew [imit.].

whim·per (hwim′·pẹr) *v.i.* and *v.t.* to cry, or utter, with low, fretful, broken voice; *n.* low peevish, or plaintive cry. **-er** *n.* **-ing** *n.*

whin (hwin) *n.* whinstone; low, coarse evergreen.

whine (hwīn) *n.* drawing, peevish wail; unmanly complaint; *v.i.* to utter peevish cry; to complain in childish way. *n.* **whining** *n.* **whiningly** *adv.* **whiny** *a.* [O.E. *hwinan*].

whinny (hwin′·i·) *v.i.* to neigh; *n.* sound made by horse [O.E. *hwinan*, to whine].

whin·stone (hwin′·stōn) *n.* basaltic or hard unstratified rock. Also **whin.**

whip (hwip) *v.t.* to strike with lash; to flog; to overcast edges of seam, etc.; to bind ends of rope with twine; to snatch or jerk (away); to beat into froth, as cream or eggs; (*Colloq.*) to defeat decisively; *v.i.* to start suddenly. *pr.p.* **-ping.** *pa.t.* and *pa.p.* **-ped.** *n.* lash attached to handle for urging on or correction; legislative manager appointed to ensure fullest possible attendance of members of his party at important debates, etc. **-cord** *n.* worsted fabric with bold, diagonal ribbing. **— hand** *n.* hand which holds whip; mastery, upper hand.**-like** *a.* **-per** *n.* **-per-snapper** *n.* *n.* insignificant person; impertinent young fellow. **-ping** *n.* flogging. [M.E. *whippen*].

whip·pet (hwip′·it) *n.* cross-bred dog of greyhound type, for racing [prop. fr. *whip*].

whip·poor·will (hwip′·pẹr·wil) *n.* nocturnal American bird [echoic].

whir (hwur) *v.i.* to dart, fly, or revolve with buzzing or whizzing noise. *pr.p.* **-ring.** *pa.t.* and *pa.p.* **-red.** *n.* buzzing or whizzing sound [Dan. *hvirre*, to twirl].

whirl (hwurl) *v.t.* to turn round rapidly; to cause to rotate; *v.i.* to rotate rapidly; to spin; to gyrate; to move very rapidly; *n.* rapid rotation; anything which whirls; bewilderment. **-igig** *n.* spinning toy; merry-go-round. **-ing** *n.* and *a.* **-pool** *n.* vortex or circular eddy of water. **-wind** *n.* forward-moving column of air revolving rapidly and spirally around low-pressure core [ON. *hvirfila*, ring].

whish (hwish) *v.i.* to move with soft, rustling sound; *n.* such a sound [echoic].

whisk (hwisk) *n.* rapid, sweeping motion; small bunch of feathers, straw, etc. used for brush; instrument for beating eggs, etc. *v.t.* to sweep with light, rapid motion or with a whisk. **-er** *n.* thing that whisks; *pl.* hair on a man's face; long stiff hairs at side of mouth of cat or other animal. **-ered** *a.* [Scand. *visk*, wisp].

whis·key (hwis′·ki·) *n.* distilled alcoholic liquor made from various grains. Also **whisky** [Gael. *uisge beatha*, water of life].

whis·per (hwis′·pẹr) *v.t.* to utter in low, sibilant tone; to suggest secretly or furtively; *v.i.* to speak in whispers, under breath; to rustle; *n.* low, soft, sibilant remark; hint or insinuation. **-er** *n.* **-ing** *n.* **-ingly** *adv.* [O.E. *hwisprian*].

whist (hwist) *n.* card game for four players (two a side) [fr. *whisk*].

whis·tle (hwis′·l) *n.* sound made by forcing breath through rounded and nearly closed lips; instrument or device for making a similar sound; form of horn; *v.i.* to make such sound; *v.i.* and *v.t.* to render tune by whistling; to signal, by whistling. **-r** *n.* one who whistles. **whistling** *n.* [O.E. *hwistlian*].

whit (hwit) *n.* smallest part imaginable; bit [O.E. *wiht*].

white (hwīt) *a.* of the color of snow; light in color; hoary; pale; pure; clean; bright; spotless; (*Colloq.*) honest; just; *n.* color of pure snow; albuminous part of an egg; white part of eyeball surrounding iris. **— alloy, — metal** *n.* alloy containing lead or tin, as pewter, resembling silver. **—ant** *n.* termite. **-bait** *n.* newly hatched young of sprat, herring, and related fishes, used as table delicacy. **-cap** *n.* wave with crest of white foam. **—collar** *a.* of clerical or professional workers. **— corpuscle,** leucocyte. **— elephant,** sacred elephant of Siam; gift entailing bother and expense; object valueless to the owners. **— feather** *n.* symbol of cowardice. **—fish** *n.* non-oily food fish. **— flag,** sign of truce or surrender. **— gold** alloyed gold with platinum appearance. **—heat** *n.* temperature at which substances become incandescent; state of extreme excitement or passion. **—hot** *a.* **—lead** *n.* compound of lead carbonate and hydrated oxide of lead, used as base and pigment for paint. **— lie,** harmless fib. **-n** *v.t.* and *v.i.* to make or turn white. **-ner** *n.* **-ening** *n.* making white. **-ness** *n.* **— slave,** woman or girl enticed away for purposes of prostitution. **-wash** *n.* mixture of whiting, water, and size, for coating walls; *v.t.* to cover with whitewash; to clear reputation of; to conceal errors, faults, etc. **whitish** *a.* somewhat white [O.E. *hwit*].

whith·er (hwiTH′·ẹr) (*Poetic*) *adv.* to which, or what, place? [O.E. *hwider*].

whit·ing (hwīt′·ing) *n.* edible seafish; pulverized chalk, for making putty and whitewash [fr. *white*].

whit·low (hwit′·lō) *n.* inflammatory sore affecting fingernails; [for *whickflaw* i.e. *quick*, sensitive part under fingernail, *flaw*, crack].

Whit·sun·day (hwit′·sun·di·) *n.* seventh Sunday after Easter, festival day of Church, kept in commemoration of descent of Holy Ghost. **Whitsun, Whitsuntide,** week containing Whitsunday [so called because newly baptized appeared in white garments].

whit·tle (hwit′·l) *v.t.* and *v.i.* to cut off thin slices or shavings with knife; to pare away [O.E. *thwitan*, to cut].

whiz, whizz (hwiz) *v.i.* to make hissing sound, as arrow flying through air. *pr.p.* **-zing.** *pa.t.* and *pa.p.* **-zed.** *n.* violent hissing and humming sound; person or thing regarded as excellent. **-zingly** *adv.* **—bang** *n.* (*Slang*) high-velocity, light shell whose explosion occurs almost immediately after its flight through the air is first heard [imit.].

who (hȯȯ) *pron.* relative or interrogative, referring to persons. **-ever** *pron.* whatever person; any one, without exception. **-m** *pron.* objective case of *who.* **-msoever** *pron.* objective of **-soever** *pron.* any person, without exception. **-se** (hȯȯz) *pron.* possessive case of *who* or *which.* **-dunit** (hȯȯ·dun′·it) *n.* (*Slang*) a detective story [O.E. *hwa*].

whoa (wō, hwō) *interj.* stop! [var. of *ho*].

whole (hōl) *a.* entire; complete; not defective or imperfect; unimpaired; healthy; sound; *n.* entire thing; complete system; aggregate; gross; sum; totality. **-hearted** *a.* earnest; sincere. **-heartedly** *adv.* **-heartedness** *n.* **—hog** *n.* completeness; without any reservations. **-ness** *n.* **-sale** *n.* sale of goods in bulk to retailers; *a.* selling or buying in large quantities; extensive; indiscriminate. **-saler** *n.* **-some** *a.* tending to promote health; healthy; nourishing; beneficial. **-someness** *n.* **wholly** *adv.* completely [O.E. *hal*].

whom See **who.**

whoop (hwȯȯp, hȯȯp) *n.* loud cry or yell; hoot, as of owl; convulsive intake of air after cough; *v.i.* to utter loud cry; to hoot; to make the sound characteristic of whooping cough. **-ee** *interj.* exclamation of joy or abandonment. **-er** *n.* one who whoops; bird with a loud harsh note. **-ing cough** *n.* infectious disease marked by fits of convulsive coughing, followed by characteristic loud whoop or indrawing of breath. **to make whoopee** (*Slang*) to celebrate uproariously [O.Fr. *houper*, to shout].

whop (hwȧp) *v.t.* (*Arch.*) to beat severely. *pr.p.* **-ping.** *pa.p., pa.t.* **-ped. -per** *n.* (*Colloq.*) anything unusually large; monstrous lie. **-ping** *a.* (*Colloq.*) very big [fr. *whip*].

whore (hōr) *n.* harlot; prostitute; *v.i.* to have unlawful sexual intercourse [O.N. *hora*].

whorl (hwurl, hwawrl) *n.* spiral of univalve shell; ring of leaves, petals, fingerprints, etc. **-ed** *a.* [O.E. *hweorfan*, to turn].

whor·tle·ber·ry (hwurt′·ạl·ber·i·) *n.* huckleberry [O.E. *wyrtil*, dim. of *wurt*, wort].

whose (ho͝oz) *poss.* of *who, which.* **whosoever, whomsoever** See **who.**

why (hwī) *adv.* and *conj.* for what reason? on which account? wherefore? *interj.* expletive to show surprise, indignation, protest; *n.* reason; cause; motive [O.E. *hwi*].

wick (wik) *n.* cotton cord which draws up oil or wax, as in lamp or candle, to be burned. **-less** *a.* [M.E. *wicke*, fr. O.E. *weoce*].

wick·ed (wik′·id) *a.* addicted to vice; evil; immoral; mischievous. **-ly** *adv.* **-ness** *n.* [M.E. *wikke*, evil].

wick·er (wik′·ẹr) *n.* small flexible twig; wickerwork; withe; *a.* made of pliant twigs. **-work** *n.* basketwork [Cf. O.E. *wican*, to bend].

wick·et (wik′·it) *n.* small door or gate, adjacent to or part of larger door; arch; one of wire arches used in croquet; box-office window [O.Fr. *wiket*].

wide (wīd) *a.* broad; spacious; distant; comprehensive; missing the mark; *adv.* to a distance; far; astray; to the fullest extent. **—angle** *a.* of motion picture system using one or more cameras and projectors and a wide curved screen. **—awake** *a.* fully awake. **-ly** *adv.* **-n** *v.t.* to make wide or wider; *v.i.* to grow wide or wider; to expand. **-ness** *n.* width. **-spread** *a.* extending on all sides; diffused; circulating among numerous people. **width** *n.* wideness; breadth. **widthwise** *adv.* [O.E. *wid*].

widg·eon, wigeon (wij′·ạn) *a.* fresh-water duck [O.Fr. *vigeon*].

wid·ow (wid′·ō) *n.* woman who has lost husband by death; *v.t.* to bereave of husband; to be a widow to. **-er** *n.* man whose wife is dead. **-hood** *n.* **grass widow,** wife temporarily separated from husband; divorcee. [O.E. *widwe*].

width See **wide.**

wield (wēld) *v.t.* to use with full command or power; to swing; to handle; to manage; to control. **-able** *a.* **-er** *n.* **-iness** *n.* **-y** *a.* manageable; controllable [O.E. *gewieldan*, to govern].

wie·ner (wē′·nẹr) *n.* smoked sausage in casing; frankfurter. Also **weenie** [Ger. *Wiener wurst*, Vienna sausage].

wife (wīf) *n.* married woman; spouse; (*Colloq.*) woman. *pl.* **wives. -hood** *n.* **-less** *a.* **-lessness** *n.* without wife; unmarried. **-ly** *a.* as befits a wife [O.E. *wif*].

wig (wig) *n.* artificial covering for head which imitates natural hair. **-ged** *a.* [for *periwig*].

wig·gle (wig′·l) *v.i.* to waggle; to wriggle; *n.* a wriggling motion. **-r** *n.* wiggling thing; mosquito larva. [var. of *waggle*].

wig·wag (wig′·wag) *v.t.* to move back and forth; to signal with flags, etc. *pr.p.* **-ging.** *pa.p., pa.t.* **-ged. -ger** *n.* [fr. *wag*].

wig·wam (wig′·wȧm) *n.* Amer. Ind. conical shelter [N. Amer. Ind. *Wigiwam*, their dwelling].

wild (wīld) *a.* living in state of nature; not domesticated or cultivated; native; savage; turbulent; *n.* uncultivated, uninhabited region. **-cat** *n.* medium-sized, undomesticated feline; experimental oil well; *a.* reckless; financially unsound; highly speculative. **-fire** *n.* anything which burns rapidly or spreads fast; sheet lightning; **—goosechase** *n.* foolish, futile pursuit or enterprise. **-ly** *adv.* **-ness** *n.* **to sow wild oats,** to be given to youthful excesses [O.E. *wilde*].

wil·de·beest (wil′·dạ·bēst) *n.* gnu [Dut.].

wil·der (wil′·dẹr) (*Arch.*) *v.t.* to cause to lose the way; to bewilder [fr. *bewilder*].

wil·der·ness (wil′·dẹr·nạs) *n.* tract of land uncultivated and uninhabited by human beings; waste; desert; state of confusion [O.E. *wildor*, wild animal].

wile (wīl) *n.* trick or stratagem practiced for ensnaring or alluring; artifice; lure; ruse; *v.t.* to entice; to pass (time) lazily. **wilily** *adv.* **wiliness** *n.* artfulness; guile; cunning. **wily** *a.* [O.E. *wil*].

will (wil) *n.* power of choosing what one will do; volition; determination; discretion; wish; desire; (*Law*) declaration in writing showing how property is to be disposed of after death; *v.t.* to determine by choice; to ordain; to decree; to bequeath; to devise; *v.i.* to exercise act of volition; to choose; to elect; *v.* used as an auxiliary, to denote futurity dependent on subject of verb, intention, or insistence. *pa.t.* **would. -able** *a.* **-er** *n.* **-ing** *a.* favorably inclined; minded; disposed; ready. **-ingly** *adv.* readily; gladly. **-ingness** *n.* **— power** *n.* strength of will. **at will,** at pleasure. **with a will,** zealously and heartily [O.E. *willan*].

will·ful (wil′·fạl) *a.* governed by the will without yielding to reason; obstinate; intentional. **-ly** *adv.* **-ness** *n.* [fr. *will*].

will·o'·the·wisp (wil′·ạ·thạ·wisp) *n.* ignis fatuus, flickering, pale-bluish flame seen over marshes; anything deceptive or illusive.

wil·low (wil′·ō) *n.* name of number of trees of genus Salix, having flexible twigs used in weaving; machine for cleaning cotton. **-er** *n.* **— pattern,** design used in decorating chinaware, blue on whte ground. **-ware** *n.* china of this pattern. **-y** *a.* abounding in willows; pliant; supple and slender. **weeping willow** *n.* tree with pendent branches [O.E. *welig*].

wil·ly-nil·ly (wil′·i·nil′·i·) *a.* indecisive; *adv.* whether or not [fr. *will I, nill I*].

wilt (wilt) *v.i.* to fade; to droop; to wither; *v.t.* to depress; *n.* weakness; plant disease.

Wil·ton (wil′·tn) *n.* velvet-pile carpet [*Wilton*, town in Wiltshire].

wil·y See **wile.**

wim·ble (wim′·bl) *n.* tool for boring; *v.t.* [O.Fr.].

wim·ple (wim′·pl) *n.* covering for neck, chin and sides of face, still retained by nuns; *v.i.* to ripple; to lie in folds [O.E. *wimpel*].

win (win) *v.t.* to gain by success in competition or contest; to earn; to obtain; to reach, after difficulty; *v.i.* to be victorious; *pr.p.* **-ning.** *pa.p., pa.t.* **won.** *n.* (*Colloq.*) victory, success. **-ner** *n.* **-ning** *n.* act of gaining; *pl.* whatever is won in game or competition; *a.* attractive; charming; victorious. **-ningly** *adv.* [O.E. *winnan*, to strive].

wince (wins) *v.i.* to shrink or flinch, as from blow or pain; *n.* act of wincing. **-r** *n.* [O.Fr. *guinchir*, to shrink].

winch (winch) *n.* hoisting machine; a wheel crank; a windlass [O.E. *wince*, pulley].

Win·ches·ter (win′·ches·tẹr) *n.* lever action repeating rifle [fr. *maker*].

wind (wind) *n.* air in motion; current of air; gale; breath; power of respiration; flatulence; idle talk; hint or suggestion; (*Naut.*) point of compass; *pl.* wind instruments of orchestra; *v.t.* to follow by scent; to run, ride, or drive till breathless; to rest (horse) that it may recover wind; to expose to wind; *v.t.* (wind) to sound by blowing (horn, etc.). *pa.p.* **-ed.** **-bag** *n.* leather bag, part of bagpipe, filled with wind by mouth; (*Slang*) empty, pompous talker. **-breaker** *n.* a warm sports jacket. **ed** *a.* breathless. **-fall** *n.* anything blown down by wind, as fruit; unexpected legacy or other gain. **-flower** *n.* the anemone. **-ily** *adv.* **-iness** *n.* **— instrument** *n.* musical instrument played by blowing or air pressure. **-jammer** *n.* (*Colloq.*) merchant sailing ship; crew member. **-less** *a.* calm; out of breath. **-mill** *n.* mill worked by action of wind on vanes or sails. **-pipe** *n.* trachea; cartilaginous pipe admitting air to lungs. **—shield** *n.* protection against wind for driver or pilot. **— sock** (or **sleeve**) cone-shaped bag to show direction of wind. **-storm** *n.* **— tunnel** in aviation, tunnel-shaped chamber for making experiments with model aircraft in artificially created atmospheric conditions. **-ward** *n.* point from which wind blows; *a.* facing the wind; *adv.* toward the wind. **-y** *a.* consisting of, exposed to wind; tempestuous; flatulent; empty; **before the wind,** with the wind driving behind. **in the wind,** afoot; astir; in secret preparation. **second wind,** restoration of normal breathing. **to get wind of,** to be secretly informed of [O.E.].

wind (wīnd) *v.t.* to twist around; to coil; to twine, to wrap; to make ready for working by tightening spring; to meander; *v.i.* to twine; to vary from direct course—*pa.t.* and *pa.p.* **wound.** **-er** *n.* one who, or that which, winds; step, wider at one end than the other. **-ing** *a.* twisting or bending from direct line; sinuous; meandering; *n.* turning; twist. **-ing-sheet** *n.* sheet in which corpse is wrapped. **—up** *n.* conclusion; closing stages; baseball pitcher's preliminary swing of arm before delivery.**to wind up,** to coil up; to bring to conclusion. **wound-up** *a.* highly excited [O.E. *windan*].

wind·lass (wind′·lạs) *n.* form of winch for hoisting or hauling purposes, consisting of horizontal drum with rope or chain, and crank with handle for turning [O.N. *vindill*, winder; *ass*, pole].

win·dow (win′·dō) *n.* opening in wall to admit air and light, usually covered with glass. **— box** *n.* box for growing plants outside window. **— dressing** *n.* effective arrangement of goods in shop window. **— sill** *n.* flat portion of window opening on which window rests [O.N. *vindauga*, wind-eye].

wine (wīn) *n.* fermented juice of grape; similar liquor made from other fruits; *v.t.* to entertain by serving wine; *v.i.* to drink much wine at a sitting. **—bibber** *n.* one who drinks much wine. **— cellar,** stock of wine. **-press** *n.* apparatus for pressing juice out of grapes. **-ry** place where wine is made [O.E. *win*, fr. L. *vinum*].

wing (wing) *n.* organ of flight; one of two feathered fore limbs of bird; flight; main lifting surface of airplane; extension or section of a building; right or left division of army or fleet; section of team to right or left of center or regular scrimmage line; sidepiece; *pl.* the side parts of a stage; *v.t.* to furnish with wings; to enable to fly or hasten; to wound in wing, arm, or shoulder; *v.i.* to soar on the wing. **-ed** *a.* furnished with wings; wounded in wing; swift. **-less** *a.* **-spread** *n.* distance between tips of outstretched wings of bird or of airplane [O.N. *vaengr*].

wink (wingk) *v.t.* and *v.i.* to close and open eyelids; to blink; to convey hint by flick of eyelid; to twinkle; *n.* act of winking; hint conveyed by winking. **forty winks,** short nap. **to wink at,** to connive at; to pretend not to see [O.E. *wincian*].

win·kle See **periwinkle.**

win·ner, win·ning See **win.**

win·now (win′·ō) *v.t.* to separate grain from chaff by means of wind or current of air; to fan; to separate; to sift; to sort out. **-er** *n.* **-ing** *a.* and *n.* [O.E. *windwian*].

win·some (win′·sạm) *a.* cheerful; charming; attractive. **-ly** *adv.* **-ness** *n.* [O.E. *wynsum*, fr. *wynn*, joy].

win·ter (win′·tẹr) *n.* fourth season; (*Astron.*) in northern latitudes, period between winter solstice and vernal equinox (22nd Dec.—20th-21st March); any dismal, gloomy time; *a.* wintry; pert. to winter; *v.t.* to keep and feed throughout winter; *v.i.* to pass the winter. **-er** *n.* **-green** *n.* aromatic evergreen plant from which is obtained oil of wintergreen, used in medicine and flavoring. **-ize** *v.t.* ready for winter. **-ly** *adv.* **wintriness** *n.* **wintry** *a.* of or like winter [O.E.].

wipe (wīp) *v.t.* to rub lightly, so as to clean or dry; to remove gently; to clear away; to efface; *n.* act of wiping. **-r** *n.* one who, or that which, wipes; in motoring, automatically operated arm to keep part of windshield free from rain or dust. **wiping** *n.* act of wiping. **to wipe out,** to erase; to destroy utterly [O.E. *wipian*].

wire (wīr) *n.* metal drawn into form of a thread or cord; a length of this; telegraphy; a telegram; string of instrument; a rabbit snare; *v.t.* to bind or stiffen with wire; to pierce with wire; to fence with wire; to install (building) with wires for electric circuit; (*Colloq.*) to telegraph; to snare; *a.* formed of wire. **-d** *a.* **—gauze** *n.* finely woven wire netting. **—haired** *a.* having short, wiry hair. **-less** *a.* without wires; pert. to several devices operated by electromagnetic waves. *n.* wireless telegraphy or telephony; (*Brit.*) a radio; *v.t.* and *v.i.* to communicate by wireless. **-less operator** *n.* one who receives and transmits wireless messages. **— netting** *n.* galvanized wire woven into net. **-photo** *n.* method of sending photographs by means of electric impulses; the photograph so reproduced. **-puller** *n.* one who exercises influence behind scenes, esp. in public affairs. **-r** *n.* one who installs wire. **— tapping** act of tapping telephone wires to get information. **-worm** *n.* larva of various click beetles, very destructive to roots of plants. **wirily** *adv.* **wiriness** *n.* **wiring** *n.* system of electric wires forming circuit. **wiry** *n.* stiff (as hair); lean, sinewy and strong, **a live wire,** wire charged with electricity; enterprising person [O.E. *wir*].

wis·dom (wiz′·dạm) *n.* quality of being wise; knowledge and the capacity to make use of it; judgment. **— tooth** *n.* posterior molar tooth, cut about twentieth year [O.E.].

wise (wīz) *a.* enlightened; sagacious; learned; dictated by wisdom. **-acre** *n.* a foolish know-it-all. **-crack** *n.* concise flippant statement; *v.i.* to utter one. **-ly** *adv.* **-ness** *n.* [O.E. *wis*].

wise (wīz) *n.* way; manner [O.E. *wise*].

wise (wīz) *adv. suffix.* in the way or manner of, arranged like, as in *clockwise, likewise, crosswise*, etc.

wish (wish) *v.t.* to desire; to long for; to hanker after; to request; *v.i.* to have a desire; to yearn; *n.* expression or object of desire; longing; request. **(ing)-bone** *n.* forked bone of fowl's breast. **-er** *n.* **-ful** *a.* desirous; anxious; longing; wistful. **-fully** *adv.* **-fulness** *n.* [O.E. *wyscan*].

wish·wash (wish′·wȧsh) *n.* thin, weak, insipid drink. **-y** *a.* morally weak; watery; diluted [redupl. of *wash*].

wisp (wisp) *n.* twisted handful, usually of hay; whisk or small broom; stray lock of hair. **-like** *a.* **-y** *a.* [M.E. *wisp*, *wips*, Cf. **wipe**].

wis·te·ri·a (wis·tir′·i·ạ) *n.* hardy climbing

leguminous shrub, with blue, purple, white or mauve flower clusters [*Wistar*, Amer. anatomist, 1761-1818].
wist·ful (wist′·fal) *a.* pensive; sadly contemplative; earnestly longing. **-ly** *adv.* **-ness** *n.* [*var.* of wishful].
wit (wit) *n.* intellect; understanding; (one with) ingenuity in connecting amusingly incongruous ideas; humor; pleasantry; *pl.* mental faculties. **-less** *a.* lacking wit or understanding; silly; stupid. **-lessly** *adv.* in all innocence. **-lessness** *n.* **-ticism** *n.* witty remark.**-tily** *adv.* **-tiness** *n.* **-tingly** *adv.* with foreknowledge or design; knowingly; of set purpose. **-ty** *a.* possessed of wit; amusing. **at one's wits' end,** baffled; perplexed what to do. **to wit,** namely [O.E. *witan*, to know].
wit·an (wit′·an) *n.pl.* members of the witenagemot [O.E. *wita*, wise man].
witch (wich) *n.* woman who was supposed to practice sorcery; ugly old woman; hag; crone; *v.t.* to bewitch; to enchant. **-craft** *n.* black art; sorcery; necromancy. **— doctor** *n.* medicine man of a savage tribe. **-ery** *n.* arts of a witch; sorcery. **—hunt** search for, and trial of subversives. **-ing** *a.* fascinating. **-ingly** *adv.* [O.E. *wicca*].
witch haz·el (wich·hā′·zal) *n.* shrub with yellow flowers and edible seeds; of dried bark and leaves of the tree used, in distilled form, as astringent drug [O.E. *wice*, drooping].
wit·e·na·ge·mot (wit′·a·na·ga·mōt) *n.* national council of England in Anglo-Saxon times [O.E. *wita*, wise man; *gemot*, meeting].
with (wiTH, with) *prep.* in company or possession of; in relation to; against; by means of; denoting association, cause, agency, comparison, immediate sequence, etc. [O.E.].
with·al (wiTH·awl′) *adv.* (*Arch.*) besides.
with·draw (wiTH·draw′) *v.t.* to take away; to recall; to retract; *v.i.* to go away; to retire; to retreat; to recede. *pa.t.* **withdrew.** *pa.p.* **-n, -al** *n.* **-ment** *n.*
withe (with, wīTH) *n.* tough, flexible twig, esp. willow, reed, or osier. Also **withy. withy** *a.* (*Chiefly Brit.*) made of withes; flexible and tough [O.E. *withig*, willow].
with·er (wiTH′·er) *v.t.* to cause to fade and become dry; to blight; to rebuff; *v.i.* to fade; to decay; to languish. **-ing** *a.* **-ingly** *adv.* scathingly; contemptuously [var. of *weather*].
with·ers (wiTH′·erz) *n.pl.* ridge between horse's shoulder blades [O.E. *wither*, resistance].
with·hold (with·hōld′) *v.t.* to hold or keep back. *pa.p., pa.t.* **withheld.**
with·in (wiTH·in′) *prep.* in the inner or interior part of; in the compass of; *adv.* in the inner part; inwardly; at home.
with·out (wiTH·out′) *prep.* on or at the outside of; out of; not within; beyond the limits of; destitute of; exempt from; all but; *adv.* on the outside; out of doors.
with·stand (with·stand′) *v.t.* to oppose; to stand against; to resist. *pa.t.* and *pa.p.* **withstood. -er** *n.*
with·y See **withe.**
wit·ness (wit′·nis) *n.* testimony; one who, or that which, furnishes evidence or proof; one who has seen or has knowledge of incident; one who attests another person's signature to document; *v.t.* to be witness of or to; *v.i.* to give evidence; to testify. **— stand** *n.* place where witness gives testimony in court of law. **-er** *n.* [O.E. *witnes*, evidence].
wit·ti·cism, wit·ty, etc. See **wit.**
wive (wīv) *v.t.* to provide with or take for a wife; *v.i.* to take a wife [fr. *wife*].
wi·vern (wī′·vern) *n.* (*Her.*) imaginary monster, with two clawed feet, two wings and serpent's tail [O.Fr. *wivre*, viper].
wives (wīvz) *pl.* of **wife.**
wiz·ard (wiz′·erd) *n.* one devoted to black art; sorcerer; magician; conjurer; a skillful person; *a.* with magical powers. **-like** *a.* **-ly** *a.* **-ry** *n.* magic [fr. *wise*].
wiz·en, wiz·ened (wiz′·n, wiz′·nd) *a.* dried up; withered [O.E. *wisnian*, to wither].
woad (wōd) *n.* plant yielding blue dye derived from pounded leaves [O.E. *wad*].
wob·ble, wabble (wab′·l) *v.i.* to rock from side to side; (*Colloq.*) to vacillate; to be hesitant; *n.* rocking; unequal motion. **-r,** *n.* **wobbly, wabbly** *a.* shaky; unsteady.
woe, wo (wō) *n.* grief; heavy calamity; affliction; sorrow. **-begone** *a.* overwhelmed with woe; sorrowful; **-ful** *a.* sorrowful; pitiful; paltry. **-fully** *adv.* [O.E. *wa*].
woke. alt. *pa.t.* of **wake.**
wold (wōld) *n.* wood; open tract of country; low hill [O.E. *weald, wald*, a forest].
wolf (woolf) *n.* carnivorous wild animal, allied to dog; rapacious, cruel person; (*Slang*) lady-killer. *pl.* **wolves** (woolvz). *v.t.* (*Colloq.*) to devour ravenously. **— dog** *n.* animal bred from wolf and dog; large dog for hunting wolves. **-hound** *n.* dog bred for hunting wolves. **-ish** *a.* rapacious, like wolf; voracious; fierce and greedy. **-ishly** *adv.* **-ishness** *n.* [O.E. *wulf*].
wolf·ram·ite (wool′·fram·īt) *n.* the mineral, ferrous tungstate, the chief source of the metal tungsten. Also **wolfram** [Ger].
wol·ver·ine, wol·ver·ene (wool·va·rēn′) *n.* a carnivorous mammal inhabiting northern region; the glutton [fr. *wolf*].
wolves *pl.* of **wolf.**
wo·man (woom′·an) *n.* adult human female; the quality of being a woman. *pl.* **women** (wim′·in). **-hood** *n.* adult stage of women; the qualities of women. **-ish** *a.* like a woman; effeminate. **-ishness** *n.* **-kind, womenkind** *n.* female sex. **-like** *a.* like, or characteristic of, a woman. **-liness** *n.* **-ly** *a.* befitting a mature woman; essentially feminine; *adv.* in manner of a woman [O.E. *wifmann*].
womb (wòòm) *n.* female organ of conception and gestation; uterus [O.E. *wamb*, belly].
wom·bat (wam′·bat) *n.* group of Australian and Tasmanian fur-bearing, burrowing marsupial animals [Austral. *womback*].
wo·men (wim′·in) *pl.* of **woman.**
won (wun) *pa.t.* and *pa.p.* of **win.**
won·der (wun′·der) *n.* astonishment; surprise; amazement; admiration; prodigy; miracle; *v.i.* to feel wonder; to marvel; to speculate. **-er** *n.* **-ful** *a.* very fine; remarkable; amazing. **-fully** *adv.* **-fulness** *n.* **-ing** *a.* **-ingly** *adv.* in a wondering and expectant manner. **-land** *n.* land of marvels; fairyland. **wondrous** *a.* wonderful. **wondrously** *adv.* **wondrousness** *n.* [O.E. *wundor*].
custom; use; v.i. fe·alrfl·fl,
wont (wawnt, wunt) *a.* accustomed; used; *n.* habit; custom; use; *v.i.* (*Poetic*) to be accustomed. **-ed** *a.* accustomed; habitual; usual. **-edness** [O.E. *gewun*, usual].
won't (wōnt) *v.i.* a contr. of **will not.**
woo (wòò) *v.t.* to make love to; to court; to endeavor to gain (sleep, etc.) **-er** *n.* **-ing** *n.* [O.E. *wogian*].
wood (wood) *n.* (usu. *pl.*) land with trees growing close together; grove; forest; hard, stiffening tissue in stem and branches of tree; timber; wood-wind instrument; *v.t.* to supply with wood; to plant with trees; *v.i.* to take in good. **— alcohol** *n.* methyl alcohol, product of dry distillation of wood, esp. beech and birch. **-bine,** *n.* wild honeysuckle; Virginia creeper. *n.* **-chuck** *n.* small burrowing rodent; ground hog. **— coal** *n.* wood charcoal; lignite or brown coal. **-cock** *n.* migrant gamebird of snipe family. **-craft** *n.* expert knowl-

edge of woodland conditions; art of making objects of wood. **-cut** *n.* engraving on wood; impression from such engravings. **-cutter** *n.* a woodsman. **-ed** *a.* covered with trees. **-en** *a.* made of wood; expressionless; stiff; stupid. **— engraver** *n.* **— engraving** *n.* art or process of cutting design on wood for printing; impression from this; woodcut. **-enhead** *n.* (*Colloq.*) a numbskull; a blockhead.**-enly** *adv.* stiffly. **-enness** *n.* **-enware** *n.* articles of wood. **-iness** *n.* **-land** *n.* and *a.* (of) wooded country. **— louse** *n.* the slater, prolific in damp places, esp. under decaying timber. **-man** *n.* or **-sman. — nymph** *n.* goddess of woods, a dryad; a moth. **-pecker** *n.* bird which taps and bores with bill the bark of trees in search of insects. **— pulp** *n.* wood crushed and pulped for paper making. **-sman** *n.* forest dweller; forester; woodcutter. **— sorrel** *n.* perennial herb of geranium order with small white flowers and acid leaves. **-shed** *n.* firewood storage place. **-sy** *a.* like the woods. **—wind** *n.* wooden musical instrument, as flute, oboe, clarinet, bassoon, etc. **-work** *n.* fittings made of wood, esp. interior moldings of a house. **-y** *a.* abounding with trees or wooded growth. **not out of the woods,** still in jeopardy [O.E. *wudu*, forest].

woo·er See **woo.**

woof (wŏŏf) *n.* threads which cross warp in weaving; texture [O.E. *owef*].

woof·er (woof′·ẹr) *n.* large loud-speaker that reproduces low frequency sound waves (opp. of *tweeter*).

wool (wool) *n.* soft, curled hair of sheep, goat, etc.; yarn or cloth of this; **-gather--ing** *n.* day dreaming.**-(l)en** *n.* cloth made of wool; *pl.* woolen goods; *a.* made of, pert. to, wool.**-liness** *n.* **-ly** *a.* of, or like wool; muddled and confused. **-pack** *n.* a pack of wool; a cumulus cloud resembling a fleecy woolen ball. **dyed-in-the-wool,** become inherent; unchangeable [O.E. *wull*].

word (wurd) *n.* spoken or written sign of idea; term; oral expression; message; order; password; promise; brief remark or observation; *pl.* speech; language, esp. contentious; wordy quarrel; *v.t.* to express in words; to phrase. **-ed** *a.* phrased; expressed.**-ily** *adv.* verbosely; pedantically. **-iness** *n.* verbosity; **-ing** *n.* precise words used; phrasing; phraseology. **-less** *a.* **-ly** *a.* verbose; prolix. **word for word,** literally; verbatim. **by word of mouth,** orally [O.E. *word*].

wore (wōr) *pa.t.* of **wear.**

work (wurk) *n.* exertion of strength; effort directed to an end; employment; toil; labor; occupation; production; achievement; manufacture; that which is produced; (*Phys.*) result of force overcoming resistance over definite distance; *pl.* structures in engineering; manufacturing establishment; good deeds; artistic productions; mechanism of a watch, etc.; fortifications; *v.i.* to exert oneself; to labor; to be employed; to act; to be effective; to have influence (on, upon); *v.t.* to produce or form by labor; to operate; to perform; to effect; to embroider. **-able** *a.* **-aday** *a.* commonplace. **-bag, -basket, -box** *n.* receptacle for holding work implements, esp. for needlework. **—day** *n.* day when work is done; week-day. **-er** *n.* **—house** *n.* house of correction. **-ing** *n.* act of laboring or doing something useful; mode of operation; fermentation; *pl.* a mine as a whole, or a part of it where work is being carried on, e.g. level, etc.; *a.* laboring; fermenting. **-man** *n.* one actually engaged in manual labor; craftsman. **-man-like** *a.* befitting skilled workman; skillful. **-manship** *n.* skill. **-out** *n.* practice; performance; training. **-shop** *n.* place where things are made or repaired; people meeting for intensive study in some field. **to work off,** to get rid of gradually. **to work out,** to solve (problem); to plan in detail; to exhaust (mine, etc.). **to work up,** to excite unduly; to study intensively; to advance [O.E. *weorc*].

world (wurld) *n.* earth and its inhabitants; whole system of things; universe; any planet or star; this life; general affairs of life; society; human race; mankind; great quantity or number. **-liness** *n.* state of being worldly. **-ling** *n.* one who is absorbed in the affairs, interests, or pleasures of this world. **-ly** *a.* relating to the world; engrossed in temporal pursuits; earthly; mundane; carnal; not spiritual. **-ly-wise** *a.* experienced in the ways of people. **—weary, —wearied** *a.* tired of worldly affairs. **—wide** *a.* extending to every corner of the globe. **—man (woman) of the world,** one with much worldly experience. **old-world** *a.* old-fashioned; quaint. **the New World,** N. and S. America. **the Old World,** Europe, Africa, and Asia [O.E. *weorold*].

worm (wurm) *n.* small, limbless, invertebrate animal with soft, long, and jointed body; spiral thread; small, metal screw that meshes with the teeth of a worn wheel; spiral pipe through which vapor passes in distillation; emblem of corruption, of decay, or remorse; groveling, contemptible fellow; *pl.* disease of digestive organs or intenstines of humans and animals due to parasite worms; *v.i.* to work (oneself) in insidiously; to move along like a worm; *v.t.* to work slowly and secretly; to free from worms. **— drive** *n.* system in which power is communicated by means of worm, through worm wheel. **—eaten** *a.* of wooden furniture, etc., full of holes gnawed by worms; old; antiquated. **-er** *n.* **-less** *a.* **-like** *a.* **— wheel** *n.* cogged wheel whose teeth engage smoothly with coarse threaded screw or worm. **-y** *a.* worm-like; abounding with worms; groveling [O.E. *wyrm*, serpent].

worm·wood (wurm′·wood) *n.* bitter plant, Artemisia, used in making absinthe, vermouth, etc.; bitterness [O.E. *wermod*].

worn (wōrn) *pa.p.* of **wear. —out** *a.* no longer serviceable; exhausted; tired.

wor·ry (wur′·i·)*v.t.* to cause anxiety; to torment; to vex; to plague; to tear or mangle with teeth; *v.i.* to feel undue care and anxiety; *n.* mental disturbance due to care and anxiety; trouble; vexation. **worrier** *n.* **worrisome** *a.* causing trouble, anxiety, or worry. **-ing** *a.* [O.E. *wyrgan*, to strangle].

worse (wurs) *a. comp.* of **bad, ill;** more unsatisfactory; of less value; in poorer health; *adv.* in a manner more evil or bad. **worsen** *v.t.* to make worse; to impair; *v.t.* and *i.* to make or become worse; to deteriorate. **worsening** *n.* [O.E. *wyrsa*].

wor·ship (wur′·ship) *n.* religious reverence and homage; act or ceremony of showing reverence; adoration; *v.t.* to adore; to pay divine honors to; *v.i.* to perform religious service; to attend church. **-ful** *a.* **-fully** *adv.* **-fulness** *n.* **-er** *n.* [O.E. *weorthscipe* = worth-ship].

worst (wurst) *a. superl.* of **bad, ill;** most evil; of least value or worth; *adv.* in most inferior manner or degree; *n.* that which is most bad or evil; *v.t.* to get the better of; to defeat [O.E. *wyrst, wyrsta*].

wor·sted (woos′·tid, woor′·stid) *n.* yarn spun from long-fibred wools which are combed, not carded; cloth of this yarn; *a.* made of worsted [*Worstead*, England].

wort (wurt, wawrt) *n.* plant, herb—usually appearing as the last element of a compound term, e.g. *milkwort*, etc. [O.E. *wyrt*].

wort (wurt) *n.* in brewing of beer, liquid portion of mash of malted grain produced during fermenting process before hops and yeast are added; malt extract used as a medium for culture of micro-organisms [O.E. *wyrt*, a plant].

worth (wurth) *n.* quality of thing which renders it valuable or useful; relative excellence of conduct or of character; value, in terms of money; merit; excellence; *a.* equal in value to; meriting; having wealth or estate to the value of. **-ily** *adv.* **-iness** *n.* **-less** *a.* of no worth or value; useless. **-while** *a.* **-lessly** *adv.* **-lessness** *n.* **-y** (wur′THi·) *a.* having worth or excellence; deserving; meritorious; *n.* man of eminent worth; local celebrity. *pl.* **worthies** [E. *weorth*].

wot (wȧt) (*Arch.*) *v.i.* to know; to be aware [O.E. fr. *witan*, to know].

would (wood) *pa.t.* of **will;** expresses condition, futurity, desire. **—be** *a.* desiring or intending to be.

wound (wound) *pa.t.* and *pa.p.* of **wind.**

wound (wòȯnd) *n.* injury; cut, stab, bruise, etc.; hurt (to feelings); damage; *v.t.* to hurt by violence; to hurt feelings of; to injure. **-er** *n.* **-less** *a.* [O.E. *wund*].

wove (wōv) *pa.t.* of **weave. -n** *pa.p.* of **weave. — paper** *n.* paper with no marks of wire as in laid paper.

wow (wou) *interj.* exclamation of astonishment; *n.* (*Slang*) great success.

wrack (rak) *n.* seaweed thrown ashore by waves; shipwreck; ruin. Also **rack** [var. of *wreck*].

wraith (rāth) *n.* apparition of person seen shortly before or after death; specter; ghost. **-like** *a.* [O.N. *vorthr*, guardian].

wran·gle (rang′·gl) *v.i.* to dispute angrily; to bicker; to tend horses; *n.* angry dispute; an argument. *n.* angry disputant; ranch hand who rounds up cattle. **-r** *n.* [M.E. *wranglen*, to dispute].

wrap (rap) *v.t.* to cover by winding or folding something around; to roll, wind, or fold together; to enfold; to envelop; to muffle. *pr.p.* **-ping.** *pa.t., pa.p.* **-ped** (or **-t**) *n.* a loose garment; a covering. **-per** *n.* one who, or that which, wraps; loose dressing-gown worn by women; negligee. **-ping** *n.* wrapping material [earlier *wlap*, etym. uncertain].

wrapt (rapt) *a.* alt. *pa.p., pa.t.* of wrap; rapt; ecstatic; transported.

wrath (rath) *n.* violent anger; indignation; rage; fury. **-ful** *a.* **-fully** *adv.* **-fulness** *n.* [O.E. *wrath*, angry].

wreak (rēk) *v.t.* to inflict (vengeance, etc.) **-er** *n.* [O.E. *wrecan*, to avenge].

wreath (rēth) *n.* circular garland or crown of flowers, leaves, etc. entwined together; chaplet; a similar formation, as of smoke. **wreathe** (rēTH) *v.t.* to surround; to form into a wreath; to wind round; to encircle; *v.i.* to be interwoven or entwined [O.E. *wraeth*, a fillet].

wreck (rek) *n.* destruction of vessel; hulk of wrecked ship; remains of anything destroyed or ruined; desolation; *v.t.* to destroy, as vessel; to bring ruin upon; to upset completely. **-age** *n.* remains of something wrecked. **-er** *n.* one who wrecks; one employed in tearing down buildings, salvaging or recovering cargo from, wreck [O.E. *wraec*, punish].

wren (ren) *n.* tiny song-bird about 4 in. long, with reddish-brown plumage [O.E. *wrenna*].

wrench (rench) *v.t.* to wrest, twist, or force by violence; to distort; *n.* sudden, violent twist; tool with fixed or adjustable jaws for holding or adjusting nuts, bolts, etc. [O.E. *wrenc*, twist].

wrest (rest) *v.t.* to pull or force away by violence; to extort; to get with difficulty; to twist from its natural meaning; to distort; *n.* violent pulling or twisting [O.E. *wraestan*].

wres·tle (res′·l)) *v.i.* to contend by grappling and trying to throw another down; to struggle; to strive (with). **-r** *n.* **wrestling** *n.* sport in which contestants endeavor to throw each other to the ground in accordance with rules [O.E. *wraestlian*, fr. *wraestan*, to twist about].

wretch (rech) *n.* miserable creature; one sunk in vice or degradation; one profoundly unhappy. **-ed** (rech′·id) *a.* very miserable; very poor or mean; despicable. **-edly** *adv.* **-edness** *n.* [O.E. *wraecca*, an outcast].

wrig·gle (rig′·l) *v.i.* to move sinuously, like a worm; to squirm; *v.t.* to cause to wriggle; *n.* act of wriggling; wriggling motion. **-r** *n.* **wriggling** *n.* **wriggly** *a.* [Dut. *wriggelen*, to move].

wright (rīt) *n.* one who fashions articles of wood, metal, etc., as *wheelwright* [O.E. *wyrhta*].

wring (ring) *v.t.* to twist and compress; to turn and strain with violence; to squeeze or press out; to pain; to extort; *v.i.* to turn or twist, as with pain. *pa.t.* and *pa.p.* **wrung. -er** *n.* one who wrings; machine for pressing out water from wet clothes, etc. **-ing wet,** absolutely soaking [O.E. *wringan*].

wrin·kle (ring′·kl) *n.* ridge or furrow on surface due to twisting, shrinking, or puckering; crease in skin; fold; corrugation; *v.i.* to make ridges, creases, etc. *v.i.* to shrink into wrinkles. **-ling** *n.* **wrinkly** *a.* [O.E. *wrincle*].

wrin·kle (ring′·kl) *n.* (*Colloq.*) valuable hint; novel method or approval [O.E. *wrenc*, trick].

wrist (rist) *n.* joint connecting the forearm and hand; the carpus. **-band** *n.* part of shirt sleeve covering wrist; elastic band to give support to injured wrist. **-let** *n.* band clasping wrist fairly tightly; bracelet; (*Slang*) handcuff. **-lock** *n.* wrestling hold [O.E.].

writ (rit) *n.* that which is written; in law, mandatory precept issued by a court; **Holy Writ,** the Scriptures [fr. *write*].

write (rīt) *v.t.* to set down or express in letters or words on paper, etc.; to compose, as book, song, etc.; *v.i.* to form characters representing sounds or ideas; to be occupied in writing; to express ideas in writing. *pr.p.* **writing.** *pa.t.* **wrote.** *pa.p.* **written. -r** *n.* one who writes; scribe; clerk; author. **-r's-cramp** *n.* neurosis of muscles of hand. **-up** *n.* (*Colloq.*) favorable press criticism or report. **writing** *n.* mechanical act of forming characters on paper or any other material; anything written; style of execution or content of what is written; *pl.* literary or musical works; official papers, etc. **written** *a.* expressed in writing. **to write off,** to cancel, as bad debts [O.E. *writan*].

writhe (rīTH) *v.t.* to twist or distort; to turn to and fro; *v.i.* to twist or roll about (as in pain) [A.S. *writhen*, to twist].

writ·ten *pa.p.* of **write.**

wrong (rawng) *a.* not right; incorrect; mistaken; evil; immoral; injurious; unjust; illegal; unsuitable; improper; *n.* harm; evil; injustice; trespass; transgression; error; *adv.* not rightly; erroneously; *v.t.* to treat with injustice; to injure; to impute evil to unjustly. **-doer** *n.* one who injures another; one who breaks law; offender; sinner. **-ful** *a.* **-fully** *adv.* **-fulness** *n.* **-headed** *a.* obstinate; stubborn; perverse. **-headedly** *adv.* **-headedness** *n.* **-ly** *adv.* **-ness** *n.* **in the wrong,** at fault; blameworthy [O.E. *wrang*, injustice].

wrote (rōt) *pa.t.* of **write.**

wroth (rawth) *a.* full of wrath; angry; incensed [fr. *wrath*].

wrought (rawt) *pa.t.* and *pa.p.* of **work.** *a.* hammered into shape, as metal products. **—iron** *n.* purest form of commercial iron, fibrous, ductile, and malleable, prepared by puddling. **—up** *a.* excited; frenzied [O.E. *worhte*, worked].

wrung (rung) *pa.t.* and *pa.p.* of **wring.**
wry (rī) *a.* turned to one side; twisted; distorted; crooked; askew. **-ly** *adv.* **-neck** *n.* condition in which head leans permanently towards shoulders. **-necked** *a.* **-ness** *n.* [O.E. *wrigian*, to twist].
wy·an·dotte (wī′.ạn.dȧt) *n.* breed of domestic fowls [name of N. Amer. tribe].

X

xan·tip·pe (zan.tip′.ē) *n.* a scolding, shrewish woman [*Xantippē*, wife of Socrates].
X chro·mo·some (eks′.krōmạ.sōm) *n.* (*Biol.*) chromosome which determines the sex of the future organism.
xe·bec (zē′.bek) *n.* small three-masted vessel with lateen and square sails, used formerly in the Mediterranean by pirates [Fr. *chebec*].
xe·nog·a·my (zi.nȧg′.ạ.mi.) *n.* (*Bot.*) cross-fertilization. **xenogamous** *a.* [Gk. *xenos*, stranger; *gamos*, marriage].
xen·o·gen·e·sis (zen.ạ.jen′.ạ.sis) *n.* fancied generation of organism totally unlike parent. **xenogenetic** *a.* [Gk. *xenos*, stranger; *gamos*].
xe·non (zē′.nȧn) *n.* non-metallic .element belonging to group of rare or inactive gases [Gk. *xenos*, a stranger].
xen·o·pho·bi·a (zen.ạ.fō′.bi.ạ) *n.* fear or hatred of strangers or aliens [Gk. xenos, strange; *phobos*, fear].
xe·rog·ra·phy (zē.rȧg′.rạ.fi.) *n.* a process similar to photography, but not requiring specially sensitized paper or plates, using instead a special photoconductive plate.
X rays (eks′.rāz) *n.pl.* Röntgen rays—electromagnetic rays of very short wave length, capable of penetrating matter opaque to light rays and imprinting on sensitive photographic plate picture of objects; the picture so made. *v.t.* to treat, examine, or photograph with X-rays.
xy·lo·graph (zī′.lạ.graf) *n.* a wood engraving; impression from wood block. **-er** *n.* **-ic** *a.* **-ical** *a.* **-y** *n.* the art of wood engraving. [Gk. *xylon*, wood; *graphein*, to write].
xy·loid (zī′.loid) *a.* of the nature of wood; resembling wood; ligneous [Gk. *xylon*, wood].
xy·lol (zī′.lawl) *n.* commercial name for **xylene,** dimethyl benzene—hydrocarbon de- from coal tar used medicinally and as solvent for fats [Gk. *xylon*, wood; L. *oleum*, oil].
xy·lo·phone (zī′.lạ.fōn) *n.* musical instrument consisting of blocks of resonant wood, notes being produced by striking blocks with two small hammers. **xylophonist** *n.* [Gk. *xulon*, wood; *phonē*, a voice].
xy·lo·py·rog·ra·phy (zī.lō.pī.rȧg′.rạ.fi.) *n.* production of designs in wood by charring with hot iron [Gk. *xulon*, wood; *pur*, fire; *graphein*, to write].
xys·ter (zis′.tẹr) *n.* surgical instrument for scraping bones [Gk. fr. *xuein*, to scrape].

Y

yacht (yȧt) *n.* light sailing or power-driven vessel, for pleasure or racing; *v.i.* to sail in a yacht. **-ing** *n.* art or act of sailing a yacht; *a.* pert. to yacht. **-sman** *n.* **-smanship** *n.* [Dut. *jagt*].
yah (yȧ) *interj.* exclamation of derision, defiance or disgust.
yak (yak) *n.* species of ox found in C. Asia, with a hump and long hair [Tibetan, *gyag*].
yam (yam) *n.* tuber of tropical climbing-plant; sweet potato [Port. *inhame*].
yam·mer (yam′.ẹr) *v.i.* (*Colloq.*) to whine; to wail; to shout; complain [O.E. *geomor*, sad].
yank (yangk) *v.t.* and *v.i.* (*Colloq.*) to jerk; to tug; to pull quickly; *n.* quick tug.
Yank (yangk) *n.* (*Slang*) Yankee.
Yan·kee (yang′.kē) *n.* (in U.S.A.) citizen of New England, or of Northern States; (outside U.S.A.) an American; *a.* American. **-dom***n.*
yap (yap) *v.i.* to yelp; (*Slang*) to chatter incessantly; *n.* yelp. *pr.p.* **-ping.** *pa.p.* and *pa.t.* **-ped** [imit. origin].
yapp (yap) *n.* style of bookbinding in limp leather projecting beyond edges of book [Fr. *Yapp*, the inventor].
yard (yȧrd) *n.* standard measure of length, equal to three feet or thirty-six inches; (*Naut.*) spar set crosswise to mast, for supporting a sail. **-age** *n.* measurement in yards; amount to be measured. **-arm** *n.* either half of a ship's yard. **-stick** *n.* measuring stick 36 inches long; (*Fig.*) standard of measurement [O.E. *gyrd*, a rod].
yard (yȧrd) *n.* grounds surrounding a building; enclosed space used for specific purpose as *brickyard*, a *railroad yard*, etc. [O.E. *geard*, enclosure].
yarn (yȧrn) *n.* spun thread, esp. for knitting or weaving; thread of rope; (*Colloq.*) imaginative story; *v.i.* to tell a story. [O.E. *gearn*].
yar·row (yar′.ō) *n.* plant having strong odor and pungent taste [O.E. *gearwe*].
yash·mak (yash′.mak) *n.* veil worn by Mohammedan women, covering the face from beneath the eyes down [Ar.].
yat·a·ghan (yat′.ạ.gan) *n.* Turkish dagger, without a guard and usually curved [Turk.]
yaw (yaw) *v.i.* of ship or aircraft, to fail to keep steady course; *n.* act of yawing; temporary deviation from a straight course [O.N. *jaga*, to bend].
yawl (yawl) *n.* small, two-masted sailing boat, with smaller mast at stern; ship's small boat [Dut. *jol*].
yawn (yawn) *v.i.* to open mouth involuntarily through sleepiness, etc.; to gape; *n.* involuntary opening of mouth through sleepiness, etc. a gaping space. **-ing** *a.* gaping [O.E. geonian].
yaws (yawz) *n.* tropical contagious disease of the skin, usually chronic; (*Med.*) frambesia [Afr. *yaw*, a raspberry].
y·clept (i.klept′) *a.* (*Arch.*) called [O.E. *clipian*, to call].
ye (yē) *pron.* (*Arch.*) **you** [O.E. *ge.*].
ye (yē) *a.* an *Arch.* spelling of article **the.**
yea (yā) *n.* yes; *adv.* indeed [O.E. *eag.*].
yean (yēn) *v.t.* and *v.i.* to bring forth young; as sheep or goat. **-ling** *n.* a lamb; kid [O.E. *eanian*].
year (yir) *n.* time taken by one revolution of earth round sun, i.e. about 365¼ days; twelve months; scholastic session in school, university, etc.; *pl.* age; old age. **-ly** *a.* and *adv.* happening every year; annual. **-ling** *n.* young animal, esp. horse, in second year; *a.* being a year old. **-long** *a.* **-book** *n.* reference book of facts and statistics published yearly. **leap year,** year of 366 days, occurring every fourth year. [O.E. *gear*]
yearn (yurn) *v.i.* to seek earnestly: to feel longing or desire; to long for. **-ing** *n.* earnest desire; longing; *a.* desirous. **-ingly** *adv.* [O.E. *gyernan*].
yeast (yēst) *n.* froth that rises on malt liquors during fermentation; frothy yellow fungus growth causing this fermentation, used also in bread making, as leavening agent to raise dough. **-y** *a.* frothy; fermenting. **-cake** *n.* yeast mixed with meal and formed

into small cakes for use in baking. [O.E. *gist*].

yegg (yeg) *n.* (*Slang*) criminal.

yell (yel) *v.i.* to cry out in a loud, shrill tone; to scream; to shriek; *n.* a loud, shrill cry. **-ing** *n.* [O.E. *gellan*].

yel·low (yel′·ō) *n.* primary color; color of gold, lemons, buttercups, etc.; *a.* of this color; *(Colloq.)* cowardly; mean; despicable; of newspaper, sensational; *v.t.* to make yellow; *v.i.* to become yellow. **-ish, -y** *a.* somewhat yellow. **-ishness** *n.* **-ness** *n.* **— fever** *n.* infectious, tropical disease, characterized by a yellow skin, vomiting, etc. **— jack** *n.* (*Colloq.*) yellow fever; yellow flag flown by ships, etc. in quarantine. **— jacket** *n.* a bright yellow wasp [O.E. *geolu*].

yelp (yelp) *n.* sharp, shrill bark or cry; *v.i.* to utter such a bark or cry. **-er** *n.* [O.E. *gilpan*, to boast].

yen (yen) *n.* (*Colloq.*) longing; urge.

yeo-man (yō′·mąn) *n.* (*Arch.*) officer of royal household; *(Navy)* petty officer. *pl.* **yeomen. -ly** *a.* **-ry** *n.* yeomen collectively. **— service,** long and faithful service; effective aid [contr. of *young man*].

yes (yes) *interj.* word expressing affirmation or consent. **—man** *n.* servile and obedient supporter [O.E. *gese*].

yes·ter (yes′·tẹr) *a.* (*Arch.*) pert. to yesterday; denoting period of time just past, esp. in compounds, e.g. 'yester-eve.' **-day** *n.* day before today. **-year** *n.* last year [O.E. *geostran*].

yet (yet) *adv.* in addition; at the same time; still; at the present time; now; hitherto; even; *conj.* nevertheless; notwithstanding. **as yet,** up to the present time [O.E. *giet*].

yew (ū) *n.* cone-bearing evergreen tree; its fine-grained wood, formerly used for making bows for archers [O.E. *iw*].

Yid·dish (yid′·ish) *n.* a mixture of dialectal German, Hebrew and Slavic, spoken by Jews; *a.* to or in this language [Ger. *Judisch*, Jewish].

yield (yēld) *v.t.* to produce; to give in return, esp. for labor, investment, etc.; to bring forth; to concede; to surrender; *v.i.* to submit; to comply; to give way; to produce; to bear; *n.* amount produced; return for labor, investment, etc.; profit; crop. **-ing** *a.* **-ingly** *adv.* [O.E. *gieldan* to pay].

yo·del, yo·dle (yō′·dl) *v.t.* and *v.i.* to sing or warble, with frequent changes from the natural voice to falsetto tone; *n.* falsetto warbling. **-er, yodler** *n.* [Ger. *jodeln*].

yo·ga (yō′·gą) *n.* system of Hindu philosophy; strict spiritual discipline practiced to gain control over forces of one's own being, to gain occult powers, but chiefly to attain union with the Deity or Universal Spirit. **yogi** *n.* one who practices yoga [Sans. = union].

yo·gurt (yō′·goort) *n.* a thick liquid food made from fermented milk [Turk. *yoghurt*].

yoicks (yoiks) *interj.* old fox-hunting cry.

yoke (yōk) *n.* wooden framework fastened over necks of two oxen, etc. to hold them together, and to which a plough, etc. is attached; anything having shape or use of a yoke; separately cut piece of material in garment, fitting closely over shoulders; bond or tie; emblem of submission, servitude, bondage; couple of animals working together; *v.t.* to put a yoke on; to couple or join, esp. to unite in marriage; to attach draft animal to vehicle; *v.i.* to be joined [O.E. *geoc*].

yo·kel (yō′·kl) *n.* rustic; country bumpkin.

yolk (yōk, yōlk) *n.* yellow part of egg. **-less** *a.* **-y** *a.* [O.E. *geolu*, yellow].

yon (yȧn) (*Arch.*) *a.* and *adv.* yonder.**-der** *a.* that or those there; *adv.* at a distance [O.E. *geon*].

yore (yōr) *n.* the past; old times [O.E. *geara*, fr. *gear*, year].

York·shire (yawrk′· shẹr) *n.* county in north of England. **— pudding,** batter baked in roasting tin along with meat. **— terrier,** small, shaggy terrier, resembling Skye terrier.

you (ū) *pron. sing., pl.* of second person in nominative or objective case, indicating person or persons addressed; also used indefinitely meaning, one, they, people in general. **your, yours** *a.* possessive form of *you*, meaning belonging to you, of you, pert. to you. **yourself** *pron.* your own person or self (often used for emphasis or as a reflexive). *pl.* **yourselves** [O.E. *eow, eower*].

young (yung) *a.* not far advanced in growth, life, or existence; not yet old; vigorous; immature; *n.* offspring of animals. **-ish** *a.* somewhat young. **-ling** *n.* young person or animal. **-ster** *n.* young person or animal; child. **with young,** pregnant [O.E. *geong*].

youth (yòòth) *n.* state of being young; life from childhood to manhood; lad or young man; young persons collectively. **-ful** *a.* possessing youth; pert. to youth; vigorous. **-fully** *adv.* **-fulness** *n.* [O.E. *geoguth*].

yowl (youl) *v.i.* to howl; *n.* cry of a dog; long, mournful cry [M.E. *yowlen*].

yo-yo (yō′·yō) *n.* toy consisting of flat spool with string wound round in the deep groove in its edge, which when released from hand spins up and down string. [Trade Name].

yuc·ca (yuk′·ą) *n.* genus of lilaceous plants, having tall, handsome flowers [W. Ind. name].

Yu·go·slav (yòò′·gō·slȧv) *a.* pert. to *Yugoslavia*, the country of the Serbs, Croats, and Slovenes, in the N.W. of the Balkan Peninsula; *n.* a native of Yugoslavia. Also **Jugoslav.** [Slav. *jug*, the south].

yule (yòòl) *n.* feast of Christmas. **-tide** *n.* season of Christmas. **— log** *n.* log of wood to burn on the open hearth at Christmas time [O.E. *geol*].

Z

za·min·dar (zą·mēn·dȧr′) *n.* in India, landowner paying revenue to government. Also **zemindar** [Pers. = a landowner].

za·ny (zā′·ni·) *n.* formerly, buffoon who mimicked principal clown; simpleton. *a.* comical. **-ism** *n.* [corrupt. of It. *Giovanni*].

za·re·ba (zą·rē′·bą) *n.* in Sudan, stockade of thorny bushes to protect against enemies and wild animals [Ar. *zaribah*, an enclosure].

zeal (zēl) *n.* intense enthusiasm for cause or person; passionate ardor. **zealot** (zel′·ąt) *n.* fanatic; enthusiast. **zealotry** *n.* fanaticism. **zealous** (zel′·ąs) *a.* ardent; enthusiastic; earnest. **zealously** *adv.* **zealousness** *n.* [Gk. *zēlos*, ardor].

ze·bec Same as **xebec.**

ze·bra (zē′·brą) *n.* genus of African quadrupeds of horse family, with tawny coat striped with black [W. Afr.].

ze·brass (zē′·bras) *n.* offspring of male zebra and she-ass.

ze·bu (zē′·bū) *n.* the humped Indian ox [Fr.].

zed (zed) *n.* name for letter **z.**

ze·na·na (ze·nȧ′·ną) *n.* women's apartments in Hindu household [Pers. *zan*, woman].

Zend (zend) *n.* interpretation of the *Avesta*, sacred writings of Zoroastrians; Iranian language in which Zend-Avesta is written. **—Avesta** *n.* sacred writings and commentary thereon (Zend) of Zoroastrians [Pers. *Avistak va Zand*, text and commentary].

ze·nith (zē′·nith) *n.* point of heavens directly above observer's head; summit; height of success; acme; climax. **-al** *a.* [Ar. *samt,* path].

zeph·yr (zef′·ẹr) *n.* west wind; gentle breeze; fine, soft woolen fabric [Gk. *zephuros,* west wind].

zep·pe·lin (zep′·(ạ)·lin) *n.* cigar-shaped long-range dirigible [fr. Count *Zeppelin,* inventor].

ze·ro (zē′·rō) *n.* nought; cipher; symbol, 0; neutral fixed point from which graduated scale is measured, as on thermometer, barometer, etc.; lowest point; *pl.* **-s, -es;** *v.t.* to adjust instrument to a fixed point. **—base budgeting** *n.* a method of budgeting that considers the merits of each item without regard to any previous budget. **— hour** *n.* precise moment at which military offensive, etc. is timed to begin; crucial moment. **— in** *v.i.* to adjust gun fire to a specific point. **— population growth** *n.* a balance in the average number of births and deaths of a population [Ar. *cifr,* a cipher].

zest (zest) *n.* relish; fillip; stimulus; keen pleasure. **-ful** *a.* [O.Fr. *zeste,* lemon peel].

zeug·ma (zòòg′·mạ) *n.* condensed sentence in which a word, such as a verb, is used with two nouns to only one of which it applies. **-tic** *a.* [Gk. *zeugnunai,* to yoke].

Zeus (zòòs) *n.* in Greek mythology, chief deity and father of gods and men [Gk.].

zig·zag (zig′·zag) *n.* line, with short sharp turns; *a.* forming zigzag; *v.t., v.i.* to form, or move with, short sharp turns. *pr.p.* **-ging.** *pa.p., pa.t.* **-ged** [Ger. *zacke,* sharp point].

zil·lion (zil′·yạn) *n.* (*Colloq.*) inconceivably large number [coined word].

zinc (zingk) *n.* hard bluish metal used in alloys, esp. brass, and, because of its resistance to corrosion, for galvanizing iron; *v.t.* to coat with zinc, to galvanize. **— alloys** (*Metal.*) alloys containing percentage of zinc, as brass, etc. **-ic** *a.* **-iferous** *a.* containing zinc. **-ify** *v.t.* **-ograph** *n.* waxed-zinc engraving plate for etching; print of this. **-ographer** *n.* **-ographic(al)** *a.* **-ography** *n.* process of engraving on zinc. **-oid** *a.* resembling zinc. **-ous** *a.* pert. to zinc [Ger. *Zink*].

zing (zing) *n.* the high-pitched sound of something moving at great speed; pep [echoic].

zin·ni·a (zin′·i·a) *n.* plant with bright-colored flowers [fr. *Zinn,* a German botanist].

Zi·on (zī′·ạn) *n.* hill in Jerusalem; town of Jerusalem; the Jewish people; Church of God; heaven. **-ism** *n.* movement among Jews to further the Jewish national state in Palestine. **-ist** *n.* advocate of Zionism [Heb. *tsiyon,* a hill].

zip (zip) *n.* whizzing sound, as of bullet in air; (*Slang*) energy; *v.t.* to shut with a zipper; *v.i.* to move with great speed. *pr.p.* **-ping.** *pa.p., pa.t.* **-ped. — gun** *n.* a crude homemade pistol. **-per** *n.* device of interlocking, flexible teeth opened and shut by sliding clip. **-py** *a.* lively [imit.].

ZIP code, zip code (zip′·kōd) *n.* the five-digit code of each postal area, assigned to speed up deliveries [fr. *z*one *i*mprovement *p*lan].

zir·con (zur′·kàn) *n.* silicate of zirconium occurring in crystals; transparent ones used as gems. **-ium** (zẹr·kōn′·i·ạm) *n.* metal obtained from zircon, and resembling titanium **-ic** *a.* [Ar. *zargun*].

zith·er (ziTH′·ẹr, zith′·ẹr) *n.* flat, stringed instrument comprising resonance box with strings. **-ist** *n.* [Ger.].

zlo·ty (zlà′·ti·) *n.* Polish coin and monetary unit. *pl.* **zlotys** [Pol.]

zo·di·ac (zō·di·ak) *n.* (*Astron.*) imaginary belt in heavens following path of sun, and divided into twelve equal areas containing twelve constellations, each represented by appropriate symbols, called the ***signs of the zodiac***; namely Aries (*Ram*), Taurus (*Bull*), Gemini (*Twins*), Cancer (*Crab*), Leo (*Lion*), Virgo (*Virgin*), Libra (*Balance*), Scorpio (*Scorpion*), Sagittarius (*Archer*), Capricornus (*Goat*), Aquarius (*Water-bearer*), *Pisces* (*Fishes*); a circular chart representing these signs **-al** *a.* [Gk. *zōdiakos,* fr. *zōon,* animal].

zom·bi, zom·bie (zàm′·bi·) *n.* orig. in Africa, deity of the python; in West Indies, corpse alleged to have been revived by black magic; the power which enters such a body; human being without will or speech but capable of automatic movement; intoxicating drink made with rum [W. African *zumbi,* fetish].

zone (zōn) *n.* girdle; climatic or vegetation belt; one of five belts into which earth is divided by latitude lines, as *frigid zone* of Arctic and Antarctic, *torrid zone* between Tropics of Cancer and Capricorn, *temperate zone* north of Tropic of Cancer and south of Tropic of Capricorn; division of a city, etc., for building or other purposes; *v.t.* to enclose; to divide into zones; to divide country into regional areas. **zonal** *a.* pert. to or divided into zones. **-d** *a.* having zones; distributed regionally. **zonate** *a.* striped [Gk. *zonē*].

zoo (zòò) *n.* zoological garden; place where wild animals are kept for showing.

zo·o (zō′·a) *prefix* (from Greek word *zōon,* animal) used in compound words, such as *zoochemistry, zoogeny,* etc.

zo·o·chem·is·try (zō·ạ·kem′·is·tri·) *n.* chemistry of constituents of animal body [Gk. *zōon,* animal; and *chemistry*].

zo·o·ge·og·ra·phy (zō·ạ·jē·àg′·rạ·fi·) *n.* science which treats of the regional distribution of animals in the world. **zoogeographer** *n.* **zoogeographic, -al** *a.*

zo·oid (zō′·oid) *a.* resembling an animal; *n.* organism capable of relatively independent existence; a compound organism [Gk. *zōon,* an animal; *eidos,* a form].

zo·ol·a·try (zō·àl′·ạ·tri·) *n.* animal worship. **zoolater** *n.* **zoolatrous** *a.* [Gk. *zōon,* animal; *latreia,* worship].

zo·ol·o·gy (zō·àl′·ạ·ji·) *n.* natural history of animals, part of science of biology. **zoological** *a.* **zoologically** *adv.* **zoologist** *n.* one versed in zoology, **zoological gardens, zoo,** park where wild animals are kept for exhibition [Gk. *zōon,* animal; *logos,* discourse].

zoom (zòòm) *n. v.t.* (of prices) to become inflated; (of aircraft) to turn suddenly upwards at sharp angle; to move camera rapidly toward or away from an object which thus appears to move similarly [imit.].

zo·on (zō′·àn) *n.* individual part of compound animal; complete product of fertilized germ. *pl.* **zoa, zoons, -ic** *a.* [Gk. *zōon,* animal].

zo·oph·a·gous (zō·àf′·ạ·gạs) *a.* feeding on animals; carnivorous. Also **zoophagan** [Gk. *zōon,* animal; *phagein,* to eat].

zo·o·phyte (zō′·ạ·fīt) *n.* plant-like animal, such as sponge. **zoophytic, -al** *a.* pert. to zoophytes. **zoophytology** *n.* study of zoophytes [Gk. *zōon,* animal; *phuton,* plant].

zoot suit (zòòt′·sòòt) *n.* flashy type of man's suit, generally with padded shoulders, fitted waist, knee-length jacket and tight trousers.

Zo·ro·as·tri·an (zō·rō·as′·tri·ạn) *n.* follower of Zoroaster; *a.* pert. to Zoroaster or his religion; **-ism** *n.* ancient Persian religious doctrine taught by Zoroaster, principal feature of which is the recognition of the dual principle of good and evil; religion of the Parsees [fr. L. corrupt. of Persian *Zarathustra*].

zounds (zoundz) (*Arch.*) *interj.* of anger and surprise [corrupt. of *God's wounds*].

zuc·chet·to (zòò·ket′·ō, tsòòk·ket′·ō) *n.* skull cap worn by R.C. ecclesiastics, and differing in color according to rank of wearer. [It. *zucca,* a gourd].

zuc·chi·ni (zòò.kē′.ni.) *n.* a long green-skinned squash [It. dim. of *zucca,* squash].

Zu·lu (zòò′.lòò) *n.* member of Bantu tribe of S. Africa; *a.* pert. to Zulus [Native].

zwie·back (swē′.bak, .bȧk, swī′.bȧk)*n.* a dry crisp bread, usually sweetened, that has been baked, sliced and then toasted [G. = twice baked].

zyme (zīm) *n.* ferment; disease germ. **zymic** *a.* **zymogen** *n.* any substance producing an enzyme. **zymogenesis** *n.* **zymogenic** *a.* **zymoid** *a.* resembling ferment. **zymosis** *n.* fermentation. **zymotic** *a.* pert. to or caused by fermentation. **zymotically** *adv.* **zymotic disease,** infectious or contagious disease caused by germs introduced into body from without [Gk. *zumē,* leaven].

zy·mur·gy (zì′.mur.ji.) *n.* branch of chemistry dealing with fermentation process. [Gr. *zūme* leaven + *-ourgia,* working].

THESAURUS

PLAN OF CLASSIFICATION

Class	Section	Nos.
I. ABSTRACT RELATIONS	I. Existence	1 to 8
	II. Relation	9— 24
	III. Quantity	25— 57
	IV. Order	58— 83
	V. Number	84— 105
	VI. Time	106— 139
	VII. Change	140— 152
	VIII. Causation	153— 179
II. SPACE	I. Generally	180— 191
	II. Dimensions	192— 239
	III. Form	240— 263
	IV. Motion	264— 315
III. MATTER	I. Generally	316— 320
	II. Inorganic	321— 356
	III. Organic	357— 449
	Division	
IV. INTELLECT	(I.) Formation of Ideas	450— 515
	(II.) Communication of Ideas	516— 599
V. VOLITION	(I.) Individual	600— 736
	(II.) Intersocial	737— 819
	Section	
VI. AFFECTIONS	I. Generally	820— 826
	II. Personal	827— 887
	III. Sympathetic	888— 921
	IV. Moral	922— 975
	V. Religious	976—1000

TABULAR SYNOPSIS OF CATEGORIES

CLASS I. ABSTRACT RELATIONS

I. EXISTENCE		
1°. ABSTRACT	1. Existence.	2. Inexistence.
2°. CONCRETE	3. Substantiality.	4. Unsubstantiality.
3°. FORMAL	*Internal.*	*External.*
	5. Intrinsicality.	6. Extrinsicality.
4°. MODAL	*Absolute.*	*Relative.*
	7. State.	8. Circumstance.
II. RELATION		
1°. ABSOLUTE	9. Relation.	10. Irrelation.
	11. Consanguinity.	
	12. Correlation.	
	13. Identity.	14. Contrariety.
	15. Difference.	
2°. CONTINUOUS	16. Uniformity.	16*a*. Non-uniformity.
3°. PARTIAL	17. Similarity.	18. Dissimilarity.
	19. Imitation.	20. Non-imitation.
	20*a*. Variation.	
	21. Copy.	22. Prototype.
4°. GENERAL	23. Agreement.	24. Disagreement.
III. QUANTITY		
1°. SIMPLE	*Absolute.*	*Relative.*
	25. Quantity.	26. Degree.
2°. COMPARATIVE	27. Equality.	28. Inequality.
	29. Mean.	
	30. Compensation.	
	By Comparison with a Standard.	
	31. Greatness.	32. Smallness.
	By Comparison with a similar Object.	
	33. Superiority.	34. Inferiority.
	Changes in Quantity.	
	35. Increase.	36. Decrease.
3°. CONJUNCTIVE	37. Addition.	38. Non-addition. Subduction.
	39. Adjunct.	40. Remainder.
		40*a*. Decrement.
	41. Mixture.	42. Simpleness.
	43. Junction.	44. Disjunction.
	45. Vinculum.	
	46. Coherence.	47. Incoherence.
	48. Combination.	49. Decomposition.

4°. CONCRETE	50. Whole.	51. Part.
	52. Completeness.	53. Incompleteness.
	54. Composition.	55. Exclusion.
	56. Component.	57. Extraneous.

IV. ORDER

1°. GENERAL	58. Order.	59. Disorder.
	60. Arrangement.	61. Derangement.
2°. CONSECUTIVE	62. Precedence.	63. Sequence.
	64. Precursor.	65. Sequel.
	66. Beginning.	67. End.
	68. Middle.	
	69. Continuity.	70. Discontinuity.
	71. Term.	
3°. COLLECTIVE	72. Assemblage.	73. Non-assemblage. Dispersion.
	74. Focus.	
4°. DISTRIBUTIVE	75. Class.	
	76. Inclusion.	77. Exclusion.
	78. Generality.	79. Speciality.
5°. CATEGORICAL	80. Rule.	81. Multiformity.
	82. Conformity.	83. Unconformity.

V. NUMBER

1°. ABSTRACT	84. Number.	
	85. Numeration.	
	86. List.	
2°. DETERMINATE	87. Unity.	88. Accompaniment.
	89. Duality.	
	90. Duplication.	91. Bisection.
	92. Triality.	
	93. Triplication.	96. Trisection.
	94. Quadruplication.	
	95. Quaternity.	97. Quadrisection.
	98. Five, &c.	99. Quinquesection, &c.
3°. INDETERMINATE	100. Plurality.	100*a*. Fraction.
		101. Zero.
	102. Multitude.	103. Fewness.
	104. Repetition.	
	105. Infinity.	

VI. TIME

1°. ABSOLUTE		106. Time.	107. Neverness.
		Definite.	*Indefinite.*
		108. Period.	109. Course.
		108*a*. Contingent Duration.	
		110. Diuturnity.	111. Transientness.
		112. Perpetuity.	113. Instantaneity.
		114. Chronometry.	115. Anachronism.
2°. RELATIVE	1. *to Succession*	116. Priority.	117. Posteriority.
		118. Present time.	119. Different time.
		120. Synchronism.	
	2. *to a Period*	121. Futurity.	122. Preterition.
		123. Newness.	124. Oldness.
		125. Morning.	126. Evening.
		127. Youth.	128. Age.
		129. Infant.	130. Veteran.
		131. Adolescence.	
	3. *to an Effect or purpose*	132. Earliness.	133. Lateness.
		134. Occasion.	135. Intempestivity.
3°. RECURRENT		136. Frequency.	137. Infrequency.
		138. Periodicity.	139. Irregularity.

VII. CHANGE

1°. SIMPLE	140. Change.	141. Permanence.
	142. Cessation.	143. Continuance.
	144. Conversion.	145. Reversion.
	146. Revolution.	
	147. Substitution.	148. Interchange.
2°. COMPLEX	149. Changeableness.	150. Stability.
	Present.	*Future.*
	151. Eventuality.	152. Destiny.

VIII. CAUSATION

1°. CONSTANCY OF SEQUENCE	153. { *Constant Antecedent.* Cause.	154. { *Constant Sequent.* Effect.
	155. { *Assignment of Cause.* Attribution.	156. { *Absence of Assignment.* Chance.
2°. CONNECTION BETWEEN CAUSE AND EFFECT	157. Power.	158. Impotence.
	Degrees of Power.	
	159. Strength.	160. Weakness.
3°. POWER IN OPERATION	161. Production.	162. Destruction.
	163. Reproduction.	
	164. Producer.	165. Destroyer.
	166. Paternity.	167. Posterity.
	168. Productiveness.	169. Unproductiveness.
	170. Agency.	
	171. Energy.	172. Inertness.
	173. Violence.	174. Moderation.
4°. INDIRECT POWER	175. Influence.	175*a*. Absence of Influence.
	176. Tendency.	
	177. Liability.	
5°. COMBINATIONS OF CAUSES	178. Concurrence.	179. Counteraction.

CLASS II. SPACE

I. SPACE IN GENERAL

1°. ABSTRACT SPACE		180*a*. Inextension.
	180. { *Indefinite.* Space.	181. { *Definite.* Region.
		182. { *Limited.* Place.
2°. RELATIVE SPACE	183. Situation.	
	184. Location.	185. Displacement.
3°. EXISTENCE IN SPACE	186. Presence.	187. Absence.
	188. Inhabitant.	189. Abode.
	190. Contents.	191. Receptacle.

II. DIMENSIONS

1°. GENERAL	192. Size.	193. Littleness.
	194. Expansion.	195. Contraction.
	196. Distance.	197. Nearness.
	198. Interval.	199. Contiguity.
2°. LINEAR	200. Length.	201. Shortness.
	202. { Breadth. Thickness.	203. { Narrowness. Thinness.
	204. Layer.	205. Filament.
	206. Height.	207. Lowness.
	208. Depth.	209. Shallowness.

SYNOPSIS OF CATEGORIES

2°. LINEAR—*continued*		210. Summit.	211. Base.
		212. Verticality.	213. Horizontality.
		214. Pendency.	215. Support.
		216. Parallelism.	217. Obliquity.
		218. Inversion.	
		219. Crossing.	
3°. CENTRICAL	1. *General*	220. Exteriority.	221. Interiority.
		222. Centrality.	
		223. Covering.	224. Lining.
		225. Investment.	226. Divestment.
		227. Circumjacence.	228. Interjacence.
		229. Circumscription.	
		230. Outline.	
		231. Edge.	
		232. Inclosure.	
		233. Limit.	
	2. *Special*	234. Front	235. Rear.
		236. Laterality.	237. Contraposition.
		238. Dextrality.	239. Sinistrality.

III. FORM

1°. GENERAL	240. Form.	241. Amorphism.
	242. Symmetry.	243. Distortion.
2°. SPECIAL	244. Angularity.	
	245. Curvature.	246. Straightness.
	247. Circularity.	248. Convolution.
	249. Rotundity.	
3°. SUPERFICIAL	250. Convexity.	252. Concavity.
	251. Flatness.	
	253. Sharpness.	254. Bluntness.
	255. Smoothness.	256. Roughness.
	257. Notch.	
	258. Fold.	
	259. Furrow.	
	260. Opening.	261. Closure.
	262. Perforator.	263. Stopper.

IV. MOTION

1°. MOTION IN GENERAL	264. Motion.	265. Quiescence.
	266. Journey.	267. Navigation.
	268. Traveler.	269. Mariner.
	270. Transference.	
	271. Carrier.	
	272. Vehicle.	273. Ship.
2°. DEGREES OF MOTION	274. Velocity.	275. Slowness.
3°. CONJOINED WITH FORCE	276. Impulse.	277. Recoil.
4°. WITH REFERENCE TO DIRECTION	278. Direction.	279. Deviation.
	280. Precession.	281. Sequence.
	282. Progression.	283. Regression.
	284. Propulsion.	285. Traction.
	286. Approach.	287. Recession.
	288. Attraction.	289. Repulsion.
	290. Convergence.	291. Divergence.
	292. Arrival.	293. Departure.
	294. Ingress.	295. Egress.
	296. Reception.	297. Ejection.
	298. Food.	299. Excretion.
	300. Insertion.	301. Extraction.
	302. Passage.	
	303. Overstep.	304. Shortcoming.

4°. With Reference to Direction—*cont.*...		305. Ascent.	306. Descent.
		307. Elevation.	308. Depression.
		309. Leap.	310. Plunge.
		311. Circuition.	
		312. Rotation.	313. Evolution.
		314. Oscillation.	
		315. Agitation.	

Class III. MATTER

I. MATTER IN GENERAL.......		316. Materiality.	317. Immateriality.
		318. World.	
		319. Gravity.	320. Levity.
II. INORGANIC MATTER			
1°. Solids.............		321. Density.	322. Rarity.
		323. Hardness.	324. Softness.
		325. Elasticity.	326. Inelasticity.
		327. Tenacity.	328. Brittleness.
		329. Texture.	
		330. Pulverulence.	
		331. Friction.	332. Lubrication.
2°. Fluids	1. *In General*	333. Fluidity.	334. Gaseity.
		335. Liquefaction.	336. Vaporization.
	2. *Specific*...	337. Water.	338. Air.
		339. Moisture.	340. Dryness.
		341. Ocean.	342. Land.
		343. Gulf. Lake.	344. Plain.
		345. Marsh.	346. Island.
	3. *In motion*	347. Stream.	
		348. River.	349. Wind.
		350. Conduit.	351. Air-pipe.
3°. Imperfect Fluids...		352. Semiliquidity.	353. Bubble.
		354. Pulpiness.	355. Unctuousness.
			356. Oil.
			356*a*. Resin.
III. ORGANIC MATTER			
1°. Vitality	1. *In General*....	357. Organization.	358. Inorganization.
		359. Life.	360. Death.
			361. Killing.
			362. Corpse.
			363. Interment.
	2. *Special*	364. Animality.	365. Vegetability.
		366. Animal.	367. Vegetable.
		368. Zoology.	369. Botany.
		370. Cicuration.	371. Agriculture.
		372. Mankind.	
		373. Man.	374. Woman.

SYNOPSIS OF CATEGORIES

2°. SENSATION

(1) *General*

375. Sensibility.	376. Insensibility.
377. Pleasure.	378. Pain.

(2) *Special*

1. *Touch*

379. Touch.	
380. Sensations of Touch.	381. Numbness.

2. *Heat*

382. Heat.	383. Cold.
384. Calefaction.	385. Refrigeration.
386. Furnace.	387. Refrigeratory.
388. Fuel.	
389. Thermometer.	

3. *Taste*

390. Taste.	391. Insipidity.
392. Pungency.	
393. Condiment.	
394. Savouriness.	395. Unsavouriness.
396. Sweetness.	397. Sourness.

4. *Odor*

398. Odor.	399. Inodorousness.
400. Fragrance.	401. Fœtor.

5. *Sound*

(i.) *Sound in General.*

402. Sound.	403. Silence.
404. Loudness.	405. Faintness.

(ii.) *Specific Sounds.*

406. Snap.	407. Roll.
408. Resonance.	408*a*. Non-resonance.
	409. Sibilation.
410. Stridor.	
411. Cry.	412. Ululation.

(iii.) *Musical Sounds.*

413. Melody. Concord.	414. Discord.
415. Music.	
416. Musician.	
417. Musical Instruments.	

(iv.) *Perception of Sound.*

418. Hearing.	419. Deafness.

6. *Light*

(i.) *Light in General.*

420. Light.	421. Darkness.
422. Dimness.	
423. Luminary.	424. Shade.
425. Transparency.	426. Opacity.
427. Semitransparency.	

(ii.) *Specific Light.*

428. Color.	429. Achromatism.
430. Whiteness.	431. Blackness.
432. Gray.	433. Brown.
434. Redness.	435. Greenness.
436. Yellowness.	437. Purple.
438. Blueness.	439. Orange.
440. Variegation.	

(iii.) *Perceptions of Light.*

441. Vision.	442. Blindness.
443. Dimsightedness.	
444. Spectator.	
445. Optical Instruments.	
446. Visibility.	447. Invisibility.
448. Appearance.	449. Disappearance.

SYNOPSIS OF CATEGORIES

Class IV. INTELLECT

Division (I.). Formation of Ideas

I. Operations of Intellect in General....	450. Intellect.	450*a*. Absence of Intellect.
	451. Thought.	452. Incogitancy.
	453. Idea.	454. Topic.
II. Precursory Conditions and Operations......	455. Curiosity.	456. Incuriosity.
	457. Attention.	458. Inattention.
	459. Care.	460. Neglect.
	461. Inquiry.	462. Answer.
	463. Experiment.	
	464. Comparison.	
	465. Discrimination.	465*a*. Indiscrimination.
	466. Measurement.	
III. Materials for Reasoning...........	467. Evidence.	468. Counter-evidence.
	469. Qualification.	
	Degrees of Evidence.	
	470. Possibility.	471. Impossibility.
	472. Probability.	473. Improbability.
	474. Certainty.	475. Uncertainty.
IV. Reasoning Processes .	476. Reasoning.	477. Intuition. Sophistry.
	478. Demonstration.	479. Confutation.
V. Results of Reasoning .	480. Judgement.	481. Misjudgement.
	480*a*. Discovery.	
	482. Over-estimation.	483. Under-estimation.
	484. Belief.	485. Unbelief. Doubt.
	486. Credulity.	487. Incredulity.
	488. Assent.	489. Dissent.
	490. Knowledge.	491. Ignorance.
	492. Scholar.	493. Ignoramus.
	494. Truth.	495. Error.
	496. Maxim.	497. Absurdity.
	Faculties.	
	498. Intelligence. Wisdom.	499. Imbecility. Folly.
	500. Sage.	501. Fool.
	502. Sanity.	503. Insanity.
		504. Madman.
VI. Extension of Thought — 1°. *To the Past*...	505. Memory.	506. Oblivion.
VI. Extension of Thought — 2°. *To the Future*.	507. Expectation.	508. Inexpectation.
		509. Disappointment.
	510. Foresight.	
	511. Prediction.	
	512. Omen.	
	513. Oracle.	
VII. Creative Thought..	514. Supposition.	
	515. Imagination.	

SYNOPSIS OF CATEGORIES

Division (II.). Communication of Ideas

I. Nature of Ideas Communicated

516. Meaning. — 517. Unmeaningness.
518. Intelligibility. — 519. Unintelligibility.
520. Equivocalness.
521. Metaphor.
522. Interpretation. — 523. Misinterpretation.
524. Interpreter.

II. Modes of Communication

525. Manifestation. — 526. Latency.
527. Information. — 528. Concealment.
529. Disclosure. — 530. Ambush.
531. Publication.
532. News. — 533. Secret.
534. Messenger.
535. Affirmation. — 536. Negation.
537. Teaching. — 538. Misteaching. 539. Learning.
540. Teacher. — 541. Learner.
542. School.
543. Veracity. — 544. Falsehood. 545. Deception. 546. Untruth.
547. Dupe. — 548. Deceiver. 549. Exaggeration.

III. Means of Communication

1°. Natural Means

550. Indication.
551. Record. — 552. Obliteration.
553. Recorder.
554. Representation. — 555. Misrepresentation.
556. Painting.
557. Sculpture.
558. Engraving.
559. Artist.

2°. Conventional Means

1. Language generally

560. Language.
561. Letter.
562. Word. — 563. Neology.
564. Nomenclature. — 565. Misnomer.
566. Phrase.
567. Grammar. — 568. Solecism.
569. Style.

Qualities of Style.

570. Perspicuity. — 571. Obscurity.
572. Conciseness. — 573. Diffuseness.
574. Vigour. — 575. Feebleness.
576. Plainness. — 577. Ornament.
578. Elegance. — 579. Inelegance.

2. Spoken Language

580. Voice. — 581. Aphony.
582. Speech. — 583. Stammering.
584. Loquacity. — 585. Taciturnity.
586. Allocution. — 587. Response.
588. Interlocution. — 589. Soliloquy.

3. Written Language

590. Writing. — 591. Printing.
592. Correspondence. — 593. Book.
594. Description.
595. Dissertation.
596. Compendium.
597. Poetry. — 598. Prose.
599. The Drama.

Class V. VOLITION

Division (I.). Individual Volition

I. Volition in General

1°. *Acts*

600. Will.	601. Necessity.
602. Willingness.	603. Unwillingness.
604. Resolution.	605. Irresolution.
604*a*. Perseverance. 606. Obstinacy.	607. Tergiversation.
	608. Caprice.
609. Choice.	609*a*. Absence of Choice. 610. Rejection.
611. Predetermination.	612. Impulse.
613. Habit.	614. Desuetude.

2°. *Causes*

615. Motive.	615*a*. Absence of Motive. 616. Dissuasion.
617. Plea.	

3°. *Objects*

618. Good.	619. Evil.

II. Prospective Volition

1°. *Conceptional*

620. Intention.	621. Chance.
622. Pursuit.	623. Avoidance.
	624. Relinquishment.
625. Business.	
626. Plan.	
627. Method.	
628. Mid-Course.	629. Circuit.
630. Requirement.	

2°. *Subservience to Ends*

1. *Actual Subservience.*

631. Instrumentality.	
632. Means.	
633. Instrument.	
634. Substitute.	
635. Materials.	
636. Store.	
637. Provision.	638. Waste.
639. Sufficiency.	
641. Redundance.	640. Insufficiency.

2. *Degree of Subservience.*

642. Importance.	643. Unimportance.
644. Utility.	645. Inutility.
646. Expedience.	647. Inexpedience.
648. Goodness.	649. Badness.
650. Perfection.	651. Imperfection.
652. Cleanness.	653. Uncleanness.
654. Health.	655. Disease.
656. Salubrity.	657. Insalubrity.
658. Improvement.	659. Deterioration.
660. Restoration.	661. Relapse.
662. Remedy.	663. Bane.

3. *Contingent Subservience.*

664. Safety.	665. Danger.
666. Refuge.	667. Pitfall.
668. Warning.	
669. Alarm.	
670. Preservation.	
671. Escape.	
672. Deliverance.	

II. Prospective Volition—*cont.*	3°. *Precursory Measures*	673. Preparation.	674. Non-preparation.
		675. Essay.	
		676. Undertaking.	
		677. Use.	678. Disuse.
			679. Misuse.
III. Action	1°. *Simple*	680. Action.	681. Inaction.
		682. Activity.	683. Inactivity.
		684. Haste.	685. Leisure.
		686. Exertion.	687. Repose.
		688. Fatigue.	689. Refreshment.
		690. Agent.	
		691. Workshop.	
	2°. *Complex*	692. Conduct.	
		693. Direction.	
		694. Director.	
		695. Advice.	
		696. Council.	
		697. Precept.	
		698. Skill.	699. Unskilfulness.
		700. Proficient.	701. Bungler.
		702. Cunning.	703. Artlessness.
IV. Antagonism	1°. *Conditional*	704. Difficulty.	705. Facility.
	2°. *Active*	706. Hindrance.	707. Aid.
		708. Opposition.	709. Co-operation.
		710. Opponent.	711. Auxiliary.
		712. Party.	
		713. Discord.	714. Concord.
		715. Defiance.	
		716. Attack.	717. Defence.
		718. Retaliation.	719. Resistance.
		720. Contention.	721. Peace.
		722. Warfare.	723. Pacification.
		724. Meditation.	
		725. Submission.	
		726. Combatant.	
		727. Arms.	
		728. Arena.	
V. Results of Action		729. Completion.	730. Non-completion.
		731. Success.	732. Failure.
		733. Trophy.	
		734. Prosperity.	735. Adversity.
		736. Mediocrity.	

Division (II.). Intersocial Volition

I. General		737. Authority.	738. Laxity.
		739. Severity.	740. Lenity.
		741. Command.	
		742. Disobedience.	743. Obedience.
		744. Compulsion.	
		745. Master.	746. Servant.
		747. Sceptre.	
		748. Freedom.	749. Subjection.
		750. Liberation.	751. Restraint.
			752. Prison.
		753. Keeper.	754. Prisoner.
		755. Commission.	756. Abrogation.
			757. Resignation.
		758. Consignee.	
		759. Deputy.	

II. SPECIAL	760. Permission.	761. Prohibition.
	762. Consent.	
	763. Offer.	764. Refusal.
	765. Request.	766. Depreciation.
	767. Petitioner.	
III. CONDITIONAL	768. Promise.	768*a*. Release.
	769. Compact.	
	770. Conditions.	
	771. Security.	
	772. Observance.	773. Non-observance.
	774. Compromise.	
IV. POSSESSIVE RELATIONS		
1°. *Property in General*	775. Acquisition.	776. Loss.
	777. Possession.	777*a*. Exemption.
	778. Participation.	
	779. Possessor.	
	780. Property.	
	781. Retention.	782. Relinquishment.
2°. *Transfer of Property*	783. Transfer.	
	784. Giving.	785. Receiving.
	786. Apportionment.	
	787. Lending.	788. Borrowing.
	789. Taking.	790. Restitution.
	791. Stealing.	
	792. Thief.	
	793. Booty.	
3°. *Interchange of Property*	794. Barter.	
	795. Purchase.	796. Sale.
	797. Merchant.	
	798. Merchandise.	
	799. Mart.	
4°. *Monetary Relations*	800. Money.	
	801. Treasurer.	
	802. Treasury.	
	803. Wealth.	804. Poverty.
	805. Credit.	806. Debt.
	807. Payment.	808. Non-payment.
	809. Expenditure.	810. Receipt.
	811. Accounts.	
	812. Price.	813. Discount.
	814. Dearness.	815. Cheapness.
	816. Liberality.	817. Economy.
	818. Prodigality.	819. Parsimony.

CLASS VI. AFFECTIONS

I. AFFECTIONS GENERALLY	820. Affections.	
	821. Feeling.	
	822. Sensibility.	823. Insensibility.
	824. Excitation.	
	825. Excitability.	826. Inexcitability.

II. PERSONAL

1°. PASSIVE	827. Pleasure.	828. Pain.
	829. Pleasureableness.	830. Painfulness.
	831. Content.	832. Discontent. 833. Regret.
	834. Relief.	835. Aggravation.
	836. Cheerfulness.	837. Dejection.
	838. Rejoicing.	839. Lamentation.
	840. Amusement.	841. Weariness.
	842. Wit.	843. Dulness.
	844. Humorist.	
2°. DISCRIMINATIVE	845. Beauty.	846. Ugliness.
	847. Ornament.	848. Blemish.
		849. Simplicity.
	850. Taste.	851. Vulgarity.
	852. Fashion.	
		853. Ridiculousness.
		854. Fop.
		855. Affection.
		856. Ridicule.
		857. Laughing-stock.
3°. PROSPECTIVE	858. Hope.	859. Hopelessness. 860. Fear.
	861. Courage.	862. Cowardice.
	863. Rashness.	864. Caution.
	865. Desire.	867. Dislike.
	866. Indifference.	
		868. Fastidiousness.
		869. Satiety.
4°. CONTEMPLATIVE	870. Wonder.	871. Expectance.
	872. Prodigy.	
5°. EXTRINSIC	873. Repute.	874. Disrepute.
	875. Nobility.	876. Commonalty.
	877. Title.	
	878. Pride.	879. Humility.
	880. Vanity.	881. Modesty.
	882. Ostentation.	
	883. Celebration.	
	884. Boasting.	
	885. Insolence.	886. Servility.
	887. Blusterer.	

III. SYMPATHETIC

1°. SOCIAL	888. Friendship.	889. Enmity.
	890. Friend.	891. Enemy.
	892. Sociality.	893. Seclusion.
	894. Courtesy.	895. Discourtesy.
	896. Congratulation.	
	897. Love.	898. Hate.
	899. Favorite.	
		900. Resentment.
		901. Irascibility.
		901*a*. Sullenness.
	902. Endearment.	
	903. Marriage.	904. Celibacy. 905. Divorce.

2°. DIFFUSIVE........	906. Benevolence.	907. Malevolence.
		908. Malediction.
		909. Threat.
	910. Philanthropy.	911. Misanthropy.
3°. SPECIAL..........	912. Benefactor.	913. Evil doer.
	914. Pity.	914*a*. Pitilessness.
	915. Condolence.	
4°. RETROSPECTIVE....	916. Gratitude.	917. Ingratitude.
	918. Forgiveness.	919. Revenge.
		920. Jealousy.
		921. Envy.

IV. MORAL

1°. OBLIGATIONS.......	922. Right.	923. Wrong.
	924. Dueness.	925. Undueness.
	926. Duty.	927. Dereliction. 927*a*. Exemption.
2°. SENTIMENTS........	928. Respect.	929. Disrespect.
		930. Contempt.
	931. Approbation.	932. Disapprobation.
	933. Flattery.	934. Detraction.
	935. Flatterer.	936. Detractor.
	937. Vindication.	938. Accusation.
3°. CONDITIONS........	939. Probity.	940. Improbity.
		941. Knave.
	942. Disinterestedness.	943. Selfishness.
	944. Virtue.	945. Vice.
	946. Innocence.	947. Guilt.
	948. Good Man.	949. Bad Man.
	950. Penitence.	951. Impenitence.
	952. Atonement.	
4°. PRACTICE..........	953. Temperance.	954. Intemperance.
		954*a*. Sensualist.
	955. Asceticism.	
	956. Fasting.	957. Gluttony.
	958. Sobriety.	959. Drunkenness.
	960. Purity.	961. Impurity.
		962. Libertine.
5°. INSTITUTIONS......	963. Legality.	964. Illegality.
	965. Jurisprudence.	
	966. Tribunal.	
	967. Judge.	
	968. Lawyer.	
	969. Lawsuit.	
	970. Acquittal.	971. Condemnation.
	973. Reward.	972. Punishment. 974. Penalty.
		975. Scourge.

V. RELIGIOUS

1°. SUPERHUMAN BEINGS AND REGIONS..	976. Deity.	
	977. Angel.	978. Satan:
	979. Jupiter.	980. Demon.
	981. Heaven.	982. Hell.
2°. DOCTRINES........	983. Theology.	
	983*a*. Orthodoxy.	984. Heterodoxy.
	985. Revelation.	986. Pseudo-revelation.
3°. SENTIMENTS........	987. Piety.	988. Impiety.
		989. Irreligion.

SYNOPSIS OF CATEGORIES

4°. ACTS	990. Worship.	991. Idolatry 992. Sorcery. 993. Spell. 994. Sorcerer.
5°. INSTITUTIONS	995. Churchdom. 996. Clergy. 998. Rite. 999. Canonicals. 1000. Temple.	997. Laity.

ABBREVIATIONS, &c.

Adj. *adj.* Adjectives, Participles, and Words having the power of Adjectives.
Adv. *adv.* Adverbs and Adverbial Expressions.
Int. *int.* Interjections.
Phr. *phr.* Phrases.
V. *v.* Verbs.

The numbers are those of the headings, or Categories.

Words in italics within parentheses are not intended to explain the meanings of the words which precede them, but to indicate the nature of allied group of words under the numbers which follow them.

THESAURUS

OF

ENGLISH WORDS AND PHRASES

1. Existence.—N. existence, being, entity, *ens, esse,* subsistence, quiddity.

reality, realness, actuality; positiveness etc. *adj.*; fact, matter of fact, sober reality; truth etc. 494; actual existence.

presence etc. (*existence in space*) 186; coexistence etc. 120.

stubborn fact; not a -dream etc. 515; no joke.

substance, essence, prime constituent, hypostatis.

[Science of existence], ontology.

V. exist, be; have -being etc. *n.*; subsist, live, breathe, stand, obtain, be the case; occur etc. (*event*) 151; have place, rank, prevail; find oneself, pass the time, vegetate.

consist in, lie in, reside in, inhere in.

come into -existence etc. *n.*; arise etc. (*begin*) 66; come forth etc. (*appear*) 446.

become etc. (*be converted*) 144; bring into existence etc. 161; coexist, preexist, endure etc. 141.

Adj. existing etc. *v.*; existent, subsistent, under the sun; in -existence etc. *n.*; extant; afloat, on foot, current, prevalent, rife, in force, -vogue; undestroyed.

real, actual, positive, absolute; true etc. 494; substan-tial, -tive; self-existing, -ent.

well-founded, -grounded; un-ideal, -imagined; not -potential etc. 2.

Adv. actually etc. *adj.*; in -fact, – point of fact, – reality; indeed; *de –*, *ipso-facto.*

2. Nonexistence.—N. nonexistence; inexistence, -subsistence; nonentity, *nil*; negativeness etc. *adj.*; nullity; nihil-ity, -ism; *tabula rasa,* blank; abeyance; absence etc. 187; no such thing etc. 4; nothingness, oblivion, *non esse.*

annihilation; extinction etc. (*destruction*) 162.

V. not -exist etc. 1; have no -existence etc. 1; be null and void; cease to -exist etc. 1; pass away, perish; be –, become-extinct etc. *adj.*; die out; disappear etc. 449; melt away, dissolve, leave not a rack behind, leave no trace; go, be no more; die etc. 360.

annihilate, render null, nullify; abrogate etc. 756; destroy etc. 162; take away; remove etc. (*displace*) 185.

Adj. inexistent, non-existent etc. 1; negative, blank, null and void; missing, omitted; absent etc. 187; visionary etc. 515.

unreal, potential, virtual; baseless, *in nubibus*; unsubstantial etc. 4; vain.

un-born, -created, -begotten, -conceived, produced, -made.

perished, annihilated etc. *v.*; extinct, exhausted, gone, lost, departed; defunct etc. (*dead*) 360;

fabulous, ideal etc. (*imaginary*) 515; suppositition etc. 514.

Adv. negatively, virtually, etc. *adj.*

3. Substantiality.—N. substantiality, *hypostasis*; person, thing, object, article; something, a being, an existence; creature, body, substance, flesh and blood, stuff, *substratum*; matter etc. 316; physical nature.

[Totality of existences], world etc. 318; *plenum.*

Adj. substan-tive, -tial, concrete; hypostatic; personal, bodily; tangible etc. (*material*) 316; real, corporeal, evident.

Adv. substantially etc. *adj.*; bodily, essentially.

4. Unsubstantiality.—N. un-, in-substantiality; nothingness, nihility.

nothing, naught, *nil*, nullity, zero, cipher, no one, nobody; never –, ne'er -a one; no such thing, none in the world; nothing -whatever, – at all, – on earth; not a -particle etc. (*smallness*) 32; all -talk, – moonshine, – stuff and nonsense, matter of no import.

thing of naught, man of straw, John Doe and Richard Roe; *nominis umbra,* nonentity, figurehead, lay figure; flash in the pan, *vox et praeterea nihil.*

shadow; phantasm, phantom etc. (*fallacy of vision*) 443; dream etc. (*imagination*) 515; *ignis fatuus* etc. (*luminary*) 423; 'such stuff as dreams are made of;' air, thin air; bubble etc. 353; 'baseless fabric of a vision;' mockery.

hollowness, blank; vacuity, void etc. (*absence*) 187.

inanity, fool's paradise, fatuity, stupidity, emptiness of mind.

V. vanish, evaporate, fade, sink, fly –, die –, melt- away, dissolve, disappear etc. 449; become extinct, become invisible.

Adj. unsubstantial; fleeting; base-, ground-less; ungrounded; without –, having no- foundation.

visionary etc. (*imaginary*) 515; immaterial etc. 317; spectral etc. 980; dreamy; shadowy; ethereal, airy, imponderable, tenuous, vague.

vacant, vacuous; empty etc. 187; eviscerated; blank, hollow; nominal; null; inane.

Phr. there's nothing in it.

5. Intrinsicality.—N. intrinsicality, inbeing, inherence, inhesion, immanence; subjectiveness; *ego*; essence; essentialness etc. *adj.*; essential part, essential stuff, substance, quintessence, incarnation, quiddity, gist, pith, core, kernel, marrow, sap, lifeblood, backbone, heart, soul, life, flower; important part etc. (*importance*) 642.

principle, nature, constitution, character, ethos, type, quality, crasis, *diathesis.*

habit; temper, -ament; spirit, humor, grain, disposition, streak, tendency etc. 176.

endowment, capacity; capability etc. (*power*) 157; moods, declensions, features, aspects; peculiarities etc. (*specialty*) 79; idiosyncrasy; idiocrasy; diagnostics.

V. be –, run- in the blood; be born so; be -intrinsic etc. *adj.*

Adj. derived from within, subjective; idiocratic, idiosyncratic, intrin-sic, -sical; fundamental, cardinal, normal, inherent, essential, natural; in-nate, -born, -bred, -dwelling, -grained; -wrought; radical, incarnate, thoroughbred, hereditary, inherited, immanent; congen-ital, -ite; connate, running in the blood; coeval with birth, genetic, ingenerate, -genite; indigenous; in the -grain etc. *n.*; bred in the bone, instinctive; inward, internal etc. 221; to the manner born; virtual.

characteristic etc. (*special*) 79, (*indicative*) 550; invariable, incurable, ineradicable, fixed, settled, constant, unchanging.

Adv. intrinsically etc. *adj.*; at bottom, in the main, in effect, essentially, practically, virtually, substantially, *au fond*; fairly.

6. Extrinsicality.—N. extrinsicality, objectiveness, *non ego;* extraneousness etc. 57; accident; letter of the law.

Adj. derived from without; objective; extrinsic, -sical; extraneous etc. (*foreign*) 57; modal, adventitious, additional, supervenient, fortuitous; a-, ad-scititious; incidental, casual, accidental, unessential, non-essential, accessory.

implanted, ingrafted; instilled, inculcated.

outward etc. (*external*) 220.

Adv. extrinsically etc. *adj.*

7. State.—N. state, condition, category, estate, lot, case, trim, mood, pickle, plight etc. 704; temper; aspect etc. (*appearance*) 448.

constitution, habitude, *diathesis;* frame, fabric etc. 329; stamp, set, fit, mold.

mode, modality, schesis; fettle; form etc. (*shape*) 240.

tone, tenor, turn; trim, guise, fashion, light, complexion, style, character.

V. be in –, possess –, enjoy –, labor under- a -state etc. *n.;* be on a footing, do, fare; come to pass.

Adj. conditional, modal, formal; structural, organic.

Adv. conditionally etc. *adj.;* as -the matter stands, – things are; such being the case etc. 8.

8. Circumstance.—N. circumstance, situation, phase, position, posture, attitude, place, point; terms; *régime;* footing, standing, status.

occasion, juncture, conjuncture; contingency etc. (*event*) 151.

predicament; emergen-ce, -cy; exigency, crisis, pinch, pass, push; turning point; crossroads.

bearings, how the land lies.

Adj. circumstantial; given, conditional, provisional; critical; modal; contingent, incidental; adventitious etc. (*extrinsic*) 6.

Adv. in the circumstances etc. *n.*, under the conditions etc. 7; thus, in such wise.

accordingly; that –, such- being the case; that being so, since, seeing that.

as matters stand; as -things, – times- go.

conditionally, provided, if, in case; if -so, – so be, – it be so; if it so -happen, – turn out; in the event of; in such a -contingency, – case, – event; provisionally, unless, without.

according to -circumstances, – the occasion; as it may -happen, – turn out, – be; as the -case may be, – wind blows; *pro re natâ.*

9. Relation.—N. relation, bearing, reference, connection, apposition, interconnection, concern, cognation; applicability, appositeness; correlation etc. 12; analogy; similarity etc. 17; affinity, intimacy, friendship; homology, alliance, homogeneity, association, rapport; approximation etc. (*nearness*) 197; filiation etc. (*consanguinity*) 11; interest; relevancy etc. 23; relationship, relative position; relativity; interrelation etc. 12.

comparison etc. 464; ratio, proportion.

link, tie, bond, bond of union.

V. be-related etc. *adj.;* have a relation etc. *n.;* relate –, refer- to; bear upon, regard, concern, touch, affect, have to do with; pertain –, belong –, appertain- to; have respect to; answer to; interest.

bring -into relation with, – to bear upon; connect, associate, draw a parallel; link etc. 43.

Adj. relative; correlative etc. 12; cognate; relating to etc. *v.;* relative to, in relation with, referable *or* referrible to; belonging to etc. *v.;* appurtenant to, in common with.

related, connected; implicated, associated, affiliated, akin, allied to; collateral, cognate, congenial, kindred, affinitive, *en rapport*, in touch with.

approxima-tive, -ting; approaching; proportion-al, -ate, -able; allusive, comparable.

in the same -category etc. 75; like etc. 17; relevant etc. (*apt*) 23.

Adv. relatively etc. *adj.;* pertinently etc. 23.

thereof; as -to, – for, – respects, – re-gards; about; concerning etc. *v.;* anent; relating –, as relates- to; with -relation, – reference, – respect, – regard-to; in respect of; while speaking –, *à propos*-of; in connection with; by the -way, – by; whereas; for –, in -as much as; in point of, as far as; on the -part, – score- of; *quoad hoc; pro re natâ;* under the -head etc. (*class*) 75- of; in the matter of, *in re.*

Phr. 'thereby hangs a tale.'

10. Irrelation. [Want, or absence of relation.]**—N.** irrelation, dissociation; inapplicability; inconnection; multifariousness; disconnection etc. (*disjunction*) 44; inconsequence, independence; incommensurability; irreconcilableness etc. (*disagreement*) 24; heterogeneity;

unconformity etc. 83; irrelevancy, impertinence, *nihil ad rem;* intrusion etc. 24.

V. have no -relation etc. 9 to, – bearing upon, – concern etc. 9 with, – business with; not -concern etc. 9; have -nothing to do with, – no business there; intrude, etc. 24.

bring –, drag –, haul –, lug- in head and shoulders.

Adj. irrelative, irrespective, unrelated, irrelated; arbitrary; independent, unallied; un-, dis-connected; adrift, isolated, insular; extraneous, strange, alien, foreign, outlandish, exotic.

not comparable, incommensurable, heterogeneous; unconformable etc. 83.

irrelevant; rambling etc. 279; inapplicable; not -pertinent, – to the purpose; impertinent, inapposite, beside the mark, *à propos de bottes;* away from –, foreign to –, beside- the -purpose, – question, – transaction, – point; misplaced etc. (*intrusive*) 24.

remote, far fetched, out of the way, forced, neither here nor there, quite another thing; detached, segregated, segregate.

multifarious; discordant etc. 24.

incidental, parenthetical, *obiter dictum,* episodic.

Adv. parenthetically etc. *adj.;* by the -way, – by; *en passant,* incidentally; irrespecitively etc. *adj.;* without reference, – regard- to; in the abstract etc. 87; *a se.*

11. Consanguinity. [Relations of kindred.]—**N.** consanguinity, relationship, kindred, blood; parentage etc. (*paternity*) 166; filiation, affiliation; lineage, agnation, connection, cognation, alliance; family -connection, – tie; ties of blood; blood relationship; nepotism.

kins-man, -folk; people; kith and kin; relation, -tive; connection; sib; next of kin; uncle, aunt, nephew, niece; cousin, -german; first –, second- cousin; cousin -once, – twice etc.- removed; near –, distant-relation; brother, sister, one's own flesh and blood.

family, patriarch, matriarch; fraternity; brother-, sister-, cousin-hood.

race, stock, generation; sept etc. 166 ; stirps, side; strain; breed, clan, tribe.

V. be -related etc. *adj.* – to; claim -relationship etc. *n.*- with.

Adj. related, akin, consanguineous, matrilinear, patrilineal, of the blood, family, allied, collateral; cog-, ag-, con-nate; kindred; affiliated, affine; fraternal, avuncular.

intimately –, nearly –, closely –, remotely –, distantly- related, – allied; german.

12. Correlation. [Double or reciprocal relation.]—**N.** reciprocalness etc. *adj.;* recipro-city, -cality, -cation; mutuality, correlation, correspondence, interdependence; interchange etc. 148; exchange, barter; interrelation, interconnection; alternation, see-saw.

V. reciprocate, alternate; interchange etc. 148; exchange; counterchange; interact, correspond, mutualize, give and take.

Adj. reciprocal, mutual, commutual, correlative; alternate; interchangeable; international; correspondent, complementary, analogous.

Adv. *mutatis mutandis; vice versâ;* each other; by turns etc. 148; reciprocally etc. *adj.;* to and fro etc. 314.

13. Identity.—**N.** identity, sameness, oneness, ditto, homogeneity; unity, coincidence, coalescence; convertibility; equality etc. 27; selfness, self, oneself; identification.

monotony, tautology etc. (*repetition*) 104.

synonym.

fac-simile etc. (*copy*) 21; *alter ego* etc. (*similar*) 17; *ipsissima verba* etc. (*exactness*) 494; same; self –, very –, one and the same; very –, actual-thing, no other.

V. be -identical etc. *adj.;* match, coincide, coalesce.

treat as –, render--the same , –identical; identify; recognize the identity of.

Adj. identical; self, ilk; the -same etc. *n.;* self same; synonymous; one and the same.

coincid-, coalesc-ent, -ing; indistinguishable; one; equivalent etc. (*equal*) 27; much -the same, – of a muchness; unaltered.

Adv. identically etc. *adj.;* on all fours; ibid-, -em.

14. Contrariety. [Non-coincidence.]—**N.** contrariety, contrast, foil, antithesis, oppositeness; counterpole; contradiction; antagonism etc. (*opposition*) 708; counteraction etc. 179.

inversion etc. 218; the -opposite, – reverse, – inverse, – converse, – antipodes, – other extreme etc. 237.

antonym.

V. be -contrary etc. *adj.;* contrast with, oppose; differ *toto coelo.*

invert, reverse, turn the tables etc. 218.

contra-dict, -vene; antagonize etc. 708.

Adj. contrar-y, -ious, -iant; opposite, counter, dead against; ad-, con-, reverse; opposed, antithetical, contrasted, antipodean, antagonistic, opposing; conflicting, inconsistent, contradictory, at cross purposes; negative; hostile etc. 708.

differing *toto coelo;* diametrically opposite; as opposite as -black and white, – light and darkness, – fire and water, – the poles, as different as chalk from cheese; 'Hyperion to a satyr;' quite the -contrary, – reverse; no such thing, just the other way, *tout au contraire.*

Adv. contrarily etc. *adj.; contra,* contrariwise, *per contra,* on the contrary, nay rather; topsyturvy; *vice versâ;* on the other hand etc. (*in compensation*) 30.

15. Difference.—**N.** difference, unlikeness; heterogeneity; vari-ance, -ation, -ety; diversity, dissimilarity etc. 18; disagreement etc. 24; disparity etc. (*inequality*) 28; distinction, contradistinction; distinctness; discrepancy, divergence, contrast etc. 18; nonconformity, incompatibility, antithesis.

discord etc. 713.

modification, moods and tenses.

nice –, fine –, delicate –, subtle- distinction; shade of difference, *nuance;* discrimination etc. 465; *differentia.*

different thing, something else, variant, apple

off another tree, horse of another color, another pair of shoes; this that or the other.

V. be -different etc. *adj.;* differ, vary, ablude, mismatch, contrast; diverge –, depart –, deviate- -from; divaricate; differ -*toto coelo*, — *longo intervallo*.

disagree etc. 713.

vary, modify etc. (*change*) 140.

discriminate etc. 465.

Adj. differing etc. *v.;* different, diverse, divided, heterogeneous; distinguishable; varied, modified; divergent, incongruous, diversified, various; discrepant, dissentient, differential; divers, all manner of; variform etc. 81; discordant etc. 713.

other, another, not the same; unequal etc. 28; unmatched; widely apart.

distinctive, characteristic; discriminative; distinghishing.

Adv. differently etc. *adj.*

Phr. *il y a fagots et fagots; tot nomines tot sententiae;* one man's meat is another man's poison.

16. Uniformity.—**N.** uniformity; homogeneity, -ousness; continuity, stability, consistency; connatural-ity, -ness; homology; accordance; conformity etc. 82; agreement etc. 23.

regularity, constancy, even tenor, routine; monotony, evenness, sameness, dead level; steadiness, equability, unity.

V. be -uniform etc. *adj.;* accord with etc. 23; run through.

become -uniform etc. *adj.;* conform to etc. 82.

render uniform etc. *adj.;* assimilate, level, smooth, dress.

Adj. uniform; homo-geneous, -logous; of a piece, consistent, steady; connatural; monotonous, changeless, dreary, even, invariable, equable, level, regular, stereotyped, unchanged, unvarying; methodical etc. 60; habitual etc. 613.

Adv. uniformly etc. *adj.;* uniformly with etc. (*conformably*) 82; in harmony with etc. (*agreeing*) 23; in a -rut, – groove.

always, ever etc. 112; invariably, without exception, never otherwise; by clock-work; endlessly etc. 112.

Phr. *ab uno disce omnes.*

16a. Non-uniformity. [Absence or want of uniformity.]–**N.** diversity, irregularity, unevenness; multiformity etc. 81; unconformity etc. 83; roughness etc. 256; heterogeneity, heteromorphism.

Adj. diversified, varied, irregular, uneven, rough etc. 256; multifarious; multiform etc. 81; of various kinds; all -manner, – sorts, – kinds-of.

Adv. in all manner of ways, here there and everywhere.

17. Similarity.—**N.** similarity, resemblance, likeness, similitude, semblance; affinity, approximation, parallelism; parity; agreement etc. 23; ana-logy, -logicalness; correspondence, equality etc.

connatural-ness, -ity; brotherhood, family likeness.

alliteration, rhyme, pun.

repetition etc. 104; sameness etc. (*identity*) 13; uniformity etc. 16.

analogue; the like; match, *pendant*, fellow, companion, pair, mate, twin, double, counterpart, brother, sister; one's second self, *alter ego*, chip of the old block, *par nobile fratrum*, *Arcades ambo*, birds of a feather, *et hoc genus omne*.

parallel; simile; type etc. (*metaphor*) 521; image etc. (*representation*) 554; photograph; close –, striking –, speaking –, faithful etc. *adj.* – likeness, – resemblance.

V. be -similar etc. *adj.;* look like, resemble, bear resemblance, favor; savor –, smack- of; approximate; parallel, match, rhyme with; take after; imitate etc. 19; run in pairs.

Adj. similar; resembling etc. *v.;* like, alike; twin.

analog-ous, -ical; parallel, of a piece; such as, so.

connatural, congeneric, allied to; corresponding, cognate; akin to etc. (*consanguineous*) 11.

approximate, much the same, near, close, something like, such like; a show of; mock, *pseudo*, simulating, representing.

exact etc. (*true*) 494; lifelike, faithful, realistic; true to -nature, – the life; the -very image – picture- of; for all the world like, *comme deux gouttes d'eau;* as like as -two peas, – it can stare; *instar omnium*, case in the same mold, ridiculously like.

Adv. as if, so to speak; as –, as if- it were; *quasi*, just as, *veluti in speculum*.

18. Dissimilarity.—**N.** dissimil-arity, -itude; unlikeness, diversity, disparity, dissemblance; divergence, inequality, difference etc. 15; novelty; variation, variety, originality, disguise.

V. be -unlike etc. *adj.;* vary etc. (*differ*) 15; bear no resemblance to, differ *toto coelo*.

render -unlike etc. *adj.;* vary etc. (*diversify*) 140.

Adj. dissimilar, unlike, disparate; of a different kind etc. (*class*) 75; unmatched, unique; new, novel; unprecedented etc. 83; original.

nothing of the kind; no such –, quite anotherthing; far from it, other than, cast in a different mold, *tertium quid*, as like a dock as a daisy, 'very like a whale;' as different as -chalk from cheese, – Macedon and Monmouth; *lucus a non lucendo*.

diversified etc. 16*a*.

Adv. otherwise, *alias*.

19. Imitation.—**N.** imitation; copying etc. *v.;* transcription; repetition, mimeograph, mimeotype, duplication, reduplication; quotation; reproduction.

mockery, mimicry, mime, simulation, personation; representation etc. 554; semblance, pretence; copy etc. 21; assimilation.

paraphrase, parody etc. 21.

plagiarism; forgery etc. (*falsehood*) 544.

imitator; echo, cuckoo, parrot, ape, monkey, mocking-bird, mimic, impersonator, copyist.

V. imitate, copy, mirror, reflect, reproduce, repeat, borrow; do like, echo, re-echo, catch; transcribe; match, parallel.

mock, take off, mimic, ape, simulate, personate, impersonate; forge; act etc. (*drama*) 599; represent etc. 554; counterfeit, duplicate; portray, parody, travesty, caricature, burlesque.

follow –, tread- in the- -steps, – footsteps, – wake- of; pattern after, take pattern by; follow - suit, – the example of; walk in the shoes of, take a leaf out of another's book, strike in with; take –, model -after; emulate.

Adj. imitated etc. *v.;* mock, mimic; counterfeit, false, pseudo; modelled after, molded on, paraphrastic; literal; imitative, apish; second-hand; imitable; sham etc. 545.

Adv. literally, to the letter, strictly, precisely, *verbatim, literatim, sic, totidem verbis,* word for word, *mot à mot.*

Phr. like master like man.

20. Non-Imitation.—N. no imitation, genuineness, originality; creativeness.

Adj. unimitated, uncopied; unmatched, unparalleled; inimitable etc. 33; *unique,* original, primordial, primary, pristine, underived, first-hand, archetypal, prototypal.

20a. Variation.—N. variation; alteration etc. (*change*) 140. modification, moods and tenses; modulation.

divergency etc. 291; deviation etc. 279; aberration; innovation.

V. vary etc. (*change*) 140; deviate etc. 279; diverge etc. 291.

Adj. varied etc. *v.;* modified; dissimilar etc. 18; diversified etc. 16*a.*

21. Copy. [Result of imitation.]—**N.** copy, facsimile, counterpart, *effigies,* effigy, symbol, image, form, likeness, similitude, semblance, resemblance, cast, electrotype, stereotype, tracing, ectype; imitation etc. 19; model, representation, adumbration, study; counterfeit presentment, portrait etc. (*representment*) 554.

duplicate; transcript, -ion; reflex, -ion; shadow, echo; chip of the old block; reprint, reproduction, casting, engraving, replica; transfer; second edition etc. (*repetition*) 104; *réchauffé* apograph, fair copy; revise.

parody, caricature, cartoon, burlesque, travesty, paraphrase.

servile -copy, – imitation; counterfeit etc. (*deception*) 545; *pasticcio.*

Adj. faithful; lifelike etc. (*similar*) 17.

22. Prototype. [Thing copied.]—**N.** prototype, original, model, pattern, founding, precedent, standard, scantling, type, arche-, anti-type: protoplast, copy-book, module, exemplar, example, ensample, specimen; paradigm; guide; templet; lay-figure.

text, copy, manuscript, MS., design; fugleman, keynote.

die, mold; matrix, engraving, last, plasm; pro-, proto-plasm; mint; seal, punch, *intaglio,* negative, stamp.

V. be –, set- an example; set a copy; standardize.

23. Agreement.—N. agreement; ac-cord, -cordance; unison, harmony, concord etc. 714; concordance, concert, understanding, convention, *entente -cordiale, consortium,* consensus of opinion, pact, mutual understanding, unanimity.

conformity etc. 82; conformance; uniformity etc. 16; consonance, consentaneousness, consistency; congruity, -ence; keeping; congeniality; correspondence, concinnity, parallelism, apposition, union.

fitness, aptness etc. *adj.;* relevancy; pertinence, -cy; sortance; case in point; aptitude, propriety, applicability, admissibility, commensurability, compatibility, suitability; cognation etc (*relation*) 9.

adaptation, adjustment, arrangement, graduation, accommodation; reconcil-iation - ement; assimilation; attunement.

consent etc. (*assent*) 448; concurrence etc. 178; co-operation etc. 709.

right man in the right place, very thing; quite –, just- the thing.

V. be -accordant etc. *adj.;* agree, accord, harmonize; correspond, tally, respond; meet, suit, fit, befit, do, adapt itself to; fall in –, chime in –, square –, quadrate –, consort –, comport- with; dovetail, assimilate; fit like a glove; fit to a -tittle, – T; match etc. 17; become one.

consent etc. (*assent*) 488.

render -accordant etc. *adj.;* fit, suit, adapt, accommodate; graduate; adjust etc. (*render equal*) 27; dress, regulate, readjust; accord, harmonize, reconcile; fadge, dovetail, square.

Adj. agreeing, suiting etc. *v.;* in accord, accordant, concordant, consonant, congruous, consentaneous, correspondent, corresponding, homologous, congenial; becoming; harmonious, reconcilable, conformable; in -accordance, – harminy, – keeping, – unison, etc. *n.;*-with; at one with, of one mind, of a piece; consistent, compatible, proportionate, answerable; commensurate; on all fours.

apt, apposite, pertinent, pat; to the -point, – purpose; happy, felicitous, germane, *ad rem,* in point, bearing upon, applicable, relevant, admissible.

fit, adapted, *in loco, â propos,* appropriate, seasonable, sortable, suitable, idoneous, deft; meet etc. (*expedient*) 646.

at home, in one's proper element.

Adv. *â propos of;* pertinently etc. *adj.; pro rata.*

Phr. *rem acu tetigisti,* the cap fits.

24. Disagreement.—N. disagreement, discord, -cordance; disunion, dissonance, dissidence, discrepancy; unconformity etc. 83; incongru-ity, -ence; discongruity, *mésalliance, oxymoron;* jarring etc. *v.;* clash, collision, dissension etc. 713; conflict etc. (*opposition*) 708; controversy etc. 720; falling out, wrangle, argument.

disparity, mismatch, misfit, disproportion; disproportionateness etc. *adj.;* variance, divergence, repugnance.

unfitness etc. *adj.;* inaptitude, impropriety; inapplicability etc. *adj.;* inconsistency, inconcinnity; irrelevancy etc. (*irrelation*) 10.

misjoin-ing, -der; syncretism, intrusion, interference; *concordia discors*.
fish out of water.
V. disagree; clash, quarrel, jar etc. (*discord*) 713; interfere, intrude, come amiss; not concern etc. 10; mismatch; *hymano capiti cervicem jungere equinam*.
Adj. disagreeing etc. *v.;* discordant, discrepant; at -variance, – war; hostile, antagonistic, repugnant, factious, contradictory, dissentious, incompatible, irreconcilable, inconsistent with; unconformable, exceptional etc. 83; intrusive, incongruous; disproportionate, -ed; unharmonious; unconsonant; divergent, repugnant to.
inapt, unapt, inappropriate, inept, infelicitous, improper; unsuit-ed, -able; inapplicable; un-fit, -fitting, -befitting; unbecoming; ill-timed, ill-adapted, unseasonable, *mal â propos*, inadmissible; inapposite etc. (*irrelevant*) 10.
uncongenial; ill-assorted, -sorted, -matched; mis-matched, -mated, -joined, -placed; unaccommodating, irreducible, uncommensurable, unsympathetic.
out of -character, – keeping, – proportion, – joint, – tune, – place, – season, – its element; at -odds, – variance with.
Adv. in -defiance, – contempt, – spite-of; discordantly etc. *adj.; à tort et à travers*.

25. Quantity. [Absolute quantity.]—**N.** quantity, magnitude; size etc. ((*dimensions*) 192; amplitude, mass, amount, *quantum*, measure, measurement, substance, strength.
[Science of quantity.] Mathematics, Mathesis.
[Definite or finite quantity] arm-, hand-, mouth-, spoon-, thimble-, capful; stock, batch, lot, dose, ration, quotum, quota, pittance, driblet, part, portion etc. 51.
Adj. quantitative, some, any, more or less.
Adv. to the tune of.

26. Degree. [Relative quantity.]—**N.** degree, grade, extent, measure, proportion, amount, ratio, stint, standard, height, pitch; reach, amplitude, range, scope, size, caliber; gradation, shade; tenor, compass; sphere, station, rank, standing; rate, way, sort.
point, mark, step, stage etc. (*term*) 71; intensity, strength etc. (*greatness*) 31.
V. compare, graduate, calibrate, measure.
Adj. comparative; gradual, shading off, gradational; within the bounds etc. (*limit*), 233.
Adv. by degrees, gradually, inasmuch, *pro tanto*; how-ever, -soever; step by step, bit by bit, little by little, inch by inch, drop by drop, gradatim; by -inches, – slow degrees, – little and little; in some -degree, – measure; to some extent; just a bit.

27. Equality. [Sameness of quantity or degree.]—**N.** equality, parity, co-extension, symmetry, balance, poise; evenness, monotony, level.
equivalence; equi-pollence, -poise, -librium, -ponderance; par, quits; not a pin to choose; distinction without a difference, six of one and half a dozen of the other; identity etc. 13; similarity etc. 17; isotropism; coequality.
equalization, equation, equilibration, coordination, adjustment, readjustment.
drawn -game, -battle, draw, stalemate; neck and neck race; tie, dead heat.
match, peer, compeer, equal, mate, fellow, brother; equivalent.
V. be -equal etc. *adj.;* equal, match, reach, keep pace with, run abreast; come –, amount –, come upto; be –, lie- on a level with; balance; cope with; come to the same thing; level off.
render -equal etc. *adj.;* equalize, level, dress, balance, equate, handicap, give points, trim, adjust, poise; fit, accommodate; adapt etc. (*render accordant*) 23; strike a balance; establish –, restore- equality, – equilibrium; readjust; stretch on the bed of Procrustes.
Adj. equal, even, level, monotonous, coequal, symmetrical, coordinate; on a -par, – level, – footing- with; up to the mark; equiparent.
equivalent, tantamount; quits; homologous; synonymous etc. 522; resolvable into, convertible, much at one, as broad as long, neither more nor less; much the same –, the same thing —, as good- as; all -one, — the same; equi-pollent, -ponderant, -ponderous, -balanced; equalized etc. *v.;* drawn; half and half; isochronous; isoperimetrical.
Adv. equally etc. *adj.; pari passu, ad eundem, caeteris paribus; in equilibrio;* to all intents and purposes.
Phr. it -comes, -adds up, – amounts- to the same thing.

28. Inequality. [Difference of quantity or degree.]—**N.** inequality; dis-, im-parity; odds; difference etc. 15; ill-balanced; unevenness; inclination of the balance, partiality; shortcoming; casting –make- weight; superiority etc. 33; inferiority etc. 34.
V. be -unequal etc. *adj.;* countervail; have –, give- the advantage; turn the scale; kick the beam; topple, -over; over-match etc. 33; not come up to etc. 34.
Adj. unequal, uneven, disparate, partial; un-, over-balanced; top-heavy, lop-sided.
Adv. *haud passibus aequis*.

29. Mean.—**N.** mean, medium, intermedium, average, run of the mill, normal, balance; mediocrity, generality, rule, ordinary -run, -ruck; golden mean etc. (*mid-course*) 628; middle etc. 68; compromise etc. 774; neutrality; middle point, middle course.
V. split the difference; take the -average etc. *n.;* reduce to a -mean etc. *n.;* strike a balance, pair off.
Adj. mean, intermediate; medial; middle etc. 68; average, normal, standard, neutral; middling, moderate.
médiocre, middle-class; *bourgeois*, commonplace etc. (*unimportant*) 643.
Adv. on an average, in the long run; taking -one with another, – all things together, – it for all in all; *communibus annis*, in round numbers.

30. Compensation.—**N.** compensation, equation; commutation; indemnification; compromise etc. 774; neutralization, nullification; counteraction etc. 179; reaction; measure for measure; retaliation etc. 718; equalization etc. 27; redemption, recoupment, recompense.

set-off, offset; make- casting-weight; counterpoise, equipoise, ballast; indemnity, reparation etc. 790; equivalent, *quid pro quo;* bribe, hush-money, tribute etc. 784; amends etc. (*atonement*) 952; counterclaim, counterbalance, equiponderance, countervail, cross demand.

V. make -amends, – compensation; compensate, -pense; indemnify; counter-act, -vail, -poise; equiponderate; balance; out-, over-, counterbalance; set off, offset, cancel; hedge, square, give and take; make up -for, – lee way; cover, fill up, neutralize, nullify; equalize etc. 27; make good; redeem etc. (*atone*) 952; recoup, pay etc. 973.

Adj. compensat-ing, -ory; amendatory, reparative, countervailing etc. *v.;* in the opposite scale; equivalent etc. (*equal*) 27.

Adv. in -return, – consideration; but, however, yet, still, notwithstanding; neverthe-, nathless; although, though; al-, how-beit; in spite of, despite; mauger; at -all events, – any rate; be that as it may, for all that, even so, on the other hand, at the same time, *quoad minus, quand mâme,* however that may be; after all, – is said and done; taking one thing with another etc. (*average*) 29.

31. Greatness.–N. greatness etc. *adj.;* magnitude; size etc. (*dimensions*) 192; multitude etc. (*number*) 102; immensity, enormity, infinity etc. 105; might, strength, intensity, fulness; importance etc. 642; fame etc. 873.

great quantity, quantity, deal, power, sight, pot, volume, world; mass, heap etc. (*assemblage*) 72; stock etc. (*store*) 636; peck, bushel, load, cargo; cart –, wagon –, car –, truck –, ship-load; flood, spring tide; abundance etc. (*sufficiency*) 639.

principal –, chief –, main –, greater –, major –, best –, essential- part; bulk, mass etc. (*whole*) 50.

V. be -great etc. *adj.;* run high, soar, loom up, tower, bulk large, transcend; rise –, carry- to a great height; know no bounds; scale, overtop, ascend.

enlarge etc. (*increase*) 35, (*expand*) 194.

Adj. great; greater etc. 33; large, considerable, fair, above par; big, massive, huge etc. (*large in size*) 192; ample; abundant etc. (*enough*) 639; Herculean etc. 159; full, intense, strong, sound, passing, heavy, plenary, deep, high; signal, at its height, in the zenith.

world-wide, wide-spread, extensive; wholesale; many etc. 102.

goodly, noble, precious, mighty; sad, grave, serious; far gone, arrant, downright; utter, -most; crass, gross, arch, profound, intense, consummate; rank, unmitigated, red-hot, desperate; glaring, flagrant, stark staring; thorough-paced, -going; roaring, thumping, thundering, strapping, whacking; extraordinary; important etc. 642; unsurpassed etc. (*supreme*) 33; complete etc. 52.

vast, immense, enormous, extreme; inordinate, excessive, extravagant, exorbitant, outrageous, preposterous, unconscionable, swinging, monstrous, over-grown; towering, stupendous, prodigious, astonishing, incredible; terrific, frightful; marvelous etc. (*wonder*) 870; grand.

unlimited etc. (*infinite*) 105; unapproachable, unutterable, indescribable, ineffable, unspeakable, inexpressible, beyond expression, fabulous.

un-diminished, -abated, -reduced, -restricted.

absolute, positive, stark, decided, unequivocal, essential, perfect, finished.

remarkable, of mark, marked, pointed, veriest; noticeable, uncommon, noteworthy, eminent etc. 873.

Adv. [in a positive degree] truly etc. (*truth*) 494; decidedly, unequivocally, purely, absolutely, seriously, essentially, fundamentally, radically, downright, in all conscience; for the most part, in the main.

[in a complete degree] entirely etc. (*completely*) 52; abundantly, etc. (*sufficiently*) 639; widely, far and wide.

[in a great or high degree] greatly etc. *adj.;* much, muckle, well, indeed, very, very much, a deal, no end of, most not a little; pretty, – well; enough, in a great measure, passing richly; to a -large, – great, – gigantic- extent; on a large scale; so; never –, ever- so; ever so much; by wholesale; mightily, mighty, powerfully; with a witness, *ultra,* in the extreme, extremely, exceedingly, intensely, exquisitely, acutely, indefinitely, immeasurably; beyond -compare, – comparison, – measure, – all bounds; incalculably, infinitely.

[in a supreme degree] pre-eminently, superlatively etc. (*superiority*) 33.

[in a too great degree] immoderately, unduly, monstrously, grossly, preposterously, inordinately, exorbitantly, excessively, enormously, out of all proportion, with a vengeance.

[in a marked degree] particularly, remarkably, singularly, curiously, uncommonly, unusually, peculiarly, notably, signally, strikingly, pointedly, mainly, chiefly; famously, egregiously, prominently, glaringly, emphatically, strangely, wonderfully, amazingly, surprisingly, astonishingly, incredibly, marvelously, awfully, stupendously.

[in an exceptional degree] peculiarly etc. (*unconformity*) 83.

[in a violent degree] furiously etc. (*violence*) 173; severely, desperately, tremendously, extravagantly, confoundedly, deucedly, devilishly, with a vengeance; *à –, à toute- outrance.*

[in a painful degree] painfully, sadly, grossly, sorely, bitterly, piteously, grievously, miserably, cruelly, woefully, lamentably, shockingly, frightfully, dreadfully, fearfully, terribly, horribly, distressingly, balefully.

32. Smallness.—N. smallness etc. *adj.;* littleness etc. (*small size*) 193; tenuity; paucity; fewness etc. (*small number*) 103; meanness, insignificance etc. (*unimportance*) 643; mediocrity, moderation.

small quantity, *modicum, minimum;* vanishing point; material point, electron, atom, particle, molecule, corpuscle, point, dab, fleck, speck, dot, mote, jot, iota, ace; *minutiae,* details; look, thought, idea, *soupçon,* whit, tittle, shade, shadow; spark, *scintilla,* gleam; touch, cast; grain, scruple, granule, globule, minim, sup, sip, sop, spice, drop, droplet, sprinkling, dash, smack, tinge, tincture; inch, patch, scantling, dole; scrap, shred, tag, splinter, rag, tatter, cantlet, flitter, gobbet, mite, bit, morsel, crumb, seed, fritter, shive; snip, -pet; snick, snack, snatch, slip, scrag; chip, -ping; shiver, sliver, driblet, clipping, paring, shaving, hair.

nutshell; thimble-, spoon-, hand-, cap-, mouthful; fragment; fraction etc. (*part*)51; drop in the ocean, drop in the bucket.

animalcule etc. 193.

trifle etc. (*unimportant thing*) 643; mere –, next to- nothing; hardly anything; just enough to swear by; the shadow of a shade.

finiteness, finite quantity.

V. be -shall etc. *adj.;* lie in a nutshell.

diminish etc. (*decrease*) 36, (*contract*) 195.

Adj. small, little, tiny, weeny; diminutive etc. (*small in size*) 193; minute; minikin, fine, inconsiderable, dribbling, paltry etc. (*unimportant*) 643; faint etc. (*weak*) 160; slender, light, slight, scanty, scant, limited; meager etc. (*insufficient*) 640; sparing; few etc. 103; low, so-so, middling, tolerable, no great shakes; below –, under-par, – the mark; at a low ebb; halfway; moderate, modest; tender, subtle; petty, shallow, skin-deep.

inappreciable, evanescent, infinite-simal homeopathic, very small, atomic, molecular, ultra-, -microscopic.

petty, shallow etc. 499.

mere, simple, sheer, stark, bare; near run.

Adv. [in a small degree] to a small extent, on a small scale; a -little, – wee, – tiny bit; slightly etc. *adj.,* imperceptibly; miserably, wretchedly; insufficiently etc. 640; imperfectly; faintly etc. 160; passably, pretty well, well enough.

[in a certain or limited degree] partially, in part; in –, to a certain degree; to a certain extent; comparatively; some, rather; in some -degree, -measure; some-thing, -what; simply, only, purely, merely; at –, at the- -least, – most; ever so little, as little as may be, *tant soit peu,* in ever so small a degree; thus far, *pro tanto;* within bounds, in a manner, after a fashion.

almost, nearly, well nigh, short of, not quite, all but; near –, close- upon; *peu s'en faut,* near the mark; within an -ace, – inch- of; on the brink of; scarcely, hardly, barely, only just, no more than.

[in an uncertain degree] about, therabouts, somewhere about, nearly, say; be the same - more, – little more- or less.

[in no degree] no- ways, – wise; not -at all, – in the least, – a bit, – a bit of it, – a whit, – a jot, – a shadow; in no -wise, – respect; by no -means, – manner of means; on no account, at no hand.

33. Superiority.—N. superiority, supremacy, majority; greatness etc. 31; advantage, odds, pull; preponderance, -ation; predominance, vantage ground, coign of vantage, prevalence, partiality; personal superiority; sovereignty etc. 737; nobility etc. (*rank*) 875; Triton among the minnows, *primus inter pares, nulli secundus,* superman; captain etc. 475.

supremacy, pre-eminence; primacy, lead, *maximum;* record; climax, crest, top; culmination etc. (*summit*) 210; transcendence; *ne plus ultra;* lion's share, Benjamin's mess; excess; bisque, surplus etc. (*remainder*) 40, (*redundance*) 641.

V. be -superior etc. *adj.;* exceed, excel, transcend; out-do, -balance, -weigh, -rival, -Herod, outrank, pass, surpass, surmount, get ahead of; over-top, -ride, -pass, -balance, -weigh, -match; top, o'er-top, cap, beat, win out, cut out; beat hollow; outstrip etc. 303; eclipse, throw into the shade, take the shine out of, put one's nose out of joint; have the -upper hand, – whip hand of, – advantage; turn the scale, play first fiddle etc. (*importance*) 642; preponderate, predominate, prevail; precede, take precedence, come first; come to a head, culminate; beat etc. all others, bear the palm; break the record, take the cake.

become –, render- -larger, etc. (*increase*) 35, (*expand*) 194.

Adj. superior, greater, major, higher; exceeding etc. *v.;* great etc. 31; distinguished, *ultra;* vaulting; more than a match for.

supreme, greatest, maximal, maximum, utmost, paramount, pre-eminent, foremost, crowning; first-rate etc. (important) 642, (*excellent*) 648; unrivalled; peer-, match-less; none such, second to none, *sans pareil;* un-paragoned, - paralleled, -equalled, -approached, -surpassed; superlative, inimitable, *facile princeps,* incomparable, sovereign, without parallel, *nulli secundus, ne plus ultra;* beyond -compare, – comparison; culminating etc. (*topmost*) 210; transcendent, -ental; *plus royaliste que le Roi.*

increased etc. (*added to*) 35; enlarged etc. (*expanded*) 194.

Adv. beyond, more, over; over –, above- the mark; above par; upwards –, in advance- of; over and above; at the top of the scale, on the crest, at it height.

[in a superior or supreme degree] eminently, egregiously, pre-eminently, surpassing, prominently, superlatively, supremely, above all, of all things, the most, to crown all, *par excellence,* principally, especially, particularly, peculiarly, *a fortiori,* even, yea, still more.

Phr. 'we shall not look upon his like again.'

34. Inferiority.—N. inferiority, minority, subordinancy; shortcoming, deficiency; handicap; *minimum;* smallness etc. 32; imperfection, shabbiness.

[personal inferiority] commonalty etc. 876; subordinate, substitute, sub.

V. be -inferior etc. *adj.;* fall –, come- short of; not -pass, – come up to; want.

become –, render- smaller etc. (decrease) 36, (*contract*) 195; hide its diminished head, retire into the shade, yield the palm, play second fiddle, take a back seat; bow.

Adj. inferior, smaller; small etc. 32; minor, less, lesser, deficient, minus, lower, subordinate, secondary; second-rate etc. (*imperfect*) 651; sub, subaltern; thrown into the shade; weighed in the balance and found wanting; not fit to hold a candle to.

least, smallest etc. (*see* little, small etc. 193); lowest.

diminished etc. (*decreased*) 36; reduced etc. (*contracted*) 195; unimportant etc. 643.

Adv. less; under –, below- -the mark, – par; at -the bottom of the scale, – a low ebb, – a disadvantage; short of, under.

35. Increase.—**N.** increase; augmentation, addition, enlargement, extension; dilatation etc. (*expansion*) 194; multiplication; increment, accretion; accession etc. 37; production etc. 161; development, growth; aggrandizement, aggravation, intensification; rise; ascent etc. 305; anabasis; ex-aggeration, -acerbation; spread etc. (*dispersion*) 73; flood-, spring-, -tide; gain, produce, profit etc. 618; booty, plunder etc. 793.

V. increase, augment, add to, enlarge; dilate etc. (*expand*) 194; grow, wax, mount, swell, get ahead, gain strength; advance; run –, shoot- up; rise; ascend etc. 305; sprout etc. 194.

aggrandize; raise; exalt; deepen, heighten; lengthen; thicken; strengthen; intensify, enhance, inflate, magnify, double, redouble; multiply; aggravate, exaggerate; ex-asperate, -acerbate; add fuel to the flame, *oleum addere camino,* superadd etc. (*add*) 37; spread etc. (*disperse*) 73.

Adj. increased etc. *v.;* on the increase, undiminished, additional etc. (*added*) 37; increasing etc. *v.;* growing, crescent, intensive, cumulative.

Adv. *crescendo,* increasingly.

Phr. *vires acquirit eundo.*

36. Non-Increase, Decrease.—**N.** decrease, diminution, lessening etc. *v.;* subtraction etc. 38; reduction, abatement, declension; shrinkage etc. (*contraction*) 195; coarctation; abridgment etc. (*shortening*) 201; extenuation.

subsidence, catabasis, wane, ebb-, neap-tide, decline; descent etc. 306; decrement, reflux, depreciation; erosion, wear and tear, deterioration etc. 659; anticlimax; mitigation etc. (*moderation*) 174.

V. decrease, diminish, lessen; abridge etc. (*shorten*) 201; shrink etc. (*contract*) 195; drop –, fall –, tail- off; fall away, waste, wear, erode; wane, ebb, decline; descent etc. 306; subside; deliquesce, melt –, die -away; retire into the shade, hide its diminished head, fall to a low ebb, run low, languish, decay, crumble, consume away.

bate, abate, dequantitate; discount; depreciate; extenuate, lower, weaken, attenuate, fritter away; mitigate etc.(*moderate*) 174; belittle, minimize; dwarf, throw into the shade; keep down, reduce etc. 195; shorten etc. 201; subtract etc. 38.

Adj. unincreased etc. (*see* increase etc. 35); decreased etc. *v.;* decreasing etc. *v.;* on the -wane etc. *n.;* deliquescent.

Adv. *diminuendo, decrescendo,* decreasingly.

37. Addition.—**N.** addition, annexation, adjection; junction etc. 43; super-position, -addition, -junction, -fetation; accession, reinforcement; increase etc. 35; increment, supplement; accompaniment etc. 88; interposition etc. 228; insertion etc. 300; summation etc. 85; adjunct etc. 39.

V. add, annex, adject, affix, attach, superadd, subjoin, superpose; clap –, saddle- on; tack to, postfix, append, tag; ingraft; saddle with; sprinkle; introduce etc. (*interpose*) 228; insert etc. 300.

become added, accrue; ad-, supervene; add up etc. 85.

reinforce, strengthen, swell the ranks of; augment etc. 35.

Adj. added etc. *v.;* additional; supplement, -al, -ary; suppletory, subjunctive; adjec-, adsci-, ascititious; additive, extra, spare, further, fresh, more, new, ulterior, other, auxiliary, supernumerary, accessory.

Adv. in addition, more, plus, extra; and, also. likewise, too, furthermore, further, item; and -also, – eke; else, besides, to boot, *et cetera;* etc.; and so -on, – forth; into the bargain, *cum multis aliis,* over and above, moreover.

with, withal; including, inclusive, as well as, not to mention, let alone; together –, along –, coupled –, in conjunction- with; conjointly; jointly etc. 43.

38. Non-Addition. Subduction.—**N.** sub-traction, -duction; deduction, retrenchment; removal; ab-, sub-lation; abstraction etc. (*taking*) 789; garbling etc. *v.;* mutilation, detruncation; amputation, severance; abs-, ex-, re-cision; curtailment etc. 201; minuend, subtrahend; decrease etc. 36; abrasion.

V. sub-tract, -duct; rebate, de-duct, –duce; bate, retrench; remove, withdraw; take –from, –away; detract.

garble, mutilate, amputate, sever, detruncate; cut -off, – away, – out; expurgate; abscind, excise; pare, thin, prune, decimate; abrade, scrape, file; geld, castrate, emasculate, unman, spay, caponize; eliminate.

diminish etc. 36; curtail etc. (*shorten*) 201; deprive of etc. (*take*) 789; weaken.

Adj. subtracted etc. *v.;* subtractive.

tailless, acaudal.

Adv. in -deduction etc. *n.;* less; short of; minus, without, except, excepting, with the exception of, barring, bar, save, exclusive of, save and except, with a reservation.

39. Adjunct. [Thing added.]—**N.** adjunct, addit-ion, -ament; *additum,* affix, appendage, annex; augment, -ation; increment, reinforcement, supernumerary, accessory, item; garnish, sauce; accompaniment etc. 88; adjective, *addendum,* accession, complement, supplement; continuation; extension, subscript, tag, appendix, postscript, interlineation, interpolation, insertion.

rider, codicil, off-shoot, episode, side issue, corollary; piece; flap, lapel, label, tab, strip, fold, lappet, apron, skirt, embroidery, trappings, *cortège;* tail, suffix etc. (*sequel*) 65; wing.

Adj. additional etc. 37.

Adv. in addition etc. 37.

40. Remainder. [Thing remaining.]—**N.** remainder, residue; remains, *remanet,* remnant, rest, relic, relict; leavings, heel-tap, odds and ends, cheese-parings, candle ends, orts; *residuum;* dottle, dregs, etc. (*dirt*) 653; refuse etc. (*useless*) 645; stubble, result, educt; fag-end, stub; ruins, wreck, skeleton, stump; *alluvium.*

surplus, overplus, excess; balance, complement; superfluity etc. (*redundance*) 641; surviv-al, -ance; afterglow.

V. remain; be -left etc. *adj.*; exceed, survive; leave.

Adj. remaining, left; left -behind, – over;

residu-al, -ary; over, odd; unconsumed, sedimentary; surviving; net; exceeding, over and above; outlying, -standing; cast off etc. 782; superfluous etc. (*redundant*) 641.

V. remain; be -left; left -behind, – over; redidual, -ary; over, odd; unconsumed, sedimentary; surviving; net; exceeding, over and above; outlying, -standing; cast off etc. 782; superfluous etc. (*redundant*) 641.

40a. Decrement. [Thing deducted.]—**N.** decrement, discount, rebate, defect, loss, deduction, eduction, tare; drawback; waste, wastage; reprise.

41. Mixture. [Forming a whole without coherence.]—**N.** mix-, admix-, commix-ture, -tion, mingling; commixion, immixture, interfusion, intermixture, alloyage, matrimony; junction etc. 43; combination etc. 48; entanglement, interlacing; miscegenation, interbreeding.

impregnation; in-, dif-, suf-, transfusion; infiltration; seasoning, sprinkling, interlarding; interpolation etc. 228; adulteration, sophistication.

[Thing mixed] tinge, tincture, touch, dash, smack, sprinkling, spice, seasoning, infusion, *soupçon.*

[Compound resulting from mixture] alloy, brass, bronze, pewter etc.; amalgam, *magma,* blend, half-and-half, *mélange, tertium, quid,* miscellany, *ambigu,* medley, mess, hash, hotchpotch, hodgepodge, *pasticcio,* patchwork, odds and ends, all sorts; jumble etc. (*disorder*) 59; salad, sauce, mash, *omnium gatherum,* gallimaufry, ragout, *olla podrida, olio,* salmagundi, *potpourri,* Noah's ark; texture, mingled yarn; mosaic etc. (*variegation*) 440.

half-blood, -caste, -breed, Eurasian; mulatto; terc-, quart-, quinteron etc.; quad-, octo-roon; *griffo, zambo;* cross, hybrid, mongrel etc. 83.

V. mix; join etc. 43; combine etc. 48; com-, im-, inter-mix; mix up with, mingle; com-, inter-, bemingle; shuffle etc. (*derange*) 61; pound together; hash –, stir- up; knead, brew; impregnate with; interlard etc. (*interpolate*) 228; intertwine, -weave etc. 219; associate with, miscegenate, interbreed.

be mixed etc.; get among, be entangled with.

instil, imbue; in-, suf-, trans-fuse; infiltrate, dash, tinge, tincture, season, sprinkle, besprinkle, attemper, medicate, blend, cross; alloy, amalgamate, compound, adulterate, sophisticate, infect.

Adj. mixed etc. *v.;* implex, composite, half-and-half, linsey-wolsey, hybrid, mongrel, heterogeneous; motley etc. (*variegated*) 440; miscellaneous, promiscuous, indiscriminate; miscible.

Adv. among, amongst, amid, amidst, with; in the midst of, in the crowd.

42. Simpleness [Freedom from mixture.]—**N.** simpleness etc. *adj.;* purity, homogeneity.

elimination; sifting etc. *v.;* purification etc. (*cleanness*) 652.

V. render -simple etc. *adj.;* simplify.

sift, winnow, bolt, eliminate; narrow down; get rid of, exclude etc. 55; clear; purify etc. (*clean*) 652; disentangle etc. (*disjoin*) 44.

Adj. simple, uniform, of a piece, homogeneous, single, pure, clear, sheer, neat; Attic.

un-mixed, -mingled, -blended, -combined, -compounded; elementary, undecomposed; unadulterated, -sophisticated, -alloyed, -tinged, -fortified; pure and simple.

free –, exempt- from; exclusive.

Adv. simply etc. *adj.;* only.

43. Junction.—**N.** junction; joining etc. *v.;* joinder, union; con-nection, -junction, -jugation, compendency, annex-ion, -ation, -ment; coalition; astriction, attachment, compagination, vincture, ligation, alligation; accouplement; marriage etc. (*wedlock*) 903; infibulation, inosculation, symphysis, anastomosis, confluence, communication, concatenation; concurrence, meeting, reunion; assemblage etc. 72.

copulation, coition, intercourse.

joint, joining, juncture, chiasma, pivot, hinge, articulation, commissure, seam, suture, gusset, stitch, splice; link etc. 45; miter, mortise.

closeness, tightness etc. *adj.;* coherence etc. 46; combination etc. 48.

V. join, unite; con-join, -nect; associate; put –, lay –, clap –, hang –, lump –, hold –, piece –, tack –, fix –, bind up- together; embody, re-embody; roll into one.

attach, fix, affix, saddle on, fasten, bind, secure, clinch, twist, make -fast etc. *adj.;* tie, pinion, string, strap, sew, lace, stitch, tack, paste, knit, button, buckle, hitch, lash, truss, bandage, braid, splice, swathe, gird, tether, moor, picket, harness, chain; fetter etc. (*restrain*) 751; lock, latch, belay, brace, hook, grapple, leash, couple, accouple, link, yoke, bracket; marry etc. (*wed*) 903; bridge over, span.

pin, nail, bolt, hasp, clasp, clamp, screw, rivet; impact, solder, braze, cement, set; weld –, fuse- together; wedge, rabbet, mortise, miter, jam, dovetail, enchase; graft, ingraft, inosculate; en-, in-twine; inter-link, -lace, -twine, -twist, -weave; entangle; twine round, belay; tighten; trice –, screw-up.

be -joined etc.; hang –, hold- together; cohere etc. 46.

Adj. joined etc. *v.;* joint; con-joint, -junct; corporate, compact; hand in hand.

firm, fast, close, tight, taut, taught, tense, secure, set, intervolved; in-separable, -dissoluble, -secable, -severable.

Adv. jointly etc. *adj.;* in conjunction with etc. (*in addition to*) 37; fast, firmly etc. *adj.;* intimately.

44. Disjunction.—**N.** dis-junction, -connection, -unity, -union, -association, -engagement, -sociation; discontinuity etc. 70; inconnection; abstraction, -edness; isolation; insul-arity, -ation; oasis; separateness etc. *adj.;* severalty; *disjecta membra;* dispersion etc. 73; apportionment etc. 786.

separation; parting etc. *v.;* detachment, segregation; divorce, sejunction, seposition, diduction, diremption, discerption; elision; *caesura,* division, subdivision, break, fracture, rupture; compartition; dis-memberment, -integration, -location; luxation; sever-, dis-severance; scission; re-, ab-scission; circumcision;

lacer-, dilacer-ation; dis-, ab-ruption; avulsion, divulsion; section, resection, cleavage; fission; separability; separatism.

fissure, breach, rent, split, rift, crack, slit, slot, incision.

dissection, anatomy; decomposition etc. 49; cutting instrument etc. (*sharpness*) 253; saw.

V. be -disjoined etc.; come –, fall- -off, – to pieces; peel off; get loose.

dis-join, -connect, -engage, -unite, -sociate, -pair; divorce, part, dispart, detach, uncouple, separate, cut off, rescind, segregate; set –, keep- apart; insulate, isolate; throw out of gear; cut adrift; loose; un-loose, -do, -bind, -tie, -hitch, -chain, -lock etc. (*fix*) 43, -pack, -ravel; disentangle; set free etc. (*liberate*) 750.

sunder, divide, subdivide, sectionalize, sever, dissever, abscind; cut; segment; in-cide, -cise; circumcise; saw, snip, nib, nip, cleave, rive, rend, slit, split, splinter, chip, crack, snap, break, tear, burst; rend etc. -asunder, – in twain; wrench, rupture, shatter, shiver, cranch, crunch, craunch, chop; rip up; hack, hew, slash; whittle; haggle, hackle, discind, lacerate, scamble, mangle, gash, hash, slice.

cut up, carve, quarter, dissect, anatomize; take –, pull –, pick –, tear- to pieces; tear to tatters, – piecemeal; divellicate; skin etc. 226; dis-integrate, -member, -branch, -band; disperse etc. 73; dis-locate, -joint; break up; mince; comminute etc. (*pulverize*) 330; distribute, apportion etc. 786.

part, – company; separate, leave; alienate, estrange.

Adj. disjoined etc. *v.;* discontinuous etc. 70; bipartite, multipartite, abstract; digitate; disjunctive; isolated etc. *v.;* insular, separate, disparate, discrete, apart, asunder, far between, loose, free; unattached, -annexed, -associated, -connected; distinct; adrift; straggling; rift, reft, cleft, split.

[capable of being divided] scissile, partible, divisible, separable, severable, detachable.

Adv. separately etc. *adj.;* one by one, severally, apart; adrift, asunder, in twain; in the abstract, abstractedly.

45. Vinculum. [Connecting medium.]—**N.** vinculum, link, *nexus*; connec-tive, -tion; junction etc. 43; bond of union, copula, intermedium, hyphen; bracket; bridge, stepping-stone, isthmus.

bond, tendon, tendril; fiber; cord, -age; riband, ribbon, rope, guy, cable, line, halser, hawser, painter, moorings, wire, chain; string etc. (*filament*) 205.

fastening, tie; liga-ment, -ture; strap; bowline, halliard, tackle, lanyard, rigging, shrouds; standing –, running- rigging; traces, harness; yoke; band, -age; brace, roller, fillet; inkle; with, withe, withy; thong, braid; girder, tie-beam; girt, cinch, girth, girdle, cestus, garter, braces, suspenders, halter, noose, lasso, lariat, surcingle, knot, hitch, running knot, frog.

pin, corking pin, nail, brad, tack, skewer, staple, cleat, clamp; cramp, screw, button, buckle, clasp, hasp, hinge, hank, catch, latch, bolt, ring, latchet, pawl, tag; tooth; stud; hook, – and eye; morse, lock, holdfast, padlock, rivet; anchor, grappling-iron, drawbar, coupler, drawhead, coupling, treenail, trennel, stake, pale, pile, post, bollard.

cement, glue, gum, paste, size, wafer, solder, lute, putty, bird-lime, mortar, stucco, plaster, grout.

shackle, rein etc. (*means of restraint*) 752; suspender etc. 214; prop etc. (*support*) 215.

V. bridge over, span; connect etc. 43; hang etc. 214.

46. Coherence.—**N.** co-, ad-herence, -hesion, -hesiveness; concretion, accretion; con-, agglutination, -glomeration; aggregation; consolidation, set, cementation; sticking, soldering etc. *v.;* connection.

tenacity, toughness; stickiness etc. 352; insepara-bility, -bleness; bur, remora.

conglomerate, concrete etc. (*density*) 321.

V. cohere, adhere, stick, cling, cleave, hold, take hold of, hold fast, close with, embrace, clasp, hug; grow –, hang-together; twine round etc. (*join*) 43.

stick like -a leech, – wax; stick close; cling like -ivy, – a bur; adhere like -a remora, – Dejanira's shirt.

glue; ag-, con-glutinate; cement, lute, paste, gum; solder, weld; cake, coagulate, consolidate etc. (*solidify*) 321; agglomerate.

Adj. co-, ad-hesive, -hering etc. *v.;* tenacious, tough; sticky etc. 352.

united, unseparated, sessile, inseparable, inextricable, infrangible; compact etc. (*dense*) 321.

47. Incoherence. [Want of adhesion, non-adhesion, immiscibility.]—**N.** non-adhesion; immiscibility; incoherence; looseness etc. *adj.;* laxity; relaxation; loosening etc. *v.*; freedom; disjunction etc. 44; rope of sand.

V. make -loose etc. *adj.;* loosen, slacken, relax; un-glue etc. 46; detach etc. (*disjoin*) 44.

Adj. non-adhesive, immiscible; incoherent, detached, loose, slack, baggy, lax, relaxed, flapping, streaming; dishevelled; segregated, like grains of sand; un-consolidated etc. 321; -combined etc. 48; non-cohesive.

48. Combination.—**N.** combination; mixture etc. 41; alloy; junction etc. 43; union, unification, synthesis, incorporation, amalgamation, embodiment, coalescence, crasis, fusion, blend, blending, absorption, centralization, federation.

compound, amalgam, composition, *tertium quid;* resultant, impregnation.

V. combine, unite, incorporate, alloy, intertwine etc. 41; amalgamate, embody, absorb, reembody, blend, merge, fuse, melt into one, consolidate, coalesce, centralize, impregnate; put –, lump- together; federate, associate; fraternize; cement a union, marry, wed, couple, pair, ally.

Adj. combined etc. *v.;* conjunctive, conjugate, conjoint, allied, confederate; impregnated with, ingrained, inoculated.

49. Decomposition.—**N.** decomposition, analysis, diaeresis dissection, resolution, catalysis, electrolysis, hydrolysis, photolysis, dissolution; dispersion etc. 73; disjunction etc. 44;

putrescence, caries, necrosis, corruption etc. (*uncleanness*) 653.

V. decom-pose, -pound; analyze, disembody, dissolve; resolve –, separate- into its elements; electrolyze; dissect, decentralize, break up; disintegrate; disperse etc. 73; unravel etc. (*unroll*) 313; crumble into dust; decay etc. *n.;* deteriorate etc. 659.

Adj. decomposed etc. *v.;* catalytic, analytical.

50. Whole. [Principal part.]—**N.** whole, totality, integrity; totalness etc. *adj.;* entirety, *ensemble,* collectiveness; unity etc. 87; completeness etc. 52; indivisibility, indiscerptibility; integration, embodiment; integer, integral.

all, the whole, total, aggregate, one and all, gross amount, sum, sum-total, *tout ensemble,* length and breadth of, Alpha and Omega, 'be all and end all,' lock, stock and barrel.

bulk, mass, lump, tissue, staple, body, torso, *compages;* truck, bole, hull, hulk, skeleton; greater –, major –, best –, principal –, main-part; essential part etc. (*importance*) 642; lion's share, Benjamin's mess; the long and the short; nearly –, almost- all.

V. form –, constitute- a whole; integrate, embody, amass; aggregate etc. (*assemble*) 72; amount to, come to.

Adj. whole, total, integral, entire; complete etc. 52; one, individual.

un-broken, -cut, -divided, -severed, -clipped, -cropped, -shorn; seamless; undiminished; undemolished, -dissolved, -destroyed, -bruised.

in-divisible, -dissoluble, -dissolvable, -discerptible.

wholesale, sweeping, comprehensive.

Adv. wholly, altogether; totally etc. (*completely*) 52; entirely, all, all in all, considering all things, in a body, collectively, all put together; in the -aggregate, – lump; – mass, – gross, – main, – long run; *en masse,* on the whole, as a whole, bodily, *en bloc, in extenso,* throughout, every inch; substantially.

51. Part.—**N.** part, portion; dose; item, particular; aught, any; division, ward; subdivision, section; chapter, verse; article, clause, count, paragraph, passage; phrase; number, volume, book, fascicule; sector, segment; fraction, fragment; cantle, -t; frustum; detachment, parcel, unit, class etc. 75.

piece, lump, bit; cut, -ting; chip, chunk, collop, slice, scale, shard; lamina etc. 204; moiety; small part; morsel, scrap, crumb; particle etc. (*smallness*) 32; instalment, dividend; share etc. (*allotment*) 786.

débris, odds and ends, oddments, *detritus; excerpta;* member, limb, lobe, lobule, arm, wing, scion, branch, bough, joint, link, offshoot, rami fication, twig, stipule, tendril, bush, spray, sprig; runner; leaf, -let; stump; constituent, ingredient, component part etc. 56.

compartment; department etc. (*class*) 75; county etc. (*region*) 181.

V. part, divide, break etc. (*disjoin*) 44; partition etc. (*apportion*) 786.

Adj. fractional, fragmentary; sectional, aliquot; divided etc. *v.;* in compartments, multifid, incomplete, partial, divided etc. 44.

Adv. partly, in part, partially; piecemeal, part by part; by -instalments, – snatches, – inches, – driblets; bit by bit, inch by inch, foot by foot, drop by drop; in -detail, – lots.

52. Completeness.—**N.** completeness etc. *adj.;* completion etc. 729; integration; integrality.

entirety; universality; totality; perfection etc. 650; solid-ity, -arity; unity; all; *ne plus ultra,* ideal, limit.

complement, supplement, make-weight; filling up etc. *v.*

impletion; satur-ation, -ity; high water; high –, flood –, spring- tide; fill, load, bumper, bellyful; brimmer; sufficiency etc. 639.

V. be -complete etc. *adj.*; come to a head.

render -complete etc. *adj.*; complete etc. (*accomplish*) 729; fill, charge, load, replenish; make-up, – good; piece –, eke- out; supply deficiencies; fill -up, – in, – to the brim, – the measure of; saturate etc. 869.

go the whole -hog, – length, go all lengths.

Adj. complete, entire; whole etc. 50; perfect etc. 650; full, good, absolute, thorough, plenary; solid, undivided; with all its parts.

exhaustive, radical, sweeping, thorough-going; dead.

regular, consummate, unmitigated, sheer, unqualified, unconditional, free; abundant etc. (*sufficient*) 639.

brimming; brim-, top-ful; chock –, choke-full; as full as- an egg is of meat, – a vetch, – a tick; saturated, crammed; replete etc. (*redundant*) 641; fraught, laden; full-laden, -fraught, -charged; heavy laden.

completing etc. *v.;* supplement-al, -ary; ascititious.

Adv. completely etc. *adj.;* altogether, outright, wholly, totally, *in toto,* quite; over head and ears; effectually, for good and all, nicely, fully, through thick and thin, head and shoulders; neck and -heel, – crop; all out; in -all respects, – every respect; at all points, out and out, to all intents and purposes; *toto coelo;* utterly, clean, – as a whistle; to the -full, – utmost, – backbone; hollow, stark; heart and soul, root and branch; down to the ground.

to the top of one's bent, as far as possible, *à outrance.*

throughout; from -first to last, – beginning to end, – end to end, – one end to the other, – Dan to Beersheba, – head to foot, – head to heels, – top to toe, – top to bottom; *de fond en comble; à fond, a capite ad calcem, ab ovo usque ad mala,* fore and aft; every -whit, – inch; *cap-à-pie,* to the end of the chapter; up to the -brim, – ears, – eyes; as ... as can be.

on all accounts; *sous tous les rapports;* with a -vengeance, – witness.

53. Incompleteness.—**N.** incompleteness etc. *adj.;* deficiency, short -measure, – wieght; shortcoming etc. 304; insufficiency etc. 640; imperfection etc. 651; immaturity etc. (*non-preparation*) 674; half measures.

[part wanting] defect, deficit, shortage, ullage, defalcation, omission, *caret;* interval etc. 198; break etc. (*discontinuity*) 70; non-completion etc. 730; missing link.

V. be -incomplete etc. *adj.;* fall short of etc. 304; lack etc. (*be insufficient*) 640; neglect etc. 460.

Adj. incomplete; imperfect etc. 651; unfinished; uncompleted etc. (*see* complete etc. 729); defective, deficient, wanting; failing; in -default, – arrear; short, – of; hollow, meagre, lame, half-and-half, perfunctory, sketchy; crude etc. (*unprepared*) 674.

mutilated, garbled, mangled, docked, lopped, truncated; bobtailed, cropped, bobbed, shingled.

in -progress, – hand; going on, proceeding.

Adv. incompletely etc. *adj.;* by halves.

Phr. *caetera desunt; caret.*

54. Composition.—N. composition, constitution, crasis, synthesis; make-up; combination etc. 48; inclusion, admission, comprehension, reception; embodiment, formation, conformation, production.

compilation etc. 72. (*musical*) composition etc. 415; painting etc. 556; writing etc. 590; typography etc. 591.

V. be -composed, – made, – formed, – made up- of; consist of, be resolved into.

include etc. (*in a class*) 76; subsume; synthesize; contain, hold, comprehend, take in, admit, embrace, embody; involve; implicate, drag into.

compose, constitute, form, make; make –, fill –, build- up; weave, construct, fabricate; compile; write, draw; set up (*printing*); enter into the composition of etc. (*be a component*) 56.

Adj. containing, constituting etc. *v.*

55. Exclusion.—N. exclusion, non-admission, omission, exception, rejection, repudiation; exile etc. (*seclusion*) 893; preclusion, lock out, ostracism, prohibition; disbarment, expulsion, ban.

separation, segregation, seposition, elimination, coffer-dam.

V. be excluded from etc.

exclude, bar, ban; leave –, shut –, thrust –, bar- out; reject, repudiate, spurn, blackball; ostracize, boycott; lay –, put –, set-apart, – aside; relegate, segregate; throw overboard; strike -off, – out; neglect etc. 460; banish etc. (*seclude*) 893; separate etc. (*disjoin*) 44.

pass over, omit; garble; eliminate, weed, winnow.

Adj. excluding etc. *v.;* exclusive.

excluded etc. *v.;* unrecounted, not included in; inadmissible; preventive, interdictive.

Adv. exclusive of, barring, except; with the exception of; save, bating.

56. Component.—N. component; component –, integral –, integrant-part; element, constituent, ingredient, leaven; part and parcel; contents; appurtenance; feature; member etc. (*part*) 51; personnel.

V. enter into, – the composition of; be a -component etc. *n.;* be –, form- part of; merge –, be merged- in; be implicated in; share in etc. (*participate*) 778; belong –, appertain- to.

form, make, constitute, compose.

Adj. forming etc. *v.;* inclusive; inherent etc. 5.

57. Extraneousness.—N. extraneousness etc. *adj.;* extrinsicality etc. 6; exteriority etc. 220; alienism.

foreign -body, – substance, – element; alien, stranger, intruder, interloper, foreigner, tramontane, *novus homo,* new comer, immi-, emi-grant; creole, Afrikander; outsider, outlander, tenderfoot.

Adj. extraneous, foreign, alien, ulterior; exterior, external, outside, outlandish; oversea; tra-, ultra-montane.

excluded etc. 55; inadmissible; exceptional.

Adv. in foreign -parts, – lands; abroad, beyond seas, overseas.

58. Order.—N. order, regularity etc. 80; uniformity, symmetry, *lucidus ordo;* harmony, music of the spheres.

gradation, progression; series etc. (*continuity*) 69.

subordination; course, even tenor, routine; method, disposition, arrangement, array, system, economy, discipline; orderliness etc. *adj.*

rank, place etc. (*term*) 71.

V. be –, become- in order etc. *adj.;* form, fall in, draw up; arrange –, range –, place- itself; adjust; fall into –, take- -one's place, – rank; rally round; arrange etc. 60.

Adj. orderly, regular; in -order, – trim, – apple-pie order according to Cocker, – its proper place, neat, neat as a pin, tidy, *en règle,* well regulated, correct, methodical, uniform, symmetrical, ship-shape, business-like, systematic; habitual; unconfused etc. (*see* confuse etc. 61) arranged etc. 60.

Adv. in order; methodically etc. *adj.;* in -turn, – its turn; step by step; by regular -steps, – gradations, – stages, – intervals; *seriatim,* systematically, by clockwork, *gradatim;* at stated periods etc. (*periodically*)138.

59. Disorder. [Absence, or want of Order, etc.]—**N.** disorder; derangement etc. 61; irregularity; anomaly etc. (*unconformity*) 83; anar-chy, -chism; want of method; dishevelment, untidiness etc. *adj.;* disunion; discord etc. 24.

confusion; confusedness etc. *adj.;* disarray, jumble, mix-up, huddle, litter, lumber; *cahotage;* farrago; mess, muss, mash, muddle, hash; hotchpotch; *imbroglio,* chaos, *omnium gatherum,* medley; mere -mixture etc. 41; fortuitous concourse of atoms, *disjecta membra, rudis indigestaque moles.*

complexity; complexness etc. *adj.;* com-, implication; intri-cacy, -cation; perplexity; network, maze, labyrinth, wilderness, jungle; involution, ravelling, entanglement; coil etc. (*convolution*) 248; sleave, tangled skein, knot, Gordian know, kink, web; wheels within wheels.

turmoil; ferment, etc. (*agitation*) 315; to do, trouble, pudder, pother, row, disturbance, convulsion, tumult, pandemonium, uproar, riot, rumpus, stour, scramble, *fracas,* embroilment, *mêleé,* spill and pelt, rough and tumble; whirlwind etc. 349; bear garden, Babel, Saturnalia, Donnybrook Fair, confusion worse confounded, most admired disorder, *concordia discors;* Bedlam –, hell- broke loose; bull in a china shop;

all the fat in the fire, *diable à quatre,* Devil to pay; pretty kettle of fish; pretty piece of -work, — business.

slattern, slut, sloven; draggle-tail.

V. be -disorderly etc. *adj.;* ferment, play at cross purposes.

put out of order; derange etc. 61; ravel etc. 219; ruffle, rumple; bungle, botch.

Adj. disorderly, orderless; out of -order; — place, — gear, — whack; irregular, desultory; anomalous etc. (*unconformable*) 83; acephalous, disorganized, straggling; un-, im-methodical; unsymmetric; unsystematic; untidy, slovenly, bedraggled, messy; dislocated; out of sorts; promiscuous, indiscriminate; chaotic, anarchical, lawless; unarranged etc. 60; confused, tumultuous, turbulent, tempestuous; deranged etc. 61; topsy turvy etc. (*inverted*) 218; shapeless etc. 241; disjointed, out of joint.

com-plex, -plexed; intricate, complicated, perplexed, involved, ravelled, entangled, knotted, tangled, inextricable; irreducible.

troublous; riotous etc. (*violent*) 173.

Adv. irregularly etc. *adj.;* by fits and -snatches, — starts; pell-mell; higgledy-piggledy; helter-skelter, harum-scarum; in a ferment; at -sixes and sevens, — cross purposes; upside down etc. 218.

Phr. the cart before the horse, chaos is come again.

60. Arrangement. [Reduction to Order.]—**N.** arrangement; plan etc. 626; preparation etc. 673; dispos-al, -ition; col-, al-location; disbribution; sorting etc. *v.;* assortment, allotment; grouping; apportionment, *taxis,* taxonomy, *syn-taxis,* graduation, organization, grading; re-organization, rationalization.

analysis, classification, division, digestion; systematism.

[Result of arrangement] order, orderliness, form, array; digest, synopsis etc. (compendi -um) 596; *syntagma,* table, atlas; register etc. (*record*) 551; score etc. 415; cosmos, organism, architecture.

[Instrument for sorting] sieve etc. 260; file, card index.

V. reduce to —, bring into- order; introduce order into; rally.

arrange, dispose, place, form; put —, set —, place- in order; straighten up, tidy up; set out, collocate, allocate, pack, marshal, range, size, rank, array, group, parcel out, allot, space, distribute, deal; cast —, assign- the parts; dispose of, assign places to; assort, sort; sift, riddle; put —, set- -to rights, — into shape, — in trim, — in array.

class, -ify; divide; file, string together, thread; register etc. (*record*) 551; list, catalogue, tabulate, index, alphabeticize, graduate, digest, grade, codify; orchestrate, score.

methodize, regulate, systematize, standardize, co-ordinate, organize, settle, fix.

unravel, disentangle, ravel, card; disembroil.

Adj. arranged etc. *v.;* embattled, in battle array; cut and dried; methodical, orderly, regular, systematic, tabular.

61. Derangement. [Subversion of Order; bringing into disorder.]—**N.** derangement etc. *v.;* disorder etc. 59; evection, discomposure, disturbance; dis-, de-organization; involvement; dislocation; perturbation, interruption; shuffling etc. *v.;* inversion etc. 218; corrugation etc. (*fold*) 258; insanity etc. 503.

V. derange; dis-, mis-arrange; dis-, mis-place; mislay, discompose, disorder, de-, dis-organize; embroil, unsettle, disturb, confuse, trouble, perturb, jumble, tumble; huddle, shuffle, muddle, toss, hustle, fumble, riot; bring —, put —, throw- into -disorder etc. 59; break the ranks, disconcert, convulse; break in upon.

unhinge, dislocate, put out of joint, throw out of gear.

turn topsy-turvy etc. (*invert*) 218; bedevil; complicate, involve, perplex, confound; im-, embrangle; tangle, en-tangle, ravel, tousle, dishevel, ruffle, rumple etc. (*fold*) 258; dement.

litter, scatter; mix etc. 41.

Adj. deranged etc. *v.;* syncre-tic, -tistic.

62. Precedence.—**N.** precedence; coming before etc. *v.;* the lead, *le pas;* superiority etc. 33; importance etc. 642; anteced-ence, -ency; anteriority etc. (*front*) 234; precursor etc. 64; priority etc. 116; precession etc. 280; anteposition, preference.

V. precede; come -before, — first; forerun, head, lead, take the lead; lead the -way, — dance; introduce, usher in; have the *pas*; set the fashion etc. (*influence*) 175; lead off, kick off, open the ball; take —, have- precedence; outrank; have the start etc. (*get before*) 280.

place before; prefix; premise, prelude, preface.

Adj. preceding etc. *v.;* pre-, antecedent; anterior, prior etc. 116; before; former, foregoing; before-, above-mentioned; aforesaid, said; precurs-ory, -ive; prevenient, preliminary, prefatory, introductory; prelus-ive, -ory; proemial, preparatory.

Adv. before; in advance etc. (*precession*) 280.

Phr. *seniores priores.*

63. Sequence.—**N.** sequence, coming after; going after etc. (*following*) 281; consecution, succession; posteriority etc. 117.

continuation; prolongation, order of succussion; successiveness; Elijah's mantle.

secondariness; subordinancy etc. (*inferiority*) 34.

V. succeed; come -after, — on, — next; follow, ensue, step into the shoes of; alternate.

place after, suffix, append.

Adj. succeeding etc. *v.;* sequent; sub-, consequent; sequacious, proximate, next; consecutive etc. (*continuity*) 69; alternate, amoebaean.

latter; posterior etc. 117.

Adv. after, subsequently; behind etc. (*rear*) 235.

64. Precursor.—**N.** precursor, antecedent, precedent, predecessor; forerunner, van-courier, *avant-coureur,* pioneer, prodrome, *prodromos,* outrider; leader, bell-wether; herald, harbinger; dawn.

prelude, preamble, preface, prologue, foreword, *avant-propos, protasis,* prolusion, proem, *prolepsis, prolegomena,* prefix, introduction;

lead, heading, frontispiece, groundwork; preparation etc. 673; overture, voluntary, *exordium,* symphony, *ritornello;* premises.

prefigurement etc. 511; omen etc. 512.

Adj. precursory; prelu-sive, -sory, -dious; proemial, introductory, prefatory, prodromous, inaugural, preliminary; precedent etc. (*prior*) 116.

65. Sequel.—N. sequel, suffix, successor; tail, *queue,* train, wake, trail, rear; retinue, suite; appendix, postscript, subscript; epilogue; conclusion; peroration; codicil; continuation, *sequela;* appendage etc. 39; tail –, heel-piece; tag, more last words; *colophon.*

follower, after-glow, -growth, -crop, -taste, -math.

after-part, -piece, -course, -thought, -game; *arrière pensée,* second thoughts.

66. Beginning.—N. beginning, commencement, opening, outset, incipience, inception, inchoation; introduction etc. (*precursor*) 64; *alpha;* initial; foundation; inauguration, *début, le premier pas,* embarcation, rising of the curtain; zero hour; exordium, curtain raiser; maiden speech; prelude; outbreak, onset, brunt; initiative, move, first move; gambit, narrow –, thin- end of the wedge; fresh start, new departure; forefront.

origin etc. (*cause*) 153; source, rise; bud, germ etc. 153; egg, rudiment; genesis, birth, nativity, cradle, infancy, incunabula; start, starting-point etc. 293; dawn etc. (*morning*) 125.

title-page; head, -ing, caption; van etc. (*front*) 234.

en-trance, -try; inlet, orifice, mouth, chops, lips, porch, portal, portico, *propylon,* door; gate, -way; postern, wicket, threshold, vestibule; skirts, border etc. (*edge*) 231; tee.

first -stage, – blush, – glance, – impression, – sight.

rudiments, elements, outlines, *principia,* grammar, *protasis;* alphabet, ABC.

V. begin, commence, inchoate. rise, arise, originate, institute, conceive, initiate, open, dawn, set in, take its rise, enter upon, start; enter; set out etc. (*depart*) 293; embark in.

usher in; lead -off, – the way; take the -lead, – initiative; inaugurate, head; stand -at the head, – first, – for; lay the foundations etc. (*prepare*) 673; found etc. (*cause*) 153; set -up, – on foot, – agoing, – abroach, – the ball in motion; apply the match to a train; launch, broach; open -up, – the door to; set -about, – to work; make a -beginning, – start; handsel; take the first step, lay the first stone, cut the first turf; break -ground, – the ice, – cover; pass –, cross- the Rubicon; open -fire, – the ball; ventilate, air; undertake etc. 676.

come into -existence, – the world; make one's *début,* take birth; burst forth, break out; spring –, crop- up.

begin -at the beginning, – *ab ovo,* – again, – *de novo;* start afresh, make a fresh start, shuffle the cards, resume, recommence.

Adj. beginning etc. *v.;* initi-al, -atory, -ative; inceptive, introductory, incipient; proemial, inaugural; incho-ate, -ative; embryonic, rudimental; primogenial; primeval etc. (*old*) 124; rudimentary, aboriginal; natal, nascent.

first, foremost, front, leading, head; maiden.

begun etc. *v.;* just -begun etc. *v.*

Adv. at –, in- the beginning etc. *n.;* first, in the first place, *imprimis,* first and foremost; *in limine;* in -the bud, – embryo, – its infancy; from -the beginning, — its birth; *ab -initio,* – *ovo,* – *incunabilis,* primarily, originally.

67. End.—N. end, close, termination; desinence, conclusion, *finis, finale,* period, term, *terminus,* last, *omega;* extreme, -tremity; gable –, butt –, fagend; tip, nib, point; tail etc. (*rear*) 235; verge etc. (*edge*) 231; tag, epilogue, peroration; *bonne bouche,* bitter end, tail end; terminal; *apodosis;* appendix.

consummation, *dénouement;* finish etc. (*completion*) 729; fate; doom, -sday; crack of doom, day of Judgment, fall of the curtain, wind-up; goal, destination; limit, stoppage, end all, determination; expiration, expiry; death etc. 360; end of all things; finality; eschatology.

break up, *commencement de la fin,* last stage, turning point; *coup de grâce,* death-blow; knock-out.

V. end, close, finish, terminate, conclude, be all over; expire; die etc. 360; come –, draw- to a -close etc. *n.;* have run its course; run out, pass away.

bring to an -end etc. *n.;* put an end to, make an end of; determine; get through; achieve etc. (*complete*) 729; stop etc. (*make to cease*) 142; shut up shop.

Adj. ending etc. *v.;* final, terminal, definitive, conclusive; crowning etc. (*completing*) 729; last, ultimate; hindermost; rear etc. 235; caudal.

contermin-ate, -ous, -able.

ended etc. *v.;* at an end; settled, decided, over, played out, set at rest.

penultimate; last but -one, – two, etc.

unbegun, uncommenced; fresh.

Adv. finally etc. *adj.;* in fine; at the last; once for all.

68. Middle.—N. middle, midst, mediety; mean etc. 29; medium, middle term; center etc. 222; mid-course etc. 628; *mezzo termine; juste milieu* etc. 628; half-way house, nave, navel, omphalos; nucle-us, -olus.

equidistance, bisection, half-distance; equator, diaphragm, midriff; interjacence etc. 228.

Adj. middle, medial, mesial, mean, mid; middle-, mid-most; middling; mediate; intermediate etc. (*interjacent*) 228; equidistant; central etc. 222; mediterranean, equatorial.

Adv. in the middle; in the thick; mid-, half-way; midships, *in medias res.*

69. Continuity. [Uninterrupted sequence.]—**N.** continuity; consecu-tion,, -tiveness etc. *adj.;* succession, round, suite, progression, series, train, chain; cat-, concatenation; catena; scale; gradation, course, constant flow, perpetuity.

procession, column; retinue, *cortège,* cavalcade, rank and file, line of battle, array.

pedigree, genealogy, lineage, race etc. 166.

rank, file, line, row, range, tier, string, thread, team; suit; colonnade.

V. follow in –, form- a series etc. *n.;* fall in.

arrange in a -series etc. *n.;* string together, catenate, file, thread, graduate, tabulate.

Adj. continu-ous. -ed; consecutive; progressive, gradual; serial, successive; immediate, unbroken, entire; linear; in a -line, – row etc. *n.;* uninter-rupted, -mitting; unremitting; perennial, evergreen; constant.

Adv. continuously etc. *adj.; seriatim;* in a -line etc. *n.*; in -succession, – turn; running, gradually, step by step, *gradatim,* at a stretch; in -file, – column, – single file, – Indian file.

70. Discontinuity. [Interrupted sequence.]—**N.** discontinuity; disjunction etc. 44; anacoluthon; interruption, break, fracture, flaw, fault, split, crack, cut; gap etc. (*interval*) 198; solution of continuity, *caesura*; broken thread; parenthesis, episode; rhapsody, patchwork; intermission; alternation etc. (*periodicity*) 138; dropping fire.

V. be -discontinuous etc. *adj.;* alternate, intermit.

discontinue, pause, interrupt; intervene; break, – in upon; interpose etc. 228; break –, snap- the thread; disconnect etc. (*disjoin*) 44.

Adj. discontinuous, unsuccessive, broken, interrupted, *décousu;* dis-, un-connected, discrete, disjunctive; fitful etc. (*irregular*) 139; spasmodic, desultory, intermit-ting etc. *v.;* -tent; alternate; recurrent etc. (*periodic*) 138; few and far between.

Adv. at intervals; by -snatches, – jerks, – skips, – catches, – fits and starts; skippingly, *per saltum; longo intervallo.*

71. Term.—**N.** term, rank, station, stage, step; degree etc. 26; scale, remove, grade, link, peg, round –, rung- of the ladder, *status,* position, place, point, mark, *pas,* period, pitch; stand, -ing; footing, range.

V. hold –, occupy –, fall into- a place etc. *n.*

72. Assemblage.—**N.** assemblage; col-lection, location, -ligation; compilation, levy, gathering, ingathering, mobilization, meet, foregathering, muster, *attroupement*; con-course, -flux, -gregation, -tesseration, -vergence etc. 290; meeting, *levée, réunion,* drawing room, at home; conversazione etc. (*social gathering*) 892; assembly, congress, eisteddfod; conven-tion, -ticle; gemote; conclave, etc. (*council*) 696; posse, *posse comitatus;* Noah's ark.

miscellany, *collectanea,* symposium; museum, menagerie, etc. (*store*) 636.

crowd, throng, multitude; flood, rush, deluge; rout, rabble, mob, press, crush, *cohue,* jam, horde, body, tribe; crew, gang, knot, squad, band, party; swarm, shoal, school, covey, flock, herd, drove, kennel; array, bevy, galaxy; *corps,* company, troop, *troupe;* army, force, regiment, etc. (*combatants*) 726; host etc. (*multitude*) 102; populousness.

clan, brotherhood, association etc. (*party*) 712.

volley, shower, storm, cloud.

group, cluster, Pleiades, clump, pencil; set, batch, lot, pack; budget, *dossier,* assortment, bunch; parcel; pack-et, -age; bundle, *fasciculus,* fascine, bale; ser-on, oon; faggot, wisp, truss, tuft; shock, rick, fardel, stack, sheaf, swath, gavel, haycock, stook.

accumulation etc. (*store*) 636; congeries, heap, lump, pile, *rouleau,* tissue, mass, pyramid; drift; snow-ball, -drift; acervation, cumulation; amassment, glom-, agglom-eration; conglobation; conglomeration, -ate; coacervation, coagmentation, aggregation, concentration, congestion, *omnium gatherum, spicilegium,* black hole of Calcutta; quantity etc. (*greatness*) 31.

collector, gatherer; whip, -per in.

V. [be or come together] assemble, collect, muster; meet, unite, join, rejoin; cluster, flock, swarm, surge, stream, herd, crowd, throng, associate; con-gregate, -glomerate, -centrate; center round, *rendezvous,* resort; come –, flock –, get –, pig- together; forgather; huddle; reassemble.

[get or bring together] assemble, muster, mobilize; bring –, get –, put –, draw –, scrape –, lump- together; col-lect, -locate, -ligate; get –, whip- in; gather; hold a meeting; con-vene, -voke, -vocate; rake up, dredge; heap, mass, pile; pack, put up, truss, cram; acervate; ag-glomerate, -gregate; compile; group, aggroup, concentrate, unite; collect –, bring- into a focus; amass, accumulate etc. (*store*) 636; collect in a drag-net; heap Ossa upon Pelion.

Adj. assembled etc. *v.;* closely packed, dense, serried, crowded to suffocation, teeming, swarming, populous; as thick as hops; all of a heap, fasciculated; cumulative.

Phr. the plot thickens.

73. Non-assemblage. Dispersion.—**N.** dispersion; disjunction etc. 44; divergence etc. 291; scattering etc. *v.*; dissemination, broadcasting, diffusion, dissipation, distribution; apportionment etc. 786; spread, respersion, circumfusion, interspersion, spargefaction.

waifs and estrays, flotsam and jetsam, *disjecta membra.*

V. disperse, scatter, sow, disseminate, radiate, diffuse, shed, spread, ted, bestrew, overspread, dispense, disband, disembody, demobilize, dismember, distribute; apportion etc. 786; blow off, let out, dispel, cast forth, draught off; strew, straw, strow; spirtle, cast, sprinkle, shatter; issue, deal out, retail, utter; re-, inter-sperse; set abroach, circumfuse.

turn –, cast- adrift; scatter to the winds; sow broadcast.

spread like wildfire, disperse themselves.

Adj. unassembled etc. (*see* assemble etc. 72); dispersed etc. *v.*; sparse, dispread, broadcast, sporadic, widespread; far-flung; epidemic etc. (*general*) 78; adrift, stray; dishevelled, streaming.

Adv. *sparsim,* here and there, *passim.*

74. Focus. [Place of meeting.]—**N.** focus; point of- convergence etc. 290; corradiation; center etc. 222; gathering-place, resort; haunt; retreat; *venue, rendezvous;* rallying point, head-quarters, home, club; *dépôt* etc. (*store*) 636; tryst, trysting-place; place of -meeting, – resort, – assignation; *point de –, lieu de- réunion;* issue.

V. bring to- a point, – a focus, – an issue; focus.

75. Class.—**N.** class, category, *categorema,* head, order, section; division, subdivision; department, province, domain, sphere.

kind, sort, genus, species, variety, branch, family, race, tribe, caste, sept, clan, breed; *clique, coterie;* type, kit, sect, set; assortment; feather, kidney; suit; range; gender, sex, kin.

manner, description, denomination, persuasion, connection, designation, character, stamp; predicament; conviction etc. 484.

similarity etc. 17.

76. Inclusion. [Comprehension under, or reference to a class.]—**N.** inclusion, admission, incorporation, comprehension, reception.

composition etc. (*inclusion in a compound*) 54.

V. be -included in etc.; come –, fall –, range-under; belong –, pertain- to; range with; merge in.

include, compromise, comprehend, contain, admit, embrace, receive; enclose etc. (*circumscribe*) 229; incorporate, cover, embody, encircle.

reckon –, enumerate –, number- among; refer to; place –, arrange-under, – with; take into account.

Adj. includ-ed; -ing etc. *v.;* inclusive; comprehensive, all-embracing; congen-er, -erous; of the same -class etc. 75.

Phr. *et hoc genus omne,* etc.; *et caetera.*

77. Exclusion.*—**N.** exclusion etc. 55.

* The same set of words is used to express *Exclusion from a class* and *Exclusion from a compound.* Reference is therefore made to the former at 55. This identity does not occur with regard to *Inclusion,* which therefore constitutes a separate category.

78. Generality.—**N.** general-ity, -ization; universality; catholic-ity, -ism; miscel-lany, -laneousness; drag-net.

every-one, -body; all hands, all the world and his wife; any body, N or M, all sorts; *tout le monde.*

prevalence, run.

V. be -general etc. *adj.;* prevail, obtain, be going about, stalk abroad.

render -general etc. *adj.;* generalize; spread, broadcast.

Adj. general, usual, current, generic, collective; broad, comprehensive, sweeping; encyclopedical, panoramic, widespread etc. (*dispersed*) 73.

universal; catho-lic, -lical; common, worldwide; e-cumenical; transcendental; prevalent, prevailing, rife, epidemic, besetting; all over, covered with.

every, all; indeterminate, indefinite, unspecified, impersonal.

customary etc. (*habitual*) 613.

Adv. what-ever, -soever; to a man, one and all, without exception.

generally etc. *adj.;* always, for better for worse; in general, generally speaking; speaking generally; for the most part; in the long run etc. (*on an average*) 29.

79. Speciality.—**N.** speciality, *spécialité;* individ-uality, -uity; particularity, peculairity; idiocrasy etc. (*tendency*) 176; personality, characteristic, mannerism, idiosyncrasy, attribute specificness etc. *adj.;* singularity etc. (*unconformity*) 83; reading, version, lection; state; *trait;* distinctive feature; technicality; *differentia.*

particulars, details, minutiae, items, counts.

I, self, I myself, *ego;* my-, him-, her-, it-self.

V. specify, particularize, individualize, realize, specialize, designate, differentiate, determine, define, denote, indicate, itemize, detail.

descend to particulars, enter into detail, come to the point.

Adj. special, particular, individual, specific, proper, personal, intimate, original, private, respective, definite, concrete, determinate, especial, certain, esoteric, endemic, partial, party, peculiar, marked, appropriate, several, characteristic, diagnistic, exact, exclusive; singular etc. (*exceptional*) 83; idiomatic; typical, representative, distinctive.

this, that; yon, -der.

Adv. specially etc. *adj.;* in particular, *in propriâ personâ; ad hominem;* for my part.

each, apiece, one by one; severally, respectively, each to each; *seriatim,* in detail, bit by bit; *pro hac vice,* – *re natâ.*

namely, that is to say, *videlicet,* viz.; to wit.

80. Rule.—**N.** regularity, uniformity etc. 16; clock-work precision; punctuality etc. (*exactness*) 494; routine etc. (*custom*) 613; formula; system; rut; canon, convention, maxim; rule etc. (*form, regulation*) 697; key-note, standard, model; precedent etc. (*prototype*) 22; conformity etc. 82.

nature, principle; law; order of things; normal –, natural –, ordinary –, model- -state, – condition; standing -dish, – order; normality; Procrustean law; law of the Medes and Persians; hard and fast rule.

Adj. regular, uniform, symmetrical, constant, steady; according to rule etc. (*conformable*) 82; customary etc. 613; orderly etc. 58.

81. Multiformity.—**N.** multi-, omniformity; variety, diversity; multifariousness etc. *adj.*

Adj. multi-form, -fold, -farious, -generous; multiplex, variform, manifold, many-sided, multiplicate; omni-form, -genous, -farious; polymorphic; protean; heterogeneous, motley, mosaic; epicene, indiscriminate, desultory, irregular, diversified, different, divers; all manner of; of -every description, – all sorts and kinds; *et hoc genus omne;* and what not? *de omnibus rebus et quibusdam aliis.*

82. Conformity.—**N.** conform-ity, -ance; observance.

naturalization; conventionality etc. (*custom*) 613; agreement etc. 23.

example, instance, specimen, sample, quotation; exemplification, illustration, case in point; object lesson.

conventionalist, formalist, Philistine.

pattern etc. (*prototype*) 22.

V. conform to, – rule; accommodate –, adapt- oneself to; rub off corners.

be -regular etc. *adj.;* move in a groove; follow –, observe –, go by –, bend to –, obey- -rules, – precedents; comply –, tally –, chime in –, fall in-with; be -guided, – regulated- by; fall into a -custom, – usage; follow the -fashion, – multitude; pass muster, do as others do, *hurler aves les loups;* do at Rome as the Romans do; go –, swim- with the -stream, – current, – tide; tread the beaten track etc. (*habit*) 613; rubber-stamp; keep one in countenance.

exemplify, illustrate, cite, quote, put a case; produce an- instance etc. *n.*

Adj. conformable to rule, adaptable, compliant, consistent, agreeable; regular etc. 80; according to -regulation, – rule, – Cocker; *en règle, selon les règles,* well regulated, orderly; symmetric etc. 242.

conventional commonplace etc. (*customary*) 613; of -daily, – every day- occurrence; in the natural order of things; ordinary, common, – or garden, prosaic, habitual, usual.

in the order of the day; naturalized.

typical, normal, formal; canonical, orthodox, sound, strict, rigid, positive, uncompromising, Procrustean; point device.

secundum artem, ship-shape, technical.

exemplary, illustrative, in point.

Adv. conformably etc. *adj.;* by rule; agreeably to; in -conformity, – accordance, – keeping- with; according to; consistently with; as usual, *ad instar, instar omnium; more -solito, – majorum.*

for the sake of conformity; of –, as a matter of- course; *pro formâ,* for form's sake, by the card; according to plan.

invariably etc. (*uniformly*) 16.

for -example, – instance; *exempli gratiâ; e.g.; inter alia.*

Phr. *cela va sans dire, ex pede Herculem, noscitur a sociis.*

83. Unconformity.—N. non-conformity etc. 82; un-, dis-conformity; unconventionality, informality, abnormity, anomaly; anomalousness etc. *adj.;* exception, peculiarity, etc. 79; infraction –, breach –, violation –, infringement- of -law, – custom, – usage; eccentricity, *bizarrerie,* oddity, *je ne sais quoi,* monstrosity, rarity; freak of Nature.

individuality, idiosyncrasy, singularity, oritinality, mannerism.

aberration; irregularity; variety; singularity; exemption; salvo etc. (*qualification*) 469.

nonconformist; nondescript, character, original, nonsuch, monster, prodigy, wonder, miracle, curiosity, missing link, flying fish, black swan, *lusus naturae, rara avis,* queer fish; mongrel; half-caste, -blood, -breed; *métis,* cross breed, hybrid, mule, mulatto, sacatra, marabou; *tertium quid,* hermaphrodite, gynander, androgyn.

phoenix, chimera, hydra, sphinx, minotaur; griff-in, -on; centaur; hippogriff, -centaur; sagittary; kraken; cockatrice, wyvern, roc, liver, dragon, sea-serpent; mermaid; unicorn; Cyclops, 'men whose heads do grown beneath their shoulders;, Teratolgy.

fish out of water; neither -one thing nor another, – fish flesh nor fowl nor good red herring; one in a -way, – thousand; out-cast, -law; Ishmael, pariah; oasis.

V. be -unconformable etc. *adj.;* leave the beaten -track, – path; infringe –, break –, violate- a -law, – habit, – usage, – custom; drive a coach and six through; stretch a point; have no business there; baffle –, beggar- all description.

Adj. unconformable, exceptional; abnorm-al, -ous; anomal-ous, -istic; out of -order, – place, – keeping, – tune, – one's element; irregular, arbitrary; lawless, informal, aberrant, stray, wandering, wanton; peculiar, exclusive, unnatural, eccentric, crotchety, egregious; out of the -beaten track, – common, – common run, – pale of; misplaced; funny.

un-usual, -accustomed, -customary, -wonted, -common; rare, singular, *unique,* curious, odd, extraordinary, strange, monstrous; wonderful etc. 870; unexpected, unaccountable; *outré,* out of the way, remarkable, noteworthy; queer, quaint, nondescript, none such, *sui generis;* original, unconventional, Bohemian, unfashionable; un-described, -precedented, -paralleled, -exampled, -heard of, -familiar; fantastic, newfangled, grotesque, *bizarre;* outlandish, exotic, *tombé de nues,* preternatural; denaturalized.

heterogeneious, heteroclite, amorphous, mongrel, amphibious, epicene, half-blood, hybrid; androgyn-ous, -al; unsymmetric etc. 243.

qualified etc. 469.

Adv. unconformably etc. *adj.;* except, unless, save, barring, beside, without, save and except, let alone.

however, yet, but.

Int. what -on earth! – in the world!

Phr. never was -seen, – heard, – known- the like.

84. Number.—N. number, symbol, numeral, figure, cipher, digit, integer; counter; round number; formula; function; series.

sum, total, aggregate, difference, complement, subtrahend; product; multipli-cand, -er, -cator; coefficient, multiple; dividend, divisor, factor, quotient, sub-multiple, fraction; mixed number; numerator, denominator; decimal, circulating decimal, repetend; common measure, aliquot part; reciprocal; prime number; totitive, totient.

permutation, combination, variation; election.

ratio, proportion; progression; arithmetical –, geometrical –, harmonical- progression; percentage.

figurate –, pyramidal –, polygonal- numbers.

power, root, exponent, index, logarithm, antilogarithm; modulus.

differential, integral, fluxion, fluent.

Adj. numeral, complementary, divisible, aliquot, reciprocal, prime, fractional, decimal, figurate, incommensurable.

proportional, exponential, logarithmic, logometric, differential, fluxional, integral.

positive, negative; rational, irrational; surd, radical, real, imaginary, impossible.

85. Numeration.—N. numeration, numbering etc. *v.;* pagination; tale, tally, recension, enumeration, summation, reckoning, computation, supputation; calcu-lation, -lus; algorithm, rhabdology, dactylonomy; measurement etc. 466; statistics.

arithmetic, analysis, algebra, fluxions; differential –, integral –, infinitesimal-calculus; calculus of differences.

[Statistics] dead reckoning, muster, poll, census, capitation, roll-call, recapitulation; account etc. (*list*) 86.

[Operations] notation, addition, subtraction, multiplication, division, proportion, rule of three, practice, equations, extraction of roots, reduction, involution, evolution, approximation, interpolation, differentiation, integration.

[Instruments] abacus, swan-pan, logometer, sliding –, slide- rule, tallies, Napier's bones, calculating –, adding- machine, difference engine; cash register.

arithmetician, calculator, abacist; mathematician, actuary, statistician, surveyor, geodesist.

V. number, count, tell; call –, run- over, take an account of, enumerate, call the roll, muster, poll, recite, recapitulate; sum; sum –, cast- up; tell off, score, cipher, compute, calculate, set a price, reckon, – up, estimate; suppute, add, subtract, multiply, divide, extract roots.

check, prove, demonstrate, balance, audit, overhaul, take stock; affix numbers to, page, foliate, paginate.

amount –, come- to.

Adj. numer-al, -ical; arithmetical, analytic, algebraic, statistical, numerable, computable, calculable; commensur-able, -ate; incommensur-able, -ate.

86. List.—**N.** list, catalogue, enumeration, inventory, schedule; register etc. (*record*) 551; account; bill, – of costs, syllabus; terrier, tally, file; almanac, calendar, index, table, atlas, contents, card index; rota, ticket; book, ledger; synopsis, *catalogue raisonné; tableau,* scroll, manifest, invoice, bill of lading; prospectus, *programme;* bill of fare, *menu, carte;* score, census, statistics, returns; Red –, Blue –, Domesday- book; *cadaster;* directory, gazetteer, dictionary, glossary, lexicon, thesaurus, gradus.

roll; check –, chequer –, bead- roll, – of honor; muster -roll, – book; roster, panel; cartulary, diptych.

V. list, enrol, schedule, register etc. *n.;* indent, post, docket; matriculate.

Adj. cadastral, listed etc. *v.*

87. Unity.—**N.** unity; oneness etc. *adj.;* individuality; solitude etc. (*seclusion*) 893; isolation etc. (*disjunction*) 44; unification etc. 48.

one, unit, ace; item; individual; solo, none else, no other, naught beside.

V. be -one, – alone etc. *adj.;* dine with Duke Humphrey.

isolate etc. (*disjoin*) 44.

render one; unite etc. (*join*) 43, (*combine*) 48.

Adj. one, sole, single, solitary, only- begotten; individual, apart, alone; kithless.

un-accompanied, -attended; *solus,* single-handed; singular, odd, unique, unrepeated, azygous, first and last; isolated etc. (*disjoined*) 44; insular; unitary.

lone; lone-ly, -some; desolate, dreary.

in-secable, -severable, -discerptible; compact, irresolvable.

Adv. singly etc. *adj.;* alone, by itself, *per se,* only, apart, in the singular number, in the abstract; one -by one, – at a time; simply; one and a half, *sesqui-*.

Phr. *natura il fece, e poi roppe la stampa.*

88. Accompaniment.—**N.** accompaniment; appurtenance, adjunct etc. 39; context.

coexistence, concomitance, company, association, companionship; part-, copart-nership; coefficiency.

concomitant, accessory, coefficient; companion, attendant, fellow, associate, consort, spouse, colleague, *fidus Achates;* part-, co-partner; satellite, hanger on, shadow; excort, *entourage,* suite, *cortège;* convoy, follower etc. 65; attribute.

V. accompany, coexist, attend, convoy, chaperon; hang –, wait- on; go hand in hand with; synchronize etc. 120; bear –, keep- company; row in the same boat; bring in its train, associate –, couple- with.

Adj. accompanying etc. *v.;* concomitant, fellow, twin, joint; associated –, coupled- with; accessory, attendant, *obbligato.*

Adv. with, withal; together –, along –, in company- with; hand in hand, side by side; cheek by -jowl, – jole; arm in arm; there-, here-with; and etc. (*addition*) 37.

together, in a body, collectively.

89. Duality.—**N.** dual-ity, -ism; duplicity; biplicity, -formity; span, polarity.

two, deuce, couple, couplet, doublet, brace, pair, cheeks, twins, Castor and Pollus, *gemini,* Siamese twins; fellows; yoke, conjugation, dyad, distich.

V. [unite in pairs] pair, couple, bracket, yoke; conduplicate, mate.

Adj. two, twain; dual, -istic; binary, binomial; twin, biparous; dyadic; conduplicate; duplex etc. 90; *tête-à-tête;* paired; dihedral.

coupled etc. *v.;* conjugate.

both, – the one and the other.

90. Duplication.—**N.** duplication, doubling etc. *v.;* gemi-, ingemi-nation; reduplication; iteration etc. (*repetition*) 104; renewal.

V. double; re-double, -duplicate; geminate; repeat etc. 104; renew etc. 660; duplicate, copy etc. 21.

Adj. double; doubled etc. *v.;* bicameral, bicapital, bi-fold, -form, -lateral, -farious, -facial; two-fold, -sided, -headed, -edged etc.; duplex; double-faced; twin, duplicate, ingeminate; second; dual etc. 29.

Adv. twice, once more; over again etc. (*repeatedly*) 104; as much again; twofold.

secondly, in the second place, again.

91. Bisection. [Division into two parts.]—**N.** bi-section, -partition; di-, subdi-chotomy; halving etc. *v.;* dimidiation; *hendiadis.*

bifurcation, forking, branching, furcation, ramification, divarication; fork, prong; fold.

half, moiety.

V. bisect, halve, divide, split, cut in two, cleave, dimidiate, dichotomize, divaricate.

go halves, divide with.

separate, fork, bifurcate; branch -off, – out; ramify.

Adj. bisected etc. *v.;* cloven, cleft; bipartite, biconjugate, bicuspid, bifid; bifur-cous, -cate, -cated; semi-, demi- hemi-.

92. Triality.—N. triality, trinity,* triplicity.

three, triad, triplet, trey, trio, ternion, trinomial, leash; tierce; triennium; trefoil, triangle, trident, tripod, triumvirate, *troika.*

third power, cube.

Adj. three; tri-form, -nal, -nomial; tertiary; triune.

**Trinity* is hardly ever used except in a theological sense; *see* Deity 976.

93. Triplication.—N. tripli-cation, -city; trebleness, trine, trilogy.

V. treble, triple, triplicate, cube.

Adj. treble, triple; tern, -ary; triplex, triplicate, threefold, trilogistic; third; trinal; trihedral.

Adv. three -times, – fold; thrice, in the third place, thirdly; trebly etc. *adj.*

94. Trisection. [Division into three parts.]—**N.** tri-section, -partition, -chotomy; third, – part.

V. trisect, divide into three parts, trifurcate.

Adj. trifid; trisected etc. *v.;* tripartite, -chotomous, -sulcate.

95. Quaternity.—N. quaternity, four, tetrad, quartet, quaternion, square, quadrature, quarter, quadruplet; quadrilateral, quadrangle, quatrefoil; *quadriga.*

V. reduce to a square, square.

Adj. four; quat-ernary, -ernal; quadratic; quartile, quartic, tetractic, tetrad, tetrahedral; quadrennial; quadrivalent.

96. Quadruplication.—N. quadruplication.

V. multiply by four, quadruplicate, biquadrate.

Adj. fourfold; quad-ruple, -ruplicate, -rible; quadruplex; fourth.

Adv. four times; in the fourth place, fourthly.

97. Quadrisection. [Division into four parts.]—N. quadri-section, -partition; quartering etc. *v.;* fourth; quart, -er, -ern; farthing (*i.e.* fourthing); quarto.

V. quarter, divide into four parts, quadrisect.

Adj. quartered etc. *v.;* quadri-fid, -partite.

98. Five, etc.—N. five, cinque, quint, quincunx, quintuplet, quintet, pentagon, pentameter, Pentateuch; six, half-a-dozen; sextet, hexagon, hexameter; seven, Heptarchy; eight, octet, octagon, octave; nine, three times three; ten, decade; eleven; twelve, dozen; thirteen; long –, baker's-dozen.

twenty, score; twenty-four, four and twenty, two dozen; twenty-five, five and twenty, quarter of a hundred; forty, two score; fifty, half a hundred; sixty, three score, sexagenarian; seventy, three score and ten, septuagenarian; eighty, four score, octogenarian; ninety, four score and ten, nonagenarian.

hundred, centenary, hecatomb, century; hundredweight, cwt.; one hundred and forty-four, gross; bicentenary, tercentenary etc.

thousand, chiliad; myriad, millennium, ten thousand; lac, lakh, one hundred thousand, plum; million; thousand million, *milliard.*

billion, trillion etc.

V. centuriate.

Adj. five, quinary, quintuple; fifth; senary, sextuple; sixth; seventh; octuple; eighth; ninefold, ninth; tenfold, decimal, denary, decuple, tenth; eleventh; duo-denary, -denal; twelfth; in one's 'teens, thirteenth.

vices-, viges-imal; twentieth; twenty-fourth etc. *n.*

cent-uple, -uplicate, -ennial, -enary, -urial; secular, hundredth; thousandth; millenary etc.

99. Quinquesection, etc.—N. division by -five etc. 98; quinquesection etc.; fifth etc.; decimation.

V. decimate, quinquesect.

Adj. quinque-fid, -partite; quinquarticular; octifid; decimal, tenth, tithe, teind; duodecimal, twelfth; sexagesimal, -genary; hundredth, centesimal; millesimal etc.

100. Plurality. [More than one.]—**N.** plurality; a -number, – certain number; one or two, two or three etc.; a few, several; multitude etc. 102.

Adj. plural, more than one, upwards of, some, certain; not -alone etc. 87.

Adv. *et cetera, etc.,* etc.

Phr. *non deficit alter.*

100a. Fraction [Less than one.]—**N.** fraction, fractional part, fragment; part etc. 51.

Adj. fractional, fragmentary, partial.

101. Zero.—N. zero, nothing, naught, nought, duck's egg, goose egg; cipher, none, nobody; not a soul; *âme qui vive*; absence etc. 187; unsubstantiality etc. 4.

Adj. not -one, – any.

102. Multitude.—N. multitude; numerousness etc. *adj.*; numer-osity, -ality; multiplicity; profusion etc. (*plenty*) 639; legion, host; great –, large –, round –, enormous- number; a quantity, numbers, array, sight, army, sea, galaxy; scores, peck, bushel, school, shoal, swarm, draft, bevy, cloud, flock, herd, drove, flight, covey, hive, brood, litter, farrow, fry, nest; mob, crowd etc. (*assemblage*) 72; lots, loads, heaps; all the world and his wife.

[Increase of number] greater number, majority; multiplication, multiple.

V. be -numerous etc. *adj.*; swarm –, teem –, crawl –, creep -with; crowd, swarm, come thick upon; outnumber, multiply; people; swarm like -locusts, — bees.

Adj. many, several, sundry, divers, various,

not a few; a -hundred, – thousand, – myriad, – million, – thousand and one; some -ten or a dozen, – forty or fifty etc.; half a -dozen, – hundred etc.; very –, full –, ever so- many; numer-ous, -ose; profuse, in profusion; manifold, multiplied, multitudinous, multiferous, multiple, multinomial, teeming, crawling, populous, peopled, crowded, thick, studded; galore.

thick coming, many more, more than one can tell, a world of; no end -of, – to; *cum multis aliis*; thick as -hops, – hail; plenty as blackberries; numerous as the -stars in the firmament, – sands on the sea-shore, – hairs on the head; and -what not, – heaven knows what; endless etc. (*infinite*) 105.

Phr. their name is 'Legion.'

103. Fewness.—**N.** fewness etc. *adj.*; paucity, small number; small quantity etc. 32; scarcity, sparsity; rarity; infrequency etc. 137; handfull; maniple; minority, exiguity.

[Diminution of number] reduction; weeding etc. *v.*; elimination, sarculation, decimation.

V. be -few etc. *adj.*

render -few etc. *adj.*; reduce, diminish the number, weed; eliminate, thin, decimate.

Adj. few; scarce; scant, -y; thin, rare, thinly scattered, few and far between; exiguous; infrequent etc. 137; *rari nantes*; hardly –, scarcely- any; to be counted on one's fingers; reduced etc. *v.*; unrepeated.

Adv. here and there.

104. Repetition.—**N.** repetition, iteration, reiteration, duplication, ding-dong, alliteration; *epistrophe;* harping, recurrence, succession, run; batto-, tauto-logy; monotony, tautophony; rhythm etc. 138; pleonasm, redundancy, diffuseness.

chimes, repetend, echo, *ritornello,* burden of a song, *refrain;* rehearsal; encore; *réchauffé, rifacimento,* recapitulation.

cuckoo etc. (*imitation*) 19; reverberation etc. 408; drumming etc. (*roll*) 407; renewal etc. (*restoration*) 660.

twice-told tale; old -story, – song, chestnut; second –, new- edition; reprint, new impression; return game, return match, reappearance, reproduction; periodicity etc. 138.

V. repeat, iterate, reiterate, reproduce, parrot, echo, re-echo, drum, harp upon, battologize, hammer, redouble.

recur, revert, return, reappear; renew etc. (*restore*) 660.

rehearse; do –, say- over again; ring the changes on; harp on the same string; din –, drum- in the ear; conjugate in all its moods, tenses and inflexions, begin again, go over the same ground, go the same round, never hear the last of; resume, return to, recapitulate, reword.

Adj. repeated etc. *v.*; repetition-al, -ary; recurrent, -ring; ever recurring, thick coming; frequent, incessant, redundant, pleonastic, tautological.

monotonous, harping, iterative; mocking, chiming; retold; aforesaid, -named; abovementioned, said; habitual etc. 613; another.

Adv. repeatedly, often, again, afresh, anew, over again, once more; ditto, *encore, de novo, bis, da capo.*

again and again; over and over, – again; many times over; time- and again, – after time; year after year; day by day etc.; many –, several –, a number of- times; many –, full many- a time; times out of number, year in and year out, morning, noon and night; frequently etc. 136.

Phr. *ecce iterum Crispinus, toujours perdrix,* cut and come again; 'tomorrow and tomorrow.'

105. Infinity.—**N.** infini-ty, -tude, -teness etc. *adj.;* perpetuity etc. 112.

V. be -infinite etc. *adj.;* know –, have- no -limits, – bounds; go on for ever.

Adj. infinite, immense; number-, count-, sum-, measure-less; innumer-, immeasur-, incalcul-, illimit-, intermin-, unfathom-, unapproach-able; exhaustless, inexhaustible, indefinite; without -number, – measure, – limit, – end; incomprehensible; limit-, end-, bound-, termless; un-told, -numbered, -measured, -bounded, -limited; illimited; perpetual etc. 112.

Adv. infinitely etc. *adj.; ad infinitum.*

106. Time.—**N.** time, duration; period, term, stage, space, span, spell, season; the whole -time, – period; course etc. 109.

intermediate, time, while, *interim,* interval, bit, pendency; inter-vention, -mission, -mittence, -regnum, -lude; respite.

era, epoch, eon, cycle; time of life, age, year, date; decade etc. (*period*) 108; moment, etc. (*instant*) 113; reign etc. 737.

glass –, ravages –, whirligig –, noiseless foot- of time; scythe.

V. continue, last, endure, go on, hold out, remain, stay, persist, abide, run; intervene; elapse etc. 109.

take –, take up –, fill –, occupy- time.

pass –, pass away –, spend –, while away –, consume –, talk against –, kill- time; tide over; use –, employ- time; tarry etc. 110; seize an opportunity etc. 134; waste time etc. (*be inactive*) 683.

Adj. continuing etc. *v.;* on foot; permanent etc. (*durable*) 110.

Adv. while, whilst, during, pending; during the -time, – interval; in the course of; for the time being, day by day; in the time of, when; meantime, -while; in the -meantime, – *interim; ad interim, pendente lite; de die in diem;* from -day to day, – hour to hour etc.; hourly, always; for a -time, – season; till, until, up to, yet; the whole –, all the- time; all along; throughout etc. (*completely*) 52; for good etc. (*diuturnity*) 110.

here-, there-, where-upon; then; *anno,* – *Domini;* A.D.; *ante Christum;* A.C.; before Christ; B.C.; *anno urbis conditae;* A.U.C.; *anno regni,* A.R.; once upon a time, one fine morning.

Phr. time -runs, – runs against; *tempus fugit.*

107. Neverness.—**N.** 'neverness;' absence of time, no time; *dies non;* Tib's eve; Greek Kalends.

Adv. never; at no -time, – period; on no occasion, never in all one's born days, nevermore, *sine die.*

108. Period. [Definite duration, or portion of time.]—**N.** period; second, minute, hour, day, week, sennight, octave, month, moon, quarter, semester, year, *lustrum, quinquennium,* decade, *decennium,* indiction, lifetime, generation, epoch, era, cycle.

century, age, *millennium; annus magnus.*

Adj. horary; hourly, annual etc. (*periodical*) 138.

108a. Contingent Duration.—Adv. during -pleasure, – good behavior; *quamdiu se bene gesserit.*

109. Course. [Indefinite duration.]—**N.** course –, progress –, process –, succession –, lapse –, flow –, flux –, effluxion, stream –, tract –, current –, sweep –, tide –, march –, step –, flight- of time; duration etc. 106.

[Indefinite time] aorist.

V. elapse, lapse, flow, run, proceed, advance, pass; roll –, wear –, press –, drag- on; flit, fly, slip, slide, glide, crawl; run -its course.

out; expire; go –, pass- by; be -past etc. 122.

Adj. elapsing etc. *v.;* aoristic; progressive, transient etc. 111.

Adv. in due -time, – season; in -course, – process, – the fulness- of time; in time.

Phr. *labitur et labetur; truditur dies die; fugaces labuntur anni;* 'tomorrow and tomorrow and tomorrow creeps in this petty pace from day to day.'

110. Diuturnity. [Long duration.]—**N.** diuturnity; a -long –, length of -time; an age, a century, an eternity, aeons; slowness etc. 275; perpetuity etc. 112; blue moon.

dura-bleness, -bility; persistence, lastingness etc. *adj.;* continuance, assiduity, endurance, standing; permanence etc. (*stability*) 150; survival, -vance; longevity etc. (*age*) 128; distance of time.

protraction –, prolongation –, extension- of time; delay etc. (*lateness*) 133.

V. last, endure, stand, remain, abide, continue, brave a thousand years.

tarry etc. (*be late*) 133; drag -on, – its slow length along, – a lengthening chain; protract, prolong; spin –, eke –, draw –, lengthen- out; temporize; gain –, make –, talk against- time.

out-last, -live; survive; live to fight again.

Adj. durable; perdurable; lasting etc. *v.;* of long -duration, – standing; permanent, chronic, long-standing; intransi-ent, -tive; intransmutable, persistent; life-, live-long; longeval, long-lived, macrobiotic, diuturnal, sempervirent, evergreen, perennial; unin-, ter-, unremitting; perpetual etc. 112.

lingering, protracted, prolonged, spun out etc. *v.;* long-pending, -winded; slow etc. 275.

Adv. long; for -a long time, – an age, – ages, – ever so long, – many a long day; long ago etc. (*in a past time*) 122; *longo intervallo.*

all the -day long, – year round; the livelong day, as the day is long, morning, noon and night; hour after hour, day after day, etc.; for good; permanently etc. *adj.*

111. Transientness. [Short duration.]—**N.** transientness etc. *adj.*; evanescence, impermanence, fugacity, transitoriness, volatility, caducity, mortality, span; flash in the pan, nine days' wonder, bubble, May-fly; spurt; temporary arrangement, interregnum.

velocity etc. 274; suddenness etc. 113; changeableness etc. 149.

V. be -transient etc. *adj.;* flit, pass away, fly, gallop, vanish, fade, fleet, melt away, evaporate; pass away like a -cloud, – summer cloud, – shadow, – dream.

Adj. transi-ent, -tory, -tive; passing, evanescent, fleeting; flying etc. *v.;* fug-acious, -itive; shifting, slippery; spasmodic.

tempor-al, -ary; provis-ional, -ory; cursory, short-lived, ephemeral, deciduous; perishable, mortal, precarious; impermanent.

brief, quick, brisk; cometary, meteoric, extemporaneous, summary; pressed for time etc. (*haste*) 684; sudden, momentary etc. (*instantaneous*) 113.

Adv. temporarily etc. *adj.; pro tempore;* for -the moment, – a time; awhile, *en passant, in transitu;* in a short time; soon etc. (*early*) 132; briefly etc. *adj.;* at short notice; on the -point, – eve -of; *in articulo*; between cup and lip.

Phr. one's days are numbered; the time is up; her to-day and gone tomorrow; *non semper erit aestas; eheu! fugaces labuntur anni; sic transit gloria mundi.*

112. Perpetuity. [Endless duration.]—**N.** perpetuity, eternity, timelessness; everness, aye, sempiternity, immortality, athanasia; everlastingness etc. *adj.;* perpetuation; infinite duration.

V. last –, endure –, go on- for ever; have no end.

eternize, eternify, perpetuate, immortalize.

Adj. perpetual, eternal, eterne; everlasting, -living, -flowing; continual, constant, sempiternal; co-eternal; endless, unending; ceaseless, incessant, uninterrupted, indesinent, unceasing; interminable, having no end; unfading, evergreen, amaranthine; neverending, -dying, -fading; deathless, immortal, undying, imperishable.

Adv. perpetually etc. *adj.;* always, ever, evermore, aye; for -ever, – aye, – evermore, – ever and a day, –, ever and ever; in all ages, from age to age; without end; world –, time- without end; *in saecula saeculorum;* to the -end of time, – crack of doom, – 'last syllable of recorded time;' till doomsday; constantly etc. (*very frequently*) 136.

Phr. *esto perpetuum; labitur et labetur in omne volubilis aevum.*

113. Instantaneity. [Point of time.]—**N.** instantane-ity, -ousness; sudden-, abrupt-ness.

moment, instant, second, minute; twinkling, trice, flash, breath, crack, jiffy, *coup,* burst, flash of lightning, stroke of time.

epoch, time; time of -day, – night; hour, minute; very -minute etc., – time, – hours; present –, right –, true –, exact –, correct-time.

V. be -instantaneous etc. *adj.;* twinkle, flash.

Adj. instantaneous, momentary, extempore, sudden, instant, abrupt; subitaneous, hasty; quick as- thought,* – lightning, – a flash; rapid as electricity.

Adv. instantaneously etc. *adj.*; in – in less than- no time; *presto, subito, instanter,* suddenly, at a stroke, like- a shot, – greased lightning; in a trice, in a moment etc. *n.*; eftsoons, in the twinkling of - ai eye, – a bed post; at one jump, in the same breath, *per saltum, uno saltu*; at – , all at- once; in one's tracks; plump, slap; 'at one fell swoop;' at the same -instant etc. *n.*; immediately etc. (*early*) 132; *ex tempore,* on the -spot, – spur of the moment, – dot; just then; slap- dash etc. (*haste*) 684; before you could -turn round, – say -knife, – Jack Robinson.

Phr. touch and go; no sooner said than done.

*See note on 264.

114. Chronometry. [Estimation, measurement, and record of time.]—**N.** chrono-, horo-metry, -logy; date, epoch; style, era.

almanac, calendar, ephemeris; register, -try; chronicle, annals, journal, diary, chronogram.

[Instruments for the measurement of time] clock, watch; chrono-meter, -scope, -graph; repeater, alarum; time-keeper, -piece; dial, sundial, *gnomon, pendule,* horologe, pendulum, hourglass, water clock, clepsydra.

mean –, Greenwich –, solar –, sidereal –, local –, summer- time; daylight saving.

chrono-grapher, -loger, -logist; annalist.

V. fix –, mark- the time; date, register, chronicle; measure –, beat –, mark- time; bear date.

Adj. chrono-logical, -metrical, -grammatical; isochronal.

Adv. o'clock; *a.m., p.m.*

115. Anachronism. [False estimate of time.]—**N.** ana-, meta-, para-, prochronism; *prolepsis,* misdate; anticipation, antichronism.

disregard –, neglect –, oblivion- of time.

intempestivity etc. 135.

V. mis-, ante-, post-, over-date; anticipate; take no note of time.

Adj. misdated etc. *v.;* undated; overdue; out of date; anachronous etc. *n.*

116. Priority.—**N.** priority, antecedence, anteriority, pre-existence, precedence etc. 62; precession etc. 280; precursor etc. 64; the past etc. 122; premises.

V. precede, come before; forerun; antecede, go before etc. (*lead*) 280; pre-exist; dawn; premise, presage etc. 511.

be -beforehand etc. (*be early*) 132; steal a march upon, anticipate, forestall; have –, gain- the start.

Adj. prior, previous; preced-ing, -ent; anterior, antecedent; pre-existing, -existent; foresighted; former, foregoing; afore –, before-, above-mentioned; aforesaid, said; introductory etc. (*precursory*) 64; pre-war.

Adv. before, prior to; earlier; previously etc. *adj.;* afore, ere, theretofore, erewhile, ere –, before- -then, – now; erewhile, already, yet, beforehand; aforetime; on the eve of, in anticipation.

117. Posteriority.—**N.** posteriority; succession, sequence; following etc. 281; subsequence, supervention; futurity etc. 121; successor; sequel etc. 65; remainder, reversion.

V. follow etc. 281 –, come –, go- after; ensue, result; succeed, supervene; step into the shoes of.

Adj. subsequent, posterior, following, after, later, succeeding, postliminious, postnate; successive etc. 63; postdiluvial, -an; *puisné;* posthumous; post-war, future etc. 121.

Adv. subsequently, after, afterwards, since, later; at a -subsequent, – later- period; next, in the sequel, close upon, thereafter. thereupon, upon which, eftsoons; from that -time, – moment; after a -while, – time; in process of time.

postcenal, postcibal, postprandial, after-dinner.

118. The Present Time.—**N.** the present -time, – day, – moment, – juncture, – occasion; the times, existing time, time being; twentieth century; nonce, crisis, epoch, day, hour.

age, time of life.

Adj. present, actual, instant, current, latest, existing, that is.

Adv. at this -time, – moment etc. 113; at the - present time etc. *n.;* now, at present.

at this time of day, to-day, now-adays; already; even –, but –, just-now; on the present occasion; for the -time being, – nonce; *pro hâc vice;* on the -nail, – spot; on the spur of the -moment, – occasion.

until now; to -this, – the present day.

119. Different Time. [Time different from the present.]—**N.** different –, other- time.

[Indefinite time] aorist.

Adj. aoristic.

Adv. at that –, at which- -time, – moment, – instant; then, on that occasion, upon.

when; when-ever, -soever; upon which, on which occasion; at -another, – a different, – some other, – any - time; at various times; some –, one- -of these days, – fine morning, – day; sooner or later; some time or other; once upon a time, once.

120. Synchronism.—**N.** synchronism; coexistence, coincidence; simultaneousness etc. *adj.;* concurrence, concomitance, unity of time, interim.

[Having equal times] isochronism, syntony.

contemporary, coetanian.

V. coexist, concur, accompany, go hand in hand, keep pace with; synchronize, isochronize.

Adj. synchron-ous, -al, -ical, -istical; simultaneous, coexisting, coincident, concomitant, concurrent; coev-al, -ous; contempora-ry, -neous; coetaneous; coterminous, coeternal; isochronous.

Adv. at the same time; simultaneously etc. *adj.;* together, in concert, during the same time; in the same breath; *pari passu;* in the interim.

at the -very moment etc. 113; just as, as soon as; meanwhile etc. (*while*) 106.

121. Futurity. [Prospective time.]—**N.** futurity, -ition; future, hereafter, time to come; approaching –, coming –, after- -time, – age, – days, – hours, – years, – ages, – life;

morrow, to-morrow, by and by; millennium, doomsday, day of judgment, crack of doom, remote future.

approach of time, advent, time drawing on, womb of time; destiny etc. 152; eventuality.

heritage, heirs, posterity, descendants.

prospect etc. (*expectation*) 507; foresight etc. 510.

V. look forwards; anticipate etc. (*expect*) 507, (*foresee*) 510; forestall etc. (*be early*) 132.

come –, draw- on; draw near; approach, await, threaten; impend etc. (*be destined*) 152.

Adj. future, to come; coming etc. (*impending*) 152; next, near; near –, close- at hand; eventual, ulterior; expectant, prospective, in prospect etc. (*expectation*) 507.

Adv. prospectively, hereafter, on the knees of the gods, in future; to-morrow, the day after to-morrow; in -course, – process, – the fulness- of time; eventually, ultimately, sooner or later; *proximo; paulo post futurum;* in after time; one of these days; after a -time, – while.

from this time; hence-forth, -forwards; thence; thence-forth, -forward; whereupon, upon which.

soon etc. (*early*) 132; on the -eve, – point, – brink- of; about to; close upon.

122. Preterition. [Retrospective time.]—**N.** preterition, priority etc. 116; the past, past time; days –, times- -of yore, – of old, – past, – gone by; bygone days, good old days; old –, ancient –, former -times; fore time; yesterdays; the olden –, good old- time; auld lang syne; eld.

antiquity, antiqueness, *status quo;* time immemorial; distance of time; remote -age, – time; ancient history; remote past; rust of antiquity; ancientness.

pale-ontology, -ography, -ology; palaetiology,* archaeology; archaism, antiquarianism, mediaevalism, pre- Raphaelitism; retrospection, looking back, memory etc. 505.

laudator temporis acti; mediaevalist, pre-Raphaelite; antiqu-ary, -arian; archaeologist etc.; Oldbuck, Dryasdust.

ancestry etc. (*paternity*) 166.

V. be -past etc. *adj.;*have -expired etc. *adj.;* – run its course, – had its day; pass; pass –, go- -by, – away, – off; lapse, blow over.

look –, trace –, cast the eyes- back; exhume.

Adj. past, gone, gone by, over, passed away, bygone, foregone; elapsed, lapsed, preterlapsed, expired, no more, run out, blown over, that has been, whilom, extinct, never to return, exploded, forgotten, irrecoverable; obsolete etc. (*old*) 124; extinct as the dodo.

former, pristine, *quondam, ci-devant,* late; ancestral.

foregoing; last, latter; recent, overnight; past, preterite, preter-perfect, -pluperfect, past perfect.

looking back etc. *v.;* retro-spective, -active; archaelogical etc. *n.*

Adv. formerly; of -old, –yore; erst, whilom, erewhile, time was, ago, over; in -the olden time etc. *n.;* anciently, long -ago, – since; a long -while, – time- ago; years –, ages-ago; some time -ago, – since, – back.

yesterday, the day before yesterday; last -year, – season, – month etc.; *ultimo,* lately etc. (*newly*) 123.

retrospectively; ere –, before –, till- now; hitherto, heretofore; no longer; once, – upon a time; from time immemorial; in the memory of man; time out of mind; already, yet, up to this time; *ex post facto.*

Phr. time was; the time -has, – hath- been.

*Whewell.

123. Newness.—**N.** newness etc. *adj.;* neologism, neoterism; novelty, recency; immaturity; youth etc. 127; gloss of novelty.

innovation; renovation etc. (*restoration*) 660.

modernist, neologist, neoteric.

modernism, modernity; mushroom; latest fashion, *dernier cri.*

upstart, *parvenu, nouveau riche.*

V. renew etc. (*restore*) 660; modernize.

Adj. new, novel, recent, fresh, green; young etc. 127; evergreen; raw, immature; virgin; untried, -handseled, -used, -trodden, -beaten; fledgling.

late, modern, neoteric; new-born, -fashioned, -fangled, -fledged; of yesterday; just out, brand –, span-new, up to date, topical; vernal, renovated; innovatory.

fresh as -a rose, – a daisy, – paint; spick and span.

Adv. newly etc. *adj.;* afresh, anew, lately, just now, only yesterday, the other day; latterly, of late.

not long –, a short time- ago.

124. Oldness.—**N.** oldness etc. *adj.*; age, antiquity; cobwebs of antiquity.

maturity, ripeness; decline, decay; senility etc. 128.

seniority, eldership, primogeniture.

archaism etc. (*the past*) 122; thing –, relic- of the past; megatherium.

tradition, prescription, custom, folklore, immemorial usage, common law.

V. be -old etc. *adj.;* have -had, – seen- its day; become -old etc. *adj.;* age, fade.

Adj. old, olden, ancient, antique; of long standing, time-honored, venerable; eld-er, -est; first-born.

prime; prim-itive, -eval, -igenous; primordi-al, -nate; aboriginal etc. (*beginning*) 66; diluvian, antediluvian; pre-historic; patriarchal, preadamite; paleocrystic; fossil, paleozoic, preglacial, ante-mundane; archaic, classic, mediaeval, pre-Raphaelite, ancestral, black-letter.

immemorial, traditional, prescriptive, customary, whereof the memory of man runneth not to the contrary; inveterate, rooted.

antiquated, of other times, rococo, of the old school, after-age, obsolete; fusty, moth-eaten; out of -date, – fashion; stale, old-fashioned, behind the -age, – times; exploded; gone out, – by; *passé,* outworn, run out; disused; senile etc. 128; time-worn; crumbling etc. (*deteriorated*) 659; second-hand.

old as -the hills, – Methuselah, – Adam, – history.

Adv. since the -world was made, – year one, – days of Methuselah.

125. Morning. [Noon.]—**N.** morning, morn, matins, forenoon, *a.m.*, prime, dawn, daybreak, daylight, sun-up, peep –, break- of day; aurora,

Eos; first blush –, prime- of the morning; twilight, crepuscule, sunrise, cockcrow.

spring; vernal equinox.

noon; mid-, noon-day; noontide, meridian, prime.

summer, midsummer; summer solstice.

Adj. matin, matutinal; vernal, aestival.

Adv. at -sunrise etc. *n.*; with the lark, when the morning dawns.

126. Evening. [Midnight.]—**N.** evening, eve; decline –, fall –, close- of day; eventide, evensong, vespers; candlelight; nightfall, curfew, dusk, twilight, blind man's holiday; eleventh hour; sun-set, -down; going down of the sun, cock-shut, dewy eve, gloaming, bed-time.

afternoon, *post meridiem, p.m.*.

autumn; fall, – of the leaf; autumnal equinox, Indian summer, harvest-time.

midnight; dead –, witching time- of night; winter, – solstice.

Adj. vespertine, autumnal, nocturnal, wintry, brumal, hiemal.

127. Youth.—**N.** youth; juven- -ility, -escence; juniority; infancy; baby-, child-, boy-, girl-, youth-hood; *incunabula;* minority, immaturity, nonage, teens, tender age, bloom.

cradle, nursery, leading-strings, pupilage, puberty, *pucelage*.

prime –, flower –, spring-tide –, seedtime –, golden season - of life; heyday of youth, school days; rising generation, younger generation.

Adj. young, youthful, juvenile, green, callow, budding, sappy, *puisné*, beardless, unfledged, unripe, under age, in one's teens; *in statu pupillari;* younger, junior.

128. Age.—**N.** age; oldness etc. *adj.;* old –, advanced- age; sen-ility, -escence; years, anility, grey hairs, climacteric, grand climacteric, declining years, decrepitude, hoary age, caducity, superannuation; second childhood, -ishness; dotage; vale of years, decline of life, 'sear and yellow leaf;' three-score years and ten; green old age, ripe old age; longevity; time of life.

seniority, eldership; elders etc. (*veteran*) 130; firstling; *doyen,* dean, father; primogeniture; nostology.

V. be -aged etc. *adj.;* grow –, get- old etc. *adj.;* age; decline, wane.

Adj. aged; old etc. 124; elderly, senile; matronly, anile; in years; ripe, mellow, run to seed, declining, waning, past one's prime; grey, -headed; hoar, -y; venerable, time-worn, antiquated, *passé,* effete, doddering, decrepit, superannuated; advanced in -life, – years; stricken in years; wrinkled, marked with the crow's foot; having one foot in the grave; doting etc. (*imbecile*) 499.

old-, eld-er, -est; senior; first-born.

turned of, years old; of a certain age, no chicken, old as Methuselah; gerontic; ancestral; patriarchal etc. (*ancient*) 124.

129. Infant.—**N.** infant, babe, baby; nurse-, suck-, year-, wean-ling; *papoose, bambino.*

child, bairn, little- one, – tot, – mite, chick, brat, chit, pickaninny, kid, urchin; bant-, brat-ling; elf.

youth, boy, lad, slip, sprig, stripling, youngster, cub, unlicked cub, younker, callant, whipster, whipper-snapper, schoolboy, hobbledehoy, hopeful, cadet, minor, master.

scion; sap-, seed-ling; tendril, olive branch, nestling, chicken, duckling; larva, caterpillar, chrysalis, cocoon; tadpole, whelp, cub, pullet, fry, callow; codlin, -g; *foetus,* calf, colt, pup, foal, kitten; lamb, -kin.

girl; lass, -ie; wench, miss, damsel, *demoiselle,* damozel; maid, -en; virgin; nymph; colleen; minx, baggage, school-girl; tomboy, flapper, hoyden.

Adj. infant-ine, -ile; puerile; boy-, girl-, child-, baby-, kitten-ish; baby; new-born, unfledged, new-fledged, callow.

in -the cradle, – swaddling clothes, – long clothes, – arms, – leading strings; at the breast; in one's teens; young etc. 127.

130. Veteran.—**N.** veteran, old man, seer, patriarch, greybeard, dugout, grand-father, -sire; grandam, beldam; gaffer, gammer; hag, crone; pantaloon; sexage-, octoge-, nonage-, cente-narian; old stager; dotard etc. 501.

preadamite, Methuselah, Nestor, Rip van Winkle, old Parr; elders; forefathers etc. (*paternity*) 166.

131. Adolescence.—**N.** adolescence, pubescence, majority; adultness etc. *adj.;* manhood, virility, maturity; flower of age; prime –, meridian- of life.

man etc. 373; woman etc. 374; adult, no chicken.

V. come -of age, – to man's estate, – to years of discretion; attain majority, assume the *toga virilis;* have -cut one's eye-teeth, – sown one's wild oats, settle down.

Adj. adolescent, pubescent, of age; of -full, – ripe- age; out of one's teens, grown up, mature, full- blown, – grown, in one's prime, in full bloom, manly, virile, adult; womanly, matronly; marriageable, nubile.

132. Earliness.—**N.** earliness etc. *adj.;* morning etc. 125.

punctuality; promptitude etc. (*activity*) 682; haste etc. (*velocity*) 274; suddenness etc. (*instantaneity*) 113.

prematurity, precocity, precipitation, anticipation; prevenience, a stitch in time.

V. be -early etc. *adj.;* – beforehand etc. *adv.;* keep time, take time by the forelock, anticipate, forestall; have –, gain- the start; steal a march upon; gain time, draw on futurity; bespeak, secure, engage, pre-engage.

accelerate; expedite etc. (*quicken*) 274; make haste etc. (*hurry*) 684.

Adj. early, prime, timely, in time, punctual, forward; prompt etc. (*active*) 682; summary.

premature, precipitate, precocious; prevenient, anticipatory; rathe.

sudden etc. (*instantaneous*) 113; unexpected etc. 508; impending, imminent; near, – at hand; immediate.

Adv. early, soon, anon, betimes, rathe; eft, -soons; ere –, before- long; punctually etc. *adj.;* to the minute; in time; in -good, – military, – pudding, – due- time; time enough.

beforehand; prematurely etc. *adj.;* precipitately etc. (*hastily*) 684; too soon; before -its, – one's- time; in anticipation; unexpectedly etc. 508.

suddenly etc. (*instantaneously*) 113; before one can say 'Jack Robinson,' at short notice, extempore; on the spur of the -moment, – occasion; at once; on the -spot, – instant; at sight; off –, out of- hand; *à vue d'oeil;* straight, -way, -forth; forthwith, incontinently, summarily, instanter, immediately, briefly, shortly, quickly, speedily, apace, before the ink is dry, almost immediately, presently, at the first opportunity, in no long time, by and by, in a while, directly.

Phr. touch and go, no sooner said than done.

133. Lateness.—**N.** lateness etc. *adj.;* tardiness etc. (*slowness*) 275.

de-lay, -lation; cunctation, procrastination; detention; deferring etc. *v.;* filibuster, postponement, adjournment, prorogation, retardation, respite, reprieve, stay; protraction, prolongation, moratorium; contango; demurrage; remand; Fabian policy, *médecine expectante,* chancery suit; leeway; high time.

V. be -late etc. *adj.;* tarry, wait, stay, bide, take time; dawdle etc. (*be inactive*) 683; linger, loiter, saunter, lag behind; bide –, take- one's time; hang -about, – around, – back, – in the balance; gain time; hang fire; stand –, lie-over.

put off, defer, delay, lay over, suspend; shift –, stave- off; waive, retard, remand, postpone, adjourn; procrastinate; dally; prolong, protract; spin –, draw –, lengthen- out; prorogue; keep back; tide over; push –, drive- to the last; let the matter stand over; reserve etc. (*store*) 636; temporize; consult one's pillow, sleep upon it.

shelve, table, lay on the table.

lose an opportunity etc. 135; be kept waiting, dance attendance; kick –, cool- one's heels; *faire antichambre;* wait impatiently; await etc. (*expect*) 507; sit up, – at night.

Adj. late, tardy, slow, behindhand, belated, postliminious, posthumous, backward, unpunctual; dilatory etc. (*slow*), overdue 275; delayed etc. *v.;* in abeyance.

Adv. late; late-, back-ward; late in the day; at -sunset, – the eleventh hour, – length, – last, – long; ultimately; after –, behind- time; too late; too late for etc. 135.

slowly, leisurely, deliberately, at one's leisure; *ex post facto; sine die.*

Phr. *nonum prematur in annum.*

134. Occasion.—**N.** occasion, opportunity, opening, room, scope, field; suitable –, proper- -time, – season; high time; opportuneness etc. *adj.;* tempestivity.

crisis, turn, juncture, emergency, conjuncture; turning point; given time.

nick of time; golden –, well-timed –, fine –, favorable- opportunity; clear stage, fair field; *mollia tempora; fata Morgana;* spare time etc. (*leisure*) 685.

V. seize etc. (*take*) 789 –, use etc. 677 –, give etc. 784- an -opportunity, – occasion; improve the occasion.

suit the occasion etc. (*be expedient*) 646.

strike the iron while it is hot, *battre le fer sur l'enclume,* make hay while the sun shines, take time by the forelock, *prendre la balle au bond.*

Adj. opportune, timely, well-timed, timeous, timeful, seasonable.

providential, lucky, fortunate, happy, favorable, propitious, auspicious, critical; suitable etc. 23; *obiter dicta.*

Adv. opportunely etc. *adj.;* in -proper, – due- -time, – course, – season; for the nonce; in the -nick, – fulness- of time; all in good time; just in time, at the eleventh hour, now or never.

by the -way, – by; *en passant, à propos; pro -re natâ, – hac vice; par parenthèse,* parenthetically, by way of parenthesis; while -speaking of, – on this subject; *ex tempore;* on the spur of the -moment, – occasion; on the spot etc. (*early*) 132.

Phr. *carpe diem; occasionem cognosce;* one's hour is come, the time is up; that reminds me.

135. Intempestivity.—**N.** intempestivity; unseasonableness; unsuitable –, improper-time; unreasonableness etc. *adj.;* evil hour; *contretemps;* intrusion; anachronism etc. 115.

V. be -ill timed etc. *adj.;* mistime, intrude, come amiss, break in upon; have other fish to fry; be -busy, – engaged, – tied up, – occupied.

lose –, throw away –, waste –, neglect etc. 460- an opportunity; allow –, suffer- the -opportunity, – occasion- to -pass, – slip, – go by, – escape, – lapse; waste time etc. (*be inactive*) 683; let slip through the fingers, lock the stable door when the steed is stolen.

Adj. ill-, mis-timed; untimely, intrusive, unseasonable; out of -date, – season; inopportune, timeless, untoward, *mal à propos,* unlucky, inauspicious, unpropitious, unfortunate, unfavorable; unsuited etc. 24; inexpedient etc. 647.

unpunctual etc. (*late*) 133; too late for; premature etc. (*early*) 132; too soon for; wise after the event.

Adv. inopportunely etc. *adj.;* as ill luck would have it, in an evil hour, the time having gone by, a day after the fair.

Phr. after meat mustard, after death the doctor.

136. Frequency.—**N.** frequency, oftness; repetition, etc. 104.

V. recur etc. 104; do nothing but; keep, – on.

Adj. frequent, many times, not rare, thickcoming, incessant, perpetual, continual, constant, recurrent, repeated etc. 104; habitual etc. 613; hourly, etc. 138.

Adv. often, often to be met with, oft; oft-, often-times; frequently; repeatedly etc. 104; unseldom, not unfrequently; in -quick, – rapid- succession; many a time and oft; daily, hourly etc.; every -day, – hour, – moment etc.

perpetually, continually, constantly, incessantly, without ceasing, at all times, daily and hourly, night and day, day and night, day after day, morning, noon and night, ever and anon.

most often; commonly etc. (*habitually*) 613.

sometimes, occasionally, at times, now and then, from time to time, there being times when, *toties quoties*, often enough, again and again etc. 104.

137. Infrequency.—**N.** infrequency, infrequence, rareness, rarity; fewness etc. 103; seldomness, uncommonness.

V. be -rare etc. *adj.*

Adj. un-, in-frequent; uncommon, sporadic, rare, — as a blue diamond; few etc. 103; scarce; almost unheard of, unprecedented, which has not occurred within the memory of the oldest inhabitant, not within one's previous experience.

Adv. seldom, rarely, scarcely, hardly; not often, unfrequently, infrequently, unoften; scarcely —, hardly- ever; once in a blue moon.

once; once -for all, — in a way; *pro hac vice;* like angels' visits, few and far between.

138. Regularity of recurrence. **Periodicity.**—**N.** periodicity, intermittence; beat; oscillation etc. 314; pulse, pulsation; rhythm; alternation, -nateness, -nativeness, -nity.

bout, round, revolution, rotation, turn.

anniversary, birthday, jubilee, centenary, bi-, ter-centenary.

[Regularity of return] rota, cycle, period, stated time, routine; days of the week; Sunday, Monday etc.; months of the year; January etc.; feast, fast, saint's day etc.; Christmas, Easter, New Year's Day etc. 998; quarter-, Lady-, Midsummer-, Michaelmas-day; May Day, the King's Birthday; leap year, seasons.

punctuality, regularity, steadiness.

V. recur in regular -order, — succession; return, revolve, rotate; come -again, — in its turn; come round, — again; beat, pulsate; alternate; intermit.

Adj. periodic, -al; serial, recurrent, cyclic-, -al, rhythmic-, -al, even; recurring etc. *V.;* inter-, remittent; alternate, every other.

hourly; diurnal, daily; quotidian, tertian, weekly; hebdomad-al, -ary; bi-weekly, fortnightly; monthly, menstrual, catamenial; yearly, annual; biennial, triennial, etc.; bissextile; centennial, secular; paschal, lenten, etc.

regular, steady, punctual, constant, methodical, regular as clockwork.

Adv. periodically etc. *adj.;* at -regular intervals, — stated times; at -fixed, — established- periods; punctually etc. *adj.; de die in diem;* from day to day, day by day.

by turns, in -turn, — rotation; alternately, every other day, off and on, ride and tie, round and round.

139. Irregularity of recurrence.—**N.** irregularity, uncertainty, unpunctuality; fitfulness etc. *adj.*

Adj. irregular, uneven, uncertain, unpunctual, capricious, erratic, desultory, fitful, flickering; rambling, rhapsodical; spasmodic, unsystematic, unequal, variable, halting.

Adv. irregularly etc. *adj.;* by fits and starts etc. (*discontinuously*) 70.

140. Change. [Difference at different times.]—**N.** change, alteration, mutation, permutation, variation, modification, modulation, inflexion, mood, qualification, innovation, *metastasis,* deviation, shift, turn; diversion; break.

transformation, transfiguration; metamorphosis; metabolism; transmutation; transubstantiation; metagenesis, transanimation, transmigration, metempsychosis; version, metathesis, transmogrification; catalysis; *avatar*; alterative.

conversion etc. (*gradual change*) 144; revolution etc. (*sudden or radical change*) 146; inversion etc. (*reversal*) 218; displacement etc. 185; transference etc. 270.

changeableness etc. 149; tergiversation etc. (*change of mind*) 607.

V. change, alter, vary, wax and wane; modulate, diversify, qualify, tamper with; turn, shift, veer, jibe, tack, chop, shuffle, swerve, dodge, warp, deviate, turn aside, evert, intervert; pass to, take a turn, turn the corner, resume.

work a change, modify, vamp, revamp, superinduce; trans-form, -mute, -ume, -figure etc. *n.;* metamorphose, ring the changes; convert, resolve; revolutionize; chop and change; patch, re-shape.

innovate, introduce new blood, shuffle the cards, spin the wheel; give a -turn, — color- to; influence, turn the scale; shift the scene, turn over a new leaf.

recast etc. 146; reverse etc. 218; disturb etc. 61; convert into etc. 144.

Adj. changed etc. *v.;* new-fangled; changeable etc. 149; transitional; modifiable; alterative.

Adv. *mutatis mutandis.*

Int. *quantum mutatus!*

Phr. 'a change came o'er the spirit of my dream;' *nous avons changé tout cela; tempora mutantur et nos mutamur in illis; non sum qualis eram.*

141. Permanence. [Absence of change.]—**N.** stability etc. 150; quiescence etc. 265; obstinacy etc. 606.

permanence, -cy, persistence, fixity, fixity of purpose, endurance, durability; standing, *status quo;* maintenance, preservation, conservation; conservatism; *laissez-faire;* law of the Medes and Persians; standing dish.

V. let -alone, — be; persist, remain, stay, tarry, rest; hold, — on; last, endure, bide, abide, aby, dwell, maintain, keep; stand, — still, — fast; subsist, live, outlive, survive; hold —, keep- one's ground, — footing; hold good.

Adj. stable etc. 150; persisting etc. *v.;* permanent; established, fixed; durable; unchanged etc. (change etc. 140); unrenewed; intact, inviolate; persistent; monotonous, uncheckered; unfailing.

un-destroyed, -repealed, -suppressed; conservative, *qualis ab incepto;* prescriptive etc. (*old*) 124; stationary etc. 265.

Adv. *in statu quo;* for good, finally; at a stand, -still; *uti possidetis;* without a shadow of turning.

Phr. as you were!; *j'y suis j'y reste; esto perpetua; nolumus leges Angliae mutari;* let sleeping dogs lie.

142. Cessation. [Change from action to

rest.]—**N.** cessation, discontinuance, desistance, desinence.

inter-, re-mission; sus-pense, -pension, interruption, hitch; hartal; stop; stopping etc. *v.;* closure, stoppage, halt; arrival etc. 292.

pause, rest, lull, respite, truce, armistice, drop; interregnum, abeyance.

closure etc. 261.

dead -stop, – stand, – lock; checkmate; comma, colon, semicolon, period, full stop; end etc. 67; death etc. 360; *caesura.*

V. cease, discontinue, desist, stay; break –, leave- off; hold, stop, pull up, stall, stop short, check; stick, deadlock, hand fire; halt; pause, rest.

have done with, give over, surcease, shut up shop; give up etc. (*relinquish*) 624.

hold –, stay- one's hand; rest on one's oars, repose on one's laurels.

come to a -stand, – standstill, – dead lock, – full stop; arrive etc. 292; go out, die away, peter out; wear -away, – off; pass away etc. (*be past*) 122; be at an end.

intromit, interrupt, suspend, interpel; inter-, re-mit; put -an end, – a stop, – a period- to; bring to a stand, -still; stop, cut out, cut short, arrest, avast; stem the -tide, – torrent; pull the check string; switch off.

Int. halt! hold! stop! enough! avast! have done! a truce to! soft! leave off! shut up! give over! chuck it!

143. Continuance in action.—**N.** continu-ance, -ation; run; extension, prolongation; maintenance, perpetuation; persistence etc. (*perseverance*) 604a; repetition etc. 104.

V. continue, persist; go –, jog –, keep –, carry –, run – hold- on; abide, keep, pursue, stick to; endure; take –, maintain- its course; keep up.

sustain, uphold, hold up, keep on foot; follow up, perpetuate. prolong; maintain; preserve etc. 604*a*; harp upon etc. (*repeat*)104.

keep -going, – alive, – at it, – the pot boiling, – the ball rolling, – up the ball; plod-, plug- along; slog on; die in harness; hold on –, pursue- the even tenor of one's way.

let be; *stare super antiquas vias; quieta non movere;* let things take their course.

Adj. continuing etc. *v.;* uninterrupted, unintermitting, unremitting, unvarying, unshifting; unreversed, unstopped, unrevoked, unvaried; sustained; undying etc. (*perpetual*) 112; inconvertible.

follow-up.

Int. carry on! right away!

Phr. *vestigia nulla retrorsum, labitur et labetur.*

144. Conversion. [Gradual change to something different.]—**N.** conversion, reduction, transmutation, transformation, development, resolution, assimilation; assumption; naturalization.

chemistry, alchemy; progress, growth, lapse, flux.

passage; transit, -ion; transmigration, shifting etc. *v.;* conjugation; convertibility.

crucible, alembic, caldron, retort, test tube etc.

convert, neophyte, proselyte, pervert, renegade, deserter, apostate, turncoat.

V. be converted into; become, get, wax; come –, turn- -to, – into; turn out, lapse, shift; run –, fall –, pass –, slide –, glide –, grow –, ripen –, open –, resolve itself –, settle –, merge- into; melt, grow, come round to, mature, mellow; assume the -form, – shape, – state, – nature, – character- of; illapse; assume a new phase, undergo a change.

convert –, resolve- into; make, render; mold, form etc. 240; remodel, new model, refound, reform, reorganize; assimilate –, bring –, reduce- to; transform.

Adj. converted into etc. *v.;* convertible, resolvable into; transitional; naturalized.

Adv. gradually etc. (*slowly*) 275; *in transitu* etc. (*transference*) 270.

145. Reversion.—**N.** reversion, return; revulsion; reaction.

turning point, turn of the tide; *status quo ante bellum;* calm before a storm.

alternation etc. (*periodicity*) 138; inversion etc. 219; recoil etc. 277; regression etc. 283; restoration etc. 660; relapse etc. 661; vicinism, atavism, throwback.

V. revert, turn back, return; relapse etc. 661; recoil etc. 277; retreat etc. 283; restore etc. 660; undo, unmake; turn the -tide, – scale; escheat.

Adj. reverting etc. *v.;* revulsive, reactionary.

Adv. *à rebours,* wrong side out.

146. Revolution. [Sudden or violent change.]—**N.** revolution, *bouleversement,* subversion. break up; destruction etc. 162; sudden –, radical –, sweeping –, organic- change; clean sweep, *coup d'état,* overthrow, *débâcle*; counterrevolution, rebellion etc. 742.

transilience, jump, leap, plunge, jerk, start; explosion; spasm, convulsion, throe, revulsion; storm, earthquake, eruption, upheaval, cataclysm.

legerdemain etc. (*trick*) 545.

V. revolutionize; new model, remodel, recast; strike out something new, break with the past; change the face of, unsex; revert etc. 742.

Adj. unrecognizable.

Revolutionary, Bolshevik etc. 742.

147. Substitution. [Change of one thing for another.]—**N.** substitution, subrogation, commutation; supplanting etc. *v.;* supersession, metonymy etc. (*figure of speech*) 521.

[Thing substituted.] substitute, *succedaneum,* make-shift, temporary expedient, shift, *pis aller,* stop-gap, jury-mast, *locum tenens,* warming-pan, dummy, goat, scape-goat; double; changeling; *quid pro quo,* alternative; remount; representative etc. (*deputy*) 759; palimpsest.

price, purchase-money, consideration, equivalent.

V. substitute, put in the place of, change for; make way for, give place to; supply –, take- the place of; supplant, supersede, replace, cut out, serve as a substitute; step into –, stand in- the shoes of; make a shift –, put up- with; borrow of Peter to pay Paul; commute, redeem, compound for.

Adj. substituted etc. *v.;* vicarious, subdititious; substitutional.

Adv. instead; in -place, – lieu, – the stead, – the room- of; *faute de mieux.*

148. Interchange. [Double or mutual change.]—**N.** inter-, ex-change; com-, per-, intermutation; reciprocation, transposal, transposition, shuffling; reciprocity, castling [at chess]; hocus-pocus.

interchange-ableness, -ability.

barter etc. 794; tit for tat etc. (*retaliation*) 718; cross fire, battledore and shuttlecock; *quid pro quo.*

V. inter-, ex-, counter-change; bandy, transpose, shuffle, change hands, swap, trade, permute, reciprocate, commute; give and take, return the compliment; play at -puss in the corner, – battledore and shuttlecock; retaliate etc. 718; barter etc. 794.

Adj. interchanged etc. *v.;* reciprocal, mutual, commutative, interchanged etc. *v.;* interchangeable, intercurrent.

Adv. in exchange, *vice versâ, mutatis mutandis*, backwards and forwards, by turns, turn and turn about, turn about; each –, every one- in his turn.

149. Changeableness.—**N.** changeableness etc. *adj.*; mutability, inconstancy; versatility, mobility; instability, unstable equilibrium; vacillation etc. (*irresolution*) 605; fluctuation, vicissitude; alternation etc. (*oscillation*) 314.

restlessness etc. *adj.;* fidgets, disquiet; dis-, inquietude; unrest; agitation etc. 315.

moon, Proteus, chameleon, kaleidoscope, quicksilver, shifting sands, weathercock, harlequin, Cynthia of the minute, April showers; wheel of Fortune; transientness etc. 111.

V. fluctuate, vary, waver, flounder, flicker, flitter, flit, flutter, shift, shuffle, shake, totter, tremble, vacillate, wamble, turn and turn about, ring the changes; sway –, shift- to and fro; change and change about; oscillate etc. 314; vibrate –, oscillate- between two extremes; alternate; have as many phases as the moon.

Adj. change-able, -ful; changing etc. 140; mutable, variable, checkered, ever changing, kaleidoscopic, prote-an, -iform; versatile.

unstaid, inconstant; un-steady, -stable, -fixed, -settled; fluctuating etc. *v.;* restless; mercurial; agitated etc. 315; erratic, fickle; irresolute etc. 605; capricious etc. 608; touch-and-go; inconsonant, fitful, spasmodic; vibratory; afloat; alternating; alterable, plastic, mobile; fleeting, transient etc. 111.

Adv. see-saw etc. (*oscillation*) 314; off and on.

150. Stability.—**N.** stability; immutability etc. *adj.;* unchangeableness etc. *adj.;* constancy; stable equilibrium, immobility, soundness, vitality, stabiliment, stabilization, stiffness, ankylosis, solidity, *aplomb.*

establishment, fixture; rock, pillar, tower, foundation, leopard's spots, Ethiopian's skin, law of the Medes and Persians.

stabilimeter, stabilizator.

permanence etc. 141; obstinacy etc. 606.

V. be -firm etc. *adj.;* stick fast; stand –, keep –, remain- firm; weather the storm.

settle, establish, stablish, ascertain, fix, set, stabilitate, stabilize; retain, stet, keep hold; make -good, – sure; fasten etc. (*join*) 43; set on its legs, float; perpetuate.

settle down; strike –, take- root; take up one's abode etc. 184; build one's house on a rock.

Adj. unchangeable, immutable; unalter-ed, -able; not to be changed, constant; permanent etc. 141; invariable, undeviating; stable, durable; perennial etc. (*diuturnal*) 110.

fixed, steadfast, firm, fast, steady, balanced; confirmed, valid, fiducial, immovable, irremovable, riveted, rooted; settled, established etc. *v.;* vested; incontrovertible, stereotyped, indeclinable.

tethered, anchored, moored, at anchor, on a rock, firm as a rock; firmly -seated, – established etc. *v.;* deep-rooted, ineradicable; inveterate; obstinate etc. 606.

transfixed, stuck fast, aground, high and dry, stranded.

indefeasible, irretrievable, intransmutable, incommutable, irresoluble, irrevocable, irreversible, reverseless, inextinguishable, irreducible; indissol-uble, -vable; indestructible, undying, imperishable, indelible, indeciduous; insusceptible, – of change.

Int. *stet.*

151. Eventuality.—**N.** eventuality, event, occurrence, incident, affair, transaction, proceeding, fact; matter of –, naked- fact; phenomenon; advent.

business, concern; circumstance, particular, casualty, happening, accident, adventure, passage, crisis, pass, emergency, contingency, consequence etc. 154.

the world, life, things, doings, affairs, matters; things –, affairs- in general; the times, state of affairs, order of the day; course –, tide –, stream –, current –, run –, march- of -things, – events; ups and downs of life; chapter of accidents etc. (*chance*) 156; situation etc. (*circumstances*) 8.

V. happen, occur; take -place, – effect; come, become of; come -off, – about, – round, – into existence, – forth, – to pass, – on; pass, present itself; fall; fall –, turn- out; run, be on foot, fall in; be-fall, -tide, -chance; prove, eventuate, draw on; turn –, crop –, spring –, cast- up; super-, sur-vene; issue, emanate, arrive, ensue, arise, start, hold, take its course; pass off etc. (*be past*) 122.

meet with; experience; fall to the lot of; be one's -chance, – fortune, – lot; find; encounter, undergo; pass –, go- through; endure etc. (*feel*) 821.

Adj. happening etc. *v.;* going on, doing, current; in the wind, afloat; on -foot, – the *tapis;* at issue, in question; incidental.

eventful, momentous, signal; stirring, bustling, full of incident.

Adv. eventually, ultimately, in -the event of, – case; in the course of things; in the -natural, – ordinary- course of things; as -things, – times-go; as the world -goes, – wags; as the -tree falls, – cat jumps; as it may -turn out, – happen.

Phr. the plot thickens.

152. Destiny.—**N.** destiny etc. (*necessity*) 601; hereafter, future –, post- existence; future state, next world, world to come, after life; futurity etc. 121; everlasting -life, – death; prospect etc. (*expectation*) 507.

V. impend; hang –, lie –, hover- over; threaten, loom, await, come on, approach, stare one in the face; fore-, pre-ordain; predestine, doom, foredoom, foreshadow, have in store for.

Adj. impending etc. *v.;* destined; about to -be, – happen; coming, in store, to come, going to happen, instant, at hand, near; near –, close- at hand; overhanging, hanging over one's head, imminent; brewing, preparing, forthcoming; in the wind, on the cards, in reserve; that -will, – is to-be; in prospect etc. (*expected*) 507; looming in the -distance, – horizon, – future; unborn, in embryo; in the womb of -time; – futurity; on the knees of the gods; pregnant etc. (*producing*) 161.

Adv. in -time, – the long run; all in good time; eventually etc. 151; whatever may happen etc. (*certainly*) 474; as -chance etc. 156- would have it.

153. Cause. [Constant antecedent.]—**N.** cause, origin, source, principle, element; occasioner, prime mover, engine, turbine, motor, *primum mobile; vera causa*; author etc. (*producer*) 164; main-spring, agent; dynamo, generator, battery (electric); leaven; groundwork, foundation etc. (*support*) 215.

spring, fountain, well, font; fountain –, spring- head; *fons et origo,* genesis; descent etc. (*paternity*) 166; remote cause; influence.

pivot, hinge, turning-point, lever; key; kernel, core; proximate cause, *causa causans;* last straw that breaks the camel's back.

ground; reason, – why; why and wherefore, rationale, occasion, derivation; final cause etc. (*intention*) 620; *le dessous des cartes;* undercurrents.

rudiment, egg, germ, embryo, fetus, bud, root, *radix,* radical, etymon, nucleus, seed, stem, stalk, stock, *stirps,* trunk, tap-root; latent organism.

nest, cradle, nursery, womb, *nidus,* birth-, breeding-place, hot-bed.

caus-ality, -ation; origination; production etc. 161.

V. be the -cause etc. *n.*- of; originate; give -origin, – rise, – occasion- to; cause, occasion, sow the seeds of, kindle, suscitate; bring -on, – to pass, – about; produce; create etc. 161; set -up, – afloat, – on foot; found, broach, institute, lay the foundation of, inaugurate; lie at the root of.

procure, induce, draw down, open the door to, superinduce, evoke, entail, operate; elicit, provoke.

conduce to etc. (*tend to*) 176; contribute; promote; have a -hand in, – finger in- the pie; determine, decide, turn the scale, give the casting vote; have a common origin; derive its origin etc. (*effect*) 154.

Adj. caused etc. *v.;* causal, original; prim-ary, -itive, -ordial; aboriginal; radical; inceptive, embry-onic, -otic; *in -embryo, – ovo;* seminal, germinal; formative, productive etc. 168; at the bottom of; connate, having a common origin.

Adv. because etc. 155; behind the scenes.

154. Effect. [Constant sequent.]—**N.** effect, consequence, sequela; derivative, -tion; result; result-ant, -ance; upshot, issue, *dénouement;* outcome; termination, end etc. 67; development, outgrowth, fruit, crop, harvest, product, bud, blossom, florescence, ear.

production, produce, product, finished product, work, handiwork, fabric, performance; creature, creation; offspring, -shoot; first-fruits, -lings; *prémices.*

V. be the -effect etc. *n.*- of; be -due, – owing-to; originate -in, – from; rise –, arise –, take its rise –, spring –, proceed –, emanate –, come –, grow –, bud –, sprout –, germinate –, issue –, flow –, result –, follow –, derive its origin –, accrue- from; come -to, – of, – out of; depend –, hand –, hinge –, turn- upon.

take the consequences, sow the wind and reap the whirlwind.

Adj. owing to; resulting from etc. *v.;* resultant; derivable from; due to; caused etc. by, 153; dependent upon; derived –, evolved- from; derivative; hereditary.

Adv. of course, it follows that, naturally, consequently; as a –, in- consequence; through all, all along of, necessarily, eventually.

Phr. *cela va sans dire,* thereby hangs a tale.

155. Attribution. [Assignment of cause.]—**N.** attribution, theory, etiology, ascription, reference to, rationale; accounting for etc. *v.;* imputation, derivation from.

fil-, affil-iation; pedigree etc. (*paternity*) 166.

explanation etc. (*interpretation*) 522; reason why etc. (*cause*) 153.

V. attribute –, ascribe –, impute –, refer –, lay –, point –, trace –, bring home- to; put –, set- down- to; charge –, ground- on; invest with, assign as cause, charge with, blame, lay at the door of, father upon; saddle with; affiliate; account for, derive from, point out the -reason etc. 153; theorize; tell how it comes; put the saddle on the right horse.

Adj. attributed etc. *v.;* attributable etc. *v.;* refer-able, -rible; due to, derivable from; owing to etc. (*effect*) 154; putative.

Adv. hence, thence, therefore, for, since, on account of, because, owing to; on that account; from -this, – that- cause; thanks to, forasmuch as; whence, *propter hoc.*

why? wherefore? whence? how -comes, – is, – happens- it? how does it happen?

in -some, – some such- way; somehow, – or other.

Phr. that is why; *hinc illae lachrymae; cherchez la femme.*

156. Chance.† [Absence of assignable cause.]—**N.** chance, indetermination, accident, fortune, hazard, hap, haphazard, chance-medley, random, luck, *raccroc,* casualty, fortuity, contingence, coincidence, adventure, hit; fate etc. (*necessity*) 601; equal chance; lottery, raffle, tombola, sweepstake; toss up etc. 621; turn of the -table, – cards; hazard of the die, chapter of accidents; cast –, throw- of the dice; heads or tails, wheel of Fortune, whirligig of chance; *sortes;* – *Virgilianae.*

probability, possibility, contingency, odds, long odds, run of luck; main- chance.

theory of -probabilities, – chances; bookmaking; assurance; speculation, gamble, gaming etc. 621.

V. chance, hap, turn up; fall to one's lot; be one's -fate etc. 601; stumble on, light –, blunder –, hit- upon; take one's chance etc. 621.

Adj. casual, fortuitous, accidental, haphazard, random, stray, adventitious, adventive, causeless, incidental. contingent, uncaused, undetermined, indeterminate; possible etc. 470; unintentional etc. 621.

Adv. by -chance, – accident; casually; perchance etc. (*possibly*) 470; for aught one knows; as -good, – bad, – ill-luck etc. *n.*- would have it; as it may -be, – chance, – turn up, – happen; as the case may be.

†The word *Chance* has two distinct meanings: the first, the absence of assignable *cause*, as above; and the second, the absence of *design*—for the latter see 621.

157. Power.—N. power; poten-cy, -tiality; puissance, might, force; energy etc. 171; dint; right -hand, – arm; ascendency, sway, control; pre-potency, -pollence; almightiness, omnipotence; authority etc. 737; strength etc. 159.

ability; ableness etc. *adj.;* competency; efficiency, -cacy; validity, cogency; enablement; vantage ground; influence etc. 175; horse power; dynamometer.

pressure; elasticity; gravity; attraction, repulsion; *vis -inertiae, – mortua, – viva;* friction, suction.

electricity, magnetism, galvanism, voltaic electricity, voltaism, electro-magnetism, electrostatics, electrification; electric – current, – power; potential –, dynamic –, kinetic –, electrical –, chemical –, atomic- energe; electric field, circuit, charge, discharge, shock, polarity, pole; amperage, voltage, wattage, resistance, conduction, induction, electrification, electrolysis.

electronics, radionics, electron physics, electrophysics, avionics, radiometry, photoelectronics; electron, negatron, positron, photoelectron, thermion, barytron; electronic effect; electron emission; electron –, cathode –, anode –, positive – ray; electron – current, – flow – stream, – beam, – volt; electronic circuit; conductance; electron tube, tube, vacuum tube, photoelectric tube, call; transistor.

capability, capacity; *quid valeant humeri quid ferre recusent;* faculty, quality, attribute, endowment, virtue, gift, property, qualification, susceptibility.

V. be -powerful etc. *adj.;* gain -power etc. *n.*

belong –, pertain- to; lie –, be- in one's power; can.

electrify, generate, magnetize.

give –, confer –, exercise- power etc. *n.;* empower, enable, invest; in-, en-due; endow, arm; strengthen etc. 159; compel etc. 744.

Adj. powerful, puissant; potent, -ial; capable, able; equal –, up- to; cogent, valid; effect-ive, -ual; efficient, efficacious, adequate, competent; multi-, pleni-, omni-, armi- potent; mighty, ascendent; almighty.

electric, electrical, electronic etc.

forcible etc. *adj.* (*energetic*) 171; influential etc. 175; productive etc. 168.

Adv. powerfully etc. *adj.;* by -virtue, – dint-of.

158. Impotence.—N. impotence; in-, dis-ability; disablement, impuissance, imbecility, caducity; incapa-city, -bility; inapt-, inept-itude; indocility; invalidity, inefficiency, incompetence, disqualification.

telum imbelle, brutum fulmen, blank cartridge, flash in the pan, *vox et praeterea nihil,* dead letter, bit of waste paper, dummy; scrap of paper.

inefficacy etc. (*inutility*) 645; failure etc. 732.

helplessness etc. *adj.;* prostration, paralysis, palsy, ataxia, apoplexy, syncope, sideration, *deliquium,* collapse, exhaustion, softening of the brain, emasculation, inanition, senility etc. 128; castrato, eunuch.

cripple, old woman, muff, molly-coddle, milksop.

V. be -impotent etc. *adj.;* not have a leg to stand on.

vouloir -rompre l'anguille au genou, – prendre la lune avec les dents.

collapse, faint, swoon, fall into a swoon, drop; go by the board; end in smoke etc. (*fail*) 732.

render -powerless etc. *adj.;* deprive of power; decontrol; dis-able, -enable; disarm, incapacitate, disqualify, unfit, invalidate, undermine, deaden, cramp, tie the hands; double up, prostrate, paralyze, muzzle, cripple, becripple, maim, lame, hamstring, draw the teeth of; throttle, strangle, *garrotte;* ratten, silence, sprain, clip the wings of, render *hors de combat,* spike the guns; take the wind out of one's sails, scotch the snake, put a spoke in one's wheel; break the -neck, – back; un-hinge, -fit; put out of gear.

unman, unnerve, devitalize, attenuate, enervate; emasculate, spay, caponize, castrate, geld; effeminize.

shatter, exhaust; weaken etc. 160.

Adj. powerless, impotent, unable, incapable, incompetent; ineff-icient, -ective; inept; un-fit, -fitted; un-, dis-qualified; unendowed; in-, un-apt; crippled, decrepit; disabled etc. *v.;* armless.

harmless, unarmed, weaponless, defenceless, *sine ictu,* unfortified, indefensible, vincible, pregnable, untenable.

para-lytic, -lyzed; palsied, imbecile; nerve-, sinew-, marrow-, pith-, lust-less; emasculate, disjointed, out of -joint, – gear; un-nerved, -hinged; water-logged, on one's beam ends, rudderless; laid on one's back; done up, dead beat, exhausted, shattered, demoralized; gravelled etc. (*in difficulty*) 704; helpless, unfriended, fatherless; without a leg to stand on, *hors de combat,* laid on the shelf.

null and void, nugatory, imoperative, good for nothing; dud; invertebrate; ineffectual etc. (*failing*) 732; inadequate etc. 640; inefficacious etc. (*useless*) 645.

159. Strength. [Degree of power.]—**N.** strength; power etc. 157; energy etc. 171; vigor, force; main –, physical –, brute- force; spring, elasticity, tone, tension, tonicity.

stoutness etc. *adj.;* lustihood, stamina, nerve,

muscle, sinew, thews and sinews, *physique;* pith, -iness; virility, vitality.

athlet-ics, -icism; gymnastics, feats of strength.

adamant, steel, iron, oak, heart of oak; iron grip; grit, bone.

athlete, gymnast, tumbler, acrobat; Atlas, Hercules, Antaeus, Samson, Cyclops, Goliath, Titan; tower of strength; giant refreshed.

strengthening etc. *v.;* invigoration, refreshment, refocillation.

[Science of forces] dynamics, statics.

V. be -strong etc. *adj.*, – stronger; overmatch.

render -strong etc. *adj.;* give -strength etc. *n.;* strengthen, invigorate, brace, nerve, fortify, buttress, sustain, harden, case-harden, steel; gird; screw –, wind –, set- up; gird –, brace- up one's loins; recruit, set on one's legs; vivify; refresh etc. 689; refect; reinforce etc. (*restore*) 660.

Adj. strong, mighty, vigorous, forcible, hard, adamantine, stout, robust, sturdy, hardy, powerful, potent, puissant, valid.

resistless, irresistible, invincible, proof against, impregnable, unconquerable, indomitable, inextinguishable, unquenchable; incontestable; more than a match for; over-powering, -whelming; all-powerful; sovereign.

able-bodied; athletic, gymnastic; Herculean, Cyclopean, Atlantean; muscular, husky, brawny, wiry, well-knit, broad-shouldered, sinewy, strapping, stalwart, gigantic.

man-ly, -like, -ful; masculine, male, virile, in the prime of manhood.

un-weakened, -allayed, -withered, -shaken, -worn, -exhausted; in full -force, – swing; in the plenitude of power.

stubborn, thick-ribbed, made of iron, deep-rooted; strong as -a lion, – a horse, – brandy; sound as a roach; in -fine, – high- feather; in fine fettle; like a giant refreshed.

Adv. strongly etc. *adj.*; by -force etc. *n.*; by main force etc. (*by compulsion*) 744.

Phr. 'our withers are unwrung.'

160. Weakness.—N. weakness etc. *adj.;* debility, atony, relaxation, languor, enervation; impotence etc. 158; infirmity; effeminancy, feminality; fragility, flaccidity; inactivity etc. 683.

declension –, loss –, failure- of strength; delicacy, invalidation, decrepitude, asthenia, adynamy, cachexy, *cachexia,* anemia, bloodlessness, sprain, strain.

reed, thread, rope of sand, broken reed, house -of cards, – built on sand.

soft-, weak-ling; infant etc. 129; youth etc. 127.

V. be -weak etc. *adj.;* drop, crumble, give way, totter, tremble, shake, halt, limp, fade, languish, decline, flag, fail, have one foot in the grave.

render -weak etc. *adj.;* weaken, enfeeble, debilitate, shake, deprive of strength, relax, enervate; un-brace, -nerve; cripple, unman, etc. (*render powerless*) 158; cramp, reduce, sprain, strain, blunt the edge of; dilute, impoverish; decimate; extenuate; reduce -in strength, – the strength of; invalidate; *mettre de l'eau dans son vin.*

Adj. weak, feeble, debile; impotent etc. 158; relaxed, unnerved etc. *v.*; sap-, strength-, powerless; weakly, unstrung, flaccid, adynamic, asthenic; nervous.

soft, effeminate, feminate, womanish.

frail, fragile, shattery, frangible, brittle etc. 328; flimsy, unsubstantial, gimcrack, gingerbread; rickety, cranky; creachy; drooping, tottering etc. *v.;* broken, lame, halt, game, withered, shattered, shaken, crazy, shaky, tumble-down; palsied etc. 158; decrepit; C3.

lanquid, poor, poorly, infirm; faint, -ish; sickly etc. (*disease*) 655; dull, slack, evanid, spent, short-winded, effete; weatherbeaten; decayed, rotten, worn, seedy, languishing, wasted, washy, wishy-washy, laid low, pulled down, the worse for wear.

un-strengthened etc. 159, -supported, -aided, -assisted; aidless, defenceless etc. 158.

on its last legs; weak as a -child, – baby, – chicken, – cat, – rat; weak as -water, – water gruel, – gingerbread, – milk and water; colorless etc. 429.

Phr. *non sum qualis eram.*

161. Production.—N. production, creation, construction, formation, fabrication, manufacture; building, architecture, erection, edification; coinage; organization; *nisus formativus;* putting togeher etc. *v.;* establishment; workmanship, performance; achievement etc. (*completion*) 729; effect etc. 154.

flowering, fructification fruition.

bringing forth etc. *v.;* parturition, birth, birththroe, child-birth, delivery, confinement, *accouchement,* travail, labour, midwifery, obstetrics; geniture; gestation etc. (*maturation*) 673; evolution, development, growth; genesis, fertilization, breeding, conception, germination, generation, *epigenesis,* pro-creation, -generation, -pagation; fecundation, impregnation; spontaneous generation; *arche-genesis, -biosis; bio-, abio-, homo-, xeno-genesis.*

authorship, publication; works, *oeuvre, opus.*

edifice, building, structure, fabric, erection, pile, tower, flower, fruit.

V. produce, perform, operate, do, make, gar, form, construct, fabricate, frame, contrive, manufacture; weave, forge, coin, carve, chisel; build, raise, edify, rear, erect, put together; set –, run- up; establish, constitute, compose, organize, institute, get up; achieve, accomplish etc. (*complete*) 729.

flower, sprout, blossom, burgeon, bear fruit, fructify, spawn, teem, ean, yean, farrow, drop, calf, pup, whelp, kitten, kindle; bear, lay, bring forth, give birth to, lie in, be brought to bed of, evolve, pullulate, usher into the world.

make productive etc. 168; create; beget, conceive, get, generate, fecundate, impregnate; procreate, -generate, -pagate; engender; bring –, call- into -being, – existence; breed, hatch, develop, bring up.

induce, superinduce; suscitate; cause etc. 153; acquire etc. 775.

Adj. produc-ed, -ing etc. *v.;* productive of; prolific etc. 168; creative; formative; gen-etic, -ial, -ital; fertile, pregnant; *enceinte,* big –, fraught-with; with child, in the family way, teeming, parturient, in the straw, brought to bed of; puerper-al, -ous.

architectonic; constructive.

162. Destruction. [Non-production.]—**N.** destruction; waste, dissolution, breaking up; di-, dis-ruption; consumption; disorganization.

fall, downfall, ruin, perdition, crash, smash, havoc, *délabrement, débâcle;* break -down, – up; prostration; desolation, *bouleversement*, wreck, crack-up, crash, wrack, shipwreck, cataclysm; Caudine Forks, Sedan.

extinction, annihilation; destruction of life etc. 361; knock-out, knock-down blow; doom, crack of doom.

destroying etc. *v.*; demo-lition, -lishment; biblioclasm; overthrow, subversion, suppression; abolition etc. (*abrogation*) 756; sacrifice; ravage, devastation, *sabotage, razzia*; incendiarism; revolution etc. 146; extirpation etc. (*extraction*) 301; *commencement de la fin,* road to ruin; dilapidation etc. (*deterioration*) 659.

V. be -destroyed etc.; perish; fall, – to the ground; tumble, topple; go –, fall- to pieces; break up; crumble, – to dust; go to -the dogs, – the wall, – smash, – shivers, – wreck, – pot, – wrack and ruin; go -by the board, – all to smash, – to pieces, – under; be all -over, – up- with; totter to its fall.

destroy; do –, make- away with; nullify; annul etc. 756; sacrifice, demolish; tear up; over-turn, -throw, -whelm; upset, subvert, put an end to; seal the doom of, do for, dish, undo; break -, cut- up; break –, cut –, pull –, mow –, blow –, beat- down; suppress, quash, put down; cut short, take off, blot out; dispel, dissipate, dissolve; consume.

smash, – to smithereens, quell, squash, squelch, crumple up, shatter, shiver; batter; tear –, crush –, cut –, shake –, pull –, pick- to pieces; nip; tear to -rags, – tatters; crush –, knock- to atoms; pulverize; ruin; strike out; throw –, knock- -down, – over; lay by the heels; fell, sink, swamp, scuttle, wreck, crash, shipwreck, engulf, submerge; lay in -ashes, – ruins; sweep away, erase, expunge, strike out, delete, efface, raze; level, – with the -ground, – dust.

deal destruction, lay waste, ravage, gut; disorganize; dismantle etc. (*render useless*) 645; devour, swallow up, desolate, devastate, sap, mine, blast, confound; exterminate, extinguish, quench, annihilate; snuff –, put –, stamp –, trample- out; lay –, trample- in the dust; prostrate; tread –, crush –, trample- under foot; lay the axe to the root of; make -short work, – a clean sweep, – mincemeat- of; cut up root and branch; fling –, scatter- to the winds; throw overboard; strike at the root of, sap the foundations of, spring a mine, blow up; ravage with fire and sword; cast to the dogs; eradicate etc. 301.

Adj. destroyed etc. *v.;* perishing etc. *v.;* trembling –, nodding –, tottering- to its fall; in course of destruction etc. *n.;* extinct.

destructive, subversive, ruinous, incendiary, deletory; destroying etc. *v.*; suicidal; deadly etc. (*killing*) 361.

Adv. with -crushing effect, – a sledgehammer.

Phr. *delenda est Carthago.*

163. Reproduction.—N. reproduction, renovation; restoration etc. 660; renewal; new edition, reprint etc. 21; revival, regeneration, palingenesia, revivification; apotheosis; resuscitation, reanimation, resurrection, resurgence, reappearance, atavism; Phoenix; reincarnation.

generation etc. (*production*) 161; multiplication.

V. reproduce; restore etc. 660; revive, renovate, renew, regenerate, revivify, resuscitate, reanimate, refashion, stir the embers, put into the crucible; multiply, repeat, resurge.

crop up, spring up like mushrooms.

Adj. reproduced etc. *v.;* renascent, reappearing; reproductive; resurgent; progenitive; Hydraheaded.

164. Producer.—N. producer, creator, deviser, designer, originator, inventor, author, founder, generator, mover, architect; grower, constructor, maker etc. (*agent*) 690.

165. Destroyer.—N. destroyer etc. (destroy etc. 162); cankerworm etc. (*bane*) 663; iconoclast; assassin etc. (*killer*) 361; executioner etc. (*punish*) 975; Hun, Vandal, nihilist, anarchist.

166. Paternity.—N. paternity; parentage; fatherhood; consanguinity etc. 11.

parent, father, sire, dad, daddy, papa, governor, *pater, paterfamilias, abba;* genitor, progenitor, procreator, begetter; ancestor; grandsire, -father; great-grandfather.

house, stem, truck, tree, stock, *stirps,* pedigree, lineage, line, family, tribe, sept, race, clan; genealogy, descent, extraction, birth, ancestry; forefathers, forbears, patriarchs.

motherhood, maternity; mother, dam, mamma, *materfamilias;* grand-mother; matriarch.

Adj. paternal, parental; maternal; family, ancestral, linear, matrilinear, patrilineal, patriarchal.

167. Posterity.—N. posterity, progeny, breed, issue, offspring, brood, litter, seed, farrow, spawn, spat; family, children, grandchildren, heirs; great-grandchild.

child, son, daughter; kid; infant etc. 129; bantling, scion; shoot, sprout, olive branch, sprit, branch; off-shoot, -set; ramification; descendant; heir, -ess; heir -apparent, – presumptive; chip of the old block; heredity; rising generation.

straight descent, sonship, line, lineage, filiation, promogeniture.

Adj. filial.

168. Productiveness.—N. productiveness etc. *adj.;* fecundity, fertility, luxuriance, uberty.

pregnancy, pullulation, fructification, multiplication, propagation, procreation; superfetation.

milch cow, rabbit, hydra, warren, seed-plot, land flowing with milk and honey; second crop, after-crop, -growth, -math; fertilization.

V. make -productive etc. *adj.;* fructify; procreate, generate, fertilize, spermatize, impregnate; fecund-ate, -ify; teem, pullulate, multiply; produce etc. 161; conceive.

Adj. productive, prolific; teem-ing, -ful; fertile, fruitful, frugiferous, fruit-bearing; fructiferous; fecund, luxuriant; pregnant, uberous.

procre-ant, -ative; generative, life-giving, spermatic; originative; multiparous; omnific; propagable.

parturient etc. (*producing*) 161; profitable etc. (*useful*) 644.

169. Unproductiveness.—N. unproductiveness etc. *adj.;* infertility, steril; ity, infecundity; impotence etc. 158- unprofitableness etc. (*inutility*) 645.

waste, desert, Sahara, wild, wilderness, howling wilderness.

V. be -unproductive etc. *adj.;* hang fire, flash in the pan, come to nothing.

Adj. unproductive, inoperative, barren, addle, unfertile, unprolific, arid, sterile, unfruitful, acarpous, infecund; *sine prole;* fallow; teem-, issue-, fruitless; unprofitable etc. (*useless*) 645; null and void, of no effect.

170. Agency.—N. agency, operation, force, working, strain, function, office, maintenance, exercise, work, swing, play; inter-working, -action, procuration, procurement.

causation etc. 153; instrumentality etc. 631; influence etc. 175; action etc. (*voluntary*) 680; *modus operandi* etc. 627.

quickening –, maintaining- power; home stroke.

V. be -in action etc. *adj.;* operate, work; act, – upon; perform, play, support, sustain, strain, maintain, take effect, quicken, strike.

come –, bring- into -operation, – play; have -play, – free play; bring to bear upon.

Adj. operative, efficient, efficacious, practical, effectual.

at work, on foot; acting etc. (*doing*) 680; in -operation, – force, – action, – play, – exercise; acted –, wrought- upon.

Adv. by the -agency etc. *n.*- of; through etc. (*instrumentality*) 631; by means of etc. 632.

171. Physical **Energy.—N.** energy, physical energy, force; keenness etc. *adj.;* intensity, vigor, strength, elasticity; go; pep, live wire, high pressure; backbone, mettle, fire, vim.

acri-mony, -tude, -dity; causticity, virulence, poignancy; harshness etc. *adj.;* severity, edge, point; pungency etc. 392.

cantharides; Spanish fly; seasoning etc. (*condiment*) 393, stimulant, excitant.

activity, agitation, effervescence; ferment, -ation; ebullition, splutter, perturbation, stir, bustle; voluntary energy etc. 682; quicksilver.

resolution etc. (*mental energy*) 604; exertion etc. (*effort*) 686; excitation etc. (*mental*) 824.

V. give -energy etc. *n.;* energize, stimulate, kindle, excite, activate, exert; sharpen, pep up, intensify; inflame etc. (*render violent*) 173; wind up etc. (*strengthen*) 159.

strike, – into, – hard, – home; make an impression.

Adj. strong, energetic, forcible, active; strenuous, forceful, mettlesome, enterprising, go ahead; intense, deep-dyed, severe, keen, vivid, sharp, acute, incisive, trenchant, brisk, vigorous, live.

rousing, irritating; poignant; virulent, caustic, corrosive, mordant, harsh, stringent; double-edged, – shotted, – distilled; drastic, escharotic; racy etc. (*pungent*) 392; sarcastic etc. 932.

potent etc. (*powerful*) 157; radio-active.

Adv. strongly etc. *adj.; fortiter in re;* with telling effect.

Phr. the steam is up; *vires acquirit eundo.*

172. Physical **Inertness.—N.** inertness, dulness etc. *adj.;* inertia, *vis inertiae,* inertion, inactivity, torpor, languor; dormancy, quiescence etc. 265; latency, inaction, passivity.

mental inertness; sloth etc. (*inactivity*) 683; inexcitability etc. 826; irresolution etc. 605; obstinacy etc. 606; permanence etc. 141.

V. be -inert etc. *adj.;* hang fire, smoulder.

Adj. inert, inactive, passive, pacific; torpid etc. 683; sluggish, stagnant, dull, heavy, flat, slack, tame, slow, blunt; lifeless, dead, uninfluential.

latent, dormant, smouldering, unexerted.

Adv. inactively etc. *adj.;* in -suspense, -abeyance.

173. Violence.—N. violence, inclemency, vehemence, might, impetuosity; boisterousness etc.; *adj.;* effervescence, ebullition; turbulence, bluster; uproar, riot, row, rumpus, *le diable à quatre,* devil to pay, all the fat in the fire.

severity etc. 739; ferocity, rage, berserk, fury; exacerbation, exasperation, malignity; fit, paroxysm, orgasm; force, brute force; outrage; *coup de main;* strain, shock, shog; spasm, convulsion, throe; hysterics, passion etc. (*state of excitability*) 825.

out-break, -burst; burst, bounce, dissilience, discharge, volley, explosion, blow up, blast, detonation, rush, eruption, displosion, torrent.

turmoil etc. (*disorder*) 59; ferment etc. (*agitation*) 315; storm, tempest, rough weather; squall etc. (*wind*) 349; earthquake, volcano, thunderstorm.

fury, dragon, demon, tiger, beldame, Tisiphone, Megaera, Alecto, madcap, wild beast; fire-eater etc. (*blusterer*) 887.

V. be -violent etc. *adj.*; run high; ferment, effervesce; romp, rampage; run -wild, – riot; break the peace; rush, tear; rush head-long, -foremost; run amuck, raise a storm, make a riot; make –, kick up- a row, – a fuss; bluster, rage, roar, riot, storm; boil, – over; fume, foam, come in like a lion, wreak, bear down, ride roughshod, out-Herod Herod; spread like wildfire.

break –, fly –, burst- out; bounce, shock, strain; break-, pry-, force-, prize- open.

render -violent etc. *adj.;* sharpen, stir up, quicken, excite, incite, urge, lash, stimulate; irritate, inflame, exacerbate, kindle, suscitate, foment; accelerate, aggravate, exasperate, convulse, infuriate, madden, lash into fury; fan –, add fuel to- the flame; *oleum addere camino.*

explode, go off. displode, fly, detonate, thunder, blow up, flash, flare, erupt, burst; let - off, – fly; discharge, detonize, fulminate.

Adj. violent, vehement, forcible; warm; acute, sharp; rough, rude, ungentle, bluff, boisterous, wild, vicious; brusque, abrupt, waspish; impetuous; rampant.

turbulent; disorderly; blustering, raging etc. *v.;* troublous, riotous; tumultu-ary, -ous; obstreperous, uproarious; extravagant; unmitigated; ravening, tameless; frenzied etc. (*insane*) 503; desperate etc. (*rash*) 863; infuriate, towering, furious, outrageous, frantic, hysteric, in hysterics.

fiery, flaming, scorching, hot, red-hot, ebullient.

savage, fierce, ferocious, fierce as a tiger.

excited etc. *v.;* un-quelled, -quenched, -extinguished, -repressed, -bridled, -ruly; headstrong; un-governable, -appeasable, -mitigable; un-, in-controllable; insup-, irre-pressible.

spasmodic, convulsive, explosive; detonating etc. *v.;* volcanic, meteoric; stormy etc. (*wind*) 349.

Adv. violently etc. *adj.;* amain; by -storm, – force, – main force; with might and main; tooth and nail, *vi et armis,* at the point of the -sword, – bayonet; at one fell swoop; with a high hand, through thick and thin; in desperation, with a vengeance; *à –, à touteoutrance;* head-long, - foremost, -first; like a bull at a gate.

174. Moderation.—N. moderation; lenity etc. 740; temperance, temperateness, gentleness etc. *adj.;* sobriety; quiet; mental calmness etc. (*inexcitability*) 826.

moderating etc. *v.;* relaxation, remission, mitigation etc. 834; tranquilization, alleviation, assuagement, appeasement, contemporation, pacification.

measure, *juste milieu,* golden mean etc. 29.

moderator; lullaby, sedative, lenitive, demulcent, rose-water, balm, soothing syrup, poppy, opiate, anodyne, milk, opium, laudanum, 'poppy or mandragora;' wet blanket; palliative, calmative.

V. be -moderate etc. *adj.;* keep within -bounds, – compass; sober –, settle- down; keep the pease, remit, relent; take in sail.

moderate, soften, mitigate, temper, accoy; at-, con-temper; mollify, lenify, dull, take off the edge, blunt, obtund, sheathe, subdue, chasten; sober –, tone –, smooth- down; censor, blue-pencil, weaken etc. 160; lessen etc. (*decrease*) 36; check; palliate.

tranquilize, assuage, appease, dulcify, swage, lull, soothe, compose, still, calm, cool, quiet, hush, quell, sober, pacify, tame, damp, lay, allay, rebate, slacken, smooth, alleviate, rock to sleep, deaden, smother; throw -cold water on, – a wet blanket over; slake; curb etc. (*restrain*) 751; tame etc. (*subjugate*) 749; smooth over; pour oil on the -waves, – troubled waters; pour balm into, *mettre de l'eau dans son vin.*

go out like a lamb, 'roar you as gently as any sucking dove.'

Adj. moderate; lenient etc. 740; gentle, mild; cool, sober, temperate, reasonable, measured; tempered etc. *v.;* calm, unruffled, quiet, tranquil, still; slow, smooth, untroubled; tame; peaceful, -able; pacific, halcyon.

un-exciting, -irritating; soft, bland, oily, demulcent, lenitive, anodyne; hypnotic etc. 683; sedative; assuaging.

mild as mother's milk; milk and water; gentle as a lamb.

Adv. moderately etc. *adj.;* gingerly; *piano;* under easy sail, at half speed; within -bounds, – compass; in reason.

Phr. *est modus in rebus.*

175. Influence.—N. influence; importance etc. 642; weight, pressure, preponderance, prevalence, sway, pull; predomi-nance, -nancy; ascendency; control, dominance, reign; authority etc. 737; capability etc. (*power*) 157; interest; spell, magic, magnetism.

footing; purchase etc. (*support*) 215; play, leverage, vantage ground.

tower of strength, host in himself; protection, patronage, auspices.

V. have -influence etc. *n.;* be -influential etc. *adj.*; carry weight, actuate, sway, bias, weigh, tell; have a hold upon, magnetize, bear upon, gain a footing, work upon; take -root, – hold; strike root in.

run through, pervade, prevail, dominate, predominate, subject; out-, over-weigh; over-ride, - bear, – come; gain head; rage; be -rife etc. *adj.;* spread like wildfire; have –, get –, gain- -the upper hand, – full play.

be -recognized, – listened to; make one's voice heard, gain a hearing; play a -part, – leading part- in; lead, control, rule, master; get the mastery over; make one's influence felt, cut ice with; take the lead, pull the strings; turn –, throw one's weight into- the scale; set the fashion, lead the dance.

Adj. influential; important etc. 642; weighty; prevailing etc. *v.;* prevalent, rife, rampant; dominant, regnant, predominant, in the ascendant, hegemonical; authoritative, recognized, telling, with authority.

Adv. with telling effect.

175a. Absence of Influence.—N. impotence etc. 158; inertness etc. 172; irrelevancy etc. 10.

V. have no -influence etc. 175.

Adj. uninfluential; unconduc-ing, -ive, -ting to; powerless etc. 158; irrelevant etc. 10.

176. Tendency.—N. tendency; apt-ness, -itude; proneness, proclivity, bent, turn, tone, bias, set, warp, leaning to, predisposition, inclination, conatus, propensity, susceptibility; liability etc. 177; quality, nature, temperament; characteristic, idio-crasy, -syncrasy; cast, vein, grain; humor, mood; drift etc. (*direction*) 278; conduciveness, -ducement; applicability etc. (*utility*) 644; subservience etc. (*instrumentality*) 631.

V. tend, contribute, conduce, lead, dispose, incline, verge, bend to, warp, turn, trend, affect, carry, redound to, bid fair to, gravitate towards; promote etc. (*aid*) 707.

Adj. tending etc. *v.;* conducive, working towards, in a fair way to, calculated to; liable etc. 177; subservient etc. (*instrumental*) 631; useful etc. 644; subsidiary etc. (*helping*) 707.

Adv. for, whither.

177. Liability.—N. lia-bility, -bleness; possibility, contingency; suscepti-vity, -bility.

V. be -liable etc. *adj.;* incur, lay oneself open to; run the –, stand a- chance; lie under, expose oneself to, open a door to.

Adj. liable, subject; in danger etc. 665; open –, exposed –, obnoxious- to; answerable, responsible, accountable, amenable; unexempt from; apt to; dependent on; incident to.

contingent, incidental, possible, on the cards, within range of, at the mercy of.

178. Concurrence.—N. concurrence, cooperation, coagency; coincidence, consilience; union; agreement etc. 23; consent etc. (*assent*) 488; alliance; concert etc. 709; partnership etc. 712; collaboration, conformity.

V. con-cur, -duce, -spire, -tribute; agree, unite, harmonize; hang –, pull- together etc. (*cooperate*) 709; help to etc. (*aid*) 707.

keep pace with, run parallel to; go –, go along –, go hand in hand- with.

Adj. concurring etc. *v.;* concurrent, conformable, joint, co-operative, concordant, coincident, concomitant, harmonious; in alliance with, banded together, of one mind, at one with; parallel.

Adv. with one consent.

179. Counteraction.—N. counteraction, opposition; contrariety etc. 14; antagonism, polarity; clashing etc. *v.;* collision, interference, resistance, renitency, friction; reaction; retroaction; repercussion etc. (*recoil*) 277; counterblast; neutralization etc. (*compensation*) 30; *vis inertiae;* check etc. (*hindrance*) 706.

voluntary -opposition etc. 708, – resistance etc. 719; repression etc. (*restraint*) 751.

V. counteract; run counter, clash, cross; interfere –, conflict- with; jostle; go –, run –, beat –, militate- against; stultify; antagonize, frustrate, oppose etc. 708; withstand etc. (*resist*) 719; hinder etc. 706; repress etc. (*restrain*) 751; react etc. (*recoil*) 277.

undo, neutralize, cancel; counterpoise etc. (*compensate*) 30; overpoise.

Adj. counteracting etc. *v.;* antagonistic, conflicting, retroactive, renitent, reactionary; contrary etc. 14.

Adv. although etc. 30; in spite of etc. 708; *malgré;* against.

180. Space. [Indefinite space.]—**N.** space, extension, extent, superficial extent, expanse, stretch; capacity, volume, room, accommodation, scope, range, latitude, field, way, expansion, compass, sweep, play, swing, spread.

dimension, fourth dimension; relativity, geometry.

spare –, elbow –, house- room; stowage, roomage, margin; opening, sphere, arena; lee-, sea-, head-way.

open –, free- space; wide open spaces, void etc. (*absence*) 187; waste; wild-, wilder-ness; up-, bottom-, moor -land; *campagna, veldt,* prairie, steppe.

abyss etc. (*interval*) 198; unlimited space; infinity etc. 105; world, wide world; ubiquity etc. (*presence*) 186; length and breadth of the land.

proportions, acreage; acres, – roods and perches; square -inches, – yards etc.

V. reach, extend, stretch, sweep, spread, range, cover, thrust out, reach forth.

Adj. spacious, roomy, extensive, expansive, capacious, ample; wide-spread, vast, world-wide, uncircumscribed; boundless etc. (*infinite*) 105; shore-, track-, path-less; large etc. 192.

spatial, dimensional, proportional; two-, three-, four-dimensional; stereoscopic.

Adv. extensively etc. *adj.;* wherever; everywhere; far and -near, – wide; right and left, all over, all the world over; throughout the -world, – length and breadth of the land; under the sun, in every quarter; in all -quarters, – lands; here, there and everywhere; from -pole to pole, – China to Peru, – Indus to the pole, – Dan to Beersheba, – end to end; on the face of the earth, in the wide world, from all points of the compass; to the -four winds, – uttermost parts of the earth.

180a. Inextension.—N. in-, non-extension; point; atom etc. (*smallness*) 32; pinprick; limitation etc. 229.

181. Region. [Definite space.]—**N.** region, sphere, sphere of influence, corridor, ground, soil, area, realm, hemisphere, quarter district, beat, orb, orbit, zone, belt, circuit, circle; pale etc. (*limit*) 233; com-, department; domain, tract, territory, terrain, country, canton, county, shire, province, *arrondissement,* diocese, parish, township, borough, constituency, *commune,* ward, wapentake, hundred, riding, lathe, garth, soke, tithing, bailiwick; empire, kingdom, principality, duchy, grand –, arch- duchy, palatinate, republic, commonwealth, dominion, colony, state, island.

arena, precincts, *enceinte,* walk, march; patch, plot, enclosure, etc. 232; close, *enclave,* field, court; street etc. (*abode*) 189.

clime, climate, zone, meridian, latitude.

Adj. territorial, local, parochial, provincial, insular.

182. Place. [Limited space.]—**N.** place, lieu, spot, point, dot; niche, nook, etc. (*corner*) 244; hole; pigeonhole etc. (*receptacle*) 191; compartment; premises, precinct, station, confine; area, court, yard, quadrangle, square, compound; abode etc. 189; locality etc. (*situation*) 183.

ins and outs; every hole and corner.

Adv. somewhere, in some place, wherever it may be, here and there, in various places, *passim.*

183. Situation.—**N.** situation, position, locality, *locale, status*, latitude and longitude; footing, standing, standpoint, post; stage, aspect, attitude, posture, *pose*.
place, site, base, station, seat, *venue*, whereabouts, environment, neighborhood; bearings etc. (*direction*) 278; spot etc. (*limited space*) 182.
top-, ge-, chor-ography; map etc. 554.
V. be -situated, – situate; lie; have its seat in.
Adj. situ-ate, -ated; local, topical, topographical etc. *n.*
Adv. *in -situ, – loco;* here and there, *passim;* here-, there-, whereabouts; in place, here, there.
in –, amidst- such and such- -surroundings, – *environs, – entourage.*

184. Location.—**N.** loca-tion, -lization; lodgement; de-, re-position; stow-, pack-age; collocation; packing, lading; establishment, settlement, installation; fixation; insertion etc. 300.
anchorage, roadstead, mooring, mooring mast, encampment, camp, bivouac.
plantation, colony, settlement, cantonment, encampment, reservation; colonization, domestication, situation; habitation etc. (*abode*) 189; cohabitation; 'a local habitation and a name;' indenization, naturalization.
V. place, situate, locate, localize, make a place for, put, lay, set, scat, station, lodge, quarter, post, install; storehouse, stow; extablish, fix, pin, root; graft; plant etc. (*insert*) 300; shelve, pitch, camp, lay down, deposit, reposit; cradle; moor, tether, picket; pack, tuck in; embed; vest, invest in.
billet on, quarter upon, saddle with; load, lade, freight; pocket, put up, bag.
inhabit etc. (*be present*) 186; domesticate, colonize, populate, people; take –, strike-root; anchor; cast –, come to an- anchor; sit –, settle- down; settle; take up one's -abode, – quarters; plant –, establish –, locate- oneself; squat, perch, hive, *se nicher,* bivouac, burrow, get a footing; encamp, pitch one's tent; put up -at, – one's horses at; keep house.
indenizen, naturalize, adopt.
put back, replace etc. (*restore*) 660.
Adj. placed etc. *v.;* situate, posited, ensconced, embedded, embosomed, rooted; domesticated; vested in unremoved; settled, stationed, established.
moored etc. *v.;* at anchor.

185. Displacement.—**N.** displacement, elocation, transposition.
ejectment etc. 297; exile etc. (*banishment*) 893; removal etc. (*transference*) 270; unshipment.
misplacement, dislocation etc. 61; fish out of water.
V. dis-place, -plant, -lodge, -nest, -establish; misplace, unseat, disturb; exile etc. (*seclude*) 893; ablegate, set aside, remove; take –, cart- away; take –, draft- off; lade etc. 184, unship.
unload, empty etc. (*eject*) 297; transfer etc. 270; dispel.
vacate; depart etc. 293.
Adj. displaced etc. *v.;* un-placed, -housed, -harbored, -established, -settled; house-, homeless; out of -place, – a situation.
misplaced, out of its element.

186. Presence.—**N.** presence; occupancy, -ation; attendance; whereness.
permeation, pervasion; diffusion etc. (*dispersion*) 73.
ubi-ety, -quity, -quitariness; omnipresence.
bystander etc. (*spectator*) 444.
V. exist in space, be -present etc. *adj.;* assist at; make one -of, – at; look on, attend, remain; find –, present- oneself; show one's face; fall in the way of, occur in a place; lie, stand; occupy.
people; inhabit, dwell, reside, stay, sojourn, live, room, abide, bunk, lodge, nestle, roost, perch; take up one's abode etc. (*be located*) 184; tenant, occupy.
resort to, frequent, haunt; revisit.
fill, pervade, permeate; be -diffused, – disseminated- through; over-spread, -run; run through; meet one at every turn.
Adj. present; occupying, inhabiting etc. *v.;* moored etc. 184; residential, resi-ant, -dent, -dentiary; domiciled.
ubiquit-ous, -ary; omnipresent.
peopled, populous, full of people, inhabited.
Adv. here; there, where, everywhere, aboard, on board, at home, afield; on the spot; here, there and everywhere etc. (*space*) 180; in presence of, before; under the -eyes, –nose- of; in the face of; *in propriâ personâ.*

187. Absence. [Nullibiety.]—**N.** absence; inexistence etc. 2; non-residence, absenteeism; non-attendance, *alibi.*
emptiness etc. *adj.;* void, *vacuum;* vac-uity, -ancy; *tabula rasa;* exemption; *hiatus* etc. (*interval*) 198; no man's land.
truant, absentee.
nobody; nobody -present, – on earth; no one; not a soul; *âme qui vive.*
V. be -absent etc. *adj.;* keep -away, – out of the way; play truant, absent oneself, stay away.
withdraw, make oneself scarce, vacate; go away, slip out, slip away, retreat etc. 293.
Adj. absent, not present, away, nonresident, gone, from home; missing; lost; wanted, wanting; omitted; nowhere to be found; inexistent etc. 2.
empty, void; blank, vac-ant, -uous; untenanted, -occupied, -inhabited; tenantless; desert, -ed; devoid; un-, uninhabitable.
exempt from, not having.
Adv. without, *minus,* nowhere; elsewhere; neither here nor there; in default of; *sans;* behind one's back.
Phr. the bird has flown, *non est inventus.*

188. Inhabitant.—**N.** inhabitant; habitant, resident, -iary; dweller, in-dweller; occup-ier, -ant, farmer, planter; householder, lodger, boarder, paying guest; inmate, tenant, renter, incumbent, sojourner, *locum tenens,* commorant; settler, squatter, backwoodsman, colonist; islander; denizen, citizen; burgher, oppidan, cockney, cit, townsman, burgess; villager; cottager, -tier, -ter; compatriot.
native, indigene, aboriginal, aborigines, autochthones; Briton, Englishman, John Bull; new comer etc. (*stranger*) 57.
garrison, crew; population; people etc. (*mankind*) 372; colony, settlement; household.

V. inhabit etc. (*be present*) 186; indenizen etc. (*locate oneself*) 184.

Adj. indigenous; enchorial; national, nat-ive, -al; autochthonous; British, English; colonial; domestic, domiciliated, -ed; naturalized, vernacular, domesticated; domiciliary.

in the occupation of; garrisoned —, occupied-by.

189. Abode. [Place of habitation, or resort.]—**N.** abode, dwelling, lodging, -s; diggings, domicile, residence, address, habitation, where one's lot is cast, local habitation, berth, seat, lap, sojourn, housing, quarters, headquarters, resiance, tabernacle, throne, ark.

home, fatherland, mother country, country etc. 181; home-stead, -stall; fireside, chimney corner; hearth, — stone; household gods, *lares et penates*, roof, household, housing, *dulce domum*, paternal domicile; native -soil, — land, blighty.

nest, *nidus*, snuggery; arbor, bower etc. 191; lair, den, cave, hole, hidingplace, cell, *sanctum sanctorum*, aerie, eyry, rookery, hive; *habitat*, haunt, covert, resort, retreat, perch, roost; nidification.

bivouac, camp, encampment, cantonment, castrametation; barrack, casemate, casern.

tent etc. (*covering*) 223; building etc. (*construction*) 161; chamber etc. (*receptacle*) 191.

tenement, messuage, farm, farmhouse, grange, *hacienda*.

cot, cabin, log cabin, shack, hut, *châlet*, croft, shed, booth, stall, hovel, bothy, shanty, igloo, tepee, wigwam; pen etc. (*inclosure*) 232; barn, bawn; kennel, sty, dog-hole, cote, coop, hutch, byre; cowhouse, -shed; stable, dove-cote, shippen.

house, mansion, place, villa, cottage, box, lodge, hermitage, *rus in urbe*, folly, rotunda, tower, *château*, castle, pavilion, hotel, court, manor-house, capital messuage, hall, palace, alcazar; country seat; kiosk, bungalow; temple etc. 1000; home of rest, alms-, poor-, work-house, asylum; boarding-, lodging-house; flat, maisonette, duplex, penthouse, suite of rooms, apartments, rooms, room building etc. 161; Mansion House, town hall, Capitol.

assembly-room, auditorium, coliseum, meeting-house, pump-room, spa, health resort, watering-place; club; theatre etc. 840; drill hall, gymnasium, church etc. 1000; Houses of Parliament etc. 696; school etc. 542; inn; hostel, -ry; hotel, tavern, caravansary, khan, hospice; public-, ale-, pot-, mug-house; gin-palace, gin mill; coffee-, eating-house; canteen, *restaurant*, *rotisserie*, cafeteria, grill-room, *buffet*, *café*, *estaminet*, *posada*, *bodega*; bar; saloon, speakeasy, shebeen.

hamlet, village, thorp, dorp, ham, kraal; borough, burgh, town, county-seat, — town, city, capital, metropolis; suburb, quarter, parish etc. 181; ghetto; province, country.

street, place, terrace, parade, esplanade, promenade, pier, embankment, road, villas, row, walk, lane, alley, court, quadrangle, quad, wynd, close, yard, passage, rents, mansions, buildings, mews.

square, polygon, circus, crescent, mall, *piazza*, arcade, colonnade, peristyle, cloister; gardens, grove, residences; block of buildings, market-place, *place*.

anchorage, roadstead, roads; dock, basin, wharf, quay, port, harbor; dry-, graving-, floating-dock.

garden, park, pleasure-ground, pleasance, demesne.

V. take up one's abode etc. (*locate oneself*) 184; inhabit etc. (*be present*) 186.

Adj. urban, oppidan, metropolitan; suburban; provincial, rural, rustic; countrified; regional, parochial, domestic; cosmopolitan; palatial.

190. Contents. [Things contained.]—**N.** contents; cargo, lading, freight, shipment, load, bale, burden; cart-, ship-load; cup —, basket —, etc. (*receptacle*) 191 - of; inside etc. 221; stuffing, ullage.

V. load, lade, ship, charge, fill, stuff.

191. Receptacle.—N. receptacle, container; inclosure etc. 232; recipient, receiver, reservatory.

compartment; cell, -ule; follicle; hole, corner, niche, recess, nook; crypt, stall, pigeon-hole, cove, oriel; cave etc. (*concavity*) 252.

capsule, vesicle, cyst, pod, calyx, *cancelli*, utricle, bladder, udder.

stomach, paunch, *venter*, abdomen, ventricle, crop, craw, ingluvies, maw, gizzard, bread-basket, belly, little Mary; mouth.

pocket, pouch, fob, sheath, scabbard, socket, bag, vanity bag, compact, sac, sack, saccule, despatch —, attaché-, tachy- case, wallet, scrip, card-, note-, case, billfold, poke, knit, knap-, haver-, ruck-sack, sachel, satchel, reticule, budget, net; ditty-, -box, -bag, kitbag; portfolio; saddlebags, holster; quiver etc. (*magazine*) 636.

chest, box, coffer, caddy, case, casket, pyx, pix, *caisson*, desk, *bureau*, reliquary, shrine; trunk, portmanteau, band-box, *valise*, suitcase, hand-, traveling-, overnight-, Gladstone-, carpet-bag, brief case; boot, imperial; *vache*; cage, manger, rack.

vessel, vase, bushel, barrel; canister, jar; pottle, basket, punnet, pannier, buck-basket, hopper, maund, creel, cran, crate, cradle, bassinet, wisket, whisket, *jardinière*, *corbeille*, hamper, wastepaper basket, dosser, dorser, tray, hod, scuttle, utensil, spittoon, cuspidor.

[For liquids] cistern etc. (*store*) 636; vat, caldron, barrel, cask, puncheon, keg, rundlet, tun, butt, firkin, hogshead, kilderkin, carboy, amphora, ampulla, bottle, jar, leather bottle, decanter, ewer, cruse, carafe, crock, kit, canteen, flagon; demijohn; flask, -et; stoup, noggin, vial, phial, ampoulé, cruet, caster; gourd; urn, *épergne*, salver, *patella*, *tazza*, *patera*; pig-, big-gin; tea-, coffee-pot, percolator, *samovar*; tyg, nipperkin, pocket-pistol; tub, bucket, pail, skeel, pot, tankard, jug, pitcher, toby, mug, pipkin; gal-, gall-ipot, pannikin; matrass, receiver, retort, alembic, bolthead, can, kettle; bowl, basin, jorum, punch-bowl, cup, goblet, chalice, tumbler, glass, wineglass, rummer, beaker, tass, horn, saucepan, skillet, posnet, tureen, terrine, *casserole*, sauce-, gravy-boat.

plate, platter, paten, dish, vegetable —, *entrée*-dish, trencher, calabash, porringer, potager, saucer, pan, crucible.

shovel, trowel, spoon; table-, dessert-, tea-, egg-,

salt-spoon; spatula, ladle; dipper; baler; watch-glass, thimble.

closet, commode, cupboard, cellaret, *chiffonnière*, locker, bin, bunker, *buffet*, press, safe, sideboard, drawer, chest of drawers, till, *scrutoire*, *secrétaire*, *éscritoire*, davenport, book-case, cabinet, canterbury; corner cupboard, wardrobe.

chamber, apartment, room, cabin; office, court, hall, atrium; suite of rooms, flat, story; saloon, *salon*, parlor; presence-chamber; sitting-, drawing-, reception-, state-, living-, work-room; gallery, cabinet, closet, cubicle; pew, box; *boudoir*; *adytum, sanctum*; bed-room, dormitory, dressing-room; refectory, dining-room, *salle-à-manger*; nursery, schoolroom; library, study; *studio*; billiard-, bath-, smoking-room; den, canteen, mess, officers' mess; gun-, ward-, mess-room.

attic, loft, garret, cockloft, clerestory; cellar, vault, hold, cockpit; *entre-sol*; mezzanine floor; ground-floor, *rez-de-chaussée*; basement, kitchen, cook-house, galley, pantry, scullery, offices; store-room etc. (*depository*) 636; lumber-room; dust-hole, -bin; dairy, laundry, coachhouse; *garage*; *hangar*; out-, pent-house; lean-to.

portico, porch, piazza, verandah, lobby, court, hall, vestibule, corridor, passage; ante-room, chamber; lounge; *foyer, loggia*.

conservatory, green-house, glass-house, vinery, bower, arbor, summer-house, alcove, grotto, hermitage, pergola.

lodging etc. (*abode*) 189; bed etc. (*support*) 215; carriage etc. (*vehicle*) 272.

Adj. capsular; saccu-lar, -lated; recipient; ventricular, cystic, vascular, vesicular, cellular, camerated, locular, multilocular, poly-gastric; marsupial; siliqu-ose, -ous.

192. Size.—N. size, magnitude, dimension, bulk, volume; largeness etc. *adj.*; greatness etc. (*of quantity*) 31; expanse etc. (*space*) 180; amplitude, mass; proportions.

capacity; ton-, tun-nage; caliber, scantling.

turgidity etc. (*expansion*) 194; corpulence, obesity; plumpness, etc. *adj.*: *embonpoint*, corporation, flesh and blood, lustihood.

hugeness etc. *adj.*; enormity, immensity, monstrosity.

giant, Brobdingnagian, Antaeus, Goliath, Gog and Magog, Gargantua, monster, mammoth, Cyclops; whale, porpoise, behemoth, leviathan, elephant, hippopotamus; colossus; tun, lump, bulk, block, loaf, mass, clod, nugget, bushel, thumper, whopper, spanker, strapper; Triton among the minnows.

mountain, mound; heap etc. (*assemblage*) 72. largest portion etc. 50; full-, life-size.

V. ve- large etc. *adj.*; become -large etc. (*expand*) 194.

Adj. large, big; great etc. (*in quantity*) 31; considerable, bulky, voluminous, ample, massive, massy; capacious, comprehensive; spacious etc. 180; mighty, towering, fine, magnificent.

corpulent, stout, fat, plump, squab, full, lusty, strapping, bouncing; portly, burly, well-fed, full-grown; stalwart, brawny, fleshy; goodly; in good - case. – condition; in condition; chopping, jolly; chub-, chubby-faced.

lubberly, hulky, unwieldy, lumpish, gaunt, spanking, whacking, whopping, thumping, thundering, hulking; overgrown; puffy etc. (*swollen*) 194.

huge, immense, enormous, mighty; vast, -y; amplitudinous, stupendous; monst-er, -rous; gigantic, elephantine; giant, -like; colossal, Cyclopean, Brobdingnagian, Garguantuan, Titanic; infinite etc. 105.

large as life; plump as a dumpling, – partridge; fat as -a pig, – a quail, – butter, – brawn, – bacon.

193. Littleness.—N. littleness etc. *adj.*; smallness etc. (*of quantity*) 32; exiguity, inextension; parvi-tude, -ty; duodecimo; Elzevir edition, epitome, microcosm; rudiment; vanishing point; thinness etc. 203.

dwarf, pigmy, atomy, Liliputian, midget, chit, pigwidgeon, urchin, elf; doll, puppet; Tom Thumb, Hop-o'-my thumb, Humpty-dumpty; man-, mannikin; *homunculus*, dapperling, fingerling, dandiprat, cock-sparrow, scalawag.

animalcule, monad, mite, insect, emmet, fly, midge, gnat, shrimp, minnow, worm, maggot, entozoon; *bacillus*, microbe, micro-organism, *bacteria*; *infusoria*; microbe; grub; tit, tomtit, runt, mouse, small fry; millet-, mustard-seed; barleycorn; pebble, grain of sand; mole-hill, button, bubble.

point; atom etc. (*small quantity*) 32; fragment etc. (*small part*) 51; powder etc. 330; point of a pin, mathematical point; *minutiae* etc. (*unimportance*) 643.

micro-graphy, -meter, -scope; vernier; scale.

V. be -little etc. *adj.*; lie in a nutshell; become small etc. (*decrease*) 36, (*contract*) 195.

Adj. little; small etc. (*in quantity*) 32; minute, diminutive, microscopic; inconsiderable etc. (*unimportant*) 643; exiguous, puny, tiny, wee, petty, minikin, miniature, pigmy, elfin; under sized; dwarf, -ed, -ish; spare, stunted, limited; cramp, -ed; pollard, Liliputian, dapper, pocket; port-ative, -able; duodecimo; dumpy, squat; compact, handy; short etc. 201.

impalpable, intangible, evanescent, imperceptible, invisible, inappreciable, infinitesimal, homeopathic; atomic, corpuscular, molecular; rudiment-ary, -al; embryonic.

weazen, scant, scraggy, scrubby; thin etc. (*narrow*) 203; granular etc. (*powdery*) 330; shrunk etc. 195.

Adv. in a -small compass, – nutshell; on a small scale.

194. Expansion.—N. expansion; increase etc. 35 -of size; enlargement, extension, augmentation; ampli-fication, -ation; aggrandizement, spread, increment, growth, development, pullulation, swell, dilation, dilatation, rarefaction; turg-escence, -idness, -idity; obesity etc. (*size*) 192; dropsy, tumefaction, intumescence, swelling, tumor, *diastole*, distension; puff-ing, -iness; inflation; pandiculation.

dilatability, expansibility.

germination, growth, upgrowth; accretion etc. 35.

over-growth, -distension; hypertrophy, tympany.

bulb etc. (*convexity*) 250; plumper; superiority of size.

V. become -larger etc. (large etc. 192); expand, widen, enlarge, extend, grow, increase, incrassate, swell, gather; fill out; deploy, take open order, dilate, stretch, spread; mantle, was; grow –, spring- up; bud, bourgeon, shoot, sprout, germinate, put forth, vegetate, pullulate, open, burst forth, flower, blow etc. 734; gain –, gather- flesh; outgrow; spread like wildfire, overrun.

be larger than; surpass etc. (*be superior*) 33.

render -larger etc. (large etc. 192); expand, spread, extend, aggrandize, distend, develop, amplify, spread out, widen, magnify, rarefy, inflate, puff, puff out, blow up, stuff, pad, cram; exaggerate; fatten.

Adj. expanded etc. *v.*; larger etc. (large etc. 192); swollen; expansive; wide-open, -spread; fan-shaped; flabelliform; overgrown, exaggerated, bloated, fat, turgid, tumid, hypertrophied, dropsical; pot-, swag-bellied; edematous, obese, puffy, pursy, blowzy, distended; patulous; bulbous etc. (*convex*) 250; full-blown, -grown, -formed; big etc. 192.

195. Contraction.—N. contraction, reduction, diminution; decrease etc. 36- of size; defalcation, decrement; lessening, shrinkage; collapse, emaciation, attenuation, tabefaction, consumption, marasmus, atrophy; systole, neck, hourglass.

condensation, compression, constraint, compactness; compendium etc. 596; squeezing etc. *v.*; strangulation; corrugation; astringency, constringency; astringents, sclerotics; contractility, compressibility; coarctation.

inferiority in size.

V. become -small, – smaller; lessen, decrease etc. 36; grow less, dwindle, shrink, contract, narrow, shrivel, collapse, wither, lose flesh, wizen, fall away, waste, wane, ebb; decat etc. (*deteriorate*) 659.

be smaller than, fall short of; not come up to etc. (*be inferior*) 34.

render smaller, lessen, diminish, contract, draw in, shrink, shrivel, narrow, coarctate; constrict, constringe; condense, compress, boil down, deflate, exhaust, empty; squeeze, corrugate, crush, crumple up, warp, purse up, pack, stow; pinch, tighten, strangle; cramp; dwarf, bedwarf; shorten etc. 201; circumscribe etc. 229; restrain etc. 751; fold etc. 258.

pare, reduce, attenuate, rub down, scrape, file, grind, chip, shave, shear.

Adj. contracting etc. *v.*; astringent; shrunk, contracted etc. *v.*; strangulated, tabid, wizened, stunted, tabescent; marasmic; waning etc. *v.*; neap; compact; shriveled, preshrunk.

unexpanded etc. (expand etc. 194); inswept; contractile; compressible; smaller etc. small etc. 193).

196. Distance.—N. distance; space etc. 180; remoteness, farness; far- cry to; longinquity, elongation; offing, background; removedness; parallax; reach, span, stride; drift.

out-post, -skirt; horizon, sky-line; aphelion; foreign parts, ***ultima Thule***, ***ne plus ultra***, antipodes; long range, giant's stride.

dispersion etc. 73.

V. be -distant etc. *adj.*; extend –, stretch –, reach –, spread –, go –, get –, stretch away- to; range, outrange, outreach.

remain at a distance; keep –, stand- -away, – off, – aloof, – clear of.

Adj. distant; far -off, away; remote, telescopic, distal, wide of; stretching to etc. *v.*; yon, -der; ulterior; trans-marine, -pontine, -atlantic, -pacific, -continental, -polar, -equatorial, -alpine; tramontane; ultra-montane, -mundane; hyperborean, antihodean; inaccessible, out of the way; unapproached, -able; incontiguous.

Adv. far -off, – away; afar, -off; off; away; a -long, – great, – good- way off; wide away, aloof; wide –, clear- of; out of -the way, – reach; abroad, yonder, farther, further, beyond; ***outre mer***, over the border, far and wide, over the hills and far away; from pole to pole etc. (***over great space***) 180; to the -uttermost parts, – ends- of the earth; out of -hearing, – range, nobody knows where, ***à perte de vue***, out of the sphere of, wide of the mark; a far cry to.

apart, asunder; wide -apart, – asunder; ***longo intervallo***; at arm's length.

197. Nearness.—N. nearness etc. *adj.*; proximity, propinquity; vicinity, -age; neighborhood, adjacency; contiguity etc. 199.

short -distance, – step, – cut; earshot, close quarters, brief span; stone's throw; bow –, gun –, pistol- shot; hair's breadth, span; close-up.

purlieus, neighborhood, vicinage, ***environs***, ***alentours***, suburbs, confines, ***banlieue***, borderland; whereabouts.

bystander; neighbor, borderer.

approach etc. 286; convergence etc. 290; perihelion.

V. be -near etc. *adj.*; adjoin, hang about, trench on; border-, verge upon; stand by, approximate, tread on the heels of, cling to, clasp, hug; cuddle, huddle; hang about the skirts of, hover over; burn; abut.

bring –, draw- -near etc. 286; converge etc. 290; crowd etc. 72; place -side by side etc. *adv.*

Adj. near, nigh; close-, near- at hand; close, neighboring, propinquent, bordering upon; adjacent, adjoining, limitrophe; proxim-ate, -al; at hand, handy; near the mark, near run; home, intimate.

Adv. near, nigh; hard –, fast- by; close -to, upon, – up; at the point of; next door to; within -reach, – call, – hearing, – earshot, – range; within an ace of; but a step, not far from, at no great distance; on the -verge, – brink, – skirts- of; in the -environs etc. *n.*; at one's -door, – feet, – elbow, – finger's end, – side; on the tip of one's tongue; under one's nose; within a -stone's throw etc. *n.*; in -sight, – presence- of; at close quarters; cheek by -jole, – jowl; beside, alongside, side by side, ***tête-à-tête***; in juxtaposition etc. (***touching***) 199; yard-arm to yard-arm; at the heels of; on the confines of, at the threshold, bordering upon, verging to; in the way.

about; here-, there-abouts; rougly, in round

numbers; approxim- -ately, – atively; as good as, well nigh.

198. Interval.—N. interval, interspace; separation etc. 44; break gap, opening; hole etc. 260; chasm, *hiatus,* caesura; inter-ruption,-regnum; interstice, *lacuna,* cleft, mesh, crevice, chink, rime, creek, cranny, crack, chap, slit, slot, fissure, scissure, rift, flaw, breach, fracture, rent, gash, cut, leak, dike, ha-ha.

gorge, defile, ravine, canon, *crevasse,* abyss, abysm; gulf; inlet, frith, strait, gully, gulch, nullah; pass; notch; furrow etc. 259; yawning gulf; *hiatus - maxime, – valde- deflendus*; parenthesis etc. (*interjacence*) 228; void etc. (*absence*) 187; incompleteness etc. 530.

V. gape etc. (*open*) 260; part, remove.

Adj. with an interval, far between; separated, spaced, split.

Adv. at intervals etc. (*discontinuously*) 70; *longo intervallo.*

199. Contiguity.—N. contiguity, contact, proximity, apposition, juxtaposition, touching etc. *v.*; abutment, osculation; meeting, appulse, appulsion, *rencontre*, rencounter, syzygy, coincidence, conjunction, coexistence; adhesion etc. 46.

border-land; frontier etc. (*limit*) 233; tangent.

V. be -contiguous etc. *adj.*; join, adjoin, abut on, march with, border; tick, graze, touch, meet, osculate, kiss, come in contact; coincide; coexist; adhere etc. 46.

Adj. contiguous; touching etc. *v.*; in -contact etc. *n.*, conterminous, end to end, osculatory; pertingent; tangential.

hand to hand; close to etc. (*near*) 197; with no - interval etc. 198.

200. Length.—N. length, longitude, span, extent, mileage.

line, bar, rule, stripe, streak, spoke, radius.

lengthening etc. *v.*; pro-longation, -duction, -traction; ten-sion, -sure; extension.

[Measures of length] line, nail, inch, hand, palm, foot, cubit, yard, ell, fathom, rod, pole, perch, furlong, mile, league; chain, meter, kilo-, centi-, milli- etc meter.

pedometer, perambulator, odometer, odograph, speedometer, cyclometer, log, telemeter, range finder; scale etc. (*measurement*) 466.

V. be -long etc. *adj.*; stretch out, sprawl; extend –, reach –, stretch -to; make a long arm, 'drag its slow length along.'

render -long etc. *adj.*; lengthen, extend, elongate; stretch; pro-long, -duce, -tract; let –, pay –, draw –, spin- out; drawl.

enfilade, look along, view in perspective.

Adj. long, -some; lengthy, lank, wiredrawn, outstretched; stretched, drawn out, lengthened etc. *v.*; sesquipedalian etc. (*words*) 577; interminable, no end of.

line-ar, -al; longitudinal, oblong.

as long as -my arm, –to-day and to-morrow; unshortened etc. (shorten etc. 201).

Adv. lengthwise, at length, longitudinally, endlong, along; *tandem*; in a line etc. (*continuously*) 69; in perspective.

from -end to end; –stem to stern, –head to foot, –the crown of the head to the sole of the foot, –top to toe, –head to heels; fore and aft.

201. Shortness.—N. shortness etc. *adj.*; brevity; littleness etc. 193; a span.

shortening etc. *v.*; abbrevia-tion, -ture; abridgment, concision, retrenchment, curtailment, decurtation; reduction etc. (*contraction*) 195; epitome etc. (*compendium*) 596.

abridger, abstractor, epitomiser.

elision, ellipsis; conciseness etc. (*in style*) 572.

V. be -short etc. *adj.*; render -short etc. *adj.*; shorten, curtail, abridge, abbreviate, take in, reduce; compress etc. (*contract*) 195; epitomize etc. 596.

retrench, cut short, obtruncate; scrimp, cut, chop up, hack, hew; cut –, pare- down; clip, snip, dock, lop, prune; shear, shave, mow, reap, crop; snub; truncate, pollard, stunt, nip, nip in the bud, check the growth of; [in drawing] foreshorten.

Adj. short, brief, curt; compendious, compact; stubby, scrimp; shorn, stubbed; stumpy, thickset, podgy, stocky, pug; squab, -by; squat, dumpy; little etc. 193; curtailed of its fair proportions; short by; oblate; concise etc. 572; summary.

Adv. shortly etc. *adj.*; in short etc. (*concisely*) *572.*

202. Breadth. Thickness.—N. breadth, width, latitude, amplitude; diameter, bore, calibre, radius; superficial extent etc. (*space*) 180.

thickness, crassitude; corpulence etc. (*size*) 192; dilatation etc. (*expansion*) 194.

V. be -broad etc. *adj.*; become –, render- -broad etc. *adj.*; expand etc. 194; thicken, widen.

Adj. broad, wide, ample, extended; discous; fanlike; out-spread, -stretched; wide as a church-door.

thick, dumpy, squab, squat, thickset, tubby; thick as a rope, stubby etc. 201.

203. Narrowness. Thinness.—N. narrowness etc. *adj.*; closeness, exility; exiguity etc. (*little*) 193.

line; hair's –, finger's -breadth; strip, streak, vein.

thinness etc. *adj.*; tenuity; emaciation, slenderness, macilency, *marcor.*

shaving, slip etc. (*filament*) 205; threadpaper, skeleton, shadow, scrag, anatomy, spindle-shanks, barebones, lantern jaws, mere skin and bone.

middle construction, stricture, neck, waist, isthmus, wasp, hour-glass; ridge, *ghaut*, pass; ravine etc. 198.

narrowing, coarctation, angustation, tapering contraction etc. 195.

V. be-narrow etc. *adj.*; narrow, taper, diminish, contract etc. 195; render -narrow etc. *adj.*

Adj. narrow, close; slender, thin, fine; *svelte;* thread-like etc. (*filament*) 205; finespun, taper, slim, gracile, slight, slight-made; scant, -y; spare, delicate, incapacious; contracted etc. 195; unexpanded etc. (expand etc. 194); slender as a thread, capillary.

emaciated, lean, meager, gaunt, macilent; lank, -y; weedy, skinny, scrawny, scraggy; starv-ed, -eling; attenuated, shrivelled; wizened, pinched, peaky, skeletal, spindling, spindle- -legged, -shanked; extenuated, tabid, marcid, bare-bone, raw-boned; herring-gutted; worn to a shadow, lean as a rake; thin as a -lath,—whipping post,—wafer; hatchet-faced; lantern-jawed.

204. Layer.—N. layer, stratum, course, bed, zone, *substratum*,floor, flag, stage, story, tier, slab, escarpment, table, tablet, panel, plaque; board, plank; trencher, platter.

plate; lam-ina, -ella; sheet, flake, foil, wafer, scale, coat, peel, pellicle, ply, thickness, membrane, film, leaf, slice, shive, cut, rasher, shaving, integument etc. (*covering*) 223.

V. slice, shave, pare, peel; plate, coat, veneer; cover etc. 223.

Adj. lamell-ar, -ated, -iform; laminated, -iferous; micaceous; schist-ose, -ous; scaly; filmy, membranous, flaky, squamous; folia-ted, -ceous; stratified, -form; tabular, discoid, spathic.

205. Filament.—N. filament, line; fiber, fibril; funicle, vein, hair, capillament, *cilium*, tendril, gossamer; hair-stroke; harl.

wire, string, thread, packthread, cotton, sewing-silk, twine, twist, whip-cord, cord, rope, cable, yarn, hemp, oakum, jute, wool, worsted.

strip, shred, slip, spill, list, band, fillet, *fascia*, ribbon, riband, tape, roll, lath, slat, strake, splinter, shiver, shaving.

beard etc. (*roughness*) 256; ramification; strand.

Adj. fil-amentous, -aceous, -iform; fibr-ous, -illous; thread-like, wiry, stringy, ropy; capill-ary, -iform; funicular, wire-drawn; anguilliform; flagelliform; hairy etc. (*rough*) 256; ligulate.

206. Height.—N. height, altitude, elevation, ceiling; eminence. pitch; loftiness etc. *adj.*; sublimity.

tallness etc. *adj.*; stature, procerity; prominence etc. 250.

colossus etc. (*size*) 192; giant, grenadier, giraffe.

mount, -ain; hill, butte, monticle, fell, knap; cape; head-, fore-land; promontory; ridge, hog's back, dune; rising –, vantage- ground; down; moor, -land; Alp; up-, table-, high-lands; heights etc. (*summit*) 210; knoll, hummock, hillock, barrow, mound, mole, *kopje*; steeps, bluff, cliff, craig, tor, peak, pike, clough; escarpment, edge, ledge, brae; dizzy height.

tower, pillar, column, pylon, obelisk, monument, steeple, spire, minaret, *campanile*, belfry, turret, roof, dome, cupola, pagoda, pyramid; sky scraper; Eiffel tower.

pole, pikestaff, maypole, flagstaff; mast, top—, topgallant- mast.

ceiling etc. (*covering*) 223.

high water; high—, flood—, spring-tide.

altimetry etc. (*angle*) 244; altimeter, height-finder, hypsometer, barograph.

V. be -high etc. *adj.*; tower, soar, command; hover; cap, culminate; overhang, hang over, impend, beetle; bestride, ride, mount; perch, surmount; cover etc. 233; overtop etc. (*be superior*) 33; stand on tiptoe.

become -high etc. *adj.*; grow, – higher, – taller; upgrow; rise etc. (*ascend*) 305.

render -high etc. *adj.*; heighten etc. (*elevate*) 307.

Adj. high, elevated, eminent, exalted, lofty, supernal; tall; gigantic etc. (*big*) 192; Patagonian; towering, beetling, soaring, hanging [gardens]; elevated etc. 307; upper; highest etc. (*topmost*) 210; monticulous, perching, hill-dwelling.

up-, moor-land; hilly, mountainous, alpine, subalpine, heaven-kissing; cloud-topt, -capt, -touching; aerial.

overhanging etc. *v.*; incumbent, overlying; super-incumbent, -natant, -imposed; prominent etc. 250.

tall as a -maypole, —poplar,—steeple; lanky etc. (*thin*) 203.

Adv. on high, high up, aloft, up, above, aloof, overhead; up—, above- stairs; in the clouds; on -tiptoe, —stilts,—the shoulders of; over head and ears; breast high.

over, upwards; from top to bottom etc. (*completely*) 52.

207. Lowness.—N. lowness etc. *adj.*; debasement, depression; prostration etc. (*horizontal*) 213; depression etc. (*concave*) 252.

molehill; lowlands; bottomlands; basement-ground-floor; *rez de chaussée* etc. 211; hold; feet, heels.

low water; low—, ebb—, neap—, spring- tide.

V. be -low etc. *adj.*; lie -low, —flat; underlie; crouch, slouch, wallow, grovel; lower etc. (*depress*) 308.

Adj. low, neap, debased; nether, -most; flat, level with the ground; lying low etc. *v.*; crouched, subjacent, squat, prostrate etc. (*horizontal*) 213.

Adv. under; be-, under-neath; below; down, -wards; adown, at the foot of; under-foot, -ground; down—, below-stairs; at a low ebb; below par.

208. Depth.—N. depth; deepness etc. *adj.*; profundity, depression etc. (*concavity*) 252.

hollow, pit, shaft, well, crater, abyss; gulf etc. 198; bowels of the earth, bottomless pit, hell.

soundings, sonar, depth of water, water, draught, submersion; plummet, sound, probe; sounding -rod, – line, – machine; lead; submarine, diving bell, bathysphere; diver.

V. be -deep etc. *adj.*; render -deep etc. *adj.*; deepen.

plunge etc. 310; sound, heave the lead, take soundings; dig etc. (*excavate*) 252.

Adj. deep, -seated; profound, sunk, buried; submerged etc. 310; sub-aqueous, -marine, -terranean, -terrene; underground.

bottom-, sound-, fathom-less; unfathom-ed, -able; abysmal; deep as a well, deep-sea.

knee-, ankle-deep.

Adv. beyond—, out of- one's depth; over head and ears, over one's head.

209. Shallowness.—N. shallowness etc. *adj.*; shoals; mere scratch; veneer, gloss, pinprick.

Adj. shallow, superficial; skin–, ankle–, knee-deep; just enough to wet one's feet; shoal, -y.
V. shallow, shoal, skim– over, –the surface, touch on.

210. Summit.—N. summit, -y; top, vertex, apex, zenith, pinnacle, acme, acropolis, culmination, meridian, utmost height, *ne plus ultra,* height, pitch, maximum, climax, apogee; culminating –, crowning –, turning- point; turn of the tide, fountain head; water-shed, -parting; sky, pole.

tip, -top; crest, crow's nest, cap, truck, peak, nib; end etc. 67; crown, brow; head, nob, noddle, pate, skull, cranium.

high places, heights.

top-, top-gallant mast, sky scraper; quarter –, hurricane- deck.

architrave, frieze, cornice, coping, coping-stone, zoophorus, capital, headpiece, capstone, epistyle, sconce, pediment, entablature; tympanum; ceiling etc. (*covering*) 223.

attic, loft, garret, house-top, upper story, roof.
topping, icing, frosting.

V. culminate, cap, crown, top; overtop etc. (*be superior to*) 33.

Adj. highest etc. (high etc. 206); top; top-, up-per-most; tip-top; culminating etc. *v.*; meridi-an, -onal; capital, head, polar, supreme, supernal, top-gallant.

Adv. a-top, at the top of – the tree, – the heap.

211. Base.—N. base, -ment; plinth, dado, wainscot, baseboard; foundation etc. (*support*) 215; substructure, *sub · stratum,* sump, ground, earth, pavement, floor, paving, flag, carpet, ground-floor, deck; footing, groundwork, basis; hold, bilge, orlop deck.

bottom, nadir, foot, sole, toe, hoof, keel, kelson, root.

Adj. bottom; under-, nether-most; fundamental; founded –, based –, grounded –, built- on.

212. Verticality.—N. verticality; erectness etc. *adj.*; perpendicularity; right angle, normal; azimuth circle.

wall, palisade, precipice, cliff, steep, bluff.

elevation, erection; square, plumb-line, plummet.

V. be -vertical etc. *adj.*; stand -up, – on end, – erect, – upright; stick –, cock-up.

render -vertical etc. *adj.*; set –, stick –, raise –, cock- up; erect, rear, raise, pitch, raise on its legs.

Adj. vertical, upright, erect, perpendicular, normal, plumb, straight, bolt upright; rampant; straight –, standing- up etc. *v.*; rectangular, orthogonal.

Adv. vertically etc. *adj.*; up, on end; up –, right- on end; *à plomb*, endwise; on one's legs; at right angles.

213. Horizontality.—N. horizontality; flatness; level, plane; stratum etc. 204; dead -level, – flat; level plane.

recumbency; lying down etc. *v.*; reclination, decumbence; de-, discumbency; proneness etc. *adj.*; accubation, supination, resupination, prostration; azimuth.

plain, floor, platform, bowling-green; cricket--ground; court; gridiron; base-ball diamond; hockey rink; tennis-, croquet-ground, – lawn; billiard table; terrace, estrade, esplanade, *parterre,* table-land, *plateau,* ledge.

spirit-, level; T-square.

V. be -horizontal etc. *adj.*; lie, recline, couch; lie -down, – flat, – prostrate; sprawl, loll; sit down.

render -horizontal etc. *adj.*; lay, – down, – out; level, flatten, even, raze, equalize, smooth, align; prostrate, knock down, floor, fell, ground.

Adj. horizontal, level, even, plane; flat etc. 251; flat as a -billiard table, – bowling green; alluvial; calm, – as a mill-pond; smooth, –as glass.

re-, de-, pro-, ac-cumbent; lying etc. *v.*; prone, supine, couchant, jacent, prostrate.

Adv. horizontally etc. *adj.*; on -one's back. –all fours, – its beam ends.

214. Pendency.—N. pend-, dependency; suspension, hanging etc. *v.*

pendant, drop, tippet, tassel, lobe, tail, train, flap, lappet, skirt, pig-tail, queue, pendulum, hanger, suspender, supporter.

peg, knob, button, hook, nail, stud, ring, staple, tenterhook; davit; fastening etc. 45; spar, horse.

chande-, gase-, electro-lier.

V. be -pendent etc. *adj.*; hang, depend, swing, dangle, droop, sag; swag; daggle, flap, trail, flow.

suspend, hang, sling, hook up, hitch, fasten to, append.

Adj. pend-ent, -ulous; pensile; hanging etc. *v.*; dependent; suspended etc. *v.*; lowering, overhanging, beetling, decumbent; loose, flowing.

having a -peduncle etc. *n.*; pedunculate, tailed, caudate.

215. Support.—N. support, backing, ground, foundation, base, basis; *terra firma*; bearing, fulcrum, *point d'appui*, caudex, purchase, footing, hold, *-locus standi*; landing, – stage, – place; stage, platform; block; rest, resting-place; ground--work, ***substratum***, sustentation, subvention; floor etc. (*basement*) 211.

supporter; aid etc. 707; prop, stand, anvil, fulciment; hod, stay, shore, skid, rib, sprag, truss, bandage; sleeper; stirrup, stilts, shoe, sole, heel, splint, lap; bar, rod, boom, sprit, outrigger.

staff, stick, crutch, alpenstock, bourdon; *bâton*, maulstick, colstaff, cowlstaff, staddle; stalk, pedicel, -icle, – uncle.

post, pillar, shaft, column, pilaster; pediment, pedestal; plinth, shank, leg, socle, zocle; buttress, jamb, mullion, abutment; pile, baluster, banister, stanchion, king post; balustrade.

frame, -work, body, *chassis*, *fuselage*; scaffold, skeleton, beam, rafter, girder, lintel, joist, cantilever, travis, trave, corner-stone. summer, transom; rung, round, step, sill.

columella, back-bone; key-stone; axle, -tree; axis; arch, ogive, mainstay.

trunnion, pivot, rowlock; peg etc. (*pendency*)

214; tie-beam etc. (*fastening*) 45; thole pin.

board, ledge, shelf, hob, bracket, trevet, trivet, arbor, rack, hatrack; mantel, -piece, -shelf; slab, console; counter, dresser; flange, corbel; table, trestle, teapoy; shoulder; perch; horse; easel, desk; retable, predella.

seat, throne, dais; divan, musnud; chair, bench, form, stool, camp-stool, sofa, settee, davenport, stall, miserere, arm –, easy –, elbow –, rocking-chair; couch, day bed, *fauteuil*, woolsack, ottoman, settle, squab, bench, box, dicky; saddle, pannel, pillion; side –, pack- saddle; pommel.

bed, berth, pallet, tester, crib, cot, bassinet, hammock, shakedown, camp bed, bunk, truckle-bed, cradle, litter, stretcher, bedstead; four-poster, French bed; bedding, mattress, *paillasse;* pillow, bolster; mat, rug, cushion.

stool, footstool, hassock, faldstool, *prie-dieu*; tabouret; tripod.

Atlas, Persides, Atlantes, Caryatides, Hercules.

V. be -supported etc.; lie –, sit –, recline –, lean –, loll –, rest –, stand –, step –, repose – , abut –, beat –, be based etc.- on; have at one's back; be-stride, -straddle.

support, bear, carry, hold, sustain, shoulder; hold –, back –, bolster –, shore- up; up-hold, -bear; prop; under-prop,-pin, -set; bandage, etc. 43; brace, truss; cradle, pillow.

give –, furnish –, afford –, supply –, lend- support, – foundations; bottom, found, base, ground, embed.

maintain, keep on foot; aid etc. 707.

Adj. support-ing, -ed, etc.*v.*; atlantean, columellar; sustentative, fundamental, basal.

Adv. astride on, astraddle; pick-a-back.

216. Parallelism.—N. parallelism; coextension, concentricity, collimation.

V. be –, lie- parallel to; collimate; equate, match.

Adj. parallel; coextensive, collateral, concentric, concurrent, abreast, aligned.

Adv. alongside, abreast etc. (*laterally*) 236.

217. Obliquity.—N. obliquity, inclination, skew, slope, slant; crookedness etc. *adj.*; slopeness; leaning etc. *v.*; bevel, bezel, ramp, tilt; bias, list, twist, warp, swag, cant, lurch; distortion etc. 243; bend etc. (*curve*) 245; tower of Pisa.

acclivity, rise, ascent, grade, gradient, *glacis*, rising ground, hill, bank, declivity, downhill, dip, fall, devexity; gentle –, rapid- slope; easy -ascent, – descent; shelving beach; *talus; montagne Russe; facilis descensus Averni.*

steepness etc. *adj.*; cliff, precipice etc. (*vertical*) 212; escarpment, scarp.

[Measure of inclination]clinometer, theodolite, level, sextant, quadrant, protractor; angle, sine, cosine, tangent etc. hypothenuse.

diagonal; zigzag, chevron.

V. be -oblique etc. *adj.*; slope, slant, lean, incline, shelve, stoop, decline, descent, bend, heel, careen, sag, swag, seel, slouch, cant, sidle.

render -oblique etc. *adj.*; sway, bias; slope, slant; incline, bend, crook; cant, tilt; distort etc. 243.

Adj. oblique, inclined; sloping etc. *v.*; tilted etc. *v.*; recumbent, clinal, skew, askew, slant, aslant, bias, plagiedral, indirect, wry, awry, ajee, crooked; knock-kneed etc. (*distorted*) 243; bevel, out of the perpendicular.

uphill, rising, ascending, acclivous; downhill, falling, descending; declining, declivous, devex, anticlinal; steep, abrupt, precipitous, breakneck.

diagonal; trans-verse, -versal; athwart, antiparallel; curved etc. 245.

Adv. obliquely etc. *adj.*; on –, all on- one side; askew, askant, askance, aslope, asquint, edgewise, at an angle; side-long, -ways; slope-, slant-wise; by a side wind.

218. Inversion.—N. in-, e-, sub-, re-, retro-, intro-version; contraposition etc. 237; contrariety etc. 14; reversal; turn of the tide.

overturn; upset, capsize; somer-sault, -set; summerset; *culbute*; revulsion; *pirouette.*

transposition, transposal, anastrophy, *metastasis, hyperbaton, anastrophe, hysteron--proteron,* hypallage, *synchysis, tmesis,* parenthesis; *metathesis*; palindrome; Spoonerism.

pronation and supination.

V. be -inverted etc.; turn –, go –, wheel- -round, – about, – to the right about; turn –, go –, tilt –, topple-over; capsize, turn turtle.

in-, sub-, retro-, intro-vert; reverse; up-, over-turn, -set; turn -topsy turvy etc. *adj.*; *culbuter*; transpose, put the cart before the horse, turn the tables.

Adj. inverted etc. *v.*; wrong side -out, – up; inside out, upside down; bottom –, keel- upwards; supine, on one's head, topsy turvy, *sens dessus sens dessous.*

inverse; reverse etc. (*contrary*) 14; opposite etc. 237.

topheavy, unstable.

Adv. inversely etc.*adj.*; hirdie-girdie; heels over head, head over heels.

219. Crossing.—N. crossing etc. *v.*; intersection, – lacement, – twinement, -digitation; decussation, transversion; convolution etc. 248.

reticulation, meshwork, network; inosculation, anastomosis, inter-texture, mortise.

net, *plexux*, web, mesh, twill, skein, sleeve, felt, lace; wicker; mat, -ting; plait, trellis, wattle, lattice, grating, *grille*, gridiron, tracery, fretwork, filigree, reticle; tissue, netting, mokes.

cross, crucifix, rood, crisscross, crux; chain, wreath, braid, cat's cradle,knot; entanglement etc. (*disorder*) 59.

[woven fabrics] cloth, linen, muslin, cambric, drill, homespun, tweed, broadcloth etc.

V. cross, decussate; inter-sect, -lace, -twine, -twist, -weave, -digitate, -link.

twine, entwine, weave, inweave, twist, wreathe; anastomose, inosculate, dovetail, splice, link.

mat, plait, plat, braid, felt, twill; tangle, entangle, ravel; net, knot; dishevel, raddle.

Adj. crossing etc.*v.*; crossed, matted etc. *v.*; transverse.

cross, cruciform, crucial; reti-form, -cular, -culated; areolar, cancellated, mullioned, latticed, grated, barred, streaked; textile, secant, plexal; interfretted.

Adv. across, thwart, athwart, transversely, crosswise.

220. Exteriority.—N. exteriority; outside, exterior; surface, superficies; skin etc. (*covering*) 223; *superstratum*; disk, disc; face, facet, external, the open.

excentricity; circumjacence etc. 227.

V. be -exterior etc. *adj.*; lie around etc. 227.

place -exteriorly, — outwardly, — outside; put —, turn- out.

Adj. exter-ior, -nal; extraneous, outer, -most; out-ward, -lying, -side, -door; round about etc. 227; extramural.

superficial, skin-deep; frontal, discoid.

extraregarding; eccentric; outstanding; extrinsic etc. 6.

Adv. externally etc. *adj.*; out, without, over, outwards, *ab extra*, out of doors; *extra muros.*

in the open air; *sub -Jovè, — dio; à la belle étoile, al fresco.*

221. Interiority.—N. interiority; inside, -land, interior, endocrine; interspace, subsoil, *substratum.*

contents etc. 190; substance, pith, marrow; backbone etc. (*center*) 222; heart, bosom, breast, abdomen; vitals, viscera, entrails, bowels, belly, intestines, guts, chitterlings, womb, lap; gland, cell; internal organs, *penetralia*, recesses, innermost recesses; cave etc. (*concavity*) 252.

inhabitant etc. 188.

V. be -inside etc. *adj.*, — within etc. *adv.*

place —, keep- within; enclose etc. (*circumscribe*) 229; intern; embed etc. (*insert*) 300.

Adj. inter-ior, -nal; inner, inside, intimate, inward, intraregarding; in-, inner-most; deep-seated; visceral, intestine, -tinal; inland; subcutaneous; interstitial etc. (*interjacent*) 228; inwrought etc. (*intrinsic*) 5; enclosed etc. *v.*

home, domestic, indoor, intramural, vernacular; endemic.

Adv. internally etc. *adj.*; inwards, within, in, inly; here-, there-, where-in; *ab intra*, withinside; in —, within- doors; at home, in the bosom of one's family.

222. Centrality.—N. centrality, centricalness, center; middle etc. 68; focus etc. 74.

core, kernel; nucleus, nucleolus; heart, pole, axis, pivot, fulcrum, bull's eye; hub, nave, navel; *umbilicus*, spine, backbone, marrow, pith; hot-bed; concentration etc. (*convergence*) 290; centralization; symmetry.

center of -gravity, — pressure, — percussion, — oscillation, — buoyancy etc. metacenter.

V. be -central etc. *adj.*; converge etc. 290.

render central, centralize, concentrate; bring to a focus.

Adj. centr-al, -ical; middle etc. 68; axial, pivotal, focal, umbilical, concentric; middlemost, nuclear, centric, centraidal; spinal, vertebral.

Adv. middle; midst; centrally etc. *adj.*

223. Covering.—N. covering, cover; canopy, tilt, awning, baldachin, tent, marquee, *tente d'abri,* umbrella, parasol, sunshade; veil (*shade*) 424; shield etc. (*defense*) 717; hall.

roof, dome, cupola, mansard roof; ceiling; thatch, tile; pan-, pen-tile; tiling, shingles, slates, slating, leads; shed etc. (*abode*) 189.

top, lid, covercle, door, *operculum,* eyelid, blind, curtain.

bandage, plaster, lint, wrapping, dossil, finger stall.

coverlet, counterpane, sheet, quilt, comforter, eiderdown; tarpaulin, blanket, rug, drugget, linoleum, oilcloth; housing.

in-, tegument; skin, pellicle, fleece, fell, fur, ermine, miniver, sable, sealskin etc.; fabrikoid; leather, morocco, calf, pigskin, elk, kid, cowhide etc.; shagreen, hide; pelt, -ry; cuticle, *dermis*, scarfskin, *epidermis.*

clothing etc. 225; mask etc. (*concealment*) 530.

peel, crust, bark, rind, *cortex,* husk, shell, coat.

capsule; ferrule; sheath, -ing; pod, cod; casing, case, theca; *elytron; involucrum;* wrapp-ing, -er, cellophane; envelope, vesicle; dermatology, conchology.

armor, -plate, armoring; veneer, facing; pavement; scale etc. (*layer*) 204; coating, paint, stain; varnish etc. (*resin*) 356*a*; anointing etc. *v.*; inunction; incrustation, superposition, obduction, ground, enamel, whitewash, plaster, stucco, rough cast, pebble dash, compo; rendering; cerement; ointment etc. (*grease*) 356.

V. cover; super-pose, -impose; over-lay, -spread; wrap etc. 225; incase; face, case, veneer, pave, paper; tip, cap, bind, revet.

coat, paint, varnish, pay, incrust, stucco, cement, dab, plaster, tar; wash; be-, smear; be-, daub; anoint, do over; gild, plate, electroplate, japan, laquer, lacker, enamel, whitewash; lay it on thick.

over-lie, -arch; conceal etc. 528.

Adj. covering etc. *v.*; cutaneous, dermal, cortical, cuticular, tegumentary, skinny, scaly, squamous; covered etc. *v.*; imbricated, loricated, armor-plated, iron-clad; under cover, hooded, cloaked, cowled.

224. Lining.—N. lining, inner coating; coating etc. (*covering*) 223; stalactite, -agmite.

filling, stuffing, wadding, padding, bushing.

wainscot, *parietes,* wall brattice.

V. line, stuff, incrust, wad, pad, fill.

Adj. lined etc. *v.*

225. Investment.—N. investment; covering etc. 223; dress, clothing, raiment, drapery, costume, attire, guise, toilet, *toilette,* trim; habiliment; vesture, -ment; garment, garb, palliament, apparel, wardrobe, wearing apparel, clothes, things.

array; tailoring, millinery; best bib and tucker; finery etc. (*ornament*) 847; full dress etc. (*show*) 882; garniture; theatrical properties.

outfit, equipment, *trousseau*; uniform, khaki, regimentals; academicals, canonicals etc. 999; livery, gear, harness, turn out, accoutrement, caparison, suit, rigging, trappings, traps, slops, togs, toggery; masquerade.

dishabille, morning dress, lounge suit, tea-gown, *kimono*, *négligé*, dressing-gown, *peignoir*, wrapper, undress; shooting-coat; smoking jacket, mufti; rags, tatters, old clothes; mourning, weeds; duds; slippers.

robe, tunic, dolman, *paletot*, habit, gown, coat, coatee, frock, blouse, *pelisse*, middy, sagum, *toga*, smock-frock; frock-, dress-, morning-, tail- coat; dress-suit, – clothes, swallow-tail coat, dinner-, Eton-jacket.

cloak, pall; mantle, mantlet, mantua, shawl, *pelisse*, veil, yashmak; cape, tippet, kirtle, plaid, muffler, comforter, Balaclava helmet, haik, huke, chlamys, mantilla, tabard, housing, horse-cloth, burnous, *roquelaure*, *houppelande*; sur-, top-, over-, great-coat; *surtout*, spencer, cardigan, sweater, blazer; mackintosh, waterproof, slicker, raincoat, oilskin, trench coat, ulster, monkey-, pea-, pilot-jacket, redingote; wraprascal, poncho, cardinal, pelerine, talma.

jacket, jumper, vest, jerkin, waistcoat, doublet, *camisole*, gabardine; stays, *corsage*, corset, corselet, bodice; stomacher; skirt, petticoat, slip, farthingale, kilt, jupe, crinoline, bustle, hobble skirt, *panier*, apron, pinafore; loin cloth.

trousers; breeches, trews, pantaloons, unmentionables, inexpressibles, overalls, pajamas, smalls, small-clothes; tights, pants, shorts, drawers; knickerbockers, knickers, plus fours, bloomers, divided skirt; phil-, fill-ibeg.

head-dress, -gear; cap, *béret*, tam o' shanter, glengarry, topee, sombrero; hat; cocked –, high –, tall –, top –, silk –, opera –, crush - hat, *gibus*, beaver, castor, bonnet, tile, wideawake, billy-cock; bowler; soft felt –, straw –, leghorn- hat, panama; toque; wimple; night-, mob-, skull-cap, biretta; hood, cowl, coif; capote, calach; scull-cap; kerchief, snood; head, *coiffure*; crown etc. (*circle*) 247; *chignon*, pelt, wig, front, peruke, periwig; caftan, turban, fez, *tarboosh*, taj, shako, csako, busby; *képi*, forage cap, bearskin; helmet etc. 717; mask, domino.

body clothes; linen; shirt, sark, smock, shift, *chemise*, *lingerie*; night-gown, -shirt; bed-gown, *sac de nuit*; jersey, guernsey; underclothing, -waistcoat.

neck-erchief, -cloth; tie, ruff, collar, cravat, stock, handkerchief, bandana, scarf; bib, tucker; dicky; boa; girdle etc. (*circle*) 247; cummerbund.

shoe, pump, brogue, boot, slipper, sandal, galoche, galoshes, arctics, rubber boots, overshoes, patten, clog, sabot; high-low; Blücher –, Wellington –, Hessian –, jack –, top- boot; Balmoral; legging, puttee, buskin, greave, galligaskin, moccasin, *gamache*, gambado, gaiter, spatter-dash, spat, antigropeles; stocking, hose, gaskins, trunk-hose, sock, hosiery.

glove, gauntlet, mitten, cuff, muffettee, wristband, sleeve.

swaddling cloth, baby-linen, *layette*; pocket-handkerchief.

shroud, etc. 363.

clothier, tailor, milliner, *costumier*, sempstress, seamstress, snip; dress-, habit-, breeches-, shoemaker; cordwainer, cobbler, Crispin, hosier, hatter; draper, linendraper, haberdasher, mercer.

V. invest; cover etc. 223; envelop, lap, involve; in-, en-wrap; wrap; fold –, wrap –, lap –, muffle-up; overlap; sheathe, swathe, swaddle, roll up in, shroud, circumvest.

vest, clothe, array, dress, dight, drape, robe, enrobe, attire, tire, garb, habilitate, apparel, accouter, rig, fit out; bedizen, deck etc. (*ornament*) 847; perk; equip, harness, caparison; dress up.

wear; don; put –, huddle –, slip- on; mantle.

Adj. invested etc. *v.*; habited; dight, -ed; clad, *costumé*, shod, *chaussé*; *en grande tenue* etc. (*show*) 882.

sartorial.

226. Divestment.—N. divestment; taking off, stripping, removal etc. *v.*

nudity; bareness etc. *adj.*; undress; dishabille etc. 225, altogether; nu-, denu-dation; decortication, depilation, excoriation, desquamation; molting; exfoliation.

baldness, alopecia, acomia.

V. divest; uncover etc. (*cover* etc. 223); denude, bare, strip; undress, unclothe, disrobe etc. (dress, enrobe, etc. 225); uncoif; dismantle; uncase; put –, take –, cast- off; shed, doff; husk, peel, pare, decorticate, desquamate; excoriate, skin, scalp, flay, bark, expose, lay open; exfoliate, molt, mew; cast the skin.

Adj. divested etc. *v.*; bare, naked, nude; undressed, -draped, -clad, -clothed, -appareled; exposed; in dishabille; *décolleté*; bald, threadbare, ragged, callow, roofless.

in -a state of nature, – nature's garb, – buff, – native buff, – birthday suit; *in puris naturalibus*; with nothing on, stark naked; bald as a coot, bare as the back of one's hand; out at elbows; barefoot; bareback; leaf-, nap-, hairless, shaved, clean shaven, tonsured, beardless, bald-headed, acomous.

227. Circumjacence.—N. circumjacence, -ambience; environment, encompassment; atmosphere, medium; surroundings, *entourage*.

outpost; border etc. (*edge*) 231; girdle etc. (*circumference*) 230; outskirts, *boulevards*, suburbs, purlieus, precincts, *faubourgs*, *environs*, *banlieue*, neighborhood, vicinity.

V. lie -around etc. *adv.*; surround, beset, compass, encompass, environ, inclose, enclose, encircle, circle, embrace, circumvent, lap, gird; begird, girdle, engird; skirt, twine round; hem in etc. (*circumscribe*) 229; besiege, invest, blockade.

Adj. circum-jacent, -ambient, -fluent; ambient; surrounding etc. *v.*; circumferential, suburban.

Adv. around, about; without; on -every side, – all sides; right and left, all round, round about; in the neighborhood.

228. Interjacence.—N. inter-jacence, -currence, -venience, -location, -digitation, -penetration; permeation.

inter-jection, -polation, -lineation, -spersion, -calation; embolism.

inter-vention, -ference, -position; in-, ob-trusion; insinuation; insertion etc. 300; dovetailing; infiltration; intromission.

intermedi-um, -ary; go-between, agent, middleman, medium, bodkin, intruder, interloper; parenthesis, episode; fly-leaf.

partition, *septum*, diaphragm, mid-riff; party-wall, panel, vail, bulkhead, brattice, *cloison*; half-way house.

V. lie –, come –, get- between; intervene, slide in, interpenetrate, permeate.

put between, introduce, intromit, import; throw –, wedge –, edge –, jam –, worm –, foist –, run –, plough –, work- in; interpose, -ject, -calate, -polate, -line, -leave, -sperse, -weave, -lard, -digitate; let in, dovetail, splice, mortise; insinuate, smuggle; infiltrate, ingrain.

interfere, put in an oar, thrust one's nose in; intrude, obtrude; have a finger in the pie; introduce the thin end of the wedge; thrust in etc. (*insert*) 300.

Adj. inter-jacent, -current, -venient, -vening etc. *v.*, -mediate, -mediary, -calary, -sitital, -costal, -mural, -planetary, -stellar; embolismal.

parenthetical, episodic: mediterranean; intrusive; embosomed; merged, mean, middle, medium, median.

Adv. between, betwixt; 'twixt; among, -st; amid, st; 'mid, -st; in the thick of; betwixt and between; sandwich-wise; parenthetically, *obiter dictum*.

229. Circumscription.—N. circumscription, limitation, inclosure; confinement etc. (*restraint*) 751; circumvallation, encincture; envelope etc. 232.

V. circumscribe, limit, bound, confine, restrict, enclose; surround etc. 227; compass about; imprision etc. (*restrain*) 751; hedge —, wall —, rail-in; fence —, hedge- round; embar; picket, corral.

enfold, bury, incase, pack up, enshrine, inclasp; wrap up etc. (*invest*) 225; embosom.

Adj. circumscribed etc. *v.*; begirt, lapt; circumambient; buried –, immersed- in; embosomed, in the bosom of, imbedded, encysted, mewed up; imprisoned etc. 751; land-locked, in a ring fence.

230. Outline.—N. outline, circumference; perimeter, -phery; ambit, circuit, lines, *tournure*, *contour*, profile, *silhouette*, lineaments; bounds, coastline.

zone, belt, girth, band, baldric, zodiac, girdle, tire, cingle, clasp, girt; *cordon* etc. (*inclosure*) 232; circlet etc. 247.

V. outline, delineate, *silhouette*, circumscribe etc. 229; profile, block out.

Adj. outlined etc. *v.*; circumferential, perimetric, peripheral.

231. Edge.—N. edge, verge, brink, brow, brim, margin, border, confines, skirt, rim, felloe, felly, flange, side, mouth; jaws, chops, chaps, *fauces*; lip, muzzle.

threshold, door, porch; portal etc. (*opening*) 260; coast, shore, strand, beach, bank, wharf, quay, dock.

frame, fringe, flounce, frill, list, trimming, edging, skirting, hem, selvedge, welt; furbelow, valance, exergue.

Adj. border, marginal, skirting; labial; labiated, marginated.

232. Inclosure.—N. inclosure, enclosure, envelope; package, box, crate, case etc. (*receptacle*) 191; wrapper; girdle etc. 230.

pen, fold, croft, sty; pen-, in-, sheep--fold; paddock, pound, corral, kraal; yard, compound; net, seine net.

wall; hedge, -row; *espalier*; fence etc. (*defence*) 717; pale, paling, balustrade, rail, railing, gunwale; quickset hedge, park paling, circumvallation, *enciente*, ring fence.

barrier, barricade; gate; -way; door, hatch, *cordon*; prison etc. 752.

dike, dyke, ditch, fosse, moat, trench.

V. inclose; circumscribe etc. 229.

233. Limit.—N. limit, boundary, bounds, confine, *enclave*, term, bourn, verge, kerb-stone, curbstone, but, pale; termin-ation, -us; stint, frontier, precinct, marches.

boundary line, landmark; line of -demarcation, – circumvallation; pillars of Hercules; Rubicon, turning-point; *ne plus ultra*; sluice, flood-gate.

V.limit, bound, confine, define, circumscribe, demarcate, delimit, encompass.

Adj.definite; contermin-ate, -able, terminable, limitable; terminal, frontier, border, bordering, boundary.

Adv.thus far, – and no further.

234. Front.—N.front; fore, – part; foreground; forefront, face, disk, disc, frontage, *façade*, *proscenium*, facia, frontispiece; priority, anteriority; obverse [of a medal].

fore –, front- rank, first line; van, -guard; advanced guard; outpost, scout.

brow, forehead, visage, physiognomy, phiz, features, countenance, map, mug; rostrum, beak, bow, stem, prow, prore, jib, bowsprit; forecastle.

pioneer etc.(*precursor*) 64; metoposcopy.

V. be –, stand- in front etc. *adj.*; front, face, confront, breast, brave; bend forwards; come to the -front, – fore.

Adj. fore, forward, anterior, front, frontal, head-on, leading, first, primary.

Adv. before; in -front, – the van, – advance; ahead, right ahead; fore-, head-most; in the foreground; before one's -face, – eyes; face to face, *vis-à-vis*.

235. Rear.—N. rear, back, posterior-ity; rear -rank, – guard; background, *hinterland*.

occiput, nape, scruff, chine; heels; tail, rump, croup, buttock, posteriors, bottom, seat, backside, scut, breech, *dorsum*, loin; dorsal –, lumbar-region; hind quarters.

stern poop, after-part, counter; postern, heel-, tail-piece, crupper.

wake; train etc. (*sequence*) 281.

reverse; other side of the shield.

V. be -behind etc. *adv.*; fall astern; bend backwards; bring up the rear; follow etc. 622; tail, shadow.

Adj. back, rear; hind, -er, -most, -ermost; postern, -erior; dorsal, after; caudal, lumbar; mizzen.

Adv. behind; in the -rear, – ruck, – back-

ground; behind one's back; at the -heels, – tail, – back- of; back to back.
after, -most, aft, abaft, astern, stern- most, aback, rear-, hind-, back-ward.

236. Laterality.—N. laterality; side, flank, beam, quarter, lee; hand; cheek, jowl, jole, wing; profile; temple, *parietes*, loin, haunch, hip.
gable, -end; broadside; lee side.
points of the compass; East, Orient, Levant; West, occident; orientation.
V. be -on one side etc. *adv.*; flank, outflank; sidle; skirt, border.
Adj. lateral, sidelong; collateral; parietal, flanking, skirting; flanked; sideling.
many-sided; multi-, bi-, tri-, quadri- lateral.
East-ern, -ward, -erly; orient, -al, auroral, Levantine; West-ern, -ward, -erly; occidental, Hesperian; equatorial.
Adv. side-ways, -long; broadside on; on one side, abreast, abeam, alongside, beside, aside; by, – the side of; side by side; cheek by jowl etc. (*near*) 197; to -windward, – leeward; laterally etc. *adj.*; right and left; on her beam ends.

237. Contraposition.—N. contraposition, opposition; polarity; inversion etc. 218; opposite side; antithesis; reverse, inverse; counterpart; antipodes; opposite poles, North and South.
V. be -opposite etc. *adj.*; subtend.
Adj. opposite; reverse, inverse; antipodal, subcontrary; fronting, facing, diametrically opposite.
Northern, Septentrional, Boreal, arctic; Southern, Austral, antarctic, polar.
Adv. over, – the way, – against; against; face to face, vis-à-vis; as poles asunder.

238. Dextrality.—N. dextrality; right, – hand; dexter, offside, starboard.
Adj. dextral, right-handed: ambidextral; dexterous, dextrorsal etc.

239. Sinistrality.—N. sinistrality; left, – hand; *sinister*, nearside, larboard, port.
Adj. sinistral, sinister, sinistrorsal etc., left-handed, sinistromanual, sinistrous.

240. Form.—N. form, figure, shape, physique; con-formation, -figuration; make, formation, frame, construction, design, cut, set, build, trim, cut of one's jib; stamp, type, cast, mold; fashion; contour etc. (*outline*) 230; structure etc. 329.
feature, lineament, outline, turn; phase etc. (*aspect*) 448; posture, attitude, *pose*.
[Science of form] morphology.
[Similarity of form] isomorphism.
forming etc. *v.*; form-, figur-, efform- ation; sculpture.
V. form, shape, figure, fashion, efform, carve, cut, chisel, hew, cast; rough-hew, -cast; sketch; block –, hammer- out; trim; lick –, put- into shape; model, knead, work up into, set, mold, sculpture; cast, stamp; built etc. (*construct*) 161.
Adj. formed etc. *v.*
[Receiving form] plastic, fictile, full- fashioned etc.
[Giving form] plasmic, etc.
[Similar in form] isomorphous etc.

241. Amorphism. [Absence of form.]**—N.** amorphism, informity, uncouthness; unlicked cub, rough diamond; *rudis indigestaque moles*; disorder etc. 59; deformity etc. 243.
disfigure-, deface-ment, deformation; mutilation.
V. [Destroy form] deface, disfigure, deform, mutilate, truncate; derange etc. 61.
Adj. shapeless, amorphous, malformed, formless; un-formed, -hewn, -fashioned, -shapen; rough, rude, Gothic, barbarous, rugged, in the rough; misshapen etc. 243.

242. Symmetry. [Regularity of form.]**—N.** symmetry, shapeliness, finish; beauty etc. 845; proportion, eurythmy, eurythmic, uniformity, parallelism; bi-, tri-, multi-lateral symmetry; centrality etc. 222.
arborescence, branching, ramification.
Adj. symmetrical, shapely, well set, finished; beautiful etc. 845; classic, chaste, severe.
regular, uniform, balanced; equal etc. 27; parallel, coextensive.
arbor-escent, -iform; dendr-iform, -oid; branching; ramous, ramose.

243. Distortion. [Irregularity of form.]**—N.** dis-, de-, con-tortion; knot, mop, warp, buckle, screw, twist; crookedness etc. (*obliquity*) 217; grimmace; deformity; mal-, malcon-formation; monstrosity, misproportion, want of symmetry, *anamorphosis*; ugliness etc. 846; teratology.
V. distort, contort, twist, warp etc. *n.*; wrest, writhe, make faces, deform, misshape.
Adj. distorted etc. *v.*; out of shape, irregular, unsymmetric, awry, wry, askew, crooked, sinuous; anamorphous; not -true, – straight; on one side, crump, deformed; mis-shapen, -begotten; mis-, ill-proportioned; ill-made; grotesque, crooked as a ram's horn; hump-, hunch-, bunch-, crook-backed; bandy; bandy-, bow-legged; bow-, knock-kneed; splay-, club-footed; taliped; round-shouldered; snub-nosed; curtailed of one's fair proportions; scalene, stumpy etc. (*short*) 201; gaunt etc. (*thin*) 203; bloated etc. 194.
Adv. all manner of ways.

244. Angularity.—N. angular-ity, -ness; aduncity; angle, cusp, bend; fold etc. 258; notch etc. 257; fork, bifurcation.
elbow, knee, knuckle, ankle, groin, crotch, crane, fluke, scythe, sickle, zigzag, kimbo.
corner, nook, recess, niche, oriel.
right angle etc. (*perpendicular*) 212; obliquity etc. 217; angle of 45 degrees, miter; acute –, obtuse –, salient –, re-entrant –, spherical –, solid –, dihedral- angle.

angular -measurement, – elevation, – distance, – velocity; trigon-, goni-ometry; altimetry; clin-, graph-, goni-ometer; theodolite; transit circle; sextant, quadrant; dichotomy.

triangle, trigon, wedge; rectangle, square, lozenge, diamond; rhomb, -us; quadr-angle, -ilateral; parallelogram; quadrature; poly-, penta-, hexa-, hepta-, octa-, deca-gon.

Platonic bodies; cube, rhomboid; tetra-, penta-, hexa-, octa-, dodeca-, icosa-hedron; prism, pyramid; parallelopiped.

V. bend, fork, bifurcate, crinkle, divaricate, branch, ramify.

Adj. angular, bent, crooked, aduncous, uncinated, aquiline, jagged, serrated; falc-iform, -ated; furcular, furcated, forked, bifurcate, crotched; zigzag; dovetailed; knock-kneed, crinkled, akimbo, kimbo, geniculated; oblique etc. 217.

fusiform, wedge-shaped, cuneiform; tri-angular, -gonal, -lateral; quadr-angular, -ilateral; rectangular, square, foursquare, multilateral; polygonal etc. *n.*; cubical, rhomboidal, pyramidal.

245. Curvature.—N. curv-ature, -ity, -ation; incurv-ity, -ation; bend; flex- ure, -ion; conflexure; crook, hook, bought, bending; de-, inflexion; arcuation, devexity, turn; deviation, *détour*, sweep; curl, -ing; bough; recurv-ity, -ation; sinuosity etc. 248; aduncity.

curve, arc, arch, arcade, vault, dome, bow, crescent, *meniscus*, half-moon, lunule, horse-shoe, loop, crane-neck; para-, hyper-bola; catenary, festoon; conch-, cardi-oid; caustic, instep; tracery.

V. be -curved etc. *adj.*; sweep, swag, sag; deviate etc. 279; turn; re-enter.

render -curved etc. *adj.*; bend, curve, incurvate; de-, in-flect; crook; turn, round, arch, arcuate, arch over, loop the loop, concamerate; bow, coil, curl, recurve, frizzle.

Adj. curved etc. *v.*; curvi-form, -lineal, -linear, devex, devious; recurv-ed, -ous; *retroussé*; crump; bowed etc. *v.*; vaulted; hooked; falc-iform, -ated; semicircular, crescentic; lun-iform, -ular; semilunar, meniscal; conchoidal; cord-iform, -ated; cardioid; heart-, bell-, pear-, fig-shaped; reniform; lenti-form, -cular; bow-legged etc. (*distorted*) 243; oblique etc. 217; circular etc. 247.

246. Straightness.—N. straightness, rectilinearity, directness; inflexibility etc. (*stiffness*) 323; straight –, right –, direct-, bee- line; short cut.

V. be -straight etc. *adj*; have no turning; not -incline, – bend, – turn, – deviate- to either side; go straight; steer for etc. (*direction*) 278.

render straight, straighten, rectify; set –, put- straight; un-bend, -fold, -curl etc. 248, -ravel etc. 219, -wrap.

Adj. straight; rectiline-ar, -al; direct, even, right, true, in a line; unbent etc. *v.*; un-deviating, -turned, -distorted, -swerving; straight as an arrow etc. (*direct*) 278; inflexible etc. 323.

247. Circularity. [Simple circularity.]—**N.** circularity, roundness; rotundity etc. 249.

circle, circlet, ring, washer, areola, hoop, roundlet, *annulus*, annulet, bracelet, armlet, armilla; ringlet; eye, loop, wheel; cycle, orb, orbit, rundle, zone, belt, *cordon*, band; sash, girdle, cestus, cincture, baldric, fillet, *fascia*, wreath, garland; crown, corona, coronet, chaplet, snood, necklace, collar; noose, lasso, lariat.

ellipse, oval, ovule; ellipsoid, cycloid; epicycloid, -cycle; semi-circle; quadrant, sextant, sector.

V. make -round etc. *adj.*; round.

go round; encircle etc. 227; describe -a circle etc. 311.

Adj. round, rounded, circular, annular, orbicular; oval, ovate; elliptic, -al; ovoid, egg-shaped; pear-shaped etc. 245; cycloidal etc. *n.*; spherical etc. 249.

248. Convolution. [Complex circularity.]—**N.** winding etc. *v.*; con-, in-, circum-volution; wave, undulation, tortuosity, anfractuosity; sinu-osity, -ation, sinuousness; meandering, circuit, circumbendibus, twist, twirl, windings and turnings, *ambages*; torsion; inosculation; reticulation etc. (*crossing*) 219.

coil, roll, curl, buckle, spire, spiral, helix, corkscrew, worm, volute, whorl, rundle; tendril; scollop, scallop, escalop; kink.

serpent, snake, eel, maze, labyrinth.

V. be -convoluted etc. *adj.*; wind, twine, turn and twist, twirl; wave, undulate, meander; inosculate; entwine, intwine; twist, coil, roll; wrinkle, curl, crisp, twill; frizz, -le; crimp, crape, indent, scollop, scallop; wring, intort; contort; wreathe etc. (*cross*) 219.

Adj. convoluted; winding, twisted etc. *v.*; tortile, tortive; wavy; und-ated, -ulatory; circling, snaky, snake-like, serpentine; serpent-, anguill-, vermiform; vermicular; mazy, tortuous, anfractuous, sinuous, flexuous, wavy, sigmoidal.

involved, intricate, complicated, perplexed; labyrinth-ic, -ian, -ine; circuitous; peristaltic; daedalian, curly.

wreathy, frizzly, *crêpé*, buckled; ravelled etc. (*in disorder*) 59.

spiral, coiled, helical, turbinated.

Adv. in and out, round and round.

249. Rotundity.—N. rotundity; roundness etc. *adj.*; cyclindricity; spher-icity, -oidity; globosity.

cylin-der, -droid; barrel, drum; roll, -er; *rouleau*, column, rolling-pin, rundle; chimney-pot, drain-pipe.

cone, conoid; pear-, egg-, bell-shape.

sphere, globe, orb, orbit, ball, boulder, bowlder; spher-, ellips-, ge-, glob-oid, oblong –, oblate- spheroid; drop, spherule, globule, vesicle, bulb, bullet, pellet, *pelote*, clew, pill, marble, pea, knob, pommel, knot.

V. render -spherical etc. *adj.*; form into a sphere, sphere, roll into a ball; give -rotundity etc. *n.*; round.

Adj.rotund; round etc. (*circular*) 247; cylindric, -ical, -oid; columnar, lumbriciform; conic, -al; spher-ical, -oidal; glob-ular, -ated, -ous, -ose; egg-, bell-, pear-shaped; ov-oid, -iform; gibbous; campaniform, -ulate, -iliform; fungiform, bead-like, moniliform, pyriform, bulbous; *teres atque rotundus*; round as -an orange, — an apple, — a ball, — a billiard ball, — a cannon ball.

250. Convexity.—N. convexity, prominence, projection, swelling, gibbosity, bilge, bulge, protuberance, protrusion; excrescency, camber.

intumescence; tumor; tubercle, -osity; excrescence; hump, hunch, bunch, gnarl.

tooth, knob, elbow, process, *apophysis*, condyle, bulb, node, nodule, nodosity, tongue, *dorsum*, boss, embossment, bump, clump; sugar-loaf etc. (*sharpness*) 253; bow; mamelon.

pimple, wen, wheal, *papula*, postule, pock, proud flesh, growth, goiter, *sarcoma*, caruncle, corn, bunion, wart, furnuncle, polypus, adenoid, fungus, fungosity, *exostosis*, bleb, blister, blain; boil etc. (*disease*) 655; bubble, blob.

papilla, nipple, teat, pap, breast, dug, mammilla; proboscis, .ose, neb, beak, snout, nozzle, snozzle; Adam's apple; belly, paunch, corporation; withers, back, shoulder, lip, flange.

peg, button, stud, ridge, rib, jutty, trunnion, snag.

cupola, dome, bee-hive; arch, balcony, eaves; pilaster.

relief, relievo, *cameo*; *basso-*, *mezzo-*, *alto-rilievo*; low-, bas-, high-relief.

hill etc. (*height*) 206; cape, promontory, mull; fore-, head-land; point of land, naze, ness, mole, jetty, hummock, ledge, spur.

V. be -prominent etc. *adj.*; project, bulge, protrude, bag, belly, pout, bouge, bunch; jut —, stand —, stick —, poke- out; stick —, bristle —, start —, cock —, shoot- up; swell —, hang —, bend-over; beetle.

render -prominent etc. *adj.*; raise 307; emboss, chase.

Adj. convex, prominent, protuberant, underhung, undershot; projecting etc. *v.*; bossed, bossy, nodular, bunchy; clav-ate, -ated; hummocky, *moutonné*, mammiform; papul-ous, -ose; hemispheric, bulbous; bowed, arched; bold; bellied; tuber-ous, -culous; tumorous; cornute, knobby, odontoid; lenti-form, -cular; gibbous.

salient, in relief, raised, *repoussé*; bloated etc. (*expanded*) 194.

251. Flatness.—N. flatness etc. *adj.*; smoothness etc. 255.

plane; level etc. 213; plate, platter, table, tablet, slab.

V. render flat, flatten, squash; level etc. 213.

Adj. flat, plane, even, flush, scutiform, discoid; level etc. (*horizontal*) 213; smooth; flat as -a pancake, — a fluke, — a flounder, — a board, — my hand.

252. Concavity.—N. concavity, depression, dip; hollow, -ness; indentation, *intaglio*, cavity, antrum, dent, dint, dimple, follicle, pit, *sinus*, *alveolus*, *lacuna*; excavation, trench, shaft, sap, mine, tunnel, burrow; trough etc. (*furrow*) 259; honeycomb.

cup, basin, crater, punch-bowl; cell etc. (*receptacle*) 191; socket, faucet.

valley, vale, dale, dell, gap, dingle, combe, bottom, slade, strath, glade, grove, glen, cave, cavern, cove; grot, -to; alcove, *cul-de-sac*, blind alley; gully etc. 198; arch etc. (*curve*) 245; bay etc. (*of the sea*) 343.

excavator, sapper, miner.

V. be -concave etc. *adj.*; retire, cave in.

render -concave etc. *adj.*; depress, hollow; scoop, — out; gouge, dig, delve, excavate, dent, dint, mine, sap, undermine, burrow, tunnel, stave in.

Adj. depressed etc. *v.*; concave, hollow, stove in; dished; spoon-like; retiring; retreating; cavernous; porous etc. (*with holes*) 260; cellular, spongy, spongious; honeycombed, alveolar; infundibul-ar, -iform; funnel-, bell-shaped; campaniform, capsular; vaulted, arched.

253. Sharpness.—N. sharpness etc. *adj.*; acuity, acumination; spinosity.

point, spike, spine, *spiculum*, tine; needle, pin; tack, nail; prick, -le; spur, rowel, barb; spit, cusp; horn, antler; snag; tag; thorn, bristle.

nib, tooth, incisor, tusk; spoke, cog, ratchet.

crag, crest *arête*, cone, peak, sugar-loaf, pike, *aiguille*; spire, pyramid, steeple.

beard, *chevaux de frise*, porcupine, hedgehog, brier, bramble, thistle; comb, awn, bur.

wedge; knife-, cutting- edge; blade, edge-tool, cutlery, knife, penknife, whittle, razor; scalpel, bistoury, lancet; chisel; ploughshare, coulter; hatchet, axe, pick-axe, mattock, pick, adze, bill; bill-hook, cleaver, cutter; skiver; scythe, sickle, scissors, shears; sword etc. (*arms*) 727; bodkin etc. (*perforator*) 262.

sharpener, hone, strop; grind-, whet-stone; steel, emery.

V. be -sharp etc. *adj.*; taper to a point; bristle with.

render -sharp etc. *adj.*; sharpen, point, aculeate, acuminate, whet, barb, spiculate, set, strop, grind.

cut etc. (*sunder*) 44.

Adj. sharp, keen; acute; aci-cular, -form; aculeated, -minated; pointed; tapering; conical, pyramidal; mucron-ate, -ated; spindle-, needle-shaped; spiked, spiky, ensiform, peaked, salient, cusp-ed; -idate, -idated; corn-ute, -uted, -iculate; prickly; spiny, spinous; thorny, bristling, muricated, pectinated, studded, thistly, briery; craggy etc. (*rough*) 256; snaggy; digitated, two-edged, fusiform; denti-form, -culated; toothed; odontoid; star-like; stell-ated, -iform; arrow-headed; arrowy, barbed, spurred, sagittal; spear-shaped, hastate; horned; conical.

cutting; sharp-, knife-edged; sharp —, keen- as a razor; sharp as a needle; sharpened etc. *v.*; set.

254. Bluntness.—N. bluntness etc. *adj.*; abruptness, dullness.

V. be —, render- blunt etc. *adj.*; obtund, dull; take off the -point, — edge; turn.

Adj. blunt, obtuse, dull, bluff.

255. Smoothness.—N. smoothness etc. *adj.*; polish, gloss; lubric-ity, -ation.

down, velvet, silk, satin; slide; bowling green etc. (*level*) 213; glass, ice; asphalt, pavement, flags.

roller, steam-roller; iron, flat-iron, tailor's goose; sand-, emery-paper; burnisher, turpentine and bees-wax.

V. smooth, -en; plane; file; mow, shave; level, roll; macadamize; polish, burnish, planish, levigate, calender, glaze; iron, hot-press, mangle; lubricate etc. (*oil*) 332.

Adj. smooth; polished etc. *v.*; even; level etc. 213; plane etc. (*flat*) 251; sleek, glossy; silken, silky; lanate, downy, velvety; glabrous, slippery, glassy, lubricous, oily, soft; unwrinkled; smooth as -glass, — ice, — velvet, — oil; slippery as an eel; wooly etc. (*feathery*) 256.

256. Roughness.—N. roughness etc. *adj.*; tooth, grain, texture, ripple; asperity, rugosity, salebrosity, corrugation, nodosity; arborescence etc. 242.

brush, hair, beard, shag, mane, whisker, mutton-chops, *moustache*, *mustachio*, imperial, Van Dyke, tress, lock, curl, ringlet, *fimbriae*, *cilia*, *villi*; eye-lashes, eye-brows, love-lock.

plum-age, -osity; plume, *panache*, crest; feather, tuft, tussock, fringe, toupee.

wool, velvet, plush, nap, pile, floss, fluff, fur, down; byssus, moss, bur.

V. be -rough etc. *adj.*; go against the grain.

render -rough etc. *adj.*; roughen, rough cast, knurl; ruffle, crisp, crumple, crinkle, corrugate, engrail; set on edge, stroke —, rub- the wrong way, rumple.

Adj. rough, uneven; scabrous, knotted; nodular; rug-ged, -ose, -ous; asperous, crisp, salebrous, gnarled, unpolished, unsmooth, rough-hewn; knurled, cross-grained, crag-gy, -ged; crankling, scraggy, jagged, unkempt, prickly etc. (*sharp*) 253; arborescent etc. 242; leafy, well-wooded; feathery; plum-ose, -igerous; tufted, fimbriated, hairy, bristly, ciliated, filamentous, hirsute; crin-ose, -ite; bushy, hispid, villous, pappous, bearded, pilous, shaggy, shagged; fringed, befringed; set-ous, -ose, -aceous; 'like quills upon the fretful porcupine;' rough as a -nutmeg grater, — bear.

downy, velvety, flocculent, wolly; lan-ate, -ated; lanugin-ous, ose; tomentous.

Adv. against the grain, in the rough, on edge.

257. Notch.—N. notch, dent, nick, cut; indent, -ation; serration; dimple.

embrasure, battlement, machicolation; saw, tooth, crenelle, scallop, scollop, vandyke.

V. notch, nick, cut, pink, mill, score, dent, indent, jag, scarify, scotch, crimp, scollop, crenulate, vandyke.

Adj. notched etc. *v.*; crenate, -d; dentate, -d; denticulate, -d; toothed, palmated, serrated.

258. Fold.—N. fold, plicature, pleat, plait, ply, crease; tuck, gather; flexion, flexure, joint, elbow, doubling, duplicature, wrinkle, rimple, crinkle, crankle, crumple, rumple, rivel, ruck, ruffle, dog's ear, corrugation, frounce, flounce, lapel; pucker, crow's feet.

V. fold, double, plicate, pleat, plait, crease, wrinkle, crinkle, crankle, curl, smock, cockle up, crocker, rimple, rumple, frizzle, frounce, rivel, twill, corrugate, ruffle, crimple, crumple, pucker; turn —, double- -down, — under; tuck, ruck, hem, gather.

Adj. folded etc. *v.*

259. Furrow.—N. furrow, groove, rut, *sulcus*, scratch, streak, *striae*, crack, score, incision, slit; chamfer, fluting.

channel, gutter, trench, ditch, dike, dyke, moat, fosse, trough, kennel; ravine etc. (*interval*) 198.

V. furrow etc. *n.*; flute, groove, carve, corrugate, plough; incise, chase, enchase, grave, engrave, etch, bite in, cross-hatch.

Adj. furrowed etc. *v.*; ribbed, straited, sulcated, fluted, canaliculated; bisculc-ous, -ate; trisulcate; corduroy.

260. Opening.—N. hole, foramen; puncture, blow-out, perforation; pin-, key-, loop-, port-, peep-, mouse-, pigeon-hole; eye, — of a needle; eyelet; slot.

opening; apert-ure, -ness; hiation, yawning, oscitancy, dehiscence, patefaction, pandiculation; gap, chasm etc. (*interval*) 198.

embrasure, window, casement, light; sky-, fan-light; lattice; bay-, bow-window; oriel; dormer, lantern.

out-, in-let; vent, vomitory; *embouchure*; orifice, mouth, sucker, muzzle, throat, gullet, placket, weasand, wizen, nozzle, *esophagus*.

portal, porch, gate, ostiary, postern, wicket, trap-door, hatch, door; arcade; gate-, door-, hatch-, gang-way; lych-gate.

way, path etc. 627; thoroughfare; channel, passage, tube, pipe; waterpipe etc. 350; air-pipe etc. 351; vessel, tubule, canal, gut, fistula; adjutage, ajutage; chimney, smoke stack, flue, tap, funnel, gully, tunnel, main; mine, pit, adit, shaft; gallery.

alley, aisle, glade, lane, vista.

bore, caliber; pore; blind orifice.

por-ousness, -osity; sieve, cullender, colander; grater, shredder; cribble, riddle, screen; honeycomb.

apertion, perforation; piercing etc. *v.*; terebration, empalement, pertusion, puncture, acupuncture, penetration.

opener, corkscrew, can opener, key, master-key, *passe-partout*.

V. open, ope, gape, dehisce, yawn, bilge; fly open.

perforate, pierce, empierce, tap, bore, drill; mine etc. (*scoop out*) 252; tunnel; trans-pierce, -fix; enfilade, impale, spike, spear, gore, spit, stab, pink, puncture, lance, trepan, trephine, stick, prick, riddle, punch; stave in.

cut a passage through; make -way, — room- for.

un-cover, -close, -rip; lay —, cut —, rip —, throw- open.

Adj. open; perforated etc. *v.*; perforate; wide open, agape, ajar; un-closed, -stopped; oscitant, gaping, yawning; patent.

tubular, cannular, fistulous; per-vious, -meable; foraminous; vesi-, vas-cular; porous, follicular, cribriform, honeycombed, infundibular, riddled; tubul-ous, -ated, piped.

opening etc. *v.*; aperient.

Int. *open sesame!*

261. Closure.—N. closure, occlusion, blockade; shutting up etc. *v.*; obstruction etc. (*hindrance*) 706; gag; embolism; contraction etc. 195; infarction; con-, ob-stipation; blind -alley, – corner; *cul-de-sac*, *caecum*; imperforation, -viousness etc. *adj.*; -meability; stopper etc. 263; *operculum*.

V. close, occlude, plug; block –, stop –, fill –, bung –, cork –, button –, stuff –, shut –, dam- up, obturate; blockade; obstruct etc. (*hinder*) 706; bar, bolt, stop, seal, plumb; choke, throttle; ram down, tamp, dam, cram; trap, clinch; put to –, shut- the door; batten down the hatches.

Adj. closed etc. *v.;* shut, operculated; unopened.

unpierced, imporous, caecal; imperforate, -vious, -meable; impenetrable; un-, im-passable; invious; path-, way-less; untrodden.

unventilated; air-, water-tight; hermetically sealed; tight, snug.

262. Perforator.—N. perforator, piercer, borer, auger, gimlet, stylet, drill, wimble, awl, bradawl, scoop, terrier, corkscrew, dibble, trocar, trepan, trephine, probe, bodkin, needle, stiletto, broach, reamer, rimer, warder, lancet; punch, -eon; spikebit, gouge; spear etc. (*weapon*) 727.

263. Stopper.—N. stopper, stopple; plug, cork, bung, spike, spill, stop-cock, tap; rammer; ram, -rod; piston; stopgap; wadding, stuffing, padding, stopping, dossil, pledget, tompion, tourniquet, obturator; wad.

cover etc. 223; valve, slide valve; vent-peg, spigot.

janitor, door –, gate- keeper, porter, commissionaire, *concierge*, warder, beadle, Cerberus, usher, guard, sentry, sentinel; ostiary.

264. Motion. [Successive change of place.*]—**N.** motion, movement, move; motivity, motility, going etc. *v.*; unrest.

stream, current, flow, flux, run, course, stir; conduction, evolution; kinematics.

step, rate, pace, tread, stride, gait, clip, port, footfall, cadence, carriage, velocity, angular velocity; progress, locomotion; journey etc. 266; voyage etc. 267; transit etc. 270.

restlessness etc. (*changeableness*) 149; mobility; movableness, motive power; laws of motion; mobilization.

V. be -in motion etc. *adj.*; move, go, hie, gang, budge, stir, pass, flit; hover -round, – about; shift, slide, slither, glide; roll, – on; flow, stream, run, drift, sweep along; wander etc. (*deviate*) 279; walk etc. 266; change –, shift- one's -place, – quarters; dodge; keep -going, – moving.

put –, set- in motion; move; impel etc. 276; propel etc. 284; render movable, mobilize.

Adj. moving etc. *v.*; in motion; motile, transitional; motory, motive; shifting, movable, mobile, mercurial, unquiet; restless etc. (*changeable*) 149; nomadic etc. 266; erratic etc. 279.

Adv. under way; on the -move, – wing, – tramp, – march.

*A thing cannot be said to *move* from one place to another, unless it passes in succession through every intermediate place; hence motion is only such a change of place as is *successive*. 'Rapid, swift, etc., as thought' are therefore incorrect expressions.

265. Quiescence.—N. rest; stillness etc. *adj.*; quiescence; stag-nation, -nancy; fixity, immobility, catalepsy; indisturbance; quietism.

quiet, tranquillity, calm; repose etc. 687; peace; dead calm, anticyclone; statue-like repose; silence etc. 403; not a -breath of air, – mouse stirring; sleep etc. (*inactivity*) 683.

pause, lull etc. (*cessation*) 142; stand, – still; standing still etc. *v.*; lock; dead -lock, – stop, – stand; full stop; fix; embargo.

resting-place; bivouac; home etc. (*abode*) 189; pillow etc. (*support*) 215; haven etc. (*refuge*) 666; goal etc. (*arrival*) 292.

V. be -quiescent etc. *adj.*; stand –, lie- still; keep quiet, repose, hold the breath.

remain, stay; stand, lie to, ride at anchor, remain *in situ*, mark time, tarry; bring –, heave –, lay- to; pull –, draw- up; hold, halt; stop, – short; rest, pause, anchor; cast –, come to an- anchor; rest on one's oars; repose on one's laurels, take breath; stop etc. (*discontinue*) 142.

stagnate, vegetate; *quieta non movere*; let -alone, – well alone; abide, rest and be thankful; keep within doors, stay at home, go to bed.

dwell etc. (*be present*) 186; settle etc. (*be located*) 184; alight etc. (*arrive*) 292.

stick, – fast; stand, – like a post; not stir a -peg, – step; be at a -stand etc. *n.*

quell, becalm, hush, stay, lull to sleep, lay an embargo on; put the brake on.

Adj. quiescent, still; motion-, move-less; fixed; stationary; at -rest, – a stand, – a stand-still, – anchor; stock-still; immotile; standing still etc. *v.*; sedentary, untravelled, stay-at-home; becalmed, stagnant, quiet; un-moved, -disturbed, -ruffled; calm, restful; cataleptic; immovable etc. (*stable*) 150; sleeping etc. (*inactive*) 683; silent etc. 403; still as -a statue; – a post, – a mouse, – death.

Adv. at a stand etc. *adj.*; *tout court*; at the halt.

Int. stop! stay! avast! halt! hold, – hard! whoa!

Phr. *requiescat in pace*.

266. Journey. [Locomotion by land.]—**N.** travel; traveling etc. *v.*; wayfaring, campaigning.

journey, excursion, expedition, tour, trip, grand tour, circuit, peregrination, discursion, ramble, pilgrimage, *trek*, course, ambulation, march, walk, hike, promenade, constitutional, stroll, saunter, tramp, jog-trot, turn, stalk, perambulation; noctambulation; somnambulism, sleep walking; outing, ride, drive, airing, jaunt.

equitation, horsemanship, riding, *manège*, ride and tie.

roving, vagrancy, pererration; marching and countermarching; nomadism; vagabond-ism, -age; gadding; flit, -ting; migration; e-, im-, de-, inter-migration.

plan, itinerary, guide; hand-, road- book; Baedeker, Murray, Bradshaw, time table.

procession, parade, cavalcade, caravan, file, *cortège*, column.

[Organs and instruments of locomotion] vehicle etc. 272; locomotive etc. 271; legs, feet, pegs, pins, trotters.

traveler etc. 268.

V. travel, journey, course; tour; take –, go- a journey, take –, go out for- -a walk etc. *n.*; have a run; take the air.

flit, take wing; migrate, emigrate, *trek*; rove, prowl, roam, range, patrol, pace up and down, traverse; scour –, traverse- the country; peragrate; per-, circum-ambulate; nomadize, wander, ramble, stroll, saunter, hover, go one's rounds, straggle; gad; – about; expatiate.

walk, march, step, tread, pace, plod, wend; promenade; trudge, tramp; stalk, stride, straddle, strut, foot it, stump, bundle, bowl along, toddle; paddle; tread –, follow –, pursue- a path.

take horse. ride, drive, trot, amble, canter, prance, fisk, frisk, *caracoler*; gallop etc. (*move quickly*) 274; motor, cycle, taxi; go by -car, – train, – tram, – bus, – plane.

peg –, jog –, wag –, shuffle- on; stir one's stumps; bend one's -steps, – course; make –, find –, wend –, pick –, thread –, plough- one's way; coast, slide, glide, skim, skate, ski; march in procession, file off, defile.

go –, repair –, resort –, hie –, betake oneself- to.

Adj. traveling etc. *v.*; ambulatory, itinerant, peripatetic, perambulatory, roving, rambling, gadding, discursive, vagrant, migratory, nomadic; circumforane-an, -ous; somnambular, nocti-, mundi-vagant; locomotive, automotive, self-moving.

way-faring, -worn; travel-stained.

Adv. on -foot, – horseback, – Shanks's mare; by the Marrowbone stage; *in transitu* etc. 270; *en route* etc. 282.

Int. come along!

267. Navigation. [Locomotion by water, or air.]—**N.** navigation; aquatics; boating, cruising, yachting; ship etc. 273; oar, scull, sweep, punt pole, paddle, – wheel, screw, propeller, stern wheel, sail, canvas.

natation, swimming; fin, flipper, fish's tail.

aeronautics, aviation, flying, winging, cruising, gliding, ballooning; blind –, instrument – flying; avigation, take-off.

flight, trip, run; solo –, nolo (pilotless) –, supersonic –, test – flight; air -lift, -drop; shuttle, reconnaisence, mission, dry run (coll.), search mission, combat flight, sortie, air raid, bombing mission; air – support, – cover, – umbrella; formation flying, maneuvers, aerobatics, stunt flying (coll.), diving, rolling, barrel roll, spin, tail spin, loop, buzzing.

landing, instrument –, crash – landing.

angle, center, axis, stability, load, pressure, torsion, torque, thrust, propulsion, jet propulsion, pitch, lift, dray, yaw, resistance, drift, flow, wash.

course, heading, altitude; air -route, -lane.

voyage, sail, cruise, passage, circumnavigation, *periplus*; head-, stern-, lee-way.

astro-, cosmo- nautics; space –, interplanetary – travel; space – exploration, – flight.

mariner, aeronaut etc. 269.

V. sail; put to sea etc. (*depart*) 293; take ship, get under way; spread -sail, – canvas; gather way, have way on; make –, carry- sail; plough the -waves, – deep, – main, – ocean; walk the waters.

navigate, warp, luff, scud, boom, kedge; drift, course, cruise, coast; hug the -shore, – land; circumnavigate.

ply the oar, row, paddle, pull, scull, punt, steam.

swim, float; buffet the waves, ride the storm, skim, *effleurer*, dive, wade.

fly, pilot, copilot, astronavigate, solo, take off, taxi, ascend, climb, stunt, spin, loop, roll, dive, buzz, land, descend, level off, bail out, parachute.

Adj. sailing etc. *v.*; seafaring, nautical, maritime, naval; sea-going, coasting; afloat; navigable, aquatic, natatory.

volitant, volant, aerostatic, aerial, aeronautic; alar, alate, pennate.

Adv. under -way, – sail, – canvas, – steam; on the wing.

268. Traveler.—N. traveler, wayfarer, voyager, itinerant, passenger.

tourist, excursionist, globe-trotter; explorer, adventurer, mountaineer, Alpine Club; peregrinator, wanderer, rover, straggler, rambler; bird of passage; gad-about, -ling; vagrant, scatterling, landloper, waifs and estrays, wastrel, stray; loafer; tramp, -er, hobo, beachcomber, vagabond, nomad, Bohemian, gipsy, Arab, Wandering Jew, Hadji, pilgrim, palmer; peripatetic; somnambulist; sleep walker, noctambulist; emigrant, fugitive, refugee, *émigré*.

runner, courier, King's messenger; Mercury, Iris, Ariel, comet.

pedestrian, walker, foot-passenger; cyclist; wheelman.

rider, horseman, equestrian, cavalier, jockey, rough rider, trainer, breaker, huntsman.

driver, coachman, whip, Jehu, charioteer, postilion, post-boy, carter, wagoner, drayman, truckman; cab-man, -driver; *voiturier*, *vetturino*, *condottiere*; engine-driver; stoker, fireman, guard, brakeman, conductor; chauffeur, automobilist, motorist, motor –, truck –, taxi- driver.

269. Mariner.—N. sailor, mariner, navigator, argonaut; sea-man, -farer, -faring man; yachtsman; tar, jack tar, salt, gob, sea-dog, shellback, able seaman, A.B.; man-of-war's man, bluejacket, marine, jolly; midshipman, middy, reefer; captain, commander, master mariner, skipper, mate; ship-, boat-, ferry-, water-, lighter-, barge-, longshoreman, hoveller; bargee, gondolier; oar-, -sman; rower; boat-, cock-swain; coxswain; steersman, helmsman, pilot; crew; lascar.

aerial navigator, navigator; aero-, astro-, cosmonaut; balloonist, Icarus, aviator, pilot, flyer, copilot, spaceman; fighter –, bomber – pilot; bombardier, gunner; meteorologist; stewardess, aviatrix, aviatress; ground crew, aeromechanic, aeronautical engineer; parachutist, paratrooper.

270. Transference.—N. transfer, -ence; trans-, e-location; displacement; *meta-stasis, -thesis*; removal; re-, a-motion; relegation; de-, as-portation; extradition, conveyance, draft; carrying, carriage; convection, -duction, -tagion, infection; transfusion; transfer etc. (*of property*) 783.

transit, transition; passage, ferry, gestation; portage, porterage, carting, cartage; shoveling etc. *v.*; vect-ion, -ure, -itation; shipment, freight, wafture; trans-mission, -port, -portation, -umption, -plantation, -lation; shift-, dodg-ing; dispersion etc. 73; transposition etc. (*interchange*) 148; traction etc. 285.

[Thing transferred] drift, alluvium, detritus, *moraine*; gift, legacy, bequest, lease; freight, mails, cargo, luggage, baggage, goods.

V. trans-fer, -mit, -port, -place, -plant; convey, assign, carry, bear, fetch and carry; carry —, ferry-over; hand, pass, forward; shift; conduct, convoy, bring, fetch, reach.

send, delegate, consign, mail post, relegate, turn over to, pass the buck, deliver; ship, embark; waft; switch, shunt; transpose etc. (*interchange*) 148; displace etc. 185; throw etc. 284; drag etc. 285.

shovel, lade, dip, ladle, bale, decant, draft off, transfuse.

Adj. transferred etc. *v.*; drifted; movable, portable, -ative; conductive; contagious, infectious.

transferable, assignable, conveyable, devisable, negotiable, transmissible.

Adv. from -hand to hand, — pillar to post.

on —, by- the way; on the -road, — wing; as one goes; *in transitu, en route, chemin faisant, en passant*, in mid-progress.

271. Carrier.—N. carrier, porter, red cap, bearer, messenger, postman, tranter, conveyer; stevedore; coolie; conductor, locomotive, tractor, caterpillar tractor, motor.

beast of burden, cattle, horse steed, nag, palfrey, Arab, blood horse, thorough-bred, galloway, charger, courser, racer, hunter, jument, pony, filly, colt, foal, barb, roan, jade, hack, *bidet*, pad, cob, tit, punch, roadster, goer; race-, pack-, draft-, cart-, dray-, post-horse, mount; Shetland pony, sheltie; garran; jennet, genet, bayard, mare, stallion, gelding; stud.

Pegasus, Bucephalus, Rozinante.

ass, donkey, jackass, mule, hinny; sumpter -horse, — mule; reindeer; camel, dromedary, mehari, llama, elephant; carrier pigeon.

carriage etc. (*vehicle*) 272; ship etc. 273.

Adj. equine, asinine.

272. Vehicle.—N. vehicle, conveyance, carriage, car, caravan, van, furniture van, pantechnicon; wagon, wain, dray, cart, lorry.

carriole; sledge, sled, sleigh, bob-sleigh, toboggan, *luge*, truck, tram; limber, tumbrel, pontoon; barrow; wheel-, hand- -barrow, — cart, trolley; perambulator; Bath —, wheel —, sedan-chair, jinriksha, rickshaw; ekka; chaise; palankeen, -quin; litter, horse-litter, brancard, crate, hurdle, stretcher, ambulance; velocipede, hobby-horse, coaster, scooter, go-cart; cycle; bi-, tri-, quadri-cycle; tandem, safety; skate, roller —, ice — skate; sled, sleigh; ski, snow-shoe.

equipage, turn-out; coach, chariot; *quadriga*, chaise, phaëton, break, brake, mail-phaëton, wagonette, drag, curricle, tilbury, whisky, landau, *barouche*, victoria, brougham, clarence, calash, *calèche*, britzska, *araba*, kibitka; berlin; sulky, *désobligeant*, sociable, *vis-à-vis, dormeuse*; jaunting —, outside- car; *tarantass*; runabout; shay.

post-chaise; diligence, stage; stage —, mail —, hackney —, glass- coach; stage-wagon; car, omnibus, bus, fly, *cabriolet*, cab, hansom, shofle, fourwheeler, growler, *droshki*, drosky.

dog-cart, trap, gig, whitechapel, buggy, four-in-hand, unicorn, random, tandem; shandredhan, *char-á-banc*.

automobile, motor-, auto-, touring-, racing-, cycle-, side-, steam-, electric- car; motor — cycle, — bike; motorized vehicle; bus, mini-bus; buggy, crate, tub, flivver, jalopy, wreck, clunker, dog, heap (all slang): coupe, coup, sedan, convertible, hard-top; camper, trailer, mobile home; limosine, landaulette, cabriolet, *coupé, voiturette*, runabout, electromobile, taxi, -cab.

train; passenger —, express —, freight —, subway —, special —, corridor —, parliamentary —, luggage —, goods- train, *train de luxe*; 1st-, 2nd-, 3rd- class- -train, — carriage, — compartment; Pullman —, sleeping-, club-, observation-, dining-, restaurant-car; mail-, luggage-, brake-van, coach, car, carriage; rolling stock; horse-box, cattle- truck.

273. Ship.—N. ship, vessel, sail; craft, bottom.

navy, marine, fleet, flotilla, squadron; shipping.

man of war etc. (*combatant*) 726; transport, tender, store-ship; merchant ship, merchantman; packet, liner; whaler, slaver, collier, coaster, tanker, freighter, freight steamer, cargo boat, lighter; fishing-, pilot- boat; trawler, drifter; cable ship; hulk; yacht; floating palace, ocean greyhound.

ship, bark, barque, brig, snow, hermaphrodite brig; brigantine, barquentine; schooner; topsail —, fore and aft —, three masted- schooner; *chasse-marée*; sloop, cutter, corvette, clipper, foist, yawl, dandy, ketch, smack, lugger, barge, hoy, cat-, -boat, buss; sail-er, -ing vessel, wind jammer; steamer, -boat, -ship; mail—, paddle —, screw —, stern-wheel- steamer; tug; train-ferry; line of steamers etc.

boat, pinnace, launch, motor-boat, picket-boat; hydroplane; life-, long-, jolly-, bum-, fly-, cock-, ferry-, canal- boat, dory, dugout, galliot; shallop, gig, funny, skiff, dingy, scow, cockleshell, wherry, coble, punt, cog, lerret; eight-, four-, pair- oar; randan; out- rigger; float, raft, pontoon; prame, ice-yacht.

state barge, bucentaur.

catamaran, coracle, gondola, carvel, caravel felucca, caique, canoe; trireme; galley, — foist; bilander, dogger, hooker, howker; argosy, carack; galliass, galleon; galliot, polacca, polacre, corsair, tartane, junk, lorcha, praam, proa, prahu, saick, sampan, xebec, dhow; dahabeah; nuggar, cayak, piroque; trireme.

submarine, submersible.

aircraft (*combatant*) etc. 726; flying machine, air mail, aero-, air-, mono-, bi-, tri-, hydro aeroplane, plane, cabin —, transport —, propeller — plane; *avion*, flying boat, glider; helicopter, rotor —, gyro-plane, whirlybird, autogyro, gyrodine; sea-, hydro-plane; amphibian; jet, — plane; turbo-, ram-, pulse-, subsonic —, supersonic —, strato- jet; rocket — plane, — ship,; space ship; war-, combat — plane; kamikaze, fleet, armada; trainer, fliight simulator; aerostat, dirigible, blimp (coll.), zeppelin; parachute, chute (coll.); kite.

rocket, flying —, ballistic —, guided — missile; projectile; rocket —, robot —, buzz-bomb; multistage —, step —, test — rocket; booster; satellite; flying saucer, unidentified flying object. (UFO).

nacelle, car, gondola, aileron; hangar, airport, landing field, airdrome; catwalk, controls, rudder, tail.

Adj. marine, maritime, naval, nautical, seafaring, sea-, ocean-going, sea-worthy.

aerial, aeronautical, air-worthy, flying etc. *n.*

Adv. afloat, aboard; on -board, — ship board, — board ship.

274. Velocity.—N. velocity, speed, celerity; swiftness etc. *adj.*; rapidity, eagle speed; expedition etc. (*activity*) 682; pernicity; acceleration; haste etc. 684.

spurt, rush, dash, race, steeplechase; smart —, lively —, swift etc. *adj.* —, rattling —, spanking —, strapping- -rate, — pace; round pace; flying, flight.

gallop, canter, trot, round trot, run, scamper; hand —, full- gallop; swoop.

lightning, light, electricity, wind; cannon-ball, rocket, arrow, dart, quicksilver; telegraph, express train; torrent; swallow flight.

eagle, antelope, courser, race-horse, gazelle, greyhound, hare, doe, squirrel.

Mercury, Ariel, Camilla, Harlequin.

[Measurement of velocity.] speedometer, log, -line, tachometer.

air speed, speed of sound, sonic —, subsonic —, supersonic —, ultrasonic —, hypersonic —, transonic — speed.

V. move quickly, trip, fisk; speed, hie, hasten, sprint, spurt, post, spank, scuttle; scud, -dle, scurry; scour, — the plain; scamper, sprint, dash, run, — like mad; fly, race, run a race, cut away, cut and run, shoot, tear, whisk, whiz, sweep, skim, brush; cut —, bowl- along; rush etc. (*be violent*) 173; dash -on, — off, — forward; bolt; trot, gallop, bound, flit, spring, dart, boom; march in -quick, — double-time; ride hard; et over the ground, scorch.

hurry etc. (*hasten*) 684; accelerate, put on; quicken; quicken —, mend- one's pace; clap spurs to one's horse; make-haste, — rapid strides, — forced marches, — the best of one's way; put one's best leg foremost, stir one's stumps, wing one's way, set off at a score; carry —, crowd- sail; go off like a shot, go ahead, gain ground; outstrip the wind, fly on the wings of the wind.

keep -up, — pace- with; outstrip etc. 303.

Adj. fast, speedy, swift, rapid, quick, fleet; nimble, agile, expeditious; express; active etc. 682; flying, galloping etc. *v.*; light- nimble-footed; winged; eagle-winged, mercurial, electric telegraphic; light-legged; light of heel; swift as -an arrow etc. *n.*; quick as -lightning etc. *n.*, — thought.*

Adv. swiftly etc. *adj.*; with -speed etc. *n.*; apace; at -a great rate, — full speed, — railway speed; full -drive, — gallop; post-haste, in full sail, tantivy; trippingly; instantaneously etc. 113; like a shot.

under press of -sale, — canvas, — sail and steam; *velis et remis*, on eagle's wing, in double quick time; with -rapid, — giant- strides; *à pas de géant*; in seven league boots; whip and spur; *ventre à terre*; as fast as one's -legs, — heels- will carry one; as fast on one can lay feet to the ground, at the top of one's speed; by leaps and bounds; with haste etc. 684; in- high — gear, — speed.

Phr. *vires acquirit eundo.*

*See note on *274.*

275. Slowness.—N. slowness etc. *adj.*; languor etc. (*inactivity*) 683; drawl; creeping etc. *v.*, lentor.

retardation; slackening etc. *v.*; delay etc. (*lateness*) 133; claudication.

jog-, dog-trot, walk; mincing steps; slow -march, — time.

slow -goer, — coach, — back; lingerer, loiterer, sluggard, tortoise, snail; dawdle etc. (*inactive*) 683.

V. move -slowly, etc. *adv.*; creep, crawl, lag, slug, walk, drawl, linger, loiter, saunter; plod, trudge, stump along, lumber; trail; drag; dawdle etc. (*be inactive*) 683; grovel, worm one's way, steal along; jog —, rub —, bundle- on; toddle, waddle, wabble, slug; traipse, slouch, shuffle, halt, hobble, limp, claudicate, shamble; flag, falter, totter, stagger; mince, step short; march in -slow time, — funeral procession; take one's time; hang fire etc. (*be late*) 133.

retard, relax; slacken, check, moderate, rein in, curb; reef; strike —, shorten —, take in- sail; put on the drag, apply the brake; clip the wings; reduce the speed, decelerate; slacken -speed, — one's pace, lose ground; back -water, — pedal, put the engines astern, throttle down.

Adj. slow, slack; tardy; dilatory etc. (*inactive*) 683; gentle, easy; leisurely; deliberate, gradual; insensible, imperceptible; languid, sluggish, apathetic, phlegmatic, slow-paced, tardigrade, snail-like; creeping etc. *v.*

Adv. slowly etc. *adj.*; leisurely; *piano*, *adagio*; *largo*, *larghetto*; at half speed, under easy sail; at a -foot's, — snail's, — funeral- pace; slower than molasses in January; in slow time; with -mincing steps, — clipped wings; *haud passibus aequis*; in-low —, gear, — speed.

gradually etc. *adj.*; *gradatim*; by -degrees, — slow degrees, — inches, — little and little; step by step; inch by inch, bit by bit, little by little, *seriatim*; consecutively.

276. Impulse.—N. impulse, impulsion, impetus; momentum; push, pulsion, thrust, shove, jog, jolt, brunt, booming, boost, throw; explosion etc. (*violence*) 173; propulsion etc. 284, jet propulsion; firing, launching, projection, trajection.

percussion, concussion, collision, occursion, clash, encounter, cannon, *carambole*, appulse, shock, crash, bump; impact; *élan*; charge etc. (*attack*) 716; beating etc. (*punishment*) 972.

blow, dint, stroke, knock, tap, rap, slap, smack, pat, dab; fillip; slam, bang; hit, whack, thwack, clout; cuff etc. 972; squash, dowse, whap, swap, punch, thump, swipe, jab, pelt, kick, punce, calcitration; *ruade*; arietation; cut, thrust, lunge, yerk.

hammer, sledge-hammer, mall, maul, mallet, flail; ram, -mer; battering-ram, monkey, pile-driver, punch, bat, tamper, tamping iron; cudgel etc. (*weapon*) 727; axe etc. (*sharp*) 253.

[Science of mechanical forces] mechanics, dynamics etc.

V. give an -impetus etc. *n.*; impel, push; start, give a start to, set going; drive, urge, boom; thrust, prod, foin; cant; elbow, shoulder, jostle, justle, hustle, hurtle, shove, jog, jolt, bean, encounter; run –, bump –, butt- against; knock –, run- one's head against; impinge.

fire, launch, project, traject, propel, 284.

strike, knock, hit, bash, tap, rap, bat, slap, flap, dab, pat, thump, beat, bang, slam, dash; punch, thwack, whack; hit –, strike- hard; swap, batter, dowse, baste; pelt, patter, skelter, buffet, belabor, tamp; fetch one a blow, swat; poke at, pink, lunge, yerk; kick, calcitrate; butt; strike at etc. (*attack*) 716; whip etc. (*punish*) 972; propel etc. 284.

come –, enter- into collision; collide; foul; fall –, run- foul of.

throw etc.

Adj. impelling etc. *v.*; im-pulsive, -pellent; booming; dynamic, -al; impelled etc. *v.*

277. Recoil.—N. recoil; re-, retro-action; revulsion; rebound, *ricochet*; re-percussion, -calcitration; kick, *contre-coup*; springing back etc. *v.*; elasticity etc. 325; reflexion, reflex, reflux; reverberation etc. (*resonance*) 408; rebuff, repulse; return.

ducks and drakes; boomerang; spring; reactionist, reactionary.

V. recoil, resile, react; spring –, fly –, bound- back; rebound, reverberate, repercuss, recalcitrate, echo, *ricochet*.

Adj. recoiling etc. *v.*; re-fluent, -percussive, -calcitrant, -actionary; retroactive.

Adv. on the -recoil etc. *n.*

278. Direction.—N. direction, bearing, course, set, drift, tenor; tendency etc. 176; incidence; bending, trending etc. *v.*; dip, tack, aim, collimation; steer-ing, -age.

point of the compass, cardinal –, half –, quarter- points; North, East, South, West; N by E, ENE, NE by N, NE etc; rhumb, azimuth, line of collimation.

line, path, road, range, quarter, line of march; alignment; straight shot, bee-line.

course, bearing, heading, altitude, air -route, -lane, angle, center, axis, torsion, torque, pitch, lift, drift, flow, wash.

V. tend –, bend –, point- towards; conduct –, go- to; point -to, – at; bend, trend, verge, incline, dip, determine.

steer –, make- -for, – towards; aim –, level- at; take aim; keep –, hold- a course; be bound for; bend one's steps towards; direct –, steer –, bend –, shape- one's course; align –, align- one's march; go straight, – to the point; march -on, – on a point.

ascertain one's -direction etc. *n.*; *s'orienter*, see which way the wind blows; box the compass.

Adj. directed etc. *v.*, – towards; pointing towards etc. *v.*; bound for; aligned –, with; direct, straight; un-deviating, -swerving; straightforward; North, -ern, -erly, etc. *n.*

directable etc. *v.*

Adv. towards; on the -road, – high road- to; versus, to; hither, thither, whither; directly; straight, – forwards, – as an arrow; point blank; in a -direct, – straight- line -to, – for, – with; in a line with; full tilt at, as the crow flies.

before –, near –, close to –, against- the wind; windwards, in the wind's eye.

through, *via*, by way of; in all -directions, – manner of ways; ***quaqua-versum***, from the four winds.

279. Deviation.—N. deviation; swerving etc. *v.*; obliquation, warp, refraction; flection, flexion; sweep; de-flection, -flexure; declination.

diversion, digression, departure from, aberration, drift, sheer; divergence etc. 291; zigzag; *détour* etc. (*circuit*) 629.

[Desultory motion] wandering etc. *v.*; vagrancy, evagation; by-paths and crooked ways.

[Motion sideways, oblique motion] sidling etc. *v.*; *échelon*, leeway; knight's move (at chess).

V. alter one's course, deviate, depart from, turn, trend; bend, curve, etc. 245; swerve, heel, bear off.

intervert; deflect; divert, – from its course; put on a new scent, shift, shunt, switch, wear, draw aside, crook, warp, short circuit.

stray, straggle; sidle, edge; diverge etc. 291; tralineate, digress, divagate, wander; wind, twist, meander, meander around Robin Hood's barn; veer, tack, sheer; turn -aside, – a corner, – away from; wheel, steer clear of; ramble, rove, drift; go -astray, – adrift; yaw, dodge; step aside, ease off, make way for, shy.

fly off at a tangent; glance off; turn, wheel –, face- about; turn –, face- to the right about; wabble etc. (*oscillate*) 314; go out of one's way etc. (*perform a circuit*) 629; lose one's way.

Adj. deviating etc. *v.*; aberrant, errant; ex-, dis-cursive; devious, desultory, loose; rambling; stray, erratic, vagrant, undirected; circuitous, indirect, zigzag; crab-like.

Adv. astray from, round about, wide of the mark; to the right about; all manner of ways; circuitously etc. 629.

obliquely, sideling, like the move of the knight on a chessboard.

280. Precession. [Going before.]**—N.** precession, leading, heading; precedence etc. 62; priority etc. 116; the lead, *le pas*; van etc. (*front*) 234; precursor etc. 64.

V. go -before, – ahead, – in the van, – in advance; precede, forerun; usher in, introduce, herald, head, take the lead; lead, – the way, – the dance; get –, have- the start; steal a march; get -before, – ahead, – in front of; outstrip etc. 303; take precedence etc. (*first in order*) 62.

Adj. foremost, first, leading etc. *v.*

Adv. in advance, before, ahead, in the van; fore-head-most; in front.

Phr. *seniores priores.*

281. Sequence. [Going after.]—**N.** sequence, run; coming after etc. (*order*) 63; (*time*) 117; following; pursuit etc. 622.

follower, attendant, satellite, shadow, dangler, train.

V. follow; pursue etc. 622; go –, fly- after.

attend, beset, dance attendance on, dog, be-dog; tread -in the steps of, – close upon; be –, go –, follow- in the -wake, – trail, – rear- of; trail, follow as a shadow, hang on the skirts of; tread –, follow- on the heels of, tag after.

lag, get behind.

Adj. following etc. *v.*

Adv. behind; in the -rear etc. 235, – train of, wake of; after etc. (*order*) 63, (*time*) 117.

282. Progression. [Motion forwards; progressive motion.]—**N.** progress, -ion, -iveness; advancing etc. *v.*; advance, -ment; ongoing; flood-tide, headway; march etc. 266; rise; improvement etc. 658.

V. advance; proceed, progress; get -on, – along, – over the ground; gain ground; jog –, rub –, wag- on; go with the stream; keep –, hold on- one's course; go –, move –, come –, get –, pass –, push –, press- -on, – forward, – forwards, – ahead; press onwards, step forward; make –, work –, carve –, push –, force –, edge –, elbow- one's way; make -progress, – head, – way, – headway, – advances, – strides, – rapid strides etc. (*velocity*) 274; go –, shoot- ahead; distance; make up leeway.

Adj. advancing etc. *v.*; pro-gressive, -fluent; advanced.

Adv. forward, onward; forth, on ahead, under way, *en route* for, on -one's way, – the way, – the road, – the high road- to; in -progress, – mid progress; *in transitu* etc. 270.

Phr. *vestigia nulla retrorsum.*

283. Regression. [Motion backwards.]—**N.** regress, -ion; retro-cession, -gression, -gradation, -action; *reculade*; retreat, withdrawal, retirement, remigration; recession etc. (*motion from*) 287; recess; crab-like motion.

re-fluence, -flux; backwater, regurgitation, ebb, return; resilience; reflexion (*recoil*) 277; *volte-face*.

counter -motion, – movement, – march; veering, tergiversation, recidivation, backsliding, fall, relapse; deterioration etc. 659.

turning point etc. (*reversion*) 145.

V. re-cede, -grade, -turn, -vert, -treat, -tire; retro-grade, -cede; back, – down, – out, crawl; withdraw; rebound etc. 277; go –, come –, turn –, hark –, draw –, fall –, get –, put –, run- back; lose ground; fall –, drop- astern; back water, put about; veer, – round; double, wheel, counter-march; ebb, regurgigate; *jib,* shrink, shy.

turn -tail, – round, – upon one's heel, – one's back upon; retrace one's steps, dance the back step; sound –, beat- a retreat; go home.

Adj. receding etc. *v.*; retro-grade, -gressive; regressive, -fluent, -flex, -cidivous, -silient; crab-like; reactionary etc. 277; counter-clockwise.

Adv. back, -wards; reflexively, to the right about; *à reculons, à rebours.*

Phr. *revenons à nos moutons*, as you were.

284. Propulsion. [Motion given to an object situated in front.]—**N.** pro-pulsion, -jection; *vis a tergo*; push etc. (*impulse*) 276; e-, jaculation; ejection etc. 297; throw, fling, toss, shot, discharge, shy.

[Science of propulsion] steam –, gas –, diesel –, jet –, rocket – propulsion, gunnery, ballistics, archery.

missile, projectile, ball, *discus*, javelin, hammer, quoit, brickbat, shot, bullet; arrow, shaft, gun etc. (*arms*) 727.

shooter, shot; gunner, gun-layer; archer, toxophilite; bow-, rifle-, marks- man; good –, crack- shot; sharpshooter etc. (*combatant*) 726.

V. propel, project, throw, fling, cast, pitch, chuck, toss, jerk, heave, shy, hurl; flirt, fillip.

dart, lance, tilt; e-, jaculate; fulminate, bolt, drive, sling, pitchfork.

send; send –, let –, fire- off; discharge, shoot; launch, send forth, let fly; dash.

put –, set- in motion; set agoing, start; give -a start, – an impulse- to; push, impel etc. 276; trundle etc. (*set in rotation*) 312; expel etc. 297.

carry one off one's legs; put to flight.

Adj. propelled etc. *v.*; propelling etc. *v.*; propulsive, -jectile.

285. Traction. [Motion given to an object situated behind.]—**N.** traction; drawing etc. *v.*; draft, pull, tug, haul; rake; 'a long pull, a strong pull and a pull all together;' towage, haulage.

V. draw, pull, haul, lug, rake, drag, draggle, tug, tow, trail, trawl, train; take in tow.

wrench, jerk, twitch.

Adj. drawing etc. *v.*; tractive, tractile; ductile, pulling, hauling, tugging, towing.

286. Approach. Motion towards.]—**N.** approach, approximation, appropinquation; access; appulse; afflux, -ion; advent etc. (*approach of time*) 121; pursuit etc. 622; convergence etc. 290.

V. approach, approximate; near; get –, go –, draw- near; come, – near, – to close quarters; move –, set in- towards; drift; make up to; gain upon; pursue etc. 622; tread on the heels of; bear up; make the land; hug the -shore, – land.

Adj. approaching etc. *v.*; approximative; convergent; affluent; impending, imminent etc. (*destined*) 152.

Adv. on the road.

Int. come hither! approach! here! come! come near!

287. Recession. [Motion from.]—**N.** recession, retirement, withdrawal; retreat; retrocession etc. 283; departure etc. 293; recoil etc. 277; flight etc. (*avoidance*) 623.

V. recede, go, move from, retire, ebb, withdraw, shrink; come –, move –, go –, get –, drift- away; depart etc. 293; retreat etc. 283; move –, stand –, sheer- off; swerve from; fall back, stand aside; run away etc. (*avoid*) 623.

remove, shunt, side track, switch off.

Adj. receding etc. *v.*

288. Attraction. [Motion towards, actively.]—**N.** attract-ion, -iveness; pull; drawing to, pulling towards, adduction, magnetism, gravity, attraction of gravitation; lure, bait, decoy.

lode-stone, -star; magnet, siderite, magnetite.

V. attract; draw –, pull –, drag- towards; adduce.

lure, bait, decoy.

Adj. attracting etc. *v.*; attrahent, attractive, adducent, adductive, alluring.

289. Repulsion. [Motion from, actively.]—**N.** repulsion; driving from etc. *v.*; repulse; abduction.

V. repel; push –, drive – etc. 276; from; chase, dispel; retrude; abduce, abduct; send away, repulse, dismiss.

keep at arm's length, turn one's back upon, give the cold shoulder; send packing; send -off, – away- with a flea in one's ear, – about one's business.

Adj. repelling etc. *v.*; repellant, repulsive; abducent, abductive.

290. Convergence. [Motion nearer to.]—**N.** con-vergence, -fluence, -course, -flux, -gress, -currence, -centration; appulse, meeting; corradiation.

assemblage etc. 72; resort etc. (*focus*) 74; asymptote.

V. converge, concur; come together, unite, meet, fall in with; close -with, – in upon; center -round, – in; enter in; pour in.

gather together, unite, concentrate, bring into a focus.

Adj. converging etc. *v.*; con-vergent, -fluent, -current; centripetal; asymptotical.

291. Divergence. [Motion further off.]—**N.** diverg-ence, -ency; divarication, ramification, radiation; separation etc. (*disjunction*) 44; dispersion etc. 73; deviation etc. 279; aberration, declination.

V. diverge, divaricate, radiate; ramify; branch –, glance –, file- off; fly off, – at a tangent; spread, scatter, disperse etc. 73; deviate etc. 279; part etc. (*separate*) 44; splay apart.

Adj. diverging etc. *v.*; divergent, radiant, centrifugal; aberrant.

292. Arrival. [Terminal motion at.]—**N.** arrival, advent; landing; de-, disem-barkation; reception, welcome, *vin d'honneur*.

home, goal, bourn; landing-place, -stage; resting –, stopping -place; destination, harbor, haven, port; terminal, terminus, railway station, depot, airport; halt, halting -place, – ground; anchorage etc. (*refuge*) 666.

return, recursion, remigration; meeting; ren-, encounter.

completion etc. 729.

V. arrive; get to, come to; come; reach, attain; come up, – with, – to; overtake; make, fetch; complete etc. 729; join, rejoin.

light, alight, dismount; land, go ashore; debark, disembark; put -in, – into; visit, cast anchor, pitch one's tent; sit down etc. (*be located*) 184; get to one's journey's end; make the land; be in at the death; come –, get- -back, – home; return; come in etc. (*ingress*) 294; make one's appearance etc. (*appear*) 446; drop in; detrain; outspan.

come to hand; come -at, – across; hit; come –, light –, pop –, bounce –, plump –, burst –, pitch- upon; meet; en- ren-counter; come in contact.

Adj. arriving etc. *v.*; homewardbound; terminal.

Adv. here, hither.

Int. welcome! hail! all hail! good- day, – morrow; greetings! hullo! well!

293. Departure. [Initial motion from.]—**N.** departure, decession, decampment; embarkation; take-off; outset, start; removal; exit etc. (*egress*) 295; exodus, Hejira, flight.

leave-taking, *congé*, valediction, valedictory, adieu, farewell, good-bye, stirrup-cup.

starting -point, – post; point –, place- of -departure, – embarkation; port of embarkation.

V. depart; go, – away; take one's departure, set out; set –, march –, put –, start –, be –, move –, get –, whip –, pack –, go –, take oneself- off; start, issue, march out, debouch; go –, sally- forth; sally, set forward; be gone.

leave a place, quit, vacate, evacuate, abandon; go off the stage, make ones' exit; retire, withdraw, remove; go -one's way, – along, – from home; take -flight, – wing; spring, fly, flit, wing one's flight; fly –, whip- away; take off, hop off; embark; go -on board, – aboard; set sail; put –, go- to sea; sail, take ship; hoist blue Peter; get under way, weigh anchor; strike tents, break camp, decamp; walk one's chalks, make tracks, cut one's stick; cut and run; take leave; say –, bid- -good-bye etc. *n.*; disappear etc. 449; abscond etc. (*avoid*) 623; entrain, embus, emplane; saddle –, harness –, hitch- up; inspan.

Adj. departing etc. *v.*; valedictory; outward bound.

Adv. whence, hence, thence; with a foot in the stirrup; on the -wing, – move.

Int. begone! etc. (*ejection*) 297; to horse! all aboard! farewell! adieu! good-bye, – day! *au revoir! auf wiedersehen!* fare you well! so long! God -bless you, – speed! *bon vayage!*

294. Ingress. [Motion into.]—**N.** ingress; entrance, entry; introgression; influx; intrusion, inroad, incursion, invasion, irruption; pene-, interpene- tration; illapse, import, importation, infiltration; immigration; admission etc. (*reception*) 296; insinuation etc. (*interjacence*) 228; insertion etc. 300.

inlet; way in; mouth, door etc. (*opening*) 260; path etc. (*way*) 627; conduit etc. 350; immigrant, visitor, incomer, newcomer, colonist.

V. have the *entrée*; enter; go –, come –, pour –, flow –, creep –, slip –, pop –, break –, burst- -into, – in; set foot on; burst –, break-in upon; invade, intrude, butt in, horn in, crash; insinuate itself; inter-, penetrate; infiltrate; find one's way –, wriggle –, worm oneself- into.

give entrance to etc. (*receive*) 296; insert etc. 300.

Adj. incoming, ingressive etc. *n.*; inward bound.

Adv. inward.

295. Egress. [Motion out of.]—**N.** egress, exit, issue; emer-sion, -gence; disemboguement; outbreak, -burst; e-, pro-ruption; emanation; evacuation; ex, trans-udation; extravasation, perspiration, sweating, leakage, percolation, distillation, oozing; gush etc. (*water in motion*) 348; outpour, -ing; effluence, effusion; efflux, -ion; drain; dribbling etc. *v.*; defluxion; drainage; outcome, -put; discharge etc. (*excretion*) 299.

export; expatriation; e-, re-migration; *débouche*; exodus etc. (*departure*) 293; emigrant, migrant, *émigré*, colonist.

outlet, vent, spout, tap, sluice, floodgate; pore; vomitory, out-gate, sally-port; way out; mouth, door etc. (*opening*) 260; path etc. (*way*) 627; conduit etc. 350; air-pipe etc. 351.

V. emerge, emanate, issue; go –, come –, move –, pass –, pour –, flow- out of; pass off, evacuate; migrate.

ex-, trans-ude; leak; run, – out, – through; per-, trans-colate; seep; strain, distil; perspire, sweat, drain, ooze; filter, filtrate; dribble, gush, spout, flow out; well, – out; pour, trickle etc. (*water in motion*) 348; effuse, extravasate, disembogue, discharge itself, debouch; come –, break- forth; burst- out, – through; find vent, escape etc. 671.

Adj. effused etc. *v.*; outgoing, outward bound.

Adv. outward.

296. Reception. [Motion into, actively.]—**N.** reception; admission, admittance, *entrée*, importation; initiation; intro-duction, -mission, -ception; immission, ingestion, imbibition, absorption, ingurgitation, inhalation; suction, sucking; eating, drinking etc. (*food*) 298; insertion etc. 300; interjection etc. 228.

V. give -entrance to, – admittance to, – the *entrée*; intro-duce, -mit; usher, admit, receive, import, initiate, bring in, open the door to, throw open, ingest, absorb, imbibe, inhale, infiltrate; let –, take –, suck- in; re-admit, -sorb, -absorb; snuff up; swallow, ingurgitate; enfulf, engorge; gulp; eat, drink etc. (*food*) 298.

Adj. admit-ting etc. *v.*, -ted etc. *v.*; admissible; absorbent; introductory, introceptive, intromittent, initiatory.

297. Ejection. [Motion out of, actively.]—**N.** ejection, emission, effusion, rejection, expulsion, eviction, extrusion, trajection; discharge.

egestion, evacuation, vomition, disgorgement, voidance, eruption, eruptiveness; ruc-, eruc-tation, blood-letting, venesection, phlebotomy, paracentesis; tapping, drainage; clear-ance, -age, voidance; vomiting, excretion etc. 299.

deportation; banishment etc. (*punishment*) 972; rogue's march; relegation, extradition; dislodgment.

V. give -exit, – vent- to; let –, give –, pour –, send- out; des-, dis-patch; exhale, excern, excrete, disembogue, secrete, secern; extravasate, shed, void, evacuate, egest, emit; open the -sluices, – floodgates; turn on the tap; extrude, detrude; effuse, spend, expend; pour forth; squirt, spirt, spill, slop; perspire etc. (*exude*) 295; breathe, blow etc. (*wind*) 349.

tap, draw off; bale –, lade- out; let blood, broach.

eject, reject; expel, discard; cut, send to Coventry, boycott, ostracize; *chasser*; banish etc. (*punish*) 972; throw etc. 284 -out, – up, – off, – away, – aside; push etc. 276 -out, – off, – away, – aside; shovel –, sweep- -out, – away; brush –, whisk –, turn –, send- -off, – away; discharge; send –, turn –, cast- adrift; turn –, bundle- out; throw overboard; give the sack to; send -packing, – about one's business, – to the right about; strike off the roll etc. (*abrogate*) 756; turn out- neck and heels, – head and shoulders, – neck and crop; pack off; send away with a flea in the ear; send to Jericho; bow out, show the door to, dismiss, fire, sack.

turn out of -doors, – house and home; evict, oust; exorcise, un-house, -kennel; dislodge; un-, dis-people; depopulate; relegate, deport.

empty; drain, – to the dregs; sweep off; clear, – off, – out, – away; such, draw off, extract; clean out, make a clean sweep of, clear decks, purge.

em-, dis-, disem-bowel; eviscerate, gut; unearth, root -out, – up; averruncate; weed –, get out; eliminate, get rid of, do away with, shake off; exenterate.

vomit, spew, puke, keck, retch; belch, – out, eruct, eructate; cast –, bring- up; disgorge; expectorate, salivate, clear the throat, hawk, spit, sputter, splutter, slobber, drool, drivel, slaver, slabber.

unpack, unlade, unload, unship; break bulk.

be let out; ooze etc. (*emerge*) 295.

Adj. emitt-ing, -ed etc. *v.*

begone! get you gone! get –, go- away, – along, – along with you! go your way! away, – with! off with you! go, – about your business! be off! avaunt! aroynt! get out!

298. Food. [Eating.]—**N.** eating etc. *v.*; deglutition, gulp, epulation, mastication, manducation, rumination, gastronomy, gastrology; panto-, hippo-, ichthyo-phagy etc.; gluttony etc. 957; carnivorousness, vegetarianism.

mouth, jaws, mandible, mazard, chops.

drinking etc. *v.*; potation, draught, libation; carousal etc. (*amusement*) 840; drunkenness etc. 959.

food, ***pabulum***; aliment, nourishment, nutriment; susten-ance, -tation; nurture, subsistence, provender, feed, fodder, provision, ration, keep, commons, board; commissariat etc. (*provision*) 637; prey, forage, pasture, pasturage; fare, cheer; diet, -ary; regimen; belly timber, staff of life; bread, -and cheese; proteins, carbohydrates, vitamines.

comestibles, eatables, victuals, edibles, *ingesta*; grub, prog, tack, hard tack, meat; bread, -stuffs; cereals; viands, cates, delicacy, dainty, creature comforts, contents of the larder, flesh-pots; festal board; ambrosia; good -cheer, – living.

hors-d'oeuvre; soup, pottage, *potage*, broth,

bouillon, *consommé*, *purée*, *borsch*, stock, skilly, gumbo; fish, – cakes, – pie; joint, *rôti*, *pièce de résistance*, *relevé*, hash, *réchauffé*, stew, *ragoût*, fricassee, mince, *salim*, *goulash*, *bouillabaisse*, *remove*, *entrée*, *croquette*, *rissole*, sausage, curry, bubble and squeak; haggis, collops, giblets; poultry, game etc.; biscuit, bun, scone, rusk, pancake, pie, pastry, pasty, patty, *patisseria*, tart, turnover, *vol-au-vent*, *soufflé*, dumpling, pudding, duff, *compote*, fritters, cake, napoleon, *blancmange*, custard, jelly, jam, sweets etc. 396; *entremet*; oatmeal, porridge, hasty pudding, gruel; eggs, omelet, cheese, matzoon, savory; vegetable, salad, *mayonnaise*, fruit; sauce, condiment etc. 393; kickshaws.

table, *cuisine*, bill of fare, *menu*, *table d'hôte*, ordinary, *à la carte*; cover.

meal, repast, feed, spread; mess; dish, plate, course, side dish; regale; regale-, refresh-, entertain-ment; refection, collation, picnic, feast, banquet, junket; breakfast; lunch, -eon, *déjeuner*, bever, tiffin, tea, dinner, supper, snack, whet, bait, dessert; pot-luck, *table d'hôte, déjeuner à la fourchette*; hearty –, square –, substantial –, full- -meal; blow out; light refreshment; pemmican.

mouthful, bolus, gobbet, tit-bit, morsel, sop, sippet.

drink, beverage, liquor, broth, soup; potion, dram, draft, drench, swill; nip, peg, sip, sup, gulp.

wine, champagne, spirits, *liqueur* beer, porter, stout, ale, malt liquor, julep, Sir John Barleycorn, stingo, heavy wet, bitter, lager- beer, cider; grog, toddy, flip, purl, punch, negus, cup, bishop, posset, wassail; bitters, *apéritif*, high-ball, cocktail; whisky, rum, absinthe; gin etc. (*intoxicating liquor*) 959; coffee, chocolate, cocoa, tea, *maté*, the cup that cheers but not inebriates.

eating-house etc. 189.

V. eat, feed, fare, devour, swallow, take; gulp, bolt, snap; fall to; despatch, dispatch; discuss; take –, get –, gulp-down; lay –, tuck- in; lick, pick, peck; gormandize etc. 957; bite, champ, munch, cranch, craunch, crunch, chew, masticate, nibble, gnaw, mumble.

live on; feed –, batten –, fatten –, feast- upon; browse, graze, crop, regale; carouse etc. (*make merry*) 840; eat heartily, do justice to, play a good knife and fork, banquet.

break -bread, – one's fast; breakfast; lunch, dine, take tea, sup.

drink, – in, – up, – one's fill; quaff, sip, sup; suck, – up; lap; swig; swill, tipple etc. (*be drunken*) 959; empty one's glass, drain the cup; toss -off, – one's glass; wash down, crack a bottle, wet one's whistle.

cater, purvey etc. 637.

Adj. eatable, edible, esculent, comestible, alimentary; cereal, cibarious; dietetic; culinary; nutri-tive, -tious; succulent; drinkable, pot-able, -ulent; bibulous.

omn-, carn-, herb-, frug-, gran-, gramin-, phytivorous; ichthyophagous.

prandial.

299. Excretion.—N. excretion, discharge, emanation; ejection etc. 297; exhalation, exudation, extrusion, secretion, effusion, extravasation, *ecchymosis*, evacuation, cacation, defecation, dysentery, dejection, *feces*, excrement; perspiration, sweat; sub-, exud-ation; *diaphoresis*; sewage.

saliva, spittle, rheum; ptyalism, salivation, catarrh, distemper; diarrhea; *ejecta*, *egesta*, *sputum*, *sputa*; *excreta*; lava; *exuviae* etc. (*uncleanness*) 653.

hemorrhage, bleeding; catamenia, menses; outpouring etc. (*egress*) 295; leucorrhea.

V. excrete etc. (*eject*) 297; emanate etc. (*come out*) 295.

Adj. excretory, fecal, secretory; ejective, eliminant.

300. Insertion. [Forcible ingress.]—**N.** insertion, implantation, intercalation, embolism, introduction; interpolation, insinuation etc. (*intervention*) 228; planting etc. *v.*; injection, inoculation, importation, infusion; forcible -ingress etc. 294; immersion; submersion, -gence; dip, plunge; bath etc. (*water*) 337; interment etc. 363.

V. insert; intro-duce, -mit; put –, run- into; import; inject; interject etc. 228; infuse, instil, inoculate, impregnate, imbue, imbrue.

graft, ingraft, bud, plant, implant; dovetail.

obtrude; thrust –, stick –, ram –, stuff –, tuck –, press –, drive –, pop –, whip –, drop –, put- in; impact; empierce etc. (*make a hole*) 260.

embed; immerse, immerge, merge; bathe, soak etc. (*water*) 337; dip, plunge etc. 310.

bury etc. (*inter*) 363.

insert etc. -itself; plunge *in medias res*.

Adj. inserted etc. *v.*

301. Extraction. [Forcible egress.]—**N.** extraction; extracting etc. *v.*; removal, elimination, extrication, eradication, evolution.

evulsion, avulsion; wrench; expression, squeezing; extirpation, extermination; ejection etc. 297; export etc. (*egress*) 295; distillation.

extractor, corkscrew, forceps, pliers.

V. extract, draw, pit; take –, draw –, pull –, tear –, pluck –, pick –, get- out; wring from, wrench; extort; root –, weed –, grub –, rake-up, – out; eradicate; pull –, pluck- up by the roots; averruncate; unroot; uproot, pull up, extirpate, dredge.

remove; educe, elicit; evolve, extricate; eliminate etc. (*eject*) 297; eviscerate etc. 297.

express, squeeze –, press- out; distil.

Adj. extracted etc. *v.*

302. Passage. [Motion through.]—**N.** passage, transmission; permeation; pene-, interpene-tration; transudation, infiltration; *osmosis*, osmose, endos-, exos-mose; intercurrence; ingress etc. 294; egress etc. 295; path etc. 627; conduit etc. 350; opening etc. 260; journey etc. 266; voyage etc. 267.

V. pass, – through; perforate etc. (*hole*) 260; penetrate, permeate, thread, thrid, enfilade; go -through, – across; go –, pass- over; cut across; ford, cross; pass and repass, work; make –, thread –, worm –, force- one's way; make –, force- a passage; cut one's way through; find its -way, –

vent; transmit, make way, clear the course; traverse, go over the ground.

Adj. passing etc. *v.*; intercurrent; osmotic etc. *n.*

Adv. *en passant* etc. (*transit*) 270.

303. Overstep. [Motion beyond.]—**N.** transcursion, -ilience, -gression; infraction, intrusion; trespass; encroach-, infringe-ment; extravagation, transcendence; redundance etc. 641; ingress etc. 294.

V. transgress, surpass, pass; go- beyond, – by; show in –, come to the- front; shoot ahead of; steal a march –, gain- upon.

over-step, -pass, -reach, -go, -ride- -leap, -jump, -skip, -lap, -shoot the mark; out-strip, -leap, -jump, -go, -step, -run, -ride, -rival, -do; beat, – hollow; distance; leave in the -lurch, – rear; go one better, throw into the shade; exceed, transcend, surmount; soar etc. (*rise*) 305.

encroach, intrude, trespass, infringe, invade, trench upon, intrench on; strain; stretch –, strain- a point; pass the Rubicon.

Adj. surpassing etc. *v.*

Adv. beyond the mark, ahead.

304. Shortcoming. [Motion short of.]—**N.** shortcoming, failure; delinquency; falling short etc. *v.*; de-fault, -falcation; leeway; labor in vain, no go.

incompleteness etc. 53; imperfection etc. 651; insufficiency etc. 640; noncompletion etc. 730; failure etc. 732.

V. come –, fall –, stop- -short, – short of; not reach; want; keep within -bounds, – the mark, – compass.

break down, stick in the mud, collapse, come to nothing; fall -through, – to the ground, – down; cave in, end in smoke, fizzle out, miss the mark, fail; lose ground; miss stays, slump.

Adj. unreached; deficient; short, – of; *minus*; out of depth; perfunctory etc. (*neglect*) 460.

Adv. within -the mark, – compass, – bounds; behindhand; *re infectâ*; to no purpose; far from it.

Phr. the bubble burst.

305. Ascent. [Motion upwards.]—**N.** ascent, ascension; rising etc. *v.*; rise, upgrowth; leap etc. 309; acclivity, hill etc. 217; stair, stairs, stair-case, -way, flight of -steps, – stairs; ladder, companion, – way; lift, elevator etc. 307.

rocket, lark; sky-rocket, -lark; Alpine Club.

V. ascend, rise, mount, arise, uprise; go –, get –, work one's way –, start –, spring –, shoot- up; zoom; aspire.

climb, clamber, ramp, scramble, swarm, *escalade*, surmount; scale, – the heights.

tower, soar, hover, spire, plane, swim, float, surge; leap etc. 309.

Adj. rising etc. *v.*; scandent, buoyant; supernatant, -fluitant; excelsior.

Adv. uphill.

306. Descent. [Motion downwards.]—**N.** descent, descension, declension, declination; fall; falling etc. *v.*; drop, cadence; subsidence, lapse; come-down, downfall, tumble, slip, tilt, trip, lurch; cropper, *culbute*; titubation, stumble; fate of Icarus; dive, nose-dive, *volpané*.

avalanche, *débâcle*, landslip, slide.

V. descend; go –, drop –, come-down; fall, gravitate, drop, slip, slide, glissade, dive, plunge, settle; decline, slump, set, sink, droop, come down a peg.

dismount, alight, light, get down; swoop; stoop etc. 308; fall prostrate, precipitate oneself; let fall etc. 308.

tumble, trip, stumble, titubate, lurch, pitch, swag, topple; topple –, tumble- -down, – over; tilt, sprawl, plump down, come a cropper.

Adj. descending etc. *v.*; descendent, declivitous; downcast; decur-rent, sive; labent, deciduous; nodding to its fall.

Adv. down, -hill, -wards.

307. Elevation.—**N.** elevation; raising etc. *v.*; erection, lift; sublevation, upheaval; sublimation, exaltation; prominence etc. (*convexity*) 250.

lever etc. 633; crane, derrick, windlass, capstan, winch, dredger, lift, elevator, escalator, dumb waiter.

V. heighten, elevate, raise, lift, erect; set –, stick –, perch –, perk –, tilt- up; rear, hoist, heave; up-lift, -raise, -rear, -bear, -cast, -hoist, -heave; buoy, weigh, mount, give a lift; exalt, sublimate; place –, set- on a pedestal.

take –, drag –, fish- up; dredge.

stand –, rise –, get –, jump- up; spring to one's feet; hold -oneself, – one's head- up; draw oneself up to his full height.

Adj. elevated etc. *v.*; standing up; stilted, attollent, rampant.

Adv. on -stilts, – the shoulders of, – one's legs, – one's hind legs.

308. Depression.—**N.** lowering etc. *v.*; depression; dip etc. (*concavity*) 252; abasement; detrusion; reduction.

over-throw, -set, -turn; upset; prostration, subversion, precipitation.

bow; courtesy, curtsy; genuflexion, *kowtow*, obeisance, *salaam*.

V. depress, lower; let –, take- -down, – down a peg; cast; let -drop, – fall; sink, debase, bring low, abase, slash, reduce, detrude, pitch, precipitate.

over-throw, -turn, -set; upset, subvert, prostrate, level, fell; cast –, take –, throw –, fling –, dash –, pull –, cut –, knock –, hew- down; raze, – to the ground; humiliate, trample in the dust, pull about one's ears.

sit, – down; couch, squat, crouch, stoop, bend, bow, courtsey, curtsy; bob, duck, dip, genuflect, kneel; *kowtow*, *salaam*, make obeisance, prostrate oneself; bend, bow- the -head, – knee; incline the head; bow down; cower; recline etc. (*be horizontal*) 213.

Adj. depressed etc. *v.*; at a low ebb; prostrate etc. (*horizontal*) 213; detrusive.

309. Leap.—**N.** leap, jump, hop, spring, bound, vault, saltation.

dance, caper, gambol; curvet, caracole; *gambade*, *-bado*; capriole, demivolt; buck, – jump; hop, skip and jump.

kangaroo, jerboa, chamois, goat, frog, grasshopper, flea.

V. leap; jump -up, – over the moon; hop, spring, bound, vault, ramp, cut capers, gambol, trip, skip, dance, caper, curvet, *caracole*; foot it, bob, bounce, flounce, start, frisk etc. (*amusement*) 840; jump about etc. (*agitation*) 315; trip it on the light fantastic toe, dance oneself off one's legs.

Adj. leaping etc. *v.*; saltatory, frisky.

Adv. on the light fantastic toe.

310. Plunge.—N. plunge, dip, dive, header; ducking etc. *v.*; submergence, immersion, diver.

V. plunge, dip, souse, duck; dive, plump; take a -plunge, – header, make a plunge; bathe etc. (*water*) 337.

sub-merge, -merse; immerse, douse, sink, engulf, send to -the bottom, – Davy Jones' locker.

get out of one's depth; go -to the bottom, – down like a stone; founder, welter, wallow.

311. Circuition. [Curvilinear motion.]—**N.** circuition, circulation; turn, curvet; excursion; circum-vention, -navigation, -ambulation; north-west passage; ambit, gyre, lap, circuit etc. 629.

turning etc. *v.*; wrench; evolution; coil, helix, spiral; corkscrew.

V. turn, bend, wheel; go –, put- about; heel; go –, turn -round, – to the right about; turn on one's heel; make –, describe- a -circle, – complete circle; encircle; go –, pass- through -180°, – 360°.

circum-navigate, -aviate, -ambulate, -vent; put a girdle round the earth, go the round, make the round of.

turn –, round- a corner; double a point.

wind, circulate, meander; whisk, twirl; twist etc. (*convolution*) 248; make a *détour* etc. (*circuit*) 629.

Adj. turning etc. *v.*; circuitous; circumforaneous, -fluent; devious, roundabout, circumambient, -flex, -navigable.

Adv. round about.

312. Rotation. [Motion in a continued circle.]—**N.** rotation, revolution, gyration, circulation, roll; circum-rotation, -volution, -gyration; volutation, circination, turbination, *pirouette*, convolution.

verticity; whir, whirl, swirl, eddy, vortex, whirlpool, gurge; cyclone, tornado; surge; *vertigo*, dizzy round; Maelstrom, Charybdis; Ixion; wheel of Fortune.

wheel, screw, propeller, whirligig, rolling stone, windmill; top, teetotum, merry-go-round; roller; cog-, fly-wheel, spit; jack; caster.

axis, axle, spindle, spool, pivot, pin, hinge, pole, swivel, gimbals, arbor, bobbin, mandrel, shaft.

[Science of rotatory motion] trochilics, gyrostatics.

V. rotate; roll, – along; revolve, spin; turn, – round; circumvolve; circulate; gyre, gyrate, wheel, whirl, swirl, twirl, trundle, troll, bowl; slew round.

roll up, furl; wallow, welter; box the compass; spin like a -top, – teetotum.

Adj. rotating etc. *v.*; rota-tory, -ry; circumrotatory, trochilic, vertiginous, gyratory; vortic-al, -ose.

Adv. head over heels, round and round, like a horse in a mill.

313. Evolution. [Motion in a reverse circle.]—**N.** evolution, unfolding, development; eversion etc. (*inversion*) 218.

V. evolve; un-fold, -roll, -wind, -coil, -twist, -furl, -twine, -ravel; disentangle; develop.

Adj. evolving etc. *v.*; evolved etc. *v.*

314. Oscillation. [Reciprocating motion, motion to and fro.]—**N.** oscillation; vibration, libration; motion of a pendulum; nutation; undulation; pulsation; pulse; throb; seismic disturbance.

alternation; coming and going etc. *v.*; ebb and flow, flux and reflux, ups and downs; wave, vibratiuncle, swing, beat, shake, wag, see-saw, dance, lurch, dodge; fluctuation; vacillation etc. (*irresolution*) 605.

seismometer, vibroscope, seismograph.

V. oscillate; vi-, li-brate; alternate, undulate, wave; sway, rock, swing; pulsate, beat; wag, -gle; nod, bob, courtesy, curtsy; tick; play; chatter, wamble, wabble; teeter, dangle, swag.

fluctuate, dance, curvet, reel, quake; quiver, quaver, shake, flicker; wriggle; roll, toss, pitch; flounder, stagger, totter, waddle; move –, bob- up and down etc. *adv.*; pass and repass, ebb and flow, come and go, shuttle; vacillate etc. 605.

brandish, shake, flourish.

Adj. oscillating etc. *v.*; oscill-, undul-, puls-, libr-atory; vibrat-ory, -ile; pendulous, shutterwise, seismic.

Adv. to and fro, up and down, backwards and forwards, see-saw, zigzag, wibble-wabble, in and out, from side to side, like buckets in a well.

315. Agitation. [Irregular motion.]—**N.** agitation, stir, tremor, shake, ripple, jog, jolt, jerk, shock, succession, trepidation, quiver, quaver, dance; jactit-ation, -ance; shuffling etc. *v.*; twitter, flicker, flutter.

disquiet, perturbation, commotion, turmoil, turbulence; tumult, -uation; hubbub, rout, bustle, fuss, racket, *subsultus*, staggers, megrims, epilepsy, fits, twitching, vellication, St. Vitus' dance.

spasm, throe, throb, palpitation, convulsion, paroxysm; tetanus.

disturbance etc. (*disorder*) 59; restlessness etc. (*changeableness*) 149.

ferment, -ation; ebullition, effervescence, hurly burly, *cahotage*; tempest, storm, ground swell, heavy sea, whirlpool, vortex etc. 312; whirlwhind etc. (*wind*) 349.

V. be -agitated etc.; shake; tremble, – like an aspen leaf; quiver, quaver, quake, shiver, twitter, twire, dither, dodder; twitch, writhe, toss, shuffle, tumble, stagger, bob, reel, sway; wag , -gle, wiggle; wriggle, – like an eel; squirm; dance, stumble, shamble, flounder, totter, flounce, flop, curvet, prance.

throb, pulsate, beat, palpitate, go pit-a-pat; flutter, flitter, flicker, bicker; bustle.

ferment, effervesce, foam; boil, – over; bubble, – up; simmer.

toss –, jump- about; jump like a parched pea; shake like an aspen leaf; shake to its -center, – foundations; be the sport of the winds and waves; reel to and fro like a drunken man; move –, drive- from post to pillar and from pillar to post; keep between hawk and buzzard.

agitate, shake, convulse, toss, tumble, bandy, wield, brandish, flap, flourish, whisk, jerk, hitch, jolt; jog, -gle; hostle, buffet, hustle, disturb, stir, shake up, churn, jounce, wallop, whip, vellicate.

Adj. shaking etc. *v.*; agitated, tremulous; de-, sub-sultory; shambling; giddy-paced, saltatory, convulsive, jerky, unquiet, restless, all of a twitter.

Adv. by fits and starts; subsultorily etc. *adj.*: *per saltum*; hop, skip and jump; in -convulsions, – fits, pit-a-pat.

316. Materiality.—N. material-ity, -ness; materialization; corpor-eity, -ality; substantiality, material existence, incarnation, flesh and blood, *plenum*; physical condition.

matter, body, substance, brute matter, stuff, element, principle, protoplasm, plasma, *parenchyma*, material, *substratum*, hyle, *corpus*, *pabulum*; frame.

object, article, thing, something; still life; stocks and stones; materials etc. 635.

[Science of matter] physics; somatology, -ics; natural –, experimental- philosophy; physical science, *philosophie positive*, materialism, hylism; applied –, micro-, molecular –, nuclear – physics.

atomics, atomic science, nucleonics, quantum mechanics, radiology.

atom, radical, tracer, isotope, pleiad; atomic – nucleus, – cluster; nuclear particle, neutron, protron, shell, valence electron.

materialist, physicist, atomic scientist, radiologist.

V. materialize, incorporate, incarnate, substantiate, embody.

atomize, split –, smash – the atom; radioactivate.

Adj. material, bodily; corpor-eal, -al; physical; somat-ic, -oscopic; sensible, tangible, ponderable, palpable, substantial; fleshly, incarnate.

physical, bio-, electro-, geo-physical; atomic, nuclear, thermonuclear, radio-active.

objective, impersonal, neuter, unspiritual, materialistic.

317. Immateriality.—N. immaterial-ity, -ness; incorporeity, dematerialization, unsubstantiality, spirituality; inextension; astral plane.

personality; I, myself, me; *ego*, spirit etc. (*soul*) 450; astral body; immaterialism; spiritual-ism, -ist; subliminal –, subconscious- self.

V. disembody, spiritualize, dematerialize.

Adj. immateri-al, -ate; incorpor-eal, -al; asomatous, unextended; un-, dis-embodied; extramundane, supersensible, unearthly; pneumatoscopic; spiritual etc. (*psychical*) 450; aery.

personal, subjective.

318. World.—N. world, creation, nature, universe; earth, globe, wide world; *cosmos*; terraqueous globe, sphere; macro-, mega-cosm; music of the spheres; strato-, tropo-sphere.

heavens, sky, welkin, empyrean; starry -heaven, – host; firmament; vault –, canopy- of heaven; celestial spaces.

heavenly bodies, stars, luminaries, nebulae; galaxy, milky way, galactic circle, *via lactea.*

sun, orb of day, Apollo, Phoebus; photo-, chromo-sphere; solar system; planet, -oid, asteroid; comet; satellite; moon, orb of night, Diana, Luna; aerolite, meteor; falling –, shooting-star; meteorite.

constellation, zodiac, signs of the zodiac, Charles's wain, Great Bear, Southern Cross, Orion's belt, Cassiopeia's chair, Pleiades etc.

colures, equator, ecliptic, orbit.

[Science of heavenly bodies] astronomy; uranography, -logy; cosmo-logy, -graphy, -gony; *eidouranion*, orrery; geography; geodesy etc. (*measurement*) 466; star-gazing, -gazer; astronomer; cosmogonist, geodesist, geographer; observatory.

Adj. cosmic, cosmical, mundane; terr-estrial, -estrious, -aqueous, -ene, -eous; telluric, earthly, geotic, geodetic, cosmogonal, under the sun; sublunary, -astral.

solar, heliacal; lunar; celestial, heavenly, empyreal, sphery; starry, stellar; sider-eal, -al; astral; nebular.

Adv. in all creation, on the face of the globe, here below, under the sun.

319. Gravity.—N. gravi-ty, -tation; weight; heaviness etc. *adj.*; specific gravity; ponderosity, pressure, load; bur-den, -then; ballast, counterpoise; lump –, mass –, weight- of.

lead, millstone, mountain, Ossa on Pelion.

weighing, ponderation, trutination; weights; avoirdupois –, troy –, apothecaries'- weight; grain, scruple, drachm, ounce, pound, lb., load, stone, hundredweight, cwt., ton, quintal, carat, pennyweight, tod, gram, kilogram etc.

[Weighing instrument] balance, scales, steelyard, beam, weighbridge, spring balance, weighing machine.

[Science of gravity] statics.

V. be -heavy etc. *adj.*; gravitate, weigh, press, cumber, load.

[Measure the weight of] weigh, poise.

Adj. weighty; weighing etc. *v.*; heavy, – as lead; ponder-ous, -able; lump-ish, -y; cumber-, burden-some; cumbrous, unwieldy, massive.

in-, superin-cumbent.

320. Levity.—N. levity; lightness etc. *adj.*; imponderability, imponderables, buoyancy, volatility.

feather, dust, mote, down, thistledown, flue, cobweb, gossamer, straw, cork, bubble; float, bouy; ether, air.

leaven, ferment, barm, yeast, enzyme.

V. be -light etc. *adj.*; float, swim, be buoyed up. render -light etc. *adj.*; lighten, levitate; leaven.

Adj. light, subtile, subtle, airy; imponder-ous, -able; astatic, weightless, ethereal, sublimated; uncompressed, volatile; buoyant, floating etc. *v.*; barmy, frothy; portable.

light as -a feather, – thistle down, – air.

fermenting etc. *n.*

321. Density.—N. density, solidity; solidness etc. *adj.*; impenetra-, impermea-bility; incompressibility; imporosity; cohesion etc. 46; constipation, consistence, spissitude.

specific gravity; hydro-, areo-meter.

condensation; solid-ation, -ification; consolidation; concretion, caseation, coagulation; petrifaction etc. (*hardening*) 323; crystallization, precipitation; deposit, precipitate, silt; inspissation; thickening etc. *v.*

indivisibility, indiscerptibility, indissolvableness.

solid body, mass, block, knot, lump; con-cretion, -crete, -glomerate; cake, clot, stone, curd, coagulum, grume; bone, gristle, cartilage.

V. be -dense etc. *adj.*; become –, render- solid etc. *adj.*; solid-ify, -ate; concrete, set, take a set, consolidate, congeal, coagulate; curd, -le; fix, clot, cake, candy, precipitate, deposit, cohere, crystallize; petrify etc. (*harden*) 323.

condense, thicken, inspissate, incrassate; compress, squeeze, ram down, constipate.

Adj. dense, solid, solidified etc. *v.*; cohe-rent, -sive etc. 46; compact, close, serried, thickset; substantial, massive, lumpish; impenetrable, impermeable, imporous; incompressible; constipated; concrete etc. (*hard*) 323; knot-ted, -ty; gnarled; crystal-line, -lizable; thick, grumous, stuffy.

un-dissolved, -melted, -liquified, -thawed.

in-divisible, -discerptible, -frangible, -dissolvable, -dissoluble, -soluble, -fusible.

322. Rarity.—N. rarity; tenuity; absence of -solidity etc. 321; subtility; sponginess, compressibility.

rarefaction, expansion, dilatation, inflation, subtilization.

ether etc. (*gas*) 334.

V. rarefy, expand, dilate, subtilize, attenuate, thin.

Adj. rare, subtile, thin, fine, tenuous, compressible, flimsy, slight; light etc. 320; cavernous, spongy etc. (*hollow*) 252.

rarefied etc. *v.*; unsubstantial; uncom-pact, -pressed.

323. Hardness.—N. hardness etc. *adj.*; rigidity, renitence, inflexibility, temper, callosity, durity.

induration, petrifaction; lapid-ification, -escence; vitri-, ossi-, corni-fication; crystallization.

stone, pebble, flint, marble, rock, fossil, crag, crystal, quartz, granite, adamant; bone, cartilage; heart of oak, block, board, deal board; iron, steel; cast –, wrought- iron; nail; brick, concrete; cement.

V. render -hard etc. *adj.*; harden, stiffen, indurate, petrify, temper, ossify, vitrify.

Adj. hard, rigid, stubborn, stiff, firm; starch, -ed; stark, unbending, unlimber, unyielding; inflexible, tense; indurate, -d; gritty, proof.

adamant-ine, -ean; concrete, stony, rocky, lithic, granitic, vitreous; crystalline; horny, corneous; bony; oss-eous, -ific; cartilaginous; hard as a -stone etc. *n.*; stiff as -buckram, – a poker.

324. Softness.—N. softness, pliableness etc. *adj.*; flexibility; pli-ancy, -ability; sequacity, malleability; flabbiness; duct-, tract-ility; extend-, extensibility; plasticity; inelasticity; flaccidity, laxity.

clay, wax, butter, dough, pudding; cushion, pillow, feather-bed, pad, down, padding, wadding.

mollification; softening etc. *v.*

V. render -soft etc. *adj.*; soften, mollify, mellow, relax, temper; mash, knead, squash, *massage*.

bend, yield, relent, relax, give.

Adj. soft, tender, supple; pli-ant, -able; flexible, -ile; lithe, -some; lissom, limber, plastic; ductile; tract-ile, -able; malleable, extensile, sequacious, inelastic, mollient.

yielding etc. *v.*; flabby, limp, flimsy.

flaccid, flocculent, downy; spongy, edematous, medullary, doughy, argillaceous, mellow.

soft as -butter, – down, – silk; yielding as wax; tender as a chicken.

325. Elasticity.—N. elasticity, springiness, spring, resilience, renitency, buoyancy.

india-rubber, caoutchouc, gutta-percha, whalebone, gum elastic.

V. be -elastic etc. *adj.*; spring back etc. (*recoil*) 227.

Adj. elastic, tensile, springy, ductile, resilient, renitent, buoyant.

326. Inelasticity.—N. want of –, absence of-elasticity etc. 325; inelasticity etc. (*softness*) 324.

Adj. inelastic etc. (*soft*) 324.

327. Tenacity.—N. tenacity, toughness, strength; cohesion etc. 46; sequacity; stubbornness etc. (*obstinacy*) 606; viscidity etc. 352.

leather; gristle, cartilage.

V. be -tenacious etc. *adj.*; resist fracture.

Adj. tenacious, tough, cohesive, adhesive, strong, resisting, sequacious, stringy, gristly, cartilaginous, leathery, coriaceous, tough as whit-leather; stubborn etc. (*obstinate*) 606.

328. Brittleness.—N. brittleness etc. *adj.*; frag-, friab-, frangib-, fiss-ility; frailty; house of -cards, – glass.

V. be -brittle etc. *adj.*; live in a glass house.

break, crack, snap, split, shiver, splinter, crumble, break short, burst, fly, give way; fall to pieces; crumble -to, – into- dust.

Adj. breakable, brittle, frangible, fragile, frail, friable, delicate, gimcrack, shivery, fissile; splitting etc. *v.*; lacerable, splintery, crisp, crimp, short, brittle as glass.

329. Texture. [Structure.]—**N.** structure, organization, anatomy, frame, mold, fabric, construction; frame-work, carcass, architecture; stratification, cleavage.

substance, stuff, *compages*, *parenchyma*; constitution, staple, organism.

[Science of structures] organ-, oste-, my- splanchn-, neur-, angi-, aden-ology; angi-, aden-ography.

texture; inter-, con-texture; tissue, grain, web, surface; warp and -woof, – weft; tooth, nap etc. (*roughness*) 256; fineness –, coarseness- of grain.

[Science of textures] histology.

Adj. structural, organic; anatomic, -al.

text-ural, -ile; fine-, coarse-grained; fine, delicate, subtile, gossamery, filmy; coarse; homespun; linsey-woolsey.

330. Pulverulence. [State of powder.]—**N.** pulverulence; sandiness etc. *adj.*; efflorescence; friability.

powder, dust, sand, shingle; sawdust; grit; attrition; meal, bran, flour, *farina*, spore, sporule; crumb, seed, grain; particle etc. (*smallness*) 32; thermion; limature, filings, *débris*, *detritus*, scobs, magistery, fine powder; *flocculi*.

smoke; cloud of -dust, – sand, – smoke; puff –, volume -of smoke; sand –, dust- storm.

[Reduction to powder] pulverization, comminution, attenuation, granulation, disintegration, subaction, contusion, trituration, levigation, abrasion, detrition, multure; limation; filing etc. *v.*

[Instruments for pulverization] mill, millstone, grater, rasp, file, pestle and mortar, nutmeg grater, teeth, molar, grinder, chopper, grindstone, kern, quern, muller.

V. come to dust; be -disintegrated, – reduced to powder etc.

reduce –, grind- to powder; pulverize, comminute, granulate, triturate, levigate; scrape, file, abrade, rub down, grind, grate, rasp, pound, bray, bruise; con-tuse, -tund; beat, crush, cranch, craunch, crunch, muller, scranch, crumble, disintegrate; attenuate etc. 195.

Adj. powdery, pulverulent, granular, mealy, floury, farinaceous, branny, furfuraceous, flocculent, dusty, sandy, sabulous; aren-ose, -arious, -aceous; gritty; efflorescent, impalpable.

pulverizable; friable, crumbly, shivery; pulverized etc. *v.*; attrite; in pieces.

331. Friction.—**N.** friction, attrition; rubbing etc. *v.*; erasure; con-frication, -trition; affriction, abrasion, arrosion, limature, frication, rub; elbow-grease; rosin; *massage*.

V. rub, scratch, abrade, scrape, scrub, fray, rasp, graze, curry, scour, polish, rub out, erase, gnaw; file, grind etc. (*reduce to powder*) 330; *massage*.

set one's teeth on edge; rosin.

Adj. anatriptic, abrasive.

332. Lubrication. [Absence of friction. Prevention of friction.]—**N.** smoothness etc. 255; unctuousness etc. 355.

lubri-cation, -fication; anointment; oiling etc. *v.*

synovia; lubricant, graphite, glycerine, oil etc. 356; saliva; lather.

V. lubri-cate, -citate; oil, grease, lather, soap; wax.

Adj. lubricated etc. *v.*

333. Fluidity.—**N.** fluidity, liquidity; liquidness etc. *adj.*; gaseity etc. 334; liquefaction etc. 334.

fluid, inelastic fluid; liquid, liquor; lymph, humor, juice, sap, serum, blood, serosity, gravy, rheum, ichor, sanies.

solu-bility, -bleness.

[Science of liquids] hydro-logy, -statics, dynamics, hydraulics. etc.

V. be -fluid etc. *adj.*; flow etc. (*water in motion*) 348; liquefy etc. 335.

Adj. liquid, fluid, serous, juicy, succulent, sappy; fluent etc. (*flowing*) 348.

liquefied etc. 335; uncongealed; soluble, hydrostatic etc. *n.*

334. Gaseity.—**N.** gaseity, gaseousness, vapourousness etc. *adj.*; flatulence, -lency; volatility, aeration, gasification.

elastic fluid, gas, air, vapor, ether, steam, fume, reek, *effluvium*, *flatus*; cloud etc. 353.

[Science of elastic fluids] pneumat-ics, -ostatics; aero-statics, -dynamics etc.

gas-, gaso-meter.

V. gassify, aerate, aerify; emit vapor etc. 336.

Adj. gaseous, aeriform, ethereal, aerial, airy, vaporous, volatile, evaporable; flatulent; aerostatic etc. *n.*

335. Liquefaction.—**N.** liquefaction; liquescen-ce, -cy, deliquescence; melting etc. (*heat*) 384; colliqu-ation, -efaction; thaw; de-, liquation; lixiviation, dissolution.

solution, apozem, lixivium, infusion, decoction, flux.

solvent, diluent, menstruum, alkahest, *aqua fortis*.

V. render -liquid etc 333; liquefy, run, deliquesce; melt etc. (*heat*) 384; solve; dissolve, resolve; liquate; hold in solution; leach, lixiviate.

Adj. lique-fied etc. *v.*, -scent, -fiable; deliquescent, soluble, colliquative; solvent.

336. Vaporization.—**N.** vapor-, volatilization; gasification; e-, vaporation; distillation, cohobation, sublimation, exhalation; volatility.

vaporizer, still, retort, spray, atomizer; fumigation, steaming.

V. render -gaseous etc. 334; vaporize, volatilize; distil, sublime; evaporate, exhale, smoke, transpire, emit vapor, fume, reek, steam, fumigate.

Adj. volatilized etc. *v.*; reeking etc. *v.*; volatile; evaporable, vaporizable.

337. Water.—N. water; serum, serosity; lymph; rheum; diluent.

dilution, maceration, lotion; washing etc. *v.*; im-, mersion; humectation, infiltration, spargefaction, affusion, irrigation, *douche*, balneation, bath.

deluge etc. (*water in motion*) 348; high water, flood-, spring-tide.

V. be -watery etc. *adj.*; reek.

add water, water, wet; moisten etc. 339; dilute, dip, immerse; merge; im-, sub-merge; plunge, souse, duck, drown; soak, steep, macerate, pickle, wash, sprinkle, sparge, lave, bathe, affuse, splash, swash, douse, slosh, drench; dabble, slop, slobber, irrigate, inundate, deluge; syringe, inject, gargle; infiltrate, percolate.

Adj. watery, aqueous, aquatic, lymphatic; balneal, diluent; drenching etc. *v.*; diluted etc. *v.*; weak; wet etc. (*moist*) 339.

Phr. the waters are out.

338. Air.—N. air etc. (*gas*) 334; common –, atmospheric- air; atmosphere, stratosphere, isothermal layer, troposphere, Heaviside layer.

open; – air; sky, welkin; blue, – sky; cloud etc. 353.

weather, climate, rise and fall of the barometer, isobar.

[Science of air] pneumatics, aero-logy, -scopy, -graphy; meteorology, climatology; eudio-, baro-, aero-meter; aneroid, baro-graph, -scope; weather-gauge, -glass, -cock.

exposure to the -air, – weather; ventilation; aero-station; -nautics; -naut etc. 265 and 269.

V. air, ventilate; fan etc. (*wind*) 349.

Adj. containing air, flatulent, effervescent; windy etc. 349.

atmospheric, airy; aeri-al, -form; pneumatic; meteorological; weather-wise.

Adv. in the open air, out of doors, *à la belle étoile, al fresco*; *sub -Jove, – dio.*

339. Moisture.—N. moisture; moistness etc. *adj.*; hum-idity, -ectation; madefaction, dew; *serein*; marsh etc. 345; Hygromet-ry, -er.

V. moisten, wet; humect, -ate; sponge, damp, dampen, bedew; imbue, imbrue, infiltrate, saturate; seethe, sop; soak, drench etc. (*water*) 337.

be -moist etc. *adj.*; not have a dry thread; perspire etc. (*exude*) 295.

Adj. moist, damp; watery etc. 337; undried, humid, wet, dank, muggy, dewy; roric; roscid; juicy.

wringing wet; wet -through, – to the skin; saturated etc. *v.*

swashy, soggy, dabbled; reeking, seething, dripping, soaking, soft, sodden, sloppy, muddy; swampy etc. (*marshy*) 345; irriguous.

340. Dryness.—N. dryness etc. *adj.*; siccity, aridity, drought, ebb-, neap-tide, low water.

drying, ex-, de-siccation; evaporation; dehydration; arefaction, dephlegmation, drainage.

drier, desiccator.

V. be -dry etc. *adj.*; render -dry etc. *adj.*; dry; dry –, soak- up; sponge, swab, wipe; ex-, desiccate, dehydrate, anhydrate; drain, parch.

be fine, hold up.

Adj. dry, anhydrous, arid, waterless; dried etc. *v.*; undamped; juice-, sap- less; sear; husky; rainless, without rain, fine; dry as -a bone, – dust, – a stick, – a mummy, – a biscuit; disiccated; dehydrated; water-proof, -tight.

341. Ocean.—N. sea, ocean, main, deep, brine, salt water, waters, waves, billows, high seas, offing, great waters, watery waste, 'vasty deep,' briny ocean, herring pond, steamer track, the seven seas; wave, tide etc. (*water in motion*) 348.

hydrograph-y, -er, oceanography; Neptune, Thetis, Triton, Naiad, Nereid; sea-nymph, Siren, mer-maid, -man; trident, dolphin.

Adj. oceanic; mar-ine, -itime; pleagic, -ian; sea-going, -worthy; hydrographic.

Adv. at –, on- sea; afloat, on the high seas.

342. Land.—N. land, earth, ground, dry land, *terra firma.*

continent, mainland, peninsula, delta; tongue –, neck- of land; isthmus; oasis; promontory etc. (*projection*) 250; highland etc. (*height*) 206.

coast, shore, scar, strand, beach; bank, lea; seaboard, -side, -shore, -bank, -coast, -beach; rock-, iron- bound coast; loom of the land; derelict; innings; *alluvium*, alluvion.

soil, glebe, clay, loam, marl, clodge, chalk, gravel, mold, subsoil, clod, clot; rock, crag, cliff.

acres; real estate etc. (*property*) 780; landsman, land-lubber, farmer.

geography etc. 318; agriculture etc. 371.

V. land, come to land; set foot on -the soil, – dry land; come –, go- ashore.

Adj. earthy; continental, midland; littoral, riparian, ripuarian; alluvial; terrene etc. (*world*) 318; landed, predial, territorial.

Adv. ashore; on -shore, – land.

343. Gulf. Lake.—N. land covered with water, gulf, gulph, bay, inlet, bight, estuary, arm of the sea, fiord, armlet; frith, firth, ostiary, mouth; lagune, lagoon; indraught; cove, creek; natural harbor; roads; strait, narrows; Euripus; sound, belt, gut, kyles.

lake, loch, lough, mere, tarn, plash, broad, pond, pool, lin, puddle, well, artesian well, tank, sump; standing –, dead –, sheet of- water; fish –, mill-pond; race; ditch, dike, dyke, dam; reservoir etc. (*store*) 636.

Adj. lacustrine; land locked.

344. Plain.—N. plain, table land, mesa, face of the country; open –, champaign-country; basin, downs, waste, weary waste, desert, tundra, wild, steppe, pampas, savanna, prairie, champaign, heath, common, wold, veld; moor, -land, uplands, fell; bush; *plateau* etc. (*level*) 213; *campagna.*

meadow, mead, haugh, pasturage, park, field,

lawn, green, plat, plot, grass-plat, greensward, sward, grass, turf, sod, heather; lea, ley, lay; grounds.

Adj. campestrian, champaign, alluvial.

345. Marsh.—N. marsh, swamp, morass, marish, moss, fen, bog, quagmire, slough, sump, wash; mud, squash, slush.

Adj. marsh, -y; swampy, boggy, plashy, poachy, quaggy, soft; muddy, sloppy, squashy, spongy; paludal; moor-ish, -y; fenny.

346. Island.—N. island, isle, islet, eyot, ait, holm, reef, atoll, breaker; archipelago; islander.

Adj. insular, sea-girt.

347. Stream. [Fluid in motion.]—**N.** stream etc. (*of water*) 348, (*of air*) 349.

V. flow etc. 348; blow etc. 349.

348. River. [Water in motion.]—**N.** running water.

jet, spirt, squirt, spout, splash, swash, rush, gush, *jet d'eau*; sluice, chute.

water-spout, -fall; fall, cascade, force, foss; lin, -n, ghyll, Niagara; cata-ract, -dupe, -clysm; *débâcle*, inundation, deluge.

rain, -fall; *serein*; shower, scud; downpour, cloud burst; driving –, pouring –, drenching- rain; hyeto-logy, -graphy; rainy season, monsoon; predominance of Aquarius, reigh of St. Swithin; mizzle, drizzle, *stillicidium*, plash; dropping etc. *v.*

stream, course, flux, flow, profluence; effluence etc. (*egress*) 295; defluxion; flowing etc. *v.*; current, tide, race.

spring; fount, -ain; rill, rivulet, gill, gullet, rillet; stream-, brook-let; runnel, sike, burn, beck, brook, stream, river; reach; tributary.

body of water, torrent, rapids, flush, flood, swash, spate; spring –, high –, full-tide; bore; eagre, *hugre*; fresh, -et; undertow, indraught, reflux, undercurrent, eddy, vortex, gurge, whirlpool, Maelstrom, regurgitation, overflow; confluence, corrivation.

wave, billow, surge, swell, ripple; roller, ground swell, surf, breaker, white horses; comber, beach-comber; rough –, heavy –, cross –, long –, short –, chopping –, choppy- sea, choppiness; tidal wave.

[Science of fluids in motion] Hydrodynamics; Hydraul-ics etc.; raingauge etc.

water-bearer, – carrier, Aquarius.

irrigation etc. (*water*) 337; pump; watering-pot, – cart; hydrant, standpipe, hose, sprinkler, drencher; fire engine, squirt, syringe.

V. flow, run; meander; gush, pour, spout, roll, jet, well, issue; drop, drip, dribble, plash, squirt, spurt, spirtle, trill, trickle, distil, percolate; stream, overflow, inundate, deluge, flow over, splash, swash; guggle, murmur, babble, bubble, purl, gurgle, sputter, regurgitate; ooze, flow out etc. (*egress*) 295.

rain, – hard, – in torrents, – cats and dogs, – pitchforks; come down in sheets; pour with rain, drizzle, mizzle, spit, sprinkle, set in.

flow –, fall –, open –, drain- into; discharge itself, desembogue.

[Cause a flow] pour; pour out etc. (*discharge*) 297; shower down; irrigate, drench etc. (*wet*) 337; spill, splash.

[Stop a flow] stanch; dam, -up etc. (*close*) 261; obstruct etc. 706.

Adj. fluent; dif-, pro-, af-fluent; tidal; flowing etc. *v.*; meand-ering, -ry, -rous; fluvi-al, -atile; streamy, showery, rainy, drizzly, drizzling, pluvial, pluviose, stillicidous.

349. Wind. [Air in motion.]—**N.** wind, draught, *flatus*, *afflatus*, air; breath, – of air; puff, whiff, zephyr; blow, drift; *aura*; stream, current; under-current.

gust, blast, breeze, squall, gale, half a gale, storm, tempest, hurricane, whirlwind, tornado, samiel, cyclone, typhoon; simoon; harmattan, monsoon, trade wind, sirocco, *mistral*; *bise*, *föhn*, tramontane, levanter; capful of wind; fresh –, stiff- breeze; keen blast; biizzard.

windiness etc. *adj.*; ventosity; rough –, dirty –, ugly –, stress of- weather; dirty-, windy-, mackerel- sky; mare's tail; thick –, black –, white- squall.

anemography, aerodynamics; windgauge, anemometer, weather-cock, vane.

suf-, insuf-, per-, in-, af-flation; blowing, fanning etc. *v.*; ventilation.

sneezing etc. *v.*; sternutation; hic-cup, -cough; catching of the breath; breathing etc.

Eolus, Eurus, Boreas, Zephyr, cave of Eolus.

air-pump, lungs, bellows, blow-pipe, fan, blower; pulmotor, ventilator, punkah, aspirator, exhauster, ejector.

V. blow, waft; blow -hard, – great guns, – a hurricane etc. *n.*; whistle, roar, howl, ring in the shrouds; stream, issue.

respire, breathe, in-, ex-hale, puff; whif, -fle; gasp, wheeze; snuff, -le; sniff, -le; sneeze, cough, belch.

fan, ventilate; in-, per-flate; blow –, pump- up.

Adj. blowing etc. *v.*; windy, airy, aeolian, flatulent; breezy, gusty, squally; stormy, tempestuous, blustering; boisterous etc. (*violent*) 173.

pulmon-ic, -ary.

350. Conduit. [Channel for the passage of water.]—**N.** conduit, channel, duct, watercourse, race; head –, tail- race; adit, aqueduct, canal, trough, flume, gutter, pantile; dike, canyon, ravine, gorge, hollow, main, gully, moat, ditch, drain, sewer, culvert, *cloaca*, sough, kennel, siphon, *piscina*; pipe etc. (*tube*) 260; funnel; tunnel etc. (*passage*) 627; water –, waste- pipe; emunctory, gully-hole, artery, aorta, vein, blood vessel; lymphatic; throat, alimentary canal, intestine; pore, spout, scupper; ad-, a-jutage; hose; gar-, gurgoyle; penstock, weir; flood-, water-gate; sluice, lock, valve; rose; waterworks.

Adj. vascular etc. (*with holes*) 260.

351. Air-pipe. [Channel for the passage of air.]—**N.** air-pipe, – shaft, – way, – passage, –

tube; shaft, flue, chimney, funnel, vent, blow-hole, nostril, nozzle, throat, weasand, *trachea*; *bronchus*, *-ia*; larynx, tonsils, wind-pipe, spiracle; ventiduct, -lator; louvre, Venetian blinds; blow-pipe etc. (*wind*) 349; pipe etc. (*tube*) 260.

352. Semiliquidity.—N. semiliquidity; stickiness etc. *adj.*; visc-idity, -osity; gumm-, glutin-, muc-osity; spiss-, crass-itude; lentor; adhesiveness etc. (*cohesion*) 46.

inspiss-, incrass-ation; thickening, coagulation.

jelly, aspic, mucilage, gelatin, isinglass; colloid, mucus, phlegm; pituite, lava; glair, starch, gluten, albumen, milk, cream, protein; syrup, treacle; gum, size, glue, paste; wax, bee's-wax; emulsoid, emulsion, soup; squash, mud, slush, slime, ooze; moisture etc. 339; marsh etc. 345.

V. inspiss-, incrass-ate; coagulate, gelatinize, gelatinify, gel, jell, emulsify, thicken; mash, squash, churn, beat up.

Adj. semi-fluid, -liquid; half-melted, -frozen; milky, muddy etc. *n.*; lact-eal, -ean, -eous, -escent, -iferous; emulsive, curdled, thick, succulent, uliginous.

gelat-, album-, mucilag-, glut-inous; gelatine, mastic, amylaceous, ropy, clammy, clotted; vis-cid, -cous; sticky, tacky; slab, -by; lentous, pituitous; mu-cid, -culent, -cous.

353. Bubble. [Mixture of air and water.] [Cloud.]—**N.** bubble; foam, froth, head, fume, spume, lather, suds, spray, surf, yeast, barm, spindrift.

cloud, vapor, fog, mist, haze, steam; scud, rack, *nimbus*; *cumulus*, woolpack, *cirrus*, *stratus*; *cirro-*, *cumulo-stratus*; *cirro-cumulus*; mackerel sky, mare's tail, dirty sky.

[Science of clouds] nephelognosy, nephology.

effervescence, fermentation; bubbling etc. *v.*

nebula; cloudiness etc. (*opacity*) 426; nebulosity etc. (*dimness*) 422.

V. bubble, boil, foam, froth, spume, mantle, sparkle, guggle, gurgle; effervesce, ferment, fizzle; aerate; cloud, overcast, befog.

Adj. bubbling etc. *v.*; frothy, nappy, effervescent, sparkling, *mousseux*, up, fizzy, with a head on.

cloudy etc. *n.*; vaporous, nebulous, overcast; nubiferous, nephological; foggy, brumous.

354. Pulpiness.—N. pulpiness etc. *adj.*; pulp, paste, dough, sponge, curd, pap, rob, jam, pudding, mush, fool, poultice, grume.

Adj. pulpy etc. *n.*; pultaceous, grumous.

V. pulp, pulpify, mash.

355. Unctuousness.—N. unctuousness etc. *adj.*; unctuosity, lubricity; ointment etc. (*oil*) 356; anointment; lubrication etc. 332.

V. oil etc. (*lubricate*) 332.

Adj. unctuous, oily, oleaginous, adipose, sebaceous; fat, -ty; greasy; waxy, butyraceous, soapy, saponaceous, pinguid, lardaceous; slippery.

356. Oil.—N. oil, fat, butter, cream, grease, tallow, suet, lard, dripping, margarine, oleomargarine, exunge, blubber; glycerine, stearine, elaine, oleagine; soap; soft soap, wax, cerement; paraffin, spermaceti, adipocere; petroleum, mineral –, rock –, crystal- oil, kerosene, vegetable –, colza –, olive –, linseed –, cotton seed –, rape –, nut –, fusel- oil; animal –, neat's foot –, signal –, train- oil; ointment, unguent, liniment, salve, pomade, pomatum, brilliantine, spike –, nard.

356a. Resin.—N. resin, rosin, colophony; gum; lac, shellac, sealing-wax; amber, -gris; bitumen, pitch, tar, asphalt, -e, -um; varnish, copal, mastic, magilp, lacquer, japan.

V. varnish etc. (*overlay*) 223.

Adj. resinous, bituminous, pitchy, tarry.

357. Organization.—N. organized -world, – nature; living –, animated- nature; living beings; organic remains, organism; fossils; animal and vegetable kingdom, *fauna* and *flora*, biota.

prot-oplasm, -ein; albumen; structure etc. 329; organ-ization, -ism.

[Science of living beings] biology; natural history,* organic –, bio-chemistry, anatomy, physiology, embryology, morphology, evolution, Darwinism, Lamarkism, zoology etc. 368; botany etc. 369; naturalist, biologist etc.

Adj. organ-ic, -ized.

*The term *Natural History* is also used as relating to all the objects in Nature whether organic or inorganic, and including therefore *Mineralogy*, *Geology*, *Meteorology*, etc.

358. Inorganization.—N. mineral -world, – kingdom; unorganized –, inorganic –, brute –, inanimate- matter.

[Science of the mineral kingdom] mineralogy; geo-logy, -gnosy, -scopy; metall-urgy, -ography; lithology; orycto-logy, -graphy.

V. turn to dust, pulverize.

Adj. in-organic, -animate; unorganized; azoic; mineral.

359. Life.—N. life; vi-tality, -ability; animation; vital -spark, – flame, – force.

respiration, wind; breath -of life, – of one's nostrils; life-blood; Archeus; existence etc. 1.

vivification, vitalization; revivification etc. 163; Prometheus; life to come etc. (*destiny*) 152.

[Science of life] physiology, etiology, embryology, biology; animal economy.

nourishment, staff of life etc. (*food*) 298.

V. be -alive etc. *adj.*; live, breathe, respire; subsist etc. (*exist*) 1; walk the earth; strut and fret one's hour upon a stage; be spared.

see the light, be born, come into the world; fetch –, draw- -breath, – the breath of life; quicken; revive; come to, – life.

give birth to etc. (*produce*) 161; bring to life, put into life, vitalize; vivi-fy, -ficate; reanimate etc. (*restore*) 660; keep -alive, – body and soul together, – the wolf from the door; support life.

have nine lives like a cat.

Adj. living, alive; in -life, – the flesh, – the land of the living; on this side of the grave, above ground, breathing, quick, animated, viable; lively etc. (*active*) 682; alive and kicking; tenacious of life.

vital; vivi-fying; -fied etc. *v.*; Promethean.

Adv. *vivendi causâ.*

360. Death.—N. death, dying etc. *v.*; de-cease, -mise; dissolution, departure, *obit*, release, rest, *quietus*, fall; loss, bereavement.

end etc. 67 –, cessation etc. 142 –, loss –, extinction –, ebb- of -life etc. 359.

death-warrant, -watch, -rattle, -bed; stroke –, agonies –, shades –, valley of the shadow –, jaws –, hand- of death; last -breath, – gasp, – agonies; dying -day, – breath, – agonies; swan song, *chant du cygne*; *rigor mortis*; Stygian shore; crossing the bar, the great adventure.

King -of terrors, – Death; Death, Angel of Death; mortality; doom etc. (*necessity*) 601.

euthanasia; happy release; break up of the system; natural -death, – decay; sudden –, violent- death; untimely end, watery grave; suffocation, *asphyxia*; heart failure; fatal disease etc. (*disease*) 655; death-blow etc. (*killing*) 361.

necrology, bills of mortality, obituary; death-song etc. (*lamentation*) 839.

V. die, expire, perish; meet one's -death, – end; pass away, be taken; yield –, resign- one's breath; resign one's -being, – life; end one's -days, – life, – earthly career; breathe one's last; cease to -live, – breathe; depart this life; be -no more etc. *adj.*; go –, drop –, pop -off; lose –, lay down –, relinquish –, surrender- one's life; drop –, sink- into the grave; close one's eyes; fall –, drop- dead, – down dead; break one's neck; give –, yield- up the ghost; be all over with one.

pay the debt to nature, shuffle off this mortal coil, take one's last sleep; go the way of all flesh; join the -greater number, – majority, – choir invisible, to life immortal awake; come –, turn- to dust; cross the Stygian ferry; go to -one's long account, – one's last home, – Davy Jones's locker, – the wall; receive one's death warrant, make one's will, die a natural death, go out like the snuff of a candle; come to an untimely end; catch one's death; go off the hooks, kick the bucket, pet out; go West; hop the twig, turn up one's toes; die a violent death etc. (*be killed*) 361; make the supreme sacrifice.

Adj. dead, lifeless; deceased, demised, departed, defunct; late, gone, no more; ex-, in-animate; out of the world, taken off, released; departed this life etc. *v.*; dead and gone; bereft of life, stone dead, dead as -a door nail, – a door post, – mutton, – a herring, – nits; launched into eternity, gathered to one's fathers, numbered with the dead, gone to a better land, behind the veil, beyond the grave, – mortal ken.

dying etc. *v.*; mori-bund, -ent, Acherontic; hippocratic; *in -articulo*, – *extremis*; in the -jaws, – agony- of death; going, – off; *aux abois*; on one's -last legs, – death bed; at -the point of death, – death's door, – the last gasp; near one's end, given over, booked, fey; with one foot in –, tottering on the brink of- the grave.

still-born; mortuary; deadly etc. (*killing*) 361.

Adv. *post -obit*, – *mortem*.

Phr. life -ebbs, – fails, – hangs by a thread; one's -days are numbered, – hour is come, – race is run, – doom is sealed; Death -knocks at the door, – stares one in the face; the breath is out of the body; the grave closes over one; *sic itur ad astra.*

361. Killing. [Destruction of life; violent death.]—**N.** killing etc. *v.*; homicide, manslaughter, murder, assassination, trucidation, occision; lynching, effusion of blood; blood, -shed; gore, slaughter, carnage, butchery; *battue*, gladiatorial combat.

massacre; *fussillade*, *noyade*, *pogrom*; thuggism; racketeering.

death blow, finishing stroke, *coup de grâce*, *quietus*; execution etc. (*capital punishment*) 972; judicial murder; martyrdom.

butcher, slayer, murderer, Cain, assassin, cut-throat, garrotter, *bravo*, thug, racketeer, gunman, mobster, gangster, Moloch, *matador*, *sabreur*; *guet-à-pens*; gallows, executioner etc. (*punishment*) 975; man-eater.

regicide, parricide, fratricide, infanticide, aborticide etc.

suicide, *felo de se*, *suttee*, *hara kiri*, Juggernaut; immolation, holocaust.

suffocation, strangulation, *garrotte*; hanging etc. *v.*

deadly weapon etc. (*arms*) 727; Aceldama; the potter's field, the field of blood.

fatal accident, violent death, casualty.

[Destruction of animals] slaughtering; phthiozoics;* sport, -ting; the chase, venery; hunting, coursing, shooting, fishing; pig-sticking; sports-, hunts-, fisher-man; hunter, Nimrod; slaughterer, knacker, slaughter-house, shambles, *abattoir.*

V. kill, put to death, slay, shed blood; murder, assassinate, butcher, slaughter; victimize, immolate; massacre; take away –, deprive of- life; make away with, put an end to; despatch, dispatch; burke settle, do, – to death, – for.

strangle, garrotte, hang, lynch, throttle, choke, stifle, suffocate, stop the breath, smother, asphyxiate, drown.

saber; cut -down, – to pieces, – the throat; jugulate; stab, run through the body, bayonet; put to the -sword, – edge of the sword.

shoot, – dead; blow one's brains out; brain, knock on the head; stone, lapidate; give –, deal- a death blow; give a -*quietus*, – *coup de grâce*.

behead, bowstring etc. (*execute*) 972.

hunt, shoot etc. *n.*

cut off, nip in the bud, launch into eternity, send to one's last account, bump off, rub out, sign one's death warrant, strike the death knell of.

give no quarter, pour out blood like water; decimate; run amuck, wade knee-deep –, imbrue one's hands- in blood.

die a violent death, welter in one's blood; dash –, blow- out one's brains; commit suicide; kill – -make away with –, put an end to- oneself.

Adj. killing etc. *v.*; murd-, slaught-erous; sanguin-ary, -olent; blood-stained, -thirsty;

homicidal, red-handed; bloody, -minded; ensanguined, gory, sanguineous.

mortal fatal, lethal; dead-, death-ly; mort-, lethiferous; unhealthy etc. 657; internecine; suicidal.

sporting; piscator-ial, -y.

Adv. in at the death.

*Bentham, 'Chrestomathia.'

362. Corpse.—N. corpse, corse, carcass, bones, skeleton, dry-bones; defunct, relics, *relinquiae*, remains, mortal remains, dust, ashes, earth, clay; mummy; carrion; food for- worms, – fishes; tenement of clay, this mortal coil.

shade, ghost, *manes*, apparition etc. 980.

organic remains, fossils.

Adj. cadaverous, corpse-like; unburied etc. 363.

363. Interment.—N. interment, burial, inhumation, sepulture, entombment; in-, humation; obs-, ex-equies; funeral, wake, pyre, funeral pile; cremation.

funeral -rite, – solemnity; knell, passing bell, tolling; dirge etc. (*lamentation*) 839; cypress; *obit*, dead march, muffled drum; coroner, mortician, undertaker, mute, mourner, professional mourner, pallbearer; elegy; funeral -oration, – sermon; epitaph.

grave clothes, shroud; winding-sheet, cere-cloth; cerement.

coffin, shell, sarcophagus, urn, pall, bier, hearse, catafalque, cinerary urn.

grave, pit, sepulcher, tomb, vault, crypt, catacomb, mausoleum, *Golgotha*, house of death, narrow house, long home; cemetery, necropolis, boneyard; burial-place, -ground; grave-, churchyard; God's acre; mortuary, tope, cromlech, dolmen, menhir, barrow, tumulus, cairn; ossuary; bone-, charnel-, dead-house; *Morgue*; lich-gate; crematorium.

sexton, grave-digger.

monument, memorial, cenotaph, shrine; grave-, head-, tomb-stone; *memento mori*; hatchment, stone, cross.

exhumation, disinterment; necropsy, autopsy, *post mortem* examination.

V. inter, bury, lay in –, consign to- the -grave, – tomb; en-, in-tomb; inhume; lay out, prepare for burial, embalm, mummify; conduct a funeral, hold services; toll the knell; put to bed with a shovel.

exhume, disinter, unearth.

Adj. buried etc. *v.*; burial; fune-real, -brial; mortuary, sepulchral, cinerary; elegiac; necroscopic.

Adv. *in memoriam*; *post-obit*, *-mortem*; beneath –, under- the sod.

Phr. *hic jacet, ci-git, requiescat in pace.*

364. Animality.—N. animal life; anima-tion, -lity, -lization; breath.

flesh, – and blood; corporeal nature; *physique*; strength etc. 159.

V. animalize, incorporate.

Adj. fleshly, incarnate, carnal, corporeal, human.

365. Vegetability.—N. vegetable life; vegetation, -bility; herbage.

V. vegetate, germinate, sprout, shoot; cultivate.

Adj. vegetable etc. 367; rank, lush.

366. Animal.*—N. animal, – kingdom; *fauna*; brute creation.

beast, brute, creature, created being; creeping –, living- thing; dumb -animal, – creature.

flocks and herds, live stock; domestic –, wild-animals; game, *ferae naturae*; beasts of the fields, fowls of the air, denizens of the day.

vertebrate, bi-, quadru-ped, mammal, marsupial, bird, reptile, batrachian, amphibian, fish, crustacean, shell fish, articulate, mollusc, worm, insect, zoophyte; protozoon, animalcule etc. 193.

horse etc. (*beast of burden*) 271; cattle, kine, ox; bull, -ock; steer, stot; cow, milch-cow, calf, heifer, shorthorn; sheep; lamb, -kin; ewe –, pet-lamb; ewe, ram, tup; pig, swine, boar, hog, shoat, sow; tag, teg, wether.

dog, bitch, hound; pup, -py; whelp, cur, mutt, mongrel; house-, watch-, sheep-, shepherd's, sporting-, fancy-, lap-, toy-, bull-, badger-dog; mastiff; blood-, grey-, stag-, deer-, fox-, otter-, hound; harrier, beagle, spaniel, pointer, setter, retriever; Newfoundland; water -dog, – spaniel; pug, poodle; dachshund; Pinscher; turnspit; terrier; fox –, Skye- terrier; Dandie Dinmont; colley.

cat; puss,-y; kitten; grimalkin; gib-, tom-cat; mouser; fox, Reynard, vixen, stag, deer, hart, buck, doe, roe, antelope.

bird; poultry, fowl, cock, hen, chicken, chanticleer, partlet, rooster, dunghill cock, barn-door fowl; feathered -tribes, – songster; singing –, dicky- bird; canary; finch; auk, dodo, moa, roc, phoenix.

snake, serpent, viper, adder; newt, eft; asp, vermin.

Adj. animal, zoological.

equine, bovine, vaccine, canine, feline; fishy; piscator-y, -ial; molluscous, vermicular.

*Extended lists of names of specific varieties of animals, vegetables, etc., are beyond the scope of this work.

367. Vegetable.*—N. vegetable, – kingdom; *flora*, verdure.

plant; tree, shrub, bush; creeper; vine; herb, -age; grass.

annual; per-, bi-, tri-ennial; exotic.

timber; primeval –, virgin- forest; wood, -lands; hurst; frith, holt, weald, park, chase, greenwood, brake, grove, copse, coppice, *bocage*, *tope*, clump of trees, thicket, spinet, spinney; under-, brushwood; boscage, scrub; the oak and the ash and the bonny ivy tree.

bush, jungle, prairie; heath, -er; fern, bracken, furze, gorse, whin, broom; grass, turf, grassland, greensward, green, lawn, meadow; pas-ture, -turage; turbary; sedge, rush, weed; fungus, mushroom, toadstool; lichen, moss, conferva, mold; seaweed etc.; growth, crop.

foliage, leafage, branch, bough, ramage; spray etc. 51; leaf, frond, flag, petal, shoot, tendril.

flower, blossom, bud, bloom, bine; flowering plant; tree, sapling, pollard; timber-, fruit-tree; palm-, gum-tree; pulse, legume.

Adj. veget-able, -ous; herb-aceous, -al; botanic; sylvan, silvan; arbor- ary, -eous, -escent, -ical; dendritic, dendriform; woody, grassy; ver-dant, -durous; floral, mossy; lign-ous, -eous; wooden, leguminous; end-, ex-ogenous.

*Extended lists of names of specific varieties of animals, vegetables, etc., are beyond the scope of this work.

368. Zoology. [The science of animals.]—**N.** zoo-logy, -nomy, -graphy, -tomy; anatomy; comparative anatomy; animal –, comparative-physiology; morphology.

anthrop-, ornith-, ichthy-, herpet-, ophi-, malac-, helminth-, entom-, oryct-, paleont-ology; ichthy- etc. -otomy; taxidermy.

zo- etc. -ologist.

Adj. zoological etc. *n.*

369. Botany. [The science of plants.]—**N.** botany; phyto-graphy, -logy, -tomy; vegetable physiology, herborization, dendr-, myc-, fung-, algology; flora, pomona; botanist etc.; botanic garden etc. (*garden*) 371; *hortus siccus*, *herbarium*, herbal.

herb-ist, -arist, -alist, -orist, -arian etc.

V. botanize, herborize.

Adj. botanical etc. *n.*

370. Cicuration. [The economy or management of animals.]—**N.** taming etc. *v.*; cicuration, zoohygiantics; domestication, -ity; *manège*; veterinary art; breeding, pisciculture, apiculture etc.

menagery, vivarium, zoological garden, zoo; bear-pit; aviary, apiary, hive; aquarium, fishery, fish hatchery; duck-, fish-pond; stud-farm; stock farm, dairy.

[Destruction of animals] phthisozoics etc. (*killing*) 361.

neat-, cow-, shep-herd, shepherdess; grazier; drover, cowboy, cowkeeper; trainer, breeder, groom, ostler etc. 746; veterinary surgeon, vet, horse doctor; farrier; keeper; game keeper.

cage etc. (*prison*) 752; hen-coop, bird-cage, cauf; sheep-fold etc. (*inclosure*) 232.

V. tame, domesticate, acclimatize, breed, tend, break in, train, corral, round up; cage, bridle etc. (*restrain*) 751; ride etc. 266.

drive, yoke, harness, hitch; groom, curry-comb; milk; shear; hatch; incubate.

Adj. pastoral, bucolic; tame, domestic, domesticated, broken in, gentle, docile.

371. Agriculture. [The economy or management of plants.]—**N.** agriculture, cultivation, husbandry, farming; georgics, geoponics; tillage, tilth, agronomy, gardening, spade husbandry, vintage; hort-, arbor-, silv-, citr-, vit-, flor-iculture; intensive culture; landscape gardening; forestry, afforestation.

husbandman, horticulturist, citriculturist, gardener, florist; agricult-or, -urist; yeoman, farmer, cultivator, tiller of the soil, ploughman, sower, reaper; woodcutter, backwoodsman, forester; vine grower, vintager; Boer; Triptolemus.

field, meadow, garden; botanic –, winter –, ornamental –, flower –, kitchen –, truck –, market –, hop- garden; nursery; green-, hot-, glass-house; conservatory, cucumber frame, *cloche*, bed, border, seed-plot; grass-plat, lawn; park etc. (*pleasure ground*) 840; *partere*, shrubbery, plantation, avenue, *arboretum*, pinery, *pinetum*, orchard, vineyard, vinery; orangery; farm etc. (*abode*) 189.

V. cultivate; till, – the soil; farm, garden; sow, plant; reap, mow, cut; manure, dress the ground, dig, delve, dibble, hoe, plough, plow, harrow, rake, weed, lop and top, force, transplant, thin out, bed out, prune, graft.

Adj. agr-icultural, -airan, -estic.

arable; predial, rural, rustic, country, bucolic, Boeotian; horticultural.

372. Mankind.—N. man, -kind; human -race, – species, – nature; humanity, mortality, flesh, generation.

[Science of man] anthropo-logy, -graphy, sophy; ethno-logy, -graphy; humanitarianism.

human being; person, -age; individual, creature, fellow creature, mortal, body, somebody, one; such a –, someone; soul, living soul; earthling; party, head, hand; *dramatis personae*.

people, persons, folk, public, society, world; community, – at large; general public; nation, -ality; state, realm; common-weal, -wealth; republic, body politic; million etc. (*commonalty*) 876; population etc. (*inhabitant*) 188.

cosmopolite; lords of the creation; ourselves.

Adj. human, mortal, personal, individual, national, civic, public, cosmopolitan; anthropoid.

373. Man.—N. man, male, he; manhood etc. (*adolescence*) 131; gentleman, sir, master; yeoman, wight, swain, fellow, guy, blade, *beau*, chap, gaffer, good man; husband etc. (*married man*) 903; Mr., mister, *monsieur*, *sahib*, *Herr*, *señor*, *signor*; boy etc. (*youth*) 129; Adonis.

[Male animal] cock, drake, gander, dog, boar, stag, hart, buck, horse, entire horse, stallion; gib-, tom-cat; he-, Billy-goat; ram, tup; bull, -ock; capon, ox, gelding; steer, stot.

Adj. male, he, masculine; manly, virile; unwomanly, -feminine.

374. Woman.—N. woman, she, female, petticoat, skirt, moll, broad.

feminality, feminity, muliebrity; womanhood etc. (*adolescence*) 131; feminism; gynecology, gyniatrics, gynics.

womankind; the -sex, – fair; fair –, softer- sex; weaker vessel; the distaff side.

dame, madam, *madame*, mistress, Mrs., lady, *mem-sahib*, *Frau*, *señora*, *signora*, *donna*, *belle*, matron, dowager, goody, gammer; good -woman, – wife; squaw; wife etc. (*marriage*) 903; matronage, -hood.

Venus, nymph, wench, *grisette*; little bit of fluff; girl etc. (*youth*) 129.

inamorata (love) etc. 897; courtesan etc. 962.

spinster, old maid, virgin, bachelor girl, new woman, amazon.

[Female animal] hen, slut, bitch, sow, doe, roe, mare; she-, Nanny-goat; ewe, cow; lioness, tigress; vixen.

gynecaeum, harem, *seraglio*, *zenana*, *purdah*.

Adj. female, she; feminine, womanly, ladylike, matronly, maidenly; womanish, effeminate, unmanly, gynecic.

375. Physical Sensibility.—N. sensibility; sensitiveness etc. *adj.*; physical sensibility, feeling, perceptivity, anaphylaxis, susceptibility, esthetics; moral sensibility etc. 882.

sensation, impression, effect; consciousness etc. (*knowledge*) 490.

external senses.

V. be -sensible etc. *adj.* -of; feel, perceive.

render, -sensible etc. *adj.*; excite, stir, sharpen, cultivate, tutor.

cause sensation, impress; excite –, produce- an impression.

Adj. sens-ible, -itive, -uous; esthetic, perceptive, sentient; conscious etc. (*aware*) 490; impressionable, responsive, alive to.

acute, sharp, keen, vivid, lively, impressive, thin-skinned.

Adv. to the quick.

376. Physical Insensibility.—N. insensibility, physical insensibility; obtuseness etc. *adj.*; palsy, paralysis, *anesthesia*, *analgesia*, *narcosis*, *hypnosis*, twilight sleep, stupor, coma, trance, catalepsy; sleep etc. (*inactivity*) 683; moral insensibility etc. 823; numbness etc. 381.

anesthetic agent, general –, local- anesthetic, opium, ether, chloroform, cocaine, novocaine, chloral; nitrous oxide, laughing gas; refrigeration.

V. be -insensible etc. *adj.*; have a -thick skin, – rhinoceros hide.

render -insensible etc. *adj.*; blunt, pall, obtund, benumb, deaden, paralyze; anesthetize, drug, dope; put under the influence of -chloroform etc. *n.*; hypnotize; stupefy, stun, narcotize.

Adj. insensible, unfeeling, senseless, comatose, dazed, impercipient, callous, thick-skinned, pachydermatous; hard, -ened; case-hardened; proof; obtuse, dull; anesthetic; paralytic, palsied, numb, dead.

377. Physical Pleasure.—N. pleasure; physical –, sensual –, sensuous- pleasure; bodily enjoyment, animal gratification, sensuality; hedonism, luxuriousness etc. *adj.*; dissipation, round of pleasure; titillation, *gusto*, creature comforts, comfort, ease; pillow etc. (*support*) 215; luxury, lap of luxury; purple and fine linen; bed of -down, – roses; velvet, clover; cup of Circe etc. (*intemperance*) 954.

treat; diversion, divertisement, entertainment; refreshment, regale; feast; *délice*; dainty etc. 394; *bonne bouche*.

source of pleasure etc. 829; happiness etc. (*mental enjoyment*) 827.

V. feel –, experience –, receive- pleasure; enjoy, relish; luxuriate –, revel –, riot –, bask –, swim –, wallow- in; feast on; gloat -over, – on; smack the lips.

live -on the fat of the land, – in comfort etc. *adv.*; bask in the sunshine, *faire ses choux gras*.

give pleasure etc. 829.

Adj. enjoying etc. *v.*; luxurious, voluptuous, sensual, hedonistic, comfortable, cosy, snug, in comfort, at ease.

agreeable etc. 829; grateful, refreshing, comforting, cordial, genial; sensuous; palatable etc. 394; sweet etc. (*sugar*) 396; fragrant etc. 400; melodious etc. 413; lovely etc. (*beautiful*) 845.

Adv. in -comfort etc. *n.*; on -a bed of roses etc. *n.*; at one's ease.

378. Physical Pain.—N. pain; suffering, -ance; bodily – physical -pain, – suffering; mental suffering etc. 828; dolor, ache; aching etc. *v.*; smart; shoot, -ing; twinge, twitch, gripe, head-, ear-, toothache; *migraine*, neuralgia, neuritis, lumbago, gout, sciatica; hurt, cut; sore, -ness; discomfort, *malaise*; *tic douloureux*.

spasm, cramp; nightmare, *ephialtes*; crick, stitch, kink; thrill, convulsion, throe; throb etc. (*agitation*) 315; pang.

sharp –, piercing –, throbbing –, shooting –, gnawing –, burning- pain; anguish, agony.

torment, torture; rack; cruci-ation, -fixion; martyrdom; martyr, toad under a harrow, vivisection.

V. feel –, experience –, suffer –, undergo- pain etc. *n.*; suffer, ache, smart, bleed; tingle, shoot; twinge, twitch, lancinate; writhe, wince, make a wry face; sit on -thorns, – pins and needles.

give –, inflict- pain; pain, hurt, chafe, sting, bite, gnaw, gripe, stab, grind; pinch, tweak; grate, gall, fret, prick, pierce, wring, convulse; torment, torture; rack, agonize; crucify; excruciate; break on the wheel, put to the rack; flag etc. (*punish*) 972: grate on the ear etc. (*harsh sound*) 410.

Adj. in -pain etc. *n.*; – a state of pain; pained etc. *v.*

painful; aching etc. *v.*; biting, poignant; sore, raw, tender, with exposed nerve.

379. Touch. [Sensation of pressure.] **—N.** touch; tact, -ion, -ility; feeling; palp-ation, -ability; manipulation; brush, tick, graze, contact etc. 199.

[Organ of touch] hand, finger, fore-finger, thumb, paw, feeler, *antenna*.

V. touch, feel, handle, finger, thumb, paw, fumble, grope, grabble; twiddle, tweedle; pass –, run- the fingers over, massage, rub, knead; palpate, stroke, manipulate, wield; throw out a feeler.

Adj. tact-ual, -ile; tangible, palpable; lambent.

380. Sensations of Touch.—N. itching etc. *v.*; titillation, formication, *aura*.

V. itch, tingle, creep, thrill, sting; prick, -le; tickle, titillate.

Adj. itching etc. *v.*

381. Numbness. [Insensibility to touch.] **—N.**

numbness etc. (*physical insensibility*) 376; pins and needles.

local anesthetic,cocaine novocaine etc.; morphia.

V. benumb etc. 376; freeze, dull, deaden.

Adj. numb; benumbed etc. *v.*; intangible, impalpable.

382. Heat.—N. heat, caloric; temperature, warmth, fervor, calidity; incal-, incand-, recal-, decal-escence; glow, flush, blush; fever, hectic.

phlogiston; fire, spark, scintillation, flash, flame, blaze; arc; bonfire; firework, pyrotechny; wild-fire; sheet of fire, lambent flame; devouring element; conflagration.

summer, dog-days, canicule; baking etc. 384 –, white –, tropical –, Afric –, Bengal –, summer –, blood- heat; heat wave, sirocco, simoon; broiling sun; isolation; warming etc. 384.

sun etc. (*luminary*) 423; fire worshipper etc. 991; furnace etc. 386.

geyser, hot spring, volcano.

: Science of heat. pyrology; thermology, -otics; thermometer etc. 389.

V. be -hot etc. *adj.*; glow, incandesce, flush, sweat, swelter, bask, smoke, reek, stew, simmer, seethe, boil, burn, singe, scorch, scald, grill, broil, blaze, flame; smoulder; parch, fume, pant.

heat etc. (*make hot*) 384; thaw, fuse, melt, give.

Adj. hot, heated, warm, mild, genial, tepid, lukewarm, unfrozen; therm-al, -ic; calorific; fervent, -id; ardent; aglow.

sunny, torrid, tropical, estival, canicular; close, sultry, stifling, stuffy, suffocating, oppressive; reeking etc. *v.*; baking etc. 384.

red –, white –, smoking –, bruning etc. *v.* –, piping- hot; like -a furnace, – an oven; hot as -fire, – pepper; hot enough to roast an ox.

fiery; incand-, incal-escent; candent, ebullient, glowing, smoking; on fire; blazing etc. *v.*; in - flames, – a blaze; alight, afire, ablaze; unquenched, -extinguished; smouldering; in a -heat, – glow, – fever, – perspiration, – sweat; sudorific; swelter-ing, -ed; blood-hot, -warm; warm as -a toast, – wool; recalescent, thermogenic, pyrotechnic, feverish, febrile, inflamed.

volcanic, plutonic, igneous; isother-mal, -mic, -al.

Phr. Not a breath of air.

383. Cold.—N. cold, -ness etc. *adj.*; frigidity, gelidity, algidity, inclemency, *fresco*.

winter; depth of –, hard- winter; Siberia, Nova Zembla; Ant-, arctic, North –, South- Pole.

ice; snow, – flake, – crystal – drift; sleet; hail, -stone; rime, frost; hoar –, white –, hard –, sharp- frost; icicle, thick-ribbed ice; fall of snow, snow storm, heavy fall, *avalanche*; ice-berg, -floe; floe, berg; *glacier*; *nevée*, *serac*.

[Sensation of cold] chilliness etc. *adj.*; chill shivering etc. *v.*; goose- skin, -flesh; *rigor*, horripilation, chattering of teeth; frostbite, chilblain.

V. be -cold etc. *adj.*; shiver, starve, quake, shake, tremble, shudder, didder, quiver; perish with cold; chill etc. (*render cold*) 385.

Adj. cold, cool; chill, -y; gelid, frigid, algid; fresh, keen, bleak, raw, inclement, bitter, biting, niveous, cutting, nipping, piercing, pinching; clay-cold; starved etc. (*made cold*) 385; shivering etc. *v.*; aguish, *transi de froid*; frost- bitten, -bound, -nipped.

cold as -a stone, – marble, – lead, – iron, – a frog, – charity, – Christmas; cool as -a cucumber, – custard.

icy, glacial, frosty, freezing, wintry, brumal, hibernal, boreal, arctic, antarctic, polar, Siberian, hyemal; hyperbore-an, -al; ice-bound; frozen out.

un-warmed, -thawed, -heated; isocheimal, -chimenal.

Adv. coldly, bitterly etc. *adj.*; *à pierre fendre*.

384. Calefaction.—N. increase of temperature; heating etc. *v.*; cale-, tepe-, torre-faction; melting, fusion; liquefaction etc. 335; burning etc. *v.*; kindling, combustion; in-, ac-cension; con-, cremation; scorification; cauter-y, -ization; ustulation, calcination; in-, cineration; cupellation; carbonization.

ignition, inflammation, adustion, flagration; de-, con-flagration; empyrosis, incendiarism; arson; *auto da fé*; suttee.

boiling etc. *v.*; coction, ebullition, estuation, elixation, decoction.

furnace etc. 386; blanket, flannel, fur, muffler, wrap; wadding etc. (*lining*) 224; clothing etc. 225.

match etc. (*fuel*) 388; incendiary, pryomaniac; *pétroleur, pétroleuse*; cauterant, caustic, lunar caustic, apozem, moxa.

sunstroke, *coup de soliel*; insolation, sunburn.

pottery, ceramics, crockery, porcelain, china; earthen-, stone-ware; pot, mug, *terra-cotta*, brick, clinker; cinder, ash, *scoriae*; embers, dress, slag, products of combustion, coke, carbon, charcoal.

inflamma-, combusti-bility.

[Transmission of heat] diathermancy, transcalency, diathermy.

V. heat, warm, chafe, stive, foment; make -hot etc. 382; sun oneself, bask in the sun.

fire; set -fire to, – on fire; kindle, enkindle, light, ignite, strike a light; apply the -match, – torch- to; re-kindle, -lume; fan –, add fuel to- the flame; poke –, stir –, blow- the fire; make a bonfire of; burn at the stake.

melt, thaw, fuse; liquefy etc. 335.

burn, inflame, roast, toast, fry, grill, singe, parch, bake, torrefy, scorch; brand, cauterize, sear, burn in; corrode, char, carbonize, calcine, incinerate; smelt, cupel, scorify; reduce to ashes; burn to a cinder; commit –, consign- to the flames.

boil, digest, stew, cook, seethe, scald, parboil, simmer; do to rags.

take –, catch- fire; blaze etc. (*flame*) 382.

Adj. heated etc. *v.*; molten, sodden; réchauffé; heating etc. *v.*

inflammable, burnable, inflammatory, combustible; diatherm-al, -anous; burnt etc. *v.*; volcanic.

386. Refrigeration.—N. refrigeration, infrigidation, reduction of temperature; cooling etc. *v.*; con-gelation, -glaciation; ice etc. 383; solidification etc. (*density*) 321; refrigerator etc. 387.

extincteur; fire, – engine, – extinguisher, – annihilator, – brigade, – man; sprinkler, hose, hydrant, standpipe.
incombusti-bility, -bleness etc. *adj.*
V. cool, fan, refrigerate, refresh, ice; congeal, freeze, glaciate; benumb, starve, pinch, chill, petrify, chill to the marrow, nip, cut, pierce, bite, make one's teeth chatter; damp, slack; quench; put –, stamp- out; extinguish.
go –, burn- out.
Adj. cooled etc. *v.*; frozen out; cooling etc. *v.*; frigorific.
incombustible; un-, unin-flammable; fire-proof.

386. Furnace.—N. furnace, blast furnace, fire-box, stove, incinerator, destructor, crematorium, crematory, kiln, oven, oast-house; hot-, bake-, wash-house; laundry; conservatory; hearth, focus; athanor, hypocaust, reverberatory; volcano; forge, fiery furnace; *tuyère*, brasier, salamander, heater, warming-pan, foot-warmer, hot-water bottle; radiator; boiler, geyser, caldron, seething caldron, pot; urn, kettle; chafing-dish; retort, crucible, alembic, still; saggar.
fire-place, -dog, -irons; hearth, ingle, grate, range, kitchener; kitchen range; oil-, gas-, electric, -cooker, -stove; fireless cooker; fire; galley; ca-, cam-boose; poker, tongs, shovel, hob, trivet; and-, grid-iron; frying-, stew-pan etc.
hot –, Turkish –, Russian –, vapor –, shower –, warm- bath; *calidarium*, *tepidarium*, *sudatorium*, sudatory; *hammam*.

387. Refrigerator.—N. refrigerator, -y; *frigidarium*; cold storage; refrigerating-plant, – machine; ice-house, -pail, -bag, -chest, -pack; cooler, damper; wine-cooler, freezing mixture.

388. Fuel.—N. fuel, firing, combustible, coal, wallsend, anthracite, bituminous coal, slack, culm, cannel coal, lignite, briquette, coke, carbon, charcoal; turf, peat, fire-wood, bobbing, faggot, log, yule log, ember, cinder etc. (*products of combustion*) 384; kindling wood, tinder, touch-wood; fumigator, sulphur, brimstone; incense; port-fire; fire-barrel, -ball, -brand.
fuel oil, gas, gasoline, electricity.
brand, torch, fuse; wick; spill, match, safety match, light, lucifer, congreve, vesuvian, vesta, fusee, locofoco; linstock; illuminant.
candle etc. (*luminary*) 423; oil etc. (*grease*) 356; petrol, gasoline, methylated – spirit; gas, acetylene.
Adj. carbonaceous; combustible, inflammable.
V. stoke, fire, feed, add fuel to the flames.

389. Thermometer.—N. thermo-meter, -scope, -stat, -pile, differential thermometer; pyro-, calorimeter; radio micrometer etc.

390. Taste.—N. taste, flavor, gust, *gusto*, relish, savor; sapor, sapidity; twang, smack, smatch; after-taste, tang.
tasting; de-, gustation.
palate, tongue, tooth, stomach.
V. taste, savor, smatch, smack, flavor, twang; tickle the palate etc. (*savory*) 394; smack the lips.
Adj. sapid, saporific; gusta-ble, -tory; strong; flavored, spiced, savory; palatable etc. 394.

391. Insipidity.—N. insipidity; tastlessness etc. *adj.*
V. be -tasteless etc. *adj.*
Adj. void of -taste etc. 390; insipid; jejune; taste-, gust-, savor-less; ingustible, mawkish, milk and water, weak, stale, flat, vapid, *fade*, wishy-washy, mild; untasted.

392. Pungency.—N. pungency, piquancy, poignancy, *haut-goût*, strong taste, twang, race, tang.
sharpness etc. *adj.*; acrimony, acridity; roughness etc. (*sour*) 397; unsavoriness etc. 395.
niter, saltpeter; mustard, cayenne, caviar; seasoning etc. (*condiment*) 393; brine.
dram, cordial, nip, pick-me-up, bracer, potion.
nicotine, tobacco, snuff, quid; segar; cigar, -ette, gasper, fag; cheroot; weed; fragrant –, Indian-weed; pipe, clay pipe, churchwarden, brier, meerschaum, hookah, hubble-bubble.
V. be -pungent etc. *adj.*; bite the tongue.
render -pungent etc. *adj.*; season, spice, salt, pepper, pickle, brine, devil, curry.
smoke, chew, take snuff.
Adj. pungent, strong; high-, full-flavored; high-tasted, -seasoned; gamy; sharp, stinging, rough, *piquant*, racy; biting, mordant; spicy; seasoned etc. *v.*; hot; – as pepper; peppery, vellicating, escharotic, meracious; acrid, acrimonious, bitter; rough etc. (*sour*) 397; unsavory etc. 395.
salt, saline, brackish, briny; salt as -brine, – a herring, – Lot's wife.

393. Condiment.—N. condiment, flavoring, salt, mustard, pepper, cayenne, curry, seasoning, sauce, spice, cinnamon, chillies, relish, *sauce piquante*, caviare, pot-herbs, onion, garlic, pickle, chutney, nutmeg etc.
V. season etc. (*render pungent*) 392.

394. Savoriness.—N. savoriness etc. *adj.*; relish, zest.
tit-bit, dainty, delicacy, ambrosia, nectar, *bonne bouche*; game, turtle, venison.
V. taste good, be -savory etc. *adj.*; tickle the -palate, – appetite; flatter the palate.
render -palatable etc. *adj.*
relish, like, smack the lips.
Adj. savory, well-tasted, to one's taste, tasty, good, palatable, nice, dainty, delectable; tooth-ful, -some; gustful, appetizing, lickerish, delicate, delicious, exquisite, rich, luscious, ambrosial.
Adv. *per amusare la bocca.*
Phr. *cela se laisse manger*.

395. Unsavoriness.—N. unsavoriness etc. *adj.*; amaritude; acri-mony, -tude; roughness etc. (*sour*) 397; acerbity, austerity; gall and worm-wood, rue, quassia, aloes; sickener.

V. be -unpalatable etc. *adj.*; sicken, disgust, nauseate, pall, turn the stomach.

Adj. un-savory, -palatable, -sweet; ill-flavored, un-appetizing, -eatable, inedible; bitter, – as gall; acrid, acrimonious; rough.

offensive, repulsive, nasty; sickening etc. *v.*; nauseous; loath-, ful-some; unpleasant etc. 830.

396. Sweetness.—N. sweetness, dulcitude, saccharinity.

sugar, cane-, beet-sugar; saccharine, glucose, syrup, treacle, molasses, honey, manna; confection, -ary; sweets, grocery, conserve, preserve, *confiture*, jam, marmalade, julep; sugar-candy, -plum; licorice, liquorice, plum, lollipop, *bon bon*, *jujube*, comfit, sweetmeat, caramel, toffee, butterscotch.

nectar; hydromel, mead, metheglin, honeysuckle, *liqueur*, sweet wine.

pastry, pie, tart, puff, pudding, cake.

dulc-ification, -oration.

V. be sweet etc. *adj.*

render -sweet etc. *adj.*; sugar, saccharize, sweeten; edulcorate; dulc-orate, -ify; candy; mull.

Adj. sweet, sugary; sacchar-ine, -iferous; dulcet, honied, candied, luscious, nectarious, melliferous; sweetened etc. *v.*

sweet as -a nut, – sugar, – honey.

397. Sourness.—N. sourness etc. *adj.*; acid, -ity; acetous fermentation; acerbity.

vinegar, verjuice, crab, alum.

V. be –, turn- -sour etc. *adj.*; set the teeth on edge.

render -sour etc. *adj.*; acid-ify, -ulate.

Adj. sour; acid, -ulous, -ulated; acerb; tart, crabbed; acet-ous, -ose; sour as vinegar, sourish, acescent, sub-acid; styptic, hard, rough; unripe, green.

398. Odor.—N. odor, smell, odorament, scent, effluvium; eman-, exhal-ation; fume, essence, trail, nidor, redolence.

sense of smell; scent; act of -smelling etc. *v.*

V. have an -odor etc. *n.*; smell, – of, – strong of; exhale; give out a -smell etc. *n.*; scent.

smell, scent; snuff, – up; sniff, nose, inhale.

Adj. odor-ous, -iferous; smelling, strong-scented; redolent, graveolent, nidorous, pungent.

[Relating to the sense of smell] olfactory, quick-scented..

399. Inodorousness.—N. inodorousness; absence –, want- of smell.

V. be -inodorous etc. *adj.*; not smell.

deodorize.

Adj. inodor-ous, -ate; scentless; without –, wanting- smell etc. 398.

deodoriz-ed, -ing.

400. Fragrance.—N. fragrance, aroma, redolence, perfume, *bouquet*; sweet smell, aromatic perfume.

perfumery; incense; musk, frankincense; pastil, -le; myrrh, perfumes of Arabia, chypre; otto, ottar, attar; bergamot, balm, civet, *pot-pourri*, pulvil; nosegay, *boutonnière*; scent, -bag; *sachet*, scent-bottle, smelling bottle, *vinaigrette*; toilet water, *eau de Cologne*; thurible, censer, thurification.

perfumer; incense bearer.

V. be -fragrant etc. *adj.*; have a -perfume etc. *n.*; smell sweet, scent, perfume, thurify, embalm.

Adj. fragrant, aromatic, redolent, spicy, balmy, scented; sweet-smelling, -scented; perfum-ed, -atory; thuriferous; fragrant as a rose, muscadine, ambrosial.

401. Fetor.—N. fetor, fetidness; bad etc. *adj.*; -smell, – odor; stench, stink; mephitis, foul –, mal- odor; *empyreuma*; mustiness etc. *adj.*; rancidity; foulness etc. (*uncleanness*) 653.

stoat, polecat, skunk; asafetida; fungus, garlic; stink-pot, -bomb.

V. have a -bad smell etc. *n.*; smell; stink, – in the nostrils, – like a polecat; smell -strong etc. *adj.*; – offensively.

Adj. fetid; strong-smelling; high, bad, strong, fulsome, offensive, noisome, rank, rancid, reasty, tainted, musty, fusty, frouzy; olid, -ous; nidorous; smelling, stinking; putrid etc. 653; suffocating, mephitic; empyreumatic.

402. Sound.—N. sound, noise, strain; accent, twang, intonation, tone, tune; cadence; sonority, sonorousness etc. *adj.*; audibility; resonance etc. 408; voice etc. 580.

[Science of sound] acou-, acu-stics; catacoustics; cataphonics; phon-ics, -etics, -ology, -ography; diacoustics, -phonics.

telephone, phonograph etc. 418.

V. produce sound; sound, make a noise; give out –, emit- sound; phonetize, phonate; resound etc. 408.

Adj. sounding; soniferous; sonorific; resonant, audible, acoustic, auditory, distinct; stertorous; phonic, sonant; phonetic.

403. Silence.—N. silence; stillness etc. (*quiet*) 265; peace, hush, lull, rest; muteness etc. 581; solemn –, awful –, dead –, deathlike-silence.

V. be -silent etc. *adj.*; hold one's tongue etc. (*not speak*) 585.

render -silent etc. *adj.*; silence, still, hush; stifle, muffle, gag, stop; muzzle, put to silence etc. (*render mute*) 581.

Adj. silent; still, -y; calm, quiet; noise-, sound-, speech-less; hushed etc. *v.*; mute etc. 581; aphonic.

soft, solemn, awful, deathlike, silent as the grave; inaudible etc. (*faint*) 405.

Adv. silently etc. *adj.*; *sub silentio*; in perfect silence.

Int. hush! 'sh! silence! soft! whist! tush! chut! tut! *pax!* mum's the word! hold your tongue! shut up! be silent! be quiet! stop that noise! hold your row! dry up! peace, be still!

Phr. one might hear a -feather, – pin- drop.

404. Loudness.—N. loudness, power; loud noise, din; clang, -or; clatter, noise, bombilation, roar, uproar, racket, static, grinders, hubbub, *fracas*, *charivari*, trumpet blast, blare, flourish of trumpets, fanfare, *tintamarre*, peal, swell, blast, alarum, boom; resonance etc. 408.

vociferation; pandemonium, hullaballoo etc. 411; lungs; Stentor; megaphone; siren.

artillery, cannon, gunfire, shellburst, bomb; thunder.

V. be -loud etc. *adj.*; peal, swell, clang, boom, thunder, fulminate, roar; resound etc. 408; speak up, shout etc. (*vociferate*) 411; bellow etc. (*cry as an animal*) 412; give tongue.

rend the -air, – skies; fill the air; din –, ring –, thunder- in the ear; pierce –, split –, rend- the-ears, – head; deafen, stun; *faire le diable a quatre*; make one's windows shake; awaken –, startle- the echoes; make the welkin ring.

Adj. loud, sonorous; high-, big- sounding; blatant; deep, full, powerful, noisy, clangorous, multisonous, *fortisimo*; thundering, deafening etc. *v.*; trumpet-tongued; ear-splitting, -rending, -deafening; piercing; obstreporous, rackety, uproarious; enough to wake the -dead, – seven sleepers.

shrill etc. 410; clamorous etc. (*vociferous*) 411; stentor-ian, -ophonic.

Adv. loudly etc. *adj.*; aloud; at the top of one's voice, lustily, in full cry.

Phr. the air rings with.

405. Faintness.—N. faintness etc. *adj.*; faint sound, whisper, breath; under-tone, -breath; murmur, hum, rustle, buzz, purr; plash; sough, moan, sigh, susurration; tinkle; 'still small voice.'

hoarseness etc. *adj.*; raucity.

silencer, soft pedal, damper, mute, *sourdine*.

V. whisper, breathe, murmur, purl, hum, gurgle, ripple, babble, flow; tinkle; mutter etc. (*speak imperfectly*) 583.

steal on the ear; melt in –, float on- the air.

muffle, mute, deaden, damp, stifle.

Adj. inaudible; scarcely –, just- audible; low, dull; stifled, muffled; hoarse, husky; gentle, soft, faint; floating; purling, flowing etc. *v.*; whispered etc. *v.*; liquid; soothing; dulcet etc. (*melodious*) 413.

Adv. in a whisper, with bated breath, *sotto voce*, between the teeth, aside; *pian-o*, *-issimo*; *à la sourdine*; *con sourdine*; out of earshot, inaudibly etc. *adj.*

406. Snap. [Sudden and violent sounds.]—**N.** snap etc. *v.*; rapping etc. *v.*; de-, crepitation; smack, clap, report; thud; burst, explosion, discharge, detonation, blow-out, back-fire, firing, salvo, volley, pistol-shot.

squib, cracker, gun, rifle, pop-gun.

V. rap, snap, tap, knock; click; clash; crack, -le; crash; pop; slam, bang, clap, thump, plump; toot; back-fire, explode, burst on the ear.

Adj. rapping etc. *v.*

Int. crash! bang!

407. Roll. [Repeated and protracted sounds.]—**N.** roll etc. *v.*; drumming etc. *v.*; tattoo; ding-dong; tantara; rataplan; whirr; rat-a-tat; rub-a-dub; pit-a-pat; quaver, clutter, *charivari*, racket; cuckoo; repetition etc. 104; peal of bells, devil's tattoo; reverberation etc. 408.

drumfire, barrage.

machine gun.

V. roll, drum, rumble, rattle, clatter, rustle, roar, drone, patter, clack.

hum, trill, shake; chime, peal, toll; tick, beat.

drum –, din- in the ear.

Adj. rolling etc. *v.*; monotonous etc. (*repeated*), 104; like a bee in a bottle.

408. Resonance.—N. resonance; ring etc. *v.*; ringing etc. *v.*; tintinnabulation; reflection, reverberation, clangor.

low –, base –, bass –, flat –, grave –, deep –, pedal- note; bass; *basso*, – *profondo*; bari-, bary-tone; *contralto*.

V. re-sound, -verberate, -echo; ring, ding, sing, jingle, gingle, chink, clink; tink, -le; chime; gurgle etc. 405; plash, guggle, echo, ring in the ear.

Adj. resounding etc. *v.*; resonant, tinnient; tintinnabulary; deep-toned, -sounding, -mouthed; hollow, sepulchral; gruff etc. (*harsh*) 410.

408a. Non-resonance.—N. thud, thump, dead sound; non-resonance; muffled drums, cracked bell; silencer, damper; mute, *sourdine*.

V. sound dead; stop –, damp- the -sound, – reverberations; deaden, muffle.

Adj. non-resonant, dead, muted, muffled.

409. Sibilation. [Hissing sounds.]—**N.** sibilation; hiss etc. *v.*; sternutation; high note etc. 410.

goose, serpent, snake.

V. hiss, buzz, whiz, rustle; fizz, -le, sizzle, swish; wheeze, whistle, snuffle; squash; sneeze.

Adj. sibilant; hissing etc. *v.*; wheezy.

410. Stridor. [Harsh sounds.]—**N.** creak etc. *v.*; creaking etc. *v.*; discord etc. 414; stridor; harshness, roughness, sharpness etc. *adj.*; cacophony.

acute –, high- note; *soprano*, treble, tenor, *alto*, falsetto, *voce di testa*; shriek, cry etc. 411.

piccolo, fife, penny -whistle, – trumpet.

V. creak, grate, jar, burr, pipe, twang, jangle, clank, clink; scream etc. (*cry*) 411; yelp etc. (*animal sound*) 412; buzz etc. (*hiss*) 409.

set the teeth on edge, *écorcher les orielles*; pierce –, split- the -ears, – head; offend –, grate upon –, jar upon- the ear.

Adj. creaking etc. *v.*; strident, stridulous, harsh,

coarse, hoarse, horrisonous, raucous, metallic, rough, gruff, grum, sepulchral.

sharp, high, acute, shrill, high-pitched; trumpet-toned; piercing, ear-piercing; cracked; discordant etc. 414; cacophonous.

411. Cry.—N. cry etc. *v.*; voice etc. (*human*) 580; bark etc. (*animal*) 412.

vociferation, outcry, hullaballoo, chorus, clamor, hue and cry, plaint; lungs; stentor.

V. cry, roar, shout, bawl, brawl, halloo, halloa, hail, hoop, whoop, yell, bellow, howl, scream, screech, screak, shriek, shrill, squeak, squeal, squall, whine, whinny, pule, pipe, yaup.

cheer, hurrah; hoot; grumble, maon, groan.

snore, snort; grunt etc. (*animal sounds*) 412.

vociferate; raise –, lift up- the voice; call –, sing –, cry- out; exclaim; rend the air; thunder –, shout- at the -top of one's voice, – pitch of one's breath; *s'égosiller*; strain the -throat, – voice, – lungs; give a -cry etc.

Adj. crying etc. *v.*; clam-ant, -orous; vociferous; stentorian etc. (*loud*) 404; open-mouthed.

412. Ululation. [Animal sounds.]—**N.** cry etc. *v.*; crying etc. *v.*; ululation, latration, belling; reboation; call, note; bark, howl, yelp; twittering, woodnote; insect cry, fritinancy, drone; screech; cuckoo.

V. cry, ululate, howl, roar, bellow, blare, rebellow, bark, yelp; bay, – the moon; yap, growl, yarr, yawl, snarl, howl; grunt, -le; snort, squeak; neigh, bray; mew, mewl; purr, caterwaul, pule; bleat, low, moo; troat, croak, crow, screech, caw, coo, gobble, quack, cackle, gaggle, guggle; chuck, -le; cluck; clack; cheep, chirp, chirrup, twitter, sing, cuckoo; pout, wail, hum, buzz; hiss, blatter; hoot.

Adj. crying etc. *v.*; blatant, latrant; re-, mugient; deep-, full-mouthed.

Adv. in full cry.

413. Melody. Concord.—N. melody, rhythym, measure; rhyme etc. (*poetry*) 597.

pitch, *timbre*, intonation, tone, overtone.

scale, gamut; diapason; diatonic –, chromatic –, enharmonic- scale; key, clef, chords.

modulation, temperament, syncope, syncopation, preparation, suspension, resolution.

staff, stave, line, space, brace; bar, rest; *appogiato*, *-tura*; *acciaccatura*, shake, *arpeggio*.

note, musical note, notes of a sclae; sharp, flat, natural; high note etc. (*shrillness*) 410; low note etc. 408; interval; semitone; second, third, fourth etc.; diatessaron.

breve, semibreve, minim, crotchet, quaver; semi-, demisemi- quaver; sustained note, drone, burden.

tonic; key-, leading-, fundamental-, note; supertonic, mediant, dominant; sub-mediant, -dominant, organ-, pedal-point; octave, tetrachord; major –, minor- -mode, – scale, – key; Doric mode, passage, phrase.

concord, harmony; unison, -ance; chime, homophony; euphon-y, -ism; tonality; consonance; concent; part.

orchestration; harmonization, – phrasing.

[Science of harmony] harmon-y, -ics; thorough-, fundamental- bass; counterpoint; faburden.

piece of music etc. 415; composer, harmonist, contrapuntist.

V. be -harmonious etc. *adj.*; harmonize, chime, symphonize, transpose; put in tune, tune, accord, string; score, arrange, orchestrate.

Adj. harmoni-ous, -cal; in -concord etc. *n.*, – tune, – concert; unisonant, concentual, symphonizing, isotonic, homophonous, assonant, consonant.

measured, rhythmical, diatonic, chromatic, enharmonic.

melodious, musical; tuneful, tunable; sweet, dulcet, canorous; mell-ow, -ifluous; soft; clear, – as a bell; silvery; euphon-ious, -ic, -ical; symphonious; enchanting etc. (*pleasure-giving*) 829; fine-, full-, silver-toned.

Adv. harmoniously etc. *adj.*

414. Discord.—N. discord, -ance; dissonance, cacaphony, caterwauling; harshness etc. 410; consecutive fifths.

[Confused sounds] Babel, pandemonium; Dutch –, cat's- concert; marrow-bones and cleavers.

V. be -discordant etc. *adj.* ; jar etc. (*sound harshly*) 410.

Adj. discordant; dis-, ab-sonant; out of tune, tuneless; un-musical, -tunable; un-, im-melodious; un-, in-harmonious; sing-song; cacophonous; jarring, harsh etc. 410.

415. Music.—N. music, classical –, modern –, descriptive- music; concert, recital; strain, tune, air, *motif*; melody etc. 413; *aria*, *arietta*; piece of music, *sonata*; *rond-o*, *-eau*; *pastorale*, *cavatina*, roulade, *fantasia*, *toccata*, *concerto*, overture, symphony, symphonic poem, tone poem, prelude, voluntary, *intermezzo*, variations, *cadenza*; cadence; fugue, canon, serenade, *nocturne*, *notturno*, rhapsody, romance, *aubade*, dithyramb; opera, operetta; oratorio; composition, movement, stave.

instrumental music; full-, orchestral- score; minstrelsy, tweedledum and tweedledee, band, orchestra etc. 416; concerted piece, *potpourri*, medley, *capriccio*, incidental music; improvisation; peal.

vocal music, vocalism; chaunt, chant; psalm, -ody; hymn; song etc. (*poem*) 597; canticle, canzonet, *cantata*, *bravura*, *coloratura*; lay, ballad, ditty, carol, barcarolle, pastoral, recitative, *recitativo*, *solfeggio*, tonic sol-fa.

Lydian measures; slow -music, – movement; *adagio* etc. *adv.*; minuet; siren strains, soft music, lullaby; *berceuse*, cradle song, dump; dirge etc. (*lament*) 839; pibroch; martial music, march, funeral-, dead- march; dance music; waltz etc. (*dance*) 840; rag-time, syncopation, jazz.

solo, duet, *duo*, *trio*; quartet; quintet, sextet, septet; part song, descant, glee, madrigal, catch, round, chorus, *chorale*; antiphon, -y; accompaniment, second –, alto –, tenor –, bass-part; score, thorough bass; counterpoint.

composer etc. 413; musician etc. 416.
V. compose, perform etc. 416; attune.
Adj. musical; instrumental, orchestral, vocal, choral, lyric, operatic; harmonious etc. 413.
Adv. *adagio*; *largo*, *larghetto*, *andan-te*, *-tino*; *alla capella*; *maestoso*, *moderato*; *allegr-o*, *-etto*; *spiritoso*, *vivace*, *veloce*; *prest-o*, *-issimo*; *pian-o*, *-issimo*, *fort-e*, *-issimo*, *sforzando*; *con brio*; *capriccioso*; *scherz-o*, *-ando*; *legato*, *sostenuto*, *staccato*, *crescendo*, diminuendo, *rallentando*, *affettuoso*, *arioso*; *parlante*, *cantabile*; *obbligato*; *pizzacato*, *tremolo*, *vibrato*.

416. Musician. [Performance of Music.]—**N.** musician, *artiste*, *virtuoso*, performer, player, minstrel; bard etc. (*poet*) 597; instrumental-, organ-, accompan-, pian-, violin-, flaut-, harp-ist; harper, fiddler, fifer, trumpeter, piper, drummer; catgut scraper.

band, orchestra, waits.

vocal-, melod-ist; singer, warbler; songst-, chaunt-er, -ress; *diva*, *cantatrice*, coloratura, soprano, mezzo-soprano, alto, contralto, tenor, baritone, bass, *basso*, *-profundo*.

choir, quire, chorister; chorus, – singer; choral society, festival, *eisteddfod*.

nightingale, philomel, thrush; siren; Orpheus, Apollo, the Muses, Erato, Euterpe, Terpsichore; tuneful -nine, – quire.

composer etc. 413.

performance, virtuosity, execution, touch, expression, solmization.

V. play, pipe, strike –, tune-up, sweep the chords, tickle –, paw- the ivories, vamp, tweedle, fiddle; strike the lyre, beat the drum; blow –, sound –, wind- the horn; grind the organ; touch the -guitar etc. (*instruments*) 417; thrum, strum, twang, drum, beat –, keep- time, conduct.

execute, perform; accompany; sing –, play- a second; compose, write music, set to music, arrange, harmonize, orchestrate.

sing, chaunt, chant, hum, warble, carol, chirp, chirrup, lilt, purl, quaver, trill, shake, twitter, whistle; sol-fa; intone.

have -an ear for music, – a musical ear, – a correct ear, – absolute pitch.

Adj. playing etc. *v.*; musical, lyric.
Adv. *adagio*, *andante* etc. (*music*) 415.

417. Musical Instruments.—N. musical instruments; band; string-, brass-, drum and fife-, military-, bugle-, German-, dance-, jazz-band; orchestra, string quartet; orchestration, orchestrelle.

[Stringed instruments] mono-, poly-chord; harp, lyre, lute, archlute, thearbo; mandol-a, -in, -ine; guitar; *ukulele*; psaltery, zither; bandore, cither, -n; gittern, rebeck, *bandurria*, banjo, zither banjo, *balalaika*, *samisen*; plectrum.

viol, -in, Cremona, Stradivarius; fiddle; kit; *vielle*, *viola*, – *d'amore*, – *di gamba*; tenor, *violoncello*, cello; bass, bass-, bass-viol; double-bass, *contrabasso*, *violone*, hurdy-gurdy; strings, catgut; bow, fiddlestick.

piano, -forte; grand –, concert grand –, baby –, upright –, cottage- piano; pianino, pianette; harpsi-, clavi-, clari-, mani-chord; *clavier*, spinet, virginals; dulcimer, *cymbalo*; Eolian harp; piano-organ, -player, electric piano, player-piano, pianola.

[Wind instruments] organ, church –, pipe –, American- organ; harmoni-um, -phon; accordion, seraphina, concertina; melodeon; barrel- organ; humming top.

flute, fife, piccolo, flageolet, penny-whistle, reed instrument; clari-net, -onet; bass clarionet; saxophone; basset horn, *corno di bassetto*; musette, shawm, oboe, hautboy, *cor Anglais*, *corno Inglese*, bassoon, double bassoon, *contrafagotto*; bag-, union-pipes; ocarina, Pandean pipes; calliope; sirene, pipe, pitch-pipe; sourdet; whistle, catcall.

horn, bugle, key bugle, cornet, *cornet-à-pistons*, cornopean, clarion, trumpet, trombone, ophicleide, serpent; English-, French-, bugle-, sax-, flugel-, alt-, helicon-, post-horn; sackbut, euphonium, bombardon, tuba, bass tuba.

[Vibrating surfaces] cymbal, bell, gong, peal of bells, *carillon*; tambour, -ine; drum, tom-tom, tabor, -ret, -ourine, -orin; *sistrum*, *grand caisse*, bass-, big-, side-, kettle-drum; *tympani*; war drums; tymbal, timbrel, castanet, bones; musical-glasses, -stones; harmonica, sounding– board, rattle; gramophone, phonograph.

[Vibrating bars] reed, tuning-fork, triangle, Jew's harp, musical box, harmonicon, xylophone, marimba, *celeste*.

sord-ine, -et; *sourd-ine, -et;* mute.

418. Hearing. [Sense of sound.]—**N.** hearing etc. *v.*; audition, auscultation; eavesdropping; audibility; acoustics etc. 402.

acute –, nice –, delicate –, quick –, sharp –, correct –, musical -ear; ear for music.

ear, auricle, lug, acoustic organs, auditory apparatus, ear-drum, tympanum; ear-, speaking-trumpet, megaphone; telephone, radiophone, stethoscope, phonograph, gramophone, microphone.

hearer, auditor, listener, eavesdropper; audi-tory, -ence.

V. hear, overhear; hark, -en; list, -en; give –, lend –, bend- an ear; give attention; catch a sound, prick up one's ears; give -a hearing, – audience -to.

hang upon the lips of, be all ear, listen with both ears, monitor.

become audible; meet –, fall upon –, catch –, reach- the ear; be heard; ring in the ear etc. (*resound*) 408.

Adj. hearing etc. *v.*; auditory, auricular, aural, auditive, acoustic.

Adv. *arrectis auribis*.

Int. hark, – ye! hear! list, -en! *Oyez!* attention! lend me your ears!

419. Deafness.—N. deafness, hardness of hearing, surdity; inaudibility.

V. be -deaf etc. *adj.*; have no ear; shut –, stop –, close- one's ears; turn a deaf ear to.

render deaf, stun, deafen.

Adj. deaf, earless, surd; hard –, dull- of hearing; deaf-mute, stunned, deafened; stone deaf; deaf as -a post, – an adder, – a beetle, – a trunk-maker.

inaudible etc. 405; out of hearing.

420. Light.—N. light, ray, beam, stream, gleam, streak, pencil; sun-, moon-beam; dawn, aurora.

day; sunshine; light of -day, – heaven; sun etc. (*luminary*) 432, day-, broad day-, noontide- light; noon-tide, -day; glare.

glow etc. *v.*; afterglow, sunset; glimmering etc. *v.*; glint; play –, flood- of light; phosphorescence, flush, halo, glory, nimbus, aureole, *aureola.*

spark, *scintilla*; *facula*; sparkling etc. *v.*; emication, scintillation, flash, blaze, coruscation, fulguration; flame etc. (*fire*) 382; lightning, *ignis fatuus*, etc. (*luminary*) 423, radio-activity.

luster, sheen, shimmer, reflection; gloss, tinsel, spangle, brightness, brilliancy, splendor; ef-, refulgence; ful-gor, -gidity; dazzlement, resplendence, transplendency; luminousness etc. *adj.*; luminosity; lucidity; renitency; radi-ance, -ation; irradiation, illumination, phosphorescence, luminescence.

radiation, radiant heat, infra-red rays, visible radiation, ultra-violet –, actinic- rays, actinism; X –, Roentgen- rays; phot-, heli-ography; optical instruments etc. 445.

[Science of light] optics; photo-logy, -metry; di-, cat-optrics.

[Distribution of light] *chiaroscuro*, *clair-obscur*, clear obscure, breadth, light and shade, black and white, tonality, half-tone, mezzotint.

reflection, refraction, dispersion, double refraction, polarization, diffraction, interference.

illuminant etc. 423.

V. shine, glow, glitter, phosphoresce; glis-ter, -ten; twinkle, gleam; flare, – up; glare, beam, shimmer, glimmer, flicker, sparkle, scintillate, coruscate, flash, fulgurate, blaze; be -bright etc. *adj.*; reflect light, daze, dazzle, bedazzle, raidate, shoot out beams.

clear up, brighten.

lighten, enlighten; light, – up; irradiate, shine upon; give –, hang out- a light; cast –, throw –, shed- -luster, – light- upon; illum-e, -ine, -inate; relume, strike a light; kindle etc. (*set fire to*) 384.

Adj. shining etc. *v.*; lumin-ous, -iferous; luc-id, -ent, -ulent, -ific, -iferous; illuminating, light, -some; bright, vivid, splendent, nitid, lustrous, shiny, brilliant, beamy, scintillant, radiant, lambent; sheen, -y; glossy, burnished, glassy, sunny, orient, meridian; noon-day, -tide; cloudless, clear; unclouded, -obscured.

garish; re-, tran-splendent; re-, effulgent; ful-gid, -gent; relucent, splendid, blazing, in a blaze, ablaze, rutilant, meteoric, phosphorescent; aglow.

bright as silver; light –, bright- as -day, – noonday, – the sun at noonday.

optical, actinic; photo-genic, -graphic; heliographic, radioactive.

421. Darkness.—N. darkness etc. *adj.*; blackness etc. (*dark color*) 431; obscurity, gloom, murk; dusk etc. (*dimness*) 422;, tenebrosity, umbrageousness.

Cimmerian –, Stygian –, Egyptian- darkness; night; midnight; dead of –, witching time of- night; blind man's holiday; darkness -visible; – that can be felt; palpable, obscure; Erebus.

shade, shadow, umbra, penumbra; sciagraphy; *silhouette*; radiograph, skiagraph.

obscuration; ad-, ob-umbration; obtenebration, offuscation, caligation; extinction; eclipse, total eclipse; gathering of the clouds.

shading; distribution of shade; *chiaroscuro* etc. (*light*) 420.

noctivagation, noctograph, noctuary.

obscurantist.

V. be -dark etc. *adj.*

darken, obscure, shade; dim; tone down, lower; over-cast, -shadow; cloud, eclipse; ob-, of-fuscate; ob-, ad-umbrate, cast into the shade; be-cloud, -dim, -darken; cast –, throw –, spread- a -shade, – shadow, – gloom.

extinguish; put –, blow –, snuff- out; doubt.

Adj. dark, -some, -ling; obscure, tenebrous, tenebrious, sombrous, pitch dark, pitchy, caliginous; black etc. (*in color*) 431.

sunless, lightless etc. (*see* sun, light etc. 423); somber, dusky; unilluminated etc. (*see* illuminate etc. 420); nocturnal; dingy, lurid, gloomy; murk-y, -some; shady, umbrageous; overcast etc. (*dim*) 422; cloudy etc. (*opaque*) 426; darkened etc. *v.*

dark as -pitch, – a pit, – Erebus.

benighted; noctivag-ant, -ous.

Adv. in the -dark, – shade; at night.

422. Dimness.—N. dimness etc. *adj.*; darkness etc. 421; paleness etc. (*light color*) 429.

half-light, *demi-jour*; partial -shadow, – eclipse; shadow of a shade; glimmer, -ing; nebulosity; cloud etc. 353; eclipse.

aurora, dusk, twilight, gloaming, blind man's holiday, shades of evening, crepuscule, cockshut time; break of day, daybreak, dawn.

moon-light, -beam, -shine; star- owl's-, candle-, rush-, fire-light; farthing candle.

V. be –, grow- -dim etc. *adj.*; flicker, twinkle, glimmer; loom, lower; fade; darken; pale, – its ineffectual fire.

render -dim etc. *adj.*; dim, bedim, obscure.

Adj. dim, dull, lack-luster, dingy, darkish, shorn of its beams; dark 421.

faint, shadowed forth; glassy; bleary; cloudy; misty etc. (*opaque*) 426; muggy, fuliginous; nebulous, -ar; obnubilated, overcast, crepuscular, twilight, muddy, lurid, leaden, dun, dirty; looming etc. *v.*

pale etc. (*colorless*) 429; confused etc. (*invisible*) 447.

423. Luminary. [Source of light.]—**N.** luminary; light etc. 420; flame etc. (*fire*) 382.

spark, *scintilla*; phosphorescence.

sun, orb of day, day star, Phoebus, Apollo, Helios, Phaethon, Hyperion, Ra, Aurora; star, orb, meteor; falling –, shooting- star; blazing –, dog-star; Sirius, canicula, Aldebaran; morning star, Lucifer, Phosphor, evening star; Hesperus, Venus, planet, moon etc. 318; constellation, galaxy; northern light, *aurora -borealis*, – *australis*, zodiacal light; mock sun, parhelion.

lightning; fork –, sheet –, summer- lightning, St. Elmo's fire; phosphorus; *ignis fatuus*; Jack o' – Friar's- lantern; Will o' the wisp, fire-drake, *Fata Morgana.*

glow-worm, fire-fly.

radium, luminous paint.

[Artificial light] gas; gas –, lime –, electric –, head –, search –, spot –, flash –, flood –, footlight; lamp, oil –, gas –, arc –, incandescent-lamp; flare; lant-ern, -horn; dark lantern, bull's eye, projector; candle, *bougie*, tallow –, wax- candle; dip, farthing dip; taper, rush-light; oil etc. (*grease*) 356; wick, burner; Argand, moderator, duplex; torch, *flambeau*, link, brand; cresset; gase-, chande-, electro-lier; candelabrum, *girandole*, sconce, luster, candle-stick.

firework, fizgig; pyrotechnics; Roman candle, Very light, star shell, parachute light; rocket, lighthouse etc. (*signal*) 550.

V. illuminate etc. (*light*) 420.

Adj. self-luminous, incandescent; phosphor-ic, -escent; luminescent, fluorescent, radiant etc. (*light*) 420.

424. Shade.—N. shade; awning etc. (*cover*) 223; parasol, sunshade, umbrella; screen, curtain, shutter, blind, gauze, veil, mantle, mask; cloud, mist, gathering of clouds; smoke screen; smoked glasses, colored spectacles; blinkers, blinders.

umbrage, glade; shadow etc. 421.

V. draw a curtain; put up –, close- a shutter; veil etc. *v.*; cast a shadow etc. (*darken*) 421; screen, obstruct the view.

Adj. shady, umbrageous, bowery.

425. Transparency.—N. transparen-ce, -cy; translucen-ce, -cy; diaphaneity; luc-, pelluc-, limpidity.

transparent medium, glass, crystal, mica; lymph, water.

v. be -transparent etc. *adj.*; transmit light.

Adj. transparent, pellucid, lucid, diaphanous; trans-, tra-lucent; limpid, clear, serene, crystalline, clear as crystal, vitreous, transpicuous, glassy, hyaline.

426. Opacity.—N. opacity; opaqueness etc. *adj.*

film; cloud etc. 353.

V. be -opaque etc. *adj.*; obstruct the passage of light; ob-, of-fuscate.

Adj. opaque, impervious to light.

dim etc. 422; turbid, thick, muddy, opacous, obfuscated, fuliginous, cloudy, hazy, foggy, vaporous, nubiferous, muggy.

smoky, fumid, murky, dirty.

427. Semitransparency.—N. semitransparency, opalescence, milkiness, pearliness; gauze, muslin; film; mist etc. (*cloud*) 353; frosted glass.

Adj. semi-transparent, -pellucid, -diaphanous, -opacous, -opaque; opal-escent, -ine; pearly, milky, frosted, mat; misty.

428. Color.—N. color, hue, tint, tinge, dye, complexion, shade, tincture, cast, livery, coloration, chromatism, glow, flush; tone, key.

pure –, positive –, primary –, primitive –, complementary- color; three primaries; spectrum, chromatic dispersion; broken –, secondary –, tertiary- color.

local color, coloring, keeping, tone, value, aerial perspective.

[Science of color] chromatics, spectrum analysis; prism, spectroscope.

pigment, coloring matter, paint, dye, wash, distemper, stain; medium; mordant; oil-paint etc. (*painting*) 556.

V. color, dye, tinge, stain, tint, tinct, tone, paint, wash, ingrain, grain, illuminate, emblazon, imbue; paint etc. (*fine art*) 556; daub.

Adj. colored etc. *v.*; colorific, tingent, tinctorial; chormatic, prismatic; full-, high-, deep-colored; doubly-dyed; polychromatic.

bright, vivid, intense, deep; fresh, unfaded; rich, gorgeous; highly colored; gay; variegated etc. 440.

gaudy, florid; garish; showy, flaunting, flashy; raw, crude; glaring, flaring; discordant, inharmonious.

mellow, harmonious, pearly, sweet, delicate, tender, refined.

429. Achromatism. [Absence of color.]—**N.** achromatism; de-, dis-coloration; pall-or, -idity; paleness etc. *adj.*; etoilation; neutral tint, monochrome, black-and-white.

V. lose -color etc. 428; fade, fly, go; become -colorless etc. *adj.*; turn pale, pale, whiten.

deprive of color, decolorize, bleach, tarnish, achromatize, blanch, etiolate, wash out, tone down.

Adj. uncolored etc. (*see* color etc. 428); colorless, achromatic, hueless, pale, pallid; pale-, tallow-faced; faint, dull, cold, muddy, leaden, dun, wan, sallow, dead, dingy, ashy, ashen, ghastly, cadaverous, glassy, lack-luster; discolored etc. *v.*

light-colored, fair, *blond*; white etc. 430.

pale as -death, – ashes, – a witch, – a ghost, – a corpse.

430. Whiteness.—N. whiteness etc. *adj.*; argent.

albification, albescence, albinism, etiolation.

snow, paper, chalk, milk, lily, ivory, silver, alabaster; white lead, chinese –, flake –, ivory –, zinc- white, white-wash, -ning, whiting.

V. be -white etc. *adj.*

render -white etc. *adj.*; whiten- bleach, blanch, etiolate, whitewash, silver, frost.

Adj. white; milky, milk-, snow-white; snowy, niveous, candid, chalky; hoar, -y; frosted, silvery; argent, -ine; canescent.

whitish, creamy, pearly, ivory, fair, *blond*, ash-blond, platinum blond; blanched etc. *v.*; high in tone, light.

white as -a sheet, – driven snow, – a lily, – silver; like -ivory etc. *n.*

431. Blackness.—N. blackness etc. *adj.*; darkness etc. (*want of light*) 421; swarthness, lividity, dark color, tone, color; *chiaroscuro* etc. 420.

nigrification, infuscation, denigration.

jet, ink, ebony, coal, pitch, soot, smudge, charcoal, sloe, raven, crow; black.

[Pigments] lamp –, ivory –, blue-black; writing –, printing –, printer's –, Indian- ink.

V. be -black etc. *adj.*

render -black etc. *adj.*; blacken, infuscate, denigrate; blot, -ch; smutch; smirch; darken etc. 421.

Adj. black, sable, swarthy, somber, dark, inky, ebon, atramentous, jetty; coal-, jet-black; fuliginous, pitchy, sooty, swart, dusky, dingy, murky, low-toned, low in tone; of the deepest dye.

black as -jet etc. *n.*, – my hat, – a shoe, – a tinker's pot, – November, – thunder, – midnight; nocturnal etc. (*dark*) 421; nigrescent; gray etc. 432; obscure etc. 421.

Adv. in mourning.

432. Gray.—N. gray etc. *adj.*; neutral tint, silver, pepper and salt, *chiaroscuro*, *grisaille*, grayness.

[Pigments] Payne's gray; black etc. 431.

Adj. gray, grey; steel –, iron- gray, dun, drab, dingy, leaden, livid, somber, sad, pearly; silver, -y, -ed; ash-en, -y; ciner-eous, -itious; grizzl-y, -ed; dove-, slate-, stone-, mouse-, ash-colored; mole; cool.

433. Brown.—N. brown etc. *adj.*

[Pigments] bister, ocher, sepia, Vandyke brown.

Adj. brown, adust, bay, dapple, auburn, chestnut, nutbrown, cinnamon, hazel, fawn, puce, *écru*, russet, tawny, fuscous, chocolate, maroon, foxy, tan, brunette, whitey-brown; snuff-, liver-colored; brown as -a berry, – mahogany; reddish brown; copper-, rust- colored; henna, bronze, khaki; russet, roan, sorrel.

sub-burnt; tanned etc. *v.*

V. render -brown etc. *adj.*; tan, embrown, bronze.

434. Redness.—N. red, scarlet, vermilion, cardinal, Post Office, red, carmine, crimson, pink, lake, *cerise*, cherry red, maroon, carnation, *couleur de rose*, *rose du Barry*; magenta, damask; flesh -color, – tint; color; fresh –, high- color; warmth; gules.

ruby, garnet, carbuncle; rose; rust, iron-mold.

[Dyes and pigments] cinnabar, cochineal; fuchsine; ruddle, madder, redlead; light –, Venetian- red; red ink, annotto.

redness etc. *adj.*; rub-escence, -icundity, -ification; erubescence, blush.

V. be –, become- -red etc. *adj.*; blush, flush, color up, mantle, redden.

render- red etc. *adj.*; redden, rouge; rub-ify, -ricate; incarnadine; ruddle.

Adj. red etc. *n.*; -dish; rufous, ruddy, florid, incarnadine, sanguine, bloody, gory; ros-y, -eate; blowz-y, -ed; brunt; rubi-cund, -form; lurid, stammel, blood-red; russet, murrey, carroty, sorrel, lateritious.

rose-, ruby-, cherry-, claret-, wine-, plum-, flame-, flesh-, peach-, salmon-, brick-, brickdust-colored, reddish brown etc. 433.

red as -fire, – blood, – scarlet, – a turkeycock, – a lobster; warm, hot; foxy.

435. Greenness.—N. green etc. *adj.*; blue and yellow; vert.

emerald, verd antique, verdigris, malachite, beryl, aquamarine, reseda.

[Pigments] *terre verte*, verditer, bice, chlorophyl.

greenness, verdure, verdancy; viridity, -escence.

Adj. green, verdant; glaucous, olive; porraceous; green as grass.

emerald –, pea –, grass –, apple –, sea –, olive –, bottle –, leaf- green.

greenish; vir-ent, -escent.

436. Yellowness.—N. yellow etc. *adj.*; or.

[Pigments] gamboge; cadmium –, chrome –, Indian –, lemon- yellow; orpiment, yellow ocher, Claude tint, aureolin.

crocus, saffron, topaz, gold.

jaundice; London fog; yellowness etc. *adj.*

Adj. yellow, aureate, gold, golden, gilt, gilded, flavous, citrine, fallow; fulv-ous, -id; sallow, luteous, fawny, creamy, sandy; xanth-ic, -ous; jaundiced.

gold-, citron-, saffron-, lemon-, sulphur-, amber- straw-, primrose-, cream-colored; flazen, yellowish, buff.

yellow as a -quince, – guinea, – crow's foot.

437. Purple.—N. purple etc. *adj.*; blue and red, bishop's purple; aniline dyes, gridelin, amethyst; purpure.

livid-ness, -ity.

V. empurple.

Adj. purple, violet, plum-colored, lavender, lilac, puce, *mauve*; livid.

438. Blueness.—N. blue etc. *adj.*; garter-blue; watchet.

[Pigments] ultramarine, smalt, cobalt, cyanogen; Prussian –, syenite- blue; bice, indigo, woad.

lapis lazuli, sapphire, turquoise.

blue-, bluish-ness; bloom

Adj. blue, azure, cerulean; sky-blue, -colored, -dyed; navy-blue, aquamarine, electric blue, royal blue, cyanic; bluish; atmospheric, retiring; cold.

439. Orange.—N. orange, red and yellow; gold; or; flame etc. color, *adj.*

[Pigments] ochre, Mars orange, cadmium.

V. gild, warm.

Adj. orange; ocherous; orange-, gold-, flame-, copper-, brass-, apricot-colored; warm, hot, glowing.

440. Variegation.—N. variegation; di-, tri-chromism; iridescence, irisation, play of colors, polychrome, maculation, spottiness, striae.

spectrum, rainbow, iris, tulip, peacock, chameleon, butterfly, tortoiseshell; mackerel, – sky; zebra, leopard, mother-of-pearl, nacre, opal, marble, batik.

check, plaid, tartan, patchwork; mar-, parquetry; mosiac, *tesserae*, tesselation, chess-board, checkers, chequers; harlequin; Joseph's coat; tricolor; patches, bands, stripes, spots etc of color.

V. be -variegated etc. *adj.*; variegate, stripe, streak, checker, chequer; be-, speckle, fleck; be-, sprinkle; stipple, maculate, dot, bespot; tattoo, inlay, tesselate, damascene; embroider, braid, quilt.

Adj. variegated etc. *v.*; many-colored, -hued; divers-, parti-colored; di-, poly-chromatic; bi-, tri-, versi-color; of all -the colors of the rainbow, – manner of colors; kaleidoscopic.

iridescent; opal-ine, -escent; prismatic, nacreous, pearly, shot, *gorge de pigeon*, *chatoyant*, irisated.

pied, piebald, skewbald; motley; mottled, marbled; pepper and salt, paned, dappled, clouded, cymophanous.

mosiac, tesselated, chequered, plaid; tortoiseshell etc. *n.*

spott-ed, -y; punctuated, powdered; speckled etc. *v.*; freckled, fleabitten, studded; fleck-ed, -ered; striated, barred, veined; brind-ed, -led; tabby; watered; grizzled; listed; embroidered etc. *v.*; daedal.

441. Vision.—N. vision, sight, optics, eye-sight.

view, look, espial, glance, ken, *coup d'oeil*; glimpse, peep, glint; gaze, stare, leer; perlustration, contemplation; conspect-ion, -uity; regard, survey; in-, intro-spection; *reconnaissance*, speculation, watch, espionage, *espionnage*, autopsy; ocular -inspection, – demonstration; sight-seeing.

macrography, micrography.

point of view; view-, stand- point; gazebo, loophole, *belvedere*, watchtower.

field of view; theater, amphitheater, arena, vista, horizon; commanding –, bird's eye –, panoramic- view; periscope.

visual organ, organ of vision; eye; naked –, unassisted- eye; eye-ball, retina, pupil, iris, cornea, white; optics, orbs; saucer –, goggle –, gooseberry-eyes.

short sight etc. 443; clear –, sharp –, quick –, eagle –, piercing-, –, penetrating- -sight, – glance, – eye; perspicacity, discernment; catopsis.

eagle, hawk; cat, lynx; Argus.

evil eye; basilisk, cockatrice.

spectacles, telescope etc. 445.

V. see, behold, discern, perceive, have in sight, descry, sight, make out, discover, distinguish, recognize, spy, espy, ken; get –, have –, catch- a -sight, – glimpse- of; command of view of; witness, contemplate, speculate; cast –, set- the eyes on; be a -spectator etc. 444- of; look on etc. (*be present*) 186; see sights etc. (*curiosity*) 445; see at a glance etc. (*intelligence*) 498.

look, view, eye; lift up the eyes, open one's eye; look -at, – on, – upon, – over, – about one, – round; survey, scan, inspect; run the eye -over, – through; reconnoiter, glance -round, – on, – over; turn –, bend- one's looks upon; direct the eyes to, turn the eyes on, cast a glance, make eyes at.

observe etc. (*attend to*) 457; watch etc. (*care*) 459; see with one's own eyes; watch for etc. (*expect*) 507; peek, peep, peer, pry, take a peep; play at bo-peep.

look -full in the face, – hard at, – intently; strain one's eyes; fix –, rivet- the eyes upon; stare, gaze; pore over, gloat -over, – on; leer, ogle, glare; goggle; cock the eye, squint, gloat, look askance; give the glad eye.

Adj. seeing etc. *v.*; visual, ocular, -al; ophthalmic.

far-, clear-sighted etc. *n.*; eagle-, hawk-, lynx-, keen-, Argus-eyed.

visible etc. 446.

Adv. visibly etc. 446; in sight of, with one's eyes open.

at -sight, – first sight, – a glance, – the first blush; *primâ facie*.

Int. look! etc. (*attention*) 457.

Phr. the scales falling from one's eyes.

442. Blindness.—N. blindness, anopsia, cecity, excecation, *amaurosis*, cataract, ablepsy, prestriction; dim-sightedness etc. 443.

V. be -blind etc. *adj.*; not see; lose sight of; have the eyes bandaged; grope in the dark.

not look; close –, shut –, turn away –, avert- the eyes; look another way; wink etc. (*limited vision*) 443; shut the eyes –, be blind- to; wink –, blink- at.

render -blind etc. *adj.*; blind, -fold; hoodwink, dazzle; put one's eyes out; throw dust into one's eyes; *jeter de la poudre aux yeux*; screen from sight etc. (*hide*) 528.

Adj. blind; eye-, sight-, vision-less; dark; stone-, sand-, stark-blind; undiscerning; dim-sighted etc. 443.

blind as -a bat, – a buzzard, – a beetle, – a mole, – an owl; wall-eyed.

blinded etc. *v.*

Adv. blind-ly, -fold; darkly.

443. Dim-sightedness. [Imperfect vision.] [Fallacies of vision.]**—N.** dim –, dull –, half –, short –, near –, long –, double –, astigmatic –, failing- sight; dim etc -sightedness; snow blindness; purblindness, lippitude; my-, presby-opia; confusion of vision; astigmatism; nystagmus; color-blindness, dichromism, chromato-pseudo-blepsis, Daltonism; nyctalopy; *strabismus*, strabism, squint, cast in the eye, swivel eye, goggle eyes; obliquity of vision.

winking etc. *v.*; nictitation; blinkard, albino.

dizziness, swimming, scotomy; cataract; ophthalmia.

[Limitation of vision] eye shade, blinker, blinder; screen etc. (*hider*) 530.

[Fallacies of vision] *deceptio visûs*; refraction, distortion, illustion, false light, *anamorphosis*, virtual image, *spectrum*, *mirage*, looming, phasma; phant-asm, -asma, -om; vision; specter, apparition, ghost; *ignis fatuus* etc. (*luminary*) 423; specter of the Brocken; magic mirror; magic lantern etc. (*show*) 448; mirror, lens etc. (*instrument*) 445.

V. be -dim-sighted etc. *n.*; see double; have a -mote in the eye, – mist before the eyes, – film over the eyes; see through a -prism, – glass darkly; wink, blink, nictitate; squint; look ask-ant, -ance; screw up the eyes, glare, glower.

dazzle, glare, blur, swim, loom.

Adj. dim-sighted etc. *n.*; my-, presby-opic; astigmatic; moon-, mope-, blear-, goggle-, gooseberry-, one-eyed; blind of one eye, monoculous; half-, pur-, color-blind; dichromatic.

blind as a bat etc. (*blind*) 442; winking etc. *v.*

444. Spectator.—N. spectator, beholder, observer, inspector, viewer, looker-on, onlooker, witness, eye-witness, bystander, passer by; sight-seer.

spy, scout; sentinel etc. (*warning*) 668.

v. witness, behold etc. (*see*) 441; look on etc. (*be present*) 186.

445. Optical Instruments.—N. optical instruments; lens, meniscus, magnifier, reading –, burning- glass; micro-, mega-, teino-scope; spectacles, glasses, barnacles, goggles, giglamps, eyeglass, *pince-nez*, monocle; periscopic lens; telescope, glass, lorgnette, binocular; spy-, opera-, field-glass, periscope, range finder.

mirror, reflector, speculum; looking-, pier-, cheval-, hand-glass.

prism; camera, *camera-lucida*, *-obscura*; projector, stereopticon, magic lantern etc. (*show*) 448; chro-, thau-matrope; stereo-, pseudo-, poly-, kaleido-scope.

photo-, opto-, erio-, actino-, luci-, radio-, spectro-meter; polari-, polemo-, spectro-scope, diffraction grating.

optics, optician, optometry, optometrist; microscop-y, -ist; photometry, photography; photographer.

446. Visibility.—N. visibility, perceptibility; conspicuousness, distinctness etc. *adj.*; conspicuity; appearance etc. 448; exposure; manifestation etc. 525; ocular -proof, – evidence, – demonstration; field of view etc. (*vision*) 441.

V. be –, become- -visible etc. *adj.*; appear, emerge, open to the view; meet –, catch- the eye; present –, show –, manifest –, produce –, discover –, reveal –, expose –, betray- itself; stand -forth, – out; show; arise; peep –, peer –, crop- out; start –, spring –, show –, turn –, crop- up; glimmer, glitter, glow, loom; glare; burst forth, scintillate; burst upon the -view, – sight; heave in sight; come -in sight, – into view, – out, – forth, – forward; see the light of day; break through the clouds; make its appearance, show its face, materialize, appear to one's eyes, come upon the stage, enter; float before the eyes, speak for itself. etc. (*manifest*) 525; attract the attention etc. 457; reappear; live in a glass house.

expose to view etc. 525.

Adj. visible, perceptible, perceivable, discernible, apparent; in -view, – full view, – sight; exposed to view, *en évidence*; unclouded.

obvious etc. (*manifest*) 525; plain, clear, distinct, definite; well-defined, -marked; in focus; recognizable, palpable, autoptical; glaring, staring, conspicuous; stereoscopic; in -bold, – strong, – high- relief.

periscopic, panoramic.

before –, under- one's eyes; before one, *à vue d'oeil*, in one's eye, *oculis subjecta fidelibus.*

Adv. visibly etc. *adj.*; in sight of; before one's eyes etc. *adj.*; *veluti in speculum.*

447. Invisibility.—N. invisibility, nonappearance, imperceptibility; indistinctness etc. *adj.*; mystery, delitescence.

concealment etc. 528; latency etc. 526.

V. be -invisible etc. *adj.*; be hidden etc. (*hide*) 528; lurk etc. (*lie hidden*) 526; escape notice.

render -invisible etc. *adj.*; conceal etc. 528; put out of sight.

not see etc. (*be blind*) 442; lose sight of.

Adj. invisible, imperceptible; un-, in-discernible; un-, non-apparent; out of –, not in- sight; *à perte de vue*; behind the -scenes, – curtain; view-, sightless; in-, un-conspicuous; unseen etc. (*see* see etc. 441); covert etc. (*latent*) 526; eclipsed, under an eclipse.

dim etc. (*faint*) 422; mysterious, dark, obscure, confused; indistin-ct, -guishable; shadowy, indefinite, undefined; ill-defined, -marked; blurred, fuzzy, out of focus; misty etc. (*opaque*) 426; veiled etc. (*concealed*) 528; delitescent.

448. Appearance.—N. appearance, phenomenon, sight, spectacle, show, premonstration, scene, species, view, *coup d'oeil*; look-out, out-look, prospect, vista, perspective, bird's-eye view, scenery, landscape, picture, *tableau*; display, exposure, *mise en scène*; scenery, *décor*; rising of the curtain.

phant-asm, -om etc. (*fallacy of vision*) 443.

pageant, *spectacle*; peep-, raree-, gallanty-show; *ombres chinoises*; projector, optical –, magic-lantern, phantasmagoria, dissolving views; cinema, -tograph; bio-scope, -graph; moving pictures, movies, film, screen etc.; pan-, di-, cosm-, georama; *coup –*, *jeu- de théâtre*; pageantry etc. (*ostentation*) 882; insignia etc. (*indication*) 550.

aspect, phase, *phasis*, seeming; shape etc. (*form*) 240; guise, look, complexion, color, image, mien, air, cast, carriage, port, demeanor; presence, expression, first blush, face of the thing; point of view, light.

lineament, feature, trait, lines; out-line, -side; contour, *silhouette*, face, countenance, physiognomy, visage, phiz, mug, cast of countenance, profile, *tournure*, cut of one's jib, metoposcopy; outside etc. 220.

V. appear; be –, become- visible etc. 446; seem, look, show; present –, wear –, carry –, have –, bear –, exhibit –, take –, take on –, assume- the -appearance, – semblance- of; look like; cut a figure, figure; present to the view; show etc. (*make manifest*) 525.

Adj. apparent, seeming, ostensible; on view.

Adv. apparently; to all -seeming, – appearance; ostensibly, seemingly, as it seems, on the face of it, *primâ facie*; at the first blush, at first sight; in the eyes of; to the eye.

449. Disappearance.—N. disappearance, evanescence, eclipse, occultation.

departure etc. 293; exit, vanishing point; dissolving views.

V. disappear, vanish, dissolve, fade, melt away, pass, go, avaunt; be -gone etc. *adj.*; leave -no trace, – 'not a rack behind;' go off the stage etc. (*depart*) 293; suffer –, undergo- an eclipse; be lost to –, retire from- -sight, – view.

lose sight of.

efface etc. 552.

Adj. disappearing etc. *v.*; evanescent; missing, lost; lost to -sight, – view; gone; *spurlos versenki.*

Int. vanish! disappear! avaunt! etc. (*ejection*) 297.

450. Intellect.—N. intellect, mind, understanding, reason, thinking principle; rationality; cogitative –, cognitive –, intellectual- faculties; faculties, senses, consciousness, observation, percipience, apperception, mentality, intelligence, intellection, intuition, association of ideas, instinct, flair, conception, judgment, wits, parts, capacity, intellectuality, reasoning power, brains, genius; wit etc. 498; ability etc. (*skill*) 698; wisdom etc. 498.

soul, spirit, ghost, inner man, heart, breast, bosom, ***penetralia mentis, divina particula aurae***, heart's core; ego, psyche, pneuma, subconsciousness, subconscious, subliminal self; dual personality.

organ –, seat- of thought; *sensorium*, sensory, brain, gray matter; head, -piece; pate, noddle, skull, scull, *pericranium*, *cerebrum*, *cranium*, brain-pan, -box; sconce, upper story.

[Science of mind] metaphysics; psychics, psycho-logy, -metry, -genesis, -analysis, -physics, psychi-atry, -cal research, thought reading etc. 992; ideology; mental –, moral- philosophy; philosophy of the mind; pneumat-, phren-ology; no –, craniology, -scopy.

ideal-ity, -ism; transcendental-, spiritual-ism; immateriality etc. 317.

metaphysician, psychologist etc.

V. note, notice, mark; take -notice, – cognizance- of; be -aware, – conscious- of; realize; appreciate; ruminate etc. (*think*) 451; fancy etc. (*imagine*) 515; conceive, reason, understand.

Adj. [Relating to intellect] intellectual, mental, rational, subjective, metaphysical, nooscopic, spiritual; ghostly; psych-ical, -ological; cerebral.

immaterial etc. 317; endowed with reason.

Adv. *in petto.*

450a. Absence or want **of Intellect.—N.** absence –, want- of -intellect etc. 450; imbecility etc. 499; brutality; brute -instinct, – force.

Adj. unendowed with reason.

451. Thought.—N. thought; exercitation –, exercise- of the intellect; reflection, cogitation, consideration, meditation, study, lucubration, speculation, deliberation, pondering; head-, brain-work; cerebration; mentation, deep reflection; close study, application etc. (*attention*) 457.

abstract thought, abstraction, contemplation, musing; brown study etc. (*inattention*) 458; reverie, Platonism; depth of thought, workings of the mind, thoughts, inmost thoughts; self-counsel, communing, -consultation.

association –, succession –, flow –, train –, current- of -thought, – ideas.

after –, mature- thought; reconsideration, second thoughts; retrospection etc. (*memory*) 505; excogitation; examination etc. (*inquiry*) 461; invention etc. (*imagination*) 515.

thoughtfulness etc. *adj.*

V. think, reflect, reason, cogitate, excogitate, consider, deliberate; bestow -thought, – consideration- upon; speculate, contemplate, meditate, ponder, muse, dream, ruminate; brood –, con- over; animadvert, study; bend–, apply- the mind etc. (*attend*) 457; digest, discuss, hammer at, weigh, perpend; realize, appreciate; fancy etc. (*imagine*) 515; trow.

take into consideration; take counsel etc. (*be advised*) 695; commune with –, bethink- oneself; collect one's thoughts; revolve –, turn over –, run over- in the mind; chew the cud –, sleep- upon; take counsel of –, advise with- one's pillow.

rack –, ransack –, crack –, beat –, cudgel- one's brains; set one's -brain, – wits- to work.

harbor –, entertain –, cherish –, nurture- an idea etc. 453; take into one's head; bear in mind; reconsider.

occur; present –, suggest- itself; come –, get- into one's head; strike one, flit across the view, come uppermost, run in one's head; enter –, pass in –, cross –, flash on –, flash across –, float in –, fasten itself on –, be uppermost in –, occupy- the mind; have in one's mind.

make an impression; sink –, penetrate- into the mind; engross the thoughts.

Adj. thinking etc. *v.*; thoughtful, pensive, meditative, reflective, cogitative, museful, wistful, contemplative, speculative, deliberative, studious, sedate, introspective, Platonic, philosophical.

lost –, engrossed –, rapt –, absorbed- in thought etc. (*inattentive*) 458; deep musing etc. (*intent*) 457.

in the mind, under consideration, in contemplation.

Adv. all things considered; taking everything into account.

Phr. the mind being on the stretch; the -mind, – head- -turning, – running- upon.

452. Incogitancy. [Absence or want of thought.]**—N.** incogitancy, vacancy, inunderstanding; inanity, fatuity etc. 499; thoughtlessness etc. (*inattention*) 458.

V. not -think etc. 451; not think of; dismiss from the -mind, – thoughts etc. 451.

indulge in reverie etc. (*be inattentive*) 458.

put away thought; unbend –, relax –, divert- the mind.

Adj. vacant, unintellectual, unideal, unoccupied, unthinking, inconsiderate, thoughtless; absent etc. (*inattentive*) 458; diverted; irrational etc. 499; narrow-minded etc. 481.

un-thought of, -dreamt of, -considered; off one's mind; incogitable, not to be thought of, inconceivable.

453. Idea. [Object of thought.]—**N.** idea, notion, conception, thought, apprehension, impression, perception, image, sentiment, reflection, observation, consideration; abstract idea, principle; archetype.

view etc. (*opinion*) 484; theory etc. 514; conceit, fancy; phantasy etc. (*imagination*) 515.

point of view etc. (*aspect*) 448; field of view.

454. Topic. [Subject of thought.]—**N.** subject of –, material for- thought; food for the mind, mental *pabulum*.

subject, -matter; matter, theme, topic, what it is about, *thesis*, text, business, affair, matter in hand, argument; motion, resolution; head, chapter; case, point; proposition, theorem; field of inquiry; moot point, problem, etc. (*question*) 461.

V. float –, pass- in the mind etc. 451.

Adj. thought of; uppermost in the mind; *in petto*.

Adv. under -discussion, – consideration, – advisement; in -question, – the mind; on -foot, – the carpet, – the *tapis*; before the house, relative to etc. 9.

455. Curiosity. [The desire of knowledge.]—**N.** interest, thirst for knowledge; curi-osity, -ousness; inquiring mind; inquisitiveness.

sight-seer, quidnunc, newsmonger, Paul Pry, peeping Tom, eavesdropper; gossip etc. (*news*) 532; questioner, *enfant terrible*.

V. be -curious etc. *adj.*; take an interest in, stare, gape; prick up the ears, see sights, lionize; pry, speer; dig up.

Adj. curious, inquisitive, burning with curiosity, overcurious, nosey; inquiring etc. 461; prying; inquisitorial; agape etc. (*expectant*) 507; attentive etc. 457.

Phr. what's the matter? what next?

456. Incuriosity. [Absence of curiosity.]—**N.** incuriosity; incuriousness etc. *adj.*; *insouciance* etc. 866; indifference, apathy.

V. be -incurious etc. *adj.*; have no -curiosity etc. 455; take no interest in etc. 823; mind one's own business.

Adj. incurious, uninquisitive, uninterested, indifferent, bored; impassive etc. 823.

457. Attention.—N. attention; mindfulness etc. *adj.*; intent-ness, -iveness; thought etc. 451; adverten-ce, -cy; observ-ance, -ation; consideration, reflection, perpension; heed; particularity; notice, regard etc. *v.*; circumspection etc. (*care*) 459; study, scrutiny, once-over; in-, intro-spection; revision, -al.

active –, diligent –, exclusive –, minute –, close –, intense –, deep –, profound –, abstract –, labored –, deliberate- -thought, – attention, – application, – study.

minuteness, attention to detail etc. 459.

absorption of mind etc. (*abstraction*) 458.

indication, calling attention to etc. *v.*

V. be -attentive etc. *adj.*; attend, advert to, observe, look, see, view, remark, notice, regard, take notice, mark; give –, pay- -attention, – heedto; listen in, incline –, lend- an ear to; trouble one's head about; give a thought –, animadvert- to; occupy oneself with; contemplate etc. (*think of*) 451; look -at, – to, – after, – into, – over; see to; turn –, bend –, apply –, direct –, give- the -mind, – eye, – attention- to; have -an eye to, – in one's eye; bear in mind; take into -account, – consideration; keep in -sight, – view; have regard to, heed, mind, take cognizance of, be engaged in, entertain, recognize; make –, take- note of; note.

examine cursorily; glance -at, – upon, – over; cast –, pass- the eyes over; run over, turn over the leaves, dip into, perstringe; skim etc. (*neglect*) 460; take a cursory view of.

examine, – closely, – intently; scan, scrutinize, consider; give –, bend- one's mind to; overhaul, revise, pore over; inspect, review, pass under review; take stock of; fix –, rivet –, focus –, devote- the - eye, – mind, – thoughts, – attention- on *or* to; hear –, think- out; mind one's business.

revert –, hark back- to; watch etc. (*expect*) 507, (*take care of*) 459; hearken –, listen- to; prick up the ears; have –, keep- the eyes open; come to the point.

meet with attention; fall under one's -notice, – observation; be -under consideration etc. (*topic*) 454.

catch –, strike- the eye; attract notice; catch –, awaken –, wake –, invite –, solicit –, attract –, claim –, excite –, engage –, occupy –, strike –, arrest –, fix –, engross –, absorb –, rivet-the- attention, – mind, – thoughts; be -present to, – uppermost in- the mind.

bring under one's notice; point -out, – to, – at, – the finger at; lay the finger on, indigitate, indicate; direct –, call- attention to; show; put a -mark etc. (*sign*) 550- upon; call soldiers to 'attention;' bring forward etc. (*make manifest*) 525.

Adj. attentive, mindful, heedful, observant, regardful; alive –, awake- to, alert; observing etc. *v.*; taken up –, occupied- with; engaged –, engrossed –, interested –, wrapped- in; absorbed, rapt; breathless; pre-occupied etc. (*inattentive*) 458; watchful etc. (*careful*) 459; intent on, open-eyed, breathless, undistracted, upon the stretch; on the watch etc. (*expectant*) 507.

steadfast.

Int. see! look, – here, – out, – alive, – you, – to it! mark! lo! behold! soho! hark, – ye! mind! halloo! observe! lo and hehold! attention! *nota bene*; N.B.; *, †; I'd have you to know; notice! take notice! O yes! *Oyez!*

Phr. this is –, these are- to give notice.

458. Inattention.—N. in-attention, -consideration; inconsiderateness etc. *adj.*; oversight; inadverten-ce, -cy; non-observance, disregard.

supineness etc. (*inactivity*) 683; *étourderie*; want of thought; heedlessness etc. (*neglect*) 460; *insouciance* etc. (*indifference*) 866.

abstraction; absence –, absorption- of mind; preoccupation, distraction, reverie, brown study, deep musing, fit of abstraction, woolgathering.

V. be -inattentive etc. *adj.*; overlook, disregard; pass by etc. (*neglect*) 460; not -observe etc. 457; think little of.

close –, shut- one's eyes to; wink at; pay no attention to; dismiss –, discard –, discharge- from one's -thoughts, – mind; drop the subject, think no more of; set –, turn –, put- aside; turn -away from, – one's attention from, – a deaf ear to, – one's back upon.

abstract oneself, dream, indulge in reverie.

escape -notice, – attention; come in at one ear and go out at the other; forget etc. (*have no remembrance*) 506.

call off –, draw off –, call away –, divert –, distract- the -attention, – thoughts, – mind; put out of one's head; dis-concert, -compose; put out, confuse, perplex, bewilder, fluster, muddle, dazzle; throw a sop to Cerberus.

Adj. inattentive; un-observant, -mindful, -heeding, -discerning; inadvertent; mind-, regard-, respect-less; listless etc. (*indifferent*) 866; blind, deaf; flighty, hand over head; cur-, percur-sory; giddy-, scatter-, hare-brained; unreflecting, *écervelé*, inconsiderate, off-hand, thoughtless, dizzy, muzzy, brainsick; giddy, – as a goose; wild, harum-scarum, ranipole, high-flying; heed-, careless etc. (*neglectful*) 460.

absent, absent-minded, abstracted, *distrait*; lost; lost –, wrapped- in thought, woolgathering; rapt, in the clouds, bemused; dreaming –, musing- on other things; pre-occupied; engrossed etc. (*attentive*) 457; in a -reverie etc. *n.*; off one's guard etc. (*inexpectant*) 508; napping; dreamy.

disconcerted, put out etc. *v.*; rattled.

Adv. inattentively, inadvertently etc. *adj.*; *per incuriam*, *sub silentio*.

Int. stand -at ease, – easy!

Phr. the attention wanders; one's wits gone a -woolgathering, – bird's nesting; it never entered into one's head; the mind running on other things; one's thoughts being elsewhere; had it been a bear it would have bitten you.

459. Care. [Vigilance.]—**N.** care, solicitude, heed; heedfulness etc. *adj.*; scruple etc. (*conscientiousness*) 939.

watchfulness etc. *adj.*; vigilance, *surveillance*, eyes of Argus, watch, vigil, look out, watch and ward, *l'oeil du maître*.

alertness etc. (*activity*) 682; attention etc. 457; prudence etc., circumspection etc. (*caution*) 864; forethought etc. 510; precaution etc. (*preparation*) 673; tidiness etc. (*order*) 58, (*cleanliness*) 652; accuracy etc. (*exactness*) 494; minuteness, attention to detail; meticulousness, nicety, circumstantiality.

V. be -careful etc. *adj.*; reck; take care etc. (*be cautious*) 864; pay attention to etc. 457; take care of; look –, see- -to, – after; keep -an eye, – a sharp eye- upon; keep -watch, – watch and ward; mount guard, set watch, watch; keep in -sight, – view; chaperon, play gooseberry; mind, – one's business.

look -sharp, – about one; look with one's own eyes; keep a -good, – sharp- look-out; have all one's -wits, – eyes- about one; watch for etc. (*expect*) 507; stand to; keep one's eyes –, have the eyes –, sleep with one eye- open.

take precautions etc. 673; protect etc. (*render safe*) 664.

do one's best etc. 682; mind one's Ps and Qs, speak by the card, pick one's steps.

Adj. care-, regard-, heed-ful; taking care etc. *v.*; particular; prudent etc. (*cautious*) 864; considerate; thoughtful etc. (*deliberative*) 451; provident etc. (*prepared*) 673; alert etc. (*active*) 682; sure-footed.

guarded, on one's guard; on the *qui vive*, – alert, – watch, – look-out; awake, broad awake, vigilant; watch-, wake-, wist-ful; Argus-, lynx-eyed; wide awake etc. (*intelligent*) 498; on the watch for etc. (*expectant*) 507.

tidy etc. (*orderly*) 58, (*clean*) 652; accurate etc. (*exact*) 494; scrupulous etc. (*conscientious*) 939; *cavendo tutus* etc. (*safe*) 664.

Adv. carefully etc. *adj.*; with care, gingerly.

Phr. *quis custodiet ipsos custodes?*

460. Neglect.—N. neglect; carelessness etc. *adj.*; trifling etc. *v.*; negligence; omission, laches, default; remissness, slackness, procrastination; supineness etc. (*inactivity*) 683; inattention etc. 458; *nonchalance* etc. (*insensibility*) 823; imprudence, recklessness etc. 863; slovenliness etc. (*disorder*) 59; (*dirt*) 653; improvidence etc. 674; non-completion etc. 730; inexactness etc. (*error*) 495.

paraleipsis [in rhetoric].

trifler, slacker, waster, waiter on Providence; Micawber.

V. be -negligent etc. *adj.*; take no care of etc. (take care of etc. 459); neglect; let -slip, – go; lay –, set –, cast –, put- aside; keep –, leave- out of sight; lose sight of.

overlook, disregard; pass -over, – by; let pass; blink; wink –, connive- at; gloss over; take no -note, – notice, – thought, – account- of; pay no regard to; *laisser aller*; allow to lie on the table.

scamp; trifle, fribble; do by halves; skimp; cut; slight etc. (*despise*) 930; play –, trifle- with; slur; skim, – the surface; *effleurer*; take a cursory view of etc. 457.

slur –, slip –, skip –, jump- over; pertermit, miss, skip, jump, omit, give the go-by to, push aside, throw into the background, shelve, sink; ignore, shut one's eyes to, refuse to hear, turn a deaf ear to; leave out of one's calculation; not -attend to etc. 457, – mind; not trouble -oneself, – one's head- -with, – about; forget etc. 506; be caught napping etc. (*not expect*) 508; leave a loose thread; let the grass grow under one's feet.

render -neglectful etc. *adj.*; put –, throw- off one's guard.

Adj. neglecting etc. *v.*; unmindful, negligent, neglectful; heedless, careless, thoughtless; perfunctory, remiss, slack.

inconsiderate; un-, in-circumspect; off one's guard; un-wary, -watchful, -guarded; offhand.

supine etc. (*inactive*) 683; inattentive etc 458; *insouciant* etc. (*indifferent*) 823; imprudent, reckless etc. 863; slovenly etc. (*disorderly*) 59, (*dirty*) 653; inexact etc. (*erroneous*) 495; improvident etc. 674.

neglected etc. *v.*; un-heeded, -cared for, -

perceived, -seen, -observed, -noticed, -noted, -marked, -attended to, -thought of, -regarded, -remarked, -missed; shunted, shelved.

un-examined, -studied, -searched, -scanned, -weighed, -sifted, -explored.

Adv. negligently etc. *adj.*; hand over head, anyhow; in an unguarded moment etc. (*unexpectedly*) 508; *per incuriam*.

Int. never mind, no matter, let it pass; it will be all the same a hundred years hence.

461. Inquiry. [Subject of Inquiry. Question.]—**N.** inquiry; request etc. 765; search, research, quest; pursuit etc. 622.

examination, review, scrutiny, investigation, indagation; per-quisition, -scrutation, -vestigation; inqu-est, -isition; exploration; *exploitation*, ventilation.

sifting; calculation, analysis, dissection, resolution, induction; Baconian method.

strict —, close —, searching —, exhaustive- inquiry; narrow —, strict- search; study etc. (*consideration*) 451.

scire facias, ad referendum; trial.

questioning etc. *v.*; interroga-tion, -tory; third degree; interpellation; challenge, examination, cross-examination, catechism; feeler, Socratic method, zetetic philosophy; leading question; discussion etc. (*reasoning*) 476; questionnaire, questionary.

reconnoitering, *reconnaissance*; prying etc. *v.*; espionage, *espionnage*; domiciliary visit, peep behind the curtain; lantern of Diogenes.

question, query, problem, *desideratum*, point to be solved, porism; subject —, field- of -inquiry, — controversy; point —, matter- in dispute; moot-point; issue, question at issue; bone of contention etc. (*discord*) 713; plain —, fair —, open- question; enigma etc. (*secret*) 533; knotty point etc. (*difficulty) 704; quod-libet*; threshold of an inquiry.

inquirer, investigator, experimenter, inquisitor, inspector, querist, examiner, catechist; scrut-ator, -ineer; analyst; quidnunc etc. (*curiosity*) 455.

V. make -inquiry etc. *n.*; inquire, seek, search, frisk, speer, look -for, — about for, — out for; scan, reconnoiter, explore, sound, rummage, ransack, pry, peer, look round; look —, go- -over, — through; spy, over-haul.

scratch the head, slap the forehead.

look —, peer —, pry- into every hole and corner; look behind the scenes; trace up; hunt —, fish —, dig —, ferret- out; unearth; leave no stone unturned.

seek a -clue, — clew; hunt, track, trail, shadow, mouse, dodge, trace; follow the -trail, — scent; pursue etc. 622; beat up one's quarters; fish for; feel for etc. (*experiment*) 463.

investigate; take up —, institute —, pursue —, follow up —, conduct —, carry on —, prosecute- -an inquiry etc. *n.*; look -at, — into; pre-examine; discuss, canvass, agitate.

examine, study, consider, calculate; dip —, dive —, delve —, go deep- into; make sure of, probe, sound, fathom; probe to the -bottom, — quick; scrutinize, analyze, anatomize, dissect, parse, resolve, sift, winnow; view —, try- in all its phases; thresh out.

bring in question, subject to examination; put to the proof etc. (*experiment*) 463; audit, tax, pass in review; take into consideration etc. (*think over*) 451; take counsel etc. 695.

ask, question, demand; put —, pop —, propose —, propound —, moot —, start —, raise —, stir —, suggsst —, put forth —, ventilate —, grapple with —, go into- a question.

put to the question, interrogate, catechize, pump, grill; cross-question, -examine; dodge; require an answer; pick —, suck- the brains of; feel the pulse.

be -in question etc. *adj.*; undergo examination.

Adj. inquiry etc. *v.*; inquisitive etc. (*curious*) 455; requisit-ive, -ory; catechetical, inquisitorial, analytic; in -search, — quest- of; on the look-out for, interrogative, zetetic; all-searching.

un-determined, -tried, -decided; in -question, — dispute, — issue, — course of inquiry; under -discussion, — consideration, — investigation etc. *n.*, *sub judice*, moot, proposed; doubtful etc. (*uncertain*) 475.

Adv. what? why? wherefore? whence? whither? where? *quaere?* how -comes, — happens, — is- it? what is the reason? what's -the matter, — up, in the wind? what on earth? when? who?

462. Answer.—N. answer, response, reply, replication, *riposte*, rejoinder, surrejoinder, rebutter, surrebutter, counter-evidence etc. 468, counter-charge, defence, plea; retort, repartee; contradiction etc. 536; rescript, -ion; antiphon, -y; acknowledgment; password; echo.

discovery etc. 480*a*; solution etc. (*explanation*) 522; rationale etc. (*cause*) 153; clue etc. (*indication*) 550.

Oedipus; oracle, etc. 513; return etc. (*record*) 551.

V. answer, respond, reply, rebut, retort, rejoin; give —, return for- answer; acknowledge, echo.

explain etc. (*interpret*) 522; solve etc. (*unriddle*) 522; discover etc. 480*a*; fathom, hunt out etc. (*inquire*) 461; satisfy, set at rest, determine.

Adj. answering etc. *v.*; respon-sive, -dent; oracular; antiphonal; conclusive.

Adv. because etc. (*cause*) 153; on the -scent, — right scent.

Int. *eureka!*

463. Experiment.—N. experiment; essay etc. (*attempt*) 675; research etc. (*investigation*) 461; trial, tentative method, *tâtonnement*.

verification, probation, *experimentum crucis*, proof, criterion, diagnostic test, tryout, crucial test, acid test.

crucible, reagent, check, touchstone, pix; assay, ordeal; ring.

empiricism, rule of thumb.

feeler; pilot —, messenger- balloon, *ballon d'essai*; pilot engine; scout; straw to show the wind.

speculation, random shot, leap in the dark.

analy-zer, -st; adventurer, explorer, sourdough, prospector; experiment-er, -ist, -alist; assayer.

V. experiment; essay etc. (*endeavor*) 675; try, assay, sample; make -an experiment, — trial of; give a trial to; put upon —, subject to- trial; experiment upon; rehearse; put —, bring —, submit-to the -test, — proof, prove, verify, test, touch, practise upon, try one's strength.

grope; feel —, grope- -for, — one's way; fumble; *tâttonner*, *aller à tâtons*; put —, throw- out a feeler; send up a pilot balloon; see how the -land lies, — wind blows; consult the barometer; feel the pulse; fish —, bob- for; cast —, beat- about for; angle, trawl, cast one's net, beat the bushes.

venture, try one's fortune etc. (*adventure*) 675; explore etc. (*inquire*) 461.

Adj. experimental; probat-ive, ory, -ionary; analytic, docimastic; tentative; empirical; speculative, tentive.

under probation, on one's trial, on trial, on approval.

464. Comparison.—N. comparison, collation, contrast; identification.

sim-ile, -ilitude; allegory etc. (*metaphor*) 521.

V. compare -to, — with; collate, confront; place side by side etc. (*near*) 197; set —, pit- against one another; contrast balance.

identify, draw a parallel, parallel.

compare notes; institute a comparison; *parva componere magnis.*

Adj. comparative, relative; metaphorical etc. 521.

compared with etc. *v.*; comparable.

Adv. relatively etc. (*relation*) 9; as compared with etc. *v.*

465. Discrimination.—N. discrimination, distinction, differentiation, diagnosis, diorism; nice perception; perception —, appreciation- of difference; acuteness; estimation etc. 466; nicety, refinement; taste etc. 850; *critique*, judgement, tact; insight, discernment etc. (*intelligence*) 498; *nuances*.

V. discriminate, distinguish, differentiate, severalize; separate; draw the line, sift; separate —, winnow- the chaff from the wheat; split hairs.

estimate etc. (*measure*) 466; know -which is which, — one's stuff, — one's way about, — what is what, — 'a hawk from a handsaw.'

take into -account, — consideration; give —, allow- due weight to; weigh carefully.

Adj. discriminating etc. *v.*; dioristic, discriminative, critical, distinctive; nice.

Phr. *il y a fagots et fagots*; *rem acu tetigisti.*

465a. Indiscrimination.—N. indiscrimination; promiscuity; indistinctness, -ion; uncertainty etc. (*doubt*) 475; obtuseness.

V. not -indiscriminate etc. 465; overlook etc. (*neglect*) 460- a distinction; con-found, -fuse, jumble; swallow whole.

Adj. indiscriminate, undiscriminating, promiscuous; undistinguish-ed, -able, -ing; unmeasured.

466. Measurement.—N. measurement, admeasurement, mensuration, survey, valuation, appraisment, assessment, assize; estim-ate, -ation; dead reckoning; reckoning etc. (*numeration*) 85; gauging etc. *v.*

metrology, weights and measures, compound arithmetic.

measure, yard measure, standard, rule, foot-rule, chain, tape, staff, compass, callipers; dividers; gage, gauge, planimeter; meter, line, rod, check.

volt, kilowatt, ampere, candle power; horse power; axle load; foot pound.

flood —, high water- mark; Plimsoll mark; index etc. 550.

scale; gradu-ation, -ated scale; nonius; vernier etc. (*minuteness*) 193; pedo (*length*)- 200, sounding line etc. (*depth*) 208, thermo (*heat* etc. 398)-, baro (*air* etc. 338)-, dynamo (*power*)- 276, anemo (*wind* 349)-, gonio (*angle* 244)- meter; landmark etc. (*limit*) 233; balance etc. (*weight*) 310; optical instruments etc. 445.

co-ordinates, ordinate and abscissa, polar co-ordinates, latitude and longitude, declination and right ascension, altitude and azimuth.

geo-, stereo-, hypso-metry; metage; surveying, land surveying; geo-desy, -detics, -desia; ortho-, alti-metry; *cadastre.*

astrolabe, armillary sphere.

land, -surveyor; geometer, topographer, cartographer, hydrographer.

V. measure, meter, mete; value, assess, rate, appraise, estimate, form as estimate, set a value on; appreciate; standardize.

span, pace, step; apply the -compass etc. *n.*; gauge, plumb, probe, calliper, sound, fathom etc. 208; heave the -log, — lead; weigh etc. 319; survey.

take an average etc. 29; graduate.

Adj. measuring etc. *v.*; metric, -al; measurable; geodetical, cadastral, topographical.

467. Evidence. [on one side]**—N.** evidence; facts, premises, *data*, *praecognita*, grounds.

indication etc. 550; criterion etc. (*test*) 463.

testi-mony, -fication; attestation; deposition etc. (*affirmation*) 535; examination.

admission etc. (*assent*) 488; authority, warrant, credential, diploma, voucher, certificate, docket; record etc. 551; document, muniments; *pièce justificative*; deed, warranty etc. (*security*) 771; signature, seal etc. (*identification*) 550; exhibit, citation, reference.

witness, indicator; eye-, ear-witness; deponent; sponsor.

oral —, documentary —, hearsay —, external —, extrinsic —, internal —, intrinsic —, circumstantial —, cumulative —, *ex parte* —, presumptive —, collateral —, constructive- evidence; proof etc. (*demonstration*) 478; evidence in chief; finger prints, dactylogram.

secondary evidence; confirmation, corroboration, adminicle, support; ratification etc. (*assent*) 488; authentication, verification; compurgation, wager of law, comprobation.

citation, reference.

V. be -evidence etc. *n.*; evince, show, betoken, tell of; indicate etc. (*denote*) 550; imply, involve, argue, bespeak, breathe.

have —, carry- weight; tell, speak volumes; speak for itself etc. (*manifest*) 525.

rest –, depend- upon; repose on.

bear -witness etc. *n.*; give -evidence etc. *n.*; testify, depose, witness, vouch for; sign, seal, undersign, set one's hand and seal, sign and seal, deliver as one's act and deed, certify, attest; acknowledge etc. (*assent*) 488.

make absolute, confirm, ratify, corroborate, endorse, countersign, support, bear out, vindicate, uphold, warrant.

adduce, attest, cite, quote; refer –, appeal- to; call, – to witness; bring -forward, – into court; allege, plead; produce –, confront- witnesses; collect –, bring together –, rake up- evidence.

have –, make out- a case; establish, circumstantiate, authenticate, substantiate, verify, make good, quote chapter and verse; bring -home to, – to book.

Adj. showing etc. *v.*; evidential, indica-tive, -tory; deducible etc. 478; grounded –, founded –, based- on; first hand, authentic, verifiable; corroborative, confirmatory; significant, conclusive.

Adv. by inference; according to, witness, *a fortiori*; still -more, – less; *raison de plus*; in corroboration etc. *n.* of; *valeat quantum*; under -seal, – one's hand and seal.

468. Counter-evidence. [Evidence on the other side, on the other hand.]—**N.** counter-evidence; evidence on the other -side, – hand; disproof; refutation etc. 479; negation etc. 536; conflicting evidence.

plea etc. 617; vindication etc. 937; counter-protest; *tu quoque* argument; other side –, reverse- of the shield.

V. countervail, oppose; run counter; rebut etc. (*refute*) 479; subvert etc. (*destroy*) 162; check, weaken; contravene; contradict etc. (*deny*) 536; tell another story, turn the -tables, – scale; alter the case; cut both ways; prove a negative.

audire alteram partem.

Adj. countervailing etc. *v.*; contradictory, in rebuttal.

un-attested, -authenticated, -supported by evidence; suppositious, trumped up.

Adv. *per contra*, conversely, on the other hand.

469. Qualification.—N. qualification, limitation, modification, coloring.

allowance, grains of allowance, consideration, extenuating circumstances.

condition, proviso, exception; exemption; salvo, saving clause; discount etc. 813.

V. qualify, limit, modify, affect, temper, leaven, give a color to, introduce new conditions.

allow –, make allowance- for; admit exceptions, take into account.

take exception, object.

Adj. qualifying etc. *v.*; conditional; extenuatory; exceptional etc. (*unconformable*) 83.

hypothetical etc. (*supposed*) 514; contingent etc. (*uncertain*) 475.

Adv. provided, – always; if, unless, but, yet; according as; conditionally, admitting, supposing; on the supposition of etc. (*theoretically*) 514; with the understanding, even, although, though, for all that, after all, at all events.

with grains of allowance, *cum grano salis*; *exceptis excipiendis*; wind and weather permitting; if possible etc. 470.

subject to; with this -proviso etc. *n.*

470. Possibility.—N. possibility, potentiality; what -may be, – is possible etc. *adj.*; compatibility etc. (*agreement*) 23.

practicability, feasibility; practicableness etc. *adj.*

contingency, chance etc. 156.

V. be -possible etc. *adj.*; stand a chance, have a leg to stand on; admit of, bear.

render -possible etc. *adj.*; put in the way of.

Adj. possible; on the -cards, – dice; *in posse*, within the bounds of possibility, conceivable, credible, imaginable; compatible etc. 23.

practicable, feasible, workable, performable, achievable; within -reach, – measurable distance; accessible, superable, surmountable; at-, obtainable; contingent etc. (*doubtful*) 475.

Adv. possibly, by possibility; perhaps, -chance, -adventure; may be, haply, mayhap.

if possible, wind and weather permitting, God willing, *Deo volente*, D.V.

471. Impossibility.—N. impossibility etc. *adj.*; what -cannot, – can never- be; sour grapes; infeasibility, impracticability; hopelessness etc. 859.

V. be -impossible etc. *adj.*; have no chance whatever.

attempt impossibilities; square the circle; discover the -philosopher's stone – elixir of life, – secret of perpetual motion; wash a blackamoor white; skin a flint; make -a silk purse out of a sow's ear, – bricks without straw; have nothing to go upon; weave a rope of sand, build castles in the air, *prendre la lune avec les dents*, extract sunbeams from cucumbers, set the Thames on fire, milk a he-goat into a sieve, catch a weasel asleep, *rompre l'anguille au genou*, be in two places at once.

Adj. impossible; not -possible etc. 470; absurd, contrary to reason; unlikely, at variance with facts; unreasonable etc. 477; incredible etc. 485; beyond the bounds of -reason, – possibility; from which reason recoils; visionary; inconceivable etc. (*improbable*) 473; prodigious etc. (*wonderful*) 870; un-, in-imaginable, unthinkable, not a Chinaman's chance.

impracticable, unachievable; un-, in-feasible; insuperable; un-, in-surmountable; unat-, unobtainable; out of -reach, – the question; not to be -had, – thought of; beyond control; desperate etc. (*hopeless*) 859; incompatible etc. 24; inaccessible, uncomeatable, impassable, impervious, innavigable, inextricable.

out of –, beyond- one's -power, – depth, – reach, – grasp; too much for; *ultra crepidam.*

Phr. the grapes are sour; *non possumus*; *non nostrum tantas componere lites.*

472. Probability.—N. probability, likelihood; likeliness etc. *adj.*

vraisemblance, verisimilitude, plausibility;

color, semblance, show of; presumption; presumptive —, circumstantial- evidence; credibility.
reasonable —, fair —, good —, favorable- - chance, — prospect; prospect, well-grounded hope; chance etc. 156.
V. be -probable etc. *adj.*; give —, lend- color to; point to; imply etc. (*evidence*) 467; bid fair etc. (*promise*) 511; stand fair for; stand —, run- a good chance.
presume, infer, suppose, take for granted.
think likely, dare say, flatter oneself; expect etc. 507; count upon etc. (*believe*) 484.
Adj. probable, likely, hopeful, to be expected, in a fair way.
plausible, specious, ostensible, colorable, *ben trovato*, well-founded, reasonable, credible, easy of belief, presumable, presumptive, apparent.
Adv. probably etc. *adj.*; belike; in all - probability, — likelihood; very —, most- likely; as likely as not; like enough; ten etc. to one; apparently, seemingly, according to every reasonable expectation; *primâ facie*; to all appearance etc. (*to the eye*) 448.
Phr. the -chances, — odds- are; appearances —, chances- are in favor of; there is reason to -believe, — think, — expect; I dare say; all Lombard Street to a China orange.

473. Improbability.—N. improbability, unlikelihood; unfavorable —, bad —, little —, small —, poor —, scarcely any —, no —, not a ghost of a- chance; bare possibility; long odds; incredibility etc. 485.
V. be -improbable etc. *adj.*; have a -small chance etc. *n.*
Adj. improbable, unlikely, contrary to all reasonable expectation, implausible.
rare etc. (*infrequent*) 137; unheard of, inconceivable; un-, in-imaginable; incredible etc. 485; more than doubtful.
Int. not likely! no fear!
Phr. the chances are against.

474. Certainty.—N. certainty; necessity etc. 601; certitude, certainness, surety, assurance, sureness; dead —, moral- certainty; infallibleness etc. *adj.*; infallibility, reliability.
gospel, scripture, church, pope, court of final appeal; *res judicata, ultimatum*.
positiveness; dogmat-ism, -ist, -izer; *doctrinaire*, know-all, bigot, -ry; opinionist, Sir Oracle; *ipse dixit*; zealot.
fact; positive —, matter of- fact; *fait accompli*.
V. be -certain etc. *adj.*; stand to reason.
render -certain etc. *adj.*; in-, en-, as-sure; clinch, make sure; determine, decide, set at rest, 'make assurance double sure;' know etc. (*believe*) 484; dismiss all doubt.
dogmatize, lay down the law.
Adj. certain, sure; assured etc. *v.*; solid, well-founded.
unqualified, absolute, positive, determinate, definite, clear, unequivocal, categorical, unmistakable, decisive, decided, ascertained.
inevitable, unavoidable, ineluctable, avoidless.
unerring, infallible; unchangeable etc. 150; to be depended on, trustworthy, reliable, bound.
un-impeachable, -deniable, -questionable; indisputable, -contestable, -controvertible, - defeasible, -dubitable; irrefutable etc. (*proven*) 478; conclusive, without power of appeal, final.
indubious; without —, beyond a —, without a shade or shadow or- -doubt — question; past dispute; beyond all -question, — dispute; undoubted, -contested, -questioned, -disputed; question-, dount-less.
bigoted, fanatical, dogmatic, opinionat-ed, -ive, *doctrinaire*.
authoritative, authentic; official.
sure as -fate, — death and taxes, — a gun.
evident, self-evident, axiomatic; clear, — as day, — as the sun at noonday; obvious.
Adv. certainly etc. *adj.*; for certain, certes, sure, no doubt, doubtless, and no mistake, *flagrante delicto*, sure enough, to be sure, of course, as a matter of course, *à coup sur*, to a certainty, undoubtedly; in truth etc. (*truly*) 494; at -any rate, — all events; without fail; *coûte que coûte*; whatever may happen, if the worst come to the worst; come —, happen- what -may, — will; sink or swim; rain or shine.
Phr. *cela va sans dire*; there is -no question, — not a shadow of doubt; the die is cast etc. (*necessity*) 601.

475. Uncertainty.—N. uncertainty, incertitude, doubt; doubtfulness etc. *adj.*; dubi-ety, -tation, -tancy, -ousness.
hesitation, suspense; perplexity, embarrassment, dilemma, quandary, Morton's fork, bewilderment; timidity etc. (*fear*) 860; indecision, vacillation etc. 605; *diaporesis*, indetermination.
vagueness etc. *adj.*; haze, fog; obscurity etc. (*darkness*) 421; ambiguity etc. (*double meaning*) 520; contingency, double contingency, possibility upon a possibility; conjecture; open question etc. (*question*) 461; *onus probandi*; blind bargain, pig in a poke, leap in the dark, something or other; needle in a bottle of hay; roving commission.
fallibility, unreliability, untrustworthiness, precariousness.
V. be -uncertain etc. *adj.*; wonder whether.
lose the -clue, — clew, — scent; miss one's way.
not know -what to make of etc. (*unintelligibility*) 519, — which way to turn, — whether one stands on one's head or one's heels; float in a sea of doubt, hesitate, flounder; lose -oneself, — one's head, — one's way, wander aimlessly; muddle one's brains.
render -uncertain etc. *adj.*; put out, pose, puzzle, perplex, embarrass; confuse, -found; bewilder, mystify, bother, nonplus, addle the wits, throw off the scent; *ambiguas in vulgus spargere voces*; keep in suspense.
doubt etc. (*disbelieve*) 485; hang —, tremble- in the balance; depend.
Adj. uncertain; casual; random etc. (*aimless*) 621; changeable etc. 149.
doubtful, dubious; indecisive; unsettled, - decided, -determined; in suspense, open to discussion; controvertible; in question etc. (*inquiry*) 461; insecure, unstable.

vague; in-determinate, -definite; ambiguous, equivocal; undefin-ed, -able; confused etc. (*indistinct*) 447; mystic, mysterious, veiled, obscure, cryptic, oracular.

perplexing etc. *v.*; enigmatic, paradoxical; apocryphal, problematical, hypothetical; experimental etc. 463.

fallible, questionable, precarious, slippery, ticklish, debatable, disputable; un-reliable, -trustworthy.

contingent, — on, dependent on; subject to; dependent on circumstances; occasional; provisional.

unauth-entic, -enticated, -oritative; unascertained, -confirmed; undemonstrated; un-told, -counted.

in a -state of uncertainty, — cloud, — maze; ignorant etc. 491; on the horns of a dilemma; afraid to say; out of one's reckoning, astray, adrift; as -sea, — fault, — a loss, — one's wit's end, — a *nonplus*; puzzled etc. *v.*; lost abroad, *désorienté*; dis-tracted, -traught.

Adv. *pendente lite*; *sub spe rati*.

Phr. Heaven knows; who can tell? who shall decide when doctors disagree?

476. Reasoning.—N. reasoning; ratio-cination, -nalism; dialectics, induction, generalization.

discussion, comment; ventilation; inquiry etc. 461.

argumentation, controversy, debate; polemics, wrangling; contention etc. 720; logomachy; disputation, -ceptation; paper war.

art of reasoning, logic.

process —, train —, chain- of reasoning; de-, induction; systhesis, analysis.

argument; case, plea, *plaidoyer*, opening; *lemma*, proposition, terms, premises, postulate, *data*, starting point, principle; inference etc. (*judgment*) 480.

pro-, syllogism; enthymeme, sorites, dilemma, *perilepsis*, *a priori* reasoning, *reductio ad absurdum*, horns of a dilemma, *argumentum ad hominem*, comprehensive argument.

reasoner, logician, dialectician; disputant; controver-sialist, -tist; wrangler, arguer, debater, polemic, casuist, rationalist; scientist.

logical sequence; good case; correct —, just —, sound —, valid —, cogent —, logical —, forcible —, persuasive —, persuasory —, consectary —, conclusive etc. 478 —, subtle- reasoning; force of argument; strong -point, — argument.

arguments, reasons, pros and cons.

V. reason, argue, discuss, debate, dispute, wrangle; bandy -words, — arguments; chop logic; hold —, carry on- an argument; controvert etc. (*deny*) 536; canvass; comment —, moralize-upon; consider etc. (*examine*) 461.

open a -discussion, — case; join —, be at- issue; moot; come to the point; stir —, agitate —, ventilate —, torture- a question; try conclusions; take up a -side, — case.

contend, take one's stand upon, insist, lay stress on; infer etc. 480.

follow from etc. (*demonstration*) 478.

Adj. rational; reasoning etc. *v.*; rationalistic; argumentative, controversial, dialectic, polemical; discurs-ory, -ive; disputations.

debatable, controvertible.

logical; in-, de-ductive; synthetic, analytic; relevant etc. 23.

Adv. for, because, hence, whence, seeing that, since, sith, then, thence, so; for -that, — this, — which- reason; for-, inasmuch as; whereas, *ex concesso*, considering, in consideration of; there-, where-fore; consequently, *ergo*, thus, accordingly; *a fortiori*.

in -conclusion, — fine; finally, after all, *au bout du compte*, on the whole, taking one thing with another.

rationally etc. *adj*.

477. Sophistry. [The absence of reasoning.] **Intuition.** [False or vicious reasoning; show of reason.]—**N.** intuition, instinct, association; presentiment; rule of thumb.

sophistry, paralogy, perversion, casuistry, jesuitry, equivocation, evasion, mental reservation; chicane, -ry; quiddit, quiddity; mystification; special pleading; speciousness etc. *adj.*; nonsense etc. 497; word-, tongue-fence.

false —, vicious- reasoning; *petitio principii*, *ignoratio elenchi*; *post hoc ergo propter hoc*; *non sequitur*, *ignotum per ignotius*.

misjudgment etc. 481; false teaching etc. 538.

sophism, solecism, paralogism; quibble, quirk, *elenchus*, elench, fallacy, *quodlibet*, subterfuge, subtlety, quillet; inconsistency, antilogy; 'a mockery, a delusion and a snare;' claptrap, mere words; 'lame and impotent conclusion.'

meshes —, cobwebs- of sophistry; flaw in an argument; weak point, bad case.

over-refinement; hair-splitting etc. *v.*

sophist, casuist, paralogist.

V. judge -intuitively, — by intuition; hazard a proposition, talk at random.

reason -ill, — falsely etc. *adj.*; paralogize; misjudge etc. 481.

pervert, quibble; equivocate, mystify, evade, elude; gloss over, varnish; misteach etc. 538; mislead etc. (*error*) 495; cavil, refine, subtilize, split hairs; misrepresent etc. (*lie*) 544.

beg the question, reason in a circle, cut blocks with a razor, beat about the bush, play fast and loose, blow hot and cold, prove that black is white and white black, travel out of the record, *parler à tort et à travers*, put oneself out of court, not have a leg to stand on.

Adj. intuitive, instinctive, impulsive; independent of —, anterior to- reason; gratuitous; hazarded; unconnected.

unreasonable, illogical, false, unsound, invalid; unwarranted, not following; inconsequent, -ial; inconsistent, incongruous; abson-ous, -ant; unscientific; untenable, inconclusive, incorrect; fall-acious; -ible; groundless, unproved.

deceptive, sophistical, sophisticated, casuistical, jesuitical; illus-ive, -ory; specious, hollow, plausible, *ad captandum*, evasive; irrelevant etc. 10.

weak, feeble, poor, flimsy, loose, vague, irrational; nonsensical etc. (*absurd*) 497; foolish etc. (*imbecile*) 499; frivolous, pettifogging, quibbling; finespun, over-refined.

at the end of one's tether, *au bout de son latin*.

Adv. intuitively etc. *adj.*; by intuition; illogically etc. *adj.*

Phr. *non constat*; that goes for nothing.

478. Demonstration.—N. demonstration, proof; conclusiveness etc. *adj.*; *apodixis*, probation, comprobation.

logic of facts etc. (*evidence*) 467; *experimentum curcis* etc. (*test*) 463; argument etc. 476; irrefragability.

V. demonstrate, prove, establish, make good; show; evince etc. (*be evidence of*) 467; verify etc. 467; settle the question, reduce to demonstration, set the question at rest.

make out, — a case; prove one's point, have the best of the argument; draw a conclusion etc. (*judge*) 480.

follow, — of course; stand to reason; hold -good, — water.

Adj. demonstra-ting etc. *v.*, -tive, -ble; probative, unanswerable, conclusive; apodictic, -al; irre-sistible, -futable, -fragable, undeniable.

categorical, decisive, crucial.

demonstrated etc. *v.*; proven; unconfuted, -answered, -refuted; evident etc. 474.

deducible, consequential, consectary, inferential, following.

Adv. of course, in consequence, consequently, as a matter of course.

Phr. *probatum est*; there is nothing more to be said, Q.E.D., it must follow.

479. Confutation.—N. con-, re-futation; answer, complete answer; disproof, conviction, redargution, invalidation; expos-ure, -ition; clincher; retort; *reductio ad absurdum*; knock down —, *tu quoque*- argument.

V. con-, re-fute; parry, negative, disprove, redargue, expose, show the fallacy of, rebut, defeat; demolish etc. (*destroy*) 162; over-throw, -turn; scatter to the winds, explode, invalidate; silence; put —, reduce- to silence; clinch -an argument, — a question; give one a set down, stop the mouth, shut up; have, — on the hip; get the better of; confound, convince.

not leave a leg to stand on, cut the ground from under one's feet.

be confuted etc.; fail; expose —, show- one's weak point.

Adj. confut-ing, -ed etc. *v.*; capable of refutation; re-, con-futable.

condemned -on one's own showing, — out of one's own mouth.

Phr. the argument falls to the ground, *cadit quaestio*, it does not hold water, '*suo sibi gladio hunc jugulo*.'

480. Judgment. [Conclusion.]—**N.** result, conclusion, upshot; deduction, inference, ergotism, illation; corollary, porism; moral.

estimation, valuation, appreciation, judication; di-, ad-judication; arbitr- ament, -ement, -ation; assessment, ponderation.

award, estimate; review, criticism, *critique*, notice, report.

decision, determination, judgment, finding, verdict, sentence, decree, — nisi, — absolute, — interlocutory; dictum; *res judicata*.

plébiscite, referendum, voice, casting vote; vote etc. (*choice*) 609; opinion etc. (*belief*) 484; good judgment etc. (*wisdom*) 498.

judge, jurist, umpire; arbi-ter, -trator; assessor, referee; censor, reviewer, critic; *connoisseur*; commentator etc. 524; inspector, inspecting officer.

V. judge, conclude; come to —, draw —, arrive at- a conclusion; ascertain, determine, make up one's mind.

deduce, derive, gather, collect, draw an inference, make a deduction, weet, ween.

form an estimate, estimate, size up, appreciate, value, count, assess, rate, rank, account; regard, consider, think of; look upon etc. (*believe*) 484.

settle; pass —, give- an opinion; decide, try, pronounce, rule; pass -judgment, — sentence; sentence, doom; find; give —, deliver- judgment; adjud-ge, -icate; arbitrate, award, report; bring in a verdict; make absolute, set a question ar rest; confirm etc. (*assent*) 488.

comment, criticize; review, pass under review etc (*examine*) 457; investigate etc. (*inquire*) 461.

hold the scales, sit in judgment; try —, hear- a cause.

Adj. judging etc. *v.*; judicious etc. (*wise*) 498; determinate, conclusive, censorious, critical etc. 932.

Adv. on the whole, all things considered.

480a. Discovery. [Result of search or inquiry.]—**N.** discovery, invention, detection, disenchantment, disclosure, find, ascertainment, revelation.

trover etc. 775.

V. discover, find, determine, evolve; fix upon; find —, trace —, make —, hunt —, fish —, worm —, ferret —, root-out; fathom; bring —, draw-out; educe, elicit, bring to light, invent; dig —, grub —, fish- up; unearth, disinter.

solve, resolve; un-riddle, -ravel, -lock; pick —, open- the lock; find a -clue, — clew- to; interpret etc. 522; disclose etc. 529.

trace, get at; hit it, have it; lay one's -finger, — hands- upon; spot; get —, arrive- at the -turth etc. 494; put the saddle on the right horse, hit the right nail on the head.

be near the truth, burn; smoke, scent, sniff, smell a rat.

open the eyes to; see -through, — daylight, — in its true colors, — the cloven foot; detect; catch, — tripping.

pitch —, fall —, light —, hit —, stumble —, pop- upon; come across; meet —, fall in- with.

recognize, realize, verify, make certain of, identify.

Int. *eureka!*

481. Misjudgment.—N. misjudgment, obliquity of —, warped- judgment; mis-calculation, -computation, -conception etc. (*error*) 495; hasty conclusion.

prejud-gment, -ication, -ice; foregone conclusion; pre-notion, -vention, -conception, -dilection, -possession, -apprehension, -sumption, -sentiment; fixed –, preconceived- idea; *idée fixe*; *mentis gratissimus error*; fool's paradise.

esprit de corps, party spirit, race –, class-prejudice, partisanship, clannishness, *prestige*.

bias, warp, twist; hobby, fad, whim, craze, quirk, crotchet, partiality, infatuation, blind side, mote in the eye.

one-sided –, partial –, narrow –, confined –, superficial- -views, – ideas,– conceptions, – notions; narrow mind; bigotry etc. (*obstinacy*) 606; *odium theologicum*; pedantry; hypercriticism.

doctrinaire etc. (*positive*) 474.

V. mis-judge, -estimate, -think, -conjecture, -conceive etc. (*error*) 495; fly in the face of facts; mis-calculate, -reckon, -compute.

overestimate etc. 482; underestimate etc. 483.

pre-, fore-judge; pre-suppose, -sume, -judicate; dogmatize; have a -bias etc. *n.*; have only one idea; *jurare in verba magistri*, run away with the notion; jump –, rush- to a conclusion; look only at one side of the shield; view -with jaundiced eye, – through distorting spectacles; not see beyond one's nose; *dare pondus fumo*; get the wrong sow by the ear etc. (*blunder*) 699.

give a -bias, – twist; bias, warp, twist; prejudice, -possess.

Adj. misjudging etc. *v.*; ill-judging, wrong-headed; prejudiced, prejudicial, etc. *v.*; jaundiced; short-sighted, pur-blind; partial, one-sided, superficial.

narrow-minded; confined, insular, provincial, parochial, illiberal, intolerant, narrow, besotted, infatuated, fanatical, cracked, warped, *entêté*, positive, dogmatic, dictatorial; conceited; opin-, opini-ative; opinion-ed, -ate, -ative, -ated; self-opinioned, wedded to an opinion, *opinâtre*; bigoted etc. (*obstinate*) 606; crotchety, fussy, impracticable; unreason-able, -ing; stupid etc. 499; credulous etc. 486.

misjudged etc. *v.*

Adv. *ex parte*.

Phr. nothing like leather; the wish the father to the thought.

482. Overestimation.—N. overestimation etc. *v.*; exaggeration etc. 549; vanity etc. 880; optim-, pessim-ism, -ist; megalomania.

much -cry and little wool, – ado about nothing; storm in a teacup; fine talking, rodomontade, gush, hot air, gas, bombast.

egotism etc. 880; boasting etc. 884.

V. over-estimate, -rate, -value, -prize, -weigh, -reckon, -strain, -praise; estimate too highly, attach too much importance to, make mountains of molehills, catch at straws; strain, magnify; exaggerate etc. 549; set too high a value upon; think –, make- -much, – too much- of; outreckon.

extol, – to the skies; make the -most, – best, – worst- of, eulogize, panegyrize, gush, puff, boost; make two bites of a cherry.

have too high an opinion of oneself etc. (*vanity*) 880.

Adj. overestimated etc. *v.*; oversensitive etc. (*sensibility*) 822; inflated, puffed up, exaggerated etc. 549.

Phr. all his geese are swans; *parturiunt montes*.

483. Underestimation.—N. underestimation; depreciation etc. (*detraction*) 934; pessim-ism, -ist; undervaluing etc. *v.*; modesty etc. 881.

V. under-rate, -estimate, -value, -reckon; depreciate; disparage etc. (*detract*) 934; not do justice to; mis-, dis-prize; ridicule etc. 856; slight etc. (*despise*) 930; neglect etc. 460; slur over, under-state.

make -light, – little, – nothing, – no account- of; minimize, belittle, run down, think nothing of; set -no store by, – at naught; shake off as dewdrops from the lion's mane.

Adj. depreciat-ing, -ed, -ive, -ory, etc. *v.*; unappreciated, -valued, -prized; pejorative.

484. Belief.—N. belief; credence; credit; assurance; faith, trust, troth, confidence, presumption, sanguine expectation etc. (*hope*) 858; dependence on, reliance on.

persuasion, conviction, convincement, plerophory, self-conviction; certainty etc. 474; opinion, mind, view; conception, thinking; impression etc. (*idea*) 453; surmise etc. 514; conclusion etc. (*judgment*) 480.

tenet, dogma, principle, way of thinking; popular belief etc. (*assent*) 488.

firm –, implicit –, settled –, fixed –, rooted –, deep-rooted –, staunch –, unshaken –, steadfast –, inveterate –, calm –, sober –, dispassionate –, impartial –, well-founded- -belief, – opinion etc.; *uberrima fides*.

system of opinions, school, doctrine, articles, canons; declaration –, profession- of faith; tenets, *credenda*, creed; thirty-nine articles etc. (*orthodoxy*) 983*a*; catechism; assent etc. 488; *propaganda* etc. (*teaching*) 537.

credibility etc. (*probability*) 472.

V. believe, credit; give -faith, – credit, – credence- to; see, realize; assume, receive; set down –, take- for; have –, take- it; consider, esteem, presume.

count –, depend –, calculate –, pin one's faith –, reckon –, lean –, build –, rely –, rest- upon; lay one's account for; make sure of.

make oneself easy -about, – on that score; take on -trust, – credit; take for -granted, – gospel; allow –, attach- some weight to.

know, – for certain; have –, make- no doubt; doubt not; be – rest- -assured etc. *adj.*; persuade –, assure –, satisfy- oneself; make up one's mind.

give one credit for; confide –, believe –, put one's trust- in; place –, repose- implicit confidence in; take -one's word for, – at one's word; place reliance on, rely upon, swear by, regard to.

think, hold; take, – it; opine, be of opinion, conceive, trow, ween, fancy, apprehend; have –, hold –, possess –, entertain –, adopt –, imbibe –, embrace –, get hold of –, hazard –, foster –, nurture –, cherish- -a belief, – an opinion etc. *n.*

view –, consider –, take –, hold –, conceive –, regard –, esteem –, deem –, look upon –, account –, set down- as; surmise etc. 514.

get –, take- it into one's head; come round to an opinion; swallow etc. (*credulity*) 486.

cause to -be believed etc. *v.*; satisfy, persuade, have the ear of, gain the confidence of, assure; convince, -vict, -vert; put across, sell; wean, bring round; bring –, put –, win- over; indoctrinate etc. (*teach*) 537; cram down the throat; produce –, carry- conviction; bring –, drive- home to.

go down, find credence, pass current; be -received etc. *v.*, – current etc. *adj.*; possess –, take hold of –, take possession of- the mind.

Adj. believing etc. *v.*; certain, sure, assured, positive, cocksure, satisfied, confident, unhesitating, convinced, secure.

under the impression; impressed –, imbued –, penetrated- with.

confiding, trustful, suspectless; unsusp-ecting, -icious; void of suspicion; credulous etc. 486; wedded to.

believed etc. *v.*; accredited, putative; unsuspected.

worthy of –, deserving of –, commanding- -belief, – confidence; credible, reliable, trusted, trustworthy, to be depended on, undoubted; satisfactory; probable etc. 472; fiduci-al, -ary; persuasive, impressive.

relating to belief, doctrinal.

Adv. in the -opinion, – eyes- of; *me judice*; me-seems, -thinks; to the best of one's belief; I -dare say, – doubt not, – have no doubt, – am sure; in my opinion; sure enough etc. (*certainty*) 474; depend –, rely- upon it; be –, rest- assured; I'll warrant you etc. (*affirmation*) 535.

485. Unbelief. Doubt.—N. un-, dis-, mis-belief; discredit, miscreance; infidelity etc. (*irreligion*) 989; dissent etc. 489; change of -opinion etc. 484; retraction etc. 607.

doubt etc. (*uncertainty*) 475; skepticism, misgiving, demur; dis-, mis-trust; misdoubt, suspicion, jealousy, scruple, qualm; *onus probandi.*

incredib-ility, -leness; incredulity; unbeliever etc. 487.

V. dis-believe, -credit; not -believe etc. 484; misbelieve; refuse to admit etc. (*dissent*) 489; refuse to believe etc. (*incredulity*) 487.

doubt; be -doubtful etc. (*uncertain*) 475; doubt the truth of; be -skeptical as to etc. *adj.*; diffide; dis-, mis-trust; suspect, smoke, scent, smell a rat; have –, harbor –, entertain- -doubts, – suspicions; have one's doubts.

demur, stick at, pause, hesitate, scruple, waver, stop and consider.

hang in -suspense, – doubt.

throw doubt upon, raise a question; bring –, call- in question; question, challenge, query; dispute; deny etc. 536; cavil; cause –, raise –, start –, suggest –, awake- a -doubt, – suspicion; ergotize.

startle, stagger; shake –, stagger- one's faith, – belief.

Adj. unbelieving; incredulous –, skeptical- as to; distrustful –, shy –, suspicious- of; doubting etc. *v.*

doubtful etc. (*uncertain*) 475; disputable; unworthy –, undeserving- of -belief etc. 484; questionable; sus-pect, -picious; open to -suspicion, – doubt; staggering, hard to believe, incredible, not to be believed, inconceivable.

fallible etc. (*uncertain*) 475; undemonstrable; controvertible etc. (*untrue*) 495.

Adv. *cum grano salis.*

Phr. *fronti nulla fides*; *nimium ne crede colori*; *'timeo Danaos et dona ferentes;' credat Judaeus Apella*; let those believe who may.

486. Credulity.—N. credul-ity, -ousness etc. *adj.*; gull-, cull-ibility; gross credulity, infatuation; self-delusion, -deception; blind reasoning; superstition; one's blind side; bigotry etc. (*obstinacy*) 606; hyper-orthodoxy etc. 984; misjudgment etc. 481.

credulous person etc. (*dupe*) 547.

V. be -credulous etc. *adj.*; *jurare in verba magistri*; follow implicitly; swallow, – whole, gulp down; take on trust; take for -granted, – gospel; run away with -a notion, – an idea; jump –, rush- to a conclusion; think the moon is made of green cheese; take –, grasp- the shadow for the substance; catch at straws.

impose upon etc. (*deceive*) 545.

Adj. credulous, gullible; easily -deceived etc. 545; simple, green, soft, childish, silly, stupid; over-credulous, -confident; infatuated, superstitious; confiding etc. (*believing*) 484.

Phr. the wish the father to the thought; *credo quia impossibile.*

487. Incredulity.—N. incredul-ous-ness, -ity; skepticism, pyrrhonism; want of faith etc. (*irreligion*) 989.

suspiciousness etc. *adj.*; scrupulosity; suspicion etc. (*unbelief*) 485; dissent etc. 489.

unbeliever, skeptic, aporetic; atheist, agnostic, infidel, disbeliever, misbeliever, pyrrhonist etc. 989; heretic etc. (*heterodox*) 984.

v. be -incredulous etc. *adj.*; distrust etc. (*disbelieve*) 485; refuse to believe; shut one's -eyes, – ears- to; turn a deaf ear to; hold aloof; ignore; *nullis jurare in verba magistri.*

Adj. incredulous, skeptical, unbelieving, inconvincible; hard –, shy- of belief; suspicious, scrupulous, distrustful, heterodox etc. 984.

488. Assent.—N. assent, -ment; acquiescence, admission; nod; ac-, con-cord, -cordance; agreement etc. 23; affirm-ance, -ation; recognition, acknowledgment, avowal; confession, – of faith.

unanimity, common consent, *consensus*, acclamation, chorus, *vox populi*; popular –, current- -belief, – opinion; public opinion; concurrence etc. (*of causes*) 178; co-operation etc. (*voluntary*) 709.

ratification, confirmation, corroboration, approval, acceptance, *visa*; indorsement etc. (*record*) 551.

consent etc. (*compliance*) 762.

affirmant, consenter, covenantor, subscriber, endorser, upholder.

V. assent; give –, yield –, not- assent; acquiesce; agree etc. 23; receive, accept, accede, accord, concur, lend oneself to, consent, coincide, reciprocate, go with; be -at one with etc. *adj.*; go along –, chime in –, strike in –, close- with; echo, enter into one's views, agree in opinion; vote –, give one's voice- for; recognize; subscribe –, conform –, defer- to; say -yes, – ditto, – amen; – aye- to.

acknowledge, own, admit, allow, avow, confess; concede etc. (*yield*) 762; come round to; abide by; permit etc. 760.

come to –, arrive at- -an understanding, – terms, – an agreement.

con-, af-firm; ratify, approve, endorse, countersign; visa; corroborate etc. 467.

go –, swim- with the stream, float with the current; be in the fashion, join in the chorus; be in every mouth.

Adj. assenting etc. *v.*; of one -accord, – mind; of the same mind, at one with, agreed, acquiescent, content; willing etc. 602.

un-contradicted, -challenged, -questioned, -controverted.

carried –, agreed- *-nem. con.* etc. *adv.*; unanimous; agreed on all hands, carried by acclamation.

affirmative etc. 535.

Adv. yes, yea, ay, aye, true; good; well; very -well, – true; well and good; granted; *placet*; even –, just- so; to be sure, surely, 'thou hast said;' truly, exactly, precisely, that's just it, indeed, certainly, certes, *ex concesso*; of course, unquestionably, assuredly, no doubt, doubtless, undoubtedly.

be it so; so -be it, – let it be, so mote it be; amen; with all my heart; willingly etc. 602.

with one -consent, – voice, – accord; unanimously, *unâ voce*, by common consent, in chorus, to a man, *nem. con.*; *nemine -contradicente*, – *dissentiente*; without a dissentient voice; as one man, one and all, on all hands.

489. Dissent.—N. dissent; discordance etc. (*disagreement*) 24; difference –, diversity- of opinion.

non-conformity etc. (*heterodoxy*) 984; protestantism, recusancy, schism; disaffection; secession etc. 624; recantation etc. 607.

dissension etc. (*discord*) 713; discontent etc. 832; cavilling.

protest; contradiction etc. (*denial*) 536; non-compliance etc. (*rejection*) 764; disapprobation etc. 932; hartal.

dissent-ient, -er; non-juror, -content; recusant, sectary, schismatic, protestant, non-conformist, separatist, non-co-operator, conscientious objector, passive resister.

V. dissent, demur; call in question etc. (*doubt*) 485; differ in opinion, disagree; say -no etc. 536; refuse -assent, – to admit; cavil, protest, raise one's voice against, make bold to differ; repudiate; contradict etc. (*deny*) 536; agree to differ.

have no notion of, differ *toto caelo*; revolt -at, – from the idea.

shake the head, shrug the shoulders; look -askance, – askant.

secede; recant etc. 607.

Adj. dissenting etc. *v.*; negative etc. 536; dissident, -entient; unconsenting etc. (*refusing*) 764; non-content, -juring; protestant, recusant; unconvinced, -verted.

unavowed, unacknowledged; out of the question.

discontented etc. 832; unwilling etc. 603; extorted.

sectarian, denominational, schismatic, heterodox, intolerant.

Adv. no etc. 536; at -variance, – issue- with; under protest; *non placet*.

Int. God forbid! not for the world; not on your life; I beg to differ; I'll be hanged if; never tell me; your humble servant, pardon me; tell that to the marines.

Phr. many men many minds; *quot homines tot sententiae*; *tant s'en faut*; *il s'en faut bien*.

490. Knowledge.—N. knowledge; cogn-izance, -ition, -oscence; acquaintance, experience, ken, privity, insight, familiarity; com-, ap-prehension; recognition; appreciation etc. (*judgment*) 480; intuition; consci-ence, -ousness; preception, precognition; acroamatics.

light, enlightenment; glimpse, inkling; side light; glimmer, -ing; dawn; scent, suspicion; impression etc. (*idea*) 453; discovery etc. 480*a*.

system –, body- of knowledge; science, philosophy, pansophy; theory, Etiology; circle of the sciences; pandect, doctrine, body of doctrine; cy-, ency-clopedia; school etc. (*system of opinions*) 484.

tree of knowledge; republic of letters etc. (*language*) 560.

erudition, learning, lore, scholarship, reading, letters; literature; booklearning, bookishness; biblio-mania, -latry; information, general information; store of -knowledge etc.; education etc. (*teaching*) 537; culture, attainments; acquirements, -sitions; accomplishments, proficiency; practical knowledge etc. (*skill*) 698; higher education, liberal education; dilettantism; rudiments etc. (*beginning*) 66.

deep –, profound –, solid –, accurate –, acroatic –, acroamatic –, vast –, extensive –, encyclopedical- -knowledge, – learning; omniscience, pantology.

march of intellect; progress –, advance- of -science, – learning; schoolmaster abroad.

V. know, ken, scan, wot; wot –, be aware etc. *adj.*- of; ween, weet, trow, have, possess.

conceive; ap-, com-prehend; take, realize, understand, appreciate; fathom, make out; recognize, discern, perceive, see, get a sight of, experience.

know full well; have –, possess- some knowledge of; be *-au courant* etc. *adj.*; have -in one's head, – at one's fingers' ends; know by -heart, – rote; be master of; *connaître le dessous des cartes*, know what's what etc. 698.

see one's way; learn, discover etc. 480*a*.

come to one's knowledge etc. (*information*) 527.

Adj. knowing etc. *v.*; cognitive; acroamatic.

aware –, cognizant –, conscious- of; acquainted –, made acquainted- with; privy –, no stranger- to; *au -fait*, – *courant*; in the secret; up –, alive- to; sensible of; behind the -scenes, – curtain; let into; apprized –, informed- of; undeceived.

proficient –, versed –, read –, forward –,

strong –, at home- in; conversant –, familiar- with.

erudite, instructed, learned, lettered, educated; high-brow; well-conned, -informed, -read, -grounded, -educated; enlightened, shrewd, insightful, *savant*, blue, bookish, scholastic, solid, profound, deep-read, book-learned; accomplished etc. (*skilful*) 698; omniscient; self-taught, -educated.

known etc. *v.*; ascertained, well-known, recognized, received, notorious, noted; proverbial; familiar, – as household words, to every schoolboy; hackneyed, trite, commonplace.

knowable, cogn-oscible, -izable.

Adv. to –, to the best of- one's knowledge.

Phr. one's eyes being opened etc. (*disclosure*) 529.

491. Ignorance.—N. ignorance, nescience, *tabula rasa*, crass ignorance, *ignorance crasse*; unacquaintance; unconsciousness etc. *adj.*; dark-, blind-ness; incomprehension, inexperience, simplicity.

unknown quantities, *x*, *y*, *z*.

sealed book, *terra incognita*, virgin soil, unexplored ground; dark ages.

[Imperfect knowledge] smattering, superficiality, half-learning, sciolism, glimmering; bewilderment etc. (*uncertainty*) 475; incapacity.

[Affectation of knowledge] pedantry; charlatanry, -ism.

V. be -ignorant etc. *adj.*; not -know etc. 490; know -not, – not what, – nothing of; have no -idea, – notion, – conception; not have the remotest idea; not know chalk from cheese.

ignore, be blind to; keep in ignorance etc. (*conceal*) 528.

see through a glass darkly; have a -film over the eyes, – glimmering etc. *n.*; wonder whether; not know what to make of etc. (*unintelligibility*) 519; not pretend –, not take upon oneself- to say.

Adj. ignorant, nescient; un-knowing, -aware, -acquainted, -apprized, -witting, -weeting, -conscious; wit-, weet-less; a stranger to; unconversant.

un-informed, -cultivated, -versed, -instructed, -taught, -initiated, -tutored, -schooled, -guided, -enlightened; Philistine; behind the age.

shallow, superficial, green, rude, empty, half-learned, illiterate; un-read, -informed, -educated, -learned, -lettered, -bookish; empty-headed; lowbrow; pedantic.

in the dark; be-nighted, -lated; blind-ed, -fold; hoodwinked; misinformed; *au bout de son latin*, at the end of his tether; at fault; at sea etc. (*uncertain*) 475; caught tripping.

un-known, -apprehended, -explained, -ascertained, -investigated, -explored, -heard of, -perceived; concealed etc. 528; novel.

Adv. ignorantly etc. *adj.*; unawares; for -anything, – aught- one knows; not that one knows.

Int. God –, Heaven –, the Lord –, nobody- knows.

Phr. a little learning is a dangerous thing.

492. Scholar.—N. scholar, *connoissuer*, *savant*, pundit, schoolman, professor, graduate, wrangler, moonshee; academ-ician, -ist; fellow, don, post graduate, advanced student; master –, bachelor- of arts; doctor, licentiate, gownsman; philo-sopher, -math; scientist, clerk; soph, -ist, -ister; linguist, classicist; glosso-, etymo-, philologist; philologer; lexico-, glosso-grapher; scholiast, commentator. annotator, grammarian; *littérateur*, *literati*, *dilettanti*, *illuminati*; Mezzofanti, admirable Crichton, Maecenas.

book-worm, *helluo librorum*, biblio-phile, -maniac; blue-stocking, *bas-bleu*; big-wig, learned Theban.

learned –, literary- man; *homo multarum literarum*; man of -learning, – letters, – education; high-brow, intelligentsia.

antiquar-ian, -y; archeologist; sage etc. (*wise man*) 500.

pendant, *doctrinaire*; pedagogue, Dr. Pangloss; pantologist.

teacher etc. 540; schoolboy etc. (*learner*) 541.

Adj. learned etc. 490; brought up at the feet of Gamaliel.

493. Ignoramus.—N. ignoramus, illiterate, moron, dunce, numskull; wooden spoon; no scholar.

sciolist, smatterer, dabbler, half-scholar; *charlatan*; wiseacre.

novice, griffin; greenhorn etc. (*dupe*) 547; tyro etc. (*learner*) 541.

lubber etc. (*bungler) 701; fool etc. 501; pedant etc. 492.*

Adj. bookless, shallow, simple, dense, dumb, thick, dull, ignorant etc. 491.

494. Truth. [Object of knowledge.]—**N.** fact, reality etc. (*existence*) 1; plain matter of fact; nature etc. (*principle*) 5; truth, verity; gospel; orthodoxy etc. 983*a*; authenticity; veracity etc. 543.

accuracy, exactitude; exact-, precise-ness etc. *adj.*; precision, delicacy; rigor, mathematical precision, punctuality; clockwork precision etc. (*regularity*) 80.

orthology; *ipsissima verba*; letter of the law, realism.

plain –, honest –, sober –, naked –, unalloyed –, unqualified –, stern –, exact –, intrinsic- truth; *nuda veritas*; the very thing; not an -illusion etc. 495; real Simon Pure; unvarnished tale; the truth, the whole truth and nothing but the truth; just the thing.

V. be -true etc. *adj.*, – the case; stand the test; have the true ring; hold -good, – true, – water; conform to rule.

render –, prove- -true etc. *adj.*; substantiate etc. (*evidence*) 467.

get at the truth etc. (*discover*) 480*a*.

Adj. real, actual etc. (*existing*) 1; veritable, true; certain etc. 474; substantially –, categorically- true etc; true -to the letter; – to life, – to scale, – the facts, – as gospel; unimpeachable; veracious etc. 543; unre-, uncon-futed; un-ideal -imagined; realistic.

exact, accurate, definite, precise, well defined, just, right, correct, strict, severe; close etc. (*similar*) 17; literal; rigid, rigorous; scrupulous etc. (*con-*

scientious) 939; religiously exact, punctual, mathematical, scientific; faithful, constant, unerring; curious, particular, punctilious, meticulous, nice, delicate, fine.

genuine, authentic, legitimate, pukka; orthodox etc. 983*a*; official, *ex officio*.

pure, natural, sound, sterling; un-sophisticated, -adulterated, -varnished, -colored; in its true colors.

well-grounded, -founded; solid, substantial, tangible, valid; undis-torted, -guised; un-affected, -exaggerated, -romantic, -flattering.

Adv. truly etc.*adj.*; verily, indeed, in reality; as a matter of fact; beyond -doubt, – question; with truth etc. (*veracity*) 543; certainly etc. (*certain*) 474; actually etc. (*existence*) 1; in effect etc. (*intrinsically*) 5.

exactly etc. *adj.* ; *ad amussim*; *verbatim*, *– et literatim*; word for word, literally, *literatim*, *totidem verbis*, *sic*, to the letter, chapter and verse, *ipsissimis verbis*; *ad unguem*; to an inch; to a -nicety, – hair, – tittle, – turn, – T; *au pied de la lettre*; neither more nor less; in -every respect, – all respects; *sous tous les rapports*; at -any rate, – all events; strictly speaking.

Phr. the -truth, – fact- is; *rem acu tetigisti*.

495. Error.—N. error, fallacy; misconception, -apprehension, -understanding; inexactness etc. *adj.*; laxity; misconstruction etc. (*misinterpretation*) 523; miscomputation etc. (*misjudgment*) 481; *non-sequitur* etc. 477; misstatement, -report; anachronism; malapropism.

mistake; miss, fault, blunder, boner, bloomer, howler, *quid pro quo*, cross purposes, oversight, misprint, *erratum*, *corrigendum*, slip, blot, flaw, loose thread; trip, stumble etc. (*failure*) 732; botchery etc. (*want of skill*) 699; slip of the -tongue, – pen; *lapsus -linguae*, *– calami*, clerical error; bull etc. (*absurdity*) 497.

il-, de-lusion; false -impression, – idea; bubble; self-deceit, -deception; warped notion; mists of error; superstition, exploded notion.

heresy etc. (*heterodoxy*) 984; hallucination etc. (*insanity*) 503; false light etc. (*fallacy of vision*) 443; dream etc. (*fancy*) 515; fable etc. (*untruth*) 546; bias etc. (*misjudgment*) 481; misleading etc. *v.*

V. be -erroneous etc. *adj.*

cause error; mis-lead, -guide; lead -astray, – into error; beguile, misinform etc. (*misteach*) 538; delude; give a false -impression, – idea; falsify, garble, misstate; deceive etc. 545; lie etc. 544.

err; be -in error etc. *adj.*; – mistaken etc. *v.*; be deceived etc. (*duped*) 547; mistake, receive a false impression, deceive oneself; fall into –, lie under –, labor under- -an error etc. *n.*; be in the wrong, blunder; mis-apprehend, -conceive, -understand, -reckon, -count, -calculate etc. (*misjudge*) 481.

play –, be- at cross purposes etc. (*misinterpret*) 523.

trip, stumble; lose oneself etc. (*uncertainty*) 475; go astray; fail etc. 732; take the wrong sow by the ear etc. (*mismanage*) 699; put the saddle on the wrong horse; reckon without one's host; take the shadow for the substance etc. (*credulity*) 486; dream etc. (*imagine*) 515.

Adj. erroneous, untrue, false, devoid of truth, fallacious, faulty, apocryphal, unreal, ungrounded, groundless; unsubstantial etc. 4; heretical etc. (*heterodox*) 984; unsound; illogical etc. 477; wrong.

in-, un-exact; in-accurate, -correct; indefinite etc. (*uncertain*) 475.

illus-ive, -ory; delusive; mock; ideal etc. (*imaginary*) 515; spurious etc. 545; deceitful etc. 544; perverted.

controvertible, unsustain-able, -ed; unauthenticated, untrustworthy.

exploded, refuted, discarded.

in –, under an- error etc. *n.*; mistaken etc. *v.*; tripping etc. *v.*; out, – in one's reckoning; aberrant; beside –, wide of the- -mark, – truth; astray etc. (*at fault*) 475; on -a false, – the wrong-scent; in the wrong box; at cross purposes, all in the wrong, all abroad, at sea.

Adv. more or less.

496. Maxim.—N. maxim, aphorism; apo-, apoph-thegm; *dictum*, saying, gnome, adage, saw, proverb, epigram; sentence, *mot*, motto, word, by-word, precept, moral, phylactery, *protasis*, brocard.

axiom, postulate, theorem, *scholium*, truism.

reflection etc. (*idea*) 453; conclusion etc. (*judgment*) 480; golden rule etc. (*precept*) 697; principle, *principia*; profession of faith etc. (*belief*) 484; formula.

wise –, sage –, received –, admitted –, recognized- maxim etc.; true –, common –, hackneyed –, trite –, commonplace- saying etc.

Adj. aphoristic, proverbial, phylacteric; axiomatic, gnomic.

Adv. as -the saying is, – they say.

497. Absurdity.—N. absurd-ity, -ness etc. *adj.*; imbecility etc. 499; alogy, nonsense, paradox, inconsistency; stultiloqu-y, -ence, futility.

blunder, muddle, bull; Irish-, Hibernic-ism; slip-slop; anti climax; bathos; sophism etc. 477.

farce, burlesque, *galimatias*, *amphigouri*, rhapsody; farrago etc. (*disorder*) 59; extravagance, romance; sciomachy.

joke, catch, sell, pun, verbal quibble, macaronic.

jargon, fustian, twaddle etc. (*no meaning*) 517; exaggeration etc. 549; moonshine, stuff; mare's nest.

vagary, tomfoolery, mummery, monkey trick, practical joke, *boutade*, *escapade*.

V. play the fool etc. 499; stultify, blunder, muddle; joke; talk nonsense, *parler à tort et à travers*; *battre la campagne*; be -absurd etc. *adj.*

Adj. absurd, nonsensical, preposterous, egregious, senseless, farcical, inconsistent, ridiculous, extravagant, quibbling, futile; macaronic, punning, paradoxical.

foolish etc. 499; sophistical etc. 477; unmeaning etc. 517; without rhyme or reason; fantastic.

Int. fiddle-de-dee! pish! pish and tush! pho! stuff and nonsense! rubbish! !rot! bosh! in the name of the Prophet—figs!

Phr. *credat Judaeus Apella*; tell it to the marines.

498. Intelligence. Wisdom.—N. intelligence, capacity, comprehension, understanding, intellect etc. 450; nous, parts, sagacity, mother wit, wit, *esprit*, gumption, quick parts, grasp of intellect; acuteness etc. *adj.*; acumen, subtlety, penetration; perspica-cy, -city; discernment; long-headedness, due sense of, good judgment; discrimination etc. 465; craftiness, cunning etc. 702; refinement etc. (*taste*) 850.

head, brains, gray matter, headpiece, upper story, long head; eagle -eye, – glance; eye of a -lynx, – hawk.

wisdom, sapience, sense; good –, common –, plain –, horse- sense; clear thinking; rationality, reason; reasonableness etc. *adj.*; judgment; solidity, depth, profundity, caliber; enlarged views; reach –, compass- of thought; enlargement of mind.

genius, inspiration, *geist*, fire of genius, heaven-born genius, soul; talent etc. (*aptitude*) 698.

[Wisdom in action] prudence etc. 864; vigilance etc. 459; tact etc. 698; foresight etc. 510; sobriety, self-possession, *aplomb*, ballast, mental -poise, – balance.

a bright thought, inspiration, brainwave, not a bad idea.

V. be -intelligent etc. *adj.*; have all one's wits about one; understand etc. (*intelligible*) 518; catch –, take in- an idea; take a -joke, – hint.

see -through, – at a glance, – with half an eye, – far into, – through a millstone; penetrate; discern etc. (*descry*) 441; foresee etc. 510.

discriminate etc. 465; know what's what etc. 698; listen to reason.

Adj. [Applied to persons] intelligent, quick of apprehension, keen, acute, alive, brainy, awake, bright, quick, sharp; quick-, keen-, clear-, sharp- -eyed, -sighted, -witted; wide awake; canny, shrewd, astute; clear-headed; far-sighted etc. 510; discerning, perspicacious, penetrating, piercing; argute nimble-, needle-witted; sharp as a needle; alive to etc. (*cognizant*) 490; clever etc. (*apt*) 698; arch etc. (*cunning*) 702; *pas si bête*; acute etc. 682.

wise, sage, sapient, sagacious, reasonable, rational, sound, in one's right mind, sensible, *abnormis sapiens*, judicious, strong-minded.

un-prejudiced, -biassed, -bigoted, -prepossessed; un-dazzled, -perplexed; of unwarped judgment, impartial, equitable, fair, broad-minded.

cool; cool-, long-, hard-, strong-headed; long-sighted, calculating, thoughtful, reflecting; solid, deep, profound.

oracular; heaven-directed, -born.

prudent etc. (*cautious*) 864; sober, staid, solid; considerate, politic, wise in one's generation; watchful etc. 459; provident etc. (*prepared*) 673; in advance of one's age; wise as -a serpent, – Solomon, – Solon.

[Applied to actions] wise, sensible, reasonable, judicious; well-judged, -advised; prudent, politic; expedient etc. 646.

499. Imbecility. Folly.—N. want of -intelligence etc. 498, – intellect etc. 450; shallow-, silli-, foolish-ness etc. *adj.*; imbecility, incapacity, vacancy of mind, poverty of intellect, clouded perception, poor head, apartments to let; stup-, stolidity; hebetude, dull understanding, meanest capacity; short-sightedness; incompetence etc. (*unskilfulness*) 699.

one's weak side; bias etc. 481; infatuation etc. (*insanity*) 503.

simplicity, puerility, babyhood; dotage, anility, second childishness, senile dementia, fatuity; idiocy, -tism; driveling.

folly, frivolity, desipience, irrationality, trifling, ineptitude, nugacity, inconsistency, lip-wisdom, conceit; sophistry etc. 477; giddiness etc. (*inattention*) 458; eccentricity etc. 503; extravagance etc. (*absurdity*) 497; rashness etc. 863.

act of folly etc. 699.

V. be -imbecile etc. *adj.*; have no -brains, – sense etc. 498.

trifle, drivel, *radoter*, dote; ramble etc. (*madness*) 503; play the -fool, – monkey, – goat, take leave of one's senses; not see an inch beyond one's nose; stultify oneself etc. 699; talk nonsense etc. 497.

Adj. [Applied to persons] un-intelligent, -intellectual, -reasoning; mind-, wit-, reason-, brainless; having no -head etc. 498; not -bright etc. 498; inapprehensible.

weak-, addle-, puzzle-, blunder-, muddle-, muddy-, pig-, beetle-, maggotty-, gross-headed; beef-, fat- -witted, -headed.

weak, feeble-minded; dull-, shallow-, rattle-, lack-brained; half-, nit-, short-, dull-, blunt-witted; shallow-, clod-, addle-pated; dim-, short-sighted; thick-skulled; weak in the upper story.

shallow, *borné*, weak, wanting, soft, nutty, sappy, spoony; dull, – as a beetle; stupid, heavy, insulse, obtuse, blunt, stolid, doltish, asinine; inapt etc. 699; prosaic etc. 843.

child-ish, -like; infant-ine, -ile; baby-, bab-ish; puerile; anile; simple etc. (*credulous*) 486.

fatuous, idiotic, imbecile, moronic, driveling; blatant, babbling; vacant; sottish; bewildered etc. 475.

blockish, unteachable; Boeot-ian, -ic; bovine; un-gifted, -discerning, -enlightened, -wise, -philosophical; apish.

foolish, silly, senseless, irrational, insensate, nonsensical, inept; maudlin.

narrow-minded etc. 481; bigoted etc. (*obstinate*) 606; giddy etc. (*thoughtless*) 458; rash etc. 863; eccentric etc. (*crazed*) 503.

[Applied to actions] foolish, unwise, indiscreet, injudicious, improper, unreasonable, without reason, ridiculous, silly, stupid, asinine; ill-imagined, -advised, -judged, -devised; inconsistent, irrational, unphilosophical; extravagant etc. (*nonsensical*) 497; sleeveless, idle; useless etc. 645; inexpedient etc. 647; frivolous etc. (*trivial*) 643; absurd etc. 497.

Phr. *Davis sum non Oedipus.*

500. Sage.—N. sage, wise man; pundit; master -mind, – spirit of the age; longhead, thinker, philosopher.

authority, oracle, mentor, luminary, shining light, *esprit fort*, *magnus Apollo,* Solon, Solomon, Nestor, Magi, 'second Daniel.'

man of learning etc. 492; expert etc. 700; wizard etc. 994.

[Ironically] wiseacre, bigwig.

Adj. wise, learned; authoritative, oracular; erudite etc. 490; venerable, reverenced, revered, *emeritus*.

501. Fool.—N. fool, idiot, tomfool, wiseacre, simpleton, Simple Simon, nit-wit, witling, dizzard, donkey, ass; ninny, -hammer; moron, dolt, booby, Tom Noddy, looby, hoddy-doddy, noddy, nonny, noodle, nizy, owl; goose, -cap; *imbécile*; gaby, *radoteur*, nincompoop, *badaud*, zany; trifler, babbler; pretty fellow; natural, *niais*.

child, baby, infant, innocent, milksop, sop.

oaf, lout, loon, lown, dullard, doodle, calf, colt, buzzard, block, put, stick, stock, numps, tony.

bull-, dunder-, addle-, block-, dull-, logger-, jolt-, jolter-, beetle-, gross-, thick-, giddy-head; num-, thick- skull; lack-, shallow-brain; half-, lack-wit; dunder-pate; fat-head, poor stick.

sawney, gowk; clod, -hopper; clod-, clot-poll, pate; bull-calf; men of Boeotia, wise men of Gotham.

un sot à triple étage, sot; jobbernowl, changeling, mooncalf, *gobemouche*.

dotard, driveller; old -fogey, – woman; crone, grandmother.

greenhorn etc. (*dupe*) 547; dunce etc. (*ignoramus*) 493; lubber etc. (*bungler*) 701; madman etc. 504.

one who -will not set the Thames on fire, – did not invent gunpowder; *qui n'a pas inventé la poudre*; no conjuror.

502. Sanity.—N. sanity; soundness etc. *adj.*; rationality, normality, sobriety, lucidity, lucid interval; senses, sober senses, sound mind, *mens sana*.

V. be -sane etc. *adj.*; retain one's senses, – reason.

become -sane etc. *adj.*; come to one's senses, sober down.

render -sane etc. *adj.*; bring to one's senses, sober.

Adj. sane, rational, reasonable, *compos mentis*, of sound mind; sound, -minded.

self-possessed; sober, -minded.

in one's -sober senses, – right mind; in possession of one's faculties.

Adv. sanely etc. *adj.*

503. Insanity.—N. disordered -reason, – intellect; diseased –, unsound –, abnormal- mind; derangement, unsoundness.

insanity, lunacy; madness etc. *adj.*; mania, *rabies*, *furor*, mental aliénation, paranoia, aberration; *amentia*, dementation, -tia, -cy; *dementia praecox*; *morosis*, idiocy, phrenitis, frenzy, raving, incoherence, wandering, delirium, calenture of the brain, delusion, hallucination; lycanthropy, brain storm, *delirium tremens*, D.T.'s.

vertigo, dizziness, swimming; sunstroke, *coup de soleil*, siriasis.

fanatisism, infatuation, craze; oddity, eccentricity, twist, monomania; klepto-, dipso-mania; hypochondriasis etc. (*low spirits*) 837; *melancholia*, hysteria.

screw –, tile –, slate- loose; bee in one's bonnet, rats in the upper story.

dotage etc. (*imbecility*) 499.

V. be –, become- -insane etc. *adj.*; lose one's senses, – reason, – faculties, – wits; go –, run-mad, run amuck; rave, dote, ramble, wander; drivel etc. (*be imbecile*) 499; have a -screw loose etc. *n.*, – devil; *avoir le diable au corps*; lose one's head etc. (*be uncertain*) 475.

derange, render –, drive- -mad etc. *adj.*; madden, dementate, addle the wits, derange the head, infatuate, befool; turn -the brain, – one's head.

Adj. insane, mad, lunatic; crazy, crazed, *aliéné*, *non compos mentis*; not right, cracked, touched; bereft of reason; unhinged, deranged, unsettled in one's mind; insensate, reasonless, beside oneself, demented, daft; phren-, fren-zied, -etic; possessed, – with a devil; far gone, maddened, moonstruck; shatterpated; barmy; mad-, scatter-, shatter-, crack-brained, off one's head; bug-house, *loco*.

maniacal; manic, manic-depressive; delirious, light-headed, incoherent, rambling, doting, wandering; frantic, raving, stark staring mad, amok, amuck.

corybantic, dithyrambic; rabid, giddy, vertiginous, dizzy, wild, haggard, mazed; flighty; distracted, -aught; bewildered etc. (*uncertain*) 475.

mad as a -March hare, – hatter; of -unsound mind etc. *n.* touched –, wrong –, not right- in one's -head, – mind, – wits, – upper story; out of one's -mind, – senses, – wits; not in one's right mind.

fanatical, infatuated, odd, eccentric; hypp-ed, -ish.

imbecile, silly etc. 499.

Adv. like one possessed.

Phr. the mind having lost its halance; the reason under a cloud; *tête -exaltée*, *-montée*.

504. Madman—N. madman, lunatic, maniac, bedlamite, candidate for Bedlam, raver, madcap; energumen; paranoiac; auto-, mono-, pyro-, megalo-, dipso-, klepto-maniac; hypochondriac etc. (low spirit) 837.

dreamer etc. 515; rhapsodist, seer, high-flier, enthusiast, crank, eccentric, nut, fanatic, *fanatico*; *exalté*; knight errant, Don Quixote.

idiot etc. 501.

505. Memory.—N. memory, remembrance; reten-tion, -tiveness; tenacity; *veteris vestigia flammae*; tablets of the memory; readiness.

reminiscence, recognition, recurrence, recollection, rememoration; retrospect, -ion; after-thought.

suggestion etc. (*information*) 527; prompting etc. *v.*; hint, reminder, token of remembrance, *memento*, *souvenir*, keepsake, relic, *memorandum*; remembrancer, flapper; memorial etc. (*record*) 551; commemoration etc. (*celebration*) 883.

things to be remembered, *memorabilia*.

art of –, artificial- memory; *memoria technica*; mnemo-nics, -technics; phrenotypics; Mnemosyne; memorandum-, note-, engagement-, prompt-book.

retentive –, tenacious –, green –, trustworthy –, capacious –, faithful –, correct –, exact –, ready –, prompt- memory.

V. remember, mind; retain the -memory, – remembrance- of; keep in view.

have –, hold –, bear –, carry –, keep –, retain- in *or* in the -thoughts, – mind, – memory, – remembrance; be in –, live in –, remain in –, dwell in –, haunt –, impress- one's -memory, – thoughts, – mind.

sink in the mind; run in the head; not be able to get it out of one's head; be deeply impressed with; rankle etc. (*revenge*) 919.

recur to the mind; flash -on the mind, – across the memory.

recognize, recollect, bethink oneself, recall, call up, conjure up, retrace; look –, trace- -back, – backwards; think –, look back- upon; review; call –, recall –, bring- to mind; remembrance; carry one's thoughts back; rake up the past.

suggest etc. (*inform*) 527; prompt; put –, keep- in mind; remind; fan the embers; call –, summon –, rip- up; renew; *infandum renovare dolorem*; task –, tax –, jog –, flap –, refresh –, rub up –, awaken- the memory; pull by the sleeve; bring back the memory, put in remembrance, memorialize.

get –, have –, learn –, know –, say –, repeat- by -heart, – rote; drive –, get- into -one's head; say one's lesson; repeat, – as a parrot; have at one's finger's ends.

commit to memory; memorize; con, – over; fix –, rivet –, imprint –, impress –, stamp –, grave –, engrave –, store –, treasure up –, bottle up –, embalm –, enshrine- in the memory; load –, store –, stuff –, burden- the memory with.

redeem from oblivion; keep the memory -alive, – green; *tangere ulcus*; keep up the memory of; commemorate etc. (*celebrate*) 883.

make a note of etc. (*record*) 551.

Adj. remember-ing, -ed etc. *v.*; mindful, reminiscential; retained in the memory etc. *v.*; pent up in one's memory; fresh; green, – in remembrance, still vivid; unforgotten, present to the mind; within one's -memory etc. *n.*; indelible; not to be forgotten, unforgettable, enduring; uppermost in one's thoughts; memorable etc. (*important*) 642.

Adv. by -heart, – rote; without book, *memoriter*.

in memory of; *in memoriam*; suggestive.

Phr. *manet altâ mente repostum*; *forsan et haec olim meminisse juvabit.*

506. Oblivion.—N. oblivion; forgetfulness etc. *adj.*; obliteration etc. 552, of –, insensibility etc. 823 to- the past.

short –, treacherous –, loose –, slippery –, failing- memory; decay –, failure –, lapse- of memory; memory like a sieve; waters of -Lethe, – oblivion, *amnesia.*

pardon, acquittal, amnesty, oblivion; absolution.

V. forget; be -forgetful etc. *adj.*; fall –, sink- into oblivion; have -a short memory etc. *n.* – no head.

forget one's own name, have on the tip of one's tongue, come in at one ear and go out at the other.

slip –, escape –, fade from –, die away from- the memory; lose, – sight of.

unlearn; efface etc. 552 –, discharge- from the memory; consign to -oblivion, – the tomb of the Capulets; think no more of etc. (*turn the attention from*) 458; cast behind one's back, wean one's thoughts from; let bygones be bygones etc. (*forgive*) 918.

Adj. forgotten etc. *v.*; unremembered, past recollection, bygone, out of mind; buried –, sunk- in oblivion; clean forgotten; gone out of one's -head, – recollection.

forgetful, oblivious, mindless, heedless, Lethean; insensible etc. 823, to the past.

Phr. *non mi ricordo*; the memory -failing, – deserting one, – being at (*or* in) fault.

507. Expectation.—N. expect-ation, -ance, -ancy; anticipation, reckoning, calculation; contingency; foresight etc. 510.

contemplation, prospection, look out; prospect, perspective, horizon, vista; destiny etc. 152.

suspense, waiting, abeyance; curiosity etc. 455; anxious –, ardent –, eager –, breathless –, sanguine- expectation; torment of Tantalus.

presumption, hope etc. 858; trust etc. (*belief*) 484; prognostication, auspices etc. (*prediction*) 511.

V. expect; look -for, – out for, – forward to; hope for, anticipate; have in -prospect, – contemplation; keep in view; contemplate, promise oneself; not -wonder etc. 870 -at, – if.

wait –, tarry –, lie in wait –, watch –, bargain- for; keep a -good, – sharp- look-out for; await; stand at 'attention,' abide, bide one's –, mark- time, watch.

foresee etc. 510; prepare for etc. 673; forestall etc. (*be early*) 132; count upon etc. (*believe in*) 484; think likely etc. (*probability*) 472; make one's mouth water.

lead one to expect etc. (*predict*) 511; have in store for etc. (*destiny*) 152.

prick up one's ears, hold one's breath.

Adj. expentant; expecting etc. *v.*; in -expectation etc. *n.*; on the watch etc. (*vigilant*) 459; open -eyed, -mouthed; agape, gaping, all agog; on -tenterhooks, – tiptoe, – the tiptoe of expectation; *aux aguets*; ready; curious etc. 455; looking forward to; prepared for; on the rack.

expected etc. *v.*; long expected, foreseen; in prospect etc. *n.*; prospective; in -one's eye, – view, – the horizon; impending etc. (*destiny*) 152.

Adv. expectantly; in the event of; on the watch etc. *adj.*; with -breathless expectation etc. *n.*; – bated breath, – eyes, – ears strained; *arrectis auribus*; on edge.

Phr. we shall see; *nous verrons.*

508. Inexpectation.—N. in-, non-expectation; false expectation etc. (*disappointment*) 509; miscalculation etc. 481; unforeseen contingency, the unforeseen, the unexpected.

surprise, sudden burst, thunderclap, blow, shock; bolt out of the blue; eye-opener; wonder etc. 870.

V. not -expect etc. 507; be taken by surprise; start; miscalculate etc. 481; not bargain for; come –, fall- upon.

be -unexpected etc. *adj.*; come -unawares etc. *adv.*; turn up, pop, drop from the clouds; come –, burst –, flash –, bounce –, steal –, creep- upon one; come –, burst- like a thunder-clap; -bolt; take –, catch- -by surprise, – unawares, – napping. pounce –, spring a mine- upon.

surprise, startle, take aback, electrify, stun, stagger, take away one's breath, throw off one's guard; astonish etc. (*strike with wonder*) 870.

Adj. non-expectant; surprised etc. *v.*; unwarned, -aware; off one's guard; inattentive etc. 458.

un-expected, -anticipated, -prepared for, -looked for, -foreseen, -hoped for; dropped from the clouds; beyond –, contrary to –, against- expectation; out of one's reckoning; unheard of etc. (*exceptional*) 83; startling; sudden etc. (*instantaneous*) 113.

Adv. abruptly, unexpectedly, plump, pop, *à l'improviste*, unawares; without -notice, – warning, – saying 'by your leave;' like a -thief in the night, – thunderbolt; in an unguarded moment; suddenly etc. (*instantaneously*) 113.

Int. heyday! etc. (*wonder*) 870.

Phr. little did one -think, – expect; nobody would ever -suppose, – think, – expect; who would have thought?

509. Disappointment. [Failure of expectation.]—**N.** disappointment, disillusionment; blighted hope, balk; blow; slip 'twixt cup and lip; non-fulfilment of one's hopes; sad –, bitter- disappointment; trick of fortune; afterclap; false –, vain- expectation; miscalculation etc. 481; fool's paradise; much cry and little wool.

V. be disappointed; look -blank, – blue; look –, stand- -aghast etc. (*wonder*) 870; find to one's cost; laugh on the wrong side of one's mouth; find one a false prophet.

disappoint; crush –, dash –, balk –, disappoint –, blight –, falsify –, defeat –, not realize- one's -hope, – expectation; balk, jilt, bilk; play one -false, – a trick; dash the cup from the lips; tantalize; dumb-found, -founder; disillusion, -ize; dissatisfy, disgruntle.

Adj. disappointed etc. *v.*; disconcerted, aghast; out of one's reckoning; disgruntled.

Phr. the mountain brought forth a mouse; *nascitur ridiculus mus*; *parturiunt montes*; *diis aliter visum*, the bubble burst; one's countenance falling.

510. Foresight.—N. foresight, prospicience, prevision, longsightedness; anticipation; providence etc. (*preparation*) 673.

fore-thought, -cast; pre-deliberation, -surmise; foregone conclusion etc. (*prejudgment*) 481; prudence etc. (*caution*) 864.

foreknowledge; *prognosis*; pre-cognition, -science, -notion, -sentiment; second sight; sagacity etc. (*intelligence*) 498.

prospect etc. (*expectation*) 507; foretaste; prospectus etc. (*plan*) 626.

V. foresee; look -forwards to, – ahead, – beyond; scent from afar; feel in one's bones; look –, pry –, peep into the future.

see one's way; see how the -land lies, – wind blows, – cat jumps.

anticipate; expect etc. 507; be beforehand etc. (*early*) 132; predict etc. 511; fore-know, -judge, -cast; surmise; have an eye to the -future, – main chance; *respicere finem*; keep a sharp look-out etc. (*vigilance*) 459; forewarn etc. 668.

Adj. foreseeing etc. *v.*; prescient; anticipatory; far-seeing, -sighted; sagacious etc. (*intelligent*) 498; weather-wise; provident etc. (*prepared*) 673; prospective etc. 507.

Adv. against the time when.

511. Prediction.—N. prediction, announcement; program, programme etc. (*plan*) 626; premonition etc. (*warning*) 668; *prognosis*, prophecy, vaticination, Mantology, prognostication, premonstration, augur-y, -ation; a-, ha-riolation; fore-, a-boding; bode-, abode-ment; omin-ation, -ousness; auspices, forecast; sign, presage, prognostic; omen etc. 512; horoscope, nativity; sooth, -saying; fortune-telling; divination; crystal gazing, necromancy etc. 992; prophet etc. 512.

[Divination by the stars] astrology, horoscopy, astromancy, judicial astrology.*

[Place of prediction] *adytum*.

prefigur-ation, -ement; prototype, type.

V. predict, prognosticate, prophesy, vaticinate, divine, foretell, soothsay, augurate, tell fortunes; cast a -horoscope, – nativity; advise; forewarn etc. 668.

presage, augur, bode; a-, fore-bode, -cast; fore-, be-token; pre-figure, -show; portend; fore-show, -shadow, shadow forth, typify, ominate, signify, point to, precurse.

usher in, herald, premise, announce; lower.

hold out –, raise –, excite- -expectation, – hope; bid fair, promise, lead one to expect; be the -precursor etc. 64.

Adj. predicting etc. *v.*; predictive, prophetic, fatidical, vaticinal, oracular, Sibylline, haruspical, weatherwise.

ominous, presageful, portentous; augur-ous, -al, -ial; auspici-al, -ous; prescious, monitory, extispicious, premonitory, precusory, significant of, pregnant with, big with the fate of.

Phr. 'coming events cast their shadows before.'

*The following terms, expressive of different forms of divination, have been collected from various sources, and are here given as a curious illustration of bygone superstitions:

Divination *by oracles*, Theomancy; *by the Bible*, Bibliomancy; *by ghosts*, Psychomancy; *by spirits seen in a magic lens*, Cristallomantia; *by shadows or manes*, Sciomancy; *by appearances in the air*, Aeromancy, Chaomancy, *by the stars at birth*, Genethliacs; *by meteors*, Meteoromancy; *by winds*, Austromancy; *by sacrificial appearances*, Aruspicy (*or* Haruspicy), Hieromancy, Hieroscopy; *by the entrails of animals sacrificed*, Hieromancy; *by the entrails of a human sacrifice*, Anthropomancy; *by the entrails of fishes*, Ichthyomancy; *by sacrificial fire*, Pyromancy; *by red-hot iron*, Sideromancy; *by smoke from the alter*, Capnomancy; *by mice*, Myomancy; *by birds*, Orniscopy, Ornithomancy; *by a cock picking up grains*, Alectryomancy (*or* Alectoromancy); *by fishes*, Ophiomancy; *by herbs*, Botanomancy; *by water*, Hydromancy; *by fountains*, Pegomancy; *by a wand*, Rhabdomancy; *by dough of cakes*, Crithomancy; *by meal*, Aleuromancy, Alphitomancy; *by salt*, Halomancy; *by dice*, Cleromancy; *by arrows*, Belomancy; *by a balanced hatchet*, Axinomancy; *by a balanced sieve*, Coscinomancy; *by a suspended ring*, Dactyliomancy; *by dots made at random on paper*, Geomancy; *by precious stones*, Lithomancy; *by pebbles*, Pessomancy; *by pebbles drawn from a heap*, Psephomancy; *by mirrors*, Catoptromancy; *by writings in ashes*, Tephramancy; *by dreams*, Oneiromancy; *by the hand*, Palmistry, Chiromancy; *by nails reflecting the sun's rays*, Onychomancy; *by finger rings*, Dactylomancy; *by numbers*, Arithmancy; *by drawing lots*, Sortilege; *by passages in books*, Stichomancy; *by the letters forming the name of the person*, Onomancy, Nomancy; *by the features*. Anthroposcopy; *by the mode of laughing*. Geloscopy; *by ventriloquism*. Gastromancy; *by walking in a circle*. Gyromancy; *by dropping melted wax into water*. Ceromancy; *by currents*. Bletonism.

512. Omen.—N. omen, portent, presage, prognostic, augury, auspice; sigh etc. (*indication*) 550; herald, forerunner, harbinger etc. (*precursor*) 64.

bird of ill omen, signs of the times; gathering clouds; warning etc. 668.

prefigurement etc. 511.

513. Oracle.—N. oracle; prophet, -ess; seer, soothsayer, augur, fortune-teller, palmist, medium, clairvoyant, crystal gazer, witch, geomancer, *aruspex*; a-, ha-ruspice; Sibyl; Python, -ess; Pythia; Pythian –, Delphian- oracle; Monitor, Sphinx, Tiresias, Cassandra, Sibylline leaves; Zadkiel, Old Moore; sorcerer etc. 994; interpreter etc. 524.

514. Supposition.—N. supposition, assumption, postulation, condition, pre-supposition, hypothesis, postulate, *postulatum*, theory, *data*; pro-, position; *thesis*, theorem; proposal etc. (*plan*) 626.

bare –, vague –, loose- -supposition, – suggestion; conceit; conjecture; guess, – work; rough guess, shot; conjecturality; surmise, suspicion, inkling, suggestion, suggestiveness, association of ideas, hint; presumption etc. (*belief*) 484; divination, speculation.

theorist, speculator, doctrinarian, hypothesist.

V. suppose, conjecture, surmise, suspect, guess, divine; theorize; pre-sume, -surmise, -suppose; assume, fancy, wis, take it; give a guess, speculate, believe, dare say, take it into one's head, take for granted.

put forth; pro-pound, -pose; moot; hypothesize; start, put a case, submit, move, make a motion; hazard –, throw out –, put forward- a - suggestion, – conjecture.

allude to, suggest, hint, put it into one's head.

suggest itself etc. (*thought*) 451; run in the head etc. (*memory*) 505; marvel –, wonder- -if, – whether.

Adj. supposing etc. *v.*; given, mooted, postulatory; assumed etc. *v.*; supposit-ive, -itious; gratuitous, speculative, conjectural, hypothetical, suppositional, theoretical, academic, supposable, presumptive, putative.

suggestive, allusive, stimulating.

Adv. if, – so be; an; on the -supposition etc. *n.*; *ex hypothesi*; in -case, – the event of; *quasi*, as if, provided; perhaps etc. (*by possibility*) 470; for aught one knows.

515. Imagination.—N. imagination; originality; invention; fancy; inspiration; *verve*; empathy.

warm –, heated –, excited –, sanguine –, ardent –, fiery –, boiling –, wild –, bold –, daring –, playful –, lively –, fertile- - imagination, – fancy.

'mind's eye;' 'such stuff as dreams are made of.'

ideal-ity, -ism; romanticism, utopianism, castle-building; dreaming; frenzy; ecs-, ex-tasy; calenture etc. (*delirium*) 503; reverie, brown study, trance; somnambulism.

conception, *vorstellung*, ercogitation, 'a fine frenzy,' poetic frenzy, divine afflatus; cloud-, dream-land; flight –, fumes- of fancy; 'thick-coming fancies;' creation –, coinage- of the brain; imagery, word painting.

conceit, maggot, figment, myth, dream, vision, shadow, chimera; phan-tasm, -tasy; fantasy, fancy; whim, -sey; vagary, rhapsody, romance, *extravaganza*; air-drawn dagger, bugbear, nightmare; flying Dutchman, great sea-serpent, man in the moon, castle in the air, *château en Espagne*; Utopia, Atlantis, happy valley, millennium, fairy land; land of Prester John, kingdom of Micomicon; work of fiction etc. (*novel*) 594; poetry etc. 597; drama etc. 599; Arabian nights; *le pot au lait*; dream of Alnaschar etc. (*hope*) 858; day –, golden- dream

illusion etc. (*error*) 495; phantom etc. (*fallacy of vision*) 443; *Fata Morgana* etc. (*ignis fatuus*) 423; vapor etc. (*cloud*) 353; stretch of the imagination etc. (*exaggeration*) 549.

idealist, romanticist, visionary; mopus; romancer, dreamer; somnambulist; rhapsodist etc. (*fanatic*) 504.

V. imagine, fancy, conceive; ideal-, real-ize; dream, – of; 'give to airy nothing a local habitation and a name.'

create, originate, devise, invent, coin, fabricate; improvise, strike out something new.

set one's wits to work; strain –, crack- one's invention; rack –, ransack –, cudgel- one's brains; excogitate.

give -play, – the reins, – a loose- to the - imagination, – fancy; empathize; indulge in reverie.

conjure up a vision; fancy –, represent –, picture –, figure- to oneself; envisage.

float in the mind; suggest itself etc. (*thought*) 451.

Adj. imagined etc. *v.*; *ben trovato*; air-drawn, - built.

imagin-ing etc. *v.*, -ative; original, inventive, creative, fertile, productive; ingenious.

romantic, high-flown, flighty, extravagant, fanatic, enthusiastic, Utopian, Quixotic; preposterous, rhapsodical.

ideal, unreal; in the clouds, *in nubibus*; unsubstantial etc. 4; illusory etc. (*fallacious*) 495; fictitious, theoretical, hypothetical.

fabulous, legendary; myth-ic, -ological; chimerical; imagin-, vision-ary; notional; fan-cy, -ciful, -tastic, -tastical; whimsical; fairy, -like.

dreamy, entranced, vaporous.

516. Meaning. [Idea to be conveyed.] [Thing signified.]—**N.** meaning; signific-ation, -ance; sense, expression; im-, pur-port; drift, tenor, implication, connotation, essence, force, spirit bearing, coloring; scope.

matter; subject, -matter; argument, text, sum and substance; gist etc. 5.

general –, broad –, substantial – colloquial –, literal –, plain –, simple –, accepted –, natural –, unstrained –, true etc. (*exact*) 494 –, honest etc. 543 –, *primâ facie* etc. (*manifest*) 525- meaning.

literality; literal interpretation; after acceptation; allusion etc. (*latency*) 526; suggestion etc. (*information*) 527; synonym; figure of speech etc. 521; acceptation etc. (*interpretation*) 522.

V. mean, signify, express, connote, denote; im-, pur-port; convey, imply, breathe, indicate, bespeak, bear a sense; tell –, speak- of; touch on; point –, allude- to; drive at; involve etc. (*latency*) 526; delcare etc. (*affirm*) 535.

understand by etc. (*interpret*) 522.

Adj. meaning etc. *v.*; expressive, suggestive, meaningful, allusive; signific-ant, -ative, -atory; pithy; full of –, pregnant with- meaning.

declaratory etc. 535; intelligible etc. 518; literal, metaphrastic; synonymous; tantamount etc. (*equivalent*) 27; implied etc. (*latent*) 526; explicit etc. 525; literal etc. 562.

Adv. to that effect; that is to say etc. (*being interpreted*) 522.

literally; evidently, from the context.

517. Unmeaningness. [Absence of meaning.]—**N.** unmeaningness etc. *adj.*; scrabble, scribble, scrawl, daub, (*painting*), strumming (*music*).

empty sound, dead letter, *vox et praeterea nihil*; 'a tale told by an idiot, full of sound and fury, signifying nothing;' 'sounding brass and a tinkling cymbal.'

nonsense, jargon, gibberish, jabber, mere words, hocus-pocus, fustian, rant, bombast, balderdash, palaver, patter, flummery, *verbiage*, babble, *bavardage*, *baragouin*, platitude, *niaiserie*; inanity; rigmarole, rodomontade; truism; *nugae canorae*; twaddle, twattle, fudge, trash; stuff, – and nonsense; bosh, rubbish, rot, drivel, moonshine, wish-wash, fiddle-faddle, flapdoodle; absurdity etc. 497; vagueness etc. (*unintelligibility*) 519.

V. mean nothing; be -unmeaning etc. *adj.*; twaddle; quibble, rant, gabble, scrabble etc. *n.*

Adj. unmeaning; meaning-, sense-less; nonsensical; void of -sense etc. 516.

in-, un-expressive; vacant, fatuous; not significant; insignificant,.

trashy, washy, inane, vague, trumpery, trivial, fiddle-faddle, twaddling, quibbling.

unmeant, not expressed; tacit etc. (*latent*) 526.

inexpressible, undefinable, incommunicable.

Int. rubbish! etc. 497.

518. Intelligibility.—**N.** intelligibility, clearness, clarity, explicitness etc. *adj.*; lucidity, perspicuity; legibility, plain speaking etc. (*manifestation*) 525; precision etc. 494; a word to the wise.

V. be -intelligible etc. *adj.*; speak -for itself, – volumes; tell its own tale, lie on the surface.

render -intelligible etc. *adj.*; popularize, simplify, clear up; elucidate etc. (*explain*) 522.

understand, comprehend; take, – in; catch, grasp, recognize, follow, collect, master, make out; see -with half an eye, – daylight, – one's way; enter into the ideas of; come to an understanding.

Adj. intelligible; clear, – as -day, – crystal, – noonday; lucid; per-, tran-spicuous; luminous, transparent; comprehensible.

easily understood, easy to understand, for the million, intelligible to the meanest capacity, popularized.

plain, distinct, explicit, clear-cut; positive; definite etc. (*precise*) 494.

graphic, vivid, telling; expressive etc. (*meaning*) 516; illustrative etc. (*explanatory*) 522.

un-ambiguous, -equivocal, -mistakable etc. (*manifest*) 525, -confused; legible, recognizable; obvious etc. 525.

Adv. in plain -terms, – words, – English.

Phr. he that runs may read etc. (*manifest*) 525.

519. Unintelligibility.—**N.** unintelligibility, incomprehensibility, imperspicuity; inconceivableness, vagueness etc. *adj.*; obscurity; ambiguity etc. 520; doubtful meaning; uncertainty etc. 475; perplexity etc. (*confusion*) 59; spinosity; *obscurum per obscurius*; mystification etc. (*concealment*) 528; latency etc. 526; transcendentalism.

paradox; enigma, riddle etc. (*secret*) 533; *dignus vindice nodus*; sealed book; steganography, freemasonry.

pons asinorum, asses' bridge; double –, high-Dutch, Greek, Hebrew; jargon etc. (*unmeaning*). 517.

obscurantist.

V. be -unintelligible etc. *adj.*; require -explanation etc. 522; have a doubtful meaning, pass comprehension.

render -unintelligible etc. *adj.*; conceal etc. 528; darken etc. 421; confuse etc. (*derange*) 61; perplex etc. (*bewilder*) 475.

not -understand etc. 518; lose, – the clue; miss; not know what to make of, be able to make nothing of, give it up; not be able to -account for, – make either head or tail of; be at sea etc. (*uncertain*) 475; wonder etc. 870; see through a glass darkly etc. (*ignorance*) 491.

not understand one another; play at cross purposes etc. (*misinterpret*) 523.

Adj. un-intelligible, -accountable, -decipherable, -discoverable, -knowable, -fathomable; incognizable, -explicable, -scrutable; inap-, incomprehensible; insol-vable, -uble; impenetrable.

illegible, indecipherable, as Greek to one, unexplained, paradoxical; enigmatic, -al; puzzling, baffling.

obscure, dark, muddy, clear as mud, seen through a mist, dim, nebulous, shrouded in mystery; undiscernible etc. (*invisible*) 447; misty etc. (*opaque*) 426; hidden etc. 528; latent etc. 526.

indefinite etc. (*indistinct*) 447; perplexed etc. (*confused*) 59; undetermined, vague, loose, ambiguous; mysterious; mystic, -al; transcendental; occult, recondite, esoteric, abstruse, crabbed.

incon-ceivable, -ceptible; searchless; above –, beyond –, past- comprehension; beyond one's depth; unconceived.

inexpressible, undefinable, incommunicable, unutterable, ineffable, unpronounceable.

520. Equivocalness. [Having a double sense.]—**N.** equivocalness etc. *adj.*; double - meaning etc. 516; ambiguity, *double entendre*, pun, paragram, *calembour*, quibble, *équivoque*, anagram; conundrum etc. (*riddle*) 533; word-play etc. (*wit*) 842; homonym, -y; amphibo-ly, -logy; ambiloquy.

Sphinx, Delphic oracle.

equivocation etc. (*duplicity*) 544; white lie, mental reservation etc. (*concealment*) 528.

V. be -equivocal etc. *adj.*; have two -meanings etc. 516; equivocate etc. (*palter*) 544.

Adj. equivocal, ambiguous, amphibolous, homonymous; double-tongued etc. (*lying*) 544.

521. Metaphor.—N. figure of speech; *facon de parler*, way of speaking, colloquialism.

phrase etc. 566; figure, trope, metaphor, tralatition, metonymy, enallage, *catachresis*, *synecdoche*, *autonomasia*; irony, satire, figurativeness etc. *adj.*; image, -ry; *metalepsis*, type, anagoge, simile, personification, *prosopopaeia*, allegory, apologue, parable, fable; allusion, adumbration; application; euphemism; euphuism.

V. employ -metaphor etc. *n.*; personify, allegorize, adumbrate, shadow forth, apply, allude –, refer- to.

Adj. metaphorical etc. *n.*; figurative, catachrestical, typical, tralatitious, parabolic, allegorical, allusive, anagogical; ironical; colloquial.

Adv. so to -speak, – say, – express oneself; as it were.

Phr. *mutato nomine de te fabula nattatur.*

522. Interpretation.—N. interpretation, definition; explan-, explic-ation; solution, answer; rationale; plain –, simple –, strict- interpretation; meaning etc. 516.

translation; rend-ering, -ition; reddition; literal –, free- translation; key, crib; secret; clew etc. (*indication*) 550; Rosetta stone.

exegesis; ex-pounding, -position; Hermeneutics; comment, -ary; inference etc. (*deduction*) 480; illustration, exemplification; gloss, annotation, *scholium*, note; e-, di-lucidation, enucleation; *éclaircissement*, *mot de l'énigme*.

symptomat-, semei-ology; metoposcopy, physiognomy; diagnosis, prognosis; paleography etc. (*philology*) 560.

accept-ion, -ation, -ance; light, reading, lection, construction, version.

equivalent, – meaning etc. 516; synonym; para-, meta-phrase; convertible terms, apposition; dictionary etc. 562; polyglot.

V. interpret, explain, define, construe, translate, render; do –, turn- into; transfuse the sense of.

find out etc. 480*a*- -the meaning etc. 516- of; read; spell –, figure –, make- out; decipher, decode, unravel, disentangle, puzzle out; find the key of, enucleate, resolve, solve; read between the lines.

account for; find –, tell- the cause etc. 153- of; throw –, shed- -light, – new light, – a fresh light- upon; clear up, elucidate.

illustrate, exemplify; unfold, expound, comment upon, annotate; popularize etc. (*render intelligible*) 518.

take –, understand –, receive –, accept- in a particular sense; understand by, put a construction on, be given to understand.

Adj. explanatory, expository; explica-tive, -tory; exegetical; hermeneutic, interpretive, illustrative, elucidative, annotative, scholiastic.

polyglot; literal; para-, meta-phrastic; cosignificative, synonymous; equivalent etc. 27.

Adv. in -explanation etc. *n.*; that is to say, *id est*, *videlicet*, to wit, namely, in other words.

literally, strictly speaking; in -plain, – plainer- -terms, – words, – English; more simply.

523. Misinterpretation.—N. misinterpretation, -apprehension, -understanding, -acceptation, -construction, -application; *catachresis*; cross -reading, – purposes; mistake etc. 495.

misrepresentation, perversion, exaggeration etc. 549; false -coloring, – construction; abuse of terms; parody, travesty; falsification etc. (*lying*) 544.

V. mis-interpret, -apprehend, -understand, -conceive, -judge, -doubt, -spell, -translate, -construe, -apply; mistake etc. 495.

misrepresent, pervert; garble etc. (*falsify*) 544; distort; detort; travesty, play upon words; stretch –, strain –, wrest- the -sense, – meaning; explain away; put a -bad, – false- construction on; give a false coloring, look through -rose colored –, – dark – spectacles.

be –, play- at cross purposes.

Adj. misinterpreted etc. *v.*; untranslat-ed, -able.

Adv. at cross purposes.

524. Interpreter.—N. interpreter, translator, ex-positor, -pounder, -ponent, -plainer; demonstrator.

scholiast, commentator, annotator; meta-, paraphrast.

spokesman, speaker, mouthpiece, prolocutor; diplomat etc. 758.

guide, courier, dragoman, *valet de place, cicerone*, showman; oneirocritic; Oedipus; oracle etc. 513.

525. Manifestation.—N. manifestation; unfolding; plainness etc. *adj.*; plain speaking; expression; showing etc. *v.*; exposition, demonstration, *séance*; exhibition, production; display, showing off etc. 882; premonstration. [Thing shown] exhibit, show.

indication etc. (*calling attention to*) 457; publicity etc. 531; disclosure etc. 529; openness etc. (*honesty*) 543, (*artlessness*) 703; *épachement*, prominence.

V. make –, render- -manifest etc. *adj.*; bring -forth, – forward, – to the front, – into view; give notice, express; represent, set forth, exhibit; show,

– up; expose; produce; hold up –, expose- to view; set –, place –, lay- before -one, – one's eyes; tell to one's face; trot out, put through one's paces, unfold, show off, show forth, unveil, bring to light, display, demonstrate, unroll; lay open; draw –, bring- out; bring out in strong relief; call –, bring- into notice; hold up the mirror; wear one's heart upon his sleeve; show one's -face, – colors; manifest oneself; speak out; make no -mystery, – secret- of; unfurl the flag; proclaim etc. (*publish*) 531.

indicate etc. (*direct attention to*) 457; disclose etc. 529; elicit etc. 480*a*; interpret etc. 522.

be -manifest etc. *adj.*; appear etc. (*be visible*) 446; transpire etc. (*be disclosed*) 529; speak for itself, stand to reason; stare one in the face; loom large, appear on the horizon, rear its head; give -token, – sign, – indication of; tell its own tale etc. (*intelligible*) 518; go without saying.

Adj. manifest, apparent; salient, striking, demonstrative, prominent, in the foreground, notable, pronounced.

flagrant; notorious etc. (*public*) 531; arrant; stark staring; unshaded, glaring.

defin-ed, -ite; distinct, conspicuous etc. (*visible*) 446; obvious, evident, incontestable, unmistakable, not to be mistaken, plain, clear, palpable, self-evident, autoptical; intelligible etc. 518; clear as -day, – daylight, – noonday; plain as -a pikestaff, – the sun at noonday, – the nose on one's face, – the way to the parish church.

ostensible; open, – as day; overt, patent, express, explicit; naked, bare, literal, downright, undisguised, exoteric.

unreserved; frank, plain spoken etc. (*artless*) 703; barefaced, brazen, bold, shameless, daring, flaunting, loud.

manifested etc. *v.*; disclosed etc. 529; expressible, capable of being shown, producible; in-, un-concealable.

Adv. manifestly, openly etc. *adj.*; before one's eyes, under one's nose, to one's face, face to face, above board, *cartes sur table*, on the stage, in plain sight, in open court, in the open, – streets; at the cross roads; in market overt; in the face of -day, – heaven; in -broad –, open- daylight; without reserve; at first blush, *primâ facie*, on the face of; in set terms.

Phr. *cela saute aux yeux*; he that runs may read; you can see it with half an eye; it needs no ghost to tell us; the meaning lies on the surface; *cela va sans dire*; *res ipsa loquitur*.

526. Latency.—N. latency, inexpression; hidden –, occult- meaning; occultness, occultism, mysticism, mystery, cabala, symbolism, anagoge; silence etc. (*taciturnity*) 585; concealment etc. 528; more than meets the -eye, – ear; Delphic oracle; *les dessous des cartes*, undercurrent.

allusion, insinuation, implication; innuendo etc. 527; adumbration; 'something rotten in the state of Denmark.'

snake in the grass etc. (*pitfall*) 667; secret etc. 533.

darkness, invisibility, impreceptibility.

latent influence, power behind the throne; friend at court, wire puller.

V. be -latent etc. *adj.*; lurk, smoulder, underlie, make no sign; escape -observation, – detection, – recognition; lie hid etc. 528.

laugh in one's sleeve; keep back etc. (*conceal*) 528.

involve, imply, implicate, connote, import, understand, allude to, infer, leave an inference; symbolize; whisper etc. (*conceal*) 528.

Adj. latent; lurking etc. *v.*; secret etc. 528; occult, symbolic, mystic; implied etc. *v.*; dormant.

un-apparent, -known, -seen etc. 441; in the background; invisible etc. 447; indiscoverable, dark; impenetrable etc. (*unintelligible*) 519; unspied, -suspected.

un-said, -written, -published, -breathed, -talked of, -told etc. 527, -sung, -exposed, -proclaimed, -disclosed etc. 529, -pronounced, -mentioned, -expressed; not expressed, tacit.

un-developed, -solved, -explained, -traced, -discovered etc. 480*a*, -tracked, -explored, -invented.

indirect, crooked, inferential; by -inference, – implication; implicit; constructive; allusive, covert, muffled; steganographic; under-stood, -hand, -ground; concealed etc. 528; delitescent.

Adv. by a side wind; *sub silentio*; in the background; behind -the scenes, – one's back, – the veil; below the surface; on the tip of one's tongue; secretly etc. 528; between the lines; by a mutual understanding.

Phr. 'thereby hangs a tale.' 'that is another story.'

527. Information.—N. information, enlightenment, acquaintance, knowledge etc. 490; publicity etc. 531.

communication, intimation; not-ice, -ification; e-an-nunciation; announcement; representation, round robin, presentment.

case, estimate, specification, report, advice, monition; news etc. 532; return etc. (*record*) 551; account etc. (*description*) 594; statement etc. (*affirmation*) 535.

mention; acquainting etc. *v.*; instruction etc. (*teaching*) 537; outpouring; intercommunication, communicativeness.

informant, authority, teller, announcer, annunciator, harbinger, herald, intelligencer, commentator, columnist, reporter, exponent, mouthpiece; informer, keek, eavesdropper, delator, detective, sleuth; *mouchard*, spy, stool pigeon. newsmonger; messenger etc. 534; *amicus curiae*.

valet de place, *cicerone*, pilot, guide; guide-, hand-book; *vade mecum*; manual; map, plan, chart, gazetteer; itinerary etc. (*journey*) 266.

hint, suggestion, wrinkle, innuendo, inkling, whisper, passing word, word in the ear, subaudition, cue, by-play; gesture etc. (*indication*) 550; gentle – broad- hint; *verbum sapienti*; word to the wise; insinuation etc. (*latency*) 526.

V. tell; inform, – of; acquaint, – with; impart, – to; make acquainted with, bring to the ears of, apprise, advise, enlighten, awaken.

let fall, mention, express, intimate, represent, communicate, make known; publish etc 531; notify, signify, specify, convey the knowledge of.

let one –, have one to- know; serve notice, give one to understand; give notice; set –, lay –, put-before; point out, put into one's head; put one in possession of; instruct etc. (*teach*) 537; direct the attention to etc. 457.

an-nounce, -nunciate; report, – progress; bring –, send –, leave –, write- word; tele-graph, -phone; ring –, call- up; wire; retail, render an account; give an account etc. (*describe*) 594; state etc. (*affirm*) 535.

disclose etc. 529; show cause; explain etc. (*interpret*) 522.

hint; give an inkling of; give –, drop –, throw out- a hint; insinuate; allude –, make allusion- to; glance at; tip off, tip the wink etc. (*indicate*) 550; suggest, prompt, give the cue, breathe; whisper, – in the ear.

give a bit of one's mind; tell one plainly, – once for all; speak volumes.

un-deceive, -beguile; set right, correct, open the eyes of, disabuse.

be -informed of etc.; know etc. 490; learn etc. 539; get scent of, gather from; awaken –, open one's eyes- to; become -alive, – awake- to; keep posted; hear, overhear, understand.

come to one's -ears, – knowledge; reach one's ears.

Adj. informed etc. *v.*; *communiqué*; reported etc. *v.*; published etc. 531; advisory.

expressive etc. 516; explicit etc. (*open*) 525, (*clear*) 518; plain-spoken etc. (*artless*) 703.

declara-, nuncupa-, exposi-tory; declarative, enunciative, communicat-ive, -ory; oral.

Adv. from information received; according to -rumor, – report; in the air; from what one can gather.

Phr. a little bird told me.

528. Concealment.—N. concealment; hiding etc. *v.*; occultation, mystification.

seal of secrecy; screen etc. 530; disguise etc. 530; masquerade; masked battery; hiding place etc. 530; cipher, code, crypt-, stegan-ography; invisible –, sympathetic- ink; palimpsest; freemasonry.

stealth, -iness; obreption; slyness etc. (*cunning*) 702.

latit-ancy, -ation; seclusion etc. 893; privacy, secrecy, secretness; *incognita.*

reticence; reserve; mental –, reservation, aside; *arrière pensée*, suppression, evasion, white lie, misprision; silence etc. (*taciturnity*) 585; suppression of truth etc. 544; underhand dealing; close-, secretive-ness etc. *adj.*; mystery.

latency etc. 526; snake in the grass; secret etc. 533.

V. conceal, hide, secrete, stow away, put out of sight; lock –, seal –, bottle- up.

cover, screen, cloak, veil, shroud; screen from -sight, – observation; draw the veil; draw –, close- the curtain; curtain, shade, eclipse, throw a veil over; be-cloud, -fog, -mask; mask, disguise; ensconce, muffle, smother; whisper.

keep -from, – back, – to oneself; keep -snug, – close, – secret, – dark; bury; sink, suppress; keep -from, – out of- -view, – sight; keep in –, throw into- the -shade, – background; cover up one's tracks; stifle, hush up, withhold, reserve; fence with a question; ignore etc. 460.

code, codify, use a cipher.

keep -a secret, – one's own counsel; hold one's tongue etc. (*silence*) 585; make no sign, not let it go further; not breathe a -word, – syllable- about; not let the right hand know what the left is doing; hide one's light under a bushel, bury one's talent in a napkin.

keep –, leave- in -the dark, – ignorance; blind, – the eyes; blindfold, hoodwink, mystify; puzzle etc. (*render uncertain*) 475; bamboozle etc. (*deceive*) 545.

be -concealed etc. *v.*; suffer an eclipse; retire from sight, couch; hide oneself; lie -hid, – in ambush, – low, – *perdu*, – snug, – close; seclude oneself etc. 893; lurk, sneak, skulk, slink, pussyfoot, prowl; steal -into, – out of, – by, – along; play at -bopeep, – hind and seek; hide in holes and corners.

Adj. concealed etc. *v.*; hidden; veiled, secret, recondite, mystic, cabalistic, occult, dark; cryptic, -al, private, privy, *in petto*, auricular, clandestine, close, inviolate.

behind a -screen etc. 530; under -cover, – an eclipse; in -ambush, – hiding, – disguise; in a -cloud, – fog, – mist, – haze, – dark corner; in the -shade, – dark; clouded, wrapt in clouds; invisible etc. 447; buried, underground, *perdu*; incommunicado; secluded etc. 893.

un-disclosed etc. 529; -told etc. 527; covert etc. (*latent*) 526; mysterious etc. (*unintelligible*) 519.

irrevealable, inviolable; confidential; esoteric; not ot be spoken of.

obreptitious, furtive, stealthy, feline; skulking etc. *v.*; surreptitious, underhand, hole and corner; sly etc. (*cunning*) 702; secretive, evasive, noncommittal, reserved, reticent, uncommunicative, buttoned up; close, – as wax; taciturn etc. 585.

Adv. secretly etc. *adj.*; in -secret, – private, – one's sleeve, – holes and corners; in the dark etc. *adj.*

januis clausis, with closed doors, *à huis clos*; hugger-mugger, *à la dérobée*; under the -cloak of, – rose, – table; *sub rosâ*, *en tapinois*, in the background, aside, on the sly, with bated breath, *sotto voce*, in a whisper, without beat of drum, *à la sourdine*.

in –, strict- confidence; confidentially etc. *adj.*; between -ourselves, – you and me; *entre nous*, *inter nos*, under the seal of secrecy; in -code, – cipher.

underhand, by stealth, like a thief in the night; stealthily etc. *adj.*; behind -the scenes, – the curtain, – one's back, – a screen etc. 530; *incognito*; *in camerâ.*

Phr. it -must, – will- go no further; 'tell it not in Gath,' nobody the wiser.

529. Disclosure.—N. disclosure; retection; unveiling etc. *v.*; deterration, revealment, revelation; divulgence, expos-ition, -ure; *exposé*; whole truth; tell-tale etc. (*news*) 532.

acknowledgment, avowal; confession, -al; shrift.

bursting of a bubble; *dénouement.*

V. dis-close, -cover, -mask; draw –, draw aside –, lift –, raise –, lift up –, remove –, tear- the -veil, – curtain; un-mask, -veil, -fold, -cover, -seal, -kennel; take off –, break- the seal; lay -open, – bare; expose; open, – up; bare, bring to light; evidence; make -clear, – evident, – manifest; evince.

divulge, reveal, break; let into the secret; reveal the secrets of the prison-house; tell etc. (*inform*) 527; breathe, utter, blab, peach; let -out, – fall, – drop, – the cat out of the bag; betray; tell tales, – out of school; come out with; give -vent, – utterance- to; open the lips, blurt out, vent, whisper about; speak out etc. (*make manifest*) 525; make public etc. 531; unriddle etc. (*find out*) 480*a*; split; blow the gaff; break the news.

acknowledge, allow, concede, grant, admit, own, confess, avow, throw off all disguise, turn inside out, make a clean breast; show one's -hand, – cards; unburden –, disburden- one's -mind, – conscience, – heart; open –, lay bare –, tell a piece of- one's mind; unbosom oneself, own to the soft impeachment; say –, speak- the truth; turn -King's, – Queen's, – States's- evidence.

raise –, drop –, lift –, remove –, throw off- the mask; expose; debunk; lay open; un-deceive, -beguile; disabuse, set right, correct, open the eyes of; *désillusionner*.

be -disclosed etc.; transpire, come to light; come in sight etc. (*be visible*) 446; become known, escape the lips; come –, ooze –, creep –, leak –, peep –, crop- out; show its -face, – colors; discover etc. itself; break through the clouds, flash on the mind.

Adj. disclosed etc. *v.*

Int. out with it!

Phr. the murder is out; a light breaks in upon one; the scales fall from one's eyes; the eyes are opened.

530. Ambush. [Means of concealment.]—**N.** hiding-place; secret -place, drawer; recess, hole, funk hole, holes and corners; closet, crypt, *adytum*, abditory, *oubliette*, safe, – deposit.

am-bush, -buscade; stalking horse; lurking-hole, -place; secret path, backstairs; retreat etc. (*refuge*) 666.

screen, cover, shade, blinder; veil, curtain, blind, *purdah*, cloak, cloud.

mask, vizor, visor, disguise, masquerade dress, domino; *camouflage*.

pitfall etc. (*source of danger*) 667; trap etc. (*snare*) 545.

v. ambush, ambuscade, lie in ambush etc. (*hide oneself*) 528; lie in wait for; set a trap for etc. (*deceive*) 545.

Adv. *aux aguets.*

531. Publication.—N. publication; public -announcement etc. 527; promulgation, propagation, proclamation, pronouncement, encylical, *pronunciamento*; circulation, indiction, edition, imprint, impression, printing; hue and cry.

publicity, notoriety, currency, flagrancy, cry, *bruit*; *vox populi*; report etc. (*news*) 532.

the Press, fourth estate, public press, newspaper, periodical, journal, gazette; house organ, trade publication, tabloid, daily, weekly, monthly, quarterly, annual, magazine, monograph, book; review; news sheet, special edition, supplement, feature, rotogravure, comic strips; leaflet, pamphlet; telegraphy; publisher etc. *v.*

circular, – letter; manifesto, advertisement, puff, placard, bill, *affiche*, broadside, poster; notice etc. 527; program.

V. publish; make -public, – known etc. (*information*) 527; speak –, talk- of; broach, utter; put forward; circulate, propagate, promulgate; spread –, abroad; rumor, diffuse, disseminate, evulgate; put –, give –, send- forth; emit, edit, get out; issue; cover, report; bring –, lay –, drag- before the public; give -out, – to the world; put –, bandy –, hawk –, buzz –, whisper –, bruit –, blaze- about; drag into the -open day, – limelight; voice.

proclaim, herald, blazon; blaze –, noise- abroad; sound a trumpet; trumpet –, thunder- forth; give tongue; announce with -beat of drum, – flourish of trumpets; proclaim -from the housetops, – at Charing Cross, at the cross roads; declare, declaim.

advertise, placard; post, – up; *afficher*, publish in the Gazette, send round the crier.

raise a -cry, – hue and cry, – report; set news afloat.

telegraph, cable, wireless, broadcast.

be -published etc; be –, become- public etc. *adj.*; come out; go –, fly –, buzz –, blow- about; get -about, – abroad, – afloat, – wind; find vent; see the light; go forth, take air, acquire currency, pass current; go -the rounds, – the round of the newspapers, – through the length and breadth of the land; *virum volitare per ora*; pass from mouth to mouth; spread; run –, spread- like wildfire.

Adj. published etc. *v.*; current etc. (*news*) 532; in circulation, public; notorious; flagrant, arrant; open etc. 525; trumpet-tongued; encyclical, promulgatory; exoteric.

Adv. publicly etc. *adj.*; in open court, with open doors; in the limelight.

Int. *Oyez!* O yes! notice!

Phr. notice is hereby given; this is –, these are- to give notice.

532. News.—N. news; information etc. 527; piece –, budget- of -news, – information; report, story, yarn, copy, filler, intelligence, tidings; stop press news.

word, advice, *aviso*, message; dis-, des-patch; telegram, cable, wireless telegram, radio-gram, marconi-gram, communication, errand, embassy; *bulletin*.

microphone; public address system, P.A.; walkie talkie, radio -telephone, -phone.

radio, wireless (Eng.), high fidelity, hi fi, radio set, transistor, receiver; speaker, loudspeaker, amplifier, tweeter, woofer; transmitter, broadcaster; AM –, FM –, short wave – transmitter; radio station, studio, control room, network, hookup, circuit; frequency, kilocycles, megacycles; band, channel, modulation, amplification; broadcast, program, newscast, network show, commerical announcement, serial, sound effects; signature, station – identification, – break; radio listener, audiophile.

television, TV, video, color television; television –, live – broadcast, telecast, TV show; televising, telecasting, transmission, television channel, video, audio, beam, reception, image, test pattern; rain, snow, ghost; television –, TV – station, mobile unit, TVmobile, transmitter, televisor, boost, camera; set, monitor, tube, screen.

rumor, hearsay, *on dit*, flying rumor, news stirring, cry, buzz, *bruit*, fame; talk, *oüi-dire*, scandal, eavesdropping; town –, table- talk; tittle-tattle; *canard*, topic of the day, idea afloat.

fresh –, stirring –, old – stale- news; glad tidings; old –, stale- story.

narrator etc. (*describe*) 594; news-, scandal-monger; tale-bearer; tell-tale, gossip, tattler, busybody, chatterer; informer.

broad-, news-, sports-caster; commentator, announcer, master of ceremonies, M.C., programmer, sound man, radioman, ham, radioperator.

television technician, TV man, cameraman, soundman.

V. transpire etc. (*be disclosed*) 529; rumor etc. (*publish*) 531.

broadcast, radio, transmit, send, release, beam; sign – on, – off; go on –, go off – the air, monitor; listen –, tune – in.

tele-vise, -cast; color cast.

Adj. many-tongued; rumored; publicly –, currently- -rumored, – reported; rife, current, floating, afloat, going about, in circulation, in everyone's mouth, all over the town.

Adv. as the story -goes, – runs; as they say, it is said.

533. Secret.—N. secret; dead –, profound- secret; *arcanum*, mystery; latency etc. 526; Asian mystery; sealed book, secrets of the prison-house; *le dessous des cartes*.

enigma, riddle, puzzle, nut to crack, conundrum, charade, rebus, logogriph; mono-, ana-gram; acrostic, cross-word puzzle; Sphinx; *crux criticorum*.

maze, labyrinth, Hyrcynian wood.

problem etc. (*question*) 461; paradox etc. (*difficulty*) 704; unintelligibility etc. 519; *terra incognita* etc. (*ignorance*) 491.

Adj. secret etc. (*concealed*) 528.

534. Messenger.—N. messenger, envoy, emissary, legate; nuncio, internuncio; intermediary; ambassador etc. (*diplomatist*) 758.

marshal, flag-bearer, herald, crier, trumpeter, bellman, pursuivant, *parlementaire*, *apparitor*.

courier, runner, dawk, *estafette*; Hermes, Mercury, Iris, Ariel.

postman, letter carrier, telegraph boy, messenger boy, district messenger; despatch rider, commissionaire, erand-boy.

mail; post, -office; letter-bag; mail -boat, – train, – coach, – van, aerial mail; tele-graph, -phone; cable, wire; carrier-pigeon; wireless telegraph, -phone; radiotele-graph, -phone.

journalist, newspaperman, reporter; gentleman –, representative- of the press; sob sister; penny-a-liner; special –, war –, own- correspondent; spy, scout; informer etc. 527.

535. Affirmation.—N. affirm-ance, -ation; statement, allegation, assertion, predication, declaration, word, averment.

asseveration, adjuration, swearing, oath, affidavit; deposition etc. (*record*) 551; avouchment, assurance; protest, -ation; profession; acknowledgment etc. (*assent*) 488; pledge.

vote, voice, suffrage, ballot.

remark, observation; position etc. (*proposition*) 514; saying, *dictum*, sentence, *ipse dixit*.

emphasis, positiveness, peremptoriness; dogmatism etc. (*certainty*) 474; dogmatist etc. 887.

V. assert; make -an assertion etc. *n.*; have one's say; say, affirm, predicate, declare, state, represent; protest, profess.

put -forth, – forward; advance, allege, propose, propound, enunciate, enounce, broach, set forth, hold out, maintain, contend, pronounce, pretend.

depose, depone, aver, avow, avouch, asseverate, swear; make –, take one's- oath; make –, swear –, put in- an affidavit; take one's Bible oath, kiss the book, vow, *vitam impendere vero*; swear till -one is black in the face, – all's blue; be sworn, call Heaven to witness; vouch, warrant, certify, assure, swear by bell, book and candle.

swear by etc. (*believe*) 484; insist –, take one's stand- upon; emphasize, lay stress on; assert -roundly, – positively; lay down, – the law; raise one's voice, dogmatize, have the last word; rap out; repeat; re-assert, -affirm.

announce etc. (*information*) 527; acknowledge etc. (*assent*) 488; attest etc. (*evidence*) 467; adjure etc. (*put to one's oath*) 768.

Adj. asserting etc. *v.*; declaratory, predicatory, pronunciative, affirmative, *soi-disant*; positive; certain etc. 474; express, explicit etc. (*patent*) 525; absolute, emphatic, flat, broad, round, pointed, marked, distinct, decided, confident, assertive, insistent, trenchant, dogmatic, definitive, formal, solemn, categorical, peremptory; unretracted; predicable, affirmable.

Adv. affirmatively etc. *adj.*; in the affirmative.

with emphasis, *ex cathedrâ*, without fear of contradiction.

I must say, indeed, i' faith, let me tell you, why, give me leave to say, marry, you may be sure, I'd have you to know; upon my -word, – honor; by my troth, egad, I assure you; by -jingo, – Jove, – George, – etc.; troth, seriously, sadly; in –, in sober- -sadness, – truth, – earnest; of a truth, truly, pardi, perdy; in all conscience, upon oath; be assured etc. (*belief*) 484; yes etc. (*assent*) 488; I'll -warrant, – warrant you, – engage, – answer for it, – be bound, – venture to say, – take my oath; in fact, as a matter of fact, forsooth, joking apart; so help me God; not to mince the matter.

Phr. quoth he; *dixi*.

536. Negation.—N. ne-, abne-gation; denial; dis-avowal, -claimer; abjuration; contra-diction, -vention; recusation, protest; rebuttal; recusancy etc. (*dissent*) 489; flat –, emphatic- -contradiction, – denial; *démenti*.

qualification etc. 469; repudiation etc. 610; retraction etc. 607; confutation etc. 479; refusal etc. 764; prohibition etc. 761.

V. deny; contra-dict, -vene; controvert, give denial to, gainsay, negative, shake the head.

dis-own, -affirm, -claim, -avow; recant etc. 607; revoke etc. (*abrogate*) 756.

dispute, impugn, traverse, rebut, join issue upon; bring –, call- in question etc. (*doubt*) 485.

deny -flatly, – peremptorily, – emphatically, – absolutely, – wholly, – entirely; give the lie to, belie.

repudiate etc. 610; set aside, ignore etc. 460; rebut etc. (*confute*) 479; qualify etc. 469; refuse etc. 764.

Adj. denying etc. *v.*; denied etc. *v.*; contradictory; negat-ive, -ory; revocatory; recusant etc. (*dissenting*) 489; at issue upon.

Adv. no, nay, not, nowise; not a -bit, – whit, – jot; not -at all, – in the least, – so; no such thing; nothing of the -kind, – sort; quite the contrary, *tout au contraire*, far from it; *tant s'en faut*; on no account, in no respect; by -no, – no manner of-means; negatively.

phr. there never was a greater mistake; I know better; *non haec in foedera.*

537. Teaching.—N. teaching etc. *v.*; instruction; edification; education; pedagogy; tuition; tutor-, tutel-age; direction, guidance.

qualification, preparation; train-, school-ing etc. *v.*; discipline; exer-cise, -citation; drill, practice.

persuasion, proselytism, propagandism, *propaganda*; in-doctrination, -culcation, oculation.

explanation etc. (*interpretation*) 522; lesson, lecture, sermon, homily; apologue, parable; discourse, prelection, preachment, disquisition.

exercise, task; *curriculum*; course, – of study; grammar, three R's, initiation, A.B.C. etc. (*beginning*) 66.

elementary –, primary –, secondary –, grammar school –, high school –, college –, university –, technical –, liberal –, classical –, religious –, denominational –, moral –, secular-education; technical –, vocational- training; university extension lectures; propaedeutics, moral tuition; evening classes, correspondence course.

physical education, gymnastics, calisthenics, eurythmics; *sloyd*.

V. teach, instruct, edify, school, tutor; cram, prime, coach; enlighten etc. (*inform*) 527.

in-culcate, -doctrinate, -oculate, -fuse, -stil, -fix, -graft, -filtrate; im-bue, -pregnate, -plant; graft, sow the seeds of, disseminate, propagandize.

give an idea of; put -up to, – in the way of; set right.

sharpen the wits, enlarge the mind; give new ideas, open the eyes, bring forward, 'teach the young idea how to shoot;' improve etc. 658.

expound etc. (*interpret*) 522; lecture; prelect; read –, give- a -lesson, – lecture, – sermon, – discourse; hold forth, preach; sermon-, moral-ize; point a moral.

train, discipline; bring up, – to; educate, form, ground, prepare, qualify, drill, exercise, practice, habituate, familiarize with, nurture, dry-nurse, breed, rear, take in hand; break, – in; tame; pre-instruct; initiate; inure etc. (*habituate*) 613.

put to nurse, send to school.

direct, guide; direct attention to etc. (*attention*) 457; impress upon the -mind, – memory; beat into, – the head; convince etc. (*belief*) 484.

Adj. teaching etc. *v.*; taught etc. *v.*; educational; scholastic, academic, doctrinal; disciplinal; instructive, didactic, hortative, pedagogic, tutorial.

Phr. the schoolmaster abroad.

538. Misteaching—N. mis-teaching, -information, -intelligence, -guidance, -direction, -persuasion, -instruction, -leading etc. *v.*; perversion, false teaching; sophistry etc. 477; college of Laputa; the blind leading the blind.

V. mis-inform, -teach, -direct, -guide, -instruct, -correct; pervert; put on a false –, throw off the-scent; deceive etc. 545; mislead etc. (*error*) 495; misrepresent; lie etc. 544; *ambiguas in vulgum spargere voces*, preach to the wise, teach one's grandmother to suck eggs.

render unintelligible etc. 519; bewilder etc. (*uncertainty*) 475; mystify etc. (*conceal*) 528; unteach.

Adj. misteaching etc. *v.*; unedifying.

Phr. *piscem natare doces.*

539. Learning.—N. learning; acquisition of -knowledge etc. 490, – skill etc. 698; acquirement, attainment; edification, scholarship, erudition; lore; information; self-instruction; study, reading, perusal; inquiry etc. 461.

ap-, prenticeship; pupil-age, -arity; tutelage, novitiate, matriculation.

docility etc. (*willingness*) 602; aptitude etc. 698.

V. learn; acquire –, gain –, receive –, take in –, drink in –, imbibe –, pick up –, gather –, get –, obtain –, collect –, glean- -knowledge, – information, – learning.

acquaint oneself with, master; make oneself -master of, – acquainted with; grind, cram; get –, coach- up; learn by -heart, – rote.

read, spell, peruse; con –, pore –, thumb- over; wade through; dip into; run the eye -over, – through; turn over the leaves.

study; be -studious etc. *adj.*; consume the midnight oil, mind one's book.

go to -school, – college, – the university; serve -an (*or* one's) apprenticeship, – one's time; learn one's trade; be -informed etc. 527; be -taught etc. 537.

Adj. studious; schol-astic, -arly; teachable; docile etc. (*willing*) 602; apt etc. 698; industrious etc. 682; learned erudite.

Adv. at one's books; *in statu pupillari* etc. (*learner*) 541.

540. Teacher.—N. teacher, trainer, instructor, institutor, master, tutor, don, director, Corypheus, dry nurse, coach, grinder, crammer; governor, bear-leader; governess, duenna; disciplinarian.

professor, lecturer, reader, prelector, prolocutor, preacher; Boanerges; pastor etc. (*clergy*) 996; schoolmaster, dominie, usher, pedagogue, abecedarian; schoolmistress, dame, monitor, proctor, pupil-teacher.

expositor etc. 524; preceptor, guide; mentor etc. (*adviser*) 695; pioneer, apostle, missionary, propagandist, moonshee; example etc. (*model for imitation*) 22.

professorship etc. (*school*) 542.

tutelage etc. (*teaching*) 537.

Adj. professorial, tutorial etc. 537.

541. Learner.—N. learner, scholar, student, *alumnus*, *élève*, pupil; ap-, prentice; articled clerk; school-boy, -girl, beginner, tyro, abecedarian, alphabetarian.

recruit, novice, neophyte, tenderfoot, inceptor, *débutant*, catechumen, probationer; undergraduate; freshman, frosh; sophomore, junior, senior; junior –, senior- soph; sophister, questionist, fellow-, commoner, pensioner, exhibitioner, sizar, scholar, fellow, advanced –, post graduate –, research- student.

class, form, grade, standard, remove; pupilage etc. (*learning*) 539.

disciple, follower, apostle, proselyte; fellow student, school-mate, -fellow, class mate, condisciple.

Adj. *in statu pupillari*, in leading strings, sophomoric.

542. School.—N. school, academy, university, *alma mater*, college, seminary, Lyceum; instit-ute, -ution, *conservatoire*; *palaestra*, *gymnasium*.

day –, boarding –, public –, preparatory –, elementary –, primary –, nursery –, dame's –, grammar –, Board –, County –, Council –, parochial –, denominational –, Sunday –, religious –, collegiate –, secondary –, continuation –, night –, correspondence –, secretarial –, military –, law –, medical –, business –, technical- school; technical –, training- college; Polytechnic; training ship; *Kindergarten*, nursery, *crèche*, reformatory.

pulpit, desk, reading desk, ambo, class-, lecture-room, theater, amphitheater, forum, stage, rostrum, platform, hustings, tribune.

school –, horn –, text-book; grammar, primer, abecedary, rudiments, manual, *vade mecum*, Lindley, Murray, Cocker.

professor-, lecture-, reader-ship; chair; schoolmaster etc. 540.

School Board, Council of Education; *propaganda*.

Adj. scholastic, academic, collegiate; educational.

Adv. *ex cathedrâ*.

543. Veracity.—N. veracity; truthfulness, frankness etc. *adj.*; truth, sooth, sincerity, candor, honesty, fidelity; plain dealing, *bona fides*; love of truth; probity etc. 939; ingenuousness etc. (*artlessness*) 703.

the truth the whole truth and nothing but the truth; honest –, sober- truth etc. (*fact*) 494; unvarnished tale; light of truth.

V. speak –, tell- the truth; speak by the card; paint in its –, show oneself in ones -true colors; make a clean breast etc. (*disclose*) 529; speak one's mind etc. (*be blunt*) 703; not -lie etc. 544, – deceive etc. 545.

Adj. truthful, true; ver-acious, -edical; scrupulous etc. (*honorable*) 939; sincere, candid, frank, open, straightforward, unreserved; open-, true-, simple- hearted; honest, trustworthy; undissembling etc. (dissemble etc. 544); guileless, pure; unperjured, ture blue, as good as one's word; unaffected, unfeigned, *bonâ fide*; outspoken, ingenuous etc. (*artless*) 703; undisguised etc. (*real*) 494.

Adv. truly etc. (*really*) 494; on oath; in plain words etc. 703; in –, with –, of a –, in good –, very- truth; as the -dial to the sun, – needle to the pole; honor bright; troth; in good -sooth, – earnest; unfeignedly, with no nonsense, in sooth, sooth to say, *bonâ fide*, *in foro conscientiae*; without equivocation; *cartes sur table*, from the bottom of one's heart; by my troth etc. (*affirmation*) 535.

544. Falsehood.—N. false-hood, -ness; fals-ity, -ification; misrepresentation; deception etc. 545; untruth etc. 546; guile; bad faith; lying etc. *v.*; misrepresentation; mendacity, perjury, false swearing; forgery, invention, fabrication; subreption; covin.

perversion –, suppression- of truth; *suppressio veri*; perversion, distortion, false coloring; exaggeration etc. 549; prevarication, equivocation, shuffling, fencing, evasion, fraud; *suggestio falsi* etc. (*lie*) 546; mystification etc. (*concealment*) 528; simulation etc. (*imitation*) 19; dis-simulation, -sembling; deceit.

sham; pretence, pretending, malingering.

lip-homage, – service; mouth honor; hollowness; mere -show, – outside, eye-wash, window dressing; duplicity, double dealing, insincerity, hypocrisy, cant, humbug, casuistry; jesuit-ism, -ry; pharisaism; Machiavelism, 'organized hypocrisy;' crocodile tears, mealy-mouthedness, quackery; charlatan-ism, -ry; gammon; bun-kum, -come; flam, ban, flim-flam, cajolery, flattery; Judas kiss; perfidy etc. (*bad faith*) 940; *il volto sciolto i pensieri stretti.*

unfairness etc. (*dishonesty*) 940; artfulness etc. (*cunning*) 702; misstatement etc. (*error*) 495.

V. be -false etc. *adj.*, – a liar etc. 548; speak -falsely etc. *adv.*; tell a -lie etc. 546; lie, fib; lie like a trooper; swear falsely, forswear, perjure oneself, bear false witness.

mis-state, -quote, -cite, -report, -represent; belie, falsify, pervert, distort; put a false construction upon etc. (*misinterpret*) 523.

prevaricate, equivocate. quibble; palter, – to the understanding; *répondre en Normand*; trim, shuffle, fence, mince the truth, beat about the bush, blow hot and cold, play fast and loose.

garble, gloss over, disguise, give a color to; give –, put- a -gloss, – false coloring- upon; color, varnish, cook, dress up, embroider; varnish right and puzzle wrong, exaggerate etc. 549.

invent, fabricate; trump –, get- up; forge, hatch, concoct; romance etc. (*imagine*) 515; cry 'wolf!'

dis-semble, -simulate; feign, assume, put on, pretend, make believe; play -false, – a double game; coquet; act –, play- a part; affect etc. 855; simulate, pass off for; counterfeit, fake, sham, make a show of; malinger; swing the lead; say the grapes are sour.

cant, play the hypocrite, sham Abraham, *faire pattes de velours*, put on the mask, clean the outside of the platter, lie like a conjuror; hang out –, hold out –, sail under- false colors; 'commend the poisoned chalice to the lips;' *ambiguas in vulgus spargere voces*; deceive etc. 545.

Adj. false, deceitful, mendacious, unveracious,

fraudulent, untruthful, dishonest; faith-, truth-, troth-less; un-fair, -candid; evasive; un-, dis-ingenuous; hollow, insincere, *Parthis mendacior*; forsworn.

canting; hypocrit-, jesuit-, pharisa-ical; tartuffish; Machiavelian; double-tongued, -faced, -handed, -minded, -hearted, -dealing; two-faced, bare-faced; Janus-faced; smooth-faced, -spoken, -tongued; plausible; mealy-mouthed; affected etc. 855.

collus-ive, -ory; artful etc. (*cunning*) 702; perfidious etc. 940, spurious etc. (*deceptive*) 545; untrue etc. 546; falsified etc. *v.*; covinous.

Adv. falsely etc. *adj.*; *à la Tartufe*, with a double tongue; out of whole cloth; slily etc. (*cunning*) 702.

545. Deception.—N. deception; falseness etc. 544; untruth etc. 546; impos-ition, -ture; fraud, deceit, guile; fraudulen-ce, -cy; covin; knavery etc. (*cunning*) 702; misrepresentation etc. (*falsehood*) 544.

delusion, gullery, bluff, spoof, *blague*; juggl-ing, -ery; sleight of hand, legerdemain; presti-giation, -digitation; magic etc. 992; conjur-ing, -ation; hocus pocus, jockeyship; trickery, coggery, hanky-panky, chicanery, pettifogging, sharp practice; *supercherie*, cozenage, circumvention, ingannation, collusion; treachery etc. 940; practical joke.

trick, cheat, wile, ruse, blind, feint, plant, bubble fetch, catch, chicane, juggle, reach, hocus, bite; thimble-rig, card-sharping, artful dodge, machination, swindle, hoax; tricks upon travellers; confidence trick; strategem etc. (*artifice*) 702; theft etc. 791.

snare, trap, pitfall, decoy, gin; sprin-ge, -gle; noose, hook; bait, decoy-duck, tub to the whale, baited trap, *guet-à-pens*; cobweb, net, meshes, toils, mouse-trap, bird-lime; ambush etc. 530; trap-door, sliding panel, false bottom; spring-net, -gun; mask, -ed battery; mine; booby trap.

Cornish hug; wolf in sheep's clothing etc. (*deceiver*) 548; disguise, -ment; false colors, masquerade, mummery, borrowed plumes; *pattes de velours.*

mockery etc. (*imitation*) 19; copy etc. 21; counterfeit, sham, brummagem, make-believe, forgery, fraud, fake; lie etc. 546; 'a mockery, a delusion, and a snare,' hollow mockery.

whited –, painted- sepulcher; tinsel, paste, false jewelry, scagliola, ormolu, German silver, Britannia metal, paint; jerry building; man of straw.

illusion etc. (*error*) 495; *ignis fatuus* etc. 423; *mirage* etc. 443.

V. deceive, take in; defraud, cheat, jockey, do, cozen, diddle, nab, gyp, chouse, double cross, play one false, bilk, cully, jilt, bite, pluck, swindle, victimize; abuse; mystify; blind one's eyes; blindfold, hoodwink, spoof, bluff; throw dust into the eyes, 'keep the word of promise to the ear and break it to the hope,' 'draw a herring across the trail.'

impose –, practice –, play –, put –, palm –, foist- upon; snatch a verdict.

circumvent, overreach; out-reach, -wit, maneuvre; steal a march upon, give the go-by to, leave in the lurch.

set –, lay- a -trap, – snare- for; bait the hook, forlay, spread the toils, lime; decoy, waylay, lure, beguile, delude, inveigle; tra-, tre-pan; kidnap; let-, hook-in; trick; en-, in-trap, -snare, entoil, benet; nick, springe; catch, – in a trap; sniggle, entangle, illaqueate, hocus, practice on one's credulity, dupe, gull, hoax, fool, befool, bamboozle; hum, -bug; gammon, stuff up, dope, sell; play a -trick, – practical joke- upon one; balk, trip up, throw a tub to a whale; fool to the top of one's bent, send on -a wild goose chase, – a fool's errand; make -game, – a fool, – an April fool, – an ass- of; trifle with, cajole, flatter; come over etc. (*influence*) 615; gild the pill, make things pleasant, divert, put a good face upon; dissemble etc. 544.

cog, – the dice, play with marked cards; live by one's wits, play at hide and seek; obtain money under false pretences etc. (*steal*) 791; conjure, juggle, practice chicanery; gerrymander.

play –, palm –, foist –, fob- off.

lie etc. 544; misinform etc. 538; mislead etc. (*error*) 495; betray etc. 940; be -deceived etc. 547.

Adj. deceived etc. *v.*; deceiving etc. *v.*; cunning etc. 702; prestigi-ous, -atory; decept-ive, -ious; deceitful, covinous; delus-ive, -ory; illus-ive, -ory; elusive, insidious, *ad captandum vulgus.*

untrue etc. 546; mock, sham, make-believe, counterfeit, faked, pseudo, spurious, so-called, pretended, feigned, trumped up, bogus, scamped, fraudulent, tricky, factitious, artificial, bastard; surreptitious, illegitimate, contraband, adulterated, sophisticated; unsound, rotten at the core; colorable; disguised; meretricious; tinsel, pinchbeck, plated; catch-penny; Brummagem; simulated etc. 544.

Adv. under -false colors, – the garb of, – cover of; over the left.

Phr. *fronti nulla fides.*

546. Untruth.—N. untruth, falsehood, lie, story, thing that is not, fib, bounce, crammer, taradiddle, whopper.

forgery, fabrication, invention; mis-statement, -representation; perversion, falsification, gloss, *suggestio falsi*; exaggeration etc. 549.

fiction; fable, nursery tale; romance etc. (*imagination*) 515; untrue –, false –, trumped up- -story, – statement; thing devised by the enemy; *canard*; shave, sell, hum, yarn, traveler's tale, Canterbury tale, cock and bull story, fairy tale, clap-trap.

myth, moonshine, bosh, all my eye, -and Betty Martin, mare's nest, farce.

irony; half truth, white lie, pious fraud; mental reservation etc. (*concealment*) 528.

pretence, pretext; false -plea etc. 617; subterfuge, evasion, shift, shuffle, make-believe; sham etc. (*deception*) 545.

profession, empty words; Judas kiss etc. (*hypocrisy*) 544; disguise etc. (*mask*) 530.

V. have a false meaning; not ring true.

pretend, sham, feign, counterfeit, make believe.

Adj. untrue, false, trumped up; void of –, without- foundation; far from the truth, false as dicer's oaths; unfounded, *ben trovato*, invented, fabulous, fabricated, forged; fict-, fact-, supposit-, surrept-itious; e-, il-lusory; ironical; satirical; evasive; *soi-disant* etc. (*misnamed*) 565.

Phr. *se non e vero e ben trovato.*

547. Dupe.—N. dupe, gull, gudgeon, *gobemouche*, cull, cully, victim, sucker, pigeon, April fool; laughing stock etc. 857; Cyclops, simple Simon, flat, mug, greenhorn; fool etc. 501; puppet, cat's paw.

V. be -deceived etc. 545, – the dupe of; fall into a trap; swallow –, nibble at- the bait; bite; catch a Tartar.

Adj. credulous etc. 486; mistaken etc. (*error*) 495.

548. Deceiver.—N. deceiver etc. (deceive etc. 545); dissembler, hypocrite; sophist, Pharisee, Jesuit, Mawworm, Pecksniff, Joseph Surface, Tartufe, Janus; serpent, snake in the grass, cockatrice, Judas, wolf in sheep's clothing; Molly Maguire; jilt; shuffler.

liar etc. (lie etc. 544; story-teller, perjurer, false-witness, *mentuer à triple étage*, Scapin.

imposter, pretender, capper, decoy, fraud, *soi-disant*, humbug; adventurer; Cagliostro, Fernam Mendez Pinto; ass in lion's skin etc. (*bungler*) 701; actor etc. (*stage player*) 599.

quack, *charlatan*, mountebank, saltimbanco, *saltimbanque*, empiric, quacksalver, medicaster.

conjuror, juggler, magician, necromancer, trickster, prestidigitator, medium, jockey; crimp; decoy-duck, stool pigeon; rogue, knave, cheat; swindler etc. (*thief*) 792; jobber.

549. Exaggeration.—N. exaggeration; expansion etc. 194; hyperbole, stretch, strain, coloring; high coloring, caricature, *caricatura*; extravagance etc. (*nonsense*) 497; Baron Munchausen; men in buckram, yarn, fringe, embroidery, traveler's tale; Pelion upon Ossa.

storm in a teacup; much ado about nothing etc. (*over-estimation*) 482; puffery etc. (*boasting*) 884; rant etc. (*turgescence*) 577.

figure of speech, *façon de parler*; stretch of-fancy, – the imagination; flight of fancy etc. (*imagination*) 515.

false coloring etc. (*falsehood*) 544; aggravation etc. 835.

V. exaggerate, magnify, pile up, aggravate; amplify etc. (*expand*) 194; overestimate etc. 482; hyperbolize; over-charge, -state, -draw, -lay, -shoot the mark, -praise; make -much, – the most- of; strain, – a point; stretch, – a point; go great lengths; spin a long yarn; draw –, shoot with- a long-bow; deal in the marvelous.

out -Herod Herod, run riot, talk at random.

heighten, overcolor; color -highly, – too highly; embroider, *broder*; flourish; color etc. (*misrepresent*) 544; puff etc. (*boast*) 884.

Adj. exaggerated etc. *v.*; overwrought; bombastic etc. (*magniloquent*) 577; hyperbolical, on stilts; fabulous, extravagant, preposterous, egregious, *outré*, high-flying.

Adv. hyperbolically etc. *adj.*

550. Indication.—N. indication; symbol-ism, -ization; semeio-logy, -tics; sign of the times.

lineament, feature, *trait*, characteristic, trick, diagnostic; divining-rod; cloven hoof; footfall; means of recognition; earmark.

sign, symbol; ind-ex, -ice, -icator; point, -er; marker; exponent, note, token, symptom.

type, figure, emblem, cipher, device; representation etc. 554; epigraph, motto, posy.

gest-ure, -iculation; pantomime; wink, glance, leer; nod, shrug, beck; touch, nudge; grip; dactylology, -nomy; freemasonry, telegraphy, chirology, by-play, dumb-show; cue; hint etc. 527; clue, clew, key, scent, tract etc. 551.

signal, -post; rocket, blue light; watch-fire, -tower; telegraph, semaphore, flag-staff; cresset, fiery cross; calumet; heliograph, signal-, flash-lamp; radar, radar signal, pulse –, microwave –, radar; tracing, blips, pips.

mark, line, stroke, dash, score, stripe, streak, scratch, tick, dot, point, notch, nick, blaze; asterisk, red letter, Italics, heavy type, inverted commas, quotation marks, sublineation, underlining, jotting; print; impr-int, -ess, ession; note, annotation, mark of exclamation.

[For identification] badge, criterion; counter-check, -mark, -sign, -foil, duplicate, tally; label, tab, ticket, stub, billet, letter, counter, *tessera*, card, bill, check; witness, voucher; stamp; *cachet*; trade –, Hall- mark; broad arrow; signature; address –, visiting- card; *carte de visite*; credentials etc. (*evidence*) 467; passport, identity book; attestation; hand, – writing, sign-manual; cipher; monogram, – mark, seal, sigil, signet; autograph, -y, paraph, brand; superscription; in-, en-dorsement; title, heading, rubric, docket; *mot -de passe*, – *du guet*; *passe-parole*; shibboleth; watch-, catch-, pass-word; open *sesame*.

insignia, banner, -et, -ol; bandrol; flag, colors, streamer, standard, eagle, labarum, oriflamb, *oriflamme*; figure-head; ensign; pen-non, -nant, -dant; burgee, blue Peter, jack, ancient, gonfalon, union-jack; tricolor, stars and stripes; bunting.

hearldry, crest; coat of –, arms; armorial bearings, hatchment; e-, scutcheon; shield, supporters; livery, uniform; cockade, *epaulette*, brassard, chevron; garland, chaplet, love-knot, fillet, favor.

[Of locality] beacon, cairn, post, staff, flagstaff, hand, pointer, vane, cock, weathercock; guide-, hand-, finger-, directing-, sign-post; pillars of Hercules, pharos, signal fire; land-, sea-mark; lighthouse, balize; pole-, load-, lode-star; cynosure, guide; address, direction, name; sign, -board.

[Of the future] warning etc. 668; omen etc. 512; prefigurement etc. 511. [Of the past] trace record etc. 551. [Of danger] warning etc. 668; alarm etc. 669. [Of authority] scepter etc. 747. [Of triumph] trophy etc. 733. [Of quantity] gauge etc. 466. [Of distance] mile-stone, -post. [Of disgrace] brand, fool's cap, stigma, mark of Cain. [For detection] check, tell-tale; test etc. (*experiment*) 463.

notification etc. (*information*) 527; advertisement etc. (*publication*) 531.

word of command, call; bugle-, trumpet-call; reveille, taps; bell, alarum, cry; battle –, rallying-cry.

church, bell, angelus, sacring bell; muezzin.

exposition etc. (*explanation*) 522; proof etc. (*evidence*) 463; pattern etc. (*prototype*) 22.

V. indicate; be the -sign etc. *n.*- of; denote,

betoken; argue, testify etc. (*evidence*) 467; bear the -impress etc. *n.*- of; con-note, -notate.

represent, stand for; typify etc. (*prefigure*) 511; symbolize.

put -an indication, – a mark, – etc. *n.*; note, mark, tick, blaze, stamp, earmark; set one's seal upon; label, ticket, docket; dot, spot, score, dash, trace, chalk; print; im-print, -press, surprint; engrave, stereotype, electrotype.

signal, transmit, send, radiate, beam, deflect, echo, bounce back, return.

make a -sign etc. *n.*; signalize; give –, hang out- a signal; beck, -on; gesture; not; wink, glance, leer, nudge, shrug, tip the wink; gesticulate; raise –, hold up- the-finger, – hand; saw the air, suit the action to the word.

wave –, unfurl –, hoist –, hang out- a banner etc. *n.*; wave -the hand, – a kerchief; give the cue etc. (*inform*) 527; show one's colors; give –, sound- an alarm; beat the drum, sound the trumpets, raise a cry.

sign, seal, attest etc. (*evidence*) 467; underline etc. (*give importance to*) 642; call attention to etc. (*attention*) 457; give notice etc. (*inform*) 527.

Adj. indicat-ing etc. *v.*; -ive, -ory; de-, connotative; diacritical, representative, typical, symbolic, pantomimic, pathognomonic, symptomatic, ominous, characteristic, demonstrative, diagnostic, exponential, emblematic, armorial; individual etc. (*special*) 79.

known –, recognizable- by; indicated etc. *v.*; pointed, marked.

[Capable of being denoted] denotable; indelible.

Adv. in token of; symbolically etc. *adj.*; in dumb show.

Phr. *ecce signum*; *ex ungue leonem, ex pede Herculem.*

551. Record.—N. trace, vestige, relic, remains; scar, *cicatrix*; foot-step, -mark, -print; track, mark, wake, trail, spoor, scent, *piste.*

monument, hatchment, escutcheon, slab, tablet, trophy, achievement; obelisk, pillar, column, monolith, cromlech, dolmen; memorial; *memento* etc. (*memory*) 505; testimonial, medal, ribbon, order; commemoration etc. (*celebration*) 883.

record, note, minute; *dossier*; register, -try; census, roll etc. (*list*) 86; cartulary, diptych, Domesday book; entry, memorandum, indorsement, inscription, copy, duplicate, docket; notch etc. (*mark*) 550; muniment, deed etc. (*security*) 771; document; deposition, *procès-verbal*; affidavit; certificate etc. (*evidence*) 467.

note-, memorandum-, pocket-, commonplace-book; portfolio; scoring-board, -sheet; bulletin board; card index, file; pigeon-holes, *excerpta*, *adversaria*, jottings, dottings.

gazette, -er; newspaper, magazine etc. 531; alman-ac, -ack; calendar, ephemeris, noctuary, diary, log, journal, account-, cash-, day-book, ledger.

archive, scroll, state-paper, Congressional Record, return, blue-book; statistics etc. 86; *compte rendu*; Acts –, Transactions –, Proceedings- of; Hansard's Debates; chronicle, annals; legend; history, biography etc. 594.

registration; en-, in-rolment; tabulation; entry, booking; signature etc. (*identification*) 550; recorder etc. 553; journalism.

drawing, photograph etc. 554; phonograph –, gramophone- record; music roll.

V. record; put –, place- upon record; go on record; chronicle, calendar, hand down to posterity; keep up the memory of etc. (*remember*) 505; commemorate etc. (*celebrate*) 883; report etc. (*inform*) 527; commit to –, reduce to- writing; put –, set down- -in writing, – in black and white; put –, jot –, take –, write –, note –, set-down; note, minute, put on paper; take –, make- a -note, – minute, – memorandum; make a return.

mark etc. (*indicate*) 550; sign etc. (*attest*) 467.

enter, book; post, – up; insert, make an entry of; mark –, tick- off; register, list, docket, enroll, inscroll; file etc. (*store*) 636.

Adv. on record.

552. Obliteration. [Suppression of sign.]—**N.** obliteration; erasure, rasure; effacement; interference; cancel, -lation; cassation; circumduction; deletion, blot; *tabula rasa.*

V. efface, obliterate, erase, rase, expunge, cancel; blot –, take –, rub –, scratch –, strike –, wipe –, wash –, sponge- out; wipe –, rub- off; wipe away; deface, render illegible; draw the pen through, apply the sponge.

interfere, jam, black-, block-out; clutter, screen.

be -effaced etc.; leave no -trace etc. 449; 'leave not a rack behind.'

Adj. obliterated etc. *v.*; out of print; printless; leaving no trace; intestate; un-recorded, -registered, -written.

Int. *dele*; out with it!

553. Recorder.—N. recorder, notary, clerk; regis-trar, -trary, -ter; prothonotary; amanuensis, secretary, scribe, stenographer, remembrancer, book-keeper, *custos rotulorum*, Master of the Rolls.

annalist; histori-an, -ographer; chronicler, journalist, reporter, columnist; biographer etc. (*narrator*) 594; antiquary etc. (*antiquity*) 122; memorialist.

draughtsman etc. 559; engraver 558; photographer, cinematographer, camera man.

Recording instrument, recorder, camera, phonograph, gramophone, dictaphone, telegraphone, telautograph, printing telegraph, tape recorder, ticker, time recorder, cash register, turnstile, speedometer, voting machine, seismograph, radar, oscilloscope, teletypewriter, pari-mutuel, photostat.

554. Representation.—N. represent-ation, -ment; imitation etc. 19; illustration, delineation, depictment, portrayal; imagery, portraiture, iconography; design, -ing; art, fine arts; painting etc. 556; sculpture etc. 557; engraving etc. 558; photography, radiography, skiagraphy.

person-ation, -ification; impersonation; drama etc. 599.

picture, drawing, sketch, draught, draft; tracing; copy etc. 21; photo-, helio-graph; daguerreo-, talbo-, calo-, helio-type; cabinet, *carte-de-visite*, snapshot; X-ray photograph; radio-gram, -graph, skia-graph, -gram.

image, likeness, icon, portrait; striking –, speaking- likeness; very image; effigy, fac-simile.

figure, – head; puppet, doll, *figurine*, aglet, manikin, lay-figure, model, *marionnette*, *fantoccini*, bust; waxwork, statue, -tte, automaton, Robot.

hieroglyphic, anaglyph; dia-, mono-gram, graph.

map, plan, chart; ground plan, projection, elevation; ichno-, carto-graphy; atlas; outline, scheme; view etc. (*painting*) 556.

artist, draughtsman etc. 559.

V. represent, delineate; depict, -ure; portray; picture; take –, catch- a likeness etc. *n.*; hit off, photograph, daguerreotype; figure; shadow -forth, – out; adumbrate; body forth; describe etc. 594; trace, copy; mold.

dress up; illustrate, symbolize.

paint etc. 556; carve etc. 557; engrave etc. 558.

person-ate, -ify; impersonate; assume a character; pose as; act; play etc. (*drama*) 599; mimic etc. (*imitate*) 19; hold the mirror up to nature.

Adj. represent-ing etc. *v.*, -ative; illustrative; represented etc. *v.*; imitative, figurative.

like etc. 17; graphic etc. (*descriptive*) 594.

555. Misrepresentation.—N. misrepresentation, distortion, exaggeration; daubing etc. *v.*; bad likeness, daub, sign-painting; scratch, caricature; *anamorphosis*.

V. misrepresent, distort, overdraw, travesty, parody, burlesque, exaggerate, caricature, daub.

Adj. misrepresented etc. *v.*

556. Painting.—N. painting; depicting; drawing etc. *v.*; design; perspective, skiagraphy; *chiaroscuro* etc. (*light*) 420; composition; treatment, values, atmosphere, tone, technique.

historical –, portrait –, miniature –, landscape –, marine –, flower –, scene- painting; scenography.

school, style; the grand style, high art, *genre*, portraiture; ornamental art etc. 847.

mono-, poly-chrome; *grisaille*.

pallet, palette; easel; brush, pencil, stump; blacklead, charcoal, crayons, chalk, pastel; paint etc. (*coloring matter*) 428; water-, body-, oil-color; oils, oil-paint; varnish etc. 356*a*; *gouache*, tempera, distemper, fresco, water-glass; enamel; encaustic painting; *graffito*, *gesso;* mosiac; tapestry.

picture, painting, piece, *tableau*, canvas; oil etc.-painting; fresco, cartoon; easel –, cabinet- picture; drawing, draught, draft; pencil etc. –, watercolor-drawing; sketch; outline; study.

portrait etc. (*representation*) 554; whole –, full –, half- length; kitcat, head; miniature; shade, *silhouette*; profile.

landscape, sea-piece, -scape; view, scene, prospect; interior; bird's- eye view; pan-, di-orama; still life.

picture –, art- gallery; *studio*, *atelier*.

V. paint, design, limn, draw, sketch, pencil, scratch, shade, stipple, hatch, dash off, chalk out, square up; color, dead-color, wash, varnish; draw in -pencil etc. *n.*; paint in -oils etc. *n.*; stencil; depict etc. (*represent*) 554.

Adj. painted etc. *v.*; pictorial, graphic, picturesque, decorative; classical, romantic, pre-Raphaelite, modern, cubist, futurist, vorticist.

pencil, oil etc. *n.*

Adv. in -pencil etc. *n.*

Phr. *fecit, delineavit.*

557. Sculpture.—N. sculpture, insculpture; carving etc. *v.*; statuary, ceramics, plastic arts.

high –, low –, bas- relief; relievo; *basso-*, *alto-*, *mezzo-relievo*; *intaglio*, anaglyph; medal, -lion; *cameo*.

marble, bronze, *terra cotta*; ceramic ware, pottery, porcelain, china, earthenware, faïence, enamel, *cloisonné*.

statue etc. (*image*) 554; cast etc. (*copy*) 21; glyptotheca.

V. sculpture, carve, cut, chisel, model, mold; cast.

Adj. sculptured etc. *v.*; in relief, anaglyptic, ceroplastic, ceramic; parian; marble etc. *n.*

558. Engraving.—N. engraving, chalcography; line –, mezzotint –, stipple –, chalk- engraving; dry-point, bur; etching, aquatinta; plate –, copperplate –, steel –, wood-, process-, photoengraving; xylo-, ligno-, glypto-, cero-, litho-, chromolitho-, photolitho-, zinco-, glypho- -graphy, -graph.

impression, print, engraving, plate; steel-, copper-plate; etching; mezzo-, aqua-, litho-tint; cut, woodcut, block; stereo-, grapho-, auto-, helio-type; half-tone; *photogravure*, *rotogravure*.

graver, *burin*, etching-point, style; plate, stone, wood-block, negative; die, punch, stamp.

printing; plate –, copper-plate –, intaglio –, anastatic –, lithographic –, color –, three color-printing; type-printing etc. 591.

illustr-, illumin-ation; *vignette*, initial letter, *cul de lampe*, tail-piece.

V. engrave, grave, stipple, scrape, etch; bite, – in; lithograph etc. *n.*; print.

Adj. insculptured; engraved etc. *v.*

Phr. *sculpsit, imprimit.*

559. Artist.—N. artist; painter, limner, drawer, sketcher, delineator; cartoon-, caricatur-ist, designer, engraver; draughtsman; copyist; enameller, -list.

historical –, landscape –, genre –, marine –, flower –, portrait –, miniature –, scene –, sign-painter; engraver; Apelles; sculptor, carver, chaser, modeller, lapidary, *figuriste*, statuary; Phidias, Praxiteles; Royal Academician.

photographer, retoucher.

560. Language.—N. language; phraseology etc. 569; speech etc. 582; tongue, lingo, vernacular, slang; mother –, vulgar –, native- tongue; household words; King's *or* Queen's English; idiom; dialect etc. 563.

volapuk, esperanto, ido, occidental, Ro.

confusion of tongues, Babel, *pasigraphie*; pantomime etc. (*signs*) 550; *onomatopaeia.*

phil-, gloss-, glott-ology; linguistics, chrestomathy; paleo-logy; -graphy; comparative grammar.

literature, letters, polite literature, *belles lettres*, muses, humanities, *literae humaniores*, republic of letters, dead languages, classics; genius of a language; scholarship etc. (*knowledge*) 490.

linguist etc. (*scholar*) 492.

V. speak, say, express by words etc. 566.

Adj. lingu-al, -istic; dialectic; vernacular, current, colloquial, slangy; bilingual, polyglot; literary.

561. Letter.—N. letter; character; hieroglyphic etc. (*writing*) 590; type etc. (*printing*) 591; capitals; majus-, minus-cule; alphabet, ABC, abecedary, christcross row, chrisscross row.

consonant, vowel, diphthong; mute, surd; sonant, liquid, labial, dental, palatal, gutteral.

syllable; mono-, dis-, poly-syllable; affix, prefix, suffix.

spelling, orthography; phon-ography, -etic spelling; ana-, meta-grammatism.

cipher, monogram, anagram; double – acrostic.

V. spell.

Adj. literal; alphabetical, abecedarian; syllabic; uncial etc. (*writing*) 590; phonetic, voiced, mute etc. *n.*

562. Word.—N. word, term, vocable; name etc. 564; phrase etc. 566; root, etymon; derivative; part of speech etc. (*grammar*) 567.

dictionary, vocabulary, word book, lexicon, index, glossary, thesaurus, *gradus, delectus*, concordance.

etymology, lexicology, derivation; phonology, orthoepy; gloss-, termin-, orism-ology; paleology etc. (*philology*) 560; comparative philology.

lexicograph-er, -y; glossographer etc. (*scholar*) 492; etymologist; logolept.

verbosity, verbiage, loquacity etc. 584.

Adj. verbal, literal; titular, nominal. [Similarly derived] conjugate, paraonymous; derivative.

Adv. verbally etc. *adj.*; *verbatim* etc. (*exactly*) 494.

563. Neology.—N. neolo-gy; -gism; newfangled expression; barbarism; caconym; archaism, black letter, monkish Latin; corruption; missaying, antiphrasis.

paronomasia, play upon words; wordplay etc. (*wit*) 842; *double-entente* etc. (*ambiguity*) 520; palindrome, paragram, clinch; abuse of -language, – terms.

dialect, brogue, *patois*, provincialism, broken English, *lingua franca*; Brit-, Gall-, Scott-, Hibernicism; American-ism; Gipsy lingo, Romany, pidgin English.

dog Latin, macaronics, gibberish, confusion of tongues, Babel; jargon.

colloquialism etc. (*figure of speech*) 521; byword; technicality, lingo, slang, cant, *argot*, St. Giles's Greek, thieves' Latin, peddler's French, flash tongue, Billingsgate, Wall Street slang.

pseudonym etc. (*misnomer*) 565; Mr. So-and-so; what d'ye call 'em, what's his name; thingum-my, -bob; *je ne sais quoi.*

neologist, coiner of words.

V. coin words.

Adj. neologic, -al; rare; archaic; obsolete etc. (*old*) 124; colloquial, dialectic, slang, cant.

564. Nomenclature.—N. nomenclature; naming etc. *v.*; nuncupation, nomination, baptism; orismology; *onomatopaeia*; antonomasia.

name; appella-tion, -tive; designation; title; head, -ing, caption; denomination; by-name, epithet.

style, proper name; prae-, ag-, cog-nomen; patronymic, surname; cognomination; compellation, description; empty -title, – name; handle to one's name; namesake, eponym.

synonym, antonym.

term, expression, noun; by-word; convertible terms etc. 522; technical term; cant etc. 563.

V. name, call, term, denominate, designate, style, entitle, intitule, clepe, dub, christen, baptize, nickname, characterize, specify, define, distinguish by the name of; label etc. (*mark*) 550.

be -called etc. *v.*; take –, bear –, go (*or* be known) by –, go (*or* pass) under –, rejoice in- the name of.

Adj. named etc. *v.*; hight, yclept, known as; what one may -well, – fairly, – properly, – fitly-call.

nuncupa-tory, -tive; cognominal, titular, nominal; orismological.

565. Misnomer.—N. misnomer; *lucus a non lucendo*; Mrs. Malaprop; what d'ye call 'em etc. (*neologism*) 563.

nickname, *sobriquet*, by-name, handle, moniker; assumed -name, – title; *alias*; *nom de - guerre*, – *plume*, – *theâtre*; pseudonym, pen name, stage name.

V. mis-name, -call, - term; nickname; assume -a name, – an alias.

Adj. misnamed etc. *v.*; pseudonymous; *soi-disant*; self-called, -styled, -christened; so-called.

nameless, anonymous; without a –, having no-name; innominate, unnamed.

Adv. in no sense.

566. Phrase.—N. phrase, expression, set phrase; sentence, paragraph; figure of speech etc. 521; idi-om, -otism; turn of expression.

paraphrase etc. (*synonym*) 522; periphrase etc. (*circumlocution*) 573; motto etc. (*proverb*) 496. phraseology etc. 569.

V. express, phrase; word, – it; give -words, – expression- to; voice; arrange in –, clothe in –, put into –, express by- words; couch in terms; find words to express; speak by the card.

Adj. expressed etc. *v.*; idiomatic.

Adv. in -round, – set, – good, set- terms; in set phrases.

567. Grammar.—N. grammar, accidence, syntax, *praxis*, analysis, paradigm, punctuation; parts of speech, inflexion, case, declension, conjugation; *jus et norma loquendi*; Lindley Murray etc. (*school-book*) 542; correct style; philology etc. (*language*) 560.

V. parse, analyze; decline, conjugate; punctuate.

Adj. grammatical; syntactic; inflexional.

568. Solecism.—N. solecism; bad –, false –, faulty- grammar; slip, error; slip of the -pen, – tongue; *lapsus calami-*, – *linguae*; *faux pas*; slipslop; bull.

V. use -bad, – faulty- grammar; solecize, commit a solecism; murder the -King's, – Queen's- English; break Priscian's head.

Adj. ungrammatical; in-correct, -accurate; faulty, improper, incongruous, abnormal.

569. Style.—N. style, diction, phraseology, wording; manner, strain; composition; mode of expression, choice of words, literary power, ready pen, pen of a ready writer; command of language etc. (*eloquence*) 582; authorship; *la morgue littéraire.*

V. express by words etc. 566; write.

570. Perspicuity.—N. perspicuity etc. (*intelligibility*) 518; plain speaking etc. (*manifestation*) 525; defin-iteness, -ition; exactness etc. 494; perspicuousness, logical acuteness.

Adj. lucid etc. (*intelligible*) 518; explicit etc. (*manifest*) 525; exact etc. 494.

571. Obscurity.—N. obscurity etc. (*unintelligibility*) 519; involution; hard words; ambiguity etc. 520; vagueness etc. 475, inexactness etc. 495; what d'ye call 'em etc. (*neologism*) 563; cloudiness, confusion.

Adj. obscure etc. *n.*; crabbed, involved, confused.

572. Conciseness.—N. conciseness etc. *adj.*; brevity, 'the soul of wit,' laconism; Tacitus; ellipsis; syncope; abridgment etc. (*shortening*) 201; compression etc. 195; epitome etc. 596; monostitch; portmanteau word, telescope word, protogram.

V. be -concise etc. *adj.*; condense etc. 195; abridge etc. 201; abstract etc. 596; come to the point.

Adj. concise, brief, short, terse, close; to the point, exact; neat, compact, condensed, pointed; laconic, curt, pithy, trenchant, summary; pregnant; compendious etc. (*compendium*) 596; succinct; elliptical, epigrammatic, crisp, sententious.

Adv. concisely etc. *adj.*; briefly, summarily; in -brief, – short, – a word, – few words, – a nutshell; for shortness sake; to -come to the point, – make a long story short, – cut the matter short, – be brief; it comes to this, the long and short of it is.

573. Diffuseness.—N. diffuseness etc. *adj.*; amplification etc. *v.*; dilating etc. *v.*; verbosity, *verbiage*, wordiness, cloud of words, *copia verborum*; flow of words etc. (*loquacity*) 584.

poly-, tauto-, batto-, perisso-logy; pleonasm, exuberance, redundance; thrice-told tale; prolixity; circumlocution, *ambages*; periphra-se, -sis; roundabout phrases; episode; expletive; penny-a-lining; padding, drivel, twaddle, rigmarole; richness etc. 577.

V. be -diffuse etc. *adj.*; run out on, descant, expatiate, enlarge, dilate, amplify, expand, inflate, pad; launch –, branch- out; rant.

maunder, prose; harp upon etc. (*repeat*) 104; dwell on, insist upon.

digress, ramble, *battre la campagne*, beat about the bush, perorate, spin a long yarn, protract; spin –, swell –, draw- out, drivel.

Adj. dif-, pro-fuse; wordy, verbose, largiloquent, copious, exuberant, effusive, pleonastic, lengthy; long, -some, -winded, -spun, -drawn out; diffusive, spun out, protracted, prolix, prosing, maundering; circumlocutory, periphrastic, ambagious, roundabout; digressive; dis-, ex-cursive; rambling, episodic; flatulent, frothy.

Adv. diffusely etc. *adj.*; at large, *in extenso*; about it and about it.

574. Vigor.—N. vigor, power, force; boldness, raciness etc. *adj.*; spirit, point, antithesis, piquancy; *verve*, glow, fire, warmth, ardor, enthusiasm; 'thoughts that breathe and words that burn;' strong language; punch; gravity, sententiousness; elevation, loftiness, sublimity.

eloquence; command of -words, – language.

Adj. vigorous, nervous, powerful, forcible, trenchant, mordant, biting, incisive, impressive; sensational.

spirited, lively, glowing, sparkling, racy, bold, slashing; pungent, *piquant*, full of point, pointed, pithy, antithetical; sententious.

lofty, elevated, sublime, grand, weighty, ponderous; eloquent; vehement, petulant, impassioned; poetic.

Adv. in -glowing, – good set, – no measured- terms.

575. Feebleness.—N. feebleness etc. *adj.*;

Adj. feeble, bald, tame, meager, insipid, nerve-les, jejune, vapid, trashy, cold, frigid, poor, dull, dry, languid; pros-ing, -y, -aic; unvaried, monotonous, weak, frail, washy, wishy-washy, sloppy; sketchy, slight; careless, slovenly, loose, lax; slip-shod, -slop; inexact; dis-jointed, -connected; puerile, childish; flatulent; rambling etc. (*diffuse*) 573.

576. Plainness.—N. plainness etc. *adj.*; simplicity, severity; plain -terms, – English; Saxon English; household words.

V. speak plainly; call a spade 'a spade;' plunge *in medias res*; come to the point.

Adj. plain, simple; un-ornamented, -adorned, -varnished; home-ly, -spun; neat; severe, chaste, pure, Saxon; commonplace, matter of fact, natural, prosaic, sober, unimaginative.

dry, unvaried, monotonous etc. 575.

Adv. in plain -terms, – words, – English, – common parlance; point blank.

577. Ornament.—N. ornament; floridness etc. *adj.*; turg-idity, -escence; altiloquence etc. *adj.*; orotundity; declamation, teratology; well-rounded periods; elegance etc. 578.

inversion, antithesis, alliteration, *paronomasia*; figurativeness etc. (*metaphor*) 521.

flourish; flowers of -speech, – rhetoric; euphuism, -emism.

big-, high-sounding words; macrology, *sesquipedalia verba*, sesquipedalianism; Alexandrine; inflation, pretension; rant, bombast, fustian, bunkum, balderdash, prose run mad; fine writing; Minerva press.

phrasemonger; euph-uist, -emist.

V. ornament, overlay with ornament, overcharge; smell of the lamp.

Adj. ornamented etc. *v.*; beautified etc. 847; ornate, florid, rich, flowery; euph-uistic, -emistic; sonorous; high-, big-sounding; inflated, swelling, tumid; turg-id, -escent; pedantic, pompous, stilted; high-flown, -flowing; sententious, rhetorical, declamatory; grandiose; grand-, magn-, altiloquent; sesquipedal, -ian; Johnsonian, mouthy; bombastic; fustian; frothy, flashy, flaming, flamboyant.

antithetical, alliterative; figurative etc. 521; artificial etc. (*inelegant*) 579.

Adv. *ore rotundo*; with rounded phrase.

578. Elegance.—N. elegance, purity, grace, ease, felicity, distinction, gracefulness, refinement, readiness etc. *adj.*; concinnity, euphony, numerosity, balance, rythym, symmetry, proportion; restraint; good taste, propriety.

well rounded –, well turned –, flowing- periods; the right word in the right place; antithesis etc. 577.

purist, stylist.

V. point an antithesis, round a period.

Adj. elegant, polished, classical, Attic, correct, Ciceronian, artistic; chaste, pure, Saxon, academical.

graceful, easy, readable, fluent, flowing, tripping; unaffected, natural, unlabored; mellifluous; euph-onious, -emistic; rhythmical, balanced, symmetrical.

felicitous, happy, neat; well –, neatly- -put, – expressed.

579. Inelegance.—N. inelegance; vulgarity, bad taste; stiffness etc. *adj.*; unlettered Muse; barbarism; slang etc. 563; solecism etc. 568; mannerism etc. (*affectation*) 855; euphuism; fustian etc. 577; cacophony; want of balance; words that -break the teeth, – dislocate the jaw.

V. be -inelegant etc. *adj.*

Adj. inelegant, graceless, ungraceful, unpolished; harsh, abrupt; dry, stiff, cramped, formal, *guindé*; forced, labored, awkward; artificial, mannered, ponderous; turgid etc. 577; affected, euphuistic; barbarous, uncouth, grotesque, rude, crude, halting; vulgar, offensive to ears polite.

580. Voice.—N. voice; vocality; organ, lungs, bellows; good –, fine –, powerful etc. (*loud*) 404 –, musical etc. 413- voice; intonation; tone etc. (*sound*) 402- of voice.

vocalization; cry etc. 411; strain, utterance, prolation; exclam-, ejacul-, vocifer-ation; enunci-, articul-ation; articulate sound; distinctness; clearness, – of articulation; stage whisper; delivery; attack.

accent, -uation; emphasis, stress; broad –, strong –, pure –, native –, foreign- accent; pronunciation.

[Word similarly pronounced] homonym.

orthoepy; euphony etc. (*melody*) 413.

gastri-, ventri-loquism; ventriloquist; polyphonism, -ist.

[Science of voice] phonology etc. (*sound*) 402.

V. sing, speak, utter, breathe, voice; give -utterance, – tongue; cry etc. (*shout*) 411; ejaculate, rap out; vocalize, prolate, articulate, enunciate, enounce, pronounce, accentuate, aspirate, deliver, mouth; emit, murmur, whisper, – in the ear, croon, yodel.

Adj. vocal, phonetic, oral; ejaculatory, articulate, distinct, stertorous; enunciative; accentuated, aspirated; euphonious etc. (*melodious*) 413.

581. Aphony—N. aphony, *aphonia*; dumbness etc. *adj.*; obmutescence; absence –, want- of voice; dysphony; silence etc. (*taciturnity*) 585; raucity; harsh etc. 410 –, unmusical etc. 414- voice; *falsetto*, 'childish treble;' mute, dummy, deaf mute.

V. keep silence etc. 585; speak -low, – softly; whisper etc. (*faintness*) 405.

silence; render -mute, – silent etc. 403; muzzle, muffle, suppress, smother, gag, strike dumb, dumbfound, -founder; drown the voice, put to silence, stop one's mouth, cut one short.

stick in the throat.

Adj. aphon-ous, -ic, dumb, mute; deaf-mute, –

and dumb; mum; tongue-tied; breath-, tongue-, voice-, speech-, word-less; mute as a -fish, – stock-fish, – mackerel; silent etc. (*taciturn*) 585; muzzled; in-articulate, -audible.

croaking, raucous, hoarse, husky, dry, hollow, sepulchral, hoarse as a raven.

Adv. with -bated breath, – the finger on the lips; *sotto voce*; in a -low tone, – cracked voice, – broken voice; in an aside.

Phr. *vox faucibus haesit.*

582. Speech.—N. speech, faculty of speech; locution, talk, parlance, verbal intercourse, prolation, oral communication, word of mouth, *parole*, palaver, prattle; effusion.

oration, recitation, delivery, say, address, speech, lecture, harangue, sermon, *tirade*, screed, formal speech, salutatory, peroration; prelection; speechifying; soliloquy etc. 589; allocution etc. 586; interlocution etc. 588.

oratory; elo-cution, -quence; rhetoric, declamation; grandi-, multi-loquence; burst of eloquence; facundity; talkativeness; flow –, command- of -words, – language; *copia verborum*; power of speech, gift of the gab; *usus loquendi.*

speaker etc. *v.*; spokesman, pro-, inter-locutor; mouthpiece, Hermes; ora-tor, -trix, -tress; Demosthenes, Cicero; rhetorician; stump –, platform- orator, tub-thumper; elocutionist; speechmaker, patterer, *improvisatore*.

V. speak, – of; say, utter, pronounce, deliver, give utterance to; utter –, pour- forth; breathe, let fall, come out with; rap –, blurt- out; have on one's lips; have at the -end, – tip- of one's tongue.

break silence; open one's -lips, – mouth; lift –, raise- one's voice; give –, wag the- tongue; talk, outspeak; put in a word or two.

hold forth; make –, deliver- -a speech etc. *n.*; speechify, harangue, declaim, stump, flourish, spout, rant, recite, lecture, preach, sermonize, discourse, be on one's legs; have –, say- one's say; expatiate etc. (*speak at length*) 573; speak one's mind.

soliloquize etc. 589; tell etc. (*inform*) 527; speak to etc. 586; talk together etc. 588.

be -eloquent etc. *adj.*; have -a tongue in one's head, – the gift of the gab etc. *n.*

pass –, escape- one's lips; fall from the -lips, – mouth.

Adj. speaking etc., spoken etc. *v.*; oral, lingual, phonetic, not written, unwritten, outspoken; eloquent, -cutionary; orat-, rhetorical; declamatory; grandiloquent etc. 577; talkative etc. 584.

Adv. orally etc. *adj.*; by word of mouth, *vivâ voce*, from the lips of.

Phr. quoth –, said- he etc.

583. Stammering. [Imperfect Speech.]—**N.** inarticulateness; stammering etc. *v.*; hesitation etc. *v.*; impediment in one's speech; aphasia, titubancy, traulism; whisper etc. (*faint sound*) 405; lisp, drawl, tardiloquence; nasal -tone, – accent; twang; *falsetto* etc. (*want of voice*) 581; broken -voice, – accents, – sentences.

brogue etc. 563; slip of the tongue, *lapsus linguae*.

V. stammer, stutter, hesitate, falter, hammer; balbu-tiate, -cinate; haw, hum and haw, be unable to put two words together.

mumble, mutter; maund, -er; whisper etc. 405; mince, lisp; jabber, gabble, gibber; sp-, spl-utter; muffle, mump; drawl, mouth; croak; speak -thick, – through the nose; snuffle, clip one's words; murder the -language, – King's (*or* Queen's) English; mis-pronounce, -say.

Adj. stammering etc. *v.*; inarticulate, guttural, nasal; tremulous.

Adv. *sotto voce* etc. (*faintly*) 405.

584. Loquacity.—N. loquac-ity, -iousness; talkativeness etc. *adj.*; garrulity; multiloquence, much speaking, effusion, wordiness.

jaw; gab, -ble; jabber, chatter; prate, prattle, cackle, clack; twaddle, trattle, rattle; *caquet*, *-terie*; blabber, *bavardage*, bibble-babble, gibble-gabble; small talk etc. (*converse*) 588.

fluency, flippancy, volubility, flowing tongue; flow, – of words; *flux de -bouche*, – *mots*, – *paroles*; *copia verborum, cacoëthes loquendi*; verbosity etc. (*diffuseness*) 573; gift of the gab etc. (*eloquence*) 582.

talker; chatter-er, -box; babbler etc. *v.*; rattle; ranter; sermonizer, proser, driveller; wind bag; gossip etc. (*converse*) 588; magpie, jay, parrot, poll, Babel; *moulin à paroles.*

V. be -loquacious etc. *adj.*; talk glibly, pour forth, patter; prate, palaver, prose, chatter, prattle, clack, jabber, jaw; rattle, – on; twaddle, twattle; babble, gabble; out-talk; talk oneself -out of breath, – hoarse; maunder, gush, blatter; talk a donkey's hind leg off; expatiate etc. (*speak at length*) 573; gossip etc. (*converse*) 588; din in the ears etc. (*repeat*) 104; talk -at random, – nonsense etc. 497; be hoarse with talking.

Adj. loquacious, talkative, conversational, garrulous, linguacious, multiloquous; chattering etc. *v.*; chatty etc. (*sociable*) 892; declamatory etc. 582; open-mouthed.

fluent, voluble, glib, flippant; long-tongued, -winded etc. (*diffuse*) 573.

Adv. trippingly on the tongue; glibly etc. *adj.*

Phr. the tongue running -fast, – loose, – on wheels.

585. Taciturnity.—N. silence, muteness, obmutescence; taciturnity, pauciloquy, costiveness, curtness; reserve, reticence etc. (*concealment*) 528; *aposiopesis.*

man of few words.

V. be -silent etc. *adj.*; keep silence; hold one's -tongue, – peace, – jaw; not speak etc. 582; say nothing; seal –, close –, put a padlock on- the -lips, – mouth; put a bridle on one's tongue; keep one's tongue between one's teeth; make no sign, not let a word escape one; keep a secret etc. 528; not have a word to say; lay –, place- the finger on the lips; render mute etc. 581.

stick in one's throat.

Adj. silent, mute, mum; silent as -a post, – a stone, – the grave etc. (*still*) 403; dumb etc. 581.

taciturn, sparing of words; close, – mouthed, –

tongued; laconic, costive, inconversable, curt; reserved; reticent etc. (*concealing*) 528.

Int. tush! silence! mum! hush! *chut!* hist! tut! etc. 403.

586. Allocution.—N. allocution, alloquy, address; speech etc. 582; apostrophe, interpellation, appeal, invocation, salutation; word in the ear.

[Feigned dialogue] dialogism.

platform etc. 542; audience etc. (*interview*) 588.

V. speak to, address, accost, make up to, apostrophize, appeal to, invoke; hail, salute; call to, halloo.

take -aside, – by the button, button-hole; talk to in private.

lecture etc. (*make a speech*) 582.

Int. soho! halloo! hey! hist! hi!

587. Response etc.; *see* Answer 462.

588. Interlocution.—N. interlocution; collocution, colloquy, converse, conversation, confabulation, talk, discourse, verbal intercourse; communion, oral communication, commerce; dia-, duo-, tria-logue.

causerie, chat, chit-chat; small –, table –, teatable –, town –, village –, idle- talk; tattle, gossip, tittle-tattle; babble, -ment; *tripotage*, cackle, prittle-prattle, *on dit*; talk of the -town, – village.

conference, parley, interview, audience, *pourparler*; *tête-à-tête*; reception, *conversazione*; congress etc. (*council*) 696; pow-wow.

hall of audience, *durbar*, coliseum, assembly hall, auditorium.

palaver, debate, logomachy, war of words, controversy.

talker, gossip, tattler; Paul Pry; tabby; chatterer etc. (*loquacity*) 584; interlocutor etc. (*spokesman*) 582; conversation-ist, -alist; dialogist.

'the feast of reason and the flow of soul;' *mollia tempora fandi*.

V. talk together, converse, confabulate; hold –, carry on –, join in –, engage in- a conversation; put in a word; shine in conversation; bandy words; parley; palaver; chat, gossip, tattle; prate etc. (*loquacity*) 584.

discourse –, confer –, commune –, commerce- with; hold -converse, – conference, – intercourse; talk it over; be closeted with; talk with one -in private, – *tête-à-tête*.

Adj. conversing etc. *v.*; interlocutory; conversational, -able; discursive, -coursive; chatty etc. (*sociable*) 892; colloquial, *tête-à-tête*, confabulatory.

589. Soliloquy.—N. soliloquy, monologue, apostrophe.

solilo-quist, -quizer, monologist.

V. soliloquize; say –, talk- to oneself; say aside, think aloud, apostrophize.

Adj. soliloquizing etc. *v.*

Adv. aside.

590. Writing.—N. writing etc. *v.*; chiro-, stelo-, cero-graphy, graphology; stylography; pen-craft, -script, -manship; quill-driving; typewriting.

writing, manuscript, MS., *literae scriptae*; these presents.

stroke –, dash- of the pen; *coup de plume*; line; pen and ink.

letter etc. 561; uncial writing, cuneiform character, arrow-head, Ogham, Runes, futhorc; hieroglyphic, hieratic, demotic; script; contraction.

short-hand; steno-, brachy-, tachy-graphy; secret writing, writing in cipher; crypt-, stegan-ography; phono-, pasi-, poly-, logo-graphy.

copy; tran-, re-script; draft, rough –, fair- copy; handwriting; signature, sign-manual; auto-, mono-, holo-graph; hand, fist; mark.

calligraphy; good –, running –, flowing –, cursive –, legible –, copperplate –, round –, bold-hand.

cacography, *griffonage*, *barbouillage*; bad –, cramped –, crabbed –, illegible- hand; scribble etc. *v.*; *pattes de mouche*; ill-formed letters; pot-hooks and hangers.

stationery; pen, quill, goose-quill, reed; stylographic-, fountain-pen; pencil, style, stylus; paper, foolscap, parchment, vellum, papyrus, pad, tablet, block, note book, slate, marble, pillar, table, black board.

ink-bottle, -pot, -stand, -well, -horn; typewriter.

transcription etc. (*copy*) 21; inscription etc. (*record*) 551; superscription etc. (*indication*) 550.

composition, authorship; *cacoethes scribendi*.

writer, scribe, amanuensis, scrivener, secretary, clerk, penman, copyist, transcriber, quill-driver; writer for the press etc. (*author*) 593.

shorthand writer, stenographer; typewriter, typist.

V. write, pen; copy, engross; write out, – fair; transcribe; scribble, scrawl, scrabble, scratch; interline; stain paper; write down etc. (*record*) 551; sign etc. (*attest*) 467; take down, – in shorthand; typewrite, type.

compose, indite, draw up, redact, draft, formulate; dictate; inscribe, throw on paper, dash off; concoct.

take -up the pen, – pen in hand; shed –, spill –, dip one's pen in- ink.

Adj. writing etc. *v.*; written etc. *v.*; in -writing, – black and white; under one's hand.

uncial, Runic, cuneiform, hieroglyphical etc. *n.*

Adv. *currente calamo*; pen in hand.

591. Printing.—N. printing; block –, type-printing, lino-, mono-type; plate printing etc. (*engraving*) 558; the press etc. (*publication*) 531; composition.

print, letterpress, text, matter, standing type; context, note, page, column; over-running; head-, foot-line, title.

typography; stereo-, electro-, apro-type; type,

black letter, heavy type, font, fount; pi, pie; capitals etc. (*letters*) 561; diamond, pearl, nonpareil, minion, brevier, bourgeois, long primer, small pica, pica, english, great primer.

folio etc. (*book*) 593; copy, impression, pull, proof, galley –, author's –, page- proof, revise.

printer, compositor, reader; printer's devil.

V. print; compose; put –, go- to press; pass –, see- through the press; publish etc. 531; bring out; appear in –, rush into- print.

Adj. printed etc. *v.*; in type; typographical etc. *n.*

592. Correspondence.—N. correspondence, letter, epistle, note, *billet*, post-, letter-card, missive, circular, form letter; favor, *billet-doux*; des-, dis-patch; *bulletin*, communication etc. 532; these presents; rescript, -ion; post etc. (*messenger*) 534; letter writer, correspondent.

V. correspond, – with; write –, send a letter- to; keep up a correspondence; drop a line to; despatch; communicate with; circularize.

Adj. epistolary.

593. Book.—N. book, -let; writing, work, volume, tome, opuscule; tract, -ate; *livret*; *brochure, libretto*, handbook, treatise, text-book, codex, manual, pamphlet, monograph, enchiridion, circular, publication; book of poems; novel; chap-book.

part, issue, number, *livraison*; album, portfolio; periodical, serial, magazine, *ephemeris*, annual, journal.

paper, bill, sheet, broadsheet, screed; leaf, -let; fly-leaf, page; quire, ream.

chapter, section, head, article, paragraph, passage, clause, supplement, appendix; *feuilleton*.

folio, quarto, octavo; duo-, sexto-, octo-decimo.

en-, cyclopedia, dictionary, lexicon, thesaurus, concordance, anthology, bibliography; compilation, compendium, catalogue etc. 86; library, bibliotheca; the press etc. (*publication*) 531.

writer, author, *littérateur*, essayist, journalist, publicist; scribe, penman, war –, special –, correspondent; pen, scribbler, the scribbling race; ghost, hack, literary hack, Grub-street writer; writer for –, gentlemen of –, representative of- the press; reporter, penny-a-liner; editor, subeditor; playwright etc. 599; poet etc. 597.

bookseller, publisher; biblio-pole, -polist, -grapher; librarian; book -collector, – worm.

book -shop, – club, circulating –, lending –, public- library; publishing house.

knowledge of books, bibliography; booklearning etc. (*knowledge*) 490.

594. Description.—N. description, account, statement, report; *exposé* etc. (*disclosure*) 529; specification, particulars, scenario, plot; state –, summary- of facts; brief etc. (*abstract*) 596; return etc. (*record*) 551; *catalogue raisonné* etc. (*list*) 86; guide-book etc. (*information*) 527.

delineation etc. (*representation*) 554; sketch, vignette; monograph; minute –, detailed –, particular –, circumstantial –, graphic- account; narration, recital, rehearsal, relation.

histori-, chron-ography; historic Muse, Clio; history; bi-, autobi-ography; necrology, obituary.

narrative, history; memoir, memorials; annals etc. (*chronicle*) 551; tradition, legend, saga, epic, epos, story, tale, historiette; personal narrative, journal, letters, life, adventures, fortunes, experiences, confessions; anecdote, ana, *trait*.

work of fiction, short story, novelette, novel, romance, penny dreadful, shilling, shocker, Minerva press; fairy –, nursery- tale; fable, allegory, parable, apologue.

relator etc. *v.*; *raconteur*; historian etc. (*recorder*) 553; biographer, fabulist, novelist, story teller, romancer, teller of tales, spinner of yarns, anecdotist.

V. describe; set forth etc. (*state*) 535; draw a picture, picture; portray etc. (*represent*) 554; characterize, particularize; narrate, relate, recite, recount, sum up, run over, recapitulate, rehearse, fight one's battles over again.

unfold etc. (*disclose*) 529- a tale; tell; give –, render- an account of; report, make a report, draw up a statement.

detail; enter into –, descend to- -particulars, – details.

Adj. descriptive, graphic, narrative, epic, suggestive, well-drawn; historic; auto-, biographical, realistic, expository, tradition-al, -ary; legendary; fabulous, mythical; anecdotic, storied; described etc. *v.*

595. Dissertation.—N. dissertation, treatise, essay; *thesis*, theme; tract, -ate, -ation, excursus; discourse, memoir, disquisition, lecture, sermon, homily, pandect.

commentary, review, *critique*, criticism, article; lead-er, -ing article, editorial; argument, running commentary.

investigation etc. (*inquiry*) 461; study etc. (*consideration*) 451; discussion etc. (*reasoning*) 476; exposition etc. (*explanation*) 522.

commentator, critic, essayist, pamphleteer; publicist, reviewer, leader writer, editor, annotator.

V. dissert –, descant –, write –, touch- upon a subject; dissertate; treat of –, take up –, ventilate –, discuss –, deal with –, go into –, canvass –, handle –, do justice to- a subject; comment, criticize, interpret etc. 522.

Adj. dis-cursive, -coursive; disquisitional, disquisitionary; expository, critical.

596. Compendium.—N. compend, -ium; abstract, *précis*, epitome, *multum in parvo*, analysis, pandect, digest, sum and substance, brief, abridgment, summary, *aperçu*, draft, minute, note; synopsis, textbook, *conspectus*, outlines, syllabus, contents, heads, prospectus.

album; scrap –, note –, memorandum –, commonplace- book; extracts, *excerpta*, cuttings; fugitive -pieces, – writings; *spicilegium*, flowers, anthology, miscellany, *collectanea*, *analecta*; compilation.

recapitulation, *résumé*, review.

abbrevia-tion, -ture; contraction; shortening etc. 201; compression etc. 195.

V. abridge, abstract, epitomize, summarize; make –, prepare –, draw –, compile- an abstract etc. *n.*

recapitulate, review, skim, run over, sum up.

abbreviate etc. (*shorten*) 201; condense etc. (*compress*) 195; compile etc. (*collect*) 72; edit, blue pencil.

Adj. compendious, synoptic, analectic, analytical; abridged etc. *v.*

Adv. in -short, – epitome, – substance, – few words.

Phr. it lies in a nutshell.

597. Poetry.—N. poetry, poetics, poesy, Muse, Calliope, tuneful Nine, Parnassus, Helicon, Pierides, Pierian spring, afflatus, inspiration.

versification, rhyming, making verses; prosody, scansion, orthometry.

poem; epic, – poem; epopee, *epopaea*, ode, epode, idyl, lyric, eclogue, pastoral, bucolic, georgic, dithyramb, anacreontic, sonnet, roundelay, *rondel, rondoletto, rondeau, rondo*, triolet; madrigal, canzonet, *cento*, monody, elegy, palinode; rhapsody.

dramatic –, lyric- poetry; opera; posy, anthology.

song, ballad, lay; love –, drinking –, war –, folk –, sea- song; lullaby; music etc. 415; nursery rhymes.

[Bad poetry] doggerel, Hudibrastic verse, prose run mad; macaronics; macaronic –, leonine-verse; runes.

canto, stanza, distich, verse, line, couplet, triplet, quatrain, sestet; *strophe*, *antistrophe*, refrain, chorus, burden.

verse, rhyme, assonance, crambo, meter, measure, foot, numbers, strain, rhythm; accentuation etc. (*voice*) 580; iambus, dactyl, spondee, trochee, anapaest etc.; hex-, pent-ameter; Alexandrine; blank verse, alliteration.

elegiacs etc. *adj.*; elegiac etc. *adj.* -verse, – meter, – poetry.

poet, – laureate; laureate; minor poet, bard, lyrist, scald, troubadour, *trouvère*; mistrel; minne-, meister-singer; *improvisatore*; versifier, sonneteer; ballad monger; rhym-er, -ist, -ester; poetaster.

V. poetize, sing, versify, make verses, rhyme, scan.

Adj. poetic, -al; lyric, -al; tuneful; epic; dithyrambic etc. *n.*; metrical; a-, catalectic; elegiac, iambic, trochaic, spondaic, anapest; Ionic, Sapphic, Alcaic, Pindaric.

598. Prose.—N. prose, – writer, pros-aism, -aist, -er.

V. prose, write prose.

write -prose, – in prose.

Adj. pros-y, -aic; unpoetical.

rhymeless, unrhymed, in prose, not in verse.

599. Drama.—N. drama, the -drama, – stage, – theater, – play; theatricals, dramaturgy, histrionic art, buskin, sock, *cothurnus*, Melpomene and Thalia, Thespis.

play, stage-play, piece, five-act play, tragedy, comedy, opera, comic opera, *vaudeville, comedietta, lever de rideau*, curtain raiser, interlude, afterpiece, exode, farce, *divertissement, extravaganza*, burletta, harlequinade, pantomime, mimodrama, burlesque, *opéra bouffe*, musical comedy, review, revue, intimate revue, variety, cabaret entertainment, *ballet, spectacle*, masque, *drame, comédie drame*; melo-drama, -drame; *comédie larmoyante*, emotional drama, sensation drama, tragi-, farcical-comedy; mono-drame, -logue; duologue; trilogy; charade, *proverbe*; mystery, miracle –, morality- play.

act, scene, *tableau*; in-, intro-duction; pro-, epilogue, curtain; *libretto*, book, script.

performance, representation, show, *mise en scène*, stagery, *jeu de théâtre*, stage-craft; acting; gesture etc. 550; impersonation etc. 554; stage business, gag, patter, buffoonery.

theater; play-, opera-house; house; music hall; *cabaret*; amphitheater, circus, hippodrome; puppet-show, *fantoccini*; *marionnettes*, Punch and Judy.

cinema, -tograph-, picture –, theater, the pictures, the movies, the talkies.

auditory, *auditorium*, front of the house, stalls, boxes, balcony, dress –, upper- -circle, – boxes, amphitheater, pit, gallery; *foyer*; greenroom; dressing rooms, *coulisses*.

flat; drop, – scene; wing, screen, side-scene; transformation scene, curtain, act-drop, safety –, fire- curtain; *proscenium*, forestage.

stage, revolving stage, scene, the boards; star –, grave –, trap, mezzanine floor; flies; gridiron, floats, battens, footlights; lime –, spot –, flood –, bunch-lights; scenery, set, *décor*; orchestra.

theatrical -costume, – properties, props.

part, *rôle*, character, cast, *dramatis personae*; *répertoire*.

actor, player; stage –, strolling- player; old –, stager, performer; mime, -r; *artiste*; com-, tragedian, straight man; *tragédienne*, Thespian, Roscius, star.

pantomimist, clown, harlequin, *buffo*, buffoon, *farceur, grimacier*, pantaloon, columbine; *Pierrot, Pierrette*; punch, -inello; *pulcinell-o, -a*; mute, *figurante*, general utility; super, -numerary, extra.

mummer, guiser, guisard, gysart, masque.

mountebank, Jack Pudding; tumbler, posture-master, acrobat, equilibrist, juggler, contortionist; *danseuse*, *ballerina*, ballet -dancer, – girl, *coryphée*; *bayadère*, *geisha*; chorus -singer, – girl.

company; first tragedian, *prima donna*, lead, leading lady, protagonist; *jeune premier*; juvenile lead, *débutant, -e*; light –, genteel –, low- -comedy, – comedian; *soubrette*, walking gentleman, *amoroso*, heavy, heavy father, *ingénue, jeune veuve*, *commère*, *compère*.

property man, *costumier*, machinist, stage hand, electrician, prompter, call-boy; director, manager; stage –, acting –, business- manager; *entrepreneur*, *impresario*, producer, press agent.

dramatic -author, – writer; play-writer, -wright; dramatist, mimographer; dramatic critic.

V. act, play, perform; stage, produce, put on the stage; personate etc. 554; mimic etc. (*imitate*) 19; enact; play –, act –, go through –, perform- a part; rehearse, spout, gag, rant; 'strut and fret one's hour upon a stage;' tread the -stage, – boards; come out;, star.

Adj. dramatic; theatric, -al; scenic, histrionic, anctorial, comic, tragic, buskined, farcical, tragi-comic, melodramatic, operatic; stagey spectacular; stagestruck.

Adv. on the -stage, – boards; before -the floats, – an audience; in the limelight, behind the footlights; behind the scenes.

600. Will.—N. will, volition, conation, velleity; will and pleasure, free-will; freedom etc. 748; discretion; choice, inclination, intent, purpose, option etc. (*choice*) 609; voluntariness; spontane-ity, -ousness; originality.

pleasure, wish, desire, mind; frame of mind etc. (*inclination*) 602; intention etc. 620; predetermination etc. 611; self-control etc. determination etc. (*resolution*) 604; will-power.

V. will, list; see –, think- -fit; determine etc. (*resolve*) 604; settle etc. (*choose*) 609; volunteer.

have a will of one's own; do what one chooses etc. (*freedom*) 748; have it all one's own way; have one's -will, – own way.

use –, exercise- one's discretion; take -upon oneself, – one's own course, – the law into one's own hands; do -of one's own accord, – upon one's own -responsibility, – authority; take the bit between one's teeth; take responsibility; originate etc. (*cause*) 153.

Adj. voluntary, volitive, volitional, wilful; free etc. 748; optional; discretion-al, -ary; volitient; dictatorial.

minded etc. (*willing*) 602; prepense etc. (*predetermined*) 611; intended etc. 620; autocratic; unbidden etc. (bid etc. 741); spontaneous; original etc. (*causal*) 153.

Adv. voluntarily etc. *adj.*; at -will, – pleasure; *à -volonté*, – *discrétion*; *al piacere*; *ad -libitum*, – *arbitrium*; as -one thinks proper, – it seems good to.

of one's own -accord, – free will; *proprio* –, *suo* –, *ex mero- motu*; out of one's own head; by choice etc. 609; purposely etc. (*intentionally*) 620; deliberately etc. 611.

Phr. *stet pro ratione voluntas*; *sic volo sic jubeo*.

601. Necessity.—N. involuntariness; instinct, blind –, natural- impulse; inborn –, innate- proclivity; the force of circumstances.

necessi-ty, -tation, necessarianism; obligation; compulsion etc. 744; subjection etc. 749; stern –, hard –, dire –, imperious –, inexorable –, iron –, adverse- -necessity, – fate; what must be.

desti-ny, -nation; fatality, fate, *kismet*, doom, foredoom, election, predestination; pre-, fore-ordination; lot, fortune; fatalism, determinism; inevitableness etc. *adj.*; spell etc. 993.

star, -s; planet, -s; astral influence; sky, Fates, Norns, *Parcae*, Sisters three, Clotho, Lachesis, Atropos; book of fate; God's will, will of Heaven; wheel of Fortune, Ides of March, Hobson's choice.

last -shift, – resort; *dernier ressort*; *pis aller* etc. (*substitute*) 147; necessaries etc. (*requirement*) 630.

necess-arian, -itarian; fatalist, determinist; automaton.

V. lie under a necessity; be -fated, – doomed, – destined etc., – in for, – under the necessity of; have no -choice, – alternative; be- obliged –, forced –, driven –, one's -fate etc. *n.*- to; be -pushed to the wall, – driven into a corner, – unable to help, – drawn irresistibly.

destine, doom, foredoom, devote; pre-destine, -ordain; cast a spell etc. 992; necessitate; compel etc. 744.

Adj. necessary; needful etc. (*requisite*) 630.

fated; destined etc. *v.*; fateful; elect; spell-bound.

compulsory etc. (*compel*) 744; uncontrollable, inevitable, unavoidable, irrestible, irrevocable, inexorable, binding; avoid-, resist-less; written in the book of fate.

involuntary, instinctive, automatic, blind, mechanical; un-conscious, -witting, -thinking; unintentional etc. (*undesigned*) 621; impulsive etc. 612.

Adv. necessarily etc. *adv.*; of -necessity, – course; *ex necessitate rei*; needs must; perforce etc. 744; *nolens volens*; will he nil he, willy nilly, *bon gré mal gré*, willing or unwilling, *coûte que coûte*, forcefully.

faute de mieux; by stress of; if need be.

Phr. it cannot be helped; there is no- help for, – helping- it; it -will, – must, – must needs- be, – be so, – have its way; the die is cast; *jacta est alea*; *che sarà sarà*; 'it is written;' one's- days are numbered, – fate is sealed; *Fata obstant*; *diis aliter visum*.

602. Willingness.—N. willingness, voluntariness etc. *adj.*; willing mind, heart.

disposition, inclination, leaning, *animus*; frame of mind, humor, mood, vein; bent etc. (*turn of mind*) 820; *penchant* etc. (*desire*) 865; aptitude etc. 698.

doc-ility, -ibleness, tractability; persuasi-bleness, -bility; pliability etc. (*softness*) 324.

geniality, cordiality; goodwill; alacrity, readiness, earnestness, forwardness, enthusiasm; zeal, eagerness etc. (*desire*) 865.

assent etc. 488; compliance etc. 762; pleasure etc. (*will*) 600.

labor of love, self-appointed task; volunteer, -ing, gratuitous service; unpaid worker, amateur.

V. be -willing etc. *adj.*; incline, lean to, mind, propend; had as lief; lend –, give –, turn- a willing ear; have -a, – half a, – a great- mind to; hold –, cling- to; desire etc. 865.

see –, think- -good, – fit, – proper; acquiescence etc. (*assent*) 488; comply with etc. 762.

swallow –, nibble at- the bait; gorge the hook; swallow hook, line and sinker; have –, make- no scruple of; make no bones of; jump –, catch- at; meet half way; volunteer, offer oneself etc. 763.

Adj. willing, minded, fain, disposed, inclined, favorable, favorably- minded, -inclined, -disposed; nothing loth; in the -vein, – mood, – humor, – mind.

ready, forward, enthusiastic, earnest, eager; bent upon etc. (*desirous*) 865; predisposed, propense.

docile; persua-dable, -sible; suasible, easily persuaded, facile, easy-going; amenable; tractable etc. (*pliant*) 324; genial, gracious, cordial, hearty; content etc. (*assenting*) 488.

voluntary, gratuitous, spontaneous; unasked etc. (ask etc. 765); unforced etc. (*free*) 748.

Adv. willing etc. *adj.*; fain, freely, as lief, heart and soul; with -pleasure, – all one's heart, – open arms; with -good, – right good- will; *de bonne volonté*, *ex animo*; *con amore*, heart in hand, nothing loth, without reluctance, of one's own accord, graciously, with a good grace, without demur.

à la bonne heure; by all -means, – manner of means; to one's heart's content; yes etc. (*assent*) 488.

Int. sure, -ly! of course!

603. Unwillingness.—N. unwillingness etc. *adj.*; indispos-ition, -edness; disinclination, aversation, aversion; nolleity, nolition; renitence; reluctance; indifference etc. 866; backwardness etc. *adj.*; slowness etc. 275; want of -alacrity, – readiness; indocility etc. (*obstinacy*) 606.

scrupul-ousness, -osity; qualms of conscience, delicacy, demur, scruple, qualm, shrinking, recoil; hesitation etc. (*irresolution*) 605; fastidiousness etc. 868.

averseness etc. (*dislike*) 867; dissent etc. 489; refusal etc. 764.

slacker, scrimshanker, *embusqué*, unwilling worker, forced labor.

V. be -unwilling etc. *adj.*; nill; dislike etc. 867; grudge, begrudge; not be able to find it in one's heart to, not have the stomach to.

demur, stick at, scruple, stickle; hang fire, run rusty, slack, shirk, scamp, give up, fight shy of, not pull fair; recoil, shrink, swerve; hesitate etc. 605; avoid etc. 623.

oppose etc. 708; dissent etc. 489; refuse etc. 764.

Adj. unwilling; not in the vein, loth, shy of, disinclined, indisposed, averse, reluctant, not content; adverse etc. (*opposed*) 708; laggard, backward, remiss, slack, slow to; renitent; indifferent etc. 866; scrupulous; squeamish etc. (*fastidious*) 868; repugnant etc. (*dislike*) 867; rest-iff, -ive; demurring etc. *v.*; unconsenting etc. (*refusing*) 764; involuntary etc. 601; grudging, irreconcilable.

Adv. unwilling etc. *adj.*; grudgingly, with a heavy heart; with -a bad, – an ill- grace; against –, sore against- -one's wishes, – one's will, – the grain; *invitâ Minervâ*; *à contre coeur*; *malgré soi*; in spite of -one's teeth, – oneself; *nolens volens* etc. (*necessity*) 601; perforce etc. 744; under protest; no etc. 536; not for the world, far be it from me; not if I can help it; if I must I must.

604. Resolution.—N. determination, will; iron –, unconquerable- will; will of one's own, decision, resolution, backbone, grit; strength of -mind, – will; resolve etc. (*intent*) 620; *intransigeance*; firmness etc. (*stability*) 150; energy, manliness, vigor; game, pluck; resoluteness etc. (*courage*) 861; zeal etc. 682; *aplomb*; desperation; devot-ion, -edness.

mastery over self; self-control, -command, -mastery, -possession, -reliance, -government, -restraint, -conquest, -denial; moral -courage, – strength, – fiber; perseverance etc. 604*a*; tenacity; obstinacy etc. 606; bull-dog; British lion.

V. have -determination etc. *n.*; know one's own mind; be -resolved etc. *adj.*; make up one's mind, will resolve, determine; decide etc. (*judgment*) 480; form –, come to- a -determination, – resolution, – resolve; conclude, fix, seal, determine once for all, bring to a crisis, drive matters to an extremity; take a decisive step etc. (*choice*) 609; take upon oneself etc. (*undertake*) 676.

devote oneself –, give oneself up- to; throw away the scabbard, kick down the ladder, nail one's colors to the mast, set one's back against the wall, set one's teeth, put one's foot down, burn one's bridges, take one's stand; stand firm etc. (*stability*) 150; steel oneself; stand no nonsense, not listen to the voice of the charmer.

buckle to; put –, lay –, set- one's shoulder to the wheel; put one's heart into; run the gantlet, make a dash at, take the bull by the horns; beard the lion in his den; rush –, plunge- *in medias res*; go in for; insist upon, make a point of; set one's heart, – mind- upon.

stick at nothing; make short work of etc. (*activity*) 682; not stick at trifles; go -all lengths, – the whole hog; persist etc. (*persevere*) 604*a*; go down with colors flying, die game; go through fire and water, ride in the whirlwind and direct the storm.

Adj. resolved etc. *v.* determined; strong-willed, -minded; resolute etc. (*brave*) 861; self-possessed, plucky, tenacious; decided, definitive, peremptory; un-hesitating, -flinching, -shrinking; firm, cast iron, indomitable, game to the backbone; inexorable, relentless, not to be -shaken, – put down; *tenax propositi*; inflexible etc. (*hard*) 323; obstinate etc. 606; steady etc. (*persevering*) 604*a*; unbending, unyielding, irrevocable; firm as a rock; grim.

earnest, serious; set –, bent –, intent- upon.

steeled –, proof- against; *in utrumque paratus.*

Adv. resolutely etc. *adj.*; in –, in good- earnest; seriously, joking apart, earnestly, heart and soul; on one's metal; manfully, like a man, with a high hand; with a strong hand etc. (*exertion*) 686.

at any -rate, – risk, – hazard, – price, – cost, – sacrifice; at all -hazards, – risks, – events; cost what it may; *coûte que coûte*; *à tort et à travers*; once for all; neck or nothing; rain or shine; with colors nailed to the mast.

Phr. *spes sibi quisque.*

604a. Perseverance. —N. perseverance; continuance etc. (*inaction*) 143; permanence etc. (*absence of change*) 141; firmness etc. (*stability*) 150.

constancy, steadiness; singleness –, tenacity- of purpose; persistence, plodding, patience; sedulity etc. (*industry*) 682; pertina-cy, -city, -ciousness; iteration etc. 104.

bottom, game, pluck, stamina, backbone, grit; indefatiga-bility, -bleness; bulldog courage.

V. persevere, persist; hold -on, – out; die in the last ditch, be in at the death; stick –, cling –, adhere- to ; stick to one's text, keep on; keep to –, maintain- one's -course, – ground; bear –, keep –, hold-up; plod; stick to work etc. (*work*) 686;

continue etc. 143; follow up; die -in harness, – at one's post.

Adj. persevering, constant; stead-y, -fast; undeviating, -wavering, -faltering, -swerving, -flinching, -sleeping, -flagging, -drooping; steady as time; uninter-, un-remitting; plodding; industrious etc. 682; strenuous etc. 686; pertinacious; persisting, -ent.

solid, sturdy, staunch, stanch, ture to oneself; unchangeable etc. 150; unconquerable etc. (*strong*) 159; indomitable, game to the last, indefatigable, untiring, unwearied, never tiring.

Adv. through -evil report and good report, – thick and thin, – fire and water; *per fas et nefas*; without fail, sink or swim, at any price, *vogue la galère*; in sickness and in health.

Phr. never say die; *vestigia nulla retrorsum*.

605. Irresolution.—N. irresolution, infirmity of purpose, indecision; in-, un-determination, loss of will power; unsettlement; uncertainty etc. 475; demur, suspense; hesi-tating etc. *v.*, -tation, -tancy; vacillation; ambivalence; changeableness etc. 149; fluctuation; alternation etc. (*oscillation*) 314; caprice etc. 608; lukewarmness.

fickleness, levity, *légèreté*; pliancy etc. (*softness*) 324; weakness; timidity etc. 860; cowardice etc. 862; half measures.

waverer, ass between two bundles of hay; shuttlecock, butterfly; timeserver, opportunist, turn coat.

V. be -irresolute etc. *adj.*; hang –, keep- in suspense; heave *'ad referendum*;' think twice about, pause; dawdle etc. (*inactivity*) 683; remain neuter; dilly dally. hesitate, boggle, hover, wobble, shilly-shally, hum and haw, demur, not know one's own mind; debate, balance; dally –, coquet- with; will and will not, *chasser-balancer*; go half-way, compromise, make a compormise; be thrown off one's balance, stagger like a drunken man; be afraid etc. 860; let 'I dare not' wait upon 'I would;' falter, waver.

vacillate etc. 149; change etc. 140; retract etc. 607; fluctuate; alternate etc. (*oscillate*) 314; keep off and on, play fast and loose; blow hot and cold etc. (*caprice*) 608.

shuffle, palter, blink; trim.

Adj. irresolute, infirm of purpose, double-minded, half-hearted; un-decided, -resolved, -determined; drifting; shilly-shally; fidgety, tremulous; wobbly; hesitating etc. *v.*; off one's balance; at a loss etc. (*uncertain*) 475.

vacillating etc. *v.*; unsteady etc. (*changeable*) 149; unsteadfast, fickle, unreliable, irresponsible, unstable, without ballast; capricious etc. 608; volatile, frothy; light, -some, -minded; giddy; fast and loose.

weak, feeble-minded, frail; timid etc. 860; cowardly etc. 862; facile; pliant etc. (*soft*) 324; unable to say 'no,' easy-going.

revocable, reversible.

Adv. irresolutely etc. *adj.*; irresolvedly; in faltering accents; off and on; from pillar to post; see-saw etc. 314.

Int. 'how happy could I be with either!'

606. Obstinacy.—N. obstinateness etc. *adj.*; obstinacy, tenacity; perseverance etc. 604*a*; immovability; old school; inflexibility etc. (*hardness*) 323; obdur-acy, -ation; dogged resolution; resolution etc. 604; ruling passion; blind side.

self-will, contumacy, perversity; pervica-cy, -city; indocility.

bigotry, intolerance, dogmatism; opinia-try, -tiveness; fixed idea etc.; intractibility, incorrigibility; (*prejudgment*) 481; fanaticism, zealotry, infatuation, monomania, opinionativeness.

mule; opin-ionist, -ionatist, -iator, -ator; stickler, dogmatist, die-hard, bitter-ender; bigot; zealot, enthusiast, fanatic.

V. be -obstinate etc. *adj.*; stickle, take no denial, fly in the face of facts; opinionate, be wedded to an opinion, hug a belief; have one's own way etc. (*will*) 600; persist etc. (*persevere*) 604*a*; have –, insist on having- the last word.

die -hard, – fighting, fight -against destiny, – to the last ditch; not yield an inch, stand out.

Adj. obstinate, tenacious, stubborn, obdurate, case-hardened; inflexible etc. (*hard*) 323; immovable, not to be moved; inert etc. 172; unchangeable etc. 150; inexorable etc. (*determined*) 604; mulish, obstinate as a mule, pig-headed.

dogged; sullen, sulky; un-moved, -influenced, -affected.

wilful, self-willed, perverse; res-ty, -tive, -tiff; pervicacious, wayward, refractory, unruly; head-y, -strong; *entete*; contumacious; cross-grained.

arbitrary, dogmatic, opinionated, positive, bigoted; prejudiced etc. 481; prepossessed, infatuated; stiff-backed, -necked, -hearted; hard-mouthed, hidebound; unyielding; im-pervious, -practicable, -persuasible; unpersuadable; in-, untractable; incorrigible, deaf to advice, impervious to reason; crotchety etc. 608.

Adv. obstinately etc. *adj.*

Phr. *non possumus*; no surrender.

607. Tergiversation.—N. change of -mind, – intention, – purpose; afterthought.

tergiversation, recantation; palinode, -ody; renunciation; abjur-ation, -ement; defection etc. (*relinquishment*) 624; going over etc. *v.*; apostasy; retract-ion, -ation; withdrawal, disavowal etc. (*negation*) 536; revo-cation, -kement; reversal; repentance etc. 950; *redintegratio amoris*.

coquetry, flirtation; vacillation etc. 605; backsliding, recidivation.

turn-coat, -tippet; rat, apostate, renegade, mugwump; con-, per-vert; proselyte, deserter; backslider, recidivist; black leg.

time-server, -pleaser; timist, Vicar of Bray, trimmer, ambidexter; weathercock etc. (*changeable*) 149; Janus.

V. change one's -mind, – intention, – purpose, – note; abjure, renounce; withdraw from etc. (*relinquish*) 624; wheel –, turn –, veer- round; turn a *pirouette*; go over –, pass –, change –, skip- from one side to another; go to the right about; box the compass, shift one's ground, go upon another tack; back down, crawl, crawfish.

apostatize, change sides, go over, rat; recant, retract; revoke; rescind etc. (*abrogate*) 756; recall, forswear, abjure, unsay; come -over, – round- to an opinion.

- draw in one's horns, eat one's words; eat –,

swallow- the leek; swerve, flinch, back out of, retrace one's steps, think better of it; come back –, return- to one's first love; turn over a new leaf etc. (*repent*) 950.

trim, shuffle, play fast and loose, blow hot and cold, coquet, flirt, hold with the hare but run with the hounds; straddle; *nager entre deux eaux*; wait to see how the -cat jumps, – wind blows.

Adj. changeful etc. 149; irresolute etc. 605; ductile, slippery as an eel, trimming, ambidextrous, timeserving; coquetting etc. *v.*

revocatory, reactionary.

Phr. 'a change came o'er the spirit of my dream.'

608. Caprice.—N. caprice, fancy, humor; whim, -sey, -wham; crotchet, *capriccio*, quirk, freak, maggot, fad, vagary, prank, fit, flim-flam, *escapade*, *boutade*, wild-goose chase; capriciousness etc. *adj.*; kink.

V. be -capricious etc. *adj.*; have a maggot in the brain; take it into one's head, strain at a gnat and swallow a camel; blow hot and cold; play -fast and loose, – fantastic tricks.

Adj. capricious; erratic, eccentric, fitful, hysterical; full of -whims etc. *n.*; maggoty; inconsistent, fanciful, fantastic, whimsical, crotchety, particular, humorsome, freakish, skittish, wanton, wayward; contrary; captious; arbitrary; unrestrained, undisciplined; not amenable to reason; uncomfortable etc. 83; penny wise and pound foolish; fickle etc. (*irresolute*) 605; frivolous, sleeveless, giddy, volatile.

Adv. by fits and starts, without rhyme or reason, at one's own sweet will.

Phr. *nil fuit unquam six impar sibi*; the deuce is in him.

609. Choice.—N. choice, option; discretion etc. (*volition*) 600; preoption; alternative; dilemma; *ambarras de choix*; adoption, co-optation; novation; decision etc. (*judgment*) 480.

election, poll, ballot, vote, voice, suffrage, plumper, cumulative vote; *plebiscitum, plébiscite*, *vox populi*; *referendum*, electioneering; voting etc. *v.*; franchise; ballot box; slate, ticket.

selection, excerption, gleaning, eclecticism; *excerpta*, gleanings, cuttings, scissors and paste; pick etc. (*best*) 650.

preference, prelation; predilection etc. (*desire*) 865.

V. offer for one's choice, set before; hold out –, present –, offer- the alternative; put to the vote.

use –, exercise –, one's- -discretion, – option; adopt, take up, embrace, espouse; choose, elect, co-opt; take –, make- one's choice; make choice of, fix upon.

vote, poll, hold up one's hand; divide.

settle; decide etc. (*adjudge*) 480; list etc. (*will*) 600; make up one's mind etc. (*resolve*) 604.

select; pick, – and choose; pick –, single- out, excerpt; cull, glean, winnow; sift –, separate –, winnow- the chaff from the wheat; pick up, pitch upon; pick one's way; indulge one's fancy.

set apart, reserve, mark out for; mark etc. 550.

prefer; have -rather, – as lief; fancy etc. (*desire*) 865; be persuaded etc. 615.

take a -decided, – decisive- step; commit oneself to a course; pass –, cross- the Rubicon; cast in one's lot with; take for better or for worse.

Adj. optional; co-optative; discretional etc. (*voluntary*) 600; on approval.

ecletic; choosing etc. *v.*; preferential; chosen etc. *v.*; choice etc. (*good*) 648.

Adv. optionally etc. *adj.*; at pleasure etc. (*will*) 600; either, – the one or the other; or; at the option of; whether or not; once for all; for one's money.

by -choice, – preference; in preference; rather, before.

609a. Absence of Choice.—N. no –, Hobson's- choice; first come, first served; necessity etc. 601; not a pin to choose etc. (*equality*) 27; any, the first that comes.

neutrality, indifference; indecision etc. (*irresolution*) 605.

V. be -neutral etc. *adj.*; have no choice; waive, not vote; abstain –, refrain- from voting; leave undecided; make a virtue of necessity.

Adj. neu-tral, -ter; indifferent; undecided etc. (*irresolute*) 605.

Adv. either etc. (*choice*) 609.

610. Rejection.—N. rejection, repudiation, exclusion; declination; refusal etc. 764.

V. reject; set –, lay- aside; give up; decline etc. (*refuse*) 764; exclude, except, eliminate; pluck, spin; cast.

repudiate, scout, set at naught; fling –, cast –, thrown –, toss- -to the winds, – to the dogs, – overboard, – away; send to the right about; disclaim etc. (*deny*) 536; discard etc. (*eject*) 297, (*have done with*) 678.

Adj. rejected etc. *v.*; reject-aneous, -itious; not -chosen etc. 609, – to be thought of; out of the question.

Adv. neither, – the one nor the other; no etc. 536.

Phr. *non haec in foedera.*

611. Predetermination.—N. premeditation, -deliberation, -determination, -destination; foreordination; foregone conclusion; *parti pris*; resolve, propendency; intention etc. 620; project etc. 626.

V. pre-determine, -destine, -meditate, -resolve, -concert; foreordain; resolve beforehand.

Adj. pre-pense, -meditated etc. *v.*, -designed; advised, studied, designed, calculated; aforethought; intended etc. 620; foregone.

well-laid, -devised, -weighed; maturely considered; cut and dried; cunning.

Adv. advisedly etc. *adj.*; with premeditation, deliberately, all things considered, with eyes open, in cold blood; intentionally etc. 620.

612. Impulse.—N. impulse, sudden thought; *impromptu*, improvisation; inspiration, hunch, flash, spurt.

improvisatore, *improvisatrice*, improviser, extemporizer; creature of impulse.

V. flash on the mind.

say what comes uppermost; improvise, extemporize; rise to the occasion; spurt.

Adj. extemporaneous, impulsive, indeliberate; improvis-ed, -ate, -atory; un-, unpre-meditated; *improvisé*; unprompted, -guided; natural, unguarded; spontaneous etc. (*voluntary*) 600; instinctive etc. 601.

Adv. extem-pore, -poraneously; offhand, *impromptu*, *à l'improviste*; improviso; on the spur of the -moment, – occasion.

613. Habit.—N. habit, -ude; assuetude, -faction; wont; run, way.

common –, general –, natural –, ordinary –, habitual- -course, – run, – state- of things; matter of course; beaten -path, – track, – ground.

prescription, custom, use, usage, immemorial usage, practice; tradition; prevalence, observance; conventionalism, -ity; mode, fashion, vogue; *etiquette* etc. (*gentility*) 852; order of the day, cry; conformity etc. 82.

habitué, addict.

one's old way, old school, consuetude, *veteris vestigia flammae*; *laudator temporis acti.*

rule, standing order, precedent, routine; red-tape, -tapism; pipe-clay; rut, groove.

cacoëthes; bad –, confirmed –, inveterate –, intrinsic etc. 5- habit; addiction, trick.

training etc. (*education*) 537; seasoning, hardening, inurement; radication; second nature, acclimatization; knack etc. (*skill*) 698.

V. be -wont etc. *adj.*

fall into a custom etc. (*conform to*) 82; tread –, follow- the beaten -track, – path; *stare super antiquas vias*; move in a rut, run on in a groove, go round like a horse in a mill, go on in the old jobtrot way.

habituate, inure, harden, season, caseharden; accustom, familiarize; naturalize, acclimatize; keep one's hand in; train etc. (*educate*) 537.

get into the -way, – knack- of; learn etc. 539; cling –, adhere- to; repeat etc. 104; acquire –, contract –, fall into- a -habit, – trick; addict oneself –, take- to; accustom oneself to.

be -habitual etc. *adj.*; prevail; come into use, become a habit, take root; gain –, grow- upon one.

Adj. habitual; ac-, customary; prescriptive; accustomed etc. *v.*; traditional; of -daily, – every-day- occurrence; wonted, usual, general, ordinary, common, frequent, every-day, household, jog-trot; well-trodden, -known; familiar, vernacular, trite, commonplace, banal, bromidic, conventional, regular, set, stock, officinal, established, stereotyped; pre-vailing, -valent; current, received, acknowledged, recognized, accredited; of course, admitted, understood.

conformable etc. 82; according to -use, – custom, – routine; in -vogue, – fashion; fashionable etc. (*genteel*) 852.

wont; used – given – addicted –, attuned –, habituated etc. *v.*- to; in the habit of; *habitué*; at home in etc. (*skilful*) 698; seasoned; permeated –, imbued- with; devoted –, wedded- to; never free from.

hackneyed, fixed, rooted, deep-rooted, ingrafted, permanent, inveterate, besetting; naturalized; ingrained etc. (*intrinsic*) 5.

Adv. habitually etc. *adj.*; always etc. (*uniformly*) 16.

as -usual, – is one's wont, – things go, – the world goes, – the sparks fly upwards; *more -suo*, – *solito.*

as a rule, for the most part; generally etc. *adj.*; most often, – frequently.

Phr. *cela s'entend.*

614. Desuetude.—N. desuetude, disusage; disuse etc. 678; want of -habit, – practice; inusitation; newness to; new brooms.

infraction of usage etc. (*unconformity*) 83; non-prevalence; 'a custom more honored in the breach than the observance.'

V. be -unaccustomed etc. *adj.*; leave off –, cast off –, break off –, wean oneself of –, violate –, break through –, infringe- -a habit, – a custom, – a usage; break one's fetters; disuse etc. 678; wear off.

Adj. un-accustomed, -used, -wonted, -seasoned, -inured, -habituated, -trained; new; green etc. (*unskilled*) 699; fresh, original, unhackneyed.

unusual etc. (*unconformable*) 83; unconventional, non-observant; disused etc. 678.

Adv. just for once.

615. Motive.—N. motive, springs of action.

reason, ground, call, principle; mainspring, *primum mobile*, key-stone; the why and the wherefore; *pro* and *con*, reason why; secret –, ulterior- motive, *arrière-pensée*; intention etc. 620.

inducement, consideration; attraction etc. 288; loadstone; magnet, -ism, -ic force; allect-ation, -ive; temptation, enticement, *agacerie*, allurement, witchery; bewitch-ment, -ery; charm; spell etc. 993; fascination, blandishment, cajolery; seduc-tion, -ement; honeyed words, voice of the tempter, son of the Sirens; forbidden fruit, golden apple.

persuasi-bility, -bleness; attractability; impress-, suscept-ibility; softness; persuas-, attract-iveness; tantalization.

influence, prompting, dictate, instance; impuls-e, -ion; incit-ement, -ation; press, instigation; provocation etc. (*excitation of feeling*) 824; inspiration; per-, suasion; encouragement, advocacy; exhortation, advice etc. 695; solicitation etc. (*request*) 765; lobbying.

incentive, stimulus, spur, fillip, whip, goad, rowel, provocative, whet, dram.

bribe, lure; decoy, – duck; bait, trail of a red herring; bribery and corruption; sop, – for Cerberus.

prompter, tempter; seduc-er, -tor; suggester, coaxer, wheedler; instigator, firebrand, incendiary; Siren, Circe; *agent provocateur*; lobbyist.

V. induce, move; draw, – on; bring in its train, give an -impulse etc. *n.*- to; inspire; put up to, prompt, call up; attract, beckon.

stimulate etc. (*excite*) 824; spirit up, inspirit; a-, rouse; ecphorize; animate, incite, provoke, instigate, set on, actuate; act –, work –, operate-upon; encourage; pat –, clap- on the -back, – shoulder.

influence, weigh with, bias, sway, incline, dispose, predispose, turn the scale, inoculate; lead, – by the nose; have –, exercise- influence- -with, – over, – upon; go –, come- round one; turn the head, magnetize.

persuade; prevail -with, – upon; overcome, carry; bring -round, – to one's senses; draw –, win –, gain –, come –, talk- over; procure, enlist, engage; invite, court.

tempt, seduce, overpersuade, entice, allure, captivate, fascinate, intrigue, bewitch, carry away, charm, conciliate, wheedle, coax, lure, suggest; inveigle; tantalize; cajole etc. (*deceive*) 545.

tamper with, bribe, suborn, grease the palm, bait with a silver hook, gild the pill, make things pleasant, put a sop into the pan, throw a sop to, bait the hook.

enforce, force; impel etc. (*push*) 276; propel etc. 284; whip, lash, goad, spur, prick, urge; egg –, hound –, hurry- on; drag etc. 285; exhort; advise etc. 695; call upon etc.; press etc. (*request*) 765; advocate.

set -an example, – the fashion; keep in countenance; back up.

be -persuaded etc.; yield to temptation, come round; concede etc. (*consent*) 762; obey a call; follow -advice, – the bent, – the dictates of; act on principle.

Adj. impulsive, motive; suas-, persuas-, hortative, -ory; protreptical; inviting, tempting etc. *v.*; seductive, attractive, irresistible; fascinating etc. (*pleasing*) 829; provocative etc. (*exciting*) 824.

induced etc. *v.*; disposed; persuadable etc. (*docile*) 602; spellbound; instinct –, smitten- with; inspired etc. *v.*- by.

Adv. because, therefore etc. (*cause*) 155; from - this, – that- motive; for -this, – that- reason; for; by reason –, for the sake –, on the score –, on account- of; out of, from, as, forasmuch as.

for all the world; on principle.

615a. Absence of Motive.—N. absence of motive; caprice etc. 608; chance etc. (*absence of design*) 621.

V. have no motive; scruple etc. (*be unwilling*) 603.

Adj. without rhyme or reason; aimless etc. (*chance*) 621.

Adv. capriciously; out of mere caprice.

616. Dissuasion.—N. dissuasion, dehortation, expostulation, remonstrance; deprecation etc. 766.

discouragement, damper, wet blanket; warning.

cohibition etc. (*restraint*) 751; curb etc. (*means of restraint*) 752; check etc. (*hindrance*) 706.

reluctance etc. (*unwillingness*) 603; contraindication.

V. dissuade, dehort, cry out against, remonstrate, expostulate, warn, contraindicate.

disincline, indispose, shake, stagger; dispirit; discourage, -hearten, -enchant; deter; hold –, keep- back etc. (*restrain*) 751; render -averse etc. 603; repel; turn aside etc. (*deviation*) 279; wean from; act as a drag etc. (*hinder*) 706; throw cold water on, damp, cool, chill, blunt, calm, quiet, quench; deprecate etc. 766.

Adj. dissuading etc. *v.*; dissuasive; dehortatory, expostulatory; monit-ive, -ory.

dissuaded etc. *v.*; uninduced etc. (induce etc. 615); unpersuadable etc. (*obstinate*) 606; averse etc. (*unwilling*) 603; repugnant etc. (*dislike*) 867.

617. Plea. [Ostensible motive, ground, or reason assigned.]**—N.** plea, pretext; allegation, advocation; ostensible -motive, – ground, – reason; excuse etc. (*vindication*) 937; color; gloss, guise.

loop-, starting-hole; how to creep out of, salvo, come off.

handle, peg to hang on room, *locus standi*; stalking horse, *cheval de bataille*, cue.

pretence etc. (*untruth*) 546; put off, subterfuge, dust thrown in the eyes; blind; moonshine; mere –, shallow- pretext; lame -excuse, – apology, tub to a whale; flase plea, sour grapes; makeshift, shift, white lie; special pleading etc. (*sophistry*) 477; soft sawder etc. (*flattery*) 933.

V. plead, allege; shelter oneself under the plea of; excuse etc. (*vindicate*) 937; gloss over; lend a color to; furnish a -handle etc. *n.*; make a -pretext, – handle- of; use as a plea etc. *n.*; take one's stand upon, make capital out of; pretend etc. (*lie*) 544.

Adj. ostensible etc. (*manifest*) 525; excusing; alleged, apologetic; pretended etc. 545.

Adv. ostensibly; under -color, – the plea, – the pretence- of.

618. Good.—N. good, benefit, advantage; improvement etc. 658; interest, service, behoof, behalf; weal; main chance, *summum bonum*, common weal; 'consummation devoutly to be wished;' gain, boot; profit, harvest.

boon etc. (*gift*) 784; good turn; blessing, benison; world of good; piece of good -luck, – fortune; nuts, prize, windfall, godsend, waif, treasure trove.

good fortune etc. (*prosperity*) 734; happiness etc. 827.

[Source of good] goodness etc. 648; utility etc. 644; remedy etc. 662; pleasure-giving etc. 829.

Adj. commendable etc. 931; useful etc. 644; good etc., beneficial etc. 648.

V. benefit, profit, advantage, serve, help, avail; do good to, gain, prosper, flourish.

Adv. well, aright, satisfactorily, favorably, not amiss; all for the best; to one's -advantage etc. *n.*; in one's -favor, – interest etc. *n.*

Phr. so far so good.

619. Evil.—N. evil, ill, harm, hurt, mischief, nuisance; machinations of the devil, Pandora's box, ills that flesh is heir to.

blow, buffet, stroke, scratch, bruise, wound, gash, mutilation; mortal -blow, – wound; *im-*

medicabile vulnus; damage, loss etc. (*deterioration*) 659.

disadvantage, prejudice, drawback.

disaster, accident, casualty; mishap etc. (*misfortune*) 735; bad job, devil to pay; calamity, bale, woe, catastrophe, tragedy; ruin etc. (*destruction*) 162; adversity etc. 735.

mental suffering etc. 828. [Evil spirit] demon etc. 980. [Cause of evil] bane etc. 663. [Production of evil] badness etc. 649; painfulness etc. 830; evil doer etc. 913.

outrage, wrong, injury, foul play; bad –, ill-turn; disservice; spoliation etc. 791; grievance, crying evil.

V. be in trouble etc. (*adversity*) 735; harm, injure, hurt, do disservice to.

Adj. disastrous, bad etc. 649; awry, out of joint; disadvantageous, injurious, harmful.

Adv. amiss, wrong, ill, to one's cost.

620. Intention.—N. intent, -ion, -ionality; purpose; *quo animo*; project etc. 626; undertaking etc. 676; predetermination etc. 611; design, ambition.

contemplation, mind, *animus*, view, purview, proposal; study; look out.

final cause; *raison d'être*; *cui bono*; object, aim, end; 'the be all and the end all;' drift etc. (*meaning*) 516; tendency etc. 176; destination, mark, point, butt, goal, target, bull's-eye, quintain; prey, quarry, game.

decision, determination, resolve; set –, settled-purpose; *ultimatum*; resolution etc. 604; wish etc. 865; *arrière-pensée*; motive etc. 615.

[Study of final causes] teleology.

V. intend, purpose, design, mean; have to; propose to oneself; harbor a design; have in -view, – contemplation, – one's eye, – *petto*; have an eye to.

bid –, labor- for; be –, aspire –, endeavour-after; be –, aim –, drive –, point –, level- at; take aim; set before oneself; study to.

take upon oneself etc. (*undertake*) 676; take into one's head; meditate, contemplate; think –, dream –, talk- of; premeditate etc. 611; compass, calculate; dest-ine, -inate, propose.

project etc. (*plan*) 626; have a mind to etc. (*be willing*) 602; desire etc. 865; pursue etc. 622.

Adj. intended etc. *v.*; intentional, advised, express, determinate; prepense etc. 611; bound for; intending etc. *v.*; minded, disposed, inclined; bent upon etc. (*earnest*) 604; at stake, on the -anvil, – *tapis*; in -view; – prospect, – the breast of; *in petto*; teleological.

Adv. intentionally etc. *adj.*; advisedly, wittingly, knowingly, designedly, purposely, on purpose, by design, studiously, pointedly; with -intent etc. *n.*; deliberately etc. (*with premeditation*) 611; with one's eyes open, in cold blood.

for; with -a view, – an eye- to; in order -to, – that; to the end –, with the intent- that; for the purpose –, with the view –, in contemplation –, on account- of.

in pursuance of, pursuant to; *quo animo*; to all intents and purposes.

621. Chance.†[Absence of purpose in the succession of events.]—**N.** chance etc. 156; lot, fate etc. (*necessity*) 601; luck; good luck etc. (*good*) 618; bad luck etc. 735; wheel of fortune; mascot; swastika.

speculation, venture, stake, flutter, flier, gamble, game of chance; mere –, random- shot; blind bargain, leap in the dark; pig in a poke etc. (*uncertainty*) 475; fluke, pot-luck.

drawing lots; sorti-legy, -tion; *sortes*, – *Virgilianae*; *rouge et noir*, hazard, *roulette*, pitch and toss, chuck-farthing, cup-tossing, heads or tails, cross and pile, wager; bet, -ting; risk, stake, plunge; gambling; the turf.

stock exchange, bourse, board of trade, curb exchange.

gaming-, gambling-, betting-house; hell; betting ring, totalizator; dice, – box; dicer; gam-bler, -ester, plunger, stock operator, manipulator, punter; man of the turf; adventurer, speculator; bookmaker, layer, backer.

V. chance etc. (*hap*) 156; stand a chance etc. (*be possible*) 470.

toss up; cast –, draw- lots; leave –, trust- -to chance, – to the chapter of accidents; tempt fortune; chance it, take one's chance; run –, incur –, encounter- the -risk, – chance; stand the hazard of the die.

speculate, try one's luck, set on a cast, raffle, put into a lottery, buy a pig in a poke, shuffle the cards.

risk, venture, hazard, stake; lay, – a wager; make a bet, wager, bet, gamble, game, play for; play at chuck-farthing.

Adj. fortuitous etc. 156; unintentional, -ded; accidental; not meant; un-designed, -purposed; unpremeditated etc. 612; never thought of.

indiscriminate, promiscuous; undirected, random; aim-, drift-, design-, purpose-, cause-less; without purpose.

possible etc. 470.

Adv. casually etc. 156; unintentionally etc. *adj.*; unwittingly.

en passant, by the way, incidentally; as it may happen; at -random, – a venture, – haphazard; as luck would have it, by -chance, – good fortune; un-, -luckily.

† See note on 156.

622. Pursuit. [Purpose in action.]—**N.** pursuit; pursuing etc. *v.*; prosecution; pursuance; enterprise etc. (*undertaking*) 676; business etc. 625; adventure etc. (*essay*) 675; quest etc. (*search*) 461; scramble, hue and cry, game; hobby.

chase, hunt, *battue*, race, steeplechase, hunting, coursing; ven-ation, -ery; fox-chase; sport, -ing; shooting, angling, fishing, hawking.

pursuer; hunt-er, -sman; sportsman, Nimrod, the field; hound etc. 366.

V. pursue, prosecute, follow; run –, make –, be –, hunt – prowl- after; shadow; carry on etc. (*do*) 680; engage in etc. (*undertake*) 676; set about etc. (*begin*) 66; endeavor etc. 675; court etc. (*request*) 765; seek etc. (*search*) 461; aim at etc. (*intention*) 620; follow the trail etc. (*trace*) 461; fish for etc. (*experiment*) 463; press on etc. (*haste*) 684; run a race etc. (*velocity*) 274.

chase, give chase, course, dog, hunt, hound, stalk; tread –, follow- on the heels of etc. (*sequence*) 281.

rush upon; rush headlong etc. (*violence*) 173;

ride –, run- full tilt at; make a leap –, jump –, snatch- at; run down; start game.

tread a path; take –, hold- a course; shape –, direct –, bend- one's -steps, – course; play a game; fight –, elbow- one's way; follow up; take -to, – up; go in for; ride one's hobby.

Adj. pursuing etc. *v.*; in quest of etc. (*inquiry*) 461; in -pursuit, – full cry, – hot pursuit; on the scent.

Adv. in pursuance of etc. (*intention*) 620; after.

Int. tally-ho! yoicks! so-ho!

623. Avoidance. [Absence of pursuit.]—**N.** abst-ention, -inence; forbearance; refraining etc. *v.*; inaction etc. 681; neutrality.

avoidance, evasion, elusion; seclusion etc. 893.

avolation, flight; escape etc. 671; retreat etc. 287; recoil etc. 277; departure etc. 293; rejection etc. 610.

shirker etc. *v.*; slacker; truant; fugitive, refugee; runa-way, -gate; renegade; deserter.

V. abstain, refrain, spare, not attempt; not do etc. 681; maintain the even tenor of one's way.

eschew, keep from, let alone, have nothing to do with; keep –, stand –, hold- -aloof, – off; take no part in, have no hand in.

avoid, shun; steer –, keep- clear of; fight shy of; keep -one's, – at a respectful- distance; keep –, get- out of the way; evade, elude, turn away from; set one's face against etc. (*oppose*) 708; deny oneself.

shrink; hang –, hold –, draw- back; recoil etc. 277; retire etc. (*recede*) 287; flinch, blink, blench, shy, shirk, dodge, parry, make way for, give place to.

beat a retreat; turn -tail, – one's back; take to one's heels; run, -away, – for one's life; cut and run; be off, – like a shot; fly, flee; fly –, flee –, run away- from; take –, take to- flight; desert, elope; make –, scamper –, sneak –, shuffle –, sheer- off; break –, burst –, tear oneself –, slip –, slink –, steal- -away, – away from; slip cable, part company, turn on one's heel; sneak out of, play truant, give one the go by, give leg bail, take French leave, slope, decamp, flit, bolt, abscond, levant, skedaddle, absquatulate, cut one's stick, walk one's chalks, show a light pair of heels, make oneself scarce; escape etc. 671; go away etc. (*depart*) 293; abandon etc. 624; reject etc. 610.

lead one a -dance, – a merry chase, – pretty dance; throw off the scent, play at hide and seek.

Adj. unsought, unattempted; avoiding etc. *v.*; neutral; shy of etc. (*unwilling*) 603; elusive, evasive, distant; fugitive, runaway; shy, wild.

Adj. lest, in order to avoid.

Int. forebear! keep –, hands- off! *sauve qui peut!* devil take the hindmost.

624. Relinquishment.—N. relinquish-, abandon-ment; desertion, defection, secession, withdrawal; cave of Adullam; *nolle prosequi.*

discontinuance etc. (*cessation*) 142; renunciation etc. (*recantation*) 607; abrogation etc. 756; resignation etc. (*retirement*) 757; desuetude etc. 614; cession etc. (*of property*) 782.

V. relinquish, give up, abandon, desert, forsake, leave in the lurch; depart –, secede –, withdraw-from; back – out of, – down from, leave, go back on one's word, quit, take leave of, bid a long farewell; vacate etc. (*resign*) 757.

renounce etc. (*abjure*) 607; forego, have done with, drop; write off; disuse etc. 678; discard etc. 782; wash one's hands of; drop all idea of; *nolle-pros.*; lose interest in.

break –, leave- off; desist; stop etc. (*cease*) 142; hold –, stay- one's hand; quit one's hold; give over, shut up shop.

throw up the -game, – cards; give up the -point, – argument; pass to the order of the day, move the previous question, table the motion.

Adj. unpursued; relinquished etc. *v.*; relinquishing etc. *v.*

Int. avast etc.! (*stop*) 142.

625. Business.—N. business, occupation, employment; pursuit etc. 622; what one is doing-, – about; affair, concern, matter, case, undertaking.

matter in hand, irons in the fire; thing to do, *agendum*, task, work, job, chore, errand, transaction, commission, mission, charge, care; duty etc. 926.

part, *rôle*, cue; province, function, look-out, department, capacity, sphere, orb, field, line; walk, – of life; beat, round, routine; race, career.

office, place, post, incumbency, living situation, appointment, billet, berth, employ; service etc. (*servitude*) 749; engagement; undertaking etc. 676.

vocation, calling, profession, *métier*, cloth, faculty; industry, art; industrial arts; craft, mystery, handicraft; trade etc. (*commerce*) 794.

exercise; work etc. (*action*) 680; avocation; press of business etc. (*activity*) 682.

V. pass –, employ –, spend- one's time in; employ oneself -in, – upon; occupy –, concern-oneself with; make it one's -business etc. *n.*; undertake etc. 676; enter a profession; betake oneself to, turn one's hand to; have to do with etc. (*do*) 680.

drive a trade; carry on –, do –, transact- -business, – a trade etc. *n.*; keep a shop; ply one's task, – trade; labor in one's vocation; pursue the even tenor of one's way; attend to -business, – one's work.

officiate, serve, act; act –, play- one's part; do duty; serve –, discharge –, perform- the -office, – duties, – functions- of; hold –, fill- -an office, – a place, – a situation; hold a portfolio.

be -about, – doing, – engaged in, – employed in, – occupied with, – at work on; have one's hands in, have in hand; have on one's -hands, – shoulders; bear the burden; have one's hands full etc. (*activity*) 682.

be -in the hands of, – on the stocks, – on the anvil; pass through one's hands.

Adj. business-like; work-a-day; professional; official, functional; busy etc. (*actively employed*) 682; on –, in- -hand, – one's hands; afoot; on -foot, – the anvil; going on; acting.

Adv. in the course of business, all in a day's work; professionally etc. *adj.*

626. Plan.—N. plan, scheme, design, project; propos-al, -ition; suggestion; resolution, motion;

precaution etc. (*provision*) 673; deep-laid etc. (*premeditated*) 611- plan etc.; racket.

system etc. (*order*) 58; organization etc. (*arrangement*) 60; germ etc. (*cause*) 153; Five Year Plan.

sketch, skeleton, outline, draught, draft, *ébauche*, *brouillon*; rough-cast, – draft, – draught, – copy; proof, revise.

forecast, *programme*, prospectus, scenario; *carte du pays*; card; bill, protocol; order of the day, list of agenda, *memorandum*; bill of fare etc. (*food*) 298; base of operations; platform, plank.

rôle; policy etc. (*line of conduct*) 692.

contrivance, invention, expedient, receipt, nostrum, artifice, device, gadget; stratagem etc. (*cunning*) 702; trick etc. (*deception*) 545; alternative, loophole, shift etc. (*substitute*) 147; last shift etc. (*necessity*) 601.

measure, step; stroke, – of policy; master stroke; trump-, court-card; *chaval de bataille*, great gun; *coup*, – *d'état*; clever –, bold –, good- -move, – hit, – stroke; bright -thought, – idea, great idea.

intrigue, cabal, plot, frame-up, conspiracy, complot, machination; under-, counter-plot.

schem-ist, -atist; stragetist, machinator, schemer; projector, author, builder, artist, promoter, designer etc. *v.*; conspirator; *intrigant* etc. (*cunning*) 702.

V. plan, scheme, design, frame, contrive, project, forecast, sketch; conceive, devise, invent etc. (*imagine*) 515; set one's wits to work etc. 515; spring a project; fall –, hit- upon; strike –, chalk –, cut –, lay –, map-out; lay down a plan; shape –, mark- out a course; predetermine etc. 611; concert, preconcert, preestablish; prepare etc. 673; hatch, – a plot; concoct; take -steps, – measures.

cast, recast, systematize, organize; arrange etc. 60; digest, mature.

plot; counter-plot, -mine; dig a mine; lay a train; intrigue etc. (*cunning*) 702.

Adj. planned etc. *v.*; strategic, -al; planning etc. *v.*; in course of preparation etc. 673; under consideration; on the -*tapis*, – carpet, – table.

627. Method. [Path.]—**N.** method, way, manner, wise, gait, form, mole, fashion, tone, guise; *modus operandi*; procedure etc. (*line of conduct*) 692.

path, road, route, course; line of -way, – road; trajectory, orbit, track, beat, tack.

steps; stair, -case; flight of stairs, ladder, stile.

bridge, viaduct, gauntry, pontoon, stepping stone, plank, gangway, catwalk, drawbridge; pass, ford, ferry, tunnel, subway, elevated; pipe etc. 260.

door; gateway etc. (*opening*) 260; channel, passage, avenue, means of access, approach, perron, adit, entrance; artery, lane, alley, aisle, lobby, corridor, cloister; back- door, -stairs; secret passage; covert-way.

road-, path-, stair-way; thoroughfare; highway, pike, turnpike, trail, parkway, *boulevard*; turnpike –, royal –, coach- road; broad –, King's –, Queen's- highway; beaten -track, – path; horse –, bridle- road, – track, – path; pathway; walk, *trottoir*, foot-path, pavement, flags, side-walk; by –, cross- -road, – path, – way; cut; short -cut etc. (*mid-course*) 628; *carrefour*; private –, occupation- road; highways and byways; rail-, tram-road, -way; funicular, ropeway, causeway; defile, cutting; canal etc. (*conduit*) 350; street etc. (*abode*) 189.

Adv. how; in what -way, – manner; by what mode; so, in this way, after this fashion, on these lines.

one way or another, anyhow; somehow or other etc. (*instrumentality*) 631; by way of; *viâ*; *in transitu* etc. 270; on the high road to.

Phr. *hae tibi erunt artes.*

628. Mid-course.—N. middle-, mid-course; moderation, mean etc. 29; middle etc. 68; *juste milieu*, *mezzo termine*, golden mean, *aurea mediocritas*.

straight etc. (*direct*) 278 -course, – path; short –, cross- cut; short- circuit; great circle sailing.

neutrality; half –, half and half- measures; compromise.

V. keep in –, steer –, preserve- -a middle, – an even- course; go straight etc. (*direct*) 278.

go half way, compromise, make a compromise.

Adj. neutral, average, even, impartial, moderate, straight etc. (*direct*) 278.

629. Circuit.—N. circuit, round-about way, digression, divagation, *détour*, circum-ambience, -ambulation, bendibus, *ambages*, loop; winding etc. (*circuition*) 311; zigzag etc. (*deviation*) 279.

V. perform –, make- a circuit; go -round about, – out of one's way; make a *détour*; meander etc. (*deviate*) 27; circumambulate.

lead a pretty dance; beat about, – the bush; make two bites of a cherry.

adj. circuitous, indirect, round-about; zig-zag etc. (*deviating*) 279; circum-ambient, -ambulatory.

Adv. by -a side wind, – an indirect course; in a roundabout way; from pillar to post.

630. Requirement.—N. requirement, need, wants, necessities; necessaries, – of life; stress, exigency, pinch, *sine quâ non*, matter of necessity; case of -need, – life or death.

needfulness, essentiality, necessity, indispensability, urgency, prerequisite.

requisition etc. (*request*) 765, (*exaction*) 741; run upon; demand –, call- for.

desideratum etc. (*desire*) 865; want etc. (*deficiency*) 640.

charge, claim, command, injunction, requisition, mandate, order, *ultimatum*.

V. require, need, want, have occasion for, entail; not be able to -do without, – dispense with; prerequire.

render necessary, necessitate, create a necessity for, call for, put in requisition; make a requisition etc. (*ask for*) 765, (*demand*) 741,

stand in need of; lack etc. 640; desiderate; desire etc. 865; be -necessary etc. *adj.*

Adj. required etc. *v.*; requisite, needful,

necessary, imperative, essential, indispensable, prerequisite; called for; in -demand, – request.

urgent, exigent, pressing, instant, crying, absorbing.

in want of; destitute of etc. 640.

Adv. *ex necessitate rei* etc. (*necessarily*) 601; of –, out of stern- necessity; at a pinch.

Phr. there is no time to lose; it cannot be -spared, – dispensed with.

631. Instrumentality.—N. instrumentality; aid etc. 707; subservien-ce, -cy; mediation, intervention, -mediacy, medium, inter-medium, -mediary, vehicle, hand; agency etc. 170.

minister, handmaid, servant, slave, maid, valet; midwife, *accoucheur*, obstetrician; go-between; cat's paw; stepping-stone.

key; master –, pass –, latch- key; 'open seseme;' passport, *passe partout*, safe-conduct; influence.

instrument etc. 633; expedient etc. (*plan*) 626; means etc. 632.

V. subserve, minister, tend, mediate, intervene; come –, go- between, interpose; pull the strings; be -instrumental etc. *adj.*; pander to.

Adj. instrumental; useful etc. 644; ministerial, subservient, mediatorial; inter-mediate, -vening; conducive.

Adv. through, by, *per*; where-, there-, here-by; by the -agency etc. 170- of; by dint of; by –, in-virtue of; through the -medium etc. *n.*- of; along with; on the shoulders of; by means of etc. 632; by –, with- -the aid etc. (*assistance*) 707- of.

per fas et nefas, by fair means or foul; somehow, – or other; by hook or by crook.

632. Means.—N. means, resources, revenue, wherewithal, ways and means, income; capital etc. (*money*) 800; stock in trade etc. 636; provision etc. 637; a shot in the locker; appliances etc. (*machinery*) 633; means and appliances; conveniences; cards to play; expendients etc. (*measures*) 626; two strings to one's bow; sheet anchor etc. (*safety*) 666; aid etc. 707; medium etc. 631.

V. find –, have –, possess- means etc. *n.*; provide the wherewithal.

Adj. instrumental etc. 631; mechanical etc. 633.

Adv. by means of, with; by -what, – all, – any, – some- means; where-, here-, there-with; wherewithal.

how etc. (*in what manner*) 627; through etc. (*by the instrumentality of*) 631; with –, by- the aid etc. (*assistance*) 707- of; by the -agency etc. 170- of.

633. Instrument.—N. machinery, mechanism, engineering.

instrument, organ, tool, implement, utensil, contrivance, machine, motor, engine, lathe, gin, mill, pump.

gear; tack-le, -ling, trice, rigging, gear, apparatus, appliances; plant, *matériel*; harness, trappings, fittings, accouterments; equip-ment, -age; appointments, furniture, upholstery; chattels; paraphernalia etc. (*belongings*) 780; *impedimenta.*

mechanical powers; lever, -age; mechanical advantage; crow, -bar; handspike, gavelock, jemmy, arm, limb, wing; oar, paddle; pulley, sheave; parbuckle; wheel and axle; wheel-, clock-work; wheels within wheels; pinion, gear wheel, spur –, bevel-gearing, chains, belting, crank, winch, capstan, windlass, crane, derrick, hoist, lift etc. 307; cam; pedal; wheel etc. (*rotation*) 312; inclined plane; wedge; screw; jack; spring, mainspring.

handle, hilt, haft, shaft, heft, shank, blade, trigger, tiller, helm, treadle, key; turnscrew, screwdriver, spanner, wrench.

hammer etc. (*impulse*) 276; edge tool etc. (*cut*) 253; borer etc. 262; vice, teeth etc. (*hold*) 781; nail, rope etc. (*join*) 45; peg etc. (*hang*) 214; support etc. 215; spoon etc. (*vehicle*) 272; arms etc. 727; oar etc. (*navigation*) 267.

Adj. instrumental etc. 631; mechanical, machinal, automatic, self-acting; brachial.

634. Substitute.—N. substitute etc. 147; deputy etc. 759; proxy, alternative, understudy.

635. Materials.—N. material, raw material, stuff, stock, staple; building materials, bricks and mortar; metal; stone; clay, brick; crockery etc. 384; compo, -sition; reinforced –, ferro-, concrete; cement; wood, ore, timber; gravel, cobbles, macadam, asphalt, tarmac.

materials; supplies, munition, fuel, grist, household stuff; *pabulum* etc. (*food*) 298; ammunition etc. (*arms*) 727; contingents; relay, reinforcement; baggage etc. (*personal property*) 780; means etc. 632.

Adj. raw etc. (*unprepared*) 674; wooden etc. *n.*

636. Store.—N. stock, fund, mine, vein, lode, quarry; spring; fount, -ain; well, -spring; milch-cow.

stock in trade, supply; heap etc. (*collection*) 72; treasure; reserve, *corps de réserve*, reserve fund, nest-egg, savings, *bonne bouche*.

crop, harvest, mow, vintage; yield, product, gleanings.

store, accumulation, hoard, rick, stack; lumber; relay etc. (*provision*) 637.

store-house, -room, -closet; depository, *dépôt*, *cache*, safe deposit, vault, pantechnicon, repository, -servatory, -pertory; *repertorium*; promptuary, warehouse, *entrepôt*, magazine, dump, buttery, larder, pantry, panary, lanary, still-room, spence; crib, garner, granary, silo, barn; bunker; thesaurus; bank etc. (*treasury*) 802; armoury; arsenal; dock; gallery, museum, library, conservatory, hot-house; manag-ery, -erie, aquarium, zoological gardens.

reservoir, cistern, tank, sump, pond, mill-pond; gasometer.

budget, quiver, bandolier, portfolio; coffer etc. (*receptacle*) 191.

conservation; storing etc. *v.*; storage.
dictionary etc. 562; list etc. 86.

V. store; put –, lay –, set- by; stow away; set –, lay- apart; store –, hoard –, treasure –, lay –, heap –, put –, garner –, save- up; *cache*; accumulate, amass, hoard, fund, garner, save, bank.

conserve, reserve; keep –, hold- back; husband, – one's resources.

deposit; stow, stack, load, dump; harvest; heap, collect etc. 72; lay -in, – down, – by, store etc. *adj.*; keep, file [papers] lay in etc. (*provide*) 637; preserve etc. 670; put by for a rainy day.

Adj. stored etc. *v.*; in -store, – reserve, – ordinary; spare, supernumerary.

637. Provision.—N. provision, supply; grist, – to the mill; subvention etc. (*aid*) 707; resources etc. (*means*) 632.

provising etc. *v.*; purveyance; reinforcement; commissary, commissariat.

rations; iron –, emergency- rations; provender etc. (*food*) 298; *viaticum*; ensilage.

caterer, purveyor, commissary, quartermaster, steward, housekeeper, manciple, feeder, batman, victualler, storekeeper, grocer, provision merchant, green-, grocer, *comprador*, *restaurateur*; sutler etc. (*merchant*) 797; innkeeper, publican, confectioner, baker, butcher, wine merchant, vintner.

V. provide; make -provision, – due provision for; lay in, – a stock, – a store.

sup-ply, -peditate; furnish; find, – one in; arm.

cater, victual, provision, purvey, forage; beat up for; stock, – with; make good, replenish; fill, – up; recruit, feed, ration.

have in -store, – reserve; keep, – by one, – on foot; have to fall back upon; store etc. 636; provide against a rainy day etc. (*economy*) 817.

638. Waste.—N. consumption, expenditure, exhaustion; dispersion etc. 73; ebb; leakage etc. (*exudation*) 295; loss etc. 776; wear and tear; waste; prodigality etc. 818; misuse etc. 679; wasting etc. *v.*; rubbish etc. (*useless*) 645.

mountain in labor.

v. spend, expend, use, consume, swallow up, exhaust, deplete; impoverish; spill, drain, empty; disperse etc. 73.

cast –, throw –, fling –, fritter- away; burn the candle at both ends, waste; squander etc. 818.

'waste its sweetness on the desert air;' cast -one's bread upon the waters, – pearls before swine; employ a steam engine to crack a nut, waste powder and shot, break a butterfly on a wheel; labor in vain etc. (*useless*) 645; cut a whetstone with a razor, pour water into a sieve; tilt at windmills.

leak etc. (*run out*) 295; run to waste; ebb; melt away, run dry, dry up.

Adj. wasted etc. *v.*; at a low ebb.

wasteful etc. (*prodigal*) 818; penny wise and pound foolish.

Phr. *magno conatu magnas nugas; le jeu n'en vaut pas la chandelle.*

639. Sufficiency.—N. sufficiency, adequacy, enough, withal, *quantum sufficit*, satisfaction, competence; no less.

mediocrity etc. (*average*) 29.

fill; fullness etc (*completeness*) 52; plen-itude, -ty; abundance; copiousness etc. *adj.*; amplitude, galore, lots, profusion; full measure; 'good measure pressed down, shaken together and running over.'

luxuriance etc. (*fertility*) 168; affluence etc. (*wealth*) 803; fat of the land; 'a land flowing with milk and honey;' cornucopia; horn of -plenty, – Amalthaea; mine etc. (*stock*) 636.

outpouring; flood etc. (*great quantity*) 31; tide etc. (*river*) 348; repletion etc. (*reduncance*) 641; satiety etc. 869; rich man etc. 803.

V. be -sufficient etc. *adj.*; suffice, do, just do, satisfy, pass muster; have -enough etc. *n.*; eat –, drink –, have- one's fill; roll –, swim- in; wallow in etc. (*superabundance*) 641.

abound, exuberate, teem, flow, stream, rain, shower down; pour, – in; swarm; bristle with.

render -sufficient etc. *adj.*; replenish etc. (*fill*) 52.

Adj. sufficient, enough, adequate, up to the mark, commensurate, competent, satisfactory, valid, tangible.

measured; moderate etc. (*temperate*) 953.

full etc. (*complete*) 52; ample; plen-ty, -tiful, -teous; plenty as blackberries; copious, abundant; abounding etc. *v.*; replete, enough and to spare, flush; choke-full; well-stocked, -provided; liberal; unstint-ed, -ing; stintless; without stint; un-sparing, -measured; lavish etc. 641; wholesale.

rich, luxuriant etc. (*fertile*) 168; affluent etc. (*wealthy*) 803; wantless; big with etc. (*pregnant*) 161.

un-exhausted, -wasted; exhaustless, inexhaustible.

Adv. sufficiently, amply etc. *adj.*; full; in -abundance etc. *n.*; with no sparing hand; to one's heart's content, *ad libitum*, without stint.

Phr. cut and come again.

640. Insufficiency.—N. insufficiency; inadequa-cy, -teness; incompetence etc. (*impotence*) 158; deficiency etc. (*incompleteness*) 53; imperfection etc. 651; shortcoming etc. 304; paucity; stint; scantiness etc. (*smallness*) 32; none to spare; bare subsistence.

scarcity, dearth; want, need, lack, poverty, exigency; inanition, starvation, famine, drought.

dole, pittance, mite; short -allowance, – commons; half-rations; banyan –, fast- day, Lent.

emptiness, poorness etc. *adj.*; depletion, vacancy, flaccidity; ebb-tide; low water; 'a beggarly account of empty boxes;' indigence etc. (*poverty*) 804; insolvency etc. (*non-payment*) 808; poor man etc. 804; bankrupt etc. 808.

V. be -insufficient etc. *adj.*; not -suffice etc. 639; come short of etc. 304; run dry.

want, lack, need, require; *caret*; be in want etc. (*poor*) 804; live from hand to mouth.

render- insufficient etc. *adj.*; drain of resources; impoverish etc. (*waste*) 638; stint etc. (*begrudge*) 819; put on short -commons, – allowance.

do -insufficiently etc. *adv.*; scotch the snake.

Adj. insufficient, inadequate; too -little etc. 32; not -enough etc. 639; unequal to; incompetent etc. (*impotent*) 158; 'weighed in the balance and found wanting;' perfunctory etc. (*neglect*) 460; deficient etc. (*incomplete*) 53; wanting etc. *v.*; imperfect etc. 651; ill-furnished, -provided, -stored, -off.

slack, at a low ebb; empty, vacant, bare; short –, out –, destitute –, devoid –, bereft etc. 789 –, denuded- of; dry, drained.

un -provided, -supplied, -furnished; unreplenished, -fed; un-stored, -treasured; empty-handed.

meager, poor, thin, scrimp, sparing, spare, stinted, stunted; skimpy; starv-ed, -eling; half-starved, emaciated, famine-stricken, famished, underfed, undernourished; jejune.

scant etc. (*small*) 32; scarce; not to be had, – for love or money, – at any price; scurvy; stingy etc. 819; at the end of one's tether; without - resources etc. 632; in want etc. (*poor*) 804; in debt etc. 806.

Adv. insufficiently etc. *adj.*; in default –, for want- of; failing.

641. Redundance.—N. redundance; too - much, – many; superabundance, -fluity, -fluence, -saturation; nimiety, transcendency, exuberance, profuseness; profusion etc. (*plenty*) 639; repletion, enough in all conscience, *satis superque*, lion's share; more than -enough etc. 639; plethora, engorgement, congestion, load, surfeit, sickener; turgescence etc. (*expansion*) 194; over-dose, - measure, -supply, -flow; inundation etc. (*water*) 348; *avalanche*.

accumulation etc. (*store*) 636; heap etc. 72; drug, – in the market; glut; crowd; burden.

excess; sur-, over-plus, epact; margin; remainder etc. 40; duplicate; surplusage; expletive; work of –, supererogation; *bonus*, *bonanza*.

luxury; intemperance etc. 954; extravagance etc. (*prodigality*) 818; exorbitance, lavishment.

pleonasm etc. (*diffuseness*) 573; too many irons in the fire; embarassment of riches; money to burn.

V. super-, over-abound; know no bounds, swarm; meet one at every turn; creep –, bristle- with; overflow; run –, flow –, well –, brim-over; run riot; over-run, -stock, -lay, -charge, -dose, - feed, -burden, -load, -do, -whelm, -shoot the mark etc. (*go beyond*) 303; surcharge, supersaturate, gorge, glut, load, drench, whelm, inundate, deluge, flood; drug, – the market.

choke, cloy, accloy, suffocate; pile up, lay it on, – with a trowel, lay on thick; impregnate with; lavish etc. (*squander*) 818.

send –, carry- coals to Newcastle, – owls to Athens; teach one's grandmother to suck eggs; *pisces natare docere*; kill the slain, 'gild refined gold,' 'paint the lily;' butter one's bread on both sides, put butter upon bacon; employ a steam-engine to crack a nut etc. (*waste*) 638.

exaggerate etc. 549; wallow in; roll in etc. (*plenty*) 639; remain on one's hands, hang heavy on hand, go a begging.

Adj. redundant; too -much, – many; exuberant, inordinate, superabundant, excessive, overmuch, replete, profuse, lavish; prodigal etc. 818; exorbitant; overweening; extravagant; overcharged etc. *v.*; supersaturated, drenched, overflowing; running -over, – to waste, – down.

crammed –, filled- to overflowing; gorged, stuffed, ready to burst; dropsical, turgid, plethoric, full-blooded; obese etc. 194; voluminous.

superfluous, unnecessary, needless, supervacaneous, uncalled for, to spare, in excess; over and above etc. (*remainder*) 40; *de trop*; adscititious etc. (*additional*) 37; supernumerary etc. (*reserve*) 636; on one's hands, spare, duplicate, supererogatory, expletive; *un peu fort*.

Adj. over, too, over and above; over –, too-much; too far; without –, beyond – out of-measure; with ... to spare; over head and ears; up to one's eyes, – ears; *extra*; beyond the mark etc. (*transcursion*) 303; over one's head.

Phr. It never rains but it pours.

642. Importance.—N. importance, consequence, moment, prominence, consideration, mark, materialness.

import, significance, concern; emphasis, interest.

greatness etc. 31; superiority etc. 33; notability etc. (*repute*) 873; weight etc. (*influence*) 175; value etc. (*goodness*) 648; usefulness etc. 644.

gravity, seriousness, solemnity; no -joke, – laughing matter; pressure, urgency, stress; matter of life and death.

memorabilia, *notabilia*, great doings; red-letter day.

great -thing, – point; main chance, 'the be all and end all,' cardinal point, outstanding feature; substance, gist etc. (*essence*) 5; sum and substance, *gravamen*, head and front; important –, principal –, prominent –, essential- part; half the battle; *sine quâ non*; breath of one's nostrils etc. (*life*) 359; cream, salt, core, kernel, heart, nucleus; key, - note, -stone; corner stone; trumpcard etc. (*device*) 626; salient points.

top-sawyer, first fiddle, *prima donna*, chief, bigwig; triton among the minnows.

V. be -important etc. *adj.*, – somebody, – something; import, signify, matter, be an object; carry weight etc. (*influence*) 175; make a figure etc. (*repute*) 873; be in the ascendant, come to the front, lead the way, take the lead, play first fiddle, throw all else into the shade; lie at the root of; deserve –, merit –, be worthy- -of notice, – regard, – consideration.

attach –, ascribe –, give- importance etc. *n.*- to; value, care for; set store -upon, – by; mark etc. 550; mark with a white stone, underline; write –, put –, print- in -italics, – capitals, – large letters, – large type, – letters of gold; accentuate, emphasize, lay stress on.

make -a fuss, – a stir, – a piece of work, – much ado- about; make -of, – much of.

Adj. important; of -importance etc. *n.*; momentous, material; to the point; not to be -overlooked, – despised, – sneezed at; egregious; weighty etc. (*influential*) 175; of note etc. (*repute*) 873; notable, prominent, salient, signal; memorable, remarkable; worthy of -remark, – notice; never to be forgotten; stirring, eventful.

grave, serious, earnest, noble, grand, solemn, impressive, commanding, imposing.

urgent, pressing, critical, instant.

paramount, essential, vital, all-absorbing, radical, cardinal, chief, main, prime, primary, principal, leading, capital, foremost, overruling; of vital etc. importance.

in the front rank, first-rate, A1; superior etc. 33; considerable etc. (*great*) 31; marked etc. *v.*; rare etc. 137.

significant, telling, trenchant, emphatic, pregnant; *tanti*.

Adv. materially etc. *adj.*; in the main; above all, *par excellence*, to crown all.

643. Unimportance.—N. unimportance, insignificance, nothingness, immateriality.

triviality, trivia, fribble, levity, frivolity; paltriness etc. *adj.*; poverty; smallness etc. 32; vanity etc. (*uselessness*) 645; matter of - indifference etc. 866; no object; side issue.

nothing, – to signify, – worth speaking of, – particular, – to boast of, – to speak of; small –, no great –, trifling etc. *adj.*-matter; mere -joke, – nothing; hardly –, scarcely- anything; nonentity, cipher, figurehead; no great shakes, *peu de chose*; child's play; small beer.

toy, plaything, popgun, paper pellet, gimcrack, geegaw, bauble, trinket, *bagatelle*, kickshaw, knicknack, whim-wham, trifle, 'trifles light as air.'

trumpery, trash, rubbish, stuff, *fatras*, frippery; 'leather or prunello;' chaff, drug, froth, bubble, smoke, cobweb; weed; refuse etc. (*inutility*) 645; scum etc. (*dirt*) 653.

joke, jest, snap of the fingers; fudge etc. (*unmeaning*) 517; fiddlestick, – end; pack of nonsense, mere farce.

straw, pin, fig, continental, button, rush; bulrush, feather, halfpenny, farthing, brass farthing, doit, peppercorn, jot, rap, pinch of snuff, old song.

minutiae, details, minor details, small fry; dust in the balance, feather in the scale, drop in the ocean, flea-bite, molehill; fingle-fangle.

nine days' wonder, *ridiculus mus*; flash in the pan etc. (*impotence*) 158; much ado about nothing etc. (*overestimation*) 482; storm in a teacup.

V. be -unimportant etc. *adj.*; not -matter etc. 642; go for –, matter –, signify- -little, – nothing, – little or nothing; not matter a -straw etc. *n.*

make light of etc. (*underestimate*) 483; catch at straws etc. (*overestimate*) 482.

Adj. unimportant; of -little, – small, – no- - account, – importance etc. 642; immaterial; un-, non-essential; not vital; irrelevant, incidental, indifferent.

subordinate etc. (*inferior*) 34; *médiocre* etc. (*average*) 29; passable, fair, respectable, tolerable, commonplace; uneventful, mere, common; ordinary etc. (*habitual*) 613; inconsiderable, so-so, insignificant, inappreciable, nugatory.

trifling, trivial; slight, slender, light, flimsy, frothy, idle; puerile etc. (*foolish*) 499; airy, shallow; weak etc. 160; powerless etc. 158; frivolous, petty, niggling; pid-, ped-dling; fribble, inane, ridiculous, farcical; fini-cal, -kin; fiddle-faddle, namby-pamby, wishy-washy, milk and water.

poor, paltry, pitiful; contemptible etc. (*contempt*) 930; sorry, mean, meager, shabby, miserable, wretched, vile, scrubby, scrannel, weedy, niggardly, scurvy, putid, beggarly, worthless, twopenny-half penny, cheap, trashy, catchpenny, gimcrack, trumpery, one-horse; toy.

not worth -the pains, – while, – mentioning, – speaking of, – a thought, – a curse, – a straw, – rap etc. *n.*; beneath –, unworthy of- -notice, – regard, – consideration, – contempt; *de lanâ caprinâ*; vain etc. (*useless*) 645.

Adv. slightly etc. *adj.*; rather, somewhat, pretty well, fairly well, tolerably.

for aught one cares.

Int. no matter! pish! tush! tut! pshaw! pugh! pooh, -pooh! fudge! bosh! humbug! fiddle-stick, – end! fiddlededee! never mind! *n'importe!* what - signifies, – matter, – boots it, – of that, – 's the odds! a fig for! stuff ! nonsense! stuff and nonsense!

Phr. *magno conatu magnas nugas*; *le jeu n'en vaut pas la chandelle*; it -matters not, – does not signify; it is of no -consequence, – importance.

644. Utility.—N. utility; usefulness etc. *adj.*; efficacy, efficiency, adequacy; service, use, stead, avail; help etc. (*aid*) 707; applicability etc. *adj.*; subservience etc. (*instrumentality*) 631; function etc. (*business*) 625; value; worth etc. (*goodness*) 648; money's worth; productiveness etc. 168; *cui bono* etc. (*intention*) 620; utilization etc. (*use*) 677; step in the right direction.

common weal, public good; utilitarianism etc. (*philanthropy*) 910.

V. be -useful etc. *adj.*; avail, serve; subserve etc. (*be instrumental to*) 631; conduce etc. (*tend*) 176; answer –, serve- -one's turn, – a purpose.

act a part etc. (*action*) 680; perform –, discharge- -a function etc. 625; do –, render- -a service, – good service, – yeoman's service; bestead, stand one in good stead; be the making of; help etc. 707.

bear fruit etc. (*produce*) 161; bring grist to the mill; profit, remunerate; benefit etc. (*do good*) 648.

find one's -account, – advantage- in; reap the benefit of etc. (*be better for*) 658.

render useful etc. (*use*) 677.

Adj. useful; of -use etc. *n.*; serviceable, usable, proficuous, good for; subservient etc. (*instrumental*) 631; conducive etc. (*tending*) 176; subsidiary etc. (*helping*) 707.

advantageous etc. (*beneficial*) 648; profitable, gainful, remunerative, worth one's salt; in-, valuable; prolific etc. (*productive*) 168.

adequate; ef-ficient, -ficacious; effect-ive, -ual; practicable, expedient etc. 646.

applicable, available, ready, handy, at hand, tangible; commodious, adaptable; of all work.

Adv. usefully etc. *adj.*; *pro bono publico*.

645. Inutility.—N. inutility; uselessness etc. *adj.*; inefficacy, futility; inep-, inap-titude; unsubservience; inadequacy etc. (*insufficiency*) 640; inefficiency etc. (*incompetence*) 158; unskilfulness etc. 699; disservice; unfruitfulness etc. (*unproductiveness*) 169; labor -in vain, – lost, – of Sisyphus; lost -trouble, – labor; work of Penelope; sleeveless errand, wild goose chase, mere farce.

tautology etc. (*repetition*) 104; supererogation etc. (*redundance*) 641.

vanitas vanitatum, vanity, inanity, worthlessness, nugacity; triviality etc. (*unimportance*) 643.

caput mortuum, waste paper, dead letter; blunt tool.

litter, rubbish, lumber, odds and ends, cast-off clothes; button-top; shoddy; rags, orts, trash, refuse, sweepings, scourings, off-scourings, dross, slag, waste, rubble, dottle, drast, *débris*; stubble, leavings; broken meat; dregs etc. (*dirt*) 653; weeds, tares; rubbish heap, dust hole; *rudera*, deads.

fruges consumere natus etc. (*drone*) 683.

V. be -useless etc. *adj.*; go a begging etc. (*redundant*) 641; fail etc. 732.

seek –, strive- after impossibilities; use vain efforts, labor in vain, roll the stone of Sisyphus, beat the air, lash the waves, *battre l'eau avec un bâton*, *donner un coup d'épée dans l'eau*, fish in the air, milk the ram, drop a bucket into an empty well, sow the sand; bay the moon; preach –, speak- to the winds; whistle jigs to a milestone; kick against the pricks, *se battre contre des moulins*; lock the stable door when the steed is stolen etc. (*too late*) 135; hold a farthing candle to the sun; cast pearls before swine etc. (*waste*) 638; carry coals to Newcastle etc. (*redundance*) 641; wash a blackamoor white etc. (*impossible*) 471.

render -useless etc. *adj.*; dis-mantle, -mast, -mount, -qualify, -able; unrig; cripple, lame etc. (*injure*) 659; spike guns, clip the wings; put out of gear.

Adj. useless, inutile, inefficacious, futile, unavailing, bootless; inoperative etc. 158; inadequate etc. (*insufficient*) 640; in-, un- subservient: inept, inefficient etc. (*impotent*) 158; of no -avail etc. (*use*) 644; ineffectual etc. (*failure*) 732; incompetent etc. (*unskilful*) 699; 'stale, flat and unprofitable;' superfluous etc. (*redundant*) 641; dispensable; thrown away etc. (*wasted*) 638; abortive etc. (*immature*) 674.

worth-, value-less; unsaleable; not worth a straw etc. (*trifling*) 643; dear at any price.

vain, empty, inane; gain-, profit-, fruit-less; unserviceable, -profitable; ill-spent; unproductive etc. 169; *hors de combat*; barren, sterile, impotent, unproductive; effete, past work etc. (*impaired*) 659; obsolete etc. (*old*) 124; fit for the -dust-hole, – wastepaper basket; good for nothing; of no earthly use; not worth -having, – powder and shot; leading to no end, uncalled for; un-necessary, -needed, superfluous.

Adv. uselessly etc. *adj.*; to -little, – no, – little or no- purpose.

Int. *cui bono?* what's the good!

646. Expedience. [Specific subservience.]—**N.** expedien-ce, -cy; desirableness, -bility etc. *adj.*; fitness etc. (*agreement*) 23; utility etc. 644; propriety; advantage; opportunism, pragmatism.

high time etc. (*occasion*) 134.

V. be -expedient etc. *adj.*; suit etc. (*agree*) 23; befit; suit –, befit- the -time, – season, – occasion.

conform etc. 82.

Adj. expedient; desir-, advis-, accept-able; convenient; worth while, meet; fit, -ting; due, proper, eligible, seemly, becoming; befitting etc. *v.*; opportune etc. (*in season*) 134; *in loco*; suitable etc. (*accordant*) 23; applicable etc. (*useful*) 644; practical, effective, pragmatical; suitable, handy.

Adv. in the right place; conveniently etc. *adj.*; in the nick of time.

Phr. *operae pretium est.*

647. Inexpedience.—N. enexpedien-ce, -cy; undesira-bleness, -bility etc. *adj.*; discommodity, impropriety; unfitness etc. (*disagreement*) 24; inutility etc. 645; inconvenience, inadvisability; disadvantage.

V. be -inexpedient etc. *adj.*; come amiss etc. (*disagree*) 24; embarrass etc. (*hinder*) 706; put to inconvenience; pay too dear for one's whistle.

Adj. inexpedient, undesirable; un-, in-advisable; objectionable; troublesome, in-apt, -eligible, -admissable, -convenient; in-, dis-commodious; disadvantageous; inappropriate, unsuitable, unfit etc. (*inconsonant*) 24.

ill-contrived, -advised; unsatsifactory; unprofitable etc., unsubservient etc. (*useless*) 645; inopportune etc. (*unseasonable*) 135; out of –, in the wrong- place; improper, unseemly.

clumsy, awkward; cum-brous, -bersome; lumbering, unwieldy, hulky; unmanageable etc. (*impracticable*) 704; impedient (*in the way*) 706.

unnecessary etc. (*redundant*) 641.

Phr. it will never do.

648. Goodness. [Capability of producing good. Good qualities.]—**N.** goodness etc. *adj.*; excellence, merit; virtue etc. 944; value, worth, price.

super-excellence, -eminence; superiority etc. 33; perfection etc. 650; *coup de maître*; master-piece, *chef d'oeuvre*, prime, flower, cream, *élite*, pick, A1, none such, *nonpareil*, *crême de la crême*, flower of the flock, cock of the roost, salt of the earth; champion.

tid-bit; gem, – of the first water; *bijou*, precious stone, jewel, pearl, diamond, ruby, brilliant, treasure; good thing; *rara avis*, one in a thousand.

beneficence etc. 906; good man etc. 948.

V. be -beneficial etc. *adj.*; produce –, do- -good etc. 618; profit etc. (*be of use*) 644; benefit; confer a -benefit etc. 618.

be the making of, do a world of good, make a man of.

produce a good effect; do a good turn, confer an obligation; improve etc. 658.

do no harm, break no bones.

be -good etc. *adj.*; excel, transcend etc. (*be superior*) 33; bear away the bell.

stand the -proof, – test; pass -muster, – an examination.

challenge comparison, vie, emulate, rival.

Adj. harm-, hurt-less; unobnoxious; in-nocuous, -nocent, -offensive.

beneficial, valuable, of value; serviceable etc. (*useful*) 644; advantageous, profitable, edifying; salutary etc. (*healthful*) 656.

favorable; propitious etc. (*hopegiving*) 858; fair.

good, – as gold; excellent; better; superior etc. 33; above par; nice, fine; genuine etc. (*true*) 494.

best, choice, select, picked, elect, eximious, *recherché*, rare, priceless; unpara-goned, -lleled etc. (*supreme*) 33; superlatively etc. 33- good; super-fine, -excellent; bonzer; of the first water; first-rate, -class; high-wrought; exquisite, very best, crack, prime, tip-top, gilt-edged, capital, cardinal; standard etc. (*perfect*) 650: inimitable

admirable, estimable; praiseworthy etc. (*approve*) 931; pleasing etc. 829; *couleur de rose*, precious, of great price; costly etc. (*dear*) 814; worth -its weight in gold, – a king's ransom;

matchless, peerless, invaluable, inestimable, precious as the apple of the eye.

tolerable etc. (*not very good*) 651; up to the mark, un-exceptionable, -objectionable; satisfactory, tidy.

in -good, – fair- condition; fresh; unspoiled; sound etc. (*perfect*) 650.

Adv. beneficially etc. *adj.*; well etc. 618.

649. Badness. [Capability of producing evil. Bad qualities.]—**N.** hurtfulness etc. *adj.*; virulence.

evil doer etc. 913; bane etc. 663; plague-spot etc. (*insalubrity*) 657; evil star, ill wind; snake in the grass, skeleton in the closet; *amari aliquid*, thorn in the side; Jonah, jinx, hoodoo.

malignity; malevolence etc. 907; tender mercies [ironically].

ill-treatment, annoyance, molestation, abuse, oppression, persecution, outrage; misusage etc. 679; injury etc. (*damage*) 659.

badness etc. *adj.*; peccancy, abomination; painfulness etc. 830; pestilence etc. (*disease*) 655; guilt etc. 947; depravity etc. 945.

V. be -hurtful etc. *adj.*; cause –, produce –, inflict –, work –, do- evil etc. 619; damnify, endamage, hurt, harm, scathe; injure etc. (*damage*) 659; pain etc. 830.

wrong, aggrieve, oppress, persecute; trample –, tread –, bear hard –, put-upon; overburden; weigh -down, – heavy on; victimize; run down; molest etc. 830.

maltreat, abuse; ill-use, -treat; thwart, buffet, bruise, scratch, maul; smite etc. (*scourge*) 972; do -violence, – harm, – a mischief; stab, pierce, outrage.

do –, make- mischief; bring –, get- into trouble.

destroy etc. 162.

Adj. hurt-, harm-, scath-, bane-, bale-ful; injurious, deleterious, detrimental, noxious, pernicious, mischievous, full of mischief, mischief-making, malefie, malignant, nocuous, noisome; prejudicial; dis-serviceable, advantageous; wide-wasting.

unlucky, sinister; obnoxious, untoward, disastrous.

oppressive, burdensome, onerous; malign etc. (*malevolent*) 907.

corrupting etc. (corrupt etc. 659) virulent, venomous, envenomed, corrosive; poisonous etc. (*morbific*) 657; deadly etc. (*killing*) 361; destructive etc. (*destroying*) 162; inauspicious etc. 859.

bad, ill, arrant, as bad bad can be, dreadful; horrid, -rible; dire; rank, peccant, foul, fulsome; rotten, – at the core.

vile, base, villainous; mean etc. (*paltry*) 643; injured etc., deteriorated etc. 659; unsatisfactory, exception, -able, indifferent; below par etc. (*imperfect*) 651; ill-contrived, -conditioned; wretched, sad, grievous, deplorable, lamentable; piti-ful, -able, woeful etc. (*painful*) 830.

evil, wrong; depraved etc. 945; shocking; reprehensible etc. (*disapprove*) 932.

hateful, – as a toad; abominable, detestable, execrable, cursed, accursed, confounded; damn-ed, -able; infernal; diabolic etc. (*malevolent*) 907.

inadvisable etc. (*inexpedient*) 647; unprofitable etc. (*useless*) 645; incompetent etc. (*unskilful*) 699; irremediable etc. (*hopeless*) 859.

Adv. badly etc. *adj.*; wrong, ill; to one's cost; where the shoe pinches.

Phr. bad is the best; the worst come to the worst.

650. Perfection.—N. perfection; perfectness etc. *adj.*; indefectibility; inpecc-ancy, -ability.

pink, *beau idéal*, phoenix, paragon; pink –, acme- of perfection; *ne plus ultra*; summit etc. 210.

cygne noir; philosopher's stone; chrysolite, Koh-i-noor, black tulip.

model, standard, pattern, mirror, admirable Chrichton; trump; very prince of.

master-piece, -stroke, super-excellence etc. (*goodness*) 648; transcendence etc. (*superiority*) 33.

V. be -perfect etc. *adj.*; transcend etc. (*be supreme*) 33.

bring to perfection, perfect, ripen, mature; consummate, complete etc. 729; put in trim etc. (*prepare*) 673; put the finishing touch to.

Adj. perfect, faultless, ideal; indefective, -ficient, -fectible; immaculate, spotless, impeccable; free from -imperfection etc. 651; un-blemished, -injured etc. 659; sound, – as a roach; in perfect condition; scathless, intact, harmless; seaworthy etc. (*safe*) 644; right as a trivet; *in seipso totus teres atque rotundus*; consummate etc. (*complete*) 52; finished etc. 729; complete in itself.

best etc. (*good*) 648; model, standard; inimitable, unparagoned, unparalleled etc. (*supreme*) 33; superhuman, divine; beyond all praise etc. (*approbation*) 931; *sans peur et sans reproche*.

Adj. to perfection, to the limit; perfectly etc. *adj.*; *ad unguem*; clean, – as a whistle.

651. Imperfection.—N. imperfection; imperfectness etc. *adj.*; deficiency; inadequacy etc. (*insufficiency*) 640; peccancy etc. (*badness*) 649; immaturity etc. 674.

fault, defect, weak point; screw loose; rift within the lute; fly in the ointment; flaw etc. (*break*) 70; gap etc. 198; twist etc. 243; taint, attainder; bar sinister, hole in one's coat; blemish etc. 848; weakness etc. 160; half-blood, touch of the tar brush; shortcoming etc. 304; drawback; seamy side.

mediocrity; no great -shakes, – catch; not much to boast of.

V. be -imperfect etc. *adj.*; have a -defect etc. *n.*; lie under a disadvantage; spring a leak.

not –, barely- pass muster; fall short etc. 304.

Adj. imperfect; not -perfect etc. 650; de-ficient, -fective; faulty, unsound, mutilated, tainted; out of -order, – tune; cracked, leaky; sprung; warped etc. (*distort*) 243; lame; injured etc. (*deteriorated*) 659; peccant etc. (*bad*) 649; frail etc. (*weak*) 160; inadequate etc. (*insufficient*) 640; crude etc. (*unprepared*) 674; incomplete etc. 53; found wanting; below par; shorthanded; below –, under- its full -strength, – complement.

indifferent, middling, ordinary, mediocre; average etc. 29; so-so; *così-così*, milk and water; tolerable, fair, passable; pretty -well, – good; rather –, moderately- good; good –, well-enough; decent; not -bad, – amiss; inobjectionable, admissable, bearable, only better than nothing.

secondary, inferior; second-rate, -best, one-horse.

Adv. almost etc.; to a limited extent, rather etc. 32; pretty, moderately; only; considering, all things considered, enough.

Phr. *surgit amari aliquid.*

652. Cleanness.—N. cleanness etc. *adj.*; purity; cleaning etc. *v.*; purification, defecation etc. *v.*; purgation, lustration; de-, abs-tersion; epuration, mundation, ablution, lavation, colature; disinfection etc. *v.*; drain-, sewerage.

lavatory, bath, -room; swimming pool, natatorium; public baths; hot –, cold –, Turkish –, Swedish –, Russian – vapor- bath; *hammam*, laundry, washhouse; washerwoman, laundress, laundryman; scavenger, cleaner, sweeper, goodie: crossing sweeper, white wings, dustman, sweep.

brush; broom, besom, carpet-sweeper, vacuum-cleaner, mop, squilgee, rake, shovel, sieve, riddle, screen, filter; scraper, strigil.

napkin, *serviette*, cloth, table-, carving-cloth, table-linen, napery, maukin, handkerchief, towel, sudary; doyley, doily, duster, sponge, mop, swab.

cover, drugget, mat, doormat.

soap, wash, lotion, detergent, cathartic, purgative; purifier etc. *v.*; dentifrice, tooth-powder, -paste; mouth wash; disinfectant.

V. be –, render- clean etc. *adj.*

clean, -se; mundify, rinse, wring, flush, full, wipe, mop, sponge, scour, swab, scrub, holystone, brush up.

wash, shampoo, lave, launder, buck; abs-, deterge; clear, purify; de-purate, -spumate, -fecate; purge, expurgate; Bowdlerize; elutriate, lixiviate, edulcorate, clarify, refine, rack; fil-ter, -trate; drain, strain.

disinfect, sterilize, pasteurize, fumigate, ventilate, deodorize; whitewash.

sift, winnow, screen, riddle, pick, weed, comb, rake, brush, sweep.

rout –, clear –, sweep etc.- out; make a clean sweep of.

Adj. clean, -ly; pure; immaculate; spot-, stain-, taint-less; without a stain, un-stained, -spotted, -soiled, -sullied, -tainted, -infected, -adulterated; aseptic; sweet, – as a nut.

neat, spruce, tidy, trim, gimp, clean as a new penny, like a cat in pattens; cleaned etc. *v.*; kempt.

Adv. neatly etc. *adj.*; clean as a whistle.

653. Uncleanness.—N. uncleanness etc. *adj.*; impurity; immundi-ty, -city; impurity etc. [of mind] 961.

defilement, contamination etc. *v.*; defedation; soil-ure, -iness; abomination; leaven; taint, -ure; fetor etc. 401.

decay; putre-scence, -faction; corruption; mold, must, mildew, dry-rot, *mucor*, rubigo, caries.

slovenry; slovenliness etc. *adj.*; squalor.

dowdy, drab, slut, malkin, slattern, sloven, slammerkin, scrub, draggletail, mudlark, dustman, sweep; beast.

dirt, filth, soil, slop; dust, cobweb, flue; smoke, soot, smudge, smut, grime, raff.

sordes, dregs, grounds, lees; sedi-, settle-ment; heel-tap; dross, -iness; mother, precipitate, *scoria*, ashes, cinders, recrement, slag; scum, froth.

hog-wash, swill, ditch-, dish-, bilge-water; rinsings, cheese-parings; sweepings etc. (*useless refuse*) 645; off-, out-scourings; off-scum; *caput mortuum*, *residuum*, sprue, feculence, clinker, draff; scurf, -iness; *exuviae*, morphew; fur, -fur; dandruff; tartar.

riffraff; vermin, louse, cootie, flea, bug.

mud, mire, quagmire, *alluvium*, silt, sludge, slime, slush, slosh.

spawn, offal, garbage, carrion; *excreta* etc. 299; slough, peccant humor, pus, matter, suppuration, *lienteria*; *feces*, excrement, ordure, dung; sew-, sewer-age; muck, coprolite; guano, manure, compost.

dunghill, *coluvies*, mixen, midden, bog, laystall, sink, w.c., water-, earth-closet, latrine, privy, jakes, John's, cess, -pool; sump, sough, *cloaca*, drain, sewer, common sewer; Cloacina; dust-hole.

sty, pig-sty, lair, den, Augean stable, sink of corruption; slum, rookery.

V. be –, become- unclean etc. *adj.*; rot, putrefy, fester, rankle, reek; stink etc. 401; mold, -er; go -bad etc. *adj.*

render -unclean etc. *adj.*; dirt, -y; soil, smoke, tarnish, slaver, spot, smear, daub, blot, blur, smudge, smutch, smirch; d-, dr-abble, -aggle; spatter, slubber; be-smear etc.; -mire, -slime, -grime, -foul; splash, stain, distain, maculate, sully, pollute, defile, debase, contaminate, taint, leaven; corrupt etc. (*injure*) 659; cover with -dust etc. *n.*; drabble in the mud.

wallow in the mire; slob-, slab-ber.

Adj. unclean, dirty, filthy, grimy; soiled etc. *v.*; not to be handled with kid gloves; dusty, snuffy, smutty, sooty, smoky; thick, turbid, dreggy; slimy.

uncleanly, slovenly, untidy, sluttish, dowdy, slatternly, draggletailed; un-combed, -kempt, -scoured, -swept, -wiped, -washed, -strained, -purified; squalid.

nasty, coarse, foul, impure, offensive, abominable, beastly, reeky, reechy; fetid etc. 401.

moldy, lentiginous, musty, mildewed, rusty, moth-eaten, mucid, rancid, bad, gone bad, touched, fusty, reasty, rotten, corrupt, tainted, high, fly-blown, maggoty; putr-id, -escent, -efied; purulent, carious, peccant, fec-al, -ulent; stercoraceous, excrementitious; scurfy, impetiginous; gory, bloody; rotting etc. *v.*; rotten as -a pear, – cheese.

crapulous etc. (*intemperate*) 954; gross etc. (*impure in mind*) 961.

654. Health.—N. health, sanity; soundness etc. *adj.*; vigor; good –, perfect –, excellent –, rude –, robust- health; bloom, *mens sana in corpore sano*; Hygeia; incorrupti-on, -bility; good state –, clean bill- of health, eupepsia.

V. be in health etc. *adj.*; bloom, flourish.

keep -body and soul together, – on one's legs; enjoy -good, – a good state of - health; have a clean bill of health.

return to health; recover etc. 660; get better etc. (*improve*) 658; take a -new, – fresh- lease of life; convalesce, be convalescent, recruit; restore to health; cure etc. (*restore*) 660.

Adj. health-y, -ful; in -health etc. *n.*; well, sound, strong, fit, hearty, hale, fresh, blooming, green, whole; florid, flush, hardy, stanch, staunch, brave, robust, vigorous, weather-proof; convalescent.

un-scathed, -injured, -maimed, -marred, -tainted; sound of wind and limb, safe and sound; without a scratch.

on one's legs; sound as a -roach, – bell; fresh as -a daisy, – a rose, – April; picture of health; bursting with health; fit as a fiddle; hearty as a buck; in -fine, – high- feather; in -good case, – full bloom; in fine fettle; pretty bobbish, tolerably well, as well as can be expected.

sanitary etc. (*health-giving*) 656; sanatory etc. (*remedial*) 662.

655. Disease.*—N. disease, illness, sickness etc. *adj.*; ailing etc. *v.*; 'the ills that flesh is heir to;' morb-idity, -osity; infirmity, ailment, indisposition; complaint, disorder, malady; distemper, -ature.

visitation, attack, seizure, stroke, fit, epilepsy, apoplexy, shock, shell-shock.

delicacy, loss of health, valetudinarianism, invalidism, cachexy; *cachexia*, atrophy, *marasmus*; indigestion, *dyspepsia*; decay etc. (*deterioration*) 659; malnutrition, decline, consumption, palsy, paralysis, prostration; occupational diseases.

taint, pollution, infection, contagion, septicity, septicaemia, blood poisoning, pyaemia, epi-, endemic; murrain, plague, pestilence, virus, pox.

sore, ulcer, abscess, fester, boil; pimple etc. (*swelling*) 250; carbuncle, gathering, whitlow, imposthume, peccant humor, issue; rot, canker, cancer, *carcinoma*, *caries*, mortification, corruption, gangrene, *sphacelus*, leprosy, eruption, rash, breaking out, venereal disease.

fever, calenture; inflammation.

fatal etc. (*hopeless*) 859- -disease etc.; dangerous illness, galloping consumption, churchyard cough; general breaking up, break up of the system.

[Disease of the mind] neurasthenia; idiocy etc. 499; insanity etc. 503.

martyr to disease; cripple; 'the halt, the lame and the blind;' valetudinar-y, -ian; invalid, patient, case; sick-room, -chamber, hospital etc. 662.

[Science of disease] path-, eti-, nos-ology, therapeutics, diagnosis, prognosis.

V. be -ill etc. *adj.*; ail, suffer, labor under, be affected with, complain of; droop, flag, languish, halt; sicken, peak, pine, waste away, fail, lose strength; gasp.

keep one's bed; feign sickness etc. (*falsehood*) 544; malinger.

lay -by, – up; take –, catch- -a disease etc. *n.*, – an infection; be stricken by; break out.

Adj. diseased; ailing etc. *v.*; ill, – of; taken ill, seized with; indisposed, unwell, sick, squeamish, poorly, seedy; affected –, afflicted- with illness; laid up, confined, bed-ridden, invalided, in hospital, on the sick list; out of -health, – sorts; valetudinary.

un-sound, -healthy; sickly, morbose, healthless, infirm, chlorotic, unbraced, drooping, flagging, lame, halt, crippled, halting.

morbid, tainted, vitiated, peccant, contaminated, poisoned, septic, tabid, mangy, leprous, cankered; rotten, – to, – at- the core; withered, palsied, paralytic, tuberculous; dyspeptic.

touched in the wind, broken-winded, spavined, gasping; *hors de combat* etc. (*useless*) 645.

weak-ly, -ened etc. (*weak*) 160; decrepit; decayed etc. (*deteriorated*) 659; incurable etc. (*hopeless*) 859; in declining health; cranky; in a bad way, in danger, prostrate; moribund etc. (*death*) 360.

morbific, epidemic etc. 657.

*Extended lists of different diseases are beyond the scope of this work.

656. Salubrity.—N. salubrity, salubriousness; healthiness etc. *adj.*

fine -air, – climate; eudiometer.

[Preservation of health] *hygiène*; valetudinarian, -ism, preventorium, sanitarian; *sanitarium*, *sanitorium*, immunity.

V. be -salubrious etc. *adj.*; agree with, be good for; assimilate etc. 23.

Adj. salu-brious, -tary, -tiferous, wholesome; health-y, -ful; sanitary, prophylactic, benign, bracing, tonic, invigorating, good for, nutritious, hyg-eian, -ienic.

in-noxious, -nocuous, -nocent; harmless, uninjurious, uninfectious; immune.

sanative etc. (*remedial*) 662; restorative etc. (*reinstate*) 660; useful etc. 644.

657. Insalubrity.—N. insalubrity, unhealthiness etc. *adj.*; non-naturals; plague spot; malaria etc. (*poison*) 663; death in the pot, contagion.

Adj. insalubrious; un-healthy, -wholesome; noxious, noisome, foul; morbi-fic, -ferous; mephitic, septic, azotic, deleterious; pesti-lent, -ferous, -lential; virulent, venomous, envenomed, poisonous, toxic, narcotic.

contagious, infectious, catching, taking, communicable, epidemic, zymotic, sporadic, endemic, pandemic, epizoötic.

innutritious, indigestible, ungenial; uncongenial etc. (*disagreeing*) 24.

deadly etc. (*killing*) 361.

658. Improvement.—N. improvement; a-, melioration; betterment; mend, amendment, emendation; mending etc. *v.*; advancement; advance etc. (*progress*) 282; ascent etc. 305; promotion, preferment; elevation etc. 307; increase etc. 35.

cultiv-, civiliz-ation; menticulture, culture, march of intellect; eugenics, euthenics, meliorism, telesis.

reform, -ation; revision, radical reform; second thoughts, correction, *limae labor*, refinement, elaboration; purification etc. 652; repair etc. (*restoration*) 660; recovery etc. 660.

revise; revised –, new- edition.

reformer, radical, progressive.

V. improve; be –, become –, get- better; mend, amend.

advance etc. (*progress*) 282; ascend etc. 305; increase etc. 35; fructify, ripen, mature; pick up, come about, rally, take a favorable turn; turn -over a new leaf, – the corner; raise one's head, sow one's wild oats; recover etc. 660.

be -better etc. *adj.*, – improved by; turn to -right, – good, – best- account; profit by, reap the benefit of; make -good use of, – capital out of; place to good account; take advantage of.

render better, improve, emend, make over, better; a-, meliorate; correct.

improve –, refine- upon; rectify; enrich, mellow, elaborate, fatten.

promote, cultivate, advance, forward, enhance; bring -forward, – on; foster etc. 707; invigorate etc. (*strengthen*) 159.

touch –, rub –, brush –, furbish –, bolster –, vamp –, brighten –, warm- up; polish, cook, make the most of, set off to advantage; prune; repair etc. (*restore*) 660; put in order etc. (*arrange*) 60.

review, revise, edit, redact; make -corrections, – improvements etc. *n.*; doctor etc. (*remedy*) 662; purify etc. 652.

relieve, refresh, revive, infuse new blood into, recruit, re-invigorate, renew, revivify, freshen, build -afresh, – anew; uplift, inspire.

re-form, -model, -organize; new model, civilize.

view in a new light, think better of, appeal from Philip drunk to Philip sober.

palliate, mitigate; lessen etc. 36- an evil.

Adj. improving etc. *v.*; progressive, improved etc. *v.*; better, – off, – for; all the better for; better advised.

reform-, emend-atory; reparatory etc. (*restorative*) 660; remedial etc. 662.

corrigible, improvable, curable, accultural.

Adv. on -consideration, – reconsideration, – second thoughts, – better advice; *ad melius inquirendum*; on the -mend, – up grade.

659. Deterioration.—N. deterioration, debasement; want, ebb; recession etc. 287; retrogradation etc. 283; decrease etc. 36.

degenera-cy, -tion, -teness; degradation; depravation, -ement; depravity etc. 945; demoralization, retrogression.

impairment, inquination, injury, damage, loss, detriment, delaceration, outrage, havoc, inroad, ravage, scath; perversion, prostitution, vitiation, discoloration, oxidation, pollution, defedation, poisoning, venenation, leaven, contamination, canker, corruption, adulteration, alloy.

decl-ine, -ension, -ination; decadence, -cy; falling off etc. *v.*; caducity, decreptitude, senility.

decay, dilapidation, ravages of time, wear and tear; cor-, e-rosion; mouldi-, rotten-ness; moth and rust, dry-rot, blight, marasmus, atrophy, collapse; disorganization; *délabrement* etc. (*destruction*) 162.

wreck, mere wreck, honeycomb, *magni nominis umbra.*

V. be –, become- -worse, – deteriorated etc. *adj.*; have seen better days, deteriorate, degenerate, fall off; wane etc. (*decrease*) 36; ebb; retrograde etc. 283; decline, droop; go down etc. (*sink*) 306; go -downhill, – on from bad to worse, – farther and fare worse; jump out of the frying pan into the fire.

run to -seed, – waste; swale, sweal; lapse, be the worse for; break, – down; spring a leak, crack, start; shrivel etc. (*contract*) 195; fade, go off, wither, molder, rot, rankle, decay, go bad; go to – fall into- decay; 'fall into the sear and yellow leaf,' rust, crumble, shake; totter, – to its fall; perish etc. 162; die etc. 360.

[Render less good] deteriorate; weaken etc. 160; put back; taint, infect, contaminate, poison, empoison, envenom, canker, corrupt, exulcerate, pollute, vitiate, inquinate; de-, em-base; denaturalize, leaven; de-flower, -bauch, -file, -prave, -grade; stain etc. (*dirt*) 653; discolor; alloy, adulterate, sophisticate, tamper with, prejudice.

pervert, prostitute, demoralize, brutalize; render vicious etc. 945; compromise.

embitter, ex-, acerbate, aggravate.

injure, impair, labefy, damage, harm, hurt, shend, scathe, spoil, mar, despoil, dilapidate, waste; overrun; ravage; pillage etc. 791.

wound, stab, pierce, maim, lame, surbate, cripple, hough, hamstring, hit between the wind and water, scotch, mangle, mutilate, disfigure, blemish, deface, warp.

blight, rot; cor-, e-rode, eat away; wear -away, – out; gnaw, – at the root of; sap, mine, undermine, shake, sap the foundations of, break up; dis-organize, -mantle, -mast; destroy etc. 162.

damnify etc. (*aggrieve*) 649; do one's worst; knock down; deal a blow to; play -havoc, – sad havoc, – the mischief, – the deuce, – the very devil- -with, – among; decimate.

Adj. unimproved etc. (improve etc. 658); deteriorated etc. *v.*; altered, – for the worse; injured etc. *v.*; sprung; withering, spoiling, etc. *v.*; on the -wane, – decline; tabid; degenerate; worse; the –, all the- worse for; out of -repair, – tune; imperfect etc. 651; the worse for wear; battered; weather-ed, -beaten; stale, *passé*, shaken, dilapidated, frayed, faded, wilted, shabby, second-hand, second-rate, threadbare; worn, – to- -a thread, – a shadow, – the stump, rags; reduced, – to a skeleton, skeletonized; far gone.

decayed etc. *v.*; moth-, worn-eaten; mildewed, rusty, moldy, spotted, seedy, time-worn, moss-grown; discolored; effete, wasted, crumbling, moldering, rotten, cankered, blighted, tainted; depraved etc. (*vicious*) 945; decrep-id, -it; broken down; done, – for, – up; worn out, used up; fit for the -dust-hole, – wastepaper basket; past work etc. (*useless*) 645.

at a low ebb, in a bad way, on one's last legs, washed -up; – out; undermined, deciduous; nodding to its fall etc. (*destruction*) 162; tottering etc. (*dangerous*) 665; past cure etc. (*hopeless*) 859; fatigued etc. 688; backward, retrograde etc. (*retrogressive*) 283; deleterious etc. 649; behind the times.

Adv. on the down grade; beyond hope.

Phr. out of the frying pan into the fire; *aegrescit medendo.*

660. Restoration.—N. restor-ation, -al; re-instatement, -placement, -habilitation, -

establishment, -construction; reporduction etc. 163; re-novation, -newal; reviv-al, -escence; refreshment etc. 689; re-suscitation, -animation, -vivification, -viction; Phoenix; reorganization.

renaissance, renascence, rebirth, second youth, rejuvenation, rejuvenescence, new birth; regenera-tion, -cy, -teness; palingenesis, reconversion, resurgence, resurrection.

redress, retrieval, reclamation, recovery; convalescence; resumption, *résumption*.

recurrence etc. (*repetition*) 104; *réchauffé, rifacimento*.

cure, recure, sanation; healing etc. *v.*; redintegration; rectification, instauration.

repair, reparation, mending; recruiting etc. *v.*; cicatrization; disinfection; tinkering.

reaction; redemption etc. (*deliverance*) 672; restitution etc. 790; relief etc. 834.

mender, repairer, renewer; tinker, cobbler; doctor etc. 662; *vis medicatrix* etc. (*remedy*) 662.

curableness.

V. return to the original state; recover, rally, revive; come -to, – round, – to oneself; pull through, weather the storm, be oneself again; get -well, – round, – the better of, – over, – about; rise from -one's ashes, – the grave; resurge, resurrect; survive etc. (*outlive*) 110; resume, reappear; come to, – life again; live –, rise- again; relive.

heal, skin over, cicatrize; right itself.

restore, put back, place *in statu quo*; re-instate, -place, -seat, -habilitate, -establish, -estate, -install.

re-construct, -build, -organize, -constitute; reconvert; re-new, -novate; recondition; regenerate; rejuvenate.

re-deem, -claim, -cover, -trieve; rescue etc. (*deliver*) 672.

redress, recure; cure, heal, remedy, doctor, physic, medicate; break of; bring round, set on one's legs.

re-suscitate, -vive, -animate, -vivify, -call to life; reproduce etc. 163; warm up; reinvigorate, refresh etc. 689.

redintegrate, make whole; recoup etc. 790; make -good, – all square; rectify; put –, set- -right, – to rights, – straight; set up, correct; put in order etc. (*arrange*) 60; refit, recruit; fill up, – the ranks; reinforce.

repair, mend; put in -repair, – thorough repair, – complete repair; retouch, botch, vamp, tinker, doctor, cobble; do –, patch –, plaster –, vamp-up; darn, fine-draw, heel-piece; stop a gap, stanch, staunch, caulk, calk, careen, splice, bind up wounds.

Adj. restored etc. *v.*; *redivivus*, convalescent; in a fair way; none the worse; rejuvenated, renascent.

restoring etc. *v.*; restorative, recuperative; sana-, repara-tive, -tory; curative, remedial.

restor-, recover-, san-, remedi-, retriev-, cur-able.

Adv. *in statu qho*; as you were.

Phr. *revenons a nos moutons.*

661. Relapse.—N. relapse, lapse; falling back etc. *v.*; retrogradation etc. (*retrogression*) 283; deterioration etc. 659.

[Return to, or recurrence of a bad state] backsliding, recidivation, recrudescence.

V. relapse, lapse; fall –, slide –, sink- back; have a relapse; return; retrograde etc. 283; recidivate; fall off etc. 659- again.

662. Remedy.—N. remedy, help, redress; antidote, anti-toxin, -biotic; anti-, counter-poison, prophylactic, antiseptic, germicide, bactericide, corrective, restorative, stimulant, pick-me-up, tonic; sedative etc. 174; palliative; febrifuge; alterant, -ative; specific; emetic, carminative; narcotic etc. *adj.*; Nepenthe, Mithridate.

cure; radical –, perfect –, certain- cure; sovereign remedy.

physic, medicine, patent medicine, Galenicals, simples, drug, wonder –, miracle – drugs; potion, draught, dose, pill, bolus, lozenge, tablet, tabloid, capsule; electuary; linct-us, -ure; medicament.

nostrum, receipt, recipe, prescription; catholicon, panacea, elixir, *elixir vitae*, philosopher's stone; balm, balsam, cordial, theriac, ptisan.

salve, ointment, cerate, oil, lenitive, lotion, cosmetic; plaster; epithem, embrocation, liniment, cataplasm, sinapism, arquebusade, traumatic, vulnerary, pepastic, poultice, collyrium, depilatory.

compress, pledget; bandage etc. (*support*) 215.

treatment, medical treatment, regimen; diet-ary, -etics; *vis medicatrix*, – *naturae*; *médicine expectante*; seton, blood-letting, bleeding, venesection, phlebotomy, cupping, leeches; operation, surgical operation; tonsillectomy, appendectomy; injection, electrolysis, massage.

pharma-cy, -cology, -ceutics; acology; materia medica, pharmacopoeia, therapeutics, therapy, posology, pathology etc. 655; home-, hetero-, all-, hydr-opathy; cold water –, open air- cure; dietetics; sur-, chirur-gery, osteopathy; healing art, leechcraft, practice of medicine; ortho-paedy, -praxy; dentistry, midwifery, obstetrics, gynecology.

faith -cure, – healing, Christian science; psycho-therapy, -analysis, psychiatry.

hospital, infirmary, clinic; pest-, lazar-house; lazaretto, lazaret; lock hospital; *maison de santé*; *ambulance*; dispensary; *sanatorium*, *sanitarium*, spa, baths, pump-room, well; *hospice*; Red Cross; nursing home; asylum.

doctor, physician, surgeon; medical –, general-practitioner, consultant, specialist; medical attendant; medical student, medico; chemist, apothecary, pharmacopolist, druggist; leech; Aesculapius, Hippocrates, Galen; *accoucheur*, gynecologist, midwife, oculist, aurist, dentist; operator; osteopath, bonesetter; nurse, monthly nurse, sister; dresser; *masseur*, *masseuse*.

V. apply a -remedy etc. *n.*; doctor, dose, physic, nurse, minister to, attend, dress the wounds, plaster, bandage, poultice; heal, cure, work a cure, kill or cure, remedy, stay (disease), snatch from the jaws of death; prevent etc. 706; relieve etc. 834; palliate etc. 658; restore etc. 660; drench with physic; consult, operate, extract, deliver; bleed, cup, let blood, transfuse; electrolyse; psychoanalyse.

Adj. remedial; restorative etc. 660; corrective, palliative, healing; sana-tory, -tive; prophylactic; salutiferous etc. (*salutary*) 656; medic-al, -inal; therapeutic, surgical, chirurgical, orthopedic, epulotic, paregoric, tonic, corroborant, analeptic, balsamic, anodyne, hypnotic, neurotic, narcotic, sedative, lenitive, demulcent, emollient; depuratory; deter-sive, -gent; abstersive, disinfectant, febrifugal, alternative; traumatic, vulnerary.

dietetic, alimentary; nutrit-ious, -ive; peptic; alexi-pharmic, -teric; remedi-, cur-able.

663. Bane. —**N.** bane, curse, thorn in the -side, -flesh, bugbear, *bête noire*; evil etc. 619; hurtfulness etc. (*badness*) 649; painfulness etc. (*cause of pain*) 830; scourge etc. (*punishment*) 975; *damnosa hereditas*; white elephant.

sting, fang, thorn, tang, bramble, briar, nettle.

poison, leaven, virus, venom; intoxicant; arsenic, Prussic acid, antimony, tartar emetic, strychnine, nicotine, cyanide of potassium, corrosive sublimate; curare; hyoscine etc.; poison-, mustard-, tear-gas; carbon di-, mon-oxide; ptomaine poisoning, botulism; miasm, mephitis, malaria, azote, sewer gas; pest, stench etc. 401.

rust, worm, moth, moth and rust, fungus, mildew; dry-rot; canker, -worm; cancer; torpedo; viper etc. (*evil-doer*) 913; demon etc. 980.

hemlock, hellebore, nightshade, *belladonna*, henbane, aconite; Upas tree.

drugs, dope, opium, morphia, morphine, cocaine, heroin, hashish, bhang.

[*Science of poisons*] Toxicology.

Adj. baneful etc. (*bad*) 649; poisonous etc. (*unwholesome*) 657.

664. Safety.—**N.** safety, security, impregnability; invulnera-bility, -bleness etc. *adj.*; danger -past, – over; storm blown over; coast clear; escape etc. 671; means of escape, safety-valve; safeguard, palladium, sheet anchor, rock, tower of strength.

guardian-, ward-, warden-ship; tutelage, custody, safe keeping; preservation etc. 670; protection, auspices.

safe-conduct, escort, convoy; guard, sheild etc. (*defense*) 717; guardian angel, tutelary -god, – deity, – saint; *genius loci.*

protector, guardian; ward-en, -er; preserver, custodian, *duenna chaperon*, third person.

watch-, ban-dog; Cerberus; watch-, patrol-, police-man, constable, peeler, bobby, copper, cop, bull, flat-foot, detective, armed guard; sentinel, sentry, scout etc. (*warning*) 668; garrison; guard-ship.

[Means of safety] refuge etc., anchor etc. 666; precaution etc. (*preparation*) 673; quarantine, *cordon sanitaire*. [Sense of security] confidence etc. 858.

V. be -safe etc. *adj.*; keep one's head above water, tide over, save one's bacon; ride out –, weather- the storm; light upon one's feet; bear a charmed life; escape etc. 671; possess nine lives.

make –, render- -safe etc. *adj.*; protect, watch over; take care of etc. (*care*) 459; preserve etc. 670; cover, screen, shelter, shroud, flank, ward; guard etc. (*defend*) 717; secure etc. (*restrain*) 751; intrench, fence round etc. (*circumscribe*) 229; house, nestle, ensconce; take charge of.

escort, convoy; garrison; watch, mount guard, patrol, scout, spy.

make assurance double sure etc. (*caution*) 864; take up a loose thread; take precautions etc. (*prepare for*) 673; take in a reef; double reef topsails.

seek safety; take –, find- shelter etc. 666; run into port.

Adj. safe, secure, sure; in -safety, – security; have an anchor to windward; on the safe side; under the -shield of, – shade of, – wing of, – shadow of one's wing; under -cover, – lock and key; out of -danger, – the meshes, – harm's way; in -harbor, – port; on sure ground, at anchor, high and dry, above water, on *terra firma*; unthreatened, -molested; protected etc. *v.*; cavendo tutus; panoplied etc. (*defended*) 717.

snug, sea-, air-worthy; weather-, water-, fire-, bomb-proof.

defensible, tenable, proof against, invulnerable; un-assailable, -attackable; im-pregnable, -perdible; founded on a rock; inexpugnable.

safe and sound etc. (*preserved*) 670; harmless; scathless etc. (*perfect*) 650; unhazarded; not - dangerous etc. 665.

protecting etc. *v.*; guardian, tutelary; perservative etc. 670; trustworthy etc. 939.

Adv. *ex abundanti cautelâ*; with impunity.

Phr. all's well; all clear; *salva res est*; *suave mari magno*; safety first.

665. Danger.—**N.** danger, peril, insecurity, jeopardy, risk, hazard, venture, precariousness, slipperiness; instability etc. 149; defenselessness etc. *adj.*

exposure etc. (*liability*) 177; vulnerability; vulnerable point, heel of Achilles; forlorn hope etc. (*hopelessness*) 859.

[Dangerous course] leap in the dark etc. (*rashness*) 863; road to ruin, *facilis descensus Averni*, hair-breadth escape.

cause for alarm; source of danger etc. 667. [Approach of danger] rock –, breakers- ahead; storm brewing; clouds -in the horizon, – gathering; warning etc. 668; alarm etc. 669. [Sense of danger] apprehension etc. 860.

V. be -in danger etc. *adj.*; be exposed to –, run into –, incur –, encounter- -danger etc. *n.*; run a risk; lay oneself open to etc. (*liability*) 177; lean on –, trust to- a broken reed; feel the ground sliding from under one, have to run for it; have the -chances, – odds- against one.

hang by a thread, totter; tremble on the -verge, – brink; sleep – stand -on a volcano; sit on a barrel of gunpowder, live in a glass house.

bring –, place –, put- in -danger etc. *n.*; endanger, expose to danger, imperil; jeopard, -ize, compromise; sail too near the wind etc. (*rash*) 863; put one's head in the lion's mouth.

adventure, risk, hazard, venture, stake, set at hazard; run the gauntlet etc. (*dare*) 861; engage in a forlorn hope.

threaten etc. 909- danger; run one hard; lay a trap for etc. (*deceive*) 545.

Adj. in -danger etc. *n.*; endangered etc. *v.*; fraught with danger; danger-, hazard-, peril-, parl-, pericul-ous; unsafe, unprotected etc. (safe, protect etc. 664); insecure, untrustworthy, unreliable; built upon sand, on a sandy basis.

defence-, fence-, guard-, harbor-less; unshielded; vulnerable, expugnable, unsheltered, exposed; open to etc. (*liable*) 177.

aux abois, at bay; on -the wrong side of the wall, – a lee shore, – the rocks.

at stake, in question; precarious, aleatory, critical, ticklish; slip-pery, -py; hanging by a thread etc. *v.*; with a halter round one's neck; between -the hammer and the anvil, – Scylla and Charybdis, – two fires; on the -edge, – brink, – verge of a- -precipice, – volcano; in the lion's den, on slippery ground, under fire; not out of the wood.

un-warned, -admonished, -advised; unprepared etc. 674; off one's guard etc. (*inexpectant*) 508.

tottering; un-stable, -steady; shaky, top-heavy, tumble-down, ramshackle, crumbling, waterlogged; help-, guide-less; in a bad way; reduced to –, at- the last extremity; trembling in the balance; nodding to its fall etc. (*destruction*) 162.

threatening etc. 909; ominous, ill-omened; alarming etc. (*fear*) 860; explosive; poisonous etc. 657.

adventurous etc. (*rash*) 863, (*bold*) 861.

Int. stop! look out! beware! take care!

Phr. *incidit in Scyllam qui vult vitare Charybdim; nam tua res agitur paries dum proximus ardet.*

666. Refuge. [Means of safety.]—**N.** refuge, sanctuary, retreat, fastness; stronghold, keep, last resort; ward; prison etc. 752; asylum, ark, home, almshouse, refuge for the destitute; hiding-place etc. (*ambush*) 530; *sanctum sanctorum* etc. (*privacy*) 893.

roadstead, anchorage; breakwater, mole, port, haven; harbor, – of refuge; sea-port; pier, jetty, embankment, quay.

covert, shelter, abri, screen, lee-wall, wing, shield, umbrella; splash-, dash-board, mudguard.

wall etc. (*inclosure*) 232; fort etc. (*defence*) 717.

anchor, kedge; grap-nel, -pling iron; sheet-, mushroom-anchor, main-stay; support etc. 215; check etc. 706; ballast.

jury-mast; vent-peg; safety -valve, – lamp; lightning conductor.

means of escape etc. (*escape*) 671; life-boat, swimming belt, cork jacket; life preserver, breeches buoy; parachute, plank, stepping-stone.

safeguard etc. (*protection*) 664.

V. seek –, take –, find- refuge etc. *n.*; seek –, find- safety etc. 664; throw oneself into the arms of; claim sanctuary; take to the -hills, – woods; make port, reach shelter, bar –, bolt –, lock -the door, – gete; let the portcullis down; raise the drawbridge.

667. Pitfall. [Source of danger.]—**N.** rocks, reefs, coral reef, sunken rocks, snags; sands, quicksands, Goodwin sands, sandy foundation; slippery ground; breakers, shoals, shallows, bank, shelf, flat, lee shore, iron-bound coast; rock –, breakers- ahead; derelict.

precipice; abyss, chasm, pit, crevasse; maelstrom, whirlpool, eddy, vortex, rapids, current, bore, tidal wave; storm, squall, hurricane, whirlwind; volcano; ambush etc. 530; pitfall, trap-door; trap etc. (*snare*) 545.

sword of Damocles; wolf at the door, snake in the grass, viper in one's bosom, death in the pot; latency etc. 526.

ugly customer, dangerous person, *le chat qui dort*; firebrand, hornet's nest.

Phr. *latet anguis in herbâ*; *proximus ardet Ucalegon.*

668. Warning.—N. warning, caution, *caveat*; notice etc. (*information*) 527; premoni-tion, -shment; prediction etc. 511; contraindication; symptom; lesson, dehortation; admonition, monition; alarm etc. 669.

handwriting on the wall, *tekel upharsin*, yellow flag; fog-signal, -horn; siren; monitor, warning voice, Cassandra, signs of the times, Mother Carey's chickens, stormy petrel, bird of ill omen, gathering clouds, clouds in the horizon, cloud no bigger than a man's hand, death-watch.

watch-tower, beacon, signal-post; light-house etc. (*indication of locality*) 550.

sent-inel, -ry; watch, -man; watch and ward; watch-, ban-, house-dog; patrol, vedette, picket, bivouac, scout, spy, spial; advanced –, rear-guard, lookout, flagman.,

cautiousness etc. 864.

V. warn, caution; fore-, pre-warn; ad-, premonish; give -notice, – warning; menace etc. (*threaten*) 909; put on one's guard; sound the alarm etc. 669; croak.

beware, ware; take -warning, – heed at one's peril; watch out for; keep watch and ward etc. (*care*) 459.

Adj. warning etc. *v.*; premonitory, monitory, cautionary; admonitory, -tive; ominous, threatening, lowering, minatory, symptomatic.

warned etc. *v.*; on one's guard etc. (*careful*) 459; (*cautious*) 864.

Adv. *in terrorem* etc. (*threat*) 909.

Int. beware! ware! take care! mind –, take care-what you are about; mind! look out!

Phr. *ne reveillez pas le chat qui dort*; *foenum habet in cornu.*

669. Alarm. [Indication of danger.]—**N.** alarm; alarum, larum, alarm bell, tocsin, *alerte*, beat of drum, sound of trumpet, note of alarm, hue and cry, signal of distress, S.O.S.; blue-lights; war-cry, -whoop; warning etc. 668; fog-signal, -horn; siren; yellow flag; danger signal; red -light, – flag; fire -bell, – alarm; burglar alarm, police whistle, watchman's rattle.

false alarm, cry of wolf; bug-bear, -aboo.

V. give –, raise –, sound –, beat- the *or* an -alarm etc. *n.*; alarm; warn etc. 668; ring the tocsin; *battre la générale*; cry wolf.

Adj. alarming etc. *v.*

Int. *sauve qui peut! qui vive?* who goes there?

670. Preservation.—N. preservation; safe keeping; conservation etc. (*storage*) 636; maintenance, upkeep, support, sustentation, conservatism; *vis conservatrix*; salvation etc. (*deliverance*) 672; drying etc. *v.*

[Means of preservation] prophylaxis; preserv-er, -ative; canned goods; cold pack; hygi-astics, -antics; cover, durgget; *cordon sanitaire*.

[Superstitious remedies] charm etc. 993.

V. preserve, maintain, keep, sustain, support; keep -up, – alive; not willingly let die; shore –, bank- up; nurse; save, rescue; be –, make- safe etc. 664; take care of etc. (*care*) 459; guard etc. (*defend*) 717.

stare super antiquas vias; hold one's own; hold –, stand- -one's ground etc. (*resist*) 719.

embalm, dry, cure, smoke, salt, pickle, season, kyanize, bottle, pot, tin, can; husband etc. (*store*) 636.

Adj. preserving etc. *v.*; conservative; prophylatic; preserva-tory, -tive; hygienic.

preserved etc. *v.*; un-impaired, -broken, -injured, -hurt, -singed, -marred; safe, – and sound; intact, with a whole skin, without a scratch.

Phr. *nolumus leges Angliae mutari*.

671. Escape.—N. escape, scape; avolation, elopment, flight, get-away; evasion etc. (*avoidance*) 623; retreat; narrow –, hairbreadth- escape; close –, near- shave; come off, impunity.

[Means of escape] loophole etc. (*opening*) 260; path etc. 627; secret -door, – passage; refuge etc. 666; vent, – peg; safety-valve; drawbridge, fire-escape.

reprieve etc. (*deliverance*) 672; liberation etc. 750.

refugee etc. (*fugitive*) 623.

V. escape, scape; make –, effect –, make good- one's escape, make a get-away; get -off, – clear off, – well out of; *échapper belle*, save one's bacon; weather the storm etc. (*safe*) 664; escape scot-free.

elude etc., make off etc. (*avoid*) 623; march off etc. (*go away*) 293; give one the slip; slip through the -hands, – fingers; slip the collar, wriggle out of; break -loose, – from prison; break –, slip –, get- away; find -vent, – a hole to creep out of.

Adj. escap-ing, -ed etc. *v.*; stolen away, fled.

Phr. the bird has flown.

672. Deliverance.—N. deliverance, extrication, rescue; repriev-e, -al; respite; ransom; liberation etc. 750; truce, armistice; redemption, salvation; riddance; gaol delivery; exemption, day of grace; redeemableness.

V. deliver, extricate, rescue, save, redeem, ransom, free, liberate, release, set free, redeem, emancipate; bring -off, – through; *tirer d'affaire*, get the wheel out of the rut; snatch from the jaws of death, come to the rescue; rid; retrieve etc. (*restore*) 660; be –, get- rid of.

Adj. saved etc. *v.*; extric-, redeem-, rescu-able.

Phr. to the rescue!

673. Preparation.—N. preparation; providing etc. *v.*; provi-sion, -dence; anticipation etc. (*foresight*) 510; precaution, -concertation, disposition; forecast etc. (*plan*) 626; rehearsal, not of preparation.

[Putting in order] arrangement etc. 60; clearance; adjustment etc. 23; tuning; equipment, outfit, accoutrement, armament, array.

ripening etc. *v.*; maturation, evolution; elaboration, concoction, digestion; gestation, hatching, incubation, sitting.

groundwork, datum, first stone, cradle, stepping-stone; foundation, scaffold etc. (*support*) 215; scaffolding, *échafaudage*.

[Preparation -of men] training etc. (*education*) 537; inurement etc. (*habit*) 613; novitiate; [– of food] cook-ing, -ery; brewing, culinary art; [– of the soil] till-, plough-, sow-ing; semination, cultivation.

[State of being prepared] prepared-, readi-, ripe-, mellow-ness; maturity; *un impromptu fait à loisir*.

[Preparer] preparer, teacher, coach, trainer, pioneer; *avant-courrier*, *-coureur*; sappers and miners, paver, navvy; packer, stevedore; warmingpan; precursor etc. 64.

V. prepare; get –, make- ready; make preparations, settle preliminaries, get up, sound the note of preparation; address oneself to.

set –, put- in order etc. (*arrange*) 60; forecast etc. (*plan*) 626; prepare –, plough –, dress- the ground; till –, cultivate- the soil; predispose, sow the seed, lay a train, dig a mine; lay –, fix- the -foundations, – basis, -groundwork; dig the foundations, erect the scaffolding; lay the first stone etc. (*begin*) 66.

rough-hew; cut out work; block –, hammer-out; lick into shape etc. (*form*) 240.

elaborate, mature, ripen, mellow, season, bring to maturity; nurture etc.

(*aid*) 707; hatch, cook, brew; temper; anneal, smelt; dry, cure etc. 670.

equip, arm, man; fit-out, -up; furnish, rig, dress, garnish, betrim, accouter, array, fettle, fledge; dress –, furbish –, brush –, vamp- up; refurbish; sharpen one's tools, trim one's foils, set, prime, attune; whet the -knife, – sword; wind –, screw- up; adjust etc. (*fit*) 27; put in- trim, – train, – gear, – working order, – tune, – a groove for, – harness; pack, stow away, store.

train etc. (*teach*) 537; inure etc. (*habituate*) 613; breed; prepare etc.- for; rehearse; make provision for; take -steps, – measures, – precautions; provide, – against; beat up for recruits; open the door to etc. (*facilitate*) 705.

set one's house in order, make all snug; clear -decks, – for action; close one's ranks; shuffle the cards.

prepare oneself; serve an apprenticeship etc. (*learn*) 539; lay oneself out for, get into harness, gird up one's loins, buckle on one's armor, *reculer pour mieux sauter*, prime and load, shoulder arms, get the steam up, put the horses to.

guard –, make sure- against; forearm, make sure, prepare for the evil day, have a rod in pickle, provide against a rainy day, feather one's nest; lay in provisions etc. 637; make investments; keep on foot.

be -prepared, – ready etc. *adj.*; hold oneself in readiness, watch and pray, keep one's powder dry; lie in wait for etc. (*expect*) 507; anticipate etc. (*foresee*) 510; *principiis obstare*; *veniente occurrere morbo*.

Adj. preparing etc. *v.*; in -preparation, – course

of preparation, – agitation, – embryo, – hand, – train; afoot, afloat; on -foot, – the stocks, – the anvil; under consideration etc. (*plan*) 626; brewing, hatching, forthcoming, brooding; in -store for, – reserve.

precautionary, provident; prepara-tive, -tory; provisional, inchoate, under revision; preliminary etc. (*precedent*) 62.

prepared etc. *v.*; in readiness; ready, – to one's hand, – made, cut and dried; ready for use, reach me down; made to one's hand, handy, on the table, made to order; in gear; in working -order, – gear; snug; in practice.

ripe, mature, mellow; practiced etc. (*skillet*) 698; labored, elaborate, highly-wrought, smelling of the lamp, worked up.

in -full feather, – best bib and tucker; in –, at-harness; in – the saddle, – arms, – battle array, – war paint; up in arms; armed -at all points, – to the teeth, – *cap-à-pie*; sword in hand; booted and spurred.

in utrumque –, semper- paratus; on the alert etc. (*vigilant*) 459; at one's post.

Adv. in -preparation, – anticipation of; afoot, astir, abroad; abroach.

674. Non-preparation.—N. non-, absence of –, want of- preparation; unpreparedness; inculture, inconcoction, improvidence.

immaturity, crudity; rawness etc. *adj.*; abortion; disqualification.

[Absence of art] nature, state of nature; virgin soil, unweeded garden; rough diamond, neglect etc. 460.

rough copy etc. (*plan*) 626; germ etc. 153; raw material etc. 635.

improvisation etc. (*impulse*) 612.

V. be -unprepared etc. *adj.*; want –, lack- preparation; lie fallow; *s'embarquer sans biscuits*; live from hand to mouth.

[Render unprepared] dismantle etc. (*render useless*) 645; undress etc. 226.

extemporize, improvise.

surprise, pay a surprise visit, take by surprise, drop in upon, take unawares; take pot-luck.

Adv. un-prepared etc. prepare etc. 673] without -preparation etc. 673; incomplete etc. 53; rudimental, embryonic, abortive; immature, unripe, raw, green, crude; coarse; rough, -cast, -hewn; in the rough; un-hewn, -formed, -fashioned, -wrought, -labored, -blown, -cooked, -boiled, -concocted, -cút, -polished.

callow, un-hatched, -fledged, -nurtured, -licked, -taught, -educated, -cultivated, -trained, -tutored, -drilled, -exercised; precocious, premature; un-, indigested; un-mellowed, -seasoned, -leavened.

fallow; un-sown, -tilled; natural, in a state of nature; undressed; in dishabille, *en déshabille, en négligé.*

un-, dis-qualified; unfitted; ill-digested; unbegun, -ready, -arranged, -organized, -furnished, -provided, -equipped, -trimmed; out of -gear, – order; dismantled etc. *v.*

shiftless, improvident, unthrifty, thoughtless, unguarded; happy-go-lucky; caught napping etc. (*inexpectant*) 508; unpremeditated etc. 612.

Adv. extempore etc. 612.

675. Essay.—N. essay, trial, endeavor, aim, attempt; venture, adventure, speculation, *coup d'essai, début*; probation etc. (*experiment*) 463.

V. try, essay; experiment etc. 463; endeavor, strive; tempt, tackle, take on, attempt, make an attempt; venture, adventure, speculate, take one's chance, tempt fortune; try one's -fortune, – luck, – hand; use one's endeavor; feel –, grope –, pick- one's way.

try hard, push, make a bold push, use one's best endeavor; do one's best etc. (*exertion*) 686.

Adj. essaying etc. *v.*; experimental etc. 463; tentative, empirical, probationary

Adv. experimentally etc. *adj.*; on trial, at a venture; by rule of thumb.

if one may be so bold.

676. Undertaking.—N. undertaking, compact etc. 769; engagement etc. (*promise*) 768; enter-, em-prise; venture etc. 675; pilgrimage; matter in hand etc. (*business*) 625; move; first move etc. (*beginning*) 66.

V. undertake; engage –, embark- in; launch –, plunge- into; volunteer; apprentice oneself to; engage etc. (*promise*) 768; contract etc. 769; take upon -oneself, – one's shoulders; devote oneself to etc. (*determination*) 604.

take -up, – in hand; tackle; set –, go- about; set –, fall- -to, – to work; launch forth; set up shop; put in -hand, – execution; set forward; break the neck of a business, be in for; put one's hand to; betake oneself to, turn one's hand to, go to do; begin etc. 66; broach, institute, etc. (*originate*) 153; put –, lay- one's -hand to the plough, – shoulder to the wheel.

have in hand etc. (*business*) 625; have many irons in the fire etc. (*activity*) 682.

Adj. undertaking etc. *v.*; on the anvil etc. 625; adventurous, venturesome.

Int. here goes!

677. Use.—N. use; employ, -ment; exer-cise, -citation; appli-cation, -ance; adhibition, disposal; consumption; agency etc. (*physical*) 170; usufruct; usefulness etc. 644; recourse, resort, avail, pragmatism.

[Conversion to use] utilization, service, wear.

[Way of using] usage.

V. use, make use of, employ, put to use; apply, put in -action, – operation, – practice; set -in motion, – to work.

ply, work, wield, handle, manipulate; play, – off; exert, exercise, practice, avail oneself of, profit by; resort –, have recourse –, recur –, take –, betake oneself- to; take -up with, – advantage of; lay one's hands on, try.

render useful etc. 644; mold; turn to -account, – use; convert to use, utilize, administer; work up; call –, bring- into play; put into requisition; call –, draw- forth; press –, enlist- into the service; bring to bear upon, devote, dedicate, consecrate, apply, adhibit, dispose of; make a -handle, – cat's paw- of.

fall beak upon, make a shift with; make the -most, – best- of.

use –, swallow- up; consume, absorb, expend; tax, task, wear, put to task.

Adj. in use; used etc. *v.*; well-worn, -trodden. useful etc. 644; subservient etc. (*instrumental*) 631; utilitarian; pragmatical.

678. Disuse.—N. forbearance, abstinence; disuse; relinquishment etc. 782; desuetude etc. (*want of habit*) 614.

V. not use; do without, dispense with, let alone, not touch, forbear, abstain, spare, waive, neglect; keep back, reserve.

lay -up, – by, – on the shelf, – up in a napkin; shelve; set –, put –, lay- aside; disuse, leave off, have done with; supersede; discard etc. (*eject*) 297; dismiss, give warning.

throw aside etc. (*relinquish*) 782; make away with etc. (*destroy*) 162; cast –, heave –, throw- overboard; cast to the -dogs, – winds; dismantle etc. (*render useless*) 645.

lie –, remain- unemployed etc. *adj.*

Adj. not used etc. *v.*; un-employed, -applied, -disposed of, -spent, -exercised, -touched, -trodden, -essayed, -gathered, -culled; uncalled for, not required.

disused etc. *v.*; done with; run down, used up, cast off.

679. Misuse.—N. mis-use, -usage, -employment, -application, -appropriation.

abuse, profanation, prostitution, desecration; waste etc. 638.

V. mis-use, -employ, -apply, -appropriate.

desecrate, abuse, profane, prostitute; waste etc. 638; over-task, -tax, -work; squander etc. 818.

cut a whetstone with a razor, employ a steam-engine to crack a nut; catch at a straw.

Adj. misused etc. *v.*

680. Action.—N. action, performance; doing etc. *v.*; perpetration; exercise, -citation; movement, operation, evolution, work; labor etc. (*exertion*) 686; *praxis*, execution; procedure etc. (*conduct*) 692; handicraft; business etc. 625; agency etc. (*power at work*) 170.

deed, act, overt act, stitch, touch, gest; transaction, job, doings, dealings, proceeding, measure, step, maneuver, bout, passage, move, stroke, blow; *coup*, – *de main*, – *d'état*; *tour de force* etc. (*display*) 882; feat, exploit, stunt; achievement etc. (*completion*) 729; handiwork, workmanship, craftsmanship; manufacture; stroke of policy etc. (*plan*) 626.

actor etc. (*doer*) 690.

V. do, perform, execute; achieve etc. (*complete*) 729; transact, enact; commit, perpetrate, inflict; exercise, prosecute, carry on, work, practice, play.

employ oneself, ply one's task; officiate, have in hand etc. (*business*) 625; labor etc. 686; be at work; pursue a course; shape one's course etc. (*conduct*) 692.

act, operate; take -action, – steps; strike a blow, lift a finger, stretch forth one's hand; take in hand etc. (*undertake*) 676; put oneself in motion; put in practice; carry into execution etc. (*complete*) 729; act upon.

be -an actor etc. 690; take –, act –, play –, perform- a part in; participate in; have a -hand in, – finger in the pie; have to do with; be a -party to, – participator in; bear –, lend- a hand; pull an oar, run in a race; mix oneself up with etc. (*meddle*) 682.

be in action; come into operation etc. (*power at work*) 170.

Adj. doing etc. *v.*; acting; in action; in harness; on duty; at work; in operation etc. 170; up to one's ears in work, in the midst of things.

Adv. in the -act, – midst of, – thick of; red-handed, *in flagrante delicto*; while one's hand is in.

681. Inaction.—N. inaction, passiveness, abstinence from action; non-interference; Fabian –, conservative- policy; neglect etc. 460; stagnation, vegetation; loafing.

inactivity etc. 683; rest etc. (*repose*) 687; quiescence etc. 265; want of –, in- occupation; unemployment; idle hours, time hanging on one's hands, *dolce far niente*; sinecure.

V. not -do, – act, – attempt; be -inactive etc. 683; abstain from doing, do nothing, hold, spare; not -stir, – move, – lift- a -finger, – foot, – peg; fold one's -arms, – hands; leave –, let- alone; let -be, – pass, – things take their course, – it have its way, – well alone; *quieta non movere*; *stare super antiquas vias*; rest and be thankful, live and let live; lie –, rest- upon one's oars; *laisser -aller*, – *faire*; stand aloof; refrain etc. (*avoid*) 623; keep oneself from doing; remit –, relax- one's efforts; desist etc. (*relinquish*) 624; stop etc. (*cease*) 142; pause etc. (*be quiet*) 265.

wait, lie in wait, bide one's time, take time, tide it over.

cool –, kick- one's heels; loaf, while away the -time, – tedious hours; pass –, fill –, beguile- the time; talk against time; waste time etc. (*inactive*) 683.

lie -by, – on the shelf, – in ordinary, – idle, – to, – fallow; keep quiet, slug; have nothing to do, whistle for want of thought; twiddle one's thumbs.

undo, do away with; take -down, – to pieces; destroy etc. 162.

Adj. not doing etc. *v.*; not done etc. *v.*; undone; passive; un-occupied, -employed; out of -employ, – work, – a job; fallow; *désoeuvré*.

Adv. *re infectâ*, at a stand, *les bras croisés*, with folded arms; with the hands -in the pockets, – behind one's back; *pour passer le temps*.

Int. so let it be! stop! etc. 142; hands off!

Phr. nothing doing; *cunctando restituit rem*.

682. Activity.—N. activity; briskness, liveliness etc. *adj.*; animation, life, vivacity, spirit, verve, dash, energy, go.

nimbleness, agility; smartness, quickness etc. *adj.*; velocity etc. 274; alacrity, promptitude; des-, dis-patch; expedition; haste etc. 684; punctuality etc. (*early*) 132.

eagerness, zeal, ardor, *perfervidum ingenium*, *empressement*, earnestness, intentness; *abandon*; vigor etc. (*physical energy*) 171; devotion etc. (*resolution*) 604; exertion etc. 686.

industry, assiduity; assiduousness etc. *adj.*; sedulity; laboriousness; drudgery etc. (*labor*) 686; painstaking, diligence; perseverance etc. 604*a*; indefatigation; habits of business.

vigilance etc. 459; wakefulness; sleep-, restlessness; *pervigilium, insomnia*; racketing.

movement, bustle, hustle, stir, fuss, ado, bother, pottering; fidget, -iness; flurry etc. (*haste*) 684.

officiousness; dabbling, meddling; inter-ference, -position, -meddling, butting in, intrusiveness; tampering with, intrigue.

press of business, no sinecure, plenty to do, many irons in the fire, great doings, busy hum of men, battle of life, thick of -things, – the action; the madding corwd.

housewife, busy bee; new brooms; sharp fellow, blade; hustler, devotee, enthusiast, fan, zealot, fanatic; meddler, intermeddler, intriguer, busybody, kibitzer, pickthank.

V. be -active etc. *adj.*; busy oneself in; stir, -about, – one's stumps; bestir –, rouse- oneself; speed, hasten, peg away, lay about one, bustle, fuss; raise –, kick up- a dust; push; make a -push, – fuss, – stir; go ahead, push forward; flight –, elbow- one's way; make progress etc. 282; toil etc. (*labor*) 686; drudge, plod, persist etc. (*persevere*) 604*a*; keep -up the ball, – the pot boiling.

look sharp; have all one's eyes about one etc. (*vigilance*) 459; rise, arouse oneself, get up early, hustle, push; be about, keep moving, steal a march, kill two birds with one stone; seize the opportunity etc. 134; lose no time, not lose a moment, make the most of one's time, not suffer the grass to grow under one's feet, improve the shining hour, make short work of; dash off; make haste etc. 684; do one's best, take pains etc. (*exert oneself*) 686; do –, work- wonders.

have -many irons in the fire, – one's hands full, – much on one's hands; have other -things to do, – fish to fry; be busy; not have a moment -to spare, – that one can call one's own.

have one's fling, run the round of; go all lengths, stick at nothing, run riot.

outdo; over-do, -act, -lay, -shoot the mark; make a toil of a pleasure.

have a hand in etc. (*act in*) 680; take an active part, put in one's oar, have a finger in the pie, mix oneself up with, trouble one's head about, intrigue; agitate.

tamper with, meddle, moil; inter-meddle, -fere, -pose; obtrude; poke –, thrust- one's nose in, butt in.

Adj. active; brisk, – as a lark, – as a bee; lively, animated, vivacious; alive, – and kicking; frisky, spirited, stirring.

nimble, – as a squirrel; agile; light-, nimble-footed; featly, tripping.

quick, prompt, yare, instant, ready, alert, spry, sharp, smart, slick, go-ahead; fast etc. (*swift*) 274; quick as a lamplighter, expeditious; awake, broad awake; wide awake etc. (*intelligent*) 498.

forward, eager, ardent, strenuous, zealous, enterprising, pushing, in earnest; resolute etc. 604.

industrious, assiduous, diligent, sedulous, notable, painstaking; intent etc. (*attention*) 457; indefatigable etc. (*persevering*) 604*a*; unwearied; unsleeping, sleepless, never tired; plodding, hard-working etc. 686; business-like, workaday.

bustling; restless, – as a hyena; fussy, fidgety, pottering; busy, – as a hen with one chicken.

working, laboring, at work, on duty, in harness; up in arms; on one's legs, at call; up and -doing, – stirring.

busy, occupied; hard at -work, – it; up to one's ears in, full of business, busy as a bee.

meddling etc. *v.*; meddlesome, pushing, officious, overofficious, *intrigant*.

astir, stirring; a-going, -foot; on foot; in full swing; eventful; on the alert etc. (*vigilant*) 459.

Adv. actively etc. *adj.*; with -life and spirit, – might and main etc. 686, – haste etc. 684, – wings; full tilt, *in mediis rebus*.

Int. be –, look- -alive, – sharp! move –, push-on! keep moving! go ahead! stir your stumps! *age quod agis!*

Phr. *carpe diem* etc. (*opportunity*) 134; *nulla dies sine lineâ*; *nec mora nec requies*; no sooner said than done etc. (*early*) 132; catch a weasel asleep.

683. Inactivity.—N. inactivity; inaction etc. 681; inertness etc. 172; obstinacy etc. 606.

lull etc. (*cessation*) 142; quiescence etc. 265; rust, -iness.

idle-, remiss-ness etc. *adj.*; sloth, indolence, indiligence; otiosity, dawdling etc. *v.*

dullness etc. *adj.*; languor; segni-ty, -tude; lentor; sluggishness etc. (*slowness*) 275; procrastination etc. (*delay*) 133; torp-or, -idity, -escence; stupor etc. (*insensibility*) 823; somnolence; drowsiness etc. *adj.*; nodding etc. *v.*; oscitation, -ancy; pandiculation, hypnotism, lethargy; heaviness, heavy eye-lids, sand in the eyes.

sleep, slumber; sound –, heavy –, balmy- sleep; Morpheus, dreamland; coma, trance, catalepsy, hypnosis, *ecstasis*, dream, hibernation, nap, doze, snooze, *siesta*, wink of sleep, forty winks, snore; Hypnology.

dull work; pottering; relaxation etc. (*loosening*) 47; Castle of Indolence.

[Cause of inactivity] lullaby, *berceuse*; anesthetic, sedative etc. 174; torpedo.

idler, drone, droil, dawdle, mopus; do-little, *fainéant*, dummy, sleeping partner; afternoon farmer; truant etc. (*runaway*) 623; lounger, *lazzarone*, floater, loafer, tramp, beggar, cadger; lubber, -bard; slow-coach etc. (*slow*) 275; opium –, lotus- eater; slug; lag-, slug-gard, lie-abed; slumberer, dormouse, marmot; waiter on Providence, *fruges consumere natus*.

V. be -inactive etc. *adj.*; do nothing etc. 681; move slowly etc. 275; let the grass grow under one's feet; take one's time, dawdle, poke, drawl, droil, lag, hang back, slouch; loll, -op; lounge, loaf, loiter; go to sleep over; sleep at one's post; *ne battre que d'une aile*.

take -it easy, – things as they come; lead an easy life, vegetate, swim with the stream, eat the bread of idleness; loll in the lap of -luxury, – indolence; waste –, consume –, kill –, lose time; burn daylight, waste the precious hours.

idle –, trifle –, fritter –, fool- away time; spend –, take- time in; ped-, pid-dle; potter, putter, dabble, faddle, fribble, fiddle-faddle; dally, dilly-dally.

sleep, slumber, be asleep; hibernate; oversleep; sleep like a -top, – log, – dormouse; sleep -soundly, – heavily; doze, drowze, snooze, nap; take a -nap etc. *n.*; dream; snore; settle –, go –, go off- to sleep; drop off; fall –, drop- asleep; close –, seal up- -the -eyes, – eyelids; weigh down the eyelids; get sleepy, nod, yawn; go to bed, turn in.

languish, expend itself, flag, hang fire; relax.

render -idle etc. *adj.*; sluggardize; mitigate etc. 174.

Adj. inactive; motionless etc. 265; unoccupied etc. (*doing nothing*) 681.

indolent, lazy, slothful, idle, otiose, lusk, remiss, slack, inert, torpid, sluggish, languid, supine, heavy, dull, leaden, lumpish; exanimate, soulless; listless; dron-y, -ish; lazy as Ludlam's dog.

dilatory, laggard; lagging etc. *v.*; slow etc. 275; rusty, flagging; lackadaisical, maudlin, fiddle-faddle; pottering etc. *v.*; shilly-shally etc. (*irresolute*) 605.

sleeping etc. *v.*; alseep; fast –, dead –, sound-alseep; in a sound sleep; sound as a top, dormant, comatose; in the -arms, – lap- of Morpheus.

sleep-y, -ful; dozy, drowsy, somnolent, torpescent; lethargic, -al; heavy, – with sleep; napping; somni-fic, -ferous; sopor-ous, -ific, -iferous; hypnotic; balmy, dreamy; un-, una-wakened.

sedative etc. 174.

Adv. inactively etc. *adj.*; at leisure etc. 685.

Phr. the eyes begin to draw straws.

684. Haste.—N. haste, urgency; des-, dis-patch; acceleration, spurt, spirt, forced march, rush, dash; velocity etc. 274; precipit-ancy, -ation, -ousness etc. *adj.*; impetuosity; *brusquerie*; hurry, scurry, scuttle, drive, scramble, push, hustle, bustle, fuss, fidget, flurry, flutter, splutter.

V. haste, hasten; make -haste, – a dash etc. *n.*; hurry –, dash –, whip –, push –, press- -on, – forward; hurry, skurry, scuttle along, bundle on, dart to and fro, bustle, flutter, scramble; plunge, – headlong; run, race, speed; dash off; rush etc. (*violence*) 173.

bestir oneself etc. (*be active*) 682; lose -no time, – not a moment, – not an instant; make short work of; make the best of one's -time, – way.

be -precipitate etc. *adj.*; jump at; be in -haste, – a hurry etc. *n.*; have -no time, – not a moment- -to lose, – to spare; work -under pressure, – against time.

quicken etc. 274; accelerate, expedite, put on, precipitate, urge, whip, spur, flog, goad.

Adj. hasty, hurried, *brusque*; scrambling, cursory, precipitate, headlong, furious, boisterous, impetuous, hot-headed; feverish, fussy; pushing.

in -haste, – a hurry etc. *n.*; in -hot, – all- haste; breathless, pressed for time, hard pressed, urgent.

Adv. with -haste, – all haste, – breathless speed; in haste etc. *adj.*; apace etc. (*swiftly*) 274; amain; all at once etc. (*instantaneously*) 113; at short notice etc., immediately etc. (*early*) 132; posthaste; by -express, – telegraph, – wire, – wireless, – air mail.

hastily, precipitately etc. *adj.*; helter-skelter, hurry-skurry, holusbolus; slap-dash, -bang; full-tilt, -drive; heels over head, head and shoulders, headlong, *à corps perdu*.

by -fits and starts, – spurts; hop, skip and jump.

Phr. *sauve qui peut*, devil take the hindmost, no time to be lost; no sooner said than done etc. (*early*) 132; a word and a blow.

Int. hurry up! look alive! get a move on! buck up! double march! rush! urgent!

685. Leisure.—N. leisure; spare -time, – hours, – moments; vacant hour; time, – to spare, – on one's hands; holiday etc. (*rest*) 687; *otium cum dignitate*, ease.

V. have -leisure etc. *n.*; take one's -time, – leisure, – ease; repose etc. 687; move slowly etc. 275; while away the time etc. (*inaction*) 681; be -master of one's time, – an idle man; *desipere in loco.*

Adj. leisurely; slow etc. 275; deliberate, quiet, calm, undisturbed; at -leisure, – one's ease, – a loose end.

Phr. time hanging heavy on one's hands.

686. Exertion.—N. exertion, effort, strain, tug, pull, stress, force, pressure, throw, stretch, struggle, spell, spurt, spirt; stroke –, stitch- of work.

'a stong pull, a long pull and a pull all together;' dead lift; heft; gymnastics, sports; exer-cise, -citation; wear and tear; ado; toil and trouble; uphill –, hard –, warm- work; harvest time.

labor, work, toil, travail, manual labor, sweat of one's brow, swink, operoseness, drudgery, slavery, fagging, hammering; *limae labor*.

trouble, pains, duty; resolution etc. 604; energy etc. (*physical*) 171.

V. exert oneself; exert –, tax- one's energies; use exertion.

labor, work, toil, moil, sweat, fag, drudge, slave, drag a lengthened chain, wade through, strive, strain; make –, stretch- a long arm; pull, tug, ply; ply –, tug at- the oar; do the work; take the laboring oar.

bestir oneself (*be active*) 682; take trouble, trouble oneself.

work hard; rough it; put forth -one's strength, – a strong arm; fall to work, bend the bow; buckle to, set one's shoulder to the wheel etc. (*resolution*) 604; work like a -Briton, – horse, – carthorse, – galley-slave, – coalheaver; labor –, work-day and night; redouble one's efforts; do double duty; work double -hours, – tides; sit up, burn the -midnight oil, – candle at both ends; stick to etc. (*persevere*) 604*a*; work –, fight- one's way; lay about one, hammer at.

take pains; do one's -best, – level best, – utmost; do -the best one can, – all one can, – all in one's power, – as much as in one lies, – what lies in one's power; use one's -best, – utmost- endeavor, try one's -best, – utmost; play one's best card; put one's -best, – right- leg foremost; have one's whole soul in one's work, put all one's strength into, strain every nerve; spare no -efforts, – pains; go all lengths; go through fire and water etc. (*resolution*) 604; move heaven and earth, leave no stone unturned.

Adj. laboring etc. *v.*

laborious, operose, elaborate; strained; toil-, trouble-, burden-, weari-some; uphill; herculean, gymnastic, athletic, palestric.

hardworking, painstaking, strenuous, energetic. hard at work, on the stretch.

Adv. laboriously etc. *adj.*; lustily; with -might and main, – all one's might, – a strong hand, – sledge-hammer, – much ado; to the best of one's abilities, *totis viribus*, *vi et armis, manibus pedibusque*, tooth and nail, *unguibus et rostro*, hammer and tongs, heart and soul; through thick and thin etc. (*perseverance*) 604*a*.

by the sweat of one's brow, *suo Marte*.

687. Repose.—N. repose, rest, silken repose; sleep etc. 683.

relaxation, breathing time; halt, pause etc. (*cessation*) 142; respite.

day of rest, *dies non*, Sabbath, Lord's day, holiday, red-letter day, vacation, recess.

V. repose; rest, – and be thankful; take -rest, – one's ease.

relax, unbend, slacken; take breath etc. (*refresh*) 689; rest upon one's oars; pause etc. (*cease*) 142; stay one's hand.

lie down; recline, – on a bed of down, – on an easy chair; go to -rest, – bed, – sleep etc. 683.

take a holiday, shut up shop; lie fallow etc. (*inaction*) 681.

Adj. reposing etc. *v.*; unstrained.

Adv. at rest.

688. Fatigue.—N. fatigue; weariness etc. 841; yawning, drowsiness etc. 683; lassitude, tiredness, fatigation, exhaustion; sweat.

anhelation, shortness of breath, panting; faintness; collapse, prostration, swoon, fainting, *deliquium*, syncope, lipothymy.

V. be -fatigued etc. *adj.*; yawn etc. (*get sleepy*) 683; droop, sink, flag; lose -breath, – wind; gasp, pant, puff, blow, drop, swoon, faint, succumb.

fatigue, tire, weary, bore, irk, fag, jade, harass, exhaust, knock up, wear out, prostrate.

tax, task, strain; over-task, -work, -burden, -tax, -strain.

Adj. fatigued etc. *v.*; weary etc. 841; drowsy etc. 683; drooping etc. *v.*; haggard; toil-, way-worn; footsore, surbated, weatherbeaten; faint; done –, used –, knock- up; exhausted, prostrate, spent; over-tired, -spent, -fatigued; forspent; unre-freshed, -stored.

worn, – out; battered, shattered, pulled down, seedy, altered.

breath-, wind-less; short of –, out of -breath, – wind; blown, puffing and blowing; short-breathed; anhelous; broken-, short-winded.

ready to drop, more dead than alive, dog -tired, – weary, walked off one's legs, tired to death, on one's last legs, played out, *hors de combat*.

fatiguing etc. *v.*; tire-, irk-, weari-some; weary; trying.

689. Refreshment.—N. bracing etc. *v.*; recovery of -strength etc. 159; restoration, revival etc. 660; repair, refection, refocillation, refreshment, regalement, bait; relief etc. 834.

V. brace etc. (*strengthen*) 159; reinvigorate; air, freshen up, refresh, recruit; repair etc. (*restore*) 660; fan, revocillate.

breathe, respire; draw –, take –, gather –, take a long –, regain –, recover- breath; get better, raise one's head; recover –, regain –, renew- one's strength etc. 159; perk up.

come to oneself etc. (*revive*) 660; feel like a giant refreshed.

Adj. refreshing etc. *v.*; recuperative etc. 660.

refreshed etc. *v.*; un-tired, -wearied.

690. Agent.—N. doer, actor, agent, performer, perpetrator, operator; execu-tor, -trix; practitioner, worker, stager.

bee, ant, working bee, laboring oar, shaft horse, servant –, maid- of all work, general servant, factotum.

workman, artisan; crafts-, handicrafts-man; mechanic, operative; working –, laboring- man; hewers of wood and drawers of water, laborer, navvy; hand, man, day laborer, journeyman, hack; mere -tool etc. 633; porter, docker, stevedore, beast of burden, drudge, fag.

maker, artificer, artist, wright, manufacturer, architect, contractor, builder, mason, bricklayer, smith, forger, Vulcan; black-, tin-smith; carpenter; ganger, platelayer.

machinist, mechanician, engineer, electrician, plumber, gasfitter etc.

semp-, sem-, seam-stress; needle-, char-, work-woman; tailor, cordwainer.

minister etc. (*instrument*) 631; servant etc. 746; representative etc. (*commissioner*) 758; (*deputy*) 759.

co-worker, fellow-worker, party to, participator in, co-operator, colleague, associate, collaborator, *particeps criminis, dramatis personae*; *personnel*.

Phrs. *'quorum pars magna fui.'*

691. Workshop.—N. work-shop, -house; laboratory; manufactory, mill, factory, armory, arsenal, mint, forge, loom; cabinet, *studio*, *bureau*, *atelier*; hive, – of industry; nursery; hot-house, -bed; kitchen, kitchenette; dock, -yard; slip, yard, wharf; found-ry, -ery; furnace; vineyard, orchard, farm, kitchen garden.

melting pot, crucible, alembic, caldron, mortar, *matrix*.

692. Conduct.—N. dealing, transaction etc. (*action*) 680; business etc. 625.

tactics, game, policy, polity; general-, statesman- seaman-ship; strate-gy, -gics; plan etc. 626.

husbandry; house-keeping, -wifery; stewardship; *ménage*; regimen, *régime*; econom-y, -ics; political economy; management; government etc. (*direction*) 693.

execution, manipulation, treatment, campaign, career, life, course, walk, race.

conduct; behavior; de-, com-portment; carriage, *maintien*, demeanor, guise, bearing, manner, mien, air, observance.

course –, line- of -conduct, – action, – proceeding; *rôle*; process, ways, practice, procedure, *modus operandi*; method etc., path etc. 627.

V. transact, execute; des-, dis-patch; proceed with, discharge; carry -on, – through, – out, – into effect; work out; go –, get- through; enact; put into practice; officiate etc. 625.

behave –, comport –, demean –, carry –, bear –, conduct –, acquit- oneself.

run a race, lead a life, play a game; take –, adopt- a course; steer –, shape- one's course; play one's- part, – cards; shift for oneself; paddle one's own canoe.

conduct; manage etc. (*direct*) 693.

deal –, have to do- with; treat, handle a case; take -steps, – measures.

Adj. conducting etc. *v.*; strategical, business-like, practical, economic, executive.

693. Direction.—N. direction; manage-ment, -ry; government, gubernation, conduct, legislation, regulation, guidance; steer-, pilot-age; reins, – of government; helm, rudder, controls, joy stick, needle, compass, binnacle; guiding –, load –, lode –, pole- star; cynosure.

super-vision, -intendence; *surveillance*, oversight; eye of the master; control, charge, auspices; board of control etc. (*council*) 696; command etc. (*authority*) 737.

premier-, senator-ship; director etc. 694; chair, seat, portfolio.

statesmanship; state-, king-craft.

minis-try, -tration; administration; steward-, proctor-ship; agency.

V. direct, manage, govern, conduct; order, prescribe, cut out work for; head, lead; lead –, show- the way; take the lead, lead on; regulate, guide, steer, pilot; take –, be at- the helm; have –, handle –, hold –, take- the reins, handle the ribbons; drive, tool; tackle.

super-intend, -vise; overlook, control, keep in order, look after, see to, oversee, legislate for; administer, ministrate; patronize; have the -care, – charge- of; have –, take- the direction; pull the -strings, – wires; rule etc. (*command*) 737; have –, hold- -office, – the portfolio; preside, – at the board; take –, occupy –, be in- the chair; pull the stroke oar.

Adj. directing etc. *v.*; executive, supervisory, hegemonic.

Adv. at the -helm, – head of, in charge of; under the auspices of.

694. Director.—N. director, manager, governor, rector, comptroller; super-intendent, -visor; intendant; over-seer, -looker; foreman, boss, straw boss; supercargo, husband, inspector, visitor, ranger, surveyor, aedile, moderator, monitor, taskmaster; master etc. 745; leader, ringleader, demagogue, corypheus, conductor, fugleman, precentor, bellwether, agitator.

guiding star etc. (*guidance*) 693; adviser etc. 695; guide etc. (*information*) 527; pilot; helmsman; steers-man, -mate; man at the wheel; wire-puller.

driver, whip, Jehu, charioteer; coach-, car-, cabman, jarvey; postilion, *vetturino*, muleteer, teamster; whipper in; engineer, engine driver, motorman, *chauffeur*.

head, – man; principal, president, speaker; chair, -man; captain etc. (*master*) 745; superior; dean; mayor etc. (*civil authority*) 745; vice-president, prime minister, premier, vizier, grand vizier; dictator.

officer, functionary, minister, official, red-tapist, bureaucrat; man –, Jack- in office; office-bearer; person in authority etc. 745.

statesman, strategist, legislator, lawgiver, politician, administrator, statist, statemonger; Minos, Draco; arbiter etc. (*judge*) 967; king maker, power behind the throne.

board etc. (*council*) 696.

secretary, – of state; Reis Effendi; vicar etc. (*deputy*) 759; steward, factor; agent etc. 758; bailiff, middleman; ganger, clerk of works; landreeve; factotum, major-domo, seneschal, housekeeper, shepherd, *croupier*; proctor, procurator, curator, librarian.

Adv. *ex officio*.

695. Advice.—N. advice, counsel, adhortation; word to the wise; suggestion, submonition, recommendation, advocacy, consultation.

exhortation etc. (*persuasion*) 615; expostulation etc. (*dissuasion*) 616; admonition etc. (*warning*) 668; guidance etc. (*direction*) 693.

instruction, charge, injunction.

adviser, prompter; counsel, -lor; monitor, mentor, Nestor, *magnus Apollo*, senator; teacher etc. 540.

guide, manual, chart etc. (*information*) 527.

physician, leech, archiater; arbiter etc. (*judge*) 967.

refer-ence, -ment; consultation, conference, parley, *pourparler* etc. 696.

V. advise, counsel; give -advice, – counsel, – a piece of advice; suggest, prompt, submonish, recommend, prescribe, advocate; exhort etc. (*persuade*) 615.

enjoin, enforce, charge, instruct, call; call upon etc. (*request*) 765; dictate.

expostulate etc. (*dissuade*) 616; admonish etc. (*warn*) 668.

advise with; lay heads –, consult- together; compare notes; hold a council, deliberate, be closeted with.

confer, consult, refer to, call in; take –, follow- advice; follow implicitly; be advised by, have at one's elbow, take one's cue from.

Adj. recommendatory; hortative etc. (*persuasive*) 615; dehortatory etc. (*dissuasive*) 616; admonitory etc. (*warning*) 668; consultative.

Int. go to!

696. Council.—N. council, committee, subcommittee, *comitia*, court, chamber, cabinet, board, bench, staff; consultation.

senate, *senatus*, parliament, house, – of Lords, – Peers, – Commons, legislature, legislative assembly, federal council, chamber of deputies, directory, *reichsrath*, *rigsdag*, *cortes*, storthing, witenagemote, *junta*, divan, *musnud*, *sanhedrim*, Amphictyonic council; *duma*, *zemstvo*, *soviet*, *cheka*, *ogpu*; *Dail Eireann*; caput, consistory, chapter, syndicate; court of appeal etc. (*tribunal*) 966; board of -control, – works; vestry; county –, borough –, district –, parish –, town- council, local board.

cabinet –, privy- council, royal commission; cockpit, convocation, synod, congress, congregation, convention, diet, states-general, aulic council.

League of Nations, assembly, *caucus*, conclave, *clique*, conventicle; meeting, sitting, *séance*, conference, session, hearing, palaver, *pourparler*, *durbar*, pow-wow, house; *quorum*.

senator; member, – of parliament; councilor, M.P., representative of the people.

Adj. senatorial, curule, parliamentary.

697. Precept.—N. precept, direction, instruction, charge; prescript, -ion; *recipe*, receipt; golden rule; maxim etc. 496.

commandment, rule, ruling, canon, law, code, *corpus juris*, *lex scripta*, common –, unwritten –, canon- law; the Ten Commandments; act, statute, convention, rubric, stage direction, regulation; form, -ula, -ulary; technicality; nice point.

order etc. (*command*) 741.

698. Skill.—N. skill, skilfulness, address; dexter-ity, -ousness; adroitness, expertness etc. *adj.*; proficiency, competence, craft, callidity, facility, knack, trick, sleight; master-y, -ship; excellence, panurgy; ambidext-erity, -rousness; sleight of hand etc. (*deception*) 545.

sea-, air-, marks-, horse-manship; tight-, rope-dancing.

accomplish-, acquire-, attain-ment; art, science; techn-icality, -ology, -ique; practical –, technical-knowledge; technocracy; finish, technic.

knowledge of the world, world wisdom, *savoir-faire*; tact; mother wit etc. (*sagacity*) 498; discretion etc. (*caution*) 864; *finesse*; craftiness etc. (*cunning*) 702; management etc. (*conduct*) 692; *ars celare artem*; self-help.

cleverness, talent, ability, ingenuity, capacity, parts, talents, faculty, endowment, *forte*, turn, gift, genius, flair, feeling; intelligence etc. 498; sharpness, readiness etc. (*activity*) 682; invention etc. 515; apt-ness, -itude; turn –, capacity –, genius- for; felicity, capability, *curiosa felicitas*, qualification, habilitation.

proficient etc. 700.

masterpiece, *coup de maître*, *chef- d'oeuvre*, *tour de force*; good stroke etc. (*plan*) 626.

V. be -skilful etc. *adj.*; excel in, be master of; have -a turn for etc. *n.*

know -what's what, – a hawk from a handsaw, – what one is about, – on which side one's bread is buttered, – what's o'clock, – a thing or two; have cut one's -eye, – wisdom- teeth.

see -one's way, – where the wind lies, – which way the wind blows; have -all one's wits about one, – one's hand in; *savoir vivre*; *scire quid valeant humeri quid ferre recusent*

look after the main chance; cut one's coat according to one's cloth; live by one's wits; exercise one's discretion, feather the oar, sail near the wind; stoop to conquer etc. (*cunning*) 702; play one's -cards well, – best card; hit the right nail on the head, put the saddle on the right horse.

take advantage of, make the most of; profit by etc. (*use*) 677; make a hit etc. (*succeed*) 731; make a virtue of necessity; make hay while the sun shines etc. (*occasion*) 134.

Adj. skilful, dexterous, adroit, expert, apt, slick, handy, quick, deft, ready, resourceful, gain; smart etc. (*active*) 682; proficient, good at, up to, at home in, master of, a good hand at, *au fait*, thoroughbred, masterly, crack, accomplished; conversant etc. (*knowing*) 490.

experienced, practiced, skilled; up –, well up- in; in -practice, – proper cue; competent, efficient, qualified, capable, fitted, fit for, up to the mark, trained, initiated, prepared, primed, finished.

clever, able, ingenious, felicitous, gifted, talented, endowed, cute, inventive etc. 515; shrewd, sharp etc. (*intelligent*) 498; cunning etc. 702; alive to, up to snuff, not to be caught with chaff; discreet.

neat-handed, fine-fingered, ambidextrous, sure-footed; cut out –, fitted- for.

technical, artistic, scientific, daedalian, ship-shape; workman-, business-, statesman-like.

Adv. skilfully etc. *adj.*; well etc. 618; artistically; with -skill, – consummate skill; *secundum artem*, *suo Marte*; to the best of one's abilities etc. (*exertion*) 686; like a machine.

699. Unskillfulness.—N. unskillfulness etc. *adj.*; want of -skill etc. 698; incompeten-ce, -cy; inability, -felicity, -dexterity, -experience; clumsiness; disqualification, unproficiency; quackery.

folly, stupidity etc. 499; indiscretion etc. (*rashness*) 863; thoughtlessness etc. (*inattention*) 458, (*neglect*) 460.

mis-management, -conduct; impolicy; maladministration; mis-rule, -government, -application, -direction, -feasance.

absence of rule, rule of thumb; bungling etc. *v.*; failure etc. 732; screw loose; too many cooks.

blunder etc. (*mistake*) 495; *étourderie*, *gaucherie*, act of folly, *balourdise*; botch, -ery; bad job, sad work.

sprat sent out to catch a whale, much ado about nothing, wildgoose chase.

bungler etc. 701; fool etc. 501.

layman, amateur.

V. be -unskillful etc. *adj.*; not see an inch beyond one's nose; blunder, bungle, boggle, fumble, muff, botch, bitch, flounder, loppet, stumble, trip; hobble etc. 275; put one's foot in it; make a -mess, – hash, – sad work- of; overshoot the mark.

play -tricks with, – Puck; mismanage, -conduct, -direct, -apply, -send.

stultify –, make a fool of –, commit- oneself; act foolishly; play the fool; put oneself out of court; lose one's -head, – cunning.

begin at the wrong end; do things by halves etc. (*not complete*) 730; make two bites of a cherry; play at cross purposes; strain at a gnat and swallow a camel etc. (*caprice*) 608; put the cart before the horse; lock the stable door when the horse is stolen etc. (*too late*) 135.

not know -what one is about, – one's own interest, – on which side one's bread is buttered; stand in one's own light, quarrel with one's bread and butter, throw a stone in one's own garden, kill the goose which lays the golden eggs, pay dear for one's whistle, cut one's own throat, burn one's fingers; knock –, run- one's head against a stone wall; fall into a trap, catch a Tartar, bring the house about one's ears; have too many -eggs in one basket (*imprudent*) 863, – irons in the fire.

mistake etc. 495; take the shadow for the substance etc. (*credulity*) 486; be in the wrong box, aim at a pigeon and kill a crow; take –, get- the wrong sow by the ear, – the dirty end of the stick; put -the saddle on the wrong horse, – a square peg into a round hole, – new wine into old bottles.

cut a whetstone with a razor; hold a farthing candle to the sun etc. (*useless*) 645; fight with –, grasp at- a shadow; catch at straws, lean on a broken reed, reckon without one's host, pursue a wildgoose chase; go on a fool's –, sleeveless-errand; go further and fare worse; loose –, miss-one's way; fail etc. 732.

Adj. un-skillful etc. 698; unskilled, inexpert; bungling etc. *v.*; awkward, clumsy, unhandy, lubberly, *gauche, maladroit*; left-, heavy-handed; slovenly, slatternly; gawky.

adrift, at fault.

in-, un-apt; inhabile; un-tractable, -teachable; giddy etc. (*inattentive*) 458; inconsiderate etc. (*neglectful*) 460; stupid etc. 499; inactive etc. 683; incompetent; un-, dis-, ill-qualified; unfit; quackish; raw, green, inexperienced, rusty, out of practice.

un-accustomed, -used, -trained etc. 537; -initiated, -conversant etc. (*ignorant*) 491; shiftless; unbusinesslike, unpractical; unstatesmanlike.

un-, ill-, mis-advised; ill-devised, -imagined, -judged, -contrived, -conducted; un-, mis-guided; misconducted, foolish, wild; infelicitous; penny wise and pound foolish etc. (*inconsistent*) 608.

Phr. one's fingers being all thumbs; the right hand forgets its cunning.

il se noyerait dans une goutte d'eau.

incidit in Scyllam qui vult vitare Charybdim; *out of the frying pan into the fire.*

700. Proficient.—N. proficient, expert, adept, dab; *connoisseur* etc. (*scholar*) 492; master, -hand; top-sawyer, *prima donna,* first fiddle, *chef de cuisine*; protagonist; past master; profess-or, -ional, specialist.

picked man; medalist, prizeman.

veteran; old -stager, – campaigner, – soldier, – file, – hand; man of -business, – the world.

nice –, good –, clean- hand; practised –, experienced- -eye, – hand; marksman; good –, dead –, crack- shot; rope-dancer, funambulist, acrobat, contortionist; cunning man; conjuror etc. (*deceiver*) 548; wizard etc. 994.

genius; master-mind, – head, – spirit.

cunning –, sharp -blade, – fellow; jobber; cracksman etc. (*thief*) 792; politician, tactician, diplomat, -ist, strategist.

pantologist, admirable Crichton, Jack of all trades; prodigy of learning; walking encyclopedia; mine of information.

701. Bungler.—N. bungler; blunderer, -head; marplot, fumbler, lubber, lout, oaf, duffer, stick, clown; bad –, poor- -hand, – shot; butter-fingers.

no conjuror, flat, muff, slow coach, looby, lubber, swab; clod, yokel, hick, awkward squad, novice, greenhorn, jaywalker, *blanc-bec.*

land lubber; fresh water –, fair weather- sailor; horse-marine; fish out of water, ass in lion's skin, jackdaw in peacock's feathers; quack etc. (*deceiver*) 548; Lord of Misrule.

sloven, slattern, trapes.

Phr. *il n'a pas inventé la poudre*; he will never set the Thames on fire.

702. Cunning.—N. cunning, craft; cunningness, craftiness etc. *adj.*; subtlety, artificiality; maneuvring etc. *v.*; temporization; circumvention.

chicane, -ry; sharp practice, knavery, jugglery; concealment etc. 528; nigger in the woodpile; guile, duplicity etc. (*falsehood*) 544; foul play.

diplomacy, politics; Machiavellism; jobbery, back-stairs influence, gerrymandering.

art, -ifice; device, machination; plot etc. (*plan*) 626; maneuver, stratagem, dodge, artful dodge, wile; trick, -ery etc. (*deception*) 545; *ruse, – de guerre; finesse,* side-blow, thin end of the wedge, shift, go by, subterfuge, evasion; white lie etc. (*untruth*) 546; juggle, *tour de force*; tricks -of the trade, – upon travelers; imposture, deception; *espièglerie,* net, trap etc. 545.

Ulysses, Machiavel, sly boots, fox, reynard; Scotch-, Yorkshire-man; Jew, Yankee; intriguer, *intrigant,* schemer, trickster.

V. be -cunning etc. *adj.*; have cut one's eyeteeth; contrive etc. (*plan*) 626; live by one's wits; maneuver; intrigue, gerrymander, *finesse,* double, temporize, stoop to conquer, *reculer pour mieux sauter,* circumvent, steal a march upon; overreach etc. 545; throw off one's guard; surprise etc. 508; outdo, get the better of, snatch from under one's nose; snatch a verdict; waylay, undermine, introduce the thin end of the wedge; play -a deep game, – tricks with; have an axe to grind; *ambiguas in vulgum spargere voces*; flatter, make things pleasant.

Adj. cunning, crafty, artful; skilful etc. 698; subtle, feline, vulpine; cunning as a -fox, – serpent; deep, – laid; profound; designing, contriving; intriguing etc. *v.*; strategic, diplomatic, politic, Machiavellian, time-serving; artificial; trick-y, -sy; wily, sly, slim, insidious, stealthy, foxy; underhand etc. (*hidden*) 528; subdolous; deceitful etc. 545; double-tongued, -faced; shifty; crooked; arch, pawky, shrewd, acute; sharp, – as a needle; canny, astute, leery, knowing, up to snuff, too clever by half, not to be caught with chaff.

Adv. cunningly etc. *adj.*; slily, on the sly, by a side wind.

Phr. diamond cut diamond.

703. Artlessness.—N. artlessness etc. *adj.*; nature, simplicity; innocence etc. 946; *bonhomie, naiveté, abandon,* candor, sincerity; singleness of -purpose, – heart; honesty etc. 939; plain speaking; *épanchement.*

rough diamond, matter of fact man; *le palais de vérité*; *enfant terrible.*

V. be -artless etc. *adj.*; look one in the face; wear one's heart upon his sleeves for daws to peck at; think aloud; speak -out, – one's mind; be free with one, call a spade a spade.

Adj. artless, natural, pure, native, simple, plain, inartificial, untutored, unsophisticated, *ingénu*, unaffected, *naïve*; sincere, frank; open, – as day; candid, ingenuous, guileless, unsuspicious, childlike; honest etc. 939; innocent etc. 946; Arcadian; undesigning, straightforward; unreserved, unvarnished, above-board; simple-, single-minded; frank-, open-, single-, simple-hearted; open and above-board.

free-, plain-, out-spoken; blunt, downright, direct, matter of fact, unpoetical; unflattering.

Adv. in plain -words, – English; without mincing the matter; not to mince the matter etc. (*affirmation*) 535.

Phr. *Davus sum non Oedipus*; *liberavi animam meam*.

704. Difficulty.—N. difficulty; hardness etc. *adj.*; impracticability etc. (*impossibility*) 471; tough –, hard –, uphill- work; hard –, Herculean –, Augean- task; task of Sisyphus, Sisyphean labor, tough job, teaser, rasper, dead lift.

dilemma, embarrassment; perplexity etc. (*uncertainty*) 475; involvement; intricacy; entanglement etc. 59; cross fire; awkwardness, delicacy, ticklish card to play, deadlock, knot, Gordian knot, *dignus vindice nodus*, net, meshes, maze; coil etc. (*convolution*) 248; crooked path.

nice –, delicate –, subtle –, knotty-point; vexed question, *vexata quaestio*, poser; puzzle etc. (*riddle*) 533; paradox; hard –, nut to crack; bone to pick, *crux*, *pons asinorum*, where the shoe pinches.

nonplus, quandary, strait, pass, pinch, pretty pass, stress, brunt; critical situation, crisis; trial, rub, emergency, exigency, scramble.

scrape, hobble, slough, quagmire, hot water, hornet's nest; sea –, peck- of troubles; pretty kettle of fish; pickle, stew, *imbroglio*, mess, muddle, botch, fuss, bustle, ado; false position; set fast, stand; dead -lock, – set; fix, horns of a dilemma, *cul de sac*; hitch; stumbling block etc. (*hindrance*) 706.

V. be -difficult etc. *adj.*; run one hard, go against the grain, try one's patience, put one out; put to one's -shifts, – wit's end; go hard with –, try- one; pose, perplex etc. (*uncertain*) 475; bother, nonplus, gravel, bring to a dead lock; be -impossible etc. 471; be in the way of etc. (*hinder*) 706.

meet with –, labor under –, get into –, plunge into –, struggle with –, contend with –, grapple with- difficulties; labor under a disadvantage; be -in difficulty etc. *adj.*

fish in troubled waters, buffet the waves, swim against the stream, scud under bare poles.

have -much ado with, – a hard time of it; come to the -push, – pinch; bear the brunt.

grope in the dark, lose one's way, weave a tangled web, walk among eggs.

get into a -scrape etc. *n.*; bring a hornet's nest about one's ears; be put to one's shifts; flounder, boggle, struggle; not know which way to turn etc. (*uncertain*) 475; get -tangled up, – wound up; *perdre son latin*; stick - at, – in the mud, – fast; come to a -stand, – dead lock; hold the wolf by the ears.

render -difficult etc. *adj.*; encumber, embarrass, ravel, entangle; put a spoke in the wheel etc. (*hinder*) 706; lead a pretty dance.

Adj. difficult, not easy, hard, tough; trouble-, toil-, irk-some; operose, laborious, onerous, arduous, Herculean, formidable; sooner –, more easily- said than done; difficult –, hard- to deal with; ill-conditioned, crabbed; not -to be handled with kid gloves, – made with rosewater.

awkward, unwieldy, unmanageable; intractable, stubborn etc. (*obstinate*) 606; perverse, refractory, plaguy, trying, thorny, rugged; knot-ted, -ty; invious; path-, track-less; labyrinthine etc. (*convoluted*) 248; intricate, complicated etc. (*tangled*) 59; impracticable etc. (*impossible*) 471; not -feasible etc. 470; desperate etc. (*hopeless*) 859.

embarrassing, perplexing etc. (*uncertain*) 475; delicate, ticklish, critical; beset with –, full of –, surrounded by –, entangled by –, encompassed with- difficulties.

under a difficulty; in -difficulty, – hot water, – the suds, – a cleft stick, – a fix, – the wrong box, – a scrape etc. *n.*; – deep water, – a fine pickle; *in extremis*; between -two stools, – Scylla and Charybdis; surronded by -shoals, – breakers, – quicksands; at cross purposes; not out of the wood.

reduced to straits; hard –, sorely- pressed; run hard; pinched, put to it, straitened; hard -up, – put to it, – set; put to one's shifts; puzzled, at a loss etc. (*uncertain*) 475; at -the end of one's tether, – one's wit's end, – a nonplus, – a standstill; graveled, nonplussed, stranded, aground; stuck –, set- fast; up a tree, at bay, *aux abois*, driven -into a corner, – from post to pillar, – to extremity, – to one's wit's end, – to the wall; *au bout de son latin*; out of one's -depth, – reckoning; put –, thrown -out.

accomplished with difficulty; hard-fought, -earned.

Adv. with -difficulty, – much ado; hardly etc. *adj.*; uphill; against the -stream, – grain; *à rebours*; *invitâ Minervâ*; in the teeth of; at –, upon- a pinch; at long odds.

Phr. ay there's the rub; *hic labor hoc opus*; things are come to a pretty pass.

705. Facility.—N. facility, ease; easiness etc. *adj.*; capability; feasibility etc. (*practicability*) 470; flexibility, pliancy etc. 324; smoothness etc. 255; convenience.

plain –, smooth –, straight- sailing; mere child's play, holiday task.

smooth water, fair wind; smooth – royal- road; clear -coast, – stage; *tabula rasa*; *full play* etc. (*freedom*) 748.

disen-cumbrance, -tanglement; deoppilation; permission etc. 760.

V. be -easy etc. *adj.*; go on –, run- smoothly; have -full play etc. *n.*; go –, run- on all fours; obey the helm, work well.

flow –, swim –, drift –, go- with the- -stream, – tide; see one's way; have -it all one's own way, – the game in one's own hands; walk over the course, win -at a canter, – hands down; make -light of, – nothing of; be at home in etc. (*skilful*) 698.

render -easy etc. *adj.*; facilitate, smooth, ease; popularize; lighten, – the labor; free, clear; disencumber, -embarrass, -entangle, -engage; deobstruct, unclog, extricate, unravel; untie –, cut- the knot; disburden, unload, exonerate, emancipate, free from, deoppilate; humor etc. (*aid*) 707; lubricate etc. 332; relieve etc. 834.

leave -a hole to creep out of, – a loophole, – the matter open; give -the reins to, – full play, – full swing; make way for; open the -door to, – way; prepare –, smooth –, clear- the -ground, – way, – path, – road; pave the way, bridge over; permit etc. 760.

Adj. easy, facile; feasible etc. (*practicable*) 470; easily -managed, – accomplished; within reach, accessible, easy of access, for the million, open to.

manageable, wieldy; towardly, tractable; submissive; yielding, ductile; pliant etc. (*soft*) 324; glib, slippery; smooth etc. 255; on -friction wheels, – velvet; convenient.

un-, dis-burdened, -encumbered, -embarrassed; exonerated; un-loaded, -obstructed, -trammeled, -impeded, -restrained etc. (*free*) 748; at ease, light.

at –, quite at- home; in -one's element, – smooth water.

Adv. easily etc. *adj.*; readily, smoothly, swimmingly, *ad lib.*, on easy terms, single-handed.

Phr. touch and go.

Int. all clear!

706. Hindrance.—N. prevention, preclusion, obstruction, stoppage; prohibition; inter-ruption, -ception, -clusion; hindrance, impedition; retardment, -ation; constriction; embarrassment, oppilation; coarctation, stricture, restriction; anchor etc. 666; restraint etc. 751 & 752; inhibition etc. 761; blockade etc. (*closure*) 261; picketing.

inter-ference, -position; obtrusion; discouragement, -countenance, -approval, -approbation; opposition etc. 708.

impediment, let, obstacle, obstruction, knot, knag; check, hitch, *contretemps, impasse,* screw loose, grit in the oil.

bar, stile, barrier; turn-stile, -pike; gate, portcullis; bulwark, parapet, barricade etc. (*defence*) 717; wall, dead wall, breakwater, groyne; bulkhead, block, buffer; stopper etc. 263; boom, dam, weir, burrock.

drawback, objection; stumbling-block, -stone; lion in the path; snag; snags and sawyers.

en-, in-cumbrance; clog, skid, shoe, spoke; brake, drag, – chain, – weight; stay, stop; preventive, prophylactic; contraception; load, burden, fardel, *onus,* millstone round one's neck, *impedimenta*; dead weight; lumber, pack; nightmare, Ephialtes, incubus, old man of the sea; remora.

difficulty etc. 704; insuperable etc. 471- obstacle; estoppel; ill wind; head wind etc. (*opposition*) 708; trammel, tether etc. (*means of restraint*) 752; hold back, counterpoise; damper, wet blanket, hinderer, marplot, kill-joy, dog in the manger, interloper; trail of a red herring; opponent etc. 710.

V. hinder, impede, impedite, embarrass.

keep –, stave –, ward- off; picket; obviate; a-, ante-vert; turn aside, draw off, prevent, forefend, nip in the bud; retard, slacken, check, let; counteract, -check; preclude, debar, foreclose, estop; inhibit etc. 761; shackle etc. (*restrain*) 751; restrict, restrain, cohibit.

obstruct, filibuster, stop, stay, bar, bolt, lock; block, – up; belay, barricade; block –, stop- the way; dam up etc. (*close*) 261; put on the -brake etc. *n.*; scotch –, lock –, put a spoke in- the wheel; put a stop to etc. 142; traverse, contravene; inter-rupt, -cept; oppose etc. 708; hedge -in, – round; cut off; interclude.

inter-pose, -fere, -meddle etc. 682.

cramp, hamper; clog, – the wheels; cumber; en-, in-cumber; handicap; choke; saddle –, load- with; overload, lay; lumber, trammel, tie one's hands, put to inconvenience; in-, discommode; discompose; hustle, drive into a corner; choke off.

run –, fall- foul of; cross the path of, break in upon.

thwart, frustrate, disconcert, balk, foil, baffle, snub, override, circumvent; defeat etc. 731; spike guns etc. (*render useless*) 645; spoil, mar, clip the wings of; cripple etc. (*injure*) 659; put an extinguisher on; damp; dishearten etc. (*dissuade*) 616; discountenance, throw cold water on, spoil sport; lay –, throw- a wet blanket on; cut the ground from under one, take the wind out of one's sails, undermine; be –, stand- in the way of; act as a drag; hang like a millstone round one's neck.

Adj. hindering etc. *v.*; obstr-uctive, -uent; impedi-tive, -ent; intercipient; prophylactic etc. (*remedial*) 662.

in the way of, unfavorable; onerous, burdensome; cumb-rous, -ersome; obtrusive.

hindered etc. *v.*; wind-bound, water-logged, heavy laden; hard pressed.

unassisted etc. (*see* assist etc. 707); single-handed, alone; deserted etc. 624.

707. Aid.—N. aid, -ance; assistance, help, opitulation, succor; support, lift, advance, furtherance, promotion; coadjuvancy etc. (*co-operation*) 709.

patronage, championship, countenance, favor, interest, advocacy, auspices.

sustentation, subvention, subsidy, bounty, alimentation, nutrition, nourishment, maintenance; manna in the wilderness; food etc. 298; means etc. 632.

ministr-y, -ation; subministration; accomodation.

relief, rescue; help at a dead lift; supernatural aid; *deus ex machinâ.*

supplies, reinforcements, succors, contingents, recruits; support etc. (*physical*) 215; adjunct, ally etc. (*helper*) 711.

V. aid, assist, help, succor, lend one's aid; come to the aid etc. *n*- of; contribute, subscribe to; bring –, give –, furnish –, afford –, supply- -aid etc. *n.*; render assistance; give –, stretch –, lend –, bear –, hold out- a -hand, – helping hand; give one a -lift, – cast, – turn; take -by the hand, – in tow; help a lame dog over a stile, lend wings to.

relieve, rescue; set -up, – agoing, – on one's legs; bear –, pull- through; give new life to, be the making of; reinforce, recruit; set –, put –, push- forward; give -a lift, – a shove, – an impulse- to; promote, further, forward, advance; speed, expedite, quicken, hasten.

support, sustain, uphold, prop, hold up, bolster.

cradle, nourish; nurture, nurse, dry nurse, suckle, put out to nurse; manure, cultivate, force; foster; cherish, foment; feed –, fan- the flame.

serve; do service to, tender to, pander to; ad-, sub-, minister to; tend, attend, wait on; take care of etc. 459; entertain; smooth the bed of death.

oblige, accomodate, consult the wishes of; humor, cheer, encourage.

second, stand by; back, – up; pay the piper, abet; work –, make interest –, stick up –, take up the cudgels- for; take up –, espouse –, adopt- the cause of; advocate, beat up for recruits, press into the service; squire, give moral support to, keep in countenance, countenance, patronize; lend - oneself, – one's countenance- to; smile –, shine- upon; favor, befriend, take up, take in hand, enlist under the banners of; side with etc. (*co-operate*) 709.

be of use to; subserve etc. (*instrument*) 631; benefit etc. 648; render a service etc. (*utility*) 644; conduce etc. (*tend*) 176.

Adj. aiding etc. *v.*; auxiliary, adjuvant, helpful; coadjuvant etc. 709; subservient, ministrant, ancillary, accessory, subsidiary.

at one's beck; friendly, amicable, favorable, propitious, well-disposed; neighborly; obliging etc. (*benevolent*) 906.

Adv. with –, by- -the aid etc. *n.*- of; on –, in- behalf of; in -aid, – the service, – the name, – favor, – furtherance- of; on account of; for the sake of, on the part of; *non obstante*.

Int. help! save us! to the rescue! S.O.S.!

708. Opposition.—N. opposition, antagonism, oppug-nancy, -nation; impugnation; contravention; counteraction etc. 179; counterplot.

cross-fire, under-current, head-wind.

clashing, collision, conflict, lack of harmony, contest.

competition, two of a trade, rivalry, emulation, race; war to the knife.

absence of -aid etc. 707; resistance etc. 719; restraint etc. 751; hindrance etc. 706.

V. oppose, conteract; run counter to; withstand etc. (*resist*) 719; control etc. (*restrain*) 751; hinder etc. 706; antagonize, oppugn, fly in the face of, go dead against, kick against, fall foul of; set –, pit- against; face, confront, cope with; make a -stand, – dead set- against; set -oneself, one's face- against; protest –, vote –, raise one's voice- against; disfavor, turn one's back upon; set at naught, slap in the face, slam the door in one's face.

be –, play- at cross purposes; counter-work, - mine; thwart, overthwart.

stem, breast, encounter; stem –, breast- the - tide, – current, – flood; buffet the waves; beat up –, make head- against; grapple with; kick against the pricks etc. (*resist*) 719; contend etc. 720 –, do battle etc. (*warfare*) 722- -with, – against.

contra-dict, -vene; belie; go –, run –, beat –, militate- against; come in conflict with.

emulate etc. (*compete*) 720; rival, spoil one's trade.

Adj. oppos-ing, -ed etc. *v.*; adverse, antagonistic; ambivalent; contrary etc. 14; at variance etc. 24; at issue, at war with; in opposition; 'agin the Government.'

un-favorable, -friendly; hostile, inimical, cross, unpropitious.

in hostile array, front to front, with crossed bayonets, at daggers drawn; up in arms; resistant etc. 791.

competitive, emulous.

Adv. against, *versus*, counter to, in conflict with, at cross purposes.

against the -grain, – current, – stream, – wind, – tide; with a headwind; with the wind - ahead, – in one's teeth.

in spite, in despite, in defiance; in the -way, – teeth, – face- of; across; a-, over-thwart; where the shoe pinches.

though etc. 30; even; *quand même*; *per contra*.

Phr. *nitor in adversum*.

709. Co-operation.—N. co-operation; coadju-vancy, -tancy; coagency, coefficiency; concert, concurrence, complicity, participation; union etc. 43; amalgamation, combination etc. 48; collusion.

association, alliance, colleagueship, jointstock, copartnership, trust, cartel, pool, ring, combine, interlocking directorate; confederation etc. (*party*) 712; federation, coalition, fusion; a long pull, a strong pull and a pull all together; log-rolling, freemasonry.

unanimity etc. (*assent*) 488; *esprit de corps*, party spirit; clan-, partisan-ship; reciprocity, concord etc. 714.

V. co-operate, co-adjute, concur; conduce etc. 178; combine, cartelize, unite one's efforts; keep –, draw –, pull –, club –, hang –, hold –, league –, band –, be banded- together; stand –, put- shoulder to shoulder; act in concert, join forces, fraternize, cling to one another, conspire, concert, lay one's heads together; confederate, be in league with; collude, understand one another, play into the hands of, hunt in couples.

side –, take side –, go along –, go hand in hand –, join hands –, make common cause –, strike in –, unite –, join –, mix oneself up –, take part –, play along –, cast in one's lot- with; join –, enter into- partnership with; rally round, follow the lead of; come to, pass over to, come into the views of; be –, row –, sail- in the same boat; sail on the same tack.

be a party to, lend oneself to; participate; have a -hand in, – finger in the pie; take –, bear- part in; second etc. (*aid*) 707; take the part of, play the game of; espouse a -cause, – quarrel.

Adj. co-operating etc. *v.*; in -co-operation etc. *n.*, – league etc. (*party*) 712; coadju-vant, -tant; hand and glove with.

favorable etc. 707- to; un-opposed etc. 708.

Adj. as one man etc. (*unanimously*) 488; shoulder to shoulder; in co-operation with.

710. Opponent.—N. opponent, antagonist, adversary; adverse party, opposition; enemy etc. 891; assailant.

oppositionist, obstructive; obscurantist; brawler, wrangler, brangler, disputant, extremist, irreconcilable, diehard, bitter-ender.

malcontent; Jacobin, Fenian etc. 742; demagogue, reactionist.

passive resister, conscientious objector.

rival, competitor, contestant.

711. Auxiliary.—N. auxiliary; recruit; assistant; adju-vant, -tant; adjunct; help, er, -mate, -ing hand; midwife; colleague, partner, mate, *confrère*, co-operator; coadju-tor, -trix; collaborator.

ally; friend etc. 890; confidant, *fidus Achates*, pal, chum, buddy, *alter ego*.

confederate; ac-, complice; accessory, – after the fact; *particeps criminis*.

aide-de-camp, secretary, clerk, associate, marshal; right-hand; candle-, bottle-holder; hand-maid; servant etc. 746; puppet, cat's-paw; stooge, dependent, creature, jackal; tool, *âme damnée*; satellite, adherent, parasite.

votary, disciple; secta-rian, -ry; seconder, backer, upholder, supporter, abettor, advocate, partisan, champion, patron, friend at court, mediator.

friend in need, Jack at a pinch, *deus ex machinâ*, guardian angel, fairy godmother; special providence, tutelary genius.

712. Party.—N. party, faction, side, denomination, class, communion, set, crowd, crew, band, horde, posse, phalanx; regiment etc. 726; family, clan etc. 166.

Tories, Conservatives, Unionists, Whigs, Liberals, Radicals, Labour party, Socialists, Communists etc.; Republicans, Democrats, Farmer-Labor; *Fascisti*, Revolutionaries etc. 742.

community, body, fellowship, sodality, solidarity; con-, fraternity; sorority; brother-, sisterhood.

Freemasons, Knights Templars, Odd Fellows, Ku Klux Klan etx.

knot, gang, *clique*, ring, circle; *coterie*, club, *casino*.

corporation, corporate body, guild; establishment, company, copartnership, firm, house, joint concern, joint-stock company, trust, investment trust, combine etc. 709.

society, association; instit-ute, -ution; union; trade-union; league, syndicate, alliance, *Verein*, *Bund*, *Zollverein*, combination; league –, alliance- offensive and defensive; coalition; federation; confedera -tion, -cy; junto, cabal, *camarilla*, *camorra*, *brigue*; freemasonry; party spirit etc. (*co-operation*) 709.

staff; cast, *dramatis personae*.

V. unite, join; club together etc. (*co-operate*) 709; cement –, form- a party etc. *n.*; associate etc. (*assemble*) 72.

Adj. in -league, – partnership, – alliance etc. *n.*

bonded –, banded –, linked etc. (*joined*) 43- together; embattled; confederated, federative, joint, corporate, leagued, fraternal, masonic, cliquish.

Adv. hand in hand, side by side, shoulder to shoulder, *en masse*, in the same boat.

713. Discord.—N. disagreement etc. 24; discord, -accord, -sidence, -sonance; jar, clash, shock; jarring, jostling etc. *v.*; screw loose.

variance, difference, dissension, misunderstanding, cross purposes, odds, *brouillerie*; division, split, rupture, disruption, division in the camp, house divided against itself, rift within the lute; disunion, breach; schism etc. (*dissent*) 489; feud, faction.

quarrel, dispute, rippet, spat, tiff, *tracasserie*, squabble, altercation, words, high words; wrangling etc. *v.*; jangle, brabble cross questions and crooked answers, snip-snap; family jars.

polemics; litigation; strife etc. (*contention*) 720; warfare etc. 722; outbreak, open rupture; breaking off of negotiations, recall of ambassadors; declaration of war.

broil, brawl, row, racket, hubbub, rixation; embroilment, embranglement, *imbroglio*, *fracas*, breach of the peace, piece of work, scrimmage, rumpus; breeze, squall; riot, disturbance etc. (*disorder*) 59; commotion etc. (*agitation*) 315; bear garden, Donnybrook Fair.

subject of dispute, ground of quarrel, battle ground, disputed point; bone -of contention, – to pick; apple of discord, *casus belli*; question at issue etc. (*subject of inquiry*) 461; vexed question, *vexata quaestio*, brand of discord.

troublous times; cat-and-dog life; contentiousness etc. *adj.*; enmity etc. 889; hate etc. 898; Kilkenny cats; disputant etc. 710; strange bedfellows.

V. be -discordant etc. *adj.*; disagree, come amiss etc. 24; clash, jar, jostle, pull different ways, conflict, have no measures with, misunderstand one another; live like cat and dog; differ; dissent etc. 489; have a -bone to pick, – crow to pluck- with.

fall out, quarrel, dispute; litigate; controvert etc. (*deny*) 536; squabble, wrangle, jangle, brangle, bicker, nag; spar etc. (*contend*) 720; have -words etc. *n.* with; fall foul of.

split; break –, break squares –, part company- with; declare war, try conclusions; join –, put in- issue; pick a quarrel, fasten a quarrel on; sow –, stir up- -dissension etc. *n.*; embroil, estrange, entangle, disunite, widen the breach; set -at odds, – together by the ears; set –, pit- against; rub up the wrong way.

get into hot water, fish in troubled waters, brawl; kick up a -row, – dust; turn the house out of window.

Adj. discordant; disagreeing etc. *v.*; out of tune, dissonant, inharmonious, harsh, grating, jangling, ajar, on bad terms; dissentient etc. 489; inconsistent, contradictory, incongruous, discrepant; un- reconciled, -pacified.

quarrelsome, unpacific; gladiatorial, controversial, polemic, disputatious; factious; liti-gious, -gant; pettifogging.

at odds, at loggerheads, at daggers drawn, at variance, at issue, at cross purposes, at sixes and sevens, at feud, at high words; up in arms, together by the ears, in hot water, embroiled.

torn, disunited.

Phr. *quot homines tot sententiae*; no love lost between them, *non nostrum tantas componere lites*.

714. Concord.—N. concord, accord, harmony, symphony, homology; aggreement etc. 23; sympathy etc. (*love*) 897; response; union, unison, unity; bonds of harmony; peace etc. 721; unanimity etc. (*assent*) 488; league etc. 712; happy family.

rapprochement; *reunion*; amity etc. (*friendship*) 888; reciprocity; alliance, *entente cordiale*, good understanding, conciliation, arbitration, peacemaker etc. 724.

V. agree etc. 23; accord, harmonize with; fraternize; be -concordant etc. *adj.*; go hand in hand; blend –, tone in- with; run parallel etc. (*concur*) 178; understand one another; pull together etc. (*co-operate*) 709; put up one's horses together, sing in chorus.

side –, sympathize –, go –, chime in –, fall in- with; come round; be pacified etc. 723; assent etc. 488; enter into the -ideas, – feelings- of; reciprocate.

hurler avec les loups; go –, swim- with the stream.

pour oil on troubled waters, keep in good humor, render accordant, put in tune; come to an understanding, meet half-way; keep the –, remain at- peace.

Adj. concordant, congenial; agreeing etc. *v.*; in-accord etc. *n.*; harmonious, united, cemented; banded together etc. 712; allied; friendly etc. 888; fraternal; conciliatory; at one with; of one mind etc. (*assent*) 488.

at peace, in still water; tranquil etc. (*pacific*) 721.

Adv. with one voice etc. (*assent*) 488; in concert with, hand in hand; on one's side, unanimously.

715. Defiance.—N. defiance; daring etc. *v.*; dare, challenge, *cartel*; threat etc. 909; war-cry, -whoop.

V. defy, dare, beard; brave etc. (*courage*) 861; bid defiance to; set at -defiance, – naught; hurl defiance at; dance the war dance; snap the fingers at, laugh to scorn; disobey etc. 742.

show -fight, – one's teeth, – a bold front; bluster, look big, stand akimbo; double –, shake-the fist; threaten etc 909.

challenge, call out; throw –, fling- down the -gauntlet, – gage, – glove.

Adj. defiant; defying etc. *v.*; with arms akimbo; rebellious, insolent; reckless, greatly daring.

Adv. in -defiance, – the teeth- of; under one's very nose.

Int. do your worst! come if you dare! come on! marry come up! hoity toity!

Phr. *noli me tangere*; *nemo me impune lacessit*.

716. Attack.—N. attack; assault, – and battery; onset, onslaught, charge.

aggression, drive, offence; incursion, inroad; invasion; irruption; outbreak; *estrapade*, *ruade*; *coup de main*, sally, *sortie*, *camisade*, raid, foray; run -at, – against; dead set at.

storm, -ing; boarding, *escalade*; siege, investment, obsession, bombardment, cannonade; air raid.

fire, volley; platoon –, file –, rapid-fire; *fusillade*; sharp-shooting, sniping; broadside; raking –, cross –, machine gun- fire; – volley of grapeshot, *feu d'enfer*; salvo.

cut, thrust, lunge, pass, *passado*, *carte* and *tierce*, home thrust, *coup de pied*; kick, punch, etc. (*impulse*) 276.

battue, *razzia*, *Jacquerie*, *dragonnade*; devastation etc. 162.

assailant, aggressor, invader.

base of operations, point of attack.

V. attack, assault, assail; set –, fall- upon; charge, impugn, break a lance with, enter the lists.

assume –, take- the offensive; be –, become-the aggressor; strike the first blow, fire the first shot, throw the first stone at; lift a hand –, draw the sword- against; take up the cudgels; advance –, march- against; march upon, invade, harry; come on, show fight.

strike at, poke at, thrust at; aim –, deal- a blow at; give –, fetch- one a -blow, – kick; have a -cut, – shot, – fling, – shy- at; be down –, pounce-upon; fall foul of, pitch into, launch out against; bait, slap on the face; make a -thrust, – pass, – set, – dead set- at; dunt; bear down upon.

close with, come to close quarters, bring to bay.

ride full tilt against; let fly at, dash at, run a tilt at, rush at, tilt at, run at, fly at, hawk at, have at, let out at; make a -dash, – rush at; attack tooth and nail; strike home; drive –, press- one hard; be hard upon, run down, strike at the root of.

lay about one, run amuck.

fire -upon, – at, – a shot at; shoot at, pop at, level at, let off a gun at; open fire, pepper, bombard, shell, pour a broadside into; fire -a volley, – red-hot shot; spring a mine.

throw -a stone, – stones- at; stone, lapidate, pelt; hurl -at, – against, – at the head of.

beset, besiege, beleaguer; lay siege to, invest, open the trenches, plant a battery, sap, mine; storm, board, scale the walls.

cut and thrust, bayonet, butt; kick, strike etc. (*impulse*) 276; whip etc. (*punish*) 972.

Adj. attacking etc. *v.*; aggressive, offensive, obsidional.

up in arms; on the warpath; over the top.

Adv. on the offensive.

Int. 'up and at them!'

717. Defense.—N. defense, protection, guard, ward; shielding etc. *v.*; propugnation; preservation etc. 670; guardianship.

self-defense, -preservation; resistance etc. 719.

safeguard etc. (*safety*) 664; screen etc. (*shelter*) 666, (*concealment*) 530; barrage; fortification; muni-tion, -ment; bulwark, fosse, moat, ditch, intrenchment, trench, dugout, gas mask; dike, dyke; parapet, parados, sunk fence, embankment, mound, mole, bank; earth- field-work, gabions; fence, wall, dead wall, contravallation; paling etc. (*inclosure*) 232; palisade, haha, stockade, *stoccado, laager, sangar*; barri-er, -cade; boom; portcullis, *chevaux de frise*; aba-, abat-, abba-tis; *vallum,* circumvallation, battlement, rampart, scarp; e-, counter-scarp; glacis, casemate.

mine, countermine.

buttress, abutment; shore etc. (*support*) 215.

breastwork, *banquette,* curtain, mantlet, bastion, demilune, redan, ravelin; advanced –, horn –, out- work, lunette; barb-acan, -ican; redoubt; fortelage, -alice; lines; coast defense.

loop-hole, machicolation; sally-port, postern gate.

hold, stronghold, fastness; asylum etc. (*refuge*) 666; keep, donjon, fortress, citadel; capitol, castle; tower, – of strength; fort, barracoon, pah, sconce, martello tower, peel-house, block-house, rath; wooden walls; turret, barbette.

buffer, corner-stone, fender, apron, mask, gauntlet, thimble, carapace, armor, shield, buckler; target, targe, aegis, breastplate, cuirass, plastron, habergeon, mail, coat of mail, brigandine, hauberk, lorication, helmet, helm, basinet, sallet, salade, heaume, morion, murrion, armet, cabaset, vizor, casquetel, siege-cap, head-piece, casque, steel helmet, tin hat; *pickelhaube,* csako; shako etc. (*dress*) 225; bearskin; panoply; truncheon etc. (*weapon*) 727.

garrison, picket, piquet; defender, protector; guardian etc. (*safety*) 664; trabant, body guard, champion; knight-errant, Paladin; propugner.

V. defend, forfend, fend; shield, screen, shroud; fence round etc. (*circumscribe*) 229; fence, intrench; guard etc. (*keep safe*) 664; guard against; take care of etc. (*vigilance*) 459; bear harmless; keep –, ward –, beat- off; hinder etc. 706.

parry, repel, propugn, put to flight; give a warm reception to [*ironical*] ; hold –, keep- at -bay, – arm's length.

stand –, act- on the defensive; show fight; maintain –, stand- one's ground; stand by; hold one's own; bear –, stand- the brunt; fall back upon, hold, stand in the gap.

Adj. defending etc. *v.*; defensive; mural; armed, – at all points, – *cap-à-pie*, – to the teeth; panoplied; accoutred, harnessed; iron-plated, -clad; loop-holed, castellated, machicolated; casemated; defended etc. *v.*; proof against, bomb-, bullet-proof; protective.

Adv. defensively; on the -defense, – defensive; in defense; at bay, *pro aris et focis.*

Int. no surrender! *il ne passeront pas!*

Phr. defense not defiance.

718. Retaliation.—N. retaliation, reprisal, retort; counter-stroke, -blast, -plot, -project; retribution, *lex talionis*; reciprocation etc. (*reciprocity*) 12.

requital, desert, tit for tat, give and take, blow for blow, *quid pro quo,* a Roland for an Oliver, measure for measure, an eye for an eye, diamond cut diamond, the biter bit, a game at which two can play; boomerang.

recrimination etc. (*accusation*) 938; revenge etc. 919; compensation etc. 30; reaction etc. (*recoil*) 277.

V. retaliate, retort, turn upon; pay -off, – back; pay in -one's own, – the same- coin; cap; reciprocate etc. 148; turn the tables upon, return the compliment; give -a *quid pro quo* etc. *n.*, – as much as one takes; give and take, exchange -blows, – fisticuffs; be -quits, – even- with; pay off old scores.

serve one right, be hoist on one's own petard, throw a stone in one's own garden, cathch a Tartar.

Adj. retaliating etc. *v.*; retalia-tory, -tive; retributive, recriminatory, reciprocal.

Adv.. in retaliation; *en revanche.*

Phr. *mutato nomine de te fabula narratur; par pari refero; tu quoque*; you're another; *suo sibi gladio hunc jugulo.*

719. Resistance.—N. resistance, stand, front, oppugnation; opposition etc. 708; renitence, reluctation, recalcitration, recalcitrance; repugnance; kicking etc. *v.*

repulse, rebuff.

insurrection etc. (*disobedience*) 742; strike; turn –, lock –, barring- out; *levée en masse, Jacquerie*; riot etc. (*disorder*) 59.

V. resist; not -submit etc. 725; repugn, reluctate, withstand; stand up –, strive –, bear up –, be proof –, make head- against; stand, – firm, – one's ground, – the brunt of, – out; hold -one's ground, – one's own, – out.

breast the -wave, – current; stem the -tide, – torrent; face, confront, grapple with; show a bold front etc. (*courage*) 861; present a front; make a –, take one's- stand.

kick, – against; recalcitrate, kick against the pricks; oppose etc. 708; fly in the face of; lift the hand against etc. (*attack*) 716; rise up in arms etc. (*war*) 722; strike, turn out; draw up a round robin etc. (*remonstrate*) 932; revolt etc. (*disobey*) 742; make a riot.

prendre le mors aux dents; take the bit between the teeth; sell one's life dearly, die hard, keep at bay; repel, repulse.

Adj. resisting etc. *v.*; resist-ive, -ant; refractory etc. (*disobedient*) 742; recalcitrant, re-nitent, -pulsive, -pellant; up in arms.

proof against; unconquerable etc. (*strong*) 159; stubborn, unconquered; indomitable etc. (*persevering*) 604*a*; unyielding etc. (*obstinate*) 606.

Int. hands off! keep off!

720. Contention.—N. contention, strife; contest, -ation; struggle; belligerency; opposition etc. 708.

controversy, polemics; debate etc. (*discussion*) 476; war of words, logomachy, litigation; paper war, ink slinging; high words etc. (*quarrel*) 713; sparring etc. *v.*

competition, rivalry; corrival-ry, -ship; agonism, *concours,* match, race, horse-racing, heat, steeple chase, point-to-point race, handicap; boat race, regatta; field-day; sham fight, Derby day; turf, sporting, bull-fight, tauromachy, *gymkhana,* rodeo, Olympiad.

wrestling, *ju-jitsu,* pugilism, boxing, fisticuffs, spar, mill, set-to, scrap, round, bout, event; prize-fighting; quarter-staff, single stick; gladiatorship, gymnastics; athletic-s, – sports; games of skill etc. 840.

shindy; *fracas* etc. (*discord*) 713; clash of arms; tussle, scuffle, broil, fray; affray, -ment; velitation; col-, luctation; brabble, *brique,* scramble, *mêlée,* scrimmage, stramash, bush-fighting.

free –, stand up –, hand to hand –, running-fight.

conflict, skirmish; ren-, en-counter; *rencontre,* collision, affair, brush, fight; battle, – royal; combat, action, engagement, joust, tournament; tilt, -ing; tourney, list; pitched battle, guerilla warfare.

death-struggle, struggle for life or death, Armageddon; hard knocks, sharp contest, tug of war.

naval -engagement, – battle; *naumachia,* sea-fight.

duel, -lo; single combat, monomachy, satisfaction, *passage d'armes,* passage of arms, affair of honor; triangular duel; hostile meeting, digladiation; appeal to arms etc. (*warfare*) 722.

deeds –, feats- of arms; pugnacity; combativeness etc. *adj.*; bone of contention etc. 713.

V. contend; contest, strive, struggle, scramble, wrestle; spar, square; exchange -blows, – fisticuffs; scrap, mix with, fib, justle, tussle, tilt, box, stave, fence; skirmish; fight etc. (*war*) 722; wrangle etc. (*quarrel*) 713.

contend etc. –, grapple –, engage –, close –, buckle –, bandy –, try conclusions –, have a brush etc. *n.* –, tilt- with; encounter, fall foul of, pitch into, clapperclaw, run a tilt at; oppose etc. 708; reluct.

join issue, come to blows, be at loggerheads, set-to, come to the scratch, exchange shots, measure swords, meet hand to hand; take up the -cudgels, – glove, – gauntlet; enter the lists; couch one's lance; give satisfaction; appeal to arms etc. (*warfare*) 722.

lay about one; break the peace.

compete –, cope –, vie –, race- with; outvie, emulate, rival; run a race; contend etc. –, stipulate –, stickle- for; insist upon, make a point of.

Adj. contending etc. *v.*; together by the ears, at loggerheads, at war, at issue.

competitive, rival; belligerent; contentious, combative, bellicose, unpeaceful; warlike etc. 722; quarrelsome etc. 901; pugnacious; pugilistic, gladiatorial; palestric, -al.

Phr. *a verbis ad verbera*; a word and a blow.

721. Peace.—N. peace; amity etc. (*friendship*) 888; harmony etc. (*concord*) 714; tranquility etc. (*quiescence*) 265; truce etc. (*pacification*) 723; pacificism; pipe –, calumet- of peace.

piping time of peace, quiet life; neutrality.

V. be at peace; keep the peace etc. (*concord*) 714; make peace etc. 723.

Adj. pacific; peace-able, -ful; calm, tranquil, untroubled, halcyon; bloodless; neutral.

Phr. the storm blown over; the lion lies down with the lamb.

722. Warfare.—N. warfare; fighting etc. *v.*; hostilities; war, arms, the sword; Mars, Bellona, grim visaged war, *horrida bella*, Armageddon.

appeal to -arms, – the sword; ordeal –, wager- of battle; *ultima ratio regum*, arbitrament of the sword.

battle array, campaign, crusade, expedition; mobilization; state of siege; battle-field etc. (*arena*) 728; warpath.

art of war, tactics, strategy, castrametation; general-, soldier-ship; aerial –, submarine –, naval –, chemical-, atomic-, guerilla- warfare; military evolutions, ballistics, gunnery; chivalry; poison gas; gun-powder, shot, – and shell.

battle, tug of war etc. (*contention*) 720; service, campaigning, active service, tented field; fiery cross, trumpet, clarion, bugle, pibroch, slogan; war-cry, -whoop; battle cry, beat of drum, rappel, tom-tom; word of command; pass-, watch-word.

war to the -death, – knife; *guerre a -mort*, – *outrance*; open –, internecine –, civil- war.

V. arm; raise –, mobilize- troops; raise up in arms; take up the cudgels etc. 720; take up –, fly to –, appeal to- -arms, – the sword; draw –, unsheathe- the sword; dig up the hatchet; go to –, declare –, wage –, let slip the dogs of- war; cry havoc; kindle –, light- the torch of war; raise one's banner, send round the fiery cross; hoist the black flag; throw –, fling- away the scabbard; enrol, enlist, join up; take the field; take the law into one's own hands; do –, give –, join –, engage in –, go to- battle; flesh one's sword; set to, fall to, engage, measure swords with, draw the trigger, cross swords; come to -blows, – close quarters; fight; combat; contend etc. 720; battle –, break a lance- with.

serve; see –, be on- -service, – active service; campaign; wield the sword, shoulder a musket, smell powder, be under the fire; spill –, imbrue the hands in- blood; be on the warpath.

carry on -war, – hostilities; keep the field; fight the good fight; go over the top; cut one's way through; fight -it out, – like devils, – one's way, – hand to hand; sell one's life dearly.

Adj. conten-ding, -tious etc. 720; armed, – to the teeth, – cap-à-pie; sword in hand; in –, under –, up in- arms; at war with; bristling with arms; in -battle array, – open arms, – the field; embattled.

unpacific, unpeaceful; belligerent, combative, armigerous, bellicose, martial, warlike; mili-tary, -tant; soldier-like, -ly; chivalrous; strategical, internecine.

Adv. *flagrante bello*, in the -thick of the fray, – cannon's mouth; at the -swords's point, – point of the bayonet.

Int. *vae victis!* to arms! to your tents O Israel!

Phr. the battle rages.

723. Pacification.—N. pacification, conciliation; reconcil-iation, -ement; shaking of hands, accomodation, arrangement, adjustment; terms, compromise; amnesty, deed of release.

peace-offering; olive-branch; overtures; pipe –, calumet –, preliminaries- of peace.

truce, armistice; suspension of -arms, – hostilities; breathing-time; convention; *modus vivendi*; flag of truce, white flag, *parlementaire*, *cartel*.

hollow truce, *pax in bello*; drawn battle.

V. pacify, tranquilize, compose; allay etc. (*moderate*) 174; reconcile, propitiate, placate, conciliate, meet half-way, hold out the olive-branch, heal the breach, make peace, restore harmony, bring to terms.

settle –, arrange –, accommodate- -matters, – differences; set straight; make up a quarrel, *tantas componere lites*; come to -an understanding, – terms; bridge over, hush up; make -it, – matters-up; shake hands.

raise a siege; put up –, sheathe- the sword; bury the hatchet, lay down one's arms, turn swords into ploughshares; smoke the calumet of peace, close the temple of Janus; keep the peace etc. (*concord*) 714; be -pacified etc.; come round.

Adj. conciliatory, pacificatory; composing etc *v.*; pacified etc. *v.*

Phr. *requiescat in pace.*

724. Mediation.—N. media-tion, -torship, -tization; inter-vention, -position, -ference, -meddling, -cession; parley, negotiation, arbitration; flag of truce etc. 723; good offices, peace -offering; diploma-tics, -cy; compromise etc. 774.

mediator, intercessor, peacemaker, make-peace, negotiator, go-between; diplomatist etc. (*consignee*) 758; moderator, propitiator, umpire, arbitrator.

V. media-te, -tize; inter-cede, -pose, -fere, -vene; step in, negotiate; meet half-way; arbitrate; *magnas componere lites*.

Adj. mediatory, propitiatory, diplomatic.

725. Submission.—N. submission, yielding, acquiescence, compliance; non-resistance; obedience etc. 743; submissiveness, deference.

surrender, cession, capitulation, resignation.

obeisance, homage, kneeling, genuflexion, courtesy, curtsy, *salaam*, *kowtow*, prostration.

V. succumb, submit, yield, bend, resign, defer to, accede.

lay down –, deliver up- one's arms; hand over one's sword; lower –, haul down –, strike- one's flag, – colors; deliver the keys of the city.

surrender, – at discretion; cede, capitulate, come to terms, retreat, beat a retreat; draw in one's horns etc. (*humility*) 879; give -way, – ground, – in, – up; cave in; suffer judgment by default; bend, – to one's yoke, – before the storm; reel back; bend –, knuckle- -down, – to, – under; knock under.

humble oneself; eat -dirt, – the leek, – humble pie; bite –, lick- the dust; be –, fall- at one's feet; craven; crouch before, throw oneself at the feet of; swallow the -leek, – pill; kiss the rod; turn the other cheek; *avaler des couleuvres*, gulp down.

obey etc. 743; kneel to, bow to, pay homage to, cringe to, truckle to; bend the -neck, – knee; kneel, fall on one's knees, bow submission, courtesy, curtsy, *kowtow*; make obeisance.

pocket the affront; make -the best of, – a virtue of necessity; grin and abide, shrug the shoulders, resign oneself; submit with a good grace etc. (*bear with*) 826.

Adj. surrendering etc. *v.*; submissive, resigned, crouching; down-trodden; down on one's marrow bones; on one's bended knee; weak-kneed, un-, non-resisting; pliant etc. (*soft*) 324; undefended.

untenable, indefensible; humble etc. 879.

Phr. have it your own way; it can't be helped; amen etc. (*assent*) 488.

726. Combatant.—N. combatant; disputant, controversialist, polemic, litigant, belligerent; competitor, rival, corrival; fighter, assailant, aggressor; champion, Paladin; moss-trooper, swashbuckler, fire-eater, duellist, bully, bludgeon-man, rough, fighter, fighting-man, prize-fighter, pugilist, pug, boxer, bruiser, the fancy, gladiator, athlete, wrestler; fighting-, game-cock; swordsman, *sabreur*.

warrior, soldier, Amazon, man-at-arms, armigerent; campaigner, veteran; red-coat, military man, *rajpoot*, brave.

armed force, troops, soldiery, military, forces, sabaoth, the army, standing army, regulars, the line, troops of the line, militia, territorials, yeomanry, volunteers, trainband, fencible; auxiliary –, reserve- forces; reserves, *posse comitatus*, national guard, *gendarme*, beefeater; guards, -man; yeoman of the guard, life guards, household troops.

janissary; myrmidon; Mama-, Mame-luke; spahee, *spahi*, Cossack, Croat, Pandour; irregular, free lance, *franc-tireur, bashi-bazouk, guerilla, condottiere*; mercenary.

levy, draught, commando; *Land-wehr, -sturm*; conscript, recruit, rookie, cadet, raw levies.

private, – soldier; Tommy Atkins, rank and file, peon, trooper, doughboy, sepoy, *askari*, *legionnaire*, legionary, food for powder, cannon fodder; officer etc. (*commander*) 745; subaltern, ensign, shave-tail, standard bearer, non-com; spear-

pike-man; halberdier, lancer; musketeer, carabineer, rifleman, sharpshooter, yager, skirmisher; grenadier, fusileer; archer, bowman.

horse and foot; horse –, foot- soldier; cavalry, horse, artillery, horse –, field –, heavy –, mountain- artillery, infantry, light horse, *voltigeur, Uhlan*, mounted rifles, dragoon, hussar, trooper; light –, heavy- dragoon; heavy; *cuirassier*; gunner, cannoneer, bombardier, artillery-man, matross; sapper, – and miner; engineer; light infantry, rifles, *chasseur, zouave*; military train, supply and transport, coolie.

army, – corps, *corps d'armée*, host, division, column, wing, detachment, *escadrille*, garrison, flying column, brigade, regiment, *corps*, battalion, squadron, company, platoon, battery, subdivision, section, squad; piquet, picket, guard, rank, file; legion, phalanx, cohort; cloud of skirmishers; impi.

war-horse, charger, *destrier*.

armored -train, – car; tank.

marine, man of war's man etc. (*sailor*) 269; navy, first line of defense, wooden walls; naval forces, fleet, flotilla, armada, squadron.

man-of-war, warship; H.M.S., U.S.S.; capital ship; line-of-battle ship, battle ship; super-, dreadnought, battle –, armored –, protected – light-cruiser; scout, flotilla leader; destroyer, torpedo boat; submarine, submersible, U-boat; submarine chaser, eagle boat, mystery ship, Q-boat; mine-layer, -sweeper; ship of the line, iron-clad, turret-ship, ram, Monitor, floating battery; first-rate, frigate, sloop of war, corvette, gunboat, bomb-vessel, fire-boat; flag ship, guard ship, cruiser; airplane carrier; privateer; tender; depot –, parent-ship; store –, troop- ship; transport, catamaran.

aircraft etc. 273; air force, scout, fighter, bomber, troop carrier, aerial patrol, seaplane, flying boat, torpedo plane; airship, Zeppelin; rigid –, semi-rigid –, non-rigid- airship; dirigible –, free –, captive –, kite –, observation- balloon.

anti-aircraft guns, searchlights, sound locators; catapult.

727. Arms.—N. arm, -s; weapon, deadly weapon; arma-ment, -ture; panoply, stand of arms; armor etc. (*defense*) 717; armory etc. (*store*) 636.

ammunition; powder, – and shot; explosive; propellant; gun-powder, -cotton; dynam-, melin-, cord-, lydd-ite; trinitrotoluene, T.N.T., ammonal; cartridge; ball cartridge, *cartouche*, fire-ball; dud, black Marie; 'villainous saltpeter;' poison –, mustard –, lachrymatory –, tear- gas.

sword, saber, broadsword, cutlass, falchion, scimitar, cimeter, brand, whinyard, bilbo, glaive, glave, rapier, skean, Toledo, Ferrara, tuck, claymore, creese, kris, *kukri*, dagger, dirk, hanger, poniard, stiletto, stylet, dudgeon, bayonet; sword-bayonet, -stick; side arms, foil, blade, steel; axe, bill; pole-, battle-axe; gisarm, halberd, partisan, tomahawk, bowie-knife; at-, att-, yat-aghan; yatachan; good –, trusty –, naked- sword; cold –, naked-steel.

club, mace, truncheon, staff, bludgeon, cudgel, life-preserver, shillelagh, sprig; hand-, quarter-staff; bat, cane, stick, knuckle-duster, sand bag.

gun, piece; fire-arms; artillery, ordnance; siege –, battering-train; park, battery; cannon, gun of position, heavy –, siege –, field –, mountain –, anti-aircraft –, breech loading –, quick firing-gun; field piece, mortar, trench mortar; mine –, flame- -thrower, napalm; howitzer, carronade, culverin, basilisk; falconet jingal, swivel, *pederero, bouche à feu*; smooth bore, rifled cannon; Armstrong –, Lancaster –, Paixhan –, Whitworth –, Parrott –, Krupp –, Gatling –, Maxim –, Vickers –, Hotchkiss –, Lewis –, machine- gun; tommy gun, Thompson's submachine gun; *mitrailleu-r, -se*; pompom; blow pipe.

small arms; musket, -ry, firelock, flintlock, fowling-piece, shot gun, rifle, *fusil*, caliver, carbine, blunderbuss, musketoon, Brown Bess, matchlock, harquebuss, *arquebuse*, haguebut; petronel; smallbore; breech-, muzzle-loader; Minié –, Enfield –, Westly Richards –, Snider –, Springfield –, Martini-Henry –, Lee-Metford –, Lee-Enfield –, Mauser –, Männlicher –, magazine –, repeating- rifle; needle-gun, *chassepot*; pis-tol, -et; revolver, automatic pistol, automatic; wind-, air-gun; flame –, gas- projector.

bow, cross-bow, arbalest, balister, catapult, sling; battering-ram etc. (*impulse*) 276; gunnery; ballistics etc. (*propulsion*) 284.

missile, bolt, projectile, shot, pellet, ball; grape; grape –, canister –, bar –, cannon –, langrel –, langrage –, round –, chain- shot; explosive; incendiary –, expanding –, soft-nosed –, dum-dum- bullet; slug, stone, brickbat; hand –, rifle-grenade; high explosive –, incendiary –, stink-, A-, H-, atomic –, hydrogen – bomb; petard, torpedo, carcass, rocket; congreve, – rocket; shrapnel, *mitraille*; thunderbolt; mine, land mine, infernal machine.

pike, lance, spear, spontoon, javelin, assagai, throwing stick, dart, djerrid, arrow, reed, shaft, bolt, boomerang, harpoon, gaff.

728. Arena.—N. arena, field, platform; scene of action, theater; walk, course; hustings; stage, boards etc. (*playhouse*) 599; amphitheater; Coli-, Colos-seum; Flavian amphitheater, hippodrome, circus, race-course, track, *stadium*, *corso*, turf, cockpit, bear-garden, play-ground, playing fields, *gymnasium, palaestra*, ring, lists; tilt-yard, -ing ground; *Campus Martius, Champ de Mars*; aerodrome, airport, air base, flying field.

theater –, seat- of war; battle-field, -ground; field of -battle, – slaughter; no man's land; Aceldama, camp; the enemy's camp; trysting- place etc. (*place of meeting*) 74.

729. Completion.—N. completion; accomplish-, achieve-, fulfil-ment; performance, execution; des-, dis-patch; consummation, culmination, climax; finish, conclusion, effectuation; close etc. (*end*) 67; terminus etc. (*arrival*) 292; winding up; *finale, dénouement*, catastrophe, issue, upshot, result; final –, last –, crowning –, finishing- -touch, – stroke; last finish, *coup de grâce*; crowning of the edifice; coping-, keystone; missing link etc. 53; superstructure, *ne plus ultra*, work done, *fait accompli*.

elaboration; finality; completeness etc. 52.

V. effect, -uate; accomplish, achieve, compass, consummate, hammer out; bring to -maturity, – perfection; perfect, complete; elaborate.

do, execute, make; go –, get- through; work out, enact, bring -about, – to bear, – to pass, – through, – to a head.

des-, dis-patch; knock –, finish –, polish- off; make short work of; dispose of, set at rest; perform, discharge, fulfil, realize; put in -practice, – force; carry -out, – into effect, – into execution; make good; be as good as one's word.

do thoroughly, not do by halves, go the whole hog; drive home; be in at the death etc. (*persevere*) 604*a*; carry through, play out, exhaust, deliver the goods, fill the bill.

finish, bring to a close etc. (*end*) 67; wind up, stamp, clinch, seal, set the seal on, put the seal to; give the -final touch etc. *n.* to; put the -last, – finishing- hand to; crown, – all; cap.

ripen, culminate; come to a -head, – crisis; come to its end; die -a natural death, – of old age; run -its course, – one's race; touch –, reach –, attain- the goal; reach etc. (*arrive*) 292; get in the harvest.

Adj. completing, final; conclu-ding, -sive; crowning etc. *v.*; exhaustive, complete, mature, perfect, consummate.

done, completed etc. *v.*; done for, sped, wrought out; highly wrought etc. (*preparation*) 673; thorough etc. 52; ripe etc. (*ready*) 673.

Adv. completely etc. (*thoroughly*) 52; to crown all, out of hand.

Phr. the race is run; *actum est*; *finis coronat opus*; *consummatum est*; *c'en est fait*; it is all over; the game is played out, the bubble has burst.

730. Non-Completion.—N. non-completion, -fulfilment; shortcoming etc. 304; incompleteness etc. 53; drawn -battle, – game; work of Penelope, task of Sisyphus.

non-performance, inexecution; neglect etc. 460.

V. not -complete etc. 729; leave -unfinished etc. *adj.*, – undone; neglect etc. 460; let -alone, – slip; lose sight of.

fall short of etc. 304; do things by halves; scotch the snake, not kill it; hang fire; be slow to; collapse etc. 304.

Adj. not completed etc. *v.*; incomplete etc. 53; uncompleted, unfinished; unaccomplished; unperformed, unexecuted; sketchy, addle.

in progress, in hand; going on, proceeding; on one's hands; on the fire; on the stocks; in preparation; lacking the finishing touch.

Adv. *re infectâ*.

731. Success.—N. success, -fulness; speed; advance etc. (*progress*) 282.

trump card; hit, stroke; lucky –, fortunate –, good- -hit, – stroke; bold –, master- stroke; *coup de maître*, checkmate; half the battle, prize; profit etc. (*acquisition*) 775; best seller.

continued success; good fortune etc. (*prosperity*) 734; time well spent.

advantage over; edge; upper-, whiphand; ascendancy, mastery; expugnation, conquest, victory, subdual; subjugation etc. (*subjection*) 749.

triumph etc. (*exultation*) 884; proficiency etc. (*skill*) 698; conqueror, victor, winner, champion; master of the -situation, – position.

V. succeed; be -successful etc. *adj.*; gain one's -end, – ends; crown with success.

gain –, attain –, carry –, secure –, win- -a point, – an object; put over; make a go of; manage to, contrive to; accomplish etc. (*effect, complete*) 729; do –, work- wonders.

come off -well, – successfully, – with flying colors; make short work of; take –, carry- by storm; bear away the bell; win -one's spurs, – the battle; win –, carry –, gain- the -day, – prize, – palm; climb on the bandwagon; have -the best of it, – it all one's own way, – the game in one's own hands, – the ball at one's feet, – one on the hip; walk over the course; carry all before one, remain in possession of the field; score a success, win hands down.

speed; make progress etc. (*advance*) 282; win –, make –, work –, find- one's way; strive to some purpose; prosper etc. 734; drive a roaring trade; make profit etc. (*acquire*) 775; reap –, gather- the -fruits, – benefit of, – harvest; make one's fortune, get in the harvest, turn to good account; turn to account etc. (*use*) 677.

triumph, be triumphant; gain –, obtain- -a victory, – an advantage; chain victory to one's car.

surmount –, overcome –, get over- -a difficulty, – an obstacle etc. 706; *se tirer d'affaire*; make head against; stem the -torrent, – tide, – current; weather -the storm, – a point; turn a corner, keep one's head above water, tide over; master; get –, have –, gain- the -better of, – best of, – upper hand, – ascendancy, – whip hand, – start of; distance; surpass etc. (*superiority*) 33.

defeat, conquer, vanquish, discomfit; over-come, throw, -power, -master, -match, -set, -ride, -reach; out-wit, -do, -flank, -maneuver, -general, -vote; take the wind out of one's adversary's sails; beat, – hollow; rout, lick, drub, floor, worst; put -down, – to flight, – to the rout, – *hors de combat*; – out of court.

silence, quell, nonsuit, checkmate, upset, confound, nonplus, trump; baffle etc. (*hinder*) 706; circumvent, elude; trip up – the heels of; drive -into a corner, – to the wall; run hard, put one's nose out of joint.*

settle, do for; break the -neck of, – back of; capsize, sink, shipwreck, drown, swamp; subdue; subjugate etc. (*subject*) 749; reduce; make the enemy bite the dust; victimize, roll in the dust, trample under foot, put an extinguisher upon.

answer, – the purpose; avail, prevail, take effect, do, turn out well, work well, take, tell, bear fruit; hit -it, – the mark, – the right nail on the head; nick it; turn up trumps, make a hit; find one's account in.

Adj. succeeding etc. *v.*; successful; prosperous etc. 734; triumphant; flushed –, crowned- with success; victorious; set up; in the ascendant; unbeaten etc. (*see* beat etc. *v.*); well-spent; felicitous, effective, in full swing.

Adv. successfully etc. *adj.*; with flying colors, in triumph, swimmingly; *à merveille,* beyond all hope; to some –, good- purpose; to one's heart's content.

Phr. *veni vidi vici,* the day being one's own, one's star in the ascendant; *omne tulit punctum.*

732. Failure.—N. failure; non-success, -fulfilment; dead failure, successlessness; abortion, miscarriage; *brutum fulmen* etc. 158; labor in vain etc. (*inutility*) 645; no go; inefficacy; inefficaciousness etc. *adj.*; vain –, ineffectual –, abortive- -attempt, – efforts; flash in the pan, 'lame and impotent conclusion;' frustration; slip 'twixt cup and lip etc. (*disappointment*) 509.

blunder etc. (*mistake*) 495; fault, omission, miss, oversight, slip, trip, stumble, claudication, footfall; false –, wrong- step; *faux pas,* titubation, *bévue, faute,* lurch; botchery etc. (*want of skill*) 699; scrape, jam, mess, muddle, foozle, *fiasco,* breakdown.

mishap etc. (*misfortune*) 735; split, collapse, smash, blow, explosion.

repulse, rebuff, defeat, rout, overthrow, discomfiture; beating, drubbing; *quietus,* nonsuit, subjugation; check-, fool's-mate.

fall, downfall, ruin, perdition; wreck etc. (*destruction*) 162; death-blow; bankruptcy etc. (*non-payment*) 808.

losing game, *affaire flambée.*

victim, prey; bankrupt.

V. fail; be -unsuccessful etc. *adj.*; not -succeed etc. 731; make -vain efforts etc. *n.*; do –, labor –, toil- in vain; lose one's labor, take nothing by one's motion; bring to naught, make nothing of; wash a blackamoor white etc. (*impossible*) 471; roll the stone of Sisyphus etc. (*useless*) 645; do by halves etc. (*not complete*) 730; lose ground etc. (*recede*) 283; flunk; fall short of etc. 304.

miss, – one's aim, – the mark, – one's footing, – stays; slip, trip, stumble; make a -slip etc. *n.*, – blunder etc. 495, – mess of, – botch of; bitch it, miscarry, abort, go up like a rocket and come down like the stick, reckon without one's host; get the wrong sow by the ear etc. (*blunder, mismanage*) 699.

limp, halt, hobble, titubate; fall, tumble; lose one's balance; fall -to the ground, – between two stools; flounder, falter, stick in the mud, run aground, split upon a rock; run –, knock –, dash- one's head against a stone wall; break one's back; break down, sink, drown, founder, have the ground cut from under one; get into -trouble, – a mess, – a scrape; come to grief etc. (*adversity*) 735; go to -the wall, – the dogs, – pot; lick –, bite- the dust; be -defeated etc. 731; have the worst of it, lose the day, come off second best, lose; fall a prey to; succumb etc. (*submit*) 725; not have a leg to stand on.

come to nothing, end in smoke; fall -to the ground, – through, – dead, – still-born, – flat; slip through one's fingers; hang –, miss- fire; flash in the pan, collapse; topple down etc. (*descent*) 305; go to wrack and ruin etc. (*destruction*) 162.

go amiss, go wrong, go cross, go hard with, go on a wrong tack; go on –, come off –, turn out

–, work- ill; take -a wrong, – an ugly- turn; gang agley.

be all -over with, – up with; explode; dash one's hopes etc. (*disappoint*) 509; defeat the purpose; upset the apple cart; sow the wind and reap the whirlwind, jump out of the frying pan into the fire.

Adj. unsuccessful, successless; failing, tripping etc. *v.*; at fault; unfortunate etc. 735.

abortive, addle, still-born; fruitless, sterile, bootless; ineffect-ual, -ive; inefficient etc. (*impotent*) 158; inefficacious; lame, hobbling, *décousu*; insufficient etc. 640; unavailing etc. (*useless*) 645; of no effect.

aground, grounded, swamped, stranded, cast away, wrecked, foundered, capsized, shipwrecked, non-suited; foiled; defeated etc. 731; struck –, borne –, broken- down; down-trodden; overborne, -whelmed; all up with; beaten to a frazzle.

lost, undone, ruined, broken; bankrupt etc. (*not paying*) 808; played out; done -up, – for; dead beat, ruined root and branch, *flambé,* knocked on the head; destroyed etc. 162.

frustrated, thwarted, crossed, unhinged, disconcerted, dashed; thrown -off one's balance, – on one's back, – on one's beam ends; unhorsed, in a sorry plight; hard hit.

stultified, befooled, dished, hoist on one's own petard, victimized, sacrificed.

wide of the mark etc. (*error*) 495; out of one's reckoning etc. (*inexpectation*) 508; left in the lurch; thrown away etc. (*wasted*) 638; unattained; uncompleted etc. 730.

Adv. unsuccessfully etc. *adj.*; to little or no purpose, in vain, *re infectâ.*

Phr. the bubble has burst, the game is up, all is lost; the devil to pay; *parturiunt montes* etc. (*disappointment*) 509.

733. Trophy.—N. trophy; medal, prize, palm; ribbon, blue ribbon, *cordon bleu*; citation; cup, laurel, -s; bays, crown, chaplet, wreath, civic crown; Victoria Cross, V.C., *Croix de Guerre,* Iron Cross; Distinguished Service Cross, Medal of Honor, Congressional Medal; insignia etc. 550; feather in one's cap etc. (*honor*) 873; decoration etc. 877; garland, triumphal arch.

triumph etc. (*celebration*) 883; flying colors etc. (*show*) 882.

monumentum aere perennius.

734. Prosperity.—N. prosperity, welfare, well-being; affluence etc. (*wealth*) 803; success etc. 731; thrift, roaring trade; chicken in every pot, the full dinner paid; good –, smiles of- fortune; blessings, godsend.

luck; good –, run of- luck; sunshine; fair -weather, – wind; palmy –, bright –, halcyon-days; piping times, tide, flood, high tide.

Saturnia regna, Saturnian age; golden -time, – age; bed of roses; fat of the land, milk and honey, loaves and fishes, fleshpots of Egypt.

made man, lucky dog, *enfant gâté,* spoiled child of fortune.

upstart, *parvenu, nouveau riche,* profiteer, skip-jack, mushroom.

V. prosper, thrive, flourish; be -prosperous etc. *adj.*; drive a roaring trade; go on -well, – smoothly, – swimmingly; sail before the wind, swim with the tide; run -smooth, – smoothly, – on all fours.

rise –, get on- in the world; work –, make- one's way; look up; lift –, raise- one's head, make one's -fortune, – pile, feather one's nest.

flower, blow, blossom, bloom, fructify, bear fruit, fatten, batten.

keep oneself afloat; keep –, hold- one's head above water; light –, fall- on one's -legs, – feet; drop into a good thing; bear a charmed life; bask in the sunshine; have a -good, – fine- time of it; have a run, – of luck; have the -good fortune etc. *n.* to; take a favorable turn; live -on the fat of the land, – in clover.

Adj. prosperous; thriving etc. *v.*; in a fair way, buoyant; well -off, – to do, – to do in the world; set up, at one's ease; rich etc. 803; in good case; in -full, – high- feather; fortunate, lucky, in luck; born -with a silver spoon in one's mouth, – under a lucky star; on the sunny side of the hedge.

auspicious, propitious, providential.

palmy, halcyon; agreeable etc. 829; *couleur de rose.*

Adv. prosperously etc. *adj.*; swimmingly; as good luck would have it; beyond all -expectation, – hope, – one's wildest dreams.

Phr. one's star in the ascendant, all for the best, one's course runs smooth.

735. Adversity.—N. adversity, evil etc. 619; failure etc. 732; bad –, ill –, evil –, adverse –, hard- -fortune, – hap, – luck, – lot; frowns of fortune; evil -dispensation, – star, – genius; ups and downs of life, broken fortunes; hard -case, – lines, – life; sea –, peck- of troubles; hell upon earth; slough of despond; jinx.

trouble, humiliation, hardship, curse, blight, blast, load, pressure.

pressure of the times, iron age, evil day, time out of joint; hard –, bad –, sad- times; rainy day, cloud, dark cloud, gathering clouds, ill wind; visitation, infliction; affliction etc. (*painfulness*) 830; bitter -pill, – cup; care, trial; the sport of fortune.

mis-hap, -chance, -adventure, -fortune; disaster, calamity, catastrophe; accident, casualty, cross, reverse, check, *contretemps,* rub, pinch, setback.

losing game; falling etc. *v.*; fall, down-fall, come-down; ruin-ation, -ousness; undoing; extremity; ruin etc. (*destruction*) 162.

V. be -ill off etc. *adj.*; go hard with; fall on evil, – days; go on ill; not -prosper etc. 734.

go -downhill, – to rack and ruin etc. (*destruction*) 162, – to the dogs; fall, – from one's high estate; decay, sink, decline, go down in the world; have seen better days; bring down one's grey hairs with sorrow to the grave; come to grief; be all -over, – up- with; bring a -wasp's, – hornet's- nest about one's ears.

Adj. unfortunate, unblest, unhappy, unlucky; im-, un-prosperous; luck-, hap-less; out of luck; in trouble, in a bad way, in an evil plight; under a cloud; clouded; ill –, badly- off; in adverse circumstances; poor etc. 804; behindhand, down in the world, decayed, undone; on the road to ruin, on its last legs, on the wane; in one's utmost need.

planet-struck, devoted; born -under an evil star, – with a wooden ladle in one's mouth; ill-fated, -starred, -omened; inconspicuous, ominous, doomed, unpropitious.

adverse, untoward; disastrous, calamitous, ruinous, dire, deplorable.

Adv. if the worst come to the worst, as ill luck would have it, from bad to worse, out of the frying pan into the fire.

Phr. one's star is on the wane; one's luck -turns, – fails; the game is up, one's doom is sealed, the ground crumbles under one's feet, *sic transit gloria mundi, tant va la cruche à l'eau qu'à la fin elle se casse.*

736. Mediocrity.—N. moderate –, average-circumstances; respectability; middle classes, *bourgeoisie*; mediocrity; golden mean etc. (*mid-course*) 628, (*moderation*) 174.

V. jog on; go –, get on- -fairly, – quietly, – peaceably, – tolerably, – respectably; steer a middle course etc. 628.

Adj. middling, so-so, fair, medium, moderate, mediocre, second-, third- etc. -rate.

737. Authority.—N. authority; influence, patronage, power, preponderance, credit, *prestige*, prerogative, jurisdiction; right etc. (*title*) 924.

divine right, dynastic rights, authoritativeness; absolut-eness, -ism; despotism, tyranny; *jus nocendi.*

command, empire, sway, rule; domin-ion, -ation; sovereignty, supremacy, suzerainty; lord-, head-ship; chiefdom; seignior-y, -ity, hegemony, patriarchate, patriarchy; master-y, -ship, -dom; government etc. (*direction*) 693; dictation, control.

hold, grasp; grip, -e; reach; iron sway etc. (*severity*) 739; fangs, clutches, talons; rod of empire etc. (*scepter*) 747.

reign, regnancy, *régime*, dynasty; director-, dictator-ship; protector-ate, -ship; caliphate, pashalic, electorate; presiden-cy, -tship; administration; pro-, consulship; prefecture; seneschalship; magistra-ture, -cy; raj.

empire; monarchy; king-hood, -ship; royalty, regality, autocracy, monocracy, arist-archy, -ocracy; oligarchy, democracy, demogogy; republic, -anism, federalism; socialism, collectivism; communism, bolshevism, syndicalism; mob law, mobocracy, ochlocracy, ergatocracy; *vox populi, imperium in imperio*; bureaucracy; beadle-, bumble-dom; stratocracy; martial law, military -power, – government; feodality, feudal system, feudalism.

Thearchy, diarchy; du-, tri-, heter-archy; du-, triumvirate; auto-cracy, -nomy; limited monarchy; constitutional -government, – monarchy; home rule, autonomy; self-government, -determination; representative government; Soviet government.

gyn-archy, -ocracy, -aeocracy; petticoat government, matriarchate, matriarchy.

[Vicarious authority] commission etc. 755; deputy etc. 759; permission etc. 760.

country, state, realm, commonwealth, canton, constituency, toparchy, municipality, polity, body politic, *posse comitatus.*

person in authority etc. (*master*) 745; judicature etc. 965; cabinet etc. (*council*) 696; usurper; seat of -government, – authority; head-quarters.

[Acquisition of authority] accession; installation etc. 755; usurpation.

V. authorize etc. (*permit*) 760; warrant etc. (*right*) 924; dictate etc. (*order*) 741; have –, hold –, possess –, exercise –, exert –, wield- -authority etc. *n.*

be -at the head of etc. *adj.*; hold –, be in –, fill an- office; hold –, occupy- a post; be -master etc. 745.

rule, sway, command, control, administer; govern etc. (*direct*) 693; lead, preside over, reign; possess –, be seated on –, occupy- the throne; sway –, wield- the scepter; wear the crown.

have –, get- the -upper, – whip- hand; gain a hold upon, preponderate, dominate, boss, rule the roost; over-ride, -rule, -awe; lord it over, hold in hand, keep under, make a puppet of, lead by the nose, hold in the hollow of one's hand, turn round one's little finger, bend to one's will, hold one's own, wear the breeches; have -the ball at one's feet, – it all one's own way, – the game in one's own hand, – on the hip, – under one's thumb; be master of the situation; take the lead, play first fiddle, set the fashion; give the law to; carry with a high hand; lay down the law; 'ride in the whirlwind and direct the storm;' rule with a rod of iron etc. (*severity*) 739.

ascend –, mount- the throne, take the reins, – into one's hand; assume -authority etc. *n.*, – the reins of government; take –, assume the- command.

be -governed by, – in the power of; be under -the rule of, – the domination of.

Adj. ruling etc. *v.*; regnant, at the head, dominant, paramount, supreme, predominant, preponderant, in the ascendant, influential; gubernatorial; imperious; authoritative, executive, administrative, clothed with authority, official, *ex officio*, ministerial, bureaucratic, departmental, imperative, peremptory, overruling, absolute; hegemonic, -al; arbitrary; compulsory etc. 744; stringent.

regal, sovereign; royal, -ist; monarchical, kingly; imperial, -istic; princely; feudal; aristo-, auto-cratic; oligarchic etc. *n.*; democratic, republican, dynastic.

at one's command; in one's -power, – grasp; under control; authorized etc. (*due*) 924.

Adv. in the name of, by the authority of, *de par le Roi*, in virtue of; under the auspices of, in the hands of.

at one's pleasure; by a -dash, – stroke- of the pen; *ex mero motu*; *ex cathedrâ.*

Phr. the grey mare the better horse; 'every inch a king.'

738. Laxity. [Absence of authority.]—**N.** laxity; lax-, loose-, slack-ness; toleration etc. (*lenity*) 740; freedom etc. 748.

anarchy, interregnum; relaxation; loosening etc. *v.*; remission; dead letter, *brutum fulmen*; misrule; license, licentiousness; insubordination etc. (*disobedience*) 742; lynch law etc. (*illegality*) 964; nihilism.

[Deprivation of power.] dethronement, deposition, usurpation, abdication.

V. be -lax etc. *adj.*; *laisser -faire*, – *aller*; hold a loose rein; give -the reins to, – rope enough, – a loose to; tolerate; relax; misrule.

go beyond the length of one's tether; have one's -swing, – fling; act without -instructions, – authority; act on one's own responsibility, usurp authority.

dethrone, depose; abdicate.

Adj. lax, loose; slack; remiss etc. (*careless*) 460; weak.

relaxed; licensed; reinless, unbridled; anarchical; unauthorized etc. (*unwarranted*) 925.

739. Severity.—N. severity; strictness, formalism, harshness etc. *adj.*; rigor, stringency, austerity; inclemency etc. (*pitilessness*) 914*a*; arrogance etc. 885.

arbitrary power; absolut-, despot-ism; dictatorship, autocracy, tyranny, domineering, oppression; assumption, usurpation; inquisition, reign of terror, martial law; iron -heel, – rule, – hand, – sway; tight grasp; brute -force, – strength; coercion etc. 744; strong –, tight- hand.

hard -lines, – measure; tender mercies [ironical.]; sharp practice; bureaucracy, red tape; pipe-clay, officialism.

tyrant, disciplinarian, martinet, stickler, formalist, bashaw, despot, hard master, Draco, oppressor, inquisitor, extortioner, harpy, vulture, bird of prey.

V. be -severe etc. *adj.*

assume, usurp, arrogate, take liberties; domineer, bully etc. 885; tyrannize, inflict, wreak, stretch a point, put on the screw; be hard upon; bear –, lay- a heavy hand on; be –, come- down upon; ill-treat; deal-hardly with, – hard measure to; rule with a rod of iron, chastise with scorpions; dye with blood; oppress, override; trample –, tread- -down, – upon, – under foot; crush under an iron heel, ride roughshod over; rivet the yoke; hold –, keep- a tight hand; force down the throat; coerce etc. 744; give no quarter etc. (*pitiless*) 914*a*.

Adj. severe; strict, hard, harsh, dour, rigid, stiff, stern, rigorous, uncompromising, exacting, exigent, *exigeant*, inexorable, inflexible, obdurate, austere, relentless, Spartan, Draconian, stringent, strait-laced, puritanical, prudish, searching, unsparing, ironhanded, hard-headed, peremptory, absolute, positive, arbitrary, imperative; coercive etc. 744; tyrannical, despotic, masterful, extortionate, grinding, withering, oppressive, inquisitorial; inclement etc. (*ruthless*) 914*a*; cruel etc. (*malevolent*) 907; haughty, arrogant etc. 885.

Adv. severely etc. *adj.*; with a -high, – strong, – tight, – heavy-hand.

at the point of the -sword, – bayonet.

Phr. *Delirant reges plectuntur Achivi.*

740. Leniency.—N. leni-ency, -ence, -ty; moderation etc. 174; toler-ance, -ation; mildness, gentleness; favor; indulgen-ce, -cy; clemency, mercy, forbearance, quarter; compassion etc. 914.

V. be -lenient etc. *adj.*; tolerate, bear with; *parcere subjectis*, give quarter.

indulge, allow one to have his own way, spoil.

Adj. lenient; mild, – as milk; gentle, soft; tolerant, indulgent, easy-going; clement etc. (*compassionate*) 914; forbearing; complaisant, long-suffering.

741. Command.—N. command, order, ordinance, act, *fiat*, bidding, *dictum*, hest, behest, call, beck, nod.

des-, dis-patch; message, direction, injunction, charge, instructions; appointment, fixture.

demand, exaction, imposition, requisition, claim, reclamation, revendication; *ultimatum* etc. (*terms*) 770; request etc. 765; requirement.

dictation; dict-, mand-ate; *caveat*, decree, decree -nisi, – absolute, *senatus consultum*; precept; pre-, re-script; writ, ordination, bull, edict, decretal, dispensation, prescription, brevet, placet, ukase, *firman*, hatti-sheriff, warrant, passport, *mittimus, mandamus*, summons, subpoena, *nisi prius*, interpellation, citation; word, – of command; *mot d'ordre*; bugle –, trumpet- call; beat of drum, tattoo; order of the day; enactment etc. (*law*) 963; *plébiscite* etc. (*choice*) 609.

V. command, order, decree, enact, ordain, dictate, direct, give orders.

prescribe, set, appoint, mark out; set –, prescribe –, impose- a task; set to work, put in requisition etc. 926.

bid, enjoin, charge, call upon, instruct; require, – at the hands of; exact, impose, tax, task; demand; insist on etc. (*compel*) 744.

claim, lay claim to, revendicate, reclaim.

cite, summon; call –, send- for; subpoena; beckon.

issue a command; make –, issue –, promulgate- -a requisition, – a decree, – an order etc. *n.*; give the -word of command, – word, – signal; call to order; give –, lay down- the law; assume the command etc. (*authority*) 737; remand.

be -ordered etc.; receive an order etc. *n.*

Adj. commanding etc. *v.*; authoritative etc. 737; decret-ory, -ive, -al; imperative, jussive, decisive, final.

Adv. in a commanding tone; by a -stroke, – dash- of the pen; by order, at beat of drum, on the first summons; at the word of command.

Phr. the decree is gone forth; *sic volo sic jubeo*; *le Roi le veut.*

742. Disobedience.—N. disobedience, insubordination, contumacy; infraction, -fringement; violation, non-compliance; non-observance etc. 773.

revolt, rebellion, mutiny, outbreak, rising, uprising, putsch, insurrection, *émeute*; riot, tumult etc. (*disorder*) 59; strike etc. (*resistance*) 719; barring out; defiance etc. 715.

mutinousness etc. *adj.*; mutineering; sedition, treason; high –, petty –, misprison of- treason; *premunire*; *lèse- majesté*; violation of law etc. 964; defection, secession, revolution, *sabotage*, bolshevism, *Sinn Fein.*

insurgent, mutineer, rebel, revolter, rioter, traitor, *carbonaro*, *sansculottes*, red republican, communist, Fenian, chartist, *frondeur*; seceder, runagate, brawler, anarchist, demagogue; suffragette; Spartacus, Masaniello, Wat Tyler, Jack Cade; bolshevist, bolshevik, maximalist, ringleader.

V. disobey, violate, infringe; shirk; set at defiance etc. (*defy*) 715; set authority at naught, run riot, fly in the face of, bolt, take the law into one's own hands; kick over the traces.

turn –, run- restive; champ the bit; strike etc. (*resist*) 719; rise, – in arms; secede; mutiny, rebel.

Adj. disobedient; uncompl-ying, -iant; unsubmissive, unruly, ungovernable; insubordinate, impatient of control; rest-iff, -ive; refractory, contumacious; recusant etc. (refuse) 764; recalcitrant; resisting etc. 719; lawless, mutinous, seditious, insurgent, riotous, revolutionary.

disobeyed, unobeyed; unbidden.

743. Obedience.—N. obedience; observance etc. 772; compliance; submission etc. 725; subjection etc. 749; non-resistance; passiveness, passivity, resignation.

allegiance, loyalty, fealty, homage, deference, devotion, fidelity, constancy.

submiss-ness, -iveness; ductility etc. (*softness*) 324; obsequiousness etc. (*servility*) 886.

V. be -obedient etc. *adj.*; obey, bear obedience to; submit etc. 725; comply, answer the helm, come at one's call; do -one's bidding, – what one is told, – suit and service; attend to orders, serve -devotedly, –, loyally, – faithfully.

follow, – the lead of, – to the world's end; serve etc. 746; play second fiddle.

Adj. obedient; compl-ying, -iant; law-abiding, loyal, faithful, leal, devoted; at one's -call, – command, – orders, – beck and call; under -beck and call, – control.

restrainable; resigned, passive; submissive etc. 725; henpecked; pliant etc. (*soft*) 324.

unresist-ed, -ing.

Adv. obediently etc. *adj.*; in compliance with, in obedience to.

Phr. to hear is to obey; as –, if- you please; at your service.

744. Compulsion.—N. compulsion, coercion, coaction, constraint, eminent domain, duress, enforcement, press, conscription.

force; brute –, main –, physical- force; the sword, *ultima ratio*; club –, mob –, lynch- law; *argumentum baculinum, le droit du plus fort*, martial law.

restraint etc. 751; necessity etc. 601; *force majeure*; Hobson's choice; the spur of necessity.

V. compel, force, make, drive, coerce, constrain, enforce, necessitate, oblige.

force upon, press; cram –, thrust –, force- down the throat; say it must be done, make a point of, insist upon, take no denial; put down, dragoon.

extort, wring from; put –, turn- on the screw; drag into; bind, – over; pin –, tie- down; require, tax, put in force; commandeer; restrain etc. 751.

Adj. compelling etc. *v.*; coercive, coactive; inexorable etc. 739; compuls-ory, -atory; obligatory, stringent, peremptory, binding.

forcible, not to be trifled with; irresistible etc. 601; compelled etc. *v.*; fain to.

Adv. by -force etc. *n.*, – force of arms; on compulsion, perforce; *vi et armis*, under the lash; at the point of the -sword, – bayonet; forcibly; by a strong arm.

under protest, in spite of one's teeth; against one's will etc. 603; *nolens volens* etc. (*of necessity*) 601; by stress of -circumstances, – weather; under press of; *de rigueur*.

745. Master.—N. master, *padrone*; lord, – paramount; command-er, -ant; captain; chief, -tain; *sahib*, sirdar, sachem, sheik, head, senior, governor, *duce*, ruler, dictator; leader etc. (*director*) 694.

lord of the ascendant; cock of the -walk, – roost; grey mare; mistress.

potentate; liege, – lord; suzerain, sovereign, monarch, autocrat, despot, tyrant, oligarch, overlord.

crowned head, emperor, king, anointed king, majesty, *imperator,* protector, president, stadtholder, judge.

caesar, kaiser, czar, sultan, grand Turk, caliph, imaum, shah, padishah, sophi, mogul, great mogul, khan, cham; lama, tycoon, mikado, inca, cazique; domn; vaivode; wai-, way-wode; landamman; seyyid, cacique.

prince, duke etc. (*nobility*) 875; arch-duke, doge, elector; seignior; mar-, land-grave; rajah, emir, nizam, nawab, negus.

empress, queen, sultana, czarina, princess, infanta, duchess, margravine, begum, maharani.

regent, viceroy, exarch, palatine, khedive, hospodar, beglerbeg, three-tailed bashaw, pasha, pashaw, bashaw, bey, beg, dey, scherif, tetrarch, satrap, mandarin, subhadar, nabob, maharajah; burgrave; laird etc. (*proprietor*) 779; High Commissioner.

the -authorities, – powers that be, – government; staff, *état major,* aga, official, man in office, person in authority.

[Naval authorities] admiral, -ty, – of the fleet; rear-, vice-, port-admiral; senior-, naval officer, S.N.O., commodore, captain, commander, lieutenant-commander, lieutenant, sub-lieutenant, midshipman, warrant –, petty- officer, leading seaman; skipper, mate, master.

[Military authorities] marshal, field-marshal, *maréchal*; general, -issimo; commander-in-chief, *seraskier, hetman*; lieutenant-, major-general; commandant; colonel, lieutenant-colonel, major, captain, centurion, skipper, lieutenant, second-lieutenant, officer, staff-officer, *aide de camp*, brigadier, brigade-major, adjutant, *jemidar*, ensign, cornet, cadet, subaltern, warrant officer, quartermaster, noncommissioned officer, N.C.O.; sergeant, -major; top-sergeant, color sergeant; corporal, -major; lance-, acting-corporal; drum major; shavetail.

[Air authorities] air -marshal, – commodore; group captain, squadron leader, wing commander, flight lieutenant, flying –, pilot- officer.

[Civil authorities] judge etc. 967; mayor, -alty; prefect, chancellor, archon, provost, magistrate, syndic; alcalde, alcaid; burgomaster, *corregidor*, seneschal, alderman, warden, constable, portreeve; lord mayor, sheriff; officer etc. (*executive*) 965.

746. Servant.—N. subject, liegeman; servant, retainer, follower, henchman, servitor, domestic, menial, help, lady help, *employé*, *attaché*; official.

retinue, suite, *cortège*, staff, court.

attendant, squire, usher, page, buttons, donzel, footboy; dog robber; train-, cup-bearer; waiter, busboy, tapster, butler, livery servant, lackey, footman, flunkey, valet, *valet de chambre*; boots; scout, gyp; equerry, groom; jockey, hostler, ostler, tiger, orderly, messenger, cad, gillie, caddie; *wallah*; journeyman, herdsman, swineherd.

bailiff, castellan, seneschal, chamberlain, *major-domo*, groom of the chambers.

secretary; under –, assistant- secretary; clerk; clerical staff, stenographer, subsidiary; agent etc. 758; subaltern; under-ling, -strapper; man.

maid, -servant, waitress; handmaid; *confidente*, lady's maid, abigail, *soubrette*; nurse, *bonne*, *ayah*; nurse-, nursery-, house-, parlor-, waiting-, chamber-, kitchen-, scullery-, between –, laundry –, dairy-maid; *femme –*, *fille- de chambre*; *camarista*; *chef de cuisine*, *cordon bleu*, cook, scullion, Cinderella; maid –, servant- of all work, tweeny, general servant, girl, slavey; laundress, bed-maker, goodie, char-woman etc. (*worker*) 690.

serf, vassal, slave, negro, helot; bondsman, -woman; bondslave; *âme damnée*, *odalisque*, ryot, *adscriptus glebae*; vill-ain, -ein; bead-, bede-sman; sizar; pension-er, -ary; client; dependant, -ent; hanger on, stooge, satellite; parasite etc. (*servility*) 886; led captain; *protégé*, ward, hireling, mercenary, puppet, creature.

badge of slavery; bonds etc. 752.

V. serve; minister to, wait –, attend –, dance attendance –, pin oneself- upon; squire, tend, hang on the sleeve of, char, do for; fag; valet.

Adj. in the train of; in one's -pay, – employ; at one's call etc. (*obedient*) 743; in bonds.

747. Scepter. [Insignia of authority.]—**N.** scepter, regalia, rod of empire, sword of state, mace, *fasces*, wand; staff, – of office; *bâton*, truncheon; flag etc. (*insignia*) 550; ensign –, emblem –, badge –, insignia- of authority, rank marks, brassard, badge, sash; cocked –, brass- hat.

epaulette, aiguilette, crown, star, eagle, bar, double bar, pip, stripe, chevron, curl, ring, anchor, shoulder-strap, tab.

throne, chair, musnud, divan, dais, woolsack.

toga, pall, mantle, robes of state, ermine, purple.

crown, coronet, diadem, tiara, triple crown, miter, crozier, cardinal's hat etc.; cap of maintenance; decoration; title etc. 877; portfolio.

key, signet, seals, talisman; helm; reins etc. (*means of restraint*) 752.

748. Freedom.—N. freedom, liberty, independence; license etc. (*permission*) 760; facility etc. 705.

scope, range, latitude, play; free –, full- -play, – scope; free stage and no favor; swing, full swing, elbow-room, margin, rope, wide berth; Liberty Hall.

franchise, denization; free –, freed-, liveryman; denizen.

autonomy, self-government, homerule, self-determination, liberalism, free trade; non-interference etc. 706.

immunity, exemption; emancipation etc. (*liberation*) 750; en-, af-franchisement; rights, privileges.

free land, freehold; allodium; frankalmoigne, mortmain.

independent, free-lance, -thinker, -trader.

V. be -free etc. *adj.*; have -scope etc. *n.*, – the run of, – one's own way, – a will of one's own, – one's fling; do what one -likes, – wishes, – pleases, – chooses; go at large, feel at home, paddle one's own canoe; stand on one's -legs, – rights; shift for oneself.

take a liberty; make -free with, – oneself quite at home; use a freedom; take -leave, – French leave.

set free etc. (*liberate*) 750; give the reins to etc. (*permit*) 760; allow –, give- scope etc. *n.* to; give a horse his head.

make free of; give the -freedom of, – franchise; en-, af-franchise.

laisser -faire, – *aller*; live and let live; leave to oneself; leave –, let- alone; mind one's own business.

Adj. free, – as air; out of harness, independent, at large, loose, scot free; left -alone, – to oneself.

in full swing; uncaught, unconstrained, unbuttoned, unconfined, unrestrained, unchecked, unprevented, unhindered, unobstructed, unbound, uncontrolled, untrammeled.

unsubject, ungoverned, unenslaved, unenthralled, unchained, unshackled, unfettered, unreined, unbridled, uncurbed, unmuzzled, unimpeded.

unrestricted, unlimited, unconditional; absolute; discretionary etc. (*optional*) 600.

unassailed, unforced, uncompelled.

unbiassed, unprejudiced, uninfluenced, spontaneous.

free and easy; at –, at one's- ease; *dégagé*, quite at home; wanton, rampant, irrepressible, unvanquished.

exempt; freed etc. 750; freeborn; autonomous, freehold, allodial; *gratis* etc. 815.

unclaimed, going a begging.

Adv. freely etc. *adj.*; *ad libitum* etc. (*at will*) 600.

749. Subjection.—N. subjection; depend-ence, -ance, -ency; subordination; thrall, thraldom, enthralment, subjugation, bondage, serfdom; feudal- -ism, -ity; vassalage, villenage; slavery, enslavement, involuntary servitude.

service; servi-tude, -torship; tendence, employ, tutelage, clientship; liability etc. 177; constraint etc. 751; oppression etc. (*severity*) 739; yoke etc. (*means of restraint*) submission etc. 725; obedience etc. 743.

V. be -subject etc. *adj.*; be –, lie- at the mercy of; depend –, lean –, hang- upon; fall -a prey to, – under; play second fiddle.

be a -mere machine, – puppet, – football; not dare to say one's soul is his own; drag a chain.

serve etc. 746; obey etc. 743; submit etc. 725.

break in, tame; subject, subjugate; master etc. 731; tread -down, – under foot; weigh down; drag at one's chariot wheels; reduce to -subjection, –

slavery; en-, in-, be-thral; enslave, lead captive; take into custody etc. (*restrain*) 751; rule etc. 737; drive into a corner, hold at the sword's point; keep under; hold in -bondage, – leading strings, – swaddling clothes.

Adj. subject, dependent, subordinate; feud-al, -atory; in subjection to, under control; in -leading strings, – harness; subjected, enslaved etc. *v.*; constrained etc. 751; subservient, servile, fawning, slavish, obsequious, cringing; down-trodden; overborne, -whelmed; under the lash, on the hip, led by the nose, henpecked; the -puppet, – sport, – plaything- of; under one's -orders, – command, – thumb; like dirt under one's feet; a slave to; at the mercy of; in the -power, – hands, – clutches- of; at the feet of; at one's beck and call etc. (*obedient*) 743; liable etc. 177; parasitical; stipendiary.

Adv. under.

750. Liberation.—N. liberation, disengagement, release, disenthrallment, enlargement, emancipation; af-, en-franchisement; manumission; discharge, dismissal.

deliverance etc. 672; redemption, extrication, acquittance, absolution; acquittal etc. 970; escape etc. 671.

V. liberate, free; set -free, – clear, – at liberty; render free, emancipate, release; en-, af-franchise; manumit; enlarge; dis-band, -charge, -miss, -enthral; let -go, – loose, – out, – slip; cast –, turn- adrift; deliver etc. 672; absolve etc. (*acquit*) 970; reprieve.

unfetter etc. 751; untie etc. 44; loose etc. (*disjoin*) 44; loosen, relax; un-bolt, -bar, -close, -cork, -clog, -hand, -bind, -latch, -chain, -harness; dis-engage, -entangle; clear, extricate, unloose.

gain –, obtain –, acquire- one's -liberty etc. 748; get -rid, – clear- of; deliver oneself from; shake off the yoke, slip the collar; break -loose, – prison; tear asunder one's bonds, cast off trammels; escape etc. 671.

Adj. at -liberty, – large, free, liberated etc. *v.*; out of harness etc. 748; adrift.

Int. unhand me! let me go!

751. Restraint.—N. restraint; hindrance etc. 706; coercion etc. (*compulsion*) 744; cohibition, constraint, repression; discipline, control, self-restraint etc. 604.

confinement; durance, duress; im-, prisonment; incarceration, coarctation, entombment, mancipation, durance vile, thrall, -dom, limbo, captivity; blockade; quarantine; detention.

arrest, -ation; custody, keep, care, charge, ward, restringency.

curb etc. (*means of restraint*) 752; *lettres de cachet*.

limitation, restriction, protection, monopoly; prohibition etc. 761; economic pressure.

prisoner etc. 754.

V. restrain, check; put –, lay- under restraint; en-, in-, be-thral; restrict; debar etc. (*hinder*) 706; constrain; coerce etc. (*compel*) 744; curb, control; hold –, keep- -back, – from, – in, – in check, – within bounds; hold in -leash, – leading strings; withhold.

keep under; repress, suppress; smother; pull in, rein in; hold, – fast; keep a tight hand on; prohibit etc. 761; in-, co-hibit.

enchain; fasten etc. (*join*) 43; fetter, shackle; en-, trammel; bridle, muzzle, gag, pinion, manacle, handcuff, tie one's hands, hobble, bind hand and foot; swathe, swaddle; pin –, peg- down; tether, picket; tie, – up, – down; secure; forge fetters.

confine; shut –, clap –, lock –, box –, mew –, bottle –, cork –, seal –, button- up; shut –, hem –, bolt –, wall –, rail- in; impound, pen, coop; enclose etc. (*circumscribe*) 229; cage; in-, en-cage; close the door upon, cloister; imprison, immure; incarcerate, entomb; clap –, lay- under hatches; put in -irons, – a strait waistcoat; throw –, cast- into prison; put into bilboes.

arrest; take -up, – charge of, – into custody; take –, make- -prisoner, – captive; captivate; lead -captive, – into captivity; send –, commit- to prison; commit; give in -charge, – custody; subjugate etc. 749.

Adj. re-, con-strained; imprisoned etc. *v.*; pent up; jammed in, wedged in; under -restraint, – lock and key, – hatches; serving –, doing- time; in swaddling clothes; on *parole*; in custody etc. (*prisoner*) 754; cohibitive; coactive etc. (*compulsory*) 744.

stiff, restringent, straitlaced, hide-bound.

ice-, wind-, weather-bound; 'cabined, cribbed, confined;' in Lob's pound, laid by the heels.

Adv. in captivity, under arrest, behind the bars, in -prison, – jail, – durance vile.

752. Prison. [Means of restraint.]**—N.** prison, -house; jail, gaol, cage, coop, den, death house, condemned –, cell; stronghold, fortress, keep, donjon, dungeon, *Bastille, oubliette*, bridewell, house of correction, hulks, tool-booth, panopticon, penitentiary, guard-room, clink, can, stir, tronk, jug, lock-up, hold; round –, watch –, station –, sponging-house; station; house of detention, black hole, pen, fold, pound; enclosure etc. 232; penal settlement; chain gang; debtors' prison; reformatory; federal penitentiary, state prison; criminal lunatic asylum; bilboes, stocks, limbo, quod.

Dartmoor, Newgate, Fleet, Marshalsea; King's (*or* Queen's) Bench; Sing Sing, Dannemora.

bond; strap, bandage, splint, tourniquet; irons, pinion, gyve, fetter, shackle, trammel, manacle, handcuff, bracelets, darbies, strait waistcoat, strait-jacket.

yoke, collar, halter, harness; muzzle, gag, bit, brake, curb, snaffle, bridle; rein, -s; ribbons, lines, bearing-rein; martingale, leading string; tether, picket, band, guy, chain; cord etc. (*fastening*) 45.

bolt, bar, lock, padlock, rail, wall; paling, palisade; fence; barrier, barricade.

brake, drag etc. (*hindrance*) 706.

753. Keeper.—N. keeper, custodian, *custos*, ranger, warder, jailer, gaoler, turnkey, castellan, guard; watch, -dog, -man; Charley; sen-try, -tinel; watch and ward; *concierge*, coast-guard, *guarda costa*, gamekeeper.

escort, body guard, convoy.

protector, governor, duenna; guardian; governess etc. (*teacher*) 540; nurse, *bonne*, *ayah*, *amah*.

754. Prisoner.—N. prisoner, captive, *détenu*, close prisoner.
jail-bird, ticket-of-leave man.
V. stand committed; be -imprisoned etc. 751.
Adj. imprisoned etc. 751; in -prison, – quod, – durance vile, – limbo, – custody, – charge, – chains; under -lock and key, – hatches; on *parole*; detained at his Majesty's pleasure.

755. Commission. [Vicarious authority.]—**N.** commission, delegation; con-, as-signment; procuration; deputation, legation, mission, embassy; agency, agentship; power of attorney, proxy; clerkship.
errand, charge, *brevet*, diploma, *exequatur*, permit etc. (*permission*) 760.
appointment, nomination, return; charter; ordination; installation, inauguration, investiture; accession, coronation, enthronement.
vicegerency; regency, regentship.
viceroy etc. 745; consignee etc. 758; deputy etc. 759.
V. commission, delegate, depute; consign, assign; charge; in-, en-trust; turn over to; commit, – to the hands of; authorize etc. (*permit*) 760.
put in commission, accredit, engage, hire, bespeak, appoint, name, nominate, return, ordain; install, induct, inaugurate, invest, crown; en-roll, -list.
employ, empower; give power of attorney to; set –, place- over; send out.
be commissioned, be accredited; represent, stand for; stand in the -stead, – place, – shoes- of.
Adj. commissioned etc. *v.*
Adv. *per procuratione.*

756. Abrogation.—N. abrogation, annulment, nullification; cancelling etc. *v.*; cancel; revo-cation, -kement; repeal, rescission, defeasance.
dismissal, *congé*, demission; depos-al, -ition; sack, dethronement; disestablish-, disendow-ment; deconsecration.
aboli-tion, -shment; dissolution.
counter-order, -mand; repudiation, retractation; recantation etc. (*tergiversation*) 607.
V. abrogate, annul, cancel; destroy etc. 162; abolish; revoke, repeal, rescind, reverse, retract, recall; over-rule, -ride; set aside; disannul, dissolve, quash, nullify, declare null and void; dis-establish, -endow; deconsecrate.
disclaim etc. (*deny*) 536; ignore, repudiate; recant etc. 607; divest oneself, break off.
counter-mand, -order; do away with; sweep –, brush- away; throw -overboard, – to the dogs; scatter to the winds, cast behind.
dismiss, discard; cast –, turn- -off, – out, – adrift, – out of doors, – aside, – away; send -off, – away, – about one's business; discharge, get rid of, fire out, fire etc. (*eject*) 297; jilt.
cashier; break; oust; set down, unseat, -saddle; un-, de-, disen-throne; depose, uncrown; unfrock, strike off the roll; dis-bar, -bench.
be -abrogated etc.; receive its quietus.
Adj. abrogated etc. *v.*; *functus officio*.
Int. get along with you! begone! go about your business! away with!

757. Resignation.—N. resignation, retirement, abdication, renunciation, abjuration, disclaimer, abandonment, relinquishment.
V. resign; give –, throw- up; lay down, throw up the cards, wash one's hands of, abjure, renounce, forego, disclaim, abandon, relinquish, retract, demit; deny etc. 536.
abrogate etc. 756; desert etc. (*relinquish*) 624; get rid of etc. 782.
abdicate; vacate, – one's seat; accept the stewardship of the Chiltern Hundreds; retire; tender –, send in –, hand in- one's resignation.
Adj. abdicant, renunciatory etc. *v.*
Phr. 'Othello's occupation's gone.'

758. Consignee.—N. consignee, trustee, nominee, committee.
delegate; commiss-ary, -ioner; emissary, envoy, commissionaire; messenger etc. 534.
diplomatist, diplomat, *corps diplomatique*, embassy; am-, em-bassador; representative, resident, consul, legate, nuncio, internuncio, *chargé d' affaires, attaché*.
vicegerent etc. (*deputy*) 759; plenipotentiary.
functionary, placeman, curator; treasurer etc. 801; agent, factor, bailiff, steward, clerk, secretary, attorney, solicitor, proctor, broker, underwriter, commission agent, auctioneer, one's man of business; factotum etc. (*director*) 694; caretaker.
negotiator, go between; middleman; under agent, *employé*; servant etc. 746.
salesman; commercial, – traveler; bagman, *commis-voyageur*, touter.
newspaper –, own –, war –, special- correspondent; reporter.

759. Deputy.—N. deputy, substitute, vice, proxy, *locum tenens*, delegate, representative, next friend, surrogate, secondary.
regent, vicegerent, vizier, minister, vicar; premier etc. (*director*) 694; chancellor, prefect, provost, warden, lieutenant, archon, consul, proconsul; viceroy etc. (*governor*) 745; commissioner etc. 758; plenipotentiary, *alter ego*.
team, eight, eleven; champion.
V. be -deputy etc. *n.*; stand –, appear –, hold a brief –, answer- for; represent; stand –, walk- in the shoes of; stand in the stead of.
substitute, ablegate, accredit; commission, empower, delegate etc. 755.
Adj. acting; vice, -regal; accredited to.
Adv. in behalf of, by proxy.

760. Permission.—N. permission, leave; allow-, suffer-ance; toler-ance, -ation; liberty, law, license, concession, grace; indulgence etc. (*lenity*) 740; favor, dispensation, exemption, release; connivance; vouchsafement.
authorization, warranty, accordance, admission.
permit, warrant, *brevet*, precept, sanction, authority, *firman*; pass, -port; furlough, license, *carte blanche*, ticket of leave; grant, charter, patent.
V. permit; give -permission etc. *n.*, – power;

let, allow, admit; suffer, bear with, tolerate, recognize; concede etc. 762; accord, vouchsafe, favor, humor, gratify, indulge, stretch a point; wink at, connive at; shut one's eyes to.

grant, empower, charter, enfranchise, privilege, confer a privilege, license, authorize, warrant; sanction; entrust etc. (*commission*) 755.

give -*carte blanche*, – the reins to, – scope to etc. (*freedom*) 748; leave -alone, – it to one, – the door open; open the -door to, – floodgates; give a loose to.

let off; absolve etc. (*acquit*) 970; release, exonerate, dispense with.

ask –, beg –, request- -leave, – permission.

Adj. permitting etc. *v.*; permissive, indulgent; permitted etc. *v.*; patent, chartered, permissible, allowable, lawful, legitimate, legal; legalized etc. (*law*) 963; licit; unforbid, -den; unconditional.

Adv. permissibly; by –, with –, on- -leave etc. *n.*; *speciali gratiâ*; under favor of; *pace*; *ad libitum* etc. (*freely*) 748, (*at will*) 600; by all means etc. (*willingly*) 602; yes etc. (*assent*) 488.

761. Prohibition.—N. pro-, in-hibition; *veto*, disallowance; interdict, -ion; injunction; embargo, ban, *verboten*, taboo, proscription; *index expurgatorius*; restriction etc. (*restraint*) 751; hindrance etc. 706; forbidden fruit.

V. pro-, in-hibit; forbid, put one's *veto* upon, disallow; bar; debar etc. (*hinder*) 706, forefend.

keep -in, – within bounds; restrain etc. 751; cohibit, withhold, limit, circumscribe, clip the wings of, restrict, narrow; interdict, taboo; put –, place- under -an interdiction, – the ban; proscribe, censor; exclude, shut out; shut –, bolt –, show- the door; warn off; dash the cup from one's lips; forbid the banns.

Adj. prohibit-ive, -ory; interdictive; proscriptive; restrictive, exclusive; forbidding etc. *v.*

prohibited etc. *v.*; not -permitted etc. 760; unlicensed, contraband, under the ban of; illegal etc. 964; unauthorized, not to be thought of.

Adv. on no account etc. (*no*) 536.

Int. forbid it heaven! etc. (*deprecation*) 766. hands –, keep- off! hold! stop! avast!

Phr. that will never do.

762. Consent.—N. consent; assent etc. 488; acquiescence; approval etc. 931; compliance, agreement, concession; yield-ance, -ingness; accession, acknowledgment, acceptance, agnition.

settlement, ratification, confirmation, adjustment.

permit etc. (*permission*) 760; promise etc. 768.

V. consent; assent etc. 488; yield assent, admit, allow, concede, grant, yield; come -over, – round; give in to, acknowledge, agnize, give consent, comply with, acquiesce, agree to, fall in with, accede, accept, embrace an offer, close with, take at one's word, have no objection.

satisfy, meet one's wishes, settle, come to terms etc. 488; not -refuse etc. 764; turn a willing ear etc. (*willingness*) 602; jump at; deign, vouchsafe; promise etc. 768.

Adj. consenting etc. *v.*; agreeable, compliant; agreed etc. (*assent*) 488; unconditional.

Adv. yes etc. (*assent*) 488; by all means etc. (*willingly*) 602; if –, as- you please; be it so, so be it, well and good, of course.

763. Offer.—N. offer, proffer, presentation, tender, bid, overture; propos-al, -ition; motion, invitation; candidature; offering etc. (*gift*) 784.

V. offer, proffer, present, tender; bid; propose, move; make -a motion, – advances; start; invite, hold out, place- at one's disposal, – in one's way, put forward.

hawk about; offer for sale etc. 796; press etc. (*request*) 765; lay at one's feet.

offer –, present- oneself; volunteer, come forward, be a candidate; stand –, bid- for; seek; be at one's service; go a begging; bribe etc. (*give*) 784.

Adj. offer-ing, -ed etc. *v.*; in the market, for sale, to let, disengaged, on hire.

764. Refusal.—N. refusal, rejection; non-, incompliance; denial; declining etc. *v.*; declension; peremptory –, flat –, point blank- refusal; repulse, rebuff; discountenance.

recusancy, renunciation, abnegation, negation, protest, disclaimer; dissent etc. 489; revocation etc. 756.

V. refuse, reject, deny, decline; nill, negative; refuse –, withhold- one's assent; shake the head; close the -hand, – purse; grudge, begrudge, be slow to, hang fire.

be deaf to; turn -a deaf ear to, – one's back upon; set one's face against, discountenance, not hear of, have nothing to do with, wash one's hands of, stand aloof, forswear, set aside, cast behind one; not yield an inch etc. (*obstinacy*) 606.

resist, cross; not -grant etc. 762; repel, repulse; shut –, slam- the door in one's face; rebuff; send -back, – to the right about, – away with a flea in the ear; deny oneself, not be at home to; discard etc. (*repudiate*) 610; rescind etc. (*revoke*) 756; disclaim, protest; dissent etc. 489.

Adj. refusing etc. *v.*; rest-ive, -iff; recusant; uncomplying, noncompliant, unconsenting, uncomplaisant, protestant; not willing to hear of, deaf to.

refused etc. *v.*; ungranted, out of the question, not to be thought of, impossible.

Adv. no etc. 536; on no account, not for the world; no thank you.

Phr. *non possumus*; [ironically] your humble servant; *bien obligé*.

765. Request.—N. requ-est, -isition; claim etc. (*demand*) 741; petition, suit, prayer; begging letter, round-robin.

motion, overture, application, canvass, address, appeal, apostrophe; imprecation; rogation; proposal, proposition.

orison etc. (*worship*) 990; incantation etc. (*spell*) 993.

mendicancy; asking, panhandling, begging etc. *v.*; postulation, solicitation, invitation, entreaty, importunity, supplication, instance, impetration, imploration, obsecration, obtestation, invocation, interpellation.

V. request, ask; beg, crave, sue, pray, petition, solicit, invite, pop the question, make bold to ask; beg -leave, – a boon; apply to, call to, put to; call -upon, – for; make –, address –, prefer –, put up- a -request, – prayer, – petition; make -application, – a requisition; ask –, trouble- one for; claim etc. (*demand*) 741; offer up prayers etc. (*worship*) 990; whistle for.

beg hard, entreat, beseech, plead, supplicate, implore, apostrophize; conjure, adjure; obtest; cry to, kneel to, appeal to; invoke, evoke; impetrate, imprecate, ply, press, urge, beset, importune, dun, tax, clamor for; cry -aloud, – for help; fall on one's knees; throw oneself at the feet of; come down on one's marrow-bones.

beg from door to door, send the hat round, go a begging; mendicate, mump, cadge, panhandle, beg one's bread.

dance attendance on, besiege, knock at the door.

bespeak, canvass, tout, make interest, court; seek, bid for etc. (*offer*) 763; publish the banns.

Adj. requesting etc. *v.*; precatory; suppli-ant, -cant, -catory; invoc-, imprec-, rog-atory; postulant, mendicant.

importunate, clamorous, urgent; solicitous; cap in hand; on one's -knees, – bended knees, – marrow-bones.

Adv. prithee, do, please, pray; be so good as, be good enough; have the goodness, vouchsafe, will you, I pray thee, if you please.

Int. for -God's, – heaven's, – goodness', – mercy's- sake.

766. Deprecation. [Negative request.]—**N.** deprecation, expostulation; remonstrance; intercession, mediation.

V. deprecate, protest, expostulate, enter a protest, intercede for.

Adj. deprecatory, expostulatory, intercessory, mediatorial.

deprecated, protested.

un-, unbe-sought; unasked etc. (*see* ask etc. 765).

Int. cry you mercy! God forbid! forbid it Heaven! Heaven -forefend, – forbid! far be it from! hands off! etc. (*prohibition*) 761.

767. Petitioner.—**N.** petitioner, solicitor, applicant; suppli-ant, -cant; suitor, candidate, claimant, postulant, aspirant, competitor, bidder; place –, pot- hunter; prizer.

beggar, mendicant, mumper, sturdy beggar, cadger, panhandler.

canvasser, barker, touter etc. 768.

sycophant, parasite etc. 886.

768. Promise.—**N.** promise, undertaking, word, troth, plight, pledge, *parole*, word of honor, vow; oath etc. (*affirmation*) 535; profession, assurance, warranty, guarantee, insurance, obligation; contract etc. 769.

engagement, pre-engagement; affiance; betroth, -al, -ment; marriage -compact, – vow.

V. promise; give a -promise etc. *n.*; undertake, engage; make –, form- an engagement; enter -into, – on- an engagement; bind –, tie –, pledge –, commit –, take upon- oneself; vow; swear etc. (*affirm*) 535; give –, pass –, pledge –, plight- one's -word, – honor, – credit, – troth; betroth, plight faith; take the vows.

assure, warrant, guarantee, vouch for, avouch, covenant etc. 769; attest etc. (*bear witness*) 467.

hold out an expectation; contract an obligation; become -bound to, – sponsor for; answer –, be answerable- for; secure; give security etc. 771; underwrite.

adjure, administer an oath, put to one's oath, swear a witness.

Adj. promising etc. *v.*; promissory; votive; under hand and seal; upon -oath, – affirmation.

promised etc. *v.*; affianced, pledged, bound; committed, compromised; in for it.

Adv. as one's head shall answer for; upon my honor.

Phr. in for a penny, in for a pound.

768a. Release from engagement.—**N.** release etc. (*liberation*) 750.

Adj. absolute; unconditional etc. (*free*) 748.

769. Compact.—**N.** compact, contract, agreement, bargain, deal, transaction; affidation; pact, -ion; bond, covenant, indenture.

stipulation, settlement, convention; compromise, *cartel*.

protocol, treaty, *concordat, Zollverein, Sonderbund*, charter, *Magna Charta*, Pragmatic Sanction.

negotiation etc. (*bargaining*) 794; diplomacy etc. (*mediation*) 724; negotiator etc. (*agent*) 758.

ratification, completion, signature, seal, sigil, signet.

V. contract, covenant, agree for, engage etc. (*promise*) 768.

treat, negotiate, stipulate, make terms; bargain etc. (*barter*) 794.

make –, strike- a bargain; come to -terms, – an understanding; compromise etc. 774; set at rest; close, – with; conclude, complete, settle; confirm, ratify, clench, subscribe, underwrite; en-, in-dorse; put the seal to; sign, seal etc. (*attest*) 467; indent.

take one at one's word, bargain by inch of candle.

Adj. contractual, agreed etc. *v.*; conventional; under hand and seal; signed, sealed and delivered.

Phr. *caveat emptor.*

770. Conditions.—**N.** conditions, terms; articles, – of agreement.

clauses, provisions; proviso etc. (*qualification*) 469; covenant, stipulation, obligation, *ultimatum, sine quâ non*; *casus foederis*.

V. make –, come to- -terms etc. (*contract*) 769; make it a condition, stipulate, insist upon, make a point of; bind, tie up.

Adj. conditional, provisional, guarded, fenced, hedged in.

Adv. conditionally etc. (*with qualification*) 469; provisionally, *pro re natâ*; on condition; with a reservation.

771. Security.—N. security; guaran-ty, -tee; gage, waranty, bond, tie, pledge, plight, mortgage, debenture, hypothecation, bill of sale, lien, pignus, pawn, pignoration; real security; bottomry; collateral, vadium.

stake, deposit, earnest, handsel, caution.

promissory note; bill, – of exchange; I.O.U.: personal security, covenant, specialty; *parole* etc. (*promise*) 768.

acceptance, indorsement, signature, execution, stamp, seal.

spon-sor, -sion, -sorship; surety, bail; mainpernor, hostage.

recognizance; deed –, covenant- of indemnity.

authentication, verfication, warrant, certificate, voucher, docket, doquet; record etc. 551; probate, attested copy.

receipt; ac-, quittance; discharge, release.

muniment, title-deed, instrument; deed, – poll; assurance, insurance, indenture; charter etc. (*compact*) 769; charter-poll; paper, parchment, settlement, will, testament, last will and testament, codicil.

V. give -security, – bail, – substantial bail; go bail; pawn, impawn, hock, spout, mortgage, hypothecate, impignorate.

guarantee, warrant, assure; accept, indorse, underwrite, insure.

execute, stamp; sign, seal etc. (*evidence*) 467.

let, set; grant –, take –, hold- a lease; hold in pledge; lend on security etc. 787.

Adj. secure, -ed; pledged etc. *v.*; in pawn, on deposit.

772. Observance.—N. observance, performance, compliance; obedience, etc. 743; fulfilment, satisfaction, discharge; acquit-tance, -tal.

adhesion, acknowledgment; fidelity etc. (*probity*) 939; exact etc. 494- observance.

V. observe, comply with, respect, acknowledge, abide by; cling to, adhere to, be faithful to, act up to; meet, fulfil; carry -out, – into execution; execute, perform, keep, satisfy, discharge; do one's office.

perform –, fulfill –, discharge –, acquit oneself of- an obligation; make good; make good –, keep- one's -word, – promise; redeem one's pledge; keep faith with, stand to one's engagement.

Adj. observant, faithful, true, loyal; honorable etc. 939; true as the -dial to the sun, – needle to the pole; punct-ual, -ilious; meticulous; literal etc. (*exact*) 494; as good as one's word.

Adv. faithfully etc. *adj.*

773. Non-observance.—N. non-observance etc. 772; evasion, inobservance, failure, omission, neglect, laches, laxity, informality.

infringement, infraction; violation, transgression. retractation, repudiation, nullification; protest; forfeiture.

lawlessness; disobedience etc. 742; bad faith etc. 940.

V. fail, neglect, omit, elude, evade, give the go by to, cut, set aside, ignore; shut –, close- one's eyes to, avoid.

infringe, transgress, pirate, violate, break, trample under foot, do violence to, drive a coach and six through.

discard, protest, repudiate, fling to the winds, set at naught, nullify, declare null and void; cancel etc. (*wipe off*) 552.

retract, go back from, be off, forfeit, go from one's word, palter; stretch –, strain- a point.

Adj. violating etc. *v.*; lawless, transgressive; elusive, evasive; lax, casual; non-observant.

unfulfilled etc. (*see* fulfil etc. 772).

774. Compromise.—N. com-promise, -mutation, -position; middle term, *mezzo termine*; compensation etc. 30; adjustment, mutual concession.

V. com-promise, -mute, -pound; take the mean; split the difference, meet one half way, give and take; come to terms etc. (*contract*) 769; submit to –, abide by- arbitration; patch up, bridge over, fix up, arrange; adjust, – differences; agree; make -the best of, – a virtue of necessity; take the will for the deed.

775. Acquisition.—N. acquisition; gaining etc. *v.*; obtainment; procur-ation, -ement; purchase, descent, inheritance; gift etc. 784.

recovery, retrieval, revendication, replevin; redemption, salvage, trover; find, *trouvaille*, foundling.

gain, thrift; money-making, -grubbing; lucre, filthy lucre, loaves and fishes, the main chance, pelf; emolument etc. 973; wealth etc. 803.

profit, earnings, winnings, innings, clean-up, pickings, perquisite, net profit; income etc. (*receipt*) 810; pro-ceeds, -duce, -duct; out-come, -put; return, fruit, crop, harvest, tilth; second crop, aftermath; benefit etc. (*good*) 618.

sweepstakes, trick, prize, pool.

[Fraudulent acquisition] subreption; theft, stealing etc. 791.

V. acquire, get, gain, win, earn, obtain, procure, gather, annex; collect etc. 72; pick, – up; glean, take etc. 789.

find; come –, pitch –, light- upon; scrape -up, – together; get in, reap and carry, net, bag, sack, bring home, secure, come across, derive, draw, get in the harvest.

profit; make –, draw- profit; turn to -profit, – account; make -capital out of, – money by; obtain a return, reap the fruits of; reap –, gain- an advantage; turn -a penny, – an honest penny; make the pot boil, bring grist to the mill; make –, coin –, raise- money; raise -funds, – the wind; fill one's pocket etc. (*wealth*) 803.

treasure up etc. (*store*) 636; realize, clear; produce etc. 161; take etc. 789.

get back, recover, regain, retrieve, revendicate, replevy, redeem, come by one's own.

come -by, – in for; receive etc. 785; inherit; step into, – a fortune, – the shoes of; succeed to.

get -hold of, – between one's finger and thumb, – into one's hand, – at; take –, come into –, enter into- possession.

be -profitable etc. *adj.*; pay, answer.

accrue etc. (*be received*) 785.

Adj. acquir-ing, -ed etc. *v.*; acquisitive; productive, profitable, advantageous, gainful, remunerative, paying, lucrative.

776. Loss.—N. loss; de-, perdition; forfeiture, lapse.

privation, bereavement; deprivation etc. (*dispossession*) 789; riddance.

V. lose; incur –, experience –, meet with- a loss; miss; mislay, let slip, allow to slip through the fingers, squander; be without etc. (*exempt*) 777*a*; forfeit.

get rid of etc. 782; waste etc. 638.

be lost, lapse.

Adj. losing etc. *v.*; not having etc. 777*a*.

shorn of, deprived of; denuded, bereaved, bereft, *minus*, cut off; dispossessed etc. 789; rid of, quit of; out of pocket.

lost etc. *v.*; long lost; irretrievable etc. (*hopeless*) 859; irredentist; off one's hands.

Int. farewell to! adieu to! good riddance!

777. Possession.—N. possession, seisin; ownership etc. 780; occupancy; hold, -ing; tenure, tenancy, feodality, dependency; villenage; socage, chivalry, knight service.

exclusive possession, impropriation, monopoly, corner; retention etc. 781; pre-possession, -occupancy; nine points of the law.

future possession, heritage, inheritance, heirship, reversion, fee, seigniority, feud, fief.

bird in hand, *uti possidetis*, *chose* in possession.

V. possess, have, hold, occupy, enjoy; be -possessed of etc. *adj.*; have -in hand etc. *adj.*; own etc. 780; command.

inherit; come -to, – in for.

engross, monopolize, forestall, regrate, impropriate, have all to oneself, corner; have a firm hold of etc. (*retain*) 781; get into one's hand etc. (*acquire*) 775.

belong to, appertain to, pertain to; be -in one's possession etc. *adj.*; vest in.

Adj. possessing etc. *v.*; worth; possessed of, seized of, master of, in possession of; endowed –, blest –, instinct –, fraught –, laden –, charged –, instilled –, with.

possessed etc. *v.*; on hand, by one; in hand, in store, in stock; in one's -hands, – grasp, – possession; at one's -command, – disposal; one's own etc. (*property*) 780.

unsold, unshared.

777a. Exemption.—N. exemption; exception, immunity, privilege, release etc. 927*a*; absence etc. 187.

V. not -have etc. 777; be -without etc. *adj.*

Adj. exempt from, devoid of, without, unpossessed of, unblest with, immune from.

not -having etc. 777; unpossessed; untenanted etc. (*vacant*) 187; without an owner.

unobtained, unacquired.

778. Participation. [Joint possession.]—**N.** participation; co-, joint-tenancy; possession –, tenancy- in common; joint –, common- stock; co-, partnership; communion; community of -possessions, – goods; communalism, communism, socialism, collectivism; co-operation etc. 709; profit sharing.

snacks, co-portion, picnic, hotchpotch; co-heirship, -parceny, -parcenary; gavelkind.

participator, sharer; co-, partner; shareholder; co-, joint-tenant; tenants in common; co-heir, -parcener.

communist, socialist.

V. par-ticipate, -take; share, – in; come in for a share; go -shares, – snacks, – halves; share and share alike.

have –, possess –, be seized- -in common, – as joint tenants etc. *n.*

join in; have a hand in etc. (*co-operate*) 709.

Adj. partaking etc. *v.*; communistic, socialistic, co-operative, profit sharing.

Adv. share and share alike.

779. Possessor.—N. possessor, holder; occupant, -ier; tenant; person –, man- -in possession etc. 777; renter, lodger, lessee, under-lessee; zemindar, ryot; tenant -on sufferance, – at will, – from year to year, – for years, – for life.

owner; propriet-or, -ress, -ary; impropriator, master, mistress, lord.

land-holder, -owner, -lord, -lady; lord -of the manor, – paramount; heritor, laird, vavasor, landed gentry, mesne lord.

cestui-que-trust, beneficiary, mortgagor.

grantee, feoffee, relessee, devisee; legat-ee, -ary.

trustee; holder etc.- of the legal estate; mortgagee.

right –, rightful- owner.

[Future possessor] heir, – apparent; – presumptive; heiress; inherit-or, -ress, -rix; reversioner, remainder-man.

780. Property.—N. property, possession, *suum cuique, meum et tuum*.

owner-, proprietor, lord-ship; seignority; empire etc. (*dominion*) 737.

interest, stake, estate, right, title, claim, demand, holding; tenure etc. (*possession*) 777; vested –, contingent –, beneficial –, equitable- interest; use, trust, benefit; legal –, equitable- estate; seisin.

absolute interest, paramount estate, freehold; fee, – simple, – tail; estate -in fee, – in tail, – tail; estate in tail -male, – female, – general.

limitation, term, lease, settlement, strict settlement, particular estate; estate -for life, – for years, – *pur autre vie*; remainder, reversion, expectancy, possibility.

dower, dowry, *dot*, jointure, marriage portion, appanage, inheritance, heritage, patrimony, alimony; legacy etc. (*gift*) 784.

assets, belongings, means, resources, circumstances; wealth etc. 803; money etc. 800; what one -is worth, – will cut up for; estate and effects.

landed –, real- -estate, – property; realty; land, -s; subdivision; plot, site; tenements; hereditaments; corporeal –, incorporeal- hereditaments; acres; ground etc. (*earth*) 342; acquest; messuage.

territory, state, kingdom, principality, realm, empire, protectorate, margravate, dependancy, colony, sphere of influence, mandate.

manor, honor, domain, demesne; farm, ranch, plantation, *hacienda*; allodium etc. (*free*) 748; fieff, feoff, feud, zemindary, dependency.

free-, copy-, lease-holds; chattels real; fixtures, plant, heirloom easement; folkland; right of -common, – user.

personal -property, – estate, – effects; personalty, chattels, goods, effects, movables; stock, – in trade; things, traps, rattle-traps, paraphernalia; equipage etc. 633.

parcels, appurtenances.

impedimenta; lug-, bag-gage; bag and baggage; pelf; cargo, lading.

rent-roll; income etc. (*receipts*) 810.

patent, copyright; *chose* in action; credit etc. 805; debt etc. 806.

V. possess etc. 777; be the -possessor etc. 779- of own; have for one's own, – very own; come in for, inherit; enfeoff.

savor of the realty.

be one's own -property etc. *n.*; belong to; ap-, pertain to.

Adj. one's own; landed, predial, manorial, allodial, seignorial; free-, copy-, lease-hold; feu-, feo-dal; hereditary, entailed, personal.

Adv. to one's -credit, – account; to the good.

to one and -his heirs for ever, – the heirs of his body, – his heirs and assigns, – his executors, administrators and assigns.

781. Retention.—N. retention; retaining etc. *v.*; keep, detention, custody; tenacity, firm hold, grasp, gripe, grip, iron grip.

fangs, teeth, claws, talons, nail, hook, tentacle, *tenaculum*; bond etc. (*vinculum*) 45.

clutches, tongs, forceps, pincers, nippers, pliers, tweezers, vise.

paw, hand, finger, wrist, fist, neaf, neif.

bird in hand; captive etc. 754.

V. retain, keep; hold, – fast, – tight, – one's own, – one's ground; clinch, clench, clutch, grasp, gripe, hug, have a firm hold of.

secure, withold, detain; hold –, keepback; keep close; husband etc. (*store*) 636; reserve; have –, keep- in stock etc. (*possess*) 777; enfail, tie up, settle.

Adj. retaining etc. *v.*; retentive, tenacious.

unforfeited, undeprived, undisposed, uncommunicated.

incommunicable, inalienable; in mortmain; in strict settlement.

Phr. *uti possidetis.*

782. Relinquishment.—N. relinquishment, abandonment etc. (*of a course*) 624; renunciation, expropriation, dereliction; cession, surrender, dispensation; resignation etc. 757; riddance.

derelict etc. *adj.*; jetsam; waif, foundling, orphan.

v. relinquish, give up, surrender, yield, cede; let -go, – slip; spare, drop, resign, forego, renounce, abjure, abandon, expropriate, give away, dispose of, part with; lay -aside, – apart, – down, – on the shelf etc. (*disuse*) 678; set –, put- aside; make away with, cast behind; discard, cast off, dismiss; maroon.

give -notice to quit, – warning; supersede; be –, get- -rid of, – quit of; eject etc. 297.

rid –, disburden –, divest –, dispossess- oneself of; wash one's hands of; divorce, desert; disinherit, cut off.

cast –, throw –, pitch –, fling- -away, – aside, – overboard, – to the dogs; cast –, throw –, sweep- to the winds; put –, turn –, sweep- away; jettison.

quit one's hold.

Adj. relinquished etc. *v.*; cast off, derelict; unowned, unappropriated, unculled; left etc. (*residuary*) 40; divorced; disinherited.

Int. away with!

783. Transfer.—N. transfer, conveyance, assignment, alienation, abalienation; demise, limitation; conveyancing; transmission etc. (*transference*) 270; enfeoffment, bargain and sale, lease and release; exchange etc. (*interchange*) 148; barter etc. 794; substitution etc. 147.

succession, reversion; shifting -use, – trust; devolution.

V. transfer, convey; alien, -ate; assign; grant etc. (*confer*) 784; consign; make –, hand- over; pass, hand, transmit, negotiate; hand down; exchange etc. (*interchange*) 148.

change -hands, – from one to another; devolve, succeed; come into possession etc. (*acquire*) 775; take over.

abalienate; disinherit; dispossess etc. 789; substitute etc. 147.

Adj. alienable, negotiable, transferable, reversional.

Phr. estate coming into possession.

784. Giving.—N. giving etc. *v.*; bestowal, donation; present-ation, -ment; accordance; con-, cession; delivery, consignment, dispensation, communication, endowment; invest-ment, -iture; award.

almsgiving, charity, liberality, generosity; philanthropy etc. 910.

[Thing given] gift, donation, present, *cadeau*; fairing; free gift, boon, favor, benefaction, grant, offering, oblation, sacrifice, immolation.

grace, act of grace, *bonus, bonanza.*

allowance, contribution, subscription, subsidy, tribute, subvention.

bequest, legacy, devise, will, dotation, appanage; dowry; voluntary -settlement, – conveyance etc. 783; amortization.

alms, largess, bounty, dole, sportule, donative, help, oblation, offertory, Peter's pence, *honorarium*, gratuity, Maundy money, Christmas box, Easter offering, vail, tip, *douceur*, drink money, *pourboire, trinkgeld, backsheesh*; fee etc. (*recompense*) 973; consideration.

bribe, bait, ground-bait; peace-offering, handsel.

giver, grantor etc. *v.*; donor, feoffer, settlor; almoner; testator; investor, subscriber, contributor; fairy godmother; Santa Claus, benefactor etc. 816.

V. deliver, hand, pass, put into the hands of; hand –, make –, deliver –, pass –, turn- over.

present, give away, dispense, dispose of; give –, deal –, dole –, mete –, fork –, shell –, squeeze- out.

pay etc. 807; render, impart, communicate.

concede, cede, yield, part with, shed cast; spend etc. 809.

give, bestow, confer, grant, accord, award, assign.

entrust, consign, vest in.

make a present; allow, contribute, subscribe, donate, furnish its quota.

invest, endow, settle upon; bequesth, leave, devise.

furnish, supply, help; ad-, minister to; afford, spare; accommodate –, indulge –, favor- with; shower down upon; lavish, pour on, thrust upon; tip, bribe; tickle –, grease- the palm; offer etc. 763; sacrifice, immolate.

Adj. giving etc. *v.*; given etc. *v.*; allow-ed, -able; concessional; communicable; charitable, eleemosynary, sportulary, tributary; *gratis* etc. 815.

785. Receiving.—N. receiving etc. *v.*; acquisition etc. 775; reception etc. (*introduction*) 296; suscipiency, acceptance, admission.

re-, ac-cipient; assignee, devisee; lega-tee, -tary; grantee, feoffee, donee, relessee, lessee.

sportulary, stipendiary; beneficiary; pension-er, -ary; almsman.

income etc. (*receipt*) 810.

v. receive; take etc. 789; acquire etc. 775; admit.

take in, catch, touch; pocket; put into one's -pocket, – purse; accept; take off one's hands.

be received; come -in, – to hand; pass –, fall- into one's hand; go into one's pocket; fall to one's -lot, – share; come –, fall- to one; accrue; have -given etc. 784 to one.

Adj. receiving etc. *v.*; re-, suscipient.

received etc. *v.*; given etc. 784; second-hand.

not given, unbestowed etc. (*see* give, bestow etc. 784).

786. Apportionment.—N. apportion-, allot-, consign-, assign-, appoint-ment; appropriation; dispensation, -tribution; allocation, division, deal; repartition; administration.

dividend, portion, contingent, share, allotment, lot, cut, split, measure, dose; dole, meed, pittance; *quantum*, ration; ratio, proportion, quota, *modicum*, mess, allowance.

V. apportion, divide; cut, split, divvy; distribute, administer, dispense; billet, allot, detail, cast, share, mete; portion –, parcel –, dole- out; deal, carve.

partition, assign, appropriate, appoint.

come in for one's share etc. (*participate*) 778.

Adj. apportioning etc. *v.*; respective.

Adv. respectively, each to each.

787. Lending.—N. lending etc. *v.*; loan, advance, accommodation, feneration; mortgage etc. (*security*) 771; investment.

mont de piété, pawnshop, hock shop, spout, my uncle's.

lender, pawnbroker, money lender, usurer, Jew, Shylock.

V. lend, advance, loan, accommodate with; lend on security; pawn etc. (*security*) 771.

intrust, invest; place –, put- out to interest; sink, risk.

let, demise, lease, set, under-, sub-let.

Adj. lending etc. *v.*; lent etc. *v.*; unborrowed etc. (*see* borrowed etc. 788).

Adv. in advance; on -loan, – security.

788. Borrowing.—N. borrowing, pledging, pawning.

borrowed plumes; plagiarism etc. (*thieving*) 791.

replevin.

V. borrow, desume; pawn.

hire, rent, farm; take a -lease, – demise; take –, hire- by the -hour, – mile, – year etc.

raise –, take up- money; float bonds; raise the wind; fly a kite, borrow of Peter to pay Paul; run into debt etc. (*debt*) 806.

make use of, plagiarize, pirate.

replevy.

789. Taking.—N. taking etc. *v.*; reception etc. (*taking in*) 296; deglutition etc. (*taking food*) 298; appropriation, prehension, prensation; capture, caption; ap-, de-prehension; abreption, seizure; abduction, -lation; subtraction etc. (*subduction*) 38; abstraction, ademption.

dispossession; depriv-ation, -ement; bereavement; divestment; disherison; distraint, distress; sequestration, confiscation, attachment, execution; eviction etc. 297.

rapacity, extortion, vampirism, predacity, blood-sucking; theft etc. 791.

resumption; repris-e, -al; recovery etc. 775.

clutch, swoop, wrench; grip etc. (*retention*) 781; haul, take, catch; scramble.

taker, captor, capturer; vampire; extortioner.

V. take, catch, hook, nab, bag, sack, pocket, put into one's pocket, scrounge; receive; accept.

reap, crop, cull, pluck; gather etc. (*get*) 775; draw.

ap-, im-propriate; assume, possess oneself of; take possession of; commandeer; lay –, clap- one's hands on; help oneself to; make free with, dip one's hands into, lay under contribution; intercept; scramble for; deprive of.

take –, carry –, bear- -away, – off; abstract; hurry off –, run away- with; abduct; steal etc. 791; ravish; seize; pounce –, spring- upon; swoop -to, – down upon; take by -storm, – assault; snatch, reave.

snap up, nip up, whip up, catch up; kidnap, crimp, capture, lay violent hands on.

get –, lay –, take –, catch –, lay fast –, take firm- hold of; lay by the heels, take prisoner; fasten upon, grip, grapple, embrace, gripe, clasp, grab, clutch, collar, throttle, take by the throat, claw, clinch, clench, make sure of.

catch at, jump at, make a grab at, snap at, snatch at; reach, make a long arm, stretch forth one's hand.

take -from, – away from; deduct etc. 38; retrench etc. (*curtail*) 201; dispossess, ease one of, snatch from one's grasp; tear –, tear away –, wrench –, wrest –, wring- from; extort; deprive of, bereave; disinherit, cut off with a shilling.

oust etc. (*eject*) 297; divest; levy, distrain, confiscate; sequest-er, -rate, accroach; usurp; despoil, strip, fleece, shear, displume, impoverish, eat out of house and home; drain, – to the dregs; gut, dry, exhaust, swallow up; absorb etc. (*suck in*) 296; draw off; suck, – like a leech, – the blood of.

retake, resume; recover etc. 775.

Adj. taking etc. *v.*; privative, prehensile; predaceous, -al, -atory, -atorial; rap-acious, -torial; ravenous; parasitic; all-devouring, -engulfing.

bereft etc. 776.

Adv. at one fell swoop.

Phr. give an inch and take an ell.

790. Restitution.—N. restitution, return; ren-, red-dition; reinstatement, restoration; reinvestment, recuperation; repatriation; rehabilitation etc. (*reconstruction*) 660; reparation, atonement, indemnity, compensation, recompense.

release, replevin, redemption; recovery etc. (*getting back*) 775; remitter, reversion.

V. return, restore; recondition; give –, carry –, bring- back; render, – up; give up; let go, unclutch; dis-, re-gorge; regurgitate; recoup, reimburse, repay, indemnify, reinvest, remit, rehabilitate; repair etc. (*make good*) 660.

redeem, recover etc. (*get back*) 775; take back again; revest, revert.

Adj. restoring etc. *v.*; recuperative etc. 660; in full restitution, to compensate for.

Phr. *suum cuique*.

791. Stealing.—N. stealing etc. *v.*; theft, thievery, robbery, latrociny, direption; abstraction, appropriation; plagiar-y, -ism; rape, kidnapping, depredation; raid, hold up.

spoliation, plunder, pillage; sack, -age; rapine, *brigandage*, highway robbery, foray, *razzia*; blackmail; piracy, privateering, buccaneering; filibustering, -ism; burglary; house-breaking; cattle-stealing, -rustling, -lifting.

peculation, embezzlement; fraud etc. 545; larceny, petty larceny, pilfering, shop-lifting.

thievishness, rapacity, kleptomania, Alsatia; den of -Cacus, – thieves.

license to plunder, letters of marque.

V. steal, thieve, rob, purloin, pilfer, filch, lift, prig, bag, nim, crib, cabbage, palm; abstract; appropriate, plagiarize.

convey away, carry off, abduct, kidnap, shanghai, impress, crimp; make –, walk –, run- off with; run away with; spirit away; seize etc. (*lay violent hands on*) 789.

plunder, pillage, rifle, sack, loot, ransack, spoil, spoliate, despoil, strip, sweep, gut, forage, levy black-mail, pirate, pickeer, maraud, lift cattle, rustle, poach, smuggle, run.

stick –, hold- up.

swindle, peculate, embezzle; sponge, mulct, rook, bilk, pluck, pigeon, skin, fleece, diddle; defraud etc. 545; obtain under false pretences; live by one's wits

rob –, borrow of- Peter to Paul; set a thief to catch a thief.

disregard the distinction between *meum* and *tuum*.

Adj. thieving etc. *v.*; thievish, light-fingered; furacious, -tive; piratical; pred-aceous, -al, -atory, -atorial; raptorial etc. (*rapacious*) 789.

stolen etc. *v.*

Phr. *sic vos non vobis.*

792. Thief.—N. thief, robber, *homo trium literarum*, pilferer, rifler, filcher, plagiarist.

spoiler, depredator, pillager, marauder; harpy, shark, land-shark, falcon, moss-trooper, bushranger, Bedouin, brigand, freebooter, bandit, thug, dacoit, pirate, corsair, viking, Paul Jones; buccan-eer, -ier; piqu-, pick-eerer; rover, ranger, privateer, filibuster; rapparee, wrecker, picaroon; smuggler, poacher, plunderer; racketeer.

highwayman, Dick Turpin, Claude Duval, Macheath, knight of the road, footpad, sturdy beggar; abductor, kidnapper.

cut-, pick-purse; pick-pocket, light-fingered gentry; sharper; card-, skittle-sharper; crook; thimblerigger; rook, Greek, blackleg, leg, welsher, defaulter; Autolycus, Cacus, Barabbas, Jeremy Diddler, Robert Macaire, artful dodger, trickster; swell mob, *chevalier d'industrie*; shop-lifter.

swindler, peculator; forger, coiner, counterfeiter, shoful; fence, receiver of stolen goods, duffer; smasher.

burglar, housebreaker; cracks-, mags-man; Bill Sikes, Jack Sheppard, Jonathan Wild, Raffles, cat burglar.

793. Booty.—N. booty, spoil, plunder, price, loot, graft, swag, pickings, boodle; *spolia opima*, prey; blackmail; stolen goods.

Adj. looting etc. *n.*; manubial, spoliative.

794. Barter.—N. barter, exchange, scorse, truck system; interchange etc. 148.

a Roland for an Oliver; *quid pro quo*; commutation, -position.

trade, commerce, mercature, buying and selling, bargain and sale; traffic, business, nundination, custom, shopping; commercial enterprise, speculation, jobbing, stock-jobbing, *agiotage*, brokery, arbitrage.

dealing, transaction, negotiation, bargain.

free trade.

V. barter, exchange, truck, scorse, swop; interchange etc. 148; commutate etc. (*substitute*) 147; compound for.

trade, traffic, buy and sell, give and take, nundinate; carry on –, ply –, drive- a trade; be in -

business, – the city; keep a shop, deal in, employ one's capital in.

trade –, deal –, have dealings- with; transact –, do- business with; open –, keep- an account with.

bargain; drive –, make- a bargain; negotiate, bid for; dicker, haggle, higgle; chaffer, huckster, cheapen, beat down; stickle, – for; out-, underbid; ask, charge; strike a bargain etc. (*contract*) 769.

speculate, give a sprat to catch a herring; buy in the cheapest and sell in the dearest market; rig the market.

Adj. commercial, mercantile, trading; interchangeable, marketable, staple, in the market, for sale.

wholesale, retail.

Adv. across the counter; on 'change.

795. Purchase.—N. purchase, emption; buying, purchasing, shopping; pre-emption, refusal.

coemption, bribery; slave trade.

buyer, purchaser, *emptor*, vendee; patron, employer, client, customer, *clientèle*.

V. buy, purchase, invest in, procure; rent etc. (*hire*) 788; repurchase, buy in.

keep in one's pay, bribe, suborn; pay etc. 807; spend etc. 809.

make –, complete- a purchase; buy over the counter; pay cash for.

shop, market, go a shopping.

Adj. purchased etc. *v.*

Phr. *caveat emptor.*

796. Sale.—N. sale, vent, disposal; auction, roup, Dutch auction; custom etc. (*traffic*) 794.

vendi-bility, -bleness.

seller, salesman; peddler, smous; vender, vendor, consignor; merchant etc. 797; auctioneer.

V. sell, vend, dispose of, effect a sale; sell -over the counter, – by auction etc. *n.*; dispense, retail; deal in etc. 794; sell -off, – out; turn into money; realize; bring -to, – under- the hammer; put up to auction; auction, offer –, put up- for sale; hawk, peddle, bring to market; offer etc. 763; undersell; dump, unload.

let; mortgage etc. (*security*) 771.

Adj. under the hammer, in the market, for sale.

saleable, marketable, vendible, in demand, having a ready sale; unsaleable etc., unpurchased, unbought; on one's hands.

797. Merchant.—N. merchant, trader, dealer, monger, chandler, salesman; changer; regrater; shop-keeper, -man; trades-man, -people, -folk.

retailer; chapman, hawker, huckster, higgler; peddler, smous, pedlar, *colporteur*, cadger, Autolycus; sutler, *vivandière*; coster-man, -monger; market woman; cheap jack; caterer etc. 637; tallyman.

money-broker, -changer, -lender; stock-broker, -jobber; cambist, usurer, moneyer, banker.

jobber; broker etc. (*agent*) 758; buyer etc. 795; seller etc. 796.

concern; firm etc. (*partnership*) 712.

798. Merchandise.—N. merchandise, ware, commodity, effects, goods, article, stock, produce, staple commodity; stock in trade etc. (*store*) 636; cargo etc. (*contents*) 190.

799. Mart.—N. mart; market, -place, *forum*; fair, bazaar, staple; stock –, exchange; 'change, *bourse*, Wall Street, Rialto, hall, guildhall; toll-booth, custom-house; Tattersalls.

shop, stall, booth; wharf; office, chambers, counting-house, *bureau*; coun-, comp-ter.

ware-house, -room; *dépôt*, interposit, *entrepôt*, *emporium*, establishment; store etc. 636.

open market, market-overt.

800. Money.—N. money -matters, – market; finance; accounts etc. 811; funds, treasure; capital, stock; assets etc. (*property*) 780; wealth etc. 803; supplies, ways and means, wherewithal, sinews of war, almighty dollar, needful, cash.

sum, amount; balance, -sheet; sum total; proceeds etc. (*receipts*) 810.

currency, circulating medium, specie; coin, – of the realm; piece, hard cash, dollar, sterling coin; pounds, shillings and pence; L s. d., guineas; pocket, breeches pocket, purse; money in hand; the best, ready, – money; filthy lucre, shekels, roll, jack, rhino, blunt, dust, bawbees, brass, dibs, dough, mopus, tin, salt, chink, oof, spondulics, pile, wads.

precious metals, gold, silver, copper, nickel; bullion, bar, ingot, nugget.

petty cash; pocket-, pin-money; small –, change; small coin, loose cash; doit, stiver, rap, mite, farthing, *sou*, penny, shilling, bob, tanner, tester, groat, guinea, ducat; *rouleau*; *wampum*; good –, round –, lump- sum; power –, mint –, tons- of money; plum, lac of rupees, millions, money-bags, miser's hoard, stocking, mine of wealth etc. 803.

[Science of coins] numismatics, chrysology.

paper-money; money –, postal –, Post Office-order; note, – of hand; bank –, treasury- note; Bradbury; promissory note; I.O.U., bond; bill, – of exchange; draft, check, order, warrant, *coupon*, debenture, exchequer bill, *assignat*, greenback, gold –, silver- certificate.

copper, nickel, dime, quarter, two bits, half a dollar, dollar, buck, simoleon, fiver, tenner, a twenty, a sawbuck, a century, a grand; eagle, double eagle.

gold standard, bimetallism, fiat money; rate of –, exchange; in-, de-flation.

remittance etc. (*payment*) 807; credit etc. 805; liability etc. 806; solvency etc. 803.

draw-er, -ee; oblig-or, -ee; moneyer, coiner, counterfeiter, forger.

false –, bad- money; base –, counterfeit- coin, flash note, slip, kite; Bank of Elegance.

argumentum ad crumenam.

V. amount to, come to, mount up to; touch the pocket; draw, – upon; endorse etc. (*security*) 771; issue, utter, circulate; discount etc. 813.

forge, counterfeit, coin, circulate –, pass- bad money.

Adj. monetary, pecuniary, crumenal, fiscal, financial, sumptuary, numismatical; sterling; solvent etc. 803.

801. Treasurer.—N. treasurer; bursar, -y; purser, purse-bearer; cash-keeper, banker; depositary; questor, receiver, steward, trustee, chartered –, accountant; Accountant-General, almoner, liquidator, paymaster, cashier, teller; cambist; money-changer etc. (*merchant*) 797.

financier, Chancellor of the Exchequer, minister of finance; Secretary of the Treasury, Director of the Budget, Controller of Currency.

802. Treasury.—N. treasury, bank, exchequer, almonry, fisc, hanaper, bursary; safe; strong-box, -hold, -room; coffer; chest etc. (*receptacle*) 191; depository etc. 636; till, -er; cash-box, -register, purse, pocketbook, wallet; money-bag, -belt, -box, *porte-monnaie*.

purse-strings; pocket, breeches pocket.

sinking fund; stocks; government –, public –, parliamentary- -stocks, – funds, – securities, bonds; gild-edged securities; Consols, Liberty bonds, government bonds, *crédit mobilier*.

803. Wealth.—N. wealth, riches, fortune, handsome fortune, opulence, affluence; good –, easy- circumstances; independence; competence etc. (*sufficiency*) 639; solvency, soundness, solidity.

provision, livelihood, maintenance; alimony, dowry; means, resources, substance; property etc. 780; command of money.

income etc. 810; capital, money; round sum etc. (*treasure*) 800; mint of money, mine of wealth, *El Dorado*, Pactolus, Golconda, Potosi, *bonanza*; philosopher's stone.

long –, full –, well lined –, heavy- purse; purse of Fortunatus.

pelf, Mammon, lucre, filthy lucre; loaves and fishes; fleshpots of Egypt.

rich –, moneyed –, warm- man; man of substance; capitalist, millionaire, Nabob, Croesus, Midas, Plutus, Dives, Timon of Athens; Timo-, Pluto-cracy; Danaë.

V. be -rich etc. *adj.*; roll –, wallow- in -wealth, – riches; have money to burn.

afford, well afford; command -money, – a sum; make both ends meet, hold one's head above water.

become -rich etc. *adj.*; fill one's -pocket etc. (*treasury*) 802; feather one's nest, clean up –, make- a fortune; make money etc. (*acquire*) 775.

enrich, imburse.

worship -Mammon, – the golden calf.

Adj. wealthy, rich, affluent, opulent, moneyed, monied, worth -a great deal, – much; well -to do, – off; warm; well –, provided for.

made of money; rich as Croesus; rolling in -riches, – wealth.

flush, – of -cash, – money, – tin; in -funds, – cash, – full feather; solvent, solid, sound, pecunious, out of debt, all straight; able to pay 20s in the L.

Phr. one's ship coming in.

804. Poverty.—N. poverty, indigence, penury, pauperism, destitution, want; need, -iness; lack, necessity, privation, distress, difficulties, wolf at the door.

bad –, poor –, needy –, embarrassed –, reduced –, straitened- circumstances; slender –, narrow- means; straits; hand to mouth existence, *res angusta domi*, low water, impecuniosity.

beggary; mendi-cancy, -city; broken –, loss of-fortune; insolvency etc. (*non-payment*) 808.

empty -purse, – pocket; light purse; beggarly account of empty boxes.

poor man, pauper, mendicant, mumper, beggar, starveling; *pauvre diable*.

V. be -poor etc. *adj.*; want, lack, starve, live from hand to mouth, have seen better days, go down in the world, be on one's uppers, come upon the parish; go to -the dogs, – wrack and ruin; not have a -penny etc. (*money*) 800, – shot in one's locker; beg one's bread; *tirer le diable par la queue*; run into debt etc. (*debt*) 806.

render -poor etc. *adj.*; impoverish; reduce, – to poverty; pauperize, fleece, ruin, bring to the parish.

Adj. poor, indigent; poverty-striken; badly –, poorly –, ill- off; poor as -a rat, – a church mouse, – Job's turkey, – Job; fortune-, dower-, money-, penni-less; unportioned, unmoneyed; impecunious; broke, flat; out –, short- of -money, – cash; without –, not worth- a rap etc. (*money*) 800; *qui n'a pas le sou*, out of pocket, hard up; out at -elbows, – heels; seedy, bare-footed; beggar-ly, -ed; destitute; fleeced, strapped, stripped; bereft, bereaved; reduced.

in -want etc. *n.*; needy, necessitous, distressed, pinched, straitened; put to one's -shifts, – last shifts; unable to -keep the wolf from the door, – make both ends meet; embarrassed, under hatches; involved etc. (*in debt*) 806; insolvent etc. (*not paying*) 808.

Adv. *in formâ pauperis*.

Phr. *zonam perdidit*.

805. Credit.—N. credit, trust, tick, score, tally, account.

letter of credit, circular note; duplicate; mortgage, lien, debenture, paper credit, floating capital; draft; securities.

creditor, lender, lessor, mortgagee; dun; usurer.

V. keep –, run up- an account with; entrust, credit, accredit.

place to one's -credit, – account; give –, take-credit; fly a kite.

Adj. credit-ing, -ed; accredited.

Adv. on -credit etc. *n.*; to the -account, – credit- of.

806. Debt.—N. debt, obligation, liability, indebtment, debit, score.

arrears, deferred payment, deficit, default; insolvency etc. (*non-payment*) 808; bad debt.

interest; usance, usury; premium; floating -debt, – capital.

debtor, debitor; mortgagor; defaulter etc. 808; borrower.

V. be -in debt etc. *adj.*; owe; incur –, contract-a debt etc. *n.*; run up -a bill, – a score, – an account; go on tick, put on the cuff; borrow etc. 788; run –, get- into debt; outrun the constable.

answer –, go bail- for; back one's note.

Adj. indebted; liable, chargeable, answerable for.

in -debt, – embarrassed circumstances, – difficulties; incumbered, involved; involved –, plunged –, deep –, over head and ears- in debt; deeply involved; fast tied up; insolvent etc. (*not paying*) 808; *minus*, out of pocket.

unpaid; unrequieted, unrewarded; owing, due, in arrear, outstanding.

807. Payment.—N. pay-, defray-ment; discharge; ac-, quittance; settlement, clearance, liquidation, satisfaction, reckoning, arrangement.

acknowledgment, release; receipt, – in full, – in full of all demands; voucher.

repayment, reimbursement, retribution; pay etc. (*reward*) 973; money paid etc. (*expenditure*) 809.

ready money etc. (*cash*) 800; stake, remittance, instalment.

payer, liquidator etc. 801.

V. pay, defray, make payment; pay -down, – on the nail, – ready money, – at sight, – in advance; cash, honor a bill, acknowledge; redeem; pay in kind.

pay one's -way, – shot, – footing; pay -the piper, – sauce for all, – costs; do the needful; come across; shell –, fork- out; come down with, – the dust; tickle –, grease- the palm; expend etc. 809; put –, lay- down.

discharge, settle, quit, acquit oneself of; account –, reckon –, settle –, be even –, be quits- with; strike a balance; settle –, balance –, square- accounts with; quit scores; foot the bill; wipe –, clear- off old scores; satisfy; pay in full; satisfy –, pay in full of- all demands; clear, liquidate; pay - up, – old debts.

disgorge, make repayment; repay, refund, reimburse, retribute; make compensation etc. 30.

Adj. paying etc., paid etc. *v.*; owing nothing, out of debt, all straight, clear of -debt, – encumbrance; unowed, never indebted.

Adv. to the tune of; on the nail; money –, cash-down; cash on delivery.

808. Non-payment.—N. non-payment; default, defalcation; protest, repudiation; application of the sponge; whitewashing.

insolvency, bankruptcy, failure; overdraft, overdrawn account; insufficiency etc. 640; run upon a bank.

waste paper bonds; dishonored –, protested-bills; bogus cheque.

bankrupt, insolvent debtor, lame duck, man of straw, welsher, stag, defaulter, absconder, levanter.

V. non -pay etc. 807; fail, break, stop payment; become -insolvent, – bankrupt; be gazetted.

protest, dishonor, repudiate, nullify.

pay under protest; button up one's pockets, draw the purse strings; apply the sponge; pay over the left shoulder, get whitewashed; swindle etc. 791; run up bills, fly kites.

Adj. not paying; in debt etc. 806; behindhand, in arrear; beggared etc. (*poor*) 804; unable to make both ends meet; *minus*; worse than nothing.

insolvent, bankrupt, in the gazette, gazetted, ruined.

unpaid etc. (*outstanding*) 806; *gratis* etc. 815; unremunerated.

809. Expenditure.—N. expenditure, money going out; out-goings, -lay; expenses, disbursement; prime cost etc. (*price*) 812; circulation; run upon a bank.

[Money paid] payment etc. 807; pay etc. (*remuneration*) 973; bribe etc. 973; fee, footing, garnish; subsidy; tribute, Peter's pence; contingent, quota; donation etc. 784.

pay in advance, earnest, handsel, deposit, instalment.

investment; purchase etc. 795.

V. expend, spend; run –, get- through; pay, disburse; open –, loose –, untie- the purse strings; lay –, shell –, fork- out; bleed; make up a sum, invest, sink money.

fee etc. (*reward*) 973; pay one's way etc. (*pay*) 807; subscribe etc. (*give*) 784; subsidize, bribe.

Adj. expend-ing, -ed etc. *v.*; sumptuary, liberal etc. 816; openhanded, lavish etc. 818; extensive etc. 814.

810. Receipt—N. receipt, accountable –, conditional –, binding –, return- receipt; value received, money coming in; income, incomings, innings, revenue, return, proceeds; gross receipts, net profit; earnings etc. (*gain*) 775.

rent, – roll; rent-al, -age; rack-rent.

premium, *bonus*; sweepstakes, tontine, prize, drawing.

pension, annuity; jointure etc. (*property*) 780; alimony, pittance; emolument etc. (*remuneration*) 973.

V. receive etc. 785; take money; draw –, derive- from; get, be in receipt of, acquire etc. 775; take etc. 789.

bring in, yield, afford, pay, return; accrue etc. (*be received from*) 785.

Adj. receiv-ing, -ed etc. *v.*; profitable etc. (*gainful*) 775.

811. Accounts.—N. accounts, accompts; commercial –, monetary- arithmetic; statistics etc. (*numeration*) 85; money matters, finance, budget, bill, score, reckoning, account.

books, account book, ledger; day –, cash –, pass- book; journal; debtor and creditor –, cash –, petty cash –, running- account; account-current; balance, – sheet; *compte rendu*, account settled.

book-keeping, audit; double –, single- entry; reckoning etc. 85.

chartered –, certified public –, accountant; auditor, actuary, bookkeeper; financier etc. 801; accounting party.

V. keep accounts, enter, post, book, credit, debit, carry over; take stock; balance –, make up –, square –, settle –, wind up –, cast up –, add up –, tot up- accounts; make accounts square.

bring to book, audit, tax, surcharge and falsify.

falsify –, garble –, cook –, doctor- an account.

Adj. monetary etc. 800; account-able, -ing; statistical.

812. Price.—N. price, amount, cost, expense, prime cost, charge, figure, demand, damage, fare, hire; wages etc. (*remuneration*) 973.

dues, duty, toll, tax, impost, cess, sess, tallage, levy, capitation-, poll-, income-, sur-, sales-, super-tax; gabel, *gabelle*; gavel, *octroi*, custom, tariff, excise, assessment, taxation, benevolence, tithe, tenths, exactment, ransom, salvage; broker-, wharf-, lighter-, ton-, freight-age.

worth, rate, value, valuation, appraisement, money's worth, par value; penny etc. -worth; price current, market price, quotation; what it will -fetch etc. *v.*

bill etc. (*account*) 811; shot.

V. bear –, set –, fix- a price; appraise, assess, price, charge, demand, ask, require, exact, run up; distrain; run up a bill etc. (*debt*) 806; have one's price; liquidate.

amount to, come to, mount up to; stand one in.

fetch, sell for, cost, bring in, yield, afford.

Adj. priced etc. *v.*; to the tune of, *ad valorem*; mercenary, venal.

Phr. no penny, no paternoster; *point d'argent, point de Suisse*, no longer pipe, no longer dance, no song, no supper.

one may have it for.

813. Discount.—N. discount, abatement, concession, reduction, depreciation, allowance, qualification, set off, drawback, poundage, *agio*, percentage; rebate, -ment; backwardation, contango; salvage; tare and tret.

V. discount, bate; a-, re-bate; deduct, reduce, mark down, take off, allow, give, make allowance; tax, depreciate.

Adj. discounting etc. *v.*

Adv. at a discount, below par.

814. Dearness.—N. dearness etc. *adj.*; high –, famine –, fancy- price; overcharge; extravagance; exorbitance, extortion; heavy pull upon the purse; Pyrrhic victory.

V. be -dear etc. *adj.*; cost -much, – a pretty penny; rise in price, look up.

overcharge, bleed, fleece, skin, extort.

pay -too much, – through the nose, –, too dear for one's whistle.

Adj. dear; high, -priced; of great price, expensive, costly, precious, dear bought; unreasonable extravagant, exorbitant, extortionate.

at a premium; not to be had, – for love or money; beyond –, above- price; priceless, of priceless value.

Adv. dear, -ly; at great –, heavy- cost; *à grands frais*.

Phr. prices looking up; *le jeu ne vaut pas la chandelle*.

815. Cheapness.—N. cheapness, low price; depreciation; bargain; good penny etc.- worth, *bon marché*.

[Absence of charge] gratuity; free -quarters, – seats, – admission, – warren; pass, Annie Oakley; run of one's teeth; nominal price, peppercorn rent; labor of love.

drug in the market.

V. be -cheap etc. *adj.*; cost little; come down – fall- in price.

buy for -a mere nothing, – an old song; have one's money's worth; cheapen, beat down.

Adj. cheap; low, – priced; moderate, reasonable; in-, un-expensive; well –, worth the money; *magnifique et pas cher*; good –, cheap- at the price; dirt –, dog- cheap; cheap, -as dirt, – and nasty; catchpenny.

reduced, marked down, half-price, depreciated, unsaleable.

gratuitous, *gratis*, free, for love, – nothing; cost-, expense-less; without charge, not charged, untaxed; scot –, shot –, rent- free; free of -cost, – expense; honorary, unbought, unpaid, complimentary.

Adv. for a mere song; at -cost price, – prime cost, – a reduction, – a bargain; on the cheap.

816. Liberality.—N. liberality, generosity, munificence; bount-y, -eousness, -ifulness; hospitality; charity etc. (*beneficence*) 906.

benefactor, free giver, Lady Bountiful.

V. be -liberal etc. *adj.*; spend –, bleed- freely; shower down upon; open one's purse strings etc. (*disburse*) 809; spare no expense, give -with both hands, – *carte blanche*.

Adj. liberal, free, generous; charitable etc. (*beneficent*) 906; hospitable; bount-iful, -eous; handsome; unsparing, ungrudging; open-, free-, full-handed; open-, large-, free-hearted; munificent, princely, unstinting.

overpaid.

Adv. liberally, ungrudgingly, with open hand.

817. Economy.—N. economy, frugality; thrift, -iness; prudence, care, husbandry, good housewifery, savingness, retrenchment.

savings; prevention of waste, save-all; cheese parings and candle ends; parsimony etc. 819.

V. be -economical etc. *adj.*; economize, save; retrench; cut- down expenses, – one's coat according to one's cloth, make both ends meet, keep within compass, meet one's expenses, pay one's way; keep one's head above water; husband etc. (*lay by*) 636; save –, invest- money; put out to interest; provide –, save- -for, – against- a rainy day; feather one's nest; look after the main chance.

Adj. economical, frugal, careful, thrifty, saving, chary, spare, sparing; parsimonious etc. 819.

underpaid.

Adv. sparingly etc. *adj.*; *ne quid nimis*.

818. Prodigality.—N. prodi-gality, -gence; unthriftiness, waste, -fulness; profus-ion, -eness; extravagance; squandering etc. *v.*; lavishness; malversation.

prodigal; spend-, waste-thrift; losel, play-boy, spender, squanderer, locust.

V. be -prodigal etc. *adj.*; squander, lavish, sow broadcast; pour forth like water; pay through the nose etc. (*dear*) 814; spill, waste, dissipate, exhaust, drain, eat out of house and home, overdraw, outrun the constable; run -out, – through; misspend; throw -good money after bad, – the helve after the hatchet; burn the candle at both ends; make ducks and drakes of one's money;

squander one's substance, spend money like water; fool –, potter –, muddle –, fritter –, throw-away one's money; pour water into a sieve, kill the goose that lays the golden eggs; *manger son blé en herbe*.

Adj. prodigal, profuse, thriftless, unthrifty, improvident, wasteful, losel, extravagant, lavish, dissipated, over liberal; full-handed etc. (*liberal*) 816.

penny wise and pound foolish.

Adv. with an unsparing hand; money burning one's pocket; recklessly profuse.

Int. hang the expense!

819. Parsimony.—N. parsimony, parcity; parsimoniousness, stinginess etc. *adj.*; stint; illiberality, avarice, tenacity, avidity, rapacity, extortion, venality, cupidity; selfishness etc. 943; *auri sacra fames*.

miser, niggard, churl, screw, tightwad, skinflint, crib, codger, muckworm, money-grubber, pinch-fist, scrimp, lickpenny, hunks, curmudgeon, *Harpagon*,. Silas Marner. harpy, extortioner, usurer.

V. be -parsimonious etc. *adj.*; grudge, begrudge, stint, skimp, pinch, gripe, screw, dole out, hold back, withhold, starve, famish, live upon nothing, skin a flint.

drive a -bargain, – hard bargain; cheapen, beat down; stop one hole in a sieve; have an itching palm, grasp, grab.

Adj. parsimonious, penurious, stingy, miserly, mean, shabby, peddling, scrubby, pennywise, near, niggardly, frugal to excess; close; fast-, close-, strait-handed; close-, hard-, tight-fisted; tight, sparing; chary; grudging, griping etc. *v.*; illiberal, ungenerous, churlish, hidebound, sordid, mercenary, venal, covetous, usurious, avaricious, greedy, extortionate, rapacious.

Adv. with a sparing hand.

820. Affections.—N. affections, character, qualities, disposition, nature, spirit, tone; temper, -ament; *diathesis*, idiosyncrasy; cast –, habit –, frame- of -mind, – soul; predilection, turn; natural –, turn of mind; bent, bias, predisposition, proneness, proclivity; propen-sity, -sedness, -sion, -dency; vein, humor, mood, grain, mettle; sympathy etc. (*love*) 897.

soul, heart, breast, bosom, inner man; heart's -core, – strings, – blood; heart of hearts, *penetralia mentis*; secret and inmost recesses of the –, cockles of one's- heart; inmost -heart, – soul; back-bone.

passion, pervading spirit; ruling –, master-passion; *furore*; fulness of the heart, heyday of the blood, flesh and blood, flow of soul, force of character.

V. have –, possess- -affections etc. *n.*; be of a -character etc. *n.*; be -affected etc. *adj.*; breathe.

Adj. affected, characterized, formed, molded, cast; at-, tempered; framed; pre-, disposed; prone, inclined; having a -bias etc. *n.*; tinctured –, imbued –, penetrated –, eaten up- with.

inborn, inbred, ingrained, in the grain, congenital, inherent, bred in the bone; deep-rooted, ineffaceable, inveterate; pathoscopic.

Adv. in one's -heart etc. *n.*; at heart; heart and soul etc. 821; in the -vein, – mood.

821. Feeling.—N. feeling; suffering etc. *v.*; endurance, tolerance, sufferance, supportance, experience, response; sympathy etc. (*love*) 897; impression, inspiration, affection, sensation, emotion, pathos, deep sense.

fire, warmth, glow, unction, *gusto*, vehemence; ferv-or, -ency; heartiness, cordiality; earnestness, eagerness; *empressment*, ardor, zeal, passion, enthusiasm, *verve, furore*, fanaticism; excitation of feeling etc. 824; fulness of the heart etc. (*disposition*) 820; passion etc. (*state of excitability*) 825; ecstasy etc. (*pleasure*) 827.

blush, suffusion, flush; hectic; tingling, thrill, kick, turn, shock; agitation etc. (*irregular motion*) 315; quiver, heaving, flutter, flurry, fluster, twitter, tremor; throb, -bing; pulsation, palpitation, painting; trepid-, perturb-ation; ruffle, hurry of spirits, pother, stew, ferment.

V. feel; receive an -impression etc. *n.*; be -impressed with etc. *adj.*; entertain –, harbor –, cherish- -feeling etc. *n.*

respond; catch the -flame, – infection; enter the spirit of.

bear, suffer, support, sustain, endure, brook, thole, aby; abide etc. (*be composed*) 826; experience etc. (*meet with*) 151; taste, prove; labor –, smart- under; bear the brunt of, brave, stand.

swell, glow, warm, flush, blush, change color, mantle; turn -color, – pale, – red, – black in the face; blench, crimson, whiten, pale, tingle, thrill, heave, pant, throb, palpitate, go pit-a-pat, tremble, quiver, flutter, twitter; stagger, reel; shake etc. 315; be -agitated, – excited etc. 824; look -blue, – black; wince, draw a deep breath.

impress etc. (*excite the feelings*) 824.

Adj. feeling etc. *v.*; sentient; sensuous; sensorial, -y; emo-tive, -tional; of –, with- feeling etc. *n.*

warm, quick, lively, smart, strong, sharp, acute, cutting, piercing, incisive; keen, – as a razor; trenchant, pungent, racy, *piquant*, poignant, caustic.

impressive, deep, profound, indelible; deep-, home-, heart-felt; swelling, soul-stirring, deep-mouthed, heart-expanding, electric, thrilling, rapturous, ecstatic.

earnest, wistful, eager, breathless; fer-vent, -vid; gushing, passionate, warmhearted, hearty, cordial, sincere, zealous, enthusiastic, glowing, ardent, burning, red-hot, fiery, flaming; boiling, – over.

pervading, penetrating, absorbing; rabid, raving feverish, fanatical, hysterical; impetuous etc. (*excitable*) 825; overmastering.

impressed –, moved –, touched –, affected –, penetrated –, seized –, imbued etc. 820- with; devoured by; wrought up etc. (*excited*) 824; struck all of a heap; rapt; in a -quiver etc. *n.*; enraptured etc. 829.

Adv. heart and soul, from the bottom of one's heart, *ab imo pectore*, *de profundis*, at heart, *con amore*, heartily, devoutly, over head and ears.

Phr. the heart -big, – full, – swelling, – beating, – pulsating, – throbbing, – thumping, – beating high, – melting, – overflowing, – bursting, – breaking.

822. Sensibility.—N. sensi-bility, -bleness, -tiveness; moral sensibility; impress-, affect-ibility; suscepti-bleness, -bility, -vity; mobility; viva-city, -ciousness; tender-, soft-ness; sentimental-ity, -ism.

excitability etc. 825; fastidiousness etc. 868; physical sensibility etc. 375.

sore -point, – place; where the shoe pinches.

V. be -sensible etc. *adj.*; have a -tender, – warm, – sensitive- heart.

take to –, treasure up in the- heart; shrink.

'die of a rose in aromatic pain;' touch to the quick.

Adj. sensi-ble, -tive; impressi-ble, -onable; suscepti-ve, -ble; alive to, impassion-able, -ed; gushing; warm-, tender-, soft-hearted; tender –, as a chicken; soft, sentimental, romantic; enthusiastic, highflying, spirited, mettlesome, vivacious, lively, expressive, mobile, tremblingly alive; excitable etc. 825; over-sensitive, without skin, thin-skinned; fastidious etc. 868.

Adv. sensibly etc. *adj.*; to the -quick, – inmost core.

823. Insensibility.—N. insensi-bility, -bleness; moral insensibility; inertness, *inertia, vis inertiae*; impassi-bility, -bleness; inappetency, apathy, phlegm, dulness, hebetude, supineness, lukewarmness, insusceptibility, unimpressibility.

cold -fit, – blood, – heart; cold-, cool-ness; frigidity, *sang-froid*; stoicism, imperturbation etc. (*inexcitability*) 826; *nonchalance*, unconcern, dry eyes; *insouciance* etc. (*indifference*) 866; recklessness etc. 863; callousness; heart of stone, stock and stone, marble, deadness.

torp-or, -idity; obstupefaction, lethargy, coma, trance; sleep etc. 683; suspended animation; stupor, -efaction; paralysis, palsy; numbness etc. (*physical insensibility*) 376.

neutrality; quietism, vegetation.

V. be -insensible etc. *adj.*; have a rhinoceros hide; show -insensibility etc. *n.*; not -mind, – care, – be affected by; have no desire for etc. 866; have –, feel –, take- no interest in; *nil admirari*; not care a -straw etc. (*unimportance*) 643 for; disregard etc. (*neglect*) 460; set at naught etc. (*make light of*) 483; turn a deaf ear to etc. (*inattention*) 458; vegetate.

render -insensible, – callous; blunt, obtund, numb, benumb, paralyze, chloroform, deaden, hebetate, stun, stupefy; brut-ify, -alize.

inure; harden, – the heart; steel, case-harden, sear.

Adj. insensible, unconscious; impassi-ve, -ble; blind to, deaf to, dead to; un-, in-susceptible; unimpress-ionable, -ible; passion-, spirit-, heart-, soulless; unfeeling, unmoral.

apathetic; leuco-, phlegmatic; dull, frigid; cold, -blooded, -hearted; unemotional; cold as charity; flat, obtuse, inert, supine, sluggish, torpid; sleepy etc. (*inactive*) 683; languid, half-hearted, tame; numb, -ed; comatose; anesthetic etc. 376; stupefied, chloroformed, palsy-stricken.

indifferent, lukewarm; Laodicean; careless, mindless, regardless; inattentive etc. 458; neglectful etc. 460; disregarding.

unconcerned, *nonchalant, pococurante, insouciant, sans souci*; unambitious etc. 866.

un-affected, -ruffled, -impressed, -inspired, -excited, -moved, -stirred, -touched, -shocked, -struck; unblushing etc. (*shameless*) 885; unanimated; vegetative.

callous, thick-skinned, pachydermatous, impervious; hard, -ened; inured, case-hardened; steeled –, proof- against; imperturbable etc. (*inexcitable*) 826; unfelt.

Adv. insensibly etc. *adj.*; *aequo animo*; without being -moved, – touched, – impressed; in cold blood; with -dry eyes, – withers unwrung.

Phr. never mind; it is of no consequence etc. (*unimportant*) 643; it cannot be helped; nothing coming amiss; it is all -the same, – one- to.

824. Excitation.—N. excitation of feeling; mental –, excitement; suscitation, galvanism, stimulation, piquancy, provocation inspiration, calling forth, infection; interest, animation, agitation, perturbation; subjugation, fascination, intoxication; en-, ravishment; entrancement, high pressure.

unction, impressiveness etc. *adj.*; emotional appeal; melodrama; psychological moment, crisis; sensationalism.

trail of temper, *casus belli*; irritation etc. (*anger*) 900; passion etc. (*state of excitability*) 825; thrill etc. (*feeling*) 821; repression of feeling etc. 826.

V. excite, affect, touch, move, impress, strike, interest, intrigue, animate, inspire, impassion, smite, infect; stir –, fire –, warm- the blood; set astir; a-, wake; a-, waken; call forth; e-, pro-voke; raise up, summon up, call up, wake up, blow up, get up, light up; raise; get up steam, rouse, arouse, stir, fire, kindle, enkindle, apply the torch, set on fire, inflame, illuminate.

stimulate; ex-, suscitate; inspirit; spirit up, stir up, work up; infuse life into, five new life to; bring –, introduce- new blood; quicken; sharpen, whet; work upon etc. (*incite*) 615; hurry on, give a fillip, put on one's mettle.

fan the -fire, – flame; blow the coals, stir the embers; fan, – into a flame; foster, heat, warm, foment, raise to a fever heat; keep -up, – the pot boiling; revive, rekindle; rake up, rip up.

stir –, play on –, come home to- the feelings; touch -a string, – a chord, – the soul, – the heart; go to one's heart, penetrate, pierce, go through one, touch to the quick, open the wound; possess –, pervade –, penetrate –, imbrue –, absorb –, affect –, disturb- the soul.

absorb, rivet the attention; sink into the -mind, – heart; prey on the mind; intoxicate; over-whelm, -power; *bouleverser*, upset, turn one's head.

fascinate; enrapture etc. (*give pleasure*) 829.

agitate, perturb, ruffle, fluster, flutter, shake, disturb, faze, startle, shock, stagger; give one a -shock, – turn; strike -dumb, – all of a heap; stun, astound, electrify, galvanize, petrify.

irritate, sting; cut, – to the -heart, – quick; try one's temper; fool to the top of one's bent, pique; infuriate, madden, make one's blood boil; lash into fury etc. (*wrath*) 900.

be -excited etc. *adj.*; flash up, flare up; catch the infection; thrill etc. (*feel*) 821; mantle; work oneself up; seethe, boil, simmer, foam, fume, flame, rage, rave; run mad etc. (*passion*) 825.

Adj. excited etc. *v.*; wrought up, on the *qui vive*, astir, sparkling; in a -quiver etc. 821, – fever, – ferment, – blaze, – state of excitement; in hysterics; black in the face, over-wrought; hot, red-hot, flushed, feverish; all -of a twitter, – of a flutter, – of a dither, – in a pucker; with -quivering lips, – tears in one's eyes.

flaming; boiling, – over; ebullient, seething; foaming, – at the mouth; fuming, raging, carried away by passion, wild, raving, frantic, mad, distracted, distraught, beside oneself, out of one's wits, amuck, ready to burst, *bouleversé*, demoniacal.

lost, *eperdu*, tempest-tossed; haggard; ready to sink.

stung to the quick, up, on one's high ropes.

exciting etc. *v.*; impressive, warm, glowing, fervid, swelling, imposing, spirit-stirring, thrilling; high-wrought; soul-stirring, -subduing; heart-swelling, -thrilling; agonizing etc. (*painful*) 830; telling, sensational, melodramatic, hysterical; overpowering, -whelming; more than flesh and blood can bear.

piquant etc. (*pungent*) 392; spicy, appetizing, provocative, *provaquant*, tantalizing.

Adv. till one is black in the face.

Phr. the heart -beating high, – going pit-a-pat, – leaping into one's mouth; the blood -being up, – boiling in one's veins; the eye -glistening, – 'in a fine frenzy rolling;' the head turned.

825. Excitability. [Excess of sensitiveness.]—**N.** excitability, impetuosity, vehemence; boisterousness etc. *adj.*; turbulence; impatience, intolerance, non-endurance; irritability etc. (*irascibility*) 901; itching etc. (*desire*) 865; wincing; disquiet, -ude; restlessness; fidge-ts, -tiness; agitation etc. (*irregular motion*) 315.

trepidation, perturbation, ruffle, hurry, -skurry, fuss, flurry; fluster, flutter; pother, stew, ferment; whirl; thrill etc. (*feeling*) 821; state –, fever- of excitement; transport.

passion, excitement, flush, heat; fever, -heat; fire, flame, fume, blood boiling; tumult; effervescence, ebullition; boiling, – over; whiff, gust, storm, tempest; scene, breaking out, burst, fit, paroxysm, explosion; out-break, -burst; agony.

violence etc. 173; fierceness etc. *adj.*; rage, fury, *furor*, *furore*, desperation, madness, distraction, raving, delirium, brain storm; frenzy, hysterics; intoxication; tearing –, raging- passion, towering rage; anger etc. 900.

fascination, infatuation, fanaticism; Quixot-ism, -ry; *tête montée*.

V. be -impatient etc. *adj.*; not be able to -bear etc. 826; bear ill, wince, chafe, champ the bit; be in a -stew etc. *n.*; be out of all patience, fidget, fuss, not have a wink of sleep; toss, – on one's pillow.

lose one's temper etc. 900; break –, burst –, fly- out; go –, fly- -off, – off the handle, – off at a tangent; explode; flare up, flame up, fire up, burst into a flame, take fire, fire, burn; boil, – over; foam, fume, rage, rave, rant, tear; go –, run- -wild, – mad; go into hysterics; run -riot, – amuck; *battre la campagne, faire le diable à quatre*, play the deuce; raise -Cain, – the devil.

Adj. excitable, easily excited, in an excitable state; high strung; irritable etc. (*irascible*) 901; impatient, intolerant.

feverish, febrile, hysterical; delirious, mad, moody, maggoty-headed.

unquiet, mercurial, electric, galvanic, hasty, hurried, restless, fidgety, fussy; chafing etc. *v.*

startlish, mettlesome, high mettled, skittish.

vehement, demonstrative, violent, wild, furious, fierce, fiery, hot-headed, mad-cap.

over-zealous, enthusiastic, impassioned, fanatical; rabid etc. (*eager*) 865.

rampant, clamorous, uproarious, turbulent, tempestuous, tumultuary, boisterous.

impulsive, impetuous, passionate; uncontroll-ed, -able; ungovernable, irrepressible, stanchless, inextinguishable, burning, simmering, volcanic, ready to burst forth.

excit-ed, -ing etc. 824.

Int. pish! pshaw!

Phr. *noli me tangere*.

826. Inexcitability. [Absence of excitability, or of excitement.]—**N.** inexcit-, imperturb-, inirritability; even temper, tranquil mind, dispassion; tolerance, toleration, patience.

passiveness etc. (*physical inertness*) 172; hebetude, -ation; impassibility etc. (*insensibility*) 823; stupefaction.

coolness, calmness etc. *adj.*; composure, placidity, indisturbance, imperturbation, *sang-froid*, tranquility, serenity; quiet, -ude; peace of mind, mental calmness.

staidness etc. *adj.*; gravity, sobriety, Quakerism; philosophy, equanimity, stoicism, command of temper; self-possession, -control, -command, -restraint; presence of mind.

submission etc. 725; resignation; suffer-, support-, endur-, long-suffer-, forbear-ance; longanimity; fortitude; patience -of Job, – 'on a monument,' – 'sovereign o'er transmuted ill;' moderation; repression –, subjugation- of feeling; restraint etc. 751.

tranquilization etc. (*moderation*) 174.

V. be -composed etc. *adj.*

laisser -faire, – *aller*; take things -easily, – as they come; take it easy, run on, live and let live; take -easily, – cooly, – in good part; *aequam serva e mentem*.

bear, – well, – the brunt; go through, support, endure, brave, disregard.

tolerate, suffer, stand, bide; abide, aby; bear –, put up –, abide- with; acquiesce; submit etc. (*yield*) 725; submit with a good grace; resign –, reconcile- oneself to; brook, digest, eat, swallow, pocket, stomach; make -light of, – the best of, – a virtue of necessity; put a good face on, keep one's countenance; carry -on, – through; check etc. 751- oneself.

compose, appease etc. (*moderate*) 174; propitiate; repress etc. (*restrain*) 751; render insensible etc. 823; overcome –, allay –, repress- one's -excitability etc. 825; master one's feelings.

make -oneself, – one's mind- easy; set one's mind at -ease, – rest.

calm –, cool- down; thaw, grow cool.

be -borne, – endured; go down.

Adj. in-, un-excitable; imperturbable; unsusceptible etc. (*insensible*) 823; un-, dispassionate; cold-blooded, inirritable; enduring etc. *v.*; stoical, Platonic, philosophic, staid, stayed; sober, – minded; grave; sober –, grave- as a judge; sedate, demure, cool-, level-headed; steady.

easy-going, peaceful, placid, calm; quiet, – as a mouse; tranquil, serene; cool, – as -a cucumber, – custard; undemonstrative.

temperate etc. (*moderate*) 174; composed, collected; un-excited, -stirred, -ruffled, -disturbed, -perturbed, -impassioned; unoffended; unresisting.

meek, tolerant; patient, – as Job; submissive etc. 725; tame; content, resigned, chastened, subdued, lamblike; gentle, – as a lamb; *suaviter in modo*; mild, – as mother's milk; soft as peppermint; armed with patience, bearing with, clement, forbearant, long-suffering.

Adv. 'like patience on a monument smiling at grief;' *aequo animo*, in cold blood etc. 823; more in sorrow than in anger.

Int. patience! and shuffle the cards.

827. Pleasure.—N. pleasure, gratification, enjoyment, fruition; ob-, de-lectation; relish, zest; *gusto* etc. (*physical pleasure*) 377; satisfaction etc. *(content)* 831; complacency.

well-being; good etc. 618; snugness, comfort, ease; cushion etc. 215; *sans souci*, mind at ease.

joy, gladness, delight, glee, cheer, sunshine; cheerfulness etc. 836.

treat, refreshment; frolic, fun, lark, gambol, merry-making; amusement etc. 840; luxury etc. 377; hedonism.

mens sana in corpore sano.

happiness, felicity, bliss; beati-tude, -fication; enchantment, transport, rapture, ravishment, ecstasy; *summum bonum*; paradise, elysium etc. (*heaven*) 981; third –, seventh- heaven; unalloyed - happiness etc.

honeymoon; palmy –, halcyon- days; golden - age, – time; *Saturnia regna*, Eden, Arcadia, happy valley, Agapemone; Cockaigne.

V. be pleased etc. 829; feel –; experience- pleasure etc. *n.*; joy; enjoy –, hug- oneself; be in - clover etc. 377, – elysium etc. 981; tread on enchanted ground; fall –, go- into raptures.

feel at home, breathe freely, bask in the sunshine.

be -pleased etc. 829- with; receive –, derive- pleasure etc. *n.*- from; take -pleasure etc. *n.*- in; delight in, rejoice in, indulge in, luxuriate in; gloat over etc. (*physical pleasure*) 377; enjoy, relish, like; love etc. 897; take -to, – a fancy to; have a liking for; enter into the spirit of.

take in good part.

treat oneself to, solace oneself with.

Adj. pleased etc. 829; not sorry; glad, -some; pleased as Punch.

happy, blest, blessed, blissful, beatified; happy as -a king, – the day is long; thrice happy, *ter quaterque beatus*; enjoying etc. *v.*; joyful etc. (*in spirits*) 836; hedonic.

in -a blissful state, – paradise etc. 981; – raptures, – ecstasies, – a transport of delight.

comfortable etc. (*physical pleasure*) 377; at ease; content etc. 831; *sans souci*, in clover.

overjoyed, entranced, enchanted; enraptured; en-, ravished; transported; fascinated, captivated.

with -a joyful face, – sparkling eyes.

pleasing etc. 829; ecstatic, beat-ic, -ific; painless, unalloyed, without alloy, cloudless.

Adv. happily etc. *adj.*; with pleasure etc. (*willingly*) 60; with -glee etc. *n.*

phr. one's heart leaping with joy.

828. Pain.—N. mental suffering, pain, dolor; suffer-ing, -ance; ache, smart etc. (*physical pain*) 378; passion.

displeasure, dissatisfaction, discomfort, discomposure, disquiet; *malaise*; inquietude, uneasiness, vexation of spirit; taking; discontent etc. 832.

dejection etc. 837; weariness etc. 841.

annoyance, irritation, worry, infliction, visitation; plague, bore; bother, -ation; stew, vexation, mortification, chagrin, *esclandre*; *mauvais quart d'heure*.

care, anxiety, solicitude, trouble, trial, ordeal, fiery ordeal, shock, blow, cark, dole, fret, burden, load.

concern, grief, sorrow, distress, affliction, woe, bitterness, gloom, heartache; heavy –, aching –, bleeding –, broken- heart; heavy affliction, gnawing grief; unhappiness, infelicity, misery, tribulation, wretchedness, desolation; despair etc. 859; extremity, prostration, depth of misery.

nightmare, *ephialtes*, incubus.

anguish, agony; throe, tor-ture, -ment; crucifixion, martyrdom; pang, twinge, stab; the rack, the stake; purgatory etc. (*hell*) 982.

hell upon earth; iron age, reign of terror; slough of despond etc. (*adversity*) 735; peck –, sea- of troubles; ills that flesh is heir to etc. (*evil*) 619; miseries of human life; unkindest cut of all.

sufferer, victim, prey, martyr, object of compassion, wretch, shorn lamb.

V. feel –, suffer –, experience –, undergo –, bear –, endure- pain etc. *n.*; smart, ache etc. (*physical pain*) 378; suffer, bleed, ail; be the victim of; bear – take up- the cross.

labor under afflictions; quaff the bitter cup, have a bad time of it; fall on evil days etc. (*adversity*) 735; go hard with, come to grief, fall a sacrifice to, drain the cup of misery to the dregs, sup full of horrors.

sit on thorns, be on pins and needles, wince, fret, chafe, worry oneself, be in a taking, fret and fume, take -on, – to heart.

grieve; mourn etc. (*lament*) 839; yearn, repine, pine, droop, languish, sink; give way; despair etc. 859; break one's heart; weigh upon the heart etc. (*inflict pain*) 830.

Adj. in –, in a state of –, full of- pain etc. *n.*; suffering etc. *v.*; pained, afflicted, worried, displeased etc. 830; aching, griped, sore etc. (*physical pain*) 378; on the rack; in limbo; between hawk and buzzard.

un-comfortable, -easy; ill at ease; in a -taking, – way; disturbed; discontented etc. 832; out of humor etc. 901*a*; weary etc. 841.

heavy laden, stricken, crushed, a prey to, victimized, ill-used.

unfortunate etc. (*hapless*) 735; to be pitied, doomed, devoted, accursed, undone, lost, stranded.

unhappy, infelicitous, poor, wretched, miserable, woe-begone; cheerless etc. (*dejected*) 837; careworn.

concerned, sorry; sorrow-ing, -ful; cut up, chagrined, horrified, horror-stricken; in –, plunged in –, a prey to- grief etc. *n.*; in tears etc. (*lamenting*) 839; steeped to the lips in misery; heart-stricken, -broken, -scalded; broken-hearted; in despair etc. 859.

Phr. 'the iron entered into our soul;' *haeret lateri lethalis arundo*;' one's heart bleeding.

829. Pleasurableness. [Capability of giving pleasure; cause or source of pleasure.]**—N.** pleasurable-, pleasant-, agreeable-ness etc. *adj.*; pleasure giving, jocundity, delectability; amusement etc. 840.

attraction etc. (*motive*) 615; attractiveness, -

ability; invitingness etc. *adj.*; charm, fascination, captivation, enchantment, witchery, seduction, winsomeness, winning ways, amenity, amiability, sweetness.

loveliness etc. (*beauty*) 845; sunny –, bright-side; sweets etc. (*sugar*) 396; goodness etc. 648; manna in the wilderness, land flowing with milk and honey.

treat; regale etc. (*physical pleasure*) 377; dainty; tit-, tid-bit; nuts, *sauce piquante*.

V. cause –, produce –, create –, give –, afford –, procure –, offer –, present –, yield- pleasure etc. 827.

please, charm, delight; gladden etc. (*make cheerful*) 836; take, captivate, fascinate; enchant, entrance, enrapture, transport, bewitch; en-, ravish.

bless, beatify; satisfy; gratify –, desire etc. 865; slake, satiate, quench; indulge, humor, flatter, tickle; tickle the palate etc. (*savory*) 394; regale, refresh; enliven; treat; amuse etc. 840; take –, tickle –, hit- one's fancy; meet one's wishes; win –, gladden –, rejoice –, warm the cockles of- the heart; do one's heart good.

attract, allure etc. (*move*) 615; stimulate etc. (*excite*) 824; interest, intrigue.

make things pleasant, popularize, gild the pill, sweeten.

Adj. causing pleasure etc. *v.*; pleasure-giving; pleas-ing, -ant, -urable; agreeable, cushy; grat-eful, -ifying; leef, lief, acceptable; welcome, – as the roses in May; welcomed; favorite; to one's -taste, – mind, – liking, – heart's content; satisfactory etc. (*good*) 648.

refreshing; comfortable; cordial; genial; glad, -some; sweet, delectable, nice, dainty; delic-ate, -ious; dulcet; luscious etc. 396; palatable etc. 394; luxurious, voluptuous; sensual etc. 377.

attractive etc. 615; inviting, prepossessing, engaging; win-ning, -some; taking, fascinating, captivating, killing; seduc-ing, -tive; alluring, enticing; appetizing etc. (*exciting*) 824; cheering etc. 836; bewitching; interesting, absorbing, enchanting, entrancing, enravishing.

charming; delightful, felicitous, exquisite; lovely etc. (*beautiful*) 845; ravishing, rapturous; heartfelt, thrilling, ecstatic; beat-ic, -ific; seraphic; empyrean; elysian etc. (*heavenly*) 981.

palmy, halcyon, Saturnian.

Phr. *decies repetita placebit.*

830. Painfulness. [Capability of giving pain; cause or source of pain.]—**N.** painfulness etc. *adj.*; trouble, care etc. (*pain*) 828; trial; af-, in-fliction; cross, blow, stroke, burden, load, curse; bitter -pill, – draught, – cup; waters of bitterness.

annoyance, grievance, nuisance, vexation, mortification, sickener; bore, bother, pother, hot water, sea of troubles, hornet's nest, plague, pest.

cancer, ulcer, sting, thorn; canker etc. (*bane*) 663; scorpion etc. (*evil-doer*) 913; dagger etc. (*arms*) 727; scourge etc. (*instrument of punishment*) 975; carking –, canker worm of- care.

mishap, misfortune etc. (*adversity*) 735; *désagrément, esclandre*, rub.

source of -irritation, – annoyance; wound, sore subject, skeleton in the closet; thorn in -the flesh, – one's side; where the shoe pinches, gall and wormwood.

sorry sight, heavy news, provocation; affront etc. 929; head and front of one's offending.

infestation, molestation; malignity etc. (*malevolence*) 907.

V. cause –, occasion –, give –, bring –, induce –, produce –, create –, inflict- pain etc. 828; pain, hurt, wound.

pinch, prick, gripe etc. (*physical pain*) 378; pierce, lancinate, cut.

hurt –, wound –, grate upon –, jar upon- the feelings; wring –, pierce –, lacerate –, break –, rend- the heart; make the heart bleed; tear –, rend- the heart-strings; draw tears from the eyes.

sadden; make -unhappy etc. 828; plunge into sorrow, grieve, fash, afflict, distress; cut -up, – to the heart.

displease, annoy, incommode, discommode, discompose, trouble, disquiet, disturb, thwart, cross, perplex, molest, tease, rag, tire, irk, vex, mortify, wherret, worry, plague, bother, pester, bore, pother, harass, harry, badger, heckle, bait, beset, infest, persecute, importune, be troublesome.

wring, harrow, torment, torture; put to the -rack, – question; break on the wheel, rack, scarify; cruci-ate, -fy; convulse, agonize; barb the dart; plant a -dagger in the breast, – thron in one's side.

irritate, provoke, sting, nettle, try the patience, pique, fret, rile, tweak the nose, chafe, gall; sting –, wound –, cut- to the quick; aggrieve, affront, enchafe, enrage, ruffle, sour the temper; give offence etc. (*resentment*) 900.

maltreat, bite, snap at, assail, bully; smite etc. (*punish*) 972.

sicken, disgust, revolt, nauseate, disenchant, repel, offend, shock, stink in the nostrils; go against –, turn- the stomach; make one sick, set the teeth on edge, go against the grain, grate on the ear; stick in one's -throat, – gizzard; rankle, gnaw, corrode, horrify, appal, freeze the blood; chill the spine; make the -flesh creep, – hair stand on end; make the blood -curdle, – run cold; make one shudder.

haunt, – the memory; weigh –, prey- on the -heart, – mind, – spirits; bring one's grey hairs with sorrow to the grave; add a nail to one's coffin.

Adj. causing pain, hurting etc. *v.*; hurtful etc. (*bad*) 649; painful; dolor-ific, -ous; unpleasant; un-, dis-pleasing; disagreeable, unpalatable, bitter, distasteful; uninviting; unwelcome; undesir-able, -ed; obnoxious; unacceptable, unpopular, thankless.

unsatisfactory, untoward, unlucky, uncomfortable.

distressing; afflict-ing, -ive; joy-, cheer-, comfortless; dismal, disheartening; depress-ing, -ive; dreary, melancholy, grievous, piteous; woeful, rueful, mournful, deplorable, pitiable, lamentable; sad, affecting, touching, pathetic.

irritating, provoking, stinging, annoying, aggravating, mortifying, galling; unaccommodating, invidious, vexatious; trouble-, tire-, irk-, weari-some; plagu-ing, -y; awkward.

importunate; teas-, pester-, bother-, harass-, worry-, torment-, cark-ing.

in-toler-, -suffer-, -support-able; un-bear-, -endur-able; past bearing; not to be -borne, – endured; more than flesh and blood can bear; enough to -drive one mad, – provoke a saint, – make a parson swear, – try the patience of Job.

shocking, terrific, grim, appalling, crushing; dreadful, fearful, frightful; thrilling, tremendous, dire; heart-breaking, -rending, -wounding, corroding, -sickening; harrowing, rending.

odious, hateful, execrable, repulsive, repellent, abhorrent; horri-d, -ble, -fic, -fying; offensive; nause-ous, -ating; disgust-, sicken-, revolt-ing; nasty; loath-some, -ful; fulsome; vile etc. (*bad*) 649; hideous etc. 846.

sharp, acute, sore, severe, grave, hard, harsh, cruel, biting, acrimonious, caustic; cutting, corroding, consuming, racking, excruciating, searching, searing, grinding, grating, agonizing; envenomed.

ruinous, disastrous, calamitous, tragical; desolating, withering; burdensome, onerous, oppressive; cumb-rous, -ersome.

Adv. painfully etc. *adj.*; with -pain etc. 828; deuced.

Int. *hinc illae lachrymae!* woe is me!

Phr. *surgit amari aliquid*; the place being too hot to hold one; the iron entering the soul.

831. Content.—N. content, -ment, -edness; complacency, satisfaction, entire satisfaction, ease, heart's ease, peace of mind; serenity etc. 826; cheerfulness etc. 836; ray of comfort; comfort etc. (*well-being*) 827.

re-, conciliation; resignation etc. (*patience*) 826. waiter on Providence.

V. be -content etc. *adj.*; rest -satisfied, – and be thankful; take the good the gods provide, let well alone, feel oneself at home, hug oneself, lay the flattering unction to one's soul.

take -up with, – in good part; assent etc. 488; be reconciled to, make one's peace with; get over it; take -heart, – comfort; put up with etc. (*bear*) 826.

render -content etc. *adj.*; set at ease, comfort; set one's -heart, – mind- at -ease, – rest; speak peace; conciliate, reconcile, win over, propitiate, disarm, beguile; content, satisfy; gratify etc. 829.

be -tolerated etc. 826; go down, – with; do.

Adj. content, -ed; satisfied etc. *v.*; at -ease, – one's ease, – home; with the mind at ease, *sans souci, sine curâ*, easy-going, not particular; conciliatory; unrepining, of good comfort; resigned etc. (*patient*) 826; cheerful etc. 836.

un-afflicted, -vexed, -molested, -plagued; serene etc. 826; at rest; snug, comfortable; in one's element.

satisfactory, satisfying, ample, sufficient, adequate, tolerable.

Adv. to one's heart's content; *à la bonne heure*; all for the best.

Int amen etc. (*assent*) 488; very well, so much the better, well and good; it –, that- will do; it cannot be helped.

Phr. nothing comes amiss.

832. Discontent.—N. discontent, -ment; dissatisfaction; dissent etc. 489; labor unrest.

disappointment, mortification; cold comfort; regret etc. 833; repining, taking on etc. *v.*; inquietude, vexation of spirit, soreness; heartburning, -grief; querulousness etc. (*lamentation*) 839; hypercriticism.

malcontent, grumbler, growler, croaker, *laudator temporis acti*; censurer, complainer, faultfinder, murmurer, Adullamite, Diehard, Bitterender.

the Opposition, cave of Adullam, indignation meeting, 'winter of our discontent.'

V. be -discontented etc. *adj.*; quarrel with one's bread and butter; repine; regret etc. 833; wish one at the bottom of the Red Sea; take -on, – to heart; shrug the shoulders; make a wry –, pull a long-face; knit one's brows; look -blue, – black, – black as thunder, – blank, – glum.

take -in bad part, – ill; fret, chafe, make a piece of work; grumble, croak, grouse; lament etc. 839.

cause -discontent etc. *n.*; dissatisfy, disappoint, mortify, put out, disconcert; cut up; dishearten.

Adj. discontented; dissatisfied etc. *v.*; unsatisfied, ungratified; dissident; dissentient etc. 489; malcontent, exigent, exacting, hypercritical.

repining etc. *v.*; regretful etc. 833; down in the mouth etc. (*dejected*) 837.

in -high dudgeon, – a fume, – the sulks, – the dumps, – bad humor; glum, sulky; sour, – as a crab; soured, sore; out of -humor, – temper.

disappointing etc. *v.*; unsatisfactory.

Int. so much the worse!

Phr. that –, it- will never do.

833. Regret.—N. regret, repining; home sickness, nostalgia; *mal –, maladie- du pays*; lamentation etc. 839; contrition, compunction, penitence etc. 950.

bitterness, heart-burning.

laudator temporis acti etc. (*discontent*) 832.

V. regret, deplore; bewail etc. (*lament*) 839; repine, cast a longing lingering look behind; rue, – the day; repent etc. 950; *infandum renovare dolorem*.

prey –, weigh –, have a weight- on the mind; leave an aching void.

Adj. regretting etc. *v.*; regretful; home-sick.

regretted etc. *v.*; much to be regretted, regrettable; lamentable etc. (*bad*) 649.

Int. what a pity! hang it!

Phr. 'tis -pity, – too true.

834. Relief.—N. relief; deliverance; refreshment etc. 689; easement, softening, alleviation, mitigation, palliation etc. 174; soothing, lullaby; cradle song, *berceuse*

solace, consolation, comfort, encouragement.

lenitive, restorative etc. (*remedy*) 662; poultice etc. *v.*; cushion etc. 215; crumb of comfort, balm in Gilead; aspirin.

V. relieve, ease, alleviate, mitigate, palliate, soothe, addulce; salve; soften, – down; foment, stupe, poultice; assuage, allay.

cheer, comfort, console; encourage, bear up, pat on the back, give comfort, set at ease; enliven, gladden –, cheer- the heart.

remedy; cure etc. (*restore*) 660; refresh; pour -balm into, – oil on.

smoothe the ruffled brow of care, temper the wind to the shorn lamb, lay the flattering unction to one's soul.

disburden etc. (*free*) 705; take off a load of care.

be relieved; breathe more freely, draw a long breath; take comfort; dry –, wipe- the -tears, – eyes.

Adj. relieving etc. *v.*; consolatory, soothing; assua-ging, -sive; bal-my, -samic; lenitive, palliative; anodyne etc. (*remedial*) 662; curative etc. 660.

835. Aggravation.—N. aggravation, heightening; exacerbation; exasperation; overestimation etc. 482; exaggeration etc. 549.

V. aggravate, render worse, heighten, embitter, sour; ex-, acerbate; exasperate, envenom; tease, provoke, enrage.

add fuel to the -fire, – flame; fan the flame etc. (*excite*) 824; go from bad to worse etc. (*deteriorate*) 659.

Adj. aggravated etc. *v.*; worse, unrelieved; aggravable; aggravating etc. *v.*

Adv. out of the frying pan into the fire, from bad to worse, worse and worse.

Int. so much the worse!

836. Cheerfulness.—N. cheerfulness etc. *adj.*; geniality, gaiety, *l'allegro*, cheer, good humor, spirits; high –, animal –, flow of- spirits; glee, high glee, light heart; sunshine of the -mind, – breast; *gaieté de coeur, bon naturel.*

liveliness etc. *adj.*; life, alacrity, vivacity, animation, *allégresse*; jocundity, joviality, jollity; levity; jocularity etc. (*wit*) 842.

mirth, merriment, hilarity, exhilaration; laughter etc. 838; merry-making etc. (*amusement*) 840; heyday, rejoicing etc. 838; marriage bells.

nepenthe, Euphrosyne.

optimism etc. (*hopefulness*) 858; self-complacency.

V. be -cheerful etc. *adj.*; have the mind at ease, smile, put a good face upon, keep up one's spirits; view -the bright side of the picture, – things *en couleur de rose*; *ridentem dicere verum*, cheer up, brighten up, light up, bear up; chirp, take heart, cast away care, drive dull care away, perk up.

rejoice etc. 838; carol, chirrup, lilt; frisk, rollick, give a loose to mirth.

cheer, enliven, elate, exhilarate, gladden, inspirit, animate, raise the spirits, inspire; put in good humor; cheer –, rejoice- the heart; delight etc. (*give pleasure*) 829.

Adj. cheerful; happy etc. 827; cheer-y, -ly; of good cheer, smiling; blithe; in –, in good- spirits; in high -spirits, – feather; happy as -the day is long, – a king; gay, – as a lark; *allegro*; light, -some, -hearted; buoyant, *débonnaire*, bright, free and easy, airy; janty, jaunty, canty; spright-ly, -ful; spry; spirit-ed, -ful; lively; animated, breezy, vivacious; brisk, – as a bee; sparkling; sportive; full of -play, – spirit; all alive.

sunny, palmy; hopeful etc. 858.

merry, – as a -cricket, – grig, – marriage bell; joyful, joyous, jocund, jovial; jolly, – as a thrush, – as a sandboy; blithesome; glee-ful, -some; hilarious, rattling.

winsome, bonny, hearty, buxom.

play-ful, -some; *folâtre*, playful as a kitten, tricksy, frisky, frolicsome; gamesome; jocose, jocular, waggish; mirth-, laughter-loving; mirthful, rollicking.

elate, -d; exulting, jubilant, flushed; rejoicing etc. 838; cock-a-hoop.

cheering, inspiriting, exhilarating; cardiac, -al; pleasing etc. 829; flourishing, halcyon.

Adv. cheerfully etc. *adj.*

Int. never say die! come! cheer up! hurrah! etc. 838; 'hence loathed melancholy!' begone dull care! away with melancholy!

837. Dejection.—N. dejection; dejectedness etc. *adj.*; depression, prosternation; lowness –, depression- of spirits; weight –, oppression –, damp- on the spirits; low –, bad –, drooping –, depressed- spirits; heart sinking; heaviness –, failure- of heart.

heaviness etc. *adj.*; infestivity, gloom; weariness etc. 841; *taedium vitae*, disgust of life; *mal du pays* etc. (*regret*) 833.

melancholy; sadness etc. *adj.*; *il penseroso*, *melancholia*, dismals, mumps, mopes, lachrymals, dumps, blues, blue devils, doldrums, vapors, megrims, spleen, horrors, hypochondriasis, pessimism; despondency, slough of Despond; disconsolateness etc. *adj.*; hope deferred, blank despondency.

prostration, – of soul; broken heart; despair etc. 859; cave of -despair, – Trophonius.

demureness etc. *adj.*; gravity, solemnity; long –, grave- face.

hypochondriac, seek-sorrow, self-tormentor, *heautontimorumenos*, *malade imaginaire*, *médecin tant pis*; croaker, pessimist; mope, mopus.

[Cause of dejection] affliction etc. 830; sorry sight; *memento mori*; damper, wet blanket, Job's comforter; death's head, skeleton at the feast.

V. be -dejected etc. *adj.*; grieve; mourn etc. (*lament*) 839; take on, give way, lose heart, despond, droop, sink.

lower, look downcast, frown, pout; hang down the head; pull –, make- a long face; laugh on the wrong side of the mouth; grin a ghastly smile; look -blue, – like a drowned man; lay –, take- to heart.

mope, brood over; fret; sulk; pine, – away; yearn; repine etc. (*regret*) 833; despair etc. 859.

refrain from laughter, keep one's countenance; be –, look- grave etc. *adj.*; repress a smile, keep a straight face.

depress; dis-courage, -hearten; dis-pirit; damp, dull, deject, lower, sink, dash, knock down, unman, prostrate, break one's heart; frown upon; cast a -gloom, – shade- on; sadden; damp –, dash –, wither- one's hopes; weigh –, lie heavy –, prey- on the -mind, – spirits; damp –, depress- the spirits.

Adj. cheer-, joy-, spirit-less; uncheer-ful, -y; unlively; unhappy etc. 828; melancholy, dismal, somber, dark, gloomy, adust, *triste*, clouded, murky, lowering, frowning, lugubrious, Acherontic, funereal, mournful, lamentable, dreadful.

dreary, flat; dull, – as -a beetle, – ditchwater; depressing etc. *v.*

'melancholy as a gib cat;' oppressed with –; a prey to- melancholy; down-cast, -hearted; down -in the mouth, – on one's luck; heavy-hearted; in the -dumps, – suds, – sulks, – doldrums; in doleful dumps, in bad humor; sullen; mumpish, dumpish; mopish, moping; moody, glum; sulky etc. (*discontented*) 832; out of -sorts, – humor, – heart, – spirits; ill at ease, low-spirited, in low spirits, a cup too low; weary etc. 841; dis-couraged, -heartened; desponding; chop-, jaw-, crest-fallen.

sad, pensive, *penseroso*, tristful; dole-some, -ful; woebegone, lachrymose, in tears, melancholic, hypped, hypochondriacal, bilious, jaundiced, atrabilious, saturnine, splenetic; lackadaisical.

serious, sedate, staid, stayed; grave, – as -a judge, – an undertaker, – a mustard pot; sober, solemn, demure; grim; grim-faced, -visaged; rueful, wan, long-faced.

disconsolate; un-, in-consolable; forlorn, comfortless, desolate, *désolé*, sick at heart; soul-, heartsick; *au désepoir*; in despair etc. 859; lost.

overcome; broken-, borne-, bowed-down; heartstricken etc. (*mental suffering*) 828; cut up, dashed, sunk; unnerved, unmanned; down-fallen, -trodden; broken-hearted; care-worn.

Adv. with -a long face, – tears in one's eyes; sadly etc. *adj*.

Phr. the countenance falling; the heart -failing, – sinking within- one.

838. Rejoicing. [Expression of pleasure.]—**N.** rejoicing, exultation, triumph, jubilation, heyday, flush, revelling; merry-making etc. (*amusement*) 840; jubilee etc. (*celebration*) 883; *paean*, *Te Deum* etc. (*thanksgiving*) 990; congratulation etc. 896; applause etc. 971.

smile, simper, smirk, grin; broad –, sardonic-grin.

laughter, giggle, titter, crow, cheer, chuckle, snicker, snigger, shout; Homeric laughter, horse –, hearty- laugh; guffaw; burst –, fit –, shout –, roar –, peal- of laughter; cachinnation.

risibility; derision etc. 856.

Momus; Democritus the Abderite; rollicker; Laughter holding both his sides.

V. rejoice; thank –, bless- one's stars; congratulate –, hug- oneself; rub –, clap- one's hands; smack the lips, fling up one's cap; dance, skip, caleer; sing, carol, chirrup, chirp; hurrah; cry for –, leap with- joy; exult etc. (*boast*) 884; triumph; hold jubilee etc. (*celebrate*) 883; make merry etc. (*sport*) 840; sing a paean of joy.

smile, simper, smirk; grin, – like a Cheshire cat; mock, laugh in one's sleeve; laugh, – outright; giggle, titter, snigger, crow, smicker, chuckle, snicker, cackle; burst -out, – into a fit of laughter; shout, split, roar.

shake –, split –, hold both- one's sides; roar –, die- with laughter.

raise laughter etc. (*amuse*) 840.

Adj. rejoicing etc. *v.*; jubilant, exultant, triumphant; flushed, elated; laughing etc. *v.*; risible; ready to -burst, – split, – die with laughter; convulsed with laughter.

laughable etc. (*ludicrous*) 853.

Int. hip, hip, -hurrah! huzza! aha! hail! tolderolloll! tra-la la! Heaven be praised! *io triumphe! tant mieux!* so much the better.

Phr. the heart leaping with joy.

839. Lamentation. [Expression of pain.]—**N.** lament, -ation; wail, complaint, plaint, murmur, mutter, grumble, groan, moan, whine, whimper, sob, sigh, suspiration, heaving, deep sigh.

cry etc. (*vociferation*) 411; scream, howl; outcry, wail of woe, frown, scowl.

tear; weeping etc. *v.*; flood of tears, fit of crying, lachrymation, melting mood, weeping and gnashing of teeth.

plaintiveness etc. *adj.*; languishment; condolence etc. 915.

mourning, weeds, willow, cypress, crêpe, crape, deep mourning; sackcloth and ashes; knell etc. 363; dump, deathsong, dirge, coronach, keen, *nenia*, requiem, elegy, *epicedium*; threne; mon-, thren-ody; jeremiad; ululation.

mourner, professional mourner, keener; grumbler etc. (*discontent*) 832; Niobe; Heraclitus.

V. lament, mourn, deplore, grieve, weep over; be-wail, -moan; keen; condole with etc. 915; fret etc. (*suffer*) 828; wear –, go into –, put on- mourning; wear -the willow, – sackcloth and ashes; *infandum renovare dolorem* etc. (*regret*) 833; give sorrow words.

sigh; give –, heave –, fetch- a sigh; 'waft a sigh from Indus to the pole;' sigh 'like furnace;' wail.

cry, weep, sob, greet, blubber, pipe, snivel, bibber, whimper, pule; pipe one's eye; drop –, shed- -tears, – a tear; melt –, burst- into tears; *fondre en larmes*; cry -oneself blind, – one's eyes out.

scream etc. (*cry out*) 411; mew etc. (*animal sounds*) 412; groan, moan, whine, yammer; roar; roar –, bellow- like a bull; cry out lustily, rend the air, yell.

frown, scowl, make a wry face, grimace, gnash one's teeth, wring one's hands, tear one's hair, beat one's breast, roll on the ground, burst with grief.

complain, murmur, mutter, grumble, growl, clamor, make a fuss about, croak, grunt, maunder; deprecate etc. (*disapprove*) 932.

cry out before one is hurt, complain without cause.

Adj. lamenting etc. *v.*; in mourning, in sackcloth and ashes; crying, sorrowing, -ful etc. (*unhappy*) 828; mourn-, tear-ful; lachrymose; plaint-ive, -ful, quer-ulous, -imonious; in the melting mood.

in tears, with tears in one's eyes; with -moistened, – watery- eyes; bathed –, dissolved- in tears; 'like Niobe all tears.'

elagiac, epicedial, threnetic.

Adv. *de profundis*; *les larmes aux yeux*.

Int. heigh-ho! alas! alack! O dear! ah –, woe is-me! lackadaisy! well –, lack –, alack- a day! well-a-way! alas the day! *O tempora! O mores!* what a pity! *miserabile dictu!* O lud lud! too true!

Phr. tears -standing in, – starting from- the eyes; eyes -suffused, – swimming, – brimming –, over- flowing- with tears.

840. Amusement.—N. amuse-, entertain-ment; diver-sion, -tissement; reaction, relaxation, solace; pastime, *passetemps*, sport; labor of love; pleasure etc. 827.

fun, frolic, merriment, whoopee, jollity; joviality, -ness; heyday; laughter etc. 838; jocos-ity, -eness; droll-, buffoon-, tomfool-ery; mummery, masquing, pleasantry; wit etc. 842; quip, quirk.

play; game, – at romps; gambol, romp, prank, antic, rig, lark, spree, skylarking, vagary, trick, monkey trick, *gambade, fredaine, escapade, échappée*, bout, *espièglerie*; practical joke etc. (*ridicule*) 856.

dance; round –, square –, solo –, step –, tap –, clog –, skirt –, sand –, folk –, morris-dance, *pas seul*, step, turn, *chassé*, cut, shuffle, double shuffle; hop, reel, rigadoon, saraband, hornpipe, bolero, fandango, pavan, tarantella, minuet, waltz, polka; galop, -ade; Schottische, *pas de quatre*, Boston, one-, two-step, rumba, tango, maxixe, fox-, turkey-trot, shimmy, ragtime, cakewalk, jazz, blues, Charleston; jig, breakdown, fling, strathspey; *allemande*; gavot, -te; mazurka, morisco; quadrille, lancers, country dance, *cotillon*, polonaise, Sir Roger de Coverley, Swedish dance; *ballet* etc. (*drama*) 599; ball; *bal*, – *masqué*, – *costumé*; masquerade, fancy dress ball; *thé dansant*; Terpsichore, choreography, Russian ballet, classical dancing; eurythmics; nautch dance, *danse du ventre*, cancan.

festivity, merry-making; party etc. (*social gathering*) 892; *fête*, festival, gala, *ridotto*; revel-s, -ry, -ling; carnival, brawl, saturnalia, high jinks; feast, banquet etc. (*food*) 298; regale, *symposium*, wassail; carous-e, -al; jollification, junket, wake, pic-nic, *fête champêtre*, garden party, gymkhana, regatta, track meet, field day, jamboree, treat.

round of pleasures, dissipation, a short life and a merry one, racketing, holiday making, high jinks.

rejoicing etc. 838; jubilee etc. (*celebration*) 883.

bonfire, fireworks, *feu-de-joie*, rocket, catherine wheel, roman candle etc.

holiday; gala –, red letter –, play- day; high days and holidays; high –, Bank- holiday; May –, Derby- day; Saint –, Easter –, Whit- Monday; King's birthday, Empire Day; *mi-carême*; *Bairam*; wayzgoose, bean feast, beano.

place of amusement, theater etc. 599; concert-, ball-, assembly-room; music-hall, cinema, movies, talkies, vaudeville; hippodrome, circus, rodeo; *casino*, *kursaal*; winter garden; park, pleasance, arbor; garden etc. 371; pleasure-, play-, cricket-, football-, polo-, croquet-, archery-, hunting-ground; golf links, race course, stadium, gridiron, bowl, speedway, racing track, ring; gymnasium, swimming pool; shooting gallery; tennis-, racket-court; bowling-green, -alley; croquet-lawn, rink, skating rink; roller-coaster, roundabout, carousel, merry-go-round; swing; *montagne russe*; switchback, scenic railway etc.

game, – of -chance, – skill; athletic sports, gymnastics; fencing; archery, rifle-shooting; tournament, pugilism etc. (*contention*) 720; sporting etc. 622; horse-racing, the turf; aquatics etc. 267; skating, roller skating; ski-running, -joring, -jumping, bobsleighing, luging, tobogganing, winter sports; sliding; cricket, tennis, lawn –, table –, deck-tennis, rackets, fives, squash, ping pong, trap bat and ball, battledore and shuttlecock, badminton, *la grâce*; pall mall, tip-cat, croquet, golf, curling, hockey, basketball, soccer, football, Rugby, Association, *pallone*, polo; tent-pegging, tilting at the ring, quintain, greasy pole; quoits, *discus*; throwing the hammer, putting the -weight, – shot, tossing the caber; knurr and spell; leap-frog; hop, skip and jump; French and English, tug of war; blind man's buff, hunt the slipper, hide-and-seek, kiss in the ring; snapdragon; cross questions and crooked answers; jig-saw puzzle; rounders, base-ball, *la crosse* etc.; angling; swimming, diving, water-polo.

billiards, pool, pyramids, snooker, bagatelle; bowls, skittles, ninepins, kail, American bowls.

cards; bridge, auction, contract, whist, rubber; round game, coon-can, loo, cribbage, *bésique*, pinocle, euchre, drole, *écarté*, skat, picquet, all-fours, quadrille, ombre, reversi, Pope Joan, commit; bo-, boa-ston; *vingt-et-un*; *quinze*, thirty-one, put-and-take, speculation, connections, brag, cassino, lottery, commerce, snip-snap-snorem, lift smoke, blind hookey, Polish bank, poker, banker; faro; Earl of Coventry, Napoleon, nap, patience, pairs; old maid, fright, beggar-my-neighbor; *baccarat*, *chemin de fer*, *monté*, *roulette*.

chess, draughts, backgammon, dominoes, checkers, mah jong, merelles, nine men's morris, go-bang, solitaire; game of –, fox and-goose; lotto; etc.

morra; gambling etc. (*chance*) 621.

toy, plaything, bauble; doll etc. (*puppet*) 554; teetotum; knick-knack etc. (*trifle*) 643; magic lantern etc. (*show*) 448; peep-, puppet-, raree-, gallanty-show; marionettes, Punch and Judy; toy-shop; 'quips and cranks and wanton wiles, nods and becks and wreathed smiles.'

sportsman, gamester, gambler etc. 621; reveler, master of the -ceremonies, – revels; *arbiter elegantiarum*.

V. amuse, entertain, divert, eliven; tickle, – the fancy; titillate, raise a smile, put in good humor; cause –, create –, occasion –, raise –, excite –, produce –, convulse with- laughter; set the table in a roar, be the death of one.

recreate, solace, cheer, rejoice; please etc. 829; interest; treat, regale.

amuse oneself; game; play, – a game, – pranks, – tricks; sport, disport, toy, wanton, revel, junket, feast, carouse, banquet, make merry; drown care; drive dull care away; frolic, gambol, frisk, romp; caper; dance etc. (*leap*) 309; keep up the ball; run a rig, sow one's wild oats, have one's fling, paint the town red, take one's pleasure; see life; *desipere in loco*, play the fool.

make –, keep- holiday; go a Maying.

while away –, beguile- the time; kill time, dally.

Adj. amusing, entertaining, diverting etc. *v.*; recreative, lusory; pleasant etc. (*pleasing*) 829; laughable etc. (*ludicrous*) 853; witty etc. 842; festive, -al; jovial, jolly, jocund, roguish, rompish; sporting; playful – as a kitten; sportive, ludibrious.

amused etc. *v.*; 'pleased with a feather, tickled with a straw.'

Adv. 'on the light fantastic toe,' at play, in sport.

Int. *vive la bagatelle! vogue la galère!*

Phr. *Deus nobis haec otia fecit*; *dum vivimus vivamus*.

841. Weariness.—N. weariness, defatigation, boredom, *ennui*; lassitude etc. (*fatigue*) 688; drowsiness etc. 683.

disgust, nausea, loathing, sickness; satiety etc. 869; *taedium vitae* etc. (*dejection*) 837.

wearisome-, tedious-ness etc. *adj.*; dull work, tedium, monotony, twice told tale.

bore, button-hole, proser, wet blanket; heavy hours, 'the enemy' [time].

V. weary; tire etc. (*fatigue*) 688; bore; bore –, weary –, tire- -to death, – out of one's life, – out of all patience; set –, send- to sleep.

pall, sicken, nauseate, disgust.

harp on the same string; drag its -slow, – weary-length along.

never hear the last of; be -tired etc. *adj.* -of, – with; yawn; died with *ennui*.

Adj. wearying etc. *v.*; wearing; weari-, tire-, irksome; uninteresting, stupid, bald, devoid of interest, dry, monotonous, dull, arid, tedious, humdrum, mortal, flat; pros-y, -ing; slow; soporific, somniferous, dormitive.

disgusting etc. *v.*; unenjoyed.

weary; tired etc. *v.*; drowsy etc. (*sleepy*) 683; uninterested, flagging, used up, worn out, *blasé*, life-weary, weary of life; sick of.

Adv. wearily etc. *adj.*; *usque ad nauseam*.

Phr. time hanging heavily on one's hands; *toujours perdrix*; *crambe repetita*.

842. Wit.—N. wit, -tiness; attic -wit, – salt; atticism; salt, *esprit*, point, fancy, whim, humor, drollery, pleasantry.

farce, buffoonery, fooling, tomfoolery; harlequinade etc. 599; broad -farce, – humor; fun, *espièglerie*; *vis comica*.

jocularity; jocos-ity, -eness; facetiousness; waggery, -ishness; whimsicality; comicality etc. 853.

smartness, ready wit, banter, *badinage, persiflage*, retort, repartee, *quid pro quo*; ridicule etc. 856.

facetiae, quips and cranks; jest, joke, capital joke; standing -jest, – joke; conceit, quip, quirk, crank, quiddity, *concetto, plaisanterie*, brilliant idea; merry –, bright –, happy- thought; sally; flash, – of wit, – of merriment; scintillation; *mot*, – *pour rire*; witticism, smart saying, *bon mot, jeu d'esprit*, epigram; jest book; dry joke, *quodlibet*, cream of the jest.

word-play, *jeu de mots*; play -of, – upon- words; pun, -ning; *double entente* etc. (*ambiguity*) 520; quibble, verbal quibble; conundrum etc. (*riddle*) 533; anagram, acrostic, double acrostic, *nugae canorae*, trifling, idle conceit, *turlupinade*.

old joke, Joe Miller, chestnut, hoary-headed jest.

V. joke, jest, cut jokes; crack a joke; perpetrate a -joke, – pun; make -fun of, – merry with; set the table in a roar etc. (*amuse*) 840; scintillate.

retort, flash back; banter etc. (*ridicule*) *856*; *ridentem dicere verum*; joke at one's expense.

Adj. witty, attic, salty; quick-, nimble-witted; keen, clever, smart, brilliant, pungent, jocular, jocose, funny, waggish, facetious, whimsical, humorous, gilbertian; playful etc. 840; merry and wise; pleasant, sprightly, *spirituel*, sparkling, epigrammatic, full of point, *ben trovato*; comic etc. 853.

Adv. in joke, in jest, in sport, in play.

843. Dullness.—N. dullness, heaviness, flatness; infestivity etc. 837; stupidity etc. 499; want of originality, dearth of ideas.

prose, matter of fact; heavy book, *conte à dormir debout*; platitude.

V. be -dull etc. *adj.*; prose, platitudinize, take *au sérieux*, be caught napping.

render -dull etc. *adj.*; damp, depress, throw cold water on, lay a wet blanket on; fall flat upon the ear; hang fire.

Adj. dull, – as ditch water; dry, insipid, jejune; unentertaining, uninteresting, unlively, unimaginative; heavisome, heavy-gaited; insulse; dry as dust; pros-y, -ing, -aic; matter of fact, commonplace, banal, pointless; 'weary, flat, stale and unprofitable.'

stupid, slow, flat, sluggish, ponderous, humdrum, monotonous; melancholic etc. 837; stolid etc. 499; plodding.

Phr. *Davus sum non Oedipus*.

844. Humorist.—N. humorist, wag, wit, reparteeist, epigrammatist, gag man, punster; *bel esprit*, life of the party; wit-snapper, -cracker, -worm; joker, jester, jokesmith, Joe Miller, *drôle de corps, gaillard*, spark, *persiffleur*, banterer.

buffoon, *farceur*, merry-andrew, mime, tumbler, acrobat, mountebank, charlatan, posturemaster, harlequin, punch, *pulcinella*, scaramouch, clown; wearer of the -cap and bells, – motley; motley fool; pantaloon, gipsy; jack -pudding, – in the green, – a dandy; zany; mad-cap, pickle-herring, witling, caricaturist, *grimacier*.

845. Beauty.—N. beauty, the beautiful, *le beau ideal*, loveliness.

[Science of the perception of beauty] Callaesthetics.

form, elegance, grace, beauty unadorned; symmetry etc. 242; comeliness, fairness etc. *adj.*; pulchritude, polish, gloss; good -effect, – looks; *belle tournure*; bloom, brilliancy, radiance, splendor, gorgeousness, magnificence; sublimi-ty, -fication.

concinnity, delicacy, refinement; charm, *je ne sais quoi*, style, *chic*, swank.

Venus, – of Milo; Aphrodite, Hebe, the Graces, Peri, Houri, Cupid, Apollo, Hyperion, Adonis, Antinous, Narcissus; Helen of Troy.

peacock, butterfly; flower, flow'ret gay, rose, lily, asphodel; garden; flower of, pink of; *bijou*; jewel etc. (*ornament*) 847; work of art.

pleasurableness etc. 829.

beautifying; landscape gardening; decoration etc. 847; calisthenics.

V. be -beautiful etc. *adj.*; shine, beam, bloom; become one etc. (*accord*) 23; set off, grace, flatter one.

render -beautiful etc. *adj.*; beautify; polish, burnish; gild etc. (*decorate*) 847; set out.

'snatch a grace beyond the reach of art.'

Adj. beaut-iful, -eous; handsome; pretty; lovely, graceful, elegant; delicate, dainty, refined, exquisite; fair, personable, comely, seemly; bonny; good-looking; well-favored, -made, -formed, -proportioned; proper, shapely; symmetrical etc. (*regular*) 242; harmonious etc. (*color*) 428; sightly.

fit to be seen, passable, not amiss.

goodly, dapper, tight, jimp; gimp; janty, jaunty; natty, quaint, trim, tidy, neat, spruce, smart, tricksy.

bright, -eyed; rosy-, cherry-cheeked; rosy, ruddy; blooming, in full bloom.

brilliant, shining; beam-y, -ing; sparkling, swanky, splendid, resplendent, dazzling, glowing; glossy, sleek.

showy, specious; rich, gorgeous, superb, magnificent, grand, fine, sublime, imposing; majestic 873.

artistic, -al; aesthetic; pict-uresque, -orial; *fait à piendre*, paintable; well-composed, -grouped, -varied; curious.

enchanting etc. (*pleasure-giving*) 829; attractive etc. (*inviting*) 615; becoming etc. (*accordant*) 23; ornamental etc. 847.

undeformed, undefaced, unspotted; spotless etc. (*perfect*) 650.

846. Ugliness.—N. ugliness etc. *adj.*; deformity, inelegance; disfigurement etc. (*blemsih*) 848; want of symmetry, inconcinnity; distortion etc. 243; squalor etc. (*uncleanness*) 653.

forbidding countenance, vinegar aspect, hanging look, wry face, *'spretae injuria formae.'*

eyesore, object, figure, sight, fright, specter, scarecrow, hag, harridan, satyr, witch, toad, baboon, monster, Caliban, Aesop, *'monstrum horrendum informe ingens cui lumen ademptum.'*

V. be -ugly etc. *adj.*; look ill, grin horribly a ghastly smile, make faces.

render -ugly etc. *adj.*; deface; dis-, de-figure; deform, spoil, distort etc. 243; blemish etc. (*injure*) 659; soil etc. (*render unclean*) 653.

Adj. ugly, – as -sin, – a toad, – a scarecrow, – a dead monkey; plain, bald etc. 226; homely etc. (*unadorned*) 849; ordinary, unornamental, inartistic; unsightly, unseemly, uncomely, unshapely, unlovely; sightless, seemless; not fit to be seen; unbeaut-eous, -iful; beautiless; shapeless etc. (*amorphous*) 241; course; garish, over-decorated etc. 882.

mis-shapen, -proportioned; monstrous; gaunt etc. (*thin*) 203; dumpy etc. (*short*) 201; curtailed of its fair proportions; ill-made, -shaped, -proportioned; crooked etc. (*distorted*) 243; hard-featured, -visaged; ill-, hard-, evil-favored; ill-looking; unprepossessing.

graceless, inelegant; ungraceful, ungainly, uncouth; stiff; rugged, rough, gross, rude, awkward, clumsy, slouching, rickety; gawky; lump-ing, -ish; lumbering; hulk-y, -ing; unwieldy.

squalid, haggard; grim, -faced, -visaged; grisly, ghastly; ghost-, death-like; cadaverous, gruesome.

frightful, hideous, odious, uncanny, forbidding, repellant, repulsive; horri-d, -ble; shocking etc. (*painful*) 830.

foul etc. (*dirty*) 653; dingy etc. (*colorless*) 429; gaudy etc. (*color*) 428; disfigured etc. *v.*; discolored (*blemished*) etc. 848.

847. Ornament.—N. ornament, -ation, -al art; ornat-ture, -eness; adorn-ment, decoration, embellishment; architecture.

garnish, polish, varnish, French polish, gilding, japanning, lacquer, ormolu, enamel.

cosmetics, rouge, powder, lipstick, lip salve, mascara; manicure, nail polish; permanent –, Marcel –, finger-wave.

pattern, diaper, powdering, panelling, graining, pargeting, inlay, detail; texture etc. 329; richness; tracery, molding, beading, reeding, fillet, listel, strapwork, *coquillage*, flourish, *fleur-de-lis*, arabesque, fret, *anthemion*; egg and -tongue, -dart; *astragal*, zigzag, *acanthus, cartouche*; pilaster etc. (*projection*) 250; cyma, ogee.

em-, broidery, needlework; knitting, crochet, tatting, brocade, *brocatelle*, beads, bugles; galloon, lace, gimp, *guipure*, fringe, trapping, border, edging, insertion, *motif*, trimming; *passementerie*; drapery, hanging, tapestry, arras; millinery, ermine.

wreath, festoon, garland, lei, chaplet, flower, nosegay, *bouquet*, posy, 'daisies pied and violets blue.'

tassle, knot; shoulder-knot, *épaulette*, epaulet, aigulet, *aiguilette*, frog; star, rosette, bow; feather, plume, *panache, aigrette*.

jewel, -ry, -lery; bijoutry; *bijou*, *-terie*; diadem, tiara; pendant, trinket, locket, necklace, armilla, bracelet, bangle, armlet, anklet, ear-, nose- ring, carcanet, chain, *châtelaine*, albert, brooch, torque.

gem, precious stone; diamond, brilliant, beryl, aquamarine, alexandrite, cat's eye, emerald, calcedony, chrysoprase, cornelian, jasper, bloodstone, agate, heliotrope; girasol, -e; onyx, plasma; sard, -onyx; garnet, lapis-lazuli, opal, peridot, chrysolite, sapphire, ruby; spinel, -le; balais; oriental –, topaz; turquois, -e; zircon, jacinth, hyacinth, carbuncle, amethyst; moonstone; pearl, coral.

finery, frippery, gewgaw, gimcrack, knick-knack, tinsel, spangle, sequin, *clinquant*, pinch-beck, paste; excess of ornament etc. (*vulgarity*) 851; gaud, pride, ostentation; frills and furbelows.

illustration, illumination, *vignette*; *fleuron*; head-, tail-piece; *cul-de-lampe*; flowers of rhetoric etc. 577; work of art, article of vertu, *bric-à-brac*, curio, *bibelot*.

V. ornament, embellish, enrich, decorate, adorn, beautify, adonize.

smarten, furbish, polish, gild, varnish, whitewash, enamel, japan, lacquer, paint, grain.

garnish, trim, dizen, bedizen, prink, prank; trick –, fig- out; deck, bedeck, dight, bedight, array; dress, – up, preen, spruce up, titivate; spangle, bespangle, powder; embroider, work; chase, tool, emboss, fret; emblazon, blazon, illuminate; illustrate.

become etc. (*accord with*) 23.

Adj. ornamented, beautified etc. *v.*; ornate, rich, gilt, begilt, tesselated, enamelled, inlaid; festooned; topiary.

smart, gay, tricksy, flowery, glittering; new-gilt, -spangled; fine, – as -a Mayday queen, – fivepence, – a carrot fresh scraped; pranked out, bedight, well-groomed.

in full dress etc. (*fashion*) 852; *en grande -tenue*, *– toilette*; in best bib and tucker, in Sunday best, *endimanché*; dressed to advantage.

showy, flashy; gaudy etc. (*vulgar*) 851; garish; gorgeous.

ornamental, decorative; becoming etc. (*accordant*) 23.

848. Blemish.—N. blemish, disfigurement, deformity; defect etc. (*imperfection*) 651; flaw; injury etc. (*deterioration*) 659; spots on the sun; eyesore.

stain, blot, slur; spot, -tiness; speck, -le; blur, freckle, mole, *macula*, patch, blotch, birthmark, blain, maculation, tarnish, smudge, smear; dirt etc. 653; bruise, black eye, scar, wem; pustule; excrescence, pimple etc. (*protuberance*) 250.

V. disfigure etc. (*injure*) 659; speckle; render ugly etc. 846.

Adj. pitted, freckled, discolored, bloodshot, bruised, disfigured; stained etc. *n.*; imperfect etc. 651; injured etc. (*deteriorated*) 659.

849. Simplicity.—N. simplicity; plain-, homeli-ness; undress, nudity, nakedness, beauty unadorned, chastity, chasteness.

V. be -simple etc. *adj.*

render -simple etc. *adj.*; simplify, chasten, strip of ornament.

Adj. simple, plain; home-ly, -spun; ordinary, household.

natural, unaffected; free from -affectation, – ornament; *simplex munditiis*; *sans façon, en déshabillé*, nude, naked.

chaste, inornate, severe.

un-adorned, -ornamented, -decked, -garnished, -arranged, -trimmed, -varnished.

bald, flat, dull, blank.

850. Taste. [Good taste.]—**N.** taste; good –, refined –, cultivated- taste; delicacy, refinement, fine feeling, gust, *gusto*, tact, *finesse*; nicety etc. (*discrimination*) 465; polish, elegance, grace.

virtu; dilettanteism, virtuosity; fine art; cul-ture, -ivation.

[Science of taste] esthetics.

man of -taste etc.; *connoisseur*, judge, critic, *conoscente, virtuoso, amateur, dilettante*, Aristarchus, Corinthian, *arbiter elegantarum*, stagirite, euphemist.

'caviar to the general.'

V. appreciate, judge, criticize, discriminate etc. 465.

Adj. in good taste; tasteful, tasty; unaffected, pure, chaste, classical, attic; cultivated, refined; dainty; esthetic, artistic; elegant etc. 578; euphemistic.

to one's -taste, – mind; after one's fancy; *comme il faut*; *tiré à quatre épingles*.

Adv. elegantly etc. *adj.*

Phr. *nihil tetigit quod non ornavit.*

851. Vulgarity. [Bad taste.]—**N.** vulgar-ity, -ism; barbar-, Vandal-, Gothic-ism; *mauvais goût*, bad taste; Babbittry; *gaucherie*, awkwardness, want of tact; ill-breeding etc. (*discourtesy*) 895; ungentlemanly behavior.

coarseness etc. *adj.*; indecorum, misbehavior.

low-, homeli-ness; low life, *mauvais ton*, rusticity; boorishness etc. *adj.*; brutality; rowdy-, ruffian-, blackguard-ism; ribaldry; slang etc. (*neology*) 563.

bad joke, *mauvaise plaisanterie*.

[Excell of ornament] gaudi-, tawdri-ness; false ornament; finery, frippery, trickery, tinsel, gewgaw, *clinquant*.

rough diamond, tomboy, hoyden, cub, unlicked cub; clown etc. (*commonalty*) 876; Hun, Goth, Vandal, Boeotian; vulgarian; snob, cad, bounder, gent; *parvenu* etc. 876; frump, dowdy; slattern etc. 653.

V. be -vulgar etc. *adj.*; misbehave; talk –, smell of the- shop.

Adj. in bad taste, vulgar, unrefined, gutter.

coarse, indecorus, ribald, gross; unseemly, unbeseeming, unpresentable; *contra bonos mores*; ungraceful etc. (*ugly*) 846.

dowdy, slovenly etc. (*dirty*) 653; ungenteel, shabby genteel; low etc. (*plebeian*) 876;uncourtly; uncivil etc. (*discourteous*) 895; ill-bred, -mannered; underbred; ungentleman-ly, -like; unladylike, unfeminine; wild, – as an unbacked colt.

unkempt, uncombed, untamed, unlicked, unpolished, uncouth, plebeian; incondite; heavy, rude, awkward; home-ly, -spun, -bred; provincial, hick, countrified, rustic, uncultivated, freshwater; boorish, clownish; savage, brutish, blackguard, rowdy, snobbish; barbar-ous, -ic; Gothic, unclassical, doggerel, heathenish, tramontane, outlandish; Bohemian.

obsolete etc. (*antiquated*) 124; unfashionable, old-fashioned, out of date; new-fangled etc. (*unfamiliar*) 83; fantastic, odd etc. (*ridiculous*) 853.

particular; affected etc. 855; meretricious; extravagant, monstrous, horrid; shocking etc. (*painful*) 830.

gaudy, tawdry, bedizened, tricked out, gingerbread; obtrusive, flaunting, loud, flashy, garish, showy.

852. Fashion.—N. fashion, style, *ton*, *bon ton*, society; good –, polite- society; drawing room, civilized life, civilization, town, *beau monde*, high life, court; world; fashionable –, gay- world; Vanity Fair; show etc. (*ostentation*) 822.

manners, breeding etc. (*politeness*) 894; air, demeanor etc. (*appearance*) 448; *savoir faire*; gentlemanliness, gentility, decorum, propriety, *bienséance*; conventions –, dictates- of society; Mrs. Grundy; convention, -ality; punctilio; form, -ality; etiquette, point of etiquette; custom etc. 613; mode, vogue, style, go; rage etc. (*desire*) 865; prevailing taste, *dernier cri*, dress etc. 225.

man –, woman- of -fashion, – the world; height –, pink –, star –, glass –, leader- of fashion; *arbiter elegantiarum* etc. (*taste*) 850; upper ten thousand etc. (*nobility*) 875; *élite* etc. (*distinction*) 873.

V. be -fashionable etc. *adj.*, – the rage etc. *n.*; have a run, pass current.

follow –, conform to –, fall in with- the fashion etc. *n.*; go with the stream etc. (*conform*) 82; *savoir -vivre*, – *faire*; keep up appearances, behave oneself.

set the –, bring into- fashion; give a tone to –; cut a figure in- society, rub shoulders with nobility, keep one's carriage.

Adj. fashionable; in -fashion etc. *n.*; *à la mode, comme il faut*; admitted –, admissible- in -society etc. *n.*; presentable, decorous, punctilious, conventional etc. (*customary*) 613; genteel; well-bred, -mannered, -behaved, -spoken; gentleman-like, -ly; ladylike; civil, polite etc. (*courteous*) 894.

polished, refined, thoroughbred, courtly; *distingué*, aristocratic, unembarrassed, poised, *dégagé*; ja-, jau-nty; dashing, fast, showy, high toned, toney.

modish, stylish, in the latest style, *recherché*; new-fangled etc. (*unfamiliar*) 83.

in -court, – full, – evening- dress; *en grande tenue* etc. (*ornament*) 847.

Adv. fashionably etc. *adj.*; for fashion's sake.

853. Ridiculousness.—N. ridiculousness etc. *adj.*; comical-, odd-ity etc. *adj.*; extravagance, drollery.

farce, comedy; burlesque etc. (*ridicule*) 856; buffoonery etc. (*fun*) 840; frippery; doggerel verses; Irish bull, Hibernianism, Hibernicism; Spoonerism; absurdity etc. 497; bombast etc. (*unmeaning*) 517; anticlimax, bathos; monstrosity etc. (*unconformity*) 83; laughing stock etc. 857.

V. be -ridiculous etc. *adj.*; pass from the sublime to the ridiculous; make one laugh; play the fool, make a fool of oneself, commit an absurdity.

play a joke on, make a -fool of, – sucker of, – monkey of.

Adj. ridiculous, ludicrous; comic, -al; droll, funny, laughable, *pour rire*, grotesque, farcical, odd; whimsical, – as a dancing bear; fanciful, fantastic, queer, rum, quizzical, waggish, quaint, *bizarre*; eccentric etc. (*unconformable*) 83; strange, outlandish, out of the way, *baroque*, *rocaille*, rococo; awkward etc. (*ugly*) 846.

absurd, extravagant, *outré*, monstrous, preposterous, bombastic, inflated, stilted, burlesque, mock heroic.

drollish; serio-, tragic-comic; gimcrack, contemptible etc. (*unimportant*) 643; doggerel; ironical etc. (*derisive*) 856; risible.

Phr. *'risum teneatis amici?' rideret Heraclitus.*

854. Fop.—N. fop, fine gentleman; swell; dand-y, -iprat; exquisite, coxcomb, toff, beau, macaroni, blade, blood, buck, man about town, fast man; fribble, jemmy, spark, popinjay, puppy, prig, *petit maître*; jacka-napes, -dandy; man milliner; Jemmy Jessamy, carpet-knight, masher, Dundreary, Johnnie, dude.

belle, fine lady, *coquette*, flirt.

855. Affectation.—N. affectation; affectedness etc. *adj.*; acting a part etc. *v.*; pretence etc. (*falsehood*) 544; (*ostentation*) 882; boasting etc. 884.

charlatanism, quakery, shallow profundity, humbug, pretension, airs, pedantry, purism, precisianism, euphuism, prunes and prisms; teratology etc. (*altiloquence*) 577.

mannerism, *simagrée*, grimace.

conceit, foppery, dandyism, man millinery, coxcombry, puppyism.

stiffness, formality, buckram; prudery, demureness, coquetry, mock modesty, *minauderie*, sentimentalism; *mauvaise honte*, false shame.

affector, performer, actor; pedant, pedagogue, *doctrinaire*, purist, euphuist, mannerist; shoneen; *grimacier*; lump of affectation, *précieuse ridicule*, *bas bleu*, blue stocking, poetaster; prig, hypocrite; charlatan etc. (*deceiver*) 548; *petit maître* etc. (*fop*) 854; flatterer etc. 935; *coquette*, prude, puritan; precisian, formalist.

V. affect, act a part, put on; give oneself airs etc. (*arrogance*) 885; boast etc. 884; coquet; simper, mince, attitudinize, strike a pose, pose; flirt a fan; over-act, -play, -do.

Adj. affected, full of affectation, pretentious, pedantic, stilted, stagey, theatrical, big-sounding, *ad captandum*, canting, insincere.

not natural, unnatural; self-conscious; *maniéré*; artificial; over-wrought, -done, -acted; euphuistic etc. 577.

stiff, starch, formal, prim, smug, demure, *tiré à quatre épingles*, quakerish, puritanical, prudish, pragmatical, priggish, conceited, coxcomical, foppish, dandified; fini-cal, -kin, -cky, mincing, simpering, namby-pamby, sentimental, languishing.

856. Ridicule.—N. ridicule, derision; sardonic -smile, – grin; irrision; snigger; scoffing etc. (*disrespect*) 929; mockery, quiz, banter, irony, *persiflage*, raillery, chaff, *badinage*; quizzing etc. *v.*

squib, satire, skit, quip, quib, grin.

parody, burlesque, travesty; farce etc. (*drama*) 599; caricature, take-off.

buffoonery etc. (*fun*) 840; practical joke, horseplay.

V. ridicule, deride; laugh at, grin at, smile at; snigger; laugh in one's sleeve; banter, rally, chaff, joke, twit, quiz, poke fun at, jolly, roast, rag; fleer; play –, play tricks- upon; fool, – to the top of one's bent; show up.

satirize, parody, caricature, burlesque, travesty.

turn into ridicule; make merry with; make -fun, – game, – a fool, – an April fool- of; rally; scoff etc. (*disrespect*) 929.

raise a laugh etc. (*amuse*) 840; play the fool, make a fool of oneself.

be ridiculous etc. 853.

Adj. deris-ory, -ive; mock; sarcastic, ironical, quizzical, burlesque, Hudibrastic; scurrilous etc. (*disrespectful*) 929.

Adv. in -ridicule etc. *n.*

857. Laughing-stock. [Object and cause of ridicule.]**—N.** laughing-, jesting-, gazing-stock; butt, game, fair game; April fool etc. (*dupe*) 547.

original, oddity; queer –, odd- fish; quiz, square toes; old –, fogey *or* fogy.

monkey; buffoon etc. (*jester*) 844; pantomimist etc. (*actor*) 599.

jest etc. (*wit*) 842.

858. Hope.—N. hope, -s; desire etc. 865; fervent hope, sanguine expectation, trust, confidence, reliance; faith etc. (*belief*) 484; affiance, assurance; secur-eness, -ity; reassurance.

good -omen, – auspices; promise; well-grounded hopes; good –, bright- prospect; clear sky.

as-, pre-sumption; anticipation etc. (*expectation*) 507.

hopefulness, buoyancy, optimism, enthusiasm, heart of grace, aspiration; optimist, utop-ian, -ist; Pollyanna.

castles in the air, *châteaux en Espagne*, hope chest, *le pot au lait*, Utopia, millennium; day –, golden- dream; dream of Alnaschar; airy hopes, fool's paradise; *mirage* etc. (*fallacies of vision*) 443; fond hope.

beam –, ray –, gleam –, glimmer –, dawn –, flash –, star- of hope; cheer; bit of blue sky, silver lining of the cloud, bottom of Pandora's box, balm in Gilead.

anchor, sheet-anchor, main-stay; staff etc. (*support*) 215; heaven etc. 981.

V. hope, trust, confide, rely on, put one's trust in, lean upon; pin one's -hope, – faith- upon etc. (*believe*) 484.

feel –, entertain –, harbor –, indulge –, cherish –, feed –, foster –, nourish –, encourage –, cling to –, live in- hope etc. *n.*; see land; feel –, rest- -assured, – confident etc. *adj.*

presume; promise oneself; expect etc. (*look forward to*) 507.

hope for etc. (*desire*) 865; anticipate.

be -hopeful etc. *adj.*; look on the bright side of, view on the sunny side, make the best of it, hope for the best; put -a good, – a bold, – the best- face upon; keep one's spirits up; take heart, – of grace; be of good -heart, – cheer; flatter oneself, lay the flattering unction to one's soul.

catch at a straw, hope against hope, count one's chickens before they are hatched.

give –, inspire –, raise –, hold out- hope etc. *n.*; raise expectations; encourage, hearten, cheer, assure, reassure, buoy up, embolden; promise, bid fair, augur well, be in a fair way, look up, flatter, tell a flattering tale.

Adj. hoping etc. *v.*; in -hopes etc. *n.*; hopeful, confident; secure etc. (*certain*) 484; sanguine, in good heart, buoyed up, buoyant, elated, flushed, exultant, enthusiastic; utopian.

unsus-pecting, -picious; fearless, free –, exempt from- -fear, – suspicion, – distrust, – despair; undespairing, self-reliant.

probable, on the high road to; within sight of - shore, – land; promising, propitious; of –, full of- promise; of good omen; auspicious, *de bon augure*; reassuring; encouraging, cheering, inspiriting, looking up, bright, roseate, *couleur de rose*, rose-colored.

Adv. hopefully etc. *adj.*

Phr. *nil desperandum*; never say die, *dum spiro spero, latet scintillula forsan*, all is for the best, *spero meliora*; the wish being father to the thought; 'hope told a flattering tale;' *rusticus expectat dum defluat amnis*.

859. Hopelessness. [Absence, want, or loss of hope.]—**N.** hopelessness etc. *adj.*; despair, desperation; despondency etc. (*dejection*) 837; pessimism.

hope deferred, dashed hopes; vain expectation etc. (*disappointment*) 509.

airy hopes etc. 858; forlorn hope; bad -job, – business; *enfant perdu*; gloomy –, black spots in the- horizon; slough of Despond, cave of Despair.

Job's comforter; bird of -bad, – ill-omen.

V. despair; lose –, give up –, abandon –, relinquish- -all hope, – the hope of; give -up, – over; yield to despair; falter; despond etc. (*be dejected*) 837; *jeter le manche après la cognée.*

inspire –, drive to- despair etc. *n.*; disconcert; dash –, crush –, shatter –, destroy- one's hopes; hope against hope.

Adj. hopeless, desperate, despairing, in despair, *au désespoir*, forlorn; inconsolable etc. (*dejected*) 837; broken-hearted.

out of the question, not to be thought of; impracticable etc. 471; past -hope, – cure, – mending, – recall; at one's last gasp etc. (*death*) 360; given -up, – over.

incurable, cureless, immedicable, remediless, beyond remedy; incorrigible; irre-parable, -mediable, -coverable, -versible, -trievable, -claimable, -deemable, -vocable; ruined, undone; immitigable.

unpromising, unpropitious; inauspicious, ill-omened, threatening, clouded over, lowering, ominous.

Phr. *'lasciate ogni speranza voi ch' entrate';* its days are numbered; the worst come to the worst.

860. Fear.—N. fear, timidity, diffidence, want of confidence; apprehensive-, fearful-ness etc. *adj.*; solicitude, anxiety, care, apprehension, misgiving; mistrust etc. (*doubt*) 485; suspicion, qualm; hesitation etc. (*irresolution*) 605.

nervous-, restless-ness etc. *adj.*; in-, dis-quietude; flutter, trepidation, fear and trembling, perturbation, tremor, quivering, shaking, trembling, throbbing heart, palpitation, ague fit, cold sweat; abject fear etc. (*cowardice*) 862; mortal funk, heart-sinking, despondency; despair etc. 859.

fright; affright, -ment; alarm, pavor, dread, awe, terror, horror, dismay, consternation, panic, scare, stampede [of horses].

intimidation, terrorism, reign of terror.

[Object of fear] bug-bear, -aboo; scarecrow; hobgoblin etc. (*demon*) 980; daymare, nightmare, Gorgon, Medusa, mormo, ogre, Hurlothrumbo, raw head and bloody bones, fee faw fum, *bête noire*, *enfant terrible*.

alarmist etc. (*coward*) 862.

V. fear, stand in awe of; be -afraid etc. *adj.*; have -qualms etc. *n.*; apprehend, sit upon thorns, eye askance; distrust etc. (*disbelieve*) 485.

hesitate etc. (*be irresolute*) 605; falter, funk, cower, crouch; skulk etc. (*cowardice*) 862; let 'I dare not' wait upon 'I would;' take -fright, – alarm; start, wince, flinch, shy, shrink; fly etc. (*avoid*) 623.

tremble, shake; shiver, – in one's shoes; shudder, flutter; shake –, tremble- -like an aspen leaf, – all over; quake, quaver, quiver, quail; get the wind up.

grow –, turn- pale; blench, stand aghast; not dare to say one's soul is one's own.

inspire –, excite- -fear, – awe; raise apprehensions; give –, raise –, sound- an alarm; alarm, startle, scare, cry 'wolf,' disquiet, dismay; fright, -en; affright, terrify; astound; frighten from one's propriety; frighten out of one's -wits, – senses, – seven senses; awe; strike -all of a heap, – an awe into, – terror; harrow up the soul, appal, unman, petrify, horrify.

make one's -flesh creep, – hair stand on end, – blood run cold, – teeth chatter; chill one's spine; take away –, stop- one's breath; make one - tremble etc.

haunt, obsess, beset; prey –, weigh- on the mind.

put in -fear, – bodily fear; terrorize, intimidate, cow, daunt, over-awe, abash, deter, discourage; browbeat, bully; threaten etc. 909.

Adj. fearing etc. *v.*; frightened etc. *v.*; in -fear, – a fright etc. *n.*; haunted with the -fear etc. *n.*- of.

afraid, fearful; tim-id, -orous; nervous, diffident, coy, faint-hearted, tremulous, shaky, afraid of one's shadow, apprehensive, restless, fidgety; more frightened than hurt.

aghast; awe-, horror-, terror-, panic- -struck, -stricken; frightened to death, white as a sheet; pale, – as -death, – ashes, – a ghost; breathless, in hysterics.

inspiring fear etc. *v.*; alarming; formidable, redoubtable; perilous etc. (*danger*) 665; portentous; fear-ful, -some; dread, -ful; fell; dire, -ful; shocking; terri-ble, -fic; tremendous; horri-d, -ble, -fic; ghastly; awful, awe-inspiring, eerie, weird; revolting etc. (*painful*) 830.

Adv. *in terrorem.*

Int. 'angels and ministers of grace defend us!'

Phr. *ante tubam trepidat*; *horresco referens*, one's heart failing one, *obstupui steteruntque comae et vox faucibus haesit*.

861. Courage. [Absence of fear.]—**N.** courage, bravery, valor; resolute-, bold-ness etc. *adj.*; spirit, daring, gallantry, intrepidity; contempt –, defiance- of danger; derring-do; audacity; rashness etc. 863; dash; defiance etc. 715; confidence, self-reliance.

man-liness, -hood; nerve, pluck, mettle, game; heart, – of grace; spunk, gameness, grit, face, virtue, hardihood, fortitude; firmness etc. (*stability*) 150; heart of oak; bottom, backbone etc. (*perseverance*) 604*a*.

resolution etc. (*determination*) 604; tenacity, bull-dog courage.

prowess, heroism, chivalry.

exploit, feat, achievement; heroic -deed, – act; bold stroke.

man, – of mettle; hero, demigod, paladin, heroine, Amazon, Hector, Joan of Arc; lion, tiger, panther, bulldog; game-, fighting-cock; bully, fire-eater etc. 863; dare-devil.

V. be -courageous etc. *adj.*; dare, venture, make bold; face –, front –, affront –, confront –, brave –, defy –, despise –, mock- danger; look in the face; look -full, – boldly, – danger- in the face; face; meet, – in front; brave, beard; defy etc. 715.

take –, muster –, summon up –, pluck up- courage; nerve oneself, take heart; take –, pluck up- heart of grace; hold up one's head, screw one's courage to the sticking place; come -to, – up to- the scratch; stand, – to one's guns, – fire, – against; bear up – against; hold out etc. (*persevere*) 604*a*.

put a bold face upon; show –, present- a bold front, face the music; envisage; show fight.

bell the cat, take the bull by the horns, beard the lion in his den, march up to the cannon's mouth, go through fire and water, run the gauntlet, go over the top.

give –, infuse –, inspire- courage; reassure, encourage, embolden, inspirit, cheer, hearten, nerve, put upon one's mettle, rally, raise a rallying cry; pat on the back, make a man of, keep in countenance.

Adj. courageous, brave; val-iant, -orous; gallant, intrepid; spirit-ed, -ful; high-spirited, -mettled; mettlesome, game, plucky; man-ly, -ful; resolute; stout, -hearted; iron-, lion-hearted; heart of oak; Penthesilean.

bold, – spirited; daring, audacious; fear-, daunt-, dread-, awe-less; un-daunted, -appalled, -dismayed, -awed, -blenched, -abashed, -alarmed, -flinching, -shrinking, -blenching; apprehensive; confident, self-reliant; bold as -a lion, – brass.

enterprising, adventurous; ventur-ous, -esome; dashing, chivalrous; soldierly etc. (*warlike*) 722; heroic.

fierce, savage; pugnacious etc. (*bellicose*) 720.

strong-minded, hardy, doughty; firm etc. (*stable*) 150; determined etc. (*resolved*) 604; dogged, indomitable etc. (*persevering*) 604*a*.

up to, – the scratch; upon one's mettle; reassured etc. *v.*; unfeared, undreaded.

Phr. one's blood being up.

862. Cowardice. [Excess of fear.]—**N.** cowardice, pusillanimity; cowardliness etc. *adj.*; timidity, effeminacy.

poltroonery, baseness; dastard-ness, -y; abject fear, funk; Dutch courage; fear etc. 860; white feather, faint heart.

coward, poltroon, dastard, sneak, recreant; shy –, dunghill- cock; coistril, milksop, white-liver, nidget, cur, craven, one that cannot say 'Boo' to a goose; Bob Acres, Jerry Sneak.

alarm-, terror-, pessim-ist; runagate etc. (*fugitive*) 623; shirker.

V. quail etc. (*fear*) 860; be -cowardly etc. *adj.*, – a coward etc. *n.*; funk; cower, skulk, sneak; flinch, shy, fight shy, slink, turn tail; run away etc. (*avoid*) 623; show the white feather, have cold feet, show a yellow streak.

Adj. coward, -ly; fearful, shy; tim-id, -orous; skittish; poor-spirited, spirit-less, soft, effeminate.

weak-minded; infirm of purpose etc. 605; weak-, faint-, chicken-, lily-, pigeon-hearted; yellow; white-, lily-, milk-livered; milksop, smock-faced; unable to say 'Boo' to a goose.

dastard, -ly; base, craven, sneaking, dunghill, recreant; unwar-, unsoldier-like.

'in face a lion but in heart a deer.'

unmanned; frightened etc. 860.

Int. *sauve qui peut!* devil take the hindmost!

Adv. in fear and trembling, in fear of one's life, in a blue funk.

Phr. *ante tubam trepidat*, one's courage oozing out.

863. Rashness.—N. rashness etc. *adj.*; temerity, want of caution, imprudence, indiscretion; over-confidence, presumption, audacity.

precipit-ancy, -ation; impetuosity; levity; foolhardi-hood, -ness; heed-, thought-lessness etc. (*inattention*) 458; carelessness etc. (*neglect*) 460; desperation; Quixotism, knight-errantry; fire-eating.

gam-ing, -bling; blind bargain, leap in the dark, fool's paradise; too many eggs in one basket.

desperado, rashling, mad-cap, dare-devil, Hotspur, fire-eater, bully, *bravo*, Hector, scapegrace, *enfant perdu*; Don Quixote, knight-errant, Icarus; adventurer; gam-bler, -ester; dynamitard.

V. be -rash etc. *adj.*; stick at nothing, play a desperate game; run into danger etc. 665; play with -fire, – edge tools.

carry too much sail, sail too near the wind, ride at single anchor, go out of one's depth.

take a leap in the dark, buy a pig in a poke.

donner tête baissée; knock one's head against a wall etc. (*be unskilful*) 699; rush on destruction; kick against the pricks, tempt Providence, go on a forlorn hope.

count one's chickens before they are hatched; reckon without one's host; catch at straws; trust to –, lean on- a broken reed.

Adj. rash, incautious, indiscreet, injudicious; imprudent, improvident, temerarious; uncalculating; heedless; careless etc. (*neglectful*) 460; without ballast, heels over head; giddy etc. (*inattentive*) 458; wanton, reckless, wild, madcap; desperate, devil-may-care.

hot-blooded, -headed, -brained; head-long, -strong; break-neck; fool-hardy; harebrained; precipitate, impulsive.

over-confident, -weening; ventur-esome, -ous; adventurous, Quixotic; fire-eating, cavalier; free-and-easy.

off one's guard etc. (*inexpectant*) 508.

Adv. post haste, *à corps perdu*, hand over head, *tête baissée*, head- foremost; happen what may.

Phr. neck or nothing, the devil being in one.

864. Caution.—N. caution; cautiousness etc. *adj.*; discretion, prudence, cautel, heed, circumspection, calculation, deliberation; safety first.

foresight etc. 510; vigilance etc. 459; warning etc. 668.

coolness etc. *adj.*; self-possession, -command; presence of mind, *sang froid*; well-regulated mind; worldly wisdom, Fabian policy.

V. be -cautious etc. *adj.*; take -care, – heed, – good care; have a care; mind, – what one is about; be on one's guard etc. (*keep watch*) 459; make assurance double sure; ca' canny.

bespeak etc. (*be early*) 132.

think twice, look before one leaps, keep one's weather eye open, count the cost, look to the main chance, cut one's coat according to one's cloth; feel one's -ground, – way; see how the land lies etc. (*foresight*) 510; wait to see how the cat jumps; bridle one's tongue; *reculer pour mieux sauter* etc. (*prepare*) 673; let well alone, let sleeping dogs lie, *ne pas réveiller le chat qui dort*.

keep out of -harm's way, – troubled waters; keep at a respectful distance, stand aloof; keep –, be- on the safe side.

husband one's resources etc. 636.

caution etc. (*warn*) 668.

Adj. cautious, wary, guarded; on one's guard etc. (*watchful*) 459; *cavendo tutus*; *in medio tutissimus*.

care-, heed-ful; cautelous, stealthy, chary, shy of, circumspect, prudent, canny, safe, non-committal, discreet, politic; sure-footed etc. (*skilful*) 698.

unenterprising, unadventurous, cool, steady, self-possessed; over-cautious.

suspicious, leery, vigilant.

Adv. cautiously, gingerly etc. *adj.*

Int. have a care! look out! *cave canem!*

Phr. *timeo Danaos*; *festina lente*.

865. Desire.—N. desire, wish, fancy, fantasy; want, need, exigency.

mind, inclination, leaning, bent, *animus*, partiality, *penchant*, predilection; propensity etc. 820; willingness etc. 602; liking, love, fondness, relish.

longing, hankering; solicitude, anxiety; yearning, coveting; aspiration, ambition, vaulting ambition; eagerness, zeal, ardor, *empressement*, breathless impatience, over-anxiety; solicitude, impetuosity etc. 825.

appet-ite, -ition, -ence, -ency; sharp appetite, keenness, hunger, stomach, twist; thirst, -iness; drouth, mouth-watering; itch, -ing; prurience, *cacoëthes*, cupidity, lust, concupiscence.

edge of -appetite, – hunger; torment of Tantalus; sweet –, lickerish- tooth; itching palm; longing –, wistful –, sheep's-eye.

avidity; greed, -iness; covetous-, ravenous-ness etc. *adj.*; grasping, craving, canine appetite, rapacity; voracity etc. (*gluttony*) 957.

passion, rage, *furore*, mania, *manie*; inextinguishable desire; dips-, klept-, mon-omania.

[Person desiring] desirer, lover, *amateur*, votary, devotee, aspirant, solicitant, candidate; cormorant etc. 957; sycophant.

[Object of desire] *desideratum*; want etc. (*requirement*) 630; 'consumation devoutly to be wished;' attraction, magnet, allurement, fancy, temptation, seduction, lure, fascination, *prestige*, height of one's ambition, idol; whim, -sey; maggot; hobby, -horse.

Fortunatus's cap, wishing cap, love potion.

V. desire; wish, – for; be -desirous etc. *adj.*; have a -longing etc. *n.*; hope etc. 858.

care for, affect, like, list; take to, cling to, take a fancy to; fancy; prefer etc. (*choose*) 609.

have -an eye, – a mind- to; find it in one's heart etc. (*be willing*) 602; have a fancy for, set one's eyes upon; cast a sheep's eye –, look sweet- upon; take into one's head, have a heart, be bent upon; set one's -cap at, – heart upon, – mind upon; covet.

want, miss, need, lack, desiderate, feel the want of; would fain -have, – do; would be glad of.

be -hungry etc. *adj.*; have a good appetite, play a good knife and fork; hunger –, thirst –, crave –, lust –, itch –, hanker –, run mad- after; raven –, die- for; burn to.

desiderate; sigh –, cry –, gape –, gasp –, pine –, pant –, languish –, yearn –, long –, be on thorns –, hope- for; aspire after; catch at, grasp at, jump at.

woo, court, solicit; fish –, spell –, whistle –, put up- for; ogle.

cause –, create –, raise –, excite –, provoke- desire; whet the appetite; appetize, titillate, allure, attract, take one's fancy, tempt; hold out -temptation, – allurement; tantalize, make one's mouth water, *faire venir l'eau à la bouche*.

gratify desire etc. (*give pleasure*) 829.

Adj. desirous; desiring etc. *v.*; orectic, appetitive; inclined etc. (*willing*) 602; partial to; fain, wishful, optative; anxious, wistful, curious; at a loss for, sedulous, solicitous.

craving, hungry, sharp-set, peckish, ravening, with an empty stomach, esurient, lickerish, thirsty, athirst, parched with thirst, pinched with hunger, famished, dry, drouthy; hungry as a hunter, – hawk, – horse, – church mouse.

greedy, – as a hog; over-eager, voracious; ravenous, – as a wolf; open-mouthed, covetous, rapacious, grasping, extortionate, exacting, sordid, *alieni appetens*; insati-able, -ate; unquenchable, quenchless; omnivorous.

unsatisfied, unsated, unslaked.

eager, avid, keen; burning, fervent, ardent; agog; all agog; breathless; impatient etc. (*impetuous*) 825; bent –, intent –, set- -on, – upon; mad after, *enragé*, rabid, dying for, devoured by desire.

aspiring, ambitious, vaulting, sky-aspiring.

desirable; popular; desired etc. *v.*; in demand; pleasing etc. (*giving pleasure*) 829; appeti-zing, -ble; tantalizing.

Adv. wistfully etc. *adj.*; fain.

Int. would -that, – it were! O for! *esto perpetua!* if only!

Phr. the wish being the father to the thought; *sua cuique voluptas*; *hoc erat in votis*, the mouth watering, the fingers itching; *aut Caesar aut nullus*.

866. Indifference.—N. indifference, neutrality; coldness etc. *adj.*; unconcern, *insouciance, nonchalance*; want of -interest, – earnestness; anorexy, inappetency; apathy etc. (*insensibility*) 823; supineness etc. (*inactivity*) 683; disdain etc. 930; recklessness etc. 863; inattention etc. 458.

V. be -indifferent etc. *adj.*; stand neuter; take no interest in etc. (*insensibility*) 823; have no -desire etc. 865. – taste, – relish- for; not care for; care nothing -for, – about; not care a -straw etc. (*unimportance*) 643 -about, – for; not mind.

set at naught etc. (*make light of*) 483; spurn etc. (*disdain*) 930.

Adj. indifferent, cold, frigid, lukewarm; cool, – as a cucumber; unconcerned, *insouciant*, phlegmatic, *pococurante*, easy-going, devil-may-care, careless, listless, lackadaisical, feckless; half-hearted; un-ambitious, -aspiring, -desirous, -solicitous, -attracted.

un-attractive, -alluring, -desired, -desirable, -cared for, -wished, -valued, all one to.

insipid etc. 391; vain.

Adv. for aught one cares.

Int. never mind.

867. Dislike.—N. dis-like, -taste, -relish, -inclination, -placency.

reluctance; backwardness etc. (*unwillingness*) 603.

repugnance, disgust, queasiness, turn, nausea, loathing; avers-eness, -ation, -ion; abomination, antipathy, abhorrence, horror; mortal –, rooted- -antipathy, – horror; hatred, detestation; hate etc. 898; animosity etc. 900; hydrophobia.

sickener; gall and wormwood etc. (*unsavory*) 395; shuddering, cold sweat.

V. dis-, mis-like, -relish; mind, object to; have rather not, not care for; have –, conceive –, entertain –, take- -a dislike, – an aversion- to; have no -taste, – stomach- for.

shun, avoid etc. 623; eschew; withdraw –, shrink –, recoil- from; not be able to -bear, – abide, – endure; shrug the shoulders at, shudder at, turn up the nose at, look askance at; make a -mouth, – wry face, – grimace; make faces.

loathe, nauseate, abominate, detest, abhor; hate etc. 898; take amiss etc. 900; have enough of etc. (*be satiated*) 869.

cause –, excite- dislike; disincline, repel, sicken; make –, render- sick; turn one's stomach, nauseate, wamble, disgust, shock, stink in the nostrils; go against the -grain, – stomach; stick in the throat; make one's blood run cold etc. (*give pain*) 830; pall.

Adj. disliking etc. *v.*; averse to, loth, adverse; shy of, sick of, out of conceit with; disinclined; heart-, dog-sick; queasy.

disliked etc. *v.*; uncared for, unpopular; out of favor; repulsive, repugnant, repellent; abhorrent, insufferable, fulsome, nauseous; loath-some, -ful; offensive; disgusting etc. *v.*; disagreeable etc. (*painful*) 830; unsavory etc. 395.

Adv. *usque ad nauseam*.

Int. faugh! foh! ugh!

868. Fastidiousness.—N. fastidiousness etc. *adj.*; nicety, meticulosity, hypercriticism, difficulty in being pleased, *friandise*, epicurism, *omnia suspendens naso*.

discrimination, discernment, good taste, perspicacity.

epicure, gourmet.

[Excess of delicacy] prudery, prudishness, primness.

V. be -fastidious etc. *adj.*; split hairs, discriminate, have a sweet tooth.

mince the matter; turn up one's nose at etc. (*disdain*) 930; look a gift horse in the mouth, see spots on the sun.

Adj. fastidious, meticulous, exacting, nice, delicate, *délicat*, finical, finicky, difficult, dainty, lickerish, squeamish, thin-skinned; s-, queasy; hard –, difficult- to please; querulous, particular, over-particular, straitlaced, prudish, prim, scrupulous; censorious etc. 932; hypercritical, discriminating, discerning, perspicacious.

Phr. *noli me tangere*.

869. Satiety.—N. satiety, satisfaction, saturation, repletion, glut, surfeit; weariness etc. 841.

spoiled child; *enfant gâté*; too much of a good thing, *toujours perdrix*; *crambe repetita*.

V. sate, satiate, satisfy, saturate; cloy, quench, slake, pall, glut, gorge, surfeit; bore etc. (*weary*) 841; tire etc. (*fatigue*) 688; spoil.

have -enough of, – quite enough of, – one's fill, – too much of; be -satiated etc. *adj.*

Adj. satiated etc. *v.*; overgorged; *blasé*, used up, sick of, heart-sick.

Int. enough! hold! *eheu jam satis!*

870. Wonder.—N. wonder, marvel; astonish-, amaze-, wonder-, bewilder-ment; amazedness etc. *adj.*; admiration, awe; stup-or, -efaction; stound, fascination; sensation; surprise etc. (*inexpectation*) 508; cynosure.

note of admiration; thaumaturgy etc. (*sorcery*) 992.

V. wonder, marvel, admire; be -surprised etc. *adj.*; start; stare; open –, rub –, turn up- one's eyes; gloar; gape, open one's mouth, hold one's breath; look –, stand- -aghast, – agog; look blank etc. (*disappointment*) 509; *tomber des nues*; not believe one's -eyes, – ears, – senses.

not be able to account for etc. (*unintelligible*) 519; not know whether one stands on one's head or one's heels.

surprise, astonish, amaze, astound; dumbfound, -er; startle, dazzle; strike, – with -wonder, – awe; electrify; stun, stupefy, petrify, confound, bewilder, flabbergast; stagger, throw on one's beam ends, fascinate, turn the head, take away one's breath, strike dumb; make one's -hair stand on end, – tongue cleave to the roof of one's mouth; make one stare.

take by surprise etc. (*be unexpected*) 508.

be -wonderful etc. *adj.*; beggar –, baffle-description; stagger belief.

Adj. surprised etc. *v.*; aghast, all agog, breathless, agape; open-mouthed; awe-, thunder-, moon-, planet-struck; spell-bound; lost in -amazement, – wonder, – astonishment; struck all of a heap, unable to believe one's senses, like a duck in thunder.

wonderful, wondrous; surprising etc. *v.*; unexpected etc. 508; unheard of; mysterious etc. (*inexplicable*) 519; miraculous; *foudroyant*.

in-describable, -expressible, -effable; unutterable, -speakable.

monstrous, prodigious, stupendous, marvelous; in-conceivable, -credible; in-, un-imaginable; strange etc. (*uncommon*) 83; passing strange.

striking etc. *v.*; over-whelming; wonder-working.

Adv. wonderfully etc. *adj.*; fearfully; for a –, in the name of- wonder; strange to say; *mirabile -dictu*, – visu; to one's great surprise.

with -wonder etc. *n.*, – gaping mouth, – open eyes, – upturned eyes; eyes starting out of one's head.

Int. lo, – and behold! O! hey-day! halloo! what! indeed! really! surely! humph! hem! good -lack, – heavens, – gracious! – lord! by jove! gad so! well a day! dear me! only think! lack-a-daisy! my -stars, – goodness! gracious goodness! goodness gracious! mercy on us! heavens and earth! God bless me! bless -us, – my heart! odzookens! *O gemini!* adzooks! hoity-toity! strong! Heaven save –, bless-the mark! can such things be! zounds! 'sdeath! what -on earth, – in the world! who would have thought it! etc. (*inexpectation*) 508; fancy! did you ever? you don't say so! what do you say to that! how now! where am I? well I'm blowed! etc.

Phr. *vox faucibus haesit*; one's hair standing on end.

871. Expectance. [Absence of wonder.]—**N.** expectan-ce, -cy etc. (*expectation*) 507; calmness, composure, tranquillity, serenity, coolness, imperturbability etc. 826.

nine days' wonder.

V. expect etc. 507; not -be surprised, – wonder etc. 870; *nil admirari*, make nothing of.

Adj. expecting etc. *v.*; unamazed, astonished at nothing; *blasé* etc. (*weary*) 841; unimaginative, calm, serene, imperturbable etc. 826; expected etc. *v.*; foreseen.

common, ordinary etc. (*habitual*) 613.

Int. no wonder; of course; why not?

872. Prodigy.—N. prodigy, phenomenon; wonder, -ment; genius, marvel, miracle; freak, monster etc. (*unconformity*) 83; curiosity, lion, infant prodigy, sight, spectacle; *jeu –, coup- de théâtre*; gazing-stock; sign; portent etc. 512.

bursting of a -shell, – bomb; volcanic eruption, peal of thunder; thunder-clap, -bolt.

what no words can paint; wonders of the world; *annus mirabilis*; *dignus vindice nodus*.

873. Repute.—N. distinction, mark, name, figure; repute, reputation, character; good –, high-repute; note, notability, notoriety, *éclat*, 'the bubble reputation,' vogue, celebrity; fame, famousness; renown; populairty, *aura popularis*; esteem, approval, approbation etc. 931; credit, *succes d'estime*, *prestige*, talk of the town; name to conjure with.

glory, honor; luster etc. (*light*) 420; illustriousness etc. *adj.*

account, regard, respect; reputableness etc. *adj.*; respectability etc. (*probity*) 939; good -name, – report; fair name.

dignity; stateliness etc. *adj.*; solemnity, grandeur, splendor, nobility, majesty, sublimity.

rank, standing, brevet rank, precedence, *pas*, station, place, *status*; position, – in society; order, degree, *locus standi*, caste, condition.

greatness etc. *adj.*; eminence; height etc. 206; importance etc. 642; pre-, super-eminence; high mightiness, primacy; top of the -ladder, – tree.

elevation; ascent etc. 305; super-, ex-altation; dignification, aggrandizement.

dedication, consecration, enthronement, canonization, apotheosis, deification, celebration, enshrinement, glorification.

hero, man of mark, great card, celebrity, worthy, lion, *rara avis*, notability, somebody; man of rank etc. (*nobleman*) 875; pillar of the -state, – society, – church.

chief etc. (*master*) 745; first fiddle etc. (*proficient*) 700; scholar etc. 492; cynosure, mirror; flower, pink, pearl; paragon etc. (*perfection*) 650; choice and master spirits of the age; *élite*; star, sun, constellation, galaxy.

ornament, honor, feather in one's cap, halo, aureole, nimbus; halo –, blaze- of glory; blushing honors; laurels etc. (*trophy*) 733.

memory, posthumous fame, niche in the temple of fame; immor-tality, -tal name; *magni nominis umbra*.

V. be conscious of glory; be proud of etc. (*pride*) 878; exult etc. (*boast*) 884; be vain of etc. (*vanity*) 880.

be -distinguished etc. *adj.*; shine etc. (*light*) 420; shine forth, figure; make –, cut- a -figure, – dash, – splash.

rival, surpass; out-shine, -rival, -vie, -jump; emulate, vie with, eclipse; throw –, cast- into the shade; overshadow.

live, flourish, glitter, scintillate, flaunt; gain –, acquire- honor etc. *n.*; play first fiddle etc. (*be of importance*) 642; bear the -palm, – bell; lead the way; take -precedence, – the wall of; gain –, win- -laurels, – spurs, – golden opinions etc. (*approbation*) 931; graduate, take one's degree, pass one's examination, win a -scholarship, – fellowship.

make -a, – some- -noise, – noise in the world; leave one's mark, exalt one's horn, star, have a run, be run after; enjoy popularity, come -into vogue, – to the front; raise one's head.

enthrone, signalize, immortalize, deify, exalt to the skies; hand one's name down to posterity.

consecrate; dedicate to, devote to; enshrine, inscribe, blazon, lionize, blow the trumpet, crown with laurel.

confer –, reflect- honor etc. *n.* on; shed a luster on; redound to one's honor, ennoble.

give –, do –, pay –, render- honor to; honor, accredit, pay regard to, dignify, glorify; sing praises to etc. (*approve*) 931; look up to; exalt, aggrandize, elevate, nobilitate.

Adj. distinguished, *distingué*, noted; of -note etc. *n.*; honored etc. *v.*; popular; fashionable etc. 852.

in good odor; in –, in high- favor; reput-, respect-, credit-able.

remarkable etc. (*important*) 642; notable, notorious; celebrated, renowned, in every one's mouth, talked of; fam-ous, -ed; far-famed; conspicuous, to the front; foremost; in the -front rank, – ascendant.

imperishable, deathless, immortal, never fading, *aere perennius*; time-honored.

illustrious, glorious, splendid, brilliant, radiant; bright etc. 420; full-blown; honorific.

eminent, prominent; high etc. 206; in the zenith; at the -head of, – top of the tree; peerless, of the first water; superior etc. 33; super-, pre-eminent.

great, dignified, proud, noble, honorable, worshipful, lordly, grand, stately, august, princely, imposing, solemn, transcendent, majestic, sacred, sublime, heaven-born, heroic, *sans peur et sans reproche*; sacrosanct.

Int. hail! all hail! *ave! viva! vive!* long life to! glory –, honor- be to!

Phr. one's name -being in every mouth, – living for ever; *sic itur ad astra, fama volat, aut Caesar aut nullus*; not to know him argues oneself unknown; none but himself could be his parallel, *palmam qui meruit ferat.*

874. Disrepute.—N. disrepute, discredit; ill-, bad- -repute, -name, -odor, -favor; disapprobation etc. 932; in-gloriousness, derogation; a-, debasement; abjectness etc. *adj.*; degradation, dedecoration; 'a long farewell to all one's greatness;' odium, obloquy, opprobrium, ignominy.

dishonor, disgrace; shame, humiliation; scandal, baseness, vileness; perfidy, turpitude etc. (*improbity*) 940; infamy.

tarnish, taint, defilement, pollution.

stain, blot, spot, blur, stigma, brand, reproach, imputation, slur.

crying –, burning- shame; *scandalum magnatum*, badge of infamy, blot in one's escutcheon; bend –, bar- sinister; champain, point champain; by- word of reproach; Ichabod.

argumentum ad verecundiam; sense of shame etc. 879.

V. be -inglorious etc. *adj.*; incur -disgrace etc. *n.*; have –, earn- a bad name; put –, wear- a halter round one's neck; disgrace –, expose- oneself.

play second fiddle; lose caste; pale one's ineffectual fire; recede into the shade; fall from one's high estate; keep in the background etc. (*modesty*) 881; be conscious of disgrace etc. (*humility*) 879; look -blue, – foolish, – like a fool; cut a -poor, – sorry- figure; laugh on the wrong side of the mouth; make a sorry face, go away with a flea in one's ear, slink away.

cause -shame etc. *n.*; shame, disgrace, put to shame, dishonor; throw –, cast –, fling –, reflect- dishonor etc. *n.* upon; be a -reproach etc. *n.* to; derogate from.

tarnish, stain, blot, sully, taint; discredit, degrade, debase, defile; beggar; expel etc. (*punish*) 972.

impute shame to, brand, post, stigmatize, vilify, defame, slur, cast a slur upon, hold up to shame, send to Coventry; tread –, trample- under foot; show up, drag through the mire, heap dirt upon; reprehend etc. 932.

bring low, put down, snub; take down a peg, – lower, – or two.

obscure, eclipse, outshine, take the shine out of; throw –, cast- into the shade; overshadow; leave –, put- in the background; push into a corner, put one's nose out of joint; put out, – of countenance.

upset, throw off one's center; discompose, disconcert; put to the blush etc. (*humble*) 879.

Adj. disgraced etc. *v.*; blown upon; shorn of -its beams, – one' glory; overcome, down-trodden; loaded with -shame etc. *n.*; in -bad repute etc. *n.*; out of -repute, – favor, – fashion, – countenance; at a discount; under -a cloud, – an eclipse; unable to show one's face; in the -shade, – background; out at elbows, down in the world, down and out.

inglorious; nameless, renownless, obscure, unknown to fame; un-noticed, -noted, -honored, -glorified.

shameful; dis-graceful, -creditable, -reputable; despicable; questionable; unbecoming, unworthy; derogatory; degrading, humiliating, *infra dignitatem*, dedecorous; scandalous, infamous, too bad, unmentionable; ribald, opprobrious; arrant, shocking, outrageous, notorious, shady.

ignominious, scrubby, dirty, abject, vile, beggarly, pitiful, low, mean, shabby; base etc. (*dishonorable*) 940.

Adv. to one's shame be it spoken.

Int. fie! shame! for shame! *proh pudor! O tempora! O mores!* ough! *sic transit gloria mundi!*

875. Nobility.—N. nobility, rank, condition, distinction, optimacy, blood, *pur sang*, birth, high descent, order; quality, gentility; blue blood of Castile; *ancien régime*.

high life, *haut monde*; upper -classes, – ten thousand; *élite*, aristocracy, great folks; fashionable world etc. (*fashion*) 852; salariat.

peer, -age; house of -lords, – peers; lords, – temporal and spiritual; *noblesse*; baronage, knightage; noble, -man; lord, -ling; grandee, *magnifico, hidalgo*; don, -ship; aristocrat, swell, three-tailed bashaw; gentleman, squire, squireen, patrician, laureate.

gentry, gentlefolk; squirarchy, better sort, *magnates, primates, optimates*.

king etc. (*master*) 745; prince, crown prince, *Dauphin*; duke; marquis, -ate; earl, viscount, baron, thane, banneret; baronet, -cy; knight, -hood; count, armiger, laird; sig-, seig-nior; esquire, boyar, margrave, vavasor, sheik, emir, ameer, scherif, *pasha*, effendi, sahib.

queen etc. 745; princess, begum, duchess, marchioness; countess etc.; lady, dame.

personage –, man- of -distinction, – mark, – rank; nota-bles, -bilities; celebrity, big-wig, magnate, great man, star; *magni nominis umbra*; 'every inch a king;' grand Panjandrum

V. be -noble etc. *adj.*

Adj. noble, exalted; of -rank etc. *n.*; princely, titled, patrician, aristocratic; high-, well-born; of gentle blood; genteel, *comme il faut*, gentlemanlike, courtly etc. (*fashionable*) 852; highly respectable.

Adv. in high quarters.

876. Commonalty.—N. commonalty, democracy; obscruity; low -condition, – life, – society, – company; *bourgeoisie*; mass of -the people, – society; Brown, Jones, and Robinson; Tom, Dick, and Harry; lower –, humbler- - classes, – orders; vulgar –, common- herd; rank and file, *hoc genus omne*; the -many, – general, – crowd, – people, – populace, – multitude, – million, – masses, – mobility, – peasantry; king Mob; proletariat, *fruges consumere nati*, great unwashed; man in the street

mob; rabble, – rout; chaff, rout, horde, *canaille*; scum –, *residuum* –, dregs- of -the people, – society; swinish multitude, *faex populi*; *profanum* –, *ignobile- vulgus*; vermin, riff-raff, tag-rag and bobtail; small fry.

commoner, one of the people, democrat, plebeian, republican, proletary, *prolétaire, roturier*, Mr. Snooks, *bourgeois, épicier*, Philistine, cockney; *grisette, demi-monde*.

peasant, countryman, boor, carle, churl; vill-ain, -ein; serf, kern, tyke, tike, chuff, ryot, fellah; longshoreman; swain, clown, hind; clod, -hopper; hobnail, yokel, hick, rube, cider squeezer, bog-trotter, bumpkin; ploughman, -boy; rustic, chawbacon, tiller of the soil; hewers of wood and drawers of water, groundling; gaffer, loon, put, cub, Tony Lumpkin, looby, lout, under-ling; *gamin*, guttersnipe, street arab, mudlark; rough, rowdy, ruffian, roughneck; pot-wallopper, slubberdegullion; vulgar –, low- fellow; cad, curmudgeon.

upstart, *parvenu, nouveau-riche*, skipjack; nobody, – one knows; *hesterni quirites, pessoribus orti*; *bourgeois gentilhomme*, *novus homo*, snob, gent, mushroom, no one knows who, adventurer; man of straw.

beggar, panhandler, gaberlunzie, muckworm, mudlark, *sans-culotte*, raff, tatterdemalion, caitiff, ragamuffin, Pariah, outcast of society, tramp, weary Willie, bum, vagabond, *chiffonaier*, rag-picker, Cinderella, cinderwench, scrub, jade; boots, gossoon.

Goth, Vandal, Hottentot, savage, barbarian, Yahoo; unlicked cub, rough diamond.

barbar-ousness, -ism; Boeotia.

V. be -ignoble etc. *adj.*, – nobody etc. *n.*

Adj. ignoble, common, mean, low, base, vile, sorry, scrubby, beggarly, below par; no great shakes etc. (*unimportant*) 643; home-ly, -spun; vulgar, low-minded; snobbish, *parvenu*.

plebeian, proletarian; of -low, – mean- - parentage, – origin, extraction; low-, base-, earthborn, low bred; mushroom, dunghill, risen from the ranks; unknown to fame, obscure, untitled.

rustic, uncivilized; lout-, boor-, clown-, churl-, brut-, raff-ish; rude, unlicked, unpolished.

barbar-ous, -ian, -ic, -esque; cockney, born within sound of Bow bells.

underling, menial, servile, subaltern.

Adv. below the salt.

877. Title.—N. title, honor; knighthood etc. (*nobility*) 875.

royal –, serene- highness, excellency, grace; lordship, worship, Rt. Hon., rever-ence, -end; esquire, sir; madam, *madame*; master, mistress, Mr., Mrs., *signor, señor, Mein Herr, mynheer*; your –, his- honor; handle to one's name.

decoration, laurel, palm, wreath, garland, bays, medal, ribbon, riband, blue ribbon, *cordon*, cross, crown, coronet, star, garter; feather, – in one's cap; chevron, epaulet, *épaulette*, colors, cockade; livery; order, arms, armorial bearings, shield, scutcheon, crest, reward etc. 973.

878. Pride.—N. dignity, self-respect, *mens sibi conscia recti*.

pride; haughtiness etc. *adj.*; high notions, *hauteur*; vainglory, crest; arrogance etc. (*assumption*) 885; pomposity etc. 882.

proud man, highflier; fine -gentleman, – lady; *grande dame*.

V. be -proud etc. *adj.*; put a good face on; look one in the face; stalk abroad, perk oneself up; presume, swagger, strut; rear –, lift up –, hold up- one's head; hold one's head high, look big, take the wall, 'bear like the Turk no rival near the throne,' carry with a high hand; ride the –, mount on one's- high horse; set one's back up, bridle, toss the head; give oneself airs etc. (*assume*) 885; boast etc. 884.

pride oneself on; glory in, take pride in; pique –, plume –, hug- oneself; stand upon, be proud of; put a good face on; not -hide one's light under a bushel, – put one's talent in a napkin; not think small beer of oneself etc. (*vanity*) 880.

Adj. dignified; stately; proud, -crested; lordly, baronial; lofty-minded; high-souled, -minded, - mettled, -handed, -plumed, -flown, -toned.

haughty, paughty, insolent, lofty, high, mighty, swollen, puffed up, flushed, blown; vain-glorious; purse-proud, fine; proud as -a peacock, Lucifer; bloated with pride.

supercilious, disdainful, bumptious, magisterial, imperious; high-handed, – and mighty; overweening, consequential; arrogant etc. 885; unblushing etc. 880.

stiff, -necked; starch; perked –, stuck- up; in buckram, straitlaced; prim etc. (*affected*) 855.

on one's -high horses, – tight ropes, – high ropes; on stilts; *en grand seigneur*.

Adv. with head erect, with one's nose in the air.

Phr. *odi profanum vulgus et arceo*.

879. Humility.—N. hum-ility, -bleness; meek-, low-ness; lowli-ness, -hood; abasement, self-abasement, -effacement; submission etc. 725; resignation.

condescension; affability etc. (*courtesy*) 894.

modesty etc. 881; verecundity, blush, suffusion, confusion; sense of -shame, – disgrace; humiliation, mortification; let –, set- down.

V. be -humble etc. *adj.*; deign, vouchsafe, condescend; humble –, demean- oneself; stoop, – to conquer; carry coals; submit etc. 725; submit with a good grace etc. (*brook*) 826; yield the palm.

lower one's -tone, – note; sing small, draw in one's horns, sober down; hide one's -face, – diminished head; not dare to show one's face, take shame to oneself, not have a word to say for oneself; feel –, be conscious of- -shame, – disgrace; drink the cup of humiliation to the dregs; eat -humble pie, – one's words, – dirt; be humiliated, receive a snub.

blush -for, – up to the eyes; redden, change color; color up; hang one's head, look foolish, feel small.

render humble; humble, humiliate; let –, set –, take –, tread –, frown- down; snub, abash, abase, make one sing small, strike dumb; teach one -his distance, – his place; take down a peg, – lower; throw –, cast- into the shade etc. 874; stare –, put- out of countenance; put to the blush; confuse, ashame, mortify, disgrace, crush; send away with a flea in one's ear.

get a set down.

Adj. humble, lowly, meek; modest etc. 881; humble-, sober-minded; unoffended; submissive etc. 725; servile etc. 886.

condescending; affable etc. (*courteous*) 894.

humbled etc. *v.*; bowed down, resigned; abashed, ashamed, dashed; out of countenance; down in the mouth; down on one's -knees, – marrow-bones; humbled in the dust, brow-beaten; chap-, crest-fallen; dumbfoundered, flabbergasted, struck all of a heap.

shorn of one's glory etc. (*disrepute*) 874.

Adv. with -downcast eyes, – bated breath, – bended knee; on all fours, on one's feet.

under correction, with due deference.

Phr. I am your -obedient, – very humble- servant; my service to you.

880. Vanity.—N. vanity; conceit, -edness; self-conceit, -complacency, -confidence, -sufficiency, -esteem, -love, -approbation, -praise, -glorification, -laudation, -gratulation, -applause, -admiration; *amour-propre*; selfishness etc. 943.

airs, pretensions, mannerism; egotism; prigg-ism, -ishness; coxcombery, gaudery, vainglory, elation; pride etc. 878; ostentation etc. 882; assurance etc. 885.

vox et praeterea nihil; *cheval de bataille*.

ego-ist, -tist; peacock, coxcomb etc. 854; Sir Oracle etc. 887.

V. be -vain etc. *adj.*, – vain of; pique oneself etc. (*pride*) 878; lay the flattering unction to one's soul.

have -too high, – an overweening- opinion of -oneself, – one's talents; blind oneself as to one's own merit; not think -small beer, – *vin ordinaire*- of oneself; put oneself forward; fish for compliments; give oneself airs etc. (*assume*) 885; boast etc. 884.

render -vain etc. *adj.*; inspire with -vanity etc. *n.*; inflate, puff up, turn up, turn one's head.

Adj. vain, – as a peacock; conceited, assured, overweening, pert, forward, perky; vain-glorious, high-flown; ostentatious etc. 882; puffed up, inflated, flushed.

self-satisfied, -confident, -sufficient, -flattering, -admiring, -applauding, -glorious, -opinionated; *entêté* etc. (*wrong-headed*) 481; wise in one's own conceit, pragmatical, overwise, pretentious, priggish; egotistic, -al; *soi-disant* etc. (*boastful*) 884; arrogant etc. 885.

un-abashed, -blushing; un-constrained, -ceremonious; free and easy.

Adv. vainly etc. *adj.*

Phr. how we apples swim!

881. Modesty.—N. modesty; humility etc. 879; diffidence, timidity; retiring disposition, unobtrusiveness, bashfulness etc. *adj.*; *mauvaise honte*; blush, -ing; verecundity; self-knowledge.

reserve, constraint; demureness etc. *adj.*; blushing honors.

V. be -modest etc. *adj.*; retire, reserve oneself; give way to; draw in one's horns etc. 879; hide one's face.

keep -private, – in the background, – one's distance; pursue the noiseless tenor of one's way, 'do good by stealth and blush to find it fame,' hide one's light under a bushel, cast a sheep's eye.

Adj. modest, diffident; humble etc. 879; timid, timorous, bashful; shy, nervous, skittish, coy, sheepish, shamefaced, blushing, over-modest.

unpreten-ding, -tious; un-obtrusive, -assuming, -ostentatious, -boastful, -aspiring; poor in spirit.

out of countenance etc. (*humbled*) 879.

reserved, constrained, demure.

Adv. humbly etc. *adj.*; quietly, privately; without -ceremony, – beat of the drum; *sans facon*.

882. Ostentation.—N. ostentation, display, show, flourish, parade, *étalage*, pomp, array, state, solemnity; dash, splash, glitter, strut, swank, side, swagger, pomposity; preten-se, -sions; showing off; fuss.

magnificence, splendor; *coup d'oeil*; grand doings.

coup de théâter; stage -effect, – trick; clap-trap; *mise en scène*; *tour de force*; *chic*.

demonstration, flying colors; tomfoolery; flourish of trumpets etc. (*celebration*) 883; pageant, -ry; spectacle, exhibition, procession; turn –, set- out; grand function; *fête*, gala, field-day, review, march past, promenade, insubstantial pageant.

dress; court –, full –, evening –, ball –, fancy- dress; tailoring, millinery, man-millinery, frippery; foppery, equipage.

ceremon-y, -ial; ritual; form, -ality; etiquette; punct-o, -ilio, -ilious-ness; starched-, stateli-ness.

mummery, solemn mockery, mouth honor.

attitudinarian; fop etc. 854.

V. be -ostentatious etc. *adj.*; come –, put oneself- forward; attract attention, star it.

make –, cut- a -figure, – dash, – splash; strut, blow one's own trumpet; figure, – away; make a show, – display; glitter.

show -off, – one's paces; parade, march past;

display, exhibit, put forward, hold up; trot –, hang- out; sport, brandish, blazon forth; dangle, – before the eyes.

cry up etc. (*praise*) 931; *prôner*, flaunt, emblazon, prink, set off, mount, have framed and glazed.

put a good, – smiling- face upon; clean the outside of the platter etc. (*disguise*) 544.

Adj. ostentatious, showy, dashing, pretentious, ja-, jau-nty; grand, pompous, palatial; high sounding; turgid etc. (*big-sounding*) 577; garish, gorgeous; gaudy, – as a -peacock, – butterfly, – tulip; flaunting, flashing, flaming, glittering; gay etc. (*ornate*) 847; colorful.

splendid, magnificent, sumptuous.

theatrical, dramatic, spectacular, scenic, ceremonial, ritual, -istic.

solemn, stately, majestic, formal, stiff, ceremonious, punctilious, starch-ed, -y.

en grande tenue, in best bib and tucker, in Sunday best, *endimanché*.

Adv. with -flourish of trumpet, – beat of drum, – flying colors, – a brass band.

ad captandum vulgus.

883. Celebration.—N. celebration, solemnization, jubilee, diamond jubilee, commemoration, ovation, paean, triumph, jubilation.

triumphal arch, bonfire, salute; salvo, – of artillery; *feu de joie*, flourish of trumpets, *fanfare*, colors flying, illuminations, fireworks.

inauguration, installation, presentation; *début*, coming out, birthday anniversary, bi-, ter-, centenary; silver –, golden –, diamond- wedding, -day; coronation; Lord Mayor's show; harvest home, red letter day, festival; trophy etc. 733; *Te Deum* etc. (*thanksgiving*) 990; fête etc. 882; holiday etc. 840.

V. celebrate, keep, signalize, do honor to, commemorate, solemnize, hallow, mark with a red letter, hold high festival, maffick.

pledge, drink to, toast, hob and nob.

inaugurate, install, instate, induct, chair.

rejoice etc. 838; kill the fatted calf, hold jubilee, roast an ox, fire a salute.

Adj. celebrating etc. *v.*; commemorative, celebrated, immortal.

Adv. in -honor, – commemoration, – celebration of.

Int. hail! all hail! *io -paean*, – *triumphe!* 'see the conquering hero comes!'

884. Boasting.—N. boasting etc. *v.*; boast, vaunt, crake; preten-ce, -sions; puff, -ery; flourish, *fanfaronnade*; gasconade; bluff, swank, brag, -gardism; bravado, bunkum, Buncombe; highfalutin; jact-itation, -ancy; bounce, rant, bluster; venditation, vaporing, rodomontade, bombast, fine talking, tall talk, magniloquence, teratology, heroics; jingoism, Chauvinism; exaggeration etc. 549; gas, hot air.

vanity etc. 880; *vox et praeterea nihil*; much cry and little wool, *brutum fulmen*.

exultation; glorification; flourish of trumpets; triumph etc. 883.

boaster; bragg-art, -adocio; hot air merchant; Gascon, *fanfaron*, pretender, fourflusher, *soi-disant*; windbag, blowhard, bluffer; chauvinist; blusterer etc. 887; charlatan, jack-pudding, trumpeter; puppy etc. (*fop*) 854.

V. boast, make a boast of, brag, vaunt, puff, show off, flourish, crake, crack, trumpet, strut, swagger, vapor, bluff; draw the long bow.

exult, crow over, neigh, chuckle, triumph; glory, gloat, jubilate; throw up one's cap; talk big, *se faire valoir*, *faire claquer son fouet*, take merit to oneself, make a merit of, sing *Io triumphe*, holloa before one is out of the wood.

Adj. boasting etc. *v.*; magniloquent, flaming, Thrasonic, stilted, gasconading, braggart, boastful, pretentious, *soi-disant*; vain-glorious etc. (*conceited*) 880.

elate, -d; jubilant, triumphant, exultant; in high feather; flushed, – with victory; cock-a-hoop; on stilts.

vaunted etc. *v.*

Adv. vauntingly etc. *adj.*; with a brass band.

Phr. 'let the galled jade wince.'

885. Insolence. [Undue assumption of superiority.]—**N.** insolence; haughtiness etc. *adj.*; arrogance, airs; overbearance, brashness, bumptiousness, contumely, disdain; domineering etc. *v.*; tyranny etc. 739.

impertinence; cheek, nerve, sauce; sauciness etc. *adj.*; flippancy, dicacity, petulance, procacity, bluster; swagger, -ing etc. *v.*; bounce; terrorism; jingoism, chauvinism.

as-, pre-sumption; beggar on horseback; usurpation.

impudence, assurance, audacity, self-assertion, hardihood, front, face, brass; shamelessness etc. *adj.*; effrontery, hardened front, face of brass.

assumption of infallibility.

malapert, saucebox etc. (*blusterer*) 887.

V. be -insolent etc. *adj.*; bluster, vapor, swagger, swell, give oneself airs; snap one's fingers, kick up a dust; swear etc. (*affirm*) 535; rap out oaths; roister.

arrogate; as-, pre-sume; make -bold, – free; take a liberty, give an inch and take an ell.

domineer, bully, dictate, hector; lord it over, bulldoze; *traiter de haut*, *regarder de haut en bas*; exact; snub, huff, beard, fly in the face of; put to the blush; bear –, beat- down; browbeat, intimidate; trample –, tread- -down, – under foot; dragoon, ride roughshod over, terrorize.

out-face, -look, -stare, -brazen, -brave; stare out of countenance; brazen out; lay down the law; teach one's grandmother to suck eggs; assume a lofty bearing; talk –, look- big; put on big looks, act the *grand seigneur*; mount –, ride- the high horse; toss the head, carry with a high hand.

tempt Providence, want snuffing.

Adj. insolent, haughty, arrogant, imperious, magisterial, dictatorial, arbitrary; high-handed, high and mighty; contumelious, supercilious, overbearing, intolerant, domineering; overweening, high-flown.

flippant, pert, cavalier, saucy, forward, impertinent, fresh, malapert.

precocious, assuming, would-be, bumptious.

bluff; brazen-, browed-faced, shameless, aweless, unblushing, unabashed; bold-, bare-faced; dead –, lost- to shame.

impudent, audacious, presumptuous, free and easy, devil-may-care, rollicking; janty, jaunty; roistering, blustering, hectoring, swaggering, vaporing; thrasonic, fire-eating, 'full of sound and fury.'

Adv. insolently, with a high hand; *ex cathedrâ*.

Phr. one's bark being worse than his bite.

886. Servility.—N. servility; slavery etc. (*subjection*) 749; obsequiousness etc. *adj.*; subserviency; abasement; pros-tration, -ternation; genuflexion etc. (*worship*) 990; fawning etc. *v.*; tuft-hunting, time-serving, flunkeyism; sycophancy etc. (*flattery*) 933; humility etc. 879.

sycophant, parasite, yes-man; toad, -y, -eater; tuft-hunter; snob, flunkey, lap-dog, spaniel, lickspittle, smell-feast, *Graeculus esuriens*, hanger on, stooge, *cavaliere servente*, led captain, carpet knight; time-server, fortune-hunter, Vicar of Bray, Sir Pertinax Mac Sycophant, pick-thank; flatterer etc. 935; doer of dirty work; *âme damnée*, tool; reptile; slave etc. (*servant*) 746; courtier; sponge, jackal; truckler.

V. cringe, bow, stoop, kneel, bend the knee; fall on one's knees, prostrate oneself; worship etc. 990.

sneak, crawl, crouch, cower, truckle to, grovel, fawn, toady, lick the feet of, kiss the hem of one's garment.

pay court to; feed –, fatten –, batten- on; dance attendance on, pin oneself upon, hang on the sleeve of, *avaler des couleuvres*, keep time to, fetch and carry, do the dirty work of.

go with the stream, follow the crowd, worship the rising sun, hold with the hare and run with the hounds.

Adj. servile, obsequious; supple, – as a glove; soapy, oily, pliant, cringing, fawning, slavish, groveling, sniveling, mealy-mouthed; beggarly, sycophantic, parasitical; abject, prostrate, down on one's marrow-bones; base, mean, sneaking; crouching etc. *v.*

Adv. hat –, cap- in hand.

887. Blusterer.—N. bluster-, swagger-, vapor-, roister-, brawl-er; brazen-face; *fanfaron*; braggart etc. (*boaster*) 884; bully, terrorist, rough, roughneck; hooligan, hoodlum, larrikin, ruffian; Mohock, -hawk; drawcansir, swashbuckler, Captain Boabdil, Sir Lucius O'Trigger, Thraso, Pistol, Parolles, Bombastes Furioso, Hector, Chrononhotonthologos; jingo; desperado, dare-devil, fire-eater; fury etc. (*violent person*) 173; rowdy.

puppy etc. (*fop*) 854; prig; Sir Oracle, dogmatist, *doctrinaire*, stump orator, jack-in-office; saucebox, malapert, jackanapes, minx; bantam-cock.

888. Friendship.—N. friendship, amity; friendliness etc. *adj.*; brotherhood, fraternity, sodality, confraternity, sorosis, sisterhood; harmony etc. (*concord*) 714; peace etc. 721.

firm –, staunch –, intimate –, familiar –, bosom –, cordial –, tried –, devoted –, lasting –, fast –, sincere –, warm –, ardent- friendship.

cordiality, fraternization, *entente cordiale*, good understanding, *rapprochement*, sympathy, fellowfeeling, response, welcomeness; *camaraderie*.

affection etc. (*love*) 897; favoritism; goodwill etc. (*benovolence*) 906; partiality.

acquaintance, familiarity, intimacy, intercourse, fellowship, knowledge of; introduction.

V. be -friendly etc. *adj.*, – friends etc. 890; – acquainted with etc. *adj.*; know; have the ear of; keep- company with etc. (*sociality*) 892; hold communication –, have dealings –, sympathize- with; have a leaning to; bear good will etc. (*benevolence*) 906; love etc. 897; make much of; befriend etc. (*aid*) 707; introduce to.

set one's horses together; hold out –, extend the right hand of -friendship, – fellowship; become -friendly etc. *adj.*; make -friends etc. 890 with; break the ice, be introduced to; make –, pick –, scrape- acquaintance with; get into favor, gain the friendship of.

shake hands with, fraternize, embrace; receive with open arms, throw oneself into the arms of; meet half way, take in good part.

Adj. friendly, amic-able, -al; well affected, unhostile, neighborly, brotherly, fraternal, sisterly, sympathetic, harmonious, hearty, cordial, warmhearted, devoted.

friends –, well –, at home –, hand in hand- with; on -good, – friendly, – amicable, – cordial, – familiar, – intimate- -terms, – footing; on -speaking, – visiting- terms; in one's good -graces, – books.

acquainted, familiar, intimate, thick, hand and glove, hail fellow well met, free and easy; welcome.

Adv. amicably etc. *adj.*; with open arms; *sans cérémonie*; arm in arm.

889. Enmity.—N. enmity, hostility; unfriendliness etc. *adj.*; discord etc. 713.

alienation, estrangement; dislike etc. 867; hate etc. 898; antagonism.

heartburning; animosity etc. 900; malevolence etc. 907.

V. be -inimical etc. *adj.*; keep –, hold- at arm's length; be at loggerheads; bear malice etc. 907; fall out; take umbrage etc. 900; harden the heart, alienate, estrange.

Adj. inimical, unfriendly, hostile; at -enmity, – variance, – swords points, – daggers drawn, – open war with; up in arms against; in bad odor with.

on bad –, not on speaking- terms; cool; cold, -hearted; estranged, alienated, disaffected, irreconcilable.

890. Friend.—N. friend, – of one's bosom, intimate acquaintance, neighbor, well-wisher; *alter ego*; best –, bosom –, fast- friend; *amicus usque ad aras*; *fidus Achates*; *persona grata*.

favorer, *fautor*, patron, backer, Maecenas; tutelary saint, good genius, advocate, partisan, sympathizer; ally; friend in need etc. (*auxiliary*) 711.

associate, compeer, comrade, mate, companion, *confrère*, *camarade*, *confidante*, colleague; old –, crony; side-kick; chum, buddy, bunkie, roommate, pal; play-fellow, -mate; classmate, schoolfellow; bed-fellow, -mate; maid of honor.

compatriot; fellow –, countryman, – townsman.

shop-, ship-, mess-mate; fellow –, boon –, pot-companion; co-partner.

Arcades ambo, Pylades and Orestes, Castor and Pollux, Nisus and Euryalus, Damon and Pythias, *par nobile fratrum*.

host, Amphitryon, Boniface; guest, visitor, frequenter, *habitué*; *protégé*.

891. Enemy.—N. enemy; antagonist, foeman; open –, bitter- enemy; opponent etc. 710; back friend.

public enemy, enemy to society, traitor, anarchist etc. 743.

Phr. every hand being against one.

892. Sociality.—N. soci-ality, -ability, -ableness etc. *adj.*; social intercourse; consociation; intercourse, -community; consort-, companion-, fellow-, comrade-ship; clubbism; *esprit de corps*.

conviviality; good -fellowship, – company, *camaraderie*; joviality, jollity, *savoir -vivre*, festivity, festive board, merry-making; loving cup; hospitality, heartiness; cheer.

welcome, -ness; greeting; hearty –, warm –, welcome- reception; urbanity etc. (*courtesy*) 894; intimacy, familiarity.

good –, jolly- fellow, good mixer, Rotarian; *bon enfant*.

social –, family- circle; circle of acquaintance, *coterie*, society, company.

social -gathering, – *réunion*; assembly etc. (*assemblage*) 72; party, entertainment, reception, *levée*, at home, *conversazione*, *soirée*, *matinée*, evening –, morning –, afternoon –, garden –, dinner –, tea –, cocktail- party; symposium, singsong; kettle-, drum; *partie carrée*, dish of tea, *ridotto*, rout, housewarming; ball, prom, hop, dance, *thé dansant*; festival etc. (*amusement*) 840; wedding breakfast; 'the feast of reason and the flow of soul.'

visit, -ing; round of visits; call, morning call; interview etc. (*interlocution*) 588; assignation; tryst, -ing place; appointment.

club etc. (*association*) 712.

V. be -sociable etc. *adj.*; know; be -acquainted etc. *adj.*; associate –, sort –, keep company –, walk hand in hand -with; eat off the same trencher, club together, consort, bear one company, join; make acquaintance with etc. (*friendship*) 888; make advances, fraternize, embrace; intercommunicate.

be –, feel –, make oneself- at home with; make free with; crack a bottle with; take pot luck with, receive hospitality, live at free quarters.

visit, pay a visit; interchange -visits, – cards; call -at, – upon; leave a card; drop in, look in; look one up, beat up one's quarters.

entertain; give a -party etc. *n.*; be at home, see one's friends, hang out, keep open house, do the honors; receive, – with open arms; welcome; give a warm reception etc. *n.* to; kill the fatted calf.

Adj. sociable, companionable, clubbable, clubby, conversable, cosy, cosey, chatty, conversational; homiletical.

convivial; fest-ive, -al; jovial, jolly, hospitable.

welcome, – as the roses in May; *fêté*, entertained.

free and easy, hail fellow well met, familiar, on visiting terms, acquainted.

social, neighborly; international, cosmopolitan, gregarious.

Adv. *en famille*, in the family circle; *sans -façon*, – *cérémonie*, arm in arm.

893. Seclusion. Exclusion.—N. seclusion, privacy; retirement; concealment; reclusion, recess; snugness etc. *adj.*; delitescence; rustication, *rus in urbe*; solitude; solitariness etc. (*singleness*) 87; isolation; loneliness etc. *adj.*; estrangement from the world, anchoritism, voluntary exile; aloofness.

cell, hermitage; convent etc. 1000; *sanctum sanctorum*; study, library, den; hide-out.

depopulation, desertion, desolation; wilderness etc. (*unproductive*) 169; howling wilderness; rotten borough, Old Sarum.

exclusion, excommunication, banishment, exile, ostracism, proscription; cut, – direct; dead cut.

inhospit-ality, -ableness etc. *adj.*; un-, dissociability; domesticity, Darby and Joan.

recluse, hermit, eremite, cenobite; anchor-et, -ite; Simon Stylites; Troglodyte, Timon of Athens, Santon, *solitaire*, ruralist, disciple of Zimmermann, closet cynic, Diogenes; outcast, Pariah, castaway, outsider, pilgarlic; wastrel, foundling, orphan.

V. be –, live- secluded etc. *adj.*; keep –, stand –, hold oneself- -aloof, – in the background; keep snug; shut oneself up; deny –, seclude- oneself; creep into a corner, rusticate, *aller planter ses choux*; retire, – from the world; hermetize. take the veil; abandon etc. 624.

cut, – dead; refuse to -associate with, – acknowledge; look cool –, turn one's back –, shut the door- upon; repel, blackball, excommunicate, exclude, exile, expatriate; banish, outlaw, maroon, ostracize, proscribe, cut off from, send to Coventry, keep at arm's length, draw a cordon round; boycott, blockade, lay an embargo on, isolate.

depopulate; dis-, un-people.

Adj. secluded, sequestered, retired, delitescent, private, bye; out of the -world, -way; in a backwater; 'the world forgetting by the world forgot.'

snug, domestic, stay-at-home.

unsociable; un-, dis-social; inhospitable, cynical, inconversable, unclubbable, *sauvage*, eremetic.

solitary; lone-ly, -some; isolated, single.

excluded, estranged; unfrequented; uninhabitable, -ed; tenantless; un-tenanted, -occupied; abandoned; deserted, – in one's utmost need; unfriended; kith-, friend-, home-less; lorn, forlorn, desolate.

un-visited, -introduced, -invited, -welcome; under a cloud, left to shift for oneself, derelict, outcast, outside the gates.

banished etc. *v.*; under an embargo.

Phr. *noli me tangere*.

894. Courtesy.—N. courtesy; respect etc. 928; good -manners, – behavior, – breeding; manners; politeness etc. *adj.*; *bienséance*, urbanity, comity, gentility; gentle –, breeding; polish, presence, cultivation, culture; civili-ty, -zation; amenity, suavity; good -temper, – humor; amiability, easy temper, complacency, soft tongue, mansuetude; condescension etc. (*humility*) 879; affability, complaisance, *prévenance*, amiability, gallantry, chivalry; pink of -politeness, – courtesy.

compliment; fair –, soft –, sweet- words; honeyed phrases, flattering remarks, ceremonial; salutation, reception, presentation, introduction, *accueil*, greeting, recognition; welcome, *abord*, respects, *devoir*, regards, remembrances; kind -regards, – remembrances; love, best love, duty; deference.

obeisance etc. (*reverence*) 928; bow, courtesy, curtsy, scrape, *salaam*, *kow-tow*, bowing and scraping; kneeling; genuflexion etc. (*worship*) 990; obsequiousness etc. 886; capping, shaking hands etc. *v.*; grip of the hand, embrace, hug, squeeze, *accolade*, loving cup, *vin d'honneur*, pledge; love token etc. (*endearment*) 902; kiss, buss, salute.

mark of recognition, not; 'nods and becks and wreathed smiles;' valediction etc. 293; condolence etc. 915.

V. be -courteous etc. *adj.*; show -courtesy etc. *n.*

mind one's P's and Q's, behave oneself, be all things to all men, conciliate, speak one fair, take in good part; make –, do- the amiable; look as if butter would not melt in one's mouth; mend one's manners.

receive, do the honors, usher, greet, hail, bid welcome; welcome, – with open arms; shake hands; hold out –, press –, squeeze- the hand; bid God speed; speed the parting guest; cheer, serenade.

salute; embrace etc. (*endearment*) 902; kiss, – hands; drink to, pledge, hob and nob; move to, nod to; smile upon.

uncover, cap; touch –, take off- the hat; doff the cap; pull the forelock; present arms; make way for; bow; make one's bow; scrape, curtsy, courtesy; bob a -curtsy, – courtesy; kneel; bow –, bend- the knee; salaam, *kowtow*.

visit, wait upon, present oneself, pay one's respects, pay a visit etc. (*sociability*) 892; dance attendance on etc. (*servility*) 886; pay attentions to; do homage to etc. (*respect*) 928.

prostrate oneself etc. (*worship*) 990.

give –, send- one's duty etc. *n.* to.

render -polite etc. *adj.*; polish, civilize, humanize.

Adj. courteous, polite, civil, mannerly, urbane; well-behaved, -mannered, -bred, -brought up, gently bred, of gentle -breeding, – manners, good-mannered, polished, civilized, cultivated; refined etc. (*taste*) 850; gentlemanlike etc. (*fashion*) 852; gallant, chivalrous, on one's good behavior.

fine –, fair –, soft- spoken; honey-mouthed, -tongued; oily, unctuous, bland, suave; obliging, conciliatory, complaisant, complacent; obsequious etc. 886.

ingratiating, winning; gentle, mild; good-humored, cordial, gracious, amiable, tactful, addressful, affable, genial, friendly, familiar; neighborly.

Adv. courteously etc. *adj.*; with a good grace; with -open, – outstretched- arms; *à bras ouverts*; *suaviter in modo*, in good humor.

Int. hail! welcome! well met! *ave!* all hail! good -day, – morning etc., – morrow! God speed! *pax vobiscum!* may your shadow never be less! *chin-chin!*

895. Discourtesy.—N. discourtesy; ill-breeding; ill –, bad –, ungainly- manners; insuavity; grouchiness; un-courteousness etc. *adj.*, tactlessness; rusticity, inurbanity; illiberality, incivility, displacency.

disrespect etc. 929; procacity, impudence; barbar-ism, -ity; misbehavior, brutality, blackguard-ism, conduct unbecoming a gentleman, *grossièreté*, *brusquerie*; vulgarity etc. 851.

churlishness etc. *adj.*; spinosity, perversity; moroseness etc. (*sullenness*) 901*a*.

bad-, ill-temper; sternness etc. *adj.*; austerity; moodishness, captiousness etc. 901; cynicism; tartness etc. *adj.*; acrimony, acerbity, virulence, asperity.

scowl, black looks, frown; short answer, rebuff; hard words, contumely; unparliamentary language, personality.

bear, bruin, brute, grouch, blackguard, beast; unlicked cub; frump, cross-patch; saucebox etc. 887.

V. be -rude etc. *adj.*; insult etc. 929; treat with discourtesy; take a name in vain; make -bold, – free- with; take a liberty; stare out of countenance, ogle, point at, put to the blush.

cut; turn -one's back upon, – on one's heel; give the cold shoulder; keep at -a distance, – arm's length; look -cool, – coldly, – black- upon; show the door to, send away with a flea in the ear.

lose one's temper etc. (*resentment*) 900; sulk etc. 901*a*; frown, scowl, glower, pout; snap, snarl, growl.

render -rude etc. *adj.*; brut-alize, -ify.

Adj. dis-, un-courteous; uncourtly; ill-bred, -mannered, -behaved, -conditioned; unbred; unmanner-ly, -ed; im-, un-polite; un-polished, -civilized, -genteel; ungentleman-like, -ly; unladylike; blackguard; vulgar etc. 851; dedecorous; foul-mouthed, -spoken; abusive.

un-civil, -gracious, -ceremonious; cool; pert, forward, obtrusive, impudent, rude, saucy, precocious; insolent etc. 885.

repulsive; un-complaisant, -accommodating, -neighborly, -gallant; inaffable; un-gentle, -gainly; rough, rugged, bluff, blunt, gruff; churl-, boor-, bear-ish; brutal, *brusque*; stern, harsh, austere; cavalier.

tart, sour, crabbed, sharp, short, trenchant, sarcastic, crusty, biting, caustic, virulent, bitter, acrimonious, venomous, contumelious; snarling etc., *v.*; surly, – as a bear; perverse; grim, sullen etc. 901*a*; peevish etc. (*irascible*) 901.

Adv. discourteously etc. *adj.*; with -discourtesy etc. *n.*, – a bad grace.

896. Congratulations.—N. con-, gratulation; felicitation; salute etc. 894; condolence etc. 915; compliments of the season; good –, best- wishes.

V. con-, gratulate; felicitate, compliment; give –, wish one- joy; tender –, offer- one's congratulations; wish -many happy returns of the day, – a merry Christmas and a happy new year.

congratulate oneself etc. (*rejoice*) 838.

Adj. con-, gratulatory.

897. Love.—N. love; fondness etc. *adj.*; liking; inclination etc. (*desire*) 865; regard, dilection, admiration, fancy.

affection, sympathy, fellow-felling; tenderness etc. *adj.*; heart, brotherly love; benevolence etc. 906; attachment.

yearning, tender passion, *affaire de coeur*, *amour*, gallantry, passion, flame, devotion, fervor, enthusiasm, transport of love, rapture, enchantment, infatuation, adoration, idolatry.

narcissism, Oedipus complex, Electra complex.

Cupid, Venus, Eros; myrtle; true lover's knot; love -token, – suit, – affair, – tale, – story; the old story, plighted love; courtship etc. 902; *amourette*.

maternal love.

attractiveness, charm; popularity; favorite etc. 899.

lover, suitor, follower, admirer, adorer, wooer, amoret, beau, sweetheart, inamorato, swain, young man, flame, love, truelove; leman, Lothario, gallant, paramor, *amoroso*, *cavaliere servente*, captive, *cicisbeo*; *caro sposo*, Don Juan, sheik, ladies' man, squire of dames, Knave of Hearts.

inamorata, lady-love, idol, darling, duck, Dulcinea, angel, goddess, *cara sposa*; mistress.

betrothed, affianced, *fiancée*.

flirt, *coquette*; amorette; pair of turtle doves; abode of love, *agapemone*.

V. love, like, affect, fancy, care for, take an interest in, be partial to, sympathize with; be -in love etc. *adj.*- with; have –, entertain –, harbor –, cherish- a -love etc. *n.* for; regard, revere; take to, bear love to, be wedded to; set one's affections on; make much of, feast one's eyes on; hold dear, prize, treasure; hug, cling to, cherish, pet, caress etc. 902.

burn; adore, idolize, love to distraction, *aimer eperdument*; dote -on, – upon.

take a fancy to, fall for, be stuck on, look sweet upon; become -enamored etc. *adj.*; fall in love with, lose one's heart; desire etc. 865.

excite love; win –, gain –, secure –, engage- the -love, – affections, – heart; take the fancy of; have a place in –, wind round- the heart; attract, attach, endear, charm, fascinate, captivate, bewitch, seduce, enamor, enrapture, turn the head.

get into favor; ingratiate –, insinuate –, worm- oneself; propitiate, curry favor with, pay one's court to, make a date with, *faire l'aimable*, set one's cap at, flirt, coquet.

Adv. loving etc. *v.*; fond of; taken –, struck- with; smitten, bitten; attached to, wedded to; enamored; charmed etc. *v.*; in love; lovesick; over head and ears in love.

affectionate, tender, sweet upon, sympathetic, loving, fond, amorous, amatory; erotic, uxurious, ardent, passionate, rapturous, devoted, motherly.

loved etc. *v.*; beloved; well –, dearly- beloved; dear, precious, darling, pet, little; favorite, popular.

congenial; to –, after- one's -mind, – taste, – fancy, – own heart.

in one's good -graces etc. (*friendly*) 888; dear as the apple of one's eye, nearest to one's heart.

lovable, adorable; lovely, sweet; attractive, seductive, winning; charming, engaging, interesting, enchanting, captivating, fascinating, intriguing, bewitching; amiable, like an angel, angelic, seraphic.

898. Hate.—N. hate, hatred, vials of hate; Hymn of Hate.

dis-affection, -favor; alienation, estrangement, coolness; enmity etc. 889; animosity etc. 900.

umbrage, pique, grudge; dudgeon, spleen; bitterness, – of feeling; ill –, bad- blood; acrimony; malice etc. 907; implacability etc. (*revenge*) 919.

repugnance etc. (*dislike*) 867; odium, unpopularity; loathing, detestation, antipathy; object of -hatred, – execration; abomination, aversion, *bête noire*; enemy etc. 891; bitter pill; source of annoyance etc. 830.

V. hate, detest, abominate, abhor, loathe; recoil –, shudder- at; shrink from, view with horror, hold in abomination, revolt against, execrate; scowl etc. 895; disrelish etc. (*dislike*) 867.

owe a grudge; bear -spleen, – a grudge, – malice etc. (*malevolence*) 907; conceive an aversion to.

excite –, provoke- hatred etc. *n.*; be -hateful etc. *adj.*; stink in the nostrils; estrange, alienate, repel, set against, sow dissension, set by the ears, envenom, incense, irritate, rile, ruffle, vex; horrify etc. 830.

Adj. hating etc. *v.*; abhorrent; averse from etc. (*disliking*) 867; set against.

bitter etc. (*acrimonious*) 895; implacable etc. (*revengeful*) 919.

un-loved, -beloved, -lamented, -deplored, -mourned, -cared for, -endured, -valued; disliked etc. 867.

crossed in love, forsaken, rejected, love-lorn, jilted.

obnoxious, hateful, odious, abominable, repulsive, offensive, shocking; disgusting etc. (*disagreeable*) 830.

invidious, spiteful; malicious etc. 907.

insulting, irritating, provoking.

[Mutual hate] at -daggers drawn, – swords points; not on speaking terms etc. (*enmity*) 889.

Phr. no love lost between.

899. Favorite.—N. favorite, pet, cosset, minion, idol, jewel, spoiled child, *enfant gâté*; led captain; crony; fondling; apple of one's eye, man after one's own heart; *persona grata*.

love, dear, darling, duck, honey, jewel; mopsey, moppet; sweetheart etc. (*love*) 897.

general –, universal- favorite; idol of the people; matinée idol, movie –, radio- star.

900. Resentment.—N. resentment, displeasure, animosity, anger, wrath, indignation; vexation, exasperation, bitter resentment, wrathful indignation.

pique, umbrage, huff, miff, soreness, dudgeon, acerbity, virulence, bitterness, acrimony, asperity, spleen, gall; heart-burning, -swelling; rankling.

ill –, bad- -humor, – temper; irascibility etc. 901; ill blood etc. (*hate*) 898; revenge etc. 919.

excitement, irritation; warmth, bile, choler, ire, fume, pucker, dander, ferment, ebullition; towering -passion, – rage, *acharnement*, angry mood, taking, pet, tiff, passion, fit, tantrums.

burst, explosion, paroxysm, storm, rage, fury, desperation; violence etc. 173; fire and fury; vials of wrath; gnashing of teeth, hot blood, high words.

scowl etc. 895; sulks etc. 901*a*.

[Cause of umbrage] affront, provocation, offence; indignity etc. (*insult*) 929; grudge, crow to pluck, sore subject; red rag to a bull; *casus belli.*

Furies, Erinys, Eumenides, Alecto, Megaera, Tisiphone.

buffet, slap in the face, box on the ear, rap on the knuckles.

V. resent; take -amiss, – ill, – to heart, – offence, – umbrage, – huff, – exception; take in -ill part, – bad part, – dudgeon; *ne pas entendre raillerie*; breathe revenge, cut up rough.

fly –, fall –, get- into a -rage, – passion; bridle –, bristle –, froth –, fire –, flare- up; open –, pour out- the vials of one's wrath.

pout, knit the brow, frown, scowl, lower, snarl, growl, gnarl, gnash, snap; redden, color; look -black, – black as thunder, – daggers; bite one's thumb; show –, grind- one's teeth; champ the bit.

chafe, mantle, fume, kindle, fly out, take fire; boil, – over; boil with -indignation, – rage; rage, storm, foam; vent one's -rage, – spleen; lose one's temper, stand on one's hind legs, stamp the foot, kick up a row, fly off the handle, cut up rough; stamp –, quiver –, swell –, foam- with rage; burst with anger; raise Cain, breathe fire and fury.

have a fling at; bear malice etc. (*revenge*) 919.

cause –, raise- anger; affront, offend; give -offence, – umbrage; anger; hurt the feelings; insult, discompose, fret, ruffle, nettle, heckle, huff, pique; excite etc. 824; irritate, stir the blood, stir up bile; sting, – to the quick; rile, provoke, chafe, wound, incense, inflame, enrage, aggravate, add fuel to the flame, fan into a flame, widen the breach, envenom, embitter, exasperate, infuriate, kindle wrath; stick in one's gizzard; rankle etc. 919.

put out of humor; put one's -monkey, – back-up; set –, get- one's back up; raise one's -gorge, – dander, – choler; work up into a passion; make -one's blood boil, – the ears tingle; throw into a ferment, madden, drive one mad; lash into -fury, – madness; fool to the top of one's bent; set by the ears.

bring a hornet's nest about one's ears.

Adj. angry, wrath, irate; ire-, wrath-ful; cross etc. (*irascible*) 901; sulky etc. 901*a*; bitter, virulent; acrimonious etc. (*discourteous*) etc. 895; violent etc. 173.

warm, burning; boiling, – over; fuming, raging; foaming, – at the mouth; convulsed with rage.

offended etc. *v.*; waxy, *acharné*; wrought, worked up; indignant, hurt, sore, peeved; set against.

fierce, wild, rageful, furious, mad with rage, fiery, infuriate, rabid, savage; relentless etc. 919.

flushed with -anger, – rage; in a -huff, – stew, – fume, – pucker, – passion, – rage, – fury; on one's high ropes, up in arms; in high dudgeon.

Adv. angrily etc. *adj.*; in the height of passion; in the heat of -passion, – the moment.

Phr. one's -blood, – back, – monkey- being up; *fervens difficili bile jecur*; the gorge rising, eyes flashing fire; the blood -rising, – boiling; *haeret lateri lethalis arundo*.

901. Irascibility.—N. irascibility, temper; crossness etc. *adj.*; susceptibility, procacity, petulance, irritability, tartness, acerbity, protervity; pugnacity etc. (*contentiousness*) 720.

excitability etc. 825; bad –, fiery –, crooked –, irritable etc. *adj.*- temper; *genus irritabile*, hot blood.

ill humor etc. (*sullenness*) 901*a*; asperity etc., churlishness etc. (*discourtesy*) 895.

huff etc. (resentment) 900; a word and a blow.

Sir Fretful Plagiary; brabbler, Tartar; shrew, vixen, virago, termagant, dragon, scold, Xanthippe; porcupine; spit-fire; fire-eater etc. (*blusterer*) 887; fury etc. (*violent person*) 173.

V. be -irascible etc. *adj.*; have a -temper etc. *n.*, – devil in one; fire up etc. (*be angry*) 900.

Adj. irascible; bad-, ill-tempered; irritable, susceptible; excitable etc. 825; thin-skinned etc. (*sensitive*) 822; fretful, fidgety; on the fret.

hasty, over-hasty, quick, warm, hot, testy, touchy, techy, tetchy; like -touchwood, – tinder; huffy; pet-tish, -ulant; waspish, snapp-y, -ish, peppery, fiery, passionate, choleric, shrewish, 'sudden and quick in quarrel.'

querulous, captious, mood-y, -ish; quarrelsome, contentious, disputatious; pugnacious etc. (*bellicose*) 720; cantankerous, exceptious; restive etc. (*perverse*) 901*a*; churlish etc. (*discourteous*) 895.

cross, – as -crabs, – two sticks, – a cat, – a dog, – the tongs; like a bear with a sore head; fractious, peevish, *acariâtre*.

in a bad temper; sulky etc. 901*a*; angry etc. 900.

resent-ful, -ive; vindictive etc. 919.

Int. pish!

901a. Sullenness.—N. sullenness etc. *adj.*; morosity, spleen; churlishness etc. (*discourtesy*) 895; irascibility etc. 901.

moodiness etc. *adj.*; perversity; obstinacy etc. 606; torvity, spinosity; crabbedness etc. *adj.*

ill –, bad- -temper, – humor; sulks, dudgeon, mumps, doleful dumps, doldrums, fit of the sulks, *bouderie*, black looks, scowl; huff etc. (*resentment*) 900.

V. be -sullen etc. *adj.*; sulk; frown, scowl, lower, glower, grouse, grouch, crab, gloam, pout, have a hang-dog look, glout.

Adj. sullen, sulky; ill-tempered, -humored, -affected, -disposed; in -an ill, – a bad, – a shocking- -temper, – humor; out of -temper, – humor; knaggy, torvous, crusty, crabbed; sore as a boil; surly etc. (*discourteous*) 895.

moody; spleen-ish, -ly; splenetic, cankered.

cross, -grained; perverse, wayward, humorsome; restive; cantankerous, refractory, intractable, exceptious, sinistrous, deaf to reason, unaccommodating, rusty, crust, froward.

dogged etc. (*stubborn*) 606.

grumpy, glum, grim, grum, morose, frumpish; in the -sulks etc. *n.*; out of sorts; scowl-, glower-, growl-ing.

peevish etc. (*irascible*) 901.

902. Endearment. [Expression of affection or love.]—**N.** endearment, caress; blandish-, blandiment; *épanchement*, fondling, billing and cooing, dalliance.

embrace, salute, kiss, buss, smack, osculation,

deosculation; amorous glances; ogle, side glance, sheep's eyes.

courtship, wooing, suit, addresses, the soft impeachment; love-making; an affair; serenading; caterwauling.

flirting etc. *v.*; flirtation, gallantry; coquetry, spooning.

ture lover's knot, plighted love, engagement, bethrothal; love -tale, – token, – letter; *billet-doux*, valentine.

honeymoon; Strephon and Chloe, 'Arry and 'Arriet.

V. caress, fondle, pet, dandle, nurse; pat, – on the -head, – cheek; chuck under the chin, smile upon, coax, wheedle, cosset, coddle, cocker; make -of, – much of, pamper; cherish, foster, kill with kindness.

clasp, hug, cuddle; fold –, strain- in one's arms; nestle, nuzzle, neck, embrace, kiss, buss, smack, blow a kiss; salute etc. (*courtesy*) 894.

bill and coo, spoon, toy, dally, flirt, coquet; galli-, gala-vant; philander; make love; pay one's -court, – addresses, – attentions- to; serenade; court, woo; set one's cap at; be –, look- sweet upon; ogle, cast sheep's eyes upon; *faire les yeux doux*.

fall in love with, win the affections etc. (*love*) 897; die for.

propose; make –, have- an offer; pop the question; plight one's -troth, – faith; become -engaged, – betrothed.

Adj. caressing etc. *v.*; 'sighing like furnace;' love-sick, spoony.

carressed etc. *v.*

903. Marriage.—N. marriage, matrimony, wedlock, union, intermarriage, *vinculum matrimonii*, nuptial tie, knot.

married state, coverture, bed, cohabitation.

match; betrothment etc. (*promise*) 768; wedding, nuptials, Hymen, bridal; e-, spousals; leading to the altar etc. *v.*; nuptial benediction, *epithalamium*,

torch –, temple- of Hymen; hymeneal altar; honeymoon.

bride, bridegroom; brides-maid; -man.

best –, grooms-man, page, usher.

married -man, – woman, – couple; neogamist, Benedick, partner, spouse, mate, yokemate; husband, man, consort, baron; old –, good- man; wife of one's bosom; help-meet, -mate, rib, better half, grey mare, old woman, good wife; feme, – coverte; squaw, lady; matron, -age, -hood; man and wife; wedded pair, Darby and Joan.

affinity, soul-mate.

mono-, bi-, di-, deutero-, tri-, poly-gamy; mormonism; poly-andry; Turk, Bluebeard.

unlawful –, left-handed –, companionate –, morganatic –, ill-assorted- marriage; *mésalliance*; *mariage de convenance*; an affair.

match-maker, marriage broker, matrimonial agent.

V. marry, wive, take to oneself a wife; be -married, – spliced; go –, pair- off; wed, espouse, lead to the hymeneal altar, take 'for better, for worse,' give one's hand to, bestow one's hand upon; remarry; intermarry.

marry, join, handfast; couple etc. (*unite*) 43; tie the nuptial knot; give -away, – in marriage; affy, affiance; betroth etc. (*promise*) 768; publish –, bid- the banns; be asked in church.

Adj. married etc. *v.*; one, – bone and one flesh.

marriageable, nubile.

engaged, betrothed, affianced.

matrimonial, marital, conjugal, connubial, wedded; nuptial, hymeneal, spousal, bridal.

Phr. the gray mare the better horse.

904. Celibacy.—N. celibacy, singleness, single blessedness; bachelor-hood, -ship; miso-gamy, -gyny.

virginity, *pueelage*; maiden-hood, -head.

unmarried man, bachelor, agamist, old bachelor; miso-gamist, -gynist; celibate.

unmarried woman, spinster; maid, -en; virgin, *feme sole*, old maid; bachelor girl; nun etc.

V. live single; keep bachelor hall.

Adj. un-married, -wedded; wife-, spouse-less; single, virgin, celibate.

905. Divorce.—N. divorce, -ment; separation; judicial separation, separate maintenance; *separatio a -mensâ et thoro*, – *vinculo matrimonii*.

widowhood, viduage, viduity, weeds.

widow, -er; relict; dowager; *divorcée*; cuckold.

V. live -separately, – apart; separate, divorce, disespouse, put away; wear the horns.

906. Benevolence.—N. benevolence, Christian charity; God's -love, – grace; good-will; philanthropy etc. 910; unselfishness etc. 942.

good -nature, – feeling, – wishes; kind-, kindliness etc. *adj.*; lovingkindness, benignity, brotherly love, charity, humanity, fellow-feeling, sympathy; goodness –, warmth- of heart; *bon-homie*; kind-heartedness; amiability, milk of human kindness, tenderness; love etc. 897; friendship etc. 888.

toleration, consideration, generosity; mercy etc. (*pity*) 914.

charitableness etc. *adj.*; bounty, alms-giving; good works, beneficence, the luxury of doing good.

acts of kindness, a good turn; good –, kind- -offices, – treatment.

good Samaritan, sympathizer, well-wisher, philanthropist, *bon enfant*; altruist.

V. be -benevolent etc. *adj.*; have one's heart in the right place, bear good will; wish -well, – God speed; view –, regard- with an eye of favor; take in good part; take –, feel- an interest in; be –, feel-interested- in; sympathize with, feel for; fraternize etc. (*be friendly*) 888.

enter into the feelings of others, do as you would be done by, meet halfway.

treat well; give comfort, smooth the bed of death; do -good, – a good turn; benefit etc. (*goodness*) 648; render a service, be of use; aid etc. 707.

Adj. benevolent; kind, -ly; wellmeaning; amiable; obliging, accommodating, indulgent, considerate, gracious, complacent, good-humored.

warm-, soft-, kind-, tender-, large-, broad-hearted; merciful etc. 914; philanthropic etc. 910; charitable, beneficent, humane, benign, benignant; bount-eous, -iful etc. 816.

good-, well-natured; spleenless; sympath-izing, -etic; complaisant etc. (*courteous*) 894; kindly, well-meant, -intentioned.

fatherly, motherly, brotherly, sisterly; pat-, mat-, frat-ernal; friendly etc. 888.

Adv. with -a good intention, – the best intentions.

Int. God speed! much good may it do!

907. Malevolence.—N. malevolence; bad intent, -ion; un-, dis-kindness; ill -nature, – will, – blood; bad blood; enmity etc. 889; hate etc. 898; malignity; malice, – aforethought, – prepense; maliciousness etc. *adj.*; spite, despite; resentment etc. 900.

uncharitableness etc. *adj.*; incompassionateness etc. 914*a*; gall, venom, rancor, rankling, virulence, mordacity, acerbity; churlishness etc. (*discourtesy*) 895.

hardness of heart, heart of stone, obduracy; cruelty; cruelness etc. *adj.*; brutality, savagery; ferity, -ocity; barbarity, inhumanity, immanity, truculence, ruffianism; evil eye, cloven -foot, – hoof; Inquisition; torture.

ill –, bad- turn; affront etc. (*disrespect*) 929; outrage, atrocity; ill usage; intolerance, bigotry, persecution; tender mercies [ironical]; 'unkindest cut of all.'

V. be -malevolent etc. *adj.*; bear –, harbor- -spleen, – a grudge, – malice; betray –, show- the cloven foot.

hurt etc. (*physical pain*) 378; annoy etc. 830; injure, harm, wrong; do -harm, – an ill office- to; outrage; disoblige, malign, plant a thorn in the breast.

molest, worry, harass, haunt, harry, bait, tease, throw stones at; play the devil with; hunt down, dragoon, hound; persecute, oppress, grind; maltreat; ill-treat, -use.

wreak one's malice on, do one's worst, break a butterfly on the wheel; dip –, imbrue- one's hands in blood; have no mercy etc. 914*a*.

Adj. male-, unbene-volent; unbenign; ill-disposed, -intentioned, -natured, -conditioned, -contrived; evil-minded, -disposed.

malicious; malign, -ant; rancorous; de-, spiteful; mordacious, caustic, bitter, envenomed, acrimonious, virulent; un-amiable, -charitable; maleficent, venomous, grinding, galling.

harsh, disobliging; un-kind, -friendly, -gracious; treacherous; inofficious; invidious; uncandid; churlish etc. (*uncourteous*) 895; surly, sullen etc. 901*a*.

cold, -blooded, -hearted; hard-, flint-, marble-, stony-hearted; hard of heart, unnatural; ruthless etc. (*unmerciful*) 914*a*; relentless etc. (*revengeful*) 919.

cruel; brut-al, -ish; savage, – as a -bear, – tiger; ferine, feral, ferocious; inhuman; barbarous, fell, untamed, tameless, truculent, incendiary; bloodthirsty etc. (*murderous*) 361; atrocious.

fiend-ish, -like; demoniacal; diabolic, -al; devilish, infernal, hellish, Satanic.

Adv. malevolently etc. *adj.*; with -bad intent etc. *n*.

908. Malediction.—N. malediction, malison, curse, imprecation, denunciation, execration, anathema, ban, proscription, excommunication, commination, thunders of the Vatican, fulmination, *maranatha*, aspersion, vilification, vituperation, scurrility.

abuse; foul –, bad –, strong –, unparliamentary- language, Limehouse; Billingsgate, sauce, evil speaking; cursing etc. *v.*; profane swearing, oath.

threat etc. 909; more bark than bite; invective etc. (*disapprobation*) 932.

V. curse, accurse, imprecate, damn, swear at; slang; curse with bell, book and candle; invoke –, call down- curses on the head of; devote to destruction.

execrate, beshrew, scold; anathematize etc. (*censure*) 932; hold up to execration, denounce, proscribe, excommunicate, fulminate, thunder against; threaten etc. 909; curse up hill and down dale.

curse and swear; swear, – like a trooper; fall a cursing, rap out an oath, damn, cuss.

Adj. curs-ing, -ed etc. *v.*; maledictory.

Int. woe to! beshrew! *ruat coelum!* ill –, woe-betide! confusion seize! damn! confound! blast! curse! devil take! hang! out with! a plague –, out-upon! aroynt! *honi soit!*

Phr. *delenda est Carthago.*

909. Threat.—N. threat, menace; defiance etc. 715; abuse, minacity, intimidation; fulmination; commination etc. (*curse*) 908; gathering clouds etc. (*warning*) 668.

V. threat, -en; menace; snarl, growl, gnarl, mutter, bark, bully.

defy etc. 715; intimidate etc. 860; keep –, hold up –, hold out- *in terrorem*; shake –, double –, clinch- the fist at; thunder, talk big, fulminate, use big words, bluster, look daggers.

Adj. threatening, menacing; mina-tory, -cious; comminatory, abusive; *in terrorem*; ominous etc. (*predicting*) 511; defiant etc. 715; under the ban.

Int. *vae victis!* at your peril! do your worst!

910. Philanthropy.—N. philanthropy; altruism, humanit-y, -arianism; universal benevolence; *deliciae humani generis;* cosmopolitanism, utilitarianism, the greatest happiness of the greatest number, social science, sociology.

common weal, public welfare, socialism, communism.

patriotism, civism, nationality, love of country, *amor patriae*, public spirit.

chivalry, knight errantry; generosity etc. 942.

philanthropist, altruist etc. 906; utilitarian, Benthamite, socialist, communist, cosmopolite, citizen of the world, *amicus humani generis*; knight errant; patriot.

Adj. philanthropic, altruistic, humanitarian, utilitarian, cosmopolitan; public-spirited, patriotic; humane, large-hearted etc. (*benevolent*) 906; chival-ric, -rous, generous etc. 942.

Adv. *pro -bono publico*, – *aris et focis*.

Phr. *'humani nihil a me alienum puto.'*

911. Misanthropy.—N. misanthropy, incivism; egotism etc. (*selfishness*) 943; moroseness etc. 901*a*; cynicism; defeatism.

misanthrope, misanthropist, egotist, cynic, man-hater, Timon, Diogenes.
woman-hater, misogynist.
Adj. misanthropic, antisocial, unpatriotic; egotistical etc. (*selfish*) 943; morose etc. 901*a*.

912. Benefactor.—N. benefactor, savior, good genius, tutelary saint, patron, guardian angel, fairy godmother, good Samaritan; *pater patriae*; salt of the earth etc. (*good man*) 948; auxiliary etc. 711.

913. Evil-doer. [*Maleficent being.*]**—N.** evil--doer, – worker; wrong doer etc. 949; mischief maker, marplot; oppressor, tyrant; firebrand, incendiary, pyromaniac, anarchist, destroyer, Hun, *Boche*, Vandal, iconoclast; communist; terrorist, *apache*, gunman, gangster, racketeer.
savage, brute, ruffian, barbarian, semi-barbarian, caitiff, desperado; Mo-hock, -hawk; bludgeon man, bully, rough, hooligan, larrikin, dangerous classes, ugly customer; thief etc. 792.
cockatrice, scorpion, hornet; viper, adder; snake, – in the grass; serpent, cobra, asp, rattlesnake, anaconda; canker-, wire-worm; locust, Colorado beetle; torpedo; bane etc. 663.
cannibal; Anthropophag-us, -ist; bloodsucker, vampire, ogre, ghoul, gorilla; vulture; gyr-, gerfalcon.
wild beast, tiger, hyaena, butcher, hangman; cut-throat etc. (*killer*) 361; blood-, sleuth-, hell-hound.
hag, hellhag, beldam, Jezebel.
monster; fiend etc. (*demon*) 980; homicidal maniac, devil incarnate, demon in human shape; Frankenstein's monster.
harpy, siren, vampire; Furies, Eumenides etc. 900.
Attila, scourge of the human race.
Phr. *foenum habet in cornu.*

914. Pity.—N. pity, compassion, commiseration; bowels, – of compassion; condolence etc. 915; sympathy, fellow-feeling, tenderness, yearning, forbearance, humanity, mercy, clemency, exorability; leniency etc. (*lenity*) 740; charity, ruth, long-suffering.
melting mood; ***argumentum ad misericordiam***; quarter, grace, ***locus poenitentiae***.
sympathizer, champion, partisan.
V. pity; have –, show –, take- pity etc. *n.*; commiserate, compassionate; condole etc. 915; sympathize; feel –, be sorry –, yearn- for; weep, melt, thaw, enter into the feelings of.
forbear, relent, relax, give quarter, wipe the tears, *parcere subjectis*, give a *coup de grâce*, put out of one's misery; be cruel to be kind.
raise –, excite- pity etc. *n.*; touch, soften; melt, – the heart; appeal to one's better feelings; propitiate, disarm.
ask for -mercy etc. *n.*; supplicate etc. (*request*) 765; cry for quarter, beg one's life, kneel; deprecate.
Adj. pitying etc. *v.*; pitiful, compassionate, sympathetic, touched.
merciful, clement, ruthful; humane; humanitarian etc. (*philanthropic*) 910; tender, – hearted, – as a chicken; soft, – hearted; unhardened; lenient etc. 740; exorable, forbearing; melting etc. *v.*; weak.
Int. for pity's sake! mercy! have –, cry you-mercy! God help you! poor -thing, – dear, – fellow! woe betide! ***quis talia fando temperet a lachrymis!***
Phr. one's heart bleeding for; ***haud ignara mali miseris succurrere disco.***

914a. Pitilessness.—N. pitilessness etc. *adj.*; inclemency; inexorability, hardness of heart; inflexibility; severity etc. 739; malevolence etc. 907.
V. have no –, shut the gates of- mercy etc. 914; give no quarter.
Adj. piti-, merci-, ruth-, bowel-less; unpitying, unmerciful, inclement; in-, un-compassionate; inexorable, inflexible; harsh etc. 739; cruel etc. 907; unrelenting etc. 919.

915. Condolence.—N. condolence; lamentation etc. 839; sympathy, consolation.
V. condole with, console, sympathize etc. 914; share one's misery; feel for; express –, testify- pity; afford –, supply- consolation; lament etc. 839-with; send one's condolences.

916. Gratitude.—N. gratitude, thankfulness, gratefulness, feeling of obligation.
acknowledgement, recognition, thanksgiving, giving thanks.
thanks, praise, benediction; paean; *Te Deum* etc. (*worship*) 990; grace, – before, – after-meat; thank-offering.
requital.
V. be -grateful etc. *adj.*; thank; give –, render –, return –, offer –, tender- thanks etc. *n.*; acknowledge, requite.
feel –, be –, lie- under an obligation; *savoir gré*; not look a gift horse in the mouth; never forget, overflow with gratitude; thank –, bless-one's stars; fall on one's knees.
Adj. grateful, thankful, obliged, beholden, indebted to, under obligation.
Int. thanks! many thanks! gramercy! much obliged! thank you! thank Heaven! Heaven be praised!

917. Ingratitude.—N. ingratitude, thanklessness, oblivion of benefits; unthankfulness.
'benefits forgot;' thankless -task, – office.
V. be -ungrateful etc. *adj.*; forget benefits; look a gift horse in the mouth.
Adj. un-grateful, -mindful, -thankful; thankless, ingrate, wanting in gratitude, insensible of benefits.
forgotten; un-acknowledged, -thanked, -requited, -rewarded; ill-requited.
Int. thank you for nothing! ***'et tu Brute!'***

918. Forgiveness.—N. forgiveness, pardon, condonation, grace, remission, absolution, amnesty, oblivion; indulgence; reprieve.

conciliation; reconciliation etc. (*pacification*) 723; propitiation.

excuse, exoneration, quittance, release, indemnity; bill –, act –, covenant –, deed- of indemnity; exculpation etc. (*acquittal*) 970.

longanimity, placability, forbearance; *amantium irae*; *locus poenitentiae*.

V. forgive, – and forget; pardon, condone, think no more of, let bygones be bygones, shake hands; forget an injury, bury the hatchet; clean the slate.

excuse, pass over, overlook; wink at etc. (*neglect*) 460; bear with; allow –, make allowances- for; let one down easily, not be too hard upon, pocket the affront; blot out one's transgression.

let off, remit, absolve, give absolution, reprieve; acquit etc. 970.

beg –, ask –, implore- pardon etc. *n.*; conciliate, propitiate, placate; make up a quarrel etc. (*pacify*) 723; let the wound heal.

Adj. forgiving, placable, conciliatory.

forgiven etc. *v.*; un-resented, -avenged, revenged.

Adv. cry you mercy.

Phr. *veniam petimusque damusque vicissim*; more in sorrow than in anger.

919. Revenge.—N. revenge, -ment; vengeance; avenge-ment, -ance; sweet revenge, *vendetta*, death-feud, eye for an eye, blood for blood, a Roland for an Oliver; retaliation etc. 718; day of reckoning.

rancor, vindictiveness, implacability; malevolence etc. 907; ruthlessness etc. 914*a*.

avenger, vindicator, Nemesis, Eumenides.

V. re-, a-venge; take –, have one's- revenge; breathe -revenge, – vengeance; wreak one's -vengeance, – anger; give no quarter.

have -accounts to settle, – a crow to pluck, – a rod in pickle; pay off old scores.

keep the wound green; harbor -revenge, – vindictive feeling; bear malice; rankle, – in the breast; have at one's mercy.

Adj. revenge-, venge-ful; vindictive, rancorous; pitiless etc. 914*a*; ruthless, rigorous, avenging, retaliative.

unforgiving, unrelenting; inexorable, stony-hearted, implacable; relent-, remorse-less.

aeternum servans sub pectore vulnus; rankling, immitigable.

Phr. *manet -cicatrix,– altâ mente repostum.* revenge is sweet.

920. Jealousy.—N. jealous-y, -ness; jaundiced eye, heartburning; green-eyed monster; yellows; Juno.

V. be -jealous etc. *adj.*; view with -jealousy, – a jealous eye.

Adj. jealous, – as a Barbary pigeon; jaundiced, yellow-eyed, horn-mad.

921. Envy.—N. envy; enviousness etc. *adj.*; rivalry; *jalousie de métier*.

V. envy, covet, lust after, crave, burst with envy, regard with envious eyes.

Adj. envious, invidious, covetous; *alieni appetens*.

922. Right.—N. right; what -ought to, – should- be; fitness etc. *adj.*; *summum jus*.

justice, equity; equitableness etc. *adj.*; propriety; fair play, impartiality, measure for measure, give and take, *lex talionis*, square deal.

Astraea, Nemesis, Themis.

scales of justice, even-handed justice, retributive justice, *suum cuique*; clear stage –, fair field- and no favor; Queensberry rules.

morals etc. (*duty*) 926; law etc. 963; honor etc. (*probity*) 939; virtue etc. 944.

V. be -right etc. *adj.*; stand to reason.

see -justice done, – one righted, – fair play; do justice to; recompense etc. (*reward*) 973; hold the scales even, give and take; serve one right, put the saddle on the right horse; give -every one, – the devil- his due; *audire alteram partem*.

deserve etc. (*be entitled to*) 924.

Adj. right, good; just, reasonable; fit etc. 924; equ-al, -able, -itable; evenhanded, fair, – and square.

legitimate, justifiable, rightful; as it -should, – ought to- be; lawful etc. (*permitted*) 760, (*legal*) 963.

deserved etc. 924.

Adv. rightly etc. *adj.*; in -justice, – equity, – reason.

without -distinction of, – regard to, – respect to- persons; upon even terms.

Int. all right!

923. Wrong.—N. wrong; what -ought not to, – should not- be; *malum in se*; unreasonableness, grievance; shame.

injustice; unfairness etc. *adj.*; iniquity, foul play, partiality, leaning; favor, -itism; nepotism, party spirit, partisanship; undueness etc. 925; unlawfulness etc. 964.

robbing Peter to pay Paul etc. *v.*; the wolf and the lamb; vice etc. 945.

a custom more honored in the breach than the observance.

V. be -wrong etc. *adj.*; cry to heaven for vengeance.

do -wrong etc. *n.*; be -inequitable etc. *adj.*; favor, lean towards; encroach; impose upon; reap where one has not sown; give an inch and take an ell; rob Peter to pay Paul.

Adj. wrong, -ful; bad, too bad; unjust, -fair; in-, un-equitable; unequal, partial, one-sided.

objectionable; un-reasonable, -allowable, -warrantable, -justifiable; not cricket, not playing the game; improper, unfit; unjustified etc. 925; illegal etc. 964; iniquitous, criminal; immoral etc. 945; injurious etc. 649.

in the wrong, – box.

Adv. wrongly etc. *adj*.

Phr. it will not do; this is too bad.

924. Dueness.—N. due, -ness; right, privilege, prerogative, prescription, title, claim, pretension, demand, birthright.

immunity, license, liberty, franchise; vested - interest, – right; licitness.

sanction, authority, warranty, charter; warrant etc. (*permission*) 760; constitution etc. (*law*) 963; tenure; bond etc. (*security*) 771.

deserts, merits, dues.

claimant, appellant; plaintiff etc. 938.

V. be -due etc. *adj.* to, – the due etc. *n.* of; have -right, – title, – claim- to; be entitled to; have a claim upon; belong to etc. (*property*) 780.

deserve, merit, be worthy of, richly deserve.

demand, claim; call upon –, come upon –, appeal to- for; re-vendicate, -claim; exact; insist -on, – upon; challenge; take one's stand, make a point of, require, lay claim to, assert, assume, arrogate, make good; substantiate; vindicate a -claim, – right; make out a case.

give –, confer- a right; sanction, entitle; authorize etc. 760; sanctify, legalize, ordain, prescribe, allot.

give every one his due etc. 922; pay one's dues; have one's -due, – rights; stand upon one's rights.

use a right, assert, enforce, put in force, lay under contribution.

Adj. having a right to etc. *v.*; entitled to; claiming; deserving, meriting, worthy of.

privileged, allowed, sanctioned, warranted, authorized; ordained, prescribed, constitutional, chartered, enfranchised.

prescriptive, presumptive; absolute, indefeasible; un-, in-alienable.

imprescriptible, inviolable, unimpeachable, unchallenged; sacrosanct.

due to, merited, deserved, condign, richly deserved, *emeritus*.

allowable etc. (*permitted*) 760; lawful, licit, legitimate, legal; legalized etc. (*law*) 963.

square, unexceptionable, right; equitable etc. 922; due, *en règle*; fit, -ting; correct, proper, meet, befitting, becoming, seemly; decorous; creditable, up to the mark, right as a trivet; just –, quite- the thing; *selon les règles*.

Adv. duly, *ex officio*, *de jure*; by -right, – divine right; as is -fitting, – proper, – fitting and proper; *jure divino*, *Dei gratiâ*, in the name of.

Phr. *civis Romanus sum*.

925. Undueness. [Absence of right.]—**N.** undueness etc. *adj.*; *malum prohibitum*; impropriety; illegality etc. 964.

falseness etc. *adj.*; emptiness –, invalidity- of title; illegitimacy.

loss of right, disfranchisement, forfeiture.

usurpation, assumption, tort, violation, breach, encroachment, presumption, seizure, stretch, exaction, imposition, lion's share.

usurper, pretender, Carlist; imposter.

V. be -undue etc. *adj.*; not be -due etc. 924.

infringe, encroach, trench on, exact; arrogate, – to oneself; give an inch and take an ell; stretch –, strain- a point; usurp, violate, do violence to; sail under false colors.

dis-franchise, -entitle, -qualify; invalidate.

relax etc. (*be lax*) 738; misbehave etc. (*vice*) 945; misbecome.

Adj. undue; unlawful etc. (*illegal*) 964; unconstitutional, *ultra vires*; illicit; un-authorized, -warranted, -allowed, -sanctioned, -justified; un-, dis-entitled, -qualified; un-privileged, -chartered.

illegitimate, bastard, spurious, false; usurped, tortious.

un-deserved, -merited, -earned; unfulfilled.

forfeited, disfranchised.

improper; un-meet, -fit, -befitting, -seemly; un-, mis-becoming; seemless; *contra bonos mores*; not the thing, out of the question, not to be thought of; preposterous, pretentious, would- be.

926. Duty.—**N.** duty, what ought to be done, moral obligation, accountableness, liability, *onus*, responsibility; bounden –, imperative- duty; call, – of duty.

allegiance, fealty, tie; engagement etc. (*promise*) 768; part; function, calling etc. (*business*) 625.

morality, morals, decalogue; case of conscience; conscientiousness etc. (*probity*) 939; conscience, inward monitor, still small voice within, sense of duty, tender conscience.

dueness etc. 924; propriety, fitness, seemliness, amenableness, decorum; the -thing, – proper thing; the -right, – proper- thing to do.

[Science of morals] eth-ics, -ology; deon-, aretology; moral –, ethical-philosophy; casuistry, polity.

observance, fulfilment, discharge, performance, acquittal, satisfaction, redemption; good behavior.

V. be -the duty of, – incumbent etc. *adj.* on, – responsible etc. *adj.*; behoove, become, befit, beseem; belong –, pertain- to; fall to one's lot; devolve on; lie -upon, – on one's head, – at one's door; rest -with, – on the shoulders of.

take upon oneself etc. (*promise*) 768.

be –, become- -bound to, – sponsor for; be responsible for; incur a -responsibility etc. *n.*; be –, stand –, lie- under an obligation; have to answer for, owe it to oneself.

impose a -duty etc. *n.*; enjoin, require, exact; bind, – over; saddle with, prescribe, assign, call upon, look to, oblige.

enter upon –, perform –, observe –, fulfil –, discharge –, adhere to –, acquit oneself of –, satisfy- -a duty, – an obligation; act one's part, redeem one's pledge, do justice to, be at one's post; do duty; do one's duty etc. (*be virtuous*) 944.

be on one's good behavior, mind one's P's and Q's.

Adj. obligatory, binding; imperative, peremptory; stringent etc. (*severe*) 739; behooving etc. *v.*; incumbent –, chargeable- on; under obligation; obliged –, bound –, tied- by; saddled with.

due –, beholden –, bound –, indebted- to; tied down; compromised etc. (*promised*) 768; in duty bound.

amenable, liable, accountable, responsible, answerable.

right, meet etc. (*due*) 924; moral, ethical, casuistical, conscientious, ethological.

Adv. with a safe conscience, as in duty bound, on one's own responsibility, at one's own risk, *suo periculo*; *in foro conscientiae*; *quamdiu se bene gesserit*; at one's post, on duty.

Phr. *dura lex sed lex*.

927. Dereliction of Duty.—**N.** dere; liction of duty; fault etc. (*guilt*) 947- sin etc. (*vice*) 945; nonobservance, -performance, -co-operation; neglect, carelessness, laziness, incompetence, eye-service, relaxation, infraction, violation, transgression, failure, evasion, indolence; dead letter.

slacker, loafer, striker, non-co-operator.

V. violate; break, – through; infringe; set -aside, – at naught; trample -on, – under foot; slight, neglect, evade, renounce, forswear, repudiate; wash one's hands of; escape, transgress, fail.

call to account etc. (*disapprobation*) 932.

927a. Exemption.—N. exemption, freedom, irresponsibility, immunity, liberty, license, release, exoneration, excuse, dispensation, absolution, franchise, renunciation, discharge; exculpation etc. 970; *aegrotat*.

V. be -exempt etc. *adj.*

exempt, release, acquit, discharge, quit-claim, remise, remit; free, set at liberty, let off, pass over, spare, excuse, dispense with, give dispensation, license; stretch a point; absolve etc. (*forgive*) 918; exonerate etc. (*exculpate*) 970; save the necessity.

Adj. exempt, free, immune, at liberty, scot free; released etc. *v.*; unbound, unencumbered; irresponsible, unaccountable, not answerable; excusable.

928. Respect.—N. respect, regard, consideration; courtesy etc. 894; attention, deference, reverence, honor, esteem, estimation, veneration, admiration; approbation etc. 931.

homage, fealty, obeisance, genuflexion, kneeling, prostration; obsequiousness etc. 886; salaam, *kowtow*, bow, presenting arms, salute.

respects, regards, duty, *devoirs*, *égards*.

devotion etc. (*piety*) 987.

V. respect, regard; revere, -nce; hold in reverence, honor, venerate, hallow; esteem etc. (*approve of*) 931; think much of; entertain –, bear- respect for; have a high opinion of; look up to, defer to; pay -attention, – respect etc. *n.*- to; do –, render- honor to; do the honors, hail; show courtesy etc. 894; salute, present arms; do –, pay- homage to; pay tribute to; kneel to, bow to, bend the knee to; fall down before, prostrate oneself, kiss the hem of one's garment; worship etc. 990.

keep one's distance, make room, observe due decorum, stand upon ceremony.

command –, inspire- respect; awe, impose, overawe, dazzle.

Adj. respecting etc. *v.*; respectful, deferential, decorous, reverential, obsequious, ceremonious, bare-headed, cap in hand, on one's knees; prostrate etc. (*servile*) 886.

respected etc. *v.*; in high -esteem, – estimation; time-honored, venerable, *emeritus*.

Adv. in deference to; with -all, – due, – the highest- respect; with submission.

saving your -grace, – presence; *salva sit reverentia*; *pace tanti nominis*.

Int. hail! all hail! *esto perpetua!* may your shadow never be less!

929. Disrespect.—N. dis-respect, -esteem, -estimation, -favor, -repute; low estimation; disparagement etc. (*dispraise*) 932; (*detraction*) 934.

irreverence; slight, neglect; *spretae injuria formae*; superciliousness etc. (*contempt*) 930.

vilipendency, contumely, affront, dishonor, insult, indignity, outrage, discourtesy etc. 895; practical joking; scurrility, scoffing, sibilation; ir-, derision; mockery; irony etc. (*ridicule*) 856; sarcasm.

hiss, hoot, gibe, flout, jeer, scoff, gleek, taunt, sneer, quip, fling, wipe, slap in the face.

V. hold in disrespect etc. (*despise*) 930; misprize, disregard, slight, undervalue, depreciate, trifle with, set at naught, pass by, push aside, overlook, turn one's back -on, laugh in one's sleeve; be -disrespectful etc. *adj.*, – discourteous etc. 895; treat with -disrespect etc. *n.*; set down, browbeat.

dishonor, desecrate; insult, affront, outrage.

speak slightingly of; disparage etc. (*dispraise*) 932; vilipend, call names; throw –, fling- dirt; drag through the mud, point at, indulge in personalities; make -mouths, – faces; bite the thumb; take –, pluck- by the beard; toss in a blanket, tar and feather.

have –, hold- in derision; deride, scoff, sneer, laugh at, snigger, ridicule, gibe, mock, jeer, taunt, twit, niggle, gleek, gird, flout, fleer; roast, turn into ridicule; guy, burlesque etc. 856; laugh to scorn etc. (*contempt*) 930; smoke; fool; make -game, – a fool, – an April fool- of; play a practical joke; rag; lead one a dance, run the rig upon, have a fling at, scout, hiss, hoot, mob.

Adj. disrespectful; aweless, irreverent; disparaging etc. 934; insulting etc. *v.*; supercilious etc. (*scornful*) 930; rude, derisive, contemptuous, sarcastic; scurri-le, -lous; contumelious.

un-respected, -worshipped, -envied, -saluted; un-dis-regarded.

Adv. disrespectfully etc. *adj.*

930. Contempt.—N. contempt, disdain, scorn, sovereign contempt; despi-sal, -ciency; vilipendency, contumely; slight, sneer, spurn, by-word.

contemptuousness etc. *adj.*; scornful eye; smile of contempt; derision etc. (*disrespect*) 929.

[State of being despised] despisedness.

V. despise, contemn, scorn, disdain, feel contempt for, view with a scornful eye, disregard, slight, not mind; pass by etc. (*neglect*) 460.

look down upon; hold -cheap, – in contempt, – in disrespect; think -nothing, – small beer- of; make light of; underestimate etc. 483; esteem -slightly, – of small or no account; take no account of, care nothing for; set no store by; not care a -straw etc. (*unimportance*) 643; set at naught, laugh in one's sleeve, snap one's fingers at, shrug one's shoulders, turn up one's nose at, pooh-pooh, damn with faint praise; sneeze –, whistle –, sneer- at; curl up one's lip, toss the head, *traiter de haut*; laugh at etc. (*be disrespectful*) 929.

point the finger of –, hold up to –, laugh to- scorn; scout, hoot, flout, hiss, scoff at.

turn -one's back, – a cold shoulder- upon; tread –, trample- -upon, – under foot; spurn, kick; fling to the winds etc. (*repudiate*) 610; send away with a flea in the ear.

Adj. contemptuous; disdain-, scorn-ful; withering, contumelious, supercilious, cynical, haughty, bumptious, cavalier; derisive.

contemptible, despicable; pitiable; pitiful etc. (*unimportant*) 643; despised etc. *v.*; down-trodden; unenvied.

Adv. contemptuously etc. *adj.*

Int. a fig for etc. (*unimportant*) 643; bah! never mind! away with! hang it! fiddle-de-dee!

931. Approbation.—N. approbation; approv-al, -ement; sanction, advocacy; nod of approbation; esteem, estimation, good opinion, golden opinions, admiration; love etc. 897; appreciation, regard, account, popularity, *kudos*, credit; repute etc. 873.

commendation, praise; laud, -ation; good word; meed –, tribute- of praise; encomium; eulog-y, -ium; *éloge*, panegyric; homage, hero worship; benediction, blessing, benison.

applause, plaudit, clap; clapping, – of hands; accl-aim, -amation; cheer; paean, hosannah; shout –, peal –, chorus –, thunders- of -applause etc. Kentish fire; Prytaneum; blurb.

V. approve; think -good, – much of, – well of, – highly of; esteem, value, prize; set great store -by, – on.

do justice to, appreciate; honor, hold in esteem, look up to, admire; like etc. 897; be in favor of, wish God speed; hail, – with satisfaction.

stand –, stick- up for; uphold, hold up, countenance, sanction; clap –, pat- on the back; keep in countenance, endorse, give credit, recommend; mark with a white -mark, – stone.

commend, praise; be-, laud; compliment, pay a tribute, bepraise; clap, – the hands; applaud, cheer, acclaim, acclamate, encore; panegyrize, eulogize, cry up, *prôner*, puff; extol, – to the skies; magnify, glorify, exalt, boost, swell, make much of; flatter etc. 933; bless, give a blessing to; have –, say- a good word for; speak -well, – highly, – in high terms- of; sing –, sound –, chaunt –, resound- the praises of; sing praises to; cheer –, applaud- to the -echo, – very echo.

redound to the -honor, – praise, – credit- of; do credit to; deserve -praise etc. *n.*; recommend itself; pass muster.

be -praised etc.; receive honorable mention; be in -favor, – high favor- with; ring with the praises of, win golden opinions, gain credit, find favor with, stand well in the opinion of; *laudari a laudato viro*.

Adj. approving etc. *v.*; in favor of; lost in admiration.

commendatory, complimentary, benedictory, laudatory, panegyrical, eulogistic, encomiastic, acclamatory, lavish of praise, uncritical.

approved, praised etc. *v.*; un-censured, -impeached; popular, in good odor; in high esteem etc. (*respected*) 928; in –, in high- favor.

deserving –, worthy of- praise etc. *n.*; praiseworthy, commendable, of estimation; good etc. 648; meritorious, estimable, creditable, plausible, unimpeachable; beyond all praise.

Adv. commendably, with credit, to admiration; well etc. 681; with three times three.

Int. hear, hear! well done! *brav-o! -a! -i! bravissimo! euge! macte virtute!* so far so good, that's right, quite right; *optime!* one cheer more; may your shadow never be less! *esto perpetua!* long life to! *viva! enviva!* God speed! *valete et plaudite! encore! bis!*

Phr. *probatum est.*

932. Disapprobation.—N. disappro-bation, -val; improbation; dis-esteem, -valuation, -placency; odium; dislike etc. 867; dissent etc. 489.

dis-praise, -commendation; blame, censure, obloquy; detraction etc. 934; disparagement, depreciation; denunciation; condemnation etc. 971; ostracism; boycott; black-list, -ball; *index -expurgatorius*, – *librorum prohibitorum*.

animadversion, reflection, stricture, objection, exception, criticism; sardonic -grin, – laugh; sarcasm, insinuation, innuendo; bad –, poor –, left-handed- compliment.

satire; sneer etc. (*contempt*) 930; taunt etc. (*disrespect*) 929; cavil, carping, censoriousness; hypercriticism etc. (*fastidiousness*) 868.

reprehension, remonstrance, expostulation, reproof, reprobation, admonition, increpation, reproach; rebuke, reprimand, castigation, jobation, lecture, curtain lecture, blow up, wigging, dressing, – down; rating, scolding, trimming; correction, set down, rap on the knuckles, *coup de bec*, rebuff; slap, – on the face; home thrust; hit; frown, scowl, black look.

diatribe; jeremiad; *tirade*, philippic.

clamor, outcry, hue and cry; hiss, -ing; sibilation, cat-call; execration etc. 908.

chiding, upbraiding etc. *v.*; exprobration, abuse, vituperation, invective, objurgation, contumely, personal remarks; hard –, cutting –, bitter- words.

evil-speaking; bad language etc. 908; personality.

V. disapprove; dislike etc. 867; lament etc. 839; object to, take exception to; be scandalized at, think ill of; view with -disfavor, – dark eyes, – jaundiced eyes; *nil admirari*, disvalue, improbate.

frown upon, look grave; bend –, knit- the brows; shake the head at, shrug the shoulders; turn up the nose etc. (*contempt*) 930; look -askance, – black upon; look with an evil eye; make a wry -face, – mouth- at; set one's face against.

dis-praise, -commend, -parage; deprecate, speak ill of, not speak well of, slate, condemn etc. (*find guilty*) 971.

blame; lay –, cast- blame upon; censure, *fronder*, reproach, pass censure on, reprobate, impugn.

remonstrate, expostulate, recriminate.

reprehend, chide, admonish; bring –, call- -to account, – over the coals, – to order; take to task, reprove, lecture, bring to book; read a -lesson, – lecture- to; rebuke, correct.

reprimand, chastise, castigate, lash, blow up, trounce, trim, *laver la tête*, overhaul; give it one, – finely; gibbet.

accuse etc. 938; impeach, denounce; hold up to -reprobation, – execration; expose, brand, gibbet, stigmatize; show –, pull –, take- up; cry 'shame' upon; be outspoken; raise a hue and cry against.

execrate etc. 908; exprobrate, speak daggers, vituperate; abuse, –, like a pickpocket; scold, rate, objurage, upbraid, fall foul of; jaw; rail, – at, – in good set terms; bark at; anathematize, call names; call by -hard, – ugly- names; a-, re-vile; vili-fy, -pend; bespatter; backbite; clapperclaw; rave –, thunder –, fulminate- against; load with reproaches; lash with the tongue.

exclaim –, protest –, inveigh –, declaim –, cry out –, raise one's voice- against.

decry; cry –, run –, frown- down; clamor, hiss,

hoot, mob, ostracize; draw up –, sing- a round robin; black-ball, -list.

animadvert –, reflect- upon; glance at; cast - reflection, – reproach, – a slur- upon; insinuate, damn with faint praise; 'hint a fault and hesitate dislike;' not to be able to say much for.

scoff at, point at; twit, taunt etc. (*disrespect*) 929; sneer at etc. (*despise*) 230; satirize, lampoon; defame etc. (*detract*) 934; depreciate, find fault with, criticize, cut up; pull –, pick- to pieces; take exception; cavil; peck –, nibble –, carp- at; be - censorious etc. *adj.*; pick -holes, – a hole, – a hole in one's coat; make a fuss about.

take –, set- down; snub, snap one up, give a rap on the knuckles; throw a stone -at, – in one's garden; have a -fling, – snap- at; have words with, pluck a crow with; give one a -wipe, – lick with the rough side of the tongue.

incur blame, excite disapprobation, scandalize, shock, revolt; get a bad name, forfeit one's good opinion, be under a cloud, come under the ferule, bring a hornet's nest about one's ears.

take blame, stand corrected; have to answer for.

Adj. disapproving etc. *v.*; scandalized.

disparaging, condemnatory, damnatory, denunciatory, reproachful, abusive, objurgatory, clamorous, vituperative; defamatory etc. 934.

satirical, sarcastic, sardonic, cynical, dry, sharp, cutting, biting, severe, virulent, withering, trenchant, hard upon; censorious, critical, captious, carping, hypercritical; fastidious etc. 868; sparing of –, grudging- praise.

disapproved, chid etc. *v.*; in bad odor, blown upon, unapproved; unblest; at a discount, exploded; weighed in the balance and found wanting.

blameworthy, reprehensible etc. (*guilt*) 947; to –, worthy of- blame, answerable, uncommendable, exceptionable, not to be thought of, bad etc. 649; vicious etc. 945.

un-lamented, -bewailed, -pitied.

Adv. with a wry face; reproachfully etc. *adj.*

Int. it is too bad! it -won't, – will never- do! marry come up! Oh! come! 'sdeath!

forbid it Heaven! God –, Heaven- forbid! out –, fie- upon it! away with! tut! *O tempora! O mores!* shame! fie, – for shame! out on you!

tell it not in Gath!

933. Flattery.—N. flattery, adulation, gloze; bland-ishment, -iloquence; cajolery; fawning, wheedling etc. *v.*; captation, coquetry, sycophancy, obsequiousness, flunkeyism, toad-eating, tuft-hunting; snobbishness.

incense, honeyed words, flummery; bun-kum, -combe; blarney, *placebo*, butter; soft -soap, – sawder; rose water.

voice of the charmer, mouth honor; lip-homage; euphemism; unctuousness etc. *adj.*

V. flatter, praise to the skies, puff; wheedle, cajole, glaver, coax; fawn, –, upon; humor, gloze, soothe, pet, coquet, slaver, butter; be-spatter, -slubber, -plaster, -slaver; lay it on thick, overpraise; earwig, cog, collogue; truckle –, pander *or* pandar –, pay court- to; court; creep into the good graces of; curry favor with, hang on the sleeve of; fool to the top of one's bent; lick the dust.

lay the flattering unction to one's soul, gild the pill, make things pleasant.

overestimate etc. 482; exaggerate etc. 549.

Adj. flattering etc. *v.*; adulatory; mealy-, honey-mouthed; honeyed; smooth, – tongued; soapy, oily, unctuous, blandiloquent, specious; fine-, fair-spoken; plausible, servile, sycophantic, fulsome; courtier-ly, -like.

Adv. *ad captandum*.

934. Detraction.—N. detraction, disparagement, depreciation, vilification, obloquy, scurrility, scandal, defamation, aspersion, traducement, slander, calumny, obtrectation, evil-speaking, backbiting, *scandalum magnatum*.

personality, libel, squib, lampoon, skit, pasquinade; *chronique scandaleuse*.

sarcasm, cynicism; criticism (*disapprobation*) 932; invective etc. 932; envenomed tongue; *spretae injuria formae*.

detractor etc. 936.

V. detract, derogate, decry, depreciate, disparage; run –, cry- down; minimize, make light of; belittle, sneer at etc. (*contemn*) 930; criticize, pull to pieces, pick a hole in one's coat, asperse, cast aspersions, blow upon, bespatter, blacken; vilify, -pend; avile; give a dog a bad name, brand, malign, backbite, libel, lampoon, traduce, slander, defame, calumniate, bear false witness against; speak ill of behind one's back.

'damn with faint praise, assent with civil leer; and without sneering, others teach to sneer.'

fling dirt etc. (*disrespect*) 929; anathematize etc. 932; dip the pen in gall, view in a bad light.

Adj. detracting etc. *v.*; defamatory, detractory, derogatory; disparaging, libellous; scurril-e, -ous; abusive; foul-spoken, -tongued, -mouthed; slanderous; calumni-ous, -atory; sar-castic, -donic; satirical, cynical.

935. Flatterer.—N. flatterer, adulator; eulogist, -phemist; optimist, encomiast, *laudator*, whitewasher, booster.

toad-y, -eater; sycophant, courtier, pickthank, Sir Pertinax MacSycophant; *flâneur*, *prôneur*; puffer, touter, *claqueur*; claw-back, ear-wig, doer of dirty work; parasite, hanger on etc. (*servility*) 886.

936. Detractor.—N. detractor, reprover; censor, -urer; cynic, critic, caviller, carper, word-catcher.

defamer, backbiter, slanderer, knocker, Sir Benjamin Backbite, lampooner, satirist, traducer, libeller, calumniator, dearest foe, dawplucker, Thersites; Zoilus; good-natured –, candid- friend [satirically]; reviler, vituperator, castigator; shrew etc. 901.

disapprover, *laudator temporis acti*.

937. Vindication.—N. vindication, justification, warrant; exoneration, exculpation; acquittal etc. 970; whitewashing.

extenuation; pallia-tion, -tive; softening, mitigation.

reply, defense; recrimination etc. 938.

apology, gloss, varnish; plea etc. 617; salvo; excuse, extenuating circumstances; allowance, – to be made; *locus poenitentiae*.

apologist, vindicator, justifier; defendant etc. 938.

justifiable charge, true bill.

V. justify, warrant; be an -excuse etc. *n.*- for; lend a color, furnish a handle; vindicate; ex-, disculpate; acquit etc. 970; clear, set right, exonerate, whitewash.

extenuate, palliate, excuse, soften, apologize, varnish, slur, gloze; put a -gloss, – good face- upon; mince; gloss over, bolster up, help a lame dog over a stile.

advocate, defend, plead one's cause; stand –, stick –, speak- up for; contend –, speak- for; bear out, keep in countenance, support; plead etc. 617; say in defense; plead ignorance; confess and avoid, propugn, put in a good word for.

take the will for the deed, make allowance for, do justice to; give -one, – the Devil- his due.

make good; prove -the truth of, – one's case; be justified by the event.

Adj. vindicat-ed, -ing etc. *v.*; vindicat-ive, -ory; palliative; exculpatory; apologetic.

excusable, defensible, pardonable; veni-al, -able; specious, plausible, justifiable.

Phr. *'honi soit qui mal y pense.'*

938. Accusation.—N. accusation, charge, imputation, slur, inculpation, exprobration, delation; crimination; in-, ac-, re-crimination; *tu quoque* argument; invective etc. 932.

de-nunciation, -nouncement; libel, challenge, citation, arraignment; im-, ap-peachment; indictment, bill of indictment, true bill; lawsuit etc. 969; condemnation etc. 971.

gravamen of a charge, head and front of one's offending, *argumentum ad hominem*; scandal etc. (*detraction*) 934; *scandalum magnatum*.

accuser, prosecutor, plaintiff, complainant, petitioner; relator, informer; appellant.

accused, defendant, prisoner, panel, co-, respondent; litigant.

V. accuse, charge, tax, impute, twit, taunt with, reproach.

brand with reproach; stigmatize, slur; cast a -stone at, – slur on; incriminate; inculpate, implicate; call to account etc. (*censure*) 932; take to- blame, – task; put in the black book.

inform against, indict, denounce, arraign; im-, ap-peach; have up, show up, pull up, challenge, cite, lodge a complaint; prosecute, bring an action against etc. 969.

charge –, saddle- with; lay to one's -door, – charge; lay the blame on, bring home to; cast –, throw- in one's teeth; cast the first stone at.

have –, keep- a rod in pickle for; have a crow to pluck with.

trump up a charge.

Adj. accusing etc. *v.*; accusat-ory, -ive; imputative, denunciatory; re-, criminatory.

accused etc. *v.*; suspected; under -suspicion, – a cloud, – *surveillance*; in -custody, – detention; in the -lock up, – watch house, – house of detention.

accusable, imputable; in-defensible, -excusable; un-pardonable, -justifiable; vicious etc. 945.

Int. look at home; *tu quoque* etc. (*retaliation*) 718.

939. Probity.—N. probity, integrity, rectitude; uprightness etc. *adj.*; honesty, faith; honor; good faith, *bona fides*; purity, clean hands.

fairness etc. *adj.*; fair play, justice, equity, impartiality, principle; grace.

constancy; faithfulness etc. *adj.*; fidelity, loyalty; incorrupt-ion, -ibility.

trustworthiness etc. *adj.*; truth, candor, singleness of heart; veracity etc. 543; tender conscience etc. (*sense of duty*) 926.

punctil-iousness, -io; delicacy, nicety; scrupulosity, -ousness etc. *adj.*; scruple; point, – of honor; punctuality.

dignity etc. (*repute*) 873; respectability, -bleness etc. *adj.*; gentleman; man of -honor, – his word; *fidus Achates*, *preux chevalier*; *galantuomo*; truepenny, trump, brick; true Briton, white man, sportsman.

court of honor, a fair field and no favor; *argumentum ad verecundiam*.

V. be -honorable etc. *adj.*; deal -honorably, – squarely, – impartially, – fairly; speak the truth etc. (*veracity*) 543; tell the truth and shame the devil, *vitam impendere vero*; show a proper spirit, make a point of; do one's duty etc. 944; play the game.

redeem one's pledge etc. 926; keep –, be as good as- one's -promise, – word; keep faith with, not fail.

give and take, *audire alteram partem*, give the devil his due, put the saddle on the right horse.

redound to one's honor.

Adj. upright; honest, – as daylight; veracious etc. 543; virtuous etc. 944; honorable; fair, right, just, equitable, impartial, even-handed, square; fair –, open- and aboveboard.

constant, – as the northern star; faithful, loyal, staunch; true, – blue, – to one's colors, – to the core, – as the needle to the pole; true-hearted, trust-y, -worthy; as good as one's word, to be depended on, incorruptible.

manly, straightforward etc. (*ingenuous*) 703; frank, candid, open-hearted.

conscientious, tender-conscienced, right-minded; high-principled, -minded; scrupulous, religious, strict; nice, punctilious, correct, punctual; respect-, reput-able; gentlemanlike.

inviol-able, -ate; un-violated, -broken, -betrayed; un-bought, -bribed.

innocent etc. 946; pure; stainless; un-stained, -tarnished, -sullied, -tainted, -perjured; uncorrupt, -ed; unde-filed, -praved, -bauched; *integer vitae scelerisque purus*; *justus et tenax propositi*.

chivalrous, jealous of honor, *sans peur et sans reproche*; high-spirited.

supra-mundane, unworldly, overscrupulous.

Adv. honorably etc. *adj.*; *bona fide*; on the square, in good faith, honor bright, *foro conscientiae*, with clean hands; by fair means.

940. Improbity.—N. improbity; dishon-esty, -our; deviation from rectitude; disgrace etc. (*disrepute*) 874; fraud etc. (*deception*) 545; lying etc. 544; bad –, Punic- faith; *mala* –, *Punica*, *fides*; infidelity; faithlessness etc. *adj.*; Judas kiss, betrayal; scrap of paper.

breach of -promise, – trust, – faith; prodition, disloyalty, divided allegiance, treason, high treason; apostacy etc. (*tergiversation*) 607; nonobservance etc. 773.

shabbiness etc. *adj.*; villainy; baseness etc. *adj.*; abjection, debasement, turpitude, moral turpitude, laxity, trimming, shuffling.

perfidy; perfidiousness etc. *adj.*; treachery, double-dealing; unfairness etc. *adj.*; knavery, roguery, rascality, foul-play; jobb-ing, -ery; Tammany, graft; venality, nepotism; corruption, job, shuffle, fishy transaction, barratry; sharp practice, heads I win, tails you lose; mouth-honor etc. (*flattery*) 933.

V. be -dishonest etc. *adj.*; play false; break one's -word, – faith, – promise; jilt, betray, forswear; shuffle etc. (*lie*) 544; live by one's wits, sail near the wind; play with marked cards.

disgrace –, dishonor –, demean –, degrade- oneself; derogate, stoop, grovel, sneak, lose caste; sell oneself, go over to the enemy; seal one's infamy.

Adj. dishon-est, -orable; un-conscientious, -scrupulous; fraudulent etc. 545; knavish; disgraceful etc. (*disreputable*) 874; wicked etc. 945.

false-hearted, disingenuous; unfair, one-sided; double, -tongued, -faced; time-serving, crooked, tortuous, insidious, Machiavellian, dark, slippery; questionable; fishy; perfidious, treacherous, perjured.

infamous, arrant, foul, base, vile, low, ignominious, blackguard.

contemptible, abject, mean, shabby, little, paltry, dirty, scurvy, scabby, sneaking, groveling, scrubby, rascally, pettifogging; beneath one; not cricket.

low-minded, -thoughted; base-minded.

undignified, indign; unbe-coming, -seeming, fitting; de-rogatory, -grading; *infra dignitatem*; ungentleman-ly, -like; un-knightly, -chivalric, -manly, -handsome; recreant, inglorious.

corrupt, venal; debased, mongrel.

faithless, of bad faith, false, unfaithful, disloyal; untrustworthy; trust-, troth-less; lost to shame, dead to honor.

Adv. dishonestly etc. *adj.*; *malâ fide*, like a thief in the night, by crooked paths; by foul means.

Int. *O tempora! O mores!*

941. Knave.—N. knave, rogue, villain; Seapin, rascal; Lazarillo de Tormes; bad man etc. 949; blackguard etc. 949.

traitor, betrayer, arch-traitor, conspirator, stool pigeon, Judas, Catiline; reptile, serpent, snake in the grass, wolf in sheep's clothing, sneak, Jerry Sneak, tell-tale, squealer, mischief-maker, trimmer; renegade etc. (*tergiversation*) 607; truant, recreant; sycophant etc. (*servility*) 886.

942. Disinterestedness.—N. disinterestedness etc. *adj.*; generosity; liberal-ity, -ism; altruism; benevolence etc. 906; elevation, loftiness of purpose, exaltation, magnanimity; chival-ry, -rous spirit; heroism, sublimity.

self-denial, -abnegation, -effacement, -sacrifice, -immolation, -control etc. (*resolution*) 604; stoicism, devotion, martyrdom, *suttee*.

labor of love.

V. be -disinterested etc. *adj.*; make a sacrifice, lay one's head on the block; put oneself in the place of others, do as one would be done by, do unto others as we would men should do unto us.

Adj. disinterested; unselfish; self-denying, -sacrificing, -devoted; generous.

handsome, liberal, noble; noble-, high-minded; princely, great, high, elevated, lofty, exalted, spirited, stoical, magnanimous; great-, large-hearted, chivalrous, heroic, sublime.

un-bought, -bribed; uncorrupted etc. (*upright*) 939.

943. Selfishness.—N. selfishness etc. *adj.*; self-love, -indulgence, -worship, -interest; ego-tism, -ism; egocentrism, narcissism; *amour propre* etc. (*vanity*) 880; nepotism.

worldliness etc. *adj.*; world wisdom.

illiberality; meanness etc. *adj.*

time-server; tuft-, fortune-hunter; self-seeker; jobber, worldling; egotist, egoist, monopolist, nepotist, profiteer; temporizer, trimmer; dog in the manger, charity that begins at home.

V. be -selfish etc. *adj.*; please –, indulge –, coddle- oneself; consult one's own -wishes, – pleasure; look after one's own interest; feather one's nest; take care of number one, have an eye to the main chance, know on which side one's bread is buttered; give an inch and take an ell; wangle.

Adj. selfish; self-seeking, -indulgent, -interested; wrapt up –, centered- in self; egotistic, -al; egoistical; egocentric.

illiberal, mean, ungenerous, narrowminded; mercenary, venal; covetous etc. 819.

unspiritual; earthly, -minded; mundane; worldly, -minded, -wise; time-serving.

interested; *alieni appetens sui profusus*.

Adv. ungenerously etc. *adj.*; to gain some private ends; from selfish –, interested- motives.

Phr. *après nous le déluge*.

944. Virtue.—N. virtue; virtuousness etc. *adj.*; morality; moral rectitude; integrity etc. (*probity*) 939; nobleness etc. 873.

morals; ethics etc. (*duty*) 926; cardinal virtues.

merit, worth, desert, excellence, credit; self-control etc. (*resolution*) 604; self-denial etc. (*temperance*) 953.

well-doing; good -actions, – behavior; discharge –, fulfilment –, performance- of duty; well spent life; innocence etc. 946.

V. be -virtuous etc. *adj.*; practice -virtue etc. *n.*; do –, fulfil –, perform –, discharge- one's duty; redeem one's pledge etc. 926; act well, – one's part; fight the good fight; acquit oneself well; command –, master- one's passions; keep -straight, – in the right path.

set -an, – a good- example; be on one's -good, – best- behavior.

Adj. virtuous, good; innocent etc. 946; meritorious, deserving, worthy, desertful, correct; dut-iful, -eous; moral; right, -eous, -minded; well-intentioned, creditable, laudable, commendable, praiseworthy; above –, beyond- all praise; excellent, admirable; sterling, pure, noble.

exemplary; match-, peer-less; saint-ly, -like; heaven-born, angelic, seraphic, godlike.

Adv. virtuously etc. *adj.*; *e merito*.

945. Vice.—N. vice; evil-doing, – courses; wrong doing; wickedness, viciousness etc. *adj.*; iniquity, peccability, demerit; sin, Adam; old – offending- Adam.

immorality, impropriety, indecorum, scandal, laxity, looseness of morals; want of -principle, – ballast; obliquity, backsliding, infamy, demoralization, pravity, depravity, pollution; hardness of heart; brutality etc. (*malevolence*) 907; corruption etc. (*debasement*) 659; knavery etc. (*improbity*) 940; profligacy; lust etc. 961; flagrancy, atrocity; cannibalism.

infirmity; weakness etc. *adj.*; weakness of the flesh, frailty, imperfection; error; weak side; foible; fail-ing, -ure; crying –, besetting- sin; defect, deficiency, shortcoming; cloven foot.

lowest dregs of vice, sink of iniquity, Alsatian den; *gusto picaresco*.

fault, crime; criminality etc. (*guilt*) 947.

sinner etc. 949.

V. be -vicious etc. *adj.*; sin, commit sin, do amiss, err, transgress; misdemean –, forget –, misconduct- oneself; mis-do, -behave; fall, lapse, slip, trip, offend, trespass; deviate from the -line of duty, – path of virtue etc. 944; take a wrong course, go astray; hug a -sin, – fault; sow one's wild oats.

render -vicious etc. *adj.*; demoralize, brutalize; corrupt etc. (*degrade*) 659.

Adj.* vicious; sinful; sinning etc. *v.*; wicked, iniquitous, bad, immoral, unrighteous, wrong, criminal; naughty, incorrect; undut-eous, -iful.

unprincipled, lawless, disorderly, *contra bonos mores*, indecorous, unseemly, improper; dissolute, profligate, scampish; unworthy; worth-, desert-less; disgraceful, recreant; reprehensible, blameworthy, uncommendable; dis-creditable, -reputable.

base, sinister, scurvy, foul, gross, vile, black, grave, facinorous, felonious, nefarious, shameful, scandalous, infamous, villainous, of a deep dye, heinous; flag-rant, -itious; atrocious, incarnate, accursed.

Mephistophelian, satanic, diabolic, hellish, infernal, stygian, fiend-ish, -like, hell-born, demoniacal, devilish.

mis-created, -begotten; demoralized, corrupt, depraved.

evil-minded, -disposed; ill-conditioned; malevolent etc. 907; heart-, grace-, shame-, virtue-less; abandoned, lost to virtue; unconscionable; sunk –, lost –, deep –, steeped- in iniquity.

incorrigible, irreclaimable, obdurate, reprobate, past praying for; culpable, reprehensible etc. (*guilty*) 947.

unjustifiable; in-defensible, -excusable; inexpiable, unpardonable, irremissible.

weak, frail, lax, infirm, imperfect, indiscreet; demoralizing, degrading.

Adv. wrong; sinfully etc. *adj.*; without excuse.

Int. *O tempora! O mores!*

*Most of these adjectives are applicable both to the act and to the agent.

946. Innocence.—N. innocence; guiltlessness etc. *adj.*; incorruption, impeccability.

clean hands, clear conscience, *mens sibi conscia recti*.

innocent, new born babe, lamb, dove.

V. be -innocent etc. *adj.*; *nil conscire sibi nullâ pallescere culpâ*.

acquit etc. 970; exculpate etc. (*vindicate*) 937.

Adj. innocent, not guilty, unguilty; guilt-, fault-, sin-, stain-, blood-, spot-less; clear, immaculate; *rectus in curiâ*; un-spotted, -blemished, -erring; undefiled etc. 939; unhardened, Saturnian; Arcadian etc. (*artless*) 703.

in-, un-culpable; unblam-ed, -able; blameless, inerrable, above suspicion; irrepr-oachable, -ovable, -ehensible; un-exceptionable, -objectionable, -impeachable; salvable; venial etc. 937.

harmless; in-offensive, -noxious, -nocuous; dove-, lamb-like; pure, harmless as doves; innocent as -a lamb, – the babe unborn; more sinned against than sinning.

virtuous etc. 944; un-reproved, -impeached, -reproached.

Adv. innocently etc. *adj.*; with clean hands; with a -clear, – safe- conscience.

947. Guilt.—N. guilt, -iness; culpability; crimin-ality, -ousness; deviation from rectitude etc. (*improbity*) 940; sinfulness etc. (*vice*) 945; peccability.

mis-conduct, -behavior, -doing, -deed; malpractice, fault, sin, error, transgression; dereliction, delinquency; indiscretion, lapse, slip, trip, *faux pas*, *peccadillo*; flaw, blot, omission; fail-ing, -ure.

offence, trespass; mis-demeanor, -feasance, -prision, tort; mal-efaction, -feasance, -versation; crime, felony.

enormity, atrocity, outrage; deadly –, mortal –, unpardonable- sin; died without a name.

corpus delicti.

Adj. guilty, to blame, culpable, peccable, in fault, censurable, reprehensible, blameworthy, uncommendable, illaudable; weighed in the balance and found wanting; exceptionable, objectionable.

Adv. *in flagrante delicto*; red-handed, in the very act.

948. Good Man.—N. good man, worthy.

good woman, goddess, *madonna*, virgin.

model, paragon etc. (*perfection*) 650; good example; hero, demigod, seraph, angel; innocent etc. 946; saint etc. (*piety*) 987; benefactor etc. 912; philanthropist etc. 910; Aristides.

brick, trump, rough diamond, ugly duckling.

salt of the earth; one in ten thousand; one of the best.

Phr. *si sic omnes!*

949. Bad Man.—N. bad man, wrongdoer, worker of iniquity; evil-doer etc. 913; sinner; the -wicked etc. 945; bad example.

rascal, scoundrel, villain, miscreant, caitiff; wretch, reptile, viper, serpent, cockatrice, basilisk, urchin; tiger, monster; devil etc. (*demon*) 980; devil incarnate; demon in human shape, Nana Sahib; hell-hound, -cat; rake-hell.

bad woman, jade, Jezebel, adultress, etc. 962.

scamp, scapegrace, rip, runagate, ne'er-do-well, reprobate, *roué*, rake; limb; one who has sold himself to the devil, fallen angel, *âme damnée*, *vaurien*, *mauvais sujet*, loose fish, sad, dog; lost –, black-sheep; castaway, recreant, defaulter; prodigal etc. 818; libertine etc. 962.

rough, rowdy, ugly customer, ruffian, hoodlum, bully; Jonathan Wild; hangman; incendiary; thief etc. 792; murderer etc. 361.

culprit, delinquent, criminal, melefactor, misdemeanant; felon; convict, jail-bird, ticket-of-leave man; outlaw.

blackguard, *polisson*, loafer, sneak; raps-, rascallion; cullion, mean wretch, varlet, kern, *âme-de-boue*, *drôle*; cur, dog, hound, whelp, mongrel; lown, loon, runnion, outcast, vagabond; rogue etc. (*knave*) 941; scum of the earth, riff-raff; *Arcades ambo*.

Int. sirrah!

950. Penitence.—N. penitence, contrition, compunction, repentance, remorse; regret etc. 833.

self-reproach, -reproof, -accusation, -condemnation, -humiliation; stings –, pangs –, qualms –, prickings –, twinge –, twitch –, touch –, voice- of conscience; compunctious visitings of nature.

acknowledgment, confession etc. (*disclosure*) 529; apology etc. 952; recantation etc. 607; penance etc. 952; resipiscence.

awakened conscience, deathbed repentance, *locus poenitentiae*, stool of repentance, cutty stool.

penitent, Magdalen, prodigal son, returned prodigal, a sadder and wiser man.

V. repent, be sorry for; be -penitent etc. *adj.*; rue; regret etc. 833; think better of; recant etc. 607; knock under etc. (*submit*) 725; plead guilty; sing -*miserere*, – *de profundis*; cry *peccavi*; own oneself in the wrong; acknowledge, confess etc. (*disclose*) 529; humble oneself; beg pardon etc. (*apologize*) 952; turn over a new leaf, put on the new man, turn from sin; reclaim; repent in sackcloth and ashes etc. (*do penance*) 952; learn by experience.

Adj. penitent; repenting etc. *v.*; repentant, contrite; conscience-smitten, -stricken; self-accusing, -convicted.

penitenti-al, -ary; chastened, reclaimed; not hardened; un-hardened.

Adv. *meâ culpâ*.

Phr. *peccavi*; *erubuit*; *salva res est*; *vous l'avez voulu, Georges Dandin*.

951. Impenitence.—N. impenitence, irrepentance, recusance.

hardness of heart, seared conscience, induration, obduracy.

V. be -impenitent etc. *adj.*; steel –, harden- the heart; die -game, – and make no sign.

Adj. impenitent uncontrite, obdurate; hard, -ened; seared, recusant; unrepentant; relent-, remorse-, grace-, shrift-less.

lost, incorrigible, irreclaimable.

unre-claimed, -formed; unrepented, unatoned.

952. Atonement.—N. atonement, reparation; compromise, composition; compensation etc. 30; quittance, quits; indemni-ty, -fication; expiation, redemption, reclamation, conciliation, propitiation.

amends, apology, *amende honorable*, satisfaction; peace –, sin –, burnt- offering; scapegoat, sacrifice.

penance, fasting, maceration, sackcloth and ashes, white sheet, shrift, flagellation, lustration; purga-tion, -tory.

V. atone, – for; expiate; propitiate; make -amends, – good; reclaim, redeem, repair, ransom, absolve, purge, shrive, do penance, stand in a white sheet, repent in sackcloth and ashes.

set one's house in order, wipe off old scores, make matters up; pay the -forfeit, – penalty.

apologize, beg pardon, express regret, *faire amende honorable*, give satisfaction; come –, fall-down on one's -knees, – marrow bones.

Adj. propitiatory, expiatory; sacrific, -ial, -atory; piacul-ar, -ous.

953. Temperance.—N. temperance, moderation, sobriety, soberness.

forbearance, abnegation; self-denial, -restraint, -control etc. (*resolution*) 604.

frugality; vegetarianism, teetotalism, total abstinence, prohibition; abst-inence, -emiousness, asceticism etc. 955; system of -Pythagoras, – Cornaro; Pythagorism, Stoicism.

vegetarian; Pythagorean, gymnosophist; teetotaler etc. 958; abstainer.

V. be -temperate etc. *adj.*; abstain, forbear, refrain, deny oneself, spare; know when one has had enough; take the pledge; look not upon the wine when it is red.

Adj. temperate, moderate, sober, frugal, sparing; abst-emious, -inent; within compass; measured etc. (*sufficient*) 639.

Pythagorean; vegetarian; teetotal, pussy-foot.

954. Intemperance.—N. intemperance; sensuality, animalism, carnality; pleasure; effeminacy, silkiness; luxur-y, -iousness; lap of -pleasure, – luxury.

indulgence; high-, free- living, in-abstinence, self-indulgence; voluptuousness etc. *adj.*; epicurism, -eanism; sybaritism.

dissipation; licentiousness etc. *adj.*; debauchery; crapulence.

revel-s, -ry; debauch, carousal, jollification, drinking bout, wassail, Saturnalia, orgies; excess, too much; intoxication etc. 959.

Circean cup; drug habit etc. 663.

V. be -intemperate etc. *adj.*; indulge, exceed; live -well, – high, – on the fat of the land; give a loose to -indulgence etc. *n.*; dine not wisely but too well; wallow in -voluptuousness etc. *n.*; plunge into dissipation.

revel, rake, live hard, run riot, sow one's wild oats; slake one's -appetite, – thirst; swill; pamper.

Adj. intemperate, inabstinent, intoxicated etc. 958; sensual, self-indulgent; voluptuous, luxurious, licentious, wild, dissolute, rakish, fast, debauched.

brutish, crapulous, swinish, piggish, hoggish, bestial.

Paphian, Epicurean, Sybaritical; bred –, nursed- in the lap of luxury; indulged, pampered, full-fed.

954a. Sensualist.—N. Sybarite, voluptuary, Sardanapalus, man of pleasure, carpet knight; epicure, -an; *gourm-et, -and;* gormandizer, gutling, glutton, pig, hog; votary –, swine- of Epicurus; sensualist; Heliogabalus; free –, hard- liver; libertine etc. 962; hedonist.

955. Asceticism.—N. asceticism, puritanism, sabbatarianism; cynicism, austerity; total abstinence.

mortification, maceration, sackcloth and ashes, flagellation; penance etc. 952; fasting etc. 956; martyrdom.

ascetic; anchor-et, -ite; martyr; *Heautontimorumenos*; hermit etc. (*recluse*) 893; puritan, sabbatarian, cynic.

Adj. ascetic, austere, puritanical; cynical; over-religious.

956. Fasting.—N. fasting; exrophagy; famishment, starvation; banting.

fast, *jour maigre*; fast –, banyan-day; Lent, quadragesima; Rama-dan, -zan; spare –, meager-diet; lenten -diet, – entertainment; *soupe maigre*, short -rations, – commons; Barmecide feast; hunger strike.

V. fast, starve, clem, famish, perish with hunger; dine with Duke Humphrey; make two bites of a cherry.

Adj. lenten, quadragesimal; unfed; starved etc. *v.*; half-starved; fasting etc. *v.*; hungry etc. 865.

957. Gluttony.—N. gluttony; greed; greediness etc. *adj.*; voracity.

epicurism; good –, high- living; edacity, gulosity, crapulence; gutt-, guzz-ling; over-indulgence.

good cheer, blow out; feast etc. (*food*) 298; gastronomy.

epicure, *bon vivant*, *gourmand*; glutton, cormorant, hog, belly-god, Apicius, gastronome, gormandizer.

V. gormandize, gorge; over-gorge, -eat- oneself; engorge, eat one's fill, cram, stuff, stodge, glut, satiate; gutt-le, guzz-le; bolt, devour, gobble up; gulp etc. (*swallow food*) 298; raven, eat out of house and home.

have the stomach of an ostrich; play a good knife and fork etc. (*appetite*) 865.

Adj. gluttonous, greedy; gormandizing etc. *v.*; edacious, omnivorous, crapulent, swinish, voracious, devouring.

pampered; over-fed, -gorged.

958. Sobriety.—N. sobriety; teetotalism, temperance etc. 953.

water-drinker; teetotal-er, -ist; abstainer, Good Templar, Rechabite, band of hope; prohibitionist, pussyfoot.

V. take the pledge.

Adj. sober, – as a judge; dry, on the water wagon.

959. Drunkenness.—N. drunkenness etc. *adj.*; intemperance; drinking etc. *v.*; inebri-ety, -ation; ebri-ety, -osity; befuddlement; insobriety; intoxication; temulency, bibacity, wine-bibbing; com-, potation; deep potations, bacchanals, *bacchanalia*, libations.

oino-, dipso-mania; *delirium tremens*, d.t., alcohol, -ism.

drink; alcoholic drinks, alcohol, booze; gin, blue ruin, grog, brandy, port wine; punch, -bowl; cup, rosy wine, flowing bowl; drop, – too much; dram; beer, wine, spirits etc. (*beverage*) 298; cocktail, nip, peg; stirrup cup.

drunkard, sot, toper, tippler, bibber, wine-bibber; hard –, gin –, dram- drinker; soak, soaker, sponge, tun; love-, toss-pot; thirsty soul, reveller, carouser; Bacchanal, -ian; Bacch-al, -ante; devotee to Bacchus, dipsomaniac.

V. get –, be- drunk etc. *adj.*; see double; take a -drop, – glass- too much; drink, tipple, tope, booze, bouse, guzzle, swill, soak, sot, lush, bib, swig, carouse; sacrifice at the shrine of Bacchus; take to drinking; drink -hard, – deep, – like a fish; have one's swill, drain the cup, splice the main brace, take a hair of the dog that bit you.

liquor, – up; wet one's whistle, take a whet; lift one's elbow; crack a –, pass the- bottle; toss of etc. (*drink up*) 298; go to the -ale, – public house.

make one-drunk etc. *adj.*; inebriate, fuddle, fuzzle, get into one's head.

Adj. drunk, tipsy; intoxicated; inebri-ous, -ate, -ated; in one's cups; in a state of -intoxication etc. *n.*; temulent, -ive; fuddled, mellow, cut, boosy, fou, fresh, merry, elevated, squiffy; plastered, befuddled, sozzled; flush, -ed; flustered, disguised, groggy, beery; topheavy; potvaliant, glorious; potulent; over-come, -taken; whittled, screwed, tight, primed, oiled, corned, raddled, sewed up, lushy, nappy, muddled, muzzy, bosky, obfuscated, maudlin; crapulous, dead –, blind- drunk.

inter pocula; in –, the worse for- liquor, having had a drop too much, half seas over, three sheets in the wind; under the table, blind to the world, one over the eight.

drunk as -a piper, – a fiddler, – a lord, – Chloe, – an owl, – David's sow, – a wheelbarrow.

drunken, bibacious, bibulous, sottish; given –, addicted- to -drink, – the bottle; toping etc. *v.*; wet.

Phr. *nunc est bibendum.*

960. Purity.—N. purity; decency, decorum, delicacy; continence, chastity, honesty, virtue, modesty, shame; pudicity, *pucelage*, virginity.

vestal, virgin, Joseph, Hippolytus; Lucretia, Diana; prude.

Adj. pure, undefiled, modest, delicate, decent, decorous; *virginibus puerisque*; chaste, continent, virtuous, honest, Platonic.

961. Impurity.—N. impurity; uncleanness etc. (*filth*) 653; immodesty; grossness etc. *adj.*; indelicacy, indecency; impudicity; obscenity, ribaldry, smut, bawdry, *double entendre*, *équivoque*; Aretinism; pornography.

concupiscence, lust, carnality, flesh, salacity; pruriency, lechery, lasciviency, lubricity, lewdness.

incontinence, intrigue, *faux pas*; *amour*, *-ette*; gallantry; dabauchery, libertinism, *libertinage*, fornication; *liaison*; wenching, venery, dissipation.

seduction; defloration, defilement, abuse, violation, rape; incest.

social evil, harlotry, stupration, whoredom, concubinage, cuckoldom, adultery, advoutry, *crim. con.*; free love.

seraglio, harem, zenana; brothel, bagnio, stew, bawdy-house, *lupanar*, house of ill fame, *bordel*, kip.

V. be -impure etc. *adj.*; intrigue; debauch, defile, assault, attack, seduce; prostitute; abuse, violate, deflower; commit -adultery etc. *n.*

Adj. impure; unclean etc. (*dirty*) 653; not to be mentioned to ears polite; immodest, shameless; indecorous, -delicate, -decent; loose, suggestive, *risqué*, coarse, gross, broad, free, equivocal, smutty, fulsome, ribald, obscene, bawdy, pornographic.

concupiscent, prurient, lickerish, rampant, lustful; carnal, -minded; lewd, lascivious, lecherous, libidinous, erotic, ruttish, salacious; Paphian; voluptuous; incestuous.

unchaste, light, wanton, licentious, adulterous, debauched, dissolute; of -loose character, – easy virtue; frail, gay, riggish, incontinent, meretricious, rakish, gallant, dissipated; no better than she should be; on the -town, – streets, – *pavé*, – loose.

adulterous, incestuous, bestial.

962. Libertine.—N. libertine; voluptuary etc. 954*a*; rake, debauchee, loose fish, rip, rake-hell, fast man; *intrigant*, gallant, seducer, fornicator, lecher, satyr, goat, whoremonger, *paillard*, adulterer, gay deceiver, Lothario, Don Juan, Bluebeard.

adulteress, advoutress, courtesan, prostitute, strumpet, tart, hustler, chippy, broad, harlot, whore, punk, *fille de joie*; woman, – of the town; street-walker, Cyprian, miss, piece; frail sisterhood, fallen woman; demirep, wench, trollop, trull, baggage, hussy, drab, bitch, jade, skit, rig, quean, mopsy, slut, minx, harridan; woman -of easy virtue etc. (*unchaste*) 961; wanton, fornicatress; Jezebel, Messalina, Delilah, Thaïs, Phryne, Aspasia, Lais, *lorette*, *cocotte*, *petite dame*, *grisette*; *demimonde*; white slave.

concubine, mistress, fancy woman, kept woman, doxy, *chère amie*, *bona roba*.

pimp; pand-er, -ar; bawd, *conciliatrix*, procuress, mackerel; wittol.

963. Legality.—N. legality; legitima-cy, -teness, legitimization.

legislature; law, code, *corpus juris*, constitution, pandect, charter, act, enactment, statute, rule; canon etc. (*precept*) 697; ordinance, institution, regulation; by-, bye-law, rescript; decree etc. (*order*) 741; *ordonnance*; standing order; *plébiscite* etc. (*choice*) 609.

legal process; form, -ula, -ality; rite; arm of the law; *habeas corpus*.

[Science of law] jurisprudence, nomology; legislation, codification.

equity, common law; *lex* –, *lex nonscripta*, unwritten law; law of nations, international law, *jus gentium*; *jus civile*; civil –, criminal –, canon –, statute –, ecclesiastical- law; *lex mercatoria*.

constitutional-ism, -ity; justice etc. 922.

V. legalize, legitimize; enact, ordain; decree etc. (*order*) 741; pass a law; legislate; codify, formulate; authorize.

Adj. legal, legitimate; according to law; vested, constitutional, chartered, legalized; lawful etc. (*permitted*) 760; statut-able, -ory; legislat-orial, -ive.

Adv. legally etc. *adj.*; in the eye of the law; *de jure*.

964. Illegality. [Absence or violation of law.]—**N.** lawlessness; breach –, violation- of law; disobedience etc. 742; unconformity etc. 83.

arbitrariness etc. *adj.*; antinomy, violence, brute force, despotism, outlawry.

mob –, lynch –, club –, Lydford –, martial –, drumhead- law; *coup d'état*; *le droit du plus fort*; *argumentum baculinum*.

illegality, informality, unlawfulness, illegitimacy, bar sinister.

trover and conversion; smuggling, boot-legging, rum-running, poaching; simony.

speakeasy, speakie, blind pig.

V. offend against –, violate- the law; set the law at defiance, ride rough-shod over, drive a coach and six through a statute; make the law a dead letter, take the law into one's own hands.

smuggle, run, poach.

Adj. illegal; prohibited etc. 761; not allowed, unlawful, illegitimate, illicit, contraband, actionable.

unchartered, unconstitutional; unwarrant-ed, -able; unauthorized; informal, unofficial; in-, extrajudicial.

lawless, arbitrary; despotic, -al; summary, irresponsible; un-answerable, -accountable.

null and void; a dead letter.

Adv. illegally etc. *adj.*; with a high hand, in violation of law.

965. Jurisdiction. [Executive.]—**N.** jurisdiction, judicature, administration of justice, soc; executive, commission of the peace; magistracy etc. (*authority*) 737.

judge etc. 967; tribunal etc. 966; municipality, corporation, bailiwick, shrievalty; lord lieutenant; lord –, mayor, city manager, alderman etc. 745; sheriff, bailie, shrieve, chief –, constable; police, – force; constabulary, bumbledom.

officer; proctor, high –, commissioner; bailiff, tipstaff, bum-bailiff, catchpoll, beadle; police-man, -constable, -sergeant; *sbirro*, *alguazil*, *gendarme*, kavass, *lictor*, macebearer, *huissier*, bedel.

press-gang; exciseman, gauger, custom-house officer, *douanier*.

coroner, edile, aedile, portreeve, paritor; *posse comitatus*.

V. judge, sit in judgment.

Adj. executive, administrative, municipal;

inquisitorial, causidical; judic-atory, -iary, -ial; juridical.

Adv. *coram judice*.

966. Tribunal.—N. tribunal, court, board, bench, judicatory, curia; court of -justice, – law, – arbitration; inquisition; guild.

justice –, judgment –, mercy- seat; woolsack; bar, – of justice; dock; forum, hustings, *bureau*, drum-head; jury-, witness-box.

senate-house, town-hall, theater; House of - Lords, – Commons.

assize, eyre; ward-, burgh-mote; superior courts of Westminister; court of -record, – oyer and terminer, – assize, – appeal – error; High court of -Judicature, – Appeal; Judicial Committee of the Privy Council; Star-Chamber; Court of -Chancery, – King's *or* Queen's Bench, – Exchequer, – Common Pleas, – Probate, – Arches, – Admiralty, – Criminal Appeal; Lords Justices' –, Rolls –, Vice Chancellor's –, Stannary –, Divorce –, Palatine –, ecclesiastical –, county –, police- court; sessions; quarter –, petty-sessions; court -leet, – baron, – of pie poudre, – of common council; board of green cloth.

court-martial; drum-head court-martial; *durbar*, divan; Areopagus; *rota*.

Adj. judicial etc. 965; appellate; curial.

967. Judge.—N. judge; justi-ce, -ciar, -ciary; chancellor; justice –, judge- of assize; recorder, common serjeant; puisne –, assistant –, county court- judge; conservator –, justice- of the peace, J.P.; court etc. (*tribunal*) 966; grand –, petty –, coroner's- jury; panel, juror, juryman; twelve men in a box; magistrate, police magistrate, stipendiary, the great unpaid, beak; his -worship, – honor, – lordship; deemster, moderator.

Lord -Chancellor, – Justice; Master of the Rolls, Vice-Chancellor; Lord Chief -Justice, – Baron; Mr. Justice; Baron, – of the Exchequer.

jurat, assessor; arbi-ter, -trator; umpire; refer-ee, -endary; revising barrister; domesman; censor etc. (*critic*) 480; official –, receiver.

archon, tribune, praetor, *ephor*, syndic, *podestà*, mullah, ulema, mufti, cadi, kadi; Rhadamanthus.

litigant etc. (*accusation*) 938.

V. adjudge etc. (*determine*) 480; try a -case, – prisoner.

Adj. judicial etc. 965.

Phr. 'a Daniel come to judgment.'

968. Lawyer.—N. lawyer, jurist, legist, civilian, pundit, publicist, jurisconsult, legal adviser, advocate; barrister, – at law; counsel, -lor; King's *or* Queen's counsel; K.C.; Q.C.; silk gown, leader; junior, – counsel; stuff gown, serjeant-at-law; bencher, tubman; judge etc. 967.

bar, legal profession, gentleman of the long robe; junior –, outer –, inner- bar; Inns of Court; equity draftsman, conveyancer, pleader, special pleader.

solicitor, attorney, proctor; notary, – public; scrivener, cursitor; writer, – to the signet; S.S.C.; limb of the law; pettifogger.

V. practice -at, – within- the bar; plead; call –, to called- -to, – within- the bar; take silk.

Adj. learned in the law; at the bar; forensic.

969. Lawsuit.—N. lawsuit, suit, action, cause, petition; litigation; dispute etc. 713.

citation, arraignment, prosecution, impeachment; accusation etc. 938; presentment, true bill, indictment.

apprehension, arrest; committal; imprisonment etc. (*restraint*) 751.

writ, summons, subpoena, *latitat*, *nisi prius*; *habeas corpus*.

pleadings; declaration, bill, claim; *procès-verbal*, bill of right, information, *corpus delicti*; affidavit, state of facts; answer, replication, plea, demurrer, rebutter, rejoinder; surre-butter, - joinder.

suitor, party to a suit; litigant etc. 938; libellant.

hearing, trial; verdict etc. (*judgment*) 480; appeal, – motion; writ of error; *certiorari*.

case, decision, precedent, ruling; decided case, reports.

V. go to –, appeal to the- law; bring to -justice, – trial, – the bar; put on trial, pull up; accuse etc. 938; prefer –, file- a claim etc. *n.*; take the law of, inform against.

serve with a writ, cite, apprehend, arraign, sue, prosecute, bring an action against, indict, impeach, attach, distrain, commit; arrest; summon, -s; give in charge etc. (*restrain*) 751.

empanel a jury, implead, join issue; close the pleadings; set down for hearing.

try, hear a cause; sit in judgment; adjudicate etc. 480.

Adj. litigious etc. (*quarrelsome*) 713; *qui tam*; *coram* –, *sub- judice*.

Adv. *pendente lite*.

Phr. *adhuc sub judice lis est*.

970. Acquittal.—N. acquit-tal, -ment; clearance, exculpation, exoneration; discharge etc. (*release*) 750; *quietus*, absolution, compurgation, reprieve, respite; pardon etc. (*forgiveness*) 918.

[Exemption from punishment] impunity, immunity.

V. acquit, exculpate, exonerate, clear; absolve, whitewash, assoil, discharge, release; liberate etc. 750.

reprieve, respite; pardon etc. (*forgive*) 918; let off, – scot free.

Adj. acquitted etc. *v.*; un-condemned, - punished, -chastised; recommended to mercy.

971. Condemnation.—N. condemnation, conviction, proscription, damnation; death warrant; penalty etc. 974.

attain-der, -ture, -tment.

V. condemn, convict, cast, bring home to, find guilty, damn, doom, sign the death warrant, sentence, pass sentence on, attaint, confiscate, proscribe, sequestrate; non-suit.

disapprove etc. 932; accuse etc. 938.

stand condemned.

Adj. condem-, dam-natory; condemned etc. *v.*; non-suited etc. (*failure*) 732; self-convicted.

Phr. *mutato nomine de te fabula narratur*.

972. Punishment.—N. punishment, punition; chast-isement, -ening; correction, castigation.

discipline, infliction, trial; judgment; penalty etc. 974; retribution; thunderbolt, Nemesis; requital etc. (*reward*) 973; penology; retributive justice.

lash, scaffold etc. (*instrument of punishment*) 975; imprisonment etc. (*restraint*) 751; chain gang; transportation, banishment, expulsion, deportation, exile, involuntary exile, ostracism; penal servitude, hard labor; galleys etc. 975; beating etc. *v.*; flagellation, fustigation, gantlet, *strappado*, *estrapade*, *bastinado*, *argumentum baculinum*, stick law, rap on the knuckles, box on the ear; blow etc. (*impulse*) 276; stripe, cuff, kick, buffet, pummel; slap, – in the face; wipe, douse; *coup de grâce*; torture, rack; picket, -ing; *dragonnade*; capital punishment, extreme penalty; execution; hanging etc. *v.*; de-capitation, -collation; *garrot-te*, *-to*; electrocution, lethal chamber; crucifixion, impalement; martyrdom, *auto-da-fé*; *noyade*; *hara-kiri*, happy despatch.

V. punish; chast-ise, -en; castigate, correct, inflict punishment, administer correction, deal retributive justice.

visit upon, pay; pay –, serve- out; settle with, get even with, get one's own back; do for; make short work of, give a lesson to, strafe, serve one right, make an example of; have a rod in pickle for; give it one.

strike etc. 276; deal a blow to, administer the lash, smite; slap, – the face; smack, cuff, box the ears, spank, thwack, thump, beat, lay on, swinge, buffet; thresh, thrash, pummel, drub, leather, trounce, baste, belabor; lace, – one's jacket; dress, give a -dressing, – down; trim, warm, wipe, tund, cob, bang, strap, comb, lash, lick, larrup, whallop, whop, flog, scourge, whip, birch, cane, give the stick, switch, flagellate, horsewhip, *bastinado*, towel, rub down with an oaken towel, rib roast, dust one's jacket, fustigate, pitch into, lay about one, beat black and blue; beat to a -mummy, – jelly; give a black eye; hit on the head; sandbag.

tar and feather; pelt, stone, lapidate; mast-head, keelhaul.

execute; bring to the -block, – gallows; behead; de-capitate, -collate; guillotine; hang, turn off, gibbet, bowstring, hang, draw and quarter; shoot; decimate; burn; electrocute; break on the wheel, crucify; em-, im-pale; flay; lynch; put to death.

torture; put -on, – to- the rack; picket.

banish, exile; trans-, de-port; expel, ostracize; rusticate; drum out; dismiss, -bar, -bench; strike off the roll, unfrock; post.

suffer, – for, – punishment; be -flogged, – hanged etc.; come to the gallows, dance upon nothing, die in one's shoes, be rightly served.

Adj. punishing etc. *v.*; penal; puni-tory, -tive; inflictive, castigatory; punished etc. *v.*

Int. *à la lanterne!*

973. Reward.—N. reward, recompense, remuneration, prize, meed, guerdon, reguerdon; indemni-ty, -fication, price; quittance; compensation; reparation, *ersatz*, assythment, redress; retribution, reckoning, acknowledgment, requital, amends, sop; atonement; consideration, return, *quid pro quo*; salvage, perquisite; vail etc. (*donation*) 784; *douceur*, bribe, bait, baksheesh, tip; hush-, smart-money; black-mail; carcelage; *solatium*.

allowance, salary, stipend, wages; pay, -ment; emolument; tribute; batta, shot, scot; premium, fee, *honorarium*; hire.

crown etc. (*decoration of honor*) 877.

V. re-ward, -compense, -pay, -quite; re-, munerate; compensate; fee, tip, bribe; pay one's footing etc. (*pay*) 807; make amends, indemnify, atone; satisfy, acknowledge.

get for one's pains, reap the fruits of.

Adj. remunerat-ive, -ory; munerary, compensatory, retributive, reparatory.

974. Penalty.—N. penalty; retribution etc. (*punishment*) 972; pain, pains and penalties; *peine forte et dure*; penance etc. (*atonement*) 952; the devil to pay.

fine, mulct, amercement; forfeit, -ure; escheat, damages, deodand, sequestration, confiscation, *premunire*.

V. penalize, fine, mulct, amerce, sconce, confiscate; sequest-rate, -er; escheat; estreat, forfeit.

975. Scourge. [Instrument of punishment.]—**N.** scourge, rod, cane, stick; ra-, rat-tan; birch, – rod; rod in pickle; switch, ferule, cudgel, truncheon; rubber hose.

whip, lash, strap, thong, cowhide, knout; cat, – o'-nine-tails, *sjambok*, quirt; rope's end.

pillory, stocks, whipping-post; cuck-, duck-ing stool; brank; triangle, wooden horse, maiden, thumbscrew, boot, rack, wheel, iron heel; treadmill, crank, galleys.

scaffold; block, axe, *guillotine*; stake; cross; gallows, gibbet, Tyburn tree; drop, noose, rope, halter, bowstring; electric chair, lethal chamber.

house of correction etc. (*prison*) 752.

gaol-, jail-er; executioner; hang-, heads-man; Jack Ketch; lyncher.

976. Deity.—N. Deity, Divinity; God-head, -ship; Omnipotence, Providence.

[Quality of being divine] divin-eness, -ity.

God, Lord, Jehovah, *Deus*; The -Almighty, – Supreme Being, – First Cause; *Ens Entium*; Author –, Creator- of all things; Author of our being; The -Infinite, – Eternal; The All-powerfull, -wise, -merciful, -holy; The Omni-potent, -scient.

[Attributes and perfections] infinite -power, – wisdom, – goodness, – justice, – truth, – love, – mercy; omni-potence, -science, -presence; unity, immutability, holiness, glory, majesty, sovereignty, infinity, eternity.

The -Trinity, – Holy Trinity, – Trinity in Unity, – Triune God; Three in One and One in Three.

God the Father; The -Maker, – Creator, – Preserver.

[Functions] creation, preservation, divine government; The-ocracy, -archy; providence; ways –, dealings –, dispensations –, visitations- of Providence.

God the Son, Jesus, Christ; The -Messiah, – Anointed, – Savior, – Redeemer, – Mediator,

– Intercessor, – Advocate, – Judge; The Son of - God, – Man, – David; The Only Begotten; The Lamb of God, The Word; Em-, Im-manuel; The - King of Kings and Lord of Lords, – King of Glory, – Prince of Peace, – Good Shepherd, – Way, – Truth, – Life, – Bread of Life, – Light of the World; The -Lord our, – Sun of- Righteousness.

The -Incarnation, – Hypostatic Union, – Word made Flesh.

[Functions] salvation, redemption, atonement, propitiation, mediation, intercession, judgment.

God the Holy Ghost, The Holy Spirit, Paraclete; The -Comforter, – Consoler, – Spirit of Truth, – Dove.

[Functions] inspiration, unction, regeneration, sanctification, consolation.

eon, aeon, special providence, *Deus ex machinâ*; *Avatar*.

V. create, uphold, preserve, govern etc.

atone, redeem, save, propitiate, mediate etc.

predestinate, elect, call, ordain, bless, justify, sanctify, glorify etc.

Adj. almighty, holy, hallowed, sacred, divine, heavenly, celestial; messianic; sacrosanct; all-powerful, -wise, -seeing, -knowing; omnipotent, omniscient; supreme.

super-human, -natural; ghostly, spiritual, hyper-physical, unearthly; the-istic, -ocratic, deistic; anointed.

Adv. *jure divino*, by divine right; *Deo volente*, D.V.

977. Angel. [Beneficent spirits.]—**N.** angel, archangel; heavenly host, choir invisible, host of heaven, sons of God; Michael, Gabriel etc.; seraph, -im; cherub, -im; ministering spirit, morning star; saint, *Madonna*; Our Lady, the Blessed Virgin, the Virgin Mary.

Adj. angelic, seraphic, cherubic.

978. Satan. [Maleficent spirits.]—**N.** Satan, the Devil, Lucifer, Ahrimanes, Belial; Sammael, Zamiel, Beelzebub, the Prince of the Devils; Mephistopheles, his satanic majesty.

the tempter; the evil -one, – spirit; the -author of evil, – wicked one, – old Serpent; the Prince of -darkness, – this world, – the power of the air; the -foul, – arch- fiend; the devil incarnate; the - common enemy, – angel of the bottomless pit; Abaddon, Apollyon, Mammon.

fallen agnels, unclean spirits, devils; the -rulers, – powers- of darkness; inhabitants of Pandemonium; demon etc. 980.

diabolism; devil-ism, -ship, -dom, -ry, -worship; *diablerie*; satanism, manicheism; the cloven foot; black magic etc. 992.

Adj. satanic, diabolic, devilish, infernal, hell-born.

979. Jupiter.—N. god, -dess; heathen gods and goddesses; Pantheon; Jupiter, Jove, Zeus, Apollo, Mars, Mercury, Neptune, Vulcan, Bacchus, Pluto, Saturn, Cupid, Eros, Pan; Juno, Ceres, Proserpina, Dina, Minerva, Pallas, Athenae, Venus, Aphrodite, Vesta; The Fates etc. 601.

Allah, Brahma, Vishnu, Siva, Shiva, Krishna, Juggernaut, Buddha; Ra, Isis, Osiris; Belus, Bel, Baal, Asteroth etc.; Thor, Odin; Mumbo Jumbo; good –, tutelary- genius; demiurge, familiar, – spirit; Sibyl; fairy, fay; sylph, -id; Ariel, peri, nymph, nereid, dryad, oread, sea-maid, Banshee, Benshie, Ormuzd; Oberon, Titania, Mab, hamadryad, naiad, mermaid, kelpie, Ondine, nix, nixie, sprite; denizens of the air; pixy etc. (*bad spirit*) 980.

mythology; heathen –, fairy- mythology; Lemprière, folklore.

Adj. fairy-, sylph-like; sylphic.

980. Demon.—N. demon, -ry, -ism, -ology; evil genius, fiend, familiar, – spirit, devil; bad –, unclean- spirit; cacodemon, incubus, Frankenstein's monster, succubus and succuba, Titan, Shedim, Mephistopheles, Asmodeus, Moloch, Belial, Ahriman, fury, The Furies etc. 900; harpy; Friar Rush.

vampire, ghoul; af-, ef-freet; afrite; ogre, -ss; gnome, gin, djinn, imp, deev, *lamia*; bo-gie, -gle; nis, kobold, flibbertigibbet, fairy, brownie, pixy, elf, dwarf, urchin, Puck, Robin Goodfellow; lepre-, cluri-chaune; troll, dwerger, sprite, oaf, changeling, bad fairy, nixe, pigwidgeon, Will-o'-the-wisp; Erl King.

[Supernatural appearance] ghost, specter, apparition, genie, spirit, shade, shadow, vision, phantom etc. 443; materialization (*spiritualism*) 992; hob-, goblin; wraith, spook, werwolf, boggart, banshee, *loup-garou*, *lemures*; evil eye.

nisse, necks; mer-man, -maid, -folk; siren, Lorelei; satyr, faun.

Adj. supernatural, weird, uncanny, unearthly, spectral; ghost-ly, -like; elf-in, -like; fiend-ish, -like; impish, demoniacal; haunted.

981. Heaven.—N. heaven; kingdom of - heaven, – God; heavenly kingdom; throne –, presence- of God; inheritance of the saints in light.

Paradise, Eden, abode of the blessed; Holy City, New Jerusalem; celestial bliss, glory.

[Mythological -heaven] Olympus; [– paradise] Elysium, Elysian fields, Arcadia, bowers of bliss, garden of the Hesperides, Islands of the Blessed; happy hunting-ground; third –, seventh-heaven; Valhalla (Scandinavian); Nirvana (Buddhist).

future state, eternity, eternal life, life after death, eternal home, resurrection, translation; resuscitation etc. 660; apotheosis, deification.

Adj. heavenly, celestial, supernal, unearthly, from on high, paradisiacal, beatific, elysian, Olympian, Arcadian.

982. Hell.—N. hell, bottomless pit, place of torment; habitation of fallen angels; Pandemonium, Abaddon, Domdaniel.

hell fire; everlasting -fire, – torment; lake of fire and brimstone; fire that is never quenched, worm that never dies.

purgatory, limbo, gehenna, abyss.

[Mythological hell] Tartarus, Hades, Avernus, Styx, Stygian creek, pit of Acheron, Cocytus,

Phlegethon, Lethe; infernal regions, *inferno*, shades below, realms of Pluto.

Pluto, Rhadamanthus, Erebus, Charon, Cerberus; Tophet.

Adj. hellish, infernal, stygian.

983. Theology. [Religious Knowledge.]—**N.** Theology (natural and revealed); Theo-gony, -sophy; Divinity; Hagio-logy, -graphy; Caucasian mystery; monotheism; religion; religious - persuasion, – sect, – denomination; cult; creed etc. (*belief*) 484; articles –, declaration –, profession –, confession- of faith.

theolog-ue, -ian; divine, schoolman, canonist, monotheist.

Adj. theological, religious; canonical; denominational; sectarian etc. 984.

983a. Orthodoxy.—N. orthodoxy; strictness, soundness, religious truth, true faith; truth etc. 494.

Christian-ity, -ism; Catholic-ism, -ity; 'the faith once delivered to the saints;' hyperorthodoxy etc. 984; iconoclasm.

the Holy –, the Orthodox- Church; Catholic –, Universal –, Apostolic –, Established- Church; temple of the Holy Ghost; Church –, body –, members –, disciples –, followers- of Christ; Christian, – community; true believer; canonist etc. (*theologian*) 983; Christendom, collective body of Christians, the Church Militant.

canons etc. (*belief*) 484; thirty-nine articles; Apostles' –, Nicene –, Athanasian- Creed; Church Catechism; textuary.

Adj. orthodox, sound, literal, strict, faithful, catholic, schismless, Christian, evangelical, scriptural, divine, monotheistic; true etc. 494.

984. Heterodoxy. [Sectarianism.]—**N.** heterodoxy; error etc. 495; false doctrine, heresy, schism; schismantic-ism, -alness; recusancy, backsliding, apostasy; atheism etc. (*irreligion*) 989.

bigotry etc. (*obstinacy*) 606; fanaticism, iconoclasm; hyperorthodoxy, precisianism, bibliolatry, hagiolatry, sabbatarianism, puritanism; idolatry etc. 991; superstition etc. (*credulity*) 486; dissent etc. 489.

sectar-ism, -ianism; nonconformity; secularism; syncretism, religious sects; the clash of creeds.

protestant-, advent-, Arian-, Erastian-, Calvin-, quaker-, method-, anabapt-, Pusey-, tractarian-, ritual-, Origen-, Sabellian-, Socinian-, De-, The-, mon-, material-, positiv-, latitudinairan-ism etc.

High –, Low –, Broad –, Free- Church; ultramontanism; monasticism; pap-ism, -istry; papacy; Anglican-, Catholic-, Roman-ism; popery, Scarlet Lady, Church of Rome, Greek Church; Christian Science, The Church of Christ Scientist.

pagan-, heathen-, ethic-ism; mythology; animism; poly-, di-, tri-, pan-theism; dualism; heathendom.

Juda-, Gentil-, Mahometan-, Islam-, Turc-, Brahmin-, Hindoo-, Buddh-, Lama-, Confucian-, Shinto-, Sabian-, Gnostic-. Soofee-, Hylothe-, Mormon-ism.

Theosophy; Spiritualism, Occultism.

heretic, antichrist; pagan, heathen; pai-, pay-nim; *giaour*; gentile; pan-, poly-theist; idolator; misbeliever, apostate, backslider.

bigot etc. (*obstinacy*) 606; fanatic, dervish, abdal, iconoclast.

latitudinarian, limitarian, Deist, Theist, Unitarian; positivist, materialist; agnostic, sceptic etc. 989.

schismatic; sectar-y, -ian, -ist; seceder, separatist, recusant, dissenter; non-conformist, -juror; Huguenot, Protestant; orthodox dissenter, Congregationalist, Independent; Episcopalian, Presbyterian; Lutheran, Calvinist, Quaker, Methodist, Weslayan; Ana-, Baptist; Dunker; Mormon, Latter-day Saint, Irvingite, Sandemanian, Glassite, Erastian; Sub-, Supra-lapsarian; Gentoo, Antinomian, Swedenborgian, Adventist, Plymouth Brother; Theosophist etc.

Catholic, Roman Catholic, Romanist, papist, ultramontane; Old Catholic, tractarian, Anglican, Puseyite, ritualist; Puritan.

Jew, Hebrew, Rabbist; Mahometan, Mohammedan, Mussulman, Moslem, Islamite, Osmanli; Brahm-in, -an; Parsee, Sofi, Soofee; Buddhist; Zoroastrian, Magi, Gymnosophist, fire-worshipper, Sabian, Gnostic, Sadducee, Rosicrucian etc.

Adj. heterodox, heretical; un-orthodox, -scriptural, -canonical; antiscriptural, apocryphal; un-, anti-christian; schismatic, recusant, iconoclastic; sectarian; dis-senting, -sident; secular etc. (*lay*) 997.

pagan; heathen, -ish; ethnic, -al; gentile, painim; pan-, poly-theistic; agnostic, sceptic.

Judaical, Mohammedan, Moslem, Brahminical, Buddhist etc. *n.*; Romish, Protestant etc. *n.*

bigoted etc. (*prejudiced*) 481; (*obstinate*) 606; superstitious etc. (*credulous*) 486; fanatical; idolatrous etc. 991; visionary etc. (*imaginative*) 515.

985. Revelation.—N. revelation, inspiration, *afflatus*.

Word, – of God; Scripture; the -Scriptures, – Bible, – Book of Books; Holy -Writ, – Scriptures; inspired writings, Gospel.

Old Testament, Septuagint, Vulgate, Pentateuch; Octateuch; the -Law, – Jewish Law, – Prophets; major –, minor- Prophets; Hagio-grapha, -logy; Hierographa; Apocrypha.

New Testament; Gospels, Evangelists, Acts, Epistles, Apocalypse, Revelations.

Talmud; Mishna, Masorah.

prophet etc. (*seer*) 513; evangelist, apostle, disciple, saint; the –, the Apostolical- fathers; Holy Men of old, inspired -writers, – penmen.

Adj. scriptural, biblical, sacred, prophetic; evangel-ical, -istic; apostolic, -al; inspired, theopneustic, apocalyptic, ecclesiastical, canonical, textuary.

986. Pseudo-Revelation.—N. the -Koran, – Alcoran; Ly-king, Shaster, Vedas, Zendavesta, Vedidad, Purana, Edda; Go-, Gau-tama; Book of Mormon.

[False prophets and religious founders] Buddha, Zoroaster, Zerdhusht, Confucius, Mahomet.

[Idols] golden calf etc. 991; Baal, Moloch, Dagon.

987. Piety.—N. piety, religion, theism, faith; religiousness, holiness etc. *adj.*; saintship; religionism; sanctimony etc. (*assumed piety*) 988; reverence etc. (*respect*) 928; humility, veneration, devotion; prostration etc. (*worship*) 990; grace, unction, edification; sancti-ty, -tude; consecration.

spiritual existence, odor of sanctity, beauty of holiness.

theopathy, beatification, adoption, regeneration, conversion, justification, sanctification, salvation, inspiration, bread of life; Body and Blood of Christ.

believer, convert, theist, Christian, devotee, pietist; the -good, – righteous, – just, – believing, – elect; Saint, *Madonna*.

the children of -God, – the kingdom, – light.

V. be -pious etc. *adj.*; have -faith etc. *n.*; believe, receive Christ; revere etc. 928; worship etc. 950; be -converted etc.

convert, edify, sanctify, hallow, keep holy, beatify, regenerate, inspire, consecrate, enshrine.

Adj. pious, religious, devout, devoted, reverent, godly, heavenly minded, humble; pure, – in heart; holy, spiritual, pietistic; saint-ly, -like; seraphic, sacred, solemn.

believing, faithful, Christian, Catholic.

elected, adopted, justified, sanctified, regenerated, inspired, consecrated, converted, unearthly, not of the earth.

988. Impiety.—N. impiety; sin etc. 945; irreverence; profan-eness etc. *adj.*, -ity, -ation; blasphemy, desecration, sacrilege; scoffing etc. *v.*

[Assumed piety] hypocrisy etc. (*falsehood*) 544; pietism, cant, pious fraud; lip-devotion, -service, -reverence; mis-devotion, formalism, austerity; sanctimon-y, -iousness etc. *adj.*; pharisaism, precisianism; sabbat-ism, -arianism; *odium theologicum*, sacerdotalism; bigotry etc. (*obstinacy*) 606, (*prejudice*) 481.

hardening, backsliding, declension, perversion, reprobation apostacy, recusancy.

sinner etc. 949; scoffer, blasphemer; sacrilegist; worldling; hypocrite etc. (*dissembler*) 548; Scribes and Pharisees; Tartufe, Maw-worm.

bigot; saint [ironically]; Pharisee, sabbatarian, formalist, methodist, puritan, pietist, precisian, religionist, devotee, ranter, fanatic, wowser.

the -wicked, – evil, – unjust, – reprobate; son of -men, – Belial, – the wicked one; children of darkness.

V. be -impious etc. *adj.*; profane, desecrate, blaspheme, revile, scoff; swear etc. (*malediction*) 908; commit sacrilege.

snuffle; turn up the whites of the eyes; idolize.

Adj. impious; irreligious etc. 989; desecrating etc. *v.*; profane, irreverent, sacrilegious, blasphemous.

un-hallowed, -sanctified, -regenerate; hardened, perverted, reprobate.

hypocritical etc. (*false*) 544; canting, pietistical, sanctimonious, unctuous, pharisaical, over-righteous, righteous over much.

bigoted, fanatical etc. 481 and 606; priest-ridden.

Adv. under the -mask, – cloak, – pretence, – form, – guise- of religion.

989. Irreligion.—N. irreligion, indevotion; ungodliness etc. *adj.*; laxity, quietism, apathy, indifference, passivity.

scepticism, doubt; un-, dis-belief; incredul-ity, -ousness etc. *adj.*; want of -faith, – belief; pyrrhonism; doubt etc. 485; agnosticism.

atheism, deism; hylotheism; materialism; positivism; nihilism.

infidelity, freethinking, antichristianity, rationalism.

atheist, anti-christian, sceptic, unbeliever, deist, infidel, pyrrhonist; *giaour*, heathen, alien, gentile, Nazarene; *esprit fort*, freethinker, latitudinarian, rationalist; materialist, positivist, nihilist, agnostic.

V. be -irreligious etc. *adj.*; disbelieve, lack faith; doubt, question etc. 485.

dechristianize; serve Mammon, love darkness better than light.

Adj. irreligious; in-, un-devout; devout-, god-, grace-less; un-godly, -holy, -sanctified, -hallowed; atheistic, without God.

sceptical, free-thinking; un-believing, -converted; incredulous, faithless, lacking faith; deistical; un-, anti-christian.

worldly, mundane, earthly, carnal, unspiritual; worldly etc.- minded.

Adv. irreligiously etc. *adj.*

990. Worship.—N. worship, adoration, devotion, aspiration, latria, homage, service, humiliation; kneeling, genuflexion, prostration.

prayer, invocation, supplication, rogation, intercession, orison, holy breathing; petition etc. (*request*) 765; collect, litany, Lord's prayer, paternoster, *Ave Maria*, rosary; bead-roll; latria, dulia, hyperdulia, vigils; revival; cult.

thanksgiving; giving –, returning- thanks; grace, praise, glorification, benediction, doxology, hosanna; h-, allelujah; *Te Deum*, *non nobis Domine*, *nunc dimittis*; paean.

psalm, -ody; hymn, plainsong, chant, chaunt, response, anthem, motet; antiphon, -y.

oblation, sacrifice, incense, libation; burnt –, votive –, thank-offering; offertory, collection.

discipline; self-discipline, -examination, -denial; fasting.

divine service, office, duty; morning prayer; mass, matins, evensong, vespers, compline; holy day etc. (*rites*) 998.

worshipper, congregation, communicant, celebrant.

V. worship, lift up the heart, aspire; revere etc. 928; adore, do service, pay homage; humble oneself, kneel; bow –, bend- the knee; fall -down, – on one's knees; prostrate oneself, bow down and worship, recite the rosary.

pray, invoke, supplicate; put –, offer- up -prayers, – petitions; beseech etc. (*ask*) 765; say one's prayers, tell one's beads.

return –, give- thanks; say grace, bless, praise, laud, glorify, magnify, sing praises; give benediction, lead the choir, intone, chant, sing.

propitiate, offer sacrifice, fast, deny oneself; vow, offer vows, give alms.

work out one's salvation; go to church; attend -service, – mass; communicate etc. (*rite*) 998.

Adj. worshipping etc. *v.*; devout, devotional, reverent, pure, solemn; fervid etc. (*heartfelt*) 821.

Int. h-, allelujah! hosanna! glory be to God! O Lord! pray God that! God -grant, – bless, – save, – forbid! *sursum corda.*

991. Idolatry.—N. idol-atry, -ism; demon-ism, -olatry; idol –, demon –, devil –, fire- worship; zoolatry, fetishism, Mari-, Bibli-, ecclesi-, heliolatry.

deification, apotheosis, canonization; hero worship.

sacrifices, hecatomb, holocaust; human sacrifices, immolation, mactation, infanticide, self-immolation, *suttee*.

idol, golden calf, graven image, fetish, *avatar*, Juggernaut, joss, *lares et penates*; Baal etc. 986.

idolator etc. *n.*

V. worship -idols, – pictures, – relics; put on a pedestal, bow down to, prostrate oneself before, make sacrifice to; deify, canonize, idolize.

Adj. idolatrous.

992. Sorcery.—N. sorcery; superstition; occult -art, – sciences; black –, magic; the black art, necromancy, theurgy, thaumaturgy; demon-ology, -omy, -ship; *diablerie*, bedevilment; witch-craft, -ery; glamor; fetis-hism, -ism; ghost dance; hoodoo, voodoo; Shamanism [Esquimaux], vampirism; conjuration; bewitchery, exorcism, enchantment, incantation, obsession, possession, mysticism, second sight, mesmerism, animal magnetism; od –, odylic- force; electro-biology, *clairvoyance*; spiritualism, spirit-rapping, table-turning; thought reading, telepathy, thought transference, automatic writing, *planchette*, ouija board; crystal gazing; spirit manifestation, materialization, astral body, ectoplasm etc.

divination etc. (*prediction*) 511; sortilege, ordeal, *sortes Virgiliance*; hocus-pocus etc. (*deception*) 545; oracle etc. 513.

V. practice -sorcery etc. *n.*; cast a -horoscope, – nativity; conjure, exorcise, charm, enchant; bewitch, -devil; overlook, look on with the evil eye; entrance, mesmerize, magnetize; fascinate etc. (*influence*) 615; taboo; wave a wand; rub the -ring, – lamp; cast a spell; call up spirits, – from the vasty deep; raise spirits from the dead; raise –, lay- ghosts; command genii.

Adj. magic, -al; mystic, weird, cabalistic, talismanic, phylacteric, incantatory; charmed etc. *v.*

993. Spell.—N. spell, charm, incantation, exorcism, weird, cabala, exsufflation, cantrap, runes, abracadabra, hocus-pocus, open *sesame*, countercharm, Ephesian letters, bell, book and candle, Mumbo-jumbo, evil-eye, fee-faw-fum.

talisman, amulet, periapt, telesm, phylactery, philter, wish-bone, merry-thought, mascot, scarab, swastika; fetish; *agnus Dei*.

wand, caduceus, rod, divining rod, lamp of Aladdin, magic carpet, seven-league boots; magic ring; wishing –, Fortunatus's- cap.

994. Sorcerer.—N. sorcerer, magician; thaumat-, the-urgist; conjuror, necromancer, seer, wizard, witch; fairy etc. 980; *lamia*, hag, warlock, charmer, exorcist, voodoo, mage, diviner, dowser; cunning –, medicine- man, witch doctor; Shaman, figure-flinger, ecstatica, medium, *clairvoyant*, mesmerist, hypnotist; *deus ex machinâ*; astrologer; soothsayer etc. 513.

Katerfelto, Cagliostro, Merlin, Comus, Mesmer, Rosicrucian; Hecate, Circe, Lilith, siren, weird sisters; witch of Endor.

995. Churchdom.—N. church, -dom; ministry, apostleship, priesthood, prelacy, hierarchy, church government, christendom, pale of the church.

clerical-, sacerdotal-, episcopalian-, ultramontan-ism; Theocracy; ecclesiolog-y, -ist; priestcraft, *odium theologicum*.

monach-ism, -y; monasticism, monkhood.

[Ecclesiastical offices and dignities] pontificate, primacy, archbishopric, archiepiscopacy; prelacy; bishop-ric, -dom; episcop-ate, -acy; see, diocese; deanery, stall; canon-ry, -icate; prebend, -aryship; benefice, incumbency, glebe, advowson, living, cure, – of souls; rectorship; vicar-iate, -ship; pastor-ate, -ship; deacon-ry, -ship; -curacy; chaplain, -cy, -ship; cardinal-ate, -ship; abbacy, presbytery.

holy orders, ordination, institution, consecration, induction, reading in, preferment, translation, presentation.

popedom, papacy; the -Vatican, – apostolic see, – see of Rome; religious sects etc. 984.

council etc. 696; conclave, college of cardinals, convocation, synod, consistory, chapter, vestry, presbytery; sanhedrim, *congé d'élire*; ecclesiastical courts, consistorial court, court of Arches.

V. call, ordain, induct, prefer, translate, consecrate, present, elect, bestow.

take -orders, – the veil, – vows.

Adj. ecclesi-astical, -ological; clerical, sacerdotal, priestly, prelatical, pastoral, ministerial, capitular, theocratic; hierarchical, archiepiscopal; episcopal, -ian; canonical; mon-astic, -achal; monkish; abbati-al, -cal; pontifical, papal, apostolic; untramontane, priest-ridden.

996. Clergy.—N. clergy, clericals, ministry, priesthood, presbytery, the cloth, the pulpit.

clergyman, divine, ecclesiastic, churchman, priest, presbyter, hierophant, pastor, shepherd, minister, clerk in holy orders; father, – in Christ; *padre*, *abbé*, *curé*; patriarch; reverend; black coat; confessor; sky pilot.

dignitaries of the church; ecclesi-, hier-arch; eminence, reverence, elder, primate, metropolitan, archimandrite, archbishop, bishop, prelate, diocesan, suffragan, dean, subdean, archdeacon, prebendary, canon, rural dean, rector, parson, vicar, perpetual curate, residentiary, beneficiary, incumbent, chaplain, curate, – in charge; deacon, -ess; preacher; lay reader, lecturer; capitular; missionary, propagandist, Jesuit, revivalist, field preacher.

churchwarden, sidesman; clerk, precentor, choir; almoner, *suisse*, verger, beadle, sexton, sacristan; acol-yth, -othyst, -yte; thurifer; chorister, choir boy.

[Roman Catholic priesthood] Pope, *Papa*, Holy

Father, pontiff, high priest, cardinal; ancient –, flamen; confessor, penitentiary; spiritual director.

cenobite, conventual, abbot, prior, monk, friar, lay brother, beadsman, mendicant, pilgrim, palmer; canon-regular, -secular; Jesuit, Franciscan, Friars minor, Minorites; Observant, Capuchin, Dominican, Carmelite; Augustinian; Gilbertine; Austin-, Black-, White-, Grey-, Crossed-, Crutched- Friars; Bonhomme, Carthusian, Benedictine, Cistercian, Trappist, Cluniac, Premonstratensian, Maturine; Templar, Hospitaller.

abb-, prior-, canon-ess; mother superior; *religieuse*, nun, sister, *beguine*, novice, postulant.

[Under the Jewish dispensation] prophet, priest, high priest, Levite; Rabbi, -n; scribe.

[Mohammedan etc.] mullah, ulema, imauam, sheik; so-fi, -phi; mufti, hadji, muezzin, dervish; fakir, -quir; brahmin, gooroo, druid, bonze, santon, abdal, Lama, talapoin, caloyer etc.

V. take orders etc. 995.

Adj. the –, the very –, the Right- Reverend; ordained, in orders, called to the ministry.

997. Laity.—N. laity, flock, fold, congregation, assembly, brethren, people.

temporality, secularization.

layman, civilian; parishioner, catechumen; secularist.

V. secularize.

Adj. secular, lay, laical, civil, temporal, profane.

998. Rite.—N. rite; ceremon-y, -ial; ordinance, observance, function, duty; form, -ulary; solemnity, sacrament; incantation etc. (*spell*) 993; service, psalmody etc. (*worship*) 990; liturgies.

ministration; preach-ing, -ment; predication, sermon, homily, exhortation, lecture, discourse, pastoral.

baptism, christening, chrism; immersion; baptismal regeneration; font; circumcision.

confirmation; imposition –, laying on- of hands; churching, purification, ordination etc. (*churchdom*) 995; excommunication.

Eucharist, Lord's supper, communion; the –, the holy- sacrament; celebration, high celebration; *missa cantata*; offertory; introit; consecration; con-, tran-substantiation; real presence; elements, bread and wine; mass; high –, low –, dry- mass.

matrimony etc. 903; burial etc. 363; visitation of the sick.

seven sacraments, impanation, extreme unction, last rites, *viaticum*, invocation of saints, canonization, transfiguration, auricular confession; fasting; maceration, flagellation, sackcloth and ashes; penance etc. (*atonement*) 952; absolution; telling of beads, reciting the rosary, processional; thurification, incense, holy water, aspersion.

relics, rosary, beads, reliquary, host, cross, rood, crucifix, pax, pix, pyx, *agnus Dei*, censer, thurible, patera, urceole; chalice, patten, Holy Grail, sangrail; seven-branch candle stick, monstrance, sacring bell.

ritual, rubric, canon, ordinal; liturgy, prayer-book, book of common prayer, pietas, euchology, litany, lectionary; missal, breviary, mass-book, bead-roll.

psalter; psalm –, hymn- book; hymn-al, -ology; psalmody.

ritual-, ceremonial-ism; sabbat-ism, -arianism; ritualist, sabbatarian.

holyday, feast, fast; Sabbath, Passover, Pentecost; Advent, Christmas, Noel, Epiphany, Lent, Shrove Tuesday, Ash Wednesday, Maundy Thursday; Passion –, Holy- week; Good Friday, Easter, Ascension Day, Whitsuntide; Trinity Sunday, Corpus Christi; All-Saints' –, – Souls'- Day; Candle-, Lam-, Martin-, Michael-mas; hogmanay; Ramadan, -zan; Bairam etc. etc.

V. perform service, do duty, minister, officiate, baptize, dip, sprinkle; confirm, lay hands on; give –, administer –, take –, receive –, attend –, partake of- the -sacrament, – communion; communicate; celebrate mass; administer –, receive- extreme unction; anele, shrive, absolve, confess; do penance; genuflect; cross oneself, make the sign of the cross.

excommunicate, ban with bell, book and candle.

preach, sermonize, predicate, lecture.

Adj. ritual, -istic; ceremonial, liturgic; baptismal, eucharistical; paschal.

999. Canonicals.—N. canonicals, vestments; robe, gown, Geneva gown, frock, pallium, surplice, cassock, dalmatic, scapulary, cope, scarf, tunicle, chasuble, alb, *alba*, stole; fan-on, -nel; tonsure, cowl, hood; calo-te, -tte; bands; capouch, amice, orarium, ephod; apron, lawn sleeves, pontificals, pall; miter, tiara, triple crown; shovel –, cardinal's- hat; biretta; crosier; pastoral staff; costume etc. 225.

1000. Temple.—N. place of worship; house of -God, – prayer.

temple, cathedral, minister, church, kirk, chapel, meeting-house, bethel, tabernacle, conventicle, *basilica*, fane, holy place, chantry, oratory.

synagogue; mosque; marabout; pantheon; pagoda; joss-house; dagobah, tope; kiosk.

parsonage, rectory, vicarage, manse, deanery, glebe, church house; Vatican; bishop's palace; Lambeth.

altar, shrine, sanctuary, Holy of Holies, *sanctum sanctorum*, sacrarium, -isty; communion –, holy –, Lord's- table; table of the Lord; pyx; baptistery, font; piscina, stoup; aumbry; sedile; reredos; rood-loft, – screen; jube.

chancel, quire, choir, nave, aisle, transept, lady chapel, vestry, crypt, cloisters, porch; triforum, clerestory, churchyard, *golgotha*, calvary, Easter sepulcher; stall, pew, sitting; pulpit, ambo, lectern, reading-desk, confessional, prothesis, credence, baldachin, *baldacchino*; jesse, apse, belfry; chapter-house; presbytery.

monastery, priory, abbey, friary, convent, nunnery, cloister.

Adj. claustral, cloistered; monast-ic, -erial; conventual.

INDEX

The numbers refer to the headings under which the words or phrases occur. When the same word or phrase may be used in various senses, the several headings under which it, or its synonyms, will be found, according to those meanings, are indicated by the words printed in Italics. These words in Italics are not intended to explain the meaning of the word or phrase to which they are annexed, but only to assist in the required reference.

When the word given in the Index is itself the title or heading of a category, the number of reference is printed in blacker type, thus: **abode 189.**

D

F

I

M

P

Q

T

MEDICAL DICTIONARY

—A—

Abacterial, sterile, free of bacteria.

Abalienation, mental derangement.

Abarognosis, loss of sense of weight.

Abarticular, not affecting a joint.

Abarticulation, dislocation.

Abasia, unable to walk because of loss of motor coordination.

Abatement, lessening of pain.

A.B.C. Process, purifying water or sewage by use of alum, blood and charcoal.

Abdomen, area of body between diaphragm and pelvic bones. The abdomen is lined with a smooth, transparent membrane called the peritoneum.

Abdominal, pertaining to the abdomen.

Abdominal Wall, the muscles in front of and along the sides of the abdomen.

Abduce, abduct.

Abduct, movement of an extremity away from the body or of a part from the middle of the whole.

Aberration, different from normal action.

Abevacuation, incomplete evacuation.

Abeyance, condition of suspended activity.

Abiology, study of nonliving things.

Abionarce, insanity due to infirmity.

Abiosis, absence of life.

Abirritant, soothing.

Ablactation, weaning.

Ablation, removal.

Ablepsia, blindness.

Ablucent, detergent.

Ablution, a washing.

Abnormal, not normal.

Aborad, away from the mouth.

Abortion, termination of pregnancy before the child is able to exist outside the womb. There are three types of abortions. An accidental abortion, usually referred to as a miscarriage, may be due to abnormalities of the egg or infant, glandular or nutritional problems in the mother, as well as other internal problems.
On the other hand, a therapeutic abortion is a deliberate step, taken for medical reasons, to stop a pregnancy. Therapeutic abortions are generally performed when the life or the health of the mother is threatened by the pregnancy. In this type of abortion, the decision to end the pregnancy is made and carried out by a doctor.
The third type of abortion, deliberate abortion, is performed when the mother decides that she does not wish to continue the pregnancy.

Abrachia, congenital absence of arms.

Abrade, chafe, roughen.

Abrasion, any injury which rubs off the surface skin, leaving a raw, bleeding surface.

Abreaction, a method employed in psychoanalysis to relieve a patient's feelings of guilt or hostility by reenacting the experience which brought on the feelings.

Abscess, collection of pus enclosed anywhere in the body, formed when foreign organisms destroy tissue.

Abscission, surgical removal of a growth.

Absorb, to seep in.

Abstract, to take away from.

Abtorsion, turning outward of both eyes.

Abuse, excessive use, or misuse. The term is frequently used in connection with drugs, such as in "drug abuse."

Abutment, anchorage tooth for a bridge.

Acampsia, rigidity of a part or limb.

Acapnia, decrease in carbon dioxide in the blood.

Acarbia, decrease of bicarbonate in the blood.

Acarid, tick, mite.

Acathexia, inability to retain bodily secretions.

Acceleration, increase the motion or speed.

Accident, unpleasant, unexpected happening leading to or causing an injury or death.

Acclimatize, to get used to a climate.

Accommodation, adjustment.

Accouchement, act of being delivered.

Accoucheur, an obstetrician or person trained as a midwife.

Accretion, accumulation of matter at a part.

Acedia, mental depression.

Acephalous, headless.

Acescence, sour.

Acetabulum, hollow area in the hip bone in which thigh bone fits.

Acetarsone, a drug derivative of arsenic used in the treatment of amebiasis.

Acetate, salt of acetic acid.

Acetic, sour like venegar.

Acetone, a colorless, inflammable solvent.

Acetychlorine, hormone secreted by the nervous system.

Acetylcholine, an acid found in the body. It plays an important part in nerve impluse transmissions.

Achalasia, inability of certain hollow, muscular organs to contract.

Achilles Tendon, the tendon at the back of the heel. It connects the muscles of the calf to the heel bone.

Achlorhydria, inability of the stomach wall to manufacture hydrochloric acid.

Acholic, without bile.

Achondroplasia, form of dwarfism in which the trunk is of normal size, the limbs are too short.

Achor, small skin elevation on hairy parts of body.

Achoresis, diminution of the capacity of an organ.

Achroma, absence of color.

Achromyan, antibiotic.

Achylia, absence of chyle, an emulsion of fat globules formed in the intestine.

Acicular, needle-shaped.

Acid, a sour substance that combines with metals, releasing hydrogen.

Acid Burns, burns caused by acids. Acid burns should be washed immediately to remove the acid. Treatment then consists of applying a solution of sodium bicarbonate (baking soda) or some other mild alkali to neutralize any chemical which remains on the skin. (An exception is an acid burn from carbolic acid which should be treated by washing the skin with alcohol.) The affected area is then washed with fresh water and gently dried. At this point it is treated as though it were a true burn.

Acid-forming, applied to foods, which when digested, leave a residue that is acid.

Acidity, excess of the hydrochloric acid normally found in the stomach.

Acidosis, condition in some diseases which causes more acid in the blood than normal. Acidosis can be caused by disease of or failure of the lungs or kidneys (the two body organs which help regulate acids and bases). It can also be caused by dehydration (including severe diarrhea), diabetes, and acid poisoning.

Acid Poisoning, poisoning by acid taken by mouth. The antidote for acid poisoning is usually an alkali diluted in water which is swallowed to neutralize the acid.

Acme, crisis.

Acne, skin condition found usually in adolescents in which glands of skin become infected. It is characterized by comedos (blackheads) and small skin elevations (with or without pus). Acne is caused by excessive secretions of grease from the sebaceous glands. The grease dries and blocks pore opening (blackheads) and sometimes becomes infected (skin elevations with pus, usually referred to as pimples). Treatment of acne includes a diet low in greasy foods. The diet will often prohibit chocolates and carbonated beverages. The use of astringents can be helpful. Acne will normally subside in the late teens when puberty is completed.

Acneform, resembling acne.

Acoria, insatiable appetite.

Acousma, hearing imaginary sounds.

Acoustic, relating to sound or hearing.

Acquired, obtained after birth.

Acral, affecting the extremities.

Acrid, irritating.

Acro, a prefix used to denote the hands or feet.

Acroarthritis, arthritis of the extremities.

Acrodolichomelia, hands or feet which are abnormally long.

Acromegaly, gigantism; state of excessive growth of the body caused by overactivity of the pituitary gland.

Acromion, the highest and outermost extension of the shoulder.

Acronyx, ingrowing nail.

Acropathy, disease of the extremities.

Acrophobia, fear of great heights.

Acrosphacelus, gangrene of the fingers or toes.

Acrotism, pulse defect.

A. C. T. H., Adreno-Cortico-Tropic-Hormone; hormone that stimulates one part of the adrenal gland.

Actinic, applies to those rays of sunlight beyond the violet end of the spectrum, which produce chemical change.

Actinomycosis, disease of cattle that can be transmitted to man. It is caused by the microorganism *Actinomyces bovis*. The infection forms obscesses in the neck, chest, and abdomen. It is treated with antibiotics such as penicillin.

Acuity, sharpness, clearness.

Acupuncture, one of the methods of treatment used for a variety of conditions, diseases, and disorders. The treatment is based on inserting needles into various specified points on the body.

Acute, illness which had a sudden beginning, a short course and severe symptoms.

Acyesis, female sterility.

Addiction, the condition of being physically or psychologically dependent on some foreign matter.

Addiment, complement.

Addison's Disease, condition in which adrenal glands are underactive, characterized by a deficiency of blood sugar, low blood pressure, and low temperature.

Adduct, movement of an extremity toward the body or parts toward the midline of the body.

Adenalgia, pain in a gland.

Adenase, enzyme.

Adenitis, inflammation of a gland.

Adenoidectomy, surgical removal of the adenoids.

Adenoids, lymph glands in back of nasal passage which function to trap germs and debris.

Adenoma, tumor consisting of glandular material.

Adenopathy, any disease of the glands.

Adenosine Triphosphate, a compound found in muscles which is the storage place for extra muscular energy (abbreviated ATP).

Adhesions, abnormal growing together of tissue following injury or operation.

Adiaphanous, opaque.

Adicity, valance.

Adipose, fatty.

Adipose Tissue, fatty connective tissue found under the skin and surrounding various body organs.

Adiposity, obesity.

Adjuvant, an auxiliary agent or medication.

Adneural, toward a nerve.

Adnexa, appendages or accessory parts of an organ.

Adolescence, the period of life from the onset to the conclusion of puberty.

Adrenal Gland, small gland immediately above each of the two kidneys. Each gland is approximately the size of a pea. Each gland is made up of two distinct parts, and each part has different functions. The outer layer, or adrenal cortex, is essential to life and life processes; the inner part, or adrenal medulla, while important, is not essential.

Adrenalin, hormone secreted by the adrenal gland, with many properties.

Adrenocorticotropic Hormone, a hormone secreted by the anterior pituitary. Adrenocorticotropic hormone (abbreviated ACTH) stimulates the adrenal cortex of the adrenal glands to secrete hormones. ACTH has been synthesized and has been used to replace secreted ACTH. More frequently, however, it is used as a diagnostic tool.

Adtorsion, turning inward of both eyes.

Adult, fully developed.

Adventitious, accidental or acquired; pertaining to the tough outer coat of an organ or blood vessel; occurring in unusual places.

Aeration, the process of giving off carbon dioxide and taking on oxygen, which occurs to blood in the lungs.

Aeriform, gaseous.

Aerobic, a term applied to any living organism which can live in an oxygen atmosphere.

Aeropathy, decompression sickness.

Aerophagy, air-swallowing spasms.

Afebrile, without fever.

Affect, feeling, mood.

Afferent, conducting toward a center.

Affinity, attraction.

Afterbirth, material from womb after childbirth.

After-pains, the contractions of the uterus after delivery.

Agalactia, absence of milk secretion.

Agar, form of seaweed used in treating constipation.

Age-adjusted Death Rate, death rates that have been standardized by age for the purpose of making comparisons between different populations or within the same population at various intervals of time. Also called age-adjusted mortality rate.

Agenesia, sterility; imperfect development.

Agent, something which acts upon or against something else.

Age-specific Death Rate, the ratio of deaths in a specific age group to the population of the same age group during a given period of time, such as a year. It is calculated by dividing the deaths that occurred among the specific age group during the year, by the mid-year population in the same group of the same year.

Ageusia, lack of sense of taste.

Agglutination, the part of the healing process in which the wound closes by adhesion.

Aggregation, clumping together.

Aging, the process of growing old.

Everyone is subject to aging, starting from the moment of conception. Aging is part of the growing process. As the individual matures, there takes place a constant and simultaneous tearing down of old tissue and a building up of new tissue. In children, the building up process is more rapid than the tearing down process. When the child becomes an adult, the tearing down process begins to catch up with the building up process. Throughout an individual's lifetime, he is subject to this simultaneous dual process.

Agitation, restlessness; mental illness.

Aglutition, inability to swallow.

Aglycemia, lack of sugar in the blood.

Agnail, a hangnail.

Agnogenic, of unkown origin.

Agony, extreme pain.

Agorophobia, extreme fear of open places.

Ague, an old-fashioned name for malaria or other fevers.

Ahypnia, insomnia.

Aid, assistance given to a person in need of help.

AIDS (acquired immune deficiency syndrome), a fatal disease caused by a virus known as HTLV III OR HIV (human immunodeficiency virus). AIDS is primarily transmitted through sexual intercourse, but it can also be transmitted when contaminated blood comes in contact with a cut or break in the skin. The virus attacks certain types of white blood cells, leaving the body vulnerable to some kinds of infections and to cancers such as Kaposi's sarcoma. Symptoms include fever, drowsiness, skin infections, weight loss, swollen glands, weakness, headaches, and brown or purple nodules on the lower parts of the legs (Kaposi's sarcoma). A test is available to determine the presence of the virus before symptoms develop.

Air, the gaseous mixture which constitutes the atmosphere.

Air Embolism, the blockage of any blood vessel by a bubble of air.

Air-sickness, sickness caused by high altitudes and motion during air travel.

Airway, instrument used to keep breathing passages open.

Akalamathesia, inability to understand.

Alae Nasi, nostril openings.

Alalia, speech impairment.

Alastrim, variola minor, a mild type of smallpox.

Alba, white.

Albinism, absence of pigmentation.

Albino, lack of pigment in the skin. The lack of normal pigmentation causes the skin and hair to be white and the eyes to be pink. Albinos must be careful of the amount of sun to which they are exposed.

Albumen, protein.

Albuminuria, albumin in urine.

Alcohol, a colorless liquid which can be used as an astringent or antiseptic. One type of alcohol, ethyl alcohol, is the major ingredient in wines, beers, and distilled beverages. In this form, alcohol is a colorless inflammable liquid which has intoxicating effects.

Alcoholism, drunkenness, an addictive disease characterized by a craving for alcohol and its effect in relieving psychic and physical pain.

Aldosterone, a hormone secreted by the adrenal cortex of the adrenal glands which regulates the amount of salt that is excreted by the kidneys.

Alexia, unable to read.

Algesia, sensitivity to pain.

Algid, cold.

Algogenic, causing pain; lowering temperature.

Algophobia, extreme fear of pain.

Alienist, psychiatrist.

Alignment, the act of straightening or placing in a line a body part which is out of shape or place.

Alimentary, pertaining to nutrition.

Alimentary Canal, that part of the digestive system consisting of the esophagus, stomach, and intestines.

Alimentation, act of nutrition.

Alkali, a base substance. In the body, alkalis are balanced by acids. Alkalis will turn red litmus paper blue. Lye, ammonia, and potash are alkalis.

Alkalosis, an excess of alkaline in the body and bloodstream.

Allergen, that which produces an allergic reaction.

Allergist, specialist in allergies.

Allergy, abnormal sensitivity to any substance.

Allochroism, variation in color.

Allodromy, irregular heart rhythm.

Allopathy, the method of treating diseases and conditions by using drugs which produce effects opposite those from which the patient is suffering.

Aloe, vegetable used as a laxative.

Alogia, inability to form words; senseless behavior.

Alopecia, baldness.

Alveoli, tiny air sacs found at the end of bronchioles in the lung.

Alvine, pertaining to the belly.

Alzheimer's Disease, a rare disease in which there is mental deterioration similar to senility, but the disease occurs in middle age.

Amaurosis, blindness.

Ambidextrous, proficient with each hand.

Amblyacusia, dullness of hearing.

Amblyopia, dimness of vision due to errors of refraction.

Amblyopia Ex Anopsia, a condition of reduced or dim vision in an eye which appears to be normal. It sometimes is called "lazy eye." It occurs when the two eyes do not see the same thing with the same degree of clarity, and the poorer eye is not stimulated to develop or maintain clearness of vision. An example is when the eyes are not straight or have grossly unequal vision. Amblyopia ex anopsia usually is not caused by a disease process and it can generally be corrected if discovered early enough. The condition usually begins in children during pre-school years and may go undiagnosed into adulthood.

Ambulatory, able to walk.

Ambustion, burn, scald.

Ameba, a simple single cell protozoan.

Amebiasis, an infection of the bowel caused by a microscope ameba whose technical name is *Entamoeba his tolytica.* The infection can occur in mild or severe forms. In its severe form, amebiasis is known as amebic dysentery. More rarely, the infection may spread to the liver or other parts of the body.

Amenia, amenorrhea.

Amenorrhea, stoppage of normal menstrual periods.

Amentia, mental impairment.

Amine, an organic compound that may be derived from ammonia by the replacement of one or more of the hydrogen atoms by hydrocarbon radicals.

Amino Acids, a chemical radical in all proteins.

Ammonia, colorless gas which is soluble in water.

Amnesia, loss of memory.

Amniocentesis, procedure used to withdraw amniotic fluid from the uterus in order to ascertain if the baby has certain abnormalities.

Amniotic Fluid, the fluid in which the fetus lives until birth.

Amorphous, shapeless.

Amphetamines, drugs which stimulate the central nervous system. They induce a transient sense of well-being, self-confidence, and alertness.

Ampule, container for hypodermic solutions.

Ampulla, widened end of a small passageway.

Amputation, removal of a limb or appendage. The primary reasons for amputations are trauma, death of tissues due to inadequate circulation, malignant tumors, chronic infections of bone or tissue, heat or cold injuries, uselessness in a limb, and congenital deformities.

Amyasthenic, muscular weakness.

Amyl Nitrite, a drug that has the primary purpose of relaxing smooth muscles.

Amyloid, starchlike.

Amylophagia, eating of starch.

Amylopsin, an enzyme secreted from the pancreas. Amylopsin converts partially digested starches into simple sugars such as maltose.

Amylum, starch.

Amyotonia, flaccidity of muscles.

Amyotrophic Lateral Sclerosis, a disease causing paralysis because of degeneration of spinal cord.

Amyxia, absence of mucus.

Ana, of each.

Anabolism, any body process that builds complex compounds from simple compounds.

Anadipsia, intense thirst.

Anaerobic, a term applied to any living organism that cannot live in an oxygen atmosphere.

Anal, pertaining to the anus.

Analgesic, drug used to relieve pain.

Analygesia, lack of feeling any pain.

Analysand, one undergoing psychoanalysis.

Analysis, an examination of the different parts or elements that make up the whole.

Anamnesis, patient's history.

Anandria, absence of male characteristics.

Anaphase Stage, the stage in cell division (mitosis) during which the chromosomes are pulled or drawn toward the two poles. The anaphase stage follows the metaphase stage and precedes the telophase stage (the last step in cell division).

Anaplasia, a phenomenon of tumors (benign or malignant) in which the cells composing the tumor revert to simple, unspecific cells incapable of performing the highly developed, very specific functions associated with the tumor area.

Anemic, pertaining to anemia.

Anmeophobia, extreme fear of winds and draughts.

Anepia, inability to speak.

Anesthesia, loss of sensation.

Anesthesiology, study and administration of anesthetics.

Anesthetic, drug or gas used to abolish pain.

Aneuria, deficiency of nervous energy.

Anaphia, lack of sense of touch.

Anaphrodisia, loss of sexual desire.

Anastattis, highly astringent.

Anastole, retraction.

Anatomy, science which deals with the structure of the body.

Ancipital, two-edged.

Anconal, pertaining to the elbow.

Androcyte, spermatid.

Androgen, any substance or hormone causing masculine characteristics.

Androphobia, fear of men.

Androsterone, an important male sex hormone.

Anemia, condition in which the normal amount of red blood cells is reduced. Hemoglobin is the red-colored substance in the red blood cells; it carries oxygen to the body tissues. If the amount of hemoglobin is below normal, or if there are too few red blood cells, not enough oxygen will get to the tissues.

Anesthetics, substance that artifically produces complete or partial lack of feeling.

Aneurysm, swelling in a blood-vessel arising from the stretching of a weak place in the wall. Surgery on an aneurysm generally involves the removal of the aneurysm and the damaged areas around it. The length of artery or vein that is removed is replaced by a section of vein from another part of the patient's body or by a synthetic section of tube.

Anfractuous, convoluted.

Angina, a choking, suffocating sense of pain.

Angina Pectoris, severe attacks of pain over the heart. Angina pectoris is not a disease itself, but a symptom of a disease. Chest pains may be the result of many conditions other than an insufficient flow of blood to the heart muscle.
The symptoms appear with exertion, emotion, exposure to cold, or overeating, and can be relieved by rest or nitroglycerine.

Angiogram, an examination of a blood vessel by means of X-rays.

Angitis, inflammation of a vessel.

Anhelation, shortness of breath.

Anhematosis, defective blood formation.

Anhydrous, containing no water.

Anhypnosis, insomnia.

Aniline, a poisonous substance which is the base for both phenacetin and acetanilid, two drugs used as analgesics and antipyretics.

Anility, like an old woman.

Animation, liveliness.

Anisomastia, inequality of the breasts.

Ankle, region between the foot and lower leg.

Ankylosing Spondylitis, immobility of the vertebrae similar to rheumatoid arthritis.

Ankylosis, partial or complete rigidity of a joint produced either by disease, such as arthritis, or deliberately, by surgical operation.

Ankyroid, hooklike.

Annectent, connecting.

Annular, ring-shaped.

Annulus, circular opening.

Anodmia, absence of the sense of smell.

Anodyne, pain reliever.

Anoia, idiocy.

Anomaly, abnormality.

Anopheles, a genus of mosquitoes that transmits malaria to humans.

Anopsia, defective vision.

Anorchism, absence of testes.

Anorexia, loss of appetite. Anorexia can be caused by a nervous condition. It is more of a symptom than a disease. People with high fevers often exhibit anorexia. Certain drugs will also induce it. Among those are drugs prescribed as diet aids for people who are overweight.

Anoscope, instrument used for rectal examination.

Anoscopy, examination of the anus.

Anosmia, lack of sense of smell.

Anostosis, defective formation of bone.

Anoxemia, reduction in the normal amount of oxygen in the blood.

Anoxia, insufficient supply of oxygen. This condition most frequently occurs when the blood supply to a part of the body is completely cut off. This results in the death of the affected tissue.

However, anoxia may also occur when the entire body is lacking in oxygen as a result of breathing air with a low percentage of oxygen.

Ansa, looplike structure.

Antabuse, proprietary drug used in the treatment of alcoholism.

Antacid, substance that neutralizes acids.

Antebrachium, forearm.

Antemortem, before death.

Antenatal, before birth.

Ante-Partum, before maternal delivery.

Anterior, before.

Anteversion, forward displacement of part of the body, particularly the womb.

Anthelmintic, drugs used to rid the body of worms.

Anthophobia, extreme dislike of flowers.

Anthorisma, swelling.

Anthracosis, inflammation of the lungs due to inhalation of carbon dust.

Anthrax, disease of man from animals; two forms exist, one on skin and other in lungs.

Antianemic Principle, substance which counteracts anemia.

Antiarthritic, that which relieves or cures arthritis.

Antibechnic, relieving cough.

Antibiotics, the group of drugs usually prepared from molds or mold-like organisms, which are used in treatment of specific infections. Antibiotics are either bacteriostatic or bactericidal. That is, they inhibit growth of bacteria (bacteriostats) or they destroy them (bactericides). In either case, they work with the body's own defense system to cure the illness.

Despite the remarkable effectiveness of antibiotics against a wide range of diseases caused by bacteria, antibiotics do have drawbacks. Some people are hypesensitive, or allergic, to antibiotics.

The use of antibiotics may also lead to superinfections. These are infections caused by bacteria that normally live in the body without causing illness. The action of an antibiotic may upset the natural bacterial balance within the body, causing usually harmless bacteria to multiply into infections.

Antibody, a protein produced by body which reacts specifically with a foreign substance in the body.

Antibromic, deodorant.

Anticarcinogen, an environmental agent offering some protection against a carcinogen which is similar in chemical construction.

Anticoagulants, a group of drugs which reduce the clotting tendencies of the blood.

Anticus, anterior.

Antidote, remedy given to counteract a poison.

Antiemetic, remedy to prevent vomiting.

Antigen, any protein not normally present in the body and which stimulates the body to produce antibodies.

Antihemorragic, a general term for any drug or substance that helps slow, stop, or prevent hemorrhaging.

Antihistamine Drugs, a series of drugs used in the treatment of allergy.

Antihypertensive Agents, drugs that are used to lower blood pressure.

Antilemic, counteracting plague.

Antimetabolite, a substance closely similar to an essential cell-building material. An antimetabolite will tend to replace the essential material.

Antipathic, opposite in nature.

Antipathy, dislike.

Antipyretic, anything that reduces fever.

Antirabic, counteracting rabies.

Antiseptic, substance used to inhibit growth or destroy germs. Antiseptics are used on the skin only. They are similar to disinfectants in that both kill germs, but disinfectants are too strong to apply to the human body.

Antiserum, a serum that contains antibodies. It is obtained by withdrawing blood from an animal that has manufactured the antibodies as a result of exposure to antigens.

Anti-Toxin, substance manufactured by the blood, which specifically neutralizes the poison (toxin) given off by a particular germ.

Antitussive, any drug or agent which relieves or prevents coughing.

Antixerotic, preventing dryness.

Anton's Symptom, the failure or inability of a person who is blind to recognize or accept the fact of his blindness.

Antrum, space within a bone, usually that in the maxilla or upper jaw.

Anuria, absence of urine flow.

Anus, outlet of the bowel.

Anvil, the small bone located in the middle ear, situated between the stirrup and the hammer.

Anxietas, anxiety, worry.

Anxiety, a psychological term indicating uneasiness, apprehension, and similar emotions and feelings.

Aorta, main artery leaving the heart.

Aortic insufficiency, a condition in which there is an improper closing of the valve between the aorta and the lower left chamber of the heart. This allows a backflow of blood.

Aortitis, inflammation of the aorta.

Aortography, an examination by X-ray of the aorta and its main branches. This is made possible by the injection of a dye which is opaque to X-rays.

Apandria, dislike of men.

Apanthropy, dislike of human society.

Apathic, not having sensation.

Aperient, mild laxative.

Aperture, opening.

Apex, a term used to indicate the top or uppermost part of a body organ.

The blunt, rounded end of the heart, directed downward, forward, and to the left is also referred to as the apex.

Aphagia, inability to swallow.

Aphakia, absence of a lens behind the pupil of the eye.

Aphasia, inability to form words.

Aphephobia, fear of being touched.

Aphonia, inability to speak.

Aphrodisiac, drug which produces sexual excitement.

Aphtha, white spot.

Aphthous Stomatitis, a disease that causes recurring outbreaks of blister-like sores inside the mouth and on the lips. The sores are called canker sores.

Apnea, a momentary loss of the impulse to breathe.

Apogee, state of greatest severity of a disease.

Apomorphine, an opium derivative that causes nausea and vomiting very rapidly after it has been injected. The primary use for apomorphine is to induce vomiting when the patient has swallowed a poisonous substance. It has also been used to help alcoholics and drug abusers.

Apoplexy, condition which is the result of decreased blood flow to part of brain, also called stroke.

Apostasis, abscess.

Apothecary, druggist.

Appendage, outgrowth.

Appendectomy, surgical removal of the appendix.

Appendicitis, inflammation of the appendix.

Appendix, fingerlike projection from the large intestine with no known function.

Appestat, a part of the hypothalamus which regulates hunger.

Appetite, desire for food.

Applicator, instrument used to make local application of medicine.

Apprehension, a psychological term indicating a feeling of uneasiness about future events.

Approximal, close.

Apsithyria, a nonphysical condition in which the patient is unable to speak. Apsithyria is caused by hysteria.

Apsychia, unconsciousness.

Aptyalism, lack of saliva.

Aqueous, watery.

Arachnidism, condition resulting from spider bite.

Arachnoid, fine, thin tissue.

Arbor Urinae, a burning sensation experienced during urination.

ARC (AIDS-related complex), a condition in which some of the milder syptoms of AIDS are experienced.

Arcate, curved.

Archepyon, very thick pus.

Arenoid, like sand.

Areola, ring of color around a particular point, e.g., the nipple.

Argentic, containing silver.

Arhigosis, an inability to feel cold.

Ariboflavinosis, deficiency of riboflavin.

Arm, region from shoulder to below. The arm is composed of three large bones: the humerus, the ulna, and the radius. The humerus extends from the shoulder to the elbow, where it meets the ulna and the radius. The ulna and radius extend from the elbow to the wrist.

Armamentarium, doctor's entire equipment.

Armpit, the area under the arm where it joins the shoulder. The armpit is a small, hollow area. Its proper name is axilla.

Arrest, stopping; restraining.

Arrhenic, pertaining to arsenic.

Arrhythmia, disturbance of normal rhythm.

Arrowroot, nutrient starch.

Arsenic, poisonous chemical element.

Arteria, artery.

Arterial Blood, oxygenated blood. The blood is oxygenated in the lungs, then passes from the lungs to the left side of the heart via the pulmonary veins. It is then pumped by the left side of the heart into the arteries, which carry it to all parts of the body. Arterial blood is bright red in color.

Arteriole, smallest sized artery.

Arterioplasty, operation in which the artery is reconstructed.

Arteriosclerosis, condition in which arteries of body become thickened and inelastic. Every artery throughout the body is subject to hardening, but the most often and most seriously affected vessels are the largest arteries, such as the aorta, the coronary arteries, and the arteries that feed the brain and kidneys. Arteries may harden in one part of the body more rapidly then in other areas.

Arteriostenosis, constriction of an artery.

Arteristis, inflammation of an artery.

Artery, vessel which carries blood away from the heart. Blood moves through the arteries in spurts corresponding to the contractions of the heart muscle, which is forcing blood throughout the body.

Arthralgia, pain in a joint.

Arthrifuge, remedy for gout.

Arthritis, inflammation of one or more joints. The exact cause is unknown. There are two main theories: infection, and that the body's own defenses go awry and attack its own tissues. Emotional stress is believed to play an important role.

Arthrocace, ulceration of a joint.

Arthrodesis, a surgical procedure to put a joint in a fixed, rigid position.

Arthronosos, any joint disease.

Arthropathy, any joint disease.

Arthrophyma, joint swelling.

Arthroplasty, an operation upon a joint to make it function.

Arthrosclerosis, stiffening of the joints.

Articulation, enunciation of speech; a joint.

Artificial, not natural.

Artificial Respiration, the act of restoring breathing, the best method being mouth to mouth respiration. The standard methods of artificial respiration are the mouth-to-mouth method (with variations) and several manual methods (back-pressure, arm-lift; chest-pressure, arm-lift; back-pressure, hip-lift). Of these the mouth to mouth method is considered the best. Although first advocated for infants and children, it is now the recognized method of choice.

Asbestosis, lung disease occurring in those who inhale asbestos or asbestos-like material.

Ascariasis, invasion of the body by roundworms.

Ascending Paths, term used for the paths nerve impulses take on their way to the brain.

Ascites (Dropsy), an accumulation of body fluid in the abdomen.

Asepsis, absence of infected material or infection.

Asexual, without sex.

Asexualization, castration.

Asiderosis, iron deficiency.

Asitia, dislike of food.

Aspermatism, nonformation of sperm.

Asphyxia, stoppage of breathing due to obstruction of the air passages. Drowning, electric shock, and gas poisoning are the three most common accidents likely to result in asphyxiation. Asphyxiation also occurs from such accidents as choking, hanging, and burial in materials like grain, sand, or gravel. Excessive use of alcohol or drugs may also cause breathing to stop. Also, some illnesses, such as poliomyelitis (sometimes called polio or infantile paralysis), may result in asphyxiation.

Aspirator, instrument for withdrawing fluids by suction.

Aspirin, Acetylsalicylic acid, commonly used to relieve headache.

Assay, examine.

Asteroid, shaped like a star.

Asthenia, lack or loss of strength.

Asthma, condition of lungs characterized by decrease in diameter of some air passages. The asthma sufferer has periodic attacks of difficulty in breathing, which may be mild or severe.

Astigmatism, a defect of eyesight caused by uneven curvature of the outside membrane of the eye.

Astringent, that which causes contraction and stops discharges.

Asynergy, lack of coordination.

Atactitia, loss of the sense of touch.

Ataxia, loss of co-ordinated movement caused by disease of the nervous system.

Atelectasis, noninflation or incomplete inflation of a lung or lungs at birth, and, in adults, collapse of a lung.

Atheroma, hardening of the arteries.

Atherosclerosis, form of hardening of the arteries.

Athetoid, a type of cystic fibrosis in which the patient shows constant uncontrolled motion.

Athetosis, repetitive, involuntary, slow movements.

Athelete's Foot, fungus infection of the foot. The symptoms of infection are: itching, cracking or scaling of the skin, and sometimes small blisters that contain a watery fluid. If the disease continues without treatment, there can be large blisters and raw places on the skin.

Athrombia, defective blood clotting.

Atlas, topmost vertebra in the spinal column.

Atocia, sterility in the female.

Atomization, breaking up of a liquid into a fine spray.

Atony, lack of normal tone.

Atopy, allergy.

Atoxic, not poisonous.

Atresia, absence of a normal body opening.

Atrial Septum, the muscular wall that divides the left and right upper chambers of the heart which are called atria.

Atrophy, decrease in size of a normally developed organ or tissue.

Atrichia, absence of hair.

Attack, the onset of illness.

Attenuation, weakening, thinning.

Audiogenic seizure, an attack or seizure similar to an epileptic attack but brought on by auditory stimulation. The sound is usually a very high pitch.

Audiograph, graph showing acuteness of hearing.

Audiology, science of hearing.

Audiometer, instrument for measuring acuteness of hearing.

Audiophone, hearing aid.

Auditory Canal, the outer part of the ear.

Aura, sensations experienced before the onset of a disease or convulsion.

Aural, pertaining to the ear or hearing.

Aureomycin, antibiotic.

Auricle, the part of the ear that projects out from the head.

Auris, ear.

Aurotherapy, treatment with gold salts.

Auscultation, part of physical examination which uses detection of sounds in body by use of stethescope to aid diagnosis.

Autism, morbid concentration, a mental disorder which develops in childhood. The most striking symptom of the autistic child is his almost total withdrawal into himself. Ironically, autistic children often are very intelligent.

Autoclave, sterilizer.

Autodermic, a skin graft coming from the patient's own body.

Autodigestion, self-digestion.

Autoerotism, sexual stimulation of self.

Autogenuous, self, generated.

Autoimmunity, a condition in which the body has developed a sensitivity to some of its own tissues.

Autointoxication, poisoning by toxins formed within the body.

Autokinesis, voluntary motion.

Automatic, involuntary motion.

Autonomic, independent in action or function.

Autophobia, extreme fear of solitude.

Autopsy, examination of a body after death to discover the cause of death.

Autonomic Nervous System, part of the central nervous system which supplies the internal organs. It is divided into two parts: the sympathetic and the parasympathetic nervous systems.

Avitamic Acid, vitamin C; ascorbic acid.

Autotoxin, toxin formed in the body.

Auxesis, increase in size.

Avitaminosis, disease resulting from a vitamin deficiency.

Avulsion, tearing away of a part.

Axilla, armpit.

Axillary, pertaining to the armpit.

Axillary Nerve, nerve involved in shoulder movement and general sensations in the shoulder area. The axillary nerve used to be called the circumflex nerve.

Azoospermia, absence of sperm in the semen.

Azote, nitrogen.

— B —

Baby Blues, a feeling of depression and weepiness experienced by many new mothers. There are many reasons why a feeling of depression may occur. Physical changes within the mother's body may trigger and deepen feelings of depression. Because the mind and the body are so delicately meshed, any profound physical readjustment is bound to be reflected in feelings and thoughts. The hormones secreted during pregnancy are no longer needed, and the supply of available energy may not match the increased demands of the day—and night.

Baby Teeth, the first teeth, also called primary or milk teeth. The baby teeth are formed long before birth; the permanent teeth begin to form in the baby's jaw about the time he is born. At about six months of age (earlier in some children, later in others), the first baby teeth appear, usually the lower front ones. These are followed at more or less regular intervals by the upper front teeth, the back teeth, and the cuspids (called eye or canine teeth).

Bacca, berry.

Baccate, berry-shaped.

Bacillary, pertaining to bacillus bacteria.

Bacillemia, presence of bacilli in the blood.

Bacilliform, similar to a bacillus in shape.

Bacilluria, presence of bacilli in the urine.

Bacillus, pl., Bacilli, one of the major forms of bacteria.

Bacitracin, an antibiotic drug.

Back, posterior part of the body from the neck to the pelvic girdle.

Backache, pain in spine or adjacent areas.

Backflow, fluid moving in the opposite direction from the way it should be moving. A faulty or incompetent valve will allow blood to flow back in the wrong direction.

Bacteremia, bacteria in the blood.

Bacteria, microscopic organisms.

Bacterial Endocarditis, an inflammation of the inner layer of the heart caused by bacteria. The lining of the heart valves is most frequently affected. Bacterial endocarditis is commonly a complication of an infectious disease, an operation, or an injury.

Bactericide, that which destroys bacteria.

Bacteriostatic, a term applied to any drug or agent that inhibits the growth of bacteria. Different bacteriostats act against different bacteria.

Bacteriuria, bacteria in the urine.

Bagassosis, lung disease.

Bag of Waters, the sac of fluid in which an embryo floats. The fluid keeps the fetus evenly warm and acts as a shock absorber to protect it from jolts and bumps.

Balanitis, inflammation of the tip of the penis or clitoris.

Balanus, tip of the penis or clitoris.

Balbuties, stammering.

Baldness, lack of hair.

Ballistocardiogram, a tracing of the movements of the body caused by the beating of the heart.

Ballistophobia, extreme fear of missiles.

Ballooning, distention of a cavity.

Ballottement, rebound of a part when pressure is released.

Balm, soothing ointment.

Balsam, an aromatic resin.

Bandage, piece of gauze or other material for wrapping any part of the body.

Banti's Syndrome, an anomoly of the spleen.

Barber's Itch, infection of the beard area, also known as sycosis.

Barbital, a drug used to depress the central nervous system.

Barbiturates, drugs used as a hypnotic or sleep producer. Properly prescribed and taken as directed in small doses, they relieve tension and anxiety. In larger doses (three or four times as much) they produce drowsiness and sleep. They are also used medically for such psychosomatic conditions as high blood pressure, peptic ulcer, spastic colitis, and other psychophysiologic disorders.

Barium, a toxic metallic element.

Barium Sulfate, powder used in an emulsion which a patient drinks prior to X-rays of the stomach and intestines.

Barren, sterile.

Baryecois, deafness.

Basal Ganglia, part of the nervous system located in the brain. They play an important role in the transmission of impulses involved in voluntary muscular movement.

Basal Metabolism, the processes and/or measurement of vital cellular activity in the fasting and resting state based on oxygen usage.

Basedow's Disease, a goiter (thyroid enlargement) condition which includes a rapid pulse and nervous symptoms.

Baseplate, plastic material for making dental trial plates.

Basic, opposite of an acid; fundamental.

Basilic Vein, large vein on the inner side of the upper arm.

Bastard, one born of an unwed mother.

Bath, method of cleansing; therapeutic treatment.

Bathophoia, extreme fear of high objects.

Battarism, stuttering.

Beaker, glass with a wide mouth.

Bearing Down, the expulsive effort of a woman in the second stage of labor.

Beat, throb due to the contraction of the heart or passage of blood through a vessel.

Bedbug, an insect found in temperate and tropical climates. Bedbugs are usually flat and red. They live in houses, particularly in furniture and beds, and feed on human blood.

Bedsores, lesions over pressure areas on body of a bedridden patient.

Begma, cough.

Behavior, the observable activity of an individual.

Belch, escape of gas from the stomach through the mouth.

Belladonna, drug used to help spasmodic disorders.

Bell's Palsy, paralysis of the facial nerve; shown in weakness of one side of the face. The eye on the affected side will not close properly, and it becomes impossible to blow out the cheeks or whistle.

Belly, stomach.

Bemegride, a central nervous system stimulant which is used as a respiratory stimulant and as one of the antidotes for barbiturate poisoning.

Bends, decompression sickness.

Benign, non-repeating when referring to a disease.

Benignant, not recurrent.

Benzedrine, the proprietary name of a nervous stimulant.

Benzothiadiazine, a drug used to increase the output of urine by the kidney.

Beriberi, disease, uncommon in this country, caused by eating food deficient in vitamin B.

Beryllosis, inflammation of the lungs due to beryllium oxide dust.

Bestiality, intercourse with an animal.

Beta Rays, negatively charged particles emitted by radium.

Betalin S, synthetic vitamin B.

Bex, cough.

Bicameral, having two cavities.

Biceps, major muscle of the upper arm.

Bicarbonate, salt containing two parts carbonic acid and one part basic substance.

Bicellular, composed of two cells.

Biceps, any muscle that has two heads or branches.

Bicuspid, premolar tooth.

Bifocals, eyeglasses that serve the dual purpose of correcting both near and far vision.

Bifurcate, forked.

Bile, liver secretion.

Biliation, excretion of bile.

Biliousness, mild upset of the liver caused by dietary indiscretion.

Biliuria, bile in the urine.

Binaural Hearing-Aid System, a hearing-aid system consisting of two complete hearing aids—microphone, amplifier, and receiver—one for each ear. For some people, the binaural system increases the directional sense and helps to separate wanted sounds from unwanted background noise.

Binder, broad bandage used to encircle and support.

Biochemistry, chemistry of living things.

Biologicals, medical preparations used in the treatment or prevention of disease.

Biology, science of life and living things.

Biolytic, able to destroy life.

Bion, any living organism.

Biopsy, tissue taken from a living person for study.

Biostatics, vital statistics.

Biotomy, vivisection.

Bipara, woman who has had two labors.

Birth, process of being born.

Birth Canal, the canal a baby passes through during the birth process. The canal consists of the cervix, vagina, and vulva.

Birth Control, measures used to prevent pregnancy.

Birth Injury, any injury to an infant during the birth process.

Birth-Mark, blemish on skin of new born child, which is usually permanent.

Bisexual, both sexes in one person.

Bismuthosis, poisoning due to use of bismuth, a drug formerly used in the treatment of syphilis.

Bistoury, surgical knife.

Bite, cut with teeth; puncture by an insect.

Blackblood, impure blood.

Black Death, bubonic plague.

Black Lung Disease (pneumoconiosis), occupational disease caused by inhaling coal dust. Constant exposure over a long period of time irritates the lungs, causing scar tissue to develop.

Blackout, sudden temporary loss of sight and even consciousness.

Blackwater Fever, form of malaria.

Black Widow, poisonous spider.

Bladder, collecting pouch for urine from kidneys.

Bladder Control, the ability to control the urge to urinate. From birth on, the bladder empties automatically. To empty it is the natural thing to do. To hold back is somewhat harder and takes training. Most babies are not ready to master such delicate timing until long past one year of age.

Bland, soothing; mild

Blastocyte, a cell in an embryo. Blastocytes are nonspecific or primitive cells that later become more specific or differentiated.

Blastoma, tumor.

Blear-eye, chronic inflammation of margins of eyelids.

Bleb, blister.

Bleeder, one suffering from hemophilia; an inborn incurable disease in which severe bleeding follows even a slight cut.

Bleeding, emitting blood. The term bleeding is usually used to indicate bleeding from capillaries when blood trickles or oozes from a wound. The term hemorrhaging usually indicates bleeding from an artery or from a vein. The difference is one of degree—hemorrhaging is always serious, and if unchecked it is often fatal. Bleeding can result from a small cut or wound and will usually clot of its own accord.

Bleeding Time, time necessary for the natural stoppage of bleeding from a cut, about 3 minutes or less.

Blenna, mucus.

Blennagenic, producing mucus.

Blepharitis, inflammation of the eyelids shown by redness, crusting, swelling and infection of the eyelashes.

Blepharon, eyelid.

Blindness, inability to see; blindness can be partial or total. Visual impairment may result from one or more of the following: disease, defective functioning of the various parts of the eye, defects in the shape of the eye, congenital defects, irritation, injury, and accidents.

Blister, collection of fluid under the skin.

Bloated, swollen beyond normal size.

Block, an obstruction or blockage. The term is also used to refer to an anesthesia that goes deep into the tissues but is restricted in area.

Blood, fluid contained in arteries and veins of body that carries nutrients to and waste away from all tissues. Made up of cells and plasma.

Blood Bank, storing place for reserve blood.

Blood Clot, coagulated mass of blood.

Blood Count, a procedure that determines the number and type of red and white blood cells per cubic millimeter of blood.

Blood Groups, categories under which all human blood can be classified.

Bloodletting, a very old method for treating disease. It involved cutting the patient and allowing him to bleed. The idea was that the disease would leave the body with the escaping blood. It is used today in a very few cases of heart trouble to reduce the amount of blood and hence the amount of work the heart is required to do.

Bloodshot, locally congested with blood.

Blood-Pressure, this term refers to two different pressures in the blood system; the systolic pressure, which is that existing when the heart contracts and the diastolic pressure when the heart is in full relaxation.

Blood Transfusion, a technique for replacing a patient's lost, diseased, or ineffective blood with fresh blood from a healthy donor.

Blood Type, classification of blood into different groups.

Blood Vessels, vessels that carry blood throughout the body. There are three major blood-vessel types: arteries, capillaries, and veins.

Bloody Flux, dysentery.

Blotch, a spot, usually red or pink.

Blue Baby, child born with a blue color due usually to a heart defect.

Blue Ointment, mercurial ointment.

Blushing, rush of blood to the face.

Body, the physical man; trunk.

Body Cavities, thorax, abdomen, pelvis.

Boil, infection of the skin.

Bolus, round mass; pill; food prepared for swallowing by mastication.

Bone Grafting, transplanting a healthy bone to replace missing or defective bone.

Bonelet, small bone.

Bone Onlay, portion of transplanted bone placed across a break in a bone.

Bones, framework of body, composed of calcium and elastic tissue.

Bone Wax, material used to pack bone in order to stop bone bleeding.

Booster Inoculations, shots given at intervals to maintain a level of immunity.

Boric Acid, an antiseptic used on skin to help infections.

Boss, protuberance at one side of a bone.

Botulism, the most dangerous form of food poisoning; botulism is usually the result of eating contaminated foods from cans. The bacteria that cause botulism are anaerobic. This means that they grow only in an oxygen-free atmosphere. Therefore, canned foods provide an ideal growing place for them.

Bowel, intestine.

Bowleg, a leg that curves outward, usually below the knee.

Box Splint, used for fractures below the knee.

Brachium, arm.

Bradycardia, slow heart rate.

Braidism, hypnotism.

Brain, the primary nervous structure which sends out and receives stimulations to and from the rest of the body.

Brain Fever, meningitis.

Breakbone Fever, acute epidemic febrile disease.

Breast, front of the chest; mammary gland.

Breast-Feeding, feeding a newborn child with human milk from the mother's breast. It is probably the safest and most desirable way to nourish a child, because nobody has ever improved on the formula that the breast secretes to nournish the baby. However, breast-feeding should not be relied on exclusively for complete nutrition for much longer than the first four months of life.

Breath, air inhaled and exhaled in the respiratory process.

Breathe, to inhale and exhale air.

Breathing, act of taking in air to the body and exhaling carbon dioxide.

Breech Presentation, a baby born buttocks or feet first.

Bright's Disease, kidney disease.

Broad-Spectrum Antibiotic, any antibiotic that is effective against many different types of bacteria.

Bromides, salts of bromine.

Bromidrosis, offensive body odor.

Bromide, any salt containing bromine.

Bronchial Tubes, the large tubes (bronchi) that lead from the windpipe and carry the air that has been breathed in through the mouth and nose.

Bronchiectasis, state in which the lung tissue around the end of the breathing tubes becomes infected with the formation of sac-like cavities which fill with infectious material.

Bronchiole, smallest subdivision of the breathing tubes within the lung.

Bronchitis, inflammation of the windpipe which divides and subdivides into narrower tubes making up the network of air passages within the lungs.

Bronchorrhagia, hemorrhaging in the bronchial tubes.

Brown Mixture, cough syrup containing opium and licorice.

Brucella, type of bacillus.

Bruise, any injury to the surface of the body in which the skin is discolored but not broken.

Bubonic Plague, fatal infectious disease.

Bucca, mouth.

Bug, small insect.

Buggery, sexual relations through the anus.

Bulimia, an insatiable appetite.

Bulla, large blister.

Bunion, thickened area of skin on skin on lateral side of big toe.

Burn, an injury to the body caused by high temperature. Burns are classified in several ways: by the extent of the burned surface, by the depth of the burn, and by the cause of the burn. Of these, the extent of body surface burned is the most important factor in determining the seriousness of the burn and plays the greatest role in the patient's chances for survival.

Bursa, a sac like cavity usually found in or near joints.

Bursitis, inflammation of a bursa.

Buttocks, the rounded portion of the lower back which joins the thighs.

Buttonhole, straight cut through the wall of a cavity.

Bysma, plug; tampon.

Bythus, lower abdominal region.

Byssinosis, irritation of the air passages in the lung due to inhalation of cotton dust.

— C —

Cacation, defecation.

Cachet, capsule.

Cachexia, extreme wasting and weakness found in the later stages of a severe illness or starvation.

Cachinnation, hysterical laughter.

Cacomelia, deformity of a limb. Cacomelia is congenital.

Cadaver, corpse.

Caduceus, symbol of the medical, i.e., the wand of Hermes.

Caffeine, stimulant found mainly in coffee. It is used as a stimulant, a diuretic, and in the treatment of migraine headaches.

Cainotophobia, extreme fear of anything new.

Caisson Disease, occurs in workers, such as divers, who work under high atmospheric pressure, occurs when the pressure is reduced too rapidly, and the nitrogen in the blood escapes in the form of bubbles.

Calamine, pink substance composed of zinc and iron oxides, used in the form of lotion to soothe the skin.

Calcaneus, heel bone.

Calcareous, chalky; containing calcium.

Calcicosis, inflammation of the lungs due to marble dust.

Calcification, calcium deposits within the tissues of the body.

Calcinosis, calcium deposit in the skin and its underlying tissue.

Calcium, element which is the basis of limestone, important in body skeleton and function.

Calculus, stone-like mass which may form in the body under abnormal conditions.

Calf, the fleshy part of the back of the leg.

Calibrator, instrument for measuring openings.

Callous, any thickening of the skin formed on the site of continual irritation, usually on the feet or hands.

Callus, the new tissue formed at the site of fracture when a bone heals.

Calmant, Calmative, sedative.

Calomel, mercurous chloride; formerly used in the treatment of syphilis.

Calorie, measure of energy intake and output in the body.

Calvities, baldness.

Camphor, drug obtained from the camphor tree and used to stimulate the skin.

Camphorated, containing camphor.

Camphor Test, test for liver disease. When camphor is given orally, glycuronic acid will appear in the urine Absence of this reaction indicates a disease of the liver

Canal, passage, duct.

Cancer, any malignant tumor. Malignant tumors, such as cancer, always endanger life. They choke out normal tissue as they extend to adjacent tissue layers. They may also spread to other parts of the body. New growths thus related to the original tumor are called metastases. Cancerous cells can spread throughout the body via the blood and lymph systems.
Malignant tumors are divided into two main classes: carcinomas, which develop in the lining and covering tissues of organs; and sarcomas, which develop in the connective and supportive tissues of the body. Bone cancers are sarcomas.

Cancroid, like cancer; a tumor; type of skin cancer.

Cancrum Oris, gangrene of the mouth.

Canine Teeth, four teeth (upper and lower) between the incisors and molars.

Canker, type of mouth ulceration.

Cannabis, the dried, flowering tops of the hemp plant. Also called marihuana and hashish.

Capillary, smallest blood vessel. The capillaries serve as the crossing point between the small arteries (arterioles), which carry oxygenated blood from the heart, and the small veins (venules), which return blood to the heart. The walls of capillaries are semipermeable, allowing the interchange of water, salts, glucose, etc., between the blood and tissue fluid.

Capsule, tissue covering a part; soluble coating surrounding medication.

Caput, head.

Caput Succedaneum, edema or an abnormal collection of fluid in and under the scalp of a newborn baby.

Carbo, carbon, charcoal.

Carbohydrates, the scientific name for sugars, starches and cellulose.

Carbolic Acid, coal tar derivative used as an antiseptic and disinfectant.

Carbon, element which is the characteristic constituent of organic compounds.

Carbon Dioxide (CO^2), colorless, odorless gas used with oxygen to promote respiration.

Carbon-Dioxide Poisoning, a result of an increase in the percentage of carbon dioxide in the body over six per cent. This causes the rate of respiration to increase to the point where it can strain the heart, slow reflexes, and cause unconsciousness and death. In a healthy body this is uncommon, because the body will compensate by increasing the rate of depth of breathing.

Carbon Monoxide, A colorless, odorless, tasteless gas, which is produced as a result of incomplete combustion of organic material.

Carbuncle, large boil.

Carcinogenic, causing cancer.

Carcinoma, particular type of cancer.

Cardiac, concerning the heart.

Cardiac Arrest, total loss of heart function.

Cardiac Catheter, a diagnostic device for taking samples of blood, or pressure readings within the heart chambers, that might reveal defects in the heart.

Cardiac Failure, heart failure.

Cardiac Opening, the opening between the esophagus and the upper part of the stomach.

Cardiogram, record of changes in electrical energy of heart cycle.

Cardiograph, apparatus for making a graph of heart cycle.

Cardiology, medical specialty dealing with the heart.

Cardiospasm, contraction of the muscles controlling the inlet to the stomach.

Cardiovascular, pertaining to the heart and blood vessels.

Cardiovascular Disease, any disease that affect the heart and the blood vessels.

Caries, condition of decay, usually applied to decay of the teeth.

Carminative, drug to aid digestion and relieve flatulence, e.g., ginger, peppermint.

Carnal, pertaining to the flesh.

Carnal Knowledge, sexual knowledge.

Carnivorous, flesh-eating.

Carotene, a pigment (yellow or red in color) found in carrots, sweet potatoes, leafy vegetables, milk, and eggs. The body can convert it to vitamin A.

Carotid, major artery leading to the brain.

Carotid Gland, a small gland located between the internal and external carotid arteries.

Carpal, relating to the wrist.

Carpal Tunnel, the passage in the wrist for the median nerve and the flexor tendons in the wrist.

Carpus, wrist.

Carrier, one who harbors disease germs without suffering from the disease himself.

Car Sickness, illness due to motion of a car.

Cartilage, gristle; there are three types in the human body—hyaline, fibrocartilage, and elastic cartilage. Cartilage differs from bone in that it has no blood vessels. If it is cut or torn, the damage must be repaired surgically.

Cascara, a laxative.

Case, particular example.

Caseation, conversion of tissue into a cheese-like substance by certain diseases.

Casebook, Physician's record book.

Casein, protein product of milk.

Cast, mold to hold bone rigid and straight.

Castor Oil, old-fashioned purgative.

Castrate, to remove the testicles or ovaries.

Castration Complex, extreme fear of injury to the sex organs.

Casualty, accidental injury.

Catabolism, the breaking down of complex compounds into simpler ones.

Catalepsy, general name to describe various states marked by loss of power to move the muscles.

Catalyst, agent which influences a chemical reaction without taking part in it.

Cataplasm, a poultice, usually medicated.

Catamenia, onset of first menstrual period.

Cataract, clouding of the lens of the eye which prevents clear vision; not a film growing over the lens, but a change in the lens itself.

Catarrh, any illness which causes inflammation of membranes with a discharge of mucus.

Catatonia, type of schizophrenia characterized by immobility.

Catgut, sheep's intestine twisted for use as a surgical thread.

Catharsis, purging.

Cathartic, purgative.

Catheter, tube for passage through body channels, usually to evacuate fluids.

Cathexis, emotional energy attached to an object.

Catoptric Test, a test for cataracts made by observing reflections from the eye lens and cornea.

CAT SCAN (computerized axial tomography), type of diagnostic x-ray used to give a three-dimensional picture.

Caustic, irritating, burning.

Cautery, application of a burning agent to destroy tissue.

Cauterization, application of heat or burning chemicals to the surface of the body.

Cavity, hollow space.

Cecostomy, establishing an artificial opening into the large intestine near the appendix for evacuation.

Cecum, first part of the large intestine.

Celiac, pertaining to the abdominal region.

Cell, small cavity; a mass of protoplasm containing a nucleus.

Cell Membrane, the semipermeable wall surrounding an individual cell composed of protein and fat molecules that carefully regulate admission to the cell.

Cellular, composed of cells.

Cellular Tissue, loose connective tissue that has large interspaces and is found under the skin, peritoneum, etc.

Cellulitis, deep inflammation of the tissues just under the skin caused by infection with germs.

Central Nervous System, the part of the nervous system that includes the brain and the spinal cord.

Centrifuge, a machine that rotates at high speeds and is used to separate substances according to their densities.

Cephalalgia, headache.

Cephalic, pertaining to the head.

Cephalotractor, a forceps used by an obstetrician during delivery.

Cerebellum, small part of the nervous system, situated at the back of the brain, which is concerned with coordination of movements and bodily functions such as respiration.

Cerebral Palsy, a broad term used to describe a variety of chronic conditions in which brain damage, usually occurring at birth, impairs motor function and control.

Cerebration, mental activity.

Cerebrospinal Fever, an acute infectious form of meningitis, also referred to as epidemic cerebrospinal meningitis. In addition to inflammation of the membranes of the brain and spinal cord, there is usually an eruption of hemorrhage spots on the skin.

Cerebro-Spinal Fluid, the clear fluid which surrounds the brain and spinal cord as they lie inside the skull and in the canal of the spinal column; acts mainly as a shock absorber.

Cerebrum, the brain, especially the large frontal portion, as distinct from the cerebellum and the spinal cord.

Cerumen, ear wax.

Cervical, pertaining to the neck or mouth of womb.

Cervix, the neck or that part of an organ resembling the neck.

Cervix Uteri, the narrow lower portion of the uterus.

Cesarean Operation, abdominal operation to remove a child from the womb of a pregnant woman.

Cestoid, resembling a tapeworm.

Chafing, irritation caused by the rubbing together.

Chalazion, tumor of the eyelid.

Chancre, the name given to the sore that appears on the body when infected with certain types of venereal disease organisms.

Chancroid, an infection of the genitals that is caused by *Haemophilus ducreyi*. The original sore is at the site of infection and can be quite painful. The infection can spread to the lymph nodes of the genital area. It is treated with sulphonamide drugs and sometimes with tetracycline.

Change of Life, the menopause, usually occurring in women between the ages of forty and fifty-five, and about ten years later in men.

Charcoal, a black carbon that results from the burning (or charring) of organic material.

Charley Horse, bruised or torn muscle associated with cramping pain in the muscle.

Charting, recording the progress of a disease.

Check, slow down; stop, verify.

Cheek, side of the face below the eye.

Cheilitis, inflammation of the lips.

Cheilosis, lip disorder due to vitamin deficiency.

Chemical Burn, a burn caused by acids, alkalies, or other chemicals.

Chemotherapy, the treatment of disease by chemicals or drugs.

Chest, area enclosed by the ribs and sternum.

Cheyne-Stokes Respiration, breathing that is characterized by changing depths of respiration.

Chicken Pox, relatively mild childhood disease. It is spread by secretions from the mouth and nose and by fluid from the characteristic skin blisters. The incubation period is two to three weeks.

Chilblains, painful swelling of fingers, toes and ears caused by exposure to cold.

Child, one in the period between infancy and youth.

Child Abuse, the willful injury of a child by parents or guardians.

Chill, symptoms that occur when one first becomes infected with any germs which cause fever; result of nervous stimulation.

Chin, area below lower lip.

Chiropractic, system of treatment based on the belief that all disease is caused by pressure on the nerves as they leave the spinal column.

Chiropractor, one who specializes in bone manipulation.

Chlamydia, venereal disease.

Chloasma, brownish discoloration of the skin found in patches on any part of the body; particularly apparent in some pregnant women.

Chloral Hydrate, a drug used as an hypnotic. It works as a depressant to the central nervous system. For a while the use of chloral hydrate was replaced by the barbiturates, but recently it has been used more frequently. It has a strong odor and a bitter taste and should not be taken on an empty stomach. Chloral hydrate is one of the drugs prescribed for insómnia.

Chloremia, decrease of hemoglobin and red corpuscles of the blood.

Chlorine, a yellow-green poisonous gas used in compounds as a disinfectant and antiseptic.

Chloroform, heavy, clear, colorless liquid used as an anesthetic.

Chloromycetin, antibiotic.

Chloroquine, a compound drug used in the treatment of malaria.

Chlorosis, form of anemia.

Chlorothlozide, a chemical compound that increases the output of urine.

Choke, obstruction of the pharynx or esophagus.

Cholecystis, the gallbladder.

Cholecystectomy, removal of the gall bladder.

Cholecystitis, inflammation of the gall bladder.

Cholelith, gallstone.

Cholemia, presence of bile in the blood.

Cholera, tropical intestinal disease.

Choleric, irritable.

Cholesterol, substance found in fats and oils.

Cholestasis, a condition in which the flow of bile from the liver is stopped or suppressed.

Cholinesterase, an enzyme.

Chondral, pertaining to cartilage.

Chondro, a prefix meaning cartilage.

Chondroma, a benign tumor containing the structural elements of cartilage.

Chopart's Amputation, an amputation of part of the foot.

Chorda, string, tendon.

Chordae Tendineae, fibrous chords that serve as guy ropes to hold the valves between the upper and lower chambers of the heart secure when forced closed by pressure of blood in the lower chambers.

Chorea, also known as St. Vitus' dance or Sydenham's chorea; disease of the nervous system, usually considered to be related to rheumatism or rheumatic fever.

Choriomeningitis, inflammation of the coverings of the brain.

Chorion, outermost of the fetal membranes.

Chorlocarcinoma, a cancer occurring in a part of the placenta sometimes retained in the uterus following pregnancy.

Chromatelopsia, color blindness.

Chromatic, pertaining to color.

Chromatid, one of the pair of spirals of a chromosome.

Chromatosis, pigmentation.

Chromocyte, colored cell.

Chromosome, one of several small more or less rod-shaped bodies in the nucleus of a cell.

Chronic, of long duration.

Chronological, according to time sequence.

Chrysoderma, a pigmentation of the skin resulting from deposits of gold.

Chylomicron, a minute particle of fat that is found in the blood during digestion.

Chyme, food after digestion in the stomach.

Cicatrix, scar.

Cilia, microscopic waving hairs.

Ciliary Muscle, the muscle that surrounds the eye lens and helps the eye to focus by changing the shape of the lens.

Circulation, flowing in a circular course.

Circulation Time, rate of blood flow.

Circulatory System, the system that consists of the heart, the arteries, the veins, and the capillaries.

Circumcision, operation of cutting off the foreskin of male penis.

Circumflex, a term used to denote a part of the body that winds around or bends around another part of the body.

Cirrhosis, hardening of any tissue, but particularly of the liver.

Cirsectomy, removal of a part of a varicose vein.

Citric Acid, a mild acid found in citric fruits such as lemons and grapefruit. It plays an important role in metabolism.

Clamp, surgical device for compressing a part or structure.

Claudication, lameness due to decreased blood flow.

Claustrophobia, extreme fear of enclosed spaces.

Clavicle, collar bone.

Clavus, corn.

Cleavage, division into distinct parts.

Cleft, fissure.

Cleft Palate, congenital fissure of the palate forming one cavity for the nose and throat.

Climacteric, change of life.

Clinic, bedside examination; center where patients are treated by a group of physicians practicing together.

Climax, period of greatest intensity.

Clinical, pertaining to bedside treatment.

Clinotherapy, treatment of a patient's complaints by bed rest.

Clitoris, small erectile organ of the female genitalia.

Clomiphene, a drug used to increase fertility.

Clot, to coagulate.

Clubbed Fingers, fingers with a short, broad tip and overhanging nail, somewhat resembling a drumstick.

Club-Foot, congenital deformity of the feet of unknown cause.

Clunis, buttock.

Clyster, enema.

Coagulation, formation of a blood clot.

Coaguloviscosimeter, an instrument that measures the amount of time the blood takes to coagulate.

Coalescence, fusion of parts.

Coarctation, narrowing or constricting.

Cocaine, a highly addictive drug of abuse; a local anesthetic.

Cocci, a type of bacteria that are spherical in shape. "Cocci" is used as a suffix for denoting specific bacteria.

Coccygodynia, pain in the area of the tail bone.

Coccyx, small bones at the end of the spine.

Cochlea, cavity in the internal ear.

Codeine, sedative.

Cod-Liver Oil, the chief outside source of vitamins A and D, obtained from oil of cod fish.

Cognition, processes involved in knowing.

Coitus, sexual intercourse.

Coitus Interruptus, a method of contraception in which the penis is withdrawn before semen is ejaculated.

Colchicine, drug which helps to relieve symptoms of gout.

Cold Abscess, an abscess that develops slowly and shows little sign of inflammation. A cold abscess is generally tuberculous.

Colds, common viral infection of man causing symptoms of nasal fullness, cough and fever.

Cold Sores, lesions particularly in and around mouth caused by herpes simplex virus.

Colectomy, removal of part of the large intestine.

Colic, severe abdominal pain caused by spasm of one of the internal organs, usually the intestines; pertaining to the colon or large intestine.

Colitis, inflammation of the large intestine.

Collapse, to flatten; breakdown; prostration.

Collateral, a secondary or alternative path for the flow of blood.

Colles' Fracture, a fracture of the lower end of the radius.

Collodion, drug which, when painted on the skin, forms a thin transparent protective film.

Collyrium, local eye medication, e.g., eye wash.

Coloboma, a defect. Usually used to indicate a congenital defect of the eye.

Colon, large intestine.

Color Blindness, an inborn condition in which, while ordinary vision remains normal the individual is unable to distinguish between particular colors.

Colostomy, a surgical procedure that reroutes the colon to bypass and avoid the rectum.

Colostrum, first milk from a mother's breast after childbirth.

Colpalgia, vaginal pain.

Colpatitis, vaginal inflammation.

Column, supporting part.

Coma, complete loss of consciousness, which may be the result of various causes.

Comatose, state of being in a coma.

Comedo, blackheads in glands of skin.

Commensal, a term used to denote an organism that lives on or within another organism without causing harm to the host.

Comminute, a bone shattered in several pieces.

Comminution, breaking into small fragments.

Commissurotomy, an operation to widen the opening in a heart valve that has become narrowed by scar tissue.

Commitment, placing a patient in an institution.

Common Cold, a viral infection of the throat and nasal passages.

Comparative Anatomy, human anatomy compared to that of animals.

Compensation, a change made by the body to compensate for some abnormality.

Complication, added difficulty.

Compound, substance composed of different elements.

Compound Fracture, a fracture of the bone in which the broken bone pierces the skin.

Compress, a pad for application of pressure or medication to a specific area.

Conception, fertilization of an ovum by a sperm forming a zygote or fertilized egg which develops into an embryo.

Concha, shell-like organ.

Concussion, stunning; condition of dizziness, mental confusion and sometimes unconsciousness, due to a blow on the head.

Condom, rubber covering worn over the penis to prevent conception.

Conduction, conveyance of energy.

Condyle, the rounded protuberance at the end of a bone.

Condyloma, wartlike growth near the anus or genitals.

Congenital, existing at or before birth.

Congenital Heart Defects, a defect existing at birth, resulting from the failure of an infant's heart or of a major blood vessel near the heart to develop normally during pregnancy.

Congestion, excess accumulation of blood or mucus in any part of the body.

Conjunctiva, the membrane lining of the eyelid and outer surface of the exposed portion of the eyeball.

Conjunctivitis, inflammation of the transparent membrane which covers the eyeball.

Connective, that which binds together.

Connective Tissue, one of the four main tissues of the body which support bodily structures, bind parts together and take part in other bodily functions.

Consciousness, awareness.

Constipation, failure of bowels to excrete residue at proper intervals.

Constrictive Pericarditis, a shrinking and thickening of the outer sac of the heart, which prevents the heart muscle from expanding and contracting normally.

Consumption, tuberculosis.

Contact Lenses, a substitute for or an alternative to wearing eyeglasses. Contact lenses are usually round disks, concave in shape, to fit on the convex surface of the eyeball. The disk floats on the fluid of the eye and serves the same purpose as the lenses from a pair of eyeglasses—helping to adjust impaired vision.

Contagion, (see infection.)

Contagious, easily transmitted by contact.

Contagium, agent causing infection.

Contaminate, to soil or infect.

Continence, ability to control natural impulses.

Contraception, use of mechanical devices or medicines to prevent conception.

Contractile Protein, the protein substance within the heart muscle fibers responsible for heart contraction by shortening the muscle fibers.

Contraction, a drawing together.

Contracture, a shortening of tissue, causing deformity or distortion, e.g., scar.

Contraindication, a condition or factor that indicates that a particular treatment or drug is unsuitable for use in a specific case.

Contusion, bruise.

Convalescense, the period following an injury, illness, surgery, etc., during which the patient is recuperating.

Convex, rounded and somewhat elevated.

Convolutions, curved and winding inward folds, such as the surface of the cerebrum or the intestines.

Convulsant, medicine which causes convulsions.

Convulsion, temporary loss of consciousness with severe muscle contractions due to many causes; fit or generalized spasm.

Copulation, sexual intercourse.

Cord, Spinal, that portion of the central nervous system contained in the spinal canal.

Cord, Umbilical, cord which connects the umbilicus of the fetus to the placenta.

Corium, layer of skin under the epidermis.

Corn, thickening of the skin, hard or soft, according to location on the foot.

Cornea, transparent membrane covering the eye and lying beneath the conjunctiva.

Corneum, outermost layer of skin.

Coronary Artery Bypass, major heart surgery which removes one or more veins from the leg and uses them to bypass blocked arteries in the heart.

Coronary Atherosclerosis, an irregular thickening of the inner layer of the walls of the coronary arteries.

Coronary Thrombosis, clotting of blood in the blood vessels which supply the heart.

Coroner, one who holds inquests over those dead from violent or unknown causes.

Cor Pulmonale, heart disease resulting from disease of the lungs or the blood vessels in the lungs.

Corpus, principal part of an organ; mass.

Corpuscle, blood cell.

Corpus Luteum, a yellow substance secreted by the ovary after an ovum has been released.

Corrosive, destructive; disintegrating.

Corsucation, sensation of flashes of light before the eyes.

Cortex, outer layer of the brain and other organs.

Corticosteroids, hormones secreted in the adrenal cortex.

Cortisone, a hormone produced by the adrenal glands.

Costae, the twenty-four bones (twelve on each side) that form the rib cage.

Costalgia, rib pains.

Couching, a technique used in the treatment of cataracts. Instead of stripping the lens from the eye, the surgeon displaces or moves the cataract into a position where it cannot block light rays.

Cough, an attempt on the part of the body to expel something causing irritation in the respiratory tract.

Coumarin, a class of chemical substances that delay clotting of the blood. An anticoagulant.

Counterirritation, the application of an irritant to reduce or relieve another irritation. Counterirritation can involve the use of drugs in the form of ointments or the use of heat. Counterirritants are usually applied to the skin and seem to work by producing an inflammation, thus increasing the flow of blood to the affected area.

CPR (cardiopulmonary resuscitation), type of artificial respiration which maintains heart and lungs until professional help is available.

Cradle Cap, an accumulation of a thick, greasy crust, usually on the scalp; but it may occur behind the ears, on the eyebrows or eyelashes, at the corners of the nose, on the cheeks, or even on the truck.

Cramp, painful, spasmodic contraction.

Cranial Nerves, twelve pairs of nerves directly connected to the brain.

Cranium, skull.

Creatine, a compound of nitrogen manufactured in the body.

Cremaster, muscle which draws up the testis.

Crest, ridge on a bone.

Cretinism, condition caused by the lack of or decreased secretion of the thyroid gland in a child.

Crevice, small fissure.

Cricoid Cartilage, cartilage that forms the lower and back sections of the larynx.

Crisis, the turning point of a disease.

Critical, dangerous; severe.

Crohn's Disease, chronic inflammation of the intestinal tract.

Cross-eyes, condition in which eyes do not move together.

Cross Matching, a method used to be sure that the recipient and the donor involved in a blood transfusion are compatible blood types.

Croup, a disease of children characterized by coughing and difficult breathing.

-cule, -cle (suffix), little.

Cubitus, the elbow; also the forearm and hand.

Culture, propagation of an organism.

Cure, system of treatment; restoration to health.

Cusp, point of the crown of a tooth; pointed projection on a segment of a cardiac valve.

Cuspid, canine tooth.

Cut, a wound in which the skin is broken by a sharp cutting instrument or by material.

Cuticle, outermost layer of the skin.

Cutis, the outer layers of skin, including the epidermis and the dermis (or corium).

Cyanide, one of the fastest-acting poisons.

Cyanosis, term used to describe blueness of the skin, generally caused by lack of oxygen.

Cyclarthrodial, a term applied to any joint that can rotate.

Cyclomethycaine, a chemical preparation used as a local or surface anesthesia.

Cyesis, pregnancy.

Cyst, any sac in the body filled with liquid or semi-liquid substance.

Cystic Fibrosis, an inherited disease of children and adolescents that affects the exocrine, or externally secreting, glands of the body.

Cystitis, inflammation of the bladder.

Cystoscope, a lighted tube used in the examination of the urinary bladder.

Cystoscopy, process of examining the inside of the bladder with an instrument.

Cytochrome, a group of compounds found in animal and human tissues; they play an important role in the movement of oxygen from the blood to the cells.

— D —

Dacryorrhea, excessive flow of tears.

Dactyl, digit.

Dactylion, webbing of the fingers and toes.

Dactylitis, inflammation of a finger or toe.

Dactylology, communication with the fingers, i.e., sign language.

Dactylus, finger; toe.

Daltonism, color blindness.

D. & C., dilation and curettage of uterus.

Dandruff, condition of the scalp characterized by dry scaling.

Dapsone, one of the sulfone class of drugs used in the treatment of leprosy.

Dartos, fibrous layer under the skin of the scrotum.

Deaf-mutism, inability to hear or speak.

Deafness, complete or partial loss of hearing.

Dealbation, bleaching.

Dearterialization, conversion of arterial into venous blood.

Death Rate, number of people who die each year, compared with the total number of population.

Death Rattle, gurgling noise caused by passage of air through accumulated fluid in the windpipe.

Debility, weakness.

Decalcification, decrease in the normal mineral salts content of bone.

Decalvant, making bald.

Decerebration, removal of the brain.

Decidua, membranous lining of the uterus shed after childbirth or at menstruation.

Decompensation, failure of an organ to adjust itself to changing condition.

Decompression, removal of pressure.

Decompression Sickness, a condition caused by a rapid decrease in atmospheric pressure brought on by an excess of nitrogen in the blood and body tissues.

Decripitude, senile feebleness.

Decubitus, lying down posture.

Decubation, period of convalescence from an infectious disease.

Defecation, evacuation of the bowels.

Defective, imperfect.

Defemination, loss of female and assumption of male sex characteristics.

Defibrillator, any agent or measure that stops irregular contractions of the heart muscle and restores a normal heartbeat.

Deficiency Disease, any disease caused by the lack of some essential part of the diet.

Defloration, loss in a woman of virginal characteristics, i.e., rupture of the hymen.

Defluvium, falling out of hair.

Deformity, distortion, malformation.

Degeneration, deterioration or breaking down of a part of the body.

Deglutition, act of swallowing.

Dehydration, loss of water.

Dejecta, excrement.

Dejection, melancholy.

Delactation, weaning, stopping of lactation.

Deliquesence, liquefaction of a salt by absorption of moisture from the air.

Delirium, mental disturbance, usually occurring in the course ot some infectious disease, or under the influence of poisonous drugs.

Deliver, to aid in birth.

Deltoid, triangular.

Delusion, false belief.

Demented, insane.

Dementia, deterioration of intelligence.

Dementia Praecox, the old term for schizophrenia.

Demorphinization, treatment of morphine addiction by gradual withdrawal.

Demulcent, reducing irritation; a soothing substance.

Dengue, tropical disease carried by mosquitoes, causing fever and joint pain.

Denigration, process of becoming black.

Dens, tooth.

Dentagra, toothache; forceps for pulling teeth.

Dental Caries, tooth decay. Three conditions are necessary for tooth decay. One is a susceptible individual, which includes nearly every American. This susceptibility may be related in part to hardness and other qualities of the enamel and dentin, which may influence resistance to decay. Another condition is the presence of decay-producing bacteria found in plaques, which are allowed to remain on the teeth. Equally important is a caries-producing diet with large amounts of carbohydrates, particularly sugar, taken into the mouth frequently.

Dentalgia, toothache.

Dentifrice, any substance used for cleaning teeth.

Dentin, chief substance of teeth.

Dentistry, branch of medicine dealing with teeth.

Denture, complete unit of teeth.

Deodorant, that which destroys odors.

Deontology, medical ethics.

Deorsum, downward.

Depersonalization, loss of the sense of one's own reality.

Depilate, to remove hair.

Depilatory, substance used to remove hairs.

Deplete, to empty.

Depraved, perverted.

Depressant, that which retards any function.

Depression, a feeling of melancholy, hopelessness, and dejection.

Derangement, disorder.

Dermad, toward the skin.

Dermatitis, inflammation of the skin, eczema.

Dermatologist, skin specialist.

Dermatology, branch of medicine which deals with the skin and its diseases.

Dermatosis, any skin disease.

Dermis, the true skin.

Dermoid, resembling skin.

Desensitization, a series of injections given to a patient who has an allergy.

Desiccant, a drying medicine; tendency to cause drying.

Desiccate, to dry.

Desmalgia, pain in a ligament.

Desquamation, the shedding of skin.

Detergent, cleansing.

Deterioration, the process of losing ground, or of getting worse.

Deviation, variation from the normal condition.

Dexter, right.

Dextrocardia, position of the heart in the right side of the chest.

Dextrophobia, extreme fear of objects on the right side of the body.

Dextrose, form of sugar.

Diabetes, a disease which shows itself in an inability of the body to handle glucose.

Diabetes Mellitus, a disorder of carbohydrate metabolism characterized by excessive sugar in the blood and urine and associated with a disturbance of the normal insulin mechanism.

Diagnosis, determination of a patient's disease.

Diagnostician, one skilled in determining the nature of a disease.

Di- (prefix, two.

Dialysis, a method of separating substances in solution form.

Diaphragm, large muscle which separates the inside of the chest from the inside of the abdomen; contraceptive device.

Diaphysis, shaft of a long bone.

Diarrhea, watery, loose bowel movements.

Diarticular, pertaining to two joints.

Diastole, period of relaxation of the heart during which it fills with blood.

Diastalsis, forward movement of the bowel contents.

Diastema, space, cleft.

Diathermy, treatment of disease or injury by use of heat.

Diathesis, type of constitution which makes one liable to a particular disease.

Dichotomy, division into two separate parts.

Dick Test, test to discover whether a patient is liable to or immune from scarlet fever.

Didymalgia, pain in a testis.

Diet, nutritional intake; prescription of food permitted to be eaten by a patient.

Dietetics, science of diet and nutrition.

Dietitian, specialist of diet in health and disease.

Dietotherapy, use of a diet regimen for cure.

Differentiation, a process of growth in the embryo from very general cells to very specific cells.

Diffuse, widely spread.

Digestant, that which aids digestion.

Digestion, assimilation of food by the body.

Digestive Tract, the system responsible for the body's breakdown and use of food. It is composed of the mouth, pharynx, esophagus, stomach, small intestine, large intestine (including the colon and rectum), and accessory glands.

Digit, finger; toe.

Digitalis, drug used in the treatment of heart diseases.

Dilatation, stretching; increase in diameter.

Dimercaprol, a heavy metal antagonist. Drugs such as dimercaprol are used as antidotes to heavy metal poisoning. Dimercaprol is effective against metals such as mercury and arsenic.

Dionism, homosexuality.

Diphasic, having two phases.

Diphtheria, disease causing the development of membrane in nose and throat.

Diplopia, double vision.

Dipsomania, excessive desire for drink.

Disarticulation, separation of bones at a joint.

Disc, Disk, platelike structure or organ.

Discharge, setting free; excretion.

Discipline, a body of knowledge or field of study with distinctive rules and assumptions.

Discrete, separate.

Disease, sickness; ailment.

Disengagement, liberation of the fetus from the vaginal canal.

Disinfectant, a fluid used to kill bacteria and other microorganisms.

Disinfectation, extermination of pests.

Disinfection, killing germs by antiseptics or other methods.

Disks, the pads (made of cartilage) that are located between each of the vertebrae.

Dislocation, displacement of the bones in a joint. Dislocations result from force applied at or near the joints, from sudden muscular contractions, from twisting strains on joint ligaments, or from falls where the force of landing is transferred to a joint. The joints most frequently dislocated are those of the shoulder, hip, finger, and jaw.

Dismemberment, amputation.

Dispensary, place which gives free or low cost medical treatment.

Displacement, a condition in which a body part has been moved out of its normal position.

Dissection, cutting up.

Disseminated Sclerosis, disease of the nervous system in which small patches of hard tissue (sclerosis) develop throughout the spinal cord and brain.

Distal, remote or removed from. The opposite of proximal.

Distention, widening; enlargement.

Distillation, purification of a liquid by vaporizing it and then condensing it.

Distrix, the splitting of the hairs at the end.

Diuresis, frequent urination.

Diuretic, medicine which increases the flow of urine.

Divagation, unintelligible speech.

Diverticulitis, inflammation of small pouches or diverticuli in large intestine.

Dizziness, sensation of spinning or off balance.

DNA, the abbreviation for deoxyribonucleic acid. DNA is one of the two nucleic acids found in all cells. (The other is RNA—ribonucleic acid.)

Dolorific, causing pain.

Domatophobia, extreme fear of being in a house.

Dominant Trait, a trait that can be inherited from only one parent.

Donor, one who gives blood or body tissue for the use of others.

Dope, a slang term applied to narcotic drugs when they are misused.

Doraphobia, extreme fear of fur.

Dorsal, pertaining to the back or hind part of an organ.

Dorsalgia, pain in the back.

Dorsum, back.

Dose, amount of medication to be given at one time.

Dose, Lethal, dose large enough to cause death.

Dossier, file containing a patient's case history.

Double-Blind, an experiment in which neither the patient nor the attending physician knows whether the patient is getting one or another drug.

Douche, stream of water directed into a body cavity or against the body itself.

Dowel, pin used to hold an artificial crown to a natural tooth root.

Down's Syndrome, a form of mental retardation. Also known as mongolism.

D.P.H., Department of Public Health.

DPT and Polio Injection, a shot given to develop immunity to diphtheria, pertussis (whooping cough), tetanus (lockjaw), and polio (infantile paralysis).

Dragee, large, sugar-coated pill.

Drain, channel of exit for discharge from a wound.

Drainage, a rubber tube inserted in the body, which allows excess fluid or pus to escape instead of collecting.

Dramamine, drug commonly used for seasickness.

Dreams, flowing images that occur during sleep.

Dressing, protective covering placed over a wound to aid the healing process.

Drive, basic urge.

Drop Foot, state of inability to raise the foot upwards due to paralysis of the leg muscles.

Dropper, tube for giving liquid in drops.

Dropsy, generalized accumulation of fluid in body, edema.

Drowning, suffocation and death due to filling the lungs with liquid.

Drug, any medicinal substance.

Drug Abuse, the deliberate act of taking a drug for other than its intended purpose, and in a manner that can result in damage to the person's health or his ability to function.

Drug Addiction, physical dependence on a drug. The definition includes the development of tolerance and withdrawal.

Duct, tube or channel that conducts fluid, especially the secretion of a gland.

Ductus Arteriosus, the passageway between the two major blood vessels that adjoin the heart: the aorta and the pulmonary artery.

Dumb, unable to speak.

Duodenum, first eight to ten inches of the small intestine.

Dura Mater, outermost covering of the brain and spinal cord.

Dwarf, an undersized person.

Dynamia, energy.

Dys- (prefix), bad; difficult.

Dysarthria, stammering.

Dysarthrosis, dislocation; disease or deformity of a joint.

Dysbasis, difficulty in walking.

Dyschiza, painful bowel movement.

Dysemesia, painful vomiting.

Dysentery, name given to a group of disorders in which

there is diarrhea, produced by irritation of the bowels.

Dysfunction, impairment of function.

Dysgenesis, malformation.

Dysgraphia, inability to write.

Dyskinesia, impairment of the ability to make any physical motion.

Dysmenorrhea, painful menstruation.

Dyspepsia, indigestion.

Dyspnea, labored breathing.

Dystithia, difficulty in breast feeding.

Dystocia, difficult childbirth.

Dystrophy, weakening of muscle due to abnormal development.

Dysuria, painful urination.

— E —

Ear, organ of hearing. Consists of three different sections: the outer ear, the middle ear, and the inner ear.

Earache, pain in ear usually due to inflammation.

Eat, to take solid food.

Ebullition, boiling.

Eburnation, hardening of teeth or bone.

Ecbolic, that which speeds up child birth or produces abortion.

Eccentric, peripheral, peculiar in ideas.

Ecchymosis, a discoloring of the skin caused by the seepage of blood beneath skin.

Eccysesis, extrauterine pregnancy.

Ecdemic, pertains to disease brought into a region from without.

Echinococcosis, infestation with a type of tapeworm.

Echo, reverberating sound.

Echolalia, senseless repetition of words spoken by others.

Eclampsia, form of internal poisoning and convulsions which may occur in late pregnancy.

Ecouvillonage, cleansing of a wound or cavity.

Ecphuma, outgrowth.

Ecphyadectomy, appendectomy.

Ecstasy, exaltation.

Ectal, external.

Ectasia, widening in diameter of a tubular vessel.

Ecthyma, inflammation of the skin, characterized by large pimples that rupture and become crusted.

Ecthyreosis, absence of or loss of function of the thyroid gland.

Ectocardia, displacement of the heart.

Ectoderm, outermost layer of cells in a developing embryo.

-ectomy (suffix), excision.

Ectopic, abnormal position of an organ, part of a body; pregnancy outside the uterus.

Ectropion, the turning out of a part, particularly an eyelid.

Eczema, an itching disease of the skin.

Edema, an excessive accumulation of tissue fluid.

Edentate, without teeth.

Edeology, study of the genitalia.

Edible, suitable to be eaten.

Effemination, assumption of feminine qualities in a man.

Efferent, conducting away from a center.

Effluvium, foul exhalation.

Effort Syndrome, a group of symptoms (quick fatigue, rapid heartbeat, sighing breaths, dizziness) that do not result from disease of organs or tissues and that are out of proportion to the amount of energy that is used.

Effusion, accumulation of fluid, or the fluid itself, in various spaces of the body, e.g., joints.

Egesta, body excretions or discharges.

Egg, ovum.

Ego, that part of the mind which possesses reality and attempts to bring harmony between the instincts and reality.

Egocentric, self-centered.

Egomania, morbid self-esteem.

Egotism, exaggerated evaluation of one's self.

Eiloid, coiled.

Ejaculation, ejection of semen.

Ejaculum Praecox, premature ejaculation in the male.

Ejection, the act of expelling.

Elastic, able to return to normal shape after distortion.

Elation, joyful emotion.

Elbow, juncture at which the arm and forearm meet.

Electric Cardiac Pacemaker, an electric device that can control the beating of the heart by a rhythmic discharge of electrical impulses.

Electric Shock, shock caused by electricity. Electricity causes shock by paralyzing the nerve centers that control breathing or by stopping the regular beat of the heart.

The symptoms of electric shock are sudden loss of consciousness, absence of respiration (which, if present, is slight and cannot be detected), weak pulse, and probable burns. Every second of delay in removing a person from contact with an electric current lessens the chance of resuscitating him. It is important to act quickly, but the rescuer must be careful not to come in contact with the current or a conductor.

Electricity, form of energy having magnetic, chemical and thermal effects.

Electrocardiogram, a graphic record of the electric currents produced by the heart.

Electrocardiography, a machine which records the electrical activity of the heart muscles.

Electrocoagulation, the deterioration or hardening of tissues by high-frequency currents.

Electroconvulsive Therapy, a method of treating certain types of mental illnesses. Electroconvulsive therapy (ECT) involves passing an electric current or shock through the patient's brain.

Electrode, an electric conductor through which current enters or leaves a cell, an apparatus or body.

Electroencepalogram, record of the electrical changes of the brain.

Electrolyte, any substance that, in solution, is capable of conducting electricity by means of its atoms or groups of atoms, and in the process is broken down into positively and negatively charged particles.

Electron, an elementary unit of electricity; negatively charged particle of the atom.

Electron Microscope, an optical instrument using a beam of electrons directed through an object to produce an enlarged image (up to 100,000 × magnification) on a fluorescent screen or photographic plate.

Electroshock, shock produced by electric current.

Electrotherapy, treatment of disease by use of electricity.

Electuary, soft, medicated confection.

Elephantiasis, tropical disease in which blocking of the lymph vessels by a parasite leads to great swelling of the tissues, especially in the lower part of the body.

Elimination, discharge of indigestible materials and waste products from the body.

Elixer, a sweetened, alcoholic liquid used to disguise unpleasant tasting medicines.

Emaciated, excessively thin.

Emasculation, castration.

Embalming, preservation of a corpse against decomposition.

Embolism, small clot or foreign substance detached from the inside of a blood vessel and floating free in the blood stream.

Embolus, a blood clot (or other substance such as air, fat, or tumor) inside a blood vessel, where it becomes an obstruction to circulation.

Embryo, earliest stage of development of a young organism; the human young through the third month of pregnancy.

Embryology, the study of the development of embryos.

Emedullate, to deprive of marrow.

Emesis, vomiting.

Emetic, drug that causes vomiting.

Emetine, drug that causes sweating and expectoration.

Emiction, urination.

Emission, sending forth; discharge of semen.

Emmenia, the menses.

Emmenology, that which is known about mestruation.

Emmenagogue, that which stimulates the menstrual flow.

Emollient, relaxing, soothing agent used to soften the skin or internally to soothe an irritated surface.

Emotion, mental attitude.

Empathy, understanding, sympathy.

Emphysema, lung disease characterized by the thinning and loss of elasticity of lung tissue.

Emphiric, based on experience.

Empyema, collection of pus in the lung.

Emulgent, draining out.

Emulsion, product made up of tiny globules of one liquid suspended in another liquid.

Enamel, the hard, white substance which covers and protects the tooth.

Encelialgia, pain in abdominal region.

Encephalic, pertaining to the brain.

Encephalitis, inflammation of the brain.

Encephalogram, brain x-ray.

Encephalomalacia, softening of the brain due to deficient blood supply.

Encephalon, the brain.

Encranial, located within the cranium.

Endangium, membrane which lines blood vessels.

Endeictic, symptomatic.

Endemic, a term used to describe a disease that is constantly present in or native to a particular region or locality.

Endermic, administered through the skin.

Endoblast, cell nucleus.

Endocardial, pertaining to the interior of the heart.

Endocarditis, inflammation of the inner lining of the heart, especially the heart valves.

Endocardium, tissue lining the inside of the heart.

Endochrome, coloring matter of a cell.

Endocranial, within the cranium.

Endocrine Glands, ductless glands that secrete directly into the blood stream.

Endocrinology, study of ductless glands and their secretions.

Endoderm, inner layer of cells of an embryo.

Endodontitis, inflammation of the dental pulp.

Endometritis, inflammation of the lining of the womb.

Endometrium, tissue that lines the interior wall of the womb.

Endomoeba, a single-celled parasite that lives in humans.

Endoplast, nucleus of a cell.

End-Organ, any terminal structure of a nerve.

Endothelium, the thin lining of the blood vessels.

End Pleasure, pleasure enjoyed at the height of the sexual act.

End Product, the final excretory product that passes from the system.

Endothermic, characterized by heat absorption.

Enema, an injection of liquid into the rectum, usually intended for the treatment of constipation.

Energy, ability to work.

Enervation, weakness.

Engorgement, excessive fulness.

Engram, the indelible impression which experience makes upon nerve cells.

Enomania, craving for alcoholic drink, delerium tremens.

Enstrophe, turning inward.

Ental, inner.

Entamoeba, a microscopic ameba.

Enteralgia, pain in the intestine.

Enteric, pertaining to the intestines.

Enteritis, inflammation of the intestinal tract by infection or irritating food.

Enterocolitus, inflammation of the small and large intestines.

Enteron, the intestine.

Enthetic, introduced from without.

Entopic, located in the proper place.

Entropian, turning in of the edge of the eyelid so that the lashes rub against the eyeball.

Enucleate, to remove a tumor or an organ in its entirety.

Enuresis, bed wetting.

Environment, external surroundings.

Enzyme, a substance produced by living cells which, although not participating in a chemical reaction, promotes its speed.

Ephebic, pertaining to puberty.

Ephedrine, drug used to shrink the lining of the nose in colds and in the treatment of asthma.

Ephelis, freckle.

Ephidrosis, profuse sweating.

Epibular, upon the eyeball.

Epicutaneous, on the surface of the skin.

Epicyte, wall of a cell.

Epicardium, the outer layer of the heart wall. It is also called the visceral pericardium.

Epidemic, disease that affects many people at one time in the same area.

Epidemic Pleurodynia, an epidemic disease caused by a virus. The disease causes pain in the region of the chest or abdomen, as well as fever. One of the typical symptoms of epidemic pleurodynia is a relapse occurring two to three days after the original attack. Epidemic pleurodynia is also referred to as Bornholm's disease.

Epidemiology, study of the occurrence and distribution of disease.

Epidermis, outermost layer of the skin.

Epididymitis, inflammation of the epididymis, a structure which covers the upper end of the testicle.

Epiglottis, a lid which covers the opening to the windpipe and prevents food from getting into the voice box or lungs.

Epilation, removal of hair by the root.

Epilepsy, a symptom of some disorder in the brain. The name of this condition comes from the Greek word for seizure. The brain has many millions of nerve cells, called neurons, that work together to control or guide the actions of the body. To do their work; the nerve cells build up a supply of electricity through the action of the chemicals they contain. Each cell has its own storage battery, which it discharges at the proper moment and then recharges instantaneously.

However, cells can become overactive and fire off irregularly. This distrubance can suddenly spread to neighboring areas or jump to distant ones or even overwhelm the brain. When it spreads, a seizure results. The great majority of the neurons soon begin working in harmony again, and the seizure is over.

Epilepsy is a condition in which seizures occur. A seizure itself is the sign of an abnormal release of energy within the brain.

There are three major types of epilepsy: grand mal, petit mal, and focal seizures.

Epinephrine, the active principle of one of the secretions of the adrenal gland.

Epiotic, located on or above the ear.

Epiphora, continuous overflow of tears.

Episiotomy, cutting of the wall of the vagina during childbirth to avoid tearing.

Epistasis, substance which rises to the surface instead of sinking.

Epistaxis, nose bleeding.

Epithelioma, cancer of the skin.

Epithelium, cellular substance of skin and mucous membrane.

Eponym, using the name of a person to designate a disease, organ, syndrome, etc.

Equilibrium, balance.

Equivalent, of equal value.

Erasion, abrasion.

Erection, becoming upright and rigid.

Eremophobia, extreme fear of being alone.

Erepsin, intestinal enzyme.

Erg, unit of work.

Ergasiatrics, psychiatry.

Ergophobia, extreme fear of work.

Ergosterole, substance found in the skin and elsewhere which, when exposed to sunlight, becomes converted to vitamin D.

Ergot, drug used to cause contraction of the uterus and control bleeding after childbirth.

Ergotamine, an alkaloid substance used in treatment of migraine and can produce contractions of the uterus.

Erode, wear away.

Erogenous, producing sexual excitement.

Erosion, wearing away of a substance.

Erotic, pertaining to sex.

Erotogenic, originating from sexual desire.

Erotogenic Zones, areas of the body, stimulation of which promote sexual feelings.

Erotophobia, extreme fear of sexual love.

Errhine, causing sneezing and nasal discharge.

Eructation, belching.

Eruption, rash; cutting of a tooth.

Erysipelas, infection of the skin with streptococci.

Erythema, redness of the skin.

Erythema Multiforme, one of the more severe forms of oral ulcerations. Because the skin and the mucous lining of the mouth are similar in structure, the same kind of sores will develop both on the skin and in the mouth. Erythema multiforme is common in children and young adults. It appears most frequently in the winter and spring months.

Erythroblastosis, a condition brought about by an incompatibility of Rh factors. The condition can cause severe anemia and a failing heart.

Erythrocytes, red blood cells.

Erythroderma, skin disturbance characterized by abnormal redness.

Erythromycin, an antibiotic drug with many of the same properties as penicillin.

Esbach's Method, a method of estimating quantity of albumin in urine.

Eschar, sloughed tissue due to a burn.

Esophagus, the tube that connects the stomach to the throat, about nine inches long.

Essential Hypertension, an elevated blood pressure not caused by kidney or other evident disease. Sometimes called primary hypertension, it is commonly known as high blood pressure.

Ester, compound formed by the combination of an organic acid with an alcohol.

Estrogens, female sex hormones. Estrogens have special importance at puberty, because they are responsible for the development of secondary sex characteristics—such as the growth of the breast. Estrogens also stimulate the growth of the lining of the uterus. Any hormone that affects the monthly cycle of changes taking place in the female genital tract is considered to be an estrogen.

Estrus, female sexual cycle.

Estuarium, vapor bath.

Ether, organic liquid used as an anesthetic.

Ethics, Medical, system of moral principles governing medical conduct.

Ethnic, pertaining to the races of mankind.

Etiology, study of the causes of disease.

Eucalyptus, an oil used as an antiseptic in nasal solutions and mouth washes.

Eugenics, study of inheritance.

Eunuch, castrated male.

Eupepsia, normal digestion.

Euphonia, normal clear condition of the voice.

Euphoria, exaggerated sense of well-being.

Eupnea, normal respiration.

Eusitia, normal appetite.

Eustachian Tube, the tube that connects the pharynx with the middle ear.

Euthanasia, mercy killing.

Evacuant, medicine which empties an organ; laxative.

Evagination, protusion of a part or organ.

Eversion, turning outward.

Evisceration, removal of inner parts.

Evolution, gradual transition from one state to another.

Ex- (prefix), out; away from.

Exacerbation, increase in the degree of sickness.

Examination, scrutiny of a patient's state of health.

Exanthema, any fever accompanied by a rash.

Excerebration, removal of the brain.

Excise, surgical removal.

Excitability, susceptible to stimulation.

Excitation, stimulation; irritation.

Excoriation, rubbing away of part of the skin by disease or injury.

Excrement, feces.

Excretory Systems, the several different systems that eliminate waste products that enter or are formed within the body.

Exenteration, evisceration.

Exercise, physical exertion.

Exhalation, expulsion of air from the lungs.

Exhaustion, extreme fatigue.

Exhibitionist, abnormal impulse to show one's genitals to a member of the opposite sex.

Exhilarant, cheering.

Exo- (prefix), outside; outward.

Exocardia, abnormal position of the heart.

Exocrine Glands, glands that have ducts and that deliver their secretions to a specific location.

Exodontia, tooth extraction.

Exophthalmos, bulging of the eyes, usually caused by over-activity of the thyroid gland.

Exostosis, outgrowth from the surface of a bone.

Expansion, increase in size.

Expectorant, drug supposed to have the effect of liquefying the sputum.

Expectoration, spittle.

Expire, exhale; die.

Exploration, investigation.

Expression, the act of squeezing out; facial disclosure of feeling or emotion.

Exterior, outside.

Extern, medical student who works in a hospital but lives elsewhere.

Extima, outermost covering of a blood vessel.

Extirpation, complete surgical removal or destruction of a part.

Extra- (prefix), outside of; in addition.

Extracorporeal Circulation, the circulation of the blood outside the body as by a mechanical pump-oxygenator.

Extract, to pull out; remove the active portion of a drug.

Extrasystole, a contraction of the heart that occurs prematurely and interrupts the normal rhythm.

Extremity, terminal part of anything; a limb of the body.

Extrinsic, of external origin.

Extrovert, one interested in external objects and actions.

Eye, the organ of vision. The eye is a hollow ball or globe that contains various structures that perform specific functions. The bulb of the eye, or eyeball, is composed of three layers of tissue.

Eyebrow, hair ridge above the eye.

Eyeground, the inside of the back part of the eye seen by looking through the pupil.

Evelash, hair growing on the edge of an eyelid.

Eyestrain, eye fatigue.

Eyetooth, a cuspid or upper canine tooth.

— F —

F., Fahrenheit, one gauge of measuring temperature.

Face, anterior part of the head.

Facial, pertaining to the face.

Facies, appearance of the face.

Facilitation, hastening of a natural process.

Facioplegia, facial paralysis.

Factitious, artificial.

Faculty, normal power or function; mental attribute.

Fahrenheit Scale, boiling point of water 212 degrees, freezing point, 32 degrees.

Fahr., Fahrenheit.

Fainting, temporary loss of consciousness due to insufficient blood reaching the brain. Fainting is a mild form of physical shock. It may be caused by an injury, the sight of blood, exhaustion, weakness, lack of air, and emotional shocks such as fright.
The patient feels weak and becomes dizzy, black spots appear before his eyes, his face becomes pale and his lips blue, and his forehead is covered with perspiration. He then sinks back in his seat or falls to the ground unconscious. The pulse is rapid and weak, and the breathing is shallow. The above symptoms usually occur in a few seconds.

Fallopian Tubes, tubes which connect the ovaries with the womb.

Fallout, settling of radioactive dust from the atmosphere after a nuclear explosion.

False, not true.

False Labor, early contractions over a period of several hours or even days during pregnancy.

False Ribs, lower five pairs of ribs.

Familial, pertaining to the same family.

Family, group descended from a common ancestor.

Fang, root of a tooth.

Farina, meal; flour.

Far Point, farthest point which an eye can see distinctly when completely relaxed.

Farsightedness, difficulty in close vision.

Fastigium, acme; highest point.

Fat, obese; greasy deposits in body tissue.

Fatigue, exhaustion; weariness.

Fauces, space in the back part of the mouth, surrounded by the soft palate, the tonsil arches and the base of the tongue.

Favus, contagious skin disease.

F.D., fatal disease.

Fear, emotional response to danger.

Fear Reaction, emotional illness in which anxiety is shown by the conscious fear of a particular event or object.

Febricide, that which destroys fever.

Febrifacient, producing fever.

Febrile, pertaining to fever.

Febris, fever.

Fecal, pertaining to feces.

Feces, waste matter excreted by the bowels.

Fecundity, fertility.

Feeble-mindedness, state of low development of the intelligence.

Feeding, taking of food.

Fee Splitting, unethical practice of dividing the patient's charges between the referring physician and the consultant.

Feet, the extremities of the legs on which humans stand.

Fellatio, type of sexual perversion in which the male sex organ is placed in the mouth of another.

Felon, deep skin, infection on the far end and inner surface of a finger.

Female, woman; girl; pertaining to a woman.

Feminism, possession of female characteristics by a male.

Femoral Artery, the main blood vessel supplying blood to the leg.

Femur, thighbone. It is the longest and strongest bone in the body. The femur extends from the hip joint to the knee. Its upper end is rounded to fit into the socket in the pelvis, and the lower end broadens out to help form the knee joint.

Fenestration, surgical operation designed for the treatment of certain types of deafness.

Fermentation, decomposition of complex substances under the influence of enzymes.

Ferrule, metal band applied to a tooth to strengthen it.

Fertile, capable of reproduction.

Fertilization, the union of a spermatozoa (male sex cell) and an ovum (female sex cell).

Fester, to produce pus.

Fetal, pertaining to a fetus.

Fetation, pregnancy.

Feticide, killing of an unborn child.

Fetid, having a disagreeable odor.

Fetish, that which becomes attractive because of its association with sexual pleasure.

Fetus, an unborn child from the third month until birth.

Fever, elevation of the body temperature.

Fiber, threadlike structure.

Fibrillation, state of tremor in the muscles found in certain nervous, muscular and heart diseases. When filbrillation occurs, it is often necessary to use a defibrillator, such as electric shock, to stop the uncoordinated contractions and restore the normal heartbeat.

Fibrin, protein substance produced by elements of the

blood and tissues which forms a network as the base of clots.

Fibrinogen, a soluble protein in the blood which, by the action of certain enzymes, is converted into the insoluble protein of a blood clot.

Fibrinolysin, an enzyme that can cause coagulated blood to return to a liquid state.

Fibroid, benign tumor of the womb consisting of tough, fibrous tissue.

Fibroidectomy, surgical removal of a fibroid tumor.

Fibroma, benign tumor composed of fibrous tissue.

Fibrositis, the commonest rheumatic condition that does not affect the joints directly.

Fibrous Tissue, two types of connective tissue, both composed of fibrous cells. White fibrous tissue is dense and helps form tendons and ligaments. Yellow fibrous tissue is not as dense as white fibrous tissue. It is more elastic and can be found in arterial walls.

Fibula, bone of lower leg.

Filament, small, threadlike structure.

Field, limited area.

Figure, body; shape; outline.

Filament, delicate fiber or thread.

Filariasis, tropical disease due to infection of the body with tiny worms which block the lymph vessels, causing swelling of the limbs, elephantiasis.

Filling, material inserted in the cavity of a tooth.

Filter, to pass a liquid through a porous substance to eliminate solid particles; device used in this process.

Filtrate, fluid which has passed through a filter.

Finger, digit of the hand.

First Aid, emergency, temporary medical care and treatment of an injured person. The aim of first aid is to prevent death or further injury, to relieve pain, and to counteract shock until medical aid can be obtained.

Fission, division into parts.

Fissure, groove, cleft.

Fistula, abnormal passage leading from the surface of the body to an internal cavity.

Fit, convulsion; sudden attack.

Flaccid, flabby; weak; soft.

Flagellation, to beat or whip; beating as a means of satisfying sexual desires.

Flap, mass of partly detached tissue.

Flat Foot, not having the normal arch of the sole of the foot.

Flatulence, gas in the stomach or intestines. This causes a very uncomfortable feeling. Although flatulence can be caused by diseases and by fermentation in the intestines, it is usually the result of swallowing air. The patient feels that he can relieve the discomfort by burping, but actually all he does is swallow more air. This is a very typical cycle seen in nervous patients.

Flatus, stomach or intestinal gas.

Flaxseed, linseed.

Fleas, small, wingless insects that feed on the blood of animals and humans.

Flesh, soft tissue and muscles of the animal body.

Fletcherism, thorough mastication of food.

Flex, to bend.

Flexion, bending.

Flexor, muscle that bends or flexes.

Floating, moving around; out of normal position.

Flora, plant life.

Florid, having a bright color.

Fl. Oz., fluid ounce.

Fluid, a non-solid, liquid or gaseous substance.

Fluorescent Antibody Test, a rapid and sensitive test for certain disease organisms and substances. Its value in the field of heart disease is that it speeds the recognition of harmful streptococci in a throat smear, so that immediate treatment might avert an attack of rheumatic fever. The test consists of "tagging" with a fluorescent dye the antibodies, i.e., substances in blood serum that have been built up against certain bacteria. This dyed antibody is then mixed with a smear taken from the throat of the patient. If streptococci are present in the smear, the glowing antibodies will attach to them, and they can be clearly seen in the microscope.

Fluoride, a mineral that is important for sound tooth development and for the prevention of tooth decay.

Fluoroscope, an X-ray instrument used to examine the interior of the body.

Fluoroscopy, the examination of a structure deep in the body by means of observing the fluorescence on a screen, caused by X-rays transmitted through the body.

Flush, to blush; to clean with a stream of water.

Flutter, irregular, rapid motion; agitation, especially of the heart.

Flux, a large flow of any body excretion, particularly the bowel contents.

Fly, the housefly. This fly is a danger to the health of man and animals, principally because it carries and spreads disease germs that may be in the materials it breeds in, feeds on, or walks on.

Focal Seizures, some types of epilepsy in which abnormal electrical discharges can be traced to one small area, or focus, in the brain, or to a number of such areas.

Fold, ridge; a doubling back.

Folie, mania; psychosis.

Follicle, small secretory sac or gland.

Folliculitis, inflammation of the follicles of the hair.

Fomentation, treatment of inflammation by applying heat and moisture to the affected part.

Fontanel, the soft spot of a baby's head that later is closed by the growth of bone.

Food, that which nourishes—the body's source of energy. Food is necessary to support growth, to repair constantly wearing tissues, and to supply energy for physical activity. Unless the food consumed supplies all the elements required for normal life processes, the human body cannot operate at peak efficiency for very long. If an essential nutrient is missing from the diet over very long periods of time, "deficiency diseases" such as rickets, scurvy, or certain anemias may develop.

Food Allergies, allergies caused by sensitivity to one or more foods. The symptoms, which can appear shortly after the food is eaten, affect the skin, the digestive tract, or the respiratory system.

Food Poisoning, digestive disorder due to eating foods containing poisonous substances.

Foot, terminal part of the leg.

Foot Print, impression of the foot.

Foramen, any opening or perforation.

Foramen Ovale, an oval hole between the left and right upper chambers of the heart that normally closes shortly after birth.

Forceps, two-pronged instrument for extracting.

Forearm, portion of the arm between the elbow and wrist.

Forefinger, first finger.

Forehead, portion of the head above the eyes; brow.

Forensic Medicine, aspects of medicine related to law.

Formation, structure; shape; figure.

Formula, rule prescribing the kind and quantity of ingredients in a preparation.

Fornication, sexual intercourse of persons not married to each other.

Fossa, pit; depression.

Fracture, a break in a bone. There are two main kinds of fractures. A simple fracture is one in which the injury is entirely internal—that is, the bone is broken but there is no break in the skin. In simple fractures there is no considerable displacement of the ends of the broken bone.

A compound fracture is one in which there is an open wound in the soft tissues and the skin. Sometimes the open wound is made when a sharp end of the broken bone pushes out through the tissues and skin; some-

times it is made by an object piercing the skin and tissues and breaking the bone.
Compound fractures are more serious than simple fractures. They usually involve extensive damage to the tissues, and they are quite likely to become infected.

Fragilitas, brittleness.

Fragility, characteristic of being easily broken.

Frenum, fold of skin or lining tissue that limits the movement of an organ, e.g., tissue under the tongue.

Freckles, small patches of pigmented skin more commonly found in blonde or red-headed people.

Freezing, frigidity of a limb due to severe cold.

Frenzy, maniacal excitement.

Friable, easily broken into small pieces.

Friction, rubbing.

Friedman's test, a test for pregnancy that involves injecting the woman's urine into a rabbit.

Fright, extreme, sudden fear.

Frigidity, absence of sexual desire in women, coldness.

Frons, forehead.

Frontal, relating to the front of the body or an organ; pertaining to the forehead.

Frost Bite, condition caused by long exposure to severe cold; freezing of a part of the body, usually nose, fingers, toes. At first the symptoms are burning, stinging, and then numbness. However, the victim may not be aware of frostbite of the cheeks, ears, or nose until someone tells him, or of frostbite of hands or feet until he removes his gloves or shoes.
Ice crystals in the skin cause a gray or white waxy color, but the skin will move over bony ridges. When the part is completely frozen, there are ice crystals in the entire thickness of the extremity, indicated by a pale, yellow, waxy color. The skin will not move over bony ridges. When the frozen part is thawed, it becomes red and swollen, and large blisters develop.

Frottage, rubbing, massage.

Fructose, a simple sugar that resembles glucose.

Frustration, the feeling aroused when physical or personal desires are thwarted.

Fugitive, wandering.

Fulguration, therapeutic destruction of tissue by means of electric sparks.

Fulling, kneading.

Full Term, normal end of pregnancy.

Fumes, vapors.

Fumigation, disinfecting.

Function, normal and specific action of a part.

Fundament, base; foundation.

Fundus, base of an organ.

Fundus of the Eye, the inside of the back part of the eye, seen by looking through the pupil. Examining the fundus of the eye is used as a means of assessing changes in the blood vessels. The fundus of the eye is also called the eyeground.

Fungicide, an agent that destroys fungi.

Fungus, mold.

Funny Bone, outer part of the elbow which is crossed by part of the ulnar nerve.

Fur, deposit forming on the tongue.

Furfur, dandruff.

Furibund, maniacal.

Furor, rage.

Furuncle, boil.

Furunculosis, boils on skin.

Fusiform, spindle-shaped.

Fusion, uniting.

— G —

Gait, manner of walking.

Galactic, pertaining to milk.

Galactischia, suppression of the secretion of milk.

Galactorrhea, excessive flow of milk.

Galactosemia, an inherited disorder caused by a missing enzyme necessary for the digestion of milk or lactose to convert galactose into the useful glucose of the blood.

Galeophobia, extreme fear of cats.

Gall, secretion stored in the liver which helps in emulsifying fats.

Gall Bladder, sac beneath the liver which stores bile and secretes mucus.

Gallop Rhythm, an extra, clearly heard heart sound that, when the heart rate is fast, resembles a horse's gallop.

Gall Stones, stone-like objects found in gall bladder and its drainage system, composed primarily of calcium.
If a large stone starts to move, its possessor will know that something is radically wrong. The movement of the stone may cause an attack of severe pain. One may suddenly feel a stabbing pain in the upper right portion of the abdomen. The pain may spread out—it may be felt on both sides, in the back, throughout the abdomen, where it shifts from side to side, and it may be felt in the right shoulder. This pain is often so intense that the sufferer may be in agony. He becomes wet with perspiration; he may vomit. Often he has a chill with a high fever. The upper right quarter of his abdomen may become very tender to pressure. An attack of this kind may be over in a few minutes or it may last a week.
If a gallstone is so located as to cause obstruction to the flow of bile into the intestine, the person may become yellow (jaundiced). An individual may have only one attack, or he may have several attacks at irregular intervals.

Galvanism, uninterrupted electric current.

Gamete, a female or male reproductive or sex cell; i.e., an ovum or a sperm.

Gammacism, imperfect pronunciation of **g** and **k** sounds.

Gamma Globulin, a type of protein in the blood that aids the body in resisting diseases.

Gamogenesis, sexual reproduction.

Gamophobia, extreme fear of marriage.

Ganglion, cyst-like swelling found in the region of a joint or the sheath of a tendon; area between two nerve fibers.

Ganglionic Blocking Agent, a drug that blocks the transmission of a nerve impulse at the nerve centers (ganglia).

Gangrene, death and deterioration of a part of the body, caused by interference with the blood supply.

Gapes, disease of fowls caused by a worm.

Gargle, mouth wash.

Gargoylism, a form of dwarfism with heavy facial features, damaged vision, and mental retardation.

Gastralgia, stomach pain.

Gastrectomy, the surgical removal of all or a portion of the stomach.

Gastric, pertaining to the stomach.

Gastritis, inflammation of the stomach walls.

Gastrobrosis, perforation of the stomach.

Gastrocnemius, calf muscle.

Gastroenteritis, inflammation of the stomach and intestine.

Gastroptosis, abnormal relaxation of stomach musculature.

Gastrorrhagia, stomach hemorrhage.

Gastrosis, any stomach disease.

Gatophilia, abnormal fondness for cats.

Gatophobia, extreme fear of cats.

Gaucher's Disease, a family disease, particularly found in Jewish families. The onset of Gaucher's disease occurs in infancy and consists of listlessness, bronze spots in the skin, retardation, and eventual paralysis. No specific treatment is yet available. The disease is also known as familial splenic anemia.

Gauntlet, hand bandage.

Gavagi, liquid nourishment supplied through a tube inserted into the mouth, down the gullet and into the stomach.

Gelatin, body protein in a solid state, used in manufacture of drug capsules.

Gelatinous, like jelly.

Gelosis, hard, swollen mass.

Gelotolepsy, spontaneous loss of normal muscle tension.

Geminate, in pairs.

Gen., gene.

Genal, pertaining to the cheek.

Gender, sexual category; male or female.

Gene, biological unit which transmits hereditary characteristics.

Generation, reproduction; period of family history.

Generative, pertaining to reproduction.

Generic, pertaining to genus; distinctive.

Genesis, origin and development.

Genetics, the science of natural differences and similarities in successive generations of living organisms.

Genetous, dating from fetal life.

Genial, pertaining to the chin.

Genicular, pertaining to the knee.

Genital, pertaining to the sex organs.

Genitalia, reproductive organs.

Genitourinary System, the genital and urinary system.

Genocide, race destruction.

Genu, knee; knee-like structure.

Genus, biological classification.

Geophagy, eating of soil.

Geriatic, pertaining to old age.

Geriatrics, medical study of old age.

Germ, organism that infects man; primitive beginning of a developing embryo.

German Measles, a viral infection characterized by high fever and skin rash. German measles is also known as rubella.

Germicide, agent that destroys germs.

Geroderma, wrinkling of the skin.

Gestation, pregnancy.

Gestosis, toxemia in pregnancy.

Gibbous, humpbacked.

Gigantism, abnormal height and size.

Gingiva, the gum that surrounds the tooth.

Gingivitis, inflammation of the gums.

Girdle, encircling structure.

Glabella, space between the eyebrows.

Glabrous, smooth.

Gladiolus, main portion of the sternum.

Glanders, contagious horse disease.

Glandilemma, outer covering of a gland.

Glandula, small gland.

Glands, there are three main types of glands: the lymph glands, which are found mainly at various junctions in the body, such as the armpit and the groin, and also within the body and around the base of the neck, their function being to trap germs and prevent them from reaching vital areas; larger glands, such as the pancreas and liver which produce digestive agents such as bile, enzymes, etc. and which empty their products into the intestines through a duct or tube; the endocrine glands, which are also called ductless glands because they empty their products directly into the blood stream.

Glandular, pertaining to a gland.

Glandule, small gland.

Glans, cone-shaped body that forms the tip of the penis or clitoris.

Glasses, lenses to aid vision.

Glaucoma, disease of the eyes in which the pressure of the fluid in the eye increases. Prolonged high eye pressure can kill many nerve fibers in the eyes. Once destroyed, these nerve fibers are never usuable again. The increased eye pressure, called increased intraocular pressure, strangles the optic (eye) nerve and the blood vessels that nourish it. A block in normal eye drainage is the usual cause of such increased pressure.

Gleet, discharge from the urethra found in chronic gonorrhea.

Glioma, tumor of the nerve cells.

Globular, spherical.

Globule, small droplet.

Globulicidal, destroying red corpuscles.

Globulin, the name of a group of proteins.

Globus, ball, sphere.

Globus Hystericus, imaginary lump in the throat.

Glomerulonephritis, kidney disease.

Glomerulus, small, round mass; important element of the kidney.

Glossa, tongue.

Glossalgia, tongue pain.

Glossitis, inflammation of the tongue.

Glottis, the space between the vocal cords.

Glucohemia, sugar in the blood.

Glucose, liquid which is sweet and important to body chemistry; sugar.

Gluteal, pertaining to the buttocks.

Gluten, protein, found in cereals.

Glutinous, sticky.

Glycemia, sugar in the blood.

Glycerin, clear, syrupy liquid used for medicinal purposes.

Glycolysis, digestion of sugar.

Glycosuria, sugar in the urine.

Glycyrrhyza, licorice.

Gnathic, pertaining to the jaw.

Gnosia, faculty of perception and recognition.

Goiter, an enlargement of the thyroid gland. It is usually caused by lack of iodine in the diet, but in some areas of the world goiter also may be caused by certain agents in the food. The number of cases in the United States and in many other countries has been greatly reduced in recent years by adding iodine to table salt.

Goitrogenic, causing goiter.

Gold, a heavy metal that is used as a drug to treat certain diseases and conditions.

Gomphiasis, looseness of teeth.

Gonad, ovary or testes.

Gonadotrophin, hormone which stimulates the ovary or testes.

Gonagra, gout in the knee.

Gonalgia, pain in the knee.

Gonococcus, germ which causes gonorrhea.

Gonorrhea, veneral disease.

Couge, instrument for cutting bone.

Gout, disease in which there is an upset in the metabolism of uric acid, causing symptoms of joint pain.

Gouty, pertaining to gout.

G.P., general practitioner.

Gracile, slender.

Gradatim, gradually.

Graft, piece of tissue for transplantation. The areas most frequently used to remove skin for a graft are the legs and the back of the neck.
The grafted area takes the place of the scar that would normally form. The advantage of the skin graft (aside from the cosmetic value) is that a grafted area will be more flexible than a scarred area.

Grand Mal, epileptic attack.

Granulation, process of wound healing.

Granulocytopenia, disease which reduces the defensive cells in the blood, the white blood cells.

Granum, grain.

Grave's Disease, increased activity of thyroid gland with bulging of the eyes.

Gravid, pregnant.

Gravida, pregnant woman.

Gravity, weight.

Gray Matter, a slang term used to indicate the brain. The term is applicable because most of the brain belongs to the nervous system, and most nerve tissues are gray in color.

Grip, influenza; grasp.

Groin, depression between the thigh and abdomen.

Grumous, lumpy; clotted.

G.U., genitourinary.

Gumboil, a swelling in the mouth due to an abscess at the root of a tooth.

Guilt, feeling of having committed an offense.

Gullet, passage to the stomach.

Gums, the tissues and membrane surrounding the teeth.

Gun-Barrel Vision, vision in which the field is narrow, as if the patient were looking through a tube. The visual field is the total area perceived when the eyes are focused straight ahead. This comprises both the small area on which the eyes are focused for sharp impression (central vision) and the large area that is seen "out of the corner of the eye" (indirect or peripheral vision). In gun-barrel vision, the eye loses the ability to see "out of the corner of the eye"; that is, the eye loses the peripheral vision. Gun-barrel vision is also called shaft vision or tunnel vision.

Gustation, sense of taste.

Gustatory, pertaining to the sense of taste.

Gut, bowel; intestine.

Gutta, a drop.

Guttate, like a drop.

Guttur, throat.

Guttural, pertaining to the throat.

Gymnastics, physical exercise.

Gymnophobia, extreme fear of the naked body.

Gymandromorphism, condition in which one has male and female characteristics.

Gynatrisia, condition in which there is no passageway in the vagina.

Gynecic, pertaining to women.

Gynecoid, like a woman.

Gynecologist, specialist in female diseases.

Gynecology, study of the diseases of women.

Gynecomastia, enlargement of male breasts.

Gynoplasty, plastic surgery of the female genitals.

Gyrus, one of the convolutions of the cerebral cortex of the brain.

— H —

Habit, automatic action; bodily temperament.

Habituation, becoming accustomed to a thing.

Hachement, hacking.

Hacking, chopping stroke in massage.

Hair, threadlike outgrowth from the skin.

Halazone, white powder used as drinking water disinfectant.

Halitosis, offensive breath.

Halitous, covered with moisture.

Hallucination, mistaken sense impression.

Hallucinogens, drugs capable of provoking changes of sensation, thinking, self-awareness and emotion.

Hallucinosis, condition of persistent hallucinations.

Hallux, big toe.

Ham, back part of the thigh above the knee and below the buttock; hip, thigh; buttock.

Hamarthritis, arthritis in all the joints.

Hammer, instrument for striking blows; middle ear bone.

Hammer Toe, claw-like deformity of the toe.

Hamster, rodent frequently used in laboratory tests.

Hamstring Muscles, the collection of muscles at the back of either thigh.

Hamular, hook-shaped.

Hand, terminal part of an arm.

Handedness, tendency to use a particular hand.

Hangnail, partly detached piece of skin at the root of a fingernail.

Hangover, the body's reaction to an excess of alcohol. The associated symptoms of nausea, gastritis, anxiety, and headache vary by individual.

Haphiphobia, extreme fear of contact.

Haptics, science of the sense of touch.

Hare Lip, cleft lip.

Haunch, hips and buttocks.

Haut-Mal, epileptic attack at its peak.

Hay Fever, an allergic disease caused by abnormal sensitivity to certain air borne pollens.

HB., hemoglobin.

Head, a nonmedical term used to indicate the part of the body above the neck, including the face, brain, ears, etc.

Headache, a pain that lasts several minutes or hours; it may cover the whole head, one side of it, or sometimes the front or the back of the head. The pain may be steady or throbbing, barely noticeable, or completely prostrating. To add to the confusion about a definition, some people call any dizzy, tense, or queer feeling in the head a headache. Doctors feel that headache is not a disease by itself but rather a symptom. Headache is important because it can be the symptom—perhaps the first warning—of a serious condition that probably could be controlled if detected early. Headache may be classified as acute or chronic. The acute headache occurs suddenly and occasionally and is an unpleasant part of many illnesses. Chronic headaches recur more or less frequently.

Heal, cure.

Healing, process of making well.

Health, state of having a normally active body and mind.

Hearing, perceiving sound.

Hearing Aid, device used by one who is deaf to amplify sound waves.

Hearing Impairments, hearing losses. There are two main types of hearing loss—conductive deafness and perceptive or nerve deafness. Conductive deafness exists when sound waves are blocked before they reach the inner ear. Perceptive or nerve deafness, which is much more serious, results when there is a defect in the inner ear or when there is damage to the nerve that carries the impulses to the brain, or injury to the brain itself.

Heart, the powerful, muscular, contractile organ, the center of the circulatory system.
By its pump action, the heart keeps the blood under pressure and in constant circulation throughout the body. In a healthy person, with the body at rest, the heart contracts about seventy-two times a minute. This varies with age, weight, sex, amount of exercise, and body temperature. Each contraction of the heart is followed by limited relaxation. Cardiac muscle never completely relaxes but always maintains a degree of

tone. Contraction of the heart is systole and is the period of work. Relaxation of the heart with limited dilation is called diastole and is the period of rest. A complete cardiac cycle is the time from the onset of one contraction or heartbeat to the onset of the next.

Heart Attack, a serious decrease in the flow of blood to the heart muscle.

Heart Block, disease of the heart in which the impulse of contraction is unable to pass from the auricles to the ventricles, with the result that both beat independently of each other.

Heartburn, burning sensation, either in the back of the throat or in the left side of the chest, usually occurs after eating.

Heart Failure, inability of the heart to maintain adequate body ciculation.

Heart-Lung Machine, a machine through which the bloodstream is diverted for pumping and oxygenation while the heart is opened for surgery.

Heart Murmur, abnormal heart sound.

Heart Rate, number of heart beats per minute.

Heart Transplant, an operation that replaces a severely diseased or malfunctioning heart with a healthy heart.

Heat, warmth; high temperature; form of energy; sexual excitement in certain animals; to make hot.

Heat Cramps, painful spasms of muscles, especially those of the abdomen and limbs, after prolonged exposure to high temperatures while engaged in strenuous labor.

Heat Exhaustion, collapse from the effects of heat from the sun or any other source. It occurs more frequently when the humidity is high.
The patient is seldom unconscious but may complain of feeling very weak. His face is pale and anxious-looking and covered with cold perspiration. Frequently he vomits. He may complain of feeling chilly. His pulse is rapid and weak, and his breathing is shallow, with little chest expansion.

Heatstroke, state of dizziness, nausea and spots before the eyes due to direct exposure to high temperatures.

Hebetic, pertaining to puberty.

Hebetude, mental slowness.

Hectic, habitual; constitutional.

Hedonism, devotion to pleasure.

Heel, hind extremity of the foot.

Heimlich Maneuver, method for helping a choking victim. The method involves grasping the victim from behind with the fist against the victim's abdomen and the other hand holding the fist and pressing upward into the abdominal area with a sharp movement.

Helcoid, resembling an ulcer.

Helcosis, formation of an ulcer.

Helicine, spiral.

Heliosis, sunstroke.

Heliotherapy, treatment of disease by the rays of the sun or by the use of an ultra violet-lamp.

Heliotropism, tendency of an organism to turn toward sunlight.

Helix, margin of the external ear.

Helminthiasis, presence of parasitic worms in the body.

Heloma, callosity, corn.

Helotomy, surgical removal of a corn.

Hemafacient, blood producing agent.

Hemagogue, agent which promotes the flow of blood.

Hemangiectasis, enlargement of blood vessels.

Hemarthrosis, accumulation of blood in a joint.

Hemase, blood enzyme.

Hematemesis, vomiting of blood.

Hematic, pertaining to blood.

Hematischesis, stopping of bleeding.

Hematocolpos, collection of blood in the vagina.

Hematoid, resembling blood.

Hematologist, one who specializes in the study of blood and its diseases.

Hematology, science of the blood.

Hematoma, swelling containing clotted blood, usually caused by direct violence, e.g., a black eye.

Hematometachysis, blood transfusion.

Hematonosis, blood disease.

Hematuria, the passing of blood in the urine.

Hemeralopia, day blindness.

Hemi-(prefix), half.

Hemianopsia, blindness in half of the visual field of each eye.

Hemic, pertaining to blood.

Hemicrania, headache on one side of the head only; migraine.

Hemifacial, affecting one side of the face.

Hemiplegia, paralysis of one side of the body caused by damage to the opposite side of the brain. The paralyzed arm and leg are opposite to the side of the brain damage because the nerves cross in the brain, and one side of the brain controls the opposite side of the body. Such paralysis is sometimes caused by a blood clot or hemorrhage in a blood vessel in the brain.

Hemocidal, destructive of blood cells.

Hemocyte, blood corpuscle.

Hemodynamics, the study of the flow of blood and the forces involved.

Hemofuscin, brown coloring matter of blood.

Hemoglobin, the oxygen-carrying red-colored substance of the red blood cells. Hemoglobin carries oxygen to the body tissues. If the amount of hemoglobin is below normal, not enough oxygen will get to the tissues. When hemoglobin has absorbed oxygen in the lungs, it is bright red and is called oxyhemoglobin. After it has released the oxygen load in the tissues, it is purple in color and is called reduced hemoglobin.

Hemoid, resembling blood.

Hemolysis, destruction of elements of the blood.

Hemopathy, blood disease.

Hemopericardium, blood in the heart sac

Hemopexin, blood coagulating enzyme.

Hemopexis, coagulation of blood.

Hemophilia, blood disease characterized by defective coagulation of the blood and a strong tendency to bleed.
Hemophilia, or bleeder's disease, is the commonest of a rather rare, incurable group of hereditary blood disorders occurring almost exclusively in males but transmitted through women. Females themselves generally show no signs of difficulty.

Hemophiliac, one afflicted with hemophilia.

Hemophobia, aversion to blood.

Hemophoris, conveying blood.

Hemoptysis, spitting up of blood.

Hemorrhage, severe loss of blood from a blood vessel. In external hemorrhage, blood escapes from the body. In internal hemorrhage, blood passes into tissues surrounding the ruptured blood vessel. Hemorrhage (escape of blood) occurs whenever there is a break in the wall of one or more blood vessels. In most small cuts, only capillaries are injured. Deeper wounds result in injury to veins or arteries. Bleeding that is severe enough to endanger life seldom occurs except when arteries or veins are cut.

Hemorrhagenic, causing hemorrhage.

Hemorrhoids, enlarged, dilated veins inside or just outside the rectum. Hemorrhoids are also called piles. They are somewhat like varicose veins in the legs. The veins in the rectum are not buried deep in the flesh but lie close to the surface, where they can easily be pressed on and irritated. Any pressure that slows up the flow of blood through them or that irritates can cause piles.

Hemopasia, withdrawal of blood.

Hemostasis, stopping of hemmorhage.

Hemostat, instrument which stops bleeding, clamp.

Hemotherapy, using blood to treat disease.

Hemothorax, accumulation of blood between the lungs and chest wall.

Hepar, liver.

Heparin, substance which prevents clotting of blood.

Hepatic, concerning the liver.

Hepatitis, a swelling and soreness of the liver. Two types caused by viruses—infectious and serum hepatitis—are frequently found in the United States. One is called "infectious" because a person with the disease can infect others by contact. This type is also spread by contaminated water and food, including raw clams and oysters harvested from polluted waters. "Serum" hepatitis was first recognized in people who had been given medicines or vaccines that contained human serum. A person may develop serum hepatitis after receiving a transfusion of infected blood or its derivatives or after having contaminated needles, syringes, or other skin-puncturing instruments (including tattoo needles) used on him.

Hepatogenic, produced in the liver.

Hepatoma, tumor with its origin in the liver.

Hepatomegaly, enlargement of the liver.

Hepatopathy, liver disease.

Hereditary, transmitted from one's forefathers.

Heredity, traits and characteristics transmitted from parents and other ancestors to offspring.

Heredosyphilis, congenital syphilis.

Hermaphodite, one having both male and female sex characteristics.

Hermetic, Hermetical, airtight.

Hernia, rupture; the bulging out of a part of any of the internal organs through a weak area in the muscular wall.

Heroin, morphine chemically altered to make it three to six times stronger. Heroin is an addictive narcotic (a drug that relieves pain and induces sleep).

Herpes, skin disease characterized by clusters of small blisters.

Herpes Simplex, fever blisters, mouth blisters.

Herpes Simplex Type II (genital herpes), a viral infection transmitted through sexual intercourse.

Herpes Zoster, acute, infectious, inflammatory skin disease; shingles.

Herpetiform, resembling herpes.

Heterogeneous, of unlike natures.

Heterosexuality, sexual desire for one of the opposite sex.

Hexamethonium Chloride, a drug that lowers blood pressure and increases blood flow by interfering with the transmission of nerve impulses that constrict the blood vessels.

Hiatus, fissure, gap.

Hiccups, sharp, inspiratory sound caused by contractions of the diaphragm.

Hiccups can often be stopped by increasing the amount of carbon dioxide in the system. This can be accomplished by rapidly drinking a glass of water or by breathing into a paper bag. When the underlying cause is more serious, stronger measures may have to be taken.

Hidrosis, sweating.

Hip, upper part of the thigh where it joins with the pelvis.

Hippocrates, Greek physician, the Father of Medicine.

Hippocratic Oath, oath taken by the graduating physician on which he bases his medical ethics.

Hirsute, hairy.

Histamine, bodily substance found in most tissues, released when tissue is damaged.

Histoblast, tissue cell.

Histology, science of the microscopic structure of tissues.

Histoma, any tissue tumor.

History, patient's record of past illness, present illness and symptoms.

Hitch, knot.

HIV (human immunodeficiency virus), virus which causes AIDS.

Hives, skin rash characterized by large wheals.

Hoarseness, difficulty in speaking.

Hodgkin's Disease, disease in which the lymph glands and spleen become enlarged.

Holarthritis, inflammation of all joints.

Homeopathy, a method of treating diseases that involves giving the patient a minute dose of a drug that normally causes symptoms similar to his own.

Homogeneous, of uniform structure.

Homosexuality, psychological disorder which causes one to be attracted to people of same sex.

Hook, curved instrument used for traction or holding.

Hookworm Disease, a disease caused by microscopic worms. The most common way of getting hookworm disease is by walking barefoot on infected soil or by handling such dirt. Once the hookworms are in the body, they are carried by the blood to the heart and then to the lungs. There they bore through the membranes and get into the bronchial tubes and are coughed up into the throat. Even if some are expectorated, others are swallowed. Those that are swallowed go down through the stomach to the intestines, where they stay.

Hookworm disease makes a person listless and weak, even in mild cases.

Hordeolum, sty.

Hormone, a chemical that originates in the glands and is carried to all parts of the body by the blood.

Horror, fear, dread.

Hospital, institution for the care of those in need of medical attention.

Hospitalization, placing of a person in a hospital for treatment.

Host, organism on which a parasite lives.

Hot, having a high temperature.

Hot Flashes, sudden attacks of feeling hot, flushing, and sweating, characteristic of menopause.

Hottentotism, abnormal form of stuttering.

House Physician, doctor who lives in the hospital and is available for help at all times.

House Staff, residents, interns and certain doctors of a hospital.

Humerus, arm bone.

Humidifier, device used to increase moisture in the air of a room.

Humidity, amount of moisture in the air.

Humor, body fluid.

Humpback, curvature of the spine.

Hunger, desire, especially for food.

Huntington's Chorea, a rather rare inherited disease.

Hyaline, glassy.

Hybrid, product of parents of different species.

Hydatid, cyst formed in the tissues.

Hydragogue, strong laxative.

Hydralazine Hydrochloride, a drug that lowers blood pressure. An antihypertensive agent.

Hydrarthrosis, accumulation of fluid in a joint.

Hydroa, skin disease with blisterlike patches.

Hydrocarbon, compound of hydrogen and carbon.

Hydrocephalus, abnormal enlargement of the head due to interference with the drainage of cerebral fluid.

Hydrocyst, cyst with watery contents.

Hydrogenate, combine with water.

Hydrogen Peroxide, a strong antiseptic.

Hydrophilia, absorbing water.

Hydrophobia, rabies.

Hydrops, dropsy.

Hydrotherapy, treatment of disease by means of water.

Hygiene, science of health and observance of its rules.

Hygienic, pertaining to health.

Hygiene, Mental, development and preservation of mental health.

Hygiene, Oral, proper care of the mouth and teeth.

Hygienist, specialist in hygiene.

Hymen, membrane fold located at the entrance to the female sex organs.

Hymenectomy, surgical removal of the hymen.

Hymenotomy, surgical opening of the hymen.

Hypacusia, faulty hearing.

Hypalgesia, reduced sensitivity to pain.

Hyper, a prefix meaning too much or too high.

Hyperacidity, excess of stomach acid.

Hyperacuity, sharp vision.

Hyperacusia, acute hearing.

Hyperbulia, excessive willfulness.

Hypercholesteremia, an excess of a fatty substance called cholesterol in the blood.

Hyperemesis, abnormal amount of vomiting.

Hyperglycemia, excess blood sugar.

Hyperhydrosis, excessive sweating.

Hypermastia, unusually large breasts; having more than two breasts.

Hypermotility, increased activity.

Hyperopia, farsightedness. A condition in which far vision is very good but near or close vision is poor because the focus of light rays is behind the retina.

Hyperplasia, an abnormal increase of the number of normal cells. Hyperplasia is frequently the result of a hormone imbalance.

Hyperpresia, unusually high blood pressure.

Hyperpnea, hard breathing with an increase in the depth of inhalation.

Hyperrhinolalia, marked nasal quality of the voice.

Hypersensitivity, allergy.

Hypersthenia, unusual strength or tone of body.

Hypertension, high blood pressure.
Primary hypertension, the most common kind of high blood pressure, apparently is not related to any other disease and its cause is not known. Secondary hypertension is high blood pressure caused by an underlying disease.
Treatment which varies with causes and individual cases, may include surgery, drugs, weight reduction or other dietary restriction, or a combination of these.

Hyperthermia, abnormally high temperature.

Hyperthymia, excessive emotionalism.

Hyperthyroidism, condition caused by excessive secretion of the thyroid gland.

Hypertrichosis, excessive hairiness.

Hypertrophy, the enlargement of a tissue or organ owing to an increase in the size of its constituent cells.

Hypnagogic, causing sleep.

Hypnagia, pain while asleep.

Hypnogenetic, causing sleep.

Hypnosis, trance induced through verbal suggestion or concentration upon an object.

Hypnotherapy, treatment by hypnotism.

Hypnotic, any drug that induces sleep.

Hypnotize, to put in a state of hypnosis.

Hypo, a prefix meaning too little or too low.

Hypobaropathy, decompression sickness.

Hypocalcia, calcium deficiency.

Hypochondria, undue concern about one's health; suffering with imaginary illnesses.

Hypochondriac, one who suffers from imaginary illness.

Hypodermic, beneath the skin; injection under the skin; needle used for injections.

Hypogastrium, lowest middle abdominal region.

Hypoglobulia, decrease of red blood cells.

Hypoglossal, under the tongue.

Hypoglycemia, a condition in which the level of blood sugar is abnormally low or abnormally reduced. Hypoglycemia may be caused by many different factors.

Hypogonadism, deficient activity of testis or ovary.

Hypomastia, unusual smallness of the breast.

Hypomenorrhea, deficient menstruation.

Hyponoia, mental sluggishness.

Hypophrenia, feeblemindedness.

Hypopraxia, deficient activity.

Hypophysis, pituitary gland.

Hypoplasia, incomplete tissue development.

Hyposensitization, treatment of allergy by giving small doses of the material to which the person is allergic and gradually increasing the doses until the allergic reaction is reduced.

Hypotension, low blood pressure.

Hypothalamus, the part of the brain that exerts control over activity of the abdominal organs, water balance, temperature, etc.

Hypothesis, supposition.

Hypothyroidism, a condition in which the thyroid gland is underactive, resulting in the slowing down of many of the body processes, including the heart rate.

Hypotonia, abnormally low strength or tension.

Hypoxia, a condition in which there is less than the normal content of oxygen in the organs and tissues of the body.

Hysterectomy, surgical removal of whole or part of the womb.

Hysteria, psychological state or neurosis resulting from failure to face reality.

Hysterosalpingectomy, surgical removal of the womb and fallopian tubes.

— I —

Iateria, therapeutics.

Iatric, medical.

Iatrogenic, a term that literally means "caused by the doctor." A patient's belief that he has a disease or condition that is based solely on the physician's actions, manner, or other clues belongs in this category. An iatrogenic illness is based on the power of suggestion.
The term is also used to indicate any condition that follows or results from the treatment given a patient by a physician.

Iatrogenic Disease, condition caused by a doctor's statements or procedure.

Iatrology, medical science.

Ice, frozen water.

Ichnogram, footprint.

Ichor, watery discharge from a sore.

Ichthyol, coal tar product used in the treatment of skin diseases.

Iconologny, sexual desire aroused by pictures or statues.

Icthyophobia, extreme fear of fish.

Ichthyosis, condition in which babies have dry and scaly skin.

Icterpatitis, jaundice.

Icteric, relating to or characterized by jaundice.

Icterus, jaundice.

Ictus, beat; stroke; attack.

Id, psychological term for the unconscious.

Idea, concept.

Idea, Flight of, rapid, disconnected speech characteristic of certain mental diseases.

Ideal, concept of perfection.

Ideation, thinking.

Idée Fixe, obsession.

Identical, exactly the same.

Identical Twins, twins developed from one fertilized cell.

Idiosyncrasy, peculiar characteristics whereby one person differs from another.

Idiocrasy, peculiarity.

Idiocy, mental deficiency with an I.Q. under 25.

Idiogamist, man capable of having sexual relations only with his wife, or only with a few women.

Idiot, person suffering from congenital feeblemindedness.

Idiotic, like an idiot.

Idiotypic, relating to heredity.

Idrosis, excessive sweating.

Ignis, cautery.

Ileitis, inflammation of the lower small intestine.

Ileocolitis, inflammation of the lower small intestine and the large intestine.

Ileum, lower part of the small intestine.

Ileus, intestinal obstruction.

Iliac Artery, a large artery that conducts blood to the pelvis and the legs.

Ilium, flank, upper wide part of the hipbone.

Ill, not healthy; diseased.

Illegal, not lawful.

Illegitimate, not according to law; born out of wedlock.

Illness, ailment.

Illusion, misinterpretation of a real sensation.

Imagery, imagination.

Imago, memory of a loved person formed in childhood.

Imbalance, lack of balance.

Imbecility, mental deficiency with the mental age between three and seven years and an I.Q. between 25 and 49.

Imbibation, absorption of a liquid.

Imbrication, surgical procedure for closing wounds.

Immature, not fully developed.

Immedicable, incurable.

Immersion, placing a body under a liquid.

Immersion Foot, a condition caused by exposure to cold water (50°F. and below) for twelve hours or more or to water of approximately 70°F. for several days. Inability to move about freely is also a contributing factor. These injuries are characterized by tingling and numbness, swelling of the legs and feet, bluish discoloration of the skin, and by blisters and pain.
The best treatment is to expose the affected areas to warm, dry air.

Immiscible, not able to be mixed.

Immobilization, making immovable.

Immune, protected against disease.

Immunity, ability to resist infectious disease. When an individual's own body provides immunity automatically, he is said to have a natural immunity to a specific disease.
There are two types of active acquired immunity. In one type, the person produces the antibodies (defensive agents) to defend the body. This often occurs after a person has had a particular disease—such as measles. In this type of immunity, one attack of the disease confers immunity against subsequent attacks. Another type of active acquired immunity is artificially induced. This is done by injecting the individual with weakened or dead bacteria or viruses. This method is known as vaccination or immunization. The amount of bacteria or viruses is enough to force the body to develop antibodies against the injected substance but not strong enough to actually give the individual the disease. In this way the body is prepared to defend itself against the stronger form of the same disease.
Passive acquired immunity is obtained by injecting foreign antibodies into an individual. These antibodies usually come from an animal that has been vaccinated. This form of immunity is important in cases where an individual has already been exposed to a disease and needs immediate protection. Passive acquired immunity may be used against diseases such as tetanus and diphtheria.

Immunization, the process of artificially conferring immunity to a specific disease.

Immunologist, one who specializes in the science of immunity.

Immunology, science dealing with the study of the processes by which the body fights infection.

Impacted Teeth, teeth that cannot grow properly because of the angle at which they are growing.

Impaction, firmly wedged in.

Impalpable, too weak or fine to be felt.

Impar, unequal.

Imperative, obligatory, involuntary.

Impermeable, not allowing to pass through.

Impervious, unable to be penetrated.

Impetigo, infectious disease of the skin characterized by isolated pustules.
Impetigo spreads easily from one person to another and from one part of the body to other parts. The open sores contain germs that transfer the infection.

Implant, graft, insert.

Implantation, the attachment of the fertilized egg into the lining of the uterus.

Impotence, sexual weakness in the male.

Impotent, unable to copulate; sterile.

Impregnation, fertilization; saturation.

Impulse, instinctual urge.

Inanimate, lifeless.

Inanition, starvation.

Inarticulate, without joints; not given to clear expression.

Inborn, innate; inherent.

Inbreeding, mating between close relatives.

Incest, sexual relations between those of close relationship.

Incidence, the number of new cases of a disease developing in a given population during a specific period of time, such as a year.

Incipient, beginning; about to appear.

Incision, a wound made by a sharp cutting instrument such as a knife, razor, broken glass, etc. Incisions, commonly called cuts, tend to bleed freely, because the blood vessels are cut straight across. There is relatively little damage to the surrounding tissues. Of all classes of wounds, incisions are least likely to become infected, because the free flow of blood washes out many of the microorganisms (germs) that cause infection.
The term incision is also used to indicate a surgical stroke that cuts open part of the body.

Incisor, any one of the four front teeth of either jaw.

Inclination, tendency.

Incompetent, not functioning properly.

Incompetent Valve, any valve that does not close completely and consequently allows blood to leak or flow back in the wrong direction.

Incontinency, inability to control evacuation.

Increment, increase.

Incretion, internal secretion.

Incrustation, scab.

Incubate, to provide favorable conditions for growth and development.

Incubation, stage of an infectious disease from the time the germ enters the body until the appearance of the first symptoms. During the early incubation period of a contagious disease the patient is not usually contagious; however, toward the end of the incubation period he may be highly contagious.
The incubation period of a disease varies considerably. Bacterial diseases such as diphtheria usually have shorter incubation periods than do diseases, such as chickenpox, that are caused by viruses. The two major exceptions to this are the common cold and influenza.

Incubator, a piece of equipment that is used to protect premature babies.

Incubus, nightmare.

Incurable, not able to be cured.

Index, forefinger.

Indication, any aspeet of a disease that points out its treatment.

Indigenous, native to a particular place.

Indigestion, failure of digestive function; a somewhat vague term used to indicate a wide variety of uncomfortable stomach symptoms. Flatulence, nausea, heartburn, and other similar symptoms are often classified as indigestion.
Indigestion may be a symptom of a serious disorder, or it may simply be caused by overeating. Indigestion frequently results from eating when emotionally upset or when rushed. At these times much of the blood leaves the digestive tract, as a result of strong emotion or for use by the muscles. Without a sufficient supply of blood, the digestive organs cannot perform properly. The result may be indigestion.

Indolent, inactive.

Induced, brought about by indirect stimulation.

Indurated, hardened.

Inebriation, intoxication.

Inert, inactive.

Inertia, inactivity.

In Extremis, at the point of death.

Infant, baby.

Infanticide, killing of an infant.

Infantile, pertaining to infancy; possessing characteristics of early childhood.

Infantile Paralysis, infection of central nervous system; poliomyelitis.

Infantilism, failure of development.

Infarct, an area of tissue that is damaged or dies as a result of not receiving a sufficient blood supply. The term is frequently used in the phrase "myocardial infarct," referring to an area of the heart muscle damaged or killed by an insufficient flow of blood through the coronary arteries that normally supply it.

Infarction, blockage of a vessel.

Infection, the invasion of the body by harmful microorganisms. Any break in the skin or other body membrane (such as the mucous membrane that lines the nasal passages) is dangerous, because it allows microorganisms (germs) to enter the wound. Although infection may occur in any wound, it is a particular danger in wounds that do not bleed freely, wounds in which torn tissue or skin falls back into place and so prevents the entrance of air, and wounds that involve crushing of the tissues. Incisions, in which there is a free flow of blood and relatively little crushing of the tissues, are least likely to become infected. Infections are dangerous in any part of the body but particularly so in the area around the nose and mouth. From this area infections spread very easily into the bloodstream, causing septicemia (blood poisoning), and into the brain, causing abscesses and infections there. Boils, carbuncles, and infected hair follicles just inside the nostril are perhaps the most common infections that occur in this area. The general symptoms of infection include heat, redness, swelling, and pain around the wound or site of the infection. Pus is often (although not always) visible. If the infection is severe, there may be an increase of body temperature and swelling of the glands in the neck, armpit, or groin. Infections are usually treated with antibiotics.

Infectious, liable to be transmitted by infection.

Infectious Mononucleosis, an infectious disease. The major characteristic of infectious mononucleosis is constant fatigue. In addition, possible symptoms include fever (although this may be only a low, persistent fever), headache, sore throat, swollen glands, jaundice, and upset stomach.
One of the major problems with mononucleosis is the difficulty involved in proper diagnosis. Because the symptoms are fairly general, special tests must be made to diagnose infectious mononucleosis. The problem is further complicated because not all patients have the symptoms.
The incubation period for infectious mononucleosis is between five and fifteen days. Patients are contagious for two to four weeks, but, since the method of transmission is not clear, the amount of time a patient is contagious is sometimes difficult to gauge.

Inferior, of a lower position or situation.

Infertility, sterility.

Infiltration, process by which substances pass into cells or into the spaces around cells.

Infirm, weak, feeble.

Infirmary, place for the care of the sick.

Infirmity, weakness, sickness.

Inflammation, changes that occur in living tissues when they are invaded by germs, e.g. redness, swelling, pain and heat.
When a part of the body is attacked by foreign organisms, the injured cells in the area release a substance called histamine. The histamine forces the blood vessels in the area to expand, thus increasing the flow of blood and fluid. This increase causes the redness, heat, and swelling. The additional fluid and swelling increase the pressure in the area and cause the pain associated with inflammation.

Inflation, distention.

Inflection, bending inward.

Influenza, virus infection characterized by fever, inflammation of the nose, larynx and bronchi, neuralgic and muscular pains and gastrointestinal disorder.
There are several known main types of influenza virus. Each type has various strains, and each is somewhat different from the others. Sometimes new strains develop. These are very likely to cause epidemics, because people have had no experiences with them to help build up some degree of natural immunity against them. Because existing vaccines are ineffective against new virus strains, a special vaccine has to be developed, usually on short notice, to protect the susceptible population. Single cases of influenza appear occasionally, but the disease usually occurs in epidemic form.
Influenza attacks suddenly. The symptoms can be some or all of the following: fever, chills, headache, sore throat, cough, and soreness and aches in the back and limbs. Although the fever usually lasts only one to five days, the patient is often as exhausted or weakened as if he had gone through a long illness. No known medicine will cure influenza.

Infracostal, below a rib.

Infracture, incomplete bone fracture.

Inframaxillary, below the jaw.

Infrared, beyond the red portion of the visible spectrum.

Ingestion, taking by mouth; eating; drinking.

Ingravescent, gradually becoming worse.

Inguinal, referring to the groin.

Inhalant, that which is inhaled.

Inhalation, taking of air into the lungs.

Inherent, intrinsic, innate.

Inherited, received from one's ancestors.

Inhibition, restraint.

Initial, beginning; first; commencing.

Initis, inflammation of muscular substance.

Injection, forcing a liquid into body tissue or a cavity.

Injury, hurt; damage.

Inlay, filling for a dental cavity.

Inlet, means of entrance.

Innate, hereditary; congenital.

Innervation, distribution of nerves to a part; amount of nervous stimulation received by a part.

Innocent, harmless; benign.

Innocuous, harmless.

Innominate, nameless.

Innominate Artery, one of the largest branches of the aorta.

It rises from the arch of the aorta and divides to form the right common carotid artery and the right subclavian artery.

Inoculation, immunization against disease by introducing one form of the germ or its products into the body.

Inoculum, material used in inoculation.

Inoperable, not surgically curable.

Inorganic, without organs; not of organic origin.

Inquest, medical examination of a corpse to determine cause of death.

Insanity, mental disorder.

Insatiable, not able to be satisfied.

Inscription, part of a prescription which states the names and amounts of ingredients.

Insect Bites and Stings, the injection of a toxic substance into the body by an insect. Many insects bite or sting, but few are poisonous in the sense that their bite or sting can cause serious symptoms of itself. However, there are insects that do transmit diseases; these insects act as hosts to an organism or virus of diseases. For example, certain types of mosquitoes transmit malaria, yellow fever, and other diseases; certain types of ticks transmit spotted or Rocky Mountain fever; and certain types of biting flies transmit tularemia or rabbit fever. Occasionally, stinging or biting insects have been feeding on or in contact with poisonous substances, and at the time of the sting or bite such substances may be injected into or come in contact with the wound thus made, causing a poisoned or infected wound.

Insecticide, agent which kills insects.

Insemination, fertilization of the female by introduction of male sperm.

Insensible, not perceived by the senses; unconscious.

Insheathed, enclosed.

Insidious, stealthy; applied to a disease that does not show early symptoms of its advent.

Insipid, without taste; without animation.

In Situ, in the normal place.

Insoluble, not capable of being dissolved.

Insomnia, the inability to sleep. Insomnia may be caused by external sources such as noise, an unfamiliar bed, excessive heat or cold, etc. Pain can also cause insomnia. Surprisingly, being too tired (either mentally or physically) can also interfere with getting to sleep. Overstimulation from coffee and tea keep some people awake. One of the most common causes of insomnia is emotional upset. Physicians try to cure the cause of insomnia rather than try to cure the insomnia itself.

Inspection, visual examination.

Inspersion, sprinkle with powder or fluid.

Inspiration, breathing in.

Inspissated, thickened.

Instillation, pouring a liquid by drops.

Instinct, inherent behaviour pattern.

Insufficiency, incompetency. In the term valvular insufficiency, it means an improper closing of the valves, which admits a backflow of blood in the wrong direction. In the term myocardial insufficiency, it means the inability of the heart muscle to do a normal pumping job.

Insulin, internal secretion of the pancreas concerned with metabolism of glucose in the body. When there is a lack of insulin or the body is not using insulin properly, unused sugar collects in the blood. This condition is called diabetes.

Integration, assimilation.

Integument, skin.

Intellect, mind.

Intelligence, ability to see the relationship between things.

Interatrial Septum, the muscular wall that divides the left and right upper chambers of the heart, which are called atria.

Intercellular, between the cells.

Intercostal, between two ribs.

Intercourse, communication between persons.

Intercourse, Sexual, coitus.

Intermittent Claudication, pain in legs after brief exercise caused by a defect in blood circulation.

Intern, an assistant physician of a hospital staff who is in training prior to receiving a license to practice medicine.

Internist, doctor who specializes in diseases of the internal organs.

Internship, term of service of an intern.

Internus, internal.

Interstice, space or gap in a tissue or structure.

Intertrigo, an acute skin irritation and inflammation.

Intervascular, between blood vessels.

Interventricular Septum, the muscular wall, thinner at the top, that divides the left and right lower chambers of the heart, which are called ventricles.

Intestinal, pertaining to the intestines.

Intestine, the digestive tract beginning at the mouth and ending at the anus.
The intestines are composed of two major parts: the small intestines and the large intestines. The names "small" and "large" refer to the diameter of the tubes. In a living body, the small intestine is only five or six feet long. However, after death, the contraction relaxes, and it becomes apparent that the small intestine is actually about twenty-two feet long. In contrast, the large intestine is only five feet long. The intestines finish the digestive process begun in the stomach and prepare the waste products for excretion from the body.

Intima, innermost covering of a blood vessel.

Intolerance, not able to endure.

Intoxication, drunkenness.

Intra-Abdominal, within the abdomen.

Intracapsular, within a capsule.

Intrad, inwardly.

Intramuscular; within the muscular substance.

Intravenous, within a vein.

Intravital, during life.

Intrinsic, innate.

Introvert, one whose thoughts and interests are turned inward upon himself.

Intuition, instinctual knowledge.

Intussusception, a condition in which a segment of the intestine will fold in on itself, cutting off the passageway.

Inunction, massaging the skin with an ointment.

Invagination, becoming insheathed.

Invalid, one who is sickly.

Inversion, turning inside out.

Inversion, Sexual, homosexuality.

Invertebrate, having no backbone.

Invest, enclose.

Inveterate, hard to cure.

In Vitro, process or reaction that is carried out in laboratory test tube; a term used to indicate a phenomenon studied outside a living body under laboratory conditions. In vitro literally means "in glass," hence in a laboratory vessel.

In Vivo, within the living organism.

Involution, return to normal that certain organs undergo after fulfilling their function, e.g., the breast after breast feeding; period of decline after middle age.

Iodine, chemical element used as an antiseptic and therapeutic agent in medicine; a naturally occurring mineral that is necessary for the proper functioning of the thyroid gland. People who live away from the seacoast in areas where the soil is low in iodine sometimes fail to get an adequate supply of this mineral. Getting too little iodine can cause, goiter, a swelling of the thyroid gland.
Iodized salt and seafoods are reliable sources of iodine. Regular use of iodized salt is the most practical way to assure enough iodine in the diet.

Ionizing Radiation, radiation that tears molecules apart, leaving their fragments electrically charged.

Iophobia, extreme fear of poisons.

Ipecac, died plant root used against dysentery and as an emetic; expectorant and diaphoretic.

Ipsilateral, situated on the same side.

I.Q., intelligence quotient.

Iridial, pertaining to the iris.

Iridectomy, surgical removal of the iris, the colored portion of the eye.

Iris, colored portion of the eye.

Iritis, inflammation of the iris.

Iron, chemical element found mainly in the hemoglobin of the red blood cell; a metallic element that is needed by the body in relatively small but vital amounts. Iron combines with protein to make hemoglobin, the red substance of blood that carries oxygen from the lungs to body cells and removes carbon dioxide from the cells. Iron also helps the cells obtain energy from food. Because of the normal monthly blood loss (menstruation), women need twice the amount of iron that men do. Only a few foods contain much iron. Liver is a particularly good source. Lean meats, heart, kidney, shellfish, dry beans, dry peas, dark-green vegetables, dried fruit, egg yolk, and molasses also count as good sources. Whole-grain and enriched bread and cereals contain smaller amounts of iron, but when eaten frequently they become important sources.

Iron Lung, respirator; apparatus to aid breathing.

Irritable, capable of reacting to a stimulus; sensitive to stimuli.

Irritants, substances that do not directly destroy the body tissues but cause inflammation in the area of contact.

Ischemia, a local, usually temporary, deficiency of blood in some part of the body. Ischemia is often caused by a constriction or an obstruction in the blood vessel supplying that part of the body.

Ischium, bone upon which body rests when sitting.

Ischuria, retention of urine.

Islets of Langerhans, groups of specialized cells scattered throughout the pancreas. These special cells produce insulin.

-ism, (suffix), condition; theory; method.

Isocellular, composed of identical cells.

Isolation, separation of persons having a contagious disease.

Isotope, a term applied to one of two elements, chemically identical, but differing in some other characteristic, such as radioactivity.

Issue, offspring; suppurating sore kept open by a foreign body in the tissue.

Isthmus, neck or narrow part of an organ.

Itching, annoying skin sensation relieved by scratching.

Iter, tubular passage.

-itis (suffix), inflammation.

IUD (intrauterine device), method of birth control which requires the insertion of a small piece of molded plastic or copper into the uterus.

I.V., intravenously.

Ixodic, pertaining to or caused by ticks.

— J —

Jacket, covering for the thorax; plaster of Paris or leather bandage used to immobilize spine or correct deformities.

Jacksonian Seizure, a type of focal seizure caused by some types of epilepsy. It is the result of overactive nerve cells in the part of the brain that controls the movement of muscles. The seizure usually begins in the fingers or toes of one hand or foot, or sometimes in the corner of the mouth. The affected part trembles violently or perhaps becomes numb. As more nerve cells become affected, the trembling or numbness spreads. It may stop as suddenly as it began, or it may spread to the other side of the body. When the seizure spreads, the patient loses consciousness and has an attack similar to grand mal (another type of epilepsy).

Jactitation, convulsive movements; restless tossing.

Jail Fever, typhus fever.

Jargon, incoherent speech.

Jaundice, increase in bile pigment in blood causing yellow tinge to skin, membranes and eyes; can be caused by disease of liver, gallbladder, bile system or blood.

Jaw, applied to one of two bones that form the skeleton of the mouth.

Jecur, the liver.

Jejunitis, inflammation of the jejunum.

Jejunum, middle section of the small intestine.

Jelly, thick, homogeneous mass.

Jerk, abrupt muscular movement.

Jockey Strap, suspensory, scrotum support.

Joint, the place where two or more bones or cartilage come together. There are several types of joints, but there are two major classifications: immovable joints, such as the bones in the head; and movable joints, such as the elbow.

Movable joints are protected against friction by cartilage and by special fluids. The fluid is contained in small pockets or bursae. If the cartilage or bursae are injured or diseased, movement in the joint is limited and very painful. There are four types of movable joints in the human body.

The ball-and-socket joint includes a rounded end of bone that fits into a pocket, or socket, of another bone. The joints between the thighbone and the hip and between the upper arm and the shoulder are ball-and-socket joints. A hinge joint unites two bones in an arrangement similar to a door hinge, allowing movement chiefly within an up-and-down or back-and-forth area. Examples of hinge joints are the elbow and the knee. A pivotal joint, such as in the lower arm, is one in which one bone rolls or rotates over another bone. A gliding joint permits two bones to slide or glide over each other. The ankle and wrist are two examples of gliding joints.

Jugal, pertaining to the cheek or bone.

Jugular Vein, large vein at front of throat.

Juice, body secretions.

Junction, point of meeting or coming together.

June Cold, rose fever.

Jungle Rot, tropical fungus infection.

Justo Major, larger than normal.

Justo Minor, smaller than normal.

Juvenile, pertaining to youth; young; immature.

Juxtaposition, placed side by side; close together.

Juxtaspinal, near the spinal column.

— K —

Kaif, tranquid state caused by drugs.

Kainophobia, extreme fear of new things.

Kakosmia, foul odor.

Kakotrophy, malnutrition.

Kala-Azar, disease which occurs in tropical countries and shows itself in fever, anemia, dropsy and swelling of the liver and spleen.

Kali, potash.

Kanamycin, a broad-spectrum antibiotic.

Kaolin, powdered aluminum silicate used for ulcerations, wounds that discharge freely or internally for inflammation of the intestines.

Karezza, prolonged sexual intercourse without ejaculation.

Karyogenesis, formation and development of a cell nucleus.

Karyomorphism, the form of a cell nucleus.

Karyon, cell nucleus.

Kata- (prefix), down.

Katabolism, breaking down process in metabolism.

Keloid, large scar formation.

Kelosteroid, group of chemical substances produced by the body of primary importance to normal development, body functioning and life.

Kelotomy, relief of hernia strangulation by incision.

Kenophobia, extreme fear of empty spaces.

Kephalin, commercial remedy for headache.

Kephyr, type of fermented milk.

Keratalgia, pain in the cornea.

Keratectomy, surgical removal of part of the cornea.

Keratin, the protein that is the principal component of nails, hair, and epidermis.

Keratitis, inflammation of the cornea.

Keratoiritis, inflammation of both the cornea and iris.

Keratolytic, agent that causes skin to shed.

Keratoma, horny growth.

Keratosis, any skin disease that causes an overgrowth of a horny material, e.g., multiple warts.

Kernicterus, a condition of severe mental retardation that results from a blood incompatability involving the Rh blood factor.

Sometimes the blood of a pregnant woman will start to build up immunity against any conflicting blood type of her unborn child. A couple who have a potential blood conflict can have from one to five normal children before the increasing blood-sensitivity of the mother threatens to cause kernicterus in her child.

This disorder used to be responsible for an estimated one percent of the severely retarded in institutions; yet it can usually be prevented by treatment. Through repeated blood transfusions for the baby before or at birth, the exchange transfusions can wash out the hostile sensitized blood before brain damage occurs.

Rh-negative mothers may become sensitized to Rh-positive blood from having an Rh-positive baby, an Rh-positive miscarriage, or an accidental Rh-positive blood transfusion.

Kidney, two small but vital organs of the human body. A little larger than a man's fist and roughly bean-shaped, the kidneys lie in the small of the back on each side of the spine. They remove waste products from the blood and regulate the amount of water and the delicate balance of chemical substances in the body. These intricate functions are absolutely essential to human life. The kidneys also assist in regulating the production of red blood cells, which carry vital oxygen from the lungs to all parts of the body, and in maintaining normal blood pressure. The life of every human being depends as much on his kidneys as on his lungs or his heart. About nineteen gallons of blood pass through the kidneys every hour. On the average, a person's entire blood supply is filtered through the kidneys twenty to twenty-five times per day. Within the outermost layers (the cortex) of the kidney the blood passes through an intricate network of arteries. These arteries grow progressively smaller, ending in microscopic units called nephrons. A single kidney contains almost a million nephrons, each of them part of a filtering system that removes fluid containing waste products brought from all parts of the body by the blood. This is the first step in the complex function of the kidneys.

This waste-carrying fluid, called filtrate, is still rich in minerals and protein. Passing from the nephrons into an arrangement of coiled tubes, most of the filtrate and its essential minerals and proteins are absorbed back into the blood. This process takes place in the medulla. The liquid remaining after these two steps have been completed is called urine. Urine collects in a pouch called the pelvis in the center of the kidney. From each kidney a tube called a ureter carries the urine to the bladder, where it is stored until it is discharged through another tube, the urethra. The entire system is called the urinary tract.

Kilo, one thousand.

Kilogram, one thousand grams.

Kilnemia, blood output of the heart.

Kinematics, science of motion.

Kinesia, motion sickness.

Kinesis, motion.

Kinesthesia, the muscle sense.

Kinesthetic Sensations, the electrical impulses sent to the central nervous system by the nerves in muscles.

Kinetic, pertaining to motion.

Kink, bend; twist.

Kleptomania, obsessive stealing.

Kleptophobia, fear of stealing.

Knee, the point of juncture of the femur and tibia.

Kneecap, patella.

Knock Knee, condition when legs are turned in at knees.

Knot, knoblike structure; small nodule.

Kolp- (prefix), vagina.

Kolpitis, inflammation of the vagina.

Kopiopia, eyestrain.

Kraurosis, dryness and hardening of skin.

Kreotoxism, meat poisoning.

Kresol, germicide.

Kwashiorkor, a syndrome or set of widely recognized symptoms caused by malnutrition, specifically a lack of protein and amino acids.

Kyllosis, clubfoot.

Kymoscope, apparatus for measuring blood pressure variations.

Kyogenic, causing pregnancy.

Kyphosis, a condition in which the vertebral column (the spine) is abnormally curved in the chest area.

— L —

Labial, pertaining to a lip.

Labialism, speech defect with the use of labial sounds.

Labile, changeable; unsteady.

Lability, instability.

Labiology, study of lip movements.

Labiomancy, lipreading.

Labium, lip.

Labor, the process by which a child is delivered from his mother's body. Preparations for labor go on all during pregnancy. The muscles of the uterus tighten and relax. This process of tightening and then relaxing is called a contraction. When labor begins, the contractions of the uterus become more and more frequent and intense. At first these contractions are fifteen or more minutes apart. The time between them gets shorter and shorter as labor progresses. During pregnancy, the cervix (the narrow end of the uterus) softens and relaxes. By the time labor begins, it is thin and has opened to about one half to three quarters of an inch. A small amount of mucus is usually present in this opening as a sort of plug. As the baby is pushed against the cervix by the strong contractions of the uterus, this opening gradually gets larger until it is finally about four inches wide—big enough for the baby to pass through. As the cervix opens, the mucus plug comes loose and is discharged through the vagina. This usually means that labor will begin soon.

A sudden rush of water from the vagina means that the bag of waters surrounding the baby has broken. This may happen at the beginning of labor or not until just before the baby is born. Labor is divided into three stages. In the first stage, the contractions of the uterus stretch the opening at its lower end, the cervix. This allows the baby to move into the birth canal. In the second stage, the baby passes down through the birth canal and out through the vaginal opening. In the third stage, the placenta and membranes (the afterbirth) are loosened and expelled.

Labor, Artificial, induced labor.

Labor, Induced, labor brought on by extraneous means.

Labor Pains, pains produced by the contractions of the womb during labor.

Laboratory, place for testing and experimental work.

Labrum, edge; lip.

Labyrinth, internal ear.

Lac, milk.

Lacerate, to tear.

Laceration, a wound that is torn, rather than cut. Lacerations have ragged, irregular edges and masses of torn or mashed tissue underneath. These wounds are usually made by blunt rather than sharp objects. A wound made by a dull knife, for instance, is more likely to be a laceration than an incision. Many of the wounds caused by accidents with machinery are lacerations, although they are often complicated by crushing of the tissues as well. These wounds, in which the blood vessels are torn or mashed, do not bleed as freely as wounds produced by sharp cutting edges. Lacerations are frequently contaminated with dirt, grease, or other foreign matter that is ground into the tissues; they are therefore very likely to become infected.

Lacertus, muscular portion of the arm.

Lacrimal, pertaining to tears.

Lacrimation, secretion of tears from the eye.

Lactation, the production of milk in the breasts. True milk is not released for at least three days after the birth of a baby. Colostrum, the liquid secreted by the breasts during the first few days, is rich in protein and nourishes the baby until the milk is formed.

Lacteal, relating to milk.

Lactescence, resembling milk.

Lactic Acid, an acid normal to the blood and connected with muscle fatigue.

Lactiferous, conveying milk.

Lactifuge, agent which stops milk secretion.

Lactigenous, producing milk.

Lactin, lactose; a sugar.

Lactinated, containing milk sugar.

Lactoglobulin, protein found in milk.

Lactolin, condensed milk.

Lactose, milk sugar.

Lactotherapy, treatment by milk diet.

Lacuna, small space; pit.

Lag, time between application of a stimulus and the response.

La Grippe, influenza.

Laity, non professional public.

Lake, small fluid cavity.

Laliatry, babbling.

Lalopathy, any speech disorder.

Lambdacism, inability to pronounce the l sound.

Lameness, limping or abnormal walk.

Lamina, thin layer or membrane.

Laminated, in layers.

Lancet, short, double-edged, puncturing knife.

Languor, weariness; exhaustion.

Lanolin, wool fat used in ointments and cosmetics.

Lanugo, fine hair which covers a baby before birth.

Lapactic, purgative.

Laparotomy, surgical incision into the abdominal cavity.

Lapis, stone.

Larva, first stage of an insect from the egg.

Larvate, hidden.

Larvicide, agent which kills larvae.

Laryngectomy, the surgical removal of the larynx. After this operation is performed, most patients can learn to speak again through a technique known as esophageal speech. This substitute speech is produced by expelling swallowed air from the esophagus. A well-trained and practical esophageal voice produces intelligible speech of surprisingly good quality. There are mechanical devices available for those patients who are unable to learn to use this type of speech.

Laryngismus, muscular spasm of the voice box.

Laryngitic, due to laryngitis.

Laryngitis, an inflammation of the larynx (voice box). The primary symptoms of laryngitis are hoarseness and a changed (usually strained sounding) voice. Other symptoms may be a tickling in the throat, a sore throat, and a cough. Laryngitis can be caused by a number of factors. It may follow an infection in the respiratory tract, or it may be a part of another disease such as syphilis or measles. Laryngitis may also be caused by abusing the voice, excessive smoking, breathing unclean air, etc. Additionally, laryngitis can be a symptom of a tumor.

Laryngology, study of the voice box.

Larynx, voice box; the passageway connecting the pharynx and trachea (windpipe).

The larynx is shaped like a tube. It has nine cartilages. One of these, the epiglottis, is responsible for covering the opening of the larynx when the mouth is in the process of swallowing. This closing or lid action prevents foreign material from entering the larynx and eventually reaching the lungs.

There are two pairs of folds in the larynx, but only the vocal folds (also called the true vocal cords) are involved in the production of vocal sound. The area between the vocal folds is known as the glottis.

Sound is produced when air, passing up out of the lungs through the glottis, causes a vibration in the vocal folds. The vibration is controlled by the degree of tension in the folds. A whisper requires less tension than a shout does.

Lassa Fever, a viral infection found in West Africa. Lassa fever causes very high fevers (up to 107°) and severe muscular pain. The fatality rate is high, because the virus kills faster than the body can defend itself.

Latent, hidden.

Lateral, pertaining to the side.

Latrine, public toilet.

Lattissimus, widest.

Lattissimus Dorsi, back muscle.

Latus, Lata, Latum, broad.

Laudable, healthy, normal.

Laughing Gas, nitrous oxide.

Laudanum, tincture of opium.

Lavage, cleansing out an organ.

Lax, without tension.

Laxative, substance when taken helps to evacuate the bowels.

Lazaretto, quarantine station, place for treatment of contagious diseases.

Lead Poisoning, a disease caused by the ingestion of substances containing lead. Studies indicate that children between one and three years of age are the most common victims, although older children also get the disease. Lead poisoning results in damage to the nervous system. The degree of damage is related to the amount and duration of exposure to lead. Once a child has the disease, unless his environment is changed, chances are very high that he will again be a victim. Lead poisoning is caused by consumption over a period of time (three to six months) of paint or plaster containing lead. The condition is frequently associated with pica, which is an abnormal appetite for nonedible substances. In the early stages, the existence of lead poisoning is often without marked symptoms. There may be vague, nonspecific symptoms common in children, such as stomach pain, constipation, vomiting, irritability, and twitching. Unless a high level of suspicion for lead poisoning exists in the physician's mind, the diagnosis may not be recognized. As the disease progresses, the symptoms become stronger, and an elevated amount of lead is found in the blood and urine.

Lean, emaciated; thin.

Lechery, lewdness.

Lechopyra, puerperal fever; child birth fever.

Leech, blood sucking water worm.

Left-Handedness, tendency to use the left hand.

Leg, lower extremity; part of the body from the knee to the ankle.

Leiphemia, thinness of the blood.

Leitrichous, having smooth straight hair.

Lemic, pertaining to any epidemic disease.

Lemology, study of epidemic diseases.

Lemostenosis, stricture of the esophagus.

Lens, magnifying glass; transparent, egg-shaped body behind the pupil of the eye.

Lenticular, lens-shaped.

Lenti-form, lens-shaped.

Lentigo, freckle.

Lentitis, inflammation of the eye lens.

Leper, one afflicted with leprosy.

Lepra, leprosy.

Leprology, study of leprosy.

Leprosarium, place for the care of lepers.

Leprosy, an infectious disease caused by the microorganism *Mycobacterium leprae.* It is not very contagious—only an insignificant percentage of the people who have spent their lives working with leprosy patients have ever contracted it. The method by which it is transmitted is not known.

There are two major types of leprosy: nodular and neural. In nodular leprosy there are masses of nodules that cause distortions in other tissues. In neural leprosy the nerves are affected, frequently producing a numbness and loss of feeling in the affected area; this in turn can result in loss of tissue and bone. The prognosis for patients with leprosy depends to a certain extent on the type of leprosy—patients with neural leprosy generally respond better to treatment than do patients with nodular leprosy.

The treatment for leprosy is primarily chemotherapy (treatment by drugs). The sulfone-class drugs are used with good results for many patients, although it may take up to five years to effect a cure in some types of leprosy. Another drug in use is dapsone.

Leprous, afflicted with leprosy.

Leptodermic, having a thin skin.

Leptophonia, having a feeble voice.

Leptospirosis, a bacterial infection spread to man from animals.

Animal carriers of the leptospirosis bacteria include: cattle, swine, sheep, goats, horses, mules, dogs, cats, foxes, skunks, racoons, wildcats, mongooses, rats, mice, and bats. Leptospirosis bacteria infect the kidneys of animals and are shed through their urine. People can get the disease by swimming in water or walking on moist soil that contains the infected urine. Most frequently, however, people get the disease either by handling a sick animal or by handling the kidney and other infected tissues of an animal that has had leptospirosis. This is why the disease is most prevalent among farmers and other workers who handle animals and animal products. The leptospirosis organism enters the human body through the nose, mouth, eyes, or through a break in the skin. The onset of the disease is sudden, with fever, headache, chills, muscle pains, and sometimes nausea and vomiting. Jaundice, skin rashes, blood in the urine, and a stiff neck are other common symptoms. Because of the numerous and varied symptoms, it is sometimes hard to distinguish this disease from other diseases, including non-paralytic polio, mumps, meningitis, typhoid fever, undulant fever, and influenza. Most cases are quite mild, and the patient recovers in one to two weeks. When the infection is severe, however, the kidney, liver, or heart may be damaged, and death can result.

Leresis, talkativeness in old age.

Lesbianism, homosexuality between women.

Lesion, wound; injury; tumor.

Lethal, fatal; morbid.

Lethargy, marked lack of energy; stupor.

Leucotomy, brain operation used in treatment of some mental disorders.

Leukemia, a fatal disease of the organs that manufacture blood, such as the lymph glands and bone marrow. Normally, these organs manufacture only as many white and red blood cells as the body needs. In leukemia this blood formation gets out of control and there is a tremendous overproduction of white cells. The white cells do not mature, and they are not able to fight infection. The number of red cells is reduced, and the patient becomes anemic. The blood does not clot properly. Patients may thus die from infection, from hemorrhage, or from damage to vital organs. The abnormal cells seen in leukemia resemble cancer cells in appearance and behavior. However, in leukemia the cells are present in the bone marrow and, in the majority of cases, in the blood, as well as in the tissues of the body. In other forms of cancer, the abnormal cells grow in the tissues only. Leukemia can develop at any age. Scientists believe that several factors are involved in the development of leukemia. Recent studies show that radiation can produce the disease. Leukemia can be chronic, acute, or subacute. There are two kinds of chronic leukemia. One begins in the bone marrow and the other in the lymphatic system. The bone-marrow type occurs most often in people thirty-five to forty-five years of age. The lymphatic type is found most frequently in those forty-five to fifty-four years of age. Chronic leukemia affects more men than women. It rarely occurs in children. Chronic leukemia develops slowly, without warning. Many cases are discovered accidentally during examination for some other condition. Even after changes in the blood are noticed, several years may pass before significant symptoms appear in the body. One early change is an enlargement of the blood-forming organs, such as the spleen. As the spleen gets bigger, the patient may feel a sense of fullness or pain in the upper left side of the abdomen. Other symptoms may be sweating, skin eruptions, anemia, hemorrhages, nervousness, and loss of weight. Acute leukemia most often affects children. It usually begins suddenly and progresses rapidly, often with a sore throat or other symptoms of a cold. The glands, spleen, and liver may enlarge rapidly. The child usually becomes pale and bruises easily. However, the beginning of acute leukemia can also develop slowly. In these cases pallor and bone pain are the main symptoms. Without treatment the patient lives only a short time—a few weeks or months. Subacute leukemia has some of the characteristics of both chronic and acute leukemia. The course it follows is harder to predict. Positive diagnosis of leukemia is made by microscopic study of the blood and bone marrow.

Leukoblast, immature white blood cell.

Leukocytes, white blood cells.

Leukocythemia, leukemia.

Leukocytolysis, destruction of white blood cells.

Leukocytosis, increase in the number of white blood cells.

Leukodermia, a condition in which there is a loss of skin pigment in certain areas of the body. The absence of pigment causes patches of very white skin.

Leukopenia, decreased number of white blood cells.

Leukoplakia, white, thickened patches which appear on the skin following chronic irritation.

Leukorrhea, whitish discharge from the womb.

Leukosis, abnormal pallor.

Leukous, white.

Levarterenol, one of the normal secretions of the adrenal glands.

Levoduction, movement of an eye toward the left.

Levorotation, turning to the left.

Libidinous, characterized by lewdness.

Libido, the instinctual energy of life, usually sexual energy.

Lichen, any form of skin disease.

Lichenification, thickening and hardening of the skin.

Licorice, dried root used in medication.

Lid, eyelid.

Lien, spleen.

Lienal, pertaining to the spleen.

Lienectomy, surgical removal of the spleen.

Lienitis, inflammation of the spleen.

Lientery, diarrhea with evacuation of undigested food.

Life, state of being alive.

Ligaments, fibrous bands that hold bones together in the region of a joint.

Ligamentous, pertaining to a ligament.

Ligature, thread for tying off vessels; binding or tying.

Lightening, dropping of the head of the developing infant into the mother's pelvis in the first stage of labor.

Limb, arm or leg.

Limbus, rim; border.

Liminal, barely noticeable.

Limitans, limiting.

Lingism, treatment by exercise.

Limp, impediment in walking.

Linctus, thick syrupy medicine.

Lingua, tongue.

Lingual, pertaining to the tongue.

Liniment, an oily substance rubbed into the skin to relieve pain and muscle cramps.

Linoleic Acid, an important component of many of the unsaturated fats. It is widely found in oils from plants. A diet with a high linoleic acid content tends to lower the amount of cholesterol in the blood.

Lip, external soft structure around the mouth.

Liparous, fat.

Lipemia, fat in the blood.

Lipid, fat.

Lipocyte, fat cell.

Lipogenic, producing fat.

Lipoma, fatty tumor, usually benign.

Lipoprotein, a complex of fat and protein molecules.

Liposarcoma, cancerous tumor composed of undeveloped fat cells.

Lip-Reading, understanding speech by watching the movements of the lips.

Listerism, principles and practice of antiseptic and asceptic surgical procedures.

Liquefacient, converting into a liquid.

Liquescent, becoming liquid.

Lisping, substitution of sounds due to a speech defect, e.g., th for s.

Lithiasis, formation of stone in the body, e.g., gallstones.

Lithotomy, an operation to remove a stone from the bladder.

Litmus Paper, a special, chemically prepared piece of paper that is used to test whether substances are acid or base. Acids turn blue litmus paper red; an alkali (base) will turn red litmus paper blue.

Litter, stretcher.

Livedo, discolored patch of skin.

Liver, important organ of body vitally concerned with metabolism, blood clotting and protein manufacture.

Livid, pale, ashen.

Lividity, discoloration.

Lobar, pertaining to a lobe.

Lobe, globular portion of an organ separated by boundaries.

Lobectomy, surgical removal of a lobe of an organ.

Lobites, inflammation of a lobe.

Lobotomy, cutting across of brain tissue.

Lobule, small lobe; part of a lobe.

Lobus, lobe.

Localization, limited to a definite area; determination of the place of infection.

Lochia, postnatal vaginal discharge. As the uterus grows smaller, clots of blood and tissue flow quite freely and contain a good deal of blood. The flow gradually subsides. At the end of the first week it has changed in color from bright red to dark red or brown. At the end of the second week it may be yellow or white, but it is not unusual for the dark discharge to persist for a while longer. Although this discharge from the vagina is often called menstruation, it is not.

Lochiopyra, puerperal fever.

Lock Jaw, tetanus.

Locomotion, movement from place to place.

Loculpus, small space; cavity.

Locus, place; site.

Logamnesia, inability to recall words.

Logokophosis, word deafness.

Logopathy, any speech disorder of central origin.

Logopedia, study and treatment of speech defects.

Loin, portion of back between thorax and pelvis.

Longevity, long life.

Longsightedness, farsightedness.

Lordosis, an abnormal curvature of the spine with the convexity towards the front.

Lotio, lotion.

Lotion, liquid substance for washing a part.

Loupe, convex lens.

Louse, parasite that transmits diseases.

Three kinds of lice (the head louse, the body louse, and the pubic or crab louse) infest the human body. The names of the three types indicate the areas of the body on which each is usually found. Head and body lice look alike, but their habits are different. Lack of personal cleanliness is a common cause of infestation; however, any child or adult may inadvertently acquire an infestation by contact with infested people or articles. While the lice themselves seldom cause serious trouble, the scratching they induce sometimes results in skin lesions and infections.

Loxia, wry neck.

Loxotic, slanting.

Loxotomy, oblique amputation.

Lozenge, soothing, medicated solid to be held in the mouth until it dissolves.

LSD, legally classed as a hallucinogen, a mind-affecting drug, LSD is noted mainly for producing strong and bizarre mental reactions in people and striking distortions in their physical senses—what and how they see, touch, smell, and hear.

Just how LSD works in the body is not yet known. It seems to affect the levels of certain chemicals in the brain and to produce changes in the brain's electrical activity. Animal experiments with LSD suggest that the brain's normal filtering and screening-out process becomes blocked, causing it to become flooded with unselected sights and sounds. Studies of chronic LSD users indicate that they continue to suffer from an overload of stimulation to their senses. Researchers believe this may explain the regular user's inability to think clearly and to concentrate on a goal.

Lubb-Dupp, vocal interpretation of heart sounds.

Lubricant, an agent which makes smooth.

Lucid, clear.

Lucipetal, attracted by bright light.

Lues, syphilis.

Lumbago, backache in the loin region.

Lumbar, pertaining to the loin.

Lumbodynia, lumbago.

Lumen, space within a tube.

Luminal, sedative; phenobarbital.

Lunacy, mental illness.

Lunatic, insane person.

Lungs, two cone-shaped bodies responsible for providing the body with air and with discharging certain waste products. The lungs are soft, spongy, and elastic. The outside of each lung is covered by a closed sac called the pleura. The inner part of the lungs communicates freely with the outside air through the windpipe. The outside of the lungs is protected from air pressure by the walls of the chest cavity, creating a lessened pressure within the enveloping lung sac. The air pressure within the lungs expands them until they fill almost the entire chest cavity. If any air gets through the chest wall, or if the lung is punctured so that air from the outside can communicate with the pleural sac, the lungs shrink because the air pressure is equalized outside and inside the chest cavity. The lungs are not equal in size. The right lung has three lobes, and the left lung has two lobes. These lobes are closed systems, so that any one lobe can be removed without damage to the remaining lobes. In passing to and from the lungs, air passes through the nose, throat, and the windpipe (trachea). In the nose the air is warmed and moistened. By means of the moist hairs and the moist mucous membrane of the nose, much of the dust is filtered out of inhaled air. Moreover, the sense of smell, which warns of the presence of some types of harmful gases, is situated in the nose. By the time air reaches the lungs it is much safer for them. Large bronchial tubes (bronchi) leading from the windpipe carry the air that has been breathed in through the mouth and nose. These large tubes divide into smaller and smaller ones (bronchioles) until they are the size of fine threads. At the end of each small tube there is a cluster of tiny air sacs called alveoli. These air cells resemble a bunch of grapes, except they are many times smaller. Around each air cell, which has very thin walls, is a fine network of small blood vessels or capillaries. The blood in these capillaries releases carbon dioxide and other waste matter brought from tissue activity all over the body. This takes place through the thin air-cell wall. In exchange, the blood takes on a supply of oxygen from the air breathed into the air cells. The discarded carbon dioxide and waste matter are removed from the air cells in the air that is breathed out of the lungs. This process is repeated about sixteen times every minute.

Lunula, pale crescent at root of nail.

Lupiform, resembling lupus.

Lupous, pertaining to lupus.

Lupus, disease of unknown origin affecting skin and vital organs.

Lusus Natural, freak of nature.

Luxation, dislocation.

Luxus, excess.

Lying-in, puerperal state; child-bed.

Lymph, special functioning fluid that flows through specific vessels, passing through the filter of the lymph glands before entering the blood stream.

Lymphadentis, inflammation of a lymph gland.

Lymphatic, relating to lymph or a vessel through which it flows.

Lymph System, a circulatory system of vessels, spaces, and nodes. The lymph system carries lymph, the almost-colorless fluid that bathes the body's cells. The lymph nodes are small glands that act as filters for the lymph system. They remove bacteria, etc., from the lymph as it passes through the nodes. These nodes produce white blood cells and antibodies to help the body defend against infection. Lymph nodes are scattered throughout the body in clumps. The principal areas are the hand, neck, face, armpits, chest, abdomen, pelvic region, groin, and legs. In addition to the lymph nodes, the lymph system also includes three other lymph organs. These organs are the spleen, the tonsils, and the thymus. Part of the function of the spleen is to produce white blood cells and to help the lymph nodes act as a filter. The tonsils and the thymus also manufacture white blood cells.

Lysemia, disintegration of the blood.

Lysis, gradual disappearance of a disease.

Lyssa, rabies.

Lyssoid, resembling rabies.

— M —

Maceration, soften in a fluid.

Machonnement, chewing motion.

Macies, wasting.

Macrobiosis, longevity.

Macrocephalus, having an unusually large head.

Macrocyte, large red blood cell.

Macrodont, having large teeth.

Macropodia, unusually large feet.

Macroscopic, visible to the naked eye.

Macrosonia, gigantism.

Macula, pigmented spot on the skin, spot in the retina.

Maculate, spotted.

Mad, insane; angry.

Madarosis, loss of eyelashes or eyebrows.

Madescent, damp.

Madura Foot, disease of the foot caused by a fungus infection.

Maduromycosis, an infection that is caused by fungus. Maduromycosis usually affects the foot but may also be found in the hand and other body parts. The fungus generally enters the body through a wound. Maduromycosis is most frequently found in warm climates. The fungus causes lesions and pus to form. The pus is discharged through dead tissue. If untreated, maduromycosis will destroy tissue and bone. Some forms of this disease, caused by specific molds, are treatable with penicillin and sulfonamides. However, other types will not respond to drugs, and in those cases the only treatment is amputation of the affected part. An untreated case of maduromycosis can lead to death as a result of secondary infections.

Maggot, worm.

Magnesium, a mineral that is essential to the proper functioning of the body. Large amounts are found in the bones and the teeth. Among other functions, it plays an indispensable role in the body's use of food for energy. Magnesium is found in goodly amounts in nuts, whole-grain products, dry beans, dry peas, and dark-green vegetables.

Maidenhead, hymen.

Maidism, pellagra.

Maieutics, obstetrics.

Maim, injure, disable.

Main, hand.

Main Succulente, edema of the hands.

Mal, sickness; pain; disease.

Mala, cheek; cheekbone.

Malabsorptive Disease, an inability to digest and absorb food properly.

Malacosarcosis, softness of muscle tissue.

Malacosteon, softening of the bones.

Malacostic, soft.

Malady, illness.

Malaise, uneasiness, indisposition.

Malar, pertaining to the cheek or cheek bone.

Malaria, acute, febrile, infectious disease caused by the presence of parasitic organisms in the red blood cells. The process by which malaria is transmitted requires one person already infected with malaria, one or more healthy people, and a female *Anopheles* mosquito. The cycle begins when this female mosquito bites the person who has malaria. The blood that is sucked into the mosquito's body contains the malaria parasites. The parasites develop into the infective stage within the insect's body. These parasites will develop over a two-week period. After this time any person the mosquito bites will become infected. This is because the mosquito injects the infective parasites at the same time it is sucking blood out of the person. About ten days to two weeks (although the incubation period can vary more than that) after being bitten, the infected person begins to exhibit the symptoms of malaria. The classic symptoms are a cycle of fever and chills, but they usually also include headache and nausea. Different varieties of malaria have different cycles. In one kind, the fever and chills occur every other day; in another type, they appear every third day; and others have different patterns.

Malariologist, specialist in malaria.

Malassimilation, defective assimilation.

Malaxation, kneading motion in massage.

Male, masculine; fertilizing member of the sex.

Malformation, deformity, an abnormal development.

Malignant, poisonous, threatening life.

Malignant Hypertension, a severe form of high blood pressure that runs a rapid course. It causes damage to the blood vessel walls in the kidneys, eyes, etc.

Malingerer, one who fakes illness and pretends to be suffering.

Malleolus, an extension of bone having the shape of a hammerhead on either side of the ankle joint.

Malleus, one of the three tiny, linked bones in the middle ear. The malleus (also called the hammer) is the outer bone that is attached to the eardrum. The vibrations of the eardrum are passed on to the malleus. At the other end of the malleus is the second of the three middle ear bones, the incus. The vibrations of the malleus are moved along to the incus.

Malnutrition, an impairment or risk of impairment to physical and mental health caused by failure to meet nutritional requirements. Malnutrition is the result of either the consumption of an insufficient quantity of food or of one or more essential nutrients. It may also be caused by faulty absorption or utilization of nutrients owing to physical or emotional causes. In this country the most usual consequence of deficient diet is general undernutrition of a rather mild degree. As a rule, this is caused by a diet that is low in a number of essentials, and it develops when a person eats one food to excess and gets too little of other foods. The amount of iron, calcium, and other minerals may all be insufficient, or the diet may furnish insufficient vitamins. The consumption of protein may be inadequate in quantity, or in quality, or in both for the best growth of muscles and other tissues. Malnutrition may also occur when the total food intake is not enough to supply the energy needed for bodily activities. A chronic disease or some particular physical defect may interfere with nutrition. Poor mental health, or simply unhappiness, may also be a factor. Such conditions may prevent a person from eating as much as he should or may interfere with his ability to utilize what he does eat. These situations usually result in a combination of mild symptoms of various diseases and in a general lack of well-being.

Malocclusion, a condition in which the upper and lower teeth do not meet evenly, resulting in an incorrect bite.

Malposition, abnormal position of any organ or part.

Malpractice, improper medical care due to carelessness or ignorance of the doctor.

Malpresentation, faulty fetal presentation.

Malum, disease.

Malunion, a condition in which a broken bone has healed improperly and the broken edges of the bone are not evenly matched together. Malunion occurs when the broken bone has not been properly set or has not been set at all. The condition is corrected by deliberately breaking the bone again and setting it properly.

Mamma Virilis, male breast.

Mammalgia, breast pain.

Mammary Glands, the breasts.

Mammilla, nipple.

Mammillary, resembling a nipple.

Mammogram, special type of x-ray used to examine the soft tissue of the breast to confirm or rule out the presence of cancer.

Mammose, having unusually large breasts.

Mancinism, left-handedness.

Mandible, lower jawbone.

Mandibular, pertaining to the mandible or lower jaw bone.

Manducation, chewing.

Maneuver, skillful procedure.

Mania, violent passion or desire; extreme excitement.

Maniac, one obsessed by a violent passion or desire.

Manic-Depressive, characterized by alternate excitement and depression.

Manipulation, skillful use of the hands.

Mantle, brain cortex.

Mantoux test, a simple skin test for detecting tuberculosis.

Manual, pertaining to the hands.

Manubrium, handle; top part of the breastbone.

Manus, hand.

Maple Syrup Urine Disease, a defect in the metabolism of certain protein builders. This causes a "maple syrup" odor to urine; seizures; mental retardation; and early death. A special diet may be successful for prevention.

Marasmic, pertaining to marasmus.

Marasmus, progressive wasting in infants without an obvious cause.

Mareo, seasickness.

Margo, pl., **Margines,** border, margin.

Marihuana, a dried plant material from the Indian hemp plant *(Cannabis sativa)*. The plant grows wild in many parts of the world, including the United States, and is frequently cultivated for its commercial value in the production of fiber for rope, in birdseed, and for other purposes. In its drug use it is known by such names as "pot," "grass," "weed," "Mary Jane," and many others. For use as a drug, the leaves and flowering tops of the plant are dried and crushed or broken into small fragments which are then typically rolled into thin, homemade cigarettes, often called "joints." It may also be smoked in small pipes and is occasionally incorporated into food and eaten. The smoke smells like burning rope or alfalfa. Because of its distinctive odor, users sometimes burn incense to mask the smell. Hashish ("hash") is the potent, dark-brown resin that is collected from the tops of high-quality cannabis. Because of the high concentration of resin, it is often five to six times stronger than the usual marihuana, although the active drug ingredients are the same. Basically, it is a much more concentrated form of the drug. When smoked, marihuana quickly enters the bloodstream and within minutes begins to affect the user's mood and thinking. The exact mechanisms of action and the alterations of cerebral metabolism are not well understood. Extensive research is currently underway to provide this basic information. Because it can cause hallucinations if used in very high doses, marihuana is technically classified as a mild hallucinogen.

Mark, spot; blemish.

Marrow, the spongy, porous material found in the center of a bone. Until adulthood, bone marrow is red because it is actively producing red blood cells. When adulthood has been reached and there is no further growth, many bones no longer produce red blood cells. These bones then have a yellow bone marrow, which is largely composed of fat. However, because red blood cells constantly wear out and must be replaced, some of the bones in the body continue to have red bone marrow.

Marsh Fever, malarial fever.

Marsupium, pouch.

Masculation, having male characteristics.

Masculine, pertaining to the male.

Masculinization, acquisition of male secondary sex characteristics by the female.

Masochism, sexual pleasure derived from pain.

Masochist, one who derives pleasure from pain.

Massage, treatment of disease of the tissues.

Masseur, man who massages.

Masseuse, woman who massages.

Mastadenitis, mammary gland inflammation.

Mastadenoma, breast tumor.

Mastalgia, pain in the breast.

Mastauxe, breast enlargement.

Mastectomy, surgical removal of the breast.

Mastication, the process of chewing food to reduce it to the point where it can be comfortably swallowed. Mastication is the first of the digestive processes.

Mastitis, inflammation of the breasts.

Mastodynia, pain in the breast.

Mastoid, bone situated behind the ear; nipple-shaped.

Mastoidectomy, surgical destruction of the cells in the mastoid.

Mastology, study of the breasts.

Mastoncus, breast tumor, swelling.

Masturbation, self-stimulation of the sex organs.

Materia, material; substance.

Materia Medica, pharmacology.

Maternal, pertaining to the mother.

Matrix, pl., **Matrices**, uterus, generative structure.

Maturation, achieving maturity.

Mature, fully developed.

Maxilla, bone of the upper jaw.

Maxillofacial, pertaining to the lower half of the face.

M.B., Bachelor of Medicine.

M.D., Doctor of Medicine.

Mean, average.

Measles, an infectious viral disease marked by fever, a rash of pink spots, redness of the eyes and mild bronchitis. The virus that causes measles is found in the secretions of the nose and throat of infected persons who discharge virus particles into the air when they talk, sneeze, or cough. People become infected by inhaling these virus particles. It is also possible to become infected with the virus by touching articles that have been in recent contact with an infected person's nose or mouth, such as handkerchiefs or clothes. Measles can be dangerous because of the complications that can follow it. These include bronchopneumonia, middle-ear infection, and encephalitis. The encephalitis that occurs in about one out of every one thousand cases of measles often causes permanent brain damage, resulting in mental retardation

Measles-German, an acute viral fever which is like a mild attack of measles, running a shorter course.

Meatus, opening; passage.

Mecamylamine Hydrochloride, a drug that blocks the transmission of nerve impulses at the nerve centers.

Meconium, opium; first feces of the newborn.

Medi- (prefix), middle.

Medial, pertaining to the middle.

Median, located in the middle.

Mediastinum, a term used to indicate the area between the lungs. It contains the heart, trachea, esophagus, etc.

Medicable, receptive to cure.

Medical, pertaining to medicine.

Medical Examiner, an official whose duty it is to determine cause of death in questionable cases.

Medical Jurisprudence, medicine and its relation to law.

Medicament, medicinal substance.

Medication, giving of remedies; medicinal agent.

Medicinal, of a curative nature.

Medicine, art and science of healing.

Medicolegal, pertaining to medical jurisprudence.

Medicus, doctor.

Medulla, marrow.

Medulla Oblongata, cone-shaped part of the nervous system which is at the junction between the spinal cord and the brain.

Medullary, pertaining to a medulla.

Medullispinal, pertaining to the spinal cord.

Medullitis, inflammation of marrow.

Megacephalic, having an unusually large head.

Magalgia, acute pain.

Megalocornea, bulging of the cornea.

Megalogastria, enlargement of the stomach.

Megalohepatia, enlargement of the liver.

Megalomania, delusions of personal grandeur.

Megalomelia, unusual largeness of the limbs.

Megarectum, enlargement of the rectum.

Megrim, migraine.

Meibomian Glands, glands located near the upper and lower eyelids.

Mel, honey.

Melaena, black vomit.

Melalgia, pain in the extremities.

Melancholia, depression and self pity.

Melanin, black or dark-brown pigment.

Melanoglossia, black tongue.

Melanoma, tumor arising from a pigmented mole.

Melanopathy, excessive skin pigmentation.

Melanosis, deposits of black pigment found in various parts of the body.

Melasma, dark pigmentation.

Melena, very dark bowel movements, an indication of internal bleeding.

Melitemia, excess blood sugar.

Melitis, inflammation of cheek.

Mellite, honey preparation.

Membrana, membrane.

Membrane, thin layer of tissue covering or dividing an organ.

Membranoid, resembling a membrane.

Membrum, body; part; organ.

Memory, recall of past experience.

Menacme, years of menstrual activity in a woman's life.

Menarche, onset of the menstrual period.

Meniere's Disease, a disease of the organs of balance in the inner ear in which there is deafness and sudden attacks of extreme giddiness, vomiting and loss of balance.

Meninges, three layered membranes that cover and protect the brain and the spinal cord. The three layers are: the dura mater, the arachnoid and the pia mater. The dura mater is the outermost layer and is the toughest of the three membranes. Beneath the dura mater is the arachnoid, so named because it resembles a spider's web. Beneath the arachnoid, and closest to the brain, is the pia mater, a transparent membrane that actually touches the brain and spinal cord.

Meningioma, tumor arising from membranes covering the brain.

Meningitides, inflammation of the lining membrane of the brain or spinal cord.

Meningitis, inflammation of the lining of the brain and spinal cord with both mental and motor systems usually involved.

It may be caused by any of several bacteria, viruses, or other microscopic organisms. A very serious form is caused by an organism called meningococcus. These bacteria may be present in the body with no effect, or they may cause serious illness. If meningococci reach the brain or spinal cord, they cause severe inflammation or meningitis. Without treatment, this disease is fatal in about half the cases; survivors may be left with disabilities such as deafness and paralysis. Meningitis usually begins suddenly, with severe headache and stiffness and pains in the neck, back, and shoulders. Other symptoms are a high fever and often nausea and vomiting. A skin rash of tiny, bright-red spots frequently occurs. If these conditions appear, a physician should be consulted, because prompt treatment is essential. A diagnosis of meningitis is confirmed by inserting a needle into the spinal column to withdraw fluid. This fluid is then analyzed.

Antibiotics and sulfa drugs are effective in most cases of meningococcal meningitis. With early treatment, most patients get well quickly. A few deaths result from an overwhelming infection that defies even prompt treatment.

Meningomalacia, softening of a membrane.

Meningopathy, any disease of the meninges.

Meninx, see meninges.

Meniscus, crescent-shaped piece of gristle usually found in the knee joint.

Menolipsis, temporary absence of menstruation.

Menopause, the end of menstrual periods and, therefore, the end of childbearing years. It is also called the climacteric or "change of life." The menopause usually occurs when a woman is between forty and fifty. It can occur earlier or later. It starts gradually and is recognized by the change in menstruation. The monthly flow becomes smaller in amount, then irregular, and finally ceases. Often, the time between periods becomes longer and longer—there may be a lapse of several months between them. Before and during these changes in the monthly periods, certain symptoms may appear; e.g., hot or warm flushes, dizziness, weakness, nervousness, and insomnia. Many women have very mild symptoms; some have none at all; with a few, the discomfort is very severe. The symptoms are caused by the disappearance of the female sex hormone that the ovaries produce. The same symptoms occur when the ovaries are removed surgically because of disease (surgical menopause). After a period of time ranging from a few months to a year or two, the body adjusts itself, and the symptoms disappear. While this adjustment is taking place, hot flushes, etc., can appear. The menopause is not a complete change of life. The normal sex urges remain, and women retain their usual reaction to sex long after the menopause. Medical treatment can be very successful in relieving symptoms of menopause. Medical care can help to correct nervousness and low spirits that often go along with menopause. Mental depression is not unusual at this time.

Menorrhagia, excessive bleeding during the monthly period.

Menorrhea, normal menstruation; profuse menstruation.

Menoschesis, suppression of menstruation.

Menostaxis, prolonged menstruation.

Menses, menstruation.

Menstruation, the periodic shedding of the lining of the uterus. About every twenty-eight days, midway between two menstrual cycles, changes take place in both the ovaries and the uterus. An ovary prepares to release one of its ova. At the same time, the lining of the uterus starts to grow. Tiny glands and blood vessels appear in the top half of this lining, and the whole of it becomes soft and velvety. About fourteen days before the menstrual flow, a single ovum leaves one of the ovaries, stops for twenty-four hours at the entrance to a fallopian tube, then goes on through the tube into the uterus. If conception does not take place, the lining of the uterus then gradually stops growing and comes loose. As it loosens, the blood vessels that come away with it begin to bleed. This causes the menstrual flow of blood, which lasts several days. It carries away the unused top layer of the lining of the uterus and any other waste materials that may be present. As soon as this first menstrual period ends, preparation for another one begins. This cycle repeats itself, except during pregnancy, until the menopause.

Mensuration, measuring.

Mental, pertaining to the mind; pertaining to the chin.

Mental Illness, a mental or emotional disorder strong enough to interfere in a major or minor way with daily living.

Mental disorders can be classified under four major headings: psychoses, neuroses, personality or character disorders, and psychosomatic diseases.

Psychoses (which the term "insanity" usually refers to) are generally characterized by strange feelings and behavior and by a distortion of reality. Psychoses are the most severe forms of mental illness.

The neuroses are less severe emotional disturbances, although in some cases thinking and judgment may be impaired. The trouble is mostly in the way a neurotic person feels—and often he feels very uncomfortable. Neurotics may be continually bothered by feelings of anxiety or depression, which use up their energies and fill them with nameless dread.

Character or personality disorders are difficulties in adjustment that show themselves in the kind of disturbed behavior that is seen in the drug addict, the chronic alcoholic, or the delinquent. Usually the person with a character disorder does not feel great anxiety or guilt about his behavior, whereas most other emotionally ill persons with the same symptoms do. He behaves very much as if he does not care about the standards of conduct or achievement that are important to most people in our society. Irresponsibility and immaturity are often indications of this type of disorder.

Psychosomatic diseases are those ailments in which the symptoms are primarily physical, although there may be a large emotional component.

Mental Retardation, a condition of inadequately developed intelligence that significantly impairs the ability to learn and to adapt to the demands of society. Mental retardation is present at birth or develops during childhood and usually continues throughout life. More than two hundred specific causes of mental retardation have been identified. In approximately twenty to twenty-five percent of cases the cause is known. Among the known biological factors are hereditary factors, infections, nutritional deficiencies or toxic substances in the mother's system during pregnancy, and injuries. Lack of a healthful environment, including motivation, stimulation, and opportunity, is a large factor for many children.

Some mentally retarded children are behind in various stages of their development such as sitting up, crawling, walking, and talking. Some are born with a combination of physical signs such as those in mongolism (Down's syndrome), which usually makes possible a diagnosis at birth. Other babies, born normal, develop jaundice in the first days of life. This warns the doctor that mental retardation may be threatening unless immediate steps are taken. A child with the enlarged head of hydrocephalus (excess fluid inside the skull) is in danger of mental retardation. Other retarded children are, in all obvious ways, physically healthy and normal. Their mental retardation may not even be suspected until they enter school and cannot keep up with normal children. The degree of mental retardation may range from mild to profound. In severe cases the condition is usually recognizable very early; when slight, it may require several years of observation to make the proper diagnosis. In terms of physical appearance, seventy-five percent of the retarded have the same characteristics as the rest of the population. On this basis alone only twenty-five percent are detectable through differences in head size, small stature, small hands, or slanted eyes. The overriding symptom of mental retardation is that the individual does not adapt or achieve in the same manner or degree as his contemporaries. Mental retardation is classified on the basis of measured intelligence and adaptive behavior.

Mentum, chin.

Mephitic, noxious; foul.

Meralgia, thigh pain.

Mercurial Diuretic, one of various compounds of mercury commonly used to promote the elimination of water and sodium from the body through increased excretion of urine.

Meropia, partial blindness.

Merotomy, cutting into sections.

Mesiad, toward the center.

Mesial, located in the middle.

Mesmerism, hypnotism.

Metabolism, the building-up and breaking-down processes of the body as a whole.

Metabolism, Basal, minimum amount of energy necessary to maintain life when the body is at complete rest.

Metacarpus, five bones in the palm of the hand.

Metachrosis, change of color.

Metachysis, blood transfusion.

Metacyesis, extrauterine pregnancy.

Metallophobia, extreme fear of metallic objects.

Metamorphosis, change of shape or structure.

Metaphase, the second stage in cell division.

Metastasis, movement of bacteria or a disease from one part of the body to another.

Metatarsus, part of the foot between the ankle and the beginning of the toes.

Methadone, a synthetic drug that can be given to a heroin addict to replace heroin. Methadone has the advantage of being less expensive and allowing the addict to maintain a normal life. However, methadone is also an addictive drug.

Methamphetamine, a stimulant, or a drug that stimulates the central nervous system. Methamphetamine is similar to amphetamine, but in many ways it is stronger. While methamphetamine does have important medical uses, it has become a drug of abuse, known as "speed."

Metopagus, twins joined at the forehead.

Metopic, pertaining to the forehead.

Metra, the uterus.

Metralgia, pain in the uterus.

Metrectasia, dilatation of the uterus.

Metritis, inflammation of the uterus.

Metrocarcinoma, cancer of the uterus.

Metrocyte, mother cell.

Metrodynia, pain in the uterus.

Metrology, science of measurements.

Metropathy, any uterine disorder.

Metrorrhagia, vaginal bleeding unrelated to monthly bleeding.

M.F.D., minimum fatal dose.

Miasm, Miasma, foul odor.

Mication, involuntary, rapid winking; fast motion.

Microbe, small, living organism discernible only through a microscope.

Microbicidal, destroying microbes.

Microbiologist, specialist in microbiology.

Microbiology, science dealing with microscopic organisms.

Microcardia, abnormal smallness of the heart.

Microcoria, smallness of the pupil.

Microcyst, tiny cyst.

Microcyte, small red blood corpuscle.

Microglossia, abnormal smallness of the tongue.

Microlesion, very small lesion.

Micromastia, unusual smallness of the breast.

Micronize, reduce to very small particles.

Microorganism, microscopic organism.

Microphallus, abnormal smallness of the penis.

Micropsia, defective vision; seeing things smaller than they are.

Microscope, instrument which enlarges objects for visual examination.

Microscopic, able to be seen only under a microscope.

Microscopy, observation with the microscope.

Micturition, urination.

Midget, one who does not attain full growth; very small person.

Midriff, diaphragm.

Midwife, woman who helps at childbirth.

Midwifery, obstetrics.

Midriasis, enlargement of the pupil of the eye.

Migraine, severe, periodic, onesided headache, usually accompanied by abdominal distress.

Miliaria, heat rash.

Milieu, environment.

Milk, one of the most important of all foods. Babies begin life on a milk diet because it is so rich in important proteins, vitamins, etc. Milk is also important to growing children because of the amount of calcium it provides.

Milphosis, loss of eyebrows or eyelashes.

Minerals, inorganic substances that are essential to the human body. They give strength and rigidity to certain body tissues and help with numerous vital functions. Most of the hard tissues of the human body, such as bones and teeth, are composed in part of mineral elements. In the case of bones and teeth, relatively large amounts of calcium and phosphorus are needed to make up these structures, but the body also needs many other minerals, some in very minute quantities, to carry on its life processes. For instance, in order to function properly, muscles, nerves, and the heart must be constantly nourished by body fluids containing the correct proportion of minerals such as sodium, potassium, and calcium. Similarly, red blood cells cannot be formed or function properly unless sufficient iron is supplied to the body. The consumption of small amounts of another mineral, fluorine, during the formative years prevents excessive tooth decay among young children and adolescents and during later life. Altogether, about fifteen different mineral elements are required by the body, and all must be derived from food or drink. The minerals in which diets are most likely to be low, or deficient, are calcium, iron, iodine, and fluorine.

Miocardia, heart contraction.

Miosis, contraction.

Miscarriage, loss of product of conception before age of viability; abortion.
Miscarriages may be caused by factors other than abnormalities of the egg or infant. They may also be caused by glandular or nutritional problems. Miscarriage used to be blamed on a fall or a blow to the abdomen, but doctors now know that this is an exceedingly rare cause. The baby is protected within a sac of fluid in the uterus and usually escapes injury even in the event of a serious accident to the mother. Slight bleeding may mean that a miscarriage is only threatening and that the baby may yet be saved. More severe bleeding, especially with cramps, usually means that a miscarriage is actually in progress.

Miscegenation, people of two different races that are married.

Miscible, able to be mixed.

Misogamy, hatred of marriage.

Misopedia, hatred of children.

Mite, tiny insect.

Mitosis, the process of human cell division or reproduction.

Mitral Valve, the heart valve on left side of heart between upper and lower chambers.

Mitral Valvulotomy, an operation to widen the opening in the valve between the upper and lower chambers in the left side of the heart (mitral valve).

Mittelschmerz, pain at time of ovulation.

M.M., mucous membrane.

Mnemonics, improvement of the memory.

Mobile, movable.

Moccasin, poisonous snake.

Modus, method.

Modus Operandi, method of performing an act.

Mogigraphia, writers' cramp.

Mogilalia, speech defect.

Mogitocia, difficult birth.

Moist, damp.

Molar, the teeth that grind food. The first permanent teeth are the four "6-year" molars, one on each side of the upper and lower jaws. Appearing about the sixth year, behind the primary teeth, they are often mistaken for primary teeth. The "6-year" molars are very important. They make it possible for the child to chew during the time the primary teeth are being replaced by permanent teeth. The position of the "6-year" molars largely determines the position of the other permanent teeth, which in turn influence the shape of the jaws and the child's appearance. If the "6-year" molars are lost, the shape of the jaw may be changed, and correction and alignment may later be required. There are three sets of molars. The first set is the "6-year" molars. The second set erupts at the age of twelve or thirteen. The third and final set emerges between the ages of seventeen and twenty-one. These last molars are often referred to as the "wisdom teeth."

Mold, fungus.

Molding, shaping of the fetal head at birth.

Mole, skin growth usually colored and sprouting hair.

Molecule, tiny mass of matter.

Molimen, effort to establish the monthly period.

Mollities, abnormal softening.

Molluscum, chronic skin disease with pulpy bumps.

Monarticular, pertaining to a single joint.

Mongolism, arrest of physical and mental development, with features similar to the Asiatic race.

Moniliasis, fungus infection of various areas of the body, especially mouth, throat, vagina.

Moniliform, beaded.

Monocular, pertaining to or affecting one eye; having a single lens.

Monocular Vision, a condition in which one eye is blind or one eye refuses to register images in coordination with the better eye.

Monocyesis, pregnancy with one fetus.

Monocyte, type of white blood cell.

Monodiplopia, double vision in one eye.

Monogenesis, nonsexual reproduction.

Monogenous, a sexual reproduction.

Monohemerous, lasting qnly one day.

Monomania, obsession with one subject or idea.

Monomelic, affecting one limb.

Mononucleosis, glandular fever; virus disease in which monocytes are increased beyond normal number, lymph nodes enlarged, sore throat.

Monopathy, disease affecting a single part.

Monoplegia, paralysis of a single group of muscles or one limb.

Monosexual, having characteristics of only one sex.

Mono-unsaturated Fat, a fat so constituted chemically that it is capable of absorbing additional hydrogen but not as much hydrogen as a polyunsaturated fat.

Mood, attitude; state of mind.

Mons, elevated area.

Mons Pubis, Mons Veneris, area over the symphysis pubis in the female.

Monster, abnormally formed fetus.

Monstrosity, state of being a monster.

Monthlies, menses.

Monticulus, protuberance.

Morbid, pertaining to disease; the disease itself.

Morbid Condition, condition of disease.

Morbidity Rate, the ratio of the number of cases of a disease to the number of healthy people in a given population during a specified period of time.
Incidence is the number of new cases of a disease developing in a given population during a specified period of time. Prevalence is the number of cases of a given disease existing in a given population at a specified moment of time.

Morbific, causing disease.

Morbilli, measles.

Morbilliform, like measles.

Morbus, disease.

Morbus Caducus, epilepsy.

Mores, customs.

Morgue, public mortuary.

Moria, foolishness.

Moribund, dying.

Morning Sickness, nausea and vomiting during the early stages of pregnancy.

Moron, one whose mental age is from seven to twelve years.

Morosis, feeblemindedness.

Morphine, drug used as an analgesic and sedative.
Morphine, like all narcotics, is physically addictive. A patient taking morphine over a period of time develops a tolerance for the drug and requires larger and larger doses. There is also a danger of psychological dependency developing in the case of a patient using morphine over a period of time. The size of the dose of morphine determines, to a certain extent, the degree of side effects present. As the level of the dose increases, so does the degree of the side effects. Morphine tends to make the patient drowsy, changes his mood (often to euphoria), produces constipation, and can cause nausea and vomiting.

Morphinism, addiction to morphine.

Mors, death.

Morsus, bite.

Morsus Humanus, human bite.

Mortal, deadly.

Mortise Joint, ankle joint.

Mosquito, blood sucking insect.

Mosquitocide, agent which kills mosquitoes.

Mother, female parent.

Mother's Mark, birthmark.

Motile, able to move.

Motion Sickness, a feeling of nausea that may be accompanied by vomiting and which is caused by motion. Motion sickness presents two problems. The first is the physical problem. Motion sickness is caused by an upset in the delicate balance mechanism of the inner ear. The parts of the inner ear that control balance (the semicircular canals and their appendages) have fluids in them. When the fluid moves, it touches small hairs, which in turn trigger nerve impulses to the brain. When the amount of motion and/or the kind of motion is sufficiently aggravating, the vomiting center of the brain is also triggered.
The second problem associated with motion sickness is a psychological one. The fear of flying can upset the stomach enough to cause motion sickness. Once a person has had motion sickness, whether from physical or psychological factors, he is prone to have motion sickness again. Thus, in addition to being afraid to travel, or actually having a disturbance in the balance mechanism, he also has to cope with his fear of motion sickness.

Mottling, discoloration in various areas.

Mounding, lumping.

Mountain Sickness, condition caused by low air pressure.

Mouth, the first part of the digestive system. The mouth is a cavity consisting of the hard palate and the teeth at the top, the cheeks as the side, the tongue and lower teeth as the floor, and the soft palate extending from the end of the hard palate to the pharynx.
The digestive functions of the mouth are mastication

and lubrication. The teeth reduce food to manageable size. Saliva prepares the food to move easily down the rest of the digestive tract.
The mouth, an important part of speech, is also an alternate breathing passage.

M.S., Master of Surgery.

M.T., Medical Technologist.

Muciferous, secreting mucus.

Mucilage, paste.

Mucilaginous, adhesive.

Mucin, main substance of mucus.

Mucopus, mucus mixed with pus.

Mucosa, mucous membrane; lining tissue that produces mucus.

Mucous, pertaining to mucus.

Mucus, a thick, white liquid secreted by mucous glands.

Mulatto, anyone of both Negro and White blood.

Muliebria, female genitalia.

Muliebrity, femininity.

Multi- (prefix), many; much.

Multigravida, pregnant woman who had more than two past pregnancies.

Multipara, woman who has had more than two live children.

Multiple Sclerosis, a chronic, progressive, degenerative disease of the central nervous system.
Multiple sclerosis is not contagious nor is it a mental disease. It is "multiple" in the sense that it produces multiple changes or lesions on the brain and spinal cord, which result in multiple effects in the body. More often multiple sclerosis attacks one area of the nervous system and later, after a period of improvement, the same area again or a different place. It is "sclerotic" because it leaves sclera or scars at the points where demyelination, the loss of the protective covering of the nerves, takes place. For this reason, multiple sclerosis is known as a demyelinating disease. The fatty covering called "myelin," which normally protects and insulates the nerve fibers of the spinal cord and brain, disappears in scattered patches during multiple sclerosis. Without this myelin, body signals go wrong. Hence the characteristics of multiple sclerosis may include shaking or tremor, extreme weakness, and progressive paralysis.

Mumps, infectious disease marked by swelling of the large salivary glands in front of the ears.
Signs of mumps appear between two and three weeks after exposure. The first sign is usually pain under one or both ears or under the chin. Often there is a fever, followed by swelling of one or more salivary glands—sometimes in the neck or throat, but usually just below and in front of the ears. Cases often start with chills, fever, headache, and loss of appetite for a day or two before the glands begin to swell. Most cases last about a week. A person with mumps is infectious from about a week before the glands start to swell until the swelling disappears.

Murmur, abnormal heart sound with a blowing or rasping quality.

Musca, fly.

Muscae Volitantes, spots before the eyes.

Muscle, the tissue that is responsible for body movement.
The fibers forming the muscles are bound together in bundles of different lengths, breadths, and thicknesses. Bundles of muscle tissue can shorten, lengthen, or thicken. This type of action makes possible the movements of various parts of the body. There are two types of muscles. Voluntary muscles are those over which an individual can exert control, such as the muscles in the arms and legs. Involuntary muscles are those that an individual cannot control, such as the muscles of the heart and muscles involved in digestion and breathing. Muscles are attached to bones by strong, fibrous cords called tendons. Tendons are not elastic, but the power of contraction or extension of the muscles to which they are attached causes the bones forming joints to move either by flexing or by extending. The body has over six hundred muscles. Approximately forty percent of a male's weight is muscle. A female's weight is thirty-five percent muscle. The exact percentage depends on the physical condition of the individual. An athlete's weight will have a higher muscle percentage than that of an office worker.

Muscle Cramp, involuntary contraction of muscles.

Muscular, pertaining to muscle.

Muscular Dystrophy, a group of diseases, often called the muscular dystrophies, that cause a progressive wasting and weakening of the muscles. Muscular dystrophy weakens the voluntary muscles—the muscles on the outside of the body, such as the biceps of the arm. Unlike polio, the internal muscles, such as the diaphragm, are not affected by muscular dystrophy. Also, unlike polio, it usually affects equally the muscles on both sides of the body, leading to symmetrical weakening and wasting.
Muscular dystrophy has long been recognized as a disorder that often affects several people in one family. It is now well established that in most forms of muscular dystrophy an inherited characteristic coming from either parent is responsible.

Musculus, muscle.

Musophobia, extreme fear of mice.

Mussitation, delirious muttering.

Mustard Plaster, home remedy no longer commonly used.

Mutation, change.

Mute, unable to speak; one who cannot speak.

Mutism, speechlessness; dumbness.

Myalgia, muscle pain.

Myasthenia, muscle weakness.

Myatonia, muscle limpness.

Mycetismus, mushroom poisoning.

Mycology, science of fungi.

Mycosis, infection caused by fungi.

Mydriasis, abnormal pupil dilation.

Myectomy, surgical removal of a piece of muscle.

Myectopia, muscle displacement.

Myelauxe, bone marrow increase.

Myelin, the fatty covering that normally protects and insulates the nerve fibers of the spinal cord and brain. A breakdown of myelin is the cause of difficulty in multiple sclerosis. Without myelin, body signals to and from the nerves cannot function properly.

Myelon, spinal cord.

Myelopathy, disease of the spinal cord.

Myeloplegia, spinal paralysis.

Myelitis, spinal cord inflammation.

Myeloma, bone marrow tumor that may be cancerous.

Myenteron, muscular layer of the intestine.

Myiasia, condition when larvae of flies enter eyes, ears or intestines.

Myitis, muscle inflammation.

Myocardial Infarction, the damaging or death of a part of the heart muscle. Myocardial infarction is caused by a reduction or a complete stoppage of the blood supply to that area of the heart. Myocardial infarction is also known as heart attack, coronary occlusion, coronary, and coronary thrombosis. Acute myocardial infarction is the most frequent cardiac emergency. The incidence of myocardial infarction increases with advancing age, particularly after age fifty. The incidence is six times as high in males as in females.
In about half of the cases, onset is preceded by a history of angina pectoris. There is sudden severe pain in the chest, often radiating to the left arm. It usually persists for several hours. There is a fall in blood pressure and also shock. The pain is accompanied by pallor, sweating, and shortness of breath. Recovery from myocardial infarction generally requires absolute bed rest for four to six weeks. morphone or other drugs for the relief of pain and apprehension, and an anticoagulant medication. The total treatment time averages three to four months.

Myocarditis, inflammation of the heart muscle.

Myocardium, muscle that makes up the heart.

Myoclonus, muscle spasm.

Myocyte, cell of muscular tissue.

Myoid, resembling muscle.

Myology, study of muscles.

Myoma, tumor from muscle tissue.

Myomectomy, surgical removal of a myoma.

Myopathy, any muscle disease.

Myope, one who is nearsighted.

Myopia, nearsightedness. In the nearsighted eye, distant objects produce a blurred image. This is usually caused by an abnormally long front-to-back diameter of the eye. Thus, the focal image is formed in front of the retina.
Some cases of high myopia (where great correction is required) are progressive; they result from a disease rather than merely an error of refraction. Glasses may be unable to correct vision to normal range, and there may be destructive changes in various parts of the eye (choroid, retina, or vitreous body). High myopia tends to be accompanied by other changes that may be affected by strenuous physical activities.

Myosis, construction of the eye pupil.

Myositis, muscle inflammation, usually a voluntary muscle.

Myospasm, muscle spasm.

Myotasis, stretching of muscle.

Myotonia, continuous muscle spasm not relieved by relaxation.

Myringitis, inflammation of the eardrum.

Myringotomy, incision into the eardrum.

Mythomania, habitual lying or exaggeration.

Myxedema, a form of cretinism occurring in adolescence or adulthood. The symptoms are similar—retardation, coarse hair, dry skin, and goiter. However, because it occurs after most growth has stopped, dwarfing is avoided. Like cretinism, myxedema is caused by a deficiency or a complete lack of thyroid hormone. Treatment consists of thyroid extract.

Myxoma, tumor of mucous tissue.

Myxorrhea, flow of mucus.

Myzesis, sucking.

— N —

Nail, a tough, dense modification of skin. Nails cover the ends of the fingers, thumbs, and toes. A nail grows out of its nail root. This root is embedded in the skin at the end of the nail closest to the body. The skin that covers the nail root and the sides of the nail is known as the nail wall. The tissue beneath the nail itself is referred to as the nail bed. The half-moon of white at the base of the nail is called the lunula. The rate of growth of nails is subject to individual differences. However, an individual's fingernails usually grow twice as fast as his toenails.

Nail Bed, part of a finger or toe covered by a nail.

Nail Biting, nervous tendency to bite or to chew the fingernails.

Naked, exposed to view.

Nalorphine, a drug classified as a narcotic antagonist.

Nanism, dwarfishness.

Nanus, dwarf; stunted.

Nap, short sleep.

Nape, back of the neck.

Narcissism, self love.

Narcolepsy, disease of unknown origin in which there are periodic episodes of sleep any time of day or night.

Narcomania, morbid desire for narcotics.

Narcosis, state of unconsciousness.

Narcotic, producing a state of unconsciousness; any sleep inducing drug, one addicted to the use of narcotics.

Narcotic Antagonists, a class of drugs that partially reverse the effects of narcotic drugs.
An overdose of a narcotic depresses the respiratory reflex. The narcotic antagonists are extremely effective in rapidly restoring the respiratory rate to its normal level. These drugs are also used in the detection of narcotic addiction. When a narcotic antagonist is given to a patient who is addicted to narcotics, the patient will exhibit the classical symptoms of withdrawal sickness.

Narcotize, to make unconscious.

Naris, nostril.

Nasal, pertaining to the nose; bone forming the bridge of the nose.

Nasal Cavity, the internal portion of the nose.

Nasus, nose.

Natal, pertaining to birth; pertaining to the buttocks.

Natality, birth rate.

Natant, floating.

Nathan's Test, a test for tuberculosis. A special serum, with a dressing, is applied to the surface of the arm. The dressing is removed the next day. A positive reaction will appear within six days.

Natis, buttocks.

Native, inherent; indigenous.

Natural, not artificial.

Natural Childbirth, a method of childbirth that requires the mother to be conscious and to cooperate actively with the processes of birth during labor and delivery. The expectant mother undergoes a program of education, exercise, and training (both physical and mental) in preparation for labor and delivery. The woman learns how to relax and to work in harmony with the contractions. Because natural childbirth requires little or no medication, there is little or no anesthesia in the mother's system for the baby to absorb.

Natural Immunity, the ability of a person to resist a disease without having had the disease and without being vaccinated against the disease. A natural immunity is based on the body's own defense and immunity system. The term is usually used to indicate an immunity to a disease that most people will contract when they are exposed to it.

Naturopathy, curing without drugs.

Nature Cure, any system of treatment which is based upon the belief that disease may best be cured and health maintained by the use of "natural remedies", as opposed to artificial and man-made drugs.

Naupathia, seasickness.

Nausea, stomach discomfort with the feeling of a need to vomit.

Nauseant, causing nausea.

Navel, remnant on outside of body where umbilical cord was attached at birth.

Near Point, point closest to the eye at which an object can be seen distinctly.

Nearsighted, able to see clearly only a short distance.

Nebula, haziness; cloudy urine.

Necator, hookworm.

Neck, part of the body connecting the head and trunk; narrow part near the extremity of any organ.
Located within the neck are body parts such as the pharynx, esophagus, larynx, trachea, and the thyroid gland. Thus, the neck is a continuation of both the digestive tract and the respiratory system. The organs mentioned above, as well as a number of lymph nodes, are situated in the front of the neck. The back of the neck consists of the spinal column. Within the spinal

column are the spinal cord and a large number of nerves. Seven vertebrae form the beginning of the spinal column. These vertebrae, called the cervical vertebrae, are all located in the neck. The first cervical vertebra is referred to as the atlas. The construction of the atlas allows the head to tilt up and down, or nod. The second of the cervical vertebrae is known as the axis. This vertebra permits the head to turn from side to side. The rotation of the head pivots on the axis.

When the spinal cord is cut or subjected to extreme pressure, paralysis of the body occurs below the site of the injury. Therefore, any serious injury to the back of the neck can lead to paralysis from the neck down.

Necromania, obsession with death.

Necrophilism, intercourse with a corpse.

Necropneumonia, gangrene of lung.

Necropsy, autopsy.

Necrosis, death of a part of the body due to absence of blood supply.

Needle, pointed instrument for sewing or puncturing.

Negative Afterimage, the visual phenomenon that occurs after looking at a colored object and then at a white object. The afterimage will occur in the complimentary color.

Negativism, a symptom in mental diseases in which the patient resists or is against everything.

Neogala, first milk after childbirth.

Neogenesis, new formation.

Neonatal, concerning the newborn.

Neonatal Period, a term used to describe the first month of a baby's life.

Neonatorum, pertaining to the newborn.

Neonatus, a newborn infant.

Neopathy, new disease or complication.

Neophilism, excessive love of new things.

Neophobia, extreme fear of new things.

Neoplasm, an abnormal growth.

Nephralgia, pain in a kidney.

Nephrectomy, surgical removal of a kidney.

Nephrelcus, renal ulcer.

Nephric, pertaining to the kidney.

Nephritis, inflammation of the kidneys.

Nephrolithiases, formation of kidney stones.

Nephrology, study of the kidney.

Nephroma, tumor of the outer portion of the kidney.

Nephropexy, sewing a floating kidney into place.

Nephros, the kidney.

Nephrosis, disintegration of the kidney without signs of inflammation.

Nepiology, study of newborn.

Nerve, bundle of nerve fibers existing outside the central nervous system.

There are three different types of nerves. Each type fulfills a slightly different function. A sensory nerve receives sensations and transmits them to the brain. A motor nerve transmits impulses from the brain to the muscles and glands. An associative nerve transmits impulses from sensory nerves to motor nerves. The impulse moves from the dendrites, to the main cell body, to the axon. The impulse (which is actually a minute electrical charge) then jumps the space between the axon of one nerve cell and the dendrites of the next nerve cell. The small space between two nerves is called a synapse.

There are only eighty-six nerves in the entire body: twelve pairs of cranial nerves and thirty-one pairs of spinal nerves. All the remaining nerves in the body are only branches of the original eighty-six nerves.

Nerve Block, the anesthesia, or numbing, of an area of the body. This is accomplished by injecting the anesthesia in the vicinity of the region to be affected. Nerve blocks are performed for a variety of reasons, including the relief of pain in facial neuralgia and for prevention of pain when a dentist is filling or extracting a tooth.

Nervous, highly excitable.

Nervous, a condition of being easily disturbed or distressed.

Nervous System, the system that is responsible for keeping the various parts of the body and the organs controlling the body functions in touch with each other. The nervous system actually consists of two separate but interconnected and coordinated systems: the cerebrospinal system and the autonomic system. The cerebrospinal system consists of the brain and the spinal cord. The brain is a collection of nerve centers, each a central station for some part of the body — much like a central telephone station, with trunk lines or nerves connecting the parts of the body with their particular centers. Leaving the brain, these trunk nerves are bundled into the spinal cord, which passes down through the opening in the center of the backbone or spinal column, giving off branches to all parts and organs of the body. Most of the nerves entering and leaving the spinal cord are either sensory nerves or motor nerves. Sensory nerves enter the cord conveying impressions of sensations, such as heat, cold, touch, and pain, from different parts of the body to the brain. Motor nerves leave the spinal cord conveying impulses from the brain to the muscles causing movement. The autonomic system is a series of nerve centers in the chest and abdominal cavity along the spinal column. Each of these nerve centers, although interconnected with the cerebrospinal system, presides over and controls vital organs and vital functions. This system is not under control of the will, but through it involuntary muscles are stimulated to act alike during periods of wakefulness and during periods of sleep. Thus, the heart beats, respiration continues, blood pressure is maintained, food is digested, and the excretory organs function without any conscious effort. The autonomic nervous system consists of two sets of systems: the sympathetic nerves and the parasympathetic nerves. These two sets have opposite effects on the same body organs. For example, the parasympathetic nerves constrict the pupil of the eye; the sympathetic nerves dilate the pupil of the eye.

Nervus, pl., **Nervi**, nerve.

Network, structure composed of interlacing fibers.

Neural, pertaining to nerves or nervous tissue.

Neuralgia, a painful disorder of one or more nerves. The nerve causing the pain is not necessarily damaged. Neuralgia usually causes sharp, fitful pains. Facial neuralgia attacks persons over fifty years of age more frequently than it does younger people. In this disorder, excruciating pains flash intermittently across one side of the face. Sometimes a tingling of the skin warns that an attack is due. The spasms are usually "set off" by a draft of cold air or by swallowing, yawning, chewing, shaving, or similar activities. The pain can often be induced by pressing a sensitive "trigger point" along the nerve path. After a while, the painful flashes stop, only to appear again at any time from hours to months later. If the condition is not relieved, the period between attacks becomes shorter and shorter, until pain is practically continuous. Various infections or injuries of the nerve may cause neuralgia to strike other parts of the body. Sometimes the back of the neck, the eye, the lower back, or the chest may be involved. The symptoms may suggest other diseases. Sharp chest pains, for example, may suggest heart disease or pleurisy when they are actually caused by neuralgia. An experienced physician can identify true neuralgia.

Neurasthenia, exhaustion of the nerves.

Neure, neuron.

Neurectasia, stretching of a nerve to relieve pain.

Neuritis, a disorder of one or more nerves. Neuritis usually involves inflammation of a nerve or nerves and causes a constant, burning pain.

The disorder may be localized to one nerve or may involve many. Either type may result from injuries, poisons, infections, or chilling. The localized type is more common. The path of the nerve develops a burning sensation. The flesh may have a numb or "crawling" feeling. The skin is often reddened along the course of the nerve. The condition is not usually serious unless it is allowed to continue without treatment. Sciatica is a localized neuritis of the sciatic nerve. This is the nerve that runs along the back of the leg. A generalized neuritis is far more serious than a localized neuritis. It is often caused by prolonged illness, by exposure to chemicals such as lead or arsenic, or by alcoholism. Failure to eat and absorb enough food containing the B vitamins seems to be an important cause. Usually the patient complains for several weeks of numbness, tingling in the fingers and feet, and of sensations of heat and cold. There may be a slight fever. After the initial symptoms, the patient experiences weakness and pain in the muscles. If untreated, he may lose all feeling in the "glove and stocking" areas of the arms and legs and develop paralysis. The untreated patient may eventually become bedridden. Neuritis may occasionally be relieved by an operation to remove the cause (such as a tumor). A sound, carefully planned exercise program is often prescribed in addition to a variety of drugs.

Neuroblastoma, a malignant tumor of the nervous system; it is composed of immature nerve cells.

Neurocirculatory Asthenia, a complex of nervous and circulatory symptoms, often involving a sense of fatigue, dizziness, shortness of breath, rapid heartbeat, and nervousness. Neurocirculatory asthenia is also known as effort syndrome and soldier's heart.

Neurocranium, portion of the cranium enclosing the brain.

Neurocyte, any nerve cell.

Neurodynamic, pertaining to nervous energy.

Neurogenic, a term used to indicate anything that originates from within the nervous system.

Neuroid, resembling a nerve.

Neuro-induction, mental suggestion.

Neurologist, specialist in disorders of the nervous system.

Neuroma, tumor composed of nerve substance.

Neuromuscular, pertaining to the nerves and muscles.

Neuron, nerve cell.

Neuronitis, inflammation of a neuron.

Neuropathy, any disease of the nervous system.

Neurophthisis, degeneration or wasting of nerve tissue.

Neuroplasm, protoplasm of a nerve cell.

Neuropsychiatry, branch of medicine dealing with nervous and mental disorders.

Neurosis, minor mental disorder.

Neurospasm, muscular twitching.

Neurosurgeon, specialist in surgery of the brain and nervous system.

Neurosyphilis, syphilis of the nervous system.

Neurothlipsis, nerve pressure.

Neurotrauma, nerve lesion.

Nevus, relatively small benign growths on the skin. They are commonly referred to as moles, birthmarks, freckles, etc., depending on the consistency, color of pigmentation, and degree of elevation. Some nevi have a tendency to become malignant. These are usually flat, dark moles that do not have hairs. Additionally, they are usually located in areas that receive constant friction from clothes, other skin, or foreign objects. Areas of special concern are the palms of the hands and the soles of the feet.

Nexus, a binding together.

Niche, depression; recess.

Nicotine, poisonous alkaloid of tobacco.
Nicotine affects the autonomic nervous system. It affects both the parasympathetic and the sympathetic nerves. Thus, the pupils of the eyes are first constricted and then dilated.

Nictitation, excessive winking.

Nidus, cluster, focus of infection; nerve nucleus.

Niemann-Pick Disease, a form of mental illness characterized by a defect of metabolism of fats. This disease is inherited. The symptoms include a brownish discoloration of the skin and progressive blindness. Niemann-Pick disease, sometimes known as lipoid histiocytosis, often causes early death.

Night Cry, cry of a child during sleep.

Nightmare, bad dream.

Nightwalking, sleepwalking.

Nigra, black.

Nigrities Linguae, black tongue.

N.I.H., National Institutes of Health.

Niphablepsia, snow blindness.

Nipple, protuberance in each breast from which the female secretes milk.

Nit, egg of a louse.

Nitrites, a group of chemical compounds, many of which cause dilation of the small blood vessels.
The importance of these compounds is that by dilating the blood vessels, they reduce the resistance to the flow of blood and consequently lower the blood pressure.

Nitroglycerin, a drug (one of the nitrites) that relaxes the muscles in the blood vessels. Nitroglycerin is used to relieve attacks of angina pectoris and spasm of the coronary arteries. Nitroglycerin works by relaxing and dilating blood vessels. This allows blood to flow more easily through the vessels, and consequently lowers the blood pressure and reduces the work load of the heart muscle. Nitroglycerin is probably the best and most widely used drug for the relief of pain in angina attacks. It is taken in tablet form, either under the tongue (where it quickly dissolves) or chewed. Nitroglycerin will not do its job if it is simply swallowed in tablet form. Most patients experience total cessation of pain within two minutes.

N.L.N., National League for Nursing.

Noctophobia, extreme fear of night.

Nocturia, bed wetting; frequent urination at night.

Nocturnal Emission, the involuntary ejaculation of semen during sleep.

Nocuity, harmfulness.

Node, small rounded protuberance; point of constriction.

Nodule, small node; small group of cells.

Nodus, node.

Noma, form of gangrene of the mouth found in ill-nourished or weak children.

Non Compos Mentis, not of sound mind.

Non Repetat, do not repeat.

Nonsexual, without sex, asexual.

Nontoxic, not poisonous.

Nonunion, failure of bone fragments to knit together.

Nonviable, incapable.

Noopsyche, intellectual processes.

Norepinephrine, a hormone secreted by the adrenal glands.
Norepinephrine produces a rise in blood pressure by constricting the small blood vessels.

Norm, standard.

Normal, a term used to indicate something that falls within a regular or established pattern. The concept of normalcy is a very difficult one in medicine. What is normal for one person is not necessarily normal for another person. Physicians refer to certain reactions to certain drugs as normal reactions. This means that most people have these reactions. For example, most people experience a certain amount of pain relief from aspirin. That is the normal reaction. However, some people are allergic to aspirin and their response to it may include an upset stomach or a rash, as well as more violent reactions. When compared with the average reaction, theirs is not normal, but their body is reacting normally for them. Another example is the range of individual differences in body temperature. Normal, or average, body temperature is 98.6°F. when taken orally. Anything below that is called subnormal; anything above that is referred to as a fever. However, there are people whose temperature is normally (for them) 98°F. or even lower. They are perfectly healthy, but their temperature is not normal. When people like this report a temperature of 98.6°F., they are usually running a fever, even though their temperature is normal for most people. An experienced physician is always aware of individual differences. He uses the concept of normal as a yardstick to compare an individual's reactions, not as a rule to which all patients must adhere. One of the reasons medicine is considered to be an art as well as a science is the degree to which these individual differences affect diagnosis and treatment.

Normocyte, normal sized red blood cell.

Normoptopic, normally located.

Normotensive, any condition characterized by normal blood pressure.

Nose, organ of the sense of smell.

Nosebleed, hemorrhage from the nose.

Nose Drops, medicine taken in liquid form through the nose. Nose drops are usually used to help clear the sinus passages and allow free breathing.

Nosema, sickness; disease.

Nosology, science of disease classification.

Nosophilia, extreme desire to be sick.

Nosophobia, extreme fear of illness.

Nosopoietic, causing disease.

Nostalgia, homesickness; feeling for past experiences and things.

Nostomania, extreme homesickness.

Nostril, nasal aperture.

Nostrum, patent medicine.

Notal, dorsal.

Notalgia, back pain.

Notifiable, pertaining to any disease which must be reported to health authorities.

Notochord, the first supportive structure of an embryo.

Noxious, harmful; deadly; poisonous.

Nubile, of childbearing age.

Nucha, nape of the neck.

Nucleus, pl., **Neuclei,** center of a cell.

Nudomania, extreme desire to be nude.

Nudophobia, extreme fear of being nude.

Nullipara, woman who has not given birth to a child.

Numb, insensible.

Numbness, a condition in which an area of the body is insensitive when touched. Numbness can be caused by disease, malfunctioning body parts, etc. Numbness can also be artificially induced by drugs to relieve existing pain or to prevent pain during a surgical or dental procedure. The sensation of touch and external pressure is transmitted by nerves. When the nerves are damaged or blocked (as by an anesthetic), the brain does not receive the proper information from the affected nerves. The term numbness is usually used to indicate a loss of surface and subsurface feeling. This can be very dangerous, because part of the body's warning system is lost. Thus, if a patient with a numb finger is burned, he may not realize it until the deep nerves are affected. By the time the deep nerves are alerted, very serious damage may have been sustained.

Nurse, one who is trained to care for the sick; to care for the sick; to breast feed.

Nutation, nodding.

Nutrient, nourishing.

Nutrition, the combination of processes by which a living organism receives and utilizes the materials necessary for the maintenance of its functions and for the growth and renewal of its components. From simple one-celled plants to highly complex human beings, all living things need food. Food is necessary to support growth, to repair constantly wearing tissues, and to supply energy for physical activity. Unless the food consumed supplies all the elements required for normal life processes, the human body cannot operate at peak efficiency for very long. If an essential nutrient is missing from the diet over long periods of time, deficiency diseases such as rickets, scurvy, or certain anemias may develop. Everyone needs the same nutrients throughout life but in different amounts. Proportionately greater amounts are required for the growth of a body than just for its upkeep. Boys and men need more energy and nutrients than girls and women. Large people need more than small people. Active people require more food energy than inactive ones. People recovering from illness need more than healthy people. The nutrients in food that are necessary for good health can be divided into certain groups — proteins, carbohydrates, fats, vitamins, minerals, and water. Most common foods consist of combinations of the above. Foods that are good sources of one food element usually also contribute other essential elements as well, but no one food supplies all needed nutrients in sufficient amounts. For good nutrition all essential food elements must work together. Therefore, well-balanced nutrition calls for a well-chosen variety of foods. Good nutrition is just as important for older people as it is for infants and growing teenagers. However, some of the nutritional requirements do change in elderly people. Usually, less physical work is performed in advanced age, and therefore the body's requirements for calories is lower. Dietary calories that are not used are stored in the form of body fat, and many persons who continue the richer diet of their physically more active days may become too heavy. This is the main reason why fewer carbohydrates and less fat are needed in the food of the aged.

Nutritious, giving nourishment.

Nux, nut.

Nyctalgia, pain during the night.

Nyctalopia, the inability to see at night or in a low-light level. Nyctalopia is also known as night blindness. The ability of the eye to see at night or in a dark room depends on the rods in the retina. The rods transmit black, white, and gray impulses. When the rods are not functioning properly, there is no low-light vision (color- and bright-light vision are not affected by the rods). Nyctalopia is caused by a lack of rhodopsin, a substance formed from vitamin A. Night blindness can also be an inherited condition.

Nycterine, occurring at night.

Nyctophobia, extreme fear of darkness.

Nyctotyphlosis, night blindness.

Nygma, puncture wound.

Nymphectomy, surgical removal of the small lips of the vagina.

Nymphomania, excessive sexual desire in the female.

Nystagmus, jerking movement of the eyes which may be inborn or a sign of disease of the nervous system.

Nyxis, puncture; pricking.

— O —

Oaric, concerning the ovary.

Oaritis, ovarian inflammation.

Obdormition, numbness and tingling in an arm or leg.

Obduction, autopsy.

Obesity, a bodily condition in which there is an excess of fat in relation to other body components. The condition is presumed to exist when an individual is twenty percent or more over normal weight. Obesity is caused by a persistent caloric intake that exceeds the energy output needs of the body. Causation is a complex problem, but current knowledge includes such factors as heredity, emotions, culture, diet, and lack of exercise. Reduced to simple terms, the successful treatment of obesity involves achieving a balance between diet and exercise.

Obfuscation, confusion.

Oblique, diagonal.

Obliteration, complete surgical removal of a part; total memory loss.

Obmutescence, loss of power to speak.

Obnubilation, confused state.

Obsession, all consuming emotion or idea.

Obstetrical, pertaining to obstetrics.

Obstetrician, physician who specializes in pregnant women.

Obstetrics, branch of medicine dealing with pregnancy and delivery of infants.

Obstipation, constipation due to obstruction.

Obstruction, a term indicating the blockage of a body vessel. Obstructions can occur in any body vessel. They can be very serious, and, if they occur in certain places, they can be fatal. For example, a child who swallows something solid may find his trachea obstructed or blocked. Unless the object is removed or an alternate breathing passage is made (tracheostomy), the child may die from lack of air. A blood clot formed in another part of the body may be carried to one of the arteries of the brain, where it obstructs the further flow of blood and causes a stroke. Obstructions may be caused by foreign objects, by blood clots, by naturally formed "stones" (such as gallstones), and by tumors (benign or malignant).

Obtund, to dull sensation.

Obturation, closing of an opening.

Occipital, pertaining to the bone that constitutes the back part of the skull.

Occiput, back part of skull.

Occlude, to block or obstruct.

Occlusion, shutting; the full meeting of the chewing surfaces of the upper and lower teeth.

Occult, hidden; obscure.

Occupational Disease, disease caused by one's work.

Occupational Therapy, use of an activity as treatment.

Ochlesis, disease due to overcrowding.

Ochlophobia, extreme fear of crowds.

Ochrodermia, yellowness of the skin.

Octoroon, one who is ⅛ Negro and ⅞ Caucasian.

Ocular, pertaining to the eye or vision.

Oculist, specialist in eye diseases.

Oculus, eye.

Odaxesmus, biting of tongue or skin of mouth during a fit.

Odaxitic, stinging or itching.

Odonitis, tooth inflanmation.

Odontalgia, toothache.

Odontechtomy, tooth extraction.

Odonterism, chattering of teeth.

Odontexesis, cleaning of teeth.

Odontiasis, teething.

Odontic, pertaining to the teeth.

Odontoclasis, breaking a tooth.

Odontodynia, toothache.

Odontogeny, development of teeth.

Odontology. study of the teeth.

Odontoma, tumor arising from the same tissue from which teeth are formed.

Odontoprisis, grinding teeth.

Odontotomy, incision of a tooth.

Odontotrypy, drilling of a tooth.

Odynophagia, pain with swallowing.

Odynophobia, extreme fear of pain.

Oedipus Complex, abnormal love of a child for a parent of the opposite sex, usually a boy for his mother.

Oikophobia, extreme hatred of the home.

Ointment, soft fat substance spread on skin as therapy.

Oleaginous, oily.

Olecranon, bony inner portion of elbow.

Oleum, oil.

Olfaction, smelling; sense of smell.

Olfactory, pertaining to the sense of smell.

Olfactory Nerve, the cranial nerve that transmits the sense of smell from the nose to the brain.

Oligemia, deficiency of blood.

Oligocholia, bile deficiency.

Oligogalactia, deficient milk secretion.

Oligoposy, insufficient liquid intake.

Oligotrichia, lack of hair.

Oligotrophy, insufficient nutrition.

Oliguria, decreased amount of urine production.

Omagra, shoulder gout.

Omalgia, neuralgia of the shoulder.

Omentum, large fatty membrane which acts as a cover for the bowels.

Omitis, shoulder, inflammation.

Omnivorous, eating all types of food.

Omodynia, shoulder pain.

Omphalic, pertaining to the umbilicus.

Omphalitis, inflammation of the navel.

Omphalocele, hernia around navel.

Omphalos, navel.

Onanism, complete sexual intercourse with ejaculation outside the vagina; masturbation.

Oncology, the branch of medicine that is concerned with tumors.

Oncosis, multiple tumors.

Oncocyte, tumor cell.

Oncogenous, causing tumors.

Oncoma, tumor.

Oncosis, multiple tumors.

Oncotic, pertaining to swelling.

Oneiric, pertaining to dreams.

Oniomania, excessive desire to buy things.

Onomatomania, compulsion to repeat words.

Onychia, infection and inflammation around fingernails.

Onychophagia, nail biting.

Onychosis, disease of the nails.

Onyx, fingernail; toenail.

Onyxis, ingrown nails.

Oocyesis, pregnancy in the ovary.

Oophoralgia, ovarian pain.

Oophorectomy, surgical removal of an ovary.

Oophoritis, inflammation of an ovary.

Oophoroma, malignant ovarian tumor.

Oophoron, ovary.

Oosperm, fertilized ovum.

Ootheca, ovary.

Opaque, dark; not transparent; mentally dull.

Open-Heart Surgery, surgery performed on the open heart while the bloodstream is diverted through a heart-lung machine.

Open Wound, any break in the skin. When the skin is unbroken, it affords protection from most infections, bacteria, or germs. However, when the skin is broken, no matter how slight the break, germs may enter, and an infection may develop. Any wound where the skin is broken should receive prompt medical attention, and only sterile objects should be in contact with any open wounds. If germ life has been carried into an open wound by the object causing the break in the skin, nature attempts to wash out the germs by the flow of blood; but some types of wounds do not bleed freely. A break in the skin may range from a pin puncture or scratch to an extensive cut, tear, or mash. An open wound may be only the surface evidence of a more serious injury to deeper structures, such as fractures, particularly in head injuries involving fracture of the skull. In first aid, open wounds are divided into four classifications: abrasions, incised wounds, lacerated wounds, and punctured wounds.

Operable, capable of being relieved by an operation.

Operation, surgical procedure.

Operation Major, one in which there is considerable risk to life.

Operation, Minor, one in which there is little or no danger to life.

Ophidism, snake poisoning.

Ophthalic, pertaining to the eyes.

Ophthalmia, inflammation of the eye.

Ophthalmologist, specialist in the eye and its diseases.

Ophthalmology, study of eye and its diseases.

Ophthalmoplegia, paralysis of the eye muscles.

Ophthalmoscope, instrument for examining the eyes.

Opiate, any opium derivative.

Opisthotonis, arched-back position with head and heel on the horizontal.

Opium, the powder produced by drying the seeds of *Papaver somniferum*, the poppy plant that grows in the Near East. Raw opium has been used as a pain-killer for thousands of years. It has also been used in the treatment of dysentery. However, not until the early part of the nineteenth century were the potent derivatives of opium isolated: morphine in 1803, codeine in 1832, and papaverine in 1848.
Opium and its derivatives are narcotics or pain-reducers. They are physically and sometimes psychologically addictive. Despite the dangers inherent in their use, the opium derivatives are the most effective narcotic agents known to man.

Opsialgia, pain in region of face.

Opsomania, extreme craving for a particular food.

Optic, concerning sight or eye.

Optical, pertaining to vision.

Optician, one who makes lenses or optical instruments.

Optic Nerve, the nerve that transmits sight impulses from the retina of the eye to the brain.

O.R., operating room.

Ora, border; margin.

Orad, toward the mouth.

Oral, pertaining to the mouth.

Oral Contraception (the "pill"), one of the most effective methods of birth control. Each pill contains hormones which causes the ovaries to stop releasing eggs.

Orbicular, circular.

Orbit, eyesocket.

Orchiectomy, surgical removal of a testes.

Orchiodynia, testicle pain.

Orchioncus, tumor of a testes.

Orchis, testicle.

Orchitis, inflammation of the testicle.

Orderly, a male hospital attendant.

Orexigenic, appetite stimulant.

Organ, group of tissue with specific function.

Organic Heart Disease, a heart disease that is caused by some structural abnormality in the heart or circulatory system.

Organism, individual animal or plant.

Orgasm, sexual climax.

Orifice, opening, entrance.

Oropharynx, first part of throat starting at mouth.

Orotherapy, treatment with serums.

Orrhorrhea, watery discharge; flow of serum.

Orrhology, study of blood serum.

Orthodontics, the branch of dentistry that deals with uneven bites or malocclusion.

Orthogenics, eugenics.

Orthopedics, branch of medicine dealing with the surgery of bones and joints.

Orthopedist, specialist in orthopedics.

Orthosis, correction of a deformity.

Orthostatic, concerning standing position.

Orthopnea, condition in which difficult breathing is aided by propping up head and shoulders.

Orthopsychiatry, branch of psychiatry dealing mainly with adolescents.

Orthuria, normal frequency of urination.

Os, pl., Ora, mouth opening.

Os, pl., Ossa, bone.

Oscedo, yawning; white spots in the mouth.

Oscheitis, inflammation of the scrotum.

Oscillometer, an instrument that measures the changes in magnitude of the pulsations in the arteries.

Oscitation, yawning.

Osculation, kissing; joining of two structures by their mouths.

Osculum, aperature.

Osmatic, having an acute sense of smell.

Osmesis, smelling.

Osmics, science of odors.

Osmosis, the diffusion (or movement) of a fluid through a membrane from an area of higher pressure to an area of lower pressure. The membranes through which osmosis can take place are called semipermeable membranes. These semipermeable membranes allow fluids and small molecules to pass through them, but they block the passage of larger molecules. Thus, these membranes act as a sieve. In the human body, cell membranes are semipermeable and permit this diffusion. Oxygen, blood, and digested nutrients pass through cells by osmosis, providing energy for growth and replacement as well as for regular life processes. Blood is pumped under pressure from the heart to the large arteries. From the arteries, blood passes into even smaller blood vessels, called capillaries. By the time blood reaches the capillaries, the pressure has been considerably reduced. However, the pressure of the blood in the capillaries is still greater than the fluid in the cells. Hence, through the process of osmosis, blood in the capillaries enters the individual cells. The movement of fluids, waste material, etc. through the body tissues is a result of osmosis. Waste materials are removed from the blood in the kidneys through this same process.

Osphresis, sense of smell.

Osphus, loin.

Ossa, bones.

Osseous, bonelike.

Ossicle, small bone of ear.

Ossiferous, producing bone.

Ossification, bone formation; change of tissue to bone.

Ossify, to turn into bone.

Ostectomy, surgical removal of a bone.

Osteitis, bone inflammation.

Osteoarthritis, a degenerative joint disease. Osteoarthritis seems to be caused by a combination of aging, irritation of the joints, and normal wear and tear. It is far commoner than rheumatoid arthritis, but, as a rule, it is less damaging. Older people are more likely to have osteoarthritis than are younger people. Chronic irritation of the joints is the main contributing factor. This may result from overweight, poor posture, injury, or strain from one's occupation or recreation.
The primary characteristic of osteoarthritis is degeneration of joint cartilage. This becomes soft and wears unevenly. In some areas it may wear away completely, exposing the underlying bone. Thickening of the ends of the bones may also occur. The remainder of the body is seldom affected. Except in some cases that involve the hip joints or knees, the disease seldom causes serious deformity or crippling.
Common symptoms are pain, aches, and stiffness. Pain is usually experienced when certain joints are used, especially finger joints and those that bear the body's weight. Enlargement of the fingers at the last joint often occurs. Although permanent, enlargements (nodes) of this type seldom lead to disability.

Osteocarcinoma, bone cancer.

Osteochrondritis, inflammation of both bone and cartilage from which bone is formed.

Osteochrondroma, tumor arising from bone cartilage.

Osteology, study of bones.

Osteoma, tumor composed of various parts of bone.

Osteomalacia, softening of bone.

Osteomyelitis, an inflammatory disease of bone caused usually by infection with streptococcus or staphylococcus.
Osteomyelitis can occur after a bone has been fractured and one of the broken ends of the bone pierces the skin. The open end of the bone may then be exposed to microorganisms capable of causing this infection. Before the discovery of antibiotics, osteomyelitis was often caused by a serious infection in another part of the body that spread to the bone or bones. Today, most infections are cured before they can enter the bloodstream and attack the bones. The symptoms of osteomyelitis are sudden pain in the bone and an elevated temperature. Treatment consists of chemotherapy—usually penicillin when the diagnosis is made before the infection spreads too far into the bone marrow. If the infection has spread, drainage of the affected bone may be needed in addition to the drugs. When the infection is severe, parts of the bone may have to be removed.

Osteopathy, system of treatment based on the idea that diseases are caused by minor dislocations of the spine, and, therefore, curable by bone manipulation.

Osteoporosis, a disorder that causes a gradual decrease in both the amount and strength of bone tissue. The bones usually involved first in osteoporosis are those of the spine and pelvis. Ordinarily, the disease thins individual bones of the spine, which are then compressed by the weight of the body and eventually reach the point of outright fracture and collapse. At any stage of osteoporosis the patient may have chronic low-back pain. As the disease advances, the patient's back becomes deformed, the patient grows progressively shorter, and capacity for physical activity becomes more and more limited. Also as the disease progresses, other bones become thinned, particularly those of the legs and arms. Because the affected bones are weak and porous, often breaking under even minor stress, the disease is responsible for many of the fractures experienced by elderly people. Osteoporosis is often the real cause of the numerous broken hips that hospitalize so many older people for long periods and which, in many cases, begin their physical decline. This disease is one of the major causes of physical disability in old age.

Osteosis, formation of bony tissue.

Ostium, small opening.

Ostum, vaginal, outer opening of the vagina.

O.T., occupational therapy.

Otalgia, earache.

Otic, pertaining to the ear.

Otitis, inflammation of the ear.

Otitis Media, an infection of the middle ear, frequently caused by the spread of bacterial infection from the throat.

Otolaryngology, medical specialty concerned with ear, nose and throat.

Otologist, ear specialist.

Otology, branch of medicine dealing with the ear.

Otopathy, any ear disease.

Otosclerosis, type of deafness caused by hardening of the tissues and bones in the inner ear.

Otoscope, instrument used to examine ear.

Oula, the gums.

Ouloid, scar-like.

Outer Ear, the part of the ear that includes the external ear and the external auditory canal.

Outlay, graft.

Outpatient, one who received treatment at a hospital without being admitted.

Oval, egg-shaped.

Oval Window, an opening in the wall of the bone housing the inner ear.

Ovarian, pertaining to the ovaries.

Ovariectomy, surgical removal of an ovary.

Ovary, the two small female organs that produce ova, the female sex cells or eggs. An ovary is about the size and shape of an almond. The ovaries are located at the outer end of the fallopian tubes—one to the right and one to the left.
Each ovary contains about 300,000 ova. Out of this large supply, only about 400 actually reach maturity during a woman's life. Of these 400, only a few are finally fertilized and go on to become human beings. About every twenty-eight days, midway between two menstrual cycles (about fourteen days before the menstrual flow), a single ovum leaves one of the ovaries. The two ovaries alternate: one month the ovum is released from the right ovary; the next month an ovum is released from the left ovary. This cycle repeats itself, except during pregnancies, until the menopause, when the childbearing part of a woman's life comes to an end.

Ovate, oval.

Overdose, taking more of a drug or drugs than the body can safely handle.

Overgrowth, excessive growth.

Overweight, exceeding desired weight by more than 10%.

Oviduct, tube from ovary to uterus.

Ovulation, process of discharge of egg from ovary.

Ovum, pl., **Ova,** egg cell.

Oxyblepsia, very acute vision.

Oxycinesia, pain on motion.

Oxygen, an element needed for life which is brought into the body by the process of breathing.

Oxygeusia, acute sense of taste.

Oxylalia, rapid speech.

Oxyopia, acute sight.

Oxytocic, agent used to stimulate uterus to contract.

Ozostomia, offensive breath.

Ozena, disease of nasal passage leading to the production of a foul-smelling discharge.

Ozone, a form of oxygen. Under ordinary conditions it is a colorless or pale-blue gas and has a characteristic pungent odor. In high concentrations it is extremely flammable, and in liquid form it becomes a dangerous explosive. As a strong oxidizing agent, ozone has many uses. Its greatest use is in the suppression of mold and bacterial growth, such as in the treatment of drinking-water supplies and industrial wastes, and the sterilizing of food products. Other uses of ozone include the rapid aging of wood; the aging of liquor; rapid drying of varnishes and printing ink; production of peroxides; bleaching of oils, waxes, textiles, and papers; and deodorizing of feathers. Despite its usefulness, ozone is acutely and chronically toxic to humans. Workers in enclosed spaces where ozone is produced or used should be on guard against the potential hazards to which they may be accidentally exposed.

— P —

Pabulum, food, nourishment.

Pacemaker, a small mass of specialized cells in the right upper chamber of the heart. These cells are responsible for the electrical impulses that initiate the contractions of the heart. The natural pacemaker is also called the sinoatrial node or the S-A node of Keith-Flack. The term pacemaker, or, more exactly, electric cardiac pacemaker, or electric pacemaker, is also applied to an electrical device that can be substituted for a defective natural pacemaker. The artificial pacemaker controls the beat of the heart by a series of rhythmic electrical discharges that replace the missing natural electrical impulses. If the electrodes that deliver the discharges to the heart are placed on the outside of the chest, the device is called an external pacemaker. If the electrodes are placed within the chest wall, it is called an internal pacemaker. An internal pacemaker is surgically implanted in the chest. It is a self-contained unit, requiring only periodic battery changes.

Pachyblepharon, thickening of the eyelid.

Pachycephalous, thick wall.

Pachychilla, thick lips.

Pachyderma, thick skin.

Pachyglossia, thick tongue.

Pachyhemia, thickening of the blood.

Pachymeningitis, inflammation of the outer covering of the brain and spinal cord.

Pachymeter, instrument for measuring thickness.

Pachynsis, thickening.

Pachyonychia, thickening of the nails.

Pachypodous, big feet.

Pack, a dry or wet, hot or cold blanket wrapped around the patient.

Packing, material used to fill wound or cavity.

Pad, soft cushion.

Paget's Disease; Osteitis Deformans, thickening of bones, mainly skull and shin; rash of nipple connected with breast tumor.

Pain, an elementary sensation of physical suffering. The sensation of pain is part of the protective system of the body. Pain serves as a warning of bodily damage, disease, or malfunction. When the body experiences pain and there is no apparent external cause, the pain itself is a warning to consult a physician. Frequently, there is no visible manifestation of the source of the pain—such as a burn or a wound. The lack of physical evidence indicates the possibility of disease or malfunction. Pain or the sensation of pain occurs in the brain. Consequently, if there is no brain, or if the brain is depressed by drugs (as by a general anesthetic) or by injury, there is no sensation of pain. Naturally, once the brain returns to normal, the sensation of pain returns. At the same time, if the nerves do not send a warning to the brain, the brain cannot initiate the pain sensation. Some pain has no physical (internal or external) basis. This pain is said to be psychogenic or psychosomatic. This type of pain—as intense as if it were caused by a physical stimulus—is caused by emotional disorders. Another type of pain, known as neurogenic, can be very confusing, because, like psychogenic pain, it mimics pain from a physical stimulus. Unlike psychosomatic pain, neurogenic pain has a physical basis, although not necessarily in the painful area. Neurogenic pain results from an improper functioning of one or more of the nerves.

Pain, False, false labor pains.

Palantine, pertaining to the palate.

Palate, roof of the mouth divided into hard and soft portions.

Palatitis, inflammation of the palate.

Paleontology, study of early man.

Palliate, to reduce or allay discomfort.

Palliative, relieving pain or suffering.

Pallid, lacking.

Pallor, paleness of skin.

Palm, inside portion of hand.

Palma, palm.

Palmar, pertaining to the palm.

Palpable, able to be touched.

Palpate, to examine by feeling.

Palpebra, eyelid.

Palpebra Inferior, lower eyelid.

Palpebra Superior, upper eyelid.

Palpitation, rapid pulsation in an organ, usually refers to the heart.

Palsy, impaired function or paralysis.

Paludism, malaria.

Panacea, cure for all ills.

Panarthritis, inflammation of the entire joint.

Pancarditis, infection of all parts of heart.

Panchrest, panacea.

Pancreas, gland lying behind and below the stomach which produces ferments which are passed into the intestinal tract to help in digestion; site of insulin production.

Pancreatitis, inflammation of the pancreas.

Pancreectomy, removal of pancreas in part or whole.

Pandemic, the spread of an infectious disease over a wide area. A pandemic is larger than an epidemic. The term is usually restricted to diseases that spread over all or almost all the world. Outbreaks of influenza have been pandemic.

Pandiculation, stretching and yawning.

Panesthesia, all of the sensations experienced.

Pang, spontaneous, sudden emotion or pain.

Panhidrosis, perspiration over entire body.

Panhysterectomy, complete removal of the womb.

Panic, extreme anxiety, with temporary loss of reason.

Panniculitis, inflammation of abdominal wall fat.

Panniculus, layer of tissue, fatty layer.

Pannus, abnormal membrane on the cornea.

Panophobia, extreme fear of everything in general.

Pansinusitis, inflammation of all the sinuses.

Pant, breathe fast and hard.

Pap, nipple; soft food.

Papaverine, a drug derived from opium. Papaverine is a muscle relaxant.

Papilla, nipple-like protuberance.

Papilla, Mammary, breast nipple.

Papillary Muscles, small bundles of muscles in the wall of the lower chambers of the heart to which the cords leading to the cusps of the valves (chordae tendineae) are attached.

Papilledema, swelling of optic nerve where nerve enters eye.

Papilloma, benign tumor of skin or inner membranes.

Pap Smear, a technique developed chiefly by Dr. George N. Papanicolaou (1883-1962) that involves the microscopic examination of cells collected from the vagina. The Pap smear is an excellent technique for the early detection of cancer of the uterine cervix, or neck of the womb. In fact, the Pap smear is one of the major reasons for the decrease in deaths from cancer of the uterine cervix. Gynecologists now routinely do a Pap smear as part of the annual examination of female patients.

Papule, small red raised area on skin.

Par, pair.

Para- (prefix), beside.

Paracentesis, puncture.

Parachroma, skin discoloration.

Paracusia, any hearing defect.

Paracyesis, pregnancy outside uterus.

Paralalia, speech disorder.

Paraldehyde, a drug that acts as a sedative and hypnotic.

Paralgesia, painful sensation.

Paralysis, loss of the power of movement or sensation in one or more parts of the body.

Paralytic, pertaining to paralysis.

Paralyze, to cause loss of muscle control and/or feeling.

Paramenia, irregular or abnormal menstrual period.

Parametrium, tissue surrounding and supporting the womb.

Paranoia, chronic psychosis characterized by fears, suspicion and well organized imaginery thoughts.

Paraphemia, distorted speech.

Paraphobia, mild phobia.

Paraplegia, the loss of both motion and sensation in the legs and lower part of the body. This condition is the result of a disease or injury to the spinal column. Among the diseases capable of causing paraplegia are poliomyelitis, muscular dystrophy, multiple sclerosis, and tumors of the spinal cord. Principal traumatic (or accidental) causes include birth injuries, automobile accidents, airplane crashes, gunshot or shrapnel wounds, and falls or injuries in industry and sports.
The loss of motion and sensation occurs from the site of the disease or damage to the spinal cord downward. Additionally, there may be a loss of normal control of the bowels and bladder.

Parapoplexy, slight apoplexy.

Parasite, any animal or plant which lives inside or on the body of another animal or plant.

Parasympathetic Nervous System, a subdivision of the autonomic or involuntary nervous system.

Parateresiomania, compulsion to see new sights.

Parathymia, disordered emotion.

Parathyroid Glands, group of six small glands situated around the thyroid gland concerned with calcium and phosphorus in body.
Diminished function or removal of the parathyroid glands results in a low calcium level in the blood. In extreme cases death occurs; it is preceded by strong contractions of the muscles and by convulsions.

Paregoric, derivative of opium used to help relieve pain or diarrhea.

Parenchyma, productive part of an organ.

Parent, one who begets offspring.

Parenteral, outside of digestive tract.

Paresis, paralysis due to disease of brain, usually syphilis.

Paries, wall of a cavity.

Parietal Pericardium, a thin membrane sac that surrounds the heart and roots of the great vessels.

Pareunia, sexual intercourse.

Parity, capable of bearing children.

Parkinson's Disease, a slowly progressive disorder of the central nervous system. It is characterized by tremor in muscles that are at rest, and by stiffness and slowness of movement. The exact cause of the disease in most cases is unknown. Among the known causative factors are: arteriosclerosis, cerebral vascular accidents, head injuries, syphilis, toxic agents, and drugs.
Many research people are convinced that part of the basal ganglia is the brain center for much of the tremor and stiffness of Parkinson's disease.
Parkinson's disease is slightly more common in men than women and generally occurs between ages fifty and sixty. An extreme variability characterizes the rate of development of this disease. For some, the onset of symptoms is mild, such as a slight tremor and stiffness on one side that does not impair functioning. For others the symptoms are marked, and within months of the onset the patient requires total care. There is a typical general appearance of the patient with Parkinson's disease: masklike and waxen features, rhythmic tremor of the fingers, stooped posture, and a gait in which the patient walks as if he were about to fall on his face. There may be drooling or a blank facial expression. This results from the loss of semiautomatic movements such as swallowing saliva and the movement of facial muscles. There is no cure for Parkinson's disease, but three kinds of treatment will help relieve symptoms. These are medication, physical therapy, and surgery. Stress and anxiety should be avoided as well as excitement, which causes the tremor to become worse.

Paronychia, infection of the tissues at the base of a nail.

Paroniria, frightful dreams.

Paropsis, disorder of vision.

Parorexia, craving for special foods.

Parosmia, smelling imaginary odors.

Parotid, located near the ear.

Parotid Gland, large salivary gland located over the jaw in front of the ear.

Parotitis, inflammation of the parotid gland, a large salivary gland.

Parous, having given birth to one or more children.

Parovarian, beside the ovary.

Paroxysm, sudden attack or recurrency of symptoms.

Paroxysmal Tachycardia, a period of rapid heart beats that begins and ends suddenly.

Pars, pl., **Partes,** a part.

Particulate, composed of minute particles.

Parturient, giving birth; labor.

Parturifacient, medicine which speeds up birth.

Parturition, childbirth.

Paruria, any abnormality in excretion of urine.

Passion, strong emotion.

Pasteurization, method of sterilizing foods.

Patch Test, test carried out to determine sensitivity.

Patella, knee-cap.

Patency, state of being open, e.g., ducts, hollow tubes.

Patent Ductus Arteriosus, a congenital heart defect. A small duct between the artery leaving the left side of the heart (the aorta) and the artery leaving the right side of the heart (the pulmonary artery) which normally closes soon after birth, remains open.

Patent Medicine, remedy for public use obtained without prescription.

Patent, open.

Pathetic, pertaining to the feelings.

Pathic, pertaining to disease.

Pathogens, anything capable of producing disease.

Pathogenic, pertaining to the ability to produce disease.

Pathogenesis, the chain of events leading to the development of a disease.

Pathognomonic, a symptom that is so specific or so characteristic of a particular disease or disorder that a definite diagnosis is possible from its presence.

Pathology, study of diseases for their own interest, rather than directly with an immediate view to curing them.

Pathomania, abnormal wish to commit crime.

Pathophobia, extreme fear of disease.

Pathophoresis, communication of disease.

Patient, one under medical care.

Patulous, open; exposed.

Paunch, protruding abdomen.

Pavor, fear; fright.

Peccant, unhealthy.

Pectinate, like teeth of comb.

Pectoral, pertaining to the chest.

Pectus, chest; breast.

Pectus Carination, "Chicken breast."

Pedal, pertaining to the foot.

Pederasty, sexual intercourse through the anus.

Pediatrician, specialist in diseases of children.

Pediatrics, branch of medicine dealing with the diseases of children and their cure.

Pediatrist, pediatrician.

Pedicular, infested with lice.

Pediculicide, agent which kills lice.

Pediculosis, infestation of the scalp or hairy parts of the body or of clothing with lice. Lice are transmitted by direct contact with infected persons or their personal possessions, particularly clothing or infected bedding. The symptoms of pediculosis are inflammation of the skin, itching, and white eggs (nits) on the hair. The treatment consists of dusting the body and clothing (especially along the seams) with a specially prescribed powder.

Pediculosis Capititis, head lice.

Pediophobia, extreme fear of children or dolls.

Pedodontics, branch of dentistry dealing with children.

Pedophila, abnormal fondness for children.

Peduncle, stalk or stem.

Pelada, patchy baldness.

Pelage, hair covering the body.

Pelagism, seasickness.

Pellagra, disease due to lack of vitamin B.

Pellet, small pill.

Pellicle, thin tissue; scum on a liquid.

Pellucid, translucent.

Pelvic Examination, an internal examination of the vagina. cervix, and uterus.

Pelvis, bony part of the body lying between the thighs and the abdomen.

The exact shape of the pelvis differs between men and women. The male pelvis is narrower and more compact than the female pelvis. The male pelvis is designed for strength and speed; the female pelvis is designed to support pregnancies.

The upper outer edges of the pelvis form the area known as the hip. A person whose weight is normal for his height will be able to feel the edges of the pelvis.

Pemphigus, one of the most severe and rare types of oral ulcerations. It is a recurrent disease involving the mouth and skin. There are three forms of this disease: pemphigus vulgaris, pemphigus vegetans, and pemphigus conjunctivae. The most common type that involves the mouth is pemphigus vulgaris. This form of the disease can be either acute and malignant or chronic and benign.

The onset of pemphigus is insidious. At first the blisters are not painful. The patient feels a sensation of dryness in his mouth and a slight pain or discomfort when eating hot or spicy food. He may also have difficulty swallowing. Next, bullae—large blisters—form on the lips, tongue, cheek, palate, or gums. Often these blisters are not seen, because they break easily, leaving a reddish erosion with ragged edges. It is after they break that the blisters become very itchy and painful. Salivation increases and is often tinged with blood.

In about three-fourths of the cases of pemphigus, blisters form first in the mouth. Lesions on the skin may not appear for several months, and sometimes they never appear. When they do appear, they form over the entire body—face, trunk, arms, and legs. These blisters are thin-walled and translucent and are filled with a yellow fluid. When they break, they form a foul, yellow membrane.

Another characteristic symptom is "Nikolsky's sign"—the top layer of skin can be rubbed off with slight pressure.

Treatment of pemphigus can only be palliative, because there is no known cure for this disease. Cortisone has been used to alleviate symptoms, and penicillin has been used to prevent secondary infection. Mild mouthwashes can help relieve pain in the mouth. Since the cause is unknown, treatment can be directed only to the manifestation of the disease.

Pendulous, heavy and loosely hanging.

Penicillin, an antibiotic discovered in 1928 by Sir Alexander Fleming.

Penicillinase, a drug employed in the treatment of penicillin reactions.

Penis, male sex organ.

Penitis, inflammation of the penis.

Pepo, pumpkin seed used in removal of tapeworm.

Pepsic, peptic.

Pepsin, ferment found in the gastric juice which helps in the breakdown of protein.

Peptic, pertaining to the digestive tract.

Peptic Ulcer, a noncancerous, crater-like sore (called an erosion) in the wall of the stomach or intestine. This ulcer erodes through the thin, inner mucous membrane lining and into the deeper muscular wall of the stomach or intestine. Peptic ulcers occur only in those regions of the gastrointestinal tract that are bathed by the digestive juices secreted by the stomach. These digestive juices contain hydrochloric acid and a protein-digesting enzyme called pepsin; hence the name "peptic ulcer." Almost all peptic ulcers occur either in the stomach itself or in the small intestine just below the stomach. Those in the first portion of the intestine, the duodenum, are called duodenal ulcers, and those in the stomach are called gastric ulcers.

Statistics suggest that a person who has one or more family members with ulcers is slightly more prone to develop an ulcer than someone from a family having no ulcer patients. In many cases this may be because of the anxiety-ridden environment in such a family. In general, the treatment of ulcers by a physician is directed toward decreasing the amount of acid or irritants that reach the ulcer and interfere with the normal healing process. Proper diet; emphasis on frequent, small feedings; the use of antacids and drugs; and relief of nervous tension are important ways of accomplishing this.

Peracidity, excessive acidity.

Per Anum, by anus.

Perception, awareness.

Percussion, striking body as an aid to physical examination and diagnosis.

Percutanteous, through the skin.

Perforating, piercing.

Perforation, opening or hole in any area of body.

Peri- (prefix), around; near.

Periorticular, surrounding a joint.

Perianal, situated around the anus.

Pericardiac, around the heart.

Pericarditis, inflammation of sac surrounding the heart.

Pericardium, sac surrounding the heart.

Pericolic, around the colon.

Pericytial, around a cell.

Perimetrium, covering tissue of the womb.

Perinephric, situated around the kidneys.

Perineum, area between the sex organs and the anus.

Periodicity, occurring at regular intervals.

Period of Gestation, period from conception to childbirth.

Periodontal, around a tooth.

Periodontal Disease, a disorder affecting the tissues and membranes surrounding the teeth.

There are several types of periodontal disease. In its early stages the most common type takes the form of gingivitis, or inflammation of the gums. This condition may develop into periodontitis (sometimes called pyorrhea), the chronic, destructive stage of the disease. It usually affects people over twenty-five years of age.

A major cause of periodontal disease is tartar, or calculus, that forms along the gums. This results in swelling and inflammation. As the disease progresses, the gums become more inflamed and pull away from the teeth, creating pockets between the gums and the teeth. Germs and food particles become wedged in these pockets, create more inflammation, and set up a vicious circle.

As the disease worsens, the inflammation spreads, the pockets deepen, and pus forms in them. The infected gums ulcerate and bleed, and tissue damage increases. In the final stages, the bone that supports the teeth is attacked and destroyed. Unless the person receives treatment, the teeth loosen and eventually come out.

Once periodontal disease has begun treatment will depend on the stage of the disease. If it has not progressed far, treatment may consist only of removing hardened tartar from around and under the gums. If pockets have formed between the teeth and gums, they must often be removed surgically to prevent further impaction of food.

In its final stages, periodontal disease attacks the underlying tissue that supports the teeth. Treatment at this stage may involve bone and reconstructive surgery.

Perionchyia, inflammation of area around a fingernail or toenail.

Periosteum, tissue around bone through which bone is nourished.

Periostitis, inflammation of the membrane surrounding a bone.

Periotic, located around the ear.

Peripatetic, changing from place to place.

Peripheral Nervous System, the part of the central nervous system that is composed of the twelve pairs of cranial nerves and thirty-one pairs of spinal nerves stemming from the brain and the spinal cord, respectively. The cranial nerves include voluntary fibers going to the eye muscles, the salivary glands, the heart, the smooth muscles of the lungs, and the intestinal tract. The spinal nerves send fibers to all muscles of the trunk and extremities, the involuntary fibers going to smooth muscles and glands of the gastrointestinal tract, genitourinary system, and cardiovascular system.

Peripheral Resistance, the resistance offered by the arterioles (small arteries) and capillaries to the flow of blood from the arteries to the veins. An increase in peripheral resistance causes a rise in blood pressure.

Periphery, away from center or midline of body.

Perirenal, around the kidney.

Perirhinal, around the nose.

Perish, die; disintegrate.

Peristalsis, the normal movements of the intestines which move the food along the digestive tract.

Peritoneum, the smooth, transparent membrane that lines the abdominal cavity and part of the pelvic region. The peritoneum allows the organs in the area to move against each other with little or no friction.

Peritonitis, inflammation of the lining tissue of the abdominal cavity. Peritonitis is caused by microorganisms that infect the peritoneum. This may follow a perforated ulcer, a ruptured appendix, an unsterile operation, or an abdominal wound, for instance. The chief symptoms are intense pain and tenderness. Peritonitis can be very serious if not treated promptly with antibiotics.

Peritonsillar, around the tonsil.

Perivascular, around a vessel.

Pernicious, severe; fatal.

Pernicious Anemia, a form of chronic anemia characterized by disturbances of the gastrointestinal and neurological systems. The exact cause of pernicious anemia is unknown. The disease is the result of a deficiency in the gastric juices that permit the body to absorb vitamin B^{12}. The lack of B^{12} causes premature death of red blood cells, thereby reducing the capacity of the blood to carry oxygen to the tissues. The onset of anemia is insidious. Depending on the stage of the disease, a patient may have the following symptoms: loss of appetite, fatigue, lassitude, pallor, faintness, jaundice, sore tongue and mouth, diarrhea, digestive disturbances, depression and irritability that may ultimately lead to a psychosis, numbness and tingling of the fingers, other neurological deficits, and shortness of breath on exertion. Pernicious anemia cannot be cured. It is controlled by adequate diet and injection of vitamin B^{12} every week. Lifelong treatment is required if neurological crippling is to be prevented.

Pernio, chillblain.

Per Os, by mouth.

Per Rectum, by rectum.

Perseveration, repetitive statements or answers to questions.

Perspiration, fluid produced by body at surface of the skin which helps to control body temperature.

Pertussis, whooping cough.

Pervert, one who practices abnormal behavior.

Pervigilium, abnormal wakefulness.

Pes, foot or footlike structure.

Pes Contortis, clubfoot.

Pes Planus, flatfoot.

Pessary, device used to hold uterus in proper position.

Pesticides, substances used to kill pests. The pests may be weeds, insects, rats and mice, algae, nematodes (worms), and other destructive forms of life. Pesticides that are used only for killing insects are called insecticides. Killing garden pests, ridding homes of insects or rodents, and defleaing or delousing pets are common household uses of pesticides. Guarding people's health and protecting fruits, vegetables, and forests are well-known commercial, agricultural, and governmental uses of pesticides. Improperly used, pesticides can and do cause illness and even death to human beings. To avoid improper use, it is very important that anyone who uses a pesticide understands its purpose and properties. It is most essential to understand that pesticides, by necessity, are poisons. However, there is a great variation between the different compounds in use as pesticides with regard to their toxic hazard. A few materials are dangerous in the relatively small amounts that spraymen encounter by skin contact and by breathing during their work. However, most compounds have not produced occupational poisoning. Accidental ingestion (swallowing) has been responsible for most of the deaths from pesticides. In addition to fear of accidental exposure, there is concern about possible long-term effects of pesticide contamination that may remain in the environment and—through air, soil, food, and water—may eventually adversely affect living things. The possible danger here is in inhaling or ingesting dangerous amounts through air, water, or food. This is why the Food and Drug Administration sets limits on the amount of pesticide residue that may safely remain on food crops at harvest and also polices our food supply to enforce these limits.

Pestiferous, causing pestilence.

Pestilence, epidemic of contagious disease.

Pestle, device used to break up drugs in pharmacy.

Petit Mal, type of epilepsy in which the attacks are relatively slight.

pH, concentration of hydrogen ion or acidity; Neutral = pH 7.

Phactis, inflammation of the eye lens.

Phacomatacia, soft cataract.

Phagocyte, absorbing cell.

Phalanges, bones of fingers.

Phalanx, one of the bones of the fingers or toes.

Phallectomy, amputation of the penis.

Phallic, concerning male sex organ.

Phallus, male sex organ.

Phanic, visible.

Phantom Limb, the sensation of feeling in a limb that has been amputated. This phenomenon is caused by the stimulation of nerves in the remaining part of the limb that had continued into the amputated part.

Pharm., pharmaceutical; pharmacy.

Pharmaceutical, pertaining to drugs.

Pharmacist, druggist.

Pharmacology, the science that deals with the study of drugs in all its aspects.

Pharmacopoeia, an official listing of drugs and drug standards. In this country, the U.S.P. (United States Pharmacopeia) is the legally accepted standard text.

Pharmacy, drug store.

Pharyngitis, inflammation of the pharynx.

Pharyngoscope, instrument for examining the throat.

Pharynx, membraneous tube extending from oral cavity to level of first part of esophagus.

Phatne, tooth socket.

Phenobarbital, barbiturate used to sedate or produce sleep.

Phenol, a strong antiseptic.

Phenolphthalein, purgative.

Phenylbutazone, a drug used in the treatment of arthritis and related disorders, such as gout and osteoarthritis. Phenylbutazone is very effective in treating many cases of these conditions. However, phenylbutazone can have many serious side effects (vomiting, diarrhea, insomnia, edema, anemia, etc.). Consequently, the drug is often used as a last resort, and even then it is used with great care.

Phimosis, excessive tightness of the foreskin of the penis.

Phlebitis, the inflammation of a vein. This often occurs in the leg and usually involves the formation of a blood clot in the inflamed vein. The danger of phlebitis is that the blood clot will move from the affected vein to another area of the body where it can cause more damage. If the blood clot reaches the heart or brain, it may cause death.

The usual treatment is to immobilize the affected region by putting the patient to bed. At the same time, the patient is frequently given an anticoagulant drug to help dissolve the blood clot.

Phlebosclerosis, hardening of a vein.

Phlebothrombosis, formation of a clot in a vein.

Phlebotomy, opening of a vein.

Phlegm, thick mucus from respiratory tract.

Phlegmatic, sluggish.

Phlogistic, inducing inflammation.

Phobia, an extreme fear.

Phonal, pertaining to the voice.

Phonetics, science of vocal sounds.

Photodynia, pain in the eyes due to intense light.

Photophobia, extreme fear of light.

Photosensitive, sensitive to light.

Phrenetic, maniacal.

Phrenic, pertaining to the diaphragm or mind.

Phrenitis, delirium.

Phrenology, study of the mind through the shape of the skull.

Phrenoplegia, paralysis of the diaphragm.

Phthisiology, study of tuberculosis.

Phthisis, tuberculosis.

Phylaxis, bodily defense against infection.

Phyma, skin tumor.

Physic, cathartic; art of medicine.

Physical Fitness, a measure of the body's strength, stamina, and flexibility. It is a reflection of the ability to work with vigor and pleasure, without undue fatigue, with energy left over for enjoying hobbies and recreational activities, and for meeting unforeseen emergencies. Physical fitness is important for mental health as well as for physical health. It requires proper nutrition, adequate rest and relaxation, good sleeping habits, good health practices, and especially adequate physical exercise. The human body contains more than six hundred muscles; overall, the body is more than half muscle. Muscles make possible every overt motion. They also push food along the digestive tract, suck air into the lungs, and tighten blood vessels to raise blood pressure when more pressure is needed to meet an emergency. The heart itself is a muscular pump. Muscles are meant to be used. When they are not used, or are not used enough, they deteriorate. An obvious effect of regular exercise is the firming of flabby muscles. In addition, research indicates that exercise produces beneficial changes in the functioning of internal organs—especially the heart, lungs, and circulatory system. The heartbeat becomes stronger and steadier, breathing becomes deeper, and circulation improves.

Physician, licensed medical doctor.

Physics, study of natural forces and phenomena.

Physiogonomy, face.

Physiology, science which deals with the functions of the body.

Physique, body build.

Phytin, material from plants used as stimulants.

Phytotoxin, plant poison.

Pia, one of membranous coverings of brain and spinal cord.

Pica, an abnormal craving to eat odd things.

Picric Acid, a substance used in the treatment of minor burns.

Piedra, hair disease.

Pigment, coloring substance.

Pilary, pertaining to the hair.

Pileous, hairy.

Piles, enlarged, painful veins in the rectum or around the anus.

Pill, capsule containing medication.

Pillion, temporary artificial leg.

Pilonidal, cyst containing hairs, frequently found at the base of the spine.

Pilose, hairy.

Pilus, hair.

Pimple, small pointed area on skin, at times filled with infectious material.

Pineal Gland, small gland about the size of a pea in the lower part of the brain.

Pinquecula, thickened area on edge of cornea of eye.

Pinkeye, contagious eye inflammation; conjunctivitis.

Pinna, projecting part of external ear.

Pinpoint Vision, a defect of the eye in which there is vision in the center of the eye only, with no visual field at all.

Pinworm, parasite found in intestine and around anus.

Pinworms enter the body when pinworm eggs are swallowed. The eggs hatch in the stomach, and the larvae pass through the small intestine into the large intestine. They remain there until they develop into adult worms, probably within five to six weeks. The female worms are then ready to deposit their eggs. They migrate down the rectum and out of the anus, where they deposit their eggs in the folds of skin surrounding the anus. After expelling many thousands of eggs, the female worm shrivels up and dies. The male worms may also migrate out of the anus and die. The migration and egg-laying usually occur at night, from a half hour to several hours after the person has gone to bed. In the case of heavy infections, migration may occur during the day, especially during periods of rest or relaxation. In the moist folds of the skin each egg develops to the infective stage in five to seven hours. The cycle of infection (or reinfection of the same individual) is completed when the infective eggs are swallowed. A sensation varying in intensity from a very mild tickling to severe itching or pain usually occurs when migrating female worms are on the anus or the surrounding skin. In women and girls, migrating worms may enter the vulva and vagina, frequently causing a vaginal discharge. Infected children sometimes have dark circles under the eyes and are pale. Restlessness, sleeplessness, loss of appetite, loss of weight, and sometimes nausea and vomiting occur. Infected children are apt to be irritable, hard to manage, and inattentive at school. Diagnosis of pinworm infection is based on finding the female worm or the pinworm eggs.

Pit, depression.

Pithecoid, apelike.

Pituita, phlegm.

Pituitarism, disorder of pituitary function.

Pituitary Gland, small gland at the base of the brain which affects all the other glands of the body.

Pityriasis, group of diseases in which the main symptom is a scaly skin.

Placebo, a harmless, inactive substance given to patients in controlled tests. The placebo helps the researcher to evaluate the effectiveness of the real drug by guarding against any psychological effects or reactions to the idea of the medication.

In many experiements, half the patients will be given the test drug and half will be given a placebo. The patients are not told whether they are taking the real drug or the placebo. The results are then tabulated to see if there is any difference. In a double-blind experiment neither the patients nor the physician are aware of who is getting the real drug.

Placenta, organ by which the unborn infant is attached to the inside of the womb and through which infants' body needs are supplied.

Blood from the fetus flows in and out through two arteries and a vein. These arteries and the vein are encased in the umbilical cord, which attaches to the surface of the placenta at one end and to the baby's navel at the other end. The waste products of the fetus are carried through the blood vessels of the umbilical cord into the placenta, where they are exchanged for oxygen and nutrients from the mother. The vein in the cord carries these materials back to the baby. The main purpose of the placenta is to make possible this interchange. Once the baby is born, the placenta is no longer needed. After birth the placenta starts to separate from its attachment to the lining of the uterus.

Plague, epidemic disease transmitted by fleas of rats. There are two major types of plague: bubonic plague and pneumonic plague. Pneumonic plague attacks the lungs; bubonic plague causes buboes, or swollen lymph glands.

Planocyte, wandering cell.

Planta, sole of the foot.

Plantar, pertaining to the sole of the foot.

Plantar Wart, painful wart occurring on the bottom of the foot.

Plaque, any patch or accumulation. Plaques play a major role in atherosclerosis, or hardening of the arteries, and in tooth decay and periodontal disease.

Plasma, colorless fluid part of the blood as distinct from blood cells.

Plaster of Paris, a chemical substance used to make hard casts for the immobilization of injured body parts.

Plastic, pertaining to plastic surgery; moldable; any material that can be molded.

Plastic Surgery, a special branch of surgery that is concerned with correcting disfigurements. Plastic surgery includes purely cosmetic surgery, such as restructuring unattractive noses. However, plastic surgery is also concerned with the reduction of scar tissue. This can be extremely important, because large scars (as from extensive burns) can cause a loss of mobility. The major aim of the plastic surgeon is to reduce the amount of the scar tissue to the smallest possible size. This is frequently achieved by hiding the scar within natural wrinkles.

Platelet, small disc in blood stream used for blood coagulation.

Platycrania, flattening of the skull.

Platypodia, flat foot.

Pledget, small piece of gauze soaked in antiseptic.

Pleonemia, increased amount of blood in a part.

Pleonexia, extreme greediness.

Plethora, abnormal amount of blood.

Pleura, thin tissue covering the lungs and lining the interior walls of the chest cavity.

Pleurisy, an inflammation of the pleura, the membrane that covers the lungs. The most common cause of pleurisy is infection, either viral or bacterial. Dry pleurisy is the easiest type of pleurisy to diagnose. There is sudden pain, usually during respiration. The pain is caused by the friction that results when the two layers of the pleura rub together. In cases of dry pleurisy, the protective fluid between the two pleura layers is partially replaced by a sticky substance known as fibrin. Dry pleurisy is not contagious, although the underlying cause may be. It is treated by any drugs needed to stop the infection and by bed rest. Frequently, drugs are not needed at all. Serofibrinous pleurisy, or pleurisy with effusion, is caused by an excess accumulation of fluid between the two layers of the pleura. Treatment may include the withdrawal of the excess fluid through a long needle inserted into the space between the pleura layers. Empyema is a type of pleurisy in which fluid containing pus infiltrates the area between the pleura membranes.

Pleurodynia, pain in the muscles between the ribs.

Plexor, percussion hammer.

Plexus, groups of nerves, lymphatic glands or blood vessels in the body.

Plica, fold.

Plug, obstruction.

Plumbism, lead poisoning.

Plummer-Vinson Syndrome, a wasting-away of the mucous membranes of the mouth, pharynx, and esophagus. This syndrome is caused by deficiencies in the diet and frequently precedes cancer of the mouth. It is common among women in Sweden and apparently accounts for there unusually high incidence of mouth cancer.

PMS (premenstrual syndrome), condition occurring from one to two weeks prior to a woman's normal menstrual period. Symptoms include nervousness, fatigue, and depression, as well as breast tenderness, water retention, headache, and general aches.

Pneumatic, pertaining to respiration.

Pneumococcus, germ which can attack the body, usually the lungs.

Pneumonectomy, surgical removal of a lung.

Pneumonia, a general term for infection of the lungs. It can be caused by different kinds of bacteria or virus or by the presence of foreign matter such as fatty droplets of liquids that have been inhaled. Frequently, the symptoms of pneumonia include high fever, chills, vomiting, and a cough. Difficult, rapid breathing is another symptom.
Pneumonia begins when the microbes or the foreign matter that has entered the lungs sets up an inflammation. As part of the inflammation, fluid rushes into the lungs. When the cause of the disease is a virus or bacteria, the fluid is used by the invading organisms as a culture, or growth media. When the cause is foreign matter, the fluid provides a growing place for any organisms already present in the lungs or respiratory system. Pneumonia can be classified by the causative agent or by the location of the infection.

Pneumonopathy, any lung disease.

Pneumorrhagia, lung hemorrhage.

Pneumothorax, abnormal entrance of air or gas into lung sacs, causing an imbalance of pressures and difficult respiration.

Pock, pustule.

Podagra, gout affecting foot.

Podalgia, pain in the feet.

Podiatrist, specialist in foot ailments.

Pogoniasis, excessive beard growth.

Point, tiny spot or area.

Pointillage, massage with the finger tips.

Poison, any substance that causes bodily disturbance, injury, or death by chemical rather than mechanical means. The action of a poison depends on several factors. The action will be more severe if a large dose is taken, because more of the poison will be absorbed in a short period of time. The toxicity of substances varies greatly—a few drops of one poison might be immediately fatal, while another poison might not be harmful unless taken by the tablespoonful. The age and body weight of the victim should also be considered. Infants, young children, and very old people are more likely to be killed by small doses of poison. In general, the less a person weighs, the smaller will be the fatal dose. Another factor that influences the action of poisons taken by mouth is the condition of the stomach; poisons taken on an empty stomach will act much more quickly (and therefore more violently) than those taken when the stomach is full.
The action of any poison is dependent, also, on the tolerance that the individual has for the particular substance. Some people seem to have a natural resistance to the action of certain poisons; others are so highly sensitive to them that even a small amount, such as might be given in a medicine, produces toxic effects. Habit is sometimes a factor to consider—drug addicts can tolerate doses of the habit-forming drugs that might kill the average person. The effectiveness of a poison also depends on the general health of the victim. The physical state of the poisonous substance also determines its effectiveness. Gases are absorbed more quickly than liquids, and liquids are absorbed more quickly than solids. Related to this is the fact that the way in which a poison enters the body determines to some extent the speed and effectiveness with which it acts. In general, inhaled poisons are likely to work most quickly, injected poisons next, and poisons taken by

mouth more slowly. Poisoning by skin contact usually occurs quite slowly over an extended period of time. Also, some substances are poisonous when taken in one way but not when taken in another; for example, snake venom may cause death when injected (as by a snakebite) but may be relatively harmless if swallowed.

Poisoning, ingestion of substance toxic to body.

Poison Ivy, a poisonous plant. It grows in the form of climbing vines, shrubs that trail on the ground, and erect shrubbery growing without support.
The leaves vary in length from one to four inches. They are green and glossy in summer; in the spring and fall they are red or russet. The fruit is white and waxy and resembles mistletoe. Although poison ivy assumes many forms and displays seasonal changes in leaf coloring, it has one constant characteristic that makes it easy to recognize: the leaves always grow in clusters of three. The irritating substance in poison ivy is the oily sap in the leaves, flowers, fruit, stem, bark, and roots. The plant is poisonous even after long drying, but is particularly irritating in the spring and early summer when it is full of sap. Most cases of ivy poisoning are caused by direct contact with the plant. Some are caused by handling clothing, garden implements, and pets that have been contaminated by the oily sap.

Poitrinaire, one having a chronic chest disease.

Poliomyelitis (Infantile Paralysis), a disease caused by any one of three closely related ciruses. Poliomyelitis is best known as a disease that causes paralysis. However, only the most severe form of polio (as poliomyelitis is sometimes called) causes lasting paralysis. The great majority of cases result in no lasting paralysis.
The virus causing poliomyelitis enters the body through the respiratory system. The virus attacks the cells in the central nervous system. The exact method by which the virus cells move from the respiratory system to the central nervous system is not known.

Poliosis, absence of hair coloring.

Pollen, male sex cells of plants.

Pollex, thumb or big toe.

Pollinosis, hay fever.

Pollution, making impure; discharge of semen without sexual intercourse.

Polyarthritis, inflammation of several joints.

Polycholia, excessive bile secretion.

Polyclinic, medical center treating many diseases.

Polycyesis, pregnancy with more than one fetus.

Polycythemia, condition in which there is an excess of red blood cells.

Polycytosis, excess of blood cells.

Polydactylism, having more than five fingers or five toes.

Polydipsia, excessive desire to drink.

Polyemia, excessive blood in the body.

Polyglandular, affecting many glands.

Polygraph, an instrument for simultaneously recording several different pulsations.

Polygyny, marriage to more than one woman at one time.

Polyhedral, many sides.

Polymenorrhea, unusual frequency of menstruation.

Polymyositis, inflammation of many muscles.

Polyneural, pertaining to many nerves.

Polyneuritis, inflammation of more than one group of nerves.

Polyp, outgrowths in the nose, intestines or bladder.

Polypathia, having more than one disease at a time.

Polyphagia, excessive eating.

Polyplegia, paralysis of several muscles.

Polypus, polyp.

Polyunsaturated fat, a fat so constituted chemically that it is capable of absorbing additional hydrogen. These fats are usually liquid oils of vegetable origin, such as corn oil or safflower oil. A diet with a high polyunsaturated fat content tends to lower the amount of cholesterol in the blood. These fats are sometimes substituted for saturated fat in a diet in an effort to lessen the hazard of fatty deposits in the blood vessels.

Polyuria, excessive urination.

Pons, a part of the brain which bridges several other sections of the nervous system.

Pontic, false tooth.

Popliteal, pertaining to the back of the leg and the bend of the knee.

Pore, small opening in skin or tissue.

Porous, having many pores.

Porrigo, ringworm.

Portio, part.

Portio Dura, facial nerve.

Porus, pore.

Position, placement of the body.

Positive, affirmative; indicating the presence of a disorder.

Posology, system of dosage.

Postcibal, after eating.

Postcoital, after sexual intercourse.

Postepileptic, after an epileptic attack.

Posterior, behind; at the back part.

Posthetomy, circumsion.

Posthumous, after death.

Postmortem, autopsy; after death.

Postnasal, situated behind the nose.

Postnasal Drip, relatively constant nasal discharge which drips or drains down the throat.

Postnatal, immediately after birth.

Postoperative, happening after an operation.

Postoral, in the back of the mouth.

Postpartum, after childbirth.

Postprandial, after a meal.

Postpubescent, after puberty.

Posture, the position of the body. Good posture is the correct alignment of the body and all body parts when standing, sitting, lying down, or in any phase of activity. Good posture helps to conserve energy, promotes the efficient use of muscles, and avoids back strain and fatigue.

Postuterine, behind the uterus.

Potable, adequate for drinking.

Potamophobia, extreme fear of large bodies of water.

Potency, strength; ability to perform coitus.

Potion, dose of liquid medicine.

Pouch, pocket-like cavity.

Poultice, hot, moist mass to be placed on the skin.

Pox, blisters and scars on the skin caused by certain diseases.

Practice, professional diagnosis and treatment of disease.

Practitioner, physician.

Pragmatagnosia, inability to recognize objects.

Prandial, pertaining to a meal,

Precordia, area overlying heart.

Pregnancy, state of being with child.

Pregravidic, preceding pregnancy.

Prehensile, able to grasp.

Prehension, grasping.

Preictal, preceding a stroke or attack.

Prelingual Deafness, the total or near-total loss of hearing that occurs before normal speech habits have been established. The lack of meaningful hearing during infancy and early childhood (when speech develops) has drastic effects on the development of both speech and language. Normally, speech develops as a direct result of hearing. Speech is both a way of making the sounds that are called words and a system of symbols that stand for something. Language is the system of symbols that uses words to represent objects, actions, ideas, and meanings.

The small child who cannot hear is doubly handicapped. He has difficulty acquiring the meanings for which language stands as well as difficulty in talking.

Premature, born before maturity.

Premature Infant, one weighing less than 5.5 pounds at birth.

Premenstrual, preceding menstruation.

Premonitary, warning.

Premunition, immunization by vaccination.

Prenatal, before birth.

Preoral, in front of the mouth.

Prepuce, foreskin of penis.

Presbyatry, treatment of diseases of the aged.

Presbyacusia, partial loss of hearing in old age.

Presbyopia, loss of elasticity in eyes which occurs in old age.

Prescription, written order for drug authorized by a physician.

Pressor, a substance that raises the blood pressure and accelerates the heartbeat.

Pressure, stress; strain.

Pressure Point, a place where a main artery lies near the skin surface and over a bone.

Preventive, prophylactic.

Priapism, continued erection of the penis without sexual desire.

Prickly Heat, irritations of the skin in which blisters form due to increased temperature.

Primary, principal.

Primary Hypertension, an elevated blood pressure that is not caused by kidney or other evident disease.

Primigravida, woman in her first pregnancy.

Primipara, woman who has given birth once.

Primitive, original.

Primordial, primitive.

Princeps, primary artery.

Principal, most important.

Probe, instrument for exploring the interior of the body.

Procaine, a drug used as a local anesthetic; better known as novocaine.

Proconceptive, aiding conception.

Procreate, to beget children.

Proctalgia, pain in the rectum.

Proctitis, inflammation of the rectum or anus.

Proctology, branch of medicine concerned with the rectum.

Proctoscope, an instrument used to examine the rectum.

Proctoscopy, examination of the rectum.

Procumbent, prone.

Prodrome, early symptoms of impending illness.

Progeny, offspring.

Progeria, condition causing early aging.

Progesterone, an important female hormone.

Prognathism, having projecting jaws.

Prognosis, medical name for the outlook of a disease.

Proiota, sexual precocity.

Prolapse, abnormal position of internal organ.

Proliferation, multiplication of cells.

Prominence, projection; elevation.

Prone, lying face downward.

Prootic, in front of the ear.

Propagation, reproduction.

Prophylactic, preventing disease.

Prophylaxis, prevention of disease.

Pro Re Nata, according to circumstances.

Prorrhaphy, advancement.

Prosodemic, spread from one person to another.

Prosopospasm, facial spasm.

Prostate, small gland in the male situated at the base of the bladder, concerned with preparation of the semen.

Prostatitis, inflammation of the prostate gland.

Prosthesis, substitute for missing part.

Prosthetics, branch of surgery dealing with artificial parts.

Prostigmine Test, a test for pregnancy.

Prostitution, having sexual relations for profit or gain.

Prostration, exhaustion.

Protein, the basic substance of every cell in the body.

Prothrombin, chemical substance important in blood coagulation.

Protistology, microbiology.

Protoplasm, prime material in living organism.

Protozoa, microscopic, one-celled organisms.

Protraction, the act of moving a part forward.

Protuberance, projection.

Provisional, of temporary use.

Proximate, nearest.

Pruritus, itching.

Prussiate, cyanide.

Psellism, stuttering.

Pseudocrisis, false crisis.

Pseudocyesis, imaginary pregnancy with some physical findings of the condition.

Psittacosis, disease spread by parrots, love-birds, canaries and other birds kept as pets.

Psoriasis, chronic skin disease in which red scaly patches develop.

Psychanalysis, psychoanalysis.

Psyche, mind.

Psychectampsia, acute mania.

Psychiatrist, one who specializes in psychiatry.

Psychiatry, study and treatment of mental disorders.

Psychic, pertaining to the mind.

Psychics, psychology.

Psychoanalysis, method of obtaining a patient's past emotional history.

Psychocoma, mental stupor.

Psychogenesis, mental development.

Psychognosis, study of mental and emotional activity.

Psychology, science dealing with mental functions.

Psychopath, one who has no sense of moral obligation.

Psychopathy, any mental disorder.

Psychophylaxis, mental hygiene.

Psychosis, type of insanity in which one loses almost complete touch with reality.

Psychosomatic Disease, physical ailments due to emotional causes.

Psychotherapy, treatment of mental and emotional disorders.

Ptarmic, causing sneezing.

Ptarmus, sneezing.

Ptomaine, specific poisoning caused by putrified food.

Ptosis, drooping of the upper eyelid.

Ptyalism, excess secretion of saliva.

Ptyalorrhea, excessive secretion of saliva.

Ptysis, spitting.

Puberal, pertaining to puberty.

Puberty, period of rapid growth and development between childhood and adult life.

Pubes, hairy area above the genitals.

Pubis, bone at front of pelvis.

Pudenda, the external sex organ.

Pudic, pudendal.

Puerile, pertaining to a child.

Puerilism, childishness.

Puerpera, woman who has had a child.

Puerperium, period immediately following childbirth.

Pulmonary, pertaining to the lungs.

Pulmonary Artery, the large artery that conveys unoxygenated blood from the lower right chamber of the heart to the lungs.

Pulmonic, pulmonary.

Pulpalgia, pain in the pulp of a tooth.

Pulpy, soft.

Pulsation, rhythmic throb.

Pulse Pressure, the difference between the blood pressure in the arteries when the heart is in contraction (systole) and when it is in relaxation (diastole).

Pulso, pressure variation in arteries due to action of heart; can be felt where arteries are close to skin.

Pulsus, pulse.

Pulsus Alternans, a pulse in which there is a regular alternation of weak and strong beats.

Pulverulent, powdery.

Punctum, point.

Punctum Caecum, blind spot.

Puncture, pierce.

Pupil, part of eye which opens or closes to adjust to light or object.

Pupillary, pertaining to the pupil.

Purgative, drug to relieve constipation.

Purge, to evacuate the bowels by medicine.

Purkinje Fibers, the specialized fibers that form a network in the walls of the lower chambers of the heart.

Purpura, purple areas or bruises on body due to abnormal blood clotting.

Purulent, forming or containing pus.

Pus, product of infection containing dead cell and cell debris.

Pustule, pimple.

Pyarthrosis, pus in a joint cavity.

Pyelitis, inflammation of the pelvis of the kidney, that is, the area where the kidney is connected to the ureter, the tube leading down to the bladder.

Pyemia, form of blood poisoning in which the germs are carried in the blood and produce abscesses.

Pygal, pertaining to the buttocks.

Pyknemia, thickening of the blood.

Pyloric Stenosis, an obstruction in the digestive system.

Pylorus, valve which lies at one end of the stomach and controls the entry of food into the small intestine.

Pyocele, pus around the testis.

Pyocolpos, pus in the vagina.

Pyocyst, sac of pus in body.

Pyoderma, any skin inflammation that produces pus.

Pyogenesis, formation of pus.

Pyorrhea, infection of the gums which causes the edges of the tooth sockets to bleed easily when teeth are being brushed.

Pyretic, pertaining to fever.

Pyretolysis, lowering of fever.

Pyrexia, increased body temperature, high fever.

Pyrogenic, causing fever.

Pyromania, obsessive compulsion to start fires.

Pyrophobia, extreme fear of fire.

Pyrosis, burning pain in stomach; acid taste in mouth.

Pyrotic, burning.

Pyuria, pus in urine.

— Q —

Q Fever, a disease caused by microorganisms called rickettsiae.

Quack, a faker in medical science.

Quadripara, woman giving birth to her fourth child.

Quadriplegia, paralysis of arms and legs.

Quadruplets, a pregnancy that results in the birth of four babies.

Quarantine, enforced isolation of people suffering from an infectious disease.

Quartan Fever, a type of malaria in which the patient has malarial symptoms every fourth day (counting the day the symptoms occur as the first day.)

Quassation, shattering.

Quickening, the feeling of life of a baby by a pregnant woman.

Quinidine, a drug that is occasionally used to treat abnormal rhythms of the heartbeat.

Quinine, drug used in the treatment of malaria.

Quinsy, formation of an abscess around one of the tonsils.

Quintan, every fifth day.

Quintipara, woman giving birth to her fifth child.

— R —

Rabbeting, interlocking of the splintered edges of a fractured bone.

Rabbit Fever, virus disease transmitted by eating or handling infected animals; tularemia.

Rabiate, one who has rabies.

Rabic, pertaining to rabies.

Rabid, pertaining to rabies.

Rabies, a fatal disease of man affecting the brain and spinal cord if untreated.

Race, class of people of similar inheritance and ethnic qualities.

Rachialgia, pain in spine.

Rachianalgesia, spinal anesthesia.

Rachicentesis, puncture into spinal canal.

Rachidian, pertaining to the spine.

Rachiocampsis, curvature of the spine.

Rachiodynia, painful condition of spinal column.

Rachis, spinal column.

Rachisschisis, spinal column fissure; congenital opening.

Rachitec, pertaining to rickets.

Radiation, rays that in proper dosage can be used to treat certain diseases.

Radicular, pertaining to a root.

Radiculitis, inflammation of a nerve root.

Radiectomy, removal of the root of a tooth.

Radioactivity, emitting of penetrating rays or small particles.

Radiograph, an x-ray film.

Radiography, taking of x-rays.

Radiologist, medical specialist who uses radiation for diagnosis and treatment.

Radiology, branch of medicine using radiant energy in diagnosis and treatment of disease.

Radiolus, sound; probe.

Radiotherapeutic, use of x-ray or radium for treatment.

Radium, an intensely radioactive metallic element.

Radius, short arm bone extending from elbow to wrist.

Radix, root.

Rale, abnormal sound coming from air passages of lungs.

Rami, branch.

Ramify, to branch.

Ramitis, inflammation of a nerve root.

Ramollissement, morbid softening of some organ or tissue.

Ramus, branch of an artery, vein or nerve; branchlike part.

Rancid, offensive; sour.

Range of Accommodation, difference between the least and greatest distance of clear vision.

Ranula, swelling under the tongue due to the blocking of a salivary gland.

Rape, sexual intercourse without consent of female.

Rash, skin eruption.

Raspatory, surgical file.

Rasura, Rasure, scraping; shaving.

Rat, rodent frequently used in experiments.

Rat Bite Fever, an infectious disease passed to human beings by bite of an infected animal.

Ratio, proportion.

Ration, fixed portion of food and drink for a certain period.

Rational, according to reason.

Rationalization, making an irrational thing appear reasonable.

Rattle, rale.

Rattle, Death, gurgling sound heard in the trachea of the dying.

Rauwolfia, drug which lowers blood pressure and causes relaxation in mind and body.

Rave, talk irrationally.

Ravish, rape.

Raw Milk, milk that has not been pasteurized.

Raynaud's Disease, circulatory disturbance affecting extremities.

R.C.P., Royal College of Physicians.

R.C.S., Royal College of Surgeons.

Re- (prefix), back; again.

Reaction, response.

Recall, memory.

Receptaculum, vessel or cavity which contains fluid.

Receptor, a nerve ending that is sensitive to stimuli.

Recessus, small hollow or recess.

Recidivation, recurrence of a disease.

Recipe, prescription; formula.

Recipient, one who receives a thing.

Recline, lie down.

Reconstituent, an agent which strengthens a part of the body by replacing lost material.

Recrement, secretion which is reabsorbed into the body after performing its function.

Recrudescence, reappearance of symptoms of a disease.

Rectal, pertaining to the rectum.

Rectal Reflex, normal desire to evacuate feces.

Rectalgia, rectal pain.

Rectectomy, surgical removal of the rectum or anus.

Rectified, made pure or straight.

Rectitis, inflammation of the rectum.

Rectoclysis, gradual introduction of fluid into rectum.

Rectocolitis, inflammation of the rectum and colon.

Rectostenosis, stricture of the rectum.

Rectostomy, making an artificial opening into the rectum to relieve stricture.

Rectum, lowest six inches of the intestinal tract adjoining the anus.

Rectus, straight; any straight muscle.

Recumbent, lying down.

Recuperation, restoration to health.

Recurrent, reappearing.

Recurve, bend backward.

Red Blood Cell, blood corpuscle containing hemoglobin.

Redressment, correction of a deformity; dressing a wound a second time or more.

Red Softening, hemorrhagic softening of brain and spinal cord.

Reduce, decrease.

Reduction, restoration to normal position.

Reduction Diet, diet which eliminates fat producing foods.

Reduplicated, folded back on itself.

Referred Pain, pain felt in part of the body other than its source.

Refine, purify.

Reflex, an involuntary action caused by a stimulus to the nerves.

Reflexogenic, causing a reflex action.

Reflux, backward flow.

Refracta Dosi, in divided doses.

Refraction, eye testing to determine amount of vision.

Refractory, not easily treated.

Refracture, break again.

Refrangible, capable of refraction.

Refresh, renew, revive.

Refrigerant, medicine which relieves thirst and reduces fever.

Refusion, return flow of blood to the vessels.

Regeneration, regrowth or repair of part of body.

Regimen, course of therapy to improve health.

Region, particular body area.

Registry, placement bureau for nurses.

Regression, process of going back to a prior status in physical or mental illness.

Regressive, subsiding, reverting.

Regular, normal.

Regurgitant, backward flow.

Regurgitate, to vomit.

Rehabilitation, restoration to activity of a handicapped person.

Rehalation, rebreathing.

Reichman's Disease, constant excessive gastric secretion.

Reinfection, return of infection.

Reimplantation, replacement of a part to its original location.

Rejuvenation, return to a youthful or normal state.

Relapse, recurrence of an illness.

Relapsing Fever, an infectious disease in which periods of fever alternate with periods of normal temperature.

Relaxant, agent which lessens tension or loosens bowels.

Relaxation, reduction of tension.

Remak's Axis Cylinder, conducting part of a nerve.

Remedial, curative.

Remedy, substance that is used in treatment of disease.

Remission, abatement.

Ren, the kidney.

Renal, pertaining to the kidney.

Renal Circulation, the circulation of the blood through the kidneys.

Renal Pelvis, the cavity in the middle of a kidney; it is the upper end of the ureter.

Renifieur, one who is sexually stimulated by certain odors, especially that of urine.

Reniform, kidney-shaped.

Rennin, a prominent component of gastric juices during infancy. It helps to coagulate milk protein.

Repair, replace; heal.

Repellent, reducing swelling; that which repels insects.

Repletion, full; satisfied; fullness of blood; plethora.

Reportable Diseases, diseases which must be reported to public health authorities.

Reposition, act of replacing a part.

Repositor, instrument for replacing a part.

Repression, suppression into unconsciousness of unacceptable ideas and emotion.

Reproduction, begetting of offspring.

Resection, excision of part of body tissue.

Reserpine, drug used to lower blood pressure.

Residue, that which remains after removal of a part.

Residuum, residue.

Resilience, elasticity.

Resilient, elastic.

Resistance, ability to protect self from disease.

Resolution, subsiding of an inflammation.

Respirable, suitable for respiration.

Respiration, breathing.

Respirator, mechanical device used to aid breathing.

Respiratory, pertaining to respiration.

Respiratory System, the parts of the body that together are responsible for bringing air into the lungs and for expelling carbon dioxide from the body.

Rest, period of inactivity.

Restiform, ropelike; rope-shaped.

Restitution, restoring.

Restorative, promoting health; remedy.

Restraint, forcible control.

Resuscitation, artificial respiration which is used to restore breathing after drowning, electric shock or other conditions interfering with breathing.

Resuscitator, mechanical device used for artificial respiration.

Retardation, delay.

Retarded Depression, depressed state of manic depressive psychosis.

Retching, unsatisfactory attempt to vomit.

Rete, network.

Retention, holding back.

Retention Cyst, cyst caused by retention of a secretion in a gland.

Retention of Urine, failure to urinate.

Reticular, netlike.

Reticulation, formation of a network mass.

Reticulum, network in cells.

Retina, part of the eye that receives the image and which is connected to the brain by the optic nerve.

Retinal, pertaining to the retina.

Retinitis, inflammation of the retina, the innermost coat of the eye.

Retinitis Pigmentosa, a disease, frequently hereditary, marked by progressive pigmentation and deterioration of the retina and disturbance of its nerve elements.

Retinosis, degeneration of the retina.

Retractile, able to be drawn back.

Retraction, drawing back.

Retractor, surgical instrument used to hold back the edges of an incision.

Retrocolic, behind the colon.

Retrocollic, pertaining to the back of the neck.

Retroinfection, infection transmitted by the fetus to the mother.

Retrolingual, behind the tongue.

Retronasal, behind the nose.

Retroposed, displaced backward.

Revulsant, causing transfer of disease or blood from one part of body to another; agent which draws blood to inflamed site.

Reye's Syndrome, serious and often fatal childhood complication that follows viral infections, influenza, and chicken pox which have been treated with aspirin. Symptoms appear a few days after the child has recovered from the viral illness and include: vomiting, drowsiness, lethargy, a change in mental status such as forgetfulness or disorientation, loss of consciousness, convulsions, and coma. There is no cure.

Rhachis, spinal column.

Rhagades, skin cracks.

-rhagia, (suffix), bleeding.

Rhegma, rupture, fracture, tear.

Rheum, watery discharge.

Rheumatalgia, rheumatic pain.

Rheumatic Fever, disease affecting joints, skin and sometimes the heart; believed due to an allergic reaction to specific bacteria.

Rheumatic Heart Disease, the damage done to the heart, particularly the heart valves, by one or more attacks of rheumatic fever.

Rheumatism, pain, swelling and deformity of joints of unknown cause.

Rheumatoid, of the nature of rheumatism.

Rhexis, rupture of a blood vessel or organ.

Rh. Factor, a substance found in the red blood cells; about 15% of people do not have this factor and are therefore called RH negative.

Rhinal, pertaining to the nose.

Rhinalgia, nasal pain.

Rhinesthesia, sense of smell.

Rhinitis, inflammation of the lining of the nose.

Rhinobyon, nasal plug.

Rhinocleisis, nasal obstruction.

Rhinodynia, nasal pain.

Rhinolalia, nasal voice quality.

Rhinologist, nose specialist.

Rhinology, branch of medicine dealing with the nose.

Rhinopathy, any nasal disease.

Rhinophyma, disease of the nose in which it becomes greatly enlarged.

Rhinoplasty, plastic or cosmetic surgery to remodel the nose.

Rhinorrhagia, nosebleed.

Rhinotomy, surgical incision of the nose.

Rhodocyte, red blood cell.

Rhodopsin, a red pigment located in the rods of the eye.

Rhoncus, rale; rattling sound in chest.

Rhypophagy, eating of filth.

Rhypophobia, extreme fear of filth.

Rhythm, measured time or movement; noting the periods of fertility and sterility in the female during the menstrual cycle.

Rhytidosis, wrinkling of skin or cornea.

Rib, bone and cartilage that form the chest cavity and protects its contents.

Ribosomes, large particles containing RNA. Ribosomes are found in the cytoplasm of a cell.

Ribs, False, five ribs on each side not directly attached to sternum.

Ribs, Floating, two lower ribs not attached to sternum.

Rickets, this is a disease caused by lack of vitamin D.

Ridge, narrow, elevated border.

Rigidity, stiffness.

Rigor, chill preceding a fever; rigidity.

Rigor Mortis, stiffening of muscles after death.

Rima, crack.

Rimula, minute crack.

Rind, skin or cortex of an organ or person.

Ringworm, fungus infection.

Risus, laugh; grin.

Ritter's Disease, severe skin inflammation seen in infants.

R.N., registered nurse.

RNA, single-strand molecules of a type of nucleic acid. RNA is the abbreviation for ribonucleic acid.

Roborant, tonic; strengthening.

Rocky Mountain Spotted Fever, infectious disease characterized by fever, pains in bone and muscle and reddish eruptions.

Rodent Ulcer, small, hard skin ulcer on the face in region of the inner corner of the eye or around the nose.

Roentgen, measure of radiation.

Roentgenogram, x-ray.

Rongeur, gouge forceps used to remove bone fragments.

Root, proximal end of a nerve; portion of an organ implanted in tissues.

Root Canal, pulp cavity of tooth root.

Rosacea, skin disease of the face in which there is permanent redness over the nose and cheeks.

Rose Fever, hay fever.

Roseola, red rash from various causes.

Rose Rash, any red colored eruption.

Rossbach's Disease, excessive secretion of gastric juice.

Rot, decay.

Rotate, twist; revolve.

Rotula, kneecap or patella.

Rotular, pertaining to the kneecap.

Roughage, coarse material.

Roundworm, an intestinal parasite.

Roust, delivery room nurse who carries out unsterile tasks.

Rubedo, temporary redness of skin.

Rubella, German measles.

Rubeola, measles.

Rubor, redness of skin due to infection.

Rubrum, red.

Ructus, belching.

Rudimentary, elementary; undeveloped.

Ruga, fold or crease.

Rugose, wrinkled.

Rule of Nine, a method of determining the extent of burns.

Rumination, regurgitation,

Rump, buttocks.

Run, to exude pus or mucus.

Runaround, infection extending around a finger or toenail.

Rupophobia, extreme dislike for dirt or filth.

Rupture, tearing apart; hernia.

Rutilizm, red-headedness.

Rx, symbol for "take" or "recipe."

— S —

Saburra, foulness of stomach or mouth.

Sac, pouch.

Saccharin, sugar substitute; sweetener.

Saccharum, sugar.

Sacculation, grouping of sacs.

Saccule, small sac.

Sacrificial Operation, removal of an organ for the patient's good.

Sacroiliac, relating to the juncture of the hipbone and lower part of the spine.

Sacroiliac Strain, type of backache.

Sacrum, part of vertebral column or spine.

Sadism, perversion in which sexual pleasure is obtained by inflicting pain on someone.

Sadist, one who enjoys inflicting pain on others.

St. Vitus' Dance, involuntary muscular action.

Sal, salt.

Salacious, lustful.

Salicylate, main component of aspirin.

Saline, pertaining to salt.

Saline Solution, salt water.

Saliva, fluid secreted by the glands of the mouth.

Salivant, stimulating secretion of saliva.

Salivary, pertaining to saliva.

Salivary Glands, three pairs of glands, located in the vicinity of the mouth, that secrete saliva.

Salivation, excess secretion of saliva.

Sallow, having a pale, yellowish complexion.

Sal Mirabile, purgative salt.

Salmonella, bacteria causing intestinal disorder.

Salmonellosis, infestation with Salmonella bacteria.

Salpingectomy, surgical removal of Fallopian tube.

Salpingitis, inflammation of the Fallopian tubes.

Salpinx, uterine tube; eustachian tube.

Salt, sodium chloride.

Saltation, dancing.

Saltatory, characterized by leaping or dancing.

Salt Free Diet, diet which allows no more than two grams of salt.

Saltpeter, postassium nitrate.

Salubrious, promoting good health.

Salutary, healthful; curative.

Salve, ointment.

Sanative, healing.

Sanatorium, place for preserving health or caring for a long term illness.

Sanatory, promoting health.

Sane, of sound mind.

Sanger's Operation, type of Cesarean section.

Sangucolous, inhabiting the blood.

Sanguifacient, forming blood.

Sanguiferous, conducting blood.

Sanguine, bloody.

Sanguineous, bloody; having a plethora of blood.

Sanguis, blood.

Sanitarium, place for the care and cure of those suffering from mental or physical illness.

Sanitary, pertaining to health.

Sanity, soundness of mind.

Saphena, large vein of leg.

Sapid, possessing flavor.

Sapo, soap.

Saponatus, mixed with soap.

Sapphism, lesbianism.

Sapremia, blood poisoning.

Saprodontis, tooth decay.

Sarcitis, inflammation of muscle tissue.

Sarcocele, tumor of testicle.

Sarcode, protoplasm.

Sarcogenic, forming flesh.

Sarcology, study of soft body tissues.

Sarcolytic, decomposing flesh.

Sarcoma, one of the two main types of cancer, the other being carcinoma.

Sarcophagy, practice of eating flesh.

Sarcopoietic, forming flesh or muscle.

Sarcous, pertaining to flesh or muscle.

Sartorius, muscle of thigh.

Satiety, satisfying fullness.

Saturated Fat, a fat so constituted chemically that it is not capable of absorbing any more hydrogen.

Saturnine, pertaining to lead.

Saturnism, lead poisoning.

Satyriasis, abnormal sex drive associated with mental excitement in male.

Satyromania, excessive sexual desire in the male.

Savory, appetizing.

Saw, cutting instrument.

Scab, crust formation over wound.

Scabies, disease of the skin caused by a mite which burrows under the skin surface and causes extreme discomfort and itching.

Scald, burn of skin.

Scale, small, thin, dry particle.

Scalenus, three muscles located in the vertebrae of the neck and attached to the first two ribs.

Scall, scalp disease.

Scalp, hairy component of head.

Scalpel, surgical knife.

Scanty, insufficient.

Scapula, shoulder blade.

Scapular, pertaining to the shoulder blade.

Scapulectomy, surgical removal of scapula.

Scar, end product of healed wound.

Scarfskin, epidermis.

Scarlatina, scarlet fever.

Scarlet Fever, contagious disease causing chills, high fever, sore throat, skin rash, discolored tongue.

Scatacratia, fecal incontinence.

Scatemia, intestinal toxemia.

Scatology, study and analysis of waste product of body.

Scelalgia, pain in leg.

Schick Test, test for susceptibility to diphtheria.

Schistasis, any congenital fissure.

Schizophrenia, psychiatric disorder of many and varied manifestations in which person loses contact or misinterprets reality.

Schizotrichia, splitting of hair.

Schwelle, threshold.

Sciage, sawing massage movement.

Sciatica, inflammation of or injury to the sciatic nerve in back of thigh.

Sciatic Nerve, largest nerve in body located in back of leg.

Scirrhoma, scirrhus.

Scirrhus, hard cancer.

Schlera, white of eye.

Schlerectomy, surgical removal of part of the sclera.

Schleritis, inflammation of the white of the eye.

Schleroderma, skin disease of unknown origin in which patches of skin become thickened, hard and white or yellowish.

Scleroma, sclerosis.

Sclerose, to become hardened.

Sclerosis, hardening of a tissue.

Sclerothrix, abnormal hardness and dryness of hair.

Scoliosis, curvature of the spine to one side or the other.

Scopophobia, extreme fear of being seen.

Scorbutus, scurvy.

Scordinemia, yawning and stretching.

Scotoma, blind spot.

Scotophobia, extreme fear of darkness.

Scotopia, adjustment of eyes to darkness.

Scours, diarrhea.

Scratch, superficial injury.

Scrobiculate, pitted.

Scrobiculus, pit.

Scrobiculus Cordis, pit of the stomach.

Scrofula, condition of tuberculous gland of the neck.

Scrotal, pertaining to the scrotum.

Scrotum, pouch of male containing testicles.

Scrub Nurse, operating room nurse.

Scruf, dandruff.

Scurvy, disease due to lack of vitamin C, causing bleeding, weakness and swelling of skin.

Scutum, thyroid cartilage.

Scytitis, dermatitis.

Sea Sickness, nausea, vomiting and unsteadiness due to unusual motion.

Sebaceous, pertaining to sebum.

Sebaceous Cyst, a wen; a swelling caused by the blocking of a duct of a sebaceous gland.

Sebaceous Glands, glands that are associated with the hair follicles. They secrete oil (sebum) into the hair follicles near the surfaces of the skin.

Sebastomania, religious insanity.

Seborrhagia, excessive secretion of sebaceous glands.

Seborrhea, condition of excessive oiliness of the skin caused by glandular upset.

Sebum, oily secretion of the oil glands of the skin.

Secondary, not of primary importance.

Secondary Hypertension, an elevated blood pressure that is caused by (and therefore secondary to) certain specific diseases or infections.

Secreta, waste material expelled by a gland or organ.

Secretin, a hormone produced in the small intestine. Secretin stimulates the pancreas and the liver.

Secretion, fluid discharged from gland or organ.

Secretomotory, stimulating secretion.

Section, divide by cutting.

Sectorial, cutting.

Secundigravida, woman in her second pregnancy.

Secundines, afterbirth material.

Sedative, agent used to quiet patient.

Sediment, material which settles at the bottom of a fluid.

Seed, semen.

Segment, part of a whole.

Seizure, sudden attack.

Sella, saddle-shaped depression; area within skull.

Semantic, pertaining to the meaning of words.

Semeiosis, approach to disease according to symptoms.

Semel, once.

Semen, male secretion containing sperm.

Semenuria, presence of semen in urine.

Semi- (prefix), half.

Semicircular Canals, three small tubes located in each ear.

Semilunar, wrist bone.

Seminal Vesicles, two pouches that are situated (in the male) between the bladder and the rectum. They secrete and store a fluid to be added to the secretion of the testes at the time of ejaculation.

Semination, introduction of semen into the vagina.

Seminiferous, producing or carrying semen.

Seminology, study of semen.

Semis, half.

Senescence, process of growing old.

Senile, old.

Senilism, premature old age.

Sensation, awareness of stimulus to nervous system.

Sense, perceive through nervous system; perceiving faculty.

Sensibility, sensitivity.

Sensitive, responsive; unusually receptive to stimuli.

Sensorium, any sensory nerve center.

Sensory, pertaining to sensation.

Sentient, sensitive.

Sepsis, poisoning of body by products of bacteria.

Septicemia, blood poisoning.

Septum, tissue dividing cavities.

Sequela, after affects of a disease.

Sequestrum, piece of dead bone.

Serial, arranged in sequence.

Seriate, saw-toothed.

Serology, study of serum.

Serosa, layer of tissue.

Serotonin, a naturally occurring compound that is found mainly in the gastrointestinal tract and in lesser amounts in the blood. Serotonin has a stimulating effect on the circulatory system.

Serous, thin and watery.

Serous Membrane, lining tissues of the body that are moistened by a fluid resembling the serum of the blood.

Serrate, notched.

Serrulate, minutely notched.

Serum, clear fluid which separates from blood when it clots.

Sesamoid Bone, a bone that develops within a tendon.

Sex, distinctive feature between male and female; Freud-pleasure.

Sex Hormones, the hormones that control and stimulate the growth of the secondary sex characteristics.

Sexual, pertaining to sex.

Shank, leg from knee to ankle.

Sheath, tubular case.

Shift, change.

Shigella, organism causing dysentery.

Shin, front part of lower leg.

Shingles, herpes zoster, viral infection of nerve path.

Shin Splints, a condition in which there is pain in the front of the lower part of the leg due to strained and swollen muscles, frequently caused by an excess of exercise or sports.

Ship-Fever, typhus fever.

Shiver, chill.

Shock, decreased effective circulating fluid volume.

Shortsighted, not able to see very far.

Shoulder, joint between arm and body.

Show, vaginal discharge prior to start of labor.

Shunt, a passage between two blood vessels or between the two sides of the heart where an opening exists in the wall that normally separates them.

Sialaden, salivary gland.

Sialadenitis, inflammation of a salivary gland.

Sialine, pertaining to saliva.

Sialism, increased production of saliva.

Sialogogue, causing the secretion of saliva.

Sialoporia, deficient saliva secretion.

Sialorrhea, flowing of saliva.

Sibilant, whistling; hissing.

Sibling, brother or sister.

Siccative, drying.

Sick, not in normal health.

Sickle Cell Anemia, a chronic disorder of the blood characterized by red blood cells that are sickle or crescent-shaped.

Sickness, illness.

Side Effect, an effect that is aside from or in addition to the desired effect. Side effects occur as a result of taking medicines or other kinds of treatments.

Siderodromophobia, extreme fear of train travel.

Sigh, involuntary inspiration of emotional origin.

Sight, act of seeing.

Sigmatism, faulty pronunciation of s sound.

Sign, symptom, evidence.

Signature, directions for taking medicine on a prescription.

Silicosis, condition of the lungs found in those who work among stone dust.

Sinapism, mustard plaster.

Sinciput, upper part of head.

Sinew, tendon or fibrous tissue.

Singultus, hiccough.

Sinister, left.

Sinistrad, toward the left.

Sinistral, pertaining to the left side.

Sinoatrial Node, a small mass of specialized cells in the right upper chamber of the heart that give rise to the electrical impulses that initiate contractions of the heart.

Sinuous, winding.

Sinus, hollow area of a bone.

Sinuses of Valsalva, three pouches in the wall of the aorta (the main artery leading from the left lower chamber of the heart) located behind the three cup-shaped membranes of the aortic valve.

Sinusitis, inflammation of the nasal sinuses.

Sinusotomy, incision of a sinus.

Sippy Diet, diets used to decrease acid or stomach juice.

Siriasis, sunstroke.

Sitology, study of food and its use.

Sitophobia, extreme dislike of food.

Situs, position.

Sitz-Bath, a therapeutic bath in sitting position.

Skelalgia, leg pain.

Skeleton, bones of body.

Skin, outer covering of body.

Skull, bones of head, 22 in all.

Sleep, normal loss of consciousness.

Sleeping Sickness, an infection of brain causing increased drowsiness; encephalitis.

Sling, support of arm or leg.

Slipped Disk, a vertebral disk that has slipped or been displaced.

Slough, dead tissue which separates from living tissue.

Smallpox, serious infectious disease with fever, pain, vomiting and an eruption of red spots which later become blisters and afterwards are filled with pus.

Smear, preparation of body secretions spread on a glass slide for microscopic study.

Smegma, thick, odorous secretion of certain glands.

Smog, mixture of smoke and fog.

Smell, odor; to stimulate olfactory cells.

Snakebite, the body's physical reaction to the venom injected by the bite of a snake.

Sneezing, a nose irritation which causes sudden expulsion of air from mouth and nose.

Snoring, a nose or throat obstruction causing a noise when breathing during sleep.

Snowblindness, temporary loss of sight due to glare on snow.

Snuffles, yellow discharges from nose of infants.

Soak, immerse in a solution.

Sociology, study of social relationships.

Socket, hollow into which another part fits.

Sodium, a mineral that is essential to life. It is found in nearly all plant and animal tissue.

Sodokosis, rat-bite fever.

Sodomy, unusual sexual relations, bestiality.

Soft, not hard or firm.

Soft Palate, posterior part of palate.

Solar, pertaining to the sun.

Solar Fever, infectious febrile disease.

Solar Plexus, anatomical area in upper part of abdomen.

Sole, bottom of foot.

Soleus, soft, broad muscle of calf or leg.

Solid, not hollow, gaseous or liquid.

Soluble, able to be dissolved.

Solute, substance which is dissolved in a solution.

Solution, homogeneous mixture of a solid in a liquid.

Solvent, solution used to dissolve material.

Soma, the body.

Somal, pertaining to the body.

Somatalgia, bodily pain.

Somatesthesia, bodily sensation.

Somatic, pertaining to the body.

Somnambulism, sleepwalking.

Somnifacient, causing sleep.

Somniferous, causing sleep.

Somniloquism, talking while asleep.

Somnolent, sleepy.

Soor, thrush.

Sophistication, adulteration of a product.

Sopor, coma.

Soporific, producing sleep.

Sore, an ulcer or wound.

Sore Throat, inflammation of pharynx, tonsils or larynx.

Sororiation, growth of breasts at puberty.

Soterocyte, blood platelet.

Sound, noise; auditory sensations caused by vibrations.

Space, area; region, segment.

Span, distance from fingertip to fingertip with arms outstretched.

Spanogyny, decrease in female births.

Spargosis, swelling of female breasts with milk; thickening of skin.

Spasm, contraction of any muscle that is sudden and involuntary.

Spasmodic, occurring in spasms.

Spasmophemia, stuttering.

Spasmophilia, tendency to spasms.

Spasmus, spasm.

Spastic, rigid; flexed; pertaining to spasms.

Spasticity, sustained increased muscle tension.

Spay, to remove female sex gland.

Specialists, one skilled in a particular field.

Species, category; classification.

Specimen, part of tissue or material used for analysis.

Spectacles, eye glasses.

Speculum, instrument which widens the opening of body cavities for examination.

Speech, thought expressed in words.

Sperm, male fertilizing cell.

Spermatocidal, killing sperm.

Sphacelate, to become gangrenous.

Sphacelation, gangrene.

Spheroma, spherelike tumor.

Sphincter, muscle that surrounds and closes an opening.

Sphincterismus, spasm of sphincter.

Sphygmic, pertaining to the pulse.

Sphygmomonometer, blood pressure gauge.

Spica, figure-of-8 bandage.

Spina, sharp protuberance; spine.

Spina Bifida, condition in which there is a defect in the development of the spinal column.

Spinal, pertaining to a spine.

Spinal Column, a series of bones in the back. The spinal column encloses and protects the spinal cord.

Spinal Cord, part of nervous system enclosed within the backbone; part of the nervous system which transmits impulses to and from the brain.

Spinal Curvature, condition where spine is abnormally bent forward or backward.

Spinal Fracture, broken back.

Spinal Nerves, the thirty-one pairs of nerves that start in the spinal cord and leave the spinal column through the spaces between the vertebrae.

Spine, sharp piece of bone; backbone.

Spinthecism, seeing sparks before the eyes.

Spirit, volatile liquid; alcoholic liquid.

Spirits of Ammonia, a fluid solution containing ammonia and alcohol.

Splanchnic, concerning abdominal organs.

Spleen, organ situated in the left upper part of the abdomen which manufactures, stores and destroys blood cells.

Splenalgia, pain in the spleen.

Splenauxe, enlargement of the spleen.

Splenectomy, surgical removal of spleen.

Splenic, pertaining to the spleen.

Splenitis, inflammation of the spleen.

Splenoma, splenic tumor.

Splenomegaly, enlargement of the spleen.

Splint, appliance to protect or stabilize injured part.

Spondyle, vertebra.

Spondylitis, inflammation of spine.

Sporadic, intermittent; occurring at different times and places.

Spot, blemish.

Sprain, injury of a joint caused by over-stretching of the ligaments.

Sprue, disease in which the patient is unable to absorb necessary nutrients.

Spur, pointed outgrowth.

Sputum, material that is spat out of mouth.

Squama, scale.

Squatting, sitting on the heels.

Stab, puncture with sharp object.

Stabilization, making firm and steady.

Stable, immobile.

Stactometer, device for measuring drops.

Staff, hospital personnel.

Stalagmometer, instrument for measuring drops.

Stamina, endurance.

Stammering, hesitant speech.

Stanch, to stop a flow of blood.

Stapedectomy, an operation to correct a hearing loss that has been caused by otosclerosis.

Stapes, small bone of middle ear.

Staphylococcus, bacteria causing body infection.

Staphyloma, budging of the white of the eye.

Starch, a form of carbohydrate.

Starvation, continued deprivation of food.

Stasis, stoppage of flow of blood or urine.

Stasophobia, extreme fear of standing up.

Stat., at once.

State, condition.

Statim, at once.

Status, condition; state.

Steatitis, inflammation of fatty tissue.

Steatopygia, having large buttocks.

Stillate, star-like shape.

Stenochoria, stenosis.

Stenosed, narrowed; constricted.

Stenosis, constricted; decrease in diameter.

Stercus, excrement.

Stereotypy, persistence of a single idea.

Sterile, barren; aseptic.

Sterility, inability to have children.

Sterilize, to make bacteria free; remove ability to reproduce.

Sterilizer, device for eliminating bacteria on instruments.

Sternal, pertaining to the sternum.

Sternalgia, pain in the sternum.

Sternodynia, pain in breastbone.

Sternum, breastbone.

Sternutation, sneezing.

Steroids, a collective term for a group of chemically similar compounds.

Stertor, snoring.

Stethalgia, chest pain.

Stethoscope, instrument used to listen to sounds of body.

Sthenia, force; strength.

Stigma, mark or spot on tissue.

Stigmatosis, skin disease characterized by ulcerated spots.

Stillbirth, birth of a dead baby.

Stillborn, born dead.

Stimulant, anything that increases activity.

Stimulus, exciting agent.

Stitch, localized sharp pain; sewing loop.

Stokes-Adams Syndrome, sudden attacks of unconsciousness.

Stoma, mouth.

Stomach, large pouch where food digestion begins.

Stomach Ulcers, sores or ulcer in stomach wall usually due to increased secretion of acid.

Stomachalgia, pain in the stomach.

Stomachic, gastric stimulant.

Stomatalgia, pain in mouth.

Stomatitis, inflammation of the mouth.

Stomatodynia, pain in mouth.

Stomatopathy, any mouth disorder.

Stool, feces.

Strabismus, squint, cross-eye.

Strain, overexertion; overstretching.

Strait, narrow passage.

Strangulation, choking; stopping of blood supply.

Strangury, painful urination.

Strap, bind with bandages.

Stratified, layered.

Stratum, layer of tissue nearly uniform in thickness.

Streak, line; stripe.

"Strep" Throat, a common childhood illness caused by a bacterial infection, which is treated with antibiotics.

Streptococcus, an organism infecting man.

Streptomycin, an antibiotic drug.

Stress, physical or emotional factor which causes tension in the body or in the mind. Stress is often a contributory factor in heart disease, ulcers, and elevated blood pressure, as well as other illnesses.

Stretcher, device for carrying the sick.

Stria, linear mark or line on body.

Striate, having streaks.

Stricture, narrowing of any tube in the body.

Stridor, harsh, rasping breath sound.

Stroke, apoplexy; seizure; fit.

Stroke Volume, the amount of blood that is pumped out of the heart at each contraction of the heart.

Stroma, framework of an organ.

Struma, goiter.

Strumectomy, thyroidectomy.

Strychnism, strychnine poisoning.

Stump, remaining part of limb after amputation.

Stun, momentary loss of consciousness.

Stupefacient, narcotic.

Stupemania, manic stupor.

Stupor, state of decreased feeling.

Stuttering, speech impediment characterized by repeating syllables.

Sty, infection of gland of eyelid.

Subacute, mildly acute.

Subclavian, below collar bone.

Subclavian Arteries, two large arteries that are located beneath the clavicle or shoulder bone.

Subconscious, out of awareness.

Subcostal, below a rib.

Subcutaneous, under the skin.

Subcutaneous Tissue, tissue located beneath the skin.

Subdelirium, mild delirium.

Sublatio, detachment of a part.

Sublimation, process of passing from solid to vapor state without liquifying.

Subliminal, below conscious awareness.

Sublingual Gland, salivary gland beneath tongue.

Subluxation, minor dislocation.

Submaxilla, mandible.

Submixillary Gland, salivary gland along jaw.

Submental, beneath the chin.

Subphrenic, beneath the diaphragm.

Subscription, part of a prescription giving directions for compounding the ingredients.

Substance, material of which a thing is composed.

Substantia, substance.

Subtotal, incomplete.

Sububeres, unweaned infants.

Subungual, beneath a nail.

Subvirile, lacking in virility.

Succorrhea, excessive secretion.

Succus, fluid secretion.

Sucrose, a complex sugar.

Sudation, perspiring.

Sudatorium, sweat bath.

Sudden Infant Death, the sudden, unexpected and unexplained death of an apparently healthy baby. This syndrome attacks infants between the ages of two weeks and two years.

Sudor, sweat.

Sudoresis, excessive sweating.

Suffocation, blockage of air ways.

Suffusion, spreading; diffusion.

Sugar, carbohydrate.

Suicide, self-destruction.

Sulcus, groove or furrow.

Sulfa Drugs, name referring to the group of drugs used in the treatment of various bacterial diseases.

Sulfonamides, a class of drugs used to treat infections that are caused by bacteria.

Sulfur, a pale-yellow, naturally occurring element used to treat infections or problems caused by fungus or by parasites.

Sunburn, skin inflammation from sun's rays.

Sunstroke, stroke due to excessive exposure to the sun.

Superalimentation, excessive feeding.

Superciliary, concerning eyebrow.

Supercilium, eyebrow.

Superego, conscience.

Superficial, near the surface.

Superinfection, an occasional complication that follows the use of antibiotics for the treatment of infections.

Superlactation, oversecretion of milk.

Supernumeray, more than usual.

Superscription, Rx before a prescription.

Supinate, turn hand upward.

Supine, lying flat on back.

Suppository, solid medication for insertion into a cavity other than the mouth.

Suppurate, form infection.

Sura, calf of the leg.

Sural, pertaining to the calf.

Suralimentation, overfeeding.

Surditas, deafness.

Surdomute, deaf and dumb.

Surgeon, medical specialist performing surgery.

Surgery, specialty of medicine that deals with disease and trauma by operative means.

Surgical, pertaining to surgery.

Surrogate, a substitute.

Susceptible, having little resistance, easily influenced.

Suspiration, sigh.

Suspirious, breathing heavily.

Susurration, murmur.

Suture, to stitch together.

Swab, gauze wrapped around a stick for application of medicine.

Sweat, perspiration.

Sweat Gland, a coiled, tubular gland embedded in the dermis.

Syllepsis, pregnancy.

Symbiosis, a relationship between two organisms in which one organism harbors or nourishes another organism.

Symmetry, similar parts on opposite sides.

Sympathetic Nervous System, one of two parts of the autonomic nervous system. With the parasympathetic nervous system, the sympathetic nervous system regulates tissues not under voluntary control, such as the glands, the heart, and the smooth muscles.

Symphysis, immovable joint.

Symphysis Pubis, pubic bones above the midline of the external genital.

Symptom, perceptible change from normal function.

Syndrome, any group of symptoms commonly occurring together.

Synechia, abnormal joining of parts.

Synergists, drugs that work together. The combined effect of the drugs is greater than the normal effects of the separate drugs.

Synergy, cooperation.

Syngamy, sexual reproduction.

Synizesis, contraction of the eye pupil.

Synovial Membranes, membranes that serve as linings for joints.

Synovitis, inflammation of the lining of a joint.

Syntaxis, junction of two bones.

Syphilis, serious venereal disease.

Syrinx, cavity or tube.

Systemic Circulation, the circulation of the blood through all parts of the body except the lungs.

Systole, period during which contraction of heart takes place.

— T —

Tabefacation, emaciation.

Tabes, gradual deterioration in chronic illness.

Tabes Dorsalis, a disease of the nervous system leading to paralysis and caused by syphilis.

Tablet, pill.

Tabule, pill.

Tache, spot; blemish.

Tachycardia, rapid beating of the heart coming on in sudden attacks.

Tachylalia, rapid speech.

Tachyphagia, rapid eating.

Tachyphasia, rapid speech.

Tachypnea, unusually fast rate of breathing.

Tachyrhythmia, rapid heart action.

Tactile, pertaining to sense of touch.

Tactual, pertaining to touch.

Tactus, touch.

Taenia, band-like muscle or tissue; tapeworm.

Tagma, protoplasm.

Talalgia, pain in the heel.

Talc, a powder.

Talipes, club foot.

Talipes Planus, flatfoot.

Tallus, ankle.

Tampon, round cotton plug used to close wound or cavity.

Tamponade, act of plugging.

Tannic Acid, one of the most valuable astringents (drugs that have the power to contract tissue).

Tap, puncture of body cavity.

Tapeworm, type of intestinal worm.

Taphephobia, extreme fear of live burial.

Tarsal, pertaining to the eyelid or the instep.

Tarsus, arch of foot.

Tartar, dental calculus.

Taste, sensation through nerves on tongue.

T.A.T., toxin-antoxin.

Taxonomy, science of classification of plants and animals.

Tay-Sachs Disease, an inherited disorder that destroys the nervous system and is always fatal. Tay-Sachs disease is caused by the absence of an enzyme (called hexosaminidase) that normally aids in the breakdown of fat.

Tear, saline fluid secreted by lacrimal glands.

Teat, nipple.

Technic, technique.

Technique, method; procedure.

Tectonic, pertaining to plastic surgery.

Tectum, roof-like structure.

Teeth, bony growths in jaw used for chewing.

Teeth, Milk, first set of teeth.

Teething, appearance of teeth.

Tegmen, covering.

Tegument, skin.

Teinodynia, pain in the tendons.

Tela, weblike structure.

Telalgia, referred pain.

Telangitis, inflammation of capillaries.

Telangiosis, disease of capillary vessels.

Teleorganic, vital.

Telepathist, mind reader.

Telepathy, communication of two minds at a distance through means undetectable by science.

Telergy, automatism.

Telesthesia, extrasensory perception.

Temperament, physical and mental characteristics of an individual.

Temperature, degree of heat and cold; body temperature is normally 98.6.

Temple, area in front of ear.

Temporal, pertaining to the temple or time.

Temulence, drunkenness.

Tenacious, adhesive.

Tenalgia, pain in a tendon.

Tenderness, soreness.

Tendinitis, inflammation of a tendon.

Tendinous, pertaining to or composed of tendons.

Tendo, tendon.

Tendon, fibrous tissue that connects muscles to other structures.

Tenectomy, surgical removal of a tendon.

Tenesmus, spasm of anus or bladder.

Tenia, tapeworm; band.

Teniacide, medication which destroys tapeworms.

Tennis Elbow, pain in the arm, particularly on twisting inwards, caused by excessive strain.

Tenodynia, pain in a tendon.

Tenonitis, inflammation of tendon.

Tenoplasty, surgical repair of a tendon.

Tenorrhaphy, suture of a tendon.

Tenosynovitis, inflammation of a tendon and its sheath.

Tension, condition of being strained or stretched.

Tentative, subject to change.

Tentigo, unusual sex desires.

Tephrosis, cremation.

Tepid, warm.

Tepidorium, warm bath.

Teras, fetal monster.

Teratism, fetal monster.

Teratoid, monster.

Teratology, science dealing with monstrosities and malformations.

Tere, to rub.

Terebration, boring.

Teres, round; smooth.

Term, boundary; definite period of time.

Terminal, end.

Terracing, suturing in several rows.

Terror, extreme fear.

Testicles, the male reproductive glands.

Testis, male reproductive gland.

Tetanus, infectious disease characterized by painful spasms of voluntary muscles.

Tetany, disease characterized by painful muscle spasms with convulsive movements, usually due to inability to utilize calcium.

Tetracycline, a drug and a class of drugs that are antibiotics.

Tetralogy of Fallot, a congenital malformation of the heart involving four distinct defects.

Tetraplegia, paralysis of all four extremities.

Tetter, blister; pimple.

Textural, pertaining to the constitution of tissues.

Thalamus, area in the brain concerned with many bodily functions, often called the seat of the emotions.

Thalassemia, a disease resembling sickle-cell anemia.

Thalassophobia, extreme fear of sea.

Thalidomide, a sedative drug.

Thanatobiologic, pertaining to life and death.

Thanatoid, resembling death.

Thanatomania, suicidal obsession.

Thebaism, opium poisoning.

Theca, case; sheath.

Theism, poisoning from overdose of tea.

Thelalgia, pain in nipples.

Thelerethism, erection of the nipple.

Thelitis, inflammation of nipple.

Thelium, nipple.

Thenal, pertaining to the palm.

Thenar, area beneath thumb; palm.

Theomania, delusion that one is a deity.

Theory, hypothesis.

Therapeutic, pertaining to healing.

Therapeutics, scientific treatment of disease.

Therapist, a person skilled in the treatment of disease.

Therapy, treatment of disease.

Thermal, pertaining to heat.

Thermanalgesia, inability to react to heat.

Thermesthesia, perception of heat or cold.

Thermic, pertaining to heat.

Thermofuge, reducing fever.

Thermometer, instrument to measure heat.

Thermoplegia, heatstroke; sunstroke.

Thermostat, device for controlling heat.

Thigh, part of leg above knee.

Thiocyanate, a chemical that causes the dilation of the blood vessels, thus lowering blood pressure.

Thirst, desire for liquid.

Thoracalgia, chest pain.

Thoracic, pertaining to the chest.

Thoracectomy, surgical removal of a rib.

Thoracodynia, pain in thorax.

Thoracomyodynia, pain in chest muscles.

Thoracoschisis, fissure of chest wall.

Thoracotomy, surgical opening of chest.

Thorax, chest.

Threadworm, parasitic worm.

Threpsology, study of nutrition.

Threshold, point at which an effect is produced.

Thrill, heart murmur or abnormal blood vessel tremor that can be felt.

Thrix, hair.

Throat, area between mouth and esophagus.

Throb, pulsation.

Throe, sharp pain.

Thrombectomy, an operation to remove a blood clot from a blood vessel.

Thrombin, substance in blood which aids clotting.

Thrombocytes, blood platelets.

Thrombopathy, defective blood clotting.

Thrombophlebitis, inflammation of a vein.

Thrombosin, thrombin.

Thrombosis, formation of a clot within a blood vessel.

Thrombus, blood clot.

Thrush, disease of the mouth and throat caused by a fungus.

Thumb, first digit of hand.

Thymectomy, surgical removal of thymus.

Thymona, tumor of thyroid.

Thymion, wart.

Thymitis, inflammation of thyroid gland.

Thymona, tumor of thymus.

Thymus, glandular structure in the chest having an unknown function.

Thyroadenitis, inflammation of thyroid.

Thyrocele, goiter.

Thyrogenic, originating in thyroid.

Thyroid, glandular structure in the neck secreting thyroxin, a substance vital to life.

Thyroidectomy, surgical removal of all or part of the thyroid gland.

Thyroiditis, inflammation of the thyroid gland.

Thyrotropic Hormone, a hormone that influences the thyroid gland, stimulating the thyroid gland to secrete its hormone (thyroxin).

Thyroxin, hormone secreted by the thyroid gland.

Tibia, shin bone.

Tibial, pertaining to the tibia.

Tic, muscular twitch, usually of the face.

Tick, blood sucking parasite.

Tigroid, striped.

Tilmus, pulling out of hair.

Tincture, an alcoholic or hydroalcoholic solution used either for their therapeutic content or as flavoring agents or perfumes.

Tinea, ringworm.

Tinnitus, noises in the ear which may take the form of buzzing, clicking or thudding.

Tiqueur, one afflicted with a tic.

Tire, exhaust, fatigue.

Tissue, structure of body made up of similar cells.

Tissue Culture, the technique of growing plant or animal cells in containers outside the body by using a medium that contains a variety of nutrients.

Tobacosis, tobacco poisoning.

Tobagism, tobacco poisoning.

Tocalogy, obstetrical science.

Tocophobia, extreme fear of childbirth.

Tocus, childbirth.

Toe, digit of the foot.

Toilet Training, the method by which a child learns how to control his bowels and bladder.

Tolerance, endurance.

Tongue, organ of speech and taste.

Tongue-Tie, congenital shortening of frenuum below tongue.

Tonic, muscular tightness.

Tonometer, an instrument for measuring eye pressure.

Tonsil, mass or special lymph tissue.

Tonsilla, tonsil.

Tonsillectomy, removal of tonsils.

Tonsillitis, infection of the tonsils.

Tooth, hard structure in the jaws used for chewing.

Tophaceous, gritty, sandy.

Topical, pertaining to a particular spot.

Topoalgia, localized pain.

Toponarcosis, local anesthesia.

Torpidity, sluggishness.

Torpor, inactivity; apathy.

Torsion, twisting.

Torso, trunk of body.

Torticollis, wryneck; abnormal twisting of the neck caused by injury or infection to the muscle or nerve.

Torulus, small elevation.

Touch, tactile sense.

Tourniquet, band used to control bleeding.

Toxemia, any illness due to poisons absorbed from organisms in the system.

Toxenzyme, any poisonous enzyme.

Toxic, poisonous.

Toxicant, poisonous; a poison.

Toxicity, poisonous.

Toxicohemia, toxemia.

Toxicology, science dealing with poisons.

Toxicophobia, extreme fear of poisons.

Toxin, a term used to describe the poisonous substances released by bacteria.

Toxipathy, disease caused by poisoning.

T.P.R., temperature, pulse, respiration.

Trachea, the windpipe.

Tracheal, pertaining to trachea.

Tracheitis, inflammation of the windpipe.

Trachelagra, gout in the neck.

Trachelismus, spasm of neck muscles.

Tracheofissure, incision of trachea.

Tracheostomy, an emergency procedure to open the trachea and place a breathing tube through the opening down the trachea.

Tracheotomy, cutting into windpipe to relieve obstruction.

Trachitis, inflammation of trachea.

Trachoma, infectious disease of the eyes.

Trachyphonia, roughness of the voice.

Traction, pulling or drawing.

Tragopodia, knock-knee.

Trait, distinguishing characteristic.

Trance, sleeplike state.

Tranquilizer, calming agent.

Transcalent, able to be penetrated by heat rays.

Transfix, pierce.

Transforation, perforation of the skull of a fetus.

Transfusion, giving of one's blood to another.

Transmissable, communicable.

Transmission, communication of a disease from one person to another.

Transpirable, allowing passage of perspiration.

Transplant, remove tissue from one part of the body to another.

Transplantation, the removal of a body organ or body tissue from one individual and placing that organ or tissue in another individual.

Transverse, extending from side to side.

Transvestitism, uncontrollable urge to dress in the clothing of the opposite sex.

Trapizius, muscle of back.

Trauma, injury; wound.

Trauma, Psychic, injury to subconscious due to emotional shock.

Treatment, medical care of a patient.

Tremor, shake or quiver.

Tremulous, quivering.

Trench Mouth, mouth infection caused by organism; also called Vincent's angina.

Trend, course.

Trepan, to make a hole in skull to relieve pressure on brain.

Tresis, perforation.

Triamcinolone, a drug used in treating psoriasis.

Trichangiectasis, dilation of capillaries.

Trichauxe, excessive hair growth.

Trichinosis, disease caused by the trichina organism found in raw pork.

Trichitis, inflammation of the hair roots.

Trichobezar, hair-ball found in intestinal tract.

Trichocardia, hairy heart.

Trichoclasia, brittleness of hair.

Trichocryptosis, brittleness of hair.

Trichology, science of hair care.

Trichoptilosis, hair splitting.

Trichosis, any hair disease.

Tricuspid Valve, a valve consisting of three cusps or triangular segments; it is located between the upper and lower chamber in the right side of the heart.

Trifid, divided into three parts.

Trigeminal Nerve, one of the twelve pairs of cranial nerves.

Trigonid, first three cusps of a lower molar tooth.

Trilobate, having three lobes.

Triorchid, having three testes.

Triphasic, having three phases.

Triplegia, paralysis of three extremities.

Triplets, the birth of three babies as a result of a single pregnancy.

Triquetrum, wrist bone.

Trismus, spasm of jaw muscles.

Tristimania, melancholia.

Troche, lozenge.

Trochlear Nerve, one of the twelve pairs of cranial nerves.

Trochocardia, rotation of the heart on its axis.

Trochoides, pivot joint.

Trophic, pertaining to nutrition.

Trophic Nerves, specialized nerves that are concerned with the growth, nourishment, and repair of body tissues.

Trophology, science of body nutrition.

Trophonosis, any nutritional disease.

Truncal, pertaining to the trunk.

Truncate, cut off limbs or branches.

Truncus, trunk.

Trunk, torso.

Truss, device to hold hernia in place.

Trypsin, an enzyme produced by the pancreas.

Tube, long, hollow cylindrical structure.

Tuber, enlargement; swelling.

Tubercle, small swelling; rounded elevation on a bone; change in tissue caused by the tuberculosis germ.

Tuberculated, covered with tubercles.

Tuberculin, an extract made from dead tubercle bacilli (the cause of tuberculosis).

Tuberculophobia, extreme fear of tuberculosis.

Tuberculosis, infectious disease of man and animals caused by tubercle bacilli having many and varied manifestations in lungs, brain, bone, etc.

Tuberculous, caused by or having tuberculosis.

Tuberosity, bone projection.

Tubule, small tube.

Tuborrhea, discharge from eustachian tube.

Tularemia, an infectious disease transmitted by insects or small animals caused by the pasteurella organism.

Tumefaction, swelling.

Tumesence, swelling.

Tumor, a swelling or growth.

Tunic, lining membrane.

Tunnel, enclosed passage.

Turbidity, cloudiness.

Turgesence, distention; swelling.

Turgescent, becoming swollen.

Turgid, congested and swollen.

Turgor, swelling.

Tussis, cough.

Tutamen, a protection.

Twin, one of two persons of the same birth.

Twitch, slight muscular contraction.

Tyloma, callus.

Tylosis, formation of callosities.

Tympanal, pertaining to the tympanum.

Tympanic Membrane, a tightly stretched membrane that separates the auditory canal from the middle ear.

Tympanites, abdominal distention due to gas or air.

Tympanous, distended with gas.

Tympanum, ear drum.

Typhlosis, blindness.

Typhoid Fever, an infectious fever caused by the typhoid bacillus, characterized by diarrhea and other symptoms.

Typhomania, delirium found with typhoid fever.

Typhous, pertaining to typhus.

Typhus, a term indicating any one of a group of diseases and infections caused by rickettsia (a type of microorganism).

—U—

Uberous, prolific.

Uberty, fertility.

Ulalgia, pain in the gums.

Ulatrophia, shrinkage of gums.

Ulcer, sores on skin or internal parts of body caused by various things.

Ulceration, formation of an ulcer.

Ulcerative Colitis, an inflamed condition of the colon and rectum, which are the lowermost portions of the bowel.

Ulcus, ulcer.

Ulectomy, surgical removal of part of gums; removal of scar tissue.

Ulemorrhagia, bleeding from the gums.

Ulitis, gum inflammation.

Ulna, bone of forearm.

Ulnar, pertaining to the ulna.

Ulocace, ulcer and infection of gums.

Uloid, scarlike.

Ulorrhagia, bleeding from gums.

Ulosis, scar formation.

Ultrasound, diagnostic procedure using sound waves to produce a detailed image. Particularly valuable because it is neither painful nor harmful.

Ultraviolet Rays, invisible rays that are beyond the violet end of the spectrum.

Ululation, hysterical crying.

Umbilical Cord, the cord that connects the placenta at one end and the baby's navel at the other end.

Umbilicus, site on abodomen of attachment of umbilical cord.

Umbo, funnel-shaped area of ear drum.

Unciform, hook-shaped; bone of wrist.

Unconscious, state in which person is unaware of both his external and internal environment as in a faint.

Unction, ointment.

Unctuus, oily.

Undulant Fever, an infectious disease caused by the Brucella organism; found in animals and transmitted to man.

Undulation, wave.

Ungual, pertaining to the nails.

Unguent, ointment.

Unguis, fingernail or toenail.

Unilateral, pertaining to one side.

Unigravida, woman in her first pregnancy.

Union, juncture.

Unipara, woman who has borne one live child.

Universal Antidote, an antidote that has been devised for use when a patient has taken a poison but the exact nature or type of the poison is not known.

Uracratia, inability to retain urine.

Uraniscus, palate.

Uranium, radioactive element.

Urea, one of the waste products of the body's metabolic processes.

Uredo, sensation of burning on skin.

Uremia, poisoning from urinary substances in the blood.

Ureter, the tube leading from the kidneys to the bladder.

Ureterolith, stone in the ureter.

Uretha, tube which carries the urine from the bladder to the outside.

Urethritis, inflammation of the urethra.

Uretic, promoting urination.

Uric Acid, an organic substance that is a solid waste product contained in urine.

Urinary, pertaining to urine.

Urinary Meatus, the external opening of the male urethra located in the penis.

Urinate, discharge urine.

Urine, fluid end product of kidney activity.

Urologist, medical specialist who deals with organs producing and transportating urine.

Urology, study of the urinary systen

Uroschesis, to retain urine.

Urous, urine-like.

Urticaria, hives.

Ustion, incinerate, burn.

Ustus, burned.

Uterine, pertaining to the womb.

Uterus, womb.

Utricle, one of two small sacs located next to the cochlea of the inner ear.

Uvea, tissue layer of eye.

Uvula, small tissue projecting in the middle of palate in throat.

— V —

Vaccination, injection with a germ or germ product to produce immunity and protect against disease.

Vaccine, substance used for inoculation.

Vaccinia, contagious disease as a result of inoculation with cowpox virus.

Vagina, the passage connecting the outer and inner female sex organs.

Vaginismus, painful spasm of the vagina.

Vaginitis, inflammation of vagina.

Vagus, tenth cranial nerve.

Valence, ability of a chemical agent to combine in a reaction.

Valetudinarian, person afflicted with frequent illness.

Valgus, bowlegged; knock-kneed.

Valve, structure which prevents backward flow in a passage.

Valvular Insufficiency, a term applied to valves that close improperly and admit a backflow of blood in the wrong direction.

Valvulitis, inflammation of a valve.

Valvulotomy, incision of a heart valve.

Vaporizer, a small piece of equipment that heats water and releases it into the air.

Varicella, chickenpox.

Varices, enlarged, tortuoris vein.

Varicocle, varicose veins in the area of scrotum.

Varicose Veins, swollen veins caused by improper valve function.

Varicosities, an alternate term for varicose veins.

Variola, smallpox.

Vas, vessel, passageway.

Vascular, pertaining to blood vessels.

Vas Deferens, duct in testis which transports semen.

Vasectomy, excision of vas deferens; operation to sterilize male.

Vasoconstrictor, causing a narrowing of blood vessels.

Vasodepressor, agent which relaxes the blood vessels, thus increasing diameter and lowering blood pressure.

Vasodilator, an agent or substance that causes the blood vessels to relax.

Vasospasm, sudden decrease in caliber of blood vessel.

Vasopressor, a chemical substance that causes the muscles of the arterioles to contract, thus narrowing the arteriole passage and raising the blood pressure.

Vein, blood vessels carrying blood to heart.

Vena Cava, two large veins that empty into the heart.

Venereal, pertaining to sexual intercourse.

Venereal Disease, any infectious disease that is transmitted almost exclusively from person to person through sexual intercourse.

Venery, sexual intercourse.

Venesection, puncture of a vein to remove blood.

Venipuncture, surgical puncture of a vein.

Venom, poison from an animal.

Venous Blood, unoxygenated blood.

Ventricle, small cavity; pouch.

Ventricular Septum, the muscular wall that divides the left and right lower chambers of the heart (the ventricles).

Veratrum, a drug that lowers the blood pressure and decreases the heart rate.

Vermis, worm.

Vernix, a white, creamy substance that forms on the body of a fetus at about the seventh month.

Verruca, wart.

Version, turning; changing the position of the fetus in the womb to facilitate birth.

Vertebra, bone of the spinal column.

Vertex, crown of the head.

Vertical, pertaining to the vertex.

Vertigo, dizziness.

Vesica, bladder.

Vesicant, blistering.

Vesicle, blister; small bladder.

Vessel, tube; passageway.

Vestigial, non-functioning part in body more highly developed in embryo or lower animal.

Viable, alive.

Vibex, linear spots beneath skin due to hemorrhage.

Vibrissal, stiff hairs in nose.

Vibrio, a class of bacteria.

Vicious, faulty.

Vigil, wakefullness.

Villi, the minute, hairlike projections that cover the mucous membrane lining of the small intestine.

Vincent's Angina, mouth infection; also called trench mouth.

Vinum, wine.

Virgin, one who has not experienced sexual relations.

Virile, masculine, mature.

Virilism, maleness.

Virology, study of virus and viral diseases.

Virose, poisonous.

Virulence, poisonousness; infectiousness; endangering life.

Viruses, minute organisms which cause certain diseases among which are the common cold, measles, mumps, poliomyelitis, chickenpox, smallpox.

Vis, energy, power.

Viscera, organs within body.

Visceral Pericardium, the outer layer of the heart wall.

Viscid, thick; adherent.

Vision, sight; seeing.

Visual Field, the total area perceived when the eyes are focused straight ahead.

Vitals, important body organs.

Vital Signs, the temperature, pulse, and respiration of a patient.

Vitamins, chemical substances found in foods that are necessary for proper bodily function.

Vitiligo, lack of pigment in certain areas of the skin.

Vitium, a defect.

Vitiation, injury; decrease in function of a part.

Vitreous Body, the semifluid, transparent substance that lies between the retina and the lens of the eye.

Vivisect, to cut or dissect living animal.

Vocal Cords, tissue bands whose vibration causes speech.

Voice, sounds produced by the vibration of the vocal cords.

Void, to empty bladder or rectum.

Volce, palm or sole of foot.

Volition, act of selecting.

Volkmann's Contracture, a condition in which the fingers contract.

Volvulus, twisting of the bowel causing obstruction.

Vomer, bone of nose.

Vomicose, containing ulcers.

Vomiting, dislodging the food in stomach through mouth.

Vomitus, vomited material.

Vox, voice.

Voyeur, person receiving sexual pleasure from watching activities of others.

Vril, inborn energy from birth leading to maturity.

Vulva, female genital.

Vulvitis, inflammation of the female external genitalia.

Vulnus, wound.

—W—

Waist, area between chest and hip encircling body.

Walleye, a form of strabismus. Walleye is a condition in which one or both eyes turn out (as opposed to crossed eyes, in which the eyes turn in).

Wangensteen Tube, a tube that is inserted into the stomach through the nostrils and pharynx to provide constant drainage of the gastrointestinal tract.

Wart, growth on the skin that may be cause by viruses.

Wasserman Test, test of the blood to determine if syphilis is present.

Waste Products, substances that have entered the body (usually as food or beverages) but which cannot be used by the body and are excreted in the form of feces, urine, and sweat.

Water on the Knee, a condition in which there is an inflammation of the membrane in the knees. Fluid collects in the area as part of the inflammation.

Wean, substitution of other substances for breast milk.

Webbed, connected by a thin membrane.

Weeping crying; seeping of a fluid.

Wen, a sebaceous cyst.

Wernicke's Center, an area of the cerebral cortex of the brain. Wernicke's center is responsible for the ability to understand words that are spoken.

Wheal, a red, round elevation on skin.

Wheeze, sound in chest due to abnormalities in lungs.

Whiplash, injury to the neck sustained in a car accident in which the car is hit from behind, causing the neck to snap back and then forwards.

White Blood Cells, cells that allow the body to defend itself against disease.

White Leg, swelling and blanching of the leg produced by thrombosis of the veins.

Whooping Cough, infectious disease characterized by episodes of coughing punctuated by whooping noises between episodes during periods of gasping for breath, pertussis.

Wintergreen Oil, a salve or liniment used in the treatment of strained muscles and for relief of rheumatoid conditions.

Wisdom Tooth, the most posterior teeth or molar on each side of jaw.

Withdrawal Sickness, a term used to describe the various symptoms a drug or narcotics addict experiences when the use of the addicting substance is stopped abruptly.

Woman, mature female.

Womb, uterus; organ in which developing fetus resides.

Work Classification Unit, a community facility involving a team approach to assessing the ability of a cardiac patient to work in terms of the energy requirements of the job.

Wound, an injury or break in the skin.

Wrist, joint between forearm and hand.

Wryneck, torticollis; a condition that causes the head to turn to one side in spasms.

—X—

Xanthic, yellow.

Xanthocyanopsia, a form of color blindness in which the patient cannot tell the difference between green and red colors.

Xanthoma, yellow tumor or growth.

Xanthopsia, yellow vision.

Xanthosis, jaundice.

X Chromosome, one of the two sex chromosomes.

Xenogenous, disease caused by foreign body or toxin.

Xenomenia, bleeding from other than normal site at time of menstrual period.

Xenophobia, extreme fear of strangers.

Xenopthalmia, inflammation of eye due to foreign body.

Xeransis, condition of dryness.

Xerasia, dryness of hair leading to baldness.

Xerocheilia, dry lips.

Xeroderma, a skin disease characterized by dryness.

Xerophthalmia, eye condition in which the lining membrane of the lid and eyeball is dry and thickened.

Xerosis, condition of dryness.

Xerostomia, dryness of the mouth.

Xiphoid, sword-shaped cartilage at lowest part of breast bone.

X-Ray, device used to photograph interior parts of body; also used as therapeutic tool.

Xylometazoline, a drug used as a nasal decongestant.

Xysma, membranous like material in some diarrhea stools.

Xyster, surgical instrument used to scrape bone.

— Y —

Yawn, involuntary opening mouth when fatigued.

Yaws, tropical disease.

Y Chromosome, one of the two sex chromosomes.

Yeast, a rich source of vitamin B.

Yellow Bone Marrow, ordinary bone marrow in which fat cells predominate.

Yellow Fever, infectious fever found in tropical lands.

Yellow Mercuric Oxide, an ointment used as an antiseptic in the treatment of eye infections and in certain other skin infections where antibiotics cannot be used because of sensitivity.

Youth, period of adolescence between childhood and adult life.

— Z —

Zein, protein from corn.

Zestocausis, to burn with steam.

Zinc, a metal used in medicines.

Zoanthropy, belief that one is an animal.

Zoetic, pertaining to life.

Zondal-Aschheim Test, test to determine pregnancy.

Zonesthesia, sensation of tightness around the waist.

Zooerastea, coitus with an animal.

Zooid, animal-like.

Zoonoses, diseases of animals that accidentally affect man.

Zoopsia, hallucinations involving animals.

Zoosis, disease in man carried by animals.

Zoxazolamine, a drug that is used as a skeletal muscle relaxant.

Zygoma, a part of the cheek bone.

Zygote, a fertilized ovum, formed by the union of a sperm and an ovum.

Zyme, fermenting substance.

SECRETARY'S HANDBOOK

Introduction

This book does not assume that today all secretaries are female or that all executives are male. Many modern offices have competent male secretaries as well as top-notch female executives. However, there is a need here to use singular pronouns for both positions. For purposes of clarity the secretary will be referred to in the female gender and the executive in the male gender.

Mechanization, electronic processes, and automation all have contributed to changes in office routine and procedure. Despite these time-savers of the late twentieth century, the position of the secretary is, if anything, more important than ever before. The scope of her work may have changed; for instance, she no longer has to lick postage stamps if there is an automatic stamp machine in the office. However, the secretary is still very much responsible for the contents of the letter her executive signs. A large telephone switchboard may eliminate the need for contact with the general public, but she will still be the girl Friday who greets people who want to contact her executive.

The secretary must be expert at time-management, a cordial and unhurried hostess to those waiting for an appointment, part-time bookkeeper, accountant, and purchasing agent. In short, a good secretary has at her fingertips the answers to a thousand questions — and, if she does not, she knows where to find them. Finding those answers is what this book is all about.

WHAT IS A SECRETARY?

A matter of semantics often confuses a secretary with a stenographer. A stenographer, according to the dictionary, is a person who takes dictation, usually in shorthand, and transcribes that dictation in typewriting.

A secretary, also according to the dictionary, is a person employed to keep records and take care of correspondence and other writing tasks for an organization or an individual. There is quite a difference between a stenographer and a secretary.

Frequently, a secretary functions as an executive assistant who relieves the executive of many routine and specialized details of the office. She is a link between the maker of decisions—the executive—and the person or persons who implement those decisions. Her work demands initiative, as she may be called on regularly to make decisions herself. These may be as simple as deciding whether to page her executive if he is out of his office or to take a message from the caller. They may be complex decisions that will actually affect the carrying out of business for the firm.

Today's secretary is a highly specialized and well-trained member of the office team. She has been referred to as an "executive-extender."

The National Secretaries Association (International) is an organization directed toward raising secretarial standards through continuing education. It is through them that the Certified Professional Secretary Examination is given--a test that requires high standards of expertise for those secretaries who are certified.

The philosophy of the National Secretaries Association (International) is carried out by many colleges and universities throughout the country. These offer courses in all phases of business to prepare the secretary better with knowledge of the workings of the economic world in which she will be functioning.

In short, today's secretary can and should be a highly trained person whose advancement depends on her own ability.

HOW TO IMPROVE AS A SECRETARY

Whether you are an executive secretary or a very small cog in a large wheel, you should be up-to-date on secretarial skills. The more you know, the more competent you can be. Check your skills and general education. If English grammar is your weakness, take a course in the subject. If you are involved with accounting or bookkeeping for your executive, check with an accountant to clear up any bugs in the system you are now using. Ask the bank for current information on checking accounts. Seek to improve your efficiency in your job by learning all you can about every phase of that job. You will be improving yourself with this knowledge and will become a more efficient member of your office team. You, the secretary, are important. Evaluating yourself in relation to your job will enhance your worth.

You will regularly be called on to set up work priorities — deciding what should be done when. An important letter takes precedence over a routine report. Both must be completed on time. Interruptions from the telephone must be figured into each day's work schedule. Each day is different from every other, and each day calls forth decisions, both large and small, that affect you and your executive.

Change a preposition and increase your stature as a secretary. Work "with" your executive rather than "for" him. This kind of positive thinking will increase your value.

This book will not give you all the answers. Hopefully, however, it will answer some of your questions as well as make suggestions as to where to find more detailed information.

BASIC SECRETARIAL SKILLS

Basic secretarial skills may vary from one office to another, but there are general requirements that apply to most places of business, whether large corporations or small one-man shops. Most of these basic skills are taught in a good secretarial school, and most stenographers have this knowledge, too. If it has been years since you took your secretarial training, you can improve yourself by brushing up on one or all the skills mentioned. To improve in your job, all basic skills need to be updated from time to time.

Dictation

With the increased use of machines for dictation, a secretary may not need the shorthand learned in school. However, some executives still prefer the one-to-one relationship of seated secretary with her spiral-bound notebook in hand. If your dictation is given in this way, you will be required to take down accurately the correspondence or report being dictated. This calls for intense concentration on your part. This is no time for wandering thoughts. The dictator may pause to assemble thoughts, but, once he is ready, the secretary must be ready as well.

Since secretaries are not machines, even the best may miss an occasional word or thought. When this happens, do not interrupt the dictator. When he is finished, go back over your notes before you leave, and clarify whatever is necessary.

Transcribing your notes accurately is equally as important as taking them. You must be able to understand your own shorthand to do a superior job of transcription.

Typing

It may seem elementary, but accurate typing is a basic secretarial skill. If you cannot transcribe neatly and with adequate speed, you are not competent in your basic skills. No matter how advanced your position may be as an executive secretary, you may still have occasion to type or transcribe confidential matters. Your typing skills need to be fast and accurate.

General Vocabulary

A good general vocabulary is an essential part of a secretary's tools. You must be familiar with the English language in its correct form to be of help to your executive. He may depend on you to correct grammatical errors he makes.

You cannot do this if you do not have a good command of the language.

Many of the letters you send out will represent your firm and your executive. It is important to both that these letters do not go out with grammatical errors. Good use of basic English and grammar is essential to a competent secretary.

Business Forms and Punctuation

Your office will probably have a standard form to use for letters. There are several different letter formats used in business today. These are discussed in detail in a later chapter. It is up to you to know which form your company prefers and to set up your letters in that way.

Punctuation can be a real problem for a secretary if she does not know the accepted forms used in modern business. A refresher look at the proper way to use punctuation can help you solve any problems, ranging from ellipses to periods.

Office Machines

The knowledge of how to operate and care for basic business machines is essential to a career secretary. You may not be required to type on a portable, as you will probably have an electric machine. However, you should know how to handle such things as changing typewriter ribbons and cleaning the machine.

You may or may not have to be in contact with a mimeograph operation or a duplicating machine, but you should have enough familiarity with them that you can quickly learn the quirks of your own office machines. If there is a machine in the office, you probably will at some time be required to operate it or direct someone else in its operation. Learn all you can to improve your basic skills in this area.

Telephone Manner

You have probably been answering a telephone since you were able to talk, but a specific telephone manner is required in an office. Answering telephone calls and taking messages, both discussed in depth in a later chapter, reflect on you and your executive. A pleasant telephone manner is a basic secretarial skill.

Basic Filing System

Filing systems range from small 3 by 5 card files to complete file rooms with separate filing clerks in big corporations. You may even have to set up your own filing system for your executive's correspondence. Understanding how a filing system works will help you in either event. Since you will be putting into the filing system as well as locating material from it, be sure you learn how a filing system operates, particularly that in your own office.

ADDITIONAL OFFICE REQUIREMENTS

These may or may not be considered as basic skills, but you may have to perform some of them. The previously listed skills will prepare you to deal with the following possibilities.

You may have to make rough drafts of executive correspondence. You may also be required to read, sign, and send out some correspondence. The basic skills already mentioned will help prepare you to do these jobs efficiently.

Writing speeches, memoranda, and reports may be part of your work. You may have to edit copy that was prepared and typed by someone else.

Another phase of your work may be research for facts that your executive needs. This will require your knowledge of where to go and how to look for research material.

There may be times when you are considered the purchasing agent for office equipment and supplies. You must make the decision as to when to order supplies or what machine will best fit in with your office needs.

All the previously mentioned basic skills will prepare you to deal adequately with these additional office requirements. Each office requires its own specifics as to what its secretary should be able to do. The best rule is to remember that the more you know, the more efficient you will be.

THE SPECIALIZED SECRETARY

All secretaries share a need for the basic secretarial skills already mentioned here. However, there are employment opportunities that require additional and specialized skills. These are in the fields of law, medicine, and such technical firms as engineering, where technical reports and correspondence are required.

The Legal Secretary

A legal secretary must have a knowledge of law procedure and terminology to perform her job efficiently. She will need to know how to use a standard law dictionary as well as how to type formal legal documents such as briefs, proxies, and wills. She may even be required to be a notary, so that she can officially notarize legal papers. Further specialized training may be a requirement of her position. She may work in a small law office or be employed in the law department of a large corporation. Her position is important both to her employer and to the clients he serves.

The Medical Secretary

Specialized training, sometimes on-the-job, is also required for a medical secretary. She must be prepared with medical terminology and medical shorthand, as well as the office procedures of her doctor employer. Job opportunities range from offices of doctors or dentists to hospitals, clinics, and health departments. Corporate medical departments, as well as pharmaceutical houses, also offer opportunities. The duties of a medical secretary can range from a knowledge of accounting to securing medical data from patients and even to minor medical duties, such as preparing a patient for examination. A knowledge of basic sciences is a good background for the medical secretary.

The Technical Secretary

A technical secretary may be required to type chemical formulas, mathematical formulas, or highly technical reports such as those used in the field of engineering. She will need to learn the particulars of the firm for which she works. If she works with classified information, she may require government clearance. She will have a broader knowledge of her particular field, which will enable her to function more efficiently in her work.

For All Secretaries

One last thought for *all* secretaries. No matter what your employer's business is, you can be a specialized secretary. Improving your knowledge of the business requirements of your firm will improve your ability to deal with whatever may arise. Think of yourself as special—a special person with special talents who can and does do a special job.

General Office Information

Any capable newspaperman includes the what and where of the story on which he is working. The previous chapter of this book dealt with the "what" of the secretary. What she is and what her work includes were discussed there.

This chapter is the important "where" of the secretary's job. The where is your work space in the office—your office home, if you prefer—and this work space, properly arranged, will contribute to the efficiency of your work.

Take a long, critical look at your work station. It may be a private office of your own outside of your executive's office. Perhaps you share a room with several other employees or even have a section of your executive's office. Whichever is your situation, certain office rules should apply. Your work station is where you spend the major portion of most working days. Think about it both from the standpoint of doing your work as well as the reflection of you it presents.

YOUR CHAIR

You may not be allowed to select your own chair. Most offices have furniture that outlasts its employees. However, if you should select office furniture, choose carefully. Make your selections for maximum efficiency as well as attractiveness. A plush velvet-cushioned chair may be ideal for the waiting room where visitors read magazines while waiting for their appointments. It will not suit you for ten minutes if you are transcribing important dictation. The desk chair you use should be at a height that allows you to sit erect but comfortably. It may be a swivel chair so that you can turn from your typewriter to the work area. To function best, you should feel that your desk chair is in adjunct to your own body. Your feet should touch the floor, and you should be able to work in a relaxed but alert position.

YOUR DESK

Whether you have inherited your desk from someone else or have chosen your own, the way you arrange it is strictly up to you. Your desk will undoubtedly have a place for a typewriter, a telephone, and several storage drawers. It may have a large or a limited work surface.

Your desk may be a simple typing desk with an elevator mechanism that raises and lowers the typewriter stand, or it may be a complex work center. Whatever style desk you have, the key to efficiency is how well you utilize it.

Those things you use most often should be no farther away than one arm's length. If you have to stretch to reach for the telephone, you will waste time and physical energy every time the phone rings or you make an outgoing call. Have it within arm's reach—on the right if you are left-handed and on the left if you are right-handed. Having the telephone on the correct side frees your writing hand to take accurate messages. Correct placement of the telephone is so important that it is worthwhile to have it moved if that is necessary.

Your telephone-address book, desk calendar, and memo book all should have a place on your desk. These are items in daily use and need to be easily accessible. If you keep a copy of your executive's appointment book, this too needs its place in the sun. Easy accessibility of these items is a must; exactly where you position them on the desk depends on each individual.

Of course, it is necessary to have papers, folders, and supplies on the desk surface during working hours. But do not leave a lot of loose papers scattered around to be blown away. Make good use of some kind of work organizer, such as an expanding portfolio. Look to your office supply catalog for ideas along this line. There are many organizers from which to choose—from simple desk trays to elaborate space-makers. The old adage "a place for everything and everything in its place" applies to the desk surface.

As for the desk drawers, organize them as carefully as the top. It may sound simple, but keep paper clips, rubber bands, and the like in their own place, and know where these things are. Do not reach for a clip and come up empty. Keep desk supplies orderly and at hand. The same applies to your paper and stationery supplies that go in the large storage drawers.

Allow enough space in the back of one storage drawer for your personal needs, such as your pocketbook. Since you will not be using this too often during the day, it should be relegated to a spot in the back, out of your way.

So far, your desk organization has given you a workable surface, storage space—and sterility. If you want to have a flowering begonia to add a light touch, place it in a spot where it will not be in the way of your work. Make sure that the plant is not so large that it will interfere with your work space—and enjoy it. It is a known fact that it rests the eyes to look at green leaves.

LIGHTING AND NOISE

Correct lighting and a generally quiet office both contribute to better working conditions. Most office planners take both factors into their original planning. You may not be able to control the noise, but you can be sure you have proper, adequate lighting for your work.

If the overhead lights do not zero in on your desk, ask for a desk light. There are many different styles available, and the financial investment is minimal.

THE TYPEWRITER

The typewriter is certainly one of the most important tools of a secretary's trade. This, like the chair and desk, become very personally yours. If an inanimate object can be said to have rapport with a human, that object is your typewriter. Treat it kindly.

Dust and erasure crumbs are the demons of all typewriters. Cover your machine at night to prevent dust accumulation. Move the carriage to either side when using an eraser. This will help to keep dirt out of the machine.

Clean your typewriter regularly with a soft brush. Your typewriter repairman may have other suggestions for cleaning your particular machine. Listen to his advice and follow it.

Have your typewriter checked and cleaned at regular intervals. Once a year is the minimum. A hard-working typewriter may require professional maintenance more often.

SUPPLIES

You may or may not be responsible for a supply cabinet. If you are, be sure that this is as organized as your desk. Try putting any liquid supplies—glue and ink, for instance—on a low shelf; paper goods should be easy to reach, and like paper should be stacked together. Do not mix letterheads with second sheets. Keep small things in their own boxes. Pens, pencils, and paper clips can go high in the cabinet. Label the shelves, and also keep labels on boxes.

When refilling the supply cabinet, put the new supplies to the back so that the older supplies will be used first. This system of rotation keeps you aware of what you have on hand and what you may need to reorder.

If your job includes reordering supplies, keep an eagle eye on that supply cabinet. Do not get down to your last pack of carbon paper and run the risk of running out. Checking supplies at regular intervals will enable you to order before you run out.

HOUSEKEEPING

Even if your office has a custodial service, you, as a secretary, still have some housekeeping duties to perform. Naturally, you will want to keep your own work station clean and dust-free. This does not mean scrubbing the floors, but it does include regular dusting of your own desk. You may also prefer to give your executive's desk the once-over to be sure it is clean, clear, and ready for a day's work. Empty and wash dirty ashtrays, and remove and clean used coffee cups. If you are in charge of the coffee machine, you must also be responsible for keeping it clean. Another housekeeping duty may be the plants in the office. Water them as needed, and keep them looking good. An expert secretary will cheerfully tackle these small but important details. They are the little things that pace the way to office comfort for all concerned.

You and Public Relations

There are as many different phases of you, the secretary, as there are secretaries. The range stretches from the top-brass executive secretary in a multimillion-dollar corporation to the one-man office secretary. There is one thing all secretaries, regardless of their individualized and specialized duties, have in common—public relations. The secretary is a link between the executive and the outside world.

Every time you answer the telephone, greet a visitor for your executive, or send out correspondence, you are dealing with the public. How you meet this public reflects on your executive as well as on you.

PERSONAL APPEARANCE

The day you went for your initial job interview you probably took careful stock of what you wore. It was important to you that you looked as efficient and as capable as you knew you were. You hoped that your costume and grooming reflected as much about you as did the job resumé you carried with you. You certainly scrapped the idea of wearing faded blue jeans or too-short shorts to meet your prospective employer. The care you took about your grooming for that interview must certainly extend to what you wear and how you look every single day on the job.

There is a wide range of acceptable dress in the modern office of the 1970s. The classic business suit of a jacket and skirt has not changed, although pants may complete the suit in place of the skirt. Indeed, some versatile designers have created matching slacks. In this regard what you choose to wear will depend on individual office custom.

One thing applies to any office costume—it should be clean, neat, and fashionable, but not necessarily high style. Save the extreme for after-hours. Those spike-heeled glass slippers may be fine for a cocktail party, but be a bit more conservative, with a simple pair of comfortable, plain pumps, for the workday. You will actually be more comfortable, as well as more businesslike.

Both makeup and hairstyle should be suitable for the working day—not what you wear out for a big night on the town. Simplicity in your over-all appearance will create a business atmosphere around you. From 9 to 5, you are an important part of the office team. Your basic wardrobe, well chosen, will create this impression.

One last word about personal appearance: You may not always know ahead of time when you must accompany your executive to an out-of-office meeting or a business lunch. Unexpected things do arise. Dress each day with as much care as you took for that very first job interview.

KNOW YOUR EXECUTIVE

It may not be spelled out in your job requirements, but knowing your executive is of utmost importance to both of you. Your decisions as to when to approach him with a problem or an interruption should be made on the basis of what you know about him. The executive who begins his office day with a cup of coffee will not want to make important decisions until after that. When he is preparing himself and his thoughts for an important appointment or business conference, he is not ready to discuss vacation schedules or a day off for you.

A good working relationship between executive and secretary is one of mutual respect and understanding. Because you, the secretary, work closely with the executive, you are in a good position to be aware of the tensions of his work. You may also be aware of his pressures from outside sources, such as illness at home. When you understand his problems, you are better able to assist him in the heavy responsibilities he must carry.

Loyalty to your executive is part of your job. You are part of his team. He may express opinions and ideas to you that he assumes are confidential. Be sure you respect such confidences and keep them to yourself. The trustworthy secretary is not part of any office grapevine.

When you understand the responsibilities and goals of your executive, you will be best able to serve his needs. When his work goes smoothly, the chances are that yours will also go smoothly.

TELEPHONE PERSONALITY

Every time you use the telephone, either for incoming or outgoing calls, you are representing your company. Correct use of the telephone is important not only to your personal success but to that of your executive and company as well.

Many offices have their own requirements as to how to answer the telephone. An accepted form for answering your executive's phone is: "Mr. Smith's office, Mrs. Kelly." This is a concise way of telling the caller he has made connection with the correct office, as well as the name of the person to whom he is speaking. However, there is one important thing to remember. The person calling cannot see you. His first impression is the voice he hears—that voice is your telephone personality.

When you talk on the telephone, you are actually meeting people without the benefit of any visual aids. They cannot see your neat appearance or your poise and charm. They only hear the mental picture that your voice projects. Your telephone personality comes across in your warm, friendly manner, your courtesy, and your tact.

Be alert and pleasant wnen you answer the telephone. Do not let the late television show you watched last night or the disagreement you had with a friend come through the wires. Put a smile on your face so that a smile is also in your voice. Sounding pleasant when you pick up the receiver can help solve many problems.

Speak distinctly. Demosthenes may have been able to talk with a mouthful of pebbles in ancient Greece, but you will have trouble if you are talking through a mouthful of candy.

Be natural. Simple, straightforward language is the best. Talk at a moderate, easy to understand rate. Let your natural intonations come through to vary the tone of your voice and to add emphasis to what you say.

Your telephone personality tells a great deal about you. Your courtesy begins from the minute you answer—on the first ring of the phone, if possible—until you thank the person for calling at the close of the conversation. You may talk to a great many more people by telephone than you actually meet in any one business day. In this case your telephone manner becomes another important aspect of you and public relations.

LISTENING AS WELL AS HEARING

Effective listening is not the same thing as hearing. You hear a clock strike when you are aware of the noise. You listen to that clock strike when you concentrate on the number of chimes.

In an office it is not enough simply to hear. A large part of a secretary's skill is in listening. In this case a synonym for listening might be concentrating totally. Examples of listening in a given business day show the amount of concentration that is taken for granted and which the secretary must do.

Examples of Listening

1. Accept daily oral instruction from the executive.
2. Take accurate and precise dictation.
3. Answer incoming telephone calls.
4. Locate needed, specialized information from other members of the office force.
5. Contact and carry through messages to and from people outside the office.

A competent secretary learns her listening skills well. When you are that secretary, you concentrate fully on what you are hearing. In this way you are better able to cope with the daily problems that may arise in your office, from those of the lowliest stock boy to those of the president.

Everything and everybody in your office becomes part of you and public relations, from your nicely groomed appearance to your interaction with people both within and outside the office. A good secretary is far more than a good typist. Pride in yourself and in your job make you pay careful attention to all phases of that job, and good public relations may be the steps leading up the ladder of success.

Office Forms, Manners, and Conventions

YOU—A MEMBER OF THE OFFICE TEAM

Working in an office, regardless of the size of that office, makes you a part of the office team. Your ability to get along with people enhances the efficiency of your job and promotes cooperation all along the line. A good working relationship with all personnel may seem obvious, but it is important.

Courtesy in an office is far more than just "Please" or "Thank you." It should be extended to include pleasant greetings to co-workers and office visitors, although this is no time for long personal conversations. Normal friendliness and some awareness for the feelings of others will dictate when you should use extra understanding for a co-worker. Your own instincts are your best guide.

As a member of the office team, you have certain tools and supplies that you use regularly—so do your fellow workers. If you find that you have run out of a needed supply and must borrow, be sure to return the borrowed item promptly. Replace what you are missing from the supply cabinet as soon as possible to avoid borrowing again. It is never a good idea to borrow personal things, such as money, from a fellow worker.

Cheerful cooperation in the office is a must. The proverbial helping hand has saved many a secretary from work overloads. Reciprocation of help given aids the entire office to get the work out on time.

Personal complaints are best kept to a minimum. If a legitimate complaint that affects the work of the office must be lodged, be sure to lodge it with the person best able to resolve the trouble. Do not discuss the matter generally. Treat the complaint confidentially, so as not to embarrass a fellow employee.

Confidential business matters must be kept strictly confidential. You must be trustworthy about information you are told. Do not be part of the office grapevine. A good secretary may hear many things but says nothing.

PUNCTUALITY

A dependable secretary is a punctual person. Be ready to begin work when the workday starts. This means be seated at your desk comfortably and relaxed at the appointed time—not hanging up your coat five or ten minutes after the telephone has started ringing. Your executive depends on you to be ready for work at a given time. This is also true of your lunch hour. The extra cup of coffee that makes you late getting back to the office can be the catalyst that upsets the afternoon work routine for everyone.

DICTATION

Many executives prefer a routine time of day to give dictation. Since much of your time as a secretary will be spent taking and transcribing this dictation, it is essential that you be prepared for it. You will need a spiral-bound notebook, a pen and/or several well-sharpened pencils, a file folder for papers and reference material, paper clips to mark items for special attention, and a colored pencil for insertions in the dictated copy.

Before further discussing the taking of dictation, a word should be said about machine dictation. In heavily automated offices a dictating machine may take the place of the secretary's spiral notebook. These machines range from a complex, centralized dictation system to a portable dictation unit that can fit into a pocket or handbag.

A secretary who transcribes from a dictating machine will work essentially at her own desk with little or no contact with the person dictating other than placing the finished transcribed work on his desk. However, it is important that the secretary fully understands the operation of the dictating machine to enable her to transcribe the given dictation as quickly and accurately as possible.

Even though most of your dictation may be from a machine, there are still times when your executive will dictate to you in person. These are the times you must be ready on a moment's notice to take anything from a short telegram to a long emergency report that must go out immediately.

Your spiral-bound notebook should be at hand, with a rubber band around the portion of pages already used. Date each page at the bottom. This enables you to locate old dictation quickly and easily. Some secretaries keep two notebooks ready—one for letters and reports and the other for those unexpected important things that require special and prompt attention.

Be attentive and concentrate while taking dictation. Whether your executive gives you the average 70 or rapid-fire 120 or more words a minute, it is important that you do not miss a word. Do not allow yourself any wool-gathering while taking dictation. Concentrate fully on what is being said.

If you do not understand something in the dictation, wait until the end of the letter, then clarify whatever is necessary. Never interrupt your executive in the middle of his thoughts. Ask afterwards about any points in question, then mark your shorthand accordingly. If your executive is interrupted by the telephone or a personal caller, wait quietly until he is finished, or, on his signal, go back to your own desk until he is ready to resume dictating.

TRANSCRIPTION

As there was a routine for dictation, there hopefully is a routine for transcribing notes. This should be when interruptions are at a minimum. Make up your own system, tailored to your needs, for transcribing. Clear your desk of other things, and concentrate on the work at hand.

Allow time at the end of the workday to check over your dictated material for anything that must be handled on that day. This material should have been specially noted in your shorthand book as different from routine work, and should be easily located.

REORDERING SUPPLIES

Most offices have their own system for ordering and reordering supplies. This system may range from special-purchase requisitions, to a supply department, to you, the secretary, actually purchasing everything from typewriter ribbons to carbon paper direct from the stationer. Whatever system applies in your office, you will probably have some responsibility as a purchasing agent for supplies.

Know your supplier. This representative will be able to tell you what is new in the line he sells. He can tell you the difference between a carbon set and carbon sheets. He can tell you the erasing qualities of letterhead paper and second sheets. In short, the supplier can offer suggestions as to what you need based on the performance of what you have previously used. If you want to make a change, you will be fully informed and able to present your new ideas to your executive.

Keep a record of the supplies you use, quantities usually purchased, supplier's name and address, and the minimum quantity to be kept in stock. This is a stock-control system that should prevent you from running short of important supplies and yet not overload the stock kept on hand. Some supplies, such as ink and typewriter ribbons, can deteriorate with age. Your supply records, accurately kept, can prevent this from happening.

THE FILING SYSTEM

The office you work in probably had a filing system before you were hired. However, it is essential for you, as a secretary, to understand basic filing systems. With this understanding you may be able to make suggestions that will improve the already-existing system.

Alphabetical Filing

This is by far the most usual type of filing and is particularly useful for you if you want to set up a personal telephone file, for example. Whether on 3 by 5 cards or in folders, the material to be filed is listed in 26 categories—A to Z. Your system can be kept in a file cabinet in your office or on a box on your desk. Either way you will file alphabetically according to client or firm name.

Filing by subjects or geographical areas is set up in much the same way. This may call for more organization on your part and depends on the type of business in which you are involved. A mail-order house might prefer geographical filing. Subject filing usually requires an alphabetical card index that lists headings, divisions, and subdivisions of the file. This card index makes it much easier to find needed information and can save hours of time that you might spend in searching.

Nonalphabetical Filing

This type of filing system is frequently used by professional businesses, such as a law office or an engineering firm, or by a scientist. The files are set up by number, with subdivisions under them. The division might be 000. The subdivision might be 010; if further subdivisions are needed, they can be listed 010.1.

There is no attempt here to teach you how to set up a filing system of the more-complicated type. Rather, this is a bird's-eye view of what you will find in many offices. Large businesses have completely separate files that are maintained by specialized filing clerks. It is to your advantage as a good secretary to understand how the particular system in your office works. Your understanding will help you to locate filed material that your executive may need in the shortest possible time.

Basic Do's and Don't's of Filing

Keep up-to-date with needed filing supplies. It has already been said that you should keep a running record of the supplies you need in the office. The guides and folders used in filing are no good to you if they are at the stationer's. Order more before the supply on hand is depleted.

Do not place more than 50 papers in a folder. Fifty is a nice round number and is about as crowded as most folders can be without expanding the folder so that the tab is buried. Overcrowding can cause filing errors and lost time hunting for misplaced papers. When a particular file is full, subdivide it into categories of additional folders.

Perhaps the most important "don't" about filing is—don't change a system you do not understand. Familiarize yourself with the already-established files in your office. Find out the reasons things are filed the way "they always have been." After you know all the ins and outs of what is already in use, you are ready to make suggestions for change. Make haste slowly, however. Work your new ideas in after you are sure they will work well for all concerned personnel.

THE SECRETARY'S WORKBOOK

Take stock of your own efficiency by making up a workbook that could be used by a substitute secretary in the event of your unexpected absence. This might give you a clearer perspective of your own job and offer new insight as to ways of improving weaknesses in your operation. You may have all the answers in your head, but put them down on paper anyway.

Things a Substitute Needs to Know

1. The full name and title of your executive is the first thing a substitute must know. Who is able to make important (and unimportant) decisions if he is out of the office for any reason?
2. What is the procedure for handling mail in your office? When is outgoing mail picked up? At what time is daily incoming mail delivered? How does your executive prefer that his mail be handled; i.e., do you open it and process it before the executive sees it? Do you answer routine letters for him?
3. What procedure do you use for handling incoming telephone calls? Do you screen all calls before the executive is called to the phone? Does he prefer to answer calls himself? Do you have a special place for key telephone numbers?
4. What kind of filing system is used in your office? How is general material handled? Where is the filing

system located? What particular guides are needed for the files in your own office?

5. What are your executive's rules for dictation and typing? What stationery is used? How many carbons are usually needed? What letter form does your executive prefer? Include a sample. If the executive prefers a particular time of day for dictation, make a note of this also.
6. List all directories and manuals used in the routine performance of your job. Do you keep the latest copies available? Also list those pieces of office equipment you need to know how to operate. A list of the proper people to contact for repair service on that equipment should be included.
7. How and when do you order supplies? Be sure to list any special items that you use in your routine work.
8. How is the executive's calendar handled? Do you make appointments for him? Do you check his schedule with him every day? Are you responsible for the details concerning meetings, such as room reservations, note pads, and pencils for the people attending the meeting? Do you take the minutes of those meetings?
9. Does your job include making travel arrangements for your executive? Have you listed his preferences for airlines, hotels, and car rental, for example?
10. Personal data about your own job, such as coffee breaks, lunchtime, and even smoking at your desk, should be included. In addition write down your executive's personal preference about little things such as coffee, cigars, or his lunchtime preference. You might also list any routine things you handle for him, such as Christmas gifts, reminders of special occasions (both personal and business), or even reminders of when his regular organizational meetings take place.

From time to time in the performance of your job, look back over this workbook and update it if necessary. Thinking of your job through the eyes of a possible substitute may point out weaknesses that bother you, and you may then find ways to correct them.

Communications—Lifeline of the Office

Communication, the giving and receiving of information, is truly the lifeline of the office. Every phase of your office day includes communication of one sort or another, from your first pleasant "good morning" to the last cheerful "good night."

You, the secretary, communicate in many different ways. Your pleasant, attentive manner in greeting visitors is direct personal communication. Conversations with your executive and other personnel in the office are also communication. The letters and reports you type, the directions you give, the business conferences you arrange—these are all forms of communication. Many are face-to-face communication. The people with whom you communicate have a visual aid—you and your appearance (or the appearance of the letter or report at hand) to help make communicating easier.

THE TELEPHONE

One form of communication not mentioned above is that mechanical wonder known as the telephone. The voice a caller hears when you answer your telephone is frequently the only introduction that caller has to you. Your voice communicates a mental picture of you to the caller. The caller cannot see your nice hairdo, your smart fashions, or your poise. The image created depends entirely on your voice—and your good telephone manners. Your voice is your means of communication. Your voice is you!

How to Answer the Telephone

Answer the telephone promptly. Quick service reflects on your efficiency as well as on the company's. Try to answer on the first ring if possible. Remember, the waiting time seems longer to the person calling you.

If you must leave the line, explain why and excuse yourself. When you return to the line, be sure the person knows you are back before you resume the conversation.

Identify yourself. Do not frustrate a busy caller with a plain "hello." This is not businesslike and wastes time as well. Tell the caller whom he has reached.

"Mrs. Smith's office, Mrs. Kelly" is an accepted form for answering an executive's telephone. This immediately tells the caller he has the correct office and the person to whom he is speaking.

The tone of your voice says a lot about you. When you talk on the phone, the person on the other end of the line can tell whether you are happy or dejected, excited or bored, or in a good or bad mood. If you allow emotions such as frustration or anger to creep into your voice, its tone changes and so does the picture you are projecting.

By controlling your feelings, you send across the wires as pleasing a picture of your personality as you want the person on the other end to receive. Try sending a smile across the telephone line!

The picture your voice projects is important, whether you use the phone to place an urgent business call or just for a social visit. (Be sure to limit those social calls from the office. Save them for after working hours.)

A pleasing telephone voice can do everything for you, from assuring you prompt and courteous service to selling a raffle ticket for your executive.

Any number of factors can alter your telephone voice. Emotion is a major influence, but many other things contribute, too. The speed and volume with which you speak, the clarity of your voice, and the inflections you use all combine to help form your telephone image. Make sure you are not one of the ladies mentioned below.

Miss Dreary—Is your voice so flat and expressionless that people think you look like a dreary? Remember to send a smile along the line.

Miss Bewildered—Do not know for sure what you are calling about? Before you call, be prepared!

Mrs. Bossman—A loud, rude voice never sends a pleasing picture across the wires. There is a fine and important line between sounding businesslike and sounding rude.

Mrs. Whirlwind—Do you ever send this image? Talking to someone who is trying to do ten things at the same time can be really frustrating.

Mrs. Breathless—Slow down! Talking at breakneck speed will take twice as long—because you will have to repeat everything.

Mrs. Mouthful—Are you a Mrs. Mouthful? With a pencil, a cigarette, or a piece of candy in your mouth, your voice will not come through clearly over the phone.

Miss Affected—Insincerity shows up clearly over the phone. If you are just a little bit too grateful, you may come across as being affected.

Let your telephone voice speak well for you. Show that you are alert and ready to help the person on the line. Put a smile in your voice as well as on your face. Be natural. Now is not the time to impress a caller with your large vocabulary. Use simple, straightforward language, and speak distinctly and directly into the telephone transmitter. Talk at a moderate rate and volume, but vary the tone of your voice. This will add emphasis and vitality to what you say.

Each office has its own particular form for answering the telephone. You, as a good secretary, will find out how your telephone should be answered. There are certain rules that are generally acceptable.

How to Take Messages

Be prepared! A basic rule for Boy Scouts is also good for taking telephone messages. This means keeping a pad of paper and a sharpened pencil or a pen beside the telephone at all times. You cannot record the time of your executive's business appointment if you do not have pencil and paper handy.

Be sure to include the date and the time the telephone call came, as well as the caller's name. No matter how efficient you are, do not trust important messages to your memory. Remember, you are not the judge of what is important. Be sure all messages are passed on to the intended recipient, whether or not they seem to make sense to you. In this case you must be the competent recorder who delivers the message as promptly as possible.

Telephone Message Forms

The kind of telephone message forms you should use depends on the type of messages you are called on to take in a given week. A small office with a local business will not need the elaborate setup for taking messages that a large company with constant long-distance phoning will require.

It is up to the secretary, if she is to decide on the kind of message form used, to familiarize herself with the many that are available. Again, look to your local stationery supplier for the forms that best fit your business needs.

The simplest type of message form, other than a blank piece of paper, is the message pad. These convenient pads have "WHILE YOU WERE OUT" printed on them. They have a specified place for the date, time, name of the person to be contacted, who called or came to the office, and other assorted blanks to be filled in. Naturally, they also allow blank space for your remarks as well as a place for you, the person taking the message, to sign your name. In this way, the person receiving the message has all the needed facts at his command.

There are also "LONG-DISTANCE CALL" forms which offer essentially the same blank places to be filled in. These call attention to the fact that the call was from out-of-town and therefore must be handled as quickly as possible.

For an office that receives numerous long-distance calls, there are record books set up that keep full note of all details of incoming as well as outgoing long-distance calls. These provide a very convenient method for checking telephone calls against monthly statements and are usually double-paged, leaving room for all necessary information, such as name of caller, caller's firm, party called, time, costs, and notes.

There are permanent-bound record books that provide a record of every call the office receives. Some of these have automatic duplicate sets that remain in the bound book; the original goes to the person who received the call.

One of the most convenient records of phone calls is the spiral-bound variety that also has a duplicate for a permanent record. This type takes up less space on the desk because it can be opened to the waiting blank and still offers a duplicate record that the secretary can use for referral at a later time. The original, of course, goes to the person who was called.

It is up to the competent secretary to find the best method for taking phone messages for her particular office. Even a long-established secretary should take a look at her methods from time to time and see whether the manner in which she is recording telephone messages is the most efficient way for her particular office. Check into the new things that are constantly being offered by the stationer to find out if there is a new form that might make this very important aspect of the job more efficient.

Telephone messages are very important; a well-recorded message can make the difference between a satisfied customer and the loss of business for the firm.

Your Personal Directory

Many people find it most convenient to keep a book of frequently called numbers next to the telephone. This is an ideal place for emergency numbers as well as those numbers regularly called by you or your executive.

Cross-list your telephone-number file so that you can obtain numbers for your executive as quickly as possible. You will have a listing for Harrison Tool Company under H, but, if Mr. Birmingham is the man you need to contact, list him under B also.

Another good suggestion is to list the name of Mr. Birmingham's secretary on both cards. This may seem like a duplication of listings, as the information will appear on both file cards, but a cross-file of this nature will definitely help to increase your efficiency, and you may hear your executive brag—"My secretary can find anything I need."

Before You Call

Before you place a call, do you think of what you are going to say? And in what order? Make notes so that you remember to cover every point in a logical sequence. Be sure you make sense.

Have details in front of you, such as names, addresses, and dates. If you are calling in reference to a letter or bill, have it in front of you for reference.

Outgoing Calls

When you need to make an outgoing call, be sure of the number. Before dialing, check the telephone directory of your personal call list. This will help avoid wrong numbers and save time as well.

Be sure to let the telephone ring. While most business calls are made to other businesses, allow enough time for an answer. Ten rings of the telephone equal one minute of your time. Allow this much to make your connection.

As you identified yourself for incoming calls, be sure to do the same when you are placing a call. Others may not recognize you by your voice, so begin the conversation with a good start by giving your name right away.

You may reach a switchboard operator. Be prepared to tell your story in a sentence or two, so that the operator can connect you with the proper person. If you are calling long distance, be sure to tell the operator the place from which you are calling. This extra information may get you the person you want just a little bit faster.

Giving Information

If you must leave the line to obtain information for a caller, it is courteous to say, "Will you wait? Or shall I call you back?" If the person chooses to stay on the line, use the "hold" button (if your telephone has one) or lay the receiver down gently. If it should take you longer than you expected to gather material, return to the line every 30 seconds or so to assure the caller you are working on the request. When you have the information, thank the caller for waiting.

At the close of the conversation, thank the person for calling and do your best to end the conversation in a way that will leave the caller feeling satisfied. After you say goodbye, let the caller hang up first. Then replace your receiver carefully.

Long-Distance Calls

Although much of your telephone work may be done with local calls, occasions do arise when you must make a long-distance call. The etiquette listed above applies to long-distance phoning as well as to local calls.

Remember the time differences when placing long-distance calls. It may be early on a working morning in New York, but it is before business hours in Los Angeles. This can be the difference between getting your answer or not and applies to all long-distance calls placed in the course of any office day.

There are several ways to place long-distance calls. The cost depends on the type of call placed, the day of the week, and the time of day at the location from which you are calling. The expense of the telephone call you are placing might be described as the following equation:

Time of day when call is placed plus rate mileage equals cost of the call.

Day rates apply Monday through Friday from 8:00 A.M. to 5:00 P.M.

Evening rates apply Sunday through Friday from 5:00 P.M. to 11:00 P.M.

Night and weekend rates apply from 11:00 P.M to 8:00 A.M. every night plus all day Saturday and Sunday until 5:00 P.M.

Station-to-Station Calls

When you are reasonably sure the person you want to talk with will be there, or when you will talk with anyone who answers, dial direct. It is possible to dial direct to almost any state in the United States today.

With this type of call the charge is made automatically to

the phone you are calling from as soon as the distant call is answered. Rates for direct-dialed calls are lower than operator-handled calls, especially at night and on weekends. There is no longer a three-minute minimum charge for direct-dialed calls. If you talk for a minute or less, you will be billed for only a minute.

To dial direct station-to-station, you will need the telephone number of the person being called. This includes the area code as well as the local number. A numerical list of area codes, prepared by most local telephone companies, is of help when placing long-distance calls. Include such a book or booklet with your reference material.

Operator Assistance

Because it costs more to handle them, calls requiring operator assistance are charged at a higher rate than those completed without the help of an operator. Operator-assisted calls are calls such as collect, credit card, calls billed to a third number or special-billing number, calls made from coin telephones, and person-to-person calls.

Person-to-Person—Since station-to-station rates are always cheaper, it is best to use person-to-person only when it is essential to talk to a particular person or if you know there is likely to be a delay in reaching the person, such as a paging situation.

Appointment Calls

Appointment calls involve a telephone operator who is asked to put through a person-to-person call at a specified hour. The operator makes contact with the person to be called at the specified time and then notifies the caller. This service is no more expensive than a person-to-person call but does save time for the caller.

Sequence Calls

When a number of calls are to be made to out-of-town points, the secretary can supply the telephone-company operator with a list of those calls, including the names of the persons to be called, the city and state, and the correct telephone number if known, as well as the time the executive wishes to complete each call. The operator will then place the calls as arranged.

Time Difference

In the continental United States, there are four different time zones—Eastern, Central, Mountain, and Pacific. Each zone is separated by a one-hour time differential.

Eastern time	Noon
Central time..............	11:00 A.M.
Mountain time............	10:00 A.M.
Pacific time	9:00 A.M.

The earliest a business office in New York can call a business office in California is at 12:00 noon. Conversely, California knows that at 9:00 A.M., the start of their work day, it is lunchtime in New York.

Special Equipment

A competent secretary will familiarize herself with what is available from the telephone company serving her office. Phone-company personnel are only too glad to discuss the most efficient means of implementing specific business needs. The special equipment listed here does not include such specifics as telephone aids for impaired vision or loss of hearing. Such things are available, and, if you or your executive has a problem, contact your local representative about such aids.

The Call Director

This push-button telephone can handle up to 29 lines and allows one person to see the status of all lines at all times. This has taken the place of many different and separate telephones on the desk. It is a compact unit that also offers optional features such as hold calls, speakerphone, and intercom conferences.

Speakerphone

Just push one button, then dial without lifting the handset. Speak, and your voice is picked up by a microphone sensitive enough to "hear" voices clearly anywhere in the office. Listen over a loudspeaker with volume adjustable to your preference.

Using speakerphones at multiple locations permits electronic conferences that can save substantially on time and travel expenses. This is a means of getting more done faster, with hands-free telephoning.

WATS—Wide Area Telecommunications Service

If your business interests are geographically dispersed, you need all the help you can obtain to keep in touch with prospects, customers, suppliers, and diverse sources of information.

One answer is WATS—a special telephone service that lets you expand your communications ability while keeping a lid on your telephone budget. This is a special service for wide-area telephoning and allows you to make out-of-state calls within a given geographical location. Area One is composed of those states nearest your own location. WATS gives you virtually unrestricted telephoning to your chosen areas. This is a package plan that can be arranged with the local telephone company to meet your unique operational requirements.

TELEGRAMS, CABLES, AND RADIO MESSAGES

When your executive tells you to wire certain information to a customer or supplier, you will need to know the basic facts about telegrams, cables, and radio messages. If speed is of prime importance, you must know the fastest and most economical way of transmitting that information. Western Union provides modern telegraph service and is an important part of this nation's business life.

You may not need to know that a Desk-Fax is a facsimile machine that sends your message in exact picture form unless you have such a machine available in your office. However, it is wise to learn about the different types of written communication that can be sent and how this is done.

The telegram, nightletter, and the mailgram can all be dictated to Western Union over the telephone. However, if you are a frequent user of any of these methods of communication, you will want to obtain blanks from Western Union or the post office direct. These not only give you the form preferred for sending your message but also enable you to keep copies for your files.

The Telegram

The full-rate telegram is basically a 15-word message that can usually be delivered in 3 to 5 hours. Additional words on a telegram are charged for at a low extra-word rate. There is no charge for the address and signature in a full-rate telegram.

Preparing a Telegram

To facilitate the preparation of a telegram message, use telegraph blanks provided by Western Union. These blanks provide places to check the type of service to be used—either full-rate telegram or nightletter. In addition, they provide full address space, ample lineage for the message, as well as the sender's name, address, and telephone number.

It is wise to make at least three copies of a telegram—one to be sent, one to be retained in the company file, and one as a record of the telegrams sent to facilitate checking the billing at the end of the given time period.

If you, the secretary, are responsible for actually wording the telegram, you will learn many shortcuts and word economies. Any word found in the dictionary counts as one word. Abbreviations are written with no spacing, such as "COD" for cash on delivery. Geographical names are written according to the number of words; i.e., Los Angeles is two words while LA is one word. If frequent writing of telegrams is part of your job, you will want to contact your local Western Union office for more specifics along these lines.

The Nightletter

The minimum charge for a nightletter is for 100 words. The nightletter may be sent at any time up until 2:00 A.M. and will be delivered from 7:00 A.M. until 2:00 P.M. of the following business day. As with the full-rate telegram, there is no charge for the address and signature in a nightletter.

The Mailgram

The mailgram is a message based on a minimum charge for 100 words and is transmitted over Western Union facilities to the nearest post office in the city of destination. The mailgram then proceeds through regular postal facilities for delivery the day following the post office's receipt of same. The cut-off time to effect delivery for the following regular mail delivery is 7:00 P.M.

The rules for a telegram apply as well to the mailgram. Forms are also available from Western Union and should be typed at least in triplicate as for a telegram.

INTERNATIONAL MESSAGES

Few parts of the world cannot be reached by international messages. Such messages are either cabled or sent by radio in the case of shore-to-ship communication. There is a charge for every word, including the name and address. Punctuation is charged for as well. If your office is in the habit of sending many international messages, it would be wise to call Western Union to get full particulars as to international regulations.

OTHER TELEGRAPHIC SERVICES

There is so much happening constantly in data-automated systems that it is impossible to go into all here. There are systems from Western Union called Telex and TWX. Other data systems come from all major data services. Companies such as Texas Instruments, General Electric, and the like will be happy to provide you with needed material on what their companies offer.

This chapter was called "Communications—Lifeline of the Office." It is important for you, the secretary, to know what is available along these lines and the best way for you to use them in your daily work. All forms of communication—from a local telephone call to an international message—will go across your desk. You, the informed secretary, are ready for them.

The Business Letter

The handling of mail and the writing of business letters were briefly mentioned in the chapter on communications. Any graduate of a secretarial school will have been taught most of the elements of a good business letter. However, questions do arise—and, if you have some, the following are general rules for writing business letters.

WHEN TO WRITE A LETTER

When your executive dictates a letter or a memo, you have no problem as to what to do. But there may be times when you have to make a decision yourself as to whether to write or whether to use the telephone. Naturally, the telephone is the fastest means of direct communication, but there are times when the letter is a must.

When information requires confirmation, the written form is the best. This will give you a permanent record of that message for your files and will eliminate misunderstandings in the future.

If you are trying to gather information, such as credit ratings, which may be embarrassing for the other party, a written memo or letter is preferred. Likewise, if there is difficulty in contacting a specific person for information, such as a man who travels frequently, a letter or memo will reach him when he returns to his desk.

A letter will take more time than the telephone to obtain the needed answers or material, but, since it is a written form, with copies maintained in your own files, it can be considered more accurate for normal business needs.

THE FORMAT

The business organization for which you work will probably have an established format for correspondence. Before you type your first letter, look at copies of previous letters to note the form used by your company. There are four basic forms.

The Full Block

In the full-block letter all lines begin at the left margin. The advantage of this style is its simplicity, and it is one of the most popular of business-letter forms. A minor variation of the block form is to indent the date and the complimentary close to give a more balanced appearance to the letter.

The Semiblock

In the semiblock letter paragraphs are indented as well as the date and the complimentary close. Five spaces are usually allowed for the indentation, although as many as ten spaces are considered acceptable.

Indented Style

All principal lines of the indented-style letter are indented. The lines of the inside address and the closing section of the letter are all indented five spaces from the line above.

Each paragraph of the letter begins with a five-space indentation. This style is seldom used in the United States, although it does still appear in foreign correspondence.

Hanging Indented

The hanging-indented letter style is frequently used as an advertising gimmick to attract the reader's attention. Both the date and complimentary close are indented. However, the paragraphs begin at the margin. Succeeding lines are then indented five spaces. This style gives an unusual but eye-catching appearance to the letter.

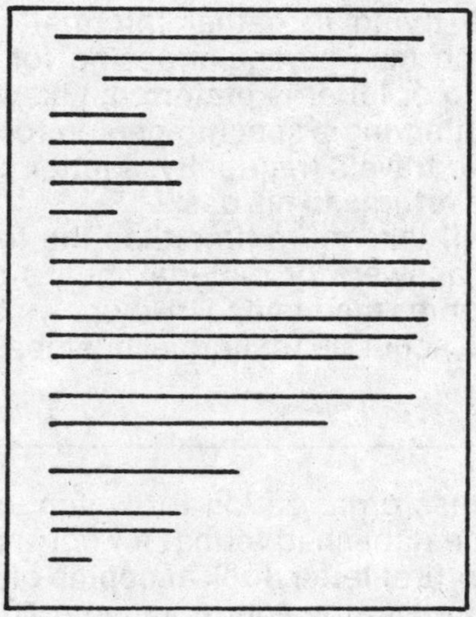

Full-block style

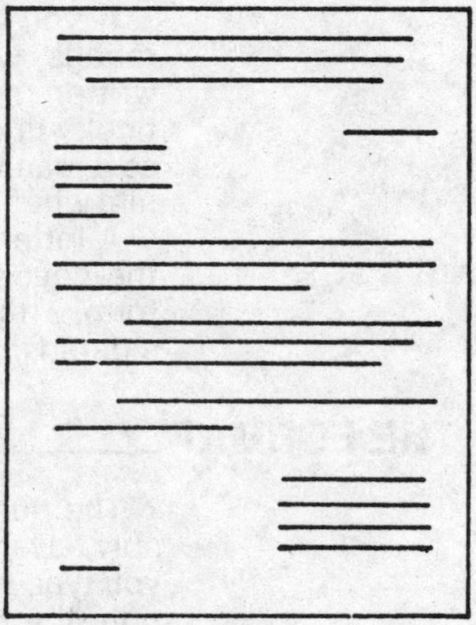

Semiblock style

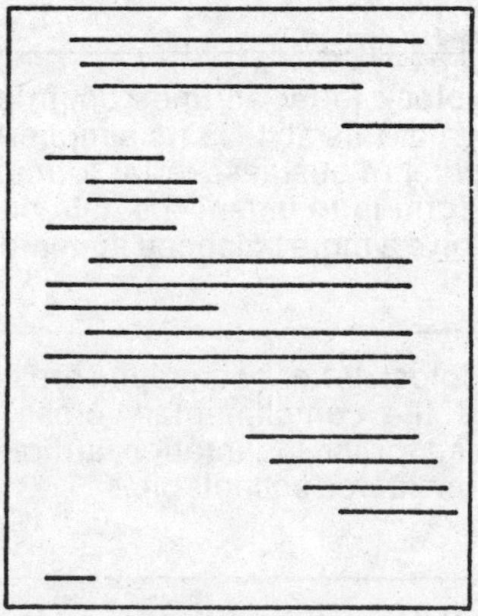

Indented style

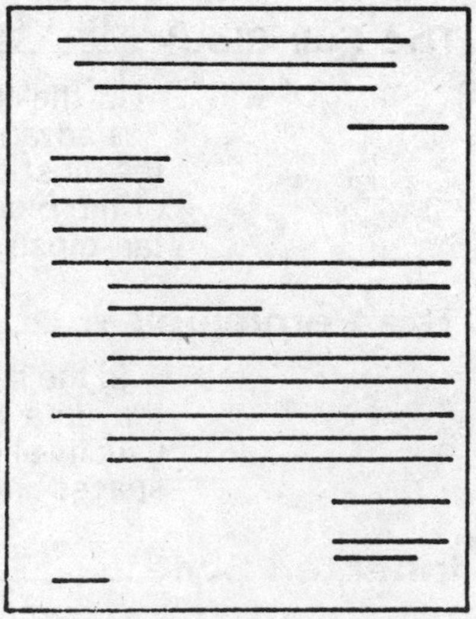

Hanging indented style

PUNCTUATION PATTERNS

Punctuation patterns vary as do the letter-format styles. Again, refer to earlier correspondence in your office to see which punctuation pattern is used.

Open

As the name implies, the ends of the lines in an open-punctuation letter are left open, without punctuation. The date, address, salutation, complimentary close, and signature—none requires a punctuation mark. While the end of the dateline is unpunctuated, the comma between day and year is still used. If an abbreviation, such as Co., is used, a period is used for that abbreviation. Any punctuation marks in the lines themselves are retained. Naturally, the body of the letter will still use punctuation to end sentences.

Mixed

With mixed punctuation a colon is used following the salutation, and a comma is used after the complimentary close. This is perhaps the most commonly used style of punctuation with any of the letter formats.

Closed

The closed-punctuation pattern is rarely used in the United States but is quite common with European businesses. A period follows the dateline. Commas are placed at the end of every line of the address except the last, which is ended with a period. A colon follows the salutation. A comma is used with the complimentary close as well as after each line of the signature block except the last, which ends with a period. After the initial and/or enclosure marks, no punctuation is used.

INDIVIDUAL PARTS OF A BUSINESS LETTER

The Letterhead

The letterhead can be defined as the printed heading on the business paper or as the paper itself. Here, letterhead refers to the printed heading that includes the name, address, and telephone number of the business. In some cases this also includes officers of the company. The letterhead is usually one and one-half to two inches in depth.

Dateline

The form in which the date is typed is fairly standard today. January 15, 1979 is the usual form. Note that the month is spelled out, not abbreviated, and that a comma follows the day. Since every business communication should be dated, this is most important. The date used by the secretary is usually the date on which the letter was dictated.

The dateline should be typed two to six lines below the last line of the letterhead. Placement on the page depends on which style of letter format your company uses.

Inside Address

The inside address includes the addressee, the street address, the city and state, and the zip code. Addresses should occupy at least three lines. If no street address is available, it is acceptable to type the city on one line and the state following. Avoid more than four typed lines for the address.

The inside address begins four to eight lines below the dateline. In the event of a very short letter on a large piece of paper, drop the inside address down several more spaces to improve the appearance of the letter. No line in the address should extend beyond the middle of the page. Two examples of correct inside address form follow:

Mr. Jonathan Wynne
Baltimore Sunpapers
2 North Calvert St.
Baltimore, Maryland 21202

Mr. Gary Hansell
Sun Life Insurance Company
New York, New York 10036

If the addressee holds several offices in the company, use the same title used on the signature line of his letter, as this is probably the one he prefers.

Salutation

The salutation is always typed underneath the inside address, with a blank line preceding and following it. It always begins at the left-hand margin. The first letter of the first word of the salutation is capitalized. Accepted forms of address for specific titles are listed elsewhere in this book.

The degree of formality used in the salutation depends on how well the writer knows the person to whom the letter is addressed. Examples of correct salutations are:

Dear Sam
My dear Senator Jones
Dear Mrs. Lewis
Dear Dr. Rogers
Gentlemen
Ladies
Mesdames

Body of the Letter

Most business letters are single-spaced. An exception can be made with a very short communication, which should be double-spaced to fill out more of the page. Double-space between paragraphs. If there is an insert in the body of the letter, such as an address or quoted material, indent ten spaces from both the left and right margins to make the insert stand out. Double-space before and after the insert.

Complimentary Close

The complimentary close, the end of the business letter, concludes the written conversation of the letter. Its placement depends on the format for the letter. The tone of it depends on the formality of the letter.

Formal closings	Respectfully
	Very respectfully yours
Less formal	Very truly yours
	Yours truly
Personal closings	Sincerely
	Cordially
	With all good wishes

Signature Line

The signature line is normally typed four spaces below the complimentary close. The signature should be typed as the writer normally signs his name, including any degrees or titles by which he wishes to be addressed in reply. A short title may be typed directly after the signature. A longer title should be placed on the line below the signature, in line with

No courtesy title is used by a man before his name, either in his written signature or on the signature line. However, a woman customarily indicates her status by using Miss or Mrs. before her typed signature. This is often done by including the status in parentheses before the name; i.e., (Miss) Lorraine Jackson.

If you are signing your executive's name to his letter, simply write his name in the space left for the signature and place your initials beside it.

The identification initials are generally typed on the left-hand side of the page, two spaces below the last line in the signature block. The dictator's initials are typed first in caps followed by a colon. This is followed by two initials of the transcriber, usually in lower case. Again, company preference as to the style to use must be considered.

TYPING NUMBERS

Numbers one through ten are usually spelled out. Numbers 11 and above should be typed as figures:

> Please send me six copies of your magazine.
> Please send me 15 copies of your magazine.

For amounts of money, use figures. Percentages are usually written, as 15 percent. Dimensions and measurements are written in figures, as 20 feet or size 4. Time is written with figures with A.M. or P.M. following, as 4 P.M.—or as four o'clock.

Where you use a series of numbers including some above and below ten, use one style to express those numbers.

My order is for three pens, five pencils, and twelve erasers.

I require 30 dresses, 15 suits, and 4 slacks.

Sorting the Mail

In most offices mail is delivered at about the same time every day. Therefore, an efficient secretary knows when she will receive mail and plans her day to include immediate handling of it.

Whether the mail comes in by the bag-load or in a reasonably small pile, the first step in handling daily mail is to sort it. The order of importance may be this:

Telegrams, first class, second class, third class, and parcel post or fourth class.

If international mail is a regular part of your incoming mail, you may want to insert this before the second-class mail. Memos may or may not deserve an early place in your sorting. The way you sort depends on the particulars of your own office.

The reason for careful sorting of the mail is to ensure that the most important matters are laid out for the executive first. It stands to reason he will want to answer an important letter before he looks over circulars, booklets, or catalogs.

Letters marked personal or confidential should be separated from the rest of the mail and given, unopened, to the executive. If they are opened by mistake, this should be noted on the envelope. In the event that the executive is away from the office for an extended time, he will give instructions as to the handling of personal and confidential mail.

Opening the Mail

Use a letter-opener carefully, so as not to tear the contents of the envelope. A light tap of the letter on the desk before opening it will ensure that the contents move down in the envelope and prevent tearing of any part of the contents.

Be sure everything is removed from the envelope. Checks and important enclosures have been lost through carelessness. When you are certain that nothing remains in the envelope, check the letter to see if it contains a return address. If this is not on the letter but is on the envelope, attach the envelope to the letter with a paper clip. Some offices prefer that this is done with all the mail. Others allow the secretary to destroy envelopes unless they are needed for return addresses.

In attaching enclosures and envelopes to the mail, use paper clips or file folders rather than staples. Staples should not be used on the punched cards that are so frequent in this data-automated age.

Dating the Mail

Many offices use a rubber stamp with the date to be sure that incoming mail is dated on the day it is received. Whether or not you have a rubber stamp, it is wise to date the mail on the day it is received. This simplifies explanations as to why a deadline was not met or why a request was not filled sooner. The date of the letter's receipt may be supplemented with the time of receipt if there is more than one regular mail delivery to the office.

Preparing the Mail

In offices where mail preparation includes the secretary's reading of the mail, the next step may be a secondary sorting. The order of importance for letters received may need to be adjusted.

An efficient secretary, when reading the mail, will underline important points for the executive's attention. It may be necessary to make notes in the margin as to action required or other points that the executive needs to know.

While reading the letters, the secretary should note any material needed from the files, such as previous correspondence. This material can be assembled either before presenting the morning mail to the executive or while he is reading the mail. Either way, it will be available to him when he needs it.

When the mail has been opened, sorted, dated, and properly prepared, it is ready to be given to the executive for his perusal. The efficiency of the secretary will make her executive's work faster and easier to complete.

If the Executive Is Away

There are times when the boss is away from the office for hours or days at a time. When these occasions occur, the executive will usually have left instructions as to the handling of his mail. The initial procedure of the secretary will be the same. When decisions are to be made as to the disposition of the mail, she will make them. This may mean taking specific problems to the next in command in the office, or it may mean drafting a letter to the writer explaining the executive's absence from the office. Either way, careful records will be kept of any action taken and will be presented to the executive on his return.

OUTGOING OFFICE MAIL

The actual letter has been discussed earlier in this chapter. However, mailing of typed letters includes a knowledge of postal rates and available fast-delivery services, as well as certain checkpoints to be made on each letter sent out.

The address on the inside of the letter should agree with

that typed on the envelope. This reduces the chance of error and delay caused by an incorrect address.

If the letter is personal or confidential, this should be noted on the envelope, as well as the type of mail delivery being used. Such things as special delivery must be noted on the mailing envelope.

Before the letter is inserted, it must be checked as to signature and enclosures. Naturally, the correct postage and correct zip code must be on the envelope.

Postal Rates and Classes

Many classes of mail are available to businesses, and, as an efficient secretary, it is your business to know what they are. The place to start is the nearest post office. There are up-to-date pamphlets available free as to postal regulations and current rates. This type of material should be part of your reference shelf in the office and you should have some knowledge of it yourself. The following is a brief summary of postal classes of mail.

First-Class Mail

First-class mail is used for handwritten and typed messages, postal cards, and the transmission of checks and money orders. First-class letter mail may not be opened for postal inspection and is determined by weight (no more than 13 ounces) without regard to distance. All first-class mail is given the fastest transportation service available.

Priority Mail

Priority mail is for fast transportation and expeditious handling of mailable matter weighing more than 13 ounces on which priority-mail rates have been paid.

Second-Class Mail

Second-class mail is generally used by newspaper and other periodical publishers who must meet certain postal-service requirements. It may also be used for mailing individual copies of magazines and newspapers.

Third-Class Mail

Third-class mail is used primarily for large mailings such as circulars, booklets, and catalogs. Because there are several categories of third-class mail, consult your postmaster for information as to your specific needs.

Fourth-Class Mail (Parcel Post)

Packages weighing one pound or more fall into the categorv of fourth-class mail. It is mainly for domestic parcel post, and there are specific regulations as to pounds, length, and girth of the packages to be sent. Consult your post office to find out the latest regulations. If you are sending packages outside of the continental United States, consult the post office for the most current regulations.

There are special mailing rates in this class for books, manuscripts, records, catalogs, etc. Again, consult the nearest post office for current regulations.

Available Fast-Delivery Services

Such things as aerograms, express mail, special delivery, and mailgrams all are services offered by the post office. There are details such as return receipts, insurance of mail, C.O.D. service, money orders, and claims for damages. You will need a speaking acquaintance with these services. The post office is continually updating its available information, and you should have available the latest copy of their rates and fees.

In addition, check the yellow pages of the telephone book for other fast-delivery services, such as United Parcel Service, local messenger services, and Federal Armored Express. All these companies will be happy to supply you with information as to how their services work. Armed with this information, you, the secretary, can make good suggestions to your executive when delivery of letters or packages is of prime importance.

Adjuncts to the Office

Certain books and materials provide great help in research for the secretary. Hopefully, this book is a start in the right direction. However, no single volume can hope to have all the answers needed. This is why it was suggested earlier to accumulate an office reference shelf that should be easily accessible to both the secretary and the executive. The list to follow will be small and compact, like this book, but it is a guide in the direction of gaining additional source material that should be in every office.

Cresci, Martha W.
Complete Book of Model Business Letters
Parker Publishing Company, Inc.
West Nyack, New York, 1976

Here is a book with over 275 actual letters that can help you find the right letter for your particular situation. The example letter may discuss an incorrect order of ceramic bowls. Your own mix-up may concern an incorrect order of stationery. You will easily adapt the ceramic-bowl letter to your own problem. The "Table of Contents" is detailed as to the many kinds of letters included, and the "Index" provides further help for specific letter problems.

Gavin, Ruth E., and Sabin, William A.
Reference Manual for Stenographers and Typists
Gregg Division/McGraw Hill Book Company
New York, 1970

While aimed for the use of the stenographer, this manual offers much help to the secretary as well. The "Table of Contents" ranges from grammar to resources, and the book is indexed fully, so that solutions to writing problems can be easily located as well as clearly understood. Both its compact size and wealth of information give this book a place on your office bookshelf of reference material.

Janis, J. Harold; Thompson, Margaret H.
New Standard Reference for Secretaries and Administrative Assistants
The Macmillan Company
New York, 1972

The authorities consulted in the preparation of this book offer the secretary in-depth research for specific business problems. Many accepted answers to problems are dealt with in the text itself. A thorough and comprehensive index as well as a quick reference table on the cover pages facilitate the use of this book.

Klein, A. E.
The New World Secretarial Handbook
Collins World Publishing Co., Inc.
Cleveland, Ohio 44111, 1968

In addition to carefully written chapters on the aspects of the secretary, written by experts in the field, this book offers a comprehensive list of words, spelled and syllabified. The complete appendix also includes such things as abbreviations, signs and symbols, and weights and measures.

Webster's Secretarial Handbook
G. & C. Merriam Company
Springfield, Massachusetts 01101, 1976

This combination of business facts includes such things as a guide to effective business English and career-path development, as well as section of suggestions for further reading. It is one of the most current (and therefore most up-to-date) of the enlarged secretarial handbooks available.

Before purchasing any of the above books for your office library, it is best to see and handle them yourself if possible. The above-listed books are available in many library systems. All are worthwhile and are well written as to accuracy and content.

OTHER REFERENCE MATERIAL (listed alphabetically)

Area-Code Booklet

This is available all over the United States as a free service from the Telephone Company. It is of great help in expediting long-distance phoning.

Atlas

A comprehensive world atlas will be especially useful to the secretary whose work goes beyond the scope of a small local area. When letters or reports go out nationally or internationally, a good atlas comes into frequent use.

Dictionary

Every office bookshelf should include a good general dictionary. An unabridged version may not be required, but a good desk dictionary is important. In law or medical offices, the secretary should add a legal or medical dictionary.

Postage Rates

This information is usually available in pamphlet form at the post office. It lists postal regulations regarding all forms of mail, from first class to parcel post. Caution: Be sure the one you use is the latest one issued by the post office.

Telephone Directory

The local telephone book with its yellow pages should be accessible, if not kept with your reference material. This book can solve many local problems.

Zip-Code Directory

Local zip codes are usually available as a service of the post office. Comprehensive directories covering all 50 states of our country are available at a nominal cost from bookstores or stationers.

USE OF THE LOCAL LIBRARY

Few secretarial positions do not include some research. A wise secretary will not wait until the executive gives a direct assignment to go to the nearest local library. Go before that assignment is issued, and familiarize yourself with the way the library is set up and what it has to offer.

Check the general library catalog. Books are listed in three ways—by author, by title, and by subject. The subject listing will also give you information that is available in periodicals.

Find out where government publications are listed and how they are available. The Federal government has written information on almost every subject, and the information is usually available from the Government Printing Office, Washington, D.C. 20402.

Take some time at the library to handle such books as *Who's Who In America, Bartlett's Familiar Quotations,* and *The Reader's Encyclopedia*. You may become interested and have a broadening experience at the same time.

Make a friend of the librarian. Ask the most efficient way to make telephone inquiries for information. Find out the regulations regarding borrowing of books (get a card for yourself, while you're there) and ascertain if the library has a copying machine. A quickly xeroxed page keeps reference material on your desk when you need it.

Never sell the library short. A good local library and full use of it may be one of the office's most useful accessories.

Tips for Secretarial Efficiency

Shortcuts become habit in handling secretarial work, and some of these time-savers are offered here as suggestions for you. They may seem obvious, or they may be real eye-openers, but they all work. Try them and see.

1. Start each day the day before. That may sound like a conundrum but it is a wise policy for efficiency. Before you leave the office at the end of the day, allow 15 or 20 minutes for planning. Check the calendar and memo pads, recording on them notes needed for the next day's work. Sort papers into their proper folders and files, and clear the desk. A well-ordered desk and a well-ordered mind will be ready to start work promptly the next morning.
2. When using carbon paper, be sure to alternate your carbons from top to bottom and from first carbon to last. This will give longer life to the carbons and ensure better copies.
3. Let a soft paint brush care for your typewriter. Daily maintenance of dusting with a soft brush will keep the exposed parts of your typewriter clean. The long handle will allow you to reach the corners. Your typewriter works hard for you. You owe it two minutes every day.
4. Tape a 3 by 5 card to your typewriter cover. List the needed minor repairs on this card as you notice them. In this way you will be ready for the serviceman when he comes; he, in turn, can do a better job for you by knowing exactly what you want.
5. In typing a two-page letter, put a light pencil mark at the left edge of your paper where you want the last line of typing to end on the first page. This will make it easier to keep the bottom margin one-inch deep. In typing a long report, mark each page in the same way with the light pencil mark. Then all pages will end at the same place. The marks can be easily erased after the page is typed.
6. Before you make an erasure on a letter in the typewriter, move the typewriter carriage to the extreme left or right. This will prevent pieces of the eraser from falling into the machine itself. Good care of your typewriter makes your work easier.
7. Erasers can and do get dirty and then they mark paper with smears. To make an ink-stained eraser work like new, rub it gently on a piece of sandpaper or an emery board. That will do the trick every time.

8. Keep a broken aspirin tablet handy to cover up erasures. A piece of white chalk rubbed on the erasure spot will do as well—but in a pinch, the broken aspirin works, too.
9. Develop a good rhythm when you type. Use a speed somewhat slower than your familiar easy letter combinations and let the less familiar catch up. A steady, moderate typing speed will improve your accuracy and save you nervous strain and fatigue.
10. To type a two-column page, newspaper style, make up a form before you begin typing. Use a dark pen (India ink is good) to draw a one-inch margin all around your guide page. This is for margins. Then draw a line down the center of the typing space. Place this guide sheet in back of your typing paper and you will have accurate margins for a two-column page.
11. If you have to make a change on a bound report, do not take the report apart. Insert a blank piece of paper into the typewriter so that an inch shows above the platen. Then insert the still-bound sheet between the platen and the plain sheet. Roll the platen backwards and you are ready to make your change.
12. To avoid tearing the contents of a letter when opening it, tap the unopened envelope on the edge of the desk. The contents will slip away from the top, and the envelope can be easily opened with a letter opener. In this way, the contents will be kept intact.
13. When making airline reservations for the executive, write down the name of the clerk making the original reservation. If changes or additions must be made later, time can be saved by not having to repeat that preliminary information.
14. If you are responsible for writing checks for your executive—either business or personal—fill out the check stub FIRST. You are then assured of never drawing a check without recording it. This helps in correct balancing of the checkbook.
15. Review your executive's appointment schedule with him at the beginning of each day. This will assure both of you that you and he have not made any conflicting dates.
16. If you must leave your desk and have no one who can cover in your absence, put a note in your typewriter stating where you have gone and when you expect to return. This thoughtfulness will tell your executive not only where you are but also that you care about his needs. Knowing when you will return will probably allow him to adjust his needs to your absence.
17. Color code your files. A small colored clip, available in most stationery stores, will allow you to keep an alphabetical file broken down into the specific needs of your office; i.e., a secretary of a company

needing machine parts from three different suppliers can alphabetize her machine parts and easily identify them and the supplier by using colored clips. Screws are under S and the supplier is known by a blue clip on the screw file.

18. Any competent secretary is well aware of most of her executive's habits—both good and bad—as well as many confidential facts that pass over his desk. Be sure the confidence placed in you by your executive is not misplaced. Learn to be a verbal football player. Carry your own ball efficiently but pass to your executive on confidential business.
19. When making long-distance calls, be aware of the time differences in different parts of the country. New York should not call California at 9:00 A.M. New York time. It is then only 6:00 o'clock in the morning in California. Check the time zones listed below before you place the call.

    Eastern Time .... Noon
    Central Time .... 11:00 A.M.
    Mountain Time .... 10:00 A.M.
    Pacific Time .... 9:00 A.M.

20. To make the rubber stamp you use easier to ink, store your stamp pad upside down when not in use. This will keep the ink at the top of the pad, ready to give you clear, sharp impressions of the stamp.
21. Open a new ream of paper on the unlabeled end. By keeping the label intact, you are assured of knowing what kind of paper is left in that ream for future use.
22. Telephone dials and receivers are dust-collectors. To keep them clean, use a cotton swab dipped in a liquid disinfectant. This is a small cleaning job that might be overlooked by the office custodian, but the telephone is one of the tools of the office trade and should be cleaned regularly.
23. Keep several paper clips attached to the side of the stenographic notebook for taking dictation. Use the clips to make any "rush" or special items that must be transcribed first. This is an easy way to mark these special items so that they can be located promptly without having to wade through all the given dictation.
24. If you need a brushup on shorthand symbols, use the slack periods of the day. Take a report from the files and practice your shorthand. It will improve your skill as well as your shorthand.
25. It you are interrupted in transcribing written notes, mark your last typed word with a colored pencil. In this way you will be able to find your place easily when you resume typing.

Forms of Address

Person	*How to Address*	*Salutation*
Ambassador	The Honorable John Doe United States Ambassador London, England	Dear Mr. Ambassador: My Dear Mr. Ambassador: My Dear Madam Ambassador:
Archbishop	The Most Reverend John Doe	Your Excellency: Most Reverend Sir: Dear Archbishop Doe:
Associate Justice of U. S. Supreme Court	Mr. Justice Doe The Supreme Court Washington, D. C. 20543	Sir: My dear Mr. Justice: Dear Mr. Justice Doe:
Bishop (Protestant)	The Reverend Bishop Doe or The Right Reverend Bishop Doe	Most Reverend Sir: My dear Bishop Doe:
Cabinet Member, U. S. A.	The Honorable John Doe Secretary of State Washington, D. C. 20520	Sir: Dear Mr. Secretary: Dear Madam Secretary:
Cardinal, U. S. A.	His Eminence, John Cardinal Doe Archbishop of New York	Your Eminence: My dear Cardinal Doe:
Chaplain	Chaplain John Doe Captain, U. S. A.	My dear Chaplain: My dear Chaplain Doe:
City Attorney	Hon. (or Mr.) John Doe City Attorney	Dear Mr. Doe:
Commissioner, City	The Honorable John Doe Commissioner of the City of St. Louis	Dear Mr. Doe:
Congressman	The Honorable John Doe House of Representatives Washington, D. C. 20515 The Honorable John Doe Representative in Congress 5214 Main Street Hometown, State 00000	Dear Representative Doe: My dear Mr. Doe: My dear Mrs. Doe:
Consul	Mr. John Doe American Consul London, England In South and Central America: Consul of the United States of America	Dear Mr. Doe:
Dean of a School	Dean John Doe School of the Arts New York University	Dear Dean Doe:
	Dr. John Doe Assistant Dean, School of Law University of Maryland	Dear Dr. Doe:
District Attorney	The Honorable John Doe District Attorney, Dade County	Dear Mr. Doe:
Governor	The Honorable John Doe Governor of North Carolina Raleigh, North Carolina	Sir: Dear Governor Doe:
Judge	The Honorable John Doe Judge of the Circuit Court	Dear Judge Doe:
Lieutenant Governor	The Honorable John Doe Lieutenant Governor of Ohio Columbus, Ohio 00000	Sir: Dear Mr. Doe: My dear Governor Doe:
Mayor	The Honorable John Doe Mayor of Chicago Chicago, Illinois 00000	My dear Mayor Doe: Dear Mr. Mayor:
Minister	The Reverend John Doe	Dear Mr. Doe:
	The Reverend John Doe, D.D., Litt. D.	Dear Mr. Doe:
	The Very Reverend John Doe, D.D. Dean of St. Mary's Cathedral	Dear Dean Doe:

Mother Superior	The Reverend Mother Superior Convent of the Sacred Heart	Reverend Mother: Dear Madam:
	Mother Mary Jane, Superior Convent of the Sacred Heart	Dear Mother Mary Jane:
Nun	Sister Mary Louise	Reverend Sister: Dear Sister Mary Louise:
Pope	His Holiness Pope Paul VI	Most Holy Father: Your Holiness:
President of a School	Dr. John Doe President, University of Texas	Dear Dr. Doe: Dear President Doe:
President of State Senate	The Honorable John Doe, President The Senate of Arizona	Sir:
President of U.S. Senate	The Honorable John Doe President of the Senate Washington, D. C. 00000	Sir:
President of the United States	The President The White House Washington, D. C. 20500	Mr. President My dear Mr. President:
	The Honorable John Doe The White House Washington, D. C. 20500	
Priest	The Reverend John Doe	Dear Reverend Father:
	The Reverend John Doe, Ph.D.	Dear Father Doe: Dear Dr. Doe:
Professor	Professor John Doe Dr. John Doe Associate Professor, Dept. of History	Dear Mr. Doe: Dear Dr. Doe: Dear Professor Doe:
Rabbi	Rabbi John Doe Dr. John Doe Rabbi John Doe, Ph.D.	My dear Rabbi Doe: My dear Dr. Doe:
Senator, U. S. or State	The Honorable John Doe	My dear Senator Doe:
	Retired: The Honorable John Doe	My dear Mr. Doe:
Speaker of the House	The Honorable John Doe Speaker of the House of Representatives Washington, D. C. 20515	My dear Mr. Speaker:
State Legislator	The Honorable John Doe	Dear Senator Doe: Dear Mr. Doe:
State Officials	The Honorable John Doe Secretary of State of Iowa	Sir: My dear Mr. Secretary: Dear Mr. Doe:
	The Honorable John Doe Director of Finance	
Undersecretary or Assistant Secretary (Federal Department)	The Honorable John Doe Undersecretary of State	My dear Mr. Doe:
	The Honorable John Doe Assistant Secretary of Labor	My dear Mr. Doe:
Vice President of the United States	The Vice President United States Senate Washington, D. C. 20510	Sir:
	The Honorable John Doe Vice President of the United States Washington, D. C. 20501	My dear Mr. Vice President:

GRAMMAR AND PUNCTUATION GUIDE

Parts of Speech

By putting words together in a meaningful combination, the writer creates sentences. A sentence basically includes a noun and a verb. Descriptive words are built around these two parts of speech. In order to understand English grammar better, the main parts of speech are included, with examples of their usage.

NOUN — A word used to name a person, place, or thing.

Proper noun — Names a particular person, place, or thing and is usually written with a capital letter: Jane, England, Baltimore, White House.

Common noun — Names any of a class of persons, places, or things: chair, letter, dog, weather.

Collective noun — Names a group or collection of single things considered as a unit: group, jury, class, board.

Noun used as an adjective — Descriptive noun, combined with another noun: potato sack, strawberry shortcake, fire engine.

PRONOUN — A substitute for a noun, referring to a person or thing already named or understood.

Personal pronouns — listed by case, singular, and plural.

Person	*Case*	*Singular*	*Plural*
1st	nominative	I	we
	objective	me	us
	possessive	my, mine	our, ours
2nd	nominative	you	you
	objective	you	you
	possessive	your, yours	your, yours
3rd	nominative	he, she, it	they
	objective	him, her, it	them
	possessive	his, her, hers, its	their, theirs

Possessive forms of personal pronouns do not require an apostrophe.

Demonstrative pronouns — point out specific things to which they refer: singular are *this* and *that*; plural are *these* and *those*.

Interrogative pronouns — used to introduce questions: *who, whose, which,* and *what* as well as the compounds *whoever* and *whatever*.

Indefinite pronouns — refer in a general manner to persons or objects. Commonly used are:

all	each	neither	other
another	either	nobody	some
any	everyone	none	somebody
anyone	everybody	no one	someone
anything	everything	nothing	something
both	few	one	such

VERBS — The grammatical center of the predicate, expressing an action, occurrence, or mode of being.

Transitive verbs — require a direct object to complete the meaning; The man raised (verb) the ladder (object).

Intransitive verbs — do not usually require an object to complete their meaning: The cat slept (verb) in the sun.

Linking verbs — intransitive verbs that make no complete statement, the most common being the verb *to be*: You are (form of verb *to be*) my friend.

Changes in Verb Forms

To go	*Singular*	*Plural*
1st person	I go	we go
2nd person	you go	you go
3rd person	he, she, it goes	they go

To be	*Singular*	*Plural*
1st person	I am	we are
2nd person	you are	you are
3rd person	he, she, it is	they are

ADJECTIVES and ADVERBS — Modifying words. An adjective modifies a noun or pronoun: red book, cool air, tired child. An adverb is a word that modifies an adjective, a verb, or another adverb: run faster, very bad, goes beyond.

PREPOSITION — Shows the relationship of the noun or pronoun to some other word: to school, among friends, concerning reading.

Commonly used prepositions

about	beside	in	since
above	between	inside	through
across	but	into	to
after	by	like	toward
against	concerning	near	until
amid	down	of	under
among	during	on	up
at	except	over	upon
before	for	per	with
below	from	regarding	within

CONJUNCTION — Connecting link that joins two or more words, phrases, or clauses of sentences: *and, but, for, or, nor,* and sometimes *yet* and *so.*

INTERJECTION — An exclamatory or parenthetic word that can stand by itself; *hello!, alas, ouch!.* The use of interjections in writing should be kept to a minimum to avoid what might seem to be an immature style.

Punctuation

Apostrophe

An apostrophe indicates possession, contraction, or plurality of different words.

Possession	John's letter
	a day's work
Contraction	it's in place of it is
	I'll in place of I will
	you're in place of you are
Plurality	p's and q's
	1's and 7's
	However: 1970s

Colon

The colon separates parts of a sentence that are almost complete and independent by themselves. The colon may also be used to introduce an extended quotation and is used after a formal salutation in a letter.

The contract said:
Mr. Jones' speech involved three principles:
Dear Sir:

Comma

A comma separates two independent clauses in a compound sentence, sets off a modifying phrase, separates words or phrases in a series of three or more.

He wrote yesterday, but you have not received the letter.
My secretary, Mrs. Black, wrote you.
We require paper, pencils, and pens. (In this example, the comma before the word "and" may be omitted.

Dash

The dash shows a break in thought, sets off a parenthetical phrase, or serves to summarize what has already been said.

I must say—before giving you details—
The anniversary sale—which was most sucessful—
Toys, puzzles, and books—all were needed.

Ellipsis

An ellipsis shows the omission of quoted material or words needed to complete a sentence.

> Friends, Romans . . . lend me your ears.
>
> Friends, Romans, and countrymen. . . . (When an ellipsis is used at the end of a sentence, a period is added.)

Exclamation Point

An exclamation point indicates strong feeling or an emphatic saying.

> Don't delay!
>
> Call at once!

Hyphen

A hyphen is used primarily to show word division at the end of a line. It also separates the parts of compound words. It is used between two or more words that serve as a single adjective preceding a noun.

> resi-dent (The letters dent will appear on the following line.)
>
> ninety-nine
>
> mother-in-law
>
> one-man office
>
> well-to-do person

Parentheses

Parentheses are used to set off explanatory or supplementary material not essential to the meaning of the sentence or to include numeric amounts in some legal documents. If they are a part of the parenthetical clause or phrase, periods, commas, and other punctuation marks belong within the parentheses. If they belong to the words outside the parentheses, other punctuation also belongs outside them.

> Included is One Dollar ($1.00) for you.

Period

A period indicates the completion of a sentence. It is also used for abbreviations.

> The sentence is over.
>
> Mrs. Jones and Mr. Smith went together.

Question Mark

A question mark is used at the end of a direct question.

> Are you ready to go?

When used in conjunction with other punctuation, such as quotations, the question mark appears like this:

> "Are you ready to go?" he asked.

Quotation Marks

Quotation marks are used to enclose a direct quotation, for some titles, and for unusual words that are not to be taken at face value.

> "Are you ready to go?" he asked.
>
> The third chapter of *Treasure Island* is titled "The Black Spot."
>
> That was some "free" service!

Semicolon

A semicolon separates two clauses not joined by a conjunction and is used before connecting adverbs. It also separates items in a series when one or more of the items contains commas.

> The agent lists the policy fee; he collects when there is a loss.
>
> The trip went all over the world; however, he stopped in Tahiti.

In conclusion, this is by no means a complete course in the correct use of punctuation. There are other books on your reference shelf that will go into more detail when you require that for special questions. Such things as capitalization, underlining, and word division can all be learned from sources of grammar such as the dictionary or English grammar you have nearby. If this is your weakness, by all means take time to brush up on your basics.

CHEMICAL TABLE OF ELEMENTS

Chemical element	Symbol	Atomic number	Relative atomic mass	Year discov.	Discoverer
Actinium	Ac	89	227	1899	Debierne
Aluminum	Al	13	26.9815	1825	Oersted
Americium	Am	95	243	1944	Seaborg, et al.
Antimony	Sb	51	121.75	1450	Valentine
Argon	Ar	18	39.948	1894	Rayleigh, Ramsay
Arsenic	As	33	74.9216	13th c.	Albertus Magnus
Astatine	At	85	210	1940	Corson, et al.
Barium	Ba	56	137.34	1808	Davy
Berkelium	Bk	97	249	1949	Thompson, Ghiorso, Seaborg
Beryllium	Be	4	9.0122	1798	Vauquelin
Bismuth	Bi	83	108.980	15th c.	Valentine
Boron	B	5	10.811	1808	Gay-Lussac, Thenard
Bromine	Br	35	79.904	1826	Balard
Cadmium	Cd	48	112.40	1817	Stromeyer
Calcium	Ca	20	40.08	1808	Davy
Californium	Cf	98	251	1950	Thompson, et al.
Carbon	C	6	12.01115	B.C.	
Cerium	Ce	58	140.12	1803	Klaproth
Cesium	Cs	55	132.905	1860	Bunsen, Kirchhoff
Chlorine	Cl	17	35.453	1774	Scheele
Chromium	Cr	24	51.996	1797	Vauquelin
Cobalt	Co	27	58.9332	1735	Brandt
Copper	Cu	29	63.546	B.C.	
Curium	Cm	96	247	1944	Seaborg, James, Ghiorso
Dysprosium	Dy	66	162.50	1886	Boisbaudran
Einsteinium	Es	99	254	1952	Ghiorso, et al.
Erbium	Er	68	167.26	1843	Mosander
Europium	Eu	63	151.96	1901	Demarcay
Fermium	Fm	100	257	1953	Ghiorso, et al.
Fluorine	F	9	18.9984	1771	Scheele
Francium	Fr	87	223	1939	Perey
Gadolinium	Gd	64	157.25	1886	Marignac
Gallium	Ga	31	69.72	1875	Boisbaudran
Germanium	Ge	32	72.59	1886	Winkler
Gold	Au	79	196.967	B.C.	
Hafnium	Hf	72	178.49	1923	Coster, Hevesy
Hahnium	Ha	105	262	1970	Ghiorso, et al.
Helium	He	2	4.0026	1868	Janssen, Lockyer
Holmium	Ho	67	164.930	1878	Soret, Delafontaine
Hydrogen	H	1	1.00797	1766	Cavendish
Indium	In	49	114.82	1863	Reich, Richter
Iodine	I	53	126.9044	1811	Courtois
Iridium	Ir	77	192.2	1804	Tennant
Iron	Fe	26	55.847	B.C.	
Krypton	Kr	36	83.80	1898	Ramsay, Travers
Lanthanum	La	57	138.91	1839	Mosander
Lawrencium	Lr	103	260	1961	Ghiorso, T. Sikkeland, A.E. Larsh, and R.M. Latimer

Chemical element	Symbol	Atomic number	Relative atomic mass	Year discov.	Discoverer
Lead	Pb	82	207.19	B.C.	
Lithium	Li	3	6.939	1817	Arfvedson
Lutetium	Lu	71	174.97	1907	Welsbach, Urbain
Magnesium	Mg	12	24.312	1829	Bussy
Manganese	Mn	25	54.9380	1774	Gahn
Mendelevium	Md	101	258	1955	Ghiorso, et al.
Mercury	Hg	80	200.59	B.C.	
Molybdenum	Mo	42	95.94	1782	Hjelm
Neodymium	Nd	60	144.24	1885	Welsbach
Neon	Ne	10	20.183	1898	Ramsay, Travers
Neptunium	Np	93	237	1940	McMillan, Abelson
Nickel	Ni	28	58.71	1751	Cronstedt
Niobium	Nb	41	92.906	1801	Hatchett
Nitrogen	N	7	14.0067	1772	Rutherford
Nobelium	No	102	258	1958	Ghiorso, et al.
Osmium	Os	76	190.2	1804	Tennant
Oxygen	O	8	15.9994	1774	Priestley, Scheele
Palladium	Pd	46	106.4	1803	Wollaston
Phosphorus	P	15	30.9738	1669	Brand
Platinum	Pt	78	195.09	1735	Ulloa
Plutonium	Pu	94	242	1940	Seaborg, et al.
Polonium	Po	84	210	1898	P. and M. Curie
Potassium	K	19	39.102	1807	Davy
Praseodymium	Pr	59	140.907	1885	Welsbach
Promethium	Pm	61	147	1945	Glendenin, Marinsky, Coryell
Protactinium	Pa	91	231	1917	Hahn, Meitner
Radium	Ra	88	226	1898	P. & M. Curie, Bemont
Radon	Rn	86	222	1900	Dorn
Rhenium	Re	75	186.2	1925	Noddack, Tacke, Berg
Rhodium	Rh	45	102.905	1803	Wollaston
Rubidium	Rb	37	85.47	1861	Bunsen, Kirchhoff
Ruthenium	Ru	44	101.07	1845	Klaus
Rutherfordium	Rf	104	261	1969	Ghiorso, et al.
Samarium	Sm	62	150.35	1879	Boisbaudran
Scandium	Sc	21	44.956	1879	Nilson
Selenium	Se	34	78.96	1817	Berzelius
Silicon	Si	14	28.086	1823	Berzelius
Silver	Ag	47	107.868	B.C.	
Sodium	Na	11	22.9898	1807	Davy
Strontium	Sr	38	87.62	1790	Crawford
Sulfur	S	16	32.064	B.C.	
Tantalum	Ta	73	180.948	1802	Ekeberg
Technetium	Tc	43	99	1937	Perrier and Segre
Tellurium	Te	52	127.60	1782	Von Reichenstein
Terbium	Tb	65	158.924	1843	Mosander
Thallium	Tl	81	204.37	1861	Crookes
Thorium	Th	90	232.038	1828	Berzelius
Thulium	Tm	69	168.934	1879	Cleve
Tin	Sn	50	118.69	B.C.	
Titanium	Ti	22	47.90	1791	Gregor
Tungsten (Wolfram)	W	74	183.85	1783	d'Elhujar
Uranium	U	92	238.03	1789	Klaproth
Vanadium	V	23	50.942	1830	Sefstrom
Xenon	Xe	54	131.30	1898	Ramsay, Travers
Ytterbium	Yb	70	173.04	1878	Marignac
Yttrium	Y	39	88.905	1794	Gadolin
Zinc	Zn	30	65.37	B.C.	
Zirconium	Zr	40	91.22	1789	Klaproth

COOKING CONVERSION TABLES

Measures in weight in the imperial and American systems are the same; measures in volume are different and the following tables show the equivalents for both imperial and metric measures. Keep to one column or the other—we hope you will use the metric one. Do not try to make comparisons between columns because they are not exact conversions from one to the other.

Solid Measures

American	**Imperial & Metric**
1 cup butter	225g(8 oz) butter or other fat
1 stick butter	115g(4 oz) butter or other fat
1 cup flour	115g(4 oz) flour
½ cup flour	55g(2 oz) flour
2½ cups brown (moist) sugar	455g(1 lb) brown (moist) sugar
1 cup brown (moist) sugar	180g(6 oz) brown (moist) sugar
1 cup castor/granulated sugar	225g(8 oz) castor/granulated sugar
1 cup confectioner's sugar	155g(5½ oz) icing sugar
1 cup corn syrup or treacle	455g(1 lb) golden syrup or treacle
1 cup rice	225g(8 oz) rice
1cup dried fruit	225g(8 oz) dried fruit
1 cup lentils/split peas	225g(8 oz) lentils/split peas
1 cup ground meat	225g(8 oz) minced meat

Spoon Measures

1 teaspoon (tsp)	1¼ teaspoons
1 tablespoon (tbsp)	1¼ tablespoons
1 level tablespoon butter	15g(½ oz) butter
1 heaped tablespoon flour	28g(1 oz) flour
1 level tablespoon flour	15g(½ oz) flour
1 level tablespoon sugar	28g(1 oz) sugar

Liquid Measures

1 cup (8 fluid oz) U.S.	275ml(10 fluid oz)
1 pint (16 fluid oz) U.S.	550ml(20 fluid oz)
1 quart (32 fluid oz) U.S.	900ml(33 fluid oz)

Oven Temperatures

	Fahrenheit	Celsius	Gas Mark
Very cool	225	110	¼
	250	130	½
Cool	275	140	1
	300	150	2
Moderate	325	170	3
	350	180	4
Moderately hot	375	190	5
	400	200	6
Hot	425	220	7
	450	230	8
Very hot	475	240	9

PRESIDENTS OF THE UNITED STATES

Name (and party)	*State of Birth*	*Born*	*Term*	*Died*
George Washington (F)	Va.	1732	1789-97	1799
John Adams (F)	Mass.	1735	1797-1801	1826
Thomas Jefferson (D-R)	Va.	1743	1801-09	1826
James Madison (D-R)	Va.	1751	1809-17	1836
James Monroe (D-R)	Va.	1758	1817-25	1831
John Quincy Adams (D-R)	Mass.	1767	1825-29	1848
Andrew Jackson (D)	S.C.	1767	1829-37	1845
Martin Van Buren (D)	N.Y.	1782	1837-41	1862
William Henry Harrison (W)	Va.	1773	1841	1841
John Tyler (W)	Va.	1790	1841-45	1862
James Knox Polk (D)	N.C.	1795	1845-49	1849
Zachary Taylor (W)	Va.	1784	1849-50	1850
Millard Fillmore (W)	N.Y.	1800	1850-53	1874
Franklin Pierce (D)	N.H.	1804	1853-57	1869
James Buchanan (D)	Pa.	1791	1857-61	1868
Abraham Lincoln (R)	Ky.	1809	1861-65	1865
Andrew Johnson (R)	N.C.	1808	1865-69	1875
Ulysses Simpson Grant (R)	Ohio	1822	1869-77	1885
Rutherford Birchard Hayes (R)	Ohio	1822	1877-81	1893
James Abram Garfield (R)	Ohio	1831	1881	1881
Chester Alan Arthur (R)	Vt.	1830	1881-85	1886
Grover Cleveland (D)	N.J.	1837	1885-89	1908
Benjamin Harrison (R)	Ohio	1833	1889-93	1901
Grover Cleveland (D)	N.J.	1837	1893-97	1908
William McKinley (R)	Ohio	1843	1897-1901	1901
Theodore Roosevelt (R)	N.Y.	1858	1901-1909	1919
William Howard Taft (R)	Ohio	1857	1909-13	1930
Woodrow Wilson (D)	Va.	1856	1913-21	1924
Warren Gamaliel Harding (R)	Ohio	1865	1921-23	1923
Calvin Coolidge (R)	Vt.	1872	1923-29	1933
Herbert Clark Hoover (R)	Iowa	1874	1923-33	1964
Franklin Delano Roosevelt (D)	N.Y.	1882	1933-45	1945
Harry S. Truman (D)	Mo.	1884	1945-53	1972
Dwight David Eisenhower (R)	Tex.	1890	1953-61	1969
John F. Kennedy (D)	Mass.	1917	1961-63	1963
Lyndon B. Johnson (D)	Tex.	1908	1963-69	1973
Richard M. Nixon (R)	Calif.	1913	1969-74 (r)	
Gerald R. Ford (R)	Nebr.	1913	1974-77	
James Earl Carter, Jr. (D)	Ga.	1924	1977-81	
Ronald W. Reagan (R)	Ill.	1911	1981-89	
George Bush (R)	Mass.	1924	1989-	

VICE-PRESIDENTS OF THE UNITED STATES

Name (and party)	*State of Birth*	*Born*	*Term*	*Died*
John Adams (F)	Mass.	1735	1789-97	1826
Thomas Jefferson (D-R)	Va.	1743	1797-1801	1826
Thomas Jefferson (D-R)	Va.	1743	1801-09	1826
Aaron Burr (R)	N.J.	1756	1801-05	1836
George Clinton (R)	N.Y.	1739	1805-12	1812
Elbridge Gerry (R)	Mass.	1744	1813-14	1814
Daniel D. Tompkins (R)	N.Y.	1774	1817-25	1825
John U. Calhoun (R)	S.C.	1782	1825-32	1850
Martin Van Buren (D)	N.Y.	1782	1833-37	1862
Richard M. Johnson (D)	Ky.	1780	1837-41	1850
John Tyler (W)	Va.	1790	1841	1862
George M. Dallas (D)	Pa.	1792	1845-49	1864
Millard Fillmore (W)	N.Y.	1800	1849-50	1874
William R. King (D)	N.C.	1786	1853	1853
John C. Breckinridge (D)	Ky.	1821	1857-61	1875
Hannibal Hamlin (R)	Me.	1809	1861-65	1891
Andrew Johnson (R)	N.C.	1808	1865	1875
Schuyler Colfax (R)	N.Y.	1823	1869-73	1885
Henry Wilson (R)	N.H.	1812	1873-75	1875
William A. Wheeler (R)	N.Y.	1819	1877-81	1887
Chester A. Arthur (R)	Vt.	1830	1881	1886
Thomas A. Hendricks (D)	Ohio	1819	1885	1885
Levi P. Morton (R)	Vt.	1824	1889-93	1920
Adlai E. Stevenson (D)	Ky.	1835	1893-97	1914
Garrett A. Hobart (R)	N.J.	1844	1897-99	1899
Theodore Roosevelt (R)	N.Y.	1858	1901	1919
Charles W. Fairbanks (R)	Ohio	1852	1905-09	1918
James S. Sherman (R)	N.Y.	1855	1909-12	1912
Thomas R. Marshall (D)	Ind.	1854	1913-21	1925
Calvin Coolidge (R)	Vt.	1872	1921-23	1933
Charles G. Dawes (R)	Ohio	1865	1925-29	1951
Charles Curtis (R)	Kan.	1860	1929-33	1936
John N. Garner (D)	Tex.	1869	1933-41	1967
Henry A. Wallace (D)	Ia.	1888	1941-45	1965
Harry S. Truman (D)	Mo.	1884	1945	1972
Alben W. Barkley (D)	Ky.	1877	1949-53	1956
Richard M. Nixon (R)	Calif.	1913	1953-61	
Lyndon B. Johnson (D)	Tex.	1908	1961-63	1973
Hubert H. Humphrey (D)	S.D.	1911	1965-69	1978
Spiro T. Agnew (R)	Md.	1918	1969-73 (r)	
Gerald R. Ford (R)	Nebr.	1913	1973-1974	
Nelson A. Rockefeller (R)	Me.	1908	1974-77	1979
Walter F. Mondale (D)	Minn.	1928	1977-81	
George Bush (R)	Mass.	1924	1981-89	
Dan Quayle (R)	Ind.	1947	1989-	

F–Federalist; D–Democratic; R–Republican; W–Whig; (r)–resigned

DECLARATION OF INDEPENDENCE

When in the Course of human events, it becomes necessary for one people to dissolve the political bands which have connected them with another, and to assume among the Powers of the earth, the separate and equal station to which the Laws of Nature and of Nature's God entitle them, a decent respect to the opinions of mankind requires that they should declare the causes which impel them to the separation.

We hold these truths to be self-evident, that all men are created equal, that they are endowed by their Creator with certain unalienable Rights, that among these are Life, Liberty and the pursuit of Happiness. That to secure these rights, Governments are instituted among Men, deriving their just powers from the consent of the governed, That whenever any Form of Government becomes destructive of these ends, it is the Right of the People to alter or to abolish it, and to institute new Government, laying its foundation on such principles and organizing its powers in such form, as to them shall seem most likely to effect their Safety and Happiness. Prudence, indeed, will dictate that Governments long established should not be changed for light and transient causes; and accordingly all experience hath shown, that mankind are more disposed to suffer, while evils are sufferable, than to right themselves by abolishing the forms to which they are accustomed. But when a long train of abuses and usurpations, pursuing invariably the same Object evinces a design to reduce them under absolute Despotism, it is their right, it is their duty, to throw off such Government, and to provide new Guards for their future security.—Such has been the patient sufferance of these Colonies; and such is now the necessity which constrains them to alter their former Systems of Government. The history of the present King of Great Britain is a history of repeated injuries and usurpations, all having in direct object the establishment of an absolute Tyranny over these States. To prove this, let Facts be submitted to a candid world.

He has refused his Assent to Laws, the most wholesome and necessary for the public good.

He has forbidden his Governors to pass Laws of immediate and pressing importance, unless suspended in their operation till his Assent should be obtained; and when so suspended, he has utterly neglected to attend to them.

He has refused to pass other Laws for the accommodation of large districts of people, unless those people would relinquish the right of Representation in the Legislature, a right inestimable to them and formidable to tyrants only.

He has called together legislative bodies at places unusual, uncomfortable, and distant from the depository of their Public Records, for the sole purpose of fatiguing them into compliance with his measures.

He has dissolved Representative Houses repeatedly, for opposing with manly firmness his invasions on the rights of the people.

He has refused for a long time, after such dissolutions, to cause others to be elected; whereby the Legislative Powers, incapable of Annihilation, have returned to the People at large for their exercise; the State remaining in the mean time exposed to all the dangers of invasion from without, and convulsions within.

He has endeavoured to prevent the population of these States; for that purpose obstructing the Laws for Naturalization of Foreigners; refusing to pass others to encourage their migrations hither, and raising the conditions of new Appropriations of Lands.

He has obstructed the Administration of Justice, by refusing his Assent to Laws for establishing Judiciary Powers.

He has made Judges dependent on his Will alone, for the tenure of their offices, and the amount and payment of their salaries.

He has erected a multitude of New Offices, and sent hither swarms of Officers to harass our people, and eat out their substance.

He has kept among us, in times of peace, Standing Armies without the Consent of our legislatures.

He has affected to render the Military independent of and superior to the Civil Power.

He has combined with others to subject us to a jurisdiction foreign to our constitution, and unacknowledged by our laws; giving his Assent to their acts of pretended Legislation:

For quartering large bodies of armed troops among us:

For protecting them, by a mock Trial, from Punishment for any Murders which they should commit on the Inhabitants of these States:

For cutting off our Trade with all parts of the world:

For imposing taxes on us without our Consent:

For depriving us in many cases, of the benefits of Trial by Jury:

For transporting us beyond Seas to be tried for pretended offences:

For abolishing the free System of English Laws in a neighbouring Province, establishing therein an Arbitrary government, and enlarging its Boundaries so as to render it at once an example and fit instrument for introducing the same absolute rule into these Colonies:

For taking away our Charters, abolishing our most valuable Laws, and altering fundamentally the Forms of our Governments:

For suspending our own Legislatures, and declaring themselves invested with power to legislate for us in all cases whatsoever.

He has abdicated Government here, by declaring us out of his Protection and waging War against us.

He has plundered our seas, ravaged our Coasts, burnt our towns, and destroyed the lives of our people.

He is at this time transporting large armies of foreign mercenaries to compleat the works of death, desolation and tyranny, already begun with circumstances of Cruelty & perfidy scarcely paralleled in the most barbarous ages, and totally unworthy the Head of a civilized nation.

He has constrained our fellow Citizens taken Captive on the high Seas to bear Arms against their Country, to become the executioners of their friends and Brethren, or to fall themselves by their Hands.

He has excited domestic insurrections amongst us, and has endeavoured to bring on the inhabitants of our frontiers, the merciless Indian Savages, whose known rule of warfare, is an undistinguished destruction of all ages, sexes and conditions.

In every stage of these Oppressions We have Petitioned for Redress in the most humble terms: Our repeated Petitions have been answered only by repeated injury. A Prince whose character is thus marked by every act which may define a Tyrant, is unfit to be the ruler of a free people.

Nor have We been wanting in attentions to our Brittish brethren. We have warned them from time to time of attempts by their legislature to extend an unwarrantable jurisdiction over us. We have reminded them of the circumstances of our emigration and settlement here. We have appealed to their native justice and magnanimity, and we have conjured them by the ties of our common kindred to disavow these usurpations which, would inevitably interrupt our connections and correspondence. They too have been deaf to the voice of justice and of consanguinity. We must, therefore, acquiesce in the necessity, which denounces our

Separation, and hold them, as we hold the rest of mankind, Enemies in War, in Peace Friends.

We, therefore, the Representatives of the united States of America, in General Congress, Assembled, appealing to the Supreme Judge of the world for the rectitude of our intentions, do, in the Name, and by authority of the good People of these Colonies, solemnly publish and declare, That these United Colonies are, and of Right ought to be Free and Independent States; that they are Absolved from all Allegiance to the British Crown, and that all political connection between them and the State of Great Britain, is and ought to be totally dissolved; and that as Free and Independent States, they have full power to levy War, conclude Peace, contract Alliances, establish Commerce, and to do all other Acts and Things which Independent States may of right do. And for the support of this Declaration, with a firm reliance on the Protection of Divine Providence, we mutually pledge to each other our Lives, our Fortunes and our sacred Honor.

INDEX GUIDE TO THE
CONSTITUTION OF THE UNITED STATES

Preamble.

ARTICLE 1.—The Legislative Department consisting of a Senate and a House of Representatives.
Organization of Congress and terms, qualifications, apportionment and elections.
Impeachment procedures.
Privileges and compensation.
Lawmaking procedures.
Congressional powers.
Limitations on the States and Congress.

ARTICLE II.—The Executive Department.
Election of the President and the Vice-President.
Presidential duties and powers.
Ratification of treaties.
Impeachment of officers.

ARTICLE III.—The Judiciary Department.
Judicial independence.
Jurisdiction of the courts.
Trial by jury guaranteed.
Definition of treason and punishment.

ARTICLE IV.—Position of States and territories.
Full faith and credit to public acts and the judicial proceedings.
Privileges and immunities of citizens of each state.
Fugitives from justice.
Congressional control over territories.
Guarantees and protection to the States.

ARTICLE V.—Methods of amending the Constitution.

ARTICLE VI.—Supremacy of the Constitution, treaties and laws. Oath of Office.

ARTICLE VII.—Method of ratification of the Constitution.

CONSTITUTIONAL AMENDMENTS

Original Ten-Bill of Rights

1. Freedom of religion, speech, press and assembly.
   Right to petition.
2. Right to keep and bear arms.
3. Quartering of soldiers.
4. Protection from unreasonable search and seizure.
5. Due process in criminal cases.
   Limitation on right of eminent domain.
6. Right to speedy trial, witnesses and counsel.
7. Right of trial by jury.
8. Excessive bail and cruel punishment forbidden.
9. Retention of rights of the people.
10. Undelegated powers belong to the States or to the people.
11. States exempted from suits by individuals.
12. New method of selecting the President and Vice-President.
13. Abolition of slavery.
14. Definition of citizenship.
    Guarantees of due process and protection against state action.
    Apportionment of Congressional Representatives.
    Certain public debts held valid.
15. Equal rights to vote for white and black citizens.
16. Authorization of income tax.
17. Popular election of Senators.
18. Prohibition of intoxicating liquors.
19. Extension of suffrage to women.
20. Change in presidential and congressional terms.
21. Repeal of the Eighteenth Amendment.
22. Limitation of President's term in office to two four-year terms.
23. Extension of suffrage to District of Columbia in presidential elections.
24. Poll tax barred in Federal Elections.
25. Succession of the Vice-President to Presidency; fill the office of Vice-President.
26. Lowering voting age to 18 years.

ENTRY OF STATES INTO THE UNION

State	Capital	Entered Union
1. Alabama	Montgomery	1819
2. Alaska	Juneau	1958
3. Arizona	Phoenix	1912
4. Arkansas	Little Rock	1836
5. California	Sacramento	1850
6. Colorado	Denver	1876
*7. Connecticut	Hartford	1788
*8. Delaware	Dover	1787
9. Florida	Tallahassee	1845
*10. Georgia	Atlanta	1788
11. Hawaii	Honolulu	1959
12. Idaho	Boise	1890
13. Illinois	Springfield	1818
14. Indiana	Indianapolis	1816
15. Iowa	Des Moines	1846
16. Kansas	Topeka	1861
17. Kentucky	Frankfort	1792
18. Louisiana	Baton Rouge	1812
19. Maine	Augusta	1820
*20. Maryland	Annapolis	1788
*21. Massachusetts	Boston	1788
22. Michigan	Lansing	1837
23. Minnesota	St. Paul	1858
24. Mississippi	Jackson	1817
25. Missouri	Jefferson City	1821
26. Montana	Helena	1889
27. Nebraska	Lincoln	1867
28. Nevada	Carson City	1864
*29. New Hampshire	Concord	1788
*30. New Jersey	Trenton	1787
31. New Mexico	Santa Fe	1912
*32. New York	Albany	1788
*33. North Carolina	Raleigh	1789
34. North Dakota	Bismarck	1889
35. Ohio	Columbus	1803
36. Oklahoma	Oklahoma City	1907
37. Oregon	Salem	1859
*38. Pennsylvania	Harrisburg	1787
*39. Rhode Island	Providence	1790
*40. South Carolina	Columbia	1788
41. South Dakota	Pierre	1889
42. Tennessee	Nashville	1796
43. Texas	Austin	1845
44. Utah	Salt Lake City	1896
45. Vermont	Montpelier	1791
*46. Virginia	Richmond	1788
47. Washington	Olympia	1889
48. West Virginia	Charleston	1863
49. Wisconsin	Madison	1848
50. Wyoming	Cheyenne	1890

*Thirteen Original States to Ratify the Constitution.

WEIGHT AND MEASUREMENT CHARTS

Linear Measure

10 millimeters (mm) = 1 centimeter (cm)
10 centimeters = 1 decimeter (dm) = 100 millimeters
10 decimeters = 1 meter (m) = 1,000 millimeters
10 meters = 1 dekameter (dam)
10 dekameters = 1 hectometer (hm) = 100 meters
10 hectometers = 1 kilometer (km) = 1,000 meters

Area Measure

100 square millimeters (mm^2) = 1 square centimeter (cm^2)
10,000 square centimeters = 1 square meter (m^2) = 1,000,000 square millimeters
100 square meters = 1 are (a)
100 ares = 1 hectare (ha) = 10,000 square meters
100 hectares = 1 square kilometer (km^2) = 1,000,000 square meters

Fluid Volume Measure

10 millimeters (mL) = 1 centiliter (cL)
10 centiliters = 1 deciliter (dL) = 100 milliliters
10 deciliters = 1 liter (L) = 1,000 milliliters
10 liters = 1 dekaliter (daL)
10 dekaliters = 1 hectoliter (hL) = 100 liters
10 hectoliters = 1 kiloliter (kL) = 1,000 liters

Cubic Measure

1,000 cubic millimeters (mm^3) = 1 cubic centimeter (cm^3)
1,000 cubic centimeters = 1 cubic decimeter (dm^3) = 1,000,000 cubic millimeters
1,000 cubic decimeters = 1 cubic meter (m^3) = 1 stere = 1,000,000 cubic centimeters = 1,000,000,000 cubic millimeters

Weight

10 milligrams (mg) = 1 centigram (cg)
10 centigrams = 1 decigram (dg) = 100 milligrams
10 decigrams = 1 gram (g) = 1,000 milligrams
10 grams = 1 dekagram (dag)
10 dekagrams = 1 hectogram (hg) = 100 grams
10 hectograms = 1 kilogram (kg) = 1,000 grams
1,000 kilograms = 1 metric ton (t)

Table of U.S. Customary Weights and Measures

Linear Measure

12 inches (in) = 1 foot (ft)
3 feet = 1 yard (yd)
5½ yards = 1 rod (rd), pole, or perch (16½ feet)
40 rods = 1 furlong (fur) = 220 yards = 660 feet
8 furlongs = 1 survey mile (mi) = 1,760 yards = 5,280 feet
3 miles = 1 league = 5,280 yards = 15,840 feet
6076.11549 feet = 1 International Nautical Mile

Liquid Measure

When necessary to distinguish the liquid pint or quart from the dry pint or quart, the word "liquid" or the abbreviation "liq" should be used in combination with the name or abbreviation of the liquid unit.

4 gills = 1 pint (pt) = 28.875 cubic inches
2 pints = 1 quart (qt) = 57.75 cubic inches
4 quarts = 1 gallon (gal) = 231 cubic inches = 8 pints = 32 gills

Area Measure

Squares and cubes of units are sometimes abbreviated by using "superior" figures. For example, ft^2 means square foot, and ft^3 means cubic foot.

144 square inches = 1 square foot (ft^2)
9 square feet = 1 square yard (yd^2) = 1,296 square inches
30-1/4 square yards = 1 square rod (rd^2) = 272-1/4 square feet
160 square rods = 1 acre = 4,840 square yards = 43,560 square feet = 1 square mile (mi^2)
1 mile square = 1 section (of land)
6 miles square = 1 township = 36 sections = 36 square miles

Cubic Measure

1 cubic foot (ft^3) = 1,728 cubic inches (in^3)
27 cubic feet = 1 cubic yard (yd^3)

Gunter's or Surveyors' Chain Measure

7.92 inches (in) = 1 link
100 links = 1 chain (ch) = 4 rods = 66 feet
80 chains = 1 survey mile (mi) = 320 rods = 5,280 feet

Troy Weight

24 grains = 1 pennyweight (dwt)
20 pennyweights = 1 ounce troy (oz t) = 480 grains
12 ounces troy = 1 pound troy (lb t) = 240 pennyweights = 5,760 grains

Dry Measure

When necessary to distinguish the dry pint or quart from the liquid pint or quart, the word "dry" should be used in combination with the name or abbreviation of the dry unit.

2 pints (pt) = 1 quart (qt) = 67.2006 cubic inches
8 quarts = 1 peck (pk) = 537.605 cubic inches = 16 pints
4 pecks = 1 bushel (bu) = 2,150.42 cubic inches = 32 quarts

Avoirdupois Weight

When necessary to distinguish the avoirdupois ounce or pound from the troy ounce or pound, the word "avoirdupois" or the abbreviation "avdp" should be used in combination with the name or abbreviation of the avoirdupois unit.

(The "grain" is the same in avoirdupois and troy weight.)

27 11/32 grains	= 1 dram (dr)
16 drams	= 1 ounce (oz) = 437 1/2 grains
16 ounces	= 1 pound (lb) = 256 drams = 7,000 grains
100 pounds	= 1 hundredweight (cwt)*
20 hundredweights	= 1 ton = 2,000 pounds*

In "gross" or "long" measure, the following values are recognized.

112 pounds	= 1 gross or long hundredweight*
20 gross or long hundredweights	= 1 gross or long ton = 2,240 pounds*

*When the terms "hundredweight" and "ton" are used unmodified, they are commonly understood to mean the 100-pound hundredweight and the 2,000-pound ton, respectively: these units may be designated "net" or "short" when necessary to distinguish them from the corresponding units in gross or long measure.

Metric Conversion Chart—Approximations

Symbol	When you know	Multiply by	To find	Symbol
		Length		
mm	millimeters	0.04	inches	in
cm	centimeters	0.4	inches	in
m	meters	3.3	feet	ft
m	meters	1.1	yards	yd
km	kilometers	0.6	miles	mi
		Area		
cm^2	square centimeters	0.16	square inches	in^2
m^2	square meters	1.2	square yards	yd^2
km^2	square kilometers	0.4	square miles	mi^2
ha	hectares ($10{,}000 m^2$)	2.5	acres	
		Mass (weight)		
g	grams	0.035	ounce	oz
kg	kilograms	2.2	pounds	lb
t	tonnes (1,000kg)	1.1	short tons	
		Volume		
mi	milliliters	0.03	fluid ounces	fl oz
l	liters	2.1	pints	pt
l	liters	1.06	quarts	qt
J	liters	0.26	gallons (U.S.)	gal (U.S.)
l	liters	0.22	gallons (Imp.)	gal (Imp.)
m^3	cubic meters	35	cubic feet	ft^3
m^3	cubic meters	1.3	cubic yards	yd^3
		Temperature (exact)		
°C	Celsius temp	9/5 (+32)	Fahrenheit temp.	°F
		Temperature (exact) to Metric		
°F	Fahrenheit temp.	(−32) 5/9 Celsius	temp. of remainder	°C
		Length		
in	inches	*2.5	centimeters	cm
ft	feet	30	centimeters	cm
yd	yards	0.9	meters	m
mi	miles	1.6	kilometers	km
		Area		
in^2	square inches	6.5	sq. centimeters	cm^3
ft^2	square feet	0.09	square meters	m^2
yd^2	square yards	0.8	square meters	m^2
mi^2	square miles	2.6	sq. kilometers	km^2
	acres	0.4	hectares	ha
		Mass (weight)		
oz	ounces	28	grams	g
lb	pounds	0.45	kilograms	kg
	short tons (2000 lb)	0.9	tonnes	t
		Volume		
tsp	teaspoons	5	milliliters	ml
tbsp	tablespoons	15	milliliters	ml
fl oz	fluid ounces	30	milliliters	ml
c	cups	0.24	liters	l
pt	pints	0.47	liters	l
qt	quarts	0.95	liters	l
gal	gallons (U.S.)	3.8	liters	l
gal	gallons (Imp.)	4.5	liters	l
ft^3	cubic feet	0.03	cubic meters	m^3
yd^3	cubic yards	0.76	cubic meters	m^3

*1 in = 2.54 cm (exactly)

Electrical Units

1. Watt — the unit of power given by the product of the voltage and the current.
2. Kilowatt hour — a unit of work or energy equal to that expended by one kilowatt in one hour.
3. Horsepower — a non-metric unit equal to 746 watts.
4. Ohm — the unit of electrical resistance equal to the resistance of a circuit in which a potential difference of one volt produces a current of one ampere.